ALA
World Encyclopedia of Library and Information Services

SECOND EDITION

AMERICAN LIBRARY ASSOCIATION   *Chicago*

1986

ADAMANTINE PRESS LIMITED   *London*

Composed by the Clarinda Company
in Linotron 202 Bembo with
Perpetua display type.

Printed on 50-pound Glatfelter,
a pH-neutral stock, and bound in
Holliston Record Buckram
by Braun-Brumfield, Inc.

Published in the United States of America
by the American Library Association,
50 East Huron Street, Chicago, Illinois 60611,
and in the United Kingdom by
Adamantine Press Ltd., 3 Henrietta Street,
London WC2E 8LU

Library of Congress Cataloging-in-Publication Data

ALA world encyclopedia of library and information
    services.

    1. Library science—Dictionaries. 2. Information
science—Dictionaries. I. Wedgeworth, Robert.
II. American Library Association.
Z1006.A18   1986   020′.3   86-10894
ISBN 0-8389-0427-0

British Library Cataloguing-in-Publication Data available.
ISBN 0-7449-0003-4

ROBERT WEDGEWORTH	*Editor*
DONALD E. STEWART	*Managing Editor*
JOEL M. LEE	*Associate Editor*
CHRISTINE ROOS	*Assistant Editor*
DONALD LUDGIN	*Copy Editor*
PAMELA HORI	*Indexing Editor*
GORDON FLAGG	*Contributing Writer*
CAROL SCHALK	*Contributing Writer*
STUART C. A. WHITWELL	*Contributing Writer*
BONNIE OBERMAN	*Contributing Picture Editor*
HARRIETT BANNER	*Production Manager and Designer*
RAYMOND S. MACHURA	*Typographic Artist*
ROBERT J. BERAN	*Proofreader*
CHARLES S. FINEMAN	*Translator for French*
EDWIN S. GLEAVES	*Translator for Spanish*
MARY NILES MAACK	*Translator for French*
THOMAS L. MANN	*Translator for Russian*
JUDY CROWLEY	*Staff Assistant for translations*

Advisers

Simeon Babasanya Aje
Director, National Library of Nigeria, Lagos.

Hedwig Anuar
Director, National Library, Singapore.

Joseph Becker
President, Becker and Hayes, Santa Monica, California.

Rebecca T. Bingham
Director of Library Media Services, Jefferson County Public Schools, Louisville, Kentucky.

George S. Bobinski
Dean, School of Information and Library Studies, State University of New York at Buffalo.

Amadou A. Bousso
Programme General d'Information (PGI), Unesco, Paris.

J. Periam Danton
Professor Emeritus, School of Library and Information Studies, University of California, Berkeley

Richard M. Dougherty
Director, University Libraries, University of Michigan, Ann Arbor.

Shirley Echelman
Executive Director, Association of Research Libraries, Washington, D.C.

Mohamed M. El Hadi
Computer Consultants, Jeddah, Saudi Arabia.

Josephine Riss Fang
Professor, School of Library Science, Simmons College, Boston, Massachusetts.

Richard K. Gardner
Professor, Ecole de Bibliotheconomié, University of Montreal, Canada.

Kenneth C. Harrison
Formerly City Librarian of Westminster, London, England.

Edward Gailon Holley
Professor, School of Library Science, University of North Carolina at Chapel Hill, Chapel Hill.

William V. Jackson
Professor, Graduate School of Library Science, University of Texas, Austin.

Ezekiel Enock Kaungamno
Director, Tanzania National Library Service, Dar es Salaam.

Dan Lacy
Formerly Senior Vice-President, McGraw-Hill Book Co., New York.

R. Brian Land
Director, Legislative Library of Ontario, Toronto.

Herman Liebaers
Consultant, Brussels, Belgium.

R. Kathleen Molz
Melvil Dewey Professor, School of Library Service, Columbia University, New York.

W. A. Munford
Formerly Director-General, National Library for the Blind, Bredbury, Stockport, England.

John Ndegwa
Librarian, University of Nairobi Library, Kenya.

Carol A. Nemeyer
Formerly Associate Librarian for National Programs, Library of Congress, Washington, D.C.

Hans Panofsky
Curator of Africana, Northwestern University Library, Evanston, Illinois.

Vladimir Popov
Deputy Director, Cyril and Methodius National Library, Sofia, Bulgaria.

Warren Tsuneishi
Chief, Orientalia Division, Library of Congress, Washington, D.C.

Robert Vosper
Professor Emeritus, Graduate School of Library and Information Science, University of California at Los Angeles.

Alfred Wagner
Archivdirector, Bundesarchiv, Koblenz, Federal Republic of Germany.

Wayne Wiegand
Professor, College of Information Science, University of Kentucky, Lexington

Margreet Wijnstroom
Secretary General, International Federation of Library Associations and Institutions, The Hague, Netherlands.

Celia R. Zaher
Director, Division of Book Promotion, Unesco, Paris.

Editor's Preface

The First Edition of this work in 1980 brought to fulfillment the long-term objective of the Editor to establish a firm basis for the comparative study of librarianship. Efforts to analyze the respective circumstances of librarianship in countries around the world are limited by the lack of factual data as a starting point for more in-depth study. For many countries there exists no readily available description of the major institutions that educate librarians and provide library and information services, including their size and scope.

The *ALA World Encyclopedia* attempts to fill this fundamental gap in the literature. Its historical articles trace the development of the field, an overview enriched by current description of library and information services in countries around the world. Professional concepts and principles are explained and analyzed in articles ranging from Abstracting and Indexing to Young Adult Services. Biographies bring to life the major activities in the lives of persons who have played a part in shaping the field.

In planning the Second Edition of this work, the editors consulted with the Advisers on its content and paid careful attention to the published reviews of the First Edition. The plan for the Second Edition called for 85 percent of the book to comprise new or completely revised contributions. When a complete revision by a contributor was not possible, the editors have revised the articles, including updated statistics and new illustrations. The editorial plan for the Second Edition continues its emphasis on the *Outline of Contents* as a guide to the organization of knowledge of the field. The Parallel Index in the margins of the text pages of the First Edition has been replaced by an expanded, conventional Index at the end of the text. The new Index also ties the *Encyclopedia* to the *ALA Yearbook of Library and Information Services;* that annual volume provides additional or continuing coverage of topics in the *ALA World Encyclopedia.*

This Second Edition of the *ALA World Encyclopedia,* whose one million words represent a 43 percent increase over the First Edition, follows the editorial plan of the First Edition.

There are six basic categories of articles:

(1) One hundred fifty-two structured articles cover the status and condition of libraries in countries of the world and provide statistics. Nine other articles cover the history and role of libraries from ancient times to the present.

(2) Eight articles cover the major types of institutions that deliver library and information services. Contributors' comprehensive articles explore the purpose, characteristic services, clientele, and patterns of governance, finance, and administration of the institutions. They represent an editorial approach to comparative librarianship that attempts to discern commonalities and differences in these institutions and their practices as they exist in many countries.

(3) Thirty articles deal with the principles and practices of librarianship and information management, explaining and analyzing the fundamental processes and basic types of services to the many different client groups.

(4) Nine articles cover the field of education and research from early apprenticeship to formal library education.

(5) Thirty-three articles describe the activities of significant international organizations, agencies, and associations.

(6) Two hundred eighteen biographical subjects (an increase of almost a third over the First Edition) are from different places of the world and different times. They were selected for inclusion from nominations made by the international advisory group. Among the editors' criteria for inclusion are: foundation of an important library, or a primary role in a major library's growth, development, and influence; author of seminal writings of great impact and lasting influence; leadership in the profession, including activity in professional associations; significant activity as a library educator; contribution to the theory of librarianship in any of the field's components; exemplary role as a practitioner, within any part of the profession; publisher of related books and periodicals; and leadership in important national and international bibliographic enterprises.

The articles, which are alphabetically arranged, vary in length from several hundred words to more than 25,000 (Academic Libraries, for example). They were designed to provide enough space to treat significant aspects of each topic; hundreds of statistical tables, charts, and illustrations enrich and enliven the text.

The 411 contributors and 31 advisers from around the world gave extraordinary cooperation in response to the editors' requests, and the knowledge, experience, and professional and scholarly achievements of the authors are reflected in the pages of this work. The editors acknowledge their contributions with sincere gratitude.

Grateful acknowledgments go especially to Joel Lee and Don Stewart, who shared major editorial responsibility, and to Christine Roos, who kept track of our progress. The editorial team of editors, translators, writers, and production specialists worked in great harmony to reach a superb level of technological efficiency and editorial achievement. I extend my highest compliments to them.

This revised and enlarged Second Edition of the *ALA World Encyclopedia of Library and Information Services* builds upon the success of the First Edition.

The editors were encouraged by the response to the original publication and hope that our efforts to improve it will be received similarly.

ROBERT WEDGEWORTH
Editor

May 7, 1986
Columbia University
School of Library Service
New York, New York

Contents

Contributors*

Constantin Ivanovich Abramov
Chief of the Department of Library Science of Moscow State Institute of Culture. *Lev Tropovsky*

Ermelinda Acerenza
Director, University School of Library Science, Montevideo. *Uruguay*

Thomas R. Adams
John Hay Professor of Bibliography and University Bibliographer, Brown University, Providence, Rhode Island. *Benjamin Franklin*

Adhana Mengste-ab
Assistant University Librarian, Addis Ababa University Libraries, Addis Ababa. *Ethiopia*

Simeon Babasanya Aje
Director, National Library of Nigeria, Lagos. *Felicia Adetowun Ogunsheye*

S. Nazim Ali
Assistant Professor, Library Services, University College of Arts, Science and Education, Bahrain. *Bahrain*

Mohammed M. Aman
Dean, School of Library and Information Science, University of Wisconsin–Milwaukee. *Egypt; Sudan*

Margaret Anderson
Associate Professor, Faculty of Library and Information Science, University of Toronto. *George Locke*

Hedwig Anuar
Director, National Library of Singapore. *Singapore*

Arie Arad
Deputy Director, Israel State Archives, Jerusalem. *Archives: Technical Aspects*

C. Wesley Armstrong
Vice President for Academic Affairs and former Director of Libraries, University of Liberia, Monrovia. *Liberia*

Allen Asaf
Cataloguer, The Grolier Club of New York. *Joseph Sabin*

Augusta Baker
Storyteller-in-Residence, College of Library and Information Science, University of South Carolina, Columbia. *Anne Carroll Moore*

F. W. G. Baker
Executive Secretary, International Council of Scientific Unions, Paris. *International Council of Scientific Unions*

John P. Baker
Chief, Conservation Division, The New York Public Library–Research Libraries. *Conservation and Preservation of Library Materials*

Leigh R. Baker
Deputy Librarian, Papua New Guinea University of Technology, Lae. *Papua New Guinea*

K. G. B. Bakewell
Principal Lecturer and Deputy Head, School of Librarianship and Information Studies, Liverpool Polytechnic. *S. C. Bradford; Shiyali Ramamrita Ranganathan*

E. Bejide Bankole
Editor, Standing Conference of African University Libraries, Western Area, Lagos. *Standing Conference of African University Libraries*

Peggy Barber
Associate Executive Director, Communications, American Library Association, Chicago. *Public Relations*

Daniel W. Barthell
Head, Search Section, Northwestern University Library, Evanston, Illinois. *Honduras*

Jean Wilfrid Bertrand
Director, National Archives of Haiti, Port-au-Prince. *Haiti*

Susan Shattuck Benson
Senior Specialist, Library and Archives Development, Department of Cultural Affairs, Organization of American States, Washington, D.C. *Organization of American States*

Russell E. Bidlack
Dean Emeritus, School of Library Science, University of Michigan, Ann Arbor. *Accreditation; Rudolph H. Gjelsness*

Judy Blackman
Director, National Library Service, Barbados. *Barbados*

George S. Bobinski
Dean and Professor, School of Information and Library Studies, State University of New York at Buffalo. *Andrew Carnegie; Edward G. Holley; Poland*

Marie Elizabeth Bouscarle
Documentation Officer, International Center for Medical Research, Gabon. *Gabon*

T. H. Bowyer
Librarian, Queen Mary College, University of London, Retired. *K. W. Humphreys*

Estelle Brodman
Librarian and Professor of Medical History Emerita, Washington University School of Medicine, Saint Louis. *Frank Bradway Rogers*

Naomi C. Broering
Medical Center Librarian, Georgetown University Medical Center, Washington, D.C. *Medical Libraries: Laws and Legislation*

Barry S. Brook
Executive Officer, Ph.D. Program in Music, City University of New York. *International Association of Music Libraries, Archives and Documentation Centres*

Gloria Primm Brown
Program Associate, Carnegie Corporation of New York. *Frederick Paul Keppel*

Robert E. Brundin
Professor, Faculty of Library Science, University of Alberta, Edmonton. *Justin Winsor*

Harrison Bryan
Director General, National Library of Australia, Canberra. *Australia*

Mary Lynn McCree Bryan
Editor, The Jane Addams Papers, Duke University, Durham. *Ernst Posner*

Redmond A. Burke
Professor, University of Wisconsin–Oshkosh. *Saint Benedict; Cassiodorus; Bartolomeo Platina*

Clifford A. Burmester
Assistant National Librarian, National Library of Australia, Canberra, Retired. *Sir John Alexander Ferguson; Edward Augustus Petherick*

Charles H. Busha
Executive Director, Pickens County (South Carolina) Council on Aging. *Censorship and Intellectual Freedom*

Ana María Magaloni de Bustamante
General Director of Libraries, Secretariat of Public Education, Mexico. *Mexico*

Robert W. Butler
Leader, Training and Education, National Agricultural Library, Beltsville, Maryland. *International*

---

*Asterisk on authors' names signed at the end of text articles denotes contributor to First Edition whose article was updated in statistics or revised by the editors for the Second Edition.

Contributors

Association of Agricultural Librarians and Documentalists

Harry C. Campbell
Library and Information Consultant, Espial Productions Ltd., Toronto. *Public Libraries: Purposes and Objectives*

Michael Carpenter
Writer, Van Nuys, California. *Seymour Lubetzky*

Ray L. Carpenter
Professor, School of Library Science, University of North Carolina at Chapel Hill. *Italy*

Genevieve M. Casey
Professor, Division of Library Science, Wayne State University, Detroit. *Public Libraries: Collections and Materials*

Edwin Castagna
Former Director, Enoch Pratt Free Library, Baltimore. *Joseph L. Wheeler*

Cordelia R. Cavalcanti
Professor, University of Brasília. *Maria Luisa Monteiro da Cunha*

Roderick Cave
Foundation Professor of Librarianship, Victoria University of Wellington, New Zealand. *Arundell Esdaile; Andrew Maunsell*

Sten Cedergren
City Librarian, Stadsbiblioteket, Göteborg, Sweden. *International Association of Metropolitan City Libraries*

Rosemary Chaït
Research Attaché, National Library of Algeria, Algiers. *Algeria*

Peter Nkangafack Chateh
Chief Librarian, University of Yaounde, Cameroon. *Cameroon*

Marc Chauveinc
Conservateur en Chef, Bibliothèque Nationale, Paris. *France*

Mary K. Chelton
Administrator, Programming and Community Services, Virginia Beach (Virginia) Public Libraries. *Margaret C. Scoggin; Young Adult Services*

Elin B. Christianson
Library Consultant, Hobart, Indiana. *Special Libraries*

Charles D. Churchwell
Dean of Library Services, Washington University Libraries, Saint Louis. *Charles C. Williamson*

Jean-Pierre Clavel
Directeur de la Bibliothèque Cantonale et Universitaire, Lausanne. *Switzerland*

Paul E. Cohen
Assistant Librarian for Reference Services, New-York Historical Society, New York. *Isadore Gilbert Mudge*

Lois Ann Colaianni
Associate Director for Library Operations, National Library of Medicine, Bethesda, Maryland. *Martin M. Cummings*

John Y. Cole
Executive Director, The Center for the Book, Library of Congress, Washington, D.C. *Archibald MacLeish;*

Herbert Putnam; Ainsworth Rand Spofford

Jean Ellen Coleman
Director, Office for Library Outreach Services, American Library Association, Chicago. *Joyce Robinson*

John P. Comaromi
Editor and Chief, Decimal Classification Division, Library of Congress, Washington, D.C. *Melvil Dewey*

Barbara Comissiong
Deputy Librarian, The University of the West Indies. *Trinidad and Tobago*

Charles William Conaway
Assistant Professor, School of Library Science, Florida State University, Tallahassee. *Iceland*

Michael G. Cook
University Archivist and Lecturer in Archival Studies, University of Liverpool. *Archives: Professional Training*

Martha Cornog
Special Projects Coordinator, National Federation of Abstracting and Indexing Services, Philadelphia. *Abstracting and Indexing*

Jeannette Fernández de Criado
Head Librarian, American School, San Salvador. *El Salvador*

Timothy J. Crist
Director, Issues Management, Prudential Insurance Company, Newark, New Jersey; former Editor, Wing Short Title Catalogue Revision. *Donald Goddard Wing*

Maria Manuela Cruzeiro
Chief Librarian, New University of Lisbon, Portugal. *Cape Verde; Guinea-Bissau; Portugal*

Clifford Currie
Librarian, The College of William and Mary, Williamsburg, Virginia, Retired. *Robert Shackleton*

Frank Kurt Cylke
Director, National Library Service for the Blind and Physically Handicapped, Library of Congress, Washington, D.C. *Handicapped, Services to*

Doris Cruger Dale
Professor, Department of Curriculum, Instruction, and Media, Southern Illinois University, Carbondale. *Sarah Bogle*

Phyllis I. Dalton
Library Consultant, Las Vegas, Nevada. *Institutionalized, Services to*

Evelyn H. Daniel
Dean, School of Library Science, University of North Carolina at Chapel Hill. *School Libraries/Media Centers: Measurement and Evaluation*

R. K. Das Gupta
Honorary Visiting Professor of English, Jadarpur University, Calcutta; former Director, National Library of India. *India*

Charles H. Davis
Professor, formerly Dean, Graduate School of Library and Information Science, University of Illinois at Urbana-Champaign. *Library and Information Science Research*

Donald G. Davis, Jr.
Associate Professor, Graduate School of Library and Information Science, University of Texas at Austin. *Mary Wright Plummer*

Anthony Debons
Professor of Information Science, University of Pittsburgh. *Information Science*

Andrew N. DeHeer
Director, Research Library on African Affairs, Accra, Ghana. *Eve Evans*

Rafael R. Delgado
Director, General Library, University of Puerto Rico, Río Piedras. *Puerto Rico*

Uthai Dhutiyabhodi
President, Thai Libraries Association, Bangkok. *Thailand*

Oumar Diouwara
Head Librarian, National Library, Nouakchott. *Mauritania*

Mahir Domi
Chairman of the Council of Libraries, Tiranë, Albania. *Albania*

Keith Doms
Director, Free Library of Philadelphia. *Ralph Munn*

J. A. Dosunmu
Deputy Director, National Library of Nigeria, Lagos. *Nigeria*

Daphne Douglas
Professor of Library Studies, University of the West Indies; President, ACURIL, 1984–85. *Association of Caribbean University, Research and Institutional Libraries*

Henry Dua-Agyemang
Sub-Librarian, Balme Library, University of Ghana, Accra. *Ghana*

Michel Duchein
Inspector General of the Archives of France, Paris. *Archives: Legislative Foundations*

Frederick Duda
Assistant University Librarian for Personnel, Columbia University Libraries, New York. *Warren J. Haas*

Martha L. P. Dukas
Deputy Director for Technical Services, Sultan Qaboos University Library, Muscat, Oman. *Oman*

Winifred E. Duncan
Director, Bureau of Libraries, Chicago Public Schools. *School Libraries/ Media Centers: Collections*

Domingos van Dúnem
Director, National Library of Angola, Luanda. *Angola*

Harry East
Senior Research Fellow, Department of Information Science, The City University, London. *Brian Vickery*

Johanna Eggert
Secretary-General of ISO/TC 46, Berlin. *International Organization for Standardization*

Mohamed M. El-Hadi
Senior Consultant, Computer Consultants, Jeddah, Saudi Arabia. *El Sayed Mahmoud El Sheniti; Jordan; Kuwait; Qatar; Saudi Arabia; Syria; United Arab Emirates; Yemen (Aden); Yemen (Sana'a)*

Roger Ellis
Consultant Editor, Public Record Office, London. *Sir Hilary Jenkinson*

Deirdre Ellis-King
Dublin City and County Librarian. *Ireland*

Hipolito Escolar-Sobrino
Director of the National Library, Madrid. *Spain*

William R. Eshelman
President, Scarecrow Press, Edison, New Jersey. *Lawrence Clark Powell*

John R. Turner Ettlinger
Professor, School of Library Service, Dalhousie University, Halifax, Nova Scotia. *Middle Ages, Libraries in the*

Charles W. Evans
Associate Professor, Department of Computer and Information Science, University of Mississippi. *Library Education: Education and Training for Library Employees*

Frank B. Evans
Deputy Assistant Archivist for Records Administration, National Archives and Records Administration, Washington, D.C. *Archives: Nature, Goals, Principles; Arrangement and Description; Theodore R. Schellenberg*

Elaine Fain
Former Assistant Professor, School of Library Science, University of Wisconsin-Milwaukee (d. 1980). *Mary Eileen Ahern*

Judith Farley
Reference Specialist, Library of Congress, Washington, D.C. *National Bibliographies*

Emily Gallup Fayen
Assistant Director for Systems, Van Pelt Library, University of Pennsylvania, Philadelphia. *Circulating Systems*

Evgeny Alekseevich Fenelonov
Deputy Director, the V. I. Lenin State Library of the U.S.S.R. *Ogan Stepanovich Chubarian*

Meyer H. Fishbein
Director, Military Archives Division, National Archives and Record Service, Washington, D.C. *Archives: Records Management and Records Appraisal*

Alice E. Fite
Formerly Executive Director, American Association of School Librarians, American Library Association, Chicago. *School Libraries/ Media Centers: Library Cooperation*

Richard Fitzsimmons
Director of the Library, the Worthington Scranton Campus, the Pennsylvania State University. *J. B. Lippincott*

Marisol Floren
Director of the Library, Central University of the East, San Pedro de Macoris, Dominican Republic. *Dominican Republic*

Edson Nery da Fonseca
Professor, University of Brasilia. *Brazil; Rubens Borba de Moraes*

Georgij Polikarpovich Fontonov
Chief Lecturer, Department of Library Science, All-Union Institute of Improvement of Skill of Cultural Workers, Lenin State Library of the U.S.S.R. *Nadezhda Krupskaya*

Jody Bales Foote
Librarian, Cornell University, Ithaca, New York. *Bangladesh*

John B. Forbes
Assistant to the Director for Networking, National Agricultural Library, Beltsville, Maryland. *Food and Agriculture Organization*

Vincent Forshaw
Director, Lesotho National Library Service, Maseru. *Lesotho*

D. J. Foskett
Director of Central Library Services, University of London, Retired. *Sir Frank Francis*

Barbara Foster
Assistant Professor, Hunter College Library, New York. *Netherlands Antilles*

Sir Frank Francis
Director and Principal Librarian, British Museum, London, Retired. *Donald John Urquhart*

Yoshika Moriya de Freundorfer
Director, School of Library Science, National University of Asuncion. *Paraguay*

Stephen E. Furth
Retired Industry Manager, Information Systems, International Business Machines Corporation. *Hans Peter Luhn*

Ervin J. Gaines
Director, Cleveland Public Library. *William Howard Brett; Public Libraries: Finance and Administration*

Ahmed M. Gallal
General Director, Garyounis University Libraries, Benghazi. *Libya*

Budd L. Gambee
Professor Emeritus, School of Library Science, University of North Carolina at Chapel Hill. *Caroline M. Hewins*

Richard K. Gardner
Directeur, École de Bibliothéconomie et des Sciences de l'Information, Université de Montréal. *Association Internationale des Écoles des Sciences de l'Information*

Barbara Gates
Head, Catalog Department, Brown University Library, Providence, Rhode Island. *Minnie Earl Sears*

Mary Virginia Gaver
Professor Emeritus, Graduate School of Library Service, Rutgers, the State University of New Jersey. *Ralph Shaw*

Stanley Gillam
Librarian of the London Library, Retired. *Thomas Carlyle*

Marion Gilroy
Formerly Associate Professor Emeritus, School of Librarianship, University of British Columbia, Vancouver (d. 1981). *Elizabeth Homer Morton*

George Glaser
President, George Glaser, Inc.; U.S. Delegate, IFIP General Assembly. *International Federation for Information Processing*

Edwin S. Gleaves
Professor and Chair, Department of Library and Information Science, George Peabody College for Teachers, Vanderbilt University, Nashville, Tennessee. *Micrographics; Spain (and others) translation; Josefa Emilia Sabor (in part)*

Margaret Knox Goggin
Professor Emeritus, University of Denver. *Certification of Librarians*

Charles A. Goodrum
Assistant Director, Congressional Research Service, Library of Congress, Washington, D.C., Retired. *National Libraries*

Henry Alfred Ian Goonetileke
Librarian, University of Peradeniya, Sri Lanka. *Sri Lanka*

Martha Gorman
Consultant, Boulder, Colorado. *Ecuador; Peru*

G. Thimme Gowda
Unesco Documentation Service Specialist, Ministry of National Planning, Mogadiscio, Somalia. *Somalia*

Else Granheim
Director, Norwegian Directorate for Public and School Libraries, Oslo. *Norway; Margreet Wijnstroom*

Chandler B. Grannis
Contributing Editor, *Publishers Weekly. Daniel Melcher*

Hans G. Gravenhorst
Director, Institute of Library Science, University of Buenos Aires. *Argentina*

Belver C. Griffith
Professor, School of Library and Information Science, Drexel University, Philadelphia. *Eugene Garfield*

Laurel A. Grotzinger
Dean and Chief Research Officer, The Graduate College, Western Michigan University, Kalamazoo. *Adelaide Hasse; Katharine Lucinda Sharp*

Seydou Gueye
Librarian, National Library, Ivory Coast. *Ivory Coast*

Hussein Habaili
Associate Professor, Faculty of Medicine of Tunis. *Tunisia*

Aida Kassantini Hafez
Director of Learning Resources Center, Beirut University College. *Lebanon*

Alfred D. Hagle
Public Resources Officer, National Library Service for the Blind and Physically Handicapped, Library of Congress, Washington, D.C. *Handicapped, Services to*

Jane Anne Hannigan
Professor, School of Library Service, Columbia University, New York. *Frances E. Henne*

Hrafn A. Hardarson
Chief Librarian, Kópavogur Town Library, Iceland. *Iceland*

Genevieve Sue Hariki
National Center for Documentation, Rabat. *Morocco*

Contributors

Helen P. Harrison
Secretary-General, International Association of Sound Archives; Media Librarian, Open University Library, Milton Keynes, England. *International Association of Sound Archives*

K. C. Harrison
Consultant Librarian; Emeritus City Librarian of Westminster, London. *D. J. Foskett; Frank Gardner; Sir Harry Hookway; Library Association; Lionel R. McColvin; W. A. Munford; W. C. Berwick Sayers; United Kingdom*

Robert M. Hayes
Dean, Graduate School of Library and Information Science, University of California at Los Angeles. *Information Science Education*

Dan C. Hazen
Berkeley, California. *Seminar on the Acquisition of Latin American Library Materials*

Kathleen M. Heim
Dean, School of Library and Information Science, Louisiana State University, Baton Rouge. *Adult Services*

John B. Hench
Associate Director for Research and Publication, American Antiquarian Society, Worcester, Massachusetts. *J. Franklin Jameson; Waldo Gifford Leland*

Helen L. Henderson
Secretary, EUSIDIC, London. *European Association of Information Services*

Donald D. Hendricks
Dean of Library Services, Earl K. Long Library, University of New Orleans. *J. Pierpont Morgan*

Dan Henke
Professor of Law and Director of the Hastings Legal Information Center, University of California, San Francisco. *Law Libraries: Services to Users*

Hernandono
Head, Reprography Division, Indonesian National Scientific Documentation Center-Indonesian Institute of Sciences, Jakarta. *Winarti Partaningrat*

M. Teresa Herrero de Alvarez
Head Librarian, Chilean-North American Institute of Culture, Santiago. *Chile*

Joe A. Hewitt
Associate University Librarian for Technical Services, University of North Carolina at Chapel Hill. *F. Wilfrid Lancaster*

Doralyn J. Hickey
Professor, School of Library and Information Sciences, North Texas State University, Denton. *Cataloguing; Paul S. Dunkin*

Harold Holdsworth
Librarian, University of the South Pacific Library, Suva. *Fiji*

Edward G. Holley
Professor, formerly Dean, School of Library Science, University of North Carolina at Chapel Hill. *American Library Association; Lester E. Asheim; Charles Evans*

Oliver W. Holmes
Former Executive Director, National Historical Publications and Records Commission, Washington, D.C. (d. 1981). *Philip M. Hamer*

Virginia H. Holtz
Director, Middleton Health Sciences Library, University of Wisconsin-Madison. *Medical Libraries: Measurement and Evaluation*

Norman Horrocks
Director and Professor, School of Library Service, Dalhousie University, Halifax, Nova Scotia. *Library Education: History*

P. Lim Pui Huen
Librarian, Institute of Southeast Asian Studies, Singapore. *Hedwig Anuar; Congress of Southeast Asian Librarians*

Sybil M. Iton
Director, Jamaica Library Service, Kingston. *Jamaica*

Toshio Iwasaru
Professor, Library Science, Kansai University, Osaka. *Keitaro Amano; Fujio Mamiya*

Sidney L. Jackson
Former Professor of Library Science, Kent State University, Kent, Ohio (d. 1979). *Alexandrian Library; Byzantine Libraries; Egypt (Ancient); Greece (Ancient); Near East (Ancient); Rome*

William Vernon Jackson
Professor, Graduate School of Library and Information Science, University of Texas at Austin. *Louise-Noëlle Malclès*

Roger F. Jacobs
Law Librarian, Supreme Court of the United States, Washington, D.C. *Law Libraries: Laws and Legislation*

J. Myron Jacobstein
Professor of Law and Law Librarian, Stanford University Law School Library, Stanford, California. *Law Libraries: Law Library Cooperation*

Louis Sydney Jean-François
Head Librarian, Mauritius Institute, Beau-Bassin. *Mauritius*

Duane F. Johnson
State Librarian, Kansas State Library, Topeka. *Extension Services*

Norman Johnson
Librarian, National Free Library of Zimbabwe, Bulawayo, Retired. *Zimbabwe*

Stephen C. Johnson
President, Behavioral Images, Inc., Bloomington, Illinois. *Audiovisual Services*

H. G. Jones
Curator, North Carolina Collection, and Adjunct Professor of History, University of North Carolina at Chapel Hill. *Robert D. W. Connor*

Milbrey L. Jones
Policy Coordinator, Center for Libraries and Education Improvement, U.S. Department of Education, Washington, D.C. *Mary Gaver*

Alma Jordan
University Librarian, The University of the West Indies. *Trinidad and Tobago*

E. J. Josey
Chief, Bureau of Specialist Library Services, New York State Education Department, Albany. *Eliza Atkins Gleason*

Gladys M. Jusu-Sheriff
Librarian, Fourah Bay College, University of Sierra Leone, Freetown. *Sierra Leone*

Paul Kaegbein
Professor of Library Science, University of Cologne. *Federal Republic of Germany; Horst Kunze; Fritz Milkau*

Lief Kajberg
Lecturer, Royal School of Librarianship, Copenhagen. *Preben Kierkegaard*

Margaret Kaltenbach
Associate Professor Emeritus, Case Western Reserve University, Cleveland. *Jesse H. Shera*

Lai-bing Kan
Librarian, University of Hong Kong Libraries. *Hong Kong*

David Kaser
Distinguished Professor of Library and Information Science, Indiana University, Bloomington. *Frederick G. Kilgour; Library Buildings; Keyes D. Metcalf*

Ezekiel Enock Kaungamno
Director, Tanzania Library Services, Dar es Salaam. *Tanzania*

B. M. Kawesa
Librarian, Makerere Institute of Social Research, Kampala, Uganda. *Uganda*

Charles Kecskemeti
Executive Secretary, International Council on Archives, Paris. *International Council on Archives*

Stella Keenan
Secretary General, International Federation for Documentation, The Hague. *International Federation for Documentation*

Dhan G. Keswani
Legon, Accra, Ghana. *Jeremias Mama Akita*

M. T. Khafagi
Director, Department of Documentation and Information, Arab League Educational, Cultural and Scientific Organization, Tunis. *Arab League Educational, Cultural and Scientific Organization*

Sha'ban Khalifa
Professor of Library Science, Cairo University, Giza, Egypt. *Egypt*

Anis Khurshid
Professor and Chairman, Department of Library and Information Science, University of Karachi. *Pakistan*

Amer Ibrahim Kindilchie
Professor and Director of Libraries, Al-Mustansiriyah University, Baghdad. *Iraq*

Mary E. Kingsbury
Professor, School of Library Science, University of North Carolina at

Chapel Hill. *Effie Louise Power*

Firmin Kinigi
Chief Librarian, University of Burundi, Bujumbura. *Burundi*

Preben Kierkegaard
Rector Emeritus, Royal School of Librarianship, Copenhagen. *Denmark*

Jendo Kiss
City Librarian, Metropolitan Ervin Szabó Library, Budapest. *Hungary*

Thérèse Kleindienst
Honorary Secretary General of the Bibliothèque Nationale, Paris. *Julien Cain*

Philip A. Knachel
Associate Director, Folger Shakespeare Library, Washington, D.C. *Henry Clay Folger*

Al Hady Koita
Writer on Mali, *Mali*

Helena Kolarova-Palkova
Head of Library Department, Ministry of Culture, Slovak Socialist Republic. *Czechoslovakia*

Madoko Kon
Professor, Faculty of Literature, Chuo University, Tokyo. *Japan*

Richard L. Kort
Slavic Cataloger, Boston Public Library. *Yugoslavia*

Cecile E. Kramer
Northwestern University School of Medicine, Chicago. *Medical Libraries: Collections*

Joe W. Kraus
Director Emeritus, Illinois State University Libraries, Bloomington. *Robert B. Downs*

Miroslav Krek
Brandeis University, Waltham, Massachusetts. *Islamic Libraries*

Larba Ali Krissiamba
Chief, Interafrican Committee for Hydraulic Studies, Documentation Center, Ouagadougou. *Burkina Faso*

D. W. Krummel
Professor of Library and Information Science, University of Illinois, Urbana. *Conrad Gesner*

Narayan H. Kulkarnee
Deputy Director of Archives, Government of India, Retired. *S. N. Prasad*

A. R. Kulkarni
Professor of History Emeritus, University of Poona, India. *Vishwanath Kashinath Rajwade*

A. W. Z. Kuzwayo
Librarian, University College of Swaziland, Kwaluseni. *Swaziland*

Luc Kwanten
Curator, Far Eastern Library, University of Chicago. *Bhutan; Tibet*

Alex Ladenson
Executive Director, Urban Libraries Council, Chicago, Illinois. *William Frederick Poole; Public Libraries: Public Library Legislation in the United States*

Fanny Lalande Isnard
Director, Camlivres, Douala, Guinea. *Amadou A. Bousso; Guinea*

F. Wilfrid Lancaster
Professor of Library and Information

Science, Graduate School of Library and Information Science, University of Illinois, Urbana. *Cyril Cleverdon*

Charles T. Laugher
Archivist, Dalhousie University, Halifax, Nova Scotia. *Thomas Bray*

Betty V. LeBus
Visiting Law Librarian and Professor of Law, University of Wyoming, Laramie. *Law Libraries: Measurement and Evaluation*

Poongsoon Lee
Seoul, Korea. *Republic of Korea*

Battiwa Lekbir
Assistant Director, National Documentation Center, Rabat. *Morocco*

Renée Lemaître
Head of the Documentation Center for the Press, United States Information Service, Paris, Retired. *Henri Lemaître*

Herman Liebaers
Grand Marshall of the Court of Belgium, Royal Library, Brussels. *Margarita Ivanovna Rudomino*

Emma Linares
Director of the Library, Center for the Study of Publications, Buenos Aires. *Carlos Victor Penna; Josefa Emilia Sabor*

Max Liniger-Goumaz
Professor, École Supérieure de Cadres pour l'économie et l'administration, Lausanne, Switzerland. *Equatorial Guinea*

R. W. Lont
Department of Librarianship, Ministry of Education and Community Development, Paramaribo. *Suriname John G. Loren*
Library Consultant, Bethesda, Maryland. *L. Quincy Mumford*

Jean E. Lowrie
Formerly Director, School of Librarianship. Western Michigan University, Kalamazoo, Michigan. *International Association of School Librarianship; School Libraries/Media Centers*

Richard A. Lyders
Executive Director, Houston Academy of Medicine, Texas Medical Center Library, Houston. *Medical Libraries: Administration, Governance, and Finance*

Beverly P. Lynch
University Librarian, University of Illinois at Chicago. *Academic Libraries: Purposes, Goals, and Objectives*

Mary Jo Lynch
Director, Office for Research, American Library Association, Chicago. *Margaret Hutchins; Public Libraries: Services to Users; Constance M. Winchell*

Mary Niles Maack
Assistant Professor, University of Minnesota, Minneapolis. *Eugène Morel; Suzanne Honoré*

Leena Maissen
Executive Secretary, International Board on Books for Young People, Basel, Switzerland. *International Board*

on Books for Young People

James J. Maloney
Marketing Representative, Dialog Information Services, Inc., Palo Alto, California. *Online Information Services*

K. A. Manley
Assistant Librarian, Institute of Historical Research, University of London. *E. W. B. Nicholson*

Julius J. Marke
Professor of Law and Director of the Law Library, St. John's University School of Law, Jamaica, New York. *Law Libraries*

Albert P. Marshall
Professor Emeritus, Eastern Michigan University, Ypsilanti. *Virginia Lacy Jones*

David J. Martz, Jr.
Head, Popular Culture Library, Bowling Green State University, Bowling Green, Ohio. *Peter Force*

A. H. H. M. Mathijsen
President, Dutch Library Association. *Netherlands*

Joseph R. Matthews
President, J. Matthews and Associates, Grass Valley, California. *Information Technologies*

Morris Matza
National Library, Caracas. *Venezuela*

Ruby S. May
Associate Director, Regional Medical Library, Library of the Health Sciences, University of Illinois at the Medical Center, Chicago. *Medical Libraries: Library Cooperation*

Elfrieda B. McCauley
Coordinator of Media Services, Greenwich Public Schools, Connecticut. *School Libraries/Media Centers: Services to Users*

Donald R. McCoy
University Distinguished Professor of History, University of Kansas, Lawrence. *Solon Justus Buck; Wayne C. Grover*

Stanley McElderry
Director, University of Chicago Library. *Herman Fussler*

Neil McHugh
Northwestern University, Evanston, Illinois. *Benin; Chad*

Brian McKeon
City Librarian, Wellington Public Library. *New Zealand*

Donald Bruce McKeon
Tallahassee, Florida. *Jacques-Charles Brunet*

Haynes McMullen
Professor Emeritus, School of Library Science, University of North Carolina at Chapel Hill. *R. R. Bowker*

Jean Médioni
Associate Director, Cantonal and University Library of Lausanne, Switzerland. *Switzerland*
Victor Ubaldo Mendieta Ortiz
University of Panama, El Dorado. *Panama*

Francis L. Miksa
Professor, Graduate School of Library and Information Science, University

of Texas at Austin. *Charles Ammi Cutter; John Eaton*

Marion A. Milczewski
Former Professor, University of Washington School of Librarianship, Seattle (d. 1981). *Carl H. Milam*

Arthur H. Miller, Jr.
College Librarian, Lake Forest College, Illinois. *Collection Development*

Marilyn L. Miller
Associate Professor, School of Library Science, University of North Carolina at Chapel Hill. *May Hill Arbuthnot; Children's Services*

Betty L. Milum
Reference Librarian, Ohio State University, Lima, Ohio. *Luther Evans*

Shanti Mishra
Chief Librarian, Tribhuvan University, Kathmandu. *Nepal*

Thornton W. Mitchell
North Carolina State Archivist, Retired. *Margaret Norton*

Ownali Nurdin Mohamedali
Head, Department of Library Studies, University of Zambia, Lusaka. *Zambia*

Foster E. Mohrhardt
Arlington, Virginia. *Fred C. Cole*

Margaret E. Monroe
Professor Emeritus, University of Wisconsin–Madison. *Adult Services; Douglas Waples*

Nick Moore
Project Officer, Research and Development Department, the British Library, London. *Public Libraries: Measurement and Evaluation*

Paul H. Mosher
Deputy Director of Libraries, Stanford University, California. *Academic Libraries: Collections*

Julie Glienna Mueller
University of Chicago, Illinois. *Henry Bliss*

W. A. Munford
Librarian Emeritus, National Library for the Blind, Cambridge, England. *Theodore Besterman; George Birkbeck; James Duff Brown; Edward Edwards; John Passmore Edwards; Richard Garnett; Sir John Young Walker MacAlister*

Gerhard Munthe
Riksbibliotekar, National Office for Research and Special Libraries, Oslo, Norway. *LIBER; Harald L. Tveterås*

Reuben Musiker
University Librarian and Professor of Librarianship and Bibliography, University of the Witwatersrand, Johannesburg. *South Africa*

Steve S. Mwiyeriwa
University Librarian, University of Malawi Libraries, Zomba. *Malawi*

Margaret Myers
Director, Office for Library Personnel Resources, American Library Association, Chicago. *Profession of Librarianship*

William Z. Nasri
Associate Professor, School of Library and Information Science, University of Pittsburgh; Copyright Consultant. *Copyright*

Ildar K. Nazmutdinov
Deputy Chief, Library Department, Ministry of Culture, U.S.S.R. *Union of Soviet Socialist Republics*

John Ndegwa
University Librarian, University of Nairobi. *Kenya*

Waly Ndiaye
Conservator, Archives of Senegal, Dakar. *Senegal*

Diane M. Nelson
Junior Research Fellow, Department of Asiatic Art, Museum of Fine Arts, Boston. *Li Ta-chao*

Robert B. Nelson
President, Wilson/Cambridge, Cambridge, Massachusetts. *Li Ta-chao*

M. Lynne Neufeld
Vice President, Network Development, Easynet, Narberth, Pennsylvania. *Abstracting and Indexing*

Donald E. Oehlerts
Director of Libraries, Miami University, Oxford, Ohio. *Stephen McCarthy*

Felicia Adetowun Ogunsheye
Professor of Library Studies, University of Ibadan, Nigeria. *Simeon B. Aje*

James G. Ollé
Lecturer in Library History, University of Technology, Loughborough, England, Retired. *Louis Stanley Jast; Gabriel Naudé; Sir Anthony Panizzi; Ernest A. Savage; A. J. Walford*

Oneida R. Ortiz
Librarian and Library Consultant, Guaynabo, Puerto Rico. *Puerto Rico*

Cyril Outerbridge Packwood
Head Librarian, The Bermuda Library. *Bermuda*

Guillermo Palma R.
Librarian, Institute of Nutrition of Central America and Panama, Guatemala City. *Guatemala*

George C. Papademetriou
Director of the Library, Hellenic College/Holy Cross Greek Orthodox School of Theology, Brookline, Massachusetts. *Greece*

Anne Pellowski
Former Director, Information Center on Children's Cultures, U.S. Committee for UNICEF, New York. *UNICEF*

Luisa Cárdenas Perez
Director, Education Library, Ministry of Education, Managua. *Nicaragua*

Trudy Huskamp Peterson
Archivist, National Archives and Records Administration, Washington, D.C. *Archives: Education and Research*

Günther Pflug
Director General, Deutsche Bibliothek, Frankfurt. *Federal Republic of Germany*

Patricia Barbara Pieterse
Principal Librarian, Estorff Reference Library, Windhoek. *Namibia*

Harold T. Pinkett
Chief, Legislative and National Resources Branch, National Archives and Records Administration, Washington, D.C. *Archives: Services to Users*

Irwin H. Pizer
University Librarian for the Health Sciences, University of Illinois at Chicago. *Medical Libraries: Purposes, Goals, and Objectives*

Peter Andrews Poole
Director, Center for International Studies, Old Dominion University, Norfolk, Virginia. *Kampuchea; Laos*

Angela I. Popescu-Brădiceni
Director, Central State Library, Bucharest. *Romania*

Vladimir Popov
Deputy Director, Cyril and Methodius National Library of Bulgaria, Sofia. *Bulgaria*

Alain-Michel Poutou
Champs sur Marne, France. *Central African Republic*

Luella Powers, O.P.
Professor Emeritus, Graduate School of Library Science, Rosary College, River Forest, Illinois. *Carleton B. Joeckel*

Luwarsih Pringgoadisurjo
Director, National Scientific Documentation Centre, Jakarta. *Indonesia*

Serafin D. Quiason
Director, National Library of the Philippines, Manila. *Philippines*

Julio Aguirre Quintero
Library Consultant, Bogotá, Colombia. *Bolivia*

Naimuddin Qureshi
Head, Periodicals Department, Huntington Park Regional Library, Los Angeles County Public Library System, Fullerton, California. *Anis Khurshid*

Winifred A. Ragsdale
Director, George G. Stone Center for Books and Lecturer in Children's Literature, Claremont Graduate School, Claremont, California, Retired. *Francis Clarke Sayers*

Ruth R. Rains
Associate Professor, University Film Center, University of Illinois at Urbana. *Audiovisual Services*

T. N. Rajan
Scientist, Indian National Scientific Documentation Centre, New Delhi. *B. S. Kesavan*

H. Kay Raseroka
University Librarian, University of Botswana, Gaborone. *Botswana*

Neil Ratliff
Secretary General, International Association of Music Libraries, Archives and Documentation Centers, College Park, Maryland. *International Association of Music Libraries, Archives and Documentation Centres*

Juliette Ratsimandrava
Chief, Documentation Service, Ministry of Scientific Research, Antananarivo. *Madagascar*

W. Boyd Rayward
Formerly Dean, Graduate Library School, University of Chicago. *International Library and Bibliographical Organizations; John Wallace Metcalfe; Andrew D. Osborn; Paul-Marie-Ghislain Otlet*

C. Reedijk
Chief Librarian, Royal Library, The Hague. *Leendert Brummel*

Marion T. Reid
Associate Director for Technical Services, Louisiana State University Libraries, Baton Rouge. *Acquisitions*

Paulina Retana
Chief Librarian, Technical Institute of Costa Rica, Cartago. *Costa Rica*

James R. Rettig
Head, Reference Department, Main Library, University of Illinois at Chicago. *Reference and Information Services*

James B. Rhoads
Honorary President, International Council on Archives, Bellingham, Washington. *International Council on Archives*

Phyllis A. Richmond
Emeritus Professor, Case Western Reserve University, Cleveland, Ohio. *Eva Verona*

Morris Rieger
Counselor to the President and Chairman, Committee on Archival Development, International Council on Archives, Bethesda, Maryland. *Archives: Nature, Goals, Principles*

Constance Rinehart
Assistant Dean and Professor, School of Library Science, The University of Michigan, Ann Arbor. *Margaret Mann*

Jane Robbins-Carter
Professor and Director, School of Library and Information Studies, University of Wisconsin–Madison. *Library Education: Curriculum*

David D. Roberson
Senior Filtration Engineer, James River Paper Company, Richmond, Virginia. *William J. Barrow*

Jean Claude Roda
Director, Central Library of Prêt des Yvehries, Versailles, France. *Seychelles*

Frank Bradway Rogers
Librarian Emeritus, University of Colorado Medical Center, Denver. *John Shaw Billings*

Samuel Rothstein
Professor, School of Library, Archival and Information Studies, University of British Columbia, Vancouver. *Canada; Elizabeth Homer Morton*

Gotthard Rückl
Director, Central Institute for Librarianship, Berlin. *German Democratic Republic*

Bendik Rugaas
Director, Royal University Library, Oslo, Norway. *Wilhelm Munthe*

James E. Rush
President, James E. Rush Associates, Inc., Powell, Ohio. *Library and Information Science Research*

Paul A. Saenger
George A. Poole III Curator of Rare Books, The Newberry Library, Chicago. *Renaissance Libraries*

William Saffady
Vanderbilt University, Nashville, Tennessee. *Micrographics*

Armando Samper
Director General, Sugar Cane Research Center of Colombia, Bogotá. *Daniel Samper Ortega*

Lars-Erik Sanner
Director of the Libraries, Stockholm University. *Scandinavian Federation of Research Librarians*

D. Gail Saunders
Director of Archives, Ministry of Education, Nassau. *Bahamas*

C. James Schmidt
Vice President, Research Libraries Group, Stanford, California. *Academic Libraries: Measurement and Evaluation*

Hans Georg Schulte-Albert
Associate Professor, School of Library and Information Science, University of Western Ontario, London, Ontario. *Gottfried Wilhelm Leibniz*

Mortimer D. Schwartz
Professor and Associate Dean for the Law Library, University of California at Davis. *Law Libraries: Administration, Governance, and Finance*

Edith Scott
Former Chief Instructor, Cataloging Instruction Office, Library of Congress, Washington, D.C. (d. 1983). *J. C. M. Hanson; Charles Martel*

JoAn S. Segal
Executive Director, Association of College and Research Libraries, American Library Association, Chicago. *Bibliographic Networks and Utilities*

Emmanuel Serugendo
Head of Reference Division, Library of the Campus of Butare, National University of Rwanda, Butare. *Rwanda*

Shmuel Sever
Director, University Library, and Chairman, Department of Library Studies, University of Haifa. *Israel*

Russell Shank
University Librarian, University of California at Los Angeles. *Charles Coffin Jewett; Robert G. Vosper*

Nasser Sharify
Dean and Professor, Graduate School of Library and Information Science, Pratt Institute, Brooklyn, New York. *Iran; Maurice Tauber*

Homayoun Gloria Sharify
Periodicals Librarian, C. W. Post College, Long Island University. *Iran*

Dennis F. Shaw
Keeper of Scientific Books, Radcliffe Science Library, Oxford University. *International Association of Technological University Libraries*

Spencer G. Shaw
Professor, Graduate School of Library and Information Science, University of Washington, Seattle. *Augusta Baker*

Jesse H. Shera
Former Dean, Case Western Reserve University, Cleveland (d. 1982). *Pierce Butler; Philosophy of Librarianship*

Gerald R. Shields
Assistant Dean, School of Library and Information Studies, State University of New York at Amherst. *David H. Clift*

Ritva Sievänen-Allen
Librarian, Central Medical Library, Helsinki. *Finland*

Ivan Sipkov
Editor-in-Chief, International Journal of Legal Information, Washington, D.C. *International Association of Law Libraries*

A. E. Skinner
Former Chemistry Librarian, University of Texas at Austin (d. 1985). *H. W. Wilson*

Elaine F. Sloan
Dean, Indiana University Libraries, Bloomington. *Academic Libraries: Library Cooperation*

Geoffrey Smith
Director, Leicestershire Libraries and Information Service, Loughborough, England. *Frederick A. Thorpe*

Malcolm Smith
Deputy Head, Document Supply, British Library Lending Division, Boston Spa, England. *Resource Sharing*

Wilfred Irvin Smith
Dominion Archivist, Public Archives of Canada, Ottawa, Ontario. *Archives: Archives Management*

Soemartini
Director, National Arhives of Indonesia, Djakarta. *Harsya W. Bachtiar*

Joseph S. Soosai
Chief Librarian, Rubber Research Institute of Malaysia, Kuala Lumpur. *D. E. K. Wijasuriya*

Jutta Sørenson
Lecturer, Royal School of Librarianship, Copenhagen. *Derek Austin*

Claud Glenn Sparks
Professor of Library and Information Science, University of Texas at Austin. *William Warner Bishop*

Francis F. Spreitzer
University of Southern California, Los Angeles. *Reprography*

David H. Stam
Andrew Mellon Director of the Research Libraries, New York Public Library. *Scholarly and Research Services*

Costas D. Stephanou
Librarian, Pedagogical Academy, Nicosia. *Cyprus*

Yvonne V. Stephenson
University Librarian, University of Guyana Library, Georgetown. *Guyana*

Gordon Stevenson
Associate Professor, State University of New York at Albany. *KarlDziatzko*

Elizabeth W. Stone
Professor Emeritus and Former Dean, School of Library and Information Science, The Catholic University of

Contributors

America, Washington, D.C. *Library Education: Continuing Profssional Education*

Margaret R. Strassnig-Bachner
Austrian National Library, Vienna. *Austria*

Basil Stuart-Stubbs
Director, School of Library, Archival and Information Studies, University of British Columbia, Vancouver. *W. Kaye Lamb; Guy Sylvestre*

Reinaldo José Suarez
Department of Technical Information, National Commission for Atomic Energy, Buenos Aires. *Argentina; Domingo Faustino Sarmiento; Aurelio Zlatka Tanodi*

John B. Sultana
Librarian, National Library of Malta, Valetta. *Malta*

F. William Summers
Dean, School of Library and Information Studies, Florida State University, Tallahassee. *Accreditation; Francis R. St.John*

Ray R. Suput
Chairperson and Professor of Library and Information Science, Ball State University, Muncie, Indiana. *E. I. Shamurin*

R. G. Surridge
Borough Librarian, London Borough of Islington. *Lorna V. Paulin*

Joan E. Swaby
Executive Secretary, COMLA, Mandeville, Jamaica. *Commonwealth Library Association*

Thein Swe
Chief Bibliographer, Louisiana State University, Baton Rouge. *Burma*

Richard J. Talbot
Director of Libraries, University of Massachusetts/Amherst. *Academic Libraries: Measurement and Evaluation*

Sönmez Taner
Information Specialist, Türdok, Scientific and Technical Research Council of Turkey, Ankara. *Turkey*

G. Thomas Tanselle
Vice President, John Simon Guggenheim Memorial Foundation, New York. *Frederic G. Melcher*

Ruth W. Tarbox
Chicago, Illinois. *Mildred Batchelder*

Betty W. Taylor
Professor of Law and Director, Law Library, University of Florida, Gainesville. *Law Libraries: Collections*

Björn Tell
Counsellor to the Swedish Unesco Commission, Lund. *Sweden/*

Marta Terry
Director, Library José A. Echeverría, Havana. *Cuba*

Dennis V. Thomison
Associate Professor, School of Library Science, University of Southern California, Los Angeles. *Theresa West Elmendorf*

James Thorpe
Senior Research Associate and former Director, Huntington Library, San Marino, California. *Henry E. Huntington*

Jacques J. Tocatlian
Director Division General Information Programme, Unesco. *Unesco*

Martha V. Tome
Senior Library Specialist, Department of Education, Organization of American States, Washington, D.C. *Jorge Aguayo; Carmen Rovira*

Anabel Torres
Subdirector, National Library, Bogotá. *Colombia*

Alphonse F. Trezza
Associate Professor, School of Library and Information Studies, Florida State University, Tallahassee. *Library Cooperative Systems*

Helen Welch Tuttle
Assistant University Librarian for Technical Services, Princeton University, Retired. *William S. Dix*

John de Belfort Urquidi
Regional Activities Consultant, International Federation of Library Associations and Institutions, The Hague. *Afghanistan*

Rosa M. Vallejo
Professor of Library Science and Dean, Institute of Library Science, University of the Philippines, Quezon City. *Gabriel A. Bernardo*

Willy Vanderpijpen
Assistant Librarian, Royal Library, Brussels. *Belgium*

Carlo Vernimb
Commission of the European Communities, Luxembourg. *Euronet*

Lawrence Vernon
Chief Librarian, National Library Service of Belize, Belize City. *Belize*

Colette Meuvret Viaux
Honorary Conservator in Chief, Forney Library, Paris. *Gabriel Henriot*

Maria Margaritha Viljoen
Deputy Librarian, Old Mutual Library, Academy, Windhoek, Namibia. *Namibia*

Ernesto de la Torre Villar
Master and researcher, Autonomous National University of Mexico. *Maria Teresa Chavez Campomanes; Juana Manrique de Lara*

Rose L. Vormelker
Adjunct Professor, Kent State University, Cleveland. *John Cotton Dana*

Robert Vosper
University Librarian and Professor Emeritus, University of California at Los Angeles. *Herman Liebaers; Foster E. Mohrhardt*

Frederick H. Wagman
Emeritus Director, University Library, The University of Michigan, Ann Arbor. *Verner W. Clapp*

Ruth W. Waldrop
Executive Secretary, Alabama Library Association, University, Alabama. *School Libraries/Media Centers: Laws and Legislation*

William D. Walker
Director, Medical Library Center of New York, New York City. *Medical Libraries: Services to Users*

Clyde C. Walton
Director of Libraries, University of Colorado, Boulder. *Academic Libraries: Laws and Legislation*

Bruno Wambi
Curator of the Library, University Library, Darien Ngouabi University, Brazzaville. *Congo*

Chen-ku Wang
Director, National Central Library, Taipei. *Republic of China*

Chi Wang
Head, Chinese and Korean Section, Library of Congress, Washington, D.C. *T'ung-li Yuan*

Ruth Warncke
Deputy Executive Director, American Library Association, Chicago, Retired. *Helen Haines*

Frances A. Weaver
Assistant University Archivist, University of North Carolina at Chapel Hill. *Louis Round Wilson*

Robert Wedgeworth
Dean, School of Library Service, Columbia University, New York. *P. T. Sevensma*

Hans H. Wellisch
Professor, College of Library and Information Services, University of Maryland, College Park. *Classification*

Leonard Wertheimer
Languages Coordinator, Metropolitan Toronto Library Board. *Bilingual and Ethnic Groups, Services to*

Herbert S. White
Dean and Professor, School of Library and Information Science, Indiana University, Bloomington. *Mortimer Taube*

John Kremers Whitmore
Program Officer, Center for South and Southeast Asian Studies, University of Michigan, Ann Arbor. *Vietnam*

Wayne A. Wiegand
Associate Professor, College of Library and Information Science, University of Kentucky, Lexington. *Daniel J. Boorstin; United States*

D. E. K. Wijasuriya
Acting Director General, National Library of Malaysia, Kuala Lumpur. *Malaysia*

Margreet Wijnstroom
Secretary General, International Federation of Library Associations and Institutions, The Hague. *International Federation of Library Associations and Institutions*

Billy R. Wilkinson
Director, Albin O. Kuhn Library and Gallery, University of Maryland Baltimore County. *Academic Libraries: Services for Users*

Alexander Wilson
Director, Reference Division, British Library, London. *Public Libraries: Library Cooperation*

Howard W. Winger
Professor Emeritus, Graduate Library School, University of Chicago, Illinois. *Leon Carnovsky*

Francis J. Witty
Professor, School of Library Science, Catholic University of America, Washington, D.C. *Jean-Paul Bignon*

Pat Woodrum
Director, Tulsa City-County Library, Tulsa, Oklahoma. *Allie Beth Martin*

H. Curtis Wright
Professor, Library and Information Sciences, Brigham Young University, Provo, Utah. *Assurbanipal; Callimachus*

Margaret Wright
Senior Sub-Librarian, Rare Books, John Rylands University Library of Manchester, England. *A. W. Pollard*

Arthur P. Young
Dean of University Libraries and Professor, University of Rhode Island. *Ernest C. Richardson; Arthur Fremont Rider; George Burwell Utley*

Ding Zhigang
President, China Society of Library Science, Beijing. *People's Republic of China*

Outline of Contents

This *Outline* is organized under five principal divisions.

Part One, on *The Library in Society,* covers the history and role of libraries from ancient times to the present. In addition to nine major articles on historical periods, 152 articles cover libraries and librarianship in separate articles on the countries of the world. The articles, which appear in alphabetical order in the text, usually include comprehensive statistical information and tables. Biographies appear in the *Outline* under major headings according to period and place.

Part Two, on *The Library as an Institution,* comprises eight major articles on the principal types of libraries and archives. Articles emphasize North America but examples and generalizations are also drawn from various systems in other sections of the world.

Part Three, on *Theory and Practice of Librarianship,* deals with the heart of librarianship. Thirty articles bring together under broad titles the principles and practices of librarianship and information management.

Part Four, on *Education and Research,* in nine major articles covers librarianship, information science, and archival administration. The articles treat the fundamentals of curriculum content and issues in research and education.

Part Five, on *International Library, Information, and Bibliographical Organizations,* comprises 33 articles that describe the growth and development of international information systems and enumerate the key organizations on the international level.

Article titles are set in CAPITAL LETTERS in the following *Outline of Contents.*

PART ONE: The Library in Society

PART TWO: **The Library as An Institution**

PART THREE: **Theory and Practice of Librarianship**

PART FOUR: **Education and Research**

PART FIVE: # International Library, Information, and Bibliographic Organizations

Abstracting and Indexing

This article covers the processes of abstracting and indexing, use of computers in the field, and major organizations. (For theories of classification, see also Classification.)

INDEXING

The American National Standards Institute defines *index* as "a systematic guide to items contained in or concepts derived from a collection (document, group of documents, or set of objects). It is arranged in a known or stated order, usually different from that of the items or concepts within the collection itself." John Rothman in *The Encyclopedia of Library and Information Science* (vol. 11, 1974) provides more of a perspective on the indexing process as "neither strictly an art nor a science, but mixes characteristics of each," and described the operations within the process as

(1) Scanning the collection, (2) analyzing its content, this content analysis being based on predetermined criteria of use of the collection and the index, (3) tagging discrete items in the collection with appropriate identifiers, and (4) adding to each identifier the precise location within the collection where the item occurs, so that it may be retrieved. Additional functions, which may but need not be performed by the same indexer, are: (1) cumulating the resulting entries into a cohesive, consistent whole, (2) establishing rules for the selection of identifiers, (3) establishing a pattern of interrelationship of identifiers (through cross references, tracings, and scope notes), (4) establishing the format of the locator, and (5) determining the physical form in which the completed index is to be published or otherwise made available for use. Note that the process of indexing does not include the actual production (for example, printing) of the completed index; and that the term is never applied to using an index.

Early History. The origins of indexing are found in the arrangement of chapter heads or summaries at the beginning of historical or other nonfiction works, and in concordances to the Bible—probably in existence by the 7th and 8th centuries. Francis J. Witty cites the "earliest approach to an alphabetic subject index" as appearing in connection with a list of the sayings of various Greek fathers on certain theological topics, published in the fifth century and arranged in alphabetical order in the sixth century. Such "indexes" were only sporadic until about the 14th century, when the rise of the university system—and, with it, the passion for scholarly debate—led to increasing need for detailed subject access to past writings. By the 17th and 18th centuries, scholarly books contained indexes more routinely, although choice of terms and order of entries often appear haphazard by modern indexing standards. At about this time, indexes to individual periodicals were also produced.

According to Harold Borko and Charles Bernier, William Frederick Poole is credited with the invention of the "modern" collective index to journal articles, although Bruce M. Manzer cites many earlier European examples. Poole's *Index to Periodical Literature* (1882) was a forerunner to the H. W. Wilson Company's *Reader's Guide to Periodical Literature,* first published in 1901.

Traditional Controlled Vocabulary Indexing Systems. Traditionally, indexing is allied with classification, and has involved a deductive method of organization. Knowledge—defined broadly or narrowly (as within the contents of one book)—is divided into disciplines or subject categories, each category is subdivided, and each subcategory is further subdivided. This process has been used for "back-of-the-book" indexing, periodical indexing, and classifying and indexing a collection of books or documents. For example, in classification systems such as the Dewey Decimal Classification and the Library of Congress Classification, classification numbers are assigned to categories and subdivisions, with allowances for the addition of new subcategories. These systems were originally developed to organize collections of books on shelves in libraries and permit browsing in shelf areas by classification number; an alphabetical list of the hierarchical subject headings used provides an index to the classification number.

As each document is added to a collection organized by a classification system, the indexer makes a decision about the subject content of the document by asking what the document is about. Subject headings and corresponding classification numbers are selected from the lists. This type of indexing is sometimes referred to as "indexing by assignment," because subject headings are assigned to the document. The vocabulary in this type of system is controlled, and subject terms are linked together (bound, or pre-coordinated) to represent a discipline or subcategory of a discipline (such as 20th-Century French Literature). The indexer selects subject headings that best describe the document and that will later be ones likely to be used by those who try to retrieve the document.

Natural Language Systems. After World War II, there was a shift from the exclusive use of traditional indexing systems with controlled vocabulary to systems using uncontrolled vocabulary in the form of natural language. It was precipitated by the large increase in the number of technical reports issued during the war, and by the need to identify quickly those reports—as well as journal articles (rather than books)—that contained current information in science and technology.

Mortimer Taube, a principal figure in the movement toward natural language systems, developed the idea of "uniterms" in the United States. Taube noted that only a portion of the documents added to a collection are ever used and argued that time and effort should be put into retrieving documents at the output stage, in response to a request, rather than into costly indexing procedures at the input stage.

In Taube's system, the choice of subject terms for a document was based on the author's words—in the title or abstract—rather than the indexer's. Thus the indexer no longer asked what the document was about, but instead extracted terms from the document itself. This type of indexing is frequently referred to as "indexing by extraction" because terms are extracted from the document, rather than being assigned by an indexer.

As the new type of indexing put the responsibility for joining or coordinating terms upon the user of the collection at the output stage, these new systems were called post-coordinate indexing, as distinguished from the traditional pre-coordinate indexing systems.

Types. Traditional controlled vocabulary indexing systems, as mentioned above, use subject headings consisting of words joined together, or pre-coordinated. Examples of this type of indexing include subject headings used for locating books in library catalogues, back-of-the-book indexes, and some collective periodical indexes that use hierarchical subject headings. Other types of indexing systems use as terms the natural language of documents; many were designed specifically for technical report collections and for indexing journal articles. They include concept coordination and rotated and permuted indexing systems.

"Concept coordination" indexing systems list document numbers grouped under the keywords that were assigned to each document. As each new document is received, the natural language keywords are extracted from it, and the number for the document is listed on the card or part of the file for that keyword. To find the documents on subjects A and B, the cards or sections of the file for A and B are examined, and the lists of document numbers are compared to see which document numbers appear in both places. The Cross Index formerly published in *Biological Abstracts* and manual concept coordination cards are two examples of this type of index.

Rotated indexes are most frequently seen as Key Word in Context (KWIC) or Key Word Out of Context (KWOC) indexes, produced by rotating each significant word in the title of a document so that it appears alphabetically in the index. This type of index is comparatively inexpensive to produce because no intellectual effort is needed and it can be produced quickly. However, there is no control over the vocabulary, and synonyms appear in different places and—because many titles are not very meaningful or complete—a subject approach only through the words in the title may be insufficient. The Institute for Scientific Information's *Permuterm Subject Index* is a classic permuted index in that each significant word in a title is linked with each "co-term," which is every other significant word in the title. However, rotated indexes do not necessarily link the words in the title with each other. Most rotated and permuted indexes are produced by computer.

Citation Indexes. Examples of completely different kinds of computer-generated indexes produced by the Institute for Scientific Information (ISI) are *Science Citation Index, Social Science Citation Index,* and *Arts and Humanities Citation Index.* A search of this type provides answers to the following inquiries: "What scholarly papers have cited paper X (or author X) in a given time period?" This kind of index is ideally suited to machine generation, because the input can be provided by a clerk who identifies the footnotes and references at the end of each document and keyboards them directly into the computer. There may be little editing of the references, and no subject decisions are necessary as to what the document is "about." This form of index is particularly useful for searches in interdisciplinary subject areas. It has its roots in the citation indexes developed for the legal profession and can be related to traditional concordances.

Thesauri. A thesaurus is a listing of terms for indexing (which have not been pre-coordinated) showing relationships among terms, specifically the generic relationship of broader and narrower terms and other relationships of synonyms and related terms. The listing may be alphabetical, hierarchical (tree-structure), or both. In a "classic" thesaurus, the terms are derived from the natural language of the documents to be indexed. The hallmark of a true thesaurus, however, is the precise definition of broader and narrower terms. This generic relationship must always be true if it is to be established as a broader-narrower relationship in a thesaurus.

Although certain lists of subject headings may look like a thesaurus (and sometimes are called "thesauri"), they differ from a true theasurus in that they use pre-coordinated subject headings that are derived by dividing a subject area into divisions; such lists are not based on natural language keywords. Other term lists sometimes called "thesauri" are based on natural language, but do not specify broader term-narrower term relationships.

Thesauri began to be built in the late 1950s and early 1960s as a means for developing term lists for post-coordinate indexing systems, term lists that would be based on natural language and would control for synonyms, but would not have a pre-coordinated structure. By the 1980s, a number of indexing systems used thesauri; however, other less rigorously developed term lists were more widely used. Thesauri are time-consuming and costly both to build and to maintain because terms need to be added, deleted, or changed.

Standards. A useful and comprehensive set of guidelines for thesauri is the American National Standards Institute standard *Guidelines for Thesaurus Structure, Construction, and Use* (ANSI Z39.19-1980). This standard presents rules and conventions for the structure, construction, and maintenance of a thesaurus of terms, and also may serve as an aid in using existing thesauri.

There is no single standard for indexing, primarily because there are so many types of indexes and indexing systems. The ANSI standard *Basic Criteria for Indexes* (Z39.4-1984) addresses a number of useful factors and guidelines, independent of any specific system. Nearly all established, long-term indexing systems have their own manuals of guidelines and standards.

ABSTRACTING

"An abstract is an abbreviated, accurate representation of the contents of a document," as defined by the American National Standards Institute. As Ben Weil and his colleagues have noted, there is a constant thread throughout many definitions of *abstract* and its synonyms of "'fewer words, yet retaining the sense'; 'condensation and omission more or less of detail, but retaining the general sense and unity of the original'; . . . 'a brief or curtailed statement of the *contents* of a topic or a work' and 'part which represents typically a large and intricate whole'" [author's emphasis].

Early History. Abstracts appear to go back to the beginning of writing. Witty makes reference to "clay envelopes enclosing Mesopotamian cuneiform documents of the early second millennium B.C. The idea of the envelope, of course, was to preserve the document from tampering; but to avoid having to break the solid cover, the document would either be written in full on the outside with the necessary signature seals, or it would be abstracted on the envelope, accompanied likewise by the seals." Early Greek plays were abstracted to give the audience a summary of the plot and, according to Borko and Bernier, abstracts were frequently written and used by politicians, religious leaders, and scientists throughout the Middle Ages and up to 1665, when the first abstract journal, *Le Journal des Sçavans,* was published. Abstract journals proliferated in Europe throughout the 18th and 19th centuries and begin in the English-speaking world in the 19th century. Some of these early journals are still being published, although not always in their original form.

Use of Abstracts. In order to sift through the large quantity of literature on any topic to identify documents of interest, a searcher often relies on abstracts to provide summaries of the literature. Abstracts are usually consulted to determine the need for obtaining or reading the complete document and are not intended to substitute for the document.

More specific uses of abstracts have been enumerated by Borko and Bernier as follows: (1) translating into languages other than that in which the original document was written; (2) facilitating selection of documents; (3) substituting for the original document (a point of disagreement between Bernier and most abstracting and indexing services); (4) time-saving; (5) organizing documents in a more convenient and less expensive fashion than can be done with the original documents; (6) retrospective searching; (7) selecting more accurately literature to be read or translated than through titles alone or titles plus annotations; (8) facilitating indexing by concentrating the indexable subjects to speed indexing and by eliminating the language problem; and (9) facilitating the preparation, acquisition, and searching of documents through ease of physically organizing (for example, copying, cutting, and pasting) abstracts. Additional uses include current awareness services and a memory-aiding device to remind a researcher of which articles have been read without need to scan the entire article again.

Types. Types of abstracts are generally defined by purpose, although Borko and Bernier also categorize them by whom they were written and by form. The three most common types are informative (or informational or comprehensive), indicative (or descriptive), and an annotation. These have been defined by Weil et al. as follows:

(1) The "informative," "informational," or "comprehensive" abstract, one that is still complete enough in its distillation "to communicate knowledge." This type of abstract contains the significant findings, arguments, and applications; states the scope; and usually at least indicates such other important aspects of the document as methods and equipment used. . . .

(2) The "indicative" or "descriptive" abstract, usually restricted to descriptive statements about the contents of the document . . .

(3) The "annotation," in which a few words or a sentence are added to a title by way of further description, explanation, or even critical comment. Annotations are usually indicative; it is difficult to make them informative.

Writing Abstracts. Weil and his colleagues provide a clear and succinct description of technical abstracting. They identify four purposes of abstracts and suggest that informative abstracts may well be the most desirable type of abstract because they transmit salient facts from the document rather than simply indicating that certain information exists in it.

They provide a list of rules and a description of techniques for writing abstracts. In summary, the first sentence of an abstract should be a topical sentence containing the most important findings, conclusions, and recommendations of the document, and it may serve as a one-sentence abstract of the abstract. If properly prepared, it will contain most of the terms needed for indexing. Brevity is essential, and stock phrases should be avoided. Direct statements in the active voice are preferred.

Standards for Abstracts. The most comprehensive official standard for abstracts is the *American National Standard for Writing Abstracts,* which was approved in 1970 and revised in 1979 (ANSI Z39.14-1979). The abstract of the revision summarizes the recommendations as follows:

Prepare an abstract for every formal item in journals and preceedings, and for each separately published report, pamphlet, thesis, monograph, and patent. Make the abstract as informative as the nature of the document will permit, so that readers may decide quickly and accurately whether they need to read the entire document. State the purpose, methods, results, and conclusions presented in the original document, either in that order or with initial emphasis on findings (results and conclusions). . . .

Make each abstract self contained, since it must be intelligible without reference to the document itself. Be concise without being obscure; retain the basic information and tone of the original document. Keep abstracts of most papers and portions of monographs to fewer than 250 words, abstracts of reports and theses to fewer than 500 words (preferably on one page), and abstracts of short communications to fewer than 100 words.

Write most abstracts in a single paragraph, except those for long documents. Normally employ complete, connected sentences; active verbs; and the third person. Use nontextual material such as short tables and structural formulas only when no acceptable alternative exists. Employ standard nomenclature, or define unfamiliar terms, abbreviations, and symbols the first time they occur in the abstract.

When abstracts are employed in access publications and services, precede or follow each abstract with the complete bibliographic citation of the document described. Include pertinent information about the document itself (type, number of tables, illustrations, and citations) if this is necessary to complete the message of the abstract; here, complete sentences need not be used.

COMPUTERS IN INDEXING AND ABSTRACTING

Computers have been used since the 1950s to produce indexes of all types, although much less work has been done in using computers to abstract. Several studies indicate that computers are being used to prepare *extracts,* rather than true *abstracts.* Results range in quality from fairly good to disappointing, primarily because of problems related to the complexity of the language itself and the need for human intervention to interpret and edit the abstracts.

Several types of indexes have been produced by

computer, including the KWIC, KWOC, and citation indexes mentioned previously. Also, many abstracting and indexing (A&I) services and freelance book indexers use computers as aids to human indexing and to detect spelling errors and perform routine functions. In most cases, however, human beings still perform the majority of the tasks associated with subject indexing.

In the 1960s new computer-driven photocomposition techniques, used for printing A&I publications, led to the development of computer-searchable A&I databases. With the capacity of making the complete abstract, title, and indexing terms available for computer searching, indexing entered a new era. The computer can provide an "index" to every word, author's name, word in a journal title, and so on, that is captured by the computer system.

Questions have arisen as to whether expensive indexing is really necessary with this new capability. Problems of synonyms, variations in spelling of the same word, and multiple-language databases are taking on new dimensions. So far, most database equivalents of print A&I publications have retained the index terms.

With the newer full-text databases, the usefulness of abstracts has also come into question. Russell J. Rowlett and others have argued that, at least in the near future, abstracts will continue to act as a "well-used filter" for the searcher.

MAJOR ORGANIZATIONS

Several organizations are involved to some extent in the fields of indexing and abstracting, including the large professional and educational associations such as the American Library Association and the American Society for Information Science. Most prominent among those organizations devoted to the field in North America are the American Society of Indexers (ASI) and the National Federation of Abstracting and Information Services (NFAIS).

ASI is a national nonprofit organization for indexers and those employing indexers, with about 550 members in 1985 throughout the U.S. and Canada. ASI is concerned with all forms of indexing, both manual and computerized. Its activities include meetings, workshops, and publications, and it presents an award in cooperation with the H. W. Wilson Company for excellence in indexing. Among its publications is the *Register of Indexers,* an annual self-selected listing of individuals available to do indexing. The Society of Indexers is a similar organization in Great Britain; ASI, the Australian Society of Indexers, and the Indexing and Abstracting Society of Canada are all formally affiliated with the British group, and all share in publishing a journal, *The Indexer.*

The National Federation of Abstracting and Information Services is an umbrella organization of nearly 50 organizations, most producing abstracting, indexing, or databases in a variety of subject areas and formats. NFAIS fosters, encourages, and improves the documentation of the world's information resources and tries to promote the exchange of information between the United States and other countries. Founded in 1958, it concentrates its activities in the area of educational seminars, an annual conference, publications (including an *Abstracting and Indexing Career Guide* and *Indexing and Searching in Perspec-*

tive), a bimonthly newsletter, active participation in standards development, and research. NFAIS is frequently called upon to represent the abstracting, indexing, and database producer community in national efforts such as the Network Advisory Committee of the Library of Congress and the CONversion of SERials (CONSER) project. The Federation also plays a role in international activities, such as the Institute for International Information Programs, headquartered at the University of Maryland. It contributed to the work of the U.S. National Committee for the Unesco/General Information Program (Unesco/PGI) and the International Council of Scientific Unions Abstracting Board (ICSU-AB).

REFERENCES
Harold Borko and Charles L. Bernier, *Abstracting Concepts and Methods* (1975).
Borko and Bernier, *Indexing Concepts and Methods* (1978).
Edward T. Cremmins, *The Art of Abstracting* (1982).
Bruce M. Manzer, *The Abstract Journal, 1790–1920: Origin, Development and Diffusion* (1977).
Russell J. Rowlett, Jr., "Abstracts, Who Needs Them?" In M. Lynne Neufeld, Martha Cornog, and Inez L. Sperr, editors, *Abstracting and Indexing Services in Perspective: Miles Conrad Memorial Lectures 1969–1983* (1983).
B. H. Weil, I. Zarember, and H. Owen, "Technical Abstracting Fundamentals," *Journal of Chemical Documentation* (1963).
Francis J. Witty, "The Beginnings of Indexing and Abstracting: Some Notes Toward a History of Indexing and Abstracts in Antiquity and the Middle Ages," *The Indexer* (1973).

M. LYNNE NEUFELD;
MARTHA CORNOG

Academic Libraries

PURPOSES, GOALS, AND OBJECTIVES

Academic libraries reflect the development of the colleges and universities of which they are a part. These libraries, integral parts of the institutions they serve, design their collections and services to meet the instructional programs of the particular institution. The program of the academic library varies depending upon whether the institution is a doctoral-granting research institution; a comprehensive university or college that offers a liberal arts program as well as several other programs such as engineering or business administration; a liberal arts college; a two-year college or institute; or a specialized institute such as a technical college, theological school, or medical, law, or other professional school. In some countries, particularly countries of the Third World, university libraries have a responsibility to serve as national libraries in addition to the role of service to the faculty and students of the institutions. They play leading roles in national library development.

The basic assumption governing the growth and development of all academic libraries is that the library plays a role of central and critical importance in the instructional and scholarly life of the college or university. In his 1966 report to the American Council on Education, *An Assessment of Quality in Graduate Education,* Allan M. Carter wrote,

> The library is the heart of the university; no other single non-human factor is as closely related to the quality of graduate education. A few universities with poor library resources have achieved considerable strength in several

University Library, Graz

Main reading room of the University Library, Graz, Austria.

T. Charles Erickson, Yale University, Office of Public Information

Circulation desk at Sterling Memorial Library, Yale University.

departments, in some cases because laboratory facilities may be more important in a particular field than the library, and in other cases because the universities are located close to other great library collections such as the Library of Congress and the New York Public Library. But institutions strong in all areas invariably have major national research libraries.

Of the some 2,800 institutions of higher education in the United States, about 200 are doctoral-granting research universities. Most of the universities were originally founded as colleges, and almost without exception each university library developed into a great central library out of the original college library. The central library was supplemented by specialized libraries serving the professional schools. The libraries in the universities offer services that facilitate the use of recorded information in all formats. The records that permit access to the collections are designed to be complete, consistent, and in conformity with national bibliographic standards. The collections in university libraries include those materials necessary for direct support of the university's instructional programs at both the graduate and undergraduate levels. The collections are also designed to be comprehensive so as to support the scholarly efforts of the students and faculty members. With the continued growth of knowledge and the rapid increase in the scholarly literature that results from such growth, no university library is now able to possess in its collections all of the recorded information that faculty members and students may need as they pursue their research; therefore, university libraries have designed formal and informal arrangements for sharing resources. Many developments at the national and international levels are aimed at providing access to library resources regardless of where they might be located.

The primary goal of every university library remains, however, to offer to those who may be said to constitute its primary clientele—the faculty, students, and academic staff of the university—collections of broad scope and depth and specialized and in-depth assistance in the use of its resources. The university library seeks to attain the level of self-sufficiency that is essential to the health and vigor of the university and its academic programs. The library also makes available to its clientele, through various cooperative programs, the resources and collections of other libraries.

The European pattern of a university composed of separate colleges or faculties has been influential in many nations, although to a lesser extent in the U.S., where many universities grew out of individual colleges. In the European structure, each college, faculty, or department might possess its own library, usually dedicated to a particular subject and often administered independently of other libraries on campus. There has been a strong trend toward centralization of university library administration in the U.S.; many departmental libraries are united with a single administrative structure, with various services performed centrally.

There are about 1,500 liberal arts colleges and comprehensive colleges and universities in the U.S., whose libraries are expected to meet the full curricular needs of undergraduate students and to provide for the students' requirements in each field in which the institution offers a Master's degree. The college library makes available standard works representing the heritage of the civilization and works that will enable faculty members to keep apprised of the latest advances in their fields. Unlike research libraries, which are required to keep and maintain retrospective holdings, college libraries tend to weed their collections regularly and systematically.

The two-year or junior college played a minor role in American higher education until about 1910, but by the end of the 1970's, more than 1,000 two-year colleges existed in the U.S. The libraries in these institutions are often called learning resources centers, reflecting the nature of the collections and the types of services provided. Books, periodicals, films, videotapes, pictures, models, kits, and realia form their collections. A much greater emphasis is placed on nonprint materials in libraries serving the two-year institutions than in other academic libraries. These institutions often serve to prepare students for later baccalaureate study or function as centers for technical training in a variety of fields. Styled often as community colleges, they may offer, in addition to training for work as technicians, preparatory courses for further higher education. The subjects taught in some instances reflect the community's particular needs for trained personnel in certain fields. The library resources in these institutions are designed to support immediate curricular needs.

In other countries universities are similarly complemented by institutions for the training of skilled personnel in specific fields. Most evident are schools for training teachers.

Historical Background. The development of higher education in the U.S., although influenced by the English and German traditions, is peculiarly American. From the beginning—1636, which marks the founding of Harvard College—colleges proliferated. In 1900 there were 977 institutions of higher education in the U.S., but 80 percent of those founded before the Civil War had not survived. Rapid growth in numbers of schools meant that only a few colleges could offer the academic leadership needed or the financial security required of a quality educational program. Before 1900 American colleges resembled more the secondary schools of Europe than the European universities; generally, the libraries in these colleges reflected the same low quality, although the library was considered an important part, if not a central part, of every college. Among the nine American colleges established before the Revolution, eight had libraries by 1800.

Unlike Harvard College, which grew and developed into one of the premier universities of the world, most American institutions of higher education have remained colleges. The Harvard College Library started with a collection of books variously estimated at from 260 to 370 volumes bequeathed to the college by John Harvard. It grew to 226,650 volumes in 1876 and 901,000 in 1900. Now a research library of the first rank, Harvard University Library has nearly 11,000,000 volumes. The collections of Harvard, like those of other major university and independent research libraries, are available to Harvard students and scholars. The collections of most research libraries are so rich, however, that the purpose of the library includes extending the use of its collections to the broad community of scholars outside the institution. Although some university libraries in the U.S. are described as great national resources, none fulfills the role of a national library as do many of the university libraries of Europe or other regions of the world.

The collections of the great American university libraries such as Harvard, Yale, and the universities of Illinois, Michigan, and California are prominent and impressive. Also impressive are the rare book collections, the special collections, and manuscript collections of some American college libraries: Oberlin has a fine anti-slavery collection; Amherst College has special collections of Robert Frost and Emily Dickinson; and Bowdoin's collections of Nathaniel Hawthorne and Henry Wadsworth Longfellow are well known. Smith College and Wellesley College have important collections of books and manuscripts relating to women.

Until the middle of the 1800's academic libraries in the U.S., and the collections in them, owed much of their existence to private donors. There was little in the way of systematic collection development. In his 1850 Annual Report, Charles C. Jewett, the Librarian of the Smithsonian Institution, had this to say:

> College libraries . . . are frequently the chance aggregations of the gifts of charity; too many of them discarded, as well nigh worthless, from the shelves of the donors. This is not true of all our college libraries; for among them are a few of the choicest and most valuable collections in the country, selected with care and competent learning, purchased with economy, and guarded with prudence, though ever available to those who wish to use them aright.

The academic library today still receives materials by gift, but the library now relies on purchase as the major source of its materials, with gifts and exchange of materials being relatively minor sources. Collection development is a major component of academic library administration.

Much of the impetus for improvement and change in academic libraries in the U.S. has been provided by private foundations. In 1928 the Carnegie Corporation of New York, seeking a program to encourage the integration of the library into the educational program of the liberal arts college, sponsored several studies of college libraries. Among these studies was a survey of the American college library by William Randall, which described major inadequacies in the book collections of college libraries, as well as in their funding, staffing, and physical facilities. His study prompted the Carnegie Corporation to award 83 grants, for a total of $1,011,000, to college libraries for the improvement of their book collections.

Standards. Randall and the librarians advising the Carnegie Corporation sought but did not find either reliable standards for college libraries or definite and comprehensive statistics, so they prepared their own sets of standards. These efforts led to further work on library standards. The *Standards for College Libraries* were first published by the American Library Association (ALA) in 1959 and were reviewed and revised in 1975 and 1985. *Standards for Junior College Libraries* were published by ALA in 1960; they were reviewed, revised, and published as *Guidelines for Two-Year College Learning Resources Programs* in 1972. *Standards for University Libraries*, prepared jointly by the Association of College and Research Libraries (ACRL, a division of ALA) and the Association of Research Libraries (ARL), were published in 1978. Each of these standards addresses the essential questions of the adequacy of library collections, services, staff, physical facilities, finance, and governance, placed in the context of the educational program and objectives of the individual institution the library serves.

The development and application of standards for academic libraries in the U.S., first promoted by the Carnegie Corporation and interested librarians, has become a major activity of the ALA and other organizations. The adoption of the standards and the voluntary use of them in the evaluation of American academic libraries have led to significant improvement in the quality of collections and services in many academic libraries. Standards have influenced the library standards developed internationally by Unesco. The International Federation of Library Associations and Institutions (IFLA) Section for University Libraries and other General Research Libraries issued "Standards for University Libraries" in 1985. In Japan and some countries of Europe, standards have been developed and adopted by Ministries of Education; the application of the standards may become a requirement for academic institutions, not a voluntary application, as in the U.S., and may be included in national legislation concerning academic institutions.

Academic librarians have sought even better and more objective methods of measurement and evaluation of library services than the expert opinion reflected in the standards. Much of the early work emphasized size of collections, staff, and budget as indicators of quality. More recently, sophisticated techniques have been applied to academic libraries to assist librarians and others in the assessment of the quality of library programs.

Support and Governance. Institutions of higher education in the U.S. are usually grouped according to whether they are funded by private or public monies. About half of the American institutions of higher education are supported by private monies; many were founded by religious groups and continue to be denominational. The constitutional requirement of the separation of church and state has prohibited the use of public funds for direct support of private colleges and universities. Public colleges and universities are supported principally by local and state taxes, and only in comparatively recent years have any federal monies been provided for support of higher education. The advent of federal support has not brought governmental control of colleges and universities to any degree approaching that of the European, African, Asian, or South American colleges and universities. While most colleges and universities in the U.S. remain independent and autonomous, local and state boards of higher education have begun to exert greater influence.

Governance. The academic nature of the college or university influences the governance of its library and the role its faculty and adminstration play in setting policy for the library. Although cooperative agreements and contractual arrangements with other institutions are increasing, and governance of these arrangements is complex, the organizational structure and governance of the library remains based in those of its parent institution. The role of the national government in relation to academic libraries in Europe, by contrast, is much stronger, and governance patterns and structures are influenced accordingly. Librarians have sought greater participation in the decision-making process, and patterns of decision making reflect growing participation. Some libraries

University of Washington Libraries, Seattle

Library of the University of Washington, Seattle, in 1896— 6,780 titles in the attic of the school's only building.

include representation from the library staff in the regular administrative staff meetings. Others have tried to eliminate administrative staff meetings and replace them with collegially based groups. Variations in these governance arrangements result as much from personalities and individual styles as from campus tradition, personal preferences, or imagination. For instance, there may be major differences in governance on the same campus among its schools, colleges, and divisions, as well as among departments or units within a school, college, or division. Librarians looking for a mode of library governance will make a studied selection from among several varieties.

The fundamental issue in the internal governance of academic libraries in the U.S. is the evolution of consensus about which issues are appropriately decided by the administration, which are decided in the forum of the whole (that is, the entire staff of librarians), and which issues are appropriately resolved in organizational units, such as reference, collection development, public services, and technical services.

Most academic libraries in the U.S. and abroad have faculty library committees designed to advise the librarian on matters pertaining to the budget and to the collections; these committees are seldom involved in any issues of internal governance.

Facilities and Growth. Between 1967 and 1975, 674 academic library building projects were completed in the U.S. at a cost of $1,900,000,000. Many of these projects were funded partially from federal funds authorized under the Higher Education Facilities Act. The stimulus of the Act led to the rehousing of a majority of college and university libraries. Private foundations and donors have made many major contributions to the construction of academic library buildings in the U.S. and continue to do so.

The academic library buildings constructed in the U.S. after World War II show a marked change in architectural style from earlier buildings. Modular planning was accepted, and a shift occurred from fixed-function buildings to buildings with functional flexibility. More space was assigned to operation than had been seen as necessary in earlier construction. Many of these changes were proposed as early as the 1930s, when a number of elements were proposed as being important to the design of the successful academic library building: functional and flexible interiors, elimination of load-bearing interior walls, open shelf arrangements, subject arrangements for books, and comfortable furniture. All of these proposals are reflected in academic libraries built since World War II. The open shelf concept continues, but as the preservation of library materials becomes a more pressing concern, academic library buildings built in the coming decades may be designed around stacks that are kept cool and dark and are closed to the public.

Growth in size of collection, staff, and budget require new and additional library space. The predictions of Fremont Rider and others that an academic library's collection would double every 15 years have been fairly accurate. New library buildings and additions to buildings built between 1950 and 1970 were designed to allow space for 20 years of additional growth, but by the beginning of the 1970s it was clear that there would be insufficient money either in the short term or the long term to build all the new academic library buildings needed to match an indefinitely growing number of books.

In the United Kingdom the University Grants Committee, in its Atkinson Report, sought to establish criteria by which the scale, nature, and relative priority of capital projects might be judged. It also proposed a principle of a "self-renewing library of limited growth"; new aquisitions of library materials would be possible only if offset by the same number of withdrawals. The self-renewing principle remains official policy in the U.K., but some change of mind occurred. Capital monies devoted to libraries rose 40 percent (£873,000 in 1976/77 to £5.7 million in 1978/79 and £4.5 million in 1979/80). German librarians sought models to be used in the design of large cooperative storage facilities.

In the U.S. academic librarians explored ways to cooperate with one another more intensively, seeking to reduce the need for more space and larger budgets while supporting the basic purposes of their libraries. One major program of cooperation has emphasized bibliographic access and development of standards of bibliographic control and the automation of bibliographic records. Another effort seeks to design programs of direct access to materials not held by the library supporting the studies of the student or scholar. The Center for Research Libraries in Chicago, the British Library Lending Division at Boston Spa, and the proposed National Periodicals Center in the U.S. are examples of programs of direct access. The private foundations in the U.S., including the Carnegie Corporation of New York, the Council on Library Resources, the W. K. Kellogg Foundation, and the Andrew W. Mellon Foundation have been active in support of these ventures. Efforts will continue to establish cooperative arrangements in academic libraries.

All cooperative activities are designed to support the academic and research libraries in the U.S. and abroad in their efforts to serve students and scholars. Specific services and aspects of collection development are described in sections that follow. Also included are detailed descriptions of the administration and finance of academic libraries, the measurement and evaluation of these libraries, cooperation among academic and research libraries, and the laws and legislation pertaining to academic libraries.

REFERENCES

William Warner Bishop, *Carnegie Corporation and College Libraries, 1929-1938* (1938).

Keyes D. Metcalf, *Planning Academic and Research Library Buildings* (1965).

William M. Randall, *The College Library: A Descriptive Study of the Libraries in Four-Year Liberal Arts Colleges in the United States* (1932).

Fremont Rider, *The Scholar and the Future of the Research Library* (1944).

Louis Shores, *Origins of the American College Library, 1638-1800* (1935).

BEVERLY P. LYNCH

SERVICES FOR USERS

The primary functions of academic libraries are to fulfill both the needs of the instructional programs of their parent institutions and the research needs of students, faculty, other staff members, and people outside the academic community. The services designed by academic libraries to serve their clienteles have developed over many years.

After first gathering a reference collection exclusively for the on-site use of officers and faculty of the academic institution, the library next allowed use by undergraduate students. Wayne S. Yenawine, writing in *Library Trends* (1957), succinctly described the developing service:

> In the pre-Civil War library, the librarian, or someone working directly under his surveillance, determined from discussion with the borrower what was needed from the library collection, charged it to the borrower, and cleared the borrower when he returned the material. Circulation service was the sole reader service. Inherent in the situation was the opportunity for the librarian to know the borrower's need. The librarian also knew his resources, and was thus able to fulfill the need within the limits of materials available and his own competence.

Services have continued to develop into the myriad of activities now found in most academic libraries. In addition to the original sole service—circulation of materials, including interlibrary loans—the other major services are reference/information services, including bibliographic instruction; all technical processes, with their objective of delivery of services for users; and provision of space and facilities.

Circulation Services. Contemporary circulation librarians may take as their archetype Otis Robinson, Librarian of the University of Rochester. In the 1876 Bureau of Education Report, *Public Libraries in the United States,* he stressed that a college library is for the use of students, writing:

> Among the first of the privileges to be granted to students is that of carrying books to their rooms, to be used there. To this there are many and serious objections which, I learn, are allowed to prevail at several colleges of good standing, viz, the books are worn out; some are never returned; they are not in the library when wanted for consultation. These and other similar objections might have been forcible when books were rare enough to be a luxury. It was doubtless wise, then, to regard the preservation of a library as the chief end of its administration. But now the chief end is its use. If properly used, the wearing out of the good books is the best possible indication.

With this major philosophical shift from conservator to purveyor, American academic librarians have loaned countless volumes to users and have devised record systems to control the daily flow. Manual systems of ledgers and card files formed the first circulation records. By the mid-1970s automated systems were available and successful automated installations were made in various types and sizes of libraries. Larger, integrated computer systems (with circulation as one module) were installed in the 1980s in large and medium-sized academic libraries. However, in both the U.S. and other countries, manual systems were still predominant. It will take a substantial reduction in costs, as well as more funding, before most small academic libraries can afford automated systems.

Academic libraries have also extended borrowing privileges to unaffiliated persons. The most formal, if not the earliest, method of serving the unaffiliated is the ALA *National Interlibrary Loan Code.* Building on the medieval European idea of the community of scholars in which each member felt the responsibility to make his own or others' works available to a serious fellow scholar, American librarians in 1917 first formally codified the process of lending unusual volumes not available in the requesting library. This interlibrary loan system, as it was designed and has developed, did place restrictions on the kinds of materials lent to other libraries (for example, manuscripts, rare books, current issues of magazines and newspapers, and low-cost in-print volumes were excluded). The system once excluded interlibrary lending to undergraduate students, reserving this particular service for faculty members and graduate students.

Perhaps learning from their users, who have developed their own informal means of access to the holdings of libraries with which they are not affiliated, contemporary academic libraries have designed simple but effective reciprocal borrowing plans. At the present stage of development, reciprocal borrowing plans are usually parochial (that is, a small number of academic libraries lend directly to all students and faculty of those nearby institutions who have joined in the plan, on presentation of proper identification). Reciprocal borrowing, like interlibrary loan, accounts for only a very small portion of the total circulation in all libraries that participate. The development of automated online bibliographic systems will lead to an even greater and more extensive direct sharing of resources, no longer tied to one city or a part of it but expanded to the state or region.

No matter how rapid, sophisticated, and universal circulation services in academic libraries become in the future, these services rest on a manual system—the exact shelving of thousands or millions of individual books and other library materials. The training and supervision of shelving staff and the maintenance of an accurate and continuous shelf reading program will always play a large and essential part in this most basic user service.

Reference/Information Services. A public librarian, Samuel Green of the Worcester Free Library, made the first formal proposal in the U.S. for a program of assistance to readers, as distinguished from occasional aid, in his paper "The Desirableness of Establishing Personal Intercourse and Relations between Librarians and Readers in Popular Libraries," read at the historic 1876 national conference of librarians. Melvil Dewey, the Librarian at Columbia University, actually appointed the first full-time reference librarians, George Baker and William G. Baker, in 1884, as members of the reference department. It is clear the "reference department" meant organized personal assistance, because in answer to a questionnaire in 1885, Columbia responded that two reference librarians were on the staff specially to aid inquirers.

Dewey, ever the prophet, called in 1901 for subject specialization in academic library service in an article in *The Library:*

> In this limited number of great libraries the comparatively modern notion of the reference librarian is bound to develop into what I think we may wisely call the "library faculty." One man cannot possibly do the reference work for a large library from lack of time, and no man since Humboldt presumes to be a specialist on all subjects. A process of evolution is inevitable. As demand and income warrant we shall have reference librarians each limited to

history, science, art, sociology, law, medicine, education, or some other topic till we shall have in the library, as in the university, a company of men each an authority in his own field. Such a corps is obviously best named a Faculty, and for a library, equipped with such a staff of specialists I propose the name of "faculty library." . . . It is certain that reference work must be closely divided if it is to be of high value.

Louis Kaplan for the period 1876–93 and Samuel Rothstein for 1850–1950 recorded the growth and development of reference services in academic libraries. Rothstein is particularly thorough, describing the practices as well as the policies and theories of service. After presenting the conservative (minimal assistance or only guidance), the moderate, and the liberal (full information service) theories of reference service and the continuing professional debate over them, Rothstein concludes that assistance on the scale of the librarian as a collaborator in the research process was not common through 1940. The chief problem was the heterogeneous nature of the demands placed on the library, making it hard to differentiate between services for scholars and services for the more numerous general users. In larger libraries, with thousands of general readers, the great service load often resulted in limited capacity for offering more than minimal aid.

The academic library community in the U.S. has come to place considerable emphasis on two services. One is bibliographic or library instruction, generally regarded as teaching the identification and use of information resources to members of the academic community by librarians in a formal classroom setting. The other is online computer searching of bibliographic or natural language databases.

These are only two of the many activities in academic reference/information services. One-on-one, in-person reference assistance; compilation of bibliographies; supervision of professional and nonprofessional staff members; telephone information service; care of periodicals, government publications, or curriculum materials; interlibrary borrowing or lending;

or one of the other assigned professional, administrative, or clerical tasks are among the responsibilities of the reference/information staff. Robert Balay, reference librarian at Yale, observed in the *1978 ALA Yearbook,* "It would appear that reference work consists of whatever it is that reference departments do."

The profession has strongly believed it was wrong to define reference work as only what goes on in a reference room. Although questions of specialization versus nonspecialization of staff and of centralization or decentralization have concerned academic librarianship and there has been some description of library systems that provide reference/information services to supplement those offered in the local unit, the profession still lacks basic knowledge about users, their information needs, and the uses to which information is put.

Technical Services. The technical processes (searching, ordering, receiving, cataloguing, and preparing library materials for use) have always been a primary service performed in academic libraries. In supporting the instructional and research needs of their students and faculty, academic librarians have attempted to provide maximum access to the collections. In earlier decades staff in technical departments were often accused of a lack of the proper service attitude and a failure to recognize the real purpose of the organization. During the 1960s and 1970s these accusations diminished as the service aspects of the technical processes became predominant. For many reasons—the brightest librarians entering the profession were attracted to the intellectual problems of controlling and gaining access to knowledge, computerization in technical services was a great attraction, or for some other reason—much creative activity occurred. Frederick Kilgour predicted well in 1966:

> The computer, then, will radically change library procedures, particularly those involved in the production of the information store so necessary to reference librarians. In addition, the computer will facilitate the reference librarians' and the users' use of the information store.

Space and Facilities for Users. The academic library building itself may be the most important service for users. The provision of an environment in which the use of library materials for instruction and research can flourish is surely a major goal for academic librarians. American academic librarians, as well as their colleagues in Canada, Japan, Scandinavia, the U.K., and other countries, engaged in truly successful expansions of facilities in the 1960s and 1970s. Many central or main academic libraries were newly designed. At many larger U.S. institutions between 1948 (when the Lamont Library at Harvard College was opened) and the mid-1970s (when funds became scarce), separate undergraduate libraries were built or old main buildings renovated for undergraduate use. There have also been facilities designed especially for undergraduates in Canada and the U.K.

In addition to separate branch libraries, special reading rooms in the central building were developed for such collections as documents, maps, rare books, curriculum materials, manuscripts, microforms, audiovisual materials, or other special types of materials or subject matter. American libraries were influenced by German research universities. Professors wished

Chulalongkorn University

Periodicals reading room, Central Library, Chulalongkorn University, Thailand.

to meet their students where the most important books and journals were available; at first, this was the professor's own private library, then the seminar library. During the late 19th and early 20th centuries, the essential works of a discipline could be contained in a personal collection or in the seminar library—whether it was in a room near the university, as in Germany, or in the central university library building, as in the U.S. With the great expansion of scholarly publishing in the mid-20th century, seminar libraries and their progeny—the branch, departmental, collegiate, and institute libraries—have found it impossible to acquire all the essential materials of their disciplines. The development of interdisciplinary studies has also brought into question the elaborate system of separate decentralized collections. These libraries do provide the basic services of seats for study, storage of, and access to the collections, as well as other services, although they vary widely in quality and sophistication. The integration of separate units into a total service plan benefiting the largest number of users is a matter for the review of each academic institution. Recent progress in automation will make the problems of bibliographic control and lack of knowledge of the holdings of branch libraries fade; in contrast, however, current and future economic constraints may not allow for any duplication of holdings. Local conditions, as well as local politics, provide the appropriate answers.

The Future. Academic libraries will plan for dramatically increased use of microcomputers on the part of users. On American campuses, people will have access to library information using microcomputers in administrative or faculty offices. Similar trends will develop for off-campus users as more faculty, staff, and students acquire microcomputers in their homes. From such workstations, library users should be able to discover library holdings, learn whether desired items are now available, request that these items be held for them, and request purchases or interlibrary loans for items not held.

Plans will also be made for delivery of textual information by microcomputers. For example, telefacsimile transmissions, either from other libraries as interlibrary loans or from local collections, can be sent to remote locations. Reference questions and responses to them can be transmitted through electronic mail systems. Data from various machine-readable databases, and not only bibliographic ones, can also be downloaded. There will be a dramatic increase in provision of specific information as opposed to provision of sources in which that information can be found. This development will be facilitated by improved data storage on digital videodisks. It will be more cost-effective for libraries to purchase large databases on videodisks for local use than to have access to information on remote computer systems. Library budgets will need to accommodate the increasing crossover between what are traditionally called *materials* and *services*. Information needs that were once satisfied by buying a book may be better satisfied by providing a terminal with access to a database. Already, online versions of major periodical indexes are competing successfully with their printed counterparts. Budgeting must be flexible enough to accommodate alternative systems for information access and retrieval.

Foto Estudio Callado

Reading room in the library of the Universidad Católica Madre y Maestra in Santiago, Dominican Republic.

Increased use of microcomputers in libraries will cause a crisis in telecommunications on American campuses. While the demand of expensive long-distance telecommunications may level off, the need for major new local communications networks will rise sharply. Recently installed library computer systems with online catalogue and other modules will be completely inundated by new demand. Within two or three years of installation, lines added to cope with this new demand will also become swamped, because of increases in availability of microcomputers and new services that can be offered to remote locations. In short, universities and colleges will be planning a major telecommunications overhaul for library service within five years.

These changes will be evolutionary, not revolutionary, in nature. They will come to the larger and more highly developed academic libraries first. They will come more rapidly and extensively in the sciences, medicine, and law and more slowly and less extensively in the humanities. For example, Nina Matheson and John Cooper, in their 1982 report, *Academic Information in The Academic Health Sciences Center: Roles for the Library in Information Management*, predict that the "modern resource library" in the health sciences will become an "information management center" where "ice is no longer delivered; instead, there is a refrigeration system for generating ice, storing it, and making it available for use."

After reviewing the current scene and the future of automated access in academic librarianship, there is another certainty—and it will also hold true for the future. As Stanley McElderry observed in a 1976 *College and Research Libraries* article,

What appears to characterize the current stage of development is the application of more rigorous methods of analysis of problems and a more critical assessment of various alternatives. We still face the need for a better understanding of the library as an instrument of instruction and research and the definition of the most efficient and effective way to meet readers' requirements.

Although academic librarians have for years attempted to measure use and to study the effects of library use on the performance of students, little progress has been made. Usually the units of measurement have not been more sophisticated than the number of items loaned, interlibrary loans and receipts, or information questions asked or answered, and have been limited to a single library. Some studies of library use, such as those of Allen Kent and colleagues, have used more sophisticated techniques. Although the results of user studies may be controversial, the late 1980s and 1990s will demand such research.

In tracing the development of services for users of academic libraries, we can notice the small but significant changes in the use of prepositions and terminology. The early writers always discussed services *to* patrons or *to* faculty and students. *Reference work* became *reference service* and then *reference/information service*. Later, the literature shows concern about services *for* readers or *for* users. It is not too much to read into this language a change in attitude from paternalism to service. We may hope that library services will be carried one preposition further as we approach the 21st century. It should be librarians *with* students and faculty—librarians really in touch and truly working *with* users.

This should be possible because of the substantial progress made in the use of computers in libraries. In 1969 Frederick Kilgour wrote in *Library Trends*

> Fortunately for users, the electronic digital computer has immense potential for individual treatment of people and events. One major ultimate goal of computerization of college libraries must be the recapturing of humanization lost when libraries grew beyond the stage of having a staff of a single librarian familiar with all materials in the collection and able to interpret those materials personally for each user. To be sure, this goal may not be achieved until the end of the century, but it may not be achieved even then if it is not defined and established now.

Perhaps the ill-defined reference/information services can join with better-defined (even minutely defined) circulation and technical services at one of the many computer terminals now (or soon to be) in evidence about academic library buildings. The academic librarian will be *with* the user at the terminal, coming full circle to the "sole reader service"; in Wayne S. Yenawine's phrase: the "recapturing of humanization," lost when academic libraries grew so rapidly, will be happening.

REFERENCES

Robert Balay and Christine Andrew, "Use of the Reference Service in a Large Academic Library," *College and Research Libraries* (1975).

Louis Kaplan, *The Growth of Reference Service in the United States from 1876 to 1893* (1952).

Nina W. Matheson and John A. D. Cooper, *Academic Information in the Academic Health Sciences Center: Roles for the Library in Information Management* (1982).

Stanley McElderry, "Readers and Resources: Public Services in Academic and Research Libraries, 1876–1976," *College and Research Libraries* (1976).

Samuel Rothstein, *The Development of Reference Services* (1955).

BILLY R. WILKINSON

COLLECTIONS

"The powerful and steady growth of book collections in individual American University libraries, particularly during the mid-twentieth century, has been a major achievement in American cultural and educational history, it has both matched and fostered the ebullient and questing intellectual life of the universities themselves, and it has been a marvel to many foreign observers."

These words of Robert Vosper are no less valid today than when they were written in 1971, and the growth of academic library collections has also paralleled an enormous increase of new colleges and universities (more than 1,400 new two- and four-year institutions have been established since 1950) and of graduate education as a central program of higher education. A 1965 study of graduate education revealed that the top 25 graduate programs in the humanities were all in the universities with the largest book collections. Scholars need good libraries, and good libraries attract, and help to retain, good scholars.

Collection Growth. The academic library collections of the U.S. are the largest and richest the world has ever known. U.S. academic libraries spent more than $535 million on library materials in 1981–82. Between 1968 and 1977, the number of book volumes held by academic libraries increased 58 percent to a total of 48,442,000 volumes and 4,670,000 periodical subscriptions. In 1984 the 93 U.S. academic members of the ARL possessed 236 million volumes—more than half the total for all U.S. academic libraries. If the 12 Canadian ARL academic libraries are added, the resources of the 105 academic library ARL members totalled 236,197,177 volumes in 1983–84. When this number is compared to estimates of total world book production by the same date (60 to 70 million volumes—no accurate figures exist), the unparallelled strength and scale of North American academic library research resources becomes evident.

The growth of academic library collections has paralleled the development of graduate programs and professionalism as major developments in American universities. These two trends have had an enormous impact on higher education, scholarship, and the evolution of knowledge as an industry in the U.S. In 1876—one hundred years after the nation's founding—collections were still very small. Yale, which now has more than 8 million volumes, then had 114,000; the University of Illinois at Urbana-Champaign and the University of California at Berkeley, each now possessing more than 6.5 million volumes, then held 10,600 and 12,000 respectively. The University of Michigan, now holding more than 5.5 million, possessed 27,500; and Minnesota, now 4.1 million, had 10,000.

By the third decade of the 20th century, graduate programs had begun to transform higher education, colleges were becoming universities, new universities—such as Chicago, Stanford, Duke, and Texas—had been founded, and pressures to expand inadequate academic library collections began in earnest. By the beginning of World War II, academic library holdings, particularly of research libraries, had increased manyfold, especially in institutions on or near the Atlantic seaboard. In the last decade before the outbreak of the war, the collections of the five oldest university libraries grew an average of more than 42 percent and the five youngest nearly 94 percent.

The postwar years continued the prewar trends of the expansion of higher education and graduate programs and the growth of academic library collections, with academic research libraries heading the way. During the 30 years between the 1950s and 1980s, more than 1,000 new two- and four-year colleges sought to build collections adequate to serve their ambitious undergraduate, graduate, or research programs—a massive development still under way. In the meantime, research libraries have continued to attempt to acquire as substantial a part of the world's new publications as possible.

Evolution of Academic Library Collections. Library collections acquire their characteristics over time as the result of many thousands of decisions, some categorical and others individual. The history and nature of collections is largely the result of the cumulation of methods by which the collections have been developed. These methods have varied depending on the public or private nature of the institution, the differing character of academic programs, the degree of local support and funding for library collection development, and the pattern and level of staff support for collection development programs.

Most academic libraries were characterized by the accretion of gifts, both great and small, and through the active guidance and contributions of faculty members. Before the 1930s, most major collections were shaped by gifts and by emphasis on European techniques of collecting, which reflected curricular need and a focus on "serious scholarly material," mostly monographic and serial in nature and quite rigidly defined. The library in this scheme was usually the passive repository of materials thus selected, though university librarians were often active participants in identifying and soliciting major gifts or purchases of materials en bloc. In addition, many academic departments developed their own library collections over the years, under more-or-less direct faculty control. These collections, since the 1950s, have increasingly devolved to the central library system.

From the 1930s on, the nature of collecting and collections changed, largely in response to the new needs of graduate and research programs in the humanities and social sciences. There was increasing emphasis on primary and original source materials, and after World War II on information that could be accumulated, abstracted, quantified, manipulated, and analyzed. Older materials were often as valuable as current materials, increased emphasis on foreign-area studies created new need for foreign titles from nontraditional sources, and the increased study of popular and traditional cultures called for collecting more ephemeral, popular, "gray," or other elusive materials previously excluded from the serious academic library's collecting purview. As the 1960 annual report of one major academic library put it, "Selection of books for a library like this calls for an attempt to foresee the future course of research and to obtain publications that, though they may seem insignificant today, will be wanted by scholars tomorrow."

The Role of Librarians and Gathering Plans. As library collections grew, so staffs grew apace, and larger academic libraries sought ways of making their collecting efforts more systematic and consistent. Most former departmental libraries were either transformed into branches of a central library system or absorbed into the main library collections.

To help the library with its increased collection development responsibilities, and to expend acquisitions budgets that often exceeded the capacity of library staff and faculty to handle wisely and systematically, many libraries developed systems of blanket orders (all books on certain subjects or from certain publishers) or approval plans (the same as blanket orders but with right of return) with experienced dealers or agents. Harvard placed the first blanket order with Otto Harrassowitz of Germany in 1882, and the system became common in the U.S. with the innovations and success of Richard Abel and Co. in the 1960s.

Since the 1960s, librarians have gradually assumed the primary responsibility for library selection, most often with the advice and counsel of interested faculty. While some libraries concentrated this responsibility in acquisitions departments, others developed cadres of library subject specialists, often called "bibliographers," to develop the collections of the central library.

This assumption of the selection function in academic libraries by library subject specialists was one of the most significant developments in librarianship in the postwar years; it has had an enormous impact on the nature and quality of library collections in the U.S., and has helped academic librarians in their quest for professional recognition. It has also helped academic libraries create closer and more reciprocal relationships with the faculties of their institutions.

From Selection to Collection Development. Qualities of entrepreneurialism, competitiveness, aggressiveness, and laissez-faire policies characterized the American academic environment for many generations, and academic libraries tended to acquire publications by wholesale and opportunistic, even piratical, methods. By contrast, European selection methodologies, such as those of Germany (often restricted by inadequate financial resources), have tended to be based on selection criteria that seek to acertain the academic worth of each title selected.

Since World War II, the development of federally supported foreign area programs in American universities and colleges brought a great increase in foreign materials in academic libraries, as well as the accumulation of much gray or ephemeral nonbook material from foreign countries. Despite the initiative of LC and the ARL, substantial amounts of foreign materials are either catalogued very slowly or remain uncatalogued.

Since the mid-1960s the increasing shift of responsibility for collection development to the library from the faculty resulted in the establishment of cadres of subject or area specialists, some of whom carry split assignments as reference or branch librarians, while others form special units or departments in the library. These bibliographers have combined American and European theories of collection development, formed collection development policies to guide their work systematically over time, and codified the links between library collecting and academic program needs. Bibliographers have made collection development in American academic libraries more conscious, selective, and consistent: they have studied, systematized, and regularized other collection management functions such as weeding, analyzing, or evaluating the utility of collections, the systematic study of collection use and users, and the allocation of acquisitions funds.

Collection Management. The evolution of collection development as a major function of academic librarianship has parallelled a concomitant growth of the concept of librarians as stewards of the collections housed in their libraries, but in quite a new way. While once librarians were regarded as the keepers of the books in their possession, they have now become managers of their collections of library materials in a wide range of formats and media including, but not limited to, books. Collection development librarians have come to apply a number of the tools of the social and behavioral sciences to the study of library collections and their users, in order to manage more effectivly not only the development of library collections, but also the collections themselves.

University Library of Uppsala

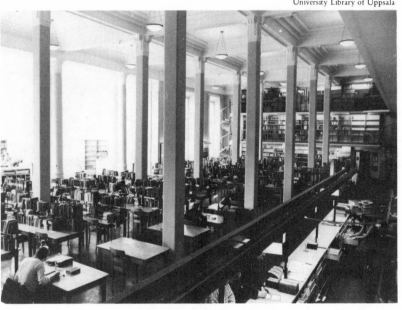

First reading room, University Library of Uppsala, Sweden.

The literature of library science now contains a substantial bibliography of studies on the functions of collection development and management, including (1) collection analysis or evaluation, (2) the preparation and use of collection development policy statements, (3) the study of library use and library users, (4) pruning collections and identifying and moving materials to auxiliary storage, (5) library materials budgeting and budget allocation, and (6) selection of materials for preservation and conservation treatment. While it is generally recognized that the most effective pruning, storage, or preservation decision is made at the time of purchase, the often unsystematic and unthought early growth of library collections and the high cost of maintaining titles in active collection

space have made review of existing collections an important part of the collection developer's job.

ALA's Resources and Technical Services Division conducted a series of collection management and development institutes in various regions of the U.S. during the 1980s to help standardize practice in these areas, and the Office of Management Studies of the ARL sponsored a series of library self-studies of collection development organization and function during the same period.

Cooperative Acquisition Plans. American academic librarians have long recognized that the concept of the entirely self-sufficient library is a myth and that the resources of any single research library cannot satisfy the entire need of that institution's researchers, either in the present or in the future. The evolution of the *National Union Catalog* and national interlibrary loan arrangements recognized this fact, but academic librarians did not begin to band together with the Library of Congress and a few other nonacademic research libraries to assume full national coverage of the foreign publishing output until World War II and its aftermath.

The Interdepartmental Committee for the Acquisition of Foreign Publications, established during the war to provide important library materials to war agencies, was followed by the Cooperative Acquisitions Project (CAP) for Wartime Publications which sought, during the immediate postwar years, to provide materials published during the war years to U.S. academic and research libraries. This project distributed nearly 820,000 book and periodical volumes to participating research libraries. It not only demonstrated the capacity of major U.S. libraries to collaborate in acquiring elusive foreign publications, but also demonstrated LC's capacity to lead such cooperative national efforts.

The ARL, which had promoted CAP, also helped form and support its successor, the Farmington Plan. Stemming from a meeting of the LC's Librarian's Council in Farmington, Connecticut, in 1942, the Farmington Plan for a division of foreign collecting among American libraries was adopted by ARL in 1947. At first limited in scope, the Farmington Plan was extended by the early 1950s to cover the entire world, with increasing emphasis on third world countries. This program continued for 24 years, until it was discontinued in 1972. Despite its significant strengthening of foreign collections in U.S. academic and other research libraries, the plan was weakened over time by growing budgetary constraints and by its inability to accommodate academic program changes on individual campuses.

The Farmington Plan was replaced by a program in which Congress, through an amendment to Public Law 480 and with the encouragement of ARL, supported the use of foreign surplus funds to acquire library materials from foreign countries for selected U.S. research libraries. The emphasis of the program was on non-Western countries, and the program sought to acquire nontrade or ephemeral items as well as trade monographs. This new program, which established the principle of direct federal funding for the support of research library acquisitions from non-Western European countries, provided academic libraries with substantial collections of publications in non-Western languages which, unfortunately, many of the receiving institutions could not catalogue. ARL sponsored discussions with both the LC and Congress itself that led to the passage of Title IIC of the Higher Education Act of 1965, establishing the National Program of Acquisitions and Cataloging (NPAC), authorizing the LC "to acquire, so far as possible, all library materials currently published throughout the world which are of value to scholarship," and to provide cataloguing for the community of academic and research libraries. This pair of programs supported the acquisition of foreign research materials and their cataloguing for another 20 years, until it began to wind down under a combination of pressures, including the exhaustion of U.S. foreign currency surpluses and Congressional efforts to reduce federal budgets during the 1980s. These pressures have all but eliminated the P.L. 480 Program and greatly reduced the LC's foreign language catalogue support for the nation's academic and research libraries. The impact these cutbacks will have on the strength of foreign area collections in U.S. academic libraries is still not fully understood.

New Approaches to Cooperation. Recognizing that past cooperative acquisitions programs and categorical collection efforts have tended to encourage a fair amount of duplication of little-used foreign materials among the nation's major research libraries, the Research Libraries Group (RLG) began a program in 1980 to map the research collections of member libraries using a common framework (based on the LC classification system) and a system of standard codes for collection intensities and languages of materials collected. This system, called the *Conspectus,* is intended to allow improved local and cooperative collection planning and management options through clearer understanding of the collections, collecting efforts, and commitments of other research libraries for more than 5,000 subjects and fields.

The RLG Conspectus has been adopted as a recommended tool for all member libraries by the ARL as the North American Collections Inventory Project (NCIP) and is in the process of implementation with the assistance and support of the Council on Library Resources (CLR) and other agencies. It differs from previous cooperative efforts in its focus on collection development and management rather than blanket acquisitions. It facilitates, supports, and encourages local and consortial planning and economies and is collectively supported by individual libraries rather than depending on federal subsidies. NACIP and the data contained in its Conspectus may also provide a basis for a variety of cooperative efforts in distributed cataloguing of less common foreign publications and in distributing preservation activity and funding among major academic and research libraries.

Collections for Undergraduates. Many early college libraries developed the concept of libraries as centers for both curricular study and self-motivated learning, but university libraries, following the growing emphasis on research and graduate study, tended increasingly to become research libraries whose size, complexity, and intensity were often bewildering for undergraduates. During the 19th and early 20th centuries, "society" or residential libraries were established at many universities and run by students to provide for recreational and basic student library needs. In the relatively clublike atmosphere of prewar academic institutions, this concept appeared to suffice but, in the postwar years, it proved inadequate for the growing legions of undergraduate students who filled U.S. universities, and whose needs seemed quite different from the research-centered requirements of faculty and graduate students. As a result of the improved academic financial atmosphere of the 1960s, a number of universities, such as Michigan, Illinois, Washington, and Stanford, built undergraduate libraries with collections designed to support undergraduate curricular, recreational, and study needs. In addition to concern for undergraduate collections, the staffs of these facilities have also developed programs of library orientation and bibliographic instruction to improve the capacity of undergraduates to study and use the library collections and services effectively.

New Formats. Academic library collections in the U.S. do not consist only of books and journals. Many academic libraries house collections of films, slides, filmstrips, maps, and sound recordings in media collections or centers, usually with equipment and facilities for their use. Recent developments in automation have seen the spread of personal computers and network terminal nodes in academic libraries, and an increasing number of libraries house and circulate software and other automated information packages in their collections. Many libraries are sharing, or even taking the lead, in providing automated information and data facilities and services on academic campuses.

As Hendrik Edelman and Marvin Tatum wrote in 1976,

> The collections of American University libraries have been built with vision, ambition, knowledge, dedication, and large amounts of money. The influence of pace-setters has been great, yet each university library reflects very much the particular academic history of its institution and especially the influence of a relatively small number of scholars and librarians. On balance, it has always been the scholar who has provided the impetus. The librarian has made it possible.

REFERENCES

Richard M. Beazley, *Library Statistics of Colleges and Universities. Trends 1968–1977; Summary Data 1977,* National Center for Education Statistics (1981).

The Bowker Annual of Library and Book Trade Information (1983).

Robert B. Downs, "The Growth of Research Collections," *Library Trends* (1976).

J. Periam Danton, *Book Selection and Collections: A Comparison of German and American University Libraries* (1963).

Hendrik Edelman and G. Marvin Tatum, Jr., "The Development of Collections in American University Libraries," *College and Research Libraries* (1976).

Robert G. Vosper, "Resources of University Libraries," *Library Trends* (1952).

Vosper, "Collection Building and Rare Books," *Essays in Honor of Robert B. Downs,* edited by Jerrold Orne (1971).

PAUL H. MOSHER

ADMINISTRATION AND FINANCE

Patterns of organization and finance for academic libraries in the U.S. tend to be more diverse and less uniform than was the case prior to 1970. A dual pattern common since World War II still predominates—all library activities are described as either reader services or technical services, and each service has in it function- or format-based departments. However, many variations can be found in the design of libraries. Columbia University Libraries underwent a widely publicized major change in 1973, organizing its activities into a resources group, a services group, and a technical support group. Other patterns, such as a subject division plan initiated at the University of Colorado, although not new, continue to be effective. Some of the new patterns of organization are similar in that reader services are no longer grouped under a single manager. The major departure from the dual organizational pattern is based on the reality in many academic libraries that the responsibilities of the public services director have become too extensive. The effect of automation on library activities also has influenced administrative structure. Another characteristic of new patterns of organization is that libraries have relatively flatter structures, with fewer levels in the administrative hierarchy.

Whether a university library should be centralized or not continues to be debated. Columbia has a highly dispersed library system, typical of many of the larger and older universities, while the library of the State University of New York at Albany is at the other extreme—a completely centralized library facility with no branches. The Brown University Library system is moderately decentralized, with five units, three of them integrated organizationally. Some libraries are experimenting with a design in which functional responsibilities transcend locations; for example, the managers who head such functions as reference and circulation are responsible for these functions in all locations. In the usual pattern, the manager in charge at a single location is responsible for all functions at that site. Whether departmental libraries should be separated from the central libraries continues to be an issue of concern, more so in countries such as West Germany and Austria, where decentralization is the predominant pattern of organization, than in the U.S.

Key Issues. The issues faced in designing the organization of academic libraries are not new, but additional insights have been provided by research since the 1960s. The issues include accountability, autonomy and professionalization, optimal use of staff, response to change, technology, and participation in decision making. Some issues can be posed as questions: Do some designs centralize authority or decision making more than others? What are the effective limits on the number of people a manager can coordinate or control? Do some designs enhance utilization of staff? Are some designs more responsive to change? What designs maximize autonomy and professionalism? How has technology affected the organization of libraries? How will it affect organization? Are some designs more hospitable to participatory decision making than others?

Among these issues accountability, in its myriad forms, has had the greatest impact on the recent patterns of organizational design of academic libraries in the U.S. In the area of personnel, formal grievance procedures instituted within the college and university, collective-bargaining agreements, equal-opportunity policies, reporting requirements imposed by the federal government, and other formalized institutional procedures have led to the creation of administrative units whose sole function is to deal with personnel matters.

In financial matters, accounting and audit standards imposed by the institution and growing demands for data supportive of budgets are resulting in the appointment of business managers and budget officers in academic libraries of all sizes in the U.S. The growth in the size and importance of institutional research and the data produced in these activities have had a corresponding effect on academic libraries, both because libraries have to produce more institutional reports and because there are more reports requiring analysis and response.

The cumulative effect of all accountability devices has been to increase the number of administrative staff positions in academic libraries. This is especially true in public institutions and in libraries where the administration has consciously attempted to buffer heads of operating units, such as technical services, public services, acquisitions, cataloguing, reference, and serials, from the encroachment of this administrative workload in order to allow these managers to focus more time and energy on operational and service issues.

Finance. In the 1950s and 1960s libraries in the U.S. received substantial increases in financial resources. By the 1970s budgetary increases were fewer and smaller, and some institutions experienced decreases. The most notable characteristic of the 1970s, however, was the uneven pattern across the country; academic libraries in the northeastern states experienced reductions in base budgets, while those in the Southeast and Southwest received substantial increases. In the Midwest, adjacent states had opposite experiences: academic libraries in one might receive an increase in resources, while in another state libraries suffered a reduction in base budget. By the 1980s most libraries in most states faced cutbacks.

Because of the declining birthrate, the typical college-age individual in the U.S. is becoming a smaller proportion of the total population. There is also some evidence that the percentage of this population that attends college may decline. Thus colleges and universities will be competing for a smaller group of traditional students, as well as reaching into other age groups for potential students. An effect of these demographic factors on finance will be to lower enrollments and to make enrollment-based formulas less workable for budgeting. Beyond the issue of formulas, however, lies the larger question of the level of funding for higher education and its libraries. It is probable that institutional budgets measured on a per-student basis will continue to rise, albeit more slowly. From the expenditure perspective, labor-intensive education will become even more so as personnel costs increase faster than capital costs. Thus, if institutional expenditures become more labor intensive, as personnel costs rise faster than budgets, expenditures in less labor-intensive areas—such as libraries—are likely to suffer.

In the decades ahead academic libraries will begin to receive income from a greater variety of funding sources. Some institutions have long dealt with endowments, alumni, individual donors, foundations, and federal and state government agencies. These sources of revenue will become even more common in more libraries, and added to these will be such others as service fees (for interlibrary loans, courtesy borrowing privileges, database searches, and photocopy and other vending machines), grants from consortia, or cooperative agreements. For librarians at publicly funded institutions this diversity will allow more flexibility than was possible in the past, when nearly all of a library's income derived from appropriated funds.

The development and application of new management tools will continue. Since the mid-1960s academic libraries have adopted various approaches and techniques—such as operations research, performance standards, management by objectives, program budgeting, and zero-based budgeting—to identify with more precision their goals and their progress toward meeting those goals.

The expectation for the rest of the 20th century is for greater variety in the organizational patterns, administrative methods, and financial circumstances of academic libraries in the U.S. than was the case in the 25 years following World War II. This in turn reflects more variety in the nation not only in economic and demographic trends but also in educational, social, and cultural attitudes and institutions.

C. JAMES SCHMIDT

MEASUREMENT AND EVALUATION

Traditionally library administrators have relied on library surveys or crude rules of thumb to measure and evaluate academic libraries. Library surveys are certainly the most popular form of library evaluation. Since Louis Round Wilson designed the first academic library survey to be conducted by an outside team in 1939, the questions addressed by the survey have not changed. They are:

1. Are the library's collections adequate to support the objectives of the university?

2. Is the staff sufficient and does it have the approriate training to carry out the library's programs?

3. Are the library's materials organized effectively?

4. How adequate are the physical equipment and plant?

5. What kinds of administrative relationships exist among the library, the faculty, and the administration?

6. Is the library adequately financed?

7. Does the library engage in cooperative ventures with other libraries in the state and region? (Today we would interpret *cooperative* to mean, at least in part, access to bibliographic utilities and databases.)

A library survey is intended to provide an authoritative assessment of a library. It is based on easily gathered countable data, on which the judgment of the surveyors is to be based. Such techniques are not to be despised; they are commonly employed in academia and elsewhere. But they are inevitably Delphic or prescriptive. They have little empirical foundation, and their credibility depends largely on the prestige of the surveyors. Very often this is what is wanted by academic or even governmental administrators, so these surveys are likely to continue to be performed, even though they provide, because of their weak empirical foundations, a very uncertain guide for library management.

Examples of rules of thumb that library admin-istrators or surveyors employ are: (1) the library should receive 6 percent of the institutional budget; and (2) its own budget should be divided into 30 percent for acquisitions, 60 percent for personnel, and 10 percent for everything else. Such measures really beg the question of measurement because they fail to justify why these rules are valid in the first place. Consequently, librarians have fallen back on comparative measures, and in those cases where they have failed to obtain the kind of institutional support they thought necessary, they have attempted to clothe their comparisons in the form of standards—preferably quantitative standards.

Quantitative Standards. The history of the effort to develop quantitative standards for libraries is long and complex, but the most obvious reason for developing them was best stated by Verner W. Clapp and Robert T. Jordan. "When . . . standardizing authorities omit or refuse to set standards in quantitative terms, the budgeting and appropriating authorities, who cannot avoid quantitative bases for their decisions, are compelled to adopt measures which though perhaps having the virtue of simplicity, may be essentially irrelevant." This statement was written in 1965; yet librarians were not much closer to developing adequate quantitative standards by the mid-1980s than they were then.

The problem is multifaceted, but it tends to resolve itself into three issues, (1) whether quantitative standards for libraries can be created at all; (2) the difficulty of obtaining adequate data; and (3) the necessity to reconceptualize the meaning of library measures to change their focus from a consideration of inputs to a consideration of outputs—that is, from additions to services and collection to measures of performance.

The resistance to the development of quantitative standards on the part of many librarians is based partly on the inadequacy of the data currently available, and partly on the fear that crude general measures will be unthinkingly applied. Typically, what tends to be a minimal standard for librarians and scholars is a sufficient standard for budget officers. The libraries of the larger, wealthier, private academic institutions and some public institutions would tend to be above any threshold level of minimal adequacy, and the application of minimum standards to them would weaken their efforts to continue to provide the services and collections to which their users have become accustomed.

It cannot be denied that presently available data are inadequate. Herman Fussler, for example, observed in his 1973 report, *Research Libraries and Technology,* "Libraries, like universities, tend to have very inadequate analytical data on their own operations and performance. Such data, especially as they relate to costs and system responses to user needs, are critically important in any effort to improve a library's efficiency and responsiveness." Others have criticized the poor quality of library recordkeeping and have challenged the utility of present library data collection, observing that it fails to measure performance or effectiveness.

In fact, the most generally used academic library formula, the Washington State formula, which was adopted in most respects by the ALA as its standard for college libraries, is statistically imperfect and generally inapplicable. It suffers from what statisticians call *multicollinearity:* the explanatory variables used in the formula cannot be isolated, so their effects overlap in ways that defy analysis. While it seems to provide results that in many cases appear acceptable, it is a defective instrument, the use of which cannot be extrapolated to the whole universe of academic libraries. Efforts to apply the formula widely demonstrate a very broad range of variability in the results obtained, so broad that its predictive value is nil. Librarians who seek quantitative standards are then faced with a dilemma. Quantitative measures are needed to analyze what libraries are and to provide a basis for communication about them, but neither presently available formulas nor existing data are completely useful for such analyses.

Comparative and Internal Measures. Two kinds of measures are necessary: a comparison between similar institutions, and a yardstick or set of yardsticks for internal measures. The first is necessary to orient the evaluation within the universe of academic libraries. It is a common habit in higher education to compare one institution with another, and libraries are usually one of the features of such comparisons. The inadequacy of comparative data is troublesome, and the counting methods used by most libraries might better be replaced by standardized sampling methods that would be both easier and cheaper to apply. Nevertheless, the Higher Educational General Information Survey (HEGIS) data, the ARL data, and the collecting efforts of various groups of libraries do provide some basis for comparison despite the limitations of the data, especially if the comparisons are carefully selected so that like institutions are compared on such indexes as size of student body, expenditure per student, and similarity of programs.

Façade of the Nicholas Murray Butler Library, home of the School of Library Service of Columbia University.

Once this comparison is made, simple inspection of the data thus isolated, aided by ranking, ranges, averages, and medians, can provide useful insights for the experienced library manager. Beyond this, a further reduction of data into ratios can occur. Some of those that provide useful insights into library operations are the ratio of professional to nonprofessional staff; expenditure for library materials as a percent of total library operating expenditures; and the ratio of salary expenditures to library material expenditures.

Most academic libraries appear to have a ratio of one professional to two nonprofessional staff members. They expend 30 percent of their total budget on library materials and twice as much on salaries. But these figures are not static; they have meaning only in relation to a comparison group. They are not benchmarks at which every institution should aim, but they do provide a relative standard, a background against which a library can begin to be evaluated, always provided that like is being compared with like.

A more extended form of ratio analysis is Allan M. Cartter's Library Resources Index, which is an average of three indexes: total volumes held, volumes added, and periodicals received. This index represents an effort to define a library factor that can be correlated with other institutional factors. In fact, when Cartter applied this technique to universities in 1963, he found a high correlation between excellence of graduate schools and a high position of the parent institution's library on the index. Anyone who bothers to compare the occasionally reported judgmental survey by scholars on the excellence of graduate schools with ARL library rankings will find that this correlation persisted in the 1980s.

Baumol and Marcus extended the comparative analysis of libraries by the use of regression techniques; Kendon Stubbs, by applying factor analysis to ARL library data, discovered a library factor that underlies most library input variables. Both regression and factor analysis provide more synthetic forms of data reduction and enable the analyst to inspect the interaction of a number of variables. Given the easy availability of computer programs to perform these statistical techniques, they should become more widely used. They remain dependent, however, on the collection of suitable and accurate data. The equations that Stubbs used to isolate his library factor or those that Baumol and Marcus derived to predict total staff, professional staff, volumes added, cost of volumes added, and total library operating costs, were largely based on the total number of volumes a library holds, expenditures per student, number of volumes added, and total expenditures. These are not necessarily the most explanatory library variables that can be determined, nor do they measure all we would like to know.

As statistical techniques, regression and factor analysis are advances over simple ratios, but they cannot provide more information than the data possess. They cannot eliminate the double inadequacy in most library data: inaccuracy of what is counted and failure to measure what is most relevant. There are no precise measures for how and why people use libraries. Library staff only dimly understand what they are trying to measure. This is true both for relative comparative measures and for what in the mid-80s were coming to be known as performance measures. As the name implies, performance measures attempt to determine how well a library performs: Can it deliver a particular item when needed? How fast can it do so? and so forth. Performance measures provide librarians with a completely new kind of measure—a feedback response mechanism that permits a standard of performance to be set, a means of comparison to determine adherence to the standard, and a method for correcting performance if it fails to meet the standard.

Every organization, especially difficult-to-manage public service organizations, would like such measures, provided they are cost-beneficial to apply. Libraries do not yet have an accepted set of them, but some are being developed; the failure to develop them more fully is probably attributable partly to the benign environment in which libraries used to exist and partly to the skepticism of library administrators about their persuasive effectiveness. The library environment is changing, however; socioeconomic and sociotechnological changes are rapidly reshaping the world in which we live. New modes of information delivery compel a reevaluation of traditional mechanisms for information storage and retrieval. These new modes of delivery challenge the existence of traditional libraries and compete for the funds that support them.

Future Trends and Goals. Changes in social objectives and economic conditions have produced a decline in the financial resources available to the parent institutions of academic libraries. Public support for higher education is eroding, and those who predicted a depression in higher education because of the decline in the numbers of college-age youth seemed to be right by the mid-1980s. Higher education faced a crisis in the 1980s, and every facet of its operations was subjected to searching scrutiny; each had to justify its existence in terms of its contribution to institutional objectives.

Libraries are not exempt from this evaluation. The typical library budget is so large a part of the institutional budget that it attracts administrative attention every time inflation moves upward or revenue downward. The persistent pressure of inflation, especially in the prices of publications, makes each library less and less able to maintain its collections, especially its serials. The buying power of library funds has been dramatically reduced, while demands for more publications and different information media have increased. Librarians are driven to ask for more funds in an effort to maintain what they have, while administrators increasingly regard libraries as a bottomless pit that can consume all the resources at their disposal.

Typically, a parent institution sets a limit on the fraction of its total budget that it devotes to the library. That fraction seldom exceeds 6 percent of the total institutional budget and is frequently less. When the parent institution is unable to raise its total budget to keep pace with the rise in the general price level, it is all the more unable to meet library demands. Two trends—the inflation of library materials at a rate greater than the general price level and the inability of most institutions to increase their budgets at the same rate as the general price level—are on a collision course. Everywhere the increase in library budgets is meeting a ceiling, a limit that the parent

Public Terminal Room, part of the student computer facilities in the Margaret Clapp Library at Wellesley College, Massachusetts.

George Don

institution must impose. All this is familiar, but what seems to be misunderstood is that these trends, together with the proliferation of other means of information delivery, will provoke a fundamental change in what libraries can be. Basically, libraries can continue to reduce their collections gradually, satisfying fewer and fewer of the demands made upon them, or they can attempt to redefine their roles, to shift their emphasis from collecting materials to providing information.

The situation demands a redefinition of what academic libraries are. Without such a redefinition it is increasingly difficult to say what is to be measured or evaluated. It is common to remark that libraries are the intellectual heart of the college or the university. Most libraries that have established objectives attempt to translate this idea into practice by defining their principal goals as the support of the educational and research needs of the parent institution. To achieve these goals the library may further specify such objectives as collecting the fraction of the world's output of printed literature that supports those goals, or having enough seats for 25 percent of the student population, or providing reference service for 80 hours a week, and so on. But the real goals of libraries, at least from the administration's perspective, are not fully describable in this way. Many institutions use their libraries as magnets to attract other publics: summer visitors, scholars of note, or potential donors who may contribute to more than the library itself. All of these purposes make it difficult to establish any uniform standard that can be applied to libraries in general. Consequently, the application to libraries of empirical measurement techniques is still in its infancy. Relatively few practitioners employ them. The literature shows only the hesitant beginnings of such applications. There is no generally accepted set of empirical standards by which libraries can be judged, no agreed-upon body of techniques yet available.

Those who have never dealt with universities may be surprised at this situation but more experienced observers will see it as merely a part of the university culture. As Howard Bowen remarked in

The Costs of Higher Education, colleges and universities are called upon to respond to so many kinds and levels of need that "no precise need . . . can be objectively defined or defended." So the skepticism of seasoned library administrators about the utility of quantitative library measures is understandable. Why should they squander precious resources in a futile effort? Perhaps they are right, but they ought to distinguish between standard measures intended to be applied to many institutions and measures that can be used internally to improve management decisions, regardless of whether such external measures exist.

Academic libraries are going to be redefined by the pressures on institutions to cope with the information revolution. If they are to survive as more than repositories for books seldom used, they must be effectively managed. Effective management of complex library processes depends on measurement. Most librarians now have personal computers and software that make measurement techniques easier to employ. Properly utilized management measures, and especially performance measures, can be one of the most effective tools librarians have to respond to the changes reshaping the academic library.

REFERENCES
William J. Baumol and Matityahu Marcus, *Economics of Academic Libraries* (1973), an examination of the available economic data on college and university libraries using and explaining regression analysis.
Verner W. Clapp and Robert T. Jordan, "Quantitative Criteria for Adequacy of Academic Library Collections," *College and Research Libraries* (1965).
P. Kantor, *Objective Performance Measures for Academic and Research Libraries* (1984).
F. W. Lancaster, *The Measurement and Evaluation of Library Services* (1977), a comprehensive review and summary of research efforts on the measurement and evaluation of libraries.
B. Lynch, "University Library Standards," *Library Trends* (1982).
R. Marvin McInnis, "The Formula Approach to Library Size: An Empirical Study of Its Efficacy in Evaluating Research Libraries," *College and Research Libraries* (1972), an analysis of the Clapp-Jordan formula.
K. Stubbs, "University Libraries: Standards and Statistics," *College and Research Libraries* (1981).

RICHARD J. TALBOT

LIBRARY COOPERATION

Cooperation, simply defined as voluntarily joining together for mutual benefit, has long been a goal of the academic library community in the U.S. Academic libraries have participated in local, statewide, national, and international cooperative programs. During recent decades the impetus for academic library cooperation has come not only from the academic community itself but also from government agencies and private foundations that have provided financial support for various cooperative programs. In addition, dramatic advances in computer and communications capabilities have supplied the technological means to accomplish some long hoped-for goals. According to data from the Association of Specialized and Cooperative Library Agencies (ASCLA), a division of ALA, the number of formal, organized cooperatives increased 61 percent from 1976 to 1982, with a 188 percent increase in the number of multi-

type cooperatives. Although *cooperation* and *network* have frequently been used synonymously, many cooperative efforts preceded the development of the telecommunications capabilities that underlie present-day library networks.

Cooperative programs in academic libraries range from informal local activities to complex formal agreements. Cooperative programs vary in scope from those that affect one aspect of library operations or services to those that impact broadly upon library operations and services and that may affect governance. Most cooperative programs are directed toward the achievement of one or more of three major goals: (1) improving bibliographic access to library materials; (2) improving physical access to library materials; and (3) engaging in cooperative collection development.

Bibliographic Access. To a large extent the availability of bibliographic information about collections is a prerequisite for other forms of cooperative activities in libraries. Unless there is adequate bibliographic information, agreements to deliver materials or to join in cooperative collection development programs can be little more than lofty goals. Not surprisingly, some of the earliest efforts in academic library cooperation, and some of the most innovative present-day techniques, involve sharing bibliographic information in order to improve bibliographic access to collections.

The standardization of bibliographic data has improved steadily since 1901, when the LC began printing its catalogue cards and making them available to others. Although the U.S., unlike many other countries, has no national library to provide bibliographic services, the LC, the nation's largest library, has assumed de facto bibliographic leadership, especially for the academic and research library community. The LC's efforts in standardizing bibliographic description have led to the development of the machine-readable format for cataloguing, the MARC II format, and to the encouragement, development, and adoption of international bibliographic standards.

The LC is involved in several cooperative projects, of which the CONSER (Conversion of Serials) project is the largest. Initiated in 1973 with funding from CLR, CONSER is designed to provide a reliable and authoritative online serials database. Since 1977 LC, the Online Computer Library Center (OCLC), and the National Library of Canada have acted as co-managers of CONSER. By 1985, 23 research libraries were participating, providing an online database for use on the international, national, regional, and local levels through OCLC. Another LC-initiated program, The Name Authority Cooperative (NACO) enables participating libraries to create authority records for LC's authority files. Additionally, the University of Chicago and Harvard University are engaged in a project in which bibliographic records and related name and subject authorities are input directly online to LC's system to be distributed as MARC records.

Cooperative cataloguing, another early interest of academic libraries, has been assisted markedly by the utilization of computer technology. Computer-based bibliographic utilities that serve academic libraries include OCLC, the Research Libraries Information Network (RLIN), the Washington Library

Network (WLN), and the University of Toronto Library Automation Systems (UTLAS).

OCLC was originally formed by a consortium of Ohio academic libraries in 1967 and is now a national network serving more than 3,500 libraries of all types. OCLC's central online database in Dublin, Ohio, contains more than 10,000,000 bibliographic records. These records, essentially catalogue records created by member libraries, serve as a major bibliographic tool in the acquisitions, cataloguing, and interlibrary loan operations of member libraries.

RLIN, previously known as BALLOTS, was developed at Stanford University. In 1978 it was selected to be the machine-based cataloguing system of the Research Libraries Group (RLG). RLG, a consortium formed in 1974 by Yale, Harvard, New York Public Library, and Columbia, addresses major issues facing research libraries, including collection development and management, shared resources, preservation, and bibliographic control. After the adoption of BALLOTS, Harvard withdrew from the consortium and membership was extended to all research universities. By 1985 RLG had 29 owner-members plus 25 associate and special members. In addition to bibliographic records, the RLIN database also contains the *Avery Index to Architectural Periodicals,* the *Eighteenth Century Short Title Catalogue,* and records of art auction catalogues.

WLN, developed by the Washington State Library Commission in 1975, serves more than 65 member libraries in the Pacific Northwest. WLN supports online cataloguing and acquisitions activities and is developing other functions. WLN has licensed its software to libraries and to a vendor for distribution.

UTLAS grew out of a consortium of Ontario libraries, developed to supply online databases in English and French. A catalogue support system is the central function, but, as in the other utilities, additional functions have been or are being added. UTLAS has more than 200 members, including some U.S. libraries, and a database of more than 8 million bibliographic records. In 1985 International Thompson, a Canadian company, acquired UTLAS.

Individual libraries have cooperated to provide full catalogue records, in place of titles only, in some of the extensive microform collections. Both contributed efforts and grant funding have been used in these cooperative projects to provide bibliographic control to these important materials. Thirteen libraries shared the responsibility for cataloguing the titles in Wright's *American Fiction* and four research libraries used federal funds in 1984 to catalogue more than 25,000 titles of early English Books, 1641–1700 (the Wing set). The ARL initiated the ARL Microform Project in 1981 and has assisted in working out the arrangements for cooperative efforts. The project established a Microform Cataloguing Clearinghouse in 1982 and has a program to investigate the current state of preservation microfilming activity and to develop a plan to increase the level of activity and make filming efforts more effective.

Another important effort is cooperative retrospective conversion projects. Retrospective conversion is the process of converting catalogue records into machine-readable form. RLG has developed a coordinated program so that retrospective conversion in individual libraries can be integrated with membershipwide efforts to minimize duplicative work. Currently, 13 RLG libraries have begun subject-based retrospective conversion projects. In 1984 CLR issued a report on issues in retrospective conversion and sponsored a conference on retrospective conversion to discuss the issues and explore options for a national conversion strategy. Following recommendations of the conference, ARL has adopted a coordinated retrospective conversion plan for its members. The plan, developed with support from CLR, entails the coordinated, systematic conversion of 6 to 7 million bibliographic records.

The bibliographic utilities have had a major impact on the operations of all academic libraries and have provided incomparable assistance to the efforts for academic library cooperation. They permit participating libraries to produce catalogue cards or store bibliographic information that is fitted to their local needs. A library's machine-readable files from the utility are often the foundation of a local online bibliographic database for circulation, public access catalogue, acquisitions, and serials control. Many cooperative activities in preservation, collection development, and resource sharing are now feasible because of these utilities. The Linked Systems Project (LSP), funded by CLR, is developing a telecommunications link among the computer systems of LC, RLG, WLN, and OCLC, beginning with name authorities, to facilitate the building of consistent files and the universal availability of bibliographic data.

Physical Access. Interlibrary lending is the most long-standing example of academic library cooperation. The first interlibrary loan code was formulated by ALA in 1917. Although interlibrary lending is widespread among academic libraries, it accounts for less than 1 percent of their recorded transactions. The cost of an interlibrary loan is many times the cost of an internal transaction. For years these costs were borne by the lending libraries but, in the late 1960s, because of increasing financial pressures, several of the largest academic libraries in the U.S. began charging fees for interlibrary loans. Most academic libraries still do not charge for interlibrary loans, but the high cost and ineffeciency of the interlibrary lending system have been of growing concern to academic librarians.

The bibliographic utilities, statewide networks, and regional networks have facilitated direct access to books and journals held in various libraries. OCLC, for example, implemented an interlibrary loan system in 1979, and more than 7 million interlibrary loan requests were sent through the system in its first six years, with usage continuing to increase each year. Other utilities have also implemented interlibrary loan systems, and RLG members provide expedited ILL and free photocopies where possible. State networks developed with federal monies provided by the Library Services and Construction Act (LSCA) were first established as public library networks. Direct borrowing and interlibrary lending were encouraged and made possible among public libraries; many of these local, regional, and statewide networks now include other kinds of libraries, and the academic libraries play important roles in these multitype cooperative networks. Many network agreements involve delivery of materials between libraries by vans or similar vehicles, reciprocal borrowing agreements that permit users from one institution to have direct access to library materials of another, photocopy service, and other special delivery or communications services such as telefacsimile.

Preservation of materials is recognized as very important for research collections, and academic libraries are beginning to cooperate in establishing conservation and preservation programs, in establishing responsibility for particular subjects, and in using the bibliographic utilities to indicate that an item has been preserved. RLG began a Cooperative Preservation Microfilming Project in 1983 with funding provided by the Andrew Mellon Foundation and the National Endowment for the Humanities (NEH). Nine libraries are filming approximately 45,000 U.S. imprints and Americana published between 1870 and 1920. Other agencies have also funded cooperative preservation activities. CLR sponsored a forum on library resources and their preservation in 1983 and

The Farmington Plan, initiated in 1947, distributed collection responsibilities for current foreign research materials among approximately 60 academic libraries. It ended in 1972, in part because of the success of both the National Program for Acquisitions and Cataloging (NPAC) and of Public Law 480 programs. Both of these projects were managed by the LC. Several hundred academic libraries have participated in these programs designed to acquire and catalogue foreign materials. In specialized areas the Latin American Cooperative Acquisitions program (LACAP) and the Center for Chinese Research Materials have been leaders in acquiring specialized materials for academic libraries.

The Center for Research Libraries is an example of formal cooperative collection development. The Center had its origins in 1949 as the Midwest Interlibrary Center, designed to be a central storage facility for little-used materials deposited by members. Now with a nationwide membership, the Center ac-

Widener Library at Harvard University, whose library system is the largest of privately endowed United States institutions.

produced a paper outlining the steps for a preservation strategy. The paper was the basis for discussion in 1984 at meetings of the ARL, the American Council of Learned Societies, and the Association of American Universities. The NEH established a separate preservation program. Beginning in the early 1980s NEH provided funding for the Midwest Cooperative Conservation Program and the Northeast Document Conservation Center as part of a nationwide effort to preserve research and historical collections in libraries and archives. The NEH preservation program was designed to fund cooperative efforts, informational materials, research and development, and institutional preservation needs.

Cooperative Collection Development. Academic librarians are increasingly aware of their inability to build comprehensive collections. Academic administrators and funding agencies have supported cooperative collection development programs, and there have been several national efforts in the U.S.

quires (by gift, deposit, and purchase) infrequently used items of research value, such as foreign dissertations, newspapers, publications of foreign governments, and journals. The Center concentrates its collections on specific subjects and specific world areas. Extensive microform collection programs and cooperative acquisitions have been established, for example, for African, Latin American, East Asian, South Asian, and Southeast Asian materials. The Center serves as a supplement to the collecting activities of member libraries, enabling a library to avoid buying infrequently used items and to borrow them instead. The Center has more than 100 full members and 60 associate members. In the mid-1980s the Center began reexamining its mission and role to determine the best way to strengthen its research resources and enhance their availability to research libraries.

Many effective cooperative collection development arrangements have been worked out among libraries that have compatible or well-recognized strengths and weaknesses. The formal agreement between the libraries of Duke University and the University of North Carolina, for example, has been in existence since 1931 and has been successful in defining collection development responsibilities for each library. Cooperation between Duke and North Carolina includes agreement not only about collection responsibilities but also about delivery of materials and reciprocal borrowing. A similar program between the libraries of the University of California at Berkeley and Stanford University, supported by a grant from the Sloan and Mellon foundations, was initiated in 1976. Both libraries strengthened and formalized existing informal arrangements and began a major effort to formulate a joint policy on collection development.

Many academic libraries consult informally about purchasing expensive items. The University of California formalized this consultation process, and 3 percent of the materials budget of the University of California libraries is allocated to a shared-purchasing program. Representatives of each of the nine University of California libraries participate in developing guidelines and in making individual selections.

The Conspectus On-Line, a summary of existing collection strengths and future collecting intensities, was developed by RLG in 1980 and is available on-line. The North American Collections Inventory Project (NCIP), sponsored by ARL and supported by CLR and the Lilly Endowment, is expanding RLG's conspectus into an inventory of collections among the major research libraries. The conspectus provides a standard tool for the identification of collection strengths and weaknesses, a mechanism to locate needed research materials more expeditiously, and the capacity to serve as the basis for cooperative collection development regionally and nationally.

Academic libraries participate in many kinds of cooperative programs that are designed to increase the services and expand the collections available to users. Computer-based systems have had great impact on the operations and services of academic libraries. More is expected in the future as the standardization of bibliographic records is extended, the size of the databases grows, and more functions are computerized. The influence of various cooperative agreements on the autonomy of individual academic libraries will lead to a reduction in autonomy, but the benefit of greater service to library users will outweigh the cost. Libraries will strive for more cooperation, not less, in the future.

REFERENCES
ASCLA, *The Report on Library Cooperation* (1982).
Council on Library Resources, *National and Regional Aspects of Collecting and Preserving Library Materials* (1983).
Dorothy Gregor, compiler and editor, *Retrospective Conversion* (1984).
Allen Kent and Thomas J. Galvin, editors, *The Structure and Governance of Library Networks* (1970).
Wilson Luquire, editor, *Library Networking: Current Problems and Future Prospects* (1983).
Susan K. Martin, *Library Networks, 1981/82* (1981).
Jutta Reed-Scott, *Issues in Retrospective Conversion* (1984).

ELAINE SLOAN

LAWS AND REGULATION

Although there is no large body of federal legislation that deals exclusively with academic libraries, two legislative acts continue to affect many academic libraries in the U.S. directly, the Library Services and Construction Act (LCSA) and the Higher Education Act (HEA) of 1965. Many other statutes affect academic libraries in part, including, for example, acts concerning civil rights; copyright; equal opportunity and affirmative action in hiring and personnel administration; occupational safety and health; and postal rates. Legislation affecting the Library of Congress (LC), the National Library of Medicine (NLM), the National Agricultural Library (NAL), and the National Endowment for the Humanities (NEH) may in turn affect academic libraries because they serve this significant constituency.

Academic librarians generally support the principles that motivated such programs as affirmative action and occupational safety but are often irritated and frustrated by local interpretations that create elaborate routines and lengthy procedures. Copyright revision was of major concern to most academic librarians, but by 1980, two years after the law went into effect, it appeared that the new statute has been less difficult to comply with than had been anticipated. Although additional recordkeeping is required, most academic librarians have been able to handle this matter without too much difficulty. Many are accumulating data that may be useful in considering possible revision; the act is reviewed every five years, but the first five-year review conducted in 1982 did not lead to changes in the law.

At the state level, legislation establishing and directing the activities of the state library agency, creating personnel classification systems in state colleges and universities, regulating union organization activities, establishing penalties for the theft or mutilation of library materials—all these and hundreds of other state legislative acts affect academic libraries. Not the least of these are the regular appropriations bills that fund state-supported academic libraries. Of more general application have been the statutes that established library systems in the individual states, in which academic libraries have come to participate along with other types of libraries.

One of the earliest federal acts concerning academic libraries was a resolution passed in the second session of the 13th Congress, on December 27, 1813. This resolution brought together a series of earlier special acts providing for the printing and distribution of the public journals of the House and Senate. Included were provisions for distributing government publications to colleges and universities. Resolutions adopted in 1857–61 formed the basis for the present Federal Depository Library System. In 1895 the General Printing Act further detailed document distribution, and 1962 amendments established the Regional Depository System. While the present provisions of Title 44 of the U.S. Code do not specifically identify academic libraries as such depositories, many academic libraries have been so designated (as provided in the statutes) by their local senator or member of the House of Representatives.

Other federal legislation in the 1960s was more directly related to academic libraries. The Academic Facilities Act of 1963 funded construction of academic buildings, including libraries, at both public and private institutions of higher education. The Vocational Education Act (1963) funded acquisition of vocational and technical material for colleges in order to encourage vocational education. Similarly, the 1965 Medical Library Assistance Act and Hospital Contruction Act funded the development of medical libraries and their collections.

The purpose of Title III of the Library Services and Contruction Act (1964) is to "establish and maintain local, regional, state, or interstate cooperative networks and for the coordination of informational services of school, public, academic, and special libraries and information centers, permitting the user of any one type of library to draw on all libraries and information centers." Academic libraries have benefited both indirectly and directly as networks have been developed and expanded and as resource centers have been identified and strengthened. For example, the University of Illinois at Urbana-Champaign and Southern Illinois University at Carbondale received LSCA funds after being designated resource centers in ILLINET, the Illinois Library and Information Network.

Higher Education Act of 1965. By far the most important of the federal acts was the Higher Education Act, passed in 1965 and subsequently amended. It is possible to view the Higher Education Act as a barometer that indicates the general status of libraries as they are viewed in Washington; the financial aid made available to libraries reflects not only the general political climate but also the ebb and flow of competing social forces. The Higher Education Act was comprehensive in scope and designed to assist all areas of higher education—including libraries—by providing through its various Titles general funds for

purposes to be decided by the granting agencies. The section of specific interest to academic libraries is Title II: College Library Assistance and Library Training and Research; it is administered through the Department of Education. A review of the evolution of funding programs under Title II mirrors with some degree of accuracy the developments, problems, and attempted solutions faced by academic libraries since 1965 in their efforts to acquire, process, and disseminate research materials for their users.

Specifically, Title II provides grants for (1) acquisition of books, periodicals, and other library materials by colleges and universities; (2) training of all types of librarians; (3) research and demonstration projects, including the development of new ways of processing, storing, and distributing information; and (4) aiding the LC to acquire and catalogue additional scholarly materials.

Under the section of Title II authorizing funds for the purchase of library materials, several types of grants were available. The most widely known of these was the basic grant of up to $5,000 for the purchase of all types of library material—books, periodicals, phonograph records, audiovisual materials, magnetic tapes, or other library-related resources. These funds were available to institutions of higher education if acquisitions budgets and total library budgets met certain criteria designed to ensure continuing financial support on the part of the institution, called maintenance-of-effort criteria. Also, the requesting institution was required to provide funds to match the grant money requested. Second, supplemental grants were offered that could equal $10 per full-time-equivalent student enrolled at the institution. Justification for these funds depended upon the "inadequacy" of the library's collections and did not

L. C. Scarborough

Rear view of the Walter Royal Davis Library, the University of North Carolina at Chapel Hill.

require matching funding from the institution. Finally, a category of special-purpose grants existed for awards to libraries on an individual need basis, requiring the requesting library to document its special need and to illustrate how the grant would expand the quality of its educational resources. Moreover, other such grants could be requested to meet specific national or regional library needs or to establish or strengthen joint-use facilities or other cooperative enterprises.

In addition to strengthening funding for acquisitions, the intent of the legislation was to improve "inadequate" academic libraries with funding to raise the level of their collections and to support institutions that could offer programs to build regional areas of strength or promote cooperation among academic libraries. In this respect, Title II seems to have been the precursor of cooperative and networking ideas now considered to be absolutely essential in day-to-day library operations.

Part B of Title II authorized federal grants for research projects and demonstrations that would assist in developing libraries and training librarians. Funding was aimed at encouraging librarians to develop new programs and innovative teaching strategies designed to cope with the dynamic changes being experienced in libraries. Funding was also available to make use of new technology to handle the production and dissemination of information.

Part C of the legislation indirectly assisted academic libraries by authorizing Title II funds to be transferred to the Librarian of Congress to acquire scholarly material and to provide prompt cataloguing for those materials. Again, there was an emphasis on expanding cooperative efforts among academic and research libraries.

There have been amendments to Title II over the years that have provided for a wider range of requests from libraries. The Education Amendments of 1972 allowed consideration of institutions that could not meet the maintenance-of-effort requirement. Other changes made it possible for both public and private institutions to apply for grants if their primary function was the provision of library and information services to higher education on a formal, cooperative basis. Perhaps the most significant amendment of 1972 was the elimination of the matching-funds requirement for basic grant requests.

Examples of grants approved under Part B of Title II in 1973 also show a broadening scope and an awareness of social concerns. Almost $2 million was awarded for projects involving studies to provide educational and library materials and services to economically disadvantaged groups and groups that had not been successful in traditional higher education settings. Successful applicants for these funds included colleges, universities, school districts, community colleges, and agencies serving ethnic or other specialized groups.

Amendments to Part C of Title II in 1976 allowed for significant grants to be awarded to major research libraries. The definition was broadened to achieve the effect of opening collections to a wider range of users, whether the library itself was a public, university, state, or independent library; the thrust was that the library make a contribution to scholarly research and open its collections and services to researchers or scholars not affiliated with that institution. Moreover, consideration of grant requests for these funds had to take into account a regional balance in the distribution of awards to ensure geographical equity in disbursing of federal dollars.

Appropriation History for College Library Programs Authorized Under Title II of the Higher Education Act (In millions of U.S. dollars)

Fiscal year	College library resources (Title II-A)	Library Career training (Title II-B)	Library research and demonstrations (Title II-B)	Research library resources (Title II-C)
1966	$10.0	$1.0	—	—
1967	25.0	3.8	$3.6	—
1968	24.5	8.3	3.6	—
1969	25.0	8.3	3.0	—
1970	9.8	4.0	2.2	—
1971	9.9	3.9	2.2	—
1972	11.0	2.0	2.8	—
1973	12.5	3.6	1.8	—
1974	10.0	2.9	1.4	—
1975	10.0	2.0	1.0	—
1976	10.0	0.5	1.0	—
1977	10.0	2.0	1.0	—
1978	10.0	2.0	1.0	$5.0
1979	10.0	2.0	1.0	6.0
1980	5.0	0.7	0.3	6.0
1981	3.0	0.7	0.3	6.0
1982	1.9	0.6	0.2	5.8
1983	1.9	0.6	0.2	6.0
1984	0.0	0.6	0.2	6.0
1985	0.0	0.9[a]	([a])	6.0

[a]FY 1985 appropriations for career training and research and demonstrations were combined.

Source: Annual Evaluation Report 1985, U.S. Department of Education, and budget documents.

Amendments to Title II enacted in 1980 reorganized Title II programs but retained most of its existing provisions. Authorizations for parts A and B were separated and a new part D was added, creating authorization for a nonprofit corporation to study the feasibility of a National Periodicals Center.

Although Title II is only one piece of legislation affecting academic libraries since the 1960s, it has surely had the greatest impact in the development of library resources. It has paralleled activities in the academic and nonacademic library communities with its emphasis on cooperative library activities and regional strengthening of resources. As those resources have become more expensive, and as comprehensive coverage of bibliographical areas has become increasingly difficult at individual libraries, cooperative efforts involving library staff, collection building, and information dissemination have been encouraged. While federal funding has not allowed individual libraries to achieve comprehensive collections to meet student and research needs in all areas, the Higher Education Act of 1965 has provided a framework for realistic library programs at a critical time in academic library history.

In the 1980s the Reagan Administration proposed ending Title II programs as part of its proposal to eliminate all federal assistance to libraries. It argued that the resource development and training problems Title II programs were originally designed to address have largely been resolved and that any remaining need for funding could be met from other sources. Congress rejected the proposals to terminate Title II programs in successive appropriation bills, but funding for Title II remained at issue.

CLYDE C. WALTON

Accreditation

Accreditation of educational institutions and programs, based on peer evaluation and judgment, developed as an American alternative to the European pattern of control of education by a government agency or the church. No provision was made in the U.S. Constitution for national involvement in education, and only in New York was there a State Board of Regents that was required to report annually to the Legislature on every college in the state.

Introduced late in the 19th century with the creation of the New England Association of Colleges and Secondary Schools, the concept of accreditation spread first to other regions of the United States and then to subject disciplines as professional associations assumed responsibility for monitoring educational programs in their respective fields. Initially, the purpose of accreditation was to improve communication between postsecondary educational institutions and secondary schools in order that students entering college might arrive with more nearly equal academic preparation. Closely allied with this purpose was the goal of standardizing the quality and measurement of learning experiences so that credits earned in one institution could be transferred to another with the assurance that the student's prior education would meet the expectations of the host school.

Another factor in the accrediting movement has been of such increasing importance that it sometimes overshadows the initial primary purposes. This is the social demand that accreditation should protect the public against incompetent and/or poorly educated graduates of educational institutions. While the health professions come most immediately to mind, the same principle applies to all professionals, including librarians. Professional self-regulation in this country begins with the accreditation of professional schools and educational programs. In no sense, however, may an association use accreditation as a device to limit access to the profession in order to reduce competition for jobs. A common misconception is that accreditation should constitute a device to control the number and the geographical distribution of educational programs within a profession. The granting of accreditation to a program signifies that that program meets or exceeds the quality expressed in the written standards for that area of study and thus meets its responsibilities to its constituency.

Accreditation falls into two categories: "regional or institutional" and "specialized or programmatic." There is much overlapping, of course, as illustrated by the fact that every library education program currently accredited in the United States exists in an institution that is recognized by one of the six regional accrediting associations. In fact, regional accreditation of the institution is a prerequisite for even the consideration of a program in library education in the United States. However, because the Canadian Library Association many years ago arranged with the American Library Association to accredit programs in Canadian library schools, this requirement does not apply in Canada, where regional accreditation does not exist.

During the early decades of the 20th century, as more and more professional associations assumed responsibility for monitoring educational programs in their fields, it was inevitable that this power to accredit would become a matter of dispute among associations. Furthermore, because much of the cost of accreditation must be borne by the institution or program seeking accreditation, university and college administrators became increasingly concerned with the number of professional associations demanding the right to accredit. In 1949 the National Commission on Accrediting (NCA), supported by some 640 institutions of higher education, was created not only to determine which professional associations would have the power to accredit educational programs but also to monitor the procedures and standards used by these associations.

In 1964, in response to a growing concern for "regionalism" in the accrediting process, the accrediting commissions of the six regional associations in the United States were brought together under the Federation of Regional Accrediting Commissions of Higher Education (FRACHE). The goal of FRACHE was to assure "quality education" on a nationwide basis.

In 1975 the National Commission on Accrediting merged with the Federation of Regional Accrediting Commissions of Higher Education to form the Council on Postsecondary Accreditation (COPA). A nongovernmental and nonprofit body, COPA fosters and facilitates the roles of both institutional and specialized accrediting agencies in promoting and ensuring the quality and diversity of American postsecondary education. COPA recognizes agencies that accredit educational programs in various fields and reviews those agencies periodically. COPA receives a portion of its financial support from the accrediting bodies that it recognizes.

The concept of accreditation developed in the United States because the founders had deliberately avoided the imposition of government control of education. It is ironic that when, beginning in the 1950s, the provision of federal aid to higher education introduced the question of institutional eligibility for aid, the U.S. Department of Education turned to the accrediting bodies to help determine that eligibility. Today, like other accrediting agencies, the ALA Committee on Accreditation (COA) is recognized by the Office of Education (OE) as the accrediting agency for programs in library education leading to the first professional degree. As with the Council on Post-secondary Accreditation, so with OE's Division of Eligibility and Agency Evaluation, the COA must undergo periodic review of its procedures and practices in order to retain its authority in the accreditation arena.

Accreditation in library education had its beginning in 1924 when the American Library Association created a Board of Education for Librarianship (BEL). This action was prompted by the publication one year earlier of the famous "Williamson Report," in which a distressingly bleak picture had been painted of the 15 library schools then in existence. Because accreditation decisions in the area of professional education must be based upon standards that have been endorsed by members of the profession, the ALA Council in 1925 approved a document entitled *Minimum Standards for Library Schools*. Like the standards for other professional schools of the time, these 1925 standards were quantitative in nature; they prescribed, for example, a minimum number of faculty members, minimum requirements for admission, and a model curriculum. New standards were adopted in 1933 that, in keeping with accreditation trends, tended to be qualitative rather than quantitative in nature. Whereas the 1925 standards had provided for four types of library schools (from the junior undergraduate school to the advanced graduate school), those of 1933 recognized only three. When in 1948 a number of major schools abandoned the fifth-year bachelor's degree in library science in favor of the master's as the first professional degree, work was begun on a new set of standards, which appeared in 1951. These standards pertained only to the first professional degree in librarianship, however, the so-called fifth-year degree. Library *schools* would no longer be accredited by the ALA; only their programs that lead to the first professional degree.

In 1956, with a general reorganization of the ALA, the COA was created to replace the Board of Education for Librarianship. It is to this committee that the Association delegates its authority in all accreditation matters. While there exists an appeal procedure through which COA decisions can be challenged before ALA's Executive Board (on grounds of procedure but not peer judgment), the Board has authority only to sustain the Committee or to direct that the Committee review the action in question. The ALA Constitution provides a mechanism for replacing the membership of a committee if it is determined that its affairs were conducted in an irresponsible manner.

The 1951 standards remained in effect for 20 years. Considering the changes in the library profession and in library education that occurred during those two decades, it is difficult in retrospect to understand how the document continued to be applied. The answer can be found in the fact that the 1951 standards were qualitative in nature—requirements expressed in quantitative terms had been avoided. Nevertheless, by the late 1960s the document was embarrassingly out-of-date.

In 1969, supported by a substantial grant from the H. W. Wilson Foundation, Inc., COA appointed a ten-member subcommittee to draft new standards. Those standards were developed after a period of open discussion, and after early drafts had been published for comments from the library community.

The six standards in the 1972 documents differ from earlier requirements in that the first and overriding standard requires that a school establish clearly defined goals and specific objectives for the program for which accreditation is sought. The standards set forth criteria by which the goals and objectives established by the school are to be judged. The interpretation of the five remaining standards depends on what the school determines to be its goals and program objectives. The latter five standards treat curriculum; faculty; students; governance, administration, and finance; and physical resources and facilities.

Between January 1, 1973, and July 1976, all but 1 of the 58 library education programs previously accredited by the ALA were visited and evaluated by the COA. Since that time COA has revisited all schools on a seven-year cycle. In addition, some new programs have been granted initial accreditation and accreditation has been withdrawn from some programs.

As of October 1985, there were 56 U.S. and Canadian schools on the list of accredited schools published by the COA. However, the closing of two additional U.S. schools had been announced and those schools were admitting no new students.

Over the years there has been serious concern in Canada over the appropriateness of Canadian library education programs receiving accreditation through the American Library Association. Both the Canadian Library Association and the Canadian Association of Library Schools had the question under discussion in the mid-1980s. Under current custom a Canadian always sits on the COA, and when a Canadian program is visited, at least one member of the visiting team is a Canadian; the Canadian Library Association is invited to send an observer.

As a standing committee of the American Library Association, the COA consists of 12 members appointed by the Executive Board. Appointments are for two years, with a second two-year term permitted. Each year one member is appointed by the Executive Board to serve as Chair. The Association's President-elect nominates individuals to fill approaching vacancies. Broad representation on the Committee is sought among practicing librarians and library educators, including two lay members to represent the public interest. The Committee's formal charge is "to be responsible for the execution of the accreditation program of the American Library Association, and to develop and formulate standards of education for librarianship for the approval of the Council."

Extensive documentation has been prepared by the COA for its own guidance in making accreditation decisions and to assist library schools in their preparation for accreditation visits. The two major documents of this nature are the *Manual of Procedures for Evaluation Visits under Standards for Accreditation, 1972,* and the *Self-Study: A Guide to the Process and to the Preparation of a Report for the Committee on Accreditation.* Both of these documents were extensively revised in 1981.

Before a site visit for either initial accreditation or reaccreditation, a library school is required to conduct a detailed self-study on which a report is then submitted to the Committee well in advance of the visitation. An annual report is required in October from each library school with an accredited program, the acceptance of which constitutes continued accreditation for that program for the next year. Schools are revisited by a COA team every seven years. A site visit lasts four days and the typical visiting team consists of four members. Special visits may be arranged to reexamine an accredited program on the initiative of either the school or the COA. The membership of a visiting team must be approved by the school, and potential site visitors are required to identify any programs in which they would find themselves in conflict of interest.

While the Committee on Accreditation has been delegated authority to make all decisions regarding accreditation, it is impossible for its 12 members to constitute the total membership of each visiting team. Many outside persons having a thorough knowledge of and keen interest in library education are called upon to assist the COA. Between 1973 and 1986, 181 individuals participated as team members. At least one current or recent COA members serves on each team, though not necessarily as Chair. The team's charge is to examine on site the program for which accreditation is sought, to prepare a detailed report that is both factual and evaluative, and to recommend an accreditation decision to the COA. The Committee must reach such a decision only by formal vote after considering all evidence, including that submitted by the school in response to the team's report. The school being visited covers the costs incurred in the accrediting process.

With the completion, in 1976, of the first round of accreditation visits under the 1972 standards, a detailed questionnaire was sent to each of the 67 schools visited, seeking their reactions to the entire process. All but five schools responded, and while there were some criticisms (most having to do with the performance of individual team members) and while a few schools tended to oppose accreditation, the general response was favorable. The 1972 standards have become widely accepted, even by the severest critics of accreditation, as has ALA's accreditation process. This conclusion was confirmed in a study made by the Task Force on Accreditation Issues of the Association of American Library Schools (AALS) in 1977.

For more than 60 years, responsibility for accreditation of American programs in library education has been held by the American Library Association. It is publicly recognized by the Council on Postsecondary Accreditation as the sole agency hav-

ing this authority. Through the years some library educators have questioned whether ALA is indeed the appropriate organization for this purpose, arguing that library education is of too little concern to ALA's membership, of which at least 90 percent are practicing librarians.

Other professional societies have also felt that their interests should be more directly represented in the accreditation process. In 1984 the Association for Library and Information Science Education (ALISE), with a grant from the H.W. Wilson Foundation, convened a conference to examine the governance, scope and finance of accreditation and to consider whether a new cooperative structure was feasible. Collaterally the COA sought and obtained from the U.S. Department of Education a grant to continue to examine the question of how other societies could be involved in the accreditation effort.

The COA/USDE project functioned during 1985 and planned to complete its work in 1986. The project was organized in a series of six working groups to address the following areas: Organization of the Accreditation Process; Finance of the Accreditation Process; Guidelines for Program Goals and Objectives; Guidelines for Faculty; Guidelines for Curriculum; Guidelines for Society Objectives. Each working group was chaired by a current or past member of the ALA Committee On Accreditation, the remaining members being representatives of the participating societies. Societies participating in the project included the American Association of Law Libraries; American Society for Information Science; Association for Library and Information Science Education; Association of Research Libraries; Canadian Library Association; Medical Library Association; and Special Libraries Association.

The outcome of the project remained to be determined in the mid-1980s. A number of societies raised questions about the possible cost of an expanded accreditation effort and their societies' willingness to support such an effort. The Association of Research Libraries questioned whether an expanded accreditation program is the best way to reach their objectives for improvement in library education. It was clear as the project neared its conclusion that further work remains to be done to bring the idea of a collaborative accreditation effort involving a number of interested organizations to fruition.

The ALA accreditation program faces many issues, some old and some new. One of the Association's oldest programs, it faces constant challenges. Many express dissatisfaction with the program but few are willing to replace it. It continues to be seen as one of the crucial activities undertaken by the American Library Association.

REFERENCES

The ALA Accreditation Process, 1973–76; A Survey of Library Schools Whose Programs Were Accredited under the 1972 Standards, 1973–76 (ALA, 1977).

Mary B. Cassata and Herman L. Totten, editors, "Standards for Accreditation, 1972," *The Administrative Aspects of Education for Librarianship: A Symposium.* (1975).

Charles A. Seavey, editor, "The Alise/ H. W. Wilson Foundation Accreditation Conference, September 16–18,

1984," *Journal of Education for Library and Information Science* (Fall 1984).

Elinor Yungmeyer, "Accreditation," *The ALA Yearbook* (1985)

RUSSELL E. BIDLACK;
F. WILLIAM SUMMERS

Acquisitions

The term acquisitions refers to the function of obtaining all materials to be added to a library's collection. This definition is limited primarily to the processes that occur after the decision on which materials are to be ordered has been made. (For the selection process itself, see Collection Development.)

In a small library one individual may handle all phases of the acquisitions process and other functions as well, while in larger libraries one person may work only on acquisitions; in the largest libraries many may be assigned acquisitions duties. Staff devoted to acquisitions are usually placed organizationally with those who handle the other technical operations required to prepare library materials for the shelf (such as cataloguing, serials check-in, and binding). They work closely with those who select the library materials, those who handle the accounting of the library materials budget, and those who catalogue and classify the material received.

Acquisitions Procedures. The acquisitions process may be divided into six major steps:

Searching. Acquisitions staff must search library files to make sure that the item to be ordered is not already in the collection, or—if it is in the collection—that an additional copy is desired. Searching includes checking the catalogue, all on-order and in-process files, and serials records. Acquisitions staff record information discovered during the searching process (such as call numbers of related editions) for later-use cataloguing.

Verification. Acquisitions staff then determine that the item to be ordered is indeed available. Such verification helps ensure accuracy in budget encumbrances. The existence of a title may be verified by finding its bibliographic description in national or trade bibliographies, locating a complete record in a bibliographic utility, or contacting the ordering source.

Placing the order. The acquisitions librarian must select the bookdealer (middleman or publisher) to receive the purchase order. The order is transmitted to the dealer as a brief bibliographic description (author, title, place, publisher, date, series) in paper or electronic format.

Receiving the piece. When the item arrives, all elements of its bibliographic description must be carefully checked against the order. The acquisitions librarian must investigate any inconsistency to be sure that the item received is indeed the item wanted. The invoice must be reviewed to make sure that the charges are correct. If the order, item received, and invoice are correct, the invoice is approved for payment and the piece is forwarded for cataloguing.

Resolving problems. Acquisitions staff must solve the problems that arise during the ordering process. They may seem to be as varied as their number, but generally can be categorized as: incorrect items received, items received damaged or incomplete, and billing inaccuracies.

Related processes. Acquisitions staff record the bookdealers' reports on why an item may be delayed or unavailable, send claims to dealers for those items not received within a specified time and for which no reports have been received, and cancel acquisitions records for those items which cannot be supplied.

The acquisitions librarian strives for an economy of effort, going into only as much detail as required for the type of library and level of specificity demanded. For example, a school librarian may be interested only in obtaining a certain work and will readily accept any English edition of it, while a research library acquisitions librarian may be concerned with obtaining a specific edition of the work defined by publisher, place, and date, as well as by author and title.

Types of Acquisitions. Most libraries obtain materials in two ways, by purchase or as gifts. In addition, some large or specialized libraries affiliated with institutions that produce publications obtain materials through exchange.

Purchases. Even the earliest libraries in the United States bought materials from booksellers in large English and western European cities. Local booksellers became their primary sources for purchase of domestic titles. Colleges and universities occasionally relied on their own professors or librarians to purchase materials as they traveled. The business for some of these local booksellers grew markedly, so that today they and newer similar firms act as middlemen in providing not only books, but also various special services tailored to library needs. Libraries find it efficient to use these bookdealers, for they can obtain through one source materials that they would otherwise have to order from many sources. Thus they can send orders to one place instead of many, process one invoice instead of many, write one check instead of many, and resolve problems with one firm instead of many. A bookdealer purchases far more titles from a publisher than most individual libraries would and, as a result of such a large volume, may receive a large discount from the publisher. Even when necessary expenses are taken into account, the bookdealer can usually pass on to the library a greater discount than the library would realize by ordering the title directly from the publisher.

Librarians can identify bookdealers through publications such as *Library Resources Market Place* (R. R. Bowker, 1981); through advertisements in library literature; through direct mailings sent to the libraries; through exhibits during state, regional, national, and international meetings; through dealer sales representatives who visit the libraries; or by communicating with colleagues responsible for acquisitions in other libraries.

It is important for an acquisitions librarian to do business with bookdealers who offer services that match the library's needs. The spectrum of bookdealer services is wide. Some dealers specialize in a particular subject matter (such as scientific and technical) or cater to a specific type of library (such as academic). Some maintain large warehouses so they are able to supply some titles immediately. A bookdealer may concentrate on certain types of materials: monographs, serials, government documents, maps, out-of-print items, rare materials, or such nonbook formats as microforms, sound recordings, slides, films, music scores, or video tapes or disks. Services may include providing customized invoices and management reports, paying shipping costs, allowing automatic returns for unmarked items, supplying processing forms, and making immediate communication possible with toll-free telephone lines.

A library may place many kinds of orders with a bookdealer. The most common are:

firm order— for a single monographic title; may be for multiple copies.

continuation or *subscription*—an order for a title that appears over a long period of time; includes titles with a specified number of volumes, not all published simultaneously, as well as serials titles, which theoretically have no end in sight.

blanket order—an order for all titles produced by a specific publisher.

approval plan—an order for current titles answering a library's customized specifications based on all or a combination of the following: subject, level of complexity, publisher, country of imprint, format, edition types, and language. Approval plan shipments may come as frequently as once a week. Only those which meet the approval of designated library staff are purchased.

The Bookdealer Library Relations Committee, a committee of American Library Association's Resources and Technical Services Division, Resources Section, produced guidelines to assist acquisitions librarians in purchasing library materials. (For published Guidelines, see References.) A guideline to aid librarians in evaluating the performance of bookdealers was in preparation from ALA (1985).

Gifts. A second source of library materials is the individual donor who wishes to give books to the library. It is important for library staff to apply their standard selection guidelines to gift materials, for the administrative cost of adding a gift title to the collection is the same as the cost for adding a purchased title. Because gifts are usually older materials, it is imperative to consider their condition as well as their subject matter. It is usually not worthwhile to go to the expense of adding a brittle book unless it is a rare or antiquarian item.

Frequently a donor asks library staff to evaluate the worth of his or her gifts. In the U.S., the Internal Revenue Service views a library's appraisal for the donor as a conflict of interest, and library staff should refrain from such evaluations. A specialist consultant or bookseller may be engaged to appraise collections donated. Written acknowledgment of the gift is not only a courtesy, but also a record of the donation for the donor.

Some donors ask the library to agree to certain stipulations placed on the gift (such as housing all the gift together or creating a special room named for the donor). Such restrictions must be carefully weighed against the real value of having the gift as a part of the library collection. It is considered good policy to accept gifts with no strings attached.

Exchanges. Some libraries use exchanges as a method of acquisition. In an exchange arrangement, a library sends publications to another library in exchange for publications which that library sends in return. Some titles are available only on an exchange basis because of the economic or political situations of the countries in which the exchange partners reside. Titles received on exchange should be selected with the same criteria used for purchased items, since processing and storage costs are identical for both; it is more economical to exchange serials than it is to barter in monographs. Care should be taken to ensure that exchanges are balanced in the sense that each half of the exchange partnership is receiving equal benefit from the arrangement, and exchanges should be reviewed periodically to assure that they are still providing valid additions to both library collections involved.

Automation. Most libraries in the mid-1980s still maintained their acquisitions files in paper format, and the organization and procedures of most acquisitions operations centered on paper files. Many more libraries will come to rely on computers to provide files in automated form. As their files evolve from paper to electronic format, acquisitions librarians will have to rethink their organizational design and procedural workflows as well.

In the 1960s several North American libraries began using computers to assist with their acquisitions processes. These acquisitions programs were costly, cumbersome batch operations run on mainframe computers and relying on punched cards for input. In the 1970s acquisitions librarians first had the opportunity to simplify their verification procedures by using bibliographic databases. Some libraries elected to use the automated acquisitions subsystems offered by the bibliographic utilities, thus relying on a large bibliographic network for computer support. In the 1980s, as microcomputer costs became within reach of more libraries, more acquisitions librarians were able to utilize automation to maintain files and produce reports.

Electronic ordering is a reality. Some libraries send their orders to vendors by electronic mail, tape transfer, or direct transmission. Some vendors in turn use similar methods of automated communication with their subsidiaries in other countries or with publishers. As more libraries, vendors, and publishers increase their own automation activities, more interfaces will be developed so that the speed of acquisition of library materials will increase in direct proportion to the increased ease of communication.

REFERENCES

American Library Association, Bookdealer Library Relations Committee, *Acquisitions Guidelines*, vol. 1: *Guidelines for Handling Library Orders for In-Print Monographic Publications*, (1973); vol. 2: *Guidelines for Handling Library Orders of Serials and Periodicals* (1974); vol. 3 *Guidelines for Handling Library Orders for Microforms* (1977); vol. 4 *Guidelines for Handling Library Orders for In-Print Monographic Publications*, 2nd edition (1984). This series sets forth practical guidelines for different components of acquisitions operations, focusing on appropriate relationships among librarians and bookdealers.

Richard W. Boss, *Automating Library Acquisitions* (1982). Assists the librarian contemplating automating the acquisitions functions when considering issues such as the relationship of acquisitions to other library functions, priorities for systems features, costs, and vendor reliability.

Stephen Ford, *The Acquisition of Library Materials,* 2nd edition (1978). A general work for students of library science and for practicing librarians on acquisitions procedures and types of materials purchased.

Alfred H. Lane, *Gifts and Exchange Manual* (1980). This volume gives a brief history of and provides practical comments on gifts and exchange procedures.

Library Acquisitions: Practice and Theory (Pergamon, Jan. 1977–) quarterly. This is the one serial devoted to library acquisitions. It addresses both philosophical approaches and practical aspects.

Andrew D. Osborn, *Serial Publications,* 3rd edition (1980). This comprehensive treatment of serials covers their selection, acquisition, cataloguing, housing, servicing, and reference.

MARION T. REID

Adult Services

Adult services, broadly construed, are all aspects of library activity directed to adults. Age categorization of services—to children, to young adults, or to adults—is a convenient compartmentalization that permits librarians to define the scope of service delivery in the context of the human life cycle. In some ways this compartmentalization, which designates one set of specialists for the early years (children's librarians) and another set for the time of adolescence and coming-of-age (young adult librarians), seems to burden the third set of specialists (adult services librarians) with a disproportionate share of humankind. Adult services librarians have responded by creating services grouped around identifiable user concerns and problems.

The broad aspects of adult service responsibilities include selection of the library's collection of resources; concern for the public's access to that collection; provision of assistance to users of the collection; activation of use of the collection with the appropriate community; and stimulation of potential users to the awareness of the relevance of library resources to their particular needs. Clearly the scope of these responsibilities includes work done by librarians with other orientations. Concern for access to information, for instance, may be viewed as within the purview of the reference librarian. Administratively, however, concerns of both reference and adult services librarians are viewed as being so interactive, for example, that the same American Library Association (ALA) unit—the Reference and Adult Services Division—provides an organizational structure for both.

For the most part "adult services" is a public library designation. In academic, school, and special libraries the parent institutional structure dictates service development. The heterogeneous and continually shifting needs of users both individually and in groups affect the shape of services to adults primarily in public libraries.

Evolution. Since the beginning of the U.S. public library movement in the middle of the 19th century, institutional goals evolved from preserving and collecting materials to organizing them for use. Samuel Swett Green's treatise on personal assistance to users in the U.S. Bureau of Education 1876 report *Public Libraries in the United States* is usually acknowledged as the first description of a role for librarians in activating collections for use.

The educational objective of public libraries emerged from 1876 to the turn of the century as evidenced by the writings of the leaders of the American Library Association. Charles Francis Adams, a trustee, declared the basic purpose of the library to be a means of continuing self-education (*Library Journal,* August 1877) and Henry Munson Utley, Librarian at the Detroit Public Library, declared the public library to be purely and wholly education—"truly the people's university" (*Library Journal,* December 1895).

During the same period that educational objectives gained ground in published accounts of library mission, librarians reluctantly began to accept responsibility for providing recreational reading. In his *Continuing Education for Adults through the American Public Library* (1966), Robert Ellis Lee observed that provision of recreational reading was generally approved by about 1920 and "associated with a theory of democratic library service which emphasized the indeterminate idea of the observance of the rights of the library user."

In this same period of the 19th century, information and bibliographic services began to emerge in the context of reference services as bibliographic indexes and reference tools were developed. The separation of reference services from the other services to adults was made clearly by 1910, with full-time reference specialists appointed to serve the student, business, and other groups of serious library users.

Children's services evolved at the turn of the century under the leadership of several public librarians who devoted their full time to such services in major city libraries, and young adult services developed as parallel special service in the 1920s and 1930s, again with full-time specialists guiding the development in the major metropolitan public libraries.

Thus public services in public libraries by the 1920s were comprised of reference services, services to children, and services to young people; the remaining services typically were called "circulation services." Innovative services to adults developed from circulation services in the 1920s, as Jennie Flexner's text on *Circulation Work in Public Libraries* (1927) documents well. Circulation services to adults comprised the activities that carried out the educational, cultural, and recreational functions of the public library until the adult services field was formalized in the mid-1940s.

Malcolm S. Knowles identified 1924 as a "distinct turning point in the library's role as an adult educational institution" in his *History of the Adult Education Movement in the United States* (1977). He contended that the Commission on Library and Adult Education established by the American Library Association in 1924, and its 1926 report *Libraries and Adult Education,* "enunciated a philosophy and set forth directional guidelines which exerted a powerful influence on the development of the library as an adult educational institution."

Library adult education provided the environment for the development of particular models of adult services: reading guidance, programming services to community organizations, and library-sponsored discussion programs. Each was introduced in its own decade (the 1920s, 1930s, and 1940s) in the context of "adult education," and each, having developed its own technique and rationale in the incubator provided by the adult education movement, survived to become a fundamental mode for public library adult services.

The term "adult services" came into use in the mid-1940s, when "adult education" was increasingly recognized as a philosophy, rather than as a set of specific services, and when the services it had generated were recognized as generic in librarianship. The New York Public Library established its first Office of Adult Services in 1946, and other major public libraries adopted similar structural coordination for services to adults at about this time.

The formal structuring of adult services in the organization of the public library gave it a place in library planning and in budget support and assured it the continuity important to the growth of evaluated programs of service. Central "offices" and system "coordinators" provided expertise throughout library systems, and the influence of talented specialists now had proper channels of influence for the exercise of leadership throughout the systems. Full-time adult services specialists were privileged to develop the individual, group, and community services needed by their adult publics. Adult services could be more than a way station for the novice librarian moving up to neighborhood library administration; now there developed specialist positions that made a career orientation for adult services librarians realistic in the major metropolitan public libraries. When in the late 1950s the New York State Legislature passed a law permitting and funding federated public library systems, leading the way in system development, adult services coordinator positions suddenly multiplied, and the field of adult services came quickly into its own on a national scale.

ALA nurtured adult services under the concept of "library adult education" continuously from the Enlarged Program at the end of World War I through the lectures and discussion groups of the People's Institute collaboratively developed in the New York Public Library in the late 1920s; the Keppel/Carnegie support of ALA projects such as the planned reading programs "Reading with a Purpose"; the work of the Subcommittee on Readable Books that initiated new forms in published books for the layman in the 1930s; the collaboration with the Ford Foundation's Fund for Adult Education in the 1950s stressing discussion of public issues, political philosophy, and humanities classics; and the sponsorship of research and development in adult services performance and community analysis in the 1950s and 1960s, such as Helen Lyman Smith's *Adult Education Activities in Public Libraries* (1954) or *Studying the Community: A Basis for Planning Adult Education Services* (1960).

For a generation ALA, in cyclical ups and downs, provided the status, the funds, the consulting expertise, and the training in workshops and conference programs that brought adult services to maturity on a national scale. John Chancellor, Grace T. Stevenson, Helen Lyman, Eleanor Phinney, Margaret E. Monroe, and Ruth Warncke are among a number of ALA leaders whose work in the field of adult services gave it the professional status needed in its developing years.

The ALA committees and boards supervising adult service projects were complemented by a growing membership structure for adult services. The Adult Education Section of the Public Library Association in the early 1950s was transformed in 1957 into the Adult Services Division, reflecting a vigorous leadership group in this field. The dominance of the information function over the educational, cultural,

and recreational functions was again reasserted strongly in ALA's structure in 1972, with the merger of the Reference Services Division with the Adult Services Division.

The preparation of public librarians for the work of adult services has taken place both in formal library education programs and in a sustained series of workshops and institutes funded by foundations and by the U.S. Office of Education since the late 1940s, such as the Allerton Park Conference, *Training Needs of Librarians Doing Adult Education Work* (1950). The teaching of Miriam Tompkins for 30 years, at Emory University and then at Columbia University, was probably a greater influence during the 1930s and 1940s than any other single educational factor in building the cadre of adult service specialists who gave leadership to the field. The early curriculum focused on reading interests of adults and later expanded to include planning reader services, community study, and special modes of public services to adults.

On the other hand, staff training in major public library systems provided significant dissemination of adult service skills and understanding throughout the nation as staff who benefited from this training in major libraries moved to other public library positions throughout the country. Such staff training included attitude development, skills training, and knowledge sharing. Often staff training was built around the learning needed to carry out staff projects in adult services. Never as successful as reference and information services in its institutionalization in formal library and information science education curricula, adult services has developed its educational preparation in the staff training programs of major public library systems. Only a handful of library schools in the 1980s offered more than a single course designed specifically for adult service preparation.

Structure. The structure of adult services is viewed here under (1) user orientation, and (2) the four major functions its service programs involve.

User Orientation. The internal structure of adult services relates directly to the structure of the broad field of public services. Analysis of the dimensions of public services had been rudimentary and scattered until in the 1970s a sustained focus on community analysis and on information-seeking behavior studies developed. This convergence on understanding the needs and interests of the community (library users and nonusers alike) is a prime element in the structure of adult services. From roots in library adult education and throughout development since the 1940s, adult services have been user-oriented and have been a major force in a greater user orientation in public services. The 1950s and 1960s saw the pioneer work of the ALA Library-Community Project centering on community analysis as a basis for adult service programs.

In the context of community analysis, attention to "special publics" has been an organizing principle for the planning of adult services, from its work with labor and foreign-born groups at the beginning of the 20th century; with the unemployed during the Depression; with leaders of community organizations in the years after World War II; with the initiation of "outreach" programs in the 1960s and early 70s to the aging, ethnic minorities, the disadvantaged, and handicapped; and with support of the Independent Learning Movement and career counseling in the 1980s. Much of the user orientation in the late 70s and early 80s focused on the needs of the adult new reader through renewed literacy programs.

Four functions of adult services. In an essay on "The Public Service Paradigm" (*The Service Imperative for Libraries,* 1982), Eliza T. Dresang noted that this paradigm, consisting of four functions—"information, instruction, guidance, and stimulation"—emerged gradually over the 20th century and was explored by Samuel Rothstein in *The Development of Reference Services through Academic Traditions* (1955) and Margaret E. Monroe in *Library Adult Education* (1963). The fourth function, stimulation of the public's awareness of the relevance of library resources to their specific needs and interests, achieved its clearest visibility in the public library outreach programs of the 1960s and early 1970s as described by Kathleen Weibel in *The Evolution of Library Outreach* (1982). Within this function, adult services librarians developed such programs as library-based career information and referral centers for adults in such libraries as Brooklyn Public, Chautauqua-Cattaraugus Library System and Onondaga County Public Library in the early 1980s. Another example of this function is the "Let's Talk About It" project, reading and discussion programs sponsored by the Association of Specialized and Cooperative Library Agencies and funded by the National Endowment for the Humanities on themes such as work, ethnicity, family, and citizenship during 1984–85.

Literacy. A renewed commitment to literacy education emerged in the adult service field in the 1980s. The renewal had strong roots in librarians' ongoing work in this area as documented in 1966 by Bernice MacDonald's *Literacy Activities in Public Libraries* and in the 1970s by Helen Huguenor Lyman's monumental three volumes published by ALA: *Library Materials in Service to the Adult New Reader* (1973), *Reading and the Adult New Reader* (1976), and *Literacy and the Nation's Libraries* (1977). Lyman's work explored formats, readability levels, and subject interests as well as cultural backgrounds and value systems of materials. It became clear that the usefulness of materials with adult new literates rose markedly when the readers' backgrounds and values were shared as background of the materials they were engaged in reading. Detailed knowledge of readers, then, became essential for librarians. Further, the definition of literacy underwent change in this five-year period, and by 1977 it was clear that library literacy efforts must include not only reading in the sense of taking words meaningfully from the printed page, but also skills in interpreting driving manuals, in completing income tax forms, in everyday mathematical computation, in use of mass media, and in gaining access to community resources for survival, for comfort in living in the community as citizens, as well as for participating in the neighborhood as a social environment. Lyman called her model of literacy services in 1976 an "active reading development program." This program had the comprehensiveness of interactive community planning, broad and diverse collection of materials in all media formats, individual information and guidance services, extensive group programs to enrich living experience and stimulate

intellectual curiosity, recruitment and training of volunteer staff, work with community agencies, extended resource centers outside the library, published evaluations of resources, and long-range plans and evaluation of service. This model is based on the needs of one "special public" and assumes that the large percentage of illiterates in major cities justified a distinctively adapted service for common backgrounds and needs.

The intellectual framework provided the basis for a new assault on the problem. The Coalition for Literacy founded in 1981 by ALA includes 11 national agencies and volunteer organizations (ALA, coordinator; American Association of Advertising Agencies; American Association for Adult and Continuing Education; B. Dalton Bookseller; CONTACT, Inc.; International Reading Association; Laubach Literacy International; Literacy Volunteers of America, Inc.; National Advisory Council on Adult Education; NCLIS; and National Council of State Directors of Adult Education). The Coalition launched a drive in 1983 to alert the public and recruit volunteer literacy program managers and tutors. A toll-free hotline staffed by CONTACT, a human service information agency, refers callers to local literacy programs and resources. Where no programs exist the Coalition helps to create them.

State and public libraries act as centers for coordination of volunteer efforts. California's Literacy Campaign, for instance, was funded by more than $2,000,000 in Library Services and Construction Act funds for demonstration projects in 1984. Adult services librarians met in 1984 at a conference in Denton, Texas ("Access to Information Through Literacy"), which focused on the role of libraries in adult literacy. Literacy persists as a central adult service, fundamental to all others.

An Enduring Learning Society. Long a staple of adult services, the concept of the library as the people's university—explored by Lynn E. Birge in *Serving Adult Learners* (1981)—emerged with new vigor after publication of the U.S. Department of Education report *Alliance for Excellence* (1984). In the *Alliance* report adult services are viewed as critical in the establishment of an enduring "learning society." The report recommends a revitalization of the Reader's Advisory Service under the title 'Learners Adviser"; targets literacy as a basic library function; and exhorts libraries to develop resources and services in support of lifelong learning and education.

The pervasiveness of adult services to the public library mission cuts across all boundaries. Whether activated on behalf of a special public—the aging, the jobless, the new reader—or topics of universal concern—citizenship, family, work—adult services enable achievement of library objectives.

REFERENCES
Catherine Suyak Alloway, "Twenty-Five Years of Adult Services," *RQ* (1985).
Suzanne Boles and Barbara D. Smith, "The Learner's Advisory Service," *Library Trends* (1979).
Kathleen M. Heim, "Stimulation," in *The Service Imperative for Libraries,* edited by Gail S. Schlachter (1982).
Margaret E. Monroe, "Adult Services in the Third Millennium," *RQ* (1979).

MARGARET E. MONROE;
revised by KATHLEEN M. HEIM

Afghanistan

Afghanistan, a republic in central South Asia, is bordered by the U.S.S.R. on the north, China and Jammu and Kashmir in two areas of the northeast, Pakistan on the east and south, and Iran on the west. Population (1984 est.) 17,650,000; area 653,000 sq.km. The official languages are Dari (Afghan Persian) and Pashto. The peasant-tribal society is composed of various ethnic groups (Pashtuns, Tadjiks, Hazaras, Uzbeks, Baluchs, Turkoman, and Kirghiz, among others), with a 90 to 95 percent nonliterate population.

History. In Afghanistan, as in many Asian countries, what libraries there were in the past were created, organized, and supported by an elite group of rulers and religious leaders for their own use. Only comparatively recently did the concept of libraries as institutions of preservation give way to a more modern concept of libraries as sources of knowledge and information service. However, the progress made in the late 1960s and early 1970s was stalled by the coup d'état of April 1978 and the Soviet occupation of the country. Reliable information about libraries thereafter was scarce.

National Library. There is no national library in Afghanistan, but some functions of one are performed by certain institutions, such as the Kabul University Library, the Ministry of Education Reference Library, and the Public Library of the Ministry of Information and Culture. A national bibliography is issued irregularly by the Kabul University Library.

Academic Libraries. The most important and largest library in Afghanistan is the Kabul University Library. Kabul University (Kabul Pohantun) was founded in 1932. Small faculty libraries came into existence but were accessible only to faculty members. In 1967 an Indiana University team reorganized the structure of the university system, and the present library was organized at that time. (Betty White, an American librarian, is remembered for organizing the present University Library.) Its collection totals about 130,000 volumes, arranged by the Library of Congress Classification. It holds special collections dealing with material on Afghanistan and Islamic civilization.

At 13 teacher training institutions, high school graduates are given one to two years of training and then sent to the provinces in a program to eradicate illiteracy. The provincial teacher training institutions have small libraries numbering at the most 500 books. These small collections were augmented regularly by small gifts of books from foreign philanthropic and cultural organizations.

Most of these collections, largely in English, were entrusted to teachers untrained in librarianship. The three teacher training institutions in Kabul fare much better. The Higher Teacher's College, a two-year institution for the training of college-level teachers, has a library of approximately 10,000 volumes with a professionally trained librarian. The Academy for Teacher Education and the Dar'ul Mo'alamein training schools have libraries of approximately 1,000 volumes. The greater portion of the collections is in English, a language not usually known by the students.

Public Libraries. The Public Library of the Ministry of Information and Culture, usually referred to as the Kabul Public Library, is in the central part of the city facing Zarnegar Park. The Library has its own Reading Garden, a pleasant plane tree grove with reading benches along the public paths, and popular with Kabul students who use the area as an outdoor reading-study room. Its collection numbers 120,000 volumes; a large portion is in English. Efforts were made to increase the books in the two national tongues, Pashtu and Dari. There is a Children's Section, an Afghan room housing material pertaining to Afghanistan, and a periodical room containing a complete collection of Afghan periodical publications. The Library is under the direct jurisdiction of the Ministry of Information and Culture. Not all books circulate, but all may be used on the premises. The Library is housed in a two-story building that was once a private mansion, and has five branches. There are 36 other public libraries in the country, but all have far smaller collections.

School Libraries. In Kabul, Habiba High School, subsidized at one time by the Americans, has a library with a collection of 5,000 books, supervised by a teacher. The Isteqlal Lycée, subsidized by the French government, has a library of approximately 10,000 volumes in French. The "Russian" Polytechnique Institute has a library, but it is not open to the public. It has approximately 10,000 volumes on science and technology. The "German" High School, subsidized to some extent by the West German government, also has a library, primarily in German. In elementary schools libraries are practically nonexistent, though a few have small collections of 50 to 100

Libraries in Afghanistan

Type	Administrative units	Service points	Volumes in collections	Annual expenditures (afghani)	Population served	Professional staff	Total staff
National	--	--	--	--	--	--	--
Academic	14	--	140,000	--	8,600	4	30
Public	37	--	200,000	--	450,000	1	25
School	4	--	30,000	--	3,000	0	5[a]
Special[b]	5	--	150,000	--	3,000	4	24

[a]Part-time.
[b]Includes embassy libraries open to the public.

Sources: Unesco, *Statistical Yearbook,* 1984, for number of public libraries and volumes (1980 data); for other data, Louis Dupree, *Afghanistan,* 1973; "Survey of Progress," Department of Statistics, Ministry of Planning, 1977.

books, usually administered by a *tawildar* (keeper), who discourages lending because he or she is held financially responsible for all books lost. There was no government assistance to libraries at the elementary school level.

Special Libraries. The Historical Society of Afghanistan Library, in the Shar-e-Nau section of Kabul, has a collection of approximately 40,000 volumes. This specialized collection deals exclusively with anthropology, ethnology, prehistory, archeology, genealogy, history, and folklore of Afghanistan. It contains all publications of the Délégation Archeologique Française en Afghanistan (DAFA), which excavated sites at Ai Khanoum and Hadda. Other special libraries include the Afghan Institute of Technology, the Anjumane Tareekh, and the Goethe Institute. All are in Kabul, and all have small collections.

The Profession. The Anjuman Ketab-khana-e-Afghanistan (Afghanistan Library Association) was organized in 1971 by a former Kabul University Librarian, Abdul Rasul Rahim, to promote literacy and libraries in Afghanistan as its basic objective; it works to improve the status of librarians and to lobby for a national library system and for a School of Library Science within Kabul University. It sponsored training workshops and seminars for teacher-librarians in the teacher training schools and irregularly published the *Afghan National Bibliography*.

JOHN DE BELFORT URGUIDI*

Aguayo, Jorge
(1903-   )

Jorge Aguayo is considered the founding father of modern library procedure and library education in Cuba. He also contributed to the library development in other parts of Latin America, to furthering library cooperation through the Pan American Union and the American Library Association, and to scholarship in Spanish-language classification.

Born in Havana, Cuba, on December 4, 1903, Aguayo received his early schooling in the capital. At the University of Havana he received degrees in Civil Law in 1925 and in Diplomatic and Consular Law in 1927. After nine years of diplomatic service, Aguayo entered the library field, following a strong interest in books and learning.

In 1937 he began a long and fruitful association with the General Library of the University of Havana, serving as Assistant Director until 1959, when he assumed the post of Director. The Rockefeller Foundation awarded him a one-year fellowship to study at Columbia University's Library School in 1941, and Aguayo took a concentrated curriculum with emphasis on cataloguing problems and university administration. In the years following his return to the University of Havana, the General Library pioneered in the use of fundamental tools such as the dictionary catalogue with subject headings translated and adapted from the Sears and Library of Congress lists, the Dewey Decimal System, the ALA cataloguing rules, the use of Library of Congress printed cards, the establishment of a separate reference collection, and many other services previously unknown to Cuban library users. The results of Aguayo's work are summarized in three manuals written in the 1940s:

Reglas para la ordenación del catálogo diccionario de la Biblioteca General de la Universidad ("Rules governing the dictionary catalogue of the General Library of the University," Havana, 1940); *Manual prático de clasificación y catalogación de bibliotecas* ("Practical manual of classification and cataloguing for libraries," Havana, 1943; 2nd ed., 1951); and *Modelos de fichas* ("Model cards," Havana, 1942; 2nd ed., 1949). The latter two have been used as textbooks by a number of Latin American library schools.

In 1940 Aguayo and three associates initiated the teaching of library science at the Havana Lyceum. All four served as Cuba's first professional faculty of library science, offering a variety of courses lasting three and six months. In 1946 the formal teaching of library science began with the establishment of Cursos de Técnica Bibliotecaria at the Summer School of the University of Havana under Aguayo's direction. He served as Director of the summer courses until 1952 and assumed the professorship of cataloguing and classification in the University's School of Librarianship from its founding in 1950 until his departure from Cuba in 1960.

Aguayo's involvement in library development in individual Latin American countries and the region as a whole went hand in hand with his ambitious program in Cuba. In 1944 the U.S. State Department, the ALA, and the Rockefeller Foundation invited him to teach the first library science course in Peru after a fire destroyed the National Library in Lima. In 1947 he accepted an offer to attend the First Assembly of Librarians of the Americas. He served as a consultant to the Regional Conference of National Commissions of the Western World, held in Havana in 1950, and to the Conference on Development of Public Library Services in São Paulo in 1951. He was President of the first Cuban Library Workshop in 1953.

Aguayo served as a prominent spokesman for Latin American librarians on cataloguing matters within the American Library Association. He was a member of the Canadian and Latin American Subcommittee of the ALA's Special Committee on Dewey Classification from 1944 to 1947. He then served on the ALA's Standing Committee on Cooperation with Latin American Catalogers and Classifiers from 1953 to 1958.

LATER CAREER
After the Castro revolution in 1960, Aguayo went to the United States and worked for a brief time at Syracuse University as bibliographer in charge of the Farmington Plan for Uruguay, Paraguay, and Argentina. In 1962 he became the Branch Librarian of the Pan American Union (PAU) and served as the Head Librarian of the PAU's central Columbus Library from 1968 until 1973. During that time he was also consultant to the Spanish translation of the Anglo-American Cataloging Rules (1970) and together with Carmen Rovira compiled the PAU-sponsored *Lista de Encabezamientos de Materia para Bibliotecas* ("List of headings for libraries," 1967), a milestone work that served libraries throughout the Spanish-speaking world as the basic subject heading list. Aguayo was named Editor and Director of the translation into Spanish of the 18th edition of the Dewey Decimal Classification System.

MARTHA TOMÉ

ALA

Jorge Aguayo

Mary Eileen Ahern

ALA

Ahern, Mary Eileen
(1860-1938)

Mary Eileen Ahern was the Editor of the journal *Public Libraries* (later just *Libraries*) from its beginning in 1896 to its demise in 1931. In its editorial pages, one can find Ahern's ideas about the public library movement, ideas that she believed in and fought for throughout her career. "There is only one solution of all social problems," she proclaimed in the opening issue, "—an increase in intelligence, a gradual education of the people." "The public library," Ahern went on to say in the same editorial, "is the broadest of teachers, one may almost say the only free teacher. It is the most liberal of schools, it is the only real people's college." She saw a librarian "as a teacher on all proper occasions."

Born in Indiana on October 1, 1860, Ahern was the daughter of Irish immigrants, William and Mary O'Neil Ahern. She attended high school and normal college in Indiana, taught in public schools in various small Indiana towns, and became Assistant State Librarian of Indiana in 1889. While in that office, she helped organize the Indiana Library Association, served as its first Secretary, and was later President. She was elected State Librarian by the Indiana Legislature in 1893, but the job ended in 1895 after the Democrats, who had supported her, lost the elections of 1894.

Aware that the State Librarian's job was a political football, Ahern mounted a campaign to take the State Library away from the Legislature and assign it to an independent Library Board. From the election until her position ended, she made special efforts to provide library materials and services to all the newly elected legislators. Each time she delivered materials and was told, "It's too bad that you cannot stay on here," she brought up her proposal for an independent library board and an independent state librarian. As it turned out, an independent library board was out of the question politically. Ahern did manage to promote a compromise in which the State Library was transferred from the Legislature to the State Board of Education. Part of that compromise was that Ahern would not seek reappointment as State Librarian, but she had already decided in any case to enroll in library school.

Ahern attended the library school at the Armour Institute of Technology in Chicago, 1895–96. During her time there, she was offered the editorship of *Public Libraries*, a new journal sponsored by the Library Bureau. The journal was subsequently taken over by the Illinois Library Association, an organization in which Ahern took an active part. A missionary for state and local library association organization and activity, she constantly urged her readers to get involved in the library movement. She was three times elected President of the Illinois Library Association (1908, 1909, and 1915), served on the ALA Council for many years, attended every ALA conference from 1893 to 1931, and was named a Charter Member of the American Library Institute. She was also Secretary for many years of the Library Department of the National Education Association, an organization whose formation she had heralded in the pages of *Public Libraries*.

The relationship between the schools and the public libraries, library training in the normal schools, the role of the school library, and the teaching function of the public librarian were topics with which Ahern was constantly concerned. She wrote on these subjects in *Public Libraries*, gave talks before library associations and civic groups, and contributed articles and reports to other publications. The school, the church, and the library were—in Ahern's view— linked together in a great mission: the education of the American people. She was an enthusiastic supporter of Andrew Carnegie's public library philanthropy. In the high-minded manner so characteristic of public librarians of her period, Ahern emphasized educational work, deplored the vulgarity of the popular newspaper press, and worried about the problems American public libraries experienced because of the publication of so many indelicate French novels.

Ahern gave up the editorship of *Libraries* in 1931; she was over 70 years of age, and her eyesight had become so poor that she could not continue in editorial work. The Illinois Library Association decided to end the journal, rather than continue it without her. In the last issue, many colleagues paid tribute to Ahern and the journal. All agreed that *Libraries* had been a voice for small public libraries and had provided an important forum for the more practical aspects of library work. "The loan desk and the field trip," commented Frank K. Walter, Librarian of the University of Minnesota, "have been nearer her heart than the private study or the complicated problem of bibliographic research."

Even after retirement, Ahern continued to travel and to take a keen interest in library affairs. She died on a train near Atlanta, Georgia, on May 22, 1938.

REFERENCE

Doris Cruger Dale, "Ahern, Mary Eileen," *Dictionary of American Library Biography* (1978)

ELAINE FAIN
(d. 1980)

National Library Association

Simeon Babasanya Aje

Aje, Simeon Babasanya
(1927–)

Simeon Babasanya Aje, Director of the National Library of Nigeria, contributed in no small measure to the national public image of the librarian and put Nigeria on the international librarianship map. He worked for professional development through IFLA and Unesco activities.

Aje was born on June 11, 1927, in Ondo State, Nigeria. He attended primary schools in his hometown, Ijurun, and Ijero in Ekiti from 1935 to 1941 and attended Christ's School, Ado-Ekiti, from 1942 to 1945, after which he took the Cambridge School Certificate and a Nigerian teachers' examination in 1948. From 1946 to 1954 Aje was a teacher in primary and secondary schools in what was then the Western Region.

He was a teacher/librarian in the Iwo District Council in 1955 and 1956. In 1957 he moved to the Western Regional Library and obtained leave and a scholarship to study at Loughborough College in England. At Loughborough Aje successfully completed the Great Britain Associateship of the Library Association Examination and obtained the Fellowship of the Library Association in 1959. Before returning to Nigeria, Aje was an Assistant Librarian at the National Central Library London (January–April 1960) and a cataloguer at the British National Bibliography later in the year. He then returned to the Western Regional Library.

Aje went to the United States for postgraduate professional education in 1962 at the University of Chicago Graduate School of Library Science, where he obtained an M.A. in 1963. During his stay in Chicago, Aje was also Social Science and Documents Librarian and Head of the Modern Languages Library at the University of Chicago Libraries. He returned as a Librarian in Western Regional Library services in 1964 and became Senior Librarian in 1967. In his post as Regional School Librarian, he was instrumental in promoting school library service and ran training programs for library assistants in primary and secondary schools. In the same year Aje was appointed Principal Librarian in the National Library of Nigeria, in Lagos. He was Acting Deputy Director from May 1967 to November 1969 and was then appointed Deputy Director. He became Director of the National Library in September 1971.

As Director of the Library, Aje contributed significantly to the development of librarianship at the national level. He initiated considerable expansion of the National Library services with the establishment of branches located in the states. He also initiated the process for recognition of the profession of librarianship and the publication of a decree establishing a register of librarians. Aje also introduced the application of national standards in bibliographical description and the use of standard book numbers and standard serial numbers. He continued the publication of the *National Bibliography of Nigeria,* which was taken over in 1970 from the University of Ibadan Library.

Aje also made available his wealth of professional experience in the area of library education and training in Nigeria. He was a Visiting Lecturer at the University of Ibadan from 1960 to 1976 and Associate Lecturer from 1977. He helped to develop programs and courses on the National Library and on national bibliographic control.

Aje became well known in professional library circles in Britain, Western and Eastern Europe, and the U.S. He served as a regular member at IFLA and attended Council meetings from 1971. He served as a member of various IFLA-connected committees. Aje also contributed to the work of Unesco through membership in various conferences and councils.

As Director and President of the Nigerian Library Association, Aje influenced the acceptance of library boards and the establishment of state libraries as an essential service to the Nigerian public.

Aje wrote *A Biography of Dr. Albert Schweitzer* in Yoruba and prepared a Yoruba translation of Chinua Achebe's *Things Fall Apart.* He also contributed to the library professional literature.

F. A. OGUNSHEYE

Akita, J. M.
(1921-   )

During the three decades of his stewardship of the National Archives of Ghana (1949–76), Jeremias Mama Akita, more than any other individual, shaped the development of the archival profession in his country in particular and Africa in general. He attacked almost all the problems that confront the modern archivists and invariably found happy and logical solutions.

Born on May 11, 1921, in Teshi, Accra, Akita had his initial schooling in Ghana. He then proceeded to the Queen's College, Cambridge, in 1945 and graduated in 1948. He did a year's training in Archives Administration at the School of Librarianship and Archives, University of London. Back in Ghana in 1949, he became Chief Archivist of Ghana, a post he held till his retirement in 1976.

His most signal service to Ghana was the founding of the National Archives. He started concentrating the records that were lying about, scattered in the government offices, corridors, and attics. At the same time he drew up plans for a new archival building. The construction work, which started in 1959, was completed by 1962. Akita went on to establish regional archival offices in Kumasi (1959) and in Cape Coast (1964), for which permanent buildings were constructed later. He also made building plans for other regional archives offices at various administrative capitals of Ghana.

To give his archival establishments legitimacy and security, he was instrumental in piloting an archival law through the then colonial legislature in 1955. The law envisages taking over all record groups and documents, both historical and administrative, and also those of the future. The procedures of evaluation and appraisal of records before their transfer to the National Archives have also been clearly enunciated.

Akita was elected a member of the Executive Committee of the International Council on Archives from 1968 to 1976. In recognition of his contributions to the International Council on Archives, he was made an honorary member of the Council for life.

When the question of establishment of a Unesco-sponsored training center for archivists for anglophone countries of Africa was mooted in 1967, Akita was naturally closely associated with the project. He was in no small measure responsible for the location of the center at the Department of Library and Archival Studies of the University of Ghana in 1975. On retirement from the National Archives in 1976, he was invited to head the center. He thereafter worked as Senior Lecturer and Acting Director of the training center.

Akita's professional knowledge and extensive travels made him uniquely qualified to write on archival and ancillary problems, and he wrote numerous articles in professional journals.

Akita shared his specialized skills generously with the neighboring countries. He was appointed Archival Adviser by the Commonwealth Secretariat to the UN Institute for Namibia in Lusaka, Zambia, in 1977 and drew up a report on the establishment of an archival service for Namibia. In 1978 Unesco sent him on a consultancy mission to Uganda to prepare short- and long-term plans for the development of archival services there.

D. G. KESWANI

Albania

Albania, a People's Socialist Republic, lies on the Balkan Peninsula in southeastern Europe. It is bounded by Yugoslavia on the north and east, by Greece on the south, and by the Adriatic and Ionian seas on the west. Population (1984 est.) 2,906,000; area 28,748 sq.km. The official language is Albanian.

National Library. The National Library was founded in Tirana on December 10, 1922, with a stock of 6,000 volumes. The liberation of the country in 1944 found it with a stock of 15,000 volumes. In 1982 it had 843,340 volumes.

Under law the National Library receives free of charge 15 copies of all publications produced in the country. Its stock is also enriched with purchases, exchanges, and loans of books and periodicals from other countries.

Library service is free. The National Library keeps readers informed about its stock through a wide information network including reference files, catalogues, bibliographies, and bulletins. The annual circulation of books among readers is about 250,000 copies. The National Library is also the archive for Albanian books, preserving one copy of each publication. It is also the center for study of practice and methods of library science and bibliography.

As the bibliographical center of the country, the National Library publishes the national bibliography on Albanian books (quarterly; first published in 1959) and the national bibliography of articles in Albanian periodicals (monthly; it appeared as a quarterly from 1961 to 1964 and as a bimonthly in 1965). The Library also publishes an annual catalogue of the foreign periodicals entering the country.

The National Library has a stock of about 30,100 publications on the history, linguistics, ethnography, and folklore of Albania. Its collections of books and manuscripts on Albanology are considered the richest and most important in the world. It also has a rich stock of books on the history and culture of the other countries of the Balkans.

The National Library has an exchange system with the other libraries of the country and with many libraries abroad. In 1982 it had such relations with 480 foreign libraries, institutions, and international organizations and with scholars in the sciences from some 70 countries.

Academic Libraries. The Library of the Academy of Sciences of Albania is the country's largest academic library. It was founded in January 1975 with a stock of about 10,000 volumes. It annexed the stock of the Albanological branch of the University of Tirana in 1976, increasing the number of volumes to about 117,000, and in 1982 the whole stock of that library numbered 540,000 volumes. It covers all branches of science and has incunabula on history and linguistics. The library increases by about 4,000 books a year through purchases, exchanges, or borrowings. The Library receives three copies of each publication of the Academy free of charge.

The Library of the Academy provides free service for students and scholars in all fields of science; it also maintains relations with and serves district libraries. The circulation of books among readers is more than 50,000 volumes a year. It publishes informative bulletins on the foreign literature entering the country, covering history, geography, and economics. It also publishes the catalogue of foreign scientific magazines received by the library as well as a number of other informative lists.

The Library of the Academy of Sciences maintains relations with 820 foreign academies, universities, scientific institutions, and libraries, and persons in the sciences and friends of Albania.

Other important academic libraries are those of the University of Tirana and of the Higher Agricultural Institute of Tirana.

The Scientific Library of the University of Tirana was founded on September 16, 1957, with an initial stock of about 40,000 volumes. In 1982 its stock numbered 500,000 volumes, 80 percent of which are technical and scientific books in foreign languages. The library receives three copies of all scientific, teachers', and periodical publications of the University free of charge. Its stock is enriched with Albanian and foreign books purchased, exchanged, or borrowed at a rate of 10,000 a year. It maintains relations with 422 foreign university libraries and scientific institutions and with individuals in 90 countries.

The Library of the University provides free service for the teachers, scientific workers, and students of the University as well as for all the specialists and workers of the country, maintaining regular contact with the libraries of the districts, scientific institutions, and production centers.

The Library of the University keeps the readers informed about its stock through reference files, informative bulletins, reference bulletins, catalogues, bibliographies, lists of new books, and other ways. It publishes periodical informative bulletins on the en-

Libraries in Albania (1982)

Type	Administrative units	Service points	Volumes in collections	Annual expenditures (lek)	Population served	Professional staff	Total staff
National	1	6	843,340	- -	9,200	69	111
Academic	3	13	755,200	- -	13,678	45	70
Public	42	49	2,175,248	- -	106,910	75	105
School	1,778	1,778	4,146,728	- -	411,861	10	1,778
Special	519	519	1,107,736	- -	74,495	60	519
Others	1,803	1,803	2,674,651	- -	199,869	- -	105

tire technical-scientific literature entering the country for 12 fields of science and reference bulletins on foreign literature for eight main fields of science and production.

The Library of the Higher Agricultural Institute is the main library specializing in agriculture. It was founded in 1951 with a limited bookstock. By 1955 its stock had grown to 27,898 volumes, in 1959 to 41,260, and in 1976 to 88,000. In 1982 the library stock numbered 105,200 volumes. The library receives three copies of each publication of the Higher Agricultural Institute free of charge and enriches it stock with about 3,000 Albanian and foreign books and periodicals a year through purchases, exchanges, or borrowings. It provides free service for the teachers, scientific workers, and students of the University as well as for all the specialists and working people of the agricultural institutions of the country. It maintains regular contact with district libraries, scientific agricultural institutions, and centers of production. In 1982 the Scientific Library of the Higher Agricultural Institute had regular relations with 111 foreign agricultural libraries and institutions in 29 countries. The Library keeps the readers informed about its stock through bulletins, bibliographies, catalogues, and other methods comparable to those of the other major libraries. Each year it publishes the bibliographical bulletin "Agricultural Science and the Advanced Experience in Our Country"; a bulletin on new foreign agricultural literature entering the country; reference bulletins on foreign agricultural literature for branches of agriculture; a catalogue on the foreign agricultural periodicals entering the country; and a series of subject bibliographies on the various branches of agriculture.

Public Libraries. Public libraries function in all the districts of the country. The first public library was opened in Elbasan in 1934. In 1935 another was opened in the city of Shkodra, and in 1938 a similar one was opened in Korça. After the liberation of the country in 1944, three public libraries were opened in 1945 in the cities of Durrës, Vlora, and Berat. Four public libraries were opened in 1950 in Gjirokastra, Peshkopia, Fier, and Pogradec. Another five were set up in 1958 in Lushnja, Kukës, Erseka, Saranda, and Tepelena. In 1966 the number of public libraries reached 25 (new ones were opened in Kruja, Lezha, Puka, Tropoja, Përmet, Gramsh, Burrel, Rrëshen, Skrapar, and Librazhd). In 1980 there were 42 public libraries altogether, with a stock of 2,175,248 volumes as against 202,000 volumes in 1950. The biggest public libraries by the mid-1980s were in the cities of Shkodra (more than 210,000 volumes), Korça (141,000 volumes), Elbasan (133,000 volumes), Berat (107,000 volumes), and Durrës, including Shijak and Kavaja (234,000 volumes). The increase of the public library stocks is subsidized by the state. Service in these libraries, as well as the postal service for remote zones, is free.

Excluding the National Library and the Library of the Academy of Sciences, the library of the city of Shkodra is the richest in works on Albania and the Balkans, and collections of manuscripts for the study of the development of Albanian nation history.

School Libraries. In 1982 there were 1,778 school libraries with 4,146,728 volumes in Albania (both in city and countryside). They provide free service for the teachers and students and lend both Albanian and foreign books. The stocks are subsidized by the state.

Special Libraries. A network of specialized libraries has been set up for each institution and work center. In 1982 there were 519 such libraries with 1,107,736 volumes. They provide free service for the specialists and employees of the institution or enterprise and offer publications in Albanian and foreign languages. Subsidized by the state, these libraries regularly increase their stock with the specialized literature they need.

Other Libraries. Each House and Hearth of Culture in the city and the countryside has its own library rich in all kinds of literature. In 1982 there were 1,803 such libraries with 2,674,651 volumes. Subsidized by the state, these libraries increase their stocks mainly with Albanian books of all kinds. The libraries of the Houses and Hearths of Culture provide free service for all the residents of towns and villages. They have the right to exchange books with all the libraries of the country free of charge in order to serve their readers.

MAHIR DOMI

Alexandrian Library

The Eastern Mediterranean coast and the Near East generally were divided after the death of Alexander the Great (323 B.C.) among his generals, who, along with many of their associates and successors, were educated individuals. Committed to maintaining Greek culture, which they regarded as justification for their rule over other peoples, they stressed a well-rounded education called *paideia*; by 323 B.C. the written word was vital to it. When faced with a foreign cultural tradition, despite whatever merits it had, the occupying Greek community felt obliged to demonstrate the superiority of its own. Such was the purpose of the Museum and the libraries in Alexandria, Egypt, initiated by Ptolemy I Soter with the help of the Athenian scholar Demetrius of Phaleron.

The collections seem to have been developed on the principle that the library should have a proper copy of every title in Greek; before long that objective was expanded with efforts to acquire translations of significant works in other languages, such as the Hebrew Torah. The procurement process embraced not only the standard dealings with book collectors and book dealers but also the practice notorious in the days of Ptolemy III Euergetes (as related by Galen) of obliging ships dropping anchor in the harbor to yield their books so that copies could be made for the library. There is some evidence of the existence of a rapid-copying shop to do the royal bidding, and Galen also notes that the books copied were identified as being "from the ships." Assembled were not only classic and other literary materials but also cookbooks, magic books, and oddities. A case can certainly be made for regarding the Alexandrian Library as the national library of Greek Egypt, not dominated by the publications or commitments of any one school of philosophy as had been common in the scholarly collections in Greece.

According to the most informative witness—the 12th-century Byzantine savant John Tzetzes, whose reports were critically reviewed by modern authority Rudolf Blum—the library in the Brucheion founded by Ptolemy I Soter was enlarged most significantly by his son, Ptolemy II Philadelphus. Demetrius of Phaleron was brought from Athens in the early 3rd century B.C. to develop the collection in Greek tragic and comic poetry, a responsibility that also included preparation of scholarly correct editions. Maintenance of the collections and supervision of library service soon became tasks of equal importance and were placed in the hands of Zenodotus of Ephesus—a Homer scholar and initially junior to Demetrius. Zenodotus seems to have been the first, around 291 B.C. to have been designated Director (*bibliophylax*), at a time when cataloguing and translation were recognized as part of the library routine under the beneficent eye of Ptolemy II Philadelphus.

Just as Zenodotus apparently made his mark first as a textual critic and then as an administrator, the cataloguing achievements of Callimachus, 25 years his junior, evidently enhanced the luster of his literary skills in about 250 B.C. His high repute may have facilitated the appointment of his fellow-Cyrenian, Eratosthenes, scholar in several fields and celebrated by posterity as a geographer, as the next Director. During the ensuing century the library continued to be managed by a succession of persons distinguished in science, Fellows of the Museum as it were. After 145 B.C. the record is silent.

When the first of several catastrophes struck, the fire at the Alexandria docks in 47 B.C. during Caesar's invasion, the Brucheion and its "daughter" library (possibly built for overflow), the Serapeum, held jointly some 532,800 rolls. The normal papyrus roll constituting a book was about 20 feet long unrolled and 10 to 12 inches high. Such a roll would contain, for instance, Plato's *Symposium* inscribed on 56 "pages" of 36 lines apiece, each line being 3.4 inches long. Quite a few papyrus rolls had writing on both sides. They were probably arranged in subject groups and utilized only on the premises. There is no proof of that arrangement or of how anything was located; available data are scattered and frequently incomplete. From the *Pinakes* of Callimachus it is known that subject, descriptive, and even evaluative features had been developed rather elaborately. Other surviving testimony is much more limited; notable is the inscribed catalogue found on Rhodes, taken to be the library of a gymnasium of the 2nd century B.C. In this catalogue the writers' names are in alphabetical order, but what order (if any) prescribes the listing of individual titles is not clear.

Information on architecture or furnishings does not exist beyond what archaeologists and chroniclers estimate on the basis of reputations and remnants of other Hellenistic library sites. Strabo the geographer visited Egypt about 24 years after the Brucheion fire and later mentioned the Museum's area with seats for discussion and mess hall for the scholarly staff, but he said nothing of books or library activities. From other sources, such as archaeological studies at Pergamum, it can be deduced that the large central area originally provided for sacred or prestige purposes gradually disappeared from libraries; by the time of the Romans all was practical, and libraries comprised a group of rooms of moderate size.

Alexandrian scientists flourished during the Roman Empire and perhaps utilized the library as before. Not very clear is the possible relationship between the library and the university developed in Alexandria by the Neo-platonists. Only too obvious, unfortunately, is the record of damage in the later 4th century, a by-product of religious conflict that went as far as street riots. By the time the Christians were finished fighting the pagans and each other, there was not a great deal left for the Islamic conquerors of the mid-7th century to maltreat.

Legacy. Yet the legacy of the Alexandrian Library was very substantial. For lack of surviving records one cannot produce details, but doubtless many writings of classical Greece and some other cultures were initially preserved for posterity by finding a home in that great repository. Indeed, the scholar hammering out the practices of textual criticism had to be working with numerous copies of many a work. And it is reasonable to assume that, with so much activity for unknown legions of scribes, there must have been considerable standardization of copying and manuscript handling, produced by supervision if not by formal instruction. We have very few precise comments by visitors and no official reports, but there are enough allusions in ancient and early medieval writings to indicate that word about many features, from architecture to the cataloguing implied by Callimachus' *Pinakes,* circulated rather widely. Moreover, for many who had no tangible data there was inspiration in the idea of the physically imposing, comprehensive scholar-library, an inspiration still voiced in Renaissance writings.

To a limited degree, the development of these traditions owed something identifiable to other libraries of the Hellenistic Age. The Attalids began in the latter half of the 3rd century B.C. to enhance their capital of Pergamum (now in northwestern Turkey, a few miles inland from Lesbos) with attractive installations, including a library. The archaeological testimony is scanty, but the literary traditions do touch on the fate of Aristotle's books on the one hand and the misadventures of the Alexandrian Library on the other. Perhaps the clearest record is the statement by late 1st century B.C. scholar Dionysius of Halicarnassus, working in Rome, that in preparing a biography he had used the *pinakes* of both Callimachus and Pergamum.

Other scholarly collections may have been established in the last two centuries of the Roman Republic in the Hellenistic East, because at least three turn up regularly in the histories of Roman conquest as war booty: at Pella, Macedonia, taken by Aemilius Paulus after the battle of Pydna in 168 B.C.; at Athens, whence about 86 B.C. Sulla carried off "Aristotle's Library"; and at Sinope, on the Black Sea, after Lucullus defeated Mithridates in 70 B.C. Scraps of archaeological and literary evidence indicate that there were founded also during that epoch, if not earlier, numerous secondary schools, *gymnasia,* teaching the seven liberal arts and a few medical schools and law schools; all have been thought likely to have had book collections, but proof is rare.

The institutions built during the Roman Empire have understandably left more traces, and certain features, such as housing in a temple, can be attributed at least partly to the influence of Egypt and the ancient East. One cannot assume, however, that the numerous libraries established in all parts of the Empire were shaped decisively, let alone exclusively, by Hellenistic models; Roman and local influences were present as well.

SIDNEY L. JACKSON
(d. 1979)

Algeria

Algeria, a republic in northern Africa, is bordered by the Mediterranean Sea on the north, Tunisia and Libya on the east, Niger, Mali, and Mauritania on the south, and the Spanish Sahara and Morocco on the west. Population (1984 est.) 20,841,000; area 2,381,741 sq.km. The official languages are Arabic and French.

History. Algeria possesses a variety of written documents for each epoch of its history from the most distant past to the present. On the rocks in the Tassili Mountains and in the Saharan Atlas Mountains there are paintings and stone engravings that bear witness to the life and culture of the first inhabitants of the country. Later the Carthaginians and Numidians left written messages on stone throughout the regions where they lived. These epigraphs in the Lybico-Berber alphabet are valuable resources for scholars. Even the Romans who colonized Algeria from the 2nd century B.C. to the 5th century A.D. used stone for writing. The ruins of Roman cities such as Djamila, Timgad, and Tipaza still contain many inscriptions.

The rarest documents are perhaps the Tablettes Albertini, private transactions from the period of Vandal rule in Algeria (429-533). These tablets of cedar wood are covered with a cursive Latin script written with a sharpened reed dipped in ink made from a base of dried carob. In 1928 these 45 tablets, which make up 34 documents, were discovered in a sealed terra cotta jar buried in the Tebessa region.

Following the Arab conquest of Algeria in 682, paper was incontestably the most used writing material, although vellum and parchment were also used in rare instances. The arts and sciences flourished by the 11th century, when two Berber dynasties, the Almoravides and later the Almohades, ruled in North Africa. Great kings such as Ibn Tumart and Abd al Mumin owned important private libraries. Much later, Ibn Khaldoun (1332-1406), an Arab historian famous for his *Mugaddima (Prolegomena),* maintained a large library during the many years he lived in Algeria. The Emir Abdelkader (1808-1883), an Algerian statesman who fought against France for 17 years, also possessed a remarkable personal library.

From their earliest existence in Algeria, the mosques and schools *(medersas)* played the role of libraries. Mosques and schools thus became the veritable guardians of manuscripts thoughout many centuries, until the time when France colonized Algeria and created libraries in the modern sense.

National Library. The National Library of Algeria, a public institution under the Ministry of Culture from 1982, was established in 1835 on the initiative of the civil administrator of the Regency of Algiers, Genty de Bussy. The National Library is the country's oldest cultural institution. Its first home

B. Ben

Façade of the National Library of Algeria, constructed in 1958. Established in 1835, the Library is Algeria's oldest cultural institution.

was a state-owned building, then it was moved into the Janissaries' barracks in 1838. After other moves, it settled in 1863 in the palace of the Dey (Janissarry commander) of Algiers, Mustafa Pasha. The National Library moved into the building it now occupies, a building constructed for it, in 1958.

The first four directors of the National Library were remarkable individuals. Adrien Berbrugger, who served from 1835 to 1869, was the author of several works including *L'Algérie historique, pittoresque et monumentale.* He was also in charge of the *Revue africaine* and the Algerian Historical Society. Oscar MacCarthy (1869–1890) was a geographer and an explorer. Thanks to him, the explorer and missionary Father Charles de Foucauld (1858–1916) was able to launch his Moroccan expedition. Émile Maupas (1890–1916), a biologist, was known in Europe for his work on the sexuality of the Rotifera, a class of microscopic animals with moving cilia, and the reproduction of Infusoria. Gabriel Esquer (1916–1948) was known for his works on Algerian history.

Although the Library collects in all fields, its humanities holdings are the strongest. Two notable private donations were the personal libraries of archaeologist Stéphane Gsell (1864–1932) and African explorer Pierre Sovorgnan de Brazza (1852–1905).

The National Library has a special collection of approximately 70,000 volumes on Algeria, Morocco, and Tunisia called the Maghreb Collection. In the 1950s, manuscripts concerning the history of Algiers in the 17th and 18th centuries (such as Pétis de la Croix's 1695 work "Description abrégée de la ville et estat d'Alger" and General O'Reilly y las Casas's 1709 work "Nuevo topographía de Argel") were acquired at sales of private libraries. The printed works in the Maghreb Collection include works of the 17th, 18th, and 19th centuries on the history of Algeria before 1830, when it became a French colony. Post-1830 materials are gathered together and include rarities such as the "Tableau de la situations des établissements français dans l'Algérie, 1838–1868" and "L'Exploration scientifique de l'Algérie," a 32-volume work (1844–54). Also included are certain old periodicals such as the *Moniteur algérien* and *El-Akbar*. Since the independence of Algeria in 1962, the National Library has brought together in this collection extensive documentation on the War of National Liberation (1954–62).

The Library also has a loan collection of approximately 25,000 books and a large reading room seating 450.

The Library's 3,500 manuscripts, mostly in Arabic, cover various disciplines such as theology, legislation, Arabic grammar and language, poetry, history and geography, medicine, philosophy, and astronomy. These manuscripts are valuable because of their age (11th–13th centuries), their rarity, or their illustrations. Examples are "Al-Muwatta," a collection of moral precepts in a magnificent copy executed in 1194 by the Almohad Abu Yusuf Yakub; and the Qur'an (Koran) in minuscule octagonal script, gilt-edged with blue and gold border, written in 1607 by the Persian Imad ben Ibrahim.

In 1958 the National Library owned a collection of 400,000 volumes and 1,200 current periodicals. By 1966 the collection had grown to 600,000 and by 1976 to 700,000 volumes, most in French, plus 150,000 Arabic-language works as well as 1,504 current periodicals in all languages. In 1981 the collections of the National Library numbered 765,850 volumes in foreign languages, 181,739 volumes in the national language (Arabic), 2,000 reels of microfilm, 4,250 phonodiscs, 360 maps, and 2,000 periodicals, of which 980 were current. The Library served 5,868 readers.

The National Library, as the beneficiary of legal deposit, publishes the *Bibliographie de l'Algérie,* a twice-yearly publication that registers publications received by the Office of Legal Deposit. The Library also publishes certain specialized bibliographies. The Library runs a large exchange service and participates in interlibrary loan.

Academic Libraries. The law pertaining to higher education in Algeria (December 20, 1879) led to the creation of the Library of the University of Algiers. It is the major academic library in Algeria of the 75 academic libraries surveyed in 1982.

After occupying several buildings, the University Library found a permanent home in 1888 in the main part of the building of the University of Algiers. At that time the library owned 15,000 volumes. At the end of the Algerian War, in June 1962, the University Library burned down, destroying 112,510 volumes. The Library was rebuilt and officially reopened in 1968. The Library of the University of Al-

giers is foremost among the various departmental and institute libraries. It is rich in foreign dissertations and has major humanities, legal, scientific, medical, and pharmacy collections. By 1976 its collections comprised 600,000 works and 1,550 periodical titles, as well as 12,326 Arabic-language works on microfilm or fiche. By the end of 1982, the library contained 641,800 volumes.

Special Libraries. Almost every ministry, firm, bank, and institution has its own library or documentation center for its own specific purposes. A national survey (1975–76) showed 300 in the country.

School Libraries. More and more primary and secondary schools are equipped with libraries serving students and teachers. The National Library assists by sending them gifts of books (500 volumes on the average). No statistics were published on the number or size of such libraries in the mid-1980s.

Public Libraries. Since independence, Algeria has built city libraries in all the *wilayate* (*départements,* or "counties"). These libraries, like the cultural center libraries, report to the Ministry of the Interior through the *wali* (prefects). In Algiers there are at present 12 city libraries, the oldest and biggest of which was opened in 1951. In 1976 it had 68,182 works and 30 current periodicals; by 1982 the collection had increased to 80,100 volumes.

The Profession. The training of research assistants and documentalists and the granting of a technical diploma in libraries and archives is regulated by decree 64-135 (April 24, 1964). Each candidate must have a high school diploma and take a 12-month program of theory and practice. The directorate of books, libraries, and public reading is in charge of this program.

The training of librarians occurs at two levels. Persons with a high school diploma take a four-year program at the University's Library Science School and receive a library science degree (decree 75-90, July 24, 1975). Research assistants may take a professional examination after five years of experience and receive the title of Librarian.

The same procedures are used for *conservateurs,* or curators. After five years of experience, a librarian may take a professional examination in order to become a curator. If not successful, the librarian must study for two more years before obtaining an advanced library degree.

Algeria did not have a library association in the mid-1980s.

R. CHAIT;
translated by CHARLES S. FINEMAN
and MARY NILES MAACK

Libraries in Algeria (1983)

Type	Administrative units	Service points	Volumes in collections	Annual expenditures (dinar)	Population served	Professional staff	Total staff
National	1	1	965,000	500,000	30,200[a]	9	82
Academic	75	12[a]	650,000[b]	250,000[a]	--	--	--
Public	35	--	--	--	--	--	--
School	--	--	--	--	--	--	--
Special	183	--	--	--	--	--	--

[a]Estimated
[b]University of Algiers only (1985) data.

Amano, Keitaro

(1901-   )

Keitaro Amano is recognized by many as the creator of modern bibliography in Japan. Born in November 1901 in Kyoto, Amano took a position in the Law Library of Kyoto University in 1922. In 1927 he published *Hosei, Keizai, Shakai Ronbun Soran* ("Index of Articles on Law, Politics, Economics, and Sociology"), which showed at once his brilliant ability as a bibliographer. It was followed by *Honpo Shoshi no Shoshi* ("A Bibliography of Japanese Bibliographies; 1933), which won him a leading position in the Japanese bibliographical world.

In 1948 Amano moved to the Kansai University Library, where he took an active part in the processing work as the head of the Technical Service Division. He also compiled a great variety of bibliographies; among them were "A Bibliography of Dr. Hajime Kawakami" (1956), "Bibliography of the Classical Economics" (1961-64), "Index of All Contents of Journals" (1966), and "A Bibliography of Max Weber in Japan" (1969). Articles collected in his *Shoshi Sakuin Ronko* ("A Study on Bibliography and Index"; 1979) represent his deep knowledge of the subjects.

Also an excellent cataloguing theorist, Amano wrote many books and articles on cataloguing, including *Yosho-Mokuroku no Tsukurikata* ("Guide to Cataloguing Books in European Languages"; 1949) and *Yosho-Mokurokuho Nyumon* ("Introduction to Cataloguing Books in European Languages"; 1951). In 1959 he represented Japan at the Preliminary Meeting of the International Cataloguing Conference held in London under the auspices of IFLA.

He retired from the Kansai University Library in 1967 and served as a professor in the Social Science Department of Toyo University until 1971. After returning to his hometown, Kyoto, he continued his life work, *Nihon Shoshi no Shoshi* ("A Japan Bibliography of Bibliographies"), the completely revised and augmented edition of *Honpo Shoshi no Shoshi,* published in 1933. The first volume, "Part Generalia," was published in 1973 and the fourth in 1984.

A detailed chronology and comprehensive list of his works appear in a book issued in honor of his 70th birthday, *Toshokan- gaku to sono Shuhen* ("On and around Library Science"; 1971).

TOSHIO IWASARU

American Library Association

The American Library Association (ALA) was founded in Philadelphia, Pennsylvania, in 1876, the centennial year of the United States. Among its founders were three major figures in American librarianship: Justin Winsor, William Frederick Poole, and Melvil Dewey, the latter relatively young and unknown at the time. The first Conference numbered 103 persons, 90 men and 13 women. From these small beginnings the Association had grown to a membership of more than 42,000 by 1985. The ALA annual summer conferences have also grown to an average of more than 12,000 persons, with the largest attendance being 14,566 at the New York City Conference in 1980. Summer Conferences are primarily

American Library Association

Reception hall of ALA Chicago Headquarters at 50 E. Huron in late 1940s.

devoted to educational and professional programs. The business of the Association has become a responsibility of the Midwinter Meetings, usually held in January.

The ALA has had its headquarters in Chicago, Illinois, since 1909. In 1946 ALA occupied its own building at 50 East Huron Street. A new building was constructed on that site in 1963. Further expansion occurred in 1981 when the Association occupied additional space in a newly built adjoining building, Huron Plaza, in which it owns an interest.

In addition to the Chicago headquarters, the Association has a Washington Office, which provides legislative liaison with the Congress and departments in the executive branch of government, and editorial offices in Middletown, Connecticut, for *Choice,* the book selection guide for academic libraries.

Total staff in the three locations numbered more than 230 in 1985. The chief operational officer of the Association is the Executive Director. In 1985 the Association had total revenues of more than $12,000,000.

Purposes. According to the 1879 Charter, the ALA was founded for "the purpose of promoting the library interests of the country by exchanging views, reaching conclusions, and inducing cooperation in all departments of bibliothecal science and economy; by disposing the public mind to the founding and improving libraries; and by cultivating good will among its own members . . . ." This charter has been amended only once, in 1942, when (1) "promoting library interests of 'the country'" was changed to read "throughout the world," thus giving a broader dimension to the Association's work, and (2) the phrase "and such other means as may be authorized from time to time by the Executive Board and Council of the American Library Association" was added.

The ALA Constitution states that the "object of the American Library Association shall be to promote library service and librarianship." This objective is further elaborated in a series of "Goals and Priorities" in the ALA Policy Manual; priorities are listed as (1)

Access to Information, (2) Legislation/Funding, (3) Intellectual Freedom, and (4) Public Awareness.

History. Since its founding ALA has promoted libraries and librarianship in various ways. During its first quarter-century the Association grew slowly. Often its major problem was staying alive. Justin Winsor served as President for the first nine years, followed by William Frederick Poole and Charles A. Cutter for two years each. Only two subsequent Presidents served more than one term: Melvil Dewey and Herbert Putnam, both for a year and a half-year on separate occasions. Dewey was also Secretary of the Association from 1879 to 1890 and in 1897 and 1898. He was, and is, the best known librarian among the American public generally.

Much was accomplished in the first 25 years despite the small membership. The Association launched a publications program; encouraged the cooperative development and publication of catalogues, indexes, and book selection guides; and promoted libraries at the World's Columbian Exposition in Chicago in 1893. Perhaps its greatest political accomplishment was the appointment of Herbert Putnam as Librarian of Congress in 1899, a position he would hold for the next 40 years and from which he would develop the Library of Congress into a truly national library.

As academic, public, and school libraries expanded, the need for trained librarians became more pressing. Dewey opened the first library school at Columbia University in January 1887. While not an ALA project, the school under Dewey's leadership was tied closely to the Association and its graduates had a far-reaching influence on the profession.

The second quarter-century was marked by Association growth and consolidation. The 1904 conference in St. Louis reflected dynamism, missionary zeal, and scholarship that, together, would continue throughout the next 75 years. This period also saw the rapid expansion of Carnegie libraries and the emergence of women as a major factor in American librarianship. ALA elected its first woman President, Theresa West Elmendorf, in 1911–12. World War I saw the ALA involved in an effort to provide books and library services to the U.S. armed forces, a highly successful effort that resulted in the permanent establishment of military libraries. Publishing was expanded with the establishment of the *ALA Bulletin* as the Association's official publication in 1907 and the *ALA Booklist,* with Carnegie help, in 1905.

Other library professional associations also began to emerge. A few state library associations had developed in the late 19th century. Some groups that began meeting informally at ALA conferences became independent: The Bibliographical Society of America (1904), the American Association of Law Libraries (1906), and the Special Libraries Association (1909). Subunits of ALA had earlier come into existence, including state librarians and college and reference librarians (1889), trustees (1890), and children's librar-

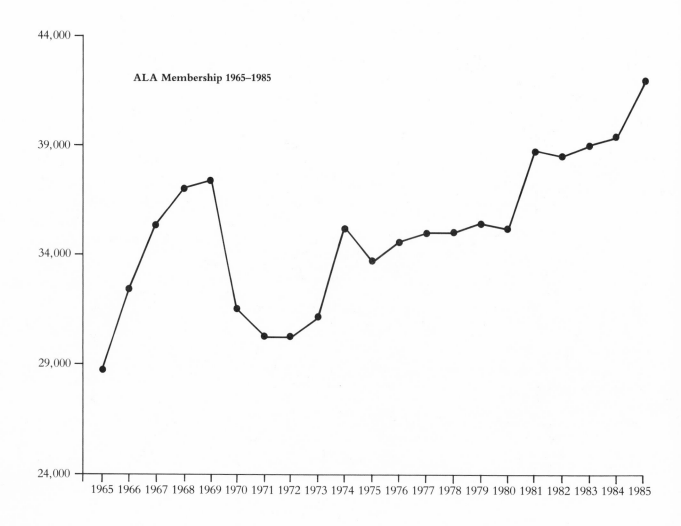

ians and catalogue librarians (1900).

At the celebration of ALA's 50th anniversary in 1926, the Carnegie Corporation announced a $4,000,000 program in grants to improve library education and to place ALA on a sound financial footing. Major topics for ALA in the next two decades would be adult education, library education, further development of library and professional standards, library legislation, and intellectual freedom.

In the years that followed, Carl H. Milam, who served as Executive Secretary from 1920 to 1948, dominated the Association as no one had since Melvil Dewey's time. His biographer, Peggy Sullivan, notes that Milam became ALA Secretary in a time of controversy and postwar unrest and left the position in a similar climate. Like his successors, he was a strong leader and an articulate spokesperson for library development and the library profession.

The Great Depression saw not only decreased revenues for libraries and for the Association, but also internal dissension. A Junior Members Round Table was formed in 1931, the Association of Research Libraries was established as a separate organization in 1932, and a far-reaching Third Activities Committee report set the Association on a path to providing more autonomy for its various units, especially the academic librarians, whose Association of College and Research Libraries (1938) was to become the largest of all ALA Divisions (9,158 members in 1985).

Three activities of the '30s became major foci for ALA during the rest of the century: a push for federal (national) aid for libraries, support of intellectual freedom, and movement toward racial equality.

Many academic and public libraries benefited from federal funding through various relief agencies of the Roosevelt administration. ALA became heavily involved in national planning, but the only result of a permanent nature was a library position in the U.S. Office of Education. Public library funding had to await passage of the Library Services Act (1956) under the Eisenhower administration. Other federal legislation for libraries was the product of Lyndon B. Johnson's Great Society programs (1963–68).

The coming of World War II, especially events in Europe, brought the issues of censorship and propaganda to the fore. ALA adopted its first Library Bill of Rights in 1939. Concern for free access was to become a major topic for the Association in the postwar years during attacks upon library materials by Sen. Joseph McCarthy. In 1953 ALA and other organizations issued a "Freedom to Read Statement" which had a significant impact on the defense of intellectual freedom. Further battles for freedom of the mind would be fought by the Association in the '60s and '70s.

Racial issues in the Association became a concern at the Richmond, Virginia, conference in 1936, as a result of hotel discrimination against ALA's black members. Afterward ALA adopted a policy that it

Chart 1. ALA Membership Organization

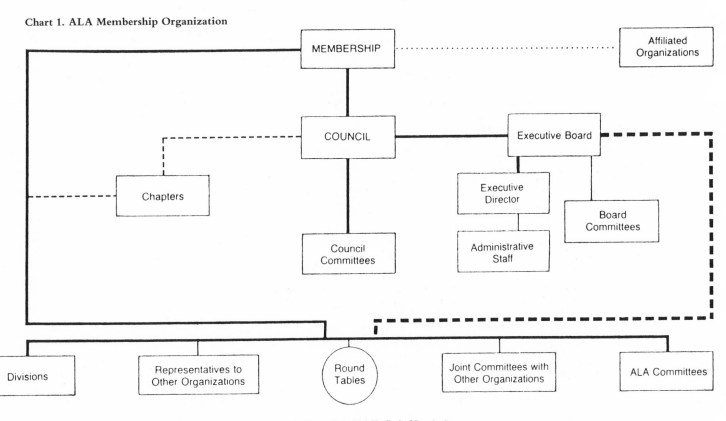

■ ■ ■ ■ ■ Central management. For explanation, see Constitution, Article VII, sec. 3, in *ALA Handbook of Organization*.

· · · · · · · · · · Special relations. For explanation, see Constitution, Article X.

- - - - - - - Representation on Council. For explanation, see Bylaws, Article IV, Sec. 2.

Carl Turk Photography

ALA constructed this building in 1963 on the 50 E. Huron site of its former headquarters in Chicago. It was connected to Huron Plaza in 1981.

addressed such issues, along with problems posed by declining fiscal resources and an inflation rate that threatened all voluntary organizations. In 1974 the membership approved a change in the personal dues structure that gave Divisions more control over their own programs. Publishing was revitalized. New space was acquired. And the Association celebrated its centennial in 1976 with a mixture of cultural events, intellectual substance, nostalgia, and more unity than it had enjoyed for a number of years.

The decade 1976–85 saw all parts of the Association grow and develop. Crucial issues remain: the professionalism of librarianship in the face of attacks on credentials; the right of every citizen to have maximum access to information in a democratic society; the improvement of opportunities for women and minorities; the continued attacks on intellectual freedom; the change in sources of financial support for libraries; the emergence of information science as a discipline; and the need for revitalization of professional education to meet needs posed by the new technology. These challenges continue as ALA promotes the cause of librarians and librarianship "throughout the world."

Organization and Structure. The ALA has been described as a "collaborative organization" or "an association of associations."

The policy making or legislative body of the Association is the Council, presided over by a President elected for a one-year term. The Council in 1985 consisted of 100 members elected at large by a mail ballot of personal members for four-year terms; one member elected by each of the 11 ALA Divisions; a chapter representative elected by each of the 51 state and regional associations; eight members of the Executive Board elected by the Council; the Association's elected officers (President, Vice-President and President-Elect, Past President, and Treasurer); and the Executive Director, a nonvoting member.

The Executive Board acts for the Council in the administration of policies and programs, serves as the ALA management board, and oversees headquarters operations.

would not again meet in cities where Conference accommodations could not be provided equally for all its members. For another 20 years ALA did not meet in the U.S. South. Progress was painfully slow. Even by the late '60s few blacks had achieved prominence in ALA positions. In the 1970s Robert Wedgeworth became the first black chosen as Executive Director (1972) and Clara S. Jones became the first black to be elected President (1976–77).

At the end of the 1960s the Association went through another period of turmoil and reorganization. Members were unhappy that the Association had not addressed the issues of a changing society. There was also a concern that the large organization was remote and impersonal. Divisions—membership units of the Association that serve special professional interests—were restive and wanted more autonomy. The new Executive Director and the Executive Board

Table 1. ALA Divisions: Membership* 1975–1985

	1985[a]	1980[a]	1975[a]
American Association of School Librarians (AASL)	6,447	4,770	7,315
American Library Trustee Association (ALTA)	1,644	1,724	2,178
Association for Library Service to Children (ALSC)	3,112	3,534	4,935[b]
Association of College and Research Libraries (ACRL)	9,158	8,915	9,324
Association of Specialized and Cooperative Library Agencies (ASCLA)	1,428	1,924	1,104[c]
Library Administration and Management Association (LAMA)	4,250	4,205	3,911[d]
Library and Information Technology Association (LITA)	4,925	4,059	3,228[e]
Public Library Association (PLA)	5,354	4,233	5,274
Reference and Adult Services Division (RASD)	4,661	4,747	6,228
Resources and Technical Services Division (RTSD)	5,922	5,916	6,464
Young Adult Services Division (YASD)	2,078	2,660	4,487

*Note: ALA members may belong to one or more divisions or to none.
[a] August 31.
[b] Children's Services Division
[c] Association of State Library Agencies
[d] Library Administration Division
[e] Information Science and Automation Division

Sources: ALA Administrative Services; *ALA Yearbook* (1976, 1981).

Eleven divisions exercise responsibility in their own designated areas. They are listed in Table 1. Each of these Associations or Divisions has its own officers, plans its own programs, manages its own budget, and has its own Executive Director. They all publish newsletters or journals. Much of the work of these units, as of ALA, is accomplished through a committee structure of volunteers who are rarely reimbursed by the Association for their expenses.

In addition to the Divisions, there are 15 Round Tables, "established to promote a field of librarianship not within the scope of any single division." They are listed in Table 2. Round Tables have no formal authority to act for the Association, but they exercise considerable unofficial power. Each has a staff liaison person, officers, and committees. Many issue newsletters, reports, and other publications.

There are also other small groups, such as Membership Initiative Groups and ALA Student Chapters (at library schools). Formal ALA Chapters are state and regional library associations, which are independent organizations. There are also 21 affiliated organizations, among them the American Association of Law Libraries, Association of Research Libraries, and Medical Library Association.

Carrying out general ALA programs that cut across divisional lines is the responsibility of major Offices at ALA headquarters. These offices, which have membership advisory committees to assist them, are the Office for Intellectual Freedom, Office for Outreach Services, Office for Library Personnel Resources, Office for Research, and the Washington Office. Other major units at headquarters include Administrative Services, Communication Services, Fiscal Services, and Publishing Services. ALA also has a Headquarters Library and an Accreditation Officer who administers the process for accreditation of library education programs.

Critics have often charged that ALA's structure is too complex. As an umbrella organization, the ALA has had difficulty creating structures that can

Arthur Plotnik

In 1981 the Association occupied new space in Huron Plaza, adjoining the 50 E. Huron building.

accommodate both general programs of benefit to all librarians and specialized programs of benefit to particular groups of librarians. Charts 1 and 2 show the organizational structure for governance and the organizational structure for the ALA staff.

Programs. The wide range of programs carried out by the ALA has been suggested in the review of its history and structure. Throughout its history the Association has promoted an awareness of libraries through its standards, publications program, legislative activities, defense of intellectual freedom, and preparation of library personnel. Priorities of the 1980s reflect that historic tradition: access to information, legislation and funding, intellectual freedom, and public awareness. Cooperative enterprises in cataloguing and classification, bibliographic control, in-

Table 2. ALA Round Tables: Membership

	1985[a]	1980[a]	1975[a]
Continuing Library Education Network and Exchange Round Table (CLENERT)	212	--	--
Ethnic Materials Information Exchange (EMIERT)	422	--	--
Exhibits Round Table (ERT)	279	308	381
Federal Librarians Round Table (FLRT)	546	513	398
Government Documents Round Table (GODORT)	1,340	1,457	965
Independent Librarians Exchange Round Table (ILERT)[b]	--	--	--
Intellectual Freedom Round Table (IFRT)	1,312	761	835
International Relations Round Table (IRRT)	608	581	515
Junior Members Round Table (JMRT)	1,251	1,079	879
Library History Round Table (LHRT)	358	438	--
Library Instruction Round Table (LIRT)	1,057	871	--
Library Research Round Table (LRRT)	713	761	554
Maps and Geography Round Table (MAGERT)	416	--	--
Social Responsibilities Round Table (SRRT)	876	773	877
Staff Organizations Round Table (SORT)	246	229	103

[a]August 31.
[b]Organized July 1985

Sources: ALA Administrative Services; *ALA Yearbook* (1976, 1981).

ALA

ALA

ALA posters promote libraries and reading, a principal objective of the Association since its inception.

dexing, bibliographic tools, automation, and networking have been encouraged and promoted by various units of the Association. Divisions and Round Tables address the specific concerns indicated by their titles. Most libraries in the U.S., and many libraries in other countries, have been affected by the activities of ALA.

The larger world of libraries outside the United States has actually involved relatively few members of the Association (except the Canadians, a large number of whom have long been ALA members). Nonetheless, international librarianship has been a concern of the ALA leadership since the beginning. The 1877 London International Conference, from which the Library Association of the United Kingdom (LA) emerged, had a large representation of librarians from America. Still, what had begun auspiciously did not take hold until the St. Louis Conference in 1904, which attracted large numbers of foreign visitors. World War I stimulated American interest in other countries and the 50th anniversary Conference of ALA in 1926 marked the first steps toward an international library organization. The following year the International Federation of Library Associations (IFLA) came into being at the 50th anniversary Conference of the LA, with ALA as one of the founding members.

Dennis Thomison, in his history (1978), describes ALA's international role as "strong and significant . . . with an almost missionary spirit in carrying the American methods of librarianship to other nations . . . ." Much of this ALA activity has been funded by American foundations or the U.S. government. An office devoted to international relations existed for quite a long time—1943–49 and 1956–72—but it was financed in large part by outside grants and was closed because of ALA's fiscal problems in the early 1970s. Still, ALA committees and boards on international relations have been and continue to be important avenues for the promotion of library interests in the areas of bibliographic control, library educa-

tion, librarian exchanges, and sharing of ideas about professional development. These activities are coordinated through the Committee on International Relations and promoted by the International Relations Round Table.

The IFLA Conference in Chicago, August 19–24, 1985, was a cooperative enterprise of the six IFLA member associations (American Association of Law Libraries, ALA, Art Libraries Society/North America, Association of Research Libraries, Medical Library Association, and Special Libraries Association), the U.S. IFLA member libraries, and NCLIS. Delegates from more than 86 countries attended programs of intellectual substance and practical significance. They toured special exhibits of products and services available to libraries primarily in North America.

Publications. One of ALA's significant contributions to the profession is its publishing program. At first ALA publications were printed and distributed by other organizations, including Dewey's Library Bureau, Houghton Mifflin, and the U.S. Government Printing Office. Early in the 20th century the Association began developing its own publishing services and now has one of the strongest publications programs of any library association. The first edition of *Guide to Reference Books* appeared in 1902. Under the editorships of Alice B. Kroeger, Isadore G. Mudge, Constance Winchell, and Eugene Sheehy, the *Guide* became known by the names of its editors ("Check its listing in Sheehy"), and over the past eight decades has been the best selling and most profitable of the ALA publications. *American Libraries,* successor to the *ALA Bulletin,* with a circulation of more than 42,000, is one of the most widely read general library periodicals. The Divisional journals are major contributors to the research literature in their fields. Through *The ALA Yearbook* (first edition, 1976; retitled *The ALA Yearbook of Library and Information Services* in 1984) the Association provides "an annual review of information about library events, activities, and personalities." *The ALA World Encyclopedia* (first edition, 1980), now in its second edition, provides "background information essential for comprehension of current issues and problems." *Booklist* is an important selection journal for thousands of libraries. The Association and its units also publish a variety of books, pamphlets, bibliographic tools, standards, and reading and audiovisual lists.

In the mid-1980s ALA Publishing Services was

Table 3. Personal and Organization ALA Members

Year	Personal	Organization	Total
1965	21,658	6,939	28,597
1975	28,754	4,762	33,516
1976	30,061	4,430	34,491
1977	30,898	4,221	35,119
1978	31,855	3,241	35,096
1979	32,723	3,075	35,798
1980	32,323	3,110	35,433
1981	35,422	3,374	38,796
1982	34,994	3,336	38,330
1983	36,104	3,020	39,124
1984	36,554	2,923	39,477
1985	39,073	2,944	42,017

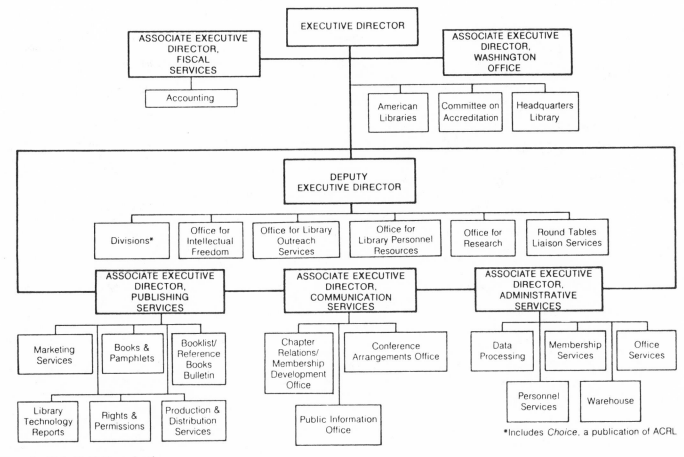

Chart 2. ALA Staff Organization

responsible for publication of almost 300,000 copies of books and pamphlets. The Association produced about 2,000 audiocasettes, 120,000 posters, 2,750,000 bookmarks, and 47 periodicals with a combined circulation of 360,000. Publishing revenue, including that of Divisional publications, was about $6,000,000.

Relations with Other Organizations. Chapters have a special relationship to the Association because they elect voting members of the ALA Council. Yet they are independent organizations and some—California, New York, and Texas—have memberships larger than some ALA Divisions.

Affiliates, including library associations in information science, library education, law, medicine, music, and theater, may share a kindred purpose with ALA, but their participation in ALA is less direct than that of the chapters.

The Association has for many years sent representatives to organizations outside the library and information science field, such as the American Council on Education, the National Council of Teachers of English, and the U.S. National Commission for Unesco.

Relations with other major national library associations can best be described as "cooperative." ALA worked closely with the Association of Research Libraries, the American Association of Law Libraries, the Medical Library Association, the Music Library Association, and the Special Libraries Association on copyright legislation in the 1970s. Through the ALA Washington Office the Association maintains liaison with many organizations that have common interests in federal legislation.

REFERENCES
Edward G. Holley, *Raking the Historic Coals: The ALA Scrapbook of 1876* (Beta Phi Mu, 1967).
Holley, "ALA at 100," *The ALA Yearbook,* Centennial Edition (1976).
Kathleen Molz, *National Planning for Library Service, 1935–1975* (1984).
Peggy Sullivan, *Carl H. Milam and the American Library Association* (1976).
Dennis Thomison, *The American Library Association, 1876–1972* (1978).
ALA *Annual Report,* 1983–84.
ALA Handbook of Organization (issued annually).
Joel M. Lee, "ALA Report," *The ALA Yearbook of Library and Information Services* (1984   ).

EDWARD G. HOLLEY

Angola

Angola, a people's republic in southwestern Africa, is bordered by Zaire on the north and northeast, Zambia on the east, Namibia on the south, and the Atlantic Ocean on the west. Population (1984 est.) 8,553,000; area 1,246,700 sq.km. The official languages are Portuguese and various Bantu languages.

National Library. Angola gained it independence on November 11, 1975, and in May 1977 the

Hedwig Anuar

National Department of Libraries was created, with the task of forming a national network of libraries, archives, and documentation centers. (Academic and school libraries, of the Ministry of Education, were excluded.) In that reorganization of the information community, the National Central Library in Luanda was founded, taking advantage of the collection and facilities of the former National Libary (1968), a part of the National Library of Lisbon, Portugal. Its collection was formed in part from materials outside the areas of specialties of the Library of the National Museum of Angola and the Institute for Scientific Investigation of Angola, and also included the Library of Education of the Provincial Secretariat of Education. Legal deposit functioned from Lisbon, which distributed materials through the national libraries of its provinces. The National Central Library was enriched by the recovery of various private and official libraries that had been abandoned. In 1978 a statute was approved to organize and regulate the National Department of Libraries and to establish the National Central Library, and in 1979 a legal deposit law was passed.

The national network also covers archives and documentation centers, with the exception of those in history, which are the charges of the National Department of Museums and Monuments. The most important center for archives is in the Museu de Angola, in Luanda.

Academic Libraries. The University of Angola maintains a General Library, which also serves as a center for documentation and as the National Center for Scientific Investigation. The Library's holdings are divided into special collections and are distributed in the cities of Luanda, Lubango, and Huambo. Individual departments of Biology, Botany, Geology, and Human Sciences maintain their own specialized collections. Taken together, the several university libraries contain several thousand volumes. At Luanda, the Library holds about 75,000 volumes.

Public Libraries. The largest public library is the Municipal Library in Luanda. After independence the National Department of Libraries moved, in keeping with a national literacy campaign, to extend the network of libraries to the rural areas, further expanded by the creation of committees of party militants functioning in such production units as farms and factories. Through these efforts people's libraries had been established in more than 50 locations by the late 1970s, serving a literate population of more than 2,500,000 (plus a student population of 2,000,000). Whether this progress continued during the country's political problems is not known.

School Libraries. School libraries are under the direction of the Ministry of Education.

Special Libraries. Under the direction of the National Department of Libraries, Angola's special libraries are administratively linked to the ministries they serve, such as Agriculture, Industry and Energy, Justice, and Petroleum. The largest, in Huambo, Luanda, and Lubango, specialize in agriculture and animal husbandry. Others are in localities throughout the country.

DOMINGOS VAN-DÚNEM*

Anuar, Hedwig
(1928-)

Hedwig (Aroozoo) Anuar, Singapore librarian and administrator, did much to promote and shape the development of Singapore libraries. Her career and interests involved her in many aspects of library development as well as library-related fields. She brought an intellectual quality and sense of vision to her work as head of the National Library and to other interests that proved unique.

She was born in the Malaysian town of Johor Bahru on November 19, 1928, and was graduated from the University of Malaya, Singapore, in 1951 with first class honors. She joined the University of Malaya Library in 1952 and was awarded an Inter-University Council Fellowship to study at the Northwestern Polytechnic in London. She obtained the Associateship of the Library Association in 1956 and the Fellowship two years later. She returned to the University of Malaya Library at its new campus in Kuala Lumpur, was assigned to the National Library of Singapore, and evenutally became its Director in 1965, a position she held thereafter.

The Library had its beginnings in colonial Singapore as the Raffles Library, a subscription library serving a largely expatriate and English reading public. It became the Raffles National Library in 1957 but was unable to break into a new pattern of service until 1962, when the New Zealand government sent A. Priscilla Taylor and J. R. Cole to Singapore as library consultants under the Colombo Plan. Taylor subsequently stayed on as Director until 1964 to do the initial planning and lay the groundwork for the development of the National Library. Under Anuar's directorship, these plans were realized and further extended.

Book collections amount to more than 2,000,000 volumes and include material in all four official languages—English, Chinese, Malay, and Tamil. Extension services were first provided through mobile libraries but later through the establishment of branch libraries housed in attractive new buildings, as in Queenstown (1970), Toa Payoh (1974), and Bukit Merah (1982). Two more branch libraries opened in 1985.

National bibliographical activities include the publication of the *Singapore National Bibliography* (1967–) and the *Singapore Periodicals Index* (1969-70–). The National Library acts as the Singapore center for regional projects such as the International Serials Data System (ISDS) and the National Libraries and Documentation Center, Southeast Asia Consortium (NLDC-SEA). It is also reponsible for the continuation of the *Masterlist of Southeast Asian Microforms* (Singapore University Press, 1978).

Her report *Blueprint for Public Library Development in Malaysia* (1968) was accepted as the basis for the development of public library services there. She served the Library Association of Singapore in many capacities, including the office of President. She chaired the LAS Joint Standing Committee on Library Cooperation and Bibliographical Service, 1965–75, and continued as the Vice-Chairman of its successor, the Committee on Bibliographical and Library Cooperation.

Other positions include Director (concurrent),

National Archives and Records Centre, 1969–78, and Honorary Secretary, National Book Development Council of Singapore, from 1965 to March 1980 and Chairman of the Council from April 1980. She was granted Honorary Fellowship of the Library Association (London) in 1985.

LIM PUI HUEN

Arab League Educational, Cultural and Scientific Organization

The Arab League Educational, Cultural and Scientific Organization (ALECSO) was established on July 25, 1970, after the first meeting of the Organization's General Conference in Cairo. Its Information Department plays an active role in the development and promotion of information services in the Arab region. At the beginning the work was planned to include collecting selected documents; facilitating the exchange of information; supporting the research work of other departments of ALECSO; publishing journals, newsletters, guides, bulletins, and bibliographies; holding meetings, seminars, and conferences; and preparing statistics related to the fields served by ALECSO.

Four main activities took place in 1971 that paved the way for the Information Department of ALECSO to fulfill its goals. The first was a Seminar on Promoting Library Services in the Arab World, held in Damascus in October 1971. The second was the Seminar on Cultural Statistics held in Khartoum in December 1971. The third was the formulation of several questionnaires covering the fields of education, culture, and science to collect relevant data related to those fields in the Arab world. Fourth, great effort was exerted to encourage the Arab states to apply legal deposit laws to their national libraries or other institutions with similar functions and roles.

As a result of those efforts, the Information Department carried out several projects in 1972–73, including (1) preparing guides and directories containing available data on information institutions, publishing houses, and periodicals in the Arab region; (2) issuing annual bulletins on Arab publications and educational statistics, a periodical entitled *The Arab Culture Magazine,* and a newsletter in Arabic and English; (3) holding a conference on the development of information services in the Arab region, the First Arab Bibliographical Conference (Riyadh, 1973), and a seminar on the Circulation of the Arabic Book (Doha, Qatar, 1972); and (4) organizing three-month training courses for librarians and documentation officers in the Arab world.

In 1974 ALECSO moved to a further stage. Programs and projects were planned to cover four major areas of activities: (1) developing technical, traditional, and mechanized tools used in information; (2) providing advanced bibliographical services in the fields covered by ALECSO; (3) raising the standards of personnel through training courses; and (4) collecting and publishing basic information on the Arab states in the fields of interest to ALECSO.

Several projects were initiated, including the *Bibliographical Guide to Reference Books in the Arab World;* a subject bibliography; new issues of the bulletins of statistics, Arab publications, *Arab Culture,* and the *ALECSO Newsletter;* organizing training courses; and holding a seminar on the use of computers in bibliographical works. The recommendations of the Riyadh Conference were carried out through a manual of Arab cataloguers, including Arabization of ISBD; a list of unified entries of Arab authors; studies on Arabic amendments to the Dewey Decimal Classification System; and experiments with an Arab classification system for Islamic disciplines. An experimental study was conducted on the rules to be adopted in preparing and using an Arab subject heading list. A model part of this list related to Islamic disciplines was produced and tried in some specialized libraries in the Arab states.

According to the results of these programs and the evaluation of the work achieved through them, ALECSO planned further projects that included a meeting on mechanical techniques in the field of information, held in Cairo in November 1976, and the Second Arab Bibliographical Conference, in Baghdad in 1977. Several studies on information sciences and the application of modern techniques were published in Arabic. A subject bibliography in education was prepared, covering Arab specialized periodicals, and a bibliographical guide to Arab works in library science and documentation was also compiled. Training courses were continued, and a meeting of Arab experts in educational statistics was held in Baghdad in 1977. This meeting played an important role in developing the annual bulletin of educational statistics.

In 1978 the new information program included preparing the draft Arabic subject heading list, the Arabization of the modified edition of ISBD, and a manual containing models for the application of the Arabized rules. A guide to Arab works in social sciences and anthropology and a guide to documentation centers were also prepared, along with a new bulletin, the *Arab Journal of Information Sciences.*

The project FRARABI (First Arab Bank of Information) was completed by mid-1985. Three data bases serve the objectives of the Organization: (1) the SAIB database deals with statistical information and research studies relating to education, culture, and science; (2) the SADOC database serves library and documentation functions; and (3) the SAFA database covers financial and administrative matters.

All three bases were to be connected with relevant databases of organizations and bodies related to the Arab League or ALECSO offices present in most Arab countries. Interconnections with international as well as inter-Arab national commissions affiliated to ALECSO, which operate in all the Arab countries, were to follow.

M. T. KHAFAGI

Arbuthnot, May Hill
(1884–1969)

May Hill Arbuthnot was not a librarian but, because of her contributions to education, as teacher, lecturer, children's literature specialist, reading consultant, and writer, children's librarianship in the United States is richer. In recognition of her efforts on behalf of literature and libraries for children, the Children's Services Division (now Association for Library Service to Children) of the American Library Association es-

May Hill Arbuthnot

51

tablished in 1969 the May Hill Arbuthnot Honor Lectureship, sponsored by Scott, Foresman and Company.

Born in Mason City, Iowa, on August 27, 1884, May Hill Arbuthnot received a baccalaureate degree from the University of Chicago in 1922 and her Master's degree from Columbia University in 1924. In 1927 she joined the faculty at Western Reserve University, Cleveland, Ohio (now Case Western Reserve University), from which she retired in 1949 as Associate Professor. Her teaching interests were in the general fields of nursery school and elementary education and the special field of children's literature. Her contributions in these areas were substantial. During her early years at Western Reserve, she was a pioneer in the nursery school movement. In 1929 she opened the University Nursery School, which became a successful model of a laboratory for teachers, doctors, nurses, parents, and other adults concerned with child development. Thousands of American children learned to read from the "Basic Curriculum Readers," which she wrote with William Scott Gray in 1951. Many of these children undoubtedly remember those readers as the "Dick and Jane" books.

Arbuthnot was a popular teacher on children's literature. A sought-after speaker throughout the country on children's books and reading, she spoke out firmly on topics related to the evaluation and selection of good books to meet children's developmental needs and reading tastes. In acknowledging the creation of the Honor Lectureship in 1969, she remembered "that long stretch of years when I was dashing from one end of the country to the other, bringing children and books together by way of the spoken word." She also offered her opinion that "a forthright, vigorous lecture can set fire to a piece of literature that had failed to come to life from the printed page."

She wrote extensively about children's books. For ten years she was Review Editor of children's books for *Childhood Education* and later for *Elementary English* (now *Language Arts*). In 1947 the first edition of her exhaustive textbook for children's literature courses, *Children and Books,* was published by Scott, Foresman and Company; she provided historical background on the development of children's literature, giving many examples of the best books of each genre and type, selections from illustrators, and advice on developing a child's reading tastes. While her textbook emphasized excellence in its approach to selecting and using books with children, she also stated as a cautionary, "Two facts we need to keep constantly before us: a book is a good book for children only when they enjoy it; a book is a poor book for children, when adults rate it a classic, if children are unable to read it or are bored by its content." This text, which reached its sixth edition in 1981, was rewritten and reorganized by Zena Sutherland and other contributors.

Her other books include many anthologies in which she brought together, by genre, excellent examples of fine children's literature and provided advice on its selection and use with children. Those anthologies, all published by Scott, Foresman, include *Time for Poetry* (with Shelton L. Root, Jr; 3d ed., 1968), *Time for Stories of the Past and Present* (with Dorothy M. Broderick, 1968), *Time for Biography*

(with Dorothy M. Broderick, 1969), *Time for Old Magic* (1970), *Time for New Magic* (with Mark Taylor, 1971), and *Time for Discovery* (with Evelyn Wenzel, 1971). Three of her other books—*The Anthology of Children's Literature* (4th ed. rev., 1976, by Zena Sutherland); a bibliography, *Children's Books Too Good to Miss* (7th ed., 1979); and *Children's Reading in the Home* (1969)—are still used in college courses and by others concerned with children's reading.

Arbuthnot's honors included the Constance Lindsay Skinner Award (1959) and the Catholic Library Association's Regina Medal (1964).

Arbuthnot died October 2, 1969, in Cleveland. Three months before her death, the May Hill Arbuthnot Honor Lectureship was announced. It provides for the annual selection of an outstanding author, critic, librarian, historian, or teacher of children's literature to prepare and give a lecture in the United States "which shall be a significant contribution to the field of children's literature." The lecture is presented annually, usually in April, and is subsequently published in an issue of *Top of the News*. (For lecturers, see *The ALA Yearbook,* 1976– , "Awards" and "Biographies.")

REFERENCE
Marilyn Miller, "Arbuthnot, May Hill," *Dictionary of American Library Biography* (1978).

MARILYN L. MILLER

Archives

NATURE, GOALS, PRINCIPLES

Nature of Archives. Archives constitute one of the world's primary information sources. They arise and grow uniquely out of the activities of any organization or institution, a family or even an individual. *Records* are the sum total of all documentary materials—regardless of their physical form or characteristics—created or received, and maintained, by an organization or other entity in connection with the transaction of its business and its other activities. An entity's records are the whole, the universe, from which its archives are selected. *Archives,* then, are those records of an organization, institution, or other entity that have been selected for preservation because they possess enduring value.

Physically, a wide variety of media have been used for record keeping during the course of human history. Included are cuneiform tablets, papyrus, palm leaves, and parchment; in modern times paper documentation of various kinds has evolved from the medieval parchments—the so-called "textual" records. In addition, many nontextual documentary forms have been brought into being by the new technologies of the 19th and particularly the 20th centuries: still photographs, motion picture films, videotapes, sound recordings, magnetic tapes, and related machine-readable forms. All of these, regardless of their special physical characteristics, are considered to be records, and therefore are potentially archives, if used by an organization or other entity for record-keeping purposes.

Types of Archival Agencies. The term *archives* is used to refer not only to records of archival value but also to the agencies—generally public or private institutions or organizational units—that are responsible for selecting, preserving, and making these records available. These agencies, as a rule, correspond to and serve the various types of record-creating and record-keeping organizations. Chief among the latter are public bodies, governmental agencies at every level (national or federal, regional, state or provincial, and local), attached to which, in a pattern that varies according to the structure of government in various countries, are the public archival agencies. The National Archives and Records Administration and the 50 independent state archives in the United States, and the Archives de France, a centralized system encompassing both the Archives Nationales and the archives services of all the departments, are examples. The term *archives* also has a third meaning; it is used to refer to a building, or part of a building, where archives are housed.

Nonpublic archival agencies consist mainly of "institutional archives" attached to and providing archival services for business firms, trade unions, universities, scientific and philanthropic organizations, religious bodies, and other institutions, both profit and nonprofit. Related to these are archival agencies, unassociated with particular creating institutions, that serve as custodians of the archives of classes of such institutions, such as businesses, unions, and churches. Archives of institutions are also to be found among the manuscript holdings of public or private libraries and historical societies. Family and personal archives are usually maintained informally by the families concerned but, when prominent people are involved, are often deposited in and administered by libraries and historical societies as "papers" or manuscript collections. Similarly, such papers may find their way to public or private archival agencies attached to organizations with which the families or individuals have been connected.

Purposes and Functions. Among archival agencies those serving public organizations were the first to emerge and still make up the predominant category. Today, as in the past, the overriding purpose of these public archival agencies is to identify the relatively small proportion of government records having archival value and to effect their regular transfer to archival custody, so they may be preserved for future use. Such preservation is justified by the information contained in the archival sources, which are valuable alike (1) to the government entities that initially produced them as evidence of their origin, organization, policies, programs, and principal operations over time and for long-term legal, financial, and other administrative purposes; (2) to private individuals and unofficial bodies in order to safeguard rights of various kinds and to assist in meeting their obligations; and (3) to scholars working in the fields of history, the other humanities, and the social sciences primarily, but also in the physical sciences, in pursuing their research.

Having developed programs for the systematic acquisition of records of archival value, based upon the application of professionally determined evaluation or appraisal standards, the archival agency provides for their physical preservation under the best possible conditions; perfects their organization and arrangement; describes them in guides, inventories, lists, and other finding aids designed to open them to

Hugh Talman/National Archives and Records Administration (NARA)

The National Archives in Washington, D.C., the National Archives and Records Administration Service (NARA) became an independent agency in 1985.

potential users; and, finally, makes them available for consultation—either directly, or through the medium of publication, originally by letterpress exclusively but later in microform as well—by the government itself and by the scholarly and general public.

Since World War II public archival agencies, led by those in the U.S., have increasingly expanded their function to the closely interconnected field of records management. Here the archival agency establishes standards of good practice with respect to the creation, organization, maintenance, and retrieval of the current records of government, as well as to their eventual disposition when they cease to be current by transfer to archival custody or by destruction; and seeks to promote the adoption of these standards by government bodies. Although the involvement of archival agencies in records management was initially motivated by the need to facilitate the transfer to them of the archival core of government records, there has been the concomitant result of more efficient and effective administration of government that is also vitally important.

Institutional archives of all kinds have the same basic purposes and functions as public archival agencies, although they generally operate on a smaller scale and are usually little, if at all, involved in the records management practices of the organizations they serve. Similarly, archival agencies, including archives, libraries, and historical societies, unassociated with the organizations, families, and individuals that created the archives they hold, play no records management role. Otherwise, however, they share the essential purposes and functions associated with other archival agencies.

Basic Principles and Terminology. A key characteristic of archives, as of the records from which they have been selected, is their organic character. This refers to the fact that they are not collected, in the usual sense of the term, by the originating organization or other entity but rather grow naturally—are created or received—out of its own activities and operations. Thus the individual documents that make up an organization's archives do not exist independently but instead are integrated within an overall structure of documentation that is essential to their significance.

The organic character common to all archival documentation leads logically to the fundamental principle of *provenance,* or *respect des fonds* in its original French formulation. This concept, which implies "belonging," holds that since the archives of a given organization belong to and constitute an organic whole, they must not be intermingled with those of any other organization. For the same reason, the corollary principle of *respect for original order* (or the "registry principle") requires that the archives of an organization should be maintained in their original internal structural pattern, and in their original filing arrangement (as in European registry offices), in order to preserve intact the close interrelationships between the individual component units. Otherwise, the meaning of the substantive informational content that they share as an organic whole would be seriously impaired or even destroyed. The implications of these principles for archival arrangement and classification on the one hand, and for archival description (that is, the preparation of finding aids) on the other, are most important: they have resulted in practices in these areas that are fundamentally different from analogous library practices, which are typically concerned with discrete items.

For purposes of control within the archival agency, all of the records, and the archives subsequently selected therefrom, of an organization compose its *fonds* (a classic French term used widely in Europe) or, in Anglo-Saxon parlance, its *record group* or *archives group.* (While there exist certain technical differences between the fonds and the record/archives group concepts, they are essentially comparable.) The contents of a record/archives group normally subdivide into *subgroups,* corresponding to the primary subordinate administrative branches of the organizations concerned. Where an organization has inherited records of a predecessor organization, these would also form a subgroup. There may be other special situations within a given record/archives group that call for the recognition of subgroups.

The primary physical unit within the record/archives group and its constituent subgroups is the *document,* a single item on which information is recorded that may take one of many varied forms, such as a letter or memorandum, a report, the minutes of a meeting, a map or chart, a photograph, a sound recording, or a reel of microfilm or magnetic tape. Documents rarely exist alone; they tend to be associated with other related documents in *file units* (for example, the folder, the dossier or case file, the bound volume in earlier centuries), which themselves are grouped in series.

As the basic archival grouping for all purposes, particularly for arrangement and description as well as reference control purposes, the *series* is of paramount importance. It consists of a body of file units, multi-document and/or single document in nature, which are interdependently linked together (1) in accordance with a particular filing scheme or other filing system of any kind, or (2) because they concern a particular physical character, or share a mutual relationship arising out of their creation, accumulation, or use. Within the record/archives group and its subgroups, the pattern of association of the constituent series reflects the hierarchical structure of the originating organization.

Against this background the following sections deal with the principal functional aspects of archives administration, preceded by a description of their legislative foundations. The functional aspects covered are: records management and records appraisal; arrangement and description; services to users; archives management; technical aspects (building, custodial services, and technical services); and professional training for archivists.

REFERENCES

Frank B. Evans, Donald F. Harrison, and Edwin A. Thompson, compilers, "A Basic Glossary for Archivists, Manuscript Curators, and Records Managers," *American Archivist* (July 1974).

Sir Hilary Jenkinson, *A Manual of Archive Administration,* 2nd edition (1965).

T. R. Schellenberg, *Modern Archives: Principles and Techniques* (1956).

Frank B. Evans, François-J. Himly, and Peter Walne, compilers, *Dictionary of Archival Terminology,* ed. by Peter Walne (1984).

MORRIS RIEGER;
revised by FRANK B. EVANS

LEGISLATIVE FOUNDATIONS

What Is Archival Legislation?. Archival legislation is probably as old and universal as archives themselves. Since archives are, according to a Unesco definition, "all noncurrent records of an institution or organization (those no longer needed in the conduct of current business) that are or should be preserved because of their permanent value," their preservation and use have long been regulated by the public powers. We know of the existence of laws on the subject as early as ancient Greece and the Roman Empire. In medieval Europe even the Popes and their Councils issued regulations on church archives, with threats of excommunication for offenders.

But the idea of comprehensive, systematic legislation on the whole matter of the conservation and use of archives is comparatively recent. The first country to conceive of it was France, in 1789–96, as a consequence of the French Revolution. Even now several countries throughout the world (especially developing countries) have no general archival legislation but only partial regulations of limited scope. Such differences from country to country can be explained by the fact that archives are closely linked with the entire legal, administrative, and socioeconomic system of each country. For example, in England and other countries with Anglo-Saxon legal traditions, documents derive legal value from the fact that they are kept in a public archival respository, whereas this is not the case in countries of Latin culture; legislation thus varies on this point. Another difference in the scope of archival laws is whether they are concerned with archives only after they have been transferred from the agency where they originated or also deal with the management of current records; the American and Canadian records management legislation has no equivalent in many countries. For all these reasons, it would be unrealistic to propose an "ideal" model for archival legislation. Many parts of a Russian or Chinese archival law would be meaningless in the U.S. or in Japan, while many requirements, useful in industrialized countries, would be useless in developing ones.

Public and Private Archives. In the eyes of the legislator, the distinction between public and private (that is, "nonpublic") archives is fundamental. Unfortunately, there is no consensus of definition in this matter. Definitions differ widely from one country to another, according to differences in socioeconomic and political systems. In socialist countries private ownership of archives is strictly limited to personal and family papers, whereas in other countires most business, society, trade union, university and school, hospital, church, and other institutional archives are largely considered private archives, with many variations from one country to another.

In nonsocialist countries one of the main points of uncertainty is the legal status of papers of heads of state, ministers, and senior public servants. A certain amount of confusion is inevitable between the private, personal correspondence and official papers of these individuals. In some countries the law enables the government to seize the papers of deceased or dismissed ministers and senior public servants, but this is seldom fully implemented, except for top-ranking army officers and diplomats.

The designation "public" applies to the legal status of these archives and not necessarily to their accessibility. Some public archives may not be accessible to the public (for example, "security-classified" diplomatic or military records), while some private archives may be freely open to inspection. Nor do "private" archives always become public when they are given, bequeathed, or sold to the state or to public institutions. In many countries they retain their private status even when they are public property, the distinction between private and public archives being more in their origin than in their actual ownership.

Public archives are universally declared to be imprescriptible (that is, not subject to claims or the assertion of customary rights by private parties) and inalienable. They can never cease to be public property, and they can be destroyed only according to official regulations. In some countries, such as the U.S., the legal designation of "archives" is even limited to documents that have a permanent value, while in some others, such as France, it applies to all documents, whether of permanent or temporary value. (There the distinction made between "records" and "archives," in the section *Archives: Nature, Goals, Principles,* does not exist.)

As to private archives (which in the U.S. are frequently referred to as manuscript collections or papers), the law really began to be interested in them, with a few exceptions, only at the end of the 19th century and the beginning of the 20th. Even now there is no legal protection for them in some countries, but generally there are at least laws prohibiting the exportation of private archives of historical interest and giving to the government a right of preemption should they be sold.

Administative Organization of Public Archives. Always a matter of legislative concern, the organization of public archives is closely related with the administrative system of each country. In countries with a centralized system, such as France, Italy, Spain, or the Scandinavian counties, archives also are generally centralized under one supreme authority (or a limited number of authorities). In such cases there is an integrated hierarchy of national (central), regional (provincial, departmental, or district), and local archives, as well as of specialized archives such as audiovisual, scientific, literary, diplomatic, military, and educational archives, all subordinate to a central governmental office.

On the other hand, in noncentralized countries, especially in countries with a federal constitution such as the U.S., Brazil, the Federal Republic of Germany, Switzerland, and Yugoslavia, each level of archival responsibility is independent of every other level (for example, the federal and state levels in the U.S.). For this reason it is very difficult to compare archival organization, for example, in France and the U.S., as in the first case there are laws and regulations applicable to the whole of archives in the country, while in the latter case separate federal and state laws and regulations exist.

In the past, archives and libraries were often confused with each other and placed under one single authority. In the 20th century advanced countries became aware of the basic differences that exist between archives and libraries and consequently created separate organizations for each of them. This was not the case everywhere, however, and in a number of countries there still remains a confusion that is highly prejudicial both to archives and to libraries, since the nature and use of the holdings of each, and the requirements for their administration, are significantly different.

The governmental authority under which archives are placed will also differ from one country to another. In the U.S.S.R. the General Directorate of State Archives depends directly on the Council of Ministers; in England the Public Record Office is under the Lord Chancellor; in France, Italy, and some other countries, archives are a responsibility of the Minister of Culture; elsewhere they belong to other ministries such as Education, Interior, or Justice, or they come directly under the authority of the President or the Prime Minister.

No system can be said to be ideal, but it seems that, at least in developing countries, only placement at the highest level of authority can give to the archival administration a sufficient degree of legal and administrative effectiveness.

Accessibility of Public Archives. Public access to archives is a relatively modern concern; it is linked with the progress of both democracy and objective historical research. The French law of 1794, which opened all public archives to public investigation, was, for a long time, nothing more than window dressing. The duration of the period during which access is restricted has been steadily diminishing. The term has come to be, in most countries, from 30 to 50 years, with special provisions to ensure the protection of individual privacy and state security. In several countries there are no time restrictions at all on access to public archives, except for certain categories and bodies of archives for which limited access is deemed a public necessity. However, despite an evident (but not universal) trend toward liberalization, access to public archives is still restricted in many countires, either by specific laws and regulations (especially when the searcher is a foreigner) or by sheer inertia and bureaucratic red tape. Of course, the "Freedom of Information" laws enacted in a number of countries in recent years have resulted in the opening of many recent records to public inspection. But these laws sometimes conflict with "right of privacy" legislation, so that the matter of accessibility has become one of the most controversial and complex of issues in the archival field.

Basic Elements of Archival Legislation. This broad survey of archival legislation and its background throughout the world enables us now to define what basic elements should figure in any archival legislation, regardless of the national political, administrative, and/or socioeconomic systems involved:

(a) Definitions of archives (and of records where the distinction is relevant), both public and private,

and of the nation's responsibility concerning their preservation for legal, administrative, evidential, and research needs. Special emphasis, where necessary, should be put on the distinction between archives, libraries, and documentation centers.

(b) Definitions of the organization and functions of public archival agencies, whether centralized or not, including their right to inspect public archives and records wherever they are located, to establish standards (preferably mandatory) of good current records management practice, and to operate intermediate records centers for the storage and maintenance of noncurrent records.

(c) Provisions granting to the archival agency the sole power and responsibility to appraise the value of public records for purposes of disposition (either destruction or preservation).

(d) Provisions governing the controlled destruction of noncurrent public records that have been appraised as lacking further value.

(e) Provisions governing (i) the transfer of noncurrent public records, selected as permanently valuable in the appraisal process, to the custody of archival repositories, and (ii) their subsequent arrangement and description.

(f) Standards for access to public records.

(g) Definitions of the duties and responsibilities of record managers and archivists and the requirements for their professional training.

(h) Provisions for the protection of private archives having historical interest.

REFERENCES
The archival legislation of more than 90 countries throughout the world has been published in vols. 17, 19–21, and 28 of *Archivum.*

MICHEL DUCHEIN

RECORDS MANAGEMENT AND RECORDS APPRAISAL

Before the Great Depression of the 1930s, records management was limited, with rare exceptions, to

National Archives of Zimbabwe

Librarians in the map room of the National Archives of Zimbabwe.

The reading room of the National Archives of Zimbabwe in Salisbury provides workspace for researchers.

National Archives of Zimbabwe

systems for controlling correspondence and devising methods of classifying centralized files. Chief clerks, then the administrative officers of most governmental agencies, and corporate secretaries or comptrollers in business and other private organizations, rarely concerned themselves with the disposition of noncurrent records. Though World War I had generated large volumes of records in most national governments, the problems of disposition were barely perceived. Filing operations were delegated to poorly paid clerks, and the cost of space for files was not deemed sufficiently high to justify managerial attention.

The public officials and archivists who were influential in establishing modern archives in France, England, Germany, Holland, and several other European countries had scant conceptions of records retirement and neglected any systematic approach to the appraisal of records values. Disposition was limited to the transfer of very old records to the archives. As these records had been produced when documentation was relatively scarce, archivists were inclined to accept all that were offered by the departments. Even records relating to housekeeping activities (personnel management, supplies, and minor fiscal operations) were accepted for preservation. By the latter half of the 19th century, however, small quantities of routine records were being culled from accessions. This weeding operation was not given much professional attention until World War I. During the war, waste paper was used for the manufacture of bullets, and occasionally important records were reduced to pulp without any oportunity for archival intervention. This loss alerted European archivists to the problem of preserving recent records; nonetheless, they failed to develop an appropriate methodology.

One exception to this neglect of systematic records disposition appeared in Poland in the early 1930s. As a result of the country's partition in the late 18th century, old and valuable Polish records were in the custody of Austria, Germany, and the U.S.S.R. Archivists, in order to establish a prestigious institution, were compelled to concentrate on providing for the preservation of valuable recent records. As a result, Poland pioneered in developing a theoretical approach by scheduling records disposition, that is, the itemization of discrete bodies of records, each accompanied by specific retention or disposal recommendations. The other European nations did not adopt similar programs until the end of World War II.

In the United States, railroads, banks, and insurance companies were among the first to try to rationalize records programs. They produced relatively large accumulations of records, many required for a number of years for administrative needs and regulatory compliance. Railroads led the reforms at the turn of the century because of the need to manage effectively information about real estate, right-of-way, rolling stock, train movements, and the administation of extensive networks. Furthermore, the Interstate Commerce Commission issued regulations concerning the maintenance of their varied records. Thus, by World War I railroads had adopted prescribed filing systems and designated records for permanent or long-term retention. Banks and insurance companies instituted similar procedures and practices in the years immediately after the war. With the exception of a few railroads, these firms did not, however, establish

institutional archival units like those emerging in Europe between 1901 and 1930.

The U.S. National Archives. When the U.S. National Archives began operations in 1935, the Archivist of the United States recruited, in addition to a managerial and an advisory staff, persons deemed qualified to appraise records for permanent preservation. These appraisers were selected on the basis of some experience with manuscript materials but, more important, because of their subject matter expertise; for example, scholars who specialized in diplomatic and military history and in the westward movement were delegated responsibility for appraising noncurrent records of the defense agencies, the Department of State, and the Department of the Interior, respectively. These archivists (Deputy Examiners) found that the records were in a chaotic state. Trivial materials were intermixed with records required to conduct essential public business, to protect the rights of individuals, and to serve scholarly research needs. Storage areas were inadequate for efficient access to records; some lacked even elemental fire protection.

To avoid uneconomical large-scale weeding operations, the appraisers had to accept or reject massive files of both temporary and permanent records. As the National Archives Building was empty, they could, in good conscience, lean heavily in the direction of conservation. They nevertheless deplored the state of records management and provided some counsel for reforms.

Enabling legislation authorized the Archivist of the United States to submit to Congress proposals by agencies for the destruction of specific bodies of noncurrent records that he deemed unworthy of permanent preservation by the federal government. The task of reviewing the proposals was delegated to the Special Examiners. The Deputy and Special Examiners thus gained considerable experience in past and current records management methods. While most agencies lacked any systematic control over their documentation, the departments of State, War, Navy, and the Treasury had developed classification schemes for some logical arrangement of their records. They had not yet devised rational systems for retiring or destroying records, though units with certain archival functions had been established.

With the start of World War II in 1939, the national archivists took an increasingly active role in advising agencies about reforms. They were especially effective, first, in the War and Navy departments and, later, in the war regulatory agencies. Some of the leading archivists actually transferred to records management positions in these agencies after they demonstrated how to organize files for more efficient access and how to rid files of records that were no longer needed for administrative purposes. They formed the nucleus of the records management profession that was to develop during and after the war.

These professional records managers worked in close association with their colleagues in the National Archives in developing efficient methods of providing for the orderly retirement of records. Together they successfully petitioned Congress in 1943 to authorize the National Archives to process agency recommendations for scheduling disposal of records after specific periods of time or after the occurence of specific events. Two years later Congess authorized the National Archives itself to propose to Congress the disposal of records common to all or several agencies (General Records Schedules). The 1950s saw the emergence of the comprehensive records control schedule by means of which agencies or major subdivision of agencies proposed the retirement of all of their records, either by disposal or by transfer to archives custody.

Growth of the Profession. During this period, about 1943 to 1970, the records management profession expanded greatly its responsibility for generally controlling records and communication channels. The Hoover Commission of 1948 gave considerable attention to efficient means for reducing the costs of managing records. It proposed centralizing responsibility for developing records management standards. Agencies would be required to appoint records management staffs to implement the standards. The recommendations led in 1950 to the incorporation of the National Archives into the National Archives and Records Service (NARS) within the newly established General Services Administration. NARS was delegated the centralized responsibility for records management recommended by the Commission.

This broad mandate led to the expansion of records management from simply developing filing techniques and retiring records to the management of mail, reports, directives, forms, reprography, and correspondence. To facilitate records retirement NARS organized Regional Records Centers based upon agency-controlled centers established during World War II for the temporary storage of noncurrent records. While the records in the centers remained under the legal custody of the creating agencies, reference service and the destruction of disposable records were carried out by center personnel. The centers also facilitated transferring to the National Archives the records designated for preservation.

As records managers and archivists became familiar with the rapidly changing technology for processing information, they promoted the use of various microfilm techniques and the use of electronic devices. They were thus in the forefront of the emerging information revolution. Some, in fact, are now designated information managers rather than paperwork or records managers.

Most of the information-oriented efforts of these managers concerned miniaturization of records. Roll microfilm had been the leading form of miniaturization for storage of records, but in the 1970s they experimented with and increasingly used microfiche and computer output microfilm (COM). Though there was an initial separation between managers of records and of automated equipment, some are cooperating to deal with the massive quantities of information in machine-readable form and in the resultant increases in hard-copy documentation and printouts. Like other types of records, machine-readable records and their by-products are being scheduled for preservation or disposal. Under recently passed legislation, NARS was separated from the General Services Adminstration and became an independent agency, the National Archives and Records Administration (NARA); it now shares with the General Services

Administration responsibility for goverment-wide records management.

These innovations had significant domestic and foreign spinoffs. The several states developed similar programs, and numerous foreign governments sent archivists and records managers to the United States to study techniques for managing current and noncurrent records. Most states and many foreign governments organized records centers, adapted to their special needs. The practice of scheduling the disposal of valueless records, as well as the transfer of permanent records to the archives, became common first in the industrialized nations and more recently in developing nations. Many private organizations, such as businesses, labor unions, universities, and churches, have to a greater or lesser extent developed similar records management and archival programs.

For the most part, public archives in other countries and private institutions generally do not differentiate between records managers and archivists. There, records management is still limited largely to advising on file management and retirement methods. In most private institutions, on the one hand, the records managers serve as archivists to the degree that they store records that are deemed of sufficient value for preservation as long as the organization exists. In certain foreign countries, on the other hand, archivists have become directly involved in making decisions about the disposition of public records. The activity common to all these organizations, now recognized as essential to efficient operations of agencies and for preservation of resources of research, is the disposition process whereby a valuable core of records is selected for permanent retention and the remainder is eventually destroyed.

Appraisal. In their initial experience in appraising records the founders of the National Archives benefited to some extent from the theories and practices of senior archivists elsewhere. The Polish archivist who recommended scheduling as a retirement technique, Gustaw Kalenski, also wrote of a selection process based on the values of records for continuity in government and for scholarly and other research. German archivists emphasized records that are required as evidence of the origin and administration of major governmental activities (evidential values). Other records deserve preservation for secondary purposes, that is, for the information of substantial value they contain for studies about people, places, events, and things (informational values).

The Archivist of the state of Illinois in the 1930s, Margaret Cross Norton, stressed the legal value of certain records as an essential element in selecting records for permanent preservation. Her emphasis on legal values was a direct extention of Germanic concerns about evidential values of basic records. About the same time Sir Hilary Jenkinson, Keeper of the Public Record Office in London, averred that records must have remained in unbroken official custody to assure their legal and evidential values. He also asserted that archivists should not intervene in records management and that archives should simply accept or reject the noncurrent records offered by administrative agencies.

While these views were helpful in developing their appraisal policies, the archivists in the Nationl Archives decided that new concepts were desirable or necessary. The long neglect of records had left them in a poor state, and the frequent alienation of important documentation led these archivists to the conclusion that unbroken custody was secondary to the need to bring valuable records under archival control. While they agreed that archivists are obligated to preserve records that document important governmental policies and decisions, they became more concerned about the value of records for research in history and the other humanities, the social sciences, and, to a lesser extent, the physical sciences. While the identification of records having evidential value for the history of governmental or private organizations is based on specific or concrete criteria, the appraisal of records for their informational values depends on subjective judgments about the likelihood of important research use of them in the future.

Records having evidential value may be classified, in the main, as follows: (1) those that show the origin and organization of agencies and their programs; (2) delegations of authority; (3) regulatory materials; (4) minutes of meetings and other records that document policy determinations; (5) documentation on the allocation of resources; and (6) selected records that deal with the procedures and the general administration of basic functions. It should be noted that these kinds of records can also be used for research on topics other than the history of the agency; for example, regulatory materials may provide valuable information about business operations, and policy records of the Department of State may be sources for research on foreign countries, as well as on U.S. relations with them.

Few concrete criteria for selecting records of informational value have evolved. Basically, archivists seek records containing unique data for research on important topics. Within reason, they should be convinced that researchers will eventually avail themselves of the records. Generally speaking, to judge informational values appraisal archivists must, by extensive study, master broad subject matter fields and familiarize themselves with related research needs and trends. In many countries they must have the concurrence of leading academicians before approving disposal.

While all records by their nature contain information of some evidential and informational value, more often than not it may be of such marginal interest that the costly preservation of the records involved is unwarranted. Furthermore, the preservation of records relating to minor subjects would so burden researchers as to impede research on significant ones. American and, increasingly, other archivists use aggregate techniques to deal with massive accumulations of records. They judge the values of each series or file on the basis of the total content. Among voluminous records on minor topics there may be some documents of interest. Seeking them would normally not be cost-effective, but records of certain agencies are so significant that an effort to find key documents is justified. In the case of large subject-classified central files, it is often possible to eliminate by class most housekeeping records and other papers that concern minor transactions.

A leading problem in appraisal involves decisions regarding voluminous case and survey files, also known as dossiers in France and as single-instance files in England. Many such files contain unique information for demographic, social, economic, and genealogical research. For research other than that which requires data about all individuals, institutions, or places documented in the series, archivists have used sampling techniques. This methodology assumes that the preservation of significant, typical, or random case files will provide sufficient information on the most important research topics to which the series relates. For functionally significant programs that generate quite routine documentation in the form of case files, appraisers have authorized the retention of another type of sample—a procedural one consisting of only a few cases to illustrate the performance of program operations.

Most sampling criteria for the disposal of case and survey files involve subjective judgments about the number of files to be retained and about their contents. To achieve objectivity archivists and records managers have increasingly used statistical sampling based on a random selection of cases to reflect the contents of the aggregate files. This solution also has its limitations, since certain files with significant research value may not be part of the sample selected for preservation. One method used to overcome this deficiency is to create a stratified sample that includes all files at the high level of a scale and reduced percentages at lower levels of the scale. Sampling has also been used as the appraisal technique itself for case files of a governmental investigative body. Concerned researchers have challenged the proposed disposition in a judicial proceeding, and the rulings to date—the case has not yet been decided—constitute one of the most copiously documented explanations of the selection process.

The information and computer revolution has greatly increased pressures on archivists for the preservation of source documents for social, economic, and political research. Before the widespread use of electronic media, detailed research about individuals, institutions, and phenomena generally in large numbers was impeded by the slowness and tedium of manual tabulations. But with computers, researchers can easily undertake the kind of research involving voluminous data that had not been envisioned during the early years of the 20th century.

Social and economic data of great variety are now being recorded in machine-readable form. The electronic media used for the purpose have the advantage of miniaturizing the information and of providing it to researchers in a mode susceptible of rapid, efficient manipulation. Evaluation of these media for permanent preservation, or disposal by erasure of the media, is conducted in Canada, Sweden, the United Kingdom, and the United States according to the same standards as for conventional records—that is, that records should have sufficient evidential or informational value to justify permanent retention. As a consequence, librarians, archivists, and records managers are increasingly including substantial training in electronic data processing as part of their professional education and training.

REFERENCES

M. H. Fishbein, "Appraisal of Twentieth Century Records," *Illinois Libraries* (February 1970), explains to nonarchivists the principles of appraisal.

Gustaw Kalenski, "Record Selection," *American Archivist* (January 1976), edited by M. H. Fishbein, from *Archiwwum Dawynch* (1934), a seminal essay by a Polish archivist.

P. Lewinson, "Archival Sampling," *American Archivist* (October 1957), the first and still best explanation of sampling techniques.

Theodore R. Schellenberg, *The Appraisal of Modern Records,* National Archives Bulletin No. 8 (1956), the standard archival text on appraisal principles and techniques.

National Archives and Records Service, *Appraisal of the Records of the Federal Bureau of Investigation,* 2 vols. (1981) includes and explains standards proposed to the U.S. District Court of the District of Columbia by NARS and the FBI.

C. P. Waegemann, *Handbook of Records Storage and Space Management* (1983) explains the effects of technology on recordkeeping and recommends standards for the retention of business records.

MEYER H. FISHBEIN

National Photography Collection, Public Archives of Canada

The enormous volume of governmental records creates special challenges in housing, processing, and using public archives.

ARRANGEMENT AND DESCRIPTION

The theory and practice of archival arrangement and description are of relatively recent origin. Historically, neither the volume, complexity, nor use of archives posed particular problems for either their custodians or their users. When no longer needed for the conduct of current business, most older documents, such as charters or treaties, were maintained in a basic chronological arrangement, while other noncurrent records, such as accounts and correspondence, tended to be maintained in the order in which they were transferred to the treasuries and strong rooms that served as archival repositories. Archives were conceived of primarily as "arsenals of law" for their parent institutions, and no general principles were needed to govern their arrangement.

During the 18th century, however, the holdings of archival repositories were subjected to a variety of reorganizations. In accordance with the predominant ideas of the Age of Reason, the merits of chronological, subject matter, and geographical arrangement of all documents were vigorously debated, and archives were frequently rearranged with no regard for their organic structure or functional relationships. With the development of the historical sciences, archives had come to be regarded primarily as "arsenals of history," and their custodians, intending to facilitate their use for historical research, adopted various schemes derived chiefly from library experience. Individual dossiers and documents were removed from the series in which they had originally been filed as part of administrative transactions (and for which they furnished the evidence) and were artificially rearranged, usually under specific subject headings.

The results of this policy were disastrous for many archives. The removal of documents and files from the organizational and functional context in which they were created or received, and from the administrative context in which they had been maintained and used, not only obscured or compromised the official and legal character of the records but also destroyed the context necessary for their evaluation and effective use as historical sources. In addition, such rearrangement rendered useless or seriously impaired the value of already existing finding aids, such as indexes and lists, and required that the archival repository undertake the expensive and time-consuming preparation of new and detailed classification schemes and indexes in order to locate and retrieve the incidental subject content that was the focus of many of the new systems. During the last half of the 19th century, however, the unfortunate consequences of artificial subject arrangement, as well as the development of a fuller understanding of the nature and character of archives, led to the formulation of the two basic principles that today are universally recognized as the sole appropriate basis for the arrangement of archives: the principle of provenance, or "respect des fonds," and the principle of respect for original order, or the "registry principle." (See *Archives: Nature, Goals, Principles* for definitions of these principles.)

Arrangement. Because the arrangement and description of archives are so closely related to the administrative structures and procedures and the record-keeping systems of the institutions in which they originated, and because these vary so greatly from country to country and historically within the same country, even a brief account for each country would require a treatise far beyond the scope of this article. The following summary is therefore limited to current arrangement/description practice in the United States and, to a lesser extent, in Canada.

The Record Group. In modern archival practice the function of arrangement refers to the process and the results of organizing archives in accordance with the principle of provenance and the principle of respect for original order at as many as necessary of the following levels: repository, record group (or comparable control unit), subgroup(s), series, file unit, and document. The process is intended to achieve physical (or administrative) control and basic identification of the total holdings of a repository, and usually also includes the packing of arranged archives into containers and the labeling and shelving of the containers. This summary of the function assumes a general archival repository that receives the permanently valuable noncurrent records of many different administrative units or offices of a parent institution, such as a government. Although hierarchically the repository level precedes the record group level, in practice the record group level must be given priority in arrangement. The process then proceeds from the repository level down to the individual item or document level.

Arrangement at the record group level consists of allocating new accessions of records on the basis of provenance to existing record groups or, if necessary, to newly established record groups. However, in establishing a record group, the concept of provenance, though fundamental, may be modified by other pragmatic considerations, particularly the administrative history, the complexity, and the volume of the records involved. In the U.S. National Archives, for example, all archives of the Department of State, on the grounds of common provenance, could theoretically be established as a single record group, but their considerable volume and complexity would serve to impede effective arrangement, description, and reference service. Thus these records have been divided into a number of record groups generally corresponding to the former bureaus of the Department, which exercised considerable autonomy in their operations. The records of the office of the head of the Department, the records of other units concerned with matters such as finance and personnel that affected the Department as a whole, and, in some cases, the records of predecessor agencies that had been incorporated into central files are then usually allocated to a separate "general" record group for the entire Department.

A further modification of the record group concept is the "collective" record group. To avoid creating an unmanageable number of record groups, the records of a number of small or short-lived, though separate, agencies that have an administrative or functional relationship (such as records of district courts or claims commissions) are assigned to a single record group. Within such a record group the records of each constituent agency form a separate and distinct subgroup. Under the record group concept, any particular body of records can belong to only one record group, and, except for subgroups or series consisting predominantly of cartographic, audiovisual, machine-readable, or other special physical types, an effort is made to keep together in the stack areas all records belonging to the same record group.

The value and flexibility of the record group concept have been demonstrated by its adaptation not only to the complex archives of governments at every level and for every period, but also to the archives of a wide range of private institutions and organizations and to the holdings of manuscript repositories, including artificially constituted collections (those that did not grow organically, as do archives in the true sense). Although broadly defined, the concept, when consistently applied, enables a repository to establish effective control over documentary materials of every type received from many different agencies, offices, and other sources.

The Repository. Once a decision has been made at the record group level, the records constituting that group are then allocated to an appropriate custodial unit for placement within the stacks of the repository. This is arrangement at the repository level, which necessarily will vary with the type of repository and, within the same repository, with the growth in the volume and character of its holdings. Allocation of record groups to custodial units may be made initially on the basis of a distinction between public records and nonpublic manuscripts (including personal papers), or it may be based, in a public repository, upon broad functional or hierarchical divisions. Legislative and judicial archives are frequently maintained separately from those of executive agencies; diplomatic and military archives are frequently maintained as separate units; and county and municipal record groups are generally separate from the records of state agencies in a state archival repository. Another basic division may be made between "open" and "closed" record groups, the latter consisting of the records of discontinued agencies to which no further accessions are expected. As indicated above, separate custodial units are generally established for significant holdings of cartographic, audiovisual, and machine-readable records. Other basic considerations that play a part in arrangement at the repository level include the size and physical layout of the stack areas, the number and type of personnel needed to work with certain bodies of records, the degree of security required for particular holdings, and the characters and frequency of reference and research use of certain record groups.

Subgroups. The third level of arrangement is that of subgroups within each record group. The subgroup concept is intended to distinguish between and to control the records of all primary subordinate offices or other administrative units that together constitute the record group, including any records of predecessor agencies. Each subgroup, in turn, is divided into as many levels as are necessary to accommodate the successive subordinate organizational units that make up the administrative hierarchy of the subgroup. For example, a bureau may be divided into divisions, each of which has several branches, each of which has several sections, and so on. The typical arrangement of subgroups is thus by administrative structure—the hierarchy of the offices of origin of the records—but where successive reorganizations or the consolidation of records series between offices obscures hierarchical origins, subgroups and subordinate levels therein may be established in terms of functional, geographical, or chronological relationships, or, if necessary, on the basis of the physical forms of the records.

The Series. Arrangement at the series level then takes place within the framework of subgroups within each record group. A series in the archival sense consists of documents in file units that normally are already structured or arranged, by the office that originated, maintained, and used them, in accordance with a filing system, or that were otherwise maintained as a collective unit by that office because they relate to a particular function or subject, result from the same activity, have a particular form, or have some other unifying relationship arising out of their creation, receipt, or use. Their hierarchical provenance ordinarily determines the specific subgroups within which series are included, but in cases where subgroups have been formed on nonhierarchical bases (see above), the subgroup position of affected series varies accordingly. Since modern decentralized record-keeping systems do not establish a set order of series within agencies or their individual offices, the archivist, on the basis of study of the administrative history, structure, and functions of the institution concerned, and also on the basis of study of the records themselves, must give to the series a meaningful physical order within the subgroup structure.

There is thus no one perfect or correct arrangement sequence for all series, but generally within each subgroup level, series relating to policy formulation and program direction are placed before series documenting program execution, and series of program or substantive records are placed before series of housekeeping or facilitative records. Particular attention is given to the functions of the organization corresponding to the subgroup: as far as possible the series are grouped according to the logical order of those functions and, with respect to each function, according to the logical sequence of actions taken to carry it out. However, regarding older records, which tend to provide more centralized and general coverage of the organization's functions and actions, it may be necessary to group and arrange series in accordance with major breaks in the filing system or according to chronological periods. In each case agency-created indexes or other finding aids are placed close to and usually precede the series to which they apply. Arrangement at the series level is thus intended to facilitate the use of archives while at the same time preserving their integrity within the organizational and functional context out of which they emerged.

File Units. Once the series have been arranged within the subgroup structure of a particular record group, arrangement then proceeds to the file unit level. Since most series are already arranged in accordance with filing systems used by the originating agencies, arrangement at this level usually consists of simply verifying the correct placement of each file unit within that system and of correcting obvious misfiles. Only where there is no original arrangement, or where it has been irretrievably lost, or where it cannot be reconstructed without an excessive expenditure of time, is the archivist justified in imposing a new internal arrangement on the series, and in such cases a full explanation of what has been done and the reasons for it should be included in the appropriate finding aid to inform and assist the users of the records.

Documents. The final level of arrangement is the document level. This involves the checking, and the correction of their placement when necessary, of the individual documents, enclosures, and annexes, and of the individual pieces of paper making up multipage documents, that collectively constitute the file unit. Because of the volume of modern archives, arrangement at this level remains an ideal rather than actual practice in most major repositories. It is a necessary preliminary, however, for series involved in microfilming or other photoduplication.

This summary of the sequence of actions involved in arrangement eventually culminates in the transfer of the records from temporary to permanent containers, which are then labeled with the designations of the appropriate record group, subgroups, se-

ries, and contents, and finally shelved. Control down to at least the series level must first be achieved before descriptive work is possible, since finding aids must refer to specific units in an established arrangement and the series is the basic unit of description.

Description. The theory and practice of archival description—the process of establishing intellectual control over holdings through the preparation of what are collectively called finding aids—is less developed than that of arrangement. In addition to the finding aids prepared for their own use by the offices of origin—which are properly part of the records and are accessioned and maintained with them—archival repositories produce a wide variety of published and unpublished finding aids that exhibit a lack of general agreement on either terminology or descriptive methodology. Published finding aids generally include guides and catalogues, inventories and registers, special lists, calendars, and indexes. In addition to such published finding aids, most archival repositories also prepare unpublished checklists, accession and location registers, and box and shelf lists. Finally, there are appraisal reports, record and manuscript group registration statements, and, for machine-readable records, software documentation, which serve incidentally as finding aids. In recent years, however, there has been a trend toward the development of three basic types of published finding aids in which an increasing uniformity of descriptive practice may be discerned. The three types are inventories (registers for manuscript groups and collections), guides, and what may be called detailed lists.

Inventories. Just as the record group level provides the critical key to the collective arrangement of archives, the inventory is the basic finding aid in their collective description. An inventory is prepared for each record group, or major subgroup thereof, in which the unit of entry is the series. An introduction defines the limits of the record group and provides a general description of the structure and functions of the agencies and offices whose records are involved and of the characteristics and general contents of the records themselves. The body of the inventory or register consists of individual series entries organized within the framework of the subgroups within the record group. Since the terms used by offices of origin to identify their "files" are usually meaningless to anyone outside that office, archivists must devise series titles that are unique and that convey the maximum information to the user about the types of records that constitute the series, the functions and activities they reflect or to which they relate, the inclusive dates within which the series was created, and its quantity. Under each series title there is usually a brief descriptive paragraph that indicates the arrangement of the constituent file units, any gaps in the series, further details of importance on the functions and activities that produced or are documented by the series, an indication of the major subject content of the records, and an indication of any restrictions on access and use. Inventories and registers frequently include in an appendix indexes, lists, or file titles or headings relating to particular series that would facilitate their use.

Guides. When holdings have been placed under basic intellectual control through a series of inventories or registers, the repository is then in a position to prepare and publish a general guide to its holdings. In such a guide the basic unit of entry is the record group. The administrative history, structure, and functions of the particular agency that corresponds to each record group are summarized, and the records that constitute the record group are collectively characterized in terms of physical types and forms, inclusive dates, quantity, and general subject content. Emphasis is also placed on organizational and functional relationships between record groups in order to provide a general orientation to the scope and character of the total holdings of the repository. For the same reason attention is directed to any restrictions on access or use of the records, and the entries also contain bibliographical data on published finding aids and relevant documentary or other publications.

In addition to repository guides, the term *guide* is also used to refer to finding aids that describe the holdings of one or more repositories relating to a particular geographical region, chronological period, or historical event, or to holdings of a particular physical type, such as cartographic or audiovisual. Although they are also called guides, finding aids that briefly describe the holdings of all repositories on the national, regional, or state level might more appropriately be termed directories.

Detailed Lists. The third type of finding aid, detailed lists of various kinds such as catalogues, calendars, and indexes, is usually prepared for records whose historical significance or research value and use justify the time and expense involved in their preparation. They may describe individual file units or documents from more than one record group, subgroup, or series that relate to particular subjects, but they are usually confined to the contents of single series or subseries. Such detailed lists are of particular value in assisting users of series whose original arrangement is unknown or that lacked any original arrangement. It should be noted, however, that microfilm publication has largely superseded the calendaring of archives.

As in the arrangement of archives, the principle of provenance remains the basis for all archival descriptive work. Faced with the wealth of major and peripheral subject content in modern public and institutional archives, obviously unable to foresee all future research trends and interests, and lacking the staff and budget necessary to create special subject-oriented finding aids to serve even the present range of research interests, archivists place primary reliance and emphasis upon the structure and functions of the creating agencies in the closely related tasks of collectively arranging and describing archival holdings. In so doing they preserve the integrity of archives and protect their official and legal character. They also make it possible for any present or future researcher on any subject to use archives effectively, because the experience of both archival repositories and users attests that knowledge of the organization and functions of their originating agencies serves as the best guide to the widely varied subject content of archives. As archivists experiment with automated techniques to establish better administrative and intellectual control over their holdings, it has become increasingly clear that the techniques devloped by related disciplines must be adapted and modified to accommodate the unique and organic character of ar-

chives if automation is to improve or replace existing controls.

REFERENCES

Frank B. Evans, "Modern Methods of Arrangement of Archives in the United States," *American Archivist* (1966), traces the development of the concept of collective arrangement to replace the earlier item-oriented manuscript tradition.

David B. Gracy II, *Archives and Manuscripts: Arrangement and Description* (1977), attempts to reconcile collective arrangement and description with the idiosyncratic practices of manuscript repositories.

National Archives, *The Control of Records at the Record Group Level,* Staff Information Circular 15 (1950); *The Preparation of Preliminary Inventories,* Staff Information Paper 14 (1974); *The Preparation of Inventories,* Staff Information Paper 14 (revised) (1982); and *The Preparation of Lists of Record Items,* Staff Information Paper 17 (revised) (1960), constitute manuals on the subjects with which they deal.

T. R. Schellenberg, *Principles of Arrangement,* Staff Information Paper (1951), is expanded upon more fully and related to the arrangement and description of personal papers and manuscripts in the same author's *The Management of Archives* (1965).

Richard C. Berner, *Archival Theory and Practice in the United States: A Historical Analysis* (1983), notwithstanding its title, deals almost exclusively with arrangement and description and proposes a unifying theory for the creation of finding aids.

FRANK B. EVANS

SERVICES TO USERS

Types of Service. The fundamental purpose of archival work is to preserve valuable records permanently and make them available for use. Together, the activities involved in providing access to records constitute the archival institution's reference service, which consists of furnishing records for use in search rooms, providing information from or concerning records, making copies of records, lending records to certain users, and exhibiting records. Complementing these direct reference services is the provision of indirect access by means of documentary publication.

Search Rooms. In the search rooms of archival repositories, which are analogous to library reading rooms, inquirers are able to examine records under the supervision of repository staff members. The inquirers are usually asked to complete an identification form giving their names and addresses and the purposes of their examination of the records. If necessary, repository personnel can advise inquirers about records that seem pertinent to their research and explain to them how the records are arranged and what guides, inventories, lists, or other finding aids are available. They can also make recommendations concerning information that should be included in footnotes or other references to records being examined and indicate what facilities exist for reproduction of records. Search room regulations governing the use of records typically require that their arrangement be left undisturbed; that they not be mutilated or destroyed by improper handling; that users avoid any actions likely to damage them, such as smoking, eating, or drinking; and that they be returned to search room attendants after their use. There are also regulations to prevent theft of records by requiring examination of objects carried out of the search room.

These security measures, however, are often accompanied by increasingly liberal arrangements for the use of search room facilities during hours when repository stack areas are closed.

Information Services. On a limited basis, archivists provide information from the records in response to written and oral inquiries. They often furnish specific facts, such as the date or place of an event and the names of principal participants. More extensive information may be furnished for administrative and legal purposes to the agencies that created the records and as a courtesy to high-ranking public officials. Efforts are made to keep written replies reasonably concise and responsive to the inquiries, and replies to recurrent types of inquiries are often made by form letters or by use of standard wording.

Information about records may also be provided orally or in writing, and inquirers are encouraged to seek such information before visiting archival search rooms. If their requests involve consultation of large bodies of records, they are informed of the titles of the pertinent record groups or other subdivisions of the records and of the inclusive dates and quantities thereof. Often such information can be furnished by supplying copies of published finding aids or reproductions of pertinent pages of finding aids. Archivists may feel obliged to furnish more information to inquirers engaged in major research that will be useful to the general public. In supplying any information from or concerning records, they strive to make factual statements and to avoid interpretation.

Copying. Photoreproduction has increasingly expanded the availability of records for research and other uses. Reproduction services often make it unnecessary for archivists to cull information from records and for inquirers to transcribe or take detailed notes on them. These services generally provide electrostatic, photostatic, or microphotographic copies of records at nominal cost. Electrostatic and photostatic methods are especially useful for furnishing full-size paper copies and reproducing selected records from scattered file locations. Such copies offer advantages in that they can be easily read; arranged, like research notes, in various ways; and examined together with related sources of information. Photographic and diazo prints of nontextual (that is, other than conventional paper documents) records are also furnished by an increasing number of archival repositories. Microphotography is generally preferred and used for the reproduction of a great quantity of records arranged in sequence. This process produces copies that are less expensive per item than full-size paper copies and have the great advantage of compactness. Such copies, however, require the use of reading devices. In recent years copies of sound recordings and machine-readable records are increasingly being made, in keeping with the growth of these forms among archival holdings.

In the United States the copyright status of records, as defined under the Copyright Law of 1976, determines whether or how copies of them can be made in reference service. Records of the U.S. government, with some exceptions, have no copyright protection and can be freely reproduced by archival repositories. Such reproductions can also be certified if required. Copyrighted materials that have found their way into the custody of public repositories can be reproduced in limited quantities for research purposes, provided there is no contrary agreement with the copyright holders. Such copies must carry a notice of the copyright status of the originals. This arrangement is supported by the accepted legal rule of "fair use," whereby certain uses are not considered an infringement of copyright.

Lending. The lending of records by archival repositories takes place only under special circumstances. Normally it occurs when organizations that created the records, or their successors, need them for administrative or legal purposes or exceptionally when such organizations give related organizations official permission to use them. Regulations usually provide that requests for loans be made only by specific officials of the creating organization, and for relatively short periods. Archivists oppose the lending of records in fragile condition and normally, in such cases, will provide photocopies instead. Records in public archival repositories may be lent to nongovernment organizations for exhibit purposes only under what are considered to be fully protective conditions. Loans are not made to individuals outside of repositories. Some American state archival agencies have established a network of regional archival repositories, usually at state universities, where state records may be sent on loan to be used for research purposes. Archival loans are also made in response to subpoenas but, as far as possible, certified photocopies are furnished instead.

Exhibits. Exhibiting records is still another way of making them available to users. Archival repositories plan both long-term and short-term exhibits as an important part of their public outreach programs. The National Archives Building in Washington, for example, has on permanent display the three fundamental charters of the United States: the Declaration of Independence, the Constitution, and its first ten amendments (the Bill of Rights). This repository also mounts temporary exhibits celebrating the anniversary of historical events in American history or documenting unusual national or international developments. In general, exhibits enable archival institutions to publicize their holdings and develop popular appreciation of historical records as cultural resources.

Documentary Publication. Documentary publication is an extension of reference service because it disseminates in published form a part of the holdings of archival institutions. Originally, publication was by printing exclusively, the contents consisting of documents of importance selected from larger bodies of archives or manuscripts. Since World War II there has developed the concept of complete publication of these larger bodies in order to preclude the danger of subjectivity in selection. A concomitant development has been the adoption of microfilming as an alternative, and far less costly, means of publication by the national archives of such countries as the U.S., Canada, the U.K., and Spain. Microfilm publication involves the preparation of a master negative microcopy of the concerned body of records, usually a series, within which is incorporated an extensive editorial apparatus analogous to that to be found in the conventional printed publication. Upon receipt of orders, positive prints are run off. In recent decades it has been U.S. National Archives policy to publish by microfilm all of the principal series in its custody for worldwide sale through a periodically updated catalogue.

Policies Governing Service. The use of records in the several types of archival reference service described above is controlled by access policies that vary nationally and, to some extent, within nations. As indicated in *Archives: Legislative Foundations,* the basic closed period has been considerably reduced over the years to the current level of 30 to 50 years. For this development much credit must go to the International Council on Archives, whose 1966 and 1968 Congresses in particular made strong recommendations for such liberalization of access. Also under the stimulus of ICA, archivists in many countries are working to ensure access for foreigners on equal terms with nationals.

In making records available to a growing variety of users, archivists must consider two competing rights: the right to know and the right to privacy. In the United States the first right is protected by a national Freedom of Information Act (1966, amended in 1974), which provides free public access to information in the records of federal executive agencies except for specified categories exempted from disclosure, primarily relating to national defense and foreign policy secrets, confidential commercial and financial data, investigations, personal affairs, and other matters specifically restricted by law.

Similarly, Canadian national government records more than 30 years old are open to the public unless they fall into specifically exempted areas, such as records whose release would constitute a breach of faith with a foreign government, be contrary to law, violate individual privacy, or be harmful to national security. The 30-year rule for access to public records has also been adopted in the U.K., with exempted records similar to these in Canada. Many U.S. states have enacted "sunshine" or open record laws, which make information in state records more liberally available to the public.

The Federal Privacy Act of 1974 limits access to records relating to individuals in the federal agencies generally but does not apply to the holdings of the National Archives. However, with respect to the latter, the right of privacy is upheld by certain of the exempted categories in the Freedom of Information Act, as well as restrictions imposed by the Archivist of the United States. These restrictions deny general access to records less than 75 years old containing information concerning the physical or mental health or medical or psychiatric treatment of individuals, and records concerning investigations of persons or groups of persons by investigative authorities of the federal executive branch. Efforts to protect privacy are also being made by archivists in administering nonfederal records containing personal data on such matters as medical treatment, legal representation, labor management relations, and welfare benefits. Similar concern for protection of privacy is evident in regulations of the Public Record Office of the U.K., which restrict access to certain records less than 75 years old, such as land revenue records concerning confidential transactions with private individuals and certain classes of police records. Also exemplifying this concern is the regulation of the Public Archives of Canada providing that personnel records may be used for research only 90 years after the birth of the individual involved.

Trends in Service. Archival reference service makes records available for several principal purposes. For the creators of the records, or their successors, it furnishes information needed to show administrative or legal precedents and fiscal accountability. For citizens it provides documentary evidence often essential for the protection of various rights. For the researcher, official and academic alike, it supplies data extensively used in all branches of learning—traditionally history and the other humanities; increasingly the social sciences; and, to a more limited extent, the physical sciences as well. Reference for these purposes constitutes by far the greatest part of all reference service, and the records involved are preponderantly in the custody of public archival institutions.

These government sources have long been used in the writing of political, diplomatic, and military history, since they were early recognized as basic for the purpose. As government functions and activities have expanded, especially in the 20th century, in various ways that touch closely the day-to-day life of the people and the operations of the national economy, government records have become more highly valued and more greatly used for research not only in social and economic history but also in political science, economics, sociology, anthropology, geography, and other social sciences. These studies have in recent decades been facilitated by the development of automation and automated records processes, symbolized by the computer and the machine-readable record. Increased use of public records has also been stimulated in recent years by mass media presentations of genealogical subjects, such as Alex Haley's *Roots* (1976), emphasizing the value of these records as sources for personal and family history.

Reference service in nongovernment archival repositories also supports important research. In such repositories records of educational, religious, business, labor, professional, civic, and other organizations are being relied upon increasingly for studies (of, for example, intellectual trends, population characteristics, urban and industrial life, and humanitarian causes) in a way similar to the expanded and unconventional use of public records today.

Archival repositories customarily maintain certain statistics on the quantity and performance of reference service. In providing records to the search room, on loan, for reproduction, or for exhibit, the unit employed for reporting purposes is an item such as a single document, folder, bound volume, roll of microfilm, or archival container. In furnishing written information from or concerning records, the unit is the transmitting letter or report. In supplying oral information the unit is the telephone call or personal conference. In most archival repositories statistics of reference service tend to show increases year after year. At the U.S. National Archives, for example, since about 1940 total units of reference service have increased annually from a few thousand to some 3,000,000. The increases result largely from expanded and diversified holdings of repositories, liberalization of access to them, and publicity given to their subject matter and value by publications, archives-sponsored scholarly conferences, and other informational methods. This trend seems likely to continue, since there is a growing appreciation of archives not only as cultural resources but also as major components of national and international information systems.

REFERENCES
Robert L. Clark, Jr., editor, *Archive-Library Relations* (1976), a seminal work dealing with the joint interests of the library and archival professions; includes treatment of these interests in reference service and in handling issues of copyright, literary property rights, and access.
Sue E. Holbert, *Archives and Manuscripts: Reference and Access* (1977), a publication in the basic manual series of the Society of American Archivists explaining principles and practices in providing access to records and manuscripts, types of reference service, and legal problems in access and use of these materials; especially useful for archivists in small and medium-size repositories.
William L. Joyce, "Archivists and Research Use," *American Archivist* (1984), an essay describing how archivists can best identify research values in records and promote the research use of records.
Ernst Posner, *American State Archives* (1964), a critical survey of practices in American state archival repositories that includes a brief description of prevailing reference service activities and recommendation of desirable standards in these activities.
Mary Jo Pugh, "The Illusion of Omniscience: Subject Access and the Reference Archivist," *American Archivist* (1982), a critique on current information retrieval methods in archival reference service.
Alfred Wagner, "The Policy of Access to Archives: From Restriction to Liberalization," *Unesco Bulletin for Libraries* (1970), a useful historical summary of access policies followed by public archives in the western world with special attention to the efforts of the International Council on Archives since 1966 to liberalize these policies.

HAROLD PINKETT

TECHNICAL ASPECTS

The technical aspects of archives administration help to fulfill the main obligation of the archivist: to preserve archival material for posterity and to make it available for use by the administration, by the scholarly community, and by the public. These aspects are necessarily based on the nature of archival materials and on the functions served by archives. Archival materials—stores of information now predominantly recorded on paper—accumulate, organically, within an administration or other organization as a by-product of its activities. Consequently documents are physically heterogeneous and exist either uniquely or in only a few copies each. Unlike modern books issued in planned editions and prepared by professionals, documents accumulate over time with little control over their physically diverse properties. Moreover, the modern media increasingly introduced by administrations, such as the various audiovisual forms and the magnetic tapes associated with data processing, bring about even greater diversity.

Archives must serve their parent administrations as well as the scholarly and general publics, and thus have to absorb materials for both their administrative and legal values on the one hand and their informational values on the other. Since materials possessing such values are being created constantly and must be presrved permanently by archival institutions, the potential for the latter's physical expansion is unlimited. The uniqueness of records, the diversity of forms, the duties to the administration and the public, and the unlimited growth—all leave their mark on archival buildings and facilities, conservation of materials, microphotography, and automation.

Archival Buildings and Equipment. The need to provide suitable housing for archives has played an important role in the establishment and design of archival buildings. This need is evident in the report of the parliamentary committee of 1836 in the U.K. as well as in the discussions leading to the establishment of the U.S. National Archives in 1934. The main purposes of an archival building are: to provide safe storage for an ever-increasing amount of valuable material, to keep the material indefinitely, and to make it available for use.

Safety and security considerations, as well as the prospect of unlimited growth, have in the 20th century led to a clear-cut separation between storage space and public reading rooms. Modern archives should be planned with an eye to expansion or decentralization. The need for expansion as well as the high cost of urban properties tends to drive archives to the urban periphery (as in the case of the new Public Record Office in the U.K.). The developed countries may have to choose between separating the urban service areas from the extraurban storage areas and decentralizing the archives themselves. In both cases, transportation and communication problems will have to be solved.

Storage specifications are dictated by the need to store vast amounts of material and to protect it from damage, natural or man-caused. In some countries the tendency is to build underground storage facilities, probably as a result of World War II experience (for example, the Riksarkivet in Oslo and the National Archives in Tokyo). Underground storage requires artificial lighting and air conditioning and thus larger expenditure. It also makes construction dependent on soil conditions. In other countries construction is both above and below ground. Some of the underground specifications are also applicable to above-ground construction, including artificial lighting and climate control.

It is now widely recognized that control of temperature, humidity, and radiation is most important for inhibiting deterioration caused by factors inherent in the documents, while filtering of the air is necessary to protect against pollution. Temperatures of 10°–14° C and 40 percent relative humidity are believed to be optimal conditions for most kinds of archival material. These conditions are, however, unsuitable for humans, and material kept under these conditions has to be preconditioned before it is transferred to reading-room environments. The accepted compromise is, therefore, 18°–20° C and about 50 percent relative humidity. Dust, aerosol, and hydrosol filtering should be introduced in most regions. In some countries, mostly tropical, the air-conditioning systems are used for fumigation. Light should be free from ultraviolet rays, since they are harmful to paper (and to other polymers). The issue of incandescent versus fluorescent lighting is still undecided; safety and economy of both are still under discussion.

Fire protection is a cardinal problem of planning. To facilitate isolation of fires, storage areas are divided into compartments no larger than 200 square meters (about 2,000 square feet) and no higher than

2.4 meters (about 8 feet). Electrical wiring, switches, and outlets should be reinforced (the European term is "Panzer"); metal fuse boards with automatic fuses are preferable. Fire detection and alarm systems are considered essential, and a direct alarm connection to a fire station is desirable. Water-sprinkler extinguishing systems are not universally recommended since water may cause considerable damage to archival material. Automatic extinguishing systems employing nontoxic gases, aerosols, and hydrosols (such as Freon or BCF) are gradually being introduced.

Efficient use of storage space leads to rectangular compartments with shelves usually running parallel to the long side of the rectangle. Internal planning depends on shelf size and aisle size. Though bodies of archives are heterogeneous, and many still consist of large series of bound volumes in various sizes, most

modern archival material is loose and boxed in containers, usually of standard cardboard, corrugated cardboard, and lately of plastics. The size of such containers varies, ranging from about 30 by 40 by 28 centimeters (about 12 by 16 by 10 inches, or a volume of about 1 cubic foot) to one-third that amount. This requires a shelf size of around 80 centimeters (32 inches) deep and a length of some multiple of 35 centimeters (13 inches). Aisle width runs from 80 centimeters for side aisles to 100 centimeters (3 feet) for main aisles. Mobile stacks or compact stacks (known as "compactus") are becoming widely used, and although they are considerably more expensive than stationary shelves, they save space up to almost 50 percent. Floor load is around 700 kilograms per square meter (145 pounds per square foot) for stationary stacks and as high as 1,000 kilograms per square meter (about 200 pounds per square foot) for mobile or compact stacks. All shelving nowadays is metal and is rustfree or properly protected.

Since archival materials sometimes include extremely valuable documents and classified records, most institutions therefore have vaults for protection against fire and theft. The large amounts of nonpaper documentation, such as tapes, films, microforms, and sound recordings, call for metal cans, small boxes, racks, air conditioning, and other special facilities.

Many archival institutions place documents on exhibition, posing the specially complex problem of preserving documents while making them accessible to the public. One of the most elaborately protected exhibits is the American Declaration of Independence and the Constitution at the National Archives in Washington; it is displayed in a case that is simultaneously a vault and an elevator.

While search rooms in archives are not essentially different from reading rooms in libraries, they have certain requirements of their own: readers' desks should be large enough to accommodate archives and

Oklahoma Department of Libraries

A 1968 warehouse fire at the Oklahoma Department of Libraries challenged archivists with smoke and water damaged records. Separate leaves had to be dried, and records repacked for storage.

records; special research rooms for researchers working on long-term projects are needed; more room for micro-readers is required; and space and equipment for playing sound recordings and for viewing films should be provided. Appropriate facilities must eventually be made available for use of the growing accumulation of machine-readable records on magnetic tapes.

Record centers are, in their essence, physically similar to archives buildings. However, they are generally smaller than the latter because they do not require as much reading room space and, given their function of accepting materials for limited periods only, are not meant to expand indefinitely. A typical feature of record centers is the loading platform needed for receiving (and sending out) large consignments of records. Adjacent to the loading platforms are usually rooms for the cleaning and fumigation, the primary arrangement, and, in some centers, the boxing and labeling of records. These features have all been inherited from the modern archives building.

Conservation of Archival Material. Conservation comprises *preservation,* preventative measures, and *restoration,* remedial measures. Preservation starts with the arrival of records at the archives. Unlike books, usually bought in new condition, records are deposited in the archives after years of frequent handling. Preliminary treatment (dry cleaning and fumigation) is necessary before they can be transferred to the stacks. Other preventative measures have been described above.

Document conservation presents some problems not encountered in book conservation. For instance, black printing ink, used in books, has remained virtually unchanged since the invention of printing. Documents, on the other hand, were first written with india ink (similar in stability to printing ink), then with ferrous ink—a stable material whose acidity, however, weakened the paper and even corroded it. The 20th century brought unstable and washable fountain-pen inks, and in the 1940s, the ball-point pen was introduced. The typewriter (patented in 1714 and put on the market in 1874) and carbon paper produced additional forms of unstable writing found in documents. Other features contributing to the problems of documentary conservation are paper clips, seals, and rubber bands and the most recent nuisance, adhesive tapes used for repairs.

In the 1930s the process of silking (to prevent documentary damage or to stabilize it once it has occurred) gave way to lamination by cellulose acetate, first practiced on a large scale by the U.S. National Archives. Yellowing and brittleness of the first laminates led to William J. Barrow's work, which resulted in the recognition of the importance of paper acidity and the necessity of deacidification. In the 1950s polyethylene was introduced for lamination in Eastern Europe, and in the 1960s Kathpalia initiated "cold lamination" (by cellulose acetate and acetone) in India. Lamination raised the problem of the reversibility of restoration where required. It is still a controversial issue, as are some new techniques that have been developed, such as encapsulation, introduced in the 1970s.

The vulnerability of modern inks encouraged research into nonaqueous deacidification, such as Bains-Cope's barium hydroxide in methanol. Gaseous dea-

cidification by ammonia has been practiced in Germany since the 1950s but is not widely accepted since it is considered unstable. Various vapor-phase-deacidification methods have been rejected, either because of unsatisfactory results or because of toxicity (for example, cyclohexilamine-carbonate). While experimentation goes on, the important problem of nonliquid deacidification has not yet been solved satisfactorily.

Paper casting, introduced in the 1960s, is not suitable for documents with unstable inks. The only way to reduce damage to ink is to fix it, the most popular fixer being soluble nylon sprayed on the document. The results of such fixing, however, are not altogether satisfactory.

The International Council on Archives, through its Conservation Committee, is trying to set standards for archival conservation and to help train archival conservators.

Microphotography. Microphotography may be applied in archives for a number of purposes: (1) Security copies: copying of the most valuable documents to insure against loss or destruction. These copies are usually deposited in vaults, preferably separate from the main storage area. (2) Supplementary material: copying records in other custody, mainly in foreign countries, of interest to the copying institution; this is especially important for countries formerly under colonial rule. (3) Publication: microphotography is considered, nowadays, the cheapest way to publish documents, especially in limited editions (see Archives: Reference Services). (4) Preservation: microcopies of documents in bad physical condition are substituted in reference service for the originals, thus protecting the originals from further damage.

Microforms present special preservation problems. The silver halide films, although the most durable of photographic materials (if properly processed), are not durable enough on the archival timescale; periodic film-to-film copying is considered essential for long-term preservation until more lasting materials are introduced. Past problems concerning the admissibility of microcopies as legal evidence of the existence of the originals have been solved in most countries.

The earlier notion that microphotography automatically solves archival space problems, once widely believed, is now regarded more skeptically since the cost of filming is often greater than that of storing the originals, even for a long period.

The International Council on Archives' Microfilm Committee is concerned with the archival aspects of microfilming and publishes a bulletin on the subject.

Computers and Archives. Archives are affected by the "electronic revolution" in two ways. Being themselves information systems, archives first use the new tool for more efficient information retrieval. Many archives employ automated techniques for the registration and indexing of archival material, though online systems are still rare in search rooms.

Second, since automation has penetrated into administration, records are increasingly kept on magnetic media, and archives have to preserve the valuable part of such records. Machine-readable archives present some serious problems—tapes are extremely unstable, and even when kept under optimal conditions (that is, complete environmental control, dust control, and protection from magnetic fields), they do not last more than about 15 years. Regular recopying procedures are therefore essential. It is hoped that Computer Output Microfilm (COM) and Computer Input Microfilm (CIM) may ease the problem to some extent.

In order to make effective use of the magnetic media, it is necessary to preserve, together with them, the complete documentation associated with their creation. The International Council on Archives Automation Committee is guiding archivists in these subjects by conducting seminars, publishing manuals, and issuing a bulletin.

REFERENCES
Yash Pal Kathpalia, *Conservation and Restoration of Archives: A Survey of Facilities* (Unesco, 1978).
Louis A. Simon, "Some Observations on Planning Archives Buildings," in *Building and Equipment for Archives,* Bulletin of the National Archives no. 6 (1944).

A. ARAD

ARCHIVES MANAGEMENT

Archives management is a subject that has been virtually ignored in archival literature, but there is some evidence that its importance is beginning to be recognized. Management is the utilization of human, financial, and material resources to perform the functions for which an organization exists. Indeed, good management is particularly important for archives. Because of the traditionally low priority given to archives in the allocation of public funds, it is necessary to make the most effective use of the resources available, and, if additional resources are required, the justification should be documented and presented in a manner that will convince legislators, budget officials, and the general public that such expenditures will produce measurable benefits to the community that is served.

While archives are universal in the sense that all human activity produces them, there exist a wide variety of archival institutions concerned with various types of archives: government archives (national, state, and municipal); the archives of businesses, universities, and other corporate bodies; and specialized archives for particular subject-matter areas (labor, immigration, or science) or particular physical types of archival material (films or sound recordings). The place of archives in an administrative structure varies even for similar types of archives. For example, some state archives are a part of a government department, while others are a part of state libraries or historical societies. Whatever the place of an archives in an administrative structure, it is desirable that it have a distinct identity, with a separate budget, staff, accommodation, and direct relationships with creators of records; and that the director have authority to control the complete operations of the archives and its available resources.

The main functions of management are planning, evaluation, organization, staffing, and external relations.

Planning. While the general objectives of archives are formulated in legislation, they are not precise enough to meet planning needs. Long-term plans should include objectives and goals to be achieved in, for example, a period of five years. For each year operational plans should have precise targets and the allocation of precise resources that can be translated into an operating budget. While managers are subject to constraints such as regulations and management systems that apply to an entire government jurisdiction or other organization of which the archival institution is a part, they have the primary responsibility for the definition of objectives for the archives and the development of plans to meet them. The approval of long-term plans implies a commitment of the resources that are necessary to attain them, and annual budgets as stages in the implementation of an approved plan are more likely to be adopted than if they were based on ad hoc increments to programs antedating the plan. Planning is a cooperative exercise in which all concerned managers should participate, but the particular objectives and plans of subunits should be in the context of a comprehensive plan for the institution as a whole. Factors that are important in archival planning are: the requirements for services to users; necessary accommodation, including space for expansion; the emphasis on conservation; the adaptation of technology to archival operations; and the commitment of a rational allocation of resources that will ensure the execution of all archival operations.

Evaluation. Plans are based on priorities at a point in time and on the information that is available at that time. Even if the elements in the plan are valid and conditions that affect its implementation do not change, it is essential to be able to assess and measure the progress in achieving the objectives for which the plan was developed. This requires performance measurement, based on quantifiable indicators that will indicate production or work accomplished. On the basis of information obtained by monitoring implementation, of changing priorities, and of other modifications arising from the allocation of resources, plans must be evaluated periodically and appropriate changes made in objectives and programs. To use the example of conservation, if all the resources called for in a particular year are not provided, if production is more or less than was projected, or if technological innovations affect the original program, these factors, considered in the evaluation of the program, will result in the revision of the original plans. Management control, then, requires a plan, the measurement of activity, the comparison of actual to planned activity, analysis of results, and corrective action. Important elements in evaluation are the promotion of economy, efficiency (the ratio of input to output), effectiveness (the extent to which the objectives are achieved), and the quality and level of service (which user surveys should test).

It is recognized that statistics are essential for planning, organizing, directing, and controlling. Most archives compile statistics for their own purposes on holdings, accessions, arrangement and description, reproduction, and reference services. But they tend to lag behind libraries in the standardization of statistics (which is necessary for comparison with similar activities in other institutions) and in using statistical data for planning purposes. For example, a plan for protective microfilming should take into consideration all the elements in the program and

National Archives of Zambia

National Archives Building in Lusaka, Zambia.

their costs. Although the quantity of material and salaries of the various types of staff involved are known, it is difficult to project the cost of such a program without information concerning time norms for prefilming preparation of material and microfilming rates. The use of statistical information is necessary not only in the costing of programs and decisions on various options but also in planning every aspect of an archival service from accommodation to reference services, establishing priorities, ensuring the most effective utilization of available resources, and justifying additional resources.

Organization. While libraries and archives have, in the words of Robert L. Clark, Jr., a common purpose, "to collect, maintain and make available the written and graphic record of man's intellect and experience," differences in the origin and nature of the sources with which they are concerned impose differences in organization and methodology. Since archives are the official records of a corporate body, the relationship between the originating body and the archival institution is an essential concern of archives management. Indeed, archives are not collected but are accumulated, as records, through a process of creation or reception by the originating body. The doctrine of continuous custody (between the originating body and the archival instituion that serves it), which has been put forward by Sir Hilary Jenkinson, a former Director of the English Public Record Office, has been extended, particularly in North America, to the concept of the integrated records/archives life cycle that encompasses the entire existence of records from the creation to permanent preservation of their valuable nucleus as archives and destruction of the valueless remainder.

Under the general direction of the chief archivist there are two distinct major operational units in the archival institution, one for current records management and retirement, and the other for archival operations, each with appropriate subdivisions. Separate units also exist for conservation, reprography, and general administration. There are two basic elements in records management operations: advisory services to originating departments, and services for records centers, intermediate repositories housing noncurrent records prior to their destruction upon expiration of residual values, or to transfer of their valuable segments to the archival institution.

Several factors, including the unique nature of archival materials, the principle of respect des fonds,

and the need for knowledge of the content of records, affect the organization of internal archival operations. While libraries are usually organized on functional lines with divisions and separate staff for accessioning, cataloguing, and reference, it is not unusual for individual archivists to be involved in all functions with respect to particular bodies of archives: appraisal, acquisition, arrangement, description, reference, and even the preparation of publications and exhibitions. Subdivisions are usually established on the basis of broad subject-matter areas—for example, foreign or military affairs—deriving from the functions of the originating bodies, or of significant chronological periods, or a combination of both. When an archival institution, in addition to receiving the official records of its parent body, accepts related corporate or personal records from external sources, these records should be maintained in a separate section or division. Other special units are required for nontextual types of archival materials—machine-readable archives, maps, photographs, films, and sound recordings. Special units are required for conservation and reprography. The institution should also have its own archival reference library.

No special organization is required for basic administrative functions such as personnel, financial, and materials management. Arrangements depend to some extent on the degree of autonomy of individual institutions, which ranges from separate archives departments, with all the staff required for administration, to archives divisions within a government department or library that provides administrative services for the archives as well as its other components. These services, however, must be responsive to the special requirements of archives with regard to specialized staff and training, special accommodation and equipment, and the essential purposes of the archival institution: records disposition, preservation, and service to the public.

Staffing. The most important resources in archival operations are human. Since these operations are labor-intensive in nature, a major proportion of a budget (perhaps 75 percent) is for salaries. One could gain the impression from publications relating to archival functions that most of these functions are carried out uniformly by professional archivists. On the contrary, in any archival organization that has a staff of more than one there is a degree of specialization that increases with its size and scope. Indeed, the operations of an archival institution require a variety of specialized skills, and an important task of its management is the recruitment and allocation of personnel possessing these skills—at the appropriate levels and in the appropriate numbers—in order to ensure the collective achievement of the objectives of the institution.

For statistical as well as functional purposes the archival staff usually comprises professional, professional support, clerical, technical, and administrative categories. While in North America the qualifications of a professional archivist are not as precise as in European countries, which typically have uniform preappointment training, a minimum educational qualification is a university degree, usually in history or a related field. Professional functions require a combination of academic knowledge, professional skills, and the exercise of judgment. To make the most effective use of staff, a "professional support" category (the archives assistant), between the professional and clerical categories, is most important. A proportion of two professional, one professional support, and three clerical positions has been suggested as most suitable for archival operations. As mentioned earlier, specialists are required to deal with such record media as maps, photographs, film, and machine-readable materials. It is advisable, however, to train professional archivists to work in the first and last of these media areas rather than to recruit the corresponding media specialists, that is, cartographers and computer programmers. The reason is that substantive archival considerations are more important in these areas than are technical ones. On the other hand, conservation and reprography are entirely technical support areas for which trained technical specialists are essential. Similarly technical specialists are needed in such areas of administration as financial and personnel management. But in all of these areas it is indispensable that senior management direct all operations, approve policies, set priorities, and ensure the maintenance of acceptable standards. Staff requirements should be identified in the context of the budgetary cycle.

External Relations. A former Archivist of the United States, Robert H. Bahmer, insisted that one of the most important functions of archival management is the interpreting of the archives to "a variety of publics." This is more than public relations in the conventional sense. An archives does not operate in isolation, and the effectiveness of its operations depends to a considerable extent on the quality of its relationships with many elements in society. The archival manager should miss no opportunity to interpret "archival work to the public as a necessary factor in an enlightened society" through speeches, interviews, conferences, publications, and so on.

A number of specific "publics" require special attention. One is the authority from which the financial resources supporting the archives are obtained, usually a legislature, and particularly the responsible minister. Another is the officialdom throughout the records-creating departments responsible for the management of records there; still another, in the case of archival institutions that accession materials from the private sector, is the body of donors, potential donors, or friends of potential donors. The users of archives and their professional associations make up another important public with which close relationships must be maintained. Among them are the historians concerning whom a great deal has been said and written, but the support and approval of many other bodies of users, in academic and nonacademic fields alike, is also vital. Close connections must be cultivated as well with related institutions such as libraries and historical societies, and with national and international professional archives associations.

REFERENCES
Robert E. Bahmer, "The Management of Archival Institutions," *The American Archivist* (1963).
B. Delmas and J. A. d'Olier, *Planning National Infrastructures for Documentation, Libraries and Archives* (1975).
Frank B. Evans and Eric Ketelaar, *A Guide for Surveying Archival and Records Management Systems and Services: A RAMP Study* (1983).
James B. Rhoads, *The Role of Archives and Records Management in National Information Systems* (1983).
Michael Swift, "Management and Technical Resources," Paper, 10th International Council on Archives, Bonn (1984).

W. I. SMITH

PROFESSIONAL TRAINING

Professional training for archivists in the strict and formal sense began in Western Europe in the first half of the 19th century. Five types or traditions have developed.

The European Tradition. Here the training offered was originally based mainly on the historical auxiliary sciences, in particular paleography and diplomatics (generally relating to the study, deciphering, and authentication of old historical documents and manuscripts), which during the 19th century and after were among the central disciplines of "scientific" history. The first formal training schools for archivists were the École National des Chartes in Paris and the Bayerische Archivschule München (Munich), both founded in 1821. These were followed during the next half-century by eminent schools in many European countries, such as the Institut für Österreichische Geshichtsorschung, Vienna, founded in 1854. Some of the leading institutes of this period no longer exist, but all those remaining were radically reorganized in the period immediately after World War II, at which time a number of new schools were set up. Today virtually all European countries have centers of some type in which the archivists for their national archives services at least (if not for other institutions) are trained. The older traditions are still carried on to a certain extent by most of the countries of Central and Eastern Europe, for example by the State Institute of History and Archives at Moscow.

The training schools of the European tradition are usually either autonomous institutes, financed by government (like the French École des Chartes), or are attached to principal archives services (like the Archivschule Marburg, West Germany), or are associated with the historical faculty of a university (like the Institute of History and Archivistics, Nicholas Copernicus University, Torun, Poland). Among

Riksarkivet/Solly Sannerud

Strongroom in the solid rock, four-story underground National Archives of Norway. The stacks on either side of the passageway are mobile.

these training schools a distinction is possible between those in which students are already staff members of the national archives services, or in which successful graduates are guaranteed appointments in those services on completion of the course, and those in which the students compete in an open job market. A distinction is also possible between those schools that take students at about the age of 18 years, on completion of their secondary school education, and those that take students on completion of their university education. The former courses are naturally longer than the latter, usually three or four years as opposed to one or two years, but there are great variations from country to country both in the length and the weight of courses, practical requirements, and so on. The most extreme case of prolonged training is found in Germany, where students are recruited at the postdoctoral stage and then given another two years of training. Such students will be at least 27 years old before starting employment. The average starting age in most European countries, however, would be 22 or 23.

Relatively little attention was given until recent years to professional subjects, as distinct from the historical sciences, so much so that in France the National Archives has had to institute a second training course, known as the Stage Technique International des Archives. This course must be attended by all its new staff members and may be attended by external and foreign students also. It has had a potent influence in disseminating professional standards and knowledge in many countries.

The Italo–Hispanic Tradition. The second of the main traditions in archival training may be termed the Italo-Hispanic. In Italy there are no fewer than 17 government-financed schools of archivistics, paleography, and diplomatics, one in each province. Together, these turn out more than 3,000 students per year, only a tiny proportion of whom actually become archivists. In Spain, and even more in Latin America, there is a similar phenomenon. In the latter continent there are at least 18 archival schools or courses in 12 countries, most of them attached to universities. Particularly notable is the Interamerican Center for Archival Development at the Escuela Nacional de Archiveros in Córdoba, Argentina, which acts as a regional training school. Most courses in this tradition offer first degrees in archival science or in librarianship and archival science. In the Spanish and Portuguese traditions, a close link is maintained between archival and library training; indeed it is difficult to differentiate them in such schools as that of the Faculty of Letters, University of Coimbra (Portugal), or the School of Documentalists, National Library of Spain, Madrid. In these first-degree courses, a large number of the students do not intend to follow archival careers.

The British Tradition. A third model is provided by the British tradition. Here there is no specialization until students have taken their first degree, usually at the age of 21, by which time they have completed their general education. They may then be recruited into an established archive service and trained by apprenticeship in-house, or, more usually, will follow a one-year postgraduate course leading to a Diploma (in some cases a Master's degree) in Archives Administration. These courses are offered by four universities (Dublin, Liverpool, London, and Wales). They concentrate on technical and professional subjects, give practical instruction, and can be closely associated with historical researchers and research methodology. Small numbers of students (between six and twenty per course) are normal. A similar pattern of training may be seen elsewhere in the world where the British tradition in education is important, particularly in the Commonwealth countries, in Africa, Asia, and Australasia, and, most recently, in Canada. For Britain itself, the Society of Archivists has a system of distance education for unqualified archivists who are in post.

North America. In the U.S. and Canada there is no universally established method of initial training. The Society of American Archivists issues an *Education Directory,* periodically updated, which lists courses and institutes in archival subjects. The 1983 issue lists 43 multi-course offerings, 19 single-course offerings, and 6 institutes and workshops at universities, archival institutions, or historical societies. None of these courses constitutes a full-time specialized training program, and many of them are not accredited academically. Normally, locally based archivists provide the teaching staff. Professionals in North America complain about the inability of the region to establish either a professional training institute on the European model, or a regular full-time course on the British model, but despite this the U.S. has achieved a flexible and economic system, which makes maximum use of the teaching potential of practicing archivists and local archives services and

Theodore F. Welch

Entrance to the Yomei Bunko, Kyoto, containing historical records of the Fujiwara-Konoye families.

which can respond quickly to local demand. In many cases the academic and professional standing of these courses is high, and they have made substantial contributions to the theory and practice of archives administration. The development of short, comprehensive summer institutes—often held in library schools, open to all comers, and a very characteristic feature of North American training methods—is associated initially with Ernst Posner (who taught 1939–61) and later with T. R. Schellenberg (who taught 1963–70). In recent years the Society of American Archivists has promoted studies of training requirements and is seeking to develop systems of accreditation of training programs and of certification of qualified archivists.

The Third World. In the Third World there has been a natural tendency to continue the traditions of the former imperial countries. This is particularly true in Latin America. The 1970s saw the emergence of a movement towards regional training, sponsored in large part by Unesco and the International Council on Archives. In Senegal (University of Dakar), the regional school for French-speaking African countries runs a two-year course to train archives assistants; students at a higher level must seek training overseas, mainly in Europe. A one-year postgraduate program has been set up at the University of Ghana, but has not succeeded in giving a training provision for English-speaking countries.

Proposed regional schools for Southeast Asia, first mooted in 1968, and for the Caribbean, were planned to start in 1983, but as of the mid-1980s they had failed to take shape. In South Asia, by contrast, the Indian national training school at New Delhi caters to students from the region as a whole and from other regions. Despite the initiative of Iraq's training school in Baghdad, which operated for some years in the late 1970s, there is no regional facility for the Arab world. The tendency now is for the more advanced countries to propose new training courses to cover their own needs; such proposals exist for Nigeria, Kenya, Zambia, the Philippines, Indonesia, and no doubt others. Although the Indian training school is associated with the National Archives, the tendency today is for new schools to be projected as components of established university schools of librarianship.

Unesco has directed much effort to promoting the harmonization of curricula between the archives courses and those provided for students of library or information studies.

World Problems. The variety of these traditions notwithstanding no country or region has as yet achieved a system of archival training that meets with general approval. There is a widespread feeling that existing facilities are inadequate and, at least in part, inappropriate. In particular, even when established training schools produce a sufficient number of trained archivists to staff the public, government-supported archives services, they frequently do not attempt to serve the archives services in the private sector. The curriculum is frequently directed toward old-fashioned and inappropriate goals, that is, biased toward the teaching of historical sciences at the expense of professional subjects, modern methodology, and practical training. Where courses are attached to

National Archives of Japan

Underground stacks area of the Japanese Cabinet Library.

library schools, there are complaints that library subjects predominate unduly.

A new directory of archival training courses published by the ICA in 1985 lists 80 such courses, but there is as yet no satisfactory list. An informed guess might be that there are some 150 worldwide. The number of student places they provide is certainly in excess of 3,000 (excluding the Italians mentioned previously). An attempt made in 1979 to calculate the numbers of archivists at work produced an estimate, certainly much too low, of some 7,000; a guess here might be that there are perhaps twice that number. The same survey suggested that there was an immediate training need of 6,000 places, worldwide. The evident immediate shortage does not necessarily mean that the long-term requirement is anything like so great. Calculations of the provision of student places is made more difficult by the numbers of general students who do not intend to enter the profession. There is a serious imbalance from region to region. Latin America is relatively well supplied with schools of indifferent reputation, while the remaining regions of the Third World are seriously undersupplied. For them, the places available in the training schools of the Third World itself, plus those of the developed countries of Europe, North America, and Australia, amount only to about 25 professional and 40 subprofessional trainees per year—about enough to supply the archival needs of one large country.

An important characteristic of archival training schools is the wide variety of subjects that must be taught. There are three main subject areas: professional studies (archives administration, records management, managerial and administrative studies, research methodology); auxiliary historical or interpretative sciences; and administrative or institutional history. It is probable that a complete course of training that limits itself strictly to these subjects and does not include any element of general education or languages would require about eight professors. To render a teaching body of this size possible, there would have to be a student enrollment of 80 to 100, but so large a training school would exceed the requirements of most countries and would demand a considerable investment. Hence there exists the problem of providing professional training to a student body of beginning archivists that typically numbers only between 10 and 30.

Consequently, most specialized archival training schools are associated with larger institutions. These are usually (1) a large archives service, such as that to which the West German Archivschule Marburg is attached; (2) a school of historical studies at a university; (3) a library school. There is much debate within the profession as to the relative merits of association with each of these. Schools dependent on archival services are probably the most effective in terms of teaching practical skills, and they can provide, better than others, for periods of supervised practical laboratory work. But few national or other archives services have the standing or the resources to undertake this work (although many larger archives systems do in fact offer training programs, and these are not usually strictly limited to their own novice staff members). Archives schools associated with historical studies have the advantage that archivists trained there may easily become, in their professional practice, members of the research communities of their countries. In the exercise of their professional skills archivists should represent research interests in the world of administration and should apply their knowledge of research methodology and of research findings to the basic archival function of appraisal. The main drawback of the association of archival training with historical studies, however, is the tendency of the archivists so trained to withdraw from active administration and from involvement in the fundamental day-to-day professional, as opposed to scholarly, functions of the archival institution.

The tendency today, and one that was given powerful backing by the leading theorist of archival science, T. R. Schellenberg, is to associate archival with library training. This has been done in the most recently established archival schools, in Senegal, Ghana, and Australia (University of New South Wales, Sydney). The benefits to be obtained from this association are considerable, and particularly so since the likely future development of technology in both archives and libraries is likely to increase the area of common skills. Conservation, reprography, computer technology, and documentation services are important fields in which both professions are operating increasingly. However, there are and will remain considerable differences in methodology inherent in the different media with which archivists and librarians work, and so far no attempt to devise common curricula for training has been practicable. Apart from technical areas shared with librarians, such as conservation, reprography, and automation, archival training courses that are situated within library schools will still have to maintain a distinct syllabus and teaching staff and inculcate a distinct professional ethos.

Technical Training. So far only peripheral mention has been made of the technical fields of conservation, reprography, and automation with the fundamentals of which professional archivists must be familiar if they are to plan and administer the technical aspects of archival programs and operations.

The degree of attention professional training schools give these subjects varies considerably, but generally speaking it can be described as inadequate. Similarly, facilities for training the actual practitioners—the technicians themselves—are inadequate as well; most technicians either learn on the job or receive prior training in a nonarchival setting. In recognition of this deficiency initiatives are being taken, both in the archivally advanced countries and in the developing world, to provide improved technical training. In particular, concrete efforts are being made to organize technical training centers on the Third World regional level.

REFERENCES

Statistical data are from a report by Michael Cook, *The Education and Training of Archivists,* made to the Unesco meeting of experts on archival training programs, November 1979.

Frank B. Evans, "Post-Appointment Archival Training: A Proposed Solution for a Basic Problem," *American Archivist* (1977), surveys history and problems of training in the U.S. and proposes solutions.

"La formation des archivistes en Europe," *Archives et Bibliothèques de Belgique* (1975); articles on archival training in East and West Germany, Spain, Austria, Holland, Italy, Britain, and the Vatican; in German, Spanish, English, and Italian.

Conseil International des Archives, *Annuaire des Ecoles et des Cours de Formation Professionnelle d'Archivistes* M. le Moel, editor, for the Committee on Professional Education and Training (1985), is the only recent published survey and analysis of training schools to date; in French.

Morris Rieger, "The Regional Training Center Movement," *American Archivist* (1972); background to development of the Third World schools.

MICHAEL COOK

Archives: Education and Research

Training to be an archivist is like training to be struck by lightning, remarked J. Franklin Jameson, one of the early leaders of the archival profession. The 20th century saw the professionalization of archival management in the United States, but training for the profession remains a vexing problem. Archivists have argued for decades over the relative merits of preappointment and postappointment training, the values of short-term institutes and graduate degree programs, and the relationship between training in archival practices and training in the correlative fields of history and library science.

Although some historical and antiquarian societies existed during the early and mid-19th century, the modern archival institutions, and with them the archival profession, are a direct result of the interest in "scientific" history that developed late in the century. This type of historical scholarship depended on access to original source materials, and proponents of the new method urged that archives be established to preserve, protect, and make valuable historical materials permanently available. Consequently, in 1899 the young American Historical Association (AHA) established a Public Archives Commission to locate source materials and publish guides to them. In 1909 the Association sponsored the first Conference of Archivists.

Historians in the forefront of this movement for archival institutions were familiar with archives and archival training in Europe, where much training took place in a university or institute affiliated with an archival institution. This preappointment training usually culminated in an examination, and only those persons who passed were appointed to archival positions in state archives. History, historical methods, and such auxiliary subjects as paleography, sigillography (the study of seals), and diplomatics (the study of documents) were emphasized. In Scandinavia and the United Kingdom the continental models of preappointment training had not gained acceptance by the end of the 19th century; instead, the archival institutions hired university graduates and gave them postappointment training that varied greatly in content, aim, and efficiency.

Drawing on the continental experience, American historian and archival proponent Waldo Gifford Leland told the 1909 Conference of Archivists that American archivists should have historical and legal training. He proposed that university history departments and library schools introduce courses on archives, but no such courses developed from his initial proposal. During the next quarter-century, Leland and other historians devoted themselves to the task of establishing a national archives. The National Archives eventually was founded in 1934, employing the largest number of archivists on the North American continent and inaugurating a new need for programs to train archivists. Two years later the Conference of Archivists, which had been a feature of AHA conventions since 1909, split from AHA and became an independent organization, the Society of American Archivists. The Society quickly established a Committee on the Training of Archivists, composed of five academic historians and chaired by Samuel Flagg Bemis. The report of that committee reaffirmed the need for historical training for archivists, rejected librarianship as an appropriate background, and suggested that specialized courses in archives be "grafted on" to graduate programs in history in "first-class" American universities.

This report profoundly affected the nascent profession's psyche but negligibly affected its practice. Solon J. Buck did teach an archives course at Columbia University in 1938–39, but the University was uninterested in continuing the program. In 1941 the first major program in archives was established by Buck and Ernst Posner at American University in Washington, D.C. Posner, trained in the German archival tradition, attempted to institute a similar program at American.

It was soon clear to Posner, however, that a single graduate program could not supply trained archivists in sufficient numbers to meet the staffing needs of growing archival institutions. Furthermore, it was apparent that institutions would continue to employ untrained persons and then either train them within the institution or seek an external source for short-term training in archival theory. To meet this need, Posner began in 1945 a summer institute in archival administration and preservation, securing the cooperation of the National Archives, the Maryland Hall of Records, and later the Library of Congress. The program was designed to meet the instructional needs of those persons without formal training who were already employed by archival institutions. This institute has been offered with modifications one or more times each year since, while sponsorship has shifted from the university to the National Archives.

European training was thus brought to the United States: the continental practice of preappointment academic training was reflected in the formal American University credit offerings, while the British practice of postappointment training was reflected in the short-term institute. During the 1950s and 1960s both models spread beyond the American University programs. The Colorado State Archives and the University of Denver began offering both academic courses and summer institutes; Wayne State University developed an academic program; and by 1984 more than 40 colleges and universities offered two or more courses in archives administration. A number of additional schools offered single courses in archives.

The expansion of graduate programs in archives education fostered a debate that was part of the larger, unresolved controversy over the relative merits of preappointment or postappointment training. This time the issue was whether the most appropriate university preappointment archival training was in history departments or in schools of library science. (Given the small numbers of students, independent archival departments seemed unrealistic.) The debate was especially heated in the mid-1960s; as of the mid-1980s it had abated but had not been resolved. Archival courses continue to be offered in history departments, in library schools, and, increasingly, in joint programs carried by both departments. In addition, some courses, especially those related to records management, are offered in public administration departments.

A series of moves to develop some nationwide standards for archival education began in the 1970s. In March 1973 ten teachers of archives courses attended a two-day meeting sponsored by the Society of American Archivists and prepared draft guidelines for credit courses and institutes. They were approved by the Council of the Society and were published for comment by the membership. Next, the Society's Committee on Education and Training produced curriculum standards for multicourse programs of archival education that would lead to a minor or concentration in a graduate degree program. Those guidelines were adopted by the Council, as were subsequent guidelines for the practicum component of graduate programs.

With the adoption of these guidelines the debate over preappointment and postappointment training may seem to have been tacitly resolved, but such is not the case. An effort in the late 1970s and early 1980s to have the Society approve programs of archival education in graduate schools failed to gain support and was dropped. Major archival institutions continue to conduct postappointment training for their new archivists; the National Archives, in particular, has a two-year career intern development program for entering archivists. Members of religious orders, employees of various businesses and institutions, and staff members of local governments continue to find themselves suddenly saddled with records management and archival responsibilities for which they are unprepared, and most of these persons turn to appropriate postappointment training. University archival education programs are not yet the sole answer to the profession's training needs.

By 1985 the Society of American Archivists, the National Archives, and several universities regularly offered short-term postappointment training. In addition, regional and local archival organizations often provided workshops in conjunction with annual meetings. Basic training remained the principal focus of these offerings, but the demand for specialty and intermediate-level short courses is increasing. In 1985 the Society hired an education director to foster and develop mid-career training opportunities for archivists, a clear indication of a new emphasis in short-term education.

Because the profession lacks a sizable academic professoriat with regular opportunities to pursue research and publication, research in archives has been undertaken either by the staffs of archival institutions as part of their regular programs (particularly in technical areas), or by archivists acting independently, often conducting their research after completing a full 40-hour work week. In the 1980s a number of funding agencies provided some formal support for research projects, particularly in the area of the theory of appraisal. Grants have made possible a number of summer research fellowships at the University of Michigan and three annual internships in archival management for young archivists. Encouraging as these developments are, they are all dependent upon the availability of grants and, as such, have a precarious future.

Pre- and postappointment training, education in history departments or schools of library science: the old issues are not resolved. In addition, in the mid-

1980s the profession was, for the second time in a decade, seriously debating whether to institute a program of certification for archivists. The effect that such a program would have on archival education, if adopted, is unclear, but the discussion fostered by the proposal has again raised fundamental questions of who an archivist is, what an archivist knows, and at what stage in an archivist's career this knowledge should be obtained. The decision made on certification opens the possibility of establishing the very shape of the profession for the remainder of this century and into the next. (See also *Professional Training in Archives.*)

REFERENCES
Frank B. Evans, "Educational Needs for Work in Archival and Manuscript Depositories," *Indian Archives* (1972).
"Postappointment Archival Training: A Proposed Solution for a Basic Problem," *American Archivist* (1977).
H. G. Jones, "Archival Training in American Universities, 1938–68," *American Archivist* (1968).
Ernst Posner, *Archives and the Public Interest* (1967).
Theodore R. Schellenberg, "Archival Training in Library Schools," *American Archivist* (1968).
Society of American Archivists, *Education Directory* (1983).

TRUDY HUSKAMP PETERSON

Argentina

A federal republic and the second largest country of South America, Argentina is bounded by Bolivia on the north, Paraguay and Brazil on the northeast, Uruguay and the Atlantic Ocean on the east, and Chile on the west. Population (1984 est.) 30,097,000; area 2,791,810 sq.km on the continent; Argentina also claims 969,464 sq.km. in Antarctica and the islands of the southern Atlantic. The official language is Spanish.

History. The majority of the national libraries in Latin America had their origins in collections of the Jesuits, the order expelled from the Spanish colonies in 1767. These collections later became the bases for the first public libraries of the region; when the colonies became independent, most of them designated these libraries as their national libraries. In 1810 the First Junta, which had arisen from the Revolution of the 25th of May, founded the public library with its decree of September 7 published September 13. (This date is observed in Argentina as "Librarian's Day" in accordance with a resolution adopted by the first librarians' congress in 1942.) The library was inaugurated on March 16, 1812; its first librarians were Fray Cayetano Rodríguez and the priest Luis José Chorroarín, who served as director until 1821. When Chorroarín died in 1823, the government ordered a tombstone that recognized him as the founder of the library.

National Library. On August 29, 1884, the library was nationalized, and from September 9 it was called the National Library. Its first collections consisted of works from the libraries of the Colegio San Carlos, the Jesuit library of Córdoba, the library of Bishop Manuel de Azamor y Ramírez, and donations from General Manuel Belgrano and others. The public also provided assistance in the form of books and financial contributions.

Materials are acquired through purchase, donations, exchange, and especially legal deposit. Its hold-

ALA

The Bernardino Rivadavia Public Library in Bahia Blanca, Argentina.

ings consist primarily of books, pamphlets, newspapers, manuscripts, copies from the Indian Archives, maps, illustrations, musical compositions, and photographs. Among its special collections are the library of Mariano Balcarce, son-in-law of José de San Martín, and the libraries and archives of Ezequiel Leguina, Pedro Denegri, Félix Frias, and Pastor Obligado, as well as manuscripts of Rubén Darío and other well-known writers. Paul Groussac, who served as director from 1885 to 1929, was succeeded by José Luis Lanza, Carlos F. Melo, Gustavo Martínez Zuviría, Jorge Luis Borges, Vicente Sierra, José Edmundo Clemente, Horacio H. Hernández, Gregorio Weinberg, and, beginning in July 1985, the writer Dardo Cúneo.

The National Library has operated since 1901 from a building constructed for the National Lottery. A new building was planned in 1960. In 1986 work was in the last stages of construction.

The National Library functions as a national exchange center. Since 1958 it also has served as headquarters for the National School of Librarians, coordinating its work with that of the National Commission on Popular Libraries. Until 1956 it published the national bibliography. That role was assumed by the Argentine Book Council, which also serves as the official agency for registering International Standard Book Numbers (ISBN). It published *Argentine Books: ISBN,* which lists all books registered during 1982–84.

Academic Libraries. In 26 universities approximately 200 libraries were reported in the early 1980s. They constitute the National University Library Network and are coordinated by the Council of Libraries of National Argentine Universities (JUBIUNA). The Council's programs include professional organization, interlibrary loan, exchange, purchasing, periodicals, union catalogues, catalogues of university publications, microfilming, user education, and similar functions.

The Institute of Library Sciences, now called the Library of the University of Buenos Aires, was founded in 1941. Its purpose is to coordinate activities of the libraries of the University of Buenos Aires, working through the appropriate council of librarians. Its centralized catalogue, which contains more than 900,000 entries covering more than 3,000,000 volumes, is the largest of its kind in the country. In 1970 the Institute began to compile a catalogue of the libraries in the interior of the country, another important source of information. Other functions of the Institute include maintaining and updating catalogues, library education courses in the university (which are attended by librarians from other universities as well), and services rendered through its specialized library. It published until December 1984 a quarterly *Information Bulletin* that was suspended after number 76. It also publishes the research record for the university, along with career guides, course listings in librarianship and documentation, theses, and catalogues of the Institute. In 1980 G. K. Hall of Boston published an important compilation of the Institute: *Argentine Bibliography: A Union Catalog of Argentine Holdings in the Libraries of the University of Buenos Aires* (7 volumes).

Public Libraries. Public libraries are known in Argentina as popular libraries. These libraries began in 1870, during the tenure of President Domingo F. Sarmiento, and the law which brought them into being is known as the Sarmiento Law for the Development of Popular Libraries. Sarmiento believed strongly in a close relationship between public and school libraries and saw the two as complementary.

The coordinating organization for public libraries is the National Commission on Popular Libraries, established in Buenos Aires in coordination with the National Library. Public libraries are found throughout the country and, for sake of classification, are divided into categories according to the numbers of volumes they possess. Though most of the approximately 1,500 public libraries are supported by private institutions, official support for operating expenses is provided through the provision of books, salaries for librarians, and purchase of equipment and furniture. There is a national culture plan under the National Secretary of Culture and a national reading campaign.

Popular libraries are grouped into federations, and these, in turn, constitute the Argentine Confederation of Popular Libraries. In some cases, these libraries serve as school libraries. In the province of Buenos Aires, a law provides for centralization of planning, coordinating, and control of libraries and, at the same time, decentralization of executive responsibility through a system of sharing between the province and local communities. Since all libraries that serve the public are considered public libraries, municipal libraries, school libraries, pilot libraries, and even libraries of private institutions belong to the provincial system of public libraries.

Libraries in Argentina (1977)

Type	Administrative units	Service points	Volumes in collections	Annual expenditures (peso)	Population served[a]	Professional staff	Total staff
National	1	1	1,880,000	37,116,000	--	8	116
Academic	--	--	--	--	--	--	--
Public	1,230	--	9,532,000	--	4,201,244	--	--
School	--	--	--	--	--	--	--
Special	699	--	11,026[b]	--	--	--	--

[a]Registered borrowers.
[b]Meters of shelving.

Source: Unesco, *Statistical Yearbook,* 1984. Contributor's estimate for public (called popular) libraries.

Some popular libraries in the province of Buenos Aires are more than a hundred years old; the Popular Library of Baradero was founded in 1872 and the Museum and Popular Library of San Fernando, which possesses more than 70,000 volumes, was established in 1873. Also, the Bernardino Rivadavia Popular Library of Bahía Blanca was established in 1882 and has a collection of more than 110,000 volumes. In Buenos Aires, the 22 libraries that belong to the the General Directorship of Municipal Libraries maintain the character of public libraries. Their collections of newspapers and magazines cover local history.

School Libraries. In spite of Sarmiento's ideas for cooperation, public and school libraries tend to go their own ways. No one agency coordinates school libraries, and action is not coordinated between school and public libraries. Nevertheless, in Buenos Aires and other parts of the country, teachers' libraries serve as research and documentation centers in the field of teaching and educational technology; these libraries serve not only as action centers but as centers for organizing all the material produced in the country in this field.

The library headquarters of Buenos Aires Province maintains a register of libraries that function exclusively in educational institutions and that meet the educational and recreational needs of both teachers and students. To take advantage of the benefits offered by this provincial organization, the people in charge of the school libraries, in addition to being teachers, must possess professional librarian certificates. To this end, the province provides training through its Superior Institute of Teacher Training in Librarianship and Museology, headquartered in La Plata.

There are more than 23,000 schools in the country, but detailed statistical information on school libraries was unavailable in the mid-1980s. A study published in 1979 by the Central Library of the University of Tucumán, which listed 5,451 schools in Buenos Aires Province, sampled 534 in 1970–71, and reported that 359 of those sampled had school libraries.

Special Libraries. These libraries include both governmental libraries and those found in the private sector in banks, hospitals, museums, institutes, planning offices, and business and industry. Characteristically, these libraries serve as documentation and information centers in such specialized areas as municipal affairs, biomedicine, biochemistry, science and technology, agricultural sciences, social sciences, development and planning, nuclear science and technology, pharmacology, law, metallurgy, and industrial technology. Most of them belong to the Argentine Association of Scientific and Technical Libraries and Information Centers, with headquarters in Buenos Aires. The Association of Argentine Biomedical Libraries includes 80 member institutions.

A guide to special libraries covering the years 1978–83 listed 846 bibliographic and documentation centers, including university libraries and databases. The Argentine Center for Scientific and Technical Information (CAICYT), which belongs to the National Council for Scientific and Technical Research (CONICET), maintains an updated union catalogue of periodicals received in the nation's special libraries. It also maintains a register of the International Standard Serial Numbers (ISSN) of the journals published in the country. With the support of the cooperating libraries, it maintains the national information system, making possible the acquisition and photocopy of material of interest to users. The service is fee-based through a Telex hookup with participating libraries.

Some special libraries, such as those of the Faculty of Agronomy of the University of Buenos Aires and the National Atomic Energy Commission, act as national centers of international cooperative information systems in the field of agriculture (AGRIS) and science and technology (INIS). The Argentine Institute for Standardization of Materials (IRAM), as a form of support to special libraries, has been working since 1972 on standards in the area of documentation. Through the efforts of the Secretary of Science and Technology, a major project for a national cooperative information system in science and technology (SIDCYT) was planned in 1985.

The Profession. The Association of Graduate Librarians of the Argentine Republic (ABGRA) was founded November 5, 1953, first calling itself the Association of Librarians of the Federal Capital. It can be considered a continuation of the Center for Library Studies of the Argentine Social Museum, which was founded October 12, 1943, and ceased operation at the time ABGRA began. The year 1943 marked the beginning of the Argentine library movement, which has, over the years, dealt with questions of professionalism in librarianship, documentation, and information through such means as meetings, conferences, publications, and graduate courses of continuing education. ABGRA is a member of the International Federation of Library Associations (IFLA). To become a member of ABGRA—which had more than 800 members in 1985—one must be an officially recognized professional librarian.

ABGRA's primary activities are concentrated on its national meetings, the first of which took place in 1962; the 21st took place in August 1985. It publishes an *Information Bulletin* (first series, 1968-1975; second series, 1984-), as well as occasional documents and proceedings of meetings. In 1979 it began publishing a journal, *Library Science and Documentation*. At the international level, it sponsored the Eleventh National and First Ibero-American Meeting of Librarians in Buenos Aires, August 14-23, 1974, as well as the Regional Meeting of the Professional Library and Information Science Associations of Latin America and the Caribbean, which took place in Buenos Aires, April 19-23, 1983, with the special participation of the Committee on Latin America of IFLA. Other library associations dedicated to professional concerns can be found in Córdoba, La Plata, Buenos Aires, Rosario, Santa Fe, and other localities throughout Argentina.

REFERENCES
Augustín Millares Carlo, *Introducción a la historia del libro y de las bibliotecas* ("Introduction to the History of Books and Libraries") (Mexico, 1971).
Investigación sobre bibliotecas escolares de la Provincia de Buenos Aires, 1970-1971 ("Study of School Libraries in Buenos Aires Province") (Tucumán, 1979).
HANS GRAVENHORST; REINALDO JOSÉ SUAREZ; translated by EDWIN S. GLEAVES

Asheim, Lester E.
(1914–)

Lester Eugene Asheim contributed to librarianship in many ways, through writing, teaching, and work with the American Library Association. He helped to define the principles of book selection, to establish criteria for library education and personnel, and to foster communication among librarians in all parts of the world.

Asheim was born in Spokane, Washington, on January 22, 1914. Except for a short period in Idaho, he grew up in Seattle, where he received from the University of Washington an A.B. in English in 1936, along with a Phi Beta Kappa key; a B.A. in Librarianship in 1937; and an M.A. in American Literature in 1941. Asheim began library work as a page in the Seattle Public Library, and from 1937 to 1941 he served as Junior Reference Assistant at the University of Washington while he continued his work on his Master's degree.

For the year 1941–42, Asheim served as Librarian of the Prison Library at McNeill Island, Washington. During World War II he served for three years in the U.S. Army Signal Intelligence Corps, chiefly in Alaska.

Upon his return to civilian life in 1945, Asheim organized a library for the Federal Public Housing Authority in Seattle. Taking advantage of a fellowship and the G.I. Bill, he enrolled at the Graduate Library School (GLS) of the University of Chicago, from which he received a Ph.D. in 1949. His doctoral dissertation, *From Book to Film: A Comparative Analysis of the Content of Novels and the Films Based on Them*, demonstrated his interest in both literature and nonprint media, an interest that he maintained throughout his career. His dissertation was published in an edited version in four installments of *Hollywood Quarterly* (1951) and *The Quarterly of Film, Radio and Television* (1951–52).

At the GLS Asheim's talents were early recognized. He assisted Bernard Berelson in writing *The Library's Public: A Report of the Public Library Inquiry* (1949) and then edited the papers of the GLS conference on the Inquiry, *A Forum on the Public Library Inquiry* (1949). This was only the first of a number of GLS conference volumes for which he was to serve as Editor, including *The Core of Education for Librarianship* (1954), *The Future of the Book* (1955), *New Directions in Public Library Development* (1957), *Persistent Issues in American Librarianship* (1961). and *Differentiating the Media* (1975).

Asheim was appointed Assistant Profesor at the GLS, 1948–52; Dean of Students, 1951–52; and Dean and Associate Professor, 1952–61. During the decade of his deanship he continued to study library education, but his most important work was probably his now classic article "Not Censorship but Selection" (1953), which has been widely reprinted. *Wilson Library Bulletin* published his reappraisal of this landmark article in November 1983. In 1957 he published *The Humanities and the Public Library*, which has been widely used in library schools as a guide to selection and use of humanities materials.

In 1961 Asheim became Director of the International Relations Office (IRO) of the American Library Association. In his five years in that post he visited 44 countries and shared his experience in American librarianship with students and practicing librarians throughout the world. One result of his IRO activities was an invitation to deliver the Phineas Lawrence Windsor Lectures at the University of Illinois. These lectures, subsequently published as *Librarianship in the Developing Countries* (1966), were a major contribution to the study of comparative librarianship and brought him the Scarecrow Press Award for "an outstanding contribution to library literature" in 1968.

In 1966 Asheim resigned his IRO post to accept the directorship of ALA's new Office for Library Education. The rapid expansion of libraries during the period of the Great Society programs placed serious strains on library education, which was urged to produce not only more librarians but also better-trained librarians. Much of Asheim's work was concentrated on the development of a statement defining the titles, basic requirements, and responsibilities of library personnel—both professional and supportive. His statement on "Library Education and Manpower" (often known as the Asheim Paper or Statement) was adopted as the official policy of the American Library Association on June 30, 1970. In the spring of 1976 that document, without substantive change, was renamed "Library Education and Personnel Utilization." It remains the major position on personnel development of the American library community.

While Director of the ALA Office of Library Education, Asheim continued to write and speak on library education and other topics. He had earlier chaired ALA's Committee on Accreditation and over the years frequently served as a consultant for library education programs. He was President of the Library Education Division of ALA, 1976–77.

In 1971 Asheim returned to the University of Chicago as Professor in the Graduate Library School and in 1972 became the Editor of the *Library Quarterly*, the major scholarly journal in American librarianship, a post he held for the next three years. He was William Rand Kenan, Jr., Professor of Library Science at the University of North Carolina at Chapel Hill from January 1975 until he retired in June 1984.

In honor of Asheim's 65th birthday, colleagues presented him with a Festschrift, *As Much to Learn as to Teach* (1979). As is apparent from the topics treated in this series of essays—such as intellectual freedom, library service to the public, library education, professional associations, international and comparative librarianship, and mass communications—Asheim showed interest in many areas of librarianship, and to most he has made significant contributions. Many testify that this diligent researcher and writer is an excellent teacher and a delightful colleague.

Asheim was selected as the 1973 recipient of the Beta Phi Mu Award for Distinguished Service to Education for Librarianship. At the ALA Centennial Conference he was given the Joseph W. Lippincott Award for distinguished service to the profession of librarianship. The University of Washington School of Librarianship gave him its Distinguished Alumnus Award in 1966 and the Illinois Library Association its Intellectual Freedom Award the same year. He was named a member of the Advisory Committee to the Center for the Book at the Library of Congress in

University of North Carolina
Lester E. Asheim

1978. At the time of his retirement ALA conferred on him its highest award, Honorary Membership.

REFERENCE
Joel M. Lee and Beth A. Hamilton, editors, *As Much to Learn as to Teach: Essays in Honor of Lester Asheim* (1979), includes biographical information and a bibliography of Asheim's writings.

EDWARD G. HOLLEY

Asociación Latinoamericana de Escuelas de Bibliotecología y Ciencias de la Información

The Asociación Latinoamericana de Escuelas de Bibliotecología y Ciencias de la Información (ALEBCI, the Latin American Association of Schools of Library and Information Science) was founded in September 1970 during the International Congress of Documentation in Buenos Aires, Argentina, to promote library education in Latin America. The Association was temporarily housed in the mid-1980s at the Colegio de Bibliotecología, Universidad Nacional Autónoma de México.

Membership is open to individuals and institutions interested in sharing information and exchanging publications related to library education in Latin American countries. The entire membership meets every two years.

The official journal is *ALEBCI: Boletín Informativo,* published four times a year. The Association is affiliated with IFLA and FID.

Association Internationale des Ecoles des Sciences de l'Information

The international association of schools of information science (AIESI) was founded in 1977 in Geneva, Switzerland; representatives from library and information science schools in eight countries were present at the founding meeting: France, Belgium, Switzerland, Tunisia, Algeria, Morocco, Senegal, and French Canada (Quebec). The original impetus for the creation of this organization came from the Université de Montréal's École de Bibliothéconomie, the one French-language library school that was accredited by the American Library Association and that had experienced the benefits of participating in the work of the English-speaking Association for Library and Information Science Education (ALISE). Membership in AIESI is limited to those schools, university departments, and other organizations engaged in the education of librarians, documentalists, and information scientists at the university level (or its equivalent) that use French, entirely or in part, as their language of instruction. Other schools or organizations that do not meet all of these requirements may be admitted as associate members. Most of the associate members in the mid-1980s did not offer university-level instruction. A change (1984) in the bylaws created the category of individual member. French-speaking professors at non-French-language schools may join as individuals along with their colleagues from AIESI-member schools. The Association attempted through this change to broaden participation in its activities without losing its French-language character.

AIESI is formally attached to the Association des universités partiellement ou entièrement de langue française (Association of French-language Universities), which provides assistance to it in the form of secretarial help and financial aid, largely from funds obtained from FICU (International Fund for Inter-University Cooperation). The Association's administrative structure consists of a General Assembly in which each institutional member has one vote. The Assembly meets every two years. An Executive Board, consisting of five elected members, who in turn choose their own President, Vice-President, Secretary, and Treasurer, runs the affairs of the Association between Assembly meetings.

The Association has the following objectives: to encourage the development of library and information science education and to assist in raising the quality of persons engaged in such activities; to establish and maintain continuing liaison among the various institutions offering French-language instruction in library and information science; to encourage cooperative programs among these institutions; to plan and organize periodic international meetings (colloquia, seminars, and workshops); to stimulate original French-language research in the area; to encourage by all possible means, financial and otherwise, the publication in French of needed textbooks, journals, and the results of research undertaken; to act as a spokesman on topics of mutual interest; and to issue opinions and recommendations, as an association, on questions having to do with the education of librarians and information scientists.

In conjunction with the meetings of its General Assembly every two years, the Association sponsors three- or four-day workshops. They covered the teaching of management (Lyons, France, 1978); the teaching of information science (Montreal, 1980); nonbook materials and documentation (Liége, Belgium, 1982); teaching methods and the information sciences (Rabat, Morocco, 1984); and continuing education (Bordeaux, France, 1986). The proceedings are published by the Association. In 1979 and again in 1985 the Association published a directory of French-language library and information science programs throughout the world. The 1985 edition included all known programs, whether their host institutions were members of AIESI or not. Furthermore, detailed information about the content of the individual programs was given, much more than is to be found in the average directory, so that each member might understand better the elements to be found in the programs of schools in other countries where the educational systems might be different.

The creation of the Association has greatly stimulated the exchange of information and expertise throughout the French-speaking world. No longer do individual schools exist in a vacuum. Increasing amounts of funds have been obtained from various governmental agencies (international and national) to facilitate such exchanges. An expansion in the French-language research and publications program was seen as much needed in a discipline in which 80 percent of the publications used in French-langauge schools are in the English language.

RICHARD K. GARDNER

Association of Caribbean University, Research and Institutional Libraries

The Association of Caribbean University, Research and Institutional Libraries (ACURIL) originated as part of a movement for Caribbean cooperation at the university level that was initiated during the 1960s by Sir Philip Sherlock, the Vice-Chancellor of the University of the West Indies.

In 1967, when the Association of Caribbean Universities (UNICA) was formed, the need for close cooperation among university and research libraries in the region was also recognized. The Association therefore sponsored the first Conference of Librarians in University and Research Libraries of the region in Puerto Rico in 1969. At that conference, an independent Association of Caribbean University and Research Institute Libraries (ACURIL) was voted into existence. Prime movers were Alma Jordan, then Deputy Librarian of the University of the West Indies Library at the St. Augustine Campus, Trinidad, and Albertina Perez de Rosa, then Chief of the Department of Latin American Studies and Exchange at the José M. Lazaro Library of the University of Puerto Rico, San Juan. Jordan was elected the first President and Perez de Rosa the first Vice-President of the Association.

Although adhering to the original proposal for collaboration among university and research libraries within the framework of UNICA, the Association early recognized that it should embrace all kinds of libraries that traditionally functioned as research libraries. Public libraries, in particular, were effectively basic providers of information in many of the small Caribbean countries. There also were a growing number of special libraries in government and other institutions that should be allowed to participate in the Association. Thus a variety of libraries enjoyed membership in ACURIL from the beginning.

There are three categories of membership: (1) institutional: open to university, research, and institutional libraries and archives in the Caribbean archipelago, the mainland countries or the states of the United States that border on the Caribbean Sea or Gulf of Mexico and the Guianas; (2) associate: open to libraries and archives with interests and collections pertinent to the Caribbean area, and qualifying for membership, but outside the specified geographic region; and (3) personal: open to persons holding professional posts in member libraries.

In 1985 the membership stood at 150 institutional members, 3 associate members, and 80 personal members. The Association has been considering ways to widen its membership to include (1) national and other regional library associations serving special interest groups, (2) library-related agencies, such as national library planning agencies and library schools, (3) personal members in their own right, that is, those independent of service in member libraries, and (4) associate institutions and associate personal members for institutions and persons outside the geographic area. A new structure would provide for sections related to types of libraries and also allow for a broad representation on the Executive Council.

Its constitution outlines the aims of the Association: To facilitate the development and use of libraries and archives and the identification of library collections in support of the whole range of intellectual and educational endeavors throughout the Caribbean area; to strengthen the profession of librarianship in the region; and to promote cooperative library activities in pursuit of these objectives. In addition the Association supports areas of national, regional, and international concern in the library and information field.

Originally, the full name of the Association (in English) was the "Association of Caribbean University and Reasearch Institute Libraries" (ACURIL). The delimiting word "Institute" was dropped from the full title but the acronym remained unchanged. Justification for the letter "I" was reintroduced when the body was renamed the "Association of Caribbean University, Research and Institutional Libraries" in 1976.

The Constitution provides for an 11-member Executive Council. Two of six ordinary members are elected for three-year terms at each annual general meeting. The Vice-President is elected by the Executive Council from among its members and is the President-elect. The Executive Council meets twice at the time of the annual conference, immediately before and after; the second is a joint meeting of the outgoing and incoming Executive Council members. It also holds one mid-term meeting during the intervening year, usually in November. This is often held in the home country of the President but some countries which might not mount the annual conference are more and more being selected for the November meeting.

Standing Committees exist for each of the following eight areas of activity: Acquisitions, Bibliography, Indexing, Constitution and Bylaws, Education, Microforms, Planning and Research, and Publications. The first three Committees operate in language groups: English-, Spanish- and French-speaking. The activities of these Committees, which have been set up in order to realize some of the objectives of the Association, are planned, reviewed, and developed during the annual conference.

The Secretariat of the Association is in San Juan at the Caribbean Regional Library in the José M. Lazaro Library of the University of Puerto Rico. Oneida Ortiz served as Executive Secretary from the establishment of the Secretariat in 1973.

An ongoing feature of the annual conference is the development of a program around a theme of interest to library and information services in the Caribbean. Papers are presented and workshops held while provision is made for discussion of the various subtopics. This feature meets the aims to which ACURIL is committed by promoting studies of topical issues in the profession and facilitating improved communication and exchange of information.

Some of ACURIL's activities and programs include the promotion of cooperation among librarians and all information personnel in the region, the organization of regional projects aimed at improving access to information produced or published in the region, among them microfilming archives and newspapers, increasing the availability of documents and publications in the region, and indexing journals in the social sciences produced in the region. The index CARINDEX facilitates access to journal articles. ACURIL also provides a forum for the presentation of research papers. Generally speaking, common problems are identified, solutions are discussed, and ideas are shared on general trends in library development and growth of the profession.

The Association publishes the proceedings of its annual conference. All of the unpublished proceedings were in varying stages of editorial preparation in the mid-1980s. The Association also publishes an occasional bilingual newsletter, *ACURIL Carta Informativa/Newsletter*.

ACURIL has retained its affiliation with the Association of Caribbean Universities (UNICA). It is also affiliated with the Seminar on the Acquisition of Latin American Library Materials (SALALM) and is a member of the International Federation of Library Associations (IFLA).

DAPHNE DOUGLAS

Assurbanipal
(fl. 7th century B.C.)

Assurbanipal (Ashurbanipal), King of Assyria, warrior, administrator, and pragmatic librarian, assembled a National Library at Nineveh. He personifies Assyrian civilization, the peak of an older Mesopotamian culture that nourished successive civilizations from the Sumerians through the Chaldeans. After Babylon fell to Cyrus the Great in 539 B.C., this

Assurbanipal   British Museum

complex culture was combined with its Egyptian counterpart by Persian foreigners who created a comprehensive synthesis of cultural influences from all the near eastern civilizations. The combined influence of the Persian cultural synthesis has been enormous. Mitigated somewhat in Hellenistic times, it nevertheless affected Alexandrian civilization, overwhelmed the Greco-Roman tradition in late antiquity, and sustained the Middle Ages for nearly a thousand years. It also created the ambivalence of modern thought by confronting humanism with theological presuppositions.

The Sumerians were cultural innovators who pioneered the Mesopotamian tradition and invented its form of writing. Subsequent innovations were largely confined to military, administrative, and artistic improvements. The tradition went through a long period of cultural stagnation under the Old Babylonians. It was preserved, organized, and consolidated by the Assyrians, whose originality was confined to administrative and military matters. The Chaldeans, who tried to revive the Old Babylonian culture, substantially altered the tradition itself. It was further diluted by the Persians, who ended its political existence, and by the Greeks, who resented its otherworldliness; but its cultural influence has never been completely lost.

The Assyrians were bristling warlords with a flair for culture. They were a pragmatic people who made war as brutal and effective as possible. They created centralized government on a large scale, the first sprawling empire to rule the world with iron claws. The bureaucratic machinery they created survived the wreckage of their empire to rise again in the Persian Empire, where it served as a model for the Roman Empire, the precursor of Western administrative procedures. Poets and scholars were sponsored by the early kings of Ur, Isin, Larsa, and Babylon; Tiglath-Pileser I, Sargon II, and Esarhaddon were addicted to Babylonian literature, and Assurbanipal systematically rescued the whole inheritance of the past. Virtually everything we know of Mesopotamian history derives from the cultural interests of these kings and their attendants.

Assurbanipal, the last important king of Assyria (7th century B.C.), helped create both its Golden Age of literature and its sudden destruction. He organized coteries of scribes, sending them to all parts of the empire to find and copy Sumero-Babylonian documents, and even learned the scribal art himself, in order to assemble the Assyrian "Library of Congress" at Nineveh. The resulting library operation represents the basic content, and possibly the complete corpus, of the Mesopotamian scribal tradition. But it does not represent the realities of librarianship for several reasons.

Assurbanipal was first of all a warrior, then an administrator, and finally a librarian. Like most imperialists, he was overly pragmatic, preferring to manage things and people rather than ideas. Accordingly, he reduced librarianship to housekeeping routines for creating and maintaining the order arrangements of clay tablets in the only library of Mesopotamia. The literatures of Sumer and Old Babylon were thus preserved by "the Assyrian gift for arranging and systematizing," not by any "marked advance in thought." There was no contemporary literature or science because the Assyrians were better consumers than producers of information. Their only original contributions were archival grist for the future historians of Assyria, but the Assyrians themselves were not concerned with "scholarly accuracy" or with "the truth."

Assurbanipal was the first ultrapragmatic librarian to exhibit "a complete absence of any speculative or reasoning effort." Not ability, mind you, but *effort*. When his bibliographical methods arrived in Alexandria, the Greeks simply accepted them as folksy procedures for running a library and turned to substantive issues—like inventing the higher and lower criticisms for managing the literary tradition itself. Thus, they avoided the unresolved problems of bibliographic organization and control, which passed through the Romans to Western Europe. The resultant utter lack of Greek influence in bibliographical matters is essentially what is wrong with librarianship today: it has never been able to get Assurbanipal off its back.

The weary Assurbanipal cried out: "Why has sickness, woe of heart, misery and destruction bound me? In the land is battle, in the house is intrigue; they are never taken from my side. Destruction and an evil word are lined up against me; ill of heart and ill of body have bowed down my form. With 'Alack' and 'Alas' I end my day; [even] on the day of the city god, the feast day, I am destroyed. Death is bringing upon me my end, I am oppressed; in want and sorrow I grieve day and night. I wail: 'O God, give this to those who do not fear the gods; may I see thy light! How long, O God, wilt thou do this unto me? As one who fears not god or goddess have I been afflicted'" (Olmstead, *History of Assyria,* 414, adding: this is "far indeed . . . from the hero . . . who brought in the millennial dawn!").

H. CURTIS WRIGHT

Audiovisual Services

The single constant in audiovisual services seems to be the continuing need for, and appreciation of, their special roles: certainly not much else about them stays the same. They are characterized by changing formats, changing delivery modes, changing administrative structures, and changing terminology.

TECHNOLOGY

Visual Technology. An overview of the history of the visual component of audiovisual services could begin in the informal sort of "show and tell" that goes on in classrooms, when individual teachers build their own collections of realia: seashells, rocks and fossils, plants, and small animals. Extra enterprise and talent produces models, dioramas, kits, and other variants. With the invention of photography and the growth of magazine publishing, pictures in black and white, and then in color, were available in great abundance, as were art reproductions and slides.

Much instruction remains aural-oral, but lecturers realize increasingly the value of illustrative materials in sharing with audiences of some size, and most schools and universities continue to provide assistance in the production and display of such materials as can be used with overhead and opaque projectors.

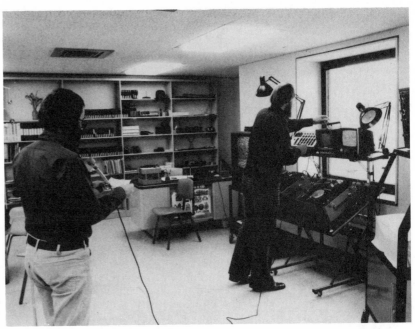

St. Paul Public Library

Editing room at the St. Paul Public Library's Video Communications Center. The Center lends equipment and offers training in production.

The invention of moving pictures saw the development of motion picture industries—theatrical (standardized at 35mm) and nontheatrical (standardized for a considerable period at 16mm; 8mm, once thought a threat to 16mm, stayed largely within the home market). Moving images are now available in a bewildering array of video formats, presenting new problems in their variety and in the ease with which they can be duplicated, the newest forms on computer screens.

Microcomputers are often considered to fall within the domain of audiovisual departments in libraries because they are similar to other machine-and-software systems already located there, and it is presumed that the audiovisual library professional is more likely than others to know how to administer them. In most types of libraries, microcomputers can be found in a variety of other places as well—such departments as systems, cataloguing, children's, and public service often find themselves the exclusive or cooperative "home" for microcomputers and manage access to them by staff and patrons. Patrons use microcomputers for information about library holdings, of course, but the primary other uses involve purchased software either for an application such as word processing or for learning, as in instructional programs. In addition, games of various sorts have been added to some library holdings, as have a variety of programming languages for specific instruction and drill.

The computer's graphic capability provides not only new modes for visualizing complex mathematical concepts but also new forms for artistic expression just beginning to be mastered by enough artists to capture the awareness of the general public. These pioneering programs where art and science meet will one day be in considerable demand in the educational environment, however they are packaged.

One packaging mode which has generated considerable interest is interactive video, though much remains to be learned about its most effective use. According to experts, interactive video has the potential to transform our current information delivery system in libraries as well as in schools, colleges, churches, and businesses. It can facilitate remote learning in stand-alone systems (replacing some professionals) and may be transmitted from satellites and cable systems, rather than borrowed physically from libraries. It has especially attractive applications in promoting products, services, and ideas and when instructing learners, training employees, and persuading people to buy, vote, and believe a certain way. It is cost-effective, standardized, realistic, flexible, adaptable, and innovative.

Interactive video is computer-controlled video instruction that tailors itself to the individual. It creates a degree of interaction never before possible with individualized (especially video) instruction. It is not just a televised lesson or a new form of programmed instruction. It combines the best of audiovisual electronic instruction with the educational technology that tutors, individualizes, and allows interaction between the learner and what is to be learned. Single-frame and moving pictures, computer graphics, text, sounds—all can be inserted anywhere within interactive video lessons.

An interactive video system for use both in creating and presenting interactive video lessons consists of a microcomputer and a video recorder connected by a relatively inexpensive interface. Software is a video program in which the sequence and selection of messages is determined by the viewer's responses to the material itself. The rate, sequence, and selection of information is a function of the viewer's active involvement with the program.

The future holds special technological promise, not the least of which is holography, a still or moving picture photograph that appears as a three-dimensional image when projected by a laser beam, without lens or screen as we currently know them. Holographic publishing and direct computer output publishing will continue and sustain the rapid evolution in audiovisual services, which may soon be recognized as a revolution in cost-effective libraries.

Audio Technology. The "audio" component, though not quite as spectacularly troublesome in its changing formats, has evolved through 78, 45, and 33-1/3 rpm records, reel-to-reel tape, and cassettes, to run parallel to video in availability on compact, easy-to-store, virtually indestructible laser disks.

Librarians are challenged with the task of judging the cost effectiveness of obtaining, cataloguing, storing, maintaining, and circulating this bewildering array of support mechanisms, both hardware and software, often in the face of mixed faculty, patron, and administrative acceptance. In an environment of this nature it is not surprising that their presence has generated mixed emotion and varied solutions to the problems their availability presents.

The advent of *AACR2* suggests that cataloguing theorists of the book tradition and the pragmatists of the audiovisual tradition have achieved a workable set of compromises. Chapter 12 moves in the direction of the *Standards for Cataloging Non-Print Materials* of the Association for Educational Communication and Technology (AECT) and is offering solutions reached

in dealing with real problems: the usual lack of a single author-creator and the frustrations of title changes and variants. In addition there is good monitoring on these and similar problems by the American Library Association, in close contact with both OCLC, Inc., and the Library of Congress. OLAC, On-Line Audiovisual Catalogers, has its own newsletter as well. Its workshops are often run in conjunction with those concerned primarily with problems of audio cataloguing, in particular, music.

ORGANIZATIONS

Organizations formed as interest groups or task forces around the various types of audiovisual media have, over the years, reflected in their names the historical changes of AV formats and delivery modes.

ALA and its units have used, alternatively, "nonbook," "nonprint," and the more conservative "media"—a serviceable term with the possible drawbacks that its literal connotation includes books, and that for some it may suggest the journalistic forms of mass communications.

EFLA. The earliest organization formed to support the interest of libraries in nonprint media is the Educational Film Library Association (EFLA), sponsor of the annual American Film Festival in New York. EFLA's extensive critical evaluations of films and video, together with its international program of publications, training, and other membership services to institutions and individuals in public libraries and schools and colleges are well known. The relationships developed by EFLA for librarians with both the commercial film production-distribution community and the government-arts-foundation community are significant.

AECT and ALA. One of the principal national organizations began as the Department of Audio Visual Instruction of the National Education Association, became independent of that association, grew in size, and chose the name Association for Educational Communications and Technology (AECT), leaving headroom for the assimilation of computers and computer-aided instruction now underway.

The high cost of conventions has led AECT to a joint venture with NAVA, the International Communications Industries Association (formerly the National Audio Visual Association, an organization representing principally the marketing and maintainance aspects of equipment for communicating images (with and without sounds). Jointly they sponsor COMMTEX, the communications technology "showcase" exhibit, and the combination helps members maximize shrinking travel budgets.

Several of ALA Divisions have ongoing committees whose focus is audiovisual. The American Association of School Librarians (AASL) has the *School Library Media Quarterly* Editorial Board, a committee on video communications and committees concerned with evaluating programs, selecting materials, instructing professionals, and standardizing access to materials. The Association of College and Research Libraries (ACRL) maintains a nonprint media publications editorial board and an audiovisual committee. The Library and Information Technology Association (LITA) includes a group concerned with video and cable communications and follows new techniques in data, voice, and video transmission over satellite and other networks. The Young Adult

Services Division (YASD) has a committee concerned with liaison with audiovisual producers and distributors, one with media selection and use, and a jury which annually identifies selected films for young adults.

AECT has four Divisions concerned either directly or peripherally with audiovisual materials. The Division of Technology (DOT) sponsors such workshops as the January 1985 program on "A Model for Planning and Implementing an Integrated Cost-Effective Campus Communication Instructional System." The Division of Instructional Development (DID) sponsored a January 1985 workshop on "the development of training courses using computer-based interactive video" and "the development of effective curriculum-correlated guide materials for classroom use of television programs, computers, and interactive video." There are in addition the Division of Educational Media Management (DEMM) and the Association for Special Education Technology (ASET).

Groups under the umbrella of AECT include the Consortium of University Film Centers (CUFC), the National Association of Regional Media Centers (NARMC), and the Association of Media Educators in Religion (AMER). While small in membership, such groups have brought some meaningful community effort to cooperation and standardization. Particularly noteworthy is the *Educational Film Locator,* appearing in its third edition (60,000 titles) in Spring 1986. It represents an effort to apply AECT cataloguing standards, to furnish full bibliographic data, and to identify sources for rental of film titles held by member libraries.

CUFC is made up of about 50 campus-based centers furnishing film and video resources for on- and off-campus use, some being national rental agencies. NARMC arose around the trend of state governments to establish and support such centers, for the purpose of providing "resources and services not technically or financially feasible at the individual system's level of support." In spite of some overlap in the service areas of CUFC and NARMC, their respective memberships have held joint meetings and engaged in idea exchange and constructive dialogue. AMER serves primarily as an interest group to identify suitable films for various religious environments. There has been expression of interest in, but a lack of resources for, updating the aging (1972) 9th edition of the AVRG, the *Audio Visual Resources Guide* of the National Council of Churches.

Other Organizations. The American Society for Information Science (ASIS) provides a national forum for those professionals in the library world who work with both the theory and applications of computers, instructional technology, and video-cable-satellite systems. ASIS has chartered 22 special interest groups that reflect the diversity of interest in its members, including arts and the humanities, behavioral and social sciences, law, medicine, and office information systems.

Other organizations concerned with the cogent presentation of information on media availability include the National Video Clearinghouse, whose publication *Video Sourcebook* is one of the most valuable and up-to-date reference listings, including 10 formats and 10 acquisition modes. The sixth edition included 40,000 titles. The NICEM (National Information Center for Educational Media) database, now produced in Albuquerque, New Mexico, and available through DIALOG as well as in print, features 50,000 titles in its film index and the same number in its video index, with no indication of the degree of overlap. The OCLC database of July 1, 1985, contained 298,806 AV items and 339,753 sound recordings.

SETTINGS FOR AV SERVICES

Academic and Public Libraries. While the use of audiovisual materials has met with wider and more casual acceptance at the junior college and technical training level, academic libraries continue to make such items available also, and to integrate them into their service programs and collections. A recent thesis surveying 400 randomly selected four-year academic institutions (and receiving a 67 percent response) found that approximately 85 percent had attempted some integration of print and nonprint resources and that nearly 50 percent had staff working closely together on both. Some still had separate print and nonprint facilities with separate directors, but none failed to provide nonprint resources.

Public librarians likewise are still divided in their approach, some "mainstreaming" media and others keeping them separate in cataloguing, classification, indexing, shelving, and use. A recent thesis surveying 1,000 public libraries or library systems having sizable nonbook media collections (and receiving a 50 percent response) found that 83 percent provided bibliographic access to nonbook media materials, though only 38 percent of these do so by means of an integrated, omnimedia catalogue as allowed by *AACR2.* In spite of the fact that only 38 percent actually had them, 73 percent approved integrated catalogues over divided catalogues. Several thought the availability of both an advantage.

School Libraries. Audiovisual media have always played an important role in school libraries and have only recently been separated in some institutions for administrative purposes as special collections away from books and other nonprint materials, ostensibly because of their unique need for machines. The recent trend toward re-integrating all kinds of learning materials into a single learning resources center has provided new challenges to library professionals, especially when they are asked to be librarians as well as media specialists, administrators of special service programs in school organizations, and experts on curriculum and instruction.

In even the smallest school media centers, the primary concerns of librarians are often technological and financial. Technology, represented primarily by computers, has forced re-thinking both in new media formats and in using computers to operate media centers. Financial problems have significantly changed the funding patterns of school audiovisual programs and will certainly be the major problems for library professionals in schools in the future.

School media programs are currently undergoing a comprehensive, professionwide self-analysis that will result in new curricula for training school media professionals as well as new standards for the development and operation of programs, including financing, staffing, and legal aspects. Experts predict that

Music room of the Audiovisual Center at the Pontificia Universidad Católica de Chile.

Fernandez C. Rodrigo/Biblioteca Central Pontificia, Universidad Catolica de Chile

the school media professional must become a "knowledge manager" in order to survive the waves of financial and technological changes affecting society, the schools, and the media program.

Special Libraries. Audiovisual services in special libraries have kept pace with similar services in other types of libraries, often leading schools and public libraries in the acquisition of specialized visual materials for such purposes as management training and public relations, in addition to archival and other needs.

Special libraries, especially those in business environments, and sometimes in government agencies, often have access to in-house specialists to develop cost- and time-effective responses to the needs of their institutions for information storage, transfer, and retrieval. In addition, the patrons of special libraries, although usually more specialized than the publics of other types of libraries, are often change-oriented and more accepting of the newer formats, including interactive video.

Federal Audiovisual Activity Report for 1984 (1985)showed audiovisual activity in 46 of 66 agencies. Total expenditures for the purpose (production, duplication, and purchase) decreased slightly in the early 1980s. Department of Defense expenditures are just over half of this figure; civilian departments and agencies make up the rest. Purchases of motion pictures had decreased 56 percent; videotape-disk had increased 28 percent. In-house production and duplication had increased, reflecting a similar trend in private industry.

This trend is reflected in the sales of blank videocassettes, which increased 81.5 percent in units and 40 percent in dollar volume in 1984 as compared to 1983. International Tape and Disk Association figures gave combined VHS and Beta sales as 157,900,000 units, representing $913,700,000 wholesale value. While no particular standardization is in sight, visible trends show that improvements Beta II and III are replacing Beta I and that 1/2-inch is gaining over 3/4-inch as a preferred size. VHS represents about 80 percent of the market.

The familiarity of the VHS format to the general public, its close resemblance to the book in matters of convenience, portability, size, and shape, the increasing availability of players, ease of playback, and variety of offerings all have generated a demand that has won the attention of commercial and private suppliers, including public libraries, many of whom view it as a new way of stimulating library patronage.

ISSUES

Current and future issues are related primarily to the power, cost, and control of technology for creating, storing, retrieving, and displaying information, regardless of format—issues such as bibliographic control, censorship, and how to pay for fee-based information services—as well as the increased need for continuing education for audiovisual specialists to remain abreast of developments in the field.

Censorship. Societal pressures have forced the recognition once more of the power inherent in well-produced media to persuade and to inform. Thus they are often prime objects of criticism from those who do not agree with the positions taken by their creators. Because of their power, particularly when combined with confusion about how to evaluate, classify, and fund them in a library, media often seem to invite censorship.

Fees. Some public, academic, and special libraries have begun to charge certain of their patrons for services, often based on the patron's ability to pay. In audiovisual service programs, where information about media tends to be difficult to obtain and where the materials themselves are often offered to patrons at some commercial-use fee, the issue of offering information for a fee influences potential access to the media in a new way.

Bibliographic Controls. Constants in the problem of bibliographic control of nonprint media are the relatively short lifespans of some formats and the strong tendency of many producers and marketers to be both inexact and changeable about titles. The title, as default main entry in cataloguing, is the key access point for tracking the item, and is of critical importance. Convincing producers that following the basic conventions and requirements of bibliographic control of nonprint media will not restrict, inhibit, damage, or in anyway affect their art (except to make it available to a wider public) is a job that must be constantly repeated by audiovisual library professionals.

The bibliographic control of audiovisual media consists of two kinds of information, descriptive and evaluative. Descriptive information continues to be a concern for many, in that no single institution or organization sets, and few organizations maintain, cataloguing standards for media. Less and less evaluative information has been forthcoming from reviewing sources, professional cooperatives, and membership associations in the field.

In certain subject areas where the information is of critical importance, such as medicine, funds are readily available for the necessary bibliographic controls to permit ready storage and retrieval. MEDLINE, the national medical data bank, has an audiovisual component known as MEDAV, probably the most comprehensive database of its kind.

Because recorded media often contain dynamically related current topics in mixed media, traditional subject control often proves inadequate. One possible solution to this problem exists, and has been perfected over 10 years. Devised by Derek W. Austin, the PREserved Context Index System (PRECIS) uses computers to generate, file, and print index entries. PRECIS is particularly suitable for bibliographic control of media. It allows the use of the item's own terminology, building an appropriate set of terms without the time lag involved in official endorsement for subject codes. It preserves the grammatical relationships of these terms as they exist within each item throughout the creation of multiple access points. And it allows all index entries to be meaningful, even for concepts that may appear only in the visual aspect of a recording, without loss of information or distortion.

PRECIS is widely used in Canada and the United Kingdom. The cost of retrocataloguing and retraining have thus far delayed the recognition of its great potential elsewhere. However, the move toward the information conglomerate concept, as well as the capabilities of the PRECIS system itself, augur well for its future, and for the future of bibliographic control of media.

There is every evidence that a small group of concerned individuals in the audiovisual field is working toward the dream of some sort of "AV in Print" that would provide for comprehensive retrieval. With the capabilities computerization provides, the dream may some day be a reality.

REFERENCES
Deirdre Boyle, *Expanding Media* (1977).
Margaret Chisholm, editor, *Reader in Media, Technology, and Libraries* (1975).
American Library Association, *Guidelines for Audio-Visual Services in Academic Libraries* (1968).
Sheila S. Intner, "Access to Media: Attitudes of Public Librarians," *RQ* (1984).
Constance Ryan, *A Survey of Print and Nonprint Materials in College Libraries* (Unpublished M.S. Thesis, 1984).
RUTH R. RAINS;
STEPHEN C. JOHNSON

Austin, Derek

(1921-   )

Derek William Austin made significant contributions to the field of indexing through his work with the Classification Research Group and the development of the PRECIS (PREserved Context Index System).

He was born in London on August 11, 1921. He started his library career in 1938, joining the staff of his local public library directly from grammar school. He spent most of the period 1941–46 on army service in India, Burma, China (with a commando unit), and Germany. After being demobilized he applied for an ex-serviceman's grant to study at Loughborough Library School and achieved the Associateship of the Library Association in 1948, passed the LA final examination (with honors) in 1949, and was elected a Fellow of the Library Association in 1950.

Most of his early career was spent in public libraries (Enfield, Hertfordshire, and Tottenham), usually in the capacity of reference librarian, readers' adviser, or subject specialist. Service of this kind,

requiring a constant use of indexes as tools for relating queries to answers, is a necessary background, Austin became convinced, for anyone who intends to produce an index or attempts to design an indexing system.

He became involved in index production when he joined the staff of the *British National Bibliography* as a Subject Editor in 1963. He was seconded from *BNB* in 1967 to work on the NATO-supported research, directed by the Classification Research Group (London), into a new library classification based on faceted principles. Although the CRG classification had not materialized when the NATO funds ran out, Austin came to consider that such an innovation was no longer necessary. The general principles of subject analysis formulated during that research were the critical starting point for his later research into subject indexing.

The need for a fresh approach to indexing arose when the editors of *BNB* decided that all its issues from the start of 1971 should be produced by computer from MARC records. With just over a year to go, Austin was appointed to lead a team with the task of designing a new subject index. The goal was a controlled-language, precoordinated indexing system conceived from the outset with the computer in mind. The system had to satisfy the following main criteria: (1) all index entries, and their supporting cross-references, should be generated, filed, and printed entirely by the computer; (2) the indexer would prepare only an input string of terms and coded instructions, which would then be manipulated by standard algorithms into index entries under any selected term; and (3) all entries should be meaningful and equally coextensive, and the mechanical generation of entries should not entail any loss of information, nor any distortion of the subject. All these goals were achieved by PRECIS—a name that has become almost a synonym for Derek Austin.

Although Austin's work on classificatory theory formed a necessary basis for his later ideas on indexing, PRECIS has taken the concept of subject analysis and concept organization in a new direction: away from relative significance as the organizing principle and toward general linguistic principles and an order of terms in index entries which is directly concerned with the clear expression of meaning. Thus, an explanation of PRECIS mainly calls for reference to grammatical categories and general logical relations.

Although PRECIS is still a relatively young system (what might be called the definitive version for the English language was adopted by *BNB* in 1974), it is now employed by a number of indexing agencies in Britain, Australia, and Canada, and experimental indexes were produced in several other countries. The logic on which the system is based, and on which the production of meaningful entries depends, appears to be language-independent, and the system has been applied successfully in a range of European languages.

In the course of his researches, Austin necessarily had to reexamine many facets of the total indexing operation. Several of the techniques developed originally for PRECIS are capable of standing in isolation, and many indexers who have no intention of adopting PRECIS have nevertheless benefited from a study of its approach to concept analysis, the treatment of compound terms, and the construction of a machine-held thesaurus. The general applicability of these techniques is mentioned only occasionally in Austin's own writing on PRECIS, but they appear, nevertheless, in two documents that would otherwise, by their very nature, remain anonymous; Austin was the principal author of a Draft International Standard on techniques for document analysis and of the current British Standard on the construction of a monolingual thesaurus.

In 1976 Austin received the first Ranganathan Award presented by the FID for original contributions to classification (defined in its widest sense). This was followed by the Margaret Mann Citation for 1978.

REFERENCES

Hans Wellisch, editor, *The PRECIS Index System: Principles, Applications, and Prospects* (1977).
Derek Austin, *PRECIS: A Manual . . .* (1974).

JUTTA SØRENSON

Australia

Australia, a federal parliamentary state and a member of the Commonwealth of Nations, is both the world's largest island and its smallest continent. It lies in the Southern Hemisphere, between the Pacific and Indian oceans. European settlement dates from 1788. Australia comprises six States—New South Wales, Queensland, South Australia, Tasmania, Victoria, and Western Australia—and two Territories—the Australian Capital Territory and the Northern Territory. The Northern Territory is, to all intents and purposes, a seventh state. Population (1984 est.) 15,462,000; area 7,682,300 sq.km. The official language is English.

History. Library development in Australia has been dominated by the size of the country, its small population, and the concentration of that population in cities and overwhelmingly on the southeast coast of the continent. In addition, the history of Australian settlement in separate colonies is perpetuated in the Australian Constitution, in which residual power re-

sides in the states; that, combined with the relative recency of Federation (1901), has imparted a strong state element into the pattern of library services and the planning of library development.

State Libraries. Until the mid-1950s the central libraries of the states, especially those of New South Wales and Victoria, were the nation's outstanding libraries. The rapid growth of the National Library and the explosive development of academic libraries, however, reduced the relative contribution of the state libraries to the bibliographic resources of the nation; as a group, they have shifted their emphasis increasingly away from research collecting to coordinating and supplementing public library services within their states. Yet, with their long history and their function as libraries of record for their respective states, they are still significant elements of the national resource, especially in the area of Australiana. The oldest and largest two, the State Library of New South Wales and the State Library of Victoria, each have book collections in excess of a million volumes and substantial holdings of manuscript and pictorial material.

National Library. The National Library of Australia was established in 1902 as the Library of the Commonwealth Parliament but, as early as 1907, the Parliamentary Library Committee recommended that it should take the Library of Congress as its model in all respects. From 1923 the title "Commonwealth National Library" came into use to cover the Library's non-Parliamentary services. In 1935 it began to compile and publish the basis for a national bibliography and from the early 1940s it undertook the development of the national archives.

In 1960, on the recommendation of a Commonwealth Government Committee of Enquiry (the Paton Committee), the National Library of Australia was established by statute as a separate institution, distinguished from both the Parliamentary Library and the Archives, the latter to become ultimately the Australian Archives.

From that time increasingly and especially with the great advantage since 1968 of a major building, the Library has been accepted in a proper position of

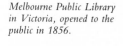

Melbourne Public Library in Victoria, opened to the public in 1856.

national leadership, resting in large part on its provision of national bibliographical services. The most significant services are regular publication of the national bibliography (*Australian National Bibliography, Australian Government Publications, Australian Maps,* and so on) and the major subject index to Australian periodicals *Australian Public Affairs Information Services (APAIS);* the maintenance of national union catalogues, originally as separate manual files but increasingly as spin-offs from the national bibliographic database which it has developed; the provision of central cataloguing services (the Australian card service and the Australian MARC Record Service, AMRS) and the operation of a nationwide, online resource-sharing network, the Australian Bibliographic Network (ABN). Together with the Commonwealth Department of Health, the Library operates the Australian MEDLINE Service and provides batch-mode support, under contract to the World Health Organization (WHO), to countries in the Western Pacific.

The Library participates in international programs, both generally and as a national bibliographic agency, and has pursued a vigorously outgoing policy in Southeast Asia and Oceania through its Regional Cooperation Program.

The Library's holdings in 1982 comprised 2,100,000 volumes together with 1,300,000 microform equivalents for a total of 3,400,000 volumes in the collections. There were approximately two million nonbook items. Significant collections and strengths in various fields are described in C. A. Burmester's four-volume *Guide to the Collections* published by the Library. The Library has also published its *Selection Policy.*

Academic Libraries. Massive Commonwealth funding for universities, colleges of advanced education, and institutes of technical and further education led to a major library phenomenon—the multiplication and expansion of academic libraries in Australia. Federal funding for universities began in earnest as a result of the report of a Committee of Inquiry (the Murray Committee) set up by the government in 1957. At that time there were nine university institutions, the libraries of which had a total stock of 1,500,000 volumes, employed 270 staff and accounted for a combined expenditure in the region of $A1,000,000. By 1982 there were 19 universities, and the comparative figures were 15,400,000 volumes (including microform equivalents), more than 2,300 staff, and more than $A74,000,000 expenditure.

The oldest of the university libraries, the University of Sydney Library (founded 1851), with 2,300,000 volumes and 700,000 microform equivalents in 1982, is easily the largest, but seven other university libraries now have collections (including microforms) in excess of one million volumes or volume equivalents.

Colleges of advanced education resulted from the recommendation of yet another Commonwealth Government Committee (the Martin Committee) in 1965. They have been described as "equal to but different from" universities, and their library collections reflect their practical and nonresearch orientation. There were more than 50 colleges in 1982, including many former teacher training institutions. Generous federal funding revolutionized their libraries in the late 1960s and early 1970s but a general decline in

State Library of New South Wales

General reference library reading room of the State Library of New South Wales, one of Australia's largest libraries.

support for tertiary education in the late 1970s left many significantly below the interim standards set in 1969 for their development by the library subcommittee of the Commission of Advanced Education, the government body coordinating the funding and growth of the colleges. The largest college library—that of the South Australian College of Advanced Education (an amalgamation of several formerly independent colleges)—held 714,000 volumes (including microform equivalents) in 1982.

Technical and further education libraries, based on the collections of former technical colleges, were also the subject of a government inquiry (the Kangan Report) in the 1970s that revealed substantial deficiencies. Although considerable progress had been achieved by the mid-1980s, funds were not forthcoming to address the deficiencies adequately.

Resource sharing, addressed nationally by the National Library, especially through the Australian Bibliographic Network, has also been a considerable concern of academic libraries. CAVAL (Cooperative Action by Victorian Academic Libraries) in Melbourne and the Office of Library Cooperation (OLC) in Sydney are university resource-sharing consortia. In each case the university libraries are joined by the state library. In the college library field, CLANN Ltd. (College Library Activity Network in New South Wales) has drawn together 19 college and other libraries in a cooperative network.

Public Libraries. The provision of local library service to the public is largely the responsibility of local government authorities in Australia. In the Australian Capital Territory, in the absence of any such authority, the Canberra Public Library Service, formerly a branch of the National Library, is operated by the Commonwealth Department of Territories and Local Government. In Tasmania all public libraries are, in effect, branches of the state library.

Elsewhere the state governments supplement local government expenditure on libraries in a variety of ways. At one extreme, in New South Wales, support is basically a financial subsidy to local authorities who provide services that meet appropriate standards; at the other, in Western Australia, the State Library Board provides the bookstock for all public libraries and the local authorities are responsible for the staff and accommodation. The other three states and the Northern Territory assume positions along this spectrum; a substantial trend in the 1980s was toward joint services, regionalization, and other devices for integration, together with increasing participation by the state authority.

Though Australia's first library, the Wesleyan Library established in Hobart, Tasmania, in 1825, was at least in some sense a public library, modern public library services date from the passage of the first State Library Act (New South Wales, 1939). It was the outcome of community action following the recommendations of a Carnegie-funded survey of Australian libraries (the Munn-Pitt Report) undertaken in 1934. Rapid development followed, but a Commonwealth Committee of Inquiry (the Horton Committee) reported in 1976 that public library services, though available to 93 percent of the population, still presented grave inadequacies. It recommended federal funding as the only remedy. After much delay the government finally announced in 1981 that it was not prepared to provide direct funding for public libraries. It pointed to measurable improvements over the preceding five years and noted its heavy commitment, directly and indirectly, to the support of libraries in educational institutions at all levels.

School Libraries. Federal assistance in the 1960s and 1970s brought dramatic improvement. From a very bleak situation indeed, school libraries in Australia were developed to the point in the 1980s where they are clearly of world class. They make a significant impact not only on Australian education but also within the Australian library community generally.

The pattern of school library provision reflects two political facts: education is a state, not a federal, preserve; the private sector, especially as represented by the various religious denominations, maintains schools at all levels in parallel with the state systems. The unifying element is Commonwealth government funding, which applies to both streams. An example of cooperation is ASCIS, an Australia-wide, shared cataloguing scheme for school libraries.

Special Libraries. In general, Australian special libraries are not well documented and their importance as a national bibliographic resource is probably considerably underrated. This situation may be remedied by the rapid rate at which they were becoming participants in the Australian Bibliographic Network, as a result of which their holdings were beginning to appear in the national bibliographic database by the mid-1980s.

The most important groups of special libraries are the libraries of the parliaments of the Commonwealth of Australia and of the states, the libraries of the departments and other instrumentalities of the federal and state governments, and the libraries of business and industry.

Parliamentary libraries present a wide range, in both functions and services. The Commonwealth Parliamentary Library survived the separate establishment of the National Library in 1960 to become the leader in establishing legislative research services in addition to more conventional reference support for members of parliament. The library of the Parliament of Queensland has developed a fully integrated automated operation, a parliamentary library network was being developed in the mid-1980s, and Australian parliamentary libraries actively support the development of sister institutions in the emerging nations of the Pacific.

Unique among a second group of special libraries is the library service of the Commonwealth Scientific and Industrial Research Organization (CSIRO). CSIRO's nationwide network of more than 60 branch libraries, serving the Organization's various divisions and laboratories, provides considerable support to library services generally. The service pioneered the union listing of serials in Australia with the publication, in 1935, of the first edition of the forerunner of *Scientific Serials in Australian Libraries (SSAL)*. Until the early 1970s, the CSIRO libraries constituted a de facto national science library. Thereafter that role was taken over gradually by the National Library; for example, *SSAL* was absorbed in 1985 into the National Union Catalogue of Serials (NUCOS), which the National Library publishes as a spin-off from the national bibliographic database. In

---

Libraries in Australia (1982)

Type	Administrative units	Service points	Volumes in collections	Annual expenditures (Australian dollar)	Population served	Professional staff	Total staff
National	1	--	3,400,000	19,600,000	15,000,000	135	628
State	7	--	4,500,000	75,300,000	15,000,000	770	1,970
University	19	--	15,400,000	74,000,000	182,000	684	1,608
Colleges of Advanced Education	53	--	7,600,000	39,100,000	201,000	576	1,612
Public	350	1,300	24,500,000	11,300,000	14,250,000	1,400	4,500
School	10,000[a]		10,000,000[a]				
Special	513	1,428	7,000,000	53,000,000	--	801	1,976

[a]Estimates.

Sources: Australian Advisory Council on Bibliographical Services, *Second Census of Library Services,* (unpublished), 1984; *The Work of AACOBS 1981–82,* Canberra, 1983; *Australian Academic and Research Libraries. Supplement, Library Statistics, 1982,* Melbourne, 1983.

1983 the two organizations published a joint statement on their functions.

Libraries of business and industry vary greatly in size and sophistication—and, indeed, in longevity in periods of business recession. But well-established library and information services, such as those maintained by Australian Consolidated Industries, operate at a high level in both conventional and computer-based services.

The Profession. Education for librarianship in Australia developed originally on the British pattern of an examination system conducted by the professional association. The Australian Institute of Librarians (AIL, founded 1937) held its first examinations in the late 1940s. Its successor, the Library Association of Australia (LAA), finally phased out the examination system in 1981, with the intention of accelerating the development of library schools in education institutions. The first of these schools was established at the University of New South Wales in 1961. By 1982, 19 institutions conducted courses for librarians or teacher librarians; two were universities and the remainder, colleges of advanced education. The vast majority of the courses were recognized (that is, accredited) by the LAA. Most courses are either at the bachelor's level or are (one-year) diplomas following first degrees in other fields. Master's degrees (which constitute second professional awards) and Doctorates are also offered. Eleven institutions of technical and further education offered courses for library technicians in 1985.

The Library Association of Australia, established in 1949 in succession to the Australian Institute of Librarians, was incorporated by Royal Charter in 1963. The LAA welcomes all interested in libraries but provides also for professional membership by associates (who must be university graduates with recognized professional qualifications) and fellows (associates recognized for distinguished contributions to the theory or practice of librarianship in Australia). Membership of the LAA in the mid-1980s stood at 6,500, including about 2,500 professional members.

The Australian School Libraries Association (ASLA) is a federation of state associations of school librarians. Although there is no formal link with the LAA, there is a joint standing committee to facilitate cooperation and there is considerable common membership. The Australian Advisory Council on Bibliographical Services (AACOBS) is a unique voluntary association of major library, archive, and information services. Through its state and regional committees it provides a mechanism for day-to-day consultation and a device for expression of group criticism and advice to governments and to the National Library. The National Library provides the secretariat for AACOBS and supports the activities of its four working parties: on bibliography, information resources, user needs, and research and development. There is a joint LAA/AACOBS Committee on Information and Technology and representatives of AACOBS, the LAA, and the National Library form the Australian Committee on Cataloguing.

In 1981 the Commonwealth Government established the Australian Libraries and Information Council (ALIC) to advise governments at all levels on the planned development of libraries and related information services. ALIC comprises the Director-General of the National Library, the six state librarians and the director of the Northern Territory Library Service, three nominees of the Commonwealth Minister for Education and Youth Affairs, and one nominee of the Commonwealth Minister for Science and Technology. ALIC is required to consult widely and indicated its intention to seek the advice of AACOBS, which has long been committed to securing both the enunciation of a national information policy and government support for planning of the kind entrusted to ALIC.

REFERENCES

Peter Biskup, *Australian Libraries*, 3rd edition (1982), is a standard work.

Dietrich H. Borchardt and J. I. Horacek, *Librarianship in Australia, New Zealand, and Oceania: a Brief Survey* (1975), makes some interesting comparisons.

Harrison Bryan and R. M. McGreal, *The Pattern of Library Services in Australia* (1972), though rather dated, is a useful brief introduction.

Harrison Bryan and G. Greenwood, editors, *Design for Diversity: Library Services for Higher Education and Research in Australia* (1977), is a major work with historical and other detail not found elsewhere.

Harrison Bryan and J. I. Horacek, editors, *Australian Academic Libraries in the Seventies* (1983), updates *Design for Diversity* to some extent.

HARRISON BRYAN

Austria

A federal republic in central Europe, Austria is bounded by the Federal Republic of Germany and Czechoslovakia on the north, Hungary on the east, Yugoslavia and Italy on the south, and Switzerland and Liechtenstein on the west. Population (1984 est.) 7,551,000; area 83,855 sq.km. The official language is German.

History. The Austrian library scene, as well as that of other old European nations, originates in a few monastic centers—Salzburg (founded around 700), the oldest library on Austrian territory, and Mondsee (748). More than 100 others followed. The most famous still are Kremsmünster (777), St. Florian (1071), Admont (1074), Göttweig (1083), Melk (1089), St. Paul (1091), Klosterneuburg (1108), Heiligenkreuz (1136), Zwettl (1138), and Altenburg (1144). Their significance lies in their abundant and precious stock of manuscripts (up to 1,300) and incunabula (up to 2,000) and in their wonderful baroque library halls.

The early Hapsburgs laid the basis for the Imperial Court Library in the 14th century. It soon became an outstanding collection and a great resource for research. In 1365 the University Library of Vienna was founded; Graz, Innsbruck, and Salzburg followed.

Decisive turning points in the administration of Austrian libraries occurred in the 18th century: The Empress Maria Theresa (ruled 1740–80) effected a series of library reforms. Later on many monasteries were dissolved and the Jesuit Order was dissolved in Austria. Many rare book collections were transferred to already existing university libraries. Other collections went to newly established research libraries (Studienbibliotheken). Library affairs were centralized

Austrian National Library

Prunksaal (State Hall) in Austrian National Library. It dates from the 14th century.

devoted to the arts and sciences and successful book collectors. In 1575 the first full-time librarian was appointed: Hugo Blotius. Around 1590 the collection held 9,000 volumes, and it grew to be the largest library of the German-speaking world, a position it held up to the 19th century.

After the dissolution of the Austro-Hungarian Empire in 1918, the Library became the property of the Republic and gradually was transformed into a modern research library. Efforts were made to meet the new requirements in library and information services up to the contemporary computer age.

With its 2,430,000 printed works and periodicals, but especially with its wealth of manuscripts (97,000, more than 16,000 of which are dated before 1600), incunabula (about 8,000), autographs (277,653), maps (221,769), globes (142), printed music (98,545), papyrus (88,162), portraits (715,961), photographs (670,212), and theatrical items (figures included in other counts), it ranks among the first libraries of the world.

As the central library of the nation it houses the Planning Center for Research Libraries, the Union Database for Periodicals (Österreichische Zeitschriftendatenbank, ÖZDB); a Union Catalogue for all new foreign monographs since 1930 acquired by research libraries (Büchernachweisstelle); the Austrian National Bibliography (since 1946), fortnightly, which listed for 1982 a total of 9,181 titles; the final stage of the professional education for research librarians; the Institute for Conservation; the Association of Austrian Librarians (Vereinigung Österreichischer Bibliothekare, VÖB); and the Austrian Institute for Library Research, Documentation and Information (Institut für Bibliotheksforschung, Dokumentations- und Informationswesen). Moreover, it is a depository library for all Austrian publications. The Library building was developed on the premises of the court from 1723 and is still expanding to the Neue Hofburg (New Imperial Palace). Its brilliant core is the State Hall (Prunksaal), a library hall of magnificent baroque splendor.

Academic Libraries. In Austria university libraries have taken a prominent role since 1975 with the passage of the UOG. There are four full universities, at Vienna, Graz, Innsbruck, and Salzburg; two general technical universities, at Graz and Vienna; 14 technical universities; and academies for the study of special fields such as theology, educational sciences, social sciences, design, music, art, commerce, mining, agriculture, and veterinary medicine. The oldest academic library is the University Library of Vienna (founded 1365). Under the terms of the UOG, it is the largest library of Austria, with combined holdings of 4,147,112 volumes, including those of more than 100 faculties and institutes; next is Graz (1573), with a total of 1,783,907 volumes.

Public Libraries. Public library services are about 100 years old in Austria. Initiated by religious and political bodies in Vienna, the center of the Danubian monarchy, they developed to quite an extent after World War II. There are more than 2,000 such libraries. The main groups are: municipal libraries (616 branches), with 2,873,583 volumes serving 8,523,672 readers; religious libraries (Österreichisches Borromäuswerk) (729), with 1,030,135 volumes serving 702,109 readers; trade unions (462), with

and a nationwide library network was created. The Ministry of Education took responsibility for research libraries, also including the Austrian National Library in 1918.

During the 19th and 20th centuries a great variety of new ministries, governmental bodies, universities, unions, chambers, institutes, and associations developed and with them new libraries with rapidly growing book collections. It has been necessary to remodel and adapt old buildings and to found a number of new ones. Present trends are toward the preservation and conservation of the old stock, employing microforms, and above all towards the implementation of an integrated, computerized library system.

The legal basis for research libraries was defined under two laws. The Universitäts-Organisationsgesetz (UOG) of 1975 altered the structure of university libraries. The main libraries became the managerial centers also for faculty- and institute-libraries (formerly independent units), controlling coordination of acquisition of library material, cataloguing, and the creation of documentation and information systems. The Forschungsorganisationsgesetz (FOG) of 1981 defines the main objectives of the Austrian National Library: the collection of "Austriaca" of the country and worldwide, central planning of library concerns for the country, and training of research librarians.

National Library. The beginnings of the Austrian National Library (Österreichische Nationalbibliothek), the former Imperial Court Library (Kaiserliche Hofbibliothek), are closely linked with the Hapsburgs. Its earliest manuscript was acquired by Duke Albrecht III in 1368. Emperor Frederick III (1440–93) and his son Maximilian I (1493–1519) were

1,310,745 volumes serving 2,027,825 readers; and smaller groups such as reading societies, provincial libraries, infirmaries, and prisons. Only a small proportion of these libraries are handled by professional librarians, often assisted by honorary personnel.

Special Libraries. Austria has a great variety of special libraries. Each of the nine provinces has a main library (Landesbibliothek) with the legal right for deposit and ranging in size from 70,000 to 300,000 volumes. A number of libraries serve governmental bodies, ministries, chambers, museums, and scientific agencies, the most comprehensive collections of which are those of the Ministry of Defense (520,000 volumes), the Federal Chancellery (430,000), the Ministry of Education and the Ministry of Science and Research (325,000), the Patent Office (265,000), the Austrian Academy of Science and Research (nearly 500,000), and the Museum of Natural History (373,000). Nongovernmental agencies and industrial and commercial enterprises also have significant collections. A modern special library is that of the International Atomic Energy Agency (100,000).

School Libraries. There are a number of pedagogical academies, some of them under the aegis of the church. They range in size from 30,000 to 175,000 volumes. Most school libraries (about 6,000) are maintained by teachers. Some of them are used by teachers and pupils alike; some of them function as public libraries.

The Profession. Austria has no library school, nor is there an opportunity to study library science at the university. Only when employed by a library is a candidate admitted to the training for the academic level (A) or for the high school level (B) (*Matura*), according to regulations of 1979. The first stage of training, mainly practical, comprises exercises in cataloguing and bibliography at six training libraries plus an examination; a second stage comprises mainly theoretical lectures on all fields of modern library and information sciences at the Austrian National Library. Training for the A level lasts 40 weeks, for the B level 27 weeks, and for a newly created C level (*Fachdienst*) 7 weeks. Instruction ends with oral and written examinations.

Public librarians have one-year training programs at training libraries and also take examinations.

Austrian National Library

Main reading room, National Library of Austria in Vienna.

Continuing education is offered in the form of seminars, symposia, and various programs at professional meetings.

The Association of Austrian Librarians dates back to 1896. It had 752 certified members in 1982. Its official journals are *Mitteilungen der Vereinigung Österreichischer Bibliothekare* and *Biblos,* in which the proceedings of the biannual meetings are published.

The Association of Austrian Public Libraries and Public Librarians (Verband der Österreichischen Volksbüchereien und Volksbibliothekare) had 799 members. It issues *Erwachsenenbildung* (formerly *Neue Volksbildung*). Other important associations are: Austrian Institute for Library Research, Documentation and Information; Austrian Association of Archivists (Verein Österreichischer Archivare), with about 300 members; Austrian Society for Documentation and Information (Österreichische Gesellschaft für Dokumentation und Information); and Austrian Society for Public Affairs of the Information Sciences (Österreichische Gesellschaft für Öffentlichkeitsarbeit des Informationswesens).

MARGARET R. STRASSNIG-BACHNER

Libraries in Austria (1982)

Type	Administrative units	Service points	Volumes in collections	Annual expenditures (schilling)	Population served	Professional staff	Total staff
National[a]	1		2,464,688	5,673,932	440,533	164	264
Academic[a]	20[d]	868	12,165,925	116,277,034	2,339,362[f]	654	--
Public[b]	799	2,118	6,043,129	--	13,135,110	--	4,582[e]
School[c]	5,600	--	9,500,000	--	--	--	--
Special[c]	512	--	7,675,000	--	--	--	--

[a]*Biblos* Heft 4, Jahrgang 32 (1983).
[b]Association of Austrian Public Libraries.
[c]Unesco, *Statistical Yearbook*, 1982.
[d]Universitäts Organisationsgesetz (UOG) (1975) altered the structure of university libraries. Formerly independent institute and faculty libraries were incorporated as managerial units with main libraries. The First Edition of the *ALA World Encyclopedcia* reported 742 academic libraries; there are 20 under reorganization.
[e]4,582 is the total number of public librarians; 506 as professionals, 392 part-time, and 3,684 without pay.
[f]For 13 libraries no figures were available.

Bachtiar, Harsya W.
(1934-)

Harsya Wardhana Bachtiar, Indonesian educator, sociologist, anthropologist, and historian, was Dean of the Faculty of Letters, University of Indonesia, 1969–75. Concerned about the acquisition, storage, and accessibility of information, he actively involved himself in programs to increase the capacity of library, documentation, and archival centers in Indonesia to provide improved services.

Born in Bandung, Indonesia, on May 3, 1934, he studied at the Faculty of Social and Political Science, University of Amsterdam, 1953–55; at the College of Arts and Sciences and then Graduate School of Arts and Sciences, Cornell University, 1955–59; and later at the Graduate School of Arts and Sciences, Harvard University, 1963–67. Bachtiar earned a Ph.D. in sociology from Harvard with a dissertation on "The Formation of the Indonesian Nation." He lectured at the Faculty of Letters, University of Indonesia, from 1959, becoming a full Professor of Sociology and Social History in 1976.

He served as Acting Director of the National Institute of Economic and Social Research (LEKNAS), Indonesian Institute of Science (LIPI), 1969–75. On the national level, he took an active part in the development of higher education and research in the social sciences as Coordinator of the Consortium of Social Sciences and Humanities, an advisory body to the Minister of Education and Culture, 1971–75, and then, among other work, as Executive Secretary of the Interdisciplinary Consortium, one of 11 consortia maintained to assist the Director General of Higher Education. Bachtiar served as a member of various official Indonesian delegations, such as the delegation to the annual conferences of the Southeast Asian Ministers of Education Organization (SEAMEO) at Kuala Lumpur, 1971, Saigon, 1972, and Vientiane, 1973, the delegation to the Unesco General Conference in Paris, 1974, when he was elected Vice-Chairman of Commission V (Social Science, Humanities, and Culture), in Nairobi, 1976; in Paris, 1983; and in Sofia, 1985. From 1975 he also served as Chairman of the Indonesian Steering Committee, Dutch-Indonesian Cooperation for the Promotion of Indonesia Studies.

He participated in many conferences on archives and worked closely with the Director of the National Archives of the Republic of Indonesia, particularly in matters of archival professional training, archival cooperation among Southeast Asian countries, archival cooperation between Indonesia and the Netherlands, and oral history.

In 1983 he became Head of the Office of Educational and Cultural Research and Development, Ministry of Education and Culture, Republic of Indonesia.

Among his many publications is a *Directory of Social Scientists in Indonesia* (Jakarta, 1976).

SOEMARTINI

Bahamas

An independent state off the southeast coast of the United States in the Atlantic Ocean, the Bahamas comprises 700 islands, of which only about 30 are inhabited. The islands basically parallel Cuba's north coast. Population (1984 est.) 227,000; area 13,939 sq.km. The official language is English.

History. Public libraries, which operate as independent units under their respective boards of trustees, were established under the Nassau Public Library Act (1847) and the Out Island Public Library Act (1909). The public libraries were included in the portfolio of the Minister of Education from 1964. In February 1972 a committee was appointed by the Government for the purpose of raising funds to establish a Public Library Service. There was no national library service in late 1985.

National Library Plan. Plans called for a library that would maintain a national union catalogue, national bibliography, national and international loan service, and strong local history collection. Arrangements were envisaged in 1985 for the library to become the official depository for all government and other publications of the Bahamas, as well as for copyrighted works. It would also possess audiovisual material and equipment, periodicals, and microforms and would include a high percentage of children's materials, according to plans in the mid-1980s. The national library, it was hoped, would open with a minimum of 440,000 volumes (or 2 volumes per capita), with an increase of 100,000 over a 20-year period. The National Archives in 1985 had holdings totaling about 2,300 linear feet and a staff of 21, including seven professionals.

Academic Libraries. The College of the Bahamas Library is the principal academic library in the Bahamas. It was established in 1975 and incorporated the Bahamas Teachers' College Library (now defunct), the Technical College Library, and the San Salvador Teachers' College Library. Its general col-

Libraries in The Bahamas (1982)

Type	Administrative units	Service points	Volumes in collections	Annual expenditures (dollar)	Population served	Professional staff	Total staff
National	--	--	--	--	--	--	--
Academic	1	--	30,000	40,000	1,650	4	12
Public	37	37	60,000	115,000	209,000	4	82
School	--	--	--	--	--	--	--
Special	--	--	--	--	--	--	--

lection numbers about 30,000 volumes and three special collections and includes Bahamian, African, and West Indian works; materials on teaching practice; and theses by students.

Public Libraries. There are five public libraries in Nassau and some 32 in the Family Islands (those outside Nassau).

School Libraries. The majority of the schools in the Bahamas (both government and private) possess libraries; comparative information and statistics on their collections were not available in 1985.

Special Libraries. The Ranfurly Out Island Library, founded in Nassau in 1954, is a branch of an international charitable and voluntary organization with headquarters in London and branches in 63 countries. It is a nonsectarian and nonracial organization, primarily interested in building up school libraries. It sends free boxes of both adults' and children's books to Family Island head-teachers, who make them available to the community. Approximately 200,000 volumes were donated in some 25 years. Some government departments have libraries in their agencies that serve the department and the Public Service (such as the Department of Statistics and the Public Service Training Centre).

REFERENCES
Enid Baa and Mary Heneghan, "Report to the National Library Committee on the Proposal for Establishing a Public Library Service in the Bahama Islands" (1973).
D. G. Reid, *Bahamas—Public Library Service* (Unesco, 1973).

D. GAIL SAUNDERS

Bahrain

Bahrain, an independent monarchy in the Middle East, lies between Saudi Arabia and the Qatar Peninsula. Population (1984 est.) 409,000; area 678 sq.km. The official language is Arabic, though English is widely used.

Bahrain does not possess a national library. For the small population of the island, there were 198 libraries of all descriptions in 1985, of which 13 were public, 4 academic, 149 school, and 32 special libraries. A total of 300 personnel were employed in the libraries, of whom only 40 held diplomas or degrees in library science. A majority of libraries are involved in increasing their professional staffing and in reorganizing and building their collections technically. Modern technology, including microcomputers in libraries and electronic library security systems, have already been introduced by libraries in Bahrain.

Academic Libraries. There are four academic libraries attached to various colleges and universities on the island: the University College of Arts, Science, and Education (UCB), Gulf Polytechnic (GP), College of Health Sciences (CHS), and Arabian Gulf University (AGU).

The UCB library, the largest academic library, was established in 1978, succeeding the Teachers Training College library, founded in 1962). The library has more than 55,000 volumes of Arabic and non-Arabic material. It subscribes to about 700 periodical titles, both Arabic and non-Arabic. UCB library has the largest Arabic collection among the academic libraries on the island, approximately 20,000

Arabian Gulf University

Arabian Gulf University College of Medicine and Medical Sciences Library, where Bahrain's first library computer was installed in September 1985.

volumes. A separate Arabic author/title catalogue has been created.

In 1968 Gulf Technical College was founded to support technical training for citizens of the Gulf and became in 1981 the Gulf Polytechnic (GP). The GP library has 22,000 volumes of Arabic and non-Arabic material. It subscribes to 220 Arabic and non-Arabic periodicals. UCB and GP libraries have a reciprocal borrowing system. The UCB and GP libraries were merging in the mid-1980s to form the Bahrain University Library System. The new library's capacity was planned for 315,000 volumes and seating capacity for 1,500 readers.

The CHS was founded in 1976 as the School of Nursing. The CHS library has 16,000 catalogued volumes and 425 subscriptions and is a depository library for WHO publications.

The Arabian Gulf University is an institution supported and sponsored by all Gulf Cooperative Council (GCC) countries. AGU began in 1982 with its College of Medicine and Medical Sciences (CMMS) located in Salmaniya Medical Center. AGU's permanent campus was to be at Zallag, with a new central library building scheduled for completion in 1986. CMMS Library had 10,000 volumes and 450 subscriptions in the mid-1980s. It offers online database retrieval services through DIALOG.

Most libraries depend on the British Library Lending Division for photocopying because of insufficient backruns of material. The *Bahrain Union List of Serials and Standing Orders,* prepared by UCB staff, includes academic, special, and school libraries. Handling textbooks for use in classrooms takes a major part of each professional academic librarian's time.

Public Libraries. The first public library was established in 1946. Today Bahrain has a Central Public Library and 12 branch libraries; 2 branch libraries serve hospital patients, and another contains special musical material. There is a bookmobile. In 1982 there were more than 28,000 registered borrowers in the library system. The Ministry of Education has established a Directorate of Libraries for overall public library operations.

In 1982 W. G. Alison recommended that the public library should assume the function of National

Library because of the size of the population and limited geographical area. The Manama Public Library (MPL) requested thereafter that all publishers and institutes in Bahrain deposit five copies of each book published in Bahrain. The MPL is the Central Public Library and the headquarters for all public libraries. Centralized purchasing and processing is done for all public libraries from that headquarters. The MPL is a depository for Unesco and Bahrain government publications. The MPL contains two specialized music libraries for listening and use of instruments.

Separate children's sections are available in most public libraries. These are equipped with TV, 16mm projectors, and 16mm films consisting of stories and dramas.

About 15 librarians were working in public libraries in the mid-1980s, of whom 4 had professional library training. As of 1984 there were 196,355 volumes and 575 periodical subscriptions in all public libraries. During 1984, 356,215 people visited the libraries and borrowed a total of 294,215 books.

School Libraries. There are 135 elementary and secondary government schools with more than 80 persons staffing the libraries; 12 had diplomas or degrees in library science from Saudi Arabia, Qatar, or Egypt. All schools have some sort of libraries, ranging from 100 volumes (Tariq Ibn Zayed Primary School) to 10,000 volumes (Manama Secondary School for Girls). Among the government schools the best libraries are found in secondary schools. Most schools run their libraries, especially in elementary schools, without any staff. Some voluntary part-time workers help.

The Ministry of Education has a centralized acquisition and processing department that distributes books to various schools. Individual schools can also purchase material if they have money available.

Among the 26 private schools are some that meet excellent international standards. Bahrain School, an American school, received the U.S. Presidential award of 1985 as one of the outstanding overseas American educational institutions. Its library contains 22,000 volumes and 150 periodicals. The library has a media center equipped with audio and video equipment. The Indian school library contains about 9,000 volumes. Ibn Khuldun School library has about 2,000 volumes.

Special Libraries. There are more government libraries than any other type in the category of special libraries. Each government Ministry has its own library to provide services for its personnel. Bahrain Center for Studies and Research (BCSR) is a

government institute which supports research in economics and social and applied sciences. The BCSR library has 2,000 volumes and subscribes to 200 journals. Bahrain Defence Forces (BDF) has a Central Library and three branch libraries, with a total collection of 12,000 volumes. Bahrain Document Center comes under the Crown Prince's Office and has a collection of 3,000 to 4,000 volumes and a large collection of manuscripts and documents related to Bahrain and other Gulf countries.

The British Council Library (BCL) has more than 10,000 volumes and several journals of wide interest. In 1977 a regional United Nations Information Center (UNIC) was established in Bahrain. Its aim is to provide information on the UN and its agencies to Bahrain, Qatar, and United Arab Emirates, which all gained UN membership in 1971. UNIC is open to the general public as well. It has 10,000 items and a selected periodical collection of all UN agencies and a film library with a large section of documentary films.

There are a number of libraries and information centers attached to the majority of the banks. The Bahrain Monetary Agency (BMA) library has a collection of 5,000 volumes and subscribes to 50 periodicals. Gulf International Bank has a library with 2,000 volumes and 110 periodical subscriptions. The National Bank of Bahrain, Arab Banking Corporation and Bahrain Bankers Training Center, and Management Consulting Group also have libraries and information centers.

Bahrain Petroleum Company (BAPCO) has two libraries: technical and recreational. The recreational library has 11,860 volumes and 65 periodical subscriptions. The Bahrain Historical and Archaeological Society Library has 1,300 items and 90 percent of them are about Bahrain archaeology. The Bahrain Society for Engineers and the Bahrain Writers Association also have libraries. Beit Al-Qur'an (Koran) (Qur'an House) Library was started with a collection of 2,000 items of Holy Qur'an and associated literature. Plans were under way in 1986 to collect monographs, manuscripts and Qur'an related material including translation of the meaning of the Qur'an from all over the world in various languages.

The Profession. Since the early 1980s most libraries have begun to see the importance of professional librarians and have appointed expatriate librarians in key positions. The UCB with six professional librarians had more than any other library. Not very much local library staffing is by professionals. Utilizing expatriate librarians, often on short-term assign-

Libraries in Bahrain (1981)

Type	Administrative units	Service points	Volumes in collections	Annual expenditures (dinar)	Population served[a]	Professional staff	Total staff
National	--	--	--	--	--	--	--
Academic	--	--	--	--	--	--	--
Public	1	10	140,000	323,000	50,000	4	70
School	--	--	--	--	--	--	--

[a]Registered borrowers.

Source: Unesco, *Statistical Yearbook,* 1984.

ments, creates problems in library operations. When there is a hiatus between terms of professional librarians, there are not enough adequately trained local staff to continue operations. Therefore, library authorities in Bahrain should give serious consideration to building their local library manpower. A few libraries have sponsored their staff to study for Master's degrees in library science in North America and Britain. In the absence of a librarianship program in Bahrain, a few staff members from public, school, and other libraries have been trained in Saudi Arabia and Egypt. Saudi Arabia and Egypt offer Bachelor's and Master's degree programs in library science, all in Arabic.

Until 1985 there was no professional body or association of librarians. Under discussion was consideration of forming a Bahrain Library Association, and bylaws and activities were outlined. Also under consideration was establishment of a Library Council to coordinate future activities and address library issues. Plans were under way to implement creation of such bodies.

The Middle East Book Fair (MEBF), held annually from 1982, stimulates interest in reading and helps local booksellers. Along with MEBF, the first library conference was held in 1982, the second in 1983, and the third in 1984. Speakers included scholars and librarians from the Middle East, United States, and Great Britain.

REFERENCES

Directorate of Public Libraries, *Bahrain Public Libraries and Publications Directory* (1977).

Directorate of Public Libraries, *Facts and Figures About Public Libraries, 1982* (1983).

S. NAZIM ALI

Baker, Augusta
(1911-)

Augusta Baker, distinguished librarian, administrator, educator, author, raconteur, and folklorist, won a preeminent place in library service to children. She was born April 1, 1911, in Baltimore, Maryland, and received a Bachelor of Arts in Education from the State University of New York in 1933 and a Bachelor of Science in Library Science from the same institution in 1935. From 1937 to 1974 Baker was a staff member of the New York Public Library, where her career was marked with notable contributions in service to children in the areas of administration, collection development, programs, and services.

As a children's librarian in the Countee Cullen Regional Branch from 1937 to 1953, she pioneered in the momentous task of bringing to the children of Harlem a knowledge of and appreciation for their cultural heritage and background. Working closely with Arthur Schomburg, whose unique collections of materials relating to the black experience were housed in the Branch Library, and with certain Harlem women interested in black culture, she established the James Weldon Johnson Memorial Collection for children because of Johnson's interest in the children and the Library. Enriching experiences for children and adults were made possible and augmented through her programs of storytelling, concerts, reading clubs, visits of school classes, and guest appearances of eminent black artists, writers, dramatists, and other specialists from various professions.

Entering into the administration of library service to children in the New York Public Library, Baker served as Assistant Coordinator and Storytelling Specialist from 1953 to 1961. Her established reputation as a storyteller and folklorist enabled her to continue the great tradition of the Library in utilizing the art form of storytelling in bringing together children and books. Creative and gifted, she shared her talents with others within and outside the Library through inspired instruction and guidance.

Administratively, she furthered the work of library service to children with the renowned Coordinator of the Children's Department, Frances Lander Spain. Recognized as an authority in the field of black literature for children, Baker continued her research in the area with a Dutton-Macrae Award, given to her in 1953 by the American Library Association. Her subsequent publication, *Books about Negro Life for Children* (1963), was a landmark and became a prototype for several revised editions under the new title *The Black Experience in Children's Books*. During this same year she accepted an invitation to organize children's library service for the Trinidad Public Library, Port of Spain, Trinidad. She began a teaching career in 1955 as a Visiting Lecturer in the Columbia University School of Library Service.

The year 1961 was significant for the New York Public Library when Baker was appointed Coordinator of Children's Services. The Library's administrators established a precedent for large urban library systems by elevating a member of an ethnic minority group to a high-level, policy-making position. Extending the traditional boundaries of service in the Library's 82 branches and six bookmobiles in Manhattan, the Bronx, and Staten Island, Baker expanded the children's collections to include recordings and cassettes; she enlarged the annual bibliography of children's books to include special juvenile materials. Utilizing the media of television and radio, she initiated the series of weekly broadcasts "The World of Children's Literature" on WNYC in 1971 and moderated the television program "It's Fun to Read." She also served as a consultant and bibliographer of materials for the television program "Sesame Street" and later produced programs for South Carolina instructional and educational television.

A member of the adjunct faculty in the College of Library and Information Science, the University of South Carolina, she was appointed Storyteller-in-Residence in 1980. Her activities include giving statewide lectures and workshops related to the art of storytelling, the preservation of the oral tradition, and the study of folklore for all age and interest groups.

Baker's influence as a librarian, storyteller, and authority in materials for children is national and international in scope. She lectured or taught in many universities, including Rutgers (1965–67), Syracuse (1955–60), and Texas Woman's University (1975–), and the universities of Nevada at Las Vegas, Southern Florida, and Washington. She lectured before the Australian Library Association in 1973 and participated in conferences of the International Board on Books for Young People (IBBY). Active in the ALA from 1953, she served as Councillor (1965–68, 1968–72), President of the Association for Library Service

Ronald Bright

Augusta Baker

to Children (1967–68), Chairperson of the Newbery-Caldecott Awards Committee (1966), and member of the ALA Executive Board (1968–72). She was a member of the Hans Christian Andersen Award Committee (1974–78) and representative to UNICEF for the ALA/IBBY. Recognizing her many years of service, ALA extended to her its highest award of Honorary Membership in 1975.

Other professional affiliations include membership in the Women's National Book Association, South Carolina Library Association, and the South Eastern Library Association. Baker was a delegate to the 1970 White House Conference on Children. She also served as a consultant to the Council on Library Resources, the Teen Age Book Club of the Scholastic Book Service, and the *Children's Digest* magazine. In 1975 she was one of the co-founders and co-chairperson of the Friends of (New York Public Library) Children's Services.

Baker received many awards and honors, including the *Parent's Magazine* Medal Award (1966) "for outstanding service to the nation's children"; the ALA Grolier Award (1968) "for outstanding achievement in guiding and stimulating the reading of children and young people"; and the Clarence Day Award (1974) "for leadership given to the world of children's books." She also received the Distinguished Alumni Award, State University of New York, Albany. In 1978 she received the honorary Doctor of Letters from Saint John's University, Queens, New York. In 1981 the Catholic Library Association presented her with the Regina Medal "for distinguished contributions to children's literature."

Among the publications she edited are *Talking Tree* (1955), *Golden Lynx* (1960), *Young Years* (1960), and *Readings for Children* (New York Library Association, 1964). She wrote *The Black Experience in Children's Books* (New York Public Library, 1971) and was co-author with Ellin Green of *Storytelling: Art and Technique* (1977). She wrote other articles and reviews for professional periodicals and the press.

SPENCER G. SHAW

Bangladesh

Bangladesh, a people's republic and member of the Commonwealth in the northeastern Indian subcontinent on the Bay of Bengal, is one of the most densely populated countries in the world. Population (1984 est.) 97,488,000; area 143,998 sq.km. The official language is Bangla (Bengali).

History. Prior to 1972, the area was East Pakistan, and before the partition of India in 1947, it was the province of East Bengal and the Sylhet district of Assam. Libraries suffered great losses during the Bangladesh War in 1971, and the young country, hindered by lack of financial resources, is still struggling to rebuild its collections.

Only 5 percent of the people in Bangladesh live in Dhaka, the capital, yet more than 75 percent of the library resources are there. Dhaka houses the premier academic library, the National Library, and nearly all of the special libraries. Most of the libraries in Bangladesh have noncirculating collections, limiting their use to nearby residents.

A key factor in the development of libraries in Bangladesh is the infusion of support from donors in the developed countries. Most Western nations have active aid programs operating in Bangladesh and a few of those resources are directed to libraries. The most sophisticated libraries in the country are those specialized collections financed partly from external sources. While modern technology was available in the mid-1980s to only a few libraries in Bangladesh, professional librarians, especially those with training from abroad, were eager to automate and computerize their operations.

National Library. In 1972 the Directorate of Archives and Libraries established the Bangladesh National Library and the Bangladesh National Archives. Both were still small and developing in the mid-1980s, but the Bangladeshi government targeted the National Library as one of its core projects.

The Copyright Ordinance of 1974 mandated that the National Library receive copies of all books published in Bangladesh. (Only 616 books were published in Bangladesh in 1983.) The 75,000-volume collection consists of Bengali, Urdu, and English-language materials. The Library also collects journals and newspapers published in Bangladesh. No circulation of materials is permitted. From 1973 the Library published the annual *Bangladesh National Bibliography* in both English and Bengali.

The Archives of East Pakistan were housed in Lahore (West Pakistan). Therefore, after independence the new country of Bangladesh was left with virtually no official records. In the 14 years after 1971, the National Archives surveyed materials from the divisional government offices around the country and trained archivists to prepare the materials. In November 1985 the National Library and the National Archives moved to a seven-story air-conditioned permanent building that provides 60,000 square feet of working space.

Academic Libraries. Six academic libraries serve Bangladesh's 42,800 university students: Dhaka University (established 1921), 500,000 volumes; Rajshahi University (1953), 230,000 volumes; Bangladesh University of Engineering and Technology (1962), 87,781 volumes; Chittagong University (1966), 117,000 volumes; Mymensingh Agricultural University (1966), 123,711 volumes; and Jahangirnagar University (1970), 50,000 volumes. All six libraries are staffed with professional librarians, have varied collections of foreign and domestic journals and newspapers, and offer reference services and bibliographic instruction to their patrons. There is no formal interlibrary loan arrangement among the university libraries, but materials are made available to students and faculty through informal contacts. Most of the academic libraries have established interlibrary loan arrangements with the British Library Lending Division.

Because textbooks are expensive and not readily available in Bangladesh, most of the university libraries have large textbook collections. At Bangladesh University of Engineering and Technology, students rent textbooks from a rental library. Circulation of nontextbooks is limited in most libraries to faculty and graduate students. The majority of materials are in English, with Bengali, Urdu, Arabic, and Persian comprising the remainder of the collections.

The Dhaka University Library is the premier library in the country. Its collection of 500,000 volumes is the largest in Bangladesh and covers all academic disciplines except engineering, technology, and medicine. The Library has a professional staff of 57 librarians and a total budget of 9,200,000 taka (approximately $300,000). In addition to its direct role in serving Dhaka University faculty and students, the library has assumed a significant role in collecting and preserving the archives of Bangladesh. It houses 25,000 handwritten manuscripts, many from the 14th and 15th centuries, reflecting the literature and culture of Bengal. Among its rare book collection is the periodical *Dhaka Prakash,* a major periodical of local news from 1890 to 1914. The Library also microfilms local journals and newspapers.

Public Libraries. The Bangladesh Central Public Library (BCPL), Dhaka, is the headquarters of the Public Library Department and administers the government-sponsored divisional and district public libraries. Part of the Dhaka University Library before 1963, BCPL has a collection of 100,00 volumes and is the focal point of all public libraries in Bangladesh. It also sponsors cultural exhibits and has a children's library.

In addition to the Central Public Library in Dhaka, divisional public libraries of approximately 30,000 volumes each are located in Chittagong, Khulna, and Rajshahi. There are 65 district level public libraries around the country, each with approximately 4,000 volumes. Thirty-six professional librarians staffed the 69 public libraries in the country in the mid-1980s.

The focus of the public libraries in Bangladesh is on textbooks, because the majority of patrons are students. Public libraries do not allow books to circulate, nor did they offer bookmobile or audiovisual services in the mid-1980s.

School Libraries. Library services to the 8,900,000 pupils attending 44,000 primary schools and 2,600,000 students attending the 9,000 secondary schools are limited. Most primary schools have no libraries; some secondary schools have library facilities, with teachers serving as librarians. The government was making a strong effort to train school librarians in the 1980s. The school library collections range in size from 500 to 5,000 books, but most libraries are at the lower end of the scale. English, Bengali, and Urdu materials can be found in the libraries. Because audiovisual materials are not available and because media centers do not exist in school libraries, the Dhaka Teacher Training College Audio-Visual Education Center provides a mobile unit of

audiovisual services to visit schools around the country.

Special Libraries. Special Libraries, both government and privately funded, play an important role in Bangladesh and are an integral part of the library system of the country. Most are associated with scientific organizations, research institutes, and government departments, and are staffed by professional librarians. The libraries of the Bangladesh Agricultural Research Council (BARC) and the International Centre for Diarrhoeal Disease Research (ICDDR) are two examples of well-staffed special libraries receiving resources from Western countries. They offer reference services, literature searching, compilation of bibliographies, current awareness service, indexing and abstracting, and selective dissemination of information to their patrons.

BARC had eight professional librarians (1985), five of whom had training abroad. The Library uses a microcomputer database management system to publish subject bibliographies. BARC created the National Agricultural Library and Documentation Centre (NALDOC), which serves as the national center for AGRIS (Agricultural Research Information Service) and CARIS (Current Agricultural Research Information Service).

The ICDDR Library, part of a well-financed internationally acclaimed medical institute, has an 18,000-volume collection, collects 525 medical journal titles, and has a reprint collection of more than 12,000 articles, reports, and documents. The BARC and ICDDR libraries represent the most sophisticated operations in the country and show how external support can substantially upgrade collections and services in a developing country. Other special libraries of interest are the Bangladesh National Scientific and Technical Documentation Centre (BANSDOC) and the National Health Library and Documentation Centre and libraries of the Bangladesh Institute of Development Studies, Bangladesh Atomic Energy Commission, and Bangladesh Bank.

Some foreign governments also provide library services in Bangladesh. Most are in Dhaka and are heavily used by college and university students. The British Council Library has a collection of 50,000 volumes and more than 100 subscriptions to British journals and newspapers. More than a third of its collection are textbooks for the use of college and university students. In addition, the Council offers English-language classes, cultural programs, and scholarships for study abroad. The American Cultural Center Library's 6,300-volume collection and 150 journals and 4 newspapers are used by about 175

Libraries in Bangladesh (1984)

Type	Administrative units	Service points	Volumes in collections	Annual expenditures (taka)	Population served	Professional staff	Total staff
National	1	1	75,000	800,000	--	25	73
Academic	6	14	1,108,492	--	42,800	--	--
Public	69	69	500,000	7,000,000	--	36	346
School	--	--	--	--	--	--	--
Special	125	--	--	--	--	--	--

students daily. Like the British Council, the American Cultural Center sponsors films, speakers, and cultural presentations, and promotes the idea of free public library services in Bangladesh.

The Profession. The Department of Library Sciences at Dhaka University, founded in 1959 with the introduction of a Diploma in Library Science, offered the only academic program for professional librarians in Bangladesh. In 1962 the Master of Arts degree program began. The Department offers the following degrees: Post-graduate Diploma in Librarianship, Master of Arts in Library Science, and Master of Philosophy in Library Science. As of 1983, 831 Diplomas had been awarded for the one-year course, and 445 Masters degrees for the two-year course.

Nearly all librarians in Bangladesh are graduates of the Dhaka University program. The curriculum is traditional, but efforts are being made to expand it into several new areas of information science.

The Library Association of Bangladesh, founded in 1956, is the professional organization of librarians in the country. Total membership was 560 in 1985, with approximately 500 holding professional degrees. Meetings are held monthly. The association's journal, *The Eastern Librarian,* discontinued publication in 1978. While continuing education ooporunities are limited for librarians in Bangladesh, several librarians have been awarded grants and fellowships from private sources for advanced training and education in other countries.

REFERENCES

East Pakistan Library Association and the British Council, *The Need for Public Library Development* (Dacca, 1966).

M. A. Syed, *Public Libraries in East Pakistan: Yesterday and Today* (1967).

JODY BALES FOOTE

Barbados

Barbados, an independent parliamentary state and member of the Commonwealth in the southern Caribbean Sea, is the easternmost island of the West Indies. Population (1984 est.) 252,000; area 430 sq.km. The language spoken is English.

History. The history of librarianship begins in the 18th century with subscription libraries. In 1847 an act was passed establishing a Public Library and the Barbados Museum, but the system did not begin to be developed until the 1920s. The entire library service was undergoing changes in the mid-1980s, particularly libraries that are government-funded.

In 1980 a National Council on Libraries, Archives, and Documentation Centres (NACOLAD) was set up by the Minister of Information to develop plans and make recommendations for a National Library Service. Two reports were eventually submitted to the Government—*A National Library and Information Service System in Barbados* (1981), by a consultant, Carl Keren, and the NACOLAD *Final Report* (1982). The Barbados Library, Archives, and Information Centre Network (BLAIN) was established in November 1982 as a result.

Network. BLAIN, an island-wide grouping of all libraries and information centers, operates at two levels with a Central Directorate. The first level involves all public-funded libraries (except academic libraries) and the library of the Department of Archives. The second level consists of quasi-government and privately funded libraries.

The Central Directorate has responsibility for purchasing, technical services, processing, binding, and microfilming for the first-level libraries. Book selection and readers' services remain the responsibility of the libraries at that level. The second-level libraries' contribution is in the areas of interlibrary cooperation and lending.

In addition to providing specific services to public-funded libraries, the Central Directorate has responsibility for network coordination, planning, and development; establishment and maintenance of links with regional and international organizations; staff development and training; publications; construction of databases; and public relations.

The Directorate conducts database literature searches for users and publishes the *National Bibliography of Barbados*.

National Library Services. The Public Library formerly performed the functions of a national library. The National Council on Libraries, Archives, and Documentation Centres, however, decided against designating any library as the national library or establishing a new one. It distributed the functions and services of a national library among existing institutions, taking areas of strength of collections into consideration.

Libraries in Barbados (1982)

Type	Adminstrative units	Service points	Volumes in collections	Annual expenditures (Barbados dollar)	Population served	Professional staff	Total staff
National	--	--	--	--	--	--	--
Academic	3	3	166,800	1,320,000[a]	1,550[a]	11	30[a]
Public (Includes Central Directorate, school mobile service)	2	89	174,728	1,449,941[b]	67,094	10	76
Special	4	5	112,786	117,000	328[c]	8	12

[a]Applies to two libraries.
[b]Expenditures for Central Directorate not given.
[c]Figures given for three service points.

Academic Libraries. The University of the West Indies (U.W.I.) group of libraries comprise the major academic libraries. They are the Main Library (established 1963), the Library of the Faculty of Law (1971), the Library of the Institute of Social and Economic Research (Eastern Caribbean) (1962), and the Library of the School of Education (1973). Other academic libraries are the Barbados Community College Library; the Medical Library of Queen Elizabeth Hospital, a teaching hospital for medical students of the University of the West Indies; Erdiston Teachers' Training College Library; and the Library of the Samuel Jackman Prescod Polytechnic.

Public Libraries. These consisted in the mid-1980s of a main library, seven branches, and two mobile libraries. Services are free to all residents over six years of age. The Public Library has a strong West Indian collection. Its focus of activity is on lending and reference services.

School Libraries. This was still a neglected area in the mid-1980s. There were 114 primary and 21 secondary schools, serving 57,000 pupils, and each secondary school in theory has a library. The reality is that pupils rely on the Public Library; among the primary schools, no provision was made for library services in school buildings. From 1968 the Public Library provided a basic service to 81 primary schools with two mobile units. Visits made to each school fortnightly, however, fell short of remedying the deficiencies of the service. NACOLAD recommended that the Ministry of Education assume responsibility for school libraries.

Special Libraries. Most of the special libraries are well run. Included among them are the libraries of the Caribbean Development Bank (1970) and the Central Bank of Barbados (1974). Others of note are CADEC Documentation Centre, sponsored by Christian Action for Development in the Carribean (1971); Caribbean Meteorological Institute (1967); Barbados Development Bank (1980); and the Barbados Museum (1933). Some government departments have sizable collections, and BLAIN was working on a program for that sector in the mid-1980s. No comprehensive information was available on the status of private libraries.

The Profession. The profession has gradually gained acceptance and the number of recruits has steadily risen. Emphasis is being given to continuing education, and professionals routinely attend workshops, seminars, and summer schools. The Organization of American States (OAS) offers annually a one-year scholarship to a university in the United States. A number of professionals pursued master's programs under OAS auspices.

Education is provided principally by the University of the West Indies (U.W.I.), which offers two programs: a three-year course for nongraduates and a post-graduate one-year course. Almost all entrants to the profession in the 1970s and 1980s were graduates of U.W.I. The cost of this training is borne by the government.

Associations. The Library Association of Barbados (1968) is the sole organization for the profession. It includes librarians, archivists, documentalists, and others interested in librarianship. Publications are *Bulletin of the Library Association* (annual) and *Update* (occasional).

Barbados Government Information Service

The headquarters of the Public Library in Bridgetown, Barbados.

REFERENCES

A National Library and Information Service System . . .: Report of a Consultancy Mission by Carl Keren (1981).
E. L. V. Ifill, "Public Library Movement in Barbados and Jamaica from the Mid-Nineteenth Century to the Present Day" (Fellowship thesis. Library Association, Great Britain, 1968).
Sylvia G. Moss, "A History of the Library of the University of the West Indies (1948–66)" (Fellowship thesis, Library Association, Great Britain, 1969).
National Council on Libraries, Archives, and Documentation Centres, *Final Report* (1982).
Chalmer St. Hill, "School Libraries in Barbados," *International Library Review* (1978).

JUDY BLACKMAN

Barrow, William J.
(1904–1967)

William James Barrow's research into the factors that cause paper to deteriorate resulted in the development of processes to restore and preserve precious library and archival materials. His work forms the basis for the increasing attention to the conservation and preservation of library resources.

Barrow was born December 11, 1904, in Brunswick County, Virginia, the son of a rural physician. After graduation from Randolph-Macon Academy in 1923, he attended Randolph-Macon College. For a time he was employed by a relative's company that manufactured overalls, but when the business faltered he turned his attention elsewhere.

In 1932 he became interested in document preservation and began to study bookbinding and the preservation techniques then in use at the Library of Congress. The Virginia State Library gave him workshop space and document restoration assignments.

During the late 1930s Barrow operated a shop at the Mariners Museum in Newport News, Virginia, where he developed the first practical roller-type laminator for the lamination of weakened and disintegrating documents, using the cellulose acetate film

William J. Barrow Restoration Shop

William J. Barrow

that had been approved for the purpose by the National Bureau of Standards. In this laminator the document and the acetate film were preheated together and fed through the nip of two synchronously driven steel rolls. Not long after, Barrow began to add strong long-fibered tissue to his laminates, which made them stronger without sacrificing legibility. The acetate filled the interstices of the tissue in such a way that there was little light scattering, and the added layers were quite transparent.

In 1940 Barrow was back at the Virginia State Library operating a restoration shop and speculating on the causes of deterioration. It seemed likely that degradation of the paper would continue even after lamination if it were not stopped. Concluding that the major cause was acidity in the paper itself, he completed by the end of 1945 the development of a deacidification process in which solutions of calcium hydroxide and calcium and/or magnesium bicarbonate are used to neutralize acidity. Subsequent events have substantiated his judgment that paper acidity is the most important single cause of paper deterioration. Barrow now had the means of greatly reducing paper's rate of deterioration and restoring integrity and strength to paper already damaged. His laminators and techniques have since been obtained by more than 30 institutions throughout the world.

Barrow recognized early that much of his restoration work was on papers manufactured after 1875 and that many papers, much older, had no need of it. This was often ascribed to the use in modern papers of wood pulp, which came into fairly common use about that time, while some blamed it on an increasingly polluted industrial atmosphere. In 1957, with the sponsorship of the Virginia State Library and the support of the Council on Library Resources, he undertook a testing program involving papers from 500 books published between 1900 and 1949. Although it is true that the early wood pulps were not as good as they could have been and that atmospheric pollution is a deteriorative factor, this study showed that the poor condition of most of the papers examined was caused by acidity resulting from the use of alum-rosin sizing in their manufacture.

With the continued involvement of CLR and VSL and the advice of A. L. Rothschild and other paper industry people, Barrow planned a series of experiments, begun in the laboratories of the Herty Foundation in Savannah, Georgia, to determine whether modern methods and materials could be used to make an affordable long-lasting paper. This work culminated in December 1959 in the production of such a paper at Standard Paper Manufacturing Company in Richmond. Only chemical wood pulps were used; Aquapel sizing, which is compatible with mild alkalinity, replaced alum and rosin, and calcium carbonate was added to ensure that the paper would remain alkaline for many years.

Barrow then published tentative specifications for long-life paper, setting minimum performance at high but demonstrably attainable levels. At that time only his paper met those criteria, but in 1972 eight commercially available papers were identified that could meet similar requirements. Such papers have the physical strength to withstand handling and use (durability) and the chemical stability that makes their deterioration very slow (permanence).

In 1961 the CLR under the leadership of Verner W. Clapp, who was always interested and involved in Barrow's research, provided a grant that made possible the establishment of the W. J. Barrow Research Laboratory in the Virginia Historical Society Building. There Barrow studied polyvinyl acetate binding adhesives and defined the properties required for long useful life. Testing equipment was designed, and experimental work for the development of library binding performance standards was performed for the American Library Association. One study resulted in better catalogue card stock. Archival materials are protected from the migration of impurities by the acid-free file folders developed there. Barrow's test facilities and experience were brought to bear in the selection of paper for the ALA National Union Catalogue.

Barrow believed the two physical tests most relevant to printing and records paper durability were folding endurance and tear resistance. Extensive testing of a variety of papers at many temperatures showed that these two properties usually decline according to a predictable pattern and that the rate of decline is related to temperature in a specific and consistent way. This work gives credibility to predictions of paper's useful life at natural temperatures, which are based on test results from oven-aged samples. The research was also the basis of his suggestion that materials of great lasting value should be stored at low temperature.

The results of Barrow's research and the techniques he developed were reported in a number of publications. The restoration process is described in *The Barrow Method of Restoring Deteriorated Documents* (1965), and the research into the structure and materials of books was published in the five-part *Permanence/Durability of the Book* (1963–65). These and other publications form the basis for contemporary practice in restoration of deteriorating print materials.

Barrow died in Richmond, Virginia, August 25, 1967. The Laboratory continued its research until 1977. The Restoration Shop in the Virginia State Library was still in operation in the mid-1980s (Barrow's son, James A. Barrow, President).

DAVID D. ROBERSON

Batchelder, Mildred
(1901-)

In July 1966 the Grolier Award was presented to Mildred Leona Batchelder, children's librarian and library association executive, the citation praising her years of "devoted attention to children's reading and books for younger readers. Throughout her career she has emphasized the values of selectivity in books. . . . Her influence has been an international one, reaching children's and school librarians, and through them the children from coast to coast in America and also in foreign lands where she has lectured and traveled. Her judgment, her knowledge, her wit, her persuasive leadership have made her a national figure in the world of books."

Batchelder was born September 7, 1901, in Lynn, Massachusetts. She received a B.A. degree from Mt. Holyoke College in 1922 and a B.L.S. from New York State Library School, Albany, in 1924.

ALA

Mildred Batchelder

She began her professional career as Head of the Children's Department, Omaha Public Library, Nebraska (1924–27), and served as Children's Librarian, State Teachers College, Saint Cloud, Minnesota (1927–28). She was Elementary and Intermediate School Librarian at the Haven School in Evanston, Illinois (1928–36).

In 1936 she joined the headquarters staff of the American Library Association as School Library Specialist, becoming Chief of the School and Children's Library Division in 1938. In 1946 she was named Acting Chief, Department of Information and Advisory Service, and a year later Chief of that department, a position she held until 1949, when a headquarters reorganization took place. Batchelder then became Executive Secretary of the Division of Libraries for Children and Young People (DLCYP), which included the School Librarians Section. When the School Libraries Section achieved division status in 1951, Batchelder became half-time Executive Secretary for the DLCYP and half-time Special Assistant to the ALA Executive Secretary on Special Membership Promotion. She held those positions until 1954, when the DLCYP executive secretaryship was made a full-time position. With reorganization in 1957, she became the Executive Secretary of the Children's Services Division (CSD) and the Young Adult Services Division (YASD); she retired from that position in 1966.

During 30 years of service on the ALA staff, Batchelder made many significant contributions to the profession. The development, growth, and accomplishments of the units she worked with are evidence of her skill as a leader. A division president described her as "a catalyst of magical proportions." Many programs and projects begun under her direction were continued, including the Frederic G. Melcher Scholarship and the divisional journal, *Top of the News*.

Batchelder initiated working relationships with many people and organizations outside the library profession in the U.S. and abroad that continue to benefit libraries and librarians today. In 1960 the first edition of *Let's Read Together*, a family reading list, was published by ALA, the work of a Special Committee of the National Congress of Parents and Teachers and the Children's Services Division.

She represented ALA at the White House Conference on Children and Youth in 1950 and 1960 and participated in the planning. An active member of the Council of National Organizations for Children and Youth (CNOCY), she served as its Secretary and was a member of the National Committee on Children and Youth (NCOCY).

At a ceremony in 1966 held during the annual National 4-H Club Conference in Washington, D.C., Batchelder was one of seven leaders in business, education, and industry commended for outstanding contributions to 4-H Club work.

Batchelder held that children's books can be an aid to international understanding and worked toward that end in many ways. In 1949 the International Youth Library was established in Munich by Jella Lepman. The U.S. portion of the funds given during the launching of that unique project was a Rockefeller Foundation grant, administered by the CSD Office (1949–57).

She recognized the need for thoughtful selection of books to be translated, and a list of 100 children's books published from 1930 to 1954 "recommended for translation" was prepared by CSD in 1955 and distributed to Unesco, the U.S. Information Agency, library contacts in other countries, publishers, and others. Annual lists were prepared from 1955.

During a five-month sabbatical in 1964, Batchelder visited 11 European countries and studied the translation of children's books. She wrote later, "To know the classic stories of a country creates a climate, an attitude for understanding the people for whom that literature is a heritage. . . . Interchange of children's books between countries, through translation, influences communication between the people of those countries, and if the books chosen are worthy books, the resulting communication may be deeper, richer, more sympathetic, more enduring. I accept and believe these assumptions."

CSD established the Mildred L. Batchelder Award in 1966; the first award was given in 1968. A citation to an American publisher, the award is intended to encourage international exchange of quality children's books by recognizing publishers of such books in translation.

The Constance Lindsay Skinner Award of the Women's National Book Association was given to Batchelder in 1967.

RUTH TARBOX

Belgium

Belgium, a constitutional monarchy of Europe, is bounded by the North Sea on the northwest, the Netherlands on the north, the Federal Republic of Germany and Luxembourg on the east, and France on the south and southwest. Population (1984 est.) 9,859,000; area 30,521 sq.km. Languages are Dutch, French, and German. The Flemings of the northern provinces speak Dutch, the Walloons of the southern provinces speak French, and a small group in the southeast speak German. The capital, Brussels, is officially bilingual (Dutch and French).

History. The earliest library collection in what is now Belgium is probably the collection of illuminated manuscripts known as the *librarie de Bourgogne,* which became part of the holdings of the royal library, established in 1559. But there were probably significant collections in Antwerp around 1480, when printing was established in the city. In 1772 the Royal Library was made accessible to the public Three popular libraries were established in the 1840s (at Furnes, Antwerp, and Andenne), precipitating a sudden desire for this sort of collection; by 1884 there were 571 in the country. University libraries were also well established by this time, having taken over the collections of the city libraries in the cities of Ghent and Liège at the beginning of the 19th century.

National Library. The National Library in Brussels (Koninklijke Bibliotheek Albert I; Bibliothèque Royale Albert Ier) originated from the 15th-century library of the Dukes of Burgundy and was established as the Royal Library of Belgium in 1837. It performs the twofold function of a national library and a central research library. The act of Parliament instituting the Copyright Deposit (April 8, 1965), obligating each Belgian publisher to deposit one copy of each work, enables it to operate as a national library. The monthly issues of the Belgian Bibliography *(Belgische Bibliografie; Bibliographie de Belgique)* are published on the basis of the deposit copies. As a central research library, the Royal Library in Brussels has a number of specialized divisions and documentation centers. The divisions cover prints, manuscripts, precious works, music, the numismatic collection, and the collection of maps. The documentation centers are the National Center for Scientific and Technical Documentation, the Center for American Studies, the Center for African Documentation, and the Documentation Center for Tropical Agriculture and Rural Developmental Works. The Royal Library holds about 3,362,000 volumes, 26,000 current periodicals, 43,000 precious works, 305,000 government documents, 37,000 manuscripts, 180,000 coins and medals, 700,000 prints, 35,000 rare books, and 4,000 records. Although the Royal Library is a library of attendance—all documents can be used for reference only—it participates in interlibrary loans with Belgian and foreign research libraries.

Academic Libraries. The six great universities in Belgium all have general academic libraries, each of them possessing a fairly extensive collection. The universities of Ghent and Liège are state universities founded in 1816. The central library of the University of Liège contains 1,700,000 volumes, 4,682 current peiodicals, and 4,072 manuscripts, that in Ghent 2,000,000 volumes, 5,900 current periodicals, and 5,060 manuscripts. The Catholic University of Louvain, founded in 1425, the oldest university in Belgium, was split into two separate, autonomous universities in 1968: the Katholieke Universiteit Leuven (KUL) and the Université Catholique de Louvain. Since 1970 the original library has also been split. The Dutch section possesses 1,000,000 volumes, the French section 1,300,000. The Faculteit der Godgeleerdheid library at the KUL also has an important collection of archives from Vatican II in its library of 500,000 volumes.

The Free University of Brussels was established in 1834. Since 1970 this institution has been split into two autonomous universities. The library of the Dutch section, the Vrije Universiteit Brussel, contains 160,000 volumes; the French section, the Université Libre de Bruxelles, 1,414,000.

Apart from the six complete universities in Belgium, there exist also a number of college insitutions with one or more integral or partial faculties. Antwerp has three such centers. The Universitaire Faculteiten Sint-Ignatius (the University Faculties Saint Ignatius) were founded in 1852. The disciplines taught are philosophy and arts, social and political sciences, law, and economics. The Rijksuniversitair Centrum Antwerpen (Antwerp State University) was established in 1965 and specializes in applied economics and exact sciences. In these institutions, only the first study-cycle is taught (two years of "candidatures"). In the Universitaire Instelling Antwerpen (Antwerp University Institution), founded in 1971, the second study-cycle (two years of "licentiate" studies) and the third study-cycle (doctorial studies) are taught in the sciences, medicine, philosophy and arts, law, and social and political sciences. The number of volumes in the specialized libraries of the three institutions amounts to 700,000.

A department of the faculties of medicine, exact sciences, law, and philosophy and arts of the KUL was founded in 1965 in Courtray (first cycle). Its library possesses 56,000 volumes. From 1968–69 economics was taught in the Limburgs Universitair Centrum (Limburg University Center) in Diepenbeek near Hasselt (three cycles). From 1971–72 the first study-cycle of sciences and medicine could also be followed there. The library of that university possesses 50,000 volumes. The Facultés Universitaires Saint Louis (the University Faculties Saint Louis), founded in 1858, specializes in philsophy and arts, law and economics, and social and political sciences (first study-cycle). The library contains 120,000 volumes.

The library of the Universitaire Faculteiten Sint Aloysius (University Faculties Saint Aloysius), where from 1968 the first study-cycles in law, philosophy and arts, and economics were taught, has 69,000 volumes. Mons has three university institutions: the Université de l'Etat à Mons (the State University Mons), founded in 1965, offering lectures in sciences, applied economics, psychology, and pedagogy; the Faculté Polytechnique de Mons (the Mons Polytechnic Faculty), founded in 1837 and specializing in applied sciences; and the Faculté Universitaire Catholique de Mons (the Mons Catholic University Faculty), founded in 1965 and specializing in economics. Volumes in the libraries of the three colleges in Mons total 540,000. The Facultés Universitaires Notre Dame de la Paix in Namur, founded in 1831, teaches philosophy and arts, law, economics, exact sciences, and medicine. The library holds collection of 720,000 volumes.

The Faculté de Sciences Agronomiques de L'Etat (the State Faculty of Agronomic Sciences) in Gem-

Libraries in Belgium (1980)

Type	Administrative units	Service points	Volumes in collections	Annual expenditures (franc)	Population served[a]	Professional staff	Total staff
National	1	1	3,366,000	345,952	8,099	--	265
Academic	--	--	--	--	--	--	--
Public	2,351	--	24,140,000	--	1,731,256	--	--
School	--	--	--	--	--	--	--

[a]Registered borrowers.

Source: Unesco, *Statistical Yearbook,* 1984.

bloux, established in 1947, has 32,000 volumes. The Faculté de Théologie Protestante de Bruxelles (the Faculty of Protestant Theology of Brussels), founded in 1942, possesses about the same number.

Many university colleges are institutions of a comparatively recent date, and their libraries, more than others, employ modern and economical library techniques. In applications of modern automation they are unrivaled. Online services such as DIALOG, ESA, QUESTEL, INKA, SDC, LIBIS, and EURONET are all used.

Public Libraries. As is the case with Belgian librarianship viewed as a whole, Belgian public librarianship is not well organized. Considerable improvement was anticipated, however, under two decrees that passed both the Dutch and French Councils of Culture in 1978. Up to that time all public libraries in Belgium came under the "Law Destrée" (1921), which did not effectively deal with the obligation to establish public libraries, the definition of such institutions, their financial support, and their general organization. The two decrees of 1978, however, defined a logical structure that meets contemporary demands for local public libraries. Their activities and operations are coordinated by central public libraries. A national center of public libraries (in both Flanders and Wallonia) studies problems concerning the public library and provides for some special (noncommercial) central services. The decree promulgated by the Dutch Council of Culture requires the municipalities to establish public libraries. This obligation is less rigidly formulated in the decree of the Frech Council of Culture (the king *can* put the municipalities under an obligation to establish public libraries). Subsidization is satisfactory.

The method used for shelving books in public libraries is nearly always open-access. Works are arranged in classified order: usually UDC in French libraries; in Dutch libraries a system called SISO (system for the arrangement of the classified catalogue in public libraries). The important public libraries have special departments: record library, media center, a center for pictures, and even a department of toys.

There was a 50 percent increase in the number of readers at public libraries over a single decade (1965–1975) while the population grew at only 3 percent during that time. This trend was more marked among Dutch-speaking Belgians than among French-speaking Belgians.

School Libraries. School librarianship in Belgium remains underdeveloped. On the level of secondary education, few schools have librarians. At best there were a few class libraries set up by teachers of subject specialties. On the level of higher, nonuniversity education are some important libraries, many of them administered by librarians. Most of them are inadequately catalogued, however. The Royal Conservatory in Brussels, for example, possesses a significant library containing 700,000 volumes, but it was not adequately staffed for cataloguing.

Special Libraries. The government departments have libraries containing documents related to their specific subjects. The Ministry of Economic Affairs, for instance, possesses an important collection of 630,000 volumes (Fonds Quetelet). This library takes a leading position in Belgium in automation.

The parliamentary library, containing 1,500,000 volumes on law and social and political sciences, possesses a significant collection of documents of several European parliaments.

Various research institutions have well-organized libraries. The Royal Institute of Natural Sciences of Belgium, for example, possesses about 800,000 volumes.

Many libraries of business companies are well-structured centeres of documentation. The best example can be found in the library and documentation service of Agfa-Geevaert in Mortsel, where books and articles in the field of photography and related sciences are abstracted.

Some cities also have "city-libraries" operating independently of the public libraries. Usually they are very old, humanistic, books-preserving libraries that perform some of the functions of "national libraries" in their own regions. The city-library of Antwerp, for example, which was founded in 1607, possesses 650,000 volumes.

The Profession. Belgium has a great number of associations of librarians and libraries. The Vereniging van Archivarissen en Bibliothecarissen van België—Association des archivistes et bibliothécaires de Belgique (the Belgian Association of Archivists and Librarians), founded in 1907, serves all persons who perform scientific functions in a record office or library. The Association publishes *Archief- en Bibliotheekwezen in België—Archives et Bibliothèques en Belgique*.

The Vlaamse Vereniging van Bibliotheek-, Archief-, en Documentatiepersoneel (the Flemish Society of Archive, Library, and Documentation Staff) was founded in 1921 and assembles the staff of libraries and archives in Flanders. Its organ is *Bibliotheekgids*. The monthly publication *Bibinfo* contains up-to-date information on the society and on activities outside it.

The Katholiek Centrum voor Lektuurinformatie en Bibliotheekvoorziening (the Catholic Center for Reading-Information and Library-Supplies) publishes criticism in its monthly annotated bibliographical review *Boekengids en Jeugdboekengids*. Its monthly publication *Openbaar* includes general information.

The Nationaal Bibliotheekfonds (National Funds of Libraries) groups Flemish socialist libraries and librarians and publishes criticism in *Lektuurgids*.

Librarians in the French-speaking part of the country are chiefly grouped in three associations: the Association Nationale des Bibliothécaires de'Expression Française (the National Association of French-speaking Librarians), the Association des Bibliothécaires-Documentalistes de l'Institute Supérieur d'Etudes Sociales de l'Etat (the Association of Librarian-Documentalists of the Higher State Institution for Social Studies), and the Association Professionelle des Bibliothécaires et Documentalistes (the Professional Association of Librarians and Documentalists). The Belgische Vereniging voor Documentatie (the Belgian Society for Documentation) serves Dutch-speaking documentalists.

The Vlaamse Bibliotheek Centrale (the Flemish Library-Center) is a central service that provides a large assortment of library-technical and bibliographical material.

WILLY VANDERPIJPEN*

Belize

Belize, a former colony of Great Britain, and an independent nation since September 1982, lies on the eastern seaboard of the Central American isthmus, bounded by Mexico on the north and by Guatemala on the west and south. Its coastline to the east is fringed by the second largest coral reef in the world. Population (1984 est.) 159,000; area 22,965 sq.km. The official language is English.

History; National and Public Library. Library services in Belize revolve around the National Library Service, which in 1960 came under the direction of the Minister of Education. As early as 1825 a library service existed, and between that time and 1902 there were seven libraries and reading rooms. The Jubilee Library, from which the public library concept commenced in Belize, opened in 1935 with assistance from the Carnegie Corporation of New York. The central government undertook to provide an annual subvention for the library service. A statutory library board administers the service. The Service's bookstock totals 113,000 (1984).

The main lending library, which is also the headquarters of the National Library Service, is in the Bliss Institute in Belize City and offers some 15,000 volumes in English. A National Collection comprises about 2,000 volumes and includes books primarily on Belize or by Belizeans, a West Indian collection, and a Central American Collection including works on the Maya civilization. Apart from the Bliss Institute, which is only partly designed for library purposes, there are only three other purpose-designed library buildings in the country. These are in three main towns: Punta Gorda, Orange Walk, and Corozal. All other accommodation is either rented or borrowed.

There are 58 service points or sub-libraries throughout the country, administered by a staff of 2 professional librarians, 14 paraprofessionals, 15 clerical, a bookbinder, and a host of voluntary part-time workers in the villages (1984). A bookmobile service has been in operation since 1979. Other sections of the service include a children's library and a reference library. The National Library Service has extended full library services to all government departments and other institutions, and the nominal role it is unofficially playing is that of a national library.

Membership at any service point of the National Library Service is free. Any child who is able to read may join a library and on reaching age 16 may register as a member of the adult library. Members total

21,600, of which the majority are children; books issued average 78,000 annually.

Academic Library. The University of the West Indies maintains a university center in Belize. Its library consists of some 3,000 volumes and other printed material.

Special Libraries. All departments and ministries of government have collections of printed materials, and many private industrial firms also have libraries.

L. G. VERNON

Benedict, Saint
(*c.* 480–*c.* 546)

Saint Benedict, Abbot of the monastery at Monte Cassino, who is considered the father of Western monasticism, made his main contribution through the constitution of monasticism, the Benedictine Rule, written at Monte Cassino (*c.* 530–540). It became the most influential factor in the spread of Western monasticism. He also made provision for the care of books, and it is difficult to overestimate his contributions to reading.

In the 6th century A.D. all was in a state of civil war, confusion, and looting, on the decline of the Roman Empire. Benedict provided the will, the means, and the men to bring some degree of cultural order out of chaos. After spending 35 years at Subiaco, he founded a monastery at Monte Cassino, about 70 miles southeast of Rome. The Rule of Benedict rapidly circulated among European monasteries with far-reaching cultural influence and has been practiced ever since.

In the tradition of Eastern monasticism, the individual monk's career was largely of a solitary kind, whereas under the Benedictine Rule the labors of the community were determined not only for its collective good but likewise for service to the world at large. Monasticism was no longer regarded so much as a life of austerity but as one of service, philanthropy, and Christian charity. The main occupations of the monks were the work of God, devotion, and physical labor. Benedict made special provision in his Rule for the illiterate but imposed the obligation of devotional reading upon the literate monks.

Reading was not so much an intellectual activity as a means to the contemplation of God and self-improvement in the life of grace. As a remedy for idleness, the life of the monk was to be devoted to phys-

Libraries in Belize (1982)

Type	Administrative units	Service points	Volumes in collections	Annual expenditures (Belize dollar)	Population served	Professional staff	Total staff
National[a]	1	69	113,000	300,000	153,000	2	32
Academic	1	--	3,000	--	--	--	1
Public[a]							
School	200	--	30,000	--	38,000	--	--
Special	17	--	13,000	--	5,500	--	17

[a]Public and national libraries are synonymous.

ical labor and the study of sacred subjects. The Rule added:

> From Easter to the Calends of October, . . . From the fourth hour until close upon the sixth let them apply themselves to reading.

The Rule mentioned the siesta following the sixth hour, important to Italians during the hot season of the year. Those who preferred to read were encouraged to do so, but in a low voice. After the seasonal labors in the fields were concluded in October, work was concentrated inside the monastery. The Rule canceled siestas and set out changes in the manual labor and in the time for reading. From morning until the close of the second hour, the monks were to devote their time to reading.

During the third and final period of the year, the Lenten season, the Rule made some changes in the daily schedule and paid special attention to a systematic program of additional reading. Benedict reflected a certain severity when communal ownership did not permit personal property ("neither a book, nor tablets, nor a pen . . ."), but in no way did he intend privation for any monk. Provisions were to be made for an adequate collection of manuscript codices so that each monk could have one for his personal reading. Though Benedict was silent on intellectual study or scribal work, the reading requirements of his Rule necessitated a monastic book collection that was essentially spiritual. The monastic library was to have sufficient books for the ceremonial distribution of books at the beginning of Lent.

The reading program discouraged skipping through pages or reading at random in a perfunctory manner. The Rule did not prescribe a definite time for loans, nor did it seem to imply that the book must be completely read by the close of Lent. But certain disciplinary measures were established to encourage individuals who felt little attraction for deciphering or other distractions. Surely some preferred working in the field to reading sermons or biblical commentators. These points are carefully detailed in the following passage:

> Let one or two seniors be deputed to go round the monastery at the hours when the brethren are engaged in reading, and see that there be no slothful brother . . . not applying himself to his reading.

On Sundays the monks did only essential work such as kitchen duty. The most desirable use of time was to be spent in reading books of devotion, but monks who found the task too difficult were to be assigned other duties so they would not be idle. Bible reading was mentioned several times in the Rule. Benedict also recommended biblical commentaries of the Church Fathers to help the monks devotionally. This was an impressive list for monks of the 6th century, and latitude on the selection of other books was also expressed in the Rule: "or something else that may edify the hearers," for those public readings were to be held every evening.

The monks assembled in the oratory at stated hours of the day and night for choral recitation of the Divine Office. The service was fixed in its general outlines, and the recitation of the psalms was its main substance.

The Rule set forth Benedict's program for beginners in the monastic life. Only the final chapter of it opens up horizons beyond the elementary reading program for monks aspiring to the advanced stages of perfect life. For such members of the monastic community he intended that his Rule would be complemented by a range of books that were the special heritage of monastic ideals and that would bring his followers to the summit of Christian perfection. Among prescribed books were the *Rule* of Saint Basil; the *Conferences* and *Institutes* of John Cassian, an author from Gaul who wrote around 435; and the "Lives of the Fathers," that is to say, the biographies of Anthony of Egypt, Pachomius, and Macarius of Alexandria.

The Rule of Silence.   It was the monastic idea that silence was golden. Benedict laid down rules on the subject and, for the most part, only three hours of speaking time was allowed in each day. This severe rule was mitigated by the provision that a brother could read aloud from a "common book." Singing was differentiated from speaking and thus allowed, provided the singer not sit too near a silent reader. Such restraints were, in practice, softened somewhat. An elaborate code of signs to allow silent communication was developed, for example; it was essentially the same for all monasteries and indispensable to the monk who used the library in a silent hour. Examples follow.

> If one wants a book, he shall make the general sign, *i.e.,* extend his hand in a movement of turning the leaves of a book. For the sign of a missal, make the same movement adding the sign of the fingers as though flying. For the sign of a tract, lay one hand on the abdomen and the other across the mouth. For the sign of a sequence or hymn, raise the hand bent and, moving it away from the breast, invest it so that what was before up shall be under. For a book containing a lesson for Sundays and feast days make the sign of a book, add the sign of reading, and, clenching the fist, place the arm over the shoulder, imitating the action of him that carries a burden, on account of the size of the book.

The books called for above are strictly liturgical. For a secular author such as Ovid, the sign was different. For such pagan authors, after making the general sign, "Scratch your ear with your finger, even as a dog when itching does with his foot, for pagans may be compared with such an animal." It is not necessary to read library catalogues to infer that monkish ears itched often.

REFERENCES
The Rule of Saint Benedict, translated by Dom Justin McCann (1961), best English translation.
E.C. Butler, *Benedictine Monachism,* 2nd edition (1961).
L. J. Daly, *Benedictine Monasticism* (1961).
Jean Decarreaux, *Monks and Civilization,* translated by Charlotte Haldane (1964).

REDMOND A. BURKE

Benin

Benin, a people's republic in West Africa, is bordered by Togo on the west, Burkina Faso on the northwest, Niger on the northeast, Nigeria on the east, and the Gulf of Guinea on the south. Population (1984 est.) 3,856,000; area 112,600 sq.km. The official language is French.

National Library. The Bibliothèque Nationale was established in the capital, Porto Novo, in 1961 and was reorganized in 1975. Under the jurisdiction of the Ministry of Youth, Popular Culture, and Sports, it houses 35,000 volumes and more than 20 periodicals.

Academic Libraries. The University of Benin Library, founded in 1970, is housed in two buildings, one on the Abomey-Calavi campus serving the departments of Letters, Linguistics, and Social Sciences; Law and Economics; Physical Sciences; and Agronomy; the other in Cotonou serving the Department of Medical and Para-Medical Studies. Also in the university system, the Centre de Formation administrative et de pefectionnement handles books and periodicals in its documentation center (Cotonou).

The teacher training colleges for women (Abomey) and men (Parakou) and the École pastorale évangelique (Porto Novo) furnish basic libraries in the relevant fields.

Public Libraries. A Central Library Service under the Ministry of Youth, Popular Culture, and Sports established provincial libraries at Abomey, Natitingou, Ouidah, Parakou, and Porto Novo.

Special Libraries. There are a number of research libraries associated with government agencies and institutes that are responsible for the study of society, education, agriculture, industry, and mining in Benin. The Institut de Recherches appliquées du Bénin, in Porto Novo, supplanted the local branch of IFAN (Institut français d'Afrique noire) in 1961 and offers a collection of 8,500 works as well as an information service. It published *Etudes dahoméennes* from 1963 to 1970. Also in Porto Novo, the CNRST (Centre nationale de la recherche scientifique et technique) keeps a collection of 6,000 volumes, 50 current periodicals, and 2,600 photographs. Libraries specializing in agriculture and textiles are those of Niaouli's Institut de Recherches agronomiques tropicales et des cultures vivrières (established 1970) and Cotonou's Institut de Recherches du coton et des textiles exotiques (1970). ORSTOM (Office de la Recherche scientifique et technique Outre-Mer) maintains a center in Cotonou. Other libraries serve the Chamber of Commerce, research institutes in education and palm oil, the Laboratoire d'Agropédologie, the Ministry of Rural Development, and the geology division of the Ministry of Industry, Commerce, and Tourism.

The Profession. Benin is a member of the Association internationale pour le développement de la documentation, des bibliothèques et des archives en Afrique (AIDBA).

NEIL MCHUGH*

Bermuda

Bermuda is a self-governing colony of the United Kingdom and comprises a group of islands in the western part of the North Atlantic Ocean. Population (1984) 56,652; land area 46 sq.km. The official language is English.

History. Library service in Bermuda is provided by the Bermuda Library, a department of the Bermuda Government, and by a number of smaller, specialized libraries. The Bermuda Library was officially established in 1839 as a subscription library, but there were at least two "public" libraries in existence before that. In 1765 the families living around Somerset Bridge got together a collection of useful books and formed a social society that circulated reading materials; it was known as the Somerset Bridge Club. Some of its books can still be found on the shelves of the Bermuda Library, as can books from the Hamilton Club, another "public" library.

The act establishing a public library (1839) provided for a Board of Trustees, which was presided over by the Governor until the passing of the Library Act in 1921. Under that act, the President of the Legislative Council became Chairman, with the Speaker of the House of Assembly his Deputy. Besides these ex officio members, there were two elected members from the Assembly and two from the Corporation of Hamilton Council. The Head Librarian acted as Secretary to the Board. With little change, this system remained in operation until the implementation of the new Bermuda Constitution in June 1968. Today the Head Librarian serves under the policy direction of the Minister for Community and Cultural Affairs. The Board of Trustees, renamed the Library Committee, acts in an advisory capacity only.

National and Public Libraries. The Bermuda Library provides both national and public library services, including legal deposit. Headquarters are at Par-la-Ville in Hamilton, the capital city, with the Youth Library a few blocks away and small branches at St. George's and Somerset. The service is free to all, including visitors. A free mailing service has operated since 1855. In 1984 total bookstock stood at 150,606 and the annual circulation was 122,705. While adult circulation figures declined, demands on the reference service rose steadily and a dramatic increase in library use by children and young people followed the relocation in 1982 of the renamed Youth Library to new quarters.

Phonograph records, a telescope, and slides with a projector may be borrowed, and a talking-books

---

Libraries in Benin (1982)

Type	Administrative units	Service points	Volumes in collections	Annual expenditures (C.F.A. franc)	Population served[b]	Professional staff	Total staff
National[a]	1	8	32,000	16,657,000	15,427	2	42
Academic	12	12	49,000	8,000,000[c]	--	3	50

[a]1980 data.
[b]Registered borrowers.
[c]Acquisitions only.

Source: Unesco, *Statistical Yearbook*, 1984.

service is provided. With the reorganization of a local radio station in 1984, the Bermuda Library Concert Hour was discontinued after some 25 years on the air. The Youth Library holds regular story hours and film shows and presents seasonal and special programs.

The Bermudiana collection includes all available books and other materials of local interest; there is a nearly complete file of the *Royal Gazette* newspaper.

The Bermuda National Bibliography, published quarterly with annual cumulations and available on a subscription basis, was launched in 1984. Microform and photocopy services are offered. A union list of serials was computerized and in the process of updating in 1985. A Rare Book Room was set up in 1982 and a modest start was made on a conservation program.

Academic Libraries. Bermuda does not have a university. Undergraduate extension students are served by the Bermuda Library and the libraries of the Bermuda College and the U.S. Naval Air Station. The Bermuda College Library holds 20,584 volumes and offers more than 80 periodicals and is geared to the courses offered by the departments of Academic Studies, Commerce and Technology, and Hotel Technology.

School Libraries. There are libraries in all government secondary schools and most primary schools, although a few of the latter are still only classroom collections. Standards of the Library Association (U.K.) in accommodation and stock are attempted, but there is a need for more professionally qualified staff. Library service in private schools is comparable.

Special Libraries. Among the larger and more formally organized government libraries are those of the Supreme Court, the departments of Education, Agriculture and Fisheries, and Health and Social Services, and the two hospitals. The E. L. Mark Memorial Library at the Bermuda Biological Station provides research facilities in marine and environmental sciences; it has a stock of 16,000 volumes and 200 current periodicals acquired by subscription, gift, and exchange. Large professional and business office libraries specialize in such areas as banking, accounting, insurance, and oil and gas.

The Bermuda Archives houses Bermuda's historical records and provides a records management service to government. Its holdings are listed in the

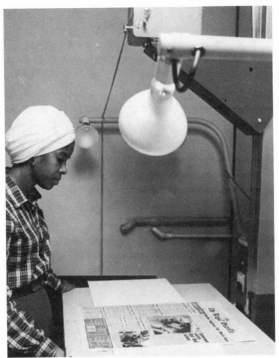

Bermuda Archives

At the Bermuda Archives in Hamilton, microfilm operator photographing the Royal Gazette.

Guide to the Records of Bermuda (1980), which also includes Bermuda-related documents in overseas repositories.

Bermuda boasts a number of significant private libraries and some rare book collectors. Community organizations such as churches and youth centers also maintain small collections.

The Profession. The first Bermudian known to have undertaken formal training in librarianship was Kate Seon, Librarian-Secretary of the Bermuda Library from 1912 to 1940. She studied children's work at Southern School in Atlanta, Georgia. By the mid-1960s the Bermuda Library had a professional staff of four librarians. The total number of professionally trained librarians on the Island was at least ten by 1983, all of diverse training. Bermudians wishing to enter the profession study abroad; usual destinations are the United States, the United Kingdom, and Canada.

Libraries in Bermuda (1985)

Type	Administrative units	Volumes in collections	Annual expenditures (Bermudan dollar)	Population served	Professional staff	Total staff
National and Public	1	149,224	723,400	56,652[a]	7	20[b]
Academic	1	22,170	99,042	586[c]	1	3
School	23	75,471	38,195	6,560	1	23
Special	22	- -	- -	- -	- -	- -

[a]Excludes tourist use.
[b]Excludes three part-time workers.
[c]Excludes two part-time students.

Sources: The Head Librarian; "Annual Report of Ministry of Education; Estimates of Revenue and Expenditure 1985–86," Bermuda Government.

The Library Association of Bermuda was formally inaugurated in 1983 and Bermuda maintains ties with such international and national professional bodies as the International Federation of Library Associations and Institutions, the Commonwealth Library Association, the International Council on Archives, and the national associations of Great Britain, Canada, the United States, and the Caribbean. In 1983 K. C. Harrison was commissioned to survey the country's resources with a view to establishing a national library and information systems network. The recommendations made in his report were under consideration by the government and the institutions concerned in the mid-1980s. Continuing development of automated processes on the Island promised to bring such a project closer to reality.

CYRIL O. PACKWOOD

Bernardo, Gabriel A.
(1891–1962)

Gabriel Adriano Bernardo, father of Philippine librarianship, was a bibliographer, scholar, librarian, writer, folklorist, and teacher and mentor of Filipino librarians for half a century. Bernardo was interested in everything Philippine: its language and literature, paleography, Tagalog literature, music and fine arts, numismatics, archives, and history. His works, both published and unpublished, show the wide spread of his interest.

Bernardo was born in Barasoain, Malolos, on March 14, 1891, during the last decade of the Spanish rule in the Philippines. The second of six children of Mauricio Bernardo, a carriage-maker and painter, and Engracia Adriano, a meat dealer in the Malolos market, he spent his elementary schooling at the Malolos Elementary School and his secondary education at the Bulacan High School. He studied at the University of the Philippines and, working his way through college, earned the Bachelor of Arts degree in 1916. He attended the University of Wisconsin from 1918 to 1920 as a government scholar in library science and bibliography and was awarded the Certificate in General Library Services. When he returned to the Philippines, he resumed his studies while working at the Philippine Library and Museum as Assistant Librarian and Researcher. In 1923 he earned the Master of Arts in English and Bibliography. At the same time, he was a lecturer in library science and bibliography at the University of the Philippines, where he taught various courses. Later he became a full-time member of the University library staff as a cataloguer, and successively became Assistant Librarian and Instructor of Library Science. When Mary Polk, then university librarian, died in 1924, Bernardo became the Librarian of the University of the Philippines Library and head of the Department of Library Science, which was then under the College of Liberal Arts.

In 1929, as a University of the Philippines Fellow, he went to Germany and took advanced courses in library science at the University of Berlin. He also worked in various library departments at the University of Leipzig and the Prussian State Library in Berlin. While he was in Germany his initiative led to the Philippine Library Association's joining the International Federation of Library Associations in 1930.

Bernardo's career as a librarian was almost totally spent in the service of the University of the Philippines Library, where he served as University Librarian from 1924 until he retired in 1957. He was responsible for the construction of the library building in Manila, the first building planned and equipped solely for library purposes there. When it was destroyed in the battle of Manila in 1945, he immediately went to work on the construction of another library building, a bigger one on a new site in Diliman, Quezon City.

In 1945 he made a survey of the destruction of libraries in the Philippines wrought by World War II. His report became the basis for the creation of a special committee to draw up specific plans for the rehabilitation of war-devastated libraries and other cultural agencies in the Philippines. In 1946 Bernardo went to the United States as technical adviser to the Philippine Foundation of America to campaign for overseas aid for the rehabilitation of libraries and cultural agencies. As a result of that campaign, book donations from America poured in.

Bernardo's far-reaching influence was expressed not only through the classroom, where he trained hundreds of librarians, but also in his leadership of the Philippine Library Association. He was cofounder and charter member and served as Vice-President and Acting President (1927–31), then as President (1933–34, 1949–53, and 1957–62). He was responsible for abolishing voting by proxy and helped raise the association's professional standards.

BIBLIOGRAPHICAL WORKS
Bernardo pursued bibliography vigorously up to his death. He believed that bibliographies are important to research and deplored the absence of an up-to-date national bibliography for the Philippines. He engaged himself in producing exhaustive studies of individual titles and subject bibliographies representing his main interests—folklore, history, anthropology, language and literature, and librarianship. He always insisted on accuracy in entries and annotations. Of the many bibliographical works he produced, noteworthy are *Bibliography of Philippine Bibliographies, 1593–1961* (1968) and *Philippine Retrospective National Bibliography, 1523–1699* (1974). Both works were published after his death in Quezon City on December 5, 1962. He produced some 88 works and, at the time of his death, left 13 bibliographical works unfinished. Tributes from public figures, scholars, and librarians recognized his special contributions as "doyen of Filipino librarians" (*Manila Times*) and "pioneer, a devoted professor" (Carlos P. Romulo).

REFERENCES
Mauro Garcia, editor, *Gabriel A. Bernardo: Librarian, Bibliographer and Scholar* (Bibliographical Society of the Philippines, 1974).
Carlos P. Romulo, "In Memoriam: Gabriel A. Bernardo; March 14, 1891–December 5, 1962, *University of the Philippines Library Bulletin* (April 15, 1963).
Natividad P. Verzosa, "Gabriel A. Bernardo: A Memoir," *Philippine Studies* (October 1963).

ROSA MENGUITO VALLEJO

Besterman, Theodore
(1904–1976)

Theodore Deodatus Nathaniel Besterman became well known as a bibliographer and Voltaire scholar, but his approach to these specialties was prolonged and gradual.

He was born in Poland on November 18, 1904, and, after his family had moved to London, was educated mostly at home, receiving little formal education at school and none at college or university. A teenage flirtation with youth movements coincided with interest in and membership of the theosophical movement and, initially, with admiration for its leader at the time, Annie Besant (1847–1933). Besterman's first book, published at the age of 20, was *A Bibliography of Annie Besant.* She had been prominent in and had published widely on a succession of interests prior to theosophy, including secularism, birth control, the status of women, and trade unionism, all, including theosophy, leading to her later concern for Indian nationalism; Besterman's bibliography included more than 400 items. His *Mind of Annie Besant,* an appreciation by a devoted admirer in honor of her 80th birthday, came in 1927. But his *Mrs. Annie Besant: a Modern Prophet* (1934) was the work of a disillusioned and lapsed theosophist who condemned her "monstrous authoritarianism."

Besterman's involvement with theosophy had encouraged a near-parallel interest in the paranormal, and from 1927 until 1935 he was one of the investigating officers of the Society for Psychical Research; he became editor of its journal and its librarian, publishing a catalogue and four supplements between 1927 and 1935. Further consequences were his *Some Modern Mediums* (1930), his editorship of and contribution to BBC talks, "Inquiry into the Unknown" in 1934, and his *Bibliography of Sir Oliver Lodge* in 1935. Prior to these, however, had come more specialist books introduced by *Crystal Gazing: a Study in the History, Distribution, Theory and Practice of Scrying* in 1924, which suggested "a latent and unknown faculty of perception." *The Divining Rod: an Experimental and Psychological Investigation,* prepared when Besterman was assistant to Sir William Barrett but published in 1926 after Barrett's death, was partly supplemented by *Water-Divining: New Facts and Theories* (1938), the books together claiming, rather more plausibly, "the impossibility of finding any normal explanation of the phenomena of dowsing."

Another interest, this time in anthropology, manifested itself in Besterman's revised 1927 edition of Ernest Crawley's *The Mystic Rose: a Study of Primitive Marriage,* first published in 1902 but now provided with a much more comprehensive index and a new bibliography of some 800 references. The revision was dedicated to Sir J. G. Frazer, of *Golden Bough* fame: Besterman's *Bibliography of Sir James George Frazer* followed in 1934. The success of the revision encouraged him to bring together a number of Crawley's essays, previously unpublished in book form, as *Studies of Savages and Sex* (1929) and *Dress, Drinks and Drums* (1931). He then attempted to bridge the gap between primitive and modern with *Men against Women: a Study of Sexual Relations* (1934), a brief historical survey based on the surely unremarkable contention that "most of the psychological manifestations of sexual life may be traced back to a fundamental and deep-lying antagonism between the sexes." His interest cannot be regarded as unconnected with his own first marriage and divorce.

Besterman displayed a more explicit interest in bibliography by becoming a lecturer in the School of Librarianship at University College, London, in 1931 and by publishing, four years later, *The Beginnings of Systematic Bibliography* (second edition 1936, third edition; in French, *Les Débuts de la Bibliographie Méthodique,* 1950). This book, which examines bibliographies published up to and during the 17th century, may be regarded as one introduction to his *World Bibliography of Bibliographies* but there were others. Prominent among them was his paper "A New Bibliography of Bibliographies," read at the (British) Library Association's conference in 1936: a slightly revised version was published separately later that year and a further revision prefaces the first volume of the *World Bibliography.* Meantime, however, there were other publications of bibliographic interest. *The Publishing Firm of Cadell and Davies: Select Correspondence and Accounts 1793–1836, Edited with an Introduction and Notes* (1938), is a revealing presentation of the company that published Robert Burns and rejected Jane Austen's *Pride and Prejudice.* In 1938 came *The Travellings and Sufferings of Father Jean de Brébeuf among the Hurons of Canada as Described by Himself, Edited and Translated from the French and Latin,* an account of the checkered life and martyrdom by the Iroquois in 1649 of the French Jesuit missionary. A year later came *The Pilgrim Fathers: a Journal of Their Coming to the Mayflower to New England and Their Life and Adventures There, Edited with Preface and Notes,* and reprinted from the rare 1622 edition, which "remains the only detailed source of information for the first settlement of New England." A further Anglo-American link was provided by Besterman's own Guyon House Press—named after his London house in Hampstead, set up in 1937 but destroyed by a bomb in 1940—which published a translation of *Magna Carta and other Charters of English Liberty:* a copy was exhibited at the Library of Congress during World War II, together with the original Charter sent to the United States for safety.

Besterman's World Bibliography of Bibliographies and of Bibliographical Catalogues, Calendars, Abstracts, Digests, Indexes and the Like was first published in 1939–40, the second edition in 1947–49 (reprinted 1950), the third in 1955–56 (reprinted in reduced facsimile 1960), and the fourth in four volumes with a separate volume of index in 1965–66. It is arranged alphabetically by subjects and, in the fourth edition, is brought down to 1963. It is limited to separately published bibliographies, aims at internationality and completeness, and excludes only lists in but not on oriental languages: it contains more than 117,000 entries. Compilation of the immense work involved the personal handling of more than 80,000 volumes in the Library of Congress and the Library of the British Museum; the work is dedicated to the staff of the latter. Entries for African and Oriental subjects, published also separately from 1939 onward, were updated to 1973 by J. D. Pearson and published in 1975; the main arrangement here is by geographical division. A decennial supplement to the *World Bibliography* is planned: the first, covering the years 1964–74 and published in two volumes in New Jersey in 1977, was compiled by Alice F. Toomey.

The time gap between the first and second editions of the *World Bibliography* was explained by Besterman's British war service and, afterward and until 1949, by a period at Unesco, where he became head of a department for the international exchange of information. He had, perhaps, prepared the way for this activity by his work for Aslib during the 1930s, by his general editorship of its publications from 1944 to 1946, by the establishment and temporary editorship in 1945 of its *Journal of Documentation,* and by the planning of the *British Union Catalogue of Periodicals (BUCOP).*

Besterman expressed his feeling for Voltaire, the great French philosopher and man of letters, at the end of the preface to his own ambitious biography published in 1960 (third revised edition 1976): "I have been his lifelong admirer this side idolatry. I have spent many years in close and critical study of his life and works, for over a decade I lived in his house, worked in his library, slept in his bedroom. It would be absurd for me to pretend to cold impartiality." He had been collecting Voltaire material for many years and, after an abortive attempt to establish a Voltaire center in France, turned alternatively—and so appropriately in view of Voltaire's own experience—to Switzerland. Following prolonged negotiations the Institut et Musée Voltaire was created in Voltaire's own house, Les Délices, in Geneva, and officially opened in 1954. From it, under Besterman's personal direction, poured an amazing output of impeccably produced books, including in particular 107 volumes of the correspondence, edited for the first time mostly from manuscript sources. Other notable publications included the first "Studies on Voltaire and the 18th century," which total nearly 200 volumes.

Besterman eventually moved his Voltaire publishing activities to England and established in Oxford the Voltaire Foundation, which he bequeathed to the Taylor Institution of the University, with the residue of his estate. The primary aims of the Foundation are to continue his work and notably to complete the definitive edition of the collected works, including the correspondence, in approximately 150 volumes, and to undertake other publications and related research on 18th-century studies and the Enlightenment.

There is an attractive Voltaire Room in the Taylorian building; publishing is directed and controlled from offices nearby.

In his Arundell Esdaile lecture, "Fifty Years a Bookman," read to a joint meeting of the Library Association and the English Association in 1973, Besterman referred to himself as "a man who has conducted a life-long and passionate affair with books," an appropriate epitaph for one whose bibliographical and literary activities verge on the unbelievable. He died on November 10, 1976, at Banbury, near Oxford.

Honorary degrees had been conferred on him by Oxford and other universities. The Library Association, which had made him an Honorary Fellow in 1969, remembers him through its Besterman Medal, awarded annually for an outstanding bibliography or guide to the literature first published in the United Kingdom during the preceding year.

REFERENCES
Theodore Besterman. *Fifty Years a Bookman* (1974).
Edward J. Carter, "Theodore Besterman: A Personal Memoir," *Journal of Documentation,* 1977.

W. A. MUNFORD

Bhutan

In the Himalayan chain, Bhutan is bounded by China on the north and India on the south. Its population, primarily of Tibetan extraction, was estimated at about 1,417,000 in 1984; the area is approximately 46,100 sq.km. Its remoteness and near inaccessibility kept Bhutan for many years outside the mainstream of cultural and political developments in the world. Only comparatively recently, under the administration of the Wangehuk dynasty, were steps taken to bring Bhutan into the 20th century. In the 1960s Bhutan was estimated to have a 95 percent illiteracy rate.

No libraries other than Tibetan monastic libraries existed in Bhutan until, in the early 1960s, with the support of the Indian government, the Bhutanese ruler, Druk Gyalpo Jigme Dorji Wangchuk, initiated the creation of elementary and high schools in the country, an effort continued by his successor, Druk Gyalpo Jigme Sinye Wangchuk. Most of the schools are in the three principal cities, Thimpu, Paro, and Phun Tsoling.

No detailed statistics dealing with libraries had been published by the mid-1980s. The education budget does not provide a breakdown for the acquisition of library materials. It is doubtful, however, that significant numbers of books—other than basic ones for support of classes—are acquired. English was used as the principal language until the mid-1980s, but it was to be replaced by Dzongkha, the national language and a Tibetan dialect, according to a decision made in 1975.

An effort was undertaken to collect the country's archives in the former royal palace in Pharo.

LUC KWANTEN*

Bibliographic Networks and Utilities

In the library context, *network* may have several meanings: (1) The informal links that help people make contacts, transact business, and find out what they need to know. It may be used as a verb, "to network," and is most frequently seen in its gerund form, "networking." (2) *Bibliographic "utilities,"* probably most accurately called networks, since they are the most complete networking systems, including database, hardware, and telecommunications systems. (Perhaps the term ought to be reserved for them alone.) (3) *Systems for online bibliographic searching,* such database vendor systems as DIALOG, BRS, or SDC. (4) *Telecommunications system(s)* used to link libraries with utilities and database vendor systems. (5) *Organizations of libraries for assistance in the use of computerized library services,* such as utilities and database vendor systems. These usually involve several types of libraries and may be organized on a single- or multi-state basis. (6) *Organizations of libraries in a single area of specialization,* such as law or medicine, similarly linked to each other and to one or more national databases for the retrieval of technical and reference information. (7) *Library cooperatives of any kind.* This increasingly common usage for years seemed to be inaccurate, but more and more cooperatives, systems, and consortia are adding telecommunications links to improve their service to members, making the synonymous use more appropriate.

In the 1970s, a reference to library networks usually involved definition 5 above; specifically, the affiliates of OCLC, the Online Computer Library Center; AMIGOS, BCR, CAPCON, FEDLINK, ILLINET, INCOLSA, MLNC, MINITEX, MLC, NEBASE, NELINET, OHIONET, PALINET, PRLC, SOLINET, SUNY, and WILS; plus the OCLC service center, PACNET; and CLASS (see accompanying box). Norman D. Stevens's definition of networks is limited to those meeting the following criteria: *geographical level:* state, multistate, or national; *(financial) support:* primarily from payments for services from participating libraries; *direction:* having a full-time, specialized staff; *governance:* by an independent body including a high level of involvement by members, usually through a board of directors or trustees; and *services:* use of a large-scale cooperative database in machine-readable form, available through a telecommunications network.

The use of the term "bibliographic utility," disliked as it has been by those to whom it has been applied, has become increasingly standardized in the library community. A *bibliographic utility* is a nonprofit organization serving as a source of bibliographic data stored in machine-readable form, which data are available to those affiliated with the utility (usually library members) for such purposes as online cataloguing and interlibrary loan through a telecommunications network. Commercial vendors have been "designated" as utilities by at least one state government for contractual purposes, but, in 1985, the generally accepted list of utilities included only four organizations in North America—OCLC, Dublin, Ohio; The Research Libraries Information Network (RLIN), Stanford, California; UTLAS (formerly the University of Toronto Library Automation System) Toronto, Ontario; and the Washington Library Network (WLN), Olympia, Washington. UTLAS, which started as a nonprofit operation, later moved into the private sector, indicating that flexibility in the definition may be necessary.

This article covers the utilities and networks cited in definitions 2 and 5. See further articles on Library Cooperative Systems, Online Information Services, and Resource Sharing.

FUNCTIONS

The differentiation between "utilities" and "networks" is historically defined at a functional level.

Utilities. The organizations that would be called utilities came into being in various ways: OCLC as a cooperative endeavor among academic libraries in Ohio; WLN as a state-library-sponsored automation system in Washington; and RLIN and UTLAS as single library systems that grew and expanded in California and Ontario respectively. The historical development of these organizations altered their original functions and led to the use of the term "utility" to define them.

OCLC's origins as a cooperative of Ohio academic libraries is legendary. Its development through the affiliation of networks representing libraries in other regions of the country, and its subsequent addition of its own service centers in the United States and abroad, led to a demand for a governance structure representative of all users. By the time that had been accomplished, the organization's functions had been transformed from providing cataloguing information, cards, and interlibrary loan locations to a homogeneous group of libraries in a small geographical region, to that of providing a giant national, multitype library network with an increasing variety of products and services.

The Washington Library Network's state library origins defined its functions: to serve libraries in the state of Washington with high-quality cataloguing information and related products for resource-sharing. The function has not altered significantly, although the region served has been enlarged to include the Pacific Northwest, and the sale of WLN software has carried the system to the Southeastern U.S. through SOLINET; to Missouri, Arizona, and other regions of the United States; and to Australia as well.

RLIN is based on BALLOTS, the automated system of the Stanford University Libraries. Acquired by the Research Libraries Group (RLG) in 1978, BALLOTS sharply changed in function from a single library's automation system with a few regional users into a vehicle to support the sharing of cataloguing, acquisitions, interlibrary loans, preservation, and other activities among a selected group of research libraries throughout the United States.

Similarly, the University of Toronto Library Automation System was later called UTLAS and began to make its services available throughout Canada and internationally, providing a gigantic database supporting cataloguing and acquisitions. Purchased by the International Thompson Organization (ITO) in November 1984, UTLAS was the first utility to surrender its nonprofit status.

Networks. The function networks have commonly shared has been the brokering of automated services to libraries, usually in a geographically defined area. Each of the networks has had unique functions, however, depending on its origins. These functions generally fall into five categories:

1. Older cooperatives linked with a utility to replace an inefficient manual union catalogue; for example, BCR and PALINET

2. Organizations formed to automate their library members, then joined with a successful utility; for example, NELINET and SOLINET

3. Organizations formed with another purpose, for whom brokerage was a means to reach that end; for example, MINITEX and WILS

4. Organizations formed explicitly for automation brokerage; for example, AMIGOS and MLC

5. Independent organizations affiliating only loosely with a utility, such as CLASS.

Despite the historical differences among the OCLC-affiliating networks, they developed similarly in relation to OCLC. At first (PRLC was the trailblazer) they entered into innovative joint ventures; but before long they took on responsibility for serving as

Computer room at UTLAS, Inc., Toronto. UTLAS provides a database supporting cataloguing and acquisitions.

the link between their members and OCLC. Because individual libraries outside Ohio had no rights of membership in OCLC before 1978, the networks and their directors had a primary role in representing the user-members' interests. After the 1978 change in governance, when all user libraries were designated OCLC members, the liaison function altered perceptibly. Furthermore, shifts in management at OCLC and technological developments made it increasingly difficult for OCLC and networks to agree on network functions and roles, leaving the networks in a state of transition.

At the same time, the networks had been developing their range of products and services, occasionally offering competition to OCLC (such as SOLINET's LAMBDA system). Several networks also entered into brokerage relationships with other vendors, sometimes competing with OCLC (such as REMARC). In a few cases, OCLC entered into competition with networks in markets they first entered (as in the case of database brokerage, which OCLC later abandoned).

Finally, increasing attention to member needs has become the driving motivation of most networks. Indeed, for almost all of them, the primary goal is the satisfaction of member needs.

TYPES AND STRUCTURES

Governance. The governance of library networks has been defined by Huntington Carlile as "the structure and administration of the power relationships among the various organizational stakeholders (members or constituents) within the shared activity or network."

Types. Three major network types are: (1) governmentally affiliated agencies, including state-government related agencies such as INCOLSA and NEBASE; the federal agency FEDLINK; and organizations that are part of a state's higher education structure, such as MINITEX and SUNY; (2) quasi-governmental agencies, such as CLASS; and (3) not-for-profit corporations, including small-regional networks, covering parts of several states but relatively

small geographical areas (such as CAPCON, PRLC); single-state networks (MLNC and OHIONET); and multi-state regional networks (such as AMIGOS and BCR).

Carlile extolled the benefits of the nonprofit corporate form, citing advantages (among others) such as relative ease of creation, existence of a separate legal entity, availability of central management, continuity of life or existence, limited liability, a favorable tax structure, and flexibility.

Boards. A significant role in the governance of a network is played by its board. Stevens cites the importance of the board as a member-representative body with close control over the network's operations. Boards have responsibility for identifying network mission, goals, and objectives, approving long- and short-range plans, and setting and monitoring network budgets. The board also hires—and fires—management.

Members who serve on network boards have fiduciary responsibility and most are covered by liability insurance. Although they do have responsibility to their immediate constituents, most serve at-large, rather than as representatives of narrow constituencies. They may face serious conflict-of-interest problems, in that they are both governors of the network and users of its service. Their sizable time commitment and their loyalty represent major assets of library networks.

Levels of Networking. Because of technological, economic, and political developments, networking activity has become increasingly common, and libraries have tended to group together at various geographical levels:

Institution. A number of decentralized libraries at one institution may be linked for various purposes, including catalogue searching and resource sharing; multi-campus institutions are particularly appropriate examples.

Consortium. A group of institutions, usually geographically close, may link databases for shared acquisitions, circulation, or interlibrary loan, and for broadened bibliographic access.

Sub-state. Libraries in one region within a state may join a library system for shared cataloging, interlibrary loan, sharing of special collections (such as film, materials for the blind and physically handicapped, and audiovisual materials and equipment.)

State. Government-related or independent systems may be created to broker database searching, to use a bibliographic utility, or to perform any of the functions cited above.

Multi-state. Government-related, quasi-governmental, or private not-for-profit networks may exist for contracting with a bibliographic utility, brokering online searching, and providing technical assistance and training.

National. These may consist of single types of libraries, such as the Regional Medical Library Network, or may include many types of libraries with some common feature (for example, the FEDLINK network, comprised of federal libraries of all types and sizes throughout the United States). These networks may similarly offer a broad range of services.

Relationships among networks at different levels pose an interesting problem in library cooperation. Deciding what services are appropriately provided at each level is exceedingly important, because trends toward decentralization lead to proliferation of networks and to potentially counterproductive duplication of services. It is reasonable for a library to expect to receive certain services at the institution level, others from a local cooperative, still others from a substate system, further ones at the state level, and still more from a regional network. Identifying the services that should be provided at each level is an important task.

Financing. One of the principles of networking is that the affiliation should work to the financial benefit of the library members. This means that—at least for the nonprofit networks—the libraries should pay less than if they operated independently, and the vendor should find it advantageous to use the network to market and distribute its services and products, but the network should also receive sufficient revenue to operate successfully.

The financial savings obtained by government-subsidized networks mean that they can offer their members a great bargain. They represent a sizable investment on the part of the agencies that underwrite them. Where they operate in direct competition with nonprofits, they have the advantage (much as the nonprofits have some advantage over tax-paying businesses), because networks must first justify their prices to their members; indeed, many require member approval of prices on a regular basis.

In its financial aspects, a nonprofit network is more like a small business than like a library. It is a revenue-driven operation, dependent on market forces, with little leeway in which to operate. With neither allocations nor free overhead from a parent institution, the network must pay from its revenues rent, salaries, and other operating costs, a hard reality not always understood by members. Libraries must fare better within the network than outside it, or they will withdraw their membership; unless vendors continue to see an advantage in using networks to distribute their products and services, they will cease to do so. Thus, networks must try to persuade their members of the value of the entire package represented by their membership, rather than offer only products on which they can make enough revenue to support themselves. And, increasingly, they must convince vendors that networks are successful marketing and promotional agents for their products and services.

SERVICES AND BENEFITS

Program Development. Networks must constantly plan for services they will offer and both the governing body—the board—and management—the staff—must be involved in this process. Selection of a package of products and services suited to the particular network will be based on a knowledge of the field and of products and services available and on a familiarity with the market of present and future network members.

Financial considerations also rank high in decisions about service offerings. Start-up costs of new services may include staff (regular, part-time, and consultants); capitalization; market surveys; promotion; space; and support services and equipment. Therefore, new products and services often require several years to break even. Some valuable network services may be offered as part of the service package even if they never contribute to equity. Decisions about discontinuing unsuccessful services may be based on financial considerations alone, but may also take other factors into account.

Networks, however, must be able to move quickly to fill perceived gaps, to provide needed services on relatively short demand, and to gear up (or down) with flexibility; flexibility in comparison with its member institutions is one of the network's major strengths.

Services. Specific services provided by the networks considered in this article—and not all networks provide all these services—include: shared cataloguing, acquisitions, serials control, union listing, and interlibrary loan, via brokerage of a major bibliographic utility's services and products; database access, via brokerage of major database vendors; technical assistance and service in the use of the various brokered services; training and continuing education activities directly and indirectly related to brokered services; consulting services in library automation and related fields; direct provision of certain computerized services (such as SOLINET's LAMBDA System and AMIGOS' SHARES program); document delivery, either from a central collection at a parent institution or among member institutions; microcomputer hardware and software sales, service, and training; advocacy in the library networking and government environment for all types and sizes of member libraries; and provision of information about library cooperation and technology, through a newsletter or program of publications for members.

Benefits of Network Membership. Libraries that belong to networks receive certain benefits in addition to the specific products they purchase. They share the costs of developing products and services, can save money through group contracts, and have a forum in which to interact with other libraries. They enjoy the advantage of network flexibility, especially in financing. The network can order items quickly and submits to the library a single bill for a variety of services. Finally, having the network handle all contractual arrangements with all vendors, while the library has one contract with the network, is a great advantage, especially in view of the increasingly complex contracts for computerized services.

TECHNOLOGY

Library networking is based on three major areas of technology: encoding of bibliographic information in machine-readable format for storage and retrieval (database building and management); machines (hardware) and instructions (software) to manipulate the information; and telecommunications mechanisms for transmission of the information.

Database Building and Management. Although there were successful computerized library projects earlier, the development of networking only began with the creation of the MARC communication format in 1966, by Henriette Avram and others at the Library of Congress. This format instructs the computer how to read and retrieve bibliographic information.

The MARC record identifies the elements that may be used, to the level of detail desired, by librarians and others to perform such library operations as cataloguing, acquisitions, and interlibrary loan, without any need for operators to be highly sophisticated about computers. Users must follow a set of rules supplied by the utility (and often learned in training sessions offered by networks) for entering and modifying data.

One of the problems of networks and utilities is to control the quality of the records input, to see that they adhere to cataloguing standards, such as the *Anglo-American Cataloguing Rules,* Second Edition, and that exact duplicates and errors are eliminated. Efforts at quality control range from RLIN's dependence on institutional prestige to WLN's daily revision of member input. OCLC's Bibliographic Maintenance Section revises records upon notice from members, who are enjoined to report errors. Networks use peer councils, advanced training sessions, and even rewards for low error rates to encourage quality database building.

Hardware and Software. The MARC record for a typical mongraph is some 550 characters in length—rather long. Libraries also usually want a great number of access points to each record, and database indexes also tend to be very large. Library systems, therefore, tend to require very large amounts of computer storage. For years, this meant that a mainframe computer was needed to computerize even a moderate-sized library. By 1985, however, most network nodes used minicomputers, and laser disk technology was almost ready for wide use in storing large bibliographic databases on microcomputers.

The trend in computers in and out of libraries in the mid-1980s seemed to be toward a mix of centralized databases of up-to-the-minute currency, with microcomputer work stations capable of "downloading data," operating on it locally, and "uploading" the altered records or additional data into the main database. OCLC's MicroEnhancers are a good example of this trend—software packages that allow the user to retrieve records from the OCLC Online Union Catalogue, load them into the microcomputer to be manipulated offline, and later upload the records to OCLC in batch mode.

Telecommunications. Telecommunications technology allows the movement of voice and data from one point to another by means of electrical and optical transmission systems. The most common systems move data from remote terminals to a central point, where it can be operated upon by a computer, stored, and later retrieved. For libraries, this technology has primarily allowed the sharing of bibliographic information and the speedy transmission of interlibrary loans.

Several network configurations have been used by libraries. The *star* network is the most common form for a centralized network. A *tree,* or hierarchical, network has been common among noncomputerized library networks. With trends toward decentralization, configurations like the *ring,* or mixed networks, are becoming more common.

Whatever the configuration, data transmitted via the network must be transformed from ordinary language into a machine-readable form, so that the computer at the other end of the transmission channel can read it. It must then be put into a form the transmission channel can handle. In the case of bibliographical data, first the MARC communications format translates the data into machine-readable format; then the machine-readable (digital) data is changed into analogue (wave) form for transmission over communication lines (using a modem); finally, the signal is demodulated so that it can be read in its digital form by the computer at the other end of the line.

Earlier in the development of library networking, telecommunications were relatively inexpensive. More recently, however, and especially since the breakup of AT&T, increasing telecommunications costs have pushed toward decentralization. New techniques in telecommunications, such as more sophisticated multiplexing, satellite refinements, and increased use of fibre optics, may have a strong influence on the library networks of the future.

While these three technologies form the basis of library networking, others will have an impact on its future. Remote laser printing may allow printing at remote sites of accession lists, orders, shelf lists, or other centrally produced products. Telefacsimile, which was declining in price in the 1980s, may yet prove successful in transmitting interlibrary loans, while videotex will probably be used for broadcast messages within networks.

Specific library applications facilitated by networks include online catalogues, interlibrary loan bulletin board and message systems, and shared processing. Future possibilities include library management systems based on shared statistical information, cooperative consortium development, and availability on home computers of library databases including community information, popular databases such as the Wilson indexes, and catalogues of neighboring libraries.

ISSUES

Issues of importance in library networking include levels of networking and the importance of identifying levels appropriate for certain kinds of activity; home delivery of services and the need for library networks to satisfy the needs of the computer-sophisticated user; and decentralization in political and economic life and its implications for library resource sharing and cooperation.

Several other key issues can also be identified. Networks and their constituents are concerned about the respective roles of the private and public sectors and about the provision of information to those who cannot afford to pay for it. They wish to overcome the delays in actually delivering information to users, since one can now immediately identify and locate materials online and transmit interlibrary loan requests electronically. Networkers want to make their services available to all types and sizes of libraries. New barriers to cooperation can also be observed, including an individualistic attitude fostered by the availability of microcomputers, which relieve the economic pressure to share computer resources. Such attitudes could lead to short-sighted isolationism on the part of libraries. Another issue concerns competencies needed for library networking, not only to develop a cadre of professionals to work in networks, but also to educate librarians so that they can provide informed leadership in the use and governance of networks.

Networks will survive and prosper to the extent

that they provide needed services to their members at an affordable price. Technological developments, broad swings in the library automation marketplace, inter-vendor conflict, and rapid changes in the information profession characterize their highly volatile environment. To survive, networks must be soundly based upon the needs of their members, but their responses to member needs must reflect judgments about the future that, in turn, grow out of a well-founded understanding of library technology, economics, and politics. The most significant trend facing the networks in the late 1980s will be the centrifugal pull toward decentralization. To the extent that they can create reasonable service configurations, combining both political and technological separateness and the strong library tradition of cooperation, then the networks and their constituent libraries will move successfully into the next phase of library networking.

REFERENCES

Norman D. Stevens, "Network Organization: Current Status and Concerns," *Resource Sharing and Library Networks* (1981).

Huntington Carlile, "The Diversity Among Legal Structures of Library Networks," *Networks for Networks: Critical Issues in Cooperative Library Development* (1980).

JO AN S. SEGAL

Bignon, Jean-Paul
(1662–1743)

Jean-Paul Bignon oversaw the Royal Library during the reign of Louis XV, and, as *Bibliothècaire du Roi* (King's librarian), introduced a new golden age into the history of the collection.

He was born at Paris, September 19, 1662, to a family prominent in public affairs and closely associated with the management of the Bibliothèque du Roi. He received his early formal education at the College of Harcourt, where Bossuet directed his thesis in philosophy. Since his cultural tastes seemed to point toward the priesthood, he began his sacerdotal studies at the Séminaire de S. Magloire. In 1684 he was received as a priest into the Congregation of the Oratory, where, in the same year, he published his first work, a life of a Father Levêque of the same order. Seeking a retreat where he could pursue the primary sources for his literary and historical studies, the Abbé Bignon retired first to a country manor, but because of its lack of resources he returned to Paris, where he found a suitable residence and library in the Maison de S. Honoré.

In 1691 he left the Oratory so that he could pursue his scholarly interests completely. In that year he was appointed to the Académie Royale des Inscriptions et Belles-Lettres. Ten years later he was named Conseiller d'État, although he continued both his scholarly and priestly activities, even acquiring a reputation for his occasional sermons.

His extensive studies, of course, led him to acquire a sizable library; thus it is not surprising that in 1718 he was appointed by Louis XV to oversee the Royal Library. Shortly after his appointment he saw to it—like Naudé with the Bibliothèque Mazarine—that the Library was opened to the public (1720).

Thus, as Hessel observes, the leading scholars of the Enlightenment were able to utilize the collection for their studies.

Under the Abbé's direction the Library was divided into five sections: printed books, manuscripts, genealogical titles, engravings, and medals, and the holdings were significantly enlarged. During his administration the 6,645 manuscripts acquired by Colbert, along with the Louvre and Fontainebleau collections, were added. Following the precedent of Colbert, he acquired books and manuscripts through the diplomatic corps on an even larger scale than did his predecessors. In 1739 he supervised the initial publication of the printed catalogue, which was completed 10 years after his death, in six folio volumes. His four-volume catalogue of Oriental, Greek, and Latin manuscripts (1739–44) prefigured similar undertakings of the late 19th and early 20th centuries. During his term as *Bibliothècaire du Roi* he continued his wide-ranging studies, producing an extended commentary on the *Bibliotheca* of Apollodorus, a primary source for the study of Greek mythology.

His personal life seems to have been austere; rising at 4:00 A.M. to pursue his scholarly interests until 8:00 A.M., he then went to his regular duties as librarian and academician. In 1741, about to enter his 80th year, he began to suffer from a violent abdominal disorder and surmised that death was close at hand. Accordingly he had his Royal Library position transferred to his nephew, Jérôme Bignon. The Abbé's health steadily deteriorated and, on March 14, 1743, he died. To the day of his death, according to Fréret, he retained his "reason, not to mention the sweetness and equanimity that he had displayed" throughout his life.

FRANCIS J. WITTY

Bilingual and Ethnic Groups, Services to

While the meaning of *bilingual* is adequately conveyed in this article through the paragraphs dealing with it, the same may not be assumed about "ethnic." It has already become a platitude to say apologetically, "After all, everybody is an ethnic." But in some contexts in which the word appears, it often means *they* as against *we*, and *they* are people with one or more of such characteristics as coming from another country, speaking another language, or having a different color and a different way of life

Lubomyr Wynar gives for America the following definition:

> The difference between the non-ethnic American and the ethnic American is that while the former has lost the link with his past heritage, the latter has chosen to retain it, to take pride in it, and to enrich it, by adding to it American created cultural forms ("History of Services to Ethnic Communities," *Catholic Library World*, 1977).

For the purpose of this article, ethnicity is in most cases identified with a language different from that of the majority in any one country, but the realities of the demands on libraries and services given by them do not permit a rigid interpretation. It has seemed necessary, for instance, to recognize the existence of Afro-American culture and black librarian-

UNESCO/Dominique Roger

School library in Colombo, Sri Lanka, books are provided in Sinhalese, Tamil, and English.

ship among speakers of English; similarly, West Indians, who are white and black and in-between and who, as immigrants in Canada, Britain, and the U.S. ask for specialized service, are also treated in this article.

In Europe and North America, libraries, originally and for a long time, provided their services solely in the official language or languages of their own countries, and providing for other language groups was an acknowledged concern in relatively few countries. On the assumption that all citizens should know the national language, such service as was provided seldom went beyond a small collection of "foreign" books. An understanding that the responsibility to provide library service equally to all involves going beyond the official languages developed only recently. In examining the services offered today, a distinction has been made, therefore, between countries where a mixed population goes back far into history (the established multilingual countries) and those where the traditional composition of population was changed by immigration or influx of migrant workers in more recent years.

Established Multilingual Countries. In Europe most of the countries with more than one language group have been created over the centuries by wars and their peace agreements. The degree of cultural and language amalgamation varies considerably and so consequently do their libraries' services, as the following examples illustrate.

Belgium. In Belgium live two culturally, linguistically different groups who are also territorially separated, the Dutch-speaking Flemings in the north and the French-speaking Walloons in the south, with both languages spoken only in Brussels; this strict division is also followed in the libraries.

Switzerland. Less rigidity is exercised in Switzerland, where in different areas French, German, Italian, and Romansch are spoken. In each area public libraries, while organized for service to the dominant group, also provide a reasonable quantity of books in the other languages.

South Africa. Two official languages, Afrikaans

and English, are taught in schools and are used equally in all spheres of life. Library personnel must be bilingual in them as a condition of employment in most if not all provincial and municipal institutions, and the collections reflect, of course, language policy as well as reading needs. There are also about eight other large language groups, both African and Asian, in South Africa, but they are regarded as "nonofficial." Limited library service is available to their groups.

Finland. Finland is an example of how the foreign language of a larger and dominant nation persists even after political ties have been broken. Besides the Finnish language, Swedish is spoken and read by a large minority, and, accordingly, public libraries in large centers, such as Helsinki, provide material in both languages.

Yugoslavia. Yugoslavia is inhabited by many ethnic and linguistic groups, each residing mainly within a well-defined area and therefore not presenting communication problems. It is normal practice for a large library in an area where several languages are spoken to provide some material in those languages, even for minority groups.

North America. In North America the history of bilingualism is of more recent date. Canada is often described as a bilingual country, but the description is not entirely accurate, since French is spoken primarily in the province of Quebec. The Official Languages Act accords equal status to English and French in Parliament and in the federal civil service. Public libraries, while intent on meeting the needs of the majority groups in their environment, also provide books in the other language. Many libraries in the English-speaking provinces consider it a patriotic as well as a cultural duty to promote the reading of French, especially works by French Canadian authors.

Although the U.S. is officially unilingual, cultural pluralism has been a fact for a long time. Recently concerns with ethnicity, bilingual personnel, and foreign books have been mainly, though not exclusively, directed to the Spanish-speaking, and when one speaks of bilingualism in the U.S., one thinks of Spanish as the "other" language. It predominates in the Southwest, where it has always been a feature of the linguistic map. During the 1940s public libraries in the U.S. were inevitably affected by bilingual education, if not by the sheer presence of ethnic groups. Progress in the provision of services to the Spanish-speaking is reported in successive issues of *The ALA Yearbook.* Development was stimulated with funds from the Library Services and Construction Act.

The need of Chicanos and other Spanish-speaking groups for service in their own language resulted in the demand for and eventually the creation of library positions for bilingual personnel, and libraries frequently owe their success to their Spanish-speaking staff. Library services to the Spanish-speaking, Afro-American, and American Indian populations have had a continuous period of growth, which is well documented in library literature. The same is not true of other ethnic groups.

Multinational Minorities after World War II. World War II and its aftermath caused massive demographic changes in many countries and presented libraries with new and difficult tasks. Two variants

118

of the population movement are clearly distinguishable and should be treated separately because they impinge somewhat differently on the functions of libraries. They are the migrant workers, more common in Europe, and the immigrants who move to a country to live their permanently.

Migrant workers. These workers have had profound impact in many central and western European countries. When the postwar expansion of industry in Germany, Belgium, Switzerland, Denmark, and Sweden—to name the countries most affected—depleted the reservoir of indigenous labor, workmen were recruited from the southern European countries, notably Yugoslavia, Italy, Greece, Spain, Turkey, and Algeria.

The theory was that the *Gastarbeiter* (guest workers) would stay a few years in the host country and then return home. This theory also served as an excuse for withholding cultural, educational, and some social services from them. Contrary to expectations, it turned out that though a certain number of workers went home when their contracts expired, others arrived to take their place, and a growing number remained when immigration regulations permitted. Eventually libraries took notice of the new challenge, for which most if not all were largely unprepared. The newcomers did not at first know the indigenous languages, were in many cases illiterate, and were in most cases ignorant or distrustful of the public library as an institution. Libraries, on the other hand, usually lacked bilingual or multilingual staff and lacked books in foreign languages and the means of getting them. Faced with such difficulties, they had to look for good reasons for providing materials and services for foreign readers, and they had to instill motivation in staffs.

The support for special services was not, however, difficult to justify. Migrant workers contributed to the national wealth not only through their work but also through taxes and therefore had a claim on public services. In the interest of general economic and social welfare, it was important to help them adapt to prevailing circumstances; through knowledge of the national language the newcomers could not only better understand their daily work and the living conditions but also improve their vocational knowledge and their participation as citizens. Furthermore, it was unavoidable that families followed or were started by the workers. Children who went to school and were taught in the indigenous language could become estranged from their parents. When the time came to return to their home country, both old and young might have become completely assimilated and unable to resume, or, in the case of children born abroad, unable to enter into the prevailing way of life there.

Immigrants. Immigrants must be considered in the majority of cases as permanent additions to a nation, although again exceptions are possible. The types of immigrants—and consequently the role of libraries—differ from country to country, and from one period to another. The largest group of immigrants to Great Britain arrived after World War II from countries of the Commonwealth—India, Pakistan, the West Indies—but that immigration had virtually stopped by the late 1970s. Immigrants to France come from northern and western Africa and usually have at least some speaking knowledge of English and French. The United States has always attracted immigrants from Europe. Since the wars in Korea and Vietnam, immigrants to the U. S. from Southeast Asia have been more numerous. About one of every ten Americans is descended from an Hispanic background representing all of Latin America and the Caribbean. Canada has accepted immigrants from non-English, non-French backgrounds for 300 years. Recently many West Indians have immigrated to Canada. Only after World War II did Australia relax its preference for white immigrants.

BEGINNINGS

In North America at the turn of the 19th century, honest attempts were made by librarians to provide books to immigrants in non-English languages. The ALA established in 1917 the Committee on Work for the Foreign Born, which published in 1929 a special handbook, *Reading Services for the Foreign Born*. In 1948 the Committee was renamed Committee on Intercultural Relations and nothing more was heard of it. At the same time, the long and honorific history of services to ethnic groups, as exemplified by the public libraries of Cleveland, Detroit, and New York, showed signs of stagnation. Wynar and C. B. Joeckel cite as reasons declining immigration, better-educated immigrants with greater demands on library material, and declining circulation. The emphasis then shifted to the "disadvantaged"; i.e., the Afro-Americans, Spanish-Americans, and the American Indians. The influx of immigrants after World War II, greater in Canada than in the U.S., revived consciousness of the centuries-old ties between the Old and the New World.

The so-called melting-pot theory never reached fruition; immigrant communities were transformed into American ethnic communities in the U.S., while in Canada the government declared a policy of multiculturalism, i.e., one nation based on cultural pluralism.

U.S. libraries began in the 1970s to concern themselves with ethnic reading needs once more, a decade after their Canadian counterparts. When Congress passed the Educational Amendment of 1972, which provided for an Ethnic Heritage Studies Program, it noted that "in a multiethnic society a greater understanding of the contribution of one's own heritage and those of one's fellow citizens can contribute to a more harmonious, patriotic, and committed populace."

More and more public libraries provide funds, either from their own budget or out of special grants, for the selection and purchase of books in *community* languages. (This term is preferred to *foreign,* which is imprecise and also offensive to many ethnic citizens.) Encouraging signs of deepening concern for the objectives as much as for the difficulties have been noted in the literature as well as in personal communications to the author from many countries. Even so, the difficulties are enormous: problems of selection and bibliographic aids; problems of acquisition from faraway countries; problems of processing; and, finally, problems of promoting the resources to the intended user groups. Library associations in Britain, France, Germany, and Sweden, among others, are grappling with the problem. In 1975 the American

*Chinese library reading
room of central California,
Fresno, c. 1910.*

Library Association's Public Library Association constituted a Multilingual Services Committee, which met for the first time during ALA's Midwinter Meeting in Chicago in 1978.

LIBRARY SERVICES IN INDIVIDUAL LIBRARIES

Objectives and Standards. Even before the practical problems are tackled, philosophy for service should be stated and goals set. It is not enough merely to start a "foreign" or "multilingual" collection; some thought must be given to general library objectives, reading habits of the target groups, and the extent to which special (and invariably costly) resources for minority readers should be developed. Are they to be helped in order to assimilate? This would entail their need to receive language manuals and books descriptive of their new country. Are they to be helped to maintain and hand down their cultural traditions through judiciously selected works by their national authors? Or will the whole point be "books in your language," irrespective of author and content? Other issues include literacy of new citizens and attitudes toward institutions such as libraries, toward book buying, and toward book borrowing habits, and personal preference for or against retention of the mother tongue.

Selection. The implication for careful selection is obvious. It is difficult, if not impossible, to plan a complete, effective service to minority groups from scratch. Census figures are inadequate guides; one has to proceed by educated guesses, trial and error.

Standards for bibliographic records and book reviewing and reporting vary considerably from country to country. As a general rule, however, one feature is almost universal: most of them are written in the language of the country of production. Knowledge of that language is, to say the least, helpful in order to consider titles for ordering. Failing that, one

has to rely on booksellers at home and abroad or, worse, restrict purchases to translations of easily identified titles.

Booklists are relatively easy to obtain from publishers and booksellers; occasionally they are annotated. Critical reviews can often be found in literary or general magazines, but it is doubtful, given the language problem, whether the average library would subscribe to them except for the use of their ethnic readers. The ALA *Booklist* carries annotated lists of foreign books with addresses of some appropriate booksellers in the U.S. Some libraries issue acquisition lists at regular or irregular intervals, with or without annotations in English and vernacular (Cumberland County Library System, New York Public Library, Cleveland Public Libraries, and others). A comprehensive guide to selection aids and suppliers was published in 1979 by the Canadian Library Association and K. G. Saur as *Books in Other Languages.*

The frequently asked question "How many volumes?" is more difficult to answer. It depends on many factors, such as number of readers, rate of adoption of the host country's language, rate of retention of their own language, and limit on book stock imposed by budget or library policy. IFLA standards recommend distinction between national minorities with fixed residence who should have "adequate quantity of their national literature" and non-resident groups, who should have service when they number at least 500. It is suggested that for a population of 2,000, 1 volume per migrant worker is appropriate; for over 2,000, 1 for 10. There should be a minimum of 100 volumes.

Acquisition. It is axiomatic that the best source of supply is in the country of production, and the source gets poorer in direct proportion to distance from that country. Immigrants, unless heavily concentrated in a particular area or town, do not offer a lucrative market for bookshops, but those shops that do exist have stocks that are usually limited in quality and quantity; nevertheless, librarians should not bypass them entirely. An alert and knowledgeable bookseller can provide valuable guidance on books and take orders for transmission to publishers abroad, who often are not equipped to deal with customers from other countries.

Conversely, many librarians cannot deal with booksellers and publishers in foreign countries and in foreign languages. The languages problem can be aggravated by unusual local commercial practices concerning, for example, terms of payment or means of conveyance. In some countries publishing is carried on by many small enterprises, each of which sells only its own product. Only a capable jobber on the spot or a staff member on a buying trip can ensure timely purchase, for the press runs are usually limited and there is no reprinting. By far the best, reliable, and under ideal circumstances even the most economical way to purchase foreign books in other languages is to buy them personally in the country of publication; an adequate volume of ordering is necessary to justify the expense of a buying trip. This suggests cooperation on regional, national, and international levels.

Processing. Books in foreign languages, often also in different scripts, find most librarians unprepared. The difficulty begins when checking the bill against the consignment, especially when the bill is in a different language *and* in a non-Roman script. When non-Roman material is catalogued and classified, the standard aids for checking authors and authorities and for interpreting content are often inadequate or unavailable.

Staff. Mere knowledge of a language is not in itself sufficient qualification; of course, it is important when assisting those ethnic users who do not as yet speak the language of the country. In order to select books, a good education and cultural background is essential. This does not mean that the staff member must be a native of the country whose cultural heritage is to be promoted, but it helps. In the promotion of books and contact with users, the employment of members of ethnic groups is useful and frequently recommended.

Cooperation, Coordination, Networks. If ever words like these can be justified, it is in the realm of book service in community languages, since the unit cost is invariably higher because of the smaller number of copies per title ordered and processed. Because book-producing countries have had to adjust to higher costs for paper and rising wages, inexpensive books are no longer to be had. It is therefore to the advantage of library systems to have a central acquisition system to relieve the individual library of the difficult tasks of book selection, ordering, and cataloguing. Foremost among such organizations is the Swedish Bibliotekstjänst at Lund, a state enterprise founded in 1951. In response to the large numbers of migrant workers from southern and southeastern Europe, Swedish public libraries were confronted with the task of providing reading material. Bibliotekstjänst obtains books from appropriate countries by sending staff members regularly on buying trips, where they also advise or instruct reliable booksellers or publishers, and attend book fairs.

Successful Projects. The Birmingham (England) Public Library administers a central collection of books in Indian and Pakistani languages that are lent in batches on a fee basis to libraries throughout Great Britain.

Since 1975 an imaginative project has been operating in Canada. While many libraries in large cities have paid attention to the needs of ethnic groups and have built up substantial collections in various languages since the 1950s, the smaller towns and communities have been less successful. Much of the population remained unserved except by interlibrary loans (and then only if adequate bibliographic data were at hand). In order to remedy this situation the National Library of Canada established the Multilingual Biblioservice, a department staffed and equipped to purchase books in some 25 languages for rotating loans throughout the country. These features can be usefully adapted to requirements in other countries.

In Australia the Victoria government granted some money in 1974 for a rotating collection of books for migrants residing in the western suburbs of Melbourne, the Westfund Project. The Project was very successful, creating an awareness of the minorities' need for books in their languages. Monash University, in Clayton, Victoria, gives courses on library service to migrants. In 1978 the Ethnic Affairs Commission of New South Wales published a report, *Library Service to Ethnic Groups,* which in part recom-

Arthur Plotnik

Student interest in ethnic studies is sustained at the University of New Mexico Library, Albuquerque.

mended the expansion of existing services and the setting up of a cooperative acquisition and processing unit.

Service to Children. Children of ethnocultural minorities present a somewhat different task to libraries. Again, there is a distinction between children of migrant workers and those of immigrants or their descendants and between children arriving in the host country at preschool age or at schoolgoing age. In the latter case, learning of language, culture, and way of life comes easily, more so than for children who during the primary years of growth are confined to their home, where that knowledge is inadequate.

It normally happens that the children receive a good education in the country where their parents work but are then expected to return with their parents to their home country when the work contract expires. It is essential, then, that they be educated in their native tongue and learn about the history and culture of their native country in order to ease social and psychological problems that might be faced by the children in the host country or at their repatriation. An additional reason for all children, whether temporary or permanent residents, to retain language and feeling of identity of their ethnic group is the need to prevent estrangement between parent and children, which can and does occur very easily when children assimilate completely into the society of the host country while their parents alone retain language and way of life to which they have been accustomed.

Awareness of the need for library services to ethnic and cultural minorities in many countries has led to earnest investigation of ethnicity, of acquisition problems, and in many cases to the development of interesting projects. Given the uncertainty of human mobility in the future and the inevitable consequences of acculturation, the possibility and desirability of long-term plans cannot be taken for granted. For the present, however, most libraries have still much inducement for developing, even creating, a useful service to ethnic groups.

REFERENCES

John D. Buenker and Nicholas C. Burckel, *Immigration and Ethnicity: A Guide to Information Sources* (1977).

Eric Clough and Jacqueline Quarmby, *A Public Library Service for Ethnic Minorities in Great Britain* (1978).

Monteria Hightower, "Serving Our Ethnic Publics," *PLA Newsletter* (1976).

W. F. Mackey, *Bilingualism as a World Problem* (1967).

Silva Simsova, "Marginal Man," *Journal of Librarianship* (1974).

Lubomyr Wynar, "History of Services to Ethnic Communities," *Catholic Library World* (1977).

Marie F. Zielinska, "Multiculturalism and Library Services to Ethnic Communities," *Unesco Bulletin for Libraries* (1978).

Christobel Mattingley, "Ethnic Connections," *Australian Library Journal* (1976).

LEONARD WERTHEIMER

Billings, John Shaw
(1838–1913)

ALA

John Shaw Billings

John Shaw Billings, physician and librarian, was active in many fields and played a leading role in most of them. He made significant contributions in hospital design and construction, in the public hygiene and sanitation movement, in the reform of medical education, and in the development of vital statistics. His most enduring accomplishments were in the field of librarianship and bibliography, as the creator of two great U.S. research libraries—what became the National Library of Medicine and the New York Public Library.

Billings was born in Switzerland County, Indiana, on April 12, 1838. His family moved to Rhode Island in 1843 and returned in 1848 to Allensville, Indiana, where his father, James Billings, ran a country store and served as postmaster and shoemaker. The young Billings attended a country school for three months each winter and read everything he could lay his hands on; by the age of eight he had read the Bible through verse by verse and had finished *Pilgrim's Progress, Plutarch's Lives, Robinson Crusoe*, and *The Deerslayer*. With the help of a grammar, a dictionary, and the local clergyman, he taught himself Latin and a little Greek and managed to pass the entrance examination for the subfreshman class at Miami University, Oxford, Ohio, in the fall of 1852. Miami was a typical western college of the period, with a small faculty and student body, a fixed and limited curriculum, a religiously oriented administration, and a library of 8,000 volumes that was open on Sundays from 9 A.M. to 12 noon. Billings graduated in 1857, second in his class.

He then spent an interim year as a tutor and as a lecturer with a traveling lantern show, saving his earnings to enter the Medical College of Ohio at Cincinnati in 1858. "In those days," he said later, "they taught us medicine as you teach boys to swim, by throwing them in the water." He attended a course of lectures for five months and then attended the identical course of lectures for another five months in the following year, graduating with his M.D. degree in 1860. He said that he practically lived in the dissecting room and in the clinics; when he wrote his thesis on the *Surgical Treatment of Epilepsy*, he found that even after ransacking public and private libraries in Cincinnati and searching in the libraries of Philadelphia and New York, he was unable to make a complete survey of the pertinent literature. This experience formed the kernel of his resolve to try to establish a fairly complete medical library with catalogues and indexes to match, should the opportunity appear.

After graduation he stayed on at the school—one of a faculty of nine—as demonstrator of anatomy. On the April day in 1861 when the guns fired on Fort Sumter, Billings was celebrating his 23rd birthday. In September 1861 he went to Washington and took the three-day examination for admission to the Medical Corps of the Army; he passed first on the list and was immediately hired as a contract surgeon until his commissioning as First Lieutenant and Assistant Surgeon in April 1862. He was placed in charge of Cliffburne Hospital, which he set up in an old cavalry barracks on the hill above Georgetown. In August 1862 he was transferred to Philadephia as Executive Officer of the West Philadelphia Hospital. On September 3, 1862, he married Katherine Mary Stevens of Washington.

In March 1863 he reported for duty with the Army of the Potomac; by May he was performing field surgery at Chancellorsville; in July he joined the 7th Regiment of the Second Division, V Corps, at Gettysburg; and in August he was in New York City in the aftermath of the Draft Riots.

He eventually was reassigned to hospital duty on Bedloe's Island, and in February 1864 he was given command of an extraordinary secret expedition to Haiti to rescue some 371 survivors of a group of freed slaves who had been resettled there and swindled in the process. The rescue was successful, and by the end of March Billings had been reassigned as Acting Medical Inspector of the Army of the Potomac. In August he was reassigned to duties in Washington, and in December 1864 he was transferred to the Surgeon General's Office.

The war over, Billings settled down to a routine of office duties involving "arid drudgery among invoices and receipts, requisitions and bills of lading, treasury drafts and auditors' decisions. His days were filled with routine office work, with questions of bookkeeping and pecuniary responsibility." He also began to study German and undertook to teach himself something about microscopy, eventually publishing four papers on fungi between 1869 and 1872. He was detailed to the Secretary of the Treasury to conduct a survey of the Marine Hospital Service, 1869–70, and he prepared a reorganization plan that set the Service, later renamed the Public Health Service, on a new course.

During the period 1870–75 he prepared long reports on army hospitals and army hygiene. Beginning in 1875 he became closely involved in the development of the new Johns Hopkins Hospital and Medical School. His plans were chosen for the new Hospital, which was begun in 1877 and opened in 1889. He arranged the curriculum of the school and was instrumental in bringing William H. Welch and William Osler to the faculty. Shuttling by train back and forth to Baltimore, he gave his advice and delivered his lectures in the history of medicine—which he repeated in Boston, New York, and abroad.

Billings served as Vice-President of the National Board of Health in 1879, and in that year surveyed and reported on the sanitary condition of Memphis following that summer's devastating yellow fever epidemic. In 1880 he served as President of the American Public Health Association and began his long consulting association with the U.S. Census Bureau, stressing the need for collecting statistics on disease, not just mortality, and striving for standardized reporting. In that capacity he suggested to Herman Hollerith the desirability of developing a mechanical tabulating machine. In the decade or so after 1880 Billings published dozens of papers on vital statistics, on sanitation and sewage disposal, and on heating and ventilation. He also found time to be President of the Philisophical Society of Washington in 1886; Treasurer of the National Academy of Sciences from 1887 to 1898; and Treasurer of the Cosmos Club, 1878–79, and its President, 1886–87.

The wonder is that in the midst of all these activities his major task for the 30 years from 1865 to 1895 was directing the Library of the Surgeon General's Office, which he organized and developed into the foremost medical library in the world. For a staff Billings had a dozen civilian employees, most of them former army hospital stewards; they were dependable and reliable, if not learned, and Billings trained them in the rudiments of bibliographic procedure. Exchanges were instituted with medical societies and institutions; begging letters were written to private individuals at home and abroad; and duplicates were amassed for exchanging. Reference services were not neglected; Billlings and his small staff answered in a typical year about 2,000 inquiries. He also instituted an interlibrary loan system; physicians were required to make a deposit before borrowing books. And the collections kept growing—1,800 volumes in 1865, 6,000 volumes in 1868, 50,000 titles in the three-volume catalogue of 1873–74.

In 1876 Billings published the renowned *Specimen Fasciculus of a Catalogue of the National Medical Library*. The title itself is noteworthy, with "National Medical Library" appearing in large, bold type. (The letterheads of the Library at this time bore the same legend, foreshadowing the transformation to the National Library of Medicine in 1956.) The *Specimen* set forth in dictionary order both books and periodical articles; the books were listed by author and by subject, the periodical articles by subject only, in a single alphabet. On this model the first volume of the great *Index-Catalogue of the Library of the Surgeon General's Office* appeared in 1880; the first series in its 16 volumes was completed in 1895, having listed 300,000 books and pamphlets and 500,000 periodical articles during that period.

The bibliographic workflow was arranged so that library clerks copied out titles on cards, which then went to Billings and to Robert Fletcher, his assistant from 1876, who penciled a single appropriate subject rubric across the top of each card. Those cards dealing with current materials were utilized, beginning in 1879, as the substance of the *Index Medicus,*

"A Monthly Classified Record of the Current Medical Literature of the World," published by Frederick Leypoldt. Thus Billings provided both a bibliographic service for current awareness, the *Index Medicus,* and a service designed primarily for retrospective search, the *Index-Catalogue,* from the same database.

From 1876 to 1896 Billings made eight European trips. In 1884 he received the degree of LL.D. from the University of Edinburgh, in 1889 the degree of Doctor of Civil Laws from Oxford, in 1892 an honorary M.D. from Dublin. Especially noteworthy are the address he gave at the 7th International Medical Congress, London, 1881, on "Our Medical Literature," and his address before the British Medical Association in 1886, "Medicine in the United States, and Its Relations to Co-operative Investigation."

In 1895 Billings retired from the Army and went to Philadephia to become Professor of Hygiene at the University of Pennsylvania and Director of its laboratory of hygiene, which he had opened in 1892. In November 1895 his English and American friends held a great banquet in his honor, at which they presented him with a check for $10,000 and the Surgeon General announced that Billings's portrait was to be painted and hung at the Library. Just at that time he was offered the directorship of the New York Public Library, which had been formed earlier that year through a merging of the Astor Library, the Lenox Library, and the Tilden Trust. Billings remained in Philadelphia through spring 1896, then went to London as a delegate to the Royal Society's International Conference on a Catalogue of Scientific Literature. When he returned at the end of summer, he settled in New York, where he was to remain for the last 17 years of his life as Director of the New York Public Library.

In its emergent and as yet indeterminate state, the New York Public Library presented some heavy challenges. Billings set to work. He drew up a classification scheme; he reorganized the chaotic cataloguing situation and brought in a system that was much like that of the *Index-Catalogue,* with periodical articles carded among the books. He set up two miles of temporary wooden shelving in the Astor building and installed artificial lighting in both buildings. He successfully bargained for a site for a new building on the land occupied by the old Croton Reservoir at Fifth Avenue and 42nd Street. The cornerstone of the new building was laid in 1902 and the building opened to the public in May 1911. The staff was augmented and reorganized; the collections grew from 500,000 volumes in 1901 to over 1,000,000 in 1913; and the 40 branch libraries that Billings established held another million volumes.

In 1902 Billings was President of the American Library Association. From the founding of the Carnegie Institution of Washington in 1902 Billings served on its Executive Committee and from 1903 on as Chairman of its Board of Trustees. Between 1905 and 1908 Billings was engaged in drawing up plans for the Peter Bent Brigham Hospital in Boston.

On March 11, 1913, Billings died in New York City. He was buried at Arlington National Cemetery.

REFERENCES

Fielding H. Garrison, *John Shaw Billings, a Memoir* (1915).

Harry M. Lydenberg, *John Shaw Billings, Creator of The National Medical Library and Its Catalogue, First Director of the New York Public Library* (1924).

Dorothy Schullian and Frank B. Rogers, "The National Library of Medicine," *Library Quarterly* (1958).

Selected Papers of John Shaw Billings, compiled, with a life of Billings, by Frank Bradway Rogers (1965), contains a bibliography of Billings.

Phyllis Dain, "Billings, John Shaw," *Dictionary of American Library Biography* (1978).

FRANK BRADWAY ROGERS

Birkbeck, George
(1776–1841)

George Birkbeck was a "founding father" of the Mechanics' Institutes, which were the closest predecessors of public libraries in Britain.

He was born at Settle, North Yorkshire, on January 10, 1776. He came of a Quaker banking family but, having decided on a scientific career, was trained in what was then the only satisfactory medium, medicine. By the time he received his degree at the University of Edinburgh in 1799, he had rubbed shoulders with Walter Scott, Francis Jeffrey, and many of the other great literary figures then associated with "the Athens of the North." At the age of 23 he was appointed Professor of Natural Philosophy at the Glasgow Institution and began to lecture there on physics and chemistry.

The Glasgow Institution, which had been founded as a rival to the University of Glasgow, was functioning at the beginning of the 19th century as a kind of early technical college. Birkbeck was impressed by the keen interest in scientific and technical matters displayed by some of the *mechanics,* the skilled and semiskilled manual workers employed to make his medical apparatus, and he organized an eve-

George Birkbeck   Courtesy of The Newberry Library

ning class in elementary science for them. He moved to London, however, in 1804 and established himself there, not as a scientist, but as a medical man in general practice. That practice was soon fashionable and successful and included many of his distinguished neighbors, such as the Grotes, the Mills, and the Ricardos.

In the meantime, his class at the Glasgow Institution was kept going by his successor, Andrew Ure. It continued to flourish, and its members built up a small scientific library; in 1823 it was reestablished as a semiautonomous association, the Mechanics Class of the Glasgow Institution, which by head-and-tail abbreviation became known as the Mechanics' Institute. Birkbeck continued to be keenly interested and supported the movement to establish a similar institution in central London despite his earlier opinion that the lower standards of elementary education ill-prepared students for mechanics' classes. The London Mechanics' Institute, of which Birkbeck became and remained President until his death on December 1, 1841, started classes and began to accumulate a small scientific library in temporary premises. It then built its own new headquarters, but these proved much too ambitious for its finances, since its only income, apart from the gifts of a few wealthy benefactors, was from the small subscriptions of its members. Birkbeck himself lent nearly £4,000 toward the building fund. Thus, the library grew slowly and was heavily dependent on gifts.

The mechanics' institute movement spread rapidly; by the middle 1830s institutes had been established in such provincial towns as Birmingham, Dundee, Liverpool, Manchester, and Newcastle-upon-Tyne, and in other districts of London. The classes and library facilities, however limited, began to appeal more to middle-class than to working-class people. Subjects such as English grammar, elementary mathematics, and foreign languages were soon included in the London Institute's curriculum. Birkbeck continued his interest in the national expansion and visited many of the provincial institutes. By the time of his death there were institutes in many of the smallest towns and villages throughout the country. It was abundantly obvious, of course, that if those in the larger towns found financial viability difficult, the situation elsewhere was nearly hopeless. Dickens satirized small MIs in his *Uncommercial Traveller*.

Despite the continuing problems of the institutes, influential people in addition to Birkbeck continued to interest themselves in them, notably Lord Brougham and his Society for the Diffusion of Useful Knowledge. The Society was responsible for the publication of *A Manual for Mechanics' Institutes* in 1839, which was especially interesting and revealing because, following a careful survey of existing institutes, it included a model building plan with two rooms for a library. The library was to be systematically arranged and catalogued and satisfactorily administered with the aid of a model code of rules and regulations. Several paragraphs were devoted to the bookstock, and in these the risks of relying on gifts were suitably emphasized and the risks to readers relying on "miscellaneous perusal of books" suitably underlined. The fiction problem raised its ugly head as it has continued to do during the succeeding century and a half; the manual expressed the view that persistent novel reading was "an abuse of the library of a M.I." The select list of recommended subjects, authors, and titles appended nevertheless included some fiction, although no works by the questionable if standard 18th-century novelists such as Fielding, Richardson, Smollett, and Sterne. The nonfiction subjects and authors included were heavy, although a few lighter books on such perennially popular subjects as disasters at sea had managed to creep in. The MI's had always sought most assiduously to exclude any political or religious books that might be regarded as in any way controversial; most of their libraries must have been extremely dull places.

The available evidence suggests that by 1850, the beginning of the movement for public libraries supported by *rates* (local taxes) in Britain, only a small number of MI's had been able to build up bookstocks likely to attract many readers. There were happy exceptions; the Brontë sisters, for example, made good use of the library of nearly 2,000 volumes accumulated by the Keighley MI. Some of these MI's, with or without their bookstocks, were taken over by the early public libraries, and the debt of the latter to the former should not be underestimated.

Birkbeck's own pioneer institute in central London, popularly known as the Birkbeck Institute, grew finally, after a long period of stagnation, into Birkbeck College of the University of London. It has continued to provide evening classes and lectures, supported by a good library, for several generations of students employed during normal working time.

REFERENCES
T. Kelly, *George Birkbeck: Pioneer of Adult Education* (1957).
W. A. Munford, "George Birkbeck and Mechanics' Institutes" in C. B. Oldman and others, *English Libraries 1800–1850: Three Lectures Delivered at University College, London* (1958).

W. A. MUNFORD

Bishop, William Warner
(1871–1955)

Through his writings and speeches, William Warner Bishop furthered the adoption of enlightened practices in libraries and promoted ideals of technical performance, new in the early part of the 20th century but now taken for granted. He promoted international intellectual cooperation and, as an articulate advocate of cooperative and specialized acquisitions, union catalogues, and other forms of cooperation, he led his contemporaries in thinking of library adequacy for research on a regional and national basis.

Bishop was born on July 20, 1871, in Hannibal, Missouri. When his father, William Melancthon Bishop, died in 1878, his mother, Harriette Anna Warner Bishop, returned to her native Detroit with young Warner and his two sisters. Bishop attended the University of Michigan, where he earned the A.B. degree in classics in 1892 and the Master's degree a year later. He taught one year at Missouri Wesleyan College and one year at the Academy of Northwestern University before spending three years as Instructor of Greek and Assistant Librarian at Garrett Biblical Institute in Chicago.

A year at the American School of Classical Studies in Rome (1898–99) was followed by service as Li-

brarian and Latin teacher at the Polytechnic Preparatory School in Brooklyn (1899–1902) and five years at Princeton, first as Cataloguer (1902–05) and then as Reference Librarian (1905–07). At Princeton he began to mature professionally, laying foundations under the tutelage of Head Librarian Ernest Cushing Richardson for his later prominence in national and international library affairs. His professional growth continued (1907–15) during service as Superintendent of the Reading Room at the Library of Congress, then ably administered by Herbert Putnam.

From 1915 until he retired in 1941, Bishop was Director of Libraries at the University of Michigan. During his administration the library grew into one of the largest and best selected research collections in the country. His efforts in promoting library education culminated in 1926 in the formation of the Department of Library Science, which he administered as Chairman until 1941. A thorough scholar himself, Bishop insisted on a scholarly approach to education for librarianship at Michigan and elsewhere.

Bishop joined the American Library Association in 1896. He was Chairman of the Cataloging Section (1906–07) and of the College and Reference Section (1908–09; 1917–18); for five years beginning in 1912 he served on Council. These, along with some committee work, were his major ALA activities until he was elected President for 1918–19, the fifth academic librarian to serve in that capacity since formation of the organization in 1876. During his tenure the ALA War Service received much of his attention, but the end of World War I came during his year in office; the net effect of Bishop's presidency was a strong effort to set the stage for postwar organizational change and progress.

Having served as President comparatively early in his career, before the age of 50, Bishop had many years left to provide leadership in the ALA as a knowledgeable senior statesman. Chief among his assignments were those related to the international affairs of the organization, and for over two decades he played a multifaceted role in that realm. He was active in the 1920s on the Executive Board (as Chairman of the Subcommittee on Foreign Affairs), on the Committee on Library Cooperation with Other Countries, and in the planning groups concerned with the celebration in 1926 of ALA's 50th anniversary. He was Chairman of the Committee on International Relations (1926–34) and a committee member (1935–37), then consultant to the ALA Board on International Relations from 1942 to 1949. From 1928 to 1945 he was ALA's first representative in the International Federation of Library Associations, serving as President of IFLA (1931–36). He gave stimulating, responsive leadership to IFLA, both in the formation and conduct of the organization itself and in the action taken on matters that came before it for consideration.

Bishop saw in the entire area of international intellectual cooperation an opportunity and duty to influence library development worldwide, to diminish the influence of nationalism in the library field, to promote the pursuit of knowledge, and to advance research in the world at large. He did not, therefore, limit his efforts to ALA assignments with international import. At the request of League of Nations officials, he served on their Library Planning Com-

ALA
William Warner Bishop

mittee (1928–37). As a frequent adviser to the Carnegie Endowment for International Peace, the Carnegie Corporation, and the Rockefeller Foundation, he took part in a number of the international projects sponsored by those organizations in the 1920s, 1930s, and early 1940s. One of the most significant and interesting of his foundation activities resulted in his being the principal adviser to the Vatican Library in its reorganization and modernization, financed by the Carnegie Endowment for International Peace. Under his general direction, from 1927 through 1934, bibliographic records for the Vatican Library were planned and initiated, opening its great manuscript and printed-book collections for modern scholarship.

Throughout the United States significant improvements resulted from his work as Chairman of several advisory groups formed by the Carnegie Corporation to help selected college libraries with gifts of suitable books and by endowment of several college librarianships. From 1928 through 1943, Bishop headed advisory groups concerned with four-year liberal arts colleges, junior colleges, teachers colleges, Negro colleges, state colleges, and technological colleges. In all, grants totaling more than $2,000,000 were made. Out of the project grew the first qualitative standards for libraries in four-year colleges and junior colleges, as well as lists to be used for selection of basic books for collections in them. The body of doctrine on college libraries, inadequate in the literature of librarianship, was substantially increased. The books distributed under Bishop's guidance no doubt helped to raise standards of teaching in many institutions, to promote the development of reading habits among college students, and to inform college administrators of the real significance of their institutional libraries.

Bishop died in Ann Arbor, Michigan, on February 19, 1955, at the age of 83.

REFERENCES

Claud Glenn Sparks, "William Warner Bishop: A Biography," Ph.D. dissertation, University of Michigan, 1967. Includes complete bibliographies of sources of information about Bishop and of Bishop's writings.
Sparks, "Bishop, William Warner," *Dictionary of American Library Biography* (1978).
Sparks, *William Warner Bishop: A Tribute* (1941).
CLAUD GLENN SPARKS

Bliss, Henry
(1870–1955)

Henry Evelyn Bliss, a notable figure in library classification, was associated with the City College of New York for more than half a century. He devoted his life to the development, testing, and implementation of the Bibliographic Classification system (Bliss Classification). He wrote several significant works on library classification theory and practice and many journal articles. He was also Editor of the *Bliss Classification Bulletin.*

Bliss was born in New York City on January 29, 1870, the son of Henry Hale and Evelina Matilda Davis Bliss. The family lived for several years in New York and later at the Davis's New Jersey estate. Bliss settled in New York, where in 1901 he married Ellen de Koster (d. 1943), a teacher at Hunter College.

Bliss received no formal education until he was 15. He was educated at home by his mother, who taught him to read and write, and by governesses who taught him French, Latin, arithmetic, and grammar. Bliss entered the classics department of CCNY in 1885 but was dissatisfied with the program. In 1889, at his father's suggestion, he left college without finishing to pursue a business career.

For the next three years, he embarked on a variety of clerical positions in merchandising houses in New York. Following that, he taught school in New York until he accepted a position as Assistant Librarian at CCNY in 1892. Bliss had found his true vocation and began his life's work. He devoted the remaining 63 years of his life to librarianship and to library classification.

His work culminated in the Bibliographic Classification system, popularly known as the Bliss Classification. Bliss was a thoughtful and conscientious librarian and his ideas were carefully developed and constantly tested against the College's collection. Bliss was a contemporary of John Dewey, Charles A. Cutter, and S. R. Ranganathan, and of the development of their classification systems, but his aspirations and goals for library classification were different. Bliss saw relationships between things—and saw that the key to these relationships was classification. His classification system reflects a profound study of knowledge and library theory.

Bliss began working on his classification scheme in early 1900. He found none of the currently available classification systems adequate for his library's needs, so he proceeded to develop his own system. In 1908, when the College moved to its present location, Bliss had an opportunity to reclassify the entire collection using his Bibliographic Classification. In 1910 he published an article entitled "A Modern Classification for Libraries with Simple Notation, Mnemonics, and Alternatives," the first public description of his scheme. Over the next few years Bliss contributed articles to library literature while on leave from his position at the College. He presented some of his views on classification. His criticism of the Dewey Decimal Classification system, the most widely used system at the time, was considered shocking by some of his more conservative colleagues.

In 1928 he returned to active duty and was appointed Associate Librarian. In 1929 he published his theoretical work, *The Organization of Knowledge and the System of the Sciences,* which John Dewey lauded as "monumental." This laid the groundwork for his major publication in 1935 of *A System of Bibliographic Classification.* The two-volume work outlined the techniques for implementing the system, including instructions for using the main schedules and subdivisions. Bliss's work met with favorable response in the library community. Scholars called the classification system "truly impressive" and suggested that his work would help to establish librarianship as a true scholarly discipline. For the next 20 years, Bliss continued to develop, refine, and publish schedules to the classification scheme. He remained active at the College until he retired in 1940. His other activities at the College included the consolidation of several department libraries and work as coeditor of the *City College Quarterly.* He also published a small volume of his poems, *Better Late Than Never* (d1937). His finished classification scheme was published in 1953.

In early 1954 the *Bliss Classification Bulletin* was established to improve cooperation among libraries using the system. The *Bulletin* provides librarians with updated schedules and corrects some of the minor defects of the system. Bliss served as the first editor of the *Bulletin*, and his estate ensured the future of the publication.

The Bliss Classification scheme emphasizes a subject approach to information. The main outline of the scheme clusters topics under broad headings, then subdivides those headings hierarchically. It makes use of facet analysis and was one of the first systems to have alternative placements of some subjects. For this reason, it is considered one of the most flexible classification systems ever developed. Bliss favored short notation. The notation was designed so that book numbers rarely exceed four digits. A comprehensive index with more than 20,000 entries provides access to the main classes as well as to the subdivisions. This classification system compares most closely with the Library of Congress system, but has greater flexibility.

The Bliss Classification system has been used successfully in school, government, and special libraries, primarily in Britain and the Commonwealth. More than 80 libraries in Australia, Nigeria, and New Zealand use this scheme. The editorship of the *Bulletin* was continued in Britain. Many of the schedules have been updated and republished. An abridged edition of the system was published in 1967 for British school libraries.

Although the system continues to be used and updated, it is not included on LC or British Library MARC records. This is unfortunate because Bliss Classification may have interesting computer applications. In his late years, Bliss was intensely interested in computer applications of his classification system. Facet indexing, a major feature of the Bliss Classification system, is implicit in most, if not all, machine systems. Schedule revisions are being developed around many of the principles underlying the automated PRECIS system, which emphasizes subject access and has been proven to be easily manipulated by computer.

Bliss died in Plainfield, New Jersey, on August 9, 1955.

His major publications include *The Organization of Knowledge and the System of the Sciences* (1929), *A System of Bibliographic Classification* (1936), *The Organization of Knowledge in Libraries and the Subject Approach to Books* (1939), and *A Bibliographic Classification*, Vols. 1–4 (1940, 1947, 1952, 1953).

JULIE GLIENNA MUELLER

Bodley, Sir Thomas
(1545–1613)

Thomas Bodley, English diplomat, was the founder of the Bodleian Library of Oxford University. He wrote in his autobiography of the elements that made the establishment of the Library possible: knowledge of literature, ability to finance the project, friends for assistance, and the leisure in which to work. He had all of those elements under his control and established

Sir Thomas Bodley

Bodleian Library

the Library on a strong foundation that has allowed it to continue as a strong center of learning and research.

He was the son of John Bodley, a Protestant who fled to Germany and Switzerland during the reign of the Catholic Queen Mary I. The family lived among other Protestant refugees until 1558, when they returned to London. In 1559 Bodley entered Magdalen College, Oxford, where he was tutored by Lawrence Humphrey, another former Protestant refugee. Bodley earned his B.A. in 1563 and went on to Merton College, where he was elected Fellow and began lecturing in Greek and natural philosophy. In 1566 he received his M.A. and was elected a Proctor, a chief university administrative officer elected annually by colleges in rotation. He also acted as Deputy Public Orator.

Bodley's ambition was to be in state service, so he left Oxford in 1576 to become fluent in foreign languages. He traveled in Italy, France, and Germany for four years, then returned to England to accept an appointment at Court. Beginning in 1585 he was in the diplomatic service on missions to Denmark, Germany, and France, and in 1588 he became English Resident in the United Provinces. He retired in 1596 after gaining a high reputation for his service in Holland.

In 1598 Bodley wrote to the Vice-Chancellor of Oxford to explain his plan for restoring the former public library to use by the university. He rarely visited Oxford during his project but kept up a detailed correspondence with Librarian Thomas James, beginning in December 1599; they discussed, among other details, whether to chain books and how to combat woodworms, as well as more general topics such as classification and cataloguing. He also corresponded on questions of building and furnishing. Bodley acquired books through his public service contacts, including such men as the Earl of Dorset, Sir Walter Raleigh, Lord Hunsdon, and Lord Southampton, who contributed money for their purchase. The Earl of Essex contributed the Bishop of Faro's library, which he had seized in 1596 when he landed the English army in Portugal. Notable antiquarians and collectors, such as William Camden, Sir Robert Cotton, and Lord Lumley, gave gifts of manuscripts. Other manuscripts were received from ecclesiastical bodies, among them the Chapters of Exeter and Windsor.

The Library was also furnished with standing presses of a medieval pattern, similar to those in Merton College Library. (They are still in use.) By 1602 the original library room had been refurnished and housed books by major Protestant writers. On November 8, 1602, it opened to serve the University.

Bodley's great success in acquiring books for the Library led to a need for expansion. The year 1610 marked the opening of the Arts End extension, which Bodley supervised and financed. He also saw that there would be further need for book storage room, so he urged the University to restore the lecture rooms adjacent to the Library. On his death in 1613, Bodley left his fortune to the Library, in part to build the storage extensions he had proposed. The top floor of the Schools Quadrangle was the first to be completed, in 1620. It now contains the main series of reading rooms.

Bogle, Sarah
(1870–1932)

Sarah Comly Norris Bogle, Assistant Secretary of the American Library Association from 1920 to 1931, was an influential figure in the activities of the ALA, in library development overseas, and in the growth of library education.

She was born in Milton, Pennsylvania, on November 17, 1870, to John Armstrong Bogle, a chem-

Sarah Bogle

ALA

ical engineer, and Emma Ridgway Norris Bogle. Harrison Craver, in a tribute to her at the 1932 annual conference of the American Library Association in New Orleans, described her education as "the typical training then in vogue for women of leisure." This consisted of attendance at Miss Stevens' School in Germantown, Pennsylvania, and extensive foreign travel. She attended Drexel Institute Library School in Philadelphia, receiving a certificate of proficiency in 1904; that year she joined the American Library Association.

She began her library career as Librarian at Juniata College in Huntingdon, Pennsylvania, where she remained for three years. After another year of study she became a branch librarian for the Queens Borough Public Library. In spring 1909 she was invited by Craver to join the staff of the Carnegie Library of Pittsburgh, where she spent the next 10 years, first in a branch library, then as the Principal of the library school and as the chief children's librarian.

In 1920 she joined the staff of the ALA in Chicago and soon became Assistant Secretary to Carl Hastings Milam. Her work at Headquarters reflected her previous interests in library education and library services for children. Her writings also reflected these interests; of the 16 articles written by her and indexed in the first two compilations of *Library Literature* (1921–32 and 1933–35), over half express her thoughts and experiences in library education and her work as Secretary to the Temporary Library Training Board and its successor, the Board of Education for Librarianship. Sample titles are: "A Survey of the Library School Situation in the Southern States," "Training for Negro Librarians," "Trends and Tendencies in Education for Librarianship," and "Education of School Librarians in America." Two articles reflect her interest in children's library services: "The Child and the Book," and "A Conception of the Children's Librarian." Three relate her experiences as Director of the Paris Library School and her interest in the library movement in France: "The Fascination of the New Library Movement in France," "Library Development in France," and "The Future of the Paris Library School."

She traveled extensively, attending 18 ALA annual conferences and many state library association conferences, as well as library meetings abroad, such as those of the British Library Association and the British Institute of Adult Education. Besides her interest in library development in France, she conducted a survey of library needs for the Virgin Islands under a Carnegie Corporation grant in 1929 and represented ALA at the meetings of the International Library Committee in Stockholm in 1930.

At Headquarters Bogle was second in command to Milam and remained loyal to him and ALA. She had a special competence in supervising staff and dealing with people. Harold Brigham called her the "balance wheel" and the "power behind the throne." Milam called her his "tower of strength." Emily Danton said: "They were a great team during the twenties. Her vision and her personal connections, antedating her service at headquarters, must never be forgotten. She knew her way around in international relationships and she did much to help her younger chief gain background in these aspects of his work. They supplemented each other in many ways, and both were highly stimulating to their associates.''

Her special interests at ALA included the selection of staff; work with foundations, especially the Carnegie Corporation; education for librarianship; and the direction of the Paris Library School. In addition there was the daily routine of work at Headquarters.

Everett Fontaine, ALA publishing officer, described her as a grande dame—erect, well-groomed, with perfectly set blond-gray hair, and with a velvet or beaded band high up on her throat.

She served on the ALA Council (1917–20) and was a member of many library and educational groups, including the Association of American Library Schools (she was President, 1917–18), the Keystone State Library Association, the Pennsylvania Library Association, the Illinois Library Association, the Illinois Chapter of the Special Libraries Association, the American Library Institute, the American Woman's Association, the American Association for Adult Education, the National Education Association, and the Chicago Library Club (President 1922–23)

Bogle died on January 11, 1932, in White Plains, New York, and was buried in Milton, Pennsylvania. In 1951 she was selected by *Library Journal* for a "Library Hall of Fame for the 75th Anniversary" of the American Library Association.

REFERENCES

Harrison Warwick Craver, "Sarah C. N. Bogle: An Appreciation," *ALA Bulletin* (1932).
Emily Miller Danton, "Mr. ALA: Carl Hastings Milam," *ALA Bulletin (1959).*
Peggy A. Sullivan, *Carl H. Milam and the American Library Association* (1976).
Peggy A. Sullivan, "Bogle, Sarah Comly Norris," *Dictionary of American Library Biography* (1978).

DORIS CRUGER DALE

Bolivia

Bolivia, a republic in central South America, in bounded by Brazil on the north and east, Paraguay on the southeast, Argentina on the south, and Chile and Peru on the southwest and west. Population (1984 est.) 6,253,000; area 1,098,581 sq.km. The official language is Spanish.

National Library. The National Library— founded on June 23, 1821, by Mariscal Andrés de Santa Cruz and reorganized in 1938—is in Sucre, the official capital of the country (La Paz in the political capital). It houses about 150,000 volumes. The main part of the collection is made up of 19th-century publications. The National Archive, founded in 1883, is at the National Library. The National Depository Library is in La Paz and functions as the legal depository.

Academic Libraries. Libraries are located in all 10 Bolivian universities. During the colonial period the most important academic library was at the Universidad San Francisco Javier, founded in Sucre in 1624. It housed the Colonial Academy, founded in 1776, which provided much of the intellectual stimulus for the independence of Latin America.

The most important academic libraries are the Universidad Mayor de San Andrés, with 150,000 volumes, 1,300 current periodicals, 2,500 manuscripts, and a complete collection of the country's leading newspapers; and the Universidad Mayor de San Simón, with 45,000 volumes, 510 current periodicals, 800 dissertations, and 900 audiovisual materials. Collections in the other university libraries range from 10,000 to 35,000 volumes, with strengths in the humanities and the social sciences. Cataloguing in all the academic libraries is deficient because there are so few library school graduates in the country.

Public and School Libraries. In 1968 the Book Bank (Banco de Libro) was created to organize public and school libraries throughout the country. The Organization of American States began to provide technical assistance to the Book Bank in 1976 in its effort to establish a National Technical Processes Center in La Paz. In all, 55 branches of the Book Bank were founded throughout the country, with pilot centers in Sucre, Tarija, Cobija, and Trinidad. The branches serve both students and the general public. Book Bank branches are in each town's House of Culture, and cooperation between the local community and the Bolivian Institute of Culture is a necessary link in providing Book Bank services. Collections in the branches range from 800 to 1,500 volumes.

The largest public library in Bolivia is the Municipal Library in La Paz, founded in 1838 by Mariscal Andrés de Santa Cruz, with current holdings of

---

Libraries in Bolivia (1982)

Type	Administrative units	Service points	Volumes in collections	Annual expenditures (peso)	Population served	Professional staff	Total staff
National	1	--	150,000	61,000,000	60,000	1	10
Academic	17	--	220,000	20,000[a]	750,000[b]	1	70
Public and School[c]	70	--	345,000	--	1,000,000	2	72
Special[c]	15	--	450,000	--	75,000	3	48
Non-specialized	13	--	220,000	--	--	--	--

[a]Excludes expenditure for employees.
[b]Registered borrowers.
[c]1976 data.

Source: Universidad Boliviana, *Catalog General*, La Paz; Unesco, *Statistical Yearbook*, 1984.

90,000 volumes. The Municipal Library set up 12 branches in the poorer sections of the city. Another branch serves as a special library for the students at the Medical School at the Universidad Mayor de San Andrés, and a book bus serves the schools in zones without libraries.

A unique aspect of Bolivia's municipal library system is a procedure whereby bookstores pay their municipal taxes with books selected by staff of the municipal library in amounts equal in value to what the stores would have otherwise paid in taxes.

Special Libraries. Most of Bolivia's special libraries are located in La Paz. The largest is the Biblioteca de la Dirección General de Cultura, with a collection of about 130,000 volumes. Libraries are also found in the Documentation Center, Ministry of Mines and Hydrocarbons; Documentation Center, National Office of Standards and Technology, Ministry of Industry and Tourism; Military School; and Central Bank.

The Profession. The Bolivian Association of Librarians is headquartered in La Paz. Its members include both practicing librarians and students enrolled in the country's only library school, at the Universidad Mayor de San Andrés.

JULIO AGUIRRE QUINTERO*

Daniel J. Boorstin

Boorstin, Daniel J.

(1914–)

Daniel Joseph Boorstin, author and 12th Librarian of Congress, built a national and international reputation as a teacher, scholar, and historian with an attractive writing style and an army of fresh, provocative ideas.

Boorstin was born on October 1, 1914, in Atlanta, Georgia. When Boorstin was two his parents moved to Tulsa, Oklahoma, where his father, Samuel A. Boorstin, practiced law and the family prospered in the midst of the local oil boom. The precocious younger Boorstin also did well, excelling in academic studies at Tulsa Central High School. Largely at the prompting of his mother, Dee Olson Boorstin, who "was extremely ambitious for me," he entered Harvard in 1930. There his mentor was F. O. Mathiessen, internationally known professor of history and English literature. Boorstin wrote editorials for the Harvard *Crimson,* was elected to Phi Beta Kappa, and wrote a senior honors thesis on Gibbon's *Decline and Fall of the Roman Empire* that won the Bowdoin Prize. He was graduated *summa cum laude* in 1934.

The next three years he spent studying law in England as a Rhodes Scholar at Balliol College, Oxford, where he earned first-class honors in two degrees, a B.A. in jurisprudence in 1936 and a Bachelor of Civil Laws in 1937. In 1937 he returned to America as a Sterling Fellow at Yale Law School. He received a Doctor of Juridical Science degree in 1940 and was admitted to the Massachusetts bar in 1942. In the interim he began teaching American history and literature at Harvard; he published his first book, *The Mysterious Science of the Law,* in 1941.

After a few months as senior attorney in the U.S. Lend-Lease Administration in 1942, Boorstin returned to academe as Assistant Professor of History

at Swarthmore. Two years later he accepted an offer from the University of Chicago to join the faculty of an experimental interdisciplinary program in the social sciences. In the next 25 years his reputation as a scholar and writer grew, and he eventually became Preston and Sterling Morton Distinguished Professor of American History at Chicago.

Certain themes connect Boorstin's many publications. At the center is a conviction that the United States is unique because the social and political institutions it built over the centuries were a practical response to its peculiar environment, not to a set of abstract ideas that European countries experienced. This belief surfaces in *The Lost World of Thomas Jefferson* (1948) and *The Genius of American Politics* (1953), but finds its fullest development in a trilogy entitled *The Americans.* The first volume, subtitled *The Colonial Experience* (1958), concentrates on scores of previously slighted subjects in everyday life, including the "Culture" and "Decline of the Book," the "Rise of the Newspaper," and "The Publick Printer." *The Colonial Experience* won the Bancroft Prize in 1959. A second volume, subtitled *The National Experience* (1965), extends coverage from the Revolutionary to the Civil War. It received the Parkman Medal in 1966. The third volume, *The Democratic Experience* (1973), won the Pulitzer Prize for History in 1974.

Boorstin's return to this theme frequently led him to laud the entrepreneurial spirit evident in American history and to admire "the unprecedented opportunities" presented by American democracy. Conservative thinkers applaud this spirit. J. W. Lukacs, for example, once called Boorstin one of a "small but honorable group of principled, liberty-loving American thinkers who aim to restore American conservative cornerstones." But liberal thinkers often question his interpretations and criticize him for glossing over some of the sinister episodes in American history and undervaluing the power of ideology.

In *The Image* (1962), he argues that the mass media invent events and create illusions that rob Americans of the reality of national experience. In an essay entitled "The New Barbarians" (1968), he draws a distinction between *disagreement,* which he believes is a constructive way to reform society from within, and *dissent,* which he thinks is destructive of the consensus necessary to strengthen the nation. He criticizes dissenters for retarding rather than accelerating social progress. He openly criticized University of Chicago student anti-war demonstrators in 1968.

These views and actions did little to endear Boorstin to liberal critics, who also recalled his 1953 testimony before the House Un-American Activities Committee. When the Committee questioned him about a membership he had held in the American Communist Party in 1938 and 1939, he blamed youthful exuberance and a misplaced hope that the Soviet Union could check Nazi anti-Semitism. But the German-Soviet Non-Aggression Pact of 1939 had permanently soured him on Communism, he said. He also identified other people who were party members at the time and agreed with several committee members that active party members should not be allowed to teach in American schools and colleges because membership militated against intellectual freedom. "The most effective way to fight communism

. . . [and] the one effective way in which I may have some competence," he told the Committee, "is by helping people to understand the virtues of our institutions and their special values as these emerged from our history, and that I have tried to do."

In 1969 Boorstin left Chicago to become Director of the National Museum of History and Technology of the Smithsonian Institution. There he reconfigured an entire floor to consolidate a group of exhibits on printing, photography, and postal history into a coordinated "communications" display, then added a "news reporting" exhibit at the center. He also rebuilt the Hall of Numismatics and Medallic Arts and renamed it the Hall of Money and Medals. He pressed the Smithsonian to concentrate a Bicentennial display called "A Nation of Nations" on American pluralism, improved the museum's collecting policy and acquisitions procedures, and encouraged scholars to study museum objects. He expanded the museum's public services by reconstructing an old but still functional post office inside the Smithsonian and by negotiating an agreement with McGraw-Hill to fund and run the Smithsonian Bookstore. In 1973 he was appointed Senior Historian, which allowed him more time to research and write.

In the spring of 1975 President Gerald R. Ford asked Boorstin if he would accept a nomination as Librarian of Congress, a post recently vacated by the retiring L. Quincy Mumford. Boorstin asked for a month to think it over. While contemplating the offer, Boorstin visited the Library's Manuscript Reading Room, which coincidentally had an exhibit on the selection of previous Librarians of Congress. A letter from Felix Frankfurter to Franklin D. Roosevelt in 1939 caught Boorstin's eye. In response to FDR's question about whom he should pick to succeed Herbert Putnam, Frankfurter wrote, "What is wanted in the directing head of a great library [is] imaginative energy and vision. He should be a man who knows books, loves books, and makes books." Roosevelt picked poet Archibald MacLeish, who eventually became an excellent Librarian. The precedent was instructive. ". . . to be *the* Librarian, you don't have to be *a* librarian," Boorstin later concluded. On June 20, 1975, Ford nominated Boorstin to succeed Mumford.

The hearings on Boorstin's nomination were hardly routine. While many influential Congressmen supported Boorstin precisely because of his scholarly credentials and his desire to bring what he perceived as the best in American culture to a much wider audience, several important groups objected. The American Library Association argued that Boorstin did not have enough experience as an administrator and that the Library of Congress needed a professional librarian who understood the world of librarianship. Members of the Capital Area Council of Federal Employees, the American Federation of State, County, and Municipal Employees, and the Black Employees of the Library of Congress objected that Boorstin's past showed soft attitudes toward affirmative action. Since the Library had traditionally been slow to correct discriminatory hiring and promotion practices, they argued, Boorstin would not be an appropriate nominee. Others pointed to Boorstin's brief flirtation with Communism, his 1953 testimony before the House Un-American Activities Committee, and a Jack Anderson column accusing him of

misusing $65,000 in taxpayers' money for manuscript preparation on the last volume of his *Americans* trilogy. Since Boorstin owned the copyright, he was also awarded royalties, and thus the government had not been reimbursed, Anderson had charged.

Undaunted, Boorstin directly addressed all objections, emphasized his intention to be a full-time Librarian, and noted that he would probably continue to research and write in his free time. That he was sufficiently convincing, on the one hand, and that his credentials were a match for Congress's perceptions of what its Librarian ought to be, on the other, was obvious from Congressional reaction. The Senate's Committee on Rules and Administration unanimously reported the nomination to the Senate floor, where Boorstin was promptly confirmed on September 26, 1975, as the nation's 12th Librarian of Congress.

Librarian of Congress. Within months of becoming Librarian, Boorstin appointed a staff Task Force on Goals, Organization, and Planning, and supplemented it with eight outside advisory groups to review Library activities and recommend improvements. The groups reported a year later. In the interim Boorstin took several steps that forecast the direction he wished to take and that capitalized on the strength of his convictions and the influence of his scholarly contacts. He quickly opened the front doors to the Library and provided the public with direct access to the impressive Great Hall (where he had been sworn in) and replaced a guard's office with an orientation room. He placed tables on the Neptune Plaza in front of the Library and scheduled lunchtime cultural events to entertain visitors and staff. He also made the reference staff more accessible to users of the Library's domed Main Reading Room. He invited prominent members of the scholarly, publishing, and cultural communities to a series of formal dinners in the Great Hall to enlist their support as LC "ambassadors." He created a Council of Scholars to advise him on improving links with the scholarly world. In 1977 he persuaded Congress to authorize the Library to establish a Center for the Book to help concentrate more attention on the book's role in the process of communication. Since its creation, the Center has arranged various programs and seminars, promoted a series of "Read More About It" television spots after CBS television specials, sponsored an ABC cartoon character named O. G. Readmore, conducted a survey entitled "Books Make a Difference," and helped persuade the U.S. Postal Service to issue a commemorative stamp in 1984 that celebrated "A Nation of Readers."

Boorstin also altered the way in which the Library approached its holdings by promoting them as a "multimedia encyclopedia" and structuring lines of Library services to introduce users to all information formats within the Library's collections. He moved a substantial performing arts collection to Washington's Kennedy Center, inaugurated a series of traveling exhibits based on Library holdings, and expanded the LC publications list. Several of his proposals failed. He was not allowed to turn the LC Law Library into a subject department, and his recommendation that the Library move its foreign language collections to ethnic population centers around the nation was rejected for fear of damaging the Library's value as a central source for all types of materials. Another suggestion—to permit outside library access to databases created by the Congressional Research Service—was tabled; the technology was not yet sufficiently advanced.

It is still too early to measure Boorstin against his 11 predecessors at the Library of Congress. Some perceive his administrative style as arrogant, but most objections raised at the hearings on his nomination have quieted, and he formed working relationships with all communities vitally interested in the LC. In addition, he raised the institution's profile and forged new ties with scholars, cultural leaders, and various sectors of the communications industry. Problems remain, however. Perhaps the most serious is preventing further deterioration of LC materials printed on acid-bearing paper. Boorstin may not solve such problems, but he is addressing them. And at the same time he continues to research and write. *The Discoverers* (1983), a 700-page tome, became a best seller.

REFERENCE

United States Congress. Senate. Committee on Rules and Administration, *Nomination of Daniel J. Boorstin of the District of Columbia to Be Librarian of Congress* (1975).

WAYNE A. WIEGAND

Botswana

Botswana, a landlocked republic in southern Africa, shares its borders with South Africa on the south and southeast, Namibia on the west and north, Zambia on the north, and Zimbabwe on the northeast and east. Population (1984 est.) 1,047,000; area 581,700 sq.km. Major population concentrations are along the eastern escarpment, which has good communication links. The Kgalagadi (Kalahari) is dry and sandy; covered with grass and acacia thorn scrub, it occupies about 80 percent of the country and contributes to the poor communication links across the country and a library service that has concentrated on the densely populated areas. The official languages are English and Setswana.

History. The people of Botswana, then Bechuanaland, were first introduced to reading through the translation of parts of the Bible by Robert Moffat in 1826. In 1841 David Livingstone took 500 copies of the New Testament in the Tswana language to the country. The written literature of the Tswana, however, was produced only in the middle of the 20th century.

The first known reading room was provided by the London Missionary Society, in Serowe, probably for the use of students and converts. In 1938 the administration of the then Bechuanaland Protectorate asked the Carnegie Trust to establish libraries for Africans in the Territory, in keeping with its activities in neighboring South Africa. The Trust provided a grant of U.S. $1,000, which was used to finance the Travelling Library consisting of book boxes distributed to seven centers around the country. Each book box contained 25 titles, of which a third were reference and the rest were for loan. The service was free and was administered by the Education Department. The exchange of book boxes among the centers, which was supposed to take place every fourth month, ceased in 1941, though the service was not formally terminated until 1950.

From 1950 to 1963 there were many attempts to establish public library facilities. They failed because they lacked financial and administrative support. Libraries were available only in government departments or in schools and colleges.

Residents of Lobatse built and maintained a subscription library, and participants in the Operation Crossroad Scheme helped to build three public libraries, in Serowe, Mochudi, and Kanye, during the period.

The Government of Bechuanaland in 1963 requested assistance from the British Council, which prepared a blueprint for library development in Botswana. That plan was accepted and a financial commitment for capital, administration, and recurring book cost was also made.

National and Public Library Services. The Botswana National Library Services (BNLS) is both the national library and the national public library service. Its headquarters are in the capital, Gaborone. It was established by the National Library Service Act in 1967 and officially opened on April 8, 1968. BNLS is an administrative, planning, and advisory center for all matters connected with the development of library services in Botswana. The Administrative Section is responsible for policy formulation, financial

Libraries in Botswana (1982)

Type	Administrative units	Service points	Volumes in collections	Annual expenditures (pula)	Population served	Professional staff	Total staff
National*	1	17	221,957	573,320	39,477[a]	85	177
Academic	1	1	71,169	255,000[b]	1,684	14	37
Public*	--	--	--	--	--	--	--
School and Teacher[c] Training Colleges	1	11	4,000[d]	--	7,271	11	--
Special	4[e]	4	--	--	--	4	--

*Public libraries reported as part of national library.
[a]Registered borrowers only.
[b]Books and journals only.
[c]*Botswana: Education Statistics*, 1981.
[d]Average per institution.
[e]Excludes archives—one unit, 9,506 volumes, 700 shelf-meter files, six professional staff (eight total).

planning, and liaison with the Ministry of Home Affairs, under which library, archives, museums, and documentation services in the country fall. Under this Section are four Divisions. (1) The Technical Services Division is the acquisition, technical processing, and book allocation center for all branch libraries. (2) The External Services Division is responsible for the coordinated use of all collections in the 17 public branch libraries. It is also responsible for interlibrary loans and operates a postal service and a mobile library that services villages around Gaborone. (3) The School and College Libraries Division is responsible for library services to 12 educational institutions in the country and operates a book-box service that provides selected supplementary reading materials to a selected number of primary schools in five out of ten districts (1982). (4) The National Reference and Information Service Division has as its core collection legally deposited printed materials published or produced in Botswana as well as those titles published outside the country whose subject is or is related to Botswana. The latter are acquired through purchase. It incorporates the UN collection and specialized collections located in ministries and government departments. The Division compiles the triennial *National Bibliography of Botswana* (NABOB), first published in 1969.

The BNLS, though well organized, suffered from staff shortages at the supervisory professional level. The paraprofessional cadre, locally trained at the Department of Library Studies in the University of Botswana, increased to 30 in 1984 as compared to 18 in 1980.

Academic Libraries. The University of Botswana in Gaborone was inaugurated in October 1982, having been a college of the University of Botswana and Swaziland (1975–82) and of the University of Botswana, Lesotho, and Swaziland (1971–75). The Library supports four-year undergraduate programs in the humanities, sciences, education, and social sciences that include three years of a five-year law program. Master's programs in selected subjects have been introduced. The collection consisted of 71,000 volumes and 1,038 periodical titles for use by 1,300 readers and 218 academic staff in 1982 as compared to 55,659 volumes and approximately 400 periodical titles in 1980.

Within the university, but independent of the university library, is the Documentation Unit and Library of the National Institute of Development and Cultural Research. Its collection of 5,500 documents (1980) consists mainly of documents on social, economic, and cultural development relevant mainly to Botswana, and secondarily to southern African countries. It publishes a number of series: Working Papers, Research Notes, Working Bibliographies, and Seminar Proceedings.

The BNLS provides trained staff and professional advice for all school and college libraries. The establishment of librarian positions in each school, however, is dependent upon the priorities of the Ministry of Education, which administers and finances educational institutions. Out of a total of 46 schools and teacher training colleges, 12 had librarians in 1982. Thus most schools continue to utilize teachers of English as part-time librarians.

A few primary schools have libraries or book corners. Under the BNLS book-box scheme, books are selected and distributed by branch librarians while teachers are responsible for its operation.

Special Libraries. All libraries located in state-related organizations fall under this category. Previously ministerial or governmental departmental libraries serving specialized needs were included. The latter were incorporated in the National Reference collection. Special libraries are independent both financially and administratively. They are generally staffed with trained staff, most possessing nongraduate two-year diplomas. Most collections are in report and research paper format with selective reference collections.

The Profession. The Botswana Library Association was inaugurated in 1978 and its headquarters are in Gaborone. Membership is open to practising librarians, information specialists, students of librarianship, persons interested in libraries, and institutions. Its major aim is to develop libraries and protect the interests of librarianship. Individual members numbered 38 out of a total of 73 in the early 1980s. From 1979 it published, twice a year, the *Botswana Library Association Journal*.

All graduate professional librarians are trained outside Botswana, mainly in British institutions. In 1978 the then University College of Botswana established a library studies program which offers a nongraduate one-year certificate course and a two-year diploma program. The minimum entrance qualifications are a Cambridge Overseas School Certificate, with passes in three subjects including English, and at least one year of experience in library work.

There was no established program for continuing education in the mid-1980s. The National Library Service conducts workshops for selected staff from time to time.

REFERENCES
S. M. Made, *Reading—Library Facilities in Botswana*, F.L.A. thesis, University of Botswana, Lesotho, and Swaziland, Luyengo (1977).
Nick Moore, *Library and Information Manpower Needs: a Study of the Situation in Botswana* (British Council, 1984).
KAY RASEROKA

Bousso, Amadou A.

(1933–)

Amadou Alassane Bousso initiated and organized formal library education in Senegal and worked for professional training and support in other African countries.

He was born in 1933 at Kenel in the Senegal Valley to a family with a tradition of Islamic learning. His postprimary education was at the Ponty school, the only full teacher-training school for the whole of French West Africa, from which he was graduated in 1956. He then taught in primary and secondary schools in the Dakar area and attended Dakar University, where he took a degree in literature.

Appointed counterpart to the Unesco expert in charge of setting up EBAD (Ecole de Bibliothécaires, Archivists et Documentalistes) in 1963, he undertook 18 months of specialized studies in library science in France, Switzerland, Denmark, and England and was appointed Director of the Centre Régional de Formation de Bibliothécaires (CRFB, 1963–1967) and then Director of EBAD, which replaced the Centre (1967–81). The school was intended to address the need for trained librarians in former French colonies of Africa; before independence, none had been trained locally or overseas. It first took as students existing library personnel, most of whom had certificates for four years of secondary school education, which was the level Africans were usually allowed to reach, and some younger trainees with full secondary schooling. The first program crammed training into one school year. Bousso participated in a number of international meetings and traveled extensively in other countries, persuading a number of governments to send students to the school and urging them to organize the profession of librarianship so that the graduates could find suitable posts on returning home. His work proved difficult because library support by various governments often lagged.

EBAD in 1979 offered a two-year course and annually enrolled 50 or more pupils with full secondary education. It became part of Dakar University, was housed in handsome new buildings, and, more important, established a full-time staff of teachers. A Master's degree course was available in the mid-1980s.

Bousso chaired various national commissions on library science, archives, and documentation, and held numerous international positions before being appointed to Unesco, where he became Assistant to the Director of the General Information Programme. Chairman of the African branch and Chairman of the Division of Regional Activities of the International Federation of Library Associations and Institutions (IFLA), Chairman of the Committee on Professional Training and Education of the International Council on Archives (ICA), and a member of the Management Committee for the Prix Noma du Livre Africain, he often acted as adviser to African states in the development of their national information policy.

He wrote a sociological study on the Toucouleur family and various articles on library science and technical reports for Unesco, the Association of Partially or Wholly French-Language Universities (AUPELF), and IFLA.

F. LALANDE ISNARD

Bowker, R. R.

(1848–1933)

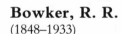

Richard Rogers Bowker, Publisher and Editor of *Library Journal* and *Publishers' Weekly*, was noted as a friend of libraries and as a political reformer.

He was born September 4, 1848, in Salem, Massachusetts, to proper and prosperous parents, Daniel and Theresa Maria Savory Bowker. The panic of 1857 brought business reverses to his father, who was never really successful afterward despite a move to New York City and several attempts to start again. Before Rogers was 20, he provided the main financial support for his mother, father, and younger sister, Carolyn.

Bowker enrolled as a student at the Free Academy in New York City in 1863; it became the City College of New York before he graduated in 1868. He had an excellent academic record and formed several lasting friendships. For a while he operated single-handedly one of the first student newspapers in the country and was influential in establishing one of the earliest student government organizations. Neither of these enterprises found favor with the college administration; when Bowker helped start a chapter of Phi Beta Kappa, the President of the College prevented the young activist's membership.

Bowker's experience in operating the student newspaper led directly into one of his several careers. While he was still in college, he reported some events for the New York *Evening Mail* and he began working full-time for that paper on the day after his commencement. He became Literary Editor of the *Mail* in 1870; as one of the many pieces he wrote for outside papers and periodicals, he contributed a series of articles reviewing American literature in 1871 that appeared early in 1872 in Frederick Leypoldt's *Publishers' and Stationers' Weekly Trade Circular* and in the third edition of Leypoldt's *Annual American Catalogue*. The *Weekly Trade Circular* became *Publishers' Weekly* in 1873 with Bowker as part-time Assistant; he began to work on it full-time in 1875 and bought it from Leypoldt in 1878. He owned *PW* until his death, exercising varying degrees of editorial control through the years, and was listed as its Editor for most of his life.

In his early years Bowker was intensely interested in the contemporary literary scene. Since many authors and publishers were his friends, he was deemed the perfect choice when the Harper firm needed a representative in London to make contacts with British authors and to launch a transatlantic version of *Harper's Magazine*. He spent two happy and successful years in England, from 1880 to 1882, but wished to come home for many reasons; he missed his family, his friends, and the chance to take part in liberal political movements.

One of his favorite causes was closely related to his work in the book world: the movement for international copyright. Bowker's innate sense of fairness and his lifelong habit of expressing his convictions through actions made it natural for him to support this cause through the pages of *Publishers' Weekly*, through his position as Chairman of the Executive Committee of the American Copyright League, and through continual efforts at personal persuasion. He was perhaps as influential as any other individual in obtaining the copyright acts in 1891 and 1909.

It is difficult to determine when Bowker first became interested in libraries. Leypoldt's *Publishers' and Stationers' Weekly Trade Circular* had carried some news of libraries before Bowker's association with the firm, and *Publishers' Weekly* continued this practice after Bowker became a member of its staff. He joined Leypoldt and Melvil Dewey in 1876 in establishing the *Library Journal* and in the planning that preceded the meeting at which the American Library Association was formed.

The *Library Journal* lost money regularly in the early years, partly because Dewey, its Editor, had struck a hard financial bargain, demanding 20 percent of gross receipts from subscriptions and advertisements. Publishing the periodical was a great nuisance to Leypoldt and Bowker because Dewey was dilatory and careless. Bowker, however, continued to support the library movement, keeping the *Library Journal*

R. R. Bowker

alive after Dewey's departure in 1881 and Leypoldt's death in 1884. Bowker wrote editorials and articles for *LJ* throughout his life; they were always informative, positive in tone, and sometimes quite laudatory of good works. Typical of the articles are "The Work of the Nineteenth-Century Librarian for the Librarian of the Twentieth" (September–October 1883), in which he saw the librarian as a liberator rather than a keeper of books; "The Formation and Organization of Public Libraries" (March 1887), in which he demonstrated a good knowledge of library legislation and suggested some practical ways to start a public library; "Making the Most of the Small Library" (March 1915), practical advice on the operation of a public library too small to hire a professional librarian; and "Women in the Library Profession," a three-part article in 1920, in which he pointed out gains made by women in the profession and described the contributions of a number of leading women librarians.

Bowker's friendship for libraries was expressed in another way: he was an active member of the ALA, serving on the Council for more than 20 years and as Chairman of the Committee on Public Documents for some time. He refused the presidency of the Association three times, believing that a librarian should hold the post, but was made Honorary President when he was in his seventies.

He promoted the welfare of several individual libraries in a number of ways. He was one of the two people who were most influential in persuading President McKinley to appoint Herbert Putnam as Librarian of Congress and later gave several thousand dollars to the LC Trust Fund. In Brooklyn, where he lived for many years, he worked hard in the movement that culminated in the formation of the Brooklyn Public Library in 1902; he then served as one of its trustees until his death. He was also President of the Library Association in Stockbridge, Massachusetts, where his summer home was located, from 1904 until 1928. He wrote articles for the *Library Journal* about the work of public library trustees.

Bowker's bibliographic work also helped libraries. He carried on Leypoldt's *Publishers' Weekly* and *American Catalogue* and inaugurated a few bibliographic enterprises of his own, most notably three features added to the *American Catalogue* that he felt were needed by librarians: a list of federal government publications (1885), a list of society publications (1885), and a list of state publications (1891). But Bowker was not the innovative bibliographer that Leypoldt had been, nor was he in his later years as inventive and as quick to sense the needs of librarians as was his younger rival, H. W. Wilson.

Perhaps Bowker did not change or develop his bibliographical work further because throughout his life his basic interest had been broadly humanitarian, not bookish and bibliographic, and he directed much of his tremendous energy into fighting bravely and intelligently for almost every liberal cause. He was a part of a small group of men who founded the "Mugwumps," a liberal group in the Republican Party, though he may not have been, as some have said, *the* founder of that movement. He fought against corrupt politicians and for civil service. A supporter of tariff reform, he felt that existing U.S. tariffs protected special interests at the expense of the public. His concern for the welfare of mankind in general led him to oppose imperialistic and militaristic tendencies in the government. He also worked for the benefit of minorities within the United States. He wrote articles strongly advocating the establishment of settlement houses, vigorously opposed tendencies toward anti-Semitism at City College, gave generously to colleges for blacks, and opposed the persecution of conscientious objectors in World War I.

Bowker held liberal, humanitarian views about the conduct of business and put them into practice. He believed that owners and managers should voluntarily hold down profits and should show concern for their employees and for consumers. He accepted the position as Executive Officer of the Edison Electric Illuminating Company in New York in 1890 partly in order to put his ideas about the proper conduct of a business into practice on a larger scale than he could at the *Publishers' Weekly* office. For a while he was successful, managing to reduce the cost of electricity to consumers while raising wages and paying a fair return to stockholders, but he resigned in 1899 when a group of stock manipulators, planning to establish a monopoly, managed to gain control of the company.

When Bowker left Edison, he was beginning to have serious eye trouble, and he became completely blind in a few years. His failing sight would have prevented him from giving close personal supervision to the development of new bibliographic or indexing services, a situation that may have prevented the diversification of the Bowker Company's services during his later life.

Around the time Bowker was adjusting to the loss of his eyesight, he surprised his friends by marrying Alice Mitchell on New Year's Day, 1902, when he was 53 and she was 38. The couple had known each other for several years.

Although Bowker had lost his sight, his general health was good, and his concern for other human beings was undiminished; for many years he wrote and spoke in favor of a variety of causes. He remained active until November 12, 1933, when he died, after a short illness, at the age of 85. At the time of his death, Herbert Putnam surely expressed the feeling of librarians when he wrote in the special December 1, 1933, issue of *Library Journal,* "Our profession has had no friend who, without the professional obligation, has aided so greatly to define its aims, maintain its dignity, and promote its fellowship."

REFERENCE

E. M. Fleming, *R. R. Bowker, Militant Liberal* (1952), is an excellent book-length biography of Bowker. The largest depository of Bowker's manuscripts is in the New York Public Library; others are listed in the bibliography of the Fleming volume.

HAYNES McMULLEN

Bradford, S. C.

(1878–1948)

Samuel Clement Bradford, British librarian and writer on the classification of scientific literature, was a supporter of moves to improve the control of scientific and technical information and contributed to the development of the field of documentation.

Bradford was born in London, England, on January 10, 1878. He trained as a chemist, and a former colleague related that Bradford obtained his degree by study at night school and his doctorate by research in his office in the Science Museum Library. He was fond of roses, and sandwiched between his many writings on chemistry and documentation was a book on the science of roses.

He joined the staff of the Science Museum in 1899 and worked in its library from 1901 until his retirement in 1938, becoming Assistant Keeper in 1922, Deputy Keeper in 1925, and Keeper in 1930. During his tenure he devoted his vision and energy to turning the Science Museum Library into the National Science Library. D. J. Urquhart observed that his great achievement was that he managed to change a small scientific library into the largest collection of scientific literature in Europe.

Bradford enthusiastically supported the adoption of the Universal Decimal Classification (UDC) throughout the world, with a view to the production of a world bibliography, and is well remembered for his advocacy of UDC as superior to any other system of classification and to alphabetical systems. He introduced UDC into the Science Library and was a keen supporter of the International Institute of Bibliography, later to become the International Federation for Documentation (FID). Largely to further the use of UDC, Bradford formed, in 1927, with A. F. C. Pollard, the British Society for International Bibliography (BSIB) as the British Committee of FID, and BSIB became one of the main channels of communication about UDC in Britain. He edited the *Proceedings of the British Society for International Bibliography* from its inception in 1939 until the amalgamation of BSIB with Aslib (then the Association of Special Libraries and Information Bureaux) in 1948. He followed Pollard as President of BSIB in 1945 and was elected a Vice-President of FID and Chairman of its International Committee on Classification in 1947.

One of the reasons for Bradford's strong support of UDC was his concern that scientific literature should be fully documented and well organized. In *Documentation* (1948), he refers to experiments conducted at the Science Library that showed that less than half the useful papers published were being covered by abstracting journals. He then investigated the manner in which articles on one subject would often appear in periodicals not primarily concerned with that subject. He deduced a common pattern in this "bibliographical scatter," which led to the formulation of Bradford's "Law of scatter." "Bradford's Law" has received a great deal of attention from writers on scientific documentation—too much, according to Bradford's successor, Urquhart, who wrote, "Bradford's Law . . . was but a small element in his propaganda war," and suggested that "Bradford would be appalled by the academic discussion which has taken place about his law. He was interested in much more practical things."

Bradford published 35 contributions to documentation, but he also wrote many papers on chemistry and other scientific subjects. He will be best remembered by librarians as a writer for the collection of essays published as *Documentation*, which Margaret Egan, reviewing the book in *Library Quarterly* (1950), said "should be useful in directing the attention of American librarians to the importance of bibliographic control in some form and the need for further investigation of this neglected aspect of librarianship." The conclusion to her review showed that Bradford was human and that he did not always practice what he preached: "One cannot conclude, however, without expressing surprise that Mr. Bradford, who argues so convincingly for more adequate indexing services, should be so inconsiderate as to give us this book without an index, organized according to either the UDC or even the abhorred concealed classification of subject headings." It is interesting to note that an index *was* provided for the reprint, published five years after Bradford's death, to which Egan and Jesse Shera contributed a 35-page introductory essay calling for librarianship and documentation to be regarded as a unity.

Urquhart remarks that Bradford seemed to him at first "a very fussy man." The official support given to the National Lending Library for Science and Technology (now incorporated in the British Library Lending Division) owed a great deal to the pioneering propaganda efforts of Bradford, and Urquhart observes, "That to me is how Bradford should be remembered—as one who sought to convince others of the importance of scientific information and who did a great deal despite the odds against him to make scientific information available. The fussy little man I once met was really a giant in disguise."

REFERENCES
E. M. R. Ditmas, "Dr. S. C. Bradford," *Journal of Documentation* (1948).
D. J. Urquhart, "S. C. Bradford," *Journal of Documentation* (1977). M. Gosset, "S. C. Bradford, Keeper of the Science Museum Library 1925–1937," *Journal of Documentation* (1977).

K. G. B. BAKEWELL

Bray, Thomas
(1658–1730)

Because of his own activities and those of the societies he founded, Thomas Bray was one of the greatest single cultural influences at work in the American colonies during the 18th century.

He was born in Marton, Shropshire, England, in 1658. Edward Lewis, Vicar of the nearby town of Chirbury, noticed Bray's aptitude for learning and made available his notable collection of chained books. Through Lewis's influence, Bray's parents sent him to Oswestry Grammar School. He matriculated at All Souls College, Oxford, in 1674 as a *puer pauper,* supporting himself through service to the fellows, and receiving his Bachelor of Arts degree in 1678. He later took Bachelor of Divinity and Doctor of Divinity degrees from Magdalen College.

Bray's first appointment was to a parish near Bridgnorth, Warwickshire, in 1681. A few months later he was asked to preach the annual assize sermon. One of the members of the congregation was Simon, Lord Digby. Impressed with the young priest's presentation, he persuaded his brother, William, to offer Bray the parish of Over Whitacre. In 1690 William presented Bray with the living at Sheldon, which he continued to hold until his death, although an appointed curate actually served the parish for over 25 years while Bray labored in London on his various schemes.

Through his friendship with the Digbys, Bray came to the notice of Bishop Compton of London, who had been concerned for some time with the lack of spiritual leadership in the colonies. He had appointed James Blair as Commissary of Virginia in 1689, and in 1696 he offered Bray a comparable position in Maryland.

Bray, who was concerned with the intellectual as well as the spiritual life of the colonists, developed a scheme to provide libraries for all the parishes of Maryland; he agreed to accept the position if Compton would support his plan. With Compton's approval, he began collecting books and interviewing missionaries for service in the colony. He was so successful that Governor Nicholson suggested Compton appoint Bray Commissary for New York, Pennsylvania, and New England as well.

At the start, Bray's primary concern was for Maryland, but as he began to hear from ministers in the New World about the lack of books in other colonies, he expanded his plan to provide libraries for each of the colonies. By 1697, 16 libraries had been established in Maryland and 7 in the other colonies, and plans were under way for 6 more.

In his *Bibliothecae Americanae Quatripartidiae,* Bray outlined his colonial library system. A large provincial library would be established in the major city of each colony. A parochial library would be established in each parish. And a layman's library would be comprised of certain religious books that would be loaned by the minister. A number of tracts would be given free to the people.

When he presented his final report on the libraries to the Society for the Propagation of the Gospel in Foreign Parts in 1704, Bray could claim the establishment of provincial libraries in Boston, New York, Philadelphia, Annapolis, Charleston, and Bath, North Carolina. He had provided 29 parochial libraries for Maryland and at least one such library in each of the other colonies, as well as providing more than 35,000 volumes for the layman's libraries in all the colonies.

Some of Bray's library ideas were surprisingly modern. In his *Memorial to the Clergy of Maryland,* published in 1700, he outlined two ideas for increasing and preserving the libraries. First, each library would provide a catalogue of its collection to the others so that they might exercise a primitive system of interlibrary loan. Second, a small annual subscription would be assessed on the borrowers to enlarge the collections.

Given his personal involvement in establishing libraries, it is certain that had Bray been able to return to America, he would have promoted their growth and development. Because he could not return, they were left to struggle on their own. Without support and encouragement from the colonists, they gradually diminished as an intellectual force in the life of the people.

In addition to providing libraries and missionaries for the colonies, Bray steered a bill through Parliament for the establishment of the Church of England in Maryland. At the same time, in order to further his library plans, he founded the Society for the Promotion of Christian Knowledge, the Society for the Propagation of the Gospel in Foreign Parts, and the Bray Associates. The Act of Establishment of the Church remained in force throughout the colonial period, and the societies still exist today, active in missionary enterprise, publishing, and education.

Bray died in London on February 15, 1730. Although Bray had the satisfaction of seeing legislative protection given to libraries in three colonies during his lifetime, he failed in his attempts to secure public support for their growth and continued development. Nearly a century and a half had to pass before the support necessary for the growth of the library as a public institution would develop. Had he lived in the 19th century, Bray would have been one of the driving forces in that development.

REFERENCES

Charles T. Laugher, *Thomas Bray's Grand Design* (1973).
Henry Thompson, *Thomas Bray* (1954).

CHARLES T. LAUGHER

Brazil

Brazil, a federal republic, is the largest country in South America. It is bordered on the north, east, and south by every South American country except Chile and Ecuador; the Atlantic Ocean borders on the west. Population (1984 est.) 135,564,000, area 8,512,000 sq.km. The official language is Portuguese.

History. The first libraries in Brazil were school libraries, maintained by the Jesuits in the schools they founded in São Vicente (1550), Rio de Janeiro (1567), and Bahia (1568). The most important was that of Bahia, which had European librarians. One of them was a Portuguese-Brazilian author, Father Antônio Vieira. Another important school library was that of the Seminary of Olinda, founded by Bishop Azeredo Coutinho in 1798, which both educated future priests and admitted the lay elite.

The Royal Library (now the National Library of Rio de Janeiro) was founded in 1810. When Portugal was invaded by Napoleon's armies in 1807, the Portuguese King, Don João VI, transferred the royal court to Brazil and settled in Rio de Janeiro in 1808. During that year various centers of higher education, together with the Royal Press, were established.

Even before the Royal Library opened to the public in 1814, a public library was inaugurated in the state of Bahia in 1811, modeled along the lines of the subscription public libraries that arose in the United States and in England in the 18th century. During the 19th century 12 other Brazilian states followed that model and opened public libraries.

By the beginning of the 20th century, most state capitals and various smaller cities had opened libraries. An important movement of the 1930s was the creation of a Department of Culture, which attempted to combine libraries with cultural services, particularly children's libraries and music libraries. Brazil followed the tradition of constructing large libraries in imposing cultural centers in major cities, (like the Pompidou Centre in Paris). In 1982 one such cultural complex was opened in São Paulo, which includes three libraries. Library activity in Brazil in the 1980s emphasized library and information system automation and the establishment of a national program for interlibrary bibliographic exchange.

Pedro Lobo

Periodicals collection at the National Library, Rio de Janeiro.

National Libraries. Brazil has two national libraries: the National Agricultural Library in Brasília was established at the end of 1978; the other is much older, and like many national libraries originated as a royal library and is made up of many collections. The Royal Library began with a collection of books and manuscripts that had been brought from Portugal and numbered more than 60,000 volumes. When Don João VI returned to Portugal, leaving his son Don Pedro as Prince Regent of Brazil, the cultural and educational institutions, including the Library, remained in Rio de Janeiro.

In 1822 the Portuguese Prince Regent himself, guided by José Bonifácio de Andrade e Silva, declared Brazil's independence, and the Library became the property of the Brazilian government. In 1825 it became known as the Imperial and Public Library; since 1878 its official title has been the National Library of Rio de Janeiro. When the last emperor, the scholarly Don Pedro II, left Brazil after the proclamation of the Republic, he donated his personal collection of some 50,000 volumes to the National Library.

Throughout its history the National Library has enriched its holdings and has undergone various reforms to adapt itself to the advances in library science. The Library's holdings include approximately 3,6000,000 volumes, 650,000 manuscripts, 40,000 periodicals, 100,000 musical scores, 200,000 iconographic pieces, and 60,000 volumes of rare books.

The Library has received financial aid from government agencies, Unesco, and the Ford Foundation. The Library receives, as the legal depository in Brazil since 1847, all publications printed in the country and issues semiannually, in its *Boletim Bibliográfico,* the current national bibliography. Recent volumes of the *Boletim Bibliográfico* are computer-produced through an agreement between the National Library and the Center for Informatics of the Ministry of Education and Culture (CIMEC). The National Library also acts as the Brazilian agency for the International Standard Book Number (ISBN).

Academic Libraries. Higher education in Brazil began rather late in comparison with other Latin American countries; students usually attended the University of Coimbra or French universities. It was only during the second decade of the 19th century that schools of higher education were founded in Brazil: two Law Schools (in São Paulo and Olinda), two Schools of Medicine (Rio de Janeiro and Bahia), and one Polytechnic School (Bahia). The first university was created by the federal government in Rio de Janeiro in 1920. In 1934 São Paulo established the first state university. Almost without exception their library collections and technical processes are decentralized, and duplication arises from such a system.

The University of Brasília, maintained by a foundation, was established in 1962 and has only one centralized library, thus avoiding the duplication that occurs in the majority of the other libraries. The library possesses 500,000 volumes and 7,080 periodicals and is open to the public 23 hours a day. Its modern building was constructed with funds from the Interamerican Development Bank at a cost of $1,500,000 and with a capacity of 1,000,000 volumes. The example of the University of Brasília was a model for newer institutions, such as the Federal University of Paraíba, that have centralized library administration and collections.

Libraries in Brazil (1979)

Type	Administrative units	Service points	Volumes in collections	Annual expenditures (cruzeiro)	Population served	Professional staff	Total staff
National[a]	1	--	3,574,623	--	94,714	154	360
Academic	1,029	--	11,496,000	--	--	1,725	6,160
Public[a]	2,333	--	13,894,006	--	13,240,561	--	6,859
School	9,479	--	14,495,000	--	3,628,273	817	14,883
Special	572	--	10,513,012	--	3,745,259[b]	--	2,534

[a]1974 data.
[b]Registered borrowers.

Source: Unesco, *Statistical Yearbook,* 1984; *Annuário Estatístico do Brasil*; Director of the National Library (Rio de Janeiro).

Public Libraries. Public libraries in Brazil are all state libraries with the exception of the Municipal Library of São Paulo, founded in 1925. This public library—today called the Mario de Andrade Library, in honor of one of the greatest Brazilian authors—became one of the best libraries of its kind in Latin America. Recognizing this, Unesco chose São Paulo in October 1951 as the site of the Conference on the Development of Public Library Services in Latin America. The reorganization of the Municipal Library of São Paulo was accomplished by the faculty members and students of an American oriented course in library science sponsored by the College of Sociology and Political Science. This framework also influenced the reorganization of the old public libraries in the states of Maranhão (1947) and Paraná (1954); they are considered among the best of their kind in Brazil.

In 1977 the National Book Institute began the National System of Public Libraries, comprising the states of Pernambuco, Minas Gerais, Ceará, Rio Grande do Sul, and the Federal District. The system was created through a pilot project in Pernambuco with financial support from Unesco to improve library services outside major cities. By the early 1980s, about half of the state libraries had joined this system.

School Libraries. The early tradition of the development of school libraries did not continue into the modern era. Although the Ministry of Education and Culture adopted a priority policy to improve primary education, there were still very few adequate school libraries in the educational system in the early 1980s. For the most part, schoolchildren use the local public library as their school library. Only a very small number of well-equipped schools have significant collections.

Special Libraries. Some of the most important special libraries in the country are in the universities since they are connected with schools of medicine, engineering, and agronomy. The Regional Library of Medicine (BIREME) is a Latin American subsystem of the National Library of Medicine of the United States. BIREME is maintained in São Paulo by the São Paulo School of Medicine, in cooperation with the World Health Organization and the Pan American Health Organization. With subcenters in several Brazilian universities, it maintains an efficient biomedical information system. The Oswalde Cruz Institute Library, maintained by the Federal University of Rio de Janeiro, possesses the country's largest collection of periodicals in the biomedical sciences.

In the agricultural sciences there is a national system for agricultural information administered by the Brazilian Agency for Technical Assistance and Rural Extension (EMBRATER); it is a component of such international systems as the International Information System for the Agricultural Sciences and Technology (AGRIS). Begun in 1975, under an agreement between the Ministry of Agriculture and FAO, this system gave rise to the founding of the National Agricultural Library (BINAGRI) at the end of 1978. It also introduced SDI (Selective Dissemination of Information) services to Brazil. The special libraries form a network coordinated by the Brazilian Institute for Information in Science and Technology (IBICT), which maintains, among other services, a national union catalogue of books and periodicals.

The Profession. The São Paulo Librarians Association, founded in 1938, was the first in the country. There are 14 librarians' associations, most of them at the state level, and the one municipal association is in São Paulo. In 1959, on the occasion of the Second Brazilian Congress of Library Science and Documentation, the Brazilian Federation of Librarians' Associations (FEBAB) was founded, with headquarters in São Paulo. FEBAB works through permanent commissions for public and school libraries, documentation in agriculture, biomedical sciences, law, and technology, and technical processes. At Belo Horizonte in 1967 the Brazilian Association of Schools of Library Science and Documentation (ABEBD) was founded to work toward the improvement of library education.

Library science and documentation in Brazil are served by four primary publications: *Ciência da Informação* (IBICT, 1972–, semiannual); *Revista da Escola de Biblioteconomia da UFMG* (Federal University of Minas Gerais, 1972–, semiannual); *Revista Brasileira de Biblioteconomia e Documentação* (FEBAB, 1973–, quarterly); and *Revista de Biblioteconomia de Brasília* (Federal District Librarians' Association and Department of Library Science of the University of Brasília, 1973–, semiannual). There is an additional irregular publication, the *Bibliografia Brasileira de Documentação,* published by IBICT.

REFERENCE

Edson Nery da Fonseca, *A biblioteconomia brasileira no contexto mundial* (1979).

Bibliotecas brasileiras (Rio de Janeiro, Fundação Instituto Brasileiro de Geografia e Estatística/Instituto Nacional do Livro, 1980).

Cavan M. McCarthy, "Achievements and Objectives in Brazilian Librarianship," *International Library Review* (1983).

EDSON NERY DA FONSECA*

Brett, William Howard
(1846–1918)

William Howard Brett was librarian of the Cleveland Public Library and a library educator. Few librarians, even among that remarkable group who were his contemporaries, displayed more virtuosity or made more contributions to disparate parts of the profession than Brett.

Brett was born in Braceville, Ohio, on July 1, 1846. Shortly after his birth the family moved to the banks of the Mahoning River in Warren. There as a boy he frequented the bookshop of William Porter, who by example and counsel influenced his choice of career. Brett attended public schools in Warren and became the school librarian in the Warren High School at the age of 14. He enlisted and fought with Ohio infantry in the Civil War before entering the University of Michigan and later Western Reserve University (Cleveland), but was forced by poverty to abandon his academic studies.

Brett settled in Cleveland. He worked for a Cleveland bookdealer, Cobb and Andrews Company, and expanded his acquaintanceship among bibliophiles, including John Griswold White, who was instrumental in appointing him Librarian of the

ALA

William Howard Brett

Cleveland Public Library in 1884.

Brett soon distinguished himself for his contributions to cataloguing in the traditions set by Cutter and Dewey. By 1890 he was developing the concept of the open-shelf library, which led among other things to his being invited to London to deliver a paper on his ideas of free access to library collections.

Brett continued to grow and expand in almost every aspect of librarianship. Andrew Carnegie depended much on Brett's advice during the most fruitful years of his philanthropy. Brett was expert in the design of buildings. He published the first issue of his *Cummulative Index to the Selected List of Periodicals* in 1896, a publication that after several metamorphoses became the familiar *Reader's Guide to Periodical Literature*. In the same year he was elected President of the American Library Association.

Brett campaigned vigorously for libraries for children and established an alcove for juvenile books in the Cleveland Public Library. Under his leadership the first branch libraries were opened in Cleveland.

Staff training came to occupy a large place in Brett's thinking, and he came to realize the importance of specialized education to the work of librarians. His interest in this idea developed eventually into a plan for a library school at Western Reserve University, where in 1904 he was present at the birth of that school. He was its first dean even as he remained head of the public library.

Brett died on August 24, 1918, in Cleveland. During his last years, he developed plans for the main library building on Superior Avenue in Cleveland, which, although not opened until 1925, bears the imprint of his thought.

REFERENCES

Linda A. Eastman, *Portrait of a Librarian: William Howard Brett* (1940).
C. H. Cramer, "Brett, William Howard," *Dictionary of American Library Biography* (1978).

ERVIN J. GAINES

Brown, James Duff

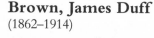

(1862–1914)

From about 1890 until 1914 the best-known initials in British librarianship were those of J. D. B., James Duff Brown. Brown was a library pioneer of outstanding importance.

Brown was born November 6, 1862, in Edinburgh into a working-class family that was unusually musical and in which books counted for much. He was educated at an excellent normal school but only up to the age of 12, when he was apprenticed to a local bookselling firm. Moving with his family in 1876 to Glasgow, he found temporary employment there with another bookseller but began his real library career at the age of 16 when appointed to a junior post in the Mitchell Library. The library, named after its founder, Stephen Mitchell, a Glasgow tobacco magnate, had opened its doors for the first time only one year before Brown joined its staff. Its founder had endowed it with the then very large sum of £70,000 to enable it to function as a large public library. Its origins were therefore comparable with those of the New York Public Library and, like its

American counterpart, it provided an outstanding reference service that did not originally form part of a normal municipal system.

J. D. B. spent 10 formative years at the Mitchell and saw its bookstock increase to 80,000—a period of growth that provided good bibliographical training for a young librarian. In 1888 he was appointed the first Librarian of Clerkenwell, one of the increasing number of London parishes that were adopting the Public Libraries Acts and initiating municipal libraries. Brown's early years at Clerkenwell established him as an apparently orthodox but unusually gifted librarian of the period, but in 1894 he became a pioneer by converting his library to "safe-guarded open access."

Prior to this date British public libraries, unlike many American ones, had not admitted readers to the shelves; books were requested at counters and fetched for readers by members of the staff. Although J. D. B. manifested throughout his life a marked antipathy to American library methods and indeed to American librarianship generally, there can be little doubt that his attendance at the ALA Congress at Chicago (1893) and visits to many libraries in the eastern states prepared the way for "open access." It remained a highly controversial issue for many years following 1894, although after 1920 British public libraries remaining "closed" could be safely regarded as extremely old-fashioned.

In 1905 J. D. B. moved from Clerkenwell, or rather from the Metropolitan Borough of Finsbury, into which his London parish had been absorbed, and became Borough Librarian of next-door Islington. His years at Clerkenwell/Finsbury had been very happy—an exceptional librarian being supported and encouraged by an understanding, progressive, and forward-looking committee. Although by contrast his governing body at Islington proved obstructive, unsympathetic, and parsimonious, J. D. B., struggling with every conceivable discouragement, built up a public library service that was regarded at the time as a model.

Despite the excellence of the two municipal library systems for which J. D. B. was successively responsible and for which, to avoid using the much disliked Dewey Decimal, he created no fewer than three systems of "Brown" classification, much of his reputation was gained outside London, mostly as journalist and author. He was the main public library contributor to MacAlister's *The Library* from 1890, and when it became clear that the Library Association would be discontinuing its recognition as the "official organ" and instead establishing its own *Library Association Record,* he ensured his own continuing independence by founding another monthly magazine, *The Library World;* the first number appeared in 1898.

This new journal not only provided a useful medium in which many librarians began and continued their journalistic careers but also enabled J. D. B. himself to write and print his own material, which he could subsequently revise and use in one or another of his many books. The best known of these was his *Manual of Library Economy.* This should have provided British librarianship, and particularly British public librarianship, with its basic textbook. The second and substantially revised edition of 1907 assuredly did; the first edition of 1903 was excessively

James Duff Brown

opinionated. The third (1920) and subsequent editions were edited and rewritten by W. C. Berwick Sayers and others.

Other notable books by J. D. B. were his *Subject Classification* (first edition, 1906; second edition, 1914; third edition [by J. D. Stewart], 1939); *Library Classification and Cataloguing* (1912), the successor to his *Manual of Library Classification and Shelf Arrangement* of 1898; *The Small Library: A Guide to the Collection and Care of Books* (1907); and *Manual of Practical Bibliography* (1906) based primarily on lectures delivered at the pioneer school of librarianship at the London School of Economics. J. D. B. was always a keen advocate of better education and better opportunities for young librarians and was also largely responsible for beginning the system of correspondence courses and classes upon which most British librarians depended for their professional studies until at least the later 1930s.

Brown's membership in a musical family had lifelong influence. He published *Biographical Dictionary of Musicians* (1886) and *British Musical Biography* (1897) and edited *Characteristic Songs and Dances of All Nations* (1910). This special musical interest also manifested itself in his keen desire to encourage and improve the provision of music and musical literature in public libraries, early symbolized by his *Guide to the Formation of a Music Library* (1893).

He exercised profound influence on British public library thinking during his lifetime and long after his death in London on February 26, 1914. That influence had at least two shortcomings; it stimulated irrational prejudice against the methods of American librarianship and against the methods of types of British librarianship other than the municipal. He was a keen admirer of the pioneer work of Edward Edwards (1812–86), the great British librarian of the mid-19th century, and ranks with him as one of the makers of modern British librarianship.

REFERENCE

W. A. Munford, *James Duff Brown 1862–1914: Portrait of a Library Pioneer* (1968).

W. A. MUNFORD

Brummel, Leendert

(1897–1976)

Leendert Brummel was Chief Librarian of the Royal Library at The Hague, Netherlands, from 1937 to 1962.

Brummel was born on August 10, 1897, at Arnhem. He received his grammar school education at The Hague and in 1916 enrolled as a student at Leiden University, where he read history and Dutch literature. Under the supervision of the famous historian Johan Huizinga, he wrote a thesis on the philosopher Franciscus Hemsterhuis, on the strength of which he received his doctorate *cum laude*. His book, *Frans Hemsterhuis: een filosofenleven* ("Frans Hemsterhuis: a Philosopher's Life," 1925), has proved to be a contribution of lasting value to the history of European thinking in the later decades of the 18th century.

In 1926 Brummel was appointed Librarian of the Royal Netherlands Academy of Sciences and Letters at Amsterdam. In 1927 he joined the staff of the

Leendert Brummel

Koninklijke Bibliotheek

Royal Library and on September 1, 1937, he succeeded P. C. Molhuysen as Chief Librarian.

When he took over, Brummel could in reason count on 25 years in which to strengthen the potential of the library and to enhance its usefulness to the community. In the event, he had considerably less time at his disposal. During the German occupation all he could do was to improvise measures for protecting the most valuable collections and to evade ideological interference on the part of the Germans and their Dutch henchmen. The war was followed by a period of great national poverty, in which libraries were decidedly not regarded as a priority.

Nevertheless, during his remaining, more prosperous years of office, Brummel succeeded in carrying out the major part of the improvements he had had in mind from the outset. He established a more efficient division of labor by freeing members of the academic staff from clerical duties. Thanks to this and to an increase of the number of subject specialists and of the budget, the quality and diversity of acquisitions were improved. The effectiveness of the union catalogue was raised. Many valuable items were added to the collections of manuscripts and early printed books. A severe lack of space was alleviated—for the time being—by the construction of an annex.

As Chairman of the State Advisory Committee on Library Affairs, of which both university librarians and the directors of some of the larger public libraries were members, Brummel did much to reconcile the sometimes conflicting views of his colleagues. His efforts to further a reasonable degree of harmony within the profession at large were sustained by the healthy mixture of idealism and pragmatism characteristic of his personality.

As Superintendent (*Hoofdbestuurder*) of the Rijksmuseum Meermanno-Westreenianum in The Hague, another ex-officio function of the Royal Librarian, Brummel brought about a symbiosis of that venerable institution and a new creation of his own: the Museum of the Book.

In 1953 the Museum and Documentation Center for Dutch Literature was founded. Brummel was its first Director and contributed much to its success.

Brummel felt very much at home on the international scene. His first contact with IFLA took place in July 1939, when the International Library Committee met in The Hague, just before the outbreak of the war. He was greatly impressed by Marcel Godet's courageous speech on the ideological rift that for years had been dividing German librarians from their colleagues. After the war he played an active role in IFLA. He was a Vice-President from 1961 to 1964 and in 1965 was made Honorary Vice-President. Together with E. Egger he published a *Guide to Union Catalogues and International Loan Centers* (1961), and he was the moving force of the team who prepared *Libraries in the World, A Long-term Programme for the International Federation of Library Associations* (1963).

Brummel was a prolific writer. His *Geschiedenis der Koninklijke Bibliotheek* ("History of the Royal Library," 1939) is still regarded as one of the best examples of library history ever produced in the Netherlands. He advocated the principle that library history should not limit itself to a mere recording of facts and events, but should include research into the political, social, and cultural forces that may have influenced the destiny of a library. Applying this principle to his own work, Brummel succeeded in producing a well-balanced and very readable work.

The dilemmatic role of the librarian as a scholar, the debate on the fundamentals of library science—those were theoretical problems which interested him to a certain extent without unduly disturbing him. In his paper *The Librarian as a Scholar,* read as a special University Lecture at the University of London in 1956 and published in *Miscellanea Libraria,* a selection from his studies presented to him on the occasion of his 60th birthday (1957), he wrestled manfully with these and related problems; yet one is left with the impression of having witnessed a mimic battle ending in a draw. When he gave his inaugural address after being appointed in 1960 to the chair of library science at the University of Amsterdam, he declared his preference for a pragmatic approach.

He retired as Royal Librarian in 1962, but continued to teach with great enthusiasm. After retiring from teaching, he kept on writing and publishing. Until a few months before his death in The Hague on February 1,1976, he was an assiduous visitor of the Royal Library.

C. REEDIJK

Brunet, Jacques-Charles

(1780–1867)

A bookseller and bibliographer, Jacques-Charles Brunet was born November 2, 1780, the son of Thomas Brunet, in Paris, where he would spend virtually his entire life. His formal education was scanty even by the standards of his day and was terminated by the revolutionary events of 1792; thereafter he was self-educated.

His private life and work in bibliography and classification are so entwined that to separate them is to falsify them. He never married, and his close friends were few; although created Chevalier of the Legion of Honor in 1845, he functioned largely outside the literary and political worlds. The sole biography devoted to Brunet was done for an antiquarian book exposition in 1960—a pastiche of obituaries and contemporary literary commentaries.

Brunet's current reputation is founded upon two complementary aspects of his bibliographical work: he was a pioneer in library classification from literary warrant and, more concretely, he compiled a massive, meticulously detailed, and often charming rare-book bibliography (each edition expanding its predecessor) that has become a mainstay of rare-book librarians and dealers.

To supplement this work and provide an ordering for lesser works, Brunet conceived a classification set forth most fully in the final volume of his *Manuel du libraire et de l'amateur de livres* ("Bookdealer's and Book Lover's Handbook"). This scheme, reportedly based upon the commerce-tested logic of the successful bookseller, was taken up and used with various modifications by many libraries. The entire scheme, along with Brunet's historical introduction (a somewhat biased history of cataloguing), was made available for the first time in English in 1976.

The most salient feature of Brunet's scheme is its a posteriori character; in contrast to most of his predecessors, he eschewed a priori theoretical structures and founded his arrangements on pragmatism. Although the weighting of the divisions (Theology: 7.3 percent; Jurisprudence: 3 percent; Arts and Sciences: 22.7 percent; Literature; 28.2 percent; History: 38.8 percent) is quite inappropriate today and reflects the tastes of his classically educated clientele, its principle that a library's content and purpose should govern its arrangement was a forerunner of modern library classification for use.

The first known direct use of the Brunet scheme in the United States was at Harvard College in 1830. At various times, it was also used by the Saint Louis Mercantile Library, the Philadelphia Library, and others.

Among Brunet's publications, his *Manuel* perpetuates his name (a reprint edition is currently available); his remaining production consisted chiefly of contemporary articles. He was perhaps the last of the individual polyhistors to work alone on such massive works of bibliography. The last expansion of his *Manuel* was completed after his death by his friends P. Deschamps and Gustave Brunet.

He passed away peacefuly in his own armchair on November 17, 1867, in his 87th year, surrounded by the books that had been the friends of his life.

REFERENCE
D. B. McKeon, *The Classification System of Jacques-Charles Brunet* (Louisiana State University Graduate School of Library Science Occasional Papers no. 1, 1976).
DONALD BRUCE McKEON

Buck, Solon Justus

(1884–1962)

Solon Justus Buck, Archivist of the United States and writer, achieved outstanding success as a scholar, teacher, archivist, and historical administrator.

He was born in Berlin, Wisconsin, August 16, 1884. Buck received B.A. and M.A. degrees from the University of Wisconsin in 1904 and 1905 and took a

Louisiana State University Library
Jacques-Charles Brunet

Ph.D. at Harvard University in 1911.

A leading protégé of the eminent historian Frederick Jackson Turner, Buck early reached prominence as a publishing scholar. In quick succession he produced *The Granger Movement* (1913), *Illinois in 1818* (1917), and *Agrarian Crusade* (1920), all of which were widely and favorably noted. Buck taught at Indiana University, 1908–09, and indeed was an outstanding teacher during much of his life, but his career was basically that of a historical administrator. From 1910 to 1914 he was a Research Associate at the University of Illinois on the "Illinois Centennial History" project. From 1914 to 1931 Buck served as Superintendent of the Minnesota Historical Society, transforming that institution into a model state historical society, greatly expanding and professionalizing its library and manuscript collections, launching a journal, editing other historical publications, and promoting the formation of county historical societies. He also found time to become the prime fund-raiser for the American Historical Association, to publish *Stories of Early Minnesota* (1925) with his wife, Elizabeth, whom he had married in 1919, and to serve as Professor of History at the University of Minnesota. From 1931 to 1935 Buck served as Director of the Western Pennsylvania Historical Survey and Professor at the University of Pittsburgh. From this period came Solon and Elizabeth Buck's *The Planting of Civilization in Western Pennsylvania* (1939).

In 1935 Buck became one of the four chief assistant administrators of the new National Archives. His title was Director of Publications, but that belied the scope of his activities. He had found a new stage upon which to act out his career and took full advantage of it. He became the chief envoy of the National Archives to historical associations, especially as Treasurer of the American Historical Association (1936–57) and a representative in 1938 to the International Committee of Historical Sciences. He was one of the founders of the Society of American Archivists in 1936 and was active in the formation of the American Documentation Institute. At Columbia University in 1938 he inaugurated the first professional course in archival administration in the United States; he refined this instruction at the American University in 1939, so that it became the model for archival courses offered over the country during the following generation. Among the many other successful projects he initiated or headed at the National Archives was the Finding Mediums Committee of 1940–41, the report of which greatly changed archival administration with its recommendations for organizing archives on the basis of record groups and for providing a variety of guides to them, most notably the preliminary inventory. Ironically, Buck was unable to make any significant progress as Secretary of the National Historical Publications Commission (NHPC), his most visible job at the Archives.

As a result of Buck's imaginative and usually successful work at the National Archives, President Franklin D. Roosevelt appointed him to head the agency as Archivist of the United States in 1941. Buck's work during his almost seven years in that position was often brilliant, though mixed in results. Despite severe shortages of staff and equipment, he expanded the services of the National Archives. Buck plunged his agency into the work of records management, achieving more efficient and economical government control over its burgeoning records. One by-product of this work was the Archives' role in developing the new records management profession and in encouraging archivists to take a broader view of their work. Buck also played the leading role in founding the International Council on Archives (1948). In addition to his continuing interest in archival training and professional organization, he found a variety of war-related research, technical, and consulting tasks for archivists to perform. He forwarded the earlier programs of his agency, especially the accessioning of older federal archives, the microfilming program, the *Federal Register,* and the Franklin D. Roosevelt Library.

Buck's frequent experiments with reorganizing the National Archives made the agency more efficient but at the cost of considerable staff unhappiness and congressional criticism. He made the Archives into a more nearly perfect servant of the state, but only at the price of the agency's becoming too acquiescent in restrictions on the private use of federal records. Buck's authoritarian leadership and his sometimes abrasive personality, moreover, contributed to problems among his staff and with Congress, in effect jeopardizing appropriations for the support of the National Archives. By 1948 it was clear that Buck—tired, aging, and having recently suffered serious illness—was unlikely to improve his staff's morale and to gain appropriations for new programs.

LATER CAREER

Buck resigned that year as Archivist of the United States and accepted the position of Chief of the Manuscripts Division of the Library of Congress. Three years later he became Assistant Librarian, a job he held until his retirement in 1954. Although his vitality was gone, he functioned satisfactorily at the Library of Congress, performing a number of administrative and intellectual tasks as an elder statesman of research and information management, including membership on the reinvigorated NHPC. He served as Acting Director of the Minnesota Historical Society, 1954–55, and occasionally as a consultant to the Library of Congress.

The University of Minnesota conferred an honorary LL.D. degree upon him in 1954. Throughout his career he had been an officer in a variety of historical, archival, and research organizations, serving as President of the Mississippi Valley Historical Association, the Agricultural History Society, and the Society of American Archivists. In addition to his several books, he was the author of numerous historical and archival articles. His was a remarkably broad career. Buck died in Washington, D.C., May 25, 1962.

Records of the National Archives
Solon Justus Buck

REFERENCES

Donald R. McCoy, *The National Archives: American's Ministry of Documents, 1934–1968* (1978).

Theodore C. Blegen, "Solon Justus Buck—Scholar–Administrator," *The American Archivist* (1960).

Ernst Posner, "Solon Justus Buck—Archivist," *The American Archivist* (1960).

DONALD R. McCOY

Bulgaria

Bulgaria, a people's republic in southeastern Europe, lies in the eastern Balkan Peninsula. Romania lies to the north, the Black Sea to the east, Turkey and Greece to the south, and Yugoslavia to the west. Population (1984 est.) 8,969,000; area 110,912 sq.km. The official language is Bulgarian.

History. The first Bulgarian state was created in 681, in the northeastern part of the Balkan Peninsula. It rapidly developed and expanded. In the second half of the 10th century it was one of the mightiest states in Europe. After the acceptance of Christianity as the official religion in A.D. 864 and following the introduction of the Cyrillic alphabet (A.D. 893), invented by the learned brothers Cyril and Methodius, Bulgaria experienced a period known as the Golden Age of Bulgarian Literature. Two great cultural centers emerged: one in the capital, Preslav, the other in the region of Ochrid. In those areas evolved the so-called Preslav Literary School and Ochrid Literary School sponsored by the Bulgarian sovereigns.

The first Bulgarian libraries of significance were created at those centers of medieval culture. One of them, perhaps the largest of all, was established in the King's palace under the direct supervision of King Simeon. It contained a large collection of old Greek and Byzantine manuscripts and all Bulgarian writings produced at the time. The literature created in the 10th century spread to other countries, especially to Russia (Kiev), thus fostering its cultural development.

After the liberation of Bulgaria from Byzantine domination, which lasted for almost two centuries (1018–1186), Bulgaria experienced a new period of cultural revival and expansion, reaching a climax in the 14th century during the reign of King Ivan Alexander. A flourishing literary school emerged in the capital, Tărnovo, and several major libraries were established in the King's palace, at the Patriarchate of the Bulgarian Orthodox Church, at monasteries and churches, and in the palaces of feudal rulers.

During the five centuries of Ottoman domination (1393–1878), all Bulgarian libraries were destroyed, with the exception of the libraries of some 300 monasteries. The monastic librarians preserved the literary heritage of Bulgaria, copied Bulgarian manuscript books, and translated foreign books and compiled historical chronicles. The most important were those of the Rila, the Bachkovo, and the Zograph monasteries.

The first Bulgarian public libraries within the Ottoman Empire began to appear after 1840 during the Bulgarian national and cultural revival. They were school libraries and libraries of the so-called *chitalishta* ("reading clubs"), and they rapidly increased in number. Thanks to them, Bulgarian writings and cultural traditions have been preserved.

After liberation from Ottoman domination (1878), public libraries played an important role in assisting the nation's education and were the most important cultural centers in the country. Research libraries also began to appear, the first being the Library of the Bulgarian Literary Society (which developed into the Bulgarian Academy of Sciences) and the National Library. The revolutionary changes after World War II gave a strong impetus to the development of libraries.

National Management. In January 1970, a decree of the Council of Ministers promulgated the Unified Library System of Bulgaria. It is governed by the Committee (or Ministry) of Culture and professionally guided and coordinated by the National Library. The Director of the National Library is simultaneously head of the Library Directorate of the Committee of Culture. The National Library, the Library of the Bulgarian Academy of Sciences, the Library of the University of Sofia (the country's largest university library), as well as the central research libraries of medicine, science and technology, and agriculture form a closely integrated group of libraries, functionally managed by a Council of Directors of Central Research Libraries and aimed at providing an overall high-quality comprehensive library and documentation service. Each of these central research libraries guides and coordinates the activities of the libraries within its respective network. Regional libraries guide the public libraries and coordinate all library activities in the regions. The directors of the regional libraries are simultaneously directors of the library directorates of the Regional People's Councils (the highest organs of local government).

Among the needs that new legislation was ex-

Libraries in Bulgaria (1982)

Type	Adminstrative units	Service points	Volumes in collections[a]	Annual expenditures (lev)	Population served[c]	Professional staff	Total staff
National	1	--	2,298,581	2,562,000[d]	23,125	296	382
Academic	27	--	5,040,150	3,379,000[e]	107,413	422	--
Public	5,731	--	41,514,690	17,965,000[d]	1,861,407	3,834	4,834[d]
School	3,587	--	15,684,025	--	866,534	743	--
Special	677	--	24,782,940[b]	--	207,048	811	--
Regional (District)	27	--	9,156,787	--	324,743	761	--

[a]Library registration units.
[b]Includes 18,500,000 patents, standards, and special technical publications.
[c]Registered readers only.
[d]Unesco, *Statistical Yearbook*, 1984. 1980 data.
[e]Ibid., 1981 data.

Source: *Bibliotekite v Balgaria: Statisticheski danni* ("Libraries in Bulgaria: Statistical Data")(Sofia: National Library, 1983).

pected to address in the mid-1980s were revision and improvement of the organization and functions of the Unified Library System of the country, introducing measures such as compulsory norms for funding libraries by parent bodies; stricter requirements for creation of new libraries; compulsory centralization of public library services; and establishment of a National Library Council at the Committee of Culture, presided over by the first Deputy Chairman of the Committee and consisting of prominent public figures and library experts with advisory and guiding powers.

National Library. The Cyril and Methodius National Library (founded 1878) in Sofia possesses a complete collection of the national production of printed materials, an important selection of foreign publications in all fields, and the country's largest collection of foreign periodicals—about 9,500 current titles in the early 1980s. It has a full collection of UN publications and the basic publications of other international organizations. Its basic holdings total more than 2,000,000 library registration units. In addition, it has a large collection of Bulgarian and foreign manuscripts and old and rare books. It also preserves over 1,500,000 historic documents and serves as National Archives for documents pertaining to Bulgarian history to the end of the 19th century. (The State Archives is responsible for the preservation of documents relating to the 20th century.)

Since 1897 it has been the national center of legal deposit, and it has published the national bibliography. The national bibliography consists of separate registration bulletins for books, maps, sheet music, and other items (issued biweekly); official publications and dissertations (monthly); articles from journals and collective works (biweekly); articles from newspapers (monthly); Bulgarian periodicals (annually); "Bulgarica" (quarterly); and the "Bibliography of Bulgarian Bibliography" (annually). There are also four annual cumulations (books and other materials, dissertations, disks, and "Bulgarica").

The National Library is an active bibliographic information center and functions as a research institute in the fields of library science, bibliography, and book science. It employed about 40 full-time research fellows in 1985.

As a national methodological center it provides help and guidance to regional and central research libraries and their networks. Since 1970 it has coordinated the basic library processes in the country's library system.

Academic Libraries. Twenty-seven academic libraries at universities and other institutions of higher education held more than 5,000,000 volumes in the early 1980s. The largest libraries are the Library at Sofia University and the Central Medical Library at the Higher Medical Institute in Sofia.

Public Libraries. *Chitalishta* libraries, those in village or town reading clubs or houses of culture, number about 3,800. Each town or village community has one or more of them serving the entire population free of charge. The second largest group consists of more than 1,800 libraries organized at industrial and trade enterprises and public agencies, which serve their staffs. They are sponsored by the trade unions and funded by their parent bodies. There are also several city libraries directly governed by the

Bulgarian Academy of Sciences Central Library

Main reading room at the Bulgarian Academy of Sciences Central Library in Sofia, one of the country's leading libraries.

state. The most important trend in the development of public libraries in the 1980s has been their gradual centralization. In order to preserve the autonomy of the *chitalishta* organizations, the centralization follows the line of functional concentration of the basic library processes within the main *chitalishta* libraries of the town communities. The second important trend has been the steady reduction of the number of public libraries, mainly affecting very small and unviable libraries.

District Libraries. The 27 district (or regional) libraries are in practice the largest widely accessible libraries, but they should not be considered public libraries because they have assumed the status and functions of central research libraries of the districts. They have large holdings of indigenous and foreign publications and unique collections of publications and other documents pertaining to the respective regions.

Special Libraries. Special scientific libraries are organized in academies of sciences, other research institutes, learned societies, industrial enterprises, business firms, museums, and editorial boards, with total holdings of about 24,000,000 library units (including 18,500,000 patents, standards, and other special technical publications). The most important are the Library of the Bulgarian Academy of Sciences (with a central library and over 40 branch libraries), the Central Agricultural Library (heading a network of specialized agricultural libraries), and the Central Technical Library (coordinating the work of specialized technical libraries).

A notable trend is the constant reduction in the number of special libraries (704 in 1976 and 677 in 1982), which reflects a policy of centralization of special libraries and abolishing unviable institutions.

School Libraries. Every school in Bulgaria has its own library. There are more than 3,500 school libraries with total holdings of 15,680,000 volumes (about 30 percent of which are children's books). About 80 percent of the country's enrolled students are registered readers of the school libraries.

The Profession. Three institutions provide courses of formal library education: the University of Sofia (which has a chair of library science and information science), the State Institute of Librarians (two years after secondary education), and the National Library (six-month training courses upon completion of university education). The University of Sofia and the National Library also provide postgraduate doctoral dissertation programs.

The National Library, the central research libraries, and the regional libraries regularly organize short courses, seminars, and other undertakings to improve the professional qualification and skills of librarians.

A library association had not been organized in Bulgaria by 1985, though one was planned.

VLADIMIR POPOV

Burkina Faso

Burkina Faso, a republic of West Africa, is bounded on the northwest by Mali, on the northeast by Niger, and on the south by Benin, Togo, Ghana, and the Ivory Coast. Population (1984 est.) 6,733,000; area 274,200 sq.km. The official language is French; the dialect More is widely spoken. The country, called Upper Volta when it became independent in 1960, was renamed Burkina Faso in August 1984.

Burkina Faso does not have a national library. A National Commission for Libraries, Archives and Documentation was established in 1969 but little was accomplished. The Centre National de la Recherche Scientifique et Technologique (CNRST), founded in 1950, receives copies of all publications on and about the country, including those published outside Burkina Faso Faso. Its Library specializes in research in the humanities and natural sciences and holds more than 6,000 volumes. The Centre publishes a quarterly "Notes and Documents" and other publications on an irregular basis, and is responsible for the compilation of a current national bibliography. The first volume was issued in 1967, the *Bibliographie générale de la Haute-Volta,* covering the years 1956 through 1965.

A National Center for Archives was organized in 1973. It conducted a survey of the archives of all administrative districts of the country and drew plans for a central depository at Ouagadougou.

Burkina Faso has one university. The Université de Ouagadougou was founded in 1970 and attained university status in 1974. The university's Library holds approximately 55,000 volumes, 100 periodicals, and 1,400 maps. There are many smaller libraries affiliated with colleges in Ouagadougou. The academic library of the Lycée Philippe Zinda Kabore de Ouagadougou has a small library primarily for the use of teachers and secondary students.

There is no public library system in Burkina Faso. Library facilities are available to the public primarily through the cultural centers in Ouagadougou, most notably those of Germany, the United States, France, Libya, and the Soviet Union.

The Documentation and Information Center of the Interafrican Committee for Hydraulic Studies (CIEH) in Ouagadougou houses 11,000 documents, including books, technical reports, proceedings of conferences, maps, aerial and satellite photographs, and periodical articles. The Center receives approximately 135 journals and compiles bibliographical bulletins, which are sent to more than a thousand recipients on five continents. The Center published two catalogues in 1977: *An Index of Authors* and a *Geographical Index* representing a total of 6,000 documents. Bulletins deal with documents selected and analyzed after the 1977 publication date.

Other documentation centers include one in Bobo-Dioulasso, which specializes in public health and tropical medicine; the Institut national de la statistique et de la démographie in Ouagadougou, with 2,200 volumes, primarily in the field of economics, 50 periodicals, and statistical bulletins from various countries; and the Institut national d'education in Ouagadougou, with approximately 15,000 volumes and 237 periodicals on educational theory and psychology.

In 1972 the Association Voltaïque pour le développement des bibliothèques, des archives et de la documentation (AVDBAD) was founded at Ouagadougou. Its primary purpose is to aid in the development of libraries, archives, and documentation centers in the country. The Association is governed by an executive committee elected by its members and is affiliated with IFLA.

KRISSIAMBA LARBA ALI*

Burma

Burma, a republic of Southeast Asia, is bounded by China on the north, Thailand and Laos on the east, the Bay of Begal and Bangladesh on the west, and India on the northwest. To the southwest and south lie the Gulf of Martaban and the Andaman Sea. Population (1984 est.) 36,368,000; area 676,577 sq.km. The official language is Burmese.

History. The history of Burma's libraries begins with King Anawrahta's violent seizure of Buddhist texts from Thaton in the late 11th century. This act established Pagan as a center for Buddhism over many centuries, and monastry libraries grew up around it. The collection of scriptures, in palm-leaf manuscript form, was housed in the Pitaka Taik. In 1795 a British envoy estimated that the Royal Library in Amarapura was the largest royal library between the Danube and China. And in Mandalay a library of 729 alabaster tablets, each 5 feet by 3 feet, was erected in 1857. It has been called "the most permanent library in the world."

National Libraries. There are two national libraries in Burma, one in the capital city, Rangoon, the other in Mandalay. Their combined strength approximated 100,000 volumes, with about a third of the materials in English. The library in Rangoon provides author and title indexes to leading Burmese periodicals from their dates of publication. The strength of holdings lies predominantly in primary source materials on Colonial Burma; however, both libraries receive books and periodicals under the Press Registration Act of 1962 and are thus depository libraries. In addition to periodicals and newspapers, the libraries also contain several thousand books in manuscript form. Although open access is not allowed, spacious reading room are available. The rate of acquisition exceeds several thousand titles a year and is primarily reflective of the quantity of publications in Burma. Burma also has its National Archives, whose holdings include the entire run of the *Burma Gazette.*

Academic Libraries. Major academic libraries are those of Rangoon University, Mandalay University, and Moulmein College. At Rangoon the Central Universities Library is responsible for acquisition of foreign materials except for medical literature, acquired by the Department of Medicine Research Library. The Central Universities Library has a collection of about 250,000 volumes. The three Institute of Medicine libraries (in Rangoon and Mandalay) house about 45,000 volumes among them. The libraries conduct literature searches, maintain union catalogues of holdings on campuses, and prepare and publish bibliographies. A notable activity is the library orientation program at Rangoon Institute of Technology (about 35,000 volumes), where library training has also been incorporated into the curriculum. A major research library is the Library of the Central Research Institute, which completed a Union List of Scientific Serials covering some 20 libraries. The Library has an exchange program with the British Library Lending Division. Burma's academic libraries are decentralized; there are several departmental and institute libraries such as the Library of the Institute of Veterinary Science. The Arts and Science University Library in Mandalay (103,000 volumes) should also be mentioned, as well as the Institute of Economics Library and the Institute of Education Library. Both are in Rangoon and both have collections of about 35,000 volumes. The college libraries in Bassain, Magwe, and Moulmein are somewhat smaller.

Public Libraries. Three or four major state libraries provide the bulk of library service to the general populace. Perhaps the most outstanding public library is the Sarpay Beikman, or "House of Literature" Institute Library (Rangoon), which has its own publishing house and which administers reading rooms in many Burmese villages. It has about 74,000 volumes, 17,670 of them in English. The bulk of Burma's domestic interlibrary loan activities are carried out by this library.

Special Libraries. Special libraries are found in the industries and institutes of various ministries. A special library of significance is the Research Library of Buddhistic Studies, whose holdings are world renowned.

Burma's libraries receive high-level government understanding and available support but are faced with the common problem of a shortage of funds.

REFERENCES

G. Miller, "Notes on Libraries in Burma," *International Library Review* (July 1978), an excellent overview.

G. Raymond Nunn, "Libraries in Burma," *International Library Review* (October 1975), emphasizes activities of libraries in Burma.

THEIN SWE*

Burundi

Burundi, a republic in central eastern Africa, is bordered by Rwanda on the north, Tanzania on the east and south, Lake Tanganyika on the southwest, and Zaire on the west. Population (1984 est.) 4,525,000; area 27,834 sq.km. The official languages are Kirundi and French.

Université du Burundi, Bibliothèque

Library at the University of Burundi/in Bujumbura. It was built in 1981 and formally dedicated in 1985.

Academic Libraries. Burundi's library resources are primarily concentrated in the Université Officielle and a few smaller, mainly government-supported schools. All institutions of higher learning along with their library holdings are in the capital city of Bujumbura.

The Official University's library system consists of a Central Library and five independent departmental libraries. Aggregate holdings of all facilities amount to about 110,000 titles and 1,270 current periodicals. The Central Library's collection of more than 60,000 volumes covers all major subjects.

The staff, trained in France and Senegal, generally maintains an acquisition rate of 3,000 titles a year through expenditure of funds provided, gifts, and exchanges with foreign universities. Departmental libraries are provided for administrative and economic sciences, letters and humanities, medicine, psychology and education, and physical sciences.

In addition to those at the Official University, libraries are maintained at the Theological College of Bujumbura, the Military High Institute, and the École Normale Supérieure du Burundi; only the last, a college for teachers, possesses a collection in the range of 11,000 volumes, which serves to emphasize the central importance of Burundi's single university among academic libraries.

Public Libraries. The Ministry of Education maintains a single public library facility, in Bujumbura, with a collection of approximately 26,000 volumes. As with academic libraries, no services or supplies exist outside the capital.

Special Libraries. A number of government-supported institutes and government departments maintain important technical and historical collections. The Institut des Sciences Agronomiques du Burundi (Burundi Institute of Agronomy) maintains a 1,500-volume collection on scientific agriculture in the capital and four field stations in other parts of the country. The Institute Library supports services vital to Burundi's future growth and prosperity. The Laboratoire de Recherches Vétérinaires in Bujumbura provides access to 200 volumes on animal husbandry and health care, topics closely related to the future success of agriculture. The Ministry of Economy and Finance's Department of Geology and Mines pos-

Libraries in Burundi (1978)

Type	Administrative units	Service points	Volumes in collections	Annual expenditures (franc)	Population served	Professional staff	Total staff
National	--	--	--	--	--	--	--
Academic	4	6	92,000	92,000[a]	--	7	36
Public	--	--	--	--	--	--	--
School	--	--	--	--	--	--	--

[a]Excludes expenditure for employees.

Source: Unesco, *Statistical Yearbook*, 1984.

sesses a 100-volume library that provides valuable information on another important factor in Burundi's future development. Historical materials and recorded folklore are available at the Institut Burundi d'Information et de Documentation in the capital.

Also in Bujumbura are two foreign libraries in cultural missions. The Alliance Française (French Cultural Center) contains more than 1,500 volumes; the American Cultural Center maintains a 3,000-volume collection. Both libraries are available to any citizen, although in practice only those living in the capital have an opportunity to utilize them.

FIRMIN KINIGI*

Butler, Pierce
(1886–1953)

Pierce Butler, library educator and scholar, was not concerned with the technology of librarianship, which he left to others, but with its philosophy, the basic principles that give it unity and cohesiveness. He was a historian and humanist, though he did not discredit the contribution that science has made to our culture and could make to librarianship. This point of view was the central theme of Butler's major course on the history of scholarship and of his *Introduction to Library Science* (1933).

The work begins with an introductory essay on the nature of science followed by an analysis of three major problem areas in librarianship—the sociological, the psychological, and the historical. The book concludes with a summary chapter on "Practical Considerations." In the literature of librarianship, which is characterized mainly by its ephemera, Butler's little volume stands out as a true landmark in the development of library thought.

Pierce Butler was born December 19, 1886, at Clarendon Hills, Illinois. As a child he suffered a severe attack of scarlet fever that left him with seriously impaired hearing, and he relied on a hearing aid throughout his lifetime. He received a Ph.B. from Dickinson College, Carlisle, Pennsylvania, in 1906, taught for one year at the Virginia Military Academy, and from 1907 to 1909 studied at the Union Theological Seminary, New York. The following year he returned to Dickinson for an A.M., and he received the B.D. from the Hartford Theological Seminary, in Connecticut, that same year. He was also a Fellow in Medieval History at Hartford, and in 1912 he was awarded the Ph.D.

Butler joined the Newberry Library staff in 1916, after holding a clerical position in the offices of the Burlington Railroad. For the first year at Newberry he was a Reference Assistant. Within a year he was promoted to Head of the Order Department and Bibliographer and Custodian of the John Wing Foundation on the History of Typography and the Printed Book. He continued in those capacities until his resignation in 1931. While at the Newberry he published a checklist of its holdings of books printed in the 15th century, issued in revised form in 1924. In 1926 he married Ruth Lapham, who was the Newberry's Curator of the Ayer Collection on the American Indian and a productive scholar in her own right.

In 1928 Butler was appointed part-time lecturer on the history of books and printing at the University of Chicago's Graduate Library School. In 1931, at the insistence of Douglas Waples and William Randall, he joined the full-time faculty of the School. He spent the remainder of his professional life at the GLS, until his retirement in 1952.

Butler's books are relatively few in number, the *Check List,* the *Introduction,* and *The Origin of Printing in Europe* (1940). In his unorthodox study of printing, he espoused the belief that Gutenberg was not the inventor of printing from movable type but that the technology was the product of many men working in various cities beginning as early as the 1440s. Butler saw Gutenberg as a shadowy figure whose primacy in the printing craft was the result of myth and the tendency of earlier generations to attribute innovation to a single figure who had caught the popular imagination.

His little pamphlet *Scholarship and Civilization,* "Published as Proof" by the University of Chicago in 1944, is a synopsis of his course on the history of scholarship and a tantalizing essay—tantalizing because it shows what a major work on that subject the pamphlet could have been had he but persisted in carrying it to completion. It still remains valuable to all who would seek insight into the sociological and anthropological relationships to the development of the library. One gains from it a deepening understanding of the origins of the library and its intellectual roots.

At the time of his death he was working on a treatment of the management and administration of rare book collections, a subject on which he was well qualified to speak. He wrote many articles on librarianship and its philosophy and was a popular speaker. He was an excellent raconteur and always enjoyed a good story.

During his Chicago years he made an impression on cultural thought and the philosophy of librarianship that, as he confessed, exceeded his expectations.

He was convinced that it was his role to recognize and interpret the social history of the library in terms that would validate it for our own age. Thus he linked the philosophical approach to the intellectual and technical problems of librarianship. "I wrote my *Introduction*," he said, "to persuade my professional colleagues to be more scientific. Now I have to struggle to keep them from being too damned scientific."

Butler's breadth of knowledge was little short of phenomenal—a true polyhistor of the 20th century. He was a superior teacher. The other teachers at Chicago's Graduate Library School taught students how to *be* librarians, and they taught well. However, Butler taught what librarianship *could be*. In his favorite course on the history of scholarship he gave students, almost without their knowing it, an intellectual heritage to which many have returned as experience has reinforced its significance.

Within the library profession, Butler was as controversial a figure as was his intellectual antagonist, Douglas Waples. Despite the handicap of defective hearing, he enjoyed a fruitful social life. He reveled in an audience and was at his best on a public platform.

Jesse Shera, writing in the First Edition of this Encyclopedia, told the following story about his relation with Butler: "The writer's own association with him was marked by frequent arguments. These discussions were often heated but never acrimonious, and were always suffused with mutual respect and the warmth of friendship. At the end of the summer quarter of 1952, when Butler was retiring and the writer was leaving Chicago for another academic post, he finally burst out, 'Pierce, before we part company I do hope you will realize that I *am* on your side. I, too, am a humanist, despite my defense of science.'

"'Oh, I know that, Shera; I know that,' he replied, 'but I sometimes feel about you as I do about Bob Hutchins; your heart is in the right place, but you are forever saying things that give aid and comfort to the enemy.'"

Less than a year later, on March 28, 1953, Butler died in an automobile crash while returning from the dedication of a new library building in Winston-Salem, North Carolina.

REFERENCE

Lee Ash, "Butler Pierce," *Dictionary of American Library Biography* (1978).

JESSE H. SHERA
(d. 1982)

Byzantine Libraries

Knowledge of the Byzantine libraries is scattered and uncertain. Because of turbulent political change and major fires and even earthquakes, there is hardly any archaeological evidence pertaining to the major centers. The student is heavily dependent upon inferences from such literary testimony as the 5th-century writings of Stobaeus (John of Stobi, Macedonia), the 9th-century "Library" of Patriarch Photius, the 10th-century encyclopedic miscellany known to the admiring West as Suidas, and the massive collection of quotations presented in poetic form by John Tzetzes in the 12th century. Some direct documentation,

mainly theological, is extant in either the original locations or Western research collections, in the form of Greek codices from the Byzantine era, presumably used for study and argumentation in the churches and monasteries of the Near East, Egypt, Greece, and the Aegean islands.

The outstanding library was reportedly the imperial collection in Constantinople (capital of the Eastern Empire, 395–1453); it was founded in 353 and favored administratively by such steps as were ordered in 372 by Emperor Valens, incorporated in the Theodosian Code. It may have held 100,000 "volumes," the largest assemblage at that time known to Western records; most, if not all, were apparently consumed in the fire of 475(?). There are references to higher studies in the 6th and 7th centuries with tantalizingly unclear hints of book collections. It is indeed known that in the years 607–10 the Patriarch of Constantinople built a library in his palace—burned in 870. Further, it is plausible that library support existed during the 8th century despite the discouragements of the Iconoclasts because a renaissance flowered in the 9th century. In any case, Benedictine-like copying began in 789 at the Constantinople abbey directed by the reformer Theodore of Studium.

The "Library" of Patriarch Photius helps to illuminate the question of what reading matter was apparently available to career men and able women of privilege in 9th-century Constantinople and the Eastern Empire, although not such particulars as where one obtained a desired book or whether it could be borrowed. Concerning Stobaeus, for example, Photius reports the author's stated purpose, the contents of the 208 chapters organized into four books, and the numerous philosophers, poets, orators, historians, kings, and generals from whom he has drawn his material. The list of "philosophers" includes Aristotle, Euclid, and Zoroaster; among the poets are Homer and Sappho. The last list, more varied, includes orator Demosthenes, physician Hippocrates, and historian Thucydides. Photius recommends Stobaeus's encyclopedia as "obviously" a great help for those who have read the writings referred to, as a painless way for others to get acquainted with their essential contributions, and as a bag from which a speaker or writer can pull an apt quotation. R. Henry, who edited Photius (Paris, 1960), can vouch for Photius's care with attributions and copying from some 300 texts but withholds any assurance as to what the Patriarch read in the original and what was picked up in anthologies. Nor is there a shred of evidence as to contacts between Photius and any library.

Hellenic culture continued to be promoted in both the new imperial schools at the capital and several established elsewhere. Considering the centralization that so sharply differentiated Byzantine civilization from Western conditions, benefit likely flowed from the advances at the imperial court. The 10th century was marked by the broad interests of Constantine Porphyrogenitus (i.e., "of the breed of Porphyry," influential promoter of Aristotle); the 11th by Constantine Monomachos, reorganizer of the university, and the philosopher Michael Psellos; and the 12th by several dictionary and encyclopedia compilers and by Princess Anna Comnena, who reputedly took good advantage of her opportunities in learning.

The Crusaders arrived in the early 13th century.

Driving out the existing regime, they also wrecked its libraries on some infamous days in 1204. The defeated retired to Nicaea and assembled, among other things, a new library. By 1263 they were able to return to Constantinople, where they remained for two centuries. When the Turks ended Christian domination in 1453, the Greek mansuscript treasures, with their remarkable illumination and bindings, had long since migrated westward. The copying still conducted in the East had settled in monasteries such as those at Patmos and Mount Athos; around 1200, at least, many libraries of the North Aegean borrowed liturgical items from Patmos. The city of Byzantium, renamed Istanbul, later regained fame for its wealth in book collections. Its Suleiman Library cherished thousands of Arabic, Persian, and Turkish codices.

REFERENCES

S. K. Padover, "Byzantine Libraries," in J. W. Thompson, *Medieval Libraries* (1939).

Handbuch der Bibliothekswesen III-1 (1955).

SIDNEY L. JACKSON
(d. 1979)

Cain, Julien
(1887–1974)

As director of the Bibliothèque Nationale for 34 years, Julien Cain exerted an enormous influence on the development of modern librarianship in France. His contributions touched virtually every aspect of the field, from modernizing library buildings and creating new services to increasing the public's appreciation for the rich artistic and literary heritage contained in French books. Cain's own deep knowledge of art also gained him the friendship of writers and artists and assured his reputation as a leading figure in the world of cultural affairs.

Cain was born in Montmorency (Val d'Oise), France, on May 10, 1887. He was descended from printers through his maternal grandfather, Napoléon Alexandre, a Parisian, and through his father, Sylvain Cain (1865–1937), who had left Lorraine after the Franco-Prussian War in 1870. Julien Cain attended secondary school in Paris, first at the Collège Rollin, then at the Lycée Condorcet, where he studied under the philosopher Alain (Emile Chartier, 1868–1961). After completing his military service in Amiens in 1907, Cain had his interest in bibliography awakened at the Sorbonne by Charles-Victor Langlois, the author of a well-known textbook on historical bibliography (*Manuel de bibliographie historique*, 1896). In 1911, after qualifying as a teacher in history, Cain taught for a year at the Lycée de Toulon (Var). He then obtained a leave to study at the École du Louvre, where he undertook research on the painter Jean-François Millet (1814–1875).

During World War I, Cain was serving as a lieutenant when he was gravely wounded on February 12, 1916. Not able to return to military service, he was assigned to the Information Office (then attached to the Ministry of War but later made part of the Ministry of Foreign Affairs). There he was involved with editing daily and periodic *Bulletins* of the foreign press as well as editing collections of foreign documents (*Recueils de documents étrangers*). In 1918 he also published the second edition of the guide to periodicals used in compiling those bulletins.

From June 10, 1919, to September 30, 1920, Cain received another leave to complete his studies at the École du Louvre. He was then assigned to the Ministry of Foreign Affairs, where he worked for several years in the cultural relations division. Cain left his post in the ministry in 1927 to take over the direction of the Cabinet of the President of the Chamber of Deputies.

Appointed Administrator-General of the Bibliothèque Nationale on May 1, 1930, Cain undertook the physical renovation of the buildings—notably the construction of an annex in Versailles (1934) and the construction of two basement floors for stacks in the department of printed books in the central library (1936). He also began the interior renovation of the 17th-century Hôtel Tubeuf for the department of engravings (1937). Between 1930 and 1939 there was also an increased pace of production of the printed catalogue (*Catalogue général des livres imprimés*); 61 volumes appeared (or one-quarter of the total set issued between 1897 and 1981). A microfilm department was also created (1937–39) and in 1938 a national record library, the Phonothèque Nationale,

was established. The Bibliothèque Nationale also began to meet the needs of other French libraries through the creation of joint services to provide for information, purchase, and cataloguing of periodicals and through the establishment of the Catalogue Room (Salle des catalogues), which was conceived in 1935 as a national center for documentation and bibliography. In addition, Cain served as President of Class II (Libraries and Literary Manifestations) of the 1937 International Exposition in Paris, where he set up a Museum of Literature. He also edited volume 8, "Written Civilization," of the topical *Encyclopédie française*.

In November 1939, the writer Jean Giraudoux (1882–1944), then commissioner general of information, called upon Cain to become secretary general of the Ministry of Information on April 9, 1940; in June he had to leave Paris with the government. Dismissed from his duties at the Bibliothèque Nationale on July 23, 1940, he nonetheless returned to Paris. The following February he was arrested by the Germans and was deported to Buchenwald in 1944. Liberated by the American army, he returned to Paris on April 18, 1945.

By October 1945 he had effectively resumed his duties as Administrator-General of the Bibliotèque Nationale; on April 18, 1946, he was also placed in charge of the national directorate of libraries created at the time of the liberation. As head of the Direction des Bibliothèques, Cain carefully followed the elaboration of civil service statutes for library personnel, which served as a key element in standardizing appointment and advancement procedures in French libraries. Between 1948 and 1963 Cain also oversaw important construction projects that affected nearly 200 municipal libraries, including the war-damaged libraries in Douai (opened in 1956) and in Brest, Tours, Chartres, and Lorient (in progress in 1963). At the same time, construction work was undertaken for many academic libraries; in some instances departments (*sections*) of the university library were moved to the central campus (as in Bordeaux-Talence, Lyon-La Doua, Toulouse-Rangueil), while in other cases they were newly created, as in Nice and Reims.

Always in favor of coordination, Cain set up a union list of foreign works (*Catalogue collectif des ouvrages étrangers*) in 1952 and created an ongoing inventory of current foreign periodicals (*l'Inventaire permanent des périodiques étrangers en cours*) in 1953. That same year he got the *Bibliographie annuelle de l'histoire de France* established under the auspices of the Centre national de la recherche scientifique (CNRS) and got the future center for research on the conservation of graphic records set up with the sponsorship of CNRS and the Muséum national d'histoire naturelle. Cain also had several directories of libraries and agencies for documentation published (1950–1951, 1963) and in 1958 he served as the first President of the Association for the Conservation and Photographic Reproduction of the Press (l'Association pour la conservation et la reproduction photographique de la presse).

At the Bibliothèque Nationale, Cain carried out 15 construction projects between 1945 and 1964; among them were the installation of the map library division in the central portion of the Hôtel Tubeuf and the construction of a second building in Versailles

Bibliothèque Nationale, Paris
Julien Cain

in 1954. Other building projects undertaken during that period included the extension of the central stacks in the department of printed books (1958); the excavation of Sully hall at the Bibliothèque de l'Arsenal (1959); and the construction of quarters for the music department and the national record library at 2 rue Louvois.

Many private collections had been acquired by the national library, and in 1960 an exhibit presented the notable acquisitions of the Bibliothèque Nationale during the preceding 15 years. On display were items drawn from the legacy of Atherton Curtis (which contained 7,000 engravings); manuscripts, drawings and valuable editions of French authors bequeathed by Henri de Rothschild (1872–1934); and items on the history of photography drawn from a collection assembled by Nadar (1820–1910).

Altogether Cain inaugurated more than a hundred exhibits, including the great retrospective exhibits on the history of the book, such as those on French manuscript painting (the 7th to the 12th century in 1954 and the 13th to the 16th century in 1955–56). Other exhibits commemorated specific artists from Pisanello, the engraver of medals (1932), to the painter Georges Braque (1960), or honored writers and composers from François Rabelais (1932) to Maurice Maeterlinck and Claude Debussy (1962).

Cain's activities extended beyond libraries to participation in many societies concerned with the book arts (Amis de la Bibliothèque Nationale; Peintres-graveurs français; La Reliure originale) and included service on national committees that dealt with illustrated French books and with engraving. As director of the Bibliothèque Nationale, Cain also served as ex officio member of national boards and commissions that dealt with archives and archival training; museums; belles-lettres; research; historical monuments; and radio and television broadcasting. In 1952 Cain was chosen a personal member of the Académie des Beaux-Arts (one of the five Académies of the Institut de France) and in 1961 he became a member of the advisory board of the Comédie française.

Cain also served on the French National Commission to Unesco until 1972; he became President in 1967 and chaired the Committee on Libraries and Museums. In addition he served as a member (1958–) and then as Vice-President (1960–1962) of the Executive Council of Unesco; he presided over the Consultative Committee on Bibliography, which became the International Consultative Committee on Documentation, Libraries and Archives in 1967. He also served as Vice-President of both the International Federation of Library Associations (1949–51) and of the International Federation for Documentation (1954–56). The creation of the International Association of Bibliophily (1959–1963) was one of Cain's last initiatives in his capacity as head of the Bibliothèque Nationale and of the Direction des Bibliothèques. He retired in 1964.

In 1963 Cain began serving as curator of the Musée Jacquemard-André, which was administered by the Institut de France. There he organized many important exhibits from 1964, when he presented the works of Millet, to 1974, when he opened an exhibit on the designer Paul Poiret. Beginning in 1964 Cain presided over the national commission charged with preparing a general inventory of the monuments and artistic treasures of France, and in 1971 he became President of the French national committee for International Book Year.

He died in Paris on October 9, 1974. His honors had included Knight of the Legion of Honor (World War I); the Grand-Croix of the Legion of Honor (1957); designation as Knight Commander of the Order of the British Empire; and honorary doctorates from the University of Glasgow (1950) and the University of Stockholm (1960). His guiding principle was "to maintain a well considered balance between two equally necessary points of view—the respect for the values of the past and the willingness to respond to the exigencies of the present."

REFERENCES
"Hommage à Julien Cain," *Gazette des Beaux-Arts* (1966).
Bernard Gavoty, *Notice sur la vie et les travaux de Julien Cain* (1976).
"Hommage à Julien Cain," *Bulletin de la Bibliothèque Nationale* (1976).

THÉRÈSE KLEINDIENST;
Translated by MARY NILES MAACK

Callimachus
(fl. 3rd century B.C.)

Callimachus, who rose from the obscurity of schoolteaching to become the lynchpin of Hellenistic poetry in its Golden Age (290–240 B.C.), worked as a bio-bibliographer at the Alexandrian Library, where he compiled the *Pinakes*, a *catalogue raisonné* of Greek literature in 120 volumes. Beyond that we know only a few details of his life, mostly of his childhood; a critical biography cannot be written.

Homer and Callimachus represent the traditional and modern viewpoints of ancient Greece. The traditional culture, which prevailed from Homer through Aristotle, was born of the Greek oral past; it was created in the absence of writing and maintained against the encroachments of literacy as long as possible. But Callimachus, less than 20 years after Aristotle, stood on the threshold of a new age whose culture was created by the book. The oral and literary cultures of Greece thus found expression in the two differing poetries of Homer and Callimachus.

Homer produced poetry spontaneously in live performances before a native audience; his was an oral art addressed to the ear, a matter of arranging preestablished musical formulas without fishing for the right word or adjusting it to the meter. Callimachus, however, composed poetry in the study, carefully selecting his words and working them into a few impeccable lines each day. He strove for technical perfection, regarding the ideal poem as a tiny jewel to be cut, polished, and admired by experts, and addressed an esoteric audience of educated connoisseurs in the artificial climate of Alexandria. He always looked things up before rehashing them.

Callimachus, finally, should not be regarded as the patron saint of cataloguers, even though he completed the bibliographical projects initiated by Zenodotus, which culminated in the higher and lower criticisms and in exegesis. The result of his work was a massive catalogue, the *Pinakes,* based on the *pinax,* the annotated list underlying all antiquarian writing in the 5th century B.C. It contained much more information than a library catalogue, providing for each writer a brief biographical sketch and a list of each writer's works, including lost ones. Any doubts about the authenticity of the book were also noted, and it was apparently arranged according to large categories such as epic, oratory, and history. Not merely a library catalogue, the *Pinakes* was actually a critical inventory of Greek literature, the first scientific literary history, attempting no less than a complete record of all Greek literature as it then existed.

Despite the availability of Oriental cataloguing techniques, Callimachus had no real model for his immense project because his bibliographical aims were typically Western: he wanted to make the *ideas* of Greek literature available for the use of scholars. The Orient, on the other hand, which regarded books as *things*, had invented a complicated system of cataloguing for keeping track of them, but it focused not on scholarship but on descriptive notes and parallel glossaries, which served only the practical needs of the archives, libraries, and schools of temples. These conflicting aims have created permanent bibliographical ambivalence. Do cataloguers deal primarily with the physical "body" of a book, or with its metaphysical "spirit" as a complex of meanings? Should they perpetuate the ancient cataloguing practices devised for managing things, or invent new procedures capable of managing ideas? The *Pinakes* of Callimachus constitutes an experiment that failed, for its influence on libraries is difficult to trace beyond the Byzantine period. But the work does raise for the Western cataloguer the bothersome question of bibliography as bookology—an issue that helps to explain, at least partially, why the problems of bibliographic organization and control continue unresolved.

REFERENCES

K. J. McKay, *The Poet at Play: Kallimachos, the Bath of Pallas* (1962).

H. Curtis Wright, *The Oral Antecedents of Greek Librarianship* (1978).

H. CURTIS WRIGHT

Cameroon

Cameroon, a republic in western Africa, is bounded on the north and east by Chad and the Central Africa Republic, on the south by Congo, Gabon, and Equatorial Guinea, and on the west by the Gulf of Guinea and Nigeria. Lake Chad links it to Niger. Population (1984 est.) 9,500,000; area 495,755 sq.km. The official languages are English and French, but there are more than 200 Cameroonian languages.

History. Oral tradition will have a key role to play for a long time to come. The Regional Centre for the Collection of Oral Traditions and Literatures collects and stores much "knowledge" from the "old wise people." It is said that "when an old man dies, it is a library burning." Before the coming of the written word, people passed on stories, messages, and other information by word of mouth. The drum was also used to a large extent. In the evenings, in the villages, old men would gather their children and tell them stories. Many of these were descriptions of wars and other adventures.

Victor Delocko

Expansion under way at the library of the University of Yaoundé in Cameroon (left).

After the partition of Africa in 1884, the Germans introduced their language as the lingua franca in Cameroon. Writing was then introduced in this language when schools were opened. There is now very little German spoken except by the old men who still pride themselves in it. In 1971 Max Dippold published a bibliography of documents in the German language in Cameroon that lists 6,216 titles. Most of these are in the National Archives in Yaounde. But a student using documents in the German language still has to go to Germany. The Germans left fortresses and archives in Cameroon but no libraries. After World War I, the French and British ruled parts of Cameroon. The French colonial administrators established *bibliothèques de brousse* (rural libraries) but these libraries served only as reading centers for officers who had to work far out of the urban centers. There is no evidence in the French-speaking part of Cameroon to show that there was any deliberate aim to open libraries for the people.

In the English-speaking part of the country, following the English tradition, all secondary schools had libraries. Some of these have grown but have not reached the dimensions of real school libraries. Many people still pride themselves today by saying, "I was the school librarian." In fact, these people were students in charge of the libraries. Even though the libraries did not receive many books and although the growth has been rather slow, all the secondary schools, especially those run by missionary bodies, have libraries.

It would be an overstatement to say that all secondary schools had or have libraries in English-speaking Cameroon. Before independence (1961), only missionary bodies ran secondary schools, besides the government. Thereafter, private secondary schools were also opened, the number of which has multiplied with time. Most or almost all of those run privately do not have libraries.

In big towns throughout the country some public libraries existed, although in the capital city these were opened (around 1960) mostly by foreign bodies. Those opened by foreign embassies are called cultural centers. The few public libraries that were of any reputation were those of Garoua and Douala in French-speaking Cameroon and Bamenda and Limbe (formerly Victoria) in English-speaking Cameroon. None of the libraries had more than a few hundred volumes, and they were badly kept. Urban centers had a great influx of people after about 1968 because of increases in schooling and more and more opportunities for jobs there. A major hurdle in the development of public libraries had been the lack of trained librarians. A few dedicated librarians can do much to encourage library development in the country.

National Library. The Cameroon National Library was established in 1966. It is attached to the Ministry of Information and Culture. It has three sections: Acquisition and Legal Deposit, Classification and Cataloguing, and National Bibliography. It had as of August 1984 1,400 books, 120 periodicals, and 50 reports. The National Archives was also attached to the Ministry of Information and Culture. The National Bibliography is supposed to be produced by the National Library, but no volumes had been issued as of mid-1985.

Academic Libraries. The largest academic library is that of the University of Yaounde. It was established in 1966 when the University (founded in 1962–63) moved to the present site. It thus brought together a number of small book depots scattered over the whole campus. It did not comprise a large collection; in 1973 it totaled 52,000 books, 620 serials, and small collections of slides, tapes, and microfilms. By 1977 the book collection had increased to 65,000, but the number of serial holdings had not changed significantly.

Two other libraries existed on the campus until 1974: the Library of African History, with holdings of 4,000, and Centre de Recherches et de Documentation Africain with 500 books, mainly intended to serve law and economic research fellows. When these libraries ceased to exist, their collections disappeared with them.

In 1975 the President announced the creation of four University Centers, at Buea, Douala, Dschang, and Ngaoundéré. Those of Douala, Dschang, and Ngaoundéré were functioning as specialized universities in 1985.

Efforts were made to increase reading facilities for the students in the University of Yaounde. The Librarian started planning for construction in 1975, and construction of a new building started in August 1983. It was planned to be a modern library. The University had an IBM 4331 computer in 1985 and library services were to be hooked to it. Twenty-four terminals, a micrographics department, and facilities for about 600 reading places and at least 500,000 books were planned. There were 90,000 books and 900 serials (August 1984).

Other academic libraries include those of the School of Journalism, opened in 1971 to train journalists for work in central Africa (as of August 1984, 4,000 books, 100 journal titles, and 320 reports); the Polytechnic School, opened in 1971 to train engineers mainly in road construction, building construction, architecture, and electrical engineering (about 90 sitting places, 5,330 books, and 60 current serials); the Advanced Teacher College, opened in 1961, the oldest institute within the University of Yaounde (8,500 books, 170 serial titles; it receives 50 reports a year); the Medical School, opened in 1969 (20,000 books, 100 journal titles, and 320 reports, the largest outside the main University Library); the School of International Relations, opened in 1972 (10,000 books, 160 serials, and some 100 reports; it receives United Nations documents); and libraries at University Centers.

Public Libraries. The few that exist are in Bamenda, Limbe, Kumba, and Garoua. Libraries attached to certain foreign cultural centers should also be included because the general public has access to them.

Dates and statistical data are difficult to obtain. A public library existed in Bamenda long before 1960. Although most of the books are old, the seating space has helped some patrons to study and relax. It was transferred to what is called the Cultural Center attached to the Ministry of Information.

The Douala Library exists only in name. The French Cultural Center (Centre Culturel Français) in Douala, Cameroon's largest city, however, has a large library with a children's section. The French Cultural Center in Yaounde was created in 1960, just after independence. With 16,000 volumes, 49 journal titles, and 50 reports, it was the largest public library in the country in the mid-1980s. It became the first library in the country to have a children's section. Besides children and adults, it serves students of all grades. It carries out book exhibitions quite frequently. The Garoua library staff have been trained, but the number of books is unknown. The Limbe Public Library is attached to the Youth Center. Built by the Presbyterian Mission in Cameroon in a busy

Libraries in Cameroon (1984)

Type	Administrative units	Service points	Volumes in collections	Annual expenditures (C.F.A. franc)	Population served	Professional staff	Total staff
National	1	1	1,400	1,200,000[a]	500,000	2	17
Academic	9	9	135,830	50,356,317[a]	12,000	12	110
Public	5	5	--	--	--	--	--
School	43[b]	43	68,420	--	--	--	--
Special	5	5	--	27,500,000[a]	13	--	35

[a]1984–85 budget.
[b]Schools visited by compiler.

part of the town, it would ordinarily be heavily used.

Cultural centers were being created in all 10 provincial headquarters in the mid-1980s, and a rapid development of public libraries by the Ministry of Information was foreseen.

School Libraries. Libraries in secondary schools are more developed in the English-speaking than the French-speaking parts of Cameroon and vary greatly in holdings. Almost all the secondary schools run by religious organizations have rooms set apart called the "library." The number of books range from a few hundred to a few thousand. Those with more than 4,000 books include St. Joseph's College, Sasse; Queen of the Holy Rosary College, Okoyong, Mamfe; Cameroon Protestant College, Bali; St. Augustine's College, Nso; and Sacred Heart College, Mankon Bamenda (perhaps the only one in the country using AV material in 1985).

In French-speaking Cameroon, libraries are less developed. Most secondary and technical schools are not organized for them. Very few have more than 200 books. Those that have more than 3,000 books are Lycée de Bagangte, Lycée de Foumban, and Lycée de Bafoussam.

St. Pius Teacher Training College, Tatum, has about 10,000 books, although the stock is not renewed regularly. Others include the Yaounde Institute of Statistics and the School of Social Affairs.

Special Libraries. Research libraries are likely to have a rapid development in the near future; they fall under the Ministry of Higher Education and Scientific Research.

The oldest of the special libraries, the Library of the Institute of Social and Human Sciences, was founded in 1935 (25,000 books and 60 current journals). This library has some rare material on the social sciences in Cameroon. There were plans to build an entirely new library for the institute.

Other libraries that fall under the Ministry of Higher Education are: the Library of the Institute of Man and Biosphere (MAB), founded in 1977 (about 1,100 books); the Library of the Institute of Zootechnical Research (IRZ), founded in 1979 (350 books and 98 journals); and the Library of the Institute of Medicinal Plants (IMPM), founded in 1981 (650 books and 89 serial titles). Plans were under way in the mid-1980s to build entirely new buildings for these institutes, and libraries occupy a large place in them.

Library of the National Assembly and Ministries. It is difficult to classify these libraries. Although their holdings are not large, they play a key role both in the administrative set-up and the economic development of the country.

The Library of the National Assembly was opened in 1960. It covers the human sciences, politics, economics, law, and literature. It moved to a new building built specifically for it. Although the Library had only about 4,000 books in 1985, it was hoped that it would soon begin to grow faster. It is used not only by legislative members but also by university students.

Another important library is that of the Ministry of Planning and Industry, mainly concerned with economics. Its 3,900 volumes are used by those who work on national economic plans and also by university students. It is the single biggest library of any ministry in Cameroon.

The Profession. There was no library school in Cameroon in 1985. Librarians are trained in Britain, Canada, France, Nigeria, and the United States. Because of the increasing demand for trained librarians, the necessity for a library school was felt, and plans were afoot to establish one.

There were almost 30 graduate librarians in Cameroon in 1985 and about the same number of sublibrarians in the country. Practically all of them were trained at Dakar.

In July 1975 the Cameroon Association of Librarians, Archivists, Documentalists, and Museum Curators (ABADCAM) was founded. The main aims of the Association were the encouragement of the establishment of libraries at all levels and in all parts of the country and the promotion of the training of personnel for libraries, archives, museums, and documentation centers. Peter N. Chateh was its founder and President in the three founding years. By late 1978, at the end of his term, there were just over 40 members. There were more than 120 potential candidates as members, with about half trained in the profession, but the Association's activities lapsed.

On a limited basis, junior staff are trained in the University Library to work in various ministries in Yaounde. The duration of the training has been generally three to six months, but a few have stayed on for a year and even two years.

PETER NKANGAFACK CHATEH

Canada

Canada is a federal parliamentary state of North America bounded by the Arctic Ocean on the north, the Atlantic Ocean on the east, the United States on the south, and the Pacific Ocean and Alaska on the west. Population (1984 est.) 25,082,000; area 9,976,139 sq.km. Official languages are English and French. It is a member of the Commonwealth.

HISTORICAL OVERVIEW

In Canada, as in any other country, library development has depended on the interaction of five main factors: geography, demography, economics, political and governmental organization, and history. To this list must be added a special factor of profound importance—the influence of the U.S. Directly or indirectly, Canadian libraries have largely patterned themselves on U.S. counterparts; at the same time, they have significantly departed from those models. Thus Canadian libraries are recognizably "American" but they are "American with a difference."

In the context for Canadian library service, the most easily discernible element is geography—and its corollaries, settlement and communications. Canada is the second largest country in the world, but only seven percent of the land is arable, and the climate is severe. Accordingly, the entire population is comparatively small, and the vast majority live within a 4,000-mile-long corridor extending some 200 miles north of the U.S. border. This combination of distance, formidable terrain, and harsh climate has meant that access is a perennial problem, particularly for those living outside the cities. The effect for li-

The National Library of Canada in Ottawa. Established with the passage of the National Library Act of 1952, it did not occupy these permanent quarters until 1967.

The National Library of Canada

braries is that Canada has experienced unusual difficulty in providing service for all its inhabitants. Conversely, Canada has learned to be more than ordinarily resourceful in finding solutions for problems of library outreach. Indeed, in some instances, such as the development of regional libraries or service to native peoples in the far north, it has made innovations of world interest.

The example of regional libraries may also serve to illustrate the way in which political and historical factors have produced distinctively Canadian problems and responses. In Great Britain and the U.S., the county library had proved to be an effective means of serving people in smaller towns and rural areas. In Canada the county did not exist as a unit of government in most regions; where it did, it was too small to serve as a practicable basis of operation. In the province of British Columbia, therefore, pioneering librarians had to invent "a special and suitable library district," which was a combination of school districts and small municipalities cooperating specifically for regional library purposes.

British Columbia's version of the regional library is only one of many in Canada. The diversity reflects two more central facts of Canadian life: the profound linguistic, cultural, and economic differences between the various parts of Canada, and the federal form of government. The differences between French-speaking and English-speaking Canada are well known; what is less well known is that the differences *within* these two blocs are nearly as great as those between them. Some Canadian historians have thus found it reasonable to speak of "five or even ten Canadas." A familiar metaphor describes Canada as a "mosaic," in contrast with the idea of the U.S. "melting pot."

Given the diversity imposed by geography, language, history, and socioeconomic conditions, Canada inevitably began and has continued as a federation rather than a unitary state. Under the Canadian constitution, powers are divided among the national government (which also governs the Yukon and Northwest Territories) and ten provincial govern-

ments. Libraries fall mainly within provincial jurisdiction and therefore reflect the differing interests, conditions, and capacities of the provinces.

The result is a pattern of markedly uneven library development; Canada is unable to plan and enact country-wide measures for library improvement. In such vital areas as research, cooperation, and maintenance of standards, the progress of Canadian librarianship is largely dependent on extragovernmental action.

Fortunately for Canadian libraries, if the factors of geography, demography, and constitutional law have made for difficulties, there have been more than compensating advantages in the socioeconomic sphere. The country's abundance of natural resources and considerable technological advancement have combined to produce a standard of living that has long been among the highest in the world. The Canadian people have had the means and willingness to give generous support to educational and cultural enterprises, and this disposition has been markedly enhanced by the growing Canadian nationalism since the 1960s. Thus Canadian libraries of all types have, compared with other countries, enjoyed keen public interest and excellent financial backing. In buildings, equipment, advanced technological methodology, and extent of use, they rank very high by world standards. Their collections, though seldom notable for rarities or scholarly distinction, warrant a very favorable rating when measured by more utilitarian considerations. Perhaps most important, Canada's affluence and concern for educational standards have placed the practice of librarianship on a high professional level. Most Canadian libraries require, as a minimum qualification for positions of professional responsibility, a Master of Library Science degree, representing six years of university education. This is probably the longest preparation demanded anywhere in the world for the first professional degree in librarianship.

Beginning as cultural colonies of Britain and France, coming later under very strong American influence, Canadian libraries have matured into their own distinctive amalgam of borrowed and indigenous characteristics. The relationship of Canadian libraries to those of the U.S. is now not so much a matter of following as of proceeding along parallel lines. Canadian librarianship has acquired maturity, its own identity, and often a position of leadership.

Recent developments on the Canadian library scene indicate technological progress and sociocultural concern. The development of TELIDON, a Canadian videotex system featuring advanced technology in the interactive use of databases, was enthusiastically supported by Canadian libraries and has been the subject of many experimental applications. The Canadian Institute for Historical Microproduction, a nonprofit organization created largely through librarians' urging, has worked to preserve Canada's cultural heritage through the reproduction and dissemination of older materials in microform. The Freedom of Information Act, finally enacted in 1983 only after many years of lobbying, promises to make government information far more accessible to the public than ever before and thus constitutes a landmark in the Canadian intellectual freedom movement.

NATIONAL LIBRARIES

National Library of Canada. Although the idea of a national library was espoused as early as 1883 by Canada's first Prime Minister, Sir John A. Macdonald, the National Library of Canada was not actually established until 1953 and did not occupy permanent quarters until 1967. The long delay is probably chiefly attributable to the lack of a strong sense of national cultural consciousness. It was customary and convenient to draw upon the collections of U.S. university libraries and upon the bibliographical services of the Library of Congress. Moreover, in the absence of a national library association, there was no organization prepared to exert sustained pressure for the creation of a national library.

Shortly after its formation in 1946, the Canadian Library Association, in conjunction with other groups, presented a brief urging the establishment of a bibliographic center as the first step toward a national library. The government responded by appointing W. Kaye Lamb as Dominion Archivist, with the specific additional responsibility of preparing the way for a national library. In 1950 the Canadian Bibliographic Centre was formed under Lamb's direction, and work began on the preparation of the national bibliography *(Canadiana)* and the National Union Catalogue. Finally, with the passage of the National Library Act in 1952, the National Library of Canada at last came into being, with Lamb serving in the dual role of National Librarian and Dominion Archivist.

Operating in temporary quarters, the National Library staff began developing collections, drawing initially on a large quantity of material transferred from the Library of Parliament. The enactment of the legal deposit requirement brought in current Canadian publications, and a purchasing program, relatively small but carefully designed to avoid unwarranted duplication with other libraries' holdings, added significant older and foreign publications.

Lamb retired in 1968 and was succeeded as National Librarian by Guy Sylvestre. A separate appointment was made to the directorship of the Dominion Archives, the two positions having by now grown too large in responsibilities to be held by the same person. A period of very rapid expansion and change followed. In 1969 a new National Library Act came into force; it extended the powers of the National Library to coordinate the work of all federal government libraries and to assume a role of leadership in establishing a network of bibliographic systems and services for the nation. The National Library was to be, in Sylvestre's phrase, "the prime mover."

In the next six years no fewer than 14 new divi-

Libraries in Canada (1982)

Type	Administrative units	Service points	Volumes in collections	Annual expenditures (Canadian dollar)	Population served	Professional staff	Total staff
National							
National Library of Canada	1	1	912,000 (2,200,00 microfilms)	27,847,000	24,634,000	215[a]	545[a]
CISTI[b]	1	1	700,000	16,792,000	24,634,000	70[a]	208[a]
Academic							
University	108	--	48,837,000	250,242,000	421,839[c]	1,671	6,554[d]
College[e]	86	--	3,758,000	35,323,000	143,056[c]	245	977[d]
Public	1,005	3,179	50,765,000	379,887,000	24,634,000	2,231[a]	11,095[a,d]
School[f]	7,984	--	47,617,000	30,819,000[g]	24,634,000	425[h]	4,634[d]
Special	1,700 (est.)	--	--	--	--	--	--

[a]Calculated in terms of full-time equivalents or "person-years."
[b]Canada Institute for Scientific and Technical Information.
[c]Full-time students only.
[d]Full-time staff only.
[e]Regional or community colleges not granting degrees. Data does not include Quebec.
[f]Data does not include Quebec.
[g]Materials only; staff costs excluded.
[h]Full-time librarians; 2,695 other professionals not included.

Source: Culture Sub-Division, Education, Culture and Tourism Division, Statistics Canada, 1984.

sions and service units were added, and the National Library conducted or sponsored extensive studies on federal government libraries, the National Union Catalogue, and automation. By the end of the 1970s, the period of rapid growth had come to an end. It was an appropriate time to review the role, services, and objectives of the Library, and a large-scale study was undertaken toward that end. In-house research and briefs from outside bodies such as the Canadian Library Association indicated that the National Library, for all its recent progress, still had serious limitations. The main problems were that it provided too little direct service to the libraries of Canada and that it lacked a "presence" outside Ottawa. The National Library was not yet, as had originally been hoped for, the Canadian "libraries' library."

In his subsequent report, *The Future of the National Library of Canada* (1979), the National Librarian proposed solutions for these and other problems but saw the main mission of the National Library as harnessing computer technology in establishing a decentralized bibliographic network for Canada. Accordingly, DOBIS (Dortmunder Bibliothekssystem), an integrated, automated system originally acquired in 1976, was developed to operational status for use in the Canadian Union Catalogue and many other services and functions. Similarly, the National Library prepared protocols for bibliographic data interchange and performed experiments for the application of an open-systems interconnection model.

In 1984, following the retirement of Guy Sylvestre, Marianne Scott, formerly director of libraries at McGill University, was named National Librarian of Canada—the first woman to hold the position. Amid indications that the federal government would lend it strong support, a new era had begun for Canada's national library.

Canada Institute for Scientific and Technical Information (CISTI). Although no longer called the National Science Library, CISTI does in fact serve as such, thereby enabling the National Library to concentrate its efforts on the humanities and social sciences. The history of the national science library service goes back to 1924 when the National Research Council of Canada (NRC) formed its library with the express intention of serving not only the NRC staff

but also scientific workers elsewhere in Canada. Under the direction of Madge Gill and later of Jack Brown, an impressive collection was developed, and services, such as the publication of a national union list of scientific serials, were provided. The NRC was de facto a national library, and its status as such was legally recognized in 1966 when it was officially named the National Science Library. A formal agreement made in 1959 with the National Library defined the division of responsibilities between them.

In addition to serving as the principal "backstop" collection of materials in its field (readily available through a photocopying and interlibrary loan service), the Library made a notable contribution, which attracted international attention, in the development of an automated STI (scientific and technical information) service. Its CAN/SDI (selective dissemination of information) Service provided subscribers with inexpensive batch delivery of bibliographic citations based on searches of machine-readable databases. The companion online service (CAN/OLE) is available through terminals in various parts of the country.

In 1974, as announced at the dedication of the impressive new building of the National Science Library, the NRC reorganized its information services, amalgamating the National Science Library with the NRC's longstanding Technical Information Service, which provided advice, information, and field assistance to Canadian industry, so as to constitute the Canada Institute for Scientific and Technical Information.

CISTI continues to carry on the various activities of its two predecessor units, including the operation of a Resource Centre for the Health Sciences. It also holds responsibility, formally assigned by the federal government to the NRC, for developing a national network of scientific and technical information. An advisory body (ABSTI: Advisory Board for Scientific and Technical Information) provides CISTI with proposals and consumer reactions for the latter purpose.

Library of Parliament. The Library of Parliament, which in various antecedent forms goes back as far as 1792, was the major national collection until the establishment of the National Library, and served as a quasi-national library. It carried responsibility for acquiring and storing copyright deposit materials and was the agent for international exchange agreements. Its collections were of a scope going well beyond the needs of the legislators.

Since the inception of the National Library, some 250,000 seldom-used volumes have been transferred to that institution, and the latter also took over responsibilities for deposit and exchange. The Library of Parliament became primarily a legislative reference service for the House and Senate. Its collections, however, are still so extensive and of such general scholarly importance as to warrant ranking the Library of Parliament as a national rather than a departmental library.

Bibliothèque Nationale du Québec. Established under a Quebec law of 1968, the BNQ, as the name implies, is based on the assumption that culturally the people of Quebec constitute a nation. The BNQ accordingly goes well beyond the usual scope of a provincial library. With collections derived originally from its predecessor library—the Bibliothèque

Canada Institute for Scientific and Technical Information, which has developed a national automated information network.

Canada Institute for Scientific and Technical Information

Saint-Sulpice—the BNQ undertakes to acquire all materials relating to Quebec and French Canada (it has the right of legal deposit for Quebec imprints). It issues a bibliography of current publications *(Bibliographie du Québec);* maintains a union catalogue of all important holdings in the province; publishes a Quebec periodical index; and provides reference, interlibrary loan, and bibliographic services. It also operates an extensive program of international exchanges, notably with the Bibliothèque Nationale de France.

ACADEMIC LIBRARIES

In Canada, unlike the U.S., "academic libraries" are more or less synonymous with the libraries of publicly supported universities. With the exception of the two-year community colleges, a recent and an increasingly important addition to Canadian higher education, there are very few undergraduate institutions in Canada and almost none that are really private in respect of governance and funding. This situation reflects the historical development of higher education in Canada. Although some older institutions (all in eastern Canada) go back to the first half of the 19th century, a third of the some 60 major degree-granting institutions were not founded until after World War II, and the others acquired their present character and dimensions only since the 1950s. The creation or marked expansion of universities required funding on a scale that only provincial governments could command, and they wanted multipurpose institutions that would offer professional and graduate studies as well as undergraduate programs.

Most of the growth and change in Canadian higher education was concentrated in the 1960s. A combination of affluence and substantial population increase swelled enrollments. Perhaps more important, the need to produce highly trained people for the Canadian economy and the desire to cast off "cultural colonialism" led the universities to establish programs of specialization and research. Before World War II it was generally assumed that Canadians wanting to do advanced studies would go abroad (mainly to the U.S.); later Canada sought to become self-sufficient academically.

Not surprisingly, the development of Canadian university libraries closely paralleled that of the parent institutions. As late as 1949 only McGill University Library in Montreal had more than 500,000 volumes, and only two others had more than 300,000. As the institutions changed, in effect, from colleges to universities, their libraries were forced to expand at a rate wholly unprecedented for them and impressive by any standard. Alerted by such persuasive and well-timed studies as the Williams Report (1962) to the severe inadequacy of existing holdings, Canadian universities supported their libraries in a program of simultaneous collection, at an intensive level, of both older materials and current publications. At Queen's University in Kingston, Ontario, for example, the acquisitions budget grew from $20,788 in 1947 to just about $1,000,000 in 1966, and that rise was by no means exceptional. In the ten-year period from 1961 to 1971, total Canadian academic library holdings increased from some 7,000,000 volumes to more than 24,000,000.

The growth in collections was only the most dramatic of the changes that transformed Canadian

National Library of Quebec, established in 1968.

university libraries in the 1960s. The percentage of institutional budgets devoted to the library averaged (median) over 7.5 percent, nearly twice the percentage usually obtained in the larger U.S. university libraries. This degree of support enabled the libraries to multiply service outlets, double and triple their staffs, and put up imposing new buildings. Homemade or antiquated classification schemes were replaced by the use of the Library of Congress classification, and the same impetus for modernization led to a surprisingly early and widespread use of automation. Canadian university libraries such as those of the University of Toronto, Laval University in Quebec, and the University of British Columbia in Vancouver could well claim continental and even world significance for their leadership in this area.

As in the U.S., the "golden years" for Canadian university libraries ended with the 1960s, but the falloff was at first not felt so severely in Canada. "Steady-state budgets" (which, of course, in the light of rapid inflation meant a considerable reduction in purchasing power) led to sizable declines in the rate of acquisition, but in the 1970s staff losses were modest, and they were almost entirely in the nonprofessional ranks. The total Canadian university library holdings rose by 72 percent in the 1970s, reaching a total of 48,837,000 volumes in 1982–83.

Even so, it would be fair to say that many of the new developments since 1970 reflected a sense of mounting economic difficulty. Concern over their financial position led support staffs to unionize, while librarians tended to join with their teaching colleagues in some form of collective bargaining. Both library groups also sought greater power in administration, and staff participation in management became the norm rather than the exception.

For their part, the directors of Canadian libraries looked increasingly to cooperation as a means of effecting economies in acquisitions and processing. While libraries were not able to achieve "rationalization of collecting" on any large scale, such cooperative groups as OULCS (Ontario Universities Library Cooperative System) and TRIUL (Tri-University Libraries, British Columbia) could point to successes in interavailability of borrowing rights, interuniversity

Metropolitan Toronto Library

Five-story Metropolitan Toronto Library, opened in 1977, one of the largest libraries in North America in seating capacity.

transit, and shared cataloguing. However, the eventual disbandment of OULCS and TRIUL illustrated the difficulty of maintaining cooperative operations among autonomous institutions.

By the mid-1980s the most significant factor in the development of Canadian research libraries—indeed of every type of library—was the creation of a major Canadian bibliographic utility. The University of Toronto Library Automation System (UTLAS), originally a unit of the University of Toronto Library but later an independent organization, became the principal supplier of computer-based cataloguing products and services to Canadian libraries. Rapidly expanding since its creation in 1973, UTLAS came to supply over 600 customers and served in effect as Canada's "unofficial national bibliographic network."

UTLAS, which serves customers in Japan and the U.S. as well as Canada, may also be taken as an indicator of the maturity Canadian university libraries had reached. With 14 Canadian institutions as members of the Association of Research Libraries (1984), with rates of circulation consistently higher than American norms, and with buildings such as the Sedgewick Undergraduate Library (UBC) and the Robarts Research Library (Toronto) attracting international attention, Canadian university libraries were no longer the "poor relations" of 35 years ago.

The maturity of Canadian university libraries will, however, undoubtedly be put to severe test and constraint during the latter 1980s. After a decade of retrenchment following a severe economic recession and double-digit inflation, the emphasis is no longer on expansion but on how to achieve the most effective consolidation and remarshaling of existing resources. Canadian university libraries must learn to devise strategies to adapt themselves to their new environment of fast-changing technology, rising service demands, and declining financial support.

College Libraries. In Canada the term "college libraries" has taken on a new connotation. There are only a very few colleges in the sense of four-year, degree-granting institutions. Some 145 non-degree-granting institutions, however, offer postsecondary programs. Such programs, usually of two or three years' length, cover three main areas: academic courses designed for university transfer, technical and vocational programs, and continuing education programs directed to the needs of the local community.

In Quebec and Ontario, colleges do not offer university transfer courses.

The great majority of Canadian "colleges" have been founded since 1965. Typically the colleges were organized in haste and used improvised community facilities. Their libraries reflect that sense of haste and improvisation. Although they grew rapidly, they had still not been able by the mid-1980s to catch up to the demands imposed by booming college enrollments.

The Canadian college libraries are much more than just newish, developing academic libraries, however. They offer several distinctive features. The emphasis on audiovisual materials is noteworthy. College librarians have stressed bibliographic instruction since so many students (especially immigrants and returning older students) often have little idea of how to use a library. The college librarians have also tended to work more closely with the teaching faculty than has usually been true in the university libraries and nearly always have full faculty status. Finally, the college libraries have frequently offered borrowing privileges to the local community, thus constituting a useful link between the general public and academe.

Like the university libraries, the Canadian college libraries suffered severely from the economic retrenchment that beset the entire Canadian academic world with increasing force from the end of the 1970s. With small hope of expansion of service in the foreseeable future, Canadian college libraries in the mid-1980s were concentrating on making the best of their present resources in stock and personnel.

PUBLIC LIBRARIES

The British North America Act of 1867, the basis for Canada's present constitution, assigned jurisdiction over education to the provinces. Libraries, without being actually mentioned in the BNA Act, were assumed to be covered by that provision; hence public libraries in Canada have been established and are governed under the legislation of ten different provinces and two territories. While provincial governments thus have, legally, the ultimate controlling power over public libraries, their actual participation and influence in the development of Canadian public libraries was until recently rather small. No province has enacted mandatory legislation requiring the provision of public library service. Few provinces have promulgated public library standards, and even fewer have made serious efforts to enforce their observance. The financial support rendered by provincial governments, while considerably larger recently, has with few exceptions accounted for only a minor share of public library funding.

What happened, in effect, was that the provincial governments, while responsible for the overall enabling legislation, left the operation and financing of the public libraries in the hands of local authorities—boards of trustees appointed by municipal councils. The development of public libraries in Canada has thus been very much a matter of local initiative, local control, and local support. Canadian public libraries are as various as the interests, character, and capacity of the communities they serve.

Yet the differences among Canadian public libraries are not as great as the complete lack of centralized direction would suggest. There are indeed substantial variations depending on whether communities are rich or poor, rural or urban, new or old, Anglophone or Francophone. Still, the settlers in one part of Canada usually came from another and brought with them familiar patterns of organization. Some British precedents (notably the mechanics' institutes) and the strongly influential American pattern were known to all. Moreover, schooling itself, both in level and kind, was remarkably similar from province to province.

Trends. The result is that one can distinguish several large-scale themes or trends that have dominated the history of Canadian public libraries. Until after World War II library extension was probably the chief concern; then the majority of Canada's rural population had no public library service. The extension movement was spurred by provincial development agencies such as the Public Library Commission of British Columbia and was usually achieved by some form of regional library organization. For the towns and smaller cities, the problem was that the population and tax base were too small to permit more than minimal service; a "larger unit" than the individual municipality had to be found. In the metropolitan areas—such as Toronto, Winnipeg, and Vancouver—coordination and cooperation between the various governmental units was the problem; "systems," whether "federated," as in the case of the Greater Vancouver Library Federation, or "unified," as in the case of the Metropolitan Toronto Library Board, were seen as the answer. And everywhere in Canada, as the inadequacy of local support and initiative became apparent, the role of the senior governments became progressively more important. Provincial government agencies eventually gave substantial grants, employed field workers and consultants, and in several provinces, notably Saskatchewan, provided a whole array of direct services such as centralized processing and backup collections.

The most notable instance of the intervention of a provincial government was in Quebec. In the 1960s the whole public library scene there was virtually transformed. The percentage of the population served by public libraries increased from some 20 percent in 1959 to 60 percent by 1974, and per-capita support rose by nearly 500 percent in the same period.

While no other province could show the extent or speed of improvement so dramatically demonstrated in Quebec, the 1960s brought very considerable progress everywhere. From 1961 to 1971 book stocks increased by 63 percent, the number of personnel by about 50 percent, and operating expenditures by just over 100 percent. The most visible part of the transformation was in the many new or remodeled library buildings; that of the Metropolitan Toronto Library (1977) attracted world attention for its size and design.

In the 1970s and first half of the 1980s, Canadian public libraries seemed to be resting on a high plateau. They mostly escaped some of the problems that had beset many large cities of the U.S.—deteriorating cores, declining circulation, and actual cuts in funds. Still, Canadian public libraries have had plenty of problems to contend with: budgetary pressures, learning to adapt to the unionization of staff, the effects of large-scale immigration on service demands and capabilities, and longstanding but unsuccessful attempts to secure federal funding. The traditional structure, based on local control and local support, still dominated the Canadian public library scene and was serving reasonably well, but strains were showing, and major changes were clearly inescapable.

To provide help with such problems, the Canadian Library Association sponsored the preparation of a large-scale study of Canadian public libraries—the first such since the Ridington Report of 1933. The subsequent publication—*Project Progress: A Study of Canadian Libraries* (1981)—provided a large stock of practical information for use in planning and decision making, and made a number of recommendations. It pointed up Canadian public libraries' need to emphasize and improve their public relations and marketing functions, to take better advantage of computer and video technology, to make themselves more "accountable," and to improve their personnel administration. The reactions to *Project Progress* were mostly favorable but there is yet some question as to just how much long-term effect it will have.

SCHOOL LIBRARIES

Canadian school libraries range from modern, even lavishly equipped, media centers to ragbag collections in the back of a classroom; the school librarian may have a Master's degree in Library Science or (far more frequently) no library training whatsoever. The unevenness derives from a central fact of Canadian education. Coming as education does under provincial jurisdiction, there is no unified national policy. Each province sets its own policy, and indeed within each province there is much variation arising from the very considerable autonomy held by the boards of the school districts.

Some generalizations are, however, reasonably accurate. Before the end of World War II, centralized

The National Film Board of Canada

Library of Parliament in Ottawa primarily, which serves as a legislative reference service, and also houses extensive scholarly collections.

school libraries were uncommon outside the larger cities. The function of the school library was mainly to supply "good reading" as a supplement to the teaching program in English literature and to serve as a study hall. In a textbook-centered, prescribed curriculum, the library was a marginal element in the Canadian school, and its facilities, staff, and collections all reflected that fact.

In the 1950s and especially in the 1960s, many Canadian schools adopted a "child-centered" approach that gave greater emphasis and opportunity to individual learning; the school library became important as the learning laboratory and chief means of independent study. With accompanying expansion of collections to include much more audiovisual material, many school libraries changed character and name to become variously known as learning resource centers, materials resource centers, or instructional materials centers.

Another factor for progress was the employment, generally by provincial departments of education, of supervisors or consultants specifically to plan and oversee the development of school libraries on the provincial level. Much the same kind of approach was taken in the wealthier areas at the district level. "School district librarians" provided advisory, coordinating, and centralized technical services in assistance of the individual school libraries.

Nevertheless, as the 1970s neared their end, problems were still more apparent than progress. *Statistics Canada* data for 1978–79 indicated that (excluding Quebec and the Territories) centralized libraries existed in only 85.8 percent of elementary and secondary schools. (Such schools did, however, enroll 95.4 percent of the pupils; clearly, the larger schools were very likely by now to have centralized libraries.) Even more disturbing, of those schools that did have centralized libraries, only 8.7 percent of the full-time staff were professionals with library degrees. Obviously, a highly qualified librarian was not yet considered an indispensable part of the Canadian school library.

With a tightening economic squeeze affecting school funding in every province and with libraries still frequently regarded as something of a "frill," Canadian school librarians have felt increasingly hard

pressed over the last decade. Many teacher-librarians have been dismissed or not replaced. However, several important studies promised to provide beneficial long-term effects. The Canadian Book Publishers' Council survey (*School Libraries in Canada,* 1982) demonstrated the importance of the school principal in making for effective collection development. The Ontario Ministry of Education's *Partners in Action: The Library Resource Centre in the School Curriculum* (1982) made a strong case for the school library's key role in self-directed learning. The *Report of the Nova Scotia Task Force on School Library Service* (1981) argued persuasively for special commitment to school libraries as a basic support service in education.

SPECIAL LIBRARIES

Although the existence of special libraries in Canada can be traced back as far as 1725, their chief development has been comparatively recent. Beryl L. Anderson's definitive study, "Special Libraries in Canada," in *Canadian Libraries in Their Changing Environment* (1977), indicates that 75 percent of Canadian special libraries had been established since World War II. Perhaps half the present total date from the end of the 1960s.

A "branch plant economy" that historically characterized Canada probably accounts for the late development of special libraries. With so many Canadian firms being subsidiaries of foreign companies, the research operations and head offices of these firms were often not in Canada, suggesting lack of need for special library services in Canada itself. Much the same considerations account for the fact that the great majority of special libraries that have been established in Canada are in Ottawa, Toronto, and Montreal—the headquarters cities for Canadian government, industry, and finance.

From 1968 to 1978 the combination of population increases, industrialization, emphasis on economic nationalism, and regional development (notably the concentration of oil companies in Alberta) made for an unprecedented demand for special library services. Special libraries have been the "growth sector" in contemporary Canadian librarianship, with several library schools reporting that more of their graduates took jobs in special libraries and information services than in any other field. Anderson estimated that there were some 1,700 special libraries in 1982 as compared with her estimate of about 1,100 in 1977.

Predictably, however, Canadian special libraries are still rather small. Anderson indicates that, as of 1975, more than one-half had under 10,000 volumes; more significantly, only just over one-half had more than one full-time staff member and then usually not more than two. It is important to note, nevertheless, that those one-person libraries were more likely to be under professional direction as the 1970s ended. Canadian special libraries have registered substantial increases in quality, range, and professionalization of service.

Other noteworthy trends of the late 1970s and early 1980s were the countrywide spread of special libraries (they are now to be found in some numbers outside of the Ottawa-Montreal-Toronto triangle); the rapid growth in the number of freelance librarians ("special librarians without a library"); the employ-

Architecture of the Robarts Research Library at the University of Toronto has attracted international attention.

University of Toronto Library

ment of librarians by many law firms; and the formation of several associations specifically to serve the needs of Canadian special librarians. While the latter continue to belong to such American organizations as the Special Libraries Association, which has chapters in Montreal and Toronto, the Medical Library Association, and the American Association of Law Libraries, they have also started organizations of their own. The establishment and growth of the Association of Canadian Map Libraries (1967), the Association of Parliamentary Librarians in Canada (1975), the Canadian Association for Information Science (1970), the Canadian Association of Law Libraries (1960), the Canadian Association of Music Libraries (1972), the Canadian Association of Special Libraries and Information Services (1972), and the Canadian Health Libraries Association (1976)—to name only some associations of national scope—testify to the expansion and increasingly professional character of special libraries in Canada.

THE PROFESSION

As in the U.S., the Canadian library profession is distinguished from other professions in that there are no legal or even generally accepted mechanisms governing qualifications, standards, and quality control in the practice of librarianship at a professional level. Informally, however, there is a country-wide understanding that a professional librarian must be a graduate of an accredited library school. The library associations, which act as the voice of Canadian library interests, are not limited to library school graduates but are in fact dominated by them. The library schools and the library associations thus together constitute the library profession in Canada.

Education. Library schools in Canada, like the Canadian libraries themselves, began by emulating counterparts in the U.S. and have since developed their own distinctive characteristics while still remaining very much in the general American pattern. This generalization applies almost as well to the institutions in Francophone Quebec as it does to the English-speaking areas of Canada.

Although the first library school course in Canada goes back as far as 1904 (McGill University), the first full-year, postgraduate program did not begin until 1931 (McGill) and the second (University of Toronto) not until 1937. Other programs came to be offered in Ottawa, Montreal, and Halifax (Nova Scotia), but McGill and Toronto dominated Canadian library education until the 1960s. In that period of library expansion, the need for librarians was clearly greater than Toronto and McGill could meet, and new graduate library schools were started at the University of British Columbia (1961), the University of Montreal (1961; French-language), the University of Western Ontario in London (1968), the University of Alberta in Edmonton (1968), and Dalhousie University in Halifax (1969). In general, these institutions offered the Bachelor of Library Science (B.L.S.) as the first professional degree (equatable with the M.L.S. in the U.S.). The Canadian schools named above were accredited by the Committee on Accreditation of the American Library Association.

In the early 1970s, a notable departure from the American pattern occurred. Seeking additional room in their programs to accommodate expanding profes-

Metropolitan Toronto Library

Metropolitan Toronto Library (above), which attracted wide interest for its grand proportions of size and its design (completed in 1977).

Gerry Cairns

Winnipeg Public Library, Manitoba.

163

sional knowledge, recognizing the growing need for specialization while not willing to have such specialization come at the expense of generalist preparation, Canadian library schools made the first professional degree the M.L.S., to be obtained by a two-year program (four terms) of study. McGill had already instituted the two-year M.L.S. in 1964; by 1972, Toronto, Montreal, the University of Western Ontario, the University of British Columbia, and Dalhousie had followed; Alberta did so in 1976. Canadian library education programs are now thus significantly longer than most of those in the U.S. and perhaps, indeed, than anywhere else.

Other noteworthy developments in the graduate library schools were the inception of doctoral programs in the early 1970s at Toronto and the University of Western Ontario; the demise of the University of Ottawa school, which had offered the only bilingual program in Canada; the remarkable growth of the Toronto and University of Western Ontario schools, now two of the very largest in North America; and the erection of what may well be the most impressive library school building (Toronto) on the continent.

The seven graduate library schools awarded approximately 500 master's degrees in 1981–82, of which Toronto accounted for 92 and the University of Western Ontario for 148.

In addition to the graduate library school programs, undergraduate courses in librarianship are offered by the faculties of education in many Canadian universities; these courses are intended for the training of school librarians. Other undergraduate programs, of a more general character, are offered by Concordia University (Montreal) and Lakehead University (Thunder Bay, Ontario).

On the nonprofessional level, library technician training programs are very well developed in Canada. The first such Canadian program was established in Winnipeg in 1962; by 1982 such training programs were being offered in 22 institutions in Canada. In the four Western provinces, the parent institutions are community colleges; in Ontario, colleges of applied arts and technology (CAATS); in Quebec, *collèges d'enseignement général et professionel* (CEGEPs). No library technician training programs were offered in the Atlantic Provinces in the mid-1980s.

In general, the library technician programs are of two years' duration, one-half of which is given over to courses in librarianship. Apart from Quebec, all programs follow the well-designed *Guidelines for the Training of Library Technicians,* issued by the Canadian Library Association. The CLA also sponsors frequent surveys of the library technician training programs, which have had a strongly beneficial influence in the maintenance of standards. The ninth CLA survey (1981) reported that the 18 institutions described enrolled about 650 students.

Library Associations. *The Directory of Library Associations in Canada* (1979) lists no fewer than 149 library associations operating in Canada. The high number for Canada's comparatively sparse population reflects the diversity and regionalism that have characterized Canadian library development. Ninety percent of these associations have been established since 1960, which shows how recent and rapid that development has been.

The senior library associations in Canada are all provincial organizations. The Ontario Library Association, the oldest, was founded in 1900; the British Columbia Library Association began in 1911, and by 1936 there were provincial or regional associations in every area of the country. The national library association—the Canadian Library Association/Association Canadienne des Bibliothèques (CLA)—was not formed until 1946. Until that time Canadian librarians wishing to meet together on a national basis did so by meeting at the American Library Association conferences.

Canadian Library Association and ASTED. With an increasing sense of national identity (and much greater ease in communication through air travel), Canadian librarians have tended to make the CLA their principal medium for further professional interests. Since 1968, however, CLA no longer presumes to be bilingual; in an amicable recognition of linguistic, cultural, and political realities, CLA left the representation of Francophone librarians to the national French-speaking library association, ASTED (Association pour l'avancement des sciences et des techniques de la documentation). ASTED is itself a reorganization (1973) of the older ACBLF (association canadienne des bibliothècaires de langue française), which in turn was originally a Roman Catholic association. The changes of association name and outlook represent almost a capsule history of the development of librarianship in French Canada.

The Canadian Library Association (4,000 personal and 1,000 institutional members in 1982) resembles the American Library Association in its breadth of activities and complexity of organization. There are major divisions—almost autonomous associations—for the different library types, and many committees to represent special interests. CLA maintains an active publications program and speaks for librarians' concerns in public relations and politics. The lobbying function is, however, far more limited in the CLA than in the ALA, and the same is true for the Canadian provincial library associations, as compared with their state association counterparts in the U.S. The Canadian governmental system does not allow much opportunity for direct political pressure by smaller groups. The national, provincial, and regional associations are "open" in the sense that anyone may belong, though the great majority of members are in fact professional librarians. The associations thus act as umbrella organizations, trying simultaneously and not wholly successfully to work for both the advancement of libraries and the self-interest of librarians.

A type of association quite prominent in Canada but not known widely elsewhere in North America— the professional librarians' association, limiting membership to those holding stated professional qualifications—undertook the representation of librarians' self-interests. The Institute of Professional Librarians of Ontario (IPLO) was the largest and most influential of such purely professional groups; others were established in British Columbia, Alberta, and Quebec. Of these only the Corporation des bibliothècaires professionels de Québec/Corporation of Professional Librarians of Quebec and the Institute of Victoria Librarians (British Columbia) survive. The professional associations lacked sufficient numbers and failed to secure licensing powers. Unions and faculty associations, moreover, were increasingly seen as the most effective vehicles for protecting librarians' self-interests.

With their small memberships and inadequate funding, Canadian library associations seldom saw achievements match their aims. Nevertheless, they serve a vital function in Canadian librarianship. In a country of marked regional and cultural diversity whose librarians work largely in comparative isolation from each other, the library associations serve as indispensable means of communication and informal continuing education.

REFERENCES
Canadian Library Handbook/Guide des Bibliothèques Canadiennes 1979–1980 (1979).
Beryl Anderson, "Canada, Libraries in, 1970 to 1979," *Encyclopedia of Library and Information Science,* vol. 36 (1983).
Laurent Denis, editor, "Libraries and Librarianship in Canada," *IFLA Journal* (1982).
F. Dolores Donnelly, *The National Library of Canada* (1973).
Loraine Spencer Garry and Carl Garry, editors, *Canadian Libraries in Their Changing Environment* (1977).
Librarianship in Canada, 1946 to 1967: Essays in Honour of Elizabeth Homer Morton, edited by Bruce Peel (1968).
Project Progress: A Study of Canadian Public Libraries, Prepared by the Canadian Library Association (1981).
John Wilkinson, "Canada," in *International Handbook of Contemporary Developments in Librarianship,* edited by Miles Jackson (1981).

SAMUEL ROTHSTEIN

Cape Verde

Cape Verde, an independent African republic, is an island archipelago in the Atlantic Ocean approximately 620 km. off Africa's west coast. Population (1984 est.) 300,000; area 4,033 sq.km. The official language is Portuguese.

National Library. Cape Verde gained its independence from Portugal in July 1975. A National Library, with headquarters in the capital of Praia, was established to play an important role in coordinating educational activities and directing new initiatives. Coordination is especially crucial because the nation is spread among a collection of small islands.

Public Libraries. Facilities for the general public center in the nation's two major cities; both the capital of Praia on the island of Santiago and Mindelo on the island of São Vicente operate relatively small libraries.

School Libraries. Libraries in the public schools provide the boradest coverage in library service to the islands. Fifteen school libraries are found in all the major islands of the archipelago.

Special Libraries. The Government Statistics Service maintains a technical library for the use of government administrators. The Service's library serves as a center for documentation, maintaining census and other statistical records.

MARIA MANUELA CRUZEIRO*

Carlyle, Thomas

(1795–1881)

Thomas Carlyle, British essayist and historian, was responsible for founding the London Library.

Carlyle was born at Ecclefechan, Dumfriesshire, Scotland, on December 4, 1795. He entered Edinburgh University in 1809 and studied mathematics, of which he became a teacher. Later on he also read law at Edinburgh, but he is best remembered today as a writer.

Carlyle moved to London in 1834, but two years earlier he had written in his journal: "What a sad want I am in of libraries, of books to gather facts from! Why is there not a Majesty's library in every county town? There is a Majesty's gaol and gallows in every one." This cry from the heart came almost 20 years before the Public Libraries Act of 1850 was passed. Carlyle's only source of books in London was the British Museum, but to one who was extremely sensitive to physical discomforts, the Museum was an unfriendly place and its principal librarian, Sir Anthony Panizzi, totally unhelpful. Moreover, the journey from Chelsea to Bloomsbury was tedious, the Museum closed at five in the afternoon, and books could not be taken away.

Carlyle, therefore, decided to explore the possibility of forming a library containing the sorts of books that would be useful to him and that he could take home. He canvassed his many influential friends and acquaintances, called a public meeting, and formed a committee. The London Library opened its doors on May 3, 1841, with 500 subscribers and 3,000 books.

The Earl of Clarendon was elected President, and he persuaded the Prince Consort to become patron of the Library, which has enjoyed the privilege of royal patronage ever since. Once the Library was on its feet, Carlyle took little interest in its day-to-day affairs, although he was greatly concerned about finding the right librarian. Eventually he secured the election of John George Cochrane, already 60 years of age and with no library experience, although he had recently compiled the catalogue of the Scott library at Abbotsford. Cochrane died after 11 years in office and Carlyle, who in the intervening years had seldom attended committee meetings, once more became active. There were more than 200 candidates for the vacant post. Gladstone, who was on the Library Committee, supported the application of Neapolitan emigré Giacomo Lacaita, but Carlyle was determined that he should not be appointed. In the end he had his way. The committee chose William Bodham Donne, who received 16 votes, while Lacaita received only 4.

Carlyle's final appearance in the Committee Room took place five years later when Donne resigned and the question of a successor arose, but no record remains of the discussions that took place. Carlyle remained on the Committee until 1870, when he was invited to fill the vacancy on the death of the President, the Earl of Clarendon. He accepted on the strict understanding that he must never be asked to preside, and he remained in office until his death in London, February 5, 1881.

REFERENCES
Frederic Harrison, editor, *Carlyle and the London Library* (1907).
Simon Nowell-Smith, "Carlyle and the London Library," in *English Libraries 1800–1850* (1958).

STANLEY GILLAM

Courtesy of The Newberry Library

Thomas Carlyle

Andrew Carnegie

Carnegie, Andrew
(1835–1919)

Andrew Carnegie, often referred to as the "Patron Saint of Libraries," made new library buildings available to hundreds of communities in all parts of the world. He donated $56,162,622 for the construction of 2,509 library buildings throughout the English-speaking parts of the world. He gave more than $41,000,000 of this amount for the erection of 1,679 public library buildings in 1,412 communities in the United States. And he gave another $4,283,000 toward the construction of 108 academic library buildings in the U.S. After 1911 library grants were made by the Carnegie Corporation rather than by Andrew Carnegie personally, although he was president of the Corporation until his death.

This library philanthropy was actually only a small part of Carnegie's benefactions. The "Steel King" spent more than $333,000,000 (90 percent of his fortune) for what he termed "the improvement of mankind." The range of Carnegie's philanthropy was great and included the Simplified Spelling Board, more than 7,000 church organs, the Carnegie Hero Fund, the Carnegie Institute in Pittsburgh, the Carnegie Institution of Washington, the Foundation for the Advancement of Teaching, and the Carnegie Endowment for International Peace.

Andrew Carnegie was born on November 25, 1835, in a weaver's cottage in Dunfermline, Scotland. Because of the rapid industrialization of the textile trade, his father was forced to sell out his business, the boy's formal education came to an end, and the family moved to the United States in 1846. They settled in Allegheny, Pennsylvania, a suburb of Pittsburgh.

Carnegie's first job, at the age of 13, was that of a bobbin boy for $1.20 per week. After a year he became a messenger boy for a local telegraph company, where he taught himself the art of telegraphy and met important people. Carnegie eventually worked his way up in the Pennsylvania Railroad, made many wise investments, and built up the Carnegie Steel Company until he sold it to J. P. Morgan in 1901 for nearly $500,000,000. Then at the age of 66—healthy, alert, and keenly interested in politics and literature—Carnegie retired to devote the rest of his life to philanthropy and to securing international peace. He had married Louise Whitfield in 1887 and their daughter, Margaret, was born in 1897. Carnegie died in New York City on August 11, 1919.

A memorandum found among Carnegie's papers after his death revealed that as early as 1868, at the age of 33, he made plans to use the surplus of his income for the benefit of others. But he did not formally declare his philosophy of the trusteeship of wealth or, as it came to be called, the Gospel of Wealth, until 1889.

In his first essay on the subject, "Wealth," Carnegie declared that wealthy men were to live without extravagance, provide moderately for the legitimate needs of their dependents, and then consider all the remainder as surplus funds that they as trustees should distribute in their lifetime for the best promotion of welfare and happiness of ordinary people. The main consideration was to help those who would help themselves—but only to assist and never or rarely to do all, because neither the individual nor the group was improved simply by almsgiving.

In his second essay, entitled "The Best Fields for Philanthropy," Carnegie lists seven fields to which the wealthy could devote their surplus in the following order: universities, libraries, medical centers, public parks, meeting and concert halls, public baths, and churches. The best gift that could be given to a community was a free library, "provided the community will accept and maintain it as a public institution, as much a part of the city property as its public schools, and, indeed, an adjunct to these."

Carnegie Public Library Philanthropy. Why did Carnegie select libraries to be among his first and foremost benefactions? One reason was given by a friend of the philanthrophist who said that all of Carnegie's gifts were dedicated to causes and movements with which he was personally concerned. Libraries and books seemed to be of special importance to him. His father had led his fellow weavers in Dunfermline to pool their contributions for the purchase of books and delegated one of their number to read aloud while the others worked. This collection became the first circulating library in town. And Carnegie gave his first library to Dunfermline in 1881.

In 1850, while Carnegie was still a working boy in Pittsburgh, a Colonel Anderson of Allegheny established the J. Anderson Library of Allegheny City to furnish reading matter for the mechanics and workingmen in the trades. Young Andrew wrote a letter to the newspaper requesting that the library be opened to all working boys, and he was invited to use it. In later years he recalled awaiting Saturday afternoons with intense longing, "and it was when reveling in the treasures which he opened to us that I resolved, if ever wealth came to me, that other poor boys might receive opportunities similar to those for which we were indebted to that noble man."

Carnegie's confidence in the value of free libraries as a wise object of philanthropy may also have been stimulated by earlier and contemporary library philanthropists. He praised Ezra Cornell for beginning the distribution of his wealth by establishing a public library in Ithaca, New York, in 1857. He also had a high regard for Enoch Pratt's gift to Baltimore of $1,000,000 with a requirement that the city pay 5 percent of this sum annually to the library trustees for the support of the main library and branches.

Perhaps Carnegie's library philanthropy was also influenced by his business background. He once told an audience that far from being a philanthropist he was making the best bargains of his life. For instance, when he gave money to a city for library buildings, he succeeded in obtaining a pledge that the city would furnish sites and maintain the libraries forever. The city's investment was greater than his. "This was not philanthropy but a clever stroke of business." To all of these motivations must be added one with which Carnegie was frequently charged. His accusers claimed that he built libraries as monuments to himself for posterity.

Evaluation. The procedure for obtaining a Carnegie public library building grant was fairly simple. A community in need of a library structure had to have its mayor and council promise to provide a site. The city pledged to support the new library through local taxation in an annual amount that would be at least 10 percent of the sum given for the library building. That sum was usually based on about $2 per capita of local population.

The importance of Carnegie public library philanthropy lies in its perfect timing, coming in the best possible period—during the height of library expansion in the U.S. Beginning in the 1890s, states began to play active roles in organizing public libraries in each community. The need for library buildings was desperate, and Carnegie's gifts helped to fill the void. The provision of new buildings created an avid interest in and enthusiasm for libraries in their early, crucial years of development. Carnegie dramatized the value of libraries and stimulated other philanthropists to provide library benefactions.

An even more important point is that Carnegie's philanthropy widened the acceptance of the principle of local government responsibility for the public library. The method of giving was not perfect; many poor sites were selected, and the 10 percent support pledge was sometimes broken or more often not surpassed. Nevertheless, it was a wise provision, placing indirect pressure on government and the public to accept the organization and maintenance of the public library as a governmental service.

Actually, about two-thirds of the communities receiving funds for one or more Carnegie library buildings already had free public libraries or were in the process of organizing them when the Carnegie gift was offered. To be sure, many had just been organized or were being organized as a result of the stimulation of Carnegie benefactions and with the hope of obtaining new buildings. The incentive of Carnegie's gifts was enough to accelerate the library movement to a stampede. Some 188 public libraries in 1876 grew to 3,873 by 1923.

Carnegie's philanthropy continued to benefit public libraries and librarianship long after the formal termination of building grants. This extended library philanthropy is still in evidence today; in many ways it is even more important than the original bequest of Carnegie buildings, which ended after World War I.

Carnegie Corporation and Libraries. In 1918 the Carnegie Corporation asked Charles C. Williamson to make a study of library training. His report recommended that librarians should receive their education in universities rather than in training schools sponsored by public libraries and other agencies. Williamson also recommended the establishment of a graduate library school for advanced study, a national accrediting and certification system for library schools, and numerous fellowships. His study was a monumental work that resulted in a complete revision of the curriculum in library schools.

A Carnegie Corporation-sponsored study in 1924 by William S. Learned centered on the role of the library as a medium for spreading information. It called for expanded services to be provided by the American Library Association and for local and regional experiments and demonstrations leading to better ways of getting books to the people.

In 1926 the Corporation embarked on a 10-year Library Service Program, for which the trustees approved $5,000,000 in financial support. The aim of this program was to strengthen the library profession by supporting the activities of the ALA, by improving training opportunities, and by supporting certain centralized library services and projects.

ALA. Carnegie provided $100,000 in endowment funds to the ALA in 1902, and the Corporation gave $549,500 for the general support of the Association from 1924 to 1926; in 1926 it added $2,000,000 in endowment funds. During this period the Corporation also provided financial assistance to the Library of Congress and to bibliographic centers and regional catalogues such as those at the Denver and Philadelphia public libraries.

Other Benefactions. Gifts for the endowment and support of library schools and the establishment of the first graduate library school at the University of Chicago totaled $3,359,550. Fellowships for library training and the sponsorship of conferences, studies, and publications were also provided.

The Corporation also provided funds for several demonstrations of methods and techniques for bringing books to people of all ages who were living in rural areas far from the major population centers.

Following World War II, the Corporation provided $212,170 to the Social Science Research Council for the Public Library Inquiry. The idea of a study of the library's actual and potential contribution to American society was suggested by the ALA. The appraisal was made in sociological, cultural, and human terms.

Again, financial assistance from the Carnegie Corporation helped the ALA in 1956 to formulate and publish what popularly became known as the Public Library Standards. The Public Library Inquiry discovered the failings of the public libraries, and the Standards presented what they should be doing by setting up minimum guidelines for good service. Public libraries were urged to cooperate, federate, or consolidate into library systems for better library service. The Corporation's financial support of demonstration centers for extension of library service in rural areas, of the Public Library Inquiry, and of the Standards was an important factor in bringing about federal aid for public libraries beginning in 1956.

Carnegie's benefactions have played a major role in American public library development and have had a significant impact in all areas of American librarianship as well as those throughout the English-speaking world.

REFERENCES

Andrew Carnegie, *Autobiography of Andrew Carnegie* (1920).
Burton Hendrick, *The Life of Andrew Carnegie* (1932).
George Bobinski, *Carnegie Libraries: Their History and Impact on American Public Library Development* (1969), contains extensive bibliography.
Bobinski, "Carnegie, Andrew," *Dictionary of American Library Biography* (1978).
Carnegie Corporation of New York, *Carnegie Corporation Library Program, 1911–1961* (1963).

GEORGE S. BOBINSKI

Carnovsky, Leon
(1903–1975)

Leon Carnovsky, a member of the faculty of the Graduate Library School of the University of Chicago, excelled in teaching, writing, editing, and service to the profession of librarianship.

Leon Carnovsky

ALA

Carnovsky was born to Isaac and Jennie Stillman Carnovsky in St. Louis, Missouri, on November 28, 1903. Appointed Instructor at Chicago in 1932, he advanced to the rank of Professor in 1944. He continued active service until 1971 when as Professor Emeritus he moved to his retirement home in Oakland, California. He died there on December 6, 1975.

From early boyhood, his parents fostered his intellectual interests. His father had been a Talmudic scholar before emigrating from Lithuania, and his mother also came from a rabbinical family. In St. Louis they ran a small grocery store, which provided for them and their seven children, and they encouraged Leon to frequent the public library. After high school he worked for two years as a secretary, then entered the University of Missouri. Graduating with an A.B. in philosophy in 1927, he entered the training school of the St. Louis Public Library, going on in 1928 to become Assistant to the Librarian at Washington University. In 1929 he received a fellowship in the newly established Graduate Library School at the University of Chicago, where he earned his Ph.D. in 1932, the same year he joined the faculty.

As a teacher he conducted courses in the library and society, research methods, public libraries, comparative librarianship, and education for librarianship. His lectures, logical and coherent, were presented in a vibrant and resonant voice. He exerted a warm and dynamic presence within and without the classroom, and large numbers of his students regarded him as a confidant and friend. Foreign students were particularly drawn to him. He was both rigorous and skillful in directing theses and dissertations, and he was exceptionally adept at eliciting publishable papers from members of his classes.

His bibliography of published writings includes more than 160 items, all clearly and gracefully written. Their quality matches their quantity, and their range is far-reaching. Lester Asheim described the scope of this writing in a memorial tribute rendered Carnovsky in 1976:

> His doctoral dissertation was only one of his many contributions to the seminal studies of reading that marked the early years of GLS's innovative research program. His many library surveys, and studies of public libraries, became guides to action, as well as models for other professional appraisals. His writings on intellectual freedom, which anticipated by many years the themes which are now watchwords on this always contemporary issue, led to his chairmanship of ALA's Committee on Intellectual Freedom and subsequently built upon that experience. His long list of writings on library education cover developments from the early defensive days . . . through his chairmanship of the ALA's Committee on Accreditation, and after. His studies and reports on aspects of international librarianship reflect his foreign travels, as a Fulbright Fellow and on assignments for ALA, Unesco, and the American government.

Through 18 years, from 1943 to 1961, Carnovsky edited *The Library Quarterly*. In this work he maintained a standard of content and style that made the *Quarterly* the leading learned journal in its field, a model for both creative and careful editing. The work absorbed a huge amount of his energy and concentration. He devoted detailed attention to every phase of the publication process, from judging and editing manuscripts to proofreading and surveying the subscription list. Equally well edited were the many conference volumes he planned and prepared for the Graduate Library School.

His many library surveys and consultations throughout the world strongly represent his service to the profession. A notable example of their influence is his *Report of a Programme for Library Education in Israel,* prepared for Unesco in 1957, which led to the founding of the library school at Hebrew University. Also active in library associations, he was President of the Association of American Library Schools (1942–43) and Chairman of the ALA Committee on Intellectual Freedom (1944) and of the Committee on Accreditation (1963–65). He received the Melvil Dewey Medal in 1962 "for creative professional achievement of a high order," the Beta Phi Mu Award in 1971 for "distinguished service to education for librarianship," and the Joseph W. Lippincott Award in 1975 for "distinguished service in the profession of librarianship."

Carnovsky was a connoisseur of music, the ballet, drama, literature, and fine food. He married Marian Satterthwaite, a librarian and author of a book on public libraries, in August 1939. She died in January 1965. In June 1967 he married Ruth French Strout, a colleague on the Graduate Library School faculty. His homes were distinguished by their genial hospitality.

REFERENCES

"The Brothers Carnovsky: A Profile, a Monologue," *University of Chicago Magazine* (January/ February 1970); his brother, Morris, gained public notice as a distinguished actor.

William Converse Haygood, "Leon Carnovsky: A Sketch," *Library Quarterly* (October 1968).

Frederick A. Schlipf, "Leon Carnovsky: A Bibliography" *Library Quarterly* (October 1968).

Howard W. Winger, "Carnovsky, Leon," *Dictionary of American Library Biography* (1978).

HOWARD W. WINGER

Cassiodorus
(c. 485–after 580)

Flavius Cassiodorus Senator, writer and monk, was noted for his direction of his library at Vivarium. He was born in southern Italy around 485 and died after 580. Though his contemporaries called him Senator, later writers refer to him as Cassiodorus. From the scholarship displayed in his writings it can be inferred that he received the customary liberal arts training for public service. Besides giving orations, he found time while in public service at Ravenna to produce a number of writings: *A History of the Goths,* his *Chronicle,* and several other treatises.

The Gothic kingdom virtually came to a close in 540, when the royal city Ravenna fell before the onslaught of Belisarius. About the same time, and possibly as a result of it, Cassiodorus relinquished his position. He first proposed to Pope Agapetus the creation of a university at Rome on the pattern of the schools of Alexandria and of Nisibus in Syria, a plan that had to be abandoned because of unfavorable conditions. Evidently it caused the Pope to create a library in Rome.

Cassiodorus then returned to southern Italy, where he found time to establish and govern a monastery. The sacred retreat established by Cassiodorus was by no means a cheerless prison. At his estate, Squillace, overlooking a beautiful bay, it included luxuries and various attractions, such as elaborate baths and fishponds. From the latter extravagance the monastery derived its name; it was called *Vivarium,* or the fish pond. Cassiodorus's ideal was complete literacy among the monks, because he believed reading was basic to education. The written word was an instrument to develop one's individual perfection and to lead to a deeper understanding of the Bible. His *Introduction to Divine and Secular Readings* outlined the general monastic educational program. Devotional reading naturally held the highest place and comprised the content of the first of two books. The goal was a thorough knowledge of the Bible, and because the Psalms were recited in common, the Psalter was to be memorized. The total number of 1,399 lines is divided as follows: logic (dialectics) 37 percent, rhetoric 17 percent, arithmetic 16 percent, music 14 percent, astronomy 7.5 percent, grammar 5 percent, and geometry 3.5 percent. The proportion of emphasis probably reflects the chiefly literary content that constituted the curriculum of schools of his day.

Special provisions were made for those not intellectually gifted to follow the regular liberal arts program of study. It would be sufficient for them to study the outlines and usefulness of the seven liberal arts. For them Cassiodorus recommended practical training on the material needs of the monastery, including a reading program of such selected writers as Gargilius Martial, Columella, and Emilianus on the cultivation of farms, gardens, bees, birds, and fish and the study of herbs.

These two books constituted training in the correct understanding of the Bible, an art in which the liberal arts led the way. Cassidorus drew up his study program to develop methods in appreciation of the Bible: how to read it, how to understand it, how to interpret it in the light of recommended commentators, how to treat the manuscript text, and how to edit and transcribe it so that authentic writings could be preserved intact and passed on to coming generations. The last portion of the first book treated the techniques of literary transcriptions.

Cassiodorus saw the possibility of including intellectual labor within the sphere of monastic duties. Under his direction the multiplication, translation, and correction of manuscript texts was to become part of the daily routine of qualified monks. The Scriptorium was equipped with mechanical devices such as a sundial and a water clock to indicate the hours for the convenience of copyists, editors, and binders. It was lighted by self-filling lamps so that not even a cloudy day or nightfall should interrupt their tasks. Through his methodical directives, Cassiodorus made available for copyists a guidebook with rules for scribal work.

In addition to furnishing practical rules, he provided complete bibliographical references to allied fields in the reproduction of manuscripts. He recommended some knowledge of geography, abbreviations, and other secular studies as an aid to correct reading and understanding of handwritten texts. And because correctness of spelling was of high importance, he reminded them of the standard works and of his own separate book on the subject, *De Orthogra-*

phia. Some monks were trained for more advanced work in the Scriptorium. Since not all the monks could read Greek, some undertook Latin translations. Questions of textual criticism were reserved for emendators (*notarii*), who compared variant copies and added rubric notes and punctuation marks.

The craft of bookbinding was viewed as important to manuscript book production. Cassiodorus equipped a staff of binders to attire the books or, as he phrased it, provide "wedding garments for the heavenly feast," for the external decoration was intended to express the beauty of its content. Those assigned to the bindery were provided with a manual of sample bindings to assist them in selecting appropriate bindings.

Though our knowledge of the library collection at Vivarium is limited, a key to the reconstruction of its holdings is to be found in his Manual. Cassiodorus referred to 123 authors, including the Greek classical writers such as Artistotle, Homer, Hippocrates, Dioscorides, Euclid, Archimedes, Galen, Plato, Ennius, Terence, Lucretius, Varro, Cicero, Virgil, Horace Columellam Fortunatius, Valerius Probus, Seneca, Pliny, Quintilian, and Macrobius. Some of the manuscript books that lined the shelves of the library at Vivarium are extant; these are listed by D. M. Cappuyns. The library was arranged in nine bookcases with all Greek books put together in the eighth case. The classification scheme was based upopn subject matter rather than authors. Several works on the same subject were sometimes bound together in a single volume.

REFERENCES

D. M. Cappuyns, "Cassiodore," *Dictionaire d'Histoire et Geographie Ecclesiastiques* (1948), vol. 2, pp. 1349–1408, excellent for identification and location of books housed in the Library of Cassiodorus.

Cassiodorus, *Institutiones,* edited by R. A. B. Mynors (1937).

L. W. Jones, *Cassiodorus Senator: An Introduction to Divine and Human Readings* (1946), superb introduction to Cassiodorus in English and a translation of his *Institutes.*

REDMOND A. BURKE

Cataloguing

The users of libraries sometimes assume that the staff who serve them should be able to recall immediately whether any particular book, recording, or magazine is in the library's collection. Because librarians cannot in reality remember the authors, titles, and subjects of all the materials in their care, they create lists of the materials. The process of preparing such lists is called cataloguing.

Curators of ancient as well as modern repositories have regularly developed at least rudimentary lists of their holdings, if only to serve as an inventory device to determine whether all the materials that are supposed to be in the collection are actually present. Most early lists recorded the title or *incipit* (first words of the text) of a work, its author (if known), the extent of the work (such as the number of scrolls, tablets, or codices required to transcribe it), its location in the library, and perhaps its provenance (history of creation and ownership) and the name of the scribe who copied it. In addition to an inventory of

Catalogue card production in 1907: a library assistant works the press.

Cataloguing Department, Main Library, University of Pittsburgh, in the 1920s.

holdings, librarians eventually found it useful to have a fuller description to help their clientele determine accurately what materials were available and what they contained. The resulting more comprehensive lists became known as catalogues.

Defining *cataloguing* as the production of lists of library holdings serves to distinguish it from the more general discipline called *bibliography*. While bibliographers attempt to identify all items relevant to a particular subject field, produced in a given nation, or issued during a certain period of time, cataloguers normally direct their attention to the contents of a single repository. The two disciplines were often almost indistinguishable during the Middle Ages, but the separation of cataloguing from bibliography became common with the development of printed books that could be duplicated in large numbers and become parts of many libraries. During the mid-20th century the two disciplines have moved closer together again. The impact of computer and photocopying technologies and the development of comprehensive library collections, particularly at the national level, combined to cause some large library catalogues to function also as major bibliographies.

Types of Catalogues. Over the centuries various types of library catalogues were devised, with formats and arrangements dictated mainly by the context that they were designed to serve. Broad groupings of materials by their form (such as literature or music) or by the discipline represented (such as philosophy, religion, or science) were used to organize certain catalogues; others were designed to emphasize such characteristics as authorship and titles of the works and specific topics covered. The amount of detail shown in these catalogues and the order in which descriptive elements were presented, however, often differed, sometimes quite markedly, from library to library.

Even the cultural setting of the library influenced the kinds of catalogues that appeared. In Europe, for example, they tended especially in the wake of the Renaissance to focus upon personal authorship as the primary access to each item in the collection and to use the Roman alphabet as the principle of arrangement. In contrast, many of the catalogues in the Orient used the title of the work as the key element and arranged the records in a sequence according to the number of strokes in the initial character of the title.

Subject Catalogues. Library catalogues organized according to subject or topic proved to be popular, especially when only fragmentary or inconsistently developed subject bibliographies were available. Such catalogues have the distinct advantage of revealing materials immediately accessible to library users, whereas bibliographies identify but often do not specify a location for the items listed.

One form of subject catalogue, called *classified* or *classed,* gained popularity especially in Europe. Although subject catalogues can be sequenced alphabetically according to the words or phrases chosen to express the topics of the material, classed catalogues are arranged according to symbols representing a logical, hierarchical system that moves from general classes to specific subclasses in an orderly fashion. To make use of such a catalogue, a person must either recognize and be comfortable with the classification pattern or begin with the alphabetical index that will lead to the relevant sections of the classed catalogue. One strength of the classed catalogue is its "browsability," in that it can display a variety of materials either broadly or more specifically pertinent to a field of interest, without forcing its user to move back and forth among entries that are juxtaposed merely because they begin with the same letter of the alphabet. A weakness, however, is that many classification systems used to organize the catalogue are unfamiliar to the library's clientele and thus may be awkward to use.

In an effort to make the classified catalogue easier to consult, the *alphabetico-classed* list was invented. In it, materials are categorized first by the name of a general discipline, then further by the names of classes and subclasses. The general disciplines, classes, and subclasses, however, are not arranged according to a classification system. The subclasses are listed alphabetically within each class; the classes are arranged alphabetically within each discipline; and the disciplines themselves are sequenced alphabetically. This system requires some understanding of hierarchical relationships among subject fields but has the advantage of lessening the user's dependence upon knowledge of a particular classification scheme and to some degree reduces the need to consult a separate index to the catalogue.

Dictionary Catalogues. A popular catalogue during the first half of the 20th century was the *dictionary* list, in which all types of entries are arranged in a single alphabetical sequence. Such a catalogue generally includes a unit of descriptive information about each item in the collection; the unit can then be reproduced as many times as required to provide access to various aspects of the material: names of individuals and of groups associated with the work, its title, and the subject or form in which it appears. Dictionary catalogues do not need separate indexes. Because the dictionary principle was mainly used to arrange card catalogues, its popularity began to wane toward the middle of the 20th century as the increasing complexity and size of the card files caused problems for the easy location of appropriate cataloguing information.

Divided Catalogues. In an effort to overcome the filing problems of the large dictionary catalogue, a number of libraries constructed *divided* catalogues in which various types of entries were separated according to their function. Some combined author and title entries in one section, placing subject entries in another; others created a three-part file: author (or name), title, and subject. These same patterns of division have subsequently been utilized for other types of catalogues, such as those issued as books, as microforms, or as computer printouts.

Forms of Catalogues. In one ancient library, workers are reported to have inscribed its catalogue on the walls of the building. More commonly, the catalogue is recorded in a form similar to that of the library materials themselves: on clay tablets, on scrolls, or in a book (called a *codex*). After the invention of movable type, it became common to issue catalogues in printed form. During the latter part of the 19th century, however, many librarians abandoned these expensive printed book catalogues for a more easily updated loose-leaf format (including sheaf catalogues and guard books). During the first

Buffalo and Erie County Public Library

In the 1970s, cataloguers at the Buffalo and Erie County Public Library using OCLC data.

half of the 20th century, cards—eventually standardized to 7.5 × 12.5 centimeters (3 × 5 inches)—became the dominant medium for transmitting cataloguing information.

Although improvements in photographic and duplication techniques made the production of cards easier and faster, which in turn led to the development of centralized services that permitted many libraries to benefit from the cataloguing performed by one library or commercial organization, these same techniques also encouraged the reintroduction of the book catalogue, since photolithography provided a flexible and relatively inexpensive means of reproducing cataloguing data. By the 1960s, librarians began to take advantage of data processing techniques to produce catalogues as printouts or in microform. Many of these data processing systems were later supplanted by computerized systems that could produce both online (interactive) and offline (batch processed) catalogues.

This almost unlimited variety of catalogue formats has also stimulated experimentation with new configurations of data. The card catalogue in dictionary form has, in a number of libraries, been replaced or supplemented by a new form: electronic codes in a computer that can be displayed on a screen or printed, in whole or in part, as needed. Research and development in the 1980s are focusing in particular on ways in which the online catalogue can be made more responsive than its earlier counterparts to the needs of library users.

Standardization. Increased emphasis on the sharing of cataloguing data has stimulated the development of systems that can result in greater uniformity in the recording of such data. Standardization of basic descriptive data elements—their order, content, and punctuation style—has been seen as a way to enable cataloguers in one library to construct records usable by a variety of others and permit a library user

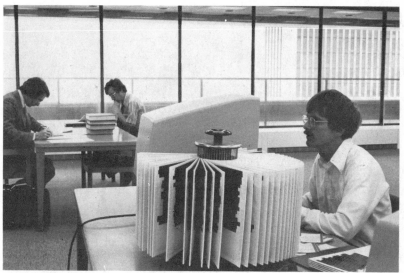

Microfiche catalogue at the State University of New York at Albany.

Arthur Plotnik

Book catalogues in the National Archives of Japan.

National Archives of Japan

to obtain information from several facilities without having to learn the cataloguing peculiarities of each. Such efforts as the International Standard Bibliographic Description (ISBD) developed by the International Federation of Library Associations and Institutions (IFLA) during the 1970s (currently under revision), the Cataloging-in-Publication (CIP) program utilized by a number of national libraries throughout the world, and the increasing dependence of individual libraries on regional and national bibliographic utilities (organizations that provide online cataloguing as well as other services for individual libraries and groups of libraries) have encouraged the standardization of descriptive cataloguing information. International agreement about standards for subject analysis (subject terminology and classification procedures) has been much more difficult to achieve.

Standardization that demands uniformity of cataloguing practice may produce undesirable consequences if it obscures the special purposes of a library by requiring it to conform to a procedure detrimental or irrelevant to the needs of its clientele. Inflexible adherence to established rules and procedures can also impede the effective cataloguing of new types of materials because specific procedures for handling them may not yet have been devised or sanctioned. The tension between the values of uniformity, on the one hand, and those of spontaneity and flexibility, on the other, continues to occasion much debate, although it appears that the use of the computer in cataloguing may not only encourage uniformity when needed but also allow for the adjustment of local catalogues to individual requirements.

Cataloguing Codes. In order to bring about standardization of cataloguing practice, a number of individuals as well as groups of librarians developed manuals detailing their procedures. These manuals specified what data should be included in the cataloguing record (such as name of author, title, edition, place of publication, publisher, date, extent and characteristics of the physical item, and series relationship), how to select access points (such as names of persons or groups, titles of works, and series connections), and how to regularize the heading forms by which the access points are listed (authority work). Some guides also offered rules for determining subject access and for the physical construction of the cataloguing medium.

A few of these cataloguing manuals, though initially designed for limited purposes, became the basis of later cataloguing codes. Such noted works as the 1791 *Instruction pour proceder a la confection du catalogue . . .* issued from Paris for those libraries taken over during the French Revolution, the "91 Rules" of Antonio Panizzi designed in the 1830s for the printed book collection of the British Museum, and the "Prussian Instructions" of 1908 were crucial in establishing cataloguing standards.

Anglo-American Cataloguing Rules. The contributions in Britain of Panizzi and in the United States of such imaginative thinkers as Charles C. Jewett, Melvil Dewey, and Charles A. Cutter led the way to the cooperative development of the first Anglo-American rules, published as *Catalog Rules: Author and Title Entries* in 1908 under the auspices of the American Library Association and the Library Association of Britain. Although the effects of World War II prevented much meaningful cooperation in the production of the preliminary second edition in 1941 (issued as *A.L.A. Catalog Rules*) or the 1949 *A.L.A. Cataloging Rules for Author and Title Entries*, with its companion volume, *Rules for Descriptive Cataloging in the Library of Congress*, Anglo-American efforts were again stimulated in the completion of the *Anglo-American Cataloguing Rules* (AACR) of 1967. At the multi-national level, IFLA sponsored a seminal conference in 1961 to try to achieve some compromise among rule differences, particularly between the Anglo-American and German traditions. The results of this International Conference on Cataloguing Principles held in Paris seemed to bode well for reducing the differences, but an American review of the expected consequences for the card files in large libraries caused dissension. Lack of agreement concerning especially the rules for the formation of corporate entry headings finally resulted in the publication of two versions of AACR: the North American text and the British text.

AACR was adopted in the United States in partial fashion, following the principle of *superimposition* used by the Library of Congress; under this principle only entries established and materials described after 1967 conformed to AACR. The North American text also perpetuated entry of certain institutions and governmental bodies under the name of the place in which they are located, while the British text supported entry directly under the name of the body.

Stimulated by the International Meeting of Cataloguing Experts (Copenhagen, 1969), IFLA, through its cataloguing secretariat, promulgated ISBDs for a variety of materials. This development in concert with the increased utilization of computer-based systems in many national libraries (initially developed by the Library of Congress as its Machine-Readable Cataloging System: MARC) suggested that AACR might be revised to bring the two texts together and introduce the ISBD as a coordinating principle for the description of all types of library materials produced anywhere in the world.

AACR 2. The introduction of the Second Edition of the *Anglo-American Cataloguing Rules* in December 1978 occasioned a break with traditional entry patterns and heading forms and caused considerable agitation among librarians using the older cataloguing codes. Some libraries decided to close (or "freeze") their card files and add or substitute machine-based cataloguing systems. The appearance of *AACR 2* did, nonetheless, help to advance international cooperation by encouraging the extension of "shared cataloguing," whereby one country can use the cataloguing output of another without significant alteration. A universal MARC (UNIMARC) program was created along with the design of an international "authority" system so that access points to library materials might be equated among the various languages and national practices.

While the basic intent of cataloguing has not been essentially altered by advancements in technology and standardization, the methods of constructing catalogues and presenting them to the public have been significantly transformed. Such transformations are likely to continue, especially as the capability for mass storage of data increases with the use of such devices as the optical disk. It may be expected that the combination of traditional descriptive and subject cataloguing data with preservation information and with the storage and indexing of text will constitute one of the next frontiers in achieving the effective bibliographic control of library materials.

REFERENCES

Kathryn Luther Henderson, " 'Treated with a Degree of Uniformity and Common Sense': Descriptive Cataloging in the United States, 1876–1975," *Library Trends* (1976), a detailed recounting of American cataloguing history, with some reference to the international scene.

Library Catalogs: Changing Dimensions (1964), the 28th Annual Conference of the Graduate Library School, University of Chicago, August 5–7, 1963, edited by Ruth French Strout, papers reviewing the function of the catalogue in the United States and Europe.

The Making of a Code: The Issues Underlying AACR 2 (1980), papers given at the International Conference on AACR 2, Florida State University, Tallahassee, March 11–14, 1979, edited by Doris Hargrett Clack, analyses of the principles expressed in AACR 2 and the expected effects of the new code on libraries.

The Nature and Future of the Catalog: Proceedings of the ALA's Information Science and Automation Division's 1975 and 1977 Institutes on the Catalog (1979), edited by Maurice J. Freedman and S. Michael Malinconico, papers discussing the changes in cataloguing and catalogue format being implemented or proposed for the 1970s and 1980s, including the automated catalogue.

Prospects for Change in Bibliographic Control (1977), Proceedings of the 38th Annual Conference of the Graduate Library School, University of Chicago, November 8–9, 1976, edited by Abraham Bookstein, Herman H. Fussler, and Helen F. Schmierer, papers considering cataloguing as part of national and international efforts toward achievement of bibliographic uniformity.

Mary Ellen Soper and Benjamin F. Page, editors, "Trends in Bibliographic Control: International Issues," *Library Trends* (1977), articles surveying cataloguing and bibliographic systems from a variety of perspectives.

Toward a Better Cataloging Code (1957), papers presented before the 21st Annual Conference of the Graduate Library School, University of Chicago, June 13–15, 1956, edited by Ruth French Strout, contributions from American and British cataloguing experts, treating the history and development of cataloguing codes and particularly the Anglo-American tradition.

DORALYN J. HICKEY

Censorship and Intellectual Freedom

In a general sense censorship is placing restrictive controls on the dissemination of ideas, information, or images transmitted through any communication medium. More specifically, censorship is commonly a prohibitive act directed against the original forms of information or materials conveyed—or intended to be conveyed—on the printed page, on television, in motion pictures, on the radio, in works of art, in voice recordings, or in a variety of electronic data transfer or communication devices. Censorship is also sometimes directed toward the contents of such live events as staged plays, musicals, dances, public speeches, or art exhibits. Some restraint is applied before the objectionable content is disseminated and is called *preventive* censorship. Restraint applied after publication is called *punitive* censorship.

Throughout recorded history censorship has been used in many attempts to bolster existing institutions, political systems, religions, or social systems. It has often been practiced to restrain free discussion, criticism, or analysis of doctrines or systems that particular censors have attempted to sustain, protect, or preserve. Censorship played a major role in the conflict between scientific inquiry and religious doctrines. Scientific inquiry won, marking a significant turning point in intellectual history.

The most prevalent type of censorship found in the United States today is based on moral grounds, occurring when private individuals or groups attempt to impose their own moral values on others. Censorship has been practiced in the United States in wartime to protect military operations and secrets from various enemies of the nation. In periods of peace, military censorship is also used to prevent such information from falling into the hands of potential adversaries. When military censorship is carried to an extreme, however, the public may be denied access to information that it ought to have to fulfill its democratic obligation to keep informed and to vote intelligently on critical issues.

Censorship for political or state reasons is common in nondemocratic societies at both ends of the political spectrum: military dictatorships and "people's democracies." After the Nazis took control of Germany in 1933, they rigidly censored books by Jewish and communist authors. They also staged public book-burnings of works they objected to as another type of political censorship. Religious or church-sponsored censorship may be practiced when ecclesiastical bodies are allowed to control certain public communications. The Roman Catholic Church maintained the *Index Librorum Prohibitorum,* a list of publications Catholics were not supposed to read.

Historical Background. There is evidence that censorship in one form or another has been practiced in almost all civilizations. Assurbanipal (c. 668–627 B.C.), the Assyrian librarian who developed a collection of more than 30,000 clay tablets that formed one of the greatest libraries of the ancient world, practiced censorship by removing from the library whatever the king found disagreeable.

Censorship also existed in Roman public libraries, where the works of Julius Caesar were removed on order of the Emperor Áugustus (63 B.C.–14 A.D.). The Emperor Julian (361–363), founder of Roman libraries in Constantinople and Antioch, attempted to destroy Christian texts. As a result of censorship in the classical world, many works by some authors were lost forever.

The term *censor* is rooted in Roman antiquity. Various magistrates were selected to take censuses of the Roman population and to determine citizens' responsibilities. These officials, called censors, were also charged with protecting traditional values. Among the renowned censors of the Roman Empire was Cato the Elder, elected to his office in 198 B.C., who worked diligently to erase immorality and promote the prevailing understanding of what virtuous Roman character should be. His great-grandson, Marcus Porcius Cato, or Cato the Younger, also functioned as an effective Roman censor after 65 B.C.

The censors of antiquity were regarded by Roman officials as protectors of high moral principles, integrity, and acceptable lifestyles among the citizenry. Thus, the modern concept of censorship derived from an ancient office of responsibility. It is significant to note, however, that free speech in the Roman Empire was primarily a privilege of members of the Senate and that many ordinary citizens who spoke out too freely were prosecuted and punished by officials of the government. Some poets, notably Ovid (43 B.C.–17 A.D.) and Juvenal 65–128 A.D.), were even banished from their homeland because of their unorthodox literary works. Ovid's *Ars Amatoria,* devoted to the art of making love, and Juvenal's remarkable satires, which dealt with the follies and vices of imperial Roman society, became objects of the censors' scorn.

Johann Gutenberg's introduction of a new technique of printing from movable type in the mid-15th century in Germany stimulated the censorship of books, when Roman Catholic authorities initiated prepublication censorship of printed books in an effort to control heretical ideas. In the 16th century the Reformation was a period of intense censorship activity, when Roman Catholic and Protestant church leaders sought to control the spread of those religious ideas that were in conflict with their favored theological teachings. The punishment of heresies was quite common during the Reformation. In England the Act of Supremacy (1534) gave Henry VIII authority to punish heretics. Church authorities were required to submit their books to higher officials for prior approval before publication; John Milton's *Areopagitica* (1644) was a protest against such licensing of printed books. The dissolution of monasteries and religious orders in England during the Reformation resulted in the wanton destruction of many thousands of irreplaceable manuscripts and books.

Philosophies of Intellectual Freedom. Ironically, the philosophers who first formulated both a theory of censorship and a theory of intellectual freedom lived as contemporaries in ancient Greece, where democracy was first conceptualized and initially practiced in Athens. Socrates (c. 470–399 B.C.) promoted freedom of the mind and refused to allow his teaching to be censored. Although Socrates respected Athenian law, the philosopher was regarded with suspicion by some public officials because he attributed vice to ignorance and promoted the notion that virtue is knowledge. Falsely charged with neglecting traditional Greek gods and of corrupting the morals of the young by alienating them from their government, the philosopher was convicted and executed. By promoting his faith in the value and benefits of free discussion, Socrates became the first person to express a profound philosophy of intellectual freedom.

On the other hand, Plato (c. 428–347 B.C.), a disciple of Socrates, formulated a defense of censorship for the control of certain undesirable religious, artistic, and intellectual ideas. In the *Republic,* Plato discussed the nature of justice and the presumed benefits of certain kinds of censorship. He argued that artistic works believed to be capable of undermining morality should be banned, that supposedly promoted heresy should be censored, and objectionable folktales should not be told to young persons.

Although dictatorships have routinely practiced censorship, most nations with democratic forms of government have limited such repressions through laws and have established legal reviews and appeals for certain repressive censorship decisions handed down by courts. For example, the Constitution of the United States outlines citizens' free-speech guarantees. The Supreme Court has ruled on many cases where constitutional law has been violated by restraints on freedom of speech or freedom of the press.

When citizens are allowed to govern themselves, intellectual freedom—freedom of the mind—takes on the role of the major sustaining right for that self-government. In a democracy, freedom of speech and of the press are sustained by the belief that citizens desire the actual truth and that, once truth has been found, it will guide human action. Citizens have the legal right in a truly free society to write articles or books for publication without first having to obtain a censor's approval. Of course, freedom of speech and intellectual freedom are not without their risks; they can be used to convey and sustain both truth and distortions of truth. However, freedom of speech and intellectual freedom have been used many times to expose falsehoods and other distortions of truth.

In the Declaration of Independence, Thomas Jefferson expressed the notion that natural right takes precedence over prescriptive law. That idea was embedded in the French Declaration of the Rights of Man and the Citizen (1789) and it became the preamble of the French Constitution of 1791. The emphasis on natural right was also incorporated in the basic laws that govern the United States. For example, it is implicit in the First Amendment to the Constitution:

> Congress shall make no law . . . abridging the freedom of speech, or of the press; or the right of the people peaceably to assemble, and to petition the government for a redress of grievances.

Freedom of the mind is the right of all people to speak or disseminate their thoughts about all subjects, accepting full responsibility, at the same time, for any related abuses of freedom of speech. When citizens have intellectual freedom, they can collect and disseminate whatever information they choose without official or unofficial restraints. In a nation founded on principles of democracy as commonly conceptualized in the western world, citizens have the right to communicate their sentiments in whatever medium they may select, whether it be a newspaper, periodical, pamphlet, book, video tape, film, musical score, computer printout, painting, or some other communication vehicle. Likewise, citizens have the right to freedom of access to all these communication media. In the library profession, the term intellectual freedom is used as the antithesis of censorship. Operationally, the term means the library user's right to read, to watch, or to listen to whatever he or she wants to read, see, or hear without any kind of official restraint. The librarian's concept of intellectual freedom is based on the conviction that freedom and ease of access to collections of information in libraries are imperative if citizens are to exercise their individual rights.

The Obscenity Problem. For the purpose of controlling publications and other materials deemed to be obscene or pornographic, all state legislatures in the United States have enacted legislation restricting sexually oriented public expression. Furthermore, federal laws currently prohibit the importation of obscene materials, their shipment across state lines, and their transmission through the mails.

Some critics of laws designed to regulate so-called obscene, lascivious, or immoral materials in the United States feel that such controls are acts of censorship and, when enforced, violate First Amendment provisions for freedom of expression or freedom of the press. In the opinion of these critics, both the lack of a precise legal definition for obscenity and the vague and indefinite nature of many laws passed to control sexually oriented materials fail to ensure due process of law for persons accused of crimes relating to such materials. Moreover, critics of obscenity legislation claim that it is often difficult—if not impossible—to prove that alleged offensive materials of a sexual nature cause criminal behavior; thus, they claim that free-press guarantees can be violated in some cases that involve the censorship of so-called obscenity. Another objection is that obscenity laws violate freedom of speech; however, it should be noted that obscene expression is presently not protected by the First Amendment, according to interpretations of constitutional law handed down in recent decades by the Supreme Court.

Many incidents of censorship are currently based on the assumption that exposure to certain ideas, words, images, or sounds will produce undesirable or illegal behavior on the part of persons who have read, seen, felt, or heard them. But the results of many scientific studies have failed to provide definitive answers to this question. Responses and reactions to materials deemed to be objectionable or obscene have often been unique; they have varied from one group of research subjects to another. Moreover, many complex sociological and psychological variables have been shown to be associated with both the desirable and undesirable internal meanings that many research subjects have gleaned from exposure to various sexual materials. Furthermore, only inconclusive research data have been produced relating to the degree and permanence of deviant behavior attributed in a cause-and-effect relationship to exposure to highly questionable sexual materials.

In the United States, many of the cases involving the censorship of books or other publications, films, videotapes, or other media presently focus on, or relate to, the alleged obscene nature of media content. Another characteristic of contemporary censorship is that printed materials are usually allowed greater latitude or freedom of content than some of the newer electronic media, particularly television. Some observers have explained this difference by noting that television is a popular vehicle of mass communication and entertainment—and that the more popular or pervasive a communication vehicle is, the more closely its contents are likely to be scrutinized by censors and would-be censors. The motion picture industry in the United States practices some degree of self-censorship, rating popular, mass-produced films according to their intended audience. As another popular entertainment and communication medium, films have long been vulnerable to the watchful eyes of censors.

In 1970, the President's Commission on Obscenity and Pornography, having responded to its charge to study the obscenity problem, and having examined results of many scientifically conducted research studies, concluded that no substantial evidence existed to link obscene materials to criminal behavior. But President Richard M. Nixon rejected the commission's conclusions and recommendations for both legislative and nonlegislative action. In addition, the Senate rejected the commission's report by a vote of 60 to 5. Almost three years after the commission's report was released, the Supreme Court issued a decision on obscenity that also reflected the Court's legal and philosophical disagreement with the commission.

In its report, the Commission on Obscenity and Pornography observed that the inability or reluctance of people in the United States to deal with sexual matters in an open and direct manner was responsible for many contemporary problems relating to sexually explicit materials. As to its recommendations, the commission also stated that "accurate, appropriate sex information provided openly and directly through legitimate channels and from reliable sources in healthy contexts can compete successfully with potentially distorted, warped, inaccurate and unreliable information from clandestine, illegitimate sources." But these conclusions and recommendations on sexual materials have remained quite controversial; they have also generated a 15-year-long debate about the question of obscenity and its real or assumed effects on people. The Department of Justice authorized a new commission on obscenity in 1985 to conduct another investigation of how obscenity and pornography might be better controlled. The national debate about whether sexually explicit materials produce adverse social effects and whether obscenity laws should be strengthened is likely to continue for many years.

In 1973 and 1974, the Supreme Court strengthened the censorship powers of governments of the 50 states by allowing the states to tighten their controls on so-called obscene works. The Court's decision delegated to the local area, rather than to the national level, the responsibility for deciding what is or is not obscene—a question that eluded the nation's highest tribunal for many years. At the same time, the states were put on notice by the Court to rewrite their censorship laws concerning sexually oriented materials. For more than a decade since the Court's last major decision on obscenity laws, state legislatures have been trying to reform their obscenity and pornography laws to bring them into conformity with the Supreme Court's three-part test for obscenity: (1) whether the average person, applying contemporary community standards, would find the work, taken as a whole, as an appeal to prurient interests; (2) whether the work depicts or describes, in a patently offensive way, sexual conduct specifically defined by the applicable state law; and (3) whether the work, taken as a whole, lacks serious literary, political, or scientific value.

Recent Censorship Trends. Since 1980, incidents of censorship and related assaults on freedom of speech and the press have been increasing in the United States. Some observers now claim that many of these new threats to intellectual freedom have been facilitated, if not encouraged, by a nationwide political shift to the right. Furthermore, activities of a number of recently founded politico-religious organizations appear to be undergirding a variety of efforts to restrict freedom of expression and to promote censorship. Increasingly, censorship is being viewed by these groups as a tool to control such objectionable materials as pornography and to trample out "amoral secular humanism," which some conservatives view as a chief source of society's contemporary ills and problems.

Collectively, ultraconservative pressure groups, aligned with moderate conservatives and right-wing politicians, various television evangelists ("electronic preachers"), and various fundamentalist religious bodies, have activated a wave of intolerance in the United States. That movement is stimulating more and more censorship in all areas of the nation. Recent efforts to place restriction on both the traditional and new technology communication and information channels, as well as on other older and newer techniques of literary and artistic expression, have been attributed to the growing climate of repression. Thus, the rise to political prominence of certain elements of restriction—coupled with the founding of such private lobbying groups as the Moral Majority,

Citizens for Decency Through Law, Coalition for Better Television, Christian Voice, The 700 Club, The Roundtable, and similar organizations of the New Christian Right—are viewed by most civil libertarians as an expanding threat to freedom of speech and intellectual freedom. On the other hand, some ongoing activities of these organizations have focused more public attention on the signifance of intellectual freedom in our pluralistic society with its democratic form of government.

Resisting Censorship. The Library Bill of Rights, adopted in 1939 by the American Library Association and systematically reviewed and revised since that time by the organization's Intellectual Freedom Committee, outlines philosophical guidelines for the protection of library users' freedom of access to uncensored library collections. It is ALA's official policy statement regarding the right of citizens to both current and historical information on all subjects and issues. The intellectual freedom statement serves as a guide to the desired professional behavior of librarians regarding freedom of speech; it also challenges librarians to resist "abridgments of free expression and free access to ideas." Although widely viewed in the profession as a standard by which practicing librarians can gauge their actions concerning the preservation of intellectual freedom and the resistance to censorship, the Library Bill of Rights is not a binding legal document, such as the Bill of Rights of the Constitution of the United States. The complete text of ALA's fundamental statement on intellectual freedom is provided below.

Library Bill of Rights

The American Library Association affirms that all libraries are forums for information and ideas, and that the following basic policies should guide their services.

1. Books and other library resources should be provided for the interest, information, and enlightenment of all people of the community served. Materials should not be excluded because of the origin, background, or views of those contributing to their creation.

2. Libraries should provide materials and information presenting all points of view on current and historical issues. Materials should not be proscribed or removed because of partisan or doctrinal disapproval.

3. Libraries should challenge censorship in the fulfillment of their responsibility to provide information and enlightenment.

4. Libraries should cooperate with all persons and groups concerned with resisting abridgments of free expression and free access to ideas.

5. A person's right to use a library should not be denied because of origin, age, background, or views.

6. Libraries which make exhibit spaces and meeting rooms available to the pulbic they serve should make such facilities available on an equitable basis, regardless of the beliefs or affiliations of individuals or groups requesting their use.

Various written interpretations of the Library Bill of Rights have been adopted by the ALA Council to bolster the maintenance of intellectual freedom in libraries. These carefully developed and widely publicized statements are as follows: How Libraries Can Resist Censorship; Free Access to Libraries for Minors; Sexism, Racism, and Other -isms in Library Materials; Exhibit Spaces and Meeting Rooms; Expurgation of Library Collections; Reevaluating Library Collections; Resolution on Challenged Materials; Intellectual Freedom Statement; The Freedom to Read; School Library Bill of Rights; and Resolution on Government Intimidation.

The ALA's Office for Intellectual Freedom works to implement ALA policies on intellectual freedom as embodied in the Library Bill of Rights. It publishes the *Newsletter on Intellectual Freedom* and the *Intellectual Freedom Manual*.

Many attempts to censor library collections have become public issues, and many librarians have struggled vigorously to maintain the rights of library users to intellectual freedom. On the other hand, there is evidence that some librarians tend to compromise and cooperate with censors. But the Library Bill of Rights and related interpretative statements are designed to help all librarians resist the forced curtailment of the purchase, use, or circulation of library materials, simply because someone finds them to be objectionable. Similarly, these principles are designed to prevent self-censorship by librarians, whereby negative selection policies are applied to screen purchases so carefully that anything likely to become the object of public controversy is not acquired or made available.

In the United States, librarians have a professional obligation to help citizens interpret and implement our democratic way of life. Thus, the library profession is committed to resisting censorship and to promoting the maximum use of libraries as institutions of freedom where citizens can seek truth without restriction in an uncensored repository of information, knowledge, and entertainment.

REFERENCES

Charles H. Busha, editor, "Censorship in the Eighties" (1982).
Robert B. Downs and R. E. McCoy, editors, *The First Freedom Today: Critical Issues Relating to Censorship and Intellectual Freedom* (1984).
Intellectual Freedom Manual, 2nd edition, Compiled by the Office for Intellectual Freedom (1983).

CHARLES H. BUSHA

Central African Republic

The Central African Republic, a former territory of French Equatorial Africa, is bounded by Chad on the north, the Sudan on the east, Zaire and Congo on the south, and Cameroon on the west. Population (1984 est.) 2,502,000; area 622,436 sq.km. The official language is French. The national language is Sango.

History. The location of Ubangi–Shari, the earlier name of the Central African Republic, in the heart of Africa was an obstacle for the first French explorers. As a result, modern institutions were established quite late in what had been an oral tradition society. Libraries, archives, and documentation services are fairly recent in the Central African Republic.

The first libraries came into being with educational institutions at the beginning of the 20th century. They were not separate institutions, just collections of books that supported the curriculum. Several decades were to pass and independence achieved (1960) before small libraries were set up in high schools and professional schools.

Archives first appeared with the French colonists who kept daily records and logs, sent reports to France, and received directives back. Ubangi–Shari was one of the countries of French Equatorial Africa (F.E.A.) that did not keep its historical archives. The capital of F.E.A. was Brazzaville, and the government's records were held there. Before the countries achieved independence, the archives were in large part transferred to Aix-en-Provence. The aim of the Central African Republic was the repatriation of those parts of the archives that concern the country.

The establishment of colonial institutions in the French Overseas Territories was followed by various local studies aimed at resource development. The accumulation of such research led gradually to the creation of documentation services, first in Brazzaville, then in Ubangi–Shari. The setting up of an agricultural research center in Boukoko and of others in the early 1940s marks the beginning of documentation services.

National Library. A decree of October 31, 1981, signed by the President of the Republic, created a National Library in the Central African Republic. The government department in charge of culture had taken steps to ensure that this institution will come into being and the draft of a legal deposit law was about to be adopted by 1985.

Public and Private Archives. The National Archives, which reports to the office of the President of the Republic, was created by a law of June 27, 1969. Legislation establishing an archives law in the Central African Republic was signed on August 20, 1983.

A large draft conservation plan exists for historical archives still dispersed throughout the country, but no real work had been started as of the mid-1980s because of a lack of funds. In the meantime, the Director of the National Archives undertook a campaign of public talks, radio interviews, and other public activities, in order to increase public awareness of the problems of archives.

The most important private archives are those of members of the clergy, former political figures, and old business firms. These remain the exclusive property of their owners.

University Library. Since 1981 the University Library, founded in 1970, at the same time as the University of Bangui, has been in a building that houses its science, literature, and law collections; the medical school has its own library. The same is true for certain other segments of the University: the Institut supérieur de développement rural at M'Bai'ki and the École Normale Supérieure, which became a university institute on March 2, 1982. There is seating for only 100 (out of a student body of 2,000) in the main building of the University Library.

Public Libraries. The public library system in the country is run by the government's Culture Department, assisted by the towns and cultural institutions such as the Protestant Youth Center and the cultural centers of certain embassies in Bangui. An objective of a new National Library is to play a major role in the promotion of reading throughout the country. In certain areas of Bangui and in the larger towns outside of Bangui, youth centers offer art programs and set space aside for reading. There was, in fact, no building housing a public library in 1985. Users are for the most part elementary and secondary school students.

School Libraries. School libraries have not been developed for a good number of years. In the larger schools there are small libraries, but they do little more than distribute books to students at the beginning and the end of the school year. Nevertheless, small reading rooms were being created here and there in the 1980s.

Special Libraries. Special libraries are connected with international organizations whose main offices are in Bangui and with research institutes. Among these are the libraries of the Organisation Commune Africaine et Mauricienne (O.C.A.M.), the Central African Customs and Economic Union (U.D.E.A.C.), and the Bureau Interafricain des Sols et de l'Économie Rurale.

Profession. In 1985 the Central African Republic had no library, archives, or documentation school. Training in those fields was given by schools elsewhere in Africa and in Europe, notably the University of Dakar (Senegal), the École Nationale Supérieure de Bibliothécaires, the École des Chartes, and the Institut National des Techniques Documentaires in France, and the École des Sciences de l'Information in Morocco.

There was no librarians', archivists', or documentalists' association in the Central African Republic in the mid-1980s.

ALAIN-MICHEL POUTOU;
translated by CHARLES S. FINEMAN

Certification of Librarians

A major characteristic of any profession is the concern its members exhibit for the quality of the services provided to its clientele. Every field sets standards of quality for those practicing in the profession and establishes some means by which those entering the profession can be qualified to practice. Several means for establishing credentials have been developed.

DEFINITIONS

Accreditation, licensure, and certification are three ways in which professions recognize the competency of those practicing in professional fields.

Accreditation is the process of examining the educational programs that prepare persons for entrance into the profession and attesting that the programs meet certain predetermined and prescribed standards. The professional association has the responsibility for setting standards and for designing the process whereby individual programs are examined and reviewed. By publicly acknowledging that the program is accredited, the profession, through its professional accreditating agency, states that the education is of sufficient quality to develop practitioners qualified to perform acceptably the functions of the profession. For the United States and Canada, the American Library Association (ALA) has chosen accreditation as the method to establish credentials for librarians, and through its Committee on Accreditation (COA) has set standards for the accreditation of graduate educational programs leading to the first professional degree. The COA regularly examines

schools and accredits those programs which measure up to its standards.

Licensure is the legal requirement that each person wishing to practice in a profession must obtain a license. A license gives the person the right to perform the duties of that profession, and anyone who attempts to perform them without a license can be prosecuted. Issued by government agencies, licenses are most often required in fields in which the health and welfare of the public might be affected by unqualified practitioners; medical doctors and dentists, for example, are required to obtain licenses to practice in a given state.

Certification is the process by which a professional organization or an independent agency recognizes a person who has successfully completed certain prescribed requirements of education and experience and has demonstrated certain skills or competencies, and declares that person qualified to practice that profession. Certification is accorded to the individual, rather than to the program of study or the institution. More than 425 professional associations have established standards and certification processes for their members in the United States.

Certification of librarians may be *mandated* by state laws or regulations; it may be *permitted* by state law, but not required; or it may be *voluntary* under a plan developed by a professional group on a nationwide basis or by professionals working at the state, regional, or local level. In general, school librarians/media specialists are certified under state law or state education department regulations; public librarians may have certification that is required, permitted, or voluntary within each state; academic librarians may be certified under state law applying to all librarians employed by the state or, more generally, are not certified but rather are employed as graduates of ALA-accredited library science programs; and librarians working in specific special library groups, such as law and medicine, are certified nationally through voluntary certification programs developed by their professional associations.

SCHOOL LIBRARIANS/ MEDIA SPECIALISTS

The certification of those who provide library and audiovisual services in elementary and secondary schools has for many years been linked with the teaching profession and governed by state education departments in each state of the United States. Generally, the requirements for library certification are attached as endorsements to teaching certificates and in most states carry a certification to practice for kindergarten through 12th grade rather than one limited to practice in only elementary or secondary schools.

There is little consistency or uniformity in certification requirements for professionals in school libraries or learning resource centers. School librarians are certified under a wide variety of titles, from "school librarian" to "media generalist," "media professional," "learning resource specialist," and "school media specialist (library)." As varied as the nomenclature is, the same variety is evident in the number of hours of course work required and the subject content of the program. Requirements range from six semester hours of preparation in librarianship to be certified to work in a school with fewer than 75 pupils, to education at the master's degree level and beyond. A majority of states require 27 or more semester hours for regular certification, and many require the master's degree.

Most states do specify certain required courses, often stipulating that they be at the graduate level. While the subjects may vary, there is some consensus that the study should include courses in administration, cataloguing and classification, reference, selection of materials, and audiovisual/instructional media production or use. Twenty-two states require a practicum.

There has recently been increased activity within state library and media associations in reviewing and updating certification requirements. Results can be seen in the added requirement of computer study in some states and a course in public relations in another. Some states have introduced tests as a part of the certification process, such as the California Basic Education Test, the Criterion Referenced Test in Georgia, and the National Teacher Exam in Virginia and South Carolina. By the mid-1980s, one state also recognized the movement toward competency-based programs for certification.

At the national level, the American Association for School Librarians, a Division of ALA, has for many years taken an active role in developing model certification programs for school/media specialists and in working with the Association for Educational Communications and Technology to raise the standards of school library/media services.

PUBLIC LIBRARIANS

Certification of public librarians can be traced back to a 1909 California law requiring certification of the head librarian of each county library, and to similar laws in Texas in 1919 and in Wisconsin in 1921. Some form of certification for librarians occupying certain positions in public library systems has since been adopted into law in about half of the states. Certification plans may be either mandatory or voluntary; in a few states, voluntary certification plans have been developed and implemented by state library associations.

Because there is no clear pattern, it is difficult to generalize on the qualifications required for certification of public librarians or on the positions that require certified librarians. Some states (such as Georgia, Virginia, and Washington) require certification of all librarians in public libraries serving populations of more than 5,000, and in every library operated by the state or its authority, including institutions of higher learning; county or city law libraries and public schools are specifically exempt. In states with this inclusive certification the law generally provides for withholding state funds from libraries that do not comply.

A larger number of states exempt the libraries of educational institutions, applying certification to public libraries supported by public funds. Other states (Maryland, for example) require each appointee to a professional library staff of a county library to hold a certificate, while other states restrict the requirement to heads of county libraries or library systems. The law may briefly state that certification is required, or

it may, as in New Mexico and Michigan, describe in detail the degrees and experience that earn the certificate. In states where the public librarians are part of the state civil service system, there is specific attention to grades or ranks and their appropriate requirements. In some states, certification is given automatically or by library school verification to those who possess a library degree from an ALA-accredited program. Other candidates for certification may offer equivalencies for consideration.

Whatever the certification requirements, most plans also provide for equivalencies to be presented for the educational requirements, often substituting experience for education, or a test over courses in specified subjects. In many states, persons with degrees from unaccredited programs may authenticate their studies with examinations, while those with foreign degrees or study in countries outside the United States may request an analysis of their credits for equivalency.

State library agencies, divisions of library service within state governments, and state professional library associations were in the mid-1980s reexamining certification rules and regulations. Wisconsin, for example, replaced the lifetime certificate with a five-year one, renewable upon evidence of suitable continuing education and professional development activity. Tests were added to the certification requirement in some states, while in others specific courses were identified.

ACADEMIC LIBRARIANS

A few states of the U.S. have general library certification plans for all librarians in libraries receiving state money; in those states, the basic requirement is the master's degree from an ALA-accredited program. The majority of states have no provision for certification of academic librarians, so requirements for employment are determined according to the needs of the library or the personnel regulations of the university or college system.

SPECIAL LIBRARIANS

Medical librarianship has led the way toward special certification in a library specialty. As early as 1948 the Medical Library Association (MLA) adopted a Code of Training and Certification of Medical Librarians. This voluntary certification, developed and implemented by the professional association rather than by an outside authority, was directed toward improving medical librarianship through basic standards for education and training and by certifying qualified librarians. This Code, with revisions, remained in effect from 1949 to 1977, and 3,200 individuals were certified.

MLA adopted a new Code for the Certification of Health Sciences Librarians in 1978, with revisions in 1981. The librarian seeking MLA certification must not only have graduated from a ALA-accredited program, but also pass an examination administered by the Association to test the entry-level competencies required of health sciences librarians; two years' post-library-degree experience as a health sciences librarian within the past ten years is also required, but provisional certificates may be issued to candidates lacking only the two years' experience. Recertification by

MLA is required every five years and is obtained through continuing education activities approved by the Association or by successful completion of the current certification examination.

Another example of a national voluntary certification plan for a special area within librarianship is that adopted in 1965 by the American Association of Law Libraries (AALL). The AALL preferred standard for all law librarians is Category I, which requires the library science degree from an ALA-accredited program, an accredited law degree or admission to the Bar, and two years of professional library experience, half of which must be in a law library. Category II substitutes four years of library experience for the library degree, and Category III substitutes six to ten years of library experience for the law degree.

The programs in both law and health sciences are examples of successful voluntary national certification that have raised the standards of library service in these special fields.

NATIONAL CERTIFICATION

One national plan for certification of librarians, in the United Kingdom, was extensively revised in the late 1970s. It offers at least a model for the planning process if not for a certification plan itself. The Library Association formed a Working Party on the Future of Professional Qualifications to "determine appropriate levels of registration and certification in relation to the present and future needs of the profession; to consider and define the nature of and to identify the principles underlying professional education and registration and how these should be attained and regulated, in the light of available evidence; and to assess the resources required from employers, training boards, educational institutions, and the Association, and to determine priorities." The document the Working Party produced, referred to as the Paulin Report, was the result of more than four years of study, work, and discussion. After its adoption in 1977 by the Library Association Council, an Implementation Board was formed to develop a plan of action and implement the program by the beginning of 1981.

The Paulin Report affirms the belief that the Library Association should "formulate a positive education policy aimed at producing the kinds of staff needed to operate the library and information services required by the community in the latter part of the twentieth century." While the plan as accepted by the Library Association Council retains two-year undergraduate courses, it recommends that "all those wishing to enter schools of librarianship should be clearly advised of the advantages of achieving graduate status." After completing the course of study, students must spend a year in a planned and supervised training program in a library agency. Candidates who complete this year with positive written assessments from their supervisors are admitted to the Library Association as Licentiates.

For the next step, the Licentiate must complete three additional years of appropriate service and professional development and submit a written report to the Association. If successful, the Licentiate becomes an Associate of the Library Association (A.L.A.) and a Chartered Librarian.

"Fellow" is the Library Association's highest classification. While retaining the requirement of a thesis and five years of library service as an Associate, the Paulin Report adds alternative routes to achieve this classification, such as submission of published work demonstrating original thought, or a carefully written account of professional achievement contributing to the field of librarianship.

With the implementation of the recommendations of the Paulin Report, the LA abolished external examinations, becoming more a validating agency than an examining one. In each classification the Association clearly affirms its belief in the importance of continuing education. The longer and more carefully prescribed period of training for chartered librarians was expected to strengthen library services, give prestige to the profession, and possibly bring the added benefit of improving salaries.

TRENDS

Certification of librarians has been discussed within the profession for many years. The Williamson Report of 1923, commissioned by the Carnegie Foundation to examine the preparation of librarians for professional practice, recommended the establishment of a national certification plan. After much discussion, ALA chose to accredit library education programs, leaving certification for the states to address.

The library literature of the 1980s reveals a growing interest in reexamining the potential of national certification for the profession. The interest in this possibility comes in part from a concern that the MLS degree has been weakened by events outside the profession.

The Civil Rights Act of 1964 and the Equal Employment Opportunity Act of 1972 led to a number of court cases that challenged educational requirements for jobs as being discriminatory. Events such as these raised the question of the validity of the MLS degree requirement for employment as a librarian. The ALA's 1970 policy *Library Education and Personnel Utilization* recommended the master's degree as the basic requirement for those holding positions designated as librarian, but in 1980 ALA's Office for Personnel Resources Advisory Committee modified that position by advising that the MLS was desirable, but that "court decisions necessitate careful consideration before requiring applicants to possess these credentials." The ALA's decision in 1984 not to testify in *Merwine v Mississippi State University,* in which the MLS was questioned as a job requirement, added to the concern of some librarians about the future credibility of its professional degree.

Some states provide for the alternate routes of examination or years of experience as qualifications for entry into the profession. The Library of Congress withdrew its recognition of the MLS as an entry-level requirement for employment in a professional capacity in its library, and a few public libraries in California, Colorado, and Ohio followed suit. The U.S. Office of Personnel Management proposed in 1983 to reclassify library positions downward for work in the federal service and to de-emphasize the MLS as an entry-level requirement. These actions represented to many librarians clear signals of the beginning of an erosion of the MLS's stature as the degree necessary for entry into professional practice.

Some librarians felt that the response to this trend must come through ALA actions toward validation of the degree through the costly process that validation requires. These people pointed to the studies of task analysis and competencies conducted by the Illinois Task Analysis Project, to the Selection Consulting Center in Sacramento, California, and to work by Susan Mahmoodi in Minnesota. Others proposed national certification, pointing to the diversity of state certification regulations and employment practices and the even greater variances among local libraries; they argued that only a national certification plan could bring cohesion to the profession, quality to the preparation of practitioners, quality of service to the community at large, and recognition and prestige to librarianship in the U.S.

Proponents of certification identify a number of advantages from a national certification plan. First, certification would guarantee to the public that the practitioners have attained a certain accepted code of professional behavior and ethics, a recognizable level of knowledge and job responsibility, and standards of acceptable performance. By developing competency-based exams, the profession would clearly define the characteristics of the professional librarian and would provide a national uniform standard of competency. Such exams might be instrumental in validating the MLS degree.

Certification would further provide employers with objective criteria by which to measure those applying for beginning professional positions, thereby reducing biased and discriminatory hiring practices. Some assert that certification could improve the public image of librarians and, therefore, help to recruit a high level of intelligent, qualified persons into the profession. It could improve the quality of professional education and provide incentives for continuing education and professional advancement. It could also enhance job security for librarians by preventing the hiring of unqualified persons.

Those opposing national certification observe that there are many incompetents in fields that do have certification as an entry requirement. They point to the high cost of developing and implementing certification programs and to the belief that librarianship is too diverse a profession to be entered through one certification plan.

One organization was formed in part to promote the idea of national certification. The National Librarians Association, established in 1975, has been persistent in its advocacy of certification and has developed a model for discussion among its members.

Whether national certification could or would become a reality for librarians in the United States was still unclear by the mid-1980s. It was certain that discussions of certification would continue at state and national levels and within the entire profession.

REFERENCES

Barry Bratton and Myrene Hildebrand, "Plain Talk about Professional Certification," *Instructional Innovator* (1980).

Holly G. Willet, "Certification and Education for Library and Information Science," *Journal of Education for Library and Information Science* (1984).

Elizabeth H. Woellner, "Requirements for Certification, for Elementary Schools, Secondary Schools, Junior Colleges," 49th ed. (1984).

The Library Association, "Working Party on the Future of Professional Qualifications: Recommendations and Implementation " (1977).

MARGARET KNOX GOGGIN

Chad

Chad, a republic in central western Africa, is bordered by Libya on the north, Sudan on the east, the Central African Republic on the south, and Cameroon, Nigeria, and Niger on the west. Population (1984 est.) 4,880,000; area 1,284,000 sq.km. The official language is French.

Academic Libraries. The library of the University of Chad, in N'Djaména, was founded with the university itself in 1971 and consists of three collections: the central University Library with just over 12,000 volumes and 41 current periodicals; the Library of the Institut universitaire des sciences, in Farcha, which offers some 1,500 volumes relating to the physical and biological sciences; and the collection of the Institut universitaire des techniques de l'élevage with its 500 volumes and 20 periodicals.

Public Libraries. While there is no centralized and uniform system of public libraries, most of the major towns have at least one library, falling within one of several classifications. Cultural Centers are in Abéché, Am Timan, Ati, Biltine, Doba, Fianga, and Oum Hadjer. Mission libraries with general collections number about 30 throughout the country. Five other larger libraries are particularly noteworthy: the Municipal Library of Sarh, the library established by the Alliance Française in Moundou, the American Cultural Center (a bilingual collection in English and French), the Libyan Cultural Center (Arabic), and the French Cultural Center (the largest collection in Chad—some 24,847 volumes with a lending rate of 8,000 per month) in the capital. The French Cultural Center also offers a film collection.

Special Libraries. The Institut National pour les Sciences Humaines, primarily a research institution, was founded in 1961 and has a library of some 3,000 volumes and 3,000 documents relating to Chadian ethnology, archaeology, geography, history, and linguistics. A similar range of subject matter is covered in the collection of the Bibliothèque Afrique et Tchad of the Archdiocese of N'Djaména. The Office de la Recherche Scientifique et Technique Outre-Mer (ORSTROM), also in the capital, has a library of 3,100 volumes, with 100 current periodicals, 713 manuscripts, and 230 maps.

Materials on problems of development are housed in the library of the Centre d'Etude et de Formation pour le Développement (CEFOD). The Centre de Documentation Pédagogique (3,300 volumes), founded in 1962, offers materials on education in French and Arabic. The American Cultural Center keeps about 4,500 volumes, with some current periodicals, records, and tapes. Other small library collections are those of the Institut d'Élevage et de Médecine Vétérinaire du Pays Tropicaux (in Farcha), the Central Hospital, and the Laboratoire de Recherche Vétérinaires et Zootechniques.

NEIL McHUGH

*Maria Teresa Chavez
Campomanes*

Chavez Campomanes, Maria Teresa
(1890-   )

Mexican library educator Maria Teresa Chavez Campomanes contributed significantly to the education of Mexican librarians, the improvement of teaching methods, and steps toward the goal of making libraries an extension of the classroom.

Born in Puebla de los Ángeles, Mexico, on August 1, 1890, Maria Teresa Chavez studied at the School for Librarians in Mexico City under the direction of Emilio Baz. She traveled to the United States for further study, graduating from Pratt Institute, and did postgraduate work in library science in Detroit and at Columbia. Later she was employed in the New York Public Library and the Library of Congress in Washington.

After returning to Mexico, she continued to study Spanish literature in the Faculty of Philosophy and Letters of the National University. She received the degree of Doctor of Literature in 1953 with a thesis on books that became classics. She was director of the Franklin Library and Subdirector (later Director) of the Library of Mexico from its establishment under José Vasconcelos, a philosopher. The progress of that library was due in great measure to her perseverance, and she became one of the few to serve youth of the metropolis with vigor and efficiency.

Chavez Campomanes came to be regarded as the very foundation of teaching at the National School of Archivists and Librarians of the Secretariat of Education and a similar school of the Faculty of Philosophy and Letters of the National University. The great majority of Mexican librarians learned at her side, gaining as much from her teaching as from the effective manuals of classification and cataloguing that she wrote. As a teacher, she was a model of clarity and patience. She was named Teacher Emeritus of the Secretariat of Education and won wide respect as one of the most distinguished women of Mexico.

ERNESTO DE LA TORRE VILLAR

Children's Services

Children in most industrialized countries have access to two kinds of libraries: one in their schools and one they call the public library. In some countries that public library may be administratively and physically separated from the library that serves adults, as in the U.S.S.R. In other countries, among them Japan and the United States, service to children is provided in a department of the local public library. Although that department may be physically housed in a special area, it is part of the larger, totally integrated administrative unit. When both public and school library systems exist in a country, the systems usually complement each other philosophically. Book collections in the two systems usually overlap in subjects covered and specific titles available. But unique mission statements of the two systems do shape differences in collection development, services, programming, and children's means of access.

The school library (now called in many countries the school media center, or school library media center) ideally serves the child's basic instructional and curricular demands for books, audiovisual materials, and other instructional resources. The public library, on the other hand, seeks to serve the child's broader and highly individualized desires for materials to serve educational, recreational, and personal developmental needs. Both library systems offer children access to the materials that will help them become literate citizens who will remain involved in lifelong learning. Therefore, in communities or countries where one system is nonexistent or poorly developed, it is crucial for the child's education and desire to read that the other system be strong.

PATTERNS OF CHILREN'S LIBRARY DEVELOPMENT
Library service to children has developed differently in each country of the world. However, the motives for providing library service to children are universal: the need to provide books to support a rising rate of literacy, the desire to enhance the social, cultural, and intellectual welfare of the children, the need to provide a variety of materials to meet the individual learning needs of the child, and the demands of the children themselves.

United States.   In the United States, public library service to children is little more than 100 years old. The earliest public libraries in the United States served children by placing collections in the schools. By 1891 some library leaders could affirm that nearly all public libraries were trying in some way to be of assistance to the schools. In many places, teachers were issued special cards for borrowing a specified number of books for a specified loan period, after which time books could be exchanged. Collections were kept in an individual classroom or housed in a central location to which children came in an organized class group at appointed times to check out books. The early cooperation was mostly with the grammar school (grades 7–9) and the high school, so younger children were left out.

Slowly, however, public libraries began providing unique facilities for the children. Concerned adults began to speak out for children's needs and rights to books. Gradually, seating space was provided; small collections of specially selected materials were made available; and attempts to provide programs, clubs, and other activities were successful in attracting the attention of children.

In the first half of the 20th century in the United States, children's work in public libraries developed as a vital and important part of total library operations and service. Children's work was established on a departmental basis in most libraries of any size and was becoming a part of branch library service as well. Children's librarians assumed responsibility for identifying and producing bibliographical aids. Service to schools through the traditional deposit of books issued to teachers and the eventual establishment of bookmobile service hastened the development of school libraries that became more prevalent after World War I.

By the 1950s, a variety of methods of reading guidance were being developed and described in the literature by a growing, talented, and dedicated new generation of children's librarians. Storytelling, puppetry, library instruction, and eventually preschool programs were acknowledged as important programs to provide for children. Forward-looking librarians in

Library Association

the late 1960s and 70s developed relationships with community agencies interested in the education, social welfare, and guidance of youth, thus setting an important trend for the future.

Libraries serving children in elementary schools were not to develop in substantial numbers in the United States until the 1960s and 70s. The substantial increase in numbers that occurred then was a result mainly of tremendous efforts made by national and state professional library and educational organizations and community groups. These efforts were supported by an outpouring of federal funds aimed at providing better educational opportunities for the so-called educationally disadvantaged and at increasing the quantities of resources available to all children. In 1960 only 31.2 percent of the public elementary schools had library media centers; by 1978, the number of facilities had risen to 82.7 percent of the schools.

When professional school librarians were added to elementary school staffs, and more money was provided to build facilities and buy materials, many of the former patterns of public library services to schools were no longer as necessary. Indeed, as school libraries became stronger in the late 60s and early 1970s, some questioned the need for two systems, advocating instead that school libraries take over all library service to children. As that debate entered its second decade, a new set of conditions had begun operating. The economy had improved, but the pattern of federal allocations for public schools had shifted. In that shift, direct categorical funding for school library resources disappeared, leaving the status of elementary school libraries throughout the nation in disarray. Salaries continued to lag for public children's librarians, and recruitment to either field had slowed dramatically. All of these conditions were exacerbated by the relentless development of expensive information technologies. The result was a dialogue that still continues within the profession about how and where the information needs of children can be most effectively met.

International Survey. The development of children's services in other countries has been uneven. Public library development depends on such things as legislation, governmental funding ability, a concern for universal education, a corps of educated librarians to lead library development, and many times on mothers and their children. These elements have been present in differing degrees in various parts of the world.

Independent children's libraries began to be developed in the U.S.S.R. early in the 20th century. Interrupted by major social and military upheavals, progress was slow in the early years, but since World War II serious efforts have been made to provide all children with access to public and school libraries. Government statistics report 8,400 independent libraries for children under the Ministry of Culture and more than 156,000 school libraries under the Ministry of Education. Once independent administratively as well as physically, many of the larger children's public libraries are now integrated administratively into general networks or systems of public libraries. Children's library needs are also served through organized programs in Pioneer Palaces, trade union libraries, and libraries in state nurseries and kindergartens. In addition, many of the Soviet republics have established republican children's libraries and juvenile libraries. These libraries collect works by writers of the Soviet Union and foreign countries. Most will also collect works of local authors in indigenous languages and dialects. The republican libraries are also valuable

183

Children watching chicks hatch at Woodson Regional Library, Chicago, part of a farm study project planned with the assistance of Illinois 4-H Cooperative Extension Service.

Phil Moloitis

Sculptor Samuel Cashwan's "Tom Thumb Relates His Adventures", in the Children's Library of the Detroit Public Library.

Theodore F. Welch

Detroit Public Library

Children's library, with its own separate entrance, attached to Japan's Osaka Municipal Library.

demonstration facilities for library development in the republics.

Activities in the Arabian Gulf area are similar to patterns in other developing countries and demonstrate the opposite extreme in the provision of library service to children. Vast wealth is available in many Arab countries for social services, but tradition, inadequate publishing structures, and the lack of good professional education programs have delayed the development of modern public library systems. In March 1980, library staff members from Kuwait, United Arab Emirates, Qatar, Iraq, and Saudi Arabia drafted goals and objectives for the modernization of library service in their countries. One of the goals which all public library representatives agreed upon was that of improving library service to children. As reported by Ken Shearer in the *International Library Review* (1981), they agreed that libraries must: "buy children's films and tapes, conduct story-telling hours, present exhibitions of children's own writings and art work, provide prizes for children who read ten books and tell the librarian about them, make children's games available for use and circulation, hire a children's librarian . . . , to concentrate on children's needs in each branch, and train such specialists." These goals were set in response to two facts: (1) children use existing public libraries almost exclusively to study prior to exams and (2) "the dearth of Arabic text for children indicates that the collection of alternative learning resources should be assigned a high priority."

In the Far East library service to children has developed slowly, and until recently little literature has been easily accessible in English about its status in those countries. In Japan the devastation of war, coupled with the traditional view that libraries were for scholars, slowed the establishment of public libraries, a remarkable occurrence in a country with a high literacy rate and an abundance of printed materials. As of March 1976, there were only 1,083 individual public libraries to serve more than 100,000,000. Japanese librarians attribute their development in part to the demands of children who would be the first to make use of any newly opened public library.

Japan is an excellent example of a country in which communities have made great efforts to make books available for their children. In 1958 Momoko Ishi, author-translator of children's books, started the *katei bunko,* a small collection of books housed in a private home for the use of neighborhood children. The popularity of the katei bunkos created such a demand for books that some communities developed the *chikki bunko,* the community library. These libraries, often managed cooperatively by groups of mothers, are supported by private contributions, in some cases a small membership fee, and fundraising activities. Many chikki bunkos have begun to receive small circulating collections from local public libraries. These home and local community efforts are credited with supporting a growing demand for more general access to public libraries for children and adults.

LIBRARY SERVICES AND PROGRAMMING FOR CHILDREN

Traditional library services to children are built around providing circulating materials, answering reference questions, teaching children how to retrieve materials and to use them, and promoting the love of reading. In the mid-1970s, librarians began to consider the role of the children's librarian in providing access to information. In 1973 the Task Force on Children's Services stated in a working paper to the ALA:

> Libraries, together with other community agencies, should provide and ensure access by all children to information services that include a diversity of media, both print and nonprint; stimulate interest in reading and the use of all types of media; and provide opportunities to develop and use communication skills that will enhance the enjoyment of life. Media and services should be offered in an atmosphere conducive to the creative and informational pursuits of children and with an awareness of the developmental needs of children.

Materials Collection. The book collection is the heart of traditional library service in every country of the world. And in every country, while technological advances in the transmission of information are acknowledged, bringing good books and children together and fostering a love of reading and learning are still the major goals of children's librarians. In addition to the general book collection, a good reference collection is necessary to help children answer questions stemming both from their school assignments and from their own active curiosity.

In more affluent countries, the basic book collection will include quantities of picture books for the very young, classics, modern favorites, folk and fairy tales, and informational books. Developing countries face tremendous problems in providing basic collections. Many developing countries do not have indigenous publishing industries, and many times librarians in these countries must pay more for postage than for the books themselves. But within these awesome restrictions, usually added to severe limitations on funds, librarians will seek to provide the same types of collections for children.

Today's libraries also collect periodicals, microcomputer software, filmstrips, audio and video tape recordings, toys, maps, globes, and other items to form a total collection of contemporary information.

In developing collections for children, no less than for adults, librarians face problems and decisions relating to demand for and interest in a wide array of subjects: accuracy of presentation; usability; intellectual freedom; and the qualities of technical workmanship, production, and design. The much discussed information explosion has not bypassed the production of materials for children. The need for bilingual materials is growing in all parts of the world. In countries where immigration is high, new populations must be served. In developing countries where publishing has not met the needs of a multilingual population, that goal must be met. Continued curriculum change in schools, more research into the ways children learn and use resources, and continued experimentation with resources to teach the learning disabled provide multiple options for the collection developer. Continued strong interest in the education of very young children creates a continued demand for a large variety of resources for that age group.

The variety of information formats poses challenges as well as opportunities for developing collections. Children's librarians in public libraries have not always been as quick as their colleagues in the schools to add audiovisual media to their collections. Many are now realizing, however, the importance of making quality audiovisual formats available in public libraries. As librarians continue to recognize that all formats have integrity, and as they become more comfortable in teaching the use of the requisite hardware and using it themselves, multimedia collections will expand.

Services and Programming. Depending on the tradition of a specific country, librarians will serve children through story hour programs and other reading guidance activities for both parents and children. They provide school related services by helping with reference questions, by teaching students how to use the library and its resources, and by assisting children in locating needed information in adult departments or other agencies. Children are voracious users of information, and for many of them the children's department is but a beginning point in their search.

Newer services have begun to be described widely in the literature, and these programs demand additional materials. Preschool and early-early childhood programs (one's and two's, or programs for toddlers as they are called in the United States) are becoming more popular in libraries of all sizes. Craft and hobby programs, audiovisual programs, drama, music, and dance materials, resource speakers, and participatory activities are provided in many libraries. Many children's librarians are developing programs for adults—parents and other adults who work with children such as recreation workers, scout leaders, health care providers, and social workers. In other libraries, the observer will note that there are meeting places for children who have no other place to meet after school, literacy development activities, and space for special services for the handicapped and the bilingual. Multiethnic and multicultural collections and programming also are becoming more typical of the variety of services and programs offered through children's departments in many countries.

Children's librarians deliver services largely through programming of various kinds. Margaret M. Kimmel states the rationale for library programming for children this way: "If children's service goes beyond housing materials, if indeed it is to provide an opportunity for an individual child to go beyond what he thinks he wants to what he might want, stimulating, effective programs should be developed as a basic part of a library's service. And the program must be regularly evaluated and revised, because the program itself is a service, not an end." Amy Kellman gives three reasons for doing programs: (1) because they give the library visibility; (2) because they stimulate the use of materials in the library; and

(3) the third reason . . . defies evaluation; if this is romantic, unscientific and unbusinesslike, so be it. Librarians do not know if the dancer brought in to move and talk to children in the intimate and comfortable setting of the library will touch the individual child or not. They do know that they are providing an experience the child might not have had otherwise. Expanding a child's world contributes positively to the quality of his or her life. It may be years before the impact of that program is felt. However, there is enough testimonial literature from suc-

cessful adults about the effects of seeing an artist, hearing someone speak or reading a book as a young child to know that such programming is worth pursuing.

Indeed, library service to the young is not based on a body of serious research. Statistics consistently indicate that children's borrowing accounts for a substantial percentage of all circulation in public libraries. This fact, added to experience with children's attendance and performance at programs, the enthusiasm of parents, faith in the efficacy of establishing sound patterns in reading, social education, and the like, has formed the basis for children's librarians' belief that their work is of value to the children and, in the end, to society itself.

Programming Around the World. Some types of library programs are provided universally: storytelling, booktalking, cultural events, and the celebration of the book through fairs, contests, and other special events. Countries differ in the time allotted to types of programming. Emphasis varies both with available resources and with assessed needs. Finland, for example, provides more bibliographic instruction than storytelling activities. In some African countries, on the other hand, storytelling in local languages helps to preserve traditional culture and to familiarize children with stories they then must read in English, since more than 90 percent of available material is in English. There are shortages of professionally educated staff and material resources, but part-time assistants and volunteers, sometimes using stories tape recorded by adults in the villages, help provide this service. In most Scandinavian countries, librarians make impressive alliances with other cultural agencies, made possible in part by their governmental organization and support. The concern for children's cultures is a constant; the means of enriching it vary.

In Ghana, new children's libraries have grown from 3 in Accra in 1950 to 50 nationwide in the early 1980s, serving a registered membership of 48,000. Only eight of these libraries are housed separately from adult lending libraries. The facilities for programs, observes Juliana V. Stackey in Colin Ray's international survey, "range from open verandas to circular shared summer huts with thatched roof" and "the exhibition halls of the main library buildings." The staff attempt to address both children and the general public, calling attention to the library through booktalks to parent-teachers associations, day-care proprietors, and other groups, through radio and television programs, and newspaper articles, and by providing advisory services to vacation schools and camps. Book exhibits and children's art shows in libraries, an International Children's Book Day that is celebrated all through April, and storytelling festivals also help meet this objective. In addition, library programs are designed to assist with language development and reading. Learning native dances, watching experienced native dancers and other artists and artisans help fill this need. Book discussions, readers' clubs, and meetings with authors are some of the techniques used by Ghanaian librarians to encourage the fun of reading just as they are by librarians in other countries.

Most Scandinavian countries, except Sweden, have library legislation that encourages the development of library service to children. The purposes of children's library service have been defined similarly in these countries and speak to meeting the needs of children's culture, a concern with the quality of materials, and the need to provide instruction in how to use public libraries. Danish and Swedish goals and objectives note that children's library activities should be of high quality and be coordinated with all of a community's leisure-time activity programming for children.

In Finland the LAKU project (LAKU an acronym for Working Group on the Muscial Development of Children) experimented directly in nine libraries and cooperated with nearly 20 others and the Sibelius Academy in 1982–83, with the object of trying to get children to listen to better and more varied music. Children listened to music, illustrated it, and used their illustrations on record jackets in the hope that the familiar illustrations would motivate other children to listen to the music. The results indicated that illustrated jackets alone did not promote listening, but the accompanying exhibits, publicity, and programs were found to be important motivators.

PERSONNEL

The desirable abilities, knowledge, and personal characteristics for children's librarians universally include respect for children, knowledge of children's developmental patterns, and competence in applying those professional abilities and knowledge. Professional librarians the world over indicate that children's librarians have taken these requirements seriously. Programs that respond to the growth and developmental needs of children, the creation of a body of children's literature that is an exciting part of world literature, and the initiation of services that keep pace with technological advances and research are evident in many fine libraries in all parts of the world. Problems result not from lack of a knowledge base but rather from understaffing, underfunding, the lack of universally available professional education preparatory programs, and a failure of the general population in specific countries to recognize the importance of chil-

Special children's section in India's National Library, Calcutta.

National Library of India

dren's libraries to the development of a literate citizenry.

In countries with well-established library education programs, children's librarians are learning to be concerned with all aspects of the school or public library operation because every governance decision and every major change in the work environment, economics, or public attitude has an impact on library service to children. Beginning librarians are urged to develop a knowledge of the fields of management and administration, information management, and the application of technology to library organization and to the collection, storage, retrieval, and dissemination of information. They are urged to demonstrate abilities in budgeting and program and staff evaluation as well as in materials evaluation and the traditional aspects of activity planning and administration. Last, but not least, children's librarians are expected to be knowledgable about child development and psychology so that they can work more effectively with all children—gifted, average, or learning disabled. Worldwide they are still a long way from providing every community with staff who are well prepared to assume such professional responsibilities. Millions of children are served by volunteers, paraprofessionals, and librarians whose professional education has been gained abroad. But the role and function of the children's library have been defined, and the job description has been outlined as a goal for all to meet.

CONTINUING ISSUES IN SERVICE TO CHILDREN

Staffing. As the latter half of the decade of the 1980s began two issues stood out as particularly deserving special attention of professional leaders. In the early 1980s, it became apparent that there was a growing shortage of children's librarians in the United States. This shortage has continued to develop, exacerbated by continued low salaries in public libraries, the lack of upward mobility within children's services, the extremely low recruitment rate of new persons entering the field, and career exhaustion. One study of library personnel needs in New England, for the period 1980–83 reported that job vacancies in youth services amounted to 25 percent of the total. A growing demand for school librarians to replace the expected surge of retirements over the next decade and to fill positions being reinstated as the economy improves may further affect recruitment, since salaries and the length of the working year are often more attractive than in the public library.

A trend in library education programs has caused further worry to leaders in the children's field. Many library schools, responding to lower enrollments, have reduced offerings in the youth services specialization and have replaced retiring staff in this field with adjunct appointments. The situation in the United States is not unique; lack of easy access to training, the high cost of studying abroad, and the demands of working in a service area that is usually understaffed are among those factors, added to the same types of problems faced in the United States, that keep the supply of professional children's librarians low in many countries.

Access to Information. Guaranteeing access to information by children remains a challenge for li-

Amman Public Library

Children's reading hall in the Amman Public Library, Jordan.

brarians. Censorship is ubiquitous and will always be an issue. Other aspects of access are of equal concern, however. One is the cost of the new technology. Electronic storage and retrieval of information pose a special problem. The costs of providing online reference service to children are being widely discussed; as public catalogues go online and as home electronic access becomes more common, youth advocates will need to call attention to children's special access needs. The growing availability of microcomputers adds additional economic pressures to those already faced by libraries serving children. Many children now take computers for granted. Studies report wide access to computers in the schools; nearly 50 percent of the elementary schools in the United States have computers, and many of the children in those schools have computers at home. Public libraries lag, however, in providing computers for their patrons. Where computers are available to children in public libraries, studies reveal that they take advantage of them. A survey taken in the Madison (WI) Public Library revealed that 54 percent of their microcomputer users were children ages 6–13. At the Chicago Public Library, the first public library to go online to the PLATO system, even preschool children can use the learning modules on the touch screens.

Publishing Trends. The lack of availability of children's books from publishers is another access problem for children's librarians. There are problems in collection development and maintenance as standards and "old favorites" are not kept in print. Costs of warehousing, the need for subsidiary sales, and the changing patterns of federal funding have affected the availability of resources from publishers. The need for materials in many languages other than English poses yet another availability problem for publishers and librarians in the United States, while the need for materials in native languages and dialects poses similar problems for children's librarians in developing countries.

187

Worldwide, community leaders need to assess the health of library service to children. It is specious to advocate good library service to children according to the belief that they will grow into adults who will or will not support public libraries. Rather, it should be argued that children need good library service for their personal, educational, and cultural development. Nevertheless, habits that are developed at a young age are harder to overcome. The future health of public libraries does depend, in part, on developing a citizenry that needs library service.

REFERENCES
Richard Ashford, "Jobs Gone Begging: Personnel Needs and Youth Services," *School Library Journal* (1984).
Amy Kellman, "Services of Medium-Sized Public Libraries," in Selma K. Richardson, editor, *Children's Services of Public Libraries* (1978).
Margaret M. Kimmel, "Library—Program—Storehouse?" *Top of the News* (1975).
Colin Ray, editor, *Library Service to Children: An International Survey* (1983).
Scandinavian Public Library Quarterly (1983) contains articles on children's services in Scandinavian libraries.
K. Shearer, "The Arabian Gulf Plans Its Library Future," *International Library Review* (1981).

MARILYN L. MILLER

Chile

Chile is on the southern Pacific coast of South America. Comprising about 750,000 sq.km. in its continental zone, and claiming 1,250,000 sq.km. in Antarctica, it is bounded by Peru, Bolivia, and Argentina. Pop. (1984 est.) 11,878,419. The inhabitants are distributed between the Andes Mountains and the Pacific Ocean. About one-third of the population live in the capital city, Santiago. The official language is Spanish.

History. The primitive inhabitants of Chile kept no written records. The Spaniards entered the area in 1535, but they were not interested in books or reading—they were constantly at war with the Araucanian Indians. Some few written works, mainly epic poems and chronicles, were published in Europe. During the 17th and 18th centuries, the influence of religious orders on the cultural life of the colony was evident and many private libraries were formed. Ec-clesiastical collections were the largest. In 1767, when the Jesuits left Chile, they had 20,000 books in their schools throughout the country.

Book trade was started in 1807 by Manuel Riesco. The National Library was created in 1813; the government gave its first impulse to public libraries under President Manuel Montt (1851–1861) by creating 43 public libraries annexed to schools. In 1863 an educational reform required the creation of school libraries.

During the 1900s Chilean governments have shown a marked interest in the development of both school and public libraries. However, geographical configuration and economic conditions have hindered a steady progress. The introduction of new technologies has meant an accelerated development of academic and special libraries.

José Toribio Medina (1852–1930), distinguished bibliographer, was commissioned by the government to visit archives and libraries in South America and Europe in order to obtain historical documents related to Chile. His works and his own library are preserved in the National Library.

National Library. The National Library was founded on August 13, 1813, during the first years of Chile's independence. Its basic collection consisted of 8,000 volumes that belonged to the ancient colonial library of the Jesuits and had been preserved in the University of San Felipe until they were transferred to the National Library. Ten years later, its holdings had increased to 12,000 volumes. By 1984 its collection totaled 4,000,000 volumes. One of the most important sources for the increase has been the legal deposit requirement established by decree in 1825. Publishers are required to deliver 15 copies of every book or pamphlet printed to the National Library.

The Library is distinguished for its collection of Chilean literature. It maintains a manuscript collection and is a depository library of United States government publications. Since 1877, it has published the important national bibliography, the "Yearbook of the Chilean Press" (Anuario de la Prensa Chilena), which changed its name to "Chilean Bibliography" (Bibliografía Chilena) in 1976.

The National Library began implementing the NOTIS (Northwestern Total Integrated System) in the 1980s. Using MARC tapes (Machine Readable Cataloging), the project planned to include its own

Libraries in Chile (1982)

Type	Administrative units	Service points	Volumes in collections	Annual expenditures (peso)	Population served	Professional staff	Total staff
National	1	1	4,000,000	36,588,000[d]		49	131[a]
Academic	37	131	2,569,055	--	127,462	470[b]	1,213[a]
Public	188	--	1,189,987	--		--	--
School	634	--	2,148,842	--		--	--
Special	182	--	2,088,664	--		346[c]	644[a]

[a]1983.
[b]Includes 410 librarians and 60 other professionals.
[c]Includes 239 librarians, 107 other professionals.
[d]Unesco, *Statistical Yearbook,* 1984. 1980 data.

Source: Conicyt, *Guía de Bibliotecas Especializadas y Centros de Documentación,* 1984.

collection as well as the collections from Chilean universities.

Academic Libraries. A decree of 1981 introduced a profound reform in the higher educational system. This disposition allows for the creation of autonomous and private universities, as well as professional and technical institutes of higher education. Careers considered not university professions were transferred to technical institutes.

Up to 1981 there were 8 universities, some of them with branches in major cities. By 1983, there were 24 institutions of higher education in the country: 11 universities, 2 academies of pedagogical sciences, 5 professional institutes receiving government support, and 6 private establishments. These institutions have well-organized libraries that served more than 127,350 students in the early 1980s.

The University of Chile, created in 1738, has 64 autonomous libraries that serve the university community and the general public. The Pablo Neruda Library (donated by the poet), Andrés Bello manuscripts, and Chilean imprints to 1849 are among the special collections maintained at the main library. Libraries of the faculties of Agriculture, Medicine, and Sanitary Engineering and Environmental Sciences are active participants in national and international information programs. The Information Systems Service provides access to several national and international databases and compiled, in a joint venture with the School of Library Science, a "Union Catalog of Periodical Publications" at the University of Chile.

The Catholic University has a centralized library administration with 21 libraries. In a new building, the main library had modern audiovisual resources and excellent facilities in the 1980s. The central administration was engaged in creating a bibliographic database using the MARC format and automating the circulation processes. They also had access to the Dialog retrieval service.

Public Libraries. The public library system is administered by the Department of Libraries, Archives, and Museums, within the Ministry of Education. In 1977 the government initiated a National Plan for Libraries to create more public libraries. A coordinating office establishes agreements with municipalities, rural community centers, and penitentiaries for the creation of new libraries. The Coordinating Office provides books and technical assistance and the institutions, their facilities and personnel. These libraries extend free borrowing privileges to patrons living in their areas. The increase of this type of library has been remarkable. Up to 1976, there were 56 public libraries. By 1982 there were 188, with more than 3,344,000 registered borrowers.

School Libraries. A decree of 1813 stated that every school should have funds for books to serve students. In 1863 a decree ordered that a library be established in the main school of every major city. Although the legal evidence shows that since Chile's independence government authorities have understood the importance of school libraries, development has been poor and slow. In 1962 only 259 out of 5,831 schools had library facilities. In 1972 there were 7,845 schools, yet only 295 had some kind of library service. In 1982 there were 9,848 schools, with 2,819,000 enrolled students, but only 634 had library service.

La Biblioteca Central de la Universidad de Chile

Central Library of the University of Chile, Santiago.

School libraries in Chile can be classified as those in public schools that possess a small book collection and offer a few hours of library service and those that have a well-rounded book collection with at least one person—a teacher or a librarian—in charge of the library.

In 1976 the Ministry of Education designed and approved a national system of school libraries, which was being developed in the 1980s.

Special Libraries. Special libraries are well organized and equipped in Chile. They offer their services to patrons in the government, national and international organizations, professional and learned societies, industry, banks and binational institutes. They showed a significant development in services. In 1976 there were 299 and in 1983, 272, excluding the special university libraries.

The use of computers in the libraries of the Institute of Natural Resources, National Development Corporation, Ministry of Housing, National Telecommunications Company, and others has allowed them to create databases and participate in a nationwide information and documentation network designed and coordinated by the National Commission for Science and Technology (CONICYT).

The National Commission of Nuclear Energy and international organizations such as the United Nations Economic Commission for Latin America (ECLA), the Center for Latin American Demographic Studies (CELADE), and the Institute of Latin American Iron and Steel (ILAFA) maintain databases providing information in their fields.

The Institute of Technology (INTEC), the Corporation of Computer and Information Technology (ECOM), and the Chilean North American Institute provide online information from international commercial databases.

The Profession. In 1946 the University of Chile retained Edward Martin Heiliger of the U.S. to help establish a school of library science program. In 1947 the Central Library for the University of Chile inaugurated a Library School, which was officially sanctioned by a Ministry of Education decree in 1959. Approximately 940 students were graduated from

1947 to 1980.

Ten continuing education courses on automation, information systems, organization of archives, statistics, and *American Cataloguing Rules,* Second Edition, were offered to practicing librarians from 1977 to 1981. Similar courses are offered by the Colegio de Bibliotecarios and the National Center for Information and Documentation.

Library students developed various projects, among them a University Union Catalogue, a survey of national and international databases, and a national bibliography entitled *Bibliografía de Chile* (Chilean Bibliography), published in 1982.

The University of Chile also offered courses in some of its southern and northern headquarters during the period 1965–80. The University of Concepción offered a Library Science program from 1975 to 1979.

Chilean librarians are represented by the Colegio de Bibliotecarios, an organization that superseded the Asociación de Bibliotecarios, established in 1953. The Colegio de Bibliotecarios, created by a 1969 law, had 1,331 members in 1984 and has prepared several publications, including a "Code of Professional Ethics," "Standards for Chilean Public and School Libraries," and "Chilean Standards for Documentation."

REFERENCES

Alejandro Burgos and Héctor Gómez, *Bases de Datos Bibliográficos en Chile* (1982).

Juan R. Freudenthal and Héctor Gómez, *Library Education in Chile* (Libri, 1983).

M. TERESA HERRERO DE ALVAREZ

China, People's Republic of

The People's Republic of China covers a total area of about 9,600,000 square kilometers in eastern Asia on the western shores of the Pacific Ocean with a continental land boundary of more than 20,000 kilometers. China adjoins Korea in the east, the U.S.S.R. in the north, Afghanistan, Pakistan, India, Nepal, Sikkim, and Bhutan in the southwest, and Burma, Laos, and Vietnam in the south. The continental coastline is more than 18,000 kilometers long. More than 4,000 islands are scattered along China's coastline. Taiwan is the largest one and Hainan Island the next. For administration, China is divided into 22 provinces, 5 autonomous regions, and 3 municipalities. According to the census of 1982, the total population of China was 1,031,882,511 on July 1, 1982; (1984 est.) 1,075,195,000. China is a unified multi-national country with 56 ethnic groups, among which the Han nationality is the largest. The official language is Chinese.

History. Ancient inscriptions, cast, engraved, or impressed on permanent materials are hardly to be considered "books." But we may say Chinese books originated from ancient literal records and archives.

The oracle-bone inscriptions are the earliest known Chinese documents preserved in their original form today. They were inscribed on tortoise shell and ox bone about 3,500 years ago. Early inscriptions cast or engraved on bronze have also been found; some have been preserved for about 3,200 years. As for the inscriptions on stone, some ancient stone drums with inscriptions engraved on them were made about 2,200 years ago.

The direct ancestors of Chinese books are believed to have been the tablets made of bamboo or wood that were connected by strings and used like paper books. They appeared from the 14th century B.C. to the 3rd or 4th century A.D. and prospered from the 8th century B.C. to the 2nd century A.D. Another kind of book written on silk rolls appeared in the 5th or 4th century B.C. down to the middle of the 3rd century A.D. In A.D. 105 paper made from the bark of trees, old rags, and fishing nets was invented by T'sai Lun, a man of talent in charge of government manufacture of the East Han Dynasty. During the 2nd and 3rd centuries A.D., paper was more and more used as a writing material. During that period, bamboo, silk, and paper were simultaneously used as writing materials. Writing tools, such as various forms of Chinese brush-pens and black ink, had been used, of course, along with the various writing materials.

The technique for multiplication of written works before the invention of block printing was the process of taking inked impressions from stone or other inscriptions by pressing paper on their surfaces. Moreover, seals, cast from metal or cut in stone or jade, were impressed on soft and sticky clay— and later, on silk and paper—to make duplicate inscriptions. Such techniques have been considered forerunners of mass production of early writings and eventually led to the invention of block printing.

Printing from engraved wood block appeared in the first years of the T'ang Dynasty or even earlier (about the 8th century A.D.). At the beginning of the 9th century, calendars were printed in that way. And an extant book, the *Diamond Sutra,* which was printed in 868, with the printing date in it, shows very nice printing technique. Therefore, it can be presumed that the invention of block printing must have been much earlier than the time the book was printed.

In the middle of the 11th century, during the Northern Sung Period, Bi Sheng invented movable type for printing. It was not necessary to print many copies of books at that time, so the former method of printing from engraved wood block was still often used. With the further development and application of movable-type printing, the number of books printed by the method grew in successive generations.

In 213 B.C. the first emperor of China of the Chin Dynasty ordered the burning of a great many books except those in certain categories and in the possession of learned officials. Large-scale recovery of ancient works was not begun until the reign of Emperor Wu (ruled 180–140 B.C.) during the Han Dynasty. And for the first time in Chinese history a centralized imperial library was established where a wide range of materials was systematically collected and well kept.

In 26 B.C., under the reign of Emperor Cheng of the Han Dynasty, a special decree was issued to collect books again and also designate Liu Hsiang (81–80 B.C.), a state counselor, to examine the collection with his assistants. Liu recorded the headings of the chapters and wrote a summary for each book to be presented to the emperor. The result of these summaries was a collection of critical bibliographies known as *Pieh-lu,* or "Separate Record." After he died with the task unfinished, his son, Liu Hsin (d. A.D. 23) succeeded him in the work. He arranged all the books then in the imperial library into seven categories and compiled a classification catalogue known as *Chi-lüeh,* or seven summaries. Liu Hsian's work is the earliest known bibliography in China and Liu Hsin's scheme is the first system of subject classification and descriptive cataloguing of Chinese books.

A modified fourfold scheme made in the 3rd century A.D. and revised again and again afterward has been used by Chinese bibliographers for more than 1,500 years. Even now many libraries in China still use such a revised scheme to classify the ancient Chinese books in their collections.

In A.D. 1407, under the decree of the Emperor Cheng Zu of the Ming Dynasty, the compilation of the famous *Yong Le Encyclopedia* was finished and the imperial library called the Wen Yuan Pavilion was founded. *Yong Le Encyclopedia* was the largest encyclopedia in China, including a total of 11,919 volumes. They were arranged according to phonetic rhymes, reproduced from more than 7,000 extant books. At that time only one set of a handwritten master copy was prepared; afterward another set was copied. The original set was unfortunately destroyed and of the second set only a little more than 200 volumes were preserved, most of which are kept in the National Library of China.

Wen Yuan Pavilion was the imperial library of the Ming Dynasty (1369–1644). The remainders of the ancient books from the preceding Sung (960–1279) and Yuan Dynasties (1279–1368) provided its basic collection. There also were the books of the Ming Dynasty that were especially rich in local chronicles.

In the last years of the Emperor K'ang-hsi (ruled 1661–1722) in the Ch'ing (Qing) Dynasty, compilation of another encyclopedia, "A Collection of Books of Ancient and Modern Times," was begun. It was completed in 1725 and was later printed with movable type. This giant work consisted of 10,000 volumes with about 100,000,000 words together with many fine pictures. At the end of Ch'ing Dynasty it was copied twice.

During the rule of the Emperor Tsien Long (1736–1795) in the Ch'ing Dynasty, "The Complete Library of the Four Treasures" had its beginning in 1772 and was completed a decade later. It consisted of 3,502 titles bound into 36,000 volumes. It was the largest collection of books in the history of China. It was copied by hand in four copies at first and three more copies afterward. Now there are only four copies left.

The collection of the Wen Yuan Pavilion of the Ming Dynasty was inherited by the Cabinet Library of the Ch'ing Dynasty, but a lot of the collection was lost. In 1910 the remaining part was transferred to the Metropolitan Library of Peking and thus it became the first collection of rare books for the National Library of China.

National Library. The National Library's predecessor was the Metropolitan Library of Peking, opened in 1912. Apart from inheriting the books from the imperial libraries, the National Library, when opened, got a number of important and famous publications collected and donated by the government. All these laid the foundation for the collection of books. Up to 1949, it had already had more than 1,400,000 volumes (items) and 120 staff members. After the establishment of the People's Republic of China in 1949, its collections were mainly augmented through channels such as sample copies from domestic publishers, selective purchase of both old and new domestic publications, donations and allocations from institutions and individuals, selection and ordering of foreign publications, international exchange of publications, and so on. At the end of 1984, the National Library of China had 12,396,807 books, magazine issues, and other items, and more than 1,100 staff members. It is a comprehensive research library under the leadership of the Ministry of Culture of China. It seeks to perform the functions required of other national libraries throughout the world. A new building of the library covering a floor space of 140,000 square meters and capable of providing for modern equipment was under construction in the mid-1980s. The computer had begun to be used in some professional work by the mid-1980s and further applications of computer technology to library service were anticipated for the near future.

Academic Libraries. Under the leadership of the National Commission of Education of the State Council and relevant administrative offices of the provincial governments or those of the same level, the Commissions of University and College Libraries lead the nationwide or regional university and college libraries respectively. There are about 900 such libraries in all parts of the country. Some of them belong to the national key universities, such as the Library of Beijing (Peking) University and the Library of Qinghwa (Tsinghua) University. The former was established as early as 1902. In the early years of the 20th century, the Chinese revolutionary pioneers and Marxists Lee Da-zhao and Mao Tse-tung worked in it. In 1985 the Library had a total collection of more than 3,500,000 volumes (items). A new building was founded in 1975, with the floor space of 24,500 square meters. In 1985 the Library of Qinghua University held more than 2,100,000 volumes (items) in its collection, concentrating on natural science and technology. These two libraries and some other university or college libraries used computers in their work in the mid-1980s.

Public Libraries. Under the leadership of the Ministry of Culture, the libraries of the cities, including those of their streets and lanes, and the libraries of counties or districts, including those of their inferior districts and villages, are all public libraries. They serve many readers, offering help in various subjects and striving to raise their working abilities in production and management. Although the libraries of provinces, autonomous regions, and municipalities and other large cities or some medium-sized cities with comparatively large populations also serve the public, their main service is seen as meeting the needs of economic construction and scientific research. They are research libraries or in some degree close to research libraries.

The Shanghai Library (about 6,500,000 items) is a notable city library; the largest public library in China, it is renowned for its collection of 1,500,000 classical Chinese books. Others include Nanking Library (about 4,700,000 items) for Jiangsu (Kiangsu) Province and Wuhan for Hubei (Hopei) Province.

School Libraries. Apart from the many libraries or reading rooms of primary and middle schools, separate children's libraries were established in some places. Under the leadership of the Ministry of Culture alone, there were 45 city or regional children's libraries in the mid-1980s and most of the county, district, and city libraries have children's reading rooms, large or small. Children's Palaces or Children's Activities Centers in some cities also have their own libraries or reading rooms. All of the children's libraries or reading rooms outside the schools are used by students and their teachers and sometimes they are open for children before school age.

Special Libraries. Libraries in the system of the Chinese Academy of Sciences, including the Academy Library, the regional Libraries of the Academy, and the institutional libraries, total 142. The Library of the Chinese Academy of Sciences is a major comprehensive scientific and technological library. It collects books, periodicals, scientific reports, patents, proceedings, professional publications, and other materials. In 1985 it had a collection of 5,000,000 volumes (items) and a staff of more than 400. In that library the Scientific Information Office was established in order to combine library service with information service. This library and others in the system of the Chinese Academy of Sciences have used computer technology to process and retrieve data from foreign source documents in the sciences.

Other academic or special libraries are under the leadership of the Chinese Academy of Social Sciences and the ministries and commissions of the State Council, such as the Library of the Chinese Academy of Agricultural Sciences, the Library of Medical Sciences, the Library of Geology, and the Library of Nationalities.

The Profession. Some 50 universities or colleges have departments or specialities of library science. One of the two oldest departments of library science was established in Wuhan University (now merged into the College of Library and Information Science of that university). The other is in Beijing University. In some universities and a few research libraries, graduate students continue to study for the master's degree and some students are sent abroad to study as graduate or undergraduate students or visiting scholars. Many libraries established schools or classes for vocational training: for example, the Spare-time Professional College for Staff Members in the National Library of China has enrolled classes of students through entrance examination. The National Library, other libraries, and the Administrative Bureau of Library Affairs of the Ministry of Culture also run many short training classes for staff members on various subjects. In addition, there are some library vocational middle schools or library vocational classes in the middle schools.

The China Society of Library Science was established in July 1979. The members of its second council were elected for a term of four years by the representatives at the second plenary session in November 1983. Its journal is the "Bulletin of China Society of Library Science" (quarterly). The Society often holds meetings for discussion on library science or exchange of experience and provides seminars or training classes on special topics. The Society had registered more than 4,000 members on the national level by the mid-1980s. Under the Society, 30 more Societies of Library Science are scattered in provinces, autonomous regions, and municipalities. They are enthusiastic in pursuing professional activities and most of them publish society journals of their own. Sometimes the societies of several neighboring areas unite to carry on their professional activities.

DING ZHIGANG

China, Republic of (Taiwan)

Taiwan, an island in eastern Asia off the southeast coast of the People's Republic of China, became the seat of the Republic of China in 1949. Population (1984 est.) 18,735,000; area 35,981 sq.km.

Library History. The history of Chinese document collection can be traced back to prehistorical time. Archaeological excavation found that people in Shang dynasty (c. 1800–1400 B.C.) stored oracle bones equivalent to modern archives and books in separate pits that were forerunners of libraries. Throughout Chinese history, there were not only official imperial collections but also private collections. However, the major modern libraries did not come into existence in China until the Provincial Hu Nan Public Library was founded in 1905. Since then, library work has attracted more and more attention and kept on growing in spite of disturbances of the times. In 1947 there were 2,702 libraries in the mainland of the Republic of China. After the move of the republic's government to Taiwan (1949), where there were only about 100 libraries at that time, the library profession was developed vigorously. By 1982 there were about 3,080 libraries in Taiwan, according to the *Library Survey of the Republic of China* (1982) and the *Publications Yearbook* (1984). These include a national Library, a branch national library, 245 public libraries, 139 university and college libraries, 2,456 school libraries, and 239 special libraries and information centers.

National Library. The National Central Library (NCL), under the jurisdiction of the Ministry of Education, renders national library services, serves as a research library, and leads and coordinates all library-related activities in the Republic of China. The NCL was established in 1933 at Nanking. At the time of its relocation to Taiwan in 1948, its collection numbered 140,000 volumes. As of February 1985, the total collection of the NCL and its branch had grown to 1,274,107 volumes. The NCL main library planned to move to a new building and offer extended services (1986). The new building has an area of 431,500 sq.ft. and accommodates 2,500,000 volumes and 4,000 readers.

In October 1973 the Provincial Taipei Library was converted into a branch of the NCL. The Branch Library has 486,652 volumes in its holdings, including an outstanding collection on Taiwan and southeastern Asia, such as gazetteers and other works published during the time Taiwan was governed by the Dutch and Spaniards.

Public Libraries. Public libraries can be found throughout Taiwan. There are 2 municipal libraries, 1 provincial library, and 20 libraries in Taiwan's county and cultural centers. The county libraries are dispersed throughout the island. In addition, there are 185 town and branch libraries.

University Libraries. At the beginning of Taiwan's restoration under the Republic of China, one university and three colleges existed, with a total of 2,022 students. As a result of the government's promotion of higher education, there were 105 public and private universities and colleges in the mid-1980s; most of the university libraries and the better-equipped colleges have independent libraries directly under the supervision of the presidents.

School Libraries. Approximately 99 percent of school-age children are enrolled in schools. There are 2,456 school libraries, including 370 senior high school libraries, 358 junior high school libraries, and 1,728 elementary school libraries.

Special Libraries. This is an important segment of the republic's library services. There are a number of organizations or groups that collect materials for their business or research. Currently there are well over 200 special libraries in Taiwan. They include the Academia Sinica, with 14 departmental libraries and some of the best collections in their subject fields; the National Palace Museum, with one of the largest collections of archives and a collection of rare books second only to the NCL; and the Agricultural Science Information Center, devoted to editing an agricultural thesaurus and processing agricultural information.

The Profession. The rapid development of libraries in Taiwan has elicited a demand for qualified librarians. They have been trained by six universities and colleges in Taiwan, as well as two graduate library studies programs. There are approximately 350 library science graduates every year. In addition, the NCL and the Library Association of China (LAC) annually sponsor a summer workshop for librarians.

There has been no shortage of professional librarians at all levels in Taiwan; moreover, the quality of library service has been continually upgraded, and many professional librarians have been sent abroad for advanced studies under various exchange programs and with government grants.

The LAC was incorporated in 1953. Membership is open to everyone who has studied library science or who is interested in library work. Major accomplishments of the LAC include the summer workshops, formulation of library standards, and the annual publication of the *Bulletin of the Library Association of China* since 1954, as well as the quarterly *Library Association of China Newsletter* since 1975.

National Chengchi University Library

Chung-Cheng Library, founded in 1977, the main library of National Chengchi University in Taipei.

The Library Automation Planning Committee, created by the LAC and the NCL in 1980, formulated the National Library Automation Project. This project in turn organized the Chinese MARC Working Group, the Chinese Cataloguing Working Group, and the Chinese Subject Heading Working Group. The Chinese MARC format was completed in 1982 and made available to libraries both locally and abroad as a basis for processing Chinese-language data, and also as a reference for processing data in other languages. *Chinese Cataloguing Rules* and *Chinese Subject Headings* are in print.

The NCL has provided strong leadership, too, in the development of library automation. Together with seven large academic libraries in Taiwan, the NCL has established a Chinese bibliographical database. In early 1985 it consisted of 31,000 entries on Chinese publications. The *Union List of Chinese Serials in the Republic of China* was to be revised to make it compatible with the new Chinese bibliographic database.

In addition, several university libraries and information centers have undertaken their own automation projects. National Taiwan Normal University developed the Chinese Educational Resource Information System, the Agricultural Science Information Center developed the Agricultural Science and Technology Information Management System, and the

Libraries in the Republic of China (1982)

Type	Administrative units	Service points	Volumes in collections	Annual expenditures (NT dollar)	Population served	Professional staff	Total staff
National[a]	1	1	1,274,107	257,071,000	18,912,690	150	249
Academic	135	--	10,221,208	245,000,050	375,889	623	1,419
Public	176	41	4,491,538	346,734,860	18,135,508	228	910
School[b]	2,456	0	13,438,240	--	3,904,762	1,325	2,610
Special	219	11	4,035,908	179,388,359	--	268	917

[a]February 1985 data.
[b]1979 data.

Science and Technology Information Center developed the Domestic Science and Technology System (which includes a union list of scientific and technical serials in the republic and Sci-Tech Research Reports). Other universities have created Western-language control projects, serial control and acquisition packages, and circulation systems. For foreign information searching, some libraries have opened online information retrieval services via the satellite communications network to complement conventional reference services.

The Taiwan government launched a Cultural Development Project to build a cultural center for each county or city and to include in each a library, museum, and music hall. Twenty such cultural centers had been established by 1985; 17 were open to the public.

Utilizing the Chinese MARC format and the Chinese Cataloging Rules, the Library Automation Committee developed the NCL Automated Information Service system. A library and information network was under study, and eventually that network was to include the public and academic library systems and the information center system.

CHEN-KU WANG

Chubarian, O. S.
(1908–1976)

Ogan Stepanovich Chubarian was a specialist in library science who greatly stimulated the development of library science and practice in the U.S.S.R. through his many-sided scientific, pedagogical, and administrative activities.

He was born in Rostov-on-Don on October 8, 1908, and received professional training at Advanced Bibliographic Courses, which functioned at the State Book Chamber of the R.S.F.S.R. Chubarian prepared a candidate dissertation on "The Technical Book in Russia during the Reign of Peter the Great." He was granted a Doctor's degree for his monograph "General Library Science."

Chubarian began his career as a rank-and-file librarian and in 1963 became one of the senior officers of the National Library of the Soviet Union. He published over a hundred works dealing with various problems of librarianship, bibliography, and bibliology. "General Library Science," one of his most important works, gives contemporary interpretations of the role of librarianship in Soviet society. This work formulates and reveals in detail the main principles of library development in the U.S.S.R.: the state character of librarianship, the availability of libraries for all, planned organization of the library network, centralization, and the drawing of representatives of the population into the work of libraries and their management. Chubarian was the first Soviet library specialist to cover the essence and place of library science in the general system of sciences from a Marxist standpoint.

Many works by Chubarian were devoted to the study of current problems of library development and the activities of libraries, such as problems of central-

ization of librarianship, cooperation of libraries and information centers, surveys of readership, development of national libraries of the Union republics, and acquisitions. Chubarian laid stress on the common goals and tasks of libraries that should not be ignored by any library institution regardless of its specific character.

Chubarian gave much of his time and effort to bibliography; he advocated the recommendatory bibliography as an efficient instrument in the guidance of reading. His idea that library and bibliographic activities should be carried out in close cooperation represents one of the leading concepts in defining the role of Soviet libraries. In his studies theoretical propositions and pragmatic conclusions interlace, and the examination of problems is closely connected with the practice and tasks of libraries.

For many years he guided the activities of important Soviet library institutions such as the Moscow State Institute of Culture, the State Public Technical and Scientific Library, and the State Lenin Library. He was also Vice-Chairman of the Council for Coordination of Research in Library Science and Bibliography attached to the U.S.S.R. Ministry of Culture.

He was one of the founders of two periodicals—*Sovetskoye bibliotekovedeniye* ("Soviet Library Science") and *Nauchniye i tekhnicheskiye biblioteki SSSR* ("Scientific and Technical Libraries of the U.S.S.R."), which greatly stimulated research in the field.

He had many students, whom he helped to write dissertations and become library specialists. He also directed many important surveys, and through his efforts the following studies were published: *The Soviet Reader* (1968), *The Book and Reading in the Life of Towns* (1973), and *The Book and Reading in the Life of the Soviet Village* (1978).

He edited many collections of articles such as *Lenin and Contemporary Problems of Library Science; History of Librarianship in the U.S.S.R.: Documents and Materials; Problems of Sociology and Psychology of Reading;* and a *Dictionary of Library Terms.*

O. S. Chubarian did much in the way of acquainting foreign librarians with the state of library science and practice in the Soviet Union. He persistently endeavored to develop the exchange of information on problems of library development; he took part in the organization of many international conferences, discussions, and joint research projects and the development of international book exchange. He participated in many IFLA sessions and worked on a number of reports. In 1966 he was elected Chairman of the IFLA Bibliographic Committee, and later he headed the Committee on Library Science.

His works have been translated into many foreign languages. The U.S.S.R. Ministry of Culture and party and state authorities of the country frequently invited him to act as adviser when important documents concerning librarianship were drawn up.

Chubarian was granted the title of Professor and the honorary title "Merited Worker of Culture of the R.S.F.S.R." He was also granted state awards and a Library in Artashat in the Armenian S.S.R. was named after him. He died in Moscow on January 7, 1976.

E. A. FENELONOV

Circulating Systems

The circulating library as we know it is a relatively recent development in the history of libraries. While the building of book collections has been important for centuries, actual use of these collections was much more restricted than it is now. It must be remembered in this day of comparatively inexpensive, expendable paperbacks in the western world that books, especially before Gutenberg, were a nearly priceless possession. The library once could more accurately be described as a safe repository for them than as a facility designed to foster use of the collections. A common name for the library in the early monastic or cathedral libraries was *armorium,* literally the book chest or press where the books were kept. The librarians of the day were known as the *bibliothecarius* and *custos librorum* or keeper of the books.

Books could be loaned for copying and also just for reading. Interlibrary loan also was not unknown in those early days, and although materials were usually exchanged between neighboring collections, loans were sometimes made between countries such as France and Greece or England and Austria.

The librarian's primary duty in caring for these collections of books was to protect the volumes, to increase the number of holdings, and to ensure that no volumes be lost or damaged. Volumes were loaned, of course, but the librarian was admonished to "Let not a book be given to anyone without a proper and sufficient voucher and let this be entered on the roll."

As the number of volumes making up a library's collection increased, the armoria gave way to shelves and later to reading rooms. In many cases the collection was separated into two parts, one for public use and another for private or reference use. Books in the public collections were the first to be chained to the desks, rather than the more valuable reference volumes. By the 18th century, after the printed book became more common, the manuscript volumes were often chained solely for their protection.

Early Systems. Circulation rules varied widely from place to place but in general followed guidelines set by the monastic libraries. In the Sorbonne Library in the 14th century, for example, books were to be used only in the building in which the library was housed, and if taken from the library had to be returned the same day. If anyone other than a student or professor took a book from the library, a deposit of equal value was required. In some other libraries, students could check out a book for a year, while in others the more valuable books were kept under triple lock and key so that the presence of more than one keeper of the books was required before a volume could even be seen.

The first of the more public circulating libraries were the commercial circulating libraries and subscription libraries that arose in England and on the Continent in the 18th century. The commercial circulating libraries were generally established by booksellers or groups of readers and would generally be called "rental collections" today. Most of these collections consisted of popular fiction and nonfiction. At about the same time, the subscription libraries came into being. These were often started by readers in a community who formed a society with a library

Guelph University

Circulation attendant at Guelph University Library, Ontario, Canada, scanning a patron's badge to charge out a book.

for use by members only; in general, the quality of the materials available in these collections was much better than in the commercial collections.

The modern public library began in about 1850 with the establishment of free public circulating libraries. By this time, collections were larger, the number of patrons had increased, and the need to manage borrowing records became more pronounced. (See also Public Libraries.)

Virtually all of the early libraries used some sort of ledger system or daybook to keep track of borrowers and the materials they checked out. The daybook consisted of a set of line entries to record each day's transactions. Thus one entry would be made in the daybook for each item checked out to a patron. When a book was returned, either a new entry would be made for it or the old one crossed out. The ledger system usually involved creating a page for each patron on which the charges and discharges could be recorded. The borrower's identification number was then attached to the book so that the proper ledger sheet could be located when it came to record the discharge.

The ledger system made it possible to monitor use of the collection, to know a patron's preferences, and to suggest other materials which might be of interest. Today, at a time of concern about privacy, such detailed records of a patron's library use are almost never kept. Instead, patrons who wish to do so may have interest profiles created for them to guide the library staff both in acquiring new material and in recommending items from the collection.

The main problem with the ledger system was the difficulty encountered in searching for overdue materials, or in placing holds on items checked out to other patrons. In spite of those drawbacks, however, the ledger system had some advantages and remained a popular way to handle circulation. Aside from its simplicity and ease of use, the ledger system provided quite a bit of additional information to the librarian. Because of its archival nature, the ledger made it possible to monitor use of the collection and to know something about patrons' preferences. Although ledger systems and daybooks have largely been replaced by more modern methods, they are still occasionally used in small, specialized collections.

Another early method of keeping track of circulating materials was the "dummy", whereby a piece of paper or block of wood was inserted in place of the item on loan, and the name of the borrower was written in a diary. This method is still sometimes used to indicate blocks of material that are shelved in another location and occasionally in vertical files to indicate materials that are on loan.

Modern Systems. As the size of the collection, number of patrons, and volumes of transactions grew and these systems became unwieldly, other more flexible systems were developed. Temporary slips containing the borrower's name, address, and registered number were made for each item checked out. These could be filed by call number, due date, or borrower's name. The slip was destroyed when the item was returned. In some libraries, multiple slips were made using carbon paper, each of which could be stored in a separate file. Obviously, these systems required careful discharging to make sure that returned items were properly credited. While these systems made it somewhat easier for libraries to detect overdues and place holds, they created additional paperwork and are seldom used today, except in some non-automated libraries.

The permanent slip or card, prepared at the time the book is processed, is an outgrowth of the temporary slip. Identity information for the book is printed on the card and the card is stored in a pocket in the book. In order to charge out a book, the patron's name, address, and registration number are entered on the card, which is then filed by due date. This approach is still often used in libraries, although some problems may result from illegible or forged patron information, but it is quick and efficient. It is particularly widely used at academic library reserve desks, where transaction volume is high and the circulation period is short.

An extension of this basic idea was developed by the Newark Public Library in 1900 and is now mar-

keted by several vendors. When a patron registers at a library, a metal plate is created showing the borrower's name, address, registration number, and any other information that the library wants to keep such as borrower class (such as J for Juvenile), expiration date, and so forth. This information is imprinted on the book card at the time it is checked out. The process works exactly like the permanent card system except that there is less chance for error in recording the borrower information and the device can set the due date automatically for various classes of materials and borrowers. One drawback of this method is that the anonymity provided by recording only the patron's registration number is lost. The saving in library staff time resulting from not having to look up the patron names and addresses is considerable.

There have been several other variations on the permanent card system primarily designed to provide additional access points and to save labor. Among them are the Bro-Dart *Sysdac System,* designed to give the library staff easy access to the patron identification information, but preserve anonymity in the permanent record; the McBee Key Sort System, with edge punched cards that assisted library staff in detecting overdue materials; and several photographic charging systems that again provide staff with easy access to borrower information but remove that information at the time the item is discharged.

System Requirements. It becomes obvious, little by little, that the requirements for a library circulation system are based on tradition, philosophy of library service, and the need to expedite the circulation process. Where collections are large, patrons numerous, and the number of daily transactions high, manual systems had to give way to more powerful methods. But these new techniques had to meet certain basic requirements. They had to be convenient for both patron and library. They had to provide the necessary access points to support easy charge and discharge, to place reserves or holds, to facilitate renewals, and to notify the library about overdue materials. They had to enable the library to keep accurate and up-to-date patron records and be flexible enough to accommodate changes in loan periods, fine structures, borrowing privileges, holds, and reserves.

Automated Systems. With the advent of electronic data processing systems in the late 1940s, it was natural that libraries should investigate and apply this technology to the circulation system problem. Virtually all of the early efforts at automating circulation were batch processing systems, in many cases using punched cards. These systems were fast and reliable, eliminated the need for filing, and could produce overdue notices on demand. But helpful as they were, they did not meet all of the libraries' needs for circulation information. It was still not possible to tell patrons what titles were charged out to them without a special computer run and, because the systems operated in batch mode (usually overnight), it was not possible to know the status of an item between runs.

Further, many of the early circulation systems were *exception systems*—that is, records were kept in the circulation system only for those materials that were checked out. There was no information about other materials that were supposedly on the shelf, and it was still difficult to locate items in order to place holds and reserves.

Laminated card with individual bar code, part of the computerized circulation system in the Queens Borough Public Library.

Queens Borough Public Library

Libraries are still concerned about issues of privacy, and today's online circulation systems are generally designed to preserve the item-patron links only while the material is actually charged out. Nevertheless, most automated circulation systems are able to provide much better management information than the previous manual systems could deliver. Although no item-patron link is preserved, aggregate statistics on collection use can be generated according to a variety of criteria such as patron types, call numbers, collections, locations, and so forth.

Great advances in computer power, rapid decline in the cost of data storage, and much more sophisticated techniques of file handling and time sharing gave rise to the development of the first online circulation systems in the early 1970s. Some were developed by libraries themselves, while others were developed and marketed by vendors such as Computer Library Systems, Inc. (CLSI). CLSI pioneered turnkey, online circulation systems, and by the mid-1980s had installed about 90 percent of the systems in use worldwide. Since then, many other vendors have developed online circulation systems for libraries using a wide range of computer equipment. They range from extremely simple microcomputer-based systems designed to meet the needs of the smallest elementary school library to highly complex mainframe-based systems that meet the needs of large networks of highly sophisticated libraries.

Use of Optical Character Recognition (OCR) labels and bar codes to mark library materials and to identify library patrons has revolutionized the charge and discharge process. It is quick, easy, and almost totally error-free, so simple in fact that in some cases patrons can even check out their own materials. Some indications (still in the early stages in the mid-1980s) suggest that there will be much more direct user involvement in the circulation activity with the development of simpler terminals, better systems dialogue, and telephone connections from home, office, dormitory room, and other places. Some circulation systems now allow patrons to place holds and recalls, and electronic mail may make it possible to notify patrons of materials that have been received on interlibrary loan or from recalls or to notify patrons that materials are overdue.

Although many library circulation systems were designed and developed as relatively straightforward single-function systems, they should be considered as just one component of much larger systems. Libraries found that they needed systems that would enable them to keep track of a book throughout its life in the library system, from the time it was ordered until it was lost or discarded. In addition, libraries needed support for other services such as online public access, serials control, and acquisitions. These needs gave rise to the development of the so-called integrated library system encompassing many functions.

The characteristics of such systems change rapidly. *Library Technology Reports* commissions studies of the available systems every few years and publishes periodic updates. The current trend is toward systems that run on microcomputers or minicomputers and, in addition to circulation, support acquisitions, cataloguing, online public access, serials receipt control, materials booking, and authority control.

As the cost of online data storage decreases, more systems are designed to handle the full Library of Congress MARC record format and are able to accept and transmit MARC formulated records. Furthermore, most circulation systems are now able to accept bibliographic records from utilities such as OCLC and the Research Libraries Group (RLG) and some have interfaces to auxiliary systems that support acquisitions and serials receipt control. There is also a trend emerging now that links one circulation system with another—perhaps different—circulation system so that library patrons can have access to circulation information for neighboring collections as well as their own. CLSI's DATALINK product, for example, links CLSI systems with GEAC and DATAPHASE systems.

REFERENCES
Elmer D. Johnson, *A History of Libraries in the Western World* (1965).
Joseph R. Matthews, *Choosing an Automated Library System: A Planning Guide* (1980).
Joseph R. Matthews, and Kevin Hagerty, editors, *Automated Circulation: An Examination of Choices* (1980)

EMILY GALLUP FAYEN

Clapp, Verner W.
(1901–1972)

One of the most influential and productive librarians of his generation, Verner Warren Clapp was a Library of Congress administrator, writer and consultant, leader in professional organizations, and foundation head.

Clapp was born on June 3, 1901, in Johannesburg, South Africa. His father, George Herbert

Arthur Plotnik

Verner W. Clapp

Clapp, was a native of New Hampshire who had gone to Johannesburg on business. His mother, May Sybil Helms, was of Danish descent. The Clapps met in Johannesburg and were married there in 1898 but left Johannesburg for Poughkeepsie, New York, in 1905, after the Boer War.

Clapp attended the public schools in Poughkeepsie and earned an A.B. at Trinity College in Hartford, Connecticut, where he captained the track team, joined Sigma Nu fraternity, and was elected to Phi Beta Kappa. Following his graduation in 1922, he joined his parents in Washington, D.C., where they then lived, and found temporary summer employment cataloguing manuscripts at the Library of Congress. In the fall he left the Library to study philosophy at Harvard, but at the close of the academic year he decided to return to the Library of Congress and was employed as a reference librarian in the main reading room. His great energy, intelligence, and wide-ranging interests impressed his superiors, and in 1928, when the Library's Congressional Unit was organized, he was placed in charge. At that time he also met Dorothy Devereux Ladd; they were married on August 24, 1929. She shared many of his diverse interests.

In 1931 Clapp was promoted to the post of Special Assistant to the Superintendent of the Reading Rooms. Six years later he became Assistant Superintedent of the Reading Rooms and was given additional responsibility for the Division for the Blind. Under his administration the production of braille and talking books was increased, and regional libraries were established to improve services to the blind.

In 1940, shortly after Archibald MacLeish's appointment as Librarian, the Library of Congress was reorganized and a Department of Administrative Services was established. Clapp became its first Director and undertook a reform of the Library's fiscal management. When the United States entered World War II, he was given responsibility for the evacuation to Fort Knox of the nation's cherished documents—the Declaration of Independence, the Constitution of the United States, and the Articles of Confederation—and, also, the copy of Magna Carta which the British Government had sent to Washington for safekeeping.

After helping plan the organization of an Acquisitions Department in 1943, Clapp was named its first Director. With his usual vigor and vision he revamped the Library's acquisitions program to make it more comprehensive and responsive to the new and increased informational needs of the government. His contributions during this period were not limited to development of the Library's collections, however. His ideas were influential in the organization of the Library's Reference Department, in the shaping of its personnel policies, in proposals for the revision of the Copyright Act, in efforts to develop interlibrary cooperation in microfilming, and in various other areas of library activity.

Immediately after World War II, Clapp entered into a new period of noteworthy and varied activity. During the war years the flow of publications to the U.S. from Germany and other countries of Europe had been cut off. With the cessation of hostilities, Clapp helped plan, and was made responsible for, a vast undertaking, the Cooperative Acquisitions Project, which involved the procurement of some 2,000,000 European publications for the Library of Congress and 112 other American research libraries and the distribution of these publications on an equitable basis. Additionally, in 1946 his talent for diplomacy was tested in successful negotiations in Berlin with representatives of the U.S.S.R. to effect the release of books and journal issues that had been ordered before the war by U.S. libraries and were being held in storage in East Germany. In 1945 and 1946 he was given the assignment of collecting and making useful disposition of a vast quantity of books published in special wartime editions for the use of the military. Even finding temporary storage for these publications was a monumental task, but the project was carried out to the satisfaction of all concerned. The books were distributed to colleges and universities, whose rapidly increasing enrollments were creating a demand for scarce teaching materials.

Of quite a different order was his assignment in 1945 to organize a library and provide a reference service for the United Nations Conference at San Francisco; he did so with great skill, working under extreme pressure. The United Nations turned to him on many occasions thereafter for advice on UN library matters, and from 1959 to 1962 he served, with three other librarians, as a consultant to the Secretary General of the United Nations and the architects employed in planning the UN Library building.

In 1947 the Librarian of Congress decided to appoint a deputy, and it was no surprise to anyone in the profession when, on March 5 of that year, Clapp was named Chief Assistant Librarian of Congress. Before he had been in that position a year, he was asked to chair a U.S. Library Mission to Japan to assist in the establishment of a National Diet Library. In two months he and Charles Harvey Brown, Director of the library of Iowa State College, produced a plan for the organization and services of the proposed library as well as drafts of the legislation needed for its implementation. Their ideas were accepted, and the necessary legislation was enacted promptly by the Diet. At the celebration of the 20th anniversary of the National Diet Library in 1968, he was honored by Japan with the Order of the Sacred Treasure.

When Luther Evans resigned as Librarian of Congress to become Director General of Unesco, Clapp assumed the duties of Acting Librarian and served in that capacity from July 4, 1953, until September 1954.

Over the years of its existence the Ford Foundation had been the recipient of many grant requests from research libraries. In 1955 it asked Louis B. Wright (Director of the Folger Library), Leonard Carmichael (Secretary of the Smithsonian Institution), and L. Quincy Mumford (Librarian of Congress) to call a meeting of librarians and scholars to advise it on how it might assist in the solution of library problems. Two conferences were held at the Folger Library that year on the problems of research libraries and the possibility of using new scientific and technological developments in solving them. At the second meeting it was decided that a new and independent organization was needed. In September 1956 the Council on Library Resources, Inc., was established with a $5,000,000 grant from the Ford Foundation, and, on the advice of many librarians and others whose opinions had been solicited, Clapp was persuaded to serve as President. He threw himself into the work of the Council with all the energy and enthusiasm he had displayed throughout his career for every venture that engaged his interest.

Under his direction the Council sponsored a variety of highly productive projects. Among many other undertakings, it supported: the study that stimulated the automation of the Library of Congress; the preliminary work that led to the mechanization of the production of the *Index Medicus;* the work of the Barrow Laboratory on the deterioration of book paper, the development of a formula for "permanent/durable" paper, an aerosol process for the deacidification of deteriorating books, and performance standards for library binding; development of the *National Union Catalog of Manuscript Collections;* the third edition of *The Union List of Serials;* production by the American Historical Association of a *Guide to Photocopied Historical Manuscripts;* the establishment of the *National Register of Microform Masters;* the production of the International Inventory of Musical Sources; a system for searching statute law by computer; the American Library Association's Library Technology Project; the book-selection journal *Choice; Books for College Libraries;* and Cataloging in Publication.

Clapp was quick to assist, through Council grants, various national and international library conferences, as well as cooperative library undertakings, surveys, studies, and extensions of worthwhile existing programs. Council support made possible the first publication of a scientific journal exclusively in microform and the production of such notable publications as Keyes Metcalf's *Planning Academic and Research Library Buildings* and Robert Hayes and Joseph Becker's *Handbook of Data Processing for Libraries.*

In 1967 Clapp retired from the Presidency of the Council on Library Resources but continued until 1972 to give the Council, as a full-time consultant, the benefit of his long experience and encyclopedic knowledge.

The range of Clapp's interests is exemplified by the many varied organizations in which he maintained membership: the American Antiquarian Society; the American Association for the Advancement of Science; the American and Canadian Bibliographic Societies; the American Institute of Graphic Arts; the American, Canadian, and District of Columbia Library Associations; the Abstracting Board of the International Council of Scientific Unions; the American Society for Information Science; the Columbia Historical Society (Washington, D.C.); the National Microfilm Association; and the Special Libraries Association.

He was also a member of the National Advisory Commission on Libraries and the Science Information Council. He served for 18 years as a Director of the Forest Press, Inc., and, for the last 12 years of his life, as its President. He was a Trustee of the Lake Placid Club Education Foundation from 1955 until his death. It is not entirely coincidental, perhaps, that one of the most important contributors to librarianship since Melvil Dewey should have had such close affiliation with projects that continued Dewey's work.

Clapp served during his career on many committees and published extensively. His writings, always lucid and lively, exhibit an astonishing range of knowledge. They number more than 200 but represent only a fraction of the subjects that engaged his interest.

Few librarians have been as honored as he in their lifetimes, nor have many been so nobly eulogized in death. The American Library Association awarded him the Lippincott Award and the Melvil Dewey Medal and made him an Honorary Life Member. The Special Libraries Association gave him a Special Citation, and the Association of Research Libraries, at the time of his retirement from the Council on Library Resources, honored him with a citation for his "selfless dedication to the cause of librarianship and the service of scholarship," his service "to the United Nations and to foreign governments, to library organizations" and "to scholarly associations." It called him "an honored spokesman for the library profession" who had exerted "a more beneficent influence on research librarianship" than any other man of our time, and it named him the "Librarian's Librarian."

When Clapp retired from the Library of Congress, Mumford said of him, "His contributions to the Library of Congress and to the library world are so varied and numerous that one is staggered at the knowledge that a single person in his lifetime could accomplish this and at the same time manage to be a loving husband, father, and friend." He died on June 15, 1972, in Virginia. At the memorial tribute to him held in the Coolidge Auditorium of the Library of Congress on June 20, David C. Mearns, the former Assistant Librarian of Congress and Honorary Consultant in the Humanities, said of him, "Verner was . . . indomitable, exuberant, prodigious, passionate, inexhaustible, a polymath, and a fellow of infinite zest. . . . He was generous with his patience, with his counsel, with his consideration. . . . his friends were legion; his admirers a mighty host."

REFERENCES

Verner W. Clapp, 1901–1972: A National Tribute (Library of Congress, 1977).
Foster E. Mohrhardt, "Clapp, Verner Warren," *Dictionary of American Library Biography* (1978).

FREDERICK H. WAGMAN

Classification

The book of Genesis tells us that the world was created out of chaos when "God divided the light from the darkness." Thus the idea of classification, literally "the making of classes," was thought to be the origin and essence of the world since ancient times. The ability to classify is indeed a fundamental faculty without which no living organism can function. We must, for example, distinguish between edible and inedible things, or animals that are (or may be) dangerous to us and those that are not. Everyone goes through life constantly making distinctions between things that are like and those that are unlike while at the same time also grouping them into larger containing classes or into smaller subclasses and perceiving relationships between classes. The farmer keeps cattle, horses, and poultry apart, but together thinks of them as livestock, and each class of animals may at times have to be further subdivided into milch and

Morgan Library of Amherst College, whose classification scheme was devised by Melvil Dewey in 1873.

beef cows, riding and draft horses, and chickens, turkeys, and geese. The mechanic sorts fasteners into nuts and bolts and puts each of these into separate bins according to shape, size, threading, and so on. All our physical sense impressions are transformed into concepts by a process of classification, and abstract ideas as well do not float haphazardly in our minds but are thought of as being related to each other in an orderly way.

The human race's greatest achievement was the discovery that concepts expressed by words could be transmitted to other people in distant places and preserved for those living in other times by means of writing. Ever since human knowledge was first recorded in more or less durable form, the resulting documents have been gathered to form collections, but such collections become libraries only when they are arranged in systematic patterns. In a larger sense, all arrangements of documents, whether by author, title, subject, or physical form, are based on some kind of classification, but in a more restricted sense only the systematic arrangement of documents by *subject* is commonly understood to be the purpose of library classification.

It is important to distinguish between three different but interrelated meanings of the term *classification* in library practice: in its most literal and basic sense it is the act of *classifying* or *making a classification scheme* (the resulting scheme often being called a classification for short); second, it is the act of *classing* or assigning class marks to documents that indicate subject content; third, it is the resulting *physical arrangement* of documents (books as well as other materials) on shelves or the related but not necessarily identical arrangement of document surrogates (catalogue entries) in a classified subject catalogue.

The first of these, making a classification scheme, is obviously the fundamental one, the others being dependent on it. It has been defined by the International Federation for Documentation (FID) as follows:

> By classification is meant any method creating relations, generic or other, between individual semantic units, regardless of the degree of hierarchy contained in the systems and of whether those systems will be applied in con-

nection with traditional or more or less mechanized methods of document searching.

A classification scheme consists generally of three interrelated parts:

(1) A *schedule* or *table* listing the classes in a sequence perceived by the makers of the scheme as a logical or useful one, normally subdivided in hierarchical order from the most general to the most specific topics. The phrase "relations, generic or other" in the FID definition means that a classification scheme should be able to express not only hierarchic (genus-species) relations but also others, such as whole-part or agent-action. These are known as *paradigmatic* relations—that is, they follow a known pattern and are independent of the treatment of the subject in a document. For example, a book on cars deals implicity also with motor vehicles and vehicles in general. There are also associative and correlative or *syntagmatic* relations, namely those dealt with in specific documents in a relationship determined by the author (such as a book on accidents caused by cars in the U.S. versus the U.K.), and classification schemes should allow for the clear and specific expression of such relations. Recurrent features, such as place-names, time periods, languages, personal characteristics, or forms of presentation (such as "bibliography" or "periodical"), which are applicable throughout all or most of a scheme, may be listed separately in *auxiliary schedules*.

(2) A *notation* that mechanizes the order of schedules by means of symbols which have a generally known order, namely either numerals or letters, or a combination of both; other marks, such as mathematical symbols or punctuation marks, may also be used, although those do not have a universally agreed-upon and known order.

(3) An *alphabetical index* that lists subjects by their names and synonyms and shows distributed aspects (their relationship to other subjects), in each case indicating through the notation their place in the schedules. Nineteenth-century classification schemes were arranged almost entirely on enumerative hierarchical principles, resulting in fixed "pigeonholes" for preconceived subjects. Modern classification schemes are both hierarchical and synthetic, providing for individual "facets" or aspects of subjects that can be combined at will to express the conceptual content of a document, thus avoiding the rigidity of older schemes and readily accommodating entirely new subjects and their various relationships.

Early Library Classifications. The clay tablets found in one of the world's oldest libraries, the large royal archives of Assurbanipal (7th century B.C.), contained a catalogue that divided the works into main classes (Grammar, History, Law, Natural History, Geography, Mathematics, Astronomy, Magic, Religion, and Legends), each being subdivided into several subclasses. No actual classification scheme from Greek and Roman libraries has survived, but the catalogue of the great Alexandrian library, the *Pinakes* ("tables") compiled by Callimachus (3rd century B.C.) was apparently classified into Poets, Lawmakers, Philosophers, Historians, Rhetoricians, and Miscellaneous writers; further subdivisions were by form, subject, and time. The libraries of China at the end of the Western Han period (1st century A.D.) were classified into seven large groups: Encyclopedias, the Six Arts, Philosophy, Poems and Songs, Military Art, Soothsaying, and Medicine. During the later Wei and Tsin dynasties (3rd to 5th centuries), a system was designed that survived practically unchanged until the 20th century. It consisted of four main classes, retaining several of the older classes as subdivisions: (1) Classics; (2) Philosophy, Military Art, Mathematics, and Theology; (3) History, Government, and Miscellanea; and (4) Literature.

Medieval Library Classification. Early monastic libraries were so small that they had no need for a classification, but later it became common practice to divide the holdings of such libraries into three large groups, Theological Works, Classical Authors of Antiquity, and Contemporary Authors on the Seven Arts. The latter were also the backbone of classification in the university libraries, where books were arranged according to the classical division of the curriculum into the Trivium (Grammar, Rhetoric, and Logic) and the Quadrivium (Arithmetic, Geometry, Music, and Astronomy).

Philosophical and Pragmatic Classifications. Since the Renaissance two main types of classifications can be distinguished: those that are based on a philosophical scheme or an ideal order of knowledge, and those that aim merely at a practical arrangement of books on shelves. Outstanding among the former is the Swiss polyhistor Conrad Gesner's *Pandectarum . . . libri xxi,* the classified part of his *Bibliotheca universalis* that listed most learned books known at the time (1548). The system arranged books according to their subjects by 21 major classes, each with a number of subdivisions. Gesner's scheme marked the beginning of modern library classification and served as a model for the arrangement of many libraries until the end of the 18th century. Another philosophical scheme was contained in Francis Bacon's *Advancement of Learning* (1605); though it was not intended for library use, it influenced many later classifiers, among them Thomas Jefferson and Melvil Dewey. A practical scheme, first developed in the mid-17th century by the Paris booksellers and ascribed to Ismael Bouilleau, was further elaborated by the French bibliographer Jacques-Charles Brunet in the early 19th century; the scheme was quite simple and had only five main classes—Theology, Jurisprudence, Sciences and Arts, Literature, and History—each with a moderate number of subdivisions. It is still used in part by the Bibliothèque Nationale and some other large French libraries, and an adaptation of the scheme is used in the British Library.

A classification scheme that combined philosophical principles of arrangement with practical applicability was designed in the 1840s by the German Orientalist and librarian A. A. E. Schleiermacher for the court library at Darmstadt. It comprised 25 main classes (A/Z) with some 13,000 subdivisions and was the most detailed scheme of the 19th century. It was remarkably modern in its use of auxiliary tables for recurrent geographical and other features, and it had a fully developed relative index. The scheme was used in some German national and university libraries well into the 20th century.

The Dewey Decimal Classification (DDC). Melvil Dewey designed his scheme for the small library at Amherst College (Massachusetts) in 1873 and first published it in 1876. It grew from a slim booklet containing less than 1,000 subdivisions on 12 pages (at the time criticized as excessively detailed!) and an alphabetical index of 18 pages to a three-volume work of more than 3,400 pages, comprising schedules for several thousands of classes and their subdivisions, supplemented by seven auxiliary tables and a comprehensive relative index. It had gone through 19 full and 11 abridged editions by the end of the 1970s. A 20th edition will appear in the late 1980s. DDC has been translated into several dozen languages, including seven in non-Roman scripts by the mid-1980s, and it is used in thousands of libraries throughout the world. It is also used for the arrangement of a number of national bibliographies, foremost among them the *British National Bibliography*.

The success of DDC results from several features. It has a simple notation that is independent of language or script and based on the principle of decimal fractions (incorrectly called "numbers") as class marks, which are infinitely expandable for further subdivision of any existing class, "horizontally" (though "vertical" expansion, the intercalation of a new subject into a hierarchy, is not possible when all nine subdivisions at the same notational level are already utilized). The notation has excellent mnemonic features and has some flexibility through auxiliary tables for forms, areas, literatures, languages, racial, ethnic, and national groups, and persons, which are applicable throughout the schedules (though not for all class marks). The principle of "number building" allows subdivision of one basic class mark by all or part of another, thus indicating certain aspects of relationships between subjects, while at the same time not burdening the schedules with an excessive number of subdivisions. These last two features are Dewey's most important contribution, and they formed the nucleus for the later development of faceted classifications. Finally, and perhaps most important, the DDC is backed by its own organization, the Forest Press, and is supported by the Library of Congress, thus assuring its continued existence and revision to keep the scheme up to date.

Among the shortcomings of the scheme are its sequence of main classes, reflecting the world outlook of the late 19th century; the allocation of only one main class each to science and technology, resulting in overcrowding and long notations and in separation of the basic sciences from their technological applications; the separation of history from social sciences; the separation of political geography from other geographical topics; and the strict adherence to the principle of "integrity of numbers," which often prevents the restructuring of old schedules to accommodate new topics and sometimes even the proper application of general facets. To a certain extent, the latter deficiency has been remedied by the successive introduction of so-called Phoenix schedules, which are completely redesigned sections of the schemes.

In the U.S. the DDC is used almost exclusively for shelf classification of books, mainly in school, public, and college libraries. Some subject bibliographies, notably the *American Book Publishing Record,* are also classified by DDC. The Library of Congress provides DDC class marks for some 70 percent of books catalogued in the MARC data base. In the U.K. and several European countries, and also in many Asian and African libraries, the DDC is widely used not only for shelf classification but also for the construction of classified subject catalogues and bibliographies, in which the detailed (and sometimes long) notations made possible by number building can be used to much better advantage than as mere call numbers on the spines of books.

With the increasing use of online catalogues in the U.S. it has been recognized that searching a DDC classified sequence is an important complement to searching by keywords or subject headings, especially for generic searches ("up" or "down" a hierarchy). For this purpose, too, long notations, far from being a hindrance, become useful in pinpointing specific subjects.

The Universal Decimal Classification (UDC). In the 1890s two Belgian lawyers, Paul Otlet and Henri LaFontaine, conceived the idea of a worldwide bibliography on cards of all recorded knowledge, not only in book form but also in articles, reports, patents, and so on. To achieve this goal they needed a highly specific classification. The DDC had by then become known in Europe, and the two men considered it suitable for their project, although it was not sufficiently detailed. In 1895 they asked for and received Dewey's permission to adopt, translate, and further develop his scheme (then in its fifth edition). Otlet and LaFontaine proceeded to translate the schedules into French, made some changes in religion, the social sciences, and technology, and thus developed with the help of subject specialists the *Classification décimale universelle* (for some time known as the "Brussels Expansion").

Although the UDC was and still is based on the DDC, it differs from it in several respects. The basic structure of 10 main classes and most of the first 1,000 three-digit notations were retained (except for final 0's, which were dropped), but a much larger number of sometimes very minute subdivisions were introduced. Dewey's form and place auxiliaries were indicated by means of mathematical symbols or punctuation marks. Finally, the colon sign was introduced to link two or more UDC codes so as to indicate relationships, a device that makes the notation highly flexible: a document on "Use of computers in the management of hospital personnel" is classed as 362.1:658.3:519.68 (Hospitals: Personnel management: Computers); each of the three codes can be used as an access point.

The full UDC tables were first published in 1905 under the title *Manuel du repertoire bibliographique universel*, followed later by full editions in German, English, Russian, Spanish, Japanese, and eight other languages. These full editions contain about 150,000 subdivisions. Medium editions (about 30 percent of the full tables) exist in English, German, French, Japanese, and 13 other languages. Abridged editions (about 10 to 15 percent of the full tables) exist in 17 languages and 5 alphabets. In addition there are special editions for certain subject fields in which the codes for the special subjects are given in full, while codes for fringe subjects are listed only in abbreviated form.

Although the idea of a worldwide bibliography had to be abandoned in the 1920s as impractical, the UDC was rapidly adopted throughout the world by many libraries, abstracting services, and journals, especially for scientific and technical subjects, and it is still a widely used general system of classification, with an estimated 100,000 institutional and individual users. In the U.S. the UDC is used by several specialist subject bibliographies, a large abstracting service, and several libraries. In the Soviet Union, the UDC has been made mandatory since 1963 for all scientific and technical libraries, as well as for abstracting services, foremost among them *Referativnyi Zhurnal;* all scientific and technical books also carry a UDC number. Consequently, in Eastern European countries the UDC is also widely used, and is employed on a large scale in Japan, in Brazil, and in other Latin American countries.

Although the basic structure of the UDC still follows DDC's 10 main classes (except for class 4, which is presently empty, Language having been amalgamated with Literature in class 8), it is no longer fully compatible with the DDC because many subjects are now classed by notations that are quite different. The responsibility for the revision and development of the UDC lies with the FID, working through committees of specialists or interested individuals. *Extensions and Corrections* are published semiannually; each issue contains many hundreds of new, corrected, or deleted codes, thus keeping the scheme continuously up to date. Because of its highly faceted structure and largely expressive notation, the UDC is the only one of the large general classification schemes that has been used successfully in computerized information retrieval, and it has also been employed as a switching language between subject heading lists and thesauri.

The Expansive Classification (EC). While Dewey conceived the DDC in the traditions of the pragmatic classifications, his older colleague Charles Ammi Cutter designed in the 1880s a scheme that was influenced by the then current philosophy of "evolutionary order in nature." The EC consisted of seven different but related schemes (the last of which remained unfinished). The first was rather broad, comprising only seven classes, each subsequent "expansion" being more finely subdivided and intended to be used by increasingly larger libraries. The notation for main classes consisted of letters, while auxiliary tables used digits; a period or full stop was also used as a notational device. Unfortunately, EC's notation had to be changed throughout the seven expansions, necessitating constant reclassification when a library grew and wished to move from one expansion to the next. Only a small number of American libraries ever used the scheme, and after its inventor's death in 1903 it was soon almost entirely abandoned. Both Cutter's notation and his ideas of an order of subjects suggested by a scientific consensus had a decisive influence on two other American schemes—the Library of Congress Classification and Bliss's Bibliographic Classification.

The Library of Congress Classification (LC). When the Library of Congress moved into its present main building in 1897, it needed a new classification scheme because the one originally devised by Thomas Jefferson (an adaptation of the Baconian scheme) had become inadequate. In 1899 the DDC was considered, but Dewey could not agree to some major changes the Library requested. The Library then decided to design its own scheme, taking many features from Cutter's EC but essentially producing a pragmatic system primarily based on its own holdings. The LC is in fact not one system but a loosely coordinated series of 21 special classifications, each with its own structure, notation, auxiliary tables, and index, occupuying 34 volumes with a total of more than 10,600 pages. One class, P (Language and Literature), occupies more than 3,200 pages (30 percent of the whole scheme), whereas all of science and technology constitutes only 13 percent; Class K (Law) is still incomplete.

The notation is mixed, consisting of one or two letters for main classes followed by ordinal numbers up to a maximum of four digits for subdivisions. Gaps are left between numbers for future expansion, but where these have been filled, decimal subdivision, generally by one or two digits, is used. Beyond (or instead of) decimal subdivision, further subdivision of a subject is alphabetical, often by the English name of a subject expressed by "Cutter numbers" (a letter plus one or more digits); this feature results in dispersion of closely related subjects. No use is made of synthesis or mnemonics. Where geographical, historical, or form subdivisions are necessary, they are specially developed for each subject without regard to similar subdivisions in the same or in other classes.

Revision of the schedules is carried out individually for each class; whole blocks of numbers may be canceled, the subjects classed there moved to an entirely different schedule, and the former numbers used for different subjects. Sometimes added subjects are arbitrarily inserted just where a vacant number exists and without regard to collocation of related subjects.

Several hundred American libraries have switched from DDC to LC since the 1960s, primarily because of the administrative advantages of centralized classification and the universal availability of LC class marks on cards and in machine-readable (MARC) catalogue records. A few university libraries outside the U.S. also adopted LC for similar reasons, though they often make their own adaptations and expansions for topics not covered by the scheme at all or not in sufficient detail.

The Bibliographic Classification (BC). Henry Evelyn Bliss, the most eminent of American classification theorists, devoted a lifetime to the design of a scheme that would reflect the "scientific consensus" on the order of things and ideas. It was considered by many to be far superior to all other general schemes both in structure and notation, but by the time it was published by the H. W. Wilson Co. (1935–53), most American libraries had already been classified by either DDC or LC and could not or would not change to a new and unproved system. In the U.K., however, about a hundred libraries adopted the BC. The scheme consists of 26 main classes (A/Z) and an "anterior class" (1/9) for form subdivisions that are applicable throughout the schedules. A characteristic feature is the provision of alternative locations or treatments for many subjects, depending on the point of view of the book or the needs of a particular library. Thus a book on economic history may be classed under History at LGE or under Economics at T9. The notation uses all let-

DIVISIONS.

0		500	Natural Science.
10	Bibliography.	510	Mathematics.
20	Book Rarities.	520	Astronomy.
30	General Cyclopedias.	530	Physics.
40	Polygraphy.	540	Chemistry.
50	General Periodicals.	550	Geology.
60	General Societies.	560	Paleontology.
70		570	Biology.
80		580	Botany.
90		590	Zoology.
100	**Philosophy.**	**600**	**Useful Arts.**
110	Metaphysics.	610	Medicine.
120		620	Engineering.
130		630	Agriculture.
140	Anthropology.	640	Domestic Economy.
140	Schools of Psychology.	650	Communication and Commerce.
150	Mental Faculties.	660	Chemical Technology.
160	Logic.	670	Manufactures.
170	Ethics.	680	Mechanic Trades.
180	Ancient Philosophies.	690	Building.
190	Modern Philosophies.	**700**	**Fine Arts.**
200	**Theology.**	710	Landscape Gardening.
210	Natural Theology.	720	Architecture.
220	Bible.	730	Sculpture.
230	Doctrinal Theology.	740	Drawing and Design.
240	Practical and Devotional.	750	Painting.
250	Homiletical and Pastoral.	760	Engraving.
260	Institutions and Missions.	770	Photography.
270	Ecclesiastical History.	780	Music.
280	Christian Sects.	790	Amusements.
290	Non-christian Religions.	**800**	**Literature.**
300	**Sociology.**	810	Treatises and Collections.
310	Statistics.	820	English.
320	Political Science.	830	German.
330	Political Economy.	840	French.
340	Law.	850	Italian.
350	Administration.	860	Spanish.
360	Associations and Institutions.	870	Latin.
370	Education.	880	Greek.
380	Commerce and Communication.	890	Other Languages.
390	Customs and Costumes.	**900**	**History.**
400	**Philology.**	910	Geography and Description.
410	Comparative.	920	Biography.
420	English.	930	Ancient History.
430	German.	940	Europe.
440	French.	950	Asia.
450	Italian.	960	Africa.
460	Spanish.	970	North America.
470	Latin.	980	South America.
480	Greek.	990	Oceanica and Polar Regions.
490	Other Languages.		

(940–990 Modern)

Amherst College Archives

Reproduced page from Dewey, A Classification and Subject Index for Cataloguing and Arranging of Books and Pamphlets of a Library, 1876.

ters of the alphabet (as many as four capital letters), lowercase letters for geographical subdivisions, and digits for forms. For example, BOV3 is History of broadcasting; JCAe is Educational research in England.

After Bliss's death in 1955, upkeep and revision of the BC ceased for almost 15 years, and several libraries abandoned the scheme. In the 1970s it was revived in England under the editorship of Jack Mills; the first new BC2 schedules began to appear in 1976, but progress has been slow, and by mid-1985 only about a third of the new BC2 schedules had been published. BC2 is in fact a new classification based on BC1 but with a faceted structure and a revised notation. Whether it will meet with more success than BC1 remains to be seen.

The Colon Classification (CC). This is the last universal scheme designed by one person and actually used in libraries. The Indian mathematician-turned-librarian S. R. Ranganathan published the first version of the CC in 1933. It constituted an almost complete break with traditional methods of classifying, relying on an analytico-synthetic approach. Instead of enumerating classes of things and ideas and their ever more minute subdivisions, the CC lists only relatively simple objects and ideas as well as general properties and characteristics, or "facets," whose class marks can be combined to express exactly the subject of a document. It thus abandoned the method of creating fixed "pigeonholes" for preconceived and precoordinated subjects that had bedeviled earlier classification schemes. The backbone of the scheme is formed by 43 main classes (denoted by one or two capital letters and two Greek letters), roughly corresponding to traditional disciplines but not extensively subdivided. All detail is provided by the facets, which are combined according to the formula PMEST, where P stands for Personality (generally the primary or central aspect of a subject), E for Energy (any kind of action or process and their results), M for Material, S for Space (Place), and T for Time. Each facet is set off from others by punctuation marks (originally only the colon sign from which the scheme takes its name and which was itself adopted from the UDC). When constructing a class mark, not all facets may have to be used, whereas others may appear more than once. Thus a work on "Attempts to eradicate poverty in Scotland in the 1940s" would first of all be put into main class Y Sociology, because it deals with a social phenomenon. Analyzing the work, we find that it is concerned with Poverty, :434 in the E facet and its Eradication, :64, also in E; Scotland is .563 in S, and the 1940s are 'N4 in facet T, so that the complete class mark becomes

Y : 434 : 64 .563 'N4
(P   E   2E   S   T
(In this case, no Material facet is involved, but two Energy facets are used.)

The alphabetical index to the scheme is also constructed along new lines, the "chain indexing" principle invented by Ranganathan.

Though the seeds of generally applicable facets were sown by Dewey, and the idea was further developed in the UDC, it was fully applied and systematized only in the CC, which reached its sixth edition in 1960; in the mid-1980s, a completely revised seventh edition was in preparation by the Documentation Research and Training Centre in Bangalore, India. Schedules for specific topics not dealt with in sufficient detail in the general scheme are also published from time to time. Although the CC is used in relatively few libraries in its homeland, and almost nowhere else, its underlying theory has had a major impact on classification. Since the 1950s, the structure and revision policy of all existing or newly devised classification schemes (with the exception of the LC) have been more or less affected by Ranganathan's ideas.

Rider's International Classification. The last attempt by one person to construct a universal scheme was made by A. Fremont Rider, an eminent American librarian. In 1960 he published a scheme intended strictly for shelf arrangement of books in general libraries, consisting of 26 main classes and 676 subclasses, all having a three-letter notation, such as PGI Passenger cars. The scheme was "printed as manuscript for the receipt of corrections . . . " but the author died one year after publication and it was never used.

The Bibliothecal-Bibliographic Classification (BBK). A classification system for the libraries of the U.S.S.R., the BBK was elaborated by the Lenin Library in Moscow and published in 30 volumes from 1960 to 1968. An abridged edition in six volumes was published, 1970–75, and a one-volume abridgment for very small libraries appeared in 1975. The BBK consists of 21 main classes, each of which is indicated by one of the 28 letters of the Cyrillic alphabet. First is Marxism-Leninism, followed by the Sciences, Technology (eight classes), Agriculture, Medicine, Social Sciences (seven classes), Literature, Art, Religion, Philosophy, and Generalia. The 21 classes are further subdivided into a total of about 45,000 main headings. The notation is mixed, the letter of the main class being followed by digits expressed in decimal fractions, with points after every three digits. General auxiliary tables are provided for geographical areas and for other facets, most of which are modeled on those in the UDC (though the notation is different). Each class has its own index, and there is no general index. Most class marks are enumerative and they are often precoordinated (similar to LC), but some combinations are possible.

The BBK has been made mandatory in general and university libraries in the Soviet Union and in those dealing primarily with the social sciences. It has also been introduced in other Eastern European countries; in the German Democratic Republic, it is used for the classified arrangement of the *Deutsche Nationalbibliographie.*

Modern Chinese Classification Schemes. In the early years of the 20th century the classification scheme used for almost 2,000 years proved to be unsuitable for modern Chinese literature. Some libraries began to use DDC in 1907, and during the 1920s LC was also tried. Neither scheme was adequate for Chinese topics, and local adaptations were made. After the establishment of the People's Republic of China, an entirely new general classification scheme was designed, the first version of which was published in 1953. It had 17 main classes with many subdivisions, the first of which in each class was always devoted to the Marxistic-Leninistic and Maoist view of a subject, and its notation used only Arabic digits. A revised version, *Zhongguo Tushu Ziliao Fenlei Fa* ("Classification System for Chinese Libraries"), appeared in 1975 and a second updated edition appeared in 1980. A third edition, which will become the standard classification scheme of the PRC, was in preparation in the mid-1980s. The scheme has more than 25,000 main headings in 22 main classes with a notation consisting of one or two Roman capital letters; subdivisions have a decimal numerical notation, general auxiliaries use lowercase Roman letters, and special auxiliaries are expressed by hyphens and digits (such as -0). Complex subjects can be expressed by coloning (as in UDC); for example, O29: TB11 is Mathematics for engineering (the first unit is the letter O, not the digit zero). The index follows traditional Chinese methods—the logograms expressing the names of the subjects are arranged by number of strokes.

The Broad System of Ordering (BSO). The most recent general classification scheme, commissioned by Unesco in 1971 and elaborated by FID as a "roof classification," was published in 1978. It was intended to be used as a "switching language" between existing classification systems, thesauri, and other information-retrieval systems, centers, or organizations, not in order to supplant any of these, but to make them mutually compatible on a general level. As its name implies, it provides only about 4,000 not very detailed subdivisions. BSO features an entirely new system of notation based on digits that are used in groups of millesimal and centesimal fractions, separated by commas, thus ensuring a maximum of hospitality and flexibility in a pattern of 3,2,2 digits. For example:

716   Building construction & services
  .40   Parts of buildings
    .45   Walls

Complex subjects can be expressed by combinations of class marks from different parts of the scheme, separated by a hyphen; under BSO, for example, "Environmental aspects of building construction" is 716-390, where 390 is Environment.

Although the BSO was not designed for classification of books in libraries, it could very well be employed for broad shelf classification, which is all that is needed in many open-shelf browsing collections. It did not, however, achieve its stated goal as an international switching language, and no further development of the BSO has taken place.

Special Classification Schemes. The universal classifications described above are useful for general collections, but many specific subject collections or databases require special classifications that provide detailed subdivisions and other features not offered by any of the general schemes. Some examples are the W schedules for Medicine developed by the National Library of Medicine (employing a letter not used in LC), a scheme for physics designed by the American Institute of Physics, and one designed for the *British Catalogue of Music* by E. J. Coates.

Research on Classification. In 1952 a Classification Research Group (CRG) was founded in England to study the theoretical foundations of classification. Members of the CRG subsequently constructed several special classification schemes, and some were also instrumental in the design of the BSO. Similar research groups were founded in other countries during the 1960s, and their work attracted much interest on the part of philosophers and linguists, resulting in several international study conferences that took place in Dorking, U.K. (1957), Elsinore, Denmark (1964), Bombay (1975), and Augsburg (1982).

The FID has a standing Committee on Classification Research (FID/CR), concerned with maintaining a register of current research on classification, the education and exchange of researchers, the organization of meetings, and the publication of research reports. The American Society for Information Science has a Special Interest Group on Classification Research (SIG/CR) whose members are active in research on classification and indexing by human beings and machines. The journal *International Classification*, founded in 1974, carries articles and research reports on classification and indexing and contains a current awareness bibliography of books, reports, and papers on these subjects.

REFERENCES

K. G. B. Bakewell. *Classification and Indexing Practice* (1978).
"Classification: Theory and Practice," *Drexel Library Quarterly* (1974).
Ingetraut Dahlberg, "Major Developments in Classification," *Advances in Librarianship* (1977).
International Classification and Indexing Bibliography (Frankfurt a.M., 1982–85) 5 volumes. Volume 1 lists 2,250 general and special classification schemes.
Leo La Montagne, *American Library Classification* (1961).
W. C. B. Sayers, *A Manual of Classification for Librarians,* 5th edition, revised by Arthur Maltby (1975).
E. I. Shamurin, "History of Library and Bibliographical Classification" (Moscow, 1955–59). In Russian. German translation: *Geschichte der bibliothekarisch-bibliographischen Klassifikation* (Munich, 1967–68).
Who Is Who in Classification and Indexing (Frankfurt a.M., 1983).

HANS H. WELLISCH

Cleverdon, Cyril
(1914–)

Cyril Cleverdon, British librarian and information scientist, is best known for his work in information retrieval.

Cleverdon was born in Bristol, England, September 9, 1914, and served on the staff of Bristol Public Libraries from 1932 to 1938. From 1938 to 1946 he was the Librarian of the Engine Division of the Bristol Aeroplane Co. Ltd. In 1946 he was appointed Librarian of the College of Aeronautics at Cranfield (later the Cranfield Institute of Technology), where he remained until his retirement in 1978. He also served there as Professor of Information Transfer Studies from 1976 to 1978. He later became Executive Secretary of the European Association of Information Services (EUSIDIC).

Cleverdon became a leader in the evaluation of information systems. In 1957 the National Science Foundation awarded a grant to Aslib for an evaluation of indexing systems, to be undertaken under Cleverdon's direction at the College of Aeronautics. Thus began the Aslib Cranfield Research Project. "Cranfield 1," 1957–62, compared the performance of four index languages: UDC, alphabetical subject catalogue, Uniterms, and a special faceted classification. The study was large, involving 18,000 documents and 1,200 search topics. The twin measures of recall ratio and precision ratio assumed major significance for the first time in the experiments. In comparing the systems, many performance variables were studied, including type of document, indexing time, qualifications of the indexers, and the number of index terms assigned. The results indicated surprisingly little difference in the performance of the systems. Human errors in indexing and searching were more serious than failures due to file organization. Cleverdon concluded that specificity of vocabulary and exhaustivity of indexing are much more important than file organization as factors affecting the performance of information systems.

Cranfield 1 was important because it revealed which factors importantly affect the performance of retrieval systems and which do not. It also developed methodologies that could be applied successfully to evaluation of experimental, prototype, and fully operating information systems. The Cranfield techniques were subsequently used in the evaluation of a number of operating systems, including the extensive evaluation of MEDLARS conducted in the period 1966 to 1968.

The second stage of the studies ("Cranfield 2")

began in 1963. The major objective was to investigate the components of index languages and their effects on the performance of retrieval systems. In Cranfield 2 the various index language devices were each evaluated according to their effect on the recall and precision of a retrieval system. Altogether 29 index languages, consisting of various combinations of the several devices, were evaluated, using a test collection of 1,400 documents and 221 test searches. The results again were rather unexpected because the index languages that performed best were natural-language systems based on words occurring in document texts.

Cleverdon wrote many reports and journal articles on information retrieval, the most important being the detailed reports on the two phases of the Cranfield studies: *Report on Testing and Analysis of an Investigation into the Comparative Efficiency of Indexing Systems* (College of Aeronautics, 1962) and *Factors Determining the Performance of Index Languages* (Aslib Cranfield Research Project, 1966), the latter written with Jack Mills and E. Michael Keen.

Cleverdon served on the Council of Aslib for most of the period from 1952 to 1967 and was its Chairman in 1958, 1975, and 1976. He became a Fellow of the Library Association, an Honorary Fellow of the Institute of Information Scientists, and an Honorary Member of Aslib.

Cleverdon's contributions were widely recognized in North America, Europe, and elsewhere. He received the Professional Award of the Special Libraries Association in 1962 and the Award of Merit of the American Society for Information Science in 1971.

F. W. LANCASTER

Clift, David H.

(1907–1973)

David H. Clift

David Horace Clift served as the chief executive of the American Library Association from 1951 to 1972. He led the association in expanding its membership and program and in organizing its headquarters.

Born on June 16, 1907, in the bluegrass hills of Washington, Kentucky, the eldest of six children, Clift was a reader all his life. He loved books and went out of his way to be involved with them. By the time he had finished high school in 1925, he had decided to attend the University of Kentucky in Lexington. He saved money by boarding with friends of the family while taking any part-time job he could find. By his junior year he had won a student assistant job in the university library. Using that experience as a springboard, he was able to obtain summer work in the Lexington Public Library.

He knew where he wanted to go by then. At that time the evolving library profession offered a fifth-year Bachelor's degree. Clift secured a loan from the Masonic Order of DeMolay and went to New York City in 1930 to attend the Columbia University School of Library Service. He found part-time work in the university library until he finished his degree in mid-1931.

Instead of returning to Kentucky during the Great Depression, he stayed in New York, working in the famous "reference" Room 315 of the New York Public Library. He was among many famous librarians to emerge from the same room; Keyes D. Metcalf, L. Quincy Mumford, Robert B. Downs, and Ed Freehafer are just a few of the people with whom he worked. He married Eleanore Flynn, a children's librarian for the Brooklyn Public Library. Their six years in the New York system were happy ones for both of them, but Clift could not resist the blandishments of Charles C. Williamson, Director of the Columbia University Library, and joined him as his assistant at Columbia in 1937. For the next five years Clift sharpened his personnel skills and managerial talent; Frederick G. Kilgour came to know Clift at Columbia and to appreciate his quiet and sure way with organization and personnel supervision.

In 1942 Clift was drafted into the Army and assigned as an orderly in a hospital. He was soon transferred into the Office of Strategic Services (OSS), where intelligence-gathering activity was growing under the Interdepartmental Committee for the Acquisition of Foreign Publications. Clift became the Deputy to the Executive Director—who happened to be Frederick G. Kilgour. Clift soon found himself supervising a staff of 140 people.

Following his honorable discharge in 1945, Clift became Associate Librarian at Yale. There he became a Fellow of Trumbull College and developed for the library a position classification and pay plan that was an admired model of academic librarians.

During this period he led a delegation of the Library of Congress Mission to Germany (1945–46) and served as President of the Connecticut Library Association (1950–51).

Clift became Executive Secretary of ALA in September 1951. He moved into the crowded old McCormick Mansion on Huron Street in Chicago, which had been serving as headquarters for the Association for far too long. The membership was 19,701 and the general funds budget was $191,129. The outlook was bleak, but Clift's strong points were administration, personnel work, and subtlety. When once asked what he felt was required of an association executive, he replied that it was to administer the policies decided by membership and leave the leadership to those elected by the membership. He went to work on reorganizing headquarters staff and creating an equitable pay plan that enabled ALA to recruit some of the most able and dedicated people in the field.

Successful dealings with the professional leadership contributed to his long tenure as ALA chief. He was able to encourage consensus and compromise, thus avoiding some of the divisive in-fighting that had marked some previous headquarters administrations. When Clift retired in 1972 as Executive Director of ALA, the membership stood at 30,592 and the general funds budget was $2,262,971. During his 20 years of service some $15 million in grants came to ALA, making possible the establishment of national library standards and advances in professional library education. Among other achievements were advances in making a place for libraries in schools. *Choice* was founded as a review medium for undergraduate collection development, under the auspices of the Association for College and Research Colleges, an ALA division. The official *ALA Bulletin* changed from a journal primarily of record to a lively magazine called *American Libraries*. A series of nationwide adult education programs were conducted in libraries, and goals set for public library service. New emphasis was placed on the defense of intellectual freedom in library service. Further, the ALA Washington Office emerged as an important agency, resulting in the successful involvement of the federal government in support and assistance programs for libraries.

Clift was returning from a European trip collecting data for a study on comparative librarianship when he died on October 12, 1973. Grace Stevenson, his long-time associate at ALA, said of Clift, "He was never selling a bill of goods—or himself—just libraries."

REFERENCE
Gerald R. Shields, "Clift, David Horace," *Dictionary of American Library Biography* (1978).

GERALD R. SHIELDS

Cole, Fred C.
(1912-   )

Fred Carrington Cole, educator and university president, is most closely identified with libraries through his work with the Council on Library Resources. Few individuals whose primary careers have been in fields other than librarianship have had as strong an influence as he had on library development. His long and distinguished career in education always emphasized libraries and the role of libraries in academic work. His ultimate opportunity for promoting libraries arrived when he helped organize, advise, and then administer the Council on Library Resources.

Cole was born in Franklin, Texas, April 12, 1912. His first close connection with libraries came when he occupied an office in the Louisiana State University Library while serving as an editor for activities connected with the university. L.S.U. awarded him an A.B. degree in 1934 and an A.M. in 1936. He so impressed the faculty with his scholarship and his writing ability that he was chosen to serve as Editorial Associate of the *Journal of Southern History,* 1936–41, and Managing Editor, 1941–42, and as Co-editor of the Southern Biography Series, 1938–45. He was History Editor for the Louisiana State University Press (1938–42). During those years he also worked on his Ph.D. in history, which he received in 1941. During World War II he saw extensive sea duty as a gunnery officer with the U.S. Navy. Later, at the Office of the Surgeon General of the Navy, he revised the Manual of the Medical Department. Before leaving the Navy in 1946, he was awarded a special commendation by the Surgeon General. A brief period as a civilian historian and editor for the Air Force followed.

He resumed his academic career in 1946 at Tulane University. He was associate professor, professor, dean, and vice-president there, and in 1959 he became President of Washington and Lee University, Lexington, Virginia. He received national recognition for his success in raising academic standards at both universities and in stimulating the integration of the libraries into the educational programs.

Within and without higher education, he won notice as a leader in academic administration, and he was called upon to serve as an adviser to many gov-ernment and nongovernmnent organizations, including the College Entrance Examination Board, the American Council on Education, various foundations, and the National Science Foundation.

A strong proponent of international cooperation in education and in the broad field of information, he served as an official U.S. representative to international conferences in Europe and Asia and was a leader in international library activities. The American Library Association in 1976 presented him with a special Centennial Award for, in part, his "skill in making Ford Foundation dollars for libraries achieve maximum impact," and for "his support of the best in the past in librarianship as well as his interest in the world of the future." He was also honored with the medal of the International Federation of Library Associations and the medal of the International Council on Archives.

In 1954–55, on leave from his post as Vice-President of Tulane University, Cole served as a full-time consultant to the Ford Foundation. He joined with other scholars, educators, and librarians in developing plans for the Council on Library Resources, which was established in 1956 with Ford Foundation funding. Cole became a member of the CLR board in 1962. When Verner Clapp, the first President of the Council, retired in 1967, Cole succeeded him. In 1977, when Cole retired from CLR, Whitney North Seymour, for many years Chairman of the CLR Governing Board, said: "Dr. Cole has shown extraordinary imagination and skill in marshaling the Council's efforts to meet the problems of libraries head-on. Under his leadership, the Council has engaged in several long-range programs aimed at increasing the effectiveness of academic library management, enhancing library services to undergraduates, and improving the skills of librarians in their own and other scholarly fields. Such programs as the Academic Library Management Intern Program, the College Library Program, the Fellowship Program, and the Library Service Enhancement Program in large measure owe their existence and success to Fred Cole."

The ALA Citation of 1976 pointed out that Cole's contributions were accomplished by a gentleman of dignity and vision whose "quiet manner and self-effacing personality belie a progressive attitude and serious concern with the library's role in the future of American society."

FOSTER MOHRHARDT

Council on Library Resources, Inc.

Fred C. Cole

Collection Development

The term collection development describes a cluster of functions that, together, shape the holdings of materials in a library: funding, self-study and evaluation, selection, weeding, and maintenance. This article focuses on the shaping and management of the collection, the decision-related aspects of the process, rather than on techniques of acquisitions or preservation. Also beyond the scope of this discussion are censorship, media, and resource sharing.

CONCEPT
Central to collection development is the art of selection. The 1970s and 80s saw both unprecedented

challenges to those who would practice this art and also the appearance of useful tools to assist practitioners. The environment for selection has often been a hostile one, with forces seriously out of equilibrium. At the same time, though, automation has put new quantitative techniques within the reach of almost all selectors.

In the 1970s selection as a branch of librarianship was attacked both from within and without; outside the library, information exploded while sources for support evaporated. Inside the profession, colleagues adopted techniques that seemed to demote selection from an art to a craft. By the 1980s a new equilibrium could be seen. The external challenges were real and acknowledged, yet the new tools became an aid to decision making. The selection process remained essentially subjective: ". . . suitability . . . is finally determined on the basis of a context that can only be privately assembled and applied" (Ross Atkinson).

The kind of choice and judgment called for in adding materials to the collection has been extended increasingly into other areas of the library: preservation, deselection, collection arrangement, format decisions, and more. In all of these areas, decisions are based on three needs described in an important 1984 article on the theory of selection by Atkinson: understanding of the collection, insight into user needs, and awareness of subject fields in question.

More than in previous generations, selection or collection development decision making in the 1980s poses a broad range of challenges, at the same time requiring from the selector an increasingly formidable background in subject, management, quantitative, and interpersonal skills. Yet at a time when so much is being asked of selectors, their personalities also need to include a humility that allows for shared decision making, integration of a range of relevant perspectives, and development of community consensus.

ENVIRONMENT
Decisions about selection, maintenance, and weeding of collections are determined by a wide range of factors: as (1) support, or the means available to acquire and maintain a collection (most often funding); (2) the quantity of materials available for acquisition; (3) the accessibility of other collections; and (4) the needs of the library's user clientele. In about 1970 in the developed Western countries, major shifts in the funding and information situations led librarians to put new emphasis on access to other collections through resource sharing, and to a comprehensive review of the user needs. Background for understanding the 1980s' substantial shift in approach toward libraries' own collections is considered here.

Support. An analysis of libraries' means for obtaining materials and the relation of these to public policy will characterize the social foundation of library collecting. Materials selection and collection building have the greatest role in identifying acquisitions to be purchased, but it is useful to keep in mind such other sources as gifts, deposits, and copying. The backbone of the great modern national collections is deposit. Great research libraries have been built on gifts of collections and, to a lesser extent, by exchanges. The monastic libraries were built by copying from borrowed texts. Each of these means survives today; often they are less frequently used as

dominant collecting vehicles, but they are nearly always significant. After World War II, for example, the National Library of the Philippines was rebuilt through copying resources available in Chicago's Newberry Library. Later, the Genealogical Society of the Church of Jesus Christ of Latter-day Saints amassed greater quantities of copies of early records for access and preservation through an international program of microfilming. But most library collecting is done through purchase and can be viewed as a reflection of public policy, directly or indirectly.

Public policy provides for library collections in four major ways: tax authority, direct appropriation, tax incentives and exemptions, and copyright deposit requirements. A key element of the modern library movement has been the passage into law of these means of support. The history of library legislation has shown a growing commitment to the values of libraries, learning, and book collections. This commitment is an aspect of broader historical trends.

Cultural, Social, and Political Determinants. Even a very brief history of library collecting cannot overlook the point that the modern state's commitment to collecting is the successor to earlier forms of patronage. The copying carried out for the monastic collections reflects the central role of the medieval church in the preservation and management of information, learning, and knowledge. The church's major partner in patronage was the aristocracy. Universities, too, housed libraries, often decentralized among colleges. Hierarchical religious and governmental institutions fostered limited access, centralized collections for the purpose of preserving those institutions. The social changes and reforms that began with the Renaissance and the Reformation and included the Age of Revolutions dramatically altered the means of distributing and collecting information. By the mid-19th century, radicals and progressive conservatives were united in working toward creating an informed and educated electorate, to make aristocrats of the masses in order to preserve institutions and culture. Library collections were one of the key means of achieving these ends, and for over a century they have prospered, as the trend toward social equality has continued. Along with the rise of democracy, the growth of capitalism and technology created new demands for libraries. In the quarter century after World War II, rapid growth in technology and Western influence in the world led to specialization and to an information explosion.

Later Changes. The transition from the 1960s to the 1970s demonstrated how much the collecting of library materials was tied to external factors, national and international social or political trends, and library responses. Around the world, the post-World War II era of librarianship had seen broad expansion, the recovery from Depression austerity and from war, the reaching of new publics, and a new and firmer partnership with technology. The economy was expanding while inflation was moderate. The new American world role brought new collection building demands. But as the 1960s drew to a close, the environment changed dramatically. The American optimism of the early 1960s was reversed, and a critical mass of new circumstances arose with significance for the planning and management of collections of library materials.

Emergence of New Subject Demands. Building

throughout the 1960s was a worldwide interest in scientific and technical subjects. Later, social topics (such as independence, ethnicity, radicalism, and feminism) in quick succession generated demand on limited library resources. In the 1970s and 1980s, health and psychological topics and interest in careers, computer science, and business caused additional expansion of libraries. Increased specialization was characteristic of both books and users. At the end of the 1970s, the typical university press print run for a new title was about as large as at the beginning of the century, even though the number of titles had grown tremendously.

Information Explosion. Reflecting the increase in specialization and the expanded learning of the post-Sputnik Western world, there was a marked growth in journal literature, book publication, and the production of government documents. By the 1970s this was followed by the expansion of index and abstract sources, made possible in part by computer technology; by the 1980s access to this new capability was available, directly or indirectly, to a great number of patrons in the form of online databases.

Energy. In the mid-70s and early 80s the shortage of energy and the premium to be paid for it caused major reallocations of funds, inevitably diverting money away from collection building, and creating intense pressure to limit collection growth by resorting to storage, deaccessioning, and resource sharing. Conversely, the resulting redistribution of wealth stimulated into the 1980s collecting in new, energy-rich regions—to support rapid economic development efforts.

Funding Constraints. Beginning in the late 1960s, academic libraries encountered slowed growth of budgets and even budget decline as institutions reached their income limits and as graduate enrollments dropped. The first crunch, around 1970, was felt in slashed library budgets, leaving permanent gaps in many American research and high technology collections. By the late 1970s, academic librarians were preparing, as well, for a decline in undergraduate enrollments. Taxpayer resistance reduced taxes supporting libraries at local and federal levels. Corporate special libraries struggled in the face of uneven profits throughout the 1970s; their fortunes improved with the economy by the mid-1980s.

Inflation. The cost of books and periodicals rose more rapidly than the costs of many other goods during the 1970s. Periodicals rose most strikingly and claimed greater and greater shares of library materials budgets. High interest rates penalized publishers and jobbers who carried large inventories. The results were short press runs and growing numbers of sought-after out-of-print titles. Thus, many books which had been "selected" never became parts of library collections. Currency values experienced major fluctuations, with grave consequences for library collections in English-speaking countries in the 1970s and outside the U.S. in the 1980s.

Library Response. As the basic social conditions around library collecting changed from the 1960s to the 1980s, the professional response took two main directions: toward resource sharing and toward improved management skills to support the functions relating to collecting. These new thrusts were reactions to changes from the external environment.

Resource Sharing. Related closely to the development of resource sharing was the effort on the part of librarians, and those who depend most on libraries to affect public policy, to provide adequate funds to meet increased costs, new demands, and a broader range of materials. When those who form public policy and the library community had worked together long enough to understand each other's limitations, proposals for resource sharing began to emerge. On state, local, and regional levels concrete consortium projects began to emerge that would profoundly affect the collecting environment of individual libraries. Linking mechanisms between libraries developed, most notably union catalogues (card files were rapidly succeeded by microfilm and by online circulation and bibliographic databases).

The idea of cooperative collecting, long a hope of the profession and more recently a panacea grasped by some funding sources, was almost totally impractical in the absence of effective bibliographic control, but the new linking mechanisms opened the way to renewed serious consideration of the potential and problems of this idea. Nevertheless, the problem of bibliographic control has been less complex for periodicals, where the task is broken up between the location devices (such as union lists) and the indexes. A limited amount of effort and resources could create a holdings list of journal titles so the articles found in indexes could be traced easily in remote locations. Libraries responded to spiraling journal costs both by creating union lists and by turning to centers for periodical servicing. The largest-scale example of the latter is the British Library Lending Division (BLLD) in Boston Spa, England. Materials available at BLLD are accessible internationally within days, via OCLC and other networks.

In the United States, the importance of Chicago's Center for Research Libraries grew, as member research libraries came to call more and more on this central source for less frequently needed titles. Also in Chicago the Periodical Bank of the Associated Colleges of the Midwest showed in the later 1960s and early 1970s that smaller academic and other libraries could meet their journal needs by relying on a central, dedicated collection of more frequently called-for titles that still might be beyond the needs of each individual library. The idea was successfully demonstrated in Illinois's North Suburban Library System, where the Central Serials Service provides a comprehensive backup to member public and affiliated libraries. In the 1980s, U.S. libraries of all types united to share journals access, often via online systems such as OCLC, RLIN, and LCS. The drive for a National Periodicals Center in the U.S. was derailed in part by federal indifference but also by the success of decentralized cooperative and other supply methods.

Management Methods. As the quantity of materials, the demands, and the funds for collecting all went out for synchronization to a significant degree, the skills needed to make collecting decisions began to grow and diversify. The bibliographer, or person knowledgeable about developments in a particular field or fields, needed to be familiar with the collections of nearby libraries as well. Both those who provided the funds and those who used the library began to hold the library accountable to develop a new

209

range of quantitative and qualitative tools for collection development: needs assessment, planning, and evaluation.

CURRENT PRACTICE
The tasks of selection and collection building, supplemented by the relatively newer emphasis on collection maintenance and weeding, depend on the results of self-study.

Managing the Collection. Functions relating to planning and managing collections have assumed roles equal in importance to those traditionally held almost exclusively by selection and collection building. In the recent literature librarians have turned much of their attention to the means available to organize scarce resources in new ways to meet demands. The idea of self-study is not new. John Cotton Dana's *Library Primer* (1899), which sums up a generation of library throught, begins by discussing what good a library does generally. Dana's chapter on selection is subtitled "Fitting the Library to Its Owners." A number of principal factors are considered: proximity to other libraries, broadly stated purposes, funds available and projected, and the characteristics of the user public (including level of education and use habits or patterns). Old wisdom has gained new sophistication. As already indicated, librarians have been able to redefine the "proximity" of other libraries through new linking devices. In addition, they have given greater attention to analyzing the characteristics of the user public. In another chapter, on general library policy, Dana begins by admonishing, "Remember always (1) that the public owns its public library, and (2) that no useless lumber is more useless than unused books." Many user studies have included the goal of narrowing the gap between usage patterns and holdings.

Needs Assessment. What are the needs of those who place demands on the library? This is not a new question, but a century ago there appears to have been more consensus about the answer than is found today. Once again Dana illustrates the nature and tenor of earlier discussion:

> Don't buy a novel simply because it is popular. If you follow that line you will end with the cheapest kind of stuff. Some librarians pretend that they must buy to please the public taste; that they can't use their own judgment in selecting books for a library . . . Why these librarians don't supply the Police Gazette is difficult to understand. 'The public' would like it—some of them . . . The silly, the weak, the sloppy, the wishy-washy novel, the sickly love story, the belated tract, the crude hodgepodge of stilted conversation, impossible incident, and moral platitude or moral posh for children—these are not needed.

Dana traces the roots of his material back to *Public Libraries in the United States of America,* a report published by the U.S. Bureau of Education in 1876, and particularly an article by William Frederick Poole. But the report contained a variety of articles and a diversity of views. F. B. Perkins argued strongly in favor of supplying the books that people wanted to read, rather than collecting those things people should want to read. Charles A. Cutter thought there would be money enough to buy only perfect books when people themselves had been perfected.

A study at the University of Pittsburgh, widely discussed in the late 1970s and early 1980s, found that many of the books acquired and housed in the university's library never were used. In rebuttal of these findings, Jasper Schad (in "Pittsburgh University Studies of Collection Usage: A Symposium," *Journal of Academic Librarianship,* 1979) reiterated Dana's earlier conviction: "In the last analysis, need, not use, should determine what libraries contain."

In general, needs assessment has encompassed the whole range of factors. The need to know the users well—the "owners"—has prompted community analysis projects in many areas to assist public library programming. What people want, certainly, is a factor, and surveys of the most popular young adult literature have been carried out by many public libraries. Academic libraries have placed new emphasis on liaison with faculty and students. Curricular demands are related to collection goals. Daniel Gore and Richard Trueswell have observed also that academic (particularly undergraduate) users often want the same books at the same time.

Planning. As librarians have measured needs against funds for collecting, they have added a range of strategies, many beyond collecting. In response to the perceived clustering of demands, some academic libraries (such as Northwestern University's) have set up "core collections," not unrelated to the undergraduate collections founded before the great period of expansion. In some cases, loan periods have been shortened to provide better turnover. At the same time, U.S. public libraries found themselves serving more and more part-time and commuting postsecondary students, and certain operations of public and academic libraries became more similar.

For collections, inadequate funds and better prospects for cooperation led to more formal collecting policies. Larger collections, following leadership from Stanford University librarians, sought to articulate the level of collecting intensity in various fields. This process generated internal consensus on collecting issues and provided a framework for future effective cooperative collecting. Consortia—from the Research Libraries Group (RLG) to the Chicago area LIBRAS colleges and often states such as Colorado and Illinois—have embarked on significant programs for coordinated cooperative collecting, based on a conspectus of subjects developed by RLG with support from the Council on Library Resources and the Office of Management Studies of the Association of Research Libraries (ARL).

Large public library systems and other cooperative systems have tended to define carefully the levels of collecting in units of the whole, dividing subject and sophistication responsibility.

Evaluation. The selector's judgment is aided increasingly as new tools for review of materials or for appraisal of past collecting performance are developed.

When needs are ascertained and profiled, they can serve to gauge collection quality. Qualitative tools, such as standard lists and bibliographies, provide a useful measure for most types of libraries. Needs—by type of clientele, by type of material, or by subject—can be compared to actual holdings. If deficiencies are found, collections can be upgraded. Public libraries can rely on lists of recommended titles, from landmarks such as the *Public Library Catalog* to more specialized lists appearing in *Library Journal, Booklist,* and elsewhere. *Magazines for Libraries,* as well as the titles indexed in the *Reader's Guide,* provides direction in choosing periodicals.

The American Library Association had issued lists of basic book collections for various levels of school libraries, and for colleges it publishes *Books for College Libraries.* Research and special libraries can use either comprehensive tools *(Ulrich's International Periodicals Directory* or MARC tapes, for example) or specialized bibliographies. The availability of the latter improved in the 1970s and 1980s, partly due to computer assistance. Still another tool in highly specialized areas is citation checking, to determine whether or not research or a monograph could have been done in the collection under study.

Consideration of the optimum size for a collection has also been a topic of discussion. Is the collection large enough to meet reasonable needs, but not so large as to impede other library and/or institutional functions?

Size standards set in the 1960s and 1970s for academic libraries reflect projections tied to the recommendations implied by lists such as *Books for College Libraries.* The Clapp-Jordan formula prescribed size goals, with other variables factored in; a smaller collection could be assumed to be unable to meet some needs. But studies by Richard Trueswell and at the University of Pittsburgh suggested that not all of the books bought or on hand were being used. Particularly in light of current resource sharing capabilities, collection growth could be seen as counterproductive—in some cases—to collection and institutional effectiveness.

In the face of an entire range of issues, a comprehensive approach to building consensus on collecting policy is necessary. The introduction of management techniques to gain an overview has been noticed. A major leadership effort of the ARL's Office of Management Studies has been the creation of a package of self-study and analysis tools, a key component of which was the Collection Analysis Project (CAP). Aimed first at large, but later also at small, academic libraries, CAP provides carefully designed and tested modules for considering a wide range of issues relating to collection development: goal setting, allocation, resource sharing, staffing, and so on. The process enables the library staff and the community it serves and to which it is accountable to take stock of the library's situation in light of the profound changes which have taken place in its environment. For smaller academic libraries the Associated Colleges of the Midwest manual for a book collection use study, also issued by OMS, integrates both the use study quantitative methodology and the process-centered, OMS approach in order to facilitate effectiveness and efficiency in collection decision making.

Periodic evaluation will tend to restructure the formal or informal collecting policy of the library. From this will come efforts in selecting new materials, maintaining needed materials, and removing less vital items.

Selection. The collecting policy will result in procedures for selecting material—who will make the final decision, how funds will be allocated, how items will be identified, and so on. Who decides on partic-

ular titles will depend on the size and type of library and other factors. For Dana, it is clear that the librarian should select, and the tendency in academic libraries has been away from faculty and toward the librarians as the scale has increased.

In 1899 Dana offered a guide for fund allocations. While specific percentages are given, local considerations are seen as the controlling factors. As quantitative tools for evaluating need and collection effectiveness improve, librarians may find themselves looking more and more at allocation, the directing of resources. The emergence of approval plans in larger libraries in the 1960s reflected this need, and these plans have become important in the operations of many libraries.

The task of selecting individual titles, guided by careful planning and evaluation, must reflect a balance of need versus want. Review media exist at all levels and inevitably reflect more potential user need than can be accommodated. In some subject areas, large or small, a library may want all of the material on a local controversy or on the pet topic of Professor X. Selection implies that some titles are "bad," and reviewers confirm that. Will the user, tracing a citation, accept this judgment? How many interlibrary loan requests result from decisions not to buy "bad" books?

Censorship is the dark side of ferreting out bad books. It is the librarian's function to maintain a pluralistic outlook on all matters. Thus librarians have led the movement to establish balance when considering works on various topics—racial, feminist, political, ideological, and academic—for their collections. This approach reflects the fundamental social roots of library collecting.

The searching out of relevant and high-quality new material is critical to the selector's role, especially with today's rapid changes. The selector must be widely read. In high technology situations, recourse to online searching will supplement traditional sources. Often the challenge will be to make items available before they are obsolete.

Weeding. During the austerity of the 1930s and under the growth pressures of the 1960s, the task of weeding items from collections for disposal or storage gained importance. But the combined pressures of the last quarter of the 20th century—funding, continued collection growth, and energy—have confronted growing and mature libraries with stubbornly inelastic buildings. Resource sharing makes direct access to marginal items less compelling. And, finally, the Trueswell and Pittsburgh studies raise questions about the utility of larger collections. In some cases, the failure to weed judiciously puts at jeopardy the library's mission to its users.

Choosing items for removal from the collection is not an inexpensive process. The decision making and recordkeeping are labor intensive, not to mention the physical work involved. Community consensus on policy and on particulars is essential to the task, and the involvement of users often builds a sense of common purpose.

Storage is costly in capital, in labor, and in utility. Movable stacks maximize the use of space and hold down heating and air conditioning costs. But this equipment expense is considerable. Microform storage provides even more compactness and more potential for incremental growth. But both of these means of storage place special physical demands: movable shelving, with the accompanying density of volumes, brings a heavy weight to bear on the floor and equipment's structure and, according to standards, should not be stored at over 70 degrees F (21°C). These arrangements, along with remote storage, necessitate delay or inconvenience for the user and expense (capital, labor, and energy) for the library. How substantial these are, along with cost and lack of access to other collections, will determine the value of storage over disposal.

The decision to store or dispose of an item should rest on a clear consensus—among those who use, serve, and fund—on need and purpose, both for the task and for the item in question. Increasingly cooperative arrangements will affect disposal decision making. Reference to standard lists and to union catalogues and bibliographic databases should provide guidance on more important issues. Many persons and viewpoints should be represented in the process.

Maintenance. Careful selection and weeding based on a comprehensive planning and evaluation process will result in a detailed and accurate profile of those elements of the collection that are essential to the library's users. At some point the librarian necessarily comes to the conclusion about some item or another that "this I want to keep!" Alas, this may be the hardest choice of all to implement. Many materials will be on paper and in bindings that defy preservation, and these may represent, for example, as much as two-thirds of the circulation of a liberal arts college library. Climate control in its ideal form exists in no known library and is approached in only a few. Many collection librarians, then, face the certainty of some materials wearing out physically long before they cease to be of value intellectually. In addition, many of the libraries that were designed well in terms of climate create other preservation problems. For the open-stack plan so popular in the 1950s and 1960s, many libraries were built in ways that make security for material difficult, and books are stolen or mutilated as a result. Decay and abuse, especially in light of rising cries to keep on hand those most-called-for items, place another encumbrance on limited materials budgets as needed items are identified and replaced.

COMPREHENSIVE COLLECTING: WHOSE RESPONSIBILITY?

Changing Collection Profiles. Collections of the 1960s may have reflected the goals of academic researchers or standard qualitative guides more than they will in the 1980s; new additions more and more reflect current demand. The "core collection" concept of Trueswell's circulation study tends to prevail, formally or informally, in many types of libraries, while at the same time subject specialities and subject-special collections will continue to flourish. Resource sharing capabilities allow even relatively small libraries to pursue without guilt the special local interests that result in demand from and the orientation of the primary clientele. The rising cost of journals, combined with the increased access from online searching, signals continuing pressure to keep down the size of the book collection. But resource sharing also makes journal material available; thus books and journals may be acquired to a greater extent than previously around current—primarily local—considerations of need and use.

At the same time that libraries will tend to develop core collections and special subject collections, their bibliographic holdings will grow in size and sophistication. The advent of computer-based bibliographic tools coincides with the emergence of online location identification networks. When an item can be obtained for research even if it is held at a distance, a new premium is placed on knowing that the specialized item even exists. Since Sputnik in the late 1950s, research literature has grown tremendously, and index and abstract tools have adjusted to the increase. Tools that became unwieldy split or changed format; online access has developed dramatically in the last decade. Sources that had become prohibitively expensive as subscriptions for smaller libraries now are available on a per-use basis online. In addition, more specialized and focused access sources have emerged. The result is an increased share or allotment of collection budgets for new tools overall. But there have been some countertrends: online access has permitted the elimination of some hardcopy subscriptions and expensive cumulations. Still, the increased emphasis in all types of libraries on knowing what exists, not just what is on hand, has altered allocation and collecting patterns.

National and International Changes. At a time when large and small libraries are carefully scrutinizing their collecting policies with pressure to limit or reduce commitments, the issue of a collecting policy for the nation emerges. Who will be responsible for seeing that everything is to be collected and maintained somewhere? How much can we afford to service hypothetical, "elite" requests in an era of broadly based heavy demand and uncertain prospects for funding?

In the mid-1980s considerable attention in the U.S. was given to work toward coordinated cooperative collection development. The growth of decentralized resource sharing via online systems has met previously unserved needs. As this national database expands, the potential for coordination in selecting and collecting improves.

Resource sharing was a first-wave response to online networks. But the online RLG conspectus points the way to online collection decision making, as selectors can call up orders by other partner-selectors or see which partner is most committed to the sub-field in which a new title appears. This second wave of library interaction will integrate selection decision making in a practical way.

Independent research libraries, along with national libraries, continue to have a key role, even as the great decentralized automated database takes shape. These libraries have defined their missions more around their collections and less around demand. Libraries such as the Huntington, the Newberry, the American Antiquarian Society, and the New York Public now function as national resources for scholarship and learning—building and preserving great collections and, when possible, attracting researchers who will address their priorities. In humanities and historical fields especially, independent libraries act as "libraries of record" in the U.S., along with the Library of Congress and the largest academic libraries, to preserve an aggregate inheritance of culture and learning. This essential mission received important support from the Higher Education Act Title II-C program to encourage research collection development. The grants, few and small each year, still provide evidence of significant recognition by the shapers of public policy.

The emergence of telefacsmile transmission points toward the potential for greater international cooperative collecting. U.S. reliance on the British Lending Library provides an important example of international cooperation. In the 1980s OCLC expanded to include Europe. Growing cooperation and trust at the level of the International Federation of Library Associations and Institutions and in preparing the Anglo-American cataloguing codes point to continued mutual activities.

REFERENCES
American Library Association, *Guidelines for Collection Development* (1979).
Ross Atkinson, "The Citation as Intertext: Toward a Theory of the Selection Process," *Library Resources & Technical Services* (1984).
Dorothy E. Christiansen, C. Roger Davis, and Jutta Reed-Scott, "Guide to Collection Evaluation Through Use and User Studies," *Library Resources & Technical Services* (1983).
Arthur Curley, *Building Library Collections* (1985).
F. Wilfred Lancaster, *The Measurement and Evaluation of Library Services* (1977), especially chapter on collection evaluation, pp. 165–206.
Barbara B. Moran, *Academic Libraries: The Changing Knowledge Centers and Universities* (1984).
Paul H. Mosher and Marcia Pankake, "A Guide to Coordinated and Cooperative Collection Development," *Library Resources & Technical Services* (1983).

ARTHUR H. MILLER, JR.

Colombia

Located on South America's northwest tip, Colombia is a republic bordered on the north by the Caribbean Sea, on the east by Venezuela and Brazil, on the south by Ecuador and Peru, on the west by the Pacific Ocean, and on the northwest by Panama. Population (1984 est.) 28,248,000; area 1,141,748 sq.km. Spanish is the official language. About 50 indigenous tongues and dialects are still in use.

History. During the 18th century, under Spanish rule, the capital, then Santa Fé de Bogotá, was a thriving cultural center. It had universities, women's private schools, printing houses, the first newspaper worth mentioning (the *Papel Periódico Ilustrado*, 1791), and the Royal Library, now Biblioteca Nacional (BN; National Library). Leaders of the movement for independence, among them Simón Bolívar, Francisco Santander, Camilo Torres, and Antonio Nariño, all born in the Western Hemisphere, were without exception highly educated men, familiar with European enlightenment ideas, and booklovers.

Academic and private libraries developed first, and, except for the BN, were always open to the public. Public libraries historically sprang from scattered local efforts, generally on a small scale, and frequently with government support. Today there are few adequately serviced towns, and hardly any lending libraries. As a result, most books are acquired by a selected few. Sometimes private collections are donated to found public libraries, yet there is an almost total absence of reading materials in many homes.

Efforts made by the Instituto Colombiano de Cultura (COLCULTURA, 1969; Colombian Institute of Culture), the government office that runs the NB and coordinates public libraries, achieved unparalleled development of public libraries during the decade 1976–85. In 1976 Colombia had 200 public libraries in 174 towns (out of a total of 990 towns and cities). The number was increased to 436 in 341 towns in 1983. By 1985 there were 780 libraries, counting Casas de Cultura (Cultural Centers) that have book collections, in 537 towns.

Colombia was the first Latin American country to create a Sistema Nacional de Información (SNI; National Information System, 1973), coordinated by the Fondo Colombiano de Investigaciones Científicas y Proyectos Especiales "Francisco José de Caldas" (COLCIENCIAS). Even though it has not fulfilled its original expectations, the SNI has promoted the creation of several subsystems and networks, mainly scientific and technical, and contributed to the development and preservation of public libraries and archives.

The Asociación Nacional de Bibliotecas Públicas (National Public Library Association), created during the Seminario Nacional de Bibliotecas Públicas (National Public Library Seminar) in Bogotá in 1985, announced that it would work to promote local and regional networks and eventually achieve national integration. COLCULTURA planned a national program for the use of 33 bookmobiles and 37 jeeps with lending libraries bought in Spain to cover areas, mainly rural, with few library services.

National Library. The BN was founded in 1777 with books confiscated from the Jesuits when they were ordered to leave by Charles III of Spain. Francisco Moreno y Escandón, Royal Auditor Fiscal,

Libraries in Colombia (1982)

Type	Administrative units	Service points	Volumes in collections	Annual expenditures (peso)	Population served	Professional staff	Total staff
National	1	--	540,000	14,750	--	10	100
Academic	--	--	--	--	--	--	--
Public	--	--	--	--	--	--	--
School	--	--	--	--	--	--	--

Source: Unesco, *Statistical Yearbook,* 1984.

is considered its founder. The first Director of great merit was a Cuban, Manuel del Socorro Rodríguez, also the father of Colombian journalism. The BN has about 600,000 volumes, with 28,000 in the Rare Books Section, including 40 incunabula. Its Newspaper and Magazine Room receives around 1,000 titles and is the country's most complete collection, dating to Colonial times. In the early 1980s the budget was 5,000,000 pesos, not counting regular staff and running costs.

The 1946 Book Law contributed to accumulation of a representative national bibliography, although not everyone complies with it. The one person who contributed the most to the BN's progress in the 20th century was Daniel Samper Ortega, BN Director from 1931 to 1938. Samper persuaded the national government to build the headquarters occupied in Bogotá, the capital. During his administration the BN published a collection of books called *Biblioteca Aldeana* ("Village Library") and *Senderos,* ("Paths"), a magazine. Jorge Eliécer Ruiz was Director of the BN from 1979 to 1982, when Eddy Torres succeeded him. Torres put in motion a plan to reorganize the BN, involving its automation, microfilming, and space and service expansion. He managed to obtain from the town government land adjoining the present building that would allow the BN to grow substantially. Torres died in January 1983. Conrado Zuluaga, writer and professor, who succeeded him, took up the plans outlined in 1982 and advanced them with enthusiasm, in spite of great financial difficulties.

The Archivo Nacional de Colombia (Colombian National Archive), directed by Pilar de Angel, is lodged temporarily in the BN. Its headquarters were under construction in the mid-1980s. It has a Colonial document collection. The Instituto Caro y Cuervo, another independent official institute, publishes the "Colombian Bibliographical Annual" and also edits works of historic, linguistic, or literary merit. COLCULTURA launched important publications from the time it was founded.

Academic Libraries. The Instituto Colombiano para el Fomento de la Educación Superior (ICFES; Colombian Institute for the Promotion of Higher Education) is the government office in charge of coordinating actions, services, and technical processes in academic libraries by means of the University Libraries Network. All higher education centers, whether universities, technological schools, or intermediate professional ones, private or public, must provide information services to their students. There are 300 information units, sponsored by some 225 schools. One-third of these services are run by professional librarians, especially in universities. There is uneven distribution and low mobility of professionals; about three-quarters work in Bogotá, Medellín, and Cali.

National average per enrolled student is four books. A great number of these libraries have no separate budgets, and almost all the funds they receive are spent for managing and personnel. Very few have adequate buildings. The services offered vary, but the most common are reading rooms, book circulation, reservations, interlibrary loans, bibliographic guidance, instructions on how to use information, and selective dissemination of information. There are central libraries, specialized faculty libraries, and information centers. Most use manual means, but about a fourth of them, especially at universities, had undergone or were in the process of undergoing automation in the 1980s. The Library of the Universidad de Antioquia, for example, automated control of its 1,500,000 books.

The Sistema de Información y Documentación para la Educación Superior (SIDES; Higher Education Information and Documentation System) is the government's major effort toward the development of modern means of controlling and using scientific and technical information. One of its aims is to create a bibliographical database to register national production and all previous documents owned by the libraries making up the network. To implement the program, the Sistema Colombiano de Información Bibliográfica (SCIB; Colombian Bibliographic Information System) was developed.

Public libraries. In May 1978 the Red Colombiana de Bibliotecas Públicas (Colombian Public Library Network) came into being as a component of SNI and coordinated, though not financed, by COLCULTURA and its Public Library Section. Starting point was a National Inventory of Information Resources and Services in Public Libraries. COLCULTURA began training, consultancy, library furnishing, and centralized technical processes in 1977. A development plan for 1979–82 was made to broaden the range of the network. Its aim was to have direct participation in structuring and running departmental networks. The most advanced are in Antioquia, Bogotá, Valle, and Tolima.

One of the three best public libraries is the Biblioteca Pública Piloto para Latinoamérica (Pilot Public Library for Latin America), founded in 1954 with Unesco support; it offers the greatest variety of services to readers and has branches in Medellín, where it is headquartered, and in some nearby towns in Antioquia. Another is the Biblioteca Luis Angel Arango (BLAA), founded and funded by the Banco de la República (the National Bank of Colombia), also with branches in several cities. The BLAA bought the NOTIS system from Venezuela and Northwestern University. The Biblioteca Gabriel Turbay, the most recent of the three leading libraries (1982), is in Bucaramanga, Department of Santander, where it has been crucial in the region's development. Its creation is almost entirely the work of its founder, Jorge Valderrama.

There are few children's library services in Colombia. The work carried out by the Cajas de Compensación Familiar (compulsory, privately run organizations that must be created for the social benefit of all kinds of workers) in library development is outstanding, and they often make up for government deficiencies.

School Libraries. The public school system is run by the Ministerio de Educación Nacional (MEN; National Ministry of Education), which also coordinates and supervises private schools and regulates curriculum. Libraries are required by law in secondary and vocational schools, but many schools do not have them. MEN itself has insufficient funds to equip and run libraries in all its schools. Many of the reported libraries do not exist, and MEN did not establish the financial means to change conditions. Perhaps the plight of school libraries is the most dramatic in the country. There is no census to determine the number of public and private school libraries. The Programa de Bibliotecas Escolares (School Library Program) began as part of the broader Plan de Mejoramiento Cualitativo de la Educación (1976; Qualitative Improvement of Education). It is geared to communities with less access to sources of information and attempts to cover the greatest number possible of underprivileged groups, rural zones, and sparsely populated areas.

Despite national efforts, most public libraries are still forced by the circumstances to double as school libraries, sometimes assigning to school users practically all resources. Even the BN has a 70 percent school reader frequency rate. This still leaves many students without library services at all, both in primary and secondary schools.

Special Libraries. There are about 300 special library and information centers, favored in funding and recognition. The network is run by COLCIENCIAS and has developed subsystems in the areas of agriculture, health, education, industry, marine studies, and environment. Its principal sites are in Bogotá, Medellín, and Cali. The Servicio Nacional de Aprendizaje (SENA; National Craftsman Service) created a technical information network in metalworking, welding, and small industries. The Departamento Administrativo Nacional de Estadísticas (DANE; National Administration Statistics Department) has a database that supports the work of many government offices. Many of the existing organizations are recognized throughout Latin America and form part of international information programs such as AGRINTER or UNISIST.

The Profession. Three library science schools have contributed to the development of libraries. The Escuela Interamericana de Bibliotecología (Interamerican Library School), attached to the Universidad de Antioquia, was founded in Medellín (1956), the city with the highest development of library networks. The Facultad de Bibliotecología y Archivística (Library and Archives Faculty), of the Universidad de La Salle, Bogotá, was founded in 1971, and the Facultad de Ciencias de la Información (Information Science Faculty), Universidad Javeriana, Bogotá, in 1972. The President of the Republic inaugurated in 1982 the Centro Latinoamericano de Informatica (Latin American Computerized Information Center), across the street from the Presidential Palace; grade and high school students may receive free training in computers there.

There are several associations, among them the Asociación Colombiana de Archivistas (ACAR; Archive Association of Colombia), and the Asociación Colombiana de Bibliotecarios (ASCOLBI, 1958; Colombian Association of Librarians), which played a significant role in getting the profession approved and regulated by law. Perhaps the most interesting one to appear in the 1980s is the Asociación Colombiana del Libro Infantil y Juvenil (ACLIJ; 1982), which serves librarians, writers, teachers, editors, and bookdealers concerned with children and books. This Children's and Juveniles' Book Association is a national chapter of the International Board on Books for Young People (IBBY), and its most ambitious project, inaugurated in 1985, is the Centro Experimental del Libro Infantil y Juvenil, an experimental center that planned to sponsor workshops, a children's library, publications, and research.

ANABEL TORRES

Commonwealth Library Association

The Commonwealth Library Association (COMLA) was inaugurated in 1972 in Lagos, Nigeria, with 20 founder members—national library associations in the countries of what was formerly the British Commonwealth. There were 52 full members in 1984–85, comprising national library associations in 33 Commonwealth countries and major library organizations in 19 others that did not yet have national associations. Affiliate members (Commonwealth) and subscribers (non-Commonwealth) numbering 125 include university schools of librarianship, libraries, and related organizations.

The principal objects of COMLA are to improve libraries in the Commonwealth; to forge, maintain, and strengthen professional links between librarians; to encourage and support library associations; to promote the education and status of librarians and reciprocal recognition of qualifications in librarianship; and to initiate research projects designed to promote library provision and to further the technical development of libraries in the Commonwealth.

COMLA is one of more than 20 Commonwealth Professional Associations (CPAs) founded since 1966 under the aegis of the Commonwealth Foundation, the agency established that year by the Commonwealth Heads of Government for the "nurturing of professional activity throughout the Commonwealth as an important component of the developmental process." The Foundation has expanded its purview to embrace funding the more practical activities of the CPAs, with emphasis on innovation and on cementing intra-Commonwealth cooperation for the greater benefit of the professions. Regional and pan-Commonwealth meetings on matters of common professional concern are supported along with joint studies of problems related to standards, ethics, discipline, and recognition. COMLA is one of the CPAs to benefit from this program.

Organization. The Commonwealth Library Association is governed by a General Council representing the members proportionately (it meets every three or four years) and an Executive Committee that meets more frequently. After Nigeria (1972), the Council met in Jamaica (1975), Fiji (1979), and Kenya (1983) and was scheduled to meet in Canada (1986–87). The Executive Committee met in Britain (1974, 1977, and 1980), in Jamaica (1976), and in Singapore (1985).

K. C. Harrison (UK) was the first and founder President of COMLA from 1972 to 1975. He was succeeded by J. C. Harrison (Canada) from 1975 to 1978. Paul Xuereb (Malta) was President from 1978 to 1983 and was followed by John Stringleman (New Zealand). The first Executive Secretary, Mrs. C. P. Fray, served from 1973 to 1979. She was succeeded by K. C. Harrison from 1980 to 1983 and thereafter Joan E. Swaby (Jamaica) occupied the position.

The Executive Committee comprises the three officers elected by the General Council (President,

215

Vice-President, and Honorary Treasurer); six Vice-Presidents elected regionally (representing East, Central, and Southern Africa; West Africa; the Americas and the Caribbean; Asia; Europe; and the South Pacific); and the immediate Past-President. Members hold office for the period between meetings of the General Council. Under the chairmanship of its Vice-President, each region has a Council that arranges its program and submits it for approval to the Executive Committee.

Programs. COMLA's activities fall into four categories: conferences, including training seminars and workshops in various regions in turn; practical projects; occasional publications; and maintaining professional contacts throughout the Commonwealth, chiefly through its quarterly *COMLA Newsletter*. There is an annual subscription, kept low to encourage membership but thereby insufficient to cover costs of these activities. When members host conferences, COMLA relies on regional support funds and on grants from agencies such as the Commonwealth Fund for Technical Cooperation (CFTC). In Jamaica the government supports the COMLA secretariat, which was located there from its inception, the first of the CPAs to be accommodated in a developing country.

COMLA conferences have included an Asia region workshop in Singapore on research methodology in librarianship (1977); a South Pacific region seminar in Brisbane on electronic systems for librarians (1984, in association with the Library Association of Australia); and a Europe region workshop in Malta on bibliography (1984).

Publications. COMLA publications have resulted from conferences other than those mentioned. They include reports on *National Bibliographies for the English-speaking Caribbean* (1974); *Exchanges, Attachments, and Internships* (1975); *Reciprocity of Qualifications and Training for Librarianship* (1975); and *Information for Development* (1984). In Fiji COMLA cooperated with CFTC in a workshop that resulted in publication by the Commonwealth Secretariat of *Training Modules for Non-Professional Library Staff* (1981). *COMLA Newsletter* was published continuously from 1973.

Ties with Other Associations. The Commonwealth Library Association is a member of the International Federation of Library Associations and Institutions (IFLA) and of the Association of Caribbean University Research and Institutional Libraries (ACURIL). It has close relations with the Standing Conference of East, Central, and Southern African Librarians (SCECSAL), the Conference of Southeast Asian Librarians (CONSAL), the Standing Conference of Pacific Librarians (SCOPAL), and the Cooperative Association of Librarians in the Mediterranean (CALM).

REFERENCES
Ken Williams, editor, *A Guide to Commonwealth Professional Associations* (1983).
The Commonwealth Foundation, *Aims and Achievements 1966–1984* (1984).

JOAN E. SWABY

Congo

The People's Republic of the Congo (République Populaire du Congo; not to be confused with Zaire, formerly Belgian Congo) was, up to 1960, a French colony as part of French Equatorial Africa. Located on the equator, the country is bounded by the Central African Republic on the north, Zaire on the east and south, Angola on the southwest, the Atlantic Ocean and Gabon on the west, and Cameroon on the northwest. Population (1984 est.) 1,745,000; area 342,000 sq.km. The official language is French; Bantu dialects are spoken. The national languages—Lingala and Kikongo—do not possess any real written literature.

History. Before independence, the library of the General Government of French Equatorial Africa (FEA) had a collection of some 2,500 volumes; the library of the Institute of Central African Studies, a collection of 8,000 volumes and approximately 250 periodical titles; and the library of the Institute of Congo Studies, about 3,040 volumes. All these libraries specialized in the ethnology, history, geography, and economy of FEA as well as in botany, entomology, soil science, and sociology.

The Board of Libraries, Archives, and Documentation (D.S.B.A.D.) is the central management, coordination, and supervision organ for library, archive, and documentation services in the Congo. The D.S.B.A.D., which reports to the Ministry of Culture and Arts, was created by decree on September 27, 1971. It has the basic functions of planning and organizing the development of all documentary structures in the country and setting national standards suited to ensure the efficacy of those structures. However, contrary to the spirit of the decree, the D.S.B.A.D. at present supervises only the People's National Library, the National Documentation Center, or the National Archives, which are the core of the Center. The D.S.B.A.D did not control other documentary units as of the mid-1980s, whether they be certain public libraries, the University Library, or other special libraries. Furthermore, its budget is woefully inadequate.

National Library Services. The People's National Library, established in 1971, is not a national library in the classical sense. It is a deposit and research library but at the same time serves as the main locus of public reading, whence its title as a people's library. The People's National Library benefits from a type of legal deposit obligation placed on bookstores that import books. (There are no publishing houses.) Its collections (some 5,500 volumes) comprise principally novels, paperback books, and some research or popular works. The library also has 53 periodical titles, plus some films and prints. The areas represented are literature, humanities, social sciences, and science.

The National Documentation Center was established in 1971 but began real operation only in 1978. It plans and carries out the national documentary policy. It is charged with research, collecting, processing, and use of all information relating to the Congo, with setting up and coordinating all documentary activity within the country, and with organizing documentation centers and furthering international cooperation through exchanges. It publishes an analytic guide to the articles it reviews.

The National Archives Service was established in 1971. It has as its task the preservation of files from all central services, territorial organizations, and state enterprises as well as the supervision of municipal archives and, according to appropriate rules, of notarial papers and certain other private archives. In 1974 the National Archives received on deposit a segment of the archives of the General Government of F.E.A., most of the colonial archives being housed in the French National Archives in Aix-en-Provence. The Archives also received on deposit the archives of retired civil service employees and contract workers.

Public Libraries. Generally speaking, the D.S.B.A.D., cultural centers of foreign countries, and certain private individuals look after public reading. However, national efforts still remain weak. There are public libraries in Makelekele (2,241 volumes), Moungale (2,234), and Ouénzé (3,557), and a pool regional library (1,500 volumes), all administered by the D.S.B.A.D.

Private libraries include those of the Abraham de Bacongo Home (3,500 volumes), of the American Cultural Center (2,450 volumes, 28 periodical titles), of the Angolan Cultural Center (632 volumes), of the French Cultural Center in Brazzaville (25,000 volumes), of the French Cultural Center in Pointe-Noire (13,331 volumes), and of the Russian Cultural Center (18,500 volumes). All but two of these libraries are located in Brazzaville; there is free access.

University Library. Open to students, university teachers, and researchers, the University Library is the largest in the country. It receives most of its support from the state and employs the most professionals. After the breakup of F.E.A., the collection of the old library of the general government of F.E.A. as well as the collection of the Alliance Française library (5,000 volumes) became the basis of the Library of the Center for Higher Education in Brazzaville (1959), which then became the Foundation for Higher Education in Central Africa (1961), the University of Brazzaville (1971), and Marien Ngouabi University (1977). Marien Ngouabi University does not have a single campus; parts of it are scattered throughout Brazzaville and indeed throughout the entire country. Each part of the university has its own library, resulting in ten libraries; the Library of the School of Letters and Humanities and of the Advanced Institute of Economic, Juridical, Administrative, and Management Sciences (which is still called the Central Library) is the most important. It arose from the ashes of the library of the general govermnment of F.E.A. and the Alliance Française. The law, economics, literature, humanities, and social science library houses an encyclopedia collection. The collections of the Central Library cover colonial literature and accounts of explorers and missionaries as well as various scientific studies on Central Africa (45,000 volumes and 252 current periodical titles). The Library of the School of Science has 11,200 volumes and 141 current periodical titles. There is a special science library. The Library of the Advanced Institute of Education contains 12,665 volumes and 41 current periodical titles. The Library of the Advanced Institute of Health Sciences has 3,890 volumes and 55 current periodical titles; it collects in the areas of medicine and pharmacy and receives grants from the World Health Organization. The Library of the Institute of Physical and Sports Education contains 400 volumes and 8 journal titles. The Library of the Institute of Rural Development has 3,750 volumes and 32 current periodicals; it collects predominantly in the fields of agronomy, education, and management. The Library is a depository for FAO publications. The Library of the Management Department has 2,500 volumes. The Library of the Advanced Normal School of Technical Education (400 volumes) covers mostly applied sciences. The 400 volumes of the Library of the National Administration and Magistrateship School cover political economy, public finance, and law. The Library of the Advanced Education Institute of Loubomo is a general education and polytechnic library. Many schools are quite new and their libraries are new.

Special Libraries. Most are organized and run by international groups. The Library of the National Institute of Research and Educational Action was established in July 1962 and has 8,500 volumes and 35 current periodical titles. The ORSTOM library in Brazzaville, established in 1947, in 1961 received as a gift the collection of the defunct library of the Institute of Central African Studies. (ORSTOM—Office pour la recherche scientifique Outre-Mer—is a French research organization.) There are 17,000 volumes and 831 periodicals, 1,400 microfilms, and 2,000 topographic maps. Principal subjects covered include botany, entomology, ethnology, psychology, sociol-

---

Libraries in the Congo (1982)

Type	Administrative units	Service points	Volumes in collections	Annual expenditures (CFA franc)	Population served	Professional staff	Total staff
National	1	3	5,528	2,000,000	3,739	8	28
Academic	1	10	80,184	35,000,000	86,545	11	56
Public	10	10[a]	between 1,500 and 25,000	--	between 1,200 and 31,000	11	61
School	--	--	--	--	--	--	--
Special	5	--	between 2,600 and 45,000	--	between 100 and 400	10	22

[a]Unesco, *Statistical Yearbook*, 1984. 1981 data.

Source: Secrétariat général du Comité Central, *Reflexion sur la politique de développement Des Archives, Des Bibliothèque et de la Documentation en République Populaire du Congo*, Bibliothèque Universitaire (Annual Report).

ogy, geography, soil science, and hydrology. The ORSTOM library at Pointe-Noire contains 6,000 volumes; its main subject is oceanography. The Library of the World Health Organization was established in 1963 and contains 45,000 volumes and 200 current periodicals; its main interest is medicine and pharmacy. The Library of the National Economic Documentation Center contains 1,100 volumes and 30 periodicals. The Library of the General Scientific and Technical Research Board has 2,600 volumes and 45 periodicals.

School Libraries. These are almost nonexistent. High schools are supposed to have libraries, but they are poor and out-of-date. School libraries contain mainly textbooks. The staffs of such libraries are generally not credentialed.

The Profession. The Congo has neither a library school nor a professional training center. Its professional workers receive their education at the library, archives, and documentalists school in Dakar, in the Soviet Union, and in France. The Congolese Association for the Development of Documentation, Libraries, and Archives (A.C.D.B.A.) was established in 1984. The Congo in 1984 had 70 trained professionals: 15 archivists, 15 documentalists, and 40 librarians, though all were not employed in libraries. Many change to other professions after earning their professional diplomas.

BRUNO WAMBI

Congress of Southeast Asian Librarians (CONSAL)

The Congress of Southeast Asian Librarians (CONSAL) was founded at the First Conference of Southeast Asian Librarians in Singapore, August 14–16, 1970. Sponsored by the Library Association of Singapore and the Library Association of Malaysia, the Conference was attended by delegates from Cambodia, Indonesia, Malaysia, Philippines, Singapore, Thailand, and Vietnam, as well as observers from other countries. The conference theme was regional cooperation and the delegates resolved to establish a regional library organization to facilitate such cooperation. Its aims are: to establish and strengthen relations among librarians, libraries, library schools, library associations, and related organizations in the region; to promote cooperation in the fields of librarianship, library education, documentation, and related activities in the region; and to cooperate with other regional and international organizations and institutions in the fields of librarianship, library education, documentation, and related activities.

CONSAL conferences range over a broad spectrum of topics reflecting an equal interest in regional problems and in matters of broader professional concern. CONSAL II was held in Manila, December 10–14, 1973, with library education as its theme. CONSAL III in Djakarta, Indonesia, December 1–5, 1975, focused on integrated library and documentation services and changed the organization's name to the "Congress" of Southeast Asian Librarians. CONSAL IV in Bangkok, Thailand, June 5–9, 1978, discussed the development of national information services. CONSAL V in Kuala Lumpur, Malaysia, May 25–29, 1981, was concerned with access to information.

CONSAL VI in Singapore, May 30–June 3, 1983, continued the discussion on the library in the information revolution. CONSAL VII was scheduled for Manila, February 15–21, 1987, and would, according to plans, return to regional problems and look at the role of libraries in rural development.

The proceedings of each conference are published and comprise CONSAL's contribution to the literature of librarianship.

The original constitution envisaged a loosely structured organization. CONSAL would meet at least once in three years; the CONSAL Committee was based in the host country with a mandate to carry out the resolutions of the preceding conference. While there were no formal memberships or subscriptions, the Committee had the authority to raise funds for its activities. The Chairman is nominated by the succeeding host country and endorsed by the delegates present, but the remaining Committee members are nominated by the respective library associations.

By CONSAL IV, in 1981, members felt that CONSAL ought to be placed on a firmer footing. While its aims and basic structure remained unchanged, the constitution was revised to provide for national membership comprising national library associations and national and other libraries and related organizations in the member countries and for associate membership comprising libraries and related organizations of nonmember countries, as well as individuals interested in the objectives of CONSAL. Membership rates were set, the duties and powers of the Executive Board (formerly the CONSAL Committee) defined, and affiliation with other regional bodies made possible. A rotating secretariat is attached to the current Chairman.

CONSAL continued in the 1980s to suffer from the lack of a secure financial base. Anticipated income from membership subscriptions did not materialize. Until the problem of funding is solved, CONSAL will continue to function largely as a conference organizing association.

CONSAL's closest relationship is with its archives counterpart, SARBICA (Southeast Asian Regional Branch of the International Council on Archives). Together they have successfully completed a major project to compile a *Masterlist of Southeast Asian Microforms* (Singapore, 1978; supplement on microfiche, 1985). Another continuing joint program is the Regional Microfilm Clearing-House, which publishes the *Southeast Asia Microfilms Newsletter,* distributed by the SARBICA Secretariat in Kuala Lumpur.

CONSAL has no official relationship to Unesco, but its members are involved in a number of Unesco projects such as ISDS (International Series Data System). Other members are involved in the FAO project AGRIS. Again, CONSAL is not a member or branch of IFLA but its members actively support and implement many IFLA projects such as ISBD, ISSD, and UBC. Its conferences provide a forum for the discussion of these and other international programs. Attendance at CONSAL Conferences continues to grow with increasing numbers of nonregional participants. CONSAL thus provides a means of professional communication and generates a climate conducive to cooperative activities. In that way it fulfilled the hopes of its founders—to act as a focus and catalyst for library development and cooperation in Southeast Asia and to promote professional development in the context of the larger world community.

REFERENCES
P. Lim Pui Huen, "CONSAL: the First Decade," *Access to Information* edited by D. E. K. Wijasuriya, Yip Seong Chun, Syed Salim Agha. (CONSAL V, 1982).
See also *Proceedings* of CONSAL conferences (available through national libraries).

P. LIM PUI HUEN

Connor, Robert D. W.
(1878–1950)

Robert Digges Wimberly Connor, historian and educator, was the first Archivist of the United States.

Connor was born in Wilson, North Carolina, September 26, 1878, one of 12 children of Henry Groves and Kate Whitfield Connor. He attended the local public schools and in 1899 received a Ph.B. from the University of North Carolina at Chapel Hill. For four years he was engaged in public school work; then from 1904 to 1907 he served as Secretary of the state educational campaign committee. In 1903 Connor was appointed by Governor Charles B. Aycock to membership on the newly created North Carolina Historical Commission; for four years he served as the Commission's unpaid Secretary.

In 1906 Connor published a booklet, *A State Library and Department of Archives and Records,* an ambitious plan for the revitalization of the State Library and the establishment of a state archival agency. In response to his prodding, the General Assembly the following year broadened the authority of the Historical Commission and gave it an increased appropriation. Thereupon Connor accepted the salaried secretaryship and during the next 14 years developed one of the nation's outstanding state historical agencies. In addition, he was Secretary of the North Carolina Teachers Assembly for six years, President of the North Carolina Literary and Historical Association for a year and its Secretary for seven, member of the University of North Carolina's Board of Trustees for seven years and its Secretary for five, President of the General Alumni Association of the University from 1917 to 1921, and member of the National Board of Historical Service during World War I.

After a leave of absence to study at Columbia University, 1920–21, Connor resigned from the Historical Commission to accept the Kenan Professorship in History and Government at the University of North Carolina. His lectures, characterized by their clarity and wit, made him an unusually popular teacher.

In 1934, with the strong endorsement of the American Historical Association, Connor was appointed the first Archivist of the United States by President Franklin D. Roosevelt. His tasks were monumental: the National Archives building was unfinished; a 150-year backlog of public records crowded offices throughout the federal government; and there were only a few people in the entire country acquainted with European archival principles. For the next six years Connor presided over the completion and occupation of the new building, the organization and training of a large staff, and the establishment of policies and procedures for the transfer, repair, arrangement, description, and use of the nation's archives. He gathered around him other historians of high standing, encouraged the formation in 1936 of the Society of American Archivists (SAA), and insisted that the National Archives share its growing expertise with records custodians at the state level. He also worked closely with the President in establishing the Franklin D. Roosevelt Library, the first of a number of similar archival institutions administered by the National Archives.

Connor resigned as Archivist in 1941 and returned to Chapel Hill as Craige Professor of Jurisprudence and History. He maintained his interest in archival administration, however, serving as President of the SAA, 1941–43, and as Chairman of the North Carolina Historical Commission and its successor, the Executive Board of the State Department of Archives and History, from 1942 until his death.

Connor's most notable published work was his two-volume history, *North Carolina: Rebuilding an Ancient Commonwealth, 1584–1925* (1929). Among other books were *History of North Carolina: The Colonial and Revolutionary Periods, 1584–1783* (1919); *The Life and Speeches of Charles Brantley Aycock* (1912); *Race Elements in the White Population of North Carolina* (1920); and *The Story of the United States, for Young People* (1916). *The North Carolina Manual 1913,* which he compiled, was for 60 years a standard reference work.

He died February 25, 1950, in Durham and was buried in the Chapel Hill Cemetery. The Historical Society of North Carolina presents each year the Robert D. W. Connor Award for the best article published in the *North Carolina Historical Review*.

H. G. JONES

North Carolina State Archives
Robert D. W. Connor

Conservation and Preservation of Library Materials

Preservation of library materials is part of a broader concern that is sometimes referred to as the preservation of cultural property. Some authorities trace the beginnings of preservation to the Age of Enlightenment and the discoveries of Pompeii and Herculaneum. Others claim that preservation is as old as civilization itself, rooted in the idea that mankind learns from what has gone before, and that the evidence of earlier times is important and worth saving. Libraries and other institutions whose collections serve an archival function play a primary role in collecting and preserving the human record; not everything worth preserving is collected by libraries, nor is everything they collect necessarily worth preserving.

Preservation and *conservation* are often used interchangeably, and there seems to be no clearcut distinction between the two terms. Conservation seems more specific and object-oriented, whereas preservation is a broader concept that embraces conservation as well as protection, maintenance, and restoration in its meaning. It also carries a connotation of official policy and perhaps for that reason is the preferred term to describe the entire constellation of administrative and technical activities that bear on collection management in libraries and archives.

Conservation

(1) Examining and documenting the condition of the untreated leaves.

(2) Testing the stability of the inks in order to determine the most appropriate deacidification treatment.

With the encouragement of several professional organizations, government agencies, and private foundations, the early 1980s witnessed a proliferation of preservation programs in the United States and abroad. In the U.S., important contributions are being made by the Society of American Archivists (SAA), the American Library Association (ALA), the Association of Research Libraries (ARL), the Council on Library Resources (CLR), and the National Preservation Program Office of the Library of Congress. Additional impetus is provided by direct grants to individual libraries in support of specific projects from such agencies as the National Endowment for the Humanities (NEH), the National Historic Publications and Records Commission (NHPRC), and the Department of Education (under Title II-C of the Higher Education Act). The Andrew W. Mellon Foundation has provided generous support to libraries in such areas as internships for conservators and preservation program administrators, establishment of treatment facilities, and support for cooperative microrecording programs.

In 1984 alone, a dozen major libraries and library consortia established administrative positions to guide expanding institutional programs; among them were Northwestern University, the University of Chicago, Cornell University, Ohio State University, the New York State Library, and the Southeastern Library Network (SOLINET). In 1983 the British Library consolidated its preservation activities under one administrative officer, and in 1984 created a National Preservation Office to promote the better conservation of library collections throughout the United Kingdom. Landmark legislation in New York State in 1984 provided annual grants of $90,000 for five consecutive years to 11 comprehensive research libraries in the state.

Preservation of library and archival materials was not viewed by most research libraries as a matter of great urgency until the 1960s. Perhaps the greatest influence on the future development of the field within the U.S. was William J. Barrow's alarming assertion—based on his investigations reported in *Deterioration of Book Stock: Causes and Remedies: Two Studies on the Permanence of Book Paper* (1959)—that most library books printed in the first half of the 20th century will be in unusable condition by the next century. Further stimulus came from two disasters that occurred in 1966—a fire at the Jewish Theological Seminary in New York City that consumed 70,000 volumes and damaged an additional 150,000, and the flood of the Arno River in Florence, Italy, that inundated a million volumes stored in the cellar and ground floor of the Biblioteca Nazionale Centrale, including 150,000 volumes in the Magliabecchiana Collection, gathered during the 17th century by Florentine Humanists to create Italy's first public library. These events, vivid reminders of the vulnerability of books, particularly those that are also cultural artifacts, contributed to the development of emergency salvage techniques for water-damaged materials and jolted libraries into action in such areas as planning for disaster preparedness and formulating recovery procedures for water-damaged materials.

Characteristics of the Field. Library preservation may be characterized as follows. (1) It is highly technical and is concerned with such complicated topics as the chemistry of materials, the monitoring of environmental control systems, and the design of book structures. (2) The ethical and philosophical framework within which preservation decisions must be made is not well developed. (3) The problems of library preservation are highly diverse as a result of the wide range of physical formats found in library collections and the difficulty of distinguishing materials of an artifactual nature from those of value solely for their intellectual content. (4) The need for preservation of library materials is both massive and urgent. (5) Preservation is expensive—given the quantity of material that is deteriorating, microfilming and conservation treatment are frighteningly costly, as is the development, testing, and implementation of such alternate technologies as mass deacidification and optical disk storage. (6) Library preservation is a developing field—there are few comprehensive training programs; the literature of the field is growing rapidly, and some of it is redundant or of varying quality; there are few standards; and numerous technical questions still demand solution. (7) Preservation is an interdisciplinary enterprise and demands close cooperation of the library profession, the conservation profession, the suppliers of materials and services, and the scientific community, including chemists and computer specialists.

Nature and Extent of Deterioration. Present-day collections are composed largely of books printed on unstable paper, and libraries will continue to acquire significant works printed on poor paper.

Scientists have defined deterioration as a process of transition from a higher to a lower energy level. Cellulose, the principal component of most library materials, is remarkably stable in its pure form, but under certain conditions it tends to break down into simpler molecules, returning eventually to carbon dioxide. Natural oxidation is accelerated by two chemical reactions—hydrolytic attack on cellulose fibers by acid in the paper itself, and photochemical degradation caused by light and other forms of radiant energy. Environmental factors (such as the polluted air present in most urban centers and widely fluctuating levels of temperature and relative humidity) and biological factors (mold, insects, and even human beings) also contribute to the process of deterioration.

In order to quantify the extent of deterioration in their collections, and to develop resources and strategies for addressing the problem, several research libraries in the U.S. had completed surveys by the early 1980s, among them Yale University Libraries, the Library of Congress (LC), and the New York Public Library (NYPL). Results of these surveys corroborated Barrow's predictions; for example, Yale determined that 44.3 percent of the books sampled had brittle paper that broke after four folds or less, and 82.7 percent had highly acidic paper and would eventually require some form of treatment. The LC and NYPL surveys yielded similar findings.

Preventive Measures. Preventive preservation—that is, action taken *before* damage has occurred, that will retard further deterioration—has emerged as a basic concept in the field. The single most effective measure libraries can take to slow the deterioration process is to reduce the temperature in book storage areas. The higher the temperature, the faster chemical reactions accelerate; conversely, paper scientists generally agree that for every 10 degrees Celsius the storage temperature can be reduced, the life of paper can be approximately doubled.

There are several immediate steps libraries can take to prolong the useful life of their collections. Smaller libraries with limited funds and small staffs can identify brittle books that are too poor to rebind and insert them into acid-free paper wrappers until they can be repaired or replaced. Such flat paper objects as manuscripts and drawings can be interleaved with alkaline-buffered tissue available from conservation supply houses and stored in archival-quality folders and boxes. Extremely fragile paper objects in single-sheet format can be placed in envelopes of

(3) A single leaf, deacidified, mended, and encapsulated in stable polyester film (Mylar) preparatory to being placed in a post binding.

(4) The completed volume.

(5) The project completed: bound volumes of the encapsulated leaves preserved for scholarly research.

Schomburg Center for Research in Black Culture, New York Public Library

221

Conservation

Orszagos Széchényi Konyvtar

Library employee restoring maps at the National Széchényi Library, Budapest, Hungary.

Fumigation station used in the preservation at the National Library of Japan.

polyester film available in the U.S. under such trade names as Mylar, Scotchpar, and Melinex; it is essential that order specifications clearly indicate that film appropriate for preservation uses is required. Volumes can be cleaned and a program of minor repairs begun using procedures such as those described in Carolyn C. Morrow's *Conservation Treatment Procedures* (1982).

Spurred by a dialogue that began in the mid-1970s between preservation librarians, representatives of library binding firms, and members of the Library Binding Institute, a growing number of firms offer a wide variety of binding methods and other preservation treatment options. For example, several firms now supply custom-made preservation cases that may be used as an alternative to rebinding for volumes that have become brittle.

National Library of Japan

In large libraries faced with massive deterioration problems, a preservation program can be developed using a phased approach, doing the easier, less expensive things first and leaving costlier and more complex tasks until later. A key element is to undertake administrative planning *before* embarking on a course of action. Initial steps should include inspecting the physical storage facilities to identify particular problems, conducting a survey to determine the extent of deterioration among the various formats of material in the collection, framing a realistic plan of action tailored to the budgetary and staffing realities of the particular library, and planning a disaster preparedness and recovery program.

Early in 1980 the Association of Research Libraries embarked on an ambitious preservation project designed to encourage individual libraries to expand and improve preservation efforts. A number of planning tools and procedural manuals were produced, and a planning procedure was developed that provides a structured approach to the numerous administrative and organizational decisions that must be made, consistent with the libraries' service goals and present and potential resources.

Training. Within the library preservation field, development of educational programs is needed in four areas: programs for new and practicing librarians, archivists, and curators; programs for training professional conservators; programs for educating administrators of preservation programs; and programs for training conservation technicians who work under the supervision of professional conservators.

A growing number of library schools in the U.S. offer courses on preservation of library materials for academic credit; the *Preservation Education Directory*, published by ALA's Resources and Technical Services Division, is an important source of information.

Outside the limited number of conservation facilities that occasionally have openings for qualified apprentices, few training centers in the U.S. offer intensive programs for conservation technicians. The Center for Book Arts in New York City and the Capricornus School of Bookbinding and Restoration in Berkeley, California, offer a number of short courses and workshops on such topics as paper deacidification techniques, paper cleaning and repair, bookbinding, and box making.

Before 1981 no academic degree-granting institutions in the U.S. offered training programs in book conservation and preservation administration. In that year, Columbia University's School of Library Service established programs in both subjects under the direction of Paul N. Banks. The programs are described in *The History and Future Directions of Conservation Training in North America* (1984).

Research. Despite growing awareness of the magnitude of the preservation problem, expenditures for basic and applied research have been disturbingly small. The high cost of staffing and equipping research facilities has obliged most libraries to place their emphasis on microrecording and physical treatment programs rather than on analysis and research. Such laboratories as do exist are usually within a museum or other institution caring for a wide variety of cultural properties.

A world-wide directory of conservation research centers was still not available in 1985, although such facilities were known to exist in several countries. An indirect means of identifying such facilities, as well as individuals conducting research and the areas of their investigations, is available through journals serving the field. Among them are *The Abbey Newsletter: Bookbinding and Conservation, Conservation Administration News, Art and Archaeology Technical Abstracts, Conservation Studies,* and the *Journal of the American Institute for Conservation.*

The Preservation Research and Testing Office of the Library of Congress, the only facility in the U.S. devoted exclusively to problems of library preservation, made significant advances in developing a large-scale method of deacidifying books at a low unit cost. A mass deacidification facility was under construction in the mid-1980s in Ft. Detrick, Maryland, where some half-million volumes a year from the Library's collections were to be treated with diethyl zinc vapor in twin chambers, at a projected cost of $3.48 per volume.

Future Technologies and Trends. Significant strides are being made in the development of new technologies and in the adaptation of existing technologies to alleviate the preservation problems of libraries and archives. Typical of recent progress is the work of Todor Stambolov and others at the Central Research Laboratory for Objects of Art and Science, Amsterdam, The Netherlands, in the conservation of leather; the investigations of Bruce J. Humphrey of the Nova Tran Corporation, Clear Lake, Wisconsin, into the application of parylene conformal coating technology as a means of strengthening paper; the achievement of Richard D. Smith in developing the Wei T'o Nonaqueous Book Deacidification System in use in the Public Archives of Canada; and of Chicago book restorer William Minter, who, with Peter Malosh, pioneered in the development of an ultrasonic welder for polyester encapsulation that seals and protects fragile documents more efficiently than traditional techniques.

The British Library in cooperation with the Optronics Group of Cambridge, England, developed a book scanner and digitizer that allows the conversion of books and other library materials into digital electronic form for storage in computers and transmission to remote destinations. This conversion is quick and is accomplished without damage to the original material.

Through its Optical Disk Pilot Program, begun in 1982, the Library of Congress is evaluating the use of optical disk technology for the preservation and management of its collections and is determining the cost and benefits of such technology when used in a production setting. The first of six analogue videodisks with its player and video monitor is now installed in the Prints and Photographs Reading Room; with it, a library patron can sort quickly through or study any one of almost 40,000 photographs, posters, and other high-use pictorial items.

In another phase of the program, a system is now being implemented on an experimental basis that uses digital optical disks for computerized mass storage, preservation, and retrieval of printed materials, including text and halftone illustrations.

An important landmark in the development of standards was set with publication of the American National Standard "Permanence of Paper for Printed Library Materials" (American National Standard Z39.48-1984). It grew out of the work of the Committee on Production Guidelines for Book Longevity, sponsored by the Council on Library Resources (1979–82), with funding from the Andrew W. Mellon Foundation. Work on a second important standard, "Standard Practice for Storage of Paper-Based Library and Archival Documents," neared completion in 1985. It was sponsored by the National Institute for Conservation under a grant from the National Historical Publications and Records Commission.

The Council on Library Resources (CLR) and the Association of American Universities (AAU) are only two of several agencies concerned with preservation as a national issue. In December 1981 an AAU/CLR Task Force issued its *Final Report on Preservation,* which stresses the need for national planning and a systematic distribution of preservation responsibilities organized and shared on a national or possibly international basis. The Task Force recommendations were undergoing further scrutiny by CLR's National Preservation Strategy Committee, which was drafting a document in 1985 that would articulate national activities and identify potential sources of large-scale funding.

At the end of 1984, the National Endowment for the Humanities established a separate Preservation Office with anticipated national funding of $4,000,000 to $5,000,000. This development was a helpful step in furthering a principal objective of the CLR Committee, to identify funding amounting to at least $10,000,000 a year for preservation activities in the United States.

REFERENCES

A National Preservation Program: Proceedings of the Planning Conference (1980).
Book Longevity: Reports of the Committee on Production Guidelines for Book Longevity (1982).
Carolyn Clark Morrow, *The Preservation Challenge: A Guide to Conserving Library Materials* (1983).

JOHN P. BAKER

Copyright*

LEGAL NATURE OF COPYRIGHT

The term "copyright" has a double meaning stemming from its etymology. It denotes the right "to own and control a work of authorship" in addition to the right to "copy it." The English term does not, for historical reasons, identify the beneficiary in the rights; the beneficiary is clearly identified, however, in usage in other languages, such as the French *droit d'auteur,* the German *Urherberrecht,* and the Spanish *derecho de autor,* all of which mean "the right of the author."

Copyright is a part of what is known as intellectual property, which also includes patents and trademarks. In general, copyright is a unique property right that rewards authors for their contributions to society and entices them to contribute to the advancement of knowledge. Copyright protects only the independently created words and arrangements of an

---

author in relation to any idea. Copyright does not extend its protection to the idea itself; thus, ideas are free and can be built upon and be expressed differently, and the expression can be protected even if it discusses a subject that is already in existence and in fact protected. Patents, in contrast, protect both the idea and its expression in any given invention, provided that the invention is novel, useful, and nonobvious to an expert in the field. A patentee has a monopoly right (for 17 years in the U.S.) to prevent others from using the invention, in part or in entirety, even if others made the same discovery independently. Trademark protection is not based on creative authorship but on the investment and skill in creating a symbol the public will readily identify with a particular goods or service.

There are two major schools of thought concerning the legal nature of copyright. One considers copyright as a type of alienable property such as real stock and goods; this school advocates unlimited, perpetual rights to the owner of copyright. The second school believes that copyright is a monopoly and since monopoly, in any form, has bad economic and social implications, the author should be given as little protection as possible. Some Western European countries (for example, France) recognize copyright as a unique form of property right with strong personal elements at its base. These countries recognize this personal right in their laws and grant the author an inalienable "Moral Right" that assures his identification with the work and protects against its distortion or any alteration that might be prejudicial to the author's reputation or honor. This approach underlies what is known today as the Berne Convention.

HISTORY OF COPYRIGHT

The copyright concept began in England after the printing press was brought there from Germany. Before that historic event, ideas had to be recorded by hand on parchment or paper. This recordation was done by scribes, often monks. These efforts produced one copy of the work, which was sometimes so valuable that it had to be chained in place for security measures. When William Caxton introduced the technique of printing with movable type to England in 1476, the production of books was revolutionized. As a result, any given work could easily be produced in quantity. The printing press thus came to have religious, social, and economic impact that has been well documented. The printing press also created a threat for the publisher of the works, whose original work could be reproduced easily by "pirates" who incurred none of the costs involved in the production of the first copy of it.

To protect themselves publishers, booksellers, and printers created a trade association, the Stationers' Company, chartered in 1557 by Queen Mary. In accordance with this Charter, the Stationers maintained a register in which the members recorded the title of each book they bought from an author or from another member. An entry in the register granted the registrant perpetual rights in the registered book and determined claims of piracy. A decade later, most regulations—including the Stationers' rules to control the press—were proved ineffective and unenforceable. By 1710 the Statute of Anne was enacted as the first English copyright law. This stat-

ute granted protection against unauthorized printing or copying of published works for a limited period of time. Unpublished works were covered by common law and not protected by the Statute of Anne.

U.S. Copyright Laws. One might consider the Statute of Anne to be the prototype of all subsequent copyright laws. For example, it was in concept the basis for Article 1, Section 8 of the U.S. Constitution, which vested in the Congress power to create a law that gives the authors and inventors, for a limited time, exclusive rights to their writings and discoveries, for the purpose of the "advancement of science and useful arts." In 1790 the first U.S. copyright law was enacted; it applied only to books, maps, and charts. Since it granted protection only to U.S. citizens, foreign authors—Charles Dickens is an example—were so fully pirated by U.S. publishers that more costly American authors were excluded. In 1891 the Chase Act was passed by Congress, granting protection to foreign authors under certain conditions, and thus protecting American authors from the unfair competition of royalty-free, pirated English works.

The 1790 law was amended several times, mainly to expand the subject matter protected by its provisions; for example, in 1802 Congress extended copyright protection to prints; in 1831 public performances became protected; and in 1870, fine arts, in addition to the rights to dramatization and translation, were included. A major revision took place in 1909. It included still more categories of protected work, such as "plastic works of scientific or technical character." The right of the author to make derivations (for example, abridgments) from an original work was also added to the author's several rights. In 1947 the law was codified and enacted as Title 17 of the U.S. Code. In 1971 the sound recording was added as the seventh category of protected works of authorship. The period of protection under the 1909 law was 28 years, renewable to a similar period.

Copyright Act of 1976. Dramatic changes in society and the vast advancement in technology after World War II dictated the necessity to review the 1909 law. On October 17, 1976, the Congress passed a general revision that had a profound effect on the copyright system. The 1976 revision, which took effect in 1978, preemtped common law copyright (that is, unpublished works are now protected for a period of 100 years from the date of creation and not in perpetuity). The period of protection for works created after 1978 was changed to the life of the author in addition to 50 years to the heirs after the author's death, thus eliminating the renewal system for such works. As to corporate ownership, copyright protection extends to 75 years from date of publication. The new law also created a Copyright Royalty Tribunal to deal with compulsory licensing for public broadcasting, cable television, and juke boxes.

In addition, two important amendments were included: (1) the concept of "fair use," a 19th-century court-created rule of reason (Section 107); (2) specific provisions pertaining to library photocopying and use of copyrighted works (Section 108). Section 108 applies only to libraries whose collections are accessible to the public or to researchers in their specialized fields, and when the reproduction of copyrighted material is made for no direct or indirect profit. The new law liberalized also the strict requirements and formalities of the copyright notice. As it stands now, the omission of the notice (© or the abbreviation "copr.") does not result in the forfeiture of statutory copyright protection, provided that the unintentional omission is corrected within five years.

The revision included also a provision that would have abolished the Manufacturing Clause in 1982. The Clause deals with works in the English language produced abroad by U.S. citizens/residents. Initially the Manufacturing Clause was included in the 1981 revision of the copyright law to protect American printers against the competition of cheap printing abroad. The Manufacturing Clause's deadline was extended to July 1986. The American Library Association and publishers favored abolishment, but strong lobbying by the American printers, who feared loss of U.S. jobs, gained congressional support for extension.

Despite the significant revisions in the copyright law, Congress fell short of dealing with the issues relating to computers and technology in general. Section 117 of the new law in essence preserved the protection status quo of information systems and reflected a lack of sufficient knowledge at the time of passage to deal with technological issues. Therefore, a National Commission on New Technological Uses of Copyright Works (CONTU) was created to look into the questions relating to interlibrary loans, computer software, and databases. CONTU was instrumental during its three-year existence in securing an agreement on guidelines between copyright owners (publishers and authors) and librarians on permissible amounts of copying for interlibrary loan purpose and on what constitutes the aggregate quality of copies obtained through interlibrary loans that are not permissible (*i.e.,* copying anything beyond five copies of one title within a year is generally not permissible without permission of the copyright owner). CONTU recommended that computer software programs should be accorded statutory copyright protection. As a result, Congress amended the copyright law in 1980 by including software under the category of "literary works" (Section 102). It also amended section 117 to include certain provisions to allow the purchaser of any software package to modify it to fit its intended use and to copy it for preservation purposes.

In passing the new revised law, the Congress acknowledged in its Report (House Report No. 94–1476) that the concept of "Fair Use" is vague and eludes precise definition and that the parties involved should come to an agreement as to what constitutes fair use of copyrighted material. As a result, representatives of publishers, authors, and an Ad Hoc Committee of Educational institutions and Organization on Copyright Law Revisions met several times and reached agreement on guidelines for classroom copying of copyrighted works for nonprofit educational insitutions. Under these guidelines, it is permissible for a teacher or teacher's agent (for example, a librarian) to make one copy of a copyrighted work for research or teaching. Multiple copying for classroom use is allowable only if it meets tests of *brevity, spontaneity,* and *cumulative effect.* Similar guidelines were developed first with music educators and later with educators in general regarding taping copy-

righted programs off the air for educational purposes. These various guidelines, however, are not a part of the copyright law, and therefore are technically not enforceable. Yet they would carry substantial weight in litigation, since the Congress included them in the published House Report and considered them to be representative of the legislative intent regarding fair use. While the CONTU guidelines for interlibrary loans are applicable to all types of libraries, the guidelines for educational uses of copyrighted material are only applicable to libraries in nonprofit educational institutions.

INTERNATIONAL COPYRIGHT LAW

Before the 19th century, national copyright laws of countries throughout the world were concerned mainly with the protection of the works of the country's own nationals and denied foreign authors any protection. Some exceptions did exist, based on bilateral treaties derived from reciprocal treatments. In 1852 France extended its copyright protection to all works regardless of nationality, a move that led to the establishment of the Association Littéraire et Artistique Internationale. This group actively campaigned for and presented in 1883 a treaty to different countries for a multilateral system of international copyright. This paved the way and provided the basis for the Berne Convention of September 9, 1886.

The Berne Convention. The objective of the Berne Convention was to give foreign authors in any of the 14 original countries that signed the Convention the same protection accorded to their native authors in signatory countries. The Convention was revised and amended more than seven times, the latest in 1971. The Berne Convention broadened its terms to include, among other items, motion pictures, architecture, choreography, pantomime, and photographs. In the 1948 revision, known as the Brussels Protocol, the author's "moral right" was introduced as a mandatory part of the author's right to be protected among the signatories. Two additional major requirements were also introduced: (1) the establishment of a minimum term of copyright protection for the life of the author plus 50 years after the author's death (a "Unionist Treatment") and (2) the abolition of any registration formalities as prerequisites for copyright protection. Therefore, according to the Berne Convention, any published work, regardless of nationality or membership, receives copyright protection automatically without the need for registration or for a copyright notice—© or the word "copyright"—affixed to it, provided the work is first published in a "Berne Union" country or published in a nonmember country and simultaneously in a member country.

It is interesting to note that the United States and the Soviet Union are not members of the Berne Convention. However, according to its rules, U.S. works are protected under the Berne Convention if they are published simultaneously (within approximately 30 days) in Canada, England, or other member countries. This partially explains why U.S. publishers often maintain offices in Berne Union countries and affix their names on the title pages of their publications.

Universal Copyright Convention. In the late 19th century, many attempts were made to secure copyright agreements in the Western Hemisphere. These attempts produced several "Pan-American" copyright conventions. The United States was a signatory only to the Buenos Aires Convention in 1910, which provides that the copyright in a work will be protected in a member country if it was copyrighted in another member country and bears a copyright notice to that effect. It became obvious during the following years that a middle ground has to be established between the Pan-American Convention and the Berne Convention; this led to the establishment of the Universal Copyright Convention (UCC) in 1952.

The U.S. was one of the original members of the UCC and in fact the moving force behind its development. The convention, signed by more than 70 countries including the U.S.S.R., which joined in 1973, recognizes registration and copyright notice requirements. It recognizes also the difference in copyright term between member countries and recognizes the U.S. Manufacturing Clause, which requires that English-language works be produced in the United States to be protected to the full extent under the U.S. copyright law. In a sense, the UCC is based on the principle of "national" treatment, as opposed to the Berne "Union" treatment. Both conventions, however, held conferences in Paris in 1971, which resulted in allowing developing countries to translate member countries' works into native languages of the developing countries if they have not been published in those countries.

The UCC includes many compromises that were concessions to the U.S. copyright system; these have been the main stumbling block for the U.S. joining the Berne Convention. The U.S.'s arguments against signing the Berne Convention merit reconsideration, since the differences have almost been eliminated by the 1976 general revision of the U.S. copyright law. The new law changed the term of protection to the life of the author plus 50 additional years; relaxed the formalities of registration and copyright notice to the extent that unintentional omission of either does not result in immediate forfeiture of copyright; and attempts have been made to abolish the Manufacturing Clause. Many observers in the mid-1980s held that the U.S. should seriously consider joining the Berne Convention. One of the difficult problems that will have to be resolved, however, is a retroactive effect of joining the Berne Union that might require copyright protection for works that are already in the public domain in the U.S. since their term of protection (28 years plus one 28-year renewal, or 56 years) has already expired according to the 1909 U.S. Copyright law.

CURRENT ISSUES

Reproduction and Distribution of Copyrighted Material. The copyright law states that the librarian's right to reproduce and distribute copies of copyrighted material extends only to the isolated and unrelated production or distribution of a single copy of the same material on separate occasions (Section 108d). Therefore, the librarian is not permitted to engage in multiple copying of the same material if the librarian or other members of the library staff have reason to believe that they are doing the same. The "one copy at a time rule" is extended only to libraries, and it seems that this rule exemplifies fair use as

practiced by librarians. Consequently, substantial and/or multiple reproduction of a copyrighted work is not considered fair, and therefore is not permitted. The "one copy at a time rule" does not extend to the parent institution which the library serves, whose copying practice is governed by sections 106 and 107 and not by section 108 of the copyright law.

Though there have been numerous court decisions regarding the violation of copyright through duplication of protected material, it was not until 1972 that for the first time a library was sued for copyright infringement. Williams and Wilkins, a medical journal publisher in Bethesda, Maryland, sought damages for copyright infringement, in the U.S. Court of Claims, based on photocopying as practiced by the National Library of Medicine (NLM) and the National Institues of Health (NIH). Several arguments were raised by the defendants (NLM and NIH): (1) whether Williams and Wilkins owns proprietary rights on the articles being copied, (2) whether or not library photocopying (with no intended profit) violates copyright, and (3) whether or not photocopying by libraries is "fair use." On February 16, 1972, Commissioner James Davis of the Court of Claims decided in favor of Williams and Wilkins, stating that the copyright law (1909 Copyright Act) does not excuse libraries from liability for the kind of copying "praticed by the defendants." On appeal, the full Court of Claims ruled on November 27, 1973, in favor of the defendant libraries by a close vote of 4-3, based on "fair use." These findings were based on a balancing of three elements: (1) that Williams and Wilkins did not show substantial harm resulting from the photocopying in question, (2) that medical science would be seriously harmed if NLM and NIH's photocopying were to stop, and (3) that the court would not put any risk or harm on medical science during a period when the copyright law was being reviewed by Congress. Nevertheless, Williams and Wilkins took their case to the U.S. Supreme Court, where the appellate decision was once more affirmed in favor of the library, by an equally divided court (4-4 vote).

The Supreme Court decision in this case predated the enactment of the new copyright law and the Court did not want to involve itself in accommodating competing interests at the time when legislative guidance was in the making. Libraries in other settings should note, however, that NLM is a unique national library that is not analogous in mission or scope to any other type of library, so that a deduction based on perceived similarity for NLM in library practice would be false and misleading. Furthermore, the equally divided Supreme Court in essence issued no opinion in the Williams and Wilkins case, thus rendering its decision a legally non-binding precedent in future cases. Moreover, "fair use" cases are judged individually, and every case is determined on its own merits. It behooves librarians to observe the law as it stands, and in the meantime lobby for amendments to it if they deem it necessary from their professional veiwpoint to do so.

Interlibrary Loans. The Library's right of copying and distribution as stated in Section 108d does not extend to cases in which the library "engages in systematic reproduction or distribution of single or multiple copies" of copyrighted material.

Though "systematic reproduction" is not formally defined, the phrase does not seem to apply to a library's "system" for handling copying requests from its own patrons. Rather, the clause seems to be intended for interlibrary loan transactions that might substitute photocopies for subscriptions or purchases. The Senate Judiciary Committee supported such an interpretation by stating in its Report (issued September 29, 1976) that systematic reproduction and distribution occurs when a library makes copies of copyrighted material available to other libraries, to the effect that the reproducing library actually becomes the primary source of such material, substituting these copies for purchased subscription. However, sensing the potential chilling effect on interlibrary loans and networking, Congress added a proviso (108g2) allowing a library to obtain copies through interlibrary loan if these copies are not in such aggregate quantities as to substitute for purchases.

Realizing the difficulty in defining an "aggregate quantity" in this context, Congress asked the National Commission on New Technological Uses of Copyrighted Works (CONTU) to develop and report to Congress a working definition of an "aggregate quantity." After several meetings, and with the concurrence of representatives of librarians, authors, and publishers, CONTU developed a set of guidelines for interlibrary loan photocopying. In summary, the guidelines allow a library to receive five photocopies per calendar year from periodicals published within the preceeding five years, provided that the requesting library states in writing that it is in compliance with section 108g2 and with the guidelines. The same applies to books, with the one exception that the library receive no more than five photocopies per year per title for as long as the book is protected by copyright. However, the guidelines do allow the requesting library to disregard the "rule of five" if the library has a subscription or purchase for the work in force or on order. They also require that the requesting library retain its records on interlibrary loans for three calendar years.

Three important points need to be emphasized in this respect. First, though the guidelines are not a part of the copyright law itself, the mere fact that they were acknowledged by Congress as representing the legislative intent in Section 108g2 and are included in the Conference Report of September 29, 1976, lend considerable weight to their importance and applicability in interlibrary loan photocopying transactions. Second, the guidelines are not limiting and are not an end in themselves, because they deal with an evolving situation that will undoubtedly require continual re-evaluation and adjustment. Finally, the "rule of five" applies only to interlibrary loan photocopying, and the CONTU guidelines in general are only applicable to libraries that are governed by Section 108 (i.e., that are not for profit and open to the public).

It is interesting to note that after passage of the law publishers indicated that they were not totally happy with the guidelines they had previously agreed upon. Based on the claim that all copyright guidelines are presently insufficient, publishers have argued that additional regulatory measures are necessary. There have been suggestions, for example, that the permissible five interlibrary loans copies be reduced to two. Whether such a notion would be agreed upon by the several parties involved remained unclear.

Section 108. The current U.S. Copyright law mandates in Section 108(i) that the Register of Copyright review the accomplishments of Section 108 (which pertains to library and archival photocopying) and submit a report to the Congress every five years about such accomplishments, and that the Report might include suggestions for changes in the law. For the first Five-Year Review, the Register commissioned a national survey, and at open meetings held by several national associations such as the American Library Association, American Chemical Society, and the Association of American Publishers, the staff of the Copyright Office listened to testimony presented by educators, library users, librarians, publishers, and authors regarding their assessment of the situation after the implementation of the 1976 copyright law.

On January 3, 1983, the Register of Copyright submitted to Congress the first Report on what was called "his best judgment about possible solutions to the copyright issue relating to libraries." The Report included "Non-statutory" and "Statutory" recommendations. The former includes recommendations such as sharing "new collective library agreements" between libraries and copyright owners and "new guidelines" in light of the new technology and the present photocopying practice in libraries. The Report suggested adding a surcharge to fees for use of copying equipment and presumably passing the proceeds to the copyright owners. It recommended a study to examine the impact of technology on library use of copyrighted material, and suggested another national study to approximate the number of photocopies made on equipment in different kinds of institutions and in different locations, to help establish a system for compensation for the copyright owners. The nonstatutory recommendations called the government's attention to the need to help publicly funded libraries pay the recommended royalties and fees.

The statutory recommendations included such suggestions as the enactment of an "Umbrella Statute" to limit the penalties for infringement provided that both the library and the owner of copyright (e.g., publishers) join a "qualified licensing system." (One might assume that the recommendation was suggested to boost membership in the Copyright Clearance Center, a clearinghouse for handling blanket agreements with users and fees to publishers for copies of their materials. The statutory recommendations also suggested that libraries, through the amendment of Section 108, should be compelled to reproduce the work's copyright notice every time they make a photocopy of any copyrighted work. Finally, the Report made clear the Register's view that the balance between copyright owners' rights and those of libraries had not been achieved in practice. It referred also to evidence suggesting that 25 percent of the photocopying done by libraries exceeds that permitted by law. Many in the library community argued that the Five Year Review report reflected a bias toward the publishers' interest at the expense of libraries' statutory priviledges. It seemed that by 1986 there was little pressure on Congress to respond promptly.

Technology. Technology is another issue with great implications for copyright and libraries.

The 1976 U.S. copyright law passed virtually without any provisions concerning the emerging technology. Section 117 maintained the status quo and the National Commission on New Technological Users of Copyrighted Works (CONTU), as noted previously, was created and asked among other things to look into the question regarding technology (e.g., computer software and databases). Many points for and against the copyrightability of computer software were argued. The main objection was that a computer program (i.e., object code) is a part of the computer hardware and lacks communicative ability. However, the 1979 CONTU final report recommended extending statutory copyright protection to computer software. In 1980 Congress passed an amendment to Sections 101, 102, and 117 under which computer software would enjoy the same copyright protection provided the category of "literary works." The amendment allows the user of a lawfully owned software package to adapt it for the purpose of its intended use and to duplicate it for archival purposes. Though there have been a few court decisions regarding computer software, this area of copyright can be expected to develop through litigation and case law throughout the 1980s.

One area of concern, for example, is the "shrink wrap agreement," often used by the industry, whereby the package containing the software is wrapped in clear plastic through which the purchaser can read a statement that opening the package constitutes an acceptance of the terms listed. The validity of such "agreements" (which are unilaterally imposed by the producer) is questionable, and case law is lacking on the point. Until questions about such agreements are legally challenged and resolved, one should assume that they are in fact binding and act according to their terms and conditions.

To prohibit computer chip piracy, Congress passed the Semiconductor Chip Protection Act (1984), which created for the first time in the world a new form of industrial intellectual property and explicitly protected the patterns on semiconductor chips against unauthorized reproduction. The act grants ten-year proprietary protection to "mask works" for semiconductor chips products and authorize the use of an Ⓜ as a notice of copyright on such chips. Congress opted for a *sui generis* rather than a copyright approach for protecting computer chips, and incorporated these provisions in the Federal District Court Organization Act (PL 98–620), signed into law on November 8, 1984. This law covers only the "mask work" itself, not the computer program on the chip, which is protected under the copyright law.

Nonprint Material. Another issue of special concern to librarians is the reproduction and use of audiovisual works and other nonprint materials. Under the current copyright law, librarians' right to reproduce copyrighted material according to Section 108(h) does not apply to audiovisual works in general, other than works dealing with news. This provision raised a number of questions about the use of audiovisual works in classroom teaching and about off-air taping. Because the law is silent on these questions, and since Congress has encouraged all parties to discuss issues of concern among themselves, representatives of audiovisual professionals, teachers and producers of media met several times over a two-year

period to resolve their differences. On September 28, 1981, the agreed upon "Guidelines for Off-Air Taping for Educational Use" were presented to the House of Representatives and were officially recognized by insertion in the *Congressional Record* on October 14, 1981. The guidelines permit taping off the air for educational purposes at nonprofit educational institutions. The recorded tape may be used once by the teacher in class teaching within 10 days of the date of recording; it may be retained by the institution for evaluation purposes for no more than 45 calendar days, after which it must be erased. The consensus is that these guidelines are in the spirit of fair use because they represent an appropriate balance between the rights of the copyright owner and the instructional needs of educational institutions.

The Betamax Case. Another question remains unsolved, however, as to whether an individual can record off the air a program for one's own enjoyment at a later time. The issue was brought to court when Universal City Studios sued Sony Corporation of America for producing video recording equipment (its Betamax®), which is capable of reproducing copyrighted programs off the air. On January 17, 1984, the U.S. Supreme Court held in a close decision that noncommercial home videotaping of television programs does not constitute copyright infringement because such home taping is generally done for the purpose of "time-shifting," i.e., for later viewing, and thus is a legitimate fair use. The Court found also that the manufacturing and selling of videotape recorders to the general public does not constitute contributory infringement. Though the decision permits home videotaping, it does not extend the same permission to libraries unless they are a part of a nonprofit educational institution and provided that they abide by the conditions of the guidelines for off-air taping. Public, special, and for-profit libraries must therefore obtain permission before taping and using off-air taped programs unless they deal with news.

Databases. Still another issue of interest to librarians concerns databases and the legal implications of their use, mainly the "downloading" issue, that is, an individual user's recording onto an in-house computer all or part of a commercial database that has been accessed through outside sources. (See also Online Information Services.) The copyright law of 1976 and revisions did not deal with databases. The issue was, however, referred by the Congress to CONTU for an answer; in its final report CONTU recommended that a database is nothing more than a compilation that might be protected by copyright under the category of literary works (Section 102), such as dictionaries and encyclopedias. Compilations are subject to copyright because they are arranged in such a way that the resulting work, as a whole, constitutes an original work. Though the component parts of a compilation may be copyrighted individually, the compilation as a whole has its own separate copyright which extends only to the format and the arrangement of its component parts. The view is that such reformatting is an original effort, without which the user would not be able to search the data easily. Conversely, the copyright on the compilation as a whole does not extend to its component parts. Databases may be numeric, bibliographic, or textual. Regardless of their nature, databases involve three different entities: the producer, the supplier or vendor, and the user.

The user makes a contract with a producer, but often the vendor, to use the database. Payment for the service is based mainly on connect time in addition to other charges. Some subscribers may wish to search a given file and record some or all of the data to the memory of their own microcomputers (downloading); while the most frequent use of downloading is to facilitate the preparation of edited and formatted search results, it may also be used to preserve search results in personal databases or subfiles. This practice can save money by avoiding repetitive searches and maximizing future connect time with the main database. Since the practice seems to imply loss of revenues to the producer and supplier and raises questions about proprietary rights, downloading is an issue of concern to all parties involved.

Who owns the database? Obviously, if it is created by a private producer such as Chemical Abstracts Service, then the latter owns it and can obtain a copyright on it. However, there are also situations in which the supplier—not the creator—of the data claims a copyright on the database. In such a situation (unless there are agreements to the contrary) the copyright pertains to the formatting and not the content of the database. A case in point is OCLC's claim of copyright of its bibliographic database. While OCLC files consist mainly of the Library of Congress MARC tapes, which contains bibliographic information produced or acquired by the Library of Congress, and as such is in the public domain because it is a United States Government work (Section 105 of Copyright Law), the remainder of the OCLC database consists of data created by libraries participating in the OCLC cooperative. This part of the OCLC file is owned by the local libraries that provided it. OCLC, however, claimed copyright on the entire file, creating a heated debate as to its ownership. It should be realized that OCLC's copyright pertains only to the format of its data file, not to its content (which is mainly in the public domain or owned by the local libraries). Some OCLC participants (e.g., Cleveland Public Library), have claimed ownership of their own original cataloguing records that they contributed to the OCLC database.

A second question relates to whether downloading is in violation of copyright law. Unless there is an explicit agreement to permit it, downloading is construed by some as a violation. However, since downloading is hard to monitor or detect, many database producers began in the late 1970s and early 1980s to rely on a variety of contractual arrangements to permit their subscribers to download for a fee.

Many, however, believe that downloading can be considered fair use in certain circumstances. The purpose of the downloading becomes very important. Downloading for noncommercial teaching and research, provided the downloaded data is erased from the computer memory after the research project is over, might be permissible as fair use. The nature of the original data file might also be considered in deciding whether downloading is fair or unfair. A specialized database with a limited market might be judged differently from one that is mass-marketed. Another criterion to consider is the substantiality or quantity of the downloaded data, perhaps viewed in relation to the entire database; however, there is no working definition of a permissible "fair" amount of downloaded data. Finally, the hardest criterion to apply in fair-use judgments is the effect of downloading on the actual and potential market of the database.

Since fair use is an ambiguous concept, negotiations and agreements, particularly collective ones, are often used. While the issue, is a complicated one, the literature in the mid-1980s began to suggest a developing balance between subscription arrangements for high-volume downloading and unrestricted downloading for other applications, with adjustments in database pricing providing for compensation (i.e., per-record charges in addition to connect-time charges).

Public Lending Right. Another potential concern is Public Lending Right (PLR), a legal concept that has been adopted in several European countries, starting in Denmark (1946) and later in England (1982). PLR is a payment to an author based upon the number of his or her books that are among the holdings of any given library, and upon annual sampling of loans of the author's books to the general public. PLR was advocated initially in response to authors' need for income from their chosen profession, but this notion was abandoned in favor of a claim that PLR is a natural, just, and fair payment for the use of the authors' books through circulating libraries, along with the royalties received from direct sales.

PLR became a controversial issue when many of its proponents compared it with copyright and royalty payment. This argument suggests that PLR legislation should be an integral part of the copyright law. Others believe that PLR is best suited as a separate piece of legislation.

Grave concern was raised by librarians in the U.S. and in the ten countries that had adopted PLR as of the mid-1980s. Many librarians saw the concept as dangerous to the idea of free public libraries, and they feared that the financial support to the author might come from government funds that would otherwise go to supporting library services. Librarians also asserted that lending services in public libraries promote reading and book buying among the general public. Further, library book purchases are the backbone of the publishing industry. In short, they held that library lending does not interfere with the sale of books.

PLR drew attention in the United States when an unsuccessful bill was introduced in Congress in 1973. In the 1980s it gained renewed attention, and Senator Charles Mathias of Maryland proposed a national study of public lending right; by early 1986 no action had been introduced in Congress regarding his proposal.

If it is determined that a certain form of Public Lending Right is desirable in the United States, there are two hypothetical models upon which PLR might be based, first, the social security model, which pays the author regardless of the extent of use of their work and (2) a copyright model, which pays authors only on the basis of the extent of use of their works in public libraries. Under either model, the author would receive payments from tax monies and not from the library operating budget.

If adopted and incorporated into the copyright law, the latter model conflicts with the first-sale doctrine, one of the main principles of the U.S. copyright law. According to Section 109 of the law, the sale of a copy of any given work conveys no copyright interest to the buyer; however, such sale will exhaust the author's economic interest in that copy once it has been sold. Therefore, incorporating PLR in the copyright law would necessitate a change in that provision.

Proponents of the PLR concept base it on a European legal concept known as the *droit de suite* (the right to follow), which is essentially an "art proceeds right" that requires payment to artists for the resale of their original work (e.g., paintings). The intent was to protect the artist from economic exploitation by dealers and collectors. The *droit de suite* became a part of the U.S. legal system in 1976 when California enacted the Resale Royalty Act; the Act was challenged in 1978 in *Morseburg* v. *Baylon* when an art dealer (Morseburg) refused to pay royalty on resale of a painting because, as a federal law, the copyright law and its first sale doctrine (Section 109) preempt the State of California Resale Royalty Act. Nevertheless, the 9th Circuit Court of Appeal found for the artist on the basis that the California Act is within the spirit of copyright.

Conclusion. Librarians must be informed about the copyright law because of its serious implications for their professional objectives and functions. Copyright is a dynamic issue that will remain an important concern for the foreseeable future. The emergence of computers will continue to intensify the controversy with the fast advancement in technology. Nevertheless, in forming the basis for any potential solution, the U.S. democratic system preserves its slow legislative and judicial process by trying to solve a complex 21st-century issue with a 19th-century concept and law. The only practical and possible solutions will be in the hands of the many parties involved, and in their willingness to adjust conflicting viewpoints for the benefit of the advancement of science and the useful arts and for the interest of the general public.

REFERENCES

Daniel T. Brooks, and Michael S. Keplinger, *Computer Programs and Data-bases: Perfecting, Protecting and Licensing Proprietary Rights after the 1980 Copyright Amendments* (1981).
John Cole, "Public Lending Right: A Symposium at the Library of Congress," Appendix to *Library of Congress Information Bulletin* (1983); summarized in *ALA Yearbook of Library and Information Service* (1984), Special Report.
Nicholas Henry, *Copyright, Congress and Technology: The Public Record* (1978), 4 vols.
Donald F. Johnston, *Copyright Handbook* (1978).
Allen Kent and Harold Lancour, Copyright: Current Viewpoints on History, Laws, Legislation (1972).
"Manufacturing Clause Extension Basis," *Copyright Management* (1982).
John Martyn, "Software Protection, Piracy and the Library . . . A Discussion Paper," *Aslib Proceedings* (1985).
Jerome Miller, *U.S. Copyright Documents: An Annotated Collection for Use by Educators and Librarians,* Colorado: Libraries Unlimited, 1981.
"Public Lending Right," *Library Trends* (1981).
William Z. Nasri, "A Balancing Act: Can Librarians and Users Afford It?" *Journal of Library Administration* (Summer 1983).
Juri Stratford, "Library Photocopying: A Legislative History of Section 108 of the Copyright Law Revision of 1976," *Government Publications Review* (1984).
Thomas S. Warrick, "Large Databases, Small Computers and Fast Modems . . . An Attorney Looks at the Legal Ramifications of Downloading," *Online* (1984).
Mary Wolfe, "Copyright and Machine Readable Databases," *Online* (1982).

WILLIAM Z. NASRI

Costa Rica

Costa Rica, a Central American Republic on the isthmus between North and South America, lies between the Pacific Ocean and the Caribbean Sea and is bounded by Nicaragua on the north and Panama on the southeast. Population (1984 est.) 2,460,226; area 51,100 sq.km. The official language is Spanish.

History. The indigenous Indians in the northwest, under Meso-American influence, wrote in hieroglyphs on deerskin parchment. They used vegetable inks in red and black. They also traced their inheritances. After discovery and conquest by the Spaniards (1563), the few Indian survivors came under strong European influences. Independent from 1821 and a republic from 1848, Costa Rica achieved recognition for its democratic tradition.

National Library. Created in 1887, the library that later became the National Library in the capital of San José was the Library of the University of Saint Thomas. When that university was closed, it was converted into the National Library. Under a law instituted in 1910, the National Library became the depository for the national bibliography, and publishers were required to deposit their publications with the Library. From 1980 the National Library became the center of a system of libraries forming part of a national plan designed to centralize cataloguing and classification. Access is provided within the Library, through loans between the various libraries of the system, and through loans for home use. The National Library maintains a National Register of authors' rights and associated matters as well as the National ISBN Agency. It publishes an "Index of Newspapers and Weeklies" and a "National Analytic Index of Periodicals."

Public Libraries. By the mid-1980s there were 83 public libraries. Before 1980, there were only 18. The newer public libraries are canton and district libraries whose collection growth depends on community effort and the help of the national system. In 1983 a law providing financing for the libraries was approved and the construction of 15 buildings for public libraries was planned. Efforts were also made to provide adequate library staff.

Public materials are available for internal use within a library and are lent among libraries.

The system uses two mobile units that visit distant zones of the Central Valley.

School Libraries. Under the Development Plan for the School Library System of 1975, programs for these libraries were initiated and a department was established under the Ministry of Public Education. Initial actions emphasized technical services through organization of a center for processing materials. Attention was also given to improving qualifications of library personnel through courses offered by the Asesoría Nacional de Bibliotecas Escolares in coordination with the state universities.

In 1978 Costa Rica began a school library pilot study under auspices of the Multinational Project of School Libraries OEA–MEP (Organización de Estados Americanos–Ministerio de Educación Pública). Costa Rica's experience provided information for Latin American librarians on concerns about school libraries. The goal has been to transform the libraries into resource centers, so that the school library can be integrated totally in the curriculum.

Children's Libraries. In 1971 the Municipality of San José established the Carmen Lyra Library for Children. In 1978 and in 1983 two new libraries for children opened. Besides offering books for use within the library and lending books for home use, children's libraries have other activities, such as storytelling hours, film programs, and puppet shows. Costa Rican librarians provided help to other Latin American librarians on the organization of libraries for children.

University Libraries. The country has four state universities. The Commission of Directors of University Libraries was founded in 1983 in order to coordinate contacts between them. The commission works to rationalize the use of resources, especially in the acquisition of bibliographic material. In these libraries, plans and projects of automation are developed.

Special Libraries. Hospital libraries, which numbered five in the 1970s, were combined into one, the Biblioteca Nacional en Ciencias de la Salud (The National Library of Health Sciences). Many specialized libraries had been consolidated by the mid-1980s, offering their special services in different areas. Examples are the Library of the Legislative Assembly, the Documentation Center of the Latin American Institute of the United Nations for the Prevention of Crime, the Library of the Central Bank, and the Documentation Center of the National Council of Scientific and Technological Investigations. Some of these have developed automation in support of their work.

The Profession. The Colegio de Bibliotecarios de Costa Rica, established in 1971, is the professional umbrella association for all librarians. Its role is to improve professional qualifications of members through courses, seminars, and various programs,

and to represent and protect professional interests of librarians.

PAULINA RETANA

Cuba

The Republic of Cuba is the largest island in the Greater Antilles. The Cuban archipelago consists of several thousand small islands, islets, and cays. Population (1984 est.) 9,945,000; area 110,922 sq.km., including the Cuban archipelago. The official language is Spanish.

History. The Biblioteca de la Sociedad Económica de Amigos del País (Library of the Economic Society of the Friends of the Country) was founded in 1793 with the main objective of "contributing to the promotion of the moral and economic interests of Cuba and to stimulate culture and popular instruction in all their manifestations." The Library has the most important collection of Cuban books and periodicals.

The Real y Pontificia Universidad de San Jerónimo was created on January 5, 1728, by Pope Innocent XIII with provision for a Library, though it took many years for the Library to work as such.

The Constitution of the Republic issued in 1940 called for a public library in each municipality, but complementary law needed to enforce that obligation was never passed. A Decree of 1954 created the Organización Nacional de Bibliotecas Ambulantes (ONBAP) with the goal of founding 50 small public libraries; each library was to have a collection of approximately 1,000 volumes; by 1958, 21 of those libraries were created with modest monthly allocations.

Before the Revolution of 1959 little can be said about librarianship and libraries in Cuba. As an underdeveloped country, Cuba found it hard to achieve even a measure of fair library and information documentation service.

In 1958, out of a population of 6,700,000, a million were illiterate, 600,000 children had no opportunities to obtain any kind of education, and 10,000 teachers were jobless. Very few libraries existed during the pre-revolutionary period.

During the 19th century and the first half of the 20th, some academic libraries were founded such as those of the Academy of Sciences, Academy of Arts, and Academy of History. Some professional societies, such as the Engineers Society and the Architects

---

Libraries in Costa Rica (1981)

Type	Administrative units	Service points	Volumes in collections	Annual expenditures (colón)	Population served	Professional staff	Total staff
National[a]	1	1	300,000	5,506,000	– –	10	98
Academic	1	205	205,000	– –	16,000[b]	– –	– –
Public[a]	18	18	707,000	– –[c]	254,500	0	31
School[b]	175	– –	1,700,000	400,000	140,000	51	180
Special[b]	21	– –	142,000	750,000	– –	14	58

[a]1976 data.
[b]Registered borrowers.
[c]Included in National Library Budget.

Source: Unesco, *Statistical Yearbook,* 1984; *ALA World Encyclopedia,* First Edition (1980).

Society, also founded important libraries.

The sugar industry has been the main economic resource of Cuba, and one of the first research libraries of the country was that of the industry's Asociación de Técnicos Azucareros.

In 1959 there were about 30 public libraries, and in December 1983 there were more than 300. Nevertheless, those libraries did not provide any of the features nor meet the standards of service that make an adequate modern public library. Only two of those libraries could be counted as such—The Lyceum Lawn Tennis Club Public Library and the Sociedad de Amigos del País Public Library.

The Lyceum Lawn Tennis Club was a women's liberal and cultural society whose public library made contributions toward shaping the literary taste of the young generations of the decades of the 1930s through the 1950s. It also supported interest in librarianship among a large group of persons.

In 1953 Unesco helped develop a School for Library Education. Another School of Librarianship had already existed at the University of Havana. Both schools survived with very few students during those times.

In 1959 Unesco also helped in the creation of a pilot project for a school library; it helped this project lead to development of the system of school libraries that was undertaken in 1960 by the Ministry of Education. By the mid-1980s, about 2,900 school libraries had been developed, each with holdings of about 2,000 volumes.

National Library. In 1901, by a military order during the United States occupation of Cuba, a director to the National Library was appointed. In 1936 a Cuban writer and historian, Emilio Roig de Leuchsenring, who was Historian of the City of Havana, denounced through his articles in the weekly magazine *Carteles* the poor condition of the Cuban National Library and the urgent need for improvement. The Asociación de Amigos de la Biblioteca Nacional (Association of Friends of the National Library) was founded. Among the many members were distinguished writers and historians such as Elías Entralgo, Emeterio S. Santovenia, Joaquín Llaverías, Manuel I. Mesa Rodríguez, Nicolás Guillén, José Antonio Ramos, and Emilio Roig de Leuchsenring, who acted as President of the Association.

In 1935 the Foreign National Association from New York published a report entitled "Problems of the New Cuba," which cited the National Library's "shameful conditions. Its shelves were drawn off during the President Machado administration and the books were packed into boxes and stored in a facility

belonging to a state prison, and even though they have already been returned to the library, the deplorable state of the building and the shelves made possible the unpacking [of only] a few volumes; in addition a fire took place in the building and a great deal of books were burned to ashes."

In 1938 another episode worked against the insitution's life and the preservation of the national heritage. The government decided to move it to the Castillo de la Fuerza (La Fuerza Castle) and also to tear down the building that housed the Library and build a police station instead. The books were packed again with haste and transferred to their new place.

The lack of resources and qualified personnel led to deteriorating conditions that became obvious to such an extent that the government was obliged to appoint a Cuban writer and diplomat, José Antonio Ramos, as the library technical adviser, giving him power over cataloguing and classification. Ramos implemented a system of classification on his own, based on the Universal Decimal System, and adapted it to Cuban and Latin American needs. It was undoubtedly the most significant attempt to organize systematically the bibliographic resources of the institution up to that time. Ramos, after a continued and difficult struggle to improve the overall conditions at the National Library, had to resign from his post in 1946. Shortly afterward he died.

In 1941 the government imposed a one-half cent tax on each 325-pound sugar bag in order to raise funds to build a National Library. A committee to manage the fund was appointed, and on January 28, 1952, the construction of the National Library's new building began. It was named after José Martí (1853–95), the Cuban national hero who was a poet, a thinker, a warrior, and a "symbol of the National Liberation against colonialism and imperialism."

After January 1, 1959, when the Cuban Revolution led by Fidel Castro triumphed, deep changes took place in the Library as well as in the rest of the country. María Teresa Freyre de Andrade, Cuban librarian and long a fighter for the development of librarianship in Cuba, was appointed Director of the institution. She started intense efforts to make libraries reach everyone and started to move the National Library toward modern goals. She also encouraged the reform of library science studies at both university and technical levels.

The revolutionary government resolved that all the books that belonged to dictator Fulgencio Batista (1901–73), to his associates, and to people leaving the country should be transferred to the National Library. These books become the so-called rescued li-

Libraries in Cuba (1984)

Type	Administrative units	Service points	Volumes in collections	Annual expenditures (U.S. dollar)	Population served	Professional staff	Total staff
National	1	--	1,352,592	1,180,300	--	207	342
Academic	19	46	1,869,091	2,538,052	213,269	119	266
Public	368	5,164	--	8,450,160	8,722,400	1,052	1,690
School	2,933	--	10,802,100	--	5,109,435	354	4,366
Special	--	--	--	--	--	--	--

braries that played an important role in filling out the collections of the National Library as well as starting collections in the new libraries in various parts of the country.

The National Library has played many outstanding roles in the cultural area. Because of the shortage of libraries in the capital city as well as in the rest of the country, and the need for encouraging people to use books, the National Library has acted also as a public library.

The Department of Bibliographic Research created a Union Catalogue of Scientific and Technological periodicals. More than 270 institutions contribute to that catalogue, which had 26,000 titles in 1984. The Department of Bibliographic Research also compiled the Union Catalogue of Social Sciences and Humanities.

Various attempts have been undertaken to provide a Cuban National Bibliography since the 19th century when the Cuban scholar Antonio Bachiller y Montes published his *Apuntes para la historia de las letras y la instrucción pública en Cuba*. The second volume of that work includes the first account of periodicals edited in Cuba; the third makes the most important contribution to the field of bibliography of that time. It was titled *Catálogo de libros y folletos publicados en Cuba desde la introducción de la imprenta hasta 1840*.

Some attempts were made by Cuban and foreign authors to compile the national bibliography during the first half of the 20th century, but Carlos M. Trelles became the most important bibliographer of the group, because of the completeness and accuracy of his work *Bibliografía Cubana del Siglo XX,* published in 1917. From 1937 to 1958 the *Anuario Bibliográfico Cubano,* compiled and edited by Fermín Peraza, tried to continue the work of Trelles and kept the record of the books published in Cuba.

In 1959 the Cuban National Library was appointed officially to make the compilations and editions of the Cuban National Bibliography. It published the bibliographies for the following years: 1917 to 1920 (published 1960); 1921 to 1936 (1979); 1959 to 1962 (1968); 1963 and 1964 (1967); and yearly from 1965.

A special service of the National Library is the Children and Young Adult Department. Its activities, including storytelling, painting, literature, philately, and others, have been the model for the rest of children's and juvenile libraries of the country.

At the international level, the National Library has an information exchange agreement with the Centro de Información Científica Técnica Humanística (CICH) of the Universidad Nacional Autónoma de México. It participates also as the coordinating center for the country of the System for Information on Culture (INFORMKULTURA) of the socialist countries. It coordinates the cultural information exchange work of several cultural institutions in Cuba.

On January 28, 1840, the Archivo General de la Isla de Cuba was founded by an order of the Queen of Spain. In 1888 the Captain General of the Island, by order of the Madrid government, sent to Spain 2,300 documents of great historical value. An official decree of December 20, 1904, established the island institution as National Archives.

From 1921 to 1956 an outstanding Cuban historian, Joaquín Llaverías y Martínez, was its Director.

ALA

Havana University Library, founded in 1728. This building was constructed in 1937.

He had "a constant preocupation [with] the search and conservation of valuable documents that are in the collection of the institution." From 1945 to 1958 it published the periodical *Memorias.* In 1963 the National Archives was attached to the Academia de Ciencias de Cuba. It succeeded in forming a network of provincial and regional archives.

Academic Libraries. The history of the Library of the University of Havana reflects the history of the main institution, which had scant resources until the late 1930s, when a new building was constructed and a new organization was adopted as a result of the revolutionary movement of that time. After 1959, the University of Havana Library evolved toward the concept of a Central Library (Biblioteca Central), providing the conditions for better development of the particular libraries of the University Faculties.

The Central Library of the University of Havana was named after Rubén Martínez Villena, a revolutionary leader of the '30s. The complete holdings of the Central Library total 150,500 volumes with a reference collection of 10,209 volumes and a natural sciences periodical collection with 10,794 titles. During the academic year 1981–82, 58,002 books and 105,690 periodicals were loaned and 89,665 pages were copied.

Higher education was expanded in order to reach more people and improve its overall quality. In 1976 a scientific and technical information network for higher education was organized to serve the universities and research centers attached to the Ministry of Higher Education. The system includes 19 scientific and technical information centers and 46 libraries. The network provides a system of information storage and retrieval of unpublished documents such as theses and papers (*informe de investigación*), and a printed union catalogue of scientific and technical periodicals in the network. The connection among the components of the network was established through a Telex system, and microcomputers were introduced in the 1980s.

Public Libraries. In 1961 the Dirección General de Bibliotecas (General Library Board) was created as part of the National Council for Culture with the task of establishing a national network of public libraries under the technical guidance of the Cuban National Library. In 1977 the Ministry of Culture was established, and within it was created the Dirección de Bibliotecas with the aim of continuing and broadening public libraries' work. There are about 274 libraries of this kind in all parts of the country. The system of public libraries in Cuba is organized as follows: the National Library as the head of the system, the provinces' main libraries, the municipalities' libraries, and the branch libraries.

There were 135 municipal branch libraries in 1985, 65 of which were in sugar mill areas and 12 in new rural communities. The system also has charge of six bookmobiles that make almost 300 stops in rural communities without libraries and about 1,500 minilibraries in factories, mass organization offices, hospitals, and other institutions.

Main libraries in the provinces comprise the second level of the system. They are in the capitals of the provinces and are financed by the Provincial Body of People's Power. Their main objectives are the compilation of the provincial bibliography, reference services, and loan services to the users of the region as well as methodological help to the municipal and branch libraries. There are 13 libraries of this kind, one for each of the provinces with the exception of the City of Havana province, which did not have its own provincial library as of 1985.

The municipal libraries comprise the third level of the system and are situated in the main town of each municipality and are financed by the Municipal Body of People's Power. Their principal functions are the compilation of the municipal bibliography and reference, loan, and other services to the users of the area as well as giving methodological help to the branch libraries. Both the provincial and municipal libraries have proved to be a helpful tool for students of all levels and for the general public. There were 96 of these libraries in the early 1980s and 8,722,400 persons visited them during 1982.

The Dirección de Bibliotecas works to create new libraries and foster their use; to establish systems and standards; to contribute to the training of personnel; and to represent Cuba in joint projects at the national and international levels in librarianship.

It elaborated a plan up to 1990 based on the principles of methodological (system) centralization and administrative decentralization of library work in the country. Some of the standards issued concern library buildings, selection and acquisition of library materials, and official regulations for the public library system. It also facilitates cooperation among socialist countries on acquisition and exchange problems, library catalogues, music libraries, and other matters.

School Libraries. There are no available statistical data on school libraries prior to the coming to power of the Revolution in 1959. A statute issued on July 6, 1960, mandated that a school library service was to be organized. It was the first official step toward reaching the goal of having a library in every primary and secondary school. Unesco had helped in the late 1950s with technical assistance through a School Library Pilot Project. After that experience was adapted to the new and growing demands of Cuban society, the school library system started to work.

The main objectives of the school library are to contribute to the formation of "a scientific conception of the world and a communist morale" in the students through "systematic reading of socio-politic as well as scientific and recreational literature linked to the curricula."

The school libraries have circulation and reference services. By the early 1980s, school libraries reported that their home lending services had lent almost 11,000,000 books.

Special Libraries. Special libraries constitute a distinctive feature of the Cuban library system. Each of the central administrative bodies of the government, research institutes in the various branches of the economy, and the services has its own information center or special library. Among them are the ministries of the Sugar Industry, Foreign Commerce, Public Health, Agriculture, and Construction, and the Central Planning Board, and there are many others.

The National Information Center for Medical Sciences, founded in 1965, is the main body for the scientific information system in the field of public health in Cuba. The whole system is structured into a network formed by the national center, 13 provincial centers, and 150 libraries, among other information resources, including small libraries in hospitals. The provincial centers are the most important units of this system; they can achieve retrospective searches up to 15 years back by traditional means and they can translate documents from three languages.

The National Center provides special services for administrative and technical leaders and for the scientists and research personnel of the 13 research centers on medical disciplines. It also has the National Medical library for physicians, students, and other users.

Hospital libraries usually have in their collections books on the various specializations of medicine as well as three or more titles of international specialized periodicals. Provincial centers have from 150 to 200 titles of international specialized periodicals and also all the books and periodicals issued in Cuba.

The personnel requirements for the various levels are as follows: For minilibraies at the "bookcase" level are nontechnically qualified employees with minimum training. At hospital library level, the personnel must be graduated from the Medium Technical Medical Librarianship School. At the provincial centers, the qualifications include both Medium Technical graduates and university graduates. The Technical and Scientific personnel at the National Center must have university degrees not only in librarianship but also from medical specialty fields.

The José A. Echeverría Library is part of the Casa de las Américas, an institution devoted "to put into practice measures and initiatives which would contribute to the cultural unity among the Latin American and Caribbean countries, as well as situating these regional cultural expressions in the context of universal culture." This institution was guided and directed until her death in 1980 by Haydée Santamaría, one of the two women who participated in the attack on Moncada Barracks (July 26, 1953), later a member of the Central Committee of the Cuban Communist Party and the country's Council of State. The Library serves the information needs of the specialists of the institution; at the same time it is a specialized public library for professionals, researchers, writers, and artists, and all those interested in Latin American culture, history, and sociology. The book collection amounts to almost 100,000 volumes and its periodical titles collection is more than 6,000. From 1968 to 1982, a technical staff of 15 persons served 156,000 users, lending 190,000 books and 80,000 periodicals.

The Institute of Scientific and Technical Information was founded in 1963 with the principal aim of establishing the National Scientific and Technical Information System. Its multisector Scientific and Technical Centers are located in each of the 14 provinces and the special municipality of Island of the Youth.

The Institute for Documentation organizes national meetings. The Pedagogic Documentation Centers form a network that was founded in 1960. It is composed of the Centro Nacional de Documentación e Información Pedagógicas, 162 centers, and 15 Provincial Departments of Research, Documentation, and Pedagogic Information.

The Junta Central de Planificación (Central Planning Board), the Cuban government institution that deals with the main economic affairs of the country, has a Scientific and Technical Information Center. At the first experts' meeting held at Havana in 1979 under the auspices of the Comité de Desarrollo y Cooperación del Caribe (CDCC) (Caribbean Committee on Development and Cooperation), it was clear that information on economic and social matters needed to be improved. It was agreed to establish an information network whose coordinating center would be the Centro de Documentación del Caribe (CDC). The International Development Research Center (ICRD) of Canada granted financial aid for the project. In June 1979 the Scientific and Technical Information Center of Junta Central de Planificación started its participation in the program as the Cuban national focus for the network. It coordinates the work of the economic institutions of the country as participants. Among those intitutions are the Banco Nacional de Cuba, Comité Estatal de Estadística, Comité Estatal de Finanzas, Instituto de Investigaciones Económicas, Ministeria de Comercio Exterior, and Oficina Nacional de Diseño Industrial. Among the main accomplishments were advances in bibliographic indexing and abstracting, the use of a thesaurus for economic information indexing, and the definition of the kinds of documents the system should process.

The Profession. Many attempts were made to establish the study of library science in Cuba prior to 1960. The most significant of them was the foundation in 1950 of the Escuela de Bibliotecarios (Library School), annexed to the Faculty of Philosophy and Letters of the University of Havana. Many of the librarians holding leading positions in the professional activities of Cuba of the 1980s were graduated from what might be regarded as the pioneer center of library education in Cuba at the university level. From an enrollment of about 10 students with five professors in 1956, the school grew to 400 students and

Biblioteca Nacional José Martí

Children's Room at the Biblioteca Nacional "José Martí" in Havana.

more than 20 professors by 1982.

The Department of Scientific and Technical Information was created in 1970 by the Ministry of Higher Education at the University of Havanna as a part of new approaches to university studies. This Department played a very important role in fostering scientific research among professors and students and the publishing of textbooks written by Cuban authors. Among the new subjects that have been added to the traditional ones and integrated within the curriculum are computing, bibliographic research, information storage retrieval systems, and the organization and management of information institutions. After passing the five-year university course, the graduate receives the degree of Licenciado. Within the national system of scientific degrees, the university graduate may obtain the Doctor in Library Science degree.

For school librarians, the pedagogic schools offer a three-year regular course and in-service training at the Institute de Superación Educacional.

For library technicians, undergraduate programs are conducted at the Escuela de Técnicos Medios under the Ministry of Culture. By examination, graduates may enroll as students in the evening courses (Workers' university courses) offered by the University of Havana.

The Dirección de Bibliotecas of the Ministry of Culture also organizes seminars and in-service courses for public library personnel. Seven hundred and fifty of the 1,300 librarians working in 274 public libraries of Cuba studied in those courses by the early 1980s. Special courses are offered also for the directors of those libraries.

MARTA TERRY

Cummings, Martin M.
(1920-)

As its 18th director, Martin Marc Cummings expanded the National Library of Medicine (NLM) from a conventional medical research library into an institution pioneering the most sophisticated technology in information exchange and established it as an international biomedical communications center. Under his leadership medical library resources through-

Martin M. Cummings

out the United States were enhanced, specialized information and medical audiovisual services were developed, and an international online bibliographic retrieval network was created. Cummings's vision and direction created and expanded the information resources that provided the biomedical research community with the necessary tools to transfer the results of their research effectively and efficiently to health care practitioners.

Cummings was born in Camden, New Jersey, on September 7, 1920. After graduating with a B.S. degree from Bucknell University, Pennsylvania, in 1941, he received his M.D. degree in 1944 from Duke University, where he became interested in microbiology and infectious diseases, especially tuberculosis. He accepted a Public Health Service (PHS) internship followed by a residency at the Boston Marine Hospital, after which the PHS provided him with specialized training programs in pulmonary medicine at the Grasslands Hospital in Valhalla, New York; at the University of Minnesota; at the Michigan State Department of Health; and at the State Serum Institute of Denmark. On his return from Denmark he was given the responsibility of establishing the first tuberculosis laboratory in the Public Health Service at the Communicable Disease Center in Atlanta, where he pursued his research interests and held a faculty appointment in medicine at Emory University. Two years later the Veterans Administration invited him to head the Tuberculosis Service at Lawson VA Hospital in Atlanta, where he organized a control laboratory for tuberculosis studies. He also developed a systematic methodology for the analyses of large numbers of medical records of veterans with pulmonary diseases.

In 1953 the Veterans Administration selected him to become Director of Research Services in Washington, D.C. He was responsible for the administration of the VA's extensive medical research program and its coordination with research initiatives at the National Institutes of Health (NIH), the Department of Defense, and the National Science Foundation. In addition to his administrative duties, he continued his research, saw patients, lectured in microbiology at George Washington University School of Medicine, and continued a growing interest in medical history.

In 1959 he accepted the position of Professor and Chairman of the Department of Microbiology at the University of Oklahoma. He was persuaded by James Shannon, Director of NIH, to return to Washington in 1961 as Chief of the Office of International Research at NIH and Shannon's principal staff adviser. That position provided an important opportunity to examine medical problems internationally, as well as nationally, and to learn firsthand the powerful and positive impact that the political process can have on public health. During these years of rapid growth at NIH, he took on the additional duties of Associate Director for Research Grants, advising the Director on related policy and administrative matters.

In 1963, following the resignation of Frank Bradway Rogers as Director of NLM, Surgeon General Luther Terry selected Cummings for the directorship. Cummings brought to the position a background of diverse and relevant experiences as a user of medical information, an understanding and familiarity with how public policy is made, a respect for the contribution of individual researchers, and a vision for the age of new communication technologies and their potential application to libraries. In his remarks to the NLM Board of Regents following his introduction at the December 1963 meeting, he noted that "The Library has an unmatched opportunity to serve national and international needs in the health communications areas. It will be my responsibility to maintain the very high standards of this Library. At the same time I recognize a need to broaden our interests to provide a creative, imaginative contribution to the increasing complexities of communications."

On January 1, 1964, when Cummings officially assumed the directorship, the Library was already engaged in the pioneering effort of implementing MEDLARS, the MEDical Literature Analysis and Retrieval System. The Library had been engaged in indexing the medical literature since 1897, but publication was a laborious process. MEDLARS was designed to store the indexed citations of the current literature in electronic format. The data on magnetic tape could then be manipulated by a computer, producing an output designed to be used by a high-speed photocomposition device for preparing copy for *Index Medicus*, recurring bibliographies, and special individual subject searches. The initial implementation of MEDLARS required many internal changes at NLM as computerized processing replaced some of the Library's well-established manual traditions with a state-of-the-art automated system.

In the Library's external relationships, extensive change also occurred under Cummings's leadership. John Shaw Billings, the Library's first director, had personally selected the journals to be included in *Index Medicus*, and journal selection had been continued through the years by a small number of library staff. Cummings sought advice from consultants, researchers, educators, administrators, and practitioners on many areas of the Library's operations, including the journals selected to be indexed in *Index Medicus* and the subject headings used in indexing. He was quick to seek the recommendations of his staff and outside experts as the Library continued to use the newest technology to upgrade its overall operation and MEDLARS specifically. Searches of the MEDLARS databases were originally run in batch mode at the Library. Advances in telecommunications technology enabled remote users with terminals, modems, and telephones to access the databases online. Up-to-date medical bibliographical information became available throughout the entire United States and many other parts of the world through international MEDLARS centers in 14 countries.

In the 1960s most medical libraries had insufficient facilities, staff, or budgets to acquire, process, house, or provide access to the information needed by users. Progress toward federal legislation authorizing grants to aid medical libraries had developed under Rogers. One of the areas receiving Cummings's immediate attention was a much-needed grant program. His articulate advocacy resulted in the introduction and passage of the Medical Library Assistance Act of 1965 (MLAA). The MLAA legislation was extended over the years and has been used to finance construction of medical libraries, training librarians and other information specialists, expansion and improvement of medical library resources, stimulation of research and development in medical library sciences, biomedical publications, and the establishment of a resource-sharing network of more than 4,000 health science libraries through the regional medical library program.

Spurred on by the awareness of the unexpected adverse effects of drugs such as thalidomide and the harmful effects of chemical contaminants in the environment, the Library undertook programs for collecting, organizing, and disseminating information on drugs and the toxic effects of chemicals. Cummings established a major division at the Library, the Specialized Information Services, to take responsibility for such activities.

Through the National Medical Audiovisual Center, the Library cooperated with professional societies and medical schools to improve instruction. Audiovisuals were produced and a database listing peer-reviewed audiovisuals (AVLINE) was developed and added to the MEDLARS family of databases.

Cummings had a vision of the Library as an active information center that was part of a network for communicating biomedical information. In 1965 he proposed the establishment of a Center for Biomedical Communications at the Library, set up in 1968 as the Lister Hill National Center for Biomedical Communications. The Lister Hill Center building was dedicated in 1980 as the research and development division of NLM. Projects at the Lister Hill Center pioneered in such areas as Abridged Index Medicus-Teletypewriter Exchange System (AIM-TWX) and those involving computer-assisted instruction, educational television, satellite communications, medical informatics, and interactive videodisks.

Cummings listened carefully to teachers and colleagues over the years. He evidenced a deep appreciation of the people whose accomplishments resulted in medical progress. This philosophy is most evident in the History of Medicine Division of the Library, especially in the oral history program and modern manuscript collections.

Cooperation among the U.S. national libraries was encouraged. Cummings met often with the directors of the Library of Congress and the National Agricultural Library to discuss issues of mutual interest and ways to avoid redundancy. In 1965 the directors of the three national libraries established the Federal Library Committee, an ongoing mechanism through which to pursue their common goals. His interest in biomedical communication also extended beyond the U.S. He established the position of Special Assistant to the Director for International Programs, providing both a focus and an impetus for NLM to expand its international cooperation.

During his tenure at the Library, Cummings addressed many public policy issues, two of which consumed considerable time and energy: (1) copyright and (2) the role of a tax-supported institution in providing information services. In 1968 a petition was filed against the government alleging that the NLM and NIH Library had infringed on a company's copyright by photocopying articles from its journals. The case was finally decided in the government's favor in 1975. (The U.S. Supreme Court allowed a decision by the U.S. Court of Claims to stand.) In this long legal battle Cummings championed the rights of scholars and libraries everywhere for the judicially created doctrine of "fair use."

The appropriate role of NLM in providing information to health professionals is an equally complex public issue. Cummings considered that biomedical information was a public resource and should not be treated solely as a market commodity. He argued forcefully that NLM was "fulfilling its Congressionally mandated function . . . when the fees the Library charged for its products and services recover only the costs of providing access to them".

Cummings complemented his administrative achievements with superb scholarship; he published more than a hundred scientific and historical publications. He gained a reputation as a forceful and articulate speaker and received seven honorary degrees and many special awards. He retired in January 1984 after 20 years as Director to pursue his interest in reviewing the papers of the first Director of the Library, John Shaw Billings, the economics of libraries, and other professional and personal interests.

REFERENCES
Wyndham D. Miles, *A History of the National Library of Medicine* (1982).
N. E. Davies and E. J. Huth, "Martin M. Cummings and the National Library of Medicine," *Annals of Internal Medicine* (December 1983).

LOIS ANN COLAIANNI

Cunha, Maria Luisa Monteiro da
(1908–1980)

Maria Luisa Monteiro da Cunha, librarian and Brazilian cataloguing specialist, was active in national and international library activities. Brazil came to rely heavily on her expert advice.

She was born in Santos (São Paulo) on September 14, 1908. She received a Bachelor's degree in Dentistry (1928); later, she registered at the Library School of the Fundação Escola de Sociologia e Política (São Paulo) and received a Bachelor's degree in library science in 1940. She won a special scholarship granted by the American Library Association and, during the academic year of 1946–47, studied at Columbia University School of Library Service. She prepared a term paper that, translated into Portuguese, contributed to the development of cataloguing practice in Brazil. She represented Columbia University at the First Conference of Librarians of the Americas (Washington, D.C., 1947).

From 1942 to 1949 she worked at the São Paulo Municipal Public Library. She was Director of the University of São Paulo Central Library from 1949 to 1970 and of the Documentation and Library Division from 1970 to 1978.

In 1965 she was appointed one of the members of a Special Committee nominated to study the creation and organization of an Institute devoted to the professional teaching of communication media, including journalism, theater, the movies, radio, television, librarianship, documentation, and public relations. The Committee activities resulted in the Communications and Arts School. A member of its Faculty from 1967 to 1972, she gave courses on librarianship and cataloguing.

Cunha became an active member of specialized committees, mainly the Brazilian Committee on Library Technical Services. She was one of the members of the Working Group on Coordination of Cataloguing Principles (created in 1959 by IFLA under a grant from the Council on Library Resources) for the organization and follow-up of the International Conference on Cataloguing Principles (Paris, 1961). She participated in the first Seminar on University Libraries (Monticello, Illinois, 1961), the International Meeting of Cataloguing Experts (Copenhagen, 1969), and the Revision Meeting for International Standard Bibliographic Description-M (Grenoble, 1973).

From 1954 she was an invited participant at Brazilian library conferences. In 1973 she received a gold medal from the Seventh Brazilian Documentation and Librarianship Congress (Belém, Pará). Cunha died in São Paulo on July 28, 1980.

She wrote *Treatment of Brazilian and Portuguese names* (Paris, IFLA, 1961), *Formación profesional* ("Professional Training," 1965), *Controle bibliográfico universal* ("Universal Bibliographical Control," Brasíla, 1975), and *Bibliotecas universitárias em sistemas nacionais de informaçao* ("University Libraries in National Information Systems," Porto Alegre, 1977).

CORDELIA R. CAVALCANTI

Cutter, Charles Ammi
(1837–1903)

One of the most important of all contributors to U.S. librarianship, Charles Ammi Cutter was librarian of the Boston Athenaeum, 1869–93, a leader of the developing U.S. library profession in the second half of the 19th century, and the author of notable works on cataloguing and classification.

Cutter was born on March 14, 1837, in Boston. He lived with his grandfather and his three aunts in West Cambridge, Massachusetts, where he was raised in a strong Unitarian religious atmosphere. He was sent to the Hopkins Classical School, a school designed to prepare young men for Harvard College. By 10 he had also become acquainted with the West Cambridge town library as both a patron and occasional assistant to his aunt, Charlotte Cutter, who served as its Librarian from 1849 to 1851.

Cutter enrolled in the fall of 1851 at Harvard College, where he applied himself diligently to his studies, winning several prizes and graduating third in his class. He studied French literature, science, and mathematics with great interest and was thoroughly exposed to the mental philosophy of Scottish Common Sense Realism through the teaching of Francis Bowen. His interest in scientific studies was such that for a semester after he graduated in 1855 he attended the Lawrence Scientific School as a special student in mathematics.

Cutter was ambivalent about pursuing a scientific career, however, and in the fall of 1856 he enrolled in the Harvard Divinity School, again distinguishing himself in scholarship by winning the Bowdoin prize dissertation competition in 1857. Although his course of studies trained him for the Unitarian ministry, the experience that had the most influence on him while in the Divinity School was his tenure as the School's student librarian for the period 1857–59. He not only discharged his regular duties but also directed the writing of a new catalogue and

ALA

Charles Ammi Cutter

the complete rearrangement of the books on the shelves. His work as a librarian also brought him into contact with Ezra Abbot, the College Library's cataloguer. This relationship was significant, not only for the personal influence that Abbot had over Cutter, but also because several months after Cutter graduated from the School in 1859, Abbot successfully obtained Cutter's appointment as his assistant in the College Library. Thus, on May 11, 1860, Cutter formally entered the career that would occupy him throughout the remainder of his life.

Cutter's years at the Harvard College Library from 1860 to the end of 1868 were formative in several ways. He experienced first-hand the growth and administrative problems of a large academic library, then under the direction of John Langdon Sibley. He learned from Abbot a systematic approach to the organization of knowledge in catalogue form, the chief characteristic of which was its basis in the classificatory theory that was inherent in the Scottish realists' view of mental processes. He also learned the techniques of cataloguing, for he not only helped Abbot to plan the alphabetico-classed card catalogue that bears Abbot's name but also assumed supervisory control over the project.

In May 1863 Cutter married Sarah Fayerweather Appleton, and by the summer of 1868 three sons had been born to them. His growing family responsibilities made it necessary for him to supplement his regular wages through a variety of special projects. These included assisting Joseph Sabin as a bibliographer on the *Bibliotheca Americana;* working as a part-time cataloguer at the Boston Public Library (1866–68), where he came into personal contact with Charles Coffin Jewett; indexing scholarly books in preparation for their publication; and writing reviews and articles for the *North American Review* and for the *Nation.* He was able to dispense with much of that activity, however, when he accepted the position of Librarian of the prestigious Boston Athenaeum on January 1, 1869.

Years of Success, 1869–80. The years from 1869 to 1880 were for Cutter ones of great success and undoubted personal satisfaction. His work at the Athenaeum consisted of a thoroughgoing and continuous systematization of the library's programs. His ideal, gained from his scientific and philosophical training, was that all elements and processes of the library should together form an integrated whole that efficiently reached stated goals at the most reasonable cost—much like a finely tuned machine. In carefully reaching toward that systematization, Cutter captured not only the confidence of his trustees but also the admiration of the new but advancing profession of librarianship.

The confidence and admiration that he gained was due in no small part to his special accomplishments; the most notable were in the realm of cataloguing. He planned and published between 1869 and 1882 a monumental five-volume dictionary catalogue of the Athenaeum's collections that was not only a testament to his ideals of systematization but also so artfully executed and convenient to use that it brought general esteem to both Cutter and the library. Moreover, Cutter presented to the wider library world both the theory and procedures he used in making the catalogue in the form of an essay, "Library Catalogues," and his *Rules for a Printed Dictionary Catalogue,* both important parts of the Bureau of Education's important special report of 1876, *Public Libraries in the United States of America, Their History, Conditions, and Management.* The *Rules* were afterward published in three more editions, the last and most notable issued posthumously in 1904. The second of his accomplishments consisted of his classification work; by the end of 1880 he had circulated the first copies of his author tables, later published in three separate formats (a two-figure author table, 1887; the *Cutter-Sanborn Three-Figure Author Table,* 1896; and Cutter's own three-figure expansion of his earlier two-figure table, 1901). By 1880 Cutter had also worked out the general plan and had circulated the first schedules of his "Boston Athenaeum Classification."

Concurrent with the foregoing activities and accomplishments, Cutter also took part directly in the formal rise of the library profession. He worked closely with Melvil Dewey and others in the establishment of the American Library Association in 1876. Preferring the shadows more than the limelight, he became one of ALA's most active committee workers, chairing the very important Cooperation Committee from its inception in 1877.

His literary contributions also increased in number. Though he was shy and somewhat reticent in public, he was able in his writing to express with great logic and clarity, as well as with occasional sharpness, the forcefulness of his views. His writings included major articles and reviews on library matters in the *Library Journal;* many literary pieces in the *Nation,* notable for their pithiness and wit; and the bibliography columns that he compiled and edited for the *Library Journal.* Finally, Cutter also joined with Dewey and others in 1879 in the formation of the Readers' and Writers' Economy, a speculative business venture of Dewey's designed to profit from the new commercial market arising with the growing library field. But that venture proved to be short-lived and engendered a financial imbroglio that cast a pall over an otherwise bright and energetic period.

ALA Leadership from 1881. One important result of the financial imbroglio of 1880 was the realignment of some of the ALA leadership responsibilities. For example, Dewey—the forceful if unofficial leader of the ALA—relinquished his editorship of the *Library Journal,* which Cutter then assumed in January 1881 and eventually continued until late in 1893. Cutter also worked on most of the Association's important new committees during the following decade and, from 1887 to 1889, served as its President. But Cutter, along with others, represented an essentially conservative approach to professional library leadership. He was content to view the meetings of the ALA and the pages of the *Journal* as a forum in which librarians shared their insights, debated their differences, and gained general inspiration. Colleagues could then apply to their own situation whatever techniques seemed appropriate. Dewey, however, represented a rising bureaucratic spirit who saw the future of the profession in the exercise of its organizational power; the formation of explicit standards; centralized control of library processes, methods, and leadership where possible; and simple, pragmatic solutions to library programs.

From his vantage point in New York, Dewey offered an increasingly attractive alternative to the regular leadership of the profession. The force with which he presented his program not only brought him the presidency of the Association twice during the early 1890s but also changed the character of the Association and its general purposes.

Cutter's response to the changes taking place, especially after 1885, was ambivalent. On the one hand, he agreed with Dewey in many matters, particularly those related to classification and education. And because of his good-natured humor, his patience, and the esteem in which others held his judgment, he was able to play a mediating role, defending Dewey's work and standing between Dewey and others who opposed him. On the other hand, Cutter found himself increasingly uncomfortable with Dewey's tendency to oversimplify library problems and their solutions and with his emphasis on the exercise of organizational power to achieve what were clearly Dewey's own goals. By the early 1890s Cutter was taking decided stands against some of Dewey's measures and in the editorials of the *Journal* increasingly emphasized the more conservative interpretation of the role of the Association. But he recognized that the ALA was changing dramatically and, as bewildering as it may have appeared, accepted it as inevitable.

Changes in the Association during that period were paralleled by changes at the Athenaeum. Cutter finished the dictionary catagloue and began the arduous task of applying his classification scheme to the Athenaeum's collections. The latter dragged on for 10 years, however, and its cost and disruption brought criticism from Athenaeum members. Furthermore, the Board of Trustees of the Athenaeum underwent a significant turnover in membership during the mid-1890s. The new members, bringing with them a growing sense of protectiveness against outsiders, criticized Cutter's openness in administration and willingness to use the Athenaeum for what they considered expensive experiments on behalf of the wider library world. In 1892 the conflict over administration priorities broke into the open when Cutter was unofficially censured by the trustees. Cutter began to search for another library position, but his search was unsuccessful. In April 1893 he resigned his Athenaeum post and traveled to Europe for a rest. He returned in the summer to attend the Columbian Exposition library meetings, but his subsequent search for a new position was likewise unsuccessful. In October 1893 he again returned to Europe, severing most of his ties with the American library scene until the following summer.

Forbes Library, 1894–1903. While in Europe, Cutter was asked by the trustees of the new Forbes Library in Northampton, Massachusetts, to purchase books for their library. After subsequent negotiations, he moved to the Forbes in August 1894 as its first Librarian. Cutter's accomplishments during the next 10 years were considerable; he increased the Forbes collections to nearly 90,000 carefully selected volumes, built large circulating collections of art reproductions and music, and began a medical collection for the area's physicians, a children's section within the Library, and a branch library system for the area surrounding Northampton. But the administration of the Forbes brought him grief as well, for while generous funds were available for purchases and building needs, severe limitations were constantly imposed on the funds necessary for the administration of the Library. As a result, Cutter was unable to hire highly trained assistants, and those he trained himself regularly left the Forbes for better-paying positions elsewhere. This factor made it impossible, for example, to catalogue and classify the collection in any more than a rudimentary manner.

The application of the shelf classification was of great concern to Cutter. During the late 1890s, he had remodeled his Boston Athenaeum classification into his much better known *Expansive Classification.* By 1893 he had published the first six expansions of the scheme. Believing it to be the best arranged and most adaptable classification available, he hoped that it might overtake Dewey's Decimal Classification as the scheme most used by all libraries. To that end he promoted his classification scheme tirelessly, presenting its merits whenever he could. In 1897 this effort took him as far as the International Conference of Librarians in London and the Institut Internationale de Bibliographie in Brussels. But his inability to apply it fully to the Forbes and the enormous work of single-handedly editing it, supervising its printing, promoting it, and distributing it slowed to a snail's pace his progress on the seventh and final expansion. At his death it remained unfinished, although its use as a fundamental pattern for the Library of Congress's classification extended its influence immeasurably.

Cutter's last years brought, as a result, a mixture of accomplishments and frustrations. Given to selfless labor on behalf of libraries, he constantly took on arduous projects. Between 1901 and early 1903, besides his Forbes work, he participated without reserve in the demanding work of the catalogue code revision committee of ALA, addressed local library groups, and lectured at library schools. He died in New Hampshire on September 6, 1903.

REFERENCES

W. P. Cutter, *Charles Ammi Cutter* (1931).

W. E. Foster, "Charles Ammi Cutter: A Memorial Sketch," *Library Journal* (1903).

Francis L. Miksa, editor, *Charles Ammi Cutter: Library Systematizer* (1977).

Miksa, "Cutter, Charles Ammi, *Dictionary of American Library Biography* (1978).

Miksa, *The Subject in the Dictionary Catalog from Cutter to the Present* (1983).

FRANCIS L. MIKSA

Cyprus

Cyprus, the third largest island of the Mediterranean Sea, lies in the eastern Mediterranean, south of Turkey and close to Syria and Israel. Population (1984 est.) 657,000; area 9,251 sq.km. The official languages are Greek and Turkish. English is the second language widely spoken. Cyprus is a member of the Commonwealth of Nations.

History. The history of Cyprus goes back to the 6th millennium B.C. with remains of Neolithic settlements. In ancient and classical times, Cyprus shared Greek culture, and libraries can be traced back to those days. The earliest were attached to the temples and kept archives, such as the sanctuary of Aphrodite at Paphos, the temple of Apollo at Curium, the temple of Cybele at Soli, and others.

The earliest known public library (*bibliophylakion*, "place where books are kept") in Cyprus was in the city–state of Soli: a man called Apollonius was in charge. Nicocrates the Cypriot is also mentioned for his famous private library.

During the Christian period Cyprus was among the first places to be converted to Christianity. With the spread of Christian literature one can assume that libraries were created and books were kept in churches and monasteries. No trace of such a library has been found, but there are many codices and manuscripts from Cyprus related to the Christian era in several major libraries abroad (including libraries at the Vatican and in Paris, Venice, and elsewhere.)

In the Frankish period (1191–1571), there were libraries in the court of Lusignan kings and in churches, monasteries, and abbeys. During the Turkish occupation (1571–1878), nearly all works of art were destroyed and the Catholic cathedrals of Saint Sophia (Holy Wisdom) in Nicosia and Saint Nicolas in Famagusta were converted to mosques. The books kept in churches and other places were destroyed. Only a few books were saved in isolated small churches and monasteries.

After 1821 a small library was formed by the Archbishopric in Nicosia, where most of the books saved from ancient collections in various churches, monasteries, and bishoprics were collected. The library of the Archbishopric of Cyprus originates from those collections. In 1982 the library of the Makarios III Foundation was amalgamated with the library of the Archbishopric of Cyprus in Nicosia.

At the beginning of the 19th century a small library known as the library of Sultan Mahmut II was set up by the Ottoman government at Cyprus with Turkish, Arabic, and Persian works. Originally housed in a medieval building behind Saint Sophia Cathedral in Nicosia, it is now in a building owned by Evkaf, a Turkish charitable trust.

After the cession of Cyprus to England in July 1878, there was an increase in book imports, mainly from Greece and England. New libraries were started, mainly in Government offices. In July 1878 operation of the first printing press was begun by a Greek Cypriot at Larnaca, and the first newspaper in Cyprus was issued at that time.

In 1887 a legal deposit law was passed and a depository set up in the office of the Chief Secretary. Two copies of each book were also sent to the Keeper of the Department of Printed Books at the British Museum. After independence (1960), the law was amended and three copies are kept in the library of the Public Information Office at Nicosia.

Nearly all libraries in Cyprus, except those already mentioned, started functioning after 1927 and mainly after independence in 1960.

In July 1974 Turkey invaded Cyprus and occupied 40 percent of the island. Many library collections were either damaged or destroyed. Two big and famous private libraries with many codices and rare books about Cyprus, which took their owners years to collect, were seized also, and no information is available about their fate. The library service thereafter faced many difficulties, including a reduction of stock and library facilities. The situation had improved by the mid-1980s as library facilities and stock were later replaced.

National and Public Libraries. Before the State Library of Cyprus started functioning in late 1985, the Public Library of Nicosia, established in 1927 and transfered to Nicosia Municipality in 1936, acted as a kind of National Library. It has its own building in the center of Nicosia. It was closed in 1953 and reopened in 1977. In the same building is housed the library of the Ministry of Education (established 1960). These two libraries are run by the same library committee and administration. The library is open to every citizen of Cyprus. Patrons can borrow books in person or by mail. The library has two regional libraries in other parts of Nicosia—one is an educational library and the other a children's library. The library has about 60,000 volumes of bound books and periodicals, mainly in Greek and English. A good stock is also kept in other languages.

The main towns of Cyprus have public libraries run by the municipalities. There are also 120 communal libraries in large villages, run by the Cultural Service of the Ministry of Education. The Cultural Service also runs three mobile libraries serving the population of the districts of Nicosia, Larnaca, Limassol, and Paphos.

There was no national bibliography before 1985. Since 1960 the Cyprus Bibliographical Bulletin has been published by C. D. Stephanou; it records the publications of Cyprus in the original language and is classified according to Dewey Decimal Classification. In 1985 the Bibliographical Society of Cyprus in Nicosia started publishing a bibliographical bulletin that records all published books of Cyprus of the previous year.

Academic Libraries. Cyprus, with many students studying abroad, has no university of its own. The country's five tertiary-level government-run institutions of higher education are the Pedagogical Academy (College of Education), the Higher Technical Institute, the Forestry College, the School of Nursing, and the Hotel and Catering Institute. Each of these institutions has its own specialized library, with from 10,000 to 30,000 volumes. There are also eight private institutions of third-level education that have their own special libraries.

School Libraries. All 435 primary schools of Cyprus had their own lending libraries of varying size in 1985. All 119 secondary schools (high schools and technical schools) had libraries ranging from 3,000 to 45,000 volumes. Most of the high-school li-

Press and Information Office, Nicosia

The library at the Nicosia Pedagogical Academy.

braries are run by assistant librarians or teachers who act as part-time librarians. School libraries are supported by the Ministry of Education, which contributes an allowance for the purchase of books based on the number of pupils.

Special Libraries. All ministries and departments of the Government have special libraries. Among them are the library of the Archeological Museum, with an excellent collection of books on the archeology of Cyprus; the Cyprus Research Center, with a fine collection on Cyprus history and folklore; and the library of the Institute of Agriculture Research.

The Public Record Office library, opened in 1972, houses all public records and archives.

The Profession. The Cyprus Library Association in Nicosia was founded in 1962. It is a member of IFLA and a founding member of the Commonwealth Library Association (COMLA), established in 1972.

COSTAS D. STEPHANOU

Czechoslovakia

Czechoslovakia, a socialist republic in central Europe, is bounded by the German Democratic Republic on the northwest, Poland on the northeast, the U.S.S.R

Libraries in Cyprus (1982)

Type	Administrative units	Service points	Volumes in collections	Annual expenditures (Cyprus pound)	Population served	Professional staff	Total staff
National	--	--	--	--	--	--	--
Academic	13	--	130,000	--	3,000	2	15
Public	130	--	180,000	--	350,000	3	130[b]
School	119[a]	--	355,000	--	40,000	--	119[b]
Special	15	--	100,000	--	--	3	15

[a]Excludes elementary schools.
[b]Most are part-time.

on the east, Hungary on the southeast, Austria on the southwest, and the German Federal Republic on the west. Population (1984 est.) 15,459,000; area 127,896 sq.km. The official languages are Czech and Slovak.

The system of libraries in Czechoslovakia consists of two independent systems—the Czech and the Slovak. Organizational structure of the whole system and its management are determined by the Library Act of 1959. According to their functional purpose or specialization, the libraries are loosely incorporated in the national systems. On principle, the services of the libraries are provided free of charge. The national systems are headed by central libraries that function as national libraries.

National Libraries. *State Library of the Czech Socialist Republic, Prague.* Origins of the Library date back to 1348. Its activities comprise the functions of both the Czech National and Central Library and that of the General Research Library.

The Library serves as the national center of research and methodology and of interlibrary lending service on an international scale and as a Unesco and UN depository library. The Library publishes the Czech national bibliography in four basic series (books, periodicals, articles, and printed music). It also provides research and lending services to specialists. Being the oldest depository library, it has vast collections (5,188,150 units in 1982); among them are unique holdings of manuscripts, incunabula, rare printed items, printed music, and other special collections.

Matica Slovenská, Martin. Founded in 1863, the Slovak National and Central Library is charged with care and protection of historical collections and is a center for bibliography and methodology, education, theory of libraries, and research.

The Library also serves as the Central Library Publishing House and fills the role of the central museum and archives of the literature. A depository for copyright copies for the whole country from 1945, it is the national center for interlibrary loans. Publishing activities include the Slovak national bibliography in four basic series (books, periodicals, articles, and printed music), from 1977 prepared with the aid of computers. The Library provides research and lending services to specialists. The collections of Matica Slovenská (4,425,775 units in 1982) include manuscripts, incunabula, and rare printed items, the archival collection (1,400,000 units), printed music, posters, postcards, and special records.

Academic Libraries. These are specialized libraries attached to the research centers and institutes of the Czechoslovak and Slovak academies of science. Library, bibliographic, documentary, research, and other types of activities support the demanding scientific research and education of research workers. The central library in the Czech Socialist Republic is the Basic Library–Science Information Center of the Czechoslovak Academy of Science, founded in 1786 (869,995 volumes in 1982). It is the specialized information center for social sciences. In Slovakia the same functions are executed by the Central Library of the Slovak Academy of Science in Bratislava, founded in 1942 (509,595 volumes in 1982).

Public Libraries. These provide educational and cultural services, as well as services for specialists in a region. They are open to all and are used by more than 50 percent of the inhabitants in rural and more than 70 percent of those in urban areas. In 1982 their collections comprised 29 percent nonfiction, 40.6 percent fiction, and 29.1 percent literature for children and youth. Sixty percent of the whole amount of library lendings in the ČSSR were by public libraries (regional, municipal, district, and local). According to the Library Act of 1959, regional and district public libraries are the centers of methodology, bibliography, information, and interlibrary lending services in a region.

Research Libraries. Research libraries are universal or specialized, with central or regional functions. They provide bibliographic and information services to specialists in science, research, management, and education.

The most important research libraries are the University Library in Bratislava (general collection of 1,808,939 volumes in 1982), the Center of Scientific Technological and Economic Information–the State Technical Library in Prague (specialized collection of 1,600,000 volumes in 1982), the Slovak Technical Library in Bratislava (specialized collection of 2,617,284 volumes in 1982), the Library of the National Museum in Prague (specialized historical collection of 1,448,450 volumes in 1982), and the State Scientific Library in Brno (universal collection—2,214,844 volumes in 1982). Specialized services are also provided by central agricultural and forestry libraries in Prague, Nitra, and Zvolen, and by central biological, medical, pedagogic, and economic libraries in Bratislava and Prague.

School and Special Libraries. Within the national library systems are school and pedagogic libraries that serve the needs of education. They are found at primary and secondary schools. Other libraries include technical, agricultural, and medical li-

Libraries in Czechoslovakia (1982)

Type	Administrative units	Volumes in collections	Annual expenditures	Population served	Total staff
National	2	9,613,927	--	52,434	896
Academic	125	6,619,794	--	60,123	912
Public	11,775	69,177,629	--	2,922,983	7,254
High School	73	13,651,422	--	283,023	805
Research	16	18,777,789	--	231,620	1,332

ªRegistered readers.

Source: Statistics of libraries.

braries (at factories and other appropriate institutions), special libraries of museums, galleries, and archives, and trade union libraries, all of which have an educational role. Statistical data are surveyed every 10 years.

Library Councils. In the Czech Socialist Republic, the Central Library Council of the CSR is an advisory, initiative, and coordinating body of the Ministry of Culture. In Slovakia the same functions are executed by the Slovak Library Council. These bodies follow and evaluate the activity of the library systems, consider their development and long-term plans of activity, and supervise the advancement of political and professional development of library workers, their social appreciation, and their remuneration. The councils cooperate with international library associations and are members of IFLA. Members of the councils are executives and experts in the field of librarianship and information science.

The Profession. In Czechoslovakia education of specialists and information workers begins at secondary librarian schools at Prague, Brno, and Bratislava. The course of study lasts four years, after basic education is finished.

Education of advanced specialists is secured at universities (the Department of Information Science and Librarianship of the Faculty of Arts of Charles University in Prague and the Department of Librarianship and Information Science of the Faculty of Arts of Comenius University in Bratislava). Information Science is also taught at the Economical High School in Prague. Study lasts eight terms, after secondary school study is finished.

Further education of workers and specialists is offered at the Center for Further Education of Librarians attached to the Slovak National Library in Martin, at the Center attached to the Slovak Technical Library in Bratislava, and under similar arrangement at the State Library in Prague. Continuing professional education is also secured at the Departments of Librarianship and Information Science in Prague and Bratislava.

Association. The Association of Slovak Librarians and Information Scientists is a voluntary organization of librarians, bibliographers, and information workers. Headquartered in Bratislava, with branch offices in Banská Bystrica and Košice, it was founded

State Library of the Czech Socialist Republic

Baroque Hall of the State Library, Prague.

in 1968. It had 2,452 members in 1982. The Association is concerned with the advancement of the profession; with state cultural and scientific policies in the fields of libraries, bibliography, and information science; and with international cooperation among libraries. The Association organizes conferences, meetings, courses, and other events, and it publishes specialized materials. It is the national member of IFLA. The bodies of the Association are the General Assembly (convened every three years), the Committee and the Board, the Control Commission, and the Secretariat. Sections include the Library Section (committees for public libraries, children and school libraries, research libraries, university libraries, and historical collections), the Section on Bibliography, and the Information Section. The Association publishes a bulletin, library and information manuals, and proceedings of conferences and meetings.

HELENA KOLAROVA-PALKOVA

Dana, John Cotton
(1856–1929)

John Cotton Dana, public librarian for four decades, notable for his innovations in offering and promoting library services and public education, was a leader of the library profession who served as President, and sometimes critic, of ALA and was an organizer and President of the Special Libraries Association.

Born on August 19, 1856, in Woodstock, Vermont, Dana spent his early life in Woodstock, where he was reared in a home in which education and reading were emphasized. He received an introduction to business there also, working in his father's general store "on the green," a store originally opened by his grandfather in 1802. He maintained strong ties with Woodstock throughout his life and spent many summer vacations there. In 1874 Dana entered Dartmouth College. There he made a good academic record and was elected to Phi Beta Kappa in 1878.

In June 1878 he returned home and began the study of law in the firm of French and Southgate in Woodstock. In addition to his study of law, he found time to read widely from the classics, biography, travel, and metaphysics. Less than two years later, threatened with tuberculosis, he sought a higher and drier climate. One of his college friends, Frank Wadleigh Gove, had gone to Colorado in 1879 and had become a deputy United States land and mineral surveyor in the mining section of the state. Dana joined him at Rico, Colorado, in 1880 and continued his study of law there. He was admitted to the Colorado bar later that year. Mostly, however, he worked with Gove as a surveyor until 1882.

Dana returned to Woodstock for a brief time before moving to New York City. There he lived with his brother Charles, a doctor, while he continued his study of law and also did some tutoring. Dana passed the New York State Bar examinations in May 1883. About the same time health problems surfaced again, and in March 1884 he went to Fergus Falls, Minnesota, where another college friend, William D. Parkinson, lived. From there he moved to Ashby, Minnesota, where he practiced law and in July 1884 became Editor, for a short time, of the local newspaper, the *Avalanche*. After a few months he returned to Colorado and again engaged in work as a surveyor and later as construction superintendent for the Colorado Midland Railroad, living in construction camp tents a good deal of the time. He also began to make public appearances as a lecturer on religious and social questions. For one month he occupied the pulpit in a Unitarian church, and there he met Adine Rowena Waggener, a native of Russellville, Kentucky, whom he married in November 1888.

For a while after marriage the couple lived on a Colorado ranch, where Dana began to write articles for publication on a variety of subjects including travel and educational and sociological matters. He also wrote letters to the editors of newspapers. An article entitled "The Public School," critical of the public school system in the United States, was published in the *Denver Arbitrator* for February 16, 1889, and attracted wide attention. To a degree it may well have been this very article that was responsible for Dana's eventual entrance into the library profession. Other influences, however, may have played a part

ALA

John Cotton Dana

also. Aaron Gove, Superintendent of the Denver Public School system, was Frank Wadleigh Gove's brother. For some time he and his Board had hoped to establish a library for the high school that could be open to the public and function as a public library also. The tax levied for educational purposes in Colorado included a provision that made this plan legal. Dana's article in the *Denver Arbitrator* spurred Gove on toward accomplishment of that hope. Gove made the recommendation to his Board to vote for the establishment of the library to serve the school and the public and to appoint John Cotton Dana as the Librarian. It was so voted. Dana accepted and in 1889 began a career in librarianship that lasted four decades.

Denver. Dana began at once to organize the Denver Public Library, gather a staff, acquire materials in books, magazines, newspapers, and pamphlets, supplementing the 2,000 books in the school library, which he inherited upon his appointment, and to initiate service. Most significant of all, he began to advertise it. His idea about libraries was to get them used. He sent notices about the new library to the editors of every newspaper in Colorado and to national educational and religious journals, and he made personal visits to many of the editors. He sought their cooperation and help in making the services, planned for everyone, known and specifically indicated to them how he was sure the library could be of use to them too.

Advertising a library had not been the custom in the profession, and Dana's first moves in that direction were frowned upon by many in it. Other libraries were giving many of the services Dana inaugurated for Denver, but publicizing and advertising them was Dana's unique contribution. He also sought a sharing of experiences from fellow librarians.

He proceeded at once to issue a monthly library bulletin entitled *Books* (the first issue was dated October 1889); he invited educational and civic leaders to give lectures in the public library open to the public; and he gave many talks himself before business, educational, and other professional groups, many of which have been published. He followed William Howard Brett's innovative policy of open access to shelves. In 1894 Dana opened the very first children's room in a public library—a room with suitable furniture, decoration, and a supply of children's literature for their enjoyment, information, and personal development.

His library flourished. Its resources and use, as determined by circulation figures, grew significantly. Visitors numbered a thousand daily. He assembled a collection of business books and related materials and placed it in the Chamber of Commerce, thus becoming one of the entrepreneurs, among librarians, attempting to provide service in the field of business information. A special collection of medical books was developed in cooperation with the Colorado Medical Library Association that later formed the nucleus of the Denver Medical Library.

With all this he also started a library training class for his staff. As procedures and forms became established, he took great pains to put them in writing for frequent review. Some of these became part of a book, the *Public Library Handbook,* in 1893. He took an active part in professional associations as a member and also officer, being elected President of the Colorado Library Association in 1895 and Chairman of its Convention Committee for the forthcoming conference of the American Library Association to be held in Cleveland the next year.

Dana began to look elsewhere for an opportunity to pursue his vocation. A controversy had arisen concerning his policy of providing library materials on both sides of the free silver matter, a policy Dana defended earnestly; the School Board was criticized by Denver's Chamber of Commerce for using part of its tax appropriation to finance the business library there, even though the action was definitely within the law. Dana became the Librarian of the City Library of Springfield, Massachusetts, effective January 1, 1898.

Springfield. The City Library of Springfield, Massachusetts, was already established with a collection over four times larger than the one Dana left in Denver and a staff already organized and at work. Dana saw possibilities for making the library better known in the community and more usable and inviting physically. He put into effect policies found successful in Denver, such as providing easier access to the shelves and a special corner for children's books and removing all devices—bars, gates, or anything else—that deterred direct contact of the public with the library staff. Because the library building was on a hill, and access to the entrance necessitated climbing flights of stairs up that hill, he had an elevator installed. He also started library training classes to provide qualified assistants for the library. The interest shown in his classes prompted him to invite the librarians in the northwestern part of the state to a meeting to discuss mutual library problems. An outgrowth of these sessions was the organization of the Western Massachusetts Library Club.

Dana wrote a series of articles entitled "A Library Primer," which were published in the first six issues of *Public Libraries* in 1896. Later he revised, rewrote, and extended the original draft for publication in book form. He included additional material selected from many sources, written by other library pioneers, for *A Library Primer* (the same title as his 1893 book), published in 1899.

Dana resigned his post in Springfield on December 18, 1901, to become Librarian of the Free Public Library of Newark, New Jersey, succeeding his friend and fellow Dartmouth graduate, Frank P. Hill.

Newark. Dana joined the Free Public Library of Newark, New Jersey, as Librarian, on January 15, 1902, and remained there the rest of his life. The new building had been completed the year before. The resources for reference and lending were comprehensive. The staff was capable, qualified, and interested. Beatrice Winser, who had been Assistant Librarian under Hill, and who was appointed Acting Librarian when Hill left, had administered the Library capably for seven months. Dana with Winser as Assistant Librarian formed a dynamic team. He did much writing, planned policies, edited Newark library publications, e.g., *The Newarker, The Library,* prepared broadsides, gave numerous talks to alert the public on the contribution the Library could and did make to the social structure of the community, and directed preparation of various book lists. He provided new activities for the Library, such as the hospital library

service, a special collection of foreign language books for the immigrants coming to the city, and branch libraries. All of these developments provided news items for the newspapers and business, professional, and other journals, and gave Dana opportunities to keep the library in the public eye. He was spectacularly successful in doing so.

Always searching for new ways to make the Library more meaningful, he became deeply involved in museums. His philosophy, expressed in one of the Library's booklists, was, "Libraries and museums exist to furnish the knowledge that leads to understanding." Though there were no museums in Newark, he saw possibilities in creating some museum activities within the Library, e.g., preparing exhibits that could be displayed there, and proceeded to borrow materials from citizens of Newark, from department stores, and from other museums for that purpose. He organized exhibits on American art and on science.

On April 29, 1909, the Newark Museum Association was formed with Dana as its Secretary. Almost four years later he was appointed the Association's first Director, holding that position as well as his Library post until his death. In this capacity he began to see his dream of a museum building and museum service for Newark come true. And so it did, but not without controversy over location and other delays. Finally, on March 17, 1926, the Newark Museum of Art, Science, and Industry was opened near the Library.

Perhaps Dana's most famous contribution to the library profession was establishment of what became the Business Library of the Newark Public Library. He had been aware of the possibilities of library service to the business community in Denver and in Springfield and initiated services there, working with business groups such as Chambers of Commerce and with community business leaders. But the information needs of business were not very clearly defined at that time, and very little printed documentation of what was defined was available to libraries. In Newark, he was fortunate in recognizing a member of his staff, Sarah B. Ball, who shared his enthusiasm for seeking ways to make the Library of genuine use to business. She was the Librarian of Branch 1, opened in October 1904 and located in Newark's business district. In reporting to him of the use being made of the branch by businessmen, she suggested a change of name to Business Men's Library and began collecting as much material as could be found on anything relating to business. No one could have been happier about this than Dana. The Business Men's Library flourished largely because of the tremendous dedication and enthusiasm of Ball, who had the wholehearted support of Dana and Richard C. Jenkinson, one of the Trustees, and also because the flood of business print had started from the presses.

At the Business Men's Library emphasis was put on providing exact information needed—specific facts and figures. Lists of book and periodical references for specific business subjects were issued frequently, and a regular bulletin entitled "Business Literature" had subscribers throughout the country. The Library became a model for other public libraries seeking to extend similar services for their communities.

Dana's work as Librarian of the Denver Public Library brought him to the attention of members of the American Library Association, some of whom stopped on the way to a San Francisco convention to meet Dana and see the Denver Public Library. The visit led to his first ALA Conference, and in 1895 he became its President-Elect.

Association Leadership. His concern with some of the country's and world's great problems made a number of the ALA's topics for discussion seem puerile to him, and he was soon in controversy with some of its members and officers. Dana, however, was willing and anxious to identify with library and education associations as a member even when he differed with them or was actively opposed to some of their activities. He was elected or appointed to many committees of national, state, and local organizations: President of the American Library Association, 1895–96; member of its Council, 1896–1902; and President of the New Jersey Library Association, 1904–05 and 1910–11. He also became President of the Special Libraries Association, which he helped organize, 1909–10.

The group whose efforts finally resulted in the formation of the Special Libraries Association had started really with Sarah B. Ball and Anna Sears, Librarian of the Merchant's Association of New York. They had invited librarians doing special library research work outside public libraries, as well as those specializing in business information and other specialties within public libraries, to meet together informally while they were in attendance at ALA meetings. When this fact was brought to Dana's attention, he started the action that brought together about 56 librarians working in such fields as law, insurance, chambers of commerce, engineering, public utilities, museums, and municipal research.

Largely through Dana's help, this group organized themselves into the Special Libraries Association (1909), a name suggested by Dana.

Dana hoped to get the new Association under the umbrella of the ALA, and his failure to accomplish this because of reluctance, or misunderstanding on both sides, increased his dissatisfaction with the ALA. He remained an active member of the Association, however, and continued vocal in his criticism when he disagreed in its decisions.

Shortly before his death on July 21, 1929, he wrote to Matthew S. Dudgeon of the Milwaukee Public Library:

> I have been for years, now and then, the down-right critic of the A.L.A. During these same years I hope I have been of assistance to A.L.A. in all its good work. My criticism is what I'm remembered for, I assume, and I cannot help feeling that I have been, not infrequently, unfairly judged concerning it (Chalmers Hadley, *John Cotton Dana—A Sketch*, ALA, 1943).

Dana had many interests in his life—politics, education, business, art, music, printing: in fact, anything that affected mankind concerned him.

Publications. Dana was a prolific writer and speaker. Many of his talks and addresses were printed in library, business, and other professional journals, often in more than one. A comprehensive list, chronologically arranged, compiled by Hazel Johnson and Beatrice Winser, was published with Hazel Johnson's article on Dana in *The Library Quarterly* (1937). *Literature of Libraries in the Seventeenth and Eighteenth*

Centuries (1906–07), edited by J. C. Dana and Henry W. Kent, was reprinted in 1967 by Scarecrow.

His family's Elm Tree Press in his home in Woodstock, Vermont, operated mainly by two of his brothers, was used frequently to print works written or edited by him or in collaboration with others. Edmund Lester Pearson's *The Old Librarian's Almanack* (1909) was printed there for many years, as were Dana's translations of 17th- and 18th-century classics on librarianship.

Newark recognized him as "the First Citizen of Newark" and celebrated the 100th anniversary of his birth with a Centennial Convocation on October 17, 1956.

Dana's philosophical approach to librarianship is best revealed in his book *Suggestions*, published by F. W. Faxon in 1921. It consists of extracts from his papers and essays. They were selected by him to help the beginner in library work look at the profession with fresh interest and make it seem deserving of careful thought. They contain those nuggets of thought that, through the years, have been quoted over and over again on reading, books, and business.

ROSE L. VORMELKER

Denmark

Denmark, a constitutional monarchy, lies between two bodies of water—the North and the Baltic seas—in north central Europe. Denmark includes the greater part of the Jutland Peninsula and approximately 100 inhabited offshore inslands in the Kattegat and the Skagerak straits. Population (1983 est.) 5,116,464; area 43,075 sq.km. The official language is Danish.

History. The first organized book collections appeared in the country districts in the mid-18th century when the clergy in particular pioneered rural education. The earliest collected statistics of public libraries in Denmark reveal that in 1885 there were 1,068 in the country's 1,697 parishes. Nearly all of them were small and rudimentary in terms of equipment, but they clearly indicate a widespread ability to read among the general population, together with an appreciation of books as a suitable medium for general education. In 1882 the state began to make grants to the smaller libraries that otherwise were maintained by voluntary contributions, often with supplementary local authority grants. The men behind the first public library law were A. S. Steenberg, H. O. Lange, chief of the Royal Library, and Th. Døssing, who became the first director of the State Inspectorate for Public Libraries.

National Library. The National Library of Denmark, in the capital city of Copenhagen, is the Royal Library. It can be traced back to the early 16th century when the King founded his private library in the Castle of Copenhagen. From the 17th century the Royal Library has served as the Danish national library, including the obligation to establish and maintain a national bibliography. Danish publications have been provided through legal deposit from 1697, and the present legal deposit act was passed in 1927. In addition to these functions the Royal Library has subject responsibility within the national research library network in the fields of the humanities, theology, and the social sciences, and acts as the main library for the University of Copenhagen in those disciplines.

Among the library's principal departments is the Danish Department, which holds the most complete collection of Danish imprints in existence as well as of all material printed outside Denmark that deals with Denmark and translations of Danish works into foreign languages. The Manuscript Collection, the Department of Maps and Prints, the Department of Oriental Manuscripts, the Collection of Judaica and Hebraica, the Music Department, and the Foreign Department all possess rich collections. The Royal Library's collection totaled 2,500,000 volumes in 1982. To these holdings can be added manuscripts, recordings, musical scores, maps, prints, and other materials.

Denmark's one principal and four provincial archives, according to the Danish National Archives' *Library Yearbook 1982* and *Statistical Yearbook 1984*, had holdings that occupied 173,535 running meters in 1982. Total staff numbered 153 (43 professionals), and annual expenditures totaled 28,617,000 Danish kroner. The Danish Business History Archives held about 86,000 volumes and had a total staff of 13 (6 professionals).

Academic and Research Libraries. The principal academic libraries in Denmark include the University Library in Copenhagen; founded in 1482, it is divided into two sections, one for the humanities and one for science and medicine. Another important library is the State and University Library of Aarhus, which serves the University of Aarhus and other educational institutions in the Aarhus region and is a focal point in the national interlibrary lending system, providing specialized literature to the public libraries. This general library was established in 1902; its general collection numbered 1,683,000 volumes in 1982.

The present network of research libraries is to a great extent based on a library reform of 1926, which introduced a scheme of subject specialization among 29 libraries. The National Technological Library of Denmark and the Royal Veterinary and Agricultural University Library are examples of major research libraries with nationwide subject responsibilities. The research library network also includes the university libraries in Odense, Roskilde, Aalborg, and Esbjerg founded in the 1960s and 1970s. Its central bodies are the Office of the National Librarian, set up in 1943 to promote cooperation among the various units of the research library system, and the National Advisory Council of Danish Research Libraries, created in 1970

Royal Library of Denmark

The Royal Library, which serves as Denmark's national library and traces its beginning to the 16th century. It also serves as the main library of the University of Copenhagen for the humanities, theology, and social sciences.

to deal with a variety of issues relating to the structure, policy, planning, and technology in the research library field.

Public Libraries. The modern public libraries organized in each of the 277 local government areas are influenced in form and aims by the Anglo-American free public libraries, which since the turn of the 20th century have formed the pattern of a large-scale development of the Danish library service.

The first public library law dates from 1920. It made available an annual government allocation to each library, subject to provision of books of quality and all-round character, acceptable premises, and regular service hours. As the subsidy was automatically calculated in proportion to the local contributions, it was an important stimulus to the development of libraries generally. The principle of Government grants was maintained in many subsequent revisions and amendments.

As a consequence of the revisions of the law in 1983, the principal outline for traditional library activities was maintained, but considerable change resulted in the economic relations between the state and the individual local library. The percentage of the local budget that previously had been granted by the state was converted into a part of the total treasury allocation to all the individual communes in accordance with a set of general rules related to the num-

Libraries in Denmark (1982)

Type	Administrative units	Service points	Volumes in collections	Annual expenditures (krone)	Population served	Professional staff	Total staff
National	1	--	2,500,000	54,048,000	--	127	297
University	5	--	4,663,000	145,800,000	--	233	546
Public	281	--	31,857,000	1,466,735,000	5,111,464	2,204	5,846
School	1,891	--	17,920,000	329,379,000	--	--	3,277
Special	23[a]	--	3,198,000	75,190,000	--	186	436

[a]Major libraries with technical and scientific literature.

Sources: *Library Yearbook*, 1982; *Statistical Yearbook*, 1984.

ber of inhabitants, total length of the streets, and many other quantitative factors. The commune became the body responsible for providing the economic basis for library activities.

The first library law of 1920 set up a State Inspectorate for Public Libraries (Bibliotekstilsyn) charged with the responsibility of distributing the state grants to the various public libraries and ensuring that their standards complied with the statutory requirements. The inspectorate has developed an extensive advisory and planning service that has been of great importance in promoting uniform development of the public library system.

Following administrative amalgamations, there were 247 free public libraries in 1984, 14 of which functioned as county libraries (amtsbiblioteker) with special duties in relation to the smaller libraries in their counties. The public libraries, with children's and school libraries, at the end of 1982 had a combined stock of 50,432,000 volumes; the number of annual borrowings (high for its population) totaled 125,6000,000 volumes. In addition to their general lending activities and reference and other services, the public libraries provide comprehensive services to hospitals, schools, and many other social institutions. Many libraries use bookmobiles where the population is too scarce to maintain branches.

In summary, Danish libraries have developed a wide measure of cooperation partly between the research libraries and the public libraries, partly among the public libraries themselves with a view to providing scholars, students, and ordinary readers with maximum service.

School Libraries. In Denmark the term "school library" generally refers to those in primary schools. Primary school libraries are required by the Public Libraries Act. Libraries in secondary schools are an emerging type of library that expanded during the mid-1980s, but they lack the legislative basis of primary school libraries. School libraries are developing into media centers offering a wide range of learning resources and audiovisual aids.

Special Libraries. Special libraries in Denmark form a heterogeneous group of about 300 ranging from libraries in museums, independent research institutions, technical schools, and teacher training colleges to commercial firms.

The Profession. The Royal School of Librarianship, Copenhagen, was reorganized in 1956 under an act of Parliament and established as an independent state institution. It provides a four-year basic course in librarianship, advanced education, and research in library science. A branch was established in 1974 in cooperation with the University Center at Aalborg.

The Danish Library Bureau is a central institution for library cooperation. It provides centralized cataloguing, issues printed cards, edits the *Danish Book List,* and compiles numerous catalogues. It is also the center for automation work in public libraries and maintains the central database for these libraries.

The Danish Library Design Bureau assists all libraries with planning and acquisition of library furniture and technical equipment and with the design of library interiors.

The Danish Library Binding Center provides fast delivery of bound volumes of library literature and supplies public libraries with information about and

review of current literature.

The Danish Library Association is the oldest and main organization, with branches in all counties. The Danish Research Library Association has a section for the libraries and one for the library staff. The Union of Danish Librarians is a trade union concerned with salaries and working conditions for professional librarians. Other associations include the Danish Society for Scientific and Technological Information and Documentation, the Danish Association of Music Libraries, and the Danish School Library Association.

REFERENCES
Danish National Archives, *Library Yearbook*
The Royal Library Today (Copenhagen, 1982) Leif Thorsen, *Public Libraries in Denmark* (Copenhagen, 1972)
Danish School Libraries (Copenhagen, 1982)

PREBEN KIRKEGAARD

ALA

Melvil Dewey

Dewey, Melvil
(1851–1931)

At an early age Melvil Dewey concluded that knowledge was better than ignorance, that education was the surest means to knowledge, and that beyond schooling reading was the surest means to an education—to reach understanding one needed only diligence and a book. He also concluded that he would have to see to it that the best means to bring person and book together be found and employed. Librarianship did not exist when Dewey set out on his self-assigned task. To be sure, there were libraries and people worked in them, but no unified body of purpose and practice (which we call librarianship) existed to guide them.

From 1873 to 1906 he was to devise and construct almost singlehandedly the forms and substance of librarianship (Charles Ammi Cutter providing the other hand on occasion). To achieve what he did Dewey had to play many roles:

organizer: of the ALA and other professional associations; of a classification scheme (the Dewey Decimal Classification); and of a library school.

advocate: for professionalism in librarianship; for the education of its members; for an equal role for women.

standardizer: of supplies, equipment, tools, methods, education.

librarian: of one of the first modern university libraries (Columbia); of the foremost state library of its day (New York).

teacher: through editing and writing for *Library Journal* and *Library Notes;* through the establishment of apprentice programs and a library school; through promoting the role of the college library in academic pursuits; through pursuing always the role of the library as the "People's University"; and through inspiration and example.

Melville Louis Kossuth Dewey was born on December 10, 1851, in Adams Center, New York, to Joel and Eliza Dewey. He gathered his early education in bits and pieces, entering Amherst College, Amherst, Massachusetts, in 1870. While there he launched his career in librarianship, the first step being to examine exemplary libraries of the Northeast in order to determine the methods libraries should use in carrying out their roles. This quest led him to his most lasting achievement in librarianship.

Libraries normally arranged their collections by the fixed location method—a book's physical location was fixed on a specific shelf in a specific range. Dewey pondered the inevitable costs of such a system: works on the same subject did not shelve near each other, and when a library grew beyond its four walls, its collection had to be renumbered on book and in catalogue—an expensive business. (Two cornerstones of Dewey's lifelong activities were his concerns for time and cost.) To prevent the unwanted effects of fixed location, Dewey conceived relative location, using decimal fractions to number the contents of books rather than the physical books themselves. That stroke of genius led to the Dewey Decimal Classification, published in 1876, in its 19th edition in the mid–1980s and the most widely used library classification in the world. From it was to stem the Universal Decimal Classification, also widely used, and itself one of the bases of information science through S. C. Bradford's *Documentation* (1948).

The year 1876 saw Dewey lay other foundations for the profession. (1) He was the motive force in bringing together the Conference of Librarians in Philadelphia at which the American Library Association was born (and dominated by him for 30 years). (2) By approaching Frederick Leypoldt and Richard R. Bowker on the need for a journal in librarianship, Dewey assured the future publication of the *Library Journal* and subsequently helped direct it for its first five years (1876–81). (3) He established the Library Bureau, a firm that took major steps toward standardizing supplies, equipment, and library methods.

Dewey moved to Boston in 1876 and for six years cultivated his slowly growing garden. During this time the DDC was being developed toward the epochal second edition; the Library Bureau was founded; and he contributed greatly to the modernization of the profession through the *Library Journal.* He also suggested, and with Cutter and Justin Winsor guided, the abortive but brilliant idea of cataloguing data accompanying a book—title-slip registery. We have the idea in practice today—the justly appreciated Cataloging-in-Publication. Dewey had taken that idea originally from one suggested by Natale Battez-

zati in 1871—colored catalogue cards would accompany a book to booksellers so that they could compile various catalogues of their inventory and better serve their patrons. Dewey's borrowing here is a good example of his capacity to recognize a useful idea when he saw one and to meld it with other ideas to produce a method or tool that, though not original in its parts, was new in its totality. Predictably, some resented this capability as much as Dewey's orginality.

On October 26, 1878, Dewey married Annie Godfrey, his companion and adviser for the next half century and mother to his only child, Godfrey Dewey (1887–1977), himself important in librarianship (primarily in his assocation with the DDC). He also contributed to the success of the 1932 Winter Olympics in Lake Placid, New York.

In 1883 Columbia College offered Melvil Dewey the opportunity to develop its library. In doing so he epitomized the schism between scholar and librarian that lasts to this day in strongly centralized academic libraries. Dewey believed—and convinced Columbia's administration—that the library is the heart of the college. His belief led to the growth of the central library that gathers as many books (and therefore as much power) to itself as it can. Many scholars believe, on the other hand, that books in their specialty (preferably just down the hall) promote the scholarship of a faculty that in turn is the heart of a college. The Columbia faculty waited as Dewey combined the diverse subject collections and integrated them through the DDC, created a classed catalogue, extended library service to other users, initiated instruction of users through the reference department, and formulated strict and often restrictive rules for the use of the library. When, in the establishment of a library school at Columbia, 17 of the 20 students to matriculate in the first class in 1887 were women, Dewey's critics saw the chance to rid themselves of the pest in the library. Late in 1888 the trustees voted to suspend him from his duties in the Library but not in the school.

His work done at Columbia, Dewey moved to the next opportunity awaiting him. After being impressed by Dewey's views on the educational role of the library delivered in a speech before them, and being in need of a state librarian, the Regents of the University of the State of New York offered him the post. They were so impressed by his vigor and accomplishments that they also offered him the responsibilities of another vacant post—thus he became both Secretary and Treasurer of the Board, as well as Director of the State Library.

If there was one aspect of life that Dewey loved more than work, it was power. His new positions gave him power and the means to gain more. He used power not primarily for personal gain (except to the extent that he equated himself with his projects) but to further the role of the library as the "People's University." Every action Dewey took furthered the library's role in the schools, colleges, cities, states, and nation (the Library of Congress).

One of Dewey's first acts at Albany was to obtain permission for the transfer of his library school from Columbia to the State Library. There instruction and supervision could be given the students for the work they did in the Library, thus maintaining the means to develop a unified profession through standard methods and a cadre of people to convey them, as well as facilitating the development of the collection and services of the State Library.

While at Albany, Dewey continued to develop the purposes and methods of the profession. (1) Just as he had founded the New York Library Club in 1885, he now was the prime mover in establishing the New York Library Assocation in 1890, the first of the state associations and the model for those to come. (2) The State Library became a reference center and "collection of last resort." (3) He instituted special collections and services for physicians, the blind, women, children, individuals with an interest in social matters and concerns, and even traveling libraries to provide support to libraries throughout the state and to carry libraries to people otherwise without access to books. He also proposed bookmobiles ("book-wagons") for the isolated, especially farmers. (4) He extended acquisitions to materials other than books; pictures, slides, and other media began to flow into the Library. (5) He advocated depository libraries for seldom-used books, centralized cataloguing by the Library of Congress, and national library status for the Library of Congress, to which the nation's libraries could turn for guidance. (6) He pioneered and advocated the use in libraries of such new equipment as the typewriter and the telephone. (7) He served in many professional offices, among them as President of the Association of State Librarians from 1889 to 1892 and as President of ALA in 1890 and 1892–93. For ALA he was instrumental in the success of an excellent library exhibit at the World's Columbian Exposition of 1893. (8) And with his able lieutenants—Walter Stanley Biscoe, Evelyn May Seymour, and Dorcas Fellows—he developed the DDC through its sixth edition. With them he was instrumental in producing the *A.L.A. Catalog: 8,000 Volumes for a Popular Library, with Notes* (1904), yet another standardized and standardizing tool for the profession.

Many of his dreams achieved and many dawning, the profession now well on its way to success in bringing education to the people who cherished and sought it, Dewey was forced to resign his positions as Director of the State Library, the Home Education Department, and the Library School. He had lost a power struggle with Andrew S. Draper, a man who admired neither Dewey nor his views and who had become his superior in 1904. The ostensible cause for his resignation on January 1, 1906, was the flap over the anti-Semitism of the Lake Placid Club, an organization that Dewey had been instrumental in founding and guiding. The actual cause, however, was that Draper sought to strengthen the position of schools at the expense of libraries regardless of the role Dewey wanted them to fulfill. Dewey had to leave or be discredited. Though he did not bring on the adverse criticism himself, Draper did let the criticism take its course, and Dewey was forced to leave.

Dewey was a visionary. Capable of perseverance and extreme dedication, he cared more for results than the particular means and not only was willing to adopt readily new materials and methods but also expected such things to change continually. (Note his attitude toward books and other media for communicating ideas to people and his adoption of the typewriter, the telephone, and other mechanical improvements. He would have equally easily adopted the computer if he were working now. It is important to note that he would have used mechanical means for his ends—he did not adapt his ends to suit the exigencies of the means, a response seen too often in today's library world.) In his writings and speeches he advocated virtually every process that librarianship has come to or is coming to: standardization and cooperation in cataloguing (he envisioned networking); standardization of cataloguing rules (the rules not to be changed unless overwhelming improvement results); the Library of Congress to be the national library; centralized storage; and "fee for service."

Dewey stood for the needs of the user above all; these included the need for information, education, and recreation. Libraries, though they change in nature, should tell the news, answer what and how and why, tell a story, and sing a song.

Scholars of library history have not truly grasped the nature of Melvil Dewey. They refer to him as being complex, charismatic, and any of a host of other terms that tell us little about anyone. The matter is not so complex: Dewey was simply a genius confident in his capacity, a demon for work, and one who took pleasure in acquiring and using power. Those who would be leaders resented or hated him; those who would follow admired or adored him. He was a master politician despite his abrasive nature; rarely did he not bring people to do what he wanted them to do—the battles he lost (Columbia, Albany) were to overwhelming odds. Nor did he accept defeat or frustration ungraciously. He did not like to lose, but he was too smart to let it show; there would always be another day. But after January 1, 1906, there was not another day. Dewey died in Lake Placid, New York, December 26, 1931.

Though Dewey never fully left his work in librarianship, his semiretirement to the Lake Placid Club removed from librarianship its strongest advocate, its most original designer, and its most effective organizer. Perhaps his leaving was not so great a loss as it was a shame; his work may have been done. One may believe, however, that had he continued, libraries would have become more central to education than they were to come to be. Dewey knew that knowing was better than not knowing, that any means to knowledge were good means if they produced enlightened leaders and citizens, and that the profession had to work hard and together to bring knowledge through books or other media. Where we work hard and together, Dewey lives.

REFERENCES

The only biography of Dewey worth consulting is Sarah K. Vann's in *Melvil Dewey, His Enduring Presence in Librarianship* (1978), from which for this article most of the facts of Dewey's life have been drawn. The book presenting the full impact of Dewey upon librarianship and other undertakings has not been written.

Melvil Dewey: The Man and the Classification (Forest Press, 1983), while adding nothing new biographically, fills a great gap regarding Dewey's professional life.

Sarah K. Vann, "Dewey Melvil," *Dictionary of American Library Biography* (1978).

JOHN P. COMAROMI

Dix, William S.
(1910–1978)

William Shepherd Dix, Librarian of Princeton University from 1953 until 1975, was honored widely for contributions to library and academic communities. He did not have a library science degree, but he *became* a librarian by *being* one. His character and scholarship fitted him peculiarly to bridge the gap between the user and the library. He matched the tradition of gentleman with a strong sensitiveness to each individual's needs.

Born on November 19, 1910, in Winchester, Virginia, Dix grew up in Berryville, Virginia, and Hagerstown, Maryland. In 1931 he graduated with honors from the University of Virginia and took his M.A. in English there the following year.

He began his career in the Darlington School for Boys in Rome, Georgia, as a teacher of English from 1932 to 1939 and went on to teach at Western Reserve University (now Case Western Reserve University), Cleveland, and Williams College, Williamstown, Massachusetts, before going to Harvard in 1944 on the staff of the wartime Radio Research Laboratory. When the Laboratory was disbanded in 1946, he taught for one year at Harvard and completed his Ph.D. in American Literature at the University of Chicago.

In 1947 Dix became an English instructor at Rice Institute (now Rice University) in Houston and the next year accepted the additional assignment of directing the school's library. He was an Associate Professor of English and Librarian when he left Rice in 1953 to head the Princeton University Library. He was Princeton's 22d Librarian and had served 22 years when he retired in 1975.

Dix's considerable activities outside his daily obligations were apparent early. During his two years at Western Reserve he became Director of the Committee on Private Research. His book, *The Amateur Spirit in Scholarship* (Western Reserve University Press, 1942), describes the work of that body, whose purpose was to promote amateur activities in scholarly and creative research.

During the Princeton years, he served the campus, the Association of Research Libraries, the American Library Association, the New Jersey Library Association, library causes in Washington and in other countries, and other libraries in advisory capacities. In 1970 he was called on to preside over disciplinary hearings at Princeton following campus disruptions protesting U.S. involvement in the Vietnam War. He kept the hearings on course through angry turmoil with a clear sense of the fundamental purposes of a university.

He served the Association of Research Libraries in a variety of capacities, including a part-time appointment from 1957 to 1959 as its first Executive Secretary when it was moving toward permanent headquarters and a full-time Executive Director. In the 1960s, in a service of lasting importance to library users, he chaired the ARL Committee on Shared Cataloging, which influenced Congress to include Title II-C in the Higher Education Act of 1965. This provision enables the Library of Congress under the National Program for Acquisitions and Cataloging to assist libraries by acquiring and cataloguing promptly the world's scholarly publications. His skill in appearing as a witness before Congressional committees was useful on other occasions in fostering legislation of value to library service.

Dix carried out a wide range of assignments in ALA and its units. As Chair of the ALA Intellectual Freedom Committee during the divisive and fearful McCarthy period, he was the principal drafter of the Association's declaration on "The Freedom to Read," a statement adopted jointly by the American Book Publishers Council (now the Association of American Publishers) and subsequently endorsed by 21 other organizations. The importance he attached to a free society is stated there:

> Freedom has given the United States the elasticity to endure strain. Freedom keeps open the path of novel and creative solutions, and enables change to come by choice. Every silencing of a heresy, every enforcement of an orthodoxy, diminishes the toughness and resilience of our society and leaves it the less able to deal with stress.

His chairing of the ALA International Relations Board was the beginning of a number of international assignments: Consultant to the Ford Foundation, Baghdad, 1958; member of the U.S. Delegation to the Unesco General Conference, Paris, 1958 and 1960, serving as Vice-Chairman of the Delegation, 1960; U.S. Delegate to the Conference of Asian National Commissions for Unesco, Manila, 1961; Asian-American Assembly, Kuala Lumpur, 1963; and U.S. Department of State Government Advisory Committee on International Book and Library Programs, 1967–69.

Dix's long-time involvement in library matters reached a climax with his service as the ALA President, 1969–70, a crucial year. It was a time of national conflict between the complacency of the old ways and the new demands for meeting social obligations. To the task of preserving the Association while providing for change, he brought his propensity to see each side of a controversy, his firmly based belief in tolerance for differing viewpoints, his concern for the individual, and his evenhanded leadership.

He was a member of the American Council of Learned Societies committee to propose programs to meet the needs of American research libraries and of the Boards of Directors of the H. W. Wilson Company and of the Franklin Book Programs. He served on advisory bodies for the New Jersey State Library, Rutgers University Graduate School of Library and Information Studies, the libraries of Duke and Harvard Universities, and the Association of American University Presses. At the time of his death, he was a member of the Board of Directors of the Council on Library Resources and of the National Commission on New Technological Uses of Copyrighted Works, the latter body working for agreement among divergent interests relating to copyright.

Dix's deportment and his public addresses probably influenced his colleagues as much as his many published articles, convincing others through the force of his well-reasoned positions. Although ill with terminal cancer during the last ten months of his life (he died in Princeton on February 22, 1978), he worked diligently on his retirement project of writing the history of the Princeton University Library—work that he had often put aside to meet his com-

Princeton University Library
William S. Dix

mitment to public groups. He was able to complete "The Princeton University Library in the Eighteenth Century," which was published as volume 40, number 1 (Autumn 1978), of *The Princeton University Library Chronicle,* and as a separate monograph by the Library. It is a worthy legacy, embodying his scholarship and his felicitous way with words.

Many honors came to him: honorary doctorates from the University of Florida and Washington College; the New Jersey Library Association's Distinguished Service Award; ALA's Melvil Dewey and Lippincott Awards and its highest honor, an Honorary Membership.

HELEN WELCH TUTTLE

Djibouti

The Republic of Djibouti, formerly French Somaliland and subsequently the French Territory of the Afars and the Issas, became independent in June 1977. It lies south of a narrow strait linking the Gulf of Aden to the Red Sea and is bordered on the southeast by Somalia and on the south, west, and northwest by Ethopia. Population (1984 est.) 324,000; area 23,000 sq.km. The official language is Arabic, and French is widely spoken.

The only significant libraries open to the public are one in the French Cultural Center and the Arab Maritime Academy library. The former opened in the capital of Djibouti in June 1978 with a collection of 8,000 books. The Arab Maritime Academy has about 8,500 volumes and 180 current periodicals. There is also a Documentation Center with a collection of materials relating to Djibouti; the collection consists primarily of periodical articles. There are small working library collections in some government ministries.

Dominican Republic

The Dominican Republic occupies the eastern section of the island of Hispaniola in the Caribbean Sea. Haiti occupies the western section, with a chain of mountains in between. Population (1984 est.) 6,102,000; area, 48,442 sq.km. The official language is Spanish.

History. The Spaniards were the first Europeans to inhabit the Caribbean Islands, and many people assume that they first used the printing press there, but such was not the case. In all probability, they utilized the printing facilities on the mainland or in Spain itself. Nothing related to the colonies at that time could be printed without the permission of the Indies Council.

No one knows for sure the date of the introduction of the printing press on the island of Hispaniola. Some historians believe that a press was used in the 17th century, but no evidence exists to that effect. The first references come from Moreau de Saint-Mery, who, in 1783, mentioned the existence of a printing press, located in the Royal Court of Justice, "the place designated by law as the residence of the President of the Royal Court of Justice, depository of the royal seal, the archives of the Secretariat, and also the printing press and the prison." The first extant imprint dates from the year 1800 and was produced by a Frenchman, Andres Josef Blocquerst, who had come to the island around 1782: *Novena para implorar*

la protección de María Santísima por medio de su imagen de Altagracia

Little is known of libraries during the colonial era. The first reference to a public library appeared in 1860, slightly more than 15 years after the founding of the Republic (1844). The library in question was organized in the Government Palace through the donation of the private library of Rafael María Baralt, a Venezuelan jurist and writer who lived for a time in the city of Santo Domingo. But his bibliographical treasures were not destined for good fortune: in 1876 they were removed to the Saint Thomas Aquinas Seminary, under the protection of the "Friends of the Nation Society," and by 1904 its contents had been scattered.

That public library was followed in the city of Santiago de los Caballeros by the libraries of the Amantes de la Luz Atheneum (1874) and the Alianza Cibaeña (1888), and by the library of the atheneum in San Pedro de Macorís (1890).

In June 1884 the National Congress created a depository for the conservation of editions produced by the state—the first known reference to a legal depository law. On September 26 of the same year, the National Congress created the position of Public Archivist based on the principle that "it was necessary to create a public office through which could be deposited all of the works, documents, and certificates that constitute the Archives of the Secretariats of State and of the other offices." The Archives were located in the main hall of the Municipal Council Building.

The founding of libraries throughout the country continued in the 20th century. The Gabriel A. Morillo Public Library was established in the town of Moca (1904), followed in other cities by the Baní Public Library (1920), the Santo Domingo Municipal Library (1922), and the Restoration Society Public Library in Puerto Plata (1928). The year 1927 saw the founding of the National Museum and Library, considered as one unit.

The period from 1930 to 1960, encompassing the 30-year dictatorship of Rafael L. Trujillo, was an important one for library development in the country. The General Archives of the Nation appeared in 1935. In 1939 the first professional librarian arrived in the Dominican Republic: the Spaniard Luis Florén Lozano (1913-1973). Florén lived in Santo Domingo from 1939 until 1953, during which he was Director of the Library of the University of Santo Domingo. He gave a technical stamp to library development in the Dominican Republic. With his arrival came a resurgence of public libraries, bibliographic activities that resulted in the first national bibliographies, the first training courses for archivists and librarians, and the first book fairs in the country.

By 1956 there were 110 public libraries in the country that served 425,874 users. The period of greatest growth was in 1959, which saw a total of 136 libraries serving 569,903 users.

The 1960s saw a period of political and economic instability in the Dominican Republic. After the death of Trujillo in 1960 and the civil war that followed in 1965, the country underwent a recession that was keenly felt in the nation's libraries. The number of libraries decreased and their collections deteriorated rapidly—heavy use and looting characterized the period. The lack of economic assistance made it difficult to keep book collections up to date.

The decade of the 1970s marked a new era for Dominican librarianship. Beginning in 1970, the first group of Dominican professional librarians, 10 in number, returned to the country. Florén, who had directed the Inter-American School of Librarianship in Medellín, Colombia, from 1959, was named as adviser to the recently created National Library. Courses for library assistants were begun and the Dominican Association of Librarians was created. The first special libraries began to emerge, but public and school libraries continued without support because of lack of interest on the part of the government. All in all, this was one of those crucial periods in library development when, little by little, the importance of library services in national development came to be appreciated.

The National Library and National Archives. The National Library was originally founded in 1927 as the National Museum and Library. From its beginning it maintained a precarious existence; it was the National Library in name only because its functions were actually carried out by the Library of the University of Santo Domingo for the period 1947-71. The Copyright Law of 1948 required the deposit of two copies of all printed materials in the Central Library of the University of Santo Domingo and two copies in the General Archives of the Nation.

In 1969 the National Library received authorization to construct its own building, which was inaugurated in 1971. A law on Legal Deposit was promulgated in 1971, overturning the law of 1948 and designating the National Library as the only depository for the national printed output. The law mandates the deposit of two copies of periodicals, monographs, and similar printed materials, and one copy of phonograph records, under penalty of fine. In 1982 the National Congress modified the legal deposit law to include the Libraries of the National Congress and the National Archives in addition to the National Library.

The National Library reports to the Presidency of the Republic. It is organized into five departments: Administrative Services, Technical Processes, Periodicals, National Bibliography, and Public Services. It maintains a collection of 345,424 volumes and publishes a current national bibliography entitled *Anuario Bibliográfico* (No. 1, 1978-).

Although the position of General Archivist dates from the year 1884, the modern organization of the General Archives of the Nation began with the promulgation in 1935 of a law designed to ensure the orderly conservation of all documents published by the state, which constitute an important source of historical data on the country.

The mission of the General Archives is the conservation, organization, and diffusion of all documents and certificates emanating from the archives of the various offices and branches of the state, as well as all the relevant historical documents that can be acquired. Its role is determined by decrees that establish the system of organization and conservation of its holdings and regulate the transfer of documents to it.

The Archives consists of seven departments: Administration, Research, Dissemination, Archives, Pre-Archives, Library and Periodicals, and Technical Services. The dates of its holdings range from 1600 to 1979. Colonial documents are represented by the valuable collections of the Royal Archives of Bayaguana and Higüey. The Periodicals Section contains a valuable collection of Dominican newspapers, including the first to be published in the country: *El Telégrafo Constitucional de Santo Domingo* (1821) and *El Duende* (1821). The Archives publishes the *Boletín del Archivo General de la Nación* (No. 1, March 1938-).

Two other important archives should be mentioned: the Historical Archives of Santiago, located in the city of Santiago de los Caballeros and containing documents pertaining to that city, and the National Archives of Music.

Academic Libraries. There are eight institutions of higher learning with libraries. The largest and oldest is the Autonomous University of Santo Domingo (UASD), formerly the University of Santo Domingo, which was founded as far back as 1538, although its present library dates from 1927. As of 1983, the library contained 260,000 volumes of books and pamphlets and 5,000 periodical titles. Its period of greatest growth was from 1940 to 1960, due in part to the Copyright Law of 1948 that called for the deposit of two copies of all works published in the Dominican Republic. From 1948 to 1971 it functioned, for all practical purposes, as the National Library. During the period 1944-52 it averaged 40,000 titles in annual acquisitions. It maintains an exchange program with the Library of Congress of the United States and is the official depository for U.S. government publications.

Under the direction of Florén, the UASD library became the National Bibliographic Center, publish-

Libraries in Dominican Republic (1983)

Type	Administrative units	Service points	Volumes in collections	Annual expenditures (peso)	Population served	Professional staff	Total staff
National	1	--	345,424	500,000	131,782	12	143
Academic	8	6	488,300	1,408,409	985,996	25	194
Public	15	--	9,377	271,587	97,255	0	54
School	55	--	53,053	--	--	0	--
Special[b]	7	--	51,160	361,666	71,546	19	58

[a]In some library budgets, the only information provided is the amount allocated for materials.
[b]Statistics based on those provided by seven libraries: CEDOPEX, INDOTEC, the Dominican Financial Company, CENADOA, the Dominican Society of Bibliophiles, the Central Bank, and the Panamerican Health Office.

ing a number of bibliographies, including the *Bibliografía dominicana, Bibliografía histórica dominicana,* and *Bibliografía de los profesores universitarios.* Its collection of journals, newspapers, books, theses, and pamphlets is one of the richest in the country, especially in materials relating to the Dominican Republic.

Of the 65 employees in the UASD library, 7 were professionals in 1985. In addition to the Central Library, the university has five other departmental libraries: Economics, Engineering and Architecture, Agronomy and Veterinary Science, Humanities, and Law and Political Science. The university also maintains libraries at the four regional campuses: the Northwest Regional University Center (CURNO), located in Mao, with an extension in the city of Santiago Rodríguez; Southwest Regional University Center (CURSO) in Barahona; Northeast Regional University Center (CURNE) in San Francisco de Macorís; and Eastern Regional University Center (CURE) in Higüey.

Some 60 percent of the nation's professional librarians work in university libraries, and this concentration is reflected in both the services offered by the university libraries and the importance assigned to them. A good sign is the increasing number of library buildings that have already been constructed or are under construction; these buildings represent large investments in furniture and equipment. The most notable of these is the modern building of the Central Library of the Eastern Central University (UCE) in San Pedro de Macorís. Inaugurated in 1981, this library had a collection of 45,000 volumes in 1985 as well as modern audiovisual equipment.

The library of the Pedro Henríquez Ureña University (UNPHU), founded in 1966, has 45,000 volumes and publishes an acquisitions bulletin entitled *Biblionotas.* The Santo Domingo Technical Institute (INTEC) maintains a collection of 35,000 volumes, and the quality of both materials and services of the library is considered outstanding. Among those services is selective dissemination of information (SDI) in the areas of pure sciences, technology, humanities, social sciences, and biomedical sciences. Three other institutions—the Catholic University, Mother and Teacher (UCMM); the World University; and the Institute of Advanced Studies—maintain collections of 70,000, 5,300, and 12,000, respectively.

Public Libraries. The government of the Dominican Republic showed little interest in the creation and development of public libraries, with the exception of the city of Santo Domingo. The mayor in the early 1980s, José Francisco Peña Gómez, promised to build 50 public libraries for the *barrio.* After assuming office, Peña Gómez created an Office for Public Libraries in the municipal government to carry out his electoral promises. In 1982 and 1983, 15 such libraries were founded in various neighborhoods, with collections ranging from fewer than 400 to more than 1,000 volumes. The Office for Public Libraries is responsible for planning, organizing, and directing this system of libraries. All materials are centrally processed by a classification system developed by the new unit. The collections consist of school textbooks ranging from the first grade through the first year of college, as well as small general collections made up of encyclopedias and dictionaries.

The private sector contributed to library devel-

opment through the founding, in 1979, of the Children's Pilot Library, directed by a women's group called the Bibliophile Circle. It has a collection of 3,900 volumes and by 1983 had been visited by 27,600 children. It has a small permanent staff.

In the city of Puerto Plata the Restoration Society carries out a number of cultural activities involving the public library, including the preservation of the city's historical monuments.

School Libraries. The Dominican Republic is almost completely lacking in school libraries. The few there are tend to be small and dependent on the goodwill of donors, and therefore do not relate to the curricula or reflect principles of good selection. Those who tend these libraries rely, in large part, on their own experience; since they have had no training in library science, both technical processes and public services suffer accordingly. Of the 5,200 educational institutions in the country, only 115 (2.2 percent) had libraries in the mid-1980s.

In 1983 the State Secretary of Education, Fine Arts, and Culture carried out a study that provided the following results: (1) not a single collection can be considered up to date; (2) without specially constructed facilities of their own, the libraries have to operate out of classrooms or administrative offices; (3) the collections consist almost entirely of textbooks, most of them ranging between 125 and 5,000 volumes with only one at more than 7,000 volumes; (4) no library has adequate furniture or open stacks; and (5) the librarians have no professional preparation. As for technical processes, no collection is processed systematically; no library maintains a file of users; and no one maintains control over book acquisitions. As for services, the basic function of these libraries is to lend books only within the reading room.

A national system of school libraries was proposed as a project of international technical assistance. A beginning point has been that of providing school library training to 276 persons, who will assume responsibility for organizing and providing modern services in the proposed network. Also under way in 1985 was a system of movable libraries designed to reach unserved populations and to support curriculum and teaching in the frontier areas of the country.

Special Libraries. This type of library began to appear in the Dominican Republic around 1975 and since then a number of important special libraries have emerged. One of them is the Scientific and Technical Information Center (CENICIT) of the Dominican Institute of Industrial Technology (INDOTEC), which is part of the Central Bank of the Dominican Republic, specializing in industrial technology with special emphasis on the technology of food production. CENICIT consists of two divisions: the Library, with 6,000 books and 600 periodical titles; and the Division of Technical Information, which contains documents, a database, reference services for technical questions, an area on standards and patents, an area on publications, and a section dealing with catalogues and directories of equipment and machinery. CENICIT is the Dominican representative of the National Technical Information Service (NTIS).

The Dominican Center for Export Promotion (CEDOPEX), which specializes in international commerce, maintains an information center with 8,104 books and 400 periodical titles and uses the commercial information system of the International Commerce Center of the United Nations.

The National Center for Agricultural Information (CENADOA) belongs to the Department of Information, Statistics, and Computation under the Secretary of Agriculture and was created in 1978. CENADOA is the national coordinator of the Interamerican System for Agricultural Information on Latin America and the Caribbean (AGRINTER/IICA) and the International Information System on Agricultural Science and Related Technologies (AGRIS/FAO). Its information center has a collection of 4,575 volumes and 712 journal titles. It offers a program of training and technical assistance to agricultural libraries belonging to the National Network of Agricultural Information.

The Enrique Apolinar Henríqez Library of the Dominican Society of Bibliophiles maintains a collection consisting of 3,279 volumes, specializing in Dominican history, literature, and related fields. The Society publishes a collection on Dominican culture, featuring previously unpublished works and first editions that have special significance for Dominican history and culture.

The Dominican Financial Company maintains a library that specializes in finance and agro-industry, with a collection of 2,463 books and 6,789 documents and journals.

Libraries also exist in the National Office of Statistics (ONE), the Advanced Institute of Agriculture (ISA) in Santiago, the Central Bank of the Dominican Republic, the Dominican Electric Corporation (CDE), and the Reserve Bank of the Dominican Republic.

The Profession. Library education in the Dominican Republic dates from the decade of the 1940s, when the Faculty of Philosophy of what is now the Autonomous University of Santo Domingo included librarianship as an area of study in the undergraduate and graduate studies in philosophy. A number of outstanding professionals set out on the long road of organizing the nation's libraries and compiling bibliographies. A large number of them were concentrated in the library of the Autonomous University of Santo Domingo.

A School of Librarians and Archivists was created as part of the Faculty of Philosophy and Education in 1960. It was abolished in 1966 as one of a number of changes in academic units. Although the School never actually functioned, its creation reflected an awareness of the need for such a program.

Beginning in 1967 the same university and the Catholic University sponsored the professional training of a group of young people to study at the Interamerican School of Librarianship in Medellín, Colombia, thus providing the first large group of professional librarians for the country.

In the 1970s formal courses were offered at the national level by the Catholic University, the Eastern Central University, the National Office of Personnel Administration, and the Dominican Association of Librarians. In addition, the School of Librarianship was created in the Dominican World University in 1979. It offers the Licenciate in Librarianship.

A total of 17 courses were offered for library

paraprofessionals for no less than 450 persons by the mid-1980s. The General Archives of the Nation offered two courses for paraprofessionals in archives for some 40 persons. They attained the title of Technical Assistant in Archives.

The Dominican Association of Librarians, Inc. (ASODOBI), was founded on November 28, 1974. Its primary objective is to promote the extension of library services throughout the country. It consists of a General Assembly and an Executive Committee of five persons. As of 1978 it had 32 members. It publishes *El Papiro* (1976-) and has its headquarters in the National Library. Membership is open to both paraprofessionals and professional librarians.

The Association of University Libraries was formed upon a resolution of the National Council of Institutions of Higher Education (CONIES) on October 3, 1978. Its objective is the creation of a system to coordinate the development of university library collections by avoiding duplication of effort and resources and establishing channels of communications among the member libraries.

MARISOL FLORÉN;
translated by EDWIN S. GLEAVES

Downs, Robert B.
(1903–   )

Robert Bingham Downs combined the careers of library administrator and library educator with outstanding leadership in professional library organizations and a remarkable publication record of books and articles.

Downs was born May 25, 1903, on a farm near Lenoir, North Carolina, where he attended a one-room country school for seven years. In 1917 his family moved to Asheville, North Carolina, where he discovered the Asheville public library and started a lifelong addiction to reading. But a career in librarianship had no place in his plans then, and formal education was abandoned after one year of high school. After a variety of jobs—including construction worker, fire ranger, telephone repairman, and ranch hand in Wyoming—he returned to graduate from Trinity High School in Durham.

He entered the University of North Carolina at Chapel Hill in 1922. As a student assistant in the University Library, he came under the influence of Louis Round Wilson. Receiving his A.B. in 1926, Downs enrolled in the School of Library Service at Columbia, where he received his B.S. in L.S. degree in 1927 and the M.S. in 1929. From 1927 to 1929 he was a reference assistant in the New York Public Library.

In 1929 he became Librarian of Colby College and two years later returned to the University of North Carolina to become Assistant Librarian under Louis Round Wilson. When Wilson became Dean of the Graduate Library School at the University of Chicago in 1932, Downs was made Acting Librarian and the following year was appointed University Librarian and Professor of Library Science. During the next five years he developed strong library collections, instituted a program of duplicate exchanges, and taught bibliography, history of books, and reference in the library school. He also began his studies in the cooperative development of library resources

ALA

Robert B. Downs

255

and, with Harvie Branscomb of Duke University, developed a plan for sharing responsibility for collecting research materials between the neighboring university libraries. His first major book, *The Resources of Southern Libraries,* was published in 1938.

The same year he was appointed Director of Libraries of New York University with the task of coordinating seven quasi-independent libraries of the University. There he centralized the technical services departments, developed a union catalogue, and reorganized the staff and services of the Washington Square Library. During this period he published his *Resources of New York City Libraries* (1942), a series of three annual surveys of "Notable Materials Added to American Libraries" in *Library Quarterly* (1940–42), and *Union Catalogs in the United States* (1942).

In 1943 he was appointed Director of Libraries and of the Library School at the University of Illinois, a dual appointment he held until his retirement 27 years later. He was designated Dean of Library Administration in 1958. At Illinois he reorganized the library staff and secured faculty rank and status for librarians, a task that earlier directors had attempted unsuccessfully. The book collection, already a notable one in many fields, grew to more than 4,000,000 volumes. Under his direction, the Library School introduced a doctoral program, a series of Windsor Lectures (honoring Director-Emeritus P. L. Windsor) to bring outstanding bookmen to the campus, the annual Allerton Park Institutes, and two serial publications, *Library Trends* (1952–) and *Occasional Papers* (1949–).

Downs served the University in many extralibrary activities: Chairman of the Land Grant Centennial Committee, Vice-Chairman of the University Centennial Committee, Chairman of the Senate Committee on Honorary Degrees, Chairman of the University Concert and Entertainment Board, and President of the University Chapters of Phi Beta Kappa and Phi Kappa Phi.

Downs's continuing interest in the definition and description of library resources led to the publication of his *American Library Resources: A Bibliographical Guide* in 1951, with supplementary volumes in 1962, 1972, and 1981. *Resources of Canadian Academic and Research Libraries* appeared in 1967, and after his retirement a Guggenheim Fellowship enabled him to spend a year in England to gather information for his *British Library Resources* (1973). A similar survey of Australian and New Zealand library resources was published in 1979.

Downs conducted more than 30 surveys of libraries and groups of libraries, beginning with the survey of Cornell University Libraries (with Louis R. Wilson and Maurice F. Tauber) in 1948. He was responsible for surveys of the libraries of the University of Utah (1965), the University of Georgia (1966), Purdue University (1967), and Brigham Young University (1969). He conducted state library surveys for North Carolina, Missouri, Arkansas, and Illinois and shorter reports on libraries ranging from the Library Company of Philadelphia (1940) to the libraries of the Kansas City Regional Council for Education (1964).

At the end of World War II Downs served as a consultant to libraries and library schools overseas. In 1948 he went to Japan as adviser to the U.S. Military Government on the establishment of the National Diet Library and two years later returned to help establish a library school at Keio University. In Mexico he was consultant to the National Library and the University of Mexico in 1952. He served in a similar capacity in Turkey in 1955, 1968, and 1971; in 1963 he was consultant for a new library at Kabul University, Afghanistan. He lectured at Brazilian libraries and library schools at São Paulo, Rio de Janeiro, and Belo Horizonte in 1961 and was adviser to the Interamerican Library School at Medellín, Colombia, in 1964. He was consultant to the Library of the University of Puerto Rico for the establishment of its library school, 1964–65, and in 1973 he was consultant for the University of Tunis.

Active in professional organizations throughout his career, Downs served as President of the Association of College and Research Libraries (1940–41) and as President of the American Library Association (1952–53). He was also President of the Illinois Library Association (1955–56).

In addition to his professional writings, which cover most areas of librarianship, Downs wrote eight popular books, all of which link books and reading with notable persons. His *Books That Changed the World* (ALA, 1956) was translated into a dozen languages. Later books include *Famous Books Ancient and Modern* (1964), *Books That Changed America* (1970), *Books That Changed the South* (1977), *In Search of New Horizons* (1978), *Landmarks in Science* (1982), and *Memorable Americans* (1983, with John T. Flanagan and Harold W. Scott).

His interest in American humor and folklore led to an early booklet on *American Humor* (1938), written with Elizabeth Downs; one on *American Humorous Folklore* (1950); one of the Windsor Lectures published in 1958 as *The Family Saga;* and a collection of stories, *The Bear Went Over the Mountain* (1964). Later he wrote *Horace Mann* (1974), *Heinrich Pestalozzi* (1975), *Henry Barnard* (1977), and *Friedrich Froebel* (1978). *The First Freedom Today,* a revision of his 1960 book, was published by ALA in 1984.

Honors came to him from many quarters. The Association of American Publishers gave him the Clarence Day Award in 1963. The ALA conferred its Joseph W. Lippincott Award in 1964 and its Melvil Dewey Award in 1974. He received the Illinois Library Association's Librarian of the Year Award in 1972 and the Syracuse University Centennial Medal. He was awarded honorary degrees by Colby College, the University of North Carolina, Ohio State University, Southern Illinois University, and the University of Illinois. In 1979 he shared the first ACRL Academic Research Librarian of the Year Award with Keyes D. Metcalf.

REFERENCES
Jerrold Orne, editor, *Research Librarianship: Essays in Honor of Robert B. Downs (1971),* contains a biography by Robert F. Delzell and a bibliography of Downs's publications.
Arthur Young, "Bestriding the Profession; Robert Bingham Downs and Academic Librarianship," *Leaders in American Academic Librarianship* (1983).
Robert B. Downs, *Perspectives on the Past; an Autobiography* (1984).

JOE W. KRAUS

Dunkin, Paul S.
(1905–1975)

As a library practitioner of merit, a philosopher of cataloguing theory and practice, a writer of pithy commentary, and a stimulating teacher, Paul Shaner Dunkin earned the recognition and respect of the library profession. His ability to strip away pretense and lay bare a problem in simple, direct fashion served the profession well during the period of library growth after World War II.

Born on September 28, 1905, in Flora, Indiana, he eventually traveled throughout the United States and abroad, and lived much of his life on the Atlantic Coast. But Dunkin remained true to his midwestern heritage, returning finally to Indiana to live after retirement from his active career. Dunkin's undergraduate work at DePauw University in Indiana led to an A.B. degree in 1929. As a Phi Beta Kappa student, he found his greatest interests to lie in English literature and the classics. Dunkin pursued classical studies further in the completion of an M.A. in 1931 and a Ph.D. in 1937, both awarded by the University of Illinois. The relatively long interval between those two advanced degrees is explained by Dunkin's move in 1935 from Graduate Assistant in classics to Cataloger for the University of Illinois Library. He obtained the B.S. in Library Science from the University in that year.

Dunkin was able to combine his classical scholarship and love of English literature with his interest in librarianship through an appointment in 1937 as Senior Cataloger at the Folger Shakespeare Library in Washington, D.C., a position he held until 1950, when he was promoted to Chief of Technical Services. Those who recognized Dunkin's continued interest in academe were perhaps not so startled as some of his other colleagues when he decided to leave the Folger Library in 1959 to assume responsibilities as Professor in the Graduate School of Library Service at Rutgers. Although the move signaled a dramatic change in focus, Dunkin's scholarly bent continued to be served as he directed masters' studies and doctoral research at Rutgers. He taught during the deanship of Ralph R. Shaw, as well as during portions of the terms of Lowell Martin and Neal Harlow. Under Shaw's leadership, the Ph.D. program in library service was initiated at Rutgers, thus allowing the Dunkin imprint to be felt by a number of the subsequent administrators and teachers in librarianship and information services.

In addition to his teaching, Dunkin became increasingly active in the work of the library profession, especially through his responsibilities in the American Library Association. While still at the Folger Library, he had completed his first library monography, *How to Catalog a Rare Book* (1951), and had begun his critique of the approach proposed by Seymour Lubetzky for the development of the *Anglo-American Cataloging Rules* while Lubetzky was serving as Editor of the code. Dunkin's 1956 paper, "Criticisms of Current Cataloging Practice," written for the 21st conference of the Graduate Library School of the University of Chicago, initiated a series of discussions and reflections that appeared under his name during the 1950s and 1960s.

Among the more significant of Dunkin's writings were his commentary on Lubetzky's *Code of Cataloging Rules* (1960), his "year's work" papers in *Library Resources & Technical Services* reviewing the developments in cataloguing and classification (1958–66), and his book *Cataloging U.S.A.* (1969). Although his commentaries tended to focus on the American scene, he participated in the International Conference on Cataloguing Principles in Paris in 1961 and continued to reflect on the impact of the "Paris Principles" throughout his subsequent writings.

Dunkin's style was filled with classical allusions as well as references to homely, everyday events. He was especially fond of making satirical comments about the pretensions of librarians and the preoccupations of cataloguers—a predilection that endeared him to some and caused others to react in annoyance and sometimes hostility. Despite the sharpness of his wit and the barbs ever present in his papers, Dunkin was a gentle companion and in later life gave the impression of being somewhat frail. The keen analytical mind was sometimes betrayed by the body; for example, a badly broken bone caused by a fall prevented him from serving an active term as President of the Resources and Technical Services Division of ALA.

As a result of his visibility in the field of cataloguing, Dunkin was elected and appointed to many posts in the ALA. When Esther Piercy, the founding editor of *Library Resources & Technical Services,* died in 1967, Dunkin was selected to assume her responsibilities. Meanwhile, he was also contributing the "Viewpoint" column for *Library Journal.* Not surprisingly, then, Dunkin became the recipient of the Margaret Mann Citation in 1968, awarded by the Cataloging and Classification Section of ALA. Noted as "elder statesman with a refreshingly young perspective," Dunkin was commended for his "modestly-worn erudition, grace and wit."

There is some difficulty in assessing the peculiar quality of Dunkin's contributions to library service and particularly to cataloguing. He was more of an interpreter than an innovator. He tried to codify, simplify, and encourage iconoclasm among his students and colleagues. By sometimes amusing and occasionally outraging his readers, he hoped to make them reflect upon their activities and avoid taking themselves too seriously. Dunkin also rejected the "cataloguing manual" mentality, preferring to recapture the philosophical approach that he so much appreciated in the works of Charles Ammi Cutter. Interestingly, in *Cataloging U.S.A.* Dunkin quietly avoided mention of the plethora of cataloguing texts published in the 1940s and 1950s, perhaps in the hope that they might not even warrant a footnote in cataloguing history.

After retiring in 1971, Dunkin was designated Professor Emeritus at Rutgers. He told his friends, however, that he intended to take no further role in professional organizations and to make no postretirement speeches. His collected essays, *Tales of Melvil's Mouser; or Much Ado about Librarians,* had appeared in 1970 at the end of his teaching career. In 1973 the second edition of *How to Catalog a Rare Book* was published. Then, in 1975, his final work, *Bibliography: Tiger or Fat Cat?,* was released; Dunkin's death in Indianapolis, Indiana, on August 25, 1975, preceded the official publication of that last volume.

Carleton F. Smith

Paul S. Dunkin

REFERENCES

Doralyn J. Hickey, "Paul Shaner Dunkin, 28 September 1905–25 August 1975: An Appreciation," *Library Resources & Technical Services* (1975).

Doralyn J. Hickey, "Dunkin, Paul Shaner," *Dictionary of American Library Biography* (1978).

Norman D. Stevens, "The Writings of Paul S. Dunkin: A Review Article," *Library Resources & Technical Services* (1978).

DORALYN J. HICKEY

Dziatzko, Karl
(1842–1903)

Karl Franz Otto Dziatzko was a prominent figure in the reform of Prussian librarianship that took place under the aegis of Friedrich Althoff (1839–1908), the Prussian Minister of Culture. The centralized authority of the libraries of the 10 Prussian universities was such as to facilitate cooperative projects such as union catalogues, cataloguing standards, interlibrary loan networks, standard administrative procedures, and requirements for the education and certification of professional librarians. Besides doing extensive research in the history of the book, printing, and philology, Dziatzko was deeply involved in these library developments.

Dziatzko was born on January 27, 1842, in Neustadt, a small town in Upper Silesia, then part of Prussia. He was educated at the Catholic Grammar School (*Gymnasium*) in Oppeln (now Opole in Poland). An early enthusiasm for language and mathematics gave way to what was to become a lifelong devotion to classical philology. He entered the University of Breslau (now University of Wroclaw) in 1859. After three years he moved to the University of Bonn, where he was influenced by the philologist and librarian Friedrich Ritschl (1806–76). A student in Ritschl's seminar, Dziatzko also worked in the library under Ritschl's direction. Graduating in 1863, with a dissertation on Plautus and Terence, he began his professional career as a teacher.

His early academic career was a restless one that first took him back to Oppeln and then to Lucerne, Switzerland. For a very brief period he was Director of the University Library at Freiburg (Baden) and then Director of a grammar school in Karlsruhe. The decisive turning point in his career came in 1872 when he was appointed Director of the University Library in Breslau. In 1886 he was appointed Director of the Library and Professor of Library Science at the University of Göttingen.

His administrative reforms at Breslau were regarded as a model for other German universities. His rules for the revision of the catalogue at Breslau subsequently became the basis of the *Prussian Instructions (Preussische Instruktionen),* which was first published in 1899, revised in 1908, and reprinted by Harrossowitz in 1966. It was translated into English by Andrew D. Osborn (University of Michigan Press, 1938). He was a key figure in the founding of the German Library Association (Verein Deutscher Bibliothekare) in 1900. His lectures and seminars on librarianship at Göttingen were the beginning of library education in Germany. He founded and edited the series *Sammlung Bibliothekswissenschaftlicher Arbeiten,* which was remarkable for the broad scope of its definition of library sciences. When, in 1893, by Althoff's decree, professional certification became mandatory in Prussia, Dziatzko was appointed Chairman of the examining committee.

Dziatzko's interests and reputation were international. He visited London and toured Italy to study methods of library organization. In 1900 he became a contributing editor to *The Library,* an English periodical. He died in . . . . on January 13, 1903. With a singular dedication to the intellectual and scholarly dimension of librarianship that, at the same time, took into account practical matters of administration, service, and bibliographic control, Dziatzko made contributions in his lifework—the perfection of librarianship and the advancement of learning—that are still a part of modern German librarianship.

REFERENCES

Alfred Schneider, bibliography in *Sammlung Bibliothekswissenschaftlicher Arbeiten,* (1904).

Robert Langker, "The Earliest Professor of Librarianship: Karl Dziatzko of Göttingen," *The Australian Library Journal* (1960), on his role in library education.

Joseph Becker, "Karl Dziatzko," in *Der Schlesier des 17. bis 18. Jahrhunderts* (Breslau, 1928) (*Schlesische Lebensbilder,* vol. 3) on his life and times; includes references to other sources.

GORDON STEVENSON

Eaton, John
(1829–1906)

John Eaton served as U.S. Commissioner of Education from 1870 to 1886. During his tenure he provided support for libraries through the compilation of statistics and the publication of reports and library aids, including the landmark 1876 *Public Libraries in the United States of America.*

Eaton was born on December 5, 1829, near Sutton, New Hampshire, the oldest in a family of nine children. His early formal education was at first delayed and scanty, but he eventually earned his way through Dartmouth College, from which he received an A.B. in 1854. Between 1854 and 1859 he worked as a public school administrator, first in Cleveland, and afterward in Toledo, Ohio (1856–59), where he served as the Superintendent of public schools. In 1859 he enrolled at the Andover Seminary. When he graduated in 1861, he entered the Civil War as a chaplain with the 27th Ohio Volunteer Infantry. In 1862 U. S. Grant placed him in charge of the many ex-slaves who were coming to the Union Army for refuge. He continued that work until the end of the war, earning the rank of Brigadier General. While in that post Eaton developed educational and humanitarian ideals that coalesced into a strong overall view of the central importance of public education as the key agency of social renewal that would ensure an enlightened democracy. After five postwar years of newspaper and educational work in Tennessee, Eaton won another appointment from Grant, now President, as the U.S. Commissioner of Education, a position in which he was able to promote his educational goals.

Eaton viewed the proper work of the Bureau of Education to be the promotion of general education through gathering and publishing educational statistics, informative reports, and other writings; presenting educational programs at public expositions; and exchanging information with other countries on the establishment of educational systems. Eaton also considered libraries to be a component of the national educational program, as essential auxiliary aids to education and culture. He had first been involved in library work in Ohio. As Superintendent of Public Instruction in Tennessee (1867–69), he insisted that each school district have a library for the aid of teachers and campaigned for each county to have a library for the general citizenry.

As Commissioner of Education he began immediately to incorporate library statistics in the annual reports of the Bureau. Between 1874 and 1876 his interest in compiling a library census led him to publish and distribute freely the special Bureau report, *Public Libraries in the United States of America: Their History, Condition and Management,* in which a variety of statistical tables were combined with a large number of general articles written by librarians to form what served for years as a fundamental handbook of library management. Eaton also correlated the issuance of the report with the initial meeting of the American Library Association in 1876, which he helped to promote.

Between 1876 and 1885 he provided annual supplements to the 1876 library statistical data and in the Bureau's 1884–85 annual report issued a fully revised library census. During this period the Bureau also published and freely distributed special circulars of information on college libraries (1880), library buildings (1881), and general library aids (1882), each written by prominent librarians. In 1884 he committed the Bureau to issuing the *A.L.A. Catalog,* a promise that kept alive the Association's interest and work on the project.

By 1885 Eaton's work had set a pattern of cooperation between the library profession and the Bureau that would continue permanently. Eaton, however, found the greatly expanded work of the Bureau to be overtaxing, and in 1886 he resigned his post. He remained active in educational concerns until his death in Washington, D.C., on February 9, 1906.

REFERENCES

P. W. Alexander, *John Eaton, Jr.—Preacher, Soldier, and Educator,* Ph.D. dissertation, George Peabody College for Teachers (1939).

Francis L. Miksa, "The Making of the 1876 Special Report on Libraries," *Journal of Library History* (1973).

Miksa, "Eaton, John," *Dictionary of American Library Biography* (1978).

G. Smith, "John Eaton, Educator, 1829—1906," *School and Society* (1969).

M. S. Williams, "The Library Work of the Bureau of Education," *Library Journal* (1887).

FRANCIS L. MIKSA

Ecuador

The Republic of Ecuador lies on the west coast of South America, with Colombia on the north and Peru on the east and south. Population (1984 est.) 8,451,000; area 281,334 sq.km. The official language is Spanish, but Indian languages are common.

History. The earliest libraries in Equador were the extensive collections of Jesuit and Franciscan monks. When a royal ordinance from Spain resulted in the confiscation of Jesuit property in 1776, these libraries became the property of the state. Universities and even a printing press had been established by Jesuits and these were taken over, also. But a demand for libraries did not spread until the middle of the 19th century. Between 1862 and 1925 40 public libraries were established in cities around the country. In 1869 a decree for public support of the National Library was issued.

The year 1968 marked a renewed effort to upgrade libraries in general, much of the momentum having been derived from the Universidad Central, which hired its first professional librarian as Director of the General Library. Decisions were made to prepare a national union catalogue, to promote the Unesco UNISIST Project, to create a NATIS (National Technical Information System), and to update the professional statutes, revise the salaries of professionals, and prepare a Professional Defense Law.

National Library. The Biblioteca Nacional del Ecuador, in Quito, was founded in 1792. It contains about 60,000 volumes, many dating from the 16th and 17th centuries. A number of cooperative programs with the 97 municipal or public libraries have been insituted. The National Bibliography is published by the Biblioteca General of the Universidad Central on a bimonthly masis and cumulated annually. Support was given by the professional community and the Asociación Ecuatoriana de Bibliotecarios (Ecuatorian Library Association).

Academic Libraries. There are 51 academic libraries serving more than 200,000 students and faculty in Ecuatorian institutions of higher education. Perhaps the largest and most noteworthy of these is the Biblioteca General de la Universidad Central (General Library of the Central University), founded in 1826 and possessing a collection of more than 170,000 volumes. Almost all academic libraries have closed stacks; most give only registered students borrowing privileges.

Public Libraries. Public libraries in Ecuador are called bibliotecas municipales, or municipal libraries, and many regions lack them, because of limited resources and lack of trained personnel. The Biblioteca Pública Municipal de Cuenca (Cuenca Public Library) has offered many short courses to train personnel for public and school libraries, as has the Ecuatorian Library Association, which has sponsored 42 multileveled training programs in the capital of each province. The Biblioteca Municipal de Quito was founded in 1886 and possesses more than 13,000 volumes; the Biblioteca Municipal de Guayaquil, founded in 1862, offers a collection of more than 120,000 volumes.

Other major libraries open to the public are the Biblioteca Ecuatoriana Aurelio Espinosa Pólit, in Quito, with about 120,000 volumes, 2,880 current periodicals, 14,000 manuscripts, 83 incunabula, 7,000 government documents, and 20,000 other materials; and the Biblioteca de Autores Nacionales Fray Vincente Solano in Cuenca, with about 40,000 volumes in its collection.

Of the 97 public libraries presently serving the Ecuatorian population, the majority struggle to survive and offer minimal services that generally do not include borrowing privileges. Most are closed collections that depend heavily on donations for growth. Many public libraries must double as school libraries in the absence or inadequacy of such institutions.

School Libraries. School libraries constitute more than 80 percent of all libraries in Ecuador, numbering almost 1,600. The majority are in private schools or offer rudimentary collections and services. Many double as public libraries, and most have irregular and insufficient hours. Generally speaking, one or several teachers with full-time class activities are assigned to library work. The government is actively promoting improvements in the public schools, but funding continues to be a problem. The Library Association has done much to promote the concept of school libraries, and training courses are directed toward the teachers in charge of these libraries.

Special Libraries. As in the majority of Latin American countries, special libraries and information centers are the most advanced in information management and enjoy the best funding and personnel. The largest are probably the Biblioteca Hispano-Americana in Cuenca (55,000 volumes) and the library of the Instituto Nacional Mejia in Quito (25,000). CIESPAL, the Centro Internacional de Estudios Superiores de Comunicación para América Latina (International Center of Higher Studies in Communications for Latin America) deserves special mention, having pioneered in modern information-handling techniques. CENDES, a technical informa-

tion center specializing in food industry documentation, has also played a major role in the field. The Junta Nacional de Planificación (National Planning Department) has endeavored to set up a National Technical Information System. It organized the Seminario Nacional de Información Científica y Técnica (National Seminar on Scientific and Technical Information) in 1975.

The Profession. The Asociacíson Ecuatoriana de Bibliotecarios was founded in 1944 by Alfredo Chávez Granja, the first professional librarian in Ecuador. It has its headquarters at the Casa de Cultura Ecuatoriana (Ecuatorian Cultural Center) and has received a great deal of support from it. The Universidad Católica (Catholic University) has also been a staunch supporter of the AEB. After a number of periods of little activity after its inception, the AEB was revived in 1965 when four professional librarians returned from the Interamerican Library School in Colombia and initiated the publication of the *Bolitín Bibliográfico Ecuatoriano*. Many courses and conferences have been offered, and the Association has been very active in promoting the development of the profession in Ecuador.

MARTHA GORMAN*

Edwards, Edward
(1812–1886)

Edward Edwards, British librarian and author, held posts at the British Museum, 1839–50, in the Manchester municipal library system, 1851–58, and thereafter at Oxford. His permanent library reputation derives, however, not from work done in salaried posts held; Melvil Dewey put his finger on basic essentials when he referred to him as "foremost writer and thinker." During March 1877 Dewey wrote to Edwards— a lonely, unemployed, and impecunious librarian living in Oxford—inviting him to become the new *American Library Journal*'s Associate Editor for England:

> It seems eminently fitting that you to whom we have so long looked as the foremost writer and thinker in the library world should be associated with the leading librarians of the country in carrying forward this work. . . . I feel a strong personal interest in the matter because on several vital points I agree wholly with you and differ from most of our American librarians. . . . Your name on our list will vouch for your interest in our work. (Dewey's unpublished letter is now in the Edwards collection in Manchester Central Library.)

Edwards was born in Stepney, in the East End of London, on December 14, 1812. His father, Anthony, was a bricklayer. Probably encouraged by his wife, Charlotte, a woman of some education, he unsuccessfully expanded his business activities to become "builder, chapman, and dealer" and was adjudged bankrupt in 1832. Mrs. Edwards's encouragement of her only son was more successful. She was very ambitious for him and probably taught him much herself; no record of his attendance at any school has been traced. Edwards also owed much to Thomas Binney, who became Minister of King's Weigh House Chapel in the City of London in 1829, and to Edwin Abbott, a teacher who was appointed

Headmaster of Marylebone Grammar School in 1827. Edwards's education obviously continued steadily and successfully during his seven years' apprenticeship to his father, and by his early 20s he was easily able to hold his own with men of similar age who had been more formally educated.

In 1834 Edwards became a reader in the library of the British Museum, then the only large and freely available library open to the general public in London, and remained closely associated with it for the next 16 years. Following commissioned authorship on such varied subjects as coins, seals, and medals, and the state, constitution, and future of New South Wales, he joined the library staff in 1839 as one of the additional cataloguers temporarily employed to prepare a new catalogue.

Until 1850 his professional life was lived on three levels. He worked on the catalogue; became extremely active in the movement to establish free public libraries, publishing numerous pamphlets and articles in periodicals; and during at least the later years of the period did little or nothing to alleviate what would now be termed a serious personality clash with the head of his department in the British Museum, Antonio Panizzi. This clash was regrettable, not only because it led ultimately to Edwards's dismissal from his post but even more because both he and Panizzi were deeply concerned with making vast improvements in the Library's service to readers.

Although various proposals to establish freely available public libraries, supported wholly or in part from public funds, had been made in England earlier in the 19th century, the task of providing the authorizing legislation fell to a private Member of Parliament, William Ewart (1798–1869). Edwards acted as his information officer and was the chief witness to testify before a Select Committee of the House of Commons, chaired by Ewart, in 1849. The Committee's Reports prepared the way for the first Public Libraries Act in 1850. This Act, which, with numerous safeguards, empowered town councils to establish libraries and to finance them up to the limit of a local rate of one halfpenny in the pound (raised to one penny by the amending Act of 1855), was adopted most readily in large towns with substantial industrial populations.

The lead was taken by Manchester, which appointed Edwards as its first Principal Librarian in 1851. He did much during the next seven years to lay sound foundations for what has become one of the greatest of British municipal library systems but, once again, did little or nothing to alleviate serious personality clashes with the members of his own governing body; Manchester dismissed him in 1858. During the remaining 30 years of his life he found salaried occupation mostly in Oxford. He was employed, primarily as a cataloguer, in the library of Queen's College from 1870 to 1876 and in the Bodleian Library from 1877 to 1883.

While in Manchester Edwards had also been working assiduously on *Memoirs of Libraries, Including a Handbook of Library Economy,* which was published in London by Trübner three months after his dismissal. It provides a history of libraries from the earliest evidences in Egypt and Assyria up to 1857, the second volume including an account of American libraries from the beginnings at Harvard in 1632 to the New York Public Library and the Smithsonian of 1854. Edwards's approach may also be regarded as propagandist, the libraries of the past being viewed as the predecessors of what the author regarded as the highest and most socially significant form, the municipal free public library. The second half of the second volume, "Economy of Libraries," covers book acquisition, buildings, classification and cataloguing, and "internal administration and public service," and provided librarians of the second half of the 19th century with their most comprehensive treatise. *Memoirs* can be regarded also as visionary because Edwards not only pioneered scientific book classification in England, but also speculated on such possibilities as national bibliographies, library associations, and even staff pension schemes.

References and discussions at the ALA's inaugural conference at Philadelphia in 1876 and at the LA's in London in 1877 make clear the continuing high reputation of *Memoirs* 20 years after first publication. By 1876, however, Edwards had supplemented it with two later works, both also published by Trübner in London: *Free Town Libraries* (1869), a mostly historical treatment in 14 chapters of which 6 cover the libraries of North America; and *Lives of the Founders of the British Museum* (1870). These two later publications may be regarded also as contributions toward the second and substantially revised edition of *Memoirs,* which the author earnestly desired but of which only a few other chapters ever found their way into print.

During the years between his dismissal from Manchester Public Library and his appointment to Queen's College, Oxford (from 1858 until 1870), Edwards had to earn his living mostly by authorship and journalism and to take advantage of whatever opportunities came his way. His publications were mostly on subjects other than librarianship. Outstanding among them was the two-volume life of *Sir Walter Raleigh* (1868), which still holds its place in the bibliography of the great Elizabethan because, as an eminent 20th-century Elizabethan scholar, A. L. Rowse, has explained: "It is admirable for its steady good judgment and is still indispensable for it contains the Letters" (*Raleigh and the Throckmortons,* [London, 1962]).

Edwards also edited a volume in the Rolls Series, *Liber Monsaterii de Hyda; Comprising a Chronicle of the Affairs of England from the Settlement of the Saxons to the Reign of King Cnut; and a Chartulary of the Abbey of Hyde in Hampshire, A.D. 455–1023,* which was welcomed on its publication as a scholar's book for scholars. He was responsible for a variety of articles in the later volumes of the Eighth Edition of the *Encyclopaedia Britannica* (1852–60) on subjects as diverse as Police, Post Office, Alexis de Tocqueville, and Wool. His *Britannica* article on Libraries had been written while he was still at Manchester.

Edwards was an outstanding example of Victorian "self-help." But he was always opinionated and frequently arrogant; he made enemies much too easily and often of people who, handled differently, might have befriended and helped him. He was a bad manager, of his own life, of his personal finances, and certainly of his own writing since he was seldom able to conform to limits and patterns previously agreed with his publishers. He married Margaretta Hay-ward, who was nine years older than himself, in 1844. Their marriage was tolerably happy for the most part, granted that Margaretta was a much more gregarious person than her husband. They had no children. He died in poverty at Niton, on the Isle of Wight, on February 7, 1886, 10 years after his wife, and is buried in the parish churchyard at Niton. The Library Association maintains his grave.

REFERENCE

W. A. Munford, *Edward Edwards 1812–1886: Portrait of a Librarian* (1963).

W. A. MUNFORD

Edwards, John Passmore
(1823–1911)

John Passmore Edwards, businessman, philanthropist, and library benefactor, became a successful publisher of newspapers and periodicals, including a pioneer halfpenny daily, and *Mechanics Magazine,* which had itself helped to pioneer mechanics institutes, regarded in Britain as the most important and influential predecessors of public libraries.

He was born of poor parents in Blackwater, Cornwall, on March 24, 1823. Edwards was much influenced by the Transcendentalism of Channing and Emerson, became a disciple of Cobden and Bright, and supported the full program of their Manchester School. He advocated moderate liberal reform throughout his life and by the age of 60 was a rich man with much money to spend on causes appealing to him. He decided to spend largely on the welfare of the working class.

Mostly during the 1890s he presented hospitals, homes for the handicapped, museums and art galleries, a public park, schools of art and science (including a notable gift to the then new London School of Economics), and even an Oxford scholarship. But he remains best known for his public library benefactions. His library gifts were given mostly to places in his native Cornwall, where, in the later 19th century, a substantial working class population was still dependent on the declining extractive industries of tin and copper mining, and to the working class areas of east and southeast London. Towns in Cornwall benefiting included Camborne and Redruth, Falmouth, Truro, Bodmin, and Launceston; and in London, Limehouse, Poplar, Whitechapel, Southwark, West Ham, Shoreditch, and Edmonton. Edwards presented approximately 30 library buildings and also gave public and other libraries nearly 100,000 books. His British library benefactions may be regarded as standing midway between those of local philanthropists such as Michael Bass at Derby, John Gulson at Coventry, Edmund Harris at Preston, and William Brown at Liverpool and the much greater, nationwide contribution of Andrew Carnegie.

Edwards died in London on April 22, 1911.

REFERENCES

J. Passmore Edwards, *A Few Footprints* (1905).

T. Kelly, *A History of Public Libraries in Great Britain 1845–1975* (1977).

J. J. Macdonald, *Passmore Edwards Institutions* (1900).

W. A. MUNFORD

John Passmore Edwards

Library Association

Egypt (Ancient)

The principal known, written records of ancient Egypt were fixed as inscriptions, paintings, or reliefs on the walls of tombs and columns of temples; those that were portable were first entered on rolls of papyrus (or leather) but were customarily restricted to tombs and temple archive rooms. The main practices were developed in the 3rd millennium B.C. under the Old Kingdom. They may account for such testimony as the sandstone stele declaration by Neferhotep (18th century B.C.) that before dispatching agents up the Nile to Thebes to begin building a temple, he consulted the ancient writings in the Atum Temple at Heliopolis (in the Delta).

The use of papyrus for writing also may have begun during the Old Kingdom, but because of its fragility nothing is extant older than the 3rd century B.C., and little has been determined beyond doubt. Ernest C. Richardson (1860–1939) thought he had identified 21 libraries in the texts of the Book of the Dead and other sources, but Karl von Vogelsang and others, after checking the originals, concluded that Richardson had misunderstood or mistranslated key terms. There were indeed archives but no known libraries before the Ptolemaic period. (As Mogens Weitmeyer put it in *Libri* (1955–56), archival materials were stored by their nature and date; library materials were gathered into subject-related series, bore colophons including regulations of a library character, and were listed in separate catalogues.)

The three "houses of writings" and the House of the Chief of Taxation in the care of a principal courtier in the 4th and 5th dynasties (c.2613–c.2345 B.C.) have not been shown to be more than archives. The same holds for the celebrated 370 cuneiform tablets found at El-Amarna, mainly international correspondence of the busy 14th century B.C., in Akkadian. Verification of a sort is provided by the wall painting in the late-13th-century grave of a Ramesside high official: scribes are depicted at work in the left panel, checking and signing of documents by the chief in the center, and the wooden storage chests of the "Records Depository" occupy the right—all under the supervising eye of Thoth, god of knowledge and patron of scribes, who is represented as a baboon.

Ramses himself (II, 1304–1237 B.C.) figures in the venerable tales of the "sacred library" of "King Osymandias," renowned for its entrance inscription, "Nourishment of the Soul." Portions of the story appear to go back to the historian Diodorus Siculus (1st century B.C.), as well as later authorities such as Galen, philosopher-physician of the 2nd century A.D.

Diodorus' recital was studied in the mid-19th century by Karl R. Lepsius, who found near the tomb of Ramses II the graves of two "librarians," father and son, which apparently encouraged him to identify the "sacred library" and "King Osymandias" with Ramses. No "sacred library" has been established beyond doubt, but the suppositions are considered reasonable because there were by that time numerous temple "libraries." The "Nourishment of the Soul" inscription, however, has never had archaeological support and is perhaps to be explained by Galen's remark that he found in the "sacred library" a medical recipe he described in terms of "nourishment."

The origins of the temple of Isis on the island of Philae, near the First Cataract, are not certain, but it is known that the building was further developed by the Ptolemies and Romans partly to attract pilgrims. A doorpost inscription referred to a bookroom designed to preserve the life-giving writings of Isis, and below the wall recesses for papyrus rolls—or for wooden jars containing them—was a life-size relief of Thoth-as-baboon with a papyrus roll.

Possibly owing something to the ideas of Imhotep, 27th-century B.C. architect-courtier, reputedly expressed in the original temple of Edfu, somewhat north of Philae, was the new Horus temple built there by the Romans as an instrument of reconciliation with the Egyptian priests. Its library is the only one in Egypt whose existence enjoys archaeological verification. The titles of 37 works were painted on a wall; their presence has been established. They are regarded as having been a sort of ready-reference collection for the staff.

SIDNEY L. JACKSON
(d.1979)

Egypt

The Arab Republic of Egypt in northeast Africa is bounded on the west by Libya, on the south by The Sudan, on the northeast by Israel, on the north by the Mediterranean Sea, and on the east by the Gulf of Aqaba and the Red Sea. Population (1984 est.) 47,120,000; area 997,667 sq.km. The official language is Arabic; French and English are widely spoken.

History. Libraries in Egypt can be traced back to the time of the Pharaohs, and are reported to have existed for 6,000 years. Small private collections were housed in schools, palaces, and temples. The library of King Ramses II (Ozymandyas), c. 1304–1237 B.C., may have been the largest in Egyptian antiquity, numbering as many as 20,000 papyrus rolls, including works on agriculture, astronomy, history, and irrigation, as well as poetry and fiction.

During the Arab-Islamic Renaissance, mosque libraries were founded in Cairo, and supported by princes and private persons for the preservation of Islamic culture. In the 9th century, the mosques became inadequate to house the growing collections and

to accommodate students. The *madrasah,* a school or college resembling medieval European colleges, came into existence. The first madrasah and its library were founded in Cairo by the Fatimid Caliph al-Hakim. The library collection included works on mathematics, astronomy, medicine, and grammar.

The Seljukian period (10th to 11th centuries) was one of great prosperity in Egypt, and important colleges and university libraries were founded. This tradition continued under the Ayyubid emirs and during the Mameluke period. In 1517 Egypt came under Ottoman rule and was isolated from the rest of the world until the late 18th century. This intellectual isolation ended with the introduction of French and English publications and particularly with the introduction of the printing press.

The beginning of modern librarianship in Egypt began with the establishment of the Khedieval Library (now the National Library) in 1870. Library activity expanded in Egypt between 1945 and 1965 when many libraries, as well as the first Arab library school, were established in Cairo. The post-1967 war era witnessed declines in the library movement in Egypt.

National Library. The National Library of Egypt (Dar el-Kutub Al-Misriyyah) was established in 1870 through the endeavors of Ali Moubarak, the Minister of Education at that time. Moubarak collected the scattered manuscripts and printed books from mosques, schools, archives, ministries, and other governmental departments. The formation of this library helped preserve what was left of Arabic books, manuscripts, and rare books from being lost or sold to foreign collectors. The library was in the palace of Khedive Isma'il until transferred to a new building in 1904.

In 1971 the National Library was combined with the National Archives and the National Publishing House to form the General Egyptian Book Organization. In 1970 the National Library ceased to be a circulation library. It concentrates on scholarly collections, research, and preservation programs. The National Library is the legal deposit for every publication printed in Egypt. It is also responsible for compiling and publishing the *Egyptian Publications Bulletin,* which can be considered the official national bibliography of the country. Since 1955 the Library has been serving as the secretariat for the Egyptian National Committee for Bibliographic Services, which is responsible for developing plans for a national bibliographic organization.

There are about 1,000,000 volumes in the National Library. Only a small number of the Library's staff of approximately 800 have library science degrees.

Academic Libraries. Egypt has 9 national universities and about 100 technical colleges and teacher training institutes. Cairo University, which was established in 1908, is the oldest of national universities. It has an enrollment of 113,800 students. Ain Shams University, just east of the center of Cairo, has an enrollment of 122,000. In addition to national universities there are two institutions that are not part of the national system: al-Azhar University, the world's oldest university, established in A.D. 970; and the American University in Cairo, a private institution established in 1920.

There are approximately 120 academic libraries in the country. Most of the universities have a main library to house the large library collections in the humanities and social sciences and many faculty libraries, which contain the more specialized materials in science and technology. Cairo University has a special building designed basically to be a library, and it is the sole exception of all university libraries. The average student enrollment ranges from 30 to 50 students.

All the university and college libraries in Egypt suffer from a shortage of qualified librarians. The country often loses its finest librarians to institutions in other Arab countries that offer better positions and salaries. A lack of cooperation is evident among university and college libraries. There is minimal interlibrary loan. Libraries at the same university do not share library resources, and no central processing exists. Students suffer from library regulations that are restrictive. Open access is very limited, with libraries usually open only during the hours when students are attending classes.

Staffing patterns in most academic libraries depend on the size of the institution. The library can have from 25 to 200 workers, divided into professionals, staff, library assistants, and technicians. Most libraries are inadequate for the number of students and faculty they serve.

Public Libraries. Although there are 223 public libraries in Egypt, only one-third have holdings of 25,000 to 100,000 volumes and are supervised by qualified librarians. The rest are in cultural centers, which were set up to attract young men and women who may be interested in reading or in any other social or cultural activities. These centers also usually include a theater, film projection room, music room, and a reading room with a small collection of books ranging from 500 to 3,000 volumes. At least one professional librarian is in charge of each cultural center.

Public library services have been extended to farmers and the rural populace in an attempt to reduce illiteracy and to educate the villagers to the best ways of maintaining healthy communities. Other public library services do not go far beyond the very traditional services, such as lending books outside the library and allowing readers to read inside the building. Reader assistance is limited. The libraries come under several jurisdictions, so there is no general or

systematic plan for developing public libraries in the country and no way to coordinate their services.

School Libraries. The systematic establishment of school libraries in Egypt began in 1955, when the Ministry of Education founded the Department of School Libraries to supervise and promote school libraries all over the country. This department recommends to the Minister of Education new regulations to improve school library service; it inspects school libraries all over the country and provides standards for furniture and equipment to be used in school libraries. Until 1970 the Department of School Libraries in the Ministry of Education also operated a centralized acquisition and book-processing center that selected, purchased, and distributed books for all the school libraries in the country. Each library thereafter purchased its own books, but most of these were chosen from the selection tools prepared by the Department. Therefore, there is a kind of similarity between collections in all school libraries of the same level not only in the quality of books but also in the quantity. In many instances the collections do not correspond with the needs of pupils or teachers. School library services are very traditional. They are restricted to lending books. Collections comprise only books and a very few local newspapers and magazines. In 1961 the concept of school-community libraries was introduced in Egypt, and they provide services to the general public as well as to the students.

There are about 4,500 school libraries, with holdings of approximately 8,150,000 volumes. These estimates, provided by the government, include all schools that have even a handful of books. The actual number of school libraries is closer to 1,000, and they serve only about 14 percent of the population.

Special Libraries. Egypt entered the 1980s with 7 information centers and 313 special libraries: 170 in ministries and other governmental agencies, 72 in learned societies, and 71 in institutions and corporations. The special library in Egypt corresponds in collections and size with the needs of the institution it serves. The size of the collections depends entirely upon the history of the institution and the available budget. Governmental libraries contain government documents, laws, archives, and foreign materials not easily available elsewhere. In many instances services are limited to lending materials only to those who work in the institution. Information centers were es-

Libraries in Egypt (1982)

Type	Administrative units	Service points	Volumes in collections	Annual expenditures (pound)	Population served	Professional staff	Total staff
National[a]	1	--	1,000,000	83,000[b]	24,490[c]	160	800
Academic[a]	120	--	2,591,000	--	441,000	432	805
Public[a]	223	--	1,329,000	--	6,000	--	--
School[a]	4,565	--	8,150,000	1,220,000	1,100,000[c]	--	--
Special	320	--	1,605,000	--	--	--	851

[a]1980 data.
[b]Acquisitions only.
[c]Registered borrowers.

Source: Unesco, *Statistical Yearbook*, 1984; *ALA World Encyclopedia*, First Edition (1980).

tablished to serve researchers and scientists in government and semigovernment organizations. They are considered special libraries, although they form a superior quality of special libraries. They go beyond traditional services and provide new kinds of services that represent modern thinking in special librarianship and information services. Among the services provided by these centers are indexing and abstracting, translation, bibliographic activities, and current awareness services, and some provide computerized information storage and retrieval. Information centers are recognized at the Institute of Public Administration, Iron and Steel Company, Atomic Energy Establishment, National Information and Documentation Center (NIDOC), Education Documentation and Research Center—Ministry of Education, National Planning Institute, and Ministry of National Planning. Each special library or information center varies. A library may have as few as 4 staff members, or it may have a staff of 100. Some libraries or centers concentrate their holdings on books, others on periodicals or documents. They may have from 3,000 to 180,000 volumes in their collections.

The Profession. The Egyptian Library and Archives Association (ELAA), established in 1946 as the Cairo Library Association, works toward improvement of professional standards of librarianship. Other activities include the development of library collections and increased publication of Arabic library literature. The Association is affiliated with IFLA.

MOHAMMED M. AMAN;
SHA'BĀN KHALIFA*

Elmendorf, Theresa West
(1855–1932)

In March 1951 the *Library Journal* selected Theresa West Elmendorf for its new Library Hall of Fame in recognition of her long contribution to the field. In commenting on her selection, *Library Journal* took note of her exceptional knowledge of books and of her ability to interest others in reading literature. Her selection was a fitting reminder of an early library pioneer with rare ability, vision, and high ideals.

Theresa Hubbell West was born in Pardeeville, Wisconsin, on November 1, 1855; six years later her family moved to Milwaukee, primarily to ensure educational opportunities for the four children. She graduated from Milwaukee's public schools and then from a school for girls in 1874. In 1877 she began her long library career as an assistant at the Young Men's Association of Milwaukee, a library that was soon to form the basis for a new municipal library. While waiting for the state legislature to pass the enabling act effecting this transfer, she kept the library open as a reading room and found time to read the 1876 report of the U.S. Bureau of Education, *Public Libraries in the United States of America.* This milestone in library literature was to form the basis of her knowledge of library theory and practice, and perhaps even the inspiration for her ideas about library service. She was appointed to the staff of the new Milwaukee Public Library and in 1880 became Deputy Librarian. Following a scandal involving the embezzlement of city funds by the head Librarian, K. A. Linderfelt, West was appointed to the post in 1892. Her four

years at the helm of Milwaukee's library were important, at a time when a new library-museum was planned and built. She also developed her executive abilities, and the library became known as a carefully administered, patron-oriented institution.

She resigned her position in 1896 upon her marriage to Henry L. Elmendorf, then Librarian of the public library at Saint Joseph, Missouri, and a Vice-President of the American Library Association. For about a year the couple lived in London, where he managed the branch of the Library Bureau. The library profession beckoned, however, and in mid-1897 Henry Elmendorf became the head of the newly established Buffalo Public Library, a position he held until his death nine years later. While having no official connection with the library during this time, Theresa Elmendorf acted as a silent partner and frequent adviser. She had had more experience as an administrator than he, and it seems likely she was instrumental in developing the library. At a time when public libraries traditionally closed their bookshelves to the public, Buffalo began what was called the Open Shelf Room. The Elmendorfs also started the "Buffalo Plan," a program that included public library service to the schools of the city. Evidence of her role in the plan is her address for the New York State Teachers Association, which was later expanded into a booklet called *Buffalo's System of Public School and Public Library Cooperation.*

As an unpaid worker, she found time to do research, to write, and to serve in various organizations. She produced a *Descriptive Catalogue of the Gluck Collection of Manuscripts and Autographs in the Buffalo Public Library* in 1899 and in 1904 served as the Selection Editor of the ALA's *Catalogue of Books for Small Libraries.* Elmendorf as Editor was a logical choice since she was recognized as an authority on book selection. Her contributions appeared in *Library Journal* and *Public Libraries,* as well as magazines outside the profession. In 1903–04 she served as President of the New York Library Association, at which time she was also a member of the American Library Institute.

The death of her husband in 1906 forced Theresa Elmendorf to end her unpaid status, and for the next 20 years she held the position of Vice-Librarian at the Buffalo Public Library. Her new role also meant an increased participation in ALA; in 1911–12 she served as its President, the first woman to hold that position. She presided at the Ottawa conference, the second meeting held by the Association in Canada. Although she made the political mistake of suggesting a closer alliance between the two countries—at a time when Canadians were especially sensitive to such a suggestion—ruffled feelings were smoothed over, and the meetings resulted in increased cooperative library development.

She probably made her greatest contribution in the area of popular bibliography. Her exceptional knowledge of books, and her enthusiasm in encouraging appreciation of reading in others, led her to produce a variety of reading lists and bibliographies. In 1917 *Poetry: The Complementary Life,* a selection made for Buffalo's Open Shelf Room, was published, and in 1921 a short reading list of popular books entitled *The United States* was reprinted by ALA. Her *Classroom Libraries for Public Schools,* published by the

Buffalo Library in 1923, was a valuable selection aid. Even mandatory retirement in September 1926 failed to bring a halt to her efforts. In 1928 she prepared the bibliography of poems and poets for Joseph Auslander and F. E. Hill's *Winged Horse,* published by Doubleday, Doran. This was enlarged three years later into the ALA publication *Poetry and Poets: A Readers List.* Appreciation of poetry was one of her strongest characteristics, and so it was especially appropriate that this would be her last contribution to the world of books. She died at her home in Buffalo on September 4, 1932.

Theresa Elmendorf was a woman of unusual ability who made a major contribution to the profession and to its Association. She had high ideals and a vision of expanding library service well before its time. After her death, Mary E. Hazeltine of the University of Wisconsin Library School wrote, "Many librarians in important positions today have carried on because she awakened their appreciation of books and opened up for them insight into new realms. She was a stimulating guide and a vitalizing teacher, as well as a great librarian."

DENNIS THOMISON

El Salvador

El Salvador, a republic in Central America, is bordered by Honduras on the north and east, the Pacific Ocean on the south, and Guatemala on the west. Population (1984 est.) 5,337,000; area 21,041 sq.km. The official language is Spanish.

National Library. The National Library of El Salvador, in the city of San Salvador, was created by presidential decree in 1870 with an initial collection of 6,000 works on theology, philosophy, law, and classical literature purchased from Rome by the family of the librarian of Pope Gregory xvi. A year later it was transferred to the National University and was under university administration until 1887, when it was opened to the general public. The Mobile Libraries, operating under the National Library, were founded in 1923, bringing books to amusement parks, fairs, and 226 rural communities. In 1962 the National Li-

brary became the General Directorate of Libraries and Archives and together with the holdings of the National Archives moved to the first library building constructed in El Salvador.

The National Library is the depository library under Salvadoran copyright law; it also holds documents of international organizations. The majority of books contained in the Library come from donations and exchanges with Latin American countries and with learned societies of the United States and Europe. The Library's principal departments are the Exchange Center, the International Organizations Department, Special Services for Children, and the Center for Documentation on Education. Its substantial collection includes microfilm of important historical documents of El Salvador in Spanish archives.

Academic Libraries. The principal academic library is the Central Library of the University of El Salvador. Established in 1854, it was destroyed in 1865 and started again in 1889 with a collection of books on general subjects, while the University faculties founded their own libraries. The University Library was the best stocked and most important library in the country, but in 1955 a fire destroyed 60 percent of its holdings, and the remaining items were divided among faculty collections.

In 1963 the University Rector established a Central Library and in 1966 initiated a university library system that aimed at the centralization of all library resources of the University. Civil war caused a disruption of this system.

The Central Library collection numbers about 100,000. The size of the whole University Library, including the faculty collections, is 205,000 volumes, and it serves a population of 45,000 readers.

There are three other university libraries with varied collections, which include former private libraries and new bibliographic resources purchased with funds loaned by regional and international banks. The private Catholic University is well stocked and staffed.

Public Libraries. Until 1973 free library services were provided by the National Library and by a few municipal libraries concentrated around the capital, but their collections were small and limited.

Libraries in El Salvador (1980)

Type	Administrative units	Service points	Volumes in collections	Annual expenditures (colón)	Population served	Professional staff	Total staff
National	1	1	80,000	529,000	22,780[a]	2	63
Academic[b]	13	--	190,960	645,975[c]	53,750	16	150
Public[b]	113	--	110,500[d]	279,750[d]	2,460,857	--	193[e]
School[b]	150	--	245,000[f]	260,000[f]	855,329	1	140[g]
Special[b]	30	--	147,032	80,000[h]	43,955	11	78[e]

[a]Registered borrowers.
[b]1976 data.
[c]Nine libraries only.
[d]61 libraries only.
[e]25 with some training in library science.
[f]75 schools only.
[g]10 with some training in library science.
[h]Two libraries only. All special libraries reported no specific budget but one included in the general budget of their respective institutions.

Source: Unesco, *Statistical Yearbook,* 1984; *ALA World Encyclopedia,* First Edition (1980).

In 1973 a project called National Network of Houses of Culture was approved by the government, and 60 public libraries were founded in important cities and rural towns from 1973 to 1977 alone. These Casas de la Cultura extend their services to surrounding communities, serving a total population of 200,000. This network of libraries has centralized processing and trains its own librarians.

School Libraries. Public and private school libraries developed rapidly in the 1960s because of educational reforms. In 1972 the Ministry of Education approved a five-year plan for public school libraries providing for 330 libraries to serve a population of 218,000 students; the number of libraries remains insufficient. Most private school have good basic collections in accordance with their curricula, some surpassing 25,000 volumes. Audiovisual materials were introduced but costs prevented the public schools from making significant use of other than book materials.

Special Libraries. Special libraries are important in the country because of the variety and richness of their holdings and because they are better funded and invariably open to the public. The oldest special library began in 1883 as the library of the National Museum. From the 1960s such libraries developed, together with their supporting organizations, in almost every bank, learned society, professional association, ministry, embassy, hospital, church, museum, and commercial and industrial firm. The libraries of the National Coffee Company serve the many people interested in this important crop. Banks have opened their libraries to students and researchers, and the Library of the Electric Company is one of the best organized.

Two of the largest special libraries are those in the Academia Salvadoreña de la Historia (8,600 volumes) and Allianza Francesca (9,000 volumes). However, there are many excellent collections belonging to private individuals who open their libraries part-time to university students or the general public. The Gallardo Collection in the city of Nueva San Salvador surpasses 80,000 volumes.

The Profession. The Association of Salvadoran Librarians, founded in 1947 and composed mainly of librarians without graduate training, conducts such activities as conferences, meetings, and the sporadic publication of a bulletin.

JEANNETTE FERNANDEZ DE CRIADO*

El Sheniti, El Sayed Mahmoud

(1920-)

El Sayed Mahmoud El Sheniti, Egyptian library educator and administrator, participated in many important library projects and conferences around the world and contributed to significant library achievements in Egypt.

El Sheniti was born in Egypt on November 25, 1920. He earned a B.A. degree from Cairo University in 1940, a higher diploma in social sciences from Alexandria University in 1953, and a Ph.D. in Library Science from the University of Chicago in 1960.

El Sheniti served the Egyptian and international library profession in several capacities. He was Librarian of Alexandria University Library, 1949–51; Assistant Librarian of the Unesco Fundamental Education Center in Sirs El Layyan, Egypt, 1952–54; Director of the American University in Cairo Library, 1958–63; Unesco Documentation and Publications Expert Stationed at the Unesco Regional Center of Community Development for the Arab States in Sirs El Layyan, Egypt, 1963–68; Under Secretary of State for the Egyptian National Library and Archives, 1968–71; Senior Under Secretary of State for the Ministry of Culture and Chairman of the General Egyptian Book Organization, 1971–77; and Deputy Minister of Culture and Chairman of the GEBO, a post he held until his retirement in December 1978.

El Sheniti contributed largely to library education in Egypt as a visiting professor to the Department of Librarianship and Archives of the Faculty of Arts, Cairo University. He also worked as an expert and consultant to numerous organizations in Egypt and in other Arab countries. From 1964 to 1970 he presided over the Egyptian Library Association.

He contributed to several Unesco meetings. From 1966 to 1974 he served as a member and Chairman of the Unesco International Advisory Committee for Libraries, Documentation and Archives. He was elected President of the Unesco Intergovernmental Conference on National Planning of Documentation, and Archives Infrastructure, Paris, 1974; Vice-President of the International Congress on National Bibliography, Paris, 1977; and member of the International Book Committee and the International Book Year Support Committee.

El Sheniti wrote or edited numerous articles and books dealing with various aspects of library science. Noteworthy are "Book Cataloging Rules for Arabic Materials" (Cairo, 1961), "Authority List of Arabic Names" (Cairo, 1962), and "Arabic Adaptation of Dewey Decimal Classification" (Cairo, 1961).

As an administrator, El Sheniti contributed to library achievements in Egypt. Among them are centralized library activities focused around the book, i.e., public library services, national library and archives, and the state publishing industry under the umbrella of the General Egyptian Book Organization; a new modern building for the National Library and Archives; and the establishment of various centers within the framework of the GEBO, such as the Arabic Book Development Center, the Bibliographic Center, the Arab Heritage Center, and the Computer and Microfilming Center.

MOHAMED M. EL HADI

Equatorial Guinea

Equatorial Guinea is a republic in West Africa, comprising Rió Muni—between Cameroon on the north and Gabon on the south and bordered by the Atlantic Ocean on the west—and the islands of Fernando Po (Bioco) and Annobon, which lie offshore from the mainland territory. Population (1984 est.) 325,000; area 28,051 sq.km. The official language is Spanish.

History. Equatorial Guinea, former Spanish Guinea, became independent in October 1968. The few libraries left by Spain were closed or had been evacuated by 1979 when Macías Nguema's dictatorship was ended in a military coup d'etat led by Obiang Ngueme. Few were reopened during the second dictatorship, 1981–85. No official sources documenting library services in Equatorial Guinea after 1968 are available.

Oral tradition—arising out of legends—has not yet been documented in any detail. The first accounts on the area go back to the 15th century. From 1827, with Protestant missions, and from 1856 with Catholic missionaries, some small libraries were started and maintained.

An American, Sanford Berman, published the first annotated bibliography of the country in 1961.

National Library. The country had no National Library until 1982. In that year, the Biblioteca Pública of Santa Isabel (Malabo) was transformed into the National Library. Most documents published on Spanish Guinea are available in Spanish libraries. In the mid-1980s, the main Equatoguinean sources could be found in libraries in Madrid, among them the Biblioteca Nacional, Biblioteca del Instituto de Estudios Africanos, Hemeroteca Nacional, Centro de Documentación Africana, and Biobiblioteca de los Misioneros Claretianos; in Rome, at the Biblioteca del Vaticano; in Geneva, Switzerland, at the United Nations Library; and in the United States at Northwestern University (Evanston, Illinois), at its Melville J. Herskovits Library of African Studies, and at the Library of Congress.

Academic Libraries. In 1963 the Escuela de Magisterio (Teacher Training College) in Bata was created with a library for students' use only. In 1971 the library's collection numbered about 3,000 volumes, covering mostly Spanish literature, books on pedagogy, and almost all publications on Guinea of the Instituto de Estudios Africanos. In 1973 the library was absorbed by the Centro de Desarrollo de la Educación, a teacher-training center created with Unesco's assistance (after many books had been burned by the Youth Movement of Macías Nguema). In 1974 there were 2,400 volumes. The government closed the library; it was reopened partially in 1976, but after deportation or exile of most of the students and the departure of Unesco's experts, the library was not in use from 1978 to 1982.

In Santa Isabel the Library of the Escuela Superior Indígena (later called Escuela Superior Provincial) was established in 1946 for training auxiliary primary school teachers and auxiliary administrators. In 1946 its stock numbered 1,400 volumes, for students' use only.

Shortly before independence, the Dirección General de Enseñanza y Inspección began to organize a pedagogical library with the help of the Spanish Dirección General de Plazas y Provincias and the Instituto Pedagógico San José de Calasanz (Madrid). Its aim was to create circulation libraries for teachers and pupils in remote districts, but they did not work.

There were also some small libraries in the four Catholic seminaries, two seminarios mayores (clerical training colleges) in Banapa and Nkuefulan, and two seminarios menores (clerical staffed secondary schools) in Concepción and Mikomeseng.

Public Libraries. The Biblioteca Pública of Santa Isabel was created in 1942 by the Ministry of Education and opened to the public in 1945. It counted 3,000 volumes at inception; the Library is in the building of the Instituto Cardenal Cisneros (presently Instituto Rey Malabo, the main secondary school of the country, also created in 1942). Books were supplied by the Gobierno General de la Colonia, the Administración de Intercambios y Compras de Libros (Madrid), the Dirección General de Marruecos y Colonias (later de Plazas y Provincias), and the Ministry of Foreign Affairs, as well as by private sources. Under the supervision of the Governor General of the Colony (later Province), the Library was directed by the Archivist of the Gobierno General. The Library administered two small circulation libraries in San Carlos (Fernando Po) and Bata (Río Muni). In 1967 (the last year for which statistics are available), for 11,600 volumes there were 25,750 loans. In 1984 there was no air conditioning in the Library, in spite of the need in the very humid climate. The Director in 1984 was Juan Chema Mijero.

Other Libraries. In 1955 Father Jesus Morras founded a small private library in the Claretian Mission (Hijos del Inmaculado Corazon de Maria—missionaries established in Spanish Guinea from 1883). The Library collected rare documents on archaeology, history, ethnology, and natural sciences, and complete collections of various newspapers. The Library's African Museum preserved some 5,000 prehistoric stones. In response to opposition to Roman Catholicism under the Macías Nguema government, the whole Library was evacuated from Fernando Po in 1974, then out of the country.

The library of the Museo Etnográfico of Santa Isabel (about 500 volumes), managed by the Ministry of Education, was abandoned after the Ministry of Education was closed in 1977 and the Minister and other officials were assassinated. From 1981, an expert of the Baha'i Faith worked toward restoring the Museum and the Library.

The French Cultural Center (Santa Isabel) offers

Type	Administrative units	Service points	Volumes in collections	Annual expenditures	Population served	Professional staff	Total staff
National	1	--	12,000	--	--	--	--
Academic	7	--	7,000	--	1,000	--	--
Public[a]							
Special	3	--	5,000	--	500	--	--
Parliament[b]	1	--	--	--	50	--	--

Libraries in Equatorial Guinea (1982)

[a]The Public Library of Santa Isabel (Malabo) became the National Library in 1982.
[b]1984 data.

a library for children and students of about 500 books, and Spain projected a Biblioteca Infantil with 2,000 volumes (1985).

The Dirección de Archivos, also in Santa Isabel and a very understaffed service since independence, was supported by the Ministry of Education (closed in 1977, reopened in 1980). Most Equatoguinean archives have to be consulted in Spain and in other countries, principally the Archivo de las Cortés, Archivo del Consejo de Estado, Archivo de la Dirección General de Promoción del Sahara, Archivo del Ministerio de Asuntos exteriores, and Archivo Histórico Nacional, all in Madrid; Archivo General de Simancas, in Valladolid; and Archivo de Indias, in Sevilla. Besides Spanish archives are the colonial archives of Portugal, France, the United Kingdom, and Germany. The Berlin archives are famous for the study of the Fang, the indigenous people of the mainland of Equatorial Guinea. Finally, the Vatican archives are also a rich resource. In the mid-1980s there were no library associations.

REFERENCES

Max Liniger–Goumaz, *Guinea Ecuatorial, Bibliografía General,* 5 volumes (1974–1985); *Historical Dictionary of Equatorial Guinea* (1979).

Eléments pour le dossier de l'afro-fascisme. De la Guinée Equatoriale (1983).

MAX LINIGER–GOUMAZ

Esdaile, Arundell
(1880–1956)

An exemplar of the old style of scholar-librarian who spent his whole professional career in the service of the British Museum, Arundell James Kennedy Esdaile made significant contributions to bibliography, library practice, and library education both in Britain and internationally.

Born in London April 25, 1880, and educated at Lancing and at Magdalene College, Cambridge, Esdaile joined the staff of the British Museum Department of Printed Books in 1903. Under the inspiration of Robert Proctor and the direction of Alfred Pollard, work on the BM *Catalogue of XVth Century Books* had recently begun, and for the next few years, in company with such scholars as Henry Thomas and Victor Scholderer, Esdaile was occupied with the cataloguing of incunabula. His own research interests were much more concerned with English literature, and with time his duties became concentrated on the purchase and particularly the cataloguing of early English books. Besides his Museum work, he was engaged in work for the Malone Society, the Bibliographical Society, and others, contributing the section on "The Age of Elizabeth" to *English History Source Books* (G. Bell & Sons Series, 1912) and assisting Caroline Spurgeon with her *Five Hundred Years of Chaucer Criticism and Allusion (1914–25)*. His authority in this field was recognized in his invitation in 1926 to give the Sandars Lectures at Cambridge, published as *The Sources of English Literature* (Cambridge, 1928).

Relations between the British Museum and the Library Association, though at one time close, had become very weak by the time of World War I. Esdaile was one of the first Museum men to strive to bring the National Library and the profession closer together. He was closely associated with the first British School of Librarianship at University College London from its establishment in 1919, creating the course in Bibliography and Historical Bibliography, which he taught for the next 20 years. His *Students Manual of Bibliography*, first published in 1931 as the first volume in the "Library Association Series," was for many years an essential textbook. His work in library education did much to change the negative attitudes toward formal library education that had been prevalent in learned libraries in Britain.

From 1923 until an illness in 1935 compelled him to resign the editorship, he directed the *Library Association Record*, injecting a new, more professional, and more scholarly tone into the journal. He was responsible for the Library Association's starting publication of the *Year's Work in Librarianship*, himself editing the annual volumes from 1928 to 1938. His work in setting up the University and Research Section of the Association in 1927 helped ensure that the gap between learned libraries and other parts of the profession could not reopen.

In 1926 Esdaile moved out of the Department of Printed Books to the Director's office at the British Museum, to the post of Secretary which had lain dormant for many years. In that position he was able to represent the Museum in many external activities, including the Library Committee of the League of Nations Institute of Intellectual Cooperation. He was closely involved in the formation of the International Library and Bibliographical Committee, later to become IFLA, at the Library Association's 50th conference, Edinburgh 1927. He subsequently served as a Vice-President of IFLA from 1931, taking an active part in its deliberations until ill health caused him to resign in 1936.

Esdaile was elected President of the Library Association in 1939. His term in office was much longer than the normal one-year period. As a consequence of the outbreak of war that year, normal conduct of the Association's affairs was suspended, and he remained as President until 1945, working unobtrusively with the Emergency Committee to consolidate the Association's progress after the end of hostilities. An Honorary Fellowship of the Association was conferred on him in 1946, in recognition of this and his earlier services for the library world.

With "ambassadorial" visits to North American libraries in 1933 and again in 1941, his work with IFLA and publication of his important *National Libraries of the World* (1934) Esdaile did much sound work to improve international links in the library world. A second volume, which he had planned as a sequel to his *National Libraries,* surveying some of the great non-national libraries (Bodleian, Boston Public Library, El Escorial, and others) was completed by Margaret Burton as *Famous Libraries of the World* (1937). His final substantial book was his excellent study *The British Museum Library,* written in retirement (1946). His interest in libraries and the health of the library profession continued right up to his death in London on June 22, 1956.

Esdaile's role in bringing together the British Museum and the library profession in Britain and in forging links with libraries abroad was of key importance in the interwar years. He may not have been a

Edmond Esdaile

Arundell Esdaile

269

National Library of Ethiopia

Main reading room of the National Library, Addis Ababa.

profound scholar, but his skills as a teacher, his friendliness, and his enthusiasm in building bridges were of real importance for facilitating the significant changes and major improvements in library service after World War II.

RODERICK CAVE

Ethiopia

Ethiopia, in northeastern Africa, is bordered by Sudan on the west and north, Djibouti and the Red Sea on the east, Somalia on the southeast, and Kenya on the south. Population (1984 est.) 42,200,000; area 1,223,600 sq.km. The official language is Amharic.

History. Ethiopia's ancient civilization had a script of its own that goes back as far as the 5th century B.C. The Ethiopian civilization is a genuine African civilization born and developed on African soil, and not transplanted from the other side of the Red Sea. The Hamitic peoples that have inhabited Ethiopia since ancient times lived on both sides of the Red Sea. Their settlements in the coastal lands of ancient southern Arabia were known and called by the Arabs of the time as Habashat, from the word *habash,* signifying individuals or tribes not organized in the usual Arab, Semitic tribal organization they were familiar with. There were constant and prolonged economic, social, cultural, and physical contacts between the peoples of the two continents. The resultant cultural and linguistic mix gives an Afro-Asian or Ethio-Semitic flavor to the present day literary culture of Ethiopia. Added is the rich centuries-old heritage of the peoples of Ethiopia.

Ethiopia developed its own ancient alphabet, which manifested itself first in its Sabean form, followed in the Geez (liturgical language), Amharic, Tigrigna, Tigre, Oromo, and other languages and now in the various vernaculars. It was restricted to the temple and the court before Christianity and to church and court afterward up to the threshhold of the 20th century.

The earliest literary records consist of inscriptions written on hard surface, mainly stone and some metal and clay. Monumental writings on walls of rock and granite steles, religious votive writings on clay vessels, iron implements, gold, silver, bronze, and iron coins were the main media, during both the pre-Christian and Christian eras. When Christianity was introduced to the country in the 4th century A.D., the Bible was translated into Geez from Greek. Gradually other religious texts were translated and adapted from Greek, Coptic, and Arabic. Parchment, imported by Christian missionaries from the Hellenized Middle East, was developed for writing as the only soft medium and spread at the end of the 5th century when a group of missionaries arrived in northern Ethiopia to found monasteries. Manuscript (known as *branna* from the Greek *membrana*) collections flourished with the growth and strength of Christian monasticism. There are tens of thousands of churches and monasteries throughout the country, mainly in the northern half plus southern Showa, holding all kinds of manuscript collections and manuscripts. The worth and full extent of these has not yet been established despite Unesco and other projects to begin to microfilm and catalogue collections in the second half of the 20th century. The manuscripts are scattered throughout some estimated 12,500 churches and 800 monasteries. The content is not exclusively religious, and the literary, linguistic, and historical importance, among other things, should not be underestimated. Royal collections were also important and a number of emperors were great manuscript collectors and patrons of religious and scholarly arts and centers.

Hundreds of Ethiopian manuscripts were expropriated by adventurers, diplomats, missionaries, and soldiers and taken to libraries in Europe. The tradition of gathering and maintaining collections was carried forward in modern times by the Emperor Yohannes IV (1871–1889), Menelik (1889–1913), and Haile Selassie (1930–1974). Menelik collected manuscripts in his palace by copying ancient manuscripts found in the Zway island monastery, by recovering some from Europe, and by other methods. There was a good scriptorium in his palace in Addis Ababa.

Before the printing press was introduced in the country in the 19th century, Geez and Amharic books were printed in Europe. A book of Psalms was printed in Geez in Rome (1513) by a German typographer from Cologne with the active help of Ethiopian monks. Learned religious men, such as Abba Tesfatsion of Malabso, an Ethiopian pilgrim monk who settled in a hospice provided to pilgrims by the Pope, were instrumental in making type fonts for small printing machines with Geez characters. They aroused European curiosity in Ethiopian studies and Ethiopia, and they made scholarly contributions on their own. Various linguistic and literary works were printed in Europe, chiefly in Rome. A missionary bishop, Lorenzo Biancheri, of the Lazarists, imported a small printing press to Massawa in October 1863. It became not only the first permanent printing press on Ethiopian soil (Massawa was then under Egyptian suzerainty) but the first in Eastern Africa (the press was introduced into Tanzania in 1875 and Kenya in 1877). The press of Biancheri began operation on May 10, 1867. It was transferred to Keren in 1879 and on to Asmara in 1912. There were other famous missionary presses, such as the Swedish Evangelical Mission's at Emkullu and a Roman Catholic press at Harar. Menelik imported a government printing press from Europe in 1906, and the Ethiopian Printing Press started production in 1908. Private commercial presses came soon to the scene and began to produce much needed literature, newspapers, government ordinances, regulations, religious texts, textbooks, journals, and pamphlets. Gradually their impact was felt, printed books for libraries were produced, and public interest in literacy and knowledge was increased.

The first modern library was established under Haile Selassie and was inaugurated on the occasion of his coronation in 1930. Named the National Library of Ethiopia, it consisted of a sort of a national and public library cum museum. The collections included fine selected Geez manuscripts and printed books in French, English, and Russian. The museum section included priceless ancient objects from various parts of the country. A prestige showpiece to impress European dignitaries during the coronation festivity, it was not much frequented by the public. The Library did not survive after Italian forces entered Addis Ababa on May 5, 1936. The Italians set up a public library for themselves in Massawa that later was transferred to Asmara. That Library grew to be comparatively large, its collection at one time reaching 10,000 volumes. During the Italian occupation there were several well run school and special libraries for the colonial community, and in Addis Ababa an Italian East Africa Central Library was set up for Italians in 1936. It too reached 10,000 volumes. But the Italian occupation brought a halt to Ethiopian education and modern librarianship. Damage to cultural and intellectual property was considerable. Fires in Addis Ababa and expropriation of irreplaceable treasures to Italy proved a severe loss to the country.

National Library. Founded, together with a National Museum, by Haile Selassie in 1944, the National Library offers loan and reference facilities to the public, acting as a central public library and as the national repository of Ethiopiana. A proclamation conferring depository privileges was enacted in 1975, a year after the Revolution.

The Library's valuable collection of several hundred Ethiopian Christian Orthodox manuscripts, some finely illuminated and dating from as early as the 14th century, also includes Ethiopian "incunabula" from the period when local printing began in the 19th century. In the 1960s the Library opened branches in several provincial centers, notably Debre Zeit, Yrgalem, and Harar, stocking them with volumes from its own collection. Collections total more than 90,000 volumes. A national bibliography had not been issued by the mid-1980s, though efforts toward its creation had been made, and plans were under way to house a national archives at the National Library.

Academic Libraries. The principal resource is the library system of the University of Addis Ababa. Founded in 1961 and building on the collections of the University College of Addis Ababa established 11 years earlier, the University Library has a number of branches, including law, medical, engineering, science, agriculture, and public health. The collections were developed extensively with Ford Foundation and U.S. AID assistance. Exceeding 500,000 volumes in the early 1980s, they include a unique library of Ethiopiana at the Institute of Ethiopian Studies,

where the holdings of more than 25,000 volumes are made up of a comprehensive collection of books about Ethiopia and the Horn of Africa; some 10,000 books, mostly in Amharic, printed in the country; and a collection of about 1,000 manuscripts and scrolls. The Library, together with the Institute, publishes *Ethiopian Publications* (1965–), a classified list of books and periodical articles published in Ethiopia.

The University of Asmara Library was founded by Italian nuns and added collections in English after the institution gained university status in 1967.

Although events of the 1970s and early 1980s—including increasing enrollments not matched by sufficient growth of collections—led to a system weakened by pressures of demand and insufficient support, academic library service remained by far the best of the library sector in the mid-1980s.

Public Libraries. Responsibility for public library service is carried by the National Library, with its inadequate funding. A number of municipal and community libraries have grown, in addition, mainly through local initiative. In 1973 a books-by-mail service was launched by the University Library, initially to provide recreational paperback reading to students on university service in the provinces, but it was later made available to the public. The service expanded after the 1974 Revolution, in cooperation with the Ethiopian Library Association, to serve students and teachers on the National Campaign for Development and Work 1974–1976, which included intensive literacy drives. Books were distributed through school or public libraries wherever these existed.

Generally speaking, the public library system is poor and the least developed service. There are only a small number of libraries but more than 6,000 reading rooms. Libraries range from one-room collections to reasonably well organized small ones. Detailed statistics are not available.

School Libraries. Modern secular education was advanced significantly in Ethiopia by Emperor Menelik, who opened the first modern government school in 1908. The Teferi Makonnen school, opened in 1925, was a landmark in educational history; it was the first school provided with a library in accord with a plan based on a European model.

In the 1960s and 1970s the Ministry of Education attempted to improve library services in secondary schools. Courses were held to train school librarians and, with AID assistance, books were purchased and distributed. School libraries continued to lack adequate bookstocks and qualified staff in the 1980s.

Special Libraries. The most important special library in Ethiopia is that of the UN Economic Commission for Africa (1958). It has a strong collection of African government and agency documents, periodicals, and some 60,000 books on African development. Other libraries serve government agencies. The National and Commercial banks, the Institute of Public Administration, and the Police and Air Force colleges have libraries of long standing. Among libraries sponsored by other countries are the British Council Library and the libraries of the French, German, Italian, and Russian cultural centers.

After the Revolution of 1974, many new special libraries were created. Several organizations imported computers in the 1980s, but modern information systems had not been widely applied by the mid-1980s.

For centuries thousands of churches and monasteries in Ethiopia have served as repositories of religious manuscripts used in services, teaching, and scholarship. It is estimated that some 50,000 manuscripts are housed in these churches. A project for recording them on film, initiated in 1973 by the Ethiopain Orthodox Church and Saint John's University, Collegeville, with funding from the National Endowment for the Humanities, led to microfilming thousands of manuscripts. They are kept in the Ethiopian Manuscripts Microfilm Library, Addis Ababa, and the Hill Monastic Manuscripts Microfilm Library, Collegeville (1976–).

The Profession. The Ethiopian Library Association, founded in 1967, achieved official status as a registered society in 1969. It has been active in campaigning for better public library facilities and in training librarians. Training is provided by a small staff with limited resources at Addis Ababa University, which offers diplomas in library science.

ADHANA MENGSTE-AB

Euronet

The Euronet communications network, jointly set up by the European Commission and the Post, Telegraph, and Telephone Departments of the member states of the European Economic Community (EEC), provides access to more than 500 databases. Thanks to work done on the Euronet system as a result of three triennial scientific and technical information and documentation action plans (1975–83), the Community developed the basis of an information industry. Euronet's functions have been assumed by interconnected national networks. The Community has largely reduced the disparity between the comparatively few EEC databases and those available in the United States by encouraging the development of an access system, most of which is used by private industry.

The European Commission worked in the mid-1980s to encourage further development of computer-based information services that could supplement Euronet in the EEC. DIANE (network for direct access to information for Europe) is the acronym under which online information services in Europe are being promoted. Trends in the development of the Euronet DIANE network include: developing new aids to assist the large community of network users (who numbered more than 8,000 by the end of 1984) to make the greatest possible use of the system and to encourage new users; exploring prospects for export; and developing the infrastructure of an information industry concerned with document delivery, multilingual problems, and other matters.

A complete guide to databases is issued by Euronet DIANE, Luxembourg. A database containing information on all the databases is made available by ECHO, the organization of the European Community's host computer.

CARLO VERNIMB

European Association of Information Services (EUSIDIC)

The European Association of Information Services (EUSIDIC) was founded in 1970. Membership is open to any organization involved in the electronic transfer of information. Those based in Europe are eligible for full membership; Associate membership is available to organizations outside the geographic region of Europe. In 1985 there were some 200 members from 27 countries.

The purpose of the Association is stated in its constitution: "to promote the unimpeded and efficient flow of information in machine-readable form both within Europe and between Europe and the rest of the world." When first established it was very much involved in the batch processing of bibliographic files, but since then its interests have grown and broadened so that it has become an international platform for information producers, hosts, users, and all groups interested in the handling, production, and dissemination of information in electronic form. These interests include online services (both bibliographic and nonbibliographic), telecommunications, economic aspects of information processing, microcomputing, office systems, transborder data flow, and other topics.

The Association is managed by its officers (Chairman, three Vice-Chairmen, and Treasurer) and its Council, all of whom are elected annually by the members. Only full members have voting rights and only representatives from full-member organizations may serve as officers and on Council. The Association employs an administrative secretary at its headquarters in London.

The annual conference is held normally in October. The spring technical meeting is aimed primarily at discussing in depth topics of immediate interest to members.

A regular newsletter (*NEWSIDIC*) is published with distribution restricted to members. In addition a variety of ad hoc reports are produced, some of which may be made available to other organizations. An ongoing series of "Guidelines" and "Codes of Practice" covering the fields of interest to EUSIDIC members is also published.

EUSIDIC is a member of INTUG (the International Telecommunications User Group) and has established close links with the European Commission. Regular contact is also maintained with other organizations in the field.

HELEN HENDERSON

Evans, Charles
(1850–1935)

Charles Evans, U.S. librarian and bibliographer, served a number of libraries from 1866 to 1901; from 1902 he devoted the rest of his life with single-minded dedication to his *American Bibliography,* the fundamental resource for early American imprints which secures his place in library history.

Evans was born on November 13, 1850, in Boston. After the deaths of both parents, he was placed in 1859 in the Boston Asylum and Farm School, where he received rigorous training in religion, manual labor, and academic studies. At the age of 16 Evans became an assistant at the Boston Athenaeum, the distingiushed private library then under the direction of William Frederick Poole. The Athenaeum proved to be Evans's bibliographical "alma mater" and Poole his life-long mentor.

ALA

Charles Evans

Evans was an effective library organizer and internal administrator and a leader in developing library services. But he failed to work well with supervising boards and administrators. That failure led to an uneven career as a librarian despite his achievements. He was the first Librarian of the new Indianapolis Public Library from late in 1872 until disagreements led to the end of his employment in August 1878. (He was to serve in Indianapolis again, from 1889 to 1892, but he again failed to sustain his board's support.)

Evans worked outside the library profession from 1878 to 1884. The following year he went as Assistant Librarian to the Enoch Pratt Free Library in Baltimore, but he resigned in December 1886 after difficulties with the Head Librarian. At the Newberry Library in Chicago, he worked in classification and reference from July 1892 to January 1895 and in the next year began to organize the collections of the Chicago Historical Society on a part-time assignment. Evans was Secretary and Librarian of the Society from July 1896 until the trustees dismissed him in 1901. His career as a librarian ended, but a new one was to begin.

In January 1902 Evans announced to a skeptical library community an ambitious project—a chronological, annotated record of publications printed in the U.S. from the beginning of printing in 1639 through 1820. Thereafter Evans set about achieving his objective with total commitment. By that time he had married Lena Young (1884), and they had three children (one of whom, Chick, became a golfer). But family and all ordinary social obligations and pleasures were to be displaced by his relentless pursuit of his goal. He took on not only the editorial and scholarly roles that the work demanded but also all production and printing—selecting his own paper, looking for the most economical printer, and directly overseeing all the work, including his own order fulfillment from his home. His plan was to offer separate volumes at $15 each to an initial 300 subscribers.

He began his editorial work for each period in the Newberry and Chicago Public libraries, carefully preparing annotated slips from bibliographies and printed catalogues. Then he would visit the Library of Congress and many other libraries in the East, often discovering stacks of publications that had not been previously organized. He worked long hours to bring out his first volume (covering the years 1639–1729), published in November 1903, and did not let up in his prodigious efforts in subsequent years. With characteristic energy and devotion, he managed to issue at fairly regular intervals the next eight volumes, carrying the work through the period 1790–92 by 1915. He had about 375 subscribers at the beginning of World War I. Evans won a reputation for his bibliographical achievement and benefited from cooperation with other bibliographers and librarians who provided information. He saw his work recognized by professional peers when he was elected to membership in the American Antiquarian Society in 1910.

Increased costs and the loss of foreign subscribers during World War I interrupted his publishing program for the next decade. With the support of Theodore Wesley Koch, Northwestern University Librarian, and an ALA committee, enough sales were generated to permit continuation of the work—volume 9 (1793–94), priced now at $25, was published

in 1926 and volume 10 (1795–96) in January 1929. During the Depression of the 1930s grants from the American Council of Learned Societies made possible publication of volume 11 and volume 12, covering the years 1796 and through the letter M of 1799. He had given up his original goal of 1820 to settle for 1800, but he did not live to complete the final volume in his revised plan. He died in Evanston, Illinois, on February 8, 1935.

Evans attended the first meeting of the American Library Association in October 1876. He served as ALA's first Treasurer until 1878, but he was not active in the Association thereafter. ALA named him an honorary member at its Conference in 1926, and in 1934 Brown University awarded him an honorary Doctor of Letters degree.

Evans's revised plan was eventually completed in 1955 when volume 13 (N 1799–1800) was published by the American Antiquarian Society under the editorship of Clifford K. Shipton. The American Antiquarian Society also issued volume 14, a cumulative Index, by Roger P. Bristol, in 1959. Bristol's index to printers, publishers, and booksellers in the series appeared in 1961. After another decade of work, Bristol issued his *Supplement to Charles Evans' American Bibliography* (1970). adding 11,000 titles to Evans's original 39,000. Thus Evans's original work continues to serve as the foundation stone of American bibliographic effort.

REFERENCES
Edward G. Holley, *Charles Evans, American Bibliographer* (1963), includes a complete list of Evans's works and other Evans materials.
Edward G. Holley, "Evans, Charles," *Dictionary of American Library Biography* (1978).

EDWARD G. HOLLEY

Evans, Eve

(1910-   )

Evelyn Jane Alice Evans, public librarian, developed the national library service of Ghana and contributed to library service in many other developing countries.

Born March 22, 1910, in Coventry, England, she served the Public Library there from 1927 to 1941. She became an Associate of the Library Association (LA) in 1931 and a Fellow in 1933. She worked in the University of Michigan Library in Ann Arbor in 1935 and 1936.

Evans was British Council Librarian in the then Gold Coast from 1945 until 1949, when she was transferred to the Gold Coast Library Board. The Board became a statutory body in 1950, and she became its first Chief Librarian and later its first Director of Library Services.

In 1945 there were no significant public library services in the Gold Coast. By 1965, when she left Ghana, there were 21 libraries and various services, including mobile units. Her philosophy was to use local resources when possible, and she early saw that she would one day have to make way for indigenous librarians. She also gave emphasis to the development of children's libraries.

In November 1961 Evans made a world tour to study library cooperation and national libraries. She traveled extensively in Africa and other developing areas, served as an expert on public libraries for Unesco, and advised Nigeria and Sierra Leone. In Ghana she was one of the pioneers who formed the West African Library Association in 1954, and she became its President in 1959.

In 1955 she was decorated as a member of the Order of the British Empire (M.B.E.) and in 1960 as a Commander of the Order (C.B.E.). She was made Honorary Fellow of the LA in 1965.

A Unesco consultant to Liberia in 1967, Evans was in Ceylon from 1967 to 1970, and she drew up legislation for the Ceylon National Library Services Board.

In 1975 she was invited by the Ghana Library Board to participate in the 25th anniversary celebration of the service that she had created from scratch and which she left intact, a monument to herself, to Ghana, and to African librarianship.

ANDREW N. DEHEER

Library of Congress
Luther Evans

Evans, Luther

(1902–1981)

Luther Evans, tenth Librarian of Congress and third Director-General of Unesco, is remembered especially for his wide participation in international activities.

He was born near Sayersville, Texas, on October 13, 1902. After earning a B.A. in 1924 and an M.A. in 1925 at the University of Texas, he completed a Ph.D. at Stanford in Political Science in 1927 with a dissertation on the mandate system of the League of Nations. Short-term instructorships ensued, at New York University (1927) and Dartmouth (1928–30), followed in 1930 by an appointment as Assistant Professor of Politics at Princeton, where he remained until 1935.

In October 1935 Evans was appointed Director of the Historical Records Survey in the Washington office of the Works Progress Administration. The American Imprints Inventory was perhaps its most significant project, as later edited by the Library of Congress and incorporated into the *National Union Catalog*. Evans remained with that office until joining the staff of the Library of Congress in 1939 as Director of the Legislative Reference Service. He was soon promoted to Chief Assistant Librarian under Archibald MacLeish and served concurrently as Director of the Reference Department. He served as Acting Head (1940–45) during MacLeish's frequent wartime absences and after his resignation in 1944. Evans succeeded MacLeish in December 1945 as the tenth Librarian of Congress. His was one of the rare appointments to be made from within the ranks.

Most significant of Evans's many accomplishments at the Library include the program to publish the *Cumulative Catalog of Library of Congress Printed Cards* (1947), the issuance of *Rules for Descriptive Cataloging in the Library of Congress* (1949) and *New Serial Titles* (1953), a greatly expanded readership, a 28 percent collection increase despite mounting budgetary restraints, and a democratic philosophy of management that greatly expanded the involvement of library staff in advisory groups.

In November 1945 MacLeish, then Assistant Secretary of State, invited Evans to join the U.S. delegation to the London Conference, which was ultimately responsible for the establishment of Unesco, the United Nations Educational, Scientific and Cultural Organization. In July 1953 Evans was elected Director-General of Unesco and resigned from the Library of Congress. This move brought an end to mounting congressional criticism of Evans's continuing extension of services to noncongressional patrons and of his heavy participation in international affairs. He served Unesco until 1958 and was actively involved in such major issues as the 1956 agreement on the protection of cultural property in wartime, peaceful use of nuclear energy, and the establishment of the Universal Copyright Convention.

After leaving Unesco, Evans served as an international studies consultant at the University of Texas and directed studies for the Brookings Institution on federal department libraries and the National Education Association on educational implications of automation. He assumed directorship of the international and legal collections at Columbia University in 1962, retiring in 1971 to an ongoing professional involvement in the American Library Association, World Federalists U.S.A., the United States Committee for Refugees, U.S. People for the United Nations, and the United Nations Association of the United States of America.

Evans died in San Antonio, Texas, on December 23, 1981.

REFERENCE
William J. Sittig, "Luther Evans: Man for a New Age," *Librarians of Congress, 1802-1974* (1977).

BETTY L. MILUM

Extension Services

Extension service is the activity of lending or delivering books and other forms of information to users who are distant from a library or who may be relatively near it but unable to travel to it. Effective extension has been developed through the commitment and experimentation of librarians in a variety of types and sizes of libraries, but the larger units of service have been encouraged to implement the most ambitious programs. Urban and rural systems, state library agencies, and, in at least one notable example, a federal library agency have pioneered in extension service. The concept and practice of library extension received dramatic support in the federal Library Services Act of 1956, for the extension of service to rural areas. Extension support continued when LSA was renewed and expanded by Congress in 1964 as the Library Services and Construction Act.

In a well-developed urban, suburban, or rural library system, extension is provided as a convenience to user populations for whom travel to a central library is difficult or expensive. Extension service may be a necessity to significant numbers of users who find travel to the central library impossible because they have physical disabilities, are institutionalized or homebound, or lack transportation. Because of these human and economic considerations, extension is a necessary and important specialization in public library service. Extension may also be provided within special, academic, and school district libraries, but the service is most frequently associated with public library operations.

Extension service is a part of many library organizations, but it does have limitations. Because of logistic and financial considerations it is difficult to provide complete information service in this manner. Compared to centralized service, on a per user basis extension is usually an expensive means of providing information delivery. Funding required for branch operations will often reduce the funding otherwise available for central library services. In spite of these limitations, extension is accepted as an essential component of effective library and information service.

Special considerations include the logistics and mechanical means for delivery, human and safety factors related to delivery systems, achieving balance between the expense of the information resources to be made available and their relative value to extension users, and the application of information and communications technology to assist extension.

Library extension began as a means of delivery of traditional lending service to users in growing cities and to dispersed populations in rural areas. Extension techniques were further developed to respond to the needs of special populations such as the visually handicapped, the homebound, and the economically disadvantaged. In the 1980s the concept of library extension took on additional new meaning as library uses of computers and improved telecommunications were employed to meet the demands of increasingly sophisticated information users.

Branch Libraries. Strategically located branch libraries form the network through which traditional library services have been most effectively extended in major city and suburban areas. The services of each branch library in the network are designed to meet the cultural and information needs of the people in the neighborhood. The cultural background of the branch's staff and other factors that affect the staff's ability to relate to users in the community should be strong considerations in the branch's design.

A branch network may be organized around a large central library, or the system may be composed entirely of relatively strong branches with central support functions performed in an administrative center or in one or more of the individual branches. There are advantages for users in having at least one library in a system where they can have access to a comprehensive materials collection and reference service; this encourages a system organization comprised of a central library with carefully planned branch locations. While such a system will have special adult collections and specialized reference services centralized, basic adult services will continue to be a feature in the branch program. Children's and young adult services are likely to be emphasized in the branch locations convenient to the younger users, who are less likely to be able to travel to the central library.

The ideal branch location would be a carefully designed, permanent library building with convenient patron access, ample parking, on a well selected site. As this ideal is frequently not achievable, there have been relatively successful branch locations in storefront buildings originally designed for uses other than as libraries, in portable buildings designed for library service but movable as changing demographics require, and even in accessible, visible areas of operat-

Library Association of Finland

Library Association of Finland

One of more than 200 Finnish bookmobiles that serve the rural countryside. Bookmobiles provide a popular service for public library lending in Finland.

ing businesses or in shopping malls where pedestrian traffic is high. A branch emphasizing reference information service as well as lending may be supported with terminals for computer communications with the central library and with other specialized information sources.

The service area of a branch is usually defined geographically, but it may also be identified as the center for a special subject or service emphasis. Each branch will rely upon the support services of a central library or administrative center, but there should also be the capability for communication and exchange of materials between branches. Thus effective communications and courier service are important to the successful operation of a branch system. These features must be added to the administrative, staff development, facility maintenance, technical service, public service, and public relations responsibilities that are basic components of any individual library's operation. The complete effectiveness of extension through a branch network will depend upon the integration of all branches with these basic support services.

Service extension through branch libraries is also characteristic of large colleges and universities and school districts. The outlying libraries may operate

Gothenberg City Library

A bookboat from the county library in Gothenberg, Sweden, visiting islands off Sweden's west coast.

of special programs for neighborhood children. Librarians have shown much creativity in the development of bookmobile story hours, puppet plays, exhibits, and other interest-generating outreach programs. In some jurisdictions a bookmobile and its staff have served as a voter-registration site.

An effective bookmobile operation is complex because it requires all of the basic support services from the administrative center and, in addition, vehicle maintenance, facilities for the exchange and loading of materials, a specially trained staff, and a process of public relations and communications with the administrators of the sites visited. A special electrical supply may be required at each stop if the vehicle is not equipped with an onboard generator. The bookmobile staff must maintain intense awareness for the safety of all users around the vehicle.

Other less-frequently used forms of mobile service include rotating book collections and deposit book collections. Rotating collections are a support for small community libraries provided by a library system or cooperative. A rotating service librarian using a truck or van moves collections of books from one community library to the next on a specified schedule and in a regular sequence until the individual collections have been held for the deposit period in all libraries of the cooperative. The rotating service van usually carries new materials for the librarian to add to the individual collections as they are left at each community library. Books still on loan to patrons at the collection change date are placed in the collection on hand as the books are returned to the library.

In an alternative form of extension, a rural library cooperative may maintain a central collection from which deposit collections of a few dozen to several hundred titles may be selected by community librarians participating in the cooperative. The deposit collection is held at the borrowing library for a period of several months to supplement the small library, until the deposit collection is returned and exchanged for another deposit. The objective of rotating book service or deposit collections is to give a small community library a variety of library materials it otherwise could not afford to buy and that may not have lasting value to the small population of users. In extension to a community without a library, system staff may place a deposit collection in a store or other business where it will be visible and where a volunteer will be on hand at least part-time to process loans from and into the collection.

Librarians use whatever affordable systems are at hand for the delivery of service. An example of determination to provide service is shown by the airplane delivery used by the State Library of Alaska to reach outlying areas.

Books by Mail and Telephone As extension service has been developed to reach widely dispersed populations in rural areas, it has become common practice to use the mail and the telephone to receive requests from users and to deliver books and other forms of information in response to those requests. It is not unusual for materials to be loaned through the mail with only minimal lending records and circulation control.

Books-by-Mail is a lending service to rural families, people in institutions, and the homebound based upon a "department store catalogue" approach to

under a designation other than "branch," but the basic service objective and many of the support service relationships are the same as those that occur among the units of a city or suburban library system. The important differences are primarily in the background and training of staff and in the specialized nature of the information resources and services maintained for the special clientele.

Mobile Services. Librarians motivated by their concern to provide service to citizens without access to central or branch libraries have devised an interesting variety of delivery methods.

The bookmobile, with a one-person or several-person staff, carrying a few hundred volumes or several thousand, has proven to be an effective means of delivering materials for loans to areas where a complete branch library is not affordable. City and suburban library systems have used bookmobile service, with scheduled stops at specified locations, as service test sites, or as a permanent but flexible method of extension. Bookmobile stops can be changed as traffic patterns and demographics change, and in developing suburban areas a bookmobile can provide service until the installation of a branch can be justified. Bookmobile service has been used as a principal form of extension for large rural areas.

A bookmobile has the advantage of being driven to a shopping center, nursing home, community center, or other location convenient to groups of users. Over a period of time, its staff can learn and supply materials for the personal interests of those who consistently visit the bookmobile at its various stops. Books for study and popular reading are the materials most frequently supplied, but requests for special interest materials such as recorded music, videocassettes, or talking books are not unusual. The staff may also provide limited reference services or convey patron requests back to central reference staff, who can then respond to the patron by telephone or mail, or through the bookmobile staff at the next scheduled visit.

The bookmobile can also be used for the delivery

merchandising. A family or individual receives a catalogue of books with a brief description of each item available for loan. A request card in the catalogue is used to mail in the book request. The central library packages the book or books requested in a protective mailer, includes a return mailing label and perhaps promotional information about available library services, and then sends the package to the borrower; books are usually returned by mail in the same mailer. Attractive catalogues for this service and related book collections and mailing supplies are available from commerical library suppliers, or, with considerable effort, can be produced locally.

Dial-A-Book and Dial-A-Fact have also been formalized as extension services. Dial-A-Book is more likely to be used in rural service extension where a library or library system is willing to receive an information request by telephone and then respond to that request with a book or other material returned to the borrower by mail along with a return mailing label. Dial-A-Fact is an extension of reference information service by telephone; it allows a patron to call the library for needed statistics, bibliographic information, recipes, or other forms of factual information. Availability of call-in reference service of this kind has come to be a standard and well-used service in many types of libraries.

Special Populations. The extension service best known in the U.S. is the recorded book and braille book distribution program of the National Library Service for the Blind and Physically Handicapped, Library of Congress (see Handicapped, Services to), popularly known as the Talking Book Service. The National Library Service, working with state and local libraries throughout the U.S., has operated an effective extension service to visually and physically handicapped users that has also served as a model for other forms of library service extension. The materials of this program are identified to users in large print and on recorded catalogues. Requests for materials are received from users by telephone and mail. Materials and the special equipment to use them are supplied to the user by mail or by personal delivery by a librarian or trained volunteer.

Extension service by personal delivery can also be effective in reaching homebound individuals who are temporarily ill, elderly, or physically handicapped or who for other reasons have limited mobility. It is not unusual for a public library to have a well-organized group of trained volunteers, or of assigned library staff, to give personalized extension service to the homebound or to individuals in institutions.

New Technology and Library Extension
As the uses of microcomputers and other computer systems in homes and libraries become commonplace, it is inevitable that these technologies, supported by improved telecommunications, will influence the traditional approaches to library service extension. Communication with online library catalogues was made possible for personal computer users at home and in offices over telephone lines. Full-text databases of reference and research information promised to be available online to more and more home users and others away from the library, as well as to users at the library.

There has been experimentation in the provision of full-text video from the library to home users, in support of reference information service. Improvements in local mass data storage will eventually allow large databases of bibliographic or textual information to be loaned by mail in disk or cassette units for use at home on personal computers.

All of these refinements in new information technology indicate that information users will see a growing capability to use library resources from remote, or home and business, locations. Librarians and the library's extension services will be important participants in these new, developing information systems.

REFERENCES
Eleanor F. Brown, *Modern Branch Libraries and Libraries in Systems* (1970).
Laura M. Janzow, editor, *The Library Without Walls, Reprints of Papers and Addresses* (1927). With its interesting and extensive collection of articles, this volume is possibly the earliest to gather together the varied concepts in library service extension.
Carleton B. Joeckel, editor, *Reaching Readers: Techniques of Extending Library Services* (1949).
Robert T. Jordan, *Tomorrow's Library: Direct Access and Delivery* (1970).

DUANE F. JOHNSON

F

Ferguson, Sir John Alexander
(1881–1969)

Sir John Alexander Ferguson, bibliographer and book collector, compiled the great *Bibliography of Australia 1784–1900*. The *Bibliography* is an important tool of the historian, the book collector, the librarian, and the dealer in rare and out-of-print books. Ferguson was by training a lawyer and industrial court judge.

Ferguson was born in Invercargill, New Zealand, December 15, 1881. His family went to Australia when his father was appointed as minister to Saint Stephen's Church in Sydney. Attending William Street Superior Public School and later studying with a private tutor, Ferguson matriculated to the University of Sydney and earned a B.A. with First Class Honours and the University Medal in Logic and Mental Philosophy. In his law school he earned the George Wigram Allen scholarship for most distinguished arts graduate entering the school and later was awarded the Pitt Cobbet Prize for international law.

Admitted to the Bar on May 27, 1905, he practiced first in equity and continued in that jurisdiction despite a developing and important practice in industrial law. By the early 1930s he was regarded as the leading barrister in the industrial jurisdiction in New South Wales and was appointed Lecturer in Industrial Law at the University of Sydney. In 1936 he was elevated to the bench of the Industrial Commission of New South Wales. During the 17 years before his retirement he made an important contribution to the industrial affairs of his state.

Early in life Ferguson began to collect and to describe materials relating to Australia, New Zealand, and the Pacific Islands, regarding collection and description as complementary activities. His personal and scholarly interests found emphasis in collections on bibliography, law, imaginative literature, social reform, military history, church affairs, the mission fields, and publishing. The influence of his father and his own lifelong association with the church led to a collecting interest in the church and missions in the Pacific areas and to the development of one of the most comprehensive collections of its vernacular publications. His *Bibliography of the New Hebrides* appeared in three parts between 1917 and 1945.

Ferguson set aside a number of other biblio-

graphical compilations to devote himself to the *Bibliography of Australia 1784–1900*, the first volume of which appeared in 1941; his work on the seventh and final volume continued, despite frailty of health, into his 80th year, the checking of the proofs completed just a week or so before his death.

As a bibliographer and collector, Ferguson saw his primary purpose to be the service of scholarship and research. Neither vanity nor greed led him to depart from a rational attitude to collecting by purchasing unique items at outrageous prices; his object was not to ornament his collection with priceless gems but to gather a substantial body of material of value for research.

As early as 1909 Ferguson had begun a relationship with the National Library that continued throughout his life. In 1937 he made the first transfer to the Library of part of his collection: "newspapers and periodicals illustrating the growth of all forms of political, social, economic and industrial thought in the Commonwealth." Further transfers included a large group of pamphlets in the same subject area, his "sociological pamphlets," arranged in the chronological order that he regarded as being of great importance. The collection finally totaled some 34,000 items; even with continuing transfers of other subject groups, there was still a considerable amount in his home in Sydney at his death on May 7, 1969. The Library purchased it from the Ferguson Estate and some time later, in 1975, acquired the copyright of the *Bibliography of Australia*, of which it published a new edition between 1975 and 1977. The Ferguson Room in the National Library is named in his honor.

Ferguson served from 1935 to 1965 as a Trustee of the Public Library of New South Wales. His university honored him in 1955 with the degree of Doctor of Letters, and in 1961 he was knighted for services to Australian literature, bibliography, and history.

C. A. BURMESTER

Fiji

Fiji, an independent parliamentary state, comprises a group of islands in the South Pacific Ocean. It lies approximately 3,200 km. east of Australia and 5,200 km. south of Hawaii. Population (1984 est.) 680,000; area 18,272 sq.km. The official language is English.

History. British sugar interests established Fiji's first lending libraries on a subscription basis, beginning in 1882. The Ramakrishna Library of books in South Indian languages (1928) long served with Suva's Carnegie Library as the islands' major source of reading material. Before 1944 little was achieved in establishing a library system. Even the period 1944–62, though full of plans and proposals, produced almost nothing.

National Library Service. The most significant step toward a National Library was the founding of the Fiji Library Service (FLS) in 1962 as a department of the Ministry of State for Social Welfare. The FLS operates public branches in all major townships, two bookmobiles, postal loan services (more than 1,000 correspondents), and a book box project (90 stations). A widely spread chain of islands creates geographical obstacles to this operation.

National Library of Australia

Sir John Alexander Ferguson

The University of the South Pacific Library in Suva, established in 1967, Fiji's largest library.

Caines Janniff, Ltd.

By extending its influence over technical operations and professional standards, the FLS looked toward obtaining statutory independence with its own Library Board and ultimately national library status. An FLS administrative headquarters was established in the capital city of Suva under a British grant.

Academic Libraries. The only university, the University of the South Pacific, established in 1967 in Suva, has the nation's largest single library, with 220,000 volumes, 8,605 current periodicals, 2,153 maps, 1,200 microforms, more professionals than in the rest of Fiji combined, and a regional clientele of 11 South Pacific nations. The University is augmented by smaller collections housed in the Pacific Theological College (25,000 volumes), Nasinu Teacher Training College (16,000), and the Fiji School of Medicine's Medical Research Library (8,000). The library at the Fiji Institute of Technology, connected to the Ministry of Education, has a library of 21,000 volumes and 50 current periodicals.

Public Libraries. Predominant libraries are the Western Regional (120,000 volumes) and Suva City (38,000). After World War II, when reading provision became more widely acknowledged as a public concern, Suva's private Carnegie Library (1909) was transformed into a public institution under city control. The Library's single professional librarian introduced a children's section and a bookmobile serving 25 city schools. But rural library service remains inadequate; public libraries, the FLS network, and bookshops are all confined to the towns. The Ramakrishna Mission is open to the public and houses about 20,000 volumes, with 150 current periodicals. However, books in general, and Hindi and Fijian language books in particular, are in limited supply.

School Libraries. Before 1940 no school libraries existed; 20 of Fiji's nearly 800 public schools support libraries containing from 1,000 to 7,000 volumes. The shortage of trained teacher-librarians, however, remains a problem.

Special Libraries. Special libraries number about 20, including academic and government holdings.

The 15,000-volume Indian Cultural Centre serves as a vital source of material for and about ethnic Indians, who comprise about half of Fiji's total population.

The government has maintained archives since 1954, and an official National Archives was established in 1969. An exceptional 10,000-volume local history and records library housed in the Archives and under professional control contains rich documentary materials dating well into the 19th century. Government departments also maintain notable collections, particularly the Ministry of Education's Educational Research Centre (13,000 volumes), the Supreme Court (12,000), and the Department of Agriculture (6,000).

Growing awareness of the importance of information has led to the creation of new special libraries such as those of the Fiji Electricity Authority, the Fiji Development Bank, and the Trades Union Congress.

The Profession. The Fiji Library Association (FLA) was founded in 1972. Its membership stood at 106 (including all 29 major libraries). It has a small library of its own.

The FLS pursues a professional staff training program for government libraries and organized an annual Fiji Certificate in Librarianship course for the training of subprofessionals.

HAROLD HOLDSWORTH*

Finland

Finland, a republic in northern Europe, is bounded by Norway on the north, the U.S.S.R. on the east, and the Gulf of Bothnia and Sweden on the west. Population (1984 est.) 4,880,000; area 338,145. The official languages are Finnish and Swedish.

History. Finland's geopolitical site between East and West, the Soviet Union and Sweden, has strongly influenced its culture. In the 12th century people were baptized into the Roman Catholic religion by the Swedes, and the country became a Swedish province. In 1810, as a result of the Russo-Swedish War, Finland was made into a Grand Duchy of the Russian Empire, and in 1917 it became independent: a Western-European democracy with a President and a Diet with 200 members.

Accordingly, the history of Finnish libraries and librarianship can be divided into three periods: from the Middle Ages to the 1820s, from the 1820s to 1917, and from 1917 onward.

The first library established in Finland was the library of Turku Academy, the first university in the country, founded in 1640. There were book collections in the churches, schools, and monasteries before

Libraries in Fiji (1978)

Type	Administrative units	Service points	Volumes in collections	Annual expenditures (Fiji dollar)	Population served	Professional staff	Total staff
National	--	--	--	--	--	--	--
Academic[a]	5	--	201,000	75,000	6,000[b]	13	50[b]
Public	9	9	91,000	--	33,044[c]	--	3
School[a]	300	750	235,000	52,000[d]	--	--	70
Special	11	--	82,000	--	--	--	--

[a]1977 data.
[b]Estimate.
[c]Registered borrowers.
[d]Acquisitions only.

Source: Unesco, *Statistical Yearbook,* 1984; *ALA World Encyclopedia,* First Edition (1980).

Finland

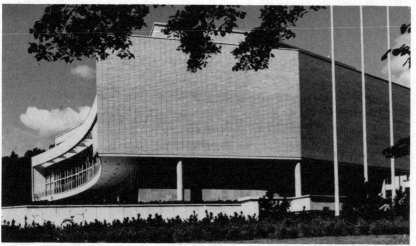

Töölö Library

Töölö branch of the Helsinki City Library, designed by Aarne Ervi, opened in 1970.

of the scientific societies, and new institutions of higher education, such as the Institute of Technology (Helsinki Technical School), founded in 1849.

The public library movement in Finland started in the middle of the 19th century on the initiatives of the clergy and the students and was linked with nationalistic ideas and achievements. The beginning of Finnish literature dates from the period of the Lutheran reformation, when the first books were printed in the vernacular. The educational system was part of the church, and the clergy played a central role in the spread of reading. During the Swedish regime, however, Finnish book production was small: only about 1,500 titles altogether. The main language was Swedish; Finnish gained its leading position toward the end of the 19th century. At that time almost the total population was literate: 97.9 percent in 1890, thanks to the public school system, which was established by the Public Education Decree in 1866.

When the country became independent, the educational level was significantly raised. New schools and universities were founded, statutes governing compulsory education were issued, and in 1921 public libraries began to receive regular government aid.

World War II interrupted the development, but in the later 1940s and the 1950s a new boom took place. More resources were given to the libraries and several new library buildings were designed and constructed. The most important example of Finnish library architecture, Viipuri Public Library, designed by Alvar Aalto and built in the late 1930s, was surrendered, however, to the Soviet Union.

A new Library Law was passed in 1962, supporting small libraries and libraries in institutions in particular. The law, however, covers only public libraries (as a law passed in 1928). There was no library legislation common to all types of libraries in the mid-1980s.

Most academic and special libraries are parts of other organizations. Their development is mainly the result of so many new universities being founded after World War II and of international information networks that have been established.

National Library. The National Library of Finland is the Helsinki University Library, established in 1640 in Turku as the Turku Academy Library and transferred to Helsinki in 1828 together with the Academy, which then became the Helsinki

that time, but they were modest in size. The academy library grew slowly, but, thanks to donations and deposit copies, it had a collection of about 3,500 volumes by the middle of the 18th century. The most important librarian was Henrik Gabriel Porthan (1739–1804), a prominent scholar, who also introduced the idea of a national "Fennica" collection. The library grew to 40,000 volumes, and it was a great loss when the collections were almost totally destroyed in the Great Fire of Turku in 1827.

When Finland became a Grand Duchy, Helsinki was made the capital of the country and the university was moved there. It was given many more resources than before, such as new buildings in the heart of the city. Even the university library received a building of its own. Designed by Carl Ludwig Engel, it is considered one of the most representative Neo-Classical buildings in the country. The Chief Librarian, Fredrik Wilhelm Pipping (1783–1868), worked hard to reestablish and organize the collections, which grew quickly thanks to liberal gifts and allowances. In 1844, when the new building was ready, there were more than 50,000 volumes, and in 1857 about 100,000.

By the beginning of the 20th century the building was too crowded, and an annex was built. Other scientific libraries were formed in the 19th century, mainly to serve the publishing and exchange activities

Libraries in Finland (1983)

Type	Administrative units	Volumes in collections	Annual expenditures (finnmark)	Population served	Professional staff[a]	Total staff[a]
National	1	2,381,200	4,692,300[b]	--	79	180
Academic	23	8,334,200	36,284,000[c]	90,500[d]	282	700
Public	1,543	27,484,502	548,577,542	4,841,700	4,150	4,850
Special	19[e]	1,770,000[e]	9,379,000[f]	--	95[e]	191[e]

[a]Full-time equivalents.
[b]Personnel expenses excluded.
[c]Incomplete data.
[d]Students and teachers only. Academic libraries are open to the public.
[e]Major libraries only. There are approximately 300 research (academic and special) libraries.
[f]Estimated from incomplete data.

Note: Official figures in Finland do not include all libraries. Real figures are higher than those in the table.

University. Its tasks include those of a national library and of a general research library. It collects all publications printed in Finland and publications written by Finns or dealing with Finland but published elsewhere, in addition to foreign literature for the study and research needs of Helsinki University. It also collects manuscripts dealing with Finnish cultural history and compiles the Finnish national bibliography and the union catalogue of Finnish research and university libraries. It receives publications on legal deposit and distributes them to other libraries. Among its resources is a special collection of Slavonic literature, started in 1820 when Finland became a grand duchy of Russia and the library received deposit copies of publications printed in that country. The library's holdings totaled 2,381,200 in 1983, making it not only the oldest but also the largest library in Finland.

The National Archives of Finland, administered by 45 professional staff members (153 total), includes seven Provincial Archives. Holdings in 1983 occupied some 77,640 linear meters of shelving, and annual expenditures were about 16,890,000 Finnmarks.

Academic Libraries. There are 23 academic libraries in Finland, a great number for a small country. Helsinki University was the only university until 1919, when Åbo Akademi, a Swedish university, was founded in Turku. Two years later a Finnish university was also founded in Turku. From their beginnings they were both remarkable, with national as well as foreign collections. In 1983, there were 1,360,724 volumes in Turku University Library and 1,263,577 volumes in the Åbo Akademi Library.

The first technical library in Finland was founded in 1849 in the Helsinki Technical School; it later became the Helsinki Technical University, and its library had a collection of 560,500 volumes in 1983. The Helsinki School of Economics Library was founded in 1911; it had 207,900 volumes in 1983.

After World War II several institutions of higher education were founded, among them the universities of Jyväskylä, Oulu, and Tampere. Only the Oulu University was actually a new institution; in Jyväskylä the Teachers' College was made into a university, and Tampere got a university when the School of Social Sciences was transferred from Helsinki and later became a university. In 1983 the Jyväskylä University Library had a collection of 905,800 volumes, the Oulu University Library 999,680 volumes, and the Tampere University Library about 681,400. These universities and other academic institutions have worked together with special libraries to provide new forms of information service, and some function as central libraries in their respective fields according to a Cabinet Statute of 1972.

A special feature in the history of Finnish academic libraries was the student libraries. The student unions established libraries of their own; some of them, such as the Library of the Student Body of Helsinki University, were quite remarkable. Founded in 1858, it had its own building and a collection of 200,000 volumes when in 1974 it became a part of the Helsinki University Library. The student libraries have merged with university libraries.

Public Libraries. The oldest public library in Finland is the library of the Regina School in Anjala, established in 1804. Its collection is now in a museum

at the Central Board of Schools, where the government office for public libraries is housed. Public libraries, in the true sense of the word, came into being in the middle of the 19th century through the initiative of students and clergy. From the beginning public libraries were local municipal institutions, and state aid was not given to them until 1921. The State Library Bureau was set up with Helle Kannila (1896–1972) as its energetic and effective Director, and a group of library inspectors was elected to direct library activities. The first Public Library Act was passed in 1928 and the second in 1962, giving strong support to rural municipalities and to libraries in hospitals and social institutions. The second act also made it possible to found central regional libraries, whose main task is to serve as interlibrary lending centers, borrowing material from research and university libraries for the public libraries. Many small public libraries have been replaced by bookmobiles; thus the number of public libraries was 4,007 in 1960 and 2,903 in 1970, while the number of home loans was 15,300,000 in 1960 and 32,400,000 in 1970. There were 1,541 public libraries in 1983. Public libraries in Finland have taken on the functions of cultural centers, arranging, for example, for concerts, exhibitions, and puppet theater performances. A new act was in preparation in 1984.

School Libraries. There is no organized system of school libraries in Finland, although school libraries were included in plans for a comprehensive school system; these plans had not been carried out by the mid-1980s.

Special Libraries. The oldest special libraries in Finland were the libraries of the scientific societies, founded in the early and middle 19th century. Most special libraries are now part of private firms and institutions. Typical of their activity are information service and documentation; documentation started in Finland in the 1940s in industrial libraries, where the first documentalists were engineers. Among Finland's special libraries are such large libraries as the Parliament Library, founded in 1872 and having a collection of 467,500 volumes, and the remarkable Central Medical Library, established in 1966 and holding some 300,000 volumes. Most of the special libraries are small, however, forming a part of bigger organizations. Several of these libraries belong to an international information network and compile special bibliographies in their fields.

The Profession. The Finnish Library Association dates back to 1910; it publishes a Finnish library journal, *Kirjastolehti*. The Finnish Research Library Association dates from 1929; together with the Finnish Association for Documentation (1948) it publishes the journal *Signum*. All three associations arrange meetings, seminars, and courses; national meetings of librarians are held every second year. There are other associations in the field of librarianship and documentation, including professional unions.

Financed by funds from a private cultural foundation, the first professional course in librarianship was organized in 1920. When the State Library Bureau was founded, it took upon itself the responsibility for training librarians. In 1945 the professional education of librarians was started on a regular basis at the School of Social Sciences, later Tampere Univer-

Henry Clay Folger

sity, where a course leading to a librarian's certificate was included in the curriculum. It was valid for service in all public libraries and in most scientific libraries. At the Helsinki University Library an Amanuensis Examination was arranged as early as the beginning of the 20th century; later it was also offered at other academic libraries.

In 1971 a remarkable change took place: a professorship of library and information science was founded at Tampere University, the Faculty of Social Sciences, and thereafter it was possible to include library and information science in programs leading to Master's and Doctor's degrees. In 1982 another professorship, at the Swedish University of Turku, Åbo Akademi, was established; the training of librarians for the Swedish-speaking minority takes place there.

Continuing education is partly organized by the Finnish Library Association, the Finnish Research Association, the Finnish Association for Documentation, and other library associations. Centers for continuing education at Tampere University and Helsinki Technical University also offer courses for librarians; the latter is responsible for the training of information scientists for libraries, information services, and various posts in industry, business, and administration. In spite of the many-sided supply of courses and degrees in librarianship, many libraries were without professional staff in the mid-1980s, legislative support lagged, and libraries were still in many cases seen as little more than book depositories. Modern methods of information service have not yet been accepted in many places.

RITVA SIEVÄNEN-ALLEN

Folger, Henry Clay
(1857–1930)

Henry Clay Folger, U.S. businessman who headed Standard Oil Company of New York, was one of the great book collectors of the late 19th and early 20th centuries. With invaluable assistance from his wife, he brought together a remarkable collection of books, manuscripts, art objects, and other materials relating to Shakespeare, his works, and his age. Folger and his wife founded the Folger Shakespeare Library in Washington, D.C., to house their collection and to make it accessible to an international community of researchers.

Folger belonged to a family with distinguished American antecedents. Peter Folger, the first of the name to settle in America, emigrated from England and settled on Nantucket Island in 1635; his daughter was the mother of Benjamin Franklin. Several generations later another descendant, Charles James Folger, served President Chester Arthur as Secretary of the Treasury. Henry Folger's father was a resident of New York City who built up a prosperous wholesale millinery business and sent his son to grammar and high school in the New York area.

Folger entered Amherst College in 1875. For a time his continuation at Amherst was threatened by his father's financial reverses, but timely loans from two classmates permitted him to complete his course of studies there, and he graduated in 1879. A career in business seemed tempting; with the help of his college roommate, Charles Pratt, whose father headed one of the affiliates of Standard Oil, Folger accepted a clerkship in the company. He also enrolled in the Columbia University Law School and two years later obtained an LL.B. degree. A steady climb up the corporate ladder rewarded Folger for his shrewd business sense and industrious dedication to the growth of the company. He became President of Standard Oil of New York and held that post until 1923, when he was made Chairman of the Board. He retired from active involvement in the company in 1928.

Despite his corporate responsibilities, Henry Folger retained a keen interest in the world of letters. The published address by Ralph Waldo Emerson on the "Tercentenary of Shakespeare's Birth," which Folger had read as an undergraduate, fired him with an enthusiastic appreciation for Shakespeare that never waned. Indeed, his marriage to Emily Clara Jordan intensified it. She was a Vassar graduate who went on to graduate school after her marriage and wrote a Master of Arts thesis on "The True Text of Shakespeare."

Their shared interest in Shakespeare led the Folgers quite early into book collecting. They started in 1885 with a relatively cheap facsimile of the 1623 First Folio edition of Shakespeare's works, and their pursuit of Shakespeareana accelerated as their financial means to satisfy their hobby increased. Soon they were combing bookshops on both sides of the Atlantic. Rare quarto editions of Shakespeare's plays and the first folio edition of his collected works were those most sought by the Folgers, but they also looked for later editions of the plays and materials reflecting Shakespeare production down to modern times, including printed texts, promptbooks, playbills, paintings and illustrations, costumes, and memorabilia of all sorts. They wisely realized that Shakespeare could best be understood in the context of the times in which he lived; they purchased books that reveal the sources for plots and ideas contained in his plays, the works of his contemporaries in the literary world, and a wide spectrum of rare books and manuscripts depicting the society of Elizabethan and Jacobean England and, more generally, Western Europe and America in the early modern period.

The Folgers amassed a collection of some 93,000 books, 50,000 prints and engravings, and thousands of manuscripts that, for lack of space, they carefully inventoried and then stored in bank vaults and warehouses. Shortly after World War I they determined to unite their collection in a library dedicated to Shakespeare. The site they selected in Washington, D.C., was directly across from the Library of Congress, whose resources they knew would enhance the value of their own Library. The cornerstone for their Library was laid May 28, 1930. Two weeks later, on June 11, Folger died in Brooklyn, New York.

Mrs. Folger was present for the opening of the Library on April 23, 1932, and she was involved closely with its operation until her death in 1936. Under the terms of Folger's will the administration of the Library was entrusted to the Trustees of Amherst College. Folger and his wife left the bulk of their estates to serve as endowment to defray the operating costs of their Library.

Following the lines laid out by its founders, the Folger Shakespeare Library has become an international center for the study of Shakespeare and of the

Renaissance and early modern period. The Library's exhibition gallery attracts thousands of visitors each year to view items from the original Folger Collection as well as many later acquisitions. An Elizabethan theater, which is an integral part of the Library, provides thousands more with an opportunity to enjoy theatrical productions both Shakespearean and modern, concerts of Renaissance music, lectures, and conferences.

REFERENCE

Betty Ann Kane, *The Widening Circle—the Story of the Folger Shakespeare Library and Its Collections* (Folger Library, 1976).

PHILIP A. KNACHEL

Food and Agriculture Organization

The Food and Agriculture Organization of the United Nations is an autonomous agency of the UN. It is made up of 156 member nations pledged to raising the levels of nutrition and standards of living of their peoples, to improving the production and distribution of all food and agricultural products, and to improving the condition of rural people. FAO functions simultaneously as a development agency, an information center, an adviser to governments, and a continuing forum for the discussion of food and agriculture issues.

Established in October 1945 at a conference in Quebec, Canada, FAO has headquarters in Rome. It established regional offices for Africa in Accra, Ghana; for Asia and the Pacific in Bangkok, Thailand; for Europe in Rome; for Latin America and the Caribbean in Santiago, Chile; and for the Near East in Rome. There is an FAO Liaison Office for North America in Washington, D.C., and a Liaison Office with the UN in New York.

The work of the organization is conducted by an international Secretariat under the leadership of a Director-General. The supreme governing body is the Conference, which meets every two years and elects as an interim governing body a Council of 49 member nations.

As a development agency, the FAO gives direct help in the developing world through technical assistance projects in all areas of food and agriculture. These projects strengthen local institutions, assist research and training, and develop and demonstrate new techniques. The technical assistance projects are financed chiefly by the UN Development Program and trust funds of national governments.

Investment in agriculture is covered by FAO's Investment Support Program, which helps developing countries find the external capital needed to build up their agriculture. The World Bank is the single most important financing institution for investment projects prepared by FAO.

As a focal point for world agriculture, FAO serves as a clearinghouse for information and makes it available in almost every medium: print, film, radio and TV, video, filmstrips, and computer tapes.

Major periodical publications include yearbooks on world production, trade, fertilizers, forest products, and fishery statistics. Others include reports on world food supply, commodity reviews, and the *FAO Plant Protection Bulletin* and *FAO Monthly Bulletin of Statistics.* Ideas and Action is a publication of the Freedom from Hunger/Action for Development program.

Major databases and systems include AGRIS (International Information System for the Agricultural Sciences and Technology), a bibliographic database online in the U.S. since November 1, 1985 (also used to produce the monthly bibliography *AGRINDEX*); CARIS (Current Agricultural Research Information System), data on current research projects; ICS (Interlinked Computer Storage and Processing System of Food and Agricultural Commodity Data); ASFIS (Aquatic Sciences and Fisheries Information System); FISHDAB (Fisheries Database); and FORIS (Forest Resources Information System).

JOHN B. FORBES

Force, Peter

(1790–1868)

Peter Force compiled historical documents and was a bibliophile and collector, printer, editor, bibliographer, librarian, and archivist. Research tools he created became models for subsequent generations.

Force was born near Little Falls, Essex County, New Jersey, November 26, 1790. His family moved several times before settling in New York City in 1794, where he received limited schooling. Early in his teens he became an apprentice in the printing business of William A. Davis and assumed the responsibilities of printshop foreman at about the age of 16. The New York Typographical Society elected him its President in 1812. He won a militia commission during the War of 1812 and served as marshal of printers.

Force moved to Washington, D.C., in 1815, when Davis secured a government printing contract, and they operated a lending library of more than 3,000 volumes out of their printery until debts compelled them to sell the books in 1825. From 1823 to 1831 Force published a newspaper, the *National Journal,* aligned with Adams's administration. A Whig, Force participated in District of Columbia politics, sitting on the city council and winning the mayorality for two terms (1836–40). He also edited directories of government personnel, commercial statistics, and historical data intermittently from 1820 to 1836. His industriousness notwithstanding, creditors in 1830 nearly seized his property, which already included another substantial library.

Financial motives, along with a genuine veneration of America's past, inspired Force to propose in 1831 publishing for the federal government a multi-volume compilation of historical documents. The idea was not original, but Force and his partner, Clerk of the House Matthew St. Clair Clarke, promised unprecedented thoroughness. Congress authorized the project in 1833. Sadly, the lucrative contract left unclear the exact scope and cost of the work and the *American Archives,* as it became known, thus suffered repeated attacks by the frugal as well as by the politically antipathetic.

Force supervised researchers and dealers dispersed through the 13 original states and England in transcribing or purchasing pamphlets, books, newspapers, maps, government documents, and manuscripts. His preference for printed sources may reflect his lack of scholarly training. His eye for ephemeral

Courtesy of The Newberry Library

Peter Force

283

pieces, however, preserved a number of texts from historical oblivion. Copyists received instructions on careful handling of archival materials that were exemplary for their time. Publication commenced in 1837; showing a canny sense of patriotic appeal, Force started with the fourth and fifth series (covering 1774–76) of the six (1492–1787) he scheduled to complete the work. In 1853 the Democrats deprived the Whigs of the presidency, and Secretary of State William L. Marcy refused to approve the contents of the next two volumes, and subsequent changes of administration failed to revive the *American Archives*. Truncation of the project left Force holding a huge collection of rare Americana, with obligations to match.

Even in its abbreviated form the *American Archives* was an impressive undertaking. Major bibliographies on colonial America still cite its more than 16,000 folio pages as a basic resource. Historians also continue to use Force's *Tract and Other Papers Relating . . . to . . . the Colonies of North America* (1836–46). This four-volume work reproduced 52 pamphlets, some of which Force had already reprinted separately. Most were 17th-century London imprints, scarce even by 1836, when the *Tracts* began to appear. The set reveals Force's personal bibliophilic leanings better than the *American Archives*. "Whenever I found a little more money in my purse than I absolutely needed," he later recalled, "I printed a volume of Tracts."

Loss of income from the *American Archives* transformed Force's matchless collection into a passion he could ill afford during the last 15 years of his life. Librarian of Congress Ainsworth R. Spofford for years visited the reclusive old man, surrounded in his Washington residence by crude tables and shelves bearing his treasures. Spofford and others yearned to relieve the owner of them; Force finally agreed for a price of $100,000. The New-York Historical Society could not raise the sum, but Spofford managed with difficulty to extract the money from a wartime Congress. So the "Force Library" in 1867 became a primary foundation for future development of Americana holdings at the Library of Congress. Force died less than a year after the collection left his home, on January 23, 1868, in Washington, D. C.

Force made several noteworthy contributions to library and archival science. He created research tools that remain useful almost a century and a half later. With Spofford's good offices, he furthered the growth of the Library of Congress. Most importantly, he communicated to a young nation the vitality of his concern about collecting and preserving records of its past. His *American Archives* mark a giant step toward federal recognition of a public responsibility to assist in the dissemination of historical information. Force's publications became models that local governments and historical organizations before long emulated with happy results.

Library Association

D. J. Foskett

REFERENCES

The main body of Force's personal papers now resides in the Manuscript Division of the Library of Congress.

Newman F. McGirr, compiler, *Bio-Bibliography of Peter Force 1790–1868* (1941), especially useful in locating works by Force and government document citations.

Ainsworth R. Spofford, "The Life and Labors of Peter Force, Mayor of Washington," *Records of the Columbia*

Historical Society (1899).

Richard W. Stephenson, "Maps from the Peter Force Collection," *Quarterly Journal of the Library of Congress* (1973), an illustrated, specialized study that includes a good general overview.

DAVID J. MARTZ, JR.

Foskett, D. J.
(1918-   )

One of the most prominent figures in contemporary British library and information science, Douglas John Foskett made many, varied, and important contributions to library and information science. Classification was always one of Foskett's major interests, and in 1952 he was one of the founders of the Classification Research Group in Britain. But he proved equally influential in the fields of comparative librarianship and library education and in the development of the Library Association.

Foskett was born in London on June 27, 1918. He had hardly begun his professional career in the Ilford (Essex) Public Libraries when World War II intervened; from 1940 to 1946 he served first in the Royal Army Medical Corps and later in the Intelligence Corps.

In 1948 Foskett left Ilford to become Librarian of the Metal Box Co. Ltd., a post he held until 1957. He served as Librarian of the University of London Institute of Education (1957–1978), then was promoted to the position of Director of Central Library Services of the University of London (1978-1983). He thus had a wide experience in public, special, and academic libraries.

A member of the Council of the Library Association for many years, he was Chairman (1962–63), a Vice-President (1966–73), an Honorary Fellow (1975), and President (1976). A vigorous protagonist for the unity of the profession, he consistently supported the idea of a confederation among the LA, Aslib, the Institute of Information Scientists, and other related bodies. He was for some time Chairman of the LA Education Committee.

Foskett also became an internationalist, undertaking numerous missions for Unesco and the British Council and traveling on lecture and observation study tours in most parts of the world. From 1968 to 1973 he was a member and rapporteur of Unesco's International Advisory Committee on Libraries, Documentation, and Archives; he also was a consultant on documentation to the International Labour Organisation. He was later a committee member of the UNISIST/Unesco and the EUDISED/Council of Europe projects. An engaging speaker, Foskett served as Visiting Professor at the Universities of Michigan, Ghana, Ibadan, and Iceland and at the Brazilian Institute of Bibliography and Documentation. He made observation tours to Czechoslovakia and the People's Republic of China.

A prolific writer on library and information topics, he wrote, among other works, *Assistance to Readers in Lending Libraries* (1952), *Information Service in Libraries* (1958), *Classification and Indexing in the Social Sciences* (1963), *Science, Humanism and Libraries* (1964), *Reader in Comparative Librarianship* (1976), and *Pathways to Communication* (1984). With B. I. Palmer he edited *The Sayers Memorial Volume* (1961).

K. C. HARRISON

France

France, a republic in northwestern Europe, is bounded by the English Channel, Belgium, and Luxembourg on the north, Germany, Switzerland, and Italy on the east, Spain and the Mediterranean Sea on the south, and the Atlantic Ocean and the Bay of Biscay on the west. Population (1984 est.) 54,872,000; area 550,000 sq.km. The official language is French.

History. *Middle Ages.* During the Middle Ages, in France as well as in other countries of Europe, the first libraries were included in monasteries and reserved for the monks. They were linked to copyists' workshops where manuscripts, borrowed from other monasteries, were transcribed by hand. This manual reproduction was the only means by which Latin and Greek texts were brought from classical antiquity to modern times.

Monastic libraries had very small collections—for example, 300 at Saint Riquier (Somme)—and were housed in single rooms or in wall niches near the *scriptorium*, such as those in Le Thoronet (Var), Silvanès (Aveyron), Luxeuil (Vosges), and Saint Martin de Tours.

From the 13th century, the development of universities led to the creation of university libraries. Each had its own *scriptorium*. In those libraries, books were kept on a lectern and chained to it. The Sorbonne was one of the largest, with 1,017 books in 1290. The library of the Chapitre (Chapter House) du Puy is the last remaining example of this type of library in France. At the same time, private libraries flourished, created by the king, princes, dukes, and other noblemen. The Comte d'Angoulême, for example, had a rich library that was later partly transferred to the king's library.

Naudé and the Bibliothèque Mazarine. When Cardinal Mazarin, Richelieu's successor as first minister of France, arrived in Paris in 1640, he brought with him a personal library of 5,000 volumes that he had collected in Rome. In 1642 he purchased the Hôtel Tubeuf on the corner of the Rue Neuve des Petits Champs and Rue de Richelieu and decided to establish a large library on the premises. To carry out the project he chose Gabriel Naudé (1600–53), who had been Richelieu's Librarian. Naudé was a scholar and a book lover. Although his studies had been in medicine, his career was in books: he was, in turn, the Librarian of Cardinal Bagni, of Cardinal Barberini, and in 1642 of Cardinal Richelieu. After Richelieu's death that same year, Naudé became Mazarin's librarian, buying large collections of books (12,000 volumes and 400 manuscripts) and compiling a catalogue. In 1627 he published *Advis pour dresser une bibliothèque* (*Advice on Establishing a Library*), in which he put forward the first rules of modern librarianship.

The library at the Hôtel Tubeuf (where the Bibliothèque Nationale is now) was opened to the public every Thursday beginning in 1643 and every day beginning in 1647, with 100 readers each open day. Naudé traveled far and wide in Europe buying for the collection, and Mazarin built several additions to house the 40,000 volumes handsomely bound and emblazoned with his arms.

During the Fronde (civil war, 1648–1653), however, the collection was dispersed in public sales. Naudé died in 1653. After Mazarin's return to France that year, he rebuilt his library with the help of François Lapoterie, his new Librarian. Mazarin's library was reconstituted and new collections, including Naudé's personal library, were bought. Mazarin, who died in 1661, left his library to the Collège des Quatre Nations, founded, according to his will, for students from four provinces conquered by France; thus began the Bibliothèque Mazarine.

Bibliothèques Communales and Impact of the French Revolution. Other than the Bibliothèque Mazarine and a few collections of the 13th and 14th centuries, which were available only to scholars, there were only private libraries in France before the Revolution. The first network of public libraries was established by the Revolution. Property that had belonged to the aristocracy and to the Church, including numerous libraries, was confiscated; from dispersed private collections, the Revolution made a national patrimony; the libraries thus created became the nucleus of a widespread public library system. Clerical properties were put "at the Nation's disposal" on November 2, 1789, and some months later the property of émigrés and of persons condemned by the Terror was sequestered. The total number of confiscated books was estimated at 10,000,000 by the Abbé Grégoire in a report to the Convention dated April 11, 1794; there were also 26,000 manuscripts. (For comparison, the Royal Library contained 300,000 volumes.)

In order to classify the mass of documents, an inventory had to be taken. The catalogue was actually written on playing cards. Then a Conservation Committee picked out for sale a certain number of books on theology, religion, and "ascetics." Books not put

Libraries in France (1982)

Type	Administrative units	Service points	Volumes in collections[a]	Annual expenditures (French franc)	Population served	Professional staff	Total staff
National	1	15	12,000,000[a]	88,973,593[a]	--	548	1,276[a]
Academic	61	182	18,000,000	130,000,000	975,000	1,641	3,349
Public	1,029	1,734	45,000,000	1,119,818,000	--	2,300	7,200
School	3,500	3,500	12,000,000	--	--	--	--
Special	4,000	--	--	--	--	--	--
Central Lending (BCP)	94	--	13,000,000	1,540,000	24,000,000	550	1,124

[a]1983 data.

The main reading room of France's Bibliothèque Nationale in Paris, originally the Royal Library dating to the 14th century.

up for sale were stocked in "literary depots" in Paris and other cities, then divided among existing libraries (the Bibliothèque Nationale received 300,000 volumes). They also served to create new libraries (for example, that of the Assemblée Nationale). The rest was given to "Central schools" formed in each département in 1795. After the suppression of those schools in 1803, the books were given to the communes to create municipal libraries.

But there was a contradiction between the intentions of the authorities and their methods. The Revolutionary project was to set up libraries to serve as "a school for all citizens," but the collections confiscated from the nobility and the Church mainly consisted of works on theology, jurisprudence, and ancient literature—not what was required for popular education. Inertia prevailed, however, and the public library system that could have come into being did not. Libraries were oriented toward conservation and learned studies. No acquisitions policy came to balance the enormous mass of ancient documents for which the public authorities became responsible.

At the end of the Revolutionary period, many large libraries in France had not been inventoried, and they were concerned more about ensuring the security of their collections than increasing them or opening them to the public. The librarians of those collections, so rich in history, literature, and theology, were bound to look toward the past—the paradoxical heritage of the French Revolution. This predominating influence of the past was the most striking feature of French public libraries until the 20th century.

Some private initiatives, however, attempted to encourage reading among the masses: the *Cabinets de lectures* were shops lending books at a nominal fee, and the *Bibliothèques populaires* were opened by the bourgeoisie to educate the workers and save them from "bad reading."

Bibliothèque Nationale. The Bibliothèque Nationale is an outgrowth of the Royal Library, which dates back to the reign of Charles V (1364–80).

Appreciating the manuscript treasures he inherited from his royal ancestors, he put them in the Louvre and appointed a scholar, Gilles Malet, to catalogue them; the first catalogue of the Bibliothèque Nationale is a manuscript dated 1380. During the fluctuations of royal history, the king's library became dispersed, but it was enthusiastically rebuilt by Francis I (reigned 1515–47), who, with the help of his ambassadors (notably in Germany, Venice, and the Middle East), bought numerous manuscripts. He housed them in Blois, then in Fontainebleau, and named Guillaume Budé *Maître de la Librarie du Roy* ("Master of the King's Library"). The King's Library comprised around 2,000 volumes; only 200 were printed books.

Budé's successors continued to buy collections, to receive gifts (for example, that of Gaston de France, duc d'Orléans [1608–1660]), and to seize private libraries, among them the libraries of Nicolas Fouquet (finance minister of Louis XIV imprisoned for embezzlement), La Vallière (a mistress of Louis XIV who fell into disfavor), and of the Jesuits, who were the object of frequent attacks in France. But the largest intake came during the Revolution.

So, after a number of vicissitudes, the King's Library found a permanent home on the Rue de Richelieu in 1743. It was renamed the Bibliothèque Nationale by the Revolution. Large improvements in the building and its reading room were made from 1856 to 1868 by the architect Henri Labrouste. It was opened to the public in 1720 and possessed 300,000 volumes in 1789.

Copyright Deposit. Legal deposit in France stems from Francis I, who in his Montpellier regulation of September 28, 1537, provided that one copy of every book published in France be deposited in the Royal Library to qualify for the King's authorization. Several texts modify this ruling, the latest being a law of June 21, 1943, when two deposits were established. Printers must send two copies to the municipal library in their region, one of which is passed on to the Bibliothèque Nationale; publishers must send four copies to the Bibliothèque Nationale and one to the Ministry of the Interior.

All types of documents in addition to books are subject to the legal deposit rule, including postcards, periodicals, brochures, prints, engravings, posters, music, films, records, and photographs. A decree of July 30, 1975, added audiovisual materials. Copyright deposits for a single year (1982) totaled: printed books, 42,318; brochures, 15,822; official publications, 15,734; serials, 32,000 titles or 1,717,466 issues; maps, 1,785; engravings, 8,790; posters, 5,652; coins, 557; musical works, 2,417; and records, 12,632.

Organization. A decree of March 22, 1983, appreciably modified the administrative structure of the Bibliothèque Nationale, taking into account a decree of July 1975, which withdrew the management of French university and public libraries from the Administrator of the Bibliothèque Nationale, who had also been, for 30 years, Director of French libraries.

The Bibliothèque Nationale is a public institution with financial autonomy under the control of the Ministry of Culture. Its objectives are described in the decree: collection, cataloguing, and preservation of the national production, collection and cataloguing of any document (manuscripts, coins, rare and precious books, audiovisual items) of national interest, and encyclopedic documentation and research in the humanities. The General Administrator is assisted by a 25-member Board of Trustees and by a Scientific Council, which gives advice on research activities of the Bibliothèque Nationale. The library is divided into departments and services: the Administrative service includes finances, personnel, publications, and buildings; the Departments include Printed Books, Periodicals, Manuscripts, Coins and Medals, Maps and Charts, Official Publications, Prints, Music, Performing Arts, Records (Phonothèque Nationale), and the Bibliothèque de l'Arsenal. The services are the National Bibliography, Acquisitions, the Lending Center, Exchanges, the Photographic service, and Conservation.

The Library is funded through the Ministry of Culture. It also relies on gifts, legacies, and the sale of documents. In 1986 the budget amounted to 126,095,972 French francs, of which 14,300,000 francs were for acquisitions and 14,000,000 francs for maintenance of collections. The staff comprised 1,276 persons, 291 of whom were professional librarians (*conservateurs*) and 257 assistant librarians. Others were 345 stack attendants, 131 technicians, and 137 administrative staff members.

Collections. The main collections in 1983 were as follows: 12,000,000 books, 450,000 periodical titles, 300,000 manuscripts, 12,000,000 prints, engravings, and photographs, 1,500,000 maps, 800,000 coins and medals, and 500,000 records.

Services. The Bibliothèque Nationale is open for postgraduate research. It seats 884 and, in 1982, served 322,993 readers. The Reference Room contains general reference works, bibliographies, and the Bibliothèque Nationale's catalogues. Except for special exhibitions, the Library's collections do not circulate. Facilities for photocopies, microfilms, and other forms of reproduction are provided. A Consultative Committee exists through which readers may express their wishes and complaints. Moreover, the Library has a lending center (Centre de prêt de la Bibliothèque Nationale, formerly called the Service Central des prêts) with its own collection, including every title received by legal deposit since 1980. Its function is to make French publications available to other libraries in France and abroad in accordance with the IFLA universal availability of publications principles.

In 1897 the Library launched the publication of its general catalogue of authors; the final volume was published in 1981. Subsequently a new catalogue was issued covering the period 1960–1970; the period 1970–1980 is being automated and will be published. Various specialized catalogues have been published concerning manuscripts, maps, engravings, and other materials. In 1931 the BN took over the weekly publication of the *Bibliographie de la France* (1811). This national bibliography became automated in 1975.

The Bibliothèque Nationale had three main projects in the mid-1980s: (1) to enlarge its premises with the building of an annex in the Rue Vivienne and the development of several centers in the country (Avignon, Sablé, Provins, Troyes, and Saint Dizier); (2) to protect its collections by a large program of microcopying and deacidification (in Sablé and Provins); and (3) to create a new online bibliographic database

for its readers, staff, and other libraries. This database, using the GEAC system, was scheduled to start in the middle of 1986 and to be open to the public in 1987.

Central Administration in Paris. Since Napoleon, France has always been an extremely centralized country, and the organization of the library system reflects this pattern. In 1945, a Direction des Bibliothèques et de la Lecture was created within the Ministry of Education; it controlled the National Library, university libraries, département lending libraries, and some important municipal libraries. The Direction was divided in 1975 and again in 1981. University libraries remained under the Ministry of Education and the Bibliothèque Nationale and public libraries came under the Ministry of Culture. Its Direction du Livre (the book) et de la Lecture (reading) (DLL) is completely responsible for provincial lending libraries, for the Bibliothèque Publique d'Information (BPI) at the Centre Georges Pompidou, and for the Bibliothèque Nationale, and partly responsible for municipal libraries. In the Ministry of Education, the Direction des Bibliothèques, des Musés, et de l'Information Scientifique et Technique (DBMIST) is fully responsible for university libraries and for libraries in some public research institutes, such as the Museum d'Histoire Naturelle and the Musée de l'Homme. The government provides from 80 to 90 percent of the national, university, and provincial libraries' budgets and partly subsidizes the municipal libraries. The DBMIST is responsible for personnel management, since about 80 percent of library staff is composed of civil servants. These civil servants include librarians, assistant librarians, and stack attendants who are recruited only through competitive national examinations. Civil service staff are able to move from one library to another (public, university, or national) without losing seniority.

Together, the DLL and the DBMIST define the library policy of France through decisions, grants, buildings, and personnel allocation. One example of centralization is the automation of libraries. Although two university libraries (Grenoble and Nice) created their own computerized catalogues, the main automation effort has been made at the central level by the Bureau for Library Automation, which in 1975 became the Division of Cooperation and Automation and, in 1981, was included in the DBMIST. This office is responsible for the automation of university libraries. In that capacity, it has built up an online union catalogue of periodicals (CCN) and has installed in Montpellier the Swiss system SIBIL for several libraries in the south of France. This office has also given terminals to enable libraries to search medical and scientific databases. The DLL is preparing new software for public libraries (LIBRA), and in 1980 the Bibliothèque Nationale was allowed to develop its own system based on GEAC.

The DBMIST and the DLL entirely control the Bibliothèque Nationale, the university libraries, and the central lending libraries; they also help other libraries outside their jurisdiction. The DBMIST appoints and pays the professional librarians of scientific institutions, such as the École Polytechnique, the Observatoire de Paris, the Institut de France, and others, thus ensuring library services at a professional level. The DLL gives grants to municipalities to help them build new libraries. It may also give special status (bibliothèque municipale classée) to some municipal libraries that harbor collections coming from the confiscations of the French Revolution. Professional civil servant librarians are in such cases appointed to these libraries and grants are given to maintain the quality of the collections and guarantee the preservation of the old books and manuscripts they hold.

Finally, the central administration directs General Inspectors who visit libraries of all categories, both to check the quality of their operation and the efficiency of their staff, to advise communes on building projects, to assess requests for grants, and to provide other services.

Special Libraries (Documentation Centers). Besides scientific sections of university libraries, which are entirely state-supported, there are numerous scientific and technical libraries for which state participation varies from total to none. Some are managed by other government departments, such as the Army, others are entirely private, while a few receive subsidies from both the government and private industries (such as the libraries at the Institut Pasteur or the Electricité de France). Most are called Documentation Centers and are linked to laboratories in private industries.

Parliamentary Libraries. The Library of the Assemblée Nationale, founded in 1789, received its first collection of books from the Revolutionary "literary depots." It holds about 650,000 books, 1,500 periodicals, and 1,800 manuscripts. It is open to members of the Assemblée Nationale and to authorized readers. Bibliographies and reports are prepared on request.

Use of the Senate Library is reserved for its members. Like the Library of the Assemblée Nationale, it contains mostly works on law, economics, and history, though it also has a number of special collections coming from donations. It, too, goes back to the Revolution, and it possesses 500,000 books and 600 periodicals.

University Libraries. These were created by a decree of 1879 that merged the libraries of the faculties and institutes. A circular letter of 1886 determined their structure and their rules of procedure. Until 1970, universities comprised four faculties (law, humanities, science, and medicine) to which were attached specialized institutes (chemistry and mathematics among others). In 1970 the former large universities (30,000 students) were split into several smaller specialized universities and new universities with their own libraries were created in small towns. The old encyclopedic university libraries had already been split into "sections" during the period 1950–70 when numerous buildings were erected on new campuses.

There were 61 university libraries in 1984, of which 14 were inter-university libraries serving two or more universities in one town. Taken as a whole, there were 169 sections and 13 subsections by subject in those libraries, offering 61,000 seats to 905,000 students and 70,000 faculty members.

A typical university library contains sections in humanities, law, sciences, and medicine. A Director (a professional librarian) is in charge, aided, since 1970, by a Board including faculty members, students, and library staff. The budget is paid for—up to 80 percent—by a grant from the Ministry of Education, the remainder coming from students' fees and various other small resources. A decree of 1970 determined the new functions and situation of the library within the university. These were to be modified by a decree of July 1985 that creates a unique documentation source within the university, bringing together university libraries and institute libraries into one system.

Organization. Since 1962, university libraries have been divided into (1) an active and up-to-date collection, classified according to UDC, on free-access shelves in the reading rooms, and (2) a somewhat less active one in closed stacks and available only on loan. Before 1962, the whole collection was in closed stacks. These libraries also are on two levels: one contains textbooks for undergraduates in the first two years of college; the other is for research only.

Buildings. France has experienced notable ex-

University of Grenoble Library.
Photopress

pansion in library construction. From 1950 to 1974 new campuses were created throughout France, each having its own library building—one per section, as in Grenoble, Bordeaux, Orsay, Orléans, and Lille. In the older, established universities, such as the Sorbonne in Paris, library buildings were renovated and enlarged. During that favorable period, 120 library buildings were constructed, totaling 4,500,000 sq.ft. (the total university library space being 6,610,546 sq.ft.).

Staff. In 1982 the total personnel in university libraries was 3,349 posts, 1,641 of which were professionals (both librarians and assistant librarians), or a ratio of one professional to 594 students.

Collections. Varying in quantity and quality, some collections have several millions books plus incunabula and manuscripts (the Sorbonne library has 2,600,000 books, the Medical Library of the University of Paris has one million, and the Bibliothèque Sainte Geneviève has three million), whereas the more recent ones, such as Mulhouse, Toulon, and Avignon have fewer than 100,000 volumes. But none has the old, rich collections typical of the municipal libraries created by the Revolution. University libraries totaled 18,000,000 volumes in 1982, not counting theses and periodicals (270,982 titles). Their annual intake of books runs roughly to 382,000 and of periodicals to 96,000 titles. Their annual expenses for documentation are 55 French francs per student.

Municipal Libraries. Created and operated by the communes, more than 1,000 municipal libraries exist in France. Ninety-nine percent of French cities with more than 20,000 inhabitants and 93 percent with more than 10,000 have their own libraries.

Many municipal libraries were created by a decree of January 28, 1803, that handed the old central schools libraries over to the cities. Thus was created the first national library network. Many of those libraries, however, were not well maintained by the communes, and some were completely abandoned. Therefore, the central government instituted tighter control over them in 1839, and in 1897 a regulation was issued proclaiming that the pre-1789 books and manuscripts were state property and that none could be sold or removed without government permission. The decree of 1897 introduced the concept of classification of municipal libraries—libraries were called "classées" when they contained collections belonging to the state, that is, coming from the former "literary depots." Today municipal libraries are divided into two categories, "classées" and "nonclassées." There are 54 libraries of the first kind. Library inspectors visit all municipal libraries, but their influence is greater on the "classées" because there they may make decisions on problems of conservation or acquisitions, advise on management, and report to the central administration. Thus the state has real control over libraries housing state collections. The most significant difference remains in the selection of personnel. Professional librarians with degrees from the École Nationale Supérieure des Bibliothèques (ENSB) are appointed by the government to manage the "classées". The other municipal libraries are staffed by personnel appointed by the municipalities.

Beside their main research collections housed downtown, the large, long-established libraries in major cities have set up networks of branches or have started bookmobiles in order to stimulate reading among the population in their areas. Bordeaux, Toulouse, and Grenoble each have 14 such branch libraries and Paris has 86.

From 1945, new buildings went up at a brisk pace; municipal library floor surfaces have doubled in a 10-year period, totaling 7,310,400 sq.ft. by 1980. Mulhouse, Nevers, Sedan, Belfort, and Annecy are among the cities where new library buildings were erected in the 1980s. Some towns have preferred to renovate old buildings, such as churches, monasteries, or even palaces, in order to obtain working libraries. Colmar, Troyes, and Avignon are examples.

The municipalities pay for their libraries, but they can receive grants from the state (the DLL) of about 20 percent toward their current budgets (from 1981), and of 50 percent for the construction and equipment of a new library. In 1983 subsidies amounted to 300,000,000 French francs. The total library budget for municipal libraries was 1,119,818,000 francs for running expenses — 39.41 francs per inhabitant (compared with 4.43 francs in 1967).

The remarkable richness of French municipal libraries was shown in a study in the late 1970s reporting that they possessed 161,200 manuscripts, 9,158 incunabula, and 69,599 16th-century books. In 1980 ten had more than 500,000 volumes. The total collection of municipal libraries amounts to 45 million books. Collections of special significance are in Dijon, Toulouse, Carpentras, Troyes, Grenoble, and Lyons.

French municipal libraries do not possess only old books and manuscripts. From 1945, the Direction des Bibliothèques et de la Lecture Publique and, from 1975, the Direction du Livre et de la Lecture have placed a new emphasis on developing reading interests among the public by creating modern collections in new buildings and by launching branch libraries and bookmobiles. The figures cited previously for expenditure per inhabitant in 1982 speak for themselves. Loans totaled 66,000,000 (2.42 per inhabitant).

Libraries tend to form centers for cultural activities within towns. In the newer peripheral towns around Paris, for instance, the libraries are integrated with other cultural equipment and collaborate closely with organizers of plays, exhibitions, and concerts. Writers are periodically invited to come and meet library users. Branches have been opened in railway stations in Evry and Saint Quentin en Yvelines and even in the Metro of Paris.

Paris. In Paris, municipal libraries have a special status. Having been created in 1865, well after the Revolution, they have no state collections, and, despite their location at the center of a centralized state, the capital's libraries are not under state control. Their funds are allocated by the city of Paris—40 French francs per inhabitant or 86,566,375 francs for a population of 2,176,000. Their collections amount to 3,000,000 books, their staff to 796, and their floor space to 430,400 sq.ft. They are administered by a Library Bureau, and their professional staff is recruited through a special competitive examination, and the Paris municipality maintains a corps of inspectors to oversee them.

Parisian libraries are of two kinds: (1) research libraries such as the Historical Library of the City of Paris, in the Hôtel Lamoignon, or the Forney Li-

Bibliothèque Nationale

*Municipal library at
Pantin, France.*

brary, in the Hôtel de Sens, specializing in arts and crafts techniques, and (2) standard public libraries. Since 1971, a network of lending libraries has been organized by the city around a central technical service responsible for acquisitions, catalogues, buildings, and other matters. These libraries are created in accordance with a plan for constructing one large district library (20,000 to 22,000 sq.ft. of floor space) in each of the Paris *arrondissements* and, around these, "sector" libraries (5,000 to 7,500 sq.ft.) for each group of 35,000 inhabitants. The first large library was opened in the 18th arrondissement in 1969, with four sector libraries. They were followed by libraries in the 5th (Buffon) and 15th (Beaugrenelle) arrondissements. There are now 6 main libraries and 34 sector libraries, to which can be added 9 children's libraries and 25 branches. In 1983 they lent out 5,668,716 documents.

Of note is the Bibliothèque Publique d'Information (BPI) at the Pompidou Center in Paris, although it is not, strictly speaking, a municipal library. The BPI depends directly on the Direction du Livre et de la Lecture. Opened in 1977, it offers a new style of library service—anyone can enter without a card and can use freely, on the premises only, its open-stack collection of 500,000 volumes and a large collection of audiovisual materials, including slides, films, and tapes. More than 14,000 visitors use it daily.

Provincial Lending Libraries. Because smaller towns cannot support libraries, the government decided in 1945 to establish Central Lending Libraries in each of the administrative jurisdictions known as *départements* (more or less the equivalent of counties). These libraries, usually set up in the département capital city, were intended to serve, with bookmobiles, communes of fewer than 20,000 inhabitants. Ninety-four Central Lending Libraries served 24,000,000 persons in the mid-1980s. Each of them operates one or more bookmobiles that circulate out from a central store, distributing books at various depots in the district, which are either the local school or the town hall. The people in charge of the depots are usually teachers or some other volunteers. Books are either left at the depots in boxes (but less and less so) or chosen by the person in charge or by local readers from the shelves of the bookmobile itself.

Book deposits are also made in factories, homes for the elderly, and cultural centers. Bookmobiles visit each town four times a year, with stocks of 3,000 books on their shelves. In 1982 there were 300 bookmobiles, with a staff of 1,124 (550 professionals), giving access to 13,000,000 books and 170,000 records. Loans numbered 25,000,000 in 1977 and 34,000,000 in 1982.

School Libraries. Before 1958, high-school libraries existed, but only for teachers or for classroom use. From 1958, and mainly from 1968 on, teachers' and classroom libraries were progressively brought together to form larger units, one for each school, called, since 1974, Centres de Documentation et d'Information (CDI).

Among France's 7,150 high schools, 3,500 have CDIs. Most CDIs are managed by teachers who, at best, may have received short introductory courses in library work. The position of high-school librarian is not officially established, and those in charge retain their teaching status. Support comes from the regular budget under the Director of the school.

The Profession. *Associations.* There are five library associations in France. The Amicale des Directeurs de Bibliothèques Universitaires (ADBU; Association of Directors of University Libraries), founded in 1971, consists of the Directors of all university libraries, plus one section chief per library. It is thus a closed association, comprising about 100 members.

After the university reform of 1968 and the establishment of new statutes for university libraries in 1970, the Directors became aware of the need to organize in order to (1) defend university libraries vis-à-vis the public authorities, (2) study problems specific to the organization and administration of university libraries, and (3) coordinate policies and technical procedures on matters not well covered by the Direction des Bibliothèques (such as photocopies and interlibrary loans). Membership fees are the only source of funds. The ADBU meets once a year; its general assembly elects a board, who select a President. The ADBU issues technical reports from time to time according to the needs of the profession, such as a "Guide for Interlibrary Lending."

The Association des Bibliothécaires Français (ABF; Association of French Librarians), founded in 1906, is the oldest and the largest association of professional librarians in France (2,500 members in 1984). Its funds come from membership fees and from grants from the government. Its objectives are to defend the profession in a very broad sense; to further librarianship by promoting studies, conferences, and reports; and to bring together all persons interested in librarianship, whatever their work. The association is open not only to professional librarians but also to those professionally concerned with libraries, such as publishers, bookdealers, and documentalists. There are individual and institutional members.

The Association is organized in sections and regional groups. There are four sections by type of library—national, university, general public, and special. There are 17 regional groups. Sections and groups elect their own councils, which choose a Board (President, Vice-Presidents, Secretary, and

Treasurer). They also elect the National Council of 30 members, which, in turn, select a Board of seven to ten persons: President, four Vice-Presidents, Secretary, Assistant Secretaries, and Treasurer. The Council members are elected for three years.

The Association's inadequate resources do not permit it to undertake extensive activities at the national level, but the regional groups are very active. They conduct regional professional activities such as organizing conferences and cooperating on union catalogues, participating in training courses, and compiling directories of libraries. Nationally, the Association organizes colloquia, working groups, and the Annual Congress on a professional theme. The Association serves as a link between state-supported and private libraries, and between all libraries and the government. It is associated in policy decisions and provides a neutral forum for discussion and proposals to the government.

The Association publishes a quarterly *Bulletin d'Information,* an informal *Note d'Information,* and professional monographs (such as a handbook of librarianship and a book on serials in public libraries).

The Association des Documentalistes et Bibliothécaires Spécialisés (ADBS; French Association of Documentalists and Special Librarians) was founded in 1963 to bring together information and documentation specialists. It had about 2,000 members in 1984, mainly from private documentation centers. Funding comes from membership fees and grants. The Association is structured in sections by subject—electronics, transportation, and so forth—and in seven regional groups. A council elects the Board, which is composed of the President, two Vice-Presidents, the Secretary General, and the Treasurer. Activities emphasize the improvement of information handling and transfer by means of visits, round tables, seminars, and the national congress every two years. The ADBS publishes a quarterly bulletin, *Le Documentaliste,* a monthly information sheet, and a series of monographs. It has also developed a large program of training courses.

The Association de l'École Nationale Supérieure des Bibliothèques (AENSB; Association of the National School for Libraries), founded in 1967, is composed, as its name indicates, of alumni of the École Nationale Supérieure des Bibliothèques in Lyons. It had about 500 members in 1984. Its funds come from membership fees and from grants. It is concerned with all aspects of library education, especially with maintaining the ENSB at the level of equivalent higher-level educational institutions in France. It also seeks improvements in the status of civil service librarians. The Association publishes an internal *Note d'Information* and is a founding member of the Presses de l'ENSB, which publishes professional librarianship books. The annual General Assembly elects a Council of 21 members for three-year terms. The Board is composed of eight members.

The Association des Diplômés de l'École des Bibliothécaires Documentalistes (ADEBD; Association of Graduates of the School of Librarian Documentalists), founded in 1936, is composed of alumni of the École des Bibliothécaires Documentalistes of the Catholic Institute in Paris. The Annual General Assembly elects a Council of 12, which then elects the President. Both council and President serve three-

year terms. It had 500 members in 1984; their fees constitute the main financial resources of the Association. It finds employment for new graduates of the School and shares with the other associations in the promotion of librarianship. It publishes a semiannual information bulletin.

Library Education. The teaching of librarianship in France cannot be understood without keeping in mind the two categories of professional librarians: (1) civil servants in most of the state-supported libraries and (2) "the others" in private and municipal libraries.

Another distinction is typical of France: (1) librarians (*bibliothécaires* or *conservateurs*) who are supposed to preserve books but, more and more, use modern techniques and (2) "documentalists" who have the reputation of using modern information tools, but also have to preserve books. Professional education is divided along these lines.

One school prepares civil servants for the position of conservateur. The École Nationale Supérieure des Bibliothèques (ENSB) in Lyons is organized, managed, and financed by the DBMIST. It is not part of the university system. Each year, a competitive examination is open for a fixed number of posts to students with Master's degrees. Successful candidates receive salaries during their stay and are guaranteed employment when they leave. The curriculum lasts one year; a paper and another examination are required at the end. A few librarians may also come from the École des Chartes. This school, located in the Sorbonne and entered through a competitive examination at the "baccalauréat" (end of high school) level, offers a three-year course for the training of archivists. Some of them may choose to work in libraries.

The ENSB also offers another diploma—the *Certificat d'aptitude aux fonctions de bibliothécaires* (CAFB). Teaching (one year) for this diploma is given in regional centers, mostly in university and large municipal libraries with their own staffs. The objective is to prepare professionals for small public libraries and for private libraries. The examination is national, with the same questions for all candidates.

There are other ways to enter the private sector. One is through study at the École des Bibliothécaires Documentalistes of the Catholic University in Paris (EBD). The curriculum lasts two years after the *baccalauréat*, with several periods of practice in documentation centers.

The Conservatoire National des Arts et Métiers has also established a training program for documentalists, the Institut National des Techniques de la Documentation (INTD), oriented toward industrial documentation centers. The Fondation Nationale des Sciences Politiques also offers a one-year course in documentation.

Within universities, several courses in documentation and in information sciences (but not in librarianship) were created from the mid-1970s to the mid-1980s. At the lower level, the Institut Universitaire de Technologie (IUT) offers a two-year course in documentation. At the upper level, some universities, such as Lyons, Paris, Grenoble, and Lille, offer graduate degrees in documentation and information sciences—Diplome d'études supérieures (DESS) and the doctorate.

REFERENCES

"Library and Information Science in France, A 1983 Overview," in *Journal of Library History* (Winter, 1984).

"Bibliothèques municipales: statistiques 1982," in *Bulletin des Bibliothèques de France* (1984).

La Bibliothèque nationale en 1982 (1983).

Henri Comte, *Les Bibliothèques publiques en France* (1977).

"Enquêtes statistiques générales auprès des bibliothèques universitaires 1981 et 1982," in *Bulletin des Bibliothèques de France* (1984).

John Camp, "Bibliothèques et universités en France, 1789–1881," *Bulletin des Bibliothèques de France* (1983).

La Lecture publique en France: rapport du Groupe détudes (1968).

Les Bibliothèques en France: rapport au Premier Ministre (1982).

André Masson and Denis Pallier, *Les Bibliothèques* (1982).

Françoise Parent-Lardeur, *Les Cabinets de lecture: la lecture publique à Paris sous la Restauration* (1982).

MARC CHAUVEINC

Library Association
Sir Frank Francis

Francis, Sir Frank

(1901–)

Sir Frank Francis, one of the oustanding figures on the British library scene for many years, contributed to the library profession and to scholarship over an unusual range as bibliographer and editor, teacher, administrator, and statesman.

Francis was born October 5, 1901, in Liverpool. After graduating from Liverpool and Cambridge, he became a schoolmaster in 1925. The following year he entered the service of the British Museum, where he spent the whole of his career. In 1946 he became Secretary in succession to Arundell Esdaile, whose contributions to bibliographical scholarship he had already followed with his own. Promoted to Keeper in the Department of Printed Books in 1948, he became in 1959 Director and Principal Librarian, holding that office until his retirement in 1968. He was created Companion of the Order of the Bath (C.B.) in 1958 and knighted (K.C.B.) in 1960.

Bibliographical and editorial work came early in his career with a regular flow of studies for the Library Association, the Bibliographical Society, and the British Museum; in 1936–53 he edited *The Library,* and in 1947–68 he jointly edited the *Journal of Documentation.* During those years he laid the foundations of his renowned course in bibliography at the School of Librarianship of University College, London (1945–59), and also for the numerous lectures he gave throughout the world. As Keeper and Director of the British Museum, he initiated and successfully carried out a number of projects for publications based on its unique collections, culminating in the third edition of the *General Catalogue of Printed Books,* which marked an epochal advance in printing technology. He was a leading figure in the discussions that led to the founding of the *British National Bibliography* within the British Museum and lent it the full weight of his support in its early years; his authority and influence were instrumental in ensuring its success.

As a statesman of the profession, Francis set a record that is unmatched. He was President of the major associations: the LA, the Museums Association, Aslib, the Bibliographical Society, and the International Federation of Library Associations. He helped to set up the advisory committee on bibliography and documentation in Unesco and, as Chairman of the Trustees of the National Central Library, guided its course until its merger with the British Museum and other libraries to form the new British Library.

In addition he proved an enthusiastic and energetic member of many committees and working parties, and many leading British librarians have had cause to be grateful for his friendship and wise counsel. In long and controverisal discussions about the nature and role of librarianship and information work, Francis constantly strove for unity among professional bodies and their members. His assertion of the value of professional qualifications was recognized by the award of the Honorary Fellowship by the LA, but he never neglected the value of high scholarship for all librarians. Thus, he was able in the early 1950s to give full recognition to the growing importance of information services in science and technology and played a significant role in the Committee of the Science Advisory Council.

His own interests demonstrated the same extraordinary range, testified by his membership and honorary rank in many scholarly bodies and his collection of honorary doctorates. Perhaps his major attention was given to the classics and especially to Scandinavian studies, in which he achieved international fame. Even in retirement his activity continued unabated. As Consultant to the Council on Library Resources, he became a familiar figure in the United States and, as Master of the Clockmakers' Company, he fulfilled a role in the functions of the City of London.

D. J. FOSKETT

Franklin, Benjamin

(1706–1790)

Benjamin Franklin stands at the beginning of the history of America's public libraries. As founder of the Library Company of Philadelphia, he initiated the first subscription library in the United States, a precursor to the modern public library.

Franklin was born on January 17, 1706, in Boston, which had the largest concentration of bookshops in British America; over half of the booksellers active between 1700 and 1725 were within a quarter-mile of his birthplace. Ideally situated for one who was to be almost entirely self-educated, he received two years of formal schooling. At the age of 12 he was apprenticed to his brother James, a printer. Franklin, who said of himself, "I do not remember when I could not read," began with his father's "little library consisting chiefly of Books in polemic Divinity," which he found of little use. Lending libraries were unknown, but Matthew Adams, a merchant, gave him access to his "pretty Collection of Books." Franklin went one step further, persuading fellow apprentices to borrow books from their masters' book shops, which he read and returned. His reading was eclectic, ranging from classical authors in translation through philosophy, logic, grammar, navigation, and arithmetic. *The Spectator* especially pleased him, and he used it as a model for his own writing. Franklin was vigorous in mind and body and developed a high opinion of his own ability.

In 1722 a series of letters signed Silence Dogood appeared in James Franklin's *The New England Cour-*

ant. Written by Benjamin, the letters were favorably received, much to James's annoyance. On two occasions when James was in trouble with the authorities, Benjamin had the full responsibility for the newspaper. The already existing strain between the two grew to the point where Benjamin was eager to break his apprenticeship, which still had three years to run. In the autumn of 1723 he secretly left Boston for New York.

Printer. Unable to find work with William Bradford in New York, Franklin continued on to Philadelphia. There he was employed by Samuel Keimer, who had opened a printing shop in competition with Bradford's son Andrew. Once settled, Franklin "began now to have some acquaintances among young people of the Town, that were Lovers of Reading with whom I spent my Evenings very pleasantly." His abilities attracted the attention of Governor William Keith, who promised him assistance and arranged for him to go to London to buy a press and type to open a shop of his own. Franklin arrived in England in 1724, only to find himself a victim of Keith's habit of making promises he did not keep. He found employment almost immediately with Samuel Palmer, a printer of some note, and later moved to John Watts's shop, where many successful printers had been trained. Franklin satisfied his need for books by making "an Aquaintance with one Wilcox a Bookseller. . . . Circulating Libraries were not then in Use; but we agreed that on certain reasonable Terms . . . I might take, and return any of his Books."

When he returned to Philadelphia in 1726 at the age of 20, Franklin had completed what amounted to his formal education, although he never stopped learning. He taught himself French, Italian, Spanish, and Latin. Opening his own printing shop in 1728, he embarked on one of the most successful business careers of any printer in pre-Revolutionary America. He started a stationer's store, made arrangements with binders, bought a lampblack house, set up as a wholesale paper merchant, and imported books. The business arrangements he entered into with printers in Newport, New Haven, New York, Charleston, and the West Indies provided a network for distributing his work. The largest part of his printing was for colonial governments; at various times he was printer to Pennsylvania, Philadelphia, Delaware, and New Jersey. Of almost equal importance were his publications on religious subjects, many of which were also subsidized. These two groups make up more than half of the output of his press between 1728 and 1748, when he went into partnership with David Hall and retired from active participation in the business.

His most successful publications were the Poor Richard's almanacs and the *Pennsylvania Gazette;* the distribution of the latter was greatly helped in 1737 when Franklin became Deputy Postmaster at Philadelphia. He scarcely ever undertook the publication of a book or pamphlet on his own. His most successful such venture was the 16 editions of George Whitefield's writing and other controversial tracts occasioned by his visit to America in 1740.

Franklin's best-known and handsomest piece of printing, James Logan's translation of *M. T. Cicero's Cato Major,* was a financial loss. Franklin could exe-

cute a piece of fine printing when he felt he could afford it, but in general he confined himself to sound workmanlike productions at reasonable prices. At one time he boasted of having the smallest typeface in America.

The Library Company. Parallel and frequently a part of his business career was Franklin's role in founding institutions and organizations for the public good. The first was the Library Company of Philadelphia. The Junto, which he had formed in 1727 for "mutual Improvement," failed in its attempt to form a small library. Soon afterward, in 1731, Franklin created the Library Company. The inspiration for it may have had its origins in Franklin's practice of borrowing books from booksellers in Boston and London, but the idea of a subscription library, owned by its members, for the purpose of circulating books of general interest to those who could not afford to build their own collections, seems to belong to Franklin. There was no counterpart in Great Britain during his stay there; the first British subscription library appeared in Scotland in 1741, the year in which Franklin printed the second *Catalogue* of the Library Company with 375 titles, and the London Library was not founded until 1785. Circulating books was not a new idea, but it had been narrowly oriented, usually around some religious interest.

The founders of the Library Company were almost all in trade, practical men who wanted useful information for self-improvement. Most of the original books were in English, and theology was held to a minimum. The Library's functions were soon expanded; it was given an air pump, followed by electrical instruments, a telescope, artifacts from the Arctic, a cabinet of fossils, and other objects appropriate to a museum. On a number of occasions its rooms were used for demonstrations and lectures. The directors saw their Library as taking an active part in making practical and scientific knowledge readily and cheaply available. Until he left for England in 1757, Franklin played an active role in the Library's affairs. He was briefly acting librarian when in 1734 the Library was opened to all who would pay a rental fee. From 1746 to 1757 he was the Secretary, the principal officer. By 1776 there were at least 18 subscription libraries in America, almost all of which bore some trace of influence from the Library Company.

Other Contributions. Although a number of other institutions with which Franklin's name is associated developed libraries, he was not closely involved. He was on the committee that selected the first books for the College of Philadelphia in 1750, but various factors, including the hostility between Provost William Smith and Franklin, meant that he had little to do with its small library. The American Philosophical Society, which he founded in 1743, did not take its present form until 1769, when Franklin was in England; until 1800 its books were all donated. After the appearance of the first volume of the Society's *Transactions* in 1771, Franklin used it to solicit gifts from the scientific writers of Europe and, even more important, to establish exchange arrangements with learned societies in Britain and on the Continent, to 20 of which he belonged. Likewise the Pennsylvania Hospital, founded in the early 1750s, did not decide to develop a medical library until 1762, and Franklin's only participation seems to have been an offer to seek gifts in England. His part in beginnings of the Pennsylvania State Library was more direct; in 1752 he was the member of the Assembly who was directed, along with the Speaker, to purchase books for the newly erected library room.

With the exception of two brief periods, Franklin spent the 28 years between 1757 and 1785 in England or France representing the interests of his country. His achievements, particularly his electrical experiments, made him a welcome addition to the literary and intellectual worlds of both countries. He continued to encourage the bookish interests of the organizations he left behind and acted as their agent in acquiring books. In London he became a close friend of England's leading printer, William Strahan, and in Paris picked up his old craft, establishing his own press in Passy. As always he bought and was given books.

On his return to Philadelphia in 1785, he set about putting his library in order and designed a ladder-chair and an arm to reach books on high shelves. At his death there on April 17, 1790, he left his library of 4,276 volumes to his family. They sold it at an 1803 auction that was the largest and most important to have taken place in America.

Appraisal Franklin's position in the history of American public libraries is well known; that some of the ideas he brought to librarianship may have predated their appearance in the mother country is not as widely recognized. Certainly the Library Company's view of itself as an active force in the educational and intellectual life of Philadelphia would seem to be one of the earliest examples of what is now taken for granted—that libraries have a responsibility that goes beyond passively providing books.

REFERENCES

Quotes and other material are from Franklin's *Autobiography*, edited by Leonard W. Labaree *et al.* (1964).

Austin K.Gray, *Benjamin Franklin's Library: A Short Account of the Library Company of Philadelphia* (1937), the standard history.

Margaret Barton Korty, "Benjamin Franklin and Eighteenth Century Libraries," *Transactions of the American Philosophical Society* (1965), a discursive attempt containing useful data.

Carl Van Doren, *Benjamin Franklin* (1938), the best complete biography.

Michael H. Harris, "Franklin, Benjamin," *Dictionary of American Library Biography* (1978).

THOMAS R. ADAMS

The University of Chicago
Herman Howe Fussler

Fussler, Herman Howe

(1914-)

Herman Howe Fussler, university library administrator, scholar, and teacher, made major contributions to the improvement of library services to scholars and labored successfully to increase the general understanding of the tasks and problems of research libraries.

A practicing library administrator for 35 years (23 of them as Director of the University of Chicago Library), he pioneered in the development and application of new technologies and service concepts, beginning with his early contributions to library microphotography and culminating in the conception and design of the Joseph Regenstein Library of the University of Chicago (opened in 1970). The Regenstein Library is widely recognized as an attractive and efficient environment remarkably well adapted to the activity of scholarship. Known as a stimulating and provocative teacher, Fussler gained a comprehensive familiarity with the literature of librarianship and with the library practitioners of his generation, and as a student and scholar distinguished himself for penetrating and balanced analyses of the major issues confronting the academic research library. He wrote or edited many significant books, articles, and reports on academic libraries, on the technologies applicable to libraries, on the ways in which the products of scholarship are disseminated, and on the management of scholarly resources. He was frequently consulted by librarians, scholars, academic administrators, and foundation officers because of his experience and perspective.

Fussler was born in Philadelphia on May 15, 1914, the son of a physics professor. His family, after living in various parts of the country, settled in Chapel Hill, where Fussler attended the University of North Carolina. He received an A.B. degree in mathematics in 1935 and, a year later, a bachelor's degree in library science. Shortly thereafter he began studies at the Graduate Library School (GLS) of the University of Chicago, where he earned the M.A. degree in 1941 and the Ph.D. in 1948.

He began his library career in 1936 at the New York Public Library as a library assistant in the Science and Technology Division. After a brief period of service there he was invited to the University of Chicago Library to establish and direct its pioneering Department of Photographic Reproduction, with the specific mission of developing operating and technical processes, particularly in microreproduction, that would be of utility to research libraries generally. He served in that capacity from 1936 to 1946, added concurrent responsibilities as Science Librarian in the University Library from 1943 to 1947, became Assistant Director and then Associate Director, 1947–48, and later in 1948 was appointed Director, serving in that position until 1971, when he resigned to devote full time to research and teaching in the GLS. Twice during his service in the University Library his abilities were made available to other important enterprises: during 1937 he served as Head of the Demonstration of Microphotography at the Paris International Exposition, under the auspices of the Rockefeller Foundation and the American Library Association; and from 1942 to 1945 he was detached from his primary responsibilities to serve the Manhattan Project as Assistant Director of the Information Division and Librarian of the Metallurgical Laboratory.

His career in library research and in education for librarianship paralleled his career in the University Library. He became an Instructor in 1942, was promoted to Assistant Professor in 1944, and was made Professor in 1948, the year he became Director of the Library. For the period 1961–63 he served, in addition, as Acting Dean of the GLS. His contributions to library scholarship and to the scholarly work of the University were formally acknowledged in 1974 when he was named the Martin A. Ryerson Distinguished Service Professor of Library Science. In 1977 he was Visiting Professor at Monash University in Australia.

Fussler influenced thought and action in many areas through his diligent and effective service on the boards and committees of library associations and learned societies. He served on the ALA Council from 1956 to 1959 as well as on a number of committees. He was a member of the board of the Association of Research Libraries from 1961 to 1964 and in 1970 and 1971. He was one of the initial three-man team selected to study the feasibility of a Midwest storage facility for academic libraries and was active in the planning and establishment of the resulting Midwest Interlibrary Center (now the Center for Research Libraries), served on its board from 1950 to 1967, was Vice Chair of the board in 1954–55, and was Chair, 1959–60. He was a member of the Board of Regents of the National Library of Medicine (1963–67) and served on the visiting committees of various academic libraries. He was appointed by President Lyndon B. Johnson to the National Advisory Commission on Libraries in 1966.

Fussler received the Melvil Dewey Medal from ALA in 1954 and the Ralph R. Shaw Award for library literature in 1976.

Fussler served as Associate Editor for the *Journal of Documentary Reproduction* (1938 to 1942) and the *Library Quarterly* from 1949. His principal publications include *Photographic Reproduction for Libraries: A Study of Administrative Problems* (1942) and *Characteristics of the Research Literature Used by Chemists and Physicists in the United States* (1949); he edited *Library Buildings for Library Service* (1947), *The Function of the Library in the Modern College* (1954), and *The Research Library in Transition* (1957); he was co-author, with Julian L. Simon, of *Patterns in the Use of Books in Large Libraries* (revised edition 1969) and editor of *Management Implications for Libraries and Library Schools* (1973) and *Research Libraries and Technology* (1973).

STANLEY MC ELDERRY

Gabon

On the west coast of Africa, Gabon is a republic bounded on the north by Equatorial Guinea and Cameroon, on the east and south by the Congo, and on the west by the Atlantic Ocean. Population (1984) 1,148,000; area 267,667 sq.km. The official language is French.

History. Among the 40 ethnic groups of Gabon, oral traditions kept alive the social codes and taboos, the tales, proverbs, and riddles, and the family-by-family genealogies of the people. The Gabonese were once matrilinear in the south and patrilinear in the north, but they have become more and more patrilinear. Local language and traditions, including the oral transmission of cultural history, have receded in the face of the Westernized French model, with village life and older people dying out.

National Library. In 1969 the National Archives in Libreville was begun, including a library department that serves as the National Library. In 1972 it became the official depository for Gabonese documents; it also receives dissertations dealing with the country.

In 1978 Amoughe M'Ba Pierre returned from study overseas as the first highly trained Gabonese librarian. He developed and catalogued the National Library collections. While the population served increased, the shortage of space worsened.

In 1982 the government decided to establish CICIBA, a Bantu civilizations international institute. Amoughe was named a member of the advisory board. The ambitious scheme, some observers felt, may impede library development in Gabon.

Academic Libraries. The largest university library, the Bibliothèque Centrale of the Université Omar Bongo, was established in 1972. Special collections are located off campus at the Medicine Faculty, Law School, and Teachers' College, and at the Computer Sciences and Forest Studies Institutes.

Public Libraries. There were no public libraries in Gabon in the mid-1980s. Experiments in providing services in working-class districts of Libreville and Port Gentil were conducted between 1968 and 1975. The National Library and the Gabonese Librarians Association in the mid-1980s plan reading facilities for everyone by the year 2000.

School Libraries. Four schools in Libreville and two denominational schools in the country maintain small libraries.

Special Libraries. Among the 26 special libraries in 1984, the oldest one was established in 1938 at the Chamber of Commerce of Libreville. Ten are attached to research institutions and four to ministries. Both the French and the American Cultural Centers have special libraries, as does the United Nations office in Libreville. The most advanced library, opened in 1979 at Franceville, with the International Center for Medical Research (CIRMF), specializing in human reproduction.

The Profession. Trained archivists or librarians numbered 35 in 1984 and most of them belong to the Gabonese Librarians Association, initiated in 1981 by Amoughe M'Ba Pierre. Most of them went to a Unesco-sponsored school in Dakar, Senegal. But in 1981 Amoughe organized a three-year professional course with university teachers and librarians. In 1984 eight archivists and librarians were graduated in Libreville. In 1985 a master's degree in information sciences was offered on the opening of a fourth-year course.

REFERENCES

Hubert Deschamps, *Traditions orales et archives du Gabon* (Paris, 1962).

Danielle Haeringer, *Documentation et planification au Gabon* (Libreville, 1981).

Marie Elizabeth Bouscarle, *Les Bibliothèques au Gabon* (1982).

MARIE ELIZABETH BOUSCARLE

Gambia, The

The Republic of Gambia, on the Atlantic coast in West Africa, is the smallest country on the African continent. It lies on a strip of land on the banks of the Gambia River; Senegal surrounds The Gambia on the north, east, and south. Population (1984 est.) 725,000; area 11,569 sq.km. The official language is English.

History; National and Public Library Services. The Gambia government did not have a public or national library service of its own until

---

Libraries in Gabon (1982)

Type	Administrative units	Service points	Volumes in collections	Annual expenditures (CFA franc)	Population served	Professional staff	Total staff
National	3	1	15,000[a]	10,000,000	2,540	8	12
Academic	6	6	31,000	34,890,000[c]	788[e]	6	18
Public	0	--	--	--	--	--	--
School	6	6	17,000[d]	1,220,000[d]	2,846[f]	0	--
Special	24	24	--	--	--	3	14
Other	3[b]	4	--	--	--	1	6

[a]Figures for the National Library only.
[b]French, U.S. Cultural Centers, United Nations office in Libreville.
[c]Unesco, *Statistical Yearbook*, 1984. 1981 data.
[d]Ibid. 1981 data for five schools.
[e]Ibid. Registered borrowers.
[f]Ibid. 1981 data for five schools. Registered borrowers.

April 1962, when the British Council closed its office and handed its library in the capital city of Banjul to the government.

The British Council, which ran a subscription library service in The Gambia from 1946, had provided the only public library in the country apart from smaller libraries in schools, government departments, mission houses, and clubs, whose materials were loaned only to members or clients. When the book stock was transferred, it numbered 25,000 volumes, excluding phonograph records, films, and filmstrips, which totaled 500.

On May 1, 1971, the name was changed from the British Council Library to The Gambia National Library. Before the change, Roy Flood had been sent from the British Council in London to evaluate and recommend a library service suitable for The Gambia. His recommendations for a complete reorganization of The Gambia library service were accepted.

In 1974 the British government, through the British Council and the Ministry of Overseas Development, provided 300,000 dalasis (£75,000) for the building, books, furniture, and equipment. On December 15, 1976, when the new library was opened, the collection numbered 54,620—it had doubled in the period 1962–76. Books, manuscripts, films, recordings, and other items added thereafter made the collection more extensive.

Under an act of Parliament, the National Library was made the depository library and also the Bibliographic Centre. More than 2,000 volumes of archival material are stored there. Its six departments are the National Collection (mainly materials by and about The Gambia and the Gambians); Adult Lending; School Library Service (bulk loans to primary schools); and Mobile and Book-box services. The National Library, in summary, serves dual purposes—as a National Reference and Lending Library and also as the public library of the nation.

Academic Libraries. The only academic institution is the Teachers' Training College at Yundum, which also trains agricultural officers. Only primary school teachers are trained there. For higher education, Gambians go abroad.

An acute shortage of teachers, particularly in the provincial schools, prompted the setting up of a training center at Georgetown. Initially the training was for one year, until the demand for staff in the schools sufficiently eased. The first college building was opened on March 7, 1949.

S. P. C. N'JIE*

Gardner, Frank
(1908–1980)

Frank Matthias Gardner, British public librarian, editor, and writer, was a leader of the Library Association (LA) and was noted for his international library service.

Gardner was born in Sheffield, Yorkshire, on January 13, 1908, and throughout his life he demonstrated the tough, hardy, blunt determination characteristic of Yorkshire folk of the North Country. But he gained his professional successes and reputation in London and the south of England.

Gardner was educated at Firth Park Grammar School in Sheffield. In 1927 he became an assistant in the Sheffield Public Libraries, staying there for three years before moving on to a more senior position in the Leeds Public Libraries, where he remained until 1933. Sheffield and Leeds were, and still are, rival Yorkshire cities, vying with each other in the fields of industrial, social, and municipal progress. During his formative years in librarianship, Gardner served under two dynamic city librarians, J. P. Lamb of Sheffield and Richard Gordon of Leeds, and these early professional experiences colored his whole future. He never forgot the library philosophies and techniques inculcated into him at Sheffield and Leeds between 1927 and 1933.

From the industrial north of England, where unemployment was rife in the 1930s, many young people were beckoned by the more affluent London and the south. Gardner was one of those who responded to the call, and in 1933 he became a branch librarian at Willesden, then a municipal borough in northwest London and now part of the London borough of Brent. He remained there from 1933 to 1938, a period that witnessed the flowering of his professional life. His new job not only widened his experience but brought him into contact with many other librarians in London and the south, librarians of his own and earlier generations. He became a member of the Council of the Association of Assistant Librarians and soon was editor of its official monthly journal, *The*

ALA

Frank Gardner

Libraries in The Gambia (1980)

Type	Administrative units	Service points	Volumes in collections	Annual expenditures (dalasi)	Population served[a]	Professional staff	Total staff
National	1	1	3,000	94,000	711	--	--
Academic	--	--	--	--	--	--	--
Public	1	5	67,000	94,000	--	1	19
School[b]	129	129	--	9,000[c]	35,196	2	--
Special							
Other (Describe)							

[a]Registered borrowers.
[b]1978 data.
[c]Acquisitions only.

Source: Unesco, *Statistical Yearbook,* 1984.

Library Assistant, now *The Assistant Librarian.* Through it he became friendly with other contemporary library journalists, among them Stanley Snaith, F. Seymour Smith, T. E. Callander, W. B. Stevenson, and J. T. Gillett. Among them, and under Gardner's editorship, they gave *The Library Assistant* a reputation and a readability second to none in the 1930s.

By 1938 Gardner had carved for himself a considerable reputation and it came as no surprise when, in that year, he was appointed borough Librarian of Luton, a town of more than 100,000 about 30 miles north of London. Two years earlier he had married a children's librarian, Lysobel Margaret Watt-Smith. The war came just at the wrong time for Gardner: it prevented him from carrying out many much-needed reforms in the Luton Public Libraries, and it also meant that by 1945 he had missed many opportunities for professional advancement. He stayed on at Luton until his retirement in 1972. By that time, however, he had not only provided Luton with new branch libraries, but also with a fine new central library, which Queen Elizabeth II opened in 1962.

During and after the war Gardner became a member of the Council of the LA. He was Chairman of the LA Publications Committee for a number of years, later becoming Chairman of the Association's Executive Committee and finally President in 1964.

Before that time, he had become interested in international library affairs. In 1950 Unesco asked him to direct the Delhi Public Library pilot project, which he did successfully, and his name will long be honored in India. In 1954 he revisited Delhi to direct a Unesco seminar on public libraries in Asia. Meanwhile, at home, he was one of the leaders of the LA's efforts to secure much-needed legislation for public libraries in England and Wales. It was very fitting that his efforts were rewarded during his LA Presidential year with the passing of the Public Libraries and Museums Act, which came into force on April 1, 1965.

During his Presidential year Gardner inaugurated "The President's Page" in the *LA Record,* presided over a memorable LA Conference at Rothesay in Scotland, and visited Nigeria and other Commonwealth countries in Africa. From then on he attended IFLA General Council meetings on a regular basis, and from 1969 to 1973 was chairman of the Public Libraries Section Commitee of IFLA. He pressed for the adoption and publication of international standards for public libraries during his term of office. This meant the formation of a special committee to study and prepare the standards, and involved additional meetings in London, Luton, Bremen, East Berlin, Lund, Liverpool, and elsewhere. As chairman, Gardner handled a difficult task with great finesse, with the result that the IFLA *Standards for Public Libraries* were published in time for the IFLA General Council meeting in Grenoble in 1973. Since then they have been widely adopted, and revisions have already taken place.

At home Gardner was a member of the Libraries Advisory Council from 1965 to 1971 and chairman of the Books and Libraries Panel of the British Council from 1966 to 1972. He remained on the LA Council until his retirement in 1972. He was also prominent in the field of library cooperation, having served as

honorary secretary of the South Eastern Regional Library System, and was also a member of the Executive Committee of the National Central Library until it was merged into the British Library in 1973. Gardner was also a great supporter of the idea of National Library Weeks and was a member of the Joint Organizing Committee for NLW in the 1960s.

Gardner contributed many articles to the British and overseas library press, though his books were relatively few. He compiled *Sequels* in 1947, which came out in revised editions periodically, and he followed it with *Junior Sequels,* produced in 1977 in collaboration with Lisa-Christina Persson. He also wrote *Letters to a Younger Librarian* (1948), *Public Library Legislation: A Comparative Study* (1971), for Unesco, and *Reading Round the World* (1969), in collaboration with M. Joy Lewis. He was made an Honorary Fellow of the LA in 1966 and was honored by the Queen with the award of the CBE (Companion of the Order of the British Empire) in the following year.

Gardner was in later life in demand as a lecturer at library schools and contributed to many conferences, national and international. He mingled freely and happily with librarians from other countries, but they sometimes found his low-pitched voice and his flat Northern accent difficult to understand. He remained a popular and certainly an influential figure in British and international library circles.

REFERENCE
K. C. Harrison. "Frank Gardner: Internationalist." *IFLA Journal* (1980).

K. C. HARRISON

Garfield, Eugene
(1925-)

The library and information world has many entrepreneurs; Eugene Garfield earned a special place in that his success was based upon early and deep insights regarding the structure of science literatures and the nature of scientific communication.

Eugene Garfield was born September 16, 1925, in New York City. He was raised in a Jewish-Italian family in which he, in retrospect, rejoiced, according to his warm memoir (1978) relating his experiences with his Italian stepfather to those with his intellectual mentor, Chauncey Leake. He was educated at Columbia University, earning a B.S. in Chemistry in 1949 and an M.S. in Library Service in 1954 while working at a variety of jobs to pay for his education. Self-employment began almost immediately after the last degree, first as a consultant to Smith, Kline and French, the pharmaceutical company, and then as the founder of a tiny company producing the predecessor to *Current Contents,* started first as a cottage industry in a converted chicken coop.

Critical years were 1960 and 1961; his small firm took on its current name, Institute for Scientific Information (ISI). He received a Ph.D. in Structural Linguistics from the University of Pennsylvania (1961). (His dissertation applied modern linguistics to the indexing of chemical information.) The most important event in 1961 was that he brought out the first citation index to a broad spectrum of science literature, genetics.

A variety of products, ideas, and special tech-

Eugene Garfield

niques and services can be identified with Garfield and his associates, but just two products, *Current Contents* and *Science Citation Index,* and their conceptualization and development, their implementation and successful management, would stand alone as major monuments to his skills, energy, and intellect. *Current Contents* capitalizes upon the researcher's urgent needs for current research information, particularly in the life sciences, and a person's enormous capability to scan text skillfully. *Science Citation Index* identified citation behavior, a means of acknowledging intellectual debt and assigning credit, as the key to a basic organizational feature of the scientific literatures, useful for retrieval, for research on the nature of science, and for science policy.

ISI marketed many products and employed hundreds of people in the 1980s; Garfield continued as an active scholar, writer, and advocate.

REFERENCES

Eugene Garfield, *Essays of an Information Scientist* (1977), provides a basic introduction to the man and his ideas.
Eugene Garfield, *Citation Indexing* (1979), an extensive treatment of techniques.

BELVER GRIFFITH

Garnett, Richard

(1835–1906)

Richard Garnett, English librarian and man of letters, was born on February 27, 1835, at Lichfield, near Birmingham, where his father, Richard (1789–1850), was then Priest-Vicar of the Cathedral and already a distinguished Celtic scholar. In 1838 the family moved to London, where the elder Garnett took up a new post as Assistant Keeper of Printed Books in the British Museum. He served in that capacity until his death; as a compliment to him, his son was appointed to an assistantship at an unusually early age.

The younger Garnett became an expert cataloguer and classifier and gained thereby, and through exceptionally wide personal reading, vast knowledge of his library's stock. This knowledge earned him unprecedented renown following his promotion to Assistant Keeper of Printed Books and Superintendent of the Reading Room in 1875. As an example, at the Library Association's inaugural conference in 1877 he arranged to facilitate Charles Ammi Cutter's researches in connection with his bibliography of the devil.

Garnett became an outstanding, active, and highly valued member of the LA and served as President in 1893, after he had succeeded George Bullen (1816–1894) as Keeper of Printed Books. His LA activities brought him into the controversies of the late 1870s and early 1880s on the various proposals for universal and specialist bibliographies, never overlooking the desirability of printing the B.M.'s own catalogue—the manuscript version in more than 2,000 pasted-up volumes was becoming increasingly unmanageable. Once the decision had been taken to print the catalogue (subsequently famous as GK1) Garnett, if at first unofficially, became its editor and in 1884 was relieved of his Reading Room responsibilities to concentrate on the vast task; it was eventually completed nearly two years after his retirement in 1899.

David Garnett, in his *Golden Echo* (1953), described his grandfather, whom he could remember only from, say, 1895 onwards, as

> tall, round-shouldered, stooping . . . by no means a well-dressed man . . . with gentleness, perfect courtesy and slyly hidden humour.

He was also a great cat lover and something of an amateur astrologer. He built up a second reputation as a man of letters with his own poems and translations of poetry from several languages; with contributions to many periodicals and to the *Dictionary of National Biography* and the *Encyclopaedia Britannica;* with numerous short biographies—for example Milton (1887), Emerson (1888), William Blake (1895); with prefaces and introductory essays to many reprints of English classical works; with a history of Italian literature (1897); and mostly, and lastingly, with *The Twilight of the Gods,* first published in book form in 1888 with a new and enlarged edition in 1903. This is a beguiling collection of 28 satirical stories of East and West which originally appeared in a wide variety of periodicals and in *The Yellow Book.* The first story provides the book with its title. It concerns the release of Prometheus from his rock at a time when the old Gods were being dethroned by the early Christians and his subsequent adventures in the company of the maiden Elenko. Others of the stories have titles such as "The Demon Pope," "Alexander the Ratcatcher," and "The Philosopher and the Butterflies." In his introduction to an illustrated reprint of 1924, T. E. Lawrence rightly insisted:

> It wants not learning to enjoy *The Twilight of the Gods* but the more learning you have the more odd corners and hidden delights you will find in it.

Garnett edited George Allen's "Library Series," which provided British librarianship at the turn of the century with some of its best working textbooks and other guides. Titles included were Henry Ogle's *The Free Library* (1897), F. J. Burgoyne's *Library Construction: Architecture, Fittings and Furniture* (1897), and his own *Essays in Librarianship and Bibliography* (1899)— he was also a member of the Bibliographical Society and served as its President from 1895 to 1897. His book contains 24 pieces, half of them reprinted papers read originally at LA meetings and conferences between 1877 and 1898. Those on the B.M.'s catalogues are specially revealing in that they trace, indirectly, the evolution of his own thought on printing—initially cautious and critical, and then assured, supportive, and determined. Others on such subjects as the future of municipal libraries, mobile shelving, the practical applications of photography, and even the possibilities of Telex are exceptionally far-sighted. The book ends with brief biographies and appreciations of the three Principal Librarians under whom Garnett had served—Sir Anthony Panizzi (1797–1879), the creator of the modern B.M., John Winter Jones (1805–1881), and Sir Edward Bond (1815–1898), under whose auspices GK1 was produced and financed, together with a biography of Henry Stevens (1819–1885), the "Green Mountain Boy," whose "happy union of bibliographical attainments and social qualities," as Garnett aptly put it, did much to link the librarians of America and Europe.

Garnett's *Essays of an Ex-Librarian* (1901) com-

The British Library

Richard Garnett

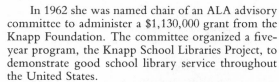

prises 12 contributions to literary history and criticism on Emerson, Shelley, Coleridge, Thomas Love Peacock, and other writers. An occasional footnote reminds the reader that the author also wrote *The Twilight of the Gods:*

> Though the scenic resources of Shakespeare's age were limited, they were sufficient to be troublesome on a private stage. Tombs, rocks, hell-mouths, beacons and trees are found in lists of properties.

Garnett died at his Hampstead home in London on April 13, 1906.

REFERENCE
Barbara McCrimmon. *Power, Politics and Print: The Publication of the British Museum Catalogue, 1881–1900* (1981)
W. A. MUNFORD

Gaver, Mary
(1906-   )

Mary Virginia Gaver, librarian, educator, researcher, editor, writer, and publisher, developed school library programs that were far in advance of the times, conducted major research on effectiveness of school libraries, assisted in development of standards for school libraries, and conceived and organized a brilliant effort to facilitate the implementation of those standards.

Gaver was born in Washington, D.C., December 10, 1906. She received an A.B. degree from Randolph-Macon Woman's College in 1927, where she earned a Phi Beta Kappa key, and the B.S. and M.S. at Columbia in 1932 and 1938. She was a Carnegie fellow in 1937 and continued graduate study at Teachers College, Columbia (1947–50). Her early professional experience included service as an English teacher and librarian, George Washington High School, Danville, Virginia (1927–37); Technical Director, State-Wide Library Project, W.P.A. of Virginia (1938–39); Librarian, Scarsdale (New York) High School (1939–42); Librarian and Associate Professor of Library Service, New Jersey State Teachers College, Trenton (1942–54); Visiting Professor, University of Teheran and leader-specialist, International Information Administration in Iran (1952–53). Between 1934 and 1942, she was a Visiting Professor at the University of Virginia and Emory University.

During her years as Associate Professor (1954–60) and Professor (1960–71) at the newly established Graduate School of Library Service at Rutgers University, Gaver made her most important contributions for the advancement of libraries. In 1959–60, under the sponsorship of the U.S. Office of Education, she directed a major research project, *Effectiveness of Centralized School Library Services (Phase I)*. She assisted Frances Henne in completing *Standards for School Library Programs* (published by the American Library Association in 1960). The 1960 standards were enormously influential in individual schools and school districts, primarily because of the extensive and highly successful national promotion campaign Gaver conceived. She chaired the advisory committee to the School Library Development Project of the American Association of School Librarians, which worked through state associations to improve professional leadership among school librarians.

In 1962 she was named chair of an ALA advisory committee to administer a $1,130,000 grant from the Knapp Foundation. The committee organized a five-year program, the Knapp School Libraries Project, to demonstrate good school library service throughout the United States.

Gaver's greatest impact during her Rutgers years was felt through the students who came from far and wide to attend her classes on school library administration, collection building for libraries, and children's literature. She taught and advised many doctoral students and directed a number of dissertations, and later maintained a wide correspondence with her former students.

Gaver worked productively for her objectives through professional organizations, including IFLA. She represented the New Jersey Library Association (NJLA) on the ALA Council (1956–60) and served as a member at large (1961–65). She served NJLA as Vice-President (1947–48) and President (1954–55). The New Jersey School Library Association honored her with a testimonial luncheon in March 1965 in appreciation of her 20 years of achievement in the development of the state's libraries. She served as President of ALA's Library Education Division (1949–50); President of the American Association of School Librarians (1959–60); and President of ALA (1966–67). In 1980 the American Association of School Librarians presented Gaver with the third annual President's Award, cosponsored by AASL and the Baker and Taylor Company, to honor an individual for "outstanding work in school librarianship and school library development."

Other recognitions include the Rutgers Research Council Award, conferred in 1962, which recognized her "outstanding contributions to the development of service to children and young people in school and public libraries"; the Randolph-Macon Woman's College Achievement Award; and the Beta Phi Mu Award of Good Teaching in 1964. One of the highest honors in librarianship, the Herbert Putnam Honor Award of the ALA, conferred only rarely since its inception in 1939, was presented to Gaver in 1963. The citation referred to her "significant contributions to the profession of librarianship in the areas of professional leadership in library development and organization, research, children's and school library work, library education, and her professional and educational writing."

Other awards include the Constance Lindsay Skinner Award of the Woman's National Book Association (1973) and research grants from the Rutgers University Research Council (1968–69 and 1969–70). C. W. Post College awarded her an honorary LL.D. in 1967; Mount Holyoke College gave her an LL.D. in 1968.

In addition to *Effectiveness of Centralized School Library Services (Phase I)* (2nd edition, 1963), Gaver published *Every Child Needs a School Library* (1957); *The Research Manual* (3rd edition, 1963) with Lucille Hook; *School Libraries of Puerto Rico, A Survey and Plan for Development* (privately published, 1963) with Gonzalo Velasquez; *Libraries for the People of New Jersey; or Knowledge for All* (1964) with Lowell A. Martin; *Patterns of Development of Elementary School Libraries Today* (3rd edition, 1969); *Services of Secondary School Media Centers* (1970); and *A Survey of the Edu-*

Compson
Mary Virginia Gaver

cational Media Services of Calgary Public Schools (with others) (1971).

She retired from the faculty of the Rutgers Graduate School of Library Science in 1971 and joined Bro-Dart, Inc., as Consultant for Library and Publisher Relations. She was named a Vice-President of the firm in 1973. She was General Editor of *The Elementary School Library Collection* (ESLC) (1st–8th editions, Bro-Dart Foundation, 1965–73), and continued to evaluate fiction for the ESLC until 1984.

In 1975 she moved back to Danville, Virginia. She organized a local arts association and Friends of the Public Library there, and also developed a Book Review series for the local Young Women's Christian Association.

In 1976, at the American Library Association Centennial Conference, Gaver received the highest award of the American Library Association, Honorary Membership.

MILBREY L. JONES

German Democratic Republic

The German Democratic Republic (GDR) is a socialist state in central Europe. It was established October 7, 1949. The GDR is bounded on the north by the Baltic Sea, on the east by Poland, on the south by Czechoslovakia, and on the west by the Federal Republic of Germany. Population (1984 est.) 16,700,000; area 108,333 sq.km. The language is German. About 100,000 Sorbs live in two counties.

History. A leading industrial and agricultural state in the 1980s, the GDR pays great attention to the production, dissemination, and utilization of literature. In 1984 78 publishers produced more than 6,000 titles annually (about eight books per capita). The development of librarianship started in 1945, immediately after fascism had been smashed. Library work had to start anew both in content and in organization after World War II.

Before 1945 Germany had large and efficient academic libraries but few general public libraries, and there was only very limited state planning or guidance in library work. As a result there were no libraries in a majority of towns, villages, and enterprises. Further, many library buildings and installations were destroyed or badly damaged during the war.

After the establishment of the GDR in 1949, development took place in several stages. In the period between 1949 and 1957 a library network was created in the towns and rural communities, in the large en-

terprises, in all universities and colleges, and in the research institutes of the academies.

The next stage involved attaining higher quality in all fields of librarianship and all phases of library work. An important step was the foundation in 1964 of the Library Association of the German Democratic Republic, open to libraries in all fields and of all types.

In 1968 the Library Ordinance of the GDR was promulgated by the Council of Ministers. The first inclusive legal instrument for the whole library system of a German state, it laid down the basic tasks for all libraries in the GDR. The ordinance also summarized the principles and requirements necessary for the further development of the branches and types of libraries and for individual libraries.

In the following years library development was marked by the implementation of the Library Ordinance. Public discussion preceded the publication of the 11 implementation regulations issued by the mid-1980s. The integrated library system, working in close connection with the information and documentation systems of the GDR, consists of various sectors with division of labor. They include libraries with state-wide functions; state public libraries and other public libraries; libraries of universities, colleges, and academies; libraries in enterprises (specialized and trade union libraries); and specialized libraries for research, administration, and other activities. Libraries in the GDR embrace a wide range of objectives, among them contributing to development of scientific-technical progress; greater efficiency in production; research work in all fields and the rapid implementation in practice of research findings; development of a rich intellectual-cultural life; increase in the educational standard of citizens; and "molding of socialist personalities and socialist modes of life."

About 32,000 libraries of various types and sizes made some 110 million volumes available to readers in the mid-1980s. More than one-third of the citizens of the GDR are regular library users, and both this number and the number of loans increases every year. Bookstocks and facilities in the libraries increase in proportion.

Every citizen is entitled to borrow books, to use library reading rooms, and to use the many library services. No fee is charged for borrowing books and other library stock, for using reading rooms, or for playing records or tapes. A small fee is charged for some services, such as photocopying and the provision of bibliographical information.

German State Library. The German State Li-

Libraries in the German Democratic Republic (1984)

Type	Administrative units	Service points	Volumes in collections	Annual expenditures (DDR mark)	Population served	Professional staff	Total staff
National	3	3	11,904,116	--	74,889	609	1,238
Academic	29	504	22,781,308	--	222,897	1,041	1,907
Public	9,002	18,772	52,730,843	148,760,000	4,820,991	6,499	7,325

Source: Alle Zahlenangaben betreffen die Staatlichen Allgemeinbibliotheken und die Gewerkschaftsbibliotheken.

German Democratic Republic

Tschuschke

The German State Library in East Berlin, founded in 1661 as the court library of the Elector of Brandenberg. It serves primarily as a reference library.

brary in East Berlin, capital of the German Democratic Republic, dates back to 1661 and serves as the central academic library of the GDR. Together with the German Library (Deutsche Bücherei) in Leipzig, it performs the tasks of a National Library, including the complete collection of German literature up to 1913. It serves various aspects of national study and research, and its 6,550,000 titles in the mid-1980s included many treasures of German-language literature from many centuries. It holds the largest collection of foreign literature in the GDR. Apart from books and periodicals, the German Library collects manuscripts and autographs, sheet music, maps, portraits, and other nonprint material. Stocks are enlarged through deposit copies and wide-ranging exchange agreements with libraries and institutes in some 85 countries; in addition, it is library of deposit for UN publications.

Access is facilitated by an alphabetical and a systematic catalogue, in addition to a variety of special catalogues and printed listings. About 1,800,000 books were evacuated from the stores during World War II, and they are still held in West Berlin.

The German State Library includes departments for music, Asia, Africa, maps, incunabula, and books for children and young people; the manuscript department/literature archive; the department for rare and precious prints; and, in addition, the Theodor Fontane Archive in Potsdam. The effectiveness of the German State Library as a center for domestic and foreign literature is shown by its annual loan figure of more than 1,000,000 titles. The bookstocks are utilized both through loans and by reprography. The library provides 454 desks for readers and extensive reference libraries.

In the framework of the library system of the GDR, the German State Library performs central functions particularly in the fields of interlibrary loan, union catalogues, and manuscripts and incunabula. In addition, it works closely with other libraries in various fields, particularly in the coordination of new acquisitions. Among its publications, the union catalogue of incunabula, a register of all known incunabula in the world, takes a special place.

German Library. The German Library (Deutsche Bücherei) in Leipzig was established in 1912 by the German Book Trade Association (Börsenverein der deutschen Buchhändler). From 1913 it collected all German publications and after 1945 con-

tinued to do so, covering the GDR, the Federal Republic of Germany, and West Berlin, as well as all varieties of German-language writing appearing in all parts of the world. In addition to books and periodicals, collections include university theses, music, art, prints, cards, patent specifications, and other classes of publications. From 1976 it collected musical records produced in the GDR. The Museum of Books and Writings is part of the German Library. The Library holds about 7,000,000 titles. It also supports restoration facilities.

As the bibliographic information center for German-language literature, the Library publishes the *Deutsche Nationalbibliographie* ("German National Bibliography") and basic bibliographies on music and translations, among others. It coordinates bibliographical work in the GDR, registers all bibliographical projects, and prepares an annual plan.

Academic Libraries. These libraries are closely linked with the functions and tasks of the bodies responsible for them in the fields of science, research, teaching, and education. In addition, they place their bookstocks and services, as a part of the national library system, at the disposal of all social sectors in the interests of the universal availability of publications and information. They take an active part in national and international lending and serve as regional and specialized information and documentation centers.

University Libraries. The seven university libraries are among the oldest libraries in the GDR and hold wide-ranging and valuable historic bookstocks in addition to modern scientific literature. They are University Library of Humboldt University, Berlin, founded 1831 (4,100,000 bound volumes in early 1980s); University and Sachsen-Anhalt Province Library of Martin Luther University, Halle-Wittenberg, founded 1696 (3,700,000); University Library of Karl Marx University, Leipzig, founded 1543 (3,300,000); University Library of Friedrich Schiller University, Jena, founded 1858 (2,500,000); University Library of Ernst Moritz Arndt University, Greifswald, founded 1604 (2,100,000); University Library of Wilhelm Pieck University, Rostock, founded 1569 (1,800,000); and University Library of the Technical University, Dresden, founded 1828 (1,300,000).

Each university library is organized as a unitary system, integrating services for literature, information, and documentation. In structure the university libraries consist of a main library to which are attached the branch libraries in the departments and other academic sections of the university.

College and Technical College Libraries. The following are among the most important of the more than 60 college libraries: the libraries of the Technical College, Karl-Marx-Stadt (580,000 titles); the Mining Academy, Freiberg (482,000); the College of Transport, Dresden (330,000); the College of Economics, Berlin (232,000); the College of Architecture and Civil Engineering, Weimar (204,000); and the College of Physical Training and Sport, Leipzig (100,000). The structure and mode of work of these libraries are, in principle, the same as that of the university libraries.

The approximately 240 technical and specialized colleges of the GDR maintain libraries that conform with their specialist requirements and the functions and educational tasks of the responsible bodies.

Academy Libraries. The libraries of the six academies of the GDR—Academy of Pedagogic Science, Academy of Architecture, Academy of Agricultural Science, Academy of Arts, Academy for Advanced Medical Training, and Academy of Sciences—hold an important stock of scientific literature amounting to about 3,000,000 titles.

The library of the Academy of Sciences, as the most important academy library, holds about 1,700,000 titles. It consists of a main library and, attached to it, 70 branch libraries in the institutes and establishments of the academy.

Saxonian Regional Library (Sächsische Landesbibliothek). This library, in Dresden, which comes directly under the Ministry for Higher and Technical Education, is a scientific general library and a specialized central library for the arts. It maintains the regional central catalogue for Dresden, Karl-Marx-Stadt, and Cottbus counties. It was founded in 1556 as the Saxonian Court Library, and has valuable historic bookstocks, including incunabula. The total bookstocks amount to 1,200,000 titles.

Special Libraries. *State Bodies.* All ministries, central state departments, and institutions maintain specialized libraries, which support the theoretical and practical work of the staffs of those organizations. The most important special libraries of state bodies are the Library of the People's Chamber (Parliament), the Central Library in the House of the Ministries, the Library of the Supreme Court of the GDR, the Library of the Office for Inventions and Patents, and the Central Library of the Ministry of Transport.

Enterprises. In the industrial combines and production firms a large potential in the form of scientific-technical specialized libraries was being developed in the 1980s, closely linked with the construction of a comprehensive system of information and documentation. This is equally true for the development of special libraries in the fields of agriculture, education, health services, and other social areas.

Social Organizations. The parties, mass organizations, and other associations maintain specialized libraries, some of which are of importance. They serve the staffs and members of these organizations, and they are often made available to a wider public.

In addition, the museums of the GDR, more than 600 in number, have specialized libraries, some of considerable importance, and the same is true for archives and for the many scientific societies.

Networks. It is characteristic of the whole range of specialized libraries that cooperative networks of technical libraries were growing up in the 1980s, specialized both by theme and bookstocks; such changes were taking place in concord with the general development of information and documentation and independent from their institutional or territorial assignment. Such thematic or subject-oriented networks are generally headed by central specialized libraries or information and documentation centers.

Developed networks exist in the fields of heavy engineering, mining and metallurgy, the chemical industry, agriculture, education, and medicine. For instance, the more than 400 medical libraries in the state hospitals, medical research centers, and training centers work together in one specialized network with the medical information centers. The network is directed by the Institute for Scientific Information in Medicine (IWIM). The network is organized on a territorial basis for medical care and on a subject basis for medical research. In medical installations, the special libraries also work closely with the libraries for patients.

State General Libraries (StAB). The State General libraries (StAB) are the basic type of library in the national library system of the GDR; they are the most comprehensive type, and have the broadest effect. Their functions and their tasks extend to all sections of the population and to all parts of the country with differing population densities and differing settlement patterns. They provide public library services under the organization of the socialist society of the GDR. For the StAB as a whole the ruling principle is that they serve, for all citizens of the socialist society, their general and special needs for literature and information services.

The mission of the StAB is to awaken, foster, and satisfy the needs of adults, young people, and children for educational, recreational, and vocational or professional information and library services. The StAB as a whole are marked by a universality in the profile of their bookstocks. Through interlibrary cooperation and loans, they can also provide readers with literature from the bookstocks of all libraries.

The StAB are installations of the local authority, entrusted with fulfilling the responsibility of those authorities to supply citizens with literature and services according to need. StAB are located in all communities and towns. As a rule, in communities with more than 3,000 inhabitants, libraries are administered and directed by full-time staff; in smaller communities, staffing is on a part-time basis. The StAB are organized in local networks on the pattern of main library, branch library, lending center. The StAB also work together in territorial networks.

Territorial networks exist for each of the 190 rural districts. The urban and rural libraries in each district center function as the advisory center and bookstock center for the library network in the district. In the framework of the district library network, there are, as a special type of library, rural central libraries, with extended bookstocks and full-time staff, which serve as bookstock centers for a number of communities with part-time libraries. Libraries in the rural districts of the 14 counties work cooperatively together. The network of StAB in a county is headed by the city and county library located in the county capital or by the scientific general library of the county. That library performs the function of a scientific book stock center and a scientific-methodical guidance center. The library network in East Berlin maintains a main library in each of the nine city boroughs; the Berlin City Library acts as the bookstock center and scientific-methodical guidance center.

In 1982 the GDR had a total of 14,450 StAB. The full-time staffed libraries consisted of 1,012 main libraries, 737 branch libraries, and 5,377 lending stations. The part-time staffed libraries consisted of 6,221 community libraries and 1,103 lending stations.

The following summary indicates the growth and performance of the StAB in the GDR: Bookstock increased from about 3,678,000 in 1949 to 11,400,000 by 1959, 18,767,000 by 1969, and 35,144,000 by 1979. It was 39,672,000 in 1982. During the same periods, readers increased from 790,770 (1949) to 2,156,600 (1959), 3,096,000 (1969), and 3,793,000 (1979). There were 3,835,000 readers in 1982. Loans increased sharply—12,000,000 (1949), 36,947,000 (1959), 51,918,000 (1969), and 76,185,000 (1979). Loans exceeded 81,500,000 in 1982. About 25 percent of the citizens of the GDR use the StAB. Among those in education and training, about 70 percent use these libraries.

Children's Services. Two-thirds of all children and young people up to the age of 18 use these libraries. For children between 6 and 14, special separate bookstocks are made available, in accordance with the abilities and knowledge of the age groups. They cover all fields of knowledge and include both print and audiovisual material. Available either in special branch libraries or in separate departments, they are sorted according to varying age groups and school grades. At branch libraries or children's departments, children can borrow books, read in the library, and play records and tapes. Guided tours of the library and instruction on library use are provided for the various ages and school grades.

An agreement between the Ministry of Culture and the Ministry of Education, concluded in 1975, provided that library services for children in the GDR should be provided solely by the StAB. As a result the ten-grade general polytechnical schools in the GDR do not maintain their own school libraries, but only grade selections with materials pertaining to the curriculum. However, many children's branches of the StAB are established in schools.

Young Adults. For young people above the age of 14 who use the StAB, certain selections particularly suited for that group are offered in the adult section of the library. Apart from that, young people are free to use the entire bookstock of the adult library.

Other Services. A considerable part of the work of the StAB cannot be expressed statistically, for instance, in the field of bibliographical work, publicity, and information work aimed at a paticular group of readers.

All StAB provide intensive advice for readers, and exhibitions and cultural events also form part of the field of activity of these libraries. Many libraries provide literary clubs and youth clubs. The quantity and quality of services offered by the StAB were anticipated to continue to grow.

Trade Union Libraries. There are many trade union libraries in all sectors of the economy, and also in state institutions, administrative offices, houses of culture, and holiday homes. The trade union libraries perform, in the factories and offices, functions similar to those of the StAB. The main task of the trade union libraries, which work in all fields, is to provide all-around delivery of and information about materials among those employed in an enterprise, in trade union groups, and in work teams. As literature dissemination installations, the trade union libraries contribute to the political, economic, and cultural tasks of their enterprises. The basic tasks of the trade union libraries and the general rules for their activities are determined by the central board of the Federation of Free German Trades Unions (FDGB). The detailed tasks and plans are worked out in the enterprises, in

particular by the enterprise trade union committee. In enterprises with more than 1,000 employees, the trade union libraries have full-time staff and in smaller enterprises, part-time staff.

There were 4,390 trade union libraries in the GDR in the early 1980s. Of them, 632 were full-time staffed libraries, with 185 branch libraries and 3,552 lending stations; there were 1,174 part-time staffed libraries with 47 lending stations.

In 1982 the trade union libraries had about a million regular readers. The bookstocks of all trade union libraries amounted to 9,300,000 titles, and there were 13,900,000 million loans.

The trade union libraries are not organized in a general library network, but they work closely with the state general libraries in their territory under an agreement between the Ministry of Culture and the central board of the Federation of Free German Trades Unions. In enterprises that have a technical library in addition to the trade union library, the aim is to achieve close cooperation between the two libraries in tackling their tasks.

The Profession. Trained library personnel in the GDR are classified in three groups: trained library workers (prepared through vocational training), librarians (training college), and graduate librarians and specialized librarians (university). Trained library workers receive two years of theoretical and practical training in a teaching library and vocational school. The profession of librarian entails either three years' full-time study at a training college or four and a half years' part-time study. Graduate librarians must complete a four-and-a-half-year university course with librarianship as the main subject.

Graduates who have taken their degrees in other disciplines can become specialized librarians on completing a two-year postgraduate course in librarianship. Completed training in one of the professional groups opens the door to full-time or part-time study in the next group.

A wide and varied system of advanced training is available for trained personnel working in libraries. The Minister of Culture honors library staff with long service and particular achievements with the titles of Senior Librarian, Library Counselor, and Senior Library Counselor (Oberbibliothekar, Bibliotheksrat, Oberbibliotheksrat). Institutions that provide library training are the Vocational School for Trained Library Workers in Sondershausen; the Erich Weinert Training College for Librarians in Leipzig; the Training College for Scientific Information and Scientific Librarianship in Berlin; the Training College for Scientific Librarianship in Leipzig; and the Institute for Library Science and Scientific Information of the Humboldt University in Berlin.

Central Scientific–Methodical Institutions and Central Institutions. Scientific-methodical institutions have been established for important areas of the library system of the GDR. They are organs of the relevant state or social bodies and work on the basis of statutes or regulations. The central scientific-methodical institutions of the library system of the GDR are the Central Institute for Librarianship; the Methodical Center for Scientific Libraries and Information and Documentation Institutes of the Ministry of Higher and Technical Education; and the Central Library of the Trades Unions.

The Central Institute for Librarianship (ZIB), established in 1950, is an agency of the Ministry of Culture for basic questions on the development of the library system in the GDR and the network of the StAB. It is also the supervisory body for coordinating scientific-methodical work in the library system and for working out basic questions such as prognosis and planning, structural questions, the construction of regional networks, library statistics, and standardization. The Central Office for Information and Documentation in Librarianship is subordinated to the ZIB.

The Methodical Center for Scientific Libraries and Information and Documentation Institutes is the scientific-methodical institute for scientific libraries and for institutes of information and documentation in the sphere of the Ministry of Higher and Technical Education. It is the supervisory body for subsections of the library system of the GDR, and it supports the relevant organs in the development of central special libraries and the organization of specialized library networks. The Central Library of the Trades Unions works as methodical center for the trade union libraries of the GDR. All three central scientific-methodical institutions work closely together on the basis of coordinated plans.

Central supervisory bodies have been formed for the coordination of library work in important subsections. These supervisory bodies are: the Institute for Interlibrary Loans and Union Catalogues, attached to the German State Library in Berlin; the Supervisory and Coordination Body for Bibliography and Bibliographic Work, attached to the German Library in Leipzig; the Institute for Library Science and Scientific Information of the Humboldt University in Berlin, coordinating library research; and the Central Supervisory Body for Manuscripts and Incunabula attached to the German State Library in Berlin. These supervisory and coordination institutes cooperate closely with the central scientific-methodical institutes.

Research. Various institutions in the library system participate in library research in the GDR. Primarily the research is undertaken in the scientific-methodical centers, central libraries, and training centers. The Institute for Library Science and Scientific Information of the Humboldt University in Berlin is the supervisory center responsible for drawing up the plans for library research and coordinating the activities of the research committees for the main research complexes. The results of library research find their expression in dissertations, diploma theses, training college theses, research reports, and publications.

Publications. There are many library publications in the GDR, issued by publishing houses, library institutions, libraries, and the Library Association of the GDR. The VEB Bibliographisches Institut in Leipzig is the specialized publishing house for most of the monographs on library subjects and on information/documentation. Library monthlies are *Zentralblatt für Bibliothekswesen* and *Der Bibliothekar.* Both periodicals have a joint editorial staff in Berlin and both of them publish in addition supplements related to special themes. Periodically the Central Institute for Librarianship, the Library Association of the GDR, and other institutions publish information bulletins. Specialized library information is provided in the GDR by the annotated *Informationsdienst Bibliothekswesen,* published every two months by the Central Office for Information and Documentation in Librarianship and attached to the Central Institute for Librarianship.

Library Association. The Library Association of the GDR (BV), established in 1964, has roughly 2,000 organization members—full-time libraries and information centers, central institutes of the library system, and the book and information branches, together with the training and advanced training institutes of the GDR library system. The Library Association is divided into 15 county groups on a territorial basis (the basic organizations of the association) and into sections for libraries with the same specialization.

The highest organ of the Library Association is the General Assembly, held every five years; it is a delegate conference of all members. The Assembly decides on the working program of the Association and elects the Executive Committee, which directs the Association between general assemblies. To deal with permanent or temporary tasks, expert groups and working groups are attached to the Executive Committee.

Through its work among its members, the Library Association helps to ensure that standards of work of the libraries and information institutes are maintained, and it supports initiatives taken for development of the socialist library system. The BV works closely with the Ministry of Culture and other central and regional government bodies and with state institutions and the leading bodies of social organizations. The Association encourages all forms of cooperative relations and teamwork in the library system and also technical exchanges of experience. It drafts proposals and recommendations for the development of the library system for state bodies, and advises those directing these bodies. In addition it undertakes wide-ranging popular educational publicity work.

The members of the Association come together at meetings, conferences, deliberations, and further-education sessions.

The BV of the GDR conducts wide-reaching international activities. It has considerable and varied working relationships with the library associations of other countries, represents the library system of the GDR as national member of IFLA, and, under the auspices of the Unesco Commission of the GDR, works for the implementation of the aims of Unesco.

State Management and Planning. Final responsibility for library service lies with the central state bodies. The Council of Ministers sets the basic policy. It delegates to the Ministry of Culture responsibility for coordination of the whole system. An Advisory Council on Librarianship, with representatives of various fields and library interests, including the Library Association, advises the Ministry of Culture.

The German State Library, the German Library, and the Saxon Province Library, as well as academic libraries, are under the Ministry for Higher Education. It also has an advisory council. Other state libraries—enterprise libraries and various special libraries—are directly or indirectly responsible to the relevant ministries of their fields.

The Ministry of Culture issues basic Implementation Regulations on the Library Ordinance covering tasks of various library types and also issues detailed regulations on use, interlibrary lending, and other operational matters.

REFERENCES

Horst Kunze and Gotthard Rückl, with Hans Riedel and Margit Wille, *Lexikon des Bibliothekswesens* ("Lexicon of Librarianship") 2nd rev. ed. (Leipzig), vol. 1, A–N. (1974), vol. 2, O–Z. (1975).

Wilfried Kern, *Librarianship in the German Democratic Republic* (1981).

Helga Klinger and Michael Peschke, Compilers, *Das Bibliothekswesen in der Deutschen Demokratischen Republik: Jahresbericht* ("The Library System in the German Democratic Republic: Annual Report"), published by the Central Institute for Librarianship, Central Office for Information and Documentation in Librarianship; Methodical Center for Scientific Libraries and Information and Documentation Institutes of the Ministry for Higher and Technical Education; Central Board of the Federation of Free German Trades Unions, Central Library and Archive; Library Association of the GDR (1983 and 1984).

Bibliotheksarbeit in der Deutschen Demokratischen Republik: ausgewählte Beirträge ("Library Work in the GDR: Selected Contributions") (1982).

GOTTHARD RÜCKL

Germany, Federal Republic of

The Federal Republic of Germany, in central Europe, is bordered by Denmark and the Baltic Sea on the north, the German Democratic Republic and Czechoslovakia on the east, Austria on the south, Switzerland on the southwest, France, Luxembourg, Belgium, and the Netherlands on the west, and the North Sea on the northwest. Population (1984 est.) 61,313,000; area 248,687 sq.km. The official language is German.

History. The foundation of contemporary librarianship in Germany dates back to the Reformation, but the development of modern librarianship in Germany—as well as in other large European nations—began in the early 19th century, a result of attempts during the Romantic period to maintain ecclesiastical libraries that had been abandoned because of political events. Rare book collections, particularly from monasteries, were generally transferred to libraries of ruling nobilities, and in turn became part of regional and state libraries—the central research libraries of the individual states of the German Empire—in the course of the 19th century. Meanwhile, university libraries gained greater prominence after the reform of German universities during the first decades of that century. The University of Göttingen—already in possession of an efficient library during the 18th century—was a model for new university libraries in already established and newly founded universities. Regional, state, and university libraries assumed guiding functions in library work in Germany.

During most of the 19th century a university library was run by a university professor, but later it was headed by a library professional, as library science came into being. However, the *professor-librarian*, as represented by Friedrich Ritschl (classical philology), Karl Richard Lepsius (Egyptology), and Adolf von Harnack (theology), still existed into the beginning of the 20th century.

In addition to academic and research libraries, public libraries, originally financed by private contributions, were established in the 19th century. Later the Anglo-American model influenced German public library development with the *Bücherhalle* ("bookhall"). During the second decade of the 20th century, the Bücherhalle's emphasis on instruction was replaced by an emphasis on the education of its readers, as shown especially in the work of Walter Hofmann. After World War II German libraries again turned toward the Anglo-American public library tradition.

World War II marked a significant turning point in the Germany library system. In the course of the ravages of war, many libraries were destroyed. The largest German library, the Preussische Staatsbibliothek (Prussian State Library) in Berlin, was divided among both German states after the German partition. The reconstruction of academic and research libraries after 1945 was based on the traditional patterns of library administration as described in the *Handbuch der Bibliothekswissenschaft* ("Handbook of Library Science;" 2nd ed. 1952–65), edited by Fritz Milkau and Georg Leyh (1931–42). It guided academic and research libraries for almost 40 years.

German university libraries at the end of the 19th century felt restricted because of the better-financed libraries of the university institutes, which the directors of the university libraries could not influence. Also the number of personnel in academic libraries

---

Libraries in the Federal Republic of Germany (1983)

Type	Administrative units	Volumes in collections	Annual expenditures[a] (mark)	Population served	Total staff
National and Central Special Libraries	7	14,096,342	27,171,639	--	1,522
Academic	166	70,760,414	155,236,798	--	6,546
Public	11,147	83,302,516	93,469,355	61,546,101	8,941
Regional and State Research Libraries	30	11,104,181	13,869,463	--	843
Special	573	30,342,596	47,217,778	--	1,911

[a]For stock additions.

Source: *Deutsche Bibliotheksstatistik 1983*, Pts A–D, Berlin, 1984.

was generally insufficient up to the middle of the 1960s. Central services, such as cataloguing by a national library, did not exist in Germany, so that libraries with only a small number of employees had to handle a considerable amount of work.

The reestablishment of German sciences after the World Wars created a strong demand for foreign literature. In order to assure that the required literature for research would be available in the Federal Republic of Germany, the Deutsche Forschungsgemeinschaft (German Research Society) founded a system of special collections in the German academic and research libraries whereby approximately 40 libraries collect newly published foreign literature relevant for scientific research in their specific field of science. Since 1949 this literature has been made available to all users through a more and more developed interlibrary loan system.

In the early 1960s a trend toward new universities brought about changes in academic libraries. These changes included open access and the building up of centralized library systems in these universities, along with the participation of professors in the book selection done by special consultants and the introduction of electronic data processing. Data processing also led to the establishment of regional library centers in the 1970s, which provide data processing services for the libraries of individual regions.

After the war the public libraries became oriented to the Anglo-American library system. In a very short period the public library replaced the German *Volksbücherei* ("people's library") first in the large cities and somewhat later in smaller cities and towns. Closed stacks were opened and comprehensive information services were developed. Efficient library centers with large collections were founded, and the collections of the Volksbüchereien, which had been restricted mainly to belles lettres, were significantly enlarged with other types of informational materials.

National Libraries. A comprehensive single national library has never existed in Germany; however, beginning in 1912 the Deutsche Bücherei ("German Library") in Leipzig collected all German publications and published a national bibliography. After the partition of Germany into two states, a new library for these tasks, the Deutsche Bibliothek, was founded in 1946 for the Federal Republic of Germany. It became a federal state institution on March 31, 1969. One of its tasks is the comprehensive collection and bibliographic registration of German literature—not only publications of the Federal Republic but also the German-language publications of the German Democratic Republic, Austria, Switzerland, and Luxembourg, as well as of the non-German-speaking countries in all parts of the world.

Besides collection and bibliographic registration, the Deutsche Bibliothek handles central services for all libraries. It maintains the German office of the International Serials Data System, a CIP-Service for central cataloguing of new German publications, and the online database Biblio-Data for bibliographic search which contains all German titles since 1972.

Central Special Libraries. There are four central special libraries—for medical sciences in Cologne, technology in Hannover (TIB), worldwide economics in Kiel, and agricultural sciences in Bonn. Orga-

Staatsbibliothek Preussischer Kulturbesitz

Staatsbibliothek Preussischer Kulturbesitz, Berlin, one of the nation's largest and most ambitious post-World War II library buildings, completed in 1978.

nized step by step from 1959, they were modeled after similar national libraries in the United States, with foremost construction on foreign literature.

State Libraries. There are two large state libraries, the Bayerische Staatsbibliothek ("Bavarian State Library") in Munich and the Staatsbibliothek Preussischer Kulturbesitz (State Library "Prussian Cultural Heritage") in Berlin, which handle certain central services for the Federal Republic. The Staatsbibliothek Preussischer Kulturbesitz is jointly financed by the federal government and the states; the Bayerische Staatsbibliothek is a library of the state of Bavaria. These two libraries handle the supply of ancient and foreign literature and are the largest German libraries. Along with the Deutsche Bibliothek they carry out central functions for all German libraries. The ISBN-agency is affiliated with the Staatsbibliothek Preussischer Kulturbesitz, which established the serials database for German libraries. The Bayerische Staatsbibliothek takes care of the German communications format for electronically stored title entries and the cataloguing of 15th- and 16th-century publications.

Other State Libraries. There are state libraries in the individual German states (Staats- und Landesbibliotheken), which supply materials within a federal state or a region. Some of these libraries additionally serve as university libraries, such as the Staats- und Universitätsbibliothek Hamburg ("State and University Library of Hamburg"). All of these libraries have the right of legal deposit for their respective regions and in most cases publish regional bibliographies.

Regional Library Centers. In order to meet the data processing needs of libraries, specific regional library centers were established, such as those in North-Rhine Westphalia (University Library Center), in Lower Saxony (Göttingen), and in Berlin, where the Deutsches Bibliotheksinstitut ("German Library Institute") performs these tasks also at the supra-regional level. These centers operate online databases for the libraries of their respective regions, make their

Bayerische Staatsbibliothek

Bayerische Staatsbibliothek, Munich, constructed in 1840.

services available to all libraries, and are responsible for centralized planning of data processing for the region's libraries.

City Libraries. The city research libraries in Germany have a very old tradition, traceable to the late Middle Ages in many cases. But the largest and most important ones received new responsibilities in the 20th century because of their integration into universities, as in Cologne, Frankfurt, Hamburg, Bremen, and Düsseldorf. The trend toward public libraries after World War II also affected city research libraries, and in many cases they were consolidated with public libraries to create new and efficient library systems, as in Hanover, Essen, Munich, and Wuppertal.

Academic Libraries. University libraries play a dominant role in German librarianship; next to the public libraries of the large cities, they have the greatest number of readers. The expansion of universities in the Federal Republic from 1960 had a considerable influence on the number and structure of university libraries. The number of universities and technical institutes in 1964 totaled 25. By 1984 the number had more than doubled. In addition, a completely new type of university, the *Fachhochschule* ("professional university"), specializing in more practical education, was created. There are approximately 60 of these institutions in the Federal Republic, so the number of academic libraries has increased to about 165 during the last 20 years.

The structure of university libraries has also changed. The library system of the old universities was characterized by a central university library and a number of independent institute libraries (often more than a hundred in one university). Recent developments now favor a university library that simultaneously manages a few departmental libraries; this type is referred to as a "single-line" university library.

Public Libraries. This type of library developed to quite an extent after World War II. Today all cities have big city-financed libraries with many branches that house comprehensive literature selections for the public. Since the beginning of the 20th century, the library development in smaller towns and provinces has been supported by advisory offices for public libraries ("Staatliche Büchereistellen"); these institutions have advising functions and keep bookstocks that are available for smaller libraries for completing their collections.

Special Libraries. The Federal Republic has a great number of special libraries, many with quite comprehensive holdings. About 1,500 important special libraries range in size from several thousand to several hundred thousand volumes. The parliamentary and administrative libraries exist at state as well as federal level, the largest being the Bibliothek des Deutschen Bundestages ("Library of the House of Parliament").

Larger industrial firms and business associations also maintain significant libraries. Both of the established churches (Roman Catholic and Protestant) also maintain library systems that include public and research libraries.

Since 1962 the Federal Republic has developed a documentation and information system, financed jointly by the federal and state governments. Under the Government Program for Advancement of Information and Documentation (I & D Program), a central institution for research and development was established, the Gesellschaft für Information und Dokumentation ("Institute for Information and Documentation") in Frankfurt. In addition, some central documentation centers in specific fields work jointly with their area libraries to supply needed materials.

The Profession. Most librarians are in the civil service and paid according to rank on three levels: as subject specialists, certified librarians, and library assistants. They prepare for service in public libraries, and for service in academic and research libraries as well as in documentation centers. Passing a state examination is a prerequisite to entering the service. Certificates for state examinations are provided by library schools after a study of three or two years respectively. The library schools mostly belong as so-called *Fachhochschulen* to the lower level of German universities, which award only the Diploma degree to their students. Library science can be studied at the University of Cologne leading to the master's degree (in a four-year course) and the doctorate (with at least two supplementary years).

Continuing education is offered by the library schools in close cooperation with library associations.

Associations. *Deutsche Bibliothekskonferenz* (German Library Conference). The six large library associations of the Federal Republic are united in the German Library Conference, which is the official partner of the federal government and the federal states regarding all general library affairs. The President is the chairman of one of the member associations and serves a one-year term.

Deutscher Bibliotheksverband (German Library Association). This association comprises libraries and their financing institutions. Until the foundation of the German Library Institute in 1978 this association was responsible for all library development in the Federal Republic.

Up to now the library foreign office (Bibliothekarische Auslandsstelle) has been part of this association. This office is responsible for international contacts, particularly for invitations to foreign librarians to visit German libraries and for trips by German librarians to foreign countries.

Verein Deutscher Bibliothekare and *Verein der Diplombibliothekare an Wissenschaftlichen Bibliotheken* (Association of German Librarians and Association of Certified Librarians in Research Libraries). Librarians in academic and research libraries are members of these two associations. The Verein Deutscher Bibliothekare has been particularly responsible for the official work of academic and research libraries for almost 75 years. The new German cataloguing rules (RAK) and new rules for interlibrary loan are examples of these initiatives. These associations also organize meetings of the Deutsche Bibliothekartag (German Librarian's Conference). Since some work has been assumed by the Deutsches Bibliotheksinstitut, the work of these associations has been somewhat more restricted to professional tasks. The official periodical of these associations is the *Zeitschrift für Bibliothekswesen und Bibliographie.*

Verein der Bibliothekare an Öffentlichen Bibliotheken (Association of Librarians in Public Libraries). This association is a personnel-oriented organization for librarians of public libraries. It deals mainly with professional matters and publishes the journal *Buch und Bibliothek* (Book and Library).

Arbeitsgemeinschaft der Spezialbibliotheken (German Special Libraries Association). This association represents the special libraries in the Federal Republic. It holds a congress every two years that deals with problems of special libraries.

National Planning. Germany's system of federal, state, and local governments precludes a single statute or administration governing libraries, and regulations concerning them are issued by individual states or local jurisdictions. For example, each federal state has its own legal deposit regulations. There are, however, several organizations which coordinate library-related activities.

Matters of concern on the federal level are addressed by the Federal Government-Federal State Commission for Educational Planning and Advanced Research, which is among the organizations responsible for libraries financed jointly by the federal government and states. This Commission was also responsible for founding the German Library Institute in Berlin in 1978; it is also devoted to library research. The Deutsche Forschungsgemeinschaft (German Research Society) has supported the work of academic and research libraries. Among the federal states, a committee within the Permanent Conference of Ministries of Culture and Education considers the problems and needs of public libraries. In 1973 several library and information-related organizations, supported by the Federal Ministry for Education and Science, developed a plan for library development in the Federal Republic that contains standards for all types of libraries.

REFERENCES
Gisela von Busse, Horst Ernestus, and Engelbert Plassmann, *Libraries in the Federal Republic of Germany,* 2nd ed. (1983), the most comprehensive handbook.
Studies on the Organizational Structure and Services in National and University Libraries in the Federal Republic of Germany and in the United Kingdom (1979) contains various important articles.

GÜNTHER PFLUG;
PAUL KAEGBEIN

Conrad Gesner

The Newberry Library

Gesner, Conrad
(1516–1565)

Conrad Gesner, Swiss humanist scholar, discovered in bibliography an appropriate expression for his profound intellectual adventurousness. It is hardly correct to see Gesner as the "father of bibliography," since Tritheim, Erasmus, Nevizzano, Leland, and Champier all did important work before him, but the dimensions of Gesner's achievements are many times more vast. The logical planning that was called for, no doubt, was conspicuous in first inspiring the monumental efforts behind the *Bibliotheca universalis,* his best-known work.

Born into a large Zurich family on March 16, 1516, he was assigned to live with two family friends, both of whom encouraged his studies. One was Johann Jacob Amman, a friend of Erasmus. Amman taught him Latin. The Battle of Kappel in 1531, which took the life of Zwingli, also claimed Gesner's father, and Conrad returned home to support his mother. In 1533 he traveled to Bourges on a fellowship but returned home the next year following the strong French reaction to Protestantism. He married in 1535, at the age of 19.

His first published book, a Greek-Latin dictionary (1537), coincided with his appointment as Professor of Greek at the newly founded university in Lausanne. Four years later he left for a chair in physics and natural history at the Collegium Carolinum in Zurich, where he resided until his death. Honors were bestowed on him by nearby royalty; scholars visited him and contributed to his vast correspondence. He died on December 13, 1565, during one of the frequent plagues of Zurich.

Gesner produced 72 "books" that were published in his lifetime and left 18 more unfinished. Alongside the *Bibliotheca universalis* is the *Historia animalium,* four volumes of which appeared 1551–58 and a fifth posthumously in 1587. His work in botany began with an edition of Valerius Cordus of 1561 and was not completed in print until the *Opera botanica* of 1751–71. In both zoology and botany, his work was mostly that of a collector and organizer; he remains the leading modern scholar up to the time of Linnaeus. In philology, his several dictionaries take second place to the *Mithridates* of 1555, in which parallels in 130 languages are presented and the Romany language is discussed for the first time. His medical studies were collected in the *Epistolarum medicinalium* of 1577, while his culinary insights are seen in his 1563 edition of Willich's cookbook, *Ars magirica*. He also worked and published extensively in geology and mineralogy; his studies of fossils were probably the result of his love for mountain climbing, the reports that he did the latter for exercise and amusement notwithstanding.

Gesner's *Bibliotheca universalis* was issued in four folio volumes by a friend, the Zurich publisher Christopher Froschauer. The first volume (1545) is the author catalogue. Next come the *pandects*, a classified subject-index to the first volume, with 21 subdivisions of the world of knowledge. The second volume (1548) contains 19 subjects; theology alone comprises the third volume (1549); while the material on medicine was never published. The fourth volume (1555) is an appendix with additional titles. Gesner's colleagues soon discovered the importance of this work. Two abridgments quickly appeared (1551, 1555); supplements were issued as early as 1555; and expanded new editions were assembled by his pupils Josias Simler (1574) and Johann Jacob Frisius (1583). Gesner's entries include not only author and title information but also in many cases imprints, chapter and section headings or other contents descriptions, and occasional critical observations. Gesner both cites the published editions he knew about and in many cases gives credit to authors for their unpublished or unfinished works, even for works that were known to have been projected.

REFERENCES

J. Christian Bay, "Conrad Gesner (1516–1565), the Father of Bibliography: An Appreciation," *Papers of the Bibliographical Society of America* (1916).

Hans Fischer, "Conrad Gessner [sic] (1516–1565) as Bibliographer and Encyclopedist," *The Library*, 5th series (1966).

D. W. KRUMMEL

Ghana

Ghana, known before independence in 1957 as the Gold Coast, is a republic of West Africa on the coast of the Gulf of Guinea. It is bounded by Burkina Faso on the northwest and north, Togo on the east, the Atlantic Ocean on the south, and the Ivory Coast on the west. Population (1984 est.) 12,206,000; area 238,533 sq.km. The official language is English.

History. All libraries in Ghana look back to two founding collections. One was that of the Bishop of Accra, kept in the Bishop's Boy's School, but opened to the public in 1928. It was 6,000 volumes strong. It was later taken over by the British Council and finally became part of the Public Library Service of Ghana. The other was the collection held by the Achimota College Library. At one time it was the center for training library students from all parts of British West Africa, possessing a general collection of more than 11,000 volumes. In time this collection became dispersed, but it formed the basis of many other collections. Ghana was the first black African country to create a nationwide public library system.

National Library Services. A National Library does not exist in Ghana. In 1961 the Padmore Research Library was founded by the Ghana Library Board in memory of the West Indian Pan-Africanist, George Padmore, to support research on African affairs. The board intended that the Library should form the nucleus of the country's national library. Thus from its birth the Research Library on African Affairs, as it was called from 1966, has been performing functions usually performed by national libraries.

The Research Library on African Affairs is in the capital, Accra, and is administered by the Ghana Library Board. A building extension designed to increase the capacity of the library from 20,000 to 50,000 volumes was completed. Services include compilation of the *Ghana National Bibliography,* for which the Library acquires everything written or published in or about Ghana, including materials not normally mentioned in the press and other media. Staff are sent to all parts of the country to fulfill this responsibility. The Library is the national agency for the administration of the ISBN system.

The Research Library cooperates actively with other Africana libraries in Ghana in order to pool library resources. Union lists of certain types of library materials are kept so that each library is aware of their existence.

The Library has an active program for the collection and preservation of oral tradition. It covers not only oral literature but also history, music, and dance, on film, tapes, and records.

Academic Libraries. The genesis of academic librarianship in Ghana can be traced to the foundation of Achimota College in 1948. Its facilities extended to other institutions of comparable nature throughout Ghana. In 1951 the Achimota Training College moved with its library to Kumase to become a department of the Kumase College of Technology, now

Libraries in Ghana (1977)

Type	Administrative units	Service points	Volumes in collections	Annual expenditures (cedi)	Population served[a]	Professional staff	Total staff
National	--	--	--	--	--	--	--
Academic	--	--	--	--	--	--	--
Public	7	40	929,000	1,825,000	70,000	50	520
School	--	--	--	--	--	--	--

[a]Registered borrowers.

Source: Unesco, *Statistical Yearbook,* 1984.

the University of Science and Technology. From Kumase College of Technology the Achimota stock continued to circulate to form the basis for the libraries of the University College of Cape Coast, now University of Cape Coast; the School of Administration of the University of Ghana; and the Teachers' Training College at Winneba.

Each academic library is supervised by a committee of its university's academic board, chaired by the Vice-Chancellor of the university. The libraries are allocated a portion of the funds provided by the central government.

The Balme Library, the main library of the University of Ghana, is the largest academic/research library in Ghana. It grew up with the foundation of the University College of the Gold Coast in 1948. When the library moved into its permanent building at Legon in 1959, the collection totaled 119,000 volumes. The new building was designed to accommodate 350 readers and 250,000 books. But when the University College became a full-fledged University of Ghana, the Library also had to grow. An Africana Library was established to support the work of the Institute of African Studies and a Students' Reference Library was created to meet the increased demand for basic textbooks. Between 1961 and 1965 the Balme Library expanded rapidly in staff, materials acquired, and services provided. The bookstock increased to more than 200,000 volumes. The collection comprises about 300,000 volumes and more than 5,000 periodical subscriptions.

The Balme Library maintains a union catalogue of its departmental libraries: the Law Library and the libraries of the Faculty of Agriculture and the departments of physics, chemistry, zoology, biochemistry, and nutrition and food science. Since 1963 the Balme Library has been a repository for United Nations documents, especially material produced by the UN, Unesco, FAO, and Economic Commission for Africa. Publications of all other agencies of the UN are kept in the main library.

The University of Science and Technology succeeded the Kumasi College of Technology, which was established in 1951 and was opened officially in January 1952 with some 200 teacher training students transferred from Achimota. The Library was started with the collection of books that formed the library of the Teacher Training College at Achimota. It has a collection of 115,000 volumes, with 1,700 current periodicals and 1,200 dissertations.

The Library of the University of Cape Coast started as a college library when the University College of Cape Coast was established in 1962 to train teachers. The library began with some 650 volumes transferred from Kumase. When the college achieved university status in 1971, the stock stood at 65,000 volumes, excluding unbound volumes of periodicals. By the mid-1980s the stock had reached more than 115,000. More than 1,100 serial and periodical titles are received through subscription and donations.

Public Libraries. The coming of the British Council to Ghana in 1943 marked an important phase in library development in the country. The Council started at the outset to develop a countrywide service, initiating a pattern adopted by the Ghana Library Board when it was established in 1950. The Council made available to the Board the services of its Librar-

Jean E. Lowrie

The Balme Library of the University of Ghana, Legon, Accra, is the largest academic library in Ghana.

ian, Evelyn J. A. Evans. With the 27,000 books inherited from the British Council, the Board set out to establish temporary libraries in the regional capitals and to lay the foundation for building permanent regional and branch libraries throughout the country. Branches with children's facilities were opened at Cape Coast and Kumasi (1950), at Sekondi (1952), at Ho (1955), and at Koforidua and Tamale (1955). By 1955 the volume of books had risen from 27,000 to 120,000 and in 1960 the bookstock stood at 266,666.

The aim of the Board is, first, to provide general reading material for the literate population not enrolled in any formal education program and, second, to acquire materials that will satisfy the information needs of the literate public. Textbooks similar to those used in schools are provided in fairly large numbers. The Board has a total stock of about 900,000 volumes.

The Board maintains a Children's Library Service. Beginning with only 3 children's libraries in Accra in 1950, the Board established 30 children's branch libraries throughout the country. Wherever the Board opened a branch library for adults, it also opened one for children.

Rural people comprise 63 percent of the population and many were illiterate in the early 1980s. About 31 percent of the adult population is literate (men 43 percent, women 18 percent). The Board could not include service to the illiterate majority in its operations because of limits of finance, books, and staff.

The rural library service dates back to 1945, when the British Council provided a postal service to subscribers in rural areas. By 1959 this system had developed into the mobile library service with the provision of book boxes. The Book Box Service was open to anyone who lived in a place without a library. For an annual fee, subscribers could receive a box of 50 books of their own choice, and they could subscribe to as many boxes as they could afford. This service attracted many schools, community and social centers, mines and other enterprises, hospitals, and individuals.

School Libraries. School and college libraries also come under the authority of the Ghana Library Board. In 1968–69 the Board in association with the Ministry of Education and the British Council appointed a committee to study school library service in the country. The committee reported in 1970 that it found unsuitable accommodations, poor furniture, and a dependence on the interest and enthusiasm of the headmaster or principal. The greatest defect was the lack of proper organization. Practices varied widely, and there was no consistency of library procedure. A total bookstock of 350,000 volumes was found in the 245 schools in the country.

Following these revelations, the committee recommended that the Ghana Library Board be asked to run the libraries in these schools with additional grants for the acquisition of books and services. The School and College Department of the Board was established in 1972. This department is responsible for the order, supply, and cataloguing of books to schools. It also arranges regular visits to advise and offer professional guidance and assistance in the use of the library and prepares booklists and conducts seminars for teacher/librarians and library clerks in the schools and colleges in the country.

Special Libraries. In industrialized countries such as the United Kingdom and the United States, special libraries are found in industries, but in developing countries such as Ghana such libraries support scientific and social research in various institutions or are built around special collections. The Central Reference and Research Library of the Council for Scientific and Industrial Research (CSIR) identified 71 such libraries.

The most important group of special libraries serves the research institutions of the CSIR. Its Central Reference and Research Library, founded in 1964, with a collection of its own numbering about 12,000 volumes, coordinates and supplements collections and services of the Council's institute libraries. Such libraries are the Animal Research Library (founded in 1964), the Building and Road Research Institute Library (1951), the Coca Research Institute Library (1937), the Crops Research Institute Library (1950), the Food Research Institute Library (1963), the Forest Products Research Institute Library (1960), the Industrial Research Institute Library (1967), the Institute of Aquatic Biology Library (1965), the Soils Research Institute Library (1945), and the Water Resources Research Unit Library (1968). These libraries have collections ranging from 2,500 volumes to nearly 14,000 volumes.

Among the other special libraries is the Ministry of Agriculture Library, established in 1926. There are 18 government libraries, the largest of which belong to the Ministry of Lands and Mineral Resources (31,500 volumes), the Central Bureau of Statistics (35,000 volumes), and the Ghana Armed Forces (40,000 volumes). The Volta River Authority Library (1964) covers water resources, hydroelectric power generation and distribution, dams, inland water transportation, and irrigation.

The Ghana Institute of Management and Public Administration Library was founded in 1961 to serve the postgraduate professional training and research institution. The scope of the Library, whose stock totals more than 50,000 books and monographs, covers management, public administration and finance, law, economic and development planning, local government, and international relations.

The University of Ghana Medical School Library was founded in 1964. The stock grew from 2,000 volumes to more than 23,000, including resources of the Ministry of Health and the National Institute of Health and Medical Research.

All the banks in the country have libraries, including the Bank of Ghana library, the Ghana Commercial Bank library, and the Capital Investment Bank library. A number of corporations and institutions run small special collections, but most of these have not been developed to any great extent.

REFERENCES

L. Agyei-Gyane, compiler, *Directory of Special and Research Libraries in Ghana* (1977).

Evelyn J. A. Evans, *A Tropical Library Service: The Story of Ghana's Libraries* (1964), an authoritative work on public library development by the first Director of the Ghana Library Board.

Ghana Library Board, *The Ghana Library Board Silver Jubilee Brochure 1950–1975* (1975), analyzes the place of the Board in the public library system in Ghana.

John Harris, *Patterns of Library Growth in English-speaking West Africa* (1970), gives statistics on libraries in Ghana and other West African countries.

H. DUA-AGYEMANG*

Gjelsness, Rudolph H.
(1894–1968)

Rudolph H. Gjelsness, library educator, consultant, and scholar, was the first recipient (1954) of the Beta Phi Mu award for distinguished service to education for librarianship.

He was born in Reynolds, North Dakota, on October 18, 1894. Following his graduation from the University of North Dakota in 1916, Gjelsness became a high school principal in Adams, North Dakota, but resigned a year later to join the American Expeditionary Force. His interest in librarianship had its origin following the Armistice in 1918 when he was detached from the Army to serve as Reference Librarian with the AEF in Beaune, France.

Returning to the United States in 1919, Gjelsness enrolled in the University of Illinois's library school and received the B.L.S. degree in 1920. His first professional library position was as Order Librarian for the University of Oregon; in 1922 he became Senior Bibliographer at the University of California. A fellowship from the American Scandinavian Foundation in 1924 permitted him to spend a year in Norway, the home of his ancestors.

Gjelsness's first contribution to library literature appeared in the July 1925 issue of *Public Libraries* and was entitled "A Librarian's Year in Norway." Writing from Norway, he closed the article with, "When I return, I shall be interested in a position where I could develop or organize something." That oppor-

ALA
Rudolph H. Gjelsness

tunity came quickly with his appointment by William Warner Bishop as Assistant Librarian and Chief Classifier for the University of Michigan. In the summer of 1927 Gjelsness was given his first opportunity to contribute to library education, teaching a course in national and regional bibliography in Michigan's new library school.

From 1929 to 1932 Gjelsness was Chief of the Preparation Division of the New York Public Library and a Lecturer in library science at Columbia University. From 1932 to 1937 he was Head Librarian at the University of Arizona. In 1937 he consented to return to Michigan as Professor of Library Science with the tacit understanding that in due course he would succeed Bishop as head of the Library School, a position he held from 1940 until his retirement in 1964. During the 24 years that Gjelsness chaired the Department of Library Science, the University conferred 2,269 degrees in Library Science, including 47 doctorates.

Active in association work, Gjelsness chaired the ALA Committee on Cataloging and Classification from 1930 to 1933, and from 1935 to 1941 he headed the Catalog Code Revision Committee. He was Editor-in-Chief of the *A.L.A. Catalog Rules: Author and Title Entries* (1941). He was Treasurer of ALA from 1941 to 1947, and he served as President of the Association of American Library Schools, 1948–49.

Strongly committed to international librarianship, Gjelsness co-directed a summer school at Bogotá, Colombia, in 1942 and spent a year away from Michigan (1943–44) as Director of the Benjamin Franklin Library in Mexico City. A sabbatical year (1962–63) was spent as Library Consultant to the President of the University of Baghdad in Iraq.

Following his retirement in 1964, Gjelsness returned to the University of Arizona Library to head its Special Collections Division. After a summer teaching assignment at Michigan in 1968, he went to the University of Puerto Rico to assist in the founding of the Graduate School of Librarianship. He was killed by an automobile in a hit-and-run accident on his second day in Rio Piedras, August 16, 1968.

Luther College and the University of North Dakota awarded him honorary degrees, and in 1966 a Festschrift was published in his honor by the University of Virginia, *Books in America's Past*. His articles and books, which number more than 80, pertain largely to issues in library education, international and comparative librarianship, cataloguing and classification, the history of books and printing, and Norwegian literature. He translated a number of Norwegian short stories and novels into English.

REFERENCE

Russell E. Bedlack, "Gjelsness, Rudolph H.," *Dictionary of American Library Biography* (1978).

RUSSELL E. BIDLACK

Gleason, Eliza Atkins

(1909-)

Eliza Atkins Gleason, librarian and educator, was the first Dean of the School of Library Service, Atlanta University, and the architect of a library education program that trained more than 90 percent of all black librarians in the United States.

She was born in Winston-Salem, North Carolina, on December 15, 1909, to Simon Green and Oleona Pegram Atkins. Her father was the founder and first President of Slater State College, now Winston-Salem State University, and her mother was a teacher.

After graduating from Fisk University in 1930 as a member of Phi Beta Kappa, Eliza Atkins received the Bachelor of Science degree from the Library School of the University of Illinois in 1931. In 1936 she received the Master of Arts in Library Science from the University of California at Berkeley. She studied at the University of Chicago Graduate Library School and in 1940 became the first black person to receive the Ph.D. in Library Science. She was married to Maurice F. Gleason, a physician, in 1937.

The Dean of the School of Library Service, Atlanta University (1940–46), which opened in 1941, Gleason was aware that the success of the program, even in a period of segregation and rampant discrimination against black persons, depended on a philosophy that was responsive to current human needs but at the same time capable of being remodeled and reshaped when necessary. She wrote, "these objectives are enunciated with the full recognition that no institution can long remain an active force unless it is sensitive to contemporary life, which implies a willingness to accept change. A program of this kind, therefore, predisposes that the objectives of the School of Library Service of Atlanta University are not static but that they may be altered according to the best judgment of the school in what seems to be the present and long-term needs of library service with special reference to the Negro" (*Library Quarterly*, July 1942).

Gleason's professional career was distinguished, wide, varied, and productive. In 1931 and 1932 she was Librarian of the Louisville Municipal College. In 1932 she accepted the position of Head of the Reference Department and Assistant Professor at Fisk and served there until 1936. In 1936–37 she was Director of Libraries at Talladega College, where she became aware of the lack of public library service to black people in the South and began to open the college library resources to black citizens in the surrounding communities. Her interest in access to public libraries for black Americans is reflected in her landmark dissertation, *The Southern Negro and the Public Library* (1941).

In 1953 Gleason became Head of the Reference Department of the Wilson Junior College Library in Chicago. In 1953–54 she was Associate Professor and Head of the Reference Department of the Chicago Teachers College Library. She was Associate Professor of Library Science, Illinois Teachers College, Chicago, from 1954 to 1963. From 1964 to 1967 she was Assistant Librarian at John Crerar Library in Chicago. She was Professor of Library Science, Illinois Institute of Technology, from 1967 to 1970. In 1970 she became Assistant Chief Librarian in charge of the regional centers, Chicago Public Library.

Writing in *Illinois Libraries* (April 1972) about the establishment of the Chicago Public Library's regional library centers, Gleason manifests her continuing interests in students and education:

In planning for Regional Center service, what potential users did the Chicago Public Library have in mind? It had

Atlanta University Center Library Archives Department, Atlanta University

Eliza Atkins Gleason

in mind "students"—students of all kinds. Can one imagine a greater boon for the high school teen-agers who are in honors or accelerated courses, or for junior college students whose programs are terminal, or for junior and senior college students whose own college libraries may be inadequate or on the wrong side of town when they have time to study? And finally, there is that vast hoard of "students" who are not enrolled in formal courses but who wish to pursue a subject in depth.

In the 1974–75 academic year she again returned to library education and served as Professor of Library Science at Northern Illinois University.

Active in professional associations, Gleason was the first Afro-American to serve on the ALA Council; she was a member from 1942 to 1946. In 1964 Fisk bestowed upon her its Alumni Award for outstanding accomplishments.

In addition to her book on *The Southern Negro and the Public Library: A Study of the Government and Administration of Public Library Service to Negroes in the South* (1941), she wrote *A History of the Fisk University Library* (1936) and a large number of journal articles.

A woman of great energy and resourcefulness, Gleason led an active community life. She was elected and appointed to many positions of leadership. In 1978, for example, she was appointed to the Chicago Public Library Board. While most people are in or considering retirement as they begin their 70th year, she demonstrated her vitality by beginning a new career for the benefit of humankind—in the fall of 1978 she was appointed Executive Director of the Chicago Black United Fund.

E. J. JOSEY

Greece (Ancient)

Libraries of public character are attributed by ancient writers to certain 6th-century tyrants of Greek cities, notably Polycrates of Samos and Peisistratus of Athens. Much more is known of the latter than of the former, but we lack the original documents that might have described Peisistratus' supposed library of papyrus rolls of contemporary poetry and drama. Leading scholars believe that any progress in library organization that may have been made under Peisistratus can be determined only by checking the practices of the later libraries of the Ionian cities, which were so important in Greek commerce and culture. Of note during the 5th century were such private libraries as those of the celebrated playwright Euripides, who collected works of poets, dramatists, and philosophers. His passion for books was ridiculed publicly by his rival, Aristophanes. Some writers argue that at least the theater public of that day was conscious of the book but nothing certain is known about these libraries.

By contrast, when one considers philosophical schools, some encouraging deductions become possible. Socrates is understood to have worked exclusively through oral discourse. His pupil Plato likewise believed that the written word was a burden on free discussion and creative thinking, although it seems probable from the testimony of his writings that much material referred to by him and his students was being checked in a book collection of some sort even though none is mentioned. Besides, Plato's own prose is indebted to some of the very poets he

banned from his ideal society, and at least one of his (and Isocrates') students established a library.

Furthermore, if one relies on a modern translation (McKeon edition), Aristotle, speaking briefly of writers on husbandry and household economy in *The Politics*, explains that he did not go into detail because "any one who cares for such matters may refer to their writings." This seems to imply the presence of one or more libraries accessible to the student, or of stores selling such works at prices within student means, but this is not certain. The sole established fact is that Aristotle's personal library was not a part of his Lyceum in either a physical or legal sense.

In the later case of Zeno, the founder of Stoicism, the personal library may have been perceived as an integral part of teaching. In any case, Antogonos Gonatas, who seized power in Macedonia in 276 B.C., tried to attract the septuagenarian Zeno to court and offered him slaves to copy books; but, reportedly, Zeno felt physically unable to leave Athens.

The question of libraries arises also in connection with a number of other educational institutions of pre-Alexandrian Greece. Medical teaching was established by Hippocrates and his associates early in the 4th century, and the early 3rd century witnessed the intellectual enrichment of the gymnasium curriculum. Both enterprises may have had "book" collections among their resources, but there is no evidence as yet.

Most vexing are the uncertainties regarding the books owned by Aristotle, thanks to his prominence and the gaps and contradictions in the record. That he left them (d. 323 B.C.) to his disciple Theophrastus is accepted by scholars on the basis of ancient writers' testimony; it is also known that Theophrastus (d. 288 B.C.) bequeathed his collection (including the Aristotle legacy) to his pupil Neleus. Though these facts promote little argument, one must be cautious, since Aristotle's will says nothing of either his school or books, while his legal status as a "metic" (alien resident) prevented him from owning real property in Athens. Did Neleus take the books (which ones?) to his hometown, Skepsis, less than 50 miles north of Pergamum? Were they hidden in a cellar to conceal them from energetic agents seeking books for Pergamum? Did they deteriorate from neglect until found and bought by a rich young Athenian, Appelicon, or were they actually stolen by him right in Athens or were they in the meantime purchased by representatives of Ptolemy II Philadelphus (reigned 285–247 B.C.) for the great library in Alexandria? It seems fairly clear that when Sulla conquered Athens in 86 B.C., he took to Rome what came to be labeled "Aristotle's library," which was confiscated from the late Appelicon's property; that some blundering efforts were made to restore the documents and the texts they contained; and that sometime in the middle of the 1st century B.C. they were properly edited by the scholarly Andronicus of Rhodes, usually referred to as the 11th Director of the Lyceum. Finally, it is clear—and distressingly important—that a danger of misinterpretation awaits every step, thanks to the dual meaning of *biblia*: when did the author refer to the writings of Aristotle or Theophrastus and when to their entire libraries?

SIDNEY JACKSON
(d. 1979)

Greece

Greece, a republic on the southern Balkan Peninsula, is bounded by Albania on the northwest, Yugoslavia and Bulgaria on the north, and Turkey on the northeast; it extends into the Mediterranean Sea, lying between the Ionian Sea on the west and the Aegean Sea on the east, and occupies most of the islands in the Aegean. Population (1984 est.) 9,908,000; area 131,957 sq.km. The official language is Greek.

History. From ancient times the Greeks were interested in the collection of manuscripts and papyri. In Athens Peisistratus (d. 527 B.C.) was the first to build a collection of Homeric epics and other works of literature to preserve for future generations. Aristotle followed in collecting manuscripts for his private use and systematically catalogued them for more efficient use. The Roman Emperor Hadrian later created a large and beautiful library in Athens in the old Agora.

During the Middle Ages, a great number of libraries were established in Byzantium by individual and religious institutions. After the fall of Constantinople (A.D. 1453), many important manuscripts found their way to the West.

During the Turkish occupation of Greece (1453 to 1821), many libraries were founded to preserve the culture of the Greek nation. After the 16th century and the introduction of the printing press, many monastic libraries were enriched with rare editions of important works in theology and other disciplines that are preserved until the present day.

In modern Greece, since independence in 1821, the first public library created for research and public use was that of the National Library of Greece, which was donated by the wealthy Cephallonian brothers Vallianos in 1828–29 and was designed by the Danish architect Christian Hansen. The second library to be created in modern Greece was that of the Parliament in 1845.

In 1914 the General Archives of the Nation was established and is housed in the Academy of Athens. It has a rich collection of archives of eminent personalities of 1821 and the following period.

National Library. The inspiration to establish a national library in modern Greece was John Mager, the Swedish publisher of the Greek Chronicles of Messologhi. The first Prime Minister, John Kapodestrias, was instrumental in establishing what became the National Library. He was assisted by the great educator and bibliophile George Gennadius. The first collection was housed in the National Museum and the Center for Educational Institutions of Greece in Aegina. In 1832 it moved to Naphlion and through

Arthur Plotnik

National Library of Greece, established in 1829 in Aegina and moved to Athens in 1834.

legislation was named Public Library. It had a collection of 1,844 volumes, and the first Librarian was George Gennadius. The National Library was moved to Athens in 1834. A law was passed that required one copy of all published books to be given to the National Library. In 1867 by law it was named "National Library."

In 1888 groundbreaking took place for the erection of a new library edifice. This magnificent, beautiful building was completed in 1903. The Library is open to the public on all working days. It contains books in Greek and several European languages, ancient and modern, and Asian languages. The strength of the library is in the area of papyri, Byzantine manuscripts, manuscripts in several European and Asian languages, Byzantine documents, Patriarchal sigillia, a great wealth of historical archives of the Turkish domination, the revolution for independence and modern Greece, first-edition printed books, including the famous Greek grammar by Laskaris printed in Milan in 1476, and many old and rare books from the 16th century. The Library collection was especially enriched by gifts from Greeks and philhellenes who endowed the National Library with their collections. It contains more than 2,000,000 volumes and 4,500 manuscripts.

Library of Parliament. The second library to be created in modern Greece is that of the Parliament (Vivliotheke tes Voules). It was established by law in 1845. In the beginning the collection was housed in

Libraries in Greece (1982)

Type	Administrative units	Service points	Volumes in collections	Annual expenditures (drachma)	Population served	Professional staff	Total staff
National	1	--	1,800,000	35,000,000	--	--	--
Academic	--	--	--	--	--	27	75
Public	498	--	--	70,000,000	--	--	--
School	--	--	--	--	--	--	--
Special	--	--	--	--	--	--	--

the Old House of the Parliament. In 1935 the greater part of the collection was moved to the second floor of the Old Palace. The Library of the Parliament is open to the public on all working days and is partially a lending library. By special permission of the Director, students may borrow books. It sponsors lectures and book displays. The strongest collection is that of law. It has the most complete collection of periodicals and newspapers in Greece.

Academic Libraries. The University of Athens does not have a central library but each school or department has its specialized collection to support its curriculum.

The University of Thessaloniki, created in 1926, has an academic central library that has more than 1,000,000 volumes.

The University of Crete was created in 1977 and organized its library according to the Library of Congress cataloguing system, the only institution in Greece that is completely organized on the basis of the LC classification.

In addition, there are many special archaeological libraries of various archaeological institutions such as the American, Austrian, British, French, German, and Italian, among others. Also, many local libraries throughout Greece are of significant importance.

Public and School Libraries. In Greece the idea of school libraries and modern public libraries did not exist until after World War II. There were attempts to create media centers for the schools in Greece.

Special Libraries. The most important special library in Athens is the Gennadius Library. It was established by the generous gift of 24,000 volumes by John Gennadius to the American School of Classical Studies. The Greek government donated the land and the Carnegie Corporation provided the funds for the construction of the library building. The collection is specialized in Greek history and culture, mainly before 1900. It is a research library and well organized with more than 60,000 volumes. In 1985 it published a *Guide to the Gennadius Library*.

Religious Collections. The most significant collections in Greece are those of the religious institutions. Some of these libraries, especially in monasteries, were established during the Byzantine era. One of the oldest libraries in Greece was established in 1088 in the monastery of St. John the Evangelist on the island of Patmos. The monk Christodoulos willed his library to the monastery in 1093. Valuable collections of manuscripts are found in the monasteries of Mount Athos from the 10th century. Each of the 20 monasteries has a library of valuable manuscripts.

The libraries in Greece are making strenuous efforts toward cataloguing their rich collections. Most libraries in Greece use the Dewey Decimal System with some modification to accommodate the Greek language.

The Profession. Library personnel receive minimal training in Greece, and their preparation is not on a par with university-level education for other intellectual pursuits. Schools for technical training of librarians have been founded in several cities throughout Greece, and certification from those schools is required for employment in libraries in Greece. Many library personnel receive library science education in Europe or America, however.

In 1968 the Greek Library Association was organized in Athens to promote library science and librarianship in Greece. It also encourages bibliographic dissemination and information and keeps in close touch with international library associations. It is a member of IFLA.

Librarianship in Greece in the mid-1980s was in a state of development. Newer methods and library procedures were only slowly implemented and refined. The library profession in Greece needed to be appropriately recognized. This can be accomplished by implementing a university-level degree for librarianship. Also, librarians needed to make greater use of contemporary techniques for manuscript preservation. And finally there was need for the computerization of information about library collections through a central database that would serve scholars in and outside Greece. In some academic libraries recognition of the importance of such changes for the future of libraries led to the application of computer technology.

GEORGE C. PAPADEMETRIOU

Grover, Wayne C.
(1906–1970)

Wayne Clayton Grover, Archivist of the United States from 1948 until 1965, was the architect of the many-faceted organization that the National Archives and Records Service became.

Grover was born in Garland, Utah, September 16, 1906. Graduated from the University of Utah in 1930, he received the M.A. (1937) and Ph.D. degrees (1946) from the American University, Washington, D.C. In 1935 he married Esther Thomas, the daughter of U.S. Senator Elbert Thomas (Democrat, Utah).

Grover worked as a journalist and as a congressional aide between 1930 and 1935. He joined the staff of the National Archives in 1935, during its first year. One of the first persons to receive training as an archivist, he was given a variety of assignments at the Archives. He served as a Records Consultant in 1941–42 with the Office of Strategic Services. In 1943 Grover was commissioned a Captain in the Army, and he became Chief of its records management branch in the Adjutant General's Office. As such he was the War Department's principal staff officer for its pioneering records management program, and he inaugurated the Army's system of records centers. Although he was discharged a Lieutenant Colonel in 1946, he remained in his job as a civilian. He was decorated with the Legion of Merit for his work.

In 1947 the National Archives was confronted with a reduction in staff, a great preservation backlog, and the need to bring the records glut of the federal government under control. The Archivist of the United States, Solon J. Buck, decided to make use of Grover's demonstrated ability by naming him his deputy as Assistant Archivist. Grover was responsible for mending his agency's relations with Congress and getting the Archives to work more efficiently within its slender resources. When Buck resigned as Archivist in 1948, he proposed Grover as his successor.

During his first year as Archivist, Grover managed to improve his agency's funding and to reduce

Records of the National Archives
Wayne C. Grover

the backlog of material needing preservation. Nevertheless, the long-range outlook for proper support of the National Archives's programs was poor. Grover was able to get the Hoover Commission on the Organization of the Executive Branch of the Government to champion the establishment of a comprehensive federal records management program. Only that, he believed, would lead to efficiency, economy, and effectiveness in the use of federal records and would assure a smooth flow of records of enduring value to the Archives. The Hoover Commission, however, recommended that the National Archives lose its status as an independent federal agency and that a new bureau deal with records management. In 1949 Congress did place Grover's agency, as the National Archives and Records Service (NARS), under the General Services Administration (GSA), but Congress also clearly intended that NARS become the government's records management service and provided increased funding for that purpose.

Previously, his agency had been chiefly concerned with archives, although it also operated the Franklin D. Roosevelt Library and the Federal Register Division and was involved in promoting records management. Grover's first important step was to gain enactment of the comprehensive Federal Records Act of 1950, which officially made NARS into the government's records management agency. This step enhanced the likelihood of preserving federal archives for research use, as well as the improved management of records by government agencies. It was most important for the information sciences and for research that Grover won his fight to have records dealt with during their life span on the basis of archival as well as managerial principles.

Grover was responsible for more than the enduring—though occasionally rocky—marriage of archivists and records managers. He upgraded NARS's display program, the centerpieces of which were the Declaration of Independence and the Constitution, which he procured from the Library of Congress in 1952. He inaugurated a facsimile program and expanded his agency's outstanding micropublications and film preservation operations. In 1950 he resuscitated the National Historical Publications Commission, the work of which has enriched the nation's documentary publications.

Under Grover's sponsorship the Federal Register Division in 1957 began a valuable new series, the *Public Papers of the Presidents of the United States*. Grover guided the systematization of the acquisition and administration of the papers of recent Presidents and their associates in the Presidential Libraries Act of 1955. Moreover, under his supervision NARS made considerable progress in solving its problems of preservation and description. His agency grew from 341 employees when he became Archivist to 1,716 by the time of his retirement in 1965.

Grover did not deal easily with the General Services Administration. Although it provided NARS with increased resources, GSA, with its management orientation, was increasingly criticized for posing a threat to archival professionalism. Grover used the occasion of his retirement to argue for his agency's return to independent status. Although his campaign was unsuccessful, it resulted in better funding for NARS and expansion of its programs. The issue continued to be raised by archivists and historians. Grover remained active in other ways after his retirement, including advising President Lyndon B. Johnson on the development of his Presidential Library.

In recognition of Grover's services, Brown (Providence, Rhode Island) and Bucknell (Lewisburg, Pennsylvania) universities and Belmont Abbey College (North Carolina) bestowed honorary degrees upon him. He received the GSA's Distinguished Service Award in 1959 and one of the National Civil Service League's Career Service Awards in 1961. Grover was President of the Society of American Archivists, Vice-President of the International Council on Archives, and a member of the United States Commission of Unesco. He was the author of articles in a wide array of professional publications. Yet the real monument to his vision was the remarkably broad-based institution that NARS became during his tenure as Archivist of the United States. Grover died in Silver Spring, Maryland, June 8, 1970.

REFERENCE

Donald R. McCoy, *The National Archives: America's Ministry of Documents, 1934–1968* (1978).

DONALD R. McCOY

Guatemala

Guatemala, a republic in northern Central America, is bordered by Mexico on the west and north, Belize on the northeast, the Caribbean Sea on the east, Honduras and El Salvador on the southeast, and the Pacific Ocean on the south and southwest. Population (1984 est.) 9,908,000; area 108,889 sq.km. The official language is Spanish.

History. Although the Mayan civilization was a rich one, no evidence has been found of library collections in pre-Columbian times. The earliest collections, in fact, date from the colonial period, in convents and monasteries founded by the conquerors. The opening of the University of San Carlos in 1677 marked the first time since the arrival of printing presses (1659) that any institution cultivated special collections of books. Yet the idea of public libraries did not take root until the founding of the National Library in 1879, with its 15,000 volumes. The greatest expansion of libraries took place in the 1960s.

National Library and Archives. The National Library of Guatemala was founded in Guatemala City. A dependent of the Ministry of Public Education, it preserves the national bibliographic heritage and also functions as a public library, the largest in the country. It occasionally produces and publishes works of national significance. Service is provided to more than 125,000 readers annually and includes a special service for children. The total collection of volumes in the National Library is 350,000, including that of the periodicals in the library, which operates independently in the same building. The national archives are held in the Archivo General de Centro América in Guatemala City. It holds almost 100,000 documents relating to Costa Rica, El Salvador, Guatemala, Honduras, Nicaragua, and Chiapa (a state of Mexico). There are also periodicals pertaining to the colonial period and independence, historical volumes, and microfilm.

Central Library, University of San Carlos

Reading Room of the Central Library, University of San Carlos, Guatemala.

Public Libraries. Ninety-three small public libraries exist throughout the republic. Of these libraries, 64 in various parts of the country fall under the direction of the National Library; the remaining 29 are under the direction of the Bank of Guatemala, which sponsors them. Their total collection is about 74,000 volumes. Service is provided to approximately 232,500 readers annually throughout the republic.

Academic Libraries. The Central Library of the Universidad de San Carlos, the autonomous state university, is the largest academic library in the country. It was established at the new university city in 1966; however, as the faculties that had continued to function in other areas of the capital moved to the new site, their libraries were also incorporated into the Central Library, beginning in 1974. The collection comprises 150,000 volumes.

The Library of the Universidad Rafael Llandivar (1963) has 20,000 volumes and 60 journals and serves 30,000 readers. The library of the Universidad Francisco Marroquín (1972) has 9,788 volumes, serving 37,500 readers. The library of the Universidad José Cecilio del Valle provides service to 37,500 readers. Founded in 1966, it holds 16,555 volumes and 373

journals. The library of the Universidad Mariano Gálvez (1966) contains 5,000 volumes, serving 5,000 readers. All five of these libraries are in Guatemala City.

School Libraries. In some educational establishments, especially at the secondary level and in state schools, there are small libraries. However, the largest collection does not exceed 3,000 volumes, and they lack professional personnel. The use of these libraries is restricted to faculty and students. These institutions are not required by law to maintain libraries.

Special Libraries. The most important special libraries are in the capital. The Library of the Bank of Guatemala, founded in 1946, serves interests in banking, currency, and economics. Its collection totals 31,000 volumes and 320 journals. It provides service to 60,000 readers, including the Bank's officials and the general public. The Library of the Instituto de Nutrición de Centroamérica y Panamá (INCAP), founded in 1949, specializes in nutrition and allied sciences. Its basic functions are research, teaching, and providing technical assistance to the area countries, and it also serves the general public. Its collection numbers 70,000 volumes. Almost half of its collection was destroyed by fire resulting from the earthquake of February 1976, but this material has since been replaced.

The Library and Documentation Center of the Instituto Centroamericano de Investigación y Tecnología Industrial (ICAITI), founded in 1956, serves industry and business; it also functions as the regional coordinator of the OAS Program of Information and Technical Assistance for Business in Central America and the Caribbean. It conducts training in documentation services. Its collection totals 20,000 volumes and 300 journals. Service is provided to approximately 10,000 readers. Other institutions that contribute to the economic development of Guatemala, and whose holdings include important collections of journals and documents, are the Instituto Técnico de Capacitación y Productividad (INTECAP), the Centro Nacional de Promoción de las Exportaciones (GUATEXPRO), and the Secretaría Permanente del Tratado General de Integración Económica Centroaméricana (SIECA).

GUILLERMO PALMA R.*

Libraries in Guatemala (1981)

Type	Administrative units	Service points	Volumes in collections	Annual expenditures (quetzal)	Population served	Professional staff	Total staff
National[b]	1	--	350,000	--	700,504	4	32
Academic	1	7	818,000	272,000	45,000[a]	16	58
Public[b]	93	--	--	--	--	--	93
School	--	--	--	--	--	--	--
Special	19	--	184,500[c]	32,000[d]	600[d]	--	--

[a]Registered borrowers.
[b]1978 data.
[c]11 libraries only.
[d]INCAP Library only.

Source: Unesco, *Statistical Yearbook,* 1984.

Guinea

Guinea, a republic of West Africa, on the Atlantic Ocean, is bounded by Guinea-Bissau on the northwest, Senegal and Mali on the north and northeast, Ivory Coast on the east, and Liberia and Sierra Leone on the south. Population (1984 est.) 5,297,00; area 245,857 sq.km. The official language is French.

When Guinea obtained independence from France in October 1958, it had no professional librarians. The only library open to the general public, and the largest library in the former French territory, was the research library of the Institut Français d'Afrique Noire (IFAN) in the capital city of Conakry. It was strongest in history and natural sciences, and it served as the nucleus of the new National Library. The stock had reached 11,000 books and 300 periodicals when it was moved to another building in 1967. In early 1959 staff were recruited, and during the 1960s short training courses were introduced. Its collection remained stable thereafter.

The nation's first school at the university level, the Institut Polytechnique, appointed its first professional librarian in 1965; at that time the collection numbered 20,000 volumes. It later dwindled to about 15,000 volumes.

Efforts were made to expand public library service beyond the capital of Conakry through the Partie Démocratique de Guinée (PDG), which is responsible for certain quasi-government functions. It began its program with about 600 volumes per lot (30 lots), mostly donated by friendly governments. The national archives has a collection of about 3,000 volumes. In addition there are four research libraries in the country, all very small.

Little current information on library service is available. What there is suggests little change over the decades of the mid-1900s to mid-1980s.

F. LALANDE ISNARD*

Guinea-Bissau

Guinea-Bissau, an independent republic of West Africa, is bounded by Senegal on the north, Guinea on the east and south, and the Atlantic Ocean on the west. Population (1984 est.) 881,000; area 36,125 sq.km. The official language is Portuguese.

Before Guinea-Bissau, a former overseas province of Portugal (Portuguese Guinea), gained its independence in 1975, the Museum and Public Library of Bissau was the only significant library. Its restricted schedule of hours and out-of-date collections limited use. The Center of Scientific Investigation,

under the Ministry of Culture, was founded after independence; it received the collections previously held by the Museum and Public Library. It then entered a period of reorganization. The Biblioteca Nacional da Guiné-Bissau holds 25,000 volumes and 4,000 current periodicals.

Three secondary and eight primary schools operate libraries in the capital of Bissau.

Two special libraries are the Library of Legal Sciences, which planned to become part of a new university, and the library of the Statistics Service, under the Ministry of State for Planning. However, the only significant special libraries to date appear to be the Centro de Estudos da Guiné-Bissau (14,000 volumes) and the library at the Museu da Guiné-Bissau (10,000 volumes). The most important library activities center in Bissau.

MARIA MANUELA CRUZEIRO*

Guyana

Guyana, a republic on the Atlantic coast of South America, is bounded by Suriname on the east, Brazil on the south, and Venezuela on the west. Population (1984 est.) 934,000; area 215,000 sq.km. The official language is English.

History. The Amerindians, the earliest inhabitants of Guyana (formerly British Guiana), are associated with the marks and figures found engraved on many huge rocks in the mountainous interior of the country. These engravings, said to be several centuries old, are called Timehri writings and some are said to be expressions of thoughts, ideas, and events recorded on rocks.

Starting in the early 17th century, Guyana developed as a plantation society in which most of the people were slaves, working for Dutch and later British plantation owners. There is no evidence that the owner used books; the slaves were not allowed to learn to read. Oral communication, with a few exceptions, was the principal means of receiving or passing on information locally.

During the post-emancipation period, which started in 1834, the introduction of popular education gradually led to the development of a literate society. A few private subscription libraries such as the Berbice Reading Society (1843) and The Royal Agricultural and Commercial Society (1864) were established, but they served only exclusive groups. A few church and Sunday school libraries offered a limited service to selected groups of persons. The first public library service became available in 1909 with the opening of the Carnegie Free Library. Pioneered by

Libraries in Guinea (1980)

Type	Administrative units	Service points	Volumes in collections	Annual expenditures (syli)	Population served[a]	Professional staff	Total staff
National	1	3	66,000	693,000	711	17	80
Academic	--	--	--	--	--	--	--
Public	--	--	--	--	--	--	--
School	--	--	--	--	--	--	--

[a]Registered borrowers.

the early librarians Emily Murray (1909–1940) and Ruby Franker (1942–1962) and later significantly expanded by Stella Merriman, (1962–1972), this service laid the foundation for what has become a countrywide public library service.

General expansion of library services in the country has been blocked by a persistent lack of adequate financial resources, an inadequate supply of professional personnel, and foreign currency crises. Yet the University of Guyana Library can boast of having developed an extensive collection of research material on Guyana unsurpassed by any other known collection of material on this subject.

National and Public Library Services. The National Library of Guyana in Georgetown had its origin in the Public Free Library established in 1909 through the munificence of Andrew Carnegie. In 1950 an act of the British Guiana Legislative Council empowered the Library Authority to extend its service beyond the city of Georgetown, initiating the rapid development of a countrywide service. The Law Revision Act of 1972 created the National Library, assigning to it the responsibility for performing the functions of both a national and a public library. The Act also designated the National Library a legal deposit library entitled to one copy of every local imprint. It published the Guyanese National Bibliography from 1972.

The National Library provides countrywide service through the operation of several service units. The Adult Reference and Lending Departments, a phonograph records service, the Juvenile Department, a toy library service, and one Branch Library serve Georgetown, Two Branch Libraries outside Georgetown, the Rural Services Department comprising 17 Rural Library Centers, and 2 bookmobiles jointly provide a service to the rest of the country. The resources of the National Library totaled an estimated 195,000 items in the early 1980s; they include rare historical documents, manuscripts, and a valuable special collection of research material on Guyana. It is also a depository of Unesco publications.

The John F. Kennedy Library provides additional public library services with collections devoted exclusively to works published in the United States, including videotape recordings. It sponsors a number of public activities that include video shows, lectures, and professional and cultural discussion groups.

The National Archives of Guyana had a staff of four in 1984. Holdings totaled 510,000 linear feet, and annual expenditures were G$20,000.

Academic Libraries. The University of Guyana Library, established in 1963, is the only academic library in the country. A substantial extension to its original building was added in 1983. Organized on a subject divisional arrangement, it supports the teaching and research programs of seven faculties and one research institute with a total collection of some 158,000 items including manuscripts and nonprint materials. The Library is a partial depository for the publications of the United Nations and its several agencies, and in 1972 it was designated a legal deposit library for Guyanese imprints.

Of special importance is the Library's Caribbean Research Collection. An extensive collection of material on Guyana and the Caribbean, it is considered, because of its many unique holdings, perhaps the world's largest collection of material on Guyana.

The University Library operates an international gifts and exchange program and is the local center for international lending activities relating to the British Lending Library. It conducts international loan activities.

Special Libraries. The Medical Science Library, the Public Service Ministry Library, the State Planning Secretariat Library, and the Department of Mines and Surveys Library are about the largest and best organized special libraries in the country; although primarily committed to serving the organizations to which they are attached, these libraries also provide a limited service to the wider community. The Library of the State Planning Secretariat is responsible for coordinating the local contributions of libraries in Guyana to the regional development planning database CARISPLAN. Most other special libraries are small units of unorganized collections attached to government departments and to corporations. In 1985 efforts toward developing those libraries were under way. The Library of the Caribbean Community Secretariat (CARICOM) in Georgetown is a regional institution that supports the needs of an estimated 80 specialists and researchers concerned with the development of the English-speaking Caribbean. Limited service is given to researchers and students in the Guyanese community. Its stock comprises an estimated 19,000 monographs and pamphlets and a large unnumbered collection of unpublished reports and conference documents.

School Libraries. The organized libraries in 14 of the largest secondary schools in the country indicate a modest increase in the development of libraries at that level, but it could still be said that school libraries were still in their formative years in the 1980s, particularly in the primary level of the educa-

Libraries in Guyana (1984)

Type	Administrative units	Volumes in collections	Annual expenditures (Guyanese dollar)	Population served	Professional staff	Total staff
National	1	195,000[a]	673,958	192,000	4	66
Academic	1	158,000	685,000	3,000	13	65
Public	1	10,000	--	175,000	1	4
School	18	--	--	--	--	--
Special	24	130,000	--	20,000	9	69

[a]1983 data.

tion system. There were six libraries in the post-secondary colleges such as colleges of education, most of which are relatively small collections of books, journals, and, in some cases, audiovisual materials.

The Profession. Professional librarians in Guyana were trained exclusively in the United Kingdom, the U.S.A. or Canada, until the Department of Library Studies was established at the University of the West Indies, Jamaica in   . Continuing education programs follow a pattern similar to that of courses pursued in the U.K., U.S. and Canada. In addition, some short courses are also pursued in European countries, among them Denmark, the Soviet Union, and Yugoslavia. Programs with a focus on regional activities are sometimes available under the sponsorship of organizations such Unesco, and the Organization of American States (OAS).

The Guyana Library Association (GLA), established in 1972 with a membership of 17 professionals and 42 non-professionals, promotes the professional interests of all personnel in libraries. It sponsors lectures, seminars, and workshops on a range of topics concerning the library and information field. Its principal publications is the *Guyana Library Association Bulletin,* published twice a year. The Association also publishes a *Directory of Library and Information Services.*

YVONNE V. STEPHENSON

H

Haas, Warren J.
(1924-)

Warren James Haas, U.S. university library director and administrator and President of the Council on Library Resources (CLR) from January 1978, served at the center of some of the most innovative and successful efforts to reshape research libraries in an era marked by revolutionary technological change. At the CLR he gained increased support of private foundations in the research library enterprise, particularly in the areas of computer and communications technology; scholarly communications; library resources, preservation, and access; and library education, management, and cooperation.

Born on March 22, 1924, in Racine, Wisconsin, Haas received a B.A. degree from Wabash College, in Indiana, in 1948, after serving in the U.S. Air Force from 1943 to 1946. He received a B.L.S. degree from the University of Wisconsin in 1950. His first library position was as Head of Branch Libraries for the Racine Public Library. In 1952 he went to Johns Hopkins University, where he served first as Acquisitions Librarian and then as Assistant Librarian. In 1959 and 1960 he was Library Consultant for the Council of Higher Educational Institutions of New York. In 1961 he began his first association with Columbia University, when he was appointed Associate Director of Libraries, a position he held until he was appointed Director of the University of Pennsylvania Libraries in 1966.

Haas returned to Columbia as University Librarian in 1970. In 1972 he was made Vice-President for Information Services with responsibilities for both libraries and the university's computer center, the first such designation in a major university. The Columbia that Haas returned to in 1970 had been the scene of massive student demonstrations, the resignation under fire of senior university administrators, and the unionization of supporting staff in the Library. Haas faced serious fiscal constraints. He was among the first administrators of major resarch libraries to experience drastic budgetary cuts at a time when user demands were increasing and emerging technology was promising many advantages but at enormous costs.

Recognizing the need for a reorganization and redefinition of academic librarianship, he devised a two-track system of professional ranks and position categories that recognized both the management responsibilities of librarian positions and the professional achievements of the individual. He subtly modified the structure introduced for the Columbia Libraries after a pilot management study by the Association for Research Libraries. The success of these organizational ventures was directly attributable to Haas's personal philosophy of upgrading the profession of research librarianship by raising the sights of individual members, encouraging higher standards of performance, and identifying ways for librarians to contribute effectively to the academic purposes of higher education.

With Douglas Bryant of Harvard, Richard Couper of the New York Public Library, and Rutherford Rogers of Yale, Haas was a major force in the establishment of the Research Libraries Group in 1974. RLG's transformation from a regional association of four major research libraries into a national partnership of some 30 owner-members and a number of associate and special members and associates owes much to Haas's vision and to his early recognition of the need to promote a comprehensive computerized bibliographic system for the U.S.

As President of the Council on Library Resources from 1978, Haas introduced a number of new projects while continuing to support major programs in networking, preservation, and library management and education. His view of the role of the Council is that it is "one of a few library organizations focused on the future rather than the past." In carrying on the traditions of the Council, Haas attracted the interests of a growing number of private foundations.

Haas's memberships on the American Library Association's International Relations Advisory Committee on Liaison with Japanese Libraries and on the Library subcommittee of the Japan–U.S. Conference on Cultural and Educational Interchange indicate active involvement on the international library scene. The Council assisted the International Federation of Library Associations and Institutions for many years, an effort that Haas continued. In November 1984 the CLR, along with the NATO Scientific Affairs Division, the Commission of the European Communities, the European Cultural Foundation, and the Council of Europe, sponsored an advanced research workshop in Luxembourg on the impact of new information technologies on library management, resources, and cooperation. The reports presented at that workshop cover cooperative efforts, education and training, and a European equivalent of the CLR. The Haas imprimatur is evident.

Haas was a workshop leader in Beijing and Shanghai in 1980, providing some 300 Chinese librarians with their first exposure to advances in librarianship after 30 years of dissociation from the U.S. He also presented a paper at the Kanazawa Institute in Japan in 1984 on the preservation of library materials. In 1980 he was awarded the Henry Elias Howland Memorial Prize from Yale University. In 1983 Wabash College conferred an honorary Doctor of Literature, and in 1984, the Melvil Dewey Medal was awarded to him by the American Library Association. The citation says, in part: "Combining originality of method and vigorous leadership, Warren James Haas is invariably at the center of the most successful efforts to mould new information systems. A zealous amateur birdwatcher, he seems as perpetually airborne as his feathered friends, advancing projects in Los Angeles, New York, The Hague, Peking, and Tokyo . . . He is a spokesman with sensible solutions and an imaginative creator of the building blocks of the information systems of the future."

FREDERICK DUDA

Haines, Helen
(1872–1951)

Helen Elizabeth Haines, teacher, reviewer, and advocate of intellectual freedom, influenced generations of students of librarianship through her book *Living with Books: The Art of Book Selection* (1935, 1950).

A native of New York City, Haines was born on February 9, 1872. Privately educated, she held

Warren J. Haas   ALA

only one degree, an honorary M.A. conferred by the University of Southern California in 1945.

After undertaking freelance work as an indexer and writing *The History of New Mexico from the Spanish Conquest to the Present Time, 1530–1890* (New Mexico Historical Publishing Company, 1891), Haines was employed by R. R. Bowker, publisher of library indexes and journals, in 1892 on the recommendation of Mary Wright Plummer, library educator and family friend. She held a number of editorial positions before she was appointed Managing Editor of *Library Journal* in 1896, a position she held until ill health forced her resignation in 1908.

The *Proceedings* of the American Library Association were published annually in *Library Journal,* and Haines became the Association's recorder. She served on the Council and the Executive Board; in 1906 she was elected Second Vice-President.

In Pasadena, California, where Haines moved in search of health, she began a career as book reviewer and activist in library affairs. She began a book review column, "The Library Table," in the *Pasadena News* in 1910 and continued it for 40 years. Her reviews appeared in other newspapers and periodicals, including the *New York Herald Tribune,* the *Nation,* and the *Saturday Review of Literature,* and she gave series of book talks for the Pasadena, Long Beach, and Los Angeles public libraries. Her articles on library legislation, book selection, and other topics appeared in state and national library journals.

Haines's advocacy of high literary standards in the selection of materials for libraries was brought to the attention of library educators, and in 1914 she began to teach book selection and the history of books and libraries at the training class of the Los Angeles Public Library. When the class became a library school and, in 1932, part of the University of Southern California, Haines became a full-time faculty member. She lectured to book selection classes at the University of California at Berkeley and prepared and conducted correspondence courses in book selection for the American Correspondence School of Librarianship and the Columbia University Home Study Department. She taught at Columbia University during summer sessions.

Columbia University Press gave Haines a grant that enabled her to write *Living with Books: The Art of Book Selection* (1935), which, published by Columbia, became a standard text in library schools and a reference tool in libraries. Appreciative of contemporary as well as traditional literature, comprehensive, liberal in outlook, and delightfully readable, it became the book-oriented librarian's bible. *What's in a Novel,* also published by Columbia (1942), an analysis and appreciation limited to contemporary literature, largely of the more or less popular mainstream, did not serve as broad a purpose.

By 1950, when a new edition of *Living with Books* was published, again by the Columbia University Press, the climate had changed. Haines, then 78 years old, again exhibited an open, liberal attitude toward the books of the period, including those on politics, religion, and science. It was inevitable that she should be accused of a pro-Soviet bias, and not surprising that many librarians should timidly reject the book. Long a defender of intellectual freedom, and one of the founders of the Committee on Intellectual Freedom of the California Library Association in 1940, Haines had foreseen and warned against censorship from within libraries.

Recognized as an outstanding library educator, a brilliant speaker and author, and a principal force in encouraging in librarians a love of books and high critical standards, Haines was given the Joseph W. Lippincott Award for outstanding achievement in librarianship by ALA in 1951. Her eloquent speech of acceptance measured the power of the book in the past and foretold its continuing influence in the future. Helen Haines died in Altadena, California, on August 26, 1951.

REFERENCES
Helen E. Haines, "Living with Books," *Library Journal* (1951).
Everett T. Moore, "Innocent Librarians," *ALA Bulletin* (1961), describes attacks on Haines as "a propagandist for the Stalinist way of life" by Oliver Carlson in *The Freeman* (1952), and the point-by-point answer given by Elinor S. Earle in *ALA Bulletin* (1952).
Everett T. Moore, "The Intellectual Freedom Saga in California," *California Librarian* (1974), an account of Haines's activities and leadership in intellectual freedom.
Robert D. Harlan, "Haines, Helen Elizabeth," *Dictionary of American Library Biography* (1978).
RUTH WARNCKE

Haiti

Haiti, a republic in the Caribbean Sea, occupies the western part of the island of Hispaniola, which lies between Puerto Rico and Cuba. It shares the island with the Dominican Republic on the east. Population (1984 est.) 5,197,000; area 26,833 sq.km. The official language is French; the national language is Creole.

History. Haiti's first libraries were created during the French colonial period (1625–1803). Some private collections and a type of library called *cabinet de lecture* existed in Port-au-Prince, Cap-Haitien, and Cayes, but these books did not survive the war for independence. In 1825 a national library (with 444 books) was founded by President Jean-Pierre Boyer. In 1920 the library of L'Amicale du Lycée Pétion was established, followed by the library of the École Pratique de Damien (1926) and the Faculty of Medicine Library (1927). In 1940 the present National Library was built with branches in Jacmel, St-Marc, Jérémie, Cayes, and Port-de-Paix by President Sténio Vincent.

National Library. The National Library was organized in 1940. It was directed by Max Bissainthe, who published the Haitian current and retrospective bibliographies, compiled in his *Dictionnaire de bibliographie hiatienne (1804–1949)* and its *Supplement* covering the period 1950–70. After Bissainthe's administration (1942–57), the collection of 6,000 books was reduced to about 4,000.

This institution was later reorganized under new legislation, with a new building and more modern equipment. From 1984 it received depository copies of Haitian imprints. It had no acquisition budget as of the mid-1980s. The Haitian Society of History and Geography gave it a deposit of 5,000 books and microfilmed rolls of Haitian colonial archives. The library was planned as the nucleus of a public libraries network under the Institut National Haitien de la Culture et des Arts (INAHCA).

The National Archives of Haiti has old documents from 1779 (civil registers). Precious and rare documents were transferred in 1922 to the present building. The bad conditions of conservation and management of those papers resulted in great losses. There are about 20 archives depositories in Port-au-Prince and many others in the provinces.

Academic Libraries. There are 17 schools of higher education in Haiti; in 1985, 9 of them had their own libraries. The best libraries were the Faculty of Medicine Library (9,896 volumes), National Institute of Management and International High Studies (INAGHEI) Library (3,958 volumes), and Faculty of Agriculture Library (7,000 volumes). Only the INAGHEI Library had an acquisition budget and had made a great part of its collections available on loan. Some collections for the period 1920–34 are available in the libraries of the faculties of Medicine and Agriculture.

Public Libraries. There are no state public libraries in Port-au-Prince. Small public libraries exist in seven towns in the country, supported by the National Library, which pays only for limited staff, some books, and elementary equipment.

The best public libraries are the French Institute (about 29,000 volumes) and the Haitian American (4,500 volumes), which provide free access to their bookstocks and make loans.

School Libraries and Media Centers. There is no school library service at the Ministry of National Education. Some of the public schools have libraries. According to certain regulations of the Ministry, all private schools on opening must have libraries, yet the regulation is fulfilled only in some of them. According to the latest data available in the mid-1980s, schools with libraries numbered 21 public and 115 private. Schools without libraries numbered 71 public and 332 private (data published 1975).

Special Libraries. Thirteen special libraries have between 500 and 4,000 volumes; managed in many cases by professionally unqualified employees, they offer services to small numbers of users. The most important is the Saint Louis Gonzague Library, with its 20,000 documents, the richest Haitian collection in the country, followed by the Jean Fouchard collection, owned by the Central Bank of Haiti

(BRH). The Ministries of Commerce and Planning have many official documents and technical reports.

The Profession. There is no library school in Haiti. Courses in general librarianship are offered by the Faculty of Ethnology. Continuing education is given by Haiti's section of the Association of French Caribbean Librarians, Archivists and Documentalists, founded in 1979 at Fort-de-France (Martinique). It publishes *Notes bibliographiques Caraïbes* and *Bulletin d'Information de l'A.A.B.D.F.C (section Haiti)*.

Haiti had six professional librarians, 12 paraprofessionals, and 14 archivist assistants in 1985.

REFERENCE

Association des Archivistes, bibliothécaires et documentalistes francophones de la Caraïbe (Section Haiti), *Répertoire commenté de la législation haitienne relative aux unités documentaires* (1983).

JEAN WILFRID BERTRAND

Hamer, Philip M.
(1891–1971)

Historian and teacher of history, librarian and archivist, Philip May Hamer served on the staff of the National Archives from 1935 and was Executive Director of the National Historical Publications Commission from 1951 to 1961.

Hamer was born in Marion, South Carolina, November 10, 1891. He received a B.A. from Wofford College in Spartanburg, South Carolina; an M.A. from Trinity College (now Duke University); and a Ph.D. in History (1918) from the University of Pennsylvania in Philadelphia. After a year as Professor of History at the University of Tennessee at Chattanooga, he went to the University of Tennessee at Knoxville, where he served as Associate Professor of History, 1920–26, Professor of History, 1926–35, and Chairman of the Graduate School, 1930–34.

Hamer was popular as a teacher, but he also loved research and writing history, and he published many articles on East Tennessee, the Revolution, Indian relations, the southwestern frontier, and a four-volume history of Tennessee (1933). He helped organize the East Tennessee Historical Society, of which he was President, 1926–28. Later, he was a founder of the Southern Historical Association, Editor of its *Journal of Southern History*, and in 1938 its President. His presidential address, delivered at New

Libraries in Haiti (1982)

Type	Administrative units	Service points	Volumes in collections	Annual expenditures (gourde)	Population served	Professional staff	Total staff
National	1	6	23,535	426,600	--	3	43
Academic	11	11	29,534[a]	--	5,950[a]	4	38
Public	3	3	35,900	--	8,500	4	11
School	9	9	--	--	--	1	11
Special	14	14	--	--	--	5	27
Other[b]	1	1	9,000	10,000	--	0	1

[a]Estimate.
[b]Private collection open to researchers.

Source: Dorsainvil Joseph, *Les exigences socio-économiques de l'établissement d'un réseau de bibliothèques publiques à Port-au-Prince*, 1985, supplemented by data collected through interviews.

Philip M. Hamer

Records of the National Archives

Orleans, "The Records of Southern History," was published in volume 5 of the Association's *Journal*.

Hamer joined the staff of the newly established National Archives in 1935 as a deputy examiner of records and was assigned to survey the records of the Interior Department, which had in its file rooms, basements, and attics much that intrigued him. But not only records in the District of Columbia were of interest to him. On January 1, 1936, he became the National Director of the Survey of Federal Records outside the District of Columbia, a project supported by Works Progress Administration funds. Hamer accepted this responsibility without special compensation, depending on the $3,500 a year he was receiving as Deputy Examiner. He prepared *The Manual of the Survey of Federal Archives,* a mimeographed pamphlet of 29 numbered leaves, which was sent to appointed regional directors, members of advisory committees, and some of the key workers.

When the Survey of Federal Records was legally terminated on June 30, 1937, most of the records of the federal government in the 48 states had been surveyed and reported, but the work of compiling and making available the information thus secured remained unfinished. Responsibility for such activity was transferred to the Historical Records Survey, of which Luther H. Evans was National Director, and members of the staff of the Survey of Federal Records both in the field and in Washington were also transferred. Hamer was appointed, again without pay, as Associate National Director. The intended *Inventory of Federal Records* in the states got out of hand because records of the federal agencies were stored in 58,840 rooms in 24,536 buildings and in volume amounted to 5,080,694 linear feet. By the end of 1940, 333 volumes with a total of 36,168 pages had been published in mimeograph form and distributed to libraries throughout the country. Hamer's interesting reports on the problems of the Survey of Federal Records from 1936 to 1940 may be found as appendices in the second to sixth Annual Reports of the Archivist of the United States. He also gave a number of speeches, one of them to the newly organized Society of American Archivists.

In April 1936 he was appointed Chief of the Division of the Library in the National Archives. It was expected that the Library would consist of some 50,000 or 60,000 volumes—mainly American history and biography—printed government documents, and many pamphlets and journals. Many older copies of printed documents could be secured from federal agencies that no longer needed them. His achievement—a good, working library—is still evident, for next to the Library of Congress the National Archives Library is the best and most convenient American history repository in the District of Columbia.

In 1938 Hamer was appointed Chief of the Reference Division, into which the Library Division had been merged, a position he held until 1944. During those years his staff members not only took care of the Library but also ran the central search room, requesting records from the custodial divisions for historians wishing to examine federal records.

From 1944 to 1951 Hamer was Director of Records Control. The change in title indicated that Hamer and his staff members, while still handling reference work, had become increasingly concerned with the preparation of guides, inventories, and other finding aids, and had taken over much of the work of the Classification and Cataloguing Divisions, which had been abolished in 1939 and 1941. The first adequate *Guide to the Records in the National Archives* (684 pages), published by the Government Printing Office in 1948, was "prepared under the immediate direction and editorial supervision of Philip M. Hamer." He was also responsible for planning and directing a special guide in two volumes to *Federal Records of World War II* (1950).

Hamer had also been serving as Secretary of a National Historical Publications Commission, 1946–51, established as part of the Act of 1934 creating the National Archives. Not much had been done before 1946 because of the demands of World War II, but Hamer, who had always been interested in making documentary sources more available, felt it was time to get that program going. He had the support of Solon J. Buck, the Archivist, who by law chaired the Commission. President Harry S. Truman, on being presented with volume one of Julian Boyd's *The Papers of Thomas Jefferson,* asked the Commission to canvass scholars and plan a similar program for publishing the papers of other American leaders. The Federal Records Act of 1950 gave the Commission additional authority, and in 1951 Hamer was made Executive Director, a full-time assignment that he held until his retirement in 1961.

In 1954 he transmitted to the President the Commission's *A National Program for the Publication of Historical Documents* (106 pages), which he had prepared after discussions with history teachers, historical societies, and others interested in the publication of source documents. The Commission also proposed the preparation of a guide to the archival and manuscript collections of the nation, which Hamer and his staff planned, prepared, and published in 1961. It describes the holdings of more than 1,000 archival agencies, historical societies, and libraries in the United States and is still a basic tool of the scholarly historian.

The Commission labeled as priority projects the publication of the papers of Benjamin Franklin, John and John Quincy Adams, Alexander Hamilton, and James Madison. Hamer helped to get all of them started, along with a project for the "Documentary History of the Ratification of the Constitution and First Ten Amendments." He worked with certain scholars and universities to start additional projects for John C. Calhoun, Henry Clay, John Jay, Andrew Johnson, John Marshall, James K. Polk, and Woodrow Wilson, among others.

In October 1960 Hamer was elected the 16th President of the Society of American Archivists, and in 1961 he gave the presidential address at the annual meeting in Kansas City. His subject was "Authentic Documents Tending to Elucidate Our History" (published in *The American Archivist*, volume 25).

Hamer wanted to see published the papers of Henry Laurens, who had represented South Carolina in the Continental Congress and served two years, 1777–78, as its President. Hamer felt that he had been one of the forgotten Revolutionary leaders. Upon Hamer's retirement from the Commission on November 30, 1961, he continued to work on the project in the National Archives building, where the papers of the Continental Congress were preserved. He chose as his Associate Editor Professor George C. Rogers, Jr., of the University of South Carolina, which was another repository for many papers. Much collecting and editing had been done, and two volumes were published by the University of South Carolina Press, before Hamer died on April 10, 1971. A third volume, on which he had worked, was published in 1972; others followed.

OLIVER W. HOLMES (d. 1981)

Handicapped, Services to

The gravity of the loss of reading ability is directly related to the great importance of the written word in contemporary daily life. Also, advances in publishing technology are rapidly increasing the flow of the printed word from the presses of the world. Because access to the printed word has, at best, been limited for blind and other handicapped persons, and because, to read, these individuals usually must depend on the assistance and intervention of others, print-handicapped persons will find it more and more difficult to gain the information they need in their educational and professional lives. In addition, as the proportion of print-handicapped people in society increases, particularly among those of advanced age, the need to find alternative solutions and accommodations to their lack of access to the printed page will become more urgent.

Access to the printed page is essential for entry into educational and professional life. More handicapped persons are becoming more mobile and less sedentary than in earlier years. They are eager to become independent and contributing members of society. It is thus becoming axiomatic that attention to and support of access to print for handicapped persons have become a public investment.

This article deals with several aspects of efforts in the United States and other countries to increase reading access for handicapped individuals. In the decade 1975–84 in particular, public librarians became more aware of the need for quality service for all seg-

ments of their communities, including the handicapped. Libraries have made encouraging accommodations, ranging from staff members learning sign language to having buildings designed or remodeled to provide barrier-free access. Libraries have become deposit stations to house and circulate books in special format (for example, braille, spoken word recordings, and large print) and have installed a variety of reading machines. Library schools across the United States have instituted classes to acquaint future librarians with library service for handicapped persons, and library associations are lending support and assistance to the development of standards in this field of library service. The work of the American Library Association (ALA) and the International Federation of Library Associations (IFLA) has been particularly noteworthy.

Outstanding advances have also been made in modern technology. For example, computers and miniaturization can now provide a direct reading of a page through synthesized speech, and modern technology is also helping improve the timeliness of the circulation of reading materials and related equipment. Technology is helping handicapped individuals meet the demands and challenges of an industrialized society and is facilitating their participation in community life.

Handicapped Readers and the Public Library. The terms *handicap* and *impairment* have no legal or medical definition. For the library, however, they do indicate persons in the community or service area who usually require special assistance or special equipment and who often must meet eligibility or certification requirements not usually sought from others in the general public. Determining the various handicapping conditions (such as visual impairments, deafness, mental retardation, paralysis, or mobility impairment) is not difficult. Problems arise in the application of statistics concerning these handicaps. Figures on requirements and the population to be served in a particular community are available in abundance. Numerous agencies and organizations, whether providing rehabilitation, educational help, or financial assistance, collect and compile statistics that conform to the specific functions or objectives of the agency or organization doing the compiling. Frequently, the agencies and organizations providing services, materials, or equipment will restrict the availability of that aid to people who meet the criteria established by such agencies. Such practices may not meet the needs of all handicapped persons to be served by a library. More often, information must come from surveys conducted locally, by or on behalf of the library.

National statistics can give some indication of the extent and prevalence of various handicaps. These figures can be the basis on which to build reasonably good estimates. For example, in its survey on "Prevalence of Selected Impairments, United States, 1977," the National Center for Health Statistics (NCHS) numbered 11,400,000 (53.8 per 1,000) persons as having visual impairment and 1,400,000 as having "severe visual impairment, defined as an inability to see newsprint with corrective lenses, or, with no useful vision in one or both eyes." NCHS reported that 14,200,000 (70.2 per 1,000) had trouble hearing in one or both ears, and 7,200,000 of these had trouble hearing in both ears. Severe bilateral hearing problems occurred in 3,200,000, and 367,000 reportedly could hear no speech at all. These hearing statistics exclude persons under three years of age and those whose sole hearing impairment was tinnitus (ringing in the ears).

Paralysis may affect travel to or access to the library building or possibly to the use of the printed book (that is, holding it or turning its pages). Says NCHS, about 1,500,000 (7.2 per 1,000) suffer from complete or partial paralysis; approximately 358,000 had a major extremity missing. Nonparalytic orthopedic impairments of the back or spine occurred in 9,000,000; 7,000,000 had paralysis of a lower extremity or hip and 2,500,000, paralysis of an upper extremity or shoulder. Other nonparalytic orthopedic impairments of the limbs, back, or trunk were reported in a million people. Of the persons paralyzed, about 52 percent had cerebral palsy or partial paralysis of the extremities or trunk.

The statistics for mentally retarded persons in the general population were not readily available in the mid-1980s. The federal government's annual collection and publication of numbers of the mentally retarded in state institutions ended in 1971. Statistics for later years are the result of several private and federally sponsored efforts. According to available statistics, mentally retarded residents of public and community residential facilities in 1977 numbered 214,397 (99 per 100,000), with another 5,000 in foster homes (*Digest of Data on Persons with Disabilities,* Congressional Research Service, p. 12).

Other disabling conditions may affect the scope of the library's outreach program, dependent—as in all disabling conditions—on their degree of severity and limitation on activity. These include arthritis (26,800,000; 123 per 1,000); heart disease (16,400,000; 76 per 1,000); and cerebrovascular condition (1,900,000; 9 per 1,000).

Few countries fail to provide some kind of library or reading service for their handicapped citizens. Such service varies widely depending on whether it is centralized solely under the auspices of the central or federal government or is decentralized among public libraries and charitable organizations. A trend also exists toward more cooperation among libraries in sharing resources that are scarce and expensive to produce. Following are a few examples of library service in various countries on the continents of Europe, Asia, Australia, and North America.

United States. *National Library Service.* In the United States, a free national library service authorized by an act of Congress (P.L. 71-787, March 3, 1931) is available to residents, as well as eligible American citizens living abroad, who are certified by competent authority as being unable to see a page of print, hold a book, or turn its pages. Examples of disabling conditions that may make a person eligible include cerebral palsy, blindness, severe arthritis, multiple sclerosis, muscular dystrophy, and quadriplegia. Mailing to and from the cooperating network of 56 regional libraries and more than 100 subregionals is free. The cooperating network, made up largely of state and local public libraries, serves blind and other physically handicapped persons within its service area. Four multistate service centers (MSCs) provide backup, such as duplicating services, interlibrary loan coordination, storage for publication and equip-

Institute for Perception Research

At the Institute for Perception Research in the Netherlands, a boy scanning a barcode with a light pen. The barcode indicates which word is to be produced by the sound synthesizer.

ment reserves, and housing for multiple copies of books in all media. Each MSC serves regional libraries in 13 to 15 contiguous states.

Full-length books and magazines of general interest are produced by the Library of Congress, National Library Service for the Blind and Physically Handicapped (LC-NLS), in braille as well as on disk and cassette tapes. This material, along with related equipment to play the recordings, is provided to the regional libraries as a basic collection. Magazines are a large proportion of the material circulated in recorded form. More than 70 popular titles are recorded on flexible disks and mailed directly from the producer to the readers. From 1980 to 1984, the number of blind and physically handicapped readers throughout the country grew from over 605,000 to almost 635,000 and circulation from approximately 16,888,700 units (volumes and containers) to over 19,000,000. The network collection is supplemented by single-copy transcriptions and recordings by local volunteers. The music collection at NLS is the major national resource for music scores, textbooks, and instructional materials in a format usable by blind and handicapped persons.

Other Programs. NLS cooperates with educational, vocational, and nonprofit organizations that provide materials to disabled persons. One such organization, Recording for the Blind (RFB), with headquarters in Princeton, New Jersey, lends free textbooks on cassettes to medically certified visually, physically, or perceptually handicapped students and professional persons. The RFB Master Tape Collection contains approximately 60,000 titles covering all educational levels, from elementary school through the university level.

Public libraries in the United States have taken initiatives to provide easier access to the buildings and to printed collections so that disabled persons can take their place in the cultural and social life of their communities on equal terms with everyone else.

The Phoenix, Arizona, Public Library, while not

typical, nevertheless illustrates a public library's extensive use of technology to benefit handicapped persons without dependence on sighted people. It has a Special Needs Center where the staff can communicate with deaf persons in sign language. Equipment in the Center includes a Versabraille computer for telephone communication with deaf-blind persons and a Kurzweil reading machine, a computer-assisted device that scans a printed page through an optical character recognition system and reads the page aloud in synthesized speech. The Kurzweil machine, coupled with a paperless braille machine, a computer with synthetic speech, and a letter-quality printer, enables blind persons to read and write braille or printed material electronically, edit manuscripts, and print out corrected copies. The center also has a TDD (a telephone device for the deaf), a video print enlarger, a microfiche enlarger, and a braille fingerspelling program.

Versabraille, the trade name for one of several machines known as "cassette braille" or "paperless braille," is a specially designed cassette recorder/player that receives and stores braille characters on a cassette tape. The user reads the braille displayed as a line of metal pins that are advanced on command. This machine and others, such as the Optacon, which converts letters into vibrating points that can be felt on the fingertips, are in use in libraries around the country.

Librarians and others, such as those in educational and rehabilitation agencies and volunteer organizations, bring newspapers and other timely and topical information to handicapped persons through radio reading services. Using both paid professionals and volunteers, FM stations broadcast news and interpretive reports, often from daily and weekly newspapers, to handicapped persons who listen over specially adapted receivers. Some libraries and volunteer groups record selected articles from newspapers onto cassettes. These papers are not usually recorded in their entirety because of the cost and time involved, but they are usually recorded on a weekly basis.

Tactile maps, often called "braille maps," convey geographic location information through the use of raised lines and braille notation. Such maps are receiving increased attention in the United States and abroad. The first International Symposium on Maps and Graphics for the Visually Handicapped was held in Washington, D.C., in March 1983 and was attended by more than 100 cartographers, geographers, and educators working with blind persons. In April 1984 more than 200 persons from 40 countries gathered in East Berlin, German Democratic Republic, to discuss international cooperation and technological advances in tactile map production. The International Federation of Library Associations' Section of Libraries for the Blind was developing an international registry of maps to be located in the Netherlands Library for the Blind. In 1984 the NLS published a bibliography with more than 475 entries relating to maps and graphics and covering such diverse topics as spatial perception and map design.

Video is being used for deaf persons the same way audio tapes are used for the blind—that is, to make already existing print material available in another medium. The videotapes are also used for sign language training. Some libraries, through grants under the Library Services and Construction Act, have purchased telecaption decoders. Such decoders make it possible for deaf persons to view some 30 hours of educational and commercial television programs a week

Until comparatively recently, public libraries had not made special attempts to serve mentally retarded individuals adequately. The term *mentally retarded* covers those with a wide range of abilities. Some of the more severely retarded may have difficulty reading and be able to speak only with difficulty. Changes in public attitudes and improved and enlightened care, training, and psychological evaluation have led to greater efforts to bring mentally retarded people into community life. These efforts include library service as well. According to some librarians, mentally retarded children have problems in book selection common also to dyslexic children. Libraries have been stocking toys for both groups on the theory that toys can lead to improved interaction between handicapped and nonhandicapped children. For dyslexic children, spoken-word recordings are believed by educators to be beneficial, and are viewed as a complement to, rather than a substitute for, the printed form. The spoken-word recordings available from libraries around the country are often helpful; however, few recently published books are available on such recordings.

Outside the U.S., Dutch researchers began developing a recorded book in the mid-1980s that could turn out to be an important reading and teaching aid for dyslexic children. Each work in the book has below it a combination of black and white marks making up a bar code, much like those used on products in supermarkets. A microcomputer analyzes the binary sequence that the scanner reads and converts it into speech sounds that emerge from a speaker. The project is a joint effort of Eindhoven's Technical University and the Philips Language Laboratory.

Scandinavia. In Scandinavian countries, service to handicapped persons has in the past been the responsibility of charitable associations for the blind operating centralized services. With the growth of public libraries and increased concern for the welfare of the handicapped, however, conditions favorable to decentralization are present.

Denmark. In Denmark, service is entirely the responsibility of the state. Until 1976, it was centralized in the Statens Bibliotek og Trykkeri for Blinde (SBTB), the state library and printing house for the blind. Decentralization began in 1976, the year that marked the beginning of production of talking books for Denmark's public libraries as well as the entry of commercial publishers into the talking book business.

Proposed legislative changes led to the formation of the Committee on Library Servicing of the Blind and Sight Impaired to assist in the transfer of talking book circulation from the government agency for the blind to local public libraries. By 1982, 205 of 247 public libraries were lending talking books, and the Danish government and private publishers had each produced 500 titles for public library distribution. Individual blind and visually impaired users were to have the option of selecting books from either source during the changeover period when public libraries expand their capabilities for service.

Sweden. As in most Scandinavian countries, library service for blind persons in Sweden was originally created on philanthropic initiative. The Society for the Blind began service as early as 1892 and began lending recorded books in 1955, two years before the society had received its first state grant for library activities. The Library for Talking Books and Braille (TPB) was established in January 1980. Cassette tapes are the dominant medium. TPB, a state authority under the auspices of the Ministry of Education, is responsible for almost all braille-related activity. Visually handicapped persons in Sweden obtain braille books directly from the TPB and borrow talking books, produced by TPB and the Swedish Library Service, Ltd., through public libraries. Recorded books are made available to local and regional libraries through deposit collections and interlibrary loans.

Visually impaired students at universities and colleges and professional persons have access to academic material in braille or recorded-book form through TPB's Section for Course Material. About 300 to 400 recorded book titles are produced for these readers yearly. TPB initiates the production of the majority of the 1,600 titles recorded for library use each year. The Swedish Library Service, Ltd., arranges for the recording of about 150 recorded titles a year. Along with approximately 500 of TPB's recordings, these titles are sold to public libraries.

In recent years, the public libraries have been building up their collections of recorded books using grants from county councils. About two-thirds of the 279 municipalities have recorded books. The loan of these books represents about one percent of the total annual circulation in Sweden.

Iceland. An act of Parliament in 1982 created the Icelandic Library for the Blind, bringing together the resources and services formerly provided by the Reykjavik Public Library and the Icelandic Association for the Blind. The Icelandic Association for the Blind serves blind and visually handicapped persons as well as anyone unable to read normal print. Materials are available in braille and on cassettes.

The Icelandic Library for the Blind is governed by a 10-member board appointed by the Ministry of Education and is divided into three departments. The Educational Materials Department provides students past the elementary grades with textbook support. During 1983, the library's first year of operation, it served about 1,000 people, circulated 23,000 items, and added 100 titles to its collection.

The braille collection contains 600 uncatalogued titles, mostly in Danish, which were contributed to the library by the Icelandic Association for the Blind. Danish is the first foreign language Icelandic students learn in school. For recordings, all narration (for example, reading a book onto cassette tape) is done by volunteers. Cassette readers buy their own machines. Members of the Association for the Blind are able to purchase theirs duty-free; other readers buy theirs commercially. The cassette collection contained approximately 1,300 titles in 1985, with three cassette copies each.

An agreement between the Library and the Author's Association restricts the library to recording and duplicating only three copies of each title.

Poland. Although braille libraries existed in Poland before World War II, more extensive services have been organized since then under social organizations such as the Section for the Propagation of Reading Programs for Invalids and Physically Handicapped Persons. In 1952 the Central Library of the Polish Association for the Blind was established in Warsaw to provide training assistance and library materials to six branch libraries in large city centers and nearly 20 libraries in cooperatives, schools, and community centers. Services to those with visual and physical impairments are also offered by public libraries, although on a more limited scale. These services have begun to increase, especially for persons with physical handicaps and for nonhospitalized invalids. Reading programs for the blind and physically handicapped were introduced in public libraries in 1975 as a result of an agreement between the Polish Association for the Blind and the Ministry of Culture and Art. Of the 49 regional branches of the Association of Polish Librarians, 35 have sections for recorded books, and some of them have recording studios. The Ministry of Culture and Art has steadily increased funds to purchase tape-recorded books and related equipment. All the libraries have cassette players for cassette readers on a loan basis. By the end of 1981, 35 libraries had recorded book collections amounting to just over 12,000 titles, not including titles purchased for the libraries by the Polish Association for the War on Disability, which are deposited in the libraries but not listed in the catalogues.

Japan. Of the 83 braille libraries throughout Japan, the Japan Braille Library has the largest collection. In 1981 it contained about 104,000 braille volumes and 182,000 tapes; it lent more than 64,000 braille volumes and 424,000 tapes to its 12,750 registered borrowers. The Japan Braille Library was established in 1940 with a collection of 700 braille books; recorded books were added in 1958. The library produced both press-braille and single-copy, transcribed braille books.

Facilities and services vary greatly among the other 82 libraries. Some concentrate on braille books, while others focus on recorded books, personal reader or reference services, aides, training classes for daily living, or braille classes. Nineteen main braille-publishing centers provide most of the braille books

Library of Congress

The recorded books project began at the Library of Congress in 1931.

Daniel J. Boorstin, 12th Librarian of Congress, narrating his book An American Primer *in a studio of the National Library Service for the Blind and Physically Handicapped. When completed, the book was made available in 1,500 copies for the thousands of users of the LC program.*

for the braille libraries, and some have small publishing departments for special items. The Japanese Red Cross loans braille books and provides volunteer braille transcription services. Lions Clubs also provide braille and recorded books.

In Japan, volunteer narrators are an important part of the increasing reader preference for talking books. Such recording requires less training than do braille transcribers, who train from 16 to 36 months. Most braille libraries in Japan are governed by elected boards of directors. Organizations are entitled to national government funding if they are registered under the Social Welfare Law of 1963. The balance of funds comes from local and prefectural governments and fund-raising activities. The Ueda Braille Library is the only one in Japan that is government-operated.

Australia. The Royal Blind Society (RBS) of New South Wales, through five sections, provides reader services, audio production, music, and student and special request materials. Full-time and part-time employees are assisted by about 300 volunteers who do reading, proofreading, and clerical work in addition to helping with brailling.

As a braille library, RBS dates back to the early years of the 20th century. In 1961 it took over the production and distribution of recorded books, which had been a separate operation of the Blind Book Society up to that time. The Blind Book Society then became the RBS Talking Book Auxiliary. Through its Reader Services Section, RBS lends braille, recorded books, line-embossed system (Moon Type) books, and large print; it also has a circulating library of magazines. The Department of Social Security underwrites the cost of one-third of the audio and braille productions that meet certain production standards. Visually impaired persons in Australia are not directly served by RBS; instead, the society supplies

recorded cassettes at cost to public libraries serving both visually handicapped and blind readers. Submaster tapes are made available to similar agencies in Victoria and Western Australia on the same basis. In 1982 more than 2,100 titles were sold.

International Cooperation. Librarians from a number of countries have found it advantageous to work together to share resources and materials for blind persons that are both scarce and expensive to produce. Important in the field is the International Federation of Library Associations (IFLA). In 1977, at the IFLA meeting in Brussels, Belgium, a Working Group was established by the Hospital Library Section. In 1979 it was renamed the Round Table of Libraries for the Blind and later the Section of Libraries for the Blind. The many and varied activities and interests of the Section include consideration of international standards for talking book formats, recommendations on national standards for talking book formats, recommendations on national standards of library service for the blind, copyright exemption for materials for the handicapped, and international cooperation and exchange of bibliographic information.

Two useful directories have been published by the Section: the *International Directory of Libraries and Production Facilities for the Blind* and the *International Directory of Braille Music Collections*. The first lists sources for braille and recorded materials throughout the world and provides pertinent information, such as the languages in which the materials are produced. The music directory lists sources for braille music along with detailed information on the nature of the collections. Its purpose is to locate needed braille music and also to encourage future bibliographic research, to foster international cooperation among braille music organizations, and to conserve limited resources by avoiding unnecessary duplication of braille music.

Section members work with international organizations, such as the Universal Postal Union and the International Transport Association, to improve the transportation of library materials among countries. They devised a self-adhesive label bearing the word *Blindpost*. The label has black letters on an orange background for maximum visibility and is intended to help speed packages through international postal depots and customs by identifying them as materials for the blind. Certain materials for the blind, particularly braille, can now be mailed free across international borders using surface (but often slow) mail.

Standards. The *Approved Recommendations on Working Out National Standards of Library Service for the Blind (August 1983),* compiled and edited by the Standards Development Committee of the Section of Libraries for the Blind, IFLA, has received international support. It was compiled by Frank Kurt Cylke (United States), Henry Fidder (The Netherlands), William C. Byrne (Australia), and D. S. Zharkov (Soviet Union). These standards cover a wide variety of essential topics, including library administration, resource development, lending policies, and response to users.

The IFLA standards and those published under the auspices of the American Library Association, the revised *Standards and Guidelines for the Library of Congress Network Libraries for the Blind and Physically Handicapped, 1984,* indicate an important trend in upgrading the quality of library service for handicapped individuals. It should be noted that important progress has been made in this area of service since the mid-1960s. That progress can most likely be attributed to concentration on certain objectives: (1) continuity of service, so that users can request and rely on quality service at any entry point in the system; (2) fullest use of the bookstock, each title and volume of which is more expensive to produce and more limited in quantity than what is available to members of the general public; (3) increase in the use of professional personnel at all service points and the elevation of professional librarians in charge of libraries for the handicapped to administrative, policy-making positions, along with a more flexible approach to the whole organization of the service; and (4) increase in accessibility of books and information for the users of the collections, together with an increase in the breadth and range of titles and subjects from which the handicapped reader may choose.

The American Library Association standards were the first comprehensive review related to libraries serving blind and physically handicapped persons. Begun in 1977 with a contract between the NLS and the ALA Health and Rehabilitative Services Division, the standards were approved in January 1979. They were developed for service to blind and handicapped individuals provided by regional, subregional, state, public, school, academic, and institutional libraries. Subsequently, Battelle's Columbus Laboratories evaluated the NLS regional and subregional network, including NLS itself, through data collected from questionnaires, from interviews, and from site visits. Each component in the network received a detailed report on its performance as measured against the standards. Also, a comprehensive state-of-the-network report, with comparative data for libraries of similar size and scope, was issued. The study indicates an improved understanding of library services in this network. The standards were scheduled for revision again in 1989, when the network libraries, their parent agencies and organizations, state libraries, and administering and funding agencies would be provided with an excellent means of assessing the current status of library service for physically handicapped individuals.

Book Production and Distribution. The objectives of producing materials for use by handicapped individuals are to decrease costs, increase timeliness, and maintain quality. The increase in the use of computers, including microcomputers, foreshadows revolutionary developments in braille production—particularly in increasing speed, which would in turn shorten the time between the book's publication in print and its availability to the handicapped reader. Computers have been assisting publishers of braille and are also helping to increase the efficiency of transcribers. For example, complex braille codes can be input so that less transcriber training is required, and the text can be edited before it is committed to paper. Master copies can be stored on compact diskettes rather than on bulky paper or metal plates, so more material can be kept in a given amount of storage space.

The timeliness of braille production has improved with the use of compositor tapes, the storage medium that drives phototypesetting equipment for print materials. Compositor tapes can be employed to operate braille presses automatically. They eliminate the need for time-consuming manual stereographing and provide readers with braille versions of books and periodicals nearer to the time the print version is published. *National Geographic,* for example, is published using such tapes. The braille edition of Joseph Lash's *Helen and Teacher,* a biography of Helen Keller and Anne Sullivan Macy, was available to blind individuals at about the same time the print edition became available for the sighted. Except for experiments with compositor tapes in braille production in 1969, it was the first time in the United States that a book of that length—786 pages, or eight braille volumes—had been produced in that manner.

Further improvements in the quality and speed of braille production may be expected. A cooperative project was begun in 1980 between the Library of Congress and the American Foundation for the Blind (AFB) in New York. AFB contributed significantly to the development of talking books in the 1930s and became one of two major producers of sound recordings for blind and physically handicapped people. The project calls for the establishment of a production center and a developmental laboratory to examine technology in relation to the use of computers in producing high-quality braille.

Voice Indexing. Technological advances have made reference material, not previously available in recorded form, accessible to blind and handicapped individuals through voice indexing. This technique uses key words to locate specific information. Index words are audible when the cassette is played in the fast-forward mode. When the desired word or name is located, the reader stops the tape and resumes play at regular speed to hear the full entry under that heading. Recorded voice-indexed reference material includes *Access National Parks: A Guide for Handicapped Visitors;* the *Concise Heritage Dictionary,* recorded in the studios of the NLS on 55 casettes; and the 1980 *World Book Encyclopedia,* recorded on 219 cassettes at the American Printing House for the Blind in Louisville, Kentucky.

Computer Technology. Computers now perform many of the centralized functions of NLS. For example, the NLS Comprehensive Mailing List System (CMLS) is used to accomplish the massive job of mailing periodicals and catalogues to thousands of individuals. A recent development in the use of computer technology is the Reader Enrollment and Delivery System (READS), a microcomputer-based circulation system designed for long-term growth. And READS is designed to be compatible with NLSNET, a planned information system linking NLS, its multistate service centers (MSCs), and automated network libraries by computer for intercommunication and data transfer. READS was designed to handle four functions: (1) maintenance of patron records, (2) circulation, (3) inventory control, and (4) information exchange. The system was in the test phase at pilot locations in 1985 and was designed to take advantage of local area network architecture, using 2 to 12 small computers as work stations performing a variety of tasks including optical scanning. One of READS' objectives is to operate on as wide a range of devices as are available in the computer marketplace. The READS system will contain data to support activities related to book circulation, maga-

J.C.M. Hanson Collection Luther College Archives

J.C.M. Hanson

zine subscriptions, inventory of sound reproduction equipment, and patron recordkeeping. Modifications in the system will be made as required.

FRANK KURT CYLKE;
ALFRED D. HAGLE

Hanson, J. C. M.
(1864–1943)

James Christian Meinich Hanson's was perhaps the greatest individual influence on the bibliographical organization of libraries in the United States during the first half of the 20th century. Hanson was born March 13, 1894, at Sørheim, his father's farm, in the district of Nord-Aurdal in the Valdres Valley of Norway. The sixth of eight children of Gunnerius (Gunnar) and Eleanore Adamine Röberg Hansen, he was christened Jens Christian Meinich Hansen. His boyhood friends in Iowa called him Jim, which he, to his later regret, formalized as James. The change in the spelling of his surname was inconsistent. By 1897 he had adopted "J. C. M. Hanson" as his signature, although he sometimes reverted to "Jens" or "J. C. M. Hansen" in his writings for the Norwegian-American press.

Hanson's father was a government official, *lensmand* for the district of Nord-Aurdal, and the family would not ordinarily have been among those considering emigration to the United States, but Hanson's mother's half-brother, Hans Röberg, had settled in Decorah, Iowa. He offered an education to one of the boys in the family, and in the summer of 1873 Hanson, who was then only nine, left Norway in the company of the Reverend Ove J. Hjort for the trip to Iowa. He could not enroll in the preparatory department of Luther College until the following year because of his age. In 1882, at the age of 18, he received a B.A. degree.

Hanson had no definite career plans and was persuaded by the Reverend Ulrich V. Koren, a member of the college Board of Trustees, that Concordia Seminary in St. Louis was the proper goal for a Luther graduate. Hanson stayed at Concordia for only two years. He felt no real call to the ministry, and the lack of adequate financial support would have made the third and final year exceedingly difficult even had he wished to remain. Instead he accepted a position in the fall of 1884 as Principal of Our Saviour's Church school in the Norwegian community in Chicago, *Klokker* (Deacon) for the church, and Superintendent of its Sunday School. He supplemented his income by teaching English to adult Scandinavians in the Montefiore Evening School and by pitching for several commercial baseball teams. After saving enough money for a year's graduate study, he enrolled at Cornell University in 1888.

In his second year at Cornell, Hanson was awarded the President White Fellowship in history and political science. His research required extensive use of the library, which was at the time undergoing reclassification. He became acquainted with the Acting Librarian, George William Harris, whose influence, according to Hanson, led him to decide on librarianship as his life's work. Accordingly, in September 1890 Hanson joined William Frederick Poole's prestigious training ground at the Newberry Library in Chicago. Among the many benefits gained

there, the formation of his lifelong friendship with Charles Martel was not the least.

In 1893 Hanson was appointed Head Cataloguer at the University of Wisconsin. His experience in the planning and implementation of complete reclassification and recataloguing was to prove invaluable to him later at the Library of Congress.

Hanson was appointed Superintendent of the Catalogue Department at the Library of Congress in August 1897 by the newly appointed Librarian of Congress, John Russell Young. In beginning the new catalogue during Young's brief administration, Hanson laid the groundwork for the success of cooperative, later centralized, cataloguing by his carefully considered modifications of Charles A. Cutter's *Rules for a Printed Dictionary Catalogue* to conform to the best practice of the time and thereby "facilitate" the use by other libraries of the Library of Congress cataloguing. The resulting entries, printed for the copyright books in the subdivision *Books Proper* of the *Catalogue* of the Register of Copyrights, were welcomed enthusiastically in a *Library Journal* editorial.

The Montreal conference of the American Library Association in 1900 heralded an era of cooperation in cataloguing. The ALA Publishing Board established an Advisory Comittee on *Cataloging* Rules with Hanson as Chairman. (The name of the committee, which became a special committee of the ALA in 1906, varies; the predominant form was Catalog Rules Committee.) The reconciliation of the numerous divergent views on the many disputed points of cataloguing was credited by William Warner Bishop to Hanson's "thoroughness and patience." His wholehearted commitment to cooperation in cataloguing, which is dependent on agreement on rules, was a major factor in his successful leadership.

This achievement was crowned by the further cooperation with the Library Association's Catalogue Rules Committee in the mutual acceptance, with only eight differences, of *Catalog Rules: Author and Title Entries,* commonly known as the Anglo-American code of 1908. The official ALA motion thanking the Catalog Rules Committee noted that thanks were due "especially" to Hanson, who "has done more to bring the English and American committees into harmony, and has borne the burden of the final editing of the Code." The catalogue cards produced at the Library of Congress under his direction were generally acclaimed for their excellence. Their quality and the general acceptance of the cataloguing rules were major factors in the success of the Library of Congress card distribution service. The card distribution service, in turn, led to an unprecedented national standardization in cataloguing practice.

Hanson's influence on subject cataloguing in the United States was equally powerful and long-lasting. Cutter's "dictionary" principle was radically modified for the new catalogue. Because of the anticipated size of the catalogue, Hanson thought the dispersion of related headings would be too great. Subject topics were therefore subordinated extensively, and independent headings were deliberately inverted to group the headings together. Although some of the principles underlying the system have been modified over the years, the *Library of Congress Subject Headings* remains virtually the standard list of subject headings in use in the United States today.

Within two months of his arrival at the Library of Congress, Hanson was able to bring Charles Martel from the Newberry Library as one of his two chief assistants. Hanson always accorded to Martel the credit for the Library of Congress Classification, but he himself had a major role in its beginnings, primarily in its conception and notation. Hanson, too, carried the responsibility for convincing both Young and Young's successor, Herbert Putnam, of the need for a new classification scheme.

In 1910 Hanson moved to the University of Chicago as Associate Director of the library. This was his third library reorganization, and he became one of the leading voices for cooperative cataloguing to supplement centralized cataloguing as the most efficient and economical means of bibliographical organization. He was appointed to the faculty of the newly established Graduate Library School of the University of Chicago in 1928.

That same year Hanson led the team of cataloguing experts sent by the Carnegie Endowment for International Peace to assist in the reorganization of the Vatican Library. The Vatican Library's *Norme per il catalogo degli stampati* ("rules for the cataloguing of forms"), which reflected the influence of the Anglo-American code of 1908, was another step toward international agreement in cataloguing. Even after his retirement in 1934, Hanson continued to work for international cooperation in cataloguing as the only route for the future. In furtherance of this cause he compiled his monumental work, *A Comparative Study of Cataloging Rules Based on the Anglo-American Code of 1908; with Comments on the Rules and on the Prospects for a Further Extension of International Agreement and Co-operation* (1939).

Hanson was the author of numerous articles on technical library matters, book reviews, and frequent contributions to the Norwegian-American press. "Corporate Authorship versus Title Entry" (*Library Quarterly,* 1935) is perhaps his most frequently cited article, but his earlier paper on "Rules for Corporate Entry" (*Library Journal,* 1905) is especially valuable for its analysis of the problems.

Hanson's scholarship and the integrity of his character inspired respect; his kindliness, modesty, and generous spirit evoked the affection of his colleagues, staff, and students. His feeling for Luther College was strong. He was appointed to its Board of Trustees in 1920; in 1931 it bestowed on him the honorary LL.D. degree. In 1928 he was appointed Knight and Commander of the Order of Saint Olav by the Crown of Norway. Hanson died at Green Bay, Wisconsin, on November 8, 1943.

REFERENCES

The Hanson Festschrift issue of the *Library Quarterly* (1934) includes a chronological bibliography of Hanson's publications. The bibliography, with a continuation to May 1943, is also in Hanson's autobiography, *What Became of Jens?,* edited by Oivind M. Hovde (Luther College Press, 1974).

The largest collection of Hanson's papers is in the University of Chicago Libraries; a smaller collection of personal papers is in the Luther College Library, Decorah, Iowa.

The manuscript materials relating to Hanson's work at the Library of Congress are in the Library of Congress Archives. These sources, as well as secondary sources, are documented in Edith Scott, "J. C. M. Hanson and His Contribution to Twentieth-Century Cataloging" (Ph.D. dissertation, University of Chicago, 1970).

John Phillip Immroth, "Hanson, James Christian Meinich," *Dictionary of American Library Biography* (1978).

EDITH SCOTT
(d.1983)

Hasse, Adelaide
(1868–1953)

Indexer, writer, and bibliographer Adelaide Rosalie Hasse, during nearly 60 years in which she served in a variety of library and bibliographic positions, produced dozens of articles for the library and popular press as well as compiling a series of checklists and bibliographies that are unparalleled in their value and coverage.

Born in Milwaukee, Wisconsin, on September 13, 1868, she was raised in an environment shaped by individuals who challenged both her mind and her ability to do unusual things in an unusual way. Her father, Hermann Edward Hasse, was a well-known physician, surgeon, and botanist who, with other members of a distinguished family, created a noteworthy learning environment for his five children. There is no evidence that Adelaide attended any private schools or attained a college education, but from childhood she was educated to think, to examine, to challenge the obvious and the easy. As a result, she developed analytical skills and a critical acumen that played an important role in her library career.

When her family moved to the West Coast, Adelaide Hasse began her library career in 1889 under the leadership of a woman of unique character, Tessa L. Kelso, of the Los Angeles Public Library. At that time, there was no school of library science other than the prototype Dewey enterprise in New York; those who came to the field learned by example and by doing. Several decades later Hasse recalled Kelso's tremendous impact on her life as one "which gave point and direction to my natural bent." At the Los Angeles Public Library, Kelso asked her apprentice to organize the library's collection of U.S. government publications. Since there were few guidelines or procedures, Hasse applied her own logical approach, devised a classification scheme, and began a checklist of items. The success of her methods, especially in a field where so little was known, quickly came to the attention of persons in key positions in Washington, D.C. Because of the requirements of the Printing Act of January 12, 1895, an office had been organized that, among other responsibilities, was to prepare and print an index to government publications. As a result of her pioneer work in Los Angeles, Hasse was invited to serve in Washington as the first Librarian of the Office of the Superintendent of Documents.

Washington, D.C.: 1895–97. Hasse arrived in the capital in May 1895; the following year the first of her major bibliographies was published by the Government Printing Office. *The List of Publications of the U.S. Department of Agriculture* initiated a life as an indexer and bibliographer that was not concluded until Hasse, in her 80s, came out of retirement to help edit a microfilm publication of records of the United States.

Among her works are two remarkable indexes that are still key resources. The first, published in 13 volumes from 1907 to 1922, is the *Index of Economic*

Material in Documents of the States of the United States. Financed by the Carnegie Institution of Washington, it was, as R. R. Bowker noted in 1920, "a life work for any less persistent and industrious person." The second set, a three-volume *Index to United States Documents Relating to Foreign Affairs, 1828–1861,* was also funded by the Carnegie Institution and was published from 1914 to 1921.

Adelaide Hasse's arrival in Washington occasioned a burst of activity typical of her dedication and enthusiasm for her work. The duties of her position called for the collection of existing documents from all of the government departments and then for them to be organized and housed. She uncovered an amazing amount of material; in six weeks nearly 300,000 documents from all the government departments had been retrieved and roughly inventoried. Hasse's story of this experience, along with an autobiographical commentary on many aspects of her professional career, is contained in a privately published pamphlet, written in 1919, entitled *The Compensations of Librarianship.*

Although Hasse remained in Washington for only two years, 1895–97, her efforts there are especially recognized because she developed a classification for government documents. The scheme was expanded in the *Checklist of United States Public Documents, 1789–1909,* and served as the structural basis for the *Monthly Catalog.* Her organization of the Library of the Superintendent of Documents so impressed John Shaw Billings, Director of the New York Public Library, that she was offered a position "to build up what Dr. Billings wished to be a great document collection."

New York Public Library. Hasse's career in New York is divided into two distinct phases: (1) the period from 1897 until Billing's death in 1913, when she was able to develop a model public documents collection; and (2) the final six years during which, in her own eyes at least, her accomplishments and her position were destroyed. In both instances, the particular natures of her employers apparently were key factors.

John Shaw Billings was an outstanding librarian, even in an era of unusual library leaders; his vision and his administrative skills were instrumental in establishing the New York Public Library. In fact, only a man of his scholarship and achievements could have impressed Adelaide Hasse, who brought a special aptitude of her own to the library profession. Billings recognized her brilliance and dealt with her acerbic personality in such a way as to encourage and enhance her contributions. During the years of his administration, she was instrumental in building a collection of documents from an unorganized base of 10,000 items to nearly 300,000 catalogued volumes. Hasse's reputation as an expert on government publications was also evident in the contributions she made to the American Library Association; she served first as a member and later as Chair of the Committee on Public Documents, and she spoke and wrote often on the collection and administration of government publications. As life member number 779 of ALA, she regularly participated in conferences, was a member of the Committee on Library Schools, and was elected to ALA Council from 1908 through 1913.

In addition to her capable development of the documents collection, Hasse was also involved in serving the assorted publics of the Library. Her ability to retrieve specialized information from the vast resources of the government was extended to other databases as well. Since her perception of direct service to the business world predated that of many of her colleagues, Public Documents and then the Economics Division of the Library emerged as major service centers. During this productive period, the first decade of the 20th century, she also began a massive index of economic material and was able to uncover, during a trip to Europe, a copy of the "lost" *Bradford Journal,* which she later edited for publication.

Billings's death in 1913 marked the beginning of the end for much of Hasse's work in the New York Public Library, although six years elapsed before the Board of Trustees terminated her employment. The new director, E. H. Anderson, was not of the same mind and pursuits as his predecessor. Several personal and professional factors were involved, but before many months had passed, Hasse and Anderson were stubbornly set in a pattern of action and reaction that, given Anderson's power as Director, could only end in Hasse's removal. She made it clear that she considered Anderson incompetent and destructive of her work of 16 years; he, in turn, rallied the staff and the Board, charged her with insubordination, and asked for her resignation. Hasse refused and was fired in the fall of 1918.

The emotional character of the library conflict and the nature of the accusations leveled against Hasse, some of which involved rumors of pro-German sympathies in a traumatic war climate, might have debilitated a lesser personality. Hasse, however, was neither incapacitated nor silenced. *The Compensations of Librarianship* (1919) is a statement of professional interests, an accusatory and spirited explanation of the situation leading to her firing, and a credo of continuing dedication to library work. Moreover, she was able to provide positive evidence that the U.S. government perceived no treacherous tendencies, since she left New York in 1918, a few weeks after her termination, to work for the Department of State.

For the next 30 years, until she retired in 1941, Hasse was employed in a series of responsible positions in Washington including the War Labor Policies Board (1918–19), the War Industries Board (1919–21), the office of the Assistant Secretary of War (1921), the Brookings Institution (1923–32), the Works Progress Administration (1934–39), and the Temporary National Economics Committee (1939–41). After she retired, she continued to live in Washington until her death on July 29, 1953.

Appraisal. In reviewing Adelaide Hasse's long life, it is important to emphasize the amount of her publication, which includes nearly 24 monographs and some 50 articles. She was an incisive and perceptive commentator on numerous facets of library service as well as a compiler of excellent checklists and bibliographies, many of which identified difficult-to-locate government publications. Hasse was an early advocate of library service for special groups and, in Washington during the 1920s, helped to organize the local chapter of the Special Libraries Association, served as its first President, and edited the association journal, *Special Libraries*. She applied her expertise and organizational skill concerning government resources in her employment as a lecturer at George Washington University from 1933 to 1937 and, near the end of her career, at Catholic University.

Although Hasse's precise motivation and expectations cannot be interpreted exactly, it is well established that she had a confidence in the role of libraries and librarians that inspired a personal commitment that never waivered. Writing in the *New Republic* in January 1918, at a period in her life that for her was verging on the catastrophic, she posed the question to the library profession: "Why Not?" Hasse felt keenly the failure of the profession to function as a "public service organization." Yet, beneath the critical question there existed a sense of that which might be. She asked then, and throughout her career, regardless of consequences, "What is there so very incongruous about taking just one more step and by so doing galvanizing the present inert mass into a pulsating service plant?" Her life was an example of that one more step.

REFERENCE

Laurel A. Grotzinger, "Hasse, Adelaide Rosalie, *"Dictionary of American Library Biography* (1978).

LAUREL A. GROTZINGER

Henne, Frances E.
(1906–1985)

Frances Elizabeth Henne, library educator who inspired thousands of students, drew on her critical and incisive mind to create books, articles, and addresses dedicated to excellence in service to children and youth. Always willing to break with tradition, she saw beyond the usual patterns to seek new and innovative ways to make learning a joy to children and to those who work with them.

Born in Springfield, Illinois, on October 11, 1906, she received her B.A. (1929) and M.A. (1934) in English from the University of Illinois, a B.S. from the School of Library Service, Columbia University (1935), and her Ph.D. from the University of Chicago Graduate Library School (1949). In 1942 she became the first woman appointed to the faculty of the Graduate Library School at the University of Chicago; from 1947 to 1950 she was Associate Dean and Dean of Students; and in 1951–52 she was Acting Dean. In 1954 she moved to the School of Library Service at Columbia.

While at the University of Chicago, Henne established the Center for Children's Books and its *Bulletin*. Her innovation was bringing children's books into one place for analysis and then producing a reviewing medium that related books to curriculum. It included reviews of books that were not recommended. *Time* magazine (May 5, 1952), describing the Center for Children's Books as unique in U.S. education, reported that she was worried that "there was no place where all books for children were being examined and reported on." Henne brought her concern to the attention of Robert M. Hutchins, then head of the University of Chicago, telling him that her juvenile books were just as important as his Great Books. The Center still contributes to education

through its analysis of children's materials.

Book Selection and Evaluation Centers, including the Children's Book Council, were recipients of Henne's strong support and leadership. She acted as an adviser (1968–73) to the Educational Media Selection Centers Project, a joint program of the U.S. Office of Education and the National Book Committee. She established the annual Book Discussion Days at Columbia's School of Library Service, which served to influence similar activities elsewhere in the country; they offer opportunities for librarians to discuss children's books and to share their interpretations with others. In these ways her work continues to reach out to help bring children and books together.

Henne always grasped the significance of professional organizations and understood the internal dynamics of organizational life. She helped to found the American Association of School Librarians (AASL) and to define the role it could play in the lives of school librarians and in the lives of those they serve. As President of AASL (1948–49), she continued and expanded her influence. As a member of the School Library Standards Committee that prepared *School Libraries for Today and Tomorrow: Functions and Standards* (ALA, 1945) and Chairperson of the committee that prepared *Standards for School Library Programs* (ALA, 1960) and of the joint committee of AASL and the Department of Audio-Visual Instruction (DAVI) of the National Education Association that issued *Standards for School Media Programs* (ALA, 1969), Henne was a leading force in establishing criteria for excellence in school library programs in the United States.

Her research on school libraries in the U.S. contributed to the production of standards that formed the basis for most state evaluation programs in these and subsequent years. Very early Henne recognized the significance of nonprint media and the necessity to include all media in school library collections. She wrote prolifically on the role of standards in schooling and exerted influence far beyond what is usual for school librarianship with her coverage in national professional journals. Her special and unique contribution, however, was her ability to see the need for cooperative arrangements among all the institutions working with children and youth. She was the driving force, using the *Standards,* to forge the links of relationship with the Association for Educational Communications and Technology (AECT, then DAVI) and to win the recognition and support of many other national associations devoted to work with children and youth. She helped in the development of standards for school libraries for the deaf and aided individual states in their development of standards and guidelines. Her consistent belief in and championing of standards for school library media centers as a means to provide excellence in education was the most extraordinary achievement of her career; personal sacrifices and bitter attacks for her beliefs and vision never stopped her in her determination to make standards in school media programs critical to professional practice.

Henne served as a member of the Knapp School Library Development Project Advisory Board (1960–62) and was a member of the New York State Regents Advisory Council on Libraries (1965–74). She also served the U.S. Office of Education innumerable

ALA

Frances E. Henne

times as evaluator and consultant. She spoke to the profession not only through her lucid writing but also in speeches before professional meetings. She called all to follow her to the high path of quality, eschewing the path of mediocrity. The philosophy she set forth in *Youth Communication and Libraries* (ALA, 1949) was only a herald of what she was to continue to achieve in the years that followed.

Winner of the prestigious ALA Joseph W. Lippincott Award in 1963, an Honorary Citation during the Centennial of ALA (1976), and the Beta Phi Mu Award in 1978, Henne received many other national and regional awards for her outstanding scholarship and her contributions to work with children and youth. AASL gave her its President's Award in 1979 for her consistent and continuing efforts on behalf of children and schooling.

Henne recognized early in her career that the formal study of materials for children and youth is a scholarly discipline. Always a believer in interdisciplinary programs and ever hopeful of establishing a National Institute of Research on Children and Youth, she worked diligently to foster these goals. As a teacher she developed courses that met the vision and ideals she set forth. She taught one of the first courses in the history of children's literature and designed a course in the sociology of reading of children and youth. An avid book collector, particularly in the field of children's books, Henne gave her collections to the Special Collections Department of the Columbia University Libraries (the Henne Collection).

Henne retired in June 1975 after 21 years at Columbia's School of Library Service. She died in Greenfield, Massachusetts, December 21, 1985.

A Festschrift, *Frontiers of Library Service for Youth* (Columbia University, 1979), completed by some of her students, contains their tribute to her through a continuation of her ideas and ideals and includes a bibliography of her publications.

In 1947 Henne wrote, "we must provide also the ideals, the force, the zeal, the spirit, the hard work, and yes, the toughness, that form the dynamics which turn visions and plans into workable realities."

JANE ANNE HANNIGAN

Henriot, Gabriel
(1880–1965)

Gabriel Henriot, French archivist and librarian and pioneer in library professional education, was a leader in international library cooperation and became known as the "spiritual father" of the International Federation of Library Associations (IFLA).

Henriot was born on January 18, 1880, in the Bellevue district of Paris. His grandfather was a peasant from Lorraine in the region of Domremy; his father worked for the Paris-Lyons-Mediterranean railway. The family moved to the Boulevard de Picpus shortly after the boy's birth, and he never moved from the Faubourg Saint-Antoine. He was enrolled in the neighborhood nursery school, then the communal primary school. A brilliant student singled out by his teachers, he easily obtained a scholarship to continue his studies at the Lycée Charlemagne. He then entered the École des Chartes (the national school for

Gabriel Henriot

archivists) and at the same time attended classes at the École des Hautes Études. Thus he earned an advanced university degree (diplôme d'études supérieure) as well as an archivist's certificate (diplôme d'archiviste-paléographe).

In 1905 Henriot was named Librarian of the Historical Library of the City of Paris (Bibliothèque Historique de la Ville de Paris). He began working with Georges Bourgin on an edition of the proceedings of the Commune of 1871 (*Procès verbaux de la Commune de 1871*). World War I delayed the work, which was issued in parts beginning in 1924. Henriot, who had received officer training in 1901–02, was called to serve in the army in August 1914. He joined the 367th Infantry Regiment at Toul and fought for 52 months in dangerous posts (including Bois le Prêtre near Verdun, Alsace, and Picardy) without a single wound and without a day of sick leave. He became a major, with five citations and the Croix de Guerre, by the time of the Armistice. On his return to civilian life in 1920 he was named Director (*Conservateur*) at the Forney Library, a collection devoted to industrial design, arts, crafts, and related subjects. Henriot remained in this position until the general mobilization in September 1939.

The situation in the Forney Library was hardly brilliant. Since its foundation in 1886, the Library had functioned in antiquated quarters annexed to a school. Henriot refused to be discouraged by the material conditions of the Library and decided to make the Forney collection not just a resource for the artisans of the neighborhood but an arts and crafts institution for all of Paris.

At great personal effort, Henriot was able to carry out many kinds of activities with minimal funding. He opened the Library ten and a half hours a day, Monday through Saturday, and on Sunday morning. He put the telephone at the disposition of the readers. He published many reader aids; worked closely with vocational schools; participated in exhibits; and created the Society of Friends of the Library, interesting many noted individuals in the life of Forney.

Henriot preached by example, writing in journals (*Mobilier et decoration*) and publishing books (on furniture, wrought iron work, lighting, and wood carving) that were useful to those involved in contemporary arts and crafts. He also published a very beautiful book that captured the spirit of the Faubourg Saint-Antoine, where a hard-working population of artisans lovingly crafted the objects of daily life.

To carry out his innovative program, Henriot needed people, but library education was not organized in France until long after World War I. An archivist by training, he turned first to the École des Chartes. Elected President of its alumni society (1923), he unsuccessfully tried to persuade the group to promote library training. Henriot then approached the Association des Bibliothécaires Français (ABF, the French library association). First elected to the Executive Committee in 1923, Henriot was President from 1925 to 1927. During the first weeks of his presidency, he launched a survey of municipal libraries that became the basis for a report he drafted for the Minister of Public Instruction. His 1926 report was followed by a table with salaries for a proposed national corps of librarians. Published and discussed, that report finally began to bear fruit when Julien Cain became Director of the Bibliothèque Nationale.

Facing obstacles to the realization of the reforms he had specified, Henriot proposed using examples from abroad to make the French administration realize the importance of such changes. He made contact with the International Institute of Intellectual Cooperation and in 1924 undertook a survey of national library associations sponsored by ABF. At the International Congress of Librarians and Booklovers held in Prague in 1926, Henriot presented the proposal that led to the creation of a standing international library committee to serve as a liaison among library associations. Welcomed with enthusiasm, this initiative laid the foundations for IFLA. Three years later, at the first World Congress of Librarianship and Bibliography in Rome, IFLA became a reality.

Named President of the 11th section of IFLA in 1929, Henriot was charged with the task of drawing up a report on training and on library education. He took part in the IFLA Congress in Madrid in 1935, but three years earlier at the Berne Conference he had offered his resignation because of the neglect of professional education in France and because he believed that IFLA was more concerned with research libraries than with libraries for everyone. The latter were Henriot's chief preoccupation.

From 1924 on, at the same time that he was most active on the international level, Henriot also directed his efforts toward developing a specialty in library education. He in fact became an internationally known expert in this area. A meeting in Prague with Mary Parsons proved decisive for him. Parsons was the chief aide to Sarah Bogle, the Assistant Secretary of the American Library Association, who had been sent to Paris to organize a school for librarians. The school was funded for two years by the American Committee for Devastated France, a war relief agency that had set up small public libraries in Aisne and Paris. Bogle wished to adapt the American library school program to French needs. While the courses on cataloguing and classification were entrusted to Margaret Mann, then Vice-President of ALA, part of the training was delegated to French librarians such as Ernest Coyecque, Eugène Morel, and, of course, Henriot. He was entrusted with a course that covered the history of books and printing, book selection, and work with children. Henriot subsequently became chief French adviser to the school.

At the end of the second full-year course in 1926, Henriot persuaded his U.S. friends that the school should be continued. He cautioned: "If one abruptly withdraws the school's budget, it will be the end of the work for modern libraries. The Paris Library School and the libraries created through your aid will be a lost effort, without future." The school was to last for another three years. In all, 201 students from 25 countries enrolled in its program.

The Paris Library School had scarcely closed its doors when Henriot, with his characteristic tenacity, opened a municipal school for librarians. Because the national government had turned a deaf ear to his pleas, he cast his lot with the city of Paris.

In 1931 Henriot was named Inspector of Libraries for the city of Paris and the *département* of the Seine. During his inspection tours, he became aware of the urgent need to provide professional training for the haphazardly recruited, poorly paid personnel, most of whom only barely grasped the most elementary rudiments of librarianship. The new municipal library school that he created functioned for five years with no budget and without any quarters other than the reading room of the Forney Library. Classroom instruction, limited to just 24 hours, was complemented by practice work, visits to libraries, and short internships. The school was free and open not just to the municipal library staff but to anyone who wished to create popular libraries. The 200 students who benefited from this training were drawn from Paris and the provinces and from both the public and the private sector. The city, however, was indifferent to the effort. In December 1936, after failing to obtain for the instructors the modest salaries the city had promised them, Henriot decided to give up the school. A new possibility was then offered to him.

The Ligue féminine d'action catholique (Women's Catholic Action League) provided a grant enabling Henriot to create a library school at the private Institut Catholique. Although Henriot had long hoped for a national library school, he accepted the League's offer. He then set up a program of study that lasted two years and included practice work as well as a number of short internships and visits to institutions. After his second demobilization and his retirement from the Forney Library in 1940, Henriot devoted himself to teaching and to directing the school. When he died in Paris on April 21, 1965, the school had already trained 717 students from 45 countries. The creation of a national graduate library school did not overshadow the unique training program created by Henriot and adapted by his former students to meet the exigencies of modern librarianship.

COLETTE MEUVRET JACQUELINE VIAUX

Hewins, Caroline M.
(1846–1926)

Caroline Maria Hewins was a pioneer in children's library work and, for 50 years, Librarian of the Hartford (Connecticut) Public Library.

She was born October 10, 1846, in Roxbury, Massachusetts. Her paternal forebears had sailed from England to Sharon, Massachusetts, in 1656. Her father was a well-to-do Boston haberdasher. In her infancy the family moved to Jamaica Plain, and when she was seven to West Roxbury, where they occupied a five-acre estate, ample for their nine children, of whom she was the oldest.

A precocious, bookish child, Hewins was reading by the age of four and later enjoyed reading and telling stories to her younger sisters and brother. These experiences, which inculcated a life-long love of children's books, were described in her memoir, *A Mid-Century Child and Her Books* (1926). Education at home and at private schools was followed by Eliot High School in Jamaica Plain and then the Girls' High and Normal School of Boston, which prepared her for teaching.

While at Normal School Hewins was much impressed with the Boston Athenaeum, where she was required to do some research. Upon graduation she

ALA

Caroline M. Hewins

arranged to work at that library in 1866 and 1867 under the guidance of its famous Librarian, William Frederick Poole. For a number of years thereafter she taught in private schools in the Boston area and took courses at Boston University.

In 1875, learning that the Young Men's Institute of Hartford, Connecticut, needed a librarian, she applied and was accepted. The Institute, a subscription library, served a membership of about 600 with a collection of some 20,000 volumes. It was absorbed by the older Hartford Library Association in 1878. Though few children used the library, Hewins sought by means of extensive discarding of objectionable books and purchase of desirable titles to improve the children's collection and raise reading standards. Without neglecting her other duties she became a pioneering specialist in work with children. An innovative admiminstrator, she instituted many programs that later became standard practice in youth libraries, including clubs, book talks, storytelling, nature walks, a doll collection, and dramatics. She used the children's own book reviews as guides to book selection.

Membership in the library was opened to the schools; reading lists were provided for teachers; and eventually classroom libraries were sent out, making the Hartford Library a leader in the movement for cooperation between public and school libraries. A concern for disadvantaged youth led her to live for 12 years at the North Street Settlement House, where she founded a drama club and a branch library. On her frequent trips abroad Hewins wrote letters to her young patrons that were published in the *Hartford Courant* and later were published as a book, *A Traveller's Letters to Boys and Girls* (1923). Despite her prominence in the growing field of children's libraries, she was not able to persuade the trustees to establish a separate children's room until 1904, followed in 1907 by the appointment of a full-time children's librarian.

Hewins was nationally recognized as an authority on the selection of books for children. She started the quarterly *Bulletin of the Hartford Library Association,* primarily to list new acquisitions and including perhaps the first selected lists of children's books. These led in 1882 to the publication by Frederick Leypoldt of *Publishers' Weekly* of her *Books for the Young: A Guide for Parents and Children* (reprinted 1884) and later by the American Library Association of her *Books for Boys and Girls: A Selected List* (1897, rev. 1904, 1915). In these lists and elsewhere she expressed her philosophy of book selection for children. Her emphasis was heavily on the classics; modern books had to meet her exacting standards, and "series" books were rejected. She deplored an apparent tendency to denigrate the bookish child.

Although Hewins is remembered as a children's librarian, she also capably ran a growing city library. The Hartford Library Association became a free library in 1892 and the following year adopted the name of Hartford Public Library. By 1925, the last year of her administration, it had a collection of 150,000 volumes in the main library, branches, and deposit stations.

A founder in 1891 of the Connecticut Library Association, she served as President, 1912–13, and was also prominent in the Hartford Librarians' Club.

In 1893 she was largely responsible for establishing the Connecticut Public Library Committee, for which she served as volunteer Executive Secretary and "library visitor" for many years. The Educational Association, later the Parent Teachers Association, occupied her organizational abilities in 1897. She lectured at library schools and educational workshops and taught children's literature to Hartford teachers and librarians.

Hewins probably joined the American Library Association at its third Conference in Boston in 1879. Recorded as the first woman to speak from the floor of an ALA Conference, she subsequently read many papers at those meetings. She was a Councilor from 1885 to 1888 and again from 1893 to 1902 and Vice-President in 1891. In 1897 she was one of two women in the American delegation who read papers at the second International Conference of Librarians in London; she spoke on children's books as seen by children themselves. A meeting of children's librarians that she called at the Montreal Conference of ALA in 1900 resulted ultimately in the establishment of its Children's Section. Hewins published extensively in library and educational periodicals, with well over half her writings on children's library work.

In 1911 Trinity College of Hartford awarded her an honorary Master's degree, the first woman to be so honored by this men's college. On February 15, 1926, at a celebration of her 50 years of service, the Hartford Librarians' Club gave her funds to establish the Caroline M. Hewins Scholarship Fund for Children's Librarians. During the same year, though retired, she remained active at the Library until she died in Hartford on November 4 after a brief illness.

Cheerful, energetic, intelligent, and capable, she had been one of the most eloquent supporters of the public library movement, particularly as it contributed toward a fuller life for children, and an exemplar of the increasing role of women in the professions. Her collection of children's books is now in the Connecticut Historical Society. The Caroline M. Hewins Lectureship, an annual presentation at New England Library Association meetings, was established by Frederick G. Melcher in 1946. When ALA celebrated its 75th anniversary, Hewins was one of 40 persons named to the "Library Hall of Fame."

REFERENCES
Jennie D. Lindquist, "Caroline Maria Hewins," in *Notable American Women, 1607–1950* (1971).
Mary E. Root, "Caroline Maria Hewins," in *Pioneering Leaders in Librarianship,* edited by Emily M. Danton (1953).
Budd L. Gambee, "Hewins, Caroline Maria," *Dictionary of American Library Biography* (1978).

BUDD L. GAMBEE

Holley, Edward G.
(1927-)

Edward Gailon Holley contributed to the library profession as a scholar, university library administrator, and library school dean, and as President of the American Library Association.

He was born on November 26, 1927, in Pulaski (Giles County), Tennessee. His close contact with li-

State University of New York
Edward G. Holley

braries began when he started working at the local public library on Sunday afternoons during high school. It continued at David Lipscomb College, where he worked as a library assistant. Indeed, Holley became de facto Librarian during his senior year, when there was no regular librarian. After his graduation in 1949 (B.A. in English, magna cum laude) Holley was persuaded by the Dean to stay on as Librarian. He also attended George Peabody College, where he earned a Master's in Library Science and English in 1951.

Holley then went on to the University of Illinois at Urbana-Champaign to a professional position at the Photo Reproduction Library and to begin work on a library science doctorate. From 1953 to 1956 he was called into active service from the U.S. Naval Reserve. Upon his return he served as a Graduate Assistant in the University of Illinois Library Science Library, 1956–57, and as Librarian of the Education, Philosophy, and Psychology Library from 1957 to 1962.

He was awarded the Ph.D. in Library Science at Illinois in 1961; his dissertation, *Charles Evans: American Bibliographer,* was published by the University of Illinois Press in 1963 and won the Scarecrow Press Award for Library Literature the same year.

From 1962 through 1971 Holley served as Director of Libraries at the University of Houston. During his tenure 126,000 sq.ft. were added to the existing 93,000 sq.ft. of library space and the collection grew from 300,000 to 665,000 volumes, with more than double the number of periodical subscriptions.

From January 1972 to July 1985 Holley was Dean and Professor at the School of Library Science of the University of North Carolina, where he strengthened the faculty with many outstanding appointments and inaugurated a doctoral program. He remained on the faculty after his resignation as Dean.

His numerous activities included Chairperson of the U.S. Office of Education's Advisory Council on College Library Resources (1969–71); Editor for the Association of College and Research Libraries Publications in Librarianship Series (1969–72); President of the Texas Library Association (1971); Chairperson of the ALA Publishing Board (1972–73); and President of ALA (1975–76).

Holley became a member of Beta Phi Mu and in 1971 received a Council on Library Resouces Fellowship, during which he made a study of urban university libraries in the United States. Among his works are *Raking the Historical Coals: The ALA Scrapbook of*

1876 (1967), *Resources of Texas Libraries* (with Donald Hendricks, 1968), and many articles on academic libraries, copyright issues, and other topics. He contributed "ALA at 100" to *The ALA Yearbook* (1976).

He was a major contributor to, and member of the Advisory Board for, the *Dictionary of American Library Biography* (1978).

In 1983 he was awarded the Melvil Dewey Medal by ALA. The citation paid tribute to his inspiring lifetime commitment to the education of librarians, to his distinguished service on numerous professional organizations, to his prolific contributions to library literature, and to his creative leadership in state, national, and international library organizations.

GEORGE S. BOBINSKI

Honduras

Honduras, a republic in Central America, is bounded by the Caribbean Sea on the north, Nicaragua on the east and south, El Salvador on the south and west, and Guatemala on the west. Population (1984 est.) 4,135,000; area 112,088 sq.km. The official language is Spanish.

National Library. Most of the major libraries in the country are government libraries. The Biblioteca Nacional de Honduras is in the capital city, Tegucigalpa. Founded in 1880, it has holdings of about 55,000 volumes. It shares with other libraries the legal deposit of three copies of each book published in Honduras, but enforcement of the law is not rigorous. From 1961 the National Library published an *Anuario Bibliografico Hondureno.*

Academic Libraries. In higher education, the library of the Universidad Nacional Autónoma de Honduras (founded 1847) has shown significant progress. The library has grown from 25,000 volumes early in the 1970s to 110,000 volumes, with 500 current periodicals, 2,000 dissertations, 1,000 microfilms, and 3,000 government documents. Its staff performs centralized cataloguing and other services for the University's two branch campus libraries as well as for the National Medical Library and its branch library, which are part of the University.

Public Libraries. Although 32 public libraries with a total holding of 50,000 volumes were reported in the early 1970s, some of these may in fact have been primary school libraries. The largest public library is the Romulo E. Durón in Tegucigalpa, with 20,000 volumes. However, the illiteracy rate is about

Libraries in Honduras (1977)

Type	Administrative units	Service points	Volumes in collections	Annual expenditures (lempira)	Population served[a]	Professional staff	Total staff
National	--	--	--	--	--	--	--
Academic	1	6	82,000	346,000	7,849	9	57
Public	--	--	--	--	--	--	--
School	--	--	--	--	--	--	--

[a]Registered borrowers.

Source: Unesco, *Statistical Yearbook,* 1984.

50 percent and the condition of public libraries is poor.

School Libraries. In the area of primary school libraries, Honduras showed its greatest initiative. In 1967 the government began the School Library Pilot Project in cooperation with Unesco. Under the direction of a librarian, the program was designed, among other things, to teach students the use of various kinds of library materials and to provide communities with public library facilities where none existed. The project was planned to have two stages. The first, from 1968 to 1972, was under the direction of Unesco, which provided extensive technical assistance. Schools were divided into four categories, depending on enrollment. Twenty-three libraries were opened before 1970. The second stage, beginning in 1973, was directed by the Ministry of Education. Unesco ended its participation in the project at the close of the first stage. After that, progress was slow.

Special Libraries. The government also maintains several special libraries, each with a collection of a few thousand volumes, emphasizing archaeology, art, law, administration, and the humanities.

The Profession. The Association of Librarians and Archivists has its headquarters in Tegucigalpa. It sponsors courses for its 53 members and seeks ways to improve organization and service in Honduran libraries. It also publishes the monthly *Catalogo de Prestamo* and keeps a small library of its own. It is affiliated with ACURIL.

Cooperation with librarians from other countries has centered mainly in the Primary School Pilot Project. Librarians from the National University have participated in the Consejo Superior Universitario Centroamericano, a group made up of other national universities in Central America and designed to promote cooperation among them.

Overall, libraries in Honduras, where the system for publishing and distributing books is antiquated, and the political climate often stifled unapproved ideas, have been few, small, and poorly financed. They also lack professional staff. There has been little coordination among libraries, and librarians have not been well organized.

DANIEL W. BARTHELL*

Multilevel Hong Kong Polytechnic Library, one of Hong Kong's three major academic libraries.

Hong Kong Polytechnic

Hong Kong

Hong Kong, a British Dependent Territory off the southern coast of China, comprises Hong Kong Island and islets nearby; Kowloon Peninsula; and the mainland areas of the New Territories. Population (1984 est.) 5,394,000; area 1,060 sq.km. The official languages are English and Chinese.

More than 560 libraries serve Hong Kong. A comprehensive survey of library and information services in Hong Kong carried out in 1983 enumerated 97 libraries open to the general public and children, 56 government department and British Armed Forces libraries, 307 school libraries, 30 postsecondary and university libraries, 66 special libraries, and 5 club, society, and private libraries.

History. The beginnings of the library history of Hong Kong can be traced to a collection of books started at the English Factory in Canton in 1806. It later became part of the Morrison Education Society Library, which moved to Macao and then to Hong Kong in 1842.

National Services. Hong Kong has no national library or national bibliographical center. The Cultural Services Department of the Urban Services Department of the Hong Kong Government serves part of the functions of a national library in that it administers the Hong Kong Book Registration Ordinance. Under this Ordinance, publishers and printers submit five copies of every title published and printed locally to the Cultural Services Department of the Urban Services Department. Based on those deposits, *A Catalogue of Books Printed in Hong Kong* is issued quarterly.

The Public Records Office has the largest collection of official documents. From 1972 that office collected old documents and records from a number of the Government departments, some dating back to 1844.

Academic Libraries. The libraries of the University of Hong Kong, the Chinese University of Hong Kong, and the Hong Kong Polythechnic are the major academic libraries. Other academic libraries include those of the Baptist College, Lingnan College, and Shue Yan College. The new Hong Kong City Polytechnic had just begun to plan for a library in 1984. The collections at the universities each exceeded about 750,000 volumes. The University of Hong Kong Libraries system is the oldest (established in 1912) and the most comprehensive library system in Hong Kong. Online cataloguing is done at the University of Hong Kong Libraries. The three large academic libraries share the MARC database maintained at the University of Hong Kong. They also provide information retrieval services using DIALOG and SDC.

Public Libraries. The two public library systems of the Urban Council and Urban Services Department serve the general public of the urban and rural areas. The City Hall Library, opened in March 1962, is the headquarters of the Urban Council Libraries. As of March 1983, the whole network of Urban Council Libraries comprised 18 libraries (including two mobile libraries) with a total of 1,200,000 volumes. The system administered by the Cultural Services Department of the Urban Services Department comprised 12 libraries (including one mobile library) with a total of 430,000 volumes. There are plans to continue opening more branch libraries in both systems.

School Libraries. School library service improved a great deal during the decade 1976–85. More than 250 schools now employ teacher-librarians trained by the Education Department of the Hong Kong Government. Class libraries are provided for many primary schools by this Department.

Special Libraries. Many Government department libraries are specialized and serve primarily the staffs of their own departments. The Hong Kong Productivity Centre, Hong Kong Trade Development Council, Federation of Hong Kong Industries, Hong Kong Management Associations, and Hong Kong Tourist Association, among others, maintain libraries and information services to serve the commercial and industry sectors. In addition, there are several medical libraries in hospitals and other special libraries in some business firms, factories, and learned societies.

The Profession. Approximately 150 professional librarians worked in the Hong Kong libraries in the mid-1980s. From 1981 the Department of Extramural Studies of the University of Hong Kong and the Hong Kong Library Association jointly offered a three-year part-time Diploma Course in Librarianship aimed at the graduate professional level. Established in 1958, the Hong Kong Library Association had a membership of 336 in 1983, including five categories: personal, student, corresponding, institutional, and honorary. The Association publishes a *Journal* and a *Newsletter*.

REFERENCE

Hong Kong Library Association, *Directory of Special Libraries in Hong Kong* (1983).

KAN LAI-BING

Honoré, Suzanne
(1909-)

During more than four decades of service at the Bibliothèque Nationale, Suzanne Duvergé Honoré became known both in France and abroad as a specialist in cataloguing and government publications. In addition to her administrative responsibilities at the national library, she continued her early interest in historical research, contributed to the standardization of French cataloguing practices, and promoted the international exchange of bibliographic data through her work in the International Federation of Library Associations (IFLA). She also played a key role in the Association des Bibliothécaires Français (ABF, the French library association) and served for 15 years as Secretary-General of the Syndicat des Bibliothécaires, the librarians' union.

Born on July 13, 1909, in Oloron-Sainte-Marie in southwestern France, Suzanne Duvergé grew up in a household where her interest in reading and travel were encouraged. Her father was a professor of mathematics. She took a degree in history from the University of Bordeaux and entered the École des Chartes in Paris, where she received training as an archivist-palaeographer. She graduated in 1932 as valedictorian of her class—a distinction that entitled her to a place at the École française de Rome, a French institute for advanced research in medieval history.

She remained in Rome from 1932 to 1934, when she was appointed to the École des hautes études hispaniques in Madrid. There she continued scholarly work in medieval Spanish history. After two years in Madrid, she married Pierre Honoré, a French sculptor. They had three sons: Michel, Georges, and Olivier.

In 1936 she began her career at the Bibliothèque Nationale as a library assistant (auxiliaire). She was named Librarian (Bibliothécaire) six years later and subsequently served in the department of printed books and the department of official publications. In 1962 she prepared a comparative study of official publications from the perspective of their use in public relations. Her report on that topic was presented at the Congrès international des sciences administratives in 1962 and was published the following year. In 1963 Honoré became head of the department of international exchanges, which was reorganized and installed in new quarters under her direction. She left that post in 1967 to take charge of the Département des Entrées, the unit responsible for copyright deposit, the acquisition of books, and cataloguing.

In 1964 she was elected President of the ABF, the second woman to hold that office. She provided leadership at a time when the Association's statutes were being revised, and she was subsequently elected to the presidency for a second term, which expired in 1969.

In 1961 she participated in the International Conference on Cataloguing Principles held in Paris. She also took part in a second international cataloguing conference held in Copenhagen in 1969 under the sponsorship of IFLA and Unesco. Later she served as President of the Cataloguing Committee of the Association Française de Normalisation (AFNOR, the French national standards association) and participated in many meetings of the committee on documentation of the International Standards Organization (ISO). She was also active in other international bodies, serving as a member of the consultative committee of the International Office for Universal Bibliographic Control and also as Vice-President of the Association for International Libraries.

Honoré published about 35 articles and reports, ranging from scholarly studies in medieval history to the *International List of Approved Forms for Catalogue Entries of Names of States* (Unesco, 1964). She also taught cataloguing at the École des Chartes and gave courses on bibliography and on international library cooperation at the École Nationale Supérieure des Bibliothèques (the national library school).

Honoré retired from the Bibliothèque Nationale in 1978. In recognition of her many contributions, she was named to the Legion of Honor and later elevated to the rank of officer.

MARY NILES MAACK

Suzanne Hornoré

Hookway, Sir Harry
(1921-)

In 1972 Parliament passed the British Library Act, which led to the establishment of the British Library in the following year. Prior to that time the national library of the United Kingdom was the British Museum Library, which was to form the centerpiece of

Courtesy of the British Library
Sir Harry Hookway

the new British Library, together with the addition of the National Lending Library for Science and Technology, the National Central Library, and the *British National Bibliography*. The first Deputy Chairman and Chief Executive of the British Library was Harry Thurston Hookway, who occupied this signally important position from 1973 until he retired in 1984.

Hookway came to library organization rather late in life. Born in London on July 23, 1921, he obtained his B.Sc. (1941) and Ph.D. (1943) degrees from the University of London. From 1941 to 1949 he occupied several posts in industry, but from 1949 to 1965 he was with the Department of Scientific and Industrial Research (DSIR). From 1960 to 1964 he was seconded from the DSIR to direct the UK Scientific Mission (North America); during this time he was also Scientific Attaché at the British Embassy in Washington, D.C., and Scientific Adviser to the UK High Commission in Ottawa. In 1964 he returned to the DSIR and was Head of its Information Division in 1964–65. From 1966 to 1969 he was Chief Scientific Officer at the Department of Education and Science, becoming Assistant Under Secretary of State in that Department from 1969 to 1973.

The British Library was in gestation at that time, and Hookway formed an excellent working relationship with Lord Eccles, then the Minister responsible for Arts and Libraries. Hookway steeped himself in the history and problems of library organization in the United Kingdom, and with Lord Eccles he played an important role in preparing and steering through the legislation that led to the establishment of the British Library. He was careful to involve the Library Association, the National Central Library, and other interested bodies throughout this planning stage, giving them information on the broad intentions and allowing them to put forward their views to the Minister responsible.

Although British librarians had naturally hoped that the first Chief Executive of the British Library would be a professional librarian, it came as no real surprise when Harry Hookway was named for the post. From the outset he cooperated closely with professional librarians and was accepted by them. Some preparatory work on the formation of the British Library had been carried out in advance of the official starting date of July 1, 1973, including the transfer of staff and stock from the National Central Library in London to the premises occupied by the National Lending Library for Science and Technology at Boston Spa in Yorkshire to form the British Library Lending Division (BLLD). But Hookway still had many difficult tasks facing him. He had to weld together personnel of varied experience, disciplines, and levels; in 1974 he had to arrange the formal inclusion of the *British National Bibliography* into the British Library organization; and he had to ensure that the British Library had a vigorous public relations policy so that people were kept fully informed about the problems and progress of Britain's national library. All this he did with conspicuous success.

But mostly he was concerned with the future of the British Library, and particularly with the provision of the much-needed new building in London to accommodate the Reference Division and the Central Administration. Thanks to the persistence of Hook-

way and the members of his Board, the government finally agreed that a new building would be erectd on a site in the Euston Road next to St. Pancras railway station. Work began in 1982 but the date of completion could not be forecast in the mid-1980s because it was scheduled to be built in stages.

Hookway did much to further the cause of British librarianship. He chaired the Unesco Advisory Committee for Documentation, Libraries, and Archives, and from 1982 served as Chairman of the British Council Libraries Advisory Committee. He was Chairman of the Conference of Directors of National Libraries and a member of IFLA's Programme Management Committee. In 1984 he was awarded the IFLA Gold Medal.

He became an Honorary Fellow of the Institute of Information Scientists and was its President from 1973 to 1976. In 1982 he was made an Honorary Fellow of the Library Association and was its President in 1985. Meanwhile, in 1978, he was knighted by Queen Elizabeth II.

Hookway received honorary degrees from the Universities of Sheffield and Loughborough, and after his retirement from the British Library in 1983 he became Chairman of Publishers' Data Bases Ltd., a member of the Court and Common Council of Loughborough University, a Governor of Birkbeck College, and Vice-President of the National Book League.

K. C. HARRISON

Humphreys, K. W.
(1916–   )

Kenneth William Humphreys, British university librarian and paleographer, became a major figure in the provision and development of academic library and information services, both nationally and internationally, in the years after 1950.

Humphreys was born in Oxford on December 4, 1916. Obliged by family circumstances to leave school at 16, he became a junior library clerk in the Codrington Library, All Souls College, Oxford, in 1933. Three years later he joined the Bodleian Law Library as a member of "Extra Staff," an appointment which entailed some duties in the Bodleian Library itself. Studying in his free time, he obtained a B.A. degree in 1938 and was appointed an Assistant on the permanent staff of the Bodleian in the same year. With an interruption for war service in the army, he remained at the Bodleian until 1950, when he became Deputy Librarian at the Brotherton Library, University of Leeds. After only two years, Humphreys was appointed Librarian at the University of Birmingham, where he was to emerge as one of the leading librarians of his time.

In 1952 Humphreys inherited a library of 330,000 volumes housed in cramped conditions in elderly buildings and, as was the University itself, split between two sites some three miles apart. By the time he left Birmingham, the University had effectively been consolidated on one campus and the Library had grown to nearly a million volumes housed in new or completely refurbished accommodation. With its emphasis on open access for readers, full air-conditioning, and provision for a large bindery, the new building (opened in 1959) influenced subsequent university library planning in many parts of Europe; an extension was completed in 1970. A new Medical Library was also opened in 1959 and, in 1960, the Law Library was moved into the converted and renovated space formerly occupied by the Science Library.

By judicious purchases and by attracting gifts, Humphreys much improved the research capability of the bookstock. Attention was paid to official publications, older material was regularly acquired, and some valuable presentations were received, such as a collection of most of the books printed by Baskerville. The Library's status as a source of research material was enormously enhanced by the deposit of important literary and political manuscripts, the Brett Young, Galsworthy, and Harriet Martineau collections, and the papers of the Earl of Avon (Sir Anthony Eden) and the Chamberlains. At the same time, undergraduate services were improved by the introduction of a short loan collection and the duplication of titles in heavy demand.

Between 1967 and 1969 he established a small automation team; in collaboration with Birmingham's other university library at the University of Aston and with Birmingham Public Libraries, investigations were started into the cooperative use of tapes produced by the Library of Congress and the British National Bibliography (BNB), and the creation of a common machine-readable catalogue. From those beginnings, the Birmingham Libraries Cooperative Mechanization Project (BLCMP) evolved, financed by a government grant from the Office of Scientific and Technical Information (OSTI) and directed by committees representing the three libraries. BLCMP rapidly assumed national importance as other libraries became interested in its research; government financial support was extended, and there was increased collaboration with the BNB and, later, the British Library. The Project produced its first machine-generated catalogue in July 1973.

In 1975 Humphreys was appointed Librarian of the new European University Institute at Florence, where he confronted the opportunities and difficulties of building up a research library from nothing outside the Anglo-American library environment. Recruiting a multi-national staff from the countries of the European Communities, he planned a totally automated system providing online access to the Library database for staff and readers alike. Books were catalogued by the Anglo-American Cataloguing Rules, were classified by Dewey, and were available on open access.

Humphreys retired as a practicing librarian in 1981, but he was Professor of Library Studies at the University of Haifa, Israel, during 1982.

Humphreys was prominent in professional activities. He was Honorary Secretary of the Standing Conference of National and University Libraries (SCONUL) from 1954 to 1968 and Chairman from 1971 to 1973; he was a member of the Council of the Library Association from 1964 to 1975. He served on a number of committees connected with library cooperation; he was a member of the Library Advisory Council for England from 1966 to 1971 and, as a member of the Committee on Libraries set up by the University Grants Committee in 1963 to review the needs of universities for books and periodicals, made a large contribution to its *Report* published in 1967.

In the International Federation of Library Associations (IFLA), Humphreys was President of the National and University Libraries Subsection from 1967 to 1973. He was closely associated with the formation and direction of the Ligue des Bibliothèques Européennes de Recherche (LIBER) in the 1970s and was Chairman of the British Council Books Panel from 1970 to 1975. In demand as a consultant, he advised on libraries in Europe, Africa, and Asia.

Alongside his professional duties as librarian and administrator, Humphreys maintained his scholarly interests in paleography. He was himself a collector of medieval manuscripts and for many years a member of the Comité International de Paléographie. He edited a series of studies on the history of libraries and librarianship and published a number of books and articles on medieval libraries and texts.

Humphreys became an Oxford M.A. in 1943 and obtained the degree of B.Litt. in 1949; in 1967 he was awarded a Birmingham Ph.D. and, in the same year, was made an honorary Litt.D. by Trinity College, Dublin. He also became a Fellow of the Library Association (F.L.A.) in 1967 and was made an Honorary F.L.A. in 1980.

Humphreys' writings illustrate the national and international stretch of his conception of library services and, although primarily a university librarian, he comprehended all types of libraries. Yet he remained strictly practical in his ideas. He perceived that cooperation was essential to the successful development of national and international library and information networks, and practiced it from Birmingham to Tuscany. For Humphreys, academic librarianship had to be dynamic and adaptable, to take advantage of new technologies, but it also had to retain its links with scholarship if it was fully to achieve its purpose in serving education and research.

T. H. BOWYER

Birmingham University Library

K.W. Humphreys

Hungary

A people's republic in Central Europe, Hungary is bounded by Czechoslovakia on the north, the U.S.S.R. and Romania on the east, Yugoslavia on the south, and Austria on the west. Population (1984 est.) 10,700,000 (98% Hungarian); area 93,036 sq.km. The language spoken is Hungarian, which is related only to Finnish and Estonian among the European languages.

History. Hungarians, who migrated in the 9th century A.D. to their present country, used a runic script cut on wood. They soon adopted the use of the Latin-language book hand of contemporary Europe. The first record to contain Hungarian words (the foundation deed of the Tihany Abbey) dates back to 1055. From 1190 to 1200 Hungarian history was written in Latin by an author who is known as Anonymus in *Gesta Hungarorum*. The first coherent text in Hungarian, a funeral sermon, dates from about 1200.

The Library of the Benedictine Abbey in Pannonhalma was founded in 1001. The inventories of a few smaller monastery libraries remained from the end of the 11th century. One of the richest Humanist libraries of Europe, the Bibliotheca Corviniana, was

Municipal Library Szabo Ervin

*National Széchényi
Library, founded in 1802,
largest Hungarian library.*

collected by King Mátyás Hunyadi (1458–1490) from richly decorated codices. The library was destroyed during the 150 years of Turkish rule, and now only 168 codices are extant, 43 of them in Hungarian collections. The first printing office was established in Buda in 1473. The first Hungarian-language book was printed in 1533 (in Cracow). The first Hungarian translation of the New Testament was published at Sárvár in 1541.

The 16th century saw the foundation of Protestant college libraries (Sárospatak, 1531; Debrecen, 1538), followed by Catholic college libraries (Nagyszombat, 1561), which exist today. In the 18th century, academies of technology (Selmecbánya, 1735) and agriculture established their libraries. The private libraries of rich aristocrats became the bases of large public collections at the beginning of the 19th century. The endowment of Count Ferenc Széchényi laid the foundation of the national library; that of Count József Teleki played the same role for the Library of the Hungarian Academy of Sciences.

In the first decades of the 19th century, casinos and reading circles were established. Beginning from 1868 municipal libraries and popular libraries were set up. (Municipal libraries numbered 53 in 1913). The first library authority, the National Council of Museums and Libraries, was formed in 1897.

Ervin Szabó (1887–1918), one of the greatest figures in Hungarian librarianship, established the first Anglo-Saxon-type public library at the beginning of the 20th century and introduced a number of innovations—Dewey Decimal classification, bibliographical work, branch library service, and reference services.

The post-World War II period saw enormous development. Large libraries had to be modernized and public libraries almost entirely organized in four decades. Work started in 1949. The Council of Ministers issued a decree on librarianship in 1952 and the Presidential Council passed law-decrees on the subject in 1956 and 1976. Librarians held national conferences in 1952, 1955, 1970, and 1981 to define their tasks.

Hungarian librarianship is administered by the Ministry of Culture, in cooperation with the Hungarian Council for Librarianship and the National Library. The library act of 1976 assigned libraries to more than 100 systems on the one hand and to cooperation circles on the other. Their work is harmonized by coordination centers according to particular subject fields or regions.

There are more than 16,000 libraries operating in Hungary and the main problem of Hungarian librarianship is indicated by this figure itself. In spite of the intentions to cooperate and coordinate, the number of libraries could not be reduced as needed and no adequate cooperation was established among them. Consequently, in both the public and special library fields, holdings are rather fragmented, and there are strong efforts toward autarky, leading to unnecessary parallelisms and the dissipation of resources. Hungarian librarians tend to recognize up-to-date solutions, but with inadequate finances for automation and new buildings, for example, and with inadequate organizational methods, much of their practical work falls behind the solutions that have been elaborated.

National Library. The National Széchényi Library (founded 1802) is the largest Hungarian library, with a collection of 6,289,000 volumes (1983). Aiming at comprehensive coverage, it collects publications, phonograph records produced in Hungary,

Libraries in Hungary (1982)

Type	Administrative units	Service points[a]	Volumes in collections	Annual expenditures[b] (forint)	Population served	Professional staff	Total staff
National[c]	1	4	6,289,000	7,434,756	10,700,000	297	457
Academic	18	221	14,482,994	129,836,879	114,575	997	1,235
Public[c]	2,069	10,012[d]	47,766,706	136,596,072	10,700,000	4,074	4,926
School[e]	3,991	– –	20,897,161	53,611,024	1,670,017	483	483
Special	638	– –	21,897,943	336,144,953	– –	2,207	2,971

[a]Includes totals from previous column.
[b]Acquisitions budget.
[c]December 1983 data.
[d]Includes 5,201 trade union libraries (11,698,163 volumes).
[e]September 1983 data.

Sources: *Statistical Yearbook 1983,* Budapest, 1984; Statistical information of the Ministry of Culture: public libraries, 1983; special libraries, 1983, Budapest, 1984.

and works published abroad in Hungarian or pertaining to Hungary. (Some 15,000,000 Hungarians live in the world, about 1,000,000 of them in North and South America.)

The responsibilities of the national library are to collect and distribute legal deposit copies; to maintain the national union catalogues of foreign books and periodicals; to serve as the center of interlibrary lending and to conduct the international exchange of publications; to act as a central repository; to house the ISBN and ISSN bureaus; to maintain a central registry of libraries; to operate a central restoration laboratory; to perform R and D tasks; to provide professional and methodological help for all Hungarian libraries through the Center for Library Science and Methodology (1959); and, last but not least, to compile and publish current and retrospective national bibliographies. The national library is also the coordination center for public library systems.

The *Magyar Nemzeti Bibliográfia Könyvek bibliográfiája* (Hungarian National Bibliography) lists Hungarian printed publications and phonograph records (UDC division) and, under the subtitle *Időszaki kiadványok repertóriuma* (Repertory of Serials), provides a list of articles of periodical publications. Its quarterly supplements are *Hungarika irodalmi szemle* (Hungarian Publications Published Abroad in Foreign Languages) and *Külföldi magyar nyelvü kiadványok* (Hungarian Publications Published Abroad in the Hungarian Language). The *Időszaki kiadványok bibliográfiája* (Hungarian National Bibliography of Serials) is published annually, the *A magyar bibliográfiák bibliográfiája* (Bibliography of Hungarian Bibliographies) every two years. Since 1961 annual cumulations of the Hungarian National Bibliography have been published. The retrospective bibliographic ventures group compiles the bibliographies of so-far-uncovered periods; at the same time it releases the revised and enlarged editions of the great works from the last century. Under *Magyar könyvészet* (Hungarian National Bibliography), the material of the period 1945 to 1960 was published in five volumes. The material from the period 1961 to 1975 was in preparation in the mid-1980s. The period 1921 to 1944 will be covered in nine volumes (two had been published by 1985). From the series of enlarged and updated bibliographies two volumes of *Régi magyarországi nyomtatványok* (Early Hungarian Printings) were published—for the periods 1473 to 1600 and 1601 to 1635, respectively—as well as supplements to the national bibliographies of the 18th and 19th centuries.

The national library maintains two former church libraries, the old books of which have a historical value: the József Bajza Library in Gyöngyös (1473) and the Antal Reguly Library in Zirc (1720).

Archives. According to the Archives Act of 1969, general and specialized archives operate in Hungary. The duties of the national archives are performed by two collections with national responsibilities. The Hungarian National Archives (1756) holds 33,531 linear meters of written documents and 35,868,326 film frames from the beginnings to 1945. The New Central Archives (1970) collects its material from 1945. Its stock contains 8,549 linear meters of records and 102,464 microfilm frames. Council or regional archives numbered 20 in 1983, and special archives included the archives of the following: state organs, 8; social organs, 22; and churches, 37. Holdings (1983) from all archives totaled 200,500 linear meters; annual budgets (for the national and council archives only) totaled 98,500,000 forints; and staff 747 (475 professional).

Academic Libraries. Each institution of higher education has a library system of its own, the core of which is the central library, its members being institutional, faculty, clinical, and other designated libraries. University libraries generally serve as national switching centers. There are four academic library systems in science (Budapest, 1561; Debrecen, 1916; Pécs, 1774; and Szeged, 1921); three in technology (Budapest, 1848; Miskolc, 1735; and Veszprém, 1949); four in medicine (Budapest, 1828; Debrecen; Pécs; and Szeged); and nine in agriculture. The principal agricultural libraries are in the field of veterinary science (1872) and in horticulture (1894) in Budapest; in forestry (1735) in Sopron, and further in Keszthely (1797), in Debrecen (1868), in Gödöllő (1945), and in Mosonmagyaróvár (1818). The holdings of these libraries range from 500,000 to 3,000,000 volumes.

Most colleges of arts and pedagogy, founded in the last century and having the rank of universities, have libraries with more than 100,000 volumes.

The largest system serves the Loránd Eötvös University in Budapest. The main library has more than 1,300,000 units, the total system (130 libraries) 2,500,000. The system is particularly rich in old materials on the humanities.

Public Libraries. There are three types of public library systems in Hungary: council, trade union, and armed forces. There are council library systems in each of the 19 counties. Trade union library systems are also organized by counties, except in Budapest, where they are organized by 11 trades. Council libraries providing local library services play a dominant role in the delivery of library services. The centers of their systems are municipal libraries holding an average of from 200,000 to 250,000 volumes. These institutions have been called county libraries since 1952. Council libraries also provide library services for hospital patients and minority nationalities, such as Germans, Slovaks, Southern Slavs, and Romanians. To serve the minorities better, 15 so-called basis libraries assist and supply materials in the communities where national minorities live. Trade union libraries serve workers at their factories and offices. In some industrial areas they have undertaken to supply the general population too. In 1983, 10,012 council and trade union libraries contained 47,766,706 units; 2,251,000 registered readers borrowed more than 50,000,000 books a year. Public libraries have not only books and periodicals in their holdings but also audiovisual materials, primarily phonograph records and cassettes. They operate more than 100 music departments.

The Metropolitan Ervin Szabó Library (1904) in Budapest, with 106 branches and total holdings of 4,000,000 volumes, offers a variety of services and is the leading public library system in the country. Its main library, the national switching center for sociology, holds the largest local collection in Hungary. The Somogyi Library in Szeged (1880) and the county libraries of Békéscsaba and Szombathely are famous not only for their rich collections but also for their modern buildings. The Gorky State Library collects literature in foreign languages and is a coordination center for basis libraries of the nationalities.

School Libraries. In the decade 1975–84 councils spent considerable sums on school library acquisitions. Still, they are the weakest chainlinks of Hungarian librarianship. There is a library in each of the more than 3,500 general schools and about 1,000 secondary schools, but in most places they have neither their own room, nor specialist staff. School libraries belong to county and metropolitan systems headed by either the local pedagogical continuing educational institute or the county library. Their work is coordinated by the National Pedagogical Library and Museum (1867 and 1958, respectively), which serves at the same time as the information center on pedagogy. The children's libraries of public libraries also take part in the services to school children.

Special Libraries. In 1978, 1,822 special libraries were reported in Hungary. Their number was not reduced thereafter, but statistics of the 1980s covered only those with at least one full-time librarian; thus their number was 860 in the early 1980s, academic libraries included. The principal 122 libraries are qualified as national switching centers. They are authorized to organize cooperation circles in their subject fields and they hold 65 percent of the total stock of special libraries and provide most of their services. Hungarian special libraries are characterized first of all by traditional services; automation was at an initial stage in the first half of the 1980s. Some switching centers provide computerized SDI services from foreign databases. Automation of their own activities was being started in the mid-1980s.

Special libraries are organized into systems according to their supervising authorities. So, for example, the Library of the Hungarian Academy of Sciences (1826) supervises the libraries of 51 research institutes. There are health, agricultural, museum, and other special library systems as well. The work of the various systems is coordinated by large special libraries. The National Technical Information Center and Library (1883), for example, coordinates the libraries of more than 800 industrial firms and research institutes, the Information Center of the Ministry of Agriculture and Food (1951) that of 148 libraries, the National Medical Information Institute and Library (1960) that of 197 libraries. Church libraries, especially those of the Roman Catholic and Reformed churches, have rich old collections.

The Profession. Librarians can graduate from universities or academies. At the Loránd Eötvös University in Budapest, librarians have been trained since 1949. Education lasts for five years with day-time courses, for six years with study by correspondence courses; other courses qualify students for teaching in secondary schools. Graduates from other universities receive three-year post-graduate training or take a one-year course on documentation. In three teachers' training colleges (Szombathely, Nyiregyháza, and Budapest), a librarian's diploma is granted in four years, with other courses in teachers' subjects. Large libraries organize 200-hour courses for library technicians. The system of extension training, in the process of formation, relies first of all on the Center for Library Science and Methodology.

The nongovernmental organization of the library community is the Association of Hungarian Librarians (1935), of which archivists can also be members. Its work is managed by an elected board. Its President and Secretary are also elected. The 3,500 members can participate in the work of several sections (for example, children's, technical and music librarians, regional organizations). The Association safeguards professional interests and organizes extension training. A congress is held every year.

The Hungarian Academy of Sciences publishes the journal *Magyar Könyvszemle* (Hungarian Book Review) (1876) which includes mainly studies of a historical nature. The Hungarian Council for Librarianship and the Center for Library Science and Methodology compile the journal Könyvtári Figyelő (Library Review) (1955), which focuses more on current problems. Both provide summaries in English. The Hungarian specialist literature is reviewed in English by the semi-annual publication "Hungarian Library and Information Science Abstracts," edited by the Center for Library Science and Methodology.

REFERENCES

Jenő Kiss, *Libraries in Hungary.* (1972) New revised edition in press.
Peter Balázs, editor, *Guide to the Archives of Hungary.* (1976).
JENŐ KISS

Huntington, Henry E.
(1850–1927)

Henry Edwards Huntington was a leading American businessman, a premier book collector, and the founder of the Henry E. Huntington Library, Art Gallery, and Botanical Gardens in San Marino, California. According to A. S. W. Rosenbach, Huntington was "the greatest figure in the history of American book-collecting." He and his legacy have had a profound influence on the development of research libraries in the United States.

Huntington was born February 27, 1850, in the village of Oneonta, in central New York state. His father's family had moved to New England from England in the early 17th century, and his father, Solon, moved west to Oneonta from Connecticut to open a general store. The fourth of seven children, the young "Ed" Huntington, as his boyhood friends knew him, worked in the family store, but set out on his own as soon as he had finished school. First he went to New York City, where he got a job in a hardware store, then to West Virginia to manage a sawmill (of which he soon became the sole owner), then to Tennessee and Kentucky to become construction superintendent for a railroad, and later to manage another railroad that was on the brink of failing. He was wonderfully successful in all his business dealings.

When he was 42, in 1892, he answered the call of his uncle, Collis P. Huntington (who had been a junior partner in the store in Oneonta), to go to San Francisco and share the management of the Southern Pacific Railway. Eight years later, in 1900, his uncle died and left him a large legacy. Two years later Huntington decided to move to southern California, where he developed the Pacific Electric Interurban Railway for the Los Angeles area. That venture was especially successful because Huntington owned substantial amounts of land in the areas opened up, and

Henry E. Huntington

Huntington Library

the population tripled in a decade.

In 1910 Huntington retired at the age of 60. The Pacific Electric was transferred to the Southern Pacific, and Huntington gave up active business management. He retired to devote himself to his "other interests," which consisted mainly of books and manuscripts, along with paintings and other art objects, and the horticultural development of his ranch.

He was prepossessing in appearance but shy, retiring, and deferential in manner. He loved jokes and got his greatest pleasure from simple activities such as playing hearts and croquet. Business associates called him "H. E." In the family, he was "Uncle Edwards," or "Edwards," or "Edward." His dominant activity was reading.

The book-buying bug bit him in San Francisco. Soon after he arrived there, he began frequenting the bookshops, coming away first with one book, later with an armful. Often he spent his lunch hour in a bookshop. He was a reader by nature and by habit, and his principle was to buy things in which he had or could develop an interest. Through the 1890s he bought many books about the discovery of America and 19th-century fiction. In the first decade of this century, when Huntington was in Los Angeles and often in New York, his interests greatly increased, to writers such as Montaigne, Chaucer, and Izaak Walton. He began reading up on rare books and their prices and started buying first editions and small collections of rare books. He also collected such writers as Kipling, Conrad, and Wells in depth. "In depth" turned out to be the key to all his collecting.

In the great period of his collecting, from 1910 until his death in 1927, he bought dozens of large collections, important libraries, and choice rarities. These acquisitions included the E. Dwight Church Collection in 1911 (for $1,000,000), the cream of the Robert Hoe Collection (including the splendid copy of the Gutenberg Bible on vellum), the Beverly Chew Library of early English literature, the Kemble-Devonshire Collection of English plays, the Halsey Library, the Bridgewater House Library, many collections of Californiana and Americana, and many collections of English manuscripts (Loudoun, Abercromby, Battle Abbey, Hastings, and Stowe—the last alone containing some 350,000 manuscripts from the 12th century onward).

The result was a magnificent collection of great treasures (such as the Ellesmere manuscript of Chaucer and the manuscript of Franklin's *Autobiography*), but also a library of great depth (the largest collection of 15th-century printed books in the United States, for example, and firsts in many other areas). By concentrating on English and American literature and history, he was able to have strength in all periods from the medieval to the present.

Huntington early decided to found an independent institution so that his collections might continue to have useful value. In 1919 he established the Huntington Library and Art Gallery as a research institution for scholars and a cultural center for the public. The library building was completed in 1920; the collections were made freely available to qualified scholars, and exhibitions were open to the public. Huntington appointed a distinguished scholar as Director and made provision for a staff of scholars in residence in addition to the library staff.

Huntington was a builder by inclination. He built companies, and he built a Library. In addition, he built an Art Gallery and Botanical Gardens. He bought his Ranch in 1903 and immediately started building gardens. In 1910 he began building a mansion to serve as an Art Gallery after his death. His first marriage, to Mary Alice Prentice in 1873, ended in divorce in 1906, and in 1913 he married Arabella Huntington, the widow since 1900 of his uncle Collis. Arabella (who was his own age) was an important art collector, and she guided him in collecting the most significant group of British paintings of the 18th and early 19th centuries outside London; it included such masterpieces as Gainsborough's *Blue Boy,* Reynolds' *Mrs. Siddons as the Tragic Muse,* Constable's *View on the Stour near Dedham,* and Lawrence's *Pinkie.* He also completed several important gardens, such as the Desert Garden, the Japanese Garden, and the North Vista.

The last book that Huntington examined before he died, in Philadelphia on May 23, 1927, was the *Short-Title Catalogue of Books Printed in England, Scotland and Ireland, 1475–1640.* At that time, his Library consisted of about 170,000 rare books and three-quarters of a million manuscripts. Since then, the rare book collection has more than doubled, the manuscript collection has grown fourfold, and there is a reference collection of nearly 300,000 volumes. Many new areas (such as 20th-century poetry) have been developed within the framework of English and American literature and history. The art collection has greatly increased (with more than 12,000 British drawings and watercolors, for example, and a new building for American art). There are now a dozen fully developed gardens, with 15,000 kinds of plants, occupying 130 acres.

One thousand five hundred scholars work at the Huntington every year, doing research in all of the divisions. Half a million visitors each year enjoy the cultural and educational activities. Thus the Huntington continues to fulfill the purposes that its founder set forth.

JAMES THORPE

Hutchins, Margaret
(1884–1961)

Margaret Hutchins, library educator and reference specialist, made significant contributions to librarianship through outstanding practice, teaching, and a seminal monograph, *Introduction to Reference Work.*

Born in Lancaster, New Hampshire, on September 21, 1884, Hutchins was graduated from Smith College in 1906 with a Bachelor of Arts degree. After receiving a Bachelor of Library Science from the University of Illinois in 1908, she became a reference librarian there and lecturer in the library school. Together with Alice S. Johnson, who held similar positions in the library and library school at Illinois, and Margaret S. Williams, an instructor in the New York State Library School, Hutchins wrote a text published by H. W. Wilson in 1922 as *Guide to the Use of Libraries: A Manual for College and University Students.* A revised edition was published by Wilson in 1925.

Hutchins left Illinois in 1927 to become a reference specialist in the Queens Borough Public Library,

New York. In 1931 she received an M.L.S. at the School of Library Service at Columbia University and joined the faculty there. She taught for many years, retiring as an Associate Professor in 1952. While at Columbia, Hutchins wrote the monograph that is her major contribution to librarianship—*Introduction to Reference Work* (1943). Dedicated to Francis Simpson, a teacher at Illinois, and Isadore Gilbert Mudge, a teacher at Columbia and Head of the Reference Department at its library, the book expressed its aim—"to describe and interpret reference work as the reference librarian sees it for the information of administrators of libraries and other librarians and library school students."

Hutchins's monograph bears some resemblance to James Wyer's *Reference Work* (1928) in that it describes the process of reference work rather than the contents of individual reference books. Wyer's work, however, had been based on a literature survey and visits to some 50 libraries; Hutchins did not repeat such an investigation. Instead she relied on her "thirty-five years' devotion to the subject, two thirds of which were spent in actual practice of reference work" to support "an attempt to interpret the essence of reference work in its universal aspects." The 28 chapters of the work are organized into seven sections: (1) the Scope of Reference Work as a Branch of Library Service, (2) Reference Questions, (3) Selec-

tion of Reference Material, (4) Organization of Reference Materials, (5) Organization and Administration of Reference Service, (6) the Less Common Functions of a Reference Librarian (including advising readers, teaching the use of books and libraries, reporting literature searches, work in connection with interlibrary loan, and participating in public relations), and (7) In Conclusion (Evaluating and Reporting Reference Work).

Recent developments in library service, ranging from the availability of databases for online searching to the establishment of information and referral services in public libraries, make Hutchin's *Introduction to Reference Work* seem very old-fashioned, but her comments on the reference interview are noticeably modern. Indeed, she was first to use the phrase "reference interview," and her chapter on that subject anticipates much that is currently discussed in articles and dissertations on the communication skills needed by reference librarians.

Hutchins died at Bayshore, Long Island, on January 4, 1961.

REFERENCE
Frances Neel Cheney, "Hutchins, Margaret," *Dictionary of American Library Biography* (1978).

MARY JO LYNCH

Iceland

Iceland, a republic, occupies an island in the North Atlantic Ocean near the Arctic Circle. Population (1984 est.) 240,000; area 103,000 sq.km. The official language is Icelandic.

History. In the "Book of the Icelanders" Ari the Wise, who wrote in the 12th century, indicates that there were books in Iceland from the earliest days of its recorded history. Christianity was taken to the country from Norway in 1000. The Golden Age of Saga literature, at a time when the climate was probably milder and the land flourished, covered the 11th to the 13th centuries. The people of the country had fled from Norway, setting up the Albingi ("the Grandmother of parliaments") in 930. The country was under Norwegian and later Danish domination from the 14th century until independence in 1918; all ties with the Danish crown were cut in 1944. The patriotic struggles provide the substance of sonnets and songs still sung.

Even though general formal education was not introduced until 1907, Icelanders take pride in their bookish traditions and many prominent scholars were self-educated. They consider themselves a nation of readers. There were opportunities to send students to Copenhagen University before the 20th century. The University of Iceland, the only one in the country, was opened in 1911.

From 1000 to 1550, nine Roman Catholic monasteries flourished. They collected, copied, and preserved manuscripts before printing was introduced in 1534. Many manuscripts were lost (monasteries were plundered and burned) when the country became Evangelic Lutheran in the mid-16th century.

Iceland suffered volcanic devastation and epidemics in the following centuries, and little public effort toward preservation of its written literature and history was evident during those times. Yet one scholar, Arni Magnússon, saved vast numbers of manuscripts that were preserved in Copenhagen (many were lost in the great fire in that city in 1728). In 1971 Iceland celebrated the return from Denmark of the Árnasafn manuscripts (so named in his honor).

The first library in Iceland was organized in 1790 as part of "the Icelandic Library and Reading Club on the South Coast," and it operated until about 1818. The first real public library was founded in 1828 in Akureyri. Before the people of Reykjavík founded their own public library in 1923, the National Library provided those services. Iceland's "reading societies" (Lestrarfélög) were established chiefly in the early 19th century; some grew into modern public libraries.

National Library. Landsbókasafn Islands was founded in 1818, instigated by members of the Icelandic Literary Society in Copenhagen. Donations were immediately solicited in Denmark, but space was not provided in the cathedral loft in Reykjavík until 1825.. Through gifts, purchases, and a comprehensive exchange program, the Library grew. It moved first to the Althing (Parliament) building and then to its own home in 1909.

Since 1886 the National Library has received deposit copies of all works published in Iceland. Later they are distributed to libraries in Iceland and abroad, such as; the University Library, the University of Copenhagen in Denmark, and the University of Manitoba in Canada, with which Icelanders have special cultural ties.

The Library's holdings include an extensive collection of manuscripts and printed books, which in 1982 numbered about 367,000 (or about 1.5 volumes per capita). Since the founding of the University Library in 1940 and Iceland's full independence in 1944, the National Library has been responsible for acquiring materials in the humanities, while the University Library oversees collections of scientific books. In 1970 the Althing passed a resolution authorizing the building of a joint library and the eventual merging of the two collections. Among the National Library's

National Library of Iceland, founded in 1818. It moved to this building in Reykjavík in 1909.

Kenneth C. Harrison

Libraries in Iceland (1982)

Type	Administrative units	Service points	Volumes in collections	Annual expenditures (krona)	Population served	Professional staff	Total staff
National	1	1	367,000	7,183,000[a]	235,000	5.5	16
Academic	3	7	230,000[b]	6,600,000[b]		8[b]	13[b]
Public	240	244	1,385,000	37,948,000	235,000	--	--
School	c. 150	--	--	--	--	--	--
Special	c. 25	--	--	--	--	--	--

[a]1983 data.
[b]University of Iceland only.

activities are the publication in Icelandic of "The Icelandic National Bibliography" since 1974, union lists of foreign language materials, and a catalogue card distribution service in collaboration with the Iceland Library Bureau, established in 1978.

Academic Libraries. Háskólabókasafn, the University of Iceland Library, is the principal academic library in the nation, although there are libraries in some other specialized institutions. In Reykjavík, it held more than 230,000 volumes in 1983. Its collections include materials to support the full range of general curricula and numerous research programs in Icelandic studies and vulcanology. On campus, the Stofnun Árna Magnussonar (Icelandic Manuscript Institute) is the principal repository of the nation's extensive literary heritage, which includes manuscripts of the sagas from as early as the 12th century.

Public Libraries. Because of Iceland's long-standing tradition of reading, the literacy rate is virtually 100 percent. Public libraries are found in all population centers, and bookmobiles provide service in the suburbs of Reykjavík. Per capita circulation in 1982 was approximately 9.5 items from public libraries alone. Services are provided to hospitals, asylums, and other institutions, and, typically Icelandic, collections of materials ("book-boxes") are regularly prepared for ships in the country's fishing fleets. The state pays a small sum of money to Icelandic authors whose works have been acquired by libraries, to compensate for royalties not gained from direct sales; writers of Icelandic-language works have a small potential market (no more than 150,000 buyers).

School Libraries. In 1974 the Icelandic Parliament passed a law mandating libraries for all schools by 1984. In Reykjavík, by early 1976, more than half of the schools had libraries, many of them modern facilities similar to media centers in the United States. A centralized service center in Reykjavík handles acquisitions, cataloguing, and other processes. In some of the smaller towns, school and public library functions are provided by the same institution.

Special Libraries. Several small special libraries support research centers (such as the National Energy Authority and the Marine Research Institute) and the specialized training schools (such as those in marine engineering and health-related professions). An extensive collection of materials is held by the Nordic House, a cultural center supported by the Nordic countries. The U.S. International Communication Agency also maintains a modern library.

Icelandic Library for the Blind and Visually Handicapped. Blindrabókasafn Islands was founded by law in 1982 and opened in 1983. It produces and distributes braille material and talking books. Before the founding of the library, the Reykjavik City library and the Society for the Blind provided that service for the whole country. The Library is under the Ministry of Education.

The Profession. People working in Icelandic libraries become members of The Association of Icelandic Librarians, founded in 1960. It has approximately 300 members. The Association of Professional Librarians, established in 1973, has approximately 100 members with university-level training, mostly from the University of Iceland, but also from the U.S., Britain, or one of the Nordic countries. The University of Iceland provides professional training in combination with another study area in a three-year program. Graduation from it is regarded as necessary for admission to the professional library ranks.

In May 1984 the Icelandic Parliament passed a Law on Professional Librarians defining qualifications required before the Minister of Education grants a person the right to the title of bókasafnsfræðingur (professional librarian).

HRAFN A HARÐARSON;
CHARLES WILLIAM CONAWAY

India

India, a federal republic in southern Asia, lies on a peninsula that juts out into the Indian Ocean; the Arabian Sea is on the west and the Bay of Bengal on the east. It is bordered on the north and from east to west by Burma, Bangladesh, China, Bhutan, Nepal, and Pakistan. Population (1984 est.) 746,000,000; area 3,064,063 sq. km. The official languages are Hindi and English. Fifteen languages including Hindi are listed in the Eighth Schedule of the republic's constitution.

History. In ancient and medieval India, there were no public libraries: collections of books were mostly maintained in temples and palaces. There was an oral tradition in the world of learning that very largely reduced dependence on the written word. Important centers of theological and philosophical learning, however, had their libraries. The modern library movement in India began in the first half of the 19th century.

National Library. The National Library of India was established as the Imperial Library in 1903 in Calcutta, then the country's capital, by an act of the government passed in 1902. It was given its present name by the Imperial Library (Change of Name) Act passed by India's Constituent Assembly in 1948, when it moved to its 30-acre grounds at Belvedere in southeast Calcutta. The Compulsory Deposit of Books and Periodicals Act of 1954, amended in 1956, made it one of the four depository libraries in the country. The other three are the Connemara Library, Madras; the Central Library, Bombay; and the Delhi Public Library.

When the Imperial Library was founded by Lord Curzon, then Viceroy and Governor-General of India, it took over the holdings of the Calcutta Public Library (established in 1836) and the Imperial Secretariat Library (1891). Consequently it had then, as it has now, some features of both a public and a departmental library. Any Indian citizen who is at least 18 years of age can obtain a reading room ticket and a borrower's ticket free of charge. Only books in print are issued on loan against deposit of money. Central and state government officials are permitted to borrow books without deposit. The Library offers an interlibrary loan service covering libraries in India and abroad.

The National Library's collections totaled 1,730,530 in 1983. It had 804,272 Indian and foreign official documents, including the publications of the UN and other international bodies, and 75,666 maps. Among its rare items are about 2,000 books in European languages published between the 15th and 18th centuries and another 3,000 rare titles published in India. In 1982–83 it received 16,660 books and more than 15,000 periodicals under the Delivery of Books Act, purchased 3,302 books, and subscribed to 763 periodicals. During the same period, the Library received about 5,000 publications as gifts from individuals and institutions, both Indian and foreign, and 6,761 publications on exchange with foreign institutions. Its reading rooms have 500 seats for its average of 1,000 daily readers. In March 1983 the Library had 30,650 holders of borrower's tickets and 7,396 holders of reading room tickets.

The Library had a staff of 783 in 1982–83; 206 were professional librarians holding degrees or diplomas in library science. The Library is under the Union Ministry of Education and Culture. The National Library of India Act of 1976, which grants the Library statutory autonomy, had not yet come into force by 1985. The National Science and the National Law Libraries are in New Delhi.

National Medical Library. The National Medical Library, New Delhi, was established in 1966 out of the Directorate General of Indian Medical Services Library, which was renamed Directorate General of Health Services Library in 1946. It had a collection of more than 125,000 volumes in the early 1980s and subscribed to 2,000 journals. It publishes a semiannual *Index to Indian Medical Periodicals* (from 1959), and the sixth edition of its *Union List of Medical Periodicals in Indian Libraries* appeared in 1972. Its annual budget for books and periodicals exceeds 5,000,000 rupees.

Bibliography. The Indian National Bibliography, begun in 1956, is compiled and published by the Central Reference Library on the National Library grounds and is headed by its Librarian. The Central Reference Library also produces *Index Indiana,* a quarterly index of articles appearing in current Indian periodicals in major Indian languages.

Academic Libraries. The libraries of India's 130 universities and 10 institutions deemed to be universities by the University Grants Commission and another 12 learned bodies recognized by the Union Government as institutions of national importance are the country's most important academic libraries. Among the oldest university libraries are those of Calcutta, Madras, and Bombay, all founded in 1857. Among the libraries of the country's 4,500 first-degree colleges, some, like those of Presidency College, Sanskrit College, and the Scottish Church College, all in Calcutta, are more than 150 years old.

Public Libraries. Public libraries in India are as old as the introduction of the New Learning in the country in the early decades of the 19th century. Ef-

Bombay University Library

Completed in 1878, the Rajabai Tower Building Library in Bombay.

forts began after the country's independence in 1947 to establish a network of such libraries in the cities, towns, and villages in the country's 22 states and 9 union territories. Central and state governments have a policy of establishing public libraries supported by public funds and open to the public free of charge. Five of the republic's 22 states passed their library acts between 1948 and 1979, and the rest were planning to do so in the mid-1980s. In 1972, the International Book Year, the Government of India set up the Raja Rammohun Roy Library Foundation to mark the bicentenary of the birth of Rammohun Roy (1772–1833), the Father of Modern India, and its objective was to help build up a national library system. The Foundation gave assistance to more than 17,000 libraries through the Library Planning Boards of the states and Union territories. Among recipients of assistance by the mid-1980s were 27 State Central Libraries, 386 District Libraries, and 14,856 Town and Rural Libraries. The Foundation also offers counsel and funds for seminars, workshops, and exhibitions to help raise the standards of the services of the country's public libraries.

School Libraries. The libraries of India's more than 100,000 secondary and higher secondary schools are used mostly by the 1,000,000 students of their four top classes, a fairly large number of whom have to be provided with their textbooks. The new scheme of two years of preuniversity education after high school required a large number of schools to enlarge their collections to include books for students

Libraries in India (1983)

Type	Administrative units	Service points	Volumes in collections	Annual expenditures (rupee)	Population served	Professional staff	Total staff
National	6	7	1,730,530	11,500,000	40,000	206	783
Academic	4,652[a]	--	12,536,000[b]	--	--	--	--
Public	--	17,024[a]	--	--	--	--	--
School	100,000[a]	--	--	--	--	--	--

[a]Approximate figures.
[b]1977 data from Unesco, *Statistical Yearbook,* 1984.

National Library of India

The National Library of India, Belvedere, southeast Calcutta. It stands on a 30-acre grounds.

who though still in high school are actually pursuing collegiate courses.

Special Libraries. The *Directory of Special and Research Libraries,* published by the Indian Association of Special Libraries and Information Centres in 1962, lists 173 special libraries, the majority of which are supported by the government. Among these are libraries of central government institutions. They include:

The Geological Survey of India Central Library, Calcutta, established in 1851. It has a collection of more than half a million volumes and 1,500 periodicals. The Library serves the scientific and technical personnel of the department and scientists and research scholars, teachers, and students of various government and nongovernment institutions and commercial organizations. It publishes *Earth Science Abstracts* and *Indian Geological Abstracts.*

Botanical Survey of India Library, Howrah, established in 1890. It has a collection of more than 61,000 volumes and 250 periodicals. The library maintains a current information file (from 1973) and provides bibliographic and reprographic services.

Zoological Survey of India Library, Calcutta, established in 1926. It has a collection of about 50,000 books and 1,000 periodicals. It publishes *Bibliography of Indian Zoology* and maintains bibliographic and reprographic services.

The Anthropological Survey of India Central Library, Calcutta, established in 1947. It has a collection of about 30,000 volumes and 300 periodicals. It publishes *Documentation of Indian Anthropology.*

Indian Agricultural Research Institute Library, New Delhi, established in 1905. It has a collection of more than 250,000 volumes and about 3,000 periodicals. It maintains a central information file (from 1944) and bibliographic and reprographic services.

National laboratories, such as the National Physical Laboratories and National Chemicals Laboratory, and other national institutions for scientific research, such as the Bhaba Atomic Research Centre, Bombay, and the Institute of Chemical Biology, Calcutta, have large collections of books and journals in their areas

of research.

A special library of international affairs is the Indian Council of World Affairs Library, New Delhi, which has a collection of more than 100,000 books and documents, about 1,700,000 press clippings, and 12,000 microfilms. The Government of India is assisting the library to grow into a reference library of last resort for scholars specializing in international affairs. Founded by Sir William Jones in 1784, the Library of the Asiatic Society is the oldest library in Calcutta. It has a large collection of books, journals, and manuscripts relating to Indian literature, history, and philosophy. The Society has been recognized by the Union Government as an institution of national importance.

Scientific and Technical Information Services. In 1952 the Union Government set up, with assistance from Unesco, the Indian National Scientific Documentation Centre (INSDOC), New Delhi, as a central scientific and technical information service for the country's 1,500,000 scientific and technical personnel. It maintains translation and reprographic services in cooperation with other organizations of this kind, such as the Defence Science Information and Documentation Centre, Small Enterprise National Documentation Centre, Social Science Documentation Centre, Library and Information Services of the Bhaba Atomic Research Centre, and others. On an average it receives 800 requests a year involving 10,000 pages of translations. It publishes *Indian Science Abstracts,* is bringing out state-wide union catalogues of scientific and technical journals, and is compiling a union catalogue of books on science and technology in Indian libraries. Its Russian Science Information Centre publishes a current bibliography of Soviet scientific and technological literature.

National Policy. The library policy of the Union Government was stated in the *Annual Report* of its Ministry of Education and Culture (1981–82): "The Central Government has jurisdiction only over libraries established by the Central Government and institutions of national importance as declared by the Central Government. However, the Central Government takes initiative to secure the voluntary cooperation of the State Governments to promote coordinated development of national and State library systems. Funds for such integrated development are provided in the Central and State Five Year Plans." The Union Government pursued that policy through the Raja Rammohun Roy Library Foundation and by offering financial assistance to the Indian Library Association, Indian Association of Special Libraries and Information Centres, Government of India Librarians Association, and comparable groups. Although "Libraries, museums, and other similar institutions controlled or financed by the State" are included in item 12 of the State List in the Seventh Schedule of the Indian constitution, the Union Government could take such initiative in library development on a national level because education is now in the Concurrent List; it appropriately linked up its work toward the establishment and maintenance of libraries in rural and semi-urban areas throughout the country with its plans for formal and continuing education. For the last quarter of a century since the publication of the Report of the Advisory Committee for Libraries appointed by the Government of India in 1959, leading librarians and educators have been seriously reflecting on the question of a sound national library system. A national library policy is expected to emerge when all 31 states and union territories have their library acts and when an instrument of cooperation among all libraries is drawn up for the sharing and economy of library resources. That instrument may be embodied in a central government policy resolution or act.

The Profession. Some Indian universities have faculties of library and information sciences to conduct graduate courses in the subject. The minimum qualification for a professional librarian in the country is a bachelor's degree in library science. Junior posts in the profession may go to holders of certificates in library science for which courses are conducted by bodies such as the Bengal Library Association, which was more than 40 years old in the mid-1980s. S. R. Ranganathan, the first Indian professor of library science in Delhi University, gave a new dimension to teaching and research at higher levels. A fair number of India's librarians hold doctoral degrees.

Associations include the Indian Association of Special Libraries and Information Centres (IASLIC), founded in 1955 in Calcutta, and the Indian Library Association (1933); about 1,600 members in the early 1980s), publisher of *Indian Library Association Bulletin* and other works such as *Subject Headings in Hindi*. The Federation of Indian Library Associations was established in Chandigarh in 1966.

REFERENCES

S. R. Ranganathan, *Library Development Plan: Thirty-year Programme for India with Draft Library Bills for the Union and Constituent States* (1950).

Subodh Kumar Mookerjee, *Development of Libraries and Library Science in India* (1969).

Jibananda Saha, *Special Libraries and Information Services in India and the USA* (1969).

B. D. Kesavan, *India's National Library* (1961).

Indian National Scientific Documentation Centre, *Science Information Services in India* (1980).

National Library, *The National Library of India: 1903–1978: A Pictorial History* (1978).

R. K. DAS GUPTA

Indonesia

Indonesia, a republic in Southeast Asia and part of the Malay archipelago, comprises thousands of islands over an area of 1,919,443 sq.km. The most densely populated island, Java, (137,187 sq.km.) has 91,269,528 inhabitants (1980 census). Other principal islands are Sumatra, Kalimantan (Borneo), and Sulawesi (Celebes). Population (1984 est.) 164,347,000. The official language is Bahasa Indonesia, the government-sponsored form of Malay.

History. As in medieval Europe, scholarly activities in early Indonesia were intimately connected with religion. Besides writings about religion and ethics, treatises of a secular nature, such as belles-lettres and works on history, arts, and law, have been preserved. Like their medieval counterparts, however, these so-called secular works should also be seen against their cultural background, which was dominated by religions—first Hinduism and Buddhism, later by Islam (except in Bali and certain other areas).

Indonesia, with its thousands of islands, has a variety of social and cultural identities. A large number of local languages exist. Fortunately the Malay language was from the early days selected as its lingua franca. The language was used as a vehicle of communication for trade among the Chinese, the Hindus, the Arabs, the Portuguese, and later the Dutch, and also for the spread of religions. The Malay language grew to become the Indonesian language, and was later promoted to become the national language.

In the 19th century the Dutch colonial government introduced the Western style of education for the population, but it made reading available to the general public only in 1908 with the establishment of the Folk Program in 1908. Around 1918 Balai Pustaka, the office in charge of promoting reading among the people, started operating mobile libraries. People were then able to read in their own local languages. During the Dutch colonial period, the special libraries to support colonial programs were better developed than the public libraries.

National Library. The National Library was established in 1980, merging four libraries in Jakarta: the National Museum Library (established in 1778), the Library of Social and Political History, the Provincial Library of Jakarta, and the Bibliographic and Deposit Division of the Center for Library Development.

The main functions are: to preserve national imprints, to collect publications on Indonesia and written by Indonesians wherever they are published; to publish the National Bibliography; and to act as a national center for library cooperation in the country and abroad. A Legal Deposit Act had not been approved by 1984 though a draft had been submitted to the Parliament. The collection totaled 650,000 volumes in 1984. The Library was housed in temporary quarters while a new site for the National Library building was under discussion in the mid-1980s.

Academic Libraries. Most of the colleges and universities in Indonesia, and thus also their libraries, are comparatively young, especially those outside Java. Only the Faculty of Medicine of the University of Indonesia in Jakarta and the Institue of Technology in Bandung existed long before Indonesia gained its independence in 1945.

Most libraries in Indonesia are government-owned. Several private ones belong to the Islamic institutes, theological seminaries, and teachers' training colleges. More centralized university library services remained to be developed, as many universities still maintain departmental libraries. An integrated university library system is being managed by the Directorate of Higher Education, Department of Education and Culture.

In September 1984 an Open University System was opened, and it promised to give additional responsibilities and dimension to academic libraries.

Public Libraries. It is difficult to meet the demand of the reading needs of more than 150,000,000 people and to serve them properly because of the vastness of the country. An effective book publishing and distribution system was still needed in the mid-1980s; programs are hampered very much by the inadequate transport and communication system.

Indonesia's 27 provincial capitals have provincial

libraries. The public libraries are to be found in districts and villages.

About 275 public district libraries were in operation in 1984. The provincial and public libraries are managed centrally by the Center for Library Development in cooperation with the local governments. To reach people in far-away places, many of the provincial libraries started operating mobile libraries. In 1984, 104 mobile libraries were in operation.

School Libraries. Indonesia's school-age population accounts for 60 percent of the total population. The development of the state school libraries is the responsiblity of the Center for Library Development. Effective school library service is very much handicapped by the shortage of available teacher-librarians.

Most of the services given are limited to borrowing and returning books during schoolbreaks. Pilot projects were being set up in the mid-1980s to demonstrate models to teachers and also to the parent-teacher associations.

Special Libraries. Categorized as special libraries are those with collections in a special field and also those rendering active information services. Most of the special libraries or information centers belong to research institutes or universities.

Many of the special libraries, in management and collections, are better off than the other types of libraries in the country because of their history. The *Directory of Special Libraries and Information Services in Indonesia 1981* reports a total of 295 libraries. National documentation and information centers, for example, in biology and agriculture, science and technology, and health and medicine, carry out national functions in their fields of specialization. National centers also become a training ground for staff from other libraries who are in need of improving management and technical capabilities.

In Indonesian library development, the special libraries could be considered the principal innovators in and advocates of library and information services. The system still faces financial and other handicaps in making the services effective for users in far-away places. Indonesia is still far from making all levels of the community information conscious.

The Profession. The Indonesian Library Association, founded in 1954, was the only library association existing in the country in 1984. Throughout

its history it has undergone several changes of names and coverage of activities. At one time it was also an association for archivists. Later, between 1969 and 1973, workers in special libraries felt they needed their own association and formed the Indonesian Special Library Association. Although the small group flourished, many believed that the small number of professionals in the associations was not advantageous to the development of the profession and a new combined association was started in 1974. Many constraints work against making the Association strong with a voice to be heard.

REFERENCES
Central Bureau of Statistics, *Statistical Yearbook of Indonesia 1980/1981* (1982).
Philip Ward, *Indonesia: Development of a National Library Service* (1975).
Unesco, *Report on Survey. Indonesia National Survey of Scientific and Technological Information.* (1980).

LUWARSIH PRINGGOADISURJO

Information Science

Before the Soviet Union launched the Sputnik satellite in 1958, the phrase *information science* rarely appeared in encyclopedias, books, or journals. This is not to say that there was not a science of information. Human beings by necessity have always been concerned with information, but then analysis of this concern depends on what we mean by *information*.

A compilation of the areas of interest indicated in the various technical reports included in the *Journal of the American Society of Information Science,* the official publication of a society representing the professionals who work in the field, shows that the major areas of interest of information scientists lie in the logistical properties and requirements of knowledge: acquisition, storage, and retrieval. They are involved in three fundamental functions, namely, the means for *generating* new knowledge, means for *using* what is known (possibly for generating new knowledge), and means for *transferring* (disseminating or distributing) this knowledge to others. These functions occur primarily in institutions such as libraries, schools, information centers, and public or government agencies. And these functions are directed toward *objects* such as documents and reports, *services* related to doc-

Libraries in Indonesia (1982)

Type	Administrative units	Service points	Volumes in collections	Annual expenditures (rupiah)	Population served	Professional staff	Total staff
National	1	--	600,000	537,404,000	5,548[a]	61	80
Academic	26	--	--	--	--	--	168
Public	274	--	467,986	--	--	--	533
School	1,139	--	--	--	3,653,780	--	10,389
Special	295[b]	--	1,000,000	--	--	--	800
Provincial Libraries	26	--	768,137	--	--	--	1,047
Mobile Libraries	104	--	151,029	--	--	--	--

[a]Unesco, *Statistical Yearbook,* 1984. 1981 data: registered borrowers.
[b]Directory of Special Libraries and Information Services in Indonesia, 1981.

Source: Center for Library Development, National Scientific Documentation Center.

ument storage and retrieval, and *technologies* that help in dealing with such objects.

Information scientists are occupied with records; such a focus suggests that information science has two basic roots, grounded in two fundamental human properties—enterprise and experience—recording human experience so that future generations can benefit from it.

Another way of examining the development of information science as a field is provided by Alvin M. Schrader in a 1984 article. The accompanying table lists conferences in information science from 1948 to 1978. The first conference whose title in any way referred to "information science" was the Second International Congress on Information System Sciences at Hot Springs, Virginia, in 1962. This conference, sponsored by the U.S. Air Force in collaboration with the Mitre Corporation of Lexington, Massachusetts, was an important step in identifying scholars from various disciplines with common goals of understanding information and the sciences related to it.

Selected Conferences

1948	London	Royal Society Scientific Information Conference
1950	Cambridge, Massachusetts	International Congress of Mathematicians, sponsored by the American Mathematics Society
1950	Chicago	Conference on Bibliographic Organization, sponsored by the Graduate Library School, University of Chicago
1952	London	Symposium on Applications of Communication Theory
1955	London	Third London Symposium on Information Theory
1955-56	Minneapolis: Dallas	Symposium on Chemical Literature Retrieval, sponsored by the American Chemical Society
1957	Dorking, England	International Study Conference on Classification for Information Retrieval
1957	Cleveland	Symposium on Systems for Information Retrieval
1958	Washington	International Conference on Scientific Information
1959	Cleveland	International Conference on Standards for a Common Language for Machine Searching and Translation, sponsored by Western Reserve University and the Rand Corporation
1960	London	Fourth London Symposium on Information Theory
1961-62	Atlanta	Conference on Training Science Information Specialists sponsored by Georgia Institute of Technology
1962	Hot Springs, Virginia	Second International Congress on Information System Sciences
1964	Cleveland	Conference on Education of Science Information Personnel, sponsored by Western Reserve University
1964	Elsinore, Denmark	Second International Study Conference on Classification Research
1964	Washington	Study Conference on Evaluation of Document Searching Systems and Procedures, sponsored by the National Science Foundation
1964	Cleveland	Conference on Education of Scientific Information Personnel, sponsored by Western Reserve University
1965	Warrenton, Virginia	Symposium on Education for Information Science sponsored by the American Documentation Institute
1965	Syracuse, New York	Symposium on the Foundations of Access to Knowledge, sponsored by Syracuse University and the National Science Foundation
1967	London	International Conference on Education for Scientific Information Work, sponsored by the International Federation for Documentation
1968	Albany, New York	Conference on the Bibliographic Control of Library Literature, sponsored by the State University of New York at Albany and the American Library Association
1969	Tokyo	First Japan–United States Conference on Libraries and Information Science in Higher Education
1970	London	Conference on International Developments in Scientific Information Services, sponsored by Aslib
1971	Devner	Symposium on Directions in Education for Information Science, sponsored by the American Library Association and the American Society for Information Science
1971	Rome	International Conference on Training for Information Work, sponsored by the International Federation for Documentation
1972	New York	Conference on Access to Knowledge and Information in the Social Sciences and Humanities
1972	Veszprem, Hungary	International Seminar on Education for Information Science
1972	Champion, Pennsylvania	NATO Advanced Study Institute on Information Science Search for Identity
1973	Aberystwyth, Wales	NATO Advanced Study Institute on Perspectives in Information Science
1975	Moscow	Conference on Terminology of Information and Documentation, sponsored by the International Federation for Documentation Committee on Terminology of Information and Documentation
1975	London	First International Form on Information Science
1977	Copenhagen	Second International Forum on Information Science, sponsored by the Royal School of Librarianship
1977	Albany, New York	Conference on Education for Information Science Strategies for Change in Library School Programs
1977	Aberystwyth, Wales	Workshop on Curriculum Development in Librarianship and Information Science
1978	Crete	NATO Advanced Study Institute on Information Science
1978	Moscow	Conference on New Trends in Informatics and Its Terminology, sponsored by the International Federation for Documentation Committee on Research on the Theoretical Basis of Information and Committee on Terminology of Information and Documentation

Source: Alvin M. Schrader, "In Search of a Name: Information Science and its Conceptual Antecedents," *Library and Information Science Research* (1984).

Additional insights into the growth of information science as a field can be found in studying the development of educational programs for information professionals. According to Tevko Saracevic, education for information science began with courses on documentation and on storage and retrieval. The first course on documentation in the U.S. was offered in 1950 by Helen Foche of Western Reserve University, Cleveland. James W. Perry and Allen Kent of the University of Pittsburgh later offered the first course on information retrieval. Perry and Kent presented the first academic attempt to describe the role of technology in the generation, use, and transfer of knowledge.

Several conferences have tried to identify the intellectual competencies and skills needed for the profession of information science. Despite these efforts, however, the search for a structure for educational programs specifically oriented to information science continues. By and large, academic programs serving information science are generally predicated on the needs of the job market.

Academic departments in information science provide another perspective. A report by the University of Maryland biomed project in 1967 found 52 institutions offering programs leading to graduate degrees in information science. Most of these programs were affiliated or associated with schools of library science. The first separate department of information science was established that same year, offering a program leading to a graduate degree specifically identified as information science, at the University of Dayton in Dayton, Ohio.

Fifteen years later, a 1982 study found 89 universities and colleges offering such graduate degree programs. An inventory of these programs reveals that many, if not most, are directly linked with library or computer science departments or schools, although some are associated with engineering or business schools. Information science as an area of scientific and professional interest had not achieved full definition and administrative autonomy in academic departments by the mid-1980s. A major study of the competencies that can be related directly to the field was conducted in 1984 by King Research, Inc. There is a fervent debate about whether professionals in the field should be the product of education or of training. In this debate, the need for developing individuals with certain competencies (such as skills in writing computer programs or conducting online searches) seems counterpoised against the need for developing individuals who possess a broad educational base and with it the capacity to develop theories and conduct research.

Interdisciplinary Perspectives. The interests of information scientists are diverse, addressing the problems inherent in generating, using, and disseminating knowledge. In fact, several in the field have suggested that information science actually borders on being an engineering discipline; whether or not information science should really be identified as information engineering can be and has been debated. In any case, the phenomena of information can be seen as metaphenomena embracing the principles of a number of disciplines; the view that information science incorporates the interests of a number of disciplines is one that enjoys broad support. The study of information science requires an understanding of a number of disciplines; some have suggested that in-

formation science thus fulfills the role and function of a metascience.

The growing interdisciplinary approach can be discerned in the slow but gradual inclusion of scientific interests among the issues identified with information science. Topics related to information and information systems are represented in the meetings and conferences of many scientific and engineering professional associations. A National Science Foundation study of the Information Professional reported 79 professional societies that were in one way or another directly related to and involved in the scientific and technical concerns of information science and its objectives.

THEORIES OF INFORMATION AND ITS PROPERTIES

As anyone who has ever attended a meeting, conference, or symposium in information science can attest, trying to define *information* can lead to utter frustration and even a breakdown in logical discourse. Except perhaps among philosophers, who by historical reference may possess an advantage, the term *knowledge* suffers a similar difficulty of definition. Hans Wellisch in 1971 produced a seminal report on the problems of defining information. Several institutes supported by the Scientific Division of the North Atlantic Treaty Organization documented the complexity of this matter; the influence of these institutes on the definition of information and knowledge is still to be determined. It is of course difficult to deal with theories of information (or anything else, for that matter) unless we know what we are talking about. At the very least an operational definition can be attempted.

The problems with defining *information* can be stated as follows:

First, historically, the word has been used without precision or specificity in meaning. The average person seems to know what is meant by information: "it's a fact, news, some content of knowledge."

Second, at a more technical level the word is used as a noun (as in "give me that information I need"). But information can almost become synonymous with being informed, in which case it becomes a verbal form; thus, information assumes a dual nature—a commodity that a person needs or the result of an action on the commodity.

Third, the term is seen in the context of communication and seems to be linked to the method by which we obtain it. One person gives information to another, who thereby becomes informed.

Because of the various ways that information can be viewed, discussing the theory of information becomes extensive and complex. Talking about a theory of information in a context where it is synonymous with facts or news leads directly to an insight into communication, which in turn suggests the role of journalism and media, among other issues. Marshall McLuhan's exhortations about the "hot and cold media" (or information) can stand as theoretical propositions of some magnitude and as such have been discussed extensively. In addition, the theory of transporting data (signals) from one place or person to another—communication—has been identified as part of the theory of information.

The differentiation between information as a

commodity or information as a process is theoretically provocative, and a review of some of the thinking associated with a theory of information is pertinent here.

Information as a Commodity. These theories are essentially logistical, dealing with information as if it were an object that is needed to do a job; acquiring, storing, and retrieving objects identified as information are important to our jobs and daily lives. In addition to the logistics, the object has economic value, so that economic theory related to information is of interest; indeed some information scientists consider the foundations of information science to be directly related to the laws dealing with the logistics of commodities. The following formulations are examples of such laws.

Zipf's Law shows that a relationship exists between the frequency in the use of words and their distribution in books, reports, documents, and other printed matter.

Bradford's Law provides the basis for understanding, through mathematical formulation, the distribution of scientific writing. The law describes how science-related literature and its uses and users are distributed.

Lotka's Law states that there is an exponential relationship between the number of items contributed to the literature and the total contribution by those who contribute two, three, or more papers.

An extension of the position that information is a commodity is advanced by those who have discussed information as analogous to energy (or meta-energy). In part this position assumes that, because information is similar to energy, it is a resource that can be handled as a utility; as a utility, information provides a basis for commerce akin to electricity, oil, gas, and water. Information can be packaged, stored, and distributed in various forms; in this sense, information has value, and the laws of economics can be applied to it.

Information as State or Process. Another formalism, devised by Debons, Horne, and Cronenweth, defines a knowledge spectrum, wherein information is considered to be at one end of a continuum. Information as a state of being is said to be synonymous with consciousness and awareness. The view of information as a process in relation to data and knowledge is germane to information theory. Debons has proposed that information is part of a continuum of processes through which all intellectual capacities of all organisms can be represented.

One thesis is that information represents the state of an organism following the reception of energy from the environment in the form of a symbol or datum. The transformation that occurs between datum and the resulting state (information) is part of the function of all organisms, and it reaches the highest known competence in the human being through the activities of the central nervous system. Technology, in the form of electronic devices such as computers, serves to extend these capabilities. Many theories are allied to this position.

Theories of information as a cognitive process embrace the notion that much of human behavior can be seen as information processing. Thinking, memory, learning, and perception are seen as functions of processing information.

Linked to and spurred on by the theoretical work of mathematician A. Turing, who established the theoretical framework of computing machinery (automata), thus providing the basis for automata theory, scholars have applied automata theory to the study of behavior. These studies add credibility to the thesis that information can be considered as a process intrinsic to all organismic activity and can be replicated in part by machines.

Human information processing (HIP) theory, developed by cognitive scientists (psychologists), is seen by some to be the leading fundamental concept of information science. HIP has been instrumental in a careful analytical examination of the role of language in information. Building on the debate between linguists and psychologists on the nature of language, scholars have extended their interest to the role of language as a technology in the representation of knowledge, including the nature of meaning and the process of formulating questions. The importance of this activity becomes clear when we realize the extent to which acquiring, storing, and retrieving information is a function of language—the way we ask questions and the kind of language we use in working with electronic devices such as computers.

APPLICATIONS OF INFORMATION SCIENCE

The use of information science must be related to how we perceive or define such a science. Because individuals variously consider information science as akin to library science, computer science, and communication science, its applications can be quite diverse. However, two perceptions have prevailed: one stresses the accounting of commodities—a logistical orientation; the other stresses the human use of such commodities—process orientation. A still broader view that embraces both of these perceptions examines information science in the tradition of a physical science, that is, by attempting to discover the fundamental laws that govern information, be they in energy, logistics, human mental activity, or systems.

The Logistical Application—Accounting of Commodities. Basically, much of the effort in this area has been directed at improving information resources and resource sharing. The development of databases has created a new climate for the business of acquiring information. Companies have sought to profit from advances in database construction and accessibility through new technology by establishing online information services. In contrast to the commercial sector, research projects such as those undertaken by certain universities (WEBNET, for example) have attempted to organize a number of local resource outlets, including libraries and online databases, to serve the purposes of the user.

To serve further the growing and changing logistical requirements and environment of the field, new entrepreneurial vocations have also arisen, such as information brokers, information consultants, and information counselors. This movement has extended the normal reference functions associated with the library toward their inclusion as part of commercial enterprises.

A still more encompassing application of information science, but one perhaps not as often entertained by those in the public sector, is the important role that information science plays in the analysis and design of information systems—particularly in management information systems, command-control-communication systems, decision support systems, and expert systems. These systems attempt to provide cognitive enhancements to the organization through the use of machines that are particularly designed to help human diagnostic, prescriptive, and evaluative functions, with various purposes, such as management in a business or diagnosis in medicine.

LIBRARY SCIENCE AND INFORMATION SCIENCE

It has been the fashion to differentiate between library science and information science; depending on political reasons or on personal predilection, the distinction will be based on experience, educational background, or job motivations. Some of the arguments in support of these predilections assume a certain rationality, while historical perspectives could pose a different set of counter-arguments leading to a different rationality.

As we have seen, data, information, and knowledge can be seen as part of a continuous spectrum. Ultimately, librarians and information scientists are interested in the generation, use, and transfer of knowledge. Like librarians, information scientists are in the knowledge "business." Whereas the library scientist and librarian are educated and trained to ensure the efficiency and effectiveness of the *institution* of the library to serve the needs of the user, the information scientist is interested in ensuring that the capability of the library is increased through the use of available *technology*.

The term *information systems* incorporates those resources already present in the library for achieving their objectives. Information systems—or environments for which the goal is to make people aware of what is available or going on—are the products of two merging forces: the increasing abundance of an organized record of human experience (knowledge) and the technology that permits the acquisition, storage, and retrieval of such records.

Toward Knowledge Systems. There is a basic human need to study and apply whatever we have experienced and learned toward problems and decisions. If human problems could be managed solely through human endowment, it is questionable that efforts would be expended for technology to supplement this endowment, whether through the library or the computer. However, it is increasingly clear that all aspects of knowledge are vital to human existence and survival. New ways of acquiring and capturing information, new ways of transmitting data across great distances, new ways of processing and of interpreting the data received, new and better ways of conveying the data are needed. We see the emergence of the concept of knowledge systems to incorporate these needs as an outgrowth of information science.

The continuing movement to improve our capacity to store and retrieve data results from the impact of science, particularly space science, in recent history. The nature of events in our time has demanded an increased awareness of and responsiveness to such events. The library, as the traditional custodian of records of human experience, and the information system that combines this resource of records with other technologies together provide the basis for structuring a system that augments our ability to understand, apply, synthesize, and evaluate our experience—the basis for a knowledge system. (See also Information Science Education.)

REFERENCES
C. West Churchman, *The Design of Inquiry Systems* (1971).
A. Debons, "Relation between Library and Information Science, *Journal of the South African Library Association* (1985).
A. Debons, E. Horne, and S. Cronenweth, *Information Science: An Introduction* (1986).
A. Debons, D. King, U. Mansfield, and D. Shirey, *The Information Professional: Survey of an Emerging Field* (1981).
Glynn Harmon, "On the Evolution of Information Science," *Journal of the American Society for Information Science* (1971).
C. Jancks and David Riesman, *The Academic Revolution* (1969).
T. Saracevic, "An Essay on the Past and Future of Information Science Education," *Information Processing and Management* (1979).
Hans Wellisch, "From Information Science to 'Informatics': A Terminological Investigation," *Journal of Librarianship* (1972).

ANTHONY DEBONS

Information Science Education

Information science has become an established discipline within the context of each of several related fields: librarianship, computer science, management, engineering, and others. This article defines information science and reviews the status of education for it, with special emphasis on its relevance to library education.

Definitions. First, it is essential to establish definitions of terms as they will be used in this article.

Information. The term "information" is used with a variety of meanings. Some identify it with communications over transmission lines, measured by the statistical properties of signals; some identify it with recorded facts; some with the content of text; some with the experience stored in the human mind. In this article, though, the following is the operational definition of the term:

> *Information* is a property of data resulting from or produced by a process performed upon the data. The process may be simply data transmission (in which case the definition and measure used in communication theory are applicable); it may be data selection; it may be data organization; it may be data analysis.

It is important to note that, given this definition, information is dependent upon the processes that produce it. While some of the properties of information may be investigated independent of the means for performing these processes, the important and interesting ones cannot. That means that information can best be understood in the context of specific systems.

Information Systems. Any complex phenomenon encompasses a variety of aspects—physical structure, cybernetic responses to environment, chemical and metabolic balance, or information processing. Thus a person can be viewed as a physical organism made of bones and muscles, capable of performing mechanical tasks; as a chemical factory processing ingested food, water, and air and converting them to metabolic energy; or as a thinking human being, taking in sensory data, making decisions, and controlling its physical and chemical structure. A library can be viewed as a collection of physical books and records; as an administrative organization; or as an information processing system, taking in data and providing it in response to requests. If the aspects of specific interest are those that we identify as information processing, the phenomenon becomes an information system. Hence, the definition:

An *information system* is that set of aspects of a general system (a natural phenomenon, a physical construct, or a logical construct) that are identified as information producing.

That leads then to the very natural definition of information science:

Information science is the study of information producing processes in any information system in which they may occur.

This means that while information science may in principle be concerned with the analysis of pure process, it depends primarily upon the methodologies for studying phenomena in specific disciplines. For example, RNA and DNA can be studied for the information processes they embody and, as such, are information systems of vital interest to information science. But it would be impossible to study the means by which they transmit, select, organize, and analyze data (as represented by configurations of amino acids) without the methods of microbiology. It is therefore most appropriate to talk about information science in the context of specific disciplines— in genetics, in social theory, in documentation, in librarianship—instead of talking about it in isolation from specific systems.

Information Systems. What then are examples of systems with which information science is concerned?

The Computer. The computer has been an especially important context for information science, for very clear reasons. The *raison d'être* for the computer is data processing. Furthermore, those processes are well defined and measurable in very precise ways; the computer is therefore a very predictable system to study.

Computer-based Information Systems. The use of the computer in an ever increasing variety of applications has resulted in computer-based information systems that have been a major focus of information science. They embody information processes considerably more complex than those of the computer itself, since they function within organizations that provide many of the additional processes needed for data acquisition and decision making by people. Information science in this context has therefore needed to include the body of techniques by which such organizations are studied and by which alternative systems for information processing are designed and evaluated.

Libraries and Information Centers. These specific organizations exist, as institutions, for the information processing functions they provide. Those functions—cataloguing and indexing, for example—are relatively well formalized and serve as ideal subjects for study by information science. The results of such study can have direct value to the institutions, by improving their operations and extending their services. Indeed, the extent of mutual value has been so great that some have identified information science with library science.

Social Systems and Biological Systems. Each of these performs information processes. In governmental structures, the processes for selection of officials and for organizing bureaucracies all constitute information processes. Economics is concerned with processes upon symbols of capital. The genetic code, embodied in the amino acids of DNA and RNA, is transmitted and reorganized through information processes. Psychology is concerned with processes of the human mind. Each of these clearly relates to an example of an information system, which taken together have been called "living systems."

Information Science Education. Given the range of information systems within which information science must be important, it is not surprising that there is a parallel array of programs for education in information science. The result is a diversity that makes it impossible to extract a common curriculum.

The Range of Programs. Some educational programs include information science as part of computer science; in a few cases, they have even called themselves "computer and information science" programs. Some have focused on the use of computers in libraries for either internal operations or computer-based services; in a large number of cases, they have called themselves "library and information science" programs. Some have identified information science with "science information," focusing on documentation, indexing and abstracting, and mechanized information retrieval. Some have focused on the uses of computers for application to information needs in business and industry; typically, they call themselves "information management" programs.

Historical Development. The earliest identifiable recognition of the field as part of librarianship (not in name, but in fact) was at Western Reserve University, under the guidance of Dean Jesse Shera. In the mid-1950s, James W. Perry and Allen Kent established the Center for Documentation and Communication Research as an adjunct of that library school.

In the subsequent five to ten years, a number of short courses, workshops, conferences, and similar ad hoc means for instruction were launched by a number of other universities—at UCLA, American University, Drexel, Georgia Institute of Technology, and the University of Washington. In them, the several types of context listed above were thoroughly intermixed, with computer systems specialists, librarians, documentalists, and business data processing systems persons all working in all of them. The result was continuing confusion among the related fields—science information, computer science, information systems design, and information science.

The steadily increasing number of ad hoc programs, however, provided clear evidence of a real need for formal instruction. In 1961 and 1962, two conferences were held at Georgia Institute of Technology at which, for the first time, the various aspects of the field were identified and delineated and goals for formal curricula were defined.

Almost immediately, in 1964 to 1967 various schools initiated formal information science programs, but with foci representing the differing aspects of the field. The ones started at Georgia Institute of Technology (Vladimir Slamecka), Ohio State (Marshall Yovits), and Lehigh University (Robert Taylor and Donald Hillman) focused on the technological and theoretical aspects. The ones at the University of Chicago (Don Swanson), Case Western Reserve (Perry, Kent, and later Alan Goldwyn), UCLA (Robert Hayes and Harold Borko), and Pittsburgh (Allen Kent) were established as integral parts of library schools.

In the subsequent years, these programs developed variously. Those with a technological and theoretical orientation gradually became indistinguishable from computer science programs. Some of those in library schools became independent (as at the University of Pittsburgh), though with a tenuous connection to librarianship. Others associated with library schools (Chicago and UCLA, in particular) became increasingly integrated with librarianship.

In parallel, virtually every other library school in the United States added courses on one or another of the kinds of subject matter identified with information science—information retrieval, computer applications to libraries, indexing and abstracting, and so on. Many library schools changed their names to reflect the coverage of information science; some refer to "library and information science," others to "library and information studies," but all with the same intent of broadening the definition of the field.

By the middle of the 1970s, the importance of computer usage for information services in business and industry led several schools to take a new direction, related to information science and representing one of the more specific areas of interest—information management or, alternatively, information resource management. These programs (at Syracuse and the University of Southern California, for example) saw an increasing need for educated personnel to develop, manage, and serve in the information systems being created in corporate enterprises.

By the mid-1980s, there was a broad array of information science programs, with a substantial area of common concern, especially with respect to the computer, but also with substantial differences in curricula and focus.

Structure of Curricula. The curricula will to some extent include coursework in six major areas: (1) core, introductory courses, (2) formal disciplines (mathematics and linguistics, for example), (3) applied disciplines (such as statistics and operations research), (4) computer-oriented courses (database management and computer retrieval, for example), (5) management oriented courses (accounting and organization theory, for example), and (6) information organization and service courses (cataloguing and reference, for example, though frequently with differing names). These reflect the need for an educational program in information science to provide the student with the intellectual orientation and technical tools needed for professional and research work in the field. The student must learn about how information is used, how systems are designed and operated, and

about the technical tools needed for information work.

An effective information curriculum should provide a common core of technical knowledge, integrated into a framework of the total field. It should provide the basis for specialization in any one of the major components—the information specialist, concerned with utilization; the information manager, concerned with operations; the system designer, concerned with technical problems in implementation; and the theoretician, concerned with the future research in the field. While any given curriculum will emphasize one or another of these specialty areas, each should be explicitly recognized if the curriculum is properly to be characterized as one in "information science."

Information Science in Library Education. Most library schools treat information science as a component of the M.L.S. degree program, with varying degrees of integration of it into the M.L.S. curriculum. While the broad range of specialties previously identified may be represented, the emphasis is likely to be on the operational and professional aspects, and there will be minimal attention to the other components. One crucial problem faced by every library school has been how best to integrate information science with the more traditional components of the M.L.S. curriculum. If not properly handled, the information science courses can become an isolated enclave, bearing little relationship to the remainder of the curriculum; the result is a loss for faculty and students in both library science and information science. Fortunately, the progress within the decade 1976–85 in development of computer-based systems and services within libraries made it easy to incorporate at least those aspects of information science into the M.L.S. curriculum. The more theoretical and technical course work, however, is difficult to encompass within the framework of one-year M.L.S. programs, and the coverage of it, if any, tends to be superficial.

Standards. As of 1985, there were no established standards for education in information science, nor was there an accrediting body for the field. However, the American Library Association explicitly recognized information science in its *1972 Standards for Accreditation,* regarding it as an essential component of M.L.S. programs. In 1985 and 1986 the ALA Committee on Accreditation continued an investigation initiated by the Association of Library and Information Science Education (ALISE) aimed at determining how best to accommodate the needs of information science and other specialties in the field within the accreditation process.

ROBERT M. HAYES

Information Technologies

Specialized technology has, broadly speaking, been used in libraries for many years. Consider, for example, the wide range of circulation technologies: three-by-five cards, edge-punched McBee circulation systems, the Gaylord Model C charging machine, early computer batch card circulation systems, and so on. Similarly, microfilm technology has been used in libraries to help preserve library materials that are rapidly disintegrating as a result of age or the chemical content of the paper itself. Libraries have also embraced the many formats in which information is published—such as audio, video, microforms, and maps—each of which requires its own technology to view and use materials. Effective use of technology helps make libraries more than mere warehouses of books.

CURRENT INFORMATION TECHNOLOGIES

The information technologies found in libraries today can be conveniently divided into three categories: (1) computers; (2) storage media; and (3) communications devices.

Computers. A computer is an electronic device that automatically performs a specified sequence of processing operations on data to achieve a desired purpose. General purpose digital computers are used to store and retrieve information, perform calculations, process transactions, and sort data, all at great speed. Because of this speed, they can process a large volume of routine transactions efficiently and store huge amounts of information. In libraries, computers can store large files and make them quickly available to both staff members and patrons.

Digital computers come in a variety of sizes. Within each size category, a range of processing capabilities is available: hence clear distinctions are becoming blurred. Typically, computers are grouped into three broad categories:

1. Mainframe computers are the oldest, fastest, and most expensive type of digital computer. Evolving since about 1960, the mainframe is today the most versatile computer available, usually serving a large number of users simultaneously performing a variety of tasks. Mainframe computers typically require a large support staff composed of managers; systems analysts and programmers to prepare the "software;" and operators to run the "hardware." They require large air conditioning systems to maintain a consis-

tent, cool environment. The dominant force in the mainframe computer market is International Business Machines (IBM). IBM's competitors are affectionately known as "the BUNCH" (Burroughs, Univac, NCR, Control Data Corporation, and Honeywell).

2. Minicomputers, developed during the late 1960s, are slightly slower, smaller, and less expensive than mainframe computers. Minicomputers can support a large number of users at one time, but these users are limited to working on one application (such as circulation control) at a time. Minicomputers are the machine of choice for the "turnkey" vendors who supply both hardware and software as a package to library customers. "Minis," as minicomputers are usually called, require fewer support staff, and usually require only a limited amount of air conditioning. Among the many minicomputer manufacturers with which librarians may be familiar are: Digital Equipment Corporation (DEC), Data General (DG), Hewlett-Packard, and IBM.

3. Microcomputers are the smallest computer available today. Developed during the late 1970s, "micros" have become commonplace tools in the home, office, and library. The microcomputer typically serves a single user performing a single task. The Apple II, Radio Shack TRS-80, Commodore PET, and IBM PC are the most popular microcomputers available today; in fact, the IBM PC has become a de facto standard in the business community. There is more software available to run on the PC than on any other machine. Selection of the IBM PC by all the bibliographic utilities, including OCLC, RLIN, WLN, and UTLAS, as their cataloguing terminal by 1985 means that the IBM PC has also become a new library standard.

The Table provides summary comparative information about mainframe computers, minicomputers, and microcomputers.

It is important to note that distinctions between different sizes of computer are convenient but not precise. It is not uncommon for some manufacturers

Computer Capability and Applications

	Microcomputer	Minicomputer	Mainframe Computer
Number of Terminals			
1–8	X		
8–120		X	
120 +			X
Number of Tasks	One	Limited	Many
Hardware Capability			
CPU word size	8–16	16–32	32–64
CPU memory	Limited	Modate	Large
Speed of CPU	Slow	Medium	Fast
Input/Output Speed	Slow	Medium	Fast
Type of processing	Serial	Overlapped	Parallel
Auxiliary Storage	Small floppy diskettes	Small-medium hard disks	Large hard disks
Type of Application			
Low cost	X	X	
Transaction		X	
Major computing		X	X
Batch computing			X

to talk about thier "super micro" or "super mini."

The basic units of any computer memory are *bits* (a contraction of two words, "binary digit"). Bits, when combined in groups, form *bytes*. A byte is equivalent to one character of data—for example, the letter "J" or the number "6." The storage capacity of the computer's primary storage unit (usually called the central processing unit or CPU) is expressed in bytes. One block of 1,024 bytes is abbreviated by the letter *K*. Thus, a computer with 256 K memory has 262,144 bytes of main memory. A *megabyte* is one million bytes. Even microcomputers can now have one megabyte or more of memory.

Based on the most recent data available, it is safe to say that by 1985 more than 2,500 libraries had at least one computer, whether a mainframe, mini, or microcomputer, in use.

The computer itself has limited capabilities. It might be compared to a stereo amplifier without the speakers, tuner, tape deck, and turntable. Therefore, additional equipment, called peripherals, is necessary to take advantage of the processing power of the computer.

The majority of peripheral devices are designed to provide either a means by which data can be entered into the computer (input) or a means by which data can be retrieved from the computer (output). Common input devices include keyboards, magnetic tape readers, magnetic disk drives, bar code readers, and optical character scanners. Data output from the computer can be displayed on a visual display unit, usually called a cathode ray tube (CRT) terminal, recorded on a magnetic tape or disk, printed out on paper or cardstock, typeset on film or paper, or used to produce a computer output microform (COM) product.

Storage Media. Since the CPU has a finite amount of data storage capacity the computer requires additional or auxiliary storage. Among the traditional data storage media are magnetic disk, magnetic tape, and audio tape. Some storage media, such as magnetic tape, provide access to the information only in a sequential manner, which is adequate for infrequently accessed information. Magnetic disks provide random access to the stored information, and must be used for data that is frequently updated or reviewed.

A *disk* is the most common auxiliary storage device. The computer disk is a hard metal or soft plastic platter that closely resembles a phonograph record. The soft disks, often called "floppy disks" or "diskettes," are handled singly. Hard disks are usually stacked one on top of another, separated by spacers, in "disk packs." Disk capacity is measured in megabytes (*MB*); for example, a 300 MB disk has 307,200,000 bytes of disk storage capacity. Of this amount, between 80 and 90 percent is available for data storage. An overview of the capabilities of various auxiliary storage devices is shown in Table 2.

Communications Devices. Peripheral devices located more than 3,000 feet from the computer require additional equipment to allow communications. (Devices located less than 3,000 feet from the computer can be wired directly to the CPU). For example, a group of libraries sharing an automated library system, several branch libraries linked to a computer at the main library, or libraries using the

OCLC system must all communicate with the computer from a distance, usually over telephone lines.

This area of communications, called *telecommunications,* requires a *modem* (a contraction of the terms "modulate-demodulate") to enable the computer and the peripheral devices to exchange signals. A pair of modems is required for each peripheral device—one at the site where the peripheral is located, and one at the CPU. The modem at one end translates the *digital* signals of the computer into the *analog* signals understood by the telephone system; the modem at the other end translates them back again. Heavy users lease the phone lines (called "dedicated lines") instead of making a separate phone call for each use.

Since the breakup of AT&T in 1984, competing telephone services have gained national recognition. Many of these services use alternative technologies to complete the telecommunications process.

Coaxial cable, commonly used to carry television signals, can also carry large amounts of computer data, but the signal must be amplified every 4 to 5 miles. Coaxial cables are used in *local area networks (LANs),* designed to link terminals, printers, and other peripheral equipment to a computer or group of computers in the same building or in nearby buildings.

Microwaves can also carry telecommunication signals, but the signal must be amplified and refocused every 25 or 30 miles. Microwave is a line-of-sight technology; microwave towers must be placed so that hills and trees cannot interfere with the signal.

Satellite transmission is similar to microwave. In this case, the "tower" is a satellite in orbit 22,500 miles above the earth; any antenna or "dish" within the satellite's receiving area on earth can pick up the signal. The primary advantage of satellite transmission is that its cost is not based on the distance the signals must travel. Satellite antenna costs are falling and the size of the dishes is also coming down, making this technology an affordable option for libraries. The University of California, for example, is installing satellite communications as a part of its campus-wide online union catalogue.

Value-added networks, such as Tymnet and Telenet, provide systems that collect and transmit large volumes of messages over telephone lines in an efficient manner. Their attraction for libraries is that they charge a flat rate, regardless of the distance traveled.

Fiber optics technology employs thin glass fibers which, in combination with optical (light) technology, can now handle the telecommunication load that used to require traditional copper wire telephone lines several inches thick.

Telex/TWX, a fairly old technology, has been used by libraries for a number of years. Telex/TWX provides a paper copy of each message, but it is relatively expensive primarily because of its low transmission speeds. The many libraries that continue to rely on Telex/TWX should consider the cost-effectiveness of other technologies.

Telefacsimile or "fax" is essentially a long-distance copying machine, but by 1985 this technology was still not widely used in libraries. Fax suffers from three principal limitations: (1) only single sheets can be fed into the machine, so that some materials must be photocopied before they can be transmitted; (2) the transmission speeds for library materials have been fairly slow because of the high density of the text, making the cost per page high; and (3) the resolution of the received text is not always satisfactory, so that some pages may have to be retransmitted.

APPLICATION OF INFORMATION TECHNOLOGIES

Needs Assessment. The first and most important step in considering the application of technology to a library setting is to perform a needs assessment or needs analysis. The objective of this process is to understand current operations and to determine how frequently a particular activity is performed. Computer systems are especially effective when asked to do frequently occuring tasks. As a part of the assessment, it is important to understand the "why" of the library's operations; if it is not clear why a particular task is currently being done, then that task might be eliminated, rather than automated. The major benefits of considering a new technology often come not from the technology itself but from examining and changing existing procedures and operations.

Tools used to help complete this step in the process are systems analysis, work/flow analysis, and time/activity surveys. *Systems analysis* describes current operations, often using flowcharts and other tools, by breaking complex activities down into simple steps. *Work/flow analysis* charts the movement of both information and physical materials, such as books, memos, and documents, within an organization. A *time/activity survey* provides detailed information about the time and associated costs for a variety of activities. This information is often used to help prepare a cost/benefit analysis.

In considering various options for the application of new technology, it is important to recognize how various services are priced. *Variably priced services* charge for each transaction, so the more they are used, the more they cost. Examples include OCLC's cataloguing or interlibrary loan modules and vendors of COM catalogues. *Fixed-price* services, such as an automated library system located in the library, have a one-time installation cost and recurring maintenance and overhead costs. When fixed-price services are used frequently, the cost per transaction actually falls; thus fixed-price services offer the greatest potential benefits to a library.

Selection. Once the library has determined that a particular technology is a candidate for implementation, there is often a bewildering variety of choices. How to choose? The first step is to prepare written specifications that document the library's requirements and can be used as a basis of comparison for the offerings in the marketplace. These specifications usually become part of a formal document, called a Request for Proposal (RFP) or Invitation for Bid (IFB). The RFP is sent to system providers for written proposals. When the proposals have been received, they are rated against the written specifications. References from existing customers should be obtained and even more detailed information can be gathered during a site visit to an existing installation. It may be prudent to invite the top three or four system providers in to demonstrate their systems in the library.

If the offerings of vendors in the marketplace are not sufficient to meet the library's needs, the library may wish to consider developing its own system. This approach is not advised, however, because of the high risks involved—the cost of machines that may not work together properly, the cost of programming, and the danger of building a system so complex and so specialized that only a few individuals can operate or maintain it.

Once the selection has been made, a written contract will be needed. The library should *not* simply sign a standard form contract provided by the vendor, but should submit a draft System Purchase Agreement and System Maintenance Agreement to the vendor as the point from which to start contract negotiations. Indeed, libraries are advised to seek outside assistance with this part of the system selection process, because any good contract must clearly spell out vendor responsibilities in many situations.

Installation. If the system to be installed is a minicomputer or mainframe computer, the system provider will give the library detailed instructions about the environmental conditions required to ensure the smooth operation of the hardware, and these instructions must be carefully followed. If terminals are to be placed in various staff and public areas, then existing furniture may need to be rearranged or new furniture acquired.

Among the many complaints heard from people who use computer terminals for long hours, two problem areas consistently emerge: lighting and furniture. The existing lighting in most buildings was not designed to be compatible with terminals, and there may be significant amounts of light reflecting off the face of a terminal screen. When terminals are simply placed on existing furniture, workers may have to assume awkward positions to read the display, with resulting muscle fatigue, backaches, and headaches. These problems may be overcome by providing chairs and desk surfaces that are adjustable, and by allowing for individual control over lighting—"task lighting."

Administration and Maintenance. All technology must be managed and maintained. Thus, someone within the organization will need to be knowledgeable about the technology and how to adapt it to the goals of the library. In addition, to achieve maximum benefits from the technology, existing manual procedures will need to be revised to complement the capabilities and limitations of the new technology. Adminstrators must also recognize that the organization becomes vitally dependent upon the technology; portions of the budget become fixed costs over which they have little or no control.

One of the principal problems library administrators face when considering the use of new technology is securing the funding required for the initial purchase of the system. Moreover, no technology—especially computer technology—will last forever; the library is likely to face the same capital accumulation problem every seven to ten years unless it develops a strategy, such as a system replacement and enhancement sinking or reserve fund, to cope with this problem.

EMERGING TECHNOLOGIES

Three emerging information technologies can be identified as having great potential for libraries: the videodisk, packet-switching radio, and instructional

363

television.

Videodisk. The great appeal of videodisk is its capacity for storing vast quantities of information and retrieving this information quickly. In addition, the preservation qualities of videodisk exceed that of microfilm. There are a number of videodisk technologies, two of them of primary interest to libraries: the digital 12-inch videodisk, which can store one gigabyte of data—1,000,000,000 characters per side; and the CD ROM (Compact Disk, Read Only Memory) audio disk, which can store 600 megabytes of data. Both use lasers to read the information from the disk, so there is no wear on the disk itself despite heavy use.

Among the videodisk products demonstrated at American Library Association conferences in 1984 and 1985 were: Carrollton Press, (12-inch videodisk) MARVLS, DisCon, and DisCat for retrospective conversion and current cataloguing; Library Corporation, Bibliofile (CD ROM disk) for current cataloguing and retrospective conversion; Library Systems and Services, MiniMARC (12-inch videodisk) for current cataloguing and retrospective conversion; Information Access Corporation, InfoTrac (12-inch videodisk) for access to periodical indexes; and International Standard Information Systems (CD ROM disk) for access to six databases, including ERIC and a subset of PsychoINFO. Additional products could clearly be expected in the future. The Library of Congress begain experimenting in the 1980s with two videodisk systems, one to store, retrieve, and print catalogue cards and one to preserve library materials.

The University of California Division of Library Automation began experimenting with the use of packet-switching radio for broadcast telecommunications by a number of terminals located within a building and among buildings on a single campus. This technology would eliminate the need to run data cables to each terminal.

The U.S. Federal Communications Commission has assigned some television frequencies for use by educational institutions for instruction, but by the mid-1980s only a few institutions had applied for permission to use them. The unused capacity of this transmission technology could be used to meet the voice and data telecommunication requirements of educational institutions, including libraries.

Market Forces. Historically, suitable technology has arrived slowly in libraries, but the pace quickened in the 1980s. Vendors began to realize that many of the needs of libraries are somewhat similar to those of automated offices. Yet even in the face of fairly stiff competition in the marketplace, the technology providers, rather than libraries themselves, were clearly driving the pace of development.

Libraries *can* have an impact on the development of technology which better meets their needs. This is illustrated by the efforts of a number of academic libraries that decided to try to shape the online catalogue, then in its infancy. This group, called CONDOC (Consortium to Develop an Online Catalog), developed a set of public access online catalogue specifications which were shared with all vendors. Over the next 18 months the vendor offerings moved quickly to include the features sought by CONDOC. Similar results are possible in other areas; a group of

libraries could similarly seek a microcomputer replacement for the Teletype.

Cooperative Programs. The high initial costs of new technology, especially computer technology, can be prohibitive. A number of libraries have found that economic and service benefits can be derived from sharing automated library systems.

Technology is here to stay; and the fact that technology is changing and affording new opportunities for libraries to play an important role in this information age should be apparent. The challenge facing libraries is in learning how to embrace and manage technology for the benefit of their patrons.

See also articles on various library operations and services (such as Cataloguing, Circulation) for details on applications of information technology.

REFERENCES
John Corbin, *Developing Computer-Based Library Systems* (1981).
Kenneth C. Dowlin, *The Electronic Library* (1983).
Journal of Library Automation (December 1979). Entire issue focuses on developing a system within the library.
James Martin, *The Computerized Society* (1981).
Joseph R. Matthews, *Choosing an Automated Library System* (1980).
William Saffady. *Introduction to Automation for Libraries* (1983).

JOSEPH R. MATTHEWS

Institutionalized, Services to the

Although there are still institutions existing in the United States that provide no library service to their residents, such service had reached an all-time high by the mid-1980s, both in the number of institutions providing the service, and in the quality of that service. The Library Services and Construction Act (LSCA) has not only provided for growth in library services to the institutionalized, but also stimulated local funding for this service.

There have been many recent changes in these libraries. The number of people reported to be in institutions in the United States in the 1980 census was 2,506,777—an increase of 346,497 over the number reported in 1970. There is, however, a change in the ratio of those people in institutions over those outside institutions. In 1980, one out of every 90 persons counted was institutionalized, while in 1970 the number was one out of every 100. The libraries providing service in institutions are directly affected by both the population trends in the institution and the general trends taking place in society, including the actions and attitudes of government concerning people who are institutionalized. A rising crime rate, the lack of new construction of correctional facilities, and the failure to expand existing ones at a pace necessary to keep up with the number of people coming into correctional institutions, all have resulted in seriously overcrowded conditions. This overcrowding has taxed all resources and services to the people in these institutions, including library services. The difficulty of providing adequate library service in overcrowded facilities is severe; libraries must provide not only materials for recreational reading at all levels, but also legal materials, in compliance with the *Younger v Gil-*

more decision that legal information must be provided in prisons and jails.

In contrast, the reverse situation is true of many others types of institutions as a result of the concepts of "mainstreaming" and independent living for the many physically and mentally disabled persons who were formerly placed in instutitions. One example is the trend away from institutionalizing the mentally retarded. The institutional libraries for these people still provide active programs of service, but they have had to alter many of them in response of the mainstreaming of those who can benefit from living in less restrictive environments. Many institutions now work only with the profoundly or severely mentally retarded. Because of these changes in the population to be served, greater emphasis is placed on the special programs introduced into the institutional libraries as well as on special collections.

Collection development still includes basic print materials, but libraries now go far beyond such basic collections in their programs. While audiovisual materials have had a prominence in institutional library programs for many years, as they have had in all libraries, they have become essential to institutional libraries. The high cost of these materials and their wide variety have led to greater sharing of audiovisual materials within a state or a region. Sometimes they are provided by the state library agency, as in West Virginia, or through a large public library, as in Kansas. Sometimes the sharing is conducted among institutional libraries themselves; one example of such a cooperative program is the cooperative film program in Missouri.

In addition, toys, games, and realia are important in libraries such as those for people who are mentally or physically disabled. An outstanding program in this area is that of the media center at the Wheat Ridge (Colorado) Regional Center for the Developmentally Disabled, where a part of its unique collection is a "sensory wall."

Because it is important that libraries meet the individual needs of the people in institutions, much research attention is being given to the information needs of the institutionalized. As a result, some libraries are conducting reader/user studies—important because, although many institutions now have professionally trained librarians, other libraries are managed by people with only in-service training and are operated under only the general supervision of a professional librarian in an outside state, regional, or local library. Patron studies help libraries ensure that their services match the needs of the people in the institutions.

Literacy programs are as much a part of library service as they are in society at large. They are perhaps even more important in institutional programs. The Library Service to Prisoners Forum, held at the ALA Annual Conference in Chicago in 1985 by the Association of Specialized and Cooperative Library Agencies, focused on the need for literacy programs outside of and within the correctional setting. Literacy needs were met at the Cambridge Mental Health and Development Center in Ohio through a project whereby the library worked with adolescent and adult students. Another creative program was Project Literacy at the Western Psychiatric Institute in Pittsburgh, Pennsylvania, where the patients' librarian di-

Stockholms Staatsbibliothek

Book-truck delivery of library materials to patients in a Swedish hospital

rected a volunteer tutoring service for deinstitutionalized patients.

Many institutional libraries now include in their programs group therapy, pre-release training and the development of skills needed to find jobs. Bibliotherapy, including poetry therapy, is also a part of many institutional library programs. Technology is apparent in library programs; the use of computers both as aids in the library program and as learning tools is incorporated into some institutional library services.

Because the many changes found in institution populations are reflected in library programs, some standards which have been applicable to institutional libraries have become outmoded. The 1980's have seen new or revised standards; some are the result of efforts within a state such as those on selecting materials for resident libraries in Texas institutions, guidelines for library services in jails and detention facilities in Maryland, and the standards for patient library services in Massachusetts. In many instances, the people developing the standards in the states have acquired the opinions and knowledge of people outside the state with an expertise in the field. In other instances, the standards have evolved as the result of evaluations of the services through the work of outside consultants who have surveyed the institutional service and have presented reports; such evaluations were made in Illinois and California in the area of library services in correctional institutions. Attention is also paid to the evaluation of library programs in institutions to determine the adequacy of library service to the institutionalized. Through these evaluations, changes can be effected as needed to remedy any inadequacies which exist.

The services provided to the institutionalized remain many and varied. Audiovisual listening and reviewing centers utilize these materials and equipment in many types of institutions. The "sensory wall" provides stimulation activities for the developmentally disabled, and the resulting auditory experiences, kinesthetic/tactile sensations, and olfactory experiences as well as visual stimuli are very effective. In institutions providing library services to children, many libraries provide materials for use by parents. Legal materials are widely available in many institutions, especially those in the field of corrections. Large print books and high-interest/low reading-level library materials, along with materials for non-English speaking people, are needed.

The materials are made in a variety of ways. Bookmobiles are a popular means of providing supplementary service, as is Books-by-Mail. Inter-library loan and rotating collections provide a means to supplement small local collections and to provide currency in the service. Computerized lists of institutional holdings facilitate coordinated acquisitions and resource sharing. Service from regional or state libraries strengthen the collections and services. Transportation from the institution to the local public library is also a means used to supplement institutional collections. Centralized acquisition of library materials, as was accomplished by the Texas State Library, ensures access to a variety of material for a group of institutions while cooperative planning in acquisitions broadens the scope of the institutional collections. Special programs in institutional libraries rival those of libraries outside of institutions. It is possible to survey readily the reading needs of an institutional population at almost any given time.

Another consideration involved in institutional library service is the freedom of the institutionalized to read. Two documents can be cited which support the right to read in relation to institutional libraries. A positive declaration on the right of prisoners to read was stated in a resolution passed by the ALA Council. The Massachusetts Board of Library Commissioners Service to Mental Health Facilities developed a policy statement on patients' rights to library service.

Library service to people in institutions continued to be provided in a variety of ways. Many institutions maintain libraries within the facility with supplemental services from other libraries. In some instances the regional libraries provide the institutional services or they are provided by library systems. Some institutional libraries are actually part of the local school system. Bookmobiles provide basic

services at times. Complete service by a public library or a community college library is often provided to the institution; this is especially true of jail library service. Institutional libraries are often a part of a cooperative which includes all types of libraries in a large geographical area.

Further research is needed in institutional library service in many areas. Some of those are the following: (1) studies of the impact of library service on people in institutions; (2) analysis of the reasons why people in institutions use the library; (3) determining whether on release from an institution library users continue to use libraries. (4) consideration of effects of specialized training on the quality of institutional library service by professional staff.

Such research will be easier to accomplish in the future; many institutional librarians were formerly isolated because of their geographical location or because there was little formal contact with other librarians available. The trend in the 1980's has been toward providing opportunities in institutions to meet formally with other librarians. The New Jersey State Library provides meetings and workshops for institutional librarians as do the Maine and New Mexico State Libraries. In North Dakota, the Governor's Council on Libraries is involved in workshops for institutional libraries, as is the Virgin Islands Bureau of Libraries, Museums and Architectural Services. The Florida Division of Library Services holds an annual Conference on Institutional Libraries in cooperation with the Florida State University's Center for Professional Development. In Louisiana an annual meeting for institutional librarians is held.

Closely related to this pattern of holding workshops is special training for librarians and other library personnel in institutional libraries, such as that provided by the Colorado State Library. A slide-tape show on institutional library services was developed by the Massachusetts Board of Library Commissioners Consultant Services. Both the Montana State Library and the New Mexico State Library offer in-service staff training programs. The Virginia Library Commission Consultant Services also provides training. Through these workshops and training sessions, the institutional library personnel learn the importance of understanding the individuals with whom they are working; that in providing the service, the emphasis is on the people being served; and that the development of collections, activities, and facilities arises from these bases of understanding.

As the movement to bring people with disabilities into the mainstream of society and as the independent living movement has taken people out of the institutional setting, or even prevented them from entering it, such people now have a need for service from libraries outside institutions. This common need brings institutional libraries closer to noninstitutional libraries because they both serve certain people with similar needs. Institutional library service is not really different in purpose from the specialized services of the noninstitutional libraries except in their setting and intensity.

While funding for institutional libraries is often insufficient to meet the need, the present and future of institutional library service is positive. The Library Services and Construction Act funds enable institutional librarians to maintain their programs through

Library service is offered to prisoners.

Stockholms Staatsbibliothek

the "maintenance of effort" requirements—that the total amount of funds expended in a given year cannot be less than the amount expended in the second preceding year. This requirement plus a greater acceptance of the need and value of institutional library service has moved such programs forward. In prior years these programs might have lost ground during difficult funding years. Library service to the institutionalized has a permanent and important place among other types of library service in local, state, and national plans for library service and in their implementation.

REFERENCES

Barbara S. Crosby, *Selecting Library Materials for Resident Libraries in State Institutions,* Texas State Library (1984).

Robert Ensley, "Synopsis: An Evaluation of System-provided Library Services to State Correctional Centers in Illinois," *Illinois Libraries* (1984).

Massachusetts Committee on Standards Patients' Library Services, *Massachusetts Standards for Patients' Library Services* (1984).

Rhea Joyce Rubin, *An Evaluation of System-provided Services to State Correctional Centers in Illinois* (1983). *Standards for Libraries at Institutions for the Mentally Retarded* (1981).

PHYLLIS I. DALTON

International Association of Agricultural Librarians and Documentalists

The International Association of Agricultural Librarians and Documentalists (IAALD) was founded in 1955 to promote agricultural library science and documentation, internationally and nationally, as well as the professional interests of agricultural librarians and documentalists. The term agriculture is interpreted in its widest sense and includes forestry, agricultural engineering, veterinary science, fisheries, food and nutrition, and agricultural and food industries.

There were more than 600 members from some 80 countries in 1985. Membership is open to agricultural librarians and documentalists as individuals, corporate bodies (national and multinational associations of agricultural librarians and documentalists), and institutions (libraries, information or documentation centers, research and educational institutions, and official bodies).

In pursuing its objectives, IAALD encourages collaboration among agricultural libraries and documentation centers in various countries, including the loan and exchange of books, journals, and reports. This exchange has been formalized by the establishment of AGLINET, a cooperative document supply system supported by the major agricultural libraries of the world. The Association assists in the coordination of activities and projects dealing with agricultural bibliographies and abstracting services. It cooperates with national, regional, and international organizations and networks in the field of agricultural information. In particular, IAALD supported and took part in the development of the FAO-sponsored international agricultural information system, AGRIS.

The organs of the Association are the General Assembly, the Executive Committee, and the Secretariat. The General Assembly of all members meets every five years in a World Congress at which it lays down general policy, amends the Constitution, appoints officers and members of the Executive Committee, and establishes membership fees. The Executive Committee consists of a President, two Vice-Presidents, a Secretary/Treasurer, at least six but not more than ten members, and a representative from each recognized national or multinational association of agricultural librarians and documentalists. The Executive Committee calls meetings of the General Assembly and directs the Association between them. The Secretariat handles current affairs of the Association under the direction of the Secretary/Treasurer. Additionally, a Working Group has been established on IAALD Education and Training.

IAALD holds a World Congress every five years. The seventh World Congress was held in 1985 in Ottawa, Canada, on the general theme, "Information for Food." The 1980 Congress, in Manila, Philippines, took up the theme of "Agricultural Information to Hasten Development." Regional congresses are held at other times.

From 1956 the Association published a *Quarterly Bulletin of IAALD* and from 1980 the *IAALD News,* an occasional President's newsletter, both free to members. In addition to the *Proceedings* of the World Congresses, it published *World Directory of Agricultural Libraries and Documentation Centres* (1960), *Current Agricultural Serials: a World List* (2 volumes, 1965 and 1967), *Primer for Agricultural Libraries* (2nd edition, 1980), and the *Proceedings* (1984) of an IAALD-sponsored regional conference, the International Conference on Education and Training for Agricultural Library and Information Work, held at Nairobi, Kenya, March 7-12, 1983.

IAALD is affiliated with the International Federation of Library Associations and the International Federation for Documentation as an international member. It has close contact with regional and national associations in its field, which are represented on its Executive Committee.

ROBERT W. BUTLER

International Association of Law Libraries

The International Association of Law Libraries (IALL), established in New York City in 1959, is a professional organization of lawyers, legal information specialists, bibliographers, and law librarians. The IALL Constitution describes the goals and objectives as follows:

> to promote on a cooperative, non-profit and fraternal basis the work of individuals, libraries, and other institutions and agencies concerned with the acquisition and bibliographic processing of legal materials collected on a multinational basis, and to facilitate the research and other uses of such materials on a world-wide basis.

IALL members represent 54 countries on 5 continents. The membership is composed of individuals and institutions specifically interested in the transmission of law-related information throughout the world and international cooperation on the level of official and private documentation. For that purpose, IALL is affiliated with other international organizations such as the International Federation of Library Associations and the International Federation for Documentation. IALL also has working relationships with such specialized organizations as the Association of Parliamentary Libraries and the Association of International Libraries.

The main purpose of IALL is to emphasize the pooling and dissemination of legal and documentary sources and publications among its members as well as other lawyers, law librarians, and legal bibliographers. It supports an active publication program and regular institutes and meetings of the membership.

For several years before the June 1959 meeting in New York City when the IALL was born, a small group of legal information specialists—William R. Roalfe, then Law Librarian and Professor of Law at Northwestern University; William B. Stern, Foreign Law Librarian at Los Angeles County Law Library; and Kurt Schwerin, Assistant Librarian and Associate Professor of Law at Northwestern University—carefully laid the groundwork for the IALL. Their work was the result of constant frustrations involved in source work on foreign and international law. Having experienced the raised standards, higher efficiency, and improved status brought about in the United States by the American Association of Law Libraries, they felt similar results could be achieved on an international level. Roalfe was elected the first President of the Association.

The IALL Board of Directors is comprised of representatives from throughout the world. IALL Headquarters migrates with the President of the Association. IALL committees include IALL regional advisory councils.

A formal program of institutes was inaugurated by IALL in 1964. Institutes address a wide range of legal research, bibliography, and documentation subjects. The following were held from 1975 to 1985:

1975: Workshop on selected problems of the European Communities in Bergisch-Gladbach, Federal Republic of Germany. Round table discussion on the law library profession, held in conjunction with the International Federation of Library Associations General Conference in Oslo.

1976: Round table conference on the significance of legal literature and documentation in developing countries in Lausanne, Switzerland.

1977: IALL course on the legal literature of socialist countries in Budapest, Hungary. Round table discussion of law library development in conjunction with IFLA meeting at Brussels.

1978: Workshop on the Japanese law and legal literature in Tokyo.

1979: Meeting on Latin-American legal literature in Quito, Ecuador.

1980: IALL week in Manila; round table discussion on development of libraries and information systems: global information for greater international understanding.

1981: Course on law librarianship in Sydney and Canberra, Australia.

1982: Participation at the 47th IFLA general conference with program presentation on international cooperation in law librarianship and legal documentation.

1983: Round table conference on admiralty and maritime law: the state of art and survey of literature in conjunction with IFLA meeting at Montreal.

1984: 25th IALL anniversary, in Freiburg im Breisgau, Federal Republic of Germany; course on courts, law libraries, and legal information in a changing society.

1985: Preliminary program of the 26th IALL conference on law in multicultural societies; the role of cultural heritage in modern legal systems (Israel as an example), in Jerusalem.

The Association's official publication, *IALL Bulletin,* began its first issue in September 1960 and lasted until December 1972 (issue no. 30), when the name was changed to *The International Journal of Law Libraries* (vol. 1, no. 1, March 1973) and then to *The International Journal of Legal Information* (vol. 10, no. 1, February 1982–). It appears three times annually and contains articles on problems and concerns of law librarianship, current surveys of legal literature, bibliographies, and book reviews, as well as reports and results of the IALL meetings. The IALL also publishes a *Newsletter* (six times a year), which contains brief review notes of recent publications and bibliographic news of interest to law librarians, and a *Directory* of its personal and institutional members (the only updated listing of specialists in international legal information throughout the world).

IVAN SIPKOV

International Association of Metropolitan City Libraries (INTAMEL)

International Association of Metropolitan City Libraries (INTAMEL), founded in 1968, is open to all public libraries in cities (or counties) of more than 400,000. City librarians or directors represent their cities at INTAMEL general assemblies. In 1976, when INTAMEL became a Round Table of IFLA, the following statement of its purpose was approved:

INTAMEL is a platform for professional communication and information for libraries of cities with 400,000 or more inhabitants. It is a Round Table of the Division of Libraries Serving the General Public.

Every year INTAMEL organizes conferences where exchanges of experience and ideas take place on library systems, library buildings, and library activities. In the Medium-Term Programme period special attention will be given to:

1. Library networks in larger cities.

2. Library buildings.

3. The formation within city libraries of special subject departments with their own collections and services.

4. Catalogues in large city libraries: their use and organization.

5. The automation of catalogues and circulation.

6. The problems of library services to ethnic and linguistic minorities in large cities.

7. Research library work in city libraries.

8. The provision and use of online information services.

INTAMEL's inaugural meeting was held in Liverpool in 1968. Venues for general asemblies were, in

1969, Gothenburg, Sweden; 1970, Tokyo; 1971, Baltimore, Maryland; 1972, Milan; 1973, Delhi; 1974, Hamburg, Germany; 1975, Lagos, Nigeria; 1976, Paris; 1977, The Hague, Netherlands; 1978, Toronto; 1979, Vienna; 1980, Glasgow and Edinburgh, Scotland; 1981, Budapest; 1982, Mexico City; 1983 Berlin; 1984, Gothenburg; and 1985, Cleveland, Ohio. Among themes were, in Cleveland, "Libraries and the Universal availability of Information." Others included, in 1981, "Research Services," in 1982, "Service to Children," in 1983, "Budget Cuts," and in 1984, "Library Services to Special Groups." Each assembly was followed by a study tour taking in an average of three other city libraries in the host country or in neighboring countries. Over a period of several assemblies, regular attendees thus have the opportunity to visit scores of metropolitan city library systems in many countries.

Presidents of INTAMEL succeeded in securing financial aid to ensure the participation of librarians from developing countries at the annual meetings in Rome (1972), New Delhi (1973), and Gothenburg (1984).

By 1985 INTAMEL had about 100 members in nearly 40 countries. Its president and secretary-treasurer are elected for three-year terms. At the inaugural meeting in 1968 George Chandler of Liverpool was elected as the first President of INTAMEL, with Godfrey Thompson of the City of London as Secretary and Lars Tynell of Stockholm as Treasurer. Vice-Presidents elected in Liverpool were Friedrich Andrae of Hamburg, Edwin Castagna of Baltimore, and Rudolf Malek of Prague. From 1974 to 1977, the President was Keith Doms (Philadelphia), with Kenneth F. Duchac (Brooklyn) serving as Secretary-Treasurer. During the next three years the President was Jürgen Eyssen (Hannover), and the Secretary-Treasurer was Friedrich Andrae (Hamburg). From 1980 to 1983, P. van Swigchem (The Hague) was President, with Piet Schoots (Rotterdam) serving as Secretary-Treasurer. From 1983 Sten Cedergren (Gothenburg) served as President, with Andrew Miller (Glasgow) as Secretary-Treasurer.

One area of special attention for INTAMEL has been compiling and presenting comprehensive comparative statistics. They cover stocks of books, periodicals, audiovisual materials, loans, budgets, book funds, staff (professional and nonprofessional), branch libraries, mobile libraries, opening hours, and other statistical data from the member cities.

Among INTAMEL publications are a final report on its project in Lagos and *Metropolitan Libraries on Their Way into the Eighties* (1982) (by M. Beaujean).

STEN CEDERGREN

International Association of Music Libraries, Archives and Documentation Centres (IAML)

The International Association of Music Libraries, Archives and Documentation Centres (IAML), known in other languages as Association Internationale des Bibliothèques, Archives et Centres de Documentation Musicaux (AIBM), and Internationale Vereinigung der Musikbibliotheken, Musikarchive und Musikdokumentationszentren (IVMB), was formed shortly after World War II to promote worldwide cooperation in all aspects of music librarianship, bibliography, and documentation, such as cataloguing, interlibrary loan, training, and the creation of new tools for research. Among its early members were many distinguished scholars and music librarians. Annual meetings, one-third of which are international congresses, have been held in various cities of the world.

The membership as of 1985 was about 1,700 individuals—music librarians, scholars, bibliographers, archivists, and documentalists from 39 countries. Each country is represented through its own national association on the IAML Council, the governing body. IAML is organized into Professional Branches and Subject Commissions, each also represented on the Council and each reflecting its primary concerns and areas of activity. The Professional Branches include Broadcasting and Orchestra Libraries, Public Music Libraries, Music Research Libraries, Libraries in Music Teaching Institutions, and Music Information Centres. The three Subject Commissions are Bibliography, Cataloguing, and Service and Training. Each commission has its own goals and projects and at the same time interacts with others to refine ideas and enhance productivity.

IAML has played a central role in the implementation and publication of the "three R's" of international musicology: Répertoire international des sources musicales (RISM); Répertoire international de littérature musicale (RILM); and Répertoire international d'iconographie musicale (RIdIM).

RISM, founded in 1952, is concerned with gathering and publishing bibliographies of all sources in music and music literature to 1800—from the writings of the Hebrew and Greek theorists, through vast repertories of monophonic and polyphonic music and writings about music through the centuries, to extant printed editions and manuscripts of Dittersdorf, Boccherini, and Michael Haydn, among others.

RILM, founded in 1966, deals with current music literature. It sponsors *RILM Abstracts* (1967-), published quarterly in New York, which contains citations to articles about music in many countries and in many languages, accompanied by a detailed computer-generated index. *RILM Abstracts* is also available online through the Dialog database. RILM has produced a series of annotated bibliographies entitled *RILM Retrospectives,* including *Thematic Catalogues in Music, French Dissertations in Music,* and *Congress Reports in Music.*

RIdIM, established in 1971, is concerned with accumulating, classifying, cataloguing, interpreting, and reproducing visual materials relating to music; training iconologists; and publishing checklists, bibliographies, iconographies, and scholarly studies. The Research Center for Musical Iconography, founded in 1972 at the City University of New York, serves as the international RIdIM center for collecting and classifying iconographical materials.

Reports on the progress of the "three R's," as well as reports of IAML congresses, conferences, and meetings, and other IAML news, reviews, and communications, are published in *Fontes Artis Musicae,* the association's quarterly journal, founded in 1954 under the editorship of Vladimir Fédorov and edited in 1985 by André Jurres. Other IAML or IAML-assisted publications include *Documenta Musicologica; Catalogus Musicus; Terminorum Musicae Index Septum Linguis Redactus; The Guide for Dating Early Published Music;* the *Directories of Music Research Libraries* (RISM, Series C); the *RIdIM Newsletter;* the *RILM International Thesaurus;* professional cataloguing manuals; and various national newsletters.

IAML cooperates with the International Musicological Society (IMS) on RISM, RILM, and RIdIM projects and with the International Council of Museums on RIdIM. In addition, it actively participates in projects with the International Federation of Library Associations (IFLA) and the Unesco-sponsored International Music Council (IMC). IAML became a member of IFLA in 1976 and is represented on several of IFLA's Standing Committees. Under the sponsorship of the IMC, IAML took the lead in collaboration with IMS, the International Society for Music Education, and the Music Information Centres Commission in implementing a new international documentation project, the *World Inventory of Sources of Music Information* (WISMI). In addition, IAML has spawned a sister organization, the International Association of Sound Archives (IASA), and has served as a model for an international association of art libraries.

In response to a changing world and as a reflection of advances in current communications, IAML is working with or experimenting with computers, information retrieval, automated photocomposition of words and music, and revolutionary methods of text and sound storage to organize and maintain vast collections of books, scores, and disks, as well as archives, documentation centers, and bibliographical projects. Future goals and projects of IAML include a Unesco-supported plan to assist Third World countries in the establishment and expansion of their music libraries and documentation centers and a service to promote exchange arrangements between the members and libraries of developing countries as well as those where currency restrictions obstruct the free acquisition of materials.

REFERENCE

Barry S. Brook, "Fontes at Twenty-five—IAML at Thirty," *Fontes Artis Musicae* (1978), covers the history of IAML.

BARRY S. BROOK; NEIL RATLIFF

International Association of School Librarianship

The International Association of School Librarianship (IASL) was founded in 1971 in Kingston, Jamaica, at the annual conference of the World Confederation of Organizations of the Teaching Profession (WCOTP). By 1985 there were just under 1,000 personal and 30 association members. Members include librarians, media specialists, educators, publishers, and interested lay persons.

During the early 1960s school librarians and educators interested in school library service who attended WCOTP meetings discussed the need for an international forum. In 1967 the American Library Association's International Relations Committee gave the American Association of School Librarians a

small grant to bring together a group of 30 educators and librarians at the Vancouver WCOTP meeting. Those present decided to establish a committee and charged it to plan a program for the 1968 meeting in Dublin and to move toward formal committee status within WCOTP. An international steering committee representing Australia, Kenya, Malaysia, Paraguay, the United Kingdom, and the United States voted in Dublin (1968) to create an ad hoc committee for school library development. Program meetings were held in Abidjan, Ivory Coast (1969), and in Sydney, Australia (1970). At Sydney the concept of an independent organization was approved in principle. A charter was drawn up; IASL was incorporated in the state of Illinois and was inaugurated in 1971 in Jamaica. The new officers were installed by the Secretary General of WCOTP, John Thompson. The first leaders were President, Jean E. Lowrie, U.S.A.; Vice-President, Margot Nilson, Sweden; Treasurer, Phyllis Hochstettler, U.S.A.; and directors representing Australia, Canada, Jamaica, Nigeria, Singapore, and the United Kingdom.

The objectives of the Association are (1) to encourage the development of school libraries and library programs throughout all countries; (2) to promote the professional preparation of school librarians; (3) to bring about close collaboration between school libraries in all countries, including the loan and exchange of literature; (4) to encourage the development of school library materials; and (5) to initiate and coordinate activities, conferences, and other projects in the field of school librarianship.

IASL has continued its pattern of growth and contact with school library/media center persons around the world. Personal and association memberships doubled. The growth of national school library associations indicates the value of support beyond the community while new program approaches are among the significant exchanges at annual conferences. The six-country Nordic School Library Association, a regional group within IASL, has become another forum for interchange. The number of Directors was expanded to include representation from East Africa as well as Southeast Asia. Membership on the board in the mid-1980s included Australia, Canada, Denmark, Japan, Kenya, Malaysia, Nigeria, the United Kingdom, the United States, and Venezuela.

The 1980s saw an expansion of the annual conference to five full days with an optional study-tour program to allow participants an opportunity for in-depth visitation in the school libraries/media centers of the host country. The conference provides opportunities for discussion on such topics as school libraries and cultural involvement, crucial issues in school library development and professional education, and educational changes and their implications for quality library service.

A conference highlight is the Association Assembly. As more associations became interested in IASL, it became evident that a more formal sharing of programs, association needs, solutions, and activities was necessary. Association members send delegates to the conferences to represent their interests and participate in meetings where they are specifically discussed. The "assembly communique" is an annual publication and provides a mechanism for sharing among all member groups. The quarterly *Newsletter* was expanded in size and continues to be the only such international publication.

The conference proceedings increased in scope to embrace new areas of interest, such as school/community libraries, networking, and computer utilization. A third revised and enlarged edition of *People to Contact for Visiting School Libraries/Media Centers,* an updated *Directory of National School Library Associations, Getting Started* (an annotated bibliography of manuals and guidelines from 10 countries), *Library Services to Isolated Schools and Communities,* and *Indicators of Quality* (a joint publication with the Illinois Association of Media Educators on evaluation techniques), are publications that were in print in the mid-1980s.

IASL continues to be responsible for the Unesco Co-Action Program #554 (Books for School Libraries in Developing Countries). It maintained its affiliation with WCOTP and issued with it an official "Policy Statement on School Libraries." IASL maintains a liaison with the School Library section of the International Federation of Library Associations, of which it is a member, cooperating with it in preparing such documents as the international guidelines for school libraries/media centers, competencies for school librarians, and other projects. IASL works informally with the International Reading Association and the International Board on Books for Young People.

A five-year plan for the future of IASL, being developed by a task force in 1985, includes an analysis for program expansion, an evaluation of objectives, and a review of implementation needs.

JEAN E. LOWRIE

International Association of Sound Archives (IASA)

The International Association of Sound Archives (IASA), a nongovernmental Unesco-affiliated organization, was established in 1969 to function as a medium for international cooperation among archives that preserve recorded sound documents. IASA was founded by a group of members of the parent organization IAML (International Association of Music Libraries). IASA and IAML maintain close links and hold joint annual conferences. IASA is actively involved in such fields as the preservation, organization, and use of sound recordings, techniques of recording, and methods of reproducing sound in all fields in which the audio medium is used; the exchange of recordings among archives and of related literature and information; and all subjects relating to the professional work of sound archives.

Membership in the Association is open to all categories of archives and other institutions that preserve sound recordings and to organizations and individuals with a serious interest in the purposes or welfare of IASA. The Association includes members representing, for example, archives of music, history, literature, drama, and folklife recordings; collections of natural history, bio-acoustic, and medical sounds; recorded linguistic and dialect surveys; and radio and television sound archives.

Membership of the Association in 1985 stood at 400 members.

Organization and Program. The Association is controlled by an elected seven-member Executive Board that serves for three years. Secretary-General in 1985 was Helen Harrison, an audiovisual librarian from England. The IASA Board is supported by a number of committees with special interests and the National and Affiliated Organizations Committee. The constitution of IASA provides for national branches. In the mid-1980s there were sufficient members in four countries and one region with common interests to form national branches: Australia, Austria, the Netherlands, the United Kingdom, and a Nordic regional branch for the Scandinavian countries. In addition the Association has affiliated organizations including AFAS (the French Association for Sound Archives) and ARSC (the American Association of Recorded Sound Collections). The national branches meet at annual conferences to exchange views and act as a forum of information and to consult with the Executive Board. Members of the group also exchange newsletters.

Committees include Cataloguing, Copyright, Discography, History of IASA, Radio Sound Archives, Technical, Training, a Joint IASA/IAML committee, and the National and Affiliated Organizations Committee. Several of the committees normally hold two meetings during the annual conference, a working meeting and an open meeting with detailed coverage of particular themes or topics.

The annual conference is held in a different venue each year and is hosted by members of IASA and IAML in the country concerned. Conferences were held in Cambridge, England, 1980; Budapest, 1981; Brussels, 1982; Washington, D.C., 1983; Como, Italy, 1984, and Berlin, DDR, in 1985. The 1986 Conference was scheduled for Stockholm in August.

At the annual conference the IASA program includes two general assemblies; at one of them the officers report the business of the Association to the members. At the second, Committee and national association reports are given.

The Association publishes a journal, the *Phonographic Bulletin,* three times a year. A cumulated Index and list of contents to the journal was published in 1985. Other publications include *Directory of Member Archives,* which is periodically revised, and a Special Publications series, including *An Archive Approach to Oral History,* by David Lance, *Sound Archives: a Guide to Their Establishment and Development,* edited by David Lance, and *Selection in Sound Archives; Collected Papers from IASA Conferences,* edited by Helen Harrison.

IASA is a member of the Round Table of Audiovisual Records, which includes representatives from Unesco, FIAF (International Federation of Film Archives), FIAT (International Federation of Television Archives) ICA (International Congress of Archives), IFLA (International Federation of Library Associations), and IFTC (International Film and Television Council). The Round Table meets annually and is normally attended by one or two officers or representatives from each Federation.

HELEN P. HARRISON

International Association of Technological University Libraries

The International Association of Technological University Libraries (IATUL) was founded in Dusseldorf in May 1955 as an international forum for the exchange of ideas relevant to librarianship in technological universities throughout the world. In September 1955 it was recognized as a subsection of the International Library Associations division of IFLA. It now works in close association with the IFLA Section of Science and Technology Libraries.

Membership is open to the libraries of universities and other higher educational institutions of science and technology. IATUL Statutes stipulate that Ordinary Membership can be accorded to the library of any university that grants doctorates in science and technology. In 1985 there were 130 member libraries from 32 countries, primarily from North America, Asia, Australia, New Zealand, and Europe. Observer status is available to institutions such as national patent offices or science and science museum libraries whose collections in science and technology are of research standard.

The Association is governed by a Board consisting of a President, Secretary, Treasurer, First and Second Vice-Presidents, and three committee members elected by member libraries; the Board meets twice each year.

The primary goal, the exchange of information among university technological libraries, is accomplished mainly through publication and written communication, although international conferences are held every two years. Eleven such conferences had been held by 1985; conferences were scheduled for Helsinki in 1987 and Kanazawe, Japan, in 1989. Important areas of interest have related to any activities concerned with scientific information, the use of information resources in science and technology, library organizations and buildings, and the use of data processing in libraries and information systems.

Publications include *IATUL Proceedings* (1966 onward), issued approximately annually from 1975. The *Proceedings* contain articles (usually in English or German), reviews of published research, and digests of lectures, as well as news of the association and bibliographic information. *IATUL Conference Proceedings* contain the papers presented at the biennial conferences.

REFERENCE

D. Schmidmaier, "The History of the International Association of Technological University Libraries (IATUL)," in *IATUL Proceedings* (1976).

DENNIS F. SHAW

International Board on Books for Young People

The International Board on Books for Young People (IBBY) is the only international organization related to professional work in all disciplines concerned with the creation, promotion, study, and reading of children's literature.

Founded in Zurich in 1953 by Jella Lepman, then Director of the International Youth Library, it grew in membership from a few Western European sections to some 50 National Sections spread throughout the world by the mid-1980s. Individual members represent IBBY in countries where there is no National Section. The United States Board on Books for Young People, Inc., was established in 1984 to combine responsibilities that were formerly shared by the U.S. National Section of IBBY and the Friends of IBBY, Inc. The U.S. Board is a nonprofit, tax-exempt organization. It publishes a semi-annual *Newsletter*.

Purpose. IBBY's aims include (1) bringing together persons concerned about good books for young people; (2) promoting the availability of such books and access to them by encouraging their production to fit worldwide needs, associating them with communications media, such as radio, television, the press, films, and recordings, and ecouraging the growth of libraries for the young; (3) encouraging translations and assisting in making available books of international quality; (4) initiating, encouraging, or advancing research in children's literature and its illustration and organizing the publication of the results of such research on an international scale; and (5) advising international or national individuals, groups, institutions, or organizations on books for the young and on the training of librarians, teachers, editors, writers, or illustrators.

Programs. *National Activities.* The National Sections present national awards, compile lists of best books of the year, organize exhibits, book weeks, seminars, and conferences, and celebrate IBBY's International Children's Book Day around April 2 (Hans Christian Andersen's birthday). For that day, National Sections serve in turn as sponsors, supplying an author's message and an artist's poster made available internationally.

International Activities. Of first significance on the international level are IBBY's biennial Hans Christian Andersen Medals, one for an author, presented first in 1956, and another for an illustrator, introduced in 1966. An IBBY Honour List presents books for a two-year period in three categories: text, illustration, and translation.

IBBY participates in the publication of the quarterly *Bookbird,* edited at the International Institute for Children's Literature in Vienna and published by the Instituto Nacional del Libro Español in Madrid. It features articles, lists of outstanding books, reviews of professional works, and news of national and international conferences and prizes. A summary in Spanish accompanies every issue.

IBBY's biennial congress moves from country to country. In 1984 the Cypriot Section of IBBY hosted the 19th congress in Nicosia, dealing with children's book production and distribution in Third World countries. The theme selected for the 20th congress (Tokyo, 1986) was "Why do you write for children? Children, why do you read?" The 1988 congress, in Oslo, planned to focus attention on the new media.

IBBY has consultative relations with UNICEF and Unesco. It is a member of the International Book Committee and the International Federation of Library Associations and cooperates with the International Reading Association in joint projects. Cooperation with the Norwegian Institute for Special Education resulted in two projects dealing with books for and about handicapped children, sponsored by Unesco. IBBY also compiled a *Directory of Children's Literature Organizations and Institutions* and a *Directory of Children's Literature Specialists* for Unesco.

LEENA MAISSEN

International Council of Scientific Unions

In 1931 the final Assembly of the International Research Council (IRC) became the first Assembly of the International Council of Scientific Unions (ICSU). The IRC had been founded in 1919 as an outgrowth of the earlier International Association of Academies, which had its first meeting in 1899. ICSU has two types of members, the International Scientific Unions, of which there were 20 in 1985; and the National Members, including academies of science and science research councils, among others, of which there were 66. There were also 19 Scientific Associates and 5 National Associates.

The principal objectives of the Council are (1) to encourage international scientific activity for the benefit of humankind; (2) to facilitate and coordinate the activities of the International Scientific Unions; (3) to stimulate, design, and coordinate international interdisciplinary scientific research projects; and (4) to facilitate the coordination of the international scientific activities of its National Members.

In addition to the International Scientific Unions, each of which has its own objectives and structure, ICSU functions through a series of 11 Scientific and Special Committees, 5 Inter-Union Commissions, one Permanent Service, and other groups. These are concerned with interdisciplinary and inter-Union activities, such as the International Geophysical Year, launched by ICSU in 1957, and the International Biological Program (1964–74), the results of which were published in a series of 30 volumes.

The ICSU meets every two years in General Assembly with representatives of the National and Scientific Union Members and of all the subsidiary bodies. The General Committee—composed of 20 representatives from the Scientific Unions, 13 from the National Members, and the Officers—meets every year. The Secretariat of ICSU is at the Hôtel de Noailles, Paris, made available by the French Ministry of Education. Secretariats of six other ICSU bodies, including those of the Committee on Data for Science and Technology (CODATA) and of the International Council for Scientific and Technological Information (ICSTI) formerly the ICSU Abstracting Board, are also housed there. The other Secretariats, of the unions, committees, commissions, and others, are spread throughout the world.

From time to time ICSU organizes meetings of representatives of the members of the ICSU family involved in scientific information, documentation, libraries, and other activities, such as CODATA, ICSTI, the Federation of Astronomical and Geophysical Services, the World Data Centres Panel (WDC), several of the Scientific Associates, and a number of other such organizations to discuss future projects, ensure cooperation, and try to avoid unnecessary duplication.

ICSU has relationships with several United Nations agencies. A feasibility study for Unesco's World Scientific and Technical Information System (UNISIST) followed a decision of the 1966 ICSU General Assembly and developed into a joint study with Unesco after the Unesco 1966 General Conference. ICSU in the mid-1980s had a joint Global Atmospheric Research Program with the World Meteorological Organization (WMO) and also a joint World Climate Research Program with WMO.

The ICSU *Year Book* provides information about the various members of the ICSU family and the addresses of the officers of these bodies. The *ICSU Newsletter* provides information about ongoing activities in the ICSU.

F. W. G. BAKER

International Council on Archives

The International Council on Archives (ICA) was founded in May 1948 at a meeting convened by Unesco to establish a worldwide organization of the archival profession. A provisional constitution was adopted, and the first International Congress on Archives met in Paris (1950) to establish the ICA formally.

ICA was created to improve the worldwide standards of archival administration and practice and to advance archival theory. The Council aids professional relations between archival institutions and organizations in order to stimulate the interchange of ideas and information, to solve archival problems, to ensure the physical preservation of mankind's archival heritage, and to support archival development and training in all countries.

The concerns and issues of the international archival community, as expressed in ICA publications and meetings, include the intellectual control of records, preservation, microreproduction, greater access to archives, and technological advances in the creation, control, and preservation of archives. The programs of the Council emanating from these goals are implemented by the ICA congresses, committees, regional branches, and the Executive Secretary.

The membership of ICA is composed of public archival authorities on international, national, and subnational levels (category A members); professional associations (category B); state, local, and private institutions (category C); individuals (category D); and honorary members (category E).

In May 1985 there were 714 members of ICA, including 131 countries represented by their national archival authorities. One hundred seventy-one archivists from 36 countries and 7 international organizations are individual members. In the early history of the Council the membership centered in Western Europe; Eastern European countries joined ICA later; then membership growth came from the Third World countries, as national archival institutions were established there.

Nine regional branches of ICA in the Third World work to develop archival institutions and staff as integral parts of the information systems in those countries. The regional branches are Asociación Latinoamericana de Archivos (ALA), Arab Regional Branch (ARBICA), Caribbean Regional Branch (CARBICA), Central African Regional Branch (CENARBICA), East and South African Regional

Branch (ESARBICA), Pacific Regional Branch (PARBICA), Southeast Asian Regional Branch (SARBICA), South and West Asian Regional Branch (SWARBICA), and West African Regional Branch (WARBICA). These branch organizations sponsor conferences, seminars, and publications to make known the need for sound archival programs, to preserve the national heritages of the member countries, and to educate archivists, librarians, government officials, and the general public.

The governing bodies of the ICA are the General Assembly, the Executive Committee, and the Bureau of the Council. The General Assembly meets once every four years during the International Congresses on Archives to conduct the business activities of the Council, elect officers, and act on resolutions and recommendations concerning the professional interests of the worldwide archival community.

The Executive Committee is vested with the governing powers for the years between General Assembly meetings. It is composed of the ICA officers, 14 elected members, and a number of ex officio members. The Bureau, a smaller governing body made up of the ICA officers, meets as often as necessary between the annual sessions of the Executive Committee to expedite the business of the Council and to advise the Secretariat of ICA. The Executive Secretary is in Paris and coordinates the programs of the Council and maintains liaison with Unesco and other international organizations.

The ICA committee structure includes commissions on Publications and Archival Development, on Professional Training and Education, on Automation, on Conservation and Restoration, on Reprography, on Sigillography, on Business Archives, and on Literature and Art Archives. Sections, which are organized around professional interests, include the Section of Archival Associations and the Section of Archivists of International Organizations. The committees and sections issue newsletters and hold annual meetings on topics of specific interest to their members.

The International Congresses on Archives are the quadrennial meetings of ICA; subjects selected by the Executive Committee and the national organizing committee are discussed. Reports, prepared by specialists on the basis of original research and international inquiries, are presented at the plenary sessions and are followed by discussions and interventions. Congresses were held in London in 1980 and in Bonn in 1984. The 1988 Congress was scheduled to be held in Paris.

In 1954 the President of ICA, Charles Braibant (France), decided to convene an annual meeting of the leaders of the profession (directors of national archival institutions and presidents of national archival associations). These meetings, called the International Round Table Conferences on Archives, are held each year when an international congress is not held to study one or two major problems of archival administration. The 1983 Round Table Conference, held in Bratislava, Czechoslovakia, discussed "The Archivist and the Inflation of Contemporary Records." The 1985 Conference met in Austin, Texas, with the theme of Freedom of Information and Privacy.

The International Council on Archives has associate and consultative relations with Unesco as a Cat-

egory A international nongovernmnental organization cooperating with Unesco. The Council receives a subvention and grants from Unesco for research and publications. Cooperation between ICA and the General Information Programme of Unesco centers around international projects, missions, and meetings and is an ongoing process aimed at assisting the archival institutions in developing countries. ICA cooperates with a number of international nongovernmental organizations operating in neighboring fields, among them IFLA and the International Federation for Documentation (FID).

The Council publishes a number of journals and volumes for the international community of archivists. *Archivum* is an annual journal devoted to special topics. The *ICA Bulletin* is a semiannual newsletter of ICA programs and meetings. The Council, with the assistance of Unesco, also publishes studies and handbooks for developing countries on such topics as microfilming, archival buildings, access policies, professional training, and restoration techniques. ICA and Unesco have also cooperated in publishing a series of archival guides entitled *Guide to the Sources for the History of Nations*. By 1985 two series were complete: 11 volumes for Latin American and 10 volumes relating to Africa south of the Sahara. Other series were being prepared for North Africa, Asia, and Oceania. They are intended to encourage and facilitate research in the histories of the developing countries, particularly when many sources for those histories are in Europe and North America. The project of a General Guide to the Archives of Asia started in 1979. Twelve Asian countries were participating in the project in the mid-1980s.

The International Archival Development Fund is the ICA instrument for financially supporting Third World archival institutions. The Fund, established in 1974, assists the world's developing countries in building effective modern national archival structures and services. Administered by the ICA Commission on Archival Development, the Fund seeks contributions from governments, international organizations, private foundations, and other sources for projects, missions, and meetings; most of the funds are used for regional and national projects on archival development.

REFERENCES
International Council on Archives Directory (1985).
Oliver W. Holmes, "Toward an International Archives Program and Council, 1945–1950," *American Archivist* (July 1976).
Morris Rieger, "The International Council on Archives: Its First Quarter Century," ibid.

JAMES B. RHOADS;
CHARLES KECSKEMETI

International Federation for Documentation

The Fédération Internationale de Documentation (FID), an international, not-for-profit, nongovernmental organization, was founded in September 1895 as the Institut International de Bibliographie (IIB). The IIB was one of the resolutions resulting from the Conférence Internationale de Bibliographie, assembled by Paul Otlet and Henri La Fontaine, the two persons regarded as the founders of FID. The objectives of that conference, held under the sponsorship of the Belgian government, were to establish the Institut, to create a Répertoire bibliographique universel (RBU) classified according to the Dewey Decimal Classification, and to form a Bibliographic Union among governments.

Membership. The members of IIB could be individuals, institutions, or associations, and there was no limit placed upon the size of the membership. This pattern of membership remained until after World War I. Today FID is composed of national members, only one being accepted from each country, and international members, being international organizations active in the field of documentation. Apart from national and international members, FID accepts associates, a type of interim membership, and institutional and personal affiliates. The membership at the beginning of 1985 was 67 national members and 1 international member. In addition there were 234 affiliates from 59 countries (15 not represented by national members).

Purpose. When the IIB was founded, its essential functions were "to provide encouragement for the study of classification in general and to promote a uniform and international system of classification in particular." The purpose of FID has broadened in the ensuing years, and the original objectives of the IIB are now only a part of the Federation's purpose. Today the aim and nature of FID, as summarized in the preamble of its statutes, is "to promote, through international cooperation, research in and development of documentation, which includes inter alia the organization, storage, retrieval, dissemination, and evaluation of information, however recorded, in the fields of science, technology, social sciences, arts, and humanities.

"The nature of the Federation has been and should continue to be principally that of a federation of national members. This means that the principal responsibility in the government of the Federation remains in the hands of bodies representative of various countries, whereas it is agreed that individuals participate as specialists in the work of the Federation."

FID cannot handle the whole range of problems of documentation and information that call for study and action within that broad aim. Priority fields and activities are defined so that FID handles them effectively, taking into account information programs of related intergovernmental and nongovernmental organizations, such as Unesco and IFLA, among others.

History. The two major interests of the founders of the IIB were the development of the Decimal Classification and the Universal Bibliographic Repertory (RBU). The two were not developed independently, and the former resulted in the subsequent development of the Universal Decimal Classification (UDC). The first complete edition of the UDC was published in French in 1905 as IIB publication 63 and bore the title *Manuel du répertoire bibliographique universel.*

Because of World War I, the IIB remained stagnant for a number of years, but 1924 marked a turning point. The Institut was reorganized and became a federation with five national members: Belgium, France, Germany, the Netherlands, and Switzerland. Up to the time of the war the IIB had remained an international organization made up of individual and organizational members. The reorganization of the Institut changed its emphasis, and the UDC became only one of its tasks. At the same time, the UDC was recognized as having achieved an enhanced importance in the affairs of the IIB. The Classification Committee, which was formed in 1921, became in 1924 the official body through which the IIB exercised its control over the UDC. The Dutch national member, Nederlands Instituut voor Documentatie en Registratuur (NIDER), assumed the Secretariat for the Committee, and Frits Donker Duyvis, who was later to serve as FID Secretary General for many years, was appointed Secretary.

In 1931 the IIB became the Institut International de Documentation (IID), a name that continued until the present name was adopted in 1938. The 1931 name change, to incorporate the word *documentation,* signaled a clear separation from the word *bibliography* (work on the RBU had long since ceased) and an emphasis on practical aspects.

For almost 30 years the FID Secretariat was housed in Brussels with the Office International de Bibliographie, a semigovernmental Belgian organization. After 1924 the Netherlands and Belgium shared the Secretariat until 1938, when it was completely taken over by The Hague, and F. Donker Duyvis became the sole Secretary General—a position he had shared with the founders from 1924 to 1938.

Organization and Structure. By the end of World War II FID had added only three new national members to the first five of 1924. With the increased interest in documentation in the postwar years, membership gradually increased, and by 1958 there were 28 national members, including 7 outside Europe, making FID truly a world organization. The first committees other than the Classification Committee and its subcommittees were also established. Ten FID committees in 1985 helped to carry out the FID professional program: FID/CCC, Central Classification Committee, along with its 30 subcommittees for revising the UDC; FID/CR Classification Research; FID/DT Terminology of Information and Documentation; FID/ET Education and Training; FID/II Information for Industry; FID/IM Informetrics; FID/LD Linguistics in Documentation; FID/PD Patent Information and Documentation; FID/RI Research on the Theoretical Basis of Information; FID/SD Social Sciences Documentation. There is a Working Group FID/BSO Broad System of Ordering and there are Task Forces on FID/IS/NW Information Systems and Network Design and Management and FID/SUN Study of User Needs.

During 1984 FID commissioned a study of the management of the UDC by an external consultant, and in September 1984 appointed a UDC Management Group for the UDC.

FID established two regional commissions, FID/CLA Latin American Commission (1960) and FID/CAO Asia and Oceania (1968). The two commissions, in turn, have several of their own committees that assist in carrying out regional programs: in Latin America CLA/UDC Universal Decimal Classification, CLA/CCN National Union Catalogues, CLA/ET Education and Training, and CLA/II Information for Industry; in Asia CAO/II Information for Secondary Industry. In the mid-1980s FID was developing a program for the African region.

The highest authority of the FID is the General Assembly, which meets biennially and is composed of representatives of national and international members. The FID Council meets twice yearly to carry out the decisions of the General Assembly.

The Council is composed of the President, 3 Vice-Presidents, the Treasurer, 14 Councillors (including the Presidents of regional commissions), and ex-officio the Secretary General. Between meetings of the Council the Executive Committee, made up of the officers and the Secretary General, may meet if there is a need. The daily operation of the Federation is handled through its Secretariat in The Hague and through the secretariats of the regional commissions.

Program. In 1978 the FID General Assembly meeting in Edinburgh accepted a new program structure for FID. Under it, the first Medium Term Program (MTP) was developed for the period 1981–84. Five priorities for action were identified in the Medium Term Program. They are: Theoretical and linguistic basis of information science (including terminology); information processing and technology; education and training of information specialists and information users; information system and network design and management; and information needs and habits of users.

A second Medium Term Program for the period 1983–86 was approved in 1982. A Program Planning Group was appointed by Council in 1984 to prepare the next MTP for the FID program up to 1990.

Publications. In addition to an active monograph publications program, FID publishes the monthly FID *News Bulletin,* the quarterly *International Forum on Information and Documentation* (in Russian and English), *R & D Projects in Documentation and Librarianship* (bimonthly), and *The Extensions and Corrections to the UDC* (annual). The *Bulletin* includes two special quarterly supplements: the "Document Delivery and Reproduction Survey" and the "Newsletter on Education and Training Programmes for Information Personnel." The biennial FID *Directory,* replacing the former *Yearbook,* provides information on membership, committees, and historical information on the Federation. Annual reports have been issued since 1983.

Relations with Other Organizations. FID cooperates with the programs of several other international organizations: the Unesco General Information Programme (PGI), the World Intellectual Property Organization (WIPO), the International Federation of Library Associations and Institutions (IFLA), the International Council of Archives (ICA), and the International Organization for Standardization (ISO).

REFERENCES

W. Boyd Rayward, *The Universe of Information: The Work of Paul Otlet for Documentation and International Organizations* (1975).

The ALA *Yearbook of Library and Information Services* and the FID *Annual Report* provide summaries of the activities of each year.

FID Publications: An 80-Year Bibliography 1895–1975 and the current list of FID's *Publications* provide a bibliographical survey of many publications.

STELLA KEENAN

International Federation for Information Processing

The International Federation for Information Processing (IFIP) is a multinational federation of professional and technical organizations representing all branches of information processing. Each member organization in IFIP represents a nation or, in cases where several nations have joined together to form a confederation, a group of nations.

The vision of IFIP was first conceived in June 1959, when Unesco sponsored the first International Conference on Information Processing. Discussions initiated at that conference led to the establishment of IFIP on January 1, 1960. At its birth, IFIP included 13 national technical societies. By the mid-1980s, 45 organizations were members of the Federation, representing 57 countries and more than 500,000 computer professionals worldwide.

As a leader in information processing, IFIP is dedicated to improving worldwide communication and increased understanding among information processing practitioners of all countries. In accordance with its international leadership role, IFIP seeks to promote all aspects of information science and technology by fostering international cooperation in the field of information processing; stimulating research, development, and the application of information processing in science and human activity; furthering the dissemination and exchange of information about the subject; and encouraging education in information processing. IFIP acts as a catalyst for the advancement of the entire information processing profession by bringing together the expertise of individuals at the leading edge of technology.

During its first quarter century, IFIP helped advance the information processing profession significantly. Technical work, the heart of IFIP's activity, gradually grew to encompass nine program areas, each under the supervision of a technical committee. They include Programming, Education, Computer Applications in Technology, Data Communication, System Modeling and Optimization, Information Systems, Relationship Between Computers and Society, Digital Systems Design, and Security and Protection in Information Processing Systems. Since IFIP's creation in 1960, Working Groups, specialized subcomponents of technical committees, also continued to increase in number and scope of activity.

Headquarters are in Geneva, Switzerland. All activities of the Federation are governed by the General Assembly. It meets once each year and consists of one representative from each member nation or confederation of nations. The General Assembly determines policy and strategy and makes decisions on such matters as the yearly program of activities. The daily activities of the organization are governed by its officers, who are elected by the General Assembly and together form the Executive Body.

One of IFIP's major activities is sponsoring international conferences. The largest is the IFIP Congress, held once every three years. During these Congresses, international audiences of up to 5,000 participants from as many as 55 countries exchange ideas with their colleagues from other countries. IFIP Congresses in the latter 1980s were scheduled for Dublin (1986) and San Francisco (1989).

IFIP also organizes a triennial series on medical informatics (MEDINFO). Many of IFIP's Technical Committees sponsor conferences on other specialized topics, such as the World Conference on Computers in Education in Norfolk, Virginia, in 1985.

Greater dissemination of knowledge about information processing is achieved through publishing and distributing the proceedings of IFIP-sponsored international conferences worldwide. IFIP's list of publications included more than 240 titles in 1985. Additionally, IFIP publishes an annual *Information Bulletin*, two quarterly journals, *Computers in Industry* and *Computers and Security*, and the quarterly *IFIP Newsletter*.

IFIP maintains both informal and formal relations with several other international organizations. Founded under the auspices of Unesco, IFIP maintains a Class B status with it. In 1972 IFIP established official relations with the World Health Organization and it maintains informal relationships with other UN family members. IFIP is a Scientific Affiliate of the International Council of Scientific Unions (ICSU) and is a member of FIACC, the Five International Association Coordinating Committee. IFIP also collaborates with the Intergovernmental Bureau for Informatics and works in an advisory capacity with the International Telegraph and Telephone Consultative Committee.

GEORGE GLASER

International Federation of Library Associations and Institutions (IFLA)

History. The 50th anniversary Conference of the American Library Association in Atlantic City and Philadelphia in 1926 marked the beginning of the concept of an international library organization. Three months earlier at the International Congress of Librarians and Booklovers in Prague, the spiritual father of IFLA, Gabriel Henriot, had voiced an appeal for a standing international library committee. The idea materialized in Edinburgh on September 30, 1927, during the celebration of the 50th anniversary of the Library Association of the United Kingdom, when representatives of library associations from 15 countries signed a resolution that can be regarded as the founding of IFLA. Isak Collijn, the Swedish National Librarian, was elected first President. The most skillful negotiator was Carl H. Milam, Secretary of ALA, who agreed to draft the statutes. The first IFLA Constitution was approved in Rome in 1929 during the first World Congress of Librarianship and Bibliography, which took place under IFLA auspices.

The new organization was predominantly an association of library associations, aiming at the organization of regular world conferences. Originally, IFLA was a meeting point for leading librarians from Europe and America and continued as such for a long time. In the early years notable personalities—true representatives of their profession—defined IFLA's profile. It became a kind of "conference family," where personal friendships led to close cooperation in such areas as international loan and exchange, bibliographical standardization, and library education.

At the only prewar IFLA session outside Europe (Chicago, 1933), the second IFLA President, William

IFLA

IFLA commemorative stamp, issued on the occasion of its 50th anniversary, Brussels, 1977.

Warner Bishop, acted as host. During five years as President, he guided IFLA through the first years of economic crisis as membership reached 41 associations from 31 countries, including several library associations from outside Europe and the U.S. (China, India, Japan, Mexico, Philippines). IFLA could not yet boast of true universal international membership, however. That was not to be achieved for 40 years.

Marcel Godet, Director of the Swiss National Library at Berne, was IFLA's third President from 1936 to 1947. Through Godet and Secretary A. C. Breycha-Vauthier, IFLA took part in the Advisory Committee on Literature for Prisoners-of-War and Internees, which distributed significant numbers of books to various camps. (Breycha-Vauthier also worked at the League of Nations Library at Geneva during the war.)

IFLA's first postwar session, at Oslo in 1947, funded by a grant from the Rockefeller Foundation, was attended by 52 delegates from 18 countries. One important result of this conference was a formal agreement between Unesco and IFLA concerning future cooperation (IFLA has Consultative Status A with Unesco). In 1948 they organized an International Summer School on Public Library Practice in Manchester, attended by 50 librarians from 21 countries who from that time worked to better public librarianship (the first standards for public libraries were a result of this cooperation). Another Oslo resolution of lasting significance was the recommendation to accept an international format for catalogue cards.

In the postwar period IFLA developed slowly, perhaps too slowly, because its structure and lack of funds hampered effectiveness. Its profile was still defined by individuals who gave their time and expertise to IFLA during meetings but turned their attention between meetings to their national duties. From 1951 a series of proposals for reorganization was launched, based on a fundamental criticism about the lack of constructive programs, but they were too vague to lead to concrete results. By 1958 IFLA had grown to 64 member associations from 42 countries. The organization was basically similar to its prewar antecedent until the International Conference on Cataloguing Principles (Paris, 1961), for which the Council on Library Resources allotted a grant of

$20,000, generated major activity for IFLA in the cataloguing field.

In 1962 IFLA's first permanent central secretariat was established by a Unesco grant; Anthony Thompson became the first full-time IFLA Secretary General. During this time IFLA began to exhibit real strength in the realm of programming; in 1963 the Federation published *Libraries in the World,* a long-term program for IFLA, which distinguished itself by an imaginative and realistic view on IFLA's possible future development. Gradually the importance of sections for types of libraries and committees for types of library activity increased, enabling IFLA to react adequately to urgent library problems. IFLA's firmness of purpose became exemplary and resulted in steady growth. When Thompson resigned in 1970, the Federation had 250 members in 52 countries.

In 1971 an energetic President, Herman Liebaers, National Librarian of Belgium, brought the Secretariat to The Hague. As President he managed to interest several funding bodies in the work of IFLA. He launched the UBC (Universal Bibliographic Control) program and brought the librarians of the Third World into IFLA. With support from the Council on Library Resources, a small, effective Secretariat was strengthened at The Hague, and a permanent office for UBC was set up in London. A regional office at Kuala Lumpur in Malaysia was founded with assistance from the Canadian International Development Agency, and a program for the various world regions was developed.

When Liebaers left IFLA and the library profession in 1974, IFLA had grown into a beehive of activity and could claim virtually universal international membership with 600 members in 100 countries. Liebaers had the vision and drive necessary to adapt IFLA to the demands of modern society. He also had the foresight to use the services of a Program Development Group, a core of experts who paved the way for some major IFLA projects (such as Universal Availability of Publications and public library development) but who also had a keen eye for smaller, but nevertheless valuable, projects. This group would later develop into a statutory Professional Board.

Organization and Structure. After years of sometimes heated discussions, a new structure for IFLA was approved by the Council in Lausanne in 1976. The new Statutes define the purpose as follows:

to promote international understanding, cooperation, discussion, research, and development in all fields of library activity, including bibliography, information services, and the education of personnel, and to provide a body through which librarianship can be represented in matters of international interest.

Membership. The name of the organization was expanded to include *institutions* (libraries, library schools, and bibliographic institutes). It became the International Federation of Library Associations and Institutions (IFLA). Since 1976 IFLA has had two main categories of members, Association and Institutional. Both have voting rights in all matters and meetings. However, in Council meetings Association Members have more votes than Institutional Members, at least 51 percent, with 7 to 22 votes for the joint Association Members in any one country. A relatively new category is the Personal Affiliate, with no voting rights. There is also the opportunity for Consultative Status for related international organizations. Among those with Consultative Status are FID (International Federation for Documentation), ICA (International Council on Archives), ICAE (International Council on Adult Education), ISO (International Organization for Standardization), IPA (International Publishers Association), and ISDS (International Serials Data System). Other international organizations, mainly concerned with librarianship, tend to join IFLA as International Association Members with voting rights; for example, IAML (International Association of Music Libraries), IATUL (International Association of Technological University Libraries), COMLA (Commonwealth Library Association), LIBER (Ligue des Bibliothèques Euro-

General Policy		Professional Programs
Council		Divisions, Sections Round Tables
Member-Associations 51 percent of the votes	Member-Institutions 49 percent votes	All members one vote

Bodies with Consultative Status
Personal Affiliates
(Participants without voting rights)

General management	Management of core programmes	Professional programs
Executive Board (EB)	Programme Management Committee (PMC)	Professional Board (PB)
President + 7 members + Chair PB (Chair PMC in attendance)	President + Chair PB + representative from Conference of Directors of National Libraries + 2 other persons	Chairman + 8 members + Chair PMC

péennes de Recherche), and ACURIL (Association of Caribbean University Research and Institutional Libraries). INTAMEL (International Association of Metropolitan Cities Libraries) functions as a Round Table in IFLA.

Steering Bodies. The main steering bodies as defined by the Statutes are the Executive and Professional boards; the first has full powers of administration and management and the second deals with coordinating and planning professional activities. The Executive Board consists of an elected President and seven elected members, with the Chairperson of the Professional Board serving as an ex-officio member. The Professional Board is composed of the Chairpersons of the eight Divisions.

In May 1979 the Executive Board—at that time headed by Preben Kirkegaard—decided to establish a Programme Management Committee to coordinate and manage IFLA's so-called core programs, including their objectives, financing, and functions, and also to facilitate the liaison of those programs with the work of the Sections and Divisions.

In 1983 the Council (since 1977 convened in odd years only) approved the *IFLA Perspectives,* a document in which the Executive Board defined six core programs, presented in more detail below. These Perspectives were a result of the deliberations of a Task Force convened by Else Granheim, IFLA President from August 1979.

The new organizational structure, effective as of September 1979, is outlined in the accompanying diagram.

time administrative staff members. They are responsible for daily management of the organization, liaison with related organizations, coordination of professional groups and units within IFLA, maintaining secretariats of the Executive and Professional Boards, and issuing periodical publications. Program support was strengthened in February 1985 by the arrival of a Programme Development Officer (also functioning as Chair of the PMC) who, with financial assistance from the Council on Library Resources, was to plan the IFLA core programs in a number of six-month consultancies.

Other program focal points can be found in London (Universal Bibliographic Control and International MARC), Boston Spa in the north of England (Universal Availability of Publications and International Lending), and Frankfurt (International MARC). Offices in Kuala Lumpur, Dakar, and Caracas serve the Third World programs.

Programs. The Medium-Term Programme 1986–1991 describes a variety of activities based on two approaches. Library operation can be looked at from two points of view, one treating all operations as elements in the functioning of an integrated whole—the library; the other viewing each operation as a separate activity with its own techniques. These approaches have been expressed in IFLA by the growth of two kinds of groups, one consisting of librarians responsible for a particular type of library and another consisting of librarians concerned with the techniques appropriate to a particular operation that is common to various types of libraries. The 31

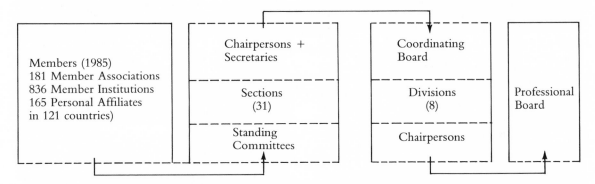

Subunits. In the new IFLA the Sections can be considered the grassroots of the organization; they are grouped together in Divisions for coordination. Members and affiliates register for the Sections of their choice and can nominate and elect persons for membership on Standing Committees, the core groups of experts that develop the program of the Section and ensure its execution. The Chairpersons and Secretaries of the Sections form the Coordinating Board of the Division to which they belong. The Chairpersons of the Divisional Coordinating Boards form the Professional Board.

In the professional field, IFLA has two other, less formal, means for the performance of professional tasks: Round Tables and Working Groups.

Headquarters. The Federation is headquartered in the Royal Library, The Hague, Netherlands. The staff consists of the Secretary General, the Coordinator of Professional Activities, an Executive Assistant also acting as Publications Officer, and three part-

Sections of IFLA, with the additional Round Tables and Working Groups, all have their own programs, ranging from sophisticated university library management studies to professional training of school librarians, from the establishment of regional braille centers in the Third World to the availability of official publications, and from improvement of the status of librarians to the development of public library work. But there are six core programs that cut across the Sections and IFLA concentrates most of its resources and efforts on them.

UBC. IFLA's international program for UBC (Universal Bibliographic Control) aims to promote the exchange and use of compatible bibliographic records. Such records must be produced in accordance with international bibliographic standards and must be interchangeable with those of other national bibliographic agencies. The main element of the program is to assist in the development and publication of ISBDs (International Standard Bibliographic Description). A five-year review of the ISBDs was completed and several new publications were planned in 1985. In addition, new ISBDs for Component Parts (ISBD(CP)) and for Machine-Readable Data Files (ISBD(MRF)) were also planned or in process in the mid-1980s. Other projects under way include those flowing from the International Cataloguing-in-Publication meeting in Ottawa, August 1982, such as the preparation of a standardized format for the Cataloguing-in-Publication (CIP) entries in books and the preparation of guidelines for CIP operation.

UAP. IFLA's international program for UAP (Universal Availability of Publications) has as its guiding principle that each country should be responsible for supplying its own publications by loan or photocopy on request to other countries. The program encompasses such matters as interlibrary lending systems, exchange of publications, legal deposit, copyright, and cooperative acquisition schemes. Publicity, research, and guidance and advice to others have played a large part in the initial development of the program. Additional research will include feasibility studies leading to implementation projects, such as the design of national availability systems for individual countries. Other projects under way in the mid-1980s include training seminars on UAP. Seminars were held in Boston Spa, in Nairobi, and in New Delhi.

IMP. The International MARC program, established officially in 1983, consists of two main project components. The first, in the Deutsche Bibliothek in Frankfurt, is concerned mainly with International MARC applications, including technical feasibility studies and UNIMARC testing. The second, housed at the British Library in London, is primarily responsible for the continuous maintenance, revision, and development of the UNIMARC format on the basis of the *UNIMARC Handbook,* for feasibility studies for the most effective methods of international transfer of bibliographic data, and for the preparation of the third edition of the UNIMARC format.

PAC. The Preservation and Conservation core program was established with the aim of promoting the search for solutions to the serious problems of physical deterioration of library and information materials. The action envisaged is oriented toward coordination and policy matters, studies and research, raising awareness, training and education, and pilot projects.

TDF. The Transborder Data Flow program deals with the promotion of the electronic transfer of data among libraries across national borders, thus ensuring that the vital interest of the library community in resource sharing is preserved. It is restricted to data publicly available, with or without charge, and encompasses both reference and source databases. Action is concentrated mainly on topics that are of primary importance to, and affect directly, the library community. The program embraces formulation of policies and guidelines, raising awareness of the subject, improvement of access to computerized databases, and cooperation with others involved in TDF.

ALP. The Advancement of Librarianship in the Third World is not a goal or problem new to IFLA, but the new and innovative aspect of the core program is the endeavor to plan a cohesive program that concentrates on the creation of the best possible conditions for self-development of library services in the Third World. Horizontal cooperation among the countries of the Third World is the main aim of ALP. Consultations starting during the 1984 IFLA Nairobi Conference resulted in a policy meeting of the Chairmen of the regional Sections in The Hague in September 1984. This ultimately led to a document meant to stimulate and facilitate the involvement of Third World librarianship in all facets of IFLA activities. The ideas formulated in this document were translated into a number of structural changes by the Executive Board, and proposals were to be voted upon by the Council in 1985.

Conferences and Meetings. Although emphasis has gradually moved from the annual meetings to continuing projects, the importance of regular personal contact must not be underestimated. IFLA holds General Conferences each year, with more than 200 professional meetings during the conferences. Every second year (in odd years) such conferences are combined with Council meetings, where IFLA business affairs (elections, budget, and rules) are dealt with. Venues were scheduled (1985) for Chicago, 1985; Tokyo, 1986; Brighton, 1987; Sydney, 1988; and Paris, 1989.

Publications. Periodical publications of the Federation are the quarterly *IFLA Journal* and *International Cataloguing; IFLA Annual,* issued yearly; and *IFLA Directory,* issued biennially.

IFLA Publications is a monograph series, published by K. G. Saur (Munich and London). Four numbers are published each year. During 1984 titles included *Guide to the Availability of Theses: II, Non-University Institutions* (IFLA Publications 29), compiled by G. G. Allen and K. Deubert, and *A Guide to Developing Braille and Talking Book Services* (IFLA Publications 30), compiled by Leslie L. Clark.

A new series, *IFLA Professional Reports,* published by IFLA Headquarters under the auspices of the Professional Board, was started in 1984 to ensure that the results of IFLA professional projects reached the wider audience for which they were intended.

Publications have also been issued under the auspices of three of the core programs. UBC's publications include the *International Standard Bibliographic Descriptions* (general, monographic publications, serials, nonbook materials, and cartographic materials) plus several publications on uniform headings, cataloging, machine-readable cataloging, serials, and *Guidelines for Authority and Reference Entries.* Publications of the UAP program include: *The Availability of Books through Commercial Channels with Particular Reference to Developing Countries* and *The Impact of New Technology on the Availability of Publications.* A *UAP Newsletter* is also issued twice yearly. In 1984 the International MARC program prepared and published the *International Guide to MARC Databases and Services* and started the regular publication of the *IMP Newsletter* to keep the library community regularly informed on new developments, activities, and projects undertaken or coordinated by the responsible bodies associated with the International MARC program.

REFERENCES

IFLA's First Fifty years: Achievement and Challenge in International Librarianship, edited by W. R. H. Koops and J.

Wieder (1977), contains eight chapters on the history of IFLA as well as views on IFLA's future.

IFLA and Contemporary Library Problems, special issue of *IFLA Journal* (1977), contains articles on IFLA's role in various fields of library work.

MARGREET WIJNSTROOM

International Library and Bibliographical Organizations

International library and bibliographic organizations now fulfill a wide range of functions. Among these functions are: (1) the lending or exchange of documentary materials; (2) the regulation of international commerce related to these materials (postal and tariff regulations, copyright agreements, publishing and distributing rights, and censorship); (3) the generation, standardization, exchange, or publication of bibliographic data in various formats for books and nonbook publications and of indexing and abstracting data for journal articles and related materials; (4) the creation, maintenance, and operation of international information systems of various kinds; (5) the provision of moral, technical, and financial assistance to developing countries to help them improve their use of existing documentary materials and information systems; and (6) the publication of reports, manuals, directories, monographs, and proceedings—a technical and general support literature about operations, systems, and procedures that represents the deliberations of expert bodies of personnel about problems of international interest.

Early History. Perhaps the first organizations to take on an international cast were the German book fairs of the 16th century, which drew buyers and sellers of books from all parts of Europe. The *Messkataloge,* begun in 1564 by Georg Willer, listed what was available and contained entries for books outside the German states, though, naturally enough, books published within them predominated. Various series of these catalogues were published until the late 19th century, though entries for non-German material began to decline in the 17th century. In 1617 John Bill began to publish an English edition of these catalogues; he soon added English titles (the catalogues already contained some), and from 1622 to 1626 these additions took the form of regular, separately titled supplements.

In the last half of the 17th century, the rise and increasingly rapid proliferation of journal literature added complexity to a bibliographic problem that, with the diffusion of printing and the widespread adoption of the vernacular, had already become serious. Nevertheless, until the latter part of the 19th century, the problem was dealt with first only by individuals and then by formal groups acting at a national level. While much individual and later corporate effort was expended on the development of national bibliographic control, where the works created reached beyond national bounds, most of them tended to seek universality of scope. Among the enormous number of works of this kind, one of the first and greatest was Gesner's *Bibliotheca Universalis* (1545). Derived from the Frankfurt *Messkataloge* were Georg Draud's *Bibliotheca Classica, Bibliotheca Exotica,* and *Bibliotheca Librorum Germanicorum Classica* (1611–

12, revised 1625). At the end of the 17th century, Raffaele Savanorola finished his *Orbis Litteraris.* Occupying some 40 folio volumes, it was never published and disappeared some time in the 19th century. Francesco Marucelli's *Mare Magnum,* a catalogue intended to list everything known to have been written, was compiled at about the same time; it, too, was never published but survives in 111 volumes copied sometime after 1751 from the now lost manuscript.

The idea of universal bibliographic control, of which these works are imperfect manifestations, exercised a potent fascination on bibliographers from the 17th through the 19th centuries. In 1631 Petrus Blanchot published his *Idea Bibliotheca Universalis,* a proposal for a universal subject index. In the 1840s and 1850s the idea sprang up more vigorously than ever, though apparently independently, in France, the United Kingdom, and the United States, in association with attempts to compile and publish library catalogues. Félix Danjou in France, Charles Wentworth Dilke, Andrea Crestadoro, and later Sir Henry Cole in the U.K., and Charles Coffin Jewett in the U.S., all had different schemes, to say nothing of the fin de siècle schemes of Ferdinand Bonnage in France and Vander Haeghen in Belgium.

The 19th Century. A major scheme for the control of scientific literature in the 19th century was the Royal Society's *Catalogue of Scientific Papers.* Universal in scope, this catalogue was almost self-consciously national in execution, though foreign academies and learned societies were consulted for recommendations as to journals to be indexed. It was published in four series between 1867 and 1925 with a supplementary volume for the period 1800–83.

A little known, more limited attempt at scientific bibliography that seems to have had some success internationally was initiated in 1889 by the Société mathématique de France, which sponsored a Congrès international de bibliographies des sciences mathématiques in Paris. The *Répertoire bibliographiques des Sciences mathèmatiques* came into being in 1893 and had two forms: a simple retrospective bibliography published in Paris from 1893 to 1912 on cards and the *Revue semestrielle des publications mathématiques d'Amsterdam.* This bibliography continued in the latter form until 1934, when it merged with the *Jahrbuch über die Fortschritte der Mathematik,* which ceased publication in 1942. Both the *Revue* and the *Jahrbuch* used the classification, revised from time to time, of the *Répertoire bibliographique des Sciences mathématiques.*

Such ventures are evidence of a growing, but incomplete, internationalism in bibliography. Two other 19th-century forms of bibliographical or bibliothecal internationalism should be mentioned: the first may be described as regulatory and involved governments; the second was essentially consultative and collegial. In 1817 a limited scheme was implemented for the exchange of dissertations among German universities, the Akademischer Tauscheverein; by the early 1880s 50 European universities and academies had become involved in this venture. In the 1840s and 1850s Alexandre Vattemare, a famous ventriloquist and quick-change artist who desired to stimulate the exchange of publications between governments, set up an Agence centrale des échanges internationaux in Paris to coordinate this work. He was eventually able, if only briefly, to interest many governments in his ideas, including 18 state legislatures and the Congress of the United States. The major development in this area, however, was an international intergovernmental conference, which culminated a number of earlier conferences, at Brussels in 1882. Here were signed two conventions governing the international exchange of documents: *Convention A* dealt with the exchange of government publications generally; *Convention B* dealt with parliamentary gazettes, journals, and annuals. While these conventions were never widely adopted, they remained in force and under scrutiny into the middle of the 20th century.

International copyright had been a subject of debate for much of the early part of the 19th century, and various bilateral agreements were concluded among European states in an attempt to protect the rights of authors internationally. As early as 1858 a major international congress in Brussels deliberated on the subject, and the movement then begun quickly gathered force leading to a convention signed in Berne in 1886. A permanent bureau directed by Henri Morel and sponsored by the Swiss government was set up in 1888 to act as the headquarters for what has since become generally known as the Berne Copyright Union.

As the 19th century progressed and as literature proliferated and libraries grew, librarians and bibliographers began locally, nationally, and internationally to seek mutual stimulation and enlightenment through formal association. In 1868 a Société bibliographique was created in Paris; in 1878 it held the first of three decennial international conferences that "in a series of reports would trace the scientific and literary movement of the ten-year period in order to provide ample materials and accurate information to all students." These gatherings, though strongly French, attracted some participants from Belgium, Italy, Luxembourg, the U.K., and elsewhere. Similar conferences were the International Conference of Librarians in London in 1877, which was enlivened by a large contingent of American librarians, and the 20th-anniversary conference of the Library Association of the United Kingdom, which had been founded at the 1877 conference. Other international conferences were held, for example, on the occasion of the international exhibitions of Paris in 1900, San Francisco in 1904, and Brussels in 1910, but no permanent organization was created either to perpetuate the conferences themselves or to allow them to undertake some corporate activity of international value. Curiously, the 1900 conference had resolved that it should reconvene every five years (it did not), and the 1910 "Congrès de Bruxelles" was organized by an avowedly "Permanent Commission for the International Congresses of Archivists and Librarians," of which no more was heard.

Before World War I. For bibliographical organization, the year 1895 is a watershed. In that year the International Institute of Bibliography was created in Brussels by Paul Otlet and Henri LaFontaine. The Concilium Bibliographicum was in the process of being set up in Zurich by Herbert Haviland Field, and the consultations with foreign academies and learned societies undertaken by the Royal Society, prior to calling an international conference to explore

the creation of an *International Catalogue of Scientific Literature,* were well advanced.

The International Conference on Bibliography, held in Brussels in 1895, created the International Institute of Bibliography (IIB), and the Belgian government undertook to support a headquarters organization for it, the International Office of Bibliography (OIB). The aim of the new organization was to create a universal bibliography or catalogue (Répertoire Bibliographique Universel) that would be organized both by author and, by means of a radical expansion of the Dewey Decimal Classification and a sophisticated development of the mechanics of the classification's notation, by subject.

The Concilium Bibliographicum had a limited goal: to compile centrally and to distribute on cards or as supplements to major journals or reviews the current bibliography of zoology and related subjects. Agreements between the Concilium and the International Institute of Bibliography were made even as both organizations completed their initial arrangements. The latter adopted the three-by-five card as the basis for its work (it had originally proposed to use a card of a quite different size), promoted its use as an international standard, and confided to Field and his colleagues the development of the UDC in the areas of the Concilium's interest. In its turn, the Concilium undertook to develop the UDC, to use it on its bibliographical notices, and to send copies of its cards and other bibliographical publications to Brussels. As well as being published in card form, the zoological portion of the Concilium's work appeared as a supplement to the *Zoologischer Anzeiger,* the physiological portion as part of the *Zentralblatt für Physiologie,* and the protozoological portion in the *Archiv für Protistenkunde.* Support for the Concilium was provided by Field himself and by local sources (the Swiss Confederation and the city and canton of Zurich principally), by international sponsors (the International Congress of Zoology and the French Zoological Society), and from revenues generated from the sale of its bibliographical services.

The first International Conference on a Catalogue of Scientific Literature was held in London in 1896, and others followed in 1898 and 1900. Sponsored by the Royal Society, these conferences led to the creation of a complex organization to govern and produce the catalogue. It was governed by an International Convention that met in 1905, 1910, and 1922 and was administered by an International Council that met regularly at more frequent intervals. A Central Bureau, supervised by the Director of the Catalogue, Henry Forster Morely, prepared the work for publication; regional bureaus in participating countries, such as the Smithsonian Institution in the U.S., transcribed references to their national scientific literature onto slips of a standard size and weight. Detailed specifications as to form of entry, content, punctuation, and abbreviation were followed in producing these slips. The first issue of the *International Catalogue of Scientific Literature,* divided into 17 subject areas, appeared in 22 volumes in 1901. Annual issues appeared until World War I.

Between the Two World Wars. The end of World War I marks a major turning point in the development of international bibliographic organization and control. A sustained period of development was abruptly terminated by the war, and the return of peace provided an opportunity for conscious choice as to whether the effort and expense of resuming prewar bibliographical ventures were worthwhile. These ventures, overlapping each other to various degrees, had involved the creation of a formal mechanism to procure the international cooperation of scholars, the centralization of publishing and consultative activities in ambiguously supported, nationally based headquarters, and the provision of conventional enumerative bibliography. After the war it seemed that new organizations for the cooperation of scholars were necessary and that conventional bibliography of the kind provided before the war was no longer enough.

The *International Catalogue of Scientific Literature* was not resumed at all after the war. Though the work of the Concilium Bibliographicum was continued for a time, and a special grant from the Rockefeller Foundation assisted the Concilium's flagging finances, it too fell rapidly into a decline from which it did not recover. Despite the German occupation of Brussels during the war, the facilities and collections of the International Institute of Bibliography were unharmed, and for a short time it seemed as if the Institute's future was secure. Nevertheless, the Belgian governmment began to withdraw its support from the vast, overextended complex of organizations (Palais Mondial or Mundaneum) of which the IIB was part, and in 1924 the IIB's members decided to reorganize the Institute, stressing its independence from the failing center in Brussels, the importance to it of national members, and the need to revise the UDC, now long out of print and out of date. The reorganizations begun in 1924 were continued under the presidencies of Allan Pollard, an Englishman (1927–30), and J. Alingh Prins, a Dutchman (1931–37). Emphasis was placed on decentralization of activity and federalism of organization. Annual congresses began in 1927, and in 1931 the Institute changed its name to International Institute of Documentation (and changed it again in 1937 to International Federation for Documentation, FID). Its work was limited to the continuous revision and translation into various languages of the UDC (the second full edition was issued in 1932), to the publication of the journal *Documentation Universalis* (1930–32) and its successor *IID Communicationes* (later *FID Communicationes*), and to the annual congresses. Bibliography, especially the preparation of a centralized universal bibliography of doubtful utility, technically inadequate and poorly supported, was subordinated first to the elaboration of a classification that, at least theoretically, could be used to bring a form of standardized access to any bibliography or catalogue anywhere, and then later, as the 1930s progressed, to the study of documentary reproduction, especially by microphotography, the techniques and uses of which the Institute had been exploring since 1906.

The League of Nations. The most important institution for the world of learning after the war took an organizational form different from any that had preceded it. Though at first not concerned with this area, the League of Nations in 1922 created an International Committee on Intellectual Cooperation and appointed to it 12 eminent scholars from a variety of disciplines and countries. Receiving inadequate financial support from the League from the start, in 1924

the Committee was given permission to appeal directly to governments for assistance. The French government offered to set up in Paris and, in part, fund what would be an executive arm and headquarters organization for the Committee, the International Institute of Intellectual Cooperation, frequently referred to as the Paris Institute. The whole was called the League Organization of Intellectual Cooperation.

Among a wide range of tasks addressed by the International Committee on Intellectual Cooperation were the organization of relief for intellectual workers in central and eastern Europe, improvement in the international exchange of publications, improvement in international copyright, and the coordination of bibliography. Indeed, one of the first subcommittees set up by the Committee was for bibliography.

Over a period the League Organization of Intellectual Cooperation arranged consultations through the Subcommittee on Bibliography, and later its Committee of Library Experts, on how the bibliography of a diverse group of subjects might be improved; it proposed major modifications in the treaties governing the protection of intellectual property and the international exchange of publications; it held conferences, conducted surveys, and issued a great many publications. Some of these were directories and some bibliographies; some, such as the *Index Bibliographicus* and the *Index Translationem,* were continued after World War II by Unesco.

Because of lack of resources and the conception of its role as primarily investigative and advisory, the League Organization of Intellectual Cooperation, as a matter of policy, did not attempt to carry out major projects. Rather, it sought to identify those that were of international importance and, whenever possible, sometimes by the provision of subsidies, to encourage other existing organizations to undertake them. From the start it had sought a viable relationship with the International Institute of Bibliography. But despite the signing of an agreement between the two bodies in 1924, the relationship between them, already delicate because of the personalities involved, gradually deteriorated to such a degree that to some outside observers, such as Ernest Cushing Richardson from the U.S., the settlement of the differences between the organizations was the crucial test of the League's ability to bring about successful international cooperation in intellectual matters.

IFLA. League cooperation with the International Federation of Library Associations (IFLA) was more successful than with the International Institute of Bibliography, partly because there could be no clash of vested interests or organizational philosophy between the two. From its inception in 1927, IFLA was deeply influenced by the League Organization and by a long-held but unfulfilled hope in the Paris Institute of setting up as part of its Section on Scientific Relations an International Library Advisory Service. In 1926 a proposal to create a permanent professional library organization, one function of which would be to work with the Paris Institute, had been made at the International Conference of Librarians and Booklovers in Prague. In 1927 at the annual meeting of the Library Association of the United Kingdom, an International Library and Bibliographical Committee was formally created. This became the

International Federation of Library Associations in 1929, and in that year the first World Congress of Librarianship and Bibliography was held. According to the statutes of the new association, its executive committee was to be called the International Library Committee, which would meet annually, while the association as a whole was to assemble at least once every five years. IFLA cooperated closely with the League Organization in the publication of several directories and guides. The *Acts* of the International Library Committee and the *Proceedings* of the 1929 Rome-Venice conference and the 1935 Madrid-Barcelona conference provide evidence of the evolution from the limited, occasional prewar library conferences of a permanent international library community, characterized by continuous if fragile links between members, sustained formal communication, and some corporate activity.

The League Organization of Intellectual Cooperation also worked closely with the International Federation of National Standardizing Associations (ISA). The latter body was formed in 1926, and in 1938 a technical committee, ISA-46, was devoted to studying standardization in documentation. This technical committee was a direct forerunner of the present ISO/TC 46.

General cooperation between the League Organization and the International Research Council was a goal pursued by both over a period of years, though its achievement was hindered in part because of the relatively long intervals between the meetings of the Council. A committee appointed by the Council in 1925 recommended in 1928 that a joint Council/League commission should be set up. In 1937 a formal agreement was reached for consultation and cooperation between the Council and the Paris Institute, which had, in any case, already referred matters to the Council for advice (including some matters of bibliography).

Thus by 1930 a pattern of international bibliographic and library organization had essentially emerged, the outlines of which can still be discerned beneath the increasing international complexity and activity characteristic of the period after World War II. At the center in the 1930s was the permanent international intergovernmental organization of the time, the League of Nations, as represented by the League Organization. Its work took a number of forms. It published, often as the result of international surveys, guides, directories, and bibliographies. It convened meetings of experts to consider issues of importance. And it tried to stimulate and coordinate the work of international nongovernmental organizations active in major areas of League interest: here lie the negotiations, successful and complete to varying degrees, between the League and IFLA, FID, ISA, and the International Council of Scientific Unions.

After World War II. As World War II drew to its close, there was no question that a new organization dealing with matters of education, culture, and science should be created as part of the United Nations family of organizations then being planned. Moreover, there was no doubt that part of the work of the new organization, which was to be called Unesco, should be concerned with libraries and bibliography. A rather grandiose plan put forward by

Theodore Besterman for an International Library and Bibliographic Clearing House within the Unesco secretariat was soon abandoned as unrealistic. Unesco's program for libraries, bibliography, documentation, archives, and related subjects has grown over the years in strength, scope, and complexity. Its early conferences on science abstracting (1949) and the improvement of bibliographic services throughout the world (1950) culminated in the UNISIST (World Scientific and Technical Information) program adopted by an intergovernmental conference in 1974. These and related programs were brought together in the General Information Program (PGI), an intersectoral program attached to the Office of the Directorate in order to facilitate coordination and development of work and to reduce duplication of effort and organizational conflict. The impact on the General Information Program of the withdrawal of the U.S. from Unesco, scheduled for December 1985, is not clear but may well be considerable.

Unesco, like the League Organization, continues to rely on the help of other organizations. IFLA has been able to bring about considerable international agreement on the standardization of cataloguing practices throughout the world, and its Universal Bibliographical Control Program (UBC), administered through a specially funded International Office for UBC, has attracted much international support, while its other programs, especially the Universal Availability of Publications (UAP), are achieving considerable impetus. FID, while continuing to support the UDC, has collaborated closely with Unesco in developing and maintaining the ISORID program (International Information System on Research and Development in Documentation) and in devising the Broad System of Ordering (BSO) within the framework of UNISIST. Like IFLA it continues to hold a range of general and special meetings, issues publications, and acts jointly with other organizations in supporting workshops, conferences, seminars, and so on. The International Council of Scientific Unions created an Abstracting Board (ICSU-AB), which first met in 1955, and this has become an important international forum for the major abstracting and indexing services in the world.

The advent of the computer as a major tool in information processing and the development of machine-readable bibliographic databases to some degree underlie aspects of UNISIST's program of systems interconnection. They have also led to the development of a number of international information systems, such as INIS (the International Nuclear Information System of the International Nuclear Energy Agency) and AGRIS (Agriculture Information System of the Food and Agriculture Organization). A number of other systems were under development in the 1980s. Such systems are similar to the *International Catalogue of Scientific Literature;* their differences, however, are crucial. The subject and scope of the present systems are specific, and the systems constitute relatively minor parts of the work of major, broadly based intergovernmental organizations. Another contemporary development predicated on the computer revolution is the emergence of regional networks for the exploitation of bibliographic databases. One of the most important of these is Euronet/Diane (Direct Information Access Network for Europe), which was developed by the Commission of the European Communities and became operational in late 1979. In terms of technical organization and the nature of the intergovernmental agreements which underlie it, it is probably unique.

International library and bibliographic organization in the last quarter of the 20th century is complex. It involves a great many nongovernmental associations—some with fairly general goals and some with quite specific ones. It involves a number of intergovernmental organizations, some maintaining international systems, some such as Unesco or ISO responsible for development, coordination, and support of the work of other organizations. There are regional organizations and global ones. Among the most notable of the former are the Association of Caribbean University Research and Institutional Libraries (ACURIL), the Ligue des bibliothèques Europeannes de Recherche (LIBER), and the Seminar on the Acquisition of Latin American Library Materials (SALAM). A curious organization, reflecting the vestigial colonial affiliations of a past era, is the Commonwealth Library Association (COMLA), which was set up in 1972. There are international agreements of various degrees of formality, ranging from intergovernmental conventions on copyright, exchange of documents, and the international flow of educational and cultural materials to expressions of approval of vaguely formulated programs of international desiderata. There are internationally drawn-up and maintained procedures and tools that are under constant scrutiny, development, and revision and that are accepted nationally with varying degrees of completeness. While much remains to be done, an established organizational basis and a widespread international awareness suggest that continuous achievement in the future is inevitable.

REFERENCES

Edward Carter, "The Birth of Unesco's Library Programmes," in *Med Boken Som Bakgrunn; Festkrift Til Harold L. Treterås* (1964).

S. Steven Falk, "The International Committee on Intellectual Cooperation: Its Work for Bibliography" (unpublished M.A. thesis, University of Chicago Graduate Library School, 1977).

Katherine Oliver Murra, "Some Attempts to Organize Bibliography Internationally," in Jesse Shera and Margaret Egan, editors, *Bibliographic Organization* (1951).

W. Boyd Rayward, *The Universe of Information: The Work of Paul Otlet for Documentation and International Organization* (1975).

W. BOYD RAYWARD

International Organization for Standardization

The International Organization for Standardization was created in 1946 following a meeting in London of the International Federation of the National Standardizing Associations. Delegates from 25 countries cooperated to create the new international organization, whose purpose would be to "facilitate the international coordination and unification of industrial standards." ISO comprised in 1985 the national standards institutes of 90 countries, of which 75 were member bodies and 15 correspondent members. Correspondent members are normally organizations in developing countries that do not yet have their own national standards bodies; most are governmental institutions, and they normally become full members after a few years. They do not take part in technical work.

The scope of ISO extends to both technical and nontechnical standards and is not limited to any particular branch, although it does not deal with the electrotechnical field, which is covered by the International Electrotechnical Commission. The object of the organization is to promote the development of world standards with a goal of facilitating the international exchange of goods and developing cooperation in intellectual, scientific, technological, and economic areas.

The technical work of ISO is accomplished through technical committees; the creation and scope of the committees are determined by the ISO Council. Within the determined scope the individual committee decides its own program and creates subcommittees and working groups. ISO had 163 technical committees by the end of 1984, with 649 attendant subcommittees and 1,460 working groups. Each technical committee and subcommittee has a secretariat assigned to an ISO member body. A new item may be introduced into an ISO working program through a proposal usually made by a member body but that may be made by some other international organization. If an item is accepted, a new technical committee may be created, or it will be referred to the appropriate existing committee. Any member body that is interested in a subject for which a committee has been authorized has the right to be represented on that committee; representatives are designated either as observers or as participating members, who have the right to vote and to participate in meetings and one of whom acts as the committee's secretariat.

ISO/TC 46. Standardization of practices relating to libraries, documentation and information centers, indexing and abstracting services, archives, information science, and publishing is the subject of ISO Technical Committee 46 (ISO/TC 46). The committee had its origins in 1938, when the German Technical Committee of librarianship within the Deutscher Normenausschuss proposed that ISA-46 be set up and took over its secretariat. The secretariat was later held by NOBIN (Nederlands Orgaan voor de Bevordering fan de Intermatieverzorging) and was reallocated in 1966 to DNA (since 1975 DIN, Deutsches Institut für Normung). Twenty-six participating members and 24 observing members, who are nominees of the respective national standards institutions, carry out the standardization work. Seven other ISO technical committees and 38 international organizations also participate. Further Technical Committees working in the field of information and documentation are ISO/TC 37—Terminology (principles and coordination); ISO/TC 97—Information Processing Systems; ISO/TC 154—Documents and Data Elements in Administration, Commerce, and Industry; and ISO/TC 171— Micrographics.

ISO publishes numerous documents and periodicals, including *ISO Catalogue,* an annual list of ISO standards that is updated quarterly, and *ISO Technical Program,* a semiannual list of all draft ISO standards.

ISO Bibliographies list all standards and draft standards in a given field. An overall view of ISO activities can be obtained in the *ISO Annual Review*, while the *ISO Bulletin* supplies monthly news. Information on technical committees is available in published Directives for the technical work of ISO. ISO also began to publish a series of handbooks containing selected ISO standards in particular fields.

ISO has granted liaison status to approximately 409 international organizations with ISO technical committees and subcommittees. Further details can be found in ISO's publication *Liaisons*.

JOHANNA EGGERT

Iran

Iran, an Islamic republic in western Asia, is bounded by the Caspian Sea and the U.S.S.R. on the north, Afghanistan and Pakistan on the east, the Gulf of Oman and Persian Gulf on the south, and Iraq and Turkey on the west. Population (1984 est.) 43,088,000; area 1,648,000 sq.km. The official language is Farsi (Persian). Iran underwent two major revolutionary changes in the 20th century: the first, the constitutional revolution 1905–09, the second, the Islamic revolution 1977–79.

History. Although 2,500 years of Iran's contributions to civilization, knowledge, and scholarship include outstanding libraries with rich collections, modern concepts of library services were not introduced until the second half of the 20th century. The first library school was established at Tehran University as recently as 1966. A shortage of professionally qualified librarians was a factor that affected the slow development of modern library services in Iran.

In its early stage, the Islamic revolution brought with it a halt in education. Dewesternization and Islamization were the goals. Libraries were no exception. The doors of many libraries were closed. A few children's libraries established by the Institute for the Intellectual Development of Children and Young Adults were burned in Tehran because of their royal connections. A number of libraries at the University of Ahvaz and Babolsar were also burned. The Islamic "cultural revolution" imposed censorship on the libraries' book collections. Many religious groups forced librarians to "purify" their collections. Certain books that did not support the Islamic government's point of view had to be discarded.

Western-inspired library education, which heavily depended on American experts and educators as well as American-educated Iranians, came to a standstill. Many American-educated Iranian librarians left Iran and practically all foreign educators and librarians were forced to leave.

During the early and mid-1980s libraries gradually returned to their normal functions, providing minimal services. Mosques and religious libraries, however, flourished everywhere in Iran. The principle of sex segregation was introduced, and libraries had to allocate certain sections of their buildings or certain days of the week for use by women only.

National Library. Ketabkhaneh Melli of Iran was established in 1937; it holds approximately 170,000 volumes and 3,000 periodicals on a wide variety of subjects. It has an outstanding manuscripts and rare books collection. It receives one copy of each publication produced in the country and publishes the "National Bibliography of Iran." Services to other libraries and participation in National Library development, which are normally considered as national library functions, were in part performed by other organizations such as the Tehran Book Processing Center and Iranian Documentation Center, both established in 1968 by the Ministry of Science and Higher Education.

Pahlavi Project. A grand and ambitious project for the establishment of a modern national library, unique in the world in concept and notable for utilization of the most sophisticated technology in information storage and transfer, was launched by the Shah in 1975. The project benefited from the contributions of more than 100 consultants from America, Europe, and Iran itself under the chairmanship of Nasser Sharify of Pratt Institute in Brooklyn, New York. The 17-volume report entitled "The Pahlavi National Library of the Future" was submitted to the government in 1976. Construction began two years later, but the project died as soon as the Islamic revolution came to life.

Academic Libraries. The first Western-style university was founded in Tehran in 1934. By 1975 there were 10 universities and 132 colleges and technical institutes in Iran, and the number increased during the late 1970s. Except for newer and smaller universities, Iranian universities have no centralized library systems; each faculty (school) within each university has its own independent library. Tehran, Tabriz, Mashhad, and Esfahan universities have created central libraries. The Central Library and Documentation Center of Tehran University holds approximately 160,000 volumes, 5,000 microfilms, 12,600

Libraries in Iran (1981)

Type	Administrative units	Service points	Volumes in collections	Annual expenditures (rial)	Population served	Professional staff	Total staff
National[a]	1	1	160,000	43,000,000	6,000[b]	4	60
Academic	198	198	3,993,000	449,446,000[c]	--	156	1.196
Public[a]	385	385	2,161,000	--	--	20	900

[a]1980 data.
[b]Registered borrowers.
[c]Acquisitions only.

Source: Unesco, *Statistical Yearbook*, 1984.

manuscripts, and 4,800 periodicals.

Tehran University as a whole holds well over 500,000 volumes. Other major university libraries in Shiraz and Mashhad each hold approximately 200,000 volumes. The University of Esfahan library holds 112,000 volumes.

Public Libraries. According to the Library Act of 1965, which authorized the establishment of public libraries in Iran, each municipality had to allocate 1.5 percent of its revenue to public library services. After 1965 more than 300 public libraries were established. Most of their users were high-school students, and book collections ranged from fewer than 500 to more than 30,000 volumes. A 1975 survey of 97 public libraries revealed that 58 libraries had fewer than 2,000 volumes each. Tehran, with a population of more than 4,500,000, is served by a main public library and 16 branches. The Municipal Library of Esfahan holds 29,000 volumes and Tabriz Public Library has approximately 13,000 volumes.

School and Children's Libraries. Through the Institute for the Intellectual Development of Children and Young Adults, founded in 1965, modern and advanced library services in Iran were provided for children. Just before the 1979 revolution a network of some 80 children's libraries in Tehran and other cities, with approximately 350,000 registered users, was functioning successfully. The Institute operated four bookmobiles serving more than 420,000 children in schools, hospitals, orphanages, and daycare centers.

A School Building Act required that one room or a section of a room in each school be allocated for a library and that a certain amount of the budget be set aside for books. Though presumably there are approximately 5,000 school libraries in the country, in fact, only a very limited number of schools, mostly in Tehran, offer library services, and those are minimal. The small collections of those libraries are built randomly through gifts rather than by purchase from public funds.

Special Libraries. The establishment of special libraries, documentation centers, and information centers is a recent development in Iran. Notable examples are the Central Bank Library with a rich collection on banking and economics; the Razi Institute Library, which holds a special collection in biology and pathology; the Oil Consortium libraries in Tehran and Ahvaz and the Iranian National Oil Company Information Center with their rich collections on petroleum engineering; and the Informatics Center of Plan and Budget Organization, which deals with data on all aspects of national development.

Among mosque libraries the Astaneh Qods Central Library in Mashhad is the oldest (it dates from the 15th century) and its rich collections include 120,000 volumes and 14,000 manuscripts. The Sepahsalar Mosque Library was founded in 1880. Mosque libraries have flourished everywhere. They include the Emam Zaman, Darol Eslam, Hazrat Mehdi, Aljavad, Hazrat Abolfazl, Shafa, and Hazrat Amir Mosque libraries.

Association. The Iranian Library Association was founded in October 1966 "to promote the adoption of more effective systems of library service and to encourage the development of librarianship as a profession." Its membership was open "to those who

Razi Institute Library

Periodicals section of the Razi State Institute Library, Tehran.

are, or have been, employed in library services or who have been enrolled in or graduated from a library school." The Association became inactive during the revolutionary period.

REFERENCES

John F. Harvey, "School Libraries in Iran" *Recent Advances in School Librarianship,* edited by Frances Laverne Carroll (1981).

Harvey, "Tehran Mosque Libraries and a Comparison with American Christian Church Libraries," *International Library Review* (October 1981).

NASSER SHARIFY;
HOMAYOUN GLORIA SHARIFY

Iraq

The Republic of Iraq, an Arab state in the Middle East, is surrounded by Turkey on the north, Iran on the east, Saudi Arabia and Kuwait on the south, and Jordan and Syria on the west. More than one-fourth of the population live in the capital, Baghdad. Population (1984 est.) 15,000,000; area 438,317 sq.km. The official language is Arabic.

History. Cultural, scientific, and educational institutions have existed in Iraq since the early history of mankind. Libraries existed in ancient Iraq—which was known as Mesopotamia—as early as 4000 B.C. The earliest written records of the Sumerians, Assyrians, and Babylonians were excavated in the form of clay tablets from various locations in Iraq. In Nippur, for example, near the city of Babylon (about 100 miles southeast of Baghdad), more than 60,000 clay tablets were excavated around the end of the 19th century. These tablets dated partly from the Sumerian period (about 4000 B.C.) and partly from the Babylonian period (about 3000 B.C.). In the ancient city of Nippur there was a huge temple collection that represents the library and archives center.

In the city of Nineveh, the Assyrian capital, in northern Iraq, another collection of clay tablets was uncovered. This collection represents a library known as the Royal Library of Assurbanipal (fl. 7th century B.C.) (see biography in this Encyclopedia on Assurbanipal).

During the Middle Ages, the Arab-Islamic civilization of the Abbasids flourished. In Baghdad, the capital of the Abbasids, there were 63 libraries housing large collections of books and manuscripts. Most were open to scholars and the public. In addition, there were libraries in the cities of Basra and Kufa.

National Library. The Iraqi National Library, established in 1920, was granted its legal status as a depository library in 1961. In 1976 it moved to its new and modern building in the center of Baghdad. The building is designed to store more than a million volumes. The collection in the mid-1980s numbered about 200,000 volumes, 1,000 titles of periodicals, and a small collection of microforms and audiovisual materials. The National Library publishes the National Bibliography as a quarterly serial.

The National Library Building houses another important information center—the National Center of Archives. It has a large collection of historical Iraqi archives, available only to scholars and graduate students.

Academic Libraries. Academic libraries are the best information centers in modern Iraq. They serve the six universities of the country and their colleges and academic institutions.

The Central Library of the University of Baghdad, founded in 1959, has a collection of more than 250,000 volumes, about 1,000 titles of periodicals, and a collection of maps, microforms, and audio recordings. The collection of this Library, like those of other Iraqi libraries and information centers, is mostly in Arabic or English. It has smaller collections in other languages. The University of Baghdad has other libraries associated with its colleges, such as the libraries of the College of Science (more than 85,000 volumes), College of Arts (60,000 volumes), College of Engineering (more than 50,000 volumes), and College of Medicine (more than 40,000 volumes).

Other central university libraries are the Library of Mosul University, in northern Iraq, which was founded in 1967 and has a collection of more than 180,000 volumes and about 2,200 titles of periodicals. The Library of Basra University, in southern Iraq, was founded in 1964 and has a collection of more than 100,000 volumes. The Library of Al-Mustansiriya University in Baghdad was founded in 1963 and has a collection of more than 100,000 volumes and about 1,000 titles of periodicals. All these libraries and other academic libraries have collections of audiovisual materials. Some, such as Mosul and Al-Mustansiriya libraries, offer additional scientific and

educational programs through closed-circuit television systems.

Public Libraries. More than 70 public libraries offer information services to the Iraqi public. Their total collection is about 1,000,000 volumes. These libraries are distributed throughout the country. There are a central public library and several branch libraries in each of the 18 provinces of Iraq. Mosul Public Library has a collection of about 100,000 volumes. Most other public libraries hold between several thousand and 25,000 volumes.

Two modern children's public libraries were established in Baghdad. One, on the east bank of the Tigris River, was founded in 1964. Another, on the west bank, was founded in 1985. They offer various activities that are attractive and useful to children aged 5 to 14, such as showing films (educational, comic, and cartoons), playing educational games, and storytelling, as well as offering collections of books and periodicals for children and young people.

Special Libraries. Libraries and information centers exist in ministries and other government institutions; for example, the Library of the Ministry of Planning was founded in 1960 and holds about 90,000 volumes. The Library of the Ministry of Foreign Affairs was founded in 1934 and holds more than 10,000 volumes, in addition to archival material, reports, and clippings.

The collections of both the Scientific Documentation Center and the Gulf States Information Documentation Center are of importance to researchers and Iraqi users. The first has a Library of 20,000 books and more than 1,300 titles of scientific and specialized periodicals and a collection of microforms and other audiovisual materials. The Gulf States Information Documentation Center, established in Baghdad in 1981 to serve Iraq and other Gulf Arab states, holds a large collection of clippings, about 800 titles of current periodicals, a large collection of microforms, audiovisual items, an information file (vertical file), and several thousand specialized books. Both centers offer various information services, such as indexing, bibliographies, abstracting, inquiry service, and other types of reference services. They also have access to computer services, using both local and international databases.

School Libraries. Although Iraqi students below college level depend heavily on public libraries for their reading, most high schools and secondary schools have their own collections. Mosul Agricultural High School, founded in 1956, has a library of about 12,000 volumes. Al-Karkh High School Library, founded in 1958, holds about 5,000 volumes. Al-Kadhimiya High School Library, founded in 1934, holds more than 5,000 volumes, and Al-Amara High

Libraries in Iraq (1980)			
Type	Administrative units	Volumes in collections	Population served
Non-specialized	15	240,000	17,452[a]

[a]Registered borrowers.

Source: Unesco, *Statistical Yearbook,* 1984.

School Library, founded in 1927, holds the same number of volumes.

In 1974 the government of Iraq issued a School Library Law. Since then, more attention has been given to these libraries; for example, both the Ministry of Education and the Ministry of Information hold one-week activities annually for publicizing school libraries.

The Profession. The Iraqi Library Association was formed in Baghdad in 1968. It has attracted several hundred professionals. It organizes and participates in meetings, lectures, book fairs, training courses, and other professional activities.

The Arab regional branch of the International Council of Archives, known as Arabica, was formed in Baghdad in 1973 to carry out archival activities in the Arab world. It has an annual professional journal, "The Journal of Arabic Archives."

The Department of Library Science at Al-Mustansiriya University was established in 1970, offering a two-year undergraduate program. In 1979 the department moved ahead to offer a four-year program. It also offered a one-year graduate course until 1983, when it discontinued that course to develop it into a graduate study program for a Master's degree, beginning in 1985. Basra University started its own four-year undergraduate course in 1984. Mosul University announced plans to open such a course.

On-the-job training courses for shorter periods are held by the Iraqi Library Association, the Gulf States Information Documentation Center, and the Central Library of the University of Baghdad.

REFERENCE
Amer Ibrahim Kindilchie, "Guide to Iraqi Libraries" (Iraqi Library Association, 1981) (in Arabic).
                                    AMER IBRAHIM KINDILCHIE

Ireland

Until 1922 the entire island of Ireland, separated from Great Britain by the North Channel, the Irish Sea, and Saint George's Channel, was a de jure part of the United Kingdom of Great Britain and Ireland. Following a rebellion (1916) and a War of Independence, self-government for the 26 counties having predominantly nationalist populations was achieved. The six northeastern counties remained part of the United Kingdom. The Republic of Ireland was declared under the relevant Act of 1948. Population (1984 est.) 3,575,000; area 70,285 sq.km. Official languages are Irish and English.

History. The early history of Irish libraries is bound up with the pursuit of learning carried out through countless monasteries and schools. The *scriptoria* or "houses of writing" of the monasteries, where the monks transcribed manuscripts, were the publishing houses of the Middle Ages. They were also the precursors of present-day interlibrary-loan centers, because the monks who traveled from monastery to monastery within Ireland and in Continental Europe carried their books with them. The international exchange of ideas was thus an important development that arose from the missionary zeal of these early Irish custodians of learning. The devastating attacks on monasteries and looting of their con-

Marsh's Library

Archbishop Marsh's Library, founded in Dublin in 1702, the first public library in Ireland.

tents during the Norse invasions of 795–1014 A.D. caused widespread damage. Total destruction was avoided, however. A National Library microfilm project carried out in 1947 showed that large numbers of manuscripts salvaged from these early monastic libraries were lodged in the libraries and archives of Europe.

Development was somewhat further retarded from the 11th century to the 17th century by continuing internal strife and the Norman invasion. These difficulties led to the development of an oral tradition of passing on information through poetry and ballads. This is still an important aspect of Irish culture. But even in difficult circumstances, some important annals and compilations were produced, including the *Annals of the Four Masters* (written between 1632 and 1636), in which the history of Ireland is recorded down to 1616.

The links between libraries and monasteries were finally ended with the Reformation, which brought about the closure of monasteries and the dispersal of their collections. After a long period in which there were few libraries in Ireland, the 19th century was notable for the foundation of some cathedral and subscription libraries.

The Mechanics' Institute libraries, founded in England during the later 18th and early 19th centuries to satisfy a demand for education, were the immediate predecessors of the public library system. With the influence of a tradition of learning promoted through early monastic libraries in the background, the retardation of library service caused by internal struggles is being overcome. Ireland now provides a wide range of library service.

National Library. The National Library of Ireland is in Dublin, the capital. It was established under the terms of the Dublin Science and Museum Act of 1877, by which the state acquired the library of the Royal Dublin Society. The library, which formed the basis of National Library collections, has been greatly expanded by bequest and purchase, and it is now the major reference resource for material related to Ireland. It is a reference library only, but photocopy service is available. *The Guide to Collections in Dublin Libraries 1982* (worth consulting about a number of libraries mentioned in this article) lists some of its major holdings; they include works by and about Jonathan Swift, some early printed music, incunabula, and some 18th- and 19th-century Irish bindings. *Manuscript Sources for the History of Irish Civilisation* (1965), published by a former Director, Richard Hayes, is an important work.

The National Library Education Division promotes awareness of the resources available. Since 1976, the Education Division has produced a number of facsimile documents relating to aspects of Irish history and culture. The series includes folders on The Land War, 1879–1903; Daniel O'Connell, 19th-century Irish political leader; and James Joyce. With the assistance of the public library system and other organizations, the Division also mounts exhibitions based on collections of the National Library in various centers throughout the country.

Academic Libraries. The most important academic libraries in Ireland are those of the two university foundations—Dublin University (Trinity College) and the National University of Ireland, which has four constituent Colleges, Dublin, Cork, Galway, and Maynooth. Of these, the oldest and most important research library in Ireland is that of Trinity College, which was established by Royal Charter under Elizabeth I in 1591. It has been a legal desposit library since 1801; although now outside the United Kingdom, it still enjoys the right to claim all British publications under British copyright laws. The library also receives all Irish publications under Irish copyright laws, alongside vast collections appropriate to the scholarly aims of the University. Trinity College Library also houses a priceless collection of ancient Irish manuscripts, chief of which is the Book of Kells. This transcription of the Four Gospels, executed by Irish monks, is considered by many experts to be the finest illuminated manuscript in the world. It is only one of the many important manuscripts and incunabula that attract scholars in immense numbers to the College. Trinity does not lend to individuals, but is committed to participation in interlibrary lending programs.

The libraries in the constituent Colleges of the National University of Ireland, which was established in 1908 under the Irish Universities Act, are of more recent origin. The collections at Dublin, Cork, and Galway are, in general, geared toward the courses taught at those Colleges. The library at University College, Dublin, the largest of the constituent Colleges, does contain notable collections of archival material, including unpublished papers of Irish historical and political importance. The Dublin library also houses an extensive collection of books and periodicals on librarianship. Saint Patrick's College, Maynooth (County Kildare), a seminary for aspirants to the Roman Catholic priesthood, was recognized as a College of the National University in 1910. It now admits lay students who follow a variety of liberal arts courses. Its library has a heavy concentration of works on philosophy and theology.

In addition to these older established academic libraries, there are others attached to the newer National Institute for Higher Education in Dublin and Limerick, and to the Regional Technical Colleges in Carlow, Galway, Athlone (Westmeath), Dundalk (Louth), Letterkenny (Donegal), Sligo, and Waterford. The Regional Technical College Libraries are organized and staffed by the local public library authority. Libraries in the constituent colleges of the Dublin Institute of Technology are also operated by staff of the Dublin Public Libraries.

Specialist academic libraries are numerous in Dublin. Particularly important is the Royal Irish Academy (R.I.A.), founded in 1785 to promote the study of science, polite literature, and antiquities. The extensive collections of the R.I.A. include part of the library of the Irish poet Thomas Moore (1779–1852). The Chester Beatty Library (Oriental arts) and the Franciscan Library, Dun Mhuire (Celtic studies and ecclesiastical history), also house material of research interest.

Public Libraries. Alongside the publicly-funded libraries established under the Public Library Ireland Act 1855 are a number of endowed public li-

Libraries in Ireland (1982)

Type	Administrative units	Service points	Volumes in collections	Annual expenditures (Irish pound)	Population served	Professional staff	Total staff
National[a]	1	2	c.750,000	--	--	7	56
Academic	28	--	3,918,000[b]	5,126,000[a]	30,860[c]	--	--
Public	31	--	7,399,000[a,e]	9,300,000[a]	718,957[d]	--	830[a]
School	--	--	--	--	--	--	--
Special	98[f]	--	303,000[g]	--	6,641[g,h]	--	--

[a]Unesco, *Statistical Yearbook,* 1984. 1980 data.
[b]Ibid. 1980 data for seven institutions of higher education.
[c]Ibid. 1980 data: registered borrowers. Access to public provided via interlibrary loan, limited personal access on application.
[d]Ibid. 1980 data: registered borrowers.
[e]Ibid. Excludes 5,886 microforms and 27,150 audiovisual items.
[f]Approximate: includes government departments.
[g]Unesco, *Statistical Yearbook,* 1984. 1977 data: reported for nine special libraries.
[h]Registered borrowers for nine libraries.

braries. Marsh's Library, founded in 1701 and thus the first public library in the country, is by far the most important. The library contains incunabula and manuscripts and is of architectural interest.

Progress in public library development was slow. The efforts of the Carnegie United Kingdom Trust, which from 1913 provided grants for public library development, proved to be an immense incentive. Until the founding of An Chomhairle Leabharlanna (The Library Council) under the Public Libraries Act, 1947, the Carnegie Trust was the single most important motivational force for public library development.

There were 31 public library authorities in Ireland in 1985. These include 23 library authorities whose area of responsiblity covers entire counties, two whose area covers adjacent counties amalgamated for library purposes, and two small areas within counties that retain separate library identities: Bray (County Wicklow) and Dun Laoghaire (County Dublin). Four of the largest cities, Dublin, Cork, Limerick, and Waterford, have independent library authorities.

The highest concentration of service is in Dublin, where nearly one-third of the total population lives. Service there is provided through 33 full-time branch libraries, 12 mobile library units, a business information center, music library, youth information center, and four prison libraries. The City Archive and Civic Museum also operate under the auspices of the Public Libraries. Professional assistance is available at all service points.

Trends in Dublin in the 1980s lean toward a concentration on service to the disadvantaged, and community information service is increasingly becoming an accepted aspect of branch library activity.

National access to service and quality of service is, generally speaking, subject to population and terrain factors. Outside the main centers of population, most towns are too small to sustain full-time professionally operated service. In many rural areas, services are available through mobile library units or small centers operated on a part-time basis by locally recruited staff.

Central government retains an overview of library services through the Department of the Environment, which is advised by The Library Council. The Council advises local authorities on library matters and recommends grants for new projects including buildings, book stock, and library vehicles. The Councils Grants Scheme (1961) has been instrumental in encouraging major development in public library service. Other major influences have been the acceptance of professional qualifications for all executive posts and the introduction, in 1970, of a scholarship system of education based on full-time release for university study for public library staffs.

School Libraries. School library provision at primary-school level is part of the public library service. In general, the service is administered by professionally qualified staff, who, although having no direct involvement with students, advise teachers who are given special responsibility for library stock and organization. In Dublin special teacher in-service training courses are organized by library staffs. The state gives special financial aid to local authorities on a per-capita basis for the national primary schools.

Subvention for schools at a higher level is not available, and library service in those schools is dependent on local initiatives. School children are encouraged to use their local public libraries, and there is extensive cooperation between school and library in the organization of group visits and the provision by the library of project material. In Dublin, a number of pilot projects involving public library staff in direct professional service to schools were monitored with the assistance of researchers from the Curriculum Development Unit of Trinity College, Dublin.

Special Libraries. Ireland has a wide variety of special libraries. Most large organizations have libraries or information centers. In noting a few—among them libraries of the Oireachtas (Parliament), Department of Education, Institute of Public Administration, Irish Management Institute, Irish Congress of Trade Unions, Federated Union of Employers, Economic and Social Research Institue, A. Guinness Son & Co. Ltd.—it is evident that special libraries relate to all aspects of Irish life. There is extensive cooperation between these libraries and the university and public library systems.

The Profession. A School of Library and Information Studies is attached to University College, Dublin. It offers a one-year post-graduate course, leading to a diploma in Library and Information Science (DLIS); and a one-year (full-time) or two-year (part-time) course, leading to a Master's degree in Library and Information Science (MLIS). Some short seminars and workshops also provide opportunities for continuing education for those already qualified. Such opportunities are extended by the Library Association of Ireland (founded in 1928), which, through a number of special interest groups, offers regular programs on subjects of professional interest, such as audiovisual services, cataloguing and indexing, youth work, and university and special libraries. Those who possess a recognized qualification in librarianship may also obtain (by thesis) a Fellowship of the Library Association of Ireland (FLAI). The Association, which had a membership of some 450 in 1984, publishes *An Leabharlann: The Irish Library*. Other professional associations include the Irish Association of Documentation and Information Services (IADIS), founded in 1967 to support special library and information work. IADIS published the *Union List of Current Periodicals in Irish Libraries* (1975). The Irish Association of School Libraries (Cumann Leabharlannaithe Scoile, CLS), founded in 1962, offers an annual summer course in school librarianship. Its official journal is the *CLS Bulletin*. Archivists further their professional interests through the Irish Association for Archives.

REFERENCES
Maura Neylon and Monica Henchy. *Public Libraries in Ireland* (1966).
Directory of Libraries in Ireland (Library Association of Ireland, 1983).

DEIRDRE ELLIS-KING

Islamic Libraries
(7th to 17th centuries)

Islam evolved early in the 7th century A.D. from an Arabic civilization that was basically nomadic but one

Interior of an Islamic library from an illuminated manuscript of al-Hariri in the Bibliothèque Nationale in Paris.

which in that century received a scripture. This development predisposed the Arabs to enrich their literary heritage with that of their Persian and Byzantine neighbors soon after they conquered them. The Qur'an (Koran), the Arabic revelation, encourages learning and knowledge. Although the word *knowledge* as used in the Qur'an has a religious connotation, later such sayings as "Seek ye knowledge from the cradle to the grave," "The search for knowledge is incumbent on every Muslim," "Seek ye knowledge even into China," and the like were broader and became commonplace. Since religion was the focal point in the Islamic state, the first library transaction can be observed in regard to the Qur'an—the deposit of a copy of this work with Hafsah, one of the Prophet Muhammad's widows.

The private library was the preponderant type of library in early Islam. Private libraries were owned mainly by scholars interested in those branches of knowledge that developed from the study of the Qur'an and the traditions of the Prophet, such as grammar, theology, law, and history. Eventually the collections of these libraries found their way into the mosques that had developed adjunct libraries rather early in their efforts to supplement religious instruc-

tion. The most famous mosque library is that of al-Azhar in Cairo, which was founded in the 9th century but gained university status in the 18th. It should also be noted that since in many instances the private libraries were accessible to other scholars and sometimes even the general public, there was a gradual transition from the private library to the later public libraries.

During the Umayyad Caliphate (661–750) scholarly interests extended to the natural sciences. This interest, particularly in mathematics, astronomy, and medicine, came to the fore during the Abbaside Caliphate (750–1258), when under al-Ma'mun (813–33) a House of Wisdom (*Dar al-Hikmah*) was established in Baghdad that was open to all. This academy contributed extensively to the understanding of Greek philosophy and science. Under its head and chief translator, Hunayn ibn Ishaq, Greek manuscripts were acquired and translated into Arabic, often through the Syriac medium. Greek works that were lost in the original were frequently preserved only through these translations.

A similar institution was founded in Cairo during the Fatimid rule (909–1171). After the dissolution of this library at the end of the Fatimid reign, much of the collection was acquired by the Secretary of Saladin, Qadi al-Fadil, and was named al-Fadiliyah after him.

The third most important library of the Middle Ages in Islam was the court library of the Umayyad rulers of Cordova, Spain (750–1031). Although apparently less accessible to the public, it had extensive holdings.

These three libraries cannot be considered national libraries in the strict sense of the word, but they were the most outstanding central institutions in these countries and were—if indirectly—financed by public revenues. Unfortunately, these libraries were often short-lived because frequent political upheavals destroyed the libraries and their collections.

During the Seljuks (1037–1300) the colleges (*madrasah*) came into prominence and with them the college library. The wazir Nizam al-Mulk, who during a period of 20 years was the virtual ruler of the realm, built numerous colleges throughout the empire; the best-known one was in Baghdad and named al-Nizamiyah. Al-Ghazzali, the famous philosopher, was one of the outstanding teachers there. At that time the monastic library also came into existence in conjunction with the rise of the dervish orders; its significance was minimal, however, compared with that of the European monastic library.

The Ottoman Turks (1299–1923) made Constantinople their capital, and consequently the principal library activity followed to that city. Giambatista Toderini, visiting the city in the early 18th century, reports on 13 major libraries, many of them open to the public, and gives an insight into their holdings.

While the strength of the Islamic library collections was first measured in camel loads, numbers do exist for later periods; these, however, cannot always be taken at face value. Volume numbers up to half a million for major libraries during the Middle Ages are probably not exaggerated, as most of these libraries had full-time manuscript copyists (*nassakh*) on their staffs. Other members of the library staff were the Superintendent (*sahib*), one or more Custodians (*khazin*), and Assistants (*farrash*). The scribes often belonged to the local guild and as such sometimes wielded considerable power; fearing for their jobs, they successfully opposed the introduction of printing into Constantinople until the beginning of the 18th century.

The arrangement of books was usually by subject, stored in compartments that could be locked. Since the books were stored on their sides, a practice that contributed to the deterioration of the outer covers and the title and colophon pages, the titles were written on labels attached to the spine and were written on the fore edge to facilitate identification. When catalogues existed, they were usually in book form. The lack of proper ventilation and the presence of vermin contributed to the damage of the manuscripts. The mosque libraries, not usually being equipped to forestall or repair deterioration, suffered most in this respect, while the caliphal libraries were financially best suited to house the collections in air-conditioned premises and to repair them when damage occured. Unfortunately the latter library bore the brunt of the attacks by the human enemy—the thieves, sectarians, and Mongol invaders.

REFERENCES
O. Pinto, "The Libraries of the Arabs during the Time of the Addasides," *Islamic Culture* (1929).
Index Islamicus provides references under "Libraries."
MIROSLAV KREK

Israel

Israel, a republic in the Middle East, is bordered on the north by Lebanon, on the northeast by Syria, on the east by Jordan, on the southwest by Egypt, and on the west by the Mediterranean Sea. Population (1984 est.) 4,197,900; area (excluding occupied territory) 21,501 sq.km. The official languages are Hebrew and Arabic.

History. Books, reading, and study have always played a central part in Judaism. However, the "People of the Book" have not necessarily been the "People of the Library." On the one hand, the Jewish tradition of learning and book appreciation provides potentially fertile soil for the growth of libraries; in fact the institution of the Beit Midrash (House of Learning attached to the synagogue in every community) contained elements of a proto-public library, serving as it did as the cultural and social center of

the community, with a book collection accessible to all. On the other hand, the strong need for books made individual acquisition and private borrowing into a social norm, reducing the need for the library as an institution.

The late 19th century saw a resurgence of Jewish settlement in Palestine. The new settlers brought with them from the Diaspora the traditional library model of the Beit Midrash as well as other library models. In relatively short order a modest system of public libraries was established, including the library that later became the Jewish National and University Library (JNUL). With the subsequent development of the JNUL and the appointment of Hugo Bergmann as National Librarian, the foundations of the Israeli library scene were laid. Bergmann adopted the American tradition of a library open to all and responsive to a variety of interests. This reader-centered library model fit the tradition of the Beit Midrash as the cultural center of the community as well as the egalitarian ideals of the democratic society being built in Palestine. On the national level, Bergmann worked to establish an informal network of small local libraries which functioned as cultural centers and were headed by the cultural leaders in each settlement—the teachers. The JNUL provided professional guidance and special services to those local libraries.

Until the early 1930s the Jewish population of Palestine numbered under 300,000 and was largely (90%) of European extraction, needing libraries mainly as an adjunct to private book acquisition. As long as this was the case, that library system was adequate. But in the 1930s the large wave of German Jewish immigration brought with it the continental European library model of learned libraries for the intellectual elite and "popular libraries" (Volksbibliotheken) for the "common" people, which changed the face of librarianship in the country entirely. This model rapidly gained favor, appealing as it did to the respect for scholarship ingrained in the Jewish tradition. The ascendency of the continental European model caused a change in the attitude toward librarianship as a profession: it began to be regarded as a technical-clerical occupation requiring minimal training (only senior staff members in research and large libraries were expected to have academic degrees, and even then not necessarily in librarianship). Professional goals were soon replaced by an emphasis on techniques, a clerical approach,

Libraries in Israel (1984)

Type	Units	Volumes in collections	Population served	Total staff
National	1	2,000,000	--	196[a]
Academic	7	4,555,000	60,685	910[a]
Public	945	6,300,000	581,000	1,060
School	1,735	--	688,200	--
Special	400	--	--	--

[a]1977 data.

Sources: surveys of National and university libraries, and of the Unit for Public Libraries at the Ministry of Education and Culture.

Elyachar Library

Elyachar Central Library on the campus of the Technion, the Israel Institute of Technology in Haifa.

and an increasing disengagement of librarians from the role of bearers of a social or cultural message.

Additional waves of immigration in the pre-1948 period brought with them the East European library tradition, which viewed the community library as a means to educating the public in the spirit of socialist ideology. This model was easily integrated with the prevailing continental-European model, since both aim at educating the masses. It is important to bear in mind that in this pre-state period the supply and the provision of books were still entirely adequate for the needs of the population (630,000 in 1947), which did not expect library services beyond those they were receiving.

When the great waves of immigration started to arrive after the declaration of Israel as an independent state in 1948, the structure of society in the country underwent a drastic change. It soon became clear that the transformations undergone by the library system and the library profession in the 1930s had rendered the libraries incapable of coping with social problems. During the first five years of statehood, when a concentrated effort was being made to absorb more than 1,000,000 immigrants, the libraries played no part. The main reason was the libraries' inability to function as community centers—the direct result of the deterioration of the profession in the 1930s.

A second reason had to do with the demographic composition of the immigration: 800,000 were refugees from Arab countries. Jews of European background were interested in reading secular literature; that interest had been fostered throughout the 18th and 19th centuries by the influence of the Haskalah (Enlightenment) movement and motivated the European Jews to apply religious norms of learning to secular learning as well. Jews from the Arab countries, on the other hand, had retained their love and respect for religious literature without necessarily extending it to secular literature. If the public libraries had had religious literature in their collections, the refugees from the Arabic-speaking countries might well have been drawn to them, but such was not the case: the prestate immigrants, the pioneers, had been for the most part rebelling against religion, and the libraries

they established were secular in nature. The library collections were irrelevant to large segments of the population in other ways, also. Many of the books were in German, a language unknown to both the eastern European Jews and the Jews from Arab countries. Even the Hebrew books were not readable by many people; the language was antiquated (Hebrew underwent drastic and rapid changes during this period), and the contents of the books reflected Central and East European Jewish culture, and as such were irrelevant to other cultural groups. In the absence of professional librarians with a sense of social mission, there was no initiative to regroup public library collections and activities in such a way that their potential as social integrators would be realized.

Furthermore, in the first years of statehood, the financial resources available for the development of libraries were being invested almost entirely in rebuilding the National and University Library, whose premises and collections on Mount Scopus had been lost as a result of the 1948 War of Independence. Only after the JNUL had been rebuilt on the new campus of the Hebrew University was professional librarianship, with Curt Wormann (JNUL Director, 1947–68) at its head, ready to turn its attention to the state of the library system in the rest of Israel.

In 1956 Wormann founded a library school at the Hebrew University, with the express intention of emphasizing the social and educational role of the librarian. This step constituted a landmark in the history of librarianship in Israel and was the beginning of a renewed professional approach.

The 1960s brought with them several additional positive developments, at a time when social integration was still one of the most pressing problems in Israeli society: C. I. Golan founded and became the first Director of the Public Library Section of the Ministry of Education and Culture. Golan saw the library as a tool for social integration; in his efforts to develop the library as an influential institution in each community, he adopted as a model the system prevalent in Denmark, where a network of independent local libraries each receiving government funding, but retain complete intellectual freedom. As a result of Golan's activities, libraries were founded in many settlements, especially in development towns populated by new immigrants.

In 1975 a Public Library Law was finally enacted. The law, whose purpose is to make mandatory the founding and maintenance of a public library by each local authority, is of central importance, although a dearth of fiscal resources prevented its widespread enforcement in the following decade.

On the academic scene the early 1960s saw a burst of activity. As a result of the increased demand for academically trained manpower, new universities were founded and the older ones underwent expansion. These developments were accompanied by increasing awareness of the role played by libraries and librarians in providing access to information. The university libraries were given higher priority than previously, and began to strike out in new directions. The new universities established libraries with centralized services and open shelves. Unfortunately, the new policies did not always work well in practice since many of the librarians, recent graduates of the Hebrew University Library School, did not have the experience to carry them out, and the new libraries did not live up to expectations. As a result, a regression to older norms took place, and faculty members in each institution began preempting responsibility for determining the nature of the library services, at the expense of the librarians' professional authority. Furthermore, many of the university library directors were scholars in other disciplines who considered their main responsibility research in their specific field rather than heading a library. A direct result was regression to fragmentation of collection and services, with many departmental libraries in each university competing for the limited funds available.

In summary, during periods when the library was perceived as a potential agent for social change, the models adopted made the reader the focus of attention, and assigned an influential role to the librarian. During periods when the library's main task was perceived as providing services to scholars and the academic elite, the book became the focus and the librarian was considered merely a clerk. The history of librarianship in Israel is, in effect, the history of the conflict between these two approaches, each of which in turn left its mark.

National Library. The Jewish National and University Library in Jerusalem serves a dual purpose as the National Library of Israel (and inherently of the entire Jewish people) and as the central library of the Hebrew University. The Library was begun in 1884 as a small collection mostly donated by European philanthropists, which merged with the library of the Bnei Brith Lodge in Jerusalem in 1892. In 1920 the World Zionist Organization took responsibility for its operation and named it "the Jewish National Library." In 1925 the Library was incorporated into the newly founded Hebrew University and was renamed the Jewish National and University Library.

The Library, which grew to more than 2,000,000 volumes by the mid-1980s, collects material about Israel, Palestine, Jews, and Judaism; material written by Jews regardless of the place of publication; and books written in Hebrew script or in a Jewish language. Priority is given to acquiring Hebrew and Jewish manuscripts, incunabula, and rare books. Private donors and organizations from all parts of the world have collected and sent books and archives to JNUL, and every effort was made to find and add to its collection material salvaged from the Jewish communities annihilated by the Nazis in Europe during World War II. Since 1938, the JNUL has received two copies of every book published in Israel as legal deposit.

The JNUL's collection of Judaica and related subjects is one of the finest in the world. The Library also contains one of the largest and best-organized collections on Arabic and Islamic subjects in the Middle East. In its permanent collection, there are 200 incunabula, 14,000 original manuscripts, 41,369 reproductions of manuscripts, and 150,000 reproductions of fragments.

The JNUL's activities include publishing *Kiryat Sefer,* an annotated bibliography which includes entries for Israeli imprints in Judaica; books about Jews, Judaica, and Israel published abroad; critical reviews of books; bibliographical research; and descriptive articles about important rare items in the JNUL's collections. The Library also publishes a bibliography of periodical literature called *Index of Articles on Jewish Studies,* which covers journals and serials from all parts of the world.

Academic Libraries. There are eight accredited universities, of which seven maintain full-fledged library services; the Open University has a small collection of its own, but it must supplement its services by making arrangements with the seven other academic institutions. The academic libraries' collections total some 4,500,000 books, with collections ranging between 270,000 and 950,000 volumes at the individual institutions. Steady growth of collections in spite of severe budgetary restraints has been ensured with the establishment of the University Grants Committee (1975) and later its Subcommittee for Libraries; nevertheless, the composite acquisition budget of all Israel's university libraries was steadily declining in the 1980s.

Available funds are dispensed without interfering with matters of academic freedom. In the absence of formal acquisition policies in most of the academic libraries, however, collection development has been dictated by faculty demand, an ad hoc process often resulting in gaps in the collections. This problem has been further aggravated by fragmentation of the collection and services between one central library and various departmental libraries, although that pattern has started to change. Economic pressures have placed a priority on internal cooperation and unification of resources. (For example, at the Hebrew University there had been some 70 departmental libraries, 25 of which were united into one library on Mount Scopus at the end of 1981.)

In the late 1960s the government, which provides some 70 percent of the academic institutions' budgets, initiated measures toward the introduction of interlibrary cooperation, in order to achieve more efficient academic library services. The committee established the Israel Standing Committee of National and University Libraries (SCONUL), which serves as a forum for discussing problems of policy and planning. The agency has no formal authority; its main accomplishment has been the efficient channeling of communications among the university libraries.

All academic libraries traditionally provide public library services to the community at large. Moreover, academic libraries fulfill national roles; for example, the Technion (Israel Institute of Technology) provides literature searches to the country's scientific and research institutions and to industrial companies; the Hebrew University houses the *Israel Union List of Serials;* Haifa University Library prepares one of Israel's main bibliographic tools, the computer-based annual *Index to Hebrew Periodicals,* as well as other computer-based bibliographic tools, and from January 1981 provided MARC-based automated cataloguing services to other universities.

Cooperation, Library Automation, and Networking Until the last few years developments in the area were slow and uncertain, and when initiative did come, it usually came from outside the library community, generally from policy-making and funding bodies of the government. The first attempt at library automation for cooperation came in the early 1970s when the JNUL received a government grant especially for the development of an automated cataloguing system. This project, costing a total of

$500,000, did not succeed and was discontinued. The next attempt to develop an automated cataloguing system, suited to local conditions, was deemed a complete technical success: MARCIS (MARC ISrael)—an automated cataloguing service based on the MARC database, which was created by the information division at one of the defense establishments in the country, became operational in 1974. In spite of its clear advantages, not every university library decided to use its services, not so much because of the official reasons stated (financial difficulties) as from the reluctance of some of the library directors to take responsibility for the required changes.

Until the end of the 1970s formal cooperation was limited to a few undertakings such as the Israel Union List of Serials; an interlibrary loan system utilizing Telex; and MARCIS. Since the beginning of the 1980s, however, there has been a recognizable acceleration in the efforts aimed at attaining cooperation. The seriousness of the financial constraints in the 1980s compelled university libraries to try to seek solutions in networking. The subcommittee for libraries of the Grants Committee initiated a program to establish a National Bibliographic Center that would serve all the university libraries.

Both the Hebrew University and the Library of the University of Haifa, having developed library automation systems for their own purposes, offered to serve as the Bibliographic Center that would operate a nationwide library network. The Hebrew University proposal was based on ALEPH—an automated system developed by its Administrative Services Department in order to unify 25 departmental libraries into one library and intended to operate on a mainframe computer. The Hebrew University proposal offered to develop a computerized bibliographic database and to provide online circulation services and an online catalogue. Later stages promised were an automated acquisition system, MARC, and other services. As opposed to the centralized model of the Hebrew University, the Library of the University of Haifa proposed a distributed processing model in which each library would have its own database that would operate on local minicomputers and provide automated cataloguing services based on MARCIS as well as information retrieval services. The program also proposed supplying software packages suited to handling specific housekeeping needs of the libraries.

The advantages and disadvantages of the two proposals were extensively debated for several years. In the meantime, the University of Haifa became the center of a de facto library network which supplies MARCIS services to the Technion, Bar Ilan, and Ben Gurion Universities, as well as computerized bibliographic services. In 1984 the Grants Committee, following a recommendation from SCONUL, decided to subsidize university library participation in ALEPH. In response to the demands of the libraries, the Hebrew University promised to adopt a distributed networking approach and to change ALEPH so that it would maintain a separate file for each library even within the Hebrew University itself and would be operational on minicomputers. It renounced quality control, however, and with the networking functions of using MARC records, a national union list, and shared cataloguing still awaiting solution, the network based on ALEPH was still in its planning

stages in 1985.

Public Libraries. The traditional attitudes of great respect toward books and reading persist in modern Israel. There is a significantly high percentage of readers—surveys reveal that more than half of the population reads at least one book a month—but only 26 percent of the population is registered at public libraries. It would seem that the public satisfies most of its information needs by using alternatives to the public library system: private lending and borrowing of books and extensive use of university libraries. In the southern region, for example, public libraries are aided by the Ben Gurion University Library, and in the north the same role is fulfilled by the Haifa University Library. In addition to their direct service to the public, the university libraries "adopt" public libraries in their region and advise them on the organization of collections, provide bibliographic service, and donate books to them.

Although Israelis were slow to recognize the importance of libraries as providers of information and as cultural and acculturation agencies, since the 1960s, when the library section of the Ministry of Education and Culture adopted measures for the active development and gradual upgrading of public library services, the trend has changed.

Also, Library Law of 1975, although implemented slowly because of financial difficulties, provided for the establishment and further development of public libraries. By 1985 only 582 settlements out of 1,060 had library services provided under the supervision of the Ministry of Education and Culture, since "recognition" and supervision also mean help in funding. In the 1960s and early 1970s government funding provided about half the budget for "recognized" libraries; in 1974, 43 percent; in 1984, only about 13 percent.

The Center for Public Libraries, founded in 1965, is another agent for the aid of public libraries, providing such services as a central cataloguing utility (in cooperation with the University of Haifa), centralized book acquisition, and book processing for libraries. The Center also publishes bibliographies, reference books, and a journal devoted to librarianship, *Yad la-Kore.*

Kibbutz Libraries. The kibbutz (collective settlement) population has access to the highest proportion of library books per capita in Israel—84,000 people (3.4 percent of the entire population) have at their disposal about 2,000,000 volumes. Some 37 percent of kibbutz residents are active readers and some 77 percent use kibbutz libraries. Until the late 1960s books were scattered throughout the settlements in small, often disorganized collections, but thereafter serious attempts were made to apply some method to kibbutz libraries. Also, an effort is being made to promote cooperation and sharing of resources between the kibbutz and the surrounding development towns and villages.

Arab Public Libraries. For the Arab minority in Israel, about 15 percent of the population, little local initiative was taken to provide adequate library service in the decades after the independence of Israel in 1948. Literacy in the Arab settlements was about 30 percent in Palestine in the 1940s, and many who spoke vernacular Arabic could not understand classical literary Arabic. Israeli newspapers and broadcast media contributed to the development of a literary language influenced by classical Arabic but rooted in the vernacular and thus comprehensible to a wider general reading public. Literacy steadily grew to 80 percent by 1980. Local leaders in the late 1970s began to give more emphasis to the establishment of community libraries or the development of school libraries initiated by the Ministry of Education. Books in Arabic were published locally and imported through open bridges from Jordan and Lebanon and later directly from Egypt. From the late 1970s the Public Libraries Section of the Ministry of Education helped establish and finance new libraries in the Arab sector. Arab settlements send teachers and high school graduates to courses of study at a level below the university and comparable to that received by elementary school teachers. The public library for Arabs in Israel was emerging as a local community institution, receiving government support but relatively free from central government interference.

In towns of mixed Jewish and Arab population, the public libraries serve both Jewish and Arab readers. Arab students and teachers make use of the Arabic collections at the university libraries.

School Libraries. Since the 1970s there has been a growing awareness of the importance of school libraries and of their potential role in education and teaching. Although this newly acquired consciousness did not result in a formal decision to upgrade school libraries, it nevertheless brought about improvement: by 1983, only 5.9 percent of the elementary schools, 3 percent of the junior high schools, and 6.4 percent of the high schools in the Jewish sector provided no library services whatsoever for their students. In the Arab sector, 22 percent of the elementary schools, 17.3 percent of the junior high schools, and 12.8 percent of the high schools had no library services.

School libraries still need much more attention: their collections are rather poor (between several hundred and several thousand volumes) and they offer only very limited services. Children receive minimal encouragement and instruction to use libraries. Although there have been recent indications of change, the need remains for much more improvement.

Special Libraries. Israel has some 400 special libraries connected to research institutions, hospitals, professional associations, government agencies, and industrial plants. They developed close ties and interlibrary loan arrangements on their own, and their readers' demand for constantly updated information brought to light the need for a central agency specifically dedicated to fostering cooperation and coordination in scientific and technical information services. The initiative for the establishment of such an agency again came from outside the profession, with the advent of government policy for industrialization in the 1960s. The National Council for Research and Development established the Center for Scientific and Technological Information (COSTI).

COSTI provides information retrieval services for special libraries by means of its subscription to the major online information services in the United States and its own information retrieval system for conducting online searches: DOMESTIC. COSTI also provides information resources for special libraries, acting as a clearinghouse between the libraries requesting the items and the university libraries or the bigger special libraries.

Other Libraries. *Parliamentary Library.* The Parliamentary Library holds a relatively small collection for the use of members of the Knesset (Israeli Parliament). It also receives deposit copies of Israeli publications, but unlike the JNUL it does not serve as a depository library; the books are distributed among other libraries.

Religious Libraries. Many libraries and book collections of religious nature are used by the orthodox segments of the population. The Jewish religious libraries are in synagogues, orthodox Jewish educational institutions, local religious councils, and rabbinical courts. There are also a number of private collections.

Christian religious libraries can be found in monasteries and missions and near churches. Although some serve the general public, many are limited to the use of researchers.

Muslim religious libraries have been founded and promoted mostly by the Muslim Religious Endowment (Waqf), although there are many private collections as well, and there are also libraries in mosques.

Foreign Libraries. Foreign libraries of a secular nature are sponsored either by foreign governments or by nongovernmental public bodies in their respective countries. Their collections fulfill a public library function to Israel's new immigrants.

The Profession. Library education in Israel has always been influenced by the vicissitudes of opinion regarding the role of the library in society. During periods when the library was thought to occupy a central position, librarians were viewed as filling a significant socio-cultural role, and their training was on an accordingly high level. But during periods when the library was considered marginal, librarians were viewed primarily as clerks, needing only technical training that could be acquired in a brief course or even on the job.

Hugo Bergmann, the National Librarian who viewed librarians as filling a vital role in the community, saw to it that the senior librarians received appropriate professional training in library schools abroad, and that even librarians in small local libraries received training beyond the technical. He enabled them to be culture-bearers to the public. In the mid-1930s, when the continental European library model gained sway, Bergmann's model of library education was replaced by a model of short, non-academic training courses that were purely technical.

The establishment of the Jewish State in 1948 brought with it a shortage of professional library personnel, as the rapidly expanding economy provided many employment opportunities for academically-trained people, all more lucrative than librarianship. In response to the shortage, the Library School at the Hebrew University was founded. The School adopted the framework of the American model of professional library education, although the content of the framework was frequently influenced by the continental European model.

In the 1970s additional academic library education programs were started. In response to the growing demand for academically-trained librarians in Northern Israel, the University of Haifa opened a graduate diploma course of library education in 1972-73 as part of the Faculty of the Humanities. The two-year course emphasizes principles over technique and attempts to develop a comprehensive approach to librarianship, stressing the role of the library in society.

In 1973 Bar-Ilan University (the only Orthodox-oriented university in the country) opened its School of Library Education. The School offers a post-B.A. diploma course similar to those of other library schools and instituted a program of librarianship as a second-major course of study for the undergraduate degree. In 1985-86 the University of Haifa instituted an undergraduate program, which is part of a general B.A. and does not lead to a professional degree.

In the 1980s there was a growing awareness among Israeli librarians that the non-academic training courses established in the 1960s are inadequate and that librarians, especially public librarians, should have a broader educational background. The Council for Public Libraries in the Ministry of Education initiated changes in the non-academic courses, making their level equivalent to that of the training programs for elementary school teachers. The first such program, leading to the degree of chartered librarian, was put into effect at Haifa University School of Education of the kibbutz movement, Oranim, in 1976.

The Israel Library Association (ILA) is the professional organization for Israeli library personnel and archivists. The number of its members grew from 150 at its foundation in 1952 to about 2,000 a quarter century later. The Israel Society of Special Libraries and Information Centers (ISLIC) was founded in 1966 to extend professional aid to special librarians and establish foreign and local contacts in the field of special librarianship. It publishes the *ISLIC Bulletin,* which deals with problems of special libraries.

REFERENCES

Central Bureau of Statistics, *Monthly Bulletin of Statistics, Vol. 35, No. 9* (September 1984).

Central Bureau of Statistics, *Statistical Abstract of Israel, No. 34* (1983).

Central Bureau of Statistics and the Ministry of Education and Culture, Culture and Arts Division, *Reading and Other Leisure Activities of the Jewish Population Ages 14 and Over, 1969-1979* (1981).

Shmuel Sever, "Integration of Immigrants and Libraries in Israel, 1948-1960," *Library Research* (Spring 1979).

Shmuel Sever, "Networking and Automation in a Small Country; Uncertain Steps Towards Networking by Israel's Universities," *Library & Information Science Research* (1983).

SHMUEL SEVER

Italy

Italy, a republic in southern Europe, comprises the Apennine Peninsula, Sicily, Sardinia, and various other islands. Italy juts out south into the Mediterranean Sea and is bordered on the north and west by France and Switzerland and on the north and east by Austria and Yugoslavia. Population (1984 est.) 56,799,000; area 301,278 sq.km. The official language is Italian.

History. Libraries in Italy may be traced back into antiquity, and are among the oldest and most famous in the world. Excavations of private houses at both Rome and Herculaneum revealed rooms that were used as libraries. A library at Herculaneum had walls fitted with bookcases. Pliny's *Natural History* describes the foundation of a public library planned by Julius Caesar.

During the Middle Ages, monastic orders, to a certain extent, performed the functions of a public library. These orders, particularly the Benedictine Order, devoted themselves to preserving manuscripts by copying them. They were then lent to other monasteries and to the public. Some of the most important collections in Italy date back to the 13th century.

Renaissance public libraries had their origins in the private collections of noble families. The Biblioteca Medicea Laurenziana in Florence began with the personal collection of manuscripts of Cosimo de' Medici and the rich collections of his sons and grandson Lorenzo the Magnificent. Many other princely libraries were established during this period.

In 1609 the Biblioteca Ambrosiana, founded by Cardinal Federico Borromeo and named after St. Ambrose, the patron saint of Milan, opened its doors to the public. This library in Milan, which consisted of Borromeo's private collection of 30,000 books and 12,000 manuscripts, is considered to be the first public library in Italy. The Biblioteca Franzoniana in Genoa, founded in the 1770s for the instruction of poorer people, reportedly is the first library in Europe to provide night lighting so that the library would be available after working hours.

With the unification of Italy in the 1860s, all libraries under the jurisdiction of the original Italian kingdom and those within universities came under the control of the Italian Ministry of Public Instruction. Between 1860 and 1866, religious corporations were suppressed, and Italian "public," or governmental, libraries, offering certain services mainly to students and scholars, received the collections of approximately 1,700 confiscated libraries. Private persons were establishing popular circulating libraries, which allowed books to be circulated to members for a small monthly fee.

The government attempted to develop a unified library system, but one had not been realized by the outbreak of World War II. The period 1940-45, when large areas of Italy became a battleground, resulted in inactivity and severe damage to Italy's libraries. The postwar years saw many improvements in Italian libraries, but progress was slow and a large portion of the population is still inadequately served in public, school, and academic libraries.

National Libraries. There are eight national libraries in Italy. The National Central Libraries in Rome and Florence are the most prominent, and both receive materials under the deposit laws of 1886 and subsequent modifications. The National Central Library in Rome, officially known as the Biblioteca Nazionale Centrale Vittorio Emanuele II, collaborates with its sister Central Library in Florence to produce bibliographies of Italian and foreign materials. Their most important bibliography is the *Bibliografia Nazionale Italiana* (BNI), the computerized version of the annual cumulative edition of the Italian National Bibliography. The BNI is primarily produced at the computer center of the National Central Library of Florence. The Central Library in Rome produced catalogue cards, but they proved to be little used by libraries in Italy owing to the retention of local classification and cataloguing procedures. The National Central Library in Rome holds over 2,800,000 books and pamphlets, 2,000 incunabula, and 6,500 manuscripts.

The National Central Library of Florence opened to the public in 1747 with 30,000 volumes and 3,000 manuscripts. It contains nearly 4,500,000 books and pamphlets, 25,000 manuscripts, and about 4,000 incunabula. As does its counterpart in Rome, this library serves the general public and acts, in fact, as the major public library in Florence.

The other six national libraries in Milan, Venice, Turin, Naples, Bari, and Palermo are also open to the public. These six libraries serve as depositories for materials printed in their respective regions.

Academic Libraries. Academic libraries have undergone great stress because of enormous increases in student enrollments, which grew from 245,000 in 1960 to more than 1,000,000 in the 1980's. Libraries in higher education reflect the fragmentation and specialization of university organizational structure. Faculties of literature, law, and medicine, among others, are quite autonomous and are subdivided into special aspects of their respective disciplines. Libraries are generally designed to serve these separate faculties and their subdivisions. Probably the largest single library is at the University of Florence, the Biblioteca di Letture e Filosofia, with over 1,300,000 books and pamphlets. There are more than 40 other institutes and similar libraries at the University. Its Central Medical Library has over 75,000 volumes in addition to 350–400 volumes in each of the 14 other special medical libraries. This characteristic pattern of specialization results in about 100 faculty and institute libraries at the University of Palermo, while the University of Rome has about 120 libraries with holdings exceeding 1,100,000 volumes. Several major university libraries are governed by the national Ministero per i Beni Culturali e Ambientali.

There are many restrictions on lending in Italy, especially in academic and special libraries, resulting in great reliance on use of materials in the library. Moreover, as many academic libraries have limited staff members, the hours of access to the collections are limited, frequently only 20 hours a week.

The European University Institute Library at San Domenico di Fiesole, Florence, a consortium affiliated with the European Economic Community, employs a fully integrated automated system. It coop-

Vera Fotografia

The Vatican Library in Rome dates from the 13th century and is open to the public, but collections are restricted to use by qualified scholars.

erates with the National Library, the Tuscan Region, and the University Library in a shared, computer-based cataloguing system. This program began in 1979. However, progress has been slow. Staff and budget reductions have hindered efforts to automate.

Public Libraries. The national government has jurisdiction over 47 libraries, all of them called *biblioteche pubbliche statali,* or state public libraries. These libraries are of various types—8 national, 12 academic, 11 annexed to national monuments, and 16 special. All are open to the public. They do not, however, include public libraries as the term is widely used, that is, libraries governed by local authorities and devoted to serving people of all levels of education with a wide variety of interests. Public libraries of this sort are known as popular or communal (municipal) libraries in Italy.

Many plans and programs were drawn up to develop library systems. One such plan would create library systems within provinces (which include many communes or municipalities). The other major approach conceives systems developed by the 20 regions of Italy, each of which includes many provinces.

The most prominent provincial system is in Bo-

Libraries in Italy (1980)

Type	Administrative units	Service points	Volumes in collections	Annual expenditures (lira)	Population served[a]	Professional staff	Total staff
National	9	16	11,655,000	3,328,071	32,749	--	1,388
Academic[b]	3,060	--	55,114,000	--	1,148,105	--	--
Public[b]	8,686	--	16,979,000	--	2,944,163	--	--
School[b]	12,042	--	22,495,000	--	3,360,510	--	--
Special[b]	3,876	--	51,047,000	--	--	--	--

[a]Registered borrowers.
[b]1972 data.

Source: Unesco, *Statistical Yearbook,* 1984; 1976.

logna. The Bologna Provincial Consortium includes 23 libraries and 21 reading rooms *(sale di lettura)*, serving about half of the 850,000 people in this province. The Consortium's libraries function as cultural resource centers; in addition to providing traditional services, such as lending books and providing reading and reference rooms, libraries are centers for musical concerts, art exhibits, and programs of lectures, discussions, and demonstrations about a wide range of issues—historical and contemporary. This broad definition of library activities is shared widely in Italy, but few public libraries are able to put the ideal into practice.

Libraries in this system hold about 181,000 volumes and 430 current periodical titles.

The city of Bologna is not a part of the Consortium. Its holdings should be considered in addition to those of the Consortium. The city has a central library and 16 branch libraries for 550,000 people. Holdings include approximately 129,000 volumes and more than 215 current periodicals.

Because it is probably the best developed municipal library, the public library of Milan merits special attention. It effectively serves 42 percent of the total population of 1,708,000 through a large central library and 33 branches. The city system has 1,747,000 volumes, including 215,000 in school libraries. The public library administers the school libraries in the city. School libraries frequently are under the jurisdiction of local public libraries, as exemplified by Milan. School libraries generally have meager resources and, like libraries of other types in Italy, are often understaffed.

Although planning for regional library systems is longstanding, no region had formed a true system or network by the early 1980s. Tuscany was developing one in the mid-1970s, but it retrenched its service to cover only six provinces—Florence, Massa-Carrara, Leghorn, Arezzo, Pistoia, and Empoli. Its objectives still constitute a model for regional systems. These include a collective regional catalogue, a special library for science and technology, bibliographic information services for the region's libraries, regional microfilm archives, guardianship of library and archival holdings, a restoration laboratory, and professional training.

Special Libraries. The thousands of special libraries in Italy serve an enormous range of needs for contemporary materials, including all of the sciences, art, and professions. Many of these are affiliated with universities and are known as institute libraries. The most important special libraries—in number and kind—are primarily devoted to serving scholars in the humanities, history, literature, and philology. Their collections are particularly strong in the Middle Ages and the Renaissance. The national government controls some of the most prominent of the world famous libraries, such as the Biblioteca Medicea Laurentiana and the Casanatense.

The Institute of Legal Documentation in Florence provides computerized bibliographic services based on about 1,000 Italian law journals to lawyers, law students, and legislators. The Central Institute for the Union Catalogue, attached to the Ministry of Cultural and Environmental Heritage, operates an online service based on the BNI file, which is available for public use.

Vatican City. The Biblioteca Apostolica Vaticana is a distinguished library with roots in the 13th century, but its modern origin more correctly dates from the 15th century. It has grown from a few hundred volumes to holdings of 900,000 printed works, 65,000 manuscripts, and tens of thousands of maps, prints, and other items. Major exhibition rooms are open to the public, but use of the collections is restricted to qualified scholars.

The Profession. Established in 1930, the Associazione Italiana Biblioteche (Italian Library Association) has about 1,300 members participating in activities covering the spectrum of interest in librarianship. Working groups and conferences on education, legislation, automation, and networks have produced reports testifying to the intense interest in solving the many problems of Italian libraries.

REFERENCES

Ray L. Carpenter, "Contrasting Developments in Italian Libraries," *International Library Review* (1976), is an analysis of selected Italian libraries and librarianship as of 1974.

Elizabeth A. Dean, "The Organization of Italian Libraries from the Unification Until 1940," *Library Quarterly* (1983), is an account of library developments in Italy from the time of the beginning of the Italian unification (1860) until World War II.

RAY L. CARPENTER*

Ivory Coast

Ivory Coast, a republic in western Africa, is bordered by Mali and Burkina Faso on the north, Ghana on the east, the Gulf of Guinea on the south, and Liberia and Guinea on the west. Population (1984 est.) 9,671,000; area 320,763 sq.km. The official language is French.

National Library. The Bibliothèque Nationale in Abidjan, the capital of Ivory Coast, was begun in 1968 with the merger of the holdings of the former territorial library and those of the Institut Français d'Afrique Noir (IFAN) in Abidjan. A decree of 1971 defined its duties as collecting, conserving, and making available all materials printed in the country or concerning it; setting up a national documentation center and furnishing readers and researchers with documentation as varied and comprehensive as possible; establishing a general bibliographic center with information on all library collections in the country and publishing a national bibliography based on copyright deposit records; and coordinating activities in the development of libraries administered by the department of libraries and publications (now known as the book promotion department).

The Bibliothèque Nationale adjoins the national museum. These two institutions are part of the government center. The building, dedicated in January 1974, includes conference and lecture rooms, reading rooms, a film library and screening rooms, a popular circulating collection, and a noncirculating research collection. In 1965 the holdings of the former territorial library numbered 6,000 volumes. By 1981, according to Unesco, the Library held 65,000 volumes. And by the mid-1980s the holdings were estimated at 100,000 volumes and 2,000 periodical titles, including 700 current periodicals.

The Bibliothèque Nationale is administered by a chief librarian who also heads the book promotion department, which is part of the Directorate for Cultural Affairs. From August 1978 the institution was directed by Seydou Gueye.

Supplementing the Bibliothèque Nationale collection are the individual libraries maintained by the Assemblée Nationale and many of the cabinet ministries.

Academic Libraries. The principal academic library is the Bibliothèque Universitaire, on the main campus of the national university in a suburb of Abidjan. The Library is open only to students, faculty, and researchers affiliated with the university; however, students of other specialized colleges as well as individuals demonstrating a bona fide need may use the library after paying nominal fees. The library can arrange international interlibrary loans with the stipulation that borrowers pay shipping costs.

Some university research institutes maintain their own specialized libraries. Examples are the Library in the Institut d'Ethno-sociologie, specializing in sociology, ethnography, and economic development, and the Institut de Linguistique Appliqué, specializing in African linguistics and oral traditions. Additional libraries at the École Nationale Supérieure de Travaux Publiques, the École Nationale Supérieure Agronomique, and the École de Statistique also provide for specialized academic needs. The library of the École Nationale d'Administration, serving both students and members of the national government, contains more than 10,000 volumes and 100 serials as well as 500 documents and studies on Ivory Coast.

Public Libraries. In 1952 the Colonial government established a municipal library in Abidjan. By 1963 it contained more than 5,000 volumes. In 1964, as part of a Unesco pilot project, the government installed a public library in one of the busiest markets in the Abidjan area. Unesco reported 25,000 volumes in one public library by 1981. The only other public library is the collection of the Centre Culturel Jacques Aqua in Bouaké, the second largest city.

Special Libraries. The holdings of larger special libraries reflect the importance of agriculture for the development of Ivory Coast. The technical libraries of the Office de la Recherche Scientifique et Technique Outre-mer (ORSTOM) and those of the Institut de Recherche Agronomique Tropicale et Cultures Vivrières (IRAT) at Bouaké, the Institut Français du Café, du Cacao, et Autres Plantes Stimulantes, and the Centre Technique Forestier Tropicale de la Côte d'Ivoire contain important works on plant and soil sciences, geology, ecology, and tropical agriculture. There is also an important geology library in the Societé pour le Developpement Minier de la Côte d'Ivoire.

Bibliothèque Nationale

The National Library of the Ivory Coast, founded in Abidjan in 1968.

Other research institutes maintain smaller libraries having for the most part fewer than 500 volumes. The library of the Institut Africain pour le Developpement Economique et Sociale, however, includes more than 30,000 volumes and 250 serials focusing on the social sciences and economic development. Also concentrating on economic development is the collection of the Bureau National d'Études Techniques du Developpement (BNETD). Finally, the American, French, and German cultural centers in Abidjan established libraries on the history and culture of their respective countries.

School Libraries. With the stated objectives of helping students with classwork, stimulating thought, and encouraging reading for pleasure, the government set up libraries in secondary schools, though most of the libraries have fewer than 1,000 volumes. Volumes are distributed unequally among the secondary school libraries, with the lion's share going to the more prestigious, though not always larger, urban schools.

The Profession. The Association for the Development of Documentation, Libraries, and Archives of the Ivory Coast (connected with the Bibliothèque Nationale) was established in Abidjan. A decree of 1971 set rules for recruitment and training. Staffs are comparatively small, and most library employees received their training on the job.

ROBERT E. HANDLOFF;
SEYDOU GUEYE

J

Jamaica

Jamaica, a parliamentary state and member of the Commonwealth, lies in the Caribbean Sea south of Cuba. Population (1984 est.) 2,141,000; area 10,991 sq.km. The official language is English.

History. The National Council on Libraries, Archives and Documentation Services (NACO-LADS) was appointed by the Prime Minister of Jamaica in 1973. Its permanent secretariat in Kingston has responsibility to advise the Prime Minister on planning and coordination in this field. The Council has been involved with producing a national plan for the development of libraries, archives, and documentation services, the establishment of a national deposit library, the stimulation and development of libraries in private organizations, and the establishment of national standards. The first plan for a national documentation, information, and library system for Jamaica was published by the Council in 1978. One objective of the Council is the establishment of a national information system, the main aims of which are to assist in the achievement of national goals and priorities, to develop human resources, and to stimulate economic activity through the provision of information.

National Library. The National Library of Jamaica was established in 1979 under Section Five of

Main building of the National Library of Jamaica, Kingston, opened in 1978 as part of the Institute of Jamaica, established in 1879.

the Institute of Jamaica Act of 1978. The Institute of Jamaica (1879) was founded mainly for the encouragement of literature, science, and art. The West Indian Reference Library (1894) forms the nucleus of the collections of the National Library. The library's collection of Caribbeana is extensive, and in 1984 its collection included 36,838 books and pamphlets, 2,631 periodical titles; 205 newspaper titles; and other items totaling 54,258. Publications include the *Jamaica National Bibliography*. The library has been used extensively by scholars for historical research on Jamaica and the other Caribbean islands.

Academic Libraries. The University of the West Indies, Mona, Kingston, has the primary academic library of Jamaica. It functions as a regional library, because it serves a regional institution. The main collection in 1983 totaled 319,146 volumes including 1,096 periodicals. Manuscripts, microforms, and maps totaling 4,331 are also included in the collection. The library is a depository for the printed publications of the United Nations. The Medical and Science Libraries, with collections of 25,409 and 59,717, respectively (1983), are its two branches.

There are also other independent libraries at the Mona University Campus: the Institute of Social and Economic Research (1948); the Documentation Centre of the School of Education (1967); the Norman Manley Law Library (1963); the Department of Library Studies (1963); the United Theological College (1967); St. Michael's Seminary (1952); and the Caribbean Food and Nutrition Institute (1968). The Library of the College of Arts, Science and Technology (1958), in Kingston, has a collection of 30,000 items. It is the largest of the academic libraries, which include the Agricultural College and eight teacher training colleges.

Public Libraries. The Jamaica Library Service, established by an act of Parliament in 1949, provides a free public library service and is responsible for the operation of the Schools Library Service. The Service is organized from a coordinating headquarters in Kingston with a network of service points consisting of 13 main libraries, one in each capital town, 160 branch libraries (102 of which are part-time), 7 book centers, and 15 bookmobiles that operate 501 bookmobile stops. Special services are provided to hospitals and correctional institutions, and a free postal service is also provided in rural areas. From March 1983 to April 1984, 2,290,127 books were circulated to 656,428 members. The stock includes 1,266,423 volumes, periodicals, pamphlets, filmstrips, slides, and

Jamaica Library Service

Libraries in Jamaica (1982–1983)

Type	Administrative units	Service points	Volumes in collections	Annual expenditures (Jamaican dollar)	Population served	Professional staff	Total staff
National	1	1	35,786	80,986	2,095,878	19	75
Academic	29	20	366,422[a]	2,448,886[a]	12,210[a]	35[a]	135[a]
Public Library Service	14	705	1,170,722	7,454,432	2,095,878	88	1,007
Schools Library Service	1	912	1,454,684	1,649,300	539,568	3	51
School[b]	55	21	92,072[a]	69,853[a]	14,565[a]	8[a]	37[a]
Special	85	51	104,338[a]	965,445[a]	14,740	27[a]	96[a]

[a]Data incomplete.
[b]High school and vocational.

records. Special collections include West Indian literature, the theatre, and foreign languages (French, Spanish, and German). Educational and cultural programs are conducted by all libraries.

School Libraries. The Schools Library Service is administered by the Jamaica Library Service on behalf of the Ministry of Education. The service for primary schools began in 1952 and was extended to the junior secondary schools in 1969. Five bookmobiles, with a stock of 2,000 books each, operating from five regional centers, visit each primary and all-age school at least three times a year. At each visit teachers may select 200 to 1,000 books, depending on the school's enrollment and other factors. The stock in 1983 totaled 1,096,626 books and periodicals and served an enrollment of 431,454 pupils.

The 80 secondary school libraries (formerly called junior secondary schools), unlike primary schools, all have organized library rooms. The total bookstock of these libraries was 422,851. There are also well-established libraries in many of the traditional high schools.

Special Libraries. The interest shown in recent years by business, industrial, and professional organizations in the provision of libraries continues. The largest of these is the Alcan Technical Information Center attached to Alcan, one of the Bauxite companies. Libraries are also attached to government ministries and agencies. These include those of Education and Agriculture, the Supreme Court, Bureau of Standards, and Scientific Research Council.

The Profession. The Jamaica Library Association (established 1950) has its headquarters in Kingston and maintains a professional collection. It has a Schools Library Section and a Special Library Section, and they sponsor seminars and workshops regularly. The Commonwealth Library Association (1972) has its headquarters in Mandeville.

SYBIL M. ITON

Jameson, J. Franklin
(1859–1937)

John Franklin Jameson—historian, teacher, editor, manuscript librarian, and administrator—was present at the beginnings of the historical profession in the United States and later of the archival profession.

Born September 19, 1859, in Somerville, Massachusetts, Jameson early showed intellectual promise and habits of hard work. He was graduated from the Roxbury Latin School and, in 1879, as valedictorian from Amherst College. While in college he set course on becoming a historian. Unable to finance graduate study in Germany, he taught high school for a year before going to the newly established Johns Hopkins University. His Ph.D. in 1882 was the first history doctorate awarded there.

Jameson had the rare opportunity to found and shape important institutions. He was one of the founders in 1884 of the American Historical Association and in 1895 of the *American Historical Review,* which he edited with great distinction until 1928 (except for 1901–05).

For the two decades after taking his doctorate, Jameson held history professorships at Hopkins (1882–88), Brown University (1888–1901), and the

University of Chicago (1901–05). But Jameson did not make his mark as a teacher.

On leaving Chicago, Jameson became the second Director of the Bureau of Historical Research of the recently founded (1902) Carnegie Institution of Washington. As an advisor to Carnegie's first President, Daniel Coit Gilman, Jameson had helped formulate Carnegie's historical programs, which centered on identifying, evaluating, and publishing guides to the archives of the federal government and of bodies of archival material abroad with bearing on American history. This work eventually made clear the abysmal state of the federal government's archival practices and the pressing need for an archives building and an appropriate agency to administer the whole enterprise. Jameson politicked actively for a quarter-century for an archival establishment and was rewarded for his efforts by the construction of the National Archives building in 1934.

In 1927 Jameson became the first incumbent of a chair of American history at the Library of Congress as well as Chief of the Manuscript Division. He actively enlarged the division's role in fostering scholarship by expanding its program of photocopying records from foreign institutions (made possible by the guides he had published at Carnegie) and by acquiring many important new collections. Jameson was responsible for the policy formulation of the Division but also supervised closely all the routine work of his staff.

Although Jameson's bibliography is lengthy, most entries were edited pieces, reports, or reviews; this remarkable historical statesman was far more intent on administering great projects than in producing large-scale interpretive works himself. Still, two of his books, *The History of Historical Writing in America* (1891) and *The American Revolution Considered as a Social Movement* (1926), were of considerable influence in their day and for some years after.

Jameson died September 28, 1937, in Washington, D.C., while still occupying his posts at LC.

REFERENCES
Elizabeth Donnan and Leo F. Stock, editors, *An Historian's World: Selections from the Correspondence of John Franklin Jameson* (American Philosophical Society, 1956). Includes biographical sketch.
Ruth Anna Fisher and William Lloyd Fox, editors, *J. Franklin Jameson: A Tribute* (1965), memoirs by 14 contributors.
Victor Gondos, Jr., *J. Franklin Jameson and the Birth of the National Archives, 1906–1926* (1981).
The major collection of Jameson's papers is in the Manuscript Division of the Library of Congress.

JOHN B. HENCH

Japan

Japan, a constitutional monarchy, lies in the shape of a bow in eastern Asia and comprises an archipelago including the four main islands of Hokkaido, Honshu, Shikoku, and Kyushu. Population (1984) 118,602,000; area 377,582 sq.km. The official language is Japanese.

History. At the turn of the 3rd century A.D., Kanji (Chinese) characters were introduced to Japan by Korean scholars. In the 4th century, a number of political refugees from Korea were naturalized in Japan. Mostly Buddhists from the higher classes and

Library Center of Kanazawa Institute of Technology, opened in 1982.

1279) were reopened and cultural and personal exchange began again. Many sutras and books on Buddhism and Confucianism were imported, stimulating the Japanese religious world. New sects of Zen and Nichiren were born. Priests were eager to study and print sutras and books on Buddhism. Non-Buddhist books, however, were made by hand as in the past. Two great libraries of Samurai clans at the time still remain today.

Kanazawa Bunko (library) was the private collection set up by the Hojo clan in the latter half of the 13th century. The collection included Buddhist materials in scrolled, folded, and printed forms numbering more than 10,000. The collection was heavily used by scholars.

Ashikaga Gakko (school) was rebuilt to educate boys of the Uesugi clan in 1432. Divination was the main subject taught, and the school's rich collection on the subject attracted scholars from all parts of the country.

The Shogun Tokugawa Ieyasu (1542–1616), who founded the last shogunate, moved the government from Kyoto to Edo (modern Tokyo) in 1590. He ruled a tranquil and prosperous country and encouraged learning to keep the country in peace. The Shogun, an enthusiastic scholar of Confucianism, invited scholars to print books, and he collected books and records that were scattered or thought lost during the civil war years. The Shogun had a private library called Momijiyama Bunko.

The third Shogun of the Tokugawa dynasty, Tokugawa Iemitsu (1604–1651), appointed an official custodian for Momijiyama Bunko to collect books and compile a catalogue of the collection. The Bunko was kept by scholar-custodians under the sponsorship of the shogunate from generation to generation until 1868, when the shogunate fell. The Bunko was full of manuscripts and rare and important materials of the country. The collection is now divided and kept in the Library of the Imperial Household Agency and the Cabinet Library for use of scholars. The Library of the Imperial Household Agency inherited another collection, from the Shoheizaka School, which was a government school to educate Samurai in Edo.

There were more than 250 feudal provinces in Japan during the Edo period (1590–1868). Feudal lords, following the Shogun's policy, established provincial schools with libraries and printed books.

Many wajuku and terakoya (small private

well educated, the Koreans brought to Japanese society their continental culture and religion, which rapidly spread over the country.

As early as the 7th century, the Japanese government sent its first messenger to China to establish direct relations. That communication accelerated the flow of Chinese culture to Japan and the Japanese utilized Kanji as a means to express their native language.

The oldest book of Japanese history was compiled in Kanji in A.D. 712 and the copperplate or wood block prints of the Buddhist sutra of Hyakumanto ("A Million Pagodas") were printed in 770. Buddhist culture was accepted by the Emperor and his courtiers and noblemen, some of whom were interested in learning and began to collect scrolls for a library. Untei-in (Nara) of Isonokami no Yakatsugu (729–81) and Kobaiden (Kyoto) of Sugawara Michizane (845–903) were private collections on Buddhism and Confucianism available to scholars. The openness of the Nara collection is often cited as evidence that it was the first public library in Japan.

Samurai Rule. After a long period of civil war, the Samurai (warrior) class gained power, taking the place of the noblemen in the Kamakura period (1185–1333). Relations with China (Sung dynasty, 960–

Libraries in Japan (1982)

Type	Administrative units	Service points	Volumes in collections	Annual expenditures (yen)	Population served	Professional staff	Total staff
National	1	36	7,531,124	11,094,529,000	117,777,000	1,128[a]	1,230
Academic	830	440	126,165,000	95,515,420,000	2,474,558	8,358[a]	12,040
Public	1,444[b]	520[c]	88,247,000	13,522,130,000	117,777,000	5,190	10,341
School	42,017[d]	--	--	18,069,000,000	23,250,072	695	17,207
Special[e]	2,023	--	50,731,702	30,863,560,000	--	1,397[a]	2,904

[a]All full-time staff; distinctions between professional and nonprofessional are not made in national, academic, and special libraries in Japan.
[b]Main and branch libraries not separated.
[c]Number of bookmobiles.
[d]Includes schools for the disabled.
[e]1981 data.

schools) gave basic education in reading, writing, and arithmetic to children of the non-Samurai classes. More than 800 terakoyas alone were reported in Edo in 1722.

In the latter part of the Edo period, the lending library became a business. Bookmen carried packs of books on their backs to customers at their homes and lent books for a fee. There were more than 2,000 publishers who had profitable businesses in Japan throughout the Edo period. Literacy of Samurai, merchants, their wives, and children appears to have been high.

Meiji Period. When the last shogun fell in 1868, the Imperial Government was restored to power. Japan opened its ports to trade with foreign countries for the first time since the 17th century. The government imported not only manufactured goods but also science, technology, and other knowledge from European countries and the United States in order to modernize and to catch up with Western civilzation in those areas.

The government established the Imperial Library in 1872. It included the collections of Shoheizaka School and other Edo governmental institutions.

In 1872, when public education was enforced, organizations of school teachers were formed in each *ken* (prefecture or province). Those libraries would become the central libraries in kens in later years.

The Japan Library Association was formed by 35 librarians and booklovers in 1892. The first Library Act was issued in 1899. In commemoration of the new building of the Imperial Library, the first annual meeting of librarians was held in 1906. The next year the Japan Library Association began to publish its journal, *Toshokan Zasshi* ("Library Journal").

Taisho Period. During the Taisho period (1912–25), the number of public libraries rapidly grew. There were 445 in the first year and 4,337 in the last year of the Taisho period, but the average number of books was as small as 2,000 volumes per library.

The Librarian's Training Institute was founded under the control of the Ministry of Education in 1921. The Institute initially produced about 40 librarians at the high-school level annually, and later developed into the National University of Library and Information Science with graduate courses.

World War II. The number of public libraries grew steadily until there were 4,794 (1,500 private) at the outbreak of World War II in 1941. During the war, most of the large cities were swept by air-raid bombing and fire. More than half of the collections of central libraries in kens and 80 percent of those in municipal libraries were destroyed.

An Education Mission from the U.S. made recommendations on reform and democratization of education to the occupation authorities. As part of education reform, some recommendations and suggestions on improvements of libraries and library services were included. Japanese libraries have risen from the ashes to develop along those recommendations.

National Library. Kokuritsu Kokkai Toshokan—the National Diet Library (NDL)—was established under law in 1948. The NDL serves the Diet members, its primary function, as well as the general public. It is the only library and bibliographic center with the privilege of legal deposit of both civil and official publications in Japan. Its six-story building and a basement (73,674 square meters) provide a stack capacity of 4,500,000 volumes.

An annex building was under construction in 1985. In addition, a plan called for establishing a Kansai (Kyoto-Osaka area) branch that would be a second service point for users in western parts of Japan.

The NDL has six divisions and a department. Its staff numbered more than 800 in the early 1980s. NDL has 36 branches, including the former Imperial Library, Toyo Bunko (Oriental Library), Library of the Supreme Court, libraries in the executive and judicial agencies of the government, and a detached library in the Diet building (a direct service point to the Diet members).

The main collection totaled 4,038,128 volumes (1,213,126 foreign), 78,660 periodical titles, 229,936 maps, 258,662 phonodisks, 127,911 reels of microfilms, and 175,852 doctoral dissertations; 1,764 braille books were maintained in the main library. Almost 500,000 readers (1,751 a day) used the collection and made about 196,000 pages of photocopies.

There is no overall interlibrary loan system for the whole country. The NDL lends books to any library whether it is a public, university, or special library. NDL loaned 5,573 books to its branches, 10,546 to university and public libraries, 1,206 to special libraries, and 136 to libraries in foreign countries (1983–84).

NDL microfilms newspapers for preservation and use by readers. The Library annually filmed 59 newspapers from 1953 under contract with the Japan Newspaper Association. The Library also has microfilmed important newspapers published in the Meiji (1868–1912) and Taisho (1912–25) periods.

NDL installed a computer system to automate certain aspects of library work in 1971 after studying its feasibility and experimenting for a decade. The first publication from the automated system was *The General Index to the Debates in Both Houses of the Diet.*

Bibliographic information on legally deposited publications was accumulated on magnetic tapes to form a central database, JAPAN MARC. Thirty-five

Central catalogue hall of Tenri University Library, Tenri, Japan.

Theodore F. Welch

libraries subscribed in the mid-1980s to JAPAN MARC tapes through the Japan Library Association. The *Japanese National Bibliography*—weekly edition, quarterly index, and annual volumes—have been compiled and printed out from JAPAN MARC.

Academic Libraries. Higher education in Japan faced great change under the Education Reform Act after World War II. A coeducational system was introduced, the number of university students greatly increased, and junior colleges for young women's education appeared as new institutions.

There were 453 universities in 1983 (93 national, 34 prefectural and municipal, and 326 private) with 1,900,000 students, of whom 22 percent were female in 1983.

There were 938 university libraries including departmental libraries and subject collections in faculty members' study rooms. Three hundred twenty-six national university libraries accounted for 44 percent of the total book resources.

The largest national university library is the University of Tokyo Library, founded in 1877. It comprises the general library and 62 libraries in faculties, departments, and research institutions with 5,129,166 volumes and 36,653 periodical titles (18,976 foreign); there were 327 librarians in all.

Keio University is the oldest private university. Its Library on the Mita campus, opened in April 1983, provides open access to faculty members and students in all parts of the building.

The Library Center of Kanazawa Institute of Technology (KIT), opened in 1982, attracted special attention because it installed a computer from the beginning to provide automated library services. It provides, for example, a bibliographic retrieval system that does not use a card catalogue. KIT planned to "bring the library to teaching programs and teaching programs to the library." It called upon subject specialists who are faculty members as well as library staffs to select materials and provide students with regular guidance on library use and bibliographic information.

In 1980 the Ministry of Education accepted "The Report on Science Information Systems" submitted by the Science Council, which calls for setting up an information retrieval system based on computer technology that effectively utilizes library resources in universities. The Ministry subsidized national university libraries for cooperative acquisition of scientific periodicals, compilation of union catalogues, and setting up interlibrary loan systems among libraries.

Three private university libraries had joined UTLAS (University of Toronto Library Automation Systems) by 1985. They use it for processing European and American books.

Junior colleges, the comparatively new higher education institutions for females, appeared in 1950. There were 542 (36 national, 51 prefectural and municipal, and 455 private) with 380,214 students in 1984.

Junior college libraries, generally speaking, are small. The average number of books was 34,400 with 2.6 staff members in a library in mid-1984. About 80 percent allow open access.

Topics discussed at annual meetings of junior college librarians in the early and mid-1980s emphasized subjects common among librarians—student in-

struction on library use and application of microcomputers to library work, for example.

Public Libraries. The concept of a public library as a tax-supported free institution whose purpose is to serve the community through books and other materials came into being after World War II. The concept was implemented in the enactment of the Public Library Law of April 30, 1950. The day has since been celebrated yearly as "Library Day" for the promotion of library service.

There are two types: the prefectural and the municipal (city, town, village, and ward) public libraries. Forty-seven prefectures have a total of 71 libraries and 63 bookmobiles. Tokyo and Kyoto have as many as six libraries in each prefecture. Libraries in Tokyo, Osaka, and Saitama prefectures have more than a million volumes, while the average number of books in each of the other 44 prefectures was 350,000 volumes. The largest amount of annual book expenditures was ¥158,000,000 in Metropolitan Tokyo in 1984 and the smallest was ¥15,000,000 in Tottori prefecture. Reorganization of six metropolitan libraries in Tokyo and computer-based rationalization of the book processing system using JAPAN MARC tapes were under way in the second half of the 1980s.

There are 3,278 municipalities, and 86 percent of the cities and 15 percent of the towns and villages had public libraries in 1984. A prefectural library, therefore, has to do double work of lending books to individual patrons via bookmobiles and to municipal libraries for interlibrary loan within the prefecture. Public libraries numbered 1,537 with 542 bookmobiles, serving a whole population of 118,602,000 in Japan in 1984.

Service to the Blind. Library services to the blind began in the 1970s. There were 92 libraries for the blind in 1984, and a large number of public libraries provided large-print books, recorded tapes, and tête-a-tête reading service by volunteers. Library buildings were remodeled to provide ramps for wheelchairs, special plumbing facilities, and dots on the floor to guide the blind in the library. Thirty-eight institutions publish braille books and five publish large-print books.

Children's Services. Library service to children is another post–World War II development. In 1955, 30 percent of public libraries had children's rooms or corners. While 24 percent of the registrants were children, only five percent of the books in public libraries were children's books. Although the importance of services to children was emphasized and the number of children's rooms grew in the 1960s, services were still inadequate and did not meet the demands of children. Through the efforts of mothers, several thousand small private collections called "home libraries" have been opened to children. In 1983, 83 percent of public libraries had children's rooms or corners, and 45 percent of total circulation was children's books.

School Libraries. The 6-3-3 system—six years primary, three middle, and three high school—was established under the postwar Education Reform Act. The first nine years of education are compulsory. After finishing compulsory education, 94 percent of the middle school students go to high school.

Before the war, there were only a few school libraries, run by some enthusiastic teachers. The School Library Law was enacted in 1953 and more than 98 percent of a total of about 41,360 schools (25,044 primary, 10,950 middle, 5,364 high schools) have libraries. Although the School Library Law required schools to employ teacher-librarians, a supplementary provision of the law held that "Schools may defer compliance concerning teacher-librarians for the present." The proviso was criticized for undermining sound development of school libraries. A new classification of librarian emerged: called "school librarians," they do not have teacher's licenses and may or may not have librarian's certificates.

A school library survey done by the Japan School Library Association in 1980 showed that primary school libraries had an average of 3,690 books (7.9 volumes per pupil) and library expenditures of ¥332,000 (U.S.$1,400); 83.3 percent of the libraries did not have card catalogues for pupils. Twenty-four percent of the schools provided posts for full-time teacher–librarians, and 10 percent of the schools provided posts for school librarians.

In a middle school library, the number of books averaged 4,699 (9.3 volumes per pupil) and library expenditures averaged ¥4,209,870 (U.S.$17,540); 75.4 percent of the libraries did not have card catalogues. Twenty-four percent of the schools had full-time teacher–librarians and 13.5 percent of the schools had school librarians.

In high school libraries, the average book collection was 12,041 volumes (15.9 volumes per student); library expenditures were ¥5,506,403 (U.S.$22,943). Public catalogues were available in 64.5 percent of the libraries. Full-time teacher–librarians were working in 45.3 percent of the high school libraries; 34.4 percent of the schools employed school librarians, 29 percent of whom had librarian's certificates.

In 1970 schools began to open their libraries to people in the community as they had done with their playgrounds outside school hours. The percentage of schools doing so, however, was still small in the 1980s.

Special Libraries and Information Centers. *A Directory of Special Libraries* (1982) listed 2,023 special libraries, of which 284 were established before 1945. Generally speaking, special libraries are small; the median was a collection of 35,000 books and 350 periodical titles and a staff of four. Most of them are closed to the public. Special libraries may be categorized as libraries in private corporations, local government councils, research institutes attached to universities, government institutions, associations and societies, and foreign government institutions.

The Japan Information Center for Science and Technology (JICST) was established as a special nonprofit organization under a legislative act in 1957. It had approximately 10,000 titles of both Japanese (40 percent) and foreign (60 percent) periodicals, 12,500 technical reports, 49,000 patent specifications, and other items in 1984. JICST compiles 12 abstract journals in Japanese from both Japanese and foreign periodicals on monthly or semimonthly bases. They include JICST File on JOIS (JICST Online Information Systems), which also includes foreign databases such as BIOSIS Previews, CAB, MEDLINE, and others.

JICST and its 10 branches are connected over lines to 2,500 terminals in private corporations, research institutes, and universities. JICST provided about 300,000 online information services in 1983.

Theodore F. Welch

Yumedono (Hall of Dreams), established on the grounds of the Horyuji Temple near Nara in A.D. 702, thought to be the earliest library in Japan.

Online copy and SDI services are available.

A hundred medical college libraries form the Japan Medical Library Association. The average medical library had 58,000 volumes of books, 1,443 current periodical titles (653 Japanese, 790 foreign), and annual expenditures of ¥61,120,000 (U.S.$250,000), with 10.5 full-time librarians.

Cooperation among medical libraries has been well organized in the most advanced ways in Japan to provide interlibrary loan and to compile a union catalogue of periodicals. Thirty-seven medical libraries had Telexes for requesting photocopies of periodical literature in 1984.

Eighty-five libraries installed computer terminals for online information services from JOIS and DIALOG of Lockheed by 1985. MEDLINE and EXCERPTA MEDICA naturally are in heavy demand.

There are two hospital library associations. A survey of hospital libraries was published in 1985 by the International Congress of Medical Librarianship in Tokyo.

Hospital libraries for patients were a new development in the mid-1980s. Volunteers who visit hospitals to lend books to patients formed the Japan Hospital Library Association to promote such services.

The Profession. *Education.* The Librarian's Training Institute was founded under the control of the Ministry of Education in 1921 in Ueno Park, Tokyo. It was the only institute to train librarians at the high school level before World War II. The Institute trained 1,530 librarians by 1964, when it was reorganized and became the National Junior College for Librarianship. The Junior College provided a two-year course in library science and a one-year course for university graduates with B.A. degrees. The junior college was reorganized again to become the National University of Library and Information Science when it moved from Tokyo to Tsukuba in Ibaraki Prefecture in 1980. Graduate courses were added in April 1984.

The Japan Library School was established in the Faculty of Letters, Keio University in 1951 with the assistance of the American Library Association and the Rockefeller Foundation. It was the first library school at the university level for professional education in Japan. During its early years, the curriculum emphasized American library science practices taught by American visiting professors with interpreters. When the grants ended, the School became part of Keio University as the Department of Library and Information Science. Graduate courses leading to the M.A. or Ph.D. in Letters were added in 1967.

In addition, 107 universities and 94 junior colleges offered minors in library science in the mid-1980s, with credits leading to librarian's certificates. Sixteen universities offered two-month summer courses and three correspondence courses for librarian's certificates in 1982.

Graduate students can specialize in library science in the Faculty of Education at the University of Tokyo and at the University of Kyoto.

A librarian must have a librarian's certificate to work in a public library, as required by the Public Library Law. It is the only qualification for librarianship that can be acquired by persons whose education ranges from high school graduation to a Ph.D. University, college, and special libraries do not require librarian's certificates, but they give preference to candidates who possess them.

A teacher-librarian's certificate is awarded after eight credits are earned in library science. Courses for teacher-librarians were offered in the mid-1980s at 91 universities and more than 50 junior colleges together with courses for librarians' certificates.

Associations. The Japan Library Association (JLA) is the only general association that covers all types and subjects of libraries. It was founded in 1892, and its membership included more than 5,000 persons and 1,812 institutions in 1984; it is a member of IFLA. *Toshokan Zasshi* ("Library Journal") is published monthly. Other publications include "Nippon Cataloging Rules," "Nippon Decimal Classification," "Basic Subject Headings," "Library Yearbook," and more than 35 other books on librarianship.

JLA has eight divisions on types of libraries and had 24 committees in 1984. JLA invited other library associations and libraries to form the Japanese Committee for IFLA in 1982. The committee became sponsor of the 52nd IFLA Conference in Tokyo, scheduled for August 1986.

Other associations include: the Association of Private University Libraries, founded in 1930 (257 member institutions); the Council on National University Libraries, founded in 1924 (93 institutions); the Japan Medical Library Association, founded in 1927 (100 institutions); the Japan School Library Association, founded in 1950 (60 regional organizations); the Japan Special Libraries Association, founded in 1952 (611 institutions); the National Council of Public Libraries, Japan, founded in 1967 (1,537 institutions); and the Private Junior College Library Association, founded in 1977 (225 institutions). All issue newsletters or journals or both and many are members of IFLA.

There are other associations in pharmaceutics, agriculture, music, law, hospitals, and library science. There also are regional and international associations such as Hokkaido Society of Library Science and La Société Franco-Japonaise des Bibliothècaires.

REFERENCES
Theodore F. Welch, *Toshokan: Libraries in Japanese Society* (1976).
Louise Watanabe Tung. "Library Development in Japan," *The Library Quarterly* (1956), for the premodern period.
MADOKO KON

Library Association
Louis Stanley Jast

Jast, Louis Stanley
(1868–1944)

Louis Stanley Jast was one of the great pioneers in the development of the British public library service. He was an inventive practicing librarian, an engaging writer on librarianship, and the best speaker in the profession in his day.

Jast was born at Halifax, Yorkshire, August 20, 1868. He was the son of an exiled Polish army officer, and his family name, which he changed in 1895, was Jastrzebski. Jast began his library career in 1887 at the Halifax public library, where he was thoroughly grounded in all the pettifogging routines that were then the very essence of public librarianship. Jast was unable to exercise his latent talents until he became his own master.

In 1892 Jast became Librarian of the small town of Peterborough. Soon afterward he discovered the Decimal Classification, which in later years he listed among the books that had most influenced his life. Under its spell he waged his first campaign, for the wider use of close classification in public libraries. He thereby gained the friendship of James Duff Brown, pioneer of open access in British public libraries. Jast joined forces with Brown not only on the platform in propagating the elements of "the new librarianship" but also in the pages of the *Library World,* the independent monthly journal that Brown had founded and also edited.

In 1898 Jast became Librarian of Croydon, a rapidly growing commuter town on the fringe of Greater London. There, with the backing of a sympathetic committee and a hard-working staff, Jast created a truly dynamic library service. Under his direction the Croydon libraries became a workshop for new ideas. Among the many novelties were the card catalogue, the reference information service, the library bulletin, lectures, reading circles, exhibitions of books and pictures, and liaison with the local schools.

Running the Croydon libraries was not enough to absorb Jast's boundless energy. From 1905 to 1915 he served as Honorary Secretary of the Library Association (LA). No one was better qualified for the post, but not even Jast's sparkle and enthusiasm could bring the LA prosperity. Its membership and resources remained obstinately small. The two major events during Jast's term of office were the inauguration in 1910 of a register of qualified librarians and the framing and publication, in collaboration with the American Library Association, of the well-known

Cataloguing Rules: Author and Title Entries (1908).

In 1915 Jast became Deputy Librarian of Manchester and in 1920 Chief Librarian. His main preoccupation as Chief was the planning of the new central library, which was long overdue. Jast's contention that one could have a useful library "with books and brains and any sort of protection against the weather" was broadly true, but for him it was rather a sour truth. The new building he planned and longed for was not opened until July 1934, by which time he had been retired for two and a half years. Throughout his service at Manchester the central library was housed in "temporary" huts.

Apart from its circular shape, resulting from the nature of the site, and its great circular reading room—modeled on the reading room of the British Museum, which Jast greatly admired—the most interesting feature of the new Manchester Central Library was the book stack. This formed the core of the building, and the public rooms were grouped around it and above it. Jast called it "an integrated stack" and was very proud of it.

Jast had given much time to studying the design of large libraries in Britain and America. His mature thoughts on the subject, first presented in a lecture in December 1926, were published in pamphlet form as *The Planning of a Great Library* (1927). Jast enunciated four principles of library planning: (1) a properly designed library should not be a building containing books but books in an appropriate setting; (2) there are limits to the value of subject departmentalization; therefore, the stock should be kept as intact as possible; (3) the book stack should be "the central nerve ganglion of the whole building"; and (4) in the collaboration between librarian and architect, the premier role should be assigned to the librarian.

With regard to the second principle, Ernest A. Savage, a zealous advocate of subject departments and busy at the time forming as many as he could in his awkward Victorian central library at Edinburgh, said that in planning the new Manchester library Jast had "raised the standard of specialization without exposing it to too strong a wind." Jast, however, had played a significant part in the development of subject specialization in Britain; at Croydon he had given some attention to the collection of local materials and had made the central library the base for an elaborate photographic survey of the county. During World War I he had made nationally a strong plea for the creation of special public library services for businessmen. In 1917 he organized a commercial library at Manchester and in 1922 followed it with a technical library.

Jast's final practical contribution to librarianship was the mobile library. In 1931 he converted a former single-decker bus (he called it a "bibliobus") to provide a library service for Manchester's new housing projects.

Jast's interest in librarianship continued throughout his retirement, when his particular interests were library cooperation, professional education, and the need for a centralized cataloguing bureau. He died in Twickenham, Middlesex, on December 25, 1944.

Jast was a successful librarian who also had ambitions to become a successful author. His poetry and plays are of little merit, but he was an agreeable belletrist, and his professional writings were often spiced with genial witticisms.

Although Jast is undoubtedly an important figure in British library history, his achievements are not as fully appreciated as they should be. This is partly because the only biography of him is too slight to do him full justice and partly because he wrote no major work on librarianship and most of his best essays and speeches remain uncollected.

REFERENCES
There is a short biography of Jast: W. G. Fry and W. A. Munford, *Louis Stanley Jast: A Biographical Sketch* (1966).
There are numerous obituary appreciations in the *Library World* (1945) and several in the *Library Association Record* (1945). Collectively they provide an excellent likeness of a librarian who was highly esteemed.
There is a vivid account of Jast's work at Croydon in Ernest A. Savage, *A Librarian's Memories* (1952).
The best account of the library Jast planned at Manchester is the one by his successor as City Librarian, Charles Nowell, "Manchester Central Library," *Library Association Record* (1934).

JAMES G. OLLÉ

Jenkinson, Sir Hilary
(1882–1961)

Charles Hilary Jenkinson was founder and leader of the British archive profession.

He was born in London, November 2, 1882, and was educated at Dulwich College and at Pembroke College, Cambridge, being a Scholar of both. At Cambridge he was placed in the First Class of the Classical Tripos. In 1905 he sat the entrance examination for the Home Civil Service and was placed in the Public Record Office.

During his earlier years in the Office, Jenkinson worked mainly on medieval records (in particular those of the Exchequer of Receipt), reducing their chaos to order and developing, from study of their vicissitudes, the principles that he was later to expound for the administration of both ancient and modern records. From 1916 to 1920 he served as an Artillery Officer and on the General Staff, then returned to the direction and reorganization of the Literary Search Room (the "Round Room") that he had undertaken in 1912 and was to continue until 1929.

In 1922 he took charge of Repairs and Binding and, relinquishing the Round Room in 1929, took charge of the Repository. In these closely related fields his most important work as an Assistant Keeper was done. Under his direction the physical care of records—not only the skilled repair of damage and decay but also their prevention through proper conditions of storage—was developed to a craft and a science, and the two departments became a center of study, experiment, and teaching.

In 1938 Jenkinson was appointed Secretary of the Public Record Office, and as its principal administrator he devised and directed the wartime program of ARP (air raid precautions), of dispersal of records and staff to improvised repositories in the country, and of their return after 1945. In 1947 he became head of the Office as Deputy Keeper; though postwar shortages frustrated many of his plans, he was able, by establishing the "intermediate repository" at Hayes, to lay the foundations for the Records Administration Division, the Office's most significant postwar development.

Though Jenkinson's official career was distinguished, his extracurricular activities gave him his unique standing and reputation. From 1911 until 1935, and again in 1938 and 1949, he was Maitland Lecturer at Cambridge. From 1920 he was Lecturer, and from 1925 to 1947 Reader, in Diplomatic and English Archives in the University of London. During the same period he published, as Charles Johnson's collaborator, *English Court Hand* (1915) and independently *Palaeography and Court Hand* (also in 1915) and *The Later Court Hands in England* (1927). These lectures and writings established Jenkinson as a leading authority on palaeography and diplomatic, and as the exponent of a new theme, already latent in his notable work for the Surrey Record Society, that the study of administrative history is the key to all work on records.

The establishment in 1932 of the British Records Association carried Jenkinson's influence and reputation into wider fields. Jenkinson was a founder of the Association and, as its joint Honorary Secretary for 15 years and thereafter as Chairman of its Records Preservation Section, he personally drafted most of the Association's influential *Reports* and *Memoranda* and led the campaigns that, among other achievements, established the *National Register of Archives* and, ultimately, a nationwide network of local record offices, besides saving countless archives from destruction.

All Jenkinson's extraofficial activities that related to archives (and few did not) were undertaken with the same boundless energy and conviction. Jenkinson was the original and most persistent advocate of the postgraduate diploma in Archive Studies at University College, London. Halfway between the official and the personal, and as important as either, was Jenkinson's appointment in 1943 as Archives Adviser to the War Office, in which capacity he planned and in part directed the rescue and preservation of archives in the war zones of Italy and Germany. In Italy the operation was successful, but in Germany a much more extensive program was less so; in both countries his work served as the basis of postwar reconstruction and greatly augmented his international reputation.

Jenkinson was a prolific writer for print, though few of his publications were in book form. The monograph upon which his fame securely rests is the *Manual of Archive Administration,* first published in 1922. This treatise, the first and the latest to be based upon English experience and practice, became at once the authoritative guide to all British archivists. Revised, reissued, and supplemented but still not superseded, the *Manual* remains required reading for archivists everywhere. Nor is it any disservice to Jenkinson's memory to recall that Charles Johnson's *The Care of Documents* preceded the *Manual* by three years and that C. G. Crump's magisterial article "Record" in the *Encylopaedia Britannica* was published in the Eleventh Edition of 1911. These men, with M. S. Giuseppi, were the young Jenkinson's mentors. Jenkinson was the youngest of the brilliant group who deduced and defined the principles of archival administration in England. He made it his task to examine these principles, to expound them with his

own prophetic fervor, and to apply them in practice with a master's hand. No less he was the first of his English colleagues to perceive the relevance to native theory and practice of the manual of Müller, Feith, and Fruin, then accessible only in a French translation.

Jenkinson was a man abounding in energy, of mind and of body, most eloquent in all his causes and equally fertile of expedient. His Protean personality was not seen by all his contemporaries in the same guise; to an opponent Jenkinson could appear obstinate, unreasonable, devious. To those who enlisted under his banner Jenkinson was their most courageous, resourceful, and inspiring leader—able to evoke deep and lasting affection. In the years since his death in 1961 old differences have been laid to rest and his stature has steadily grown.

Jenkinson was made a Commander of the Order of the British Empire (CBE) in 1943 and was knighted as Sir Hilary in 1947. He was an Honorary Fellow of University College, London, and received the honorary degree of LL.D. from the University of Aberdeen, to whose library he left the greater part of his books. He was President of the Society of Archivists, of the Surrey Archaeological Society, of the Surrey Record Society, and of the Jewish Historical Society. He was a Vice-President of the British Records Association and an Honorary Member of the Society of American Archivists. From 1947 until his death he was a Commissioner of the Royal Commission on Historical Manuscripts.

Jenkinson died at Arun House, Horsham, Sussex, on March 15, 1961.

REFERENCES

A bibliography of Jenkinson's writings (1909–56) by Roger Ellis and William Kellaway is printed in *Studies Presented to Sir Hilary Jenkinson,* edited by J. Conway Davies (1957), which includes also an important *Memoir* (unsigned, by H. C. Johnson, later Keeper of Public Records). Further "Recollections of Sir Hilary Jenkinson," by Roger Ellis, are printed in *Journal of the Society of Archivists* (1971). Jenkinson's own small archive of personal papers is accessible at the Public Record Office.

ROGER ELLIS

Jewett, Charles Coffin
(1816–1868)

Charles Coffin Jewett's contributions to American librarianship are most durable. His career spanned the earliest days of the transition from the medieval to the modern in librarianship in America. Through his ingenuity and diligence, and his service in great institutions of national prominence in America, he was one of the founders of American librarianship. He was a logical thinker and was articulate in presenting his views. His perspicacity led to major innovations in librarianship that were proved of value in practice in three of the nation's leading libraries at their earliest period of modern growth. He helped crystallize the profession, and although he did not live to see the creation of the American Library Association in 1876, his support of the librarians' conference of 1853 was a catalyst for the permanent union.

Jewett was born in Lebanon, Maine, on August 12, 1816, one of several children of Paul Jewett, a

Charles Coffin Jewett

New England minister. One of Jewett's brothers, John, achieved fame as the publisher of *Uncle Tom's Cabin*. Little is recorded about Jewett's early life, but following family influence and the normal route to education and employment, Jewett set out to gain a college education and to join the ministry. He entered Dartmouth College in 1831 but quickly transferred to Brown University, his father's alma mater, from which Charles Jewett graduated in 1835. He served briefly as preceptor at Uxbridge Academy in Massachusetts. In fall 1837 he entered Andover Seminary.

Jewett early evinced an interest in books and bibliography. As a student at Brown he and a classmate, William Lawton Brown, arranged, classified, and catalogued a collection of books belonging to one of the student societies. At Andover he assisted Oliver Alden Taylor, the Librarian, in the preparation and publication of the *Catalogue of the Library of the Theological Seminary*; as a result he was appointed Acting Librarian of the Seminary. Upon his graduation he became the Principal of Day's Academy in Wrentham, Massachusetts, but a few months later, in 1841, left to become Librarian at Brown.

Jewett was Brown's first full-time Librarian. Prior to his appointment it had been usual for a professor to hold that post. Brown's library program, however, had been expanded by its President, Francis Wayland. With an endowment of $25,000 for books and a new building, which the library shared with the University's chapel, the library program was too demanding to be managed as a part-time activity.

Jewett's first major task was to prepare and publish a new catalogue. It followed the plan of the Andover catalogue, being divided into two parts: (1) an author listing and (2) an alphabetical and classified subject index with cross references. It took two years to complete and was widely acclaimed for its arrangement and careful preparation.

The catalogue done, Jewett turned his attention to building the library collection. He traveled extensively in Europe, buying books and pamphlets and collections not only for the University but also for a few scholarly friends who entrusted him with funds to use at his discretion. Jewett was judicious and prescient in his selections, and the Brown University Library became one of the leading academic research libraries of its time.

Perhaps as important as book buying was Jewett's effort to learn more about bibliography. He spent time in England with Anthony Panizzi, Keeper of Printed Books in the British Museum. It is evident from his letters that Jewett formed important opinions about national libraries, bibliography, and all of the then-modern aspects of library science in this part of his trip.

Jewett returned to Brown in 1845. His book-buying feat placed him in the ranks of the leading scholar-bibliographers of his day. He joined the faculty at Brown and became a very popular professor of modern languages and literature.

All during Jewett's formative years as a librarian, events were transpiring in Washington, D.C., that would lead inevitably to his move to national prominence there. From 1835 to 1846 Congress had been arguing over the manner in which it could achieve the goal of the will of an English scientist, James Smithson, to operate an institution to "increase and diffuse knowledge among men." The opinion in Congress was strongly divided into two camps, one proposing the creation of a national library and the other the establishment of a scientific research and study agency. This division of opinion was transferred to the Regents of the agency, to be known as the Smithsonian Institution, when it was finally created in 1846.

The proponents of science seemed to prevail, and the Regents' choice for its Secretary and first chief operating officer of the Institution was Joseph Henry, a professor at Princeton University and then America's leading scientist. Several of the U.S. senators who were strong proponents of a national library, and who had been active in obtaining the legislation to establish the Smithsonian, served on its first Board of Regents. They kept the issue of the future of the Institution alive by promoting the appointment of an assistant secretary qualified to be the Institution's Librarian. As one of the best known and most energetic of American librarians, Jewett was the Regents' choice, and he entered their service in 1847.

The Regents were persuaded that they had full authority to spend the Institution's funds as they thought appropriate and never authorized the maximum budget for the library as allowed by congressional action. They devoted most of the funds in the early days to the construction of the first Smithsonian building, much to the dismay of both Henry and Jewett. With his usual devotion, Jewett managed to complete a list of the publications of the learned societies of the world; he established gift and exchange relationships with most of them, and by 1855, regardless of inner turmoil, the Smithsonian had thus acquired probably the finest library collection of these publications in the country.

Most of Jewett's attention, however, was focused on a novel and colossal plan for a national, centralized library catalogue production facility. In Jewett's time libraries generally printed their catalogues. Jewett devised a plan whereby the libraries could produce their catalogues from stereotype plates made and kept at the Smithsonian. Cataloguing copy would be provided by libraries, but duplicate cataloguing could be avoided by sharing the plates. The Smithsonian proposed to do the collating of entries and the printing of the catalogues.

An obvious requirement for the success of such a venture was a set of standard cataloguing rules. Here Jewett's acquaintance with Panizzi emerged, for Jewett's rules were based on Panizzi's own cataloguing rules. Along the way, in order to know his market, Jewett prepared the first major inventory of public libraries in the United States. The Smithsonian published his *Notices of Public Libraries*, prepared from descriptions provided by the libraries themselves, as an appendix to the 1851 *Annual Report* of the Regents of the Smithsonian.

Jewett described his cataloguing plan to the librarians of the United States at the 1853 librarians' conference, which he chaired. He noted that his plan could be carried out only by an agency at the national level, and that it could not be successful without the endorsement and cooperation of other libraries. The conference unanimously adopted resolutions acknowledging the need expressed by Jewett and supporting his national cataloguing plan.

His plan came to naught, however. The materials from which the stereotype plates were made warped and hence could not be made into a suitable printing surface. Of greater consequence, however, was the unwillingness of the Secretary of the Smithsonian to commit the Institution and its resources to the effort required to sustain a national library operation. In the end, with Jewett's departure from the Smithsonian, the chief advocate for a national library was without the national platform required for operating such an important national program. Still, every element of shared cataloguing and of national distribution of cataloguing copy from Washington, D.C., as it was finally put into place by the Library of Congress nearly 50 years later, was laid out in Jewett's plan.

The relationship between Jewett and Henry was never easy. Jewett assumed that he had been employed by the Regents as their direct assistant to head an independent library department. He refused to help Henry with any general duties and carried on a campaign among friends to overrule Henry's intent to make the Institution the national home for scientific research and publication. By 1854 Henry could no longer tolerate Jewett's actions, and with the Regents' approval he dismissed Jewett (January, 1855).

Jewett remained prominent in American librarianship even after leaving the Smithsonian. He was employed at the Boston Public Library, first as a cataloguer, then as an acquisitions librarian, and finally as the Library's first Superintendent from 1858 until his death 10 years later. At the Boston Public Library Jewett applied himself with his characteristic conscience, devoting his ingenuity to the problems of his library. As usual, his solutions to several key problems served as models for innovations in other libraries. Among other things he replaced the circulation record book with separate slips for each book circulated, thus introducing flexibility and management control of collections into what was formerly a cumbersome function. Under Jewett's direction the Library grew to over 150,000 volumes, second in size only to the Library of Congress. Jewett died in Braintree, Massachusetts, on January 9, 1868.

REFERENCES

Joseph A. Borome, *Charles Coffin Jewett* (1951).

Michael H. Harris, *The Age of Jewett: Charles Coffin Jewett and American Librarianship, 1841–1868* (1975).

Michael H. Harris, "Jewett, Charles Coffin," *Dictionary of American Library Biography* (1978).

Geoffrey Hellman, *The Smithsonian: Octopus on the Mall* (1967).

RUSSELL SHANK

ALA
Carleton B. Joeckel

Joeckel, Carleton B.

(1886–1960)

Carleton Bruns Joeckel, library educator, administrator, and scholar, was a unique blend of practitioner and theoretician. In his research he never lost touch with the realities of his profession. As a teacher, he was distinguished by his ability not only to impart knowledge but also to maintain fruitful contact with his students. Joeckel bequeathed a twofold legacy to the library profession: his published works, which stand as a monument to his productive scholarship, and a generation of librarians imbued with his philosophy of free public library service for everyone.

Joeckel was born in Lake Mills, Wisconsin, January 2, 1886, and attended the University of Wisconsin, obtaining his A.B. degree in 1908. Joeckel entered the New York State Library School in 1908 and completed the B.L.S. degree in 1910. His library career began in 1910 as secretary to the Librarian of the St. Louis Public Library. In 1911 he moved to Berkeley, California, where he was Assistant Reference Librarian and Superintendent of Circulation of the University of California until 1914. Writing in 1936, Sidney B. Mitchell, Founder-Director of the University of California School of Librarianship, remembered young Joeckel as leaving "a permanent impression of a quick, alert body and mind, of a habit of not talking unnecessarily and of intolerance of vague, dreamy ideas and of shams of any kind." So favorable was Joeckel's impression on the Head of the University Extension Division (who was also Chairman of the Board of the Berkeley Public Library) that in 1914 he was offered the post of Librarian. Except for a two-year leave of absence (1917–19) for service in the Army in the United States and overseas, Joeckel remained Librarian until 1927.

According to Mitchell, during Joeckel's tenure,

> he put his library on the map, built up a professional staff, made it easy for his younger untrained college graduates to go to library school, encouraged ambitious members to try out their ideas, made it evident that a humanized as well as an efficient service was to be expected by his public, extended the service by new branches, built branch buildings, and secured the passage of a building fund for a main library building (since erected), even though a bond issue for new school buildings was defeated.

Joeckel's interest in the training of librarians developed during his years as Director of the Berkeley Public Library. In his first experience in teaching, he was a lecturer in public library administration in the unit that was to become the School of Librarianship of the University of California.

Joeckel's career took a new direction when in 1927 he left California for full-time teaching at the University of Michigan. Joining the faculty of the Department of Library Science as Associate Professor, he was promoted to Professor in 1930. He strengthened the teaching faculty, chiefly in the areas of library administration and book selection. His contract with the University included the opportunity to pursue advanced study in political science, which culminated with a Master's degree in 1928.

On receiving an ALA fellowship, Joeckel took a year's leave of absence for advanced study at the University of Chicago Graduate Library School (1933–34). After obtaining his doctorate in 1934, he resumed his teaching post at the University of Michigan for another year. In 1935 he joined the faculty of the University of Chicago Graduate Library School, where he remained the next 10 years.

During his Chicago years Joeckel's career flourished. The University of Chicago was the only institution in the country offering a doctoral program in librarianship at that time, and Joeckel's dissertation, *The Government of the American Public Library* (1935), was the first comprehensive study of the public library and governmental relations. This trail-blazing treatise won for Joeckel the confidence and respect of the professional library community. It laid to rest the skepticism of some practitioners who maintained that librarianship was not a sufficiently comprehensive field in which to pursue doctoral study. A perceptive observer of the American library scene and a supporter of the Ph.D. program in librarianship, Wilhelm Munthe, Director of the University of Oslo Library, asserted, "This treatise alone is sufficient documentary evidence in justifying the existence of the [Graduate Library] school," since it "placed American library research on a higher plane."

Joeckel quickly became immersed in the spirit of research and publication that pervaded the University. Beginning in 1937 Joeckel, in collaboration with faculty colleague Leon Carnovsky, undertook a survey of the Chicago Public Library and documented the findings and recommendations in *A Metropolitan Library in Action* (1940). Their report was hailed as "a source book on the methodology of public library research" because it provided a framework for an objective approach to the study of problems in public libraries of all sizes. In 1938 Joeckel's report *Library Service,* prepared for President Franklin D. Roosevelt's Advisory Committee on Education, was released by the U.S. Government Printing Office.

Joeckel's expertise in the theory and practice of librarianship brought him in 1940 an invitation from the newly appointed Librarian of Congress, Archibald MacLeish, to serve as Chairman of the Librarian's Committee, whose charge was to make a comprehensive survey of the processing departments of the Library of Congress. MacLeish characterized the confidential report submitted by the Committee that Joeckel chaired as "one of the most important documents in the history of the Library." He used the recommendations of the Committee as the framework for a complete reorganization of the processing operations.

Of the many facets of librarianship to which Joeckel gave his attention there was none that he believed in more firmly or advocated more ardently that the concept of larger units of library service. As early as 1929 he had introduced this concept, an audacious one at that time, at the annual meeting of the Michigan Library Association. Three years later he put this perspective into sharp focus in a provocative address given before the ALA Council and published in the ALA *Bulletin* (1933):

> The typical public library unit is still so small and weak as to be seriously lacking in administrative efficiency, and the area it serves is unnecessarily circumscribed. . . . [The librarian] has been so absorbed in the library problems of his own town or city that he has overlooked the fascinating possibilities of expansion of the units of library service. . . . Sweeping changes in the complicated structure of local government are being recommended on all sides. The public library must adapt itself to them.

Throughout his career, Joeckel was actively involved in professional organizations. Recognition of his charismatic leadership came early in his career, as evidenced by the offices he held. He served as President of the California Library Association (1919–20) and of the Michigan Library Association (1930–31). He was a member of the Illinois Library Association's Executive Board (1935–45) and of the American Library Institute (1937–45). Joeckel joined the American Library Association in 1910, the year in which he

graduated from the New York State Library School. Although he was to participate in many committee activities during the next 40 years, probably the most constructive were those of the Federal Relations Committee and of the Post-War Planning Committee, of which he was Chairman.

A staunch champion of federal aid to libraries, Joeckel advocated a nationwide program of library service to be funded jointly by the federal, state, and local governments. "Without federal aid," Joeckel wrote with characteristic forthrightness, "the establishment of a national minimum standard of library service is quite simply and literally impossible."

Joeckel played a major role in the establishment in 1937 of the Library Services Division in the Office of Education, the first federal agency established with the specific responsibility for fostering a national program of library development. He was the motivating force behind the passage of the Library Services Act in 1956.

As Chairman of the Post-War Planning Committee, Joeckel was the chief architect of the *ALA Post-War Standards for Public Libraries* (ALA, 1943) and (with Amy Winslow) the author of *A National Plan for Public Library Service* (ALA, 1948), prepared for the Committee on Post-War Planning.

Some of Joeckel's most significant writing appeared as papers in the proceedings of library institutes: "Realities of Regionalism" in *Library Trends* (papers presented before the GLS Institute, 1938); "Library Extension Today" in *Library Extension: Problems and Solutions* (papers presented before the GLS Institute, 1946); and "Service Outlets as the Reader Sees Them" in *Reaching Readers: Techniques of Extending Library Services* (papers presented at the Library Institute sponsored by the University of California School of Librarianship and the ALA Library Extension Division, 1947). A noteworthy article entitled "National Leadership from Washington," written in collaboration with Willard O. Mishoff, appeared in *The Library of Tommorrow* (ALA, 1939).

Joeckel's editorial accomplishments were also impressive. They include: *Current Issues in Library Administration* (papers presented before the GLS Institute, 1938), *Library Extension, Reaching Readers, Post-War Standards for Public Libraries,* and his contributions to *The Library Quarterly* as Associate Editor from 1936 to 1945 and as Advisory Editor from 1946 to 1959.

Through his extensive writings and other professional activities, Joeckel made a notable impact on the American library scene in the 1930s and 1940s, but he contributed most significantly to the library profession through his teaching and his influence on his students. From his initial venture into teaching at the University of California in the 1920s to his return to the Berkeley campus in the mid-1940s, Joeckel concerned himself mainly with his students. His intellectual vigor and personal integrity earned their respect; his appealing and vibrant personality won their affection. A demanding professor, Joeckel expected his students to measure up to his standards. His seminars were stimulating experiences, challenging his students to critical thinking. Joeckel was major professor to many doctoral candidates who went out in all directions from Chicago to assume positions of high professional responsibility.

With the retirement of Louis Round Wilson in 1942, Joeckel was appointed Dean of the Graduate Library School, and Leon Carnovsky, a faculty colleague, was appointed Assistant Dean. In spite of war-born personnel shortages, Joeckel maintained the School's traditional strength in advanced seminars, research, and publishing. During his deanship he sponsored three summer institutes: The Library in the Community (1943); Library Extension: Problems and Solutions (1944); and Personnel Administration in Libraries (1945).

To carry out his plan of devoting some of his later years to research and writing, Joeckel resigned from his administrative post at GLS in 1945 and returned to Berkeley. Still vigorous in health, Joeckel resumed academic pursuits at the University of California by joining the faculty as Professor of Librarianship. Four years later ill health forced him to take a leave of absence, and one year later, in 1950, he retired for a second time.

Recognition of Joeckel's professional accomplishments came in the form of various honors. The American Library Association conferred upon him the first James Terry White Award for his notable professional writing (in 1938) and the Joseph W. Lippincott Award for his distinguished service to the profession (in 1958). Honorary life membership in the Association was conferred upon him in 1954. He died April 15, 1960, in Oakland, California.

REFERENCE

Thomas S. Harding, "Joeckel, Carleton Bruns," *Dictionary of American Library Biography* (1978).

MARY LUELLA POWERS
(d. 1983)

Jones, Virginia Lacy
(1912-1984)

Virginia Lacy Jones, library educator and professional leader, received many testimonies to her status in the field of library science, including the American Library Association's Melvil Dewey Award in 1973 and the Joseph W. Lippincott Award in 1977. Other recognitions indicate her profound influence on the profession as a whole. In August 1979 she was honored by the University of Michigan with a special citation for her contributions to library education. In 1980 she received the Beta Phi Mu Award and the Mary Rothrock Award. In 1981 she was cited by the Southeastern Library Association for her contributions to that organization and to the region.

Jones was born on June 25, 1912, in Cincinnati, Ohio, the daughter of Edward and Ellen Louise Parker Lacy. Her family moved shortly thereafter to Clarksburg, West Virginia, where she attended public schools. Her junior and senior high school years were spent in St. Louis, where she was sent to facilitate her entry into Stowe Teachers College. Instead of following that plan, she entered Hampton Institute in Virginia, from which she received the Bachelor of Science degree in Library Science (1933) and in Education (1936).

Her professional experience was begun at Louisville (Kentucky) Municipal College, the Negro branch of the University of Louisville. There she met Rufus E. Clement, President of the college, who was to have a significant influence on her career. In 1937

Virginia Lacy Jones

she received the first of two General Education Board fellowships which allowed her to complete her Master's degree at the University of Illinois (1938) and later her Ph.D. at the University of Chicago (1945). She was the second Afro-American to be awarded a doctor's degree in library science.

When Clement moved to Atlanta University (Georgia) as President, in 1938, he offered Jones a position as cataloguer if she would leave Louisville. She moved to Atlanta University and became a part of Clement's plan to replace the recently closed Hampton Institute Library School. Thus she became involved in the planning that led to the opening of the Atlanta University School of Library Service in 1941. She served on the faculty until 1945, when she was appointed Dean.

Her other positions included supervision of the Prairie View Regional Summer Training Center for Librarians, one of four sponsored by the General Education Board from 1936 to 1939. She was instrumental in spearheading, along with Ann Rucker, the establishment of the Library Section of the Kentucky Negro Education Association. Following her move to Atlanta, she worked in concert with Mollie Huston Lee of Raleigh, North Carolina, and Charlemae Rollins of the Chicago Public Library to raise the awareness of publishers about the negative images of Afro-Americans that appeared in many children's books. She also assisted in the establishment of a Field Service Program under the sponsorship of the Carnegie Corporation of New York that brought consultant services to libraries serving Afro-Americans in several southeastern states.

She served four terms as a member of the American Library Association Council and one term on its Executive Board. She also served as Secretary-Treasurer of the Association of American Library Schools (AALS) 1948–54, and as a member of its Board of Directors, 1960–64. She was AALS President in 1967. She became active with Beta Phi Mu (library science honorary society) and with other associations and projects related to library science. Other activities included work with the National Endowment for the Humanities, the Southern Association of Colleges and Schools, the Atlanta Area Teacher Education Service, and other professional and service organizations. She was a member of Delta Sigma Theta Sorority and of the NAACP.

On November 27, 1941, she was married to Edward Allen Jones, a professor of modern languages at Morehouse College.

She retired from the deanship of the Atlanta University School of Library Services in December 1981. From January 1982 through December 1983, she served as Director of the Robert W. Woodruff Library of Atlanta University Center. She died in Atlanta on December 3, 1984.

REFERENCES

Two autobiographical accounts of the life of Virginia Lacy Jones give excellent, though brief, insights into her life and work: "A Dean's Career," *The Black Librarian in America,* edited by E. J. Josey (1970); *Reminiscences in Library and Library Education,* a pamphlet published by the University of Michigan School of Library Science (1979) when she was awarded an honorary doctorate.

Obituaries were published in *American Libraries* (January 1985) and in *Black Caucus Newsletter* (December 1984).

ALBERT P. MARSHALL

Jordan

Jordan, a constitutional monarchy in southwest Asia, is surrounded by Syria on the north, Iraq on the east, Saudi Arabia on the east and south, the Gulf of Aqaba on the south, and Israel on the west. Population (1984 est.) 2,521,000; area (including Israeli-occupied territory from the 1967 war) 95,396 sq.km. The official language is Arabic.

History. Jordan was established in 1917, after the collapse of the Ottoman Empire. Through its association with the Ommayad, Abbassid, and Ottoman Empires, it has a rich cultural history. However, not a single public library was established until the British mandate ended in 1948. In 1955 Unesco studied library service in the country, and in 1956 the first Jordanian was sent abroad to study library science.

National Library. In 1977 the Department of Libraries, Documentation and Archives was founded to establish a national library and prepare divisions to deal with archives, documents, copyright and legal deposit, national bibliography, and a union catalogue. It has 25 staff and 16,000 volumes in its library. Until then Jordan had regulations covering the delivery of copies of all new publications to the Department of Publications at the Ministry of Information as part of its Publications Law, not legal deposit. The Jordan Library Association began registering works published in Jordan in annual lists starting in 1969. The *Bulletin of Arab Publications,* issued annually by the Arab League Educational, Cultural and Scientific Organization, lists the Arabic titles that make up Jordanian book production for any year.

Academic Libraries. The principal academic library is the Jordanian University Library, established in 1962. Its general collection numbers about 330,000 volumes and 2,700 current periodicals. The University Library is a depository for all publications issued by the UN, the Food and Agriculture Organization, and the World Health Organization. Monthly accession lists have been issued since 1969. The Bethlehem University Library, established on the West Bank in 1973, is administered by Jordanian authorities. It has a collection of 100,000 volumes. There is a university library in Irbid.

Public Libraries. Noteworthy among municipal public libraries is the one in the capital city of Amman, founded in 1960. The book collections total about 80,000 volumes in Arabic and English, some 574 current periodicals (25 for children), 1,400 Jordanian publications, 900 Palestinian case volumes, and 850 Unesco documents. It houses separate sections for children and the blind. The second major public library in Jordan is in the city of Irbid; it was founded in 1957 and possesses about 30,000 volumes.

School Libraries. The Library Section of the Ministry of Education serves school libraries in the country. Only the major secondary schools possess libraries with modest book collections. They do not have standardized procedures, furniture, and equipment. Most school libraries are managed by personnel without professional qualifications.

Special Libraries. About 25 special libraries were founded in the 1960s and 1970s, mainly in Amman. They serve the wide interests of researchers, scholars, and government officials in the country. Noteworthy are those of the Royal Scientific Society (founded in 1970), the Institute of Public Administration (1968), the Center of Building Materials (1973), the Industrial Development Bank (1969), the Jordanian Central Bank (1964), the Chambers of Commerce (1962), the National Planning Council (1965), the Ministry of National Economics (1967), the Authority of National Resources (1966), the Ministry of Industry and Commerce (1966), the Ministry of Finance (1973), and the Jordanian Petroleum Refinery Company (1962). The British Council Library, established in 1950, is the largest special library (17,100 volumes and 125 current periodicals).

A National Documentation Centre was established under the responsibility of the Ministry of Culture and Youth in Amman in 1975. The Ministry of Education established the Educational Documentation and Publication Centre to serve educators, researchers, students, administrators, and foreign organizations. Both documentation centers offer local consultation, loan, SDI, translation, preparation of bibliographies, and inquiry services through traditional methods.

The Profession. The Jordan Library Association (JLA) was founded in 1963. Considered the most active professional library association in the Arab world, it collects documents, publishes bibliographies and directories, and organizes training programs and seminars. JLA disseminates professional information through a quarterly library journal, *Rissalat Al-Maktaba,* issued since 1965. The Association published a directory of libraries in Jordan and an adaptation of the Anglo-American Cataloging Rules in 1970. The *Palestinian-Jordanian Bibliography,* compiled by the JLA, was published annually as one issue of its journal from 1970. The *Bibliography* is considered the national bibliography of Jordan.

MOHAMED M. EL HADI*

Libraries in Jordan (1981)

Type	Administrative units	Service points	Volumes in collections	Annual expenditures (dinar)	Population served[a]	Professional staff	Total staff
National	1	--	16,500	--	350	--	20
Academic	--	--	--	--	--	--	--
Public	1	3	70,000	5,013,852,000	--	60	1,261
School	--	--	--	--	--	--	--

[a]Registered borrowers.

Source: Unesco, *Statistical Yearbook,* 1984.

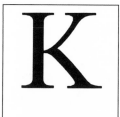

Kampuchea

Kampuchea (the Khmer Republic, formerly Cambodia) is a republic of Southeast Asia in the southwest part of the Indochinese Peninsula. It is bounded on the southwest by the Gulf of Thailand, on the west and northwest by Thailand, on the northeast by Laos, and on the east and southeast by Vietnam. Population (1984 est.) 6,118,000; area 181,035 sq.km. The official language is Khmer; French is widely spoken.

History. During the four-year period of Communist rule (1975-79) and after the Vietnamese conquest of Kampuchea in 1979, library services were reportedly effectively eliminated. There was no evidence that any were functioning at the end of the 1970s. The University of Phnom Penh was reported totally inactive in April 1979. Several public and university libraries, as well as collections in museums and temples, were destroyed. The libraries described here were in operation before 1975.

National Library. The Archives et Bibliothèque Nationales was founded in 1923 in Phnom Penh as a national deposit library that housed more than 31,000 volumes. An ordinance of 1956 required publishers to deposit five copies of all works published there. Printers were obliged to deposit three copies. No law required that every administrative document be forwarded to the National Archives, although a decree of 1918 required public departments to deposit such documents periodically. Some departments did not deposit their documents.

No national bibliography was established for Kampuchea, although the National Archives and Library compiled catalogues of its holdings, including books, pamphlets, official publications, university dissertations and theses, maps, atlases, and standards.

A national exchange center, the Bibliothèque centrale in Phnom Penh, was created in 1972 to collect works in all fields of knowledge and to establish contacts with foreign libraries. An exchange system was developed among the university libraries, which included the Université des Beaux-Arts, the Université de Phnom Penh, the Université Bouddhique, the Université des Sciences Agronomiques, and the Université Technique, all in Phnom Penh.

Other Libraries. The Bibliothèque de l'Institut Bouddhique, founded in 1923 in Phnom Penh, housed books and manuscripts in French, English, Thai, Burmese, Sinhalese, Chinese, Tibetan, and Mongolian, as well as documents in Khmer and Pali on Khmer folklore and Buddhism. The library built a collection of about 40,000 volumes and 16,200 manuscripts on palm leaves.

The Institut national de la statistique et des recherches économiques, founded in 1963 in Phnom Penh under the Ministère du Plan, became a documentation center holding more than 300 volumes. The Institut compiled national and international statistical and economic data and published the *Bulletin trimestriel de statistique, Annuaire statistique,* and *Comptes economiques.*

The Library of the Association des écrivains khmers, founded in 1962 in Phnom Penh, housed 4,525 volumes. The association was created to aid writers and promote literature in the Khmer language; it published a monthly literary review. There was no official library association, although a govern-mental department, the Office national de planification et de développement des bibliothèques, was established in 1975 to coordinate library and archival activity in Cambodia.

PETER A. POOLE*

Kenya

Kenya, an independent republic in eastern Africa, is bounded by Sudan and Ethiopia on the north, Somalia and the Indian Ocean on the east, Tanzania on the south, and Uganda on the west. Population (1984 est.) 19,536,000; area 590,367 sq.km. The official languages are Swahili and English.

History. The first recorded library in Kenya was established in 1916 by the Department of Agriculture. It was used by both officials and farmers. Other government departments then established their own libraries. The McMillan Library was a private library until 1962, when it was taken over by the Nairobi City Council. It housed a collection of 55,000 volumes, and for the first time was open to Africans. Institutions of higher education developed in the 1950s and 1960s, foremost among these being the Royal College (later the University of Nairobi). In 1984 Kenya hosted the IFLA conference in Nairobi.

National Library Service. Although Kenya has no national library in the conventional meaning of the term, the Kenya National Library Service (KNLS) runs a nationwide public library service with headquarters in Nairobi. In the early 1980s this headquarters library housed about 19,000 volumes. Most scholarly researchers use the University of Nairobi Library Service. Both libraries are legal depositories for Kenyan publications.

Academic Libraries. The major academic library is the University of Nairobi Library Service, comprising the main university library and eight sublibraries in the various campuses of the university. The main library covers commerce, social sciences, humanities, and engineering; libraries on other campuses serve the sciences, medicine, agriculture, and veterinary medicine. The total bookstock in 1981 was about 270,000 volumes and about 3,500 current periodical titles.

Kenyatta University College is a separate but constituent college of the University of Nairobi, housing the Faculty of Education. The bookstock of its library was approximately 140,000 volumes with 2,000 periodical titles.

There are in addition academic libraries of various sizes in the main postsecondary training institutions such as Egerton College (agriculture), Kenya Institute of Administration, Kenya Polytechnic, Kenya Science Teachers College, Kenya Technical Teachers College, and Mombasa Polytechnic.

Public Libraries. The KNLS operates libraries in the country and planned to start two new libraries each year until there was one in each of Kenya's 50 districts and municipalities. The bookstock of the entire Service in 1981 was about 511,000 volumes.

The Nairobi City Council operates a separate City Library Service with a main library and two branches. Other libraries open to the public are operated by foreign missions, notably the American Library in Nairobi; the British Council libraries in Kisumu, Mombasa, and Nairobi; and the French, German, and Indian information or cultural centers in Nairobi. Their stocks range from 7,000 to 16,000 volumes.

School Libraries. Expenses for formal education consume 30 percent of the country's annual budget, but the majority of schools suffer from shortages and their libraries have suffered as well. There is no organized national school library service. Of nearly 1,400 secondary schools, only about 30 percent are maintained or assisted with government grants. The older and larger libraries have 6,000 to 10,000 volumes, and many of the others have small classroom collections. The majority of the rest are Harambee (self-help) Schools, and most have no libraries at all. Practically none of the 8,500 primary schools have libraries, although some maintain small classroom collections. St. George's Primary School in Nairobi is a notable exception.

Students rely heavily on the KNLS, which has libraries in some district centers and all provincial capitals. In Nairobi the headquarters library is used extensively by students. Two provinces—Nairobi and Nyeri—provide book-box services to some schools: for a fee paid to KNLS, the schools borrow as many as 200 books at a time. These two provinces, along with Eldoret, Embu, Kisumu, and Mombasa, operate bookmobiles to serve schools in rural areas.

All primary teacher training institutions have libraries, although their sizes vary greatly, from 2,000 volumes in the smallest to 18,000 in the largest. The Kenya Institute of Education Library assists in arranging short courses for staff running libraries in schools and teacher training colleges.

Special Libraries. The *Directory of Libraries in Kenya* (1977) listed 55 special libraries, mainly in ministries and departments of government, research organizations, and training institutions of various kinds. One of the largest and oldest is the Ministry of Agriculture Library, with more than 70,000 volumes and 800 periodicals. Other notable special libraries are those in the Central Bureau of Statistics; High Court Library; Kenya Agricultural Research Institute; Mines and Geology Department; National Archives; National Public Health Laboratories; and Veterinary Research Laboratories. Collections ranged from more than 25,000 to more than 85,000 volumes.

International organizations with offices in and around Nairobi have established libraries, including the United Nations Environment Programme (UNEP), the International Laboratory for Research on Animal Disease (ILRAD), and the International Centre of Insect Physiology and Ecology (ICIPE). First established in the 1970s as modest collections, they have grown rapidly and their holdings are of great importance.

The Profession. The East African Library Association was formed in 1956, with most members located in Nairobi. In 1962 it began publishing the *East African Library Association Bulletin,* and in 1964 branches were formed in Uganda and Tanzania. At a 1972 conference it was decided that the East African Library Association should be disbanded and that each country should organize its own national association. The Kenya Library Association was founded in 1973.

At that time membership was open to all individuals and institutions connected with the administration and management of libraries or interested in the Association's aims and objectives. But in 1982 it became a strictly professional association, with a new constitution, hoping to advance professional standards more effectively. Voting rights were limited to professionals. KLA publishes a journal entitled *Maktaba* (the Kiswahili word for "libraries") and had 131 individual and 46 institutional members (1980).

REFERENCE
Anna-Britta Wallenius, *Libraries in East Africa* (1971).
JOHN NDEGWA*

Keppel, Frederick Paul
(1875–1943)

Frederick Paul Keppel, foundation administrator, was a leading figure in the growth of American libraries.

Keppel was born July 2, 1875, in Staten Island, New York, and spent most of his early years in Yonkers, New York, where he attended the public schools. His parents, Frederick and Frances Keppel, were Irish immigrants. Upon completing high school, he worked for two years in his father's print-selling shop and then entered Columbia University, graduating with an outstanding academic record in 1898. He obtained a position with Harper and Broth-

Libraries in Kenya (1981)

Type	Administrative units	Service points	Volumes in collections	Annual expenditures (shilling)	Population served[a]	Professional staff	Total staff
National[b]	1	1	19,000	765,000	- -	26	300
Academic[c]	1	8	270,000	69,000[d]	6,700	- -	127
Public[b]	2	14	511,000	835,000	97,387	28	349
School	- -	- -	- -	- -	- -	- -	- -

[a]Registered borrowers.
[b]National and public library are both organs of the Kenya National Library Services.
[c]University of Nairobi only.
[d]Acquisitions only.

Source: Unesco, *Statistical Yearbook,* 1984.

Frederick Paul Keppel

Carnegie Corporation of New York

ers in the same year but thought himself unsuited for the publishing field.

In 1900 he took a position as Assistant Secretary at Columbia University, rapidly advancing to Secretary of the University in 1902 and then to the deanship of Columbia College in 1910. Wanting to serve his country in World War I but too old at 42 to volunteer for military service, Keppel went to Washington as a confidential clerk in the War Department. His administrative talents and ability to deal with people tactfully were quickly noticed by his superiors, and within a year he was made Third Assistant Secretary of War. After the war he held administrative posts with the American Red Cross (1919–20), in Paris with the International Chamber of Commerce (1920–22), and for a brief period as Secretary of the Plan of New York. In December 1922 he was elected President of Carnegie Corporation of New York but did not actually assume his duties until October 1923.

Keppel was the fourth President of Carnegie Corporation of New York, an educational philanthropy whose name is closely associated with the early growth of libraries in the United States and abroad and with the nurturing and development of the library profession.

His earlier positions had given Keppel the understanding and skills to shape the foundation's policy, philosophy, and programs for the 18 years he was President, 1923–41. Because the Carnegie staff was quite small, he made extensive use of outside advisers and expertise. He was frank, but warm and courteous, concise, and a persuasive speaker, and he hated bores. He rarely put off decisions. His grantmaking was sometimes criticized for ranging too widely and not demonstrating any particular strategy, but he saw his role as being the administrator of a public trust, which made it incumbent upon him to dispense allocations in a variety of subject areas and projects and to do so fairly and representatively.

Libraries, particularly public libraries, he saw as among the major facilities for lifelong learning. Although he did not initiate the Corporation's relationship with the American Library Association, Keppel depended heavily on ALA to identify needs and to develop programs that would enhance librarianship and service to the public. Andrew Carnegie had

started that relationship and actually gave the Association its original endowment grant of $100,000 in 1902. During Keppel's tenure $86,000,000 was given away; of that amount, approximately $30,000,000 went for library projects, and more than $3,000,000 of that went directly to ALA for its activities. Included in this sum were additional endowment grants of $2,000,000 (paid 1926–33). This kind of support for the Association and for a diverse group of library projects was part of the Corporation's long view regarding libraries.

Three commissioned evaluative reports, two by well-known and respected scholars Alvin S. Johnson and Charles C. Williamson and one by Carnegie staff member William S. Learned, contributed immeasurably to the Corporation's ultimate decision to revise its giving policy with respect to libraries. Johnson's 1919 report carried the recommendation that the Corporation cease providing assistance to communities for the construction of library buildings and that funds instead be made available for upgrading the training of librarians and for improving services. Williamson examined the training of librarians and concluded that they needed university training instead of that provided by public libraries, and that a library school should be established to offer graduate-level courses. Learned specifically recommended that the ALA expand its services to librarians and that the foundation finance demonstration projects that would represent innovations in library service, particularly to rural communities. Accordingly, the Corporation provided the funds to set up the first graduate school of library science, at the University of Chicago in 1926, with an endowment grant of $1,000,000. It made grants for training for librarianship, for book purchases to colleges and universities, for various kinds of experimental service projects, and for the development of other library schools. The ALA, assisted by Keppel, worked closely with the colleges and other organizations to implement many of these other programs and to strengthen the Association itself.

After retiring from the Corporation in 1941, Keppel became a member of the War Relief Control Board in Washington and still later a member of the Board of Appeals on Visa Cases at the Department of State. He remained as an educational consultant to the foundation.

Throughout his life Keppel gave innumerable speeches and lectures and wrote many books. His published works include *Columbia* (1914), *The Undergraduate and His College* (1917), *Education for Adults and Other Essays* (1926), *The Foundation* (1930), *The Arts in American Life,* with R. L. Duffus (1933), and *Philanthropy and Learning* (1936). He received honorary degrees from a number of distinguished colleges and universities including Harvard, Columbia, Michigan, Pittsburgh, and Toronto.

Keppel died September 8, 1943, in New York City.

REFERENCES

Florence Anderson, *Carnegie Corporation Library Program, 1911–1961* (1963).

Peggy A. Sullivan, "Keppel, Frederick Paul," *Dictionary of American Library Biography* (1978).

GLORIA PRIMM BROWN

Kesavan, B. S.

(1909-)

Bellary Shamanna Kesavan, Indian library educator and administrator, was Librarian of the National Library, Calcutta, 1947–62, and first Director of the Indian National Scientific Documentation Centre (INSDOC), New Delhi, 1963–69.

Kesavan was born on May 10, 1909, in Mylapore, Madras, India. He was educated in Mysore and London, where he took an M.A. in English Literature at the University of London and earned a Diploma in Librarianship at the School of Librarianship and Archives, University College, London. He also had advanced training in Sanskrit and German.

Kesavan taught English at Mysore University (1929–44) and was Assistant Secretary of the Council of Scientific and Industrial Research (CSIR) in New Delhi, 1944–46. He served as educational adviser to the Ministry of Education in New Delhi in 1946 and 1947. Kesavan provided outstanding leadership to the Indian library and information community for more that two decades. The two national institutions he headed, the National Library in Calcutta and INSDOC, provide evidence of his skill for building and organization.

From 1947 to 1962 the National Library was developed from a mere storehouse of books to an active organization with national stature and international recognition. Apart from the tremendous growth of the document collection through purchase, gift, exchange, and deposit, and the generation of new services for users, the retrospective bibliographical projects of the National Library for such subjects as Indian anthropology, Indian botany, and Indian literature were significant contributions. Another important bibliographic project that was planned and brought out under the editorship of Kesavan for the Sahitya Akademi was the selective retrospective bibliography of books published from 1901 to 1953 on humanities in all the principal languages of India, including English.

Another achievement was the launching, in 1956, of the *Indian National Bibliography of Current Indian Publications,* a landmark in India's bibliographic history.

Kesavan's other major contribution was the development of INSDOC, which was established by CSIR with technical support from Unesco. In 1963 he became the first Director of INSDOC, which was until then under the administrative control of the National Physical Laboratory. Kesavan went about his new task with imagination and creativeness. The initiation of the National Science Library, the vigorous effort for the compilation of the *National Union Catalogue* of scientific serials to integrate and consolidate national resources and to create a computerized database, starting of an advanced training course in documentation and reprography, the publication of *Indian Science Abstracts,* development of programs to introduce computer-based information services, providing improved facilities for printing and reprographic services, building up translation potential, and setting up of the INSDOC Regional Centre at Bangalore were some of the major contributions during his tenure from 1963 to 1969.

He also gave leadership, direction, and advice to the development of library documentation and information services in CSIR laboratories and many research and development institutions, universities, and public sector undertakings. In effect he sowed seedlings for a national information system for science and technology.

Kesavan's international activities were also distinguished. He was the Vice-President of the International Federation of Documentation from 1964 to 1966, a member of the International Advisory Committee on Bibliography, Documentation, and Terminology of Unesco, and a member of the Expert Committee for Organizing the Library and Documentation Division in Unesco. He directed the Unesco Regional Seminar on the Development of National Libraries in Asia and the Pacific Area at Manila in February 1964.

Among his publications are a book on the national library (1961) and a small monograph on *Documentation in India* (1969), an abridged version of which was published in *Library Trends* (1969).

After retirement from his official career in 1969, Kesavan served international organizations such as the United Nations Development Programme and the World Health Organization. For publication by the National Book Trust of India, New Delhi, and under the auspices of the Indian Council of Social Science Research, New Delhi, he undertook preparation of a five-volume work, *The History of Printing and Publications in India: a Study of Cultural Reawakening.* The first volume was published in 1984.

T. N. RAJAN

Khurshid, Anis

(1926-)

Anis Khurshid, Pakistani librarian and educator, dominated the Pakistani library scene for more than 30 years and did much to promote and shape the development of Pakistani libraries.

He was born in Kamptee, India, on March 21, 1926. Khurshid started his career in librarianship in 1954 when he joined the Karachi University Library. He received a post-graduate diploma in library science from Karachi University and a Master's degree in Library Science from Rutgers University. He started teaching in the Department of Library Science, University of Karachi, in 1959 and served as Chairman of the Department from 1962 to 1964. He received an advanced certificate and a Ph.D. in Library and Information Science from the University of Pittsburgh in 1969. His dissertation ("Standards for Library Education in Burma, Ceylon, India and Pakistan") represents a landmark investigation in the field of librarianship.

From 1966 to 1969 he worked as Librarian of the International Library Information Center, University of Pittsburgh, an assignment that gave him an opportunity to learn more about librarianship in various parts of the world. On his return to Karachi, he put new life in the Library Science Department and served as Associate Professor from 1970 to 1979. From 1972 to 1975 he was Chairman of the Department. From 1979 he served Karachi University as Professor and Chairman of the Department of Library and Information Science.

University of Karachi, Pakistan
Anis Khurshid

419

Khurshid wrote several books dealing with various aspects of library science. They include *Cataloguing of Pakistani Names* (1964); *Standards for Library Education in Burma, Ceylon, India and Pakistan* (1969); *What Children Read: a Survey* (1976); and *The State of Library Resources in Pakistan* (1982). Khurshid edited many books, including reviews and *Shafi Dewey Decimal Expansions for Oriental Studies* (in Urdu; 1977); *Quaid-i-Azam Mohammad Ali Jinnah: An Annotated Bibliography* (1979); and *Library Education Across the Boundaries of Cultures: a Festschrift* (1981). Khurshid also contributed to various reference and professional publications.

Khurshid participated actively in the professional associations on local, national, and international levels. He was the founding chairman of the Karachi University Library Science Alumni Association (1957–58) and Editor of its journal, *Pakistan Library Review* (1958–62). He organized several annual conferences of the Pakistan Library Association and edited their proceedings. His other posts included Technical Chairman, Unesco Survey on Reading Habits in Pakistan (1972–73) and member, Standing Committee of Sind Educational Council (1973–); he chaired the University Grants Commission (UGC) Curriculum Revision Committee for Library Science (1979–80), the Intermediate Curriculum Committee for Library Science (1981), and the Technical Working Group for Development of a National Public Library System in Pakistan (1982–84). He also chaired the International Federation of Library Associations' Subgroup on South Asia (1976–78).

His wide range of contributions in library work, teaching, research, and writing, including comparative librarianship, qualify him for consideration as one of the outstanding librarians of his generation in the world.

NAIMUDDIN QURESHI

Kilgour, Frederick G.
(1914–)

Frederick Gridley Kilgour, library administrator, lecturer, writer, and editor, is best known as the father of OCLC—the national shared cataloguing system that pointed to a new era in librarianship.

Kilgour was born January 6, 1914, in Springfield, Massachusetts. He entered Harvard College in 1931 and received his baccalaureate degree four years later. In his senior year at Harvard he was appointed Circulation Assistant in the Widener Library, where he remained for seven years, eventually becoming Chief of the division. During the latter summers of this period he attended the School of Library Service at Columbia University.

Called to war duty in 1942, Kilgour moved to Washington, D.C., where, except for overseas service, he remained for almost six years. Until 1945 he served in the Office of Strategic Services as Executive Secretary of the Interdepartmental Committee for the Acquisition of Foreign Publications, attaining the naval rank of lieutenant (j.g.) and earning the Legion of Merit. For the following three years he was Deputy Director of the Office of Intelligence Collection and Dissemination in the U.S. Department of State.

In 1948 Kilgour returned to academic life. He

Arthur Plotnik
Frederick G. Kilgour

became Librarian of the Yale University School of Medicine, a position he held until 1965. During those years he wrote and lectured extensively in both librarianship and the history of science and technology and became active in the Medical Library Association (Secretary-Treasurer, 1950–52), the American Library Association, and other professional organizations. In 1961 he was a prime mover in one of the major early library automation efforts, the Columbia-Harvard-Yale Medical Libraries Computerization Project. As Yale's first Associate University Librarian for Research and Development between 1965 and 1967, he oversaw that library's entry into automation studies and processes.

OCLC. In 1967 Kilgour was called to what appeared to many at the time to be a most unprepossessing assignment but that later proved to be a development of great significance to American librarianship, the directorship of the Ohio College Library Center (OCLC). Technically a creature of the Ohio College Association (OCA), OCLC had actually been conceptualized by Kilgour and Ralph Parker as consultants to the OCA, and he now found himself brought West to implement his own recommendations.

Building from his successes and failures in automation at Yale, Kilgour was soon able to deliver batch-processed catalogue cards to his Ohio college library clients. By 1971 OCLC's shared cataloguing system was available online in the state of Ohio, and within two years after that it could be used elsewhere through other academic library consortia, first in the East, then the South, then the West. In 1978 it was reorganized as a national service. These developments did not come about without criticism—of both OCLC and Kilgour—but they led nonetheless to dramatic changes in academic and other library operations.

Kilgour participated actively in library professional affairs, serving as the founding Editor of the *Journal of Library Automation,* published by ALA, and as author, lecturer, and international consultant. In 1974 he received the Margaret Mann Citation and in 1978 the Melvil Dewey Award from the ALA for his distinguished service to the profession. In 1979 he was corecipient of the Academic Research Librarian of the Year Award presented by ACRL. His wife, Eleanor Margaret Beach, worked with him on many projects.

REFERENCES
Pamela S. Rogers, "Gathering Enemy Scientific Material in Wartime," *Libraries and Culture;* Proceedings of Library History Seminar VI (1981).
David L. Weisbrod, "Margaret Mann Citation, 1974: Frederick G. Kilgour," *Library Resources & Technical Services* (1974).

DAVID KASER

Kirkegaard, Preben
(1913–)

Preben Kirkegaard, Danish library leader, may be considered the father of modern Danish librarianship. He was the founding head of the Royal School of Librarianship, Denmark's recognized center for professional education and training in library and information science. The foundation of the Danish Library School (1956) was Kirkegaard's *magnum opus.* He also left his stamp on practical librarianship through his work in public libraries in Jutland. At an early stage he entered the international library scene, became involved in consultancy work abroad, and was active in IFLA.

Preben Kirkegaard was born in Aarhus, Denmark, on January 8, 1913. He passed a secondary school leaving exam in 1929, completed bookseller training in 1933, and was engaged as an assistant at the Aarhus Public Libraries on February 1, 1934. He became a trainee at the same library system on December 1, the same year. In 1936 Kirkegaard passed the final examination at the State Library School in Copenhagen. Kirkegaard was thus equipped with an all-round introduction to the booktrade and to the basics of librarianship. Kirkegaard's time in Aarhus was characterized by his involvement with county-library-operated field work, especially the assistance to the book selection process in the rural libraries, and the library-based adult education seminars.

On January 1, 1945, Kirkegaard, at the age of 31, was appointed head of the Holstebro County Library. In 1946 he was appointed Chief Librarian of the County Library in Vejle. Vejle's emerging image as a "model library," which had an impact, even abroad, was largely due to Kirkegaard.

In 1956 Kirkegaard moved from practical librarianship into library education. The Ministry of Education appointed him Director of the newly established Royal School of Librarianship in Copenhagen, an independent institution set up through a special act. The new state college replaced the formal training program named the State Library School and operated by the State Inspection of Public Libraries. During the pioneering years of the school, the Director had his hands full in building a top-notch faculty and in taking care of curriculum development, planning, and administration. Yet Kirkegaard became the architect of a large-scale and impressive expansion of the educational activities and the institutional framework of the Royal School of Librarianship during the subsequent two decades. A new act on the Royal School of Librarianship was passed in June 1966 implying a reshaped public librarianship program as well as development of curricula oriented toward the education of professional library staff for the research and academic libraries sector. A new library school building on the island of Amager, near central Copenhagen, was converted into a well-functioning, working environment for some 50 full-time faculty members, technical, and support staff and more than 1,000 students. Thanks to Kirkegaard's dynamic efforts and negotiation skills, the financial support necessary to the operation of such a large institution was secured.

In his many years as educator, planner, administrator and negotiator, Kirkegaard never concealed his visions of an upgraded and consolidated library profession and his intention to enhance the level of library education and raise the status of his school. Kirkegaard took the view that library science is an academic discipline in its own right. It may well be that Kirkegaard's views of a philosophy of librarianship and his educational ideas were inspired by distinguished American library schools such as Chicago and Columbia.

He went to England, Canada, and the United States to study, joined IFLA, as early as 1952, undertook a Unesco expert mission on library education in Greece (1962) and served on IACODLA (International Advisory Committee on Documentation, Libraries and Archives) set up by Unesco, 1971-78. But Kirkegaard's work within IFLA constitutes the apex of his activities in the field of international library cooperation.

He became a dedicated worker for IFLA over many years, served on the sections of public libraries and library schools and the Executive Board of the organization (acting as Treasurer 1965–1973) and served as President 1974–1979. During his presidency Kirkegaard exerted a clear influence on the priorities and structure of IFLA. He had a key role to play in the shaping of a new organizational structure for the Federation. The constitution was blueprinted at the General Council in Lausanne, Switzerland, August 1976.

At the IFLA Council and General Conference in Oslo, Norway, August-September 1979, the title of Honorary President of IFLA was conferred on Kirkegaard in recognition of his untiring efforts. The selection of Kirkegaard as recipient of the Professor Kaula Gold Medal for the year 1982, "in recognition of his illustrious services for the cause of Library and information science," is another appreciation of his merits.

Kirkegaard's support of the library profession is also reflected in his contribution to the work of various organizations, committees, and bodies in Denmark, including the Danish Association and the Union for Public Librarians. He has served on the Executive Committee of the Danish Library Association. In 1983 he became a honorary member of the Association. From 1957 Kirkegaard was a co-editor of *Libri,* the international journal. Kirkegaard wrote numerous articles and reviews, and his monograph on Danish public libraries (1948) has been translated into several languages.

After his retirement in 1983, Kirkegaard worked as an active freelancer, contributing feature articles and book reviews to newspapers. He continued to keep an eye on developments in the library scene, and he studied selected library history themes.

REFERENCE

The Kirkegaard Festschrift *Biblioteket,* edited by Axel Andersen and Erland Munch-Petersen, Copenhagen (1983), provides a bibliography of 291 of Kirkegaard's writings compiled through March 1982.

LEIF KAJBERG

Preben Kirkegaard

Korea, Democratic People's Republic of

North Korea, officially the Democratic People's Republic of Korea, occupies the northern half of the Korean Peninsula in eastern Asia. It is bounded on the north by China and the Soviet Union, on the east by the Sea of Japan, on the south by the Republic of Korea, and on the west by the Yellow Sea. Population (1984 est.) 19,630,000; area 121,200 sq.km. The official language is Korean.

421

The Central Library in Pyongyang, functioning as a national library, has a collection of about 1,500,000 volumes. Provincial libraries are in Chongjin, Hamhung, Shinniju, Haeju, Wonsan, Kangge, Pyonsong, Sariwon, and Hesan. The North Hwanghae Provincial Library in Sariwon is reported to have a collection of 60,000 volumes, the library in Hamhung 40,000, and the library in Haeju 33,000. In addition there are city libraries in Kaesong and Chongjin with collections of about 25,000 volumes.

The Academy of Sciences Publishing House, founded in 1953, publishes works on science, chemistry, geology, metallurgy, physics, biology, history, mathematics, meteorology, education, and economics. The Academy of Social Sciences and the Academy of Medical Sciences, both in Pyongyang, publish works in their respective fields.

The Kim Il Sung University in Pyongyang, founded in 1946, has faculties in history, philosophy, political economics, law, philology, foreign literature, geography, geology, physics, mathematics, chemistry, and biology. Its library has a collection of about 60,000 volumes. The Kim Chaek Polytechnic Institute and the Pyongyang Medical Institute are also in Pyongyang. There are institutions of higher and professional education in the main towns, including colleges of engineering, agriculture, fisheries, and teacher training. In addition, there are factory (engineering) colleges. Statistical and other detailed information was not available on library service in these institutions.

Special libraries are the Institute of Agricultural Sciences in Finjan and the Academy of Forestry, the Academy of Medical Science, and the Academy of Social Science, all in Pyongyang.

The Library Association of the Democratic People's Republic of Korea was established in 1953. The Association is affiliated with IFLA; its headquarters are in the Central Library at Pyongyang.

Korea, Republic of

The Republic of Korea in eastern Asia comprises the lower 99,022 sq.km. of a mountainous peninsula extending south from Manchuria between the Yellow Sea and the Korean Straits, and it is bounded on the north by the Democratic People's Republic of Korea. Population (1983 est.) 41,366,000. The official language is Korean.

History. Korea, throughout its history, has had a rich background of papermaking, printing, and bookmaking. Since the invention of movable metallic type in the 12th century A.D. Korea has proven a good breeding ground for libraries. Historical records prove that libraries in a variety of forms existed from ancient times. Among the early libraries were the royal palace libraries—storehouses for archival materials, classics, and government documents. Early libraries also could be found in temples and scholars' homes. The Yangban (nobility) produced the scholars of Korea and in their libraries were the manifestations of culture. The Kyujangkak (Royal Library), with some 141,000 volumes of rare books and manuscripts of literary works, fine arts, history, culture, and official documents, is one of the greatest sources for research in the entire Orient.

While much of Korean traditional literature was written in Chinese ideographic characters, Korea has an alphabet of its own—Hangul. The Hangul alphabet, comprising 24 phonological characters, was created under the learned direction of King Sejong in 1446, and it has proven a remarkable vehicle for the extension of literacy and educational growth in Korea, a country with a highly homogeneous population.

National Libraries. The Central National Library of the Republic of Korea was started in 1923 as a Japanese government library and went through reorganization in 1945 when the Japanese left Korea. Following the enactment of the Library Law of 1963, the Library became the Central National Library. It serves the country by acquisition and preservation of national literature, bibliographic services including KOMARC (Korean equivalent of MARC), and exchange services between domestic and overseas libraries. It had almost 972,600 volumes in 1983, including more than 194,000 rare books, including Chinese and Korean classics. Major publications are "The Library Journal," "Korean National Bibliography," and "Bibliographic Index of Korea."

The National Assembly Library was established in 1951 and operates in accordance with Article 11 of the National Assembly Secretariat Law. Its main duty

Libraries in the Republic of Korea (1983)

Type	Administrative units	Service points	Volumes in collections	Annual expenditures (won)	Population served	Professional staff	Total staff
National	2	1[a]	1,588,584	3,057,764,000	433,027	103	394
Academic	251	--	16,557,955	13,849,674,000	--	674	2,455
Public	143	5[a] 9[b] 35,025[c]	2,617,401	5,280,031,000	17,163,774	582	1,821
School	5,374	--	18,295,919	2,990,351,000	--	1,303	5,374
Special	230	--	3,565,428	5,915,600,000	1,417,480	372	790

[a] Branches.
[b] Mobiles.
[c] Saemaul Mungo (New Village Micro Library).

Source: Korean Library Association, *Statistics on Libraries in Korea, 1984*, Seoul, 1984.

is to serve members and committees of the Assembly, and it provides information and materials for legislative reference and research work. It also serves government officials, as well as the public, with bibliographic services, research, and technical services. The library had 616,000 volumes in 1983, including nearly 10,500 rare books. Major publications are "Korean Periodicals Index," "Theses for the Doctor's and Master's Degree in Korea," and "National Assembly Library Review."

Both libraries became depository libraries under the library law of 1963. The services rendered by the two libraries overlap in many ways, and there was a movement in the late 1970s to unify the two libraries into a single, strong national library, but it ended in vain. In the mid-1980s each library had a new building under construction, with completion for both scheduled for 1986.

Academic Libraries. University and college libraries as well as junior and teachers' college libraries supported either by the government or private institutions increased in number and were physically extended after World War II as part of the higher education systems. According to "Statistics on Libraries in Korea 1984," academic libraries served 48,679,600 users with more than 16,560,000 volumes in 1983.

Most academic libraries suffered during the Korean War, 1950–52. They were subsequently active in building up their collections and reader services. From the end of the 1970s there were trends in higher education toward independent study and changes in teaching methods, academic requirements, and library materials. Many academic libraries engaged in building new library buildings and seeking better services; among changes was that from the closed- to the open-shelf system.

The Seoul National University Library, the largest academic library in Korea, has a modern building centrally located on a campus supported by the government. The Kyujangkak, the Royal Library collection of classic literature, is preserved in a specially designed section of the Library. Eight representative national universities, one in each of eight provinces, are active in developing improved library facilities and services. Other major university libraries supported by private institutions are at Yonsei, Korea, and Ewha universities. Built in the first half of the 1980s, they have modern facilities; Ewha Woman's University Library, completed in 1984 and equipped to manage up to a million volumes, changed from a partially open-stack system to fully open-stack service for its 20,000 users.

Public Libraries. Public libraries were introduced to Korea only in the beginning of the 20th century. Because they were introduced by the Japanese during their occupation of Korea, they were considered alien institutions. A few prospered, but public libraries were not generally popular or well supported until the enactment of the Library Law of 1963. Still small in number in the 1980s, public libraries came to perform a real function in encouraging intellectual interests and filling recreational needs.

Local and city governments are financially responsible for encouraging the development of public libraries under the overall supervision of the Ministry of Education. There were 143 public libraries in Korea in 1983.

The Central National Library

Central National Library, Seoul, Korea.

Micro Libraries. The Korean Micro Library Association was inaugurated in 1961. It is a grass-roots effort to reach individuals at the village and farm level and is a part of the New Village Movement, a unique Korean community movement for better living in the rural areas. Each Saemaul Mungo (New Village Micro Library) of approximately 60 titles is self-contained in a wooden bookcase that holds upwards of 300 volumes. The original 60 titles were selected in accord with villagers' needs and interests: for example, agriculture, stock raising, gardening, fishing, or homemaking. Each recipient is responsible for adding new volumes. A Village Reading Club runs each library, and books are lent free of charge. The Association, first operated under the auspices of the Ministry of Education, came under the sponsorship of the Ministry of Home Affairs, which provided a total of 35,025 libraries. The number of the libraries will not increase, according to the Association, because its goal is to enrich the existing ones. The Association publishes Saemaul Mungo ("New Village Micro Library").

School Libraries. After the Korean War, the most notable increase in library numbers was in school libraries, which many see as indispensable in modern education. But the lack of understanding among administrators and the shortage of teacher librarians has hampered growth and presented problems of maintaining school libraries as instructional media centers. One of many wide-ranging provisions in the Library Law of 1963 is the establishment of libraries at primary, middle, and high schools. Schools have engaged in an effort to comply, but educational needs exist on all levels and the library requirement competes with the need for more classrooms, more teachers, and other basic education facilities and resources. There were 5,374 school libraries in Korea with 18,295,900 volumes in 1983.

Special Libraries. Special libraries are among the growing forces in Korean librarianship. Demands for information on sciences, technology, and business administration have increased. This growing interest among scholars, administrators, and businessmen has helped them to recognize the importance of library service in their organizations and caused the fast development of special libraries in both governmental and nongovernmental organizations. Special libraries are more adequately financed than others and are staffed by trained librarians and enjoy better interlibrary cooperation. The best example is the Science Park Complex composed of KAIST (Korean Advanced Institute of Science and Technology), KDI (Korea Development Institute), and KIET (Korean Institute for Economic Technology). Other examples are those at the Academy of Korea Studies, at the Korea Educational Development Institute, and at the Korea Research Institute for Human Settlement.

The Profession. *Education.* Training of librarians in modern librarianship is very young in Korea. In 1946 the Central National Library opened the first Library School. During the five years of its existence, 77 librarians were graduated.

The first academic library school was established in 1957 at Yonsei University in cooperation with George Peabody College for Teachers. Similar four-year programs were established at Ewha Woman's University, 1959; at Chungang University, 1963; and Sungkyunkwan, 1964. In the 1970s universities offering four-year programs increased and a number of junior colleges began offering two-year programs. Soongeui Women's Junior College was one of the first. By 1984, 25 universities offered four-year undergraduate programs at the B.A. level and six junior colleges offered the two-year program. Graduates of the four-year program receive the Ministry of Education Certificate of professional librarianship, and the junior college graduates receive the subprofessional certificate. Three universities, Sungkyunkwan, Yonsei, and Chungang, offer doctoral programs, and five universities offer postgraduate work leading to master's degrees. In addition, Sungkuyunkwan University offers a one-year program in the evenings as in-service training for library employees or college graduates desiring to work in libraries. Ministry of Education certificates are awarded to graduates.

Associations. The Korean Library Association (KLA), the first library association in Korea, was established in 1945. Its objectives are to promote library development and cooperation among individual and institutional members and to promote international library cooperation. Members in 1984 included 692 individual and 635 institutional members. The Association sponsors activities such as an annual National Library Convention, Book Week, and Library Week as well as workshops and distribution center service to member libraries. The KLA publishes "The KLA Bulletin," a "Library Science Series," revisions of

Printed courtesy of *Soviet Life*
Nadezhda Krupskaya

"The Korean Decimal Classification System," and "Korean Cataloging Rules," "Statistics on Libraries in Korea," and many other tools.

The Korean Library Science Society was started in 1970 by the members of library science school faculties and individuals interested in advanced studies in the field of libraries and information science. The Society promotes Korean librarianship through seminars, lectures, and an annual publication, *Tosogwanhak* ("Studies in Library Science").

The Korean Bibliographical Society was organized in 1968 by librarians and scholars interested in bibliographical service and archives. It also sponsors seminars and lectures and publishes a journal, *Sojihak* ("Bibliographical Studies").

REFERENCES

Pongsoon Lee, "Education for Librarianship in Korea," *Papers Presented at the FID/ET Workshop, 1982* (1983).
Ke Hong Park, "Libraries and Librarianship in the Republic of Korea," *Proceedings of IFLA Worldwide Seminar* (1976).
Pow-key Sohn, *The Early Korean Typography* (1982).

PONGSOON LEE

Krupskaya, Nadezhda
(1869–1939)

Nadezhda Konstantinovna Krupskaya Ulianova, the wife of Lenin, was prominent in Communist Party and Soviet state activities, one of the founders of the Soviet educational system, and a pioneer in the development of Soviet libraries.

Krupskaya was born February 26, 1869, in St. Petersburg (now Leningrad). She graduated from secondary school in 1887 and, in 1890, while a student of the Woman's College in St. Petersburg, she became a member of a Marxist circle. From 1891 to 1886 she taught at a Sunday evening school for workers and propagated revolutionary ideas.

She met V. I. Lenin in 1894, and soon they were married. With him she took part in the organization of the Revolution in Russia. In August 1896 Krupskaya was arrested and joined Lenin in his exile in the village of Shushenskoye and later in Ufa. At that time she wrote her first work, *The Woman-Worker*. From 1901 to 1905, together with Lenin, she lived in Germany, Great Britain, and Switzerland and was active in the revolutionary movement and the publishing of the Marxist newspapers *Iskra* and *Vperyod*. On her return to Russia in November 1905 she worked as the Secretary of the Central Committee of the Bolshevik Party. From the end of 1907 until April 1917 she again lived in exile with Lenin, continuing her revolutionary activities.

At the same time, she became interested in the study of popular education in Russia and in western European countries and in 1915–16 became a member of the Pestalozzi pedagogical society in Switzerland and the Berne and Fribourg pedagogical museums. In that period she also wrote one of her major works, *People's Education and Democracy,* which dealt with the development of popular education in the United States, a subject that she had examined in a number of her earlier works.

After the establishment of the Soviet government in Russia in November 1917, Krupskaya became one of the leaders of the Commissariat of People's Education (from 1929 serving as Deputy of the People's Commissar), where she took an active part in the preparation of the first legislative acts on people's education and became the chief organizer of cultural and educational work in the country. She taught at the Academy of Communist Education and was the founder of a number of voluntary societies, including "Away with Illiteracy" and "Children's Friend," and chaired the Society of Teachers-Marxists. She was a member of ruling bodies of the Communist Party and the Soviet government.

Krupskaya played a prominent role in activities directed toward the elimination of illiteracy, the organization of the Soviet school system, and the establishment of cultural foundations for a new society. She appreciably contributed to the formulation of the most important issues of Marxist education: the definition of the objectives of Communist education, preschool and primary education, the connection between the school and public life, professional and technical training, the content of curricula, and the education of the various nationalities of the Soviet Union. She was editor of a number of journals, including "Public Education," "People's Teacher," "Extra-Scholastic Education," and "School for Adults." Her literary production totals over 5,000 items, among which are a number of reminiscences of Lenin, representing significant primary sources for his biography.

She devoted much time to librarianship, to which she accorded an integral role in education and the development of public life. She had expert knowledge of bibliography in Russia, was acquainted with many western European libraries, and displayed a keen interest in U.S. libraries. She took part in the preparation of major legislative acts on libraries, including the decree "On the Centralization of Librarianship in the RSFSR" (1920) and the resolution of the Central Executive Committee, "On Librarianship in the USSR" (1934). The most significant meetings and conferences in the field were held under her guidance, and she gave speeches on book distribution, problems of library science, and bibliography. Such journals as "The Red Librarian," "In Aid of Self-Education," "BookBulletin," "What One Should Read," and others were founded on her initiative. She wrote hundreds of articles on librarianship, publishing, bibliography, lifelong education, and self-education.

The scope of her activities can be classified along three major lines. First, she was an ardent propagandist of the ideas of Lenin, who regarded the establishment of libraries as an inseparable part of the Socialist state policy in the field of culture and considered the establishment of an integrated system of various types of libraries, evenly distributed throughout the country and provided with all facilities required, as a necessity. Krupskaya's many speeches and articles, which were imbued with these ideas, and especially a widely known work, *What Lenin Wrote and Said about Libraries* (1929), helped to enhance the prestige of libraries in Soviet society.

REFERENCES

The collected writings of Krupskaya are *Pedagogiheskie sochineniya* ("Pedagogical Works," in Russian) 11 volumes (Moscow, 1957–63); *O Bibliotechnom Dele* ("On Librarianship") (Moscow, 1957, 1st ed.; 1976, 2nd ed.); *Reminis-*

cences of Lenin; translated by Bernard Isaacs (Moscow, 1959); *Memories of Lenin;* translated by E. Verney, 2 volumes (London, 1930–32); *Memories of Lenin* (London, 1942).

A bibliography of her works and literature about her is *Nadezhda Konstantinova Krupskaya: Bibliografia Trudov i Literatury o Zhizni i Deiatelnosti* ("Bibliography of Works and Literature about Life and Activities"), 2 volumes (Moscow, 1969–73); 4 volumes, 3rd ed., 1982–84).

Nadezhda Krupskaya, "Lenin's Work in Libraries," *Lenin and Library Organisation* (Moscow, 1983, pp. 156-164).

GEORGIJ FONOTOV

Kunze, Horst
(1909-)

Horst Kunze, one of the eminent figures of German librarianship in the 20th century, profoundly influenced the development of librarianship in the German Democratic Republic and became one of the leading librarians there.

Born in Dresden on September 22, 1909, he studied modern languages and literature, especially German, and philosophy and completed those studies in 1935 with the Ph.D. The following two years he was educated as a subject specialist in academic and research libraries at the Sächsische Landesbibliothek in Dresden and the Deutsche Bücherei in Leipzig.

Kunze's library career started in 1937 at the Deutsche Bücherei and continued in 1939 at the Landesbibliothek in Darmstadt. In 1947 he was appointed Director of the Universitäts- und Landesbibliothek Halle. Three years later, he took over responsibility for the then so-called Öffentliche Wissenschaftliche Bibliothek in Berlin. This library, successor of the former Preussische Staatsbibliothek, was named Deutsche Staatsbibliothek in 1954. Until his retirement at the end of 1976, Kunze served as Director General of that distinguished library. After the founding of the Library Association of the German Democratic Republic in 1964, Kunze was elected its first President.

He taught library science in Halle from 1948, then in Berlin at the Humboldt University as Professor from 1953, and as Director of the Institute of Library Science and Scientific Information from 1955 for a decade and a half.

His international recognition as a scholar is based, moreover, on Kunze's learned and methodology-oriented publications in library science, book science, literature, and librarianship. His textbook on library administration, *Grundzüge der Bibliothekslehre* ("Basic Library Management") (1956; 4th edition, 1977), and the "Lexikon des Bibliothekswesens" ("Encyclopedia of Librarianship") (edited together with Gotthard Rückl, 1969; 2nd edition, 1975) are outstanding publications in the field. Book science is covered, besides numerous specific research investigations and theoretical contributions, above all by Kunze's fundamental history of book illustration in Germany from the 15th to the 17th century, "Geschichte der Buchillustration in Deutschland" ("History of Book Illustration in Germany") (1975–85). Specific interest in children's literature and in the beautiful books of all ages is characteristic of his scholarly and popular writing.

In Kunze's publications, which number more

425

than 400, academic knowledge of the subjects treated is combined skillfully with the applications of historical developments and their results to the actual needs of larger groups of peoples, especially younger ones, living in the German Democratic Republic and beyond. This general attitude led Kunze to many honorary positions not only connected with his duties as librarian and library scientist but also in the publishing and editorial areas as well as in those of bibliophily. As early as 1955, he was one of the co-founders of the Pirckheimer-Gesellschaft, the association of bibliophiles in the German Democratic Republic.

Kunze was awarded many official decorations and medals and also the honorary Ph.D. degree.

PAUL KAEGBEIN

Kuwait

Kuwait, an independent constitutional monarchy, lies on the northeast coast of the Arabian Peninsula, at the northwest end of the Persian Gulf. Kuwait is bordered by Iraq on the north and west and by Saudi Arabia on the south. Population (1984 est.) 1,715,000; area 16,918 sq.km. The official language is Arabic.

History. The first library in the country was established in 1922, but although it was the National Library and its stock rose to 1,500 volumes, neglect caused the collection to dwindle to 200. In 1936 the library was started up again and attached to the Ministry of Education. School libraries were started in the early 1960s, but the turning point came with the founding of Kuwait University in 1966. Its library opened with a collection of 20,000 volumes.

National Library. The National Library of Kuwait, the National Heritage Center, is closely affiliated with and supervised by Kuwait University Libraries Department. The Center was established in 1971 on a recommendation from the Kuwaiti Cabinet. Five copies of all printed publications issued in Kuwait must be deposited in the Center according to the legal deposit law of 1972. The functions of the Center are gathering and making available all printed and nonprint materials concerning and issued in Kuwait, the Gulf States, and the Arabian Peninsula, as well as issuing national and specialized bibliographies. The library holdings of the Center total about 297,000 volumes.

Academic Libraries. The principal academic library in Kuwait is that of the Kuwait University, which was inaugurated in 1966. In the late 1970s its

growing library system comprised the Central Library, six college libraries, a separate library for periodicals, and the National Heritage Center. By 1981 the number of its service points had risen to 11. The book collections in all libraries of Kuwait University total about 340,000 volumes. Acquisitions, cataloguing, classification, compiling bibliographies, audiovisual services, reference, and other functions are performed centrally by the Department of Libraries, which administers all libraries of the University. They serve about 17,000 students and the faculty of 600.

The Kuwait University Libraries Department issued *Selected Bibliography on Kuwait and Arabian Gulf,* two volumes for foreign and Arabic sources (1969-70), the nucleus of the national bibliography; *A List of Books and Publications Received by the Kuwait University,* a computer printout from 1973; *Selected Bibliography on Arab Civilization* (1970); and other specialized bibliographies. The Kuwait Institute of Scientific Research issued editions of a union list of periodicals in the libraries of the Gulf States.

Public Libraries. Public library services in Kuwait came into existence with the establishment of the Central Public Library in 1936. The public library system consists of the Central Public Library and 23 branch libraries, mostly in the suburban shopping centers of the city of Kuwait. The public library system is administered by the Public Libraries Department of the Ministry of Education. All operations, such as acquisitions and technical processing, are done centrally by the Central Public Library. New books are distributed regularly to the branch libraries. Periodicals are acquired and processed separately. The book collections of the public library system total about 280,000 volumes.

School Libraries. The School Libraries Department of the Ministry of Education, established in 1954, is responsible for establishing and developing school libraries, providing them with library materials and personnel, and operating a book processing center for book distribution. The administration of individual school libraries is a responsibility assigned to each school principal. More than 325 school libraries serve elementary, intermediate, secondary, vocational, and technical schools.

Special Libraries. Government departments, research centers, banks, and other enterprises possess special libraries with sizable collections. Noteworthy among these libraries are those of the Ministry of Ed-

Libraries in Kuwait (1981)

Type	Administrative units	Service points	Volumes in collections	Annual expenditures (dinar)	Population served[a]	Professional staff	Total staff
National	- -	- -	- -	- -	- -	- -	- -
Academic[b]	1	11	268,000	1,288,000	12,000	28	177
Public	1	23	281,000	790,000	- -	8	170
School[c]	- -	326	1,610,000	- -	160,000	80	573

[a]Registered borrowers.
[b]Kuwait University only.
[c]1977 data.

Source: Unesco, *Statistical Yearbook,* 1984.

ucation, Ministry of Foreign Affairs, Ministry of Endowments, Kuwait Institute of Scientific Research, Arab Planning Institute, Planning Board, Kuwait Fund for Arab Economic Development, Central Bank of Kuwait, and Kuwait National Petroleum Company. The Documentation and Information Section of the Kuwait Institute of Scientific Research performs a leading role in scientific documentation, particularly in computerized bibliographies and specialized professional training.

MOHAMED M. EL HADI*

Lamb, W. Kaye
(1904-   )

William Kaye Lamb, library administrator, archivist, scholarly editor, historian, and library association leader, was first National Librarian of Canada. Born in New Westminster, B.C., on May 11, 1904, Lamb attended schools there and in Vancouver. In 1927 he earned a B.A. with first class honors in history from the University of British Columbia, followed by an M.A. in 1930. He spent the years 1928 to 1932 in France at the Sorbonne and the École Libre des Sciences Politiques. In England, at the London School of Economics, he obtained a doctorate in 1933 under the direction of Harold Laski. His appointment the next year in the dual role of Provincial Librarian and Archivist of British Columbia foreshadowed his later career and prepared him for it.

When, in two years' time, he was made the Superintendent of the British Columbia Public Library Commission, he found himself with a combination of responsibilities as unique as they were sweeping, attending to the development of the historical records of the province, serving the information requirements of the members of the Legislature and government officials, operating library services for citizens living in remote areas of a vast province, organizing regional library services in more settled areas, and generally coordinating public library services everywhere.

In 1940 he became the second of the University of British Columbia's Librarians, succeeding John Ridington. The war and post-war years presented Lamb with formidable problems: the delivery of scholarly publications from Europe was disrupted; the cost of all imported journals and books was raised by special wartime taxes; budgets were lean; and at war's end the student body increased threefold in just two years, creating heavy demands for library materials, services, and study space. Nevertheless, collections grew significantly in that period, in large part as a result of Lamb's success in increasing private donations to the Library. Most notable among these gifts were the complementary collections of F. W. Howay and R. L. Reid, which established at the University one of the continent's finest collections of Canadian and Pacific Northwest history.

Responding to the Library's physical shortcomings—there had been no change to the building since its construction in 1925—Lamb obtained a commitment to build a north wing, which was opened in the fall of 1948. This event almost coincided with his appointment as Dominion Archivist. In that post, in 1950, he established the Canadian Bibliographic Centre, which undertook the compilation of both a national union catalogue and a national bilingual bibliography, the first issue of which appeared in January 1951 under the title *Canadiana.*

Assigned special responsibility for the development of a national library, Lamb was instrumental in drafting legislation enacted by Parliament. The National Library came into official existence on January 1, 1953, with its creator as Canada's first National Librarian. Initially, the National Library had a statutory but not a separate physical existence. The Canadian Bibliographic Centre, the core of the new institution, was housed in the Public Archives Building, a 30-year-old structure too small for current needs. Lamb set out promptly to alleviate space problems, and by 1956 a new and large Federal Records Centre was constructed on the outskirts of Ottawa. The National Library was relocated there.

Planning had already commenced on a new building for the National Library and Public Archives of Canada, and although plans were completed by 1954, changes in governments and their priorities delayed construction for more than a decade. By the time the National Library finally occupied its permanent home in June 1967, it had amassed a collection of more than 600,000 volumes through legal deposit, gift, and purchase; had compiled a union catalogue of more than 10,000,000 titles; was responding to more than 80,000 location requests a year; had published 16 annual cumulated volumes of *Canadiana;* had established a microfilming service for theses written at Canadian universities; had published since 1961–62 annual lists of theses; and had increased bibliographic and reference services in many other ways. While managing the developmental years of this new institution, Lamb was also guiding the expansion of the programs of the Public Archives of Canada, which assumed responsibility for the management of all federal government records in 1956.

As a historian, Lamb wrote monographs, edited nine major edited works, wrote more than 100 articles, contributed to encyclopedias, and wrote book reviews. For 10 years he was editor of the *British Columbia Historical Quarterly,* which he founded in 1937, and for 12 years he was President of the Champlain Society, a publisher of historical texts.

After retirement as Dominion Archivist and National Librarian in 1968, he conducted further research, culminating in 1985 with his edition of Captain George Vancouver's *A Voyage of Discovery to the North Pacific Ocean and Round the World, 1791–1795,* published in London by the Hakluyt Society in four volumes. The 256-page introduction is the definitive biography of Vancouver.

Lamb served on the councils of scores of scholarly and professional organizations and as President of the British Columbia Library Association, the Canadian Library Association, the Pacific Northwest Library Association, the Canadian Historical Association, the Society of Archivists, and the Society of American Archivists. He received many honors, including doctorates from 10 Canadian universities. He was elected a Fellow of the Royal Society of Canada in 1949, served as its President in 1965–66, and was awarded its Tyrrell Medal for outstanding work in Canadian history in 1965. In 1969 he was appointed an officer of the Order of Canada.

REFERENCES

"Archives, Libraries, and the Canadian Heritage: Essays in Honour of W. Kaye Lamb," *Archivaria* (Winter 1982–83).

British Columbia, *Report of the Public Library Commission* (1936–39).

National Library of Canada, *Report of the National Librarian* (1953–67).

University of British Columbia, *Report of the Librarian to Senate* (1940–48).

BASIL STUART-STUBBS

Public Archives of Canada
W. K. Lamb

Lancaster, F. Wilfrid

(1933-   )

Frederick Wilfrid Lancaster, library educator, became a major influence in the fields of information systems and the evaluation of library services. His work deals principally with the underlying intellectual problems and conceptual frameworks of information retrieval systems, rather than technical aspects of computing and systems design. His major contributions have been in the areas of vocabulary control, interaction between system and user, evaluation of systems effectiveness, and, in his later work, the implications of advanced information systems for the future of libraries in society.

Born September 4, 1933, in Durham, England, Lancaster studied at Newcastle-upon-Tyne School of Librarianship (1950–54) and became Fellow of the Library Association of Great Britain (by thesis) in 1969. Lancaster began his professional career in 1953 as Senior Assistant, Newcastle-upon-Tyne Public Libraries. His subsequent positions include Senior Librarian for Science and Technology, Akron Public Library; Resident Consultant and Head, Systems Evaluation Group, Herner and Company, Washington, D.C.; Information Systems Specialist, National Library of Medicine; and Director of Information Retrieval Services, Westat Research, Inc. From 1970 Lancaster served on the faculty of the University of Illinois, Graduate School of Library Science, with the rank of Professor from 1972.

Lancaster's contributions have been made through writing, teaching, and consulting. Major publications include *Towards a Paperless Information Society* (1978), *The Measurement and Evaluation of Library Services* (1977; Ralph Shaw Award, 1978), *Information Retrieval Online* (1973), *Vocabulary Control for Information Retrieval* (1972), and *Information Retrieval Systems: Characteristics, Testing and Evaluation* (1968). In addition, Lancaster edited a number of books and wrote many articles and technical reports. His publications were recognized by the American Society for Information Science with best book awards in 1970 and 1975 and a best paper award in 1969.

His consulting includes work for the Central Intelligence Agency, Center for Applied Linguistics, National Library of Medicine, and National Library of Australia. He completed a set of guidelines on the evaluation of information systems and services for Unesco and the Food and Agriculture Organization.

Lancaster's strongest impact was on the development of criteria and procedures for the evaluation of systems performance, mainly through the extension, refinement, and application of concepts pioneered by the Cranfield studies, a series of investigations undertaken in the late 50s at the College of Aeronautics, Cranfield, under the direction of C. W. Cleverdon. His *Evaluation of the MEDLARS Demand Search Service* (1968) represents a landmark investigation, not particularly for its influence on the later development of the MEDLARS system, but as a demonstration of the application of refined methods for testing, analyzing, and evaluating the performance of an operational information retrieval system.

The more general significance of Lancaster's work results from his ability to combine a rigorous and thorough approach with a clarity of expression that renders advanced concepts of information retrieval accessible to the student and the practicing librarian without oversimplification. Lancaster's work, therefore, might be viewed as an attempt to bridge several important divisions in the information professions. His early work on vocabulary control and systems evaluation provides a connection between practice and theory for the technically oriented designer of information systems. His later work, particularly the *Measurement and Evaluation of Library Services,* serves to narrow the gap between the library profession at large and the growing body of research relevant to measurement and evaluation. Lancaster's most significant contribution to the literature of library and information science, assessed at a point still relatively early in his career, may well be his stimulation of interest in the possibility that theory and research may have some practical utility in the field.

JOE A. HEWITT

University of Illinois News Bureau

F. Wilfrid Lancaster

Laos

Laos, a people's democratic republic in southeast Asia, is bounded by China on the north, Vietnam on the northeast and east, and Kampuchea on the south. Population (1984 est.) 4,097,000; area 236,800 sq.km. The official language is Lao.

National Library. The National Library of Laos in Vientiane includes the National Museum and National Archives. On the grounds of the School of Fine Arts, it is under the direction of the Ministry of Education. Its holdings are about 50,000 volumes in Lao, English, and French; the degree of continuity in its operations allowed by the government is uncertain. Prior to the declaration of a people's republic in 1975, the National Library received aid from the French and U.S. governments, private foundations, and Western scholars. For example, the Rockefeller Foundation presented 9,000 volumes, mainly in French, on a wide range of subjects. Other contributions were made by the Asia Foundation and by the U.S. Library of Congress. In 1974 the former Director of the National Library, Prachit Soulisak, told a representative of the U.S. Library of Congress that he had compiled a list of 84,000 titles available in Lao at various temples and libraries throughout the country; he said the list gave the location of each item.

The National Library of Laos published *Lao National Bibliography,* 3 volumes (1968-72); *Bibliographie de Laos,* Institut Française d'Extreme Orient, with a supplement covering the years 1962-70, was compiled by the Director of the Lao National Library.

Academic Libraries. Before 1975 the Buddhist Institute in Vientiane was one of the most important centers of scholarship in Laos. It maintained a substantial collection of works, many in Pali and Sanskrit, for the use of its students and foreign scholars.

Sisavangvong University, in Vientiane, is the only university in Laos. It serves about 1,600 students. Library facilities of its faculties of medicine, law, and education were mainly provided by Western governments and foundations and are not extensive for research purposes. The libraries of the University's 10 institutes range in size from 800 to 4,200 volumes.

Public Libraries. There are not believed to be any public lending libraries, in the Western sense, in

Laos. The library of at least one major temple, the Wat That in Luang Prabang, performed some of the functions of a public library, however. It reportedly has many contemporary works in Lao and Thai and circulated about 100 books a month to residents of Luang Prabang. Most temples have teaching functions and many serve as community centers; some of the larger ones have collections of manuscripts in Pali and Sanskrit.

Prior to the Pathet Lao takeover in 1975, a number of foreign governments, including France, the United Kingdom, and the United States, operated libraries and reading rooms in Vientiane and other major towns. These were often heavily patronized. With U.S. economic assistance, a program of providing modest library facilities in rural areas also enjoyed some success.

School Libraries. The French *lycées* and the normal and technical schools in Laos had relatively modest library facilities (mainly provided through foreign-aid programs). In most schools the libraries were reserved for the use of their own students and faculties.

Special Libraries. The Directorate of Archaeology in the Ministry of Culture developed a collection of manuscripts. The U.S. Agency for International Development also maintained collections of documents on foreign assistance to Laos. (AID was expelled from Laos in 1973.)

The Profession. The Lao Library Association was closely associated with its National Library and was physically housed in a building behind the library. Little is known about the ongoing work of the Association in later years, but prior to 1974 it published a considerable number of monographs. At that time the Siaw Savath Society was also associated with the National Library and published the theses of Lao students studying abroad. Unesco helped set up national document centers under assistance grants, and along with this has contributed to a number of training programs.

PETER A. POOLE*

Lara, Juana Manrique de
(1899–1983)

Juana Manrique de Lara, Mexican librarian, introduced modern librarianship to Mexico through teaching, writing, and official duties as Inspector General of Libraries.

Born in the village of El Cubo, Guanajato, in Mexico, on March 12, 1899, she studied first in her native state and later in Puebla. A marked vocation toward teaching led her to graduate from the Normal School of Puebla. Inclined as well toward books, she enrolled in the first National School of Archivists and Librarians in Mexico City, studying there during the years of the Revolution, 1916–17.

She continued her studies in the United States to prepare as a professional librarian, one of the first Mexican women to do so. De Lara graduated from the School of the New York Public Library in 1924. Returning to Mexico, she dedicated herself to teaching library science. She taught at the early Library School of the Secretariat of Education and at the National School of Archivists and Librarians. The

Universidad Nacional Autónoma de Mexico
Juana Manrique de Lara

courses were many and the years were long, but her enthusiasm was contagious. For her pupils she published a number of valuable books such as the *Manual of the Mexican Librarian,* which she modestly described as advice for persons in charge of libraries, and which went through several editions. Other best sellers for Mexican librarians, so lacking in tools, were her *Elementary Notions concerning the Organization and Administration of a Small Library, Elements of the Organization and Administration of School Libraries,* and *Guide to Headings of Material for Dictionary Catalogues;* another work supplied a need in Mexican literature, *School Libraries and Children's Literature*—lists of books for children in primary grades and youth in secondary schools; a valuable work written in collaboration with another distinguished librarian, Guadalupe Monroy Baigen, was *Pseudonyms, Anagrams, and Initials of Mexican Authors.* She wrote numerous articles in specialized magazines of the U.S., Mexico, and countries of Central America.

She was for many years Inspector General of Libraries, Director of Libraries of the Secretariat of Education, and other specialized branches, in all of which she left her impress of positive activity totally dedicated to the culture of her country.

Juana Manrique de Lara died in Mexico City, October 8, 1983.

ERNESTO DE LA TORRE VILLAR

Law Libraries

PURPOSES AND OBJECTIVES
The dynamic growth of law library collections in the 20th century has been reflected in the changing role of the law librarian from a mere custodian of law books to an information specialist, organizing, managing, supervising, and coordinating legal research activities of the bench and bar, academia, and other institutions concerned with law.

Law in the books has always been a formidable challenge to lawyers seeking legal authority. There was a time, around the turn of the 17th century, when the English lawyer had to contend with only 5,000 reported cases. Today the American lawyer can consult millions of judicial opinions, increasing at the annual rate of approximately 80,000 published American appellate opinions alone. There is also a mass of federal and state legislation supplemented annually by hundreds of huge volumes of codes aggregating about 500,000 pages by themselves. Then there are the tens of thousands of pages of legal periodicals, government documents, administrative law and regulations, foreign law, and international law as well as topical looseleaf services.

In the years since World War II, this challenge has been heightened by the increasing relevance of economic, sociological, and scientific data in legal research so that the mere process of identifying, locating, and referring to these materials confounds not only the practicing lawyer but the legal scholar as well. It is not for naught that the late Chief Justice Arthur T. Vanderbilt of New Jersey noted in this context, "The first thing about our legal system that strikes a European or Latin American lawyer is its sheer bulk."

Law libraries have always been practitioner oriented. Lawyers generally seek legal authority in court decisions and statutes relevant to the solution of factual problems in a specific jurisdiction. These primary repositories of the law can easily be arranged chronologically on open shelves by jurisdiction or state. Hence, there was little need for the practitioner to depend on a law librarian either to arrange or organize these materials for use or to assist in locating relevant authority. We find, for example, that in England in 1646, as a result of an inquiry into the loss of books in the library of Gray's Inn, the chapel clerk was appointed Library-Keeper, with an extra annual salary of £5. In 19th-century America the title of "Librarian" was given often to the custodian of the building where the law library was located, or to its janitor. Obviously such a position did not require any special education or knowledge.

The tremendous growth of law book collections in the 20th century, however, the "information explosion," and the increasing demand for interdisciplinary materials in legal research have changed the concept that a law library is merely a collection of books in which legal authority can be found, and that can easily be arranged on shelves, alphabetically by author, or jurisdictionally under date or title.

Characteristic of this metamorphosis are innovative programs such as LEXIS, WESTLAW, and online bibliographic services that reflect the potential of the new technology. These are proving to be of value in legal research, especially in the interdisciplinary approach to law. The traditional tools of legal research are giving way to the hardware and software of this new technology to such an extent that many believe that the law library of the future could possibly be unrecognizable to the legal researchers of today.

Today law librarians function more as information specialists, coordinating the research activities of their institutions. They are more than reference assistants and bibliographers; they organize law libraries and their collections of legal materials for efficient and economic use. They suggest sources of information the lawyer can use and, even more significantly, learn to locate such sources when they are initially unknown to them.

In actual research, law librarians can find legal citations or references, suggest sources of information, verify and translate citations, interpret abbreviations, assemble materials for specific projects, prepare bibliographies, and explain the use of legal materials in the library. Law librarians, moreover, must possess judgment and legal background to anticipate the research needs of lawyers and resourcefulness to analyze legal materials and recognize their relevance to a particular subject or problem.

Law books are highly technical tools that may be difficult to use properly on occasion. Law librarians can skillfully use indexes, conversion tables, tables of cases, citations, and other technical finding tools. They provide significant assistance to legal researchers because of their thorough familiarity with legal and nonlegal bibliographies, as well as important nonlegal sources. They know where to find the answers to questions involving business, medicine, history, the social sciences, economics, and the applied sciences. Often the law librarian is the "silent part-

Supreme Court of the U.S.

Main reading room in the United States Supreme Court Library.

ner" in the research activities of lawyers, judges, and scholars.

Computers have revolutionized the art of legal research and have become an important research medium for lawyers. The adaptation of the computer for full-text searching of legal sources has broadened the role of the law librarian as a teacher and researcher in accessing these programs.

This changing role of law librarianship has been reflected in rising demands on the educational and professional qualifications held not only by head law librarians but by the rank-and-file staff members as well. Standards established by the American Bar Association (ABA) and the Association of American Law School (AALS) for law school librarians have been generally accepted as basic requirements for professional status.

With some exceptions, law school librarians are the most highly qualified in the field. Characteristically, other law librarians seek to obtain the same qualifications as law school librarians possess, to meet the test of professional acceptance. The professional careers of many law librarians suggest this trend in that they have moved from private law firm libraries, bar libraries, and the other types of law libraries to law school libraries and vice-versa. It would appear that there is a commonly accepted core of professional and educational achievement prerequisite to success in law librarianship.

The ABA standards for law librarians are part of its *Standards for the Approval of Law Schools* (1983). Its Standard 605 provides that "the law library [of an ABA accredited law school] shall be administered by a full-time law librarian whose principal activities are the development and maintenance of the library and the furnishing of library assistance to faculty and students, and may include teaching courses in the law school." Substandard 605 (c) provides that "the law librarian should have a degree in law or library science and shall have a sound knowledge of library administration and of the particular problems of a law library."

Law schools accredited by the AALS have set the most demanding professional standards, and AALS accreditation contributes significantly to a law school's standing. AALS Executive Committee Regulation 8.3(a) provides that "the librarian should have both legal and library education and . . . should have met the certification requirements of the American Association of Law Libraries."

The American Association of Law Libraries (AALL) was founded in 1906 "to promote librarianship, to develop and increase the usefulness of law libraries, to cultivate the service of law librarianship and to foster a spirit of cooperation among the members of the profession." It had 26 regional chapters in the mid-1980s and a number of Special Interest Sections. It publishes the *Law Library Journal, The Index to Foreign Legal Periodicals, The Directory of Law Librarians,* a *Biographical Directory of Law Librarians, AALL Publication Series, Current Publications in Legal and Related Fields,* and *AALL Newsletter* and a *Recruitment Checklist.* It also offers institutes, workshops, and annual meeting programs on timely and relevant topics. Its AALL Placement provides a job bank.

The AALL had approximately 3,800 members in 1985. Of that total, 1338 were law school libraries; 1085 private law firm libraries; 223 court, county, and bar libraries; 229 state law libraries; 262 company law libraries; 54 Canadian law libraries; and 90 foreign law libraries.

The AALL formerly had a certification program as a "formal recognition that a person has attained a standard of competence in law librarianship recognized by the AALL." This program was not well received and was abandoned in 1982.

Each year the AALL offers scholarships to students who plan to pursue careers in law librarianship. Scholarships were offered in the mid-1980s from each of the following categories:

Type I—*Library Degree for Law School Graduates:* Awarded to a graduate of an accredited law school who is a degree candidate in an accredited library school; Type II—*Library School Graduates attending Law School:* Awarded to a library school graduate who is in the process of working toward a law degree in an accredited law school, has no more than a certain number of credit hours of study remaining before qualifying for the law degree, and has meaningful law library experience; Type III—*Library Degree for non-law graduates:* Awarded to a college graduate with meaningful law library experience who is a degree candidate in an accredited library school; Type IV—*Special Course in law librarianship;* Awarded to law librarians for a course related to law librarianship.

The great interest in law librarianship has encouraged library schools to offer courses in the field. Among them are library schools at Columbia University, the University of Washington, the University of Illinois, Case Western Reserve, (Cleveland, Ohio), Drexel, (Philadelphia), Pratt (Brooklyn, N.Y), St. John's University (Jamaica, N.Y.), the University of California at Berkeley, Rosary College, (River Forest, Illinois), the University of North Carolina, and the University of Maryland. Many younger persons entering the profession today have both

law and library science degrees.

There are many types of law libraries that employ law librarians:

Bar Association Libraries serve practicing lawyers and are keyed to the research demands of litigation and client counseling. Among them are some of the leading law collections in the country, such as that of the Association of the Bar of the City of New York.

Company Libraries are maintained by legal departments of business enterprises. Here legal and related materials on the type of industry represented are collected—for example insurance, transportation, communications, international business transactions. Some of the larger collections of this type are held by the Prudential Insurance Company in Newark, the American Telephone and Telegraph Company in New York, and the General Motors Corporation in Detroit.

County Law Libraries are supported with public funds wholly or in part. They serve the courts, public officials, and the bar. Among this group is the Los Angeles County Law Library, the largest practitioners' collection in the country. The states with the most county law libraries are California, Ohio, Pennsylvania, Florida, Massachusetts, Maine, Michigan, Arizona, and Washington.

Court Libraries. There are more than 100 formally organized court libraries employing professional law librarians. Many more small court libraries are supervised not by professional librarians but by clerks or secretaries. The largest number of court libraries, including those of the federal courts, are concentrated in New York state.

Government Libraries comprise those of state and local governments as well as federal departmental and agency law libraries. Most of the federal law libraries are in Washington, D.C. Probably the largest law library in the world is that of the Library of Congress, with close to 2,000,000 volumes. Its divisions (American, British, European, Far Eastern, Hispanic, Near Eastern, and North African) suggest the comprehensiveness of its collection. Among other important U.S. government libraries are those of the U.S. Supreme Court, the Department of Justice, the Treasury, and the Federal Trade Commission.

Law Office Libraries. Law office collections range from a small number of volumes to approximately 60,000. Besides the usual law books, they may contain records and briefs of cases before various courts, memoranda, and forms of all types. The largest number of law office libraries are in New York, California, and Illinois.

Law School Libraries. These employ more law librarians than any other types of law libraries. Depending upon their location, resources, teaching, and research programs, law school libraries are used by law students and faculty exclusively, and when publicly funded, they are often used by the bench and bar of the area. The 1985 statistical survey of law school libraries and librarians indicates that of 174 law school libraries, 42 contain more than 200,000 volumes, and 26 more than 300,000 volumes. Harvard Law School has about 1,500,000 books in its library collection and Columbia, Michigan, Yale, and New York University more than 600,000 volumes.

State Law Libraries. Service may be provided either by independent libraries or by divisions of other state agencies. Some of them provide legislative reference services and exchanges of state legal materials, case reports, and statutes. Their primary function is to serve the state officials in all departments of state government. Their collections range in size from 30,000 volumes to more than 1,000,000 with 15 having more than 100,000 volumes. The more important state law libraries can be found in Massachusetts, Minnesota, New York, Rhode Island, New Jersey, and Wisconsin. Of course, the Law Library of Congress can be included here as well.

In essence, a law library is one of the "special libraries." A law librarian is basically a specialist in legal bibliography. In law schools, law librarians often teach courses in legal bibliography or subject courses in the law school. Professionally, law librarians also write and edit law texts and assist in the revision of statutes and the preparation of indexes. The law librarian is often called upon to act as a consultant to the Bar and other law libraries. As experts in legal bibliography, law librarians write book reviews, participate in workshops and institutes, and contribute to the professional growth of law librarianship.

REFERENCES

Julius J. Marke, and Richard Sloane, *Legal Research and Law Library Management* (1982, Suppl. 1985).

Heinz P. Mueller, Patrick E. Kehoe and Louisa Hurtado, eds., *Law Librarianship: A Handbook* (1983).

JULIUS J. MARKE

SERVICES TO USERS

The effective law library was long known as a happy combination of books and people. Today the functional legal information center is a harmonious union of people, materials, and technology. This subtle change in nomenclature is important because it implies modern service to a demanding clientele.

The raison d'être for a legal information center is service to what are probably the most influential and powerful forces in society—the executive, legislative, and judicial branches of government and the advocates of the legal profession. The role of the legal information center is vital because the missions of its users are essential in the civil and criminal matters inherent in society. Without law there would be no order; without well-organized, readily accessible legal information, Presidents and governors, legislators, judges, lawyers, and the public who must contend with law and regulation would be severely impeded in their activitites.

The traditional law library selects and acquires legal materials for the use of its audience, catalogues and classifies those materials so that many individuals may benefit from their content, and answers questions on a variety of legal and other subjects. These functions constitute the traditional role, but in an age of a rapid evolution in information they are not enough to satisfy legal professional needs properly.

Current Context. People must have information to survive in our world, and as the population increases it becomes necessary to find better ways of distributing needed information. Information is being produced faster by more people than in the past. In law this condition is reflected both in additional court decisions, because there are more people litigating, and in increased legislation, because society has be-come more complicated in human relationships and in scientific development. The number of specialized subjects is also increasing rapidly. For example, law must regulate space exploration, satellite communications, environmental pollution, toxic chemicals—areas for which there was little if any law a generation ago.

The library must become a media center that will allow its patrons communication with sources of information in various media—not only printed but also film, slides, video disks, and others—and in perhaps many different locations. Information science is concerned with discovering better ways to get the right information quickly to the person who needs it and with finding information efficiently at a later time, once it is stored in libraries and other centers of information.

The legal information system the law library profession envisions for the U.S. will deliver information to judges and lawyers, faculty and students, and the general public. To satisfy this objective it must meet three basic requirements: (1) it should be able to tell a user where to find information; (2) it should be able to deliver that information; and (3) it must respond within the time limits the user imposes.

The law library information operation will therefore be concerned with the way people create information, index or label it, store it, find it, analyze it, send and receive it, and use it. In carrying out this mission there are at least three basic tools for law library personnel: (1) computers, because they can process information in the form of words as effectively as they compute numbers; (2) telecommunications, because this technology is capable of distributing word and picture information at great speeds to widely dispersed places; and (3) micrographics, because microform technology allows large quantities of information to be condensed into a small space.

With the financial support of the AALS and the AALL, leading law libraries are working together to build a legal information network that will link the information, books, and audiovisual materials of many law libraries and legal information centers into one significant system. Using telecommunications it will then be possible to make the information resources of the whole network available to any single user in the country.

Law librarians seek to further their leadership in the application of advanced technology to law by utilizing electronic retrieval systems such as LEXIS and WESTLAW for reports of court decisions, statutes, and administrative law and by providing for the automation of library and bibliographic processes through RLIN and OCLC. The database systems developed by Lockheed, by Systems Development Corporation, and by others should provide access to subjects related to law, such as energy and the environment. Leading law firms already utilize computers and will increasingly expect new lawyers to be knowledgeable in their operation. The law library is thus the true laboratory of the law where its patrons must experiment and learn to use the new tools of the profession.

Staff. Effective service requires a professionally qualified staff. The legal profession has been slow in grasping the advantages provided to law libraries by library school graduates. Because there are no ef-

Underground structure wired for computer terminals and built below the 60-year-old gothic walls of the University of Michigan Law Library in 1982.

features often included in modern libraries. Reference services will vary among law libraries according to the institutions they serve. Law school libraries may provide more traditional academic library reference services, while in law firm libraries the staff play an integral role in research.

Access to law libraries and their materials similarly varies according to institutional setting. By national policy, the courts of last resort in each jurisdiction and accredited law school libraries with government depository status are urged to make their federal documents collections available to the general public. County law libraries are typically open to the public, while bar association and court libraries are often restricted to use by judges and attorneys. Special regulations may govern the use of law libraries in colleges and universities where space may be a factor in providing acceptable service to law students and faculty who will receive top priority. Firm law libraries are normally restricted to use by members of the firm. Relatively few public libraries maintain extensive collections of legal materials, and as library support in many communities is curtailed, this condition may be expected to continue. At the same time, however, there is a growing interest in providing access to legal materials for public library patrons.

Library personnel are not permitted to give legal advice, though they may point out standard reference sources. Legal materials may baffle the layman who has not been instructed in their use, so educational materials may be made readily available for self-instructional purposes. There is a body of literature that shows the difficulty in refraining from giving legal advice while providing access to complex legal tools.

Interlibrary loans of legal materials may be restricted to secondary materials inasmuch as primary materials—statutes and cases—are essentially reference works in sets. The procedure for interlibrary loan would be the same as in general libraries, subject to the aforementioned restrictions.

DAN HENKE;
JULIUS J. MARKE

fective or enforceable standards for personnel in many county, court, and law firm libraries, such libraries are typically quite poorly organized and maintained. With the advent of certification and accreditation procedures developed by professional associations, this situation may be expected to improve. Professional librarians are now typically the employees of choice in law firm, government, and bar association libraries. In academic libraries the personnel may be lawyer-librarians with some training in information science.

The smaller a law library collection is the more important it is that the person in charge of the library have professional training, because with a limited collection available the librarian will need knowledge of sources of information off-premises. The law firm today is backing into the 20th century by discovering the value of professional librarians as information finders and organizers on both the legal and factual sides of legal causes.

Services. Well-designed and equipped physical facilities are critical to providing law library services and access to materials. Upon entering a library the patron should see a directory upon which all service elements are mapped. Next, by various architectural techniques, the patron should notice first an information outlet where he or she may inquire about a particular problem and be directed to the proper department. Typically, provision will be made for access to the collections through card catalogues, micrographic devices, or computer terminals, and additional standard bibliographic services and indexes will be provided. Copying and typing facilities are standard. Enclosed course reserve materials areas in law school libraries, reference rooms, audiovisual and computer instructional facilities, discussion rooms, rare- or restricted-book areas, and lounges are other

COLLECTIONS

Law library collections reflect the characteristics of the clientele they are designed to serve. While core collections in sole practitioners' libraries will have contents similar to those of the larger law libraries, the expanded collections will vary in accordance with the information expectations of the users. Even within the different types of legal communities served, vast differences may be observed in the collections assembled for use. For example, one law school may teach the rudiments of the law practice and require a library primarily of the practitioners' tools, while another may emphasize research and writing requiring extensive resources for faculty and student investigation. Law firm and corporate libraries collect books in the areas of their lawyers' specialties and outside the core collection may concentrate on highly specialized titles in limited fields of practice within the firm or corporate environment. Bar associations, courts, and governmental libraries acquire resources consistent with the interests of the constituencies that they serve. The Law Library of Congress, for instance, acquires materials on a worldwide basis because of the demands for research materials and reports from Congress.

Materials. Law library collections differ from other types of special library collections in that serials comprise the largest proportion of the content, often to the extent of two-thirds of the collection. This is due to the nature of the law itself. The state legislatures produce volumes of laws, known as session laws, which when codified become "codes" or "statutes" and when reproduced by commercial vendors along with cases and notes are given titles of "annotated codes" or "annotated statutes." Courts concurrently expound their opinions in "decisions" that are published as "reports" and are later consolidated into "annotated reports," digests, encyclopedias, and eventually "annotated codes" or "statutes"; thus, the magnitude of these serial publishing programs becomes evident when 50 states and the federal system are multiplied by the number of courts and volumes that each court publishes in one year. Even the smallest library must maintain the current laws and court opinions in its state and federal law and opinions when applicable.

Beyond the primary law books, indexing tools are an essential part of legal research. As the scope of legal research activity increases, the library must parallel or exceed that activity by providing the information resources to support the demand. Growing libraries may expand toward resources of the region in which they are located—the states around them or significant states with similar legal controversies—while the larger libraries will collect nationwide and selectively in the international fields. Ultimately, the largest libraries will amass worldwide collections.

Libraries that support extensive writing projects must invest in research tools beyond the basics in laws and court reports. Law firms that have a large appellate practice, corporate legal research units, law schools that emphasize research and writing and maintain student publications, bar associations, and courts and government agencies engaged in brief writing require secondary sources of the law to assist with formulating research products and framing the final outcome of the query searched. Libraries will acquire some or all of these, depending upon their research requirements. Publications such as law reviews and legal periodicals, encyclopedias, dictionaries, and treatises fill this kind of need. Many professional associations publish legal journals and nearly every law school publishes a law review, edited by its students, with articles by leading practitioners, judges, faculty, and some student works. The *American Bar Association Journal* and the *Harvard Law Review* are but two of the approximately 500 periodicals indexed in the *Index to Legal Periodicals*.

Two national encyclopedias, the *American Jurisprudence 2nd* and *Corpus Juris Secundum,* purport to cover basic American law principles, documented with cases that have enunciated these principles. Additionally, state encyclopedias cover local law. A number of law dictionaries define legal terms citing court opinions, among them *Black's Law Dictionary* and *Ballentine's Law Dictionary*. Other legal information is published in books that exhaustively treat a legal subject with supporting documentation, referred to as treatises; often their authors are authorities in their fields, and their works are frequently cited by

name as the outstanding exposition on the law in a particular area, such as *Prosser on Torts*. *Shepard's Citations* has long served the legal profession by providing a "history" of each reported case (whether the case was affirmed, reversed, modified, or dismissed on appeal) and the "treatment" of each reported case (which indicates its value as authority by noting how other reported cases commented upon it by criticizing, distinguishing, explaining, following, limiting, overruling, or questioning its holding). Similarly, the statutory divisions of *Shepard's* provide the legislative history of statutory law and show the reported states and federal court decisions and legislative enactments construing, applying, or affecting statutory law. In the natural sciences this method of research through citation is used in *Science Citation Index*.

The passage of Public Law 95–261 in 1978 afforded law school libraries the opportunity of becoming depository libraries for U.S. government publications, and many have done so. Dramatic increases in information services, collection content, and volume count will result from this effort to secure additional resources for law libraries and will enhance the libraries' abilities to serve their patrons more effectively.

Notable Collections. Accumulation of law book collections has been an ongoing activity for many years. The first law library established in the U.S. was the Law Library Company of Philadelphia, formed in 1802 by a group of lawyers. Three years later the first law library book catalogue for this library listed 249 volumes. The Boston Social Law Library opened in 1804. Two state libraries that have excellent law collections were also established in this period, Pennsylvania in 1816 and New York in 1818. The Harvard Law School, founded in 1817, established a library with the nucleus from the college library, gifts, and some purchases; by 1826 the library had 1,752 volumes. One of the better known American bar associations is the Association of the Bar of the City of New York, which was incorporated in 1869 and within two years had acquired 6,000 volumes. From these beginnings law libraries have increased astronomically both in quality and quantity of collections as well as in numbers of libraries. The Boston Social Law Library in the mid-1980s contained more than 250,000 volumes, the State Library of Pennsylvania Law Library over 170,000 volumes, and the New York State Law Library over 310,000 volumes. Ranking among the largest law libraries in the U.S. are the Association of the Bar of the City of New York Law Library at more than 450,000 volumes in the mid-1980s and the Los Angeles County Law Library with more than 800,000 volumes. The largest law library is the Law Library of Congress at about 2,000,000 volumes and at least 200,000 more when volumes in the Library of Congress are combined with the law collection.

The most spectacular growth in law library collections has occurred in law school libraries. From its humble beginnings in 1817, the Harvard Law School Library collection has consistently ranked the largest among law schools over the years, numbering 1,500,000 volumes in 1984. A span of some 700,000 volumes separates Harvard from those following in size: Columbia, 672,000; Yale, 631,000; New York University, 620,000; and those in the 500,000-volume range—the University of California at Berkeley, the University of Texas at Austin, and the University of Minnesota.

Some early common-law collections were known to exist in England, but most law school libraries were not independent of parent universities. The Bodleian Library at Oxford enjoys a long history, but its law collection was incorporated into the main collection even though in 1878 a concession was made to shelve the law collection separately from the remainder of the collection. A new building completed in 1964 first housed a separate Bodleian Law Library with approximately 250,000 volumes, the largest law library in the British Commonwealth today. Another law library in London enjoys a worldwide reputation for excellence. Assembling a law book collection under a cooperative acquisitions policy with four colleges of the University of London, the Institute for Advanced Legal Studies possesses an extensive common-law collection in addition to holdings in the law of Western European countries; the collection holds about 200,000 volumes.

One of the most outstanding library systems with a world reputation is in West Germany. The five Max Planck Institutes, in different cities, are devoted to legal studies on foreign and international law, dealing with criminal, public, and private law, patents, copyrights, and unfair competition as well as legal history. Their combined libraries with more than 500,000 volumes form a unique law collection.

Other libraries of excellence throughout the world that deserve mention are: York University Law Library (Toronto) at more than 200,000 volumes (1984), the largest law school library in Canada; the Law Courts Library of Sydney, Australia, with 160,000 volumes; the University of Singapore Law Library with approximately 100,000; the University of Tokyo, Faculty of Law Library at more than 400,000 volumes, and the Japanese Ministry of Justice Library with approximately 300,000 volumes; and the combined libraries of the Institute of Legal Studies and the Law School Library at the University of Lagos, Nigeria, for the best law collection in Africa.

Collection Development. Budgets and space are probably the two most significant delimiters to growth in law libraries. Ideally, a library should have every law title that its clientele could possibly desire at the time the need arises, but few, if any, libraries can operate in that kind of environment. Therefore, judgment must be made in the selection of types of legal information to be furnished. In those libraries where each acquisition must be justified, a library committee of attorneys may make the selections for the library. In other libraries the librarian may have more freedom in selection of materials for the collection. In some governmental libraries a central purchasing agency must approve the acquisitions. In law school libraries, where nearly all head librarians have both legal and library degrees, the selection of materials for the collection remains largely the librarians' prerogative.

Guidelines for the contents of law school libraries are provided by the AALS and the ABA. Designated types of books are required for the normal teaching function of accredited law schools. Sufficient flexibility is permitted so that the law school libraries may acquire the basic required library tools and in

addition purchase related materials to meet the specific interests of the faculty at each school.

As a further aid to book selection the AALS sponsored the publication in 1967 of a series of 48 pamphlets of *Law Books Recommended for Libraries* in subject areas from Admiralty to Water Law and Foreign and International Law. Supplements for each were issued beginning in 1974. Books are ranked in A, B, C order for priority in ordering. The "A" ranked books are recommended for purchase in all law school libraries. Medium libraries should possess the "B" books, and the only the largest law school libraries would be expected to own the "C" books, which are primarily official government publications and materials in foreign languages. A survey conducted by the AALL Special Networks Committee concluded that these rankings are largely valid, in accordance with the holdings of libraries in the various categories that checked their collections against the list.

To determine availability of current editions and prices of law books, law librarians may refer to *Law Books in Print,* which is updated periodically, and *Law Books 1876–1981,* updated by *Law Information.* Arranged by subject and alphabetically by author, they also provide the names and addresses of law book publishers, both United States and foreign, whose books are listed. Other bibliographies cover book selection, and publishers and dealers, of course, provide advertisements, brochures, a sales slip service, and catalogues for examination. Emphasis in law book buying is generally on the most current publications; interest in retrospective collections depends upon the availability of funds beyond those required for the current collection. A survey conducted in a general university library indicated that the majority of its book buying consisted of titles more than one year on the market, whereas the vast majority of the law book buying was prepublication or current-year publications. Law libraries are constantly under pressure to stay current with new publications.

Sizable law book collections, while an asset for study and research, can become a liability where space is concerned. A general rule of thumb in the academic world points out that law library collections tend to double in ten years. Many law school libraries, having felt this pinch already, are housed in new buildings, moving into new buildings, or planning new ones. Some housed in relatively new buildings are already searching for additional space. Restrictions in funding, particularly from public sources, and the space crunch combine to challenge the resourcefulness of librarians in coping with demands for access to more information and at the same time finding places to store it.

The accelerated growth of law library collections in recent decades and the increasing lack of book storage in libraries have encouraged law librarians to substitute nonbook media for hardcopy publications. Most law libraries now consider microforms—and will eventually consider videodisks—integral parts of the collection, rather than unusual media to be purchased as a last resort. Microform not only meets the challenge of shrinking shelf space, but also plays an important roll in preservation and in acquisition of out-of-print historical materials.

Law librarians see the future law library as a

computer and audiovisual resource laboratory, with a core collection of 100,000 to 150,000 volumes. Most legal research materials will be online in a database and accessed through terminals or microcomputers installed either in library areas or in remote offices and homes of the law school community. Books stored in the law library will be those usually read cover to cover. Reports that collect bits of information will be electronically stored and retrieved. Library users, no longer limited to in-house collections, will be able to access legal databases containing reference resources from every jurisdiction in the country and even from other countries. The traditional materials presently used as part of the teaching function and curriculum in law schools and housed usually in law libraries could give way to computer programs. Computer-assisted instruction (CAI), electronic publications, and communications will become commonplace. Supplements and course books will be in the form of annual updates published in-house as printouts. Judges' opinions will be prepared so that they can be processed electronically in computer-assisted legal research programs, such as WESTLAW and LEXIS, and retrieved independently by legal researchers.

Resource Sharing. Libraries are looking toward resource sharing as budgets and space are increasingly limited. In metropolitan areas, law libraries have been cooperating in sharing resources for many years. As more law firms hire professional librarians and information managers, this activity is likely to grow. Smaller libraries will tend to lean on the larger libraries for information support in the more esoteric sources and infrequently used titles. This tendency has been evident for years, and larger libraries tend to suffer or to feel that they do, in meeting the constant demands of the smaller libraries to the detriment of their own library patrons. Consequently, many larger libraries are now imposing fees for lending materials and have thereby effectively cut off a rich source of information for less fortunate library patrons.

Two online cataloguing systems were formed originally to provide shared cataloguing data. These systems, OCLC and RLIN, are developing rapidly, and as their databases increase, so does their value for other purposes. OCLC experimented with an interlibrary loan function online to assist in the borrowing and lending of library materials. A number of law school libraries participate in OCLC, so an interlibrary loan function may become valuable for law libraries. Even if a library does not participate in the online loan system, it is possible to determine what other libraries possess law titles and to write or telephone for a book loan.

As budgets become more limited and acquisitions agreements become more prevalent, the online systems will be even more valuable in determining if a title has been purchased by another library within the geographical area, or within the same size agency or institution, or if at all in the country. Cooperative acquisitions arrangements are more realistic with a tool like online cataloguing that is within the means of most law libraries.

Audiovisual Materials. In addition to law books and information in microform, many libraries are now expanding resources to include audio cassettes, video cassettes, films, etc. Condyne and the

The University of Chicago Law School

The University of Chicago Law School Library, designed by Eero Saarinen. Five floors of stacks and reading space rise above a ground-floor lounge.

State Bar of California are two large producers and distributors of audio tapes on current topics of the law. This format has become popular with those who have cassette players in their automobiles.

Videotapes have become a very popular medium for self-instruction in trial tactics and other practical subjects. Videotaping for self-criticism has become an acceptable teaching method in law schools as well as in continuing legal education seminars for lawyers, faculty, and judges. Although collecting video equipment and software requires a sizable investment of funds and employment of skilled personnel, the results are often worthwhile. Many law schools are now providing audiovisual services, either as a library function or through a separate department created for this purpose. A number of companies are producing legal tapes, including the American Trial Lawyers Association, the National Practice Institute, the Hastings College of Trial Advocacy, and the ABA.

Databases. Computerized legal information is relatively new as compared with systems operating with general, scientific, and medical databases. A latecomer in the field, computer-assisted research and instruction are making rapid strides and gaining in popularity and momentum. In contrast to systems available to other libraries, the legal databases are searchable in full text, thus providing greater research capability and in-depth accessibility to information. LEXIS and WESTLAW are predominately case databases. LEXIS, a product of Mead Data Central, first went online in 1969 for Ohio. Subsequently, as use increased and its reputation grew, other states were added to the system. WESTLAW is a product from the West Publishing Company, the largest law book publisher in the world. WESTLAW, first offered in 1975, contains cases from all states back to 1967 and with retrospective cases in selected states.

Both systems are available at commercial rates and special academic rates. Various preferences for use prevail—some users learn how to use the systems individually, while others depend upon library staff or specially designated professionals to frame the queries and search the databases. In law schools, learning how to use the systems is heavily emphasized, whereas in law firms, courts, and other legal units, only one or two persons may become skilled in computerized searching. Autocite, a Lawyer's Cooperative Publishing Company system that displays a case history, can be leased at communication and

437

computer connect time costs through LEXIS. Databases in other subjects with applicability to law can also be added to the law library's computer capabilities. *Wilson-Line* provides an online legal periodicals index source. *Legal Resource Index* provides a similar service through DIALOG.

The advent of the personal computer, the acceptance of LEXIS and WESTLAW by the legal profession, and the success of OCLC and RLIN as cooperative computer-assisted cataloguing programs have accelerated the use of automation in law libraries.

As information accessibility increases in automated form, expertise in searching improves, equipment costs decline, and more customers are added to systems, adequate databases will develop for current, and eventually for all, research.

Computer-assisted legal instruction is gaining in popularity in law libraries. Law programs, primarily in courses for trial practice, are available in both the EDUCOM and PLATO systems.

BETTY TAYLOR;
JULIUS J. MARKE

ADMINISTRATION, GOVERNANCE, AND FINANCE

There have been changes, sometimes dramatic and frequently subtle, in how law libraries function. The causes are many. In large part the changes developed from greater dependence on law libraries, brought on by greater involvement of law and government in life itself as society becomes more complex. There has been a wider demand for law library service, stimulated by such diverse movements and trends as consumerism, equal rights, and interdisciplinary awareness. Other contributors to change include the technology explosion, the increasing availability of nonbook media, and inflation. Such factors have led to changes in varying degrees among the different types of law libraries and have resulted in alterations yet to be perceived in the nature of law librarianship.

Law school libraries, with a few exceptions, are parts of law schools that in turn are parts of universities. Authority for their existence can derive from institutional fiat, from a mandate of the university's governing board, or in the case of some tax-supported institutions, from legislative enactment. Funding can come from tuition endowment, grants, legislative appropriation, or any combination of these sources.

The label "governmental law libraries" describes an array of law libraries serving the various levels of government. On the federal level there are very large law libraries, including the Law Library of Congress and the Department of Justice Library. The states, their administrative agencies, and the county and municipal units have analogs of these federal law libraries. Most states have a "state law library," meaning that library that has the primary responsibility of meeting the law information needs of state government. The actual title, mission, and governance of this entity, which is clearly recognized by law librarians, varies widely from state to state.

The federal and state court systems frequently have law libraries serving a particular court or group of courts. These are commonly referred to as supreme court libraries, court of appeals libraries, or some other term describing the type or types of courts served.

There are hundreds of county law libraries throughout the United States, which exist primarily to assure that litigants and their attorneys have access to law books, although other persons may also use these resources. County law libraries range greatly in size. The Los Angeles County Law Library in California and the Cook County Law Library in Chicago, Illinois, are among the largest law libraries anywhere; both have comprehensive library collections and large staffs. Other county law libraries have only a few thousand volumes and are staffed part time by clerks attached primarily to other units. County law libraries will normally derive their authority from state statutes, and their funding may come from appropriations from the state or county or from a portion of the fees charged to litigants for filing required papers relating to their business with the court.

Law firm libraries have been growing in numbers and size, and the employment of professional librarians in them has been increasing. Funding comes from the firms' revenues. Corporate law libraries are quite similar to law firm libraries. They serve the attorneys in the law department of corporations. These libraries can be found among the larger manufacturers, banks, insurance companies, and public utilities.

Finally, there is a miscellaneous category of law libraries that does not fit into any of the above groupings, although resemblances may be close in some instances. Included here are bar association law libraries, such as the American Bar Foundation Cromwell Library of the ABA and the Association of the Bar of the City of New York Library. Some learned societies and other organizations devoted to law, including the American Judicature Society and the American Society of International Law, maintain law libraries. These libraries are usually funded from members' dues and sometimes additionally by grants from charitable and other foundations.

Governance. The majority of head law school librarians answer to the deans of their law schools. Less typically, the law library will be a part of the

Main reference room at the Federal Trade Commission Library in Washington, D.C.

Federal Trade Commission

campus library system, but, even in this case, logic and tradition will compel a very close relationship between the law school and library. The head librarian, in most cases, will also be a member of the faculty. Law school libraries are often referred to as "the laboratory of the law school."

The problem of autonomy (whether the law library is part of the law school) versus centralization (whether the law library is a branch of the general library) is of great concern to academic law libraries. Two of the main issues raised in this concern are the subjection of the law library budget to the approval of the law school dean, rather than to the university librarian, and a complete inhouse library, including staffing, book ordering, and processing.

The majority of county libraries are governed by boards of trustees, or boards of directors, or library committees, usually with a judge, county administrator, county commissioner, or other county official as a member. The head librarian is selected by that governing body but then exercises control over management of personnel below that position.

A similar situation exists in the law firm library. Usually there is a library committee, with one or two partners in the firm designated as "library partner," and the head law librarian reports to them. The law firm administrator and law librarian must also work closely together. In line with the trend toward compartmentalization and specialization in legal practice, firms are employing more professional law librarians to maintain their libraries, and this, at times, can cause tensions between a new professional who wants to run his or her own shop and the administrator, partner, or legal secretary who used to have control.

Government agency libraries (including court libraries) serve their respective clienteles in much the same manner as law firm libraries. Overall governance will be handled more or less formally by a library committee, a single attorney or judge, or the judges or staff of attorneys acting as a committee of the whole. The majority of state law libraries are administratively placed under the judicial branch (viz. the state supreme court). The others come under a variety of organizational arrangements, including being under the state library, the department of education, the legislature, or the attorney general, or being independent.

The library committee, whether advisory or governing, is found within all types of law libraries. The nature of the library committee's activities is determined by its function rather than by the size and type of law library, although size has an indirect relationship to the amount of authority exercised by the head law librarian. The library committee best serves the librarian by advising on matters of general policy, the development of library resources, and means of integrating the library program with the other functions of the law firm, school, agency, or other institution. On the one hand, the library is an agency whose functions and services are varied and affect many; on the other hand, it is a tight, complex agency whose inner workings are largely unknown to those it serves except for certain obvious lending and reference functions performed at the circulation desk. The law library thus needs information from the governing committee about new policies, new courses, and new instructors in the academic law library setting, and new firm members and areas of practice in the law firm setting, because almost inevitably such matters have a direct bearing on the needs of the library and the services it should be able to provide. The library committee should be advisory to the librarian.

Finance. Law school libraries are funded through tax revenues in the case of public institutions and through tuition income in the case of private universities. In both instances, such funds can be supplemented through endowments, gifts, grants, and library-use fees. County law libraries may obtain funding through earmarked portions of filing fees required of litigants or by appropriation or allocation of funds by the governmental unit of which the library is a part. Portions of bar membership dues and income from photocopy machines, investments, and book sales are also sources of funds. Law firm and corporate law libraries are allocated funds by the governing members of the law firm, frequently through the office manager or legal administrator. Other private libraries, such as a membership library or a bar association library, derive their budgetary funds through membership fees and dues. It is possible for the law librarian to supplement regular funds through creative measures such as forming a Friends of the Law Library group from a nucleus of users, or from alumni in the law school library setting.

Other ways of supplementing the library budget are through charging fees for reference work and research, for interlibrary loan requests, and for photocopying. Almost universally, however, fees are charged only to recover costs of services to secondary patrons and not as a means of raising extra revenue.

Some law libraries have initiated publication programs to supplement funding, and others exchange or sell surplus books to other libraries or to book publishers.

Administration. The administration of the law library involves planning, policymaking, budget management, and personnel management.

Goals and Policy. Each type of law library necessarily plans its policies around the clientele it serves. Law librarians tend to identify closely with their clientele. Many have law degrees or some law training, and all have an interest in the subject matter and profession of law. This fosters close and sympathetic communication between librarian and patron in setting library goals and policy. The academic or university law school librarian must, of course, accommodate the needs of students and faculty. But other problems, such as the relationship with the general library and outside use of the law library by other law patrons, must be considered. A continuing problem for the larger law school libraries in metropolitan areas is the heavy use they get from practicing attorneys and from students in smaller law schools. The government library (federal, state, municipal, county, court) must serve the needs of the local courts and practitioners and yet deal with problems generated by outside use of the facilities by the public. Only in the law firm or corporate law library is the clientele strictly defined; yet even there, sharing of resources is an important factor, and a thriving interlibrary loan activity takes place both ways among law firms and other institutions and individuals.

Organizational Structure. Administration of the

law library involves departmentalizing the activities of the library to carry out its objectives. The determination of departmental groupings is based largely on the size of the library. In the small law library—for example in a law firm or government agency—there is little need for departmentalization. All functions are performed by one person or a small number of personnel. However, since almost all law libraries are relatively small, versatility and flexibility are highly valued among law librarians. In the larger library, the organizational structure parallels that of similarly sized general libraries.

The traditional functional organization provides separate departments for cataloguing, circulation, and reference; not infrequently the last two areas are combined into a single department. In this bifurcated functional organization all library activities are considered as either reader services or technical processes.

Because of the integrating tendencies of automation, law libraries, like other libraries, are witnessing the dissolution of the old compartments of ordering, serials, binding, cataloguing, and final book processing. These units are tending to blend into one rather homogeneous technical processing section. In public services, there has always been a tendency to treat reader services as a single activity, without the usual subdivision of circulation, reference, interlibrary loan, and so on. There are several reasons for this. For one thing, circulation tends to be a less distinct activity in law libraries. Few, if any, books circulate outside the premises. Where there is any charging out, it will be to offices, carrels, or other locations on the premises. Due dates, recalls, overdues, and fines, for example, are generally not significant. Charged materials are usually quickly retrievable and therefore regarded as information location problems like any other problems a reference librarian deals with.

Personnel Administration. No administrative duty of the librarian is more important than effective selection of staff. In working with relatively small staffs conducting essentially a personalized service, the quality of each member is critical. It is important in the law library to find staff with law-related experience beyond generalized library experience or at least to place newcomers to this subject field in a position where they can learn about law materials and special needs of law library users.

The typical library staff consists of librarians and nonprofessional assistants, augmented with student or part-time help. Professionalism is a current issue in librarianship, and paraprofessionals are in the middle of the controversy. Proposed solutions include certification standards promulgated by such groups as ALA, AALL, and ACRL, and minimum requirements for professional librarian positions. Most objections to the use of paraprofessionals in the library system are centered on the argument that expanded employment of paraprofessionals will displace professionals. However, many library tasks can be performed with efficiency by paraprofessionals.

The head law librarian is usually selected by the library's governing body or library committee, which then delegates the authority of selection of lower-level library positions to the head librarian. It is common for the librarian to nominate the professional and clerical staff, and it may be required that the latter be selected from a municipal or state civil service eligibility list in certain public institutions. The governing body of the library frequently passes on the librarian's nominations of professional staff members.

In well-established organizations the practice of permitting the librarian to make all recommendations of personnel, supporting such nominations with full data and references, has been demonstrated as effective procedure. Universal to recruitment and selection is the job description, which usually includes title, salary, and minimum qualifications, and lists basic responsibilities for that position. Job descriptions are used also to organize job hierarchies within the law library and set up salary classifications. Flexibility is important in establishing minimum qualifications to allow for consideration of on-the-job training or related coursework in lieu of a job requirement. Recruitment also involves considerations of affirmative action requirements and whether the administrator must select from a civil service roster or another institutional eligibility list.

Staff size in relation to the physical size of the library will vary according to the function that the law library serves. For example, a very small law firm library may have more than one staff member because the attorneys rely on the librarian as a source of information and research. In the larger academic library, staff size in proportion to library size may be much smaller, because of a relatively greater reliance on the collection itself, rather than the personnel.

Administration of the law library involves allowing for interaction between individual personnel and the greater organization of the library. Participatory management is the style and philosophy frequently encountered in law libraries.

Budget. The budget of a law library affects nearly every major consideration in its administration. It is customary in some law libraries to classify the budget by object or type of material, thus establishing separate categories of expenditure for treatises, periodicals, continuations, supplies, equipment, and such other items that local practice may identify. Most law libraries utilize such line-type budgets, while others, especially law firm libraries, may prepare lump-sum budgets, or categorize by department or area of law rather than type of material.

Many law school libraries use comparative statistics to justify budget expenditures. The results of statistical surveys of law school libraries and librarians are published annually in the May issue of the *Law Library Journal*.

In some of the smallest law firm libraries, budgets are not yet a fixture of the law librarian's position. However, they are of growing concern as the firm realizes the impact of expenditures of its library and the need to keep track of and control over that investment.

Microform offers economies in initial cost and shelving space, and law libraries in particular are attracted to this medium because so much of their material is available in microform. But lawyers, who are used to finding their information in large, premium quality texts with all of the bibliographic and typographical conveniences, often resist this format. The economies, if any, and other impact of automation (aside from information retrieval) were comparatively late in coming to law libraries, probably because as relatively small economic units they often cannot afford the high capital costs. Law library administrators have had to look toward linking up with larger units or networks or to the purchase of commercially packaged systems. Few libraries now attempt to be "complete" in any of the broad areas. Even the largest, best-supported libraries find it difficult to cover an area such as all foreign law. All of this, of course, is not unique to law libraries but reflective of current conditions in all areas of librarianship and in society in general.

MORTIMER SCHWARTZ;
JULIUS J. MARKE

MEASUREMENT AND EVALUATION
The problem of measurement and evaluation of libraries has puzzled law librarians and those responsible for the administration and funding of law libraries during most of this century. Standards were adopted early by both the American Bar Association (ABA) and the Association of American Law Schools (AALS). Members of the American Assocation of Law Libraries (AALL) participated actively in the preparation of these standards, which were and still are largely quantitative and applicable only to law school libraries. Little had been done until the late 1970s to develop standards for court, government, bar association, or law firm libraries. The available standards have been useful especially when tied to an enforcement process, as in the accreditation of law schools; whether voluntary standards, without supporting enforcement, can be effective remains to be tested. At best, the development of standards and their application has been slow and painful.

Similarly, statistical information has been available for the law school libraries for many years but for other types of law libraries only recently. Statistical information for law libraries is useful for comparison and serves as a basis for future planning by library administrators and the profession as a whole. Librarians are able to evaluate their libraries on a quantitative basis or at least compare their libraries with others, but, in doing so, problems have arisen.

The far more difficult question, whether *qualitative* measurement and evaluation are possible, remains the subject of such argument. Because of this difficulty, library standards have tended more to be guidelines based on practices in existing institutions than to be standards in a qualitative sense. Statistical information provides a basis of comparison and in that way reinforces those standards, but many have urged the development of qualitative standards by which law libraries could be measured in terms of size, structure, clientele, resources, services, and staff. If libraries could be graded in relation to each institution's potential, each library would have a guide for the improvement of its collection and services. The argument for qualitative standards has continued steadily but without resolution. The ABA and the AALS are reviewing their law library standards with the purpose of making them qualitative rather than quantitative.

Perhaps because of the lack of qualitative standards, quantitative comparisons are made and have become qualitative by application. Thus "big becomes better" even though it is clear that volume

Leonard Parker Associates

Main Reading Room at the University of Minnesota Law Library. Glass wall looks into the adjoining undergraduate classroom building.

count alone reveals little about the quality of a collection or a library's adequacy for its mission. Volume count—absent accurate physical counting based on agreed practices and with uniform conversion of microforms and other nonbook resources to equivalent volumes—stands, at most, as a questionable basis for comparison, be it quantitative or qualitative. The AALL Committee on Bibliographic Standards prepared recommended definitions and guidelines for nonprint and nonbook library resources that, if adopted and followed, will relieve the problem but unfortunately not resolve it.

Law School Libraries. The AALS, organized in 1900, promulgated the first statement of minimum requirements for law libraries. Member schools were required to own, or have convenient access to, a library containing the reports of the state in which the school was located and of the United States. These requirements have been amended and refined as legal education has changed and the role of law libraries and law librarians in that educational process has developed. The By-laws and Executive Committee Regulations of The Association (1985) require "a library adequate for the curriculum and for research." It must also be maintained and administered as a "growing library collection capable of sustaining a modern curriculum and a full-scale student and faculty research program." It must also have a full-time librarian and an adequate staff, including professionals and clerical assistants. The librarian should be "a full participating member of the faculty."

In 1921 the ABA adopted formal standards to be used in the approval of law schools. These first standards required only that an approved law school provide an adequate library for the students. The *Standards for the Approval of Law Schools* (1983) require that a law school maintain and administer a library adequate for its program. No minimum volume count or minimum number of professional staff is specified, although a list of required titles is included.

The United States Department of Education has

recognized the ABA as the national accrediting agency for legal education. The Council on Postsecondary Accreditation similarly has recognized the ABA's program of accreditation. Law schools are inspected as part of the provisional accreditation process and after full approval are reinspected once every seven years.

Although there are differences in the ABA Standards and the AALS requirements for membership, both associations are concerned with the same basic operations. ABA and AALS have conducted joint inspections of member schools. Law librarians were included as members of the site inspection teams during the 1970s, and an ABA manual, "Suggestions for Law Library Inspectors," appeared in 1976 and is periodically updated. It contains a checklist that has proved useful in the evaluation of libraries.

Statistics on law school libraries are available in the annual *Review of Legal Education in the United States,* published by the ABA. A more detailed statistical survey is published annually in the May issue of the *Law Library Journal.* Such data are extremely helpful in comparing collections, growth rates, budgets, and staff, and in providing useful information on such subjects as hours and seating capacity. Unfortunately, the utility of this information is restricted by the lack of uniformity in reporting practices.

Law school library statistics are prepared by the office of the Statistics Coordinator of the AALL in cooperation with the Consultant on Legal Education to the ABA. Statistics pertaining to every facet of law school library organization, service, and budget are gathered annually.

Nonacademic Law Libraries. The first general study of law libraries outside the law schools appeared in 1953 as part of the Survey of the Legal Profession sponsored by the ABA, published as *The Libraries of the Legal Profession* by William Roalfe, then Law Librarian and Professor of Law at Northwestern University. The focus of this study was on all types of law libraries serving the legal profession except those in law schools. Roalfe concluded that much more information was needed about the libraries serving the legal profession, their collections, their staffs, and their funding. He emphasized the need for better libraries located throughout the nation and available to all segments of the legal profession. The availability of these libraries to the general public was not studied, and little or no attention was given to this matter for another quarter century.

Standards for nonlaw school libraries were made available only in the late 1970s. The State, Court, and County Law Libraries Special Interest Section of AALL prepared *Standards for Supreme Court Law Libraries* (adopted 1977 and revised 1978), *Federal Court Libraries* (adopted 1978), and *County Law Libraries* (adopted 1978). Their effectiveness, without an enforcement procedure, remains to be tested. Whether similar standards can, or will, be developed for other types of nonacademic libraries remains a challenge to the profession.

A report entitled "Improving the Federal Court Library System" was prepared in 1978 for the Federal Judicial Center on the libraries of the federal courts. The study, which focused on management, budget and procurement, personnel, use and facilities, and the need for future planning, was submitted to the Judicial Conference of the United States for consideration.

Statistical information on nonacademic law libraries has become increasingly available. A survey of law firm libraries and librarians first appeared in 1974, and an annual survey of law libraries serving a local bar has appeared since 1976. Both surveys seek to provide the kind of basic information on collection, income, expenditures, staffing, and salaries previously available only for law school libraries and have proved useful for comparative purposes. Unfortunately, the same problems encountered in the use of such data discussed above apply here.

Professional Qualifications. The argument over the professional qualifications for law librarians began early. Many have felt, and some still feel, that the administration of the law library is a fairly simple matter that can be learned in a short period of time and that does not require professional education. Those who argued for professionally qualified librarians generally favored law training, with only a few preferring library training. Librarians with degrees in both law and library science did not appear in any number until after World War II. Today, most head librarians in the law schools have both degrees, and in fact the AALS membership regulations state that the head librarian should have both legal and library education.

The focus of attention has now shifted to the educational requirements for supporting professional staff and to the need for continuing education for librarians at all levels of the profession. The AALL has concerned itself with both the education and continuing education of its members. The programs at annual meetings have sought to provide educational opportunities for the membership. In 1964 the Association began a series of Rotating Institutes in response to the increasing demand for education, and two series were completed before the Association discontinued them. Most head librarians, and an increasing number of supporting professional staff, enter the profession with library degrees. Librarians with advanced degrees in related areas. especially computer science, are also part of the profession today. AALL's Education Committee has presented a variety of programs to meet needs for continuing education.

BETTY LEBUS; JULIUS J. MARKE

LAW LIBRARY COOPERATION

Cooperation among law libraries occurs in various ways. There are the traditional interlibrary loan procedures, which do not differ from those of other types of libraries. Most law libraries, especially those of university law schools, will lend materials to other libraries and will borrow when needed, using standard ALA interlibrary forms. Perhaps the only distinguishing feature is that more materials in a law library are of a reference nature and do not circulate under any circumstances. Increasingly, however, law libraries are providing photocopies in lieu of lending the item itself.

But law libraries do participate in other forms of cooperation. At universities, although nearly all law school libraries are administered as part of the law school rather than as a branch of the university library, the acquisition of library materials is frequently coordinated. This occurs because of the commonality of interest among law professors and historians, political scientists, sociologists, economists, and criminologists. Moreover, agreement is frequently reached on the most effective place to house certain government documents, such as reports of administrative agencies, and other interdisciplinary materials. Sometimes the university as a whole will be better served to have some of these materials shelved in the law library with other sets shelved elsewhere on campus.

Cooperation may also occur on an interlibrary basis. In large cities law firm libraries in the same or nearby buildings will agree that one will buy one expensive set and the other another. Larger law libraries in the same metropolitan area will frequently assume responsibility to share the acquisition of foreign law. One library may assume responsibility, for example, for legal materials of Latin America, while one or more will collect European legal materials.

While there has been much discussion of a national coordinated scheme of cooperation among law libraries, in practice cooperation has been limited to local areas with informal agreements among the cooperating libraries. While much has been accomplished by such arrangements, the lack of an organized and planned program has had its effect. Cooperative schemes organized with the best of intentions have faltered with change of personnel, either at the level of the law librarian or at a higher administrative position.

Several factors, however, now point to an increased and more organized effort toward cooperation among law libraries. These factors are inflation, an ever expanding growth in the subjects of law, and the development of computer-based library networks. The extent of the growth of the law in recent years is perhaps not generally realized, even by lawyers. Society seems to feel that any new societal problem can be solved only by passing new legislation.

Some subject areas of the law developed in the decades of the mid-1960s to the mid-1980s include computer law, energy law, environmental law, fair employment practices, nuclear regulation, and pollution control, to name only a few. All of these are primarily examples of domestic law; many other examples from international and comparative law could also be cited. This growth in the law by itself has had a significant impact on the acquisitions policies of law libraries. With economic restraints, the pressure for cooperation indeed becomes urgent. Prices for legal periodicals and legal series increased steeply as a reflection of inflation of the latter 1970s.

Law libraries, therefore, perhaps even more than some other types of libraries, have the impetus to enter into cooperative agreements. As national and regional networks became operational, law libraries were quick to participate. Law school libraries frequently joined with their university libraries, although usually arranging to keep their records separately identifiable. In a few instances a law school library has joined a network different from that of its university library when it appeared the network would better meet its needs. Law libraries not connected with universities have also joined networks, either through joining a regional network or directly with a national one. However, while law libraries have taken advantage of new technology, the effect has been to diversify the cataloguing data of the various law libraries, impeding the further development of shared acquisitions and cataloguing programs among law libraries. Some of the larger law libraries, such as the University of Texas, Cornell, and the University of Florida, joined the OCLC system, while many of the larger research law libraries, such as the Los Angeles County Law Library, University of California at Berkeley and Davis, Stanford, the University of Michigan, New York University, and Columbia are in the Research Library Information Network (RLIN) of the Research Libraries Group (RLG). Others joined still other networks.

A Law Library Network. Among law librarians, however, there is a felt need for a common database for legal materials. Larger law libraries do about 50 percent original cataloguing, and records on most of this important material are not available to those law libraries not in the same network or not in any network. To remedy this situation, a number of law librarians met in the latter part of 1975 and recommended the creation of a national law library network. The concept of a network based on a subject, rather than on geography, is rather new and raised many types of problems. In order to measure the feasibility of a law network, the AALL, in cooperation with the AALS, engaged a consultant, Brett Butler, to advise on the matter. His 1978 report, *Toward a Law Network: Survey and Evaluation,* indicated that such a subject network is indeed feasible. The report recommends that the AALL sponsor the development of a law information network (LAWNET). This network, among other things, would assume the responsibility for the development of standard subject headings for law libraries, standards for the format of bibliographic records, standards for the content of a law database, and other necessary standards. The report further recommends that LAWNET should proceed to build a composite database by merging selected machine-readable files gathered from those law libraries currently inputting their records into a network. Once the database is created, and procedures have been developed for maintaining and updating it, LAWNET should arrange to have such a service available online and also available for distribution to smaller law libraries on microfiche. It further recommended the development of a "LAWNET Location Guide," which would provide listings by title and control number for all monographs and serials in the LAWNET database along with location code. The AALL is still exploring ways of implementing the recommendations for the creation of LAWNET.

This development has tremendous possibilities not only for law libraries but for other types of libraries. First, it may become a prototype for the feasibility of creating a national network by subject that may be of interest to other types of special libraries such as music, art, or engineering. Second, it will provide for an intelligent basis for shared acquisitions and cataloguing; for example, one large law library might assume all the responsibility for the original cataloguing of German materials, another for French, and still another for Italian. Under such a system all other law libraries would not have to do any original cataloguing for legal materials from those geographic areas.

Similarly, as the system grows, law libraries can start to develop coordinated acquisitions programs to ensure that all necessary legal research materials are available without unnecessary duplication. Attention will also be given to document delivery.

The significance of this program to other types of libraries should be self-evident. The need for legal materials in nonlaw libraries is growing. Large public libraries have to supply information to their patrons who may be interested in such diverse subjects as the control of the environment or of nuclear energy or even, for example, to provide information to irate citizens who want to know their rights when their reservations are not honored by an airline. Similarly, more and more undergraduate programs emphasize courses in which access to legal materials is necessary. Yet, with budget restraints, these libraries find it difficult to maintain an adequate legal collection. The development of LAWNET will make legal materials available not only to other law libraries but to other libraries in need of legal materials.

In summary, the fact that law libraries have not had a national law library comparable with the National Library of Medicine or the National Library of Agriculture has hindered the development of cooperation among law libraries. Considerable cooperation has developed and now concerted efforts are being made for cooperation on a national level. As this develops, and as law libraries increase their participation in other national plans for better bibliographic control, not only law libraries will benefit but all libraries will be better able to meet the growing demand of the public for legal information.

J. MYRON JACOBSTEIN;
JULIUS J. MARKE

LAW AND LEGISLATION

Any attempt to describe briefly the legislative foundation for U.S. law libraries is perilous indeed. First, the definition of what is a law library is subject to a criticism of being arbitrary; that criticism may be rebutted if the library is denominated a law library by its senior authority or governing rules. However, when the collection is an integral component of a larger administrative unit, or, although physically distinct, the collection is referred to as the "state library," "legislative library," or "department library," the definition of law library must be based on the nature of its collection, its services, and its primary clientele, and is necessarily subjective. Second, many law libraries cannot trace their birth to specific legislation. Rather, in many if not most instances libraries have evolved from informal office collections to major resources as an adjunct to the mission of the senior agency without initial statutory approbation. Third, the sovereign independence of 50 state legislatures as well as that of the federal government results in a variety of approaches in the formulation of law library statutes that discourage their classification and the development of broad generalizations about them.

Federal Legislation. In 1832 direct statutory action was responsible for the creation of the paramount federal law library, the Law Library of Congress. It was established as one of the two administrative units of the Library of Congress, and it was the intention of the lawmakers to form a convenient collection of law books for the use of the Supreme Court, which at that time was also located in the Capitol. As activities of the Library of Congress and the Supreme Court evolved, however, particularly when the Supreme Court was given its own building in 1935, the specific purpose of that early statute seemed to be lost. In 1977, however, under a reorganization plan proposed by the Librarian of Congress, the law library would have become one of several subject departments. The 150-year-old law was recalled as the keystone of a vigorous defense of the status quo. Focusing on the language of the early statute, supporters of the Law Library of Congress argued strongly that the special status should be maintained. Faced with these strong representations, the Library of Congress withdrew its immediate plan to reorganize insofar as the Law Library was concerned and indicated that it would subject the matter to further study and subsequent review.

The Law Library of Congress continues to stand as a distinct unit in the Library of Congress. Through its specialized organization along worldwide regional lines, the Law Library serves its primary clientele, the members of Congress. Additionally, it serves as one of the nation's capital resources in the collection of legal materials on a global scale.

A separate department in the Library of Congress was created by statute in 1946 for the analysis, appraisal, and evaluation of legislative proposals. Originally called the Legislative Reference Service, it changed its name in 1970 to the Congressional Research Service. Since this unit does not manage large book collections, it is not exactly a library; and as its interest ranges much more widely across the subject spectrum than merely the law in a narrow sense, it is not exactly a law library. Yet, because it does directly serve the legislative branch and, further, because the Service's enabling act specifically authorizes the appointment of American public law specialists, it can be asserted that a law library was created. This institution serving the federal legislature exemplifies a type of legislative law library that is frequently found in state government.

Two other most significant congressional libraries, those of the House of Representatives and the Senate, although again not specifically law libraries, have a substantial legal content and are representative of libraries that began somewhat informally. The House and Senate were no doubt collecting books, documents, and other material for their own use from the earliest days, but in the spring of 1792 both bodies passed simple resolutions that specifically charged the Secretary of the Senate and the Clerk of the House to procure or purchase library materials for their respective use. Subsequent legislative history provides ample evidence of legislative recognition of the existence of these libraries. Appropriations, debates about library space, and statutory provisions for appointment of librarians and administrative control all contribute to understanding the legislative support that has encouraged the development of two libraries.

The Library of the U.S. Supreme Court similarly evolved over a period of time without benefit of specific statutory creation. The legal collection created in 1832 for the use of the Justices ultimately developed into the Law Library of Congress. When the Court occupied the Supreme Court Building in 1935, it satisfied its law book needs by gift, with duplicates from the Library of Congress, with a small collection that had served the Court's Conference Room while it was in the Capitol, and by purchase with supplemental appropriations. The Supreme Court Building, constructed with space for a major library, is indicative of initial legislative approval and support for the nation's largest library exclusively devoted to the judicial function.

The libraries of the several courts of appeals and district courts also developed both informally and by statute. When books were necessary to carry out the legal work of the judiciary, they were acquired as a function of regular court procurement. In 1948, however, possibly in reaction to the growth of these libraries and the need for appropriate supervision, statutory authority was granted to each court of appeals to appoint a librarian and necessary library assistants. A companion statute authorized the appointment of a Marshal for the Court of Customs and Patent Appeals who would buy books and supplies and supervise the library. In 1954 the Tax Court was specifically authorized to make purchases of those library reference books and materials necessary to execute its functions.

Although no specific statutory authority seems to exist for the law libraries of the several executive departments, they have no doubt come into being either, as in the Departments of Commerce and Interior, by virtue of the authority establishing the general library of those departments or, as in the Departments of Energy and Justice, as concomitant resources to the departments' meeting their larger statutory mission. Thus the combination of explicit statutory authority to establish libraries and the implicit authority to collect library books as part of required resources provided the framework for the law libraries of the federal government to grow and prosper since their early beginnings.

Law libraries nationally have, of course, been affected by those laws that have an impact on libraries generally. Some law libraries have benefited from federal grants applicable to library building projects through the Library Services and Construction Act. Others have received some federal support for collection development. Law libraries feel the pressures of increased postage costs and regulatory limitations on the meaning of the special "library rate." But in each of these instances the law library reacts to the legislation as a library and not in any particular way because it is a law library, and thus these laws have not had any unique meaning for law libraries. One law, however, that does deserve special mention is the Depository Library Act. Although this law has been of immeasurable benefit to the general library community, and it did for many years permit state libraries and the highest state appellate court libraries to become depositories for U.S. government publications, the 1978 amendment allowing all approved law school libraries to request depository status was of substantial importance. Additionally, even though a number of law school libraries had, over time, become depositories in their own right under the historical provision of the Act, most law school libraries, including several major research centers, had never been able to take advantage of depository benefits. This extension of the Act resulted in a great

flurry of interest in documents by law librarians in the months that followed. While other laws may have been more significant in the development of the library of a particular institution, the depository law is in some measure the federal legislation that has had the single greatest impact on law libraries nationally.

State Legislation. The laws that resulted in the formation of law libraries in the several states generally follow the pattern outlined for the federal government. In general, librarians tend to classify these law libraries under three major heads: state law libraries, supreme court libraries, and county law libraries. Since state and supreme court libraries so frequently overlap in their functions and governance, joint treatment of them is appropriate.

State and Supreme Court Libraries. The respondents to a 1974 survey of state and supreme court law libraries indicated a wide disparity of organizational structures. Two libraries indicated they were units of legislative or administrative departments. Two other libraries were units of the state Attorney General's office. Two libraries were units of the legislative council, while four libraries were part of a larger, more comprehensive state library. In four instances the judicial branch shared a law library with a department of education, while there were six examples of the judicial and executive branches of government sharing the same law library. Finally, 29 law libraries were units of the judicial branch exclusively. Statutory review supports the responses from the librarians themselves. The statutes of 37 states specifically establish either a state law library, a law department of a state library, or a law library for the supreme court. Twenty-one states, including 18 of these 37, have established a legislative reference service that is also, in some instances, a department of the state library or the state law library. With this variety of organizations, some resulting from statutes that are based upon the earliest state administrative relationships and others on evolutionary development, it is difficult indeed to generalize about state law libraries. Most state statutes do, however, attempt to authorize law library service for the judicial branch. By placing superintending control in the hands of the state supreme court or a committee upon which one or more members of the supreme court sit, there is at least the opportunity that the court will receive appropriate service. The method of financing the state and court libraries is uneven, resulting in some libraries that are extremely strong, while others are of more modest circumstances. One library receives at least part of its financing from the sale of its court reports, another from a tax on newly admitted lawyers, a third from a fund composed of court fees, and a fourth from the proceeds of a state land grant. In most instances the laws are silent as to the specific services that the library is required to render, although several do specifically require that the library be open to the public.

Several libraries by statute and others, imitating the U.S. Supreme Court, by court rule prohibit the circulation of books from the court building. In one state the librarian is guilty of a misdemeanor if an unauthorized person borrows a book from the library! William B. Roalfe noted in his 1953 study, *The Libraries of the Legal Profession*, that "the service provided by state court libraries sometimes leaves a great deal to be desired and most of them operate on a level well below that maintained by the best examples." More than three decades later the statutory base of the state and court libraries had not changed substantially.

County law libraries are authorized by 35 states and consequently represent, at least potentially, a major resource for providing legal materials. Once again the minds of legislators have conceived a plethora of methods to fund county law libraries. Seventeen states use a system of filing fees and fines to support law libraries, while an additional 14 states have fixed appropriations. Five states use a combination of filing fees and appropriations, while the balance rely for funds on other miscellaneous fees.

There seems to be no particular advantage to the major types of funding in achieving a substantial level of library support. California, for example, uses the fee system; Ohio uses fines; New York relies on appropriations. In each of these states strong county law libraries have resulted, although Ohio with 44 county law libraries and California with 58 seem to provide a more extensive county law library system. In fact, the existence of substantial populations and the volume of litigation probably have a greater impact on law library development than the particular statutory method devised to support law library service. It is evident, however, that a financial support mechanism that is tied directly to litigation, such as filing fees or fines, will tend to provide a level of support that will automatically move upward as the demands increase. A survey of county law libraries in California indicates that a filing fee funding system has resulted in an array of law libraries roughly proportional to the general and lawyer populations in their respective counties. Legislative developments in most states have not matched, and probably, because of more limited means, cannot be expected to match, the resources of the great research in Los Angeles County Law Library, but the challenge of more generous funding for county law libraries in more populous counties in other jurisdictions still awaits the legislative ingenuity of many of the states.

ROGER F. JACOBS;
JULIUS J. MARKE

Lebanon

Lebanon is a republic of the Middle East on the eastern shore of the Mediterranean Sea. Population (1983 est.) 2,598,000; area 10,230 sq.km. The official language is Arabic; French and Armenian are also spoken.

History. Called Land of the Cedar in the Bible, Lebanon could also be called the land of the book. A Phoencian inscription at a tomb believed to be that of Ahiram, dated between the 13th and the 10th centuries B.C., is located at a site 25 miles north of Beirut known as Jbail, or Byblos (Greek translation), which is derivated from the word *biblio* or book. The Lebanese archaeological sites, Baalbek, Tyre, Sidon, Tripoli, and Byblos, show signs of libraries during the classical period. During the monastic period, almost every monastery had a library, but those were not organized. The best known monastic libraries were the Holy Savior, founded in 1711 near Sidon, and the Salvatorian monastery at Khonshara, founded in 1696, both belonging to the Greek Catholic sect. In 1970 a microfilming project recorded the collections of all the monasteries, and microfilms were deposited at the American University of Beirut.

Modern librarianship in Lebanon started in the 19th century with academic libraries. The American University of Beirut (AUB) was established in 1866 (as the Syrian Protestant College) and the French Saint Joseph College in 1881. Most of Lebanon's libraries were founded in the mid-1960s. However, those libraries were concentrated in Beirut, the capital, or its outskirts, leaving remote areas with few services or nothing at all.

As a result of war, the libraries declined after 1976, when many libraries were destroyed, burned, or looted. These remaining were indirectly affected by migration of personnel; frozen or cut budgets, effects of inflation, and the devaluation of the local currency (more than 100%) and loss of purchasing power. All these factors halted library services and any advancement in this field to a strict minimum in more than 80 percent of the existing libraries, leaving library service a lamentable situation in the mid-1980s.

National Library. The Lebanese National Library, also a public library but without borrowing privileges, was placed under the Ministry of National Education in 1922. It started with the personal collection of Viscount Philippe de Tarazi at the National Museum. In 1937 it moved to the Parliament building. Although a copyright deposit law (November 1941) and an amendment (1959) were passed, the Library could never enforce it.

The Library's aims and objectives were never defined, and it never had a qualified librarian. No recent inventory was taken, and its collection of 100,000 volumes and 2,000 rare manuscripts was partially burned and looted and partially saved during the Le-

Libraries in Lebanon (1984)

Type	Administrative units	Service points	Volumes in collections	Annual expenditures (pound)	Population served	Professional staff	Total staff
Academic	7	37	1,326,020	--	99,619	43	204
Public	6	6	93,550	--	4,000	2	13
School[a]	5	5	58,000	--	4,245	2	9
Special	20	20	214,839	--	9,430	13	58
Government	4	4	160,600	--	450	5	35

[a]Based on five major schools.

Source: Survey of Information Centres in Lebanon (Aida Kassantini Hafez, Ph.D. thesis, University College, London, 1984).

banese war that started in the mid-1970s and still had not ended by the mid-1980s. Approximately 20 information centers were directly damaged by the war. A National Library did not exist in the mid-1980s.

Academic Libraries. At the American University of Beirut, "the Jafet Complex," comprising four libraries, is the richest in funds and qualified staff. Beirut Arab University is academically affiliated to the University of Alexandria, Egypt. Its four libraries, holding collections mainly in Arabic, place it as best among Arabic Lebanese libraries.

At the Lebanese University the six Faculties and two Institutes were split into 16 after the Lebanese war. Thus in 1984 it had 16 libraries plus the 3 libraries of the Mohafazat (prefectorate) of Bekaa, North and South, totaling 19.

At the Beirut University College, Stolzfus Library is noted for its well-organized collection, its Documentation Center of the Institute for Women Studies in the Arab World, and its Children's Library (a multimedia learning center for education students and the only children's public Library in Lebanon). Haigazian College Library possesses a good collection on Armenology. At Saint Joseph University seven libraries possess a good collection mainly in French.

Public Libraries. A law obliging each municipality to have a public library exists, but the libraries are small and lack financial support. Libraries of foreign Cultural Centers serve as public Libraries, such as those associated with the British Council, French Cultural Center, Spanish Cultural Center, the Goethe Institute, and others.

School Libraries. There are approximately 2,460 private and public schools in Lebanon with libraries that are like storerooms for the use of the teaching staff only. The library at the International College, a private school, rates best among them.

Special Libraries. Special libraries are primarily in the private sector in research and trade organizations and banking and engineering firms. A leading special library is Beit Al Mustakbal, an automated modern library, unique in the Middle East and covering a wide range of information on Lebanon. The Oriental Institute of the German Academy of Orientalists is a well-organized library. A decree of January 1978 established an Institute of National Archives centered in Beirut and administratively and financially independent.

No statistics on archives in Lebanon were available from public sources.

The Profession. Two institutions taught Information/Library Science in the mid-1980s. Lebanese University had a four-year program leading to a B.A. in Information Science under the Faculty of Information and Documentation. Beirut University College had a two-year program leading to an Associate of Arts in Library Science, and a study was under way to develop the program into a four-year program, awarding a B.A. in information science.

Academic and special libraries have the largest number of professionals. The Lebanese Library Association was founded in 1960. The LLA is a member of IFLA. It has no government-allocated budget or its own premises. It approved the Library Science program taught at Lebanese University.

AIDA KASSANTINI HAFEZ

Gottfried Wilhelm Leibniz

Leibniz, Gottfried Wilhelm
(1646–1716)

A German philosopher, mathematician, scientist, jurist, historian, linguist, and librarian, Leibniz contributed extensively in many disciplines; this article concentrates on his contributions to librarianship and information science.

Liebniz was born in Leipzig on July 1, 1646, into a pious Lutheran family; his father was a professor and his mother the daughter of a professor at the University of Leipzig. A precocious boy, Leibniz learned to read early and widely; he taught himself Latin in the library of his father, who died when Gottfried was only six years old. From 1653 to 1661 he attended the local Nicolaischule, where among other subjects he acquired a knowledge of Greek and was impressed by the study of Aristotelian logic.

When he was nearly 15 he entered the University of Leipzig. He obtained a broad general education but concentrated on the study of philosophy and law. In 1662 he earned a Bachelor's degree and in 1664 a Master's degree of the Philosophical Faculty. A year later he obtained a Bachelor of Laws degree. Then he began to work on his doctoral dissertation, *Dissertatio de arte combinatoria (Dissertation on the Art of Combination),* which he published in 1666. His dissertation was influenced by the combinatorial logic of the Spanish mystic Raymond Lully. In this work he formulated a model that is a theoretical forerunner of modern computer logic; he saw his art of combination and permutation as a logical calculus and a logic of discovery that could lead to significant new insights. But when he wanted to obtain his Doctor of Laws degree during the same year, a majority of his faculty refused it because they felt he was still too young. Disappointed, he left his native city and moved to Altdorf, a university town close to Nürnberg, where at age 21 he earned a Doctor of Laws degree with distinction for his dissertation *On Perplexing Cases.* But he refused to accept a teaching position at the University of Altdorf.

In Nürnberg Leibniz met the retired statesman Johann Christian von Boineburg (1622–72), who had been the most prominent minister of Johann Philipp von Schönborn (1605–73), the ruling Archbishop and Elector of Mainz. With von Boineburg's recommendation, Leibniz obtained a position as legal counselor at this court and was assigned the task of revising and improving the German legal code. Von Boineburg owned a sizable private library and invited Leibniz to become his part-time librarian. Between 1668 and 1673 Leibniz had a classed catalogue prepared for this collection. The catalogue (rediscovered after World War II) consisted of four volumes with 9,840 main entries. Its major divisions corresponded to those that the German bibliographer and clergyman Georg Draud had used for his *Bibliotheca classica,* which had first appeared in 1611. A second edition was published in 1625, and both editions were available in von Boineburg's collection. The 15 main classes were further subdivided by many alphabetically arranged subject headings, several of which were sometimes used for the same work. But the death of von Boineburg brought the work to a halt; the catalogue is incomplete, and the syndetic devices are sparse. A general alphabetic author index has not been found.

In 1672 Leibniz was sent on a diplomatic mission to Paris, where he managed to stay for almost four years. In this vibrant metropolis he devoted himself to intensive studies and became acquainted with a number of the most renowned scientists. He also got to know the prominent librarians of the city, among them N. Clément, who introduced him to the rapidly growing Bibliothèque du Roi and its policies. His studies in Paris and visits to London in 1673 and 1676 broadened his intellectual horizons and established many scientific contacts for life. In 1673 he was elected a Member of the Royal Society.

Contributions to Librarianship. The need for a regular income forced Leibniz to accept a position as Counselor and Librarian at the court of Duke Johann Friedrich of Brunswick-Lüneburg, who owned in 1676 a private library of some 3,310 volumes, among them 158 manuscripts. Later Leibniz was also appointed Historiographer at the court, and he held these positions until his death in 1716. Unfortunately, the intellectual Johann Friedrich died in 1679, and his successor, Ernst August, did not appreciate libraries as much as his cosmopolitan brother. Leibniz was able to provide Ernst August with valuable historical and genealogical information that helped him to become Elector of Hanover in 1692. Nor did library support improve under Ernst August's son Georg Ludwig, who succeeded him in 1698 and became King George I of Great Britain in 1714.

In addition to his library duties at the Hanoverian Court, Leibniz was in 1690 appointed Librarian of the valuable Ducal Library at Wolfenbüttel, which was owned by another line of the Guelph dynasty. This library had been founded by the learned Duke August the Younger and held in 1661 some 28,000 volumes of printed works, including 2,000 incunabula, and about 2,000 manuscripts. Duke August had been his own librarian and had prepared a classed catalogue using 20 classes derived from Konrad Gesner's *Pandectae.* But here again the succeeding dukes did not share Duke August's enthusiasm for the library and provided little financial support for its upkeep and extension.

In Hanover and Wolfenbüttel Leibniz worked

hard to extend and improve the collections through purchases of current works and advantageous auctions. The Hanoverian collection grew rapidly and served the princes and the court. At Wolfenbüttel he ordered the production of an alphabetical author catalogue, which was completed before 1700, and he was successful in having the first separate German baroque library building constructed. It was a rectangular library topped by a cupola and a dome light. Increased shelving space was provided by means of galleries and shelving that surrounded the supporting pillars. Against Leibniz's wishes it was built as a wooden structure, and no furnace was allowed in the building to provide heat in the winter.

More important than his actual achievements were Leibniz's novel ideas, which he spread in letters, memoranda, and petitions. As a leading scholar in several disciplines, he was fully aware of the importance of libraries for the advancement of knowledge. He advocated a universal library that would contain all the original ideas of mankind that have been recorded. Such a library was not to be measured by the number, rarity, or fancy bindings of its volumes but by the balance, accuracy, and up-to-dateness of the information contained in them. The main task of the librarian was to collect works with up-to-date information, organize them efficiently, and make them readily available for use. For speedy access good catalogues would be needed; while he himself favored classed catalogues, he also stressed the need for alphabetical author and subject catalogues. He personally designed two classification schemes for libraries.

Throughout his life he was most concerned with the research needs of scientists and scholars. In order to avoid needless duplication of efforts and to make results of research speedily available, he planned and promoted the construction of abstracting and indexing tools. The abstracted information was to be indexed and integrated into a demonstrative encyclopedia that was to be organized with the help of a detailed and complex universal classificatory language, his *characteristica universalis.* For this purpose he stressed the need for division of labor and sought the help of scientific societies. He himself was the founder and first President of an academy of sciences in Berlin and the moving spirit behind the founding of the academies in Vienna and Saint Petersburg.

Contributions to Information Science. Leibniz provided important ideas and techniques for information science. He developed binary arithmetic, demonstrated its use for addition, subtraction, multiplication, and division, and praised its advantages for computation. Binary arithmetic is now generally employed in digital computers.

He was also a pioneer in symbolic and mathematical logic. He invented and used diagrams that constitute iconic representations of standard-form categorical propositions, in which spatial inclusions and exclusions correspond to nonspatial inclusions and exclusions of classes. These diagrams provided not only an exceptionally clear method of notation, but also the simplest and most direct method for testing the validity of categorical syllogisms. Usually named after the Swiss mathematician Leonhard Euler (1707–1783), who used them extensively, they were later improved by the British logician John Venn

(1834–1923), whose logical diagrams are now most commonly used.

Leibniz was much interested in developing computers that could reduce tedious and repetitive computations to mechanical operations. While we know now that Wilhelm Schickard, an astronomer and associate of Johannes Kepler who died of the plague in 1635, was the first person to construct a working model of a computer that could add, subtract, multiply, and divide, Leibniz's computer that incorporated his invention of a stepped reckoner gained much wider renown and, in spite of serious mechanical defects, laid the foundation of the modern mechanical calculator.

Beyond that, Leibniz provided seminal ideas for cybernetics. He had plans for constructing a *machina combinatoria, sive analytica* ("combining or analytical machine") which could also handle logical operations involving letters. Norbert Wiener, in his landmark work *Cybernetics* (2nd edition, 1961, page 12) says: "The philosophy of Leibniz centers about two closely related concepts—that of a universal symbolism and that of a calculus of reasoning. From these are derived the mathematical notation and the symbolic logic of the present day. Now, just as the calculus of arithmetic lends itself to mechanization progressing through the abacus and the desk computing machine to the ultra-rapid computing machines of the present day, so the *calculus ratiocinator* of Leibniz contains the germs of the *machina ratiocinatrix,* the reasoning machine."

When Leibniz died on November 14, 1716, in Hanover, he had accomplished great tasks but was keenly aware of the tremendous work that still remained to be done.

REFERENCES

Leibniz, *Sämliche Schriften und Briefe* (1923-).

Kurt Müller, *Leibniz-Bibliographie: Die Literatur über Leibniz* (1967).

Lindsay Mary Newman, *Leibniz (1646–1716) and the German Literary Scene* (1966).

Hans Georg Schulte-Albert, "Gottfried Wilhelm Leibniz and Library Classification," *Journal of Library History* (1971).

Hans Georg Schulte-Albert, "Leibniz's Plans for a World Encyclopaedia System," unpublished Ph.D. dissertation, Case Western Reserve University (1972).

HANS GEORG SCHULTE-ALBERT

Leland, Waldo Gifford

(1879–1966)

Waldo Gifford Leland, historian, archival advocate, and administrator, was a key figure in the creation of the National Archives.

Leland was born in Newton, Massachusetts, on July 17, 1879. He was graduated from Brown University in 1900 with a B.A. degree and membership in Phi Beta Kappa. Coming from a family of schoolteachers, Leland aimed at a career as a college professor. He leaned toward the social sciences, particularly sociology. Although he had studied little history at Brown, only part of a course taught by the great J. Franklin Jameson, he was persuaded by Jameson to do some graduate work in history before plunging into sociology. He went to Harvard for his advanced work, taking an M.A. in 1901 and beginning work on a Ph.D., and never did make the plunge into sociology.

Leland never completed his doctorate in history either, for in 1903 one of his professors, Albert Bushnell Hart, persuaded him to go to Washington for six months to assist Claude H. Van Tyne in compiling a report for the recently established (1902) Carnegie Institution of Washington on the condition of the archives of the federal government. His decision to accept the post started him on a lifetime of work of the highest importance in the world of scholarship, history, and archives but kept him from becoming the teacher he had set out to be.

The survey of the government's archives took the collaborators to basements and attics, warehouses and car barns, doorways and corridors all over Washington—wherever neglectful or ignorant civil servants had placed federal records when they ceased to be current. File clerks and high officials, with few exceptions, welcomed them and were cooperative. The condition of the precious records they found varied considerably, but many were in advanced stages of deterioration. The immediate result of the research by Van Tyne and Leland was the publication in 1904 of the *Guide to the Archives of the Government of the United States in Washington,* which appeared in a revised and enlarged edition three years later. This assessment of the state of the federal archives had, in the long run, a profound influence on the course of archival development in the government.

After finishing the description of the archives, Leland stayed on with the Carnegie Institution's Department of Historical Research, of which his old Brown history professor, Jameson, had become Director in 1905. One of the major projects Jameson directed was the compilation of a series of guides to source material for the study of American history in foreign archives and libraries. Leland's assignment was Paris, and he directed Carnegie's work there from 1907 to 1914 and again from 1922 to 1927. The published result was the two-volume *Guide to Materials for American History in the Libraries and Archives of Paris* (1923–43). In addition to being colleagues at the Carnegie Institution, Jameson and Leland were also close associates in the American Historical Association, Leland being the Association's Secretary (1909–20) and Jameson the Managing Editor of its journal, the *American Historical Review*.

Leland's work at the Carnegie Institution placed him center stage in the archival world, then just beginning the process of professionalization. In 1909 he spoke on "American Archival Problems" at the first American conference of archivists. Three years later he published in the *American Historical Review,* at Jameson's request, an article entitled "The National Archives: A Programme," which recited the litany of the government's neglect of and indifference to its own official records and set forth a bold plan of action to remedy the dismal situation. This article served as a public manifesto to accompany Jameson's backstage politicking for a national archives establishment. The creation of the National Archives in 1934 justified the quarter-century effort by Jameson, Leland, and others, though Leland modestly claimed no part of the credit for himself.

Many considered Leland the "dean of American

Henri Lemaître

Renée Lemaître

archivists," but Leland confessed he was "somewhat embarassed to find myself described as an archivist, a title to which I have no claim. I have never had charge of records, public or private." At most, he thought, he was an "archivist by association." Still, his colleagues in the new archival profession bestowed great honors on him. He served in 1940 as second President of the Society of American Archivists (founded in 1936, of which he was a charter member), was made an Honorary Member in 1949, and a Fellow in 1958. Leland's portrait was painted and was hung in the National Archives building in Washington, D.C.

Throughout his long career, Leland maintained an active interest in the affairs and problems of libraries, especially the Library of Congress. When he first went to Washington in 1903 to be interviewed for the job with the Carnegie Institution, the site of the appointment was the Library of Congress building. His first meal in the capital city was at the famous Round Table presided over by the Librarian of Congress, Herbert Putnam. Leland noted years later, "I was impressed to the point of being awed." Putnam was one of the two most influential men in Leland's professional life, the other being Jameson. Putnam in fact asked Leland on the day after Jameson's funeral in 1937 to succeed Jameson as Chief of the LC Manuscript Division and as occupant of the library's chair of American history. Leland refused Putnam's invitation, which "was one of the hardest things I have ever had to do." Nevertheless, Leland served LC in a number of advisory capacities and sat on numerous committees, including the planning committee that, following World War II, examined the question of the future role of LC.

On leaving the Carnegie Institution in 1927, Leland became the Secretary, or chief administrative officer, of the American Council of Learned Societies (ACLS). The ACLS had been founded in 1919 to provide United States representation in the newly established International Union of Academies, and Leland had been present as Secretary at the organizational meeting of ACLS. He remained the chief executive, his title being changed in 1939 to Director, until 1946. One of the major achievements of his administration was the sponsorship of the *Dictionary of American Biography*.

Much of Leland's work was in the sphere of national and international cooperation in the humanities. This global concern led him also to take a role as a U.S. delegate in the establishment of Unesco at the end of World War II, and he served as the U.S. representative to the third Unesco General Conference in Beirut in 1948.

Leland died in Washington on October 19, 1966.

REFERENCES

The major collection of Leland's papers is in the Manuscript Division, Library of Congress. He wrote a brief memoir, "Some Recollections of an Itinerant Historian," *Proceedings of the American Antiquarian Society* (1951).

JOHN B. HENCH

Lemaître, Henri
(1881–1946)

The library historian Noë Richter described Henri Lemaître as the man who, at the beginning of the

20th century, best embodied the modern type of librarian in France. At the same time a scholar and a man of action, Lemaître was a pioneer in many domains: technical services, libraries for children, bookmobiles, library service in business firms and hospitals, documentation, and international cooperation. Born in Valenciennes on February 17, 1881, he acquired a love for scholarship in the bookstore founded in that city by his grandfather.

A brilliant student, Lemaître entered the École des Chartes (the national school for archivists) at the age of 18 and graduated in 1903. After becoming an archivist-palaeographer, he soon joined the staff of the Bibliothèque Nationale in the department of French history. Along with his library work he also pursued his scholarly studies and published medieval texts such as *Trente Noëls poitevins* (1907) as well as articles and book reviews in scholarly journals, including the *Bibliothèque de l'École des Chartes*. His friendship with a Franciscan scholar led him to found and edit a journal entitled *Revue d'Histoire franciscaine* (1924–31).

At the Bibliothèque Nationale, Lemaître became acquainted with Eugène Morel and willingly adopted Morel's innovative ideas on the development of "Free Public Libraries" in France and on the reform of copyright deposit. In 1910 he published a work on the history of copyright practices in France (*Histoire du dépôt légal en France*), and as a result he was sent to the United States the next year to observe the operation of the Copyright Office at the Library of Congress and to study the New York Public Library. On his return he participated in a series of lectures on modern libraries organized by Morel at l'École des Hautes Etudes sociales (the Graduate School for the Social Sciences). There he discussed his experiences in the United States.

Mobilized in 1914 in a paramilitary unit of the army, Lemaître was sent to the French military mission in London, where he was assigned to the Cipher Service because of his knowledge of modern languages (English, German, Spanish, and Italian). On his return to France, he left the Bibliothèque Nationale to devote himself to working for the improvement of all types of libraries. For many years, his main source of support was an inheritance from the family bookstore.

During the period of reconstruction following World War I, Lemaître was an active member of the French Committee for the Modern Library, a group whose goal was to set up throughout France public libraries similar to the model libraries in Aisne that had been organized by the American Committee for Devastated France, a war relief agency. In the same spirit Lemaître welcomed the first library for children, l'Heure Joyeuse, which was given to the city of Paris by the Book Committee on Children's Libraries, another American philanthropic group. Lemaître wrote the first article on children's work in that library and published it in 1925 in the *Revue des Bibliothèques*. The previous year Lemaître had become Managing Editor of this journal, and under his impetus it became a mirror of library development throughout the world. After the *Revue des Bibliothèques* ceased publication in 1934, Lemaître became cofounder of a more ambitious journal, *Archives et Bibliothèques* (1935–38).

450

In 1928 Lemaître became President of l'Association des Bibliothécaires Français (ABF, the French Library Association), and in that capacity he represented France in Rome in 1929 at the first session of the International Library Committee (which was to become the International Federation of Library Associations). He represented France at all the following IFLA conferences until 1937 and directed the section on hospital libraries. Lemaître was named Honorary Vice President of IFLA at Cheltenham, England, in 1931. At the time he was the French librarian best known abroad.

That same year Lemaître launched an ambitious undertaking: organizing on behalf of ABF the Congrès international de la Lecture publique, the first international congress on reading for the public. The term *Lecture publique* was preferred over the word *bibliothèque* (library), which signified to French readers a dusty, outmoded institution. At the Congress, held in Algiers in 1931, Lemaître succeeded in attracting the interest of the Minister of Public Instruction, who promised to draft a law on public library service. This was the first success for the cause of public libraries, but unfortunately the law was never passed. The proceedings of that Congress, which Lemaître published under the title *La Lecture publique* (1931), constitute a veritable textbook on the subject. That same year, out of a desire to see a bookmobile travel on the roads of France, Lemaître persuaded the Renault firm to construct a prototype that was exhibited at the ABF stand at the Colonial Exposition in Paris. Three years later the first French bookmobile was launched in Aisne. Following these successful undertakings, Lemaître was made a member of the Legion of Honor. He then began to turn toward another goal, documentation.

Named Assistant Director of l'Institut scientifique de Recherches économiques et sociales (the Scientific Institute for Economic and Social Research), he soon set up a model documentation center for this organization. Lemaître also became President of l'Union française des Organismes de Documentation (UFOD, the French association of organizations engaged in documentation), a group of which he had been an active member since its foundation in 1931. In addition he organized training in techniques of documentation for UFOD and taught courses himself (he was already teaching library science at the École des Chartes and in other institutions). He was also President of the Committee of l'Association française de Normalization (AFNOR, the French national association for standardization), which elaborated the cataloguing code. In 1942, during World War II, he was charged with the direction of the Documentation Center for Scientific Research in the Colonies. Despite failing health, he gave many lectures to a diverse public, promoting the development of all kinds of libraries (in hospitals, in business enterprises, for the blind, and others).

The International Labor Bureau published *Bibliothèques populaires et Loisirs ouvriers,* his survey on popular libraries and leisure-time activities of workers, in 1933, and the French Ministry of National Education issued his monograph on librarians, *Les Bibliothécaires.* He devoted his remaining energy to completing a dictionary of technical library terms (in French, English, and German) sponsored by IFLA

and published by Unesco as *Vocabularium Bibliothecarii.* Lemaître died in Sceaux, France, on November 8, 1946. He was a man with little interest in material rewards who enjoyed being surrounded by his wife and four children as well as artists and writers.

REFERENCES

Andre Martin, "Henri Lemaître," *Bibliothèque de l'École des Chartes* (1947).

Renée Lemaître, "La lecture publique aux temps héroiques," *Bulletin d'information de l'Association des Bibliothécaires Français* (Spring, 1980).

RENÉE LEMAÎTRE;
translated by MARY NILES MAACK

Lesotho

Lesotho, formerly Basutoland, a British protectorate from 1868, became independent in 1966. Surrounded entirely by South Africa, the country is a monarchy. Lesotho is a purely African country, the few European residents being government officials, traders, missionaries, and artisans. Population (1984 est.) 1,474,000; area 30,355 sq.km. The languages are English and Sesotho (official).

History. The first colonial-period library was founded in 1886. It housed the National Archives. They were relocated several times and came under the jurisdiction of several authorities, but after independence they became the responsibility of the Ministry of Education. The first library offering any general services to readers was also established in 1886, in the High Commissioner's residence. By 1907 it had 3,000 volumes and was known as the Basutoland Public Library. However, it remained small and several times fell into decline. The Library at Catholic University was established in 1945. That university became the National University of Lesotho.

National Library. Work on the Lesotho National Library Service began in May 1976, and the Library opened its doors to the public in July 1978. It also serves as the center for the distribution of books to schools without collections of their own.

Public Library Service. A public library service is offered to residents of Maseru, and a free postal loan service is operated for persons outside Maseru. Books are also lent to secondary schools throughout the kingdom. Services provided include adult and children's lending and reference libraries, magazine and newspaper reading room, and a collection of material on and about Lesotho. Premises for branch libraries were acquired in Mafeteng and Leribe, the old capital. Initial funding for the library of £247,500 was provided by the British Council through the Ministry of Overseas Development.

Academic and Other Libraries. Other libraries in Lesotho include that of the National University of Lesotho, which has 118,000 books and periodicals, and the library of the National Teachers Training College in Maseru (15,000 volumes). Smaller collections exist in government departments, educational and vocational training establishments such as the Lesotho Agricultural College (7,000 volumes) and Lesotho Institute of Public Administration, and foreign agencies such as the British Council (16,000 volumes) and U.S. Information Service (2,300 volumes).

The Profession. A professional body, the Lesotho Library Association, was formed in 1979.

VINCENT FORSHAW*

LIBER (Ligue des Bibliothèques Européennes de Recherche)

The initiative for establishing an organization of European research libraries was taken at the Annual General Conference of IFLA in Frankfurt am Main in August 1968 by Jean-Pierre Clavel (Lausanne), Kenneth Garside (London), and Kenneth W. Humphreys (Birmingham), among others, all active members of the IFLA section on National and University Libraries. They saw the shortcomings of that organization. It was too comprehensive and complex, the members represented a great variety of interests and levels of professional activity, and they were not able to act continously because they only met rarely, once a year at best.

A steering committee was set up and a questionnaire was distributed to about 300 large libraries in Western Europe, asking whether they were in favor of a new and more homogeneous organization of European research libraries. Almost half answered and agreed to the establishment of the planned new asociation. The Council of Europe declared itself willing to give an initial contribution, and at a meeting in Strasbourg, March 1971, LIBER was constituted. The number of member libraries was initially about 120. It gradually increased and by 1984 was 168. Countries with the most members include Federal Republic of Germany (37), France (26), United Kingdom (24), and Italy (15).

Under its Statutes, Article 2, "The aim of LIBER is to establish a close collaboration between the general research libraries of Europe, and national and university libraries in particular. Its intention is to help in finding practical ways of improving the quality of the services these libraries provide."

Under Article 3, "It shall operate by holding conferences and congresses, calling in experts, cooperating with all bodies concerned with libraries and with other national and international governmental and nongovernmental organizations, issuing publications, conducting surveys among libraries, and by any other means appropriate to the aims of the Association."

Since the first ordinary annual general meeting in

1972 LIBER has carried out an extensive program of conferences and seminars. In addition to the annual general meeting, a number of special meetings devoted to one specific subject have been arranged: library architecture, shared cataloguing, acquisition of material from the Third World, library management, rare books and manuscripts, interlibrary lending, maps, public relations work, collection security, and library automation.

In order to stimulate work in these fields LIBER has organized a number of working groups: Acquisitions from the Third World, Exchange of Staff Members, Library Architecture, Library History, Library Management, Library Automation, Manuscripts and Rare Books, and Maps. All working groups are established and approved by the Executive Committee, which directs the activities of LIBER. Its seven members are elected for three years (renewable once) by the annual General Assembly. Since 1980 the Past-President has been an invited member of the committee.

LIBER has always faced a major financial problem. It is entirely dependent on members' subscriptions. From the beginning it had based its support partly on an annual contribution from the Council of Europe, but after some years that backing came to an end and was never renewed. The organization is run to a great extent by the efforts and enthusiasm of the Executive Committee members and the editors.

LIBER published *LIBER Bulletin* from 1972 and the LIBER *News Sheet* from 1978.

Jean-Pierre Clavel served as the first President (1971–74). He was followed by Kenneth W. Humphreys (1974–80), Gerhard Munthe (1980–83), and Franz Kroller (1983–).

GERHARD MUNTHE

Liberia

Liberia, a republic in western Africa, is bordered by Sierra Leone on the northwest, Guinea on the north, Ivory Coast on the east, and the Atlantic Ocean on the south and west. Population (1984 est.) 2,160,000; area 99,067 sq.km. The official language is English.

History. Prior to the presence of books and recorded materials in Liberia, signs, symbols, palm kernels, and the making of rice farms were used for commercial purposes and determining births and deaths and keeping records among the people of the

Libraries in Liberia (1983)

Type	Administrative units	Service points	Volumes in collections	Annual expenditures (Liberian dollar)	Population served	Professional staff	Total staff
National	--	--	--	--	--	--	--
Academic	2	6	200,526	552,718	406,833	11	75
Public	3	7	77,700	91,272	41,000	8	17
School	103	103	180,176	--	--	--	--
Special	1	1	6,000	--	--	2	4

Sources: Reports of Director of Libraries, University of Liberia; University Librarian, Cuttington University College; Deputy-Director General for Technical Services, Center for National Documents and Records; Director, Library Services, Liberian Institute of Public Administration Library, 1983.

hinterland. The age of a person, for example, was determined by the number of rice farms made; story telling was the only way of preserving oral and traditional history.

The history of the Vai Tribe shows that in the 18th century Dawlu Bokele, who lived in the area of Grand Cape Mount County, one of the political subdivisions of Liberia, invented a form of syllabic writings for the transmission of messages between various ethnic groups. Carried by couriers, the messages were attached to sticks that indicated the urgency of the communications.

National Services. Liberia does not have a national library. In 1978 legislation was passed by the National Legislature creating a Center for National Documents and Records, which merged the Public Library System and Bureau of Archives. A newly constructed archival building was dedicated in April 1984. In the absence of a national library, the Center and academic libraries provide national leadership in library development.

Academic Libraries. The University of Liberia Libraries, established in 1862 in Monrovia, is a national institution operated by the government. Cuttington University College, in Suacoco, Bong County (1888), is a private institution operated by the Protestant Episcopal Church of Liberia.

The University of Liberia Library System maintains six professional library reading rooms for law, medicine, agriculture/forestry, engineering, regional planning, and science. It holds a collection of Africana and serves as depository center for the United Nations, Unesco, and other international organizations. Cuttington University College maintains a central library.

Public Libraries. Liberia's first public library system was organized in 1826 by the American Colonization Society, but little progress was made until 1937, when the National Legislature passed the act that gave birth to the public library movement. In the early 1950s, a national library committee was formed and charged with planning the system. In 1958 the first professionally trained public librarian was employed. The system's headquarters, in Monrovia, operates and coordinates a number of branch library reading rooms in counties and territories. In 1978 the public library system was placed under the adminis-

tration of the Center for National Documents and Records.

School Libraries. By modern library standards and structure, Liberia's school library program has yet to be organized. Many schools suffer from an acute lack of funding. School librarians are not professionally trained. Few schools can afford trained library personnel, nor do they have adequate funds to build collections.

Special Libraries. Certain attempts by a few ministries and agencies of the government and private organizations are being made to organize special library services, but growth is relatively slow. Those services that exist are unstructured, because of lack of trained library personnel and funding.

The Liberian Institute of Public Administration Library (1975) does provide source materials for instructors to prepare their lectures and provides collateral readings for trainees and public civil servants. It had one professionally trained librarian in 1984 and a number of semiprofessionals. Its collection totals approximately 6,000 volumes and contains about 1,500 government documents. The Library subscribes to some 70 specialized journals. Its subject strength is in the fields of public administration and management.

The Profession. The Liberian Library Association, organized in 1977, attempts to improve and develop library services and librarianship throughout the country. Its membership includes practicing as well as professional trained librarians.

From 1972 to 1982, the Institute of Librarianship operated a Certificate Program. It was the first formal training program of its kind to be organized in Liberia. The University of Liberia offered an Associate of Arts Degree in Library Science from 1982. Plans were under consideration in the mid-1980s for a Department of Library Science at the University of Liberia that would offer a Bachelor of Science degree in Library Science.

C. WESLEY ARMSTRONG

Librarianship, Philosophy of

The Retrospective View. "The Best Books for the Most People at the Least Cost" can hardly be called a philosophy of librarianship, but for many years it was, either implicitly or explicitly, all that the

University of Liberia Libraries, Monrovia

Center for National Documents and Records, Monrovia, Liberia, dedicated in April, 1984. It was merged with the Public Library System and the Bureau of Archives.

profession had. Terms were never defined nor cultural or social relationships examined. It was a creed rather than a philosophy, a dedication to a faith. Indeed, Oliver Garceau speaks at some length about the "library faith" in *The Public Library and the Political Process* (1949):

Out of [the library's] past has come what we may call *the library faith*. It is a fundamental belief, so generally accepted as to be often left unsaid, in the virtue of the printed word, the reading of which is good in itself, and upon the preservation of which many basic values in our civilization rest. When culture is in question, the knowledge of books, the amount of reading, and the possession of a library—all become measures of value, not only of the individual, but also of the community.

Seen in the light of this faith, it may not be surprising that the present writer and his contemporaries in library school often observed that had all of us been born a generation earlier, we would likely have been ministers of the Gospel.

Pierce Butler remarked, in *The Reference Function of the Library* (1943), that librarians generally have been indifferent to a philosophical rationale for their profession:

Some librarians dislike and distrust theory. They recognize clearly that the world needs efficient library service far more than it needs theoretical opinions. They fear, not without cause, that our quest for a professional philosophy may involve a neglect of practical values. Other librarians . . . are certain that the field of librarianship is amenable to rational analysis and that this analysis will reveal basic laws and principles. . . . They believe that a sound theory of librarianship can be developed without any sacrifice of practical efficiency. Moreover, they believe that such a sound theory must be established before librarians can become even reasonably competent in certain practical areas of their activity.

There are good historic reasons for the librarians' ambivalence, not to say indifference and neglect, concerning the philosophical raison d'etre of the library as a social organism. Over the millennia libraries created, by their very existence, their own rationale, their own philosophical justification. From the time of the ancient Sumerians and Egyptians libraries have been created because they are needed. Custody of the record of the culture was necessary for the transmission of that culture from generation to generation and beyond the reach of individual human memory—for training the priesthood, for documenting important commercial and other transactions, and for carrying on affairs of state. As the medieval universities arose, libraries were necessary because the book-centered educational system required them. The early librarians were scholars who not only gave the books in their custody the needed protective care but also worked with the texts themselves. The innovation of the modern public library created the philosophical need, not only for its justification but also for its guidance as an institution.

Modern Public Library. The modern public library is rooted in those small, voluntary associations of people who banded together in England and Colonial America to acquire the books they needed in their work and for their general stimulation but could not procure in sufficient quantity for themselves. Their collections were very similar to the personal library of the gentleman scholar. These social libraries, as they were called, spread along the east coast of Colonial America and were carried into the interior as it was opened by the pioneer settlers. Some, such as the Boston Athenaeum and the Redwood Library of Newport, Rhode Island, were sufficiently strong to survive periods of severe economic stringencies, but most of them fell by the wayside as their most enthusiastic supporters either died or moved away.

By the beginning of the 19th century it was apparent that voluntary support was inadequate for the book requirements of the new nation, and readers turned to municipal funds for support. Thus the public library was born and with it the need for a pragmatic justification to elicit public support. The *public* library as a new generic institutional form that was part of the public sector (of local government specifically) created a demand for its own justification. Edward Everett and George Ticknor found themselves in sharp disagreement about the kind of book collection the new Boston Public Library should have when they set themselves the task of writing the institution's first official report. Oliver Wendell Holmes asked, "What is a library but a nest to hatch scholars?" And Horace Mann saw the public library as "the crowning glory of our public schools." All of the early advocates of legislation in support of public libraries stressed that the institution was essential to an enlightened electorate, without which a democracy could not survive.

After the Civil War and the restablilization of the federal government, public libraries spread throughout the United States and, though few of them could be called opulent, many were enriched from, if not actually created by, Andrew Carnegie's generosity. That these libraries were desirable was readily acknowledged even by those who did not use them. They played important roles in the lives of many American young people, especially in the acculturation of the immigrants who at the turn of the 20th century were flocking to U.S. shores in increasing numbers. Not until the advent of the Great Depression in the 1930s did librarians suddenly awaken to the realization that they really were a part of the public sector, that they were created by society, and that what affected the social fabric of which they were a part also had serious implications for them. It was a rude awakening, but even then not many librarians struggling against economic misfortune thought it necessary to ask themselves, "What is our function in society, and why are we here?" Librarians, by temperament and training, have always been a pragmatic breed not much given to philosophical speculation.

As a result, librarians and their libraries in recent decades have assumed a wide variety of activities in the hope that by their very diversity they will attract increased public support: adult education, service to the aged, aid to the disadvantaged, programs for the physically handicapped, and many other social functions wholly admirable in themselves. But librarians failed to ask whether the library is really the best agency to be involved with such public services. Even in the sharply defined world of bibliography librarians have not been able to resolve the argument over the *quality* or *demand* theories of collection-building. Over the centuries the library has been an elitist institution; can it, or should it, shed its heritage and strive to be as many things to as many people as possible? Questions like this are very stubborn, and no philosophical guides have evolved. The librarians talk glibly of library science, and indeed strive to endow it with scientific principles, but neglect the fact that librarianship emerged from a humanistic tradition.

Definition and Purpose. An assembly of books is not a library, nor is a library only a place where books are kept; a library in the sense we are concerned with here is an organization, a system designed to preserve and facilitate the use of graphic records. It is a social instrument created to form a link in the communication system that is essential to any society or culture. Without communication there can be no society, and without some form of graphic record and a means for the preservation of that record there can be no enduring culture. The library may from time to time assume certain marginal functions, but its basic purpose remains generically the same—a link in the communication chain that is concerned with the custody of recorded knowledge. Its fundamental concern is with the communication of knowledge, ideas, thought; but because those intangibles are embodied in physical objects—books and other graphic records—it is easy to mistake the physical object rather than its intellectual content as the reality. A book qua book is nothing more than a physical representation of what the author thought he said, and its utility varies directly with what the reader brings to it in understanding.

The modern library, in the Western world at least, is an integrated system of three interrelated and interdependent parts held together by an administrative authority, the purpose of which is to keep the triad in harmonious balance and to see that aims and objectives are adequately realized. The three parts, which may also be known as functions or operations, are: acquisition, organization, and interpretation or service.

Acquisition requires that the librarian should know what materials are to be procured to meet adequately the legitimate needs of the patron, or anticipated patron, and how these materials are to be acquired. Bibliography in the larger sense is the keystone of acquisition, because one learns about the materials to be acquired from bibliography.

Organization involves putting the materials, or the representation of those materials, together—in catalogues or other ordered files—in such a way as to make them available when needed. Organization also necessitates the analysis of the materials by subject or any other aspect that is believed to be useful to the patron. Order is essential, because the human mind can comprehend the intellectual or other aspects of the graphic record only through order and relationship. People cannot "think chaos"; order is heaven's first law, and nowhere is it more essential than in the organization of a library.

Interpretation, or service, is the rationale for the library; it is the goal for which acquisition and organization exist. Accumulating books and arranging them, no matter how expertly done, has little value if the system is not used. "Books are for use; every book its reader; and every reader his book" were the first three of S. R. Ranganathan's Five Laws of Library Science (see his biography). The fact that these are not really laws but precepts does not destroy their validity; they are the rationale of the library, no matter what kind, size, or type it happens to be.

Administration is necessary because there must be an operational focus, an authority to make decisions and impose standards. Administration is unproductive in that it does not "create" anything; it builds no collections, leaves behind it no taxonomic structures or analyses of the library's materials, and provides no direct apparent and tangible service to the user. Moreover, it should be held to a minimum. That administration is best that administers least, but this is not to say that administration is unimportant. At its best administration can achieve acceptable results under the most severe restrictions; at its worst it can leave the best library system in ruins. As libraries grow in size and complexity, the role of administration becomes increasingly important.

The library may also be viewed as operating in three spheres: the mechanistic, the one of maximum content, and the one of maximum context.

Mechanistic Sphere. This sphere encompasses all the physical operations involved in the total library process. Here are included all the "tools" the librarian uses in the performance of library tasks, including software and hardware, to borrow the terminology of the computer engineer. Such tools may be designed for either the librarian or the patron, or both.

Maximum Content. The sphere of maximum content includes the totality of the library's intellectual resources. The term maximum is used, not to suggest that the collections of the library should be as big as possible, but instead to suggest that the resources should be aligned to user needs to the greatest degree possible, given the library's available economic support. The term content also includes the resources of other libraries through various forms of interlibrary cooperation.

Maximum context refers to the social and intellectual environment in which the library operates. The library's first responsibility is to its own culture, but this mandate does not exclude consideration of other cultures and other social goals. How far the library can or should go in stimulating alterations in its culture (that is, in the social context) is a philosophical question that has not yet been answered, if indeed it can be. A serious problem for the librarian is created when the goals of society itself are unclear or when the society is in a state of flux.

Society, Culture, and the Communication System. A society, as understood by the anthropologist, is composed of people working together to achieve common ends and to satisfy common needs. Culture is that body of knowledge, understandings, and beliefs held in common by a society. The culture is interpreted, nurtured, and enforced by institutions. Institutions are those large, powerful bodies in the society, such as those associated with family, religion, law, and education, that through their agencies, such as the church, courts, and schools, implement their power. Institutions set standards of conduct, grant rewards for adherence to the culture, and exact penalties for violations. Institutions in general dominate the society, and one departs from their dicta at one's peril. Libraries, then, are molded by the culture and kept in line by such institutions as the church, state, courts, and education. Libraries are generally thought of as an agency of the institution of education, and rightly so, but they are also subjects of the state, law, and even religion.

The culture is the totality of knowledge and beliefs of a society, maintained by a trinity: physical equipment, scholarship (in the broad sense of that which is known or believed), and social organization. The physical equipment is composed of tools of any kind, from stone axes to the most sophisticated computer or other mechanical or electronic mechanism. The scholarship is the totality of the products of thought, and the social organization is the system by which the whole is held together. Language is essential to a culture, and, indeed, many anthropologists consider language the essence of culture, without which cultures cannot exist. Language, either spoken, written, or kinesic, is a system of symbolic representations commonly understood and accepted by those in the culture. It is basic to the communication system in a culture, and the library is part of that system.

Because the library is an important agent in the communication system in society, how a society, or culture, acquires, absorbs, and disseminates knowledge must find accommodation in the librarian's professional philosophy. Douglas Waples was long convinced of the importance to librarianship of the study of the social effects of reading, and though he did not find the answers he sought, he at least opened the problem through his probing and did much to reveal its importance to the philosophy of the library profession. Information science, on the other hand, seems to concern itself primarily with the effectiveness of the communication channels in society and has not as yet addressed itself to the origins and growth of knowledge and the impact of that knowledge on its coeval culture. Moreover, information scientists seem to be aligning themselves with the natural sciences, which deal with physical phenomena, things, whereas the library and librarians deal with ideas and knowledge and their communication; hence librarianship is much closer to the humanities that to the "hard" sciences.

Thus there emerges a need for a new discipline, or science, of communication. This will emphatically not be a reworking of the old area of mass communication with which we have become, it must be admitted, rather tediously familiar. We are concerned here with a body of knowledge about knowledge itself. How knowledge has developed and been augmented has long been a subject of study, but how knowledge is coordinated, integrated, and put to work is yet an almost unrecognized field of investigation. We have, from the most ancient times, our systems of logic and our formulations of systematic scientific method. We know with some exactitude how knowledge of this kind is accumulated and transmitted from one generation to another. Philosophers have speculated for generations about the nature of knowledge, its sources and methods, and the limits of its validity. But the study of epistemology has always revolved about the intellectual processes of the *individual*. Psychologists carried the philosophers' speculations into the laboratory and made some progress in examining the mental abilities and behavior of the individual. But neither epistemologists nor psychologists have developed an orderly and comprehensive body of knowledge concerning intellectual differentiation and the integration of knowledge within a complex *social* structure. The sociologists, though they have directed their attention toward the behavior of people in groups, have paid scant heed to the *intellectual forces* shaping social structures.

The new discipline that we here envisage, which for want of a better name we have called "social epistemology," will provide a framework for the effective investigation of the whole complex problem of the intellectual processes of society—a study by which society as a whole seeks to achieve a perceptive or understanding relation to the total environment. It will lift the study of intellectual life from that of the individual to an inquiry into the means by which a society, nation, or culture achieves an understanding relationship with the totality of the environment, and its focus will be upon the production, flow, integration, and consumption of all forms of communication throughout the entire social pattern. From such a discipline should emerge a new body of knowledge about, and a new synthesis of the interaction between, knowledge and social activity.

But though social epistemology will have its own corpus of theoretical knowledge, it will be a very practical discipline, too.

Because of the emerging science of information, librarianship is, for the first time in its long history, compelled to formulate, self-consciously, its role in society, to examine critically its intellectual foundations, and to view itself holistically—as an integrated system that serves people, both as individuals and as members of society, throughout life. Despite the obvious relationship of librarianship to its coeval culture, the library has been recognized as a sociological entity only within the last half century. The rise of the public library in the U.S. coincided with important new developments in sociological theory, and the beginnings of a search for status encouraged all lines of inquiry that might help to establish the librarian's claim to being professional.

Public librarians are improving their skills in working effectively with other educational and social agencies in their service areas, and they are being called upon to participate in large-scale community programs for nonreaders, the functionally illiterate, the undereducated, and the culturally deprived. In recent decades, especially within the past few years, the public library has broadened and strengthened its role in the thinking and decision making of the community. In no way do these auxiliary functions diminish the library's independence, initiative, or social prestige. Programs for the professional education of the librarian have reflected changes in educational philosophy as well as in the theory of librarianship.

Personal Knowledge. Though the library is the creature of society, it does not reach the individual as do the mass media. Individuals must seek the library and its resources out for themselves, and the library achieves its social goals through them. Therefore, for the library, "the proper study of mankind is man."

It is important to librarians that they be supported as much as possible by an understanding of those psychological and other mental processes through which the individual receives and assimilates knowledge, that they know as much as can be known, given our present limitations, of the cognitive process. For the librarian the basic questions are: What is knowledge, how do we learn, and how does the assimilation of knowledge by whatever means influence behavior? What reading, in the generic sense, does to people was long ago addressed by Waples, but we are still ignorant of the influence that knowledge exerts on our behavior. Yet the problem of the nature of personal knowledge still eludes us. We are still unable to define a book other than to say that it deals in symbolic representations of what the originator intended to say.

Because most of our communication is carried out through symbolic representations—either written, oral, or through gestures and other forms of physical representations—the problem of communication, linguistics, and symbolization lies at the very heart of what the librarian is trying to do.

Thus librarians should remember that their primary concern is with ideas rather than physical objects. But because physical objects often embody or represent conceptualizations, the one is easily mistaken for the other. Librarianship touches all subject fields and is dependent on all of them for its intellectual and professional substance.

The philosophy of librarianship, as it is evolved, must encompass all forms of human activity, both physical and mental, not only because the library's shelves hold the record of the human adventure but also because those holdings represent and can respond to the needs of all human life.

All philosophy begins in an appreciation of our own ignorance—in asking ourselves the fundamental questions. "We have all the answers," Archibald MacLeish once told his staff when he was Librarian of Congress; "it is the questions we do not know."

REFERENCES
Pierce Butler, *An Introduction to Library Science* (1933).
Conrad H. Rawski, editor, *Toward a Theory of Librarianship* (1973).
Jesse H. Shera, *The Foundations of Education for Librarianship* (1972).
Shera, *Knowing Books and Men* (1976).

JESSE H. SHERA*
(d. 1982)

Librarianship, Profession of

The emergence of librarianship as a recognized profession is a fairly modern development. Librarianship became more conscious of its status and occupational identity as did many other fields in the latter part of the 19th century. During the early part of the 20th century, definitions of what constituted a profession were formulated, and sociologists and practitioners in a variety of disciplines examined whether or not specific occupations or professions met the criteria. Although the list of characteristics of a profession varies, the following attributes are generally cited: (1) a body of theoretical and specialized knowledge; (2) a set of applied techniques for practice; (3) the establishment of formal educational programs; (4) development of a code of ethics; (5) a representative organization which monitors general standards of activity; (6) a service orientation to clients; and (7) recognition from a significant number of nonpractitioners. There have been many debates in the literature as to whether librarianship actually is a

profession, but this issue will not be considered further here.

As the numbers of libraries grew and the complexity of their operations increased, librarians found it necessary to develop new technical skills in classifying and organizing the large volume of information available. The growth of librarianship as an expanding discipline is perhaps best reflected in the changing nomenclature from the term "library economy," used in the early days, "library service" and "library science," followed by the current usage of "library/information science" to describe the field.

FUNDAMENTAL ELEMENTS

As implied above, professional practice can be seen as the application of theoretical concepts. The article on Librarianship, Philosophy of, written for the First Edition of this *Encyclopedia* by Jesse Shera and reprinted in this Edition, describes the three major functions of librarianship as acquisition, organization, and interpretation or service. The latter is seen by Shera as the rationale for the library or the goal for which the other two functions exist. In the literature on professionalism, the orientation toward service or the use of specialized expertise on behalf of others (that is, clients) is often cited as a major element. Certainly, librarianship has a long tradition of a service orientation.

Librarianship draws from many disciplines, such as management science, computer science, and communications; unique to librarianship, however, is the technical expertise involved in applying the theory of classification and indexing to the control and retrieval of information. In addition, the concept of freedom of access to information and the provision of materials on all sides of an issue are important tenets of American librarianship.

The work of librarians can be analyzed in a variety of ways. Examination can be made of the variations resulting from service in a particular type of library (for example, school, public, academic, special), different types of client or user groups (for example, children's services, adult services), or use of specialized materials (for example, maps, government documents). Public services, technical services and administration constitute yet another way of defining the broad categories within the practice of librarianship. These specific elements are discussed elsewhere in this *Encyclopedia*.

CURRENT STATE OF THE PROFESSION

Career Paths. To support the goals of quality library and information service, both professional and supportive staff are needed in libraries. As indicated in the American Library Association (ALA) policy statement "Library Education and Personnel Utilization," the library occupation is much broader than that segment of it which is the library profession; the profession has a responsibility for defining the training and education required for the preparation of all personnel who work in libraries at any level, supportive or professional.

The ALA policy recommends categories of personnel in libraries; these include three levels of supportive staff (clerk, technical assistant, and associate) and two professional levels (librarian and senior librarian, or specialist and senior specialist for those with nonlibrary related qualifications). It is recognized, however, that every type and size of library may not need all of these categories. Certainly many variations in staffing patterns exist in practice, depending on the type of library or function, size of institution, or type of environment.

Professional responsibilities are generally considered to be those that require a special background and education. Professional tasks include identification of library needs, analysis of problems, establishment of goals and objectives, and planning, organizing, and administering services to library users. Supportive staff duties are those primarily devoted to the routine application of established rules and techniques. The differentiation between professional and supportive staff responsibilities has not always been clear in practice, however. Professionals have often found themselves carrying out more routine activities, and many duties which at one time were considered professional have been shifted downward, particularly in those libraries where automation has been introduced. For example, with the advent of bibliographic databases and the availability of cataloguing data from other sources, paraprofessionals now handle a large portion of the technical processing and interlibrary loan work previously carried out by the professional staff.

Career paths for paraprofessional staff are generally limited without further formal education. Although some libraries promote paraprofessionals into librarian positions through examinations or evaluation of experience and other credentials, the mobility of these persons to professional positions in other libraries may be difficult.

Because libraries generally have hierarchical structures, career advancement is usually through movement into administrative positions. The number of these positions is limited and some librarians feel they have reached a plateau after a number of years in the profession. The ALA policy cited previously does state that the topmost classification in the professional ranks should not be limited to administrators, whose specialty is only one of several specializations of value to library service. It recommends "that a highly qualified person with a specialist responsibility in some aspect of librarianship (e.g., archives, bibliography, reference) should be eligible for advanced status and financial rewards without being forced to abandon for administrative responsibilities his/her area of major competence." This principle becomes difficult to administer in practice, particularly in libraries bound by civil service arrangements or under the jurisdiction of municipal or campus personnel departments whose practices allow for little flexibility in determining and implementing compensation policies.

Demographic Profile. A detailed demographic profile of librarians in the United States is given in the King Research, Inc., survey *Library Human Resources: A Study of Supply and Demand.* As of 1982, about 139,000 librarians were employed in 136,000 full-time equivalent positions in nearly 44,000 public, academic, and special libraries and school districts. Of these, 48 percent were in school libraries, 23 percent in public libraries, 15 percent in academic, and 14 percent in special libraries. Of a total of 307,600 library employees, 44 percent were professional librarians, 5 percent other professionals,

and 50 percent support staff. The range of professional librarians in relation to other types of staff differed by type of library—from 35 percent in academic libraries to 55 percent in school libraries. Although some have suggested libraries are substituting nonprofessional staff for librarians, the King Research survey found that librarians constituted a fairly constant proportion of the staff in all types of libraries from 1978 to 1982.

Eighty percent of employed librarians in the U.S. have some formal degree or certificate (60 percent with the master's in library science, 7 percent with a school library certificate, and 12 percent with a bachelor of library science degree). The percentage of persons with the master's degree varies by type of library—47 percent of school librarians, 63 percent of public librarians, 73 percent of special librarians, and 89 percent of academic librarians.

Librarianship in the U.S. is a predominately female profession, Women comprise approximately 85 percent of those employed. This varies by type of library, with females constituting 65 percent of academic librarians, 87 percent of public librarians, 90 percent of special librarians, and 91 percent of school librarians.

In 1982, 41,980 librarians were in the North Atlantic region, 35,340 in the Great Lakes region, 30,880 in the Southeast, and 28,320 in the West and Southwest. Although there are fewer librarians in the West and Southwest than in other geographical regions, those regions grew at a faster rate than others between 1978 and 1982 (4 percent per year v. 2 percent or less elsewhere). Predictions for the West and Southwest suggest the growth rate for librarians in the West and Southwest will increase.

Of the 23,000 librarians hired in 1981 in the United States, about 34 percent were new graduates, 44 percent were transfers from other libraries, and 22 percent came from other kinds of employment or were previously unemployed. The job market for librarians in the U.S. has followed a somewhat cyclical pattern. Following a period of expansion in the 1960s, when many new positions were created through federal funds in response to a shortage of librarians, the job market became constricted in the 1970s. This contraction was due in part to the increasing number of library school graduates at the same time that economic difficulties caused budget cuts, layoffs, and position hiring freezes in some libraries. Although in the 1980s the supply of and demand for librarians became more balanced, shortages of librarians to fill certain types of positions (for example, children's services, cataloguing, certain subject specialists) were becoming more evident.

Along with many other occupations and professions, librarianship is experiencing the movement of the post–World War II baby boom through the workforce as the number and proportion of older persons increases. The replacement rate for librarians may escalate and additional shortages occur as many persons approach retirement age in the latter 1980s and early 1990s; according to the 1980 U.S. census, 29 percent of all librarians were over the age of 50.

Status of the Profession. *United States.* Most occupations and professions, including librarianship, have stereotypes relegated to them, as certain assumed characteristics are attributed by the public to individuals belonging to specific groups. As discussed by Margaret Slater in the *Library Review* (Autumn 1983), the social image of any group exists on several levels, namely, the public image, self image, and ideal image. There may be gaps between these various images, particularly between the public and ideal image on the issue of professional status. Some writers have even claimed that librarians have *no* image because they seldom intrude on the public consciousness—they remain invisible, faceless, anonymous. The role of the professional librarian is often not visible to the public; anyone checking out books in a library is considered a librarian by many patrons.

Although concerns about the status of the profession and image of librarians have been commonplace for many years, there was an apparent upsurge of interest in these topics in the mid-70s and 80s. The move toward greater accountability and productivity in the public sector had an impact on the library profession, as government agencies and other organizations moved to cut costs and retrench in services. This occurred at the same time that librarians became more vocal in attempting to improve their economic well-being, status, and prestige.

Challenges to the use of the master's degree in library science as a hiring requirement came from some city, county, state and federal officials who have control over the classifications and salaries of library workers. In part, this was due to closer scrutiny of the application of all types of educational credentials in the employment process, as legal and regulatory procedures were established to ensure that position requirements are not artificial barriers and are indeed job related.

Library employers found it necessary to analyze and assess more realistically what is it that a librarian actually does, and to look closely at what competencies are required for performing professional jobs. Job content, job requirements, and the context in which the job is performed need to be examined, followed by delineation of the knowledge, skills, abilities, and other personal attributes related to the job and required to perform successfully. If the knowledge, skills, and abilities obtained in acquiring the library science degree are substantially correlated with the job, there is little probability of its being challenged, and the M.L.S. degree is likely to be deemed valid.

The library profession needs to do more work internally to clarify the distinction between professional and support staff duties and demonstrate which positions in libraries are best filled by librarians and which may better be filled by staff with other kinds of background. The profession may also need to be more open to the concepts of career lattices, alternatives, and equivalencies for those who can meet minimum professional qualifications by means other than an M.L.S. credential.

At the same time, the library profession needs to promote externally the librarian's role in providing quality service, thus educating legislators, government and corporate officials, and other decision makers about the complexities and demands of professional library work. In a number of instances librarians have documented discrepancies between their salaries and those of other city, campus, or corporate workers. A growing coalition of pay equity proponents, including librarians, has called for correcting the practice of paying persons in predominately female professions and occupations less than those in predominately male professions requiring comparable skill, effort, responsibility, and working conditions.

Other Regions of the World. The status of librarianship in other countries relates directly to the extent of library development existing within a specific country. Influencing the state of library development in a country are various factors, such as history, geography, patterns of government and education, population density, extent of literacy and the book industry, as well as the political environment.

Articles in this *Encyclopedia* on countries of the world cover formal education programs in library and information science developed to support demands for personnel in each country. Many developing countries have sent their personnel abroad for training, for example, to the U.S., Britain, Canada, Scandinavia, France, or other countries. A variety of levels of education and training from technician preparation to the doctorate have evolved in many countries, although some of the smaller developing countries still have no formal educational programs to prepare librarians.

In addition to education and training programs, the spread of professionalism in the library field can be linked with the founding and growth of professional library associations in each country. Most associations have as a common aim the improvement and strengthening of library service and librarianship. This is accomplished through publishing, conferences, continuing education workshops, development of standards and guidelines, and other activities. Although a number of countries, such as the U.S., Japan, and the United Kingdom, have had associations since the late 19th and early 20th centuries, the majority have founded such organizations only since 1950. As the state of library development has grown in complexity, some of the national associations have divided into separate organizations by type of library or function, as in the United States, the U.K., and elsewhere.

North American and British librarianship have influenced the development of the profession in a number of countries. In particular, characteristics such as an attitude of service, the function of the library as an educational institution, and the concept of organized information as a public resource have become aspects in the evolution of librarianship in other countries. Internationalism in librarianship has also evolved as libraries and librarians have fostered international cooperation and understanding in promoting the advancement of knowledge and availability of information. See also American Library Association, Library Association, and International Federation of Library Associations.

The image of the librarian varies in each country. In some, emphasis on education means that librarians are seen as scholars and are highly respected (although not necessarily highly paid). In others, they may be seen primarily as clerks. Lack of qualified staff still hinders the development of library service in a number of countries.

Issues and Trends. *Change in the Information Environment.* Much has been written about the increasing volume, variety, and complexity of information and the rapidly changing use of information technology in all types of professions and occupations. Growing use of automation in library management and services has been documented in the literature. Less well documented is the effect of automation on organizational structures and job content in libraries, although the literature in this area is growing. A whole range of computer products and services has been developed by library-based networks or commercial organizations for use in libraries. In some cases, these organizations' products and services are seen as competition with libraries'.

Thus, the role of the librarian in the future is the subject of debate. Some see an enhanced role as activities such as online database searching make the librarian more visible. Others suspect that the librarian's role will be deprofessionalized as users gain increased direct access to databases outside the context of the library.

The information environment is dynamic, fragmented, and fluid, creating both challenges and opportunities for librarianship. The boundaries between librarianship and other information-related professions are unclear, and one might consider librarian/information worker functions to be on a continuum. In the study *The Information Professional* by the University of Pittsburgh and King Research, Inc., approximately 1,640,000 persons in the workforce were estimated to have information functions. The majority of these are found in industry (71 percent), with 22 percent in state and local governments, 7 percent in the federal government, and 2 percent in colleges and universities. More than 1,500 different occupational titles were identified. The computer field accounts for the largest segment of information workers (42 percent); librarians and management support personnel comprise the next largest categories, with 10 percent each.

Alternative Career Paths. The extent to which librarians will be interested in and able to move into other information-related positions is still uncertain. More data are needed on the movement of personnel into and out of the information industry and traditional library settings. In the 1982 King Research study, 4 percent of the new library school graduates were reported as finding information-related jobs outside libraries, while 9 percent of practicing librarians changing jobs moved into nonlibrary information positions. A large number of these positions are found in the private for-profit sector. Some librarians are self-employed as freelancers and others established their own information businesses. A wide variety of job titles is in use by those librarians who have moved outside libraries, and their principal areas of work might include administrative duties, consulting, marketing/promotion, editing, indexing and abstracting, training, systems analysis, customer service, online searching, document delivery, research, records control, database publishing, or some other type of information management function.

Some writers have cautioned that if the library profession wants to move from its present more narrow definition of itself and become visible in the information environment, it must carefully evaluate the current situation, develop strategies and a public relations campaign to sell librarian expertise to administrators, and stake out appropriate territory within the larger information arena. Others express concern that if the information industry positions are seen as more challenging, lucrative, and exciting, then the more traditional librarian positions will suffer from difficulty in recruiting for more conventional careers. Although librarianship in the mid-1980s was in transition, librarians will no doubt continue to form an important part of the information world.

See articles on the theory and practice of librarianship, listed in Part III of the Outline of Contents, and on Education and Research, listed in Part IV of the Outline. Consult the Index for references under specific topics.

REFERENCES

Anthony Debons et al., *The Information Professional: Survey of an Emerging Field* (1981).
Library Human Resources: A Study of Supply and Demand (1983), summarized in *American Libraries* (June) (1983).
A. Robert Rogers and Kathryn McChesney, *The Library in Society* (1984).
Michael F. Winter, *The Professionalization of Librarianship,* University of Illinois Graduate School of Library and Information Science Occasional Papers, no. 160 (1983).

MARGARET MYERS

Library and Information Science Research

Library and information science comprise an interdisciplinary field concerned with all phases of the information transfer process. Library science can trace its roots to the period 669–630 B.C. and to the cuneiform inscriptions on clay tablets collected in Nineveh by the Assyrian king Assurbanipal. Information science, although derived from and indebted to many fields, achieved an identity and image of its own after World War II, when many scientific and technological advances were put to peacetime use.

Definitions and Research Process. As an interdisciplinary field, it can be viewed as a spectrum of activities ranging from information theory through information technology to service-oriented functions, such as library and information center management. In fact, it is possible to visualize it through the use of a Venn diagram (see figure), a qualitative and descriptive technique for showing the logical relationships among sets within a universe or population. If we adopt a "hard" view of information science, we might state that it is defined by the intersection of all three sets in the diagram. A "softer" viewpoint might allow for logical union. Most information scientists would probably agree that some sort of compromise would be appropriate for an emerging field of this type, and therefore the diagram is shaded to suggest the various possibilities. In any case, contributions will come from many people with a wide diversity of backgrounds, and there is no point in making arbitrary distinctions. Moreover, in attempting to classify fields or people, it is important to avoid stereotyping them. Many people possess multiple skills, although few are qualified in all pertinent aspects of information science. And, unless we are "Renaissance men or women," we will have to specialize in some aspects of the field, while trying to remain sensitive to developments in the others.

With the exception of some historical work, scientific research is an empirical process that usually involves the following steps (the steps of the scientific method): (1) state the problem under consideration; (2) formulate a hypothesis; (3) test the hypothesis; (4) predict the results of the test; (5) compare observed and predicted results; and (6) draw conclusions from the comparison.

Problem statements are concise, expository statements of some perceived problem that requires further understanding, if not solution. The statement implies a hypothesis or conjecture and may even suggest an experiment to test the validity of the hypothesis. For this reason we must be careful to state the problem in clear and accurate terms and with correct scope.

Good hypotheses generally have the following characteristics: they are testable; they are in harmony with other hypotheses in the area of investigation; their logic is no more complex than necessary; they are relevant to the problem being considered; they are susceptible of quantification; and they are as general as possible (that is, they have a large number of consequences). We do not normally speak of "proving" hypotheses; rather, we seek support for them (that is, we try to confirm or refute them). In this sense science differs from pure mathematics, wherein we often deal with logical proofs. The difference lies between the analytical thought regarding mathematical abstractions and the synthetic thought employed when working with "real" objects or events. In the latter case we can never be certain about the interpretation of observations, but must be content to express relationships between objects or events inferred from these observations in terms of relative probabilities. This is true whether we are concerned with quantum mechanics or with the social and behavioral sciences, and unobtrusive and indirect methods of measurement must be employed along with approximations that are deemed adequate to describe the relations.

Subject Areas for Research. The true scope of library and information science is as yet unclear since the discipline is really in its emergent stage. Nevertheless, indications of the scope of library science may be given by enumerating the subject areas that have been addressed thus far. The following is a brief, representative, but certainly not exhaustive, list of subject areas; the list is derived from the index in Charles H. Davis's compilation, *Doctoral Dissertations in Library Science* (1976):

Academic and research libraries
Acquisition and book selection
Alphanumeric coding
Bibliography
Book storage
Cataloguing and classification
Dewey Decimal classification
Evaluation of library science
History of books and printing
Information analysis centers

A companion work, *Computer Science, a Dissertation Bibliography* (1977) yields an equally diverse sample of subjects.

To obtain a clear picture of related dissertation topics, we would need to study not only *Dissertation Abstracts* but *American Doctoral Dissertations* and then to add lists from individual universities that do not take part in these services. There is also *Master Abstracts* for the M.L.S. works. Other publications that

report on thesis and dissertation research, such as *Library Quarterly, Library Research,* and *Journal of Librarianship,* provide insight into current research activity in the field. Research outside the library school is reported in publications of ERIC and NTIS.

Pure vs. Applied Research. Practicing librarians often think they have little or no time for research, and they are often right. But it is instructive to examine the history of scientific and technological discovery. Basic research has often come *after* technological discoveries, and the discoveries have often been made by practitioners. Archimedes came upon the famous principle that now bears his name while trying to satisfy a king's request to determine the relative amounts of gold and silver in a crown. Pasteur set forth the basic principles of bacteriology while working for the wine and silk industries. The steam engine was around long before the science of thermodynamics. And the telephone was quite well established by the time Shannon and Weaver developed a satisfactory theory of channel capacity in communication.

In a number of fields other than library and information science, there is an implicit understanding that professional and academic matters are inextricably intertwined and that they reinforce each other. In the sciences particularly, there is a substantial body of evidence suggesting that this is the case, even when we take care to differentiate properly between science and technology. But we are accustomed to thinking that basic research always precedes applications—a notion that is not discouraged by funding agencies such as the National Science Foundation. The evidence shows however, that the converse is often true and that science is frequently the beneficiary of good technology. In fact, modern science has always been heavily dependent on instrumentation because of the need for precise and accurate measurement. High technology resulting from the space programs of the 1960s, 70s, and 80s transformed aspects of astronomy from an observational to an experimental science. Did technology arise from basic research in this instance, or is science merely along for the ride?

The point is that artificial distinctions between professional and academic concerns are not useful. They may even inhibit the growth of knowledge by erecting barriers to intelligent funding by agencies who view anything "applied" as beyond the scope of their responsibilities. In the case of science and technology, the issues are fairly clear; in librarianship and

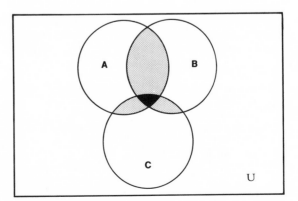

Venn Diagram of Library and Information Science Research

A Information theory, for example, cybernetics, linguistics, formal logic

B Information technology, for example, electrical engineering, computer programming

C Service-oriented functions, for example, library and information center management

U Universe of relevant fields

other professions and activities such as law, medicine, and business administration, the interdependence of theory and applications should be apparent too. What constitutes research, then? And how does it differ from management science, which often uses the same techniques and tools?

The difference seems to be the level of risk you are willing to take. Probability theory and statistics do not change from one arena to the other—that is, when you move from formal hypothesis-testing to administrative decision making. What changes is the degree of risk, or the confidence level you wish to accept before moving ahead with a given task. In research, you must be as sure as possible that enough support has been found for a hypothesis. In administration or management, you need gather only enough evidence to improve the decision-making process over more arbitrary alternative procedures. Naturally, the better the evidence, the better the decision is likely to be; however, there is often insufficient time in administration to go through all the procedures that would constitute good research—work that is publishable and that can be expected to withstand the scrutiny of long-term peer review.

Perplexing Problems. Librarians and library researchers have been using the techniques of the social and behavioral sciences increasingly, particularly when trying to find out how people use libraries and information services. Studies of the interface between the user and the reference librarian are particularly difficult, and earlier textbooks in fact refer to "library mind-reading." In order to go beyond this mind-reading stage, so that we can determine how and why people use libraries and information services, we must do one of two things. We must either alert the subjects of our study that we are going to try to find out about them, thereby running the risk of interfering with the experiment being conducted, or else we must attempt to use unobtrusive methods, perhaps hidden microphones and videotape recorders, thereby running the risk of invading the users' privacy. Reconciling such problems is a difficult task.

On a deeper level, we need to look at how people associate symbols with their referents. Among other things, we need to study the semantics and semiotics associated with indexing and classification. In addition, artificial intelligence offers hope that we can make online retrieval systems more user-friendly by programming a certain amount of apparent quasi-intelligent behavior into them. This would not obviate the need for a professional reference librarian or information specialist, but would help screen out those questions that are of such a straightforward nature that they do not require professional intervention. Such "expert systems" would clearly be of use in traditional school, academic, and public library settings as well as in special libraries and information centers.

Areas such as these, which lend themselves to research and development, should make librarianship an increasingly interesting field, and they represent a welcome addition to the historical and bibliographic scholarship that has been going on for generations.

REFERENCES

Charles H. Busha, and Stephen P. Harter, *Research Methods in Librarianship: Techniques and Interpretation* (1980).
Charles H. Davis, "Information Science and Libraries: A Note on the Contribution of Information Science to Librarianship," *The Bookmark 51 & 52* (1982).
Charles H. Davis, and James E. Rush, *Guide to Information Science* (1979).
Herbert Goldhor, *An Introduction to Scientific Research in Librarianship* (1972).
Mary Jo Lynch, "Research in Librarianship," *Library Trends* (1984).
Ronald R. Powell, *Basic Research Methods for Librarians* (1985).

CHARLES H. DAVIS;
JAMES E. RUSH

Library Association

The Library Association of the United Kingdom is the body that approves courses at British schools of librarianship and information science, awards professional qualifications, issues guidelines and sets standards, and, in short, acts as the voice of professional librarians in the United Kingdom. The Library Association (LA) was founded in 1877, the year following the formation of the American Library Association (ALA).

Early History. The Library Association was brought into existence for several reasons. First, there can be no doubt that the appearance of ALA in 1876 acted as a spur; secondly, legislation permitting the establishment of public libraries in the U.K. was over 25 years old and had already resulted in a steady growth of libraries and librarians. But the immediate impulse came from E. W. B. Nicholson, who, early in 1877, had contributed an article to *The Academy* on the Philadelphia Conference of Librarians of 1876, and later wrote to *The Times* suggesting the need for an international conference of librarians in London. With remarkable speed, the idea was taken up and arrangements for such a conference were made; it was held at the London Institution in Finsbury Square, where Nicholson was in fact the Librarian.

The conference was attended by 216, with 140 libraries represented. The international flavor was reflected by representatives from Australia, Belgium, Denmark, France, Germany, Greece, Italy, and the United States, as well as from the United Kingdom. On the last day of the conference, October 5, 1877, it was resolved "That a Library Association of the United Kingdom be founded." The original LA constitution sought to encourage a wide membership. Its main object was "to unite all persons engaged in or interested in library work, for the purpose of promoting the best possible administration of existing libraries, and the formation of new ones where desirable. It shall also aim at the encouragement of bibliographical research." Membership was open not just to practicing librarians, but also to members of the governing bodies of libraries, as well as to those expressing an interest in the furtherance of the library movement. It was for this reason that the LA could number among its early members such scholars as Benjamin Jowett, W. Stanley Jevons, Mark Pattison, Max Muller, and Alexandre Beljame.

The LA got off to a slow and tentative start, and its early years were tinted with serious differences rather than a unity of outlook. Membership was slow to gather momentum, and after 21 years' existence the total stood at a mere 582. The main cause was the paucity of library provision in the U.K. in the second half of the 19th century. Another reason was that, although the library movement could be said to be slowly growing, the profession of librarianship did not exist. It is to the credit of the early pioneers in LA that they soon set about creating such a profession.

Schisms. The first two decades were dominated by an academic, bibliographical approach, but with the growth of the public library movement during the 1880s and 1890s, there was a natural reaction. Public librarians joining LA wanted to see much more practical approaches, with more attention devoted to such topics as classification, cataloguing, and open access. It was not long before public librarians had virtually gained control of the Association. Between 1890 and 1930, LA did not become a Public Library Association, though it nearly did so. The leading figures of those times—James Duff Brown, L. Stanley Jast, James D. Stewart, W. C. Berwick Sayers, and Ernest A. Savage, to name but a few— were all public librarians who saw to it that public library affairs were prominent in LA conferences, publications, and activities generally. There was a noticeable lack of concern with nonpublic libraries, which did nothing to encourage academic and special librarians to join the Association. It was not surprising that this public library bias on the part of LA led directly to the formation in 1926 of the Association of Special Libraries and Information Bureaux (Aslib); to the start of the School Library Association in 1937; and to the establishment of the Standing Conference on National and University Libraries (SCONUL) in 1950.

By 1950 LA had learned its lesson. After observing the centenary of the passage of the Public Libraries Act of 1850, the Association began to adopt a much more universal stance to encourage the unity of the profession. The formation of many more LA Groups to cater to specialist interests has resulted in dramatic increases in membership since 1945. Aslib, SCONUL, and the School Library Association still thrive, as do the Society of Archivists and the Institute of Information Scientists (IIS), but the LA cooperates with all of them, and many people find it necessary to belong both to the LA and to other bodies appropriate to their needs. All these organizations often present a united front when it comes to making representations to the government on issues that concern librarians and information scientists. There have been moves to form a federation of all the U.K. organizations concerned with library and information science and management, but they had not come to fruition as of the mid-1980s.

Education Work. From 1880 onward the LA has been deeply interested in furthering the education and training of librarians and assistants. In that year a committee on the training of library assistants was set up. A syllabus was approved in 1884 and the first examination to be held under it took place in 1885. Correspondence courses were initiated, summer schools were held, and revisions of the syllabus occurred at intervals. During the 1920s the LA examinations consisted of six sections; passing four led to the Associateship qualification, passing six to the Fellowship.

During the 1930s a three-stage syllabus was adopted—Elementary (later Entrance), Intermediate (later Registration), and Final. The Associateship of the Library Association (ALA) was granted on completion of the intermediate stage, and the Fellowship (FLA) after the final stages. During the 1930s the LA was working toward the establishment of library schools in the U.K. and but for the outbreak of World War II these would have emerged around 1940. Before then there was only one library school in the country, the graduate school established in 1919 at University College, London.

As soon as World War II was over, library schools in the U.K. became a reality. Even so, the LA continued to hold examinations twice a year, and the library schools prepared their students for those examinations along the lines of the LA syllabus. It was but a matter of time before the schools preferred to grant their own qualifications. Educational reforms have gradually taken place, and LA examinations were finally phased out at the end of 1985. In 1986 there were 17 library schools in the U.K. The Association nevertheless maintains its interests in education and training by arranging courses for advanced students and practicing librarians, and by maintaining registers of Associates and Fellows.

Membership. LA membership was less than 400 in 1883 and by the end of the century it had grown only to 633; even in 1928, more than 50 years after its founding, LA membership was a mere 897. But the years 1928 to 1932 saw a phenomenal growth. It is perhaps no accident that this rise coincided with the appointment of the first two paid, fulltime Secretaries of the Association, Guy W. Keeling and P. S. J. Welsford. Both were instrumental in stimulating a growth in membership, but there were also other reasons for the increase. In 1895 there had been formed a Library Assistants' Association (LAA), which in 1922 changed its name to the Association of Assistant Librarians (AAL). Over the years it had concerned itself with library education and training and it had developed a considerable membership. In 1929 the LA Council decided that after January 1, 1930, candidates for LA examinations must be members of the Association. In the following year, though after protracted negotiations, AAL became a Section of LA and brought its members into the parent body.

The combination of these and other factors resulted in a membership increase from 897 in 1928 to 4,095 in 1932. The momentum continued until the outbreak of World War II in 1939, when the total had reached 6,167. Although there was a natural, though very small, decline during the war, after 1945 there were more steady increases. The 10,000 figure was passed in 1950, 15,000 in 1965, and 20,000 by 1972. By 1980 the LA had just over 25,000 members, and although the total dropped slightly thereafter, it was still over 24,000 in 1985. The main reasons for the continual rise in membership since 1945 lie in the growth in number of all types of libraries in the U.K., the ecumenical approach of the Association toward all aspects of the profession, and the LA's notable influence on central and local government. It had an international impact as well.

Presidents. The first President of the LA was J. Winter Jones, Director and Principal Librarian of the British Museum, and the second was H. O. Coxe, Bodley's Librarian. Both were dead by 1881, perhaps not a happy augury. Later Presidents have been noted for their longevity, however. From the 1880s onward there was an increasing tendency to nominate as President people outside the profession, such as noblemen, scholars, mayors, and chairmen of library governing bodies, although national and academic librarians continued to be chosen from time to time. The first public librarian to become President was Francis T. Barrett, City Librarian of Glasgow, in 1907. Among the many celebrities in the list of LA Presidents is Prince Philip, Duke of Edinburgh (1950), Earl Attlee, former Prime Minister (1959), William Temple, Archbishop of York (1937), the Earl of Elgin and Kincardine (1927), the Earl of Crawford (1898), and the Marquess of Dufferin and Ava (1894).

In 1961, however, Council decided that in future, except for special occasions, Presidents should come from the ranks of practicing librarians, a resolution that was honored thereafter with one exception. In 1977, the LA's centenary year, Sir Frederick (now Lord) Dainton was nominated; he had close library connections, having been Chairman of the Board of the British Library, which he had helped to bring into existence in 1973. The last nonlibrarian "celebrity" President was Sir Charles Snow, better known as C. P. Snow the novelist, in 1961.

In its history of more than a century, the LA had only one woman President, Lorna V. Paulin, in 1966. The previous policy of nominating celebrities from outside the profession prevented many eminent women librarians from assuming the Presidency. Among them were Kate Pierce, Marion Frost, A. M. Cooke, Ethel Gerard, and Florence E. Cook. It appears likely that the LA, which is not and never has been anti-feminist, will surely elect many women Presidents in the future.

Secretaries. In its first 85 years LA had a succession of noteworthy Honorary Secretaries, an office continued until 1961, when it was abolished after a reorganization. Well-known Honorary Secretaries of the past include Henry R. Tedder, J. Y. W. MacAlister, L. Stanley Jast, Frank Pacy, Ernest A. Savage, Lionel R. McColvin, William A. Munford, and William B. Paton, the last to hold the office. There had been instances of occasional, paid, part-time secretarial assistance as the work of the Association grew, but it was not until 1928 that the LA appointed its first full-time paid secretary, Guy W. Keeling. He had to resign due to ill health in 1931 and was succeeded by his deputy, Percy S. J. Welsford, who remained in office for 28 years. Welsford witnessed great advances in the size, influence, and work of the Association, and can take great personal credit for them.

From 1959 to 1974 the secretary was Hugh D. Barry, a barrister who quickly made his mark with proposals, which were mainly accepted, for the reorganization of the Association. He also encouraged such activities as National Library Weeks in the late 1960s and the emergence of the Commonwealth Library Association (COMLA) in 1972. He helped to instigate joint meetings at top level between representatives of the LA and Aslib, SCONUL, IIS, and the Society of Archivists. Barry also had to resign on account of ill health, and R. P. Hilliard was secretary from 1974 to 1978, during which LA celebrated its centenary year with an international conference and many other events. He was succeeded by Keith Lawrey from 1978 to 1984. In 1984 George Cunningham, a former Member of Parliament, became Chief Executive and soon proved his worth to the Association.

Headquarters. Not until 1890 was the LA able to operate from a central office; even then it was indebted to its Honorary Secretary, J. Y. W. MacAlister, for making available at a low rent a basement office at the Royal Medical and Chirurgical Society, of which he was Librarian and Secretary, at 20 Hanover Square in the West End of London. There members of the Association were able to hold monthly meetings at which papers were read and discussed. In 1899 rooms were rented in Whitcomb Street, Westminster, from Kate Reilly, who served as part-time Assistant Secretary until 1910. Council, committee, and other meetings continued to be held at 20 Hanover Square, however, until the same year.

A combination of circumstances meant that moves had to be made, and from 1910 to 1921 the LA shared office premises with the local government trade union NALGO. From 1910 to 1913 the address was 24 Bloomsbury Square and from 1913 to 1921 Caxton Hall, Westminster. There followed a one-year stay at Stapley House, Bloomsbury Square, but in 1922 Frank Pacy, then City Librarian of Westminster and Honorary Secretary of the LA, offered Buckingham Palace Road Library in Westminster as the Association headquarters. There it remained rent-free until the end of 1927. Early in the following year the LA operated from 26–27 Bedford Square, Bloomsbury, sharing the premises with Aslib and the Carnegie United Kingdom Trust (CUKT).

The year 1928 found the Association on a springboard ready for expansion. It was time to put an end to its peripatetic existence and to settle down in permanent headquarters. The CUKT, which had already given much financial help toward advancing libraries and librarianship in the U.K., was approached, and in 1931 the Trustees suggested that a property near the University of London be modernized and used partly for the National Central Library and partly for LA headquarters. The latter building was opened as Chaucer House, Malet Place, in May 1933. It afforded generous office accommodation, a members' lounge, a Council chamber and committee room, and a library. Chaucer House became a mecca for librarians visiting London, and all Council and committee meetings were held there, in addition to Branch, Section, and other professional gatherings. During World War II the headquarters moved for a time to Launceston in Cornwall. The adjacent National Central Library building suffered severe bomb damage and the LA's Chaucer House did not entirely escape.

Late in 1943 the LA office moved back to London. It continued to operate from Chaucer House for 20 years after the end of the war. In the early 1960s the University of London, whose premises practically surrounded the LA and NCL buildings in Malet Place, coveted the accommodation so much that it offered to erect a replacement building in Store Street, two blocks south of Malet Place. Agreement was reached, and toward the end of 1965 the LA moved to 7 Ridgmount Street, off Store Street. Council decided by a small majority not to retain the name Chaucer House, so the present building is simply referred to as LA Headquarters. It was never officially opened, though the neighboring National Central Library (now part of the British Library) was inaugurated by Queen Elizabeth II in March 1966, to coincide with the first National Library Week ever celebrated in the UK.

The Ridgmount Street headquarters includes a members' lounge, Council and committee rooms, and offices for the LA staff. It also has additional space on the upper floors for renting to appropriate organizations. There is also a library; it was originally the LA's own collection, but in 1974 the British Library assumed responsibility for it. The British Library staffs, maintains, and develops this professional collection more ambitiously than LA could hope to do. LA members lost no privileges, and can use the library for reference and for borrowing either on the premises or by mail.

Conferences. Since the Library Association was formed at a conference in London in 1877, it has staged an annual conference every year with the exception of the years 1914 and 1940 to 1945. World War I caused the Oxford conference of 1914 to be canceled, but conferences or annual meetings took place in London from 1915 through 1918. After World War I the first annual conference was that at Southport in September 1919, and the first after World War II was at Blackpool in May 1946. The format of conference has changed little over the years. Sometimes it has included the annual general meeting of members, sometimes this has been held separately. Sometimes there have been joint conferences, such as that with the Library Association of Ireland in Dublin in 1967, or those held jointly with Aslib and other bodies in 1980 and again in 1985. In the main, however, the LA annual conference has remained a domestic affair including in its program general and sectional meetings, the Presidential Address, an exhibition of books and library furnishings and equipment, a conference dinner, related meetings, and social gatherings. The proceedings of each conference have invariably been published subsequently. Only twice has the LA annual conference been held outside the U.K.—in Paris in 1892 and in Dublin in 1967. (It was also held in Dublin in 1884, when Ireland was not an independent republic.)

Publications. When the Association was founded, it adopted the *American Library Journal* as its official organ, with the word "American" being dropped from the title. This arrangement lasted only from 1877 to 1882. In 1880 a periodical called *Monthly Notes* had been started and in 1883 it was the only LA journal. In 1884 a *Library Chronicle* was started, which ran until 1888; then from 1889 to 1898 *The Library* was the official journal. There was much dissatisfaction with it and, impatient at the delay in producing a genuinely official periodical, James Duff Brown inaugurated his independent *Library World* in July 1898. Arrangements were already in work for the LA's own publication, however, and in January 1899 the first issue of the *Library Association Record* appeared, with Henry Guppy as editor. It has been issued regularly ever since. Between 1899 and 1975 it had a distinguished series of librarian editors, including Arundell Esdaile, R. D. Hilton Smith, Lionel R. McColvin, W. Bruce Stevenson, A. J. Walford, J. D.

Reynolds, and Edward Dudley. In January 1976 the *Record* appeared for the first time with a professional journalist as full-time paid Editor, Roger Walter, who continued until his death in 1984; then Jane Jenkins succeeded him.

As the *Record* became a more temporal and newsy journal, LA decided that a more scholarly and staid approach was also needed, so in 1969 it launched the quarterly *Journal of Librarianship*, which has longer and more detailed articles than the *Record*, and which devotes more space to reviewing professional literature.

The first *LA Year Book* came out in 1892, but it did not actually appear annually until 1932; since then there has been an unbroken series. It lists names of members of Council and committees, details of Branch and Group organizations, gives the texts of the Royal Charter and the Bye-laws, and lists all members of the Association.

Since the mid-1930s the Association has pursued a vigorous publishing program. In addition to the publications mentioned, it issues such serials as *Current Research, Library and Information Science Abstracts, British Technology Index,* and *Current Technology Index.* Among other publications with which the Association has been associated over the years are the *Anglo-American Cataloguing Rules* and Walford's *Guide to Reference Material.* For its centenary year in 1977 the Association planned a special program of centenary volumes, including W. A. Munford's *History of the Library Association 1877–1977, British Librarianship Today,* edited by W. L. Saunders, *Prospects for British Librarianship,* edited by K. C. Harrison, *The National Central Library,* by S. P. L. Filon, and other titles. A distinct organization known as Library Association Publishing Limited (LAPL) was set up to handle the increasing number of books, serials, and journals emanating from Ridgmount Street.

Branches and Groups. Branches of LA date back to 1896 when the North Western Branch came into being. In 1908 the Scottish Library Association, which became a branch of LA in 1931, was founded. Other district organizations followed, usually based on such cities as Birmingham and Bristol, but it was not until 1923 that the largest branch, London and Home Counties, was inaugurated. With the formation of the Yorkshire and the South Western Branches in 1949, the entire U.K. was covered by LA branches. Wales is covered by the Welsh Library Association, a branch of LA, and Northern Ireland by the Northern Ireland Branch. The branches have proved themselves to be necessary adjuncts to the parent body. They are active in arranging conferences, meeting programs, summer schools; they produce useful publications such as the *Scottish LA News* (SLAN), conference proceedings, and union catalogues of periodicals. The branch organization has also afforded librarians at all levels experience in committee work, chairmanships, editorial work, and organizing conferences and meetings. There are 12 LA branches, each having an elected representative on the Council of the Association.

The history of the Groups could be said to have started in 1895 when the Library Assistants' Association was formed, but it was then an independent body and remained so for many years. It was not until 1930 that, as the AAL, it became a Section of LA.

Just before that time, Sections had been started for university and research libraries, also for county libraries. After 1945 a new ecumenicalism seized hold of Council, as it appreciated the need to attract into membership librarians from all types of libraries. More Sections were formed, those for Youth Libraries, Medical Libraries, and Reference and Special Libraries among them. In 1962, following the adoption of the Barry proposals, the Sections were renamed Groups. The radical changes at that time acted as spurs in the formation of other Groups. In quick succession, Groups were set up for Hospital Libraries and Handicapped Readers, Library History, Cataloguing and Indexing, Rare Books, and International and Comparative Librarianship. Much later Groups were formed for Community Services, Information Technology, Publicity and Public Relations, and Training and Education. There were 23 Groups in LA in 1986. Like the Branches they have been busy publishing journals such as *Library History, Assistant Librarian* and *YLG News,* as well as arranging conferences and meetings all over the country. The Groups were not directly represented on Council in the mid-1980s, as were the Branches, but there was a move to change this; a report entitled *Futures,* issued to all members as a discussion document in 1985, suggested that each Group be represented on Council by a member elected by the Group.

International work. Having been born at an international conference, and having celebrated its 50th anniversary with a conference at Edinburgh (1927) which led to the founding of IFLA, it might be thought that LA has always been internationally minded, but this is not so. Before the start of IFLA (1929) there appear to have been few attempts at giving LA a leading role in world librarianship, but since 1945 onward there has been a totally different approach. Since then LA's contributors to IFLA have expanded to impressive proportions. Leaders include Sir Frank Francis, Lionel R. McColvin, Anthony Thompson, Frank M. Gardner, and others whose names came to the forefront. LA has been host to numerous IFLA meetings, including the General Councils held in Cheltenham in 1931, in London in 1948 and again in 1950, in Edinburgh in 1961, and in Liverpool in 1971. Brighton was scheduled for 1987. Another international development after World War II was the expansion of the work of the British Council in providing and encouraging library development overseas, particularly in Commonwealth countries. Edward Sydney (LA President in 1956) and Frank M. Gardner (LA President in 1964) became leading figures in the liaison between the Association and the British Council. Many British librarians went abroad either to take charge of British Council libraries overseas, or to be consultants advising the developing countries on library affairs, and LA frequently advised on the appointments. The Association gave similar help and advice to Unesco from 1946 to 1985, when the British government decided to withdraw from Unesco.

In 1971 the Library Association was approached by the Commonwealth Foundation to assist in setting up a Commonwealth Library Association (COMLA). Following an exploratory conference of librarians from 22 Commonwealth countries at LA headquarters in London, COMLA was inaugurated at La-gos, Nigeria in November 1972. Hugh D. Barry, LA Secretary and the first COMLA Acting Secretary, drew up the original draft constitution. K. C. Harrison (LA President in 1973) was the first President of COMLA from 1972 to 1975, and was also Executive Secretary from 1980 to 1983. LA continues to give full support to COMLA.

Since 1968, when it began, the International and Comparative Librarianship (ICLG) Group of LA has thrived steadily. It had about 1,500 members in 1986. It meets during the annual conference and at other times, and publishes the quarterly journal *Focus* circulated to its members. All traces of isolationism have not been eradicated from LA. There is still apathy, and sometimes downright opposition, toward international activities from some members. But it is undeniable that since the mid-1940s LA involvement and influence in world librarianship has grown enormously, and the tide of activity is still rising in the 1980s.

Influence on Government. The Library Association was granted a Royal Charter in 1898 and its text includes such phrases as "to promote the better administration of libraries" and "to watch any legislation." True to its Royal Charter the Association has lost few opportunities to make representations to government on library matters in the U.K., and this it has done with varying degrees of success. It helped to secure passage of the 1919 law that abolished legal limits on public library expenditure in England and Wales, and also gave powers to establish county libraries. The LA also played an important part in finalizing the Net Books Agreements of 1929 and 1931, by which public libraries obtained advantages, the result of a campaign begun in 1902. Over the years the Association has been represented or has given evidence to many committees, both governmental and nongovernmental. They have produced such important documents as the Kenyon Report of 1927, the Roberts Report of 1959, and the Dainton Report of 1969. Kenyon gave impetus to library cooperation in the U.K., Roberts led eventually to the passing of the Public Libraries and Museums Act of 1964, and Dainton gave rise to the British Library Act of 1972.

The Association was also prominent in the protracted debates that preceded the Public Lending Right (PLR) Act of 1979. The arguments had been going on since 1951, with LA opposing several of the schemes proposed. While the Association was not against reasonable compensation for authors, it consistently sought to ensure that library staffs would not be burdened with too much additional administrative work in connection with PLR, and also stressed that library book funds should not suffer because of the extra expenditure involved. The proposed legislation met those reservations, and PLR became operative in 1982.

Over the years as part of its efforts to live up to the high ideals of its founders, LA has kept a watchful eye on such issues as censorship and copyright and, while it is not a trade union, it tries to attend to the interests of all its members.

Future. Like most healthy bodies LA is naturally concerned with its future. It is introspective enough to continue appointing working parties which produce reports for the Council and members generally. Throughout 1984 and 1985 a Futures

Working Party looked at many aspects of LA policy and produced a report entitled *Futures,* presented to Council on October 31, 1985. In December 1985 it was circulated to all members of the Association. A readable document of 113 paragraphs summarized into 43 recommendations on LA's future, it promised to stimulate comment and debate, leading to members' decisions on the future of the Association. Members' comments were to be received through 1986 and decisions made at the 1986 annual conference.

REFERENCES

Library Association, *Year Book* (1932–   ).

William A. Munford, *Annals of the Library Association 1877–1960.*

Munford, *A History of the Library Association 1877–1977,* the Library Association Centenary Volume.

K. C. HARRISON

Library Buildings

History. The earliest library or archive facilities were associated with temples or palaces. Examples of temple libraries from the second and third pre-Christian millennia are those at Heliopolis in Egypt and at Erech in Iraq. Palace libraries include those at Ebla in Syria and at Tel-el-Amarna in Egypt. Principal differences in their physical outfitting, however, resulted more from the format of the books and records they housed than from their locations. Cuneiform tablets were usually laid up on benches or shelves, sometimes in clay or wicker containers, with their

Harvard University Science Center Library, Cambridge, Massachusetts (completed 1973).

American Institute of Architects/ALA

American Institute of Architects/ALA

Carleton College Library, Northfield, Minnesota (occupied 1983).

opening texts displayed, whereas leather or papyrus scrolls were kept either in chests, earthen jars, or wall bins with the identification tags visible.

Although primarily for proprietary use, the locations of libraries within temple or palace compounds suggest some public access as well. Certainly Assurbanipal's palace library at Nineveh and the library in the Temple of the Muses in Alexandria, both in the 1st millennium B.C., were available to the public.

In Greece and Rome public libraries came also to be built in other gathering places such as baths and forums. Usually rectangular in shape with a colonnade in the forecourt, these libraries commonly had niches in the side and rear walls where scrolls were stacked in bins. This arrangement was sometimes duplicated in upper galleries, and statues of votive deities often occupied apses facing the entry.

Information is scanty regarding early library buildings outside of Europe and the Middle East, but they too appear to have been primarily priestly or princely in origin. In old China there were imperial libraries in which written bamboo slips and silk scrolls were stored, and ancient temple collections were in the Indian Subcontinent. There are 10th- and 11th-century library buildings still standing at Angkor Wat and Banteai Srei in Kampuchea (Cambodia) that were erected as adjuncts to shrines and temples to house sacred texts written on palm leaves. At Mandalay 729 extant three-by-five-foot alabaster slabs incised with the Tripitaka still stand sheltered under separate roofs, constituting a kind of decentralized library structure spread over 13 acres. Aztec priests in pre-Columbian Mexico had very large collections of accordion-folded amate paper codices, but little is known of how they were housed.

By far the largest libraries anywhere during the Middle Ages were in the Muslim world, where collections comprising hundreds of thousands of volumes existed in university and public library buildings from Basra to Baghdad, Cairo, Cordova, and elsewhere. Manuscript codices, written on vellum or paper, were piled flat on wooden wall shelves, and some large libraries, such as the one at Bokhara, devoted different rooms to different topics in a kind of early subject divisional plan. European collections meanwhile were very small and until the 13th century were found almost solely in religious houses. These libraries were usually stored in book presses that were sometimes free-standing but were often built into the wall of the cloister walk at the end of the transept of the church.

From the Renaissance to the present time Western libraries have been engaged in a continuing struggle to house growing numbers of books. It was standard early practice for a library to chain its few books in fixed locations, first singly on lecterns and later on shelves below and above reading surfaces. By the first decade of the 17th century these bookcases were commonly arrayed either at 90 degrees from the perimeter of the library room, as was done at Leiden, or along the perimeter walls, as in the Arts End of the Bodleian at Oxford. Because of their ability to accommodate large numbers of books, these two configurations came into wide use in university, cathedral, and other large libraries, where they continued to be fashionable into the late 19th century.

Perimeter shelves, often with galleries above, were especially favored in the Rococo era and were used in such 18th-century libraries as those at St. Gallen, Wiblingen, and the Imperial Library in Vienna. In the periods of Classical and Gothic Revival, architects found especially that they could dress the alcove arrangement felicitiously in exteriors patterned upon both Greek temples and medieval churches. The narthex could serve as the foyer, the nave as the reading room with clerestory windows above, and bookcases could range inward from the buttresses through the aisles. Lancet windows could illumine the bookcases, and columns at their interior ends could support one or more galleries and a vault above. There were some aberrations, such as the round library erected as the Radcliffe Camera at Oxford in 1749.

These were the models available when libraries first came to be constructed in British North America; thus the Library Company of Philadelphia (1791) shelved its books in perimeter bookcases with galleries, whereas the Redwood Library in Newport (1750) was designed to look like a Temple to Apollo. The first library at Harvard (1841) was patterned upon a Gothic chapel with rows of bookcases in the aisles. The first library at the University of Virginia (1826) was round.

By the 1870s, however, library practice was becoming more complex, architecture was coming increasingly to regard function as at least one factor in determining form, and new structural materials were coming into use, all of which resulted in experimentation in library building design. The multi-tier structural bookstack came into widespread use, resulting also in a proliferation of large reading rooms with high ceilings to accommodate summer heat build-up and large north windows for light and ventilation. Books were thus separated from readers in inflexible, fixed-function buildings, many of which, because of the great cost of their replacement, are still in use. The temple and palace origins of libraries are still evident in many of the buildings of this vintage; the Sterling Memorial Library at Yale (1931) is an example of the former and the Boston Public Library (1896) of the latter.

As the 20th century progressed, some voices began to protest that grandiose palace and temple models were inappropriate for libraries in modern democratic settings and to call instead for simpler and more utilitarian beauty in their appearance. Andrew Carnegie, influential because his philanthropy provided some 2,617 library buildings, insisted that the buildings he funded be functional and largely unadorned. This movement toward simplicity in American library building design accelerated during the Depression and came to fruition about mid-century with the advent of modular column-and-slab construction. Structural stacks gave way to free-standing shelving, and load-bearing walls gave way to curtain walls, allowing open shelves with adjacent seating to supersede closed stacks and reading rooms. Uniform lighting, floor-loading, and air treatment, made possible for the first time by modern technology, permitted inexpensive relocation of library activities as changing service needs demanded.

The period of simplicity in library building design, however, did not last long. Although the concept of simplicity in interior layout continues today to dominate the aspirations of librarians, much new library architecture since about 1960 has tended to become increasingly complex. As a result flexibility has been reduced in the future use of much recently constructed library space.

Planning and Construction Process. Every building is designed for a purpose. The more carefully that purpose is conceptualized beforehand, the more satisfactory the building is likely to be. Since library and archive buildings often serve for a half century or more, their probable use must be envisioned over a long future before their requirements can be defined. Community surveys, either formal or informal, are frequently used to this end. For public libraries population shifts and other demographic changes must be projected, and for academic libraries enrollments must be extrapolated and curriculum changes foreseen. Patterns of future information production and use must be considered and changing service needs anticipated.

A document, usually called a "program" or "brief," can then be prepared that delineates textually all of the essential functional qualities and characteristics of the new building. It is usually considered good practice to write the same kind of building program whether the new structure is to be an expansion or a completely new building. The program is usually drafted either by the librarian or by a consultant with the counsel of a planning committee representing the owner. This document, which may run from 20 to more than 100 pages in length, can be viewed as an extension of the contract with the architect, since it defines what the architect agrees to design into the building.

The building program normally comprises at least four essential components. An introduction attempts briefly to describe the history, service philosophy, and desired ambience of the institution. A second section enumerates assumptions regarding such matters as site and cost, and it identifies "functional criteria" used to determine the amount of seating, shelf capacity, and spatial calculations specified in the document. A third section defines every functional area or department in the building, giving for each its

American Institute of Architects/ALA

Central Library, Houston, Texas (completed December 1975).

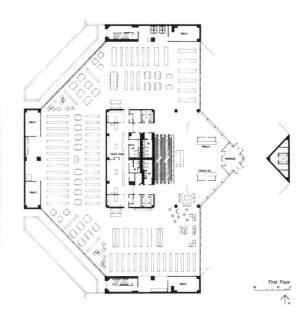

American Institute of Architects/ALA

*A. F. Parlow Library of Health Sciences, Torrance, California
(occupied 1983).*

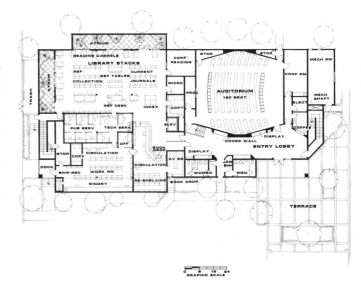

American Institute of Architects/ALA

Burling Library, Grinnel College, Grinnell, Iowa

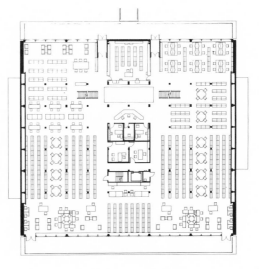

*(Top) Central Library,
Houston, Texas: first floor
plan.
(Center) A. F. Parlow
Library of Health Sciences,
Torrance, California: first
floor plan
(Left) Burling Library,
Grinnell College, Grinnell,
Iowa: first floor plan.*

469

requisite proximities, structural qualities, room configuration, equipment inventory, and spatial needs. A fourth section contains notes on such miscellanea as illumination levels, acoustics, keying systems, and ceiling heights. The preparation of a sound and thoughtful program is perhaps the most important thing the owner can do to assure a good building.

The owner must then select an architect. Questions often arise here as to the comparative advantages of local and national firms and of firms with and without previous library or archive experience. Since both good and poor buildings have been produced by any combination of these, however, such issues ought not to determine final selection. Selection should rather be based on the architect's previous work on buildings of all kinds, the firm's communication skills, its ability to keep on schedule and within budget, its experience in adhering to program, and other professional factors. The fee for architectural services is normally a percentage of the cost of construction.

The architect then converts the program's textual description of the required building into graphic representations which, together with design specifications, instruct the contractor in what is to be built. This process involves first the general articulation of the building's requisite areas into functional proximities, and aggregating them into an esthetically pleasing mass that will grace the site in harmony with its surroundings. Through a series of interchanges between architect and the planning committee, sketches are then developed laying out individual activity areas in efficient interrelationships, and necessary furniture and equipment is configured in these areas. Construction and other related costs are estimated, and a budget is prepared.

When these matters are agreed to, the architect is authorized by the owner to proceed to the preparation of working drawings and building specifications. In this stage all details must be determined, construction and finishing materials must be specified, and bid documents prepared. During this phase the architect must often draw upon a wide range of supporting expertise, including perhaps those of illumination consultants, structural as well as heating and ventilating engineers, interior designers, and others. Fulfillment of building code and other legal requirements must also be assured at this time.

By now a full year or more may have been spent just in planning the project. Although such planning is seldom begun unless the owner has some reason to expect that necessary funding will be available when needed, this period should also be spent by the owner completing financial arrangements for the project. Depending in part upon the nature of the institution, this may involve obtaining bonding authority, seeking appropriations from a government agency, solicitation of assistance from philanthropic foundations, seeking the participation of private or corporate donors, or indeed any combination of these.

When planning and funding preparations are complete, the building can be bid and construction begun. Careful planning and good architecture will facilitate these processes by keeping expensive snags and change orders minimal and by reducing unnecessary delays in the project schedule. The owner's interest during construction is protected not only by

the architect but also through the continuous oversight of a "clerk of the works" who stays on the site, checking for adherence to drawings and specifications. Payment to the contractor is normally made monthly during construction upon certification by the clerk and the architect.

Careful planning can also assure ease and efficiency in occupying the building after its completion by the contractor. Many details must be resolved just in moving the books and documents themselves and in locating them properly in the new facility. The cost of moving must be budgeted. If public service is to be maintained during the move, this will also need to be planned. Many schedules will need to be coordinated. If additional staff members will be required to operate the new facility, they will need to be recruited and trained beforehand.

Often overlooked in developing new space for archival or library purposes is the training that will be needed not only for new and old staff members but also for patrons. Library use often rises considerably when a new building is opened. Orientation to the new building will be needed, and many questions will require answering. Press releases will have to be written and dispatched. Many visitors will come to see the new building, some of whom will be architects and librarians wishing to discuss in detail many aspects of the project. Dedicatory ceremonies, sometimes very extensive, must be coordinated, and donors will have to be appropriately honored. Occupying a new building will be much easier if all of these drafts on staff time are anticipated and budgeted.

Design Considerations. From the standpoint of librarians and archivists, the most significant building design considerations may be grouped under the three elements of efficiency, economy, and effectiveness. From the standpoint of the user, the most important of these is no doubt efficiency, or the degree to which the design of the building enhances the ease with which its contents and services can be utilized.

Efficiency. The layout of a building can facilitate the movement of patrons through it, or it can impair that movement. There are natural locations for many library activities, and a well-designed building respects these natural dispositions. In nations where people habitually keep to the right, for example, circulation desks serve best when they are situated on the right of the exit, so that departing patrons may stop to check out books without crossing the flow of people entering the building. There are other "natural" locations for such things as the public catalogue and reference service which must be similarly taken into account in the placement of library functions.

Attention to layout can also accomplish efficiencies within departments as well as among them. The layout of the general stack, for example, is of great importance; much of a patron's time in seeking a book will be saved if it is immediately clear upon entering a stack area exactly where each volume is shelved, rather than ranges being distributed haphazardly or secluded in cul-de-sacs and behind stairwells. The placement of tables and chairs close to all book ranges can also save time for readers. If only ten readers a day have to go a half-dozen steps out of their way because of poor layout, more than 1,200 miles will be walked unnecessarily in the 50-year lifetime of the building.

Efficiency of layout is also very important to library operation. If the aforementioned ten walkers happen to be staff members, then the library will pay wages for the 1,200 unnecessary miles walked. Attention to traditional time-and-motion principles as well as to more recent systems analysis should precede both the layout of departments and the deployment of furniture and equipment within departments.

Economy. Two kinds of economy should be considered in planning a building: the economy with which it can be constructed and the economy with which it can be operated during its lifetime. Economy of construction can result from many factors. Obviously, the selection of building materials will impinge upon construction costs. New libraries sometimes still use sumptuous materials and finishes reminiscent of their palace and temple origins rather than cheaper, more modest materials, driving up the cost of the building.

Simplicity of design can also be a factor in the economy of construction. Rectangular structures are generally cheaper to construct than complex designs, and, since the true basic "module" of a library is the rectangular book, rectangular spaces are easier to utilize for library purposes. Irregular shapes moreover usually result in larger areas of exterior wall surface requiring expensive cosmetic treatment. Buildings with balanced ratios of height to width and depth are ordinarily cheaper to construct, and they are certainly more economical to use, than buildings that are disproportionately tall or squat. Site considerations sometimes mitigate these principles, but almost always at a cost.

The "efficiency ratio" in a design, or the relationship between its net assignable and gross areas, is also a factor in the economy of construction. This applies not only to floor area where it is ordinarily calculated, but also to vertical space. Atria and unnecessarily high ceilings, which may themselves also be vestiges of the palatial age in libraries, enlarge buildings and result in greater cubage to be maintained, heated, and cooled during the occupancy of the building. Open wells and high ceilings also create acoustical problems, increase the cost of ceiling-mounted illumination, and reduce flexibility in the future use of space. As with irregular shapes, these added costs must be evaluated when their use is being considered.

The role of design in the operating economies of library buildings has already been cited. A well-designed building will be economical to staff, and the costs of its physical maintenance will be reasonable. A good building will also be "energy efficient," so that unnecessarily high expenditures will not be required to keep it adequately lit and at comfortable temperature and humidity levels throughout its period of use.

Effectiveness. The effectiveness of a library or archives building can be of several kinds, but the most basic of these is as shelter. Even an effective shelter, however, must do more than just protect materials, readers, and services from the wind and weather; it must also aid in the preservation of the books and documents it houses. Water damage to materials, for example, is more likely to result from

American Institute of Architects/ALA

Broadneck Area Branch Library of Anne Arundel County Library, Maryland (occupied 1983).

poorly drained sites, inadequately sealed walls below grade, or bad plumbing than for leaky roofs. Water security of all kinds should therefore be considered in building planning.

Windows, important though they may be to the aesthetics of a building, can reduce the effectiveness of libraries and archives as shelter, if they are not sensitively handled. Direct sunlight is difficult to read by and bleaches the spines of books, so it should be avoided wherever possible. The ultra-violet rays of even indirect natural light, however, can also cause deterioration of paper and should therefore be filtered out of areas where preservation is important. Care should also be taken to screen deleterious ultra-violet rays out of the artificial illumination used in such areas.

Since fire security is important in virtually all kinds of buildings, it is almost always well covered in basic building code requirements. Nonetheless, because of the unusual susceptibility of books and documents to damage from combinations of fire and water, fire security should receive special attention in the planning of libraries and archives. Likewise the security of materials from theft and mutilation must also be considered in the effectiveness of a library building as shelter. Although no building can be fully theft-proof, such factors as the layout of services and equipment, the location and design of windows, and the kind and number of exits from a library building will figure in the security of its contents against theft.

REFERENCES

Aaron and Elaine Cohen, *Designing and Space Planning for Libraries* (1979)

Ralph E. Ellsworth, *Planning Manual for Academic Libraries* (1973).

Keyes D. Metcalf, *Planning Academic and Research Library Buildings* (1965); new edition by David Weber (1986).

Rolf Myller, *The Design of the Small Public Library* (1966).

Godfrey Thompson, *Planning and Design of Library Buildings,* 2nd edition (1977).

Joseph L. Wheeler and A. M. Githens, *The American Public Library Building* (1950).

DAVID KASER

471

Library Cooperative Systems

History. The first instance or example of library cooperation is impossible to identify. Joe W. Kraus in a 1975 article reports that "catalogs of manuscripts in more than one monastery library existed in the first half of the 13th century. Manuscripts in 138 English and Scottish monasteries were listed in the *Registrum Librorum Angliae*." Curt D. Wormann cites examples of an exchange agreement among the universities of Lund, Abo, and Greifswald as early as 1740, a projected union catalogue of the libraries of Weimar and Jean, a proposal for a coordinated acquistions scheme for Wolfenbüttel and Göttingen, and the ambitious attempt to establish a *Bibliographie generale* based on the millions of books confiscated during the French Revolution and gathered in the *depots littéraires*.

Suggestions for cooperative activities in the U.S. appeared in the Annual Report of the Smithsonian Institution, whose Committee on Organization proposed that the institution "become a centre of literary and bibliographical reference for the entire country . . . to procure catalogs of all the important works or bibliography so that they might be consulted by the scholar, the student, the author, the historian, from every section of the Union, and . . . inform them whether any works they may desire to examine are to be found in the United States; and if so in what library; or if in Europe only, in what country of Europe they must be sought." On September 15, 1853, Charles Coffin Jewett, the first Librarian of the Smithsonian Institution, was elected President of the first meeting of librarians ever held in the United States. The next day he spoke about the Smithsonian Catalogue System and his proposal to make general catalogues with the use of stereotype plates and his hope to publish a general catalogue of all the libraries in the country. His plan failed, not because the idea was faulty but because of inadequate technology (the impermanence of the stereotype process), inadequate financial support, and lack of an organization to support the project (the three factors necessary for any successful cooperative venture). In an 1876 *Library Journal* article Samuel S. Green proposed that librarians enter into agreements to share resources.

The first major national union list was Henry C. Bolton's *A Catalogue of Scientific and Technical Periodicals,* published in 1885. By 1901 the Library of Congress initiated cooperative cataloguing and began building the first National Union Catalog by collecting catalogue cards from government libraries in Washington, D.C., the New York Public Library, the Boston Public Library, Harvard University, the John Crerar Library, and several others. The first interlibrary lending code was drawn up by an ALA Committee on Coordination of College Libraries in 1917. The Code suggested photoreproduction in place of lending the original publications. The earliest regional union catalogue in the United States was developed by the California State Library in 1909, a card catalogue of books in public libraries in California. The first edition of the Union List of Serials (1927) located 75,000 titles in 225 libraries and in a bibliography listed 179 examples of union lists.

Major union catalogues increased in number between 1932 and 1940, when 17 catalogues were estab-

lished, many through the assistance of the Works Progress Administration (WPA). A number of these regional catalogues were added to the National Union Catalog so that by 1968 it contained more than 16,000,000 cards, representing about 10,000,000 titles and editions. Since that time, bibliographic cooperatives and networks have accelerated in pace to such an extent that resource sharing, cooperative bibliographic systems, and the formalized development of library systems, consortia, and networks are commonly accepted.

Definitions. The terms cooperative, consortium, and network are usually used interchangeably. The National Center for Education Statistics (NCES) defined the terms as follows:

> Cooperative: . . . a group of independent and autonomous libraries banded together by informal or formal agreements or contracts which stipulate the common services to be planned and coordinated by the directors of the cooperative systems.
> Consortium: . . . a formal arrangement of two or more libraries not under the same institutional control for joint activities to improve the library service of the participants by cooperation extending beyond traditional interlibrary loan as defined in the National Interlibrary Loan Code of 1968.
> Network: . . . a formal organization among libraries for cooperation and sharing of resources, usually with an explicitly hierarchical structure, in which the group as a whole is organized into subgroups with the expectation that most of the needs of a library will be satisfied within the subgroups of which it is a member [Alphonse F. Trezza, "Networks," *The ALA Yearbook* (1977)].

Raynard C. Swank defines networks as a "concept that includes the development of cooperative systems of libraries on geographical, subject, or other lines, each with some kind of center that not only coordinates the internal activities of the system but also serves as the system's outlet to, and inlet from, the centers of other systems. The concept is also hierarchical . . . . The National Commission on Libraries and Information Science (NCLIS) in its National Program Document (1975) defines a network in its glossary as

> Two or more libraries and/or other organizations engaged in a common pattern of information exchange, through communications, for some functional purpose. A network usually consists of a formal arrangement whereby materials, information, and services provided by a variety of types of libraries and/or other organizations are made available to all potential users. (Libraries may be in different jurisdictions but agree to serve one another on the same basis as each serves its own constituents. Computers and telecommunications may be among the tools used for facilitating communication among them.) (*Towards a National Program for Library and Information Services: Goals for Action.*)

Types of Networks. The earlier and more traditional cooperatives and network activity were between like types of libraries. Networking among different types of libraries received long-overdue stimulus with the passage of the Library Services and Construction Act, Title III (LSCA), and the Higher Education Act (HEA), Title II–B, which provided funds, specifically in LSCA and permissively in HEA, for intertype or multitype library cooperation. Most multitype library cooperation occurs between public libraries and academic libraries, although some experimentation and activity with school and special libraries has developed and is gradually accelerating.

Networks in the United States have developed at the local, state, intrastate and interstate, regional, and national levels. Local cooperatives or networks tend to be in metropolitan or urban areas, are voluntary, loosely organized, and minimally funded. Local networks generally consist of one single type of library—e.g., academic—or of two types—academic and public. In some urban areas metropolitan multi-type library organizations have developed; New York City, Cleveland, and Milwaukee are examples of successful efforts. Reciprocal borrowing, interlibrary loan (ILL), local delivery services, cooperative collection development, and telephone reference services are the major activities undertaken.

State networks have traditionally been in a single type of library—public, with major university collections serving as back-up resources. Funding came from state and federal (LSCA) sources. Services include resource sharing—ILL (books, periodicals, audiovisual materials)—reference, delivery service, cooperative cataloguing, collection development and consulting.

One of the most significant national trends in library development since 1970 is the creation of state-wide multitype library systems. Many states regard public library systems as transitional, expanding to become multitype systems/networks by adding university, college, junior and community college libraries, elementary and secondary school library/media centers, residential institutions, and special libraries in corporations and nonprofit organizations. Multitype library systems were first established in Illinois in 1972, in California and Colorado in 1976, in Connecticut in 1977, in Minnesota in 1983, and in Kentucky, Kansas, and New Jersey in 1984. Pilot projects also began in the early 1980s in Wisconsin, Alabama, and New York.

The first multi-state regional network was established in 1966. Six New England land-grant university libraries joined together to form the New England Library and Information Network (NELINET) whose primary purpose was to supply its members with offline computerized bibliographic sources, a machine-readable catalogue data file, catalogue data file searching, catalogue cards, and book pockets and labels. By the mid-1970s three major bibliographic utilities were established as the direct result of computerized library operations. (The utilities provide computer-based services organized by and for libraries whereby members contribute to and modify the resource databases as needed to provide various library and information services.) The Online Computer Library Center, Inc. (OCLC), began as the Ohio College Library Center. The Research Libraries Group (RLG) first consisted of the New York Public Library and the libraries of Columbia, Harvard, and Yale Universities and did not have its own network computer facilities; the entity that became RLG's Research Libraries Information Network (RLIN) was under the control of Stanford University—not an RLG member at the time—as BALLOTS (Bibliographic Automation of Large Library Operations Using a Time-Sharing System). BALLOTS was also accessible to other libraries for shared cataloguing and searching functions. The Western Library Network (WLN), formerly the Washington Library Network, had been established, although it had not yet begun full implementation of its online system.

Within the next 10 years, a number of other regional networks were established. Some of the major ones are:

AMIGOS Bibliographic Council (in the Southwest)
California Library Authority for Systems and Services (CLASS), now the Cooperative Library Agency for Systems and Services
New England Library and Information Network (NELINET)
Pennsylvania Area Library Network (PALINET)
Pittsburgh Regional Library Center (PRLC)
Southeastern Library Network (SOLINET)
State University of New York (SUNY)

They all serve as brokers for libraries of OCLC cooperative cataloguing services as well as of the many new services developed in the first half of the 1980s.

Two major subject-oriented networks at the national level developed in the 1960s with the National Library of Medicine's (NLM) mechanization of its indexing service. NLM stored citations in its computer for use in the Medical Literature Analysis and Retrieval Systems (MEDLARS), which produced 21 major indexes, including *Index Medicus,* a monthly index to more than 2,500 of the world's biomedical journals. By the early 80s more than 1,300 universities, medical schools, hospitals, government agencies, commercial organizations, and other libraries had access to MEDLARS III's 4,500,000-plus references to journal articles and books published in the health sciences since 1965. The National Library of Medicine now offers more than 15 databases online through its Medline online database service.

In 1962 the Department of Agricultural Library was designated as the National Agricultural Library (NAL). NAL developed network services with the Department's various branches and field services. Its online agricultural database, AGRICOLA, includes indexes to worldwide journals and monographic literature and U.S. government reports on general agriculture, food, nutrition, agricultural economics, and many related scientific and sociological subject fields. It has also established seven USDA Regional Document Delivery Systems serving 35 land-grant university libraries.

At the national level two major events provided both an initial impetus and lasting impact and influence on networking. In 1969 the Library of Congress began distribution of the MARC data in machine-readable form, and in 1975 national policy direction was given by NCLIS's National Program Document. The MARC database provided the resource for the establishment and development of cooperative cataloguing services by OCLC, WLN, BALLOTS (later RLIN), and other institutionally and commercially based services. NCLIS called for a nationwide library and information services network to provide access to information for all, using the best in technology and telecommunications, building on existing local, state and national resources, and raising, but not trying to resolve, the issue of governance. It provided a challenge and a framework for action. The Commission continued its efforts by engaging the library community in discussing, reviewing, and recommending actions in resource sharing, copyright issues and revision of the copyright law, and the role of government and the private sector in providing information services. It funded studies on the role of the Library of Congress in networking activity and, in cooperation with the National Bureau of Standards, initial development of computer network protocols; in addition the Commission planned and implemented the 1979 White House Conference on Libraries and Information Services, which stressed access, cooperation, sharing, network development, and effective use of technology and telecommunications.

The Library of Congress in 1976 established a Network Advisory Committee. It provides a forum for discussion of the issues involved in nationwide networking by officers and directors of state, regional, and national networks, consortia, and cooperatives. LC, with the strong support of the Council of Library Resources, developed the means and mechanisms making possible the linking of the major utilities—OCLC, RLIN, and WLN.

Organizational Structures, Governance, and Finance. Local cooperatives or consortia in most cases are informal, voluntary institutional membership organizations. They develop bylaws providing for officers, a board of directors, and committees. Members may withdraw and in many cases only participate in those cooperative services they choose. Financial support comes from modest local dues and from fees for services provided. Grants from the state library agency, foundations, or federal sources may fund feasibility studies of new services, the purchase of equipment, or studies and surveys. In a few cases—mainly in the urban areas—a small paid staff is responsible for operating the cooperative, but ordinarily the staff is voluntary and part-time.

Intrastate regional systems or networks have their organizational structures defined by state statute. They encompass the entire state, their number varying from state to state. The law provides for a formal organization and a board, makes provisions for paid staff, and specifies the system's purpose and major services. The law also usually indicates both the rights and responsibilities of the participants. The board may be a lay board representative of the member libraries of the organization; or it may include both librarians and lay members. Funding comes primarily from state appropriations and usually according to a formula, i.e., per capita and area grants. The member libraries may also contribute funding from their own budgets either for specific services or general purposes. Additional funds from LSCA and other federal sources are available through the grant process. The State Library Agency is the administrator of the intrastate regional systems and the major funding source and can exert a strong influence on statewide directions and services. However, the State Library Agencies rely on various advisory groups to assure user input in the decision-making process.

Statewide networks are also established by law and administered by a State Agency, almost always the State Library Agency. The network may be regionally organized as described previously, with the added provision of back-up resources from major research libraries, large public libraries and, in most cases, the state library agency library. This resource

sharing is hierarchial. Funding for the back-up centers may be an annual fixed sum, or be based on a formula and applied on the basis of actual use of the collection. New York, Illinois, and Texas are examples of this latter type of network structure. Overall administration of the network is the responsibility of the state agency and always includes an advisory board and user committees that address service, evaluation, financing, relationships, management, and other matters. The funding of statewide multitype networks, although primarily from state sources, is supplemented by LSCA Title III funds.

At the interstate regional level, networks are strictly membership organizations. The networks are chartered as not-for-profit agencies, have bylaws, a plan of service, a paid staff, a governing board, and advisory committees. The basic goals and objectives of the organization are included in its organizational documents. Funding comes from membership dues and service fees, although some additional support may be available from grants by foundations or state and/or federal government agencies. The regionals offer brokered services of the utilities, training, retrospective conversion, development of area union catalogues, and access to bibliographic databases, among other services.

National-level networks' organization, governance, and financing differ with each network. The Regional Medical Library Network is organized and administered by the National Library of Medicine, with funds appropriated by the U.S. government to support the network. NLM provides opportunities for institutions and librarians to offer recommendations concerning its services at both the national and regional levels.

Each of the three national utilities has a unique organizational structure. OCLC started as the Ohio College Library Center primarily to serve Ohio academic institutions, and its structure included a Board of Trustees composed of librarians elected by Ohio libraries. Its governance was restructured in 1978 to include a new Board of Trustees and a Users' Council; the board is partially self-perpetuating and partially elected by the members of the Users' Council. Users' Council members are elected by the regional network members participating in the OCLC online system. The financing of OCLC is primarily through the fees for service with additional funds from foundation and government grants. OCLC is a not-for-profit corporation and is a vendor of services to libraries.

RLIN, founded in 1974 by RLG, Inc., operates as a corporation owned and operated by its members with a Board of Governors composed of one representative from each institution. RLG derives its income from three principal sources: partnership dues, RLIN service charges, and grants or loans from foundations and other sources.

WLN was originally a state-owned operation established and operated by the Washington State Library. In 1985 it became a not-for-profit membership organization with a board of trustees and users committees. It is supported principally by service fees and grants.

Services and Functions. The *ALA Glossary of Library and Information Science* (1983) defines a bibliographic network as one "established and maintained for the sharing of bibliographic data through the use of standard communication format and authority control." A bibliographic utility is an organization that maintains online bibliographic databases, enabling it to offer computer-based support to any interested users. A bibliographic utility maintains components of a national library network data store and provides a standard interface through which bibliographic source centers and individual participants may gain access to the nationwide network. OCLC, RLIN, and WLN are considered bibliographic utilities. The bibliographic source centers serve as brokers or distributors of computer-based bibliographic processing services. A source center gains access to network resources through the facilities of a bibliographic utility; it does not necessarily contribute records directly to or maintain portions of the national library network data base. AMIGOS, CLASS, NELINET, SOLINET, PRLC, and PALINET are examples of bibliographic source centers.

Although resource sharing in its broadest definition includes all types of library materials, services, and staff expertise, the principal type of resource sharing is in library materials available through interlibrary lending or reciprocal borrowing. Identification of bibliographic information and location can be derived from the online bibliographic services of the utilities, and requests for materials may also be placed through them. Actual delivery of material may be by mail, commercial delivery services, or local—and in some cases statewide—delivery services. Many statewide resource networks provide both identification and delivery of resources with a success rate over 80 percent. Examples of effective statewide networks that have been operating for many years are ILLINET (Illinois), NYSILL (New York), and FLIN (Florida).

Trends and Issues. With the growth of the microcomputer, computerized circulation, interfacing between automated circulation systems, online catalogues and union catalogues, the communication of ILL requests has changed markedly. The electronic mailbox was replacing ordinary mail in the 1980s and the telephone for dispatching requests. The resulting reduction in the time it takes to determine the availability of an item and transmit the request to the lending institution has made ILL more attractive as a supplement to an institution's collection. Document delivery times are still longer than desirable; facsimile transmission times are more cost-effective but can only serve for limited amounts and types of materials.

The impact of improved resource sharing on an individual library's collection development policy cannot be underestimated. Size of collection may not be as important a criterion for excellence as availability and access through resource sharing. Issues and problems must be considered carefully—responsibility for collection development at the local level cannot be replaced by resource sharing no matter how efficient the services. Reproduction of documents and journal articles raise copyright issues, and new technologies such as laser disks may even aggravate copyright problems. All of these concerns are manageable if librarians, information scientists, publishers, and information entrepeneurs work toward the same goal of equal opportunity of access for all who desire it

regardless of the individual's location, social, economic or physical condition or level of intellectual achievement.

The trend in the 1970s and 80s has been toward networking for mutual benefit, whereby each participant in the cooperative effort contributes not equally but fairly and to the best of its ability. The contribution may take the form of skill, knowledge, money, resources, or technology. Success of the network depends on a clear focus of the problems and issues to be addressed, on a committment to cooperation by the participants, and on leadership by the governing authority, staff, and users groups of the network.

Shortly after the introduction of laser disks the then-Executive Director of NCLIS, Alphonse F. Trezza, in a talk on a national periodical system, speculated that the trend in the 70s and 80s would definitely be in favor of cooperation, networking, and sharing resources, but that because of the dramatic changes in technologies, the chances were excellent that the trend would shift in the 90s from centralization to decentralization. Large amounts of books, journals, and audiovisual materials will be available on laser disks at a modest cost, giving individual libraries the opportunity to enhance their on-site collections.

With the development and wide availability of microcomputers, packaged systems for circulation, acquisitions and serials control, online catalogues with union list capabilities, and other advances, a thorough review of the problems and benefits of networks will be in order. Just what are the cost benefits and trade-offs? Are the library director's time and budget better used in operating the library rather than in devoting many hours and days discussing cooperative programs and trying to work out the jurisdictional, programatic, and financial problems?

Cooperative systems can and do solve some kinds of problems, but it can be argued that the field has gone too far, looking to networking as a solution for deficiencies and problems it cannot cure. Creative use of the latest technology and people may make libraries less dependent on others and make them more self-sufficient, but, it would be a mistake to take self-sufficiency to the extreme. Interaction, mutual cooperation, and sharing and working together are essential for the survival of society; libraries and librarians are part of that process. The trend in the future, therefore, may be toward more selective networking, toward more methodical use of and interface among different technologies, and toward a different balance between the traditional, the current, and the future.

REFERENCES

Joe W. Kraus, "Prologue to Library Cooperation," *Library Trends* (1975).

Raynard C. Swank, "Interlibrary Cooperation, Interlibrary Communications and Information Networks—Explanation and Definition," in Joseph Becker, editor, *Proceedings of the Conference on Interlibrary Communications and Information Networks* (1971).

Curt D. Wormann, "Aspects of International Library Cooperation, Historical and Contemporary," *Library Quarterly* (1968).

U.S. National Commission on Libraries and Information Science, *Towards a National Program for Library and Information Services: Goals for Action* (1975).

ALPHONSE F. TREZZA

Library Education: Continuing Professional Education

Commitment to lifelong learning is important to the library and information science profession because its professionals must themselves participate in lifelong learning in order to perform competently their evolving roles in society. Further, they must be prepared to assist adults in creating a learning society.

A critical issue facing the social system of the United States—the impending obsolescence of the nation's work force, particularly in the professional sector—was underscored in the 1983 report by the National Commission on Excellence in Education, *A Nation at Risk: The Imperative for Educational Reform,* which with other reports defined the problems affecting American leaders in professional continuing education (CE) and retraining programs.

An approach to education for adults gradually emerged in the 1970s and 80s. It grew along with the realization that CE can be achieved effectively only by understanding the continuing nature of adult learning and is founded in the belief that professional education also takes place all through life. The preparatory school becomes only one provider of education. This new emphasis, which has opened up many educational opportunities, is concerned with establishing new patterns of learning described by such terms as "open learning," "independent study," "self-directed learning," "directed private study," and "distance education."

Definitions. The term *continuing professional education* (CPE) means different things to different people. A definition used here was developed by a team of six library and information science leaders who comprised the National Council on Quality Continuing Education for Information, Library, and Media Personnel (established 1980):

> Continuing education is a learning process which builds on and updates previously acquired knowledge, skills, and attitudes of the individual. Continuing education comes after the preparatory education necessary for involvement in or with information, library, media services. It is usually self-initiated learning in which individuals assume responsibility for their own development and for fulfilling their need to learn. It is broader than staff development, which is usually initiated by an organization for the growth of its own human resources.

The Council holds that regular participation in CE activities enables practitioners to refresh basic education by mastering new concepts in a constantly changing environment; keep up with new knowledge and skills; prepare for specialization in a new area; and enjoy the intrinsic satisfaction resulting from learning. In this article the term "professional" is defined as "a performer of a role." Continuing professional education therefore is concerned with the development of competent persons—those who can apply knowledge and skills in performance. Its concern with competencies, in turn, means that ways of identifying competencies needed both now and in the future should be developed, including those required for the jobs or roles practitioners wish to fill in the profession. This definition also implies that CE is more than listening to a lecture or using a new device; the learner must be able to demonstrate increased competency in actual performance.

According to Malcolm Knowles, author of a landmark work, *The Modern Practice of Adult Education: From Pedagogy to Andragogy* (1970), the first step in building a competency model is to identify three levels of competencies for the profession: (1) a core of common competencies, the basic knowledge required of everyone in the profession; (2) specialist competencies related to specific roles or jobs; and (3) stylistic competencies, the personal style the individual brings to the job.

The Need. Even though the casual observer may think that the field is cluttered with many CE opportunities, Cyril O. Houle states in his 1980 study *Continuing Learning in the Professions* that "Too few professionals continue to learn throughout their lives, and the opportunities provided to aid and encourage them to do so are far less abundant than they should be."

There is a vital need to seek out and develop practitioners who can apply knowledge, skill, and competencies that yield quality performance for the publics served and who can, and are willing to, serve as facilitators and role models for other learners. While the primary responsibility for learning rests on the individual, the profession also has a collective responsibility to integrate CPE as part of its total educational program; to understand the basic mission of the profession; to be aware of relevant new developments; to improve performance through innovative theory and practice; and to apply ethical principles in the rapidly changing environment.

Professions need to collaborate on the planning and provision of CPE for lower costs and greater quality and comprehensiveness.

Two areas of analysis are essential to needs assessment: analysis of prospective student needs and characteristics and analysis of a CPE provider's ability to meet such needs. Concerns include appropriate learning methods and tools, targeted levels of competence, delivery systems, comprehensive marketing, and forms of recognition. Surveys of both prospective learners and providers are therefore a prerequisite.

A 1982 survey of CE officers in state libraries indicated several types of desirable needs analysis at the national level for the profession as a whole: (1) identify national trends and their impact; (2) identify important recommendations for action; and (3) identify and publicize chief CE issues.

By the late 1970s CPE was considered not just desirable but indeed critical to the profession. The National Commission on Libraries and Information Science (NCLIS) even highlighted it as a priority, one of its 1975 *Goals for Action.*

CPE is a complex field with a wide array of target groups, many diverse providers and methods of producing and delivering programs, many ways for giving credit or recognition, and various means for acquiring financial support.

Target Groups. CE's goals are quality library and information service to all and maintenance of competent performance of practitioners.

A 1973 survey sponsored by NCLIS found that in librarianship there was considerable concern for the CE needs not only of professionals, but also of all levels of personnel—including support staffs and those associated with libraries. It is therefore extremely important that all CE providers identify accurately the target audience for which a particular offering is developed and to indicate the level of difficulty of each offering—beginning, intermediary, or advanced.

CE Providers. The major providers of CE opportunities in library and information science are associations; library education programs in colleges and universities; employing institutions; state library agencies; the federal government; independent suppliers of CE, such as large corporations, publishers, and suppliers of equipment and materials; and autonomous groups.

Associations. Houle emphasized the central role that the professional association should play in CE. Knowles argued that professional associations should serve as "learning communities" for their members, providing research, support, and excitement to foster their members' growth, development, and adaptation to change.

Professional societies are expected to identify needs and coming trends in the field; provide CE through conference programs, workshops, and publications; and identify CE resources for their members. They are also expected to set standards and guidelines for CE. Continuing education figures prominently in the American Library Association's 1970 "Manpower" policy, now titled *Library Education and Personnel Utilization.*

A 1972 document, revised in 1981, by the Association of American Library Schools (later the Association for Library and Information Science Education; ALISE) calls for the Association to provide leadership that encourages library, media, and information programs to provide not ony basic professional education but also an active program of CE activities in the field.

Still another example is provided by the Medical Library Association, which began its CE efforts in 1957 with national seminars; by the end of the 1970s, it had a full-scale national program. MLA advocated competency-based certification for librarians and developed and maintains a certification system for medical librarians.

At the Special Libraries Association annual meeting in June 1984, CE was identified as the *number one priority* of the Association. SLA's Professional Development Committee was directed to prepare a policy statement on CE. About 1,300 people registered for the 27 CE courses offered at that meeting—a record for SLA. At the same meeting the first graduates of SLA's Middle Management Institute completed their courses and were given certificates.

The Association of Research Libraries, through its Office of Management Studies, developed programs that have had a major impact on the quality of academic library service. Programs include basic and advanced management skills institutes, management skills institutes for directors, special focus workshops, and a management training film program.

An institute on research libraries for library school faculty, funded by the Council on Library Resources, was founded in 1983 to strengthen the dialogue among library directors and those involved in the preparation of future library staffs. Institutes on analytical skills and for personnel officers in libraries

were offered in 1985.

ALA offers CE opportunities to members in a variety of ways: through meetings at annual conferences and at pre- and post-conference workshops; through publications; and through institutes, workshops, and conferences offered by ALA offices and divisions. The strategic plan developed in 1983 by the Association of College and Research Libraries, a division of ALA, includes three objectives: "develop and coordinate CE offerings into an integrated 'curriculum' of presentations at progressive grade levels; seek out and relate ACRL CE programs to useful parallel offerings by other agencies; and develop CE packages for multiple modes of delivery (such as mail, television, individual or group use, and CAI [computer-aided instruction])."

In June 1984 the ALA Council voted to incorporate the Continuing Library Education Network and Exchange (CLENE) as a Round Table (CLENERT) within the structure of ALA. CLENE had been established in 1975 as a result of regional hearings conducted in 1972 by NCLIS. CLENE's activities included organizing annual CE workshops and tutorials; publishing directories of CE opportunities in library, media, and information science; issuing monthly updates of current programs published as the *Continuing Education Communicator;* compiling periodic directories of human resources available in the field of CPE; publishing the *CLENExchange,* a quarterly newsletter on CE activities both inside and outside the profession; sponsoring *Concept Papers* dealing with major issues in CE; and developing proposals to gain financial support for programs.

Major issues addressed by CLENE through federal funding included development of a provider-approval system to ensure quality CE and a recognition system for CE participants. During its existence as a separate organization, it was the only association in the profession that had as its *chief* mission quality CE for library and information personnel.

Professional Schools. Professional schools are gradually coming to recognize their obligation to support their graduates throughout their careers, and by the mid-1980s they were offering a wide variety of learning opportunities. They have taken increased interest in communicating with alumni about changing professional needs and in creating opportunities for alumni to develop new career patterns. Such support for alumni can help the economic position of the professional school and emphasize the importance of CE offerings in relation to the degree-granting programs. When graduate enrollments decline, providing CE for practitioners brings increased visibility to the school and can aid recruitment of students for degree programs.

State Library Agencies. State library agencies are critical to the development, provision, and coordination of CE for the profession in the U.S., because their influence reaches to all residents in each state and determines both qualitatively and quantitatively the level of library resources and services within each state. The 1970 *Standards for Library Functions at the State Level* of the American Association of State Libraries says: "The state library agency should promote and provide a program of continuing education for library personnel at all levels, as well as for trustees." This goal can be achieved through cooperation with library schools and professional associations and through sponsoring meetings and workshops.

Federal funds supported three CLENE institutes to implement or strengthen statewide systems of CE. All three had the common goal of developing, refining, or reviewing written plans that would result in statewide CE systems. CE plans were to be integrated with overall library development plans in the states. In addition, each institute planned to meet particular needs that were identified in the field during planning for it. Institute I (1976–77) developed an evaluation instrument for CE programs; Institute II (1978–79) concentrated on the development of criteria for quality CE programs and for a provider approval system; Institute III (1979–80) dealt with the management of statewide systems and with CE delivery systems.

Officials from 41 of the 50 states, plus Guam, participated in one or more of the institutes. As a result of the three institutes, there is considerable evidence that state library agencies are playing an increasingly central role in the development and provision of CE. In the "Introduction" to the Fall 1978 issue of *Library Trends* on State Library Development Agencies, editor John A. McCrossan wrote that state libraries are calling library leaders together to plan coordinated, statewide CE programs for all types of librarians. "This work," he wrote, "is the direct result of planning for statewide continuing education programs which was sponsored by the Continuing Library Education Network and Exchange (CLENE)."

In 1982 the state library agencies were asked to identify the major issues that should be faced in CE in the United States. Thirty-six percent listed the need for quality control of CE; 32 percent the necessity of finding ways to finance CE; 29 percent the need for management support of CE and the necessity of developing written CE policies; and 24 percent the need to develop computer literacy among the large percentage of professionals who have not had specific training in the new technologies.

The Federal Government. Working through the Division of Library Programs of the Department of Education and using Higher Education Act (HEA) and Library Services Construction Act (LSCA) funding, the federal government has played a significant role in the continuing education of library and information personnel.

The Library Training Institute Program—first enacted in 1968—provided both short- and long-term training and retraining opportunities. More than 16,000 librarians were trained or retrained under the program through 426 institutes between 1968 and 1980, when the appropriations ended. "Retraining" (that is, CE) constituted the bulk of institute activities, with more than 15,000 librarians being educated in new skills and techniques of library and information service.

During the first five years of the program (1968–72), two-thirds of the institutes (258) and the trainees (9,000) dealt with the improvement of school library media services, with the balance largely in the public and academic library areas. Institutes concentrated on the improvement of management and supervisory skills as well as specific speciality areas such as children's services, young adult services, and map librar-

ianship. The last five years of the program (1976–80), when program funding was being reduced, focused on retraining librarians in all types of service, but concentrated on minority groups and the economically or educationally disadvantaged. Institutes concentrated on service to minority groups and educational problem areas such as literacy, the institutionalized, human relations, and social interaction. About 3,500 librarians were retrained during this period through 107 institutes.

The Library Services and Construction Act was originally passed as the Library Services Act (1956). Many states used its funds to award scholarships or fellowships to people willing to commit themselves to working in both urban and rural areas. By 1985 the types of courses offered included seminars and workshops conducted by the state library administrative agencies; seminars, workshops, or short courses offered by multi-library or other large systems, emphasizing technology through such topics as the use of computers for acquisitions, charging, and, in some instances, online catalogues; and programs training personnel working with or serving native Americans (primarily in Arizona, New Mexico, and Idaho), personnel serving rural areas with high concentrations of disadvantaged people (Kentucky, Virginia, and Mississippi), and personnel serving the blind or physically handicapped in states where services are being decentralized or strengthened at the local system level (Michigan).

At the state level and in major metropolitan libraries, some LSCA funds have been used to develop better planning and evaluation of library programs. As an example, Florida prepared a publication called *Developing a Planning and Evaluation Process for Florida Library Service* that other states are either adapting or using in its entirety. Other states have developed exemplary materials and long-range programs, such as New York State's publication *Meeting Information Needs of the 80's: Report of the Commissioner's Committee on Statewide Library Development.*

Delivery Systems. The variety of CE delivery systems has grown rapidly, but the most used delivery system in library and information science has been and still is the workshop—it far outranked any other system cited in a 1982 survey of state library agencies (listed by 52 percent of the respondents). Other systems mentioned in that survey were: courses, 16 percent; home study, 16 percent; teleconferencing, 12 percent; and videotape, 12 percent. When these agencies were asked what new delivery systems they planned to use in their states in the near future, the chief modes mentioned were videotapes and cassettes (24 percent each); self-study learning packages (20 percent); cable combined with satellite transmission (16 percent); and teleconferencing (16 percent).

Recognizing that learning occurs most efficiently when adults study at their own pace, place, and time, an increasing number of CE providers have accepted the responsibility for developing delivery systems that have no time or geographical barriers. Many ways to achieve this goal are being examined and implemented. One is teleconferencing by satellite. At its January 1982 Midwinter Meeting in Denver, ALA tested the first one-way video, two-way audio teleconference from the site of one of its major conferences. The CE theme featured marketing library services. More than 60 libraries nationwide held viewing and "talk-back" sessions with the panel. The program demonstrated one way that a national convention can serve to bring CE to a diverse population over a large geographical area and showed that localized television delivery of satellite programs by cable has great potential.

A delivery system used increasingly by library associations, first popularized by the MLA, is a packaged series of CE programs administered first in conjunction with annual conferences and then offered repeatedly wherever there is a demand. MLA built quality control measures into its package design, implementation, and course evaluation. Similarly, the ACRL has developed courses for local presentation under sponsorship of ACRL chapters, library schools, libraries, university extension divisions, and interested professional groups. Course syllabi are available for purchase for each of the courses.

Using videotape, the Public Library Association (PLA) developed a 13-minute program, "Measure for Measure: Output Measures for Public Libraries," designed to introduce community-based performance measures to library staff members and trustees. The Catholic Library Association (CLA) has used videocassettes to provide two-hour sessions on selected CE topics.

Poster sessions for information exchange were introduced at the ALA 1982 Annual Conference in Philadelphia. The pilot project, directed by Fred M. Peterson, was so successful that this type of delivery system became a regular feature of ALA Conferences.

Credit and Recognition. The professional's real reward for participation in CE should be intellectual stimulation and an improved ability to serve the needs of users. This does not preclude the importance of public recognition for participation in CE programs, or the need to demonstrate accountability to the public for participation in lifelong learning activities. In order to give recognition for participation in the noncredit, nontraditional forms of learning in the professions, the Continuing Education Unit (CEU) was developed. A uniform measure to assist in the accumulation and exchange of standardized credit for participation in CE activities, the CEU is defined as "ten contact hours of participation in an organized continuing education activity under responsible sponsorship, capable direction, and qualified instruction."

Since 1976 associations, state library agencies, and universities have started to use the CEU to give credit for nontraditional learning experiences, and the trend will probably continue. In 1984 the Council on the Continuing Education Unit (CCEU) issued *Principles of Good Practice in Continuing Education,* the result of a three-year project to promote standards in the field of continuing education and training. *Principles* serves as a reference document for organizations developing their own CE standards and criteria. Twenty-one professionals from a wide variety of organizations assisted in drafting the final document, which consists of 18 principles, 70 additional statements of amplification and interpretation, and a discussion of each principle.

One of the last major projects of CLENE before it became an ALA Round Table was the development of a recognition system that includes the use of the CEU, the academic credit, and contact hours relative to independent learning. The concern of CLENE was to develop a compatible system that could be used nationwide. It would (1) facilitate the recognition of participation in CE in all parts of the country and in all types of libraries; (2) provide employees with a commonly understood record of CE activities; and (3) facilitate the review of the records of individuals whose CE activities take place in more than one state, institution, or association.

Criteria for Quality. The National Council on Quality Continuing Education was established in 1980 as an outgrowth of a project funded by the U.S. Department of Education Division of Libraries and Learning Resources, and carried out jointly by CLENE and the School of Library and Information Science at the Catholic University of America.

The provider approval program of the National Council was integrated with the Voluntary Recognition System (VRS) of CLENE, which incorporates the services of the National Registry of the American College Testing (ACT) program. CE providers are encouraged to use CLENE's Voluntary Recognition System, but they do not have to participate in the total system to be approved. Approval of providers and their offerings is based on how well providers meet pre-established criteria. The criteria for a CE offering cover needs assessment, objectives, design and presentation of program, timeliness of program, responsible promotion, and ongoing evaluation. Criteria for the provider cover administration, human resources, facilities, and budget.

The approval process contains initial, ongoing, retrospective, and prospective reviews of the provider's capabilities. Providers seeking approval are measured against the *Criteria for Quality,* a set of standards developed by the Council based on a careful process that included open hearings at several professional meetings. Providers are generally given a three-year term of approval, during which ongoing monitoring takes place.

Trends. Both the King Research report, *New Directions in Library and Information Science Education* (1985), and the response to the 1982 state library agency questionnaire indicate two important requirements in continuing education. First, practitioners must continually update and expand their competencies in using new technologies and in an ever-widening array of management functions. These increasingly important management, administrative, and supervisory activities include financial and resource management; standards, measures and methods for evaluating personnel; long-range and strategic planning; optimal use of information resources; marketing; and recruitment of high-potential candidates to the profession. The recognition and awareness of these needs is the responsibility of the professionals themselves, their employers, the professional societies, and the professional schools.

Second, achievement of quality service requires far more than identification, definition, description, and validation of competencies (the objectives of the King Research study). Schools and associations must design and implement competency attainment measures and evaluate them for validity and reliability. From the experience of developing such measures in other professions—and in the MLA—it is clear that these procedures will be extremely costly—too expensive for any one institution—and will probably have to be supported by foundation or government grants.

A number of emerging CE trends can be identified. One is a decentralization when the medium is a workshop, an institute, or a course before or after a larger conference; CE programs are increasingly being held at regional, state, and local levels. This pattern makes it possible for more participants to attend at less cost and enables many to participate who are unable to attend national meetings. When resources are pooled with other professional groups in one geographical area, useful CE opportunities emerge at a reasonable cost in time and finance and provide at the same time professional growth opportunities for local leadership.

John Naisbitt in *Megatrends* (1982) points out that the more technology is infused into the work setting, the more practitioners want to make connections with other people outside the work place, in part to compensate for constant involvement with technological processes at work. In spite of the technologies that now enable people to continue learning wherever they are located geographically, the most popular single delivery system for CE in the profession is still the workshop, where people can engage in dialogue and interact with others in solving problems.

Indications are that professionals will become increasingly assertive in their demands for quality CE, for assurance that what they will gain is needed now in their work or will be needed for career progress, and for greater applicability of CE offerings to solving real problems and to fulfilling their roles in their work.

Professionals will need more assistance in career planning, as more and more positions open up outside traditional library and information settings. They will also need help in identifying available CE offerings. An important aid in this field will be online CE information networks similar to the prototype developed at the Illinois State Library, whose model Online Network of Continuing Education (ONCE) is an automated clearinghouse of current and retrospective CE opportunities, including human and material resources.

As the world progresses toward a global economy, international meetings and international associations will become much more important. One example of this was the World Conference on Continuing Library and Information Science Education, held in August 1985 at the Moraine Valley Community College, near Chicago, under the auspices of ALA and the International Federation of Library Associations (IFLA). Such conferences aid in the development of communication networks and the continuing exchange of ideas with CE leaders around the world.

Finally, those organizations with the vision to declare CE as their top priority goal (as was announced by SLA in 1984) will serve as pacesetters for the whole profession and lead toward the ultimate goal of competent performance in the workplace.

INTERNATIONAL CE DEVELOPMENTS
An overview of the status of CE internationally can be gathered by examining the papers presented by participants from outside the U.S. at the World Conference on Continuing Library and Information Science Education. Questionnaires were filled out by a sampling of participants from various countries at that Conference.

Africa. The major issues in library CE were presented at the Conference in the papers from seven representatives of five African nations—Uganda, Malawi, Zimbabwe, Tanzania, and Nigeria. Although there are differences from country to country, there are recurrent situations, issues, and problems that allow for a listing of the major conditions identified.

There are continuing education seminars and workshops that cover the whole range of types of library personnel (academic, public, school, and special) at local, regional, and state levels, but their influence is marginal because of a lack of coordination and the short time during which programs are offered.

The chief providers of CE are library schools, library associations, employing institutions, and a wide array of development agencies. Especially prevalent are the German Federation for International Development, International Federation for Documentation, Unesco, the International Development for Research Center, the British Council, the Commonwealth Foundation, European Economic Community, and the United States Information Agency.

The chief delivery systems for CE are short intensive courses, workshops, seminars, and conferences. The chief teaching/learning methods used are lectures, discussions, and skill demonstrations; the greatest content interest is in technology.

Barriers to the development of CE programs are many and varied, and include in all these countries: lack of funding, lack of adequate leadership to carry on the courses (especially in information science and technology), poor coordination of the array of offerings, absence of national policies on CE, and inadequate materials, facilities, and equipment. Other problems are disruptive political conditions, lack of publicity for the programs developed, the apathy of administrators, too heavy reliance on foreign-published texts and technology, poor support for library schools, and the problems inherent for native librarians in obtaining education abroad and then adjusting to local conditions.

Future trends in CE in Africa include: (1) more practitioners participating in CE; (2) more local autonomy in program development; (3) the formulation of official policies relating to CE that would result in higher quality programming; and (4) use by government and private employers and universities of participation in CE as an evaluation tool for promotion and tenure.

South Africa. South Africa's setting in both the First and Third Worlds presents situations and problems different from those of most other African nations. Clare M. Walker summarized the history of CE in South Africa at the World CE Conference. The chief providers of CE are the library schools, library associations, and employing institutions. The South African Institute for Librarianship and Information Science (SAILIS) has a Committee on Education and Research (CER), with a subcommittee to promote and coordinate CE on a national basis. During the decade 1976–85 SAILIS offered about 50 CE courses, symposia, seminars, and workshops. Although many delivery systems are used, the most popular, by far, are short courses, workshops, seminars, and conferences.

The chief barriers to CE in South Africa are the great distances to travel and lack of sufficient funding. Other deterrents are the small percentage of librarian practitioners who are active in library association work; lack of graded, progressive CE that would lead to professional advancement; reluctance of administrators to give release time for CE; gaps in language, politics, and culture; and the high cost of foreign periodicals used to keep up to date.

Asia and Oceania. *Japan.* In Japan CE and training programs are available to those engaged in library and information work regardless of their type of pre-service education or even lack of any such professional qualification. CE is regarded as "in-service training." It therefore covers learning at all levels and in all types of libraries and information centers. The chief providers are the universities.

The chief CE methods are lectures, practical work, discussions, professional visits, and research. Library and information science are not firmly established in Japan as a profession, however, and the permanent employment system gives no incentive for CE and lifelong learning. The recommendation was made that new innovative approaches were needed for CE, such as packages for home study on automated cataloguing or database searching. Also recommended was a survey of CE needs and some sort of effective evaluation.

China. In the Peoples Republic of China, where it is estimated that fewer than two percent of 100,000 library personnel are professional, CE is viewed as supplementary or spare-time education that provides the opportunity for both young and middle-aged from other specialties (still unfamiliar with the library profession) to obtain new knowledge rather than to update previously qualified persons. Types of supplementary education are: (1) Advanced study at regular universities for a year; (2) attendance at spare-time schools (also known as night schools or adult education schools) to complete a prescribed program in two to three years; (2) short training courses, workshops, or seminars that run for a month or less (often undertaken by a cooperative body of libraries); (4) on-the-job training; and (5) correspondence schools or courses.

Correspondence school is mainly self-education, integrated with tutorials and some lectures, delivered by correspondence between the students and instructors. Courses are usually offered by the departments of a university. The advantage of correspondence education in China is great. It makes maximum use of existing faculties, equipment, and facilities, and helps the central government achieve its goal of greatest output for the least cost. Also, correspondence students can correlate on-the-job experience with text materials and apply theory to library practice while learning. China's priority is increasing the numbers of professionals to alleviate the shortage of competent library staff. CE is viewed as a way to improve standards gradually.

Philippines. A high priority is placed on professional CE in the Philippines. The University of the Philippines Institute of Library Science has received wide acclaim for pioneering in the development of a flourishing regional "Postgraduate Training Course for Science Information Specialists in South-East Asia." This program, started in 1978 with Unesco and UN Development Program funding, was in response to the growing demand for specialized manpower in the region to build information systems and provide for information needs. The Institute also offers summer institutes on information science; some 128 professional librarians participated after its initiation in 1975.

Providers of CE include the State Library, library schools, library associations, employing institutions, and various development agencies. The most popular formats, as is true almost universally, are workshops, seminars, institutes, short courses, and conferences. The modes of presentation are chiefly lectures, discussions, and audiovisual presentations.

The Philippine Library Association worked out a five-year integrated national library development plan for the years 1983 to 1988. Each of its six national chapters prepared its own development plan according to its needs, including CE opportunities.

Korea. Providers of CE in Korea include the National Library, library schools, library associations, employing institutions, and various private sector groups. In addition to the institute/workshop/meeting delivery systems for CE, there are some traveling and packaged programs. Learning methods include programmed instruction and CAI.

Barriers to the development of CE include: a low priority for CE in the profession because of the permanent employment system and promotion policies that give no recognition for CE; lack of strong leadership in the Korean Library Association for the development of CE programs; and irregularity in CE offerings and lack of provision for progression in level of opportunities.

It is anticipated that the economic impact of the new technologies will lead to intensified CE programming as the government expresses its need for information services. Professional organizations and educational institutions will join forces to provide and enhance CE opportunities.

Singapore. Singapore identifies providers of CE as the National Library, library associations, employing institutions, development agencies, and private sector groups. Chief modes are workshops, seminars, employer-sponsored courses, professional conferences, journals, and correspondence courses. The chief teaching methods used in CE programs are lectures and audiovisual. Inadequate teachers are a chief barrier to development. Future trends foreseen are greater concentration on computerized technology, use of distance learning and teleconferencing for CE, and increased use and access to data.

The Pacific Islands. Probably no area has so rapidly become dependent on the use of the new technologies in distance learning.

In 1969 the University of Hawaii established PEACESAT (Pan Pacific Education and Communication Experiment by Satellite) using the NASA Applications Technology Satellite (ATS-1), originally used as a weather satellite. Starting in 1976 regular monthly PEACESAT sessions in library science were carried out with participants from some 12 Pacific Islands. Topics covered included school libraries, children's literature, a Unesco meeting on national bibliography, literacy and libraries, training library assistants, copyright law, scientific documentation, and publishing and bookselling in the Pacific Islands.

The University of the South Pacific began using ATS-1 in 1972, when it established USPNET as a regional university to serve 11 South Pacific countries. This program includes courses in library science and consultations with resource people in the region. A certificate course was offered in library science starting in 1982. During the broadcast of these programs, local tutors are always on hand.

Australia. Australia has made increasing use of distance learning for CE, as noted by Edward R. Reid-Smith, who proposes that serious consideration be given to the recommendation that distance education is an appropriate facility for international cooperation rather than a purely local provision.

The School of Library and Information Studies at Kuring-gai College of Australia conducted imaginative learning experiments during its first decade that provided a continuum in the career development process—formal education, continuing education, staff development, and career planning.

Starting in 1984, the Library Association of Australia (LAA) established a policy of setting aside funds for activities based on the identification of priority areas by its Divisions and Branches and calling for proposals from "tenderers" to implement these priority activities. This model was an innovative approach to the organization of CE activities. The tendering system for nationally supported activities has brought with it the formalization and identification of priorities for CE activities at regional and local levels.

Another major thrust of LAA is the recommendation considered in 1985 that Associate status in LAA would not be automatically available to those who completed a recognized course at some time in the past. Those who completed a recognized course more than five years ago would need to show evidence of one of the following: renewal of qualification; a level of broad professional understanding and competence at least equivalent to that expected of graduates of courses being granted recognition against the current course recognition criteria; or an advanced level of specialization and competence directly relevant to library and information work.

Since the early 1980s LAA has shifted its focus from entrance into the profession to more active concern for the continuing professional development of members. The Association is also giving positive encouragement to individuals to take greater responsibility for their own continuing professional development.

Europe. According to Günther Dohmen, Chair of the Continuous Education Department of the University of Tübingen, West Germany, a major emphasis in Europe is "to develop a perspective for Continuing Education which helps people to live in a computerized world without transferring technical terms of thinking and categories of technical efficiency to their personal life . . . ." The challenge of CE is "to promote the creativity and the self-determination of free persons in the standardized world of modern technologies and ideologies."

Free adults should be able to carry out their objectives for personal development by means of an open, flexible modular system, by choosing the aims, contents, methods, times, conditions, and places of their learning processes. Distance learning can be an adequate delivery system for this independent self-directed lifelong learning and to "help people find a well-balanced personal and social identity which allows them to live a cultivated value-oriented human life in modern society."

Dohmen suggests that a "library model" is more adequate than a "school model" for modern, self-directed, individualized, independent lifelong learning. People working in the distance learning field are expected to be not primary teachers but tutors, advisers, animators, educational brokers, or facilitators who assist in self-learning and arrange opportunities for discussion and communication, with the aid of new technologies if necessary.

Great Britain. The Open University has become increasingly involved in post-experience courses for professionals through its Continuing Education Centre, which serves well over 100,000 adults, most of them working while studying. Students study at home, with some support from tutors and counselors in the University's 13 regions. Course components are sent by mail, radio, and television, in conjunction with the British Broadcasting Corporation (BBC). The major course components are printed and consist of books—readers, course units, and supplementary materials such as broadcast notes—to accompany radio and television programs.

The Open University offered no courses specifically in librarianship in 1985, but courses for librarians were being considered for development. Distance learning opportunities were available from the Newcastle-upon-Tyne School of Librarianship (Statistics for Librarians); Leeds Polytechnic Medical Information Research Unit (basic medical/nursing librarianship and information work); and Telford and West Bromwich Colleges (distance learning for nonprofessional staff). The National Association of Local Government Officers offers a double module in library and information science. In Scotland, there are distance learning opportunities for nonprofessional library staff.

Poland. The chief CE activities of the Polish Library Association (SBP) consist of initiating and conducting professional courses to supplement those provided in the university degree and postgraduate programs. The leading need was for programs in the area of automation of library services. Accordingly, education meetings on library electronic data processing were carried out in nonworking hours. The aim was not to train specialists, but to give librarians a general acquaintance with library automation in order to create a favorable climate for modern technology.

Overall, the chief CE delivery modes in Poland are workshops, seminars, and short courses; generally the only method used is the lecture. Barriers to CE in Poland include the need for financial support and the perception that employers are not much interested in staff development. Issues of concern include the feasibility of mandatory CE labor regulations that give preference to those engaging in CE and the inclusion of current problems of the library profession in CE.

Sweden. Sweden has CE opportunities at the national, regional, and local levels for academic, public, school, special, and information personnel, though library and information science CE has a relatively low priority in relation to other professional groups in the nation. Although there are CE opportunities available for all levels of library practitioners—professional and paraprofessional—there is need for more opportunities at all levels. The providers of CE are the National Library, library schools, library institutions, private sector groups, and employing institutions.

Chief course work modes are workshops and seminars, but short courses and traveling programs are also offered. CE is also provided through professional meetings and conferences, journals, research, and writing papers. The chief methods used are lectures and audiovisual presentations.

Motivation for CE is provided by recognition in the areas of promotion, pay raises, and fringe benefits. Certificates are also awarded for participation in CE. Chief barriers to CE include lack of funds, of leadership personnel, and of innovative ideas.

Throughout Sweden and across all professions a popular CE delivery system is the Study Circle; it is estimated that one out of three adults takes part in Study Circles. Circle members run their own small groups, assisted by trained facilitators. Generally, a Circle has 5 to 15 volunteers who meet regularly to learn more about a chosen topic; one member is trained as a facilitator. Members bring together their own shared experiences, prepared materials, and outside expertise. Study Circles may meet in libraries, community centers, business offices, or classrooms; libraries, clubs, schools, government agencies, office organizations, and all sorts of other groups sponsor Circles.

Latin America. The common denominator among Latin American countries is the need for social and economic development. The barriers to educational development include social stratification, imbalance between urban and rural areas, lack of money, irrelevant curricula, and poor teaching performance.

As long as sophisticated technology is beyond the means of most Latin American communities, the role of library and information science personnel will be to support literacy programs and the development of libraries into cultural centers to promote community development.

In Latin America, as in other developing areas, short courses, refresher courses, workshops, institutes, seminars, and demonstrations are the chief methods for CE in library and information science. Most practitioners have gained their knowledge and competency through continuing education offerings and on-the-job training and experience rather than through formal academic education. As in other developing areas, CE is the main source of modern information practice.

Many national information systems have CE as one of their chief responsibilities. An example is the Brazilian Institute for Information Science and Technology (IBICT), which in 1983 offered the following: specialization courses in Administration of Information Systems and Technological Information; a seminar on Information for Industry; a series of talks on new information technologies; 11 training courses on online information retrieval; 5 training courses on bibliographic recording for library automation; and 27 updating courses with subjects ranging from Theory of Scientific and Technical Information and Information Services Management to Applications of Mini and Micro Computers.

A serious problem for developing countries is the expense of information sources (especially in science and technology), more than 90 percent of which are produced in industrialized countries. Libraries and information centers must devote a high percentage of their budgets to these print and database sources. In trying to meet information needs in the face of high costs, libraries and information centers compromise by offering low salaries for employees, making it difficult to attract good people into careers in this field, as discussed by T. Saracevic, G. M. Braga, and M. A. Afolayan in "Issues in Information Science Education in Developing Countries," in *Journal of the American Society for Information Science* (1985).

This situation raises the question of the type of CE and formal education that is most relevant for developing nations, and results in differing points of view not only in different countries, but also in the same country. Another result is lack of coherence and progression in CE offerings.

International Organizations. Many international organizations have been active in CE in library and information science, especially in the developing countries. They have spread awareness of the value of CE by organizing short courses, giving support to the start of CE programs, providing for faculty development, developing educational guidelines, giving funds for students, and organizing conferences with CE components.

Two organizations that have been particularly active and have had great impact are Unesco, through its General Information Programme (PGI), and the International Federation for Documentation (FID). PGI activities include short courses, visiting lecturers, guidelines, faculty development, and evaluation of library and information CE programs.

FID's chief role has been as an international forum for discussion of educational issues among those concerned with the continuing education of library and information practitioners. Its Education and Training Committee (FID/ET) has been particularly active, organizing international meetings and publishing proceedings, plans, proposals, and differences of opinion. Helpful CE awareness sources are the FID/ET *Newsletter on Education and Training Programmes for Information Personnel* and the Clearinghouse of Information Education Training Materials maintained by FID/ET at Syracuse University. Further, FID has a regional commission for Latin America (FID/CLA) and for Asia and Oceania (FID/CAO). FID/CLA publishes a journal, *Revista latinoamericana de documentación,* which regularly contains announcements about courses and discussions of education activities.

During the First World Conference on CE for Library and Information Science Professionals, many people expressed the wish that IFLA would demonstrate ongoing concern for CE issues, because only IFLA has library and information science as its sole orientation. They suggested that IFLA should increase its presence in developing countries by highlighting issues and bringing them to the attention of other organizations. They also suggested that IFLA work with other library associations to change the attitude of governments and of librarians themselves to a much higher perception of the value of libraries as essential vehicles for economic and social transformation.

Activities suggested for IFLA included holding pre- or post-IFLA conferences focusing exclusively on CE; publishing a newsletter that would serve as a forum for debating CE-related issues; informing the profession of research in CE; developing needed guidelines; and especially maintaining an active worldwide communications network of those involved or interested in continuing library and information education.

The final activity at the 1985 World Conference on CE was unanimous passage of a resolution requesting IFLA to establish a Round Table on Continuing Library and Information Science Education.

REFERENCES

Barbara Conroy, *Library Staff Development and Continuing Education: Principles and Practices* (1978).
"Continuing Professional Education," in *The ALA Yearbook of Library and Information Services* (1976-).
Cyril O. Houle, *Patterns of Learning: New Perspectives on Life-Span Education* (1984).
Elizabeth W. Stone, "Continuing Education for Librarians in the United States," in *Advances in Librarianship* (1978).
Julie A. Virgo et al., *Continuing Education Needs Assessment and Model Programs* (1977).

ELIZABETH W. STONE

Library Education: Curriculum

For several decades, library education as reflected through curricula changed at a sluggish pace, with only minor adjustments to content and structure; however, fundamental and more rapid curricular revision has been characteristic of the period 1975 to 1985. Several factors precipitated curriculum change in North America:

(1) The revision adopted in 1972 by the American Library Association of its *Standards for Accreditation* of library education programs leading to the first professional degree, the Master's degree. The previous standards had been in effect since 1952. The new standards, which encourage flexibility, are more guidelines than standards; therefore, each school has great latitude in curriculum development, and most curricula reflect the predominant philosophy of librarianship at the institutions that offer them.

(2) The notable influx into library schools of library educators holding doctorates. This development resulted in large part from fellowships available for doctoral study in librarianship through the Higher Education Act of 1965. Approximately three-quarters of the full-time faculty teaching in schools holding membership in the Association for Library and Information Science Education (ALISE) have completed their doctorates. While these library educators agree that Master's education is fundamentally professional education, they bring to education for librarianship concerns and experience that encompass more than the day-to-day operational concerns of library institutions.

(3) The increasing number of undergraduate, joint-degree, sixth-year certificate, and Ph.D. programs as important components of library education programs. In the institutions where these programs exist, they affect the curriculum available to Master's degree students.

(4) The far-reaching developments in society, in technology, and in bibliography since the 1960s. One indication of the recognition of the great changes in the library environment is the trend toward changing library school names to include the broader term "information." Of the 61 American and Canadian schools admitting students and holding full accreditation from the ALA in mid-1985, 42 have changed their names to add in the word information.

In order to accommodate these and many other factors, change in curricular content and structure has come to characteristize contemporary library education programs. Some Master's programs contain specially structured required curriculum components and some extended the number of required credit hours. While the modal number of graduate-level academic credits required to complete the degree remains 36 semester hours or its equivalent in quarter hours, required courses vary from as few as 28 to more than 50 semester hours; nineteen schools require more than 36 semester equivalent credits for award of the Master's degree. Because most library educators and many practitioners agree that the basic knowledge now required for librarianship has expanded and, to a lesser degree, concur that librarians should develop a certain (although as yet undetermined) level of competence in an area of specialization prior to receiving the Master's degree, it is understandable that there appears to be a desire for, if not a trend toward, lengthening the number of credit hours required for the first professional degree. The question of program length is probably the key harbinger of fundamental curriculum change taking place in library education today.

Fundamentals in Library Education. The ALA's Committee on Accreditation (COA) gives the following as the basic content areas that all Master's programs must cover: (1) an understanding of the role of the library as an educational and informational agency; (2) an understanding of the theories of collecting, building, and organizing library materials for use; (3) a knowledge of information sources and an ability to assist the user of library materials in locating and interpreting desired items; and (4) knowledge of the principles of administration and organization to provide information services. Translated into curriculum structure in Master's programs, these four content areas constitute what has come to be known as the "core." Of 51 schools reporting for the *ALISE Statistical Report,* no school reported fewer than eight hours of course work required of all students; one school reported 24 required hours, and the typical requirement is from 12 to 15 hours (21 schools).

Because curriculum revision, especially at the level of the core, is so characteristic of today's schools, it has become difficult to describe a typical core curriculum. The required hours seem to be principally devoted to the traditional content area of librarianship that came into acceptance in the 1940's and 1950's, including courses covering reference, materials selection, cataloguing and classification, and administration. Courses or course components dealing with the library as a societal institution were introduced in the late 1960s and early 1970s and remain within the typical required core. The limitations imposed by this largely library institution-focused curriculum have come under careful scrutiny, however. Integration and expansion of core content to add course components in information science appears to be the present direction; even though there is no agreement as to the basis for an *integrated* core in librarianship, a significant number of schools are creating and implementing such curricular structures.

The first attempt at offering an integrated core curriculum was undertaken in the 1960s under the leadership of Jesse Shera at Case Western Reserve University. Since then, many schools have introduced and revised variations of an integrated core. Some include a required "foundations of librarianship" course, coupled with a small number of separate, largely skill-based courses. Another approach is a totally integrated core, usually consisting of 9 to 12 credit hours that may be taken either in a block or in a sequence of a primary 6 hours followed by 3 to 6 additional hours. These integrated core curricula subsume substantial parts of the traditional core of reference, cataloguing, materials selection, and administration and add significant components dealing with foundations, communications, the research process, media, and most notably information science. The integrated core emphasizes the view that there are elements comon to all types of libraries and other information services that include both theoretical and philosophical fundamentals, as well as skill. The central institutional focus remains the library, but other institutional and independent work settings and roles are included.

In those schools with the longest experience with integrated core curricula, notably Drexel University and the universities of North and South Carolina, the integrated core approach has had influence on the entire curriculum, especially in reducing redundancy and providing individual faculty with a shared knowledge base of those students who have completed the core.

An abbreviated, generalized outline for a hypothetical integrated core curriculum is an follows:

I. Libraries and Society

    A. Communications
        Information—its meaning, interpretation, dissemination
    B. Library role in the communication process
        User needs; comparison with other information agencies; library and information science as a profession.
    C. Social role of information institutions
        Meeting the needs of clients
    D. Political and economic context of information institutions
        Meeting the needs of clients
    D. Political and economic context of information institutions
        Library in its institutional setting, its administrative structure, means of support, legal base
    E. Freedom of information, intellectual freedom, and copyright
    F. Forms of communication media
        Film, audio tape, telecommunications, other media

II. Library Services and Materials

    A. Information institutions as service systems

A class in bibliography at Pennsylvania State University, c. 1894

    B. Mechanization of library services
        Computer usage; computer languages and programming
    C. Types of materials; types of collections; types of libraries and users; technique and principles of selection; selection tools; collection maintenance
    D. Collection access
        Bibliographic descriptions; subject analysis and description; physical access
    E. Information seeking
        Reference services; materials and automated services; reference interview

III. Research (as a means of studying concerns in library and information science)

     Problem identification, research techniques, design, data collection and treatment. Communication of research results.

IV. Management

     A. Planning, organizing, staffing, directing, controlling
     B. Systems analysis
     C. Effectiveness measurement
     D. Interlibrary cooperation and organization

Returning to the traditional core of reference, cataloguing and classification, administration, and selection, it can easily be seen that the integrated core does indeed subsume these topics, but important elements emphasizing conceptual and methodological concerns are added. Especially noteworthy are (1) the comparison of libraries and librarians with other institutions, professions, and occupations that provide information services; (2) identification of user needs and behaviors and the roles of information professionals in identifying and responding to them; (3) introduction of technology and information science to all who will become professional librarians; (4) recognition that knowledge of the content and process of research is essential to all library professionals; and (5) acknowledgement of the increasing responsibility of all professional librarians in the management of library operations.

The emphasis on the core curriculum in library education, especially the inclusion in the core of the concerns and contributions of information science and other disciplines, indicates the strong desire of library educators to maintain the traditional generalist curriculum and to head off a possible breakup of first professional degree education into specializations. However, holding together education for the information professions may well be beyond the capacity of most library education programs as they are presently structured in relatively autonomous graduate schools. It may be that mergers of related departments, as had been accomplished at Rutgers University in its School of Communications, Information and Library Studies, will be necessary to integrate education for the information professions. The 1984 ALISE/ALA initiative to bring together professionals interested in accreditation of information-related education programs may indicate whether it will be possible to integrate education for the information professions, or whether education for librarianship will remain principally education for those preparing to work in libraries.

The curriculum of librarianship, which through the 1960s had been focused almost exclusively on the library, in most cases continues to emphasize specialization in the profession by the type of institution in which the professional might expect to work—in school, public, academic, or special libraries. There are indications from curricular changes that this emphasis is declining and that specialization in the field could better focus on type of client served (such as student, researcher, or recreational user) or information function pursued (such as indexer/abstracter, collection developer, information interpreter, or information manager), disregarding the institutional setting of the professional. The development of integrated core curricula is one of the key indicators of this shift.

Specialist Areas. So long as the vast majority of Master's degree holders continue to find employment in library institutions, and so long as these institutions require only that their beginning professionals possess the degree—without much regard to the courses taken to obtain that degree—true educational specialization will be concentrated in on-the-job experience and post-Master's programs. (School/media librarianship is the only type of clearly developed library specialization offered in most schools.) Regardless of the many reasons given for continued reliance on the generalist curriculum, a growing number of library educators and practitioners concur that specialist preparation is needed. They agree that the 36-hour Master's curriculum is insufficient for the education of "real" specialists; however, if a school elects to educate only one or two types of information professional, with all courses after the core curriculum focused on selected institutional, subject, or functional areas, then specialization may be possible. Even then 36 hours may be too limited. Some library educators and employers believe that more library education programs should declare a specialty or perhaps small groups of specialty curricula. For example, a school might state that its single purpose is the education of public librarians, and perhaps include tracks for urban and rural public librarians. This type of specialization within a school might have in the curriculum, in addition to its core, such course offerings and distribution as the following:

Required of all students

Political environment of the Public Library (3)
Economics of Public Service (3)
Systems of Libraries (3)
Administration of Public Libraries (3)

Rural Track	*Urban Track*
Rural Sociology (3)	The City (3)
Regional Planning (3)	Urban Planning (3)
Rural Libraries (3)	Metropolitan and Sub-
Rural Economics (3)	urban Libraries (3)
Resources for Small	Urban Economics (3)
Public Libraries (3)	Resources for Large
Rural Library Research	Public Libraries (3)
(3)	Urban Library Research
	(3)

This type of specialist program offered totally within the library school could also be developed for academic librarianship to include tracks for univer-

A summer library school session at the University of Iowa, c. 1930.

sity, college, and community college librarians.

Another type of single-purpose curriculum that could be developed in the offerings of a single-purpose school might be the reference specialist. As in the past, many generalist librarians still decide to concentrate in reference service without regard to the type of library in which they might find employment. These students take courses in reference, totaling at least 15 semester hours, which would probably include

Introduction to Reference Service (3)
Resources for the Humanities (3)
Resources for the Social Sciences (3)
Resources for Science and Technology (3)
Government Publications (3)

In today's complex information environment, a single-purpose curriculum of some depth for a reference specialist might well include

Introduction to Reference (3)
Resources for the Humanities (3)
Resources for the Behavioral Sciences (3)
Resources for the Social Sciences (3)
Resources for the Sciences (3)
Resources for Technology (3)
U.S. Government Publications (3)
Government Publications (exclusive of U.S.) (3)
Serial Publication (3)
Nonprint Media (3)
Online Bibliographic Resources and Services (3)
Information User Studies (3)
Administration of Reference Services (3)

This hypothetical curriculum represents a total of 39 semester hours of which only 3, Introduction to Reference, might be concentrated in the core. Additional single-subject resource courses could well be added, boosting the number of credits to well over 40. Indeed, a school that chooses to be a reference specialist school could reasonably develop tracks for social science specialists, humanities specialists, and others.

Another route to specialist preparation is through cooperation with other academic departments. While the specialization program by type of library could be pursued in this manner—for example, by having those pursuing academic librarianship taking courses in schools of education and public administration—this path to specialization is especially appropriate for subject specialists. Prospective art librarians might profitably take a variety of courses in art history and fine arts as well as special courses in the library school. While many students might choose dual Master's degree programs, it would be possible to gain appropriate preparation for a specialty with fewer hours than those needed for a dual degree, provided, of course, that the specialist program is well designed.

The principal reason specializations are not more widely pursued is that library education programs continue to draw their students mainly from their local areas. The largest number of students demand education which is generalist in nature so that they can apply for a wide variety of beginning library positions. There is no national recruiting program for the field and no developed consensus on what specialization consists of; therefore, there is no clear demand for specialization except that created by state regulations for school library/media certification.

The Unesco Regional Office for Education in Asia and the Pacific

Library/documentation internship courses being conducted at the Unesco Regional Office for Education, Bangkok.

While programs of specialization are available in library schools, only a few students choose them and they vary greatly in structure. In reporting to ALISE, 26 schools indicated that they offered a total of more than 64 specialization programs. Twelve schools reported specializations in history; seven reported programs in law or business; many reported the availability of multiple specializations.

One area of specialization in the Master's curriculum that has been demanded especially by library practitioners is management. It is unclear whether practitioners are calling for an actual specialization or for an extension of the curriculum for all librarians in the area of management. There is considerable evidence, based on research studies, continuing education needs assessments, and programs held at professional meetings, that professional librarians are increasingly being used in management and supervisory positions. Traditionally, library schools offered only the core course in general library administration and taught additional administrative knowledge through type-of-library courses. A number of library schools, responding to the need to provide additional administrative knowledge, have introduced advanced general administration courses, and many offer courses in such analytical skills as systems analysis. Courses in the administration of specific library functions such as technical services and public services are also offered at some schools, and many courses dealing with library networking or cooperative systems emphasize administrative aspects. The most prevalent means for providing concentration in administrative aspects of librarianship is through cooperation with other academic departments. Master's students may be encouraged to take courses such as personnel management or organizational behavior in schools of business or public administration.

Only the schools with the largest number of faculty can hope to provide more than one or two specialization programs, although many can offer single-specialized courses such as law, map, music, or archival librarianship. The individual specialized courses do not amount to specialization in the opinion of most concerned people, and these courses are typical in most traditional library education curricula because they are offered based on the expertise available from a particular full-time or adjunct faculty member.

The future development of specialization programs within the 36-hour Master's degree is problematic. Because the COA has approved of the concept of single-purpose programs, there seems to be little compelling argument against them as long as a market exists for such specialists. However, except for some as yet not clearly defined indications from the academic library community, there does not appear to be a market for specialization at the first professional degree level. It is especially difficult for publicly supported library schools to abandon the generalist library education program, because they are expected to train librarians for all types of libraries in their states. Further, the development of specialized library education programs would best be accomplished through a national plan for library education; although a number of writers have called for such a national plan, none is on the horizon.

It appears that the most likely changes to occur in the education of librarians are that (1) curriculum content will continue to be expanded to emphasize development of competence in the technologically oriented aspects of the information environment; (2) the number of credit hours required for the first professional degree will increase slightly; and (3) undergraduate education for information professionals, including education for library support staff, will be further developed and more closely articulated with first professional degree programs.

Library education curricula in the mid-80s were in a period of scrutiny and change, and curricular change will continue to be the most characteristic element of library education throughout the decade. The inclusion of flexible course structures, such as Issues in Librarianship or Resources in Special Literatures, which will allow library educators to respond rapidly to changes in library and information science, will become essential elements in the curriculum.

Association for Library and Information Science Education. The Association, known as ALISE, was founded in 1915. Its mission is to promote excellence in education for library and information science as a means of increasing the effectiveness of library and information services. ALISE's goals are (1) to provide a forum for the active interchange of ideas and information among library educators; (2) to promote, conduct, and demonstrate research related to teaching and to library and information science; (3) to formulate and promulgate positions on matters of mutual interest to library education; and (4) to cooperate with other organizations on matters of mutual interest.

Membership in the Association is open to both institutions and personal members. Institutional memberships are granted upon request to any school in an accredited institution that offers degrees in librarianship or cognate fields, and personal membership is open to anyone interested in the goals of the Association.

The curriculum of library education programs is of vital concern to the membership of ALISE. Because this membership is principally made up of faculty of ALA-accredited schools and schools that plan to seek accreditation, the emphasis is greatest on curriculum at the Master's level. The 1977 annual meeting of ALISE was devoted to the core curriculum and the 1984 annual meeting to undergraduate preparation for the information professions. The Association supports both a general Curriculum Interest Group and several interest groups that emphasize specific curricular components such as online bibliographic services, library history, and research methods. The membership of the ALA Council's Standing Committee on Library Education (SCOLE) is largely composed of members of ALISE. Of chief concern to both SCOLE and ALISE is the continued development and availability to potential information professionals of excellent programs of library education.

REFERENCES

Association for Library and Information Science Education, *Library and Information Science Education Statistical Report* (1980–).

Richard L. Darling and Terry Balanger, editors, *Extended Library Education Programs* (1980).

Arlene T. Dowell, "The Two-Year Master's: Perspectives and Prospects," *Journal of Education for Librarianship* (1978).

King Research, Inc., *Library Human Resources: A Study of Supply and Demand* (1983).

Charles A. Seavey, editor, "Accreditation Conference," *Journal of Education for Library and Information Science* (1984).

JANE ROBBINS–CARTER

Library Education: Education and Training for Library Employees

People who work in libraries can be divided into two groups: (1) librarians and (2) people who are not librarians but work under the direction of librarians. For this article, all members of the second group are classified as *library employees*. Library employees need special knowledge in order to do their work, a need met through vocational instruction. This article recognizes three types of instruction: work experience, training, and education.

Work Experience. The simplest way to learn a job is by doing it, with exposure to the work itself, to remnants of prior work, and to the example of co-workers, and with casual instruction by colleagues and superiors. This type of instruction, long used in libraries, can be effective, but it is unreliable and inefficient because the order of instruction is dictated by the workplace rather than by the needs of the learner. It is most appropriate for teaching simple tasks, whenever inept or incorrect performance cannot inconvenience a library user or embarrass the library.

Training. Planned instruction by the library is superior to work experience as a teaching method. It may range from classroom instruction by a training officer to one-on-one instruction by a supervisor. When properly conducted, it is purposeful and combines teaching with testing and practice; job assignments are deferred until the employee attains an adequate level of proficiency. Training programs are costly to develop and administer but are more efficient and more reliable means of staff development than experience alone. Through training, employees can attain higher levels of proficiency than most can reach through work experience, and training can teach procedures that are too complex to master through work experience. In fact, there is no library technique, be it manual, mechanical, interpersonal, or bibliographic, that employees cannot learn through training programs.

Education. In this article, *education* means instruction administered by professional educators outside libraries, in scholastic or academic settings. It is most useful for teaching knowledge that is not library-specific, like that needed to discharge the professional responsibilities of librarians. Knowledge that is library-specific, such as knowledge of a circulation system or filing system, can usually be taught better through training, but in special cases superior facilities or teaching skills may make education more efficient than training, even in teaching library-specific subjects.

CLASSES OF WORK

Library work can be classified as routine or not routine; as "unskilled," skilled, or professional; and as "library work" or "not library work."

Routine or Not Routine. Any work that can be done by following a prescribed procedure is routine work. Procedures may be simple, like the process of shelving books, or they may be intricate, like the procedure for cataloguing books—but they are all routine.

Most work in libraries is routine. Apart from professional work (defined below) the only work that is not routine (or potentially so) is responding to the unexpected, something rather rare in libraries. (Even emergencies can be anticipated, and procedures developed for responding to them.) Generally speaking, work that is not routine is the responsibility of librarians, and only routine work should be assigned to employees.

"Unskilled" or Skilled. Work that is simple enough to be learned quickly through work experience, and the employees hired to do such work, are both described as "unskilled" (in quotation marks because the true meaning is "simple-skill" rather than "no-skill"). Skilled work can be learned only through special training or education, or extensive work experience. Many librarians do skilled work themselves, to avoid the costs of hiring and training employees to do it. Consequently, many people mistakenly classify work that requires a technical skill (such as classifying books) as professional work, and reserve it for librarians only. Actually, any routine work can be assigned to an employee, no matter what level or type of skill it may require, if the employee possesses that requisite skill.

Professional Work. The work of all professionals is exemplified in that of physicians, who diagnose their patients' illnesses, prescribe treatment, and then administer their prescriptions, either with their own hands or through subordinates. Physicians decide what needs to be done, decide how it is to be done, and get it done. In the business world and increasingly elsewhere, these activities are called planning and direction and are classified as managerial work, in contrast to the technical work through which plans are implemented.

Librarians are the professionals of librarianship. They "diagnose" information needs, "prescribe" library service to meet those needs, and build and operate libraries to provide that service. Library employees differ from librarians in four ways: (1) With rare exceptions, they are not members of any learned profession; they are responsible only for carrying out specific tasks assigned by librarians. (2) They are not all members of a single vocational class; they belong to various classes. Since different classes need different skills, it is inappropriate to impose a single educational program (such as the librarian's professional education) on all library employees. (3) Skills required of employees must be job-related. Librarians must be able to evaluate many services or methods that they may never provide or use, but an employee needs only the knowledge actually to be used on the job. (4) Librarians' knowledge is applicable in many library activities and in many libraries, but much of an employee's vocational knowledge applies only to the library in which he or she is employed. Consequently, while librarians are prepared better for their work by education than by training (though every librarian needs orientation training at least), employees usually can be prepared better for their work by training.

"Library Work" and "Not Library Work." Any work done in or for a library is, of course, library work, but only some work, such as repairing or cataloguing books, is peculiar to librarianship. The rest (such as typing and computer programming) is not peculiar to librarianship; skills that are specific to librarianship must be taught in libraries or in library schools, while those that are not should be acquired through vocational education outside librarianship.

INSTRUCTION FACTORS

Since employees' jobs determine what they need to know, any factor that affects those jobs may also affect employee training. Four factors that do are change in libraries, library growth, the division of work between librarians and the support staff, and the division of work within the support staff.

Change in Libraries. Libraries are not static institutions. Their environments change, the resources and technologies available to them change, and the needs and other library-related characteristics of the people they serve change. In response to these changes, libraries themselves must change, providing new services, employing new methods, and adopting new forms of organization with different jobs and different skill requirements. These changes must always be accompanied by corresponding changes in vocational instruction. Since the direction of change in libraries is, almost invariably, from the simpler to the more complex, which requires more staff expertise, vocational instruction tends to move away from dependence on work experience toward increasing reliance on training and education.

Library Growth. Growth is a special form of change common to all libraries. As a library grows its workload increases, and it must change its methods to secure economies. Its employees must not only increase in number, but also must learn new techniques and assume new responsibilities. Consequently, a library's vocational instruction must change as it grows. An instructional procedure that is satisfactory when a library is small will be less so as it grows larger.

Division of Work. As managers, librarians may choose to do technical work themselves or assign it to employees but, especially as libraries grow, they are pressed to assign such work, and increasing shares of supervisory and administrative duties too, to employees. This pressure comes from four sources, all associated with growth: (1) An increasing professional workload, inevitable as libraries become more complex, forces librarians to withdraw from technical roles. (2) A broadening range of technical duties must inevitably exceed the range of librarians' technical skills, and force them to depend on employees with the skills they lack. (3) The pursuit of efficiency (a determining factor in libraries' ability to compete against other agencies for resources) demands use of cheaper or more cost-effective methods, which often require use of employees rather than librarians. (4) Recognition that having librarians do technical work reinforces their popular image as technicians (or clerks) rather than as professionals adds impetus to dividing work between librarians and other employees.

In small libraries, librarians must do technical work (this is perhaps the origin of the librarians' nonprofessional image), but as libraries grow their options increase. In small libraries employees usually are employed only in "unskilled" tasks, which they learn through work experience. As librarians progressively assign more skilled work to them, training and education must supplant work experience in the vocational instruction of employees.

Division of Work among Employees. There are two basic ways to divide work among employees. One is to give each employee a share of every task that is assigned to all; the employees must then be generalists. This approach is most appropriate where flexibility is considered more important than a high volume of output, and where only "unskilled" work is assigned to employees. It is usually found in small libraries and is the conventional way of dividing work among library employees. It is not appropriate for large libraries, however, where employees may be limited to work in a single department, or even to a single task; such employees are de facto specialists.

The second way to divide work is to assign each employee a special group of tasks, that is, to use them as specialists rather than generalists. Generalists, all sharing the same duties and having the same skills, form a single vocational class. Specialists, with different duties, divide into many classes, each with its own instructional requirements. Specialists, if they are to be used properly, must be trained to a high degree of expertise, each one in the special skills required by his or her own job. Since any employee assigned to a specific job must be specially trained for it, use of specialists imposes a heavy training burden on the library, but one offset by a key advantage: performance improves when specialists are used. When they are employed in the same work, specialists will outperform generalist employees and librarians. (Since librarians' education in technical methods is extensive rather than intensive, they are inherently generalists with respect to technical work.) In any case, specialists must be employed when the range of tasks becomes too great or the tasks themselves too complex to be mastered by generalists.

EMPLOYEE EDUCATION AND TRAINING IN U.S. LIBRARIES

Five modes of vocational instruction have prepared employees for American libraries: apprenticeship, apprentice-schools, training classes, academic schools, and library technology training programs.

Apprenticeship. Before Melvil Dewey founded the first library school in 1887, all librarians and library employees (then called *library assistants*) learned their jobs through apprenticeship in large libraries, under the direction of the librarians. (In those days, *librarian* meant the person in charge, and no library had more than one.) Librarians were promoted from the ranks of the assistants, and small libraries with no assistants were expected to recruit their librarians from the staffs of large libraries.

Apprentice-Schools. Dewey's school was founded because the number of libraries training assistants was too small to satisfy a growing demand for librarians. That school and any others before World War I are called apprentice-schools here because they resembled apprenticeship programs more than conventional schools. Many of their graduates began their careers as library assistants.

Training Classes. In 1891 the Los Angeles Public Library began a formal apprentice program for library assistants, and during the next 25 years other large libraries followed its example. The programs, called training classes, were very much like the contemporary library schools, but were intended to produce assistants rather than librarians.

Academic Schools. After World War I C. C. Williamson's study of library schools identified two types of library personnel, which he called librarians and clerks. He recommended academic preparation for the librarians and training programs in large libraries for the clerks. The latter recommendation was ignored, but with support from the Carnegie Corporation and the American Library Association, the library schools and some training classes were gradually converted into academic institutions, each becoming part of a university and accepting only college graduates into its program.

Library school graduates were then so much preferred over employees trained by apprenticeship or in training classes that those two methods all but ceased to be used. From 1930, when economic depression reduced demand for library personnel, until after World War II, library positions that required any special skill or knowledge were reserved for library school graduates. Employees who were not library school graduates were restricted to "unskilled" tasks. Library school graduates called themselves librarians and professionals, but most actually were employed as skilled technicians—not true librarians, but library employees. The library schools, ostensibly professional schools, actually functioned primarily as technical schools. Libraries, assuming erroneously that all library school graduates were qualified for any library work, stopped training almost entirely. And they restricted themselves unnecessarily to an artificially small pool of potential employees.

Library Technology Training Programs. After World War II demand for skilled library employees far exceeded the supply of library school graduates. A few undergraduate schools then began programs to teach library skills to help meet that demand. Two or three schools began to offer such programs before 1950. Seven schools were doing so in 1960, 20 in 1965, and more than 100 in 1970. In 1975, according to a directory published by COLT (the Council on Library Media Technical Assistants), library technology programs were offered by 130 schools in the United States, 23 schools in Canada, and three more schools in American Samoa, Puerto Rico, and the Panama Canal Zone. The 1980 edition of *American Library Directory* listed 112 schools offering such programs and the 1985 edition 63 schools. (The decline in number reflects both a decline in all types of library schools and the impact of an increase in the relative number of library school graduates.)

Most of these schools are community colleges. At first their programs varied widely in quality and utility, but they have become a valuable adjunct to librarianship, teaching skills useful in libraries, in many cases with emphasis on machine skills. Beginning with audiovisual equipment, they came to include instruction in use of computers and computer-based library systems.

The contrast that these schools and their graduates offer has helped to define the professional images of graduate library schools and their graduates, and their impact on librarianship during the 1960s helped inspire the ALA to develop and to publish in 1970 its policy statement on *Library Education and Personnel Utilization* (originally *Library Education and Manpower*), which recognized again the value—obscured since 1930—of library employees without graduate library school degrees.

TRAINING THE LIBRARY STAFF

Primary responsibility for the competence of library employees does not rest on schools or even on the employees, but on libraries, because they alone know exactly what their needs are. Libraries are responsible for testing the competencies of job applicants and choosing the most competent. They are responsible for developing competencies as needed in those they employ, through either training or education programs. Training is usually the more practical choice.

Training has been so little used in libraries since 1930 that it is not part of the common image of librarianship. But in a changing world common images are always out of date and should never be used as models for planning. Training is necessary in librarianship, and will be even more necessary in the future, so much so that its absence seems prima facie evidence of poor management.

Training is required to orient new employees (and new librarians) to their library, its environment, and the people it serves. Training is necessary to teach job skills, to upgrade skills, to prepare employees for promotion or transfer, and to replace current methods with new ones. Training may be a necessary response to change or to refresh skills.

Well-planned training programs convey knowledge rather than specific job information, but that knowledge is always job related. They must be based on job descriptions and job specifications, which specify knowledge needs. They employ testing to find out what employees know and teach employees to apply knowledge. They also set performance standards. Ideally, employees who are unable to meet a standard are assigned to other work; thus training

programs also screen employees and help to fit them into the library staff.

Education is an alternative to training if a school is accessible and has the resources that a library education program requires. Reliance on education programs rather than training can be more efficient when the needed resources are available and the number of students sufficient to make education economically feasible. Libraries near a school might elect to standardize their methods, so that their employees could be educated in a single program. But libraries cannot discharge their responsibility for staff development merely by sending employees to a school; they must participate actively in developing the educational program and monitor it to make sure that it meets their needs.

Like other organizations, libraries are becoming more dependent on skilled employees, and on the education and training through which they become skilled. Librarians too are changing, becoming more like other managers who get work done through other people. Success in this art depends very much on teaching those people what their work requires them to know.

REFERENCES
Brooke E. Sheldon, *Planning and Evaluating Library Training Programs* (1976).
Charles W. Evans, "The Evolution of Paraprofessional Library Employees," *Advances in Librarianship* (1979).
Robert D. Stueart and John Taylor Eastlick, *Library Management* (1981).
William R. Tracey, *Designing Training and Development Systems* (1984).

CHARLES W. EVANS

Library Education: History

NORTH AMERICA

Formal library education began in North America in 1887 with the first classes at the School of Library Economy, Columbia University, under the direction of Melvil Dewey. Dewey had been an advocate of full-time education for a number of years, using the American Library Association (ALA), founded in 1876, as a forum to gain support for this new approach. Dewey's appointment as Librarian at Columbia in 1883 gave him the opportunity he sought. He persuaded the Annual Conference of ALA that year to endorse the concept, although some prominent members of the Association opposed the idea, notably William Fredrick Poole, John Shaw Billings, and Justin Winsor (whose biographies appear in this Encyclopedia). Essentially, their view was that experience in a good library would provide all that was needed to become a librarian, provided a person had a sound general education. At the 1877 International Conference in London, Winsor noted that libraries in the United States offered good career prospects for women and urged British librarians to train them for library work.

From 1884 to 1886 Dewey held preliminary classes at Columbia to try out his ideas. In January 1887, the School opened officially with a class of 20—17 women and 3 men—and a staff of 7, all part-time instructors, including Dewey himself. The admission of women, although supported by Columbia College (now University) President Frederick A. P. Barnard (1809–89), was opposed by the Trustees; they were relieved when, in January 1889, Dewey moved to Albany as the New York State Librarian and took the Library School with him. The School did not return to Columbia until 1926, at which time it was combined with the New York Public Library School.

While the initial programs at Columbia and Albany tended to emphasize the practical aspects of librarianship, they did offer systematic training and an opportunity to look beyond one library system. Their influence was great in that eight of the schools established in later years were founded by Dewey's graduates. Apart from Columbia, the early schools were not located in universities but in institutes of technology, such as Pratt, Drexel, and Armour (later moved to the University of Illinois), and in such large public libraries as the Los Angeles Public Library. ALA maintained a keen interest in the work of these new schools by establishing a series of committees and other units. The first committee, in 1883, was intended to serve as a liaison with Columbia but it was followed by Committees on Library Examinations and Credentials (1900), on Professional Instruction and Bibliography (1901), on Library Training (1903), on Professional Training for Librarianship (1909) and a Round Table of Library School Instructors (1911). Four years later that Round Table separated from ALA to become the Association of American Library Schools (AALS), renamed in 1983 the Association for Library and Information Science Education (ALISE).

20th Century. Over these early years, three ideas emerged that were to influence American library education as it developed in the 20th century—library schools should be affiliated with universities; college graduation should be required for admission; and an examining board with clearly defined authority should be established. While these points were still being discussed by the schools, ALA, and AALS, the influence of an outside agency provided a much needed impetus. In 1916 the Trustees of the Carnegie Corporation of New York (CCNY) had commissioned a report from Alvin S. Johnson, an economist, on its policy of providing funding for public library buildings. Johnson's *Report* focused on the need to be more concerned with the low quality of many of those staffing these libraries. He was also critical of the low standards of the library schools. A follow-up report was sought from C. C. Williamson, an economist who also taught at the New York Public Library School. In his recommendations, Williamson favored the development of a coordinated plan for library education. The CCNY Trustees then hired Williamson to undertake a major survey of library education, which he did from 1919–1921.

The subsequent Williamson *Report* is generally regarded as the most important document to have appeared in the history of library education. It was critical of current library education. Among its proposals were that library schools should distinguish between clerical and professional work and only teach the latter; such schools should be located in universities; more financial support should be provided for schools, their faculty members, and students; courses should run for two years—one year for general principles and one for specializations; a national system of

certification should be adopted; and schools should be accredited. Prior to the publication of the Williamson *Report*, ALA had established a Temporary Library Training Board drawn from all sections of the membership to look into library training, standards and an accrediting plan. In 1924 ALA replaced that temporary body with the Board of Education for Librarianship (BEL), later the Committee on Accreditation (COA). Williamson's proposal for a National Examining Body was not accepted but accreditation of schools was. To carry out the accreditation process, *Standards* were developed by the BEL, and later the COA, and adopted by ALA Council in 1925, 1933, 1951, and 1972. (See Accreditation.)

The Ten Year Program in Library Service, initiated by the Carnegie Corporation under its President F. P. Keppel as follow-up to the Williamson *Report,* provided generous support for ALA and to individual library schools. The program was based on a staff report by William S. Learned. The most significant Carnegie Corporation benefaction was to the University of Chicago to enable it to establish a Graduate Library School (GLS) in 1926, designed to be librarianship's equivalent of the Johns Hopkins Medical School and the Harvard Law School. Historian Donald G. Davis, Jr., notes that its foundation "was perhaps of greater significance to education for librarianship than was the founding 40 years earlier of the Columbia school." Its faculty was drawn from cognate disciplines in which the scholars held doctorates, and in 1928 Chicago introduced the first doctoral program in the field. The GLS emphasis on research and publications had a major impact on the program and its graduates and on library education itself.

In the years following the Williamson *Report,* library education did become the responsibility of universities as schools affiliated with large public libraries closed. Admission to the program now called for an undergraduate degree, whereas before 1924 only the New York State Library School and that at the University of Illinois required a bachelor's degree for admission. The qualifications of the faculty were improved, and more and better textbooks became available. Later reports on library education, published between 1936 and 1952 by different authors, presented varying perspectives of library education, but all tended to emphasize perceived deficiencies in the curriculum. (See also Library Education: Curriculum.) Special conferences also focused on library education, especially in the period 1940–48, and the ideas discussed and proposals made all contributed to the ferment of the times. However, the profession had recognized that the growing and increasing complexity of libraries did justify the education of its librarians at the graduate level.

The MLS. Matters came to a head with the adoption in 1951 by the ALA Council of new *Standards for Accreditation.* These had the effect of ensuring that professional librarians were those obtaining the "fifth-year" degree (i.e., one year of professional study after four years of undergraduate preparation) at graduate library schools whose programs were accredited by ALA. An unanticipated change came in the early 1950s when this fifth-year degree became a Master's degree (M.L.S) replacing the former B.L.S. as U.S. schools strengthened and, in some cases slightly lengthened, their programs.

Canada. The B.L.S. as the first professional degree remained longer in Canada, where a similar but slightly different pattern of education for librarianship developed. Dewey's influence was seen in the earliest formal instruction when his friend Charles Gould, Librarian at McGill University, offered a three-week summer school there in 1904. Short courses were offered in other years at McGill and later by the Ontario Department of Education, which established the Ontario Library School in 1919. The first full-year programs were instituted at McGill in 1927 and at the University of Toronto (taking over from the Ontario Library School) in 1928. Both schools subsequently sought and received ALA accreditation for their programs, thus setting a precedent for virtually all other library schools later established in Canada. The Canadian Library Association (CLA) was not established until 1946. (Although Provincial associations existed from 1900 onward, national gatherings of Canadian librarians were held at ALA conferences until 1946.) In the late 1960s, all but one of the Canadian schools agreed to adopt the M.L.S. as the first professional degree to be offered after four terms of study. This lengthened program became the norm for all seven Canadian schools. Periodically, since 1955, the Canadian Library Association has considered the question of a Canadian system of accreditation; in the mid-1980s it had a committee examining the issue again.

One of the seven Canadian schools (Montreal) is Francophone and CLA is an English-speaking-only organization. This alone would complicate but not be an insuperable barrier to a Canadian system of accreditation in what is officially a bilingual country. In 1985, even before the CLA Committee reported in 1986, there had already been strong support expressed for continuation of the ALA accreditation process from six of the seven schools.

Other Developments. There were other developments affecting library education in the U.S. in the 1950s apart from the adoption of new *Standards* and the introduction of the M.L.S. as the first professional degree. In 1956 the BEL was replaced by COA for accreditation matters with the Library Education Division (LED) serving as a forum for the broader participation of ALA members whether library educators or not. In 1959 ALA Council approved *Standards* for undergraduate training that have served to guide programs seeking to prepare those in teacher-training institutions. In addition, by then, several Schools had joined Chicago in offering doctoral programs.

The 1960s saw a boom in library education in the United States as enrollments grew and the number of library schools increased to meet the growing demands of the field. Four of Canada's existing seven schools also opened in the 1960s. Much of the growth in the United States was the result of increased federal and state funding for libraries at all levels. Funding was made available to support potential faculty members in doctoral programs. Recruitment of minority group students also became a more active concern. The U.S. Office of Education and its Library Service Branch proved to be a catalyst; an institute it sponsored at Western Reserve University led to ALA's establishment of a Commission on a National Plan for Library Education in 1963. It led to the creation of an

Office for Library Education within ALA in 1966 for which the H. W. Wilson Foundation provided matching funds. That Office, under Lester Asheim, produced the *Library Education and Manpower* statement designed to respond to library staffing needs at various levels. In addition to the expansion of M.L.S., Ph.D., and undergraduate teacher certification programs, the 1960s also saw the creation of library technician programs in community colleges and the introduction of sixth-year programs designed as a post-Master's program.

From 1970 the picture for library education was much less bright. In 1971 ALA closed its Office for Library Education. ALA's LED was next to go when it was unable to attract enough members to ensure its financial survival. It was replaced by a lesser unit, the Standing Committee on Library Education (SCOLE), with some of the former staff services of LED now provided by the Office for Library Personnel Resources, although its main interest lies elsewhere.

ALA initiated and the H. W. Wilson Foundation funded a major study of library education by an academic investigator, Ralph W. Conant, over the period 1972–77. When ALA released the draft report for publication, however, it stated that neither the Association nor its Advisory Committee "endorses, sanctions, or otherwise approves of the study." Conant's recommendations were not regarded as contributing greatly to the field and his research methodology was widely criticized.

There has been much enthusiasm shown in recent years in both the U.S. and Canada for changing the name of the schools in which the degree is offered. "Information science" or "information studies" are being added to, or in some instances, replacing the more traditional "library science" or "library service." This is being done to reflect the changing nature of what is being offered in these schools; indeed, a few schools have introduced undergraduate degrees in information science that do not seem to be designed for those who will later seek the M.L.S. Many schools are now offering an array of joint degrees with library science linked with another subject, for example law, or programs in information science or archives alongside the M.L.S. degree. Schools are also involved to varying degrees with continuing education offerings. A 1980 conference at Columbia University examined the case for extending the length of the M.L.S. program and generally found it wanting; only the Canadian schools and a handful of U.S. schools called in the mid-1980s for a period of study beyond one calendar year for the M.L.S. degree.

The October 1985 listing of accredited programs issued by COA included 63 schools, of which 7 were in Canada. Doctoral programs were offered at 23 schools, of which 2 were in Canada. In recent years, schools at Ball State, Case-Western Reserve, Denver, Geneseo, Minnesota, Mississippi, Southern California and Western Michigan have all closed. The status of some other schools has been threatened. While certain schools appeared to have weathered the storms of the late 1970s and mid-1980s, it would be sanguine to assume that all existing programs would survive in the United States. The annual statistical reports issued by ALISE tell their story of an overall drop in enrollments, leveling off in the mid-80s, dwindling faculty numbers, and declining financial support. Canada's schools have largely regional affiliations that may assist their survival.

UNITED KINGDOM

Education for librarianship in the United Kingdom has followed a course different from that in North America. In so doing, it has been influenced by the society in which its libraries operate and in which the pattern of higher education also differs. Until after World War II, when the number of universities increased markedly, vocational education for professional groups such as librarians, architects and accountants had been largely the responsibility of national professional associations rather than of universities. In addition, much higher education in Britain is still carried out in colleges and polytechnics, which are tertiary-level institutions with a different structure for the awarding of qualifications. When library education began in Britain in the latter half of the 19th century, the few universities that then existed—and which catered to a small, largely elite section of the population—were not considered as appropriate training agencies.

The Library Association. Three years after its establishment in 1877, the Library Association of the United Kingdom (LA) carried a motion that "it is desirable that the Council of the Association should consider how library assistants may be aided in their training in the general principles of their profession." What evolved was a system of nationwide examinations, starting in London and Nottingham in 1885, administered by the LA. Initially, the examinations sought to test both librarianship and the general education of the candidates—which was not high. Gradually the emphasis was placed almost entirely on the practical aspects of librarianship.

In 1898 the LA received its Royal Charter from the government. The awarding of a Royal Charter conveys certain privileges and powers on a body of persons for some specific purposes. In the LA's Charter were two very important clauses that authorized the LA "To promote whatever may tend to the improvement of the position and qualifications of librarians" and "To hold examinations in librarianship and issue certificates of efficiency." This was followed in 1909 by the LA's setting up a Register of qualified librarians known as Chartered Librarians. To qualify for admission to the Register, it was necessary to join the LA, complete its examination requirements, and then remain in membership by payment of annual dues. This system was favored by Williamson in his 1921 *Report* as a means of funding the proposed national certification system for the United States.

Although initial interest in taking the LA examinations was limited, the establishment of the Register and a greater awareness of the need for trained staff led to an increased number of candidates. In the absence of any system of full-time library education, the LA encouraged the holding of summer schools, evening classes in larger centers of population generally held in public libraries or colleges, advice columns in the library press, and correspondence courses. In the largely urban public libraries, whose staffs were serving virtual apprenticeships, the LA

examination system flourished as staff members sought to qualify for admission to the Register.

The London School. As in the U.S., the report of an outside surveyor to the Carnegie trustees affected the development of library education in Britain. Following the 1915 *Report on Library Provision and Policy to the Carnegie United Kingdom Trust* by Professor W. G. S. Adams, the Carnegie United Kingdom Trust (CUKT) provided initial funding for starting a full-time library school at the University of London. As a university school, London offered its own diploma, which was recognized by the LA as admitting its holders to the Register. This surrender of the LA's monopoly as an examining body was resented by many of those in the urban public libraries who had to work long hours and then were expected to study part-time for their professional qualifications. There was also unhappiness in the 1930s that too many Chartered Librarians were being produced as the LA examination system was increasingly accepted. The London School admitted both graduate and non-graduate students. Many of those completing its program found employment in academic and special libraries and also in the then newly developing county (i.e., rural) public libraries. The few university graduates entering the library profession in the years up to World War II tended to be employed in the small number of academic and national libraries where professional library qualifications were not considered essential. The London School with its largely part-time teaching staff never had the impact on the British scene that the Chicago School had in the U.S. Yet when it closed in 1939 at the outbreak of war, it had at least shown that a full-time school could exist within a British university environment.

Post-War Developments. During the years 1939–45, much post-war planning took place in Britain involving both educational institutions and the various professional associations. In 1942 the LA considered a report by its Honorary Secretary, Lionel R. McColvin, *The Public Library System of Great Britain,* funded by the CUKT. In it he proposed a national system of library schools to provide full-time education for the ex-service men and women whose careers had been interrupted. Although these schools would be small in size, McColvin foresaw that they might continue in existence to provide full-time education for new recruits to the profession. McColvin, supported by the LA Council, felt it essential that the Association remain in control of the examination system whereby national standards could be enforced. Given the many pressures on university education immediately after the war it was unlikely that, apart from London, the university authorities would have welcomed courses in librarianship, but the LA's insistence on controlling the syllabus settled the matter. Nonetheless, the LA did succeed in having seven full-time schools opened by 1947 in colleges of commerce and similar institutions of tertiary education. All prepared their students for the LA examinations which at the time offered two tiers of qualification, first the Associateship (A.L.A.) and second, the Fellowship (F.L.A.). The Schools admitted both graduates and non-graduates, with the latter numerically much larger. The introduction of these full-time schools did not mean the elimination of either part-time study or correspondence courses, although the superior success rate of those attending the schools could clearly be demonstrated.

By 1955, it was realized by the LA and the schools that a major overhaul of the system of education for librarianship was needed. From a post-war program largely designed to update ex-service people, the schools were becoming permanent fixtures seeking to control the examination of their students, providing for career paths for new recruits, and wishing to revise the syllabus which was still controlled by the LA. It took almost ten years before the various segments of the profession, which by now involved the Association of British Library Schools and also Aslib, could come to agreement. By this time other factors had entered the picture, leading to an increasing diversity in British library education.

1964 may be taken as the crucial year, as the LA then introduced a new syllabus calling for a full-time two-year program for non-graduates and a one-year post-graduate diploma for those already holding a university degree leading to the first professional qualification, the Associateship. The Fellowship now became available by thesis rather than examination. With part-time study thus eliminated, the schools were able to increase their staffing numbers to prepare for this expanded instructional program. At the same time, in 1964, the Council on National Academic Awards (CNAA) received its Royal Charter, which authorized it to grant degrees to those completing approved programs at colleges and polytechnics that were not themselves universities. Library schools, with their expanded staffs, were not slow to see the implications of this and soon moved to develop programs leading to first degrees in librarianship to be approved by CNAA or in one instance by a nearby university. Some of these schools now offer master's and doctoral degrees. Meanwhile in addition to the school at the University of London, five other schools were located in universities, all preparing for their own qualifications. As a result the LA changed from being an examining body in its own right to an agency which recognizes existing qualifications for admission to its Register.

Current Status. There were 17 schools in the United Kingdom in 1986. Most schools offer first degrees in librarianship of three or four years' duration. Post-graduate diplomas and degrees at the master's level are available at many schools, usually after one year of full-time study although it is possible to study part-time in some situations. Some schools offer higher research degrees that may be at master's or doctoral level. The great majority of the courses noted above qualify for admission to the Register of the LA. However, the LA has long required a period of supervised work experience as well as successful completion of examinations, whether its own or others. It later introduced a three-tier structure. After successful completion of an approved course, candidates for admission to the Register have to complete one year of training supervised by a Chartered Librarian, after which they may apply to become Licentiates of the LA. A further period of not less than two years as a Licentiate, again under the supervision of a Chartered Librarian, is required for the Associateship. After five years on the Register, an Associate may submit work of various kinds for election to the Fellowship.

The LA agreed to recognize, beginning in June 1986, courses taken at programs accredited by ALA and those recognized by the Library Association of Australia (LAA) as being equivalent to those taken at programs approved by the LA insofar as gaining admission to the Register is concerned. The other requirements concerning membership of the LA and its Licentiateship scheme still have to be met. The lengthy period of licentiateship before being admitted to the Register as a Chartered Librarian engendered much discussion in the LA; it is believed that an increasing number of the holders of university degrees are not persuaded of the need to follow this route. The implications to the LA are significant as there is a loss of membership and dues from those who chose not to join the Association and its Register. The Association in the mid-1980s was considering expanding its membership to seek to attract those from related professional groups. How they would be accommodated by the existing Register requirements remained to be determined. The LA also was considering a change of name to the Library and Information Association. (See also Library Association.)

At the same time the central government in the U.K., which funds virtually all undergraduate students and many graduate students, has been concerned for some time with the number of librarians being produced by this system. In 1985 it established the Transbinary Study Group on Librarianship and Information Studies, which for the first time was to look at library education in the U.K. as taught by the "public" sector (colleges and polytechnics) and the "independent" sector (the universities). Its mandate appeared to cover not only the content of library education but also the question of "supply and demand." As in North America, British schools have programs to reflect what they see as the changing nature of the field. As examples, Leeds in the 1980s offered a B.A. in Librarianship and a B.Sc. in Information Science, Sheffield changed the title of its School to the Department of Information Studies, and Strathclyde became a Department of Information Science as part of the Strathclyde Business School.

SCHOOL LIBRARIANSHIP

In general, both North American and British library schools have sought to provide a general system of education for librarians in all types of library work and now, in related fields. The exception to this in both systems has been the generally limited success in providing appropriate educational experiences for those seeking employment as school- or teacher-librarians. This calls for recognition as both a teacher and a librarian, and despite efforts over many years it seems fair to say that the ideal "mix" has not yet been achieved. In the U.S. there are often state certification requirements for employment in the school system that favor qualifications obtained from state colleges rather than ALA accredited programs. In Canada the Canadian School Library Association has sought to establish nationwide qualifications but here again Provincial requirements complicate the picture. In Britain school librarianship has traditionally had even greater difficulties in gaining recognition.

INTERNATIONAL MAIN CURRENTS

Commonwealth. The monopolistic control of library education by the LA in the U.K. has been dramatically changed by the events outlined previously. One additional aspect is the international influence of the LA through its examination system, which did not necessarily require attendance at a full-time library school. From its early days, the LA was more receptive to enabling overseas students to sit for its examinations and has made the arrangements necessary for this, enabling librarians in many parts of the world to obtain a recognized library qualification when no library school or in some cases no library association existed in their home countries. The 1964 decision to require two years of full-time attendance at library school led effectively to the cessation of this system of overseas examinations.

Some early library schools established in Colonial, later Commonwealth, countries also prepared their students for the LA examinations before moving to their own indigenous systems. In the years after World War II, many Commonwealth countries sent their students to the U.K. to obtain professional library qualifications. The fact that these were offered at first-degree level was more attractive in some cases where those being sent lacked the first degree necessary for admission to North American schools. As a result of these two approaches, some 10 percent of the LA's Register of Chartered Librarians are resident overseas, although a proportion of these are British librarians who have emigrated to other countries. In any case this percentage is likely to decline. However, British influence on library education overseas shows no sign of abating as the steady stream of faculty members serving and advising library schools in many countries, especially those of developing nations in the Commonwealth, continues with the financial support of the Government, largely through the British Council.

U.S. Influence. U.S. influence on library education overseas has also a long and historic tradition. While ALA has been involved in many cases, it has not held the same position as that of the LA because of ALA's decision, within the U.S. educational system, to accredit individual programs according to its *Standards*. As a result much of the U.S. aid has come through foundations such as the Carnegie Corporation of New York, Rockefeller Foundation, Ford Foundation, and governmental bodies such as the United States Information Agency, the Agency for International Development, and Fulbright lecturers. Writing in *Library Trends* (1972), Robert S. Burgess noted that "New library schools have been established or existing ones strengthened with U.S. assistance in, among other places, Columbia, Japan, Korea, Mexico, Nigeria, Puerto Rico, the Philippines, Thailand, Iran, Turkey, and Uruguay." An earlier example was the foundation of the Boone Library School in China in 1920 by Mary Elizabeth Wood, who graduated from Simmons. While foundation and government aid for overseas library education may have dwindled in the 1980s, the U.S. influence remains strong as many overseas faculty members hold advanced degrees from U.S. schools. U.S. faculty have held visiting appointments at overseas schools but for a variety of reasons, among them lack of external funding and development of local, trained staff,

fewer did so in the 1980s.

International Cooperation. An international library school was talked about as early as 1904, by Guido Biagi writing in *Library Journal*. More recent discussion has taken place in the International Federation of Library Associations and Institutions (IFLA) and the Federation Internationale de Documentation (FID), but there had been no really concrete progress by the mid-1980s. Unesco has been suggested as a sponsoring agency, but the location of the proposed school, language of instruction, curriculum, and recruitment of faculty present problems that so far have been and may continue to be insurmountable. On a more modest scale, a successful example of international cooperation has been the International Graduate Summer School (IGSS) held annually at the College of Librarianship Wales (CLW). CLW is a residential college devoted exclusively to librarianship. It is in Aberystwyth, which is also the home of the National Library of Wales. The faculty of the summer school changes from year to year, although there is some degree of continuity. The majority are drawn from North American schools and CLW itself, with a few from other European countries and further afield. To increase its appeal to students from North America, the IGSS is cosponsored with the School of Library and Information Science of the University of Pittsburgh. Pittsburgh issues transcripts for courses completed, thus facilitating transfer of credit to M.L.S. programs in the United States and Canada. The international flavor of the school was further enhanced by students from other overseas countries, often specially funded by the British Council.

Different examples of international cooperation in formal education for librarianship can be found in the establishment of regional schools serving more than one country. Regional schools would seem to have much to commend them, especially in those areas where resources are limited. They permit the bringing together of faculty and institutional support to meet the needs of a student body drawn in the main, although not exclusively, from the host region. The language of instruction may also be a unifying factor, as is the case of the Interamerican Library School, Medellín, Columbia, established in 1956 for Spanish-speaking countries, or the University of Dakar's School for Librarians, Archivists, and Documentalists, founded in 1963 to meet the needs of French-speaking countries in Africa. It has had strong support from the French government and Unesco; its founding Director came from France.

Other regional schools are those in Uganda and the West Indies. The East African School of Librarianship, established in 1963 at Makerere University College, Kampala, Uganda, aims to train librarians from Kenya, Tanzania, and Uganda. It has had support from Unesco, various foundations, and Scandinavia, which provided its first Director, Knud Larsen. The difficult political situation in Uganda in the 1970s and first half of the 1980s was not conducive to its development.

The West Indies School began in 1971 at the Mona campus, Kingston, Jamaica, to serve Jamaica, Trinidad and Tobago, Barbados, Grenada, Guyana, and the British Associated States and Colonies in the Caribbean. Its first two directors were supported by

Unesco, as have been other staff appointments. Additional support came from Canada through governmental agencies and with the cooperation of the library schools at Western Ontario and Dalhousie, which made faculty members available to teach at the West Indies School.

European Patterns. Most countries of the world have adopted either the North American model of graduate education or the British multi-level approach for types of librarianship. One region that is largely an exception to this is in those parts of Continental Europe in which a stratification for library education can be seen. This provides for academic level education at university level; training at a lesser level of educational institution for those to be employed in what might be termed subprofessional positions; and training for support staff at a third type of institution. As Donald E. Davinson makes clear in a survey published in 1976, it is difficult to categorize when dealing with countries as diverse and as small as Denmark with its monolithic Royal Danish School providing "programs at all levels, from advanced to those for part-time library assistants" and as vast as the Soviet Union with its tightly controlled system designed to accord with its manpower plan.

Although library schools worldwide may teach the international standards for cataloguing, there are no such standards for library education programs. The IFLA Section of Library Schools resolved in 1974 to follow up earlier work in this field by seeking to formulate global standards for library education programs.

Equivalency. The question of equivalency and reciprocity of qualifications remains. The defunct LED of ALA had a special committee to advise on these matters. It set up Country Resource Panels consisting of two North American members of ALA knowledgeable about the educational system in the country concerned together with one national resident in that country. These panels, which exist within ALA's Standing Committee on Library Education (SCOLE), give opinions on the equivalency and relationship of foreign library qualifications in relation to those offered in North America. In late 1985 the British LA decided it too would establish resource panels, as it began to recognize courses from overseas schools as qualifying for admission to its Register. The LA was also moving ahead on developing a system of equivalence of qualifications to permit the employment of non-nationals in member countries of the European Community.

REFERENCES
Robert S. Burgess, "Education for Librarianship: U.S. Assistance," *Library Trends* (1972).
Ralph W. Conant, *The Conant Report: A Study of the Education of Librarians* (1980).
J. Periam Danton, *Between M.L.S. and Ph.D.: A Study of Sixth-Year Specialist Programs in Accredited Library Schools* (1970).
Richard L. Darling and Terry Belanger, Editors, *Extended Library Education Programs; Proceedings of a Conference Held at the School of Library Service, Columbia University, March 13–14, 1980* (1980).
Donald E. Davinson, "Trends in Library Education—Europe," *Advances in Librarianship* (1976).
Donald G. Davis, Jr., "Education for Librarianship," *Library Trends* (1976).
Alvin S. Johnson, *A Report to the Carnegie Corporation of New York on the Policy of Donations to Free Public Libraries* (1917).
William A. Learned, *The American Public Library and the Diffusion of Knowledge* (1924).
John Richardson, Jr., *The Spirit of Inquiry: The Graduate Library School at Chicago, 1921–1951* (1982).
Sarah K. Vann, *The Williamson Reports of 1921 and 1923; A Study* (1971).

NORMAN HORROCKS

Libya

Libya, officially the Socialist People's Libyan Arab Jamahiriya, is in Northern Africa, bordered by the Mediterranean Sea on the north, Egypt on the east, Sudan on the southeast, Chad and Niger on the south, and Algeria and Tunisia on the west. Population (1984 est.) 3,648,000; area 1,749,000 sq.km. The language is Arabic.

History. Libya was a center of some of the outstanding civilizations of ancient times. In the Eastern Region the Greeks established a large public library in Cyrene. By Roman times many other libraries had been introduced. During Islamic rule the country benefited from the educated people who crossed the territory, traveling from one end of the Islamic world to the other. The people began to engage in scientific and literary activities. The largest library, started in Jaghboub, contained about 40,000 volumes, the great majority of which were in manuscripts; remains of that collection (over 1,000 manuscripts) are now in the Central Library of Garyounis University.

An antiquities library was founded in the capital city, Tripoli, in 1911. It is the richest library of rare books, documents, and archives in the country. Another was established in Cyrene in 1914; it holds more than 10,000 rare books in various languages. Many other libraries were founded throughout the country to serve religious and social groups where there were no public libraries. The collections of these libraries are mixed, but they cover mostly Arabic literature and Islamic interests.

National Library. From 1955, the university library acted as a national library, but in response to the need for a national library the Ministry of Education decided to establish one in Benghazi City. Construction now completed, it has been furnished and equipped. The book, manuscript, document, and periodical collections are quickly growing, and in 1984 a proclamation was issued to establish it as a depository library. Plans called for it to be open to the public.

Academic Libraries. *University of Garyounis.* The Central Library of Garyounis University, Benghazi, was founded in 1955. It started with a collection of 300 volumes. It grew at a fast rate in print and nonprint materials, and reached about 260,000 volumes by 1984. The building consists of four floors, air-conditioned, with a capacity of 3,000 seats plus facilities for a million volumes. The library has four main departments: Technical Services, Administration, Readers' Services, and Branch Libraries. It uses the Dewey Decimal Classification for non-Arabic books. An amended system is used for the Arabic collection. The Audiovisual Division is well equipped with good facilities. There are six branch libraries.

University of El-Fateh, Tripoli. The first library in this university was established in 1957 when the Faculty of Science was opened. There are seven libraries, each with a rich collection mainly in the field of the faculty. The collection totals about 155,800 volumes in addition to 3,510 periodicals and a large number of back issues.

Audiovisual departments with large collections function in each library. In 1970 a decision was made to erect a new Central Library building, but the project was delayed. The basic book collection of the Central Library is temporarily located in a part of the Faculty of Science. The Library School at this university gives good support to the faculty libraries, mainly in providing them with professional staff and technical services. The Dewey Decimal System and Anglo-American Cataloguing Rules are used.

Bright Star University of Technology, Brega. On November 25, 1981, this third university in Libya was opened in Brega, 280 km. west of Benghazi. A Central Library building was erected on the campus. The book collection totals about 35,000 volumes, mostly in English. It subscribes to 415 periodicals and has a small collection of back issues. A small audiovisual section has been established. Several departmental libraries offer quick service to the faculty, staff, and students. The library applies the technical system used in the University of Garyounis libraries.

University of Sebha. A library was established in 1977 for the Faculty of Education that was part of the University of El-Fateh in Tripoli. In 1983 a decision was made to found Sebha University, and that library became the new Central Library at Sebha. The book collection is over 35,000 volumes in various languages. The Library subscribes to 410 periodicals. It publishes a quarterly bulletin to notify readers of new additions and other news. It uses the same technical system as the other university libraries. In spite of shortages in technical manpower and other difficulties, it promised to become a dependable library serving the educated people in the Southern part of Libya.

Higher Technical Institutes. Five higher institutes for technical education were founded in various parts of the country between 1972 and 1977. Each institute has its own library; each contains about 10,000 volumes. The institutes cooperate to cover any needs that may arise among them.

Public Libraries. Public library service in the modern sense was started in the country in 1953. These libraries were under the Minister of Education. In mid-1960 the Minister of Information and Culture introduced a new service at the people's cultural centers. Both public libraries and cultural centers cooperate to provide their clientele with new books, magazines, newspapers, and government publications. They numbered 169 in the whole country in 1984. Technical services, acquisitions, and budget control are centralized in a department of the Secretary of Information.

School Libraries. From 1960 considerable efforts were made to establish libraries in secondary, preparatory, and vocational schools. By the end of 1978 almost all of them had small libraries. Services of those libraries improved when the Secretary of Education provided better support with more adequate budgets. They are still in need of proper facilities and sufficient trained personnel.

Special Libraries. These libraries have become indispensable for the main secretariats, organizations, and other establishments. Special libraries up to 1970 numbered only eight in the whole country. That number had increased to 29 by the end of 1982. Each library maintains material relating to its special activities.

AHMED M. GALLAL

Liebaers, Herman
(1919-)

Herman Liebaers, Librarian on the staff of the Royal Library of Belgium (1943–54), Director of the Library (1956–73), and Grand Marshal of the Court of Belgium (1974–81), led in strengthening IFLA and international librarianship.

Born at Tienen, Belgium, on February 1, 1919, Herman Liebaers was educated in Brussels and at the University of Ghent; like many Europeans of his generation, he was caught up in World War II. During the German occupation of Belgium, he spent most of 1943 in German captivity. On return to Brussels he came into librarianship and into his eminent career at the Royal Library by mere chance when that Library needed a staff member who had academic training in Germanic language and literature but who was, obviously, not pro-German. During his early career in the Royal Library, where his first task was to translate the existing French subject catalogue into Dutch, he not only achieved his library certification in 1944 but also continued his scholarly studies, receiving his Ph.D. from the University of Ghent in 1955. His study of the 19th-century Dutch poet Hélène Swarth, together with her correspondence, was subsequently published by the Royal Flemish Academy of Language and Literature.

Another significant element in his early career came by way of a five-month visit to the United States during 1950–51, when he was a consultant at the Library of Congress and visited many U.S. libraries, museums, and art galleries. During the next few years he conducted summer courses in Flemish art for foreign art historians under a program sponsored by the Belgian-American Educational Foundation.

In 1954 Liebaers left the Royal Library, spent half a year as Librarian of the European Council for Nuclear Research (CERN), and then returned to the U.S. until 1956 as a Fellow and Associate Secretary of the Belgian-American Educational Foundation. He returned to the Royal Library in 1956 as Director.

The Royal Library set high standards for the other ancient national libraries of western Europe in many ways under his forceful leadership. A new building, dedicated in 1959, not only functions efficiently but is also an appropriate component of the national cultural center of Brussels. In establishing an effective modern scientific and technical documentation service, Liebaers dispatched the Chief of the new facility to Kansas City to spend a term under the tutelage of Joseph Shipman at the Linda Hall Library. On quite another front, he extended the Library's rich Burgundian heritage of rare books, manuscripts, coins, and prints and brought it into public view and scholarly use through an impressive and handsome series of exhibitions and catalogs. Under his direction

EUROPALIA
Herman Liebaers

legal deposit was established for the Library, and the national bibliography was modernized.

In 1973 Liebaers took a leave of absence from the Royal Library and returned to the U.S. as Consultant to the Council on Library Resources with the intention, at least in the minds of his friends, of producing an analysis of American research libraries—sort of an update of Wilhelm Munthe's *American Librarianship from a European Angle* (1939). But before the year was out his career took a decided change of course when King Baudouin appointed him Grand Marshal of the Court of Belgium. Thus he left the Royal Library and moved, metaphorically at least, across the way to the Royal Palace. The new royal appointment recognized Liebaers's crucial role in Belgian cultural and intellectual life, his extensive international experience, and his notable diplomatic talents.

Liebaers's library career reached far beyond Belgium and the U.S., through the agency of the International Federation of Library Associations and Institutions (IFLA), to which he gave increasing attention in the years following 1956. He was Chairman of its National and University Libraries Section from 1959 to 1964, joined the IFLA Executive Board in 1963, was elected a Vice-President in 1964, became First Vice-President in 1967, and then in 1969 was elected President for the term 1969–72, succeeding Sir Frank Francis. He was elected to a second term in 1972, but it ended prematurely when he resigned in 1974 to take up his new post at the Belgian Court. At that point he was elected Honorary President of IFLA.

During his presidency IFLA was enabled to establish a permanent Secretariat in The Hague and to solidify its fiscal position, with generous support from the Council on Library Resources. It was thereby able to mount a succession of aggressive projects, notably the Universal Bibliographic Control (UBC) program and more recently that for Universal Availability of Publications.

Sir Frank Francis had grasped the international significance of the American Shared Cataloging Program, which led to the National Program for Acquisitions and Cataloging (NPAC); under Liebaers's leadership, this development was crystallized into the powerful UBC program. Similarly, Liebaers sensed the symbolic importance of Unesco's International Book Year Project of 1972 and saw to it that IFLA was the prime mover in the worldwide success of the Unesco project. For that service the Association of the German Book Trade awarded him its Interprofessional Award at the Frankfurt Book Fair in 1973. During his IFLA tenure Liebaers traveled extensively, particularly in the Third World, taking the message of books and libraries wherever he went. In these years Third World membership in IFLA expanded rapidly, and IFLA entered into an active regionalization program in order to take the IFLA program into all corners of the world.

For these and other efforts Herman Liebaers was widely honored. In 1956 he was named a Laureate of the Royal Flemish Academy of Language and Literature and in 1970 a Professor of Librarianship and Bibliography in the Free University of Brussels; the University of Liverpool awarded him an honorary doctorate in 1971, and in 1973 the Library Association of the United Kingdom named him an Honorary Vice-President; he became an Honorary Member of the Special Libraries Association in 1974 and of the American Library Association at its Centennial Conference in 1976.

REFERENCES

A bibliography of Herman Liebaers, by Robert Gabriel, appeared in the Belgian journal *Mens en Taak* (1975).
A volume of Liebaers's reminiscences, *Mostly in the Line of Duty: Thirty Years with Books,* was published by Nijhoff in 1980.

ROBERT VOSPER

Lippincott, J. B.
(1813–1886)

Joshua Ballinger Lippincott's business life as a printer, binder, publisher, bookseller, and distributor was conducted in such a way that his publishing peers referred to him as "the Napoleon of the book trade." His business philosophy is reflected in the motto of his old-line house, *Droit et Avant* ("Right and forward," or roughly, "Be sure you are right and then go ahead").

An only child, Lippincott was born in Juliustown, Burlington County, New Jersey, on March 18, 1813. Little is known of his childhood years. He had a common school education and began working at the age of 13. From all accounts, his nonbusiness life was private. Little is recorded concerning it, other than noting that the business, banking, and educational community of Philadelphia benefited from his leadership as a member of the boards of directors of the Philadelphia and Reading Railroad, the Farmers' and Mechanics' Bank of Philadelphia, the Philadelphia Saving Fund Society, the Pennsylvania Company for Insurance on Lives and Granting Annuities, and the Board of Trustees of the University of Pennsylvania.

Lippincott began his book-oriented career in 1827 as a clerk in a Philadelphia store owned by a bookseller named Clarke. Creditors subsequently closed on Clarke, and in 1832 Lippincott was designated as the store's manager. He paid close attention to the business and to his personal finances and by 1836 had saved enough from his earnings to purchase the business, thus launching J. B. Lippincott and Company.

Lippincott was energetic and increasingly successful. He was fast making his mark as a substantial publisher of bibles, prayer books, and general literature. Lippincott gave special attention to the manufacturing aspects of the book, and his interest in elegant bindings made his books popular with booksellers. He also retailed books and did contract printing.

In 1850 he made the major decision to purchase the entire stock of books and stationery of Grigg and Elliott, Philadelphia—at that time the country's largest wholesalers in the field. Although many in the trade considered it an unwise purchase, Lippincott meant it to help him become the foremost publisher in Philadelphia. This transaction more than any other occasioned people to call him "the Naopleon of the book trade."

An early business practice followed by Lippincott was to take in his assistants as partners, resulting in such imprints as Lippincott, Grambo, and Company in the first part of the 1850s. During the period 1855–85 he used the imprint J. B. Lippincott & Company.

Lippincott's early catalogue was distinguished by its comprehensiveness. Its notable works ranged from bibles, religious books, and tracts to major reference titles. In 1855 the first edition of *Lippincott's Pronouncing Gazetteer of the World* was published; subsequent editions continued in print for almost a century. In 1858 the firm began publishing Webster's *Blue-Back Speller.* Other successes under Lippincott's direction were *Allibone's Dictionary of Authors* (beginning with the second volume in 1870), a number of excellent editions of the *Unabridged Dictionary* by Webster, which the firm gave up in 1876 when it began publication of *Worcester's Dictionary,* and *Lippincott's Pronouncing Dictionary of Biography and Mythology.*

Lippincott was also a publisher of periodicals. In 1857 he began the *Medico-Chirugical Review,* edited by Samuel D. Gross. Other periodicals included *the Medical Times* and *Annals of Surgery.* In 1868, under the editorship of Lloyd Smith, Librarian of the Library Company of Philadelphia, Lippincott launched *Lippincott's Magazine.* In the years immediately following the Civil War, Lippincott expanded in the medical field, publishing textbooks and handbooks. Early examples of his success were Da Costa's three-volume *Medical Diagnosis, Principles and Practice of Surgery* by Agnew, and the *Photographic Atlas of Diseases of the Skin* by Fox. A widely used handbook is *The Dispensatory of the United States of America;* with the 27th edition in 1985 it remains the oldest continuously published reference work under private ownership in the world. He is also credited with the publication of *A Handbook of Nursing* (1878), the first nursing textbook in the United States.

Another of Lippincott's noteworthy contributions was the massive Chambers' *Cyclopaedia of English Literature.* He was the first American publisher of this title, and this nine-volume facsimile edition, illustrated with wood engravings and original maps, was important in establishing Lippincott's business with publishers in Europe.

While Lippincott was especially strong in books of reference and medicine, he also issued a sizable list of general books. Included were standard and deluxe editions of the works of Bulwer-Lytton, Scott, Thackeray, and Dickens, as well as Foster's three-volume biography of Charles Dickens. In 1871, under the editorship of Horace H. Furness, Lippincott published *Romeo and Juliet,* the first volume in its outstanding *Variorum Edition of Shakespeare.*

Important government-sponsored works were executed by him, most notably Henry Schoolcraft's *History of the Indian Tribes,* published in six folio volumes and costing nearly $100,000. Lippincott's business acumen was displayed in his securing the copyright and plates for the 15 volumes of Prescott's historical works from the Boston firm of Phillips, Sampson and Company, and from Prescott's heirs.

Some of the important works published by Lippincott were the romances of Marie Louise de la Ramé, better known by her nom de plume, Ouida; an edition of Scott's Waverley novels; *The Life of John Quincy Adams,* edited by his son Charles Francis Adams; and Bigelow's life of Benjamin Franklin. Other noteworthy publications were *The Writings of*

Albert Gallatin and an accompanying title, *Life of Gallatin,* by Henry Adams. During Lippincott's time the idea of a series of books on a common, nonfiction theme was being developed. In 1869 Lippincott produced the "Reason Why Series."

The panic of 1873 was devastating to a number of publishers and booksellers and resulted in demands for a national trade association that would regulate the retail price of books based on the cost of production. A national convention was held July 21–23, 1874, at the summer resort of Put-in-Bay on Lake Erie, and J. B. Lippincott was represented at this first American Book Trade Association (ABTA) convention at which the historic "20 percent rule" was made. The rule provided that publishers and booksellers would agree not to sell at a discount greater than 20 percent on miscellaneous books and schoolbooks to libraries, large book buyers outside the trade, professional people, and teachers, or of more than 10 percent on medical books.

Although the Lippincott firm was in attendance at Put-in-Bay, it opposed the rule, fearing that so sudden and drastic a marketing decision would adversely affect its trade. Lippincott's position subsequently moderated in objection to being called "the only holdout in the industry." Its condition for signing was that all books must be sold at the published retail price, except for a maximum discount of 20 percent to libraries, school teachers, and buyers outside the trade who purchased more than $100 net at any one time. This proposal caused much argument over a number of months, but at the second ABTA convention in July 1875 it was announced that Lippincott had finally signed the agreement. By this time Lippincott shared the distinction with Appleton of owning one of the two largest bookstores in the U.S.

In order to supply his vast empire, Lippincott developed an outstanding physical plant, moving to various locations in Philadelphia. In 1861 the firm erected a magnificent new marble building on Market Street, between Seventh and Eighth streets. Subsequent additions were built until it was the largest book publishing, distributing, and manufacturing office in the world.

In December 1879 Lippincott discussed his business with *Publishers' Weekly:*

Twenty-nine presses are kept constantly running to meet the demands of our business. The average number of books printed by them is 2,000. Our business extends from the Atlantic to the Pacific, from Newfoundland to Texas. From 25,000 to 30,000 boxes of books are annually shipped to our various customers, and about 100,000 express packages. A manuscript is brought into the establishment and comes out a bound volume. The entire book is manufactured under this roof. Here it is printed, bound, published, sold, and distributed.

In 1884 Lippincott's health began to fail. Realizing this, he reorganized the firm in February 1885. It was incorporated with a capital of $1,000,000, and he personally held 9,970 of the 10,000 shares of stock. The new name of the firm was J. B. Lippincott Company; he was the president and owner and the first publisher to incorporate in the United States. On January 5, 1886, Lippincott died at his home in Philadelphia.

REFERENCES
Stuart Freeman, *Centennial Reflections: J. B. Lippincott Company in the 1870's* (1976).
J. B. Lippincott Company, *The Author and His Audience; With a Chronology of Major Events in the Publishing History of J. B. Lippincott Company* (1967).
Charles A. Madison, *Book Publishing in America* (1966).
John Tebbel, *A History of Book Publishing in the United States,* 2 volumes (1972, 1975).

RICHARD FITZSIMMONS

Li Ta-chao
(1888–1927)

Li Ta-chao, a founder of the Chinese Communist Party, honored as China's first revolutionary martyr, is considered the father of modern Chinese librarianship.

Born on October 6, 1888, in the village of Ta-hei-t'o, Hopei, Province, Li was raised in an upper-middle-class environment. Between 1907 and 1913 he studied at the Peiyang College of Law and Political Science in Tientsin, concentrating on political economy and foreign languages. Upon graduation Li furthered his schooling at Waseda University in Tokyo.

Returning from Japan in 1916, he began several years of political activism in Peking and Shanghai. The two greatest concerns of the young Chinese intellectuals in the early 20th century were the encroachment of foreign interests, on the one hand, and the inevitable transition of a nation from the Middle Kingdom to a modern, industrialized state on the other. A leading voice of the intelligentsia was *Hsin Ch'ing-nien* ("New Youth"), for which Li wrote extensively and became a member of the editorial board in 1918. Soon after his appointment Li was asked to assume the position of Head Librarian at Peking University.

Li's career as Librarian of one of China's leading universities was to have a tremendous impact on modern history. During his tenure, from 1918 to the mid-1920s, he utilized to its fullest measure the library's potential as a center for political activism. By directing the traditional functions of a university library (such as the systematic acquisition and distribution of materials, utilization of space for private study and small discussions) toward the promulgation of the philosophies of Marxism, Li Ta-chao organized enough support to begin China's journey toward revolution.

Li's office was the center of much research and study. He collected and translated a major corpus of Marxist and Leninist works and made them available to students and faculty. His Marxist Research Society attracted many individuals to his office, which became known as the *hung-lou* or the "Red Chamber." Among his early followers was a young library assistant named Mao Tse-tung, who worked with Li and attended many sessions in the Red Chamber. Years later Mao would credit Li with his initial introduction to Marxism and the beginning of his own political development.

In 1919 a series of events known as the May Fourth Movement indicate the far-reaching importance of Li's work. For several weeks intensive riots and demonstrations occurred in several major cities as the Chinese voiced their opposition to foreign presence on their native soil. Li and the Peking University Library served a unique role during this politically volatile time, directing the earliest activities of the Marxist leaders of modern China.

Li Ta-chao's career, although vitally important, was brief. By the mid-1920s Li and other faculty members had been forced to leave the University, because the government was becoming increasingly hostile to Communists. Eventually Li was arrested in Peking and, on April 28, 1927, was executed.

The political activism of Chinese libraries in the decades following the founding of the People's Republic was strongly influenced by the work of Li Ta-chao. It has been written that if Chinese librarians study political and cultural materials, work diligently to improve their knowledge, and actively impart this information to the people, the profession will approach Li's ideal of the library after the Marxist revolution. The example of the Red Chamber, according to this view, places a responsibility upon Chinese librarians that is unique in the history of the profession.

Courtesy of The Harvard University Press

Li Ta-chao

REFERENCES
Nearly all writing on Li Ta-chao's career in librarianship is in Chinese and untranslated as of the mid-1980s. Two works that address this subject and draw from the original materials are: Maurice Meisner, *Li Ta-chao and the Origins of Chinese Marxism* (1967), the most comprehensive evaluation of Li Ta-chao in a western language, with extensive translations and historical background to Li's library years.
Diane M. Nelson and Robert B. Nelson, "The Red Chamber: Li Ta-chao and the Sources of Radicalism in Modern Chinese Librarianship," *Journal of Library History, Philosophy and Comparative Librarianship* (Spring 1979), which, in addition to tracing Li's development as political activist and librarian, presents translations of later Chinese writings concerning the impact of Li Ta-chao's career on modern practices in the People's Republic.

DIANE M. NELSON;
ROBERT B. NELSON

Locke, George
(1870–1937)

George Herbert Locke, educator and librarian, was one of two Canadians elected President of the American Library Association. He directed the fortunes of the Toronto Public Library for nearly 30 years (1908–37), during which it expanded from a small system with a staff of 26 to a major institution boasting a large central building, 16 branches, and a staff of 232.

Locke was born in Beamsville, Ontario, March 29, 1870. Educated at Victoria College, University of Toronto, he received the B.A. and M.A. degrees in classics. He then did graduate study and teaching in educational theory, first at the University of Chicago, later at Harvard. From 1899 to 1903 he was Associate Professor at Chicago, then was appointed Dean of the College of Education. He was Editor of the *School Review* (1900–06), a prestigious journal of American secondary education. After a year in Boston as an Assistant Editor with the publishing firm of Ginn & Co., Locke returned to Canada as Dean of the School of Education at McGill University, Montreal. Fron McGill he was invited to the Toronto Public Library in 1908.

Locke brought neither formal training nor prior

American Library Association

George Locke

library experience to his new position, but he had a personal concept of the public library as a social institution. Probably developed from his work in education, Locke's concept of the library contained two major components: the library should bring the pleasures of literature to the general public for recreation, and it should play a major role in continuing adult education. For him, librarianship was as educational in character as the teaching profession, although it offered no specific formal instruction and served a more varied clientele.

He used his term as ALA President (1926–27) to reiterate his conviction that the public library was an intellectual public utility that would help preserve and inspire the democratic state. Its resources, properly interpreted by librarians, would allow citizens to prepare for intelligent service to society and to become informed about workings of the democratic process. His years on the ALA Executive Board produced definite views concerning the most desirable role for the Association. Librarians served a social institution, and Locke felt their professional association needed strong personal leadership. The membership exceeded 10,000 by the mid-1920s and Locke urged alternating full membership meetings with regional meetings every second year. He also urged a two-year term for the ALA presidency to prevent erosion of the office's power by the permanent general staff.

Furthering an active professional life, Locke produced a substantial body of publications, for both educational and library journals, and works for the general public. He wrote two works of popular Canadian history and a study of English history for the ALA's "Reading with a Purpose" series. He was a member of the American Association for the Advancement of Science, the Dominion Education Association, and several Canadian and American library associations. For his services to the community the University of Toronto awarded him an LL.D. in 1927. He died in Toronto on January 28, 1937, and was mourned in three countries—Canada, the United States, and the United Kingdom—and most of all by the city of Toronto.

MARGARET ANDERSON

REFERENCE

Margaret Anderson, "Locke, George Herbert," *Dictionary of American Library Biography* (1978).

Lubetzky, Seymour

(1898-)

Seymour Lubetzky was the greatest theoretician of descriptive cataloguing in the 20th century.

He was born around 1898 in Zelwa, a town then part of Russia, later of Poland, and now in the U.S.S.R. He went to Los Angeles, California, in 1927, where he became a student at the University of California (now UCLA). Graduating in 1931, he moved to Berkeley, attended the University of California at Berkeley, and earned a Certificate in Librarianship from the School of Librarianship on that campus.

In 1936 Lubetzky went to work at the UCLA Library, eventually becoming a cataloguer. While there he wrote a number of articles questioning the

then-current library practice with respect to capitalization, the use of unnecessary title-added entries, and the division of library catalogues. These articles displayed the talent that caused the Library of Congress to hire him to look into current cataloguing practices in 1943.

In 1942 and 1943 Lubetzky worked in a shipyard in the San Francisco Bay area so that he might contribute to the war effort in a tangible fashion. By creating a uniform set of parts descriptions, he was able to reorganize the shipyard's stock and thereby save many thousands of dollars.

Lubetzky's first assignment at LC in 1943 was temporary only but later led to his being appointed Chief of the LC Catalog Maintenance Division, where he was responsible for planning for the publication of the ongoing *National Union Catalog* (the closest equivalent to an American national bibliography). Finally, he became Specialist in Bibliographic and Cataloging Policy. He made his most important theoretical contributions in this position.

Lubetzky's first major endeavor at LC was the simplification of the rules for description. His studies led to the 1949 publication of *Rules for Descriptive Cataloging in the Library of Congress (Adopted by the American Library Association)*. He turned his attention next to the rules for entry found in the *A.L.A. Cataloging Rules for Author and Title Entries, Second Edition* (1949). His analysis and critique of those rules is found in his *Cataloging Rules and Principles*, published by LC in 1953. *Cataloging Rules and Principles*, one of the classics of library literature, questions previous practice with respect to the form of heading for both personal and corporate authors as well as the very structure of previous cataloguing codes. In addition, it provides the outline for a future code.

As a result of the favorable reaction to *Cataloging Rules and Principles*, Lubetzky was appointed editor for a revised cataloguing code. The revision contemplated by Lubetzky is found in two major drafts—*Code of Cataloging Rules: Bibliographic Entry and Description* was issued in 1958; *Code of Cataloging Rules: Author and Title Entry* was issued in 1960, with its appendant *Additions, Revisions and Changes* appearing in 1961. These drafts are characterized by the clear statement of the objectives of cataloging and the rigorous pursuit of those objectives in the form of rules addressed to bibliographic conditions instead of the unsystematic case-by-case approach found in previous cataloguing codes.

Lubetzky was unable to finish work on the revised code because of the press of duties connected with his appointment as professor at the new School of Library Service at UCLA in 1961 as well as unwillingness to compromise on important points in the new code. Some of Lubetzky's major findings, however, were incorporated in the "Statement of Principles" formulated at the International Conference on Cataloguing Principles (ICCP) held in Paris in 1961. Although the 1967 *Anglo-American Cataloging Rules* (ACCR) was based on the ICCP principles, rather than the Lubetzky drafts, Lubetzky's influence is nevertheless apparent in AACR.

Probably the most definitive statment of Lubetzky's views is to be found in his 1969 report, *Principles of Cataloging; Final Report, Phase I: Descriptive Cataloging*. Among other major points, Lubetzky insists that a catalogue must deal with works, not books, as the fundamental objects to be catalogued, that main entry is a useful device for identifying works and bringing together the various editions of a work, and that corporate bodies are authors of their publications. These and other conclusions have permanent value even though they may have passed out of fashion in the Second Edition of AACR.

Lubetzky was awarded the ALA Margaret Mann Citation in 1955, a Doctor of Laws degree by UCLA in 1969, and the ALA Melvil Dewey Award in 1977. The citation for the Dewey Award states that Lubetzky's achievements assure recognition of his "position as the greatest influence on cataloging theory since Cutter."

MICHAEL CARPENTER

Luhn, Hans Peter

(1896–1964)

Hans Peter Luhn was one of the early information scientists. He came to information science by way of engineering. His interest was in the use of machines to aid in the retrieval and dissemination of information and the use of devices for the preparation of indexes and abstracts. Luhn's name will always be associated with Key Word in Context (KWIC) indexes and Selective Dissemination of Information (SDI), but beyond these two methods he pioneered in the use of mechanical—and later electronic—devices for the processing of textual material.

Luhn, known to his friends as Pete, was born in Barmen, Germany, on July 1, 1896. He completed secondary school (gymnasium) in Germany and then went to Sankt Gallen, Switzerland, to learn the printing business. His father was a well-known printer in Germany, and he was expected to join the business. At this early age, Luhn already showed an inventive mind and took great interest in technical matters, physics, and statistics.

His stay in Sankt Gallen was interrupted by World War I, in which he served in the German Army as a communications officer in France, Turkey, Romania, and Bulgaria. After the war Luhn continued his studies in Switzerland but also found time to invent a double-entry bookkeeping machine to record both debits and credits on ledger cards. In connection with that work he first became acquainted with Hollerith machines, the punched card equipment then coming increasingly into use.

In the early 1920s Luhn switched to the textile field, first as a freelance designer and then as an agent for a German textile firm, which he represented in 1924 in the United States with the hope of establishing textile plants there. Because of financial problems the mission failed, and Luhn was forced to look for a job. After working in a bank, he again joined the textile business as Assistant to the President of a company in Pennsylvania. It offered him the opportunity to show his inventiveness, and from 1927 to 1930 he was able to obtain 10 patents. One of these, the Lunometer, a device used to count threads in fabrics, is still marketed.

In 1933 Luhn established himself as an engineering consultant. The number and types of patents granted him during this period demonstrate the scope of interests and the inventiveness of the man: foldable raincoat, game table, recipe guide, apparatus to determine thickness of thread, and many others.

The recipe guide was Luhn's first invention related to information retrieval. Marketed as the Cocktail Oracle, it enables users of this "optical coincidence" system to determine quickly which cocktails they could prepare with the ingredients available on their shelves.

Luhn's interest in documentation, now called information retrieval, began in the late 1940s when he was asked by IBM to find a solution to the problem of searching chemical compounds that could be represented in coded form. Luhn's solution was to record the codes on punched cards, and he developed a machine (which became known as the Luhn Scanner) to search files of these specially encoded cards. Luhn soon recognized the limited capacity of the punched card and of the equipment used to process it if it were to be used in searching files of textual information or index terms, for example. His inventiveness was demonstrated over and over again as he came up with new schemes, such as "Super-imposed Coding" and "Row by Row Searching" to overcome the limitations of the available equipment.

With the beginning of the computer age in the early 1950s Luhn was able to find solutions to the problems he encountered in the storage and retrieval of information by using computer software, rather than having to invent machines to overcome the limitations of conventional punched-card equipment. He saw the great potential offered by computers to solve the problems created by the rapidly growing volume of scientific and technical literature. He wanted to understand these problems in depth and so participated in many meetings and conferences of librarians and documentalists.

One of the highlights of Luhn's career was his participation in the 1958 International Conference on Scientific Information in Washington, D.C. At that conference he discussed and demonstrated a method of automatically preparing abstracts of documents. Actual conference papers, the texts of which were available on Monotype tape as a by-product of publication in the conference proceedings, were abstracted automatically by a computer using a program he developed.

In 1958 Luhn wrote a paper entitled "A Business Intelligence System" in which he proposed an automatic method to provide current awareness services to scientists and engineers faced with the ever-growing volume of literature. Luhn's techniques assumed the availability of text in machine-readable form and would consist of automatic abstracting and matching of these abstracts against interest profiles of users, which he called action points. The result of a match would be a notice containing the abstract and relevant bibliographic information sent to a subscriber. Such systems of disseminating information on a selective basis, known as SDI systems, are in use today.

Another professional triumph for Luhn was the adoption by the American Chemical Society in 1960 of the Key Word in Context (KWIC) method of indexing and the publication of *Chemical Titles* by this method. Luhn had been advocating the use of computers for the preparation of permuted indexes to cut the costs and delays inherent in conventional indexing methods.

Luhn died August 19, 1964, in Armonk, New York. Throughout his career, but especially as an information scientist, Luhn always searched for the simple solution.

REFERENCES

Claire K. Schultz, editor, *H. P. Luhn: Pioneer of Information Science, Selected Works* (1968), with bibliography of Luhn's papers related to information science.

John F. Harvey, "Luhn, Hans Peter," *Dictionary of American Library Biography* (1978).

STEPHEN E. FURTH

MacAlister, Sir John Young Walker

(1856–1925)

John Young Walker MacAlister was the best known British medical librarian of his day, and he was immensely influential as a leader of others. He drove the infant Library Association (LA) at a pace comparable to Melvil Dewey's during the early years of the American Library Association.

MacAlister was born in Perth, Scotland, on May 10, 1856. He had served an appropriate double apprenticeship prior to his appointment as Librarian and Secretary of the Royal Medical and Chirurgical Society in London in 1887. He had abandoned his early medical training at Edinburgh because of illness and had instead obtained library posts in Liverpool and Leeds. From 1887 until his retirement he built up his employing society into the great Royal Society of Medicine, an achievement appropriately recognized by his Sovereign, who conferred a knighthood on him in 1919. But in 1887 he was appointed Honorary Secretary of the Library Association, and he is best remembered in this capacity and in that of Proprietor and Editor of its official organ, *The Library,* from its inception in 1889 until its supersession by *The Library Association Record* in 1899.

He provided the LA with offices and a meeting place in his employing society's headquarters in Hanover Square, London, and stimulated its members, and particularly its younger members, with ambitious ideas and untiring encouragement, both in person and through the pages of *The Library.* He was a prominent clubman at a time when the London clubs were at the height of their power and importance and persuaded his extensive and influential acquaintances to do all possible to help and support the LA. "Mac," as he was always known to his contemporaries, was almost too ambitious for the LA, since its very small membership and limited financial resources proved discouragingly restrictive. But the recollections of such prominent librarians as James Duff Brown, L. Stanley Jast, and Ernest Savage leave a later generation in no doubt as to his standing with them.

MacAlister was largely instrumental in gaining for the Library Association its Royal Charter of incorporation in 1898 but took a lesser part in its activities after his resignation from the Honorary Secretaryship in the same year. His interest and active participation in professional affairs were renewed during the years of World War I when serving as LA President from 1915 until 1919. He died in London on December 1, 1925.

REFERENCE
Shane Godbolt and W. A. Munford, *The Incomparable Mac: A Biographical Study of Sir J. Y. W. MacAlister* (1983).

W. A. MUNFORD

McCarthy, Stephen

(1908–)

Stephen Anthony McCarthy, university library director, headed the Cornell University Libraries for 21 years and was Executive Director of the Association of Research Libraries, 1967–74. Born in Eden Valley, Minnesota, McCarthy attended Saint Thomas College in Saint Paul and Gonzaga University in Spo-

kane, Washington, where he received his baccalaureate degree in 1929. After completing a Master's degree in literature at Gonzaga in 1931, McCarthy taught high school. Returning to the Midwest, he enrolled in a classics course at the University of Chicago and later enrolled at McGill University in Montreal, receiving a library degree in 1932.

He moved back to Chicago in 1934 and joined the staff of the Northwestern University Library. He also began doctoral studies at the Graduate Library School of the University of Chicago (Ph.D., 1941), then headed by Louis Round Wilson. The influence of Wilson and other faculty members and friendships with fellow students, including Ralph Ellsworth, Robert Miller, G. Flint Purdy, Benjamin Powell, and J. Periam Danton, proved important throughout McCarthy's career.

In 1937 McCarthy took the position of Assistant Director at the University of Nebraska Library, in Lincoln, then under the directorship of Robert Miller. Miller and McCarthy found a university and a library system suffering from the ravages of a prolonged depression. A small and antiquated building had forced the creation of too many small departmental libraries. McCarthy worked for seven years to improve salaries, services, and facilities. A union catalogue was created, a backlog of books was processed, and plans were made for a new building.

On the recommendation of Wilson, McCarthy was appointed one of the three Assistant Directors of the Columbia University library in 1944. His major duties included business affairs, personnel, and service as Acting Director when Carl White, the Director, was away on government assignments. The Columbia years were marked by staff shortages and frequent turnovers because of the war, but included plans for a rapid expansion of acquisitions and services after the war.

McCarthy became a candidate for the directorship of the Cornell University Libraries in 1946. However, after a visit to the campus at Ithaca, New York, he was appalled at the conditions of the library system. During a second visit, McCarthy was persuaded by the President of Cornell that the conditions in the library would be improved as quickly as possible. Fall 1946 found McCarthy in Ithaca.

During the next 21 years, McCarthy, his associates, and their staff transformed a group of poorly housed libraries with meager collections and inadequate services into one of the outstanding university library systems in the country. Cornell University was an unusual combination of endowed private colleges and state-supported professional schools. The separate colleges and schools operated almost independently of central administrative controls. It took McCarthy more than a decade to bring about a system of coooordinated libraries with more central control and budget authority.

One of McCarthy's lasting contributions to Cornell was the legacy of the Olin Library building and the other improvements made to all library facilities during his tenure. The replacement of the old 1891 library had been one of McCarthy's most urgent goals on his arrival in Ithaca. More than a decade of university committee deliberations and staff planning was frustrated by changes in both the presidency and the membership of the board of trustees, but a major

Department of Manuscripts and
University Archives Cornell
University Libraries

Stephen McCarthy

commitment by a donor and the university administration after 1955 pushed the Olin Library to a successful conclusion by 1961.

In 1967 McCarthy became the Executive Director of the Association of Research Libraries in Washington, D.C., a position he held for seven years. While at ARL he created the Office of Management Studies, presented testimony to Congress on matters affecting higher education and libraries, and advised a congressional committee on the revision of the "fair use" section of the 1976 copyright law. McCarthy retired from the ARL in November 1974.

In 1940 McCarthy served as President of the Nebraska Library Association. Later he held the same post with the New York Library Association. In 1953 he spent a year in Cairo as a Fulbright lecturer and adviser to several Egyptian university libraries. He spent part of 1967 in Great Britain surveying resources for the study of American culture. After his retirement from ARL, McCarthy served as a consultant to the Council on Library Resources. McCarthy also did a dozen or more surveys of college and university libraries during the 1950s and 60s.

REFERENCES

Director of Libraries, Cornell University, *Annual Reports* (1946/47–1967/68).

Association of Research Libraries, *Minutes of Meetings* (1950–75).

DONALD E. OEHLERTS

McColvin, Lionel R.
(1896–1976)

Lionel Roy McColvin was the outstanding public librarian of his generation in Britain. From the mid-1930s until his retirement in 1961, he dominated the public library scene, not just in his own country but internationally as well.

Born in Newcastle upon Tyne on November 30, 1896, McColvin was the son of an artist. His first library post was at Croydon, a borough of Greater London, where he worked as Reference Librarian under W. C. Berwick Sayers. Early professional advancement resulted in his becoming Deputy Librarian of Wigan Public Libraries in 1921, and in 1924 he was appointed Chief Librarian of Ipswich, in eastern England. He earned both these appointments before his 28th birthday, an early age to become a chief librarian in Britain. After seven years at Ipswich he became Chief Librarian of Hampstead, a northern suburb of London, and remained there until 1938, when he was appointed City Librarian of Westminster, one of the most important posts in British public librarianship.

Westminster was to be McColvin's final position; indeed it would have been difficult if not impossible for him to have advanced further. He was due to retire at the end of 1961, but in December 1960 he suffered a series of strokes that left him with loss of memory. He remained City Librarian of Westminster until his official retirement date on November 30, 1961, but was on sick leave for most of that year. He died in London on January 16, 1976.

McColvin was active in the Library Association (LA) all his life. He was elected to the LA Council in 1925 at the early age of 29, and it would not be far from the truth to say that he dedicated his life to the

Lionel R. McColvin

Association. He was Honorary Secretary from 1934 to 1951, a title that no longer exists but that was akin to being Prime Minister of the Association. During these years McColvin established a rapport with Percy Welsford, the full-time paid Secretary of LA, a working relationship that was to be extremely fruitful for British librarianship.

The LA Council soon recognized that it possessed an outstanding person in McColvin, and in 1936 he was sent to the United States to study library administration on behalf of the Association. At that time most public library systems in Britain had been in existence for 50 or more years, and many could be described only as Augean stables more than ready for a cleanup. To draw attention to this state of affairs, the LA sent a number of senior librarians, including McColvin, on tours of Britain with the object of investigating libraries and making recommendations for improvements.

World War II put an end to thoughts of radical improvements in libraries. McColvin, who had served in the British Army during the latter part of World War I, was too old to be called for active service in the second conflict, but he could still look after LA affairs, and he remained in close touch with Percy Welsford. During the darkest days of the war, the LA asked McColvin to undertake a one-man survey of public libraries in Britain, and to its credit the Westminster City Council agreed to release the City Librarian for that assignment.

The result of McColvin's tours, undertaken in bombed wartime Britain, often in conditions fraught with discomfort and danger, was the publication in 1942 of his report *The Public Library System of Great Britain*. It soon became known as the McColvin Report and was immediately debated at great length both inside and outside the profession.

McColvin's investigations had convinced him that there were too many public library authorities in Britain and that the majority of these were too small to function efficiently, being without the financial resources necessary for effective service. His answer was to redraw the local government map of the country, creating fewer but larger authorities, and in this respect he was years ahead of his time. Reorganization of local government finally took place in London in 1965, with similar moves in England, Wales, and Scotland in 1974 and 1975. The result of these changes was a reduction in the number of public library authorities from over 500, as there were in McColvin's day, to 170. In this way, McColvin's dream came true nearly 40 years after his report. Furthermore, the new local government boundaries bore some striking resemblances to McColvin's suggestions in 1942.

After World War II McColvin became a great library traveler, performing missions for Unesco, the British Council, and other agencies. He visited Australia, New Zealand, the Middle East, the U.S., Germany, Turkey, Scandinavia, and elsewhere. With Bengt Hjelmqvist he founded the Anglo-Scandanavian Public Library Conference, held triennially from 1958. He attended IFLA General Council meetings and in 1953 was elected Chairman of its Public Libraries Section. Alone and unaided, he drafted standards for public library service, which were printed in *Libri* in 1958; these formed the basis for the IFLA

Standards for Public Libraries, which were published in 1973.

Meanwhile, back in Britain, he still continued to serve on the LA Council, on the Executive Committee of the National Central Library, and on the British Council Advisory Panel on Libraries. A great advocate of the principle of free access to public libraries, he successfully campaigned against library charges as a member of the Roberts Committee. He was elected President of the LA in 1952 and became an Honorary Fellow in 1961.

McColvin wrote 20 books, the first being *Music in Public Libraries* in 1924. This was followed by works on book selection, assistance to readers, children's libraries, and other topics. Among his best works were *Music Libraries* (with Harold Reeves, 1937–38), *The Personal Library* (1953), and *The Chance to Read* (1956). In addition to his books he was a prolific contributor to conferences and to professional journals.

Festschrift. In 1971 the LA published a Festschrift for McColvin entitled *Libraries for the People,* edited by his former Deputy at Westminster, R. F. Vollans, and including contributions from a formidable array of international librarians such as Louis Shores, Helle Kannila, Bengt Hjelmqvist, E. Allerslev Jensen, and Anders Andreassen. It was a tribute that McColvin richly deserved.

REFERENCE
Robert L. Collison, "Lionel Roy McColvin: A Bibliography of His Writings," in *Libraries for the People: International Studies in Librarianship in Honour of Lionel R. McColvin* (1968).

K. C. HARRISON

MacLeish, Archibald
(1892–1982)

Writer and poet Archibald MacLeish was the first well-known figure from outside the library profession to be nominated and confirmed as Librarian of Congress. The controversy surrounding his nomination, especially the bitter opposition of the American Library Association, has obscured his achievements from 1939 to 1944 as Librarian of Congress and his unique role as an eloquent spokesman on behalf of libraries and librarianship. MacLeish's chief administrative accomplishments were a thorough reorganization, development of the first explicit statements of the institution's objectives (the "Canons of Selection" and a statement of reference and research objectives), and a concern for procedures and morale that brought the administration and the staff of the Library of Congress into accord for the first time in many years. Furthermore, he permanently enlarged the role of the Library of Congress as a repository of the American intellectual and cultural tradition. His contribution to the profession centered on his frequently expressed belief that librarians must play an active role in American life, particularly in educating the American public to the value of the democratic experience.

MacLeish entered public life for the first time at the age of 47 when, on July 10, 1939, the local postmaster in Conway, Massachusetts, administered his oath of office as Librarian of Congress. He was already a man of several successful careers. Born in Glencoe, Illinois, on May 7, 1892, he attended Hotchkiss preparatory school in Connecticut before entering Yale in 1911. A star athlete at Yale, he also was elected to Phi Beta Kappa. After entering Harvard Law School, he served in the U.S. Army in France during World War I, then returned to Harvard, where he was an editor of the *Harvard Law Review* before graduating in 1919. He gave up law practice with a prominent Boston firm in 1923 for Paris, where he established close ties with the American writers living on the Left Bank and published several collections of verse. He returned to the United States in 1929, joining Henry Luce's new *Fortune* magazine, for which he wrote articles on political and cultural subjects for the next nine years. During that period he continued to write verse and drama, the subjects reflecting his liberal social and political views. Such opinions consolidated MacLeish's intellectual sympathy with the New Deal and contributed to his departure from the Luce organization. They also paved the road to his nomination as Librarian of Congress.

From the start President Franklin D. Roosevelt looked outside the profession for a successor to Librarian of Congress Herbert Putnam. In choosing MacLeish, Roosevelt followed the advice of his friend Felix Frankfurter, the Supreme Court justice, who informed him that "only a scholarly man of letters can make a great national library a general place of habitation for scholars." The nomination was announced at a press conference on June 6, 1939, at which Roosevelt proclaimed that the job of Librarian of Congress required not a professional librarian but "a gentleman and a scholar."

The American Library Association was shocked. Roosevelt had not only ignored its own candidate for the job, the ALA Executive Secretary, Carl H. Milam, but also ignored all offers of ALA assistance. Even worse, in the ALA view, his nominee had no library experience. At its annual meeting in San Francisco on June 18, the ALA adopted a resolution opposing the nomination because "the Congress and the American people should have as a Librarian . . . one who is not only a gentleman and a scholar but who is also the ablest Library administrator available." The ALA testified unsuccessfully against the nomination in the Senate hearings. On June 29, 1939, by a vote of 63 to 8, the Senate confirmed the President's choice, and MacLeish became the ninth Librarian of Congress.

When the new Librarian officially began work on October 2, the Library had a book collection of approximately 6,000,000 volumes, a staff of about 1,100, and, in fiscal year 1939, a direct appropriation of approximately $3,000,000.

The new Librarian immediately tackled the most pressing internal problems left behind by Putnam. He launched studies of the Library's cataloguing, acquisitions, personnel, and budget policies. The results were distressing, and MacLeish and his senior staff asked for a substantial increase in the Library's budget request to remedy the many problems. The request was for $4,200,000 and included 287 additional positions. The Appropriations Committee approved 130 of the new positions and encouraged the new Librarian to continue his "industrious and intelligent" beginning. In response to the Appropriations Committee's report and to carry on the investigations already

Library of Congress
Archibald MacLeish

begun, MacLeish appointed on April 10, 1940, a special Librarian's Committee to analyze the operations of the Library—especially its processing activities. The report of the Committee, headed by Carleton B. Joeckel of the University of Chicago Graduate Library School, served as a catalyst for MacLeish's reorganization—a functional restructuring that served as the basis of the Library's administrative structure for the next three decades.

While the administrative reorganization was probably MacLeish's single most significant achievement, it was only one of his accomplishments. He also enhanced the Library's reputation as a major cultural institution, not only because of his own prominence as a poet but also by inaugurating the first series of poetry readings. He brought many prominent writers and poets to the Library, including the war refugees Aléxis Saint-Léger Léger (who wrote under the name Saint-John Perse) and Thomas Mann. They also included the U.S. poet Allen Tate, who served both as Poetry Consultant and as the first Editor of the newly established *Quarterly Journal of Current Acquisitions*. Relationships between the Library and scholarly and literary communities were improved through a new program of resident fellowships for young scholars and the formation of the Fellows of the Library of Congress, a group of prominent writers and poets.

MacLeish, a wartime librarian, quickly became a leading spokesman for the cause of democracy. Speaking before the ALA on May 31, 1940, he asserted that librarians "must become active and not passive agents of the democratic process." People who had bitterly opposed his nomination a year earlier applauded vigorously, and relations between the Library of Congress and ALA were on the mend. At the annual conference of the Association in June 1942, ALA President Charles H. Brown introduced MacLeish as "a man of whom we librarians are very proud," and the Librarian received a thunderous ovation before delivering his address, "Towards an Intellectual Offensive."

MacLeish and Luther H. Evans, his Chief Assistant Librarian, inaugurated a staff *Information Bulletin* and created a staff advisory committee. In April 1942 MacLeish announced the formation of the Librarian's Council, composed of distinguished librarians, scholars, and book collectors who would make recommendations about collection development and reference service. Weekly meetings with department directors were started, and in 1943 the Library administration began holding informal monthly meetings with the professional staff.

During the war MacLeish helped Roosevelt in many ways. Those activities meant that he served only part-time as Librarian of Congress, which makes the many achievements of his administration especially remarkable. In October 1941 the President directed him to assume, in addition to his duties as Librarian, supervision of the government's newly established Office of Facts and Figures. The appointment was controversial, both because of the publications produced by the new office and because the Librarian's additional duties often kept him away from the Library. In June 1942 the Office of Facts and Figures was combined with other agencies to form the Office of War Information, which MacLeish

served part-time as an Assistant Director. The Librarian also drafted speeches for the President and represented the government at various meetings, as in March 1944 when he went to London as a delegate to the Conference of Allied Ministers of Education, a forerunner of the United Nations. MacLeish apparently indicated a wish to leave the Library of Congress as early as the summer of 1943, but he stayed in office until December 19, 1944, when he resigned to become an Assistant Secretary of State, in charge of public and cultural relations.

MacLeish's relatively brief administration was one of the most fruitful in the history of the Library of Congress. The accomplishments were not his alone; in fact, as he was the first to acknowledge, his colleagues Luther H. Evans, Verner Clapp, and David C. Mearns played major roles. The style, tone, and motivation, however, came directly from the Librarian. He provided the Library of Congress and the library profession with inspiration and a badly needed sense of perspective. His succinct statement of the purpose of the Library in the first issue of the *Quarterly Journal of Current Acquisitions* (1943), for example, stands today as both a summary and a challenge: "The first duty of the Library of Congress is to serve the Congress and the officers and agencies of government. Its second duty is to serve the world of scholarship and letters. Through both it endeavors to serve the American people to whom it belongs and for whom it exists."

MacLeish died in Boston on April 20, 1982.

REFERENCES
Nancy L. Benco, "Archibald MacLeish: The Poet as Librarian," *Quarterly Journal of the Library of Congress* (1976).
Edward J. Mullaly, *Archibald MacLeish: A Checklist* (1973) contains lists of works by and about MacLeish.
Dennis Thomison, "F. D. R., the ALA, and Mr. MacLeish: The Selection of the Librarian of Congress, 1939," *Library Quarterly* (1972).

JOHN Y. COLE

Madagascar

Madagascar (Madagasikara), an island republic, lies in the Indian Ocean off the southeastern coast of Africa. Population (1984 est.) 9,642,000; area 587,051 sq.km. The official languages are Malagasy and French.

History. Madagascar's indigenous culture is essentially Indonesian, with Arabic and Islamic contributions. The London Missionary Society introduced printing in the 1820s, and the Merina dialect, in the Roman alphabet, became the official language. There is a rich written literature in the Malagasy language, which is of the Malyo-Polynesian stock, with borrowings from Bantu and Arabic as well as French and English.

Manuscripts in Arabic script have been preserved by the peoples of the southeast. The main libraries and other cultural institutions are in the capital of Tananarive (Antananarivo), where they reflect the influence of the French (Madagascar was a French colony, 1896–1945, and a member of the French Union 1946–58.)

National Library. The National Library, instituted in 1961 following the country's independence in 1960, inherited the collection of 80,000 volumes from the Library of the former General Government, created in Tananarive in 1920. The Library received its works thanks to legal trust while acting as a public library for the capital as well as a documentation center for research. From 1961 to 1973 the National Library, while fulfilling its former roles, served as national center for the promotion of books and reading and libraries. The extension of these activities led to the creation of the National Library Service in 1973. The Library Service consists of a division for the promotion of books and reading whose main role is promoting the art of writing, the rights of authors, publishing, and the pleasure of reading. It also publishes the national bibliography. The National Library is the other element; it has a collection of 170,000 printed books, manuscripts, periodicals, photos, and maps. It continues to receive printed works thanks to the legal trust; it assures the conservation of national patrimony; and it plays an important role as a public and research library because of its extensive collection on Madagascar. A new building for the service was inaugurated in 1982.

University Library. The University of Madagascar in Tananarive has a Library that specializes in the disciplines of the University. It was created in 1960 and has a collection of 180,000 works. Following decentralization of the University, five regional centers were attached to it, the oldest being the Toliara Center.

Public and School Libraries. A program to promote public libraries in the Fivondronana (subregional constituencies grouping several former communes) was launched in 1978 and was to proceed gradually over several years. It consists of stimulating the former municipal libraries and former information centers and creating new libraries: 57 small units operated in 1984. The Library Service ensures the technical training of personnel.

Furthermore, about 300 units of small libraries operate through the country. They are school libraries supported by funds from school cooperatives or private funds, or firm and association libraries. Their collections vary: most range between 1,000 and 6,000 volumes.

Special Libraries. The Malagasy Academy Library in Tananarive, created in 1905, is a specialized library in language, literature, art, social and political sciences, and fundamental and applied sciences. It had a collection of 33,000 works in the mid-1980s and received 30 periodicals. It also exchanges materials with other library systems.

Research institutions, such as the National Center of Oceanographic Research, the National Center of Pharmacological Research, and the National Center of Applied Research in Rural Development, offer studies, reports, and results of research concerning the country.

Government ministries and departments, such as Education, Agriculture, Information, Health, Justice, Industry, Economy, Telecommunication, Public Works, Development Planning, and Defense also have special libraries; most consist of 2,000 to 7,000 volumes.

The Profession. The Malagasy Books Office in Tananarive, an association created in 1971 by a few librarians, publishes and diffuses works tending to develop the pleasure of reading, promotes a book policy on a national scale, and serves as a center of information concerning books and as a resource for writers.

The Association of Archivists, Librarians, Documentalists, and Musicologists was formed in September 1976.

JULIETTE RATSIMANDRAVA

Malawi

Malawi, a republic in southeastern Africa, is bordered by Tanzania on the north, Mozambique on the east and south, and Zambia on the west. Population (1984 est.) 6,800,000; area 118,577 sq.km. The official language is English; Chichewa is the lingua franca.

History. Although some rock paintings are known to exist and to have been used in the early years of human settlement, the Maravi peoples have always communicated among themselves; the communication has been passed on from one generation to the next through oral literature.

Books were introduced into Malawi by the missionaries who, as they established their mission stations in the 1860s, also introduced printing and publishing to promote literacy and enhance the spread of the Gospel. The first mission library was created in 1890 at the Free Church Mission station in Bandawe, followed by that of the Universities' Mission to Central Africa at Likoma. A government library is known to have existed in 1890 but a public library was not established until 1950.

The main landmark in Malawi's library history was the opening of the University of Malawi in 1964. The University Library immediately became the largest library in the country and the first to be organized

---

Libraries in Madagascar (1981)

Type	Administrative units	Service points	Volumes in collections	Annual expenditures (franc)	Population served	Professional staff	Total staff
National[a]	1	--	157,000	12,116,000	--	2	66
Academic	2	6	174,000	85,530,000	14,086	3	127
Public[a]	28	28	--	7,460,000[b]	68,515	--	50
School	3	5	19,000	600,000	2,349	--	29

[a]1980 data.
[b]Acquisitions only.

Source: Unesco, *Statistical Yearbook*, 1984.

The National Library Service of Malawi

Headquarters of the Malawi National Library Service in Lilongwe, established by an act of Parliament in 1967.

along professional lines, under Wilfred Plumbe, its first Librarian. The Malawi National Library Service followed in 1968. Malawi enjoys excellent library cooperation, made possible by a good road network and an inexpensive internal book postal rate.

National Library Services. The country has no designated National Library, but the functions of a national library are performed by the National Archives of Malawi, which is the country's only legal deposit library and contains the most comprehensive collection of Malawiana in existence. It publishes an annual cumulation, *Malawi National Bibliography*.

University Library. The University of Malawi Library System is a federation of four college libraries scattered in three of the country's largest cities: Bunda College of Agriculture Library, Chancellor College Library, Kamuzu College of Nursing Library, and the Polytechnic Library. The bookstock of the Libraries has grown steadily since the mid-1960s. By 1984 the total bookstock including periodical titles stood at 241,483. Membership of the Libraries includes the staff and students of the University of Malawi, but outside borrowers are permitted upon payment of a token fee.

Public Libraries. The National Library Service was created by an act of Parliament in 1967 to operate free library services throughout Malawi. It has a main library in Lilongwe, the capital, regional Libraries and branches in the regions, and a network of library centers in such institutions as schools, prisons, community centers, and other organizations. For borrowers in far-off places and homes, it operates a nationwide postal service. In 1984 the National Library Service issued 481,500 books to readers from 253 centers.

Other public libraries include those operated by foreign governments or organizations, such as the British Council, the United States Information

Agency, and the French Cultural Center. All of these have highly regarded book collections but they are also popular for their collections of sound recordings and other nonprint media.

School Libraries. Malawi has a network of school libraries in the secondary schools, technical colleges, and teacher training colleges in all three regions of the country. The largest school library is that of the Malawi Institute of Education at Domasi.

Special Libraries. These encompass a whole range of information units in the private and public sector. Government departments, statutory organizations, and private firms operate libraries of varied strengths in book and human resources. The Central Agricultural Library and the Natural Resources College Library remain Malawi's best-known special libraries.

The Profession. The Malawi Library Association was inaugurated on April 30, 1977. From 1979 it organized Malawi Library Assistant Certificate Courses every year to train library paraprofessionals. Short seminars and workshops are also held from time to time. All of the 30 professional librarians (in 1985) were trained abroad, mainly in the United Kingdom and United States. The Malawi Library Association publishes the *MALA Bulletin*.

STEVE S. MWIYERIWA

Malaysia

Malaysia, an independent federation of 13 states in Southeast Asia, comprises two distinct land areas— Peninsular Malaysia and the states of Sabah and Sarawak on the island of Borneo. Malaysia is a member of the Commonwealth. Population (1984 est.) 15,246,000; area 329,750 sq.km. Bahasa Malaysia, the Malay language, is the official language of the country.

History. Although monastic and temple collections and state archives existed in the Indianized empires of Southeast Asia, there is little evidence of their existence in the Malay states. The earliest libraries in Malaysia were subscription libraries established by the British in the 19th and early 20th centuries to serve the needs of the European community. The planned development of libraries in Malaysia only began in the late 1960s. In that early period, the Malaysian Library Association played a leading role by initiating and submitting to the Government a *Blueprint for Public Library Development in Malaysia* (1968) which provided a plan for the development of public libraries and outlined the role of the National Library.

Libraries in Malawi (1982)

Type	Administrative units	Service points	Volumes in collections	Annual expenditures (kwacha)	Population served	Professional staff	Total staff
National	1	1	31,000	7,000	--	2	4
Academic	4	4	182,000	400,000	3,500	22	97
Public	6	259	130,000	410,141	9,922	17	--
School	59	59	--	--	9,915	--	--
Special	13	13	--	--	--	7	--

National Library. The National Library, established under provisions of the National Library Act of 1972, formed part of the Federal Department of Archives and National Library until 1977, when it was separated from the Archives and established as a Federal Department. The primary objectives of the National Library include the collection, documentation, and preservation of library materials relating to Malaysia and its people; the provision of facilities for the use of library materials; the promotion of public library development; and the coordination of the development and use of the library resources of the nation. Since 1982 The National Library has been placed under the purview of the Ministry of Culture, Youth, and Sport, and it provided mainly bibliographic, reference, and lending services. Also provided were training and conservation facilities, as well as a consultancy service.

With a collection of 380,000 volumes by 1984, acquired through purchase, exchange, donation, and legal deposit, it ranks as one of the country's major libraries. It publishes the *Bibliografi Negara Malaysia* ("Malaysian National Bibliography") issued quarterly from 1967 with annual cumulations; *Indeks Suratkhabar Malaysia* ("Malaysian Newspaper Index") from 1969 (twice yearly); and *Indeks Persidangan Malaysia* ("Malaysian Conference Index") from 1984 (annual).

Public Libraries. The National Library plays a leading role in the development of public libraries within the country. Public library services in Peninsular Malaysia, in accordance with *Blueprint* recommendations, are provided by State Public Library Corporations established under state laws. These Corporations function in all the Peninsular states. The National Library and the Malaysian Library Association are represented on these Corporations. In Sabah, public library services are constituted as a Department of the State Government, and in Sarawak they are provided by state and local government authorities. While the federal government provides funds through the National Library for public library development in Peninsular Malaysia, all recurrent expenditures are met by state governments. In Sabah and Sarawak, however, both capital development and recurrent expenditures are met by the state governments. Although public library services are now provided in all states, services are largely urban-oriented

National Library of Malaysia

Universiti Pertanian Malaysia Library, founded in 1971.

but are being actively extended to the rural areas. However, the use of public library services was still minimal in the mid-1980s, only 11 percent of the literate population being regularly served as members of the public library system. In 1983 approximately 4,500,000 books were borrowed through the country's public libraries.

Academic Libraries. Academic libraries comprise the libraries within the country's seven universities, technical colleges, colleges of further education, and teacher training colleges. Particularly outstanding are some of the university libraries. These include the University of Malaya (established 1959), Universiti Sains Malaysia (1969), Universiti Kebangsaan Malaysia (1970), Universiti Pertanian Malaysia (1971), and Universiti Teknoloji Malaysia (1972). Two newer universities are the Universiti Utara Malaysia (1984) and the International Islamic University (1983), which is co-sponsored by a number of countries. On the whole, university libraries are better funded and staffed than other libraries in the country. University library collections vary considerably in size and ranged in the mid-1980s from 730,000 volumes in the University of Malaya, 361,600 in Universiti Sains Malaysia, and 312,100 in Universiti Kebangsaan Malaysia, to 184,400 in Universiti Pertanian Malaysia and 116,400 in Universiti Teknoloji Malaysia. The collections in the two newer universities are still relatively small. Of the technical colleges, the more outstanding were the Mara Institute of Technology with 191,500 volumes and the

Libraries in Malaysia (1982)

Type	Administrative units	Service points	Volumes in collections	Annual expenditures (Malaysian dollar)	Population served	Professional staff	Total staff
National	1	3	333,962	5,102,400	607,407[a]	76	239
Academic	45	--	2,786,143	--	54,548	270	1,316
Public	58	642[b]	2,164,479	11,906,540	6,259,685[a]	83	843
School[c]	14	6,862[d]	12,336,000[e] 7,399,000[f]	6,500,000	3,392,539	156	7,202
Special	165	--	1,275,458	--	--	180	810

[a]Literate population.
[b]42 branch, 30 mobile, 570 mobile stops.
[c]1983 data.
[d]Schools.
[e]In primary schools.
[f]In secondary schools.

Tungku Abdul Rahman College with 87,000 volumes. The 16 teacher training college libraries vary in size, with collections ranging from 15,000 to 21,000 volumes.

Cooperation betwen the university libraries and the National Library is well established. The National Library and most of the university libraries are active participants in the MALMARC (Malaysian MARC) System with Universiti Sains Malaysia functioning as coordinating center. The MALMARC database contains more than 200,000 records, and the system generates institutional catalogues (in COM) and accession lists as well as the union catalogue. A serials database called PERPUNET with wider institutional participation is also maintained. Online access to national databases was planned following the introduction of a public data network by the Telecommunications Department at the end of 1984. University libraries and the National Library are also linked by telex.

School Libraries. There are over 6,000 schools in Malaysia, many with their own libraries. School library collections on the whole are relatively small and do not exceed 3,000 volumes. Malaysian school libraries are managed by teacher–librarians who have basic educational qualifications with some library training. School libraries receive an annual grant based on student enrollment; they also charge library fees. Overall supervision of school libraries is provided through school library organizers, many with both teaching and library qualifications, who are attached to State Departments of Education. National coordination and supervision is provided by the School Library Unit within the Schools Division of the Ministry of Education. In 1979 the Malaysian Library Association submitted to the government its *Blueprint for School Library Development in Malaysia*. The major recommendations of the *Blueprint* began to be progressively implemented thereafter.

Special Libraries. Special libraries represent one of the fastest-growing library sectors in the country. There were nearly 165 special libraries in the mid-1980s, although many are relatively small. About 65 percent of special libraries have collections of fewer than 5,000 volumes. The largest special libraries are found in the research institutes. They include the Rubber Research Institute (97,000 volumes), the Forest Research Institute (60,000), the Malaysian Agricultural Research and Development Institute (40,000), and the Institute for Medical Research (20,000). Other large special libraries include the Ministry of Agriculture (80,000), the Dewan Bahasa dan Pustaka (58,000), the Bank Negara Malaysia (26,000), the Asian and Pacific Development Center (25,000), and the National Institute of Public Administration (16,000). Special libraries are largely staffed by professionally qualified librarians. Special librarians in government libraries serve in a Common User Library Service under the purview of the National Library.

The Profession. The Malaysian Library Association, established in 1955 as the Malayan Library Group, is the only association for professional librarians in the country. Professional education for librarians is provided by the School of Library and Information Studies, Mara Institute of Technology.

REFERENCES

Hedwig Anuar, *Blueprint for Public Library Development in Malaysia* (1968).

Access to information: Proceedings of the Fifth Congress of Southeast Asian Librarians, Kuala Lumpur, 25–29 May, 1981, edited by D. E. K. Wijasuriya, Yip Seong Chun, and Syed Salim Agha (1982).

Lim Huck Tee, *Libraries in West Malaysia and Singapore: a Short History* (1970).

D. E. K. Wijasuriya and others, *The Barefoot Librarian: Library Developments in Southeast Asia with Special Reference to Malaysia* (1975).

B. A. J. Winslade, *Rancangan pembangunan perpustakaan sekolah di Malaysia; Blueprint for school library development in Malaysia* (1979).

D. E. K. WIJASURIYA

Malclès, Louise-Noëlle
(1899–1977)

The career of Louise-Noëlle Malclès as a bibliographer embraced the three elements of practicing, teaching, and writing. They did not, however, fall into separate or even overlapping periods of her life, but were for the most part carried on simultaneously in Paris. There is no doubt that Malclès stands as one of the most distinguished practitioners and teachers of bibliography in 20th-century Europe.

Born in the south of France on September 20, 1899, she was the daughter of a professor of physics at the Faculty of Sciences of the University of Clermont-Ferrand, where she later received her university training. Her long association with the library of the Sorbonne (now designated one of the Inter-University Libraries in the Réunion des Bibliothèques Universitaires de Paris, reflecting the restructuring of the old University of Paris) began in 1928 and lasted until 1962. Working first under the Hispanist Louis Barrau-Dihigo and later Germain Calmette, Malclès established the Salle de Bibliographie (Bibliography Room) and presided over its collections and services to students, faculty, and scholars for many years. Separate from the main reading room of the Sorbonne Library and not a main reference/reading room as found in American university libraries, this room, accommodating perhaps 20 readers, contains a carefully selected but wide-ranging group of bibliographical tools (such as bibliographies, published library catalogues, guides to the literature, and periodical indexes) both of general nature and of individual disciplines, which Malclès and her small staff used in helping a generation of persons doing research. This high-level service was geared primarily to bibliographical and documentation needs rather than to general reference questions, although the distinction often blurred in the interest of providing help. Here, too, in the 1950s—as time permitted—Malclès did some of the work on the successive volumes of *Les Sources du travail bibliographique*.

In the 1930s she spent time in Germany (Leipzig and Berlin) studying German national bibliography and union catalogues. In the 1950s she visited a number of European cities (Rome, Lisbon, Madrid, Brussels, Amsterdam, and The Hague) prior to preparing the reports on bibliographical activities for Unesco.

Attached to the Direction des Bibliothèques de France in the last years of her professional career, she had responsibility for special projects for strengthening bibliographical collections and services in French scholarly libraries. She retired in 1969 with the rank of *conservateur en chef* and returned to the south of France, spending some years in Avignon, where she died on March 27, 1977.

Her most important contribution to the field of bibliography is the monumental *Les Sources du travail bibliographique (Sources for Bibliographical Work)*, published in Geneva by Droz from 1950 to 1958. This work is not a guide to reference materials in the usual sense, but rather to all works useful in bibliographical work: bibliographies themselves, library catalogues, indexing and abstracting services, historical sets, descriptions of library resources, journals carrying reviews, and so on. Published in four physical volumes, the work consists of two parts: general bibliographies and specialized bibliographies, the latter in turn subdivided into *sciences humaines* (humanities and social sciences) and pure sciences, medicine and pharmacy. The conception, planning, style, and majority of the text remain the work of Malclès herself, although collaborators contributed some of the sections on the sciences and on countries outside of western Europe. Remarkable for clarity of exposition, precision of comments, and wealth of detail, the work nevertheless avoids the pitfall of becoming simply an elaboration of important titles. The user who still finds it helpful many years after its completion can only regret that this guide was followed by neither supplement nor later editions. It stands, however, as one of the most important syntheses of the bibliographical control achieved by the mid-20th century and assures Malclès of a permanent place in the history of the discipline to which she was so passionately devoted.

Another publication is closely related to *Les Sources:* the *Cours de bibliographie,* written primarily as a textbook for students preparing for careers in libraries and documentation centers. Published first by Droz in 1954 (before the completion of *Les Sources*), it later appeared under the title *Manuel de bibliographie.* Malclès herself prepared the first (1963) and second (1969) editions of the *Manuel;* revisions for the third (1976) and fourth (1985) were done by Andrée Lhéritier, to whom Malclès had entrusted the continuation of this work, confident that her former student and later colleague and friend would maintain her high standards for bibliographical work. The *Manuel* follows the arrangement of *Les Sources,* but has—as might be expected in a textbook—more limited coverage and greater emphasis on French titles.

In both *Les Sources* and the *Cours* Malclès had traced the history of bibliography, but full development of her ideas came several years later, when *La Bibliographie* appeared (1956) as volume 708 in the "Que sais-je" series. Three editions (1960, 1962, and 1977) followed, reaching a total of 32,000 copies sold and in print (a large number for a work in this field). There are translations into several languages.

Among Malclès' publications were two reports on *Bibliographical Services Throughout the World* (1951–52 and 1952–53), published on the recommendation of Unesco's International Advisory Committee on Bibliography. The first attempt to report on such activities in the member states of Unesco, the series was continued by others at five-year intervals.

Malclès's third, and probably least known, activ-

ity was her teaching, begun at the Sorbonne in 1933. There is no doubt that her abilities in the classroom soon led to recognition as *the* teacher of bibliography to a generation of French students. Her teaching career spanned more than three decades, most of it concurrent with her work at the Sorbonne; during that period she was also concerned with improving education for librarianship. When the École Supérieure des Bibliothèques was created in 1964 to provide higher level training, Malclès gave the first course on bibliography.

Malclès was named to the Legion d'honneur in France and was known beyond its borders (especially after the publication of *Les Sources*), but many feel that she never received the full recognition and appreciation she deserved.

REFERENCES

Richard K. Gardner, *Education for Librarianship in France: an Historical Survey* (Ph.D. dissertation, Case-Western Reserve University, 1968).

Andrée Lhéritier, "Necrologie. Louise-Noëlle Malclès (1899–1977)," *Bulletin des Bibliothèques de France* XXII (1977).

H. J. de Vleeschauwer, L'oeuvre bibiographique de L.–N. Malclès (1957).

WILLIAM VERNON JACKSON

Mali

The Republic of Mali, formerly the French Sudan, is bounded on the north by Mauritania and Algeria, on the east by Niger, on the south by Burkina Faso, the Ivory Coast, and Guinea, and on the west by Senegal. Population (1984 est.) 7,720,000; area 1,240,194 sq. km. The official language is French; more that 15 national languages are spoken, but only 5 of them are written languages.

History. Mali traces its origins to a great trading empire that flourished in West Africa (13th to 16th century). Timbuktu was a center of Islamic culture. As a French colony (French Sudan) from the 19th century, Mali was heavily influenced by French library practice. Librarians usually go to Senegal or France for their training.

National Library. Created in 1962, the Bibliothèque Nationale inherited the collection of a scientific institute created in 1944 as a branch of the Institut Fondamental d'Afrique Noire (IFAN). Its collection reached 15,000 volumes by 1985 and included many periodicals. As the depository of the national literary heritage, the Bibliothèque Nationale welcomes researchers, students, foreigners, and ordinary Malian readers. Between 1981 and 1984, 26,000 entries were recorded for users who consulted works in the library; home loan is also authorized.

Academic Libraries. There is no university in Mali, but higher education is available through advanced professional schools. The nature of the collections in the libraries of these institutions is determined by the type of training they offer. The largest of these is the library of the École Normale Supérieure (a school for training secondary school teachers created in 1962), which contains approximately 30,000 items. Other examples include the Library of the National School for Administration (created in

1966, approximately 6,000 volumes); the Library of the Rural Polytechnic Institute of Katibougou (created in 1966, about 2,000 items); the Library of the École des Hautes Études Pratiques (created in 1979, about 500 items); and the Library of the National School for Postal Service and Telecommunications (created in 1978, approximately 300 items). In addition, the library of the National School for Medicine and Pharmacy, created in 1968, contains about 3,000 items. There was a project in the mid-1980s to construct a library to hold 10,000 volumes. Other proposals included the construction of a central library for the National School for Engineers and a plan to create a library for an institute specializing in training and in applied research (Institut Supérieur de Formation et de Recherche Appliquée). All these libraries contain the theses and *mémoires* prepared by the students.

Public Libraries. For public library service there is an important network called l'Operation Lecture Publique (the Campaign for Public Reading). Between 1978 and 1983 this agency set up 46 libraries, each containing 1,200 volumes, including some works in the national languages and certain books in Arabic. These libraries, in the capitals of the administrative districts of the country, are open to young people and adults at all levels.

The Campaign for Public Reading also operates a railway-car library that serves nine communities between Bamako and the frontier of Senegal. In addition to this collection of 2,500 books for adults, there is a children's library containing 2,000 items; it serves as a practice library during the annual training program for librarians. In 1984 another railway service project for 92 *arrondissements* (two for each district) was launched.

In addition to publicly supported libraries, there are libraries and documentation centers in Bamako sponsored by the cultural centers of various foreign countries such as France, Libya, the Soviet Union, and the United States. The Catholic mission also has a public library in Bamako and sponsors many reading centers in the interior of the country.

School Libraries. There are 20 *lycees* (secondary schools) and 16 technical and vocational schools; each of these contains a library whose depth depends on the date of the creation of the school. Their collections range from a few hundred volumes to several thousand volumes. From 1984 the Campaign for Public Reading, which is a part of the Ministry of Sports, Arts, and Culture, was responsible for reorganizing all of the academic and school libraries administered by the Ministry of National Education. This responsibility includes the training of personnel and the purchase of books, periodicals, and furnishings.

Special Libraries. It is difficult to provide statistics on special libraries in both public and private agencies. Examples include scientific libraries in agencies that conduct research on topics such as rural economics (l'Institut d'Économie Rurale); the use of the Niger River (Office du Niger); mineral resources and mining (la Société Nationale de Recherche et d'Exploitation Minière); and the Sahelian environment (l'Institut du Sahel).Other specialized libraries offer materials on the social sciences and humanities; these would include the Humanities Institute, the

Ahmed Baba Study and Research Center, the National Institute for Pedagogy, and the National Museum.

There are also a large number of private family libraries.

The Profession. The Association Malienne des Bibliothécaires, Archivistes et Documentalistes (AMBAD, the Malian Association of Librarians, Archivists and Documentalists) was created in 1978.

AL HADY KOITA;
Translated by MARY NILES MAACK

Malta

The Republic of Malta, comprising the islands of Malta, Gozo, and Comino, lies in the middle of the Mediterranean Sea, about 90 km. southwest of Sicily. Population (1984 est.) 332,000; area 316 sq.km. Official languages are Maltese and English.

History. Scattered references point to the existence, from the 16th century onward, of modest collections of books in the houses of the various religious orders in Malta. In 1649 the Council of the Order of St. John, the Knights Hospitallers who ruled over Malta from 1530 to 1798, agreed to set up a library in the Conventual Church of St. John with the books recovered from the estates of deceased knights. In 1763 Fra Ludovico Guerin de Tencin, a Bailiff of the Order, donated his handsome collection of 9,700 volumes to the Order on the understanding that it should be merged with the smaller library of the Conventual Church to form a Bibliotheca Publica. He even nominated the learned Gozitan, Canon Agius de Soldanis, as the Librarian. The formal foundation of the Bibliotheca Publica was delayed until 1776, when the General Chapter of the Order also decreed the erection of a new edifice for the library. That fine building in the center of Valletta became the National Library of Malta.

National Library. The stock of the National Library of Malta (NLM) grew to around 360,000 volumes by 1985. The manuscript collections include more than 1,500 volumes; the archives of the Order of St. John from the 12th to the 18th centuries; and the records of the Municipality of Malta, known as the Universita dei Giurati from about 1450 to the early 19th century.

Among the printed books is the notable Melitensia collection, which comprises thousands of books, pamphlets, newspapers, periodicals, and other items from or about Malta. Besides 47 incunabula, the NLM has several rare editions and examples of fine and artistic bindings, as well as more modern publications. Up to 1974 the Royal Malta Library (that is, the National Library of Malta) was also Malta's only public library.

The NLM, together with the Gozo Public Library, enjoyed legal deposit from the mid-1920s, and published the first annual edition of the *Bibliografija Nazzjonali ta' Malta* ("Malta National Bibliography") in 1983.

Academic Libraries. The major academic library is that of the University of Malta, in Msida. Though the University of Malta was created in 1769, and was directly descended from the Jesuit College established in Valletta in 1592, it did not have much of an organized library until fairly recently. After World War II the University undertook the task of creating a modern undergraduate and research library, which by the mid-1980s had more than 250,000 volumes of books, pamphlets, and bound periodicals.

During the 1970s the two Teachers' Training Colleges were merged into one College of Education; it later became a Department of the Malta College of Arts, Science and Technology (MCAST). In 1978 MCAST became the New University and was subsequently merged with the University of Malta. The small libraries that belonged to those institutions now form part of the Library of the University of Malta.

The Faculty of Theology, which used to form part of the University, became an autonomous institution in 1978. The Faculty Library, at Rabat, Malta, specializes in theological and related fields of study.

Public Libraries. Early in the 1970s the Ministry of Education decided to set up a public library system separate from the Royal Malta Library, and in 1974 the Public Lending Library (PLL) was opened at Beltissebh, outside Valletta, with a substantial grant from the British Council for the purchase of new books. The new Public Library had an immediate impact on the general public and has been especially popular with children. During the first 10 years loans from the PLL exceeded 4,300,000.

In 1978 the same Ministry began to close down the small and little-used District Libraries, which had been set up in the 1930s, and to replace them by restocked part-time Branch Libraries attached to the schools in various towns and villages of Malta and Gozo. There were 50 of those branches by 1985. They cater mainly, but not exclusively, to children of school age.

The origins of the Gozo Public Library, which serves a population of about 23,000, go back to 1839, when a small group of Gozitans set up a *Gabinetto di Lettura* through gifts and subscriptions. In 1853 responsibility for the library was taken over by the state. In 1983 the lending function of the Gozo Public Library was moved to nearby premises, also in Rabat, or Victoria, the main town of the island of Gozo.

The National Library, the Public Lending Library, the Branch Libraries, and the Gozo Public Library fall under the Public Libraries Department of the Ministry of Education.

School Libraries. Simultaneously with the development of the Public Library service, the Ministry of Education undertook the provision of modern library facilities in the state schools. The New Lyceum (Sixth Form college), the technical institutes, the Junior Lyceums and other secondary schools, and the trade schools have basic reference collections as well as books for home reading. The school libraries are run on a part-time basis by teachers, while the Public Lending Library has a Schools Section that provides a centralized ordering, classification, and cataloguing service, supplies filmstrips, slides, and multi-media kits for school projects, and provides some basic library training and in-service courses for the teacher-librarians. The combined bookstock of the state school libraries exceeds 100,000. In the private schools sector, the standards of library provision vary from the adequate to the rather modest.

Special Libraries. When the Central Bank of Malta was established in 1968, immediate steps were taken to start a library and information service in its Research Department. The library specializes in economics, banking, and finance, and it includes a Trade Documentation Unit.

There are a few smaller specialized libraries: AirMalta maintains a technical library at its headquarters in Luqa; the General Workers' Union has a library in its Research Department; the Teachers' Institute Library has a wide selection of educational books; and the Social Action Movement Library specializes in books on trade unionism, cooperatives, and journalism, among other topics.

Religious libraries, which may be traced back to the 16th century, were given a new life in the 1960s. An old library of the Capuchins at Floriana was newly equipped in 1966. The Franciscan Friars Minor assembled the best books from their Maltese convents and opened a Provincial Library in 1972. In 1966 the Jesuit community started the John XXIII Memorial Library of contemporary theology, which became the headquarters of the Jesuit libraries as well as a center for cooperation among Malta's religious libraries. The Catholic Institute maintains a small library and lends books to the general public.

The Profession. Malta has its own small Ghaqda Bibljotekarji/Library Association (Valletta), which serves professional librarians, teacher-librarians, and other persons working in libraries. The

---

Libraries in Malta (1982)

Type	Administrative units	Service points	Volumes in collection	Annual expenditures (Maltese pound)	Population served	Professional staff	Total staff
National	1	2	390,000[a]	85,000[b]	--	2	26
Academic	2	2	270,000	150,000[b]	3,000	5	25
Public	2	44	210,000	115,000[b]	320,000	1	40
School[c]	1	56	88,000	15,000	24,000	1	56[d]
Special[e]	5	5	35,000	--	--	3	15

[a]Estimated. Includes reference collection of the Gozo Public Library, a depository library.
[b]Expenditure on salaries and books.
[c]Private schools excluded.
[d]Indicates teachers acting as part-time librarians.
[e]Data based on only five special libraries for which statistics are available.

Ghaqda Bibljotekarji has been a member of IFLA since its creation in 1969 and was a founder member of the Commonwealth Library Association (COMLA) in 1972. In the absence of a library school in Malta, the Association has tried to fill some of the void by organizing, from time to time, jointly with the University, subprofessional courses in basic library techniques.

REFERENCE
Paul Xuereb, "Maltese Libraries through the Ages," *The Year Book 1984* (Malta, De la Salle Brothers, 1985).
JOHN B. SULTANA

Mamiya, Fujio
(1890–1970)

National Diet Library
Fujio Mamiya

Fujio Mamiya made contributions to the Japanese library world that have much in common with some of Melvil Dewey's contributions to the American library world, and he has been called the Dewey of Japan.

Born on July 26, 1890, in Tokyo, Mamiya finished his higher primary school in 1902 and joined, as an apprentice, the Book Division of Maruzen Co., Ltd., the oldest and largest import trader of foreign books and stationery in Japan. Although his formal school education was short, he felt strongly the importance of reading as a method of self-education, and he was devoted to improvement of Japanese libraries in his later years.

In the days he worked for Maruzen, he came to the attention of a businessman in the typewriter trade who made possible a trip to the United States, a long-cherished desire. In 1915 he attended training classes of typewriter corporations in New York. He returned to Japan in 1916 and worked in the Kurosawa typewriter shop for five years.

In 1921 he left the Kurosawa shop and opened his own shop in Osaka, producing and selling library supplies. His shop developed successfully. In 1927 the League of Young Librarians, a research group for libraries, was organized under his leadership. The Japan Library Association had existed long before the League started, but the League emphasized "the standardization of norms and forms." From 1928 *Toshokan Kenkyu* ("Library Study") was published quarterly as a bulletin of the League and as the only research journal for libraries in Japan. It was forced to cease in 1943 by increasingly severe war limitations.

Mamiya made efforts to promote international standard size cards through his library supply business. In addition, he established at his office the Mamiya Library, consisting of about 3,000 volumes of foreign books on library science. Unfortunately, the Library was destroyed by fire during an air raid in May 1945 with the whole Mamiya shop . In 1950 Mamiya founded the Japan Library Bureau in Tokyo. The Japanese government recognized his long distinguished service for the Japanese library world with formal awards in 1961 and 1966. Another interest of his was the movement to promote romanization of the Japanese alphabet, to which he devoted efforts all his life. Mamiya died on October 24, 1970.
TOSHIO IWASARU

Mann, Margaret
(1873–1960)

A brilliant and imaginative teacher, Margaret Mann revolutionized instruction in cataloguing. In an obituary, the *Australian Library Journal* described her as "one of the most outstanding librarians of the twentieth century."

She was born April 9, 1873, in Cedar Rapids, Iowa. After graduating from Chicago's Englewood High School in 1893, she entered the Department of Library Economy at Armour Institute, Chicago, under the direction of Katharine Sharp. Armour was one of four library schools founded between 1887 and 1893 and the first in the Middle West. Entering students were at least 20 years of age and had to have a high school education; the entrance examination stressed a knowledge of authors and their works (in French, German, Latin, Greek, and English), some background in history, and a familiarity with current events. Students put in 40 hours a week during their year's study and were awarded certificates if successful. In addition to attending classes, they worked for various members of the library staff and gave some hours each week to the Institute.

Mann was one of 12 applicants (22 tried) to pass Armour's entrance examination. She finished the first-year course with superior grades and was employed as a cataloguer for the Institute's new 10,000-volume library. At the same time, she began a second year of study in the Armour Library School, and by 1896 she was teaching cataloguing at Armour and summer courses at the University of Wisconsin.

In September 1897 Armour moved to the University of Illinois (as the University of Illinois State Library School) with Katharine Sharp as Director of the School and Librarian of the University. Mann became an instructor; her course in the cataloguing and reference use of public documents was the first of its kind to be offered anywhere. She organized and supervised the Catalog Department in the university library and in 1900 was named Assistant Librarian.

In 1903 Mann became Head of the Cataloguing Department at the Carnegie Library of Pittsburgh, where she prepared for publication the Library's classified catalogue, a monument of its kind and a valued reference tool for many years. During her years in Pittsburgh, Mann taught cataloguing regularly in the Library's training school; offered courses at Western Reserve (Cleveland) and in Riverside, California; lectured; wrote; and began serving the American Library Association. She had become ALA member number 1,527 in 1896, when Katharine Sharp was a member of Council. In 1909 and 1910 she was Chairman of ALA's Catalog Section; from 1910 to 1913 she was a member of the Committee on Catalog Rules for Small Libraries; and she was elected to Council for the first of three five-year terms beginning in 1912. In 1914 she was appointed by the Executive Board to a Special Committee to Study Cost and Methods of Cataloging, in 1917 to the Decimal Classification Advisory Committee (for one year), and also in 1917 to the Catalog Rules Committee, where she served—except for one three-year lapse—until 1932. Her *List of Subject Headings for a Juvenile Catalog* was published by ALA in 1916.

In 1919 Harrison Craver, under whose directorship Mann had worked in Pittsburgh, employed her again in New York at the United Engineering Societies Library. From the separate catalogues and collections that had merged to form the Library, Mann created one collection arranged by a relatively brief Dewey number and a classified catalogue arranged by the Brussels (Universal Decimal) classification. During these years she was instrumental in organizing a system of regional cataloguing groups that became ALA's Council of Regional Groups. She was active on the Committee on Library Training from 1920 to 1924, was appointed to the Executive Board of ALA to fill a vacancy in 1921–22, and served on the Fiftieth Anniversary Committee in 1923–24.

In 1923 the ALA set up a library school in Paris as an outgrowth of reconstruction work with war-damaged libraries in France carried on by the American Committee for Devastated France. Sarah C. N. Bogle, Director of the École des Bibliothècaires and Mann's friend from the Pittsburgh days, asked Mann to teach in the Paris Library School in 1924. The School's international student body was taught in French and took courses for eight months, followed by a six-week summer course. Subjects were not taught in discrete parts, as in most American schools at the time, but in large groups. Mann's cataloguing course, for example, included work with the ALA and French cataloguing codes; Dewey Decimal, Brunet, Cutter, Library of Congress, and Universal Decimal classifications; shelflisting; and the making of dictionary and classified catalogues.

By the time Mann returned to the U.S. in 1926, William Warner Bishop had formed a new library school at the University of Michigan, Ann Arbor. They had met at Armour, where he was an instructor. Years later they served together on ALA Council and on the Catalog Rules Committee, where Bishop found Mann an ally against the proponents of constant change in the code. In 1923, when he left the chairmanship of the Committee (then called the Committee on Cataloging), she was appointed in his place.

Bishop's concern to find capable instructors for the school led him to Mann. By 1926 she was internationally recognized both as cataloguer and as teacher of cataloguing. Reporting to Michigan's President on Mann's qualifications, Bishop wrote: "Without exception every one in the country says that Miss Margaret Mann, now teaching cataloguing and classification . . . in Paris, . . . is the best teacher of these subjects to be found anywhere. In this opinion I heartily concur. There are certain obstacles to her appointment . . . chief of which is the fact that she has had no college work whatever. . . . Personally, I think the University of Michigan is big enough to employ the best teachers irrespective of their academic preparation. . . . Despite her lack of academic study, she is one of the best-read people I have ever met in my life." Later she was offered one of three full-time positions in the new school.

Inasmuch as Mann's fame rests chiefly on her excellence as a teacher of cataloguing, her views on the subject and methods of communicating it are worthy of attention. The organization of her Paris course does not seem unusual today until it is contrasted with other styles of teaching cataloguing. The three schools that followed Dewey's at Albany—Pratt,

Drexel, and Armour— were connected with circulating public libraries. While they could not offer students the resources of a large academic library, they could offer actual practice in library routines. Following the first plan of Dewey's school, they emphasized technique almost to the exclusion of principle. In contrast to an emphasis on activities she felt were largely clerical in nature, Mann insisted that cataloguers needed to develop critical judgment and executive ability; "emphasis on technical details," she wrote, "will never make a good cataloger." She saw the library catalogue as a service instrument for library staff and users and attempted to teach every facet of the subject in its relation to the needs of users.

In 1926 the Board of Education for Librarianship asked Mann to write the cataloguing volume in a series of seven basic textbooks sponsored by ALA and funded by the Carnegie Corporation. *Introduction to Cataloguing and the Classification of Books* was published in mimeograph form by ALA in 1928 and in bound form in 1930; a second edition came out in 1943. Regarded as a classic in its own time, it won an influence that still continues.

Mann's book followed the organization of her course. She felt cataloguing training should begin with a study of books, since students would have some familiarity with them while they lacked techniques of librarianship. Next she covered subject approach, and students learned classification and the use of subject headings. These topics were followed by cataloguing and then by subjects related to the administration of a catalogue department. Although Mann believed in laboratory practice for students, she felt card sets should be made by typists. Apparently, she was one of the first library school instructors to use audiovisuals as an aid to the teaching of cataloguing when she used a reflectoscope to display title pages on a screen.

When Bishop was immersed in problems of cataloguing the Vatican Library in the late 1920s, Mann served as an adviser on cataloguing and trained several cataloguers sent to Michigan from the Vatican. She surveyed cataloguing and classification conditions at the library of Teachers College, Columbia University; this survey led to a revision of its catalogue.

The ALA Executive Board in 1931 appointed her to a committee to study the possibilities for cooperative cataloguing among research libraries; the project begun as a result of this work was funded by the General Education Board. In 1932 she shared in a Carnegie Corporation grant and spent her sabbatical year studying library education in Europe.

Mann retired from teaching in 1938 when she was 65, although she continued to be active on ALA's Catalog Code Revision Committee until 1942. In 1945 she moved to Chula Vista, California, where she died on August 22, 1960.

REFERENCE

Laurel A. Grotzinger, "Mann, Margaret," *Dictionary of American Library Biography* (1978).

CONSTANCE RINEHART

School of Library Science,
University of Michigan

Margaret Mann

Martel, Charles
(1860–1945)

Charles Martel, the chief architect of the Library of Congress classification, was born March 5, 1860, in Zürich, Switzerland. James Bennett Childs has stated that Martel's name was originally Karl David Hanke and that he was the son of Franz and Maria Gertrud Strässle Hanke. Franz Hanke was a publisher and antiquarian bookseller, and Martel credited his education to his association with the bookstore, but he also completed the Gymnasium course in 1876 and attended the University of Zürich in 1876–77. In 1876 Martel spent five months visiting the United States. He returned to the U.S. in either late 1879 or early 1880 and became a citizen in 1887 under the name of Charles Martel. From 1880 to 1892 he taught in schools in Missouri and Nebraska and was employed in a law office in Council Bluffs, Iowa.

Martel had served as a volunteer in various libraries, and he chose librarianship as a full-time career in February 1892 when he joined the staff of the Newberry Library in Chicago. Eight months later Librarian William Frederick Poole recommended an increase in salary "because of his very great ability and enthusiasm." Poole's further evaluation in a report in October 1892 would be confirmed by others: "a quiet, scholarly man, indefatigable, and working in season and out of season." Martel was involved in both cataloguing and classification and was in charge of the Department of Arts and Letters (1893–96) and of early printed books and manuscripts (1896–97).

While at the Newberry, Martel formed a lifelong friendship with his colleague J. C. M. Hanson. Within two months after Hanson's arrival to head the bibliographical reorganization of the Library of Congress consequent to its move from the Capitol, Librarian John Russell Young appointed Charles Martel as Assistant in the Catalogue Department, one of the two top-salaried positions, effective December 1, 1897. When Martel joined Hanson, the Library of Congress acquired "a team which has never been equaled anywhere," according to William Warner Bishop (*Library Quarterly,* January 1948).

Martel's analysis of the existing classification, his first assignment, was submitted to Young by the end of the month. Although it included an outline of a new scheme, it emphasized the notation, not the scheme itself. He described the new scheme merely as an eclectic one "combining the best features of those in use in other reference libraries." Moreover, the arrangement for class Z (Bibliography and Library Science) had been "modified so as to disturb as little as possible the existing order" of the collection. These emphases may have been made in deference to the Assistant Librarian, Ainsworth Rand Spofford, an articulate foe of close classification.

Hanson always rejected any credit for the classification, as he reminded Herbert Putnam:

> Aside from some preliminary planning of the notation, I am afraid that my claims to association in the construction of the Library of Congress classification are very slight. Soon after 1898 I was forced to give almost all my time to the cataloguing, leaving the details of the classification very largely to Mr. Martel (March 25, 1915; University of Chicago Library Archives).

Work on the reclassification began in January 1898 but was suspended when, after Young's death in January 1899, Herbert Putnam was appointed to succeed him. The project was not resumed until January 18, 1901, when the reclassification of U.S. history into classes E and F, prepared by Martel in 1898–1900, was undertaken with an enlarged staff. A number of subject specialists worked with Martel in developing the other schedules.

In 1901, beginning with classes D (Universal and Old World History) and Q (Science), and in subsequent classes, a second letter for the major subdivisions was introduced to permit "the beginning of operations simultaneously at various points in the system" (Report of the Librarian of Congress . . . June 30, 1902). In 1911 Martel introduced another notational modification in subdivisions needing provision for many names, by incorporating the initial letter in the number for the subdivision and assigning the Cutter author number from the second letter in the name.

The pressure to complete and publish the classification schedules was so great that a detailed description of the philosophical basis of the system could not be written for publication until 1911. Martel first wrote it as part of a larger paper, "Classification: A Brief Conspectus of Present Day Practice," read at a meeting of the New Zealand Library Association in April 1911. The part on the Library of Congress scheme was sent for reading at the Pasadena meeting of the American Library Association in May of the same year.

Martel also made a major contribution in descriptive cataloguing. For 28 years after he was appointed Chief of the Catalog Division in October 1912 (to succeed Charles H. Hastings, who had served during the interregnum following Hanson's resignation in October 1910), Martel guided Library of Congress cataloguing on a level generally accepted as authoritative. When he reached the statutory retirement age of 70 in 1930, he filled the specially created position of Consultant in Cataloging, Classification, and Bibliography. On June 30, 1932, President Herbert Hoover, on Putnam's recommendation, exempted Martel from the provisions of the Retirement Act by Executive Order, citing Martel's "irreplaceable knowledge of the collections of the Library of Congress and his rich bibliographical and technical expertise."

In 1928 William Warner Bishop asked Martel to head a commission of cataloguers to assist in the reorganization of the Vatican Library, a project supported by the Carnegie Endowment for International Peace. Martel at first refused, but he reconsidered when Hanson, who was next approached, refused to go without him. The cataloguing rules they worked out with the Monsignors Tisserant and Mercati constituted the original draft of the Vatican Library's *Norme per il catalogo degli stampati* ("Rules for the Catalog of Printed Books"), a major step in international library cooperation. Martel also assisted in the translation into Italian of the needed parts of the Library of Congress Classification. Martel retired on May 1, 1945, and died two weeks later, on May 15.

REFERENCES

James Bennett Childs, who investigated Martel's early life as part of a planned biography, included his sources in his biography of Martel in volume 17 (1976), *Encyclopedia of Library and Information Science,* and the *Dictionary of American Biography* (3rd Supplement). In addition he wrote an article (edited for publication by John Y. Cole) for the *Dictionary of American Library Biography* (1978).

Leo E. LaMontagne, *American Library Classification with Special Reference to the Library of Congress* (1961), pp. 234–51.

Edith Scott, "J. C. M. Hanson and His Contribution to Twentieth-Century Cataloging" (Ph.D. dissertation, University of Chicago, 1970), pp. 177–227, documents manuscript sources.

Harriet Wheeler Pierson, "Charles Martel," *Catalogers' and Classifiers' Yearbook* no. 9 (1941); frontispiece is a portrait of Martel, the original of which hangs in the Descriptive Cataloging Division of the Library of Congress.

James Bennett Childs and John T. Cole, "Martel, Charles," *Dictionary of American Library Biography* (1978).

EDITH SCOTT
(d. 1983)

Martin, Allie Beth
(1914–1976)

Allie Beth Martin was an outstanding educator, a skillful politician, a talented writer, a respected leader, and a dedicated librarian. She headed the Tulsa Public Library for 13 years, and under her leadership it became well known throughout the United States for innovative and forward-looking programs.

She was born in the small town of Annieville, Arkansas, on June 28, 1914, to Carleton Gayle Dent and Ethel McCaleb Dent. She attended public schools in Seattle, Washington, and Batesville, Arkansas. While attending Batesville's high school Martin lived with her grandfather, who had a primary influence on her life and the course it would later take. It has been said that she decided as a child that she wanted to become a librarian.

Following her graduation from high school in 1932, Martin enrolled at Arkansas College in Batesville, where she majored in foreign languages and English while working part-time in the college library. She graduated in 1935 with a B.A. and became the first Librarian of the Batesville Public Library. A year later she moved to Little Rock, where she was in charge of the junior college library. The following year she joined the Arkansas Library Commission as Assistant to the Executive Secretary. She married Ralph F. Martin, a journalist, on October 6, 1937, and later resigned from the Commission. In 1939 she received a B.S. in Library Science from George Peabody College for teachers in Nashville, Tennessee. She moved with her husband to Arkansas, when he entered medical school, and she served as Director of the Mississippi County Library in Osceola, Arkansas, and later, from 1942 to 1947, returned again to the staff of the Arkansas Library Commission. In 1945 she was elected President of the Arkansas Library Association, and she served as Editor of the *Arkansas Libraries* until 1947. During her husband's internship and residency in New York, she attended Columbia University School of Library Science and received her Master's degree in 1949.

In 1949 the Martins moved to Tulsa, Oklahoma, where Dr. Martin practiced medicine until his death in 1968. She joined the Tulsa Public Library and spent her first year serving in various departments. In 1950 she worked as a children's librarian, following that with the position of extension librarian, in which she served until 1961. Martin edited the *Oklahoma Librarian* in 1953 and 1954 and was elected President of the Oklahoma Library Association in 1955. She was later honored by OLA with the Distinguished Service Award.

The condition of the Tulsa Public Library in the late 1950s was typical of many libraries of that time. The Central Library, built with Carnegie funds in 1916, was overcrowded and in a state of disrepair, as were the four branch libraries. Martin became actively involved in persuading the community of the need for new and improved facilities. A first bond issue failed, only to be overwhelmingly approved when presented the second time on November 14, 1961. The bond issue included $3,800,000 for construction of a new Central Library and building and renovation of 20 branch libraries and an annually recurring levy for the operation of the Tulsa City–County Library System. In 1963 Martin was named Director of the library system she was instrumental in creating.

Martin served as President of the Southwestern Library Association (1969–70) and led the regional association into an active leadership role in continuing education and cooperative projects.

A member of the American Library Association from 1935, she served in many capacities: on the executive boards of the Public Libraries and Children's Services Divisions, and as Chairperson of the ALA Membership Committee. *Strategy for Public Library Change: Proposed Public Library Goals* was published by ALA in 1972. She was elected to the ALA Council for the term 1972–1976 and to the Executive Board in 1973. She was inaugurated President of ALA in July 1975 at the San Francisco Conference. Three months later she underwent surgery for cancer. She continued with her work as President and as Library Director until her death in Tulsa on April 11, 1976.

Martin received many awards and honors during her lifetime and following her death; a regional library of the Tulsa System was named for her, as was a national library award and a lecture series.

Tulsa City—County Library
Allie Beth Martin

REFERENCE

Frances Kennedy, "Martin, Allie Beth," *Dictionary of American Library Biography* (1978).

PAT WOODRUM

Maunsell, Andrew
(d.1595)

Andrew Maunsell, a member of the London Drapers' Company, is remembered today almost entirely for his bibliographical work. As compiler of the first effective national bibliography on scientific principles, Maunsell is a figure of considerable importance.

Though not a member of the Stationers' Company, he obtained a license as early as 1578 to publish *The State of Swearinge and Swearers,* and thereafter until 1595 was active as a bookseller and publisher, particularly of theological works. At that time there was no general printed catalogue of English works, with the partial exception of the *Scriptorum illustrium majoris Britanniae . . . catalogus* of John Bale (Wesel, 1548; another edition Basel, 1557–59) In the *Catalogue of English Printed Books,* which occupied Maunsell in the last years of his life, he attempted the preparation of a true national bibliography, and in a form that presented many advances in bibliographical technique.

In *The First Part of the Catalogue of English printed Books: which concerneth such matters of Divinitie, as have bin either written in our owne Tongue, or translated out of anie other language,* published by Maunsell from his shop in Lothbury in 1595, he explained his purpose and method in the prefatory address to the Master of the Stationers' Company. He justified his work on the ground that it was as necessary for the bookseller to have such a catalogue "as the Apothecarie his *Dispensatorium,* or the Schoolemaster his *Dictionarie.*" In distinction to Bale and other earlier compilers, he pointed out that he was including only printed works and only works that he had personally examined, and he had arranged his entries so that books on the same subject were grouped together. Another advance was that alphabetical arrangement was by surnames, not forenames; anonymous works were listed by title and by subject. He took care to record translators, printers and publishers, date of publication, and format. Deliberate exclusions were noted: "The auncient Popish Books that have been Printed heere, I have also inserted among the rest, but the Bookes written by the fugitive Papistes, as also those that are written against the present government, I doe not thinke meete for me to meddle withall."

The First Part (which was arranged on the dictionary principle, with author, title, and subject entries in a single alphabet) was followed later in the same year by *The Second Part,* which listed works on "the Sciences Mathematicall, as Arithmetick, Geometrie, Astronomie, Astrologie, Musick, the Arte of Warre, and Navigation: And also, of Phisick and Surgerie" arranged on the same general principles. A third part was promised in the preface to this volume. It was to deal with "Humanitie," which Maunsell defined as "Grammer, Logick, Rethoricke, Lawe, Historie, Poetrie, Policie, &c. which will for the most parte concerne matters of Delight and Pleasure." However, since it was difficult to collect information, and "so tedious to digest into any good methode," Maunsell had thought it wise to publish the first two parts to test public reaction before completing his work. We must be grateful that he did so: though public reaction was favorable, Maunsell's death late in 1595 was to prevent the completion of his labors. His *Catalogue* was reprinted in 1962 as part of the Gregg/Archive Press series on English Bibliographical Sources.

RODERICK CAVE

Mauritania

Mauritania, an Islamic republic in West Africa, is bounded by Western (Spanish) Sahara on the northwest, Algeria on the north, Mali on the east and southeast, Senegal on the southwest, and the Atlantic Ocean on the west. Population (1984 est.) 1,823,000; area 1,030,700 sq.km. The official languages are Arabic and French.

The national library system in Mauritania was instituted by a law of July 10, 1962, which foresaw, in particular, the establishment of an integrated system comprised of (1) a national conservation library of all works on or printed in Mauritania and the essentials of the written civilization; (2) public and school libraries; and (3) study libraries for the use of universities, institutes, laboratories, and others.

National Library. The National Library of Mauritania in Nouakchott, the capital, was created on January 27, 1965, by decree. It comprises a conservation library, a documentation center on Mauritania, and a study and research library. The country is weak in resources, and the National Library also provides school libraries and public reading programs. It is responsible for policies on the development of libraries and documentation throughout the country. Its collection totaled 10,000 volumes and 4,000 manuscripts in the mid-1980s. The manuscript department, which had 3,500 works in 1975, was attached in 1979 to the Mauritanian Institute of Scientific Research, which had nearly 2,500 others.

Academic Libraries. Until the 1980s there was no university in Mauritania, but many schools of higher learning existed with the status of university institutes. Each had its own library. They included a School of Education (created in 1970), which had a library with nearly 10,000 volumes; a national School of Administration (1966) with a library of approximately 12,000 volumes, and a School of Elementary Education Training (1965), which had a library of more than 8,000 volumes. In 1982 the École Nationale d'Administration and the École Nationale des Sciences in Nouakchott began offering degree courses, and in 1983 the nation's first university, the University of Nouakchott, opened.

Public Library Service. The department of public reading of the National Library provides public library services, as does the Bibliothèque Publique Centrale in Nouakchott. Other libraries open to the public were those of the cultural centers of several accredited embassies in Mauritania, including Egypt, France, Libya, Syria, and the U.S.S.R., among others.

School Libraries. There is a library in each secondary school for the use of its teachers and students, but they were underdeveloped as of the mid-1980s. The 26 school libraries contain a total of some 112,000 volumes.

Special Libraries. Several special libraries or documentation centers serve various government ministries or semiprivate organizations. Among examples are the documentation services of the National Society of Mine Imports (SNIM, which has a collection of close to 13,000 titles), the National Society of Rural Development (SONADER), the Administration of Studies and Programming of the Ministry in Charge of Special Projects; and the the National Pedagogical Institute; the documentation division of the Administration of Mines and Geology; the documentation project of the Ministry of Rural Development; and the Mauritanian Institute of Scientific Research Library. There are Arab libraries at Chinguetti, Kaedi, and other towns.

The Profession. The Mauritanian section of the International Association for the Development of Libraries and Archives in Africa (AIDBA) formerly existed in the country. In May 1979 a new association was created. Continuing the work of the AIDBA and named the Mauritanian Association of Librarians, Archivists, and Documentalists (AMBAD), it established headquarters in Nouakchott; a Directory Committee included the Director of the National Library, who served as President.

OUMAR DIOUWARA*

Mauritius

Mauritius, a parliamentary state, lies east of the island of Madagascar in the Indian Ocean. It includes the island of Mauritius and the dependencies of Agalega, Cargados Carajos Shoals, and Rodrigues. Population (1984 est.) 1,823,000; area 2,040 sq.km. The official language is English.

History. Although Mauritius was colonized by the French in the early 18th century, there is no evidence of public libraries until British rule began in 1810. A subscription lending library started by the Mauritius Literary Association in the early 1800s was later opened to the public, and other public reading facilities followed. In the mid-1800s many government departments began developing libraries.

National Library. The Mauritius Institute Public Library and Museum is considered to be the national library of the island and is in the capital of Port-Louis. The library has a Natural History Museum attached to it; together they form the Mauritius Institute. The Library started in 1902 with a collection of about 7,000 books donated by the eminent lawyer Sir Virgil Naz. The Library is state-owned and has the right of legal deposit. It has a bookstock of about 52,000 volumes, lending and reference general sections, a particularly strong Mauritiana collection, and a research section on the natural sciences. The Mauritius Institute is also the depository library for Unesco publications.

Academic Libraries. The University of Mauritius, a developmental university started in 1968, has three schools: Agriculture and Sugar Technology, Industrial Technology, and Administration. The Library contains about 75,000 volumes. About 400 periodicals are acquired, and 350 are received on an exchange basis. The library of the Institute of Education started operations in 1975, though courses for the training of secondary school teachers started in 1977. The Library consists of 9,000 volumes and 60 periodicals. The Mauritius College of Education, formerly called the Teachers Training College, is concerned with the training of primary school teachers. Its Library has a bookstock of 27,000 volumes.

Public Libraries. Public library service is provided mainly in the urban areas. In Port-Louis it is provided by the Mauritius Institute and the Port-Louis city library. The latter, established in 1851, is the largest municipal library, with a bookstock of more than 80,000 volumes. There are four other municipal libraries in the district of Plaines Wilhems: the libraries of the municipalities of Beau-Bassin-Rose-Hill, Quatre-Bornes, Vacoas-Phoenix, and Curepipe.

The rural areas are not so well provided with public library service. A library in Mapou, in the north of the island, supported by the Pamplemousses-Riviere du Rempart District Council, has a bookstock of about 5,000 volumes; it is a rare example of public library service in the rural areas.

School Libraries. Among the approximately 250 government primary schools, about half have libraries, which began mainly through the efforts of parent-teacher associations. A book-box service is in operation in the schools that have no libraries, but among the many private secondary schools few have good libraries.

A Library Organizer, attached to the Ministry of Education and Cultural Affairs, is responsible for the government primary and secondary school libraries and for providing professional advice to the private school libraries. The Library Organizer also advises the Ministry generally on library matters.

Special Libraries. The Mauritius Sugar Industry Research Institute, at Reduit, promotes the technical progress and efficiency of the sugar industry in Mauritius. Its library has about 20,000 volumes. The Legislative Council Library limits its services to the members of the legislative assembly. The Supreme Court Library, which has a good collection of law books and law reports, is limited to the members of the legal profession.

There are libraries in some government departments, notably the Ministry of Agriculture, the Ministry of Economic Planning and Development, and the Ministry of Health. There are some libraries in foreign missions, the most important of which are the British Council library, situated in Rose-Hill, Le Centre d'Enseignement et de Documentation (the Library of the French embassy) in Port-Louis, and the Library of the Indian High Commission, also in Port-Louis.

Libraries for Children. Apart from the library services for children in schools, each of the five municipal libraries has a children's section. There is also a junior library in Rose-Hill run by the Ministry of Education and Cultural Affairs. The Bibliothèque Saint Joseph, which caters to children, is a Catholic Church enterprise that started in about 1968. Five parishes have children's libraries in the church precincts, open in the afternoons and run on a purely voluntary basis. A small fee is charged for the loan of books. These libraries are popular with children, and

Libraries in Mauritius (1982)

Type	Administrative units	Service points	Volumes in collections	Annual expenditures (rupee)	Population served[a]	Professional staff	Total staff
National	--	--	--	--	--	--	--
Academic	--	--	--	--	--	--	--
Public	--	--	--	--	--	--	--
School	26	26	112,000	650,000[b]	17,761	2	32

[a]Registered borrowers.
[b]Excludes expenditure for employees.

Source: Unesco, *Statistical Yearbook*, 1984.

the number of book loans is very high.

The Profession. The Mauritius Library Association, founded in 1974, numbers about 50 members of the library profession, including 15 librarians who have had their training in countries such as Australia, Canada, France, India, Jamaica, and the United Kingdom. Some members of the Mauritius Association of Booksellers are also members of the Mauritius Library Association.

S. JEAN-FRANCOIS*

Medical Libraries

PURPOSES, GOALS AND OBJECTIVES

Medical (health science) libraries form a distinct group, although they fall within the general heading of special libraries. The three main purposes of medical libraries are support of teaching (education), research, and patient care. Some libraries may be involved in all three areas, others in only one or two. Medical libraries are characterized by a high commitment to user service and have introduced many programs that have become commonly accepted in other types of libraries. Medical libraries have been in the vanguard of library automation since the late 1950s, and by the mid-1980s had become concerned with solving the problems associated with an ever-proliferating array of information files—bibliographic, text, patient and student records, and many others—by integrating them into a unified access system.

The scope of teaching that medical libraries are required to support increased enormously in the 1970s. With the greater emphasis on public health and the recognition of the impact of the environment on health, the main subjects that now fall within the scope of a medical library include almost every discipline. With an increased patient emphasis, including recovery and rehabilitation through bibliotherapy, music therapy, and art therapy, even some materials in the humanities and the arts may be collected. Medical ethics programs have become a standard part of many medical school curricula, creating a demand for humanistic studies materials in the library. As the requirements for continuing education of medical professionals in all health service areas have escalated, the demands on the library for support services and materials for such programs have also risen.

There are considerable differences of emphasis in medical libraries in developed and in developing countries. In developed countries, as the life expectancy of the population increases and as a larger percentage of the population is over the age of 40, there is a growing concern with the diseases of aging and degeneration. In developing countries the goal of much health care focuses on the pre- and post-natal period as well as on diseases related to climate and nutrition.

In the United States the 1980s have seen a shift to non-hospital-based care as a way to reduce the costs of medical care, and these shifts have led to increased needs for patients to obtain accurate and understandable medical information in a variety of settings. Medical libraries, which formerly were closed to the general public, are now making special efforts to acquire and make available health information at a nontechnical level. Many new alliances have been formed with public libraries to meet this information need, and medical librarians in larger libraries are helping to educate public librarians in this special subject area. In Illinois, for example, a number of programs for public librarians have been held, and there is a growing literature aimed at the public librarian produced by medical librarians. The concept of the patient as a consumer of health care services with recognized rights and obligations has been growing, and medical libraries have collected materials aimed at the consumer, in part to help inform the health practitioner of information available at a level that can best aid the patient.

The libraries that deal with research similarly serve a wide and varied user population, depending on their parent body. Libraries in such commercial institutions as pharmaceutical corporations may have narrowly defined roles that tie closely to specific research programs, whereas libraries supporting research in a university setting may have to provide for broad and usually heavily interdisciplinary research topics. Institutional research programs may be directed to some degree by the funds available for a given subject at a given time. For example, in the 1960s funding was available from U.S. government sources for a wide variety of research projects related to heart disease, cancer, and stroke; in the 1980s the government's research emphasis shifted to the problems of aging, and libraries are being called upon to support an increasing number of programs in gerontology and geriatrics.

Libraries primarily concerned with patient care are to be found in hospitals and such related institutions as chronic care centers, and it has been traditional to think of patient libraries as related more closely to public libraries, which may provide leisure reading for home- and hospital-bound users. In response to increasing emphasis and awareness of the problems of patient education and patient rights and responsibilities, however, the patient-care library has found a much broader and more important role. Moreover, many hospitals find it more economical to combine patient-care library services with those provided for the professional staff, although the two groups of users and the materials available to them are still kept separate.

The question of the funding of libraries in hospitals in the United States was undergoing careful scrutiny in the mid-1980s. As the government moved to reduce hospital costs by paying fees based on Diagnostic Related Group (DRG) charges, it was difficult to find a way to assign the costs of hospital libraries equitably. As a result, some hospitals moved to reduce the library services for their professional staffs.

Standards of the Joint Commission on Accreditation of Hospitals continue to follow the principle that a hospital shall provide library services to meet the informational, educational, and, when appropriate, research-related needs of the medical and hospital staffs. They call for a minimum of professional consultative services on a regular basis if the hospital is not able to employ a full- or part-time professional librarian; the qualifications for a professional specify that the librarian be graduated from a program accredited by the American Library Association (ALA) and received certification from the Medical Library

Association (MLA) or that documented equivalent training or experience or both be provided.

Medical librarians have been almost alone among professional library groups in the United States in developing certification and recertification programs by their major professional body, the MLA. A formal means for ensuring the competence of health science librarians has been one of MLA's major concerns since 1949, when its first formal certification program was implemented. Since that time, the program has been under continuous review in order to accommodate changes in the profession. The Certification Code of January 1, 1978 (revised in September 1981), calls for recertification of librarians at five-year intervals by completion of a specified number of hours of continuing education programs or by examination. The examination for certification or recertification is designed to test competency in each of three areas: public services, technical services, and administration, and is to be taken initially after two years of professional employment in a health science library. By 1984, more than 3,000 persons had been certified as health science librarians. There are questions, however, as to the value of certification that has not been recognized by employers as a measure of expertise or preparation. A review of the program was under way by the MLA in 1985.

Also as part of its professional development program, MLA sponsors an extensive program of honors, awards, scholarships, and fellowships to promote excellence in health science librarianship. The awards are presented at the Association's annual meeting, and are given only when nominees clearly meet or exceed the established criteria. The Association's highest achievement honors are the Marcia C. Noyes Award and selection as the Janet Doe Lecturer on the History or Philosophy of Medical Librarianship.

The development of national associations of medical librarians has proceeded rapidly since 1980. There are major associations in Canada, Finland, West Germany, India, Japan, New Zealand, and the United Kingdom. A multinational association was formed in Africa. All of these associations are aimed at the improvement of the provision of health information for the advancement of health care.

The MLA, the second-oldest U.S. national library association (founded in 1898), developed an extensive continuing education program to serve the needs of its more than 5,100 members. Its program was begun as early as 1964 in the present form. The programs are held annually at the Association's meetings and given regionally throughout the year, either in conjunction with its regional chapters or in cooperation with local library groups (not necessarily oriented to the health sciences). The first international presentation of its courses took place in September 1979 in Helsinki as part of the first regional meeting (for North Europe) of the Section of Biological and Medical Sciences Libraries of the International Federation of Library Associations and Institutions (IFLA). In 1985 a cycle of five courses, specially revised for an international audience, was presented as part of the program of the Fifth International Congress on Medical Librarianship, held in Tokyo.

Medical libraries vary greatly in size and run the gamut from the largest, the National Library of Medicine (NLM), located on the campus of the National

McGill University

McIntyre Medical Sciences Building, home of McGill University's Medical Library in Montreal, Canada.

Institutes of Health in Bethesda, Maryland, to small working collections in hospitals. The NLM (with 1,800,000 book, journal, and microform volumes, 1,200,000 manuscripts, and 80,000 illustrations in the history of medicine, among other materials) plays an important role in setting national and international standards for cataloguing and has a major influence on U.S. libraries in such areas as catalogue organization and the provision of cataloguing information (now available online through its CATLINE database). One of NLM's most important activities, which assists health professionals throughout the world, is the compilation and publication of the *Index Medicus,* which is available in both print and machine-readable forms.

The size of a library's collection does not necessarily guarantee its ability to serve the information needs of its users effectively; that ability is based on the degree to which the collection reflects the scope of the interests of the users. Attempts have been made to codify the purposes, and operation, and management of medical school libraries, and those guidelines were in 1985 being revised by a joint committee of the Association of Academic Health Science Library Directors and the MLA. Medical school libraries also provide a wealth of statistical information about their operations that permits comparative studies and assists other institutions in keeping pace with general trends in the field. Such statistics are published annually.

Medical libraries play a major role in biomedical information transfer. They form part of a highly structured network that provides basic library services to all health professionals and that is, in the United States, organized on a regional basis. The regionalization and cooperative interaction among medical libraries takes the form of improved and speeded document delivery services, coordinated collection development, and staff education.

Library automation began in medical libraries in the late 1950s, and medical libraries now use automated services heavily. The world's first online bibliographic information retrieval system in biomedicine began operation in 1968 (after three years of planning and development) under the aegis of the State University of New York. It was followed shortly by NLM's MEDLINE service and a number of others, both commercial and noncommercial, for searching the world's biomedical and scientific bibliographic information online. These services are used extensively in medical libraries throughout the world.

Medical libraries typically share a highly developed sense of service, in common with many other special libraries, and do more for their users than has often been considered common or proper in many libraries. The tradition that researchers themselves must perform all their own library research has passed; limited time and the volume of work have changed the perception of what a library may or can do for a user, just as medical professionals have accepted the presence and services of the nurse practitioner and midwife. Medical libraries engage in extensive outreach programs, to try to make the health professionals' task in getting and using information as easy and as rapid as possible. In recent years the highly personalized services of clinical medical librarians have become increasingly common, as have such services as LATCH (Literature Attached To Charts)—medical librarians accompany physicians on their hospital rounds and then provide the medical literature relevant to each case. For those institutions that can afford the expense of this service, the results are gratifying, and health professionals have responded enthusiastically.

On the international scene, the reorganization of IFLA resulted in the formation of a Section of Biological and Medical Sciences Libraries (1978) within the Division of Special Libraries. Besides providing substantive programs at the annual IFLA meetings, the Section works toward improving reference tools and the exchange of medical information. In 1985 the Section published the *World List of Biological and Medical Sciences Libraries,* the most comprehensive international directory of medical libraries. When published, it was not as complete as its compilers had hoped, because of the difficulties of obtaining re-

sponses from some developing countries, but plans were under way for an enlarged and revised second edition. Through the Section, IFLA is now the official co-sponsor with the World Health Organization (WHO) of the International Congresses on Medical Librarianship. The Fifth Congress was held in Tokyo in September/October 1985, and the Sixth was scheduled for New Delhi in the fall of 1990.

In 1984 NLM announced the appointment of a new Director, Donald A. B. Lindberg, M.D, whose long and distinguished career in the field of informatics portended increased emphasis on the computerization of NLM's activities in the dissemination and innovative use of medical information. NLM has played a leading role in the application of laser-disk technology for reformatting visual information coupled with minicomputer-based systems for text, and in the training of medical librarians and medical computer specialists. Lindberg noted that the research and development policies set by his predecessors, Frank B. Rogers, M.D., and Martin M. Cummings, M.D. "to support the investigation of computer-based programs to benefit information management and decision making in American health care institutions was clearly farsighted and correct. Now these programs are bearing fruit in advancing our understanding of human cognition, medical decision making, and practical interfaces to automated systems."

Medical libraries have been in the vanguard of progress in the library profession in a number of areas, such as automation, research in library management, and provision of services. There is every expectation that this progress will continue, and that the pace of change propelled by these libraries will accelerate.

REFERENCES
Annual Statistics of Medical School Libraries in the United States and Canada, 7th edition (1985).
"Code for the Certification of Health Sciences Librarians," *Medical Library Association 1984-85 Directory* (1984).
"Guidelines for Medical School Libraries," *Journal of Medical Education* (1965).
J. L. Hall, *On-line Information Retrieval Sourcebook* (1978).
Irwin H. Pizer, "The International Congresses on Medical Librarianship—Thirty Years of Evolutionary Change," *IFLA Journal* (1985).
"Professional Library Services," *AMH/84 Accreditation Manual for Hospitals* (1983).
"SUNY Biomedical Communication Network," *On-line Information Retrieval 1965-1976: a Bibliography with a Guide to On-line Data Bases and Systems,* J. L. Hall, compiler (1977).

IRWIN H. PIZER

SERVICES TO USERS

The contemporary health science library offers a myriad of innovative services designed to meet the information needs of health professionals. It has placed special emphasis on computerized information retrieval, extension and outreach programs, document delivery, library instruction, and audiovisual services. In response to societal needs, it has expanded the scope and breadth of user services to accommodate the information needs of the sophisticated health consumer who emerged in the late 1970s. An overview of the development and implementation of public services in the health science library pro-

Pan American Health Organization's Regional Library of Medicine, São Paolo, Brazil.

vides a foundation for reviewing the dynamic array of services that are available to library users today.

Before the 1920s, medical librarians were employed primarily to acquire, organize, and maintain collections of medical literature. Only the physician who provided economic support to the library was entitled to use the collection. In these libraries, then commonly referred to as "doctors' libraries," the physician independently accessed and interpreted the medical literature. As the size of medical library collections reached the point at which the typical user had difficulty in finding information, physicians learned to rely on librarians for assistance, and user-services programs evolved.

During the 1920s medical librarians, employed by private medical society libraries and in the libraries of the sizable academic institutions, provided substantial reference services to users. Noteworthy was the extraordinary library at the American College of Surgeons in Philadelphia, which in 1926 had 10 employees to handle reference services for 6,000 members.

Document delivery also received early attention. In the 1920s the American Medical Association (AMA), the American Dental Association (ADA), and other society libraries distributed "package libraries" to members. The package library consisted of selected reprints relevant to the member's information query. (The ADA's Bureau of Library Services continues to maintain this popular service on a worldwide basis to members.) In 1928 the New York Academy of Medicine began a delivery service for members living in the New York metropolitan area; thus the Academy took the library to the membership. As librarians gained familiarity with user needs, they began to investigate the resources of other medical libraries to supplement local holdings and subsequently laid the foundation for interlibrary resource sharing.

During the years following World War II, monumental progress was achieved in biomedical research and technology. New branches of medicine were born, particularly in program areas that received heavy government funding, such as aerospace medicine and nuclear medicine. A direct result of those developments was the generation of recorded information with unprecedented speed. The medical library exerted every possible resource to back up the health scientist's research efforts; it was an era of unlimited reference service. Nevertheless, the medical library community realized that in order to cope effectively with the rampant growth of biomedical literature and to render comprehensive user services to a clientele with expanding interests and needs, mechanized methods of information storage and retrieval were required.

Online Services. Health professionals were the first group of library users to realize, on a large-scale basis, the benefits of computerized information storage and retrieval systems. In response to the call in the late 1950s for improved bibliographic retrieval systems, NLM developed and mounted MEDLARS. From 1964, when MEDLARS became operational, until 1971, when MEDLINE (MEDLARS Online) became available, requests for information were searched in the database in batches. Since 1971 the number of MEDLINE terminals has increased dra-

Los Angeles County Public Library

Consumer Health Information Program and Services (CHIPS), of the Los Angeles County Public Library and the Harbor-UCLA Medical Center, uses bilingual volunteers to answer or refer health questions from the community.

matically. Much of this growth has been in direct patient care settings, which account for more than half of the total number of online terminals. From a total of 120 institutional users of MEDLINE in 1973, the user population had grown to 2,461 by August 1984. Health science libraries that serve academic institutions and major research facilities also commonly use other databases, mostly in the social, physical, and behavioral sciences.

The capability of searching the health science literature by computer has enabled the library to expand the scope of reference and interlibrary loan services. The primary application of online systems remains the production of bibliographies, tailored to the users' specific information request. Online systems have also revolutionized current awareness services: user profiles can be stored in the search system and periodic updates (usually monthly) are automatically generated. Reports furnish the user with current citations well in advance of their appearance in the printed indexes. Many databases accessed by the health science library contain abstracts of articles, helpful in deciding whether the complete article should be consulted. Abstracts are particularly popular with residents preparing for patient rounds.

Both health science librarians and library users have come to view automated search services as a tool that supplements, but does not necessarily replace, manual reference services. Computer search systems do have some other advantages over print versions of indexes in that there is often greater depth of indexing than is available in the printed form. Limitations on the size of the printed index and expenses involved with printing force the number of print terms to be limited. Thus a computer search may often identify more information than the same search done manually. In the mid-1980s, there was a trend toward training the end-user to search the online systems. This has developed, in part, because systems have become more user-friendly, and also because many users have acquired their own terminals and have achieved a new levels of capability and sophistication in information handling. It is unlikely that end-user searching will supplant the mediated search performed by the trained search analyst. The user will frequently perform the first cut in the search process and will use the library's specialists for more complex and time-consuming searches.

Reference and Outreach Services. Users of health science libraries find that reference services have been designed to furnish timely, accurate, and relevant responses to their queries. Medical librarians have formal training in health science bibliography. They communicate fluently, using concise medical terminology, and display a solid knowledge of biomedical concepts and processes when interpreting and analyzing the library's information resources. Like other types of special libraries, health science libraries provide in-depth reference services for the user. Frequently the librarian assumes the major responsibility for locating, evaluating, and summarizing the literature. Typically, library staff members verify citations, compile bibliographies, provide Selective Dissemination of Information (SDI) services, make referrals for translations, and respond to reference questions at all levels, simple to complex. The primary users of the health science library have come to expect such basic services. No review of the basic services will be given here; this article covers several newer user services that incorporate the basic reference activities.

Under the Clinical Medical Librarian (CML) program, the librarian, as a member of the health-care delivery team, interacts directly with health professionals in the patient-care setting. The CML makes patient rounds with the medical staff and assesses their information needs as they arise. Upon returning to the library, the CML searches the health science literature using manual or automated retrieval systems, evaluates articles for relevancy of content, and forwards copies of the selected articles to the health professionals. Members of the medical staff may request that the CML research a specific topic, but in many cases the CML may provide information even before it is requested. User evaluations of the CML programs reveal that interns and residents particularly find value and merit in having the information specialist readily available to assist in determining information needs and providing immediate solutions. The cost of this service is a limiting factor, however, and it is usually applied only in larger hospitals and medical centers, and then often only in selected departments.

Another user service that supplements educational efforts and relates directly to the provision of better patient care is Literature Attached to Charts (LATCH). At the medical staff's request (usually submitted by telephone), the librarian selects and locates current literature on some aspects of a patient's illness. Articles are then sent to the hospital, where they become part of a patient's chart. This program allows any individual reviewing the patient's case, whether as a primary physician, a consultant, or another member of the health care team, to have immediate access to pertinent background information.

A third example of taking library services to the health community is the Circuit Rider Librarian program. Circuit Riders travel from one library to another in order to provide reference support to the personnel in health-care institutions unable to support a full- or even part-time professional librarian. In addition, Circuit Riders provide access to the regional interlibrary loan network and collect and process materials for the individual library's collection. Usually based in large academic health science libraries, Circuit Riders also serve as liaisons between the remote user and the library sponsoring the program. Thus they can rely on comprehensive health science collections to resolve complex user questions. A further development in the 1980s was the National Biomedical Referral Network under the RML program. In this program libraries agree to accept the referral of reference questions from libraries unable to answer them, putting the human and material resources of the largest libraries at the disposal of all health professionals, no matter how far removed they may be from the referral center.

Public Services. The contemporary health science library has expanded its service population to include professional lay persons, such as lawyers and environmentalists, and the general public. The consumer health education movement has generated a strong plea from the public, often concerned about patient rights and the idea of informed consent, for access to health-related information. Health science librarians possess the expertise to disseminate biomedical information, and the provision of user services to the public appears to be a logical extension of existing activities.

The Community Health Information Network (CHIN) is a cooperative program between Mount Auburn Hospital in Cambridge, Massachusetts, and six area public library systems. By sharing collections and personnel resources, the network facilitates the dissemination of information at the appropriate level of sophistication. An individual with more complex health information needs may obtain reference services directly from the hospital library. A project coordinator, stationed at the hospital library, assists in identifying accurate health information materials for the non-health professional. Another successful program is CHIPS (Consumer Health Information Program and Services/Salud y Bienestar), a bilingual consumer health information and referral service. Two Los Angeles County libraries, the Carson Regional Library and the Harbor General Hospital Regional Medical Library, make services available to a population of more than 2,000,000 people of widely varying backgrounds. The two libraries jointly select and purchase health education materials, manage an interlibrary loan program, maintain a clearinghouse for brochures, display materials, posters, and other items, and operate a TEL-MED system. TEL-MED offers tapes on health-related topics for access by telephone. Components of both projects have been copied by health science libraries nationwide.

Hospitalized patients also need health information in order to make sound judgments related to their personal care and course of treatment. Many health science libraries offer patient education services, providing print and audiovisual materials that teach the patient and the family about pathological conditions and self-care. U.S. Veterans Administration hospital libraries conduct some of the most extensive patient-education programs in existence.

Document Delivery Services. Most users of a health science library judge its services principally on the accessibility of materials and the success of document delivery services. Failure to obtain required documents can seriously impede the progress of research projects, patient care, and educational activities. Most circulation services in the health science library closely resemble those employed by other types of libraries, although loan periods are short and, in many larger research libraries, journals are not allowed to leave the premises. There is, consequently, a heavy use of self-service photocopy machines. The exceptional component of document delivery services in a health science library is the extensive provision of interlibrary loan (ILL) services.

The bibliographies produced from online databases have stimulated users to request a huge number of items through interlibrary loan. Users have come to expect that if the library supplies the citation, it should also be able to supply the document cited. Fortunately, the advent of automated information retrieval was accompanied by the formalization of the interlibrary loan network for health science libraries in the United States. The Regional Medical Library (RML) Network of NLM filled 2,000,000 requests in 1984. The program ensures that a library user's ILL request will be routed and filled quickly under national standards established by NLM.

In addition to the RML network, health science librarians may tap many other sources and networks. Medium-sized and smaller health science libraries rely on consortium participation to improve their ability to fill user requests. Many U.S. librarians willingly forward user requests to national medical libraries in other countries when the material is not available domestically. When rapid and guaranteed delivery is crucial in supplying a user with a journal article, some librarians rely on commercial document delivery services such as the Institute for Scientific Information's OATS (Original Article Tear Sheets) program and the UMI Article Clearinghouse of University Microfilms International.

Health science libraries use a variety of methods to expedite document delivery requests. Union lists in print, microfiche, and online formats provide necessary holdings and location information. Libraries that process a large number of ILLs may transmit requests by tele-typewriter or electronic mail. The 66 member libraries of the Medical Library Center of New York (MLCNY) forward requests and documents to each other by a daily delivery service; an MLCNY request submitted by telephone is processed so quickly that the material can be in the hands of the user the next day. NLM has developed its DOC-LINE system (which first linked all the RMLs and by the end of 1985 was open to all health science libraries) for transmission and routing of requests to a predetermined group of libraries selected by the borrowing institution. The aim of the system is to fill as many requests as possible within the borrowing library's home state and then within its RML region, before an unfilled request is transmitted to NLM. Health science libraries have been experimenting for some time with high-speed telefacsimile equipment as a mode of transmitting hard copy over long geographic distances, but recent improvements in this technology offer new hopes for the development of a viable service. One remaining obstacle is the continuing need to create a photocopy for transmission. A major program linking health science, university, and public library systems in a telefacsimile network began in Illinois in 1985.

Instructional Services. A 1968 analysis of user services offered by medical school libraries indicated that instructional services were generally poorly developed. Since the initiation of public services in the health science library, instruction to users on a one-to-one basis has been commonplace. However, programs that have been developed since 1968 show that the library can and does provide effective instruction to health science students in the areas of research methodology and literature evaluation, especially when integrated in the school's curriculum. Health science librarians are also invited to deliver guest lectures preparing students for research assignments. Course content may include the detailed analysis of biomedical reference materials, application of computerized databases, use of a controlled thesaurus, and methods for conducting a review of the literature, formating a bibliography, or writing an abstract. Courses aimed at developing library skills of research assistants or other ancillary personnel, often the heaviest library users, also have proved to be worthwhile.

Audiovisual Services. As audiovisual resources assumed an increasingly important role in the education and the continuing education of the health professional, health science libraries concurrently strengthened the scope of audiovisual services offered. During the 1950s and 60s, medical librarians debated the merits of incorporating multimedia services into the library operation versus housing media in an autonomous learning resources center. In the 1970s the medical librarian came to view audiovisual and other nonprint media as important resources for providing curricular support in the education of health professionals. Multimedia services are now provided by most health science libraries, large and small, although the shift to media-based instruction has not been as extensive as many thought it would be in the 1970s.

Typically, the library user can expect comprehensive multimedia reference service including assistance with arrangements for previewing sessions, compilation of bibliographies, and selection of materials. Undergraduate and graduate students, who constitute a primary media user group, find that audiovisual materials are particularly effective in demonstrating techniques such as changing a catheter or performing periodontal surgery. Many libraries also provide users with access to computer-assisted instruction programs. The University of Illinois' PLATO system enables the student to select from numerous preclinical and clinical programmed sessions and to interact with the program to measure comprehension and to sharpen decision-making skills. This and other systems using videodisks, slides, and audiotapes appear to be the way of the future.

Libraries have recently begun to house diagnostic skill centers, where users work with models or other devices that simulate visual, tactile, or auditory manifestations of pathological conditions. Mannequins with slides projected behind the eyes teach ophthalmologic diagnosis, the "Gynne" model is used to familiarize students with the basic gynecologic examination, and Recording Resusci Anne, a life-sized model, has become an important tool in teaching cardiopulmonary resuscitation techniques. These and other materials accommodate many user needs as well as, if not better than, print sources.

To help professionals meet current requirements for recertification, AV media offer an alternative to traditional instruction. Audiovisual programs such as those of the Network for Continuing Medical Education, a videotape series, enable health professionals to earn CE credit at their local library.

The state of the art of user services in the health science library has advanced rapidly during the 20th century. Technological, professional, political, and economic factors have influenced and will continue to influence the development of these services.

REFERENCES
Estelle Brodman, "Medical Libraries around the World," *Bulletin of the Medical Library Association* (1971).
Estelle Brodman, "Users of Health Science Libraries," *Library Trends* (1974).
Louise Darling, "Changes in Information Delivery since 1960 in Health Sciences Libraries," *Library Trends* (1974).
Mildred C. Langner, "User and User Services in Health Science Libraries, 1945-1965," *Library Trends* (1974).
Gloria Werner, "Users of On-Line Bibliographic Retrieval Services in Health Science Libraries in the United States and Canada," *Bulletin of the Medical Library Association* (1979).

WILLIAM D. WALKER

COLLECTIONS

The terms *medical libraries* and *health science libraries* have been used rather loosely to define medical center libraries, hospital libraries, and medical school libraries. Although there are general statements concerning collection development that can be attributed to all types of medical libraries, there are differences in policies and methods of collection that depend upon the size and type of the library.

The purpose of any library is service to its community; an essential factor in carrying out this function is adequate resources. Although no library can acquire all of the material requested by its users, it should contain at least the primary titles needed to fulfill its mission. H. G. Weiskotten in *Medical Education in the United States* (1940) stated, "Perhaps no department is more vital to the educational and research programs of the medical school than its library. Indeed, if a medical school is to be appraised by a single criterion, the library might well serve." Although he specifically mentions medical schools, the view can be applied equally to all types of medical libraries and their parent institutions. Yet the library may be poorly financed or may be the first to have its budget cut in times of financial constraint. The librarian must be in touch with the institution's purpose, philosophy, and activities; without such current knowledge, the library cannot meet the changing needs of its users. The increase in volume of published literature and the escalating prices of materials make it imperative that the librarian use wisely the funds allotted to the library for materials.

Acquisitions Policy. An acquisitions policy is an important guide to the selection process. The policy should define any areas in which the library will collect at various levels of sophistication—for example, graduate versus undergraduate for allied health

personnel—or at various levels of support—for example, exhaustive, comprehensive, educational, or working collection. (Exhaustive collection = collect everything published in a given subject area. Comprehensive = collect all material in a given subject area to support research. Educational = collect material needed to support the teaching functions of the institution. Working collection = minimal collection in a subject area—one or two texts, a few primary journals, a reference tool.)

In many libraries the chief librarian does the major part of selection. In others, the acquisitions librarian makes the selection and carries out the actual procedures involved in acquiring the material. In larger libraries subject bibliographers do the selection, or the reference librarians, or a combination of one or more of the above. The librarian must demonstrate to the library's users that the staff has the expertise to select materials (within budgetary constraints) to support the functions of the institution the library serves. A few institutions have committees of users who approve items for purchase. Suggestions for acquisition from the library's users are always welcomed and such items are usually obtained. It is common, however, that by the time users have become aware of an item they wish to recommend, the library has already ordered it or even received it.

Weeding of the collection is an integral part of the acquisitions policy. It may be necessary not only because of space limitations, but also because out-of-date and little-used materials on the shelves tend to diminish the usefulness of the collection. Only a large library with a mission to serve as a national resource can try to collect and retain everything.

Materials. In any medical library the majority of the collection will be journal literature—about two-thirds serials and one-third books—and the bulk of the library's acquisitions budget will be used for serials. Several bibliographical aids can be used in selecting serial titles. For the small medical or hospital library there are such tools as Alfred N. Brandon and Dorothy R. Hill's "Selected List of Books and Journals for the Small Medical Library," *Bulletin of the Medical Library Association* (1985); Brandon and Hill's "Selected List of Books and Journals in Allied Health Sciences," *Bulletin of the Medical Library Association* (1984); and the list of 100 journals indexed in the *Abridged Index Medicus,* common journals that NLM expects most medical libraries to own. Each library's individual needs must be considered in the selection process. Other aids directed toward hospital, medical school, or other health science libraries will also be used and may include the American Hospital Association's *Administrator's Collection* (1978) or Fred Roper et al., *Introduction to Reference Sources in the Health Sciences* (1979).

Larger medical libraries must go beyond these tools, and for the health science library serving medicine, dentistry, nursing, and other allied health fields the task of selection becomes much more complex. Use of indexing tools, publishers' catalogues, or approval plans may be part of collection development activity.

Smaller medical libraries may have a few reference aids, but the larger medical libraries must have all the major indexing and abstracting tools in the fields they serve. Computer literature searching is now common, and many small hospital libraries have access to MEDLARS through their own terminals or through shared access with other hospital libraries. The larger libraries have access to numerous databases in addition to those of NLM. *Psychological Abstracts, BIOSIS Previews, Chemical Abstracts, Excerpta Medica,* and *Management Contents* are just a few of the databases of interest to medical library users. Use of online services leads to demands upon the library to acquire items retrieved as citations in the literature search. The librarian may initiate an interlibrary loan, but will be aware of the titles requested most frequently, to identify those that should be added to the collection.

The various professional associations issue publications that can be of great value to the hospital library, particularly those of the AHA, the AMA, and the National League for Nursing (NLN). The U.S. Department of Health and Human Services (DHHS) issues a tremendous amount of material in the health care field, as do state and local government agencies. The *Monthly Catalog of Government Publications* can be used for selection of U.S. government documents, many of them are free to libraries.

Every medical library will contain some historical, archival, or rare book material. Often the library becomes the depository for the archives of the institution, although recently institutions have realized the importance of maintaining archives in a formal way and have employed archivists to collect, maintain, and organize them. In most hospitals the archivist's position is separate from the library, but in university-affiliated health science libraries the archivist may be a member of the library staff. The archives can be a separate section in the library or part of the special collections area. Most small medical libraries have tiny historical or rare book collections, probably acquired by gift. The sizes of historical or rare book collections in larger health sciences libraries can vary depending upon the interests of users, budgets, and gifts. Many health science libraries have Friends of the Library groups that contribute single titles, collections, or funds to purchase rare books.

The acquisition of nonprint material by health science libraries increased tremendously in the 1970s, an increase evident in libraries of all sizes. In some institutions the audiovisual section is not an integral part of the library but part of a division of medical education or an AV production unit. Audiovisual materials include a variety of formats—films, slides, videotapes, videodisks, filmstrips, cassettes, audiodisks, models, and realia, and other formats in use in health care applications. Various bibliographic tools are available for selection. NLM's *AVline* lists audiovisual titles with full cataloguing information; all materials listed on *AVline* have been previewed and rated by selected previewers, and the rating for each is provided. The National Medical Audiovisual Center in Bethesda (a division of NLM) and the National Audiovisual Center in Washington, D.C., issue catalogues of AV material that can be used for selection. There are also regional online catalogues such as HAVC, Health Audio-visual Online Catalog, which serve similar purposes. A number of commercial catalogues are available, and some medical schools have developed large AV collections and issue their own catalogues, such as Southern Illinois University, the

University of Connecticut Health Center Library

University of Connecticut, and Indiana University.

Electronic publishing has begun to make an important mark on the publishing field in biomedicine, and a large number of texts and journals are now available in both electronic and print form. In 1985 the AMA announced the availability of its *Journal* and all of its clinical specialty journals in electronic format. Medical libraries are among the first libraries to have to deal with the complexities of handling material in electronic form and with attendant policy decisions regarding access, cost, and user chargeback.

Cooperation among medical libraries is described separately in this article, but is of particular importance in collection development in view of the growth in the volume of published literature, increased costs, and reduced or static budgets. The Regional Medical Library (RML) Network of the NLM has encouraged the development of consortia among hospital libraries, so these libraries could develop their collections and share resources. In the period 1986–90, the RMLs will coordinate regional acquisition and retention programs for books and journals among the resource libraries (usually academic health science libraries) in each of the seven regions. There is an increasing number of state programs for cooperative collection development on a multitype library basis. The library literature is filled with references to networks being formed by university libraries in order to share resources and cataloguing and to reduce future space needs by reducing duplication and retention of multiple copies. Cooperative acquisition and retention of periodicals is somewhat easier to achieve than cooperative acquisition of monographs, and union lists of serials are particularly helpful in deciding whether or not to acquire a given title. In some instances libraries divide the acquisition of material by subject or language. Collection rationalization programs, in place in several regions, aim to consolidate small runs of a given title into one large or complete set held in one location. By cooperating in this

A student using a slide tape presentation on dental care at the Lyman Maynard Stowe Library, part of the Health Center of the University of Connecticut in Farmington.

manner, libraries are freer to purchase what they want, and Library A can eliminate certain titles or languages knowing that Library B is responsible for obtaining and retaining them. Thus more resources are available within a given region.

Selection of quality titles requires time and a knowledge of appropriate literature. As financial resources for building collections diminish, more emphasis is being placed on analysis and evaluation of a library's existing collection. Many medical libraries are using the conspectus developed by the Research Libraries Group (RLG) to analyze their collections and integrate the collection policies into a local or regional cooperative framework. Use studies are being conducted to determine which titles are the most heavily used. The library's collection, large or small, must be made known to the users of the library so that the collection can be fully utilized. Acquisition lists, newsletters, library lectures, and online catalogues accessible from a user's desk terminal are some methods of making information about the content of the collection available.

Owsei Temkin, in his address at the opening of the Medical College of Ohio Library, said,

For a library is not only a gathering point for students, professors, practicing physicians, and others interested in medicine. It is also the point where past, present, and future meet. The library makes available knowledge accumulated up to the present day, knowledge that we assimilate with an eye to things to be done in practice or in research, be it today, tomorrow, or at some distant time. Thus, a medical library is a monument to the Hippocratic aphorism: "Life is short, the art is long." It is a monument to the short lives of those whose deeds and thoughts have passed into the stream of the medical art that flows on endlessly.

CECILE E. KRAMER

GOVERNANCE, FINANCE, AND MANAGEMENT

Governance. Health science libraries have significant roles in education, in commercial enterprises, in clinical or health research organizations, in health-related professional organizations, and in government agencies. Their governance is a function of their position and role in their parent organization.

Libraries in hospitals make up the largest group of medical libraries. In most hospitals the hospital librarian reports to the hospital administration on matters of budget, personnel, and daily operation. There is usually a library committee, made up of the hospital administrator and members from the medical and nursing staff, to determine library policy, review library effectiveness, plan continuing development, and advise on book and journal selection.

Libraries in health-related professional organizations are among the oldest medical libraries in the United States. Such a library operates within the governance structure of the medical society, and its librarian will ordinarily report to the board of the society or a designated member of it.

Libraries in medical schools are perhaps the largest employers of professional medical librarians. Most medical school libraries are parts of university systems, and they fall under one of two governance structures: (1) as integral parts of the university library systems; or (2) as libraries independent of the university library system but under the governance of the medical or health science school. Few medical school libraries exist as independent entities while at the same time serving medical or other health science schools. Of the 138 medical libraries in the U.S. and Canada, perhaps some 10 percent are independent, more than 60 percent are under the direction of medical schools, and the other 30 percent fall within university library systems.

If under the governance of a university library system, the medical library director reports to the university librarian or some other university library administrator. If under the governance of a medical school, the medical library director reports to the school administration, normally the dean or, particularly where the library also supports other health sciences programs, to a vice-president or similar administrative officer in charge of health science affairs. Neither situation is necessarily better for the medical school library. A university library may want to provide several of the medical library's functions, especially in technical processing, which may or may not cause problems; as a general rule the emphasis on currency in the medical library is much more pronounced than it is in the general university library, so the built-in delays of double processing can frustrate the medical librarian's service programs. This factor, along with other reasons to support library governance being directly under a medical school, was reported in a survey by Virginia Parker (1977):

(1) The library is responsible to, and is the responsibility of, the school it serves, which generates *better support* for the library from the medical school administration.

(2) Medical school affiliation makes possible the *recruitment of personnel* to meet the special needs of a medical library. Those on the professional staff view themselves more as health professionals than as university librarians.

(3) A library that is independent of the university library system orders, catalogues, and processes its own books in a way that serves its own users, with no time lag. It is *free to set policies* on circulation, interlibrary loan, and other services tailored to medical school needs.

(4) Being a recognized department of the medical school *improves communications with the users.*

(5) Members of *medical school faculties* are accustomed to experimentation with new methods and equipment and are, therefore, *sympathetic with a library administration that is creative.*

The governance structure of a medical school library, then, establishes its policymaking structure. The functions and goals of its advisory structure, on the other hand, are often much less understood. When the medical librarian reports to the university librarian, an advisory committee made up of members from the health sciences community can be a valuable asset. A library committee in such circumstances can assist in obtaining not only fiscal support but also support for policies, personnel, and processing. An advisory committee's role under the other structure can be much less well-defined, however. When the medical school library director reports to the health sciences administration, even such a committee's advisory functions, in the realities of faculty priorities, will demand innovation from the library director. A library advisory committee may assume a policy-making role, particularly setting external library policies such as circulation and other public services, or it may act merely as a sounding board to assist the director in determining policy for the library. An advisory committee can potentially play a significant role, yet a policy making committee—where there is competent library staff (and this is true in the hospital library as well)—is potentially a liability. The medical librarian must continue to assume responsibility for *all* of the library's policies, the committee notwithstanding.

Finance. Medical library directors are as concerned as are the executive officers of other organizations about applying current management techniques to their budgeting processes. Incremental line-item budgets are common in medical libraries, but a combination of budgeting techniques is more often used; program budgeting, zero-based budgeting, and incremental budgeting are rarely found in their pure form. Budgets and statistical data on library activities are still most commonly used in libraries as control devices—that is, the primary focus is on "how much," rather than on "what," "why," or "how." The use of a medical library budget as a tool for translating management plans into financial terms is still in its infancy. When applied in consideration of the consequences of eliminating programs, or of letting all programs compete for the library's limited resources, zero-based budgeting is a move toward answering more significant performance questions and should therefore become a much more prevalent budget tool in the future.

The medical library's budget is prepared by the library director, along with others on the library staff, and is submitted for approval to the person to whom the director reports. A budget request will normally include personnel, acquisitions (including processing), maintenance and operations (including supplies and printing), communications, travel, automation, and equipment. In the better medical school library, the three main parts of the library budget—personnel, acquisitions, and other expenses—normally fall close to a 60:30:10 percent ratio (personnel:acquisitions:other), which can be used as a guideline for standard budgeting but not as a substitute for a planned budget. In actuality, however, these ratios in most medical school libraries seem to be moving toward a heavier acquisitions budget percentage, bringing it closer to 40 percent of the total, with personnel slipping toward 50 percent. This change reflects the tremendous inflationary pressures in book and particularly journal prices. Salaries, on the other hand, have remained not only behind the inflation rate but also behind other comparable professional salaries.

In the hospital library, the major source of financial support is the hospital's operating budget. Other sources of funding may include medical staff dues or contributions, grant funds, and Medicare. Medical society libraries must rely primarily on annual dues assessed to their memberships.

Management. The AMA-MLA Guidelines for Medical School Libraries state that the purpose of the medical library is to serve its community. In both medical schools and hospitals, libraries tend to see their mission or purpose solely as furthering the mission of the institution of which they are a part. The medical school library's mission is usually stated in relation to its contributions to the teaching, research, and service goals of the institution. The hospital library's purpose is usually stated in relation to the hospital's three major functions: patient care, education, and research, with the major commitment being to patient care. Medical society libraries from their founding have played a significant role in the continuing education of practicing physicians. Even though there are still some important society libraries in the United States, this function is being assumed increasingly by hospitals and medical school libraries.

While there can be little argument with these mission statements, which have been fairly universally adopted, some medical libraries are beginning to see their mission to the user community in less reactive, more assertive terms. Contributing to the institution's teaching, research, and service goals and serving the user community in general are clearly what medical libraries do, but this statement says nothing about what they consider the desired results of these activities to be. With more and more medical libraries adopting such current management techniques as marketing, strategic planning, budgeting techniques, and Management by Objectives (all of which are taught as continuing education courses through the MLA's CE program), the ultimate goal of the medical library is being scrutinized more carefully now than ever before. Performance measurement is a concept that medical librarians are beginning to accept. With the publication of the *Annual Statistics of Medical School Libraries in the United States and Canada* beginning in 1978, comparative statistical information for medical school libraries has become readily available, and similar comparative data are being considered for hospital libraries. A next step for medical libraries will be to develop management information systems for determining their performance effectiveness. Before a medical library will be able to assess its performance fully, it first must clearly define its organizational direction.

Since the large majority of hospital libraries are small and staffed by one librarian, their internal structure is relatively simple. The librarian must function in the several roles that in larger libraries are quite distinct, from acquisitions and cataloguing to reference services and management. The medical school library or the larger medical society library, on the other hand, will have an internal organizational structure differing little from that of a general academic library. The separation into departments—cataloguing, acquisitions, serials, reference, interlibrary loan, circulation, audiovisual—is fairly standard. Some names may be changed—audiovisual departments become learning resource centers or media centers or reference departments may be called information services departments—and some units may be combined, such as acquisitions and serials. In addition, there may be some distinction given to the collection development functions in the larger medical libraries. Further differing details in organizational structure will depend upon the particular library and the management style operating in it. Some medical libraries are large and complex enough to need an associate director along with directors of the technical and public services divisions, but the two divisional directors alone are more commonly found. Some library

National Library of Medicine

*National Library of
Medicine. At left is the
Library's Lister Hill
National Center for
Biomedical
Communications.*

directors do not adopt the divisional structure at all, preferring to operate under a flat structure with each department head reporting directly to the top.

With a 1984 average of nine to ten librarians in a medical school library, there is little more than one librarian for each of the major functions; covering 54 to 57 reference desk hours each week requires the help of most of them. A pattern whereby the librarian functions as a generalist, perhaps with too many activities, is still predominant. The cataloguing librarian, when not cataloguing, handles reference desk duties and perhaps performs database searches. Some medical librarians hold that the generalist approach dilutes the quality of the service the library is capable of giving. They also believe that, with a generalist approach, the library cannot respond to anything but the most common, and too often the most superficial, needs of its community. Librarians are almost inherently activity prone; they conceive their ultimate purpose as service to their community—by definition a reactive role. All too frequently the innovative services that form the basic ingredients of an assertive and forward-looking library service are left out of the picture.

REFERENCES

Jana Bradley et al., editors, *Hospital Library Management* (1983).
Louise Darling et al., editors, *Handbook of Medical Library Practice,* 4th edition (1982–85).
Lois Ann Colaianni and Phyllis Mirsky, *Manual for Librarians in Small Hospitals* (1978).
Virginia Parker, "The Relationships of Medical School Libraries to University Library Systems," *Bulletin of the Medical Library Association* (1977).

RICHARD A. LYDERS

MEASUREMENT AND EVALUATION

Measurement and evaluation have long been an integral part of health science librarianship. The picture has been a fragmented one for an assortment of reasons, not the least of which is the great variety of agencies that harbor health-related libraries. These libraries not only span the customary library divisions of special and academic organizations but also represent within these categories the interests of host institutions that are private or public, nonprofit or for profit, and of various sizes.

Individual libraries, especially those in academic settings, are further challenged by the strikingly disparate and sometimes diametrically opposed needs of several categories of users. The classical conflict between the needs of faculty and students is well known to all academic libraries. Further, the use of materials by research scientists can be quite dissimilar from its use by those engaged in the day-to-day delivery of health care.

The factors that tie libraries in the field into a cohesive whole include not only the subject matter of the information and materials they handle but also a marked similarity in the goals they seek to achieve. The latter factor helps to provide a rationale for the strong interest in measures of *effectiveness* as a tool for evaluation. While the many differences among libraries in the field might make other common measures difficult to devise and use, shared or interlocking goals make measurement of effectiveness a satisfactory approach for health science libraries.

Over a period of years, health science libraries have used a series of complementary and overlapping mechanisms in an effort to evaluate their collections, services, and other relevant library qualities. The pattern that has emerged has been similar in many ways to that seen in other fields of librarianship, beginning with the search for acceptable standards against which to measure adequacy, followed by the collection and analysis of data to allow for comparisons among libraries, and culminating in the development and application of tools designed to assess effectiveness of library operations in meeting the needs of library users. While all of these approaches continue to be used today as circumstances require, the emphasis given to each has shifted.

Standards. The variety of standards for health-related libraries reflects the rich variety of library types within the field. In 1972 Helen Yast, then Director of Library Services at the American Hospital Association (AHA), reviewed in *Library Trends* the genesis of standards for library service in health care institutions; her study indicated the large number of organizations interested in the subject, ranging from the ALA to the Association of American Medical Colleges (AAMC). As a consequence of this great interest, a large number of standards have been produced over the years.

The Joint Commission on the Accreditation of Hospitals (JCAH) first mentioned libraries in its 1953 hospital standards. Always stated in the most general of terms, these guidelines have only recently, with the assistance of the MLA, become sufficiently specific to be meaningful to hospital administrators and helpful to hospital librarians.

During the period when many libraries were significantly out of line with what was generally considered adequate, it was expedient to provide reasonable numerical standards for bringing them up to a specified minimum level, and for hospital libraries in some geographic areas this continues to be true. Once a large number of libraries reached that level, however, the quantitative standard lost its effectiveness as an agent for change, tending instead to preserve the status quo. When a certain degree of leveling off has been reached within a field, quantitative standards become obsolete as evaluative tools.

A more recent development, intended to assist in

collection development, is lists of books and journals appropriate for libraries of various sizes and types. The most notable of these are the regularly revised Brandon and Hill list (cited previously) and the Sterns and Ratcliff "core lists." (A bibliography of 19 such lists published for health science libraries between 1967 and 1977 appeared in the July 1978 *Bulletin of the Medical Library Association*.) Small and medium-sized hospital libraries find these lists useful for evaluating and updating collections.

While it is difficult to write and apply standards for hospital libraries, the issue of complex variables is no less a problem for health science libraries in academic settings, which range from smaller libraries such as those serving schools of nursing or pharmacy alone to large multidisciplinary libraries serving several schools, clinics, hospitals, and research centers. The needs of these libraries are addressed, at least in theory, by the standards for university libraries, as well as by the now outdated guidelines sponsored by the AAMC in 1965 and prepared under a NLM contract by a distinguished panel of medical librarians. The Association of Academic Health Science Library Directors, in conjunction with the MLA, prepared a new set of "Guidelines for Academic Health Sciences Libraries" for publication in 1986.

As tools for evaluation, many standards leave much to be desired, though they may serve other useful purposes. According to F. Wilfrid Lancaster, "For evaluation purposes, standards should be precise, quantifiable, and measurable." The trend today appears to be for standards to be stated in terms of generalized goals; this approach tends to make standards appropriate starting points for evaluation, rather than tools for the evaluative process itself.

Statistics and the State of the Art. Among the additional influences that forced a search for alternatives to standards for evaluating health science libraries are the accelerated pace of research, the resulting growth of the overall body of knowledge in medical, premedical, and related subjects, the growth in the literature that reflected this knowledge, the growing interest and influence of the NLM, and the impact of the Medical Library Assistance Act (MLAA).

During the 1960s, a time of rapid change, the collection of comparative statistics assumed a new importance. While individual libraries had collected a variety of statistics as by-products of library operations for inclusion in various internal and management reports, major efforts were made in the early and mid-1960s to collect data nationwide in order to describe the general state of hospital and academic medical libraries. The MLA and other organizations conducted several major national surveys reported between 1963 and 1967, the major effect of which was to make evident the uneven profile of health-related libraries in the United States. The information provided by the studies supported the recommendations of the President's Commission on Heart Disease, Cancer, and Stroke concerning medical libraries, and to the extent that these efforts resulted in the passage of the MLAA they were successful. However, much of what was collected appeared to be redundant to other items in the surveys; the data collected were of questionable reliability and of minimal value in exploring effectiveness.

The current *Annual Statistics of Medical School Libraries in the United States and Canada* is a somewhat more carefully constructed review and is in a continuing state of refinement to ensure reliable and consistent reporting.

Evaluation for Effectiveness. In contrast to the approaches of standards and comparative statistics, some studies focused on the effectiveness of the libraries' collections and services in meeting the needs of users. These studies began by analyzing the effectiveness of individual libraries' internal abilities to meet needs, advanced to measure their capability for providing needed materials regardless of source, and later attempted to measure the success of national systems and networks in meeting users' needs

Frederick G. Kilgour's studies at Yale's Medical Library in the early 1960s, for instance, studied items circulated to determine the characteristics of library materials most in demand by users. His discovery that a very small percentage of journal titles accounted for a large percentage of the total journal circulation supported earlier findings in studies of general library collections. Kilgour later combined efforts with Thomas P. Fleming of Columbia to identify a core of biomedical journals that would satisfy 79 percent of all items circulated by the two libraries. A 1966 investigation by L. Miles Raisig and others used interviews with researchers returning monographs to determine how users had identified needed materials, the use to which borrowers had put the library materials, and how useful the materials had been. The age of the material circulated was also determined and, as in the case of the journal studies, the results supported earlier observations that most materials circulated are recent. Similar studies were conducted by other researchers. Reviews based on citation analysis had been popular as early as the mid-1940s and were also used throughout the 1960s and since, in efforts to evaluate collections of libraries, individual scientists, and hospital core collections among others.

One of the most intensive efforts in the area of measurement of satisfaction from the viewpoint of the user was that made by the Institute for the Advancement of Medical Communication (IAMC) for NLM. The intended end product of this work was not the evaluation of libraries but the development of tools whereby evaluative studies could be done. This group, led by R. H. Orr, developed methods for collecting objective data suitable for planning and guiding local, regional, and national programs. Beginning its work in 1966, the IAMC focused on the following goals: (1) to develop a method of measuring quantitatively a library's capability for providing documents its users may need; (2) to develop a standard procedure for making an "inventory" of all the services a library offers its individual users; (3) to develop a method for identifying, enumerating, and characterizing the user population that constitutes a library's primary responsibility; (4) to assess the responsibility of measuring quantitatively a library's capabilities for providing certain types of "reference service"; and (5) to evaluate alternative methods for measuring utilization of the library's services.

These studies concentrated on academic libraries serving biomedical populations. They also focused on assessing effectiveness on the basis of how well the users were served, rather than on how the library went about its business.

The user orientation of these later studies influenced, or at least foreshadowed, a persistent trend. Many recent evaluations of both traditional and innovative library services now measure success by user satisfaction rather than by numbers of units of service provided. Though Renata Tagliacozzo rightly warns of the pitfalls of oversimplified interpretations of user satisfaction studies, the trend toward measuring library effectiveness in terms of meeting user needs rather than meeting some arbitrary standards is firmly established in health science libraries.

REFERENCES

F. Wilfrid Lancaster, *The Measurement and Evaluation of Library Services* (1977).

Richard H. Orr et al., "Development of Methodologic Tools for Planning and Managing Library Services," "II. Measuring a Library's Capability for Providing Documents," "III. Standardized Inventories of Library Services," *Bulletin of the Medical Library Association* (1968).

Irwin H. Pizer and Alexander M. Cain, "Objective Tests of Library Performance," *Special Libraries* (1968).

L. Miles Raisig et al., "How Biomedical Investigators Use Library Books," *Bulletin of the Medical Library Association* (1966)

Renata Tagliacozzo, "Estimating the Satisfaction of Information Users," *Bulletin of the Medical Library Association* (1977).

VIRGINIA H. HOLTZ

LIBRARY COOPERATION

Along with their public and research library counterparts, health science libraries have been forced to recognize that they cannot be self-sufficient. Because of escalating costs, budget reductions, and the rapid accrual of information, a shift in philosophy was necessary to cope with the need to expand services while continuing to consider the quality of information added to the collection and its dissemination. As the health science community became more aware of its growing need for the world's expanding biomedical information, the resource requirements of any library to meet these needs became more challenging. Librarians could no longer be territorially possessive of their collections in even the largest libraries, nor could any library have on-site access to all materials required by its clientele. On the other hand, the reality of paring their collections and entering into cooperative arrangements was threatening to many librarians. Desperation measures such as drastic reduction of subscriptions were common before rational examination of the total acquisition program took place. Planning for cooperative activity and the incorportaion of smaller units into networks forced innovative solutions.

Medical Library Assistance Act. Historically, the responsibility for the emergence of a network concept in U.S. medical libraries must be credited to NLM under the MLAA. In 1965 the President's Commission on Heart Disease, Cancer, and Stroke studied the state of medical librarianship in the U.S. and found it wanting. The commission found poor facilities, lack of resources and services, and staff inadequately prepared to make use of advancing technology. Under the MLAA of 1965, NLM addressed the challenge and began to develop the nationwide Biomedical Communications Net-

work (BCN). The MLAA played a key role in supporting the development of the network, which had the potential of enabling NLM to fill the biomedical information needs of more than 5,000,000 health-care personnel. Approximately 8,000 health institutions, including more than 7,000 community hospitals, more than 550 colleges, universities, and professional schools in the health sciences, and some 470 medical research society, health care, and industrial organizations comprised the community of libraries to be integrated.

In addition to some 1,400 grants awarded under the MLAA for research, resources, training, construction, and publication, the Regional Medical Library Network (RMLN) was established to provide programs to meet the information needs of the health-care professional and research community. Within the Regional Medical Library Program (RMLP), grants were awarded to meet changing information needs. Developing consortia was viewed as necessary to meet the goal of adequacy for hospital

---

Table 1. Seven Regional Medical Libraries and States[a]

Region	States	Operational
1. Northeast: Greater Northeast Regional Medical Library New York Academy of Medicine (Reconfigured from former NLM Regions I, II, and III)	Connecticut Delaware Maine Massachusetts New Hampshire New Jersey New York Pennsylvania Rhode Island Vermont Puerto Rico	January 1, 1983
2. Southeast: Southeastern/Atlantic Regional Medical Library University of Maryland Health Sciences Library (Reconfigured from former NLM Regions IV and VI)	Alabama Florida Georgia Maryland Mississippi North Carolina South Carolina Tennessee Virginia West Virginia District of Columbia	January 1, 1983
3. Midwest: Greater Midwest Regional Medical Library Network University of Illinois at Chicago Library of the Health Sciences (Reconfigured from former NLM Regions V and VII)	Illinois Indiana Iowa Kentucky Michigan Minnesota North Dakota Ohio South Dakota Wisconsin	January 1, 1983
4. Midcontinent: Midcontinental Regional Medical Library University of Nebraska Medical Center Library	Colorado Kansas Missouri Nebraska Utah Wyoming	July 1970
5. South-Central: South-Central Regional Medical Library University of Texas Health Science Center Library	Arkansas Louisiana New Mexico Oklahoma Texas	February 1970
6. Pacific Northwest: Pacific Northwest Regional Medical Library University of Washington Health Sciences Library	Alaska Idaho Montana Oregon Washington	October 1968
7. Pacific Southwest: Pacific Southwest Regional Medical Library UCLA Biomedical Library Center for the Health Sciences	Arizona California Hawaii Nevada	September 1969

[a]As reconfigured January 1983.

libraries, the least tended area of medical librarianship until the early 1970s. Grants were made available to support this emerging program in 1976.

Under the initial RMLP, the country was divided into 11 regions, each with a Regional Medical Library (RML). On a decentralized basis, each RML was responsible for promoting document delivery. Selected primary libraries with major medical collections in each state were designated as Resource Libraries. Interlibrary loan requests among Resource Libraries, and from other health science libraries to Resource Libraries, for document delivery were reimbursed by NLM. This interlibrary document delivery activity had an impact on lending patterns and collection development among Resource Libraries. In the mid-1970s NLM, satisfied that the necessary steps toward filling the goal of document delivery by Resource Libraries had been taken, shifted its concern toward the limited resources or absence of health science libraries at the grass roots level. Focusing on the large segment of the U.S. where health care information needs were not being met at all, NLM began to fill the void through the Biomedical Communications Network. Prior to the contract renewals for the 1983–85 period, NLM reviewed the program and decided that a reconfigured geographic arrangement was desirable. Accordingly, the number of regions was reduced to seven (see Table) and the program emphasis was changed to provide more direct services to health professionals. For such programs as the training of online search specialists in libraries, three mega-regions (East, Midlands, and West) were

designated. In 1985, after another extensive review of the program, NLM reformulated the RML statement of work to deal with the following major areas: (1) To improve access to and delivery of information to health professionals; (2) to develop and maintain an effective and efficient network of health science libraries; and (3) to develop and maintain linkages between the network and other library/information networks or health professional organizations to share resources. The new contract period covers the years 1986–90. NLM established network maximum charges for online searches performed on MEDLINE at $25 for a minimum search and $8 for a filled interlibrary loan request (1985).

Structure. In the area of health science cooperation, three recognized configurations are in operation: the BCN hierarchy, the distributed consortium, and the star-shaped MEDLARS network (see diagram). They follow the three traditional patterns of network structure: (1) the *hierarchical network,* wherein network members share resources, with the majority of needs satisfied before requesting service to the next greater resource center and the remaining unfilled requests referred to the "library of last resort"; (2) the *distributed network,* in which network members hold different resources that are shared among members; and (3) the *star network,* wherein one network member holds all resources and all members utilize them.

Consortium development, as an example of a cooperative subregional network, was one solution to NLM's direction that RMLs develop libraries at the

Network Structure

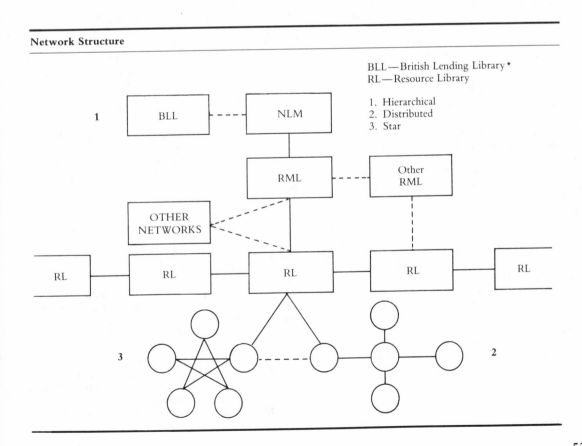

BLL—British Lending Library*
RL—Resource Library

1. Hierarchical
2. Distributed
3. Star

*Renamed BL Document Supply Centre (December 1985)

sub-Resource Library level of the BCN hierarchical structure. The success of this development can be attested to by the Greater Midwest Regional Medical Library Network's 37 consortia and local groups with 553 members. For document delivery, requests are initially sent to other members of the same group. If the request is not filled, it is sent to a Resource Library in the same state, which fills the request from its collection or refers it to another Resource Library, either in the same state or in the same region. If the request is still not filled, it is referred to the "library of last resort," the NLM. The NLM in turn has agreements with the British Library Lending Division to supply materials not in its collection. Through the BCN, a 25-bed hospital's library manager has access to the same resources as a large medical school or research organization.

Area Health Education Center (AHEC) libraries are participants in two configurations: as distributed in their AHEC to AHEC relationship, and as part of a star structure in their relationship with their local medical school library in supporting the clinical experiences for students, interns, and residents. Departmental libraries of large medical schools often work in a star configuration.

The MEDLARS/MEDLINE computerized on-line bibliographic network within the BCN can be described as a star configuration, with all terminals connected to the NLM databases through the use of two major communication networks, TYMNET and TELENET. More than 2,400,000 literature searches were performed in 1984 by 2,461 users of the network; the necessity for sharing costs of system operation requires maximum efficiency.

Governance. Medical library networks use a variety of governing structures. Within the BCN at the Regional Medical Library level, there is usually a policy-setting body as well as an advisory group in place. In varying degrees they include representatives of all levels of libraries—Basic Health Science Libraries, Resource Libraries, the Regional Medical Library, as well as sub-units of the Region—and such nonlibrarians as university faculty and medical professionals. The Regional Medical Library may be the library of last resort in a Region, and is the contracting library for NLM, administering the contractual funds for development activities including cooperative programs within the Region. Resource Libraries are libraries with large health science collections linked to the Regional Medical Library primarily for document delivery and coordinated collection development. Most Resource Libraries have assumed other resource and leadership responsibilities within their respective states. Basic Health Science Libraries are those libraries within the Region not Regional Medical Libraries or Resource Libraries.

At the consortium level a coordinator or chairperson and secretary may manage the group on an elected or rotating basis. Consortia may have formal governance with contractual agreements, bylaws, and administrative advisory councils or may be organized informally. In a majority of cooperative arrangements, monies are not involved; interlibrary loans that may require exchange of funds are generally handled with a periodic statement or balance of payment on an individual institution-to-institution basis.

Function. As an example of a wide-ranging, discipline-based, single-type form of library cooperation, health science libraries are certainly among the most advanced in the U.S. Within the single-type cooperative concept there is relative homogeneity of the network components; however, no two participants are identical in either organizational structure or needs. The 25-bed hospital obviously has information requirements different from those of the medical school or pharmaceutical research division.

At the outset of interlibrary cooperation, document delivery was the single function and principal reason for forming or joining cooperative networks. However, with recognition of the potential that cooperation holds, many cooperative ventures have developed into multi-type function networks.

The University of Pittsburgh survey of networks, cited by J. G. Williams in *The Structure and Governance of Library Networks* (1979), produced a list of 21 functions in which library networks are involved: (1) interlibrary loan, (2) reference, (3) delivery, (4) acquisitions, (5) union lists, (6) continuing education, (7) bibliographic access, (8) photocopying, (9) circulation, (10) communications, (11) publications, (12) cataloguing, (13) processing, (14) storage, (15) literature searching, (16) collection development, (17) abstracting and indexing, (18) referral, (19) consulting, (20) accounting and management, and (21) microfilming. Each of these functions has been performed by health science library networks.

The Medical Library Center of New York (MLCNY) with its 66 members (1985) is an example of a uniquely designed multifunction network. It was established for cooperative acquisition and storage of medical library materials, and further cooperation has led to the creation of the Union Catalog of Medical Periodicals (UCMP), one of the major computerized union lists of serials, and the Union Catalog of Medical Monographs and Multimedia (UCOM). OCLC, Inc., is yet another example of a multifunction network, including cooperative cataloguing, interlibrary loan transmission, and acquisition components.

Funding for cooperative activities comes in a variety of ways. The following channels are the most significant:

National Library of Medicine. Under the MLAA a portion of the NLM budget was devoted to the RML program—approximately $105,000 in 1967 rising to $3,000,000 in 1978 and settling at a level of $2,000,000 in 1984.

Regional Medical Library. RML programs are carried out under contract between NLM and the seven Regions. RMLs and Resource Libraries contribute substantial staff time, facilities, and effort over and above contract funds. Many activities are carried out voluntarily by hundreds of librarians through regional committees and projects.

Consortia. In the main, consortia are not grant-funded, with costs for activities such as printing of union lists absorbed by individual institutions. Exceptions are the NLM Resource Improvement Grants for consortium development and Resource Project Grants for large-scale consortium projects. Nonmembers may be charged fees for service. Dues, per-bed fees, and entry fees are other means of sharing the costs of consortium activities.

International Cooperation. Activities associated with international health science library cooperation have had an impact on country-to-country relationships, intracountry relationships, and the use of cooperation and exchange by varied means.

International Congresses. The First International Congress on Medical Librarianship, in 1953, enabled 317 attendees from 36 countries to share experiences and ideas on education, classification, the history of medicine, and international health science library cooperation. The Second Congress, in 1963, with 871 attendees from 58 countries, discussed health science library education, documentation, information dissemination, and MEDLARS. The Third Congress, in 1969, addressed health science library computer applications and national and regional network planning. The Fourth Congress, in 1980, focused on medical librarianship in a developing world, and the Fifth, in 1985, highlighted the unity of medical librarianship.

IFLA. The Section of Biological and Medical Sciences Libraries of IFLA, for the period 1986–91, set a program that includes: (1) updating and revision of the *World List of Biological and Medical Sciences Libraries* (1st edition 1985); (2) planning for the Sixth International Congress on Medical Librarianship in New Delhi, India, September/October, 1990; (3) conducting regional programs, including the provision of continuing education opportunities; (4) working with the World Health Organization, FID, and other relevant international bodies; and (5) working with other organizations to facilitate the international exchange of materials in biology and medicine.

Medical Library Association. The MLA's International Cooperation Committee administered an international fellowship program with a grant of $94,000 from the Rockefeller Foundation, enabling 43 Fellows from 29 countries to spend time in the U.S. on work-study-travel programs. In 1974 the Committee initiated a library-to-library project, matching 40 pairs of libraries from 28 countries. Cooperative activities in reference referral, distribution of basic lists and directories, and translation services are encouraged. The Exchange, together with Unesco, distributed duplicate materials to libraries in countries ravaged by World War II. In 1985 there were 61 overseas and 72 Canadian institutional members of the Exchange. Concerns about the manual system used to conduct the exchange had prompted several years of review, and in 1985 MLA was conducting a pilot study on a modified type of machine-based exchange. Other work on machine-based systems for facilitating exchange of materials was being conducted by the Greater Midwest Regional Medical Library Network, using microcomputers and a modified file program for integrating data on available materials. Participants exchange floppy disks for processing records.

National Library of Medicine. During John Shaw Billings's administration of the Surgeon General's Library, international exchange was initiated in 1881. NLM had 810 exchange partners in 87 countries in 1985. In response to requests for service from developing countries, NLM has provided interlibrary and audiovisual loans, as well as MEDLINE, distribution of *Current Catalog, Index Medicus,* and *Abridged Index Medicus.* Under the Special Foreign Currency Program originating in the Agricultural Trade and Assistance Act of 1954, NLM received funds to translate

biomedical literature, develop bibliographic tools, and prepare critical reviews. In 1984, 60 percent of this program was carried out in India and about 25 percent in Poland, with the remaining projects in Egypt, Israel, Pakistan, and Yugoslavia. International bilateral MEDLARS agreements to share the bibliographic database were negotiated with partners in 14 countries, and in 1985 NLM was working on arrangements with China and India for the establishment of MEDLARS centers. A number of collaborative programs are conducted with the World Health Organization in publication production and provision of photocopies of articles to users in developing countries.

NLM, in sharing its resources and expertise, has stimulated many cooperative biomedical communication activities. Mutual benefits have accrued from the collaborative efforts.

The potential impact of the efforts at the Lister Hill National Center for Biomedical Communications to marry the minicomputer, the videodisk, and speech recognition technology is exciting to consider. The Center's capability for satellite communication will continue to affect the future of health science library cooperation. Materials will be available to both individual libraries and networks in electronic form; the prospects of reduced costs through electronic document delivery begin to seem real.

In addition to biomedical information networks in such countries as Canada, Japan, and the United Kingdom, similar networks are emerging in Czechoslovakia, Germany, and Hungary. The World Health Organization, the Pan American Health Organization (PAHO), and Unesco have also provided bases for coordination of cooperative usage of health science library resources on a world spectrum.

Other Cooperative Activities. Health science library networks are moving in the direction of internetwork cooperation with non-health science library networks. Again, NLM has been in the forefront as a prime mover in initiating discussions. Through the RML program, the TALON (Texas, Arkansas, Louisiana, Oklahoma, New Mexico) and Midwest Regions have held meetings with state library directors, heads of library agencies, and other networks to discuss ways in which health science and non-health science libraries can work together to furnish maximum information to their respective patrons.

Consortia are making progress toward interconsortium sharing at the local level in each state. Interstate cooperation at the consortium level is already being experimented with.

The professional library organizations—the MLA, the Special Libraries Association (SLA), and the ALA—are working in concert to resolve problems involved with cataloguing rules, the closing of the Library of Congress card catalogue, and other programs that affect the entire library community.

Health science librarians today are far better qualified at the entry level, in view of the highly specialized training in medical librarianship and their practicum experience. Building on this increased level of professional development, perhaps the greatest impact on the success of any network has come from the contributions of individual personnel involved in network planning, management, and activities.

REFERENCES

Mary E. Corning, "National Library of Medicine International Cooperation for Biomedical Communications," *Bulletin of the Medical Library Association* (1975).

Beth A. Hamilton and William B. Ernst, Jr., *Multitype Library Cooperation* (1977).

Donald D. Hendricks, "The Regional Medical Library Program," *Library Trends* (1975).

Allen Kent and Thomas J. Galvin, editors, *The Structure and Governance of Library Networks* (1979).

RUBY S. MAY

LAWS AND LEGISLATION

International Scene. The international awareness generated by copyright revision and the trend toward developing national information systems has heightened the legislative consciousness of medical librarians throughout the world. Traditionally, library legislation made a positive impact on medical libraries by engendering public support for health information services. In the mid-1970s, however, medical librarians began to feel the negative effect of copyright revision because it threatened the freedom with which library services have usually been rendered. In the 1980s concerns about legality of public access to databases, database ownership rights (copyright), and transborder data flow raised new questions for developing national networking systems.

Legislative interest in medical librarianship already exists in the U.S. and is growing rapidly in other countries. In 1977 the MLA moved toward steady rather than spasmodic involvement in legislative affairs by expanding the role of its Legislation Committee. In 1979 the 45th IFLA Council and General Conference, in Copenhagen, chose the theme "Library Legislation and Management." The intent of the IFLA program was to share information on legislative issues affecting numerous library associations. Obviously, the concerns for legislative solutions to problems of disseminating information throughout the world extend beyond the discipline of medical librarianship. The IFLA papers raised issues that need more specific exploration in the literature and further discussion in future international meetings.

Stimulated both by national concern and by Unesco programs, a number of countries have begun establishing national networking systems for information services. In these networking systems, health and biomedicine are usually handled as an individual section. The principles for establishment of these systems usually emanate from executive decree or legislative authority. This subject remains to be explored adequately in the literature, and developing a cohesive description is beyond the limits of this article. It can be noted, however, that in a 1975 National Science Foundation report, "Scientific and Technical Information Services in Eight Latin American Countries," Scott Adams outlined the work of various technical assistance agencies, such as Unesco's Division for Scientific and Technical Information and Documentation (UNISIST), Department of Libraries, Documentation, and Archives (DBA), PAHO, and others that have achieved considerable progress in enhancing the legal and political environmental aspects of information transfer. The approaches of the countries cited vary slightly, but their ultimate purposes are to develop national organizational links for scientific and technical information in a realistic manner and to implement multilateral agreements for regional cooperation.

The PAHO attempt to create regional services at the Biblioteca Regional de Medicina (BIREME) in São Paulo, Brazil, has been reasonably effective. The NLM served as a technical consultant to assist Argentina, Peru, Chile, Colombia, Uruguay, and Venezuela to establish a regional medical library to serve as the backup resource to the member states. Services include interlibrary loans, exchange of journals, training of librarians, and access to MEDLINE bibliographic searches. With the demonstrated success of BIREME and assistance from WHO, other regional approaches are being attempted.

In a paper presented at the 1979 IFLA meeting, Estelle Brodman reported the importance for joint action of biomedical librarians through organizations such as IFLA, Unesco, the Economic and Social Commission for Asia and the Pacific (ESCAP), WHO, and MLA. In further discussion Brodman added that the major concern of developing countries is to feed and clothe the population; therefore, creating strong libraries naturally has lower priority. Regional approaches and cooperative programs seem the most economical and efficient solution for information transfer, and the trend toward creation of regional medical library groups is growing rapidly. Generally speaking, however, legislative efforts have been haphazard in the international arena, resulting in inconsistent support by individual countries and organizations.

The United States. *The National Library of Medicine.* Congress has consistently supported health and library legislation that has enabled NLM to develop networking and cooperative programs at a steady pace. It appropriates funds to conduct programs for developing national information and library services in the health sciences and for modernizing medical library services throughout the nation.

The basis for support of a national library of medicine in the U.S. dates back to 1836, with the development of a collection in the Surgeon General's Office. In 1922 that library became the Army Medical Library, and in 1952 it was renamed the Armed Forces Medical Library. As a result of legislation sponsored by Senators Lister Hill and John F. Kennedy in 1956, the Armed Forces Medical Library became the National Library of Medicine; it was then authorized as the nation's major collector and distributor of health science information. Since that time various pieces of legislation have expanded NLM's authority. After Congress authorized funds to build a new library facility on the campus of the National Institutes of Health in Bethesda, Maryland (dedicated December 14–15, 1961), it enacted the MLAA of 1965, authorizing NLM to develop a grant program to provide aid to the nation's medical libraries. In 1968 the National Medical Audiovisual Center and the Lister Hill National Center for Biomedical Communications were established by statute as part of NLM, and a new tower to house the Center was dedicated on May 22, 1980.

Funds appropriated by Congress have supported the NLM's bibliographic contributions in print and nonprint format. Most notable have been the preparation of *Index Medicus,* the comprehensive bibliography of medical literature, and the development of MEDLARS (Medical Literature Analysis and Retrieval System), the computer bibliographic service from which the major databases of NLM have been created. Another online bibliographic retrieval service, TOXLINE, is a result of the Toxicology Information Program established at NLM in 1967. Recently NLM created the Toxicology Data Bank, which stores and retrieves information about toxic substances.

The basis for the regional approach to networking and cooperation was authorized by the MLAA in 1965. This legislation set in motion a series of programs that strengthened the nation's medical libraries and enabled essential coordination and cooperation.

The Medical Library Assistance Act (MLAA) authorized NLM to administer an extramural program to upgrade medical libraries and to organize regional and local relationships by encouraging sharing of skills and resources. This legislation became the basis for more clearly defined roles and responsibilities between the medical library community and the NLM.

The soundness of the philosophy underlying this legislative program was reflected in later extensions of the MLAA with only minor amendments. To fulfill the changing needs of health professionals, the MLAA was periodically revised, consolidated, and extended. Overall, however, the act's flexibility has allowed NLM to make modifications and to implement new programs without changing the legislative language. (See Table.)

Considered non-controversial legislation, the MLAA has traditionally enjoyed strong congressional support. Extensions have been easily obtained, but full funding or even adequate appropriation levels to fulfill the expectation of the act are yet to be

Table 2. Renewals of the Medical Library Assistance Act

Years implemented	Title of acts	Dates signed
1966	Medical Library Assistance Act of 1965, P.L. 89–291	October 22, 1965
1971	Medical Library Assistance Extension Act of 1970, P.L. 92–212	March 13, 1970
1974	Health Programs Extension Act of 1973 P.L. 93–45	June 18, 1973
1975	Health Services Research, Health Statistics and Medical Libraries Act of 1974, P.L. 93–35	July 23, 1974
1977	Biomedical Research Extension Act of 1977, P.L. 95–83	August 1, 1977
1978	Biomedical Research Extension Amendments of 1978, Title II of the Community Mental Health Centers Extension Act of 1978, P.L. 95–622	November 9, 1978
1981	Omnibus Budget Reconciliation Act of 1981, P.L. 97–35	August 13, 1981
1982	Continuing Appropriations for Fiscal Year 1983	December 21, 1982
1983	Further Continuing Appropriations for Fiscal Year 1984, P.L. 98–151	November 14, 1983
1984	Making Appropriations for the Departments of Labor, Health and Human Services, and Education, and Related Agencies, for the Fiscal Year Ending September 30, 1985, and for Other Purposes, P.L. 98–619	November 8, 1984
	Making Further Appropriations, for the Fiscal Year 1985, and for Other Purposes, P.L. 98–473	October 12, 1984
1985	The Health Research Extension Act of 1985, P.L. 99–158.	

achieved. Although a good beginning was made toward achieving the tenets of the act, limited federal funds have prevented more substantial accomplishments. During the 1980s moratoria and terminations of essential library programs resulted from low funding levels. In addition, inflation multiplied the adverse effects of inadequate funding.

In administering the MLAA programs, NLM monitors the changing needs of health professionals and the medical library community to assure that they are fulfilled. Although there were relatively little fluctuation during a 19-year span, some subtle programmatic changes have in reality occurred. (See Table 2.) For example, training support has shifted from medical librarians to computer specialists in medicine and a research program for computers in medicine has been launched. NLM is also funding research proposals in the field of medical informatics and artificial intelligence. Beginning in 1983, NLM supported contract and grant programs designed to lead to integrated academic information management systems (IAIMS). Thus new precedents are constantly being established that can potentially change the manner in which the act is administered.

The programs authorized through the MLAA that most directly affect medical librarianship are the Regional Medical Library, Resource Improvement, Training, and Research Grants programs.

The Regional Medical Library Program. This program is noted for its mainstay support of information provision and document delivery to health professionals.

The Resource Improvement Grants Program. Another vital component of the MLAA, this program was originally conceived as a means of supplementing library support. Grants were awarded on a formula basis according to budget size and number of patrons served. In 1970 the program was split into Resource Improvement and Resource Project Grants. The Improvement grants were designed to assist small hospital libraries. Of the great variety of activities funded through the Resource Project Grants, probably the most innovative was consortium development for resource sharing.

The Training Program. This program has undergone a series of evolutionary steps designed to improve the skills of health professionals involved in transfer of information. In 1965 it concentrated on sponsoring medical library trainees at the undergraduate and graduate levels; in the 1970s it supported additional training programs for biomedical information personnel to assist ongoing scientific research. Eventually the medical library trainee program was phased out and replaced by training for health professionals in computer sciences and technology. In 1978 a small trial program was established to support medical library management interns.

The Research, Development, and Demonstration Program. This program supports projects to improve storage and retrieval of biomedical information, communication of biomedical research, effectiveness of biomedical teaching, and communications in health care. Largely through this program, support is given to advance the current state of the art of information sciences related to health. As a result of conferences conducted in 1974 and 1975, research goals have emphasized the need for health practitioners to retrieve actual information rather than references to documents.

The Research Support for Computers in Medicine Program. Recommended in 1978 by a task force reviewing NLM's research grant program, this program was designed to foster the growth and advance of computer sciences in the health field and to promote research in an environment conducive to interdisciplinary collaboration.

The Copyright Act of 1976, which took effect on January 1, 1978, represents one of the most controversial pieces of recent legislation to affect medical libraries. Although the antiquated copyright law of 1909 was in need of revision, ambiguities and inconsistencies of the new law created so many possibilities for varying interpretations by librarians, publishers, and producers of print and nonprint materials that guidelines representing different points of view were prepared by associations of each special-interest group. The MLA responded to the needs of its membership by drafting a copyright brochure, "The Copyright Law and the Health Sciences Librarian," to assist medical librarians in applying the law in their individual settings.

In addition, the MLA presented its position to Congress and worked with the Council of National Library Associations' (CNLA) Committee on Copyright Law Practice and Implementation to present testimony to the National Commission on New Technological Uses of Copyrighted Works (CONTU). MLA agreed to abide by the existing law until it was reviewed five years after it took effect. The review was issued in January 1983 and the MLA published its response in 1985. The MLA found that the review tended to accept the unsupported appraisal of the publishing community that photocopying under fair-use provisions still had not achieved "balance," even though studies commissioned by the Copyright Office did not bear out that position. The MLA and other library associations viewed a number of the recommendations in the report as controversial, and librarians criticized the report as biased towards the publishers' point of view. MLA argued that the issues surrounding the use of new technologies were clouded by unnecessary debate and controversy over library photocopying.

Because document delivery services in the health sciences are largely handled through photocopied articles, the current regulations may have an especially adverse effect on health libraries, their constituents, and those who subscribe to health publications. If the cooperative arrangements built by the RML network are cut because of restrictions imposed by the copyright law, the existing transfer of biomedical information will be directly impeded. This possibility has already resulted in increased serial subscription lists and operating costs for health science libraries.

Other National Health Legislation. It has become more and more apparent to American medical librarians that other health legislation can restrict or support their ability to provide information services. A selected number of acts are cited here because of their direct impact. The National Health Planning and Resource Development Act (Public Law 93-641) created Health Systems Agencies (HSA) to plan for the nation's health care system. This legislation opened the possibility for a close alliance between HSAs and RML services to sponsor innovative library programs and to prevent unnecessary duplication. Medical librarians have played a role in providing HSA staff with information related to data-gathering and research.

The National Consumer Health Information and Health Promotion Act (Public Law 94-317), administered through the Bureau of Health Education, Centers for Disease Control (CDC), authorized a program to support development of patient/consumer education materials. Although Title XVII applied to information services, it remained unfunded, and in 1979 CDC began negotiating contracts to develop resources in patient education.

The Comprehensive Health Manpower Training

Table 3. Amounts Awarded by Program under the MLAA for FY 1966–84 (dollars in thousands)

	1966	1967	1968	1969	1970	1971	1972	1973	1974	1975	1976	1977
Construction	0	0	10,000	1,250	0	0	0	0	0	0	0	0
Training	432	812	922	1,310	983	1,000	1,234	720	720	891	1,389	1,208
Special scientific projects	34	33	54	85	5	5	100	76	95	153	72	109
Research	741	1,357	1,473	1,321	990	590	640	665	900	1,292	1,353	1,180
Publications	745	588	582	300	267	280	311	389	340	614	617	738
Resource grants IAIMS	24	3,328	3,548	2,800	2,105	2,231	2,505	2,298	2,211	1,469	726	1,773
Regional medical libraries	0	105	680	2,088	1,807	1,886	2,047	2,501	3,104	2,194	3,351	3,086
SBIR[a]												
Scientific Evaluation[b]												
Total	$1,976	$6,223	$17,259	$9,154	$6,157	$5,992	$6,837	$6,649	$7,370	$6,613	$7,508	$8,094

[a]Mandated set-aside for Small Business Competitive Contracts
[b]For Review Committee expenses—not an MLAA competitive grant program

Act of 1971 (Public Law 92-157) authorized the establishment of Area Health Education Centers (AHEC). The program was designed to decentralize education and training programs for health professionals and to improve their distribution in underserved areas. Medical librarians have played a key role in providing information services to satellite facilities of university programs and in developing communications networks to link university resources to the community.

Hospital Cost Containment bills were unsuccessfully introduced beginning in the 95th Congress. Many hospital librarians argue that cost containment is already exercised to the ultimate through resource-sharing programs and that any further attempts to reduce library operating budgets would have a detrimental effect on services.

The Department of Health and Human Services (DHHS) took another approach to the problem by issuing new regulations implementing Section 223 of Public Law 92-603 (Amendment to the Social Security Act, Title XVIII), redefining criteria for Medicare reimbursements. The criteria established, based on bed size and geographic location, impose hardships on tertiary-care teaching hospitals that may ultimately affect library budgets. Another approach to this problem results from the implementation of Diagnostic Related Group (DRG) payment schedules for hospitals that make it difficult to relate hospital library costs to specific patient charges. A result of this change has been a reduction of library services and staffing in some smaller non-teaching hospitals.

General Legislation. The concern of medical librarians with respect to general legislation that affects libraries also reflects the interests and needs of health care consumers and health professionals.

The White House Conference on Libraries and Information Services, held November 15-19, 1979, and authorized as part of Public Law 93-568, was one of the major events focusing on national library issues. Medical librarians served on advisory, planning, and preconference committees at the state and national level. Important resolutions recommending national information networks and national library programs were endorsed by the conferees in 1979. A follow-up conference was tentatively scheduled for 1989.

The Postal Amendments of 1976 (Public Law 94-421) made it possible for publishers and distributors to mail materials to libraries at the fourth-class rate. However, because of an oversight, no provision was made for materials to be returned at the same rate.

The famous Williams and Wilkins suit of 1968, alleging copyright infringement by NLM and NIH, stimulated greater legislative awareness among medical librarians that was enhanced during the preparation of the Copyright Act of 1976. Although the Supreme Court found that no infringement had occurred, the impact of the suit has a chilling effect on medical libraries throughout the world. Since then, medical librarians have recognized the need to maintain vigilance over impending legislation, to sponsor supportive library legislation, and to be knowledgeable about health legislation that might affect the mission of providing health information.

REFERENCES

Scott Adams, *Scientific and Technical Information Services in Eight Latin American Countries: Developments Technical Assistance Opportunities for Cooperation* (NTIS #PB253 202, 1975), provides comprehensive background on establishment of national information systems in eight Latin American countries.

Estelle Brodman, "Biomedical Library Management and Legislation in Developing Countries in Southeast Asia," *Newsletter IFLA Section of Biological and Medical Sciences Libraries* (1980), makes numerous recommendations to IFLA on joint actions to aid biomedical libraries in developing countries.

Arthur J. Brocering, "Medical Library Resource Grants: The Past and the Future," *Bulletin of the Medical Library Association* (1971), reviews progress of the resource grants funded through the MLAA in 1970.

Martin M. Cummings and Mary E. Corning, "The Medical Library Assistance Act: An Analysis of the NLM Extramural Programs 1965-1970," *Bulletin of the Medical Library Association* (1971) includes a detailed description of the administration and implementation of the MLAA.

Department of Health, Education, and Welfare, Public Health Service, National Institutes of Health, *Communication in the Service of American Health . . A Bicentennial Report from the National Library of Medicine,* (1976), gives excellent historical background that includes establishment of the Extramural Programs and the international impact of NLM.

"Renewal of the Medical Library Assistance Act," *Bulletin of the Medical Library Association* (1978), outlines the recommendations of the MLA Legislation Committee for extension of the MLAA in 1978.

"Response of the Medical Library Association to the Report of the Register of Copyrights to Congress, Library Reproduction of Copyrighted Works (17 U.S.C. 108)," *Bulletin of the Medical Library Association* (1985).

NAOMI C. BROERING

978	1979	1980	1981	1982	1983	1984	1985
0	0	0	0	0	0	0	0
,360	1,472	1,638	1,308	930	733	786	1,091
248	215	142	290	22	34	--	0
,110	1,592	2,724	2,704	2,524	2,782	2,326	5,261
,050	764	787	818	504	440	587	403
,078	2,008	1,596	1,641	1,071	1,211	1,590	1,889
		--	--	--	--	133	1,157
,018	2,849	2,967	2,999	2,399	2,300	2,000	2,054
							60
		70	70	80	--	55	110
,864	$8,900	$9,924	$9,830	$7,500	$7,500	$7,495	$12,025

Daniel Melcher

Melcher, Daniel
(1912-1985)

Daniel Melcher, publishing executive, contributed to library service as an innovator in developing professional publications, reference services, and methods for improving book production and distribution.

Melcher was born July 10, 1912, at Newton Center, Massachusetts, the son of Marguerite Fellows Melcher and Frederic Gershom Melcher (later President of R. R. Bowker Company). Daniel Melcher was graduated from Harvard College (A.B.) in 1934. In 1934 and 1935 Melcher was a publicity assistant at the London publishing house of George Allen and Unwin and an assistant and student of publishing methods at other houses in London and Leipzig, Germany. From 1936 to 1942 he worked in a variety of sales promotion and management capactities at Henry Holt and Company, Oxford University Press, Alliance Book Corporation, and Viking Press, all in New York City. During World War II he worked in Washington, D.C., with the U.S. Treasury Department's War Finance Division, first as publishing consultant and then as National Director of its education section. In 1946 he was Director of the National Committee on Atomic Information, also in Washington.

When he joined the R. R. Bowker Company, New York, in 1947, Melcher was appointed Publisher of the firm's *Library Journal*. He quickly began developing the 70-year-old magazine into a major publication dealing with every aspect of the library profession, and in 1954 he founded, as an adjunct, *Junior Libraries (School Library Journal,* beginning 1961).

At the same time, Melcher had been working on the idea of a series of current in-print directories of American books. He devised the procedures by which the directories could be edited and produced, and in 1948 the firm launched the annual *Books in Print,* with author and title indexes. There followed, also under Melcher's vigorous direction, *Paperbound Books in Print* (1956), *Subject Guide to Books in Print* (1957), *Forthcoming Books* (advance listings), and *American Book Publishing Record* (catalogue listings, current and cumulative, in Dewey cataloguing sequence, 1961).

Meanwhile, Melcher was writing articles on library questions for *LJ* and on book distribution and book manufacturing for *Publishers' Weekly.* He contributed to the automated "belt press" concept of book manufacturing. His concern for distribution made him a major force in the mid-1960s in establishing the International Standard Book Numbering System.

Melcher became a Director and General Manager of Bowker in 1956; Vice-President, 1959; and President, 1963–68. After Bowker acquired Jaques Cattell Press, biographical directory publisher, Melcher was its Board Chairman, 1961–67. He took part in the Bowker stockholders' decision to sell the firm to the Xerox Corporation January 1, 1968, and was then Bowker Chairman under Xerox but resigned early in 1969.

He was Board Chairman of Gale Research Corporation, 1971–73, and thereafter an independent consultant. He was a member of the ALA Council,

1972–74, and from 1969 a board member of Institutes for Achievement of Human Potentials, with a special interest in the ways by which very young children can learn to read.

With Nancy Larrick, Melcher wrote a basic guide, *Printing and Promotion Handbook* (1949, 1956, 1967), and, with Margaret Saul Melcher, *Melcher on Acquisitions* (1971).

In 1937 he married Peggy Zimmerman, later a children's librarian; they had one son, Frederic G. Melcher II. After her death (1967), he married Margaret Saul, who had been editor of *School Library Journal.* Daniel Melcher died July 22, 1985, in Charlottesville, Virginia.

CHANDLER B. GRANNIS

Melcher, Frederic G.
(1879–1963)

Frederic Gershom Melcher, editor, publisher, bookseller, and book collector, became one of the most influential and respected figures in the world of books not only in the United States but throughout the world during his 45 years with the R. R. Bowker Company. Rarely has a single person had such familiarity with all the aspects of bookmaking, bookselling, and book acquisition. Melcher's devotion to books began early when as a child he read in the public libraries of Newton, Massachusetts; later (in 1947) he honored a pioneer children's librarian, Caroline M. Hewins, by establishing a lectureship on New England children's literature and naming it for her.

Born on April 12, 1879, in Malden, Massachusetts, the son of Edwin Forrest Melcher and Alice Jane Bartlett Melcher, he grew up in Newton Center and graduated from high school in 1895. He took the "Institute course," to prepare for the Massachusetts Institute of Technology, but the illness of his father and the difficult times following the depression of 1893 (combined with his own disinclination to become, as he put it, "a chemist or a civil engineer") made it necessary for him to seek a job instead.

Through the influence of his maternal grandfather, he obtained a position in the mailroom at Lauriat's famous bookstore in Boston. He remained at Lauriat's 18 years and handled its large library business for a time, built up its children's department, and eventually became one of its most successful salesmen. His discernment in judging and recommending current books earned him a reputation that began to spread beyond the Boston area; Arnold Bennett, for example, credited him with initiating the demand that led to the American success of *The Old Wives' Tale* in 1908.

His activity in professional organizations fostered his growing reputation: he was President in 1912 of the Boston Booksellers' League and delivered some rousing remarks at both the 1911 and 1912 American Booksellers Association conventions. One member of the audience, W. K. Stewart, soon after asked him to be manager of his Indianapolis store, and in March 1913 Melcher and his family (he had married Marguerite Fellows June 2, 1910) moved to Indianapolis.

The store served as the heart of Indiana's thriving literary activity. Melcher not only met Riley, Tarkington, Ade, Nicholson, Hubbard, and other writers and artists but also discussed book design and fine printing with Edwin Grabhorn, who set up his Studio Press in Indianapolis in 1915. During these years Melcher was becoming active in local and state library associations and speaking before library groups as well as writing for *Publishers' Weekly* and addressing the 1918 ABA convention. He was therefore widely known, and his knowledge of the book trade was thorough, when in 1918 an editorship of *Publishers' Weekly* became available. He joined the Bowker Company, publisher of the journal, in May 1918 as Vice-President and was associated with *Publishers' Weekly* for the next 40 years, first as Managing Editor and then, after Bowker's death in 1933, as Co-editor with Mildred C. Smith.

His intense interest in all aspects of the book and his belief in the interdependence of all parts of the book world were reflected in his handling of *PW*. One of his first actions was to institute a column on bookmaking and book design; another was to devote certain issues each year to children's books. He kept abreast of new developments and maintained personal contact with hundreds of people in the field through extensive travel, both in the U.S. and abroad, serving as a delegate to the International Publishers' Congresses and, following World War II, making trips to Europe and Japan for the State Department and the War Department. His editorials over the years amount to a compendium of informed and sensible commentary on all that was taking place.

In 1934 he succeeded R. R. Bowker as President of the company; under his direction the Bowker lists, while continuing to offer basic book trade tools for libraries and booksellers, increased their attention to bibliophilic books and works of scholarly bibliography. Bowker became the American publisher of Michael Sadleir's "Bibliographia" series, issued a series of state imprint bibliographies for the Bibliographical Society of America, and published John Carter's great *Taste and Technique in Book-Collecting* (1948—dedicated to Melcher in its 1970 printing), as well as important books on collecting by Mary Benjamin, Jacob Blanck, Howard Peckham, and Colton Storm, and *American Book-Prices Current*. The distinction of this list underlies the comment made by John Carter, one of Melcher's many English friends in the trade, in his 50th-anniversary address to the Bibliographical Society of America, when he singled out three firms, Bowker in New York and Constable and Hart-Davis in London, as having been particularly hospitable to bibliography.

In these years Melcher continued to be tireless in his professional service for such groups as the American Booksellers Association (Secretary, 1918–20), National Association of Book Publishers (Executive Secretary, 1920–24), New York Booksellers' League (President, 1924–25), American Institute of Graphic Arts (President, 1927–28), and New York Library Association (President, 1935–36) and in his work in connection with the Copyright Committee, the NRA code, the Council on Books in Wartime, and the American Civil Liberties Union, among others. As of 1959 Melcher, approaching his 80th birthday, gave up his long editorship of *PW* and presidency of Bowker and became Chairman of the Board; he remained active, however, and attended the International Publishers' Congress in Spain in 1962, the year

before he died, on March 9, 1963, in Montclair, New Jersey.

Melcher's influence, through *PW* and the Bowker Company and through his wide acquaintance, was pervasive during the second quarter of the 20th century. But his influence has been and will continue to be felt in another way—through his generosity in establishing awards and disposing of his own collections. Children's books were always one of his special interests: besides being a founder in 1919 of Children's Book Week, he set up in 1922 an annual award for excellence in children's books, the Newbery Medal, and in 1937 added to it the Caldecott Medal for children's book illustration. He commissioned and donated these medals, but with characteristic modesty he did not wish his name attached to them. As the most prestigious awards in their field, however, they will remain one of his best memorials.

Among the other awards indicative of his temperament and aims are one he established in 1940 for the Indiana library most active in promoting regional history or literature and another that he set up in 1943 for creative publishing (named after Mathew Carey and Isaiah Thomas).

His name will also be remembered for his collecting, and he often expressed his delight in the feel of a well-made book. The many friends who had the pleasure of examining his books at his house in Montclair, New Jersey, would be glad to know that much of the collection can still be consulted in libraries: his private press books are in the university libraries at Princeton and Syracuse; his Vachel Lindsay collection is in the Lilly Library at Indiana University; and his extensive collection of books about books is handsomely housed and effectively maintained (and kept up to date) in the library named for him at the R. R. Bowker Company.

A bestower of awards, he sought none for himself, but they inevitably came to him as the premier ambassador of the book world. In 1945 he was given the medal of the American Institute of Graphic Arts (in addition to being its President in 1927–28, he helped organize its Book Clinic in 1931) and in 1950 a plaque from the Children's Library Association; in 1955 at the Newbery-Caldecott dinner he was informed that a Melcher Scholarship has been established in the field of library service for children; in 1958 he was awarded an Honorary Litt.D. from Rutgers (New Brunswick, New Jersey) and the following year one from Syracuse in New York; and in 1962 the Regina Medal was presented to him by the Catholic Library Association for his work with children's literature.

Contributors to the book published in connection with the May 1945 dinner commemorating his first 50 years in the book trade were in agreement about the position he occupied; B. W. Huebsch, for instance, called him the leader "by tacit consent," and Marion E. Dodd labeled him the "number one liaison man to all the branches of the book world." The London *Bookseller* in 1954 referred to him as "the dean of the *corps diplomatique* of the American booktrade," and after his death it pronounced him "without doubt the greatest all-round bookman the English-speaking world has produced." His broad knowledge, his engaging personality and sense of humor, his infectious enthusiasm for books, his encour-

ALA

Frederic G. Melcher

agement of newcomers in the field, his skill in bringing together people of diverse interests, and his vigorous championship of professional and humanitarian causes all have combined to make him a legendary figure.

REFERENCES

Frederic G. Melcher: Friendly Reminiscences of a Half Century among Books and Bookmen, edited by Mildred C. Smith (1945). In addition to the editor's introduction, a preface by Christopher Morley, and a memoir of his early years by Melcher, this volume contains pieces by Charles E. Goodspeed, D. Laurance Chambers, Harry Hansen, Harry L. Gage, Harry M. Lydenberg, B. W. Huebsch, Bertha E. Mahony Miller, and Marion E. Dodd.

"Frederick G. Melcher—1879–1963," *Publishers' Weekly* (March 18, 1963), an unsigned biographical account written by Roger H. Smith and Chandler B. Grannis.

Helen Adams Masten, editor, "Frederic G. Melcher Memorial Issue," *Top of the News* (March 1964). In addition to an assessment by the editor and two autobiographical essays by Melcher, this issue contains articles by Storer B. Lunt, Irene Smith Green, Ruth Gagliardo, Mildred C. Smith, Anne J. Richter, Leonore St. John Power Mendelson, and Ruth Hill Viguers.

Daniel Melcher, "Fred Melcher as I Knew Him," *ALA Bulletin* (January 1967), is a reminiscence by his son.

Irene Smith, *A History of the Newbery and Caldecott Medals* (1957), contains information drawn from Melcher's correspondence files.

Chandler B. Grannis, "Melcher, Frederick Gershom," *Dictionary of American Library Biography* (1978).

G. THOMAS TANSELLE

Metcalf, Keyes D.

(1889–1983)

Keyes D. Metcalf

Keyes Dewitt Metcalf achieved international recognition for his contributions as a library administrator at the New York Public Library, as Director of University Libraries at Harvard during a period of vigorous growth, and as consultant to the library world at large. He became a leader of the profession who won the admiration of generations of librarians.

Metcalf was born April 13, 1889, in Elyria, Ohio, the son of a railroad engineer. One of 17 children, he went to work while still in high school as a page in the nearby Oberlin College Library, where his brother-in-law, Azariah Root, was Librarian. As a student at Oberlin between 1907 and 1911, he continued his work in the Library as well as playing on the college football and track teams. After graduation he served for a time as Root's Executive Assistant.

Metcalf enrolled in 1911 in the first class of the New York Public Library School, earning its certificate in 1913 and its diploma in 1915. While a student there he worked in the main reading room of the then new and still palatial building at Fifth Avenue and 42nd Street, beginning a relationship with that institution that was to extend over the next quarter-century. He served successively as its Chief of Stacks, Chief of the Order Division, Executive Assistant, and finally—from 1928 to 1937—was in charge of the entire massive operation as Chief of the Reference Department.

Metcalf's accomplishments at the NYPL alone would have been enough to assure him illustrious recognition in the annals of American librarianship. Together with its Director, Harry M. Lydenberg, he furnished a substantial measure of leadership to the library profession through his increasing involvement in the work of the American Library Association. Also during this period he married Martha Gerrish; they had two children. Widowed in 1938, he later married Elinor Gregory.

Metcalf began the second portion of his tripartite career when President James B. Conant of Harvard persuaded him in 1937 to go to Cambridge, Massachusetts, as Librarian of Harvard College and Director of University Libraries. The first person ever to fill that post who was not himself a Harvard graduate, and the first trained librarian, Metcalf instituted many significant changes in library operations between that time and his retirement 18 years later.

Faced early in his incumbency by a worsening space situation in the Widener Library, then only two decades old, Metcalf soon conceived a multifaceted library plant development program calculated to accommodate Harvard's extensive collections for almost a half-century. The program included construction of a special building for rare books and manuscripts, completed as the Houghton Library in 1942; a remote facility for joint storage of seldom-used materials, completed in the same year as the New England Deposit Library; a library for undergraduates, the Lamont Library, opened in 1949; and a structure for additional stacks and services beneath the southeast corner of the Harvard Yard, added as the Pusey Library in 1977. This network of libraries, interconnected above and below grade with Widener, created in effect a library campus within a university campus.

Another integral part of Metcalf's plan for meeting the University's spatial requirements was a calculated move toward intentional but controlled physical decentralization of libraries. All of these developments were implemented during and after Metcalf's administration in accord with the concepts described in his annual report for the year 1939–40.

Metcalf's program for housing the collections was one of many major accomplishments that took place during his tenure. Among other things, he altered markedly the character of Harvard's library staff by bringing in large numbers of men and women trained in library schools, a change that brought the library system closer to the mainstream of American librarianship and gave it a more professional, cosmopolitan cast. His concern for the collections themselves manifested itself in the remarkable accessions of rare materials, the vast increase in general holdings (from 4,000,000 to 6,000,000 volumes), and the establishment of a strong library book selection program. He also elicited important modifications in the way in which the University administered and funded its library affairs, in keeping with the needs of contemporary scholarship.

As head of the world's largest university library during this period of vigorous library growth, Metcalf thus experienced first—and frequently solved—many of the problems of sheer size that would later plague other institutions. Other libraries found it always to their benefit, when faced by a problem resulting from size, to look first at how Harvard had responded to it. In this way Metcalf and his associates, whom he was particularly adept at selecting and developing, came deservedly to be viewed as a principal fountainhead of creativity and innovation in the field of research librarianship.

In 1955 Harvard University conferred emeritus status upon Metcalf, but this meant only that he could then embark full-time upon a third career—one already well established— as adviser and consultant-extraordinary to the library world at large. Especially active in the field of planning library buildings, Metcalf traveled in the next quarter-century to all of the continents on the globe, save Antarctica, and worked on a phenomenal 600 assignments. In 1965 he produced his landmark work, *Planning Academic and Research Library Buildings,* which brought the impress of his expertise to bear upon hundreds of additional buildings.

Metcalf remained professionally active throughout his long career. He served on innumerable boards and committees of ALA and was President, 1942–43. The historian of the Association of Research Libraries, of which Metcalf was for five years Executive Secretary, rates him that Association's all-time most influential participant. He was a founding member and President of the American Documentation Institute, later the American Society for Information Science. He was Adjunct Professor of Library Service at Rutgers from 1955 to 1958. His bibliography of published writings extends to more than 180 items. These accomplishments brought him many prestigious awards and recognitions, including 13 honorary doctor's degrees and the unique 50th Anniversary Medal of Achievement from the New York Public Library in 1971.

Great industry, boundless energy, and enviable endurance pervaded his work at every point. He also became well known for his unexampled humanity, his patience, his humility, and his gentleness. A gregarious but slightly shy man, quick to smile and easy to know, Keyes Metcalf continued in the tenth decade of his life to fulfill a felicitous father-image for generations of American librarians. He died in Cambridge, Massachusetts, on November 3, 1983.

REFERENCES

Peter Hernon, "Keyes DeWitt Metcalf," *Leaders in American Academic Librarianship: 1925–1975,* edited by Wayne A. Wiegand (1983).

Keyes D. Metcalf, *Random Recollections of an Anachronism: or, Seventy-Five Years of Library Work* (1980).

Keyes D. Metcalf, "Six Influential Academic and Research Libraries," *College and Research Libraries* (1976).

Edwin E. Williams, "The Metcalf Administration, 1937–1955" and "Keyes D. Metcalf, a Bibliography of Published Writings," *Harvard Library Bulletin* (1969).

DAVID KASER

Metcalfe, John Wallace
(1901-1982)

John Wallace Metcalfe, Australian library leader and educator, won an international reputation for his contributions to the history and theory of cataloguing and classification. He was born in Blackburn, Lancashire, England, on May 16, 1901. When he was six, the family moved to New Zealand, then moved again three years later to Adelaide, South Australia. When Metcalfe was 11, they moved yet again to Sydney, New South Wales. There Metcalfe remained for the rest of his professional life, destined to play an important role in the intellectual life of the city and state.

Metcalfe attended a state school in Marrickville, a Sydney suburb, and took his first library position at the age of 16 as an Assistant in the Fisher Library of the University of Sydney. He graduated from the University with First Class Honours in History in 1923 and on December 1 of that year was appointed an Assistant in the Public Library of New South Wales, the oldest and then probably the largest and most influential reference and research library in the Australian Commonwealth. Nine years later he had risen to the position of Deputy Principal Librarian. In 1942 he was appointed Principal Librarian, a position he was to hold until 1959, when he became Librarian of the University of New South Wales.

During his years in the Public Library of New South Wales, Metcalfe was active in creating and supporting the Free Library Movement. Established in 1935 as an organization for lay persons, the Free Library Movement had as a major aim the creation of free public libraries in municipalities and shires throughout the country, supported partly by local taxes and partly by state subsidy. It was founded by Geoffrey Remington and others after the results of the Munn-Pitt survey of Australian libraries were published. Metcalfe's involvement was also intensified by his experience (1934–35) of studying libraries in Great Britain, other countries of Europe, and the United States on a grant from the Carnegie Corporation. Largely as a result of the activity of the Free Library Movement, the New South Wales Minister for Education set up a Library Advisory Committee in 1937 with Metcalfe as member and Secretary. He was responsible for much of the Committee's report and for the attached draft bill that became the basis for the Library Act of 1939. Because of the war, the provisions of the Act were not fully implemented until 1944, and in that year Metcalfe, as Principal Librarian of the Public Library of New South Wales, became ex officio Executive Member of the Library Board of New South Wales. Created under that act, the Board was to encourage and oversee the development of public libraries throughout the state and to recommend the disbursement of state subsidies to them.

In 1935 Metcalfe became the first Australian to be admitted by examination as a Fellow of the Library Association (FLA) of the United Kingdom. His interest in the education of librarians, the systematic provision of whom was also an aim of the Free Library Movement, led him to set up training classes in the Public Library of New South Wales in 1937 or 1938. The library school thus created continued for many years and enabled Metcalfe and his associates to put their stamp on a whole generation of Australian librarians. His *General Introduction to Library Practice,* part of which was prepared in collaboration with others, formed the basis for instruction in the library school and went through three editions (1940, 1943, and 1955) with various formats and supplements.

In 1937 Metcalfe organized the Australian Institute of Librarians, which became the Library Association of Australia in 1949 and which was granted a Royal Charter in 1963. A major function of the Association was that of a professional examining body

T. Dobrovits
John Wallace Metcalfe

for librarians, and Metcalfe served as Chairman of its Board of Examiners from 1943 to 1958. He was General Secretary of the Association in 1937 and 1938 and again from 1950 to 1953, President from 1946 to 1948, and again President from 1957 to 1959. He was the first Editor of the Association's journal, *The Australian Library Journal,* and wrote most if not all of the unsigned copy for many of the early issues.

After 35 years of service with the state government in the Public Library of New South Wales, Metcalfe resigned in 1959 to become the first Librarian of the University of New South Wales, a position he accepted partly because of the opportunity it gave him of creating a postgraduate School of Librarianship in the University. The School was opened in 1960 and initiated a new pattern of education for librarians in Australia.

Metcalfe wrote widely on a variety of professional subjects. His major books are *Information Indexing and Subject Cataloging: Alphabetical, Classified, Coordinate, Mechanical* (1957), *Subject Classifying and Indexing of Libraries and Literature* (1959), *Alphabetical Subject Indication of Information* (Rutgers Series on Systems for the Intellectual Organization of Information, vol 3, 1965) and *Information Retrieval, British and American, 1876–1976* (1976). He also wrote voluminously on many educational, cultural, and community matters in Australian local and national journals and newspapers, the latter of which, in his heyday in the Public Library of New South Wales, consulted him frequently for or reported his forceful, pithy, sometimes controversial views.

In 1947 Metcalfe was appointed to the Australian delegation to the Unesco General Conference in Mexico City, and upon its conclusion, at the invitation of the Carnegie Corporation and the British Council, was once again able to visit libraries in the U.S. and Great Britain. In 1956 he was a consultant to the Fisher Library at the University of Sydney. Metcalfe retired from the University of New South Wales and from professional life in 1968. He died in Sydney on February 7, 1982.

REFERENCE

W. Boyd Rayward, editor, *The Variety of Librarianship: Essays in Honour of John Wallace Metcalfe* (1976), contains a full bibliography of Metcalfe's writing together with a list of published items about him in the *Australian Library Journal.*

W. BOYD RAYWARD

Mexico

The Federal Republic of Mexico, the northernmost country of Middle America, is bounded on the north by the United States, on the east by the Gulf of Mexico, on the south by Belize and Guatemala, and on the west by the Pacific Ocean. Population (1984 est.) 76,377,000; area 1,958,201 sq.km. The official language is Spanish.

History. In Mexico, as in most Latin American countries, the history of recorded information goes back to the time before the Spanish conquest. But, speaking of books as we now know them, the New Spain had a library as early as 1534. Fray Juan de Zumárraga, Bishop of the New Spain, asked for the authorization of the King to open the first library in the Cathedral of Mexico. In 1534 King Charles V

of Spain granted permission for the first library in the recently conquered land.

During the Colonial Period the libraries opened by priests were not open to the general public; only those who belonged to the church and were educated had any access to the collections, which were continually enriched by the books that arrived from Europe. By the beginning of the 19th century, the libraries had enough books to have an influence on the people and to help spread liberal ideas that made possible the War of Independence (1810–24). The church and the state were later separated, and in the 20th century the National Library was founded.

By the end of the 19th century, many were concerned about the state of education and of libraries. Ideas looking toward improvements were prevalent among the people in charge of education after the 1910 Revolution. José Vasconcelos, the first head of the University and Fine Arts Department (later the Secretary of Public Education) tried to bring such ideas into national practice. Unfortunately, due to many cirumstances, geographical difficulties, and problems of maintaining a newly opened library, traces of most of his efforts eventually vanished, leaving only the memory of intentions unfulfilled.

National Library. The Biblioteca Nacional de Mexico (National Library of Mexico) and the Hemeroteca Nacional de Mexico (National Library of Periodicals of Mexico) are part of and are coordinated by the Instituto de Investigaciones Bibliográficas (Bibliographical Research Institute) of UNAM.

The Biblioteca Nacional de Mexico was founded by presidential decree in 1867 in Mexico City, the capital. It is a depository library for all material published in Mexico and offers information and research services to all kinds of users. The general collection has 1,500,000 volumes with a strong emphasis on the humanities. The old and rare book collection comprises approximately 41,750 books and 45,000 manuscripts. It is rich in historical material and offers a vast amount of primary source material on Mexico. The bibliography section has some 7,000 volumes of bibliographies from all parts of the world.

The Library publishes the *Anuario Bibliográfico* (Bibliographic Annual), which covers all material published in Mexico from 1958 to 1963. As of 1967 the bibliographic production of Mexico is covered in the periodical *Bibliografía Mexicana.*

The Hemeroteca Nacional is for periodical publications what the Biblioteca Nacional is for books. The collection of newspapers and journals is an important resource, especially notable for Mexico City newspapers, some of which date from the 18th century. The materials are available for internal use or through interlibrary loan. Other services available include reference, research, photocopying, and microfilming.

For many years the files of newspapers and periodicals were part of the Biblioteca Nacional. As the collection grew, it outgrew its space, and in 1944 the Hemeroteca Nacional was established.

A project to house both libraries under the same roof was begun in the late 1970s and finished by the mid-1980s.

Academic Libraries. Even though many university libraries still lack the collections, facilities, and professional staff necessary to offer adequate library service, such libraries showed important tendencies toward development during the 1970s. Collections grew and improved considerably as institutions realized the importance of the library in the university and allowed larger budgets for acquisitions and for better-paid professional librarians. The Escuela Nacional de Agricultura (National School of Agriculture), Instituto Tecnológico y de Estudios Superiores de Monterrey (Technological Institute of Monterrey), El Colegio de México, Universidad Iberoamericana, and Universidad Metropolitana were among those that designed and built new library buildings in the late 1960s and the 1970s.

Public Libraries. Throughout the modern history of Mexico public libraries have experienced varying degrees of support.

In 1982 the Secretaría de Educación Pública gave an important role to the newly created Dirección General de Bibliotecas (General Direction of Libraries). The new General Direction was given the task of implementing a National Program of Public Libraries throughout the country. The program contemplates the planning, establishment, and operation of all the public libraries run by the government. Because of the lack of human resources, it was decided to centralize the acquisitions and technical processes for supplying libraries with new and useful books and other materials. Together with the growth there were important efforts invested in organizing seminars, courses, and workshops for staff, as well as efforts to attend to public services in general, to remodel old libraries, and to provide technical assistance.

The program sees the promotion of the habit of reading as an integral part of a public library, and a whole project to promote leisure reading was implemented. The growth rate for public libraries was high: some 370 public libraries reported in all parts of the country in 1982 had increased by December 1985 to 1,022, all with modern organization and useful books. The growth rate was maintained in spite of the economic difficulties that the country experienced.

School Libraries. There is no independent school library system. Very few schools at the elementary and secondary levels have libraries, and most school children must use public libraries. The National Program of Public Libraries, taking that into account, established special areas and activities for the children. In most of the public libraries of Mexico,

Theodore F. Welch

Decorated with mosaics by Diego Rivera, the Universidad Nacional Autónoma de México, is one of the world's most striking library buildings.

children can secure assistance for their daily homework and participate in workshops, games, literary clubs, and guided visits. The public libraries provide qualified staff to work with children, and after the program started in 1983 every new public library that opened or was remodeled had this service available.

Special Libraries. There are approximately 355 special libraries and information centers in Mexico. Special libraries and information centers grew in the 1970s in response to the needs of developing technology and industry. Among the most significant collections are those at the libraries of Banco de México, Banco Nacional de México, Instituto Nacional de Energía Nuclear, and the research institutes of UNAM. There are many good and even more specialized libraries that serve highly specialized groups of users.

The Profession. AMBAC, the Asociación Mexicana de Bibliotecarios, Asociación Civil (Mexican Association of Librarians) was founded in 1954. It had 460 members in 1985. Two of its main objectives are the professional improvement of its members and the promotion of libraries, library service, and librarianship throughout the country. It has sev-

Libraries in Mexico (1982)

Type	Administrative units	Volumes in collections	Annual expenditures (peso)	Population served	Total staff
National	2[a]	2,814[a]	- -	- -	- -
Higher Education[b]	423	2,372,768	- -	15,221,017	3,072
College	280	5,816,352	- -	6,465,344	982
Public[b]	516	2,034,000	8,029[c]	- -	922[c]
School	1,621	4,128,184	460,323[d]	6,726,297	2,803
Special	355	3,123,856	- -	- -	- -

[a]Unesco, *Statistical Yearbook,* 1984. 1979 data.
[b]Excludes 219 public libraries independent of the Ministry of Public Education.
[c]Unesco, *Statistical Yearbook,* 1984. 1978 data.
[d]Ibid. 1981 data.

Biblioteca Nacional (Mexico)

Ciudad Universitaria, addition to the National Library of Mexico (1979).

eral committees, among them the Publishing Committee, which publishes a quarterly newsletter, *Noticiero de la AMBAC,* and the committee for meetings, conferences, and congresses, which organizes a yearly congress and other periodic meetings.

AMBAC has several regional associations and an affiliate, ABIESI, Asociación de Bibliotecarios en Instituciones de Enseñanza Superior e Investigación (Association of Higher Education and Research Institutions), founded in 1957. ABIESI had 60 institutional members and 120 personal members in 1985. It sets the standards for interlibrary loan in the country, organizes specialized courses and seminars of general interest for library professionals, and publishes two irregular series: *Cuadernos* and *Archivos.*

Several institutions prepare professional librarians. The oldest is the National School of Librarians and Archivists (Escuela Nacional de Biblioteconomía y Archivonomía; ENBA) founded in 1945 and under the Secretary of Public Education. The National Autonomous University of Mexico (UNAM), through the Philosophy Faculty, also offers a degree for librarians. Both are in Mexico City. At ENBA, the emphasis is on administration while UNAM emphasizes technical processes. In at least four other universities in the country, bachelor's degrees are offered in librarianship: the Autonomous University of Guadalajara, Nuevo Leon, San Luis Potosí, and the University of Guadalajara. A technician's diploma is offered through programs at ENBA and other schools.

The Division of Postgraduate Studies of the Philosophy Faculty of UNAM offered a master's degree for librarians from 1958. At the Universities of Guanajuato from 1978 and Nuevo Leon from 1980 master's degrees in librarianship were also offered.

From all schools of the country, there were fewer than 100 graduates who had completed all the requirements for master's or bachelor's degrees by late 1985.

ANA MARÍA MAGALONI DE BUSTAMANTE

Micrographics

Micrographics is the field of information management concerned with creating and utilizing *microimages,* images too small to be discerned by the unaided eye. Most microimages are representations of textual and graphic information and are produced by the highly precise photographic techniques of microphotography. Microimages are recorded on both transparent and opaque media, which collectively are called *microforms.* Transparent microforms are called *microfilm;* opaque microforms are referred to as *microopaques.*

Although experiments in microphotography were carried out as early as the mid-1800s, specialized micropublishing did not become a reality until the 1930s. During the 1960s, when American higher education was expanding rapidly, many publishers issued microfilm editions of collections that otherwise would have been unavailable to libraries. Microphotography has likewise served as an effective and relatively economical means of preserving the information content of deteriorating printed materials, especially newspapers. Computer-output microfilm (COM), a relatively new type of micrographic technology, has been widely applied to the management of library records.

Types of Microforms. Based on their physical forms, microforms are of two types: roll and flat. Roll microforms are available in several widths, only two of which—16mm and 35mm—are commonly found in libraries. By historic precedence, 35mm microfilm is the de facto standard for roll microforms in academic and research libraries. This film width permits the use of relatively low reductions that result in more legible microimages from newspapers, deteriorating manuscripts, and other difficult-to-copy materials. Even though most serials, monographs, typewritten reports, and other recently published materials can be legibly recorded on 16mm microfilm, many academic libraries have a considerable investment in 35mm microfilm and associated display equipment. For them, the acquisition of 16mm microfilm would introduce the added complications and extra costs of a mixed-media system.

On the other hand, the limited selection of new, more convenient display equipment can be a major deterrent to user acceptance of that medium. Because 16mm microfilm is widely used in business applications, many up-to-date display devices are available. Consequently, many industrial libraries prefer the 16mm width for roll film applications. Cartridges and cassettes can be used to facilitate handling of 16mm roll microfilm, with a resulting favorable effect on user acceptance.

The storage capacity of roll microfilm is impressive: two thousand letter-size pages can be recorded on a 100-foot roll of 16mm microfilm at a 24-to-1 reduction ratio (usually expressed as 24X). Flat microforms, on the other hand, are designed for applications in which smaller numbers of related images can be recorded together. Because they are often used to group a number of related images and thereby segregate them from unrelated images, flat microforms are referred to as *unitized* microforms. The dominant flat microform is the *microfiche* (often abbreviated to *fiche,*) a rectangular sheet of microfilm bearing microimages in a grid of rows and columns. Microfiche are made in a variety of sizes, but the national and international standard size is 105 by 148mm. Information capacity varies from 60 to more than 400 images, depending primarily on the reduction ratio used. A standard fiche filmed at 24X contains as many as 98 images, whereas COM fiche, with a reduction of 42 to 48X, can hold more than 400 frames.

A variant form of microfiche, called *ultrafiche,* employs proprietary technology to achieve extremely high reductions and thereby increase fiche capacity to upwards of 3,000 images. Ultrafiche has, in the main, been used for micropublishing "package libraries" and for compacting and unitizing parts catalogues.

Other flat microforms resemble microfiche but have somewhat different application characteristics. A *microfilm jacket* is a unitized, transparent carrier for strips of roll microfilm. The individual strips of film are replaceable, so jackets have been used to miniaturize vertical files and other document collections that require updating. Microprint, a proprietary product of Readex Microprint Corporation, is a unique flat microform that consists of miniaturized page images printed on both sides of an opaque card stock. Other micro-opaques, notably those sold under the trade names Microcard and Microlex, were no longer in production in the mid-1980s, although many research libraries retained large files of them. A group of hybrid microforms—aperture cards, card jackets, and jacket cards—combine transparent microimages with opaque cardstock in a single medium; the cards can contain printed or punched-card information so people or machines can read and sort them. They are used widely in business and industry but have seen little application in libraries.

A new form introduced for library applications is roll microfiche. This high-density storage medium, which consists simply of a roll of uncut fiche, is normally sold as part of a service in which the catalogue records of a library are made available on the roll fiche and are accessible through a specially made reader known as the Micro-Max.

Production of Microforms. The oldest method of producing microforms, source document microphotography, involves microfilming physical document pages. Several types of cameras are used. Rotary cameras, which have high-speed document transport mechanisms and film the documents "on the fly," have proven popular in banking and other businesses. They have only limited resolution and are impractical for books and other library materials, although they can be used to microfilm library business records. Quite a number of libraries have used rotary cameras to make security copies of their card catalogues. Planetary cameras, which microfilm stationary documents positioned on a flat surface, typically offer the high resolution required for research materials and are preferred in library applications requiring 16mm or 35mm microfilm. A special type of planetary camera, the step-and-repeat camera, is designed to create microfiche.

The silver halide process remains the dominant technology in source document microfilming. It offers excellent resolution and is the only microphotographic process that, properly applied, can assure long-term image stability. Because it requires wet chemical processing in a darkroom, it is time-con-

suming and inconvenient. As a result, several manufacturers have developed source document cameras employing alternative recording technologies. One step-and-repeat camera, for example, records microimages on dry silver microfilm that is exposed to light and developed by heat alone. Another system employs a variant of the electrostatic process used in office copiers to produce microimages on a transparent sheet of film. The resulting microfiche can later be reinserted in the camera for the addition of new images. For the duplication of existing microforms, many users prefer diazo or vesicular microfilms. Although unsuited to use in cameras, these duplicating films are less expensive and more convenient to work with than silver halide duplicating film.

The need to record rapidly the voluminous results of computer processing has led to the development of COM, a technology by which computer-processed data are converted directly to human-readable information on microfilm without the creation of intervening paper documents. In the most prevalent COM recording technique, the output of a computer is displayed as a page of eye-readable characters on the face of a cathode ray tube and automatically photographed onto silver halide microfilm by a built-in camera. Several newer COM recorders employ laser beams to write directly onto the microfilm. These recorders utilize dry silver film that, conveniently, is developed by heat as a part of the same continuous process. The speed, quality, and versatility of COM recorders compare very favorably with those of high-speed computer printers, and COM usually has a significant cost advantage when multiple copies are needed.

Interest in COM in the 1980s was stimulated by the success of OCLC and other MARC-derivative services that have enabled libraries to create machine-readable files of their holdings. An increasing number of public, academic, and special libraries replaced their card and book catalogues with COM counterparts on microfiche or 16mm microfilm. COM proved especially attractive as an economical medium for publishing the union catalogues of library systems. A number of vendors of acquisitions and cataloguing services have developed programs to create COM catalogues from library-supplied OCLC tapes

University of Toronto Library

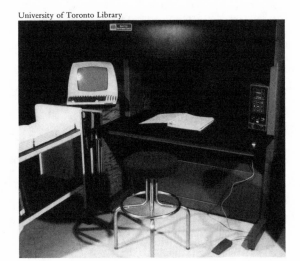

Microfiche camera available for patrons' use at the University of Toronto Library.

Micrographics

Edition of the 1850 U.S. census, in microfilm. Microform publication decreases storage space and makes materials more widely available.

Texas State Library

or other machine-readable MARC or non-MARC records. Library COM applications are not, however, limited to catalogues but include patron files, circulation records, serials listings, and other computer-generated reports.

Library Applications. The space savings offered by microforms has proved attractive to libraries, most notably special libraries, many of which operate within severe space constraints. Librarians and information specialists have employed microforms in at least five areas: (1) collection development, (2) collection management, (3) reproduction and preservation of library materials, (4) specialized information storage and retrieval systems, and (5) institutional records management. Although advances have been made in all of these areas in recent years, many libraries have augmented their collections substantially through the increased availability of micropublications. Such additions have also aggravated an already serious problem of the bibliographical control of microforms at all levels.

Micropublishing. Early library microform programs emphasized the filming of research materials by the library itself, but most libraries now purchase micropublications from *micropublishers,* broadly defined as producers of information in multiple-copy microform for sale to the public. The library market is now served by both institutional and commercial micropublishers. Institutional publishers include the Library of Congress, the National Archives, the Government Printing Office, other libraries, historical societies, and various cultural and government agencies. Their micropublishing programs are typically based on their own holdings and, in many cases, developed as a by-product of preservation microfilm-

ing and interlibrary loan activities. Commercial micropublishers include conventional book publishers, microfilm service bureaus, very small companies, and divisions of large corporations; the content and number of their offerings are equally varied. Some have extensive lists of titles, while others offer only a few.

Micropublications can be divided into three groups: original, simultaneous, and retrospective. Original micropublications contain information published for the first time in any form. University Microfilms began microfilming doctoral dissertations in 1938—probably the earliest instance of original micropublishing. Other original micropublication programs include technical reports from microfiche by ERIC and NTIS, scholarly monographs on highly specialized subjects from university presses, a relatively small number of limited circulation serials, and certain MARC-derivative bibliographies such as the *National Union Catalog,* MARCFICHE, and *Books in English*. In the late 1970s the GPO began issuing many of its publications in microfiche, a move that met with mixed reactions on the part of librarians.

Simultaneous micropublications, those issued at the same time as their paper edition counterparts, have experienced only limited acceptance, apparently because the cost differential between the two formats—paper and microforms—is usually too small to overcome the resistance many users have to microforms. The simultaneously micropublished versions of some technical journals, however, appeal to foreign subscribers, to whom they can be air-mailed at reasonable cost.

Retrospective micropublishing (or *micro-republishing,* as it is also called) is the republication in microform of material previously published on paper. It is a form of reprinting and represents the dominant type of micropublishing to the library market. The earliest retrospective micropublishing programs dealt with particular types of publications, such as serials, newspapers, or out-of-print books. These programs remain important, but more recent micropublishing projects are based on themes or established bibliographies. These collections can be viewed as anthologies, some on a grand scale; the largest of them contain tens of thousands of individual titles on roll film, fiche, or both, and cost upwards of $25,000.

Bibliographic Control. The growth of micropublishing has given rise to the need for improved bibliographic control of micropublications, and recent years have seen important developments in this area. At the national and international levels, a number of trade bibliographies and related publications are designed to enable libraries to identify and understand the offerings of various micropublishers. These publications include *Microform Review,* a leading selection aid for micropublications; *International Guide to Microforms in Print*; its companion *Subject Guide to Microforms in Print*; and *Micropublishers Trade List Annual* (MTLA), a collection of micropublishers' catalogues on microfiche accompanied by a hard copy index. In addition to these bibliographies, four Library of Congress printed catalogues facilitate the identification and location of microforms made from various research materials. The *National Register of Microform Masters,* which ceased publication at the end of 1983, is a main-entry catalogue of master microforms created by both commercial and institutional micropub-

550

lishers and reported on a voluntary basis; after 1983 microform records appeared in other LC publications. Microform masters of newspapers are reported in *Newspapers in Microform.* Locations of microform masters and use copies of archives and manuscripts are reported in the *National Union Catalog of Manuscript Collections.* Locations of microform copies of monographs available for use by library patrons are reported in the *National Union Catalog.* In addition to these tools, a number of major bibliographies developed special tools to support their offerings. These tools may take the form of catalogue card sets, bookform indexes, or both.

Bibliographic access to the major microform sets held in many research libraries continues to be a problem not directly addressed by the major published bibliographic tools. A number of research libraries have published catalogues of their microform holdings, but the best single source of information on the large microform sets themselves is the two editions of Suzanne Dodson's *Microform Research Collections* (1979 and 1983).

In 1982 the Association for Research Libraries (ARL) announced its Microform Project, funded by the Council on Library Resources, designed to improve bibliographic access to microforms in American and Canadian libraries. The purpose of the project is to coordinate the activities of libraries and other agencies, including the online bibliographic utilities, in providing bibliographic access to microform collections that are now inadequately catalogued. A subsequent survey of more than 3,600 libraries by ARL led to the creation of a Microform Cataloging Clearinghouse funded by the Mellon Foundation. The Microform Project also promoted cooperative cataloguing and assisted major research libraries in seeking grants to catalogue their microform sets and to enter the resulting records into one of the bibliographic utilities. Additional grants from the National Endowment for the Humanities to ARL have provided support for a preservation microfilming component of the Microfilm Project and for the 10 members of the Research Libraries Group (RLG) to add bibliographic records of microforms to the Research Libraries Information Network (RLIN).

One of the most ambitious microform publishing projects is Research Publications' *Eighteenth Century,* a collection of books and pamphlets published in English between 1701 and 1800. This 20-year publishing project complements the previously published collections of early English imprints based upon the two *Short-Title Catalogues.* The titles selected for the microform collection were to be made available online through RLG.

Alan Meckler's excellent work on the history of scholarly micropublishing is the only major full-length treatment of the subject—although Ashby and Campbell's *Microform Publishing* deals with all aspects of microforms as publishing media.

ALA's Reproduction of Library Materials Section (RLMS) created the Bibliographic Control of Microforms Committee to address the problem of bibliographic control through closer liaison with micropublishers and other agencies; in 1985 it published *Microforms in libraries; a manual for evaluation and management.* The Resources Section (RS) of ALA also formed a Micropublishing Projects Committee.

Display Equipment. The acceptance of microforms by library users has long suffered from the inadequacies of reading machines and other display devices. While there remains much room for further development, the quality of microform readers has improved significantly. Improvements are especially notable in newer microfiche readers, most of which are of modular design and incorporate high-quality optics, straightforward operating controls, and easily interchanged lenses. Libraries can select from a number of satisfactory models at reasonable prices. In addition, several roll microfilm readers have been developed specifically for library applications. Notable features of such readers include a screen large enough to display an entire newspaper page and simplified operation with instructions imprinted on the reader itself. Prices for these readers, however, are comparatively high.

Libraries whose users require paper enlargements of microimages can select from a number of reader–printers. Prices for this equipment remained relatively high in the mid-1980s: $1,500 to $3,000 for a microfiche reader–printer and $3,000 to $6,000 for a roll microfilm reader–printer. Even higher are the prices of high-speed enlarger–printers designed to make single or multiple plain paper copies of microfiche images.

The entire text of vendor catalogues, with access provided through a series of indexes, is available on fiche as the *International File of Micrographics: Equipment and Accessories.* Regular evaluations of display devices appear in *Micrographics Equipment Review* and occasional evaluations in *Library Technology Reports,* published by ALA.

Library Literature on Microforms. The continued interest in microform applications to libraries is evident in the abundance of secondary literature published each year in *Microform Review* and other library-related journals. The 1980s also saw a small wave of monographs on microform applications, as can be seen in the References. ALA announced publication of a two-part guide to evaluating microforms and planning microform facilities in libraries.

Microfilm reading room at the Biblioteca Nacional in Rio de Janeiro, Brazil.

Pedro Lobo

Organizational Changes. In 1983 the National Micrographics Association (NMA) became the Association for Information and Image Management (AIIM), and its publication, *Journal of Micrographics,* was changed to *Journal of Information and Image Management.* In 1982 the International Micrographics Congress (IMC) became the International Information Management Congress (retaining the initialism IMC). These changes are more than cosmetic. They reflect a change of emphasis from micrographics per se to records management and electronic information processing, with consequently greater interest in integrated systems for information handling.

Trends. Some critics of microforms claim that microforms have never reached their full potential as a publishing medium and that they are now endangered by new technologies such as videodisks, which some see as a potential alternative to microforms. Given the immense storage capacity of videodisks for text—about 50,000 video frames (or pages of text) per disk—the appeal is obvious. This technology promises to develop rapidly.

Among the fast-breaking technological developments in microform utilization are products that link computers and microform devices, such as minicomputer-controlled COM recorders and computer-assisted retrieval (CAR) systems. Still other products are designed to link CAR systems with image digitizers for the video transmission of microform images to remote monitors, printers, or both. These developments have significant potential for the improvement of information storage and dissemination in libraries. Their application, however, was not sufficiently widespread in the mid-1980s to permit accurate assessment of their likely impact.

REFERENCES
Peter Ashby and Robert Campbell, *Microform Publishing* (1979).
E. Dale Cluff, *Microforms* (1981).
Richard W. Boss and Deborah Raikes, *Developing Microform Reading Facilities* (1981).
Ralph J. Folcarelli, Arthur Tannenbaum, and Ralph C. Ferragamo, *The Microform Connection: A Basic Guide for Libraries* (1982).
Michael Gabriel and Dorothy P. Ladd, *The Microform Revolution in Libraries* (1980).
Peter Hernon, *Microforms and Government Information* (1981).
Alan Marshall Meckler, *Micropublishing: A History of Scholarly Micropublishing in America, 1938-1980* (1982).
William Saffady, *Computer Output Microfilm: Its Library Application* (1978).
Saffady, *Micrographics* (2nd edition, 1985).
S. J. Teague, *Microform, Video, and Electronic Media Librarianship* (1985).

WILLIAM SAFFADY;
EDWIN S. GLEAVES

Middle Ages, Libraries in the

The period from the extinction of the Roman Empire in the West to the discovery of America and the rise of European nation-states—from 476 to 1492—is on the whole one of the darkest in the history of culture, books, and libraries. But a tenuous connection survived between the great libraries of the ancient world and the beginning of libraries as they are understood today. This great extent of time was far from being uniform and can be subdivided into four periods that showed different characteristics of library development.

The first period, up to the end of the 6th century, witnessed the final collapse of the ancient classical heritage. The second period, up to the 9th century, saw its replacement by the Christian institution of monasticism as the refuge of a tradition of letters. The third period commenced with the slow growth of medieval cultural institutions after the devastations of the last phase of the barbarian invasions—the raids of the Vikings, the Saracens, and the Hungarians in the 9th and 10th centuries—which gravely impaired social institutions and destroyed many monasteries and their libraries. It closed with the rise of the universities in an age of increased clerical literacy in the service of church and state.

The final period of the Middle Ages showed a rapid increase in the production of books in manuscript and, at the end, in printed form, as well as rapidly growing literacy among the middle-class laity, the beginning of the new learning of the Renaissance, and the physical development of libraries in the older institutions.

Dom David Knowles, in his *Religious Orders in England* (1955), gives a relevant definition: "A library is to our thinking a large and comprehensive collection of books, gathered together according to a carefully prepared scheme to serve determined purposes, and housed from the beginning in a building designed to accommodate both the books and those who wish to consult or study them." If we are to understand the history of libraries as instruments of scholarly work or preservers of the intellectual heritage at this early period, it is necessary to put together all scraps of information that survive relating to the provision of books. Evidence is available in literary and historical references and archaeology, as well as in catalogues of medieval collections and in the books themselves that have survived the devastations caused by negligent or intentional destruction. With the caveat that literacy—even literacy in Latin—is not learning, and that learning does not predicate the existence of libraries, the thread can then be traced. There is a single constant throughout the library history of the Middle Ages: the universality of the manuscript in codex format, written on folded leaves of vellum and bound between stout wooden boards, the physical form common to the earliest liturgical manuscripts and some incunabula printed after the age of paper had begun. Provision for storage and use of the codex explains the origin of library architecture.

The format of classical pagan literature had been the papyrus roll, whose physical survival necessitated repeated copying. Neglect and damp, even more than deliberate or accidental destruction by Christians and barbarians, had probably reduced the stock of Roman literature before the beginning of the medieval period, although the tradition of collecting the classics survived among wealthy Romans and provincials in Italy and Gaul into the 6th century. Nevertheless, one of the most vital cultural services of Christian institutions throughout the Middle Ages was the preservation of pagan literary works by copying texts from decaying papyrus to permanent vellum. Christian hostility to pagan writings had been tempered even before the institution of the Christian Roman Empire by Constantine in the 4th century, through the habit of regarding them as in some sense precursors of Christian revelation, and later they were viewed as sources for grammatical teaching. Boethius (480–524), the last Roman philosopher and a Christian, furnished a link between the pagan and Christian traditions, since he studied in the library of his father-in-law, Symmachus, heir of the last great pagan family of Rome. His *De consolatione philosophiae* describes the glazed bookcases ornamented with ivory in his own library. Boethius's career as minister to the conquering Gothic king Theodoric is paralleled by that of a more significant figure in the history of libraries, Cassiodorus (502–597).

Monastery Libraries. After his retirement from the court of Ravenna and the siege of Rome in 546, Cassiodorus founded the monastery of Vivarium in southern Italy, where he established a *scriptorium* and a library. His *Institutiones* was to serve as a bibliographical guide for future monastic collections and included a detailed account of the making of books. He describes the arrangement of the library, contained in nine *armaria*, or bookcases, the majority of which held theological works and the remainder liberal arts and sciences. The *Etymologiae* of a Spanish bishop, Saint Isidore (c. 560–636), was even more influential in the organization of knowledge in the Middle Ages. This encyclopedia cites over 150 pagan and Christian writers and contains chapters on libraries, librarians, and their duties. His poem *Versus titulis bibliothecae* indicates that his private library occupied 14 to 16 cases containing from 400 to 500 volumes.

Saint Benedict (c. 480–547?) provided the key to the development of the monastic orders. His *Regula*, on which all later monastic rules were based, secured the place of writing and literacy in the Latin language. Chapter 48 mentions the word *bibliotheca*, though it is uncertain whether it means a room or a collection of books; more significant was the ample provision of time for reading sacred writings and the insistence on manual labor, later to be interpreted as including the work of the *scriptorium*. In the 500 years after Benedict, the copying of books inspired by his Rule—and consequently the survival of learning—was confined almost exclusively to monastic institutions. The root of the Benedictine traditions did not come from the schools of Christian learning in the later Roman Empire but rather from the Eastern monasticism that developed in Egypt. Originally communities of ascetic and usually illiterate hermits, Coptic monasteries, by the time of Saint Pachomius in the 4th century, had codified the place of cloistral reading of the Scriptures, the Fathers, and works of devotion. Archaeological evidence of their use of books can be traced through as late as the 13th century.

The most significant advance of Christianity in the Middle Ages was the tide of conversion that flowed from Rome to England and from the British Isles back to the pagan German lands. Its leaders, devoted to monasticism, regarded books as the lifeblood of Christianity, and the monasteries they founded developed a vital library tradition of incalculable importance in preserving and transmitting European culture. The missionaries and monasteries can be placed in a family tree that reached to and from the north of England and returned to Italy.

Courtesy of the Newberry Library

The Cloisters, Gloucester, western England.

Pope Gregory the Great dispatched Saint Augustine to the Kentish kingdom in 597. Saint Augustine, the Easterner Theodore of Tarsus, his successor as Archbishop, and Hadrian, an African monk who had been Abbot of a south Italian monastery, carried books from Rome to Canterbury. The cathedral monastery of Christ Church and the abbey of Saints Peter and Paul, later Saint Augustine's, both established libraries that existed until their destruction in the 16th century. The Northumbrian Benedict Biscop, pupil and successor of Hadrian as Abbot of Saint Peter's, journeyed to Rome several times collecting books and founded the twin monasteries of Wearmouth (674) and Jarrow (681).

Saint Ceolfrid, Abbot of both monasteries, also traveled to Rome, where he probably acquired the *Codex Grandior* that may have belonged to Cassiodorus. The *Codex Amiatinus,* written under his direction for presentation to the Pope, copied its frontispiece, a unique pictorial record of an early library bookcase. The Venerable Bede (673–735) composed his many scriptural, historical, and scientific works at Jarrow, which indicates the richness of the book collection available to him. His pupil Egbert, Archbishop of York from 732 to 766, founded a cathedral school and library, and this collection served as a source of copies made for monasteries of the Frankish Empire.

Christianity came to Northern England not only from Rome but also from the Celtic church of Ireland. Little can be conjectured about the book collections of Irish monasteries, but Saint Columbanus (543–615) provided books to the monasteries he founded in his missionary journeys to the Continent. Luxeuil in Burgundy (founded 590) and Bobbio in northern Italy (founded 612) developed great *scriptoria* and libraries, as did the houses founded by his disciples—Saint Gall, in Switzerland (founded 614), and Saint Riquier, in northern France (founded 625–645).

A 9th-century plan of Saint Gall indicates a book-room connected with a *scriptorium,* and the abbey today has one of the most magnificent of monastic libraries. The library at Bobbio transmitted some of the most ancient books of the Western world to modern times.

The Englishman Boniface, the apostle of Germany (680–755), founded the bishoprics and monasteries in the pagan areas east of the Frankish kingdom. When he was martyred by the Frisians, books were in his baggage. The sees of Mainz, Wurzburg, and Salzburg became centers of religious and political influence with schools and libraries. Boniface's monastery of Fulda (founded 744) became the most powerful in Germany, housing a *scriptorium* famous for illuminated manuscripts and a great library, of which an 8th-century catalogue survives. Charlemagne, the first of the Frankish emperors, called Alcuin of York to be master of his palace school, and Alcuin became his trusted minister. As the Abbot of Tours, he sent for books from England to add to the library. Alcuin revived Frankish monasticism under his royal patronage. Monasteries such as Fleury (7th century) and Corbie (founded 657) created collections of manuscripts that were to be matched by those in German lands, such as Reichenau (founded 724), Lorsch (founded 763), and Corvey (founded 822).

Classics copied in the Carolingian minuscule hand were to transmit their clear calligraphy to the scholars of the Renaissance. The letters of Lupus, Abbot of Ferrieres (842–860), an indefatigable collector of both classical and Christian titles, document the bibliographical cooperation between monasteries in the period before the devastation inflicted by the Northmen eliminated learning in most of the British Isles and gravely affected it on the Continent.

The period from the 10th to the 12th centuries witnessed first a slow and then a rapid recovery that brought about a rebirth of monastic institutions and their libraries. In England the efforts of Saint Dunstan (924–988) were succeeded by those of Lanfranc (1005–1089), teacher, Prior of Bec in Normandy, and Archbishop of Canterbury. His influential recension of the Benedictine Rule made specific references to the lending and reading of books. Norman prelates rebuilt English abbeys and renewed their collections. After the Saracen sack of Monte Cassino, Abbot Desiderius in the 11th century raised its library and *scriptorium* to its highest level.

The greatest age of monasticism was ushered in by the foundation of the new orders of reformed Benedictinism, the "Black Monks" of Cluny (founded 910) and the "White Monks" of Citeaux (founded 1098); both evolved international systems of daughter houses that spread over Europe. The primary concern of their monastic life was not learning but a communal spiritual life in isolation from the world. The Cluniacs placed emphasis on liturgical worship, and the early Cistercians restricted on principle the collecting and reading of books to devotional requirements. These monks regarded copying manuscripts as religious work prescribed by the Rule, rather than as a method of building up holdings, but along with their great building and economic activities, they created libraries. The first catalogue of Cluny itself in the 13th century enumerated nearly 600 works, and by this time most of the important houses of Black

Monks also had sizable collections. Cistercian foundations, such as Fountains in England and Fossa Nuova in Italy, made careful architectural provision for protecting their books, and these developed over the centuries.

The fundamental unit of monastic book storage remained the classical *armarium,* a large wooden cupboard with shelves on which the bindings were laid flat. Sometimes it was recessed into stonework, which has survived. It was usually in the east walk of the cloister, between the chapter house (where books were distributed on an annual basis during Lent for the monks' private reading) and the side door of the church. The usual location for study and writing was under the windows of the north walk of the cloister, which in the later Middle Ages was frequently glazed and fitted with wooden carrels. When space became inadequate, storage rooms were built adjoining the chapter house. The book regulations of other orders, such as the Carthusians (founded 1084) and the Premonstratensians (founded 1120), were generally similar to those of the Benedictines. The Carthusians, who lived in detached cells, were allowed to borrow two books at a time. Supervision of books and readers was the responsibility of the precentor, the official primarily responsible for the maintenance of church services, which included the care of the liturgical books used in the choir. By the end of the 12th century, the provision of libraries in large and small monastic houses was so close to universal practice that an epigram was coined: "A cloister without books is like a castle without an armory."

Episcopal establishments were frequently centers of learning throughout the Middle Ages, and the teaching of famous scholars encouraged the accumulation of books. This was particularly true in cities of northern Italy. A catalogue of the library of Cremona was made shortly after the death of Bishop Liutprand (902–972), diplomat and classicist, and other early records refer to collections at Novara, Vercelli, Monza, and Ivrea. At Verona the Capitular Library can claim lineal descent back to the 5th century, when manuscripts were written that survive to the present. North of the Alps, Archbishop Hincmar of Reims (805–822) and Gerbert, a teacher in the cathedral school there who became Pope Sylvester II (999–1003), acquired notable collections. The latter's pupil Fulbert created a library at Chartres; Beauvais and Rouen also possessed rich libraries. The see of Bamberg (founded 1007) maintained a famous school and inherited the library of the Emperor Henry II in 1024. Prior to the rise of the universities, the educational influence of the cathedral schools and their libraries had outstripped that of the monasteries. Thus when Peter Lombard, the authority on canon law, died in 1160, he bequeathed his books to the cathedral of Notre Dame in Paris.

University Libraries. Before the end of the 12th century, the University of Paris, which had its roots in the cathedral school, had become the center of the scholastic philosophy that generated a new professional literature for the clergy and largely outmoded older medieval writings. The need for books for thousands of students became pressing. The primary response of university authorities was to regulate the book trade by controlling the *stationarii* who supplied the textbooks. The many professional scribes, principally laymen, copied an *exemplar,* writing by the *pecia* for fixed prices. Public library facilites were a secondary growth. The many student hostels in Paris and the daughter university of Oxford were for the most part too small and poor to assume such a function. The growth of larger residences for masters and students, such as the Sorbonne (founded 1257), with substantial buildings and a regulated community life, made the formation of libraries possible. The Sorbonne library was organized and catalogued in 1289, and library rules exist from 1321. The collection, as was customary in monastic as well as academic institutions, was divided into two parts: books constantly referred to were chained in the great library, those available for loan or rarely used being secured in a separate room. By 1338 more than 300 volumes were in the first location and more than 1,000 in the second.

At Oxford and Cambridge during the 14th and 15th centuries, the smaller halls were gradually squeezed out by endowed colleges, which erected library facilities of a pattern that has survived to the present day. Libraries common to the university as a whole were of less importance and were founded at a relatively late date. Oxford's collection, bequeathed by Thomas de Cobham in 1327, was housed in a room above the University Church. At Cambridge a university library did not exist until the first half of the 15th century.

The new mendicant orders of friars quickly assumed a dominant role in the universities. The Dominicans (founded 1215) produced famous teachers of philosophy and were soon followed by the Franciscans (founded 1210). Their convents established working collections of books, largely academic and pastoral in content. Dominican instructions of the 1250s include precise library regulations, as do Franciscan constitutions of 1260. The catalogue of the Franciscan motherhouse at Assisi in 1381 describes a large collection carefully classified, labeled, and shelved. Substantial libraries were established by the friars in other urban centers. In England the Augustinian collection in York numbered over 600 works in 1372, and in 1429 Sir Richard Whittington built the Greyfriars' convent in London with a substantial library.

Other Libraries. Throughout the Middle Ages the popes of Rome must always have acquired books and archives, but the history of the papal library is fragmented and puzzling. Earlier collections of books and archives probably suffered destruction during the repeated sacking of the city—by the Vandals in 455, the Saracens in 846, and the Normans in 1084. The exile of the papacy to Avignon during the 14th and 15th centuries dispersed the library described in the earliest surviving catalogue of 1295, but records of the existence of libraries go back as far as Pope Damasus (366–84). Archaeological excavation has revealed remains of the building used as a library by Pope Agapetus (535–36), an associate of Cassiodorus. Gregory the Great (590–604) complained of an inadequate library, though the collection may have increased when Pope Zacharias (741–52) transferred it to the Lateran. The title of librarian existed from the time of Hadrian I (722–95), and names are known for librarians of the 11th century.

Eastern Empire. The separation between West-

Courtesy of the Newberry Library

Medieval scribe

ern and Eastern forms of Christianity was a concomitant of the division of the Roman Empire. The Eastern or Byzantine Empire, Greek in language and Orthodox in religion, maintained in isolation from the West a continuity of both cultural tradition and imperial authority. Evidence of Eastern libraries exists intermittently over the whole period. Many emperors, from Theodosius II at the end of the 5th century through the Nicaean rulers after the Latin conquest, maintained libraries that may have afforded a degree of public access. A traveler's reference of 1437 gives a glimpse of stone benches and tables used in consulting the palace collection. The contents can be presumed to have included, besides law and theology, works of Greek literature and science. Byzantine encyclopedic works and digests refer to classical works now lost. Higher educational institutions, both theological and secular, such as the academy established by Theodosius II (408–50) and those founded by the Emperors Leo the Philosopher in the 9th century and Constantine Monomachus in the 10th, must have had extensive book collections. The Patriarchate maintained schools and libraries. Monastic collections, such as those at the Lavra on Mount Athos and Saint Catherine's on Mount Sinai, were widely distributed, though usually small. About 825 Saint Theodore, Abbot of Studium, regulated his monks' reading and copying. A Greek monastery that can be singled out because its library still survives in situ and largely intact is one founded by the monk Christodoulos in 1088 on Saint John's island of Patmos in the Aegean. The looting of Constantinople by the Latins in 1204 began the flow of Greek manuscripts to Italy, and the pace accelerated until the final conquest of the city by the Turks in 1453. The acquisitions of Western travelers were supplemented by books brought by emigré Greeks, such as Cardinal Bessarion, who bequeathed his library to the Republic of Venice in 1472. Italian libraries became the home of Greek literature and philosophy, which transformed the culture of the Renaissance and superseded the medieval tradition of learning.

14th and 15th Centuries. The last two centuries of the Middle Ages witnessed greatly increased production of books and a corresponding growth in accommodation for them among collegiate and monastic institutions. The latter declined drastically in intellectual influence but maintained economic power that enabled them to erect buildings to house, not the products of their own *scriptoria,* but rather scholastic works coming to them by gift or bequest, often from their members who had attended university. At Oxford, the great abbeys of Gloucester and Durham maintained their own halls of residence. The latter was bequeathed but apparently did not receive the rich collection of Richard de Bury (1287–1345), royal civil servant and Bishop of Durham. His *Philobiblon* gives valuable insight as to the state of contemporary learning and libraries. At Canterbury, Archbishop Henry Chichele erected a library building in the early 15th century, and other English cathedral foundations did likewise, a development that was matched in France, as at Rouen. An exceptional 15th-century monastic collection was formed by John Tritheim (1462–1516), Abbot of Sponheim, who acquired 2,000 volumes, many of them printed. Incunabula from other south German monasteries have reached many modern collections, a large proportion of them having found their way into the Bavarian State Library as the result of confiscation during the Napoleonic period.

Oxford colleges had relatively small collections up to the beginning of the 14th century. Later foundations, such as New College (founded 1379), All Souls (founded 1437), and Magdalen (founded 1458), all included libraries in their building plans. These long, narrow rooms had equidistant windows on both sides between which were set lecterns, with the volumes resting on the sloping tops, either at standing height or at sitting height with benches placed between, under the windows. The books were customarily chained, and the length of the desks and the narrow shelf below limited the number of books. This system became universal in larger libraries throughout western Europe. It is exemplified in the library built by the University of Oxford over the Divinity School between 1444 and 1487 and named in honor of its benefactor, Duke Humphrey of Gloucester.

The universities had trained many clerics who possessed private libraries—Chaucer's Clerk of Oxenford, with his 20 books, must have been typical of many thousands. But country gentlemen and lawyers, too, began in the 14th and 15th centuries to acquire considerable collections, evidence of which is found in wills, inventories, and records of gifts. Like other valuables, the books were habitually stored in the stout wooden chests universally used throughout the period. Culturally, the laymen's holdings were significant because of the high proportion of books in vernacular languages, only occasionally present in institutional libraries. An outstanding German private collection was formed by the physicians Hermann

(1410–85) and Hartman (1440–1514) Schedel, burghers of the wealthy free city of Nuremberg, most of which survives in the Bavarian State Library. A number of German cities established public libraries for their citizens during the 15th century, Brunswick being the earliest in 1413.

The greatest lay libraries were in the hands of royalty, and these were to become predecessors of the national collections of the future, although bequest, sale, or plunder destroyed their continuity. Kings and emperors throughout the Middle Ages had occasionally been patrons of learning. Charlemagne installed two libraries in his capital of Aachen—as recorded by his biographer Einhard, himself a book collector—and his example was followed by his son, Louis the Pious (814–40), and his grandson, Charles the Bald (840–77). Regrettably, there is no trace of the books of the brilliant Emperor Frederick II, which must have reflected his contacts with the Greek and Muslim cultures of southern Italy and Sicily.

In the later Middle Ages kings became less peripatetic, and residence in fixed centers of government made the establishment of royal libraries feasible. Foremost among these were the collections of the French royal house, a good part of whose holdings were literary and historical works written in or translated into French. John II (1350–64) bequeathed his taste for books to both branches of his descendants—the Kings of France and the Dukes of Burgundy. His eldest son, Charles V (1364–70), installed a library of three floors in the Louvre with a resident librarian. His third son, John, Duke of Berry (1340–1416), was a munificent patron of scribes and illuminators. His fourth son, Philip the Bold (1363–1404), commenced the collection of the Dukes of Burgundy, augmented by his successors. Partially dispersed after the Netherlands passed under Hapsburg rule, the remainder became the nucleus of the Belgian Royal Library.

Two English princes of the House of Lancaster amassed book collections. John, Duke of Bedford and Regent of France (1389–1435), in 1424 bought the library formed by Charles V. Humphrey, Duke of Gloucester (1391–1447), an early patron of Humanist learning north of the Alps, gave hundreds of volumes to the University of Oxford, and after his death King Henry VI gave some of the remainder of his library to King's College in Cambridge, although only a few of his books survived the Reformation. A unique royal library was formed by Matthias Corvinus, King of Hungary (1440–90), allied by marriage with the royal house of Naples, also great collectors. His magnificent Renaissance manuscripts were looted by the Turks after the capture of Buda in 1526, and all but a tiny proportion perished through neglect.

Renaissance Italy. The libraries established by the princes of Italy were of the greatest cultural significance because their collections reflected the new learning of the Renaissance. City tyrants cooperated with the passionate enthusiasm of Humanist scholars in the discovery and copying of manuscripts of the Latin and Greek classical writers and in preserving them in libraries. Princely families, such as the Este of Ferrara and Modena, the Gonzaga of Mantua, and the Visconti and Sforza of Milan, formed sumptuous collections that had a propaganda value in reflecting the liberality and culture of the ruling house. Typical were the manuscripts of Federigo da Montefeltro,

Lord of Urbino (1444–82), commissioned from the Florentine dealer Vespasiano da Bisticci. The earliest of the great Humanists, the poet Petrarch (1304–74), possessed a library that he intended to, but never did, bequeath to form a public library in Venice.

The leading center of Renaissance learning was Florence. At the beginning of the 15th century two friaries maintained libraries accessible to the citizens, the Carmelites and the Augustinians of San Spirito, to which Petrarch's disciple Boccaccio (1313–75) bequeathed his books. The first citizen and de facto ruler of Florence, Cosimo de Medici, founded the Dominican house of San Marco, and in 1444 built a library in it designed for public use. He arranged for his donations to be supplemented by the bequest of the many classical manuscripts of the scholar and bibliophile Niccolo Niccoli (1363–1437). His fellow Humanist, Poggio Bracciolini (1380–1459), traveled in southern Germany and France from 1415 to 1417, buying, borrowing, or stealing manuscripts of classic authors from the most ancient monastic libraries. The private library of the Medici, greatly increased by Lorenzo the Magnificent (1449–92), did not find a permanent home in San Marco, but most of it—after a sojourn in Rome in the early part of the 16th century with the Medici popes, Leo X and Clement VII—returned to Florence to be incorporated in the Biblioteca Medicea-Laurenziana. It is worth noting that the library's fittings, designed by Michelangelo before 1571, are a final example of the medieval lectern system. The example of San Marco was copied by Malatesta Novella, Lord of Cesena, in a library he had built in the Franciscan convent in 1447, which survives with the original collection, desks and benches intact.

The most magnificent Renaissance library housed the papal collection, recreated by the Humanist Pope Nicholas V (1447–55) and enlarged by Sixtus IV (1471–84), who installed the Humanist Bartolomeo Platina as Librarian in 1475 and provided appropriate quarters and fittings. Though these were replaced by the present building in the 16th century, the continuity of the collection extends to the Vatican Library of today.

Reformation Losses. The libraries of Italy were to have a happier destiny than the medieval libraries north of the Alps. During the Reformation, people came to regard many libraries as representatives of an outmoded philosophy of learning and a hostile religion; some libraries fell into neglect and many others were destroyed. In England hundreds of monasteries were destroyed with the loss of almost all their books between 1536 and 1540—Durham Cathedral alone retaining an appreciable percentage—and from 1549 to 1551 the university collections were purged. In France and Germany, many libraries suffered similar dispersal and loss in the popular tumults and wars of the 16th and 17th centuries. The social and political upheavals of the French revolutionary era were hardly less destructive. While contemporaries rarely cared, posterity was to mourn the irreplaceable loss of a thousand years of cultural achievement.

REFERENCES
Anthony R. A. Hobson, *Great Libraries* (1970).
Raymond Irwin, *The Heritage of the English Library* (1964).
Burnett Hillman Streeter, *The Chained Library* (1970).
James Westfall Thompson, *The Medieval Library* (1957).
Francis Wormald and Cyril E. Wright, editors, *The English Library before 1700* (1958).
Medieval Scribes, Manuscripts and Libraries: Essays Presented to N. R. Ker (1978).

JOHN R. T. ETTLINGER

Milam, Carl H.
(1884–1963)

ALA
Carl H. Milam

Carl Hastings Milam held the principal executive position of the American Library Association from 1920 to 1948, first as Secretary and later as Executive Secretary. It may be difficult for anyone who was not involved closely with him during a considerable period of his career to appreciate his abilities as a librarian and administrator. His tenure at ALA spanned the 28 years from the end of World War I to the end of World War II and covered the period of rapid growth and change within both the Association and the profession of librarianship.

Milam was born in Harper County, Kansas, on October 22, 1884. Although a native of Kansas and resident of Illinois during most of his adult years, Milam considered himself an Oklahoman, having lived there from 1893 to 1907. He attended the University of Oklahoma, where he worked as one of two student assistants to Milton Ferguson, then the only professional librarian on the staff of the University Library. He joined the ALA and, through Ferguson's influence, decided on a career in librarianship, entering the New York State Library School after his graduation from Oklahoma in 1907. After completing his studies, he worked as a cataloguer at Purdue University (1908–09).

When Chalmers Hadley resigned in September 1909 as Secretary and organizer of the Indiana Public Library Commission to become Secretary and Executive Officer of ALA, Milam followed him at the Commission. As Secretary at a time when many public libraries were being organized and needed Commission assistance, he provided advice both in his travels throughout the state and from headquarters in Indianapolis. He prepared reports and forms, spoke to various groups on behalf of libraries, developed programs for continuing education of librarians, and initiated the founding of the first state organization of public library trustees.

Milam resigned late in 1913 to accept the post of Librarian of the Public Library of Birmingham, Alabama, the largest in the state. In 1917 he took leave to work with the Library War Service in Washington, D.C., but returned to Birmingham several times during his leave, finally resigning in 1919.

Milam was one of several assistants to Herbert Putnam, Director of the Library War Service, financed initially by the Carnegie Corporation of New York and by contributions to ALA of $50,000 from libraries and individuals. When Putnam went overseas after the Armistice in 1918, Milam became Acting Director; he succeeded Putnam as Director in 1919. Before and after the Armistice Milam worked long hours and showed his administrative abilities in recruiting, selecting, and assigning personnel, planning, policymaking, and public relations. He negotiated skillfully with army officers, government officials, nongovernmental agencies, and other representatives concerned with library service to armed service personnel in the United States and abroad.

Work with the Library War Service led Milam directly into ALA's Enlarged Program, of which he was named Director in 1919 and was thus at the same time Director of both the Library War Service, which was terminating its activities, and the Enlarged Program, which was just beginning. At its March 1920 meeting, the ALA Executive Board considered, among other matters, the resignation of George B. Utley as Secretary and a report by Milam as Director of both the Library War Service and the Enlarged Program. In his report Milam suggested the feasiblity of consolidating the two programs in Chicago. The Board abolished the Enlarged Program directorship, merged the responsibilities of that program with those of the Secretary of ALA, and offered the new post to Milam. He became the 12th Secretary but only the 4th paid, full-time executive officer of the Association.

ALA membership grew from 4,460 in 1920 when Milam took office to 18,280 when he resigned in 1948. He served under 29 Presidents of ALA and was involved in many major reorganizations of the Association—beginning in 1923, through the first three Activities Committees, and through part of the changes that resulted from the investigations and reports of the Fourth Activities Committee (see American Library Association).

Milam had to organize a growing, diverse, and increasingly specialized staff to match the growth and diversification of ALA interests and activities. His energies were also directed toward the substantive matters that concerned the Association: improved library services; welfare, salaries, and annuities for librarians; technical bibliographical improvements; publishing; education for librarianship; international relations; better statistical measurements of effectiveness of libraries; federal aid for libraries; and a host of other concerns. In pursuit of the Association's interests, Milam developed strong working relationships with many foundations, including the Carnegie Corporation of New York, Carnegie Endowment for International Peace, Laura Spelman Rockefeller Memorial, Julius Rosenwald Foundation, General Education Board, and Rockefeller Foundation, as well as with federal agencies and congressional representatives. These relationships bore fruit in support for a wide range of large and small projects, including such major ones as endowment funds for ALA, federal aid for libraries, aid for foreign libraries affected by World War II, establishment of U.S. libraries abroad, and experimentation with microfilm and cooperative cataloguing. Milam also maintained a rapport with other national associations, including the Adult Education Association, the Special Libraries Association, and the Canadian Library Council and its successor, the Canadian Library Association.

Milam left his ALA post in 1948 to become Librarian of the United Nations Library. As Librarian from 1948 to 1950, he was responsible for its development from its early beginnings at Hunter College and Lake Success to its move to new quarters at the present UN headquarters in New York City. Milam believed that a legislative reference type of service should be developed primarily for the UN Secretariat and staff but that the Library might also serve other agencies, the communications media, international governmental agencies, and affiliated nongovernmental organizations, as well as educational institutions, scholars, and writers.

In 1950 Milam and his wife, the former Nell Robinson, whom he had married in 1910, retired to their farm near Barrington, Illinois. He grew irises and Christmas trees and engaged in some professional work, but the care of his wife, who died in 1956 of a progressively debilitating disease, came to require his constant attention.

In late 1961 he returned to New York for the dedication of the new UN Library building on the invitation of UN Secretary-General Dag Hammarskjöld. Milam was praised for his contributions to the organization, functioning, and continuing direction of the UN Library, then renamed the Dag Hammarskjöld Library.

Milam died in Barrington on August 26, 1963. The Carl H. Milam Memorial Lecture was established by ALA in 1971. Visiting foreign lecturers were invited to the U.S. to speak at library schools.

REFERENCES

Doris Cruger Dale, editor, *Carl H. Milam and the United Nations Library* (1976).

Peggy A. Sullivan, *Carl H. Milam and the American Library Association* (1976).

Peggy A. Sullivan, "Milam, Carl Hasings," *Dictionary of American Biography* (1978).

MARION A. MILCZEWSKI
(d. 1981)

Milkau, Fritz
(1859-1934)

Prussian—and German—librarianship since the end of the 19th century has been shaped considerably by Fritz Milkau, leading and representative librarian, library politician, and scholar.

Milkau was born in Lötzen, in eastern Prussia, on September 28, 1859. He finished his university studies in classical, German, and Sanskrit philology with the Ph.D. in 1888. In the same year he started a highly successful library career in the University Library in Königsberg. His career led him later to Berlin, Bonn, Greifswald, Breslau, and Berlin again. His outstanding capacities as librarian were recommended early to Friedrich Althoff in the Prussian Ministry of Cultural Affairs, who at that time (1882-1907) was reforming the Prussian universities (including their libraries) and high schools. Althoff passed on to Milkau in 1895 the task of planning methods for organizing a union catalogue of Prussian libraries.

Milkau's publication *Zentralkataloge und Titeldrucke* ("Union Catalogues and Printed Catalogue Cards," 1898) presented the theoretical basis for that enormous undertaking. The *Instruktionen für die alphabetischen Kataloge der preussischen Bibliotheken und für den Preussischen Gesamtkatalog* ("Instructions for the Alphabetic Catalogue of Prussian Libraries and the Prussian Union Catalogue," 1899, the so-called Prussian Instructions) were substantially influenced by Milkau's ideas. They formed for many decades the frame not only for cataloguing principles in Germany and beyond but also for the description of titles in bibliographies—until they were replaced by the *Re-*

geln für die alphabetische Katalogisierung ("Rules for Alphabetic Cataloguing," 1977, called RAK).

From 1897 Milkau had to manage the Prussian Union Catalogue worked out on the basis of the catalogue of the Royal Library in Berlin. After three years of organizational work in the Prussian Ministry of Cultural Affairs, he was appointed Director of the University Library Greifswald in 1902 and in 1907 Director of the University Library Breslau. Both libraries flourished under his guidance and special collections for Lower German literature (in Greifswald) and Slavic literature (in Breslau) were started and enlarged under his direction. During and just after World War I, Milkau was sent to Belgium to deal with the protection of libraries from the consequences of war.

When Adolf von Harnack left office as Director General of the Prussian State Library (the former Royal Library) in Berlin in 1921, Milkau succeeded him. This was the leading position in Prussian academic and research libraries, and Milkau used it for manifold activities.

From 1911 he had been a member of the Prussian Beirat für Bibliotheksangelegenheiten (Advisory Council for Library Affairs); as its Chairman, after World War I, Milkau was in a position to strengthen considerably the central position of the Prussian State Library in Germany. Among the results was the decision to publish the Prussian Union Catalogue (1925), the manuscript of which had been completed in 1922. Milkau's *Denkschrift vom 30. Juli 1913 betr. die Kataloge der Preussischen Bibliotheken und ihre Reform durch den Druck des Gesamtkatalogs* ("Memorandum of July 30, 1913, regarding the Catalogues of the Prussian Libraries and their Reformation through the Printing of the Union Catalogue," 1925) was followed for this project. Milkau also began publishing the *Gesamtkatalog der Wiegendrucke* ("Union Catalogue of Incunabula"), in preparation since 1904; the first volume appeared in 1925.

In 1920 the Notgemeinschaft der deutschen Wissenschaft (Emergency Community for German Academic Research) was founded and Milkau became the first Chairman of its Library Committee. During and after the inflation period in the 20s, that institution provided additional funds for the purchase of foreign publications, at first for the state libraries in Berlin and Munich and later also for German university libraries.

Milkau's responsibilities thus extended beyond the borders of Prussian libraries. He expanded the Prussian interlibrary loan system to other parts of Germany on the basis of the first German *Leihverkehrsordnung* ("Regulations for Interlibrary Loan"), put into operation in 1924.

In 1925 Milkau retired from his position in the Prussian State Library. The Faculty of Arts at the University of Berlin nominated him Honorary Professor of Library Science. Milkau's lectures concentrated on library history, which he considered, together with book history, as the core of library science. Engaged for many years in the reform of the librarian's theoretical education in Prussia, he achieved in 1928 the foundation of an Institute of Library Science connected with that Faculty and stayed as its Head until 1933. The courses given there were intended especially for library candidates for the Prussian state examination, preparing them as subject specialists. New state regulations for this purpose based on Milkau's ideas were issued in 1930. But it was not possible in those years to include those studies in the regular university curricula.

Milkau laid the theoretical foundations of the discipline he taught in the *Handbuch der Bibliothekswissenschaft* ("Handbook of Library Science," 1931–42, 2nd edition 1952–65). He edited the first two volumes, on script and book (1931) and on library management (1933); the third volume, on library history, did not appear until 1940. In this huge monument of scholarship, Milkau did not intend to analyze and define library science in detail but to present in clear order knowledge of the subject from the historical and philological points of view. His emphasis on book and library history as the best way to approach library science did not survive to the present, but the "Handbook" can be considered one of the important cornerstones of the discipline.

To library history, Milkau contributed especially with a comprehensive study on libraries in the collection *Die Kultur der Gegenwart* ("The Contemporary Culture," 1906, 2nd edition 1912), in which he stressed the coherence of their history with general cultural developments. His *Geschichte der Bibliotheken im alten Orient* ("History of Libraries in the Ancient Orient," 1935) was later included in a revised version in the second edition of the "Handbook" (1953).

He died in Berlin on January 23, 1934. A lover of the book as a work of art, he had a deep sense of duty, order, thoroughness, and self-discipline. Milkau was a representative of the traditional, conservative ideas of his time. But, engaged actively in pursuing new and important developments in academic and research libraries, he was successful in achieving remarkable results through his talent to convince people with striking arguments. His eloquence and ingenious formulations gave force and authority to his writing. Milkau also stressed the importance to the public of libraries as cultural and national institutions, a result of his personal engagement. His contributions were perceived and appreciated outside Germany.

REFERENCES
Fritz Milkau zum Gedächtnis. Ansprachen, Vorträge und Verzeichnis seiner Schriften, edited by Gustav Abb (1934).
Handbuch der Bibliothekswissenschaft, 2nd edition, edited by Georg Leyh, vol. 2 (1961).
Zeitschrift für Bibliothekswesen und Bibliographie (1984).
Zentralblatt für Bibliothekswesen (1934, 1979, 1985).

PAUL KAEGBEIN

Mohrhardt, Foster E.
(1907-)

Foster E. Mohrhardt, librarian and administrator, national library director, and officer in national and international library and documentation associations, whose career stretched from junior college libraries to national and international library planning, has been called the premier librarian-diplomat of the United States.

He was born in Lansing, Michigan, on March 7, 1907. His higher education began at Michigan State University with a B.A. in 1929, as well as with stu-

Foster E. Mohrhardt

dent assistance experience that led him to Columbia for a B.S. in library science the next year. He returned for an M.A. from the University of Michigan in 1933. There he found a role model and mentor in the University's distinguished Librarian, William Warner Bishop, who had been President of ALA and of IFLA. Mohrhardt later wrote of Bishop as "our first international librarian."

In 1935 the Carnegie Corporation of New York appointed Bishop chairman of an Advisory Group on Junior College Libraries. The junior college at that time was fairly new in higher education, and the Corporation proposed to stimulate interest in its proper development by a series of support grants for book purchases. Bishop recalled Mohrhardt from a brief stint on the library and teaching staff of Colorado State College at Greeley to become his assistant on the project. Mohrhardt was involved in site visits across the country and became compiler of the Group's enduring work, *List of Books for Junior College Libraries*, published by ALA in 1937.

This task led to his appointment as Librarian of Washington and Lee University in 1938. He remained there until 1946, with an interlude of wartime service. During his tenure at Lexington the new Cyrus Hall McCormick Library was completed, and in 1942 the Trustees established the Robert E. Lee Archives Division to enhance the Library's existing collections of Lee materials. A dramatic development occurred in 1941 when the Library of Congress was seeking safe hostelry, against possible war damage, for its more valuable holdings. Washington and Lee had excess stack space which Mohrhardt made available for this evacuation service. A key LC officer at the time was Verner Clapp, and this emergency experience led to a long and close friendship between the two, who later had parallel careers as officials of national libraries, as Council on Library Resources officers, and as library advisers to the Japanese government.

Following on a 1947–48 visiting professorship at Columbia's library school, Mohrhardt began his productive Washington career. From 1948 to 1954 he was Director of Library Services for the far-flung Veterans Administration, with responsibility for 450 separate collections serving both patients and professional staff in the U.S. and abroad. There he streamlined book procurement and cataloguing systems and gained such skill in the federal service that in 1954 he succeeded the redoubtable Ralph Shaw as Director of the U.S. Department of Agriculture Library, a position Mohrhardt held until 1968.

In 1962, its centennial year, this library was rechristened as the National Agricultural Library. To some extent the change was related to developments generally in the country; the former Army Medical Library had become the National Library of Medicine (NLM) in 1956. More significant, however, in this shift of title was Mohrhardt's successful vision of the library as serving a national, even an international, role in the provision of bibliographical information and library services to the bio-agricultural community.

Reflecting in a 1967 lecture at Louisiana State University on his aspirations for NAL he listed: national library coordination with LC and NLM; development of a national library network with the land-grant colleges; a systems study, as well as the design of an agricultural-biological thesaurus, looking toward the automation of library functions, including bibliographical services; and the establishment of intensive specialized information centers. By the time he left NAL those aspirations had been realized. One of his visible monuments is the multi-volume *Dictionary Catalog* of NAL holdings 1862–1965, with the newly automated *Bibliography of Agriculture* carrying on from that point; another is the Pesticide Information Center; and towering above all this activity is the NAL building in Beltsville, Maryland, opened in 1969.

Mohrhardt's vision and forum were world-wide. In 1955 he was central to the founding of the International Association of Agricultural Librarians and Documentalists, and he became its first President, serving until 1969. Thereby he was instrumental in launching *World Agricultural Economics and Sociology Abstracts,* and in 1965 the third World Congress of Agricultural Librarians and Documentalistrs was held in Washington with Mohrhardt in the Chair.

For services of this order he was granted USDA's Distinguished Service Award in 1963 "for unusual vision, competence and accomplishment in evolving and promoting a dynamic agricultural library program for the department and the nation, and for exceptional leadership." In the same year he became the first librarian to serve as a Vice-President of the American Association for the Advancement of Science. Then in 1977 an International Symposium was convened at NAL in Morhardt's honor, resulting in the Festschrift volume *International Agricultural Librarianship: Continuity and Change* (Greenwood Press, 1979).

During those fruitful NAL years he served the profession with equal distinction: President of ARL 1966; President of ALA 1967–68, Vice-President of IFLA 1965–71, President of the National Federation of Scientific Abstracting and Indexing Services 1964–65, and Chairman of the U.S. National Commission for FID in 1965.

Early on, this librarian-diplomat's focus of international service was in Asia, especially Japan. During his tenure NAL published catalogues of its Japanese, Korean, and Chinese holdings, and he was a key figure at a number of conferences focusing on higher education, library development, and scientific and publications exchange with Japan. In consequence the Japanese government in 1980 awarded him the Order of the Rising Sun, and later he was named Honorary Librarian of the highly experimental new library of Kanazawa Institute of Technology.

Mohrhardt's diplomatic skill proved evident as well in his uncommon ability to build bridges of understanding and creative activity between the often disparate fields of librarianship and documentation. He may be the only librarian to have served as a high officer in both IFLA and FID.

In 1968 Fred C. Cole, then the new President of the Council on Library Resources, tapped Mohrhardt for appointment as Senior Program Officer, later Consultant, for the Council, a post well suited for his notable understanding of national and international library development, as well as of research and higher education.

A charming and effective American emissary to world librarianship, Mohrhardt won admiration for a sparkling manner and personal warmth and public grace, spiced with what some styled a delightfully Pickwickian appearance.

ROBERT VOSPER

Moore, Anne Carroll
(1871–1961)

Anne Carroll Moore, children's librarian, author, editor, and critic, formed the Children's Department of the New York Public Library, made many contributions to a new profession, and had significant influence on the creation and publishing of children's literature.

She was born on July 12, 1871, in Limerick, Maine, and was christened Annie. Years later, at the suggestion of her editor, she changed Annie to Anne in order to avoid confusion with Annie E. Moore, who was engaged in a related field of work. In *Roads to Childhood* (1920) she wrote about her parents, her seven older brothers, and especially the influence her father had on her childhood and youth. In her home her lawyer-father read aloud, there were vigorous family discussions, she had her own books, and there always seemed to be a family celebration. When she was ten years old, she was sent to Limerick Academy; "No doubt it was the Academy that gave Anne early control of a lucid style in speaking and writing that was to make her a distinctive critic and essayist in her day," according to her biographer, Frances Clarke Sayers. Moore entered Bradford Academy in 1889, completed her courses in two years, and graduated in 1891. She returned to Limerick to read law with her father, but the death of both parents brought that plan to an end.

In 1895 she entered Pratt Institute in Brooklyn, New York, for library training. At the end of this period Mary Wright Plummer, Director of the Pratt Institute Free Library, asked her to become Librarian of the Children's Room—"the first in the country to be included in an architect's plan, and the first to make the circulation of books subordinate to familiar acquaintance with books and pictures in a free library" (*Horn Book,* January-February 1942). Her years there were marked by bringing together children, books, and pictures. Moore was not content to know the children who came to the library; she went where they were—to the schools, settlement houses, streets. She established the Children's Library as a focal part of the community. When the room was closed to circulation, she read aloud to the children. Reading aroused an interest in storytelling and, though she never attempted to tell a story herself, she recognized its value in introducing children to stories. She was convinced of it when she heard Marie Shedlock, the great English storyteller, tell Andersen's stories.

Moore took storytelling to the New York Public Library when she was asked to form a children's department there. She reported to work on September 1, 1906. Her first responsibility was to bring together under her leadership all those who in any way had been assigned to work with children. At the same time she visited the 36 branches in Manhattan, the Bronx, and Staten Island. She began immediately to train those working with children, lecturing on such

subjects as open shelves, reading aloud, book selection, and administration—all pioneering in children's work. Five years later, May 23, 1911, the main library at 5th Avenue and 42nd Street was opened, and within it was a Central Children's Room. Over the years this room was to become nationally and internationally known for its collections, staff, programs, and influence on authors and illustrators. Meanwhile, Moore was also guiding the growth of work in the branches so that upon her retirement she had one of the strongest children's departments in the United States.

Her contributions to the profession were many. In 1900 she was chosen as President of the first Round Table organization of librarians actually in charge of children's work at the American Library Association's Annual Conference in Montreal, and in 1901, at the invitation of ALA, the Round Table became a section of ALA and Moore was its first Chairman. She had been active since her first ALA Conference in 1896. In the fall of 1918 Franklin K. Mathiews of the Boy Scouts of America and Frederic Melcher, Editor of *Publisher's Weekly,* went to Moore's office to discuss a plan to encourage authors of children's books and to interest others in the children's book world. Children's Book Week, later known as Book Week, was devised in order to celebrate books and reading. There followed the Caldecott and Newbery medals, which Frederic Melcher established under ALA auspices. In 1918 Ben W. Huebsch, a prominent publisher, asked Moore to prepare and deliver a series of lectures to a group of distinguished book people—heads of publishing firms, editors, booksellers, writers, artists—on the subject of children's books. Also in 1918 Macmillan announced the first separate department for publishing children's books under Louise Seaman Bechtel, a close associate of Moore. In the years that followed, Moore worked closely with children's editors and their authors and illustrators. She exposed her staff, through meetings and branch library visits, to many of the great literary figures of the day. Her staff and exhibits in Central Children's Room represented many nations, and she had enduring friendships with such book people as Beatrix Potter, Leslie Brooke, Walter de la Mare, Padraic Column, and Ruth Sawyer Durand.

In 1918 *The Bookman,* the chief American literary journal of its day, asked Moore to contribute articles and reviews of children's books at regular intervals. There had been frequent but sporadic reviewing of children's books by distinguished writers and illustrators, but, up to that time, there had been a lack of sustained criticism of children's books. She did so from 1918 to 1926. From 1924 to 1930 Moore edited a weekly page of criticism of children's books in *Books* of the *New York Herald Tribune.* Its logo was "The Three Owls," and subsequent books by her carried that title. In 1936 she offered "The Three Owls Notebook" as well as her editorial advice to the *Horn Book.* Her page was last published in 1960, but she continued as one of the Associate Editors. She also contributed lists and articles to journals and publications too numerous to name here. It would be difficult to measure the stimulating effect of such criticism upon the writing, illustrating, and publishing of children's books.

Moore retired from the New York Public Li-

The New York Public Library
Anne Carroll Moore

brary on October 1, 1941. She died on January 20, 1961, in New York City. According to her biographer, Frances Clarke Sayers, "One person more than any other gave shape and content to the new profession, to the greatest degree and in the fullest measure: Anne Carroll Moore, of Brooklyn's Pratt Institute and the New York Public Library. To be sure, confluence of period and place set the stage for her achievement, but the color and character of her accomplishment derived from the quality of her imagination; her courage and stubborn determination; her shrewd, New England practicality; her logical, analytical mind, which, like a pyrotechnical display, could turn and light up the sky with its rocketing commitment to joy."

Moore's books include *Nicholas: A Manhattan Christmas Story*, with drawings by Jay Van Everen (1924); *Nicholas and the Golden Goose*, with drawings by Van Everen (1932); and Introduction to *The Art of Beatrix Potter*, with an appreciation by Anne Carroll Moore (1954).

Books edited by her are *Roads to Childhood* (1920); *New Roads to Childhood* (1923); *Cross Roads to Childhood (1926); and My Roads to Childhood: Views and Reviews of Children's Books* (1939). Others include *The Three Owls: A Book about Children's Books* (1925); *The Three Owls, Second Book* (1928); *The Three Owls, Third Book* (1931); *Knickerbocker's History of New York*, by Washington Irving, illustrated by Daugherty (1928); and *The Bold Dragoon and Other Ghostly Tales*, by Washington Irving, illustrated by Daugherty (1930). "Children's Books Suggested as Holiday Gifts," published by the New York Public Library as an annual list, was edited by Anne Carroll Moore from 1918 to 1941. She issued other lists and wrote numerous articles. She received honorary degrees (Pratt, 1955; University of Maine, 1940), the Regina Medal of the Catholic Library Association (1960), and other honors, including the first Constance Lindsay Skinner Gold Medal from the Women's National Book Association (1940).

REFERENCES

Frances Clarke Sayers, *Anne Carroll Moore* (1972).
Adele M. Fasick, "Moore, Anne Carroll," *Dictionary of American Library Biography* (1978).

AUGUSTA BAKER

Moraes, Rubens Borba de
(1899-)

Rubens Borba de Moraes, General Director of the National Library of Brazil, Director of the UN Library in New York, educator, author, and editor, was responsible for significant innovations and development in Brazilian libraries.

Moraes was born in Araraquara, in the state of São Paulo, on January 23, 1899. He studied at the Collège de l'Université de Geneva, Switzerland, where he received the degree of *licencié en lettres* in 1919. His first work was written in French and published in Switzerland. When he returned to São Paulo, Moraes associated himself with a group of avant-garde writers and artists. He participated in the celebrated Week of Modern Art in 1922 and collaborated in journals of the Brazilian Modernist movement. He was one of the founders of the futurist pe-

Rubens Borba de Moraes

riodical *Klaxon* (1922–23). In 1932 he participated in the constitutionalist revolution against the federal government.

In 1934, with a fellowship from the Rockefeller Foundation, he studied library organization and operation in the United States. Returning to São Paulo in 1935, he was appointed Director of the Municipal Public Library, and in 1936 he established the first university course in library science, with a U.S. orientation. In 1938 he founded the São Paulo Librarians Association. He reorganized São Paulo's public library in a modern building, planned and built under his guidance, and directed its opening in 1942. A year later he published *O problema das bibliotecas brasileiras* (1943), a comparative essay on European, American, and Brazilian libraries in which he introduced the concept of the library network as a solution to the problems of Brazilian libraries.

From 1945 to 1947 he was the General Director of the National Library in Rio de Janeiro. He introduced the dictionary catalogue, the Dewey Decimal Classification, free access by readers to reference collections, and a more liberal philosophy in relations with the public. During this same period, he was Professor of Bibliography and Reference in the National Library course.

In 1947 he was invited by the United Nations to direct the UN Information Service in Paris, where he remained until 1951. During this time he published the *Manual bibliográfico de estudos brasileiros* (1949), which he edited with William Berrien. This collective work was the first critical survey of Brazilian studies in the fields of humanities and social sciences and contained contributions by Brazilian and foreign experts. He then became the Director of the UN Library in New York City, a position he held until 1959. From 1963 to 1970 he was a professor at the University of Brasilia, teaching the history of books and libraries and Brazilian bibliography. During his teaching career he published *Bibliografia brasileira do período colonial* (1969), a critical bibliography of Brazilian works published before 1808. In 1971 the University awarded him the title of Professor Emeritus. In 1975 he was elected Honorary President of the 8th Brazilian Congress of Librarianship and Documentation, held in Brasilia.

Moraes' other major publications include the *Bibliographia brasiliana* (1958–59; 2nd edition revised, 1979), a bibliographical essay written in English on rare books about Brazil, and *O bibliofilo aprendiz* (1965), an introductory guide for those who wish to collect rare books, ancient or modern. In addition to his important contributions to Brazilian librarianship and bibliography, Moraes translated, introduced, and edited a number of works by foreign authors about Brazil and São Paulo in two serials, the *Biblioteca Historica Brasileira* and the *Biblioteca Historica Paulista*. His *Livros e bibliotecas no Brasil colonial* (1979) covers libraries, book printing, and commerce in colonial Brazil.

EDSON NERY DA FONSECA

Morel, Eugène
(1869–1934)

Best known for his untiring efforts to promote free public libraries in France, Eugène Morel was a versatile leader whose contributions touched virtually every aspect of librarianship. His most notable achievements included the first application of the Dewey Decimal Classification in a French public library, the organization of the first course of lectures on modern librarianship, and the reform of the French copyright deposit law in 1925. He was also an ardent advocate of information services in libraries, a promoter of children's work, and one of the first French librarians to call for the employment of women in public libraries. Morel's innovative ideas extended to library mechanization, and he was always eager to experiment with the new technology of his time, from film strips and microphotographic film to mechanical processes that would facilitate research work or duplicate catalogue cards.

Born in Paris on June 21, 1869, Morel grew up in a milieu where his artistic and literary interests were encouraged. While a student at the Lycée Charlemagne, he showed a great talent for literature and for foreign languages, particularly German. At an early age he had begun to study English with his mother, who had grown up in London. In search of a profession that would allow him a certain amount of leisure to devote to writing, Morel was encouraged by his mother to study law. Just 20 when he began his law career, Morel had already published his first novel and was becoming known for his contributions to literary journals. In 1892 he abandoned law for a post at the Bibliothèque Nationale that allowed him time to continue his literary pursuits. By 1905 he had already published nine novels, and had served as Editor of the *Revue d'Art Dramatique* (1900–03). He also wrote plays for the popular theater. His potential as a writer was appreciated by such contemporaries as Romain Rolland and his work was encouraged by established authors, including Jules Verne. When an interviewer reported that Leo Tolstoy had cited Eugène Morel as "one of the most original" French novelists, the young man's literary success seemed assured. In the meantime, Morel began to turn his energies toward a new goal—the establishment of free public libraries in France.

Morel later recalled his first unpremeditated visit to a London public library on a rainy night in 1895 when a sudden storm forced him to take shelter. On his return to Paris, Morel was disappointed to find that his enthusiasm for free public libraries was not shared by his colleagues, who were either indifferent or skeptical that France would ever provide enough funding to offer the kinds of library services available in Britain. For more than a decade Morel systematically gathered data on library development abroad, which he published to stimulate public interest in improving French libraries. After publishing articles in several influential journals, he finally issued his famous and highly polemical work entitled *Bibliothèques* in 1908. This two-volume comparative "essay" dealt with all aspects of library development in France, Great Britain, and the United States. Despite the caustic style of the work, it was unquestionably well documented, with many tables, statistics, and budgets. The biting tone of Morel's work ensured that its content could not be ignored. One leading librarian charged that Morel's brilliant imagination as a novelist led him to champion reforms that were "pure utopias" while another conservative colleague described Morel's book as "passionate, highly colored, brutal and shocking."

Other library leaders were much more sympathetic to Morel's views, and he soon attracted a few colleagues, educators, and writers who were also eager to promote free public libraries. At the urging of these supporters and enthusiasts, Morel began to condense his study, eliminating discussion of academic and research libraries. The result of these efforts was *La Librarie Publique* (1910), later described as the first book in France to be devoted entirely to public libraries. In his choice of title for this pioneering work, Morel intentionally avoided the word *bibliothèque* with its scholarly connotations and attempted to repatriate the word *librairie,* which had been adopted by the English. Although Morel discussed many British libraries, which he knew first-hand, he did not hesitate to affirm that *la librarie publique* was "an American invention." Caught up by the missionary fervor of his U.S. colleagues, Morel painted an idealistic portrait of American libraries—"free, absolutely free, open all day, every day and evening . . . not waiting for the public to come, going out to [the public] . . . they are for the grown man what the school is for the child."

In order to create such libraries in France, Morel felt that propaganda was essential. He therefore organized a series of conferences aimed at the general public as well as librarians, booksellers, scholars, and bibliophiles. This lecture series, held at the École des Hautes Etudes Sociales each year from 1910 to 1914, was cosponsored by the French library association and by the publishers' society. Much to Morel's satisfaction, the conferences also attracted the interest of certain municipalities, and in 1911 he received an invitation to recatalogue the municipal library of Levallois-Perret. This working-class, industrial community on the northern outskirts of Paris offered Morel the first opportunity to introduce France to the Dewey Decimal Classification, which had been "rejected without being known." Morel's classified catalogue was published in 1913; six months after it appeared, both consultation of books and circulation figures had doubled, while the loan of nonfiction works rose from 3 to 40 percent of all books borrowed. This change—which was all the more impressive considering that the public did not have open access to the shelves—further convinced Morel that American library methods could be successfully adapted in France. Because Morel and many of his colleagues were mobilized in 1914, experimentation with open-access public libraries did not begin in earnest until after World War I. Morel's election as President of the French library association (Association des Bibliothécaires Français) in 1918 marked a softening of old antagonisms within the field at a time when there was growing public interst in modernizing and democratizing French libraries as a part of postwar reconstruction.

In 1920 when an American war relief agency, the Comité Américaine pour des Régions Devastées (CARD), prepared to inaugurate its most important model public library in Aisne, Morel was invited to participate in the ceremonies. From that point on Morel was instrumental in publicizing the success of the American model libraries; he also served on the French Committee for the Modern Library, gained

Eugène Morel

support to send young French women to study in U.S. library schools, and later became a lecturer at the Paris Library School, run by ALA from 1923 to 1929.

Morel passed more than four decades of his professional career at the Bibliothèque Nationale, where his work on the reform of the copyright deposit law was considered his most important accomplishment. Morel's influences however, extended beyond the national library, and his leadership was especially valued by an energetic cadre of public librarians who were attempting to put his ideas into practice in a handful of Parisian and provincial municipal libraries. Unfortunately, Morel did not live to see this movement extended throughout France following the creation of a national library directorate in 1945. Although not alone in the reforms he advocated, Morel was frequently ahead of his time. In a comparative study of public library development, the French scholar Jean Hassenforder remarked:

> In vitality and stature Eugène Morel of France was the equal of the great British and American pioneers, Edward Edwards and Melvil Dewey, and it was he who introduced to France the principles of modern librarianship. In all probability the reason these three were not equally influential was ascribable to the milieu more than personality. Eugène Morel was up against the French mentality of his time.

During his lifetime, Morel's reputation abroad was equal to or greater than his influence in France. In 1912 he was named an Honorary Fellow by the British Library Assistant's Association, and in 1926 he was designated the official French delegate to ALA's 50th anniversary conference. His ideas were also widely discussed in Belgium, where his book *Bibliothèques* was the inspiration for the passage of a 1921 law (*Loi Destrée*) described as the first compulsory library law on the continent. Morel was also an active member of the French affiliate of the International Institute of Bibliography created by Otlet and LaFontaine. Always interested in bibiographic control and scholarly communication, Morel submitted proposals for the improvement of international publishing and library statistics at the first IFLA conference in Rome in 1929. He further developed those ideas at the 10th Annual Conference on Bibliography in 1931 in The Hague, where he presented an important report warning against the misuse of statistics in bibliometric analysis.

When Morel died in Paris on March 23, 1934, his loss was keenly felt by a small but dynamic group of "modernist" librarians and documentalists in France and abroad.

REFERENCES

Gaetan Benoit, "Eugène Morel: 1869–1934: His Life and Work," *Libri* (1980).
Jean Hassenforder, *Développement comparé des bibliothèques publiques en France, en Grande-Bretagne et aux Etats-Unis dans la seconde moitié du XIXe siècle (1850–1914)* (1967).

MARY NILES MAACK

Morgan, J. Pierpont
(1837–1913)

The collector's role assumed by J. Pierpont Morgan evolved from several fortuitous circumstances—a

well-to-do father, an international education, and a time of economic expansion. In Morgan's time, big United States corporations were in need of capital funds; the House of Morgan arranged capital for the railroad, steel, banking, and insurance companies. Morgan was an aristocrat who dominated every situation with his powerful personality.

Morgan was born in Hartford, Connecticut, April 17, 1837, and studied in Germany at the University of Göttingen. His first acquisition was typical for a 14-year-old—a presidential signature, that of President Fillmore. The collection grew slowly during Morgan's first 45 years. Upon the death of his father, Junius Spencer Morgan (1890), and the formation of the firm of J. P. Morgan & Company in 1895, Morgan began to buy on a grand scale.

Junius Morgan had been a collector and owned a George Washington letter as well as the original manuscript of Sir Walter Scott's *Guy Mannering*. Pierpont Morgan's interest was probably stimulated by his father's possessions. That interest was further enhanced by the efforts of his nephew, another Junius Morgan, who was an ardent collector of books, prints, and manuscripts. Over the next several decades, the collection grew apace, with group and individual purchases, each adhering to the principle of selectivity first established.

Examples of the acquisitions include a Gutenberg Bible on vellum, the 1459 Mainz Psalter, the four Shakespeare Folios, and the original autograph manuscripts of Keats's *Endymion* and Dickens's *A Christmas Carol*. Collections purchased en bloc included a fine run of Aldine imprints in hand-tooled leather bindings. Several collections of manuscripts were acquired, including the Duke of Hamilton's famous "Golden Gospels" and a select group of 270 Rembrandt etchings. By 1905 Morgan had purchased some 700 incunabula, among them 40 from the press of William Caxton. Besides the printed works and manuscripts, the Morgan collections include outstanding early written records such as seals, tablets, and papyri. The collections are unusual—a high percentage of the holdings are unique copies.

In 1906 Morgan had a library building constructed adjacent to his New York home at 36th and Madison in New York City. Designed by the noted architectural firm of McKim, Mead, and White, it is styled as a Renaissance palazzo. With a grandiose interior that has been carefully preserved, the J. Pierpont Morgan Library has become a noted structural landmark. The original building was expanded with a large annex in 1928, and two additions were later made, in 1962 and 1977.

After the books and manuscripts were moved into the new building, Morgan, who died in Rome on March 31, 1913, seemed more determined to increase the scale and depth of his collection. Joining him in this effort was a talented librarian, Belle DaCosta Greene, who became a model as a private collector's librarian. She served 43 years in the post, guiding the growth of the library during the time of the transition from a private collection to an invaluable research resource.

The Library sponsors many publications and exhibits and supports an active research program; its vast resources are available at the Library to scholars. The success of the Morgan Library probably far ex-

The Pierpont Morgan Library
J. Pierpont Morgan

ceeded the founder's vision of its usefulness.

REFERENCES
An Introduction to the Pierpont Morgan Library (The Morgan Library, 1974).
Francis Henry Taylor, *Pierpont Morgan as Collector and Patron, 1837–1913* (1957).

DONALD D. HENDRICKS

Morocco

Morocco, a constitutional monarchy of Northwest Africa, is bounded on the north by the Mediterranean Sea, on the east by Algeria, on the south by Mauritania, and on the west by the Atlantic Ocean. Population (1984 est.) 21,495,000; area 458,730 sq.km. The official language is Arabic.

History and National Library Services. Founded in 1920 in Rabat, the General Library and Archives of Morocco (BGA) played an important part in the country's national library system. Originally conceived as a library of special studies on the Maghreb and Muslim west, it was first made up of collections from the Moroccan Institute of Higher Studies. The buildings were constructed and inaugurated in 1924. The acquisition of private libraries and of 1,500 manuscripts, stamps, and ancient maps built up the initial collection. At the same time, a collection of general culture developed, that of the human sciences and public reading material, which answered the needs of public users, European for the most part.

In 1926 it was established by decree as a public institution, and the decree foresaw as well the establishment of a place for the administrative archives more than 10 years old. A decree of 1931 on Moroccan public libraries authorized it to subsidize them and gave it the right to inspect them. However, the creation of a library division in the Ministry of Cultural Affairs, after independence, eliminated that role.

The BGA collection at the close of 1984 (the majority in French) totaled some 256,000 volumes, 4,500 periodicals, a quarter of which were in Arabic, and 30,000 manuscripts. These collections answer the needs of specialized researchers of ancient and modern Morocco and Islamic Spain, as well as those of the students of the School of Arts and Sciences.

Founded in 1939 by Spanish authorities, the Tetouan General Library played in the northern area a role comparable to that of the BGA before the independence and reunification of Morocco. Its specialized collection on the area, mostly in Spanish and Arabic, totals 60,000 volumes, 2,220 periodicals, and 1,500 manuscripts, and in its archives are some 20,000 historic documents, 60,000 administrative documents, and 35,000 photographs. Attached to the Library Division of the Ministry of Cultural Affairs, it supervises the public libraries in Asilah, Larache, Ksar el Kebir, and Tangier.

National Documentation Center. The National Documentation Center (CND) was created in Rabat in 1968 as a public institution attached to the Department of Planning. A decree of 1980 charged the CND to gather, index, preserve, and disseminate documentation about the economic and social development of Morocco published locally or abroad; to coordinate and promote other specialized centers (numbering 117) and public centers (numbering 61) in a national scientific and technical information system; and to coordinate this national system with other international and regional systems. The CND is associated with the European Space Agency and has a national database.

By 1984 the CND had indexed and recorded on tape approximately 110,000 references to government documents produced by the various organs of the government, the documents themselves being preserved on microfiche. The library of the CND was conceived to meet needs for special interests in the information sciences (4,400 volumes, 450 periodicals). By 1984 it had 110,000 items on microfiche. In 1982 the CND started a national investigation to record libraries, staffing, and collections in Morocco.

Academic Libraries. The famous Kairouyyin (Quaroune) University in Fez, one of the first in the world, was founded in 1400. It is now attached to the State Ministry in Charge of Cultural Affairs. At the close of 1984 its collection totaled 16,631 volumes, 426 periodicals, 1,997 manuscripts, and 5,600 microforms. Other universities include the Université Mohammed V and the Université Sidi Mohammed Ben Abdellah; the Université Mohammed I, the Université Cadi Ayyad, and the Université Hassan II are in the process of formation.

Public Libraries. More than 60 libraries are open to the public. Only 10 date to the period before independence; the first three were opened in Casablanca in 1918, in Fez in 1920, and in Marrakesh in 1923, then two in Tetouan in 1937 and 1939.

The first American library was opened in Casablanca in 1942, with the arrival of the Allies during World War II. Public library service is offered by the Ministry of Cultural Affairs, municipalities, other ministries, more than 20 foreign cultural centers, and cultural associations.

The documentary collections of the public libraries dependent on the government are almost all in Arabic, and those of the libraries of the cultural centers are mainly composed of works in the languages associated with them (French, English, Spanish, German, and Russian). French cultural centers in Rabat and Fez organized reading sections for children.

School Libraries. A survey in Rabat indicated that 80 percent of the secondary schools have libraries; the majority of the collections were estimated at 1,300 works as an average, made up chiefly of schoolbooks.

In the primary schools initiatives were undertaken, by the school directors or teachers, to build small collections of works with the financial aid of the parents or of the school cooperative, or with modest contributions from the students.

Special Libraries. There were 117 special libraries recorded in 1984. The oldest is a private library, founded in 1917 by the Association of Public Works and Buildings, followed in 1920 by the Library of the Bureau of Research and Mine Investments. Three-fourths of the special libraries have been created since independence; major subject areas are agriculture, mines and industry, education, Islam, and sociology.

The Royal Library contains a collection of historic archives and Arab manuscripts and the Libraries of Zaouias a collection of Arab manuscripts belonging to religious brotherhoods.

The Profession. In 1971 the CND and the

Cultural Affairs Department conducted a global study of Morocco's library services. The survey showed that the country was in need of 1,000 librarians. With the assistance of Unesco, a library school was opened in October 1974. The school offers two programs: a three-year graduate course and a two-year postgraduate program. The school's *informatistes* totaled 500 in the graduate program and 56 in the postgraduate program at the end of 1985. Its Library held 6,611 volumes and 181 periodicals in 1984. An Association of Information Specialists was created in July 1973.

G. HARIKI; BATTIWA LEKBIR

Canadian Library Association
Elizabeth Homer Morton

Morton, Elizabeth Homer
(1903–1977)

Elizabeth Homer Morton was the founding Executive Director of the Canadian Library Association. She was the best known Canadian librarian of her generation and perhaps the most esteemed, as much for her qualities of heart and mind as for her formal achievements.

Born on February 3, 1903, in Tunapuna, Trinidad, of Canadian parentage, Morton was privately educated until 1919. She did her high school studies in Saint John, New Brunswick, and then took an arts degree (1926) at Dalhousie University in Halifax, Nova Scotia. Brief service as a teacher in Cape Breton, Nova Scotia, convinced Morton of Canada's urgent need for better library service, and she decided to become a librarian. She took the librarian's course given by the Ontario Department of Education and then worked in the Cataloguing Department of the Toronto Public Library. Returning to New Brunswick, she was employed as a teacher and school librarian and then as Secretary of the New Brunswick Library Commission. In 1931 she rejoined the staff of the Toronto Public Library, this time as a member of the Reference Department, where she remained until 1944. From 1936 to 1943 she also served as Secretary of the Ontario Library Association.

The decisive step in Morton's career came in 1944 when she left the security of library employment to become the full-time Secretary of the Canadian Library Council, a struggling organization whose main purpose was to pave the way for the formation of a national library association. When the Canadian Library Association/Association Canadienne des Bibliothèques was actually established in 1946 (in good part because of her efforts), it was wholly logical that Morton be selected as its initial Executive Director. She held that position until her retirement in 1968.

In the fledgling years of the CLA, Morton was in effect the one-person team on whom the continued existence of the Association depended. The Association had large ambitions, a small membership, and a precarious funding, and it had to accommodate itself to a taxing diversity of regional, cultural, and professional interests. Aided by a very small staff, Morton served as initiator, organizer, lobbyist, counselor, convener, and editor. Her most visible accomplishments were the establishment and continued supervision of the *Canadian Periodical Index* (the first major index of Canadian periodicals), the *Canadian News-*

paper Microfilm Project, and the Association's two journals, *Canadian Library Association Bulletin* (now *Canadian Library Journal*) and *Feliciter*. She also edited the *C.L.A. Occasional Papers* series.

Less visible but perhaps even more important was the influence she wielded behind the scenes. Her excellent contacts in governmental and educational circles did much to muster support for the formation of Canada's National Library (1950). Her advice was sought in many library appointments and policy decisions. She was, unobtrusively, the originator as well as the executor of major developments within the Canadian Library Association itself.

To mark her retirement from the CLA in 1968, the Association published an impressive book of essays on Canadian librarianship. She was made a member of the Order of Canada in 1968 and was awarded honorary doctorates by the University of Alberta (1969) and Sir George Williams University (1970).

After leaving the CLA, Morton continued to be active for a decade. She took a Master's degree from the Graduate Library School of the University of Chicago (1969), operated her own consulting firm, assisted in the National Library's survey of resources, and acted as library consultant for Unesco in Trinidad. She lectured at various library schools and worked on several books.

Elizabeth Morton died in Ottawa on July 6, 1977.

SAMUEL ROTHSTEIN;
MARION GILROY (d. 1981)

Mozambique

Mozambique, an independent republic on the southeast coast of Africa, is bordered on the north by Tanzania, on the east by the Indian Ocean, on the south by Swaziland and South Africa, and on the west by Zimbabwe, Zambia, and Malawi. Population (1984 est.) 13,210,000; area 799,380 sq.km. The official language is Portuguese; Bantu languages are widely spoken.

The National Library of Mozambique, founded in Maputo in 1961, houses about 110,000 volumes. Mozambique does not issue a national bibliography of its own, but bibliographical references to publications of or about Mozambique are listed in the *Boletim de la Bibliografía Portuguesa*. The journal *Documentario trimestral,* issued in Mozambique from 1935, lists publications deposited under copyright law during the previous four-month period. Archival materials are kept at the Arquivo Histórico de Moçambique, Maputo, founded in 1934. The collection consists of almost 12,000 volumes. There is one university in Mozambique, the Universidade Eduardo Mondlane (formerly the Universidade de Lourenço Marques), founded in Maputo in 1962. The language of instruction is Portuguese. There are approximately 80,000 volumes in the general and departmental libraries of the university, plus 8,600 periodicals. Educational facilities in Mozambique are not highly developed. There is a city library in Maputo, the Biblioteca Municipal, which holds approximately 8,000 volumes.

The Mozambique Institute of Scientific Research, founded in Maputo in 1955, houses a library and documentation center, the Biblioteca e Centro de Documentação e Informação, established in 1977 under the Ministry of Education. The library's collection consists of approximately 3,000 scientific volumes. The Institute publishes works on ecology, natural sciences, earth sciences, and social sciences, particularly on Mozambique history. There are two other notable libraries in Maputo. The Direcção dos Serviços de Geologia e Minas, founded in 1930, specializes in mining research and geological studies. The collection consists of about 16,000 books. Research findings are published in the society's *Boletim*. The Instituto de Algodão de Moçambique (Cotton Research Institute), founded in 1962, houses 2,500 volumes and 210 journals.

Mudge, Isadore Gilbert
(1875–1957)

Isadore Gilbert Mudge was America's foremost reference librarian and for many years the author of the standard *Guide to Reference Books*. Under Mudge's editorship, the *Guide* became so well known that, as her biographer John Waddell pointed out, "'Mudge' became not merely a woman's name, but a noun, an adjective, and a verb upon the lips of librarians and students in the entire English-speaking world."

Born in Brooklyn, New York, on March 14, 1875, Mudge was the daughter of well-educated parents. Her father, Alfred Eugene Mudge, was a respected Brooklyn lawyer and the stepson of Charles Kendall Adams, who served as President of Cornell University and the University of Wisconsin and was instrumental in building important libraries at each institution. Mudge's mother, Mary Ten Brook, was the daughter of Andrew Ten Brook, a noted historian and at one time the Librarian at the University of Michigan.

Mudge was named in memory of her aunt, the name Isadore having come originally from a popular romance. Nothing is known about her early years. In 1889 she enrolled in the Adelphi Academy in Brooklyn; graduating at the top of her class in spring 1893, Mudge entered "Grandfather's university" the following fall, though by then Charles Kendall Adams had moved from Ithaca to Madison.

At Cornell, Mudge excelled in her studies and was elected to Phi Beta Kappa in her junior year. She majored in history and took classes with some of the most distinguished professors in the country, including Moses Coit Tyler and George Lincoln Burr. Of the two, Burr was the more influential. She enrolled in every course he offered and later revealed that the training she received from him started her on her career as a reference librarian.

In September 1898, 15 months after she graduated from Cornell, she enrolled in the New York State Library School at Albany, the famous school established by Melvil Dewey at the time he became State Librarian. She excelled at the Library School, completing the two-year program in 1900 and receiving the B.L.S. degree with distinction.

Mudge seems to have made a favorable impression on Dewey during her residence in Albany. Although there is no evidence of a close friendship between the two, Dewey—at the peak of his career—does appear to have recommended Mudge for her first two library positions. The first of these was at the University of Illinois, where Dewey's close friend and former star pupil, Katharine Lucinda Sharp, was the Director of the new library and the founder of an important library school in Urbana. Mudge arrived on the Urbana campus in 1900 and was put in charge of the Reference Department and made Assistant Professor in the library school. She stayed for three years, working hard to develop the reference collection and provide services for researchers. She also met Minnie Earl Sears of the Cataloguing Department, a woman who would be her companion and collaborator for several decades.

In 1903 Mudge resigned her position at Illinois to accept the directorship of the Bryn Mawr (Pennsylvania) College library. Dewey recommended her for this job as well, just as he had trained and recommended the previous two directors of the library. Accompanied by Sears, who would become Head of the Cataloguing Department there, Mudge took charge of an entire library for the only time in her life. It was a responsiblity she may not have enjoyed; nothing is known about the work she did there, and she was always reticent about the details of her Bryn Mawr experience. In 1907 she took a one-year leave of absence from the position but did not return when the year was over.

After seven years of library work, Mudge went to Europe accompanied by Sears. They traveled and worked on their *Thackeray Dictionary* (1910). After they returned to the United States they found a number of projects and part-time appointments: Mudge taught in the library school at Simmons College in Boston in 1910 and 1911, reviewed reference books for *Library Journal,* and assisted William D. Johnston in compiling *Special Collections in Libraries in the United States* (1912). Johnston was the Director of the Columbia University library, and her association with him on this project led to her eventual appointment at Columbia in 1911. She spent the rest of her professional career there.

The year before that appointment, however, Mudge began another association that would also occupy the rest of her career and would make her the best-known librarian of her generation. At the 1910 conference of the American Library Association, Mudge was asked to take over the editorship of Alice Bertha Kroeger's *Guide to the Study and Use of Reference Books*. Kroeger had brought out editions of this work in 1902 and 1908 before she died in 1909. Mudge began her editorial work by preparing a two-year supplement to the 1908 edition. Under her editorship, the *Guide* became the standard book of librarianship, and Mudge was to see it through four editions.

Columbia University. While preparing that first supplement, she was appointed to the Columbia University library by Johnston. Her first position as Gifts and Exchange Librarian (February 6, 1911) was followed a few months later by the appointment as Reference Librarian, and she remained in that position for the next 30 years. Mudge said that she had "set her mind on wanting Columbia from the days that I was at Cornell." By the time she arrived on the Morningside Heights campus, Columbia had already

ALA

Isadore Gilbert Mudge

established itself as a university of the highest quality. Under the direction of President Nicholas Murray Butler, its graduate faculties were producing more Ph.D.s than any other university in the country. But the library at Columbia was woefully inadequate to support so much advanced scholarship.

Mudge began at once to develop the reference collection and quickly won the support of Butler himself. He discovered her resourcefulness in satisfying his own bibliographical needs, and with his help Mudge was able to build the finest reference collection in existence. Moreover, she provided thorough and expert guidance to that collection for students and faculty alike. The reference service she had begun at Columbia was unique at that time. It took several years for these services to gain recognition in the Library, but gradually more and more scholars realized how helpful her knowledge could be in their research. In fact, it became clear with the passing years that her methods contributed significantly to the research and instruction at Columbia.

Throughout her years at Columbia, Mudge had the ongoing project of preparing editions and supplements to her *Guide to Reference Books,* a work that has had a distinguished history. Mudge's first edition (but the third edition since 1902) appeared in 1917, and it became the most frequently used reference book in every research library; it greatly enhanced every reference library by providing a guide to all kinds of reference books in many languages. Other editions of the *Guide* appeared in 1923, 1929, and 1936, and the tradition established by Mudge at Columbia was continued by her successors Constance Winchell and Eugene Sheehy.

During the 1920s and 1930s Mudge was the undisputed authority on reference books, and the Columbia reference department served as a model for reference departments at other institutions. Mudge-trained librarians were eagerly sought to fill newly created reference positions throughout the country. Some neophyte librarians studied with Mudge at Simmons College, where she continued to teach from time to time, and at the New York Public Library's Library School, where she also occasionally offered courses. Others studied with Mudge at Columbia after a merger in 1926 of the Albany Library School and the New York Public Library School formed the School of Library Service at Columbia. Mudge became Associate Professor there and from 1927 on regularly taught Bibliography and Bibliographical Methods, a course that made lasting impressions on the many students, who in turn spread Mudge's methods far and wide.

With Minnie Sears's death in 1933, Mudge's life began to slow down. The 1936 edition of the *Guide* was the last one she edited, and it was extremely difficult for her to complete. She had never honored deadlines, and as she grew older her habits became impossible for her publisher. Finally, ALA decided that a new editor should be sought to prepare the next edition of the *Guide.* Constance Winchell became the new editor, and Mudge retired from the Reference Department in 1941, continuing her teaching just one year longer. She moved to the Westchester home that she and Sears had purchased years before. She died on May 16, 1957, in Baltimore, Maryland.

Arthur Plotnik
L. Quincy Mumford

REFERENCES

The only full study of Mudge is John Neal Waddell, "The Career of Isadore G. Mudge: A Chapter in the History of Reference Librarianship." (unpublished Ph.D. dissertation, Columbia University, 1973).

Laurel L. Grotzinger, "Women Who 'Spoke for Themselves,'" *College and Research Libraries* (1978).

John N. Waddell and Laurel A. Grotzinger, "Mudge, Isadore Gilbert," *Dictionary of American Library Biography* (1978).

PAUL COHEN

Mumford, L. Quincy
(1903–1982)

Lawrence Quincy Mumford, 11th Librarian of Congress, directed LC during a period of great growth, from 1954 to 1974.

Mumford was born on a farm in Ayden, North Carolina, on December 11, 1903. He received his A.B. from Duke University in 1925 and the M.A. from Duke in 1928. His library career began when he was a student assistant in the Duke University Library; in 1926 he became Head of its circulation department, and in 1928 the Acting Chief of Reference and Circulation. While at Columbia University (1928–29), where he earned a graduate degree in library science, Mumford was an assistant in the library.

In 1929 he joined the staff of the New York Public Library as a reference assistant. There he served as General Assistant in charge of the Director's Office (1932–35), Executive Assistant and Chief of the Preparation Division (1936–43), and Executive Assistant and Coordinator of the General Service Divisions (1943–45). In 1940, at the request of the then Librarian of Congress, Archibald MacLeish, Mumford was granted a leave of absence to organize the Processing Department of the Library of Congress and to serve a year as its Director. In 1945 he was appointed Assistant Director of the Cleveland Public Library and in 1950 became its Director, a position he held until his appointment as Librarian of Congress in 1954 by President Dwight D. Eisenhower. He was the first Librarian to have a professional degree in librarianship. In an editorial headed "Librarians' Librarian" the *Washington Post* on April 28, 1954, applauded the selection.

The Library of Congress made remarkable progress during Mumford's 20 years as Librarian (1954–74). Congressional appropriations increased from about $10 million to almost $100 million. In 1958 the Library was authorized to use U.S.-owned foreign currencies (under the Agricultural Trade Development and Assistance Act) to acquire books for itself and other U.S. libraries and to establish acquisition offices in foreign countries such as Egypt, India, Indonesia, Israel, and Pakistan. In 1965 the Higher Education Act authorized the establishment of the National Program for Acquisitions and Cataloging (NPACP), which greatly expanded the Library's foreign procurement program and inaugurated a system to speed up the acquisition, cataloguing, and dissemination of cataloguing data for "all library materials currently published throughout the world which are of value to scholarship." Under that program the Library established additional overseas offices in Austria, Brazil, France, Germany, Great Britain, Japan, Kenya, Norway, Poland, Spain, and Yugoslavia. This improved service to the nation's libraries resulted in great savings in cataloguing costs nationally and improved access to research materials.

As a result of studies of space requirements for the Library, which began during Mumford's administration, Congress in 1965 authorized the construction of the Library's third major building, the James Madison Memorial Building. It more than doubled the space available for the Library's services and collections when it came into use in 1979.

The application of automation to the Library's processes and services began and made substantial progress during Mumford's service. Following the publication in 1964 of a feasibility study, *Automation and the Library of Congress,* the Information Systems Office was established. In 1965 the Machine Readable Cataloging (MARC) project began. It became the basis for the revolution in the rapid distribution of cataloguing information utilizing computers and communication technology.

Other notable advances at LC under Mumford include the organization of the papers of the Presidents; the beginning publication of the *National Union Catalog of Manuscript Collections* and the *National Register of Microform Masters;* the establishment with the cooperation of the Bureau of the Budget of the Federal Library Committee; the tremendous expansion of the National Books for the Blind program to include the physically handicapped; the establishment of a separate Preservation Office and expansion of preservation research and services, including motion picture preservation in cooperation with the American Film Institute; the beginning of the *Pre-1956 National Union Catalog* project, scheduled to exceed 600 volumes; the huge expansion of the Congressional Research Service under the Legislative Reorganization Act; and the establishment of the Cataloging-In-Publication program in cooperation with publishers.

Under Mumford, collections grew from about 33,000,000 items in 1954 to almost 74,000,000 in 1974, and the staff grew by more than 50 percent, to a total of more than 4,500 by 1974.

Mumford served as President of the Ohio Library Association, 1947–48, and of the American Library Association, 1954–55. He also was President of the Manuscript Society (1968–70), a member of the Lincoln Sesquicentennial Commission (1958–60), and a member on the President's Committee on Libraries (1966–68), named to review the recommendations of the temporary National Advisory Commission on Libraries. During his service as Librarian of Congress, he was a member of the Board of Advisors of the Dumbarton Oaks Research Library and Collection, the Sponsors Committee of the *Papers of Woodrow Wilson,* the U.S. National Book Committee, the National Trust for Historic Preservation, and a number of other advisory boards. He received several honorary degrees. Mumford died in Washington, D.C., August 15, 1982. On December 13, 1983, the Assembly Room on the sixth floor of the James Madison Memorial Building was named the L. Quincy Mumford Room.

JOHN G. LORENZ

Munford, W. A.
(1911-)

K. C. Harrison/
Library of Westminister
W. A. Munford

When Britain's Library Association (LA) planned its centenary celebrations for 1977, it was inevitable that W. A. Munford should be invited to become a member of the committee responsible for planning the events. It also went without saying that he was asked to write the history of the LA, designed to be published as one of several LA centenary volumes. Munford had already carved a niche for himself as a library historian *par excellence* and had been the founder of the Association's Library History Group. Add to these the further qualifications of the executive positions he had held in British librarianship, plus services as a former Honorary Secretary of the LA, and it will be obvious why he was the perfect and natural choice to advise on centenary events and to write the LA's history. He completed the book in time for publication just prior to the start of the LA centenary year.

William Arthur Munford was born in Islington, north London, on April 27, 1911. Educated first at a high school in nearby Hornsey, he later obtained the degrees of BSc (Econ.) and PhD., both gained in leisure hours, at the London School of Economics. He received his early experience in public libraries at Hornsey and at Ilford in east London before becoming the borough librarian of Dover in 1934 at the early age of 23. He remained in that post until 1945. Dover was in the firing line for most of World War II, from June 1940 to September 1944, suffering serious damage from air raids and heavy artillery shelling. Munford was Food Executive Officer for Dover from 1939 to 1945, and in 1946 he was appointed M.B.E. (Member of the Order of the British Empire) for his war services. He was City Librarian of Cambridge from 1945 to 1953.

Even before the war, Munford had evinced a deep interest in professional affairs, contributing articles to the *Library Association Record* and the *Times Literary Supplement* and chapters to issues of *The Year's Work in Librarianship.* But in the postwar years his professional work burgeoned. A strong LA supporter, he became a member of its Council and in 1947 was responsible for forming the Eastern Branch of the LA, thus ensuring the unity of the profession in the counties of Cambridge, Norfolk, and Suffolk. From 1952 to 1955 he was Honorary Secretary of the LA, a position that no longer exists but was at that time regarded as the most prominent job in the Association. If the President of the LA could be regarded as the head of state, then the Honorary Secretary was the prime minister.

In those years he formed a close friendship and working relationship with Percy Welsford, the paid secretary of the LA from 1931 to 1959, and one of those responsible for the rapid expansion of the Association during those years. Meanwhile, Munford was still working as City Librarian of Cambridge, where he did much to improve the standing of the Cambridge Public Libraries in the eyes of both town and gown. He associated with many of the academics in the Cambridge colleges, one of his particular friends being Dr. (later Sir) Sydney C. Roberts, Master of Pembroke College, Cambridge. In 1953 Roberts served as President of the LA. Munford's persuasiveness was an obvious factor, both in selling

Ralph Munn

ALA

Roberts to the LA and, perhaps more important, selling the LA to Roberts. Roberts chaired in 1957 a Ministry of Education Committee charged with investigating the structure of the public library service in England and Wales. The Roberts Committee's report, published in 1959, led to the passing of the Public Libraries and Museums Act of 1964, which remains the current legislation for public libraries in England and Wales.

Munford's first book was a bibliography called *Books for Basic Stock,* published in 1939. But in 1951 he made his name as a library historian with a book published by the Library Association called *Penny Rate: Aspects of British Public Library History.* It was rapidly taken up by the library schools as a textbook. But it was not just a textbook: it possessed readability as well. In it Munford explored the events that led to the passing of the first Public Libraries Act of 1850 and brought to life such personalities as Edward Edwards and William Ewart, both protagonists for public libraries, as well as Colonel Sibthorp, a member of Parliament notorious for his opposition to the movement.

Munford made additional contributions to library history later, with his biography *William Ewart, M.P.,* and his studies of *Edward Edwards* (1963), *James Duff Brown* (1968), *Louis Stanley Jast* (1966), and *Sir John MacAlister* (1983). The study of Jast was written in collaboration with W. G. Fry, and that of MacAlister with S. Godbolt. In 1976 Munford completed *A History of the Library Association, 1877–1977.* He next undertook work on a *Biographical Dictionary of British Librarians,* to be published in the later 1980s.

In 1954 Munford was appointed Director-General of the National Library for the Blind, which at that time was centered in Great Smith Street, Westminster, London, with a northern branch in Deansgate, Manchester. He held that post until his retirement in 1982. During his 28 years' service he initiated many improvements, notably in the braille bookstock, and culminating in the fusion of the Westminster and Manchester libraries for the blind in new premises at Bredbury, near Stockport, Cheshire. He handled the inevitable staffing problems of such an amalgamation with admirable tact and diplomacy. Munford also became an active supporter of the provision of books in large print for the hard-of-seeing, becoming a Trustee of the Ulverscroft Foundation, set up to mark the work of Frederick A. Thorpe, the founder of large print book publishing in Britain. Profits from the sales of Ulverscroft LP books are added to the funds of the Foundation, which supports hospitals, schools, and libraries.

Munford was a prolific library journalist. He contributed steadily for more than 50 years to all the British library periodicals and to some overseas as well. He served as a regional adviser to the *ALA World Encyclopedia of Library and Information Services* as well as being a contributor to Thomas Landau's *Encyclopedia of Librarianship* (1958; 3rd. ed. 1966) and to the *Encyclopedia of Library and Information Science* published by Marcel Dekker, Inc. An omnivorous reader with wide-ranging tastes, though with a preference for history, biography, literature, and detective stories, Munford writes engagingly, frequently sceptically, with a literary turn of phrase and a sense of humor.

In 1977 the Library Association made him an Honorary Fellow. Earlier, his concern for and interest in library cooperation had led to his becoming Chairman of the Executive Committee and the Regional Council of the East Midlands Regional Library System.

K. C. HARRISON

Munn, Ralph
(1894–1975)

Ralph Munn was a library administrator and educator, consultant, author, and leader in professional organizations.

Munn was born in Aurora, Illinois, on September 19, 1894, grew up in Colorado, and attended the University of Denver, where he earned an A.B. degree in 1916 and an LL.B. degree in 1917. After service with the U.S. Army in France from April 1917 to July 1919, he attended the New York State Library School at Albany, from which he received the B.L.S. degree in 1921. He was married to Anne Shepard, also a librarian, on June 6, 1922.

His first professional position was in the Seattle Public Library, where he served as Reference Librarian, 1921–25, and Assistant Librarian, 1925–26. He then became Librarian of the Flint (Michigan) Public Library, 1926–28. From 1928 to 1964 he served as Director of the Carnegie Library of Pittsburgh. He served also as Director, and later Dean, of the Carnegie Library School of Carnegie Institute of Technology, 1928 to 1962, when the school was transferred to the University of Pittsburgh.

Throughout his long and distinguished career, Munn was actively involved in international interests and concerns as a professional librarian and citizen. In 1934, commissioned by the Carnegie Corporation, he surveyed the libraries of Australia and New Zealand and made recommendations for their development and for the selections of librarians to study library practice in the United States. As a result, he became known as the "father of the modern library movement in Australia and New Zealand."

Nine years later, in 1943, he was retained by the City Planning Commission of New York City to survey library needs and select sites for new branch libraries in New York's five boroughs.

In 1947 he undertook a goodwill tour of libraries of Central and South America for the U.S. Department of State and as a representative of the American Library Association. While on that mission, he spoke in Lima, Peru, on the occasion of a presentation of 10,000 American books given to the Peru National Library, which had been rebuilt following a fire. For his work in behalf of the reconstruction of the Library, the Peruvian government awarded him the degree of Knight of the Order El Sol del Peru. In 1950 he served as Chairman of the U.S. delegation to a Unesco Library Seminar in Malmo, Sweden, to determine the needs of public libraries throughout the world.

Throughout his career Munn never deviated from his conviction that the public library's primary role was educational, informational, and cultural. This conviction brought into clear focus the issue of demand versus quality. In 1938 he implemented a revised book selection policy that sharply defined and limited the purchase of light, recreational fiction and effectively eliminated the acquisition of books that he categorized as "shopping bag fiction." As a result, the Carnegie Library of Pittsburgh gained remarkable status as a distinguished local institution, widely recognized for the quality of its collections and services.

Under his administration Carnegie Library expanded its services significantly. He frequently appeared before governmental bodies to seek necessary funds for library facilities, collections, and services. Munn sought to make libraries more responsive to the needs of young people, who, he once said, "are required to read books I never heard of until I got to college."

Through his leadership, unified library services were established in Pittsburgh with the merger of the Carnegie Free Library of Allegheny and Carnegie Library of Pittsburgh in 1956. Also in 1956 Carnegie Library contracted with the County Commissioners of Allegheny County to give service to county residents. Free borrowing privileges were extended, and bookmobile services were operated in parts of the county not served by local libraries. In his judgment, achievement of the difficult merger with the Carnegie Library of Allegheny and implementation of contractual services with the county were the most significant innovations of his administration. Previously he had established the Downtown Branch and Business Branch, and in 1958 he published his *Plan for the Federation of Libraries in Allegheny County*.

Munn was persistent in his efforts to improve public library service throughout Pennsylvania. In 1930 and 1931 and again in 1958 he served on the Governor's Commission on Public Library Development. His participation in the work of the 1958 Commission contributed to the formation of a state library system under which Pennsylvania was divided into 29 districts, with Carnegie Library of Pittsburgh as the headquarters for all of Allegheny County and parts of Butler and Westmoreland counties. As a result of its outstanding science and technology collections, the Carnegie Library became designated the resource in that field for the entire state. In 1959 he was the first recipient of the Distinguished Service Award given by the Pennsylvania Library Association for outstanding service by a Pennsylvania librarian to library development in the state.

His longtime associate, Elizabeth Nesbitt, observed that as Dean of the Carnegie Library School, Munn "insisted upon maintenance of standards in admission and performance of students, and upon honesty and fairness to employer and employee in placement of students." In 1936 the Carnegie Corporation published his *Conditions and Trends in Training for Librarianship*.

Munn was constant in his advocacy of cooperation among libraries. Cost and space factors, community needs, and the interdependence of libraries caused him to assume leadership in 1942 in coordinating the acquisition of costly research materials by the University of Pittsburgh, Carnegie Institute of Technology, and Carnegie Library. The results of this early work provided a foundation that led to the formation of the Pittsburgh Regional Library Center nearly 25 years later.

Always conscious of cost effectiveness in his management of Carnegie Library, he sought to keep overhead costs as low as possible in order to make available maximum funding for collection development and informational services. He introduced laborsaving devices and employed management techniques and principles of financial administration that were sensible and effective. He was one of a small cluster of progressive library administrators who established public relations offices in the mid-1940s.

Munn was respected universally for his professional as well as personal integrity. His unusually well-balanced judgment was combined with an unerring sense of timing that contributed greatly to his effectiveness as an administrator, planner, and strategist. His lifelong interest in young people inspired him in his work and enriched his personal life. Through his international activities, and long before the Fulbright Program was implemented, he welcomed many young librarians from abroad, including Australia, the Netherlands, and Scandinavia. They were added to the staff of the Carnegie Library, where they received the same salaries, benefits, and opportunities as their American colleagues. He took great interest in their professional development and provided many opportunities to participate in staff activities and community cultural events.

Whether writing or speaking, he had an extraordinary gift for clarity and grace. He was a keen observer, responsive, and always interested in others. His commanding and courtly presence was temporized by inner warmth and a fine sense of humor. Munn was forthright, perceptive, considerate, and kind. He possessed the qualities of a master teacher who willingly shared his insights and experience with many younger librarians.

He felt strongly that able women were too often denied equal opportunity to advance in a profession where women predominated. His concern was deepened in the years following World War II, when men were actively recruited into library schools.

A much respected leader in the American library movement throughout his long and distinguished career, he maintained active membership in professional organizations. He was the president of the American Library Association, 1939–40, and of the Pennsylvania Library Association, 1930–31. He made key addresses on many auspicious occasions, including the dedicatory address for the new ALA Headquarters building during the Association's 1963 Conference in Chicago.

Munn was honored by the University of Pittsburgh, which conferred upon him the honorary degree of Doctor of Laws in 1940. In 1960 Waynesburg College in Pennsylvania bestowed upon him the honorary degree of Doctor of Laws.

Upon his retirement, effective October 1, 1964, he was appointed Director Emeritus by the Board of Trustees of the Carnegie Library of Pittsburgh. Shortly thereafter a fund was established to support the Ralph Munn Lecture Series, subsequently a program for precollege students of the Greater Pittsburgh area. Following his death in Pittsburgh, January 2, 1975, the American Library Association adopted a resolution expressing its sense of loss and appreciation for his contribution to the library profession. The resolution characterized Munn as exemplifying "the highest ideals of the library profession in his activities as Association official, library adminis-

American Library Association
Wilhelm Munthe

trator and educator, author, consultant and citizen."

REFRENCE
Regina F. Berneis, "Munn, Ralph," *Dictionary of American Library Biography* (1978).

KEITH DOMS

Munthe, Wilhelm
(1883–1965)

Abraham Wilhelm Støren Munthe, Norwegian library director, devoted his whole life to the world of libraries. Munthe brought new ideas and stimulated professional development on the national scene in Norway; he also built bridges among the various parts of the library profession on the international level.

Born October 20, 1883, in Oslo, he passed the student's examination for the university in 1902, and while a student at the University of Oslo, he also entered the Royal University Library as an apprentice in 1903, thus starting a career that was to last for 50 years. He went through the ranks in the library, becoming Library Assistant in 1909 and Amanuensis in 1910. In 1920 he took over as Head of the Manuscript Department. In 1922 he became Director of the Royal University Library, a position in which he remained until 1953.

In the years 1913 to 1916 he studied in Berlin, Copenhagen, Stockholm, and Uppsala. He developed a lasting interest in library developments on the international scene. He also developed a keen interest in all sorts of organizational matters concerning libraries, from the very practical housekeeping details to the more general levels of library planning and library buildings. In his time Munthe came to be regarded as a specialist in library planning, called upon as consultant for a number of library projects abroad.

As the Director of Norway's largest and most important library for more than 30 years, Munthe had great influence on the whole of the Norwegian library community. He was instrumental in setting up the annual Norwegian Library Meetings, joint meetings with librarians from both the academic libraries and the public libraries. He encouraged the staff of the Royal University Library to take part in these meetings, and he pressed for programs for the meetings that included items of appeal for all types of librarians.

The Royal University Library had since 1815 served a dual function as a University Library for the University of Oslo and as the National Library for the Kingdom of Norway. In 1925 Munthe raised the question of separating the library from the University of Oslo and making it an independent national library. The time was not ready for such a change, and the suggestion created wide debate. The result was that the library remained within the University of Oslo, also serving as the national library. It so lasted until 1985, when the Ministry of Culture decided that steps should be taken to create a separate and independent national library, a process under way in the mid-1980s.

Munthe developed particularly good relations with the library community in the United States. In 1936 the Carnegie Corporation wanted a European librarian to give a critical appraisal of American librarianship, and he was given the task. From his extensive traveling in the U.S. emerged a book, *American Librarianship from a European Angle* (1939). An observant and outspoken account of the American library scene as viewed by an outsider, the book was used in American library schools for many years.

Munthe was active in the work of IFLA, and in the years after World War II he was the President of that organization, 1947–51.

His ability as a scholar and a writer can be observed, among other places, in the books *Litteraere falsknerier* ("Literary Frauds," 1942) and *Essays for bokvenner* ("Essays for Book Lovers," 1943).

A number of organizations and activities outside his professional field benefited from his knowledge and enthusiasm over the years. One organization should particularly be mentioned, the Norwegian Tourist Association (Den norske turistforening). His love for nature directed a lot of his energy toward work for nature preservation and the pleasures of mountain hiking and outdoor life.

Munthe was given honorary doctorates at the universities of Uppsala, Toronto, and Hamburg, and the Library Association made him an Honorary Member. On his 50th birthday celebration in 1933 he was given a large Festschrift with contributions from colleagues in all parts of the world. In his time the Royal University Library twice had extensions added to the original building, which made it among the more advanced and modern of the old European libraries.

Munthe died in Oslo on December 18, 1965.

BENDIK RUGAAS

Namibia

Namibia, formerly South West Africa, lies in the southwestern part of the African continent. Angola and Zambia lie to the north, Botswana to the east, South Africa to the south, and the Atlantic Ocean to the west. Almost all the land—92 percent—is classified as extremely arid to semi-arid. The capital and only city is Windhoek. The country covers 823,144 sq.km., yet is sparsely populated. According to the official census, the total population in 1981 was 1,025,324. The population is extremely heterogeneous, being a mixture of many distinct ethnic groups. The official languages are Afrikaans, English, and German. Most of the people speak either a Bantu or a Khoisan language as their mother tongue, with Afrikaans serving as the main educational medium and lingua franca.

History. The country's involved domestic political situation is complicated by its long-standing status as an international political bone of contention. A German protectorate from 1884, it was administered by South Africa under a League of Nations mandate from 1915. In 1968 the UN General Assembly gave the area the name Namibia, and the International Court of Justice declared in 1971 that South Africa was occupying it illegally. South Africa rejected a UN plan for independence by 1978. UN peace plans and election proposals in the early 1980s did not lead to peaceful settlement of hostilities nor to a stable independent government.

National Library and Archives. The Estorff Reference Library of Windhoek to some extent serves as the national library of Namibia. It was begun in 1926 with a nucleus of books originally the property of the German administration. It was known as the Library of the Legislative Assembly until 1957, when it was renamed the Administration Library. In 1968 it became part of the South West Africa Library Service, instituted by ordinance as a subsection of the Department of Education of the then South West Africa Administration. In 1980 that administration was dissolved and its functions divided up among a new first-tier Central Authority and a multiplicity of new second-tier ethnic Representative Authorities. The existing SWA Library Service fell under the Administration for Whites. Also in 1980, responsibility for the Library Service was transferred internally from the Department of Education to the newly established Cultural Promotion Section.

At the end of 1981 the Administration Library was temporarily closed down until more adequate and suitable accommodation could be provided. In October 1984 it was reopened to the public under its new name as the Estorff Reference Library. Housed in a renovated historical building dating from German colonial times, Estorff House was erected in 1891 and is one of the oldest buildings in Windhoek. It is named after Ludwig von Estorff (1859–1943), an officer of the German Schutztruppe (Colonial Troops), who occupied it.

The Library provides reference and interlibrary loan facilities both to government officials and to the general public of all races. It is a depository for publications of the United Nations and the Stockholm International Peace Research Institute. In 1951 all SWA publications were required by law to be deposited there. The Library houses an Africana collection, specializing in Namibiana, which includes both legal deposit and purchased material.

The bookstock in 1984 was approximately 33,460 volumes, excluding periodicals, newspapers, and assorted materials such as microforms. In addition, small special collections are decentralized in departmental libraries throughout the administration.

A retrospective Namibian national bibliography was independently published overseas in 1978 and 1979: *Namibische National Bibliographie (NNB), 1971–1975* and *1976–1977.*

The State Archives (or Staatsarchiv), founded in Windhoek in 1939, is the main center for historical research. Supervised by the Department of National Education, the institution contains 5,000 books, official and private documents dating from the period of German rule, 3,803 maps, 7,600 photographs, and a Namibiana collection. The Archives Service started a source publication series, called *Archeia,* and publishes diaries of missionaries, traders, and travelers, of which the first four publications were *Diaries of Carl Hugo Hahn, Missionary.*

Academic Libraries. The Library of the Windhoek College of Education opened in May 1979. The stock amounts to about 22,000 sources, featuring audiovisual material prominently. Three hundred fifty-five periodical and newspaper titles were received in the mid-1980s. The library's extensive Old Mutual Collection of educational material is worth special mention.

The Academy, Namibia's own tertiary institu-

Libraries in Namibia (1982)

Type	Administrative units	Service points	Volumes in collections	Annual expenditures (rand)	Population served	Professional staff	Total staff
National	1	1	33,460	36,000[a]	--	3	4
Academic	2	3	38,000	125,000[b]	--	10	18
Public	1	17	170,000	270,000[a]	22%	14	58
School	2	136	230,225[c]	100,000[a]	16,168	--	--
			29,000[d]	--	--	--	--

[a]Excludes salaries.
[b]Source material only.
[c]For whites.
[d]National Education.

Namibia Library Service

Estorff Reference Library of Windhoek, Namibia's national library. It is housed in one of Windhoek's oldest buildings, constructed in 1891 during German colonial times.

tion, founded in Windhoek in 1980, fulfills the needs of the Technical College, Technikon, and University. The Library, called the Old Mutual Library, contains approximately 15,700 sources, including a small audiovisual collection. The Library houses the Windhoek Branch Library associated with the University of South Africa.

Public Libraries. The first public subscription library was established in Lüderitzbucht in 1914 with a collection of donated books and periodicals. Along the same lines other public libraries were developed throughout the country. Most libraries were run by committees, funds were limited, and everybody, including the librarian, worked on a voluntary basis in most cases.

In 1968 the Library Service for South West Africa was established with the aim of providing more efficient school and public library services. Libraries were reorganized and existing books catalogued and classified according to established library standards. Local municipalities were responsible for housing, staff, and administration of public libraries, and the Library Service provided books, professional advice, and regulations. Membership in public libraries was free of charge.

At the beginning of 1980 responsibility for public libraries was allocated by legislation to representative authorities. Existing public libraries, which were until then used by whites only, were transferred to the Administration for Whites. The latter became responsible for all aspects of public libraries under its jurisdiction, such as financing, housing, staff, and administration, as well as the provision of library material. In 1984 there were 17 service points ranging from a membership of 50 to 100 in the smaller communities of the vast and sparsely populated territory up to 4,000 in the bigger places. Payment of a small membership fee by adults was introduced in 1982. Members of other representative authorities are also admitted, provided they make a financial contribution toward running the public libraries.

A Book Distribution Service mails library material to individuals who cannot make use of existing public libraries. A few smaller public libraries exist in

nonwhite communities, run by their local authority or other institutions. The total bookstock of all public libraries was approximately 170,000 in the early 1980s and served about 22 percent of the population.

The largest public library, in Windhoek, has a collection of 66,000 volumes, consisting of books in English, Afrikaans, and German, as well as a few in Dutch and French. The Library was established in 1924. Lisa Gebhardt, who died in September 1984 at the age of almost 90 years, was at its helm from 1926 to 1967. She made an important contribution toward its development from a small subscription library to an efficient modern institution.

School Libraries. The first step toward the development of school libraries was taken in early 1966 when an Organizer of School Library Services was appointed by the Department of Education of the then South West Africa Administration. With the establishment of the Library Service for South West Africa in 1968, this post fell away and new ones were created as the School Library Division of the Library Service. In 1968 all books in stock in the School Library Division were catalogued. A completely centralized system was developed whereby the Division was in charge of the selection, purchasing, classification, and cataloguing of books for school libraries.

In 1969 legislation transferred the education of blacks and Coloureds away from the SWA Administration and made it the responsibility of departments of the central government of South Africa. The SWA Administration retained control of white education.

In 1977 the Executive Committee of The SWA Legislative Assembly decided to change the structure of the school library service to white schools by divorcing it from the Library Service for SWA and placing it under the direct control of the Chief Inspector of Education. The School Library Division fell away, and new posts were created for a Subject Adviser and a Subject Inspector of School Library Services. The centralized acquisition and processing system was scrapped, and new arrangements made with the cooperation of the Transvaal Education Department Library Services of the Provincial Administration of the Transvaal.

During the 1970s three distinct school systems existed: one for whites, one for Coloureds, and a third for blacks, the black system being divided into further subgroupings to enable instruction to be given in the pupils' mother tongues in the elementary grades.

Coloured education was the responsibility of the Department of Coloured Affairs, black education that of the Department of Education and Training, both Departments being part of the central government of South Africa. Education was compulsory only for white scholars up to the age of 16 and was not compulsory for black scholars, the majority of whom entered the labor market after only a few years of schooling.

In 1980 legislation created the new first-tier, national, multi-ethnic government body, the Central Authority. Namibia then reassumed control of diverse functions that in the previous decade had been scattered among various South African government departments. The new Department of National Education was established as part of the Central Authority. It is responsible for most black government schools in the territory, and contributes per-capita pupil allowances to several multiracial church and other private schools. However, the 1980 legislation made provision for each second-tier ethnic Representative Authority to decide for itself whether it wished to undertake responsiblity for the education of its own pupils or entrust the matter to National Education. Thus the education of whites, Coloureds, Rehoboth Basters, and certain black ethnic groups (Ovambos, Damaras, and Caprivians) is controlled by their respective Representative Authorities.

In 1980 the Library Services Division of the Department of National Education was created and the first Assistant Director of Library Services appointed. The Division consists of a School Libraries Section and a Departmental Libraries Section. The School Libraries Section provides three levels of service to schools in Namibia.

The highest level of service is provided to schools directly under the control of National Education. The Section is responsible for a centralized system of book acquisition, processing, and distribution, and the supply of library furniture and equipment, as well as the provision of intensive professional guidance and training. In 1984 the Section provided such service to 4 secondary and 70 primary schools. The joint bookstock stood at 11,000 for secondary and 18,000 for primary schools. Most of the primary school bookstock is made up of small classroom collections (known as "book nooks") but a vigorous expansion program was in progress.

The School Libraries Section also provides lower levels of service to many schools that do not fall under the control of the Department of National Education. Factors such as the small number of schools involved and the lack of suitable qualified personnel have led several second-tier Representative Authorities to come to an agreement with National Education, under which the latter provides professional services on an advisory or agency basis to the Education Department staff of the respective Administration (the civil service of the Representative Authority, which is the elected legislative body). In this way the School Libraries Section assists Coloured, Rehoboth Baster, and other schools by providing professional guidance in the form of subject manuals, training courses, and school visits.

Special Libraries. The State Museum Library in Windhoek has a collection of 4,000 books and special collections in Namibiana, archaeology, entomology, ethnology, mammalogy, and ornithology; it subscribes to 200 current periodical titles. It publishes *Cimbebasia* (1962–), which reports the results of original research in the social sciences and natural history.

The South West Africa Scientific Society Library, established in Windhoek in 1925, has a collection of 8,400 books and publishes a *Newsletter, Lanioturdus* (formerly the *Ornithological Newsletter*), a *Botanical Newsletter,* and a *Journal.*

The former Museum Library in Swakopmund, founded in 1951, was incorporated into the Sam Cohen Library, a private library opened in 1977 and managed by the Society for Scientific Development. The Library contains 7,000 volumes, including the Ferdinand Stich collection of more than 2,000 volumes, a special collection of Namibian newspapers covering the period since 1898, and a considerable number of historical photographs.

In 1983 the South West Africa Broadcasting Corporation (SWABC) and Television Services started an information center mainly for the use of its own personnel. The center makes extensive use of audiovisual media and specializes in reference material, newspaper clippings, press announcements, official publications, speeches, and news commentaries.

The Library Services Division of the Department of National Education is responsible for departmental libraries of government departments under the jurisdiction of the first-tier Central Authority. In 1984 the Departmental Libraries Section was engaged in reorganizing those departmental special collections. There was a potential for 15 such libraries.

The most extensive and noteworthy of these libraries are Agriculture, Nature Conservation and Veterinary Science, Water Affairs, and the Geological Survey. Also worth mentioning are the Supreme Court library and the Weather Office library. These libraries are all mainly intended for the use of their own staffs, but are generally willing to assist bona fide researchers who have exhausted other sources of information.

The Profession. For professional library education, Namibians study either at a residential univeristy in South Africa or through the University of South Africa, a correspondence institution accepting only external students. At the Academy in Windhoek and the Windhoek College of Education, students training as teachers can take courses in school librarianship and media use. In the mid-1980s there was no full-fledged faculty of librarianship and information science offering degrees or diplomas at the Academy.

Association. The local SWA/Namibia Branch of the South African Institute for Librarianship and Information Science was founded in Windhoek at the end of 1979. In 1984 the total membership was 49. Regular meetings are organized and the Branch issues its own quarterly newsletter.

PATRICIA BARBARA PIETERSE;
MARIA MARGARITHA VILJOEN

National Bibliographies

The following list of 98 current national bibliographies was compiled from the catalogues and collections, and with assistance from the staff, of the Library of Congress. While it is as exhaustive as possible, no claim for completeness can be put forward. Some national bibliographies that are said to exist could not be traced in any of the library catalogues or holdings lists that were examined.

For this listing the editors decided, rather arbitrarily, to regard as "current" any national bibliography known to be active during the 1980s, even if its coverage lagged considerably behind the imprint date. Some of the bibliographies included on this basis may have suspended or ceased publication recently because of political changes in various parts of the world. To keep entries relatively short, each country has been limited to one title, with the exception of Czechoslovakia, which issues separate bibliographies for its two major languages. In cases where the national bibliography is issued in various parts covering different types of publications, only the part dealing with trade books is listed. With few exceptions, details about frequency, cumulations, title changes, subseries, and bibliographies that antedate the establishment of the current national bibliography have been omitted. Additional information of this kind can be found in the published sources listed under References. In the absence of a bona fide national bibliography, an entry is provided for the next best available source produced by local agencies (such as individual booksellers, book trade organizations, university or public libraries, or learned societies). It should be noted that some of these substitutes, especially in the cases of the smaller territories, include writings published elsewhere about the area in addition to items published locally. The current title and imprint are given in the vernacular, and, in most cases, a starting date is given. Titles in non-Roman alphabets have been transliterated. If the issuing agency does not appear as corporate author, as publisher, or in an "at head of title" note, its name is supplied in an additional note.

ALBANIA

Bibliografia kombëtare e Republikës Popullore të Shqipërisë: libri shqip. Bibliographie nationale de la R. P. A.: les livres albanais. 1958+ Tiranë, Botim i Bibliotekës Kombëtare.

ALGERIA

Algiers (City). al-Maktabah al-Wataniyah. *Bibliographie de l'Algérie.* 1.+ année; 1. oct. 1963+ Alger, Bibliothèque nationale.
Added title page: *al-Bibliyughrafya al)Jaza'iriyah.*

AUSTRALIA

Australian National Bibliography. Jan. 1961+ Canberra, National Library of Australia.

AUSTRIA

Oesterreichische Bibliographie; Verzeichnis der österreichischen Neuerscheinungen. Bearb. von der Österreichischen Nationalbibliothek. 1945+ Wien, Hauptverband des österreichischen Buchhandels, 1946+

BANGLADESH

Bangladesh. Directorate of Archives and Libraries. *Bamladesa jatiya granthapanji. Bangladesh National Bibliography.* 1+ 1972+ Dhaka, Bamladesa Arakaibhs o Granthagara Paridaptara, Siksha, Samskrti, o Krira Mantranalaya, Ganaprajatantri Bamladesa Sarakara.

BARBADOS

The National Bibliography of Barbados. Jan./Mar. 1975+ Bridgetown, Public Library.

BELGIUM

Bibliographie de Belgique. Belgische bibliografie. 1. + année; jan. 1875+ Bruxelles, Bibliothèque royale Albert Ier.

BENIN

Bibliographie du Bénin. 1. + année; 1976/77+ Porto-Novo, Bibliothèque nationale, 1978+

BERMUDA

Bermuda National Bibliography. v. 1+ 1983+ Hamilton, The Bermuda Library.

BOLIVIA

Bio-bibliografía boliviana. 1975+ La Paz, Editorial Los Amigos del Libro, 1977+
Compiled by W. Guttentag Tichauer.
Supersedes *Bibliografía boliviana.*

BOTSWANA

The National Bibliography of Botswana. v. 1+ 1969+ [Gaberones] Botswana National Library Service.

BRAZIL

Bibliografia brasileira. jan./jun. 1983+ [Rio de Janeiro] Biblioteca Nacional, 1984+
Supersedes *Boletim bibliográfico da Biblioteca Nacional.*

BULGARIA

Natsionalna biblografiia na NR Bulgariia. Seriia 1, Bŭlgarski knigopis: knigi, notni, graficheski i kartografski izdaniia. no. 78+ ian 1974+ Sofiia, Narodna biblioteka "Kiril i Metodiǐ."
Supersedes in part *Bŭlgarski knigopis* (1897-1973) and continues its numbering.

CANADA

Canadiana. Jan. 15, 1951+ Ottawa.
Compiled and edited by the Cataloguing Branch, National Library of Canada.

CARIBBEAN AREA

The CARICOM Bibliography. v. 1+ 1977+ Georgetown, Guyana, Caribbean Community Secretariat Library, 1977+
This is a cumulated subject list of current national imprints of the Caribbean Community member countries (Barbados, Guyana, Jamaica, and Trinidad and Tobago) and areas not yet producing national bibliographies, such as the Bahamas and Belize.

CHILE

Bibliografía chilena. 1980+ Santiago, Biblioteca Nacional, 1982+
Retrospective volume covering 1976–79 was published in 1981.
Supersedes *Anuario de la prensa chilena.*

CHINA, PEOPLE'S REPUBLIC OF

Ch'uan kuo hsin shu mu. Quan-guo xinshumu. National Bibliography. 1950+ Pei-ching, Wen hua pu, Ch'u pan shih-yeh kuan li chu, Pan-pent'u shu kuan, 1951+

CHINA, REPUBLIC OF (TAIWAN)

Chung-hua min-kuo ch'u pan t'u shu mu lu. 1970+ T'ai-pei, Kuo li chung yang t'u shu kuan.
Supersedes *The Monthly List of Chinese Books* (1960–69).

COLOMBIA

Anuario bibliográfico colombiano "Rubén Pérez Ortiz." 1951+ Bogotá.
At head of title: Instituto Caro y Cuervo. Departamento de Bibliografía.

CZECHOSLOVAKIA

České knihy. 1951 + Praha, Statni Knihovna CSR.
Supersedes *Bibliografický katalog,* pt. A, *Knihy české* (1933–50).
Slovenská národná bibliografia. Séria A: knihy. roč., 21 + 1970 + Martin, Matica slovenská.
Continues *Slovenské knihy* (1951–69) which superseded *Bibliografický katalog* pt. B, *Knihy slovenské* (1946–50).

DENMARK

Dansk bogfortegnelse. The Danish National Bibliography. Books. 1841/58 + Udarb. af Bilbiotekscentralen. Ballerup, Bibliotekscentralens Forlag, 1861 +
Det dansk bogmarked contains a weekly alphabetical list of new books.

DOMINICAN REPUBLIC

Anuario bibliográfico dominicano. 1980/82 + Santo Domingo, Biblioteca Nacional, 1984 +

EGYPT

Nashrat al-ida'. [al-Qahirah] Dar al-Kutub wa-al-Watha'iqal-Qawmiyah.
Added title page: *Legal Deposit Bulletin.*

ETHIOPIA

Ethiopian Publications. 1963/64 + Addis Ababa, Haile Selassie I University, Institute of Ethiopian Studies, 1965 +

FIJI

Fiji National Bibliography v. 1 + 1970–78 + Lautoka, Fiji, Library Service of Fiji, Ministry of Social Welfare, Dec. 1979 +

FINLAND

Suomen kirjallisuus. Finlands litteratur. The Finnish National Bibliography. 1544/1877 + [Helsinki] Helsingin Yliopiston Kirjasto, 1878 +

FRANCE

Bibliographie de la France. 1. + année; nov. 1811 + Paris, Cercle de la Librarie.

THE GAMBIA

National Bibliography of The Gambia. v. 1 + Jan./June 1977 + Banjul, National Library of The Gambia, 1980 +

GERMAN DEMOCRATIC REPUBLIC

Deutsche Nationalbibliographie und Bibliographie des im Ausland erschienenen deutschspraghigen Schrifttums. Bearb. und hrsg. von der Deutschen Bücherei. Reihe A: Neuerscheinungen des Buchhandels. 3. Jan. 1931 + Leipzig, VEB Verlag für Buch-und Bibliothekswesen.

GERMANY, FEDERAL REPUBLIC OF

Deutsche Bibliographie. Wöchentliches Verzeichnis. Amtsblatt der Deutschen Bibliothek. A: Erscheinungen des Verlagsbuchhandels. 1. März 1947 + Frankfurt am Main, Buchhändler-Vereinigung.

GHANA

Ghana National Bibliography. 1965 + Accra, Ghana Library Board, 1968 +

GREECE

Hellenike vivliographia. 1972 + Athenai, Vivliographike Hetaireia tes Hellados, 1975 +
Added title page: *Greek National Bilbiography.*

GUYANA

Guyanese National Bibliography. Jan./Mar. 1973 + Georgetown, National Library.

HAITI

Publications haitiennes et celles ayant rapport avec Haiti parues en 1980. In Association des Archivistes Bibliothecaires et Documentalistes Francophones de la Caraibe. Section Haiti. *Bulletin d'information.* no.1 + 1980 +

HONDURAS

Anuario bibliográfico hondureno (Tegucigalpa, Honduras). 1980 + Tegucigalpa, El Sistema, 1982 +
At head of title: Universidad Nacional Autonoma de Honduras. Sistema Bibliotecario.

HONG KONG

A Catalogue of Books Printed in Hong Kong. In *Hong Kong Government Gazette.* Compiled by the Chief Librarian, New Territories Public Libraries, Cultural Services Department, Hong Kong.
Published quarterly as special supplement no. 4.

HUNGARY

Magyar nemzeti bibliográfia: könyvek bibliográfiája. 32. evf. + aug. 15, 1977 + Budapest, Országos Széchényi Könyvtár.
Continues *Magyar nemzeti bibliográfia,* which began publication jan./márc. 1946.

ICELAND

Íslensk bókaskrá. The Icelandic National Bibliography. 1974 + Reykjavík, Landsbókasafn Íslands, 1975 +
A continuation of "Íslenzk rit," which appeared in *Árbok Landsbókasafns Íslands,* 1945-75, and *Bókaskrá Bóksalafélags Íslands,* 1937–73.

INDIA

Indian National Bibliography. v. 1 + Jan./Mar. 1958 + [Calcutta] Central Reference Library.

INDONESIA

Bibliografi nasional Indonesia. Okt. 1975 + Jakarta, Proyek Pengembangan Perpustakaan, Departemen Pendidikan den Kebudayaan, Apr. 1978 +
Continues Indonesia. Kantor Bibliografi Nasional. *Bibliografi nasional Indonesia.*

IRAN

Teheran. Kitabkhanah-i Milli. *Kitabshinasi-i milli.* 1 + [1963] + Tihran.
Added title page: *National Bibliography, Iranian Publications.*

IRAQ

al-Fihris al-watani lil-matbu'at al-'Iraqiyah. al-sanah 7 + al-adad 17/18 + [Baghdad] Wizarat al-I'lam, Mudiriyat al-Thaqafah al-Ammah, al-Maktabah al-Wataniyah, 1977 +
Added title page: *National Bibliography of Iraq.*
Continues *al-Bibliyughrafiyah al-wataniyah al-'Iraqiyah.*

IRELAND

Irish Publishing Record. 1967+ [Dublin] School of Librarianship, University College Dublin.

ISRAEL

Kiryat sefer, rive'on le-bibliografyah shel bet ha-sefarim ha-le'umi veha-'universita'i bi-Yerushalayim. shanah 1+ [Jerusalem, 1924]+

Added title page: *Kiryat Sefer, Bibliographical Quarterly of the Jewish National and University Library, Jerusalem.*

ITALY

Bibliografia nazionale italiana. anno 1+ genn. 1958+ Firenze, Biblioteca nazionale centrale.

With the completion of supplements covering 1982 and 1983 imprints, publication is being suspended. Efforts were being made as of 1985 to assure resumption in 1989 or 1990.

IVORY COAST

Bibliographie de la Côte d'Ivoire. 1969+ [Abidjan] Bibliothèque nationale [1970]+

JAMAICA

Jamaican National Bibliography. v. 1+ Jan.–Mar. 1975+ Kingston, Institute of Jamaica, West India Reference Library, Jan.–Mar. 1976+

Continues Institute of Jamaica, Kingston, West India Reference Library. *Jamaican National Bibliography.*

A cumulation covering 1964–1974 was published in 1981 by Kraus Thomson.

JAPAN

Nihon zenkoku shoshi. 1977+ Tokyo, Kokuitsu Kokkai Toshokan.

Continues *Zen Nihon shuppanbutsu somokuroku.*

JORDAN

al-Bibliyughrafiya al-wataniyah al-Urduniyah. 1979+ Amman, al-Jamiyah, 1980+

KENYA

Kenya National Library Service. National Reference & Bibliographic Dept. *Kenya National Bibliography.* 1980+ Nairobi, Kenya National Library Service, National Reference & Bibliographic Department, 1983+

Works published in 1979 and before constitute materials for the retrospective *Kenya National Bibliography.*

KOREA, REPUBLIC OF

Taehan Min'guk ch'ulp'anmul ch'ongmongnok. 1945/62+ [Seoul] Kungnip Chungang Tosogwan.

Added title page: *Korean National Bibliography.*

LAOS

Bannanukrom haeng chat. National Bibliography of Laos. 1968+ Vientiane, Ho Samut Haeng Chat.

LIECHTENSTEIN

Liechtensteinische Bibliographie. 1. + Jahrg. ; 1974+ Vaduz, Liechtensteinische Landesbibliothek.

LUXEMBOURG

Bibliographie luxembourgeoise. [1.]+ année; 1944/45+ Luxembourg, P. Linden.

At head of title: Bibliothèque nationale, Luxembourg.

MADAGASCAR

Bibliografie nationale de Madagascar. 1970/71+ Antananarivo, Bibliothèque universitaire.

Continues *Bibliographie annuelle de Madagascar.*

MALAWI

National Archives of Malawi. *Malawi National Bibliography: List of Publications Deposited in the Library of the National Archives.* 1965+ Zomba.

MALAYSIA

Bibliografi negara Malaysia. Malaysian National Bibliography. 1967+ Kuala Lumpur, Perkhidmatan Perpustakaan Negara, Arkib Negara Malaysia.

MAURITIUS

Mauritius. Archives Dept. *Bibliography of Mauritius.* 1955+ Port Louis.

Continues *Memorandum of Books Printed in Mauritius and Registered in the Archives Office.*

Supplements appear in the *Annual Reports of the Archives Department.*

MEXICO

Bibliografia mexicana. enero/feb. 1967+ [México] Biblioteca Nacional de México, Instituto de Investigaciones Bibliograficas.

At head of title: Universidad Nacional Autónoma de México.

MOROCCO

Morocco. Khizanah al-Ammah lil-Kutub wa-al-Watha'iq. *Bibliyughrafiya al-wataniyah al-Maghribiyah. al-ida: al-qanuni li-sanat.*

Added title page: *Bibliographie nationale marocaine.*

Continues *Bibliographie nationale marocaine.*

THE NETHERLANDS

Brinkman's cumulatieve catalogus van boeken. 1. + jaarg.; 1846+ Alphen aan den Rijn, A. U. Sijthoff.

THE NETHERLANDS ANTILLES

Caribbean Collection Quarterly Acquisition List. Curaçao, Curaçao Public Library.

NEW ZEALAND

New Zealand National Bibliography. Feb. 1967+ Wellington, National Library of New Zealand.

Supersedes in part the *Index to New Zealand Periodicals, and Current National Bibliography* (1950–65).

NIGERIA

National Bibliography of Nigeria. 1973+ Lagos, National Library of Nigeria.

Continues *Nigerian Publications: Current National Bibliography* (1950–72).

NORWAY

Norsk bokfortegnelse. The Norwegian National Bibliography. 1814/47+ Oslo, Norsk Bokhandlerforening, 1848+

PAKISTAN

The Pakistan National Bibliography. 1962+ Karachi, Govt. of Pakistan, Directorate of Archives & Libraries, National Bibliographical Unit.

PAPUA NEW GUINEA

Papua New Guinea Bibliography. Mar. 1981+ Waigan, National Library Service of Papua New Guinea, 1981+
Continues *New Guinea Bibliography.*

PERU

Peru. Biblioteca Nacional, Lima. *Bibliográfia nacional.* 1+ enero/marzo 1978+, Lima, 1981+
Continues *Anuario bibliográfico peruano.*

PHILIPPINES

Philippines National Bibliography. Jan./Feb. 1974+ Manila, National Library of the Philippines.
Preceded by *Philippine Bibliography* (1963/64–70/72), issued 1965–73 by the University of the Philippines Library in Quezon City.

POLAND

Przewodnik bibliograficzny: urzedowy wykaz druków wydawnych w Rzeczpospolitej Polskiej. [rocz. 1]+ 1944/45+ Warszawa, Biblioteka narodowa.
Supersedes *Urzedowy wykaz druków* (1928–39) and its predecessor, *Przewodnik bibliograficzny* (1878–1933).

PORTUGAL

Lisbon. Biblioteca Nacional. *Boletim de bibliografia portuguesa.* v. 1+ ano de 1935+ Lisboa, 1937+
Continued in part by *Boletim de bibliografia portugesa. Publicões em série.* Lisboa.

PUERTO RICO

Anuario bibliográfico puertorriqueño: indice alfabético de libros, folletos, revistas y periódicos publicados en Puerto Rico. 1948+ San Juan, Estado Libre Asociado de Puerto Rico, Departamento de Instrucción Pública, 1950+

ROMANIA

Bucharest. Biblioteca Centrală de Stat. *Bibliografia Republicii Socialiste România: cărţi, albume, hărţi.* 1952+ [Bucureşti]

SENEGAL

Bibliographie du Sénégal. no. 40+ 1972+ [Dakar, Archives du Sénégal]
Continues *Bulletin bibliographique des Archives du Sénégal* (1963–71).

SEYCHELLES

Bibliographical notes. In Seychelles Society. *Journal.* no. 2+ Oct. 1952+ Victoria, Mahe.
Ceased publication in Dec. 1984.

SIERRA LEONE

Sierra Leone. Library Board. *Sierra Leone Publications.* 1962/63+ Freetown, 1964+

SINGAPORE

Singapore National Bibliography. 1967+ Singapore, National Library.

SOUTH AFRICA

South African National Bibliography. Suid-Afrikaanse nasionale bibliografie. 1959+ Pretoria, State Library [1960]+
Continues *Publications Received in Terms of Copyright Act no. 9 of 1916,* issued by the State Library, Apr. 1933–1958.

SPAIN

Bibliografia española. 1958+ Madrid, Ministerio de Educación Nacional, Dirección General de Archivos y Bibliotecas.

SWAZILAND

Swaziland National Bibliography. 1973/76+ Kwaluseni University of Botswana and Swaziland.

SWEDEN

Svensk bokförteckning. The Swedish National Bibliography. jan. 1953+ Redigerad av Bibliografiska Institutet vid Kungl. Biblioteket i Stockholm. Stockholm, Svensk bokhandel.

SWITZERLAND

Das Schweizer Buch. Le livre suisse. Il libro svizzero. Hrsg. von der Schweizerischen Landesbibliothek. 1. + Jahrg.; Jan./Feb. 1901+ Zürich, Schweizerischer Buchhändler- und Verleger Verband.

SYRIA

al-Bibliyujrafiya al-wataniyah al-Suriyah. [Dimashq] al-Jumhuriyah al-'Arabiyah al-Suriyah, Wizarat al-Thaqafah, Maktabat al-Asad.
Continues *al-Nashrah al-maktabiyah bi-al-kutub al-sadirah fi al-Jumhuriyah al-'Arabiyah al-Suriyah.*

TANZANIA

Tanzania National Bibliography. 1974/75+ Dar es Salaam, Tanzania Library Service, 1975+
Continues *Printed in Tanzania.*

THAILAND

Bannanukrom haeng chat. [1962/67]+ Krung Thep, Ho Samut Haeng Chat, Krom Sinlapakon, Krasuang Su'ksathikan [1977]+

TRINIDAD AND TOBAGO

Trinidad and Tobago National Bibliography. v. 1+ Jan./June 1975+ [Port of Spain] Central Library of Trinidad and Tobago.

TUNISIA

Bibliographie nationale de Tunisie. 1. + année; 1 semestre 1969+ Tunis, Bibliothèque nationale, 1970+
Added title page: *al-Bibliyughrafiya al-qawmiyah al-Tunisyah.*
Retrospective coverage is provided by *Bibliographie Nationale: Publications non-officielles, 1956–1968,* compiled by the Bibliothèque Nationale (Dar al Kutab al-Qawmiyah) and published in Tunis by Service documentaire (1974. 167, 165 leaves).

TURKEY

Türkiye bibliyografyasi. 1934+ Ankara, Turk Tarih Kurumu Basimevi.

UGANDA

Uganda Bibliography. In *Library Bulletin and Accessions List.* no. 55+ Jan./Feb. 1965+ [Kampala] Makerere University College [Library]

Suspended publication in 1976. As of 1984, the East African School of Librarianship has plans to compile a current national bibliography with the cooperation of the legal deposit libraries.

UNION OF SOVIET SOCIALIST REPUBLICS

Knizhnaia letopis, organ gosudarstvennoi bibliografii SSSR. g. 1+ 14 iiulia 1907+ Moskva, Izd-vo "Kniga."

Issued by Vsesoiuznaia knizhnaia palata.

UNITED KINGDOM

British National Bibliography. 1950+ London, British Library, Bibliographic Services Division.

UNITED STATES

Cumulative Book Index. 1898/99+ New York, H. W. Wilson Co.

URUGUAY

Anuario bibliográfico uruguayo. 1946–49; 1968+ Montevideo, Biblioteca Nacional, 1947–51; 1969+

Bibliografía uruguaya, which began publication in 1962, is still being issued by the Biblioteca del Poder Legislativo, but its coverage is now about eight years behind.

VENEZUELA

Bibliografía venezolano. v. 1+ 1980–81+ Caracas, Instituto Autonomo Biblioteca Nacional y de Servicios de Bibliotecas, 1982+

Currently being issued only on MARC tapes. For more information, write to the Instituto, Apartado 6525, Caracas 1010A, Venezuela.

Continues *Anuario bibliográfico venezolano.*

VIETNAM

Thu'muc quoc gia Viet Nam. Ha-Noi.

At head of title: Cong Hoa Xa Hoi Chu Nghia Viet Nam, Thu'-Vien Quoc Gia.

Publications of South Vietnam were formerly covered by *Thu' tich quoc-gia Vietnam; National Bibliography of Vietnam,* issued in Saigon beginning June 1968 by Nha Van-Kho va Thu'-Vien Quoc-Gia, Bo Van-Hoa Giao-Duc va Thanh-Nien.

YUGOSLAVIA

Bibliografija Jugoslavije: knjige, brošure i muzikalije. The Bibliography of Yugoslavia: Books, Pamphlets and Music. god 1+ 1950+ Beograd.

Bibliografija Jugoslavije: knjige, brošure i muzikalije, 1950–1980, compiled by Nevenka Skendzic and edited by Venceslav Glisic, was published in Belgrade in 1981 by the Jugoslovenski bibliografski institut as part of its *Bibliografske informacije* series.

ZAIRE

Bibliographie nationale. no. 5+ 1974+ Kinshasa/Gombe, Direction des Arts et Culture, République du Zaïre.

Continues *Bibliographie nationale retrospective des publications zaïroises ou relatives à la République du Zaïre, acquises par la Bibliothèque nationale.*

ZAMBIA

The National Bibliography of Zambia. 1970/71+ Lusaka, National Archives of Zambia.

ZIMBABWE

Zimbabwe National Bibliography. 1979+ Salisbury, National Archives, 1980+

Continues *Rhodesia National Bibliography.*

REFERENCES

Beatrice S. Bankole, "Current National Bibliographies of the English Speaking Countries of Africa," *International Cataloguing* Jan.-Mar. (1985).

Marcelle Beaudiquez, *Bibliographical Services Throughout the World, Supplement, 1980* (1982).

Commonwealth National Bibliographies, An Annotated Directory, 2nd edition (1982).

G. E. Gorman, *Guide to Current National Bibliographies in the Third World* (1983).

Annemarie Nilges, *Nationalbibliographien Lateinamerikas* (1983).

A. J. Walford, "National Bibliographies," in his *Guide to Reference Material,* 3rd edition (1977).

JUDITH FARLEY

National Libraries

DEFINITIONS AND PURPOSES

There were 106 national libraries in the world by the end of 1985. These are either officially titled as the national library by their countries or are so characterized by their governments and their scholarly communities. But notwithstanding the existence of so many recognizable examples, the matter of definition—what a national library really is—remains a problem. While the national library is accepted as being a unique form of institution, and while the national library is generally perceived as being dissimilar from public, academic, or special libraries, for nearly a century the profession has been unable to agree on a single, accepted definition.

In the first half of the 20th century, library scholars tried to define the institution in terms of universals: what are the characteristics of single national libraries that are common to all national libraries? Numerous essays pursuing this approach were published before it was abandoned with the reluctant discovery that the diversity among elements was too great—scarcely a single characteristic could be described as appearing in *most* national libraries, much less *all.*

The search then shifted to broad, general descriptions rather than precise, limiting particularizations. Herman Liebaers suggested in a 1958 Unesco study:

> The main characteristic of a national library is without doubt the leading place it occupies compared with other libraries in the country. This position is due to the extent and encyclopaedic character of its collections, the variety of material held and the diversity of specialized departments and services. It thus has a general and a national responsibility: within the profession, in all cases; outside it, more often than not.

The participants in the conference for which this study was prepared rejected it in the course of the meeting, on the grounds that "there were too many exceptions" to make it useful as a working description.

Scholars then tried to define the concept in terms of fundamental functions, and K. W. Humphreys' conclusion, prepared for a study of "The Role of the National Library," met general acceptance for a time. Humphreys identified the fundamental functions of a national library as being: the possession of an outstanding and central collection of the nation's literature; the acquisition, in connection with this, of all current published material by means of a legal deposit; the extensive coverage of foreign literature for the nation's scholars; the publication of the national bibliography; and the establishment of a national bibliographic center which, as a rule, entails the publication of catalogues.

As time progressed, the Humphreys definition failed to satisfy the national librarians so that, in 1973, an IFLA colloquium on the subject tried to focus on the essential *tasks and obligations* required of national libraries. The participants sought to determine what a national library *does* rather than what it *is*. The sponsors identified the following that they believed to be typical:

Collecting and preserving the nation's literature
Collecting foreign literature for research and teaching
Caring for special forms of records such as maps, music, pictures, films, and so on.
Maintaining a collection of manuscripts and rare books bearing on the nation's heritage
Preparing appropriate bibliographic information
Indexing the national literature and publishing a national bibliography
Distributing catalogue cards
Keeping a "national central catalogue"
Controlling the nation's lending services
Participating in the international exchange of publications
Providing advisory service to other libraries
Training the nation's librarians
Coordinating acquisition policy, documentation projects, and automation at the national level
Fostering international cooperation at the "supraregional" level.

But this attempt failed to survive the conference. By the close of the meeting for which it was designed, almost every element on the list had been rejected by enough of the participating national librarians to make it inappropriate to be called a "common characteristic." Yet there was still a need for an official definition (if only to decide on who should be invited to national conferences), so the Unesco meeting noted above finally concluded that the only definition common to all was, "The national library of a country is the one responsible for collecting and conserving the whole of that country's book production for the benefit of future generations."

This description held shakily until it was finally rejected by a substantial proportion of the national librarians of the developing countries. They maintained that the quoted task was not the obligation of national libraries at all, but in most of the newer nations belonged to the state and local *universities,* and thus the hoped-for definition reached the point that Arundell Esdaille, Secretary of the British Museum, had anticipated in 1934: "Uniformity is not to be expected; the political and social traditions of one country will produce a quite different type of library service from those in another."

Three Types. Clearly the concept of the national library has meaning in the library profession and is a useful, distinctive term. Then why is it so hard to define? It seems to become workable from a taxonomic point of view if the 106 national libraries are divided into three admittedly disparate types. The majority of these provide unique services; most are recognized as holding a position of primacy among the libraries of their nation—and all share the increasing problems that face "national libraries" at the present time.

First Generation. National libraries can be grouped into three fairly clear-cut modes; the first might be called First Generation. These are the traditional, the classic national libraries that initially come to mind when the term is used in Western librarianship. Approximately 20 in number, all were

Historic Palace of the Republic, which houses special collections of the National Library of Poland, Warsaw.

founded in or before 1800 and are in the traditional mode of the Library of Congress, the British Library, and the Bibliothèque Nationale. They were originally established as an ornament of nationalism, and their collections began either with acquisition of royal holdings (as in France, Austria, and Denmark) or with the acquisition of large private libraries (as with the Library of Congress's Thomas Jefferson volumes or the British Museum's Sir Hans Sloane). Once established, they grew inexorably under forced deposit arrangements, which were in turn tied to the copyright or to permission-to-publish by the nation's book trade.

Thanks to the deposit procedures, these collections grew comprehensively. There was little selection; production of a work within the national borders gave the material standing as a part of the record of the national heritage. The vast breadth of the collections soon led to new obligations to the scholarly communities who used them. The logical first step was the development of bibliographic controls to make the holdings useful. This in turn stimulated national bibliographies, special bibliographies, union catalogues, national bibliographic standards, and finally professional training for the nation's librarians.

The very size of these founding libraries generated a reciprocal standing in their nation's cultural life. They demonstrated the nation's interest in and support of intellectual activities, and they were thus soon housed in magnificent buildings built at public expense. Private treasures were given to them, enhancing their collections and the prestige of the donors. Having brought all recorded knowledge into a single place, they became the most efficient centers for research within their countries: one-stop, million-book "encyclopedias" to explore, analyze, and then use for more writing—which would in turn be housed, catalogued, and explored. The quantity of use neither matched the size of the collections nor approached the use rate that fell on the university or municipal libraries of the time, but the quality of use reflected the highest levels of scholarship and attracted the most creative minds of the contemporary societies.

Such national libraries excelled in superlatives. The Viennese had more papyri, the Danish more Icelandic sagas, the Irish more illuminated vellum—and the Reading Room of the British Museum exceeded Saint Peter's in the breadth of its dome. They were elitist; in many of the European versions, the user had to be introduced in writing by others who had been granted access. Students were resisted everywhere, and service was frequently designed to dissuade any researcher who had any but the highest motivation to use the collections; the turnaround time between book request and book delivery almost always exceeded 24 hours and frequently involved many days. They nevertheless became the center of librarianship in each of their countries and inexorably became a major element in preserving the national memory and fostering research and scholarship. Their acceptance and tradition generated the Second Generation of national libraries.

Second Generation. This group of national libraries appeared in the period between the Napoleonic Wars and World War II; it totals approximately 50. While they may well have begun in the image of the original 20, they developed into quite different institutions along the way. Those in Latin America began as literary and historical collections, usually housed in splendid buildings, but frequent changes of government caused inadequate funding and constant variation in staffing. Their large, centrally situated buildings became involved in wars and revolutions, in which they were commandeered for purposes other than the accumulation and preservation of books; in many cases their collections were dispersed and they were forced to begin anew. Thus, when many of the Latin American national libraries arrived in the 20th century, they were old in history but new in collections and services.

Many of the Second Generation institutions began as adjuncts to the national governments and were established to support parliaments. Thus Canada, Australia, and New Zealand focused first on materials to aid the legislature and from that locus expanded to science and the humanities.

Finally, the founding of another group (such as those in Switzerland, Greece, and Israel) coincided with the development of educational and community libraries, and the national libraries therefore found themselves in competition with other institutions for funding and attention. These libraries, again, began as hopeful duplicates of the original 20, but straitened circumstances forced them to specialize in services that only a central, national collection could provide, and let many of the peripheral tasks be shifted to local universities and public libraries. Central bibliographic services were common (although the book trades in many of the countries still provided the national bibliography), and most of these libraries accumulated the history and accomplishments of the nation, but the great collections rarely materialized.

The result of major wars, frequent changes of government, and dramatic shifts of national purpose was, for most of these libraries, a selective series of targets and objectives. Instead of being all things to scholarship and the national memory, each took certain tasks as their primary purposes and built on them. Their collections vary widely in size, from Bolivia's 150,000 volumes to the U.S.S.R.'s Lenin Library at 28,200,000. Housing ranges from the National Library of Tunisia, in an old Turkish barracks that was originally used as a jail, to the splendor of the National Library of Canada.

The National libraries of the various Eastern European countries developed in a remarkably similar manner, and they became markedly similar in organization and programs. Each is typically the central book depository of its country, the central public library of the nation, and the center for professional library training.

Toward the end of the period, a new technique was developed to solve problems of use, storage, and support: the division of the national library into separate elements located in varying parts of the nation. In the British system, the National Library of Wales was established in 1909 and the National Library of Scotland in 1925. In Italy the national library was divided among fully developed institutions in Florence, Naples, Rome, Venice, Palermo, and Turin, and in Yugoslavia the national library appears in Belgrade, Zagreb, Ljubljana, Sarajevo, Skopje, and Cetinje.

Third Generation. Begun at the close of World

War II, the Third Generation comprises approximately three dozen libraries, and they are radically different from the first in their objectives. While the older states started with inherited collections and grew larger around their books, the new states picture their national libraries as integrated systems, fully developed, usually headquartered in the national capital but reaching out as a network toward the provincial and local libraries. The national library usually runs a library school, loans books, and maintains the national bibliography. Frequently they were created to meet the need for a central point for the deposit of international documents (of the United Nations, World Health Organization, Unesco, and other organizations) and for a central point for international exchange and receipt of foreign book grants.

Several began as essentially government libraries (Nigeria's, and even the National Diet Library of Japan) that then received broader responsibilities and ultimately became the center of major networks of acquisition and use.

Many of the new countries called on library specialists from the developed countries to study their needs so their systems could grow according to professional plans. Western specialists, frequently expecting to duplicate the systems of the industrial nations, soon revised their thinking and universally turned to much more integrated systems. Hans Panofsky suggested a symbolic approach would be a single building with a door labeled National Library "at one entrance, Public Library at another, University Library at a third, and perhaps Government Archives on a fourth side." Uganda, Ethiopia, Sri Lanka, and Sudan concluded that the traditional research collection of a national library more properly belonged to the universities and that the national library should be the center of a national public library network as well as supporting government activities at the national, state, and local level. Reference, research, and the record of the national experience belonged to the educational system. (This division of labor is hardly restricted to Africa and Asia; Iceland, Norway, Czechoslovakia, and Israel followed the same pattern.) A national library that forms the center of a Ministry of Education public library configuration is found in Panama, Guatemala, and Ghana. In Libya, Tunisia, and Malaysia the national library became the central warehouse for book loan and distribution, and Colombia and El Salvador opened branches of the national library in municipal centers throughout their countries.

SERVICES TO USERS

While it is obvious that, given this wide variety of institutions, one can find an example of almost every library service somewhere among the national libraries, there are certain trends that can be identified as either being common to a large number of the institutions or suggesting the way of the future.

Access. Which books are acquired and kept varies widely, but what is done with them can be safely generalized. Only in the Third Generation national libraries are loan programs common. In the more traditional institutions, books must be used either within the building or through interlibrary loan to other libraries. In Latin America use only on the premises is almost universal. Many of the major Eu-

National Library of Austria

National Library of Austria

ropean institutions limit the users themselves; while the British Library has liberalized its own rules, the traditional rules for the British Museum are typical on the Continent:

> Permission to use the reading rooms is given, not in the rooms or the departments themselves, but in the Director's office. Applicants must be 21 years of age . . . ; they must give evidence of a definite study, and of serious need for the Museum Library, and not (as is common) a mere fancy to read there rather than in a local public or special library; they must be recommended by some person in a responsible position; and they must not be reading for an examination.

Access to the Irish National Library is limited to "bona fide researchers and to graduate students."

The developing countries tend to be more liberal. The National Library of Liberia serves all members of the public over 16 years old. Ethiopia's National Library is open to all "and there is no charge for reading on premises." Two books may be borrowed at a time and kept for a month.

Hours of access vary widely. In Latin America, most national libraries are open from 9:00 to noon and then reopen from 7:00 to 10:00 in the evening. Guatemala points with pride to its 8:00 to noon, 3:00 to 9:00 service.

In Europe, book delivery to the central reading rooms is commonly on a 24-hour turnaround; a book requested at a certain time one day will be made available at approximately the same time the next. Several of these libraries permit patrons to write in advance, so the library will have a book waiting for the visitor, providing the patron has been previously approved and sufficient lead time is provided. The literature suggests that this response time is not seriously challenged by researchers in the humanities but is the source of increasing resentment by users in the scientific and technological fields. This factor, plus the increased need for specialized attendants for technological materials, accounts for a general increase of special reading rooms in many national libraries. In-

A mobile library used in the National Library of Malaysia's extension services.

deed, many national libraries are even splitting off their medical, agricultural, scientific, and governmental departments into separate institutions using different techniques of retrieval and offering different time scales of service. Examples are Canada, India, Great Britain, and the United States.

Bibliographical Services. While reader service varies markedly among the national libraries, bibliographical services are uniformly triumphant, effective, and ever expanding. Some form of deposit arrangement appears in the majority of the institutions (86 of the 106 in 1985 were primary depositories of their national publishing), and one of their earliest obligations was thus the preparation of printed cards, printed catalogues, and the ultimate preparation of the national bibliography. The latter service is the one most frequently agreed upon by the national libraries; 74 of the 106 produce national bibliographies. National bibliographies appear in either author or subject arrangements (rarely both); of the 74 identified, the subject order is the more common.

In the developed countries many national bibliographies index periodicals and newspapers as well as monographs, but this is not typical in the developing nations. In the past the traditional national libraries commonly prepared special bibliographies for their scholarly patrons and prepared printed catalogues for other libraries. Both of these services diminished in the 1960's and 1970's. Hopes for the computerization of the indexing were common in the 1970's, but one national library after another has had to delay or abandon this technique as either too expensive or too unreliable to support their plans.

Union catalogues are a common service of national libraries regardless of age. All European national libraries maintain union catalogues, but many are comparatively recent. The Dutch Union Catalogue at The Hague began in 1921, the Swiss at Bern in 1927, Yugoslavia's in 1956, Spain's in 1942, and the British Union Catalogue in 1931. When the national library produces a national bibliography, the national union catalogue in most cases contains only

"foreign" (those in other than the national) languages; the Bibliothèque Nationale's union catalogue of foreign works began in 1921 in Paris. In Germany, the union catalogues are both prepared and housed in the various provinces and therefore are in multiple parts that together add up to a single whole.

Throughout Europe the catalogues are simply location tools; few supply interlibrary loan service as well. In the developing countries, on the other hand, the union catalogues are an essential part of the interlibrary loan network and solve other problems at the same time. The National Library in Taiwan, for example, maintains four union catalogues: one of Chinese rare books, one of Chinese documents, one of Chinese serials, and one of "nonrare stitch-bound books." The union catalogue department issues Chinese catalogues for the nation's libraries and establishes the national cataloguing rules.

Photoduplication services are common among the national libraries. They are used both as an adjunct of preservation and as a substitute for loan. Older materials rarely circulate anywhere, but programs to preserve deteriorating bookstocks are still rare. The Central State Library of Romania provides a Center for "book pathology and restoration," and Taiwan's National Library is converting all its rare Chinese books to microform and distributing them to the public and university libraries. But difficulties with preservation appear everywhere. Costs are high, qualified staff are scarce, and few user groups support the search for funds.

COLLECTIONS

In no area are the national libraries' disparities more apparent than in their collections. In the classic model of a national library, the characteristics of size (enormous size, as a rule) and preoccupation with the receipt and preservation of the intellectual activities of the nation were the primary distinctions that set them apart from other libraries. They were the one national institution responsible for preserving the national memory. They were comprehensive in the extreme. But the newcomers concentrate on current, working collections, frequently linked with provincial libraries by lively interlibrary loan networks and in some cases boxes of books delivered and picked up by trucks on daily or weekly schedules. Their thrust is immediate use; eternal preservation is the least of their worries.

Some of the sharpest ironies and most difficult dilemmas fall in this area. In Peru, for example, the national library seeks to act as the nation's archive of volumes (the one place where a copy of everything needed by its scholars can be found), but the demands made on its collections are so great—indeed, the use so insatiable—that its Librarian despairs over the mutilation of the collection while watching volumes wear out from use or disappear from a dozen causes with frightening speed. The European national libraries are torn between supporting intricate interlibrary loan networks with their provincial and municipal libraries and recognizing that, as a rule, they can secure copies by airmail more quickly from other national libraries outside their own borders than rely on the domestic sources they are dedicated to fostering. Similarly, the temptation is great for these mature libraries to divide the various intellectual specializations among universities and professional associations and let these pursue, organize, and service the works in each's area of expertise—which all too quickly eliminates the national library's raison d'être.

Some of the chief ironies surrounding the national libraries come from the requirements of legal deposit, which has come to be not a boon but a millstone. The obligations of cataloguing, housing, and preserving the totality of a national print production are overwhelming. Simply because a work is published by a countryman does not guarantee its usefulness to the nation, but individual librarians are reluctant to be the agents who interrupt a tradition of comprehensive collecting carried on with vigor for centuries. The National Library of Austria represents the problem in a curiously difficult form, but its dilemma affects every national library of the West. The Austrian library was begun in the mid-14th century and has had legal deposit for over 400 years. It served an empire of 50,000,000 people with many differing national traditions until 1918, when the nation was divided and thereby reduced to a population of 7,000,000. The library, however, is still trying to collect all significant material produced that relates to the "lost" ethnic groups—not from a political context but simply to keep the early holdings of centuries in continuing use. Since these holding are so extensive, the ethnic scholars still come from all over central Europe to use them, and the present generation is reluctant to destroy the continuity of the collection.

ADMINISTRATION AND FINANCE

National libraries differ administratively from other forms of libraries in at least two ways. Most other libraries have a specific, often limited clientele or audience, as in a university community, a municipality, or a professional elite. On the other hand, the national library tends to serve as a link to the entire spectrum of the nation's literate population. It thus demands more complicated relationships outside its walls than do most libraries. It requires ties to the academic community as users, the industrial community as patrons, the government community as employer, the publishing community as producer, and so on—and the greater the number of links, the greater the support for the national library. According to David Mearns, "It seems to be a rule of life that where national libraries prosper, their activities are identifiable with and allied to the interests of many and diverse groups." The breadth of this diversity provides many advantages: national libraries tend to enjoy greater policy independence than most libraries, and they have a momentum (almost glacier-like) that protects them from attack, major elimination of funds, and certainly interruption or extinction.

Size, on the other hand, embodies serious costs for the national library. Its collections grow faster than any other collection in the nation since of all the nation's libraries it alone is collecting comprehensively. Similarly, since it attempts to preserve the nation's heritage, it can rarely weed and discard materials, and thus it grows ever larger. This, in turn, has an impact on building, which again is an especially difficult issue for national libraries. Their traditional location at the center of government, which in turn is usually in the center of the nation's largest city, makes expansion doubly difficult. Most national li-

braries have tried to solve the problems by displacing certain components of their service to satellite, suburban locations, but in doing so they have threatened the traditional advantage of the great, central ("one-stop") research collection, where the user can explore regardless of format or subject. While the U.S., Britain, France, Spain, Italy, the U.S.S.R., The Netherlands, and others have cleared central space and built new buildings to keep the central collection strong, they have at the same time moved serials, documents, motion pictures, music, newspapers, processing, or interlibrary loan units to the periphery. Ireland, Mexico, and Denmark displaced collections to adjacent universities; the U.S., Canada, Britain, and Australia cut out major parts of their collections to establish separate libraries for medicine, agriculture, science, or government. Yugoslavia, Italy, and Germany divided their collections by region or national origins, while Latin American libraries divided by age—the recent materials in the center city, older at the periphery. But all dispersion is at the expense of comparative research.

Organization. Within the walls of national libraries there is likely to be greater diversity of administrative units than in any other form of library institution. With collections covering the entire span of the nation's creative skills, most national libraries have many small, highly specialized reading rooms, units, divisions, and departments. This division, along with the library's vast size, makes it easier for the administrator to break up tasks into specializations (and thus the workers can better fit their skills, interest, and training to the particular job), but it shatters the general sense of purpose. The workers have more trouble remembering why they do a given task and how it relates to others. While such specialization was originally thought to speed up flow-through, it may well have passed the point of profit and is now becoming counterproductive in the great institutions. Each step must redo some of the preceding, reread some pages, recheck certain previous steps. In the Library of Congress this fragmentation has reached such a point that English-language materials may be touched by 65 pairs of hands between mail room and shelf, and foreign materials by as

National Library of Mexico. The building was opened in 1979.

Biblioteca Nacional (Mexico)

National Library of Peru

Biblioteca Nacional

many as 50. Similarly, the staff quickly divides into the "recorders" and the "users"—processing and reference—and it becomes increasingly easy to forget the linkage.

A corollary to the complexity of the organizational structure of a national library is its differing types of personnel. The staff is likely to be divided almost equally between librarians and technical specialists. The skills of acquisition (dealing with publishers, booksellers, and importers) and cataloguing (creating the national bibliography, preparing catalogues, and loading the bibliographic database) require professional librarians. Service to highly specialized audiences, such as social scientists, medical scientists, energy scientists, linguists, and specialists in international affairs, requires specialized training to anticipate the needs of the users and "speak their language" in serving them quickly and accurately.

While in the past the most highly trained practitioners of all these bibliographic and research arts were drawn to the great national libraries, this is no longer the case on any continent. The specialists are being pulled toward the great universities, the research laboratories of the industrial complex, the library schools, and the government agencies "where the action is." Thus, the professional literature reports in every language the failure of the national libraries to compete for the outstanding scholars in their traditional fields.

It is obviously hopeless to try to present a "typical" organizational scheme of the 106 national libraries, but a small sample might be useful.

Denmark. The Royal Library in Copenhagen has experienced a series of reorganizations and is presently tightly departmentalized into 16 sharply defined units, 10 departments organized by format and

6 by service. It has a Danish Department with its own catalogues and staff (relatively unchanged since the early 1700's and caring for a complete collection of everything printed in Denmark since the 15th century) but also two "Foreign Departments"—one concentrating on the acquisition of books (selected by a staff of 40 full-time subject specialists) and a parallel department of foreign serials. The departments of Manuscripts, Maps and Prints, Oriental Manuscripts, Judaica, Music, Rare Books, and National Bibliography are traditional.

But the Department for Public Relations is less so in European national libraries. It conducts a publicity program through radio, television, and the scientific press, carries on an intensive traveling exhibition program, and conducts courses for students on how to use the national library. Its primary purpose is to widen the circle of library users. The Department of Service to the Institute and Other Libraries is also unusual, representing a close and continuing relationship with the national universities, the Royal Academy of Music, the Scandinavian Institute for Asian Studies, and other institutions. The departments of Descriptive Cataloguing, Classification, Readers' Service, and Technical Services (primarily binding and photoduplication) are also traditional.

Brazil. The National Library of Brazil is divided into five sections: Acquisition and Processing, General Reference, Special Reference, Divulgation (publications, cultural promotions, and exchanges), and Conservation; and three services: copyright, reprography, and administration.

DDR. The Deutsche Staatsbibliothek in East Berlin has departments of Acquisition, Cataloguing, and Lending, a Reference Bureau, and departments of Manuscripts, Oriental Books, Incunabula, Music, Cartography, Children's Literature, and Reprography.

Switzerland. This national library is organized around six departments: Acquisition, Catalogues, Periodicals, Circulation, Special Collections, and the Swiss Union Catalogue. The Director's Office contains an administrative unit of personnel and accountancy and a technical services unit of reproduction and bookbinding—all four elements within the Director's immediate supervision.

Finance. There seems little unique about national libraries' budgetary needs per se. Their requirements parallel those for any large central library. Most require adequate acquisition money readily at hand so they can secure small production or regional material quickly before it is lost, but many are spared the cost of intranational purchasing since their materials come free through deposit arrangements.

Most national libraries are treated as separate entities by their parent governments, and the libraries strive to keep this independence intact, avoiding direct competition with other agencies in a ministry or department. Most receive their funds through annual budgets, and most are favorably treated. Although few get as much funding as they want, even fewer are cut back from previous levels unless the entire national budget is reduced.

LIBRARY COOPERATION

In a world of increasing international interdependency, it might be assumed that the great national libraries would be at the forefront of international library cooperation. While there has been much discussion in this area, the anticipated results have been limited. Some national librarians believe that this is less a failure in implementation than a recognition that what international cooperation was genuinely needed has already been accomplished; hoped-for additions are really linked to secondary needs, which are pushed ever further back by lack of space, resources, and the absence of demands by user elites. But real achievements have involved a number of areas.

The first area of international cooperation to be explored historically was that of documents exchange. This activity was initiated between the major national libraries as early as 1840, when the United States Congress passed a special bill to establish "a system of international exchange of public documents." These protocols grew steadily, so that by the 1950's well over 100 were operating. The national gazettes, legislative debates, and state papers were universally exchanged, and the documents of cabinet-level ministries and departments followed spottily thereafter. The majority of the programs were developed as formal diplomatic exchanges negotiated as treaties or international agreements—not as professional library dialogues.

Programs of acquisition exchange were started to repair the damage of World War II, and many of these continued into the 1960's and 1970's after the initial purpose had been satisfied. In the United States the Library of Congress's National Program for Acquisition and Cataloging was broadly active; the members of the French Union continued to support each other even after independence (with much help from the French government itself); and the traditional members of the British Commonwealth used the empire avenues to expand cooperative ventures.

Bibliographic programs expanded, notable among them the Library of Congress MARC program with its computerized database and automated union catalogues. Cooperative cataloguing built machine-readable databases, and "MARC tapes" were first exchanged with Canada and then increasingly sent to other nations. IFLA programs for the cooperative formulation of cataloguing principles were developed.

Interlibrary loan would appear to be an obvious area of cooperative potential, but this has started very slowly and shown little expansion. The original logic suggested that as national libraries are usually the primary custodians of foreign books in a country, and as national libraries are usually the source of last resort for advanced research, they are the obvious libraries to exchange materials with other national libraries dealing with institutional peers. It has not so developed. Experience has shown that from 60 to 80 percent of all interlibrary loans involve books published in the past five years; thus serious researchers tend to buy foreign books rather than rely on their national libraries to borrow them for them. While the remaining 20 to 40 percent frequently do come through international exchange from abroad, the numbers have never been as large as the potential would have suggested.

The majority of successful programs in international cooperation can be traced to the following or-

ganizations working in the field: Unesco, IFLA, the International Federation for Documentation (FID), the International Council on Archives, and the Inter-Parliamentary Union.

LAWS AND LEGISLATION

National libraries differ legally from traditional libraries in two major respects: their relation to the sovereign government and their role in the copyright or deposit system of the nation.

Authority. Other libraries are governed by a college board, a local government, or a corporation, but national libraries are usually the creation of the national government and thus may be either directly responsible to the ruling body or a part of the government's cabinet ministries. They appear in three modes. Some are independent agencies with independent authority; some have legally fixed responsibilities with "firm primacy" within larger governmental units; and some function with traditional momentum and continue without written rule but exercise authority by common consent.

The guiding charters usually spell out four elements: who appoints the chief librarian, where the money is to come from, to whom the librarian reports, and what the obligations of the institution are. Any of these elements can be missing—indeed, some national libraries can find little law relating to their institutions in any of their codes, and they find this so useful they are actively reluctant to change it.

The Swiss National Library is under the Department of the Interior. The Austrian National Library is run by the Ministry of Science and Research. The Library of El Salvador is an agency of the Ministry of Culture; the Italian National Library is under the Ministry of Fine Arts; and the National Library of Venezuela is a department of the National Institute of Culture and Fine Arts. The Royal Library of The Netherlands falls under the Department of Education and takes some pride in its lack of charter or statutes, although its internal regulations date back to 1884. This relationship to the Ministry of Education also appears in the Stockholm Royal Library, the National

Reading room in the main library building of the National Library of India in Calcutta.

National Library of India

National Library of Wales Aberystwyth.

Joel Lee

Library of Ireland, and the Tunisian National Library. The Jewish National and University Library has no link to the government of Israel at all and is financed by private contributions and university funds as an independent agency.

Deposit Laws. The first nation to use a deposit law to fill its national library with free automatically forwarded books is thought to be Austria, in 1575. Sweden in 1661, Denmark in 1697, and Spain in 1716 followed this precedent, and by the time the Library of Congress embraced the idea in 1846 it was long established. Of the 106 national libraries cited in this article, 86 are at least one of the deposit points for the product of the national publishing industry. Multiple deposit of free volumes is common; Great Britain, for example, deposits copies of all new books with the British Library, the Bodleian Library at Oxford, the University Library at Cambridge, Trinity College in Dublin, and the National Libraries of Scotland and Wales.

In some nations the printer, not the publisher, must make the deposit, thus denying the national library books printed abroad—a practice that is increasingly common with color work even in the developed countries. In the United States much material from universities, museums, and scholarly societies is deliberately published without copyright to encourage scholarly use and thus is not sent to the Library of Congress for inclusion in either its collections or its published catalogues. Most copyright and deposit laws were written in the days of books, maps, and newspapers, but they have been amended repeatedly to cover photographs, films, recordings, and now the multiple forms of electronic capture and storage. While such laws have the advantage of acquiring comprehensive collections with little cost or search effort, the disadvantages of increasing problems of space, proper preservation, and complexities of storage and retrieval are eroding the profitable trade-off.

PROBLEMS AND TRENDS
What is the future of national libraries? Once again, the future seems to vary sharply among the three

types of national libraries. The initial 20, the great institutions of the 17th and 18th centuries, are the most stressed. They are having difficulty adjusting their traditional role of encyclopedic accumulation and total preservation to a society that seems to be focusing on precise data, instantly produced. Their two primary sponsors—the scholarly and the governmental communities—seem to have changed their informational needs and turned to different ways of satisfying them.

On the university campuses of the nations, wideranging, interdisciplinary research has been replaced by precise, narrowly defined searches for specific, specialized pieces of fact. The great comprehensive collections of the initial 20 libraries have proved to be difficult to shift to the kind of quickly accessible materials, served by specially trained personnel, providing the kinds of rapidly changing bibliographic needs that are demanded by this specialized clientele.

The national libraries that supported their governmental communities found another inherent conflict. Governments needed immediate data, ephemeral, constantly changing, totally disposable, but perpetually responsive. The national libraries had developed grand skills of acquisition, careful bibliographic control, highly professional preservation and storage techniques—for materials long since discarded by their governmental users. The latter, like their scientific counterparts, have been attracted to the splitting off of their informational support facilities and thus are further weakening the central institution.

The great libraries have two powerful advantages, however—because of their size and the professional skills of their staffs, they may well be in the best possible position to take advantage of computers. If the world of automation goes to vast, centralized storage, the already encyclopedic collections of the national libraries provide the potential for exploiting automation's ability to store and manipulate great quantities of data with blinding speed.

A corollary to their comprehensive nature is the national libraries' preeminence in "foreign" (nonnational, outside-the-borders) acquisition. No institution in any nation has proved to be as efficient at accumulating research materials from around the world as the national libraries. Unfortunately, this stimulates yet another conflict that makes finding the proper role for the national libraries so difficult. Since the great libraries have the greatest concentration of stored data in their countries, they might be expected to support a major amount of the use of this material. But they are universally ill-equipped to sustain such demands and thus have had to build a wall of "last resort" around their collections—further alienating their audiences and lowering their visibility even to specialists who would be the most appropriate users of their holdings.

The Second Generation libraries, on the other hand, appear to be remarkably at peace with their roles. Having fitted their aspirations to reality along the way, they have been accepted by their nations and seem to be living comfortably with the responsibilities assigned them. The Second Generation libraries have proved to be especially adept in generating popular interest and pride in their national culture and traditions. They have cared for their national intellectual patrimony with skill and are now frequently the leading source of national programs relating to history and customs. They seem to be a major source of pride for their communities and are enthusiastically a part of their nation's cultural scene.

The Third Generation seems to be in an even healthier state. While their future seems to be "all before them," they have been recognized by their governments as a major partner in the building of the new nations and are deeply involved in the professionalization of the government cadres. They frequently are the central institution in adult education and literacy programs and are often the primary link between distant communities and provincial centers of population. Their potential impact in their nations seems to grow steadily, and their popular support is equally heartening.

Indeed, in no area of international librarianship is the national library the object of severe criticism. In this day of fashionable challenge to all public roles, librarians may take heart that the national library is firmly accepted; the only discussion is how it can be most effectively used.

National Libraries (1985)

Country	Name of library	Place	Date founded	Number of volumes	Legal depository?	Produces national bibliography?
Albania	National Library	Tirana	1922	810,000	Yes	Yes
Algeria	Bibliothèque Nationale	Algiers	1963	950,000	Yes	Yes
Angola	Biblioteca Nacional de Angola	Luanda	?	26,000	No	No
Argentina	Biblioteca Nacional	Buenos Aires	1810	1,600,000	Yes	Yes
Australia	National Library of Australia	Canberra	1902	2,073,500	Yes	Yes
Austria	Österreichische Nationalbibliothek	Vienna	1526	2,341,000	Yes	Yes
Bangladesh	National Library	Dacca	1971	16,000	Yes	Yes
Belgium	Bibliothèque Royale Albert Iᵉʳ	Brussels	1837	3,366,000	Yes	Yes
Benin	Bibliothèque Nationale	Porto Novo	?	35,000	No	Yes
Bolivia	Biblioteca y Archivo Nacional de Bolivia	Sucre	1836	150,000	Yes	No
Botswana	Botswana National Library Service	Gaborone	1968	190,000	Yes	Yes
Brazil	Biblioteca Nacional	Rio de Janeiro	1810	1,800,000	Yes	Yes
Bulgaria	Kiril i Metodij Narodna Biblioteka (Cyril and Methodius National Library)	Sofia	1878	1,982,744	Yes	Yes
Burma	National Library	Rangoon	1952	49,123	Yes	Yes
Cambodia	Archives et Bibliothèque Nationales	Phnom Penh	1923	31,000	Yes	?
Cameroon	Bibliothèque Nationale du Cameroon	Yaounde	?	10,000	?	?
Canada	National Library	Ottawa	1953	896,000	Yes	Yes
Chile	Biblioteca Nacional de Chile	Santiago	1813	1,200,000	Yes	Yes
China	National Library	Beijing	1912	10,200,000	No	No
China (Taiwan)	National Central Library	Taipei	1933	500,000	Yes	Yes
Colombia	Biblioteca Nacional	Bogota	1777	540,000	No	No
Congo	Bibliothèque Nationale Populaire	Brazzaville	?	7,000	No	No
Costa Rica	Biblioteca Nacional	San José	1888	175,000	Yes	No
Cuba	Biblioteca Nacional "José Marti"	Havana	1901	976,734	Yes	Yes
Czechoslovakia	Státni Knihovna České socialistické republiky (State Library of the Czech Socialist Republic)	Prague	1958	5,000,000	Yes	Yes
Denmark	Det Kongelige Bibliotek (The Royal Library)	Copenhagen	1657	2,500,000	Yes	No
Dominican Republic	Biblioteca Nacional	Santo Domingo	1971	153,955	Yes	No
Ecuador	Biblioteca Nacional	Quito	1792	55,000	Yes	No

Egypt	Dar el-Kutub (Egyptian National Library)	Cairo	1870	1,500,000	Yes	Yes
El Salvador	Biblioteca Nacional	San Salvador	1870	95,000	Yes	No
Ethiopia	Ethiopian National Library	Addis Ababa	1944	100,000	No	No
Finland	Helsingin Yliopiston Kirjasto (Helsinki University Library)	Helsinki	1640	2,000,000	Yes	Yes
France	Bibliothèque Nationale	Paris	1480	9,000,000	Yes	Yes
German Democratic Republic	Deutsche Staatsbibliothek	East Berlin	1661	6,814,420	Yes	No
	Deutsche Bücherei	Leipzig	1912	7,100,000	Yes	Yes
Germany, Federal Republic of	Deutsche Bibliothek	Frankfurt	1946	2,900,000	Yes	Yes
	Staatsbibliothek Preussischer Kulturbesitz	West Berlin	1661	3,200,000	No	No
	Bayerische Staatsbibliothek	Munich	1558	5,000,000	Yes	No
Ghana	Central Reference and Research Library	Accra	1964	6,500	Yes	No
Greece	National Library	Athens	1828	1,000,000	Yes	No
Guatemala	Biblioteca Nacional	Guatemala City	1879	352,000	Yes	No
Guinea	Bibliothèque Nationale	Conakry	1960	10,000	Yes	No
Guyana	National Library	Georgetown	1909	191,023	Yes	Yes
Haiti	Bibliothèque Nationale	Port-au-Prince	1940	19,000	No	No
Honduras	Biblioteca Nacional	Tegucigalpa	1880	55,000	Yes	No
Hungary	Országos Széchényi Könyvátr (National Széchényi Library)	Budapest	1802	2,193,973	Yes	Yes
Iceland	Landsbókasafn Islands (National Library of Iceland)	Reykjavík	1818	356,000	Yes	Yes
India	National Library	Calcutta	1902	1,800,000	Yes	No
Iran	National Library	Teheran	1935	169,139	Yes	Yes
Iraq	National Library	Baghdad	1963	140,000	Yes	Yes
Ireland	National Library	Dublin	1877	500,000	Yes	No
Israel	Jewish National and University Library	Jerusalem	1892	2,500,000	Yes	Yes
Italy	Biblioteca Nazionale Centrale	Florence	1747	4,000,000	Yes	Yes
	Biblioteca Nazionale "Vittorio Emanuele III"	Naples	1804	1,531,936	No	No
	Biblioteca Nazionale Centrale Vittorio Emanuele II	Rome	1876	2,800,000	Yes	No
	Biblioteca Centrale della Regione Siciliana	Palermo	1782	467,116	No	No
	Biblioteca Nazionale Marciana	Venice	1468	1,210,000	No	No
	Biblioteca Nazionale	Sagarriga-Visconti-Volpi	1865	250,000	No	No
	Biblioteca Nazionale Universitaria	Turin	1723	850,000	No	No
Ivory Coast	Bibliothèque Nationale	Abidjan	1968	30,000	Yes	Yes
Japan	National Diet Library	Tokyo	1948	7,336,386	Yes	Yes
Korea, North	State Central Library	Pyongyang	?	1,500,000	Yes	Yes
Korea, South	National Central Library	Seoul	1925	852,734	Yes	Yes
Kribati	National Library	Tarawa	1979	30,000	?	No
Laos	Bibliothèque Nationale	Vientiane	1957	50,000	Yes	Yes
Lebanon	Bibliothèque Nationale	Beirut	1921	100,000	Yes	No
Libya	National Library	Benghazi	1966	?	No	Yes
Luxembourg	Bibliothèque Nationale	Luxembourg	1798	565,000	Yes	Yes
Madagascar	Bibliothèque Nationale	Antananarivo	1961	159,200	Yes	Yes
Malaysia	National Library	Kuala Lumpur	1971	43,500	Yes	Yes
Mali	Bibliothèque Nationale	Bamako	1913	15,000	?	?
Malta	National Library	Valleta	1555	?	Yes	No

Mauritania	Bibliothèque Nationale	Nouakchott	1965	10,000	Yes	Yes
Mexico	Biblioteca Nacional	Mexico City	1833	1,000,000	Yes	Yes
Morocco	Bibliothèque Générale et Archives	Rabat	1920	230,000	Yes	Yes
Mozambique	Biblioteca Nacional	Maputo	1961	110,000	No	No
Nepal	National Library	Kathmandu	?	?	No	No
The Netherlands	Koninklijke Bibliotheek (Royal Library)	The Hague	1798	1,500,000	Yes	No
New Zealand	National Library	Wellington	1966	515,000	Yes	Yes
Nicaragua	Biblioteca Nacional	Managua	1882	70,000	?	?
Nigeria	National Library	Lagos	1962	158,000	Yes	Yes
Norway	Universitetsbiblioteket i Oslo (University Library, Oslo)	Oslo	1811	1,950,000	Yes	Yes
Pakistan	National Library	Islamabad	?	20,000	Yes	No
Panama	Biblioteca Nacional	Panama City	1892	200,000	No	No
Papua New Guinea	National Library Service	Boroko	1978	45,000	Yes	Yes
Paraguay	Biblioteca y Archivo Nacionales	Asuncion	1869	44,000	No	No
Peru	Biblioteca Nacional	Lima	1821	661,232	Yes	Yes
Philippines	National Library	Manila	?	1,296,809	Yes	Yes
Poland	Biblioteca Narodowa	Warsaw	1928	3,770,000	Yes	Yes
Portugal	Biblioteca Nacional	Lisbon	1796	1,000,000	Yes	Yes
Qatar	National Library	Doha	1963	67,217	?	Yes
Romania	Biblioteca Centrală de Stat (Central State Library)	Bucharest	1955	7,733,045	Yes	Yes
Saudi Arabia	National Library	Riyadh	1968	16,000	No	?
Singapore	National Library	Singapore	1884	1,430,753	Yes	Yes
Solomon Islands	National Library	Honiara	1974	22,000	?	?
South Africa	South African Library	Cape Town	1818	530,000	Yes	No
	State Library	Pretoria	1887	750,000	Yes	Yes
Spain	Biblioteca Nacional	Madrid	1712	3,000,000	Yes	No
Sri Lanka	Ceylon National Library Services Board	Colombo	1970	13,000	Yes	Yes
Sweden	Kungl. Biblioteket (Royal Library)	Stockholm	Early 17th century	2,000,000	Yes	Yes
Switzerland	Bibliothèque Nationale Suisse- Schweizerische Landesbibliothek	Bern	1895	1,500,000	Yes	Yes
Syria	Al-Maktabah al Zahiriah (Zahiriah National Library)	Damascus	1880	77,000	Yes	Yes
	Al-Maktabah al- Wataniah (Wataniah National Library)	Aleppo	1924	?	No	No
Tanzania	University of Dar es Salaam Library	Dar es Salaam	1961	350,000	Yes	?
Thailand	National Library	Bangkok	1905	896,671	Yes	Yes
Togo	Bibliothèque Nationale	Lomé	?	7,000	No	Yes
Tunisia	Bibliothèque Nationale	Tunis	1885	700,000	Yes	Yes
Turkey	Milli Kütüphane (National Library)	Ankara	1948	596,697	Yes	Yes
Union of Soviet Socialist Republics	V. I. Lenin State Library	Moscow	1862	28,216,000	Yes	No
United Kingdom	British Library	London	1753	20,550,000	Yes	Yes
	National Library of Scotland	Edinburgh	1682	4,000,000	Yes	No
	National Library of Wales	Aberystwyth	1907	2,000,000	Yes	No
United States	Library of Congress	Washington, D.C.	1800	20,000,000	Yes	No
	National Agricultural Library	Washington, D.C.	1962	1,700,000	No	No
	National Library of Medicine	Washington, D.C.	1836	2,000,000	No	No

Uruguay	Biblioteca Nacional	Montevideo	1816	900,000	Yes	No
Venezuela	Biblioteca Nacional	Caracas	1833	800,000	Yes	Yes
Vietnam	Vietnam National Library	Hanoi	1919	1,200,000	Yes	Yes
Yugoslavia	Narodna biblioteka Socijalističke Republike Srbije	Belgrade	1832	729,172	Yes	No
	Nacionaina i sveučilišna biblioteka (National and university library)	Zagreb	17th century	1,069,471	Yes	No
	Narodna i univerzitetska knjiznica (National and university library)	Ljubljana	1774	1,150,000	Yes	No
	Narodna i univerzitetska biblioteka Bosne i Hercegovine (National and university library of Bosnia and Herzegovina)	Sarajevo	1945	670,000	Yes	No
	Narodna i univerzitetska biblioteka "Kliment Ohridski" (National and university Library Kliment Ohridski)	Skopje	1944	1,100,000	Yes	No
	Centraina narodna biblioteka S R Crne Gore (Central National Library of the Socialist Republic of Montenegro)	Cetinje	1946	370,000	Yes	No
Zäire	Kinshasa-Gombe	Kinshasa	1949	?	Yes	Yes
Zambia	National Archives	Lusaka	1947	11,500	Yes	Yes
Zimbabwe	National Free Library	Bulawayo	1943	50,000	?	No

REFERENCES

Marcelle Beudiquez, *Bibliographical Services throughout the World, 1970–74* (1977).

Arundell Esdaile, *National Libraries of the World,* 2nd edition (1957).

International Librarianship: Surveys of Recent Developments in Developing Countries and in Advanced Librarianship, Submitted to the 1971 IFLA Pre-session Seminar for Developing Countries Sponsored by Unesco (1972).

Miles M. Jackson, editor, *Comparative and International Librarianship: Essays on Themes and Problems* (1970).

Maurice B. Line, editor, *National Libraries* (Aslib, 1979).

Line, "The Role of National Libraries: A Reassessment," *Libri* (March 1980).

David C. Mearns, "Current Trends in National Libraries," *Library Trends* (1955).

I. P. Osipova, "National Libraries in a Socialist Society," *Libri* (December 1978).

Symposium on National Libraries in Europe, Vienna, 1958, *National Libraries: Their Problems and Prospects* (1960).

CHARLES A. GOODRUM

Naudé, Gabriel
(1600–1653)

Gabriel Naudé was one of the first men to attain distinction as a professional librarian. This he achieved partly through his labors in assembling and organizing the library of Cardinal Mazarin but mainly for his celebrated treatise on library economy, *Advis pour dresser une bibliothèque (Advice on Establishing a Library)*. Strangely, the *Advis* was published when Naudé was quite young and his library experience fairly small. It was first published in Paris (1627) and dedicated to Naudé's first employer, Henri de Mesme, *President a Mortier* in the Parliament of Paris.

Naudé was born in Paris on February 2, 1600. For several years he studied medicine, but apparently he never practiced. Having become Librarian to de Mesme, he remained one—serving a succession of illustrious bibliophiles, including, for a short period, Cardinal Richelieu, and also Queen Christina of Sweden. But his most important appointment and most ambitious assignment was as Librarian to Cardinal Mazarin, for whom he assembled a magnificent and unusually large library of 40,000 volumes, which he collected himself from all parts of Europe. Mazarin fell from power in 1652, and his library was ruthlessly dispersed; some years later it was reconstituted, but Naudé did not live to see it, having died at Abbeville July 29, 1653.

The Mazarine Library reflected exactly Naudé's own enlightened views on how the library of a wealthy private collector should be organized and administered, views that he had already expressed with boldness and clarity in his *Advis*. Naudé believed that such a library should include books valuable for their content, rather than their rarity or beauty; that they should be housed with due attention to natural lighting and freeedom from dampness and household noises; and that they should be arranged by subject and made freely accessible to deserving scholars with few books of their own. These were the particular characteristics of the Mazarine Library, which was dedicated *a tous ceux qui y vouloient aller estudier* ("to all those who wish to go there to study").

Although the *Advis* was reprinted, and translated into Latin and English—the English edition, (London, 1661), was a translation by scholar diarist John Evelyn—its circulation was small. All the same, it is probable that it was of some influence in library development. It is generally agreed that it influenced the library career of Gottfried Leibniz.

To be ahead of one's time may be a disadvantage, as well as a distinction. Naudé belonged, in spirit, to the modern world of freely accessible public libraries and was, within the limitations of his day, an ideal librarian.

REFERENCES

The best modern editions of Naudé's pioneer treatise are, in French, *Advis pour dresser une bibliothèque* (Leipzig, 1963), and, in English, *Advice on Establishing a Library* (1950).

Jack A. Clarke, *Gabriel Naudé 1600–1653* (1970), a full biography that is readable and scholarly.

JAMES G. OLLÉ

Near East, Ancient

The principal Babylonian sites where written records have been found are all in southern and southeastern Iraq: Uruk (now Warka) and the ancient city of Ur (now El-Mukajjar) in southern Babylonia; Shuruppak (now Farah), almost in the middle of the area; and present-day Jamdat Nasr (ancient name unknown), north of Babylon. Oldest, heralding the new role of writing, are the tablets of the so-called Uruk-Jamdat Nasr period (3100–2700 B.C.), whose messages are clear to us about very little so far. Somewhat later are those of Ur level III, 400 tablets and many more fragments of varied content. Nikolaus Schneider studied the economic items among them, concluding (1940) that the tablets had been distributed among clay containers by subject and date and that the clay containers had tags indicating their respective contents. It is hypothesized that literary and religious texts may have been handled likewise and that the edifice in which the tablets were found had housed a school associated with the nearby temple. The temple area proper yielded religious and astronomical texts; they are ascribed to the 3rd millennium B.C., but exact dates have not been fixed.

A little later than Ur, in turn, are the Early Dynasty II and III (mid-3rd millennium) tablets recovered at Shuruppak (now Farah), some 40 miles southeast of Nippur. The numbered series among them contain lists of commodities, quantities, and persons in connection with either temple accounts or school exercises; included are lexicons and incantation texts. There are also unnumbered lists of things like writing signs, for study, and tablets bearing early examples of known Sumerian literature and lexical texts. Neither the temple nor the school tablets demonstrate the existence of a library, but they do testify to preservation of older written materials and to the development of at least rudimentary organizational devices.

Furthermore, the temple records raise the distinction between archives and libraries. Probably most widely accepted are the criteria of Mogens Weitmeyer (1955–56) that archival materials were stored by their nature and date; library materials were gathered into subject-related series, bore colophons including regulations of a library character, and were listed in separate catalogues.

Nearer the close of the 3rd millennium, it appears, are the thousands of tablets surviving from Lagash (present-day Tello), numerous enough for the site to be called "Tablet Hill" since G. C. Ernest de Sarzec found it in 1894. They are organized in individual rooms, which had plastered walls, containers along the walls, and surfaces on which to place tablets (for reading?). Of particular interest is the evidence that each room had tablets in only one corner, perhaps leaving space for additions. Access to any one of the rooms was provided only through a hole in the ceiling, which brings to mind storerooms or even graves rather than library facilities.

Second Millennium. Surviving from Ur and Nippur, particularly, and other sites are numerous tablets documenting the culture of the age of Hammurabi (18th century B.C.). The subjects were from the past: legends of ancient Sumerian gods, kings, and heroes such as Gilgamesh. The literary forms similarly derived from long practice, polished in a scholastic style. The script was cuneiform and mainly in Sumerian, but use of vernaculars was beginning, notably the Akkadian used by the Babylonians, into which Sumerian writings were increasingly being translated. Sumerian remained, like Latin in a later day, preferred for learning and literature. Serving religion were Sumerian myths, hymns, and psalms praising gods and kings; incantations and prayers of the private sort; and, most important, divination—primarily haruspicy, or prediction from entrails. Equally prominent were mathematics texts. The significance of scribes, moreover, is evident from writings about their education—both serious and humorous.

Mari, on the Euphrates, is revealed as a commercial center that flourished early in the 2nd millennium, until crushed by Hammurabi about 1750 B.C. Presently on the Syrian-Iraqi border, it is still important to the nomads. Its ancient remains cover more than 100 acres. The palace is believed to have occupied more than 6 acres, and more than 260 chambers, courtyards, and corridors have been identified. Scholars are satisfied that the building was both the king's residence and an administrative center with workshops and archives. The surviving 20,000 tablets bear mainly diplomatic and household economic records of three unconnected periods of Assyrian rule, and it is considered definite that they were shelved in separate groups.

At ancient Alalakh, a few miles northeast of Antioch, were found tablets in a western dialect of Ak-kadian constituting an archive of a state of conse-quence for perhaps 75 years soon after the fall of Mari. It seems to have benefited from trade between the sea and Aleppo, some 50 miles to the east, and the timber of the Amanus mountains north of the town. Most of the extant tablets are administrative, a few lexicographical and literary, throwing much light on Hurrian activities; but, as at Mari, nothing of a library nature has been established to date.

The world of tablets in cuneiform apparently in-cluded also, by the 16th century B.C., archives at the Hittite capitals in Anatolia. The extant data revealing bilingual dictionaries—documents such as the Hittite and Akkadian testament of Hattusili I and facilities much like those at Lagash—are interpreted by some to indicate a temple or state library. The degree to which the organized resources included known Hit-tite historical writings and supernatural or anecdotal literature is not established. Yet there are historical-critical evidences that Assyrian, biblical, and Greco-Roman historiography were influenced by the novel separation from mythology of the "Ten-Year An-nals" of a 14th-century Hittite ruler, Mursili. The ap-paratus for such influence seems likely to have in-cluded "book" collections.

The expansion of the Hittite Empire and grow-ing complexity of Near Eastern commerical and dip-lomatic activity signaled by the Amarna letters are among the events reflected in the 14th- and 13th-cen-tury tablets excavated at Ras Shamra, a Syrian coastal town about seven miles north of Latakia. Their con-tents encompass administrative, economic, ritual, and literary themes, often in more than one language and supported by bilingual word lists. They were found in buildings, both public and private, of ancient Ugarit, not just in the center but at various locations. The Baal temple is held to have had a library, not just archives. The nearby house of the chief priest pos-sessed mythological and religious texts not only in the official North Canaanite dialect but also in Hur-rian, the language of an important minority; also on hand were vocabularies and other items suggesting that the establishment performed also the functions of a seminary for training temple scribes. Not far from the palace were spacious homes of high officials, at least one of whom owned a library; the variety of its contents is perhaps implied by a surviving lexico-graphical tablet with equivalents linking Ugaritic and Hurrian with Sumerian and Babylonian. Conspicu-ous in the artisans' quarter was an imposing stone edifice that had housed a library of texts in Babylo-nian cuneiform, some astrological and some literary, perhaps used for teaching.

Fairly well documented is the 14th-century ac-tivity in Assyria-Babylonia of the Middle Kassite pe-riod. The Babylonian heritage of religious hero-poems, wisdom literature, theology, philology, prognostication, medicine, and astronomy was col-lected, edited, translated, and arranged by learned Babylonian scribes in series of numbered tablets. From the traditions of the Kassite rulers came addi-tional cults and cult literature, magic, and demonol-ogy. It seems likely that library collections played an important part in that work, which anticipates the later achievements at Alexandria.

In any case, "omens" (predictions), hymns,

prayers, and lexicographical texts from the mid-13th-century reign of Shalmaneser I of Assyria became part of a collection expanded by the conquests of Tukulti-Ninurta, the great Assyrian king of the late 13th century. According to a Sumerian-Akkadian epic, indeed, the latter carried off the tablets that dis-tinguished the libraries of Babylonia. Involved were the usual omens, prayers, and incantations, as well as medical texts. Some of them appear to have turned up among the remains of the library established at the Assur temple early in the 11th century by Tiglath-Pileser during his days as Crown Prince.

Assurbanipal's Library. For the most im-pressive legacy, testifying beyond serious challenge to a library, one jumps five centuries to Assurbanipal, "King of the World, King of Assyria" (668–c. 631). In 1850 Austen Henry Layard crowned several years' labor at Nineveh sites near Mosul, in far northern Iraq, by identifying "Chambers of Records." In 1854 Hormudz Rassam found an important portion of a library in a nearby structure. The subsequent half-century of excavations added more enlightenment. Some 20,000 tablets and fragments, preserved in the British Museum, owed their remarkable condition to the destruction of Nineveh in 612 by the Medes, so thorough that the sites had lain virtually undisturbed for more than 2,400 years. It is clear from the huge assemblage of Assyro-Babylonian and Sumerian writings and his own correspondence that Assurban-ipal built his library partly by welcoming copies from any possible source. Those sources may include the temples, whose plundering by his soldiers is noted in the records of his reign.

The library included the main works of Akka-dian literature. More particularly, Leo Oppenheim inventoried the tablets as follows: more than 300, each of which bears from 80 to 200 individual omen texts; 200 with lists of cuneiform signs and combi-nations, including Sumerian-Akkadian dictionaries; more than 100 Sumerian incantations with interlinear Akkadian translations; 100-plus with proverbs, cycles of conjuration, and others; 200 miscellaneous, includ-ing reference works for court diviners and magicians and handbooks for education, research, and the train-ing of scribes; and some 35 or 40 with epic literature. King Assurbanipal himself could read, and it may be assumed that, as elsewhere in the ancient Orient, writings could be used by priests, officials, and mer-chants, but that was probably all.

Assurbanipal's concerns presumably explain in part the directions that led to stocking his library with exceptional tablets. By comparison with many other Assyro-Babylonian survivals, they consist of notably finer and better baked clay than the usual, and the script achieved marked elegance and clarity by means of physically tight inscribing. The correct-ing and editing was of matching quality.

How the tablets were stored is not known, not from any direct evidence at the library, at any rate. Layard reported in 1853 that he had found two small rooms whose floors were piled a foot or more high with broken clay tablets and cylinders, most of which had probably fallen there from a higher room, and adjoining chambers with similar but slighter remains. Nothing further can be inferred from Rassam's nar-rative; we hear that additional fragments of the same tablets or belonging to the same series have been found scattered in various places, but thanks to the inexperience and carelessness of excavators or local handlers and arrangers we do not know from which of the two palaces involved any given fragment came. It can hardly be doubted that there were once a definite order and supervision, but we have neither knowledge of them nor any basis for reconstructing them.

Extraordinary care led to the discovery of subscripts on the tablets. Besides the ownership stamp, "Palace of Assurbanipal, King of the World, King of Assyria," precise data were furnished, the equivalent of book or manuscript description. It is now agreed that they were not created by Assurbanipal or his staff but borrowed from available models. These practices had been known at the state (?) library of the Hittites at Boghazköi, and it is no longer doubted that the seeds were planted in oldest Babylon.

That Assurbanipal was collecting systematically is plain from the tablet and series indexes, indexes that furnish at the beginning of each tablet in a series the number of lines on each tablet, and series indexes that bring together the titles of various series whose contents are related. The extant collections do not include index tablets of a bibliographical character or catalogues.

For indicators there were plain, oddly shaped little clay markers, which bear nothing but a series title, perhaps to facilitate finding the series, and which lay on the pile of series items or on the reed or clay receptacles that contained them. Such a receptacle was called *girginakku,* a designation that seems to have carried over to the whole library-like *biblio-theke;* at least the chief was called *rab girginakku,* or supervisor thereof. It may be that the scion of an old scholarly family, whose tablet collection Assurbanipal apparently acquired, was the actual organizer and first director of the royal library.

REFERENCE
Ernst Posner, *Archives in the Ancient World* (1973).

SIDNEY L. JACKSON
(d. 1979)

Nepal

Nepal, the only Hindu kingdom in the world, is a landlocked country in the Himalaya Mountains, shaped like a rectangle about 800 km. long and 200 km. wide. It lies between two powerful nations of Asia, China on the north and India on the south. Population (1984 est.) 16,104,000; area 147,181 sq.km. More than 93 percent of the total population live in rural areas and are engaged in agriculture, the

Tribhuvan University Library

Tribhuvan University Library in Kirtipur. It is Nepal's principal academic library, and the country's only library in a separate building of its own.

backbone of Nepal's economy. The official language is Nepali.

History. Nepal has been a center of learning since ancient times. The low rate of literacy (25 percent) shows Nepal's lack of development, but interest in education has a long history there. It is mentioned in ancient stone inscriptions and early records preserved in the monasteries and temples. Sanskrit education flourished in Nepal before the 6th century, and Nepal is believed to have been a repository of untold treasures of manuscripts on Tantrism, philosophy, Sanskrit grammar, astrology, rituals, religion, medicine, and Vedic literature.

Nepal can be called a country with ancient library traditions, yet education and libraries could not develop in Nepal under the autocratic Rana rule from 1846 to 1951. Books, magazines, newspapers, the radio, and other media of communication and academic study were banned for the majority. Even expressing the need for a library was forbidden and could lead to punishment. In 1929 a great Nepali poet, Laxmi Prasad Devkota, and some of his friends were punished for their decision to establish a public library in Nepal. Nevertheless, public libraries came into existence in various places in Nepal as forerunners of the revolution of 1950.

After 1950, many schools and colleges were opened and so-called public libraries were established in the hope of giving free access to knowledge. But library services in a modern sense were introduced in Nepal only in 1959 with the establishment of a Central Library under an agreement between the government of Nepal and the United States; unfortunately the agreement came to an end within a short period of time.

Tribhuvan University Central Library was established in Kirtipur, Kathmandu, and the whole collection of the Central Library was handed over to it in 1962. Tribhuvan University Central Library

Libraries in Nepal (1982)							
Type	Administrative units	Service points	Volumes in collections	Annual expenditures (rupee)	Population served	Professional staff	Total staff
National	1	--	70,000	344,500	--	3	20
Academic	120	--	495,403	3,747,000	67,518	63	339
Public	400	--	--	--	--	--	--
Special	71	--	293,944	872,000	--	13	157

played a leading role in the library movement in Nepal from 1963.

National Library and Archives. The Nepal National Library was established in 1955 with the private collection of the royal priest Pandit Hemraj Pandey bought by the royal government. It is located at Pulchok, Patan, in Kathmandu Valley. It contains 70,000 books in 11 languages. The library has not been able to function as a national library should. It is more like a museum than a library.

The Nepal National Archive has a long history. It began in the time of the Malla kings more than two centuries ago. The Bir Library, the oldest library of Nepal, was renamed the Nepal National Archive. At Thapathali, Kathmandu, it has 65,750 manuscripts; of these, 12,000 are on palm leaves. It has many valuable manuscripts that are not available in any other part of the world. These manuscripts were microfilmed under a joint Nepal–German Manuscript Preservation Project.

Academic Libraries. Schools and colleges lack library facilities. Collections of a few hundred or a few thousand books can be found at some institutions, but without much organization. Tri-Chandra Campus Library, established in 1918, is the oldest among academic libraries. It has about 23,300 volumes. Tribhuvan University, the only University of Nepal, has 69 campuses. All have library services of a sort. Their collections consist of from 5,000 to 15,000 volumes. With foreign aid projects, appreciable attention has been given to library services on technical campuses such as those on agriculture, engineering, medicine, and forestry.

Tribhuvan University Central Library in Kathmandu is the biggest systematically organized library in the country. Starting from a 1200-book collection in 1959, it had 125,000 volumes by the mid-1980s. It promotes the importance of improving library services for national development, serves as the depository library of the UN for Nepal, and cooperates in other international activities. The Library has published the *Nepalese National Bibliography* since 1981. It also issues occasional bibliographies on various topics of interest.

Public Libraries. It is said that Nepal has 400 public libraries. But they can hardly be called true public libraries judged by professional standards because of deficiencies in objectives, space, budget, books, and newspaper collections. They have only randomly-donated collections and often have difficulty in keeping open a few hours a day or a week at a time. Pradipta Library started in 1946 in Kathmandu, Dhawal Library established in 1936 in Palpa, and Adarsh Library founded in 1946 in Biratnagar are among the leading public libraries. The collections of public libraries in Nepal range from 200 to 10,000 volumes.

School Libraries and Media Centers. Most of the schools do not have libraries. The few that exist cannot be called school libraries in any real sense. Schoolchildren buy textbooks for their use. Some foreign-aided schools, such as Budhanilkantha School, St. Xavier's, and St. Mary's High Schools, give good attention to school library services.

Special Libraries. There are more than 70 libraries in various government departments, research organizations, and other organizations. Notable among them are Madan Puraskar Pustakalaya, the Library of APROSC (Agricultural Projects Services Centre), the Department of Botany Library, the Rastra Bank Library, and the Library of the Trade Promotion Centre. Madan Puraskar Pustakalaya is well known for its good collection on Nepali literature and languages. APROSC Library serves as the National Agricultural Documentation Center.

The Profession. The library profession has not been fully recognized in the country. Nepal has no library school. Professional librarians are trained from abroad. Tribhuvan University Central Library organizes training courses for working librarians. There were about 75 professional librarians in the country in the mid-1980s.

REFERENCES
E. W. Erickson, "Libraries in Nepal," *Wilson Library Bulletin,* (1961), on the library scene in Kathmandu in the late 1950s. John L. Hafenrichter, "Planning Document: Library Development Activity, Central Library," Kathmandu, 1961.

Shanti Mishra, "Library Movement in Nepal," *Unesco Bulletin for Libraries.* (January–February 1974); summarizes library history.

SHANTI MISHRA

Netherlands

The Kingdom of the Netherlands lies on the North Sea, bounded by Belgium on the south and the Federal Republic of Germany on the east. Population (1984 est.) 14,437,000; area 41,509 sq.km. Part of the country is below sea level. The official language is Dutch.

History. The contents of the many medieval monastery libraries are widely scattered and mostly known only by their contemporary catalogues; a notable exception is the library of the Carthusian monastery at Utrecht, now in the local University Library. The only late medieval library still extant is the Librije at Zutphen, built as an annex of the Walburgis church in 1563. The number of Dutch, mostly late medieval, manuscripts described in the Bibliotheca Neerlandica Manuscripta, a central catalogue in the University Library at Leiden, totals more than 12,000. The products of the earliest printing presses set up in Holland, 1566–72, are known as "prototypography." The first dated book was printed in Utrecht in 1473. Up to 1,500 Dutch presses produced 2,100 editions. The postincunabula (1501–40) are well documented.

With the coming of Protestantism, secularization of the properties of the monasteries gave rise to city libraries that in Amsterdam, Utrecht, and Groningen developed into university libraries. In the 17th century the firms of Blaeu, Elsevier, and others were the printers for the whole of Europe, specializing in scientific and cartographic works.

A national library was founded in 1798 after a political revolution. Two of its librarians, J. W. Holtrop (1806–1870) and M. F. A. G. Campbell (1819–1890), laid the foundations of incunabular studies. The number of incunabula in Dutch libraries is about 8,000. P. A. Tiele (1834–1889), who worked in the university libraries of Amsterdam, Leiden, and Utrecht, was important as a bibliographer and cataloguer. H. E. Greve (1878–1957) was the leader of the public library movement in the Netherlands. F. Donker Duyvis (1894–1961), Secretary-General of the Féderation International de Documentation (FID), was a pioneer in the fields of documentation, standardization, and efficiency.

The Dutch library landscape can be characterized as a complex of cooperative bodies, each serving its specific group but with a long tradition of service outside its own domain.

National Library. The Koninklijke Bibliotheek (Royal Library) at The Hague functions as the national library. Its starting collection was the confiscated library of Prince-Stadholder William V, which was amalgamated with some other libraries considered as common property. In 1814, after the restoration of the House of Orange, King William I renounced all claims to the confiscated collections and took great interest in the Library. It was enriched during the 19th century by the acquisition of many private collections. A representative collection of Dutch manuscripts, early editions, pamphlets, and songbooks was built. Complete coverage of Dutch literature and Dutch newspapers is attempted.

The Royal Library is not a copyright library. To compensate for the lack of a deposit system, a voluntary deposit scheme was adopted in 1974. In 1983 the depositary received 30,000 books, 11,000 periodical publications, and 3,500 maps. On the basis of these materials the Dutch Bibliography has been published. *Brinkman's Cumulative Catalogue of Books published in the Netherlands and Flanders* (since 1858) was renamed in 1983; it is now the official Dutch national bibliography. Next to it six series are published: for trade publications, for noncommercial publications, for governmental publications, for maps, for translations, and the Cataloguing-in-Publication list. In 1983 the Dutch Bibliographical Centre (NBC) was created as a consortium of the Royal Library, publishers, booksellers, and other parties; under its auspices the National Bibliography is produced. The holdings of the Library comprise about 1,800,000 printed volumes (including 6,000 printed before 1540), 1,500 medieval manuscripts, 5,000 other manuscripts, and 120,000 letters. There are many special collections, including a chess collection of 15,000 volumes. The scope of the collection of foreign publications is limited to the humanities and the social sciences; the responsibility for the other domains is the task of other libraries, especially the Library of the Royal Netherlands Academy of Sciences (biomedical sciences), the Library of the Technical University of Delft (technical sciences), and the Library of the Agricultural University of Wageningen (agricultural sciences). Two large retrospective bibliographical projects are based in the Royal Library: the Short Title Catalogue Netherlands (STCN), covering book production in the period 1540–1800 (about 300,000 titles), and the pre-Brinkman project, covering the period 1801–32. Since 1922 the Royal Library has maintained the Union Catalogue.

In 1983 the Netherlands Central Catalogue (NCC) became operational; it is the online version of the machine-readable parts of the Union Catalogue of the Royal Library (with input from the university libraries and other research libraries and of the libraries of the ministries), of the Central Technical Cata-

Royal Library

logue, maintained by the Technical University at Delft, and of the Central Agricultural Catalogue, maintained by the Agricultural University at Wageningen. The traditional cooperation in the field of interlibrary loans is further supported by this automated system. This system is one of the facilities of PICA (Project for Integrated Catalogue Automation), originally a cooperative organization of the Royal Library and the university libraries, but gradually embracing all types of libraries, the public libraries as well. PICA is evolving from a project for shared cataloguing to a truly national information network. PICA has its headquarters and its technical equipment in the Royal Library.

In 1982 the Royal Library moved into a new building next to that of the General State Archives. In its closed stacks it has a capacity for 5,000,000 volumes; there are 350 reading tables and 227 tables for consultation of reference works. Also housed in the building are the Museum and Documentation Centre for Dutch Literature, Bureau of the National Committee for Dutch History, National Bureau for the Documentation of the History of Art, Bureau of the Library Council, Headquarters of IFLA and of FID, and some other institutions.

Academic Libraries. There are 13 universities in the country, including three technical and one agricultural. The library collections reflect to a high degree the disciplines represented in the institutions. The State Universities (Leiden, founded 1575; Groningen, 1614; Utrecht, 1636); the Municipal University of Amsterdam (1877); the Free (Calvinist) University at Amsterdam, (1880); and the Catholic University at Nijmegen (1923) are complete universities with all faculties, whereas the others are more specialized. Autonomous in their administration, all universities are fully supported by the State. Collections and services are integrated in the national library services at large. The university libraries provide 40 percent of all interlibrary loans, and their collections add up to 47 percent of the total volumes outside the domain of the public libraries. There are nine insti-

Royal Library at The Hague, which functions as the national library.

597

tutes for higher learning, mainly theological schools.

In principle the central libraries form one system or network with the libraries of the faculties and the departments. The head librarians are united in a consultative, coordinating, and cooperating body, together with the librarians of the Royal Library and of the Library of the Royal Netherlands Academy of Sciences.

Public Libraries. Popular reading libraries were common from an early date, although a public library system was fully developed only in the 20th century. The denominational rift in Dutch society also split the public library world: apart from the general public libraries, both Protestants and Catholics started public library systems of their own. All received government subsidies and held the same ideal of educating the people through reading. They all gave priority to books for study and did not attract the large groups of people who wanted to read for recreation. But whereas the general libraries did not wish to select their books by other standards than inherent quality, Protestant and Catholic leaders resisted an "indiscriminate" supply of books. During the 1960s such segregation was relaxed and finally disappeared, uniting public libraries in the Nederlands Bibliotheek en Lektuur Centrum (NBLC: Dutch Center for [public] Libraries and Literature). Popular works were acquired in large quantities, branch libraries multiplied, and the reading public came to the libraries in previously unknown numbers. An annual fee is required, except for those under 18. The Public Library Act of 1975 provided that the central government was to pay all costs of staff and 20 percent of all other expenditure, the remaining 80 percent to be supplied by the provincial and local authorities. In 1983 the rule was changed: in anticipation of the decentralization of the responsibility, provincial and local authorities receive yearly a lump sum for public library work. Those authorities can decide for themselves how much they wish to pay from their own means for this work. The government announced its intention to withdraw the public library act of 1975. Only a few rules are left, but those were to be embodied in a broad social welfare act.

Until comparatively recently, research libraries were able to cope with the demand for books for study; but the increase in numbers of students, both at the universities and at the vocational colleges, required some extension of the library system. So 13 libraries were designated as regional supporting libraries; most are large public libraries, others provincial or municipal libraries. Additional government grants enabled them to buy bibliographical tools and to equip reading rooms.

School Libraries. The development of school libraries depends to a large degree on the pedagogical insights of the local school authorities. Paid professional school librarians are an exception; mostly the school libraries are managed by volunteers. But funds are available for equipment and materials. A large measure of support is given by the NBLC, the provincial library centers, or the local public libraries. This support consists of a number of special bibliographical publications, training of the volunteers, and the distribution of tools (such as an adapted classification scheme, derived from the scheme used by the public libraries). In many primary schools informative materials and audiovisual items are organized in so-called documentation centers, separated from the narrative literature; in the secondary schools both categories are found in single units.

Special Libraries. At least four groups can be distinguished: (1) libraries of learned societies and scientific institutes; (2) provincial and municipal libraries; (3) libraries of vocational colleges; and (4) special libraries in a more restricted sense.

Of the learned societies the Royal Netherlands Academy of Science in Amsterdam takes first place. It was founded in 1808 by Napoleon's brother, then King of Holland. Its importance now lies primarily in its collection of scientific and medical journals. All journals indexed by *Excerpta Medica* are kept in microfiche form. The library of the Teyler Foundation in Haarlem (1778) is celebrated for its collection in the natural sciences. An important library for the study of modern history is that of the International Institute for Social History in Amsterdam, founded in 1935, which documents with its archives, 550,000 books and 2,400 periodicals, the history of the labor movement, socialism, and anarchism. The Library of the Peace Palace in The Hague, founded in 1913 by the Carnegie Endowment for International Peace, has a comprehensive collection in the fields of international law, international organizations, and diplomatic history. It has also a fine collection of works by and

Libraries in the Netherlands (1982)

Type	Administrative units	Service points	Volumes in collections	Annual expenditures (Dutch florin)[a]	Population served	Professional staff	Total staff
National	1	1	1,798,000	7,131,000	--	65	214
Academic	22	651	16,161,000	45,061,000	--	1,268	1,630
Public	468	2,944	37,229,000	175,000,000	4,270,000	3,445	9,061
School	5,600	--	--	--	--	--	--
Special	678	824	13,979,000	55,062,000	--	1,760	2,150
Vocational Training Colleges	312	408	2,618,000	5,189,000	246,000	321	379

[a]Excludes salaries and housing.

Sources: Centraal Bureau voor de Statistiek, *Wetenschappelijke en speciale bibliotheken 1982,* 's-Gravenhage: Staatsuitgeverij, 1984; NBLC for data on public libraries; Ministry of Education for data on school libraries.

about the Dutch political scientist Hugo Grotius (1583–1645). It serves the International Court of Justice, a body of the United Nations, as well as the Académie de Droit Internationale. The library of the Royal Tropical Institute in Amsterdam (founded 1910) focused from 1950 on problems of Third World countries. It consists of 400,000 volumes and 5,000 current periodicals.

The provincial libraries of Friesland, Zeeland, and Gelderland, all dating from the middle of the 19th century, play an important role in the library service for their regions. They possess important research collections, especially on local history, but some of national importance. The same applies to city libraries. The oldest is the Athenaeum Library in Deventer (1560). The City Library of Haarlem dates from 1596; it has a fine collection on the history of typesetting. The Municipal Library of Rotterdam (1604) has a collection of works by and about the Rotterdam-born Humanist Desiderius Erasmus (1469–1536). The City Library of Maastricht was founded in 1662.

The libraries of the vocational colleges serve primarily their own students and staff. There were 54 technical colleges, 10 agricultural, 13 economic, 43 health care, 49 socio-pedagogic, 35 fine arts, and 108 pedagogic colleges in the mid-1980s.

The special libraries in a narrower sense vary enormously in scope and volume. There were 13 ministerial libraries and 263 libraries of governmental agencies and institutions, 130 business/industrial libraries, 112 libraries of foundations or associations, 90 hospital libraries, 26 museum libraries, and 38 libraries of religious organizations in the mid-1980s. Most of them participate in the interlibrary loan system with the effect that they delivered 34 percent of all interlibrary loans in the country in 1982. Some of these libraries build databases, of which some are of more than national importance, such as *Economics Abstracts International,* produced by the library of the Ministry for Economic Affairs. Also the use of online searching is heaviest in this category.

The Profession. Library and documentation/information education is offered by three types of insitutions: at the University of Amsterdam (a postgraduate course); at six Library and Documentation Academies (undergraduate courses); and through various part-time courses by the Stichting Gemeenschappelijke Opleiding (GO), which vary from the basic to a postgraduate level.

Librarians of all library types have had their professional organization, since 1912, in the Nederlandse Vereniging van Bibliothecarissen (NVB; Dutch Association of Librarians). Public librarians in 1972 organized themselves under the NBLC. The NVB, from 1974, incorporated documentalists and information specialists. It has sections for special, research, and vocational college libraries, a section for information specialists, and groups for law librarians, medical librarians, and agricultural librarians. To provide the necessary unity the Federatie van Organisaties op het gebied van het Bibliotheek-, Informatie- en Documentatiewezen (FOBID; Federation of Organizations in the Fields of Library, Information and Documentation Services) was created in 1974. Theological librarians organized their own association in 1949. Diversification in the profession led to a number of new groupings: Map librarians working group (1975), patent librarians (1976), and Association of Online Users (1977).

The Dutch library journal *Open* is published under the auspices of FOBID. The public libraries have *Bibliotheek en Samenleving* as their journal. Advisory work to the government is the task of two bodies: the Library Council and the Netherlands Organization for Information Policy. A law in preparation in the mid-1980s looked toward a new division of responsibilities: an advisory council for library and information matters and an institute with executive duties.

A. H. H. M. MATHIJSEN

Netherlands Antilles

The Netherlands Antilles, a group of six of the Leeward Islands in the Caribbean, consists of Curaçao, Aruba, Bonaire, Saint Eustatius, Saba, and the southern part of Saint Martin. Population (1984 est.) 235,000; area 993 sq.km. The official language is Dutch.

National Library Services. The Willemstad Public Library (Openbare Bibliotheek), established in Curaçao in 1922, functions as a national library for the Netherlands Antilles. There are two branch libraries, plus a bookmobile that serves suburbs. Although there is no legal deposit law, the library tries to purchase all works about, or printed in, the six islands. Its collection of Caribbeana consists of approximately 6,000 volumes. These are the only noncirculating volumes in the accumulation of more than 100,000 volumes. Holdings are mainly in Dutch, although the Library has some works in English and in Spanish. There are only a few titles in Papiamento,

Libraries in the Netherlands Antilles (1981)

Type	Administrative units	Service points	Volumes in collections	Annual expenditures (guilder)	Population served[a]	Professional staff	Total staff
National	--	--	--	--	--	--	--
Academic	--	--	--	--	--	--	--
Public	1	3	100,000	2,337,000	9,543	14	56
School	--	--	--	--	--	--	--

[a]Registered borrowers.

Source: Unesco, *Statistical Yearbook,* 1984.

the patois spoken by most people in the Netherlands Antilles.

The Central Historical Archives (Centraal Historisch Archief), founded in Willemstad in 1969, contains all archival publications of the Netherlands Antilles, concentrating on government documents. The library is in close contact with the National Library in The Hague and makes copies of all documents there that relate to the Netherlands Antilles.

Only government officials may borrow materials, but the collection is accessible to students and others during restricted hours. The library collects periodicals related to archival matters, publishes two newsletters describing old and new acquisitions, and restores and laminates Caribbeana documents.

Public Libraries. The Public Library of Aruba opened in 1944 in Oranjestad and houses approximately 140,450 books. Holdings are in Dutch, English, Spanish, French, and Papiamento. Another branch in the suburb of Saint Nicholas has been in operation for many years. The Caribbeana collection is a noteworthy feature of the Oranjestad main library. Most of the collection circulates, although a deposit is required for some of the older works. Only the rarest items must be used on the premises. Adults must pay a membership fee to join these public libraries; membership is free to children.

The main public libraries at Oranjestad and Willemstad both have special collections on music, including musical scores and works related to music, particularly that of the Netherlands Antilles.

Academic Libraries. The University of Aruba, founded in 1970, comprises colleges of liberal arts and sciences, business administration, languages, preprofession sciences, and education. The library houses more than 3,000 volumes.

The Institute of Higher Studies of the Netherlands Antilles became the University of the Netherlands Antilles in 1979. Its library was opened in 1970 and houses approximately 100,000 volumes, mainly books on law, economics, business administration, and sociology. Students are allowed to borrow books, the number of titles dependent on their class standing. The library subscribes to approximately 100 periodicals and has an active interlibrary loan operation. In addition, the library maintains a union catalogue of all library holdings in the Netherlands Antilles.

There are some special libraries in the Netherlands Antilles. The Oranjestad Sportburo was established in Aruba in 1978 as an outgrowth of a new government bureau in charge of coordinating physical activities in the schools. This circulating library has about 600 books on sports-related topics, half in English and the rest in Dutch.

The Stichting Wetenschappelijke Bibliotheek (Scientific Library Foundation), founded in 1950 in Willemstad, holds some 16,500 volumes, with an extensive music collection in addition to works on the pure and applied sciences. Holdings include musical scores, printed music, and books on music of the Netherlands Antilles, with a special collection of music by Curaçao composers. Publications of the foundation include a union catalogue of all nonfiction books in the Netherlands Antilles, plus *Curaçao Folklore, Curaçao Music,* and *Nansi Stories.*

Other special libraries connected to research institutes in Curaçao include those of the Caraibisch Marien-Biologisch Instituut, with more than 3,000 volumes, and the Meteorologische Dienst van de Nederlandse Antillen (Meteorological Service of the Netherlands Antilles).

The Association di Biblioteka i Archivo di Korsow (ABAK: Association of Libraries and Archives) was established in 1972 and is affiliated with IFLA. The association is housed in temporary headquarters in Willemstad, Curaçao. There is no official publication.

BARBARA FOSTER*

New Zealand

New Zealand, a parliamentary state and member of the Commonwealth, lies in the South Pacific Ocean; the Tasman Sea separates the country from Australia. New Zealand comprises the North and South islands and Chatham and Stewart, among other islands. Population (1984 est.) 3,265,500; area 269,057 sq.km. The official language is English.

History. The earliest libraries in New Zealand were established by European settlers at the beginning of the 19th Century. The first library for public use was the Port Nicholson Exchange and Public Library, set up in Wellington in 1840.

The first European visitors to New Zealand in the 18th century found an indigenous culture which had not devised a system of writing. The Maori had an extensive unwritten literature; the records of the people were passed from generation to generation through songs, recited genealogies, stories, and proverbs; they were inscribed in the painted and carved decorations of their wooden buildings and in cave paintings. The missionaries who worked in the country from 1814 onward established the first printing presses and endeavoured to record and publish these unwritten texts.

Books were among the household items brought to the new land by European settlers. They established libraries on the model of those in England and Scotland. The development of library services owed much initially to the influence of the English scholarly and public library systems, but American and Scandinavian practices have also been introduced as a result of overseas training and travel by New Zealand librarians.

Libraries experienced slow and uneven development up to the mid-1930s. Public libraries were established by local councils but public access was not free; university libraries were poorly funded and not adequately housed; and there was no national library.

Impetus was provided by the reformation of the Libraries Association in 1935, by the activities of the Carnegie Corporation in sponsoring surveys and providing fellowships, and by the establishment of a government library agency, the Country Library Service, in 1938. The following 30 years saw the establishment of systems for training librarians, the modernization of public library service, a better distribution of service, the establishment of strong university libraries, and the formation of a national library.

Despite the small size of its population, New Zealand has the reputation of being among the best-read countries in the world, a characteristic which owes much to the liveliness of local publishing, the large number of bookshops, and not least the quality of the library service.

National Library. The National Library was established by an act of Parliament in 1965 and came into being in 1966 by a merging of the existing National Library Service, the Alexander Turnbull Library, and the General Assembly Library. The National Librarian is an officer of the Crown, responsible to the Minister of Education. A statutory Board of Trustees advises the Minister on the state and development of the National Library and promotes the development of library services in New Zealand. The Library is financed by an annual appropriation by Parliament.

The Library provides the normal national bibliographical and interlibrary loan services and manages the national collections. Its Regional Services Division provides book loans, information services, and technical assistance to public libraries and other agencies. The School Library Service provides advisory and loan services to elementary and secondary schools. The New Zealand Bibliographic Network, established in 1982, provides a comprehensive national database of holdings and publications data. It is being expanded from an in-house system to a full nationwide cooperative network coordinated by the National Library.

The Alexander Turnbull Library, an institution for scholarly research, was founded in 1918 as the result of a bequest; its collection reflects the interests of its donor—the Pacific, New Zealand history and literature, English literature (particularly the mid-17th century and the work of John Milton)—with additional strengths in early printed books and the development of the art of printing. The General Assembly Library, established in 1858 as the library of Parliament, was for a time a library of historical research because of the strength of its holdings, but by the mid-1980s, through transfer of stock and internal reorganization, it returned to its primary role as a parliamentary information service.

The National Archives in Wellington selects, preserves, and makes available the records of central government. It may advise and assist other organizations and arrange for the preservation of specified categories of local authority records. The main record centers are in Wellington and Auckland, but some repositories of regional records also exist in nongovernmental institutions in other parts of the country. The National Archives holds 15,000 linear meters of doc-

University of Canterbury Library

University of Canterbury Library in Christchurch (opened in 1975).

uments, 400,000 maps and plans, and photographs and pictures.

Academic Libraries. The six universities, at Auckland, Hamilton, Palmerston North, Wellington, Christchurch, and Dunedin, and the agricultural college at Lincoln, finance their libraries from their government grants. The libraries have developed rapidly since 1960, following the report in 1959 by a Government Committee of Inquiry on Universities (the Parry Report). All libraries are housed in buildings erected since 1964; research collections have been built up, and salaries and conditions of employment for professional staff are competitive with those in other sectors. At the time of the Parry inquiry the holdings of all the university libraries together were some 818,000 volumes; by 1981 they held 4,120,000 volumes.

No New Zealand university library collection can match the collections of major universities in larger countries, but each library is now much more adequate for the support of postgraduate studies and research, the development of which became official policy following the Parry Report. Surveys of university library resources were carried out in 1972 and 1982 and their reports published (McEldowney, 1973 and 1983).

Libraries in New Zealand (1979)

Type	Administrative units	Volumes in collections	Annual expenditures (New Zealand dollar)	Population served	Professional staff	Total staff
National	1	4,802,641	6,456,472	3,150,900	174	366
Academic and tertiary	39	3,815,617	9,491,507	158,294	311	988
Public	276	6,076,524	22,045,462	2,902,495	409	2,469
School	1,487	8,242,508	3,435,701	699,646	130	1,681[a]
Special	241	2,516,754	6,984,971	321,565	197	734

[a]Full-time equivalent.

There are libraries in the six colleges for training elementary and secondary school teachers, financed by central government through the Department of Education.

In the 14 technical institutes and 8 community colleges (which provide education for technicians, the trades, and some professions), funding comes from central government and is based on a Department of Education formula that is not generous by overseas standards. But the holdings of these libraries (430,000 volumes in all) form a useful contribution to national resources, particularly in the area of health sciences.

Public Libraries. Public library service, other than that supplied to some isolated settlements and rural communities, is exclusively the responsibility of local government—boroughs or counties. Finance for the service is derived from a local land tax. The period of most rapid development of public libraries, 1945 onward, coincided with or was a consequence of the abandonment of the subscription and rental library systems. In 1938, local bodies operated 104 libraries; by 1959, 164; and by 1979, 276. This period has also seen the replacement of most library buildings.

All libraries in cities, most of those in boroughs, and a few in counties provide free lending and reference services to their residents. Special services in light fiction, sound recordings, and art reproductions are normally operated on a rental basis. There is a strong emphasis on lending, but increasing attention is being given to information and reference work and to services directed at particular groups, such as housebound readers, literacy students, and businesses. Services to children are strong.

The standards of public library service vary widely in various parts of the country. Local autonomy and funding and the absence of public library legislation and central government funding explain the wide disparities. The National Library and the Library Association tried to promote the reorganization of service into larger units through pilot schemes or cooperative ventures, but with little success. It was clear in the mid-1980s that the reorganization of public-library service would have to await the reorganization of local government in general.

School Libraries. Formal education at the elementary and secondary stages is the responsibility of central government, financed by annual appropriations through the Department of Education.

Most primary and secondary schools have library buildings or rooms. In many cases the library collections are improving and their scope is being widened to include a range of book and other library resources, but the emphasis continues to be on the library as a book storage area. Programs and services are very limited. The Department of Education makes no provision for the employment of professional staff in the school library resource centers, and that continues to be a major inhibiting factor.

The School Library Service, a division of the National Library of New Zealand, provides library support services to schools. Its reference services supplement the collections of school libraries and its advisory services assist and encourage the development of school-based library services.

Special Libraries. The number of special libraries has grown at a high rate since World War II.

In 1959, 98 special libraries were recorded in the Census of Libraries; by 1979 the number was 241, and the development continues. The strength of this group was such that a Special Libraries Section was formed in the New Zealand Library Association in 1971.

These libraries exist to meet the information needs of their parent bodies, but some of them—by virtue of the extent of their resources—function as national collections in their subject fields, as with the libraries of the Ministry of Works and Development, the Ministry of Agriculture and Fisheries, the Department of Scientific and Industrial Research, and the Department of Health.

The Profession. The New Zealand Library Association was founded as an association of libraries in 1910. It adopted its present name and admitted personal members in 1935, after which it became a wider forum for discussion and cultivation of library matters. It has been a powerful force in the development of library service, initiating or stimulating a wide range of activities—bibliographical projects, library training, the introduction of free library service, promotion of the National Library, interlibrary loan, publication of standards, promotion of regional library service, and sponsorship of surveys. Most recently it has been active in pressing the Government for improved school libraries, in promoting the national bibliographic network, and in developing contacts with library associations in Australia and the South Pacific. The Association publishes the monthly newsletter *Library life* and the quarterly journal *New Zealand Libraries*.

Librarians are trained in two institutions—Victoria University of Wellington and the Wellington Teachers College. The University confers a Diploma in Librarianship, a Master of Arts degree in Librarianship, and Certificates of Proficiency in individual diploma subjects. Entrants for the diploma course must normally have university degrees. The diploma course runs for an academic year. Forty-five full-time students and five part-time students were admitted each year in the mid-1980s.

The Teachers' College confers the New Zealand Library Studies Certificate. Students at the course must have the University Entrance qualification and must be working in a library throughout the course. The certificate course comprises 18 weeks of full-time studies, split into 3 sections over a period of approximately 18 months. Each course admitted 120 students in the mid-1980s.

Most continuing education is organized by the branches and sections of the Association. It takes the form of local and national courses or seminars linked with Association's annual conference.

REFERENCES
New Zealand Department of Statistics, *Census of Libraries 1979* (1981).
Sara Innis Fenwick, *Library Services for Children in New Zealand Schools and Public Libraries: a Report to the New Zealand Library Association* (1975).
Walter John McEldowney, *New Zealand Library Association 1910–1960* (1962).
Walter John McEldowney, *New Zealand University Library Resources 1982: Report of a Survey Carried Out for the Committee of New Zealand University Libraries* (1983).
Report of the Trustees of the National Library of New Zealand

and of the National Librarian. (Annual report presented to the House of Representatives).

Wilfrid Smith, *Archives in New Zealand: a Report* (1978).

BRIAN McKEON

Nicaragua

Nicaragua, a republic and the largest country of Central America, lies between the Pacific Ocean on the west and the Caribbean Sea on the east; it is bounded by Honduras on the north and Costa Rica on the south. Population (1984 est.) 2,914,000; area 127,662 sq.km. The official language is Spanish.

National Library. The National Library of Nicaragua was founded in 1882. At its inception it occupied the National Palace; it later transferred to its own building in the western sector of Managua, the capital. After the earthquake of 1972 it was transferred again, to the National Cultural Center in the northeastern section of the capital. The National Library originally contained approximately 5,000 volumes; in the mid-1980s it held 70,000, consisting of Nicaraguan bibliography, works of reference, textbooks, and other items, including works for leisure reading. The Library was named after Rubén Darío (1867–1916), the great Hispanic-American poet who in his earlier years was employed in it as Assistant Librarian. With the goal of eventually fulfilling the objectives of a truly national library, it attended in the meantime to the immediate needs of the student body of Managua. Costs of defense and economic stringency under the Sandinista government in the early 1980s led to rationing of many basic goods and deterioration in many public services, including library services.

Academic Libraries. Six major institutions have academic libraries: the Autonomous National University of Nicaragua, Central American University, National Educational Center, Polytechnic University, Autonomous Private University, and National School of Agriculture and Cattle Breeding. The principal academic libraries, in stock, organization, and function, are those of the National University in Managua and Leon, the Central American University, and the National Educational Center in Managua.

Public Libraries. From 1968 efforts were made to augment the quality and quantity of public libraries. They were established in the departments of Managua, Chinandega, Esteli, Leon, Jinotega, Bluefields, Corinto, Masaya, Ocotal, Matagalpa, Granada, and Carazo.

The public libraries in the cities of Jinotepe, Jinotega, and Chinandega were established by Rotarians and became preeminent. Others are the product of the joint efforts of municipalities, the Ministry of Education, and some citizens aware of the importance of libraries in the development of nations. All of them are in urban areas and are used largely by students at lower, intermediate, and higher levels of learning.

Special Libraries. Nicaragua's special libraries are in the capital at Managua. They include the Central American Institute of Business Administration, the Central Bank, the Supreme Court, the Ministry of Education, the National Bank, and the Bank of America. The library at the Central American Institute was established in 1968 with fewer than 500 volumes; it later acquired more than 25,000 volumes and about 500 periodicals, films, and other audiovisual items. The Library at the Central Bank, founded in 1961, was damaged in the earthquake of 1972 but thereafter largely recovered. The Library of the Ministry of Education was created in 1966; it has more than 6,000 volumes, specializing in teaching. It is used by teachers, officials of the institution, and law students. The Library of the Supreme Court was founded in 1950. The earthquake of 1972 destroyed a great portion of its books, documents, and facilities.

School Libraries. From the mid-1960s much effort went into the improvement of the libraries in educational centers. Several organizations and agencies donated books and so aided in the enlargement of those libraries—the International Development Agency, the National Institute of Spanish Books, the Central Bank of Nicaragua, and, particularly, the Organization of American States.

The Profession. The Association of University and Special Libraries of Nicaragua was created in 1969 and has some 45 personal and 20 institutional members. The Association of Librarians was established in 1965. Both associations endeavor to motivate librarians to improve service to the public within their limited financial means by offering lectures and courses, expositions, professional meetings, and workshops.

LUISA CARDENAS PEREZ*

Nicholson, E. W. B.
(1849–1912)

Edward Williams Byron Nicholson was founder of the Library Association and Librarian of the Bodleian Library.

Nicholson was born in St. Helier, Jersey, on March 16, 1849, and educated at Tonbridge School, Kent. He published a catalogue of the school library in 1866. At Oxford he studied classics but spent much time writing for undergraduate journals. He graduated B.A. in 1871 and M.A. in 1874. His involvement in Oxford Union debates revealed an excitable character, while his duties as Librarian of the union introduced him to the practical problems of librarianship.

By accepting the post of Superintendent and Librarian of the London Institution in 1873, Nicholson hoped to gain a foothold in literary circles. He completely reorganized this moribund proprietary institution; the reference library of 60,000 volumes was recatalogued and classified according to a decimal scheme, while the circulating library was increased, issues rising sixfold in five years. A letter from Nicholson to *The Times* in 1875 produced a flood of new members (and income). Popular guest lecturers were secured; in February 1876, 700 people heard John Ruskin, while 200 had to be turned away.

In 1876 the Philadelphia Conference of Librarians, resulting in the organization of the American Library Association, impelled Nicholson—aged 27 and completely unknown—to invite British librarians to support a similar venture, with the aim of establishing a Library Association of the United Kingdom. The International Conference of Librarians, held at

Library Association

E. W. B. Nicholson

the London Institution on October 2–5, 1877, and attended by 216, was a great success, particularly because of the American librarians present.

Nicholson and Henry R. Tedder were the main forces behind the Metropolitan Free Libraries Association, whose aim was promoting public libraries in London. Several violent public meetings discouraged them from continuing direct action, and Nicholson and Tedder instead drafted a public libraries bill to make the provision of libraries easier. This bill was introduced in Parliament in 1881, with the support of the Library Association Council, but unsuccessfully. Provincial public librarians resented the fact that the LA was run mainly by London-based nonpublic librarians. The provincial librarians drafted a rival bill, which also failed. These events and the growing belief that the LA was too indolent to encourage new developments in librarianship made Nicholson resign from its Council in 1881. He was never suited to work with people of opposing views.

Bodleian Library. Nicholson's election as Bodley's Librarian in 1882—which forced him to abandon his literary plans—was unexpected, since he lacked scholarship and experience. Although the Curators wanted an energetic person capable of undertaking a large-scale reorganization, their choice of an outsider was ill-received, especially by Sublibrarians Adolf Neubauer and Falconer Madan. However hard Nicholson worked at improving the Bodleian, he worked even harder at arguing against their continual opposition.

Nicholson found the Bodleian in a depressing state: "Always undermanned as it had been, always undermoneyed, and almost always underroomed, its organization, fairly advanced at some points, was in most respects absolutely rudimentary or non-existent" (Bodleian Curators papers, untitled fly-sheet by Nicholson, February 8, 1899). For years the annual income never exceeded £9,000, with expenditure only a little less. Nicholson complained about the Bodleian's poverty to the London *Daily News* in 1894 and at the Bodleian Tercentenary in 1902. His public appeals were vindicated when, from 1907, the Library was aided by Lord Brassey's Oxford University Endowment Fund.

The Bodleian's stock increased from approximately 500,000 to 1,000,000 items under Nicholson, mainly because of rigid enforcement of the legal deposit privilege (he even claimed Valentine cards and tram tickets). He was more parsimonious about purchasing books and manuscripts. Nicholson's weakness was in trying to be a perfectionist; he spent large sums on unnecessary binding and catalogued all acquisitions in detail. Notable accessions included the Saint Margaret's Gospel Book, bought for £6, and a First Folio Shakespeare, acquired after Nicholson raised a public subscription, despite opposition from Library Curators.

Nicholson's most obvious achievements were the underground bookstore—the first constructed on such a scale—and the conversion of the Picture Gallery into the Upper Reading Room, amid tremendous dissension. Nicholson published a cataloguing code in 1883 and devised an elaborate classification scheme. The latter provided the basis for producing "the greatest subject-index the world has ever seen," according to Nicholson (memorandum to the Cura-

tors, February 13, 1909), but lack of money and staff thwarted Nicholson's hopes. Much to Nicholson's mortification, his deputy, Falconer Madan, was authorized in 1890 to commence the abbreviated *Summary Catalogue of Western Manuscripts*. The Bodleian's Oriental catalogues show Nicholson's desire for detailed cataloguing.

Nicholson formed a "Select Library" of open-access reference books, exhibited manuscripts, established a photographic department, and published facsimiles. Yet he encountered opposition over minor matters, such as extending opening hours or the seating and heating arrangements. He employed boys for routine duties and undergraduates for cataloguing. Despite ingrained prejudice, he appointed a female assistant librarian. Duties were recorded in the *Staff-Kalendar,* the first published library manual of its kind.

Nicholson's tenure was marred by perpetual animosity between himself and Madan, who thought that the Library's scholarly calm had been replaced by continual disorganization. The Curators tried to "fetter" Nicholson, as he was fond of saying, but he would not be muzzled. In 1898 he threatened to take them to law if they persisted in persecuting him. Nicholson suffered his first nervous breakdown in 1901 and became increasingly incapable of administration, though he would not admit it. He died in Oxford on March 17, 1912.

REFERENCES
Henry R. Tedder, "E. W. B. Nicholson. . . In Memoriam," *Library Association Record* (March 1914); personal reminiscences by Nicholson's closest Library Association colleague.
Strickland Gibson, "E. W. B. Nicholson (1849–1912): Some Impressions," *Library Association Record* (May 1949); account, by a former colleague, of Nicholson's work at the Bodleian.
Sir Edmund Craster, *History of the Bodleian Library, 1845–1945* (1952; reprinted 1981), pp. 152–245; detailed account of Nicholson's Bodleian work.
K. A. Manley, "Edward Williams Byron Nicholson," *Encyclopedia of Library and Information Science*, volume 19 (1976), includes bibliography of Nicholson's major writings, though he published little on librarianship.
K. A. Manley, "E. W. B. Nicholson and the London Institution," *Journal of Librarianship* (January 1973).
K. A. Manley, "E. W. B. Nicholson and the Bodleian Facsimile Series," *Bodleian Library Record* (June 1977).

K. A. MANLEY

Niger

Niger, a republic of north central Africa, is bordered on the north by Algeria and Libya, on the east by Chad, on the south by Nigeria and Benin, and on the west by Burkina Faso and Mali. Population (1984 est.) 6,278,000; area 1,186,408 sq.km. The official language is French, but Sudanic dialects are widely spoken.

Niger in the mid-1980s did not have a national library, a national bibliography, or a legal deposit system, and there was no library system. There are few libraries in the country.

The Ministère du Plan, founded in February 1976 in Niamey, took over the functions of the Centre de documentation, which was under the

Commissariat général au développement. Its primary function is to gather and conserve documents on Niger, as well as the documents of other countries. Its holdings include some 23,000 items, mainly periodicals and documents. Strongest subjects in the collection are economics, statistics, technical reports of ministries and public and private organizations, and social affairs. The Centre publishes bibliographies and catalogues. The Centre does not function as a national library.

The Archives Nationales in Niamey, founded in 1913, houses a collection of documents through the 19th century.

The Institut de recherches en sciences humaines (IRSH), founded as the Centre IFAN de Niamey in 1944 and later called the Centre nigérien de recherches en sciences humaines (CNRSH), was integrated with the Université de Niamey in 1973. The Institut has a limited scholarly library of about 14,000 volumes. Approximately 60 percent of the collection is in French, and the remainder is in English, Arabic, or African languages. The Institut issues the *Études nigériennes* on an irregular basis, approximately three times a year.

The educational system has not been adequately developed. The Ministry of National Education is responsible for primary schools, secondary schools, and teacher training colleges. Literacy programs are conducted in the major African languages of the country.

There is one university. The Université de Niamey was founded in 1971 and attained university status in 1973. Its Library is that of the IRSH. In addition, it houses about 15,000 volumes.

The École nationale d'administration du Niger was founded in Niamey in 1963 to train civil servants and other officials. Its Library consists of approximately 18,000 volumes and 100 current periodicals.

Special Libraries. Two notable special libraries are those of the Centre régional de recherche et de documentation pour la tradition orale, founded in 1968 in Niamey in cooperation with Unesco, with a collection of approximately 5,000 tape recordings of songs, tales, fables, and other records in the major African languages spoken in Niger; and of the Commission du fleuve Niger (Niger River Commission), founded in 1971 in Niamey. Its documentation center provides abstracting services in agricultural production, stock farming, fish breeding, soil science and geology, and hydrology.

UNESCO/M. d'Hoop

Literacy programs in Niger are conducted in major African languages of the country.

Nigeria

Nigeria, a republic and federation of 19 states and its Federal Capital Territory (Abuja) in West Africa, is bordered by Niger on the north, Chad and Cameroon on the east, the Gulf of Guinea on the south, and Benin on the west. Population (1984 est.) 94,502,000; area 923,800 sq.km. The official language is English, but there are more than 200 indigenous languages.

History and National Library. Nigeria as a political entity emerged in 1914 from the union of Northern and Southern Provinces under the Lugard constitution. It became independent in 1960. There were libraries in the area before independence. Established under the National Library Act of 1964 (superseded by the National Library Act of 1970), the National Library holds approximately 250,000 volumes, including monographs, rare publications of the Colonial Period, and old Nigerian newspaper files, as well as official national periodicals. The Library is the nation's service center for receipt of legal deposits. It compiles and maintains the *National Bibliography of Nigeria*. The Library also maintains the *National Union Catalogue* with more than a million entries on cards (1982). The Serials Data Center, a unit in the National Library, maintains the records.

Academic Libraries. There were 24 university libraries and 65 polytechnic libraries in 1985, including libraries for several Colleges of Education and Colleges of Science and Technology.

Libraries in Nigeria (1978–1979)

Type	Administrative units	Service points	Volumes in collections	Annual expenditures (naira)	Population served	Professional staff	Total staff
National	1	3	199,610	1,679,292	16,893	70	577
Academic	89	80	1,495,764	5,408,570	87,296	258	1,128
Public	56	52	429,767	1,760,500	302,462	128	1,045
School	--	--	--	--	--	--	--
Special	162	133	524,719	1,953,833	29,733	137	589

Source: *National Digest of Library Statistics,* 1978/79.

Students in the library of the Federal Advanced Teacher's College in Lagos.

United Nations

The Ibadan University Library is the oldest and probably holds the largest collection. It contains a notable collection of Africana in addition to an unbroken run of all Nigeriana materials from 1950. Total holdings for all academic libraries were estimated at 2,500,000 in 1982.

Public Libraries. The oldest public libraries in Nigeria are the Lagos Island Local Government Library and the Lagos Subscription Library. Of these two only the Lagos Island Local Government Library still functions as an operating library, although the latter maintains some form of existence.

The real awakening in public library establishment in Nigeria occurred in 1955 with the promulgation of the Eastern Regional Library Act. Fourteen other states promulgated comprehensive library service laws setting up governing boards. All states and the Federal Capital Territory have one form or another of public library system.

Local governments maintain an estimated 300 libraries of varying sizes and quality. Services provided by public libraries include traditional lending and reference services. Mobile library systems exist where the terrain allows such systems, including boatmobile library service in the Niger Delta basin. Book-box service to schools and other institutions is featured in several library systems. Services to patrons in prisons, hospitals, institutions for the blind, and other special locations are rare. It is usual for public libraries to establish book depots that tend to be run on a commercial basis in an effort to ensure good supplies of library materials. Total population served by the public libraries is estimated at less than one million,

largely because of the low literacy rate in the country.

School Libraries. In the early 1960s the federal government inaugurated the School Library Service, and it later handed it on to the Lagos state government in 1965. This Service, which has become the Lagos State Library System, covers public and school libraries.

The University of Ibadan Department of Education founded the Abadina Media Resource Centre for School Libraries in 1970. It serves as a resource center for all school library systems in Oyo and neighboring states. Similarly, school library systems exist in Anambra and Imo states.

School library services are strong enough to form the basis for an Association in each state. In Bendel State the public library system implements the development program of school library services.

Special Libraries. There are more than 10 special libraries that are state owned or government departmental libraries and there are many libraries of private companies, research institutions, and other organizations. Notable are the Central Bank of Nigeria Research Library; the Nigerian Institute of International Affairs Library; the Library of the West African Examinations Council; the Federal Institute of Industrial Research Library, Oshodi; the Geological Survey Library, Kaduna; and libraries of the Federal Department of Forestry, Ibadan; Federal Grains Board, Badege; Veterinary Research Institute, Vom; Administrative Staff College of Nigeria, Topo, Badagry; and Centre for Management Development, Lagos.

The Profession. The Nigerian Library Association, founded in 1962, grew out of the earlier West African Library Association established during the Colonial Period. The Nigerian Library Association is governed by a Council and operates State Chapters known as Divisions. Interest groups form special sections in the Nigerian Library Association while the Council organizes Committees on subjects of interest to the membership.

The official organs of the Association are *Nigerian Libraries, Lagos Librarian,* and *N.L.A. Newsletter.*

J. A. DOSUNMU

Norton, Margaret
(1891-1984)

Margaret Cross Norton, Illinois State Archivist, during a career of more than 35 years, played a leading role in redirecting an emerging archival profession toward public service, entitled to public support, and important for public administration, at a time when many saw care of public records as an adjunct to the primary concerns of the historical profession.

Born in Rockford, Illinois, to Samuel and Jennie Adams Norton, on July 7, 1891, Margaret Norton attended Rockford College and the University of Chicago, where she received a Ph.B. in History in 1913, followed by an M.A. in History in 1914. She then enrolled in the New York State Library School at Albany; after her graduation in 1915, she became a cataloguer at the Vassar College Library. Norton became a cataloguer in the Department of History and Archives of the Indiana State Library in 1918, although she spent the early part of 1919 and the 1919–20 academic year working on a Ph.D. in History at the University of Chicago. Late in 1920 she became Cataloguer for the State Historical Society of Missouri, a position she held until April 1922.

At that time few states had archival programs, although Alabama, Delaware, Mississippi, North Carolina, and South Carolina had established state agencies with archival responsibilities. Several quasi-public state historical societies, including Minnesota and Wisconsin, served as repositories for archival materials; and some state libraries, including Pennsylvania, Texas, and Virginia, had begun to acquire and store permanently valuable public records of their states. In Illinois the Secretary of State had long been legal custodian of the state's records; a Division of Archives and Index was established in his office in 1873, but it became concerned principally with current matters and did not develop along archival lines. In 1921 the legislature created three divisions in the Illinois State Library; on April 1, 1922, Norton became Archivist of Illinois when she was designated Head of the Archives Division.

Using storage space in the state library stacks in the Centennial Building, Norton began to bring together the state's valuable records. Searching through steam tunnels, under the Capitol steps, and in attics, she acquired much of the material. During that period she contributed two volumes of *Illinois Census Returns,* published in 1934 and 1935 as volumes 14 and 16 of the *Collections of the Illinois State Historical Library.*

Norton first attended a meeting of the Public Archives Commission of the American Historical Association in 1923. Established in 1899, the Commission had as its goal the establishment of a national archives to facilitate the research of historians. Seven years later she became a member of the Commission, continuing until it was replaced by the Society of American Archivists (SAA) in 1936. A charter member of the SAA, she served as its first Vice-President, and in 1937 she became a Council member. She was elected fourth President of SAA, serving from 1943 to 1945, and in 1946 she began a two-year term as Editor of *American Archivist.*

At the same time, she became active in the National Association of State Libraries; she served as Secretary-Treasurer for five years beginning in 1933. She had served earlier as Chairman of an Archives Committee with members Charles B. Galbreath (Ohio) and George S. Godard (Connecticut). That Committee soon became inactive, and in 1935 an Archives and Libraries Committee was created with Norton first as a member and then as Chairman for 1942. Thus, for a period of more than 10 years, she was one of the links between the National Association of State Libraries and the ALA on the one hand and the Public Archives Commission of the American Historical Association and the Society of American Archivists on the other.

As early as 1930, Norton warned against allowing historians to preempt the field of archival care and preservation. She pointed out that public records were the product of governmental activity and were primarily designed to serve governmental needs. Speaking before the National Association of State Librarians in 1930, she asserted that the proper care of archives was an administrative concern of state government and not merely an adjunct to the historical field. "The archivist," she maintained, "should be a public official whose first interest is business efficiency, and only secondarily should he be interested in history. If the public records are cared for in a way that preserves their proper provenance, the historian not only of today but also of tomorrow will be as well served as the public official."

Seven years later she repeated the principle of the value of archives for administrative purposes: "An archives department is the governmental agency charged with the duty of planning and supervising the preservation of all those records of the business transactions of its government required by law or other legal implication to be preserved indefinitely."

The 1930s were doubly important to Norton's professional career. First, the state arsenal adjacent to the Capitol grounds in Springfield burned in 1934; responding to the outcry of patriotic and veterans organizations, the 1935 General Assemby appropriated money for a state archives building, and additional funds were obtained from the Public Works Administration. The building was dedicated during the Second Annual Meeting of the SAA in 1938. In the same year, the reorganization of the Illinois State Library began; it was completed in 1939 with the revision of the State Library Act. As a result of the reorganization, *Illinois Libraries,* formerly a publication of the Library Extension Division, became the official publication of the state library, and Norton became a regular contributor. The section initially entitled "The Archives of Illinois" and, after March 1942, "Illinois Archival Information" comprised what Ernst Posner called "the first American manual of archives administration." Articles were appearing elsewhere, but Norton's writings in *Illinois Libraries* specifically addressed the problems of the state archivist. Although devoted to the principles and philosophy of archival administration, they were based to a large extent on her own practical experience. She wrote at a time when the only discussions of archival practice originated in European experience, and her articles made *Illinois Libraries* essential reading for archivists. Norton also published articles in the *American Archivist* and in publications of the National Association of State Libraries and ALA.

After 1947 Norton wrote infrequently for *Illinois Libraries.* Her last article appeared in October 1956, when she discussed the relationship between the archivist and the records manager—a discussion that raised certain questions that are still debated.

Margaret Cross Norton retired as Illinois State Archivist on April 15, 1957. Her career spanned more than 35 years, the climax of which was a successful statewide records management survey. She died on May 21, 1984.

REFERENCE

Thornton W. Mitchell, editor, *Norton on Archives: The Writings of Margaret Cross Norton on Archival and Records Management* (1975).

THORNTON W. MITCHELL

Illinois State Archives
Margaret Cross Norton

Norway

Norway, a constitutional monarchy in northern Europe, lies in the western section of the Scandinavian Peninsula. The Artic Ocean lies to the north, Finland and the U.S.S.R. to the extreme northeast, Sweden to the east, and the Atlantic Ocean and the North Sea to the west. Population (1984 est.) 4,141,000; area 323,895 sq.km. The official language is Norwegian.

History. The first seeds of library activities were in the course of formation during the Age of the Enlightenment (17th and 18th centuries). First and foremost were reading associations, established mainly in towns. In the rural areas, libraries aimed at enlightening the peasants were founded.

In 1760 the Royal Norwegian Society of Sciences and Letters (Det Kongelige Norske Videnskabers Selskab) was established, and gradually the Society obtained a considerable collection of books. The Royal University Library of Oslo (founded 1812), however, later became the main library in the country.

The development of reading associations and public libraries in the rural areas was continued by the Society for the Benefit of Norway (Det kgl. Selskab for Norges Vel) and Henrik Wergeland, Ole Vig, and Eilert Sundt were among those eager to support the foundation of public libraries. A pioneer in Norway was Haakon Nyhuus. Taking inspiration from the establishment of public libraries in the United States, he transformed the Oslo City Library (Deichmanske bibliotek) into a modern public library during the years from 1897 to 1913. The library reform of 1902 laid down guidelines aimed at creating standards for public libraries. That reform also was a forerunner for the Norwegian Library Bureau (A/L Biblioteksentralen). The first Public Library Act came into force in 1935 but public libraries did not become compulsory in every municipality until the Act of 1947.

National Library Services. In Norway the tasks of a national library are dealt with by the Royal University Library in Oslo (Universitets-biblioteket i Oslo). It has had the right to legal deposits throughout its existence (from 1812) with the exception of the years between 1839 and 1882. The act of legal deposits of 1882 was revised in 1939.

The national collections contain, besides books and serials, music, maps, and materials such as manuscripts and pictures connected with the country's outstanding personalities.

The Norwegian national bibliography (*Norsk bokfortegnelse*) is published by the Royal University Library in Oslo and is also available on microfiche.

Norway's nine archival institutions, according to the Director of the National Archives, held 82,300 linear meters of materials in 1983, and annual expenditures totaled 28,250,000 kroner. The total staff numbered 131 (67 professionals). In addition, there is the Archive of the Labour Movement.

Academic Libraries. Academic libraries comprise those attached to the universities, those belonging to state colleges, and libraries serving the regional colleges. The four university libraries, in Oslo, Bergen, Trondheim, and Tromsø, have a number of branch libraries administered centrally but housed with various faculties and institutes.

The Royal University Library in Oslo dates back to 1812, when the first Norwegian university was established, but the Library only became fully operational several years later. Donations in the 1820s resulted in a collection of about 60,000 volumes, which had grown to 4,000,000 by the end of 1982.

The Library has from its beginnings served wider interests than those of the Oslo University teaching staff and students, being the largest of its kind in the country—it holds almost 40 percent of all research literature in Norway. While not officially designated as a clearinghouse, the Library handles a large number of international loans.

The main library building is far from the university campus, requiring the creation of faculty libraries at the campus. The central functions (budget, staff, and catalogue) are still in the hands of the university, which receives occasional state grants to allow it to fulfill its national tasks. A report of a departmental committee in 1984 proposed new and more comprehensive legislation on legal deposits and recommended the establishment of an independent national library.

The Tromsø University Library is the youngest and the smallest of the four university libraries. The Trondheim University Library operates two departments, one for humanities, the other for science and technology—a distinction caused by historical development. The University Library in Bergen is based on the Bergen Museum, founded in 1825 (the University was established in 1948). Large parts of the holdings in university libraries necessarily duplicate each other, but efforts toward coordinating acquisition of periodicals have been made.

Other academic libraries attached to colleges cover the fields of commerce, agriculture, and theology. Regional colleges, of which there were 13 in the country in the mid-1980s, represent a venture in decentralizing education. Their libraries had to be built up from scratch in most cases but have received increased attention, reflected in better budgets. The subjects that the libraries cover are somewhat different from traditional university subjects, which in due time should give rise to specialized collections.

Public Libraries. Through library legislation public libraries have been compulsory in every municipality since 1947. There were in all 1,373 public library units in 1984. Because of the geographical

Vestre Toten Public Library, Raufoss.

Vestre Toten Public Library

structure and the scattered population pattern, it is nevertheless difficult in practice to reach every inhabitant. Outreach service is provided through bookmobiles and a bookboat along the coast.

According to the Library Act of 1971, municipalities are obliged to give financial support to the libraries. The act also requires the fulfillment of certain requirements in order to receive Government grants (a management plan, approved premises, professional qualification, guidelines, and so on). The state grants vary according to the financial situation in the municipalities.

The act was under revision in 1984 as part of a proposed new financial system. Under the new plan, the Government would make lump-sum grants to the municipalities and counties, instead of special-purpose grants. The new plan contains no economic regulations, and guidelines and standards must henceforth be worked out separately.

County Libraries. There are 20 county libraries to supplement the public and school libraries in their districts with books either from their own collections or from other libraries through an interlibrary loan scheme. They also give professional advice to the libraries, many of which are run by part-time librarians. The county libraries in 1984 were entitled to state grants as well as financial support from the county authorities. Plans called for that to be changed in the same way as for the municipalities.

School Libraries. Such libraries are compulsory in elementary schools, and there were more than 3,700 school libraries in Norway in the mid-1980s. A certain amount per pupil for books must be granted from the municipality, which again is entitled to Government grants. The amount is given according to the same percentage scale as that for public libraries. The school libraries, according to the new proposal, would not be included in the same act but would be placed under the act for primary education. State grants would thereafter be amalgamated into the lump-sum grants for educational purposes.

Special Libraries. These belong to both state and private institutions and range in magnitude, with a few exceptions, from about 5,000 to 50,000 volumes. The best known among the exceptions are the Library of the Parliament (Stortingsbiblioteket), the Nobel Library, and the Library of the Central Bureau

of Statistics. Some of the smaller ones either endeavor to cover a more modern subject in depth, as does the Library of the Atomic Institute, or follow up a line of traditional interest, such as the library of the Whaling Museum. All are primarily oriented to serve their principal institutions, but their collections are also accessible to others through interlibrary loans.

Library Institutions. The National Office for Research and Special Libraries (Riksbibliotektjenesten) was established in 1969 and charged with coordinating the functions of academic as well as special libraries. It is headed by the National Librarian and had a staff of 14 in 1984.

The main tasks of the State Directorate for Public and School Libraries (Statens bibliotektilsyn) are to supervise, control, and advise public and school libraries in accordance with the Library Act; to assist and advise the Ministry in matters concerning public and school libraries; and to work for further development and strengthening of library activities in the whole spectrum of cultural work.

The Norwegian Library Bureau (A/L Biblioteksentralen) was inaugurated as a cooperative society on February 4, 1952. The state, the local authorities, and the Norwegian Library Association jointly own the Bureau. It is a service institution for public and school libraries of Norway, enjoined with the tasks of providing books, binding, library material and equipment, and bibliographic aids.

The Profession. The Norwegian School of Library and Information Science gives a three-year course of study at the university level. In addition it offers courses of various lengths for trained and part-time librarians.

The Norwegian Library Association (Norsk bibliotekforening), founded in 1913, has sections for various types of librarians and the various types of libraries. It had 2,800 individual members and 600 institutional members in 1983.

The Norwegian Association of Special Libraries (Norsk fagbibliotekforening), founded in 1948, had 750 members in 1984. The two Associations for Public Library Employees had 770 and 600 members respectively in 1984. The Norwegian Part-Time Librarians' Union (Norske Deltidsbibliotekarers Yrkeslag), founded in 1963, had 440 members in 1984.

ELSE GRANHEIM

Libraries in Norway (1982)

Type	Administrative units	Service points	Volumes in collections	Annual expenditures (krone)	Professional staff	Total staff
National	3	3	1,911,000	6,900,000[a]	99	149
Academic	206	--	6,092,000	29,636,000[a]	282	421
Public[d]	454	1,395	16,501,771	69,915,111[a]	--	2,868[b]
School[b,d]	454	3,777[c]	6,585,749	17,248,013[a]	--	--
Special	218	--	4,750,000	28,108,000[a]	329	537

[a]Books, periodicals, and binding only.
[b]Full-time and part-time employees.
[c]Primary schools only.
[d]1984 data.

Sources: *Annual Report: National Library Directorate and Statistical Yearbook; Statistical Yearbook*, 1983.

Ogunsheye, Felicia Adetowun
(1926-)

Felicia Adetowun Ogunsheye, educator and author, became the first Nigerian head of a library school.

She was born on December 5, 1926, in Nigeria, attended elementary school in various parts of the country, and took her secondary school education in Queen's College, Lagos, from 1939 to 1945. She proceeded to the Higher College, Lagos, where she obtained a Teaching Diploma in 1949. She attended Newham College, Cambridge, where she was graduated with a B.A. with honors in Geography in 1952, followed by an M.A. at the same university in 1956.

She married Ayo Ogunsheye, an economist and at one time a faculty member of the University of Ibadan, and started her working life as a teacher, first in high schools for girls and later in the Nigerian College of Science and Technology, 1956–57. She joined the University of Ibadan Library as Assistant Librarian in charge of maps in 1958 and took charge of the African and Map Collection in 1960.

At Simmons College, Boston, Massachusetts, she earned a Master's degree in Library Science in 1962. She returned to her post, finding time to lecture in a new Institute of Librarianship. In 1963 she became a full-time lecturer and was named Senior Lecturer. Ogunsheye was appointed Acting Director in 1970. When the Institute was redesignated the Department of Library Studies, she became the first Head, rising in rank to Professor in 1973. From 1977 she served as Dean of the Faculty of Education of the University.

In the field of bibliography, her studies and publications are extensive. She initiated the Abadina Media Research Project, a pilot library set up on the campus of Ibadan University for the children of Abadina, a satellite village created for the low-income, nonacademic staff of the University, providing direct library services and facilities for the children and offering research facilities. The center is headquarters of the Nigerian School Library Association, of which Ogunsheye became President.

A member of the Council of the Nigerian Library Association, she was Vice-President, Acting President, and President in succession in the years 1966 to 1971, which included the Nigerian Civil War years of 1967 to 1970.

She served on many committees, panels, and boards, including the National Library Board of Nigeria, and from 1971 participated regularly in the activities of IFLA, serving on some of the Standing Advisory Committees.

A tireless organizer, she played a key role in making the Department of Library Studies of the University of Ibadan an active center of the pursuit of knowledge in librarianship. She also became President of the Association of African Library Schools. She was first Secretary of the Nigerian Council of Women Societies and West African Council of Women Societies. She served as President of the Women's Improvement Society and the Nigerian Society of University Women. Simmons College awarded her an honorary doctoral degree, and she received the International Alumni Award (1979).

S. B. AJE

Daniel Bernstein, Waltham, MA

Felicia Adetowun Ogunsheye

Oman

The Sultanate of Oman occupies the southeast corner of the Arabian Peninsula and is the second largest country in that area. Population (1980 est.) 1,500,000; area 300,000 sq.km. Arabic is the official language, but English is widely understood.

History. The interior of the country remains a source of traditional cultural influence, but the coastal regions reflect the diversified and cosmopolitan interests of a mercantile people. Many of the country's mosques contain religious books deposited as endowments.

In 1977 a royal decree was issued to promote the recovery and preservation of the estimated 30,000 manuscripts in private collections. About 4,000 had been collected by 1985. They are being carefully conserved and catalogued in the Ministry of National Heritage and Culture, which also contains a Documentation Centre dedicated to preserving current sources of information about the Sultanate.

There is no designated National Library, but a 1984 royal decree promulgating a Press and Publications Law requires those who issue or import printed matter to deposit as many as five copies with the Ministry of Information.

Academic Libraries. The Library of Sultan Qaboos University in al-Khawdh was designed as the largest in the country at the time of its opening, in 1986. Its opening day collection of about 25,000 titles in European languages and Arabic included works in a variety of media. It was designed as a completely automated facility with an online public access catalogue. The Oman Technical and Industrial College Library in al-Khuwair is the only other substantial collection of academic interest.

Public Library Services. The only public library in Oman is the Islamic Library in an attractive new building in Ruwi, the main commercial center. It has a collection of about 20,000 volumes and includes a Children's Section. In the capital area both the British Council and the United States Information Service maintain well-stocked reading rooms and reference facilities.

School Libraries. Social development became a government priority with the accession of Sultan Qaboos bin Said in 1970. Thereafter the number of schools rose dramatically from three to more than 500 by the mid-1980s; adult literacy courses are taught in about 1,300 centers. The Ministry of Education distributes books to school libraries. The Sultan's School in Seeb also maintains a well-stocked library.

Special Libraries. These exist in several government ministries, such as Education and Health. There are also special library collections in other government-supported agencies, among them the Institute for Public Administration, the Development Council, the Oman Centre for Traditional Music, and the Omani Women's Association.

The Profession. There is no library association in Oman since there were, as of the mid-1980s, very few professionally trained librarians working in the country. Education for librarianship is likely to be introduced at Sultan Qaboos University by the 1990s as Oman continues its drive toward full development of its resources.

REFERENCES

Joachim Düster and Fred Scholz, *Bibliographie über das Sultanat Oman* (1980).

Bruno and Colette LeCour Grandmaison, *Contribution to a General Bibliography of Oman* (1980).

Frank A. Clements, *Oman* (1981), issued as volume 29 in the World Bibliographical Series.

"Oman," an illustrated pamphlet issued annually by the Ministry of Information.

Oman: a MEED Practical Guide, issued periodically by the *Middle East Economic Digest* in London.

MARTHA L. P. DUKAS

Online Information Services

Online information services, like general reference services, are resources that provide answers or references to answers, but with greater flexibility, precision, and speed than similar print resources can. They open comprehensive stores of information to anyone with a computer terminal. It is no coincidence that such services were first used and nurtured by libraries and are still associated with the provision of reference services in libraries.

HISTORY

Online information services were developed as a means to facilitate the search of bibliographic citations. In "Online Systems: History, Technology, and Economics," in the *Journal of the American Society for Information Science* (May 1980), Charles Bourne observed that "an investigation of online bibliographic searching was first made by Bagley in 1951" with the development of a program for the MIT computer "to search encoded abstracts." Bourne noted that "application of the computer to bibliographic searching was first demonstrated in 1954 in the form of batch searching."

Over the next 10 years, numerous research and development efforts culminated in the development of "batch" searches of bibliographic databases offered by a limited number of special libraries. Search analysts coded requests sent to them for literature searches. Several searches were then batched, or run consecutively, to make the most efficient use of the computer's time. Several weeks generally passed before the requestor received any result. One batch, retrospective search service, the Medical Literature Analysis and Retrieval System (MEDLARS) of the National Library of Medicine (NLM), was made available to the general public in 1964. Several years and a complete generation of computing ability would pass before the powerful systems that people can immediately interact with were developed.

SDC Information Services. Systems Development Corporation (SDC) demonstrated the first interactive online system, Protosynthex, developed by Robert Simons and John Olney, in 1960. Using a terminal wired directly to the computer, Protosynthex allowed access to the full text of the *Golden Book Encyclopedia* with the ability to search for the occurrence of terms in proximity with each other and to search for truncated forms of words, but not to combine terms with the use of Boolean logic.

Another online retrieval system was developed at SDC in late 1964 by Harold Borko, H. P. Burnaugh, and W. H. Moore. The system, Bibliographic Organization for Library Display (BOLD), was developed for browsing of literature citations on magnetic tapes. It was first publicly demonstrated about a year later and was one of the first systems capable of displaying an online thesaurus. In November 1964 SDC first demonstrated an online system that nearly achieved the interactive capability today's users enjoy, Language Used to Communicate Information System Design (LUCID), developed for SDC by E. Franks and P. A. DeSimone.

"The first demonstration of an online retrieval network, on a national scale," according to Bourne, "was probably made in 1965 by SDC in an experiment . . . to provide 13 organizations with access to some 200,000 bibliographic records on foreign technology." This work was done by SDC-Dayton for the Foreign Technology Division of Wright-Patterson Air Force Base, Ohio.

SDC was instrumental in the development of NLM's online information service, MEDLARS ONLINE (MEDLINE). In late 1967 NLM experimented with SDC's Online Retrieval of Bibliographic Information Timeshared (ORBIT) retrieval language to search NLM's database of 10,000 citations on neurology. In May 1970 SDC began operating the Abridged Index Medicus (AIM)/TWX online information system on behalf of NLM. In October 1970 NLM introduced MEDLINE as a free service on its own computer facilities with a database of more than 400,000 citations while allowing the AIM/TWX service to continue with SDC. In February 1972 NLM utilized TYMNET, the first public telecommunication network, for access to MEDLINE.

NLM introduced a modified version of ORBIT for the ELHILL retrieval language used in MEDLINE; the H. W. Wilson Company also adopted a version of ORBIT for the retrieval language used in its WILSONLINE service, inaugurated in 1984.

SDC Search Services was made commercially available in December 1972 as an online information service using the ORBIT retrieval language, Carlos A. Cuadra serving as its manager for several years. The service, later named SDC Information Services, offered more than 60 databases in the mid-1980s with strengths in petroleum, energy, patents, chemistry, and science and technology.

DIALOG Information Services. Roger K. Summit of Lockheed Missiles and Space Corporation first demonstrated the ability to search an in-house database of the Lockheed library catalogue file in 1961. Summit designed the DIALOG language in 1962 at the Lockheed Information Sciences Laboratory in Palo Alto, California, while "working on only the third IBM 360 produced," according to Marjorie Hlava in an article "The NASA Information System":

> In 1964, after some discussion with Mel Day of NASA, Summit prepared a proposal to NASA to use DIALOG for the automation of the NASA information system. NASA responded by issuing a Request for Proposal to develop a NASA/RECON prototype. Lockheed and several other companies bid the proposal.

Although it lost the first bid, in July 1966, Lockheed won a contract to demonstrate an online system for the search and retrieval of more than 300,000 bibliographic citations of NASA, an effort that utilized the DIALOG retrieval language. Lockheed began providing a regular online search service to the NASA Ames Laboratory in November 1966 and later to other NASA facilities. "By 1970," Bourne notes, "a version of the DIALOG system was being operated by NASA, the system serving 24 terminals in NASA facilities across the country from a file that had grown to 700,000 records." NASA's Remote Console Information Retrieval Service (RECON) was installed at its Scientific and Technical Information Facility in Maryland to serve all major NASA research centers through a telephone communication network.

Subsequent contracts resulted in application of the DIALOG language to bibliographic databases of the Atomic Energy Commission, the European Space and Research Organization, the U.S. Office of Education, and the National Technical Information Service. In March 1969, for example, the ERIC Clearinghouse at Stanford demonstrated the use of DIALOG with an ERIC database of 415,000 citations. In the same year, DIALOG was installed on the European Space Agency's online system.

Lockheed's information service became commercially available in 1972 under the name of its retrieval language, DIALOG Information Retrieval Service, with two bibliographic databases of scientific and technical information. By 1985 DIALOG had become the most comprehensive online information service in the world, with more than 200 separate databases in business and economics, chemical, patent and trademark information, science and technology, medicine and the biosciences, news and current events, education, directories, energy and the environment, law and government, computer science and microcomputers, books, the social sciences, and the humanities.

Mead Data Central (MDC). Mead is primarily associated with the full-text, online information services it created for primary sources in law and legal research. This service was introduced commercially in 1972 as LEXIS. Mead introduced NEXIS, a full text information service for news and current events, in 1980, and MEDIS, for medicine, in 1985.

LEXIS was the product of an effort funded by the Ohio Bar Association between 1968 and 1970 to make Ohio case law searchable online. This effort of the Ohio Bar Automated Research (OBAR) group and the Data Corporation developed the first extensive full-text search capability. In 1968 Data Corporation was acquired by the Mead Corporation; in 1970 Mead Data Central, Inc. (MDC), was formed as a subsidiary of the Mead Corporation with Don Wilson and Gerry Rubin as its chief executive officers.

Mead initially fostered the use of its full text databases through dedicated, custom terminals. It later allowed them to be searched with such microcomputers as the IBM PC and the Apple MacIntosh, using software it specifies.

Mead also offers full-text databases licensed from other producers such as the Encyclopaedia Britannica, the New York Times Online, and the National Automated Accounting Research System (NAARS). In 1985 Mead also introduced several bibliographic databases through its Reference Service.

Bibliographic Retrieval Services (BRS). BRS had its origins in the State University of New York (SUNY) Biomedical Communications Network (BCN). During a conference in Oxford, England, on the mechanization of library services in June 1966, Irwin Pizer described plans for the SUNY online information network. BCN began in October 1968, with online searches of the MEDLARS database for nine medical libraries, using a modified version of the IBM Document Processing System as the basis of its retrieval system. "In 1973," according to Bourne, "BCN adopted the IBM STAIRS system, added additional databases in subject areas other than medicine, and expanded to incorporate 32 member libraries." In May 1977 BRS became commercially available and BCN ceased.

BRS took a direct approach to soliciting suggestions from its user community through its User Advisory Board and its subcommittees on database selection and technical features. BRS grew by 1985 to include 73 separate databases in the life sciences, medicine and pharmacology; the physical and applied sciences; education; the social sciences and humanities; and business.

CAS ONLINE. This service is an outgrowth of the publishing efforts of one of the largest professional societies in the U.S. The American Chemical Society (ACS) began publishing its index to the chemical literature, *Chemical Abstracts,* in 1907. The Society founded the Chemical Abstracts Service (CAS) division in 1956 to manage the publication. In the late 1960s CAS developed an automated processing system and began building a database to improve text editing and formatting. CAS introduced CAS ONLINE in November 1980 as an online dictionary of chemical substances; it expanded in late 1983 to include the database of *Chemical Abstracts* citations dating back to 1967. CAS made available several million unlicensed abstracts for citations in that database on CAS ONLINE only. In 1984 ACS and West Germany's Fachinformaszentrum Energie, Physik, Mathematik (FIZ Karlsruhe) joined their online information services to form STN International (The Scientific and Technical Information Network).

Pergamon INFOLINE. In the late 1970s a consortium of British producers of scientific, technical, and patent databases created INFOLINE, unsuccessfully planning to develop it as an online information service. INFOLINE was purchased by Pergamon Press, a British publisher of scientific journals and catalogues. After its advent as Pergamon INFOLINE in 1981, the service grew to include 33 separate databases by 1985. INFOLINE's strength is patent, scientific and technical, and business information, especially for companies in the U.K. Its typesetting and index production capability have enabled it to undertake comprehensive database production, such as the conversion to a bibliographic database of the British Patent Office Archives dating back to 1910.

BIBLIOGRAPHIC AND FULL-TEXT DATABASES

The mechanics of online information services involve use of a computer terminal or microcomputer to interact with a remote database, or an organized collection of information in machine-readable form, through a telecommunications line or enhanced phone connection. The wider distribution in recent years of terminals and telecommunication services has channeled online information services into such non-library environments as offices, hospital emergency rooms, and homes. Librarians and information specialists, along with economists, financial analysts, business planners, engineers, chemists, researchers in the social sciences, educators, lawyers, physicians, and a host of other professional people, now rely on online information services.

Online information services may be defined simplistically as the use of computer technology to facilitate reference work. The service offered is unchanged from that of general reference services in libraries; expectations concerning a reference tool as set forth by William Katz in the first volume of his *Introduction to Reference Work* apply equally to online information services:

When the layman thinks in terms of a reference work, it is in terms of questions and answers. He has a question. He expects the librarian to give him an answer or, at a minimum, show him where the answer may be found. Disengaged from the necessary variables, reference work may be defined simply as the process of answering questions.

Proponents of online information services such as Ron Dunn and Harry Boyle offer the same explanation in their article "On-Line Searching: Costly or Cost-Effective?" outside the context of reference services:

Online services are not valuable in and of themselves. They merely add value to existing information through improved packaging and distribution. . . . online services are used because they provide access to information, and it is information that users want and need (*Journal of Chemical Information and Computer Sciences*, May 1984, pp 51–54).

Databases available through online information services fall roughly into the two categories of *bibliographic* databases (which at a minimum show where the answer can be found) and databases in which the source document itself can be found.

Bibliographic Databases. Bibliographic databases individually offer hundreds of thousands of references to several years of published literature in a subject discipline. References cite the author, title, and source; many include indexing and an abstract that serve to identify an article, book, or paper. Many references also cite other forms of literature, such as patents, in which the inventor serves as the author and the primary claim serves as the abstract.

An information need can sometimes be satisfied by bibliographic databases alone if sufficient summary information has been extracted from the source document into the abstract; however, document ordering services have also emerged as a growing service industry, supplying copies of original source documents to users of bibliographic databases. Presearch interviews continue to be held as a matter of policy between the librarian and the requestor to emphasize, among other things, that searches of bibliographic databases yield references to source documents rather than the source documents themselves.

The image of online information services has suffered to some extent from overidentification with bibliographic databases. For example, in his 1977 essay "Libraries in the Information Marketplace" in the book *Libraries in Post-Industrial Society*, Kas Kalba wrote:

The online retrieval services that exist today are essentially in the accessing business rather than in the convenience business. What they offer is rapid access to citations and abstracts from a particular data base.

Kalba's remark reflects the popularity and availability of bibliographic databases among search service vendors at that time. Source databases, such as numeric databases, have been equally available, but their distribution has not been as wide as that of bibliographic databases. Ching-chih Chen observed in *Numeric Databases* (1984) that "at present, librarians have not demonstrated the same acceptance and enthusiasm for numeric databases as they have expressed for bibliographic ones." Susan Meschel observed in her paper "Numeric Databases in the Sciences" that "many of the services that make numeric databases available market 1 to 5 files on the average" (*National Online Meeting Proceedings*, 1984). Other types of source databases, such as those offering directory information for business and marketing research and those offering the complete text of source documents, were emerging at the time of that observation.

Full-Text Databases. Full-text databases provide the complete text of a source document in addition to the citation and indexing found in bibliographic databases. Full-text databases offer the obvious advantage of immediate availability of the complete text of a source document. However, the ability to search the complete text of documents online for names, terms, or concepts not identified in the citation or indexing is often the greatest asset of these databases as vehicles to locate information.

Mead Data Central first made the full text of cases and statutes related to state and federal law available in 1973 through its LEXIS service. LEXIS is one of several online services that offer the complete text of important source documents in law and legal research, along with the full text of Shepard's Citations and Matthew Bender's legal treatises. The West Publishing Company offers a service, WESTLAW, with the full text of those sources and West's own indexing. The impetus for the development of such services did not arise out of a need for the ready availability of the source document, but rather, as Allan Onove explained in "A Comparison of the LEXIS and WESTLAW Databases" (*Legal Economics*, April 1983), "from the legal profession's need for more effective, less time-consuming ways of locating relevant precedents."

The demand for the complete text of sources for news and current events was first addressed by the New York Times Company. The New York Times Information Service first offered the complete text of the newspaper online with the June 1, 1980, issue, as part of its INFORMATION BANK online service. In February 1983 MDC offered the complete text of the *Times* through its NEXIS service, modeled after its full-text LEXIS service. NEXIS had been offering the full text of other newspapers, as well as magazines, wire services, and newsletters, since 1980. By 1985 the complete text of newspaper and magazine articles and newswires was offered not only by NEXIS but also by Information Access Corporation through its MAGAZINE ASAP and TRADE AND INDUSTRY ASAP databases on DIALOG. The two major wire services, UPI and AP, made the complete text of their wire services available through vendors such as DIALOG and Dow Jones.

Three major news companies, Knight-Ridder, Times Mirror, and Gannett, have produced their own online information services. Knight-Ridder's VU/TEXT contains the full text of many major newspapers, stock quote services, and bibliographic databases in business. Gannett's USA TODAY UPDATE offers national and international news, business and financial information, and industry reports in technology, banking, law, energy, insurance, and travel. In April 1985 the British Broadcasting Corporation (BBC) introduced WORLD REPORTER, which features the full text of the BBC and AP news services.

NewsNet began its venture into electronic publishing in 1982 by offering 17 online newsletters; it would be a misnomer to refer to this as a full-text service insofar as the newsletters have no printed counterparts. Approximately 250 newsletters were available by May 1985; an *IDP Report* of September 14, 1984, listed telecommunications, investment, electronics and computers, and publishing and broadcasting as the subject headings that appear most often among these newsletters.

In business and financial information, DIALOG introduced the complete text of financial research reports from leading investment banking firms through the INVESTEXT database in 1984. In the same year MDC began offering the complete text of research reports written by security analysts and economists through its EXCHANGE service. The complete text of *Commerce Business Daily,* a major publication for any business or organization that does business with the U.S. government, is available on DIALOG. The complete text of the *Harvard Business Review* dating back to 1976, with citations as far back as 1971, is produced in machine-readable form by John Wiley and Sons, and is offered by DIALOG and BRS.

In the sciences and medicine, BRS announced in April 1980 that it was experimenting with a "private test database of the full text of approximately 1,000 articles from the *Journal of Medicinal Chemistry*" in cooperation with the American Chemical Society (ACS). In 1983 BRS offered the full text of 32 medical journals in its IRCS MEDICAL SCIENCE database and the full text of 18 chemistry journals in its ACS JOURNALS FULLTEXT database. In the same year, BRS introduced the full text of the 24-volume Kirk-Othmer *Encyclopedia of Chemical Technology.*

Early in 1984 BRS began offering the complete text of reference books and journals in internal medicine, pharmacology, and critical care and emergency medicine as part of its COLLEAGUE service, targeted toward physicians and other health care professionals. The Critical Care Medical Library of COLLEAGUE contains the full texts of 18 medical textbooks.

Many standard encyclopedias, including the *Academic American, Everyman's,* and *Encyclopaedia Britannica,* are also online.

OTHER DATABASES

Numeric Databases. Numeric databases, also variously known as *fact, source,* and *non-bibliographic databases, datafiles,* and *databanks,* provide organized numeric data such as statistics, time series, demographic reports, corporate financial records, stock market quotations, chemical and physical properties, and chemical nomenclature and graphic structures. Most of these databases are used in support of business or financial research; the smaller percentage of numeric databases of physical and chemical properties are used in the physical and biological sciences.

Most numeric databases can be manipulated interactively by their users. In economic forecasting or market research, this data is *post-processed,* or manipulated after the information has been identified and captured from an online service, generally on a microcomputer. In the sciences, however, the key to retrieving the information is *pre-processing* the data, as in identifying three-dimensional structures and plotting physical data.

Business Numeric Databases. Numeric databases that support economic forecasting and market research are found on major online services and feature the ability to post-process this information. They include Dow Jones News/Retrieval, I. P. Sharp Associates Limited, Chase Econometrics/Interactive Data Corporation, Data Resources, Inc., and DIALOG.

Dow Jones News/Retrieval, which began in 1974 as a stock-quote service for brokers and professional investors, offers such information as current and historical stock quotes, current and historical Dow Jones averages, a weekly survey of U.S. money market and foreign exchange trends, and earnings forecasts for U.S. companies. Dow Jones has developed software packages to manipulate such data by collecting and storing it, performing any of 17 standard technical analyses on it, and transferring it into spreadsheet programs.

I. P. Sharp is a Canadian computer time-sharing company that began offering online databases in 1970. Sharp has more than 100 databases in aviation, economics, energy, finance, and actuarial information. The databases include text only where needed to clarify the numeric data. Sharp's software allows data to be manipulated and is also available for use on microcomputers.

Chase Econometrics/Interactive Data Corporation was established in 1971 to produce economic forecasts based on econometric models and has expanded its services to offer economic, financial, and demographic data from nearly every country in the world. Subscribers to Chase services can receive software developed by Chase for simulations, forecasting, and analysis of this data.

Data Resources, Inc. (DRI), offers national economic models of countries throughout the world and 17,000,000 time series covering U.S. national and regional, international, industrial, energy, and financial data. DRI offers its software for report writing, analytic data manipulation, and graphic display of this data. Portions of that data are sold separately on disk for manipulation with VisiCalc spreadsheet software.

Business numeric databases on DIALOG include time series, forecasts, and census-related data. Databases of time series or tables of historical data and projected forecasts of data for the economies of the U.S. and for other countries are produced by Predicasts. The Bureau of Labor Statistics offers three databases of time series for the U.S. (the producer price index, the consumer price index, and employment, hours of work, and earnings information) on DIALOG. Data from the 1980 census, current estimates, and five-year projections for demographic characterisitics of geographic regions of the U.S. are offered through the Donnelley Demographics database on DIALOG.

Non-bibliographic Databases in Chemistry. Questions raised in chemical and patent information depend heavily on non-bibliographic data for utmost precision in searching bibliographic databases. The large number of numeric databases in the physical sciences identify chemical compounds by structure, mass spectra, and other properties. In "A Review of Online Physical Sciences and Mathematics Databases. Part 2: Chemistry," (*Database,* June 1985), Donald Hawkins explained that "chemical name dictionaries and substructure searching systems are important because of the wide variety of chemical substances that exist and because classes of substances with similar structures are often of interest to chemists." Keyword searches of bibliographic databases in chemistry are effective in locating citations where the search terms are found in the title or indexing. However, the location of citations dealing with specific chemical substances is best achieved through the use of databases that serve as dictionaries of unique chemical substances, identified in the chemical literature and indexed by the American Chemical Society (ACS).

DIALOG made a significant contribution to the effective use of chemical information online as the first service to create large-scale dictionary databases containing every class of chemical substances. The registry numbers uniquely identify a substance in these dictionary databases and can be transferred to the bibliographic databases to identify citations indexed with the registry number for the substance in question.

Graphics capabilities have been introduced for sophisticated display-screen terminals, allowing for display of two- or three-dimensional chemical structure diagrams to identify chemical substances and the bibliographic citations that discuss those substances. In her previously cited paper, Susan Meschel explained the significance of graphic-display capability:

> One of the primary concerns in chemistry is identifying an active core of a compound regardless of additional groups connected to the molecules. This type of problem cannot usually be solved completely by word-segment searching. The best recent development in this area are the QUESTEL system's DARC database and CAS ONLINE marketed by Chemical Abstracts. In these files one can graphically draw the desired active core as a fragment and probabilistically match it against the over 6,000,000 compounds in these databases.

CAS has addressed the problem of online identification of indeterminate chemical substances, or those that are incapable of exact definition, known as Markush structures, previously out of reach of both print and online services. In March 1985 CAS announced the ability to identify Markush structures; as many as 20 variable groups of atoms can be combined in a single search for a structure, and a variable number and type of attachments of atoms in a molecule may also be specified.

The utility of graphics-based retrieval in chemical information is a topic of some debate, focusing on issues of speed, cost of special terminals, and technical problems. CAS ONLINE has made graphics searching possible with specific software on more common terminals and micrcomputers.

The graphics-based search services permit constructing the active core fragment of the chemical compound and matching it against the substances indexed in the dictionary databases. DARC Questal employs graphic or alphanumeric input of structures to allow each molecule to be described by a graph, the nature of the atoms, and the types of bonds, eliminating the relative ambiguity that results from the use of chemical codes and nomenclature in the identification of substances.

The largest number of science-related numeric databases are offered by the NIH-EPA Chemical Information System (CIS), a cooperative project of the National Institutes of Health, the Environmental Protection Agency, and several other U.S. and European organizations. The Structure and Nomenclature Searching System of CIS allows chemical compounds to be identified by a two-dimensional structure in addition to identification by chemical or chemical fragment name, name fragment, molecular weight, or fragment codes. Meschel observed that "through CIS it is possible to build a compound practically bond by bond graphically and request the interactive system to retrieve the partial or full formula from their field."

Among the services offered by the Mass Spectral Search System is mass spectral data and a numerical evaluation score to assess the quality of the spectra. Several databases can perform calculations on mathematical models of organic and inorganic molecules. The Man Lab-NPL Materials Databank can retrieve thermodynamic data as well as perform calculations on the thermodynamic functions, useful for chemists and metallurgists; the database can also plot phase diagrams.

To assist in the design and identification of chemical substances among local in-house databases, software producers such as Molecular Design Ltd. have developed such programs as MACCS, which allows users to draw chemical structures with light pens, add their own data, and display the results on the screen. The displays can rotate or show stereopairs.

Directory Databases. Directory databases offer the information of published directories or serve a purpose similar to that of published directories without having published equivalents. These are not full-text databases, although they may represent the complete text of a publication in machine-readable form. Nor are they numeric databases, although they contain numeric information. And they are definitely not bibliographic databases, because they provide primary sources, or source documents, for the users.

The Electronic Yellow Pages (EYP), for example, are databases created from telephone books and specialized directories in the U.S. by Market Data Retrieval, Inc. The databases cannot be said to reflect the full text of their 4,800 published counterparts. Business activity is described for each listing in the database by Standard Industrial Classification (SIC) codes. Intra-corporate relationships are identified for each listing, along with codes that represent the number of employees and net worth of the company. Potential applications exist for these databases which could not be imagined with their published counterparts. In addition to being able to search the equivalent of 4,800 yellow page directories simultaneously by the business name, state, city, or county of location, users can restrict searches to businesses with specific zip codes, telephone exchanges, or ranges of SIC codes to reflect a certain type of business activity.

The TRINET databases offer more detailed information, including a listing of the headquarters for each business, sales figures, and percentage share of the market. In addition to many of these features for locating businesses, various Dun & Bradstreet databases provide number of employees, base sales figures, intra-corporate identification numbers, Standard Metropolitan Statistical Area (SMSA) information, and sales growth and trends. The most detailed and substantive directory of U.S. businesses, DISCLOSURE II, has much of the directory information mentioned for other databases as well as information extracted from reports filed with the U.S. Securities and Exchange Commission (SEC).

Reference Directories. Databases such as the Encyclopedia of Associations, produced by Gale Research Company, correspond to the published directories of the same names. The Books in Print database corresponds to the most current edition of several published directories of books published by R. R. Bowker Company. Directories of microcomputer software directories such as .MENU– The International Software Database, or Business Software Database publish no print counterparts. The number or existence of published counterparts to these online databases is not significant; the differences in published format cannot compare to the convenience and enhanced capabilities for locating desired information that is offered by online databases.

Dictionary Databases. Dictionary databases, such as the chemical substance dictionaries mentioned earlier, are similar to directory databases insofar as each record identifies something. The purpose of some dictionary databases, such as the online version of the *Oxford English Dictionary,* is apparent to the user. Other dictionary databases serve also to provide a measure of control in the use of bibliographic databases. For example, the chemical registry numbers contained in the chemical substance dictionary files can be mapped to identify bibliographic citations that have been indexed with these numbers. The H. W. Wilson Company developed three separate databases to provide control over the bibliographic databases in WILSONLINE, including a PUBLISHERS DIRECTORY, a JOURNAL DIRECTORY, and a NAME AUTHORITY FILE, used as a means for bibliographic control of names.

ADMINISTRATION OF ONLINE SERVICES IN LIBRARIES

Pricing Structures. Of all library services, the direct costs for online information services may be among the most elusive to budget for, because they do not represent fixed costs. There are basically three charges assessed for use of online information services: connect-hour charges, print or display royalties, and telecommunication charges. The connect-hour cost for such services as DIALOG, SDC, and INFOLINE represents the combination of royalties paid to the database producer and those paid to the vendor on whose system the database is available. The full-text information services offered by MDC are priced in connect-hour units of $20 per hour (1985). An additional, separate cost for each search is added to the connect-hour price. Services such as WILSONLINE and CAS ONLINE have databases that are produced and made available through in-house online systems; prices for both are structured in connect-hour units. BRS represents the royalties paid to the database producer and those paid to itself as the vendor as separate connect-hour charges.

Lesser incremental royalty charges may also be assessed when the user displays or prints a portion or all of a record while still online or when the user requests the service to print it offline and mail it to the user.

Most vendors charge separately for telecommunication services. A majority of vendors contract with at least two and possibly three public vendors of telecommunication services, including GTE TELENET, Tymshare's TYMNET, or United Technology Corporation's UNINET. Three services— DIALOG, I.P. Sharp, and MDC—have their own dedicated networks. These services enable users to make the distant connection with a remote database more cheaply and reliably than would be possible over public telephone lines. The cost for telecommunications is usually expressed as a separate connect-hour charge paid to the database vendor.

The highest prices for online information services result from infrequent use. Discounts on connect-hour costs are available in exchange for annual subscription deposits or for commitments to a certain level of connect-hour usage throughout a year. DIALOG and SDC offer discounts through subscription or commitment agreements; SDC also offers automatic volume discounts for connect-hour usage at certain levels during a month. H. W. Wilson offers a discount for subscribtions to WILSONLINE alone, or for subscriptions to both WILSONLINE and the printed Wilson indexes. ACS, publisher of CAS ONLINE also offers lower connect-hour costs in exchange for subscriptions to print indexes. Discounts given in exchange for subscriptions to the printed *Chemical Abstracts* also apply toward the royalty charges incurred for printing or displaying citations in CAS ONLINE and toward the file entry fee for the CA file on that service. Although BRS does not use commitment agreements, it offers discounts through subscription agreements or through small group subscriptions, in which several users can consolidate their usage to obtain a discount. MDC discounts search costs according to the volume of searches per month.

The time of day that one uses a service can affect the cost of a search session. The price for MDC and Dow Jones varies during prime and nonprime hours of service; charges for an MDC search conducted during off-peak hours are half the prime-time costs. Weeknight and weekend rates for Dow Jones are significantly less than those charged during the day. BRS reduced its connect-hour rate by half for its

BRKTHRU service during off-peak hours. Dow Jones introduced DOWQUOT in mid-1984 as an off-peak service offering securities quotes and business news at a reduced flat-rate cost.

BRS and DIALOG introduced AFTER DARK and KNOWLEDGE INDEX, respectively, in late 1982 as flat-rate or lower-priced simplified versions of their more popular databases. Self-instructional manuals replaced the need for training in both cases; AFTER DARK is optionally menu-driven. Both were made available during off-peak hours, on weeknights and weekends, and with fewer system capabilities than their regular counterparts.

Contracts. Libraries most commonly contract with the vendors or producers of online services either directly or indirectly, through group contracts. Library networks make group contracts on behalf of member libraries, offering vendors substantial subscriptions in return for high rates of discount, a portion or all of which is passed on to participating libraries. These networks may be multi-type library networks on a regional, state, or local scale, such as BCR (the Bibliographical Center for Research), IN-COLSA (Indiana Cooperative Library Services Authority), or MELSA (Metropolitan Library Service Agency). Such networks may also be organized by type of library, such as the School Practices Information Network (SPIN) or the renascent Biomedical Communications Network (BCN). Group contracts are also arranged by federal or state agencies responsible for library services, such as FEDLINK. Libraries that are either unable or unwilling to make an individual commitment can obtain some discount on their costs through a network's group contract for online services.

Commercial sources of access to multiple online information services are made possible through what are commonly referred to as "gateway" services. A gateway links an online information service to such products or services as communication software or electronic mail to online information services. ITT DIALCOM is an electronic mail service that also serves as a gateway to several online databases. DIALCOM conveniently allows for use of online information services without the need for the user to secure a separate account and password for each service. Other gateways exist between online information services, such as that from MDC to DIALOG or from DIALOG to the *Official Airline Guide* and the U.S. Department of Commerce database, CEN-DATA. Communication software packages that serve as gateways to online information services also feature menu-driven prompts to obviate the need for system training and documentation among end-users of these services.

Funding. The costs described previously are all direct costs, incurred as a result of an online search session. All other expenses involved in running an online search service are indirect. Nancy Grimes, in her article "Costs, Budgets, and Financial Management" in *Online Searching Technique and Management,* (1983) divides these indirect costs into one-time expenditures and recurring costs. The purchase or lease of equipment and their maintenance contracts are only a few examples of one-time, indirect costs.

Documentation and supplies must also be purchased. System manuals, database thesauri, and other user aids will compose the search service's own reference collection, together with system newsletters and subscriptions to relevant journals. If the equipment includes a printer, paper will be needed; if the printer is an impact type, new ribbons will be needed.

Personnel, training, promotion, and overhead account for a variety of recurring indirect costs for a search service. Grimes suggests that the cost for these expenses will vary according to the specific circumstances of a library.

For example, searcher and coordinator may be one and the same person, or coordination may consume a quarter of a department head's time. Training sessions may take place onsite, or may require travel and overnight lodging. Promotion may include newsletters, brochures, or complementary searches; the facility may need modification, and so on.

Two budget options for starting an online search service, one representing a low-cost and another a more expensive approach, were developed by the Costs and Financing Committee of the Machine-Assisted Reference Section (MARS) of the Reference and Adult Services Division of ALA. The document entitled "Online Reference Services: Costs and Budgets" (1985) illustrates how the indirect costs of the service can vary according to circumstance.

Approaches to funding a search service also vary according to circumstance. The Committee observes in its "Online Reference Services: Funding Methods" (1984) that "Libraries often seek external sources of funding for start-up costs and internal sources for ongoing services." It found that the sources of funding most frequently referred to in the literature are "new money, a reallocation of existing funds, and charging end-users for searches."

New money is obtained through requests for new and ongoing funds from the budgeting agency or from outside sources such as library agencies, federal agencies, and private donors and foundations. According to the Committee, these are usually "one-time, fixed-fund sources."

Existing funds can be reallocated to support a search service in a number of ways. Funds can be transferred from other library service or material budgets to pay for the online service or can be reallocated from other units in the larger organization of which the library is a part, such as academic departments or laboratories. There is usually an implicit reallocation in the library budget for professional, clerical, and business office staff time allotted a search service and a reallocation of intangible library resources such as overhead, space, and utilities.

Charges to users for their searches may fund the online service. The amount of the assessment in a cost-recovery scheme can range anywhere from partial recovery of direct costs to full recovery of those costs plus additional charges to account for overhead. The Committee cites case studies as helpful models in deciding on a combination of funding approaches best suited to matching service goals with funding realities.

Training. There are a number of options for training in the use of online information services. Many vendors and database producers offer one-day or half-day training sessions to introduce their own services. Such courses may present instruction in the mechanics of online searching and some theory in search strategy formulation and the use of Boolean logic. Trainees should have opportunities for hands-on experience with the instructor present. In some cases, free connect time is provided through training passwords for the trainees' use after the course.

Some vendors and producers offer training databases to complement and enhance their courses. DIALOG, for example, offers several ONline Training and Practice (ONTAP) databases in a variety of subject areas at greatly reduced flat rates so users can practice economically. ONTAP databases contain small portions of regular DIALOG databases. CAS ONLINE offers a practice *Chemical Abstracts* database.

The introductory training offered by some vendors is also often complemented by one-day seminars that address more advanced search techniques and search strategy preparation. Such seminars ideally build upon prior training and search experience. Typical one-day introductory and advanced seminars may orient system instruction to the interests of people in business, the chemical industry, law, or medicine, for example.

There are various approaches to offering training. All database vendors and producers control the format and content of their training session and materials; many vendors and producers are the exclusive sources of the training. In 1983 BRS adopted a cooperative approach to the distribution of its training through qualified library networks, permitting the Bibliographical Center for Research (BCR) and the Cooperative Library Agency for Systems and Services (CLASS) to represent it as agents. BRS controls the content, materials, and price of the course and monitors the effectiveness of the presentation. DIALOG's own customer services staff, field offices, and foreign representatives train the equivalent of the total enrollment of main campuses of some state universities each year, but DIALOG has also sanctioned qualified library networks to use its training materials in network-sponsored DIALOG training.

Training is also available through qualified programs of academic instruction. Database vendors such as BRS, CAS ONLINE, DIALOG, and MDC offer most or all of their services at reduced rates to allow faculty to expose their students to the service. Graduate schools of library and information science have offered this training for many years, and professional schools in law, business, education, and the sciences have also begun to offer it as part of their instruction in research methods.

Local and regional online user groups provide continuing education in the use of online information services by hosting training seminars by database producers. These groups also foster an awareness of applications of these services through presentations by members. National associations such as the American Library Association, the Special Libraries Association, and the American Chemical Society sponsor programs, publications, and committee activity that serve as additional sources of continuing education.

Self-instruction and in-house training by experienced staff members are alternative training methods. The quality of a searcher's negotiating skills with a patron and performance online can be developed through continuous peer evaluation of searches and

through attendance at seminars or online user group meetings that highlight use of specific databases. As of the mid-1980s, WILSONLINE's Tutorial and the DIALOG Basics Manual provided opportunities for self-instruction. Computer-assisted instruction (CAI) in the use of these services, in a simulated environment, was realized by Elaine Caruso at the University of Pittsburgh through her TRAINER program, developed in the late 1970s. Observers anticipated that database vendors would develop many more CAI programs.

Enhanced communications software packages are offered by database vendors, producers, and software companies to enable online information services to be used in an environment as close to that of natural language as possible. These software packages also offer simplified ways to log on to the services, and, in many cases, the ability to build and edit personal files of information produced from online searches. SEARCH HELPER, produced by Information Access Corporation (IAC), allows for convenient log-on, search, sort, and downloading of the results of searches conducted on IAC's databases on DIALOG. Two software packages, SCI-MATE, produced by the Institute for Scientific Information (ISI), and SEARCH MASTER, produced by SDC, translate a searcher's responses to a series of questions and prompts into search statements that can be executed on any of the databases on DIALOG, BRS, SDC, or NLM. In addition to allowing a search strategy to be formulated in advance of the online connection, SCI-MATE enables search results to be downloaded and edited with additional information added by the searcher. Disclosure, Inc., offers a software package, MicroDISCLOSURE, to enable end users to conduct a menu-driven search of the DISCLOSURE-II database on DIALOG. This package also allows financial and company information to be downloaded, to analyze that information and prepare reports, and to use the data with microcomputer spreadsheet programs such as VisiCalc and Lotus 1-2-3.

In early 1984 the Menlo Coporation introduced a communication software package, In-Search, primarily to enable untrained end-users to search DIALOG. In 1985 Menlo introduced an enhanced version, Pro-Search, for experienced searchers, with the same capacity to download and edit search results, plus accounting report features, and the ability to search both DIALOG and BRS.

The Business Computer Network (BCN) sells communication software (Super-Scout) that offers electronic mail and single-keystroke access to many online services in business information. BCN offers a gateway to 14 online information services, but does not simplify search system protocols.

BRS created BRKTHRU to provide optional menu-driven prompts and instructions for searching many BRS databases during all hours of standard BRS service. BRS encouraged librarians to offer BRKTHRU to end-users "for those day-to-day searches that use your time but not your expertise."

EasyNet was introduced in 1984 as a menu-driven service offering simplified access to BRS, DIALOG, SDC, INFOLINE, Questel, VU/TEXT, and NewsNet. The service features options for those with no previous knowledge of online services, such as system selection of the databases to be searched.

Service Location and Staffing. In his overview of "Library Organizational Patterns in Online Retrieval Services" in *Online Searching Technique and Management* (1983), Peter G. Watson addressed the problems and options in deciding upon centralized or dispersed authority over the online search service in a library, describing the advantages of integrating the service with the library's full reference services or separating it from them. Physical location of the service is often a secondary question, decided in the context of the library's service goals and objectives, the degree of centralized authority, and the funding options open to the library.

The centralized authority of metropolitan public library systems is often manifest in the decision to centralize the search service in one location for all its libraries. State libraries offer centralized search services to public libraries throughout the state but in many cases also encourage development of search services among these libraries. Main and departmental libraries among academic institutions and school district offices and learning centers all face the same question of search service location in this context. Some geographically dispersed corporations have autonomous libraries with their own search service contracts, policies, and procedures. Other dispersed corporations channel search requests through central search services for all the corporate libraries.

Visibility of the service is also dependent upon the service goals and objectives of the library. The service is highly visible when all or part of it is available at the reference desk, either for ready-reference searches providing short, quick answers or for comprehensive searches. A more subtle but equally important consideration is promotion of the service. Traditionally, the service is made available in rooms closed to the public. Security considerations, the need to conduct interviews with patrons before and after the search, and the need to store documentation conveniently are strong arguments for maintaining that tradition.

Staffing is largely a matter of reallocating staff resources among those professional reference staff who are trained in the use of online services. Accommodating the service in a one-person special library involves the creative redesign of a schedule to eliminate less productive and time-consuming research activity in favor of the use of online services. Staffing for the service among libraries with reference staffs is often an extension of the subject specialization already in place. One staff person is generally appointed to coordinate the use, training, billing, and documentation activity associated with the service.

TRENDS
Growth of Online Information Services.
The growth of online information services has been consistently strong each year since their introduction. The Cuadra Associates *Directory of Online Databases* (Fall 1984) listed 2,453 databases available from 1,189 producers through 362 online information services; the Fall 1979 issue had listed only 400 databases available from 221 producers on only 59 online services. According to the *Friday Memo* of June 14, 1985, a study concluded that "the online database industry could very well maintain a 23%/year average growth rate through the next decade."

Growth of Microcomputer Applications.
The growth in the number and variety of online databases has been accompanied by an equally impressive growth in the distribution of microcomputers. In the February 1, 1985, *Library Journal,* John N. Berry concluded from the results of a research report released in late 1984 by the R. R. Bowker Company that "it is obviously safe to predict that microcomputers have found a home and utility throughout the nation's libraries. Not only are they in place, but many more will arrive in the next few months." The survey indicated that nearly 5,000 public libraries, 1,600 academic libraries, and more than 7,000 special libraries own and are using more than 45,000 microcomputers. More than 140,000 micros are in use among elementary and high school libraries in the U.S. The libraries sampled in this survey planned to purchase nearly 128,000 new micros by the end of 1986. An article in *Business Week* (August 27, 1981) had predicted a similar pattern of growth in the shipment of desktop computer systems for education. With a base rate of 70,000 units shipped in 1980, a 31 percent growth rate was predicted in shipments through 1985, when 270,000 were expected to have been shipped to educational institutions.

Microcomputers have added a significant dimension to the use of online information services by facilitating downloading, reformatting, and editing (or post-processing) of search results. Microcomputers have also introduced a new channel of distribution of online information to the library.

Distribution of Local Databases. Database producers have distributed the machine-readable versions of their products either directly to the consumer or indirectly through vendors or host services. Direct distribution has taken two forms: producers such as Chemical Abstracts Service, H. W. Wilson, and the Institute for Scientific Information (ISI) have developed their own online information services; a long-standing method is to distribute products on machine-readable tape, to be read on the user's mainframe computer.

Many in the information industry have expressed optimism about the potential of microcomputers as a distribution channel for online information services. John Blair, Jr., a columnist on microcomputer applications in *Database,* observed (December 1982) that "the microcomputer could serve as an important step toward making more of the information already stored in the large databanks or remote mainframes accessible to local centers of distribution." In his guest editorial in the September 1980 *Database,* ISI President Eugene Garfield predicted that "it is not unreasonable to expect by the end of the decade, central online databases may be replaced by local databases stored on and manipulated by microcomputers. By that time we may be sending out floppy disks or whatever, instead of printed volumes." BRS President William Marovitz voiced his optimism about the potential of videodisk and microcomputer technology to foster "a boom in local/regional database distribution" in a January 1983 column in *Online.*

A relatively recent technology, videodisk or compact disk-read only memory (CD-ROM), can make large amounts of information equivalent to large portions or all of databases available for use on sophisticated microcomputers. Applications of this technology include InfoTrac, introduced in January 1985 by IAC, a menu-driven system enabling as many as four people to search nearly half a million fully indexed citations to articles from business, technical, legal, and general-interest publications stored on a single 12-inch videodisk on a microcomputer. IAC keeps the service current with monthly updates.

The English-language portion of the complete Library of Congress MARC database is available on compact disk for use with a personal computer or an OCLC M300 Workstation. This product of the Library Corporation allows editing of catalogue records and ordering of catalogue card sets and labels.

International Thompson Information (which owns the University of Toronto Library Automation System, UTLAS), Carrollton Press (producer of the REMARC database), and Cuadra Associates (producer of the microcomputer data entry and retrieval software STAR, System To Automate Records) developed a CD-ROM, microcomputer-based system that offers the 6,500,000 records in the MARC and REMARC databases with the capacity for Boolean searching and current and retrospective cataloguing.

The video and optical disk industry showed promise in the mid-1980s as a distribution channel for database producers and suppliers. In September 1984 Reference Technology announced Clasix, which offers replicable, prerecorded optical disks and a mini-computer-based premastering system to enable publishers to organize and prepare their data for the actual mastering by 3M and other companies. In January 1985 BRS announced its commitment to produce databases on videodisk as part of a laser-optic publishing project with Reference Technology. Clasix is distributed through BRS, and the BRS Search Software, which can be used to search databases stored on videodisk, is marketed by Reference Technology.

In February 1985 SDC and Sony announced discussion of a joint venture to develop videodisk applications for online information services. In March 1985 Reference Technology announced "a complete data delivery service to publishers and information providers," a more complete premastering service that includes videodisk equipment and software. In April 1985 a Japanese firm announced a programmable version of CD-ROM that allows for the production of videodisks without an outside mastering process. The trend in this technology is toward greater convenience for database producers to provide (and distribute) their products on video or optical disk. Robert November, a managing consultant at LINK Resources, a market research firm for the information industry, predicted greater storage capacity for data on compact optical disks for use with home computers. With this technology, "publishers have the option of circumventing the costs of printing and paper for multi-volume reference works" such as encyclopedias.

Standard microcomputer floppy disks store only a fraction of the information that can be stored on video or optical disks, but represent a less complicated channel for the direct distribution of information by the producer. For example, NTIS offers portions of its complete database on 5.25-inch floppy disks for use on IBM PC's and compatible microcomputers. BIOSIS offers a similar service complete with periodic updates through its BIOSIS Information Transfer Service (BITS). Cuadra Associates made *The Directory of Online Databases* available on floppy disks. The December 1984 *Database* reported that NLM is making subsets of MEDLINE available on floppy disks defined by subject, time, language, journal title, and so on, and with optional monthly or quarterly updates to the database on disk. Companies such as Knowledge Access designed software that emulates the command logic of DIALOG's KNOWLEDGE INDEX to support the use of such databases as Microcomputer Index on floppy disk.

A rich potential for locally created databases exists among library vertical file collections. Microcomputer data entry and retrieval software such as STAR and the Micro/Mini Version of BRS/SEARCH allow for the creation and search of in-house databases on sophisticated microcomputers. The January 1981 issue of *Online* reported that STAR is also used "by publishers to support the production and management of small- to medium-sized databases that are distributed to one or more online services." A March 1981 issue of *Database* reported that firms such as Cuadra Associates and InfoMart optionally package their data-entry and retrieval software "with the small computer and all the necessary peripheral equipment" needed to enter data in-house or by data conversion companies. On a smaller scale, software packages such as Newsdex and Bookdex are used to prepare databases of literature references that one accumulates as a result of conducting research.

Online Information Services in the Home and at Work. The distribution of microcomputers outside libraries and formal education has been equally significant and has brought the technology of online information service physically closer to end users. November reported that a LINK Resources study indicated that "36.3 million modemmed computer terminals will be in approximately 95 million households" by the end of 1989. "We knew from the demographic of home computer owners that this will be the more affluent, educated . . . third of the U.S. population." Pemberton argued in his "The Linear File" column in the December 1981 *Database* that the growth in the use of online information services by the end-user will result from "propinquity," which in the context of online information searching "means that every end-user of online databases has to have his own terminal at his own desk."

Propinquity is only half of the struggle to promote the use of these services among end users. Before these services can be regarded fully as "arms-reach" references to answer the everyday questions of end-users in the manner that books on their shelf or the colleagues down the hall at work are able to do, a matter-of-fact effortlessness in their use will be achieved. The communication software packages and products that represent simplified (and in some cases menu-driven) versions of full online information services attempt to achieve this goal by reducing the training and documentation required to use these services to a minimum.

The Role of Artificial Intelligence. Seminal developments in artificial intelligence (AI) will contribute to the use of online information services by end-users. Howard Weber defined AI during the 1984 Information Industry Association conference on that subject as "a machine process that manages information so as to replicate the function of elements of human cognition more efficiently than they may function naturally." Steven Sieck observed in his article "Artificial Intelligence: Its Promise for the Information Industry" that AI will contribute to the use of natural language in the use of online information services "to allow end-users to retrieve information from databases without needing to know the specific commands used by the underlying database management software." Brattle Research applied AI to enable natural language to be used in monitoring new information added to a database. Sieck explained that "These alert rules are stored in a knowledge base—a network of attributes and relationships through which the machine can recognize and relate important concepts when they appear in incoming documents, whether or not they are expressed in the same semantic terms." The system is capable of isolating key concepts embodied in the document and automatically adding an appropriate phrase to the alert rule, once the user has identified that document as highly relevant.

Another form of AI known as *expert systems* is in use by the British chemical company ICI to give its agrochemical dealers and distributors a more sophisticated means to help farmers decide which chemicals can be used to treat crops to give the best yields. The article "Expert Systems Meet the Mass Market?" in the February 1985 issue of *Information Today* reported that the system "gives the dealer online expert help when a farmer asks him what he recommends to treat his crops." The dialog with the system is query-based, and the user can ask the system to explain why it has asked a question or made a recommendation.

In "Intelligence in the 1980s" in *The Information Society* (1981), former CIA director William Colby argued for the use of AI in the management of intelligence information "to relate not only relevant but even apparently unrelated facts." While these applications of AI are limited, they point to a trend to use computer resources to simplify the use of online information services for the end-user.

Videotex. Videotex may represent the most widespread application of online information in the home and in the office. Jeff Pemberton defined videotex in *Online* (October 1980) as "any system that stores primarily textual information in a computer and transmits specific portions of it on demand to a video terminal, usually located either in a home or office." Videotex does not bear any of the sophisticated search and retrieval features of positional association among terms, Boolean logic, or display and search of inverted indexes.

In "Consumer Videotex: Information for Everyman in *Artificial Intelligence: Its Promise for the Information Industry* (Information Industry Association, 1985) Catherine Fuller and Barry Parr describe two types of services supplied by videotex: information and transactions. "Most of the pages stored in the . . . computers supply information: breaking news, closing stock prices, movie reviews, recipes, even online encyclopedias. . ." However, "the star services of consumer videotex are home shopping and banking." For business applications, Pemberton observed that "videotex(t) is more effective right now than the printing press in the distribution of various internal directories, policy or procedure manuals, organization charts, lists of responsibilities, product descriptions, price lists, etc."

Evaluation. Online information services have come of age as a full reference tool in the library and have made significant strides toward becoming recognized as the same in the home and the office. These services are increasingly relied on as an effective and, in some cases, the only, source to satisfy the need for information conveniently. There is evidence that growth in the use of these services both in and outside the library is redefining the library's view of itself as an information provider and of the users to whom its services are delivered. At a minimum, the view that "Books Are Us," displayed on the cover of, and editiorialized in, a 1985 issue of *American Libraries,* is eroding in favor of a broader view of information and its delivery, regardless of whether the mechanism for its storage has a binding or is a silver platter.

REFERENCES

Charles P. Bourne, "On-Line Systems: History, Technology, and Economics," *Journal of the American Society for Information Science,* May 1980. The best historical overview of the emergence of the online information industry.

Greg Byerly, *Online Searching: A Dictionary and Bibliographic Guide* (1983). A standard reference work for online search services.

Carol H. Fenichel and Thomas H. Hogan, *Online Searching: A Primer* (c. 1981). A good standard text on all aspects of online searching for the library or information center.

Donald T. Hawkins, "A Review of Online Physical Sciences and Mathematics Databases," *Database,* 1985. A three-part overview of the databases in these fields written with a great deal of insight and familiarity.

Hawkins, *Online Information Retrieval Bibliography, 1964-1979* (c. 1980).

Ryan E. Hoover, with Alice H. Bahr et al., *The Library and Information Managers Guide to Online Services* (c. 1980). A good overview of online services, including management, measurement and evaluation, promotion, and training components of this service.

John E. Kinsock, *Legal Databases Online: LEXIS and WEST-LAW* (1985).

Susan V. Meschel, "Numeric Databases in the Sciences," *Online Review,* February 1984. An expert, knowledgeable overview of the complexity of numeric databases and attendant considerations in their use.

Numeric Databases, edited by Ching-chih Chen and Peter Hernon (c. 1984). An excellent overview of how numeric databases have been used among libraries and information centers.

Online Searching Technique and Management, edited by James J. Maloney (1983). A comprehensive overview of all aspects of online searching written by librarians and information specialists.

JAMES MALONEY

Organization of American States

The Organization of American States (OAS), headquartered in Washington, D.C., includes 32 member countries from the Western Hemisphere. The oldest international regional organization, it was formerly called the Pan American Union (PAU), created in 1890.

The OAS has political and technical functions. Political functions involve settling border disputes, monitoring human rights, and establishing international treaties. Technical branches of the OAS are concerned with problems basic to development in the fields of education, science, culture, economic, and social affairs. These include a wide range of projects concerned with libraries, archives, documentation centers, publishing, conservation and microfilming, and related advanced information technologies.

Background. Linked to the OAS is the world's oldest international communications association, the Inter-American Conference on Telecommunications (CITEL), which sets policies and establishes the norms for air rights. It deals with problems related to telecommunications that must be overcome for the countries to take advantage of the newer information technologies. CITEL evolved from the Inter-American Electrical Communications Commission created in 1923. During the following decades, ideas about the Inter-American Telecommunications Network (ITN) and the Inter-American Telecommunications Satellite Network (SARIT) were formulated. In 1961–62 the infrastructure of ITN was developed, and a study was undertaken of the policies and the problems of the American countries in the telecommunications field. CITEL became a permanent Specialized Conference in 1971.

The Columbus Memorial Library (endowed by Andrew Carnegie) serves the reference needs of the different OAS programs and of the public. It is also responsible for developing the catalogues of official OAS documents and publishing related bibliographic works. In the 1940s and early 1950s it began to assist the member countries. These services were separated from it when the Library Development Program (LDP) was created in the Department of Cultural Affairs under Marietta Daniels Shepard (1913–1984).

In the late 1940s and the 1950s, the PAU carried out activities related to copyright legislation and legal deposit, international exchange of publications, and free circulation of books among the members. These concerns became the responsibility of the Regional Center for Development of the Book in Latin America and the Caribbean (CERLAL), in Bogotá, Colombia.

In the 1960s the Library Development Program began assisting library schools and libraries in Latin America. To serve a large region that had little access to technical information it also granted graduate level fellowships and published important series including: *Inter-American Library Relations* in English and Spanish, *Manuales del Bibliotecario, Estudios Bibliotecarios, Reuniones Bibliotecologicas,* and *Cuadernos Bibliotecologicos*. By the 1970s, responsibility for providing technical publications shifted to projects in different countries.

Two OAS secretariats cover a broad range of subject areas dedicated to pooling Hemisphere resources for development: the Executive Secretariat for Economic and Social Affairs and the Executive Secretariat for Education, Science, and Culture; the second is most concerned with development of libraries, archives, publishing, and information systems, and this article is primarily concerned with the projects of its departments.

Libraries and Information Systems. It is difficult to generalize about Latin America and the Caribbean because of the wide diversity, but a summary of the situation and problems of the region is important to understand the context of the OAS projects.

Most governments of the region, especially the legislative and executive branches, make comparatively little use of information services, much less those delivered electronically. Almost all of the countries have serious foreign exchange problems that make purchase of computers and information (whether in book or electronic form) not only expensive but unreliable—an institution may be receiving the monthly data from a service only to miss six months for lack of foreign exchange. A greater problem is the shortage of trained personnel, especially at the mid-level in the library profession. The highly trained people in key positions do not have the support staffs they need. Research techniques and terminology are not taught widely. Librarians lack training opportunities in abstracting, indexing, and analysis, which hinders creation of national data banks.

There is a great desire for exchange of information within and between countries of the region, but the means to do so are weak. On the other hand, the means for sale and distribution of information from the United States, Europe, and Japan are strong. In the Information Age, as in the Industrial, the information-rich are getting richer and the information-poor are getting poorer. There is also frequently an imbalance within a country whereby one institution or series of institutions (such as a central bank library) commands information facilities far better than the rest. The imbalance makes collaboration within a country difficult because the inadequate institutions are seen as a drag on the advancement of the developed. In some countries, such as Brazil, Venezuela, Mexico, and Jamaica, there are several strong institutions that cover a variety of disciplines. It is in such countries that national systems and important national data banks in various fields are being developed. The resources of these countries are being used by the OAS to help the others.

Users are not experienced with traditional library use, much less with electronically delivered information and so do not demand the services, even though their need for information might be great. Most people have never used a library—school and public libraries are not common, books and paper are largely imported and expensive. Reading materials suitable for low-level readers, new literates, and children are few and poorly distributed. Large rural populations scattered throughout the region are isolated from doctors, priests, schools, books, and libraries.

Much of the OAS assistance to libraries aims to develop library staffs to the point where they can control national information, not just process data from abroad. The OAS has worked on a variety of ways to promote standardization of technical processes. It published the two Spanish versions of *Anglo-American Cataloging Rules,* 1 and 2, and translated the MARC format into Spanish. It supported the updating of the Rovira List of Subject Headings, *Lista de Encabezamientos de Materias para Bibliotecas,* which provides a common vocabulary for the Spanish-speaking countries. In these efforts it collaborated with the University of Costa Rica Library, the University of Mexico and the National Council on Science and Technology of Mexico, and the Institute for

Promotion of Higher Education of Colombia. The experts that worked on the different projects were from many different parts of Latin America.

Many library school professors received advanced training with OAS fellowships, and OAS worked to help improve the curriculum of library schools. In 1984–85, for example, it formed with the Center of Library Research at the University of Mexico a documentation center on Latin American library research and training. It supported courses for library school faculty on research techniques, abstracting, indexing, and information analysis so they could incorporate those skills in their curricula. It assisted the Department of Library Studies of the University of the West Indies (UWI) over many years, by training faculty, paying for travel to professional meetings, and providing bibliographic materials and equipment. It also helps the UWI offer extension courses in the 10 English-speaking Caribbean member states. For many years it supported the Inter-American Library School of Medellín, Colombia, by providing fellowships to students from other countries, by sponsoring advanced training to faculty, and by supporting its publishing program. It helps the University of Costa Rica to train Latin Americans in school librarianship. In the mid-1980s it was developing a series of modules to train paraprofessionals in the Caribbean that allow library assistants to take basic training without having to go abroad.

OAS also worked with university libraries on both basic library processes and advance technologies. Help to one is frequently applied to others, for example, the OAS helped the Library of the University of Costa Rica to develop computer facilities that in turn are used to train librarians from other Central American institutions. National libraries run the gamut from highly advanced centers of national information systems, as in Venezuela, to sadly neglected repositories of ragged out-of-date collections. The projects try to deal with the particular problems of each so they can assume more important roles in national information systems.

The newer OAS member states in the Eastern Caribbean have populations of under 250,000. Many have only one or two trained librarians who must serve all of the information needs of the country, with few qualified paraprofessionals to support them and low budgets. To help them, the OAS in the 1980s was trying to develop new curricula, training, and assistance tailored to the special needs of countries. It works with them to develop different and more adequate systems than models from the larger countries can provide. OAS works in these countries with libraries of all kinds, documentation centers, archives, and publishers, to maximize use of the limited resources. A committee of librarians and archivists from each country meets every two years to set priorities for OAS activities.

The fields of agriculture and science are the most advanced in use of electronic technology for information, thanks in part to the Inter-American Institute for Cooperation on Agriculture (IICA), an OAS specialized organization created in 1942. Within it is the Agricultural Documentation and Information Center (CIDIA) in Costa Rica, which supports research and technology transfer. CIDIA serves governments, the academic community, and farmers. It effectively

helped create an Inter-American system with subsystems on agriculture, "rural well-being," related production, marketing, statistical, and socio-economic information that operates throughout the Hemisphere. It set up the AGRINTER information system, which is part of the AGRIS global data network. From 1972 AGRINTER worked to establish national documentation centers in most member countries. It not only promotes dissemination of information and creation of databases on many subjects, but also the training, planning, and preparation of basic bibliographic works.

Banks and industries such as the petroleum industry are perhaps the institutions making most sophisticated use of advanced technology for their own uses. The OAS project "Scientific and Technological Information Services for Industry," which began in 1974, developed an Inter-American network of centers moving toward use of advanced information technology. The Caribbean Industrial Research Institute (CARIRI) in Trinidad and Tobago, which the OAS assists to provide information to industry, and the Scientific Research Council in Jamaica were the only English-speaking participants as of 1986.

Using the resources of ICAITI in Guatemala (the Central American Research Institute for Industry, which is assisted by the OAS), a series of workshops began in 1985 that brought many English-speaking countries into the network. The first workshop provided an overview of techniques to establish and maintain a technical information center, identify user needs, market technical information services, establish documentation centers, use online access to computerized databases, apply microcomputers in libraries and information centers. This introductory seminar was to be followed by more in-depth courses.

School libraries are becoming more widespread through a program to train teacher-librarians and to train teachers in use of books. Working through the ministries of education, many national projects in both Latin America and the English-speaking countries are helping establish basic media centers. *Flexible Model for a National System of School Libraries,* published in Spanish (1983) and Portuguese (1985), and scheduled for publication in English (1986), is used by educators throughout the Hemisphere. It reflects with its practical low-cost solutions the years of experience in many countries.

Most of the people of the region are poor and half of the poor are under 15 years of age. Information services to them have been negligible and dispersed. Public libraries have not reached many. Literacy programs have had an insignificant impact because the new readers often lapse into illiteracy within months for lack of materials to read. Few writers of fiction or of information materials in the fields of sciences, health, technology, or culture know the techniques of writing for the new reader. Few institutions such as public libraries and community cultural centers effectively reach the new reader. Not only do they lack the necessary variety and quality of culturally relevant materials at the new reader's level, they are not constituted to facilitate communication *from* the low income communities as well as *to* them.

Efforts were being made by the OAS in the

1980s to organize the services necessary to create and maintain an ambience of reading in rural and urban communities that have achieved bare literacy. Its projects in this field deal with the creation, production, and dissemination of printed materials to and from the new reader through channels independent of the formal education system. The OAS builds on existing literacy and community development projects to make use of activities that have begun and to provide the essential follow-up. Efforts are made to improve coordination between and organization of a variety of existing cultural, economic, and technical institutions at the community level as well as at the national and regional levels. Cores of people in each country are trained to write for the new reader, including journalists, fiction writers, librarians, cultural administrators, and specialists from technical, agricultural, health, science, and cultural fields. These same people are also trained in community research techniques and in distribution of information. New readers are trained in use and construction of mimeographs and in communication techniques so they can produce their own materials. Community participation in design and implementation of the projects is an important feature. Projects in Central America and the Andean countries are working together to share expertise and materials through an Inter-American network.

Publishing and Mass Media. A large potential market for children's books in Spanish is being served by publishers in Spain and Mexico whose publishing industries are well organized. Most Latin American publishers produce small editions and do not promote their books vigorously, with the result that the books are unnecessarily expensive, the writers and illustrators of Latin America have no market for their work, and Latin Americans have little access to books published in their own countries or elsewhere in Latin America. The same can be said of radio and television production for children. Between 1980 and 1985 the Proyecto Interamericano de Literatura Infantil (PILI), headquartered in Venezuela, built up 12 national documentation centers on children's literature as part of the Inter-American Network on Children's Literature, which collects and disseminates information about national publishers, writers and illustrators abroad and within each country. More are being created. These centers send information to the Banco del Libro in Venezuela. It in turn sends them relevant information. The Banco publishes current notices of recent books in catalogue format and sends this information to the countries so that potential buyers can have access to the latest Latin American publishing. The centers met in Bolivia as a group for the first time in November 1984 to plan how each could help the others improve their work. With Radionederland and the Inter-American Center for Advanced Journalism Studies for Latin America (CIESPAL), the OAS was establishing in 1986 a similar means for exchange and production of radio and television programs for children as well as for training of producers, actors, and writers. PILI promotes Latin American materials abroad through exhibits and participation in world book fairs, particularly the Bologna Book Fair, where the OAS exhibits from 1980 gave many Latin American publishers their first broad exposure. It also trains writers, illustrators, publishers, and journalists.

Archives. The member states of the OAS comprise two main archival traditions: the Hispanic and the British. The Spanish-speaking countries inherited a sophisticated, highly advanced system of record keeping from Spain that fell into disuse but that left the countries with valuable colonial archives. The English-speaking members are new countries. Many are beginning to establish national archives. (Jamaica, the Bahamas, and Barbados have well-established archives.) Their colonial records are largely in England. Their national history is short. In the Spanish-speaking countries, OAS assistance is devoted largely to improving the education level of archives staff through fellowships for basic training at the OAS Inter-American Center for Archives in Argentina, and for advanced studies in Spain, and to helping countries develop effective archives networks. In the newest English-speaking member countries, OAS helps to establish archives legislation, devise records management, and train the new staffs in archives management. Assistance to archives is closely tied with that to libraries.

Conservation. Through an Inter-American project and national projects, the OAS helps libraries and archives with storage, repair, microfilming, and architectural planning. It provides training, advice, and equipment. OAS emphasizes prevention of damage through proper storage and cleaning and provides assistance simultaneously in each country to policy makers, administrators, and "bench" people. Because the conservators of Europe and the United States are largely technicians with advanced formal education, their manuals and techniques are frequently not applicable in countries where the person doing the repair probably has not finished secondary school. Unlike the richer countries, manual labor is low cost and highly skilled in most member states while advanced mechanized methods are prohibitively expensive. The OAS therefore tries to adapt basic technical publications to appropriate levels. It emphasizes the lower-cost manual techniques that do not require expensive equipment that is frequently impossible to maintain.

SUSAN SHATTUCK BENSON

Osborn, Andrew D.
(1902–)

Andrew Delbridge Osborn, university librarian, author on library cataloguing practice, and library educator, wrote the standard treatise for librarians on serial publications.

Osborn was born in Launceston, Tasmania, Australia, on June 14, 1902. When, at the age of 17, he joined the Australian Commonwealth Parliamentary Library, it was still in Melbourne. He rose in its ranks to be Senior Cataloguer, a post he held for eight years.

In 1925 Osborn received his B.A. degree in psychology and philosophy from the University of Melbourne, and in 1927 his M.A. degree. January 1928, however, found him no longer in Australia. Looking for new professional and academic opportunities, he presented himself for employment at the Director's office in the New York Public Library. He was given a job at the information desk under the direction of

Frank A. Waite, whose daughter he was to marry. At the New York Public Library he rubbed shoulders with Robert Downs, Quincy Mumford, and David Clift, among others, who were to become, like Osborn himself, luminaries of American librarianship.

Repeating a pattern begun in Melbourne, he entered Columbia University. There he completed his Ph.D. in 1934. His dissertation was published in that same year as *The Philosophy of Edmund Husserl in Its Development from His Mathematical Interests to His First Conception of Phenomenology in Logical Investigations*. A second edition, more simply titled *Edmund Husserl and His Logical Investigations*, was issued in 1949, and this edition was reprinted by Garland Publishing in 1980. During the mid- to late 1930s, Osborn wrote a number of philosophical articles for the *Journal of Philosophy*.

But his career was to be that of librarian, not philosopher. While working at the New York Public Library, he wrote an article on the Prussian Union Catalogue for *Library Journal*. It was perhaps to plant an idea that bore fruit a few years later. In 1935–36, on a leave of absence from the Library, he completed the requirements for the A.M.L.S. degree at the University of Michigan, where his mentors were William Warner Bishop and Margaret Mann.

At the suggestion of Keyes Metcalfe, he was invited to spend the academic year 1936–37 organizing a new library school at the University of Southern California. Bishop persuaded him to spend the following academic year teaching in the Michigan Library School. There Osborn completed his masterful translation of the German cataloguing rules. His *The Prussian Instructions: Rules for the Alphabetical Catalogs of the Prussian Library* was published by the University of Michigan Press in 1938. For this work Osborn provided a comprehensive and scholarly introduction and useful footnotes to the text. Like his Husserl book, his translation of the Prussian Instructions was something of a tour de force in its mastery of German and in its grasp of the scholarship of its subject.

In 1938 Osborn followed Metcalfe to Harvard and began what might be called the first of his three major careers. He served at Harvard until 1958. He became Chief of the Serials Division, Assistant Librarian in Charge of Cataloguing, and eventually Associate Librarian. His work at Harvard was amplified by various consulting and writing assignments. He was appointed to the important committee Archibald MacLeish, Librarian of Congress, created under the chairmanship of Carleton B. Joeckel to study reorganizing the processing operations of the Library of Congress. The committee reported in 1940. Osborn's participation in this work was followed by a number of surveys, both in collaboration with others and alone, of a variety of libraries—public, state, and university—and of the Library School of the University of Illinois (1943). In 1948–49 he took a leave of absence to head the processing section of the United Nations Library in New York and continued as a consultant to that library through 1951.

His experience during this period crystallized into a number of major publications. Chief among these was his celebrated though relatively short paper, "The Crisis in Cataloging," which was published in *The Library Quarterly* in 1931. In it, Osborn describes and condemns what he calls the legalistic,

perfectionist, and bibliographic approaches to cataloguing and calls for a pragmatic approach emphasizing economy, efficiency, and common sense. Not only should catalogue codes become clearer and simpler, in Osborn's view, but library administrators should take a firm stand to ensure cost-effective, streamlined processing in catalogue departments. Osborn dealt equally bluntly with the problems of classification and subject headings, concluding that systems for intellectual access to library materials had become too cumbersome and complex to be effective. The paper was widely reviewed, reprinted, and translated. Osborn followed it up over the years with other thoughtful commentaries on and surveys of current cataloguing practice.

In 1942 and 1943 he helped with the revision of Margaret Mann's *Introduction to Cataloging and the Classification of Books*. Osborn had dedicated his translation of the *Prussian Instructions* to Mann in 1938. He was to receive the American Library Association's Margaret Mann citation in 1959.

Osborn's *Serial Publications: Their Place and Treatment in Libraries* was published by ALA in 1955. Widely reviewed, it remains the standard treatise in its field.

In 1958 Osborn began his second major career. He returned to Australia as Associate Librarian of the University of Sydney, where he soon became Librarian. He remained in Sydney four years. During that time he almost doubled the University Library's collection; created an undergraduate library; and planned and oversaw the erection of the new Fisher Library—remarkable both for its design as a library and as a building. Upon completion, it immediately won several major architectural prizes.

Osborn operated on a scale and with an energy hitherto unprecedented in Australian librarianship. Though he created considerable consternation and eventually strong criticism among academic administrators and some of his more conservative professional colleagues, he helped to dramatize the paucity of library resources throughout the country and the need for aggressive expansion if the needs of modern scholarship were to be met. Thus he was instrumental in enlarging the horizons of librarianship as a profession in Australia. Whatever difficulties his drive and style of action caused in the University of Sydney, his achievements were ultimately recognized by the University itself when it awarded him an honorary LL.D. degree in 1978. (He was the first librarian to be so honored by an Australian university.)

Osborn left Australia in 1962. After a stint of teaching at the Library School at the University of Pittsburgh, he began his third major career in 1966 when he undertook the challenge of creating a new school of library and information science at the University of Western Ontario in Canada. The rapidity of development and outstanding success of that venture are remarkable. In a period of four years, he developed the School, assembled an international faculty, indoctrinated the faculty with a special philosophy of instruction based on the repudiation of the lecture method and the use of a special seminar method that he devised, organized a large experimentally arranged library with a major rare-books and bibliography collection to serve as the School's laboratory, secured accreditation for the School, and populated it with a student body that had grown to 200 by 1970. The resonance of his powerful personality and of his educational philosophy for the new school remained perceptible within its walls for many years after his departure.

In 1970 Osborn retired to Sydney. He set up there as a bookseller, though he continued to travel, to teach occasionally, and to write (a second edition of *Serial Publications* appeared in 1973). Indomitable and indefatigable, Osborn continued his work. He bought out the third edition of *Serial Publications* in 1980.

REFERENCES

Serials Librarian (Spring 1982) is devoted to Osborn. Of special note are Keyes Metcalfe, "Andrew D. Osborn"; Harrison Bryan, "The Three Careers of Andrew Osborn"; Constantine M. Hotinsky, "Andrew D. Osborn and Education for Librarianship in Canada"; and Perry D. Morrison and Elizabeth B. Cooksey, "Andrew D. Osborn: A Bio-Bibliography."

W. BOYD RAYWARD

W. Boyd Rayward
Paul-Marie-Ghislain Otlet

Otlet, Paul-Marie-Ghislain
(1868–1944)

It is largely due to Paul-Marie-Ghislain Otlet, Belgian lawyer, bibliographer, and internationalist, in a life-long collaboration with Henri LaFontaine, that there exist the International Federation for Documentation (FID), the Union of International Associations (UIA), and a major bibliographical tool still in widespread international use, the Universal Decimal Classification (UDC). He also initiated in Europe the formal study of documentation, a term he popularized and gave its specialized contemporary meaning. His work and that of friends and followers had considerable influence in the United States, especially in the founding of the American Documentation Institute, now the American Society for Information Science.

He was born in Brussels on August 23, 1868, and his family was wealthy and of some social importance; as he grew up he was surrounded by notable figures in the literary, artistic, and intellectual circles of Brussels. His education was at first private and then in the hands of the Jesuits until he transferred in 1866 from the Université de Louvain to the Université Libre de Bruxelles, where he earned a law degree in 1890. He then married his cousin Fernande Gloner and joined an old family friend, Emile Picard, as a *stagiaire* (trainee) at the Palais de Justice.

But the law was of no vital interest to him, and he longed for some inspirational work of social and intellectual value. In 1891 he was to find both in the recently formed Société des Etudes Sociales et Politiques. At this time he began his collaboration with Henri LaFontaine, a former stagiaire of Picard's, now an international jurist of some reputation, and 15 years Otlet's senior. LaFontaine had directed a section for bibliography in the Society, and the disciplines of bibliography seemed to fire Otlet's imagination. In a seminal paper, "Un Peu de Bibliographie" ("Something About Bibliography," 1892), he addressed the question: "How can the social sciences be given the positive and documentary character of the natural sciences?" Some of the answers, he believed, could be

found in new forms of bibliography practiced on an international scale.

In 1893 the two friends expanded their work and became codirectors of what they now called the International Institute of Sociological Bibliography. Otlet's discovery of Melvil Dewey's Decimal Classification in 1895 led them to seek yet further expansion. Under the sponsorship of the Belgian government and with financial support from Ernest Solvay, industrialist and social theorist, they convened the first International Conference on Bibliography to discuss the problems involved in this expansion. The conference resolved that a catalogue truly universal in scope should be attempted, that an International Institute of Bibliography (IIB) should be formed to further the work, that the Decimal Classification should be adopted en bloc as the basis for the subject arrangement of the catalogue, and that a documentary union of governments should be created to support it. The Belgian government provided a headquarters for the Institute, and an International Office of Bibliography (OIB) was established by Royal Decree, September 17, 1895 (an official documentary union was never achieved, though the idea was raised again in 1908, 1910, and 1919).

The Universal Bibliographic Repertory (RBU) grew rapidly. By 1903 its various parts together contained over 6,000,000 notices; the number in the 1930s was variously estimated as between 12,000,000 and 15,000,000. An on-demand search service was instituted, and the service gradually expanded in the number and variety of consultations made of it. The Office began bibliographical publications of its own, directed others, and persuaded numerous bibliographical publishers to adapt their publications to meet minimum requirements for easy incorporation of entries into the RBU (thus becoming what were called "contributions" to the "Bibliographia Universalis").

The classification was to provide subject access to the RBU and was developed as the repertory grew. For Otlet and LaFontaine the Decimal Classification and the three-by-five-inch card, with its promise of indefinite intercalation, constituted a modern technology that for the first time in history made possible the creation of an up-to-date universal subject catalogue of infinite extensibility and correctability. On the one hand, they interested a cadre of prominent European scholars and scientists in developing the tables of the classification; on the other, Otlet gradually elaborated those technical features that were to make it distinctive and the first "faceted" classification. These features were a series of common subdivisions and methods for extending or elaborating classification numbers using combinatorial symbols of a prescribed function and order. The sophistication of the system was to enable it to express what Otlet called "all the nuances of ideologico-bibliographical analysis" of documents. The first full edition of the classification with a detailed discussion of principles, rules, and practices appeared in 1905 under the title *Manuel du répertoire bibliographique universel* ("Manual of the Repertoire of Universal Bibliography").

The process of expansion and revision in Belgium of the American edition of the classification was conducted in close consultation with Melvil Dewey and his assistants in the United States in Otlet's rather one-sided hope that concordance between the two versions might be maintained. As the years passed, however, divergencies inevitably increased: the purposes of the two classifications and the philosophies guiding their elaboration were too different for much mutual understanding or for accommodation to be achieved.

The first decade of the 20th century brought many developments in the IIB's work. The Institute held conferences in 1897, 1900, 1908, and 1910. In 1905 a Universal Iconographic Repertory, a "documentary repertory of pictorial material," arranged by UDC, was begun, and was intended to provide an illustrative supplement to the RBU. In 1907 came an Encyclopedic Repertory of Dossiers, in which brochures, pamphlets, and periodical and newspaper articles were assembled; its purpose was to give the RBU a substantive component, to constitute a kind of encyclopedia for which the RBU could theoretically act as a table of contents, its essential function for knowledge as a whole in Otlet's view. Also in 1907 a Collective Library of Learned Associations was opened, bringing together the libraries of a variety of national and international associations and societies, the number of which grew rapidly with the years, their collections as a whole providing a kind of documentary backup for the RBU.

Paralleling Otlet and LaFontaine's widening concern with the international organization of knowledge was their increasing interest in the problems of international organizations themselves, for, as Otlet observed, "The proper organization of documentation considered in the widest sense of the term is today one of the foremost functions to have devolved on international associations." In 1906 the two friends founded a Central Office of International Associations and mounted first a survey of those having headquarters in Belgium and then, in collaboration with Cyril Van Overbergh and the Belgian Sociological Society, a survey of international organizations more generally. In 1909 they coedited with Alfred Fried the *Annuaire de la Vie Internationale;* this directory, begun by Fried in 1904, was enormously expanded and was prefaced by a long, comprehensive analysis by Otlet of the structure, government, and functions of international organizations. They published a subsequent edition of the directory independently of Fried in 1910–11. Above all, in 1910 they organized the first World Congress of International Associations, a highly successful affair at which the Union of International Associations (UIA) was founded and for which the Central Office henceforth acted as headquarters.

A number of the associations taking part in the Congress in 1910 supported Otlet's proposal that the left wing of the Palais du Cinquantenaire should become an international museum. The Belgian government approved, and Otlet conceived of the huge building as a preliminary location for a Palais Mondial, a vast center of internationalism. In this were to be conjoined the bibliographic services of the IIB, the international library, the international museum, secretarial and publishing services for the associations, and ultimately an international university. Here, Otlet hoped, they would be developed as an integral whole with the support of governments and associations. The organization, rationalization, and propaganda for the Palais Mondial became the major preoccupations of the rest of Otlet's life. A second, even larger World Congress of International Associations was held in 1913, and plans for a third in San Francisco in 1915 were also begun. The museum had grown vigorously in the interim, and some attempt to consolidate in the Palais Mondial the collections and services originating with the RBU in 1895 was made before the outbreak of World War I put an end to such efforts.

During these prewar years Otlet had grown in importance internationally and in Belgian official and intellectual circles. The course of his personal life, however, had not been smooth. He had two sons, Marcel and Jean, the latter killed in the war, but his marriage eventually failed, and in 1908 he and Fernande were divorced. In the early years of the new century, after a series of crises, the Otlet family fortune was almost wholly lost, and Otlet was to be plagued by legal and family problems associated with its dissolution. He married in 1912 a wealthy Dutchwoman, Cato Van Nederhasselt, whose income helped support him and his institutes for the rest of his life.

During the war he lived mostly in Paris and was an active member of the European movement for a League of Nations (Société des Nations). An integral part of the international order Otlet hoped to see established after the war was the creation by the League of an organization for intellectual relations with the Palais Mondial at its center. Otlet and LaFontaine had some influence on the League's eventual creation of an International Committee on Intellectual Cooperation.

After the war the primary task confronting the two friends was to resume their work in Brussels. They found that their institutes and collections had been unharmed by the occupation government and carefully maintained by a small, devoted staff. In 1920 they held the first of what were called Quinzaines Internationales, or International Fortnights (others were held in 1921, 1922, and 1924), during which meetings of the IIB, the UIA, and other international associations were held. Otlet now called for the creation of an International University and sought for it the patronage of the League of Nations. The League, however, impoverished, politically insecure, and only recently established in Geneva, was prepared to offer no more than sympathy and encouragement for the new enterprise.

Otlet and LaFontaine's various undertakings, now increasingly identified with Otlet, at first seemed successfully recovered after the war, and they had been completed by the foundation in 1920 of what was rather extravagantly named an International University. They fell fairly soon, however, on difficult times. Otlet could not interest the League in offering them any concrete support; its Committee on Intellectual Cooperation, created in 1922, soon went in directions that he regarded as inimical to the Palais Mondial and all it stood for. Efforts to collaborate with the Committee and with its executive arm, the International Institute for Intellectual Cooperation in Paris, failed and led to bitterness on Otlet's part and suspicion of him on that of League officials. The support of the Belgian government became increasingly uncertain until, in 1924, for a short period it actually resumed occupancy of the Palais Mondial for a trade fair.

It became clear that something needed to be done for the IIB lest it be lost and buried in the Palais Mondial. Assisted by LaFontaine, the Institute gradually began to assume an independent existence. New personalities began to move it in new directions, even changing its name in 1932 to the International Institute of Documentation. Otlet disliked and resisted all of the changes that this essentially new generation of supporters effected. He restored the Palais Mondial, which he now began to call the "Mundaneum," as best he could after the dislocations of 1924, and continued to seek support for it. His opposition to the trends in the Institute toward decentralization and federalism was silenced in 1934 when the Belgian government once more closed the Palais Mondial, this time effectively for good. The UIA's last meeting was held in 1924, though Otlet continued to issue publications in its name, and the Germans tried to use it for their purposes during the occupation of Brussels in World War II.

In all of these interwar years of struggle and disappointment, Otlet continued to act as one of the Secretaries-General of the IIB along with LaFontaine and eventually Frits Donker Duyvis. While it was open, he regularly lectured at the Palais Mondial. He worked rather ineffectively and controversially on the revision of the UDC, the completed second edition of which finally appeared in 1932. He gave courses in librarianship and documentation in Brussels and wrote ceaselessly on the broad international questions that interested him. As grand old men of European documentation, he and LaFontaine were much feted at the World Congress of Universal Documentation held in Paris in 1937 jointly with the International Institute for Intellectual Cooperation. Here the IIB's name was again changed, to the International Federation for Documentation. Otlet, however, continued to speak of it as part of that vast intellectual edifice, the Mundaneum, to the elaboration of which so much of his life had been devoted, and in protest against the changes that had occurred in the IIB he cut it out of his will.

A lifetime of research and writing culminated in the publication in 1934 of *Traité de la Documentation* ("Treatise on Documentation") and in 1935 of *Monde: Essai d'Universalisme* ("The World: an Essay on Universalism"). These are large, slightly absurd encyclopedic works from which little insight seems possible because they contain no theories and offer no arguments, positions, or proof. Earlier writings, however, remain landmarks in the formal study of documentation and internationalism and have been too much neglected.

Otlet died in Brussels on December 10, 1944, a year after LaFontaine. After World War II both the FID and the UIA were resurrected. The former still issues the UDC in a variety of translations and editions though allowing it no exclusively central place in its work; the latter has taken up the *Yearbook of International Organizations* as a major task and has made of it an indispensable reference tool.

REFERENCES

Otlet's manuscript diary and the archives of the IIB are preserved in the Mundaneum in Brussels.

Samuel Bradford, "Fifty Years of Documentation," in his *Documentation* (1948).

F. Donker Duyvis, "International Federation for Documentation," *Journal of Documentary Reproduction* (1940).

A full-length study of Otlet is W. Boyd Rayward, *The Universe of Information: The Work of Paul Otlet for Documentation and International Organisation,* FID Publication 520 (1976), which contains a comprehensive but occasionally inaccurate bibliography of Otlet's writings. A translation of a selection of these and an improved bibliography by Rayward was in preparation in 1985.

W. BOYD RAYWARD

Pakistan

The Islamic Republic of Pakistan, a federal republic in South Asia, was established on August 14, 1947, as a result of partition of the subcontinent. East Pakistan broke away in December 1971 to form the independent state of Bangladesh. Pakistan is bordered by Afghanistan and the U.S.S.R. on the north, the People's Republic of China on the northeast, India on the east and southeast, the Arabian Sea on the south, and Iran on the west. Population (1984) 91,880,000; area 796,095 sq.km. The national language is Urdu, but English continues to be the official language.

History. Although Pakistan is a young country, the areas that it includes have had a long history and gained eminence for library facilities far and wide. Even in the immediate past, under British rule, Lahore, now the capital of Punjab, was regarded as a Mecca of libraries. The Punjab University inaugurated the first library course at university level in 1915 under the directorship of an American librarian, Asa Don Dickinson (1876–1960), who had taken his training under Melvil Dewey. His *Punjab Library Primer* (University of the Punjab, 1916) served as a manual and reader for librarians and library science students alike.

The Punjab Library Association, founded during Dickinson's one-year stay in Lahore, was short-lived, but the All-India Conference of Librarians, covened by the government of India in Lahore January 4–8, 1918, paved the way for the organization of the Librarians Club. The club hosted the seventh All-India Public Library Conference in Lahore in 1929. The Association was revived after the conference and began publishing a journal, *Modern Librarian,* as its official organ in 1930. It continued publication until partition in 1947.

The riots that occurred at the time of the partition and the mass influx of refugees from India in August 1947 had adverse effects on the new country's library resources. The library school, the Punjab Library Association, and its journal all closed. Four renowned libraries of Lahore, which were then the largest libraries in West Pakistan, were damaged and their services disrupted. They were the Punjab University Library (opened 1906–08, with a collection of 105,295 volumes and 15,000 manuscripts in 1947); the Punjab Public Library (founded in 1884, with a collection of 82,530 volumes and bound journals in 1947); the Punjab Civil Secretariat Library (founded 1885); and the Dayal Singh Trust Library (founded 1908, with a collection of 40,000 volumes in 1947).

Khan Bahadur K. M. Asadullah (1890–1949), the founding Secretary of the Indian Library Association and the former Librarian of the Imperial Library, Calcutta, who was born and educated in Lahore, returned to the city in 1947, but could not help the worsening library situation in the newly emerging country.

Pakistan, therefore, had to start its library development from scratch. The Karachi Library Association was founded in 1949 in Karachi, then the federal capital. A year later a locally based national organization, the Pakistan Bibliographical Working Group, was established. Also in 1950, Dickinson's school was revived in Lahore. 1950.

Library campaigns that followed and the arrival of visiting library experts helped bring about noticeable changes in attitudes to library service in the mid-1950s. Landmark events were the first post-graduate diploma course at the then federal University of Karachi in 1956, thanks to the efforts of Abdul Moid (1920–84), and the founding of the Pakistan Library Association in 1957, with Abdul Moid as the founding Secretary General.

Pakistan librarianship had yet to face many ups and downs. The publication of the Report of the Commission on National Education in 1961 helped place emphasis on much-neglected public libraries in the 1960s, but national development during that period was oriented towards research and industry, and libraries in those sectors also tended to get more development attention.

The Education Policy (1972–80) on which work was started in the later 1960s once again created enthusiasm for the development of public libraries in the country. But the separation of East Pakistan in 1971 and the political unrest in 1977 forestalled any lasting developments in public library service. The appointment of a Cabinet Committee for Reading Libraries, headed by the Federal Minister of Finance, marked a significant breakthrough in 1981.

National Library. Ad hoc functions of a national library are performed in part by the Department of Libraries in Islamabad (founded in 1949 in Karachi), the Liaquat Memorial Library in Karachi (founded in 1950), and the Central Secretariat Library in Islamabad (founded in 1951 in Karachi). Funds for the construction of the National Library of Pakistan, to be located in Islamabad, were made in each Five Year Plan from 1965, but construction of the building was not started until the later years of the Fifth Five Year Plan (1978–83). Builders hoped to complete the library in mid-1985.

By 1984 a collection of 15,000 volumes had been accumulated for the national library under the Copyright Ordinance of 1967. In addition, some 22,000 local and foreign publications were also acquired. The library was designed to have the facilities of a first-rate auditorium for cultural and educational functions in the federal capital and 15 research rooms, 500 seats for readers, and modern microfilming and computing services.

The Dr. Mohamed Husain Library, University of Karachi.

University of Karachi

The *National Bibliography,* to be published annually and also to be housed in the new library, was published in Karachi at annual but irregular intervals for the years 1962–77, with gaps for 1965–67 and 1970–71. The *Bibliography* for 1978 was published in Islamabad, but no further volumes have followed.

Archival materials in Pakistan are maintained at the federal and provincial government levels. The National Archives of Pakistan is in Islamabad. The Ministry of Foreign Affairs maintains its archives independently. The National Archives of Pakistan also collects and maintains private collections, including Quadi-e-Azam papers and a Lakha collection on Quadi-e-Azam. A number of catalogues of Quaid-e-Azam papers have been published by the National Archives. It will also house the Freedom Movement Archives, housed in the Dr. Mahmud Husain Library at Karachi University.

Academic Libraries. University libraries increased from 15 in 1978 to 20 in 1981. Two libraries (the NWFP University of Engineering and Technology, Peshawar, and the University of Azad Jammu and Kashmir, Muzaffarabad) were opened in 1980 and three (the Islamic University, Islamabad, the NWFP Agricultural University, Peshawar, and the Aga Khan University of Health Sciences, Karachi) in 1981.

Of these universities, 3 are federal, 16 are provincial or state institutions, and 1 is private. These universities (except the private Aga Khan University of Health Sciences) are funded by the University Grants Commission in Islamabad.

By and large, these university libraries constitute an advanced group of libraries in the country. Together (but excluding the University of Azad Jammu and Kashmir, which does not maintain a central library) they hold a sizeable collection of some 2,406,300 volumes (26.8 percent of the collections of all types of libraries in the country). For 34,500 students in 1978, 15 university libraries then held a collection of 1,608,500 volumes. By the early 1980s collections registered an increase of 49.6 percent in bookstock and catered to the needs of 47,400 students. Thus they had been able to catch up with the student growth of 37.4 percent over the period.

Notable central university library collections are at the Universities of Punjab (founded in 1882 and opened 1906–08; 309,970 volumes); Karachi (founded in 1952; 240,000 volumes); and Sind (founded in 1948; 137,813 volumes; with 50,000 volumes at Shah Latif Campus, Khairpur, 70,000 volumes at the Institute of Sindhology, Jamshoro; and the Agricultural University, Faisalabad (founded in 1961; 118,000 volumes).

Libraries in Pakistan (1982)

Type	Administrative units	Service points	Volumes in collections	Annual expenditures (rupee)	Population served	Professional staff	Total staff
National	1[a]	--	37,000	21,490,000	84,253,000	--	--
Academic							
University	74[b]	--	2,406,300	16,586,300[c]	47,400	223	772[d]
College	410[e]	--	3,025,300	34,747,500	472,400	246	586[f]
Public	136	18 + 11 reading rooms[g,h]	1,340,500	12,947,900	84,253,000	85[i]	547[i]
School	343[j]	--	690,500	--	235,100	18	--
Special	178[k]	--	1,368,000	--	--	90[l]	358
Pakistan National							
Center Libraries	25	--	87,500	93,800	4,300	50	121
Box Libraries	55[m]	--	15,000	--	--	--	--

[a]Part of the functions of a national library are performed on an ad hoc basis by the Department of Libraries, Liaquat Memorial Library, Karachi, and Secretariat Library, Islamabad. The building of the National Library of Pakistan was under final stages of construction in 1984.
[b]19 universities and 55 constituent colleges/institutes; the University of Azad Jammu and Kashmir has no central library.
[c]Figures for four or five universities are not available.
[d]Largely of the central library except in a few cases, such as Punjab, Quaid-e-Azam, and Aga Khan.
[e]Out of 682 colleges in Pakistan, figures for 315 colleges are given. All the colleges (69) in Karachi are included.
[f]Figures for colleges in Karachi only.
[g]Branches in Karachi.
[h]One reading room in Karachi and 10 in Peshawar.
[i]For 106 public libraries only.
[j]Out of 500 Secondary Schools in Karachi, figures for 335 Secondary Schools only are given here. Also included are 8 schools in the interior of Sind.
[k]Out of 242 libraries, figures for 178 libraries are available.
[l]Figures for 72 special libaries are given.
[m]Sponsored by the Ministry of Local Government and Rural Development in cooperation with the Asia Foundation, the experimental phase of box libraries to Union Councils was completed in 1983.

Sources: Anis Khurshid, *The Status of Library Resources,* Lahore, Student Services, 1982 [1984]; Nasim Fatima, *Secondary School Library Resources & Services,* Karachi, Library Promotion Bureau, 1984; Hasam Akhtar, *Kalyati Kutub Khanay: ek Jaeza* (Urdu; College Libraries: a Survey), Lahore, Directorate-General of Public Libraries, Punjab, 1982; and Mah Talat and Zubair Malik's unpublished master's theses submitted to the Department of Library and Information Science at the University of Karachi in November 1981 relating, respectively, to the library resources of college libraries in Karachi and those of all types of libraries of Pakistan.

The Punjab University Library had a rich collection of manuscripts (19,931) in Arabic, Gurmukhi, Persian, Sanskrit, and Urdu. A three-volume catalogue of the manuscripts in Arabic, Persian, and Urdu (1942–48), a two-volume catalogue of those in Sanskrit (1932–41), and a one-volume catalogue of those in Arabic alone (1982) have been published. The special collections of the library are renowned equally for their rarity and richness. A three-volume catalogue of the Sherwani collection was published from 1968 to 1973.

The Dr. Mahmud Husain Library at the University of Karachi is known for the size of its collection of relatively modern literature. It has also published a number of catalogues of its holdings in various forms, subjects, and areas of national interest. The Freedom Movement Archives, housed in the Library, contain about 100,000 documents and pieces pertaining to the All-India Muslim League and the Freedom Movement. These documents were in the process of transfer in the mid-1980s to the National Archives of Pakistan in Islamabad. The University has also acquired personal collections of national leaders and freedom fighters such as Sardar Abdur Rab Nashtar and Haji Abdullah Haroon that will be retained in the University. The University is also considering a proposal for the establishment and maintenance of its own university archives. The rare books and manuscripts in the Sind University Library and those of the Institute of Sindhology are also of great research value to the history and culture of the country.

The building of the Dr. Mahmud Husain Library at Karachi University, completed in 1964, stands out as the premier library building of architectural significance in the country.

Public Libraries. The concept of a public library was grossly misunderstood in the country until the 1950s. The publication of the report of the Commission on National Education in 1961, requiring local bodies to maintain public libraries and reading rooms directed toward the promotion of reading materials, resulted in a burst of enthusiasm for public libraries in the country. The Education Policy (1972–80), for which a stage was set in the mid-1960s, further promoted the idea of public libraries in the country. A broad-based system adequate to sustain even a small number of public libraries did not come about, however. An exception was the city of Karachi, where a loosely knit system had been evolved. After 1980, and especially after a Cabinet Committee for Reading Libraries was established in 1981, some positive change in the provision of public library service became apparent.

Public libraries grew from just 21 in 1951 to some 136 by the early 1980s. In 1978 there were reportedly some 240 public libraries in the country, but a good number of them were closed because of neglect in maintenance.

Many of the 136 libraries hardly merit the designation "public libraries," but still they are the only libraries accessible to the public at large. These libraries together hold a collection of 1,350,500 volumes (14.9 percent of the country's total collection). For their maintenance, support is provided by governments at the federal, provincial, and local levels. The use of these libraries is minimal.

The Punjab Public Library, Lahore (founded in 1984), holds the country's third largest collection (200,000 volumes) with 1,200 manuscripts in Arabic, Gurmukhi, Persian, and Urdu, of which printed catalogues are available. The Library also maintains a special collection, *Baituil Qur'an,* containing special materials on Qur'anic studies in the form of microfilms and tape recordings.

The Dayal Singh Trust Library (founded in 1908), also in Lahore, is the second largest public library in the country, with 100,000 volumes. It published a three-volume catalogue of its manuscript holdings (1974–82).

Good libraries maintained by the federal and provincial governments include the Liaquat Memorial Library, Karachi, run by the federal government (1950; 93,846 volumes); the Central Public Library, Bahawalpur, run by the government of Punjab (1948; 77,773 volumes); and the Khairpur Public Library, Khairpur, run by the government of Sind (1955; 43,260 volumes). In particular, the Central Public Library, Bahawalpur, is known for its good library services, including those for children. The Quaid-e-Azam Library, Lahore (1981; 30,000 volumes), in a beautiful garden, Bagh-e-Jinnah, was to be opened to the public as a research and reference library. A directorate-general of public libraries, the only provincial administrative unit of its kind in the country, was established in Lahore in 1981 to administer that library and other public libraries in the province of Punjab.

At the local government level, the Karachi Metropolitan Corporation maintains the largest number of public libraries in the country. The system, although weak in coordination of resources and services, comprises one central library, the Karachi Metropolitan City Library (1851; 42,115 volumes), and 18 branch libraries of varying sizes. These libraries together hold a collection of 158,000 volumes.

A seven-member Technical Working Group, headed by Amis Khurshid, was appointed in 1982 to conduct a survey of public library facilities in Pakistan. Under a directive of the Cabinet Committee for Reading Libraries, the group is to prepare the "design and size of a national system of public libraries in Pakistan."

School Libraries. These libraries are the most neglected libraries in the country. Libraries at the primary school level are almost nonexistent. Complete statistics for the libraries at the secondary school level are not available, and those available for the city of Karachi are only partial. Out of 500 such schools, statistics for 335 schools showed that in the early 1980s a collection of 687,900 volumes was available in the city for 235,100 students. The library collections varied from 17,000 volumes to fewer than 100 volumes; 61 libraries contained collections of 500 to 1,000 volumes and another 61 libraries between 1,001 and 2,000. The situation in other parts of the country is no better.

Special Libraries. Special libraries, in quality of resources and in accessibility, come next to academic libraries in Pakistan. They contained 1,368,000 volumes in the mid-1980s. Some of these libraries were established in the 1800s, including the Punjab Civil Secretariat Library, Lahore (founded in 1885; 60,000 volumes) and the Punjab Textbook Board Library, Lahore (1892; 32,000 volumes).

These libraries numbered 132 in social sciences

and 110 in sciences and technology. A large concentration of the libraries in both fields is in Punjab, mostly in Lahore.

The largest collections in these libraries after the Punjab Civil Secretariat Libraries are held by the State Bank of Pakistan Library, Karachi (1949; 55,000); the National Bank of Pakistan Library, Karachi (1965; 40,000); the Anjuman Taraqq-e-Urdu Library, Karachi (1952; 36,000); the High Court Bar Library and the Hamdard Foundation Library, both in Karachi (1940 and 1948, respectively; 35,000 volumes each); and the Islamic Research Library, Islamabad (1960; 30,000 volumes). Two libraries in Karachi, the Patent Office Library and the Pakistan Standards Institution Library, hold 918,957 and 25,000 patents respectively. The Sandeman Public Library, Quetta (1856) is also a depository for patents.

In the field of science and technology, the Pakistan Scientific and Technological Documentation Centre (PASTIC), replacing the former Pakistan Scientific and Technical Documentation Centre (PANSDOC), which was founded in 1957 in Karachi under a Unesco subsidy, from 1974 became a self-contained system without any defined sharing arrangement with outside libraries in the country. Strictly centralized, PASTIC plans to establish a national science reference library at its headquarters in Islamabad. The existing libraries at various regional offices will serve as branch libraries.

For the social and humanistic sciences, there is no documentation center in the country. A privately organized center, the Islamic Documentation and Information Centre (ISDIC), was established in 1982 at the University of Karachi.

The Islamic Library Information Centre (ISLIC) at the Department of Library and Information Science of the University of Karachi was established in 1974 to act as a clearinghouse for information on libraries and books in the Muslim world.

The Pakistan National Documentation Centre, established in Lahore in 1974, started collecting microfilmed materials of India Office Library records pertaining to the history and culture of Pakistan.

Other Libraries. Rental or vending libraries, popularly known as *anna* libraries, continue to grow, largely because of the absence of public libraries at easily reachable locations in cities and, more important, because most of the libraries that do exist have few reading materials that appeal to popular tastes.

The Pakistan National Centres run 25 libraries in various cities of Pakistan under the administrative supervision of the federal Ministry of Information and Broadcasting. Designed on the pattern of the American Center and British Council libraries, these libraries contain some 87,000 volumes for services to about 4,300 members. The size of collections varies from 20,100 volumes in Rawalpindi to 1,029 volumes in Muzaffarabad.

The Hatim Alavi Memorial Library in Karachi (founded in 1977; 2,000 braille books) provides valuable library services to the blind. Some college libraries in Karachi also maintain braille books in their collections.

The Profession. *Education.* There are six library schools offering courses at the university level leading to the Diploma in Library Science, Bachelor in Library and Information Science, and M.A. in Library and Information Science. The oldest school is that of the University of the Punjab (founded in 1915; suspended, 1947–50), but the University of Karachi was the first in the country to offer the post-graduate Diploma course (now called Bachelor in Library and Information Science), in 1956, and first to offer an M.A. in Library Science (now called M.A. in Library and Information Science), in 1962. It offered the Ph.D. in Library Science from 1967. The school produced more than 900 graduates.

Other universities offering the M.A. in Library Science are those of the Punjab (1974) and Sind (1974). The University of Peshawar offered a diploma course from 1960. Undergraduate courses largely designed for user education were started in junior colleges in 1976 and at the bachelor's level at one degree college in Karachi in 1982.

Associations. The first library associations to be founded in the country were the Punjab Library Association (1948) and the Karachi Library Association (1949). The former manages to survive, although it remained suspended for a number of years in the early 1950s, but the latter closed in 1969. The Pakistan Bibliographical Working Group, founded in 1950 as a result of a Unesco-Library of Congress survey of bibliographical activities throughout the world, still exists after many slack years. The *Pakistan National Bibliography (1947–61)* is its important contribution. Two fascicles of this *Bibliography*, listing materials on General Works, Philosophy, Religion, Law, and Languages, were published in 1972–73 by the National Book Centre of Pakistan.

The Pakistan Library Association (founded in 1967) is the only association in the country that is active in the profession. It rotates its headquarters every two years to one of the capital cities. It organizes annual conferences and publishes proceedings. The membership of the Association numbered more than 600 by 1982. The Association also publishes an irregular *Newsletter*. Mahmud Husain (1907–75), an eminent historian and educator of the country, led the Association until 1973 except for a few years in the mid-1960s. Under his leadership the Association was able to campaign effectively for the idea of library service in the country.

In 1960 the Society for the Promotion and Improvement of Libraries (SPIL) was established under the dynamic leadership of a noted philanthropist, Hakim Muhammed Said (1920-   ). The Society held a number of seminars, conferences, and workshops from 1961 to 1974 and published their proceedings and thus was also instrumental in creating awareness of the need for library service in the country. From 1975, however, the Society was inactive.

The Department of Libraries was founded in 1949 as a part of the Federal Ministry of Education. It was a subordinate branch of the Department of Archives and Libraries, under an archivist, and was taken over by a librarian in 1972, after the separation of East Pakistan. Thereafter, it continued to look after library affairs exclusively, but even that change failed to provide the needed library leadership in the absence of a national library.

REFERENCES

Zahiruddin Khurshid, *Ten Years' Work in Librarianship in Pakistan, 1963–1972* (1973).

Anis Khurshid, *The State of Library Resources in Pakistan* (1982).

Mahmud Husain, *Of Libraries and Librarians* (1974).

ANIS KHURSHID

Panama

Panama, a republic of Central America, is bounded by the Caribbean Sea on the north, the Pacific Ocean on the south, Colombia in South America on the east, and Costa Rica on the west. The Canal Zone bisects the Isthmus of Panama. Population (1984 est.) 2,133,000; area 76,650 sq.km. The official language is Spanish, but English is widely spoken.

History and National Library. A decree of January 31, 1942, authorized the establishment of the National Library of Panama. With initial holdings of 10,000 volumes originally at the Cólon Library, which had been donated by the Municipal Council of the Ministry of Education, it was founded on July 11, 1942. The Cólon Library of the Municipality of Panama, dating from October 12, 1892, was discontinued in 1941 by disposition of the District Council. The National Library serves as a repository of the nation's bibliographic production, including all of the literature relating to the history of Panama. Its newspaper section contains the most complete collection of the dailies of the country. The collection totals 200,000 volumes.

Academic Libraries. Academic libraries are under the aegis of the country's two universities—the University of Panama, the national university, and the Santa María La Antigua University, a private institution. The University of Panama has two libraries—the Central Library and the Simón Bolívar Inter-American Library, the latter with sections on medicine and law. Three others are independent of the Central Library—the Library of Dentistry, another at the Institute of Criminology, and a third at the Central American Institute of Administration and Supervision of Education (ICASE).

Simón Bolívar Inter-American Library was established immediately after the founding of the University of Panama in October 1935. The Library was reorganized in 1941 under the direction of Gastón Lyton. In 1951 it was transferred to La Colina, now part of University City. In 1978 it was moved again, to new facilities on the campus. The new Library was given responsibility for the acquisition and organiza-

University of Panama

The Simón Bolívar Inter-American Library, opened on the campus of the University of Panama in 1978.

tion of material from the Libraries of Medicine, Law, and five Regional University Centers at Cólon, Penome, Chitre, Santiago, and Chiriqui. The Library of ICASE was established May 11, 1970. Its collection consists of 5,000 volumes and 100 periodicals.

The Library of the University of Santa María La Antigua was established when the University was founded on April 27, 1965. The collection consists of 50,000 volumes, including imported magazines. It publishes an annual *Boletín Informativo* and bibliographies of existing material.

Public Municipal Libraries. Supported by the municipalities, these libraries are named for their sustaining organizations and not for their primary purpose or services. All offer mostly material for primary school students. There were 18, with a total of some 100,000 volumes, in 1980. The Mayor's Department of Education is in charge of the libraries of the Municipality of Panama.

School Libraries. These serve primary and middle-grade students in their own schools or groups of schools. In Panama City are libraries of the José Dolores Moscote Institute, founded in 1959 (more than 10,000 volumes), and the Octavio Méndez Pereira Library, part of the Isabel Herrera Obaldía Professional School in Paitilla (more than 10,000 books). A Unesco pilot project was organized with the cooperation and technical advice of the National Library and the Association of Librarians of Panama. It serves the following schools: Republic of Cuba, Republic of the Argentine, Republic of Peru, and Chorrillo Community.

Special Libraries. The Library of the Depart-

Libraries in Panama (1980)

Type	Administrative units	Service points	Volumes in collections	Annual expenditures (balboa)	Population served[a]	Professional staff	Total staff
National	--	43	221,000	218,351,000	49,794	6	145
Academic[b]	2	2	14,000	181,000	15,546	10	67
Public	18	18	100,000	2,337,000	9,543	14	56
School[b]	54	54	203,000	60,791,000	41,346	12	76
Special[b]	1	--	49,000	--	189,000	--	--

[a]Registered borrowers.
[b]1977 data.

Source: Unesco, *Statistical Yearbook,* 1984.

ment of the Census and Statistics of the Comptroller General of the Republic was founded in 1914. It serves the public interested in the statistics of Panama as well as other countries and is equipped to reproduce documents. Its collection totals some 55,000 volumes.

The Medical Library of the Social Security General Hospital, established March 31, 1969, contains medical information available to medical personnel working in the social security hospitals, in the city, and in the interior. Its collection consists of 600 books.

The Bio-Medical Library of the Commemorative Gorgas Laboratory is in the City of Panama. The Institute maintains an office in Washington, D.C. Its collection embraces more than 10,000 volumes and some 500 periodical titles. The contents consists of books and reviews covering preventive tropical medicine and certain facets of biology, a result of investigations conducted in the laboratory. It serves the requirements of its scientific personnel and collaborators and the scientific community of the area, in particular of the medical doctors of Saint Thomas and Children's Hospitals. It receives photocopies of articles from the U.S. National Library of Medicine and bibliographies prepared under the MEDLARS and GRACE systems.

Gorgas Hospital Medical Library, founded in 1918, is of interest to clinical medicine, with 30,000 books and periodicals.

The Smithsonian Tropical Research Institute, established in 1925, is near the Canal. It has a fairly complete collection of 22,000 volumes. It serves all persons in Panama and the Canal Zone. It is much used by patrons from the University of Panama.

The Amador Washington Library of the International Communication Agency (ICA) was created in 1952. In 1964 a fire destroyed its physical plant and its collection, and in that year it was recreated with the same staff and new books under its present name. It has a collection of 10,000 volumes and 17,000 microforms. It offers all readers service concerning books published in the U.S.

The Profession. The Panamanian Association of Librarians was established on March 6, 1951. A law approved by the National Assembly in 1956 regulated the profession of librarian and established the National Service throughout the country. Librarians created a guild. The Association participated in national and international activities contributing to the organization and improvement of the libraries in Panama. The Association publishes an annual bulletin. It has also published a bibliography of literature by Panamanian women. It addresses issues concerning the recognition of librarians' professional stature within the sanction of law; the law of 1956 was considered to have failed to achieve its goals.

VICTOR U. MENDIETA ORTIZ*

Panizzi, Sir Anthony
(1797–1879)

Sir Anthony Panizzi (Antonio before knighthood) is one of the greatest figures in library history. Posthumously, Panizzi's reputation has grown ever more lustrous. To Arundell Esdaile he was the most crea-

tive force in the history of the British Museum; to Albert Predeek he was "the greatest lawgiver the library world has known"; to Edward Miller, his biographer, he was "a librarian of librarians, perhaps the greatest we have yet seen."

He was born September 16, 1797, at Brescello, a small town in the Duchy of Modena in northern Italy. After studying at the University of Parma, he practiced law for a while at Brescello. Unfortunately, the Duchy was then under Austrian domination and virtually a police state; when it became known that Panizzi was a member of a secret society working against the government, he was obliged to flee the country. For a short time he lived in Switzerland, but in 1823, like a number of his compatriots, he found refuge in England.

For several years Panizzi eked out a living as a teacher of Italian at Liverpool. In 1828 he was appointed first Professor of Italian Language and Literature at the new University of London, but since students were few and the remuneration small, the appointment turned out to be a barren honor. In 1831 he joined the staff of the British Museum.

Although the British Museum had been founded by an act of Parliament in 1753, in 1831 it was still a random miscellany of museum specimens, books, and manuscripts, in the care of scholarly but unenterprising officials who enjoyed a peaceful but pensionless service. The Museum lacked a vital sense of purpose and its income was slender. The Department of Printed Books, which Panizzi joined as an extra assistant, was among the least regarded of the departments, even though it embraced several former private collections of considerable importance. Among them were the Old Royal Library and the King's Library. The latter, the magnificent private library of George III, was given to the BM in 1823, forcing the Trustees to provide a new building, and work had just begun on it when Panizzi joined the staff.

Although his knowledge of libraries was then slight, by dint of travel and correspondence he had become very well informed by 1836, when he was called upon to give evidence to the Parliamentary Select Committee on the condition and management of the Museum.

In 1837 Panizzi was appointed Keeper of the Department of Printed Books. In this capacity he not only did most of the things for which he is best remembered but had to endure the strongest attacks from his enemies, both within the Museum and outside it. In 1856 Panizzi was appointed Principal Librarian (i.e., Chief Officer) of the BM, but because of ill health he had to resign in 1866. He died in London, April 8, 1879.

Although Panizzi was not lacking in friends, he had to suffer virulent criticism and hatred throughout most of his career at the BM, partly because he was regarded as a foreign upstart and partly because he refused to budge an inch when he believed he was right—as he usually was.

Some librarians are remembered for the work they did for their own libraries; others are remembered for their contribution to librarianship at large. Panizzi belongs squarely to the former group. By the end of the 20th century, the great circular Reading Room of the British Museum, which to many people was Panizzi's finest achievement, probably will be

Sir Anthony Panizzi

vacated when the British Library, of which the former BM Library is now part, takes over its elaborate new headquarters at Somers Town, near London's Saint Pancras Station. No longer, then, will one be able to say, in a literal sense, *Si monumentum requiris circumspice* ("If you seek a monument, look around"). But this was never an altogether satisfactory verdict on Panizzi's achievement, which may be more profitably considered under five headings: bookstock, building, staff, service, and cataloguing.

Bookstock. The vast increase in the bookstock of the BM Library since the 1850s has been due mainly to the action taken by Panizzi, as Keeper of the Department of Printed Books, to enforce the law of legal deposit, under which the Museum was entitled to receive one copy of every new British publication. In recent years it has several times been suggested that deposit at the British Library should be selective, to prevent the acquisition of "rubbish." Panizzi, however, was unwilling to speculate on the probable needs of scholars of the future; he insisted on receiving everything. On the other hand, he recognized the disadvantage to scholars of having a national library with a stock based almost entirely on deposited publications and random donations. By securing regular and generous book funds and using them largely to acquire European and American publications, he gave the stock of the BM Library proper dimensions.

Building. Panizzi's reputation as a library planner rests securely on his successful advocacy (the conception was not entirely his own) of a great circular reading room with extensive surrounding stacks, all fabricated of cast iron, at that time little used in building construction. The addition of these desirable amenities meant the sacrifice of the Museum's inner quadrangle, but the result was accommodation for readers and books without parallel in any other library in the world.

Staff. Panizzi's particular solution to the staffing problems of the BM was to secure for its personnel civil service conditions of employment, including security of tenure. The benefits to the Library were very clear toward the end of the century, when there were several outstanding men in its service who were quite willing to make their work at the BM a lifelong career.

Cataloguing. A large part of the history of the BM Library during Panizzi's service there is concerned with his troubles with the catalogue. When Panizzi joined the BM staff, the main catalogue was urgently in need of revision; the task of preparing a new one was still in hand when Panizzi became Keeper seven years later. The problems that this catalogue generated bothered Panizzi almost continuously for the next 13 years. The main difficulty was that Panizzi and the Trustees could not agree on what kind of catalogue should be provided, but close behind it was the fact that the Trustees interfered with the day-to-day work of the cataloguers.

When he was an assistant librarian, Panizzi had made up his mind as to what was desirable and feasible: an alphabetical name catalogue in manuscript form, compiled throughout by the application of a new, comprehensive code of cataloguing rules. In the end Panizzi achieved this kind of catalogue, but only after long, bitter, and widely publicized wrangling.

The first step was to convince the Trustees that an alphabetical catalogue was preferable to a classed one; the second was to get them to approve a new catalogue code, the famous *91 Catalogue Rules,* which Panizzi drew up with the help of his colleagues. The most difficult step was the third. Panizzi realized that printing the alphabetical catalogue would be inadvisable until the entire stock had been catalogued. This proposition the Trustees would not accept, even after Panizzi had demonstrated the folly of premature printing by actually having one specimen volume printed. Panizzi won in the end, but under the worst possible conditions. The Royal Commission, which was appointed in 1847 ostensibly to "examine the constitution and government of the British Museum," was, in effect, an ill-advised attempt to impeach Panizzi for incompetence and insubordination. Unable to prove his inefficiency on any other count, Panizzi's accusers turned to his long-standing quarrel with the Trustees over the catalogue. In their final report (1850) the Commissioners accepted all Panizzi's arguments and agreed that his refusal to print the catalogue was justified. The eventual benefits of this fortunate end to a disagreeable episode were the compilation of an incomparable reading room catalogue and following it, at the end of the century, the publication of the world-famous BM *Catalogue of Printed Books*.

Service. The standard of service built up by Panizzi was, for its day, very high. One aspect of it, by itself, indicated the kind of man Panizzi was—his refusal to favor some readers more than others. His statement to the Select Committee in 1836 on this matter is his most familiar pronouncement:

> I want a poor student to have the same means of indulging his learned curiosity, of following his rational pursuits, of consulting the same authorities, of fathoming the most intricate enquiry, as the richest man in the kingdom, as far as books go, and I contend that Government is bound to give him the most liberal and unlimited assistance in this respect.

Rather less familiar is Panizzi's observation to the Royal Commission, in 1849: "I never felt the skin of any reader and they are all treated alike."

One of Panizzi's arch enemies outside the BM was the author Thomas Carlyle. Carlyle played a major role in founding the London Library in 1841, in part because Panizzi would not grant him special privileges as a reader at the BM. This quarrel therefore had the beneficial effect of enriching the metropolis with one of the finest learned subscription libraries in the world.

Evaluation. Panizzi could not have done all that he did alone. Although he was a hard taskmaster (one member of his staff described him as "a thorough-going tyrant"), he inspired in most of his lieutenants loyalty and willing cooperation. Prominent among those who helped him in all his endeavors was Thomas Watts, his right-hand man; outstanding among those who hindered him was Sir Frederic Madden, the brilliant but querulous Keeper of the Department of Manuscripts. The story of Panizzi's ceaseless arguments with Madden and the Museum's Trustees would make a volume in itself. It is a part of Panizzi's life that cannot be ignored, because the progress he made in spite of it is all the more remarkable. Furthermore, the existence of this powerful opposition led Panizzi to explain and defend his actions as he might never have done otherwise. Although he published a fair amount on language and literature, he published hardly anything on librarianship.

Most people now generally accept that the British national library should be the apex of the British library system, which is precisely what the new British Library is. But in Panizzi's day there was no national public library network; there were not even many academic libraries. Edward Edwards, who worked with Panizzi for a while, visualized a nationwide public library service and helped to prepare the way for it. Panizzi was not a protagonist in the public library movement, but this was not to his discredit; the BM's affairs absorbed him utterly.

Panizzi's name is more familiar than the names of most librarians of the past; that may be due, in some measure, to his friendship with many of the leading political figures of his day and the role he played in the struggle for the unification of Italy. Nevertheless, it is undeniable that his work for the British Museum Library was of seminal importance. He took over several valuable but static collections and left behind him a large, coherent, working library, so organized and so sustained that its continuance as a great national library was scarcely in doubt.

REFERENCES
The best full-length biography of Panizzi, which makes good use of Panizzi's official papers, is *Prince of Librarians: The Life and Times of Antonio Panizzi of the British Museum* by Edward Miller (1967). Arundell Esdaile, *The British Museum Library: A Short History and Survey* (1946), provides a concise but authoritative description of conditions at the BM before and after the Panizzi regime. It also shrewdly assesses Panizzi's reforms.
Because Panizzi himself published little on the BM Library and his work for it, the evidence he gave to the Select Committee and the Royal Commission, which was published verbatim in their respective reports, is particularly useful. Complete facsimiles of both reports were published by the Irish University Press in its British Parliamentary Papers series, *Report from the Select Committee on the Condition, Management and Affairs of the British Museum, 1836* (1968) and *Report of the Commissioners on the Constitution and Government of the British Museum, 1850* (1969).
See also the excellent symposium on Panizzi in *British Library Journal* (1979).
On the future of Panizzi's great Reading Room, see Gavin Stamp, "The British Library: Thatcher's Monument?" in *The Spectator* (1985).

JAMES G. OLLÉ

Papua New Guinea

Papua New Guinea, an independent parliamentary state in the western South Pacific, includes the eastern section of the island of New Guinea and nearby islands. The country is north of Australia and separated from it by the Torres Strait. Population (1984 est.) 3,258,000; area 462,840 sq.km. The official language is English.

National Library Service. The National Library Service (NLS), in the capital of Port Moresby, was established in 1975; by 1978 it had absorbed the Public Library Service, National Film Library, School Libraries Service, and National Archives. Under the Copyright Act of 1978 and the Statutory Deposit Act of 1979, it is one of three depository libraries. In 1978 it occupied the new National Library building, Australia's independence gift to the nation.

Research and loan services are provided to government officials and to the general public; films are loaned to government, educational, and cultural organizations throughout the country. The NLS also oversees library services to the Parliament and government departments. A central processing service is available to school and public libraries.

The NLS has about 45,000 volumes and approximately 6,000 films in the National Library building.

Academic Libraries. Papua New Guinea has two universities, the University of Papua New Guinea (UPNG) and the Papua New Guinea University of Technology (PNGUT). The UPNG Main Library, established in 1965, has 300,000 volumes, the Medical Library 17,000 volumes, and the Goroka Teachers College Branch Library 45,000 volumes. The PNGUT Library, established in 1968, has a collection of about 45,000 volumes.

The UPNG Main Library maintains an extensive New Guinea Collection, and the PNGUT Library operates a comprehensive audiovisual service. Both are depository libraries.

Public Libraries. The Commonwealth National Library of Australia established the Public Library Service of the Territory of Papua and the Mandated Territory of New Guinea in 1936. Twenty-four libraries in the urban centers serve about 20 percent of the population. The national literacy rate in English is comparatively low, and public library stocks are used mainly by nonindigenous persons. Experiments conducted with village libraries between 1949 and 1964 proved unsuccessful.

Libraries in Papua New Guinea (1982)

Type	Administrative units	Service points	Volumes in collections	Annual expenditures (kina)	Population served	Professional staff	Total staff
National	--	--	--	--	--	--	--
Academic[a]	1	1	50,000	466,000	2,615	9	30
Public[b]	24	--	186,330	--	--	1	50
School[b]	98	--	401,858[c]	--	--	--	133
Special[b]	20	--	140,248	300,000	--	4[c]	60

[a]University of technology only.
[b]1976 data.
[c]Incomplete data.

Sources: Unesco, *Statistical Yearbook*, 1984; M. Obi, *Directory of Libraries*; L. Baker, *Development of University Libraries in PNG*.

Many libraries have only part-time staff, and most collections are small and outdated. The Headquarters Library at Ela Beach provided a central selection and processing service, but devolution of national government powers in 1978 removed responsibility for library services to each of the 19 provincial governments.

School Libraries. The establishment of the School Libraries Office in 1966 facilitated book-box schemes, library subsidies, and professional advisory services, and a central processing service was introduced. Most school children do not have library services. Libraries are predominantly in the high schools and technical schools. Only in rare instances do they have trained staff or substantial collections. Responsibility for funding was placed with individual schools.

Special Libraries. Approximately 30 special libraries serve government departments. The Parliament, Department of Justice, Office of Forests, and Bougainville Copper Company, in the North Solomons Province, are among the major special libraries. The Library of the Prime Minister's Department has an extensive collection of rare historical documents, and the Research Library of the Department of Education provides a postal loan service to teachers throughout the country.

The Papua New Guinea Institute of Public Administration, established as the Administrative College in 1961, has special collections in government, New Guineana, and library science. Its collection totals more than 70,000 volumes.

The Profession. The Papua New Guinea Branch of the Library Association of Australia, established in 1967, was the forerunner of the Papua New Guinea Library Association (PNGLA), formed in 1974. Activities include an annual conference and publication of a quarterly journal, *Toktok Bilong Haus Buk.* A School Libraries Association of Papua New Guinea was formed in 1970, but it did not survive.

REFERENCES
Kwami Avafia, "Library Development in Papua New Guinea," *Libri* (1975).
Leigh Baker, *Development of University Libraries in Papua New Guinea,* Master of Philosophy thesis, PNGUT (1978), includes survey of libraries and librarianship.
Harold Holdsworth, *The Development of Library Services in Papua New Guinea* (1976).
Miles M. Jackson, "Library and Information Services in the Pacific Islands," *International Library Review* (1981), includes a section on Papua New Guinea.

LEIGH R. BAKER*

Paraguay

Paraguay, a republic of South America, is bounded by Bolivia on the north, Brazil on the east, and Argentina on the south and west. Population (1984 est.) 3,193,000; area 406,752 sq.km.

History. Very little is known about books and libraries in Paraguay before the arrival of the Spaniards. The Guaraní Indians and other indigenous inhabitants of the area were, generally speaking, nomads. Their method of communication from generation to generation was oral, not written, and the folklore of the Guaraní is rich with stories, myths, and legends.

Information Office, PNGUT

Matheson Library, Papua New Guinea University of Technology. Local artists created the mural and sculpture.

Recorded history may be said to have begun in 1537, with the arrival of the Spaniards under the command of Captain Juan de Salazar y Espinosa, founder of Asunción, who brought with him 12 books on religion. In addition to introducing books to this literary virgin territory, Salazar y Espinosa himself wrote *Los libros de romance* ("Books of Romance") during the conquest and exploration.

During the years 1538–75, a number of explorers and priests arrived, bringing their books with them. Soon after the arrival of the Jesuits in 1595, a number of well-stocked libraries were established in the Jesuit resettlement villages. Not surprisingly, the dominant themes of the works in the libraries were theology, humanistic literature, and sacred and profane theater. At that time, Paraguay remained outside the main currents of the book trade and distribution, channeled through the River Plate region (presently Argentina, Paraguay, and Uruguay), and often through Córdoba, Argentina. At times, there seems to have been actual prohibition of book importation, a product of colonial laws.

The religious orders such as the Dominicans and Franciscans that were established in the country in those early years also had their own libraries. They operated not only in Asunción, the capital of the country, but throughout the interior of the country.

Of private libraries during the Colonial Period we know very little. What information exists is often limited to pure supposition or guesses about their very existence.

During the period of Independence (1811–17), books were introduced into the country in greater variety and number than ever before. Because of the complete rupture of relations with Spain, books could be imported into Paraguay only from Buenos Aires, Montevideo, or various cities in Brazil.

From 1817 to 1840, the period of the dictatorship of Gaspar Rodríguez de Francia, the importation of books was once again restricted. During that difficult period, books made their way into the country with the help of a few intrepid travelers such as Johann Rengger, William Parish Robertson, Aimé Jacques Bonpland, the physician William Paslett, and other professionals and artisans who carried their books with them. The scarcity of books during that period makes them articles of real value today. Nevertheless,

Francia owned a well-stocked library and maintained his own library catalogue. The book was Francia's only passion and vice outside his governmental duties. After his death, his library was declared the Public Library through a resolution of the ruling *junta* on October 16, 1840. The materials in the library dealt with such areas as law, medicine and pharmacology, history, religion and ethics, and the natural sciences—clearly a collection for intellectuals.

The influx of printed materials into Paraguay resumed in a small way in 1842 and more intensely in 1853. During the period of President Don Carlos Antonio López (1841–62), books were brought in by booksellers in quantities previously unknown in the country's history. The characteristics of the works imported also changed, with preference given to novels, poetry, history, and theater, and with greater emphasis on secular than on religious literature. Other than the libraries of the religious orders, the best libraries of the day were those of Don Carlos Antonio López and Juan Andrés Gelly, with the latter collection surpassing 1,000 volumes, some of which were later given to the state.

During the López Period (1841–70)—the rule of Carlos Antonio López and his son Francisco Solano López—the French language became, in just a few years, the language of culture and social status, due primarily to the influence of Elisa Lynch and the younger López. But the War of the Triple Alliance (1864–70) caused massive losses of printed works, many of them reduced to ashes. In all likelihood, some of the books of the day were taken from the country during the war, probably to Argentina and Brazil. Among the more valuable materials that were lost were the incunabula of the missionaries, some early editions, manuscripts, and others.

Just what happened to public library services during that time is not known. It is generally believed that public services were developed through the books brought into the country by the Jesuit missionaries, enriched through the donation of Francia's library as well as those of foreigners who died while in Paraguay. What is known is that the Municipal Library in Asunción, the forerunner of the National Library, was founded in 1869, near the end of the López rule.

The National Library. The National Library of Paraguay was thus an outgrowth of the Municipal Library. Exactly when it was founded is subject to conjecture, but H. Sánchez Quell, Director General of the National Archives, Libraries, and Museums, has stated that the National Library was founded by the Paraguayan humanist Juan Silvano Godoy on May 25, 1909.

The National Library of Paraguay has not prospered since its founding. In 1984 it contained only slightly more than 40,000 volumes. Its collections are divided into four sections: international works, works of national authors, the Enrique Solano López room, and the periodicals room, in which are kept some of the most important newspapers from the 18th and 19th centuries to the present.

The collection has grown very little over the years because of the lack of funds to purchase materials. Many of the materials acquired have consisted of donations from the embassies of France, Germany, Japan, Portugal, Spain, the United Kingdom, and the United States. A team of architects was working toward remodeling the building in the mid-1980s, and a Commission of Friends is aiding in the development of appropriate cultural activities. Paraguay does not have a law requiring all works to be deposited in the National Library. The rights of the authors are protected through the Ministry of Education and Culture.

Academic Libraries. University libraries in Paraguay can be classified into two distinct administrative systems: those that belong to the National University of Asunción (UNA) and those that belong to the Catholic University, Nuestra Señora de la Asunción (UC).

The Central Library of the UNA is the administrative center of the 23 libraries of the university's various faculties, schools, and institutes. It is also the site of the union catalogue that, as of 1983, contained more than 34,000 catalogue cards. Almost all of the libraries in the system have shown improvement in their collections and services in recent years. Some of them have maintained a regular publications program of news, selective dissemination of information, and new acquisitions; those most active in such publications are the Central Library, the library of the School of Library and Information Sciences, the library of the Faculty of Veterinary Sciences, and the library of the Faculty of Agronomic Engineering.

The Library and Documentation/Information Center of the Faculty of Veterinary Sciences moved into a modern 1,400-square meter building in 1983.

Libraries in Paraguay (1983)

Type	Administrative units	Service points	Volumes in collections	Annual expenditures (guarani)	Population served	Professional staff	Total staff
National	1	--	40,000	12,250,000[a]	2,265	3	10
Academic	26	4	127,191	37,637,770	31,221	26	90
Public	15	--	44,852	--	--	4	33
School	54	--	178,483	45,087,122	47,373	25	114
Special	38	--	79,684	46,036,460	14,300	29	102

[a]Included are annual expenditures of the Library, Archives, and Museum.

Sources: Survey by the author; Riveros Ramírez, Francisca Gladys, "Guía descriptiva de bibliotecas museos y archivos del Paraguay" (thesis, Escuela de Bibliotecología, Universidad Nacional de Asunción, 1983).

The move marked the first time in the history of university libraries in Paraguay that a school made a major financial investment in its library. The library itself, which in 1979 occupied a classroom and had no more than 2,000 volumes, now boasts a collection of 8,000. Through the assistance of the embassies of Argentina, France, Germany, Japan, Spain, and the United Kingdom and the Swiss Technical Mission, the Library developed a number of projects to enrich its collection and to upgrade its equipment.

The library of the Faculty of Agronomic Engineering was being enlarged on its present site in the mid-1980s. Through the assistance of the Food and Agriculture Organization of the United Nations (FAO) and the Japan International Cooperation Agency, the Library was organizing and developing its forestry section.

The library of the Polytechnic Faculty has an exceptionally well-developed collection, except for a lack of current materials in the fields of electronics and computers.

The Pope Paul VI Central Library of the Catholic University continues in its efforts to acquire important Paraguayan books, pamphlets, and periodical publications, while coordinating the five other service points of the university library system: the libraries of the Faculty of Accounting (2,000 volumes in 1984), the Faculty of Technological Sciences (7,000 volumes), the Colegio San José (7,500 volumes), the Probatorio (pre-admission) program (7,500 volumes), and the Higher Institute of Technology on the university campus (8,000 volumes). The Central Library itself maintains a collection of more than 20,000 volumes. Because of its excellent bibliographical collection and the service of professional librarians, it is heavily used by students and researchers from Paraguay and elsewhere.

Public Libraries. There are essentially two types of public libraries in Asunción: the municipal libraries and those supported by the various embassies in the city such as the Franklin D. Roosevelt Library of the Paraguayan–American Cultural Center (6,100 volumes), the Miguel de Cervantes Saavedra Library of Spain (6,000 volumes), the Euclides da Cunha Library of Brazil (6,300 volumes), and the Juan Bautista Alberdi Library of Argentina (9,200 volumes). The Juan de Salazar Cultural Center of the Spanish embassy maintains two libraries: the Miguel de Cervantes Saavedra Library for adolescents and adults and the Children's Library, which offers weekly story hours.

Among the best-known municipal libraries are those in Asunción and in the town of San Lorenzo, 20 kilometers from Asunción; both are often filled with secondary-school and university students. A new public library of a different kind was created in 1980 by a group of dedicated librarians: the library of the National Penitentiary, with a small collection of 750 volumes that helps to meet the needs of prisoners.

Among the other libraries in the interior of the country are those of Colonia Menno, Filadelfia (the Mennonite settlement), Colonel Oviedo, Itacurubí de las Cordilleras, and the Mestre Fermín López Library (1,800 volumes) in Piribebuy, 80 kilometers from Asunción. This small-town library was founded on July 24, 1976, by the Children and Friends Association of Piribebuy and is maintained by the community. It features both children's and adult sections and is heavily used. In spite of enthusiastic support from some people in various communities in the country, public libraries in Paraguay suffered from an economic recession to the point that some of them had no funds whatsoever for the acquisition and maintenance of their collections in the mid-1980s.

School Libraries. In 1976 the Ministry of Education and Culture established a series of standards for the operation of libraries in the schools and *colegios* throughout the country. A new curriculum is also being adopted by the nation's public schools, requiring a large number of printed materials for instructional support. Many school libraries still do not meet minimum standards, however, nor do they have budgets for the acquisition of the material required to meet those standards. At best, they support a librarian and maintain a small collection. All too few of the librarians are adequately trained, with few of them having recognized degrees in librarianship. Most of them are teachers who have obtained some rudimentary introduction to the field through workshops and short courses offered for school librarians.

Among the five or six best school libraries in the country is that of the Colegio Internacional, which was founded as a modern library in 1957. From its beginning, the library has been oriented toward good information services, and for some time it has been developing into a media center which both teachers and students use as a learning laboratory. No fewer than six librarians worked there in 1984, five of them graduates of the School of Library and Information Sciences of the UNA. Teaching the use of library materials begins in kindergarten with story hours and continues through secondary school by means of courses in methods of investigation. Even teachers take advantage of some of the advanced courses.

Special Libraries. The libraries that have grown the most since 1975 are the special libraries (also called documentation centers). Few of them have adequate budgets for materials acquisition and

Yoshiko Freundorfer

Story hour at the library of the Colegio Internacional in Asunción.

not all of them are run by professional librarians. Most of the special libraries of the country are, in fact, very small.

Of the nation's special libraries, the library of the Documentation Center of Itaipú (a binational project between Paraguay and Brazil for the construction of the Usina Hydroelectric Plant on the Paraná River, said to be the largest of its kind in the world), set up in 1975, continues to be one of the best. It enjoys economic and technical support and provides excellent information services. It cooperates closely with its counterpart organization in the Itaipú project, the Brazilian Documentation Center. The Center maintains a regular program of publications, including one on its information services, another consisting of journal indexes, and still another on the library itself.

The Dr. Moisés S. Bertoni National Library of Agriculture (BINA) was established on July 17, 1979. This library, a division of the Ministry of Agriculture and Livestock, has a collection of some 7,000 books, as well as numerous pamphlets and periodicals dealing with various aspects of agriculture. It maintains cooperative relations with other national and international organizations. At the national level, BINA is developing a coordinated information service, with plans for a national information network involving the following libraries: the library of the National Agronomic Institute's Regional Center for Agricultural Research (CRIA), which has a collection of 500 volumes plus other pamphlets and documents, located in Capitán Miranda in the southern part of the country; the library of the National Seed Institute, with a basic collection exceeding 550 volumes; the library of the National Research and Extension Livestock Program (PRONIEGA), with 500-plus volumes, in San Lorenzo; the library of the Livestock Extension Service (SEAG) in San Lorenzo; and the library of the National Agronomic Institute (IAN), with more than 2,000 volumes, in Caacupé, about 50 kilometers from Asunción.

Since Paraguay is largely an agricultural nation, effective coordination and optimal operation of its agricultural libraries is especially important for the country's progress.

The Profession. *Library Education.* During the 1960s most education for librarianship was offered through short courses and workshops sponsored by such organizations as the Agency for International Development (AID); Unesco; and the Paraguayan–American Cultural Center of the American Embassy. During the period 1964–67 some special courses for school librarians were offered by the Ministry of Education and Culture. In 1968–69, four semesters of course work were offered for academic librarians under the direction of Gaston Litton. The importance of professional training for librarians that was recognized in the 1960s led to the establishment of the School of Librarianship in the National University of Asunción, reporting directly to the president of the university. The School was created by law in 1971.

During the years 1975–76 the School, through the assistance of the Organization of American States (OAS), carried out a multinational project on curriculum development. The School invited a number of visiting professors well known in the library field to take part in the project; among them were Josefa E.

Sabor (Argentina), Violeta Angulo (Peru), Emma Linares (Argentina), Edwin S. Gleaves (U.S.A.), and Omar Lino Benítez (Argentina). The School undertook further curriculum review in the mid-1980s, while offering two levels of training: técnico en bibliotecología (library technician)—two years of study—and licenciado en bibliotecología (licenciate in librarianship)—four years of study. The School was renamed the School of Library and Information Sciences. In addition to its regular courses, the School also offers continuing education programs for its graduates.

Two other Paraguayan institutions offer short courses for librarians: the Institute for Higher Education, which offers workshops for school librarians, and the Student Commission of the Honorable Government Junta of the Colorado Party, which offers a course in library techniques to university students. Both institutions offer certificates of attendance, not university degrees.

Library Associations. Two library associations are active in Paraguay: the Association of Librarians of Paraguay (ABIPAR) and the Association of University Graduated Librarians of Paraguay (ABUP). ABIPAR was created on May 27, 1961, by a group of five Paraguayan librarians and claimed 55 members in 1984. Its official publication is *Bibliotecología, Documentación Paraguaya.* ABUP, founded on July 20, 1974, by a group of 17 graduates of the School of Librarianship, had a membership of 81 in 1984. It publishes *Páginas de Contenido* and *ABUP Informaciones.*

REFERENCES

Carlos R. Centurión, *Historia de la cultura paraguaya,* 2 vols. (Asunción, 1961).

Yoshiko Moriya de Freundorfer, *Planes y programa de estudio de la Escuela de Bibliotecología y Ciencias de la Información de la Universidad Nacional de Asunción* (Asunción, 1983).

Francisca Gladys Riveros Ramírez, "Guía descriptiva de bibliotecas, museos y archivos del Paraguay" (thesis, Escuela de Bibliotecología, Universidad Nacional de Asunción, 1983).

YOSHIKO MORIYA DE FREUNDORFER;
Translated by EDWIN S. GLEAVES

Partaningrat, Winarti
(1922–1978)

Winarti Partaningrat, Indonesian librarian and government official, was one of the prominent figures who worked for the establishment and early development of special librarianship and documentation services in Indonesia.

Born on September 21, 1922, at Sragen, Central Java, she was educated at schools in Indonesia, including a medical school. In the early 1950s she went to the United States. At Columbia University she obtained a B.S. in Latin American Studies in 1957 and a Master's degree in Library Service in 1958.

From 1946 to 1951, she worked for the English Section of the Foreign Broadcasting of Radio Republik Indonesia in Jakarta. From 1951 to 1958 in New York, she worked at the Voice of America of the U.S. Information Service and United Nations Radio at UN Headquarters. After receiving her professional degree in librarianship in 1958, she worked for a year

Winarti Partaningrat

in the Science and Technology Department at the Queensborough Public Library, Jamaica, N.Y.

She returned to Indonesia in late 1959. In early 1960 she was appointed Head of the Bureau of Documentation of the MIPI (Madjelis Ilmu Pengetahuan Indonesia: Council of Sciences of Indonesia) in Jakarta. Later, in 1965, she became the first Director of the PDIN-LIPI (Pusat Dokumentasi Ilmiah Nasional–Lembaga Ilmu Pengetahuan Indonesia: Indonesian National Scientific Documentation Center–Indonesian Institute of Sciences). That Center, officially established on June 1, 1965, was formerly the Bureau of Documentation of MIPI.

She was an active member of the HPCI (Himpunan Pustakawan Chusus Indonesia: Indonesian Special Library Association), which was merged in 1973 with the APADI (Asosiasi Perpustakaan, Arsip dan Dokumentasi Indonesia: Association of Libraries, Archives and Documentation of Indonesia) to form a new association, the present IPI (Ikatan Pustakawan Indonesia: Indonesian Library Association).

Partaningrat was a leader in organizing a workshop on a National Network System of Library, Documentation and Information Services in Indonesia, held in 1971. That workshop laid basic foundations for the early development of library services of the country covering the following fields: scientific and technical information, coordinated by the PDIN-LIPI; biology and agriculture, coordinated by the PUSTAKA, the Central Library for Biology and Agriculture of the Ministry of Agriculture; health, medicine, and pharmacy, coordinated by the Ministry of Health; and social sciences and humanities, coordinated by the National Library of Indonesia.

She actively participated at several international meetings. Among them were the Unesco Seminar on Scientific Documentation in South and Southeast Asia, held in New Delhi, March 1961, where she submitted a working paper "Scientific Information Facilities in Indonesia;" the 10th Pacific Science Congress, in Tokyo, 1966, where she presented a working paper "Characteristics and History of Indonesian Scientific Periodicals;" and the Conference on Southeast Asian Research Materials, at Puncak, Indonesia, 1969. She also wrote several articles in the fields of library and documentation services. She also edited *Masterlist of Southeast Asian Microforms* (Singapore University Press, 1978), a joint project of SARBICA (Southeast Asian Regional Branch of the International Council on Archives) and CONSAL (Conference of Southeast Asian Librarians), started in the mid-1970s.

Partaningrat retired from work as a government official in 1974. She died on May 8, 1978, in Jakarta.

HERNANDONO

Paulin, Lorna V.

(1914–   )

Lorna Paulin, English public librarian, gained the presidency of the Library Association, 1966), and the award of the Order of the British Empire, only two indications of significant contributions to librarianship by an outstanding librarian. She was the first woman to hold the office of President of the LA.

Born in Bexley, Kent, in 1914, she spent her childhood in what was then the country but is now almost engulfed in London's outer suburbs. Even at

the early age of 11 she had made up her mind as to her profession, the height of which was to be the Chief Librarian of the neighboring borough.

After leaving the Grammar School for girls at Dartford, she took a B.A. degree in English in 1934 and an M.A. in English in 1936 at University College, London. The M.A. degree was combined with part-time study at the School of Librarianship, resulting in initially a Diploma in Librarianship and then, in 1938, Fellowship of the Library Association. The O.B.E. was awarded in 1970 for service to libraries, and the highest distinction of the Library Association, Honorary Fellowship, was bestowed in 1980.

She held various posts in Kent County Library from 1936 to 1948, through responsibility for student services to Branch Librarian and Deputy County Librarian. In Nottinghamshire, as County Librarian from 1948 to 1952, she saw rapid post-war library improvements in schools and in mobile services to rural areas. But she significantly influenced the librarianship of her time as County Librarian of Hertfordshire from 1952 to 1976. With enormous energy and clarity of purpose, she developed all aspects of the county's public library service. This included work with schools and developing other library services for children; setting up mobile library services for rural and suburban areas; instituting professionally run hospital library services, medical and general; a large program of providing new branch library holdings; technical library and information services in cooperation with the libraries of the colleges in the county; cooperative schemes with libraries of all types in the county; and instituting a training scheme for staff.

Paulin worked assiduously for the library profession throughout her career. She was a member of the Council of the LA from 1948 to 1978 and holder of successive offices in the County Library's Section, culminating in becoming Honorary Secretary and subsequently Chairman. In the LA, because of her strong commitment to the education of librarians, she was for many years Chairman of the Education Committee, Chairman of the Executive Committee, and Chairman of Council, becoming President in 1966. Unquestionably she will be most remembered for sterling work on professional qualifications. The report on that work, known as the Paulin Report, was implemented by a Board of which she was Chairman. It introduced far-reaching changes into the system for British professional library qualifications.

Her consistent attention to education for librarianship led her to be involved in setting up the School of Librarianship at Queen's University, Belfast. She then became an external examiner for this and other schools.

In the 1960s and 1970s no IFLA Conference seemed complete without her. She was an active member and served as Secretary of the Public Libraries Section. From their inception in Tylosand, Sweden, in 1953, she was active in Anglo-Scandinavian conferences for several years, and visited libraries in the U.S.S.R., Romania, and West Germany.

Paulin played a prominent part as public library legislation loomed in developing standards of service. She was a member of the Ministry of Education Working Party on Standards for Public Library Services in England and Wales, set up in 1961. She appended her own reservation to the published report

The Library Association

Lorna V. Paulin

in 1962 because she did not consider the recommended standards to be high enough in some respects. She was one of the first members of the Library Advisory Council (England), formed in 1966, and for six years served on it and its working parties and subcommittees.

Paulin was a leader of librarians with authority, integrity, and vision, charm, and humanity, with a delightful sense of humor never far away.

R. G. SURRIDGE

Penna, Carlos Victor
(1911-)

Carlos Victor Penna

Carlos Victor Penna, library author, educator, and administrator, worked for library advancement in Latin America as a Unesco specialist and contributed concepts of library and information service planning that led to the Unesco NATIS program.

He was born in Bahia Blanca, Buenos Aires Province, Argentina, on October 1, 1911. He attended school in Cayupán and Maza, small towns in the provinces of Buenos Aires and Pampa, and in 1927 he began studies at the Escuela de Mecánica de la Armada, which he left in 1931, unwilling to adapt to the military regimen required there.

In 1933 he began work at the Library of the Estado Mayor de la Marina as a page in charge of stack maintenance. When he was promoted to the position of Cataloguer, he applied modern cataloguing techniques for the first time in Argentina, having translated and experimented with some of the Vatican "Rules for the Cataloguing of Book Materials" and the Universal Decimal System. He later organized the centralized cataloguing of the books of more than 100 libraries in Marina—the first cooperative venture of this nature practiced in Latin America.

Penna also pioneered in the introduction of microphotographic techniques applied to the organization of the Central Catalogue of the University of Buenos Aires, which he directed in 1943 after returning from library studies at Columbia University in New York City in 1941.

Penna organized the Library School of the Social Museum of Argentina and introduced modern information management methods into the curriculum. The School had a great impact not only in Argentina but on a continental scale, and the text materials written by the faculty have been utilized by library schools in all parts of Latin America.

In 1945 Penna began traveling in a way that later enabled him to participate fully in information work on an international level. First he visited La Paz, Bolivia, together with Augusto Raúl Cortázar, to reorganize the Mariscal Santa Cruz Library. In 1947 he participated in the Assembly of American Librarians. In 1950 he traveled to Cuba to teach courses at the Library School of the Friends Society of Cuba and also made several visits to Uruguay to assist A. Gropp in the development of the Library School that the North American had organized in Montevideo. In 1951 Penna became a Unesco specialist, first assigned to the Western Hemisphere Regional Center in Havana, Cuba. From Havana, as a specialist in the area of library development, Penna worked hard for the betterment of libraries throughout Latin America. In 1964 he was transferred to the main offices of

Unesco, from which he retired in 1971 as Director of the Division for the Development of Documentation, Libraries, and Archives.

Upon leaving Unesco, Penna made his home in Palma de Mallorca, Spain, serving as an expert of the Iberoamerican Education Office. In 1974 he moved again, this time to the United States, where he taught subjects such as library and information services planning at Pratt Institute and acted in an advisory capacity with the Coordinating Commission of the National System of Library and Information Services of Venezuela.

Penna published more than 120 journal articles and professional papers. Among his many books and projects are *Catalogación y clasificación de libros* (1st ed., 1949; 2nd ed., 1964); direction of the translation of *Sears List of Subject Headings for Small Libraries* (1949); *Manual de Bibliotecología* ("Manual of Librarianship"), in collaboration with other authors (1968); direction of the Kapelusz Editorial Series, together with E. J. Sabor, *Bibliotecología: planeamiento de servicios bibliotecarios* ("Librarianship: The Planning of Library Services"; 1968), also published in English, French, Japanese, Arabic, and Turkish; *Planeamiento de servicios bibliotecarios y de documentación* (*Planning Library and Documentation Services;* 2nd ed., by Sewell and Liebaers, 1970), also published in English and French; and *Servicios de Bibliotecas e Información: nueva concepción Latinoamericana* ("Library and Information Services: A New Latin American Concept"; 1972).

Horacio Becco published *La obra bibliotecologica de Carlos Victor Penna* (1981), which covers his works and contributions to universal librarianship.

EMMA LINARES

Peru

Peru, a republic in western South America, is bordered by Ecuador and Colombia on the north, Brazil and Bolivia on the east, Chile on the south, and the Pacific Ocean on the west. Population (1984 est.) 19,198,000; area 1,285,215 sq.km. The official languages are Spanish and Quechua.

History. The Biblioteca Naciónal, the National Library of Peru, was founded in 1821 by José de San Martín. Although it was partially destroyed by fire in 1943, it was reopened in 1947, and copies of the first publications printed in Peru and the Americas are still among its most prized possessions. Public libraries in Peru were generally not developed as lending libraries, as is true in the majority of Latin American countries. In many cases public library services have been merged with the functions of the National Library, and only comparatively recently have these two types of service begun to be separate in practice. Some significant collections of manuscripts and valuable historical materials are found in convents and monasteries.

National Library. The National Library contains 706,000 volumes, 263,600 manuscripts, 11,800 maps, and 1,918,931 issues of periodical publications and newspapers. It is especially strong in Peruvian history, literature, and law.

The National Library was once called the Biblioteca Publica, or public library. However, although open to the general public, it is not permitted by law to allow borrowing privileges. It publishes the *An-*

nuario Bibliográfico Peruano ("Annual Bibliography of Peru"), as well as the *Boletín de la Biblioteca Naciónal* ("National Library Bulletin"), the *Gaceta Bibliotecaria del Perú* ("Peruvian Librarian's Gazette"), and other publications.

The Archivo General de la Nación, founded in 1861, and the Biblioteca del Instituto Nacional both complement the National Library's activities, the latter having participated closely in the identification and classification of Peruvian publications.

Academic Libraries. Academic libraries in Peru exist in almost every institution of higher learning, these numbering at least 200. They are generally closed collections offering access only through card catalogues and limiting borrowing privileges to registered students. Required text materials are usually available in multiple copies and constitute the most heavily used portions of these collections.

The Biblioteca Central of the Universidad Nacional Mayor de San Marcos (San Marcos National Higher University) was founded in Lima during the 16th century and possesses more than 450,000 volumes. It originally owned a large portion of the colonial collection presently housed in the National Library.

The Biblioteca Central of the Pontificia Universidad Nacional Católica del Perú (National Peruvian Pontifical Catholic University), although founded as recently as 1917, possesses an ample collection of more than 250,000 volumes, many of a recent, technical nature.

The Biblioteca de la Universidad Nacional de San Augustin in Arequipa deserves special mention as an example of the decentralization trend taking place in many Latin American academic libraries. The central library coordinates 12 specialized libraries that possess some 100,000 volumes above and beyond the basic collection of monographs, pamphlets, and periodical publications.

In many cases academic libraries function more as study halls than as information centers. Libraries are slowly becoming equipped to handle new demands of modern library research on their collections, services, and personnel.

Public Libraries. Public libraries in Peru are generally referred to as *bibliotecas publicas municipales* (municipal public libraries). There were about 445 such libraries in Peru in 1982, with total holdings of some 4,102,000 volumes. The majority possess small collections of donated materials and are directed by

staff members with little or no formal training in modern library methods.

Several exceptions to this broad generalization exist, principally in the major urban centers. The Lima Municipal Library, founded in 1935, has a collection of about 16,000 volumes, relatively small because of the role played by the National Library in Lima.

The Arequipa Public Municipal Library was, on the other hand, founded earlier than the Lima Public and contains more than 28,000 volumes. The Casa de la Cultura (Cultural Institute) of Peru is housed in that library, giving an indication of the humanistic nature of the collection.

The largest public library in Peru is in Callao. The Biblioteca Publica Municipal Piloto (Callao Municipal Pilot Public Library) was founded as recently as 1936 and reorganized in 1957. It offers a broad collection of some 48,000 volumes to the general public.

Public libraries in Peru receive technical assistance from the Oficina Nacional de Bibliotecas Populares Municipales, located in the National Library.

School Libraries. The majority of school libraries in Peru are found in private schools and in very large public primary and secondary schools, mainly in the major cities. Most are directed by untrained personnel, in many cases teachers with full class schedules. These factors generally lead to less than adequate collections and services and even affect access to the libraries, given usually irregular and insufficient working hours.

Audiovisual aids are generally underutilized or unavailable and many times are not considered the responsibility of the school libraries. The Dewey Decimal System is generally used for classification, but a number of school libraries are uncatalogued and unclassified because they lack trained personnel.

Special Libraries. The *Directorio de Bibliotecas Especializadas del Peru* ("Directory of Peruvian Special Libraries") was published by ABIISE (Agrupación de Bibliotecas para la Integración de la Información socioeconomica; Consortia of Libraries for the Integration of Socioeconomic Information) in 1972, serving as an update of the Peruvian Library Association's 1969 *Guia de Bibliotecas Especializadas*. The Directory lists 100 special libraries out of a total of 130 identified during the survey period. The libraries included are of three types, one-third each being in the social sciences, the applied and basic sciences, and the humanities, or geared to the broad concerns of a partic-

Libraries in Peru (1982)

Type	Administrative units	Service points	Volumes in collections	Annual expenditures (sol)	Population served[a]	Professional staff	Total staff
National[b]	1	8	2,569,000	232,278,000	--	48	191
Academic	3	7	58,000	40,742,000[c]	591	1	41
Public[d]	520	445	4,102,000	--	--	19	182
School	81	93	272,000	--	863	32	137

[a]Registered borrowers.
[b]1981 data.
[c]The University of Santa Maria only.
[d]1980 data.

ular institution. About one-third of the total, drawn from all three categories, were directly related to government offices, such as ministries.

Special libraries in Peru include INTINTEC (Instituto de Investigación Tecnológica Industrial y de Normas Tecnicas; Industrial Technology and Standards Research Institute), a fine hard-technology information and documentation center, while ESAP (Escuela Superior de Administración Publica; School of Public Administration) and ESAN (Escuela de Administración de Negocios para Graduados; Graduate School of Business Management) have specialized in the area of soft technology. Socioeconomic information sources are by far the most developed and coordinated in Peru, thanks to the efforts of ABIISE. A number of the monasteries with collections of historical interest are open to researchers and to the public.

The Profession. The two major professional associations are the APB (Asociación Peruana de Bibliotecarios; Peruvian Library Association) and ABIISE. Both have played a vital role in the development of libraries and librarianship in Peru.

A trade group, the Asociación de Empleados de la Biblioteca Nacional, was established for the employees of the National Library. The Cámara Peruana del Libro (Peruvian Book Council) worked closely with the Library Association in a number of areas and made important donations to various libraries.

MARTHA GORMAN*

Petherick, Edward Augustus
(1847–1917)

Edward Augustus Petherick, bookseller, publisher, bibliographer, and book collector, provided a collection that formed the basis of what is now the National Library of Australia's large and important body of materials relating to Australia, New Zealand, and the Pacific Islands.

Petherick was born on March 6, 1847, at Burnham, Somerset, England, the eldest of nine surviving children of Peter John Petherick, stationer-librarian, and his wife, Ann. The family sailed from Bristol to Melbourne, Australia, landing in March 1853 with, among other things, 400 books to sell. Edward attended Alfred Brunton's Public School in Melbourne part-time while working for his father. He soon began work in the bookselling and stationery firm of George Robertson, who was impressed by his precocious knowledge of books and enthusiastic application to his duties.

After 10 years' experience with the firm, Petherick was chosen in 1870 to reorganize its London office, which he quickly transformed and continued to manage until Robertson retired in 1887. That year Petherick set up his own business in London. His Colonial Booksellers' Agency at 33 Paternoster Row had a capital of $800 and was backed by a number of publishers and assisted by Australian banks supporting distributing branches in Sydney, Melbourne, and Adelaide. At this time he began publishing, issuing quarterly the *Colonial Book Circular and Bibliographical Record,* later changing its title to *The Torch,* and in 1889 launched his *Collection of Favourite and Approved Authors.*

As early as 1865 Petherick had collected titles for a catalogue or bibliography of Australiana but put it

Edward Augustus Petherick

aside when he went to England in 1870. In 1878 he made a fresh start with it, commenting, "The business of the London department being well organised, I took up the work again; but finding I could do little without the books, I began to collect them—as they came within my grasp, and the savings of a limited salary." In 1882 he won public recognition as a bibliographer by publishing the *Catalogue of the York Gate Geographical and Colonial Library.* Its success prompted William Silver, the owner, to enlarge his collection with help from Petherick, whom he commissioned to prepare a second edition, subtitled *An Index to the Literature of Geography, Maritime and Inland Discovery, Commerce and Colonisation;* it was published by John Murray in 1886. When Silver died in 1905, Petherick arranged the sale of the York Gate Library to the South Australian Branch of the Royal Geographical Society of Australasia. With tireless industry, inexhaustible energy, and bachelor freedom, he became involved with many learned societies and corporate activities—from the Royal Geographical, Hakluyt, and Linnean Societies to the Royal Colonial Institute and the Library Association—becoming a life member of all. He wrote numerous reviews, letters, and articles, many of which remain unpublished.

Petherick's publishing venture continued until 1894, when the Australian bank crisis and his own lack of financial reserves forced him into bankruptcy with debts of about $50,000. His book stocks were sold to E. W. Cole, a Melbourne bookseller, and his *Collection of Favourite and Approved Authors* was taken over by the London publishers George Bell & Sons. On March 1, 1892, in Dorset, Petherick had married a widow, Mary Agatha Annear Skeats, and mainly with her help met his financial difficulties and succeeded in saving his own collection of Australiana. Broken by business failure, he became a cataloguer with the antiquarian booksellers Francis Edwards & Co. and between 1895 and 1908 produced a series of outstanding catalogues of Australasian material. As means permitted, he continued collecting and devoted great effort to completing his *Bibliography of Australia and Polynesia;* he prepared a printed prospectus of it in 1898 but was unable to arrange publication.

As his collection grew, Petherick became anxious that it should pass to the Australian people and, even before the federation of the Australian states in 1901, he approached two premiers with an offer to present his collection to "Federated Australia," but no action resulted. Nor did anything result when he wrote to Prime Minister Barton in March 1901, his approach at that time being premature. In 1908, however, he and his wife took the collection to Australia and soon negotiated with the Federal Parliament. Its Library Committee on May 27, 1909, recommended acquisition of the collection "in consideration of an annuity of $500 a year, Mr. Petherick to render during the currency of the annuity such services in the Commonwealth Library as the Committee may from time to time prescribe." The Collection consisted of some 10,000 volumes, 232 boxes of pamphlets, and some manuscripts, maps, and pictures. It was accompanied by the sheets of the still unpublished *Bibliography* of about 100,000 entries.

Petherick tended his collection from 1909 to 1917, distressed by the casual recognition that Australians made of his overseas achievements and the small encouragement they gave him to develop his collection further, compensated only by a belated appointment as C.M.G. in 1916. Predeceased by his wife on May 10, 1915, Petherick died in Melbourne on September 17, 1917. He is commemorated today in the Petherick Reading Room of the National Library of Australia.

REFERENCE
The papers and correspondence of E. A. Petherick are held in the National Library of Australia, Canberra.

C. A. BURMESTER

Philippines

The Philippines, on the western rim of the Pacific Ocean, is an island republic of 7,107 islands. Population (1984 est.) 53,000,000; area about 300,780 sq.km. English and Filipino are the official languages, but there are more than 120 Philippine languages.

History. Philippine script can be found in specimens of writings used by the Tagbanwa of Palawan and the Mangyans of Mindoro, in early Spanish works published in the country, and in pre-Spanish artifacts such as clay pots and burial jars dating from the 14th and 15th centuries. The Filipino alphabet and script has a Hindu-Buddhist affinity but there is no extant pre-Hispanic written body of literature. Epics, poems, and songs were transmitted by oral tradition. Ancient Filipinos wrote on bamboo and other plant materials, using knives to scratch the characters.

Printing was introduced in Manila in 1593. Father Francisco de San José was the first to use a printing press in the provinces, in 1610, with Tomás Pinpin as his first Filipino printer.

The earliest libraries were the convent libraries of the Spanish missionaries, built from 1565 when the Augustinian friars began to arrive in the islands. By 1593 the Augustinian Francisco de Ortega reported a total of 72 convents and monasteries; probably all carried on the European tradition of having books and libraries in their religious houses. The Dominicans had the greatest number of books, with some 10,000 volumes besides their archives. Academic libraries began with the founding of the University of Santo Tomás in 1611. Acquisition of books for its library commenced in 1610 with the donation of volumes made by the Archbishop of Manila, Miguel de Benavides, and Diego de Soria, Bishop of Nueva Segovia. Among other libraries established were the Colegio de San Felipe de Austria, Colegio de San José, and Colegio de San Ignacio.

Nonreligious libraries were established toward the end of the 18th century. The first was the Real Sociedad Económica de Amigo del País library in 1781, the Biblioteca Militar in 1846 for the use of the Spanish soldiers, and much later the Museo Biblioteca de Filipinas in 1887 and the small library of the School of Arts and Trades in 1889. The Museo Biblioteca was in essence a national library with a scanty collection of about 1,000 volumes and with only 74 Philippine titles. Don Pedro A. Paterno, its first Director, also published the first library periodical, *Boletín del Museo Biblioteca de Filipinas,* in 1895. Paterno, a lawyer, poet, and statesman, is also the

Theodore F. Welch

The Asian Development Bank Library in Manila, an extensive book and pamphlet collection on finance and economics.

author of the law creating the Philippine Library which consolidated all government libraries.

The first library established during the American period was public in nature: a subscription library whose objective was "to create a source of instruction and profitable entertainment for the residents of Manila." The book collection of the American Circulating Library was donated to the Philippine government to become the nucleus of a public library system and a national library through a law approved in 1901. By 1903 the book collection had grown to 21,750 volumes; Nelly Young Egbert served as Librarian and James Alexander Robertson as Director. The first public school library was established in 1907 by Lois Stewart Osborn, an American teacher assigned at the Pampanga High School.

Libraries today vary widely in size, services, resources, and staff. Most libraries continue traditional library methods, but others are rapidly adopting new technology. In the late 1970s computerized information services began to appear, notably at the University of the Philippines at Los Baños (UPLB), the National Science Development Board (NSDB), and the National Library. Still, the rapid development of libraries was hindered by budget cuts, freezing of promotions and appointments, retrenchments, and other measures to combat inflation. In Central Philippines ALBASA (Academic Libraries Book Acquisition Systems Association Inc.) is a cooperative acquisitions project among 56 libraries. In metropolitan Manila the Inter-Institutional Consortium of Southern Manila Area composed of six government and private educational institutions embarked on a shared cataloguing project.

National Library and Archives. The National Library of the Philippines serves both as a repository of the nation's recorded cultural heritage and as a public library through its 493 branch libraries in various cities and towns in the country. It provides leadership among the nation's libraries; serves as a permanent depository of all publications issued in the country; maintains an up-to-date *Philippine National Bibliography,* a *National Union Catalogue,* and other bibliographical services; acquires and makes available

645

other types of reference materials; serves as a coordinating center for cooperative activities; and provides library and information services to government agencies.

The *Philippine National Bibliography,* begun in 1974, is a current listing of books published in the Philippines by Filipino authors and of books relating to the Philippines even if published abroad. It lists books, first issues of periodicals, theses and dissertations, government publications, music scores, and conference proceedings. It is published quarterly and cumulated annually.

The Decree on Intellectual Property (the copyright law of the Philippines) and two other presidential decrees are the bases of the national bibliography. The Decree on Intellectual Property (presidential decree 49) requires the deposit of at least two copies of each work published if the copyright claimant wants his work registered with the copyright office of the National Library. Presidential decree 812, known as the Decree on Legal and Cultural Deposit, designates the National Library as the prime depository library for all publications issued in the country, together with four other state institutions. The law requires each publisher to deposit at least two copies of each work at the National Library, as well as a copy each to the University of the Philippines Library in Diliman, Quezon City; the Cultural Center of the Philippines in Manila; the University of the Philippines–Cebu in Cebu City, Central Philippines; and Mindanao State University in Marawi City in Mindanao. Presidential decree 285, aimed at reducing costs and making reading materials available to the broader masses for research and study, requires the deposit of two copies of each textbook or reference book of foreign imprint intended by a publisher to be reprinted and distributed in the Philippines.

Among notable possessions in the National Library are books and manuscripts in the Rizaliana collection, by and about the national hero, José Rizal y Alonso; and original records of the Filipino-American war of 1898–1903 in Spanish and Tagalog, turned over by the United States government to the Philippine government in 1955. The President Manuel L. Quezon papers comprise an estimated 180,000 items, and the President Carlos P. Garcia papers consist of 162,000 items.

The National Archives was a division of the National Library until it was transferred to the Bureau of Records Management in 1958 as the Division of Archives. In 1982 it was renamed Records Management and Archives Office. The archival records consist of Spanish and American documents: naturalization papers, citizenship records, civil service records, notarial records, cattle brands, public works contracts, court records, and civil registers. Altogether there are about 13,321,000 items.

Academic Libraries. The Ministry of Education, Culture, and Sports requires each of the 942 institutions of higher learning to have library facilities; 75 are state-supported colleges and universities. There is, however, wide disparity in both human and financial resources as well as in facilities and book collections.

The University of the Philippines Library System, established in 1908, is the largest of the state-supported academic institutions, with a total book collection of 1,141,130 volumes, 19,247 serial titles, and 39,713 pieces of nonprint materials as of 1984. The UPLB Library is the national center for AGRIS (Agricultural Information System); the UP Law Center is the largest and most comprehensive in law literature in Southeast Asia.

The University of Santo Tomás (UST) Library is the oldest university library. It has one of the largest book collections, consisting of 280,000 books, 30,000 serials, and 8,930 nonprint materials. The Ateneo de Manila University Library, founded in 1859 by the Jesuits, also has excellent book and microform collections.

Other notable library buildings and collections are those of the De La Salle University in Manila, the St. Louis University in Baguio, the Silliman University in Dumaguete City, the University of the East in Manila and the Mindanao State University. The University of San Carlos possesses outstanding collections of Filipiniana, Cebuano materials, and the humanities. Generally, private college and university libraries are supported mainly from matriculation and library fees, gifts, and endowments from foreign agencies. The Fund for Assistance to Private Education (FAPE) also gives training grants to libraries in the private educational institutions and provides books to libraries through its Filipiniana Book Enhancement Program.

Libraries of state colleges and universities are minimal because a large portion of their budgets goes to personnel for wages and is spent on other maintenance services. Donations are also a source of funding for the libraries.

Public Libraries. In the Philippines, public libraries rely almost entirely on the financial support of their respective local governments, whether city, mu-

Libraries in the Philippines (1982)

Type	Administrative units	Service points	Volumes in collections	Annual expenditures (peso)	Population served	Professional staff	Total staff
National	1	8	439,588	9,258,600	6,914,581	155	258
Academic	--	942	5,770,522	--	1,576,500	--	--
Public[b]	--	510	1,599,228	--	24,674,000	180	764
School	--	35,793	--	--	13,464,123	--	--
Special	--	495	3,820,678	--	--	558	821

Sources: The National Library of the Philippines, *Sports Statistical Bulletin*; Directory of NEDA *Yearbook*; Ministry of Education and Culture and Special Libraries and Information Centers in the Philippines.

nicipal, or provincial. There were more than 500 public libraries in the mid-1980s, of which 493 were under the supervision and control of the National Library through its Extension Division. Some 97 public libraries are located in metropolitan Manila; the rest are scattered in the various cities and towns of the country. However, only 35 of the 72 provinces and 31 of the 61 cities have public libraries. Bookmobiles are available in seven provinces as part of the countryside development program. Yet library services to urban and rural communities are still inadequate.

School Libraries and Media Centers. School libraries and media centers both at the secondary and elementary level generally remain neglected despite the requirement that each school provide adequate library services to its students. Most are one-room affairs, others only a few shelves of discarded American books and textbooks. The national government launched in 1984 a book enhancement program wherein 77 high school libraries, chosen on the basis of population density and central location from each province and the four cities of the national capital region, were to receive 10,000 books over a four-year period from 1985 to 1988. The program was provided an annual budget of 30,000,000 pesos.

The private school libraries have some of the better resources. They include those of St. Scholastica's College in Malate, Manila; Xavier School; Ateneo de Manila; De La Salle; and the International School. They have up-to-date and excellent collections.

Special Libraries. This type of library grew from 51 special libraries in 1961 to almost 500 by the first half of the 1980s.

The International Center for Living and Aquatic Resources Management (ICLARM) was established in September 1978. Its resources as of 1984 covered 4,218 books, 490 periodical titles, and 1,919 nonprint materials dealing with fisheries and aquaculture. Philippine Aquatic Science and Fisheries Information System (PASFIS) is a networking activity of ICLARM. ICLARM has a link with the Lockheed Dialog System.

The Southeast Asian Fisheries Development Center (SEAFDEC) in Tigbauan, Iloilo City, has an excellent collection in fisheries. Its resources consist of 6,500 books, 400 periodical and serial titles, and 8,310 nonprint materials. The Aquaculture Information System became operational in October 1982.

The International Rice Research Institute (IRRI) Library and Documentation Center in Los Baños, Laguna, was established in 1960 with total resources of 62,422 books and monographs, 2,625 periodical and serial titles, and 5,658 nonprint materials in the field of rice research.

The National Scientific Clearinghouse and Documentation Service Division of the National Science and Technology Authority (NSTA) was established in 1906. Its resources consist of 26,119 books, 7,000 pamphlets, 4,990 periodical and serial titles, and 6,710 nonprint materials. The agency provides computerized information services to the science community through National Information System for Science and Technology (NISST), Current Awareness Service (CAS), and Selective Dissemination of Information (SDI).

The Philippine Council for Agriculture and Re-

sources Research (PCARR) Library in Los Baños, Laguna, was established in 1972. Its resources consist of 4,416 books, 1,100 periodical and serial titles, and 3,014 nonprint materials in the field of agriculture and allied disciplines.

The Energy Research and Development Center (ERDC) Library and Information Center of the Philippine National Oil Company was established in 1981. It has total holdings of 1,500 books.

The Dansalan Research Center in Marawi City has an extensive collection of Islamic literature, and the Cebuano Studies Center at the University of San Carlos in Cebu City has a strong collection of Bisayan literature, history, languages, and anthropology.

Other special libraries have outstanding collections in banking, management, business, and industry, including those of the Asian Development Bank (ADB), Asian Institute of Management (AIM), and San Miguel Corporation (SMC) Human Resources Library Division.

The Profession. As early as 1914, a library science course was offered at the University of the Philippines with American library pioneers such as Mary Polk and James Alexander Robertson as teachers. The U.P. Institute of Library Science offers library science course at the Master's level. Other library schools offering graduate library science courses are the University of Santo Tomás, University of the East, Philippine Women's University (all in Manila), and University of San Carlos in Cebu City.

The Philippine Library Association, founded on October 22, 1923, by Trinidad H. Pardo de Tavera, former Director of the National Library, is the umbrella organization of some 24 sectoral and local library associations. It publishes the quarterly *Bulletin of the Philippine Library Association* and the *PLA Newsletter*. The Association of Special Libraries in the Philippines publishes the quarterly *ASLP Bulletin*; the Philippine Association of Academic and Research Libraries, its quarterly *PAARL Newsletter*; and the Agricultural Libraries Association of the Philippines, its *ALAP News*, irregularly published.

REFERENCES

Concordia Sanchez, *Philippine School Libraries: Their Organization and Management* (1972).

Filomena Tann, *Philippine Librarianship: the Past and the Future* (1982).

Rosa M. Vallejo, *Philippine Librarianship: a Historical Perspective* (1981).

SERAFIN QUIASON

Platina, Bartolomeo
(1421–1481)

Italian librarian and Humanist, Bartolomeo Platina was Vatican Librarian under Pope Sixtus IV.

Born into the Sacchi family in 1421 at Piadena (thus "Platina") near Mantua, he was, in his earlier years, a tutor for the children of Marquis Ludovico Gonzaga at Mantua. From 1457 to 1461 Platina studied Greek at Florence, and the following year he became Secretary to Cardinal Francesco Gonzaga in Rome.

Two years later Platina was one of the Humanist scholars employed by the papacy to draft social letters and documents in an elegant calligraphic hand, on a staff that generally consisted of 70 "abbreviators." When Pope Paul (1464–71), dissatisfied with their work, abolished the office, the 70 picketed the papal residence for 20 days in formal protest. As organizer and leader, Platina further offended the Pope by insisting upon arbitration and drew a three-month prison sentence when he threatened to appeal before kings and princes for a public hearing of the abbreviators' problems.

Shortly after his release, Platina and other dismissed scholars formed a study group to read Latin writers, as opposed to the Greek. The Pope, however, favored the study of early Christian writers, or at least such classics as did not breathe an air of immorality and paganism, and claimed that the writings of Juvenal, Ovid, Plautus, and Terence could only corrupt children. For his contrary opinions Platina and other scholars were arrested, and he was sentenced to a year in prison.

The Vatican library at Rome was in many ways the most important of Renaissance libraries. Fifteenth-century popes were not only spiritual leaders of the world but secular rulers of territorial states. Other princes in Italy encouraged and developed manuscript and book collections; some popes also felt it a civic duty to become library patrons.

In 1474 Platina published the first part of his *Lives of the Popes,* a readable book that achieved wide circulation, and the following year Pope Sixtus IV appointed him Vatican Librarian. Pope Nicholas V (d. 1453) had initiated the idea of a library, but Platina's administrative genius made the plan feasible, causing the Pope to create an annual library budget to support book purchases, regular salaries for the librarian, two assistants, and three copyists, and the operation of a book bindery.

It was the Pope's aspiration to create in Rome the foremost library anywhere. Platina was authorized to plan a library building to hold writings collected by earlier popes and to accommodate future acquisitions. He was given a free hand in construction and in the selection of artists and craftsmen. The library, occupying the ground floor of the papal palace, consisted of four halls for books and readers: one for Latin writings; another for Greek works; a third, the *Secreta,* for valuable manuscripts; and a fourth, the *Pontificia,* for papal archives and registers. Renowned painters, such as the Ghirlandaio brothers and A. Romano, decorated walls and ceilings with paintings, while the talents of Melozzo da Forli resulted in the famous fresco "Pope Sixtus IV Appoints Platina as Vatican Librarian." Special efforts were made to accommodate patrons, including portable heating devices for their convenience during chilly Italian winters. The originality of posted regulations in Latin requesting silence and order prompted one patron in 1513 to make a copy: "When in the Library let no one speak vociferously with another nor be troublesome; and when he is going from place to place, let him not climb the steps and scrape them with his feet. Let him close the books and replace them in their proper places. Everyone may read whatever he wishes wherever he wishes. Whosoever acts otherwise will be ejected in dishonor and will henceforth be denied entrance to this place."

Three copyists (*scriptores*) were hired to reproduce Latin, Greek, and Hebrew manuscripts, and Platina also had regular funds to dispatch book agents to European countries in what a contemporary writer, Vespasiano, viewed as a new epoch in the manuscript book trade. Platina's success in developing the holdings may be measured by noting the library's growth. When he assumed his duties in 1475, his inventory listed 2,527 volumes. The materials were Latin or Greek, with none in the Italian vernacular. Though there was increasing emphasis on theology and philosophy, one-fourth of the holdings were ancient classics. Six years later, in a report prepared eight days before Platina's death, the number had increased to 3,499, an annual increase of 162 volumes. The library's only rival was the 3,000-volume collection of Matthias Corvinus of Hungary.

REFERENCE
J. W. Clark, "On the Vatican Library of Sixtus IV," *Cambridge Antiquarian Society Proceedings and Communications* (1899).

REDMOND A. BURKE

Mary Wright Plummer

ALA

Plummer, Mary Wright
(1856–1916)

Mary Wright Plummer, library educator and leader, attempted throughout her professional life to communicate her enthusiasm for broadly based liberal education and cultural experience and for practical professional training.

She was born on March 8, 1856, at Richmond, Indiana, to Jonathan W. and Hannah Ballard Plummer, who valued their Quaker heritage and passed it on to their children. Attending the Friends Academy in Richmond until she was 17, she moved about 1873 with her family to Chicago, where her father was employed as a wholesale druggist. Except for attending Wellesley College, 1881–82, she spent her early adulthood with her family—teaching, writing poetry, and generally educating herself, including mastery of several modern languages.

In January 1887 she enrolled in the first class of Melvil Dewey's new library school at Columbia College, where she first made her mark. At the September 1887 conference of the American Library Association she reported on the school to curious members in a talk that was later published in *Library Journal* as "The Columbia College School of Library Economy from a Student's Standpoint." Upon completing the program at Columbia she worked as cataloguer at the St. Louis Public Library for two years.

In the fall of 1890 she went to Pratt Institute Free Library in Brooklyn as both a librarian and an instructor for the training class. Following a year's tour of European libraries she became head of both operations in 1895—a demanding joint position she filled until 1904, when at her request she concentrated on directing the developing library school. In 1911 she became the first Principal of the new library school of the New York Public Library, where she served until her death in 1916.

Active in state and local library organizations, she was enthusiastic about the early planning that led to the establishment of the Association of American Library Schools in 1915. She had previously chaired the ALA's Committee on Library Training (1903–10). Elected the Association's second woman President for 1915–16, she did not live much beyond the end of her term; she became ill, and her presidential address of June 26, 1916, had to be read to the Conference at Asbury Park, New Jersey, in her absence. She died September 21, 1916, in Dixon, Illinois.

At both Pratt and the New York Public Library Plummer attempted to help the schools respond to the contemporary and unique needs of students and institutions, rather than to the uniform patterns of the emerging university schools. She insisted on flexible admission requirements and a greater emphasis on practice work. All the while, she hoped that the esteem in which scholarly librarianship was held in Europe could be approached in her homeland. Concerned about the status of women in librarianship, she was nevertheless patient in temperament and preferred to work for change slowly by encouraging individual achievements in the conventional manner.

During her years at Pratt, she published a book of poetry and several children's titles. Her *Hints to Small Libraries,* originally published in 1894, appeared in its fourth edition in 1911. She contributed to *Library Journal, Pratt Institute Monthly,* and the *ALA Bulletin,* as well as the "Training for Librarianship" chapter to the ALA *Manual of Library Economy* (1913). Her 1909 talk before the New York State Library Association appeared in the *Sewanee Review* (1910) as "The Seven Joys of Reading" and has been reprinted several times. Her 1916 presidential address to the ALA, "The Public Library and the Pursuit of Truth," appeared in *Library Journal* and in the conference proceedings.

REFERENCE
Robert A. Karlowich and Nasser Sharify, "Plummer, Mary Wright," *Dictionary of American Library Biography* (1978).
                    DONALD G. DAVIS, JR.

Poland

Poland, a socialist republic in eastern Europe, borders the Baltic Sea on the north, the Soviet Union on the east, Czechoslovakia on the south, and East Germany on the west. Population (1984 est.) 37,000,000; area 312,677 sq.km. The official language is Polish.

National Library of Poland

Historic Palace of the Republic, which houses special collections of the National Library.

History. The earliest mention of libraries in Poland is of cathedral and monastic libraries at the beginning of the 11th century. The oldest cathedral library, in existence since the year 1000, is in Gniezno. The library at the University of Cracow was established with the university in 1364. The art of printing came to Cracow in 1473–74; the first printed book in Polish vernacular was published in 1513.

Beginning in the 16th century, many of the Polish kings and nobles founded their own libraries. Small fragments of these private collections have survived wars and confiscations and can be found in the collections of rare books in today's Polish libraries. The first city libraries were founded in 1525 (Poznan) and 1596 (Gdansk).

National Library. Early in the 18th century the Zaluski brothers founded a library that they donated to the nation in 1747, making Poland the first country to possess a true national library. In 1780 a legal deposit law was enacted, and by 1790 the library had become one of the largest in Europe, with approximately 400,000 volumes. The history of this national library reflects the history of libraries in Poland as affected by wars, confiscation, and wanton destruction. After the partition of Poland by its big neighbors, the library was confiscated in 1794 and carried away to St. Petersburg by order of Empress Catherine II.

After World War I, when Poland regained independence, a new National Library was established in 1928. That library sustained great losses (80 percent of the collection) during World War II through deliberate destruction and looting by Nazi occupants—including 2,200 incunabula and 50,000 volumes of pre-1800 Polish books.

The Biblioteka Narodowa is in Warsaw. The collections total more than 4,000,000 volumes with strengths in the social sciences and humanities. The Library collects all Polish publications in any form, as well as foreign Polonica. As the central library of the state, the National Library also compiles statistics on publishing and library activities; coordinates activities of all Polish libraries; standardizes library procedures and technology; compiles the national bibliographies, as well as other bibliographic tools; conducts research on reading habits and the spread of knowledge about books; advises on appropriate reading materials; and prints and distributes library catalogue cards.

Academic Libraries. There are some 90 academic libraries in Poland (including main libraries and branches) with about 33,000,000 volumes. The Jagiellonian Library at the University of Cracow (founded in 1364) is preeminent among them, with a bookstock of 2,363,000 volumes and 412,300 periodicals, exceptionally strong manuscript collections, and the largest collection of incunabula in Poland. All Polish works published before 1800 are collected. The University Library in Warsaw (founded in 1817), with more than 2,000,000 volumes, is the next most important academic library.

Public Libraries. In 1980 there were about 9,315 public libraries (including branches), with collections of more than 94,500,000 volumes. All public libraries in Poland are part of a national network, which has a library in every administrative unit and rural district. Among the large public libraries are those in Warsaw, Szczecin, Torun, Lodz, Cracow, Poznan, and Bydgoszcz.

Trade-Union Libraries. Some 6,000 trade-union libraries hold collections of more than 17,000,000 volumes, mostly fiction. This network of trade-union libraries supplements the network of public libraries.

School Libraries. In Poland school libraries are found in all primary, secondary, and vocational schools—about 25,000 libraries in total. Their joint bookstocks amount to more than 100,000,000 volumes.

Special Libraries. There are about 8,000 scientific or vocational libraries and centers of scientific, technical, and economic information. They include the Main Medical Library of Warsaw, the Central Agricultural Library, the Main Communication Library, the Library of the Main School of Planning and Statistics in Warsaw, the Central Statistical Library, the Central Military Library, and the Seym (Parliament) Library.

There is a National Center for Scientific, Technical, and Economic Information. In 1974, on the recommendation of the Minister of Science, Higher Schools, and Technology, a national system of scientific, technical, and organizational information (SINTO) was established.

The Profession. The Polish Library Association was founded in 1917. It publishes works on the theory and practice of librarianship and on bibliography and two journals, *The Library Review* (from 1927) and *The Librarian* (from 1929). It has been a member of IFLA since its beginning in 1929.

REFERENCES

A. Freibish, "Polish Libraries: Their Structure, Organization and Aims," *International Library Review* (1977).

Richard Lewanski, *Guide to Polish Libraries and Archives* (1974).

R. C. Usherwood, "Rising from Ruin: Impressions of Polish Libraries," *Wilson Library Bulletin* (1976).

GEORGE S. BOBINSKI*

Pollard, A. W.
(1859–1944)

Alfred William Pollard, librarian and bibliographer of early printed books, produced with G. R. Redgrave the *Short-Title Catalogue* for the period 1475–1640.

Pollard was born in London on August 14, 1859, and was educated at an excellent London school. Taught by John Wesley Hales, he studied English literature, notably Chaucer and Shakespeare, whose texts he later reexamined and edited. His admission to the University of Oxford was a natural progression; he entered Saint John's College in 1877 with an open scholarship and earned a B.A. Honours degree in Classical Studies and Philosophy.

Pollard proved to be a brilliant addition to the staff of the Printed Books Department of the British Museum Library when he went to work there in 1883. He married a graduate of Cambridge University in 1887, who, with her own intellectual interests, constantly inspired and stimulated his work. They had two sons and a daughter; both sons were killed in World War I, a loss for which Pollard's solace was intensive scholarship and bibliographical research. He became Keeper of Printed Books in the British Museum in 1919 and in the same year was appointed honorary Professor of Bibliography at the University of London. He retired from the Museum in 1924 but remained mentally active and productive until 1935, when he suffered some brain damage after an accident.

He was associated with a bibliographical journal, *The Library,* for nearly 46 years and was officially recognized as co-editor in 1899. In the London Bibliographical Society, founded in 1892, Pollard was appointed Secretary in 1893, and under his guidance

---

Libraries in Poland (1980)

Type	Administrative units	Service points	Volumes in collections	Annual expenditures (zloty)	Population served[c]	Professional staff	Total staff
National	1	1	1,850,000	11,007,000[a]	--	96	450
Academic	1,064	--	34,220,000	475,662,000[b]	--	903	4,936
Public	9,315	26,587	94,538,000	398,203,000[a]	7,388,000	6,974	16,533
School	--	--	--	--	--	--	--
Special[d]	5,462	--	19,118,000	--	1,072	--	--
Nonspecialized	126	--	11,883,000	--	172,326		

[a]Excludes expenditure for personnel.
[b]Acquisitions only.
[c]Registered borrowers.
[d]1977 data.

Source: Unesco, *Statistical Yearbook,* 1984.

it became a prestigious organization. Eventually, *The Library* became the official publication of the London Bibliographical Society.

The high quality of Pollard's work was recognized by various institutions. In 1907 he became a Fellow of King's College, London, and in 1921 received the honorary degree of Doctor of Letters from the University of Durham. He was made a Fellow of the British Academy in 1922, and that year he was invested as a Companion of the Order of the Bath by King George V. He was also known and admired by scholars and librarians in the United States and collaborated, by mail, with the scholar Henrietta Bartlett in the compilation of a *Census of Shakespeare's Plays in Quarto* (1916). During his only visit to the U.S. he catalogued the rich library of an eccentric bibliophile, General Rush C. Hawkins, in Providence, Rhode Island. In 1921 he was elected an Honorary Foreign Corresponding Member of the Bibliographical Society of America.

All his awards cannot be listed but even those named here prove that he had a great reputation as a bibliographer. His work, however, must be assessed in historical perspective and his aims analyzed in the light of his performance. Most of his early research into 15th-century printing was done in collaboration with Robert Proctor, who joined the British Museum Library's staff in 1893. Both were keenly interested in incunabula—"fifteeners," as they were sometimes known, books produced before 1500, during printing's infancy. Proctor and Pollard cooperated in an ideal partnership. Proctor possessed the meticulous assiduity and patient precision necessary for the measurement and identification of typefaces, and Pollard concentrated on early book illustration.

Pollard condoned his partner's obsession with "fifteeners" but also, characteristically, saw the other side of the picture. Of Proctor's work at Oxford with J. G. Milne in the library of Corpus Christi he said, "I gather that the responsible librarian was a little alarmed at the enthusiasm with which the fragments of printers' or binders' waste were extracted from the old bindings, and despite the extraordinarily interesting finds which have been made in book-covers, there is much to be said on the librarian's side." Proctor had, according to Pollard, an enormous ability to labor and concentrate on bibliographical detail, but he was not an innovator. He "had one of the brains which require some outside influence to kindle them into activity."

Pollard regarded himself as a journalistic bibliographer while recognizing the importance of the work undertaken by men of the caliber of Proctor. When Proctor died suddenly in 1903, Pollard reluctantly but dutifully took on the burden of compiling a full-scale catalogue of the early printed books in the British Museum Library. Curiously, but not unnaturally, the section concerning the incunabula of the United Kingdom has not yet been completed. Pollard's ambivalent attitude toward bibliographical tasks of this nature preserved a sense of balance in the undertaking. In the words of his colleague at the Museum, Victor Scholderer, Pollard's "precision with which he kept the wood in focus could prove uncommonly disconcerting to a disciple bemused with the multitude of trees."

Although Pollard was bored by the tedious processes involved in the recognition of typefaces, he saw their importance in the training of beginners in the cataloguing of early printed books. His sense of humor was such that he could not take minutiae too seriously, and combined with this was an awareness of humanity. It is significant that his presidential address to the Edinburgh Bibliographical Society in 1923 was entitled *The Human Factor in Bibliography*.

Pollard was in a lighthearted mood at a meeting of the London Bibliographical Society in January 1918 when he made the proposal for the publication of the work that became his chief contribution to bibliography: *A Short-Title Catalogue of Books Printed in England, Scotland, and Ireland and of English Books Printed Abroad, 1475–1640*, produced in collaboration with G. R. Redgrave. The vast compilation of over 26,000 items took about nine years to prepare. Pollard received the assistance of numerous bibliographers, but in the last resort he was the editor and did much of the work himself. He believed that in the extensive bibliographical field, speed and production were more important than detail. The "S.T.C.," as it is now known, was not intended as a final product. Pollard makes this clear in his preface:

> One object of this preface is to warn all users of this book that from the mixed character of its sources, it is a dangerous work for any one to handle lazily, that is, without verification. The main workers on it on the average are septuagenarians.

Pollard's view of bibliography's function was succinctly expressed as the enumeration of books and the provision of a basis for textual criticism. Because he had an open mind, he did not expect his judgments and conclusions to be regarded as final and irrevocable, but he did expect other scholars to be stimulated by his work and to undertake further investigations. All bibliographers are indebted to him for his scientific approach to an occupation formerly regarded as a bibliophilic hobby.

Pollard died in Wimbledon, South London, March 8, 1944.

REFERENCES

G. Murphy, *A Select Bibliography of the Writings of A. W. Pollard* (1938), includes notes and an autobiographical essay, "My First Fifty Years."

J. Dover Wilson, *Alfred William Pollard, 1859–1944* (1948).

MARGARET WRIGHT

Poole, William Frederick
(1821–1894)

William Frederick Poole was Librarian of the Boston Athenaeum, of the Chicago Public Library, and of the Newberry Library. He was one of the outstanding librarians of the 19th century.

He was born in Salem, Massachusetts, on December 24, 1821, the son of working-class parents. Young Poole was compelled to abandon his studies at 12 and seek employment in a variety of occupations. Through his mother's encouragement, at the age of 17 he was able to enroll in the Leicester Academy while at the same time teaching in the local schools. He entered Yale University in 1842 but after a year was obliged to suspend his education again for financial reasons. He turned to teaching a second time

William Frederick Poole

651

and three years later resumed his college career at Yale, from which he graduated in 1849 with election to Phi Beta Kappa.

To supplement his income, during his junior year at Yale he became the Assistant Librarian of the Society of Brothers in Unity, a student literary and debating organization. The Society provided its members with a collection of books and periodicals to help them find material for their debates and other forensic exercises. Although the library maintained a catalogue of the book collection, there was no similar key to the contents of periodicals. In his desire to assist the students, Poole decided to compile an index to the periodical collection. He promptly undertook the task of preparing an index in manuscript form of some 200 volumes of magazines. Since there was only one copy of the index, Poole soon realized that it would need to be published. Through the efforts of Henry Stevens, a former Librarian of the Society, he was able to persuade G. P. Putnam to publish it. As a result of this work he received considerable recognition both at home and abroad. The first edition of the index was quickly sold out, and Poole began to compile a second edition, which was issued in 1853.

In the interim, although he indicated some leanings toward the legal profession, Poole decided to pursue librarianship as a life career. In 1851 he received a temporary appointment as Assistant Librarian of the Boston Athenaeum and shortly thereafter became the Librarian of the Mercantile Library Association of Boston, one of the leading social libraries in the country. Poole threw himself into his new responsibilities with vigor. He managed the moving of the library to new quarters, enlarged the book collection, and published a printed catalogue of its holdings. In issuing the catalogue, he introduced an innovation in that the author, title, and subject entries were listed in a single alphabetical sequence, setting a precedent that became a standard practice for many libraries to follow, popularly referred to as the dictionary catalogue. During his tenure at the Mercantile Library, he attended the first library conference, which was held in New York in 1853. Poole was treated as one of the important delegates at the conference. An advance copy of the second edition of his periodical index was on display at the meeting, and a resolution approving it was adopted by the members present.

In 1856 Poole was offered the position of Librarian of the Boston Athenaeum. The Athenaeum was one of the prestigious libraries of the country, and this appointment offered Poole considerable visibility. He remained at the Athenaeum for 13 years and was responsible for a number of important improvements in the physical quarters of the Library as well as in its services. He expanded the book collection and devised a classification scheme that was pragmatic in nature. Poole did not advocate strict subject classification, nor did he believe that it was possible. He also enlarged and trained the professional staff. Several of his assistants, among whom were Caroline M. Hewins, William I. Fletcher, and Charles Evans, later became nationally prominent librarians. In his leisure moments Poole was engaged in working on his periodical index and in writing, particularly in the field of early New England history. He published a new edition of Edward Johnson's *Wonder-Working*

Providence of Sion's Saviour in New England together with a lengthy scholarly introduction that afforded him recognition as a historian. From 1858 to 1870, he served as a member of the Visiting Committee for the Harvard Library.

Serving the reading and research needs of the intellectual elite of Boston, who were members of the Athenaeum, was doubtless an enriching experience for Poole. Nevertheless in 1869 he felt the need for greater professional opportunities and tendered his resignation to the proprietors of the Athenaeum. For the next few years he served as a consultant and adviser to a number of libraries throughout the country. In some instances his services were limited to the selection of books; in other cases it involved a complete reorganization of the library, as in the case of the Naval Academy library in Annapolis and the Cincinnati Public Library. His work in Cincinnati led to a full-time appointment as Librarian in 1871. In a short period of time he transformed a feeble institution into a strong and vibrant organization second only to the Boston Public Library. Under Poole, the Cincinnati Public Library opened its reading room on Sundays, increased the circulation of books significantly, and organized a special room for fine arts and decoration to serve commercial designers. This may well be the first subject department to have been established in a public library.

His tenure in Cincinnati was brief: in January 1874 he became Librarian of the newly established Chicago Public Library. Even before he accepted the position in Chicago, he had advised library leaders in Peoria on legislation on the legal structure of public libraries for Illinois. Poole was familiar with Ohio and Indiana library legislation, which placed public libraries under the jurisdiction of public school boards of education. He found this governing authority unsatisfactory, and he proposed the concept of a library board appointed by the mayor of a municipality that would be free from excessive political interference. The Illinois Public Library Act of 1872 , under which the Chicago Public Library was established, bore the fruits of Poole's advice.

Poole's first task upon assuming his duties was to organize a book collection and to provide suitable quarters for the Library. The people of Great Britain had sent some 8,000 volumes following the Chicago fire of 1871, but they were largely reference and scholarly works. Poole knew he needed a large collection of books to meet the reading needs of the average user. With the assistance of his staff, Poole promptly undertook the acquisition, cataloguing, and classification of the initial collection. Since Poole was essentially a pragmatist rather than a purist or a perfectionist on issues relating to cataloguing and classification, the work proceeded with dispatch. Poole designed a classification scheme that was based on utility rather than theory. It was divided into 20 major subjects or classes. Each class was assigned a letter of the alphabet. His book notation system consisted of a single letter followed by a serial number. Books in each class were numbered serially beginning with one and running continuously as books were added. Provision was made for subclasses by reserving in advance blocks of numbers for each subclass. With his characteristic flare for producing results, Poole managed to have an ample collection of circulating books ready for use within four months after he took office.

Since a printed catalogue was not possible, Poole decided on a device that he called a "finding list." This printed publication contained a sampling of the collection, with the titles arranged by subject and with the call number included. For a time the Library charged a small fee for the finding list. In later years the lists were published by a commerical firm, carried some advertising, and were distributed free.

Poole was a firm believer that the public library was an important educational institution, and he strove to make its influence felt in the community. In 1884 he expanded library service to the outlying areas of the city through a system called "station delivery." Neighborhood stores whose proprietors agreed to accept orders for library books were designated as stations. Orders were picked up by library messengers each day and the books delivered as promptly as the service would permit. The storekeepers were paid a small fee for the service they performed. Under Poole's strong leadership, the Chicago Public Library became the largest circulating library in the United States.

At this period in his professional career, Poole was undoubtedly one of the outstanding librarians of the day, if not the most eminent, second only to Justin Winsor. In 1876 he served on the organizing committee to form the American Library Association at a meeting held in Philadelphia. He was elected Vice-President of the newly established association at that historic conference, served in that capacity for eight years, then served two terms as President. Poole's proposal for the cooperative preparation of his index to periodicals was adopted at the 1876 meeting. Under his plan, librarians from both the U.S. and England would participate in the indexing project, to be coordinated by Poole and William I. Fletcher. This project came to a successful conclusion with the publication of the third edition of *Poole's Index to Periodical Literature* in 1882, receiving wide applause.

During America's centennial year Poole was also invited to contribute an article to the U.S. Bureau of Education Report on *Public Libraries in the United States of America*. His paper was entitled "The Organization and Management of Public Libraries" and can be described as a distillation of the principles and practices of library administration at that time. In 1877 he attended the International Conference of Librarians in London and served as Vice-President for the meeting.

In 1887 Poole resigned from the Chicago Public Library to become the first Librarian of the Newberry Library, which came into being under a munificent bequest of Walter L. Newberry, an early business giant of Chicago. The Newberry was to be a reference library, and Poole, at what would be retirement age for many, accepted a new challenge. Poole's contribution to this institution lay in the development of its rich collection and in his architectural plan for the building. Although this was his first opportunity to plan a completely new building, he had become a specialist in library architecture. Poole was an innovator in the field since he believed that a library building should be functional rather than monumental. Instead of the traditional large hall with a high vaulted ceiling, Poole advocated a number of large rooms, each 50 feet in width, which could accommodate a number of subject departments to be administered by subject specialists. With the use of steel beams, which were coming into general use as a result of the new Chicago school of architecture, such a building was possible. Despite the opposition of the architect, Henry Ives Cobb, the Board adopted Poole's plan. To assist him in the operation of the Library, Poole recruited an impressive array of assistants who laid the professional groundwork for the future development of the famous Library.

Poole was a dynamic person and found time to pursue the writing of history in addition to his full-time responsibilities as a librarian. He studied two major areas, Colonial New England and the early West. His writings were based on deep research into original sources and exhibited the highest degree of scholarship. For his historical studies he was elected President of the American Historical Association in 1888. Poole was also very active in the literary life of Chicago. He was a founding member of the Chicago Literary Club, and his historical bent furnished him with material for a number of papers delivered at meetings of this organization.

Poole died on March 1, 1894, in Evanston, Illinois, leaving a legacy of professional accomplishments and attainments that would be difficult to match.

REFERENCES

Annual Reports of the Board of Directors of the Chicago Public Library (1874–86).

William Landrum Williamson, *William Frederick Poole and the Modern Library Movement* (1963).

William Landrum Williamson, "Poole, William Frederick," *Dictionary of American Library Biography* (1978).

ALEX LADENSON

Portugal

Portugal, a republic on the western Iberian Peninsula, lies on the Atlantic Ocean, and is bounded by Spain on the north and east. Population (1984 est.) 10,198,000; area 91,632 sq.km. The official language is Portuguese.

History. In 1796 Queen Mary I created the Royal Public Library of the Court. The first collection was that of the Real Mesa Censória, now extinct.

National Library. The National Library, which grew out of Queen Mary's Court Library, was in the ancient Convent of Saint Francisco in Lisbon, until 1969. That year it was transferred to a new building built expressly for it.

The Library holds approximately 2,000,000 volumes, together with printed works, codified manuscripts, incunabula, collections of miscellaneous manuscripts, stamps, maps, geographic charts, and periodicals. It also has a valuable collection of medallions, coins, and other ancient items. Of special significance is its music section.

Academic Libraries. The most important university library is in Coimbra; it is the General Library of the University of Coimbra and was created in the 16th century. Its original installation, situated in a magnificent edifice on the patio of the University, is characteristic of the baroque style, typical of all the surrounding region. The Library moved to a new building expressly built for it in the university zone of the city. This Library's growth and evolution

Libraries in Portugal (1981)

Type	Administrative units	Service points	Volumes in collections	Annual expenditures (escudo)	Population served	Professional staff	Total staff
National[b]	3	4	3,263,000	80,927,000	200,916[a]	41	237
Academic	219	219	2,193,000	115,473,000	817,990	48	197
Public[b]	118	599	6,284,000	217,712,000	2,303,850[a]	38	403
School	712	712	1,658,000	- -	817,829[a]	- -	- -
Special	179	- -	2,256,000	- -	123,325[a]	- -	- -
Nonspecialized[b]	2	- -	83,000	- -	- -	- -	- -

[a]Registered borrowers.
[b]1980 data.

Source: Unesco, *Statistical Yearbook*, 1984.

give it characteristics more proper to a national library than those of a university library. Its collections consist of approximately 1,500,000 volumes, including publications, incunabula, and manuscripts, some very rare and of great value.

School Libraries. Secondary schools have libraries, some of them signally important for the antiquity and richness of their collections; an example is the one of the secondary school of Passos Manuel, in Lisbon, which inherited the library of the Convent of Jesus.

Public Libraries. Public libraries of special interest are in Porto, Evora, and Lisbon. The one in Porto, the most important, was instituted in 1833, and its first bibliographic collections were the books of convents abandoned in the face of approaching troops during the political wars of the period. It possesses approximately 1,325,000 volumes and has a valuable collection of incunabula together with a notable collection of manuscripts. It was made a Municipal Library in 1896.

Special Libraries. Of significance are the Scientific Academic Library of Lisbon, the Portuguese Academy of History, and the libraries of the National Academy of Belas Artes and those of the Geographic Society. Other special libraries notable for the richness of their collections include those associated with the Calouste Gulbenkian Foundation (art history); National Institute of Statistics (statistics); Camara Pestana Institute (biology and toxicology); Center of

Philological Studies (linguistics); National Laboratory of Civil Engineering (civil engineering); and Laboratory of Nuclear Physics and Engineering (nuclear energy). Two others are the Ajuda Library in Lisbon and the library of the Mafra Convent.

The Profession. The Portuguese Association of Librarians, Archivists and Documentalists serves the professionals in these specialties. It was instituted in 1973 with the legal recognition of its statutes.

MARIA MANUELA CRUZEIRO*

Posner, Ernst
(1892-1980)

Ernst Posner, often affectionately referred to as the Dean of American Archivists, was a major influence on the development of archival education and administration in the United States. Many archivists practicing today studied with him. But he achieved success as an archivist in Germany long before he migrated to the U.S. with his wife, Katherina, in July 1939.

Posner was born on August 9, 1892, the youngest of three children, into a cultivated, liberal German family. His father was a doctor of philosophy as well as an M.D. who practiced and taught as a urologist at the University of Berlin while he was coeditor of a journal of urology. His uncle Max, a historian recognized for his contributions to 18th-century intellectual history, was also an archivist. All family members wrote, enjoyed music and literature, and spoke and read several languages. Posner grew to manhood in this intellectual and challenging atmosphere.

He attended the University of Berlin, where he graduated in 1910. After two years of required military service in 1911 and 1912, he left the Army as a reserve noncommissioned officer to reenter the university for graduate study in auxiliary historical science and in comparative administration. World War I interrupted his studies, and he returned to the German Army to serve from 1914 to 1918, when he was mustered out as a reserve lieutenant and awarded the Iron Cross, First Class. He resumed his studies again, and in 1920 he received two degrees, one for the teaching licentiate and one for the doctorate. He was now prepared to become either a teacher or an archivist. While he eventually became both, initially he chose to pursue his career as an archivist.

In November 1920 Posner became a professional archivist at the Prussian Geheime Staatsarchiv. From

Formerly the Royal Public Library of the Court created in 1796, the National Library in Lisbon moved to this building in 1969.

Jorge Alves

the beginning he was highly regarded. Soon he became the administative assistant to the director in charge of building and personnel. He discharged this responsibility so ably that in 1930, as a 37-year-old archivist and scholar, he was among those mentioned for the position of Director.

Posner also found time to write and edit. Between 1922 and 1934 he published four papers and reports and contributed to a comprehensive bibliography of German history. He also wrote annual review articles about new literature on the history of Prussia. From 1922 until 1938 he served on behalf of the Prussian Academy of Sciences as the editor of Volumes 11 through 15 of the *Acta Borussica,* continuing the documentary publication dealing with the internal history of Prussia during the 18th century. During this period Posner became a teacher, serving from 1930 until 1935 as a faculty member of the Institute for Archival Science and Advanced Historical Studies connected with the Geheime Staatsarchiv. January 30, 1933, the date on which Adolf Hitler came to power, was the beginning of the end of Posner's archival career in Germany. As a Jew he was gradually made to resign all of his archival, editing, and teaching positions. Posner was arrested during the Krystallnacht pogrom in November 1938 and spent six weeks in Sachsenhausen concentration camp. His archival career in Germany was over.

With the help of several American historians, among them Eugene Anderson, Waldo Leland, Merle Curti, and Solon Buck, Posner and his wife made their way to the U.S. They settled in Washington, D.C., where Posner joined Buck at the American University to teach one of the first courses offered in the U.S. on the history and administration of archives. In 1942, when Buck succeeded R. D. W. Connor as Archivist of the United States, Posner was made solely responsible for teaching the course. Over the next several years he designed and added other courses to develop a major archival education curriculum. By 1957 American University could boast a certificate and degree program in archival administration and records management. The curriculum Posner developed became a model for archival education programs in other institutions throughout the U.S.

Posner's summers were busy, too. In 1945 he began the summer Institutes on Archives Administration, directing them for the next 16 years. They were designed as introductory or continuing education courses primarily for prospective archivists or for those who had on-the-job archival experience but no formal schooling in archival administration. In 1950 Posner started a summer Institute on Genealogical Research; 1954 was the start of Institutes in Records Management. With the cooperation of Colonial Williamsburg and the National Park Service, Posner presented summer Institutes on the Interpretation of Historic Sites during 1949 and 1950.

From 1939 to 1945 Posner served as a part-time member of the American University faculty, first as a Lecturer and after 1940 as an Adjunct Professor. In 1945 he became Professor of History and Archives Administration and was made Dean of the Graduate Division. Two years later he became Director of the School of Social Sciences and Public Affairs and in 1955 was appointed Dean of the Graduate School. He took time off in 1957 when he was awarded a Gug-

genheim Fellowship and Fulbright research grant to work on his history of archival development in the ancient world. After he returned from his leave in Rome, he resumed his chairmanship of the history department, which he retained until he retired from academic life in 1961.

While pursuing his career as academician, Posner also had time to participate in other professional activities. For many he was uniquely qualified by virtue of his German background and experience. In 1943 and 1944 he served, consecutively, two bodies concerned with the protection of cultural treasure in countries torn by World War II. The first was the Dinsmore Committee of the American Council of Learned Societies; the second, an official body, the American Commission for the Protection and Salvage of Artistic and Historic Monuments in Europe (the Roberts Commission). For the first time he wrote a number of reports on archival establishments in Europe and Asia. He also prepared manuals on German and Italian record practices for the U.S. War Department.

A member of the Society of American Archivists from 1939 and an honorary member from 1965, Posner served the organization long and ably. He was a member of its Council, 1947–51; Vice-President, 1953–54; and President, 1955–56. He was Chairman of several of its important committees as well as a member of the editorial board of its scholarly journal, *The American Archivist.* He often represented the Society in international archival meetings. From 1958 he served intermittently as lecturer on American archival administration and practices at the Germany Archives School at Marburg.

The last few years of Ernst Posner's life were marred by ill health. Posner and his family settled in Europe, where he continued his researches in archival history. He worked at the Vatican Archives, lived in Switzerland, and later moved to Wiesbaden. He died April 18, 1980.

In the U.S. one of his most famous works, researched and written on behalf of the Society of American Archivists between 1961 and 1964 and supported by a grant to the Society from the Council on Library Resources, was *American State Archives,* published by the University of Chicago Press in 1964. This signal work was an examination and evaluation of archival agencies throughout the United States and Puerto Rico. *Archives and the Public Interest: Selected Essays by Ernst Posner,* edited by Ken Munden, was published by the Public Affairs Press, Washington, D.C., in 1967. Posner's major work *Archives in the Ancient World* (1972), a study of the development of archives from the Tigris-Euphrates civilization to the division of the Roman Empire into eastern and western halves, appeared to acclaim in 1972.

Posner received wide recognition for his accomplishments. In 1958 he became a Fellow of the Society of American Archivists. The American Association for State and Local History honored him in 1963 by presenting him with its first Award of Distinction. The Society of American Archivists gave Posner a Certificate of Appreciation in 1964, and in 1965 *American State Archives* was awarded the Waldo Gifford Leland Prize. For *Archives in the Ancient World* he won his second Waldo Gifford Leland Prize in 1973.

MARY LYNN McCREE BRYAN

Society of American Archivists
Ernst Posner

© Cynthia Farah 1985
Lawrence Clark Powell

Powell, Lawrence Clark
(1906-)

Lawrence Clark Powell may be the last of a small but significant minority—directors of major libraries who are also bookmen. In the autobiography he wrote when he took early retirement, he characterized himself as having "a personal, autobiographical, egocentric, didactic, flamboyant, hyperbolic manner." Others have called him "the Picasso of librarianship," "one of the great eccentrics," and a "demigod." When one of his detractors, a proponent of scientific management, called him a "biblio-simpleton," he responded with "library housekeeper!"

Although he served as President of the Bibliographical Society of America, (BSA) 1954–56, he was impatient with the ponderous bureaucracy of library associations. The American Library Association nonetheless gave him the Clarence Day Award (1960) and made him an honorary member (1981)—its highest award. He was elected President of the California Library Association (1950), was a Guggenheim Fellow twice (1950–51 and 1966–67), and received, in his words, "various honorary doctorates."

Powell was born in Washington, D.C., on September 3, 1906, to Quaker parents. When he was five, the family moved to South Pasadena, California, where the public librarian waived the rules for this already voracious reader: card 3089 was good for as many books as the boy could carry.

His friend Ward Ritchie, later to be one of America's most distinguished book designers and printers, decided to enroll at nearby Occidental College. Powell also applied, but was admitted only after his mother persuaded his high school teachers to recommend him despite some low grades. There Powell came under the influence of Carlyle F. MacIntyre and Benjamin Franklin Stelter. The latter "prepared me for graduate work," he later wrote, "as Mac's courses prepared me for life and literature."

After graduation in 1929, Powell did a stint as shipping clerk in Vroman's Bookstore in Pasadena. Meantime, Ritchie's admiration for the poetry of Robinson Jeffers bolstered Powell's resolve to write a dissertation on that California poet. Few universities then considered living poets fit topics for doctoral study, so he decided to enroll at the University of Dijon. After successfully defending his dissertation, he used a legacy from his grandmother to finance his *wanderjahre* in Europe. He returned to California in 1933 and was married to Fay Ellen Shoemaker, whom he had met at Occidental.

He worked at Jake Zeitlin's bookstore in Los Angeles for the next couple of years, laying the groundwork for his life's career. To make ends meet, he found after-hours work with Primavera Press— billing, wrapping, and shipping books. During a visit to the Los Angeles Public Library with the latest offerings from Zeitlin's shop, he was surprised to have the head of the order department declare, "You should be buying for, not selling to, libraries." This man introduced Powell to the dynamic Althea Warren, LAPL's Chief Librarian, who promptly sent him to the library school at the University of California in Berkeley. Dean Sydney B. Mitchell was away on sabbatical, and Powell found the library school instructors "not inspiring."

A year later, now equipped to begin his library career, Powell found himself again in Los Angeles looking for work. Althea Warren helped out with a substitute position, and in January 1938 Dean Mitchell alerted Powell to a beginning position at the University of California at Los Angeles. Director John E. Goodwin had noted his book reviews for *Westways,* his work on Robinson Jeffers, and his experience with Zeitlin—all of which qualified Powell for an immediate task: the accessioning of the Robert Ernest Cowan collection of Californiana.

Over the next six years Powell made his presence known at UCLA. The work on the Cowan collection had revealed that the library's technical processing staff had spoiled much of it by routine treatment. Powell wrote a paper deploring insensitivity to valuable documents that caught the attention of Randolph G. Adams, Director of the University of Michigan's Clements Library and author of a controversial article, "Librarians as Enemies of Books." Further, the exhibits and book displays that Powell designed and promoted gained him powerful friends on the faculty.

In spring 1943 Powell learned that he had been recommended for the librarianship at Northwestern University in Evanston, Illinois. Characteristically, he dropped his resignation in the mailbox at Union Station when he left for Evanston. Upon his return, he found that the president of the university, Robert Gordon Sproul, had a flood of letters from the faculty urging that Powell be retained. Sproul offered Powell a choice: head the university library or direct the William Andrews Clark Memorial Library, UCLA's rare book collection, housed in its own elegant building some miles from campus. Powell suggested that he take both jobs. Sproul was persuaded by the rationale of coordination—and perhaps by the thought of filling two posts with less than two salaries. So it was done: Powell became Director of the Clark on January 1, 1944, and University Librarian six months later.

The University of California had achieved distinction as the best state university in the country on the basis of Berkeley's faculty alone. The regents took a bold step in deciding that UCLA would be built to the same strength, and rapidly. The "Southern Branch," as UCLA was then designated, was to grow from what the Berkeley folk called "a twig" to a full-sized tree. Powell's Assistant Librarian, Everett Moore, recalls:

> Larry was conscious of the remarkable role he was playing in building a library that would contribute greatly to the development of a university campus that would be a worthy part of UC. He had fought hard for the job, and he strained every nerve to make a strong library that could give appropriate support to an ambitious undertaking by this brash young campus. With the establishment of one major school or program after another, Larry in most instances was in on the ground floor in pressing for and planning new library resources. (Louise Darling's appointment as Biomedical Librarian was second only to that of Stafford Warren as dean of the new Medical School.)

During Powell's 17 years as University Librarian, he drew able people to substantiate his vision. A number went on to important careers elsewhere (Neal Harlow, Gordon Williams, Robert Vosper,

Andrew Horn, H. Richard Archer, John E. Smith); some returned; others (Page Ackerman, Everett Moore, Miriam Dudley) stayed to make national reputations at UCLA.

Powell's administrative style was "getting things done through people." It was highly personalized. Staff members got the kudos, although often he had laid the groundwork. When things went awry, Powell publicly took the blame.

The book collections Powell amassed (including the Michael Sadleir, C. K. Odgen, and Isaac Foot) raised the UCLA library from the bottom quartile to fourth in the nation. The intellectual camaraderie Powell maintained with faculty and such writers as Aldous Huxley, Henry Miller, and Lawrence Durrell helped him transform the Clark library from a mausoleum into a research institution with seminars and publications. Other strengths were his own voluminous writing and speechmaking. "Books are basic" was his theme and he spun infinite variations on it. Telephoned by a panicky program planner for the title of his upcoming speech, he said, "Oh, it's just a literary cocktail—'Shake Well and Speak.'" When introducing Powell to the audience, the same person gaily announced that he would speak on "Shakespeare and Keats." And he did.

A study by Robert D. Leigh in 1952 recommended expansion of the library schools at Berkeley and at UCLA's crosstown rival, the University of Southern California, but not a new one at UCLA. The Master Plan for Higher Education in California (1955) called for no action until 1960. With his unfailing sense of timing, Powell decided to push ahead. He pressed prominent librarians and library organizations into service, and the lobbying effort was successful: the regents approved a new library school for UCLA on August 14, 1958.

The faculty Senate, displeased that the school had been approved without its usual committee process, showed its power by insisting that Powell could be either Dean of the new school or University Librarian but not both, as Powell had anticipated. Powell moved to the library school, leaving the librarian's position open on July 1, 1961, for Robert Vosper.

As Dean, Powell drew around him an exemplary faculty (Seymour Lubetzky, Frances Clark Sayers, Betty Rosenberg) and brightened every semester with a galaxy of visiting scholars, bookmen, and librarians. Andy Horn as Assistant Dean established and maintained liaison with the Graduate Division, organized the thrust for accreditation, and set up a printer's chapel for the students. Rosenberg says, "The school was a humanistic dream. The emphasis was on books and reading and service to readers and the creation of new librarians full of zeal and enthusiasm. It was an amazing library school and still is, but not as he dreamt! The machines caught up with him and he retired while his dream still held."

When the new Research Library was completed, the collections were largely moved there, leaving the undergraduate library and the library school in the original library building. Upon Powell's retirement on his sixtieth birthday in 1966, the regents named the building after him.

After a few years of travel and writing, Powell began still another career in 1971 as consultant to Presidents Richard A. Harvill and John P. Schaefer of the University of Arizona. There he initiated a survey of the library, which resulted in the appointment of a new young librarian (W. David Laird, UCLA M.L.S., 1966) and the construction of a new building. He also helped to get the library school staffed and accredited.

Drawing new strength from his beloved Southwest, he continued writing and speaking. In Arizona, in his third career, he had written three novels by 1985, published a long piece on Ansel Adams, and worked on a "Portrait of My Father." John David Marshall planned and edited a collection of Powell quotations.

In addition to scores of articles and reviews in the library press and such journals as the *Pacific Historical Review, Southwest Review,* and the *Papers* of the Bibliographical Society of America, Powell contributed regularly to *Westways, Arizona Highways,* and *Hoja Volante.* Many of these writings were gathered in such collections as *Islands of Books* (1951), *Books West Southwest* (1957), *A Passion for Books,* (1959), *Books in My Baggage* (1960), and *The Little Package* (1964). Other titles are *Robinson Jeffers* (1932; 1934; 1940), *Philosopher Pickett* (1942), *The Alchemy of Books* (1954), and his novels, *The Blue Train* (1977), *The River Between* (1979), and *El Morro* (1984). This is only a sampling.

To understand Powell, one must see him as a Humanist, steeped in literature, music, history, and art. Sensitive and emotional on the one hand, he could also be practical, realistic, and sometimes ruthless on the other. Ahead of his time in fair treatment of women and in encouragement of ethnic minorities, he proved fiercely loyal to old friends and to institutions. His countless speeches, lectures, and writings drew many to the profession and confirmed others in their practice of it. A patron of the arts and frequent commissioner of fine printing, Powell stands as a veritable Renaissance man.

REFERENCES

Lawrence Clark Powell, *Fortune and Friendship: An Autobiography* (1968).
Wayne A. Wiegand, editor, *Leaders in American Academic Librarianship: 1925–1975,* pp. 262–287 (Beta Phi Mu, 1983).
Betty Rosenberg *Checklist of the Published Writings of LCP* (1966).
Donald C. Dickinson, et al., *Voices from the Southwest* (1976).

WILLIAM R. ESHELMAN

Power, Effie Louise
(1873–1969)

Effie Louise Power, pioneer children's librarian, educator, and author, directly influenced the development of services to children in three major cities, Cleveland, St. Louis, and Pittsburgh.

She was born February 12, 1873, near Conneautville, Pennsylvania. When she was 13, her family moved to Cleveland, where she graduated from Central High School. William Howard Brett, a neighbor of the Power family, invited her to take the Cleveland Public Library's entrance examination and thus brought to library service a protégé who caught his inspirational spark. Throughout her career, Power kindled it in others.

ALA

Effie Louise Power

Power began her library work as an apprentice in autumn 1895, then left for about three months to be school librarian at her former high school. Returning to the Public Library, she took charge of the "Junior Alcove" under Brett's supervision. His plans for a children's room materialized in 1898, and Power became the first children's librarian in the Cleveland system, a post she filled until 1902. One of her first contributions was to change the handling of nonfiction books for children. Such books had been kept out of the children's alcove on the theory that children read nonfiction only under coercion from adults. Each day Power went through the library gathering up biography, history, and nature books suited to children and arranging them on the counters in the children's alcove. Each day the books disappeared, and so did the assumption that children would check out only fiction.

Service to children profited when in late 1901 the Cleveland Library moved to new but temporary quarters that provided a large and pleasant basement room for the children's department. For the first time, Power and her two assistants had sufficient space to bring the children together for storytelling. The following year, having established the children's room on firm principles and practices, Power decided to add to her practical experience a more formal foundation of knowledge and technique. Brett noted in his annual report for 1902 that she was spending the school year studying work for children in the training program for children's librarians at the Carnegie Library in Pittsburgh. She received her diploma in 1904.

Power returned to Cleveland after a year's study only to direct her talents in new directions. Brett had long advocated that the Cleveland City Normal School introduce a course in children's literature and the use of books. At the last moment, the candidate selected to teach the course refused the invitation, and Power was given a leave of absence to fill the position. She taught at City Normal School from 1903 to 1908. During summer 1906, she earned a teaching certificate at Columbia University. Although accounts differ, some claiming she did not return to the Cleveland Public Library until 1920, certain information indicates that she returned to the Library in 1908 and stayed for a year as the children's librarian.

Power became first assistant in the children's department of the Carnegie Library of Pittsburgh in 1909 and also taught in the library school there. In March 1911 she was appointed Supervisor of Children's Work in the Saint Louis Public Library. Less than a year later, when the Library was moved to a new building, she demonstrated her belief in preparing the young to take civic pride in their library. After the general public had inspected the new building, she held a special opening; 1,000 children were taken in groups on tours of inspection and heard short talks by members of all departments.

Power stated her principles in *How the Children of a Great City Get Their Books,* first published as part of the annual report of the Saint Louis Public Library for 1913–14. Her standards for book selection were high. After being approved by the librarians, a book had to win the approval of the children before it was duplicated to any great extent. Stating the library's responsibility for books placed on open shelves, and recognizing the dependence of parents and librarians in smaller libraries on the lists put out by the Saint Louis Library, Power expressed her conviction that children's librarians must know not only "a good book but the best book for each particular need."

About this time, Power's leadership took on a national character. A member of the American Library Association since 1906, she chaired the Children's Section in 1912–13 and again in 1929–30 and served on Council (1914–19). She joined the National Education Association in 1896, serving as President of the Library Department (1916–17), and she also chaired the Committee on Elementary School Libraries from 1914 to 1918.

Power returned to Pittsburgh in 1914 as Supervisor of the Carnegie Library's schools division and later as Head of the Children's Department (1917–20). During her years in Pittsburgh, she worked for the introduction of libraries in the city's high schools and for courses in the use of books and libraries in the Teacher's Training School.

In 1920 she again returned to the Cleveland Public Library as director of work with children. She also taught at Western Reserve University, as Instructor until 1925 and as Assistant Professor (1925–29), and continued her practice begun in 1918 of teaching in library schools throughout the country. One of her contributions in these teaching stints was to help develop cooperative programs between the public library and the schools.

The American Library Association asked her to write a textbook on library work with children; this first authoritative text on the subject, *Library Service for Children* (1930), was widely used in the United States. Her revision of the work was published by ALA in 1943 under the title *Work with Children in Public Libraries*. In addition, she wrote numerous professional articles that reveal both a sense of history and a sense of humor and was the co-author, author, or compiler of several other works. In 1928 she collaborated with a Cleveland teacher, Florence Everson, in writing a collection of stories about pioneer life, *Early Days in Ohio*. In an attempt to bring to storytellers the best of world literature she compiled four collections of stories for children: *Bag o' Tales* (1934), *Blue Caravan Tales* (1935), *Stories to Shorten the Road* (1936), and *From Umar's Pack* (1937). After her retirement, she wrote another book for children, *Osceola Buddy, a Florida Farm Mule* (1941).

Allegheny College awarded Power an honorary Master's degree in 1934. Three years later when she retired from the Cleveland Public Library, Columbia University offered her a position as Instructor in the School of Library Service; she taught there until 1939. Retiring to Pompano Beach, Florida, she succeeded in inspiring the citizens to raise funds for a new library to replace one destroyed by a hurricane 20 years earlier.

Power seems in retrospect to have been the ideal librarian. In addition to her work as an influential practitioner, she, as an educator and author of professional books and articles, indirectly influenced the libraries in which her students and readers worked. She always held to essentials. Children's work would develop in direct proportion to the support given by knowledgeable administrators to well-trained and dedicated children's librarians determined to maintain the highest standards in services and collections. Throughout her long and varied career, she demonstrated a willingness to leave a comfortable position in order to meet the challenge of a new situation. Never could it be said of Effie Louise Power that she stopped growing professionally. She retired to Pompano Beach, Florida, in 1940. She died on October 8, 1969.

REFERENCE
Regina F. Berneis, "Power, Effie Louise," *Dictionary of American Library Biography* (1978).

MARY E. KINGSBURY

Prasad, S. N.
(1921-)

Sri Nandan Prasad, archivist and historian, was Director of the National Archives of India.

Prasad was born on September 18, 1921, in Varanasi, Uttar Pradesh. He obtained M.A. (History, 1944) and D.Phil. (1948) degrees from Allahabad University and entered the field of archives in 1949 as Senior Research Officer, Historical Section, in the Indian Ministry of Defence; he was later its Director (1964–69). He administered and utilized confidential military records of the government of India in those capacities.

In 1969 he was selected to head the National Archives of India as its Director. During the decade of his stewardship (1969–79) he was chiefly responsible for setting up an Institute of Archival Training and new record centers at Jaipur and Pondicherry. He also contributed to the framing and implementation of archival policy by the government of India for better records management, acceleration in acquiring documentary materials in India and abroad, better conservation, greater facilities for users by way of reference aids, publication development, easier access, and improved techniques of reproduction. As Secretary of the Indian Historical Records Commission, he provided effective leadership to Indian archivists. The expansion of the National Archives reflected his able guidance.

He joined the International Council on Archives, first as a member of its Executive Committee (1969–76), later as the only Asian member of the Committee on Archival Development (1972–76) and Vice-President (1976–80). He acted as a rapporteur at the Moscow Congress of ICA (1972) and presented a comprehensive report on "Technical Assistance: Viewpoint of Developing Countries." He represented India, the Third World, and the International Council on Archives at numerous meetings and provided expertise to Unesco as well. He took the lead in setting up the South and West Asian Regional Branch of the ICA (SWARBICA) in 1976.

Noted as a military historian, Prasad wrote *Expansion of Armed Forces and Defence Organization* (1956), *Reconquest of Burma* (1958), *Paramountcy under Dalhousie* (1964), and *Survey of Work Done on the Military History of India* (1976). Articles in professional journals cover a wide range of subjects.

N. H. KULKARNEE

Priolkar, A. K.
(1895–1973)

Bibliophile and Marathi scholar, Anant Kakba Priolkar created a consciousness for the collection and preservation of old manuscripts and incunabula, that is, Marathi books printed prior to the year 1867 when an Act of Registration of Books was passed. He also developed his own concept of an ideal library for the Marathi language. In a book entitled *Marathi Granthanche Adarsha Sangrahmalaya* (1967), he maintained that besides all the available printed books in Marathi, such a library should procure (1) all the works translated into Marathi with their originals; (2) works of Marathi authors translated into other languages; (3) the first editions of Marathi books that have gone out of print; (4) microfilm copies of Marathi books that are not available in Indian libraries; and (5) the manuscripts and correspondence of important Marathi authors.

Born in 1895 at Priol (Goa, India), he was educated at Dharwar and Sangali and obtained a B.A. at Bombay University in 1923 in Marathi language and literature. He served as a secondary teacher for a couple of years and then as a clerk for two decades in the Bombay Municipality.

In spite of his clerical position, Priolkar had a craving for literary pursuits. He composed poems under the pseudonym "Arunodaya," edited and reviewed old Marathi works, and wrote learned treatises on linguistic subjects and skits and articles of topical interest.

He made his debut as a research scholar and pioneering textual critic by bringing out an authentic critical edition of Raghunath Pandit's *Damayanti-Svayamvar* in 1935. In 1948 he became Reader and then in 1950 Director of the Marathi Postgraduate and Research Institute, Bombay. As the head of the Institute he guided Ph.D. students in Marathi and edited its prestigious quarterly, *Marathi Samshodhan Patrika,* for 12 years, bringing to light many a rare work in Marathi and its dialects. He was chiefly responsible for bringing to light Marathi and Konkani books by foreign missionaries settled in Goa in the 16th and 17th centuries. He also prepared a critically reconstructed edition of Muktesvar's *Adiparva* in four volumes (1951–59). His biographical writings on 19th-century figures indicate his interest in the history of Bombay in that century.

A work in English, *The Printing Press in India* (with an essay on Konkani printing by J. H. Da Kunha Rivara) (   ), is a scholarly and succinct account of the beginnings of printing and publishing in the various Indian languages. Priolkar always strove for authenticity, and his writings show a rare objectivity, diligence, and scrupulous accuracy. He was elected the President of the All Marathi Literary Conference at Karwar in 1951. His best-known works include critical editions on *Raghunath Panditavirachita Damayanti Svayamvar* (1935) and Mukteshvarkrit Mahabharat Adiparva, vols. 1 to 4 (1951–59); biographies of *Dadaba Pandurang* (1947) and *Bhau Daji* (1971); and, in English, a treatise on *The Goa Inquisition* (1961).

REFERENCE
Prof. A. K. Priolkar Smriti-Granth (Bombay, 1974).

S. G. MALSHE

Albany Public Library

The first readers' bureau in a U.S. public library was begun at Albany, New York (early 1920s).

Public Libraries

PURPOSES AND OBJECTIVES

Since the mid-1960s the objectives of public libraries and library systems in many parts of the world have been the subject of regular review, and they have been examined and reexamined by users and librarians alike to determine whether they respond adequately to the needs of each community. This concern can be found in countries with well-established library systems, as well as in those with few public libraries. That such an activity should be carried on in various parts of the globe is not surprising. The tide of social change that has swept through a wide variety of countries has been a powerful force, producing movements for more access by citizens to education and learning. So also has been the effect of technological advances in the production and distribution of the printed word. The need for books, information, and all types of published materials has grown constantly.

The public library has traditionally been in the forefront of the institutions that have responded to such a demand. In the 1980s the question is not "Should the public library respond?" but rather, "How can it best contribute to social change and economic development, and how can it meet the needs of a wider circle of users?" Public libraries today represent a focal point for the aspirations of many citizens, as well as for governments and public agencies.

Each decade has seen considerable changes in the goals and objectives of local, regional, and national public library systems. What has been considered as the objective of a public library system by one generation is normally revised and altered in light of the changing conditions faced by the next generation. The results achieved by public library services must also be considered at the same time as the goals and objectives of that service. If the library accomplishes little, then it can expect little support from the citizens.

This situation is not new. For more than 200 years the public library has been undergoing revision and reassessment and has developed new goals and objectives in order to meet the needs of a constantly changing pattern of demands. Such an evolutionary process has often meant the disappearance of a particular form of library service and the appearance of new services and new forms of organization. The library has been the initiator of activities later taken over by other institutions, and it has left these in their care and gone on to develop fresh approaches. The mercantile, special, technical, and business collection, the community reference information service, the continuing education course for adults, and the local history collection often had their beginnings in the public library. Along with the evolution of these and other services, there has been a constant transformation of the library's stock of materials.

Public library collections pass through many phases, from being the private possession of a few persons to being owned by a group or private association and eventually becoming the public possession of an entire nation. Public libraries' materials have alternatively found themselves hoarded and divided, fought over and bartered, suppressed and exhibited. Those in charge of the public library and its collections have had to take into account the policies set through changing social conditions in the libraries' communities. The public library will continue in this manner as long as it attempts to perform a public function. In this it is unlike its progenitor, the private library, which had often been able to maintain a fixed policy for decades.

It is not known how many public library systems exist today, and no single list of their goals and objectives can be prepared. The Union of Soviet Socialist Republics has more than 350,000 libraries in a network for the use of the public. In the United States there are more than 8,300 separate community public library systems, with an unknown number of separate branches and parts. Czechoslovakia claims 39,000 separate libraries that serve the public, and Canada reports statistics on 739 public library systems organized to meet the needs of 23,000,000 people. With such wide differences in services, and with very large differences in financial support, there can be no general statement of public library purposes and goals that applies universally.

The Unesco Public Library Manifesto, first issued in 1949 and revised in 1972 by the International Federation of Library Associations and Institutions (IFLA) on the occasion of the International Book Year, is a broad charter of public library goals. It does not cover the full variety of purposes and activities to which the public library can lend itself, but it does lay down certain basic requirements that must be met. Any statement of public library purpose that incorporates these requirements can be said to be unique for those who prepare it; yet it is unlikely that it will apply directly to other societies and to other library contexts without review and alteration.

The statements contained in this article are based on what a number of people in various countries have seen to be the scope and function of today's public library. The article deals mostly with the patterns of public library service common to North America and, in part, to several European nations. This article does not give an extensive historical appraisal of the public library, which can be found in other sources. The article is based mostly on a review of public library events of the decade 1975–1985 as seen in Europe and North America. The purposes and objectives of the public library are accordingly described in relation to three basic concerns: (1) the needs of people who use the libraries; (2) the need to ensure that the library is located in a suitable place; and (3) the need to provide for effective means of operating it and developing its services.

Needs of Library Users. The following statements, chosen from the United Kingdom, the United States, and Canadian declarations of purposes, highlight the views of public library leaders in these countries with regard to services to users.

The Public Library Research Group of the London and Home Countries Branch of the Library Association of the United Kingdom (LA) set out in 1971, under headings of education, information, culture, and leisure, the following objectives for public library services in that country:

EDUCATION: To foster and provide means for self-development of the individual/group at whatever stage of education, closing the gap between the individual and recorded knowledge.

INFORMATION: To bring to the individual/group accurate information quickly and in depth, particularly on topics of current concern.

CULTURE: To be one of the principal centres of cultural life and promote a keener participation, enjoyment and appreciation of all the arts.

LEISURE: To play a part in encouraging the positive use of leisure and providing material for change and relaxation.

The following sub-objectives were listed for those responsible for organizing public libraries:

To promote the use of public libraries as education agencies for the individual; to promote the creation of specialized resources; to promote the use of public libraries as information centres; to promote the use of public libraries as referral points to specialized sources of information; to promote and encourage the use of public libraries as centres where individuals can take part in the arts in a positive way; to encourage the public librarian to assume the role of initiator and organizer of cultural events; to encourage the public librarian to liaise with local societies and cultural organizations, fostering the creative use of leisure in the field of the arts; to promote and encourage the use of public libraries as "special library" agency for local associations and cultural organizations; to promote and encourage the use of public libraries as cultural information centres; to promote the provision of general leisure material for the individual; and to promote the provision of leisure and amenity services to special groups in the community.

In 1977 the Public Library Association of the American Library Association (ALA), having con-

ducted a review over a number of years of the standards set out a decade earlier, issued in its "Mission Statement for Public Libraries" the following statement of public library objectives:

Society needs an agency to operate as it were, in the eye of the revolutionary storm, to keep the radical new thrust in some continuity with the past. Society needs an agency to preserve and make widely accessible the record of human experience—to stimulate thoughtful people everywhere to discern positive insights and values from the past, and to assimilate them into the new order. The mass media—the press, T.V., radio, etc.—of their nature tend to concentrate exclusively on the current scene.

Because change now moves so rapidly, the majority of individuals and institutions today suffer future-shock—a sense of alienation from the world and from themselves, a sense of powerlessness in coping with, let alone controlling, the direction of life.

Therefore, society needs an agency to identify relationships in the fast-flowing river of change, to maintain the record of new ideas, technologies, values, so that individuals and institutions will be able to perceive and then control the direction of change as it relates to each person's particular life experience.

The Council of the Canadian Library Association (CLA) adopted the following statement on intellectual freedom at its Annual Conference in June 1974:

Every person in Canada has the fundamental right, as embodied in the nation's Bill of Rights, to have access to all expressions of knowledge, creativity and intellectual activity, and to express his thoughts publicly. This right to intellectual freedom is essential to the health and development of Canadian society.

Libraries have a basic responsibility for the development and maintenance of intellectual freedom.

It is the responsibility of libraries to guarantee and facilitate access to all expressions of knowledge and intellectual activity including those which some elements of society may consider to be unconventional, unpopular or unacceptable. To this end, libraries shall acquire and make available the widest variety of materials.

It is the responsibility of libraries to guarantee the right of free expression by making available all the library's public facilities and services to all individuals and groups who need them.

San Diego Public Library, one of the buildings funded by Andrew Carnegie.

San Diego Public Library

Libraries should resist all efforts to limit the exercise of these responsibilities while recognizing the right of criticism by individuals and groups.

Both employees and employers in libraries have a duty, in addition to their institutional responsibilities, to uphold these principles.

Many countries in all parts of the world have similar declarations adopted by the library profession, the governing body for library development, or the national associations of librarians. One of the main requirements of any active library development group is that it update and review on a regular basis both the statement of the purposes of public libraries and the ways in which these purposes are being carried out.

The Location of the Public Library. It is not often appreciated that the location of a public library is a key factor in determining how it will be used. For this reason, unless the library adopts as a goal that of being easily available, it will seldom reach its objective of full use by all citizens.

A basic factor in success or failure is the decision on specific location and type of service to be provided. This lesson has been well learned through experience in most of the countries that have understood the value of access to knowledge for all citizens. A related criterion is that location must be considered with respect to the other educational and cultural services of a community or nation. This includes both location in a physical setting and the relation of the library service to the planning and financing of a balanced range of social, educational, and cultural opportunities for citizens. Where there is coordination of all libraries in a country, the greatest use will result.

Examples of unified systems of public libraries can be found in most socialist countries and range from Cuba to the Ukraine. In Czechoslovakia the number and levels of libraries that made up the unified library system in 1980 were the following:

deficient in library outlets had low use. It was also shown that use decreased with the distance people had to travel to reach the public library. In Canada in 1978 the national average percentages of the adult population were 25 percent active users and 18 percent low users. The provinces with the highest percentage of active users were British Columbia and Ontario. The province of Quebec showed the lowest use, with 14 percent active users and 12 percent low users.

Those countries that are able to ensure that the locations for libraries, whether in schools or in community centers, will be readily available to adults and children reap the greatest benefits from their investment in providing books and other library materials.

Provisions for Operation and Development. The objective of a trained and qualified staff is basic to achieving success in the public library. The range and quality of resources that must be provided, the need to have up-to-date materials, and the need to select materials appropriate for users' needs have made qualified staff a prime necessity. This is why most countries provide at least 60 percent of the public library budget to secure a qualified staff and why there are increasing numbers of both professional full-time and part-time staff employed in most countries.

The situation with respect to qualified staff varies greatly among libraries throughout the world. While there are some variations between European and North American public library staff provision, there is a far greater disparity between the number of staff in Asian, African, and Latin American public libraries compared with European and North American libraries. The figures in Table 2 indicate how far many countries have to go in order to secure an adequate number of trained people to meet their public library needs, as well as to serve all of their citizens. The proper staffing for public libraries is a crucial matter for all countries, and part of the basic goals and objectives of a library must include targets for achieving

Table 1. Libraries in Czechoslovakia

	Number	Holdings (volumes) (million)	Circulation (million)	Readers (thousand)
Public Libraries	10,157	50.4	91.4	2,626
National Libraries	15	17.1	--	292
Higher Education Libraries	1,701	11.8	--	242
Special Libraries	14	14.9	--	202
Trade Union Libraries[a]	27,807	60.2	26.9	2,482
Total	39,694	154.4	118.3	5,844

[a]1975
Source: Unesco, *Statistical Yearbook,* 1983

Such a broad array of libraries within the country meant that they were used annually by 52 percent of the citizens as a whole and 70 percent of the city population.

A recent study of public library use in Canada indicated that in those provinces where there was adequate provision of library buildings and library outlets there was high use, while those areas that were

the effective use of human resources in organizing and operating public library services.

Emphasis in considering goals has been placed on meeting user needs, providing adequate facilities, and employing qualified staff. Additional objectives also prevail, set by various countries in the light of their cultural and national priorities. On a worldwide basis these objectives have been summed up in the

Table 2. Public Library Staffs and Service

Country	Year	Public library employees	Percentage of population served by public libraries
Africa			
Ghana	1977	520	30
Egypt	1980	1,029	--
Nigeria	1979	1,045	--
Uganda	1980	103	--
Latin America and the Caribbean			
Jamaica	1980	1,057	28
Cuba	1980	1,146	--
Mexico	1978	922	5
Asia			
Japan	1977	9,289	69
Malaysia	1980	503	15
Philippines	1977	816	--
Turkey	1980	2,675	30.1
North America and Europe			
U.S.A.	1978	93,335	--
Canada	1980	10,465	--
France	1980	6,984	--
Poland	1980	16,533	100
Netherlands	1980	3,272	96
Yugoslavia	1980	2,639	98

Source: Unesco, *Statistical Yearbook* 1983

General Information Programme (PGI) of Unesco, established in 1974 and implemented by a Unesco Intergovernmental Council through Unesco's worldwide program. Through the PGI there is the possibility for examining the role of the public library on a worldwide basis and for supplementing individual national efforts by cooperative action with other countries.

Within such a broad framework the task of providing access to education and cultural resources can be carried out at either the local, regional, national, or international level. Such cooperative measures are essential in order to provide for an equitable distribution of the printed and published materials of the world to all those who need them.

H. C. CAMPBELL

SERVICES TO USERS

The specific services that any particular public library offers may constitute a relatively short list, but the range of possibilities is extremely broad. This is a natural corollary of two basic characteristics of the public library: it has a broad charge, subject to multiple interpretations, and it serves, potentially at least, everyone.

In general, all statements of purpose of a public library say something to the effect that a public library supplies materials and services to a community in order to support that community's educational, information, cultural, and recreational needs. The public library, by definition, is open to everyone who lives within a particular geographic area. For a specific locality it is possible to be fairly definite about the demographic, occupational, or socioeconomic characteristics of public library users and potential users but, in general, the possibilities are limitless.

To all residents of an area, and to all on an equal basis, the public library offers library services—a phrase that once meant a circulating collection of books but that today embraces many different things, ranging from story hours for children to database searches for business. This section surveys the services offered by contemporary public libraries in the United States. Where possible and appropriate, comments will be made about practices in other countries.

Types and Range of Services. Statistics have been available for many years describing the number of public libraries in the U.S., their holdings, budget, and personnel. Counts of items circulated have also been recorded, but the range of items available is not known on a national scale. In addition, no national data exist that describe the number of other services (that is, besides circulation) available from public libraries and the use of these services. Statistics on public library services in other countries are similarly scarce. The Unesco *Statistical Yearbook* records holdings, budget, and personnel for public libraries in each nation but says nothing about services.

In 1978 the U.S. National Center for Education Statistics (NCES) convened a panel of experts to consider whether it would be feasible to gather and analyze meaningful data on public library users and public library services in the U.S. The panel concluded that a number of studies should be conducted; its report, *Approaches to the Study of Public Library Services and Users,* (1979), presents a rationale and a description of the recommended studies. One is an inventory of library services to be taken by asking a national sample of librarians to respond to an exhaustive list of possibilities. The panel considered lists of services used in several earlier studies and prepared a draft instrument that might be used.

Because the panel believed that making a collection of materials available for use is the most basic

Kyoto Prefectural Library

Theodore F. Welch

library service, the draft instrument begins with a section listing more than 40 types of material and asking the responding librarian to indicate whether a particular type is:

(1) available through the local library system
(2) available through a cooperative arrangement or federated system
(3) not available in my library system but available to anyone in the community through some other agency
(4) not available in my community

The second choice here recognizes that cooperative arrangements of various kinds supplement the collection and services of a local library. The third choice recognizes that the public library is one of a number of agencies providing print and audiovisual materials and related services to a community. Both of these factors are taken into account when planning a public library collection and service program.

From one perspective, everything a library does is a service, but it is also possible to think of services as those activities that library staff perform in direct response to client requests or in anticipation of client interest. Services in this second sense are given in Table 3, which is an adaptation of a list in the NCES panel's draft instrument. In the draft survey the respondent is asked to indicate for each service one of the four choices given for materials in the previous paragraph.

In most cases these services are available to everyone in the library service area. Frequently, however, public library staff will tailor some of these services to the needs of people sharing specified characteristics in common, thereby developing a special program for such groups as the blind or physically disabled, business people, children, deaf people, ethnic groups, government officials, homebound people, illiterate people, institutionalized people, senior citizens, and young adults.

One of the controversial issues currently facing the public library community in the U.S. is the question of whether a public library may, should, or must charge fees for expensive services such as database searches. On the one side are those who assert that it is unethical for the public library to provide special services to those who can pay; on the other are those who insist that unless the public library charges for

---

Table 3. Informational, Educational, Recreational, and Cultural Services Offered by the Public Library

Educational★
Book Reviews/Book Talks
Concerts (Live or Recorded)
Craft Demonstrations
Cultural Exhibits
Field Trips
Film Showings
Formal Courses
Lectures
Literacy Tutorials
Reading Improvement Classes
Story Hours
Training of Volunteers
Workshops on Program Planning

Informational
Advice on Use of Materials
Answers to Complex Questions
Answers to Simple Questions
Bibliographies on Specific Subjects
Community Calendar
Current Awareness Services (SDI)
Database Searches
Information on Program Resources
Referrals to Community Sources for Information
Translations

Recreational★
Concerts (Live or Recorded)
Craft Demonstrations
Cultural Exhibits
Field Trips
Film Showings
Story Hours

Cultural★
Book Reviews/Book Talks
Concerts (Live or Recorded)
Cultural Exhibits
Film Showings
Lectures

★A number of services may be considered either educational or recreational or cultural depending on the perspective of the participant or the content of the event.

technological or labor-intensive services, it will not be able to offer them at all, and other agencies will develop to fill the need.

Although the 1972 Unesco Public Library Manifesto states that a public library "should be maintained wholly from public funds, and no direct charge should be made to anyone for its services," fees are charged in many European libraries. While such a practice has not been common in the U.S., it has been suggested that public libraries will have to abandon their "information should be free in the public interest" ethic in view of the rapidly changing technological and economic forces affecting information distribution today.

Public Library Programs. Much less controversial, but still a matter of debate for public libraries in the U.S., is the extent to which public libraries should sponsor such special events as lectures, cultural exhibits, concerts, and field trips. Story hours and other events for children are usually accepted, but events for adults often raise questions. Those opposed claim that these events are the legitimate domain of other agencies in the community and should not distract staff time and energy from the services "proper" to a library. Those in favor put forth one of two arguments: (1) that these events are good public relations for the library and bring into the library people who might otherwise not come in; or (2) that these events are extensions of material on library shelves and provide needed enrichment to the life of a community. This second argument is more in keeping with the 1975 joint report of the Library Advisory Councils of England and Wales on *Public Libraries and Cultural Activities*. It is also congruent with the Unesco Public Library Manifesto, which states that

> The public library is a natural cultural centre for the community, bringing together as it does people of similar interests. Space and equipment are therefore necessary for exhibitions, discussions, lectures, musical performances, and films, both for adults and children.

In the U.S. the National Endowment for the Humanities adopted this view of the public library and supported many public library programs involving the humanities. But contradictory evidence comes from such documents as a long-range plan for the Baltimore County (Maryland) Public Library (1977), which provided that if the budget were to be cut, programming for adults would be dropped since response to it was meager.

The educational role of the public library is a more traditional one, though the present movement toward "nontraditional" education in the U.S. has encouraged libraries to develop innovative ways to respond to their public's interest in "lifelong learning" or "continuing education." At the other end of the educational spectrum are library programs to assist people who lack literacy skills. Public library interest in such programs has increased substantially during recent years and the ALA is one of the most active members of the Coalition for Literacy, which mounted a major campaign in 1985 to make people aware of the illiteracy problem and what can be done to solve it.

Other Public Library Services. In addition to these highly visible services, public library staff are regularly involved in providing a service that is often taken for granted—orientation to the library and its holdings. The orientation may provide one or more of the following to groups or individuals: an explanation of the library's catalogue; an explanation of reference sources; an explanation of machines and equipment; maps, brochures, and so on explaining the library; and tours of the library.

Another "hidden" service of the public library is the provision of space and equipment for activities related to library materials and services. A public library may provide: an auditorium or lecture room; a conference or meeting room; a facility for producing audio or visual material; a film-viewing room; photocopying equipment; space for individual reading, listening, or viewing; typewriters; and calculators. The importance of appropriate physical facilities was stressed in the Unesco document, which states that

> The public library building should be centrally situated, accessible to the physically handicapped, and open at times convenient to the user. The building and its furnishings should be attractive, informal and welcoming, and direct access by readers to the shelves is essential.

A very different perspective on the library as a place comes from C. Walter Stone, who observed in a 1967 *Library Trends* article that it was important to think of the library not as a place but as "a far-flung network composed of units of various sizes and types, each of which may perform similar as well as different functions, but all of which will be linked together electromechanically." Through this linking people everywhere will have access to the information and knowledge they need, regardless of the form it takes or its actual location.

Public libraries have not yet reached the technological level Stone sketched. Most, however, offer services far beyond those available in a particular building. Bookmobile services have been commonplace for many years in both rural and urban areas. In some countries mobile units may take the form of horse-drawn wagons or even boats. Public library units in systems routinely offer intrasystem loans to

The Research Libraries of the New York Public Library, on Fifth Avenue.

New York Public Library

Ron Davies. Courtesy Dyfed County Library.

Bookmobile in Dyfed County, Wales, offering materials in Welsh and English.

their users, and most public libraries will also go outside the system to request interlibrary loans. Many libraries send material to users by mail, and telephone reference service is available from all but the smallest libraries. A number of public libraries have begun to offer reference service and programming by cable television. Public librarians in the U.S. have recently become more conscious of the need to evaluate the way they serve their users. In 1982 ALA's Public Library Association published *Output Measures for Public Libraries,* which describes how to collect and organize data to produce 12 simple measures of service such as library visits per capita, reference transactions per capita, and turnover rate. Interest in the measures has been expressed by public librarians in several other countries.

No one public library offers all of the services just mentioned, and no one library user takes advantage of them all. Taken as a whole, however, the varied services described here constitute a rich resource for the people. Services offered by public libraries will probably change considerably in the next 10 or 20 years as the result of technological, economic, and political forces currently influencing both public services and the information community.

REFERENCES

Arthur D. Little, Inc. *Into the Information Age* (ALA, 1978), includes challenging suggestions for the future of public library service.

Lowell Martin, "Demographic Trends and Social Structure," *Library Trends* (1978), a perceptive analysis with suggestions for changes in services of public libraries.

Margaret Monroe, "A Conceptual Framework for the Public Library as a Community Learning Center for Independent Study," *Library Quarterly* (1976), a challenging view of the library's role in a learning society.

W. Boyd Rayward, editor, "The Public Library: Circumstances and Prospects," *Library Quarterly* (1978), the proceedings of a University of Chicago Graduate Library School conference. See especially articles by Thomas

Childers, Mary Jo Lynch, Mary K. Chelton, and Mae Benne.

John S. Robotham and Lydia LaFleur, *Library Programs: How to Select, Plan and Produce Them* (1976).

Douglas Zweizig and Eleanor Jo Rodgers, *Output Measures for Public Libraries* (1982).

MARY JO LYNCH

COLLECTIONS AND MATERIALS

Collections in public libraries in the U.S. range in size from the New York Public's 9,000,000 or more volumes to Elk Township, Michigan's 900 volumes. They range in form from books, periodicals, reports, and clippings through recordings, films, and microforms to databases on magnetic tape. They range in content from the most scholarly to those in basic English for the functionally illiterate. They range in focus from materials for preschool children to materials for the aged. They include special materials for the handicapped, such as talking books or braille titles. They are as diverse as public libraries themselves, but always collections are at the heart of all public library service.

Collections are the concrete expressions of the public library's mission. In the words of the *Guidelines for Public Library Service* endorsed by the ALA's Public Library Association (1979):

Materials should be selected to support the cultural, informational, educational and rehabilitative functions of the library. Relative emphases within these four objectives should be determined by analysis of individual community need and by the availability of resources in all types of libraries within the community.

Materials should be selected to meet the needs of as wide a variety of target groups as live within the community, including the literate, the illiterate, the educated, the uneducated, children, adults, aged people, majority and minority cultures.

These imperatives only reemphasize the position on collections expressed by the ALA's *Minimum Standards for Public Library Systems* (1966):

The public library as an institution exists to provide materials which communicate experience and ideas from one person to another. The function is to assemble, organize, preserve, and make easily and freely available to all people the printed and nonprinted material that will assist them to:

Educate themselves continually
Keep pace with progress in all fields of knowledge
Become better members of home and community
Discharge political and social obligations
Be more capable in their daily occupations
Develop their creative and spiritual capacities
Appreciate and enjoy the works of art and literature
Use leisure time to promote personal and social well-being
Contribute to the growth of knowledge.

Although the centrality of materials to the library's mission seems philosophically obvious, its importance is not always reflected in budget allocations. A study of 56 public library budgets made by the ALA, 1974–76, documented that materials accounted for only 9 to 11 percent of total expenditures. The skyrocketing costs of library materials, both print and nonprint, and the escalating range of materials available make this statistic even more ominous.

Selection of Library Materials. Theories of materials selection vary among public libraries from the "demand" position of the Baltimore County Public Library ("BCPL is committed to collecting, not a broad array of materials that librarians feel users should read or use, but those materials which most users do read or use") to the "should" position of many public libraries who base selection on principles of quality, authenticity, and social value. On this continuum most public libraries attempt to find a middle ground.

All public librarians agree however—in theory, if not in practice—that selection of materials should be made within the context of a written policy that articulates the objectives of the individual library or library system. The ALA Standards describe this policy statement as follows:

> This statement should be approved and supported by the governing body. It sets forth the purposes, levels of quality, and community needs to be reflected in acquiring materials. It describes the scope and emphasis and defines the limits of the collection; it affirms the institution's position on supplying resources on controversial subjects; and records the policies which govern withdrawals.

The materials selection policy is perceived by the library profession to be a guideline for the day-to-day selection and maintenance of the collections, a bulwark against attacks on intellectual freedom by community groups and individuals, and a statement to the library's public about what it can expect. However, as Ann Bender of the Brooklyn Public Library admitted during an ALA Preconference Institute on Collection Development held in June 1977,

> In most public library situations, particularly in branches, the library must be so responsive to the immediate needs of its public, needs which are often fast changing, that collection development statements may become obsolete as soon as they are written.

The ALA Standards enunciate the broad principles that should underlie materials selection policy, such as:

> Materials acquired should meet high standards of quality in content, expression, and form.

> Within Standards of purpose and quality, collections should be built to meet the needs and interests of people.

> Library collections should contain opposite views on controversial topics.

As Bender wryly comments, however:

> The preparation of a collection development policy involves more than the mere writing down of general principles. It involves:

1. Knowing the community and its needs, actual and projected.
2. Careful analysis of the existing collection and determining its strengths and weaknesses.
3. Establishing a weeding policy.
4. An estimate of possible or likely fluctuations in the materials budget.
5. Considering the rates of inflation in books and materials prices.
6. Considering which items may be deemed part of a core collection, which must be replaced continually, and how much to set aside for new materials.
7. Considering what and how much to purchase in non-print forms and what the relationship of such materials will be to the existing collection.
8. Considering factors of space, rate of deterioration of materials, optimum size of the collection and its elements, loss rates, etc.
9. Knowing what other library resources are available in the community either through other agencies in the same public system or in private, academic, and non-academic libraries in the same community and assessing the degree to which cooperation in collection development is possible.

Materials Other than Print. Most libraries agree that public library collections should include more than print materials, although it must be acknowledged that the vast bulk of the human record is still in print and that extensive nonprint collections are probably the exception rather than the rule, especially among smaller public libraries.

The ALA Standards proposed that:

> To provide a reservoir of knowledge and aesthetic enjoyment which supplies inquiring minds, library materials [should] include a variety of forms:

Books	Films, slides, filmstrips
Periodicals	Music scores
Pamphlets	Maps
Newspapers	Recordings
Pictures	Various forms of microreproduction

The later Guidelines are even more explicit and extensive in their concept of library resources:

> Library resources should include multiple forms—print, non-print, audio, visual, magnetic tape, etc.

> Human information resources in the community, as well as recorded experience should be considered part of the library's material. Community resource files, including information on organizations and agencies, their officers, activities, services, speakers, etc. should be maintained in all public libraries. Hardware to make use of microforms, audio and visual tapes, and slides, films and filmstrips, videocassettes, etc. should be available for community use.

The Audiovisual Committee of the Public Library Association published in 1975 *Guidelines for Audiovisual Materials and Services for Large Public Libraries* and *Recommendations for Audiovisual Materials and Services for Small and Medium Sized Public Libraries*. These are quantitative guidelines, proposed within the context of the following assumptions, stated in the former document:

1. Librarians are concerned with the products of imagination, intellect, and spirit.
2. All formalized communication formats are of interest to librarians.
3. Audiovisual materials and services should have equal weight, concern, familiarity, and support of library administrations and staff as those of printed materials. Integration of planning and programs, regardless of subject, format, or age level served, is required for the library to continue as a relevant agency.

These guidelines recommend that all public libraries, regardless of size,

> offer a variety of audiovisual resources [whether from their own collections or through a regional system], a minimum of 10–15 percent of the library's resources budget for audiovisual resources, and that once an audio-

visual department is established and operative, 10–15 percent of its materials budget be allocated for repair and replacements. Variables affecting basic staff and materials requirements recognized by the guidelines are:

a. population served
b. area of service in square miles
c. number of 16mm titles
d. hours open per week
e. accessibility
f. range of media

Although these guidelines would meet with little or no disagreement in principle from public libraries, the degree to which the specific, quantitative recommendations are being met is uncertain. In 1979 the Brooklyn Public Library was allocating 5 percent of its materials budget to audiovisual materials. The comment made by Lowell Martin in 1969 when he surveyed the Chicago Public Library in *Library Response to Urban Change* is probably still relevant today:

> One of the shortcomings of public libraries is a concept of resources limited to the book or at most to the book and the magazine rather than to the full range of communication media.

Increasingly, however, as Kathleen Molz has pointed out, public libraries are confronting the realities of a public who no longer depend upon print as the primary medium for news and information, who no longer have the leisure and education necessary for serious reading, and who indeed may not have mastered even basic reading skills needed for day-to-day coping. In this environment nonprint materials are certain to become increasingly emphasized in public library collections.

Intellectual Freedom and Public Library Materials. Problems relating to the preservation of intellectual freedom and guaranteeing the right to read are central to collection development in the public library. At first glance it would seem that the basic policies of materials selection are clear as enunciated in the Library Bill of Rights, first adopted by the ALA Council in 1948 and last amended in 1967:

> The Council of the American Library Association reaffirms its belief in the following basic policies.
> 1. As a responsibility of library service, books and other library materials selected should be chosen for values of interest, information and enlightenment of all the people of the community. In no case should library materials be excluded because of the race or nationality or the social, political or religious views of the authors.
> 2. Libraries should provide books and other materials presenting all points of view concerning the problems

and issues of our times; no library materials should be proscribed or removed from libraries because of partisan or doctrinal disapproval.
> 3. Censorship should be challenged by libraries in the maintenance of their responsibility to provide information and enlightenment.
> 4. Libraries should cooperate with all persons and groups concerned with resisting abridgment of free expression and free access to ideas.
> 5. The rights of an individual to the use of a library should not be denied or abridged because of his age, race, religion, national origins or social or political views.

Despite the apparent clarity of the Library Bill of Rights, it has become necessary over the years to define its application in library practice by a series of "interpretations," also adopted by the ALA Council at the recommendation of ALA's Intellectual Freedom Committee. A summary of these interpretations follows.

The statement of *Free Access to Libraries for Minors,* approved in 1972, affirms that *only* the parent may restrict *only his or her* child from access to library materials, and that the librarian is not in loco parentis. The statement opposes library procedures, such as restricted reading rooms for adults only, closed collections for adults only, and interlibrary loans for adults only, that limit access of minors to library materials. The statement affirms the *right* of children to *all* library materials rather than to only a part of a library's collection and sources.

The *Statement on Labeling,* first adopted in 1951 and amended in 1970, opposed the techniques of labeling as "a 'censor tool,' a means of predisposing readers against library materials." Librarians, the statement declares, are neither advocates of the ideas found in their library collections nor infallible about what should be considered suspicious.

Expurgation of Library Materials, adopted in 1973, defines *expurgation* as "deletion, excision, alteration, or obliteration" of any portion of any document or literary work (or film). Such expurgation is declared a violation of the Library Bill of Rights because it imposes a restriction on the rights of library users to the full ideas the work was intended to express.

Reevaluating Library Collections, adopted in 1973, while endorsing the "continuous review of library collections to remove physically deteriorated or obsolete materials," warns against the abuse of this procedure as a kind of "silent censorship" of those materials considered too controversial or disapproved of by segments of the community.

The reevaluation warning followed by two years a *Resolution on Challenged Materials,* adopted by ALA in 1971, which declared that

> as a matter of firm principle no challenged library materials should be removed from any library under any legal or extra-legal pressure, save after an independent determination by a judicial officer in a court of competent jurisdiction and only after an adversary hearing, in accordance with well-established principles of law.

Restricted Access to Library Material, adopted in 1973, opposes such library practices as closed shelves, locked cases, and "adults only" collections. While the statement recognizes that these limitations differ from direct censorship activities such as refusal to purchase

Municipal Library, Montreuil, France.

Bibliothèque Nationale, Paris

or subsequent withdrawal of controversial publications, they do constitute a form of "subtle" censorship and should be avoided.

Recognizing that maintaining principles of the Library Bill of Rights can be complicated, if not hazardous, the ALA, as early as 1962, adopted the statement *How Libraries Can Resist Censorship*. This statement recommends that public libraries as a matter of standard operating procedures:

1. Maintain a definite materials selection policy. It should be in written form and approved by the appropriate regents or other governing authority. It should apply to all library materials equally.
2. Maintain a clearly defined method for handling complaints. Basic requirements should be that the complaint be filed in writing and the complainant be properly identified before his request is considered. Action should be deferred until full consideration by appropriate administrative authority.
3. Maintain lines of communication with civic, religious, educational, and political bodies of the community. Participation in local organizations and in community affairs is desirable. Because the library and the school are key centers of the community, the librarian should be known publicly as a community leader.
4. Maintain a vigorous public relations program on behalf of intellectual freedom. Newspapers, radio, and television should be informed of policies governing materials selection and use, and of any special activities pertaining to intellectual freedom.

The public library profession recognizes its responsibilities: (1) to meet the general library and information needs of all users, actual and potential, young and old, educated and undereducated, handicapped or well; (2) to consider materials selection within the context of total available resources in a community, since no one library can provide access to the whole human record; (3) to defend the free flow of ideas against all censorship by means of a responsible, defensible selection policy; and (4) to provide materials in whatever form is appropriate to the ideas expressed and to the users to whom the ideas are disseminated.

REFERENCES

Lester Asheim, "Not Censorship but Selection," *Wilson Library Bulletin* (September 1953), a classic in its lucid consideration of the selector's role.

Ann Bender, "Allocation of Funds in Support of Collection Development in Public Libraries," *Library Resources & Technical Services* (1979).

Mary Duncan Carter, Wallace Bonk, and Rosemary Magrill, *Building Library Collections* (1974), describes the value of selection policies in all types of libraries.

Leroy Merritt, *Book Selection and Intellectual Freedom* (1970), a basic text on the theory and practice of book selection.

R. Kathleen Molz, "The Changing Capacities of Print and the Varying Utilities of Libraries," in *The Metropolitan Library*, edited by Ralph Conant and R. Kathleen Molz (1972), a thoughtful exploration of the nonprint revolution.

GENEVIEVE M. CASEY

FINANCE AND ADMINISTRATION

The public library in the U.S. has since its beginnings shown that it is adaptable to the changing social environment because it sprang from democratic idealism and not from autocratic condescension. As a vol-

Detroit Public Library

Detroit Public Library's Rare Book Room, which preserves historical materials and examples of fine printing

untary institution with no mandate in law, it flourishes on the goodwill of the citizen but for the same reason often lacks the scholarly aspirations of academic libraries. The quality of a public library's performance in the U.S. is necessarily related to the wealth of its constituents and to their attitudes toward books. In these circumstances financial support and library excellence vary greatly across the nation. Annual tax support in 1979 ranged from less than $1 per capita in the poorest jurisdictions to well over $20 in others.

Finance. The key distinguishing feature of the public library in the U.S. is its local governance. In the absence of federally imposed standards, state and local standards set the performance levels, but even so, most state library boards lack legal authority to impose penalties and are resigned to an advisory role, leaving the local library to succeed or fail as it will. Of the 50 states only Hawaii has made the public library a function of state government. Beginning in 1986, Ohio set aside 6.3 percent of the state income tax to provide basic support for local public libraries, but without disturbing traditional local government. Elsewhere the library is a creation of county, city, town, or village as permitted by state law. The diversity thus spawned by this decentralization is representative of the American preference for local decision making for human service. Reliance on local autonomy leads to an occasional jewel such as the Boston Public Library, but more often local poverty nurtures inadequate libraries and in some sparsely populated areas none at all. Local pride, however, may succeed in overcoming poverty to help local leaders form strong libraries. Some declining cities of the northeastern U.S. still boast superior institutions and support them well from a shrinking tax base in preference to other public services.

The fiscal mainstay of the local public library has long been the property tax, while taxes other than those on real property are tapped in some states. (These exceptions will not be described here, since in

Melbourne Public Library's great domed reading room, built in 1913.

general about 90 percent of library tax support originates in real estate, the remainder in grants from state or federal sources.) For most cities the property tax began to lose its reliability in the mid-1960s as taxpayers offered resistance to the mounting cost of local government. The changing climate manifested itself dramatically in California, where in 1978 a statewide referendum placed a ceiling on property tax rates. The stricture in the flow of tax revenues, whether it occurred slowly or suddenly, fostered a growing sense of pessimism about the future of the public library. Anecdotes of individual library service reductions because of budgetary stringency were numerous in the mid-1970s, and they occurred in all regions of the U.S., prompting some library scholars to gloomy prophecies of library collapse. Fiscal starvation was not the only blow dealt to public libraries in the 1960s and 1970s, since social disintegration in urban areas and the as-yet-unassessed influence of television also depressed library use, shaking the complacency, if not the confidence, of librarians. These seismic shifts in the political, social, and economic environments of the library did not occur without library response. In 1970 a group of trustees of U.S. city libraries formed the Urban Libraries Council both to publicize and to combat the declining fortunes of libraries. Later in the decade a group known as the National Citizens Emergency Committee to Save Our Public Libraries assumed a similar role.

Not all the developments in the world of public libraries were negative; certain contrary trends gave hope that fiscal defeats were isolated phenomena. Over a 15-year span beginning in the mid-1960s, the Chicago Public Library tripled its budget and by the end of the 1970s had won approval of a plan to build a new main library in the downtown area. In other regions of the U.S., state legislatures moved to appropriate additional money to compensate for the deficiencies in local budgets. Minnesota and New York both substantially raised the level of state aid in their 1978 legislative sessions. These back eddies in the general downward flow of public library fortunes suggest that by the late 1970s the limits had been

reached in effective operation of decentralized library systems and that henceforth if the public library in the U.S. is to thrive, it will come to depend more upon state and federal intervention than it has historically been willing to do. Any significant change in the budgetary mixture of libraries will inevitably bring with it a redistribution of power over them, it may be assumed. State and federal money will be followed by compulsory adherence to regulations from above, in the view of many observers, and, despite warm ideological arguments in favor of the virtues of local management, those views are not likely to prevail. The same tide that carried the victory for regionalized school systems during the period immediately following World War II was beginning to tug at the foundations of the local public library in the 1970s; how fast and how far movements toward centralized administration of public libraries will go is still conjectural. Thoughtful students of library government see an eventual partnership in the financing of libraries—an eventual partnership that would assign about 20 percent of the support to the federal government, 30 percent to the states, and the remaining half to local government. The suggested proportions may vary from observer to observer, but the consensus for a fiscal partnership is already in place.

Administration. One striking feature of public libraries in the U.S. is their historical dependence on lay boards of governors, commonly designated as trustees, even though such boards frequently have only nominal or advisory authority. Library boards symbolize the democratic character of the library, and they exemplify the original motive of founders: to keep the library at some distance from politics. The public library is analogous to the public school with respect to its governance, for both sprang from the same generous social impulse and both developed complementary missions to educate the masses. Local lay control may be somewhat anachronistic in a management-oriented society where the professional overrides the proprietor, as it were; yet the library board provides stability and continuity by slowing the rate of library adaptation to cooperative enterprises and computerized bibliographic control. Some boards had their origins in the private libraries that were the antecedents of contemporary public libraries, and it is not unusual today to find self-perpetuating boards with memberships largely confined to local elites. More commonly, boards are appointed by publicly elected officers; a few are elected by popular vote at the polls. Boards may possess taxing and budgetary authority, but just as often their control over money is nominal.

Important as they are, the governance and financing of libraries have not been all-absorbing matters for library managers in the most recent decades. There have been other preoccupations, some of them felt by all institutions, most particularly those affiliated with education. The overriding development in the library community has been the search for means to collaborate among institutions. The quest for larger and more complex combinations has been spurred both by economic necessity and by a desire to enlarge the influence and effectiveness of the library. If local control had the virtue of guaranteeing autonomy, it also threatened small libraries with impotence in a complex environment requiring machines and speedy communications. The thrust toward collaboration was fueled by the desire to equalize service by tapping the resources of the large, powerful library for the benefit of the citizen who did not have direct access to it. Coincidentally, the advantages of cost cutting through diminution of redundant operations became evident. Among the cooperative efforts most frequently advocated (and practiced) in recent years are shared cataloguing, interlibrary loan, reference referral, cooperative book buying, union lists of serials, reciprocal borrowing privileges across jurisdictional boundaries, and automated circulation-control systems.

The internal organization of public libraries is a matter of some interest, and in larger libraries with multiple buildings and services the organizational strategies call for careful planning. Aside from the housekeeping services of supplies and maintenance, public library activity falls into four major components: book selection, cataloguing, book circulation, and reference work. Variations on these basic themes are universally observable, but the four elements are the generic ingredients for all libraries. In small libraries the activities may be carried on by one librarian, while in larger libraries the activities are subdivided and allocated among many librarians.

Urban Libraries. The large urban library or the regional library system in a populous suburban area is more complex than the basic model would suggest. Many ancillary activities may flourish in the large library. Program specialists, publicists, readers' advisers, coordinators of work with young children or adolescents—all are representative of what may be found in a major institution. The urban library is normally characterized by an ample—sometimes monumental—building housing a major book collection located at the center of the commercial area of the city, accompanied by a spread of smaller, domestically oriented branches designed to serve residents in their neighborhoods. These outlying units are ordinarily further augmented by mobile services and outreach efforts within hospitals, for example, or in the homes of immobilized residents. Some big-city libraries have also assumed the more complex task of maintaining service for blind and physically handicapped readers. A typical urban library is likely to invest 50 percent of its annual budget in its downtown location; in the very largest cities the public library may, in the range and complexity of its collections, achieve the stature of a strong university library. The chief characteristic that distinguishes the city library from an equally complex suburban library system is the central building itself. By many standard measures, suburban systems perform extremely well in meeting citizen reading demands. The core city main library, however, remains a unique institution. A few of the finest research libraries in the U.S. are public: New York, Boston, Philadelphia, Cleveland. In many cities the public library is still the provider of library service with public schools, although in the 20 years after 1955, as schools tended to create and manage their own library systems, the public library withdrew.

The uniqueness of the city main library inadvertently established city-suburban rivalry for tax dollars. The flight of the middle class to the suburbs caused city libraries to serve the same people who, after leaving the taxing area, continued to patronize the library but no longer supported it. The stress caused by this demographic pattern is not unique to library services, but it poses extremely serious problems for library boards and directors trying to maintain high standards of service primarily for nonresidents. The imbalance between the tax support and library patronage has been rectified constructively in some jurisdictions through contracts designed to divert suburban tax revenues into the city. Mergers have also been a useful response. Despite these examples of success, many cities have not been able to resolve the problem. Evidences of interest in a totally different solution are beginning to appear—the designation of central city libraries as state resources, thereby giving the state government a stake in the maintenance of a city's intellectual treasures. In Michigan, for example, the state totally underwrites the cost of operating the main library of Detroit.

Public libraries, like most human institutions, develop personalities that transcend cultural and national barriers. Significant similarities from city to city or nation to nation are useful in identifying the basic imperatives that distinguish public libraries. Because the main, or central, library of a city system differs both in size and service sophistication from a branch library, the organizational structure will tacitly recognize the distinction. Typically a large public library divides its public service administration into two units, one for main library and one for all the other services. The intricacy of the web of working relationships thereafter will be determined by the relative size of the library and the city it serves. This model has become universal and is to be found in all those nations that boast public libraries.

Long before the central library became too heavy a burden for cities to carry, New York City by historical accident created a dual library system: a popular service system of branches, and a main research center. By creating, in effect, two separate libraries, the world-famous center on Fifth Avenue, privately funded, and the branch system, publicly funded,

Canadian Library Association

Winnipeg Public Library

New York actually anticipated a course of action now being imitated. In 1976 Toronto, starting from altogether different premises, divided its main library from its branch system and created a new board representing the entire district to control the main and now independent unit. The branch system continues as before under its separate board. New York City and Toronto may not be typical, but one way or another library leaders are emphasizing the distinction between main and branch libraries. A new pattern may be emerging, and it is possible that Toronto's example will be imitated.

Services. Since its inception during the years immediately preceding the Civil War, the public library in the U.S. has exhibited certain pragmatic qualities: it has shown a willingness to tinker and experiment, to seek for practical improvements in service. The public library movement is tireless in its quest for new service objectives. Service to the blind today is being augmented by use of radio broadcasts. Efforts to ease communications with deaf people through teletype are now being employed. Specialized programs to combat illiteracy are strongly advocated. Whether these techniques will survive is less important than the fact that they indicate a continuing vitality in the library world. On the larger scene, it is to be noted that migrations of populations across the globe have provided new targets of library opportunity. In English-speaking countries that heretofore were insistent on linguistic assimilation by immigrants, the tendency now is to accept polyglot populations. In the U.S. the second and growing language is Spanish; community book collections are being shaped to reflect the new demographic makeup. In Canada the interaction of French and English is important, but in Toronto, where at least 39 languages were spoken by its citizens, several library branches featured books in 23 of those languages. Melbourne, Australia, has learned to acquire books in Turkish, Greek, and Balkan languages for some of its branch libraries, a task made difficult by the enormous distance from the supply source. The Netherlands comes to grips with linguistic diversity brought in by those who migrated from the Dutch East Indies

after World War II. The U.S.S.R. faces staggering language problems with its 91 nationalities. It attempts to deal with them through bilingual publications provided through its libraries—with Russian on one page and the national language on the facing page.

Management Concerns. Automation is increasingly prevalent in the public library, and both the complexity and the high costs of computers have begun to accentuate the differences between large and small libraries. Before World War II it was reasonable to perceive a large library as differing only in scale from the smaller institution. Today the larger library performs activities, gives services, or possesses equipment not to be found at all in small independent units. Technology has increased dependence upon larger systems by small libraries, thereby fostering creative responses through the shared programs referred to earlier. Out of necessity the collaborative efforts among libraries have proliferated so that now large libraries find themselves tied into many intricate and specialized service networks.

The potential economies implicit in shared resources are increasingly attractive to library administrations hard pressed for money. Because the operating costs of large libraries tend to rise irrespective of the amount of public service rendered, the acquisition, storage, and maintenance of complex collections are not easily managed. Library administrators substitute sharing for endless growth. Many large American libraries have probably reached their practical physical growth limits and will cease to be self-sufficient. Compression of information into computers or into microforms is one substitute for costly storage space. A library of 1,000,000 volumes, expanding at the annual rate of 5 percent, would have to add 6,000 linear feet of shelving annually and would double its inventory in about 14 years if it took no action to inhibit exponential growth. Because society is less and less willing to pay for large warehouses of little-used materials stored in buildings where the economic value of the property is highest—namely the heart of the business district of the city—library administrators face difficult choices.

Collaboration among libraries may have had its origin in technology, but it is also hurried along by the world of expanding information. Libraries have also looked to common pools of stored books as a way to relieve the discomfort of growth, but more often than not book depositories have been of greater interest to academic libraries. One notable exception is the active participation of the Boston Public Library in the New England Deposit Library. Another technique of public libraries within a geographical cluster has been the assignment of major acquisition responsibilities in subject fields among its various members, at the same time increasing accessibility to those scattered collections by interlibrary loan. A national periodical center is under consideration as one more effort to inhibit collection growth. Electronic transmission of information stored in print is only beginning to be developed, but it gives promise of further relief.

The quality of the intellectual and professional capabilities of staff members has been a constant concern of library administrators. The training of staff was seen as an inescapable responsibility for public

Paphos Municipal Library, Cyprus.

Public Information Office, Nicosia, Cyprus

672

libraries as early as the 19th century. By the turn of the century major city libraries had established intramural training schools for librarianship before there was a ready supply in the academic market of graduates. Many library schools had their origins in public libraries, and over the years public library administrators have been the champions of high-quality academic preparation for librarianship. In the 1960s and early 1970s, when professionals appeared to be in short supply, library administrators advocated cultivation of paraprofessionals trained by community colleges. As a result of these efforts curricula were established to produce staff with skills at a level midway between clerical and professional.

While the many forces at work in society operate to disturb the serenity of a library administrator, those same forces are equally disturbing to the employees of libraries. Shrinking budgets have provoked inevitable disputes about remedies, and to the degree that remedies have not been agreed upon, employee dissatisfaction has risen. The growth of unions in the professional ranks has been rapid. Laws permitting bargaining between public agencies and employees have sanctioned the movement. The historical justification for unionism—pay and working conditions—has recently been augmented by rising pressure for employees to have a role in managerial decisions. Today's library administrator is likely to be less autocratic and, indeed, to possess less authority, than the administrators of the period before World War II. Increasingly, administration has come to demand as much of diplomatic art as of technical skill. Library professionalism is less deeply associated than formerly with the humanistic disciplines. As the need for technical knowledge has increased, the library profession has opened its ranks to include newer specialties: in computers, in databanks, in microforms, in measurement and evaluation. The bookish scholar is no longer the dominant personality in library administration. Managerial training is gradually displacing literary or bibliophilic scholarship as the primary qualification for library directors. The internal environment of the large city library is a rich tapestry of contrasting interests that go to make up the whole. The range of a library's programming and the demand for many specialists within the staff create a cosmopolitan environment of unusual complexity.

As previously noted, suburban libraries in the U.S. are not charged with the responsibility for maintaining massive research collections in large, monumental buildings. They perform more efficiently and at lower cost in circulating books, their chief activity. Because they also deal with clienteles of higher income and broader education than are normally to be found in cities, the suburban libraries appear as more ably managed than city libraries, intensifying political conflict for limited library tax dollars. While the social need is greater in the city than in the suburbs, the flow of money is away from the cities, thereby defeating the democratic ideal of equalization of opportunity.

It is generally true to say that important local or regional information is to be found in the public library, and most public libraries take their local history seriously. It was almost a spontaneous thing for public libraries to become a haven for documents relating to local history. Even in communities with independent academic libraries or historical societies, the public library is likely to have acquired resources not obtainable elsewhere. In the absence of competing institutions, the public library often is the sole possessor of local historical information. Libraries occasionally are called upon to play a role with respect to public archives, but archival responsibility is assigned in accordance with local initiatives, traditions, or legal structures.

National Library of Poland

Municipal library of Zielona Góra, Poland. It features mosaics and billboard-high signs for identification.

The library board, which is so important a feature of the American public library, is often absent elsewhere in the world. In Europe the library is either a function of the educational system or a department of local government under the city council or its equivalent. Library boards are, however, to be found in Canada. The decentralized Australian system has strong state libraries in all the chief cities of the nation. In New South Wales, for example, the public library of Sydney is independent of the state library, but in Western Australia the state library manages all the public libraries and, indeed, carries on all the book selection for the state's local libraries.

Soviet libraries, while numerous, are seeking to develop some autonomy under the organized supervision of the central directorate in Moscow. Book selection is governed by rigid rules, and even local budgets are set by the Ministry of Culture. In support of efforts to advance socialist thinking, the state subsidizes the publishing of children's literature, making attractive books readily available in large quantities at low prices.

The Future. The last two decades of the 20th century will put heavy pressure on library managers. The destabilizing forces of revolution and energy depletion that are agitating all institutions pose a particularly unsettling challenge to libraries. As reading declines, as illiteracy spreads, as video-telecommunications make inroads on the library's traditional clientele, how will the profession respond? Problems appear now where all was thought to be safe and secure. In the U.S. children's use of public libraries, once the staple of public library services, has been halved since the mid-1950s; in most cities children's circulation is now only about one-third of the total. Americans are using their libraries more heavily as information sources rather than as reading centers, a phenomenon also reported elsewhere in the world.

673

Libraries now have the capability of answering reference questions by means of access to remote databanks in preference to using printed sources. While faster, the service is more expensive, and it can drive up the cost of reference service to unacceptable levels. This phenomenon is bringing into question the validity of the "free" public library. Increasingly, the "free" library is being challenged by economists and politicians, many of whom advocate placing the cost burden on the beneficiary of the service rather than on the tax rolls. Such political opinions generate strong resistance among traditionalists who hold to egalitarian standards. This battleground will be fought over in the decades ahead, and in the dust of conflict the library director will require diplomatic arts to maintain a stable and safe institution. Whatever the outcome in this conflict, or any of the others, one point is indisputable: the tempo of change is speeding up, and the pressures on the managers are growing. Yet library administrators who delay decisions while awaiting a clearer view of the field will not serve their institutions well. A flexible posture is required, a willingness to move with emerging forces and still retain inviolate the fundamental principles of librarianship. It is not an easy period in public librarianship, but it may yet be the most fertile in ideas.

REFERENCES
Edward N. Howard, *Local Power and the Community Library* (1978).
Ann E. Prentice, *Public Library Finance* (1977).
Dorothy Sinclair, *Administration of the Small Public Library*, 2nd edition (1979).

ERVIN J. GAINES

MEASUREMENT AND EVALUATION
As public library systems throughout the world become more sophisticated, more time is spent on measuring and evaluating their performance. In the 1960s and early 1970s there was a tendency to centralize work within each country and to rely on ever more detailed quantitative measures. There is some evidence to show that in the 1980s the emphasis has been on decentralization and on qualitative rather than quantitative measures.

Standards. The tendency toward qualitative measures is particularly noticeable with the development of new public library standards. Traditionally, standards have been compiled centrally by a professional association or a government department. They were expressed in numerical terms and related in inputs—that is, to the number of staff, number of books, and number and size of service points. Furthermore, they were compiled with the implicit assumption that what was appropriate in one part of the country was generally appropriate elsewhere.

The newer forms of standards tend to reject this assumption and accordingly are framed in rather different ways. Modern standards start from the proposition that public library systems should themselves calculate what is appropriate in their particular circumstances. There is much more emphasis on providing a framework or methodology, which can then be used to calculate the number and proportion of inputs required for a given output, or level of service. The end results of this approach are standards that are probably more difficult to apply in individual circumstances but that take much more account of local variations.

A good example of the traditional form of library standards is the *Standards for Public Libraries* issued by IFLA in 1973. These were formulated to provide "guidance as to the levels of provision needed to maintain efficient library services . . . and should provide a basis for the formulation of national standards." They are expressed in terms of the various quantities of each input thought to be required to meet the needs of given levels of population. The standards were framed in the specific belief that "separate standards were not desirable, since the general objectives in all countries are the same."

In direct contrast to the IFLA Standards are those concerning the *Staffing of Public Libraries,* published by the United Kindgom Department of Education and Science in 1976. These standards were calculated on the basis of the detailed work study exercises that examined the various tasks undertaken in a modern public library. The result is a series of formulas that can be applied to produce information on the number of staff needed to provide a given level of service in the light of particular local circumstances.

Another example of the new way of thinking about standards was the publication in 1982 of *Output Measures for Public Libraries* by the ALA, and the wide use of *A Planning Process for Public Libraries.* The thinking behind this project was that to formulate library standards based on outputs rather than inputs it was necessary to work on information generated by a thorough review of goals, objectives, and performance in library systems. The process that was devised to facilitate this review suggests that nationally produced standards may be redundant, because standards in this process are set locally as an integral part of the review.

Statistics. Library standards and library statistics almost go hand in hand. More and more countries now collect detailed statistical information about the workings of their public library systems. In most cases the information is published for use within individual public libraries. This supply of basic data is essential for the effective planning of a national system and is recognized by many to be an important input to the management process at the local level. It can also provide an invaluable information source for research workers.

In 1970 Unesco published its *Recommendations concerning the International Standardisation of Library Statistics* in an attempt to introduce a degree of standardization and comparability into the provision of library statistics. As a result of the recommendation many countries have adopted the Unesco format as a basis for their compilations. While this has resulted in considerable improvement, much remains to be done. It is still difficult to compare the performance of public library systems in different countries, and the situation is further aggravated by the fact that not all countries collect statistics in any systematic way.

Two countries that have done much to produce full sets of public library statistics are the U.S. and Canada. In both countries central government agencies—the Library Surveys Branch of the National Center for Education Statistics, U.S. Department of Education, and Statistics Canada—have attempted to collect and publish statistics from libraries of all types, including public libraries.

The system developed for the U.S. demonstrates an interesting and profitable example of cooperation between the professional association and the government. A National Conference on Library Statistics was sponsored jointly by the then U.S. Office of Education (USOE) and the ALA in 1967. The Conference recommended that a national library data collection system be set up; this did in fact happen, and by the mid-1970s the results had begun to appear from the system. The whole operation is not without flaws, but it does represent a serious attempt to produce compatible statistics on a national basis.

A completely different situation is found in most other countries. For example, a review of library statistics in the U.K. claimed in 1976 that the provision was "uneven, uncoordinated, unsystematic and confusing." This was despite a serious attempt in the early 1970s to introduce a unified system based on the Unesco recommendation.

Much of the momentum of the early 1970s for the improvement of library statistics has been dissipated. However, much has been achieved, and the need for accurate and regular statistics should ensure that improvements continue to be made.

Public Library Research. Public library research is a rapidly growing activity. Research in one form or another has always been carried out in the larger, better-organized authorities. In the postwar years library schools throughout the world conducted research into the activities of local public libraries. The 1970s saw a noticeable increase in the involvement of central bodies—governments and professional associations. The implications of this are considerable, since the availability of support funds from these organizations can completely change the character of research.

Public libraries in the U.S. benefited from the general boom in federally funded social research that took place in the latter half of the 1960s. The benefits that accrued from this research are often hard to identify, and if the same resources were available today, they might well be used in a very different fashion.

In the U.K. funds for public library research first began to become available in 1974 when the British Library decided to include public libraries within the terms of reference of its Research and Development Department. The program began slowly, but later years show evidence that the demand for research funds, particularly from public librarians, is considerable.

In Canada there are signs that federal and provincial funds are becoming available for library research in general and for public library research in particular. There is a similar situation in Sweden, where the government decided to allocate substantial funds to support library research.

As research programs develop, there is a tendency for them to be dominated by academic researchers or, in some cases, by research consultants. While this trend is understandable, there are strong arguments for involving practitioners in the research process. Above all, there is a general move toward making the research relevant to the "real world" and oriented toward operational improvements. In the U.K. the public library research program has as its basic principle that the main thrust of the program

should be toward research into particular problems rather than toward theoretical conceptualization.

It can generally be concluded that in public libraries there is a continuing trend toward systematic management. This implies full use of statistical information, the acceptance of research as an integral part of the management process, and, it would seem, the recognition that in the matter of standards local calculations are of more value than national pronouncements. The emphasis is on using nationally provided resources to arrive at local solutions to local problems.

REFERENCES
Planning for a Nationwide System of Library Statistics (1970).
A Planning Process for Public Libraries (1980).
Frank N. Withers, *Standards for Library Services: An International Survey* (1974), the standard work reviewing library standards throughout the world.
IFLA, *International Guidelines for Public Libraries* (1986).
Unesco, *Development of Public Library Systems and Services* (1982).

NICK MOORE

PUBLIC LIBRARY LEGISLATION IN THE UNITED STATES

The earliest legislative measure in the U.S. dealing with public libraries was enacted in 1848 as a special act of the General Court of Massachusetts, authorizing the establishment of the Boston Public Library. A year later a general act was adopted by the legislature of New Hampshire authorizing cities and towns to establish free tax-supported public libraries. The other New England states adopted similar laws between 1851 and 1869. In 1872 Illinois approved a public library act that for the first time provided for separate boards to govern public libraries; the Illinois law was more comprehensive than the New Hampshire act and served as a model for many of the western states to follow.

Public Library Acts. Today every state in the Union has a public library act on its statute books that provides the legal basis for the establishment, governance, administration, and tax support of public libraries. Although these enactments are all similar, no two of them are exactly alike. In some states the public library law is so framed that it covers all types of public libraries whether they are city, village, township, county, district, regional, or school district libraries. In other states there may be a separate law for each of these various governmental units.

One of the major provisions in a public library act is a grant of authority from the legislature to the municipality empowering it to establish a public library. There are three such types of grants. In most of the states the grant is extended to the corporate authority—that is, the city council, village board, or county board of commissioners. In other states the law provides for a referendum of the voters to decide whether a public library is to be established. Finally, in a few states the statute permits the establishment of a public library initiated by a petition addressed to a municipal body and containing the signatures of a requisite number or percentage of the legal residents.

Another vital provision in a public library act is the grant of power to levy taxes for library purposes. This authorization is made to the corporate body and

Story hour in the Children's Room of the Dudley Public Library, England.

not to the library board, except in the case of certain district libraries that are expressly granted such power. Funding is made available in one of two ways: (1) through a special library tax on property, usually expressed in terms of a millage rate as, for example, one mill or more on each dollar of the assessed valuation of property; or (2) through a lump sum appropriation from the general revenue of the municipality.

A third important provision in a public library act relates to the governmental structure of the library. The law usually provides for a board of directors of a specified number, appointed or elected for a given term of years, and enumerates the powers and duties of the board.

There are a variety of other provisions. Almost all public library acts provide that use of the library shall be forever free to the inhabitants of the municipality. A provision authorizing the corporate authorities to provide suitable penalties for persons committing injury to library property or for failure to return books belonging to the library is also included. An extremely significant provision is the requirement that the proceeds from the library tax shall be kept in a separate fund, designated as the "library fund," and must not be intermingled with other funds of the corporate authority. A common provision requires the library board to submit an annual report to the corporate authority as well as to the state library agency. Finally, a large number of the laws provide for joint library service between two or more governmental units.

Boards. In general, public library boards are appointed by the mayor with the approval of the city council. In a few jurisdictions boards are elective, but the practice is chiefly in towns, villages, and townships. Library boards may have from three to nine members. At least 20 states provide for boards of five members. The term of office of board members varies, but most states provide for three-year terms.

Although for the most part library boards do not have the power to levy taxes, they do have exclusive control of the expenditure of library funds. The board has complete power over the management and care of library property, but with respect to real property there is some diversity of legal practice. Many boards enjoy the power in their own right to

purchase land and erect buildings. In some states, however, it is necessary to proceed through the city council or county board to acquire land or buildings. Library boards do not have the power to issue bonds to finance construction. This must be done by the corporate authorities, and in most cases the floating of a bond issue is subject to a referendum of the voters. In most states it is possible to acquire property for library purposes through eminent domain.

The library board also has the power to make rules and regulations covering the operation and management of the library. Under this power, the board is permitted to determine the service hours of the library and fix the schedule of fines for failure to return books, nonresident fees, and similar matters. The board has the power to accept donations of money, personal property, and real estate by gift, will, or through a trust for the benefit of the library. In the area of personnel, the board has generally complete control over the library staff, including appointments, dismissals, salaries, hours of employment, and working conditions.

Since the public library is not a legal entity in itself but merely a division or department of the municipality, a large body of municipal law impinges on the powers of the library board. For example, a municipal civil service act may limit the power of the board over personnel. A central purchasing law, requiring that purchases for city departments be handled by a central purchasing agency, may interfere with the library board's exclusive power over purchasing. A state law mandating across-the-board limitations on tax levies by municipalities may reduce the amount of revenue available for library purposes. Thus, to determine the actual legal authority of a library board, it is necessary not only to consult the public library act but also to examine a related body of municipal law.

State and Federal Legislation. To promote the extension and development of public libraries, states began to enact legislation providing for the establishment of state library agencies. Massachusetts was not only the first state to inaugurate tax-supported public library service but also the first to create a state library agency for the express purpose of promoting public libraries. In 1890 the General Court of Massachusetts passed a law establishing a State Board of Library Commissioners, whose duties were to render advice, encouragement, and a modicum of financial assistance to communities planning to organize public libraries. Within a few years several other eastern states had adopted similar measures. In 1895 the idea was taken up vigorously by Wisconsin and transmitted to many of the western states, becoming popularly known as the free public library commission movement. By 1909, 34 states had provided legislation establishing state library commissions, boards, or similar bodies designed to extend and improve public libraries. Today every state has a state library agency that is responsible by law to plan a state program of public library development, render consultative services, distribute state aid, and assume leadership in making provision for adequate public library services on a statewide basis.

In approximately 30 states, this legal responsibility is vested in a commission, board, or committee, the members of which are appointed by the governor. There is considerable diversity in the functioning of these administrative bodies, but essentially they are endowed with the power and duties to promote public library development. Operationally they act through the appointment of a state librarian or an officer who holds a similar title. In about 15 states, the responsibility to extend public library service is lodged in the state department of education through the creation of a library extension agency. Here, too, there is considerable diversity in administrative practice. In most cases, however, the head of the extension agency is under the direction of the department of education. There are notable exceptions, as in California, where the state librarian is appointed by the governor and serves at the pleasure of the governor. But even in this instance the legal power to determine policy rests with the state board of education. In the remaining jurisdictions, the state library agency reports directly to the governor or is under the office of the secretary of state or some special department of state government.

State aid is one of the key elements today in providing for the improvement of public library service. The legal rationale for state aid is based on the constitutional principle that education is a primary function of state government, and since public libraries are part of the educational establishment, it follows that the state has a direct responsibility for their financial support. In this connection the Supreme Courts of no less than nine states have declared that a public library is an educational institution. In *State ex rel. Carpenter v. St. Louis,* 318 Mo 870, for example, the Supreme Court of Missouri in 1928 ruled that a public library is an educational institution and that public library service is a state governmental function.

Although the origin of state aid for public libraries can be traced back to a New York act of 1838, this idea did not take firm root for a century. Ohio in 1935 and Michigan in 1937 were successful in enacting state-aid laws providing for the distribution of a sizable amount of state funds to public libraries. In the South a number of states adopted similar legislation at about the same time. The most ambitious state-aid program arrived several decades later, however, when New York in 1958 adopted an act providing for the establishment of cooperative library systems blanketing the entire state. In support of the system concept, New York has continued to make substantial annual appropriations for this purpose, with the appropriation in 1978 totaling approximately $35,000,000. In the 1960s and 1970s, Illinois, Pennsylvania, Massachusetts, New Jersey, Rhode Island, and Maryland likewise enjoyed large-scale state-supported public library system development programs. Other states, such as Texas, California, Indiana, Michigan, and Wisconsin, have state-aid measures for financing public library systems also.

Another form of state assistance is emerging that provides direct aid to public libraries that meet certain statutory conditions. New York, Illinois, Georgia, and West Virginia are taking the lead in this type of legislation. There are other experimental attempts at state aid such as the Michigan act undertaking to fund the Detroit Public Library completely. Another innovative measure is the California Library Services Act adopted in 1977.

The federal government was a latecomer in the field of public library legislation. More than a century and a half elapsed before Congress took any legislative recognition of public libraries. In 1956 Congress passed the Library Services Act. Designed to promote the extension of library services to rural areas, it was in essence a library demonstration program for rural communities. To participate in the program a state was required to submit a plan for extension of library service that had to be approved by the U.S. Commissioner of Education. In 1964 the Library Services Act was amended, making it applicable to all public libraries, urban as well as rural, and became known as the Library Services and Construction Act (LSCA).

LSCA now consists of four titles: Title I—Services; Title II—Construction; Title III—Interlibrary Cooperation; Title IV—Older Readers Services. In 1977 Title I was amended to provide special assistance to urban public libraries located in cities with populations of 100,000 or more. Since 1974 Congress has appropriated funds only for Titles I and III; for fiscal 1979 Congress appropriated $62,500,000 for Title I and $5,000,000 for Title III.

At the state level a most erupting event affecting public libraries occurred in 1978 with the passage of the California initiative, referred to as Proposition 13, which placed a limitation on property tax levies. This law, adopted by the voters of the state, provides that the maximum amount of any ad valorem tax on real property shall not exceed one percent of the full cash value of such property based on the 1975–76 assessed valuation. The impact of this mandate is proving to be extremely severe on public libraries. Other states moved in the same direction, and it became clear that public libraries would be required to seek other sources of revenue.

REFERENCES
Carleton B. Joeckel, *The Government of the American Public Library* (1935).
Alex Ladenson, editor, *American Library Laws,* 5th edition (1984).
Alex Ladenson, editor, "State and Federal Legislation for Libraries," *Library Trends* (1970).

ALEX LADENSON

LIBRARY COOPERATION

Cooperation is as old as libraries themselves. A basic principle has been that there should be equity in the public sector and that every individual should have the opportunity to develop to his highest potential. This approach expresses an aspiration of public librarians worldwide. Typically, the purpose of cooperation has been the interlending of monographs and serials, and the largest libraries have borne a high proportion of the administrative costs as well as the costs of being heavy net lenders. Administrative centers, union catalogues, schemes for collective acquisition, storage, and relegation have arisen as interlending became formalized, and such cooperatives have often used the new technology to improve systems with computer output microform (COM) catalogues, international standard book number (ISBN) location lists, telex and other telecommunication links, and other means.

Public Libraries

Bulawayo and District Publicity Association

Mzilikazi Memorial Library, Bulawayo, Zimbabwe.

Recent experience in a more cost-conscious age has shown the limitations of the older systems of voluntary cooperation. The small members tend to contribute little of significance; the administrative costs of maintaining union location lists are considerable. There is a tendency to abuse the facilities of the cooperative to compensate for basic weakness, ultimately hindering pressure for real improvement through consolidation of nonviable libraries and more adequate funding for units with a potential to be largely self-sufficient. Critics doubt whether such cooperatives really achieve a meaningful improvement in access to resources. There is a further problem in the metropolitan areas that are served by the greatest concentration of public libraries in that the new suburban systems of multibranch type, serving the prosperous communities, make no contribution to the major reference collections in the declining core cities.

The growing interdependence of library units, revealed by an astonishing spread of networks in North America and by administrative restructuring in the U.K., demonstrates that the public library sector needs cooperation more than ever. The reasons are

economic recession
growth and sophistication of demands on public libraries
advanced technology arising from the convergence of computers, telecommunications, and office mechanization, vastly improving the potential for data handling and transmission, and creating a need for much larger economic bases
the consequent arrival of online cataloguing systems
availablity of federal and state funds to develop networks and agencies
population changes, especially a concentration into the metropolitan areas, in which more than 70 percent of Americans now live and 85 percent will live by the year 2000
within the vast conurbations, a tendency for the core city to decline at the expense of prosperous suburbs
administrative restructuring in order to achieve economies of scale for a range of public services, including libraries.

The new generation of cooperatives and networks (which is generally taken to refer to a cooperative based on computers and telecommunications, and necessarily formal in its procedures) has to be cost-effective, not so much extending equity as offering a more economic trade-off between building up local resources and buying services or obtaining them at the expense of a higher level of government. This approach requires a wider definition of cooperation, perhaps as contractual services. The Rochester Regional Council markets a variety of services to 49 libraries of various types in which contracts are used as a convenient and formalized means for securing more services for any single library in a network of libraries. The new library networks are frequently multitype and perform brokerage for remote commercial or fee-charging public services providing bibliographic processing of information. Another characteristic, in the U.S. and Canada, is the use of cooperatives as a means of applying federal or state/provincial funds so as to reorganize and strengthen a group of autonomous public libraries, inherited from an earlier period, when the aim was for each town or city to provide itself with a general cultural facility, on a scale determined by local means and will to pay.

The complaint about "localism," that is, jealous preservation of autonomy, so often heard from network planners, derives from a conflict between the traditional assumption that the local library, with its permanent collections, is largely self-sufficient, contrasted with the planners' view that local libraries should serve primarily as public service outlets, with technical services support coming from a central service elsewhere and distributed to libraries as needed. The planners are unlikely to prevail in isolated towns and small cities unless they can "buy themselves in" with funding from other sources. Here is the fundamental structural weakness that faces public libraries in the Anglo-American and Scandinavian countries that pioneered the type. In Canada public libraries outside the metropolitan areas are inadequately funded and organized and are too small. Similar problems affect countries such as the German Federal Republic, which are trying to build up a public library network side by side with outmoded types, and such socialist countries as China, where public libraries have been established as widespread community services. There is considerable autonomy at all levels—with municipal and factory libraries much like small-town Western libraries; but the city of Shanghai has a well-developed central and branch library system. The provincial libraries are not integrated with the lower levels of provision, but they do play an important role in planning for public library modernization.

Forms of Library Cooperation. M. M. Reynold's *Reader in Library Cooperation* includes a useful typology of cooperation:

Corporate:	1 board, 1 fund
Federated:	x boards, 1 fund
Cooperative:	x boards, x funds

If we take the traditional mode already described as *cooperative networks,* a useful comparison can be made between the choice of *federated networks* in North America, with its vast distances and fragmented administrative structure, and *corporate networks* in the U.K. since the reorganization of both national and local library services in the mid-1970s. In Canada, Saskatchewan and Metropolitan Toronto illustrate a restructuring approach. New York State and Illinois are notable examples of the federated approach; in Ohio, the State Planning Committee, because of the legal, political, and attitudinal barriers to cooperation it encountered, required that cooperation be cost-effective and involve a minimum of administrative structuring and restructuring. The initiative does not always come from the top—witness Ontario's 14 regional library systems agreeing to pool their provincial grants in order to set up a network for cooperation. It is early to generalize about who is going to run the resource-sharing networks and what kind of an organization is needed. But in the U.S., where more than 350 consortia are already in existence, the trend seems to be best illustrated by Illinois, where regional networks based on major public libraries are being merged into a multitype state and interstate network, which would limit the growth of the powers of the public library systems, and which will instead provide a highly efficient service delivery mechanism. A general prediction has been made that the future public library will serve primarily for face-to-face public services and as a switching point or broker between users and information regardless of location. Illinois shows the logical result of such thinking in a statement on collection management policy that envisages that every library unit will concentrate its local resources on satisfying expressed demand, without constraints of quality or literary merit—a qualification clearly aimed at the public library sector. Others have argued the dangers of systematic shedding of less-used material, among them a loss of browsing value and of demand derived from immediate availability. In other countries different methods for getting around administrative fragmentation are used; for example, in West Germany the Einkaufzentral in Reittlingen functions as a purchasing and servicing agency for public libraries and for two research and planning bodies. In developing countries such as Malaysia and Singapore public libraries are being built up on a planned basis with strong direction by the national library.

The U.K. provides the prime example of the corporate approach. The various libraries at the national level have been integrated under the British Library Board with its divisions for reference, lending and bibliographic services, and research and development. At the local level most people in England and Wales are now served by county libraries for an average 600,000 population, with library authorities in the metropolitan areas serving populations between 250,000 and 350,000, or rather less in London. The British Library Board has a specific duty to provide support to the whole library and information community and is thus creating networks of service that are modifying existing cooperatives. The Lending Division (BLLD) serves as an example. It dominates the national interlibrary lending of serials through mass photocopying and is in the process of establishing similar preeminence in monograph loans. A recent development is the establishment of a national delivery service, achieving more than 80 percent success in document delivery in 24 hours and almost complete success in 48 hours. The individual library is still able to borrow directly from others in the region using an ISBN list of holdings or can go directly to BLLD or indirectly through the regional bureau.

Cooperation between public and school libraries had left much to be desired in the past. In the U.S., where school libraries have been professionally staffed for generations, school and public library re-

lations were still being defined as a problem in 1972 because of an unorganized ebb and flow of students, poor communications with teachers on study assignments, and a lack of role definition. The school-public library seems at first sight to have much promise for giving rural areas improved library services. Promising developments were reported from New Zealand, but Newfoundland abandoned the practice. In the U.K. dual-use libraries are growing in number after a slow start. In Adelaide, Australia, the experimental use of school audiovisual materials by the general community is one positive gain from such cooperation.

Jurisdictional boundaries between public libraries and other social agencies that have library and information needs, especially at the metropolitan and regional level, form a barrier to developing the full potential of the public library. Of 300 Regional Councils of Government (COG) in the U.S., only three had library components; Denver is cited as an admirable exception to the rule. In the U.K. the Department of Education and Science saw opportunities in the local government reorganization of 1974 for a corporate library and information service reaching out to schools, social service establishments, hospitals, and prisons, and also a special library service to local government. This was made simpler by the concurrency of powers of the new local authorities. The original British impetus in multitype cooperatives was to provide a serials interlending service, a declining need with the arrival of BLLD. Major British research-type public libraries do not have the advantages of metropolitan Toronto in that they provide services to their region generally at the cost of the local taxpayers in the core city.

Cooperation with Cultural and Technical Services. The literature of cooperation tends to ignore the role of the public library as a cultural agency. In Bulgaria public libraries are housed in cultural centers; in France a public library is an impor-

Diechmanske Public Library in Oslo, which provides listening facilities, and sound circulating collections.

Diechmanske Public Library, Oslo

tant function in the *Maisons de la Culture;* in the U.K. most metropolitan public libraries are administered as part of a leisure or cultural directorate (although this is opposed by the LA).

Participation in automated networks is of two kinds: to support internal operations and to provide user services. The latter are easily assessed, as they provide additional resources at an established cost, but participation in joint cataloguing, processing, and collection management involves in addition a partial loss of control of standards and performance. Since public libraries are minor users in most bibliographic networks, the product is not always optimal for them; hence the complaint of public libraries using the MARC files—that the search for bibliographic authority and completeness results in an unwieldy record and a loss of currency. What the public librarian wants is a brief but authoritative record, available on, or preferably before, publication, for use in an integrated order, catalogue, circulation, and stock control system—a management record rather than a bibliographic record. The OCLC Mini Catalog project and British interest in a Mini-MARC record are responses to such complaints.

Given a choice between centralized shared cataloguing and working with a regional consortium, public librarians prefer the latter because they normally have a place in policymaking. Critics of OCLC and similar systems argue that they are based on an obsolescent configuration of a remote mainframe computer, with heavy line costs, and that the new networks will be based on the chain of local minicomputers linked to one another to give a distributed national database. One side effect of using automated cataloguing is the long-delayed abandonment by North American libraries of expensive card catalogues in favor of COM output. The real gains in public library applications of automation lie in an integrated approach to all internal operations.

It should be advantageous for new users to adopt software already proved in a similar public library, and although there are many cautionary tales about the difficulty of doing this when the original program was not designed to be transportable, most of the British online cataloguing systems are based on the work of a handful of pioneers. Small public libraries should always find it better to delegate as much as possible of their internal systems to a remote agency, whose standards will be superior, and which will probably be cheaper because of subsidies. There are cooperative examples of practically every library operation from preselection of stock to staff placement, which are often substitutes for consolidating small library units.

Turning to cooperation of a service nature, interlending has already been mentioned. There is one great question: whether it is more cost-effective to establish a comprehensive national collection as a direct backup to local libraries of all types, as an alternative to the traditional interlending networks. BLLD, in direct competition with long-established cooperatives, has demonstrated a clear superiority in performance on serials; indeed, it has a world market that is growing fast. What puts these serials networks in jeopardy is the concept of intellectual property, which may cramp the scope for mass photocopying in the future. Electronic mail is now common in

North America, and Columbus (Ohio) Public Library is using facsimile transmission as a means to supply local school and public libraries with documents that they have identified from online bibliographic services. It has been demonstrated theoretically that the optimal national network should be based upon a nodal system comparable to that already mentioned for minicomputers.

Sociotechnological phenomena of the late 20th century, vastly improved communications and metropolitan living, are being encountered by a public library sector still structured on a 19th-century model. The response of government to the general situation is to create larger units of administration and to fund coordinating mechanisms, of which the fast-growing library and information networks are an example. The involvement of librarians in policy development will determine the extent of their future participation in these developing networks.

Planners see a role for the public library as an outlet for network information. But little is said about its cultural and educational roles, while the trend toward contracts and direct charges threatens the goal of serving people disadvantaged in access to knowledge.

Multitype networks are helpful in providing a corporate library and information service to the community, but one might prefer a matrix network that would help to consolidate public libraries into multipurpose units of adequate size. The public library subsystems could thereby have the capability of achieving their cultural and educational goals while subscribing wholeheartedly to information networks in order to claim their share in the "distributed national library."

REFERENCES

H. C. Campbell, *Developing Public Library Systems and Services,* (1982).
Michael M. Reynolds, editor, *Reader in Library Cooperation* (1972).
W. L. Saunders, editor, *British Librarianship Today* (1976).

ALEX WILSON

Public Relations

Public relations (PR) as a professional skill is a late-20th-century development, the outgrowth of mass communication, mass marketing, and the coupling of both to stimulate action. Simply defined, public relations is a planned and sustained effort to establish mutual understanding between an organization and its public.

The practice of public relations involves research of the attitudes and opinions of the many publics served by an organization, advising management on attitudes and responses, helping set policy that demonstrates responsiveness, communicating information about the organization, and constantly evaluating the effectiveness of all programs.

It is ironic that public relations has an image problem and is so frequently misunderstood. The term is often used interchangeably with publicity, which is just one of its tools. It is seen by some as little more than a nice attitude and a smile that create friendly relations. There is also a tinge of suspicion and distrust that may be associated with aggressive press agentry, with its stunts and puffery. Yet in spite of these misconceptions, public relations has become a powerful and indispensable tool of management. PR practitioners insist that they do not create images; a good reputation must be earned.

A public relations program may include marketing, merchandising, press agentry, promotion, publicity—rarely just one of these. PR is notably different from advertising alone, which uses paid space and time, while public relations depends on free editorial space and news or public service time.

History. Public relations was "invented" in the early 20th century when big business was forced to abandon its "public be damned" attitude. The muckrakers were fighting corruption in business and government, and the public was reading, listening, and demanding reform. Ida M. Tarbell exposed the antisocial actions of Standard Oil in her history of the company, and Upton Sinclair unmasked the horrors of the meatpacking industry in *The Jungle*. In response to such attacks, business produced a whitewash of words, one-sided communication, and little action.

In 1906 Ivy L. Lee was hired as publicity adviser by a group of anthracite producers whose aloof attitude of secrecy had angered the press and public during a labor dispute. Lee's belief in public information for business organizations made him one of the pioneers of public relations. As adviser to the Pennsylvania Railroad, he ended their policy of secrecy by inviting reporters to the scene of a train wreck to see for themselves exactly what happened; he even provided background information for their stories. His frankness generated "good press" for the railroad in reports of the wreck.

By the end of World War I, it was clear that words could be skillfully used to mold public opinion and that public understanding was necessary for the survival of institutions. One of Woodrow Wilson's first acts after the declaration of war was appointment of a Committee on Public Information, headed by journalist George Creel. Creel recruited magazine writers, advertising specialists, university professors, and a host of others for an "educational" campaign that sent American propaganda around the world; according to some historians, words won the war.

Another PR pioneer, Edward L. Bernays, who wrote the first book on the subject, *Crystallizing Public Opinion* (1922), developed the theory of specialized publics, stressing that messages should be targeted to specific audiences.

Although public relations was not defined in standard dictionaries until 1946, it has since become part of everyday vocabulary and is an accepted management function. Few business or government organizations are without a public relations department, and two of the largest public relations firms in the mid-1980s employed more than 1,200 and had annual billings in excess of $69,000,000. While most PR practitioners entered the field through training or experience as journalists, there are currently more than 150 colleges that have student chapters of the Public Relations Society of America and offer a minimum of four courses in public relations.

Library Use. Libraries have made use of the philosophy and technique of public relations vigorously but inconsistently. As early as 1910 John Cot-

ton Dana horrified some of his more staid library colleagues by using a billboard to advertise the library. He identified local interests and developed accordingly the libraries he directed in Denver, Colorado, Springfield, Massachusetts, and Newark, New Jersey, and he believed in telling the community what the library had and did. A major section of his practical guide, *Modern American Library Economy as Illustrated by the Newark, N.J., Free Public Library* (1910), was devoted to advertising and is still a useful tool. He asserts:

> Nothing is better for a public institution than publicity. The people who pay for its support are entitled to know—it is part of their education to know—all its ins and outs, its receipts, its expenditures, its methods, its plans and ambitions. Newspapers are almost invariably willing to print notes of these things. They feel that about the management of a public library there should not be, toward the public, the slightest intimation of a desire for secrecy.

His guide outlines many ways a library can involve its community and communicate effectively, from stories for the newspaper to working with local schools.

Dana said that he came to his library every day with pleasure and left it with regret. His enthusiasm was contagious, and his tradition of public relations has been continued by a profession that gives an annual John Cotton Dana Library Public Relations Award. Excellence in public relations in all types of libraries is recognized by this award program, established in 1946 by the H. W. Wilson Company and the American Library Association.

Librarians appeared progressive in embracing PR when the Library Public Relations Council (LPRC) was founded in 1939. LPRC is devoted to investiga-

U.S. library symbol, adopted by ALA in 1982.

American Library Association

Winning poster by the Australian Library Promotion Council, international poster competition (1985 IFLA conference).

tion, discussion, and promotion of every phase of library public relations. Similar organizations focusing on college and school public relations were not founded until 1949 and 1950, respectively. "Public relations of libraries" first appeared as a subject heading in *Library Literature* in the 1943–45 volume, and the articles on the subject have been numerous.

In spite of early and enthusiastic interest in public relations, librarians are uneasy about PR and are still debating its merits. A January 1974 *Library Journal* editorial, for example, protested the "selling of the public library." The writer objected to aggressive PR messages, holding that people need and will use the public library just as they use hospitals, schools, and other essential services:

> This commercial pap, when applied to an institution like the public library, may be effective to a degree, if we want to pack 'em in, but beyond its lack of dignity, it overlooks the basic justification for all public services— that people need them. No other essential public service finds it necessary to peddle its wares as if they were new appliances for a consumer public that is tired of washing dishes, preparing food from scratch, or having hair with split ends.

The editorial inspired a flurry of letters and articles on both sides of the issue. Confusion between public relations and publicity continues, and both are seen by some as undignified hucksterism. Billboards advertising libraries are still just as shocking to many librarians as they were to Dana's colleagues. A basic text on administration of the college library prefers the term *interpretation* to *public relations* "for reasons less of logic than of sensibility."

The years 1980–85 saw major growth in the numbers of libraries—even academic libraries—that make use of public relations techniques. For example, in 1979 PR consultant Alice Norton found only three college libraries with full-time PR positions. In contrast, *College and Research Libraries* (September 1985) includes a PR survey by Vikki Ford of 48 library directors at universities with student enrollments of 9,000–12,000; the response rate of 85 percent suggests a high interest in public relations. Forty of the 41 respondents said their academic libraries conduct some form of publicity, and 17 reported planned PR programs assigned to individual staff members. One of the five directors who rated his program as "highly effective" commented, "Our PR program has resulted in increased budgets, has protected funds during state-wide freezes in spending. It has made possible the purchase of more than 100,000 books in the last 10 years." Yet Ford notes that academic librarians have still not adopted PR programs wholeheartedly, and the majority (33) see their programs as only moderately effective.

While public relations has growing recognition as an important and legitimate tool of library management, many library administrators are becoming even more interested in "marketing." As defined by Philip Kotler, an expert in marketing for nonprofit organizations, marketing is "that function of the organization that can keep in constant touch with the organization's consumers, read their needs, develop products that meet these needs and build a program of communications to express the organization's purposes." In theory, marketing goes beyond public relations, in turning to the consumer for information about the products and services to be developed. Selling focuses on the needs of the seller, marketing on the needs of the buyer.

Should libraries make use of "business" skills such as marketing and public relations? A business produces goods and services, and its bottom line is profit; a nonprofit organization such as the library provides services, and its bottom line is "quality of life"; such a concept is considerably more difficult to measure than profit. It is dangerous for a library to assume that the quality of the cause will generate public support. Many organizations with that attitude fail to develop a clear statement of their service and fail to develop marketing plans and delivery systems.

In his keynote address to the combined 1978 conference of the Southeast and Southwest library associations, O. B. Hardison, Jr., Director of the Folger Shakespeare Library, stressed the "imperative of responsiveness" and described the funding realities that make research libraries "ivory towers in the arena":

> There *is* a public out there in the arena. It has legitimate needs, interests and demands. Since it pays the bills, the institutions that receive its support have a moral obligation to meet these needs and demands in ways that are appropriate, and even at times in ways that may seem odd when first seen from the barbican of the ivory tower. Lunchtime bluegrass at the Library of Congress? Well, why not if it makes the institution seem more open, less forbidding? . . . Every research library from the Library of Congress to the Folger is more in the arena today than it was even a decade ago. The problem is not whether to enter the arena but, having entered, to plot a course that is compatible with the institution's long-range interests. This situation creates stress, but I think it is basically good. It is an adjustment to current realities. The alternative is—or seems to me to be—withdrawal and decline.

The question now should not be *whether* public relations is appropriate to libraries but rather *how* every public, school, academic, and special library can best use the techniques and skills of PR to assure that its services are well defined, understood, used, and supported.

Four Basic Steps. There are four basic steps in public relations: research, planning, communication, and evaluation. These are steps in a process that can be applied to any type and size of library. They are functions of good management.

Research. The research effort involves identifying the library's publics and their attitudes toward the library. These publics may include the staff, governing board, volunteer or friends group, users and nonusers, and booksellers or other suppliers. Research should begin inside the library to determine how the staff and trustees view the library, how well they understand its goals and policies, what they see as its major strengths and weaknesses, and how they feel about their relationship with the library administration. The evaluation of the library should also include an objective view of its physical appearance, from the cold realities of access, signage, and lighting to the warmer considerations of welcoming comfort and good cheer.

Beyond the library, research involves gathering all available demographic information about the community: age, income, ethnic background, occupation, religion, interests, community groups, and whatever other formal or informal data are available. Original research should also be undertaken to discern attitudes toward the library and information needs. Librarians have used many survey techniques to gather such information, among them mail questionnaires and telephone surveys of population samples and personal contact with and responses from clubs, churches, and other local institutions. The goal is constant sensitivity to public opinion.

Planning. The planning stage should make the PR process an integral part of the total library program. There should be a written PR plan with short- and long-range goals, a clear idea of the specific publics to be reached, a timetable and reporting schedule, lists of resources such as printing facilities, artists, and volunteers, a staffing plan, and a budget. Although most libraries are not in a position to afford the large public relations staff employed by major businesses, PR does require special expertise, and it cannot be done well without sufficient funding.

In 1983 Frank Wylie, Director of Public Affairs at California State University and former President of the Public Relations Society of America, completed a national survey of library PR programs. The results were presented to the Public Relations Section of ALA's Library Administration and Management Association at the 1983 ALA Conference. The national sample included 34 percent academic libraries and 66 percent public libraries. Of all libraries surveyed, 58 percent had PR programs, but only 19 percent claimed to have formal PR plans. Wylie commented,

> We find this a rather sad commentary on the state of public relations activities in American libraries, and hope that librarians will effect a change as quickly as possible. Regardless of the size of your library, or the semi-existence of a budget, librarians should insist on, and participate in, the development of a formal plan for the public relations program. You need the organization and focus that a plan can contribute. You also need to reassess your institutional mission and establish priorities and objectives for the library before you begin to develop a PR program to help you achieve those objectives. This means the establishment of priorities for both publics and projects, and the establishment of specific goals and deadlines.

Communication. The communication element of the public relations process comprises the outreach, programming, and publicity for which the research and planning prepared. The possibilities for effective communications are great, as evidenced by the many success stories reported by libraries in the literature.

One of the first steps toward communication for the library is building a media or press list of all available publications and broadcast channels, including daily and weekly newspapers, radio and television stations, community group newsletters, school newspapers, and any other media that may reach the particular target audience. Personal contact with the people on the press list is especially important. Libraries are eligible for free public service advertising time on radio and television stations, but must compete with many other community agencies and services.

Beyond mass media, there are many other publicity tools regularly used by libraries, including newsletters (internal and external), annual reports, posters, booklists and bibliographies, exhibits and displays, special programs, audiovisual presentations, speakers bureaus, and more. The Plainedge Public Li-

brary (Massapequa, N.Y.) prepares special newsletters for expectant parents and senior citizens as well as its regular newsletter that goes by bulk mail to every household in the city; the library also has a written public relations policy approved by its board of directors. The Elmer Holmes Bobst Library at New York University introduced its new online catalogue with a mascot, "Bob Cat," who appeared on posters, T-shirts, and bookbags; it was even chosen to represent the NYU varsity basketball team. On parents' night the D. C. Everest High School Library in Schofield, Wisconsin, focused on nostalgia, featuring old football films, yearbooks, and other memorabilia. It also publishes a quarterly *I.M.C. Memo* to inform faculty and others about library activities, and distributed a special issue on parents and reading throughout the community. The Northwest Regional Library System in Panama City, Florida, reaches out to potential adult users with a series of special radio messages, including a bilingual 30-minute weekly program to help Vietnamese residents adapt to life in the United States.

Evaluation. This final step of the PR process requires that the public relations staff determine whether the communications program meets its stated objectives. One objective may have been media coverage, and a tally on how often radio and television stations carried the library messages along with a description of their audience is proof of achievement. Other means to evaluate a specific aspect of the PR program might include clips of newspaper coverage, use of evaluation forms at programs, or surveys in the library to determine how users found out about various services. It may be difficult to prove a direct cause-and-effect relationship between a communications program and increased library usage, but an attempt should be made to measure the impact of the public relations investment.

National Programs. There is a growing national effort to increase citizen use and support of libraries. Since 1945 the Children's Book Council has created posters and other promotional materials for Children's Book Week, observed each year since 1919. In 1958 National Library Week (NLW) was initiated by publishers and librarians and remains the first and only national promotion program to increase use and support of libraries. The NLW program mobilized prominent citizens and librarians at the national and local levels to focus public and media attention on libraries. Workshops, handbooks, promotional materials, and national public relations support have made NLW a means to inform the public about library services, as well as an important public relations teaching tool for the profession.

ALA. In 1975 the American Library Association's Public Information Office (PIO) assumed responsibility for National Library Week. Although long recognized as the national voice for libraries, the ALA had not previously been active in generating national media coverage. Both need and media interest were great, and the first full-fledged ALA effort—the 1975 NLW campaign—was awarded the Silver Anvil by the Public Relations Society of America and the Golden Trumpet by the Chicago Publicity Club.

ALA has continued to produce posters and other graphic materials that generate income for support of year-round PR efforts. It places radio and television

gershwin
garbo
and poe
to go

at your library

READ

Bill Cosby
and friends
for America's
Libraries

ALA

*ALA celebrity poster
promoting libraries and
reading.*

public service announcements with the networks, feature stories and print public service ads in national magazines, wire service stories, and other national publicity. In 1976 ALA also began producing a weekly syndicated book review column distributed by Newspaper Enterprise Association to more than 700 subscribing newspapers nationwide. Attached to each column is a survey of "What Americans Are Reading," compiled from tabulations of most-requested books submitted by 150 participating libraries.

In 1981 ALA launched a special marketing campaign "Call Your Library" to increase public awareness of telephone information services provided by public libraries. Entertainer Bob Newhart served as spokesperson for the campaign, which was cosponsored by the Chief Officers of State Library Agencies and included radio and TV spots, print ads, posters, and a marketing kit for local libraries. On many late evenings beginning in 1981, Johnny Carson used real questions asked of libraries on the "Tonight Show," with a positive plug for library information services. The "Call Your Library" campaign generated a second Silver Anvil for ALA from the Public Relations Society of America.

ALA/PIO's quarterly tabloid, *Openers,* "America's Library Newspaper," debuted in 1981. Combining news of books, the arts, and popular culture, *Openers* is available to libraries in bulk for distribution in local communities; by 1985 circulation had reached 228,000.

ALA's leadership in public relations received a great boost when Elizabeth W. Stone, ALA president in 1981–82, made marketing and public relations her

major program emphasis. She sponsored a video teleconference on marketing that reached more than 50 sites from ALA's Midwinter Meeting, successfully lobbied the U.S. Postal Service for a commemorative stamp honoring America's libraries, introduced a national library symbol that has since received approval from the Federal Highway Administration for use on the nation's highways, and collected and published *68 Great Ideas,* a book of promotion ideas for all types of libraries.

As ALA's public relations campaign has grown, an increasing number of celebrities have donated their fame to promote reading and library service. The ALA posters plus public service radio, television, and print ads have featured Bill Cosby, Bette Midler, Sting, Goldie Hawn, Mikhail Baryshnikov, Miss Piggy, George Burns, and others.

In recent years librarians have also put PR and marketing skills to work to raise funds for libraries. In 1983–84 ALA President Brooke E. Sheldon focused her President's Program on library fundraising. In 1983 the Gale Research Company began contributing a $2,500 annual award to recognize the most creative and successful library development projects.

The Public Relations Section of the Library Administration and Management Association, a Division of ALA, provides further national leadership in public relations. The 1,200-member section engages PR specialists from libraries across the country who work together to produce active and effective continuing education programs, workshops, and publications. Their annual "PR Swap 'n' Shop" has become one of the best-attended ALA conference programs and offers librarians a chance to sample promotional materials from libraries across the country and get expert counseling on PR matters. The Public Relations Section administers the John Cotton Dana Library Public Relations Awards.

Other Activities. The Library of Congress Center for the Book was established in 1977. Introducing the new Center, Librarian of Congress Daniel J. Boorstin said, "It is to organize, focus, and dramatize our nation's interest and attention on the book, to marshall the nation's support—spiritual, physical, and fiscal—for the book." Among its many successful programs, the Center for the Book established "Read More About It," a joint endeavor of the Library of Congress and CBS Television that has recruited more than 70 stars of major prime-time CBS specials to present 30-second messages promoting books and reading on their shows. The Center was also responsible for "Books Make a Difference," another promotion effort that built on interviews with more than 300 famous and not-so-famous Americans about the books that played a role in shaping their lives.

At the grass roots, thousands of citizen delegates participating in the state pre-White House Conferences in 1978 and 1979 asked libraries to do a better job of informing the public of their services. Almost every state conference produced a resolution similar to this one from Ohio:

Develop an aggressive, consistent, and better organized marketing, advertising, and public relations program using all available media and other agencies to increase public awareness of library and information services and their value to daily life, destroy stigmas, and improve the image of all libraries.

At the White House Conference on Library and Information Services held in Washington, D.C., November 1979, the delegates adopted as one of their major resolutions a statement on public awareness calling for "an aggressive, comprehensive national public awareness campaign coordinated at the federal level." Some of their specific recommendations, such as development of a national library symbol, have since been accomplished, but in 1985, a group of citizen and librarian activists began a campaign for a second White House Conference on Libraries projected for 1989.

Citizen support of libraries is the concern of another U.S. national group, Friends of Libraries U.S.A. (FOLUSA), founded in 1980. With more than 1,000 individual and organization members, FOLUSA works to develop and support local Friends of Library groups throughout the country.

Other Countries. U.S. libraries were pioneers in library public relations, but some of the same techniques have been used effectively elsewhere. National Library Weeks have been observed in the United Kingdom, Denmark, Australia, New Zealand, and Canada, though they are usually conducted on a more occasional basis than in the U.S. In the late 1970s, the Australian Library Promotion Council adapted the U.S. National Library Week graphics for its own week. Children's Book Week is a tradition known in the U.K. and Scandinavia. In Sweden the Library Service Ltd., started in 1951, produces a great variety of public relations materials such as posters, pamphlets, and booklists. Dutch libraries have an outstanding array of well-designed graphic materials, including a national library logo.

In connection with the 1985 conference of the International Federation of Library Associations and Institutions held in Chicago, ALA and the Department of Library Science at Northern Illinois University sponsored an International Library Poster competition that generated more than 100 entries from 60 libraries and library associations in 22 countries. The judges selected posters from the Goethe Institute in London and the Australian Library Promotion Council as top winners. The overall response to the call for posters suggests a growing interest in library promotion worldwide.

How will librarians meet the growing demand for public relations programs? More and more library schools are offering seminars and short courses in public relations. Many include PR in a general library management course, and there are many programs and workshops offered at ALA Conferences and state and regional library association meetings.

A planned communication program is a necessity for passing a bond issue, competing effectively for funds, and generating the support needed to keep the library doors open and service flowing. Libraries will have a future as primary information resources if librarians use public relations principles and techniques to find political allies and build positive public opinion. It may well be a matter of survival. Abraham Lincoln said, "With public sentiment nothing can fail; without it nothing can succeed." Lee Brawner, director of the Metropolitan Library System in Oklahoma City, observed, "People are usually down on what they ain't up on!"

REFERENCES

Marian Edsall, *Library Promotion Handbook* (1980), a practical and comprehensive guide to library public relations.
Philip Kotler, *Marketing for Nonprofit Organizations,* 2nd edition (1982), the definitive text on marketing for nonprofit organizations.
Kathleen Rummel and Esther Perica, editors, *Persuasive Public Relations for Libraries* (1983), a collection of articles on many aspects of library public relations by experts in the field.
American Library Association Public Information Office, *Publicity Book* (annual), a complete and inexpensive primer on the latest library PR ideas and opportunities.

PEGGY BARBER

Puerto Rico

Puerto Rico, a self-governing commonwealth in association with the United States since 1952, lies in the Caribbean Sea and is bounded by the Atlantic Ocean on the north and east, the Lesser Antilles on the south, and the Dominican Republic on the west. Population (1984 est.) 3,325,000; area (including the islands of Culebra and Vieques) 8,958 sq.km. Official languages are Spanish and English.

History. The first library in Puerto Rico was founded by Bishop Alonso Manso in 1512 at Caparra. During the Dutch attack on San Juan in 1625, the two existing libraries—the collection at the Dominican Monastery and the private collection of Bishop Bernardo de Balbuena—were destroyed. In the 1830s the San Juan Conciliar Seminary Library opened and later, in 1899, merged with the Bar Association Library. In 1843 La Real Sociedad Económica de Amigos del País (The Royal Society of Friends of the Island), with the donation of a book collection owned by Rufo Manuel Fernández, founded a public library; by 1885 that collection had increased to 13,000 volumes, and in 1876 a cultural group, Ateneo Puertorriqueño, took over the library. Between 1872 and 1894, the last years of Spanish rule, libraries were set up in several municipalities, including Ponce and Mayaguez. More public libraries were established following the U.S. military occupation in 1898, and in 1917 Governor Arthur Yager obtained a grant from Andrew Carnegie to establish the Carnegie Library. In that year the Department of Education was given full control of libraries, and in subsequent years more libraries, both public and private, were established.

National Library. The Biblioteca General de Puerto Rico (General Library of Puerto Rico), established in the 1970s in the General Archives building and operated by the Institute of Puerto Rican Culture, housed 75,000 books in the mid-1980s. It emphasizes book collection and preservation.

Academic Libraries. The University of Puerto Rico is the public university and comprises 11 campuses scattered on the island. Each campus has at least one library. The main library is the José M. Lázaro on the Río Piedras Campus, founded in 1905. This library held 3,800,000 books and printed documents and 64,700 bound volumes of periodicals and subscriptions in the mid-1980s. Because there is no

Puerto Rico Public Library Services

Patrons at the Villalba Public Library in Puerto Rico.

Arecibo Technological College, on the northwest coast, holds 50,900 books, 10,500 periodical volumes, 550 current periodical subscriptions, and 3,000 microforms. There are smaller libraries in regional colleges elsewhere in Puerto Rico.

The private universities have also developed extensive library collections. The Interamerican University comprises 13 campuses in San Juan, San Germán, Bayamón, Aguadilla, Arecibo, Barranquitas, Fajardo, Guayama, Ponce, and Ft. Buchanan, each with its own library and learning resource center. Holdings for Regional Colleges totaled 200,000 volumes in 1984. The main libraries are in the Metropolitan Campus with holdings of 96,700 books, 1,944 current periodicals, 16,700 bound periodical volumes, 336,100 microforms, and 4,200 audiovisual materials, and the San Germán Campus with holdings of 107,800 volumes, 1,124 periodicals, and 15,200 audiovisual materials.

The University of the Sacred Heart in Santurce has a library of 91,100 volumes, 649 periodicals, and 67,500 audiovisual materials. The Encarnación Valdés Library of the Catholic University in Ponce held 215,000 books, 1,600 periodicals, and 17,700 bound periodicals in 1983. That library serves the community also, particularly high school students from nearby towns. The Central University in Bayamón holds 51,353 books and 786 periodicals.

There are a number of private colleges in various parts of the island with small but developing library collections.

Public Libraries. The Public Libraries System is a division of the Educational Extension Area of the Commonwealth Department of Education. The System includes 73 public libraries in the municipalities, 7 bookmobiles to serve isolated and rural areas, 24 small libraries in public housing projects, and 16 in correctional institutions. It also administers the Regional Library for the Blind and Physically Handicapped located in San Juan. Some special projects of the program are: interlibrary cooperation with academic libraries, services to the elderly and to persons of limited English-speaking ability, and a community information referral center.

School Libraries. The Public School Libraries Program serves 431,655 students. All high schools have libraries, as do 89 percent of all junior high schools and 47 percent of elementary schools. Libraries include audiovisual and microform materials.

Special Libraries. The Caribbean Regional Library, housed in the José M. Lázaro Library, has a collection of more than 106,000 volumes, 4,463 periodical volumes, and 3,200 microforms to meet the needs of researchers, scholars, and users of Caribbean

large public library in the area, this library serves the general community.

The Library System of the Río Piedras Campus includes 20 libraries and collections. The special collections are the Puerto Rican collection, the Zenobia and Juan Ramón Jiménez collection, the music collection, maps and documents, the art collection, and the Library for the Blind. Libraries include collections in the graduate schools of Library Science, Natural Sciences, Public Administration, Planning, Communications, Social Work, Education, Business Administration, and General Studies. Other libraries on the campus are in the Law School (124,000 volumes) and the School of Architecture (19,000 volumes and 76,000 slides).

Libraries in other main campuses of the University of Puerto Rico include the Mayaguez Campus (176,000 books and 6,265 bound periodicals) and the Medical Sciences Campus (110,800 volumes and 1,200 subscriptions to medical journals). The Humacao University College Library in the east holds almost 72,000 volumes and 760 current periodicals. The Cayey University College, in the center of the island, holds 96,000 volumes and 1,255 periodicals as well as audiovisual materials.

Under the Regional Colleges Administration, the Ponce University College, in the south, holds 33,400 volumes, 261 periodicals, and 18,322 audiovisual materials; the Library of the Bayamón Technological College, west of San Juan, holds 41,500 volumes and 547 periodicals; and the Library of the

Libraries in Puerto Rico (1984)

Type	Administrative units	Service points	Volumes in collections	Annual expenditures (dollar)	Population served	Professional staff	Total staff
National	1	1	75,000	100,840	3,000	7	18
Academic	31	39	8,643,170	14,444,734	200,000	231	655
Public	121	121	714,621	2,770,159	3,200,000	5	125
School	722	722	--	--	692,923	--	800
Special	4	4	251,939	426,659	4,800	9	34

resources. The Legislative Library, in the Capitol, serves mainly legislators and researchers. Holdings include 50,000 books and 494 periodicals. It uses a computerized law retrieval system and computerized bibliographic utility services. The Supreme Court Library holds more than 79,200 books and 494 periodicals.

The Agricultural Experiment Station Library is the collection for agricultural research. Holdings include 16,600 books, 20,435 bound periodical volumes, and 290,800 scientific documents.

The Profession. The Puerto Rico Librarians Society (Sociedad de Bibliotecarios de Puerto Rico) was founded in 1961. A member of the International Federation of Library Associations (IFLA), it cooperates closely with the Association of Caribbean University, Research and Institutional Libraries (ACURIL). The Society publishes a journal and a newsletter. The Graduate School of Library Science on the Rio Piedras Campus of the University of Puerto Rico awards the M.L.S. The Department of Public Instruction awards a certificate of Teacher-Librarian to school teachers.

ONEIDA R. ORTIZ; RAFAEL R. DELGADO

Putnam, Herbert

(1861–1955)

George Herbert Putnam, Librarian of the Minneapolis Athenaeum (1884–87), the Minneapolis Public Library (1887–91), the Boston Public Library (1895–99), and Librarian of Congress (1899–1939), was a leading figure in the American library movement—especially during the first half of his 40-year term as Librarian of Congress. He was the first experienced librarian to hold the post of Librarian of Congress. His major contribution to the LC came directly from this experience: he linked firmly the policies of the LC with the broader interests of American librarianship. To do so he sought and obtained the support of the Congress, professional librarians, and especially the American Library Association and the American scholarly community. As a result, Putnam, more than any other Librarian of Congress, established and defined the LC's pattern of national library services to its major constituencies—the Congress, the nation's libraries, and the world of scholarship.

Putnam was born in New York City on September 20, 1861, the tenth child of Victorine Putnam and George Palmer Putnam, the founder of the Putnam publishing house. Herbert attended private schools and received his B.A. from Harvard in 1883, graduating magna cum laude. The next year he attended Columbia University Law School but was soon enticed by friends to Minneapolis as the head of the library at the Minneapolis Athenaeum. While successfully responding to the problems facing that institution, he pursued his legal studies and was admitted to the Minnesota bar. In 1887 he became Librarian of the new Minneapolis Public Library, which had absorbed the Athenaeum. After vigorously leading the Minneapolis Public Library through its fledgling years, Putnam resigned in late 1891 and returned with his family to Massachusetts to be near his ailing mother. He practiced law until he was persuaded to return to librarianship—as Superintendent of the Boston Public Library, the nation's largest public library.

He assumed those duties in February 1895.

Putnam's leadership abilities and his new position quickly involved him in the American Library Association. From November 16 to December 7, 1896, the Congressional Joint Committee on the Library held hearings on the "condition" of the Library of Congress on the eve of its move into its new building, and Putnam was one of the ALA witnesses.

The Librarian of Congress at the time, Ainsworth Rand Spofford, had served for more than 30 years and was personally responsible for the rapid growth of the Library into an institution of national significance. The ALA sent six witnesses to the hearings. Putnam and Melvil Dewey dominated, each advocating an expanded national role for the Library of Congress—a role that extended far beyond Spofford's basic concept or his accomplishments. The two library leaders offered many specific suggestions for national library service.

The 1896 hearings marked a turning point in the relations between the Library of Congress and the American library movement. For the first time ALA offered its advice to Congress, albeit cautiously, about the purpose and functions of the Library of Congress. Moreover, Congress listened; the testimony at the hearings, along with a report filed by Spofford on January 18, 1897, were major influences on the reorganization of the Library that was contained in the legislative appropriations act for fiscal year 1898, approved by President Grover Cleveland on February 19, ·1897. The restructuring and expansion of the Library simply could not wait for the report on the hearing held by the Joint Committee on the Library. Because the changes were part of the appropriations act, they became effective July 1, 1897, the beginning of the new fiscal year. On June 30, 1897, President William McKinley nominated his friend John Russell Young, a journalist and former diplomat, to be Librarian of Congress. The Senate confirmed the nomination on the same day, and Young was sworn in on July 1, the day the reorganization became effective.

Young did a remarkable job in the year and a half that he served as Librarian. After presiding over the move from the Capitol into the new building, which opened to great public acclaim on November 1, 1897, he concerned himself with organizational matters and new appointments. The new law authorized an increase in the staff of the Library proper from 42 to 108; Young was flooded with applications, and he chose well. Never a healthy man, Young did not recover from two severe falls during the winter of 1898–99, and he died on January 17, 1899. The newspapers were immediately filled with speculation regarding his successor. This time the ALA, through Richard R. Bowker and William Coolidge Lane, ALA President and Librarian of Harvard University, took the lead. Two of Young's appointees, Thorvald Solberg and J. C. M. Hanson, worked closely with the librarians. On January 23, less than a week after Young's death, Lane wrote a letter, printed in the *Library Journal,* to President McKinley urging the appointment of an experienced library administrator as the next Librarian of Congress since that library—as the national library—should "stand at the head of American libraries as the best organized and the best equipped of all."

ALA

Herbert Putnam

Within the next few days, the ALA leaders settled on Herbert Putnam as their candidate. The story of how Putnam was finally nominated is complicated, but there is no doubt that without the intervention of the ALA he would not have become Librarian. William Coolidge Lane not only persuaded President McKinley; it appears that in the end he also persuaded Putnam. On March 13, 1899, during the congressional recess, McKinley appointed Herbert Putnam to be the eighth Librarian of Congress. He took the oath of office on April 5 and was confirmed by the U.S. Senate, somewhat after the fact, on December 12.

With Putnam's appointment, the relationship between the LC and the ALA truly entered a new era. Putnam was not only a librarian's librarian but also an association spokesman. Twice he served as ALA President: from January to August, 1898, when he completed the unexpired term of the late Justin Winsor, and again in 1903–04. From 1900 to 1905, the critical years of his administration, he served on the ALA Council.

As Librarian of Congress Putnam moved quickly to expand the LC into the type of national library put forward in his 1896 testimony before the Joint Committee on the Library. He initiated a new classification scheme, the sale and distribution of printed catalogue cards, interlibrary loan, and a national union catalogue. In an appendix to his annual report of 1901, he described the organization and collection of the LC in a "manual" that came to be regarded as a model for libraries. Other Putnam actions during the first two decades of the 20th century included obtaining the support of President Theodore Roosevelt for the expansion of the LC's activities, perhaps most dramatically through an executive order transferring presidential and other state papers to the LC; revision of the 1870 coypright law, begun in 1905 and completed in 1909; the acquisiton, in 1907, of collections of Russian and Japanese books, thereby establishing the foundation of the LC's Slavic and Oriental collections; and direction of the ALA's Library War Service Committee (1917–19), which was a model of efficiency and a triumph of American librarianship.

During the first half of Putnam's administration, lasting roughly from 1899 through World War I, the Librarian had, by and large, the full support of professional librarians and the ALA. The next 20 years were not so harmonious, and the LC and the American library movement drifted apart.

One reason was that Putnam gave increasing attention to matters that did not directly concern the American library community. A separate Legislative Reference Service was created in 1914. In 1921 the Declaration of Independence and the Constitution of the United States were transferred from the State Department to the LC, enhancing the image of the Library of Congress as a symbol of American democracy. In the mid-1920s, through Putnam's efforts, the LC became a national patron of the arts; a gift from Elizabeth Sprague Coolidge provided an auditorium for the performance of chamber music, and a generous endowment from Mrs. Coolidge shortly thereafter led to the creation in 1925 of the Library of Congress Trust Fund Board, an instrument that enabled the LC, for the first time, to accept, hold, and invest gifts and bequests.

Furthermore, Putnam's personal interest in library cooperation and related technical matters was replaced with an increasing concern for the "interpretation" of the collections. Putnam had always viewed the use of the LC's collections as the prime object of the administration; in the 1896 hearings, for example, he described the national library as, ideally, the library "which stands foremost as a model and example of assisting forward the work of scholarship in the United States." After the establishment of the Library of Congress Trust Fund Board, he began to obtain private funds to support "chairs" and consultantships for subject specialists who could aid scholars in their use of the collections.

In sum, as Putnam focused on other activities, his interst in the role of the LC as a leader among American libraries lessened. For example, in 1935, in a letter to ALA Secretary Carl H. Milam, the Librarian flatly rejected the notion of locating a federal library bureau in the Library of Congress, contending that the functions of such an agency "would tend to confuse and impede the service to learning which should be the primary duty of our National Library." In Putnam's opinion, the bureau instead "should be associated with one of the executive departments of the government."

Putnam's authoritarian style presented further difficulties. He was a stern administrator, both venerated and feared. Apparently no associate ever called him by his first name, and it appears that there was no one, either inside or outside the LC, who was able to influence him to any significant degree.

By the late 1930s the LC was suffering from administrative stagnation, intensified by low staff morale and operational problems such as a large cataloguing backlog. These problems were compounded by Putnam's refusal, or inability, to delegate responsibility. By 1939 there were 35 divisions, each reporting directly to the Librarian, compared to the 16 listed in his 1901 annual report. Even Putnam, with all his gifts, could not successfully oversee 35 diverse units and 1,100 employees. In the late 1930s there were many librarians and politicians who were waiting for Putnam to decide to retire. Apparently even President Franklin D. Roosevelt chose to wait.

Such difficulties aside, Putnam was enormously respected by scholars and librarians alike. When he did retire to become, on October 1, 1939, Librarian Emeritus of Congress, his friends in the American Library Association paid him tribute as "dean of our profession" who had led LC to "its present proud position as the world's largest bibliographical institution." He continued to contribute to the LC, keeping regular office hours, for the next 15 years. He died at Woods Hole, Massachusetts, on August 14, 1955. Putnam wrote no memoirs; his 40 annual reports between 1899 and 1939 serve as the record of his achievements at the Library of Congress.

REFERENCES
John Y. Cole, "Herbert Putnam and the National Library," *Milestones to the Present: Papers from Library History Seminar V* (1978).
John Y. Cole, "Putnam, George Herbert," *Dictionary of America Library Biography* (1978).
Wayne A. Wiegand, "Herbert Putnam's Appointment as Librarian of Congress," *Library Quarterly* 49 (July 1979).
JOHN Y. COLE

Qatar

Qatar, an independent emirate, juts out from the Arabian Peninsula into the Persian Gulf. The Gulf lies to the west, north, and east; the United Arab Emirates and Saudi Arabia lie to the south. Population (1984 est.) 276,000; area 11,400 sq.km. The official language is Arabic.

National and Public Library Services. The National Library in the capital city of Doha also functions as a public library. All Qataris have access to the entire collection of the National Library. Supervised by the Ministry of Education, it was founded in the early 1960s as a merger of two former libraries: the Public Library (founded in 1956) and the Educational Library (1954). The Library preserves the Qatari heritage. Its 22-year history was published in Arabic in 1985.

The National Library of Qatar issues the annual *Bibliography of Books and Pamphlets Published in Qatar* (since 1970). The Library also has a center for exchange of publications. Its book collection totals some 56,521 volumes in Arabic, 9,396 volumes in English, and approximately 1,300 Arabic and Persian manuscripts. It published a catalogue of illustration manuscripts on microfilm, 1962-83.

Public libraries were established as branches of the National Library, following the Egyptian model. The first was opened in Khour in 1979 (more than 12,000 volumes) and the second in al- Shamaal Town in 1979 (some 4,000 volumes). There were six public library branches in 1985.

Academic Libraries. The University of Qatar, founded in 1973 as the College of Education, had some 5,200 students in 1985 (two-thirds of whom were women who attended in a separate building on a Women's Campus). Separate library buildings on the Men's and Women's Campuses held 160,000 monographs, 1,700 current periodical titles, and 14,000 units of microfiche in 1985. Monographs were acquired at the rate of 20,000 a year.

The University Libraries provide retrieval service through DIALOG, interlibrary loan with other libraries of the region, and access to the British Library Lending Service. There were four Research Centers.

School Libraries. The Ministry of Education has embarked on a plan for establishing and developing school libraries. There are 122 libraries in Qatari schools, the largest among them being in the secondary schools, the Religious Institute, and the Institute of Administration. All school libraries in Qatar are staffed with librarians recruited from other Arab countries.

Special Libraries. Government departments and ministries are planning to introduce library services to their officials. The Ministry of Education has established an Educational Documentation Center to serve administrators, teachers, and students and to aid in planning and issuing local textbooks. The British Council Library owns some 6,400 volumes.

MOHAMED M. EL HADI*

University of Qatar

University of Qatar at Doha, established in 1973. It has two campuses—one for men (above), one for women.

University of Qatar

Reading room, Men's Library, the University of Qatar.

Libraries in Qatar (1982)

Type	Administrative units	Service points	Volumes in collections	Annual expenditures (riyal)	Population served[a]	Professional staff	Total staff
National[b]	1	--	--	--	4,378	--	--
Academic[b]	2	--	98,000	--	3,000	--	--
Public[b]	6	--	--	--	1,138	--	--
School	122	--	214,000	--	13,608	--	--

[a]Registered borrowers.
[b]1981 data.

Source: Unesco, *Statistical Yearbook*, 1984.

Rajwade, Vishwanath Kashinath
(1863–1926)

Vishwanath Kashinath Rajwade is remembered principally for his monumental work in the collection, preservation, editing, and publication of primary historical source material on the history of the Marathas.

He was born June 24, 1863, in a Chitpavan Brahmin family of Varsai, a village in the Kolaba district of Maharashtra State. He studied at Elphinstone College, Bombay, and Deccan College, Pune (B.A., 1890, in history). After three years of schoolteaching, he decided to devote himself entirely to the pursuit of knowledge. At college he had read widely in European history, economics, political science, ethics, theology, logic, metaphysics, botany, and other fields, and he was influenced by the writings of Plato, Hegel, and Comte. He mastered English and acquired a working knowledge of French and Persian. But he remained a staunch protagonist of the Marathi language. He started a periodical called *Bhashantar* ("Translation") in 1894, and within a period of 37 months, Marathi translations of 23 classics, including some works of Plato and Montesquieu, had been published in the journal.

His interests were varied. He wrote on history, linguistics, grammar, etymology, philosophy, sociology, politics, anthropology, and Sanskrit and Marathi literature. His books number about 76 and his articles 343. His name, however, will ever be remembered for his work on the history of the Marathas, which embraced the source material published in 26 volumes (4 after his death) in a famous series, *Marathyanchya Itihasachi Sadhane.* The analytical introductions to volumes 1, 3, 4, 5, and 8 of this series could stand as independent monographs. His introductions to *Mahikavatichi Bakhar* and *Radha Madhav Vilas Champu* deserve special attention. An earnest collector of source material, he was his own publisher. He sought no help from government or patron.

He helped revolutionize historical methodology. According to him history should encompass social, economic, political, and intellectual activities of man irrespective of time and space. Rajwade's broad concept of history, its scope, and arrangement was comparable to that of Leopold von Ranke (1795–1886), who has been called the father of modern historical methodology. Rajwade founded the Bharat Itihas Samshodhak Mandal (1910) for promoting historical research.

He was the first to decipher the secret script of Mahanubhav literature. He was also the first to edit and publish the *Jnaneshwari,* a premier work in Marathi literature.

A contemporary historian of India, Sir Jadunath Sarkar, called Rajwade "the greatest discoverer, the life-long searcher, the exclusive devotee without a second love, the most fruitful collector of the raw materials of Maratha history, and at the same time their most painstaking editor, and their most speedy and prolific publisher" (*House of Shivaji,* p. 276).

Rajwade died on December 31, 1926, at Dhule in Khandesh (Maharashtra). The people of Dhule founded a historical research institute bearing his name—Rajwade Samshodhan Mandir.

REFERENCES
Jadunath Sarkar, "The Historian Rajwade," in *House of Shivaji,* 3d edition (Calcutta, 1955).
S. P. Sen, editor, "Vishwanath Kashinath Rajwade," *Historians and Historiography of Modern India* (Calcutta, 1973).

A. R. KULKARNI

Ranganathan, Shiyali Ramamrita
(1892–1972)

The author of *Colon Classification,* of many books and papers on classification, and of the Five Laws of Library Science, Ranganathan stands as one of the immortals of library science.

Ranganathan was born on August 9, 1892, into the Brahman community at Shiyali in the Tanjur District of Madras State. He was educated at Sabhanayaka Mudaliar's Hindu High School, Shiyali, from 1897 to 1908 and at Madras Christian College, where he majored in mathematics, from 1909 to 1916. He took a teaching diploma at the Teachers' College, Saidapet, Madras, in 1917 and became Assistant Lecturer in Mathematics at Government College (later Presidency College), Bangalore. In 1921 he was appointed Assistant Professor of Mathematics there.

In 1924 Ranganathan began a new career when he was appointed the first Librarian of the University of Madras. He was required to study for his new profession in Britain and went to University College, London, where he met and was considerably influenced by W. C. Berwick Sayers. During his two years in Britain (1924–25) he visited about 100 libraries and was confirmed in his new vocation. He received an Honours Certificate from the School of Librarianship at University College in 1925 and was elected a Fellow of the (British) Library Association in 1930.

He remained Librarian of the University of Madras until 1944, later becoming University Librarian and Professor of Library Science at Banaras Hindu University (1945–47), Professor of Library Science at the University of Delhi (1947–54), and Visiting Professor of Library Science at Vikram University, Ujjain (1957–59). He was appointed Honorary Professor and Head of the Documentation Research and Training Centre, Bangalore, which he had founded under the auspices of the Indian Statistical Institute, in 1962; in 1965 the Indian government appointed him National Research Professor in Library Science.

Contributions. Ranganathan will almost certainly be best remembered by librarians for his *Colon Classification;* had he achieved nothing else, this pioneer faceted classification would have been sufficient to place him among the giants of librarianship. The classification is hardly used outside India, though at least two quite different British libraries (at Metal Box Limited and Christ's College, Cambridge) have used it, but its influence has been tremendous: on successive editions of the Dewey Decimal classification, the Universal Decimal Classification, and, more recently, the Bliss Bibliographic Classification; on many specialist classifications; on various indexing methods; and on bibliographies such as *The British National Bibliography.* Chain indexing, developed by Ranganathan as a demonstration of the "symbiosis" between classification and subject indexing and as a technique for ensuring that aspects of a subject separated by a classification scheme are collocated in the index, is a method of subject indexing widely used in British libraries.

Apart from the *Colon Classification,* Ranganathan wrote many books and papers on classification, ranging from the introductory *Elements of Library Classification* to the monumental *Prolegomena to Library Classification.* Douglas Foskett has said that "in his writings, Ranganathan sometimes gave the impression that he was difficult or abstruse." To some extent this is true, but the *Elements* is not difficult to master, and the *Prolegomena* will repay considerable effort on the part of the reader.

But classification was only one of Ranganathan's interests, if a major one. His contributions to cataloguing include codes of rules for dictionary and classified catalogues, *Theory of Library Catalogue,* and a stimulating comparative study of catalogue codes, *Heading and Canons,* which K. G. B. Bakewell rates second only to Lubetzky's *Cataloguing Rules and Principles* as the outstanding contribution to cataloguing thought in this century. As S. S. Agraval points out, Ranganathan's influence on the *Anglo-American Cataloging Rules* of 1967 was not inconsiderable, his canons of "sought heading" and "ascertainability" being particularly relevant.

Before any of these works came his analytical study of the purpose of libraries, resulting in the Five Laws of Library Science that formed the basis of his first published books on librarianship: books are for use; every book its reader; every reader his book; save the time of the reader; a library is a growing organism. Although many today would substitute "documents" or "library materials" for "books" (and say "every reader his/her document"), these laws are as valid today as they were when first enunciated. They seem—and are—simple, but they remain fundamental objectives of the library profession; Pauline Atherton said, "these words stir students to think of and believe in library *service* above library *work* as their life goal."

Some of Ranganathan's works were specifically concerned with the development of libraries in India. Following a request from the Punjab Library Association, he produced a pamphlet in 1944 on the postwar reconstruction of libraries in India, in which he proposed a national library network of national, state, university, public, and school libraries. This was followed in 1950 by a more detailed work, *Library Development Plan,* outlining a 30-year program. Library development in India was considerably influenced by these two publications, which were followed by library development plans and draft legislation for other Indian states.

There is scarcely an area of librarianship to which Ranganathan did not turn his attention: library management, school and college libraries, the broader aspects of libraries and education, book selection, reference service, and bibliography. In addition to his own writings, he edited many works and shared with others in the authorship of more books and papers. He founded *Annals of Library Science* in 1956 and *Library Science with a Slant to Documentation* in 1965 and edited both journals until they had become firmly established. Jesse Shera said, "That one cannot properly judge the work of S. R. Ranganathan without reference to the totality of librarianship is a tribute to the breadth and depth of his contribution to the profession."

International Library Scene. V. V. Giri, then Governor of Mysore and later President of India, described Ranganathan as "the father of library science in India" when presenting him with a copy of the Ranganathan Festschrift at Bangalore on December 18, 1965. This was an apt description, for Ranganathan had done more than anyone to further library development in India, but his work transcended national barriers. As Girja Kumar said, "He was universal because his work was not confined to any geographical boundary."

H. Coblans has written about Ranganathan's contributions to international librarianship: his influence on the development of the United Nations Library; his foundation of the International Federation for Documentation (FID) Committee on General Classification and his work as Secretary and Chairman of this committee; and his work for Unesco, the International Federation of Library Associations, and the International Organization for Standardization. His fervent belief in international standardization is well known.

Offices and Honors. Ranganathan had been a librarian for only four years when he was elected the first Secretary of the Madras Library Association, which he had founded in 1928; he held that office for 25 years. Such was his energy that he managed also to hold the office of Treasurer of the Indian Mathematical Society for six of those years (1928–34). He was President of the Indian Library Association, 1944–53, and of the Madras Library Association, 1958–67.

His other offices included: Chairman of the Documentation Committee of the Indian Standards Institution (1947–66); Vice-President of the Madras Library Association (1948–57); Secretary of the Indian Adult Education Association (1949–53); Vice-President of FID (1953–56 and 1958–61); Secretary and Chairman of the FID Committee on General Classification (1954–64). He was an Honorary Fellow of FID and an Honorary Vice-President of the LA.

Among his many awards are two of special distinction that he received from the government of his country in recognition of his achievements: the title *Rao Sahib* and the distinction of *Padmashree.* He was given an Honorary Doctorate of Literature by the University of Delhi and the University of Pittsburgh. In 1970 he was awarded the Margaret Mann Citation in Cataloging and Classification by the American Library Association. His contributions to library science were recognized in 1965 by the publication of a Ranganathan Festschrift to mark his 71st birthday. He died in Bangalore on September 27, 1972, at the age of 80. After his death the FID Committee on Classification Research further recognized his achievements by establishing a Ranganathan Award for Classification Research.

The Man. What kind of man was this energetic genius who was so immersed in his work? P. N. Kaula tells us that Ranganathan never took a single day's leave during the 20 years he spent as University Librarian at Madras. The Ranganathan Memorial Number of *Herald of Library Science* contains many personal anecdotes about Ranganathan and 14

Courtesy of The Newberry Library

Shiyali Ramamrita Ranganathan

obituaries, not only containing references to his analytical mind and consideration but also noting that he could be frank, intolerant, uncompromising, and selfish. Girja Kumar refers to his sense of humor, optimism, and interest in mysticism. V. V. Giri, when presenting the Ranganathan Festschrift to him, mentioned his humility and philanthropy but said that what struck him most about Ranganathan was "his enthusiasm and ebullient spirit which even many a youth in the country could envy."

Perhaps the most moving accounts of Ranganathan as a person have come from English Librarian Bernard Palmer, who told how, inspired by reading the *Prolegomena* when he began to teach classification in 1940, he made a vow that if ever he had the money, he would go to Madras to meet the author. The opportunity came only a year later when, serving in the Royal Air Force, Palmer found himself at a camp on the outskirts of Madras. On his first free afternoon he went to the University Library and introduced himself to Ranganathan, thus laying the foundations of a friendship that lasted until Ranganathan's death. Like others, Palmer referred to Ranganathan's analytical mind, his enthusiasm, his good humor, his kindliness, and his genial personality (though admitting that he could be cold and offhand with those he believed to be fools or opponents). Palmer stated that although conscious of his unique position in Indian librarianship, Ranganathan was modest and unassuming and welcomed him, then "a quite humble member of the profession," as though he were his intellectual and cultural equal.

Ranganathan was married in 1907 and, after his wife died 21 years later, married again in 1929. In honor of his second wife and at her suggestion, he endowed all his property to the Sarada Ranaganthan Chair of Library Science in the University of Madras in 1957. He also established the Sarada Ranganathan Lectures on Library Science, the first of which was given by Palmer in 1965.

Ranganthan was passionately concerned about library science, which he saw as a vital tool for "the development of an atmosphere of peaceful co-existence among nations . . . and the evolution of One-World."

REFERENCES

Edward Dudley, editor, *S. R. Ranganathan, 1892–1972: Papers Given at a Memorial Meeting on Thursday 25th January 1973* (1974).

P. N. Kaula, "Some Less Known Facts about Ranganathan," *Herald of Library Science* (1973).

Ranganathan Festschrift, volume 1: *Library Science Today: Papers Contributed on the 71st Birthday of Dr. S. R. Ranganathan (August 1962)*, edited by P. N. Kaula; and volume 2: *An Essay in Personal Bibliography: A Bibliography of the Writings on and by Dr. S. R. Ranganathan*, compiled by A. K. Das Gupta (1965–67).

K. G. B. BAKEWELL

Reference and Information Services

The dual concept of reference *and* information services is a relatively new one. Although information service—meaning the provision of specific facts and information to library users—has always been implicit in reference service, libraries initially offered reference service for didactic reasons as a part of their broad educational role. Many definitions of reference service have been offered over the years, all of them illustrative, none definitive; it is better described than defined. The purpose of reference service is to help a library's clientele use its collections effectively to meet their information needs. The distinguishing features of reference service are a staff designated to provide the service; a collection of reference works accessible to the public in an area set aside for the provision of the service; adequate guides to the library's resources (such as a classification scheme, a catalogue, and indexes); and a high degree of interaction between the staff and the clientele. During its history in North American libraries, reference service has included reader's advisory service, bibliographic instruction, and information and referral service. These represent different developments of the service's basic purpose.

Historical Development and Definitions. The convenient and obvious place to begin any description of the history of reference service is Samuel Swett Green's article, "Personal Relations between Librarians and Readers," published in the November 30, 1876, issue of *Library Journal*. Green argued that librarians have an obligation to do more than provide a collection for their clientele, that they must also provide personal service and help readers select appropriate books from the collection. Green was most concerned with increasing use of the Worcester Public Library's "reference" collection. The term then had a different connotation; it meant serious nonfiction. In Green's day, reference works of the sort that fill today's reference collections—works offering guidance to other bibliographic works and their contents or providing easy access to factual information—were few in number. Green believed that many library users lacked the sophistication to make the best selections from serious nonfiction themselves. The purpose of reference service was to elevate their taste and improve their minds. Although this ostensible purpose included neither provision of specific bits of information nor instruction in the use of the library, Green's many examples illustrate both of these as implicit purposes of reference service.

Green's idea found favor in numerous libraries. As librarians moved beyond their original makeshift quarters in former school buildings and mansions, they designed new library buildings that included reference rooms. A paper presented at the 1882 American Library Association (ALA) conference demonstrates that public libraries were preparing special reading lists and catalogues of children's books for schools in their areas. By 1883 many libraries were giving assistant librarians special training in the techniques of reference work. The ALA Annual Conferences included reports on "Aids and Guides to Readers," and by 1891 the term "reference work" was being used in the annual index to *Library Journal;* that same year "reference work" appeared for the first time in the title of an article.

Because librarians of the day wished to improve their readers' taste in fiction, reference service developed most rapidly in the large urban public libraries. The public libraries of Boston, Brooklyn, Chicago, Detroit, Milwaukee, Newark, Providence, and Saint Louis were among the first to give particular staff members responsibility for reference service. The staff member so charged at the Saint Louis Public Library was called the "library hostess."

The textbook-based instructional methods used by colleges in the late 19th century placed the college library on the periphery of the academic program. In 1885 Melvil Dewey announced that at Columbia he was applying the "modern library idea" of reference work to the university library. He appointed two reference librarians to aid inquirers. Despite this example, academic libraries, especially in the state universities and colleges, were slower than public libraries to adopt the modern idea. Reference service did not become a regular service of academic libraries until World War I.

The purpose of reference work later broadened to include specific fact retrieval and instruction in the use of library resources. Librarians did not plan these services; they responded to needs expressed by their clients. Out of this broadening of services grew a debate about the purpose and proper function of reference work, a debate which has not yet been resolved. Some librarians have argued that the purpose of reference service is to teach library users how to use the library independently; others have argued that the librarian should provide as much service as possible to the user, illustrated by Green's example of the librarian finding appropriate books and bringing them to a patron open at the proper pages.

The first position has been labeled "conservative" or "minimum" service; the second position has been called "liberal" or "maximum" service. They have been discussed as "theories" of reference; but rather than being theories, they are attitudes about or philosophies of service. Opinion about these philosophies has been most sharply divided in academic libraries. Because of the educational role of the academic library within its parent institution, many college and university librarians believe that they have an obligation to teach students how to use library resources. It is doubtful that any library or any individual librarian applies either of these philosophies consistently.

For the sake of both the librarian's and the patron's convenience, it is simpler to give one level of service at one time and the other level at another, depending on the patron's need. For example, when a patron needs only a fact such as the longitude and latitude of a particular town, it is most efficient for both parties for the librarian simply to look up the answer in an appropriate reference source, rather than attempt to explain the complicated process to be followed to arrive at the same source. The librarian's superior knowledge of reference works makes this the preferred mode of service in such cases. On the other hand, if sources on a particular topic must be selected and judged for their relevance, it is more practical for the librarian to instruct the person needing those sources how to use the catalogue and periodical indexes, leaving the judgments to the patron. The patron's knowledge of his or her own needs makes this the preferred mode of service in such cases.

Out of these apparent inconsistencies librarians have identified a third so-called "theory" of reference service, "moderate" service, meaning that both the conservative and the liberal levels are offered in varying circumstances. The conservative level operates

Earlham College

A class discussion on bibliographic instruction in the Lilly Library at Earlham College in Richmond, Indiana.

more commonly in academic and school libraries than in public and special libraries, because of its obvious relation to the expressed original educational purpose of reference service.

Information services first flourished in special libraries. Just as the conservative philosophy agrees with the purpose of school and academic libraries' parent institutions, the liberal philosophy agrees with the purpose of special libraries' sponsors. Legislative reference libraries developed the techniques of amplified service which characterize special libraries. Melvil Dewey created the New York State Library's legislative reference section in 1890, but Charles McCarthy of the Legislative Reference Department in Wisconsin created the model of the special library, drawing information from sources outside the library, preparing digests of relevant information, and becoming a partner in the legislators' work. Both world wars further spurred the development of special libraries in business and industry.

Minneapolis Public Library

Readers' advisory services at the Minneapolis Public Library in 1940.

Applications of the techniques of special libraries have been attempted in academic and public libraries. In the early 1930s the Carnegie Corporation funded two experimental "research librarianships," one at Cornell and one at the University of Pennsylvania. At each university a designated librarian was given full-time responsibility for assisting faculty in major research projects in the humanities and social sciences. The experiment, despite initial scepticism among the faculty that a librarian could understand their research needs, was an unqualified success, but no other institution imitated it, and when funding ran out both Cornell and Pennsylvania discontinued the program. In the 1980s both public and academic libraries have offered in-depth reference and information service to business and industry. Well-known services have been developed at Rice University, the University of Michigan, Long Island University, and the Cleveland and Indianapolis public libraries. However, these services have stepped outside the tradition of free information service and charge fees for their labors. Several companies, such as Information on Demand of Berkeley, California, have also entered the information service business for profit. Often called "information brokers," these firms offer comprehensive, speedy information and document delivery services, exemplifying the liberal philosophy at its fullest.

Regardless of the type of library, the level of service, or the age of the patron, reference work possesses certain constants. When a patron asks a question, the reference librarian must clarify what the person needs. People generally ask questions too broad or too narrow to convey their needs clearly. The librarian must usually ask a series of open-ended questions until both patron and librarian are in agreement on what the patron wants. This process is called the "reference interview" or "question negotiation." It demands patience and good interpersonal communication skills on the part of the reference librarian. After determining the nature of the patron's need, the librarian must match that need with the information

Telephone reference service, of special importance to the elderly and handicapped, is provided by most public libraries.

sources available by drawing on what Green called "the habit of mental classification." In other words, the librarian categorizes the question by its subject and by the type of reference work which answers that sort of question, then identifies specific works of that type and consults them for an answer. If a question is complicated, the librarian will formulate a search strategy involving a series of reference works to be used in a particular order. After the search is completed, the patron may still not be satisfied, and further interviewing then becomes necessary until together the librarian and patron find a satisfactory answer or the librarian must make a professional judgment that the needed source is not available. In such cases the librarian recommends other approaches and may refer the patron to likely sources outside the library, including other libraries.

Reference service developed its distinguishing characteristics during its first quarter century. It acquired the trappings of a mature professional field starting about 1960. In that year the Reference Services Division of ALA began publishing *RQ,* a quarterly journal devoted to issues in the field. Other quarterlies, *Reference Services Review* and *The Reference Librarian,* followed in 1973 and 1981 respectively. Since 1959 ALA's Reference and Adult Services Division has annually presented the Isadore Mudge Citation "to an individual who has made a distinguished contribution to reference librarianship." In 1976 RASD issued "A Commitment to Information Services: Developmental Guidelines." These guidelines are the closest thing in existence to standards for reference service. The document was revised in 1979 by the addition of a statement on the ethics of reference service.

Instruction in Library Use. All libraries offer their users some form of instruction in using the library. Directories, signs, and guides to the location of sections of the classification scheme offer basic information everyone needs to make even minimal use of a library. Covered under the rubric of "library orientation," these services are often distinguished from instruction in library use. For more than a century, individualized instruction has been a feature of reference service. Many libraries, especially academic libraries, offer more extensive instructional programs, often identified as bibliographic instruction, or BI, programs. Bibliographic instruction takes many forms, including distribution of bibliographies on special topics, tours of the building, class lectures, handbooks describing library facilities and services, demonstrations of computerized information systems, printed explanations of how to use specific reference works, programmed instruction, workbooks with library exercises, separate library skills courses for credit, computer-assisted instruction, and audiovisual presentations for individual or group use. Because of variations in libraries' policies for organizing library materials, and because of the uniqueness of each library's physical facility, bibliographic instruction programs must be developed locally.

Libraries have developed BI programs for several reasons, the most common being the belief that they have an obligation to teach users, particularly students, how to use the library independently. Bibliographic instruction programs are sometimes undertaken to relieve the pressure at a busy reference desk;

the thinking is that if students are taught how to use basic library resources, they will place fewer individual demands on the reference staff. However, the experience of libraries with successful BI programs has been that the nature rather than the number of individual questions changes. As users' sophistication increases, so does the sophistication of their reference questions. Many librarians also advocate bibliographic instruction for everyone so that individuals can independently use the library throughout their lives to enrich their work and recreational activities.

Academic librarians frequently ally BI programs with the freshman English courses in which students are required to prepare term papers making use of library resources. The students hear lectures from librarians and perhaps do some written exercises or have individualized follow-up conferences during which the librarians advise them on which reference sources to use. Bibliographic instruction is generally considered to be most effective when it is integrated even more fully into a course's requirements, when students have a progressive series of assignments that require them to learn the use of a variety of library tools and skills. The bibliographic instruction program at Earlham College (Richmond, Indiana) has become a singular model of course-integrated instruction, but few other libraries have been able to approach Earlham's success.

Group and individualized instruction is also carried on extensively in school libraries. Some school districts mandate teaching of various skills at certain grade levels. Although the concept of teaching library skills in the schools receives wide support from both teachers and school librarians, the librarians, like their counterparts in colleges, face the challenge of securing the classroom teachers' cooperation in planning and implementing library instruction. The commitment to instruction has been more consistent and less subject to external trends in school libraries than in academic libraries.

One early approach to formal bibliographic instruction in some colleges was a separate course on the library required of all freshmen. The instruction program developed in the early 1950s at the library of the University of Illinois's Undergraduate Division in Chicago can be considered a precursor to the model commonly practiced today. It combined a workbook, exercises, lecture, and follow-up session to introduce the library to students in the required freshman rhetoric class. The program was imitated elsewhere, but not extensively. The greatest surge of interest in BI came in the 1970s in academic libraries. A workbook used at the University of California at Los Angeles was widely imitated, and audiovisual equipment and computers were put to the service of library orientation and instruction. Manifestations of this interest are the founding in 1977 of the Bibliographic Instruction Section within the Association of College and Research Libraries (ACRL), a division of ALA, and the creation by ACRL that same year of "Guidelines for Bibliographic Instruction in Academic Libraries." Interest remained strong enough that in 1983 *Research Strategies: A Journal of Library Concepts and Instruction,* a quarterly journal dedicated to BI, was founded. An annual award, administered by ACRL and named after Miriam Dudley, the author of the UCLA workbook, is given to recognize

Detroit Public Library

The Detroit Public Library was one of the first to designate staff responsible for reference service (1928).

an individual's contribution to the BI field.

Reader Guidance. From the earliest days reference service was concerned with improving readers' taste in reading, especially in fiction. This function was formalized in many public libraries in the 1920s through the creation of readers' advisory services, or readers' bureaus, separate from the libraries' reference departments. Readers' advisory service was the libraries' response to the adult education movement. The first readers' bureau was established at the Chicago Public Library in 1923. Others were created at the public libraries of Akron, Albany, Boston, Cincinnati, Detroit, Minneapolis, New York, and Oklahoma City.

The purpose of the readers' bureaus was to assist individual adult readers in planning systematic reading programs relating to their interests, to help casual readers select the best books, to compile lists of recommended books, and to work with adult education groups, including those concerned with adult literacy as well as those concerned with general personal improvement. The readers' advisor would meet with a patron and conduct an extensive interview to identify his or her interests, needs, and capabilities. The advisor would then draw up a bibliography of books suited to the person's purposes. The advisor would also do follow-up work with the reader to monitor progress and to learn about changes in the reader's interests or the growth of those interests in new directions. Such changes would, of course, require new recommendations. Many bureaus maintained extensive card files of readers' interests and notified them when new books relating to their interests arrived; they would be held for the readers to examine.

The heyday of readers' advisory service was the 1930s. During that decade the big cities expanded their service from the central libraries into the branches, and many small town libraries made readers' advisory work a routine part of their reference activities. It was, however, a labor-intensive service that reached relatively few people. During the 1940s

George Don

Reference service at the Margaret Clapp Library, Wellesley College, Massachusetts.

the focus of adult education efforts shifted from individuals to groups, and the service began to fade as a separate operation within libraries. The decentralization of reference service into subject departments wihtin main libraries later dispersed the readers' advisory function. Although by 1960 nearly all formal readers' advisory services had been disbanded, the function had not disappeared, and readers' advisory service is carried on to varying degrees within reference departments in all types of libraries.

Reader's advisory service has not been confined to public libraries. Perhaps the most ambitious attempt to develop it in an academic library took place between 1951 and 1955 at the library of the University of Illinois's Undergraduate Division in Chicago. The library worked with the university's student counseling service to train reference librarians in counseling techniques; the librarians were given the title "counselor librarians." To refine their counseling techniques, they spent part of each week working in the counseling center offices helping students with academic and personal problems. In the library they were to combine their library and counseling techniques to identify students' needs and satisfy them with appropriate library materials. They tried to use bibliotherapy—an intensive form of readers' guidance usually found only in prisons, hospitals, and other residential institutions—in an academic environment. The experiment ended abruptly and was not imitated by any other library.

A modern extension of readers' advisory service in public libraries has been information and referral centers, often called I & R centers. They enjoyed their greatest popularity during the 1970s. The purpose of an I & R center is to bring people with legal, medical, or personal problems into contact with social agencies that can help them solve those problems. An I & R center differs from a traditional reference department in that it makes little use of such traditional reference tools as the card catalogue. Rather, the librarian interviews a client, determines that person's need, deals with appropriate agencies to determine which ones will help, and then directs the client to the proper

person at each agency. Some proponents of I & R service have said that the librarian should also furnish transportation to the agency offices and follow up on the client's progress, staying with the case until it is resolved to the client's satisfaction. Nearly every public library has a directory of local social service agencies, and many keep in-house files to supplement these directories, but few support I & R centers. In 1979 only 13 percent of public libraries surveyed offered true I & R service.

Reference Tools. Concomitant with the development of reference service has been the development of reference works. When Green developed the idea of reference service in 1876, the universe of reference works in English consisted of little more than several general purpose encyclopedias, a few almanacs, Bartlett's *Familiar Quotations,* the *Annual Register of World Events,* and several general-purpose dictionaries. By the end of the 19th century, all of the essential features of reference service had been developed; at the same time, reference book publishing began to grow. The relationship between reference service and the reference works was synergistic. As reference service became more common, the need for reference works increased; as reference works became more common, librarians' ability to do reference work improved. Many significant reference works, still being published and in use today, date from this period. R. R. Bowker's *Publishers' Trade List Annual* has appeared since 1873. H. W. Wilson began publishing the monthly *Cumulative Book Index* in 1898; his *Reader's Guide to Periodical Literature* began three years later. The ALA promoted reference publishing with its *A.L.A. Index to General Literature* in 1901. In 1902 ALA published Alice B. Kroeger's *Guide to the Study and Use of Reference Books;* after her death in 1909, editorship of the guide passed to Isadore G. Mudge. Later editions were prepared by Constance M. Winchell and Eugene P. Sheehy. Sheehy's tenth edition of the *Guide to Reference Books,* often called "the reference librarian's bible," was scheduled for publication in 1986.

By 1928 the volume of reference publishing was such that librarians desired authoritative evaluations to guide their purchasing decisions. In response, ALA created the Subscription Books Review Committee. Two years later it published its first evaluations of subscription books and encyclopedias in the quarterly *Subscription Books Bulletin.* The committee's scope broadened to include review of single-volume reference works. Though the committee's name and the name of its journal have changed several times, its basic purpose of evaluating reference works is still carried out in the *Reference Book Bulletin,* published within the pages of *Booklist.* Other important sources of reviews of new reference books are the *Wilson Library Bulletin, RQ, Library Journal, Choice,* and *American Reference Books Annual.*

In addition to books, reference librarians since the mid-1970s have made extensive use of online databases that offer speed, convenience, and multiple access points. Most of these databases are indexes, including abstracts, to the journals of specialized fields. Some have printed counterparts; others exist only in machine-readable form.

Research. Research in reference service has addressed several key questions. These are: What is the quality of reference service? Who can do reference work? What are the interpersonal dynamics of the reference encounter? And what precisely *is* reference work? Over a number of years investigators have conducted unobtrusive tests of reference service in many types of libraries, especially public and academic libraries, to measure the quality of reference service. In an unobtrusive test, a trained surrogate poses as a library patron asking a reference question; the librarians' answers yield the test results. Results of these tests show considerable uniformity: in most unobtrusive tests, reference departments answer simple factual questions correctly only a little more than half the time. Because the results among individual libraries tested vary widely, further unobtrusive testing conducted with the purpose of isolating variables could prove fruitful in explaining what makes for quality reference service. Tests comparing librarians and nonprofessional trained library workers have shown little difference in the results of their reference work, but have indicated that the professionals answer questions in less time.

A number of researchers in reference work, particularly during the 1970s, borrowed models and methods from such fields as counseling psychology, anthropology, and sociology to elucidate what happens during the interaction between an inquirer and a reference librarian. Out of these efforts has come a good deal of practical advice on how to conduct an effective reference interview.

Many writers have attempted to define reference work. Some have depended upon a great deal of data collection and analysis; others have drawn on less formal observation and reflection on personal experience. If a definitive explanation of what reference work is should ever be developed and accepted by the profession, it will result from an amalgam of personal reflection and formal research into the diverse aspects of reference service.

Issues and Trends. A number of issues face reference librarianship. The introduction of online access to bibliographic databases in the 1970s continues to affect reference service. Their use is common in public, special, and academic libraries and is increasing in school libraries. However, public and academic libraries have tended to treat online databases as something unusual and outside the mainstream of reference work and reference publishing. Most charge fees for the searches. The increase in the number of databases during the 1980s and the introduction of nonbibliographic and full-text databases has kept the "free versus fee" debate alive. Direct patron charges for database searching has impeded the integration of online searching into routine reference service.

The debate about conservative versus liberal service has not received much attention in the reference press in recent years, but it is played out daily in every reference encounter in every library. It can still rouse passionate argument in staff meetings and classrooms. Perhaps this issue will never be laid to rest.

The question of reference librarians' job satisfaction received considerable attention in the 1980s. Despite studies showing high job satisfaction, many reference librarians complain of "burnout." Prominent among the reasons cited for reference librarians' unhappiness is their inability to give their clients optimum service because they cannot freely use online sources whenever they would be helpful unless the patron is able to pay for that help. Librarians complain of being overworked by having too many patrons to serve, and of being overwhelmed by having too many reference tools and online systems to learn. Both reference librarians and library administrators must address these problems if there is to be a stable, experienced work force in reference departments.

Perhaps the biggest issue facing reference librarianship is evaluation. No truly useful way of evaluating reference service has ever been devised. Unobtrusive tests can indicate something about the results of reference service, but few have attempted to deal simultaneously with the process which delivers those results. Evaluation, always impressionistic, will necessarily remain so until a significant breakthrough is achieved in this area.

REFERENCES

William A. Katz, *Introduction to Reference Work* (1982). The field's standard textbook, the first volume treats reference works and the second volume describes the methods and issues of reference librarianship.

Marjorie E. Murfin and Lubomyr R. Wynar, *Reference Service: An Annotated Bibliographic Guide* (1977); *Supplement 1976–1982* (1984). These two volumes comprise the definitive bibliography on reference work. The first volume covers books and articles in English from 1876 through 1975. The second volume extends coverage through 1982.

Samuel Rothstein, *The Development of Reference Services* (1955). This is the standard history of reference service in public, academic, and special libraries until approximately 1940.

JAMES R. RETTIG

Renaissance Libraries

The history of the Renaissance is inseparable from the history of its books and libraries. The expansion of knowledge within the scholastic tradition, the secularization of society, and the rekindling of interest in ancient history, literature, and art, both in Italy and in Northern Europe, placed new demands on both books and libraries from 1400 to 1700.

The intellectual achievements of the Renaissance were as complex and varied as the kinds of books and libraries that the Renaissance produced. Renaissance libraries included university libraries, since the universities founded in the Middle Ages greatly expanded during the Renaissance, and new universities with new libraries of scholastic texts were created. Other Renaissance libraries were religious libraries, many of which were established to serve the new reformed orders that spread during the period. These libraries also contained rich collections of scholastic literature. Still other Renaissance libraries were courtly libraries, assembled to preserve the new corpus of vernacular literature that expanded particularly in France under the patronage of Charles V and great noblemen such as Jean Duke of Berry and in England under the patronage of Edward IV. Other Renaissance libraries were Humanist libraries, assembled by Italian Humanists and their lay and ecclesiastical patrons to preserve the manuscripts of newly recovered ancient texts. Finally, Renaissance libraries can be said to have included theological libraries formed chiefly from printed books to serve the Protestant Reformation and the Catholic Counter-Reformation.

Rise in Literacy. Despite their remarkable variety, Renaissance libraries reflected a single and common phenomenon: a rise in the rate of literacy that, when set in the context of a moderate increase in population, yielded a dramatic increase in the number of people who were able to read and write and therefore sought to use books and to avail themselves of libraries. In the 12th century only a small, chiefly monastic, elite were able to read and write, and literate people constituted a tiny fraction of the general population. By 1533 Thomas More estimated that over half the population of England was literate in the vernacular. The rate of increase in literacy accelerated at the end of the 14th and during the 15th century. During the Renaissance, Europe was transformed from an oral culture, with a population primarily of listeners, to a population that included significant numbers of readers.

Manuscript Book Production. Monasteries had been the major centers of book production in the Middle Ages, when they also served as the major libraries. (*See* Middle Ages, Libraries in the.) Although monastic book production continued after 1300, book production generally became the domain of professional scribes, who served a varied clientele of schoolmen and lay aristocracy. Beginning in the mid-13th century Europe witnessed a growth in demand for scholastic textbooks, which stimulated a remarkable series of innovations in the way in which these books were produced. The first of these was the *pecia* system employed in the universities of Naples, Bologna, Padua, Paris, Oxford, Cambridge, and Uppsala from the 13th through the 15th centuries. Fundamental to the operation of the *pecia* system was the creation of exemplars—model manuscripts certified for their textual accuracy which were subdivided into their component quires or *pecia* of six or eight folios and rented to licensed scribes. Whereas previously a given manuscript could be copied only by one scribe at a time, the pecia system allowed a number of scribes to make copies of the same text simultaneously. The result was an increase in manuscript production combined with greater control of the textual uniformity, for the quality of the exemplars was under the control of the university. The awareness of the need for accurate textual transmission reflected in the *pecia* system was to become a hallmark of Renaissance book production.

Innovations: Imposition and Cursive Handwriting. Succeeding centuries brought continued innovation, reflecting the desire to produce standardized manuscripts with great speed. In France, the Low Countries, and England in the 14th century, scribes developed the practice of imposition, the significance of which is still being assessed by manuscript scholars. Imposition meant that texts were written on uncut quires before folding and thus out of narrative sequence, in a manner similar to the uncut pages produced by later printing presses. Another innovation that began throughout Europe in the 14th century was the adaptation of cursive handwriting to book production. Cursive scripts could be written with fewer liftings of the pen, allowing books to be made more swiftly and thus sold at lower prices.

Impact of Paper. The use of paper was also a major development. It was first introduced to book production in the 14th century but took firm hold only in the course of the 15th century when paper played a more important role in lowering the cost of books than did the introduction of printing by movable type. Paper books, written in cursive scripts, became the first truly cheap books, easily within the means of townspeople, gentry, and poor students in Italy, England, and France. In the early 1400s ordinary school manuals were being produced by *scriptoria* in editions of 200 to 300 copies, numbers comparable to the runs of printed editions a century later.

Early Standardization. While some changes in technical procedure allowed the production of cheap manuscript books, other changes increased the supply of deluxe books, which in the 15th century were becoming more uniform as they were produced in larger and larger quantities. The use of a form of tracing paper permitted the exact reproduction of miniatures and thus the standardization of iconography. Some miniatures intended for books of hours were mass-produced separately from the text. Increasing division of labor separated the copying, illustration, and decoration of the manuscript. As a result, deluxe manuscript books of the 15th century showed increased uniformity in appearance, dimensions, and length.

Impact of Printing. The invention of printing from movable type must be viewed in the light of the growing appetite in Western Europe for standardized books. The invention has traditionally been attributed to Johann Gutenberg of Mainz in 1444. Before Gutenberg, block printing was used in textile decoration, illustrations, and short texts. These processes did not play a major role in book production, however, and are of importance only insofar as they may have stimulated printers to think of the possibility of using movable type cast in molds to produce books.

The earliest printers came from *outside* the group of artisans directly concerned with manuscript book production. Gutenberg was a goldsmith, as were apparently early printers in Avignon and Basle. The secret method of *artificialiter scribere*, like other skills of goldsmiths, was initially meant to be applied to works of beauty and high cost. Many of the first printed books were printed on vellum, an indication of the luxury market to which early printers most often sought to cater. Many early printed books were illustrated with hand-painted miniatures and decorated with floral borders identical to those in contemporary manuscript codices.

Only after 1480 did printers, many of whom were former scribes, begin to produce cheap books. By 1500 printing had become an important source of cheap university textbooks, and most of the titles printed were works of proven value that had been previously disseminated in manuscript. In the first third of the 16th century, however, a new kind of author emerged who wrote with the press and its potentially wide audience in mind. Printing played an especially important role in spreading the new ideas of the Protestant Reformation and was probably a decisive factor in making Protestantism a different phenomenon from the 14th-century heresies of Wyclifism and Hussitism, which lacked a comparable means of mass communication. During the Wars of Religion in France (1562–98), printing became an important medium for the expression of political theory.

Printing had an enormous impact on the content of Renaissance libraries, since standardized and uniform books ultimately led to standardized collections. Before printing, Jerome's *De Viribus Illustribus* had on occasion been used as a model for library catalogues, but manuscript collections had remained incredibly diverse. Printing led to standardization of the texts and the definition of the corpus of ancient and medieval authors. Bibliographies such as those prepared by Conrad Gesner (1516–1565), Swiss Humanist scholar, were meant by their authors to serve as standardized catalogues of libraries of printed texts (*see* Gesner, Conrad). By the mid-16th century the corpus of cited literature was increasingly defined by what had been printed. Works that for whatever reason had escaped the press fell from the tradition of learned discourse. Whereas printing standardized the bibliographical base of 16th-century culture, it did not immediately lead to libraries larger than those of the previous century, which had been composed exclusively of manuscripts. Many printed book libraries were in fact smaller than important manuscript collections; for example, under Louis XIII the royal library of France had only 400 more printed books than the library of Charles V had manuscript books two and a half centuries earlier. Most printed books found their way into the increasing number of small personal libraries.

The Renaissance Book. In addition to changes in techniques and technology, intellectual and social changes played a major role in determining the physical appearance and content of Renaissance books and libraries. In Italy Humanism was of enormous import. Humanism developed outside the universities, which had been responsible for the greater portion of Italian book production in the 13th and 14th centuries. In general, early Humanists were not the university-trained doctors of theology, medicine, and law but laymen, often notaries, trained in the tradition of the "ars dictanimis" (the art of eloquent written expression) . The early Humanists shared a common goal: the restoration of eloquence in Latin prose. To achieve this end Petrarch, Boccaccio, and Salutati assembled collections remarkable for their richness in ancient Latin literature. The Humanists avidly collected the oldest possible manuscripts of classical authors and had them copied in order to build libraries of ancient texts in their original form, free from the corruptions in orthography and grammar introduced by medieval scribes.

For the books that they themselves copied and for their libraries, the first Humanists used the highly legible Gothic textual scripts favored in courtly and bourgeois Italian circles of the 14th century. In the first decade of the Quattrocento (1400s), however, Florentine Humanists began to produce books whose scripts and decoration were based on older manuscripts, particularly Tuscan manuscripts of the 10th to 12th centuries, which were characteristically written in Caroline script and decorated with white ivy stem motifs. Whether the Humanists really believed these manuscripts to have resembled those of the age of Cicero is not clear; nevertheless, it is certain that the Humanists believed that *littera antiqua* was the appropriate script for the classical texts. During the 15th century these scripts came to be used for other materials, including vernacular literature, and even for

Scala

Medici Library in Florence, Italy (16th century), designed by Michelangelo.

scholastic treatises and papal bulls. When printing was introduced into Italy in 1458, the dominant type fonts—Roman and Italic—were modeled on two varieties of Humanistic script.

In the second half of the 15th century, Humanists exhibited an increasing interest in epigraphy (ancient inscriptions), with particular emphasis on the inscriptions of the Roman Empire; capital letters of the Imperial period became the models for the capital letters of manuscript books and ultimately of printed books.

The link between Humanism and the physical appearance of the book, so strong in Italy, was weak in Northern Europe. In 15th-century France Humanistic script was not popular, and Humanistic texts were frequently copied in scripts wholly un-Humanistic in appearance. The major force in forming scripts and secular libraries in the early Northern Renaissance was the growth in vernacular and courtly literature under aristocratic patronage. Beginning with Charles V of France, the French-speaking aristocracy in France, the Low Countries, and England began forming libraries of vernacular texts equal in size (roughly 400 to 1,000 volumes) to those of the bibliophilic Italian Humanists. In earlier centuries princes had been read to by professional readers, who were at ease with the Gothic textual script of the universities; however, as lay readership increased, a new and more legible script became popular in aristocratic circles. *Lettre batarde,* termed *hybrida* by some modern palaeographers, achieved a dominance for the vernacular literature of Northern Europe equal to that of the forms for Humanistic texts in Italy. The vernacular chronicles, chivalric romances, and books of devotion so popular in aristocratic circles were written and printed in lettre batarde until the first third of the 16th century. In France Humanistic type fonts then replaced lettre batarde, but in Germany lettre batarde prevailed and became the model for the *fractura* type font, which remained the standard German type font until the 20th century.

Renaissance Libraries. Throughout the Renaissance the largest libraries remained university li-

699

braries; the Sorbonne, for example, in 1338 already possessed over 1,700 volumes. The holdings of university libraries were divided into reference collections, which were chained to desks for consultation only in the library, and general collections, which circulated to both students and masters. The reference collections were often freely open for consultation, and the circulating collections were, in some cases, available to even the poorest students. The university libraries were therefore the early Renaissance forerunners of public libraries. In architecture they differed greatly from the smaller monastic libraries, which had been installed in cloisters. The university libraries were centralized in halls equipped with benches and tables. They became the models for the libraries of religious houses as well as for the great princely collections of the 14th and 15th centuries.

Pope Urban V in Avignon and King Charles V in Paris founded the first of the great princely libraries in the mid-14th century. Subsequently, other important libraries were formed by Gian Galeazzo Visconti, Jean Duke of Berry, Philip Duke of Burgundy, King Alfonso the Magnanimous of Naples, and King Matthias Corvinus of Hungary. Pope Nicholas V founded the Vatican Library in Rome to take the place of the Avignon library lost during the Great Schism.

In contrast to university collections, princely libraries were considered private possessions, and admission was accorded only to the favorites of the prince. The books in princely libraries were more luxurious than those in university libraries, and new standards of cataloguing—with emphasis on description of decoration and script—were developed, in part, to prevent theft.

Princes did not always think only of themselves. Cosimo de'Medici in the mid-15th century purchased volumes and donated them, along with selected items from his own collection, to the Dominican convent of San Marco to establish a public library for the use of the citizens of Florence. Cosimo's grandson, Lorenzo the Magnificent, established the Biblioteca Medicea-Laurentiana with similar intent. Pope Sixtus IV in 1475 opened the Vatican Library to the public. During the reign of Charles IX, public access was permitted to the French Royal Library. By the 17th century many of the private libraries of the 14th and 15th centuries had become the possession, through inheritance and purchase, of the libraries of sovereign princes who permitted consultation to the public.

In the mid-16th century Europe's largest and oldest libraries still were manuscript collections. Federigo Duke of Urbino (1422–1482) was said to have been proud that he had only handwritten books and no printed books. While Paul II and Sixtus IV were patrons of printing, the Vatican appears to have retained its preference for manuscripts until the middle of the 16th century. Under Louis XIII in 1643, the Royal Library still had twice as many manuscripts as printed books.

By contrast, the new libraries of Protestant institutions were composed principally of printed volumes. Protestants, alienated from their society, built some of the first comprehensive collections of exclusively printed materials to compensate for their lack of access to the older royal and ecclesiastical collections with their great manuscript holdings. The destruction of monastic libraries during the Reformation added to the dependency of Protestants on printed sources. In Geneva the Academy of Calvin was composed entirely of printed works, as was the library of the Protestant University of Leiden at its foundation.

Protestants, who used the printing press so effectively to communicate their ideas, frequently presented copies of their works to libraries. Gifts were not the only source, however; in Geneva the law of copyright deposit of 1530 was an important aid in building the library of the Academy of Calvin.

Among Catholics the Jesuits, leaders in the Counter-Reformation, had no manuscript collection of their own and were particularly active in building large libraries of printed books and in increasing the level of bibliographic expertise. The Jesuit Library of Paris at the end of the 16th century is said to have numbered 20,000 volumes, an astounding figure when compared with libraries of the previous century.

Librarians. In the monasteries of the Middle Ages, the functions of Librarian were regularly performed by the *precentor,* who had general responsibility for liturgy, of which reading was seen as an extension. In the universities the formal office of Librarian was created, but it did not have great importance as a position of erudition, although some scholastics of note at times performed its functions. Similarly, librarians of the kings and princes of France in the 14th and 15th centuries were not known as scholars.

The first scholar-librarians in the modern sense appeared in Italy in the 15th century, when Humanist scholars such as Niccolò Niccoli built their own extensive collections. In the second half of the 15th century the Popes consistently placed scholars in charge of the Vatican Library. In the early 16th century Pope Julius II chose the renowned Humanist Tomasso Ingherami as his second Librarian; Pope Leo X chose as his Librarian Filippo Beroaldo, who in 1515 prepared the first edition of the *Annales* of Tacitus. The custom of placing libraries in the charge of scholars was emulated in France under Francis I, who chose Guillaume Budé as *maitre de la librarie du Roy* and Jacques Lefevre d'Étaples as one of his librarians. The collection of Greek manuscripts flourished under their care, and both men were responsible for a significant revival of interest in the Greek language and literature.

The modern connection between scholar-librarians and the editing of texts became clearly established in the 16th century. Marguerin de la Bigne, the first great editor of the Western Church Fathers, was Librarian of the Sorbonne and founded a tradition of entrusting the editing of patristic texts to librarians. This practice was maintained in the 17th century by Jean Mabillon and the Congrégation de Saint-Maur, to which he belonged. Under the administration of eminent scholar-librarians, libraries at the end of the Renaissance also showed an increased interest in the preservation of books, with particular emphasis on binding, which with the support of wealthy patrons evolved into an art form in its own right. With their interest in editions and textual problems, scholar-librarians also established the tradition—which endured until the 19th century—of maintaining a corps of scribes in the service of great libraries for the preparation of accurate copies for the library itself and for the benefit of scholars personally unable to consult the library's collections.

REFERENCES

Hanna H. Gray, "Renaissance Humanism: The Pursuit of Eloquence," *Journal of the History of Ideas* (1963), reprinted in Paul Oskar Kristeller and Philip P. Wiener, *Renaissance Essays* (1968).

Paul Oskar Kristeller, *Renaissance Thought: The Classic, Scholastic and Humanistic Strains* (1961).

Kristeller, *Renaissance Thought II: Papers on Humanism and the Arts* (1965).

Curt Ferdinand Bühler, *The Fifteenth Century Book* (1960).

John Willis Clark, *The Care of Books: An Essay on the Development of Libraries and Their Fittings, from Earliest Times to the End of the Eighteenth Century* (1909).

Lucian Febvre and Henri-Jean Martin, *The Impact of Printing, 1450-1860,* translated by David Gerard (1976).

Sandra Hindman and James Douglas Farquhar, *Pen to Press: Illustrated Manuscripts and Printed Books in the First Century of Printing* (1977).

Malcolm Parkes, "The Literacy of the Laity," in *Literature and Western Civilization,* edited by David Daiches and Anthony Thorlby (1972–76), volume II.

Sigfrid Heinrich Steinberg, *Five Hundred Years of Printing* (1955; revised ed. 1974).

Berthold L. Ullman, *The Origin and Development of Humanistic Script* (1960).

Berthold L. Ullman and Philip A. Stadter, *The Public Library of Renaissance Florence* (1972).

Francis Wormald and C. E. Wright, *The English Library before 1700* (1958).

PAUL SAENGER

Reprography

During the 1950s a new word, "reprography," came to be used to describe the technology of reproducing two-dimensional visual communication media in administrative, business, and institutional operations. The term appeared sporadically in the library literature of the 1960s and entered the working vocabulary of librarians in the mid-1970s, gradually replacing photoduplication, document copying, documentary reproduction and, to some extent, photocopying, although the latter term is still very much in use. Copying is uniquely important as a means of carrying out the library's mission of information transfer.

Technology. Reprographic processes are based on the differential chemical or physical changes effected in some materials by an exposure to radiant energy, which form an image that is visible, or can be made visible, and permanent. The currently used processes—photography, electrophotography, and thermography—depend on chemical systems (such as iron salts, silver halides, diazonium), electrical phenomena, or the action of heat.

The various copying processes and methods may be characterized by the tonal relationships of the copies to the original that was copied (the so-called polarity, whether positive or negative), the image orientation (right-reading, or reverse-reading), the size of copies, the method of image production (direct or transfer), the method of exposure (contact or optical), the color sensitivity (blue-sensitive, ortho, pan), speed (sensitivity to the radiant energy), and the resolving power and contrast of the sensitized materials used.

Black areas in the original image appear black, and white areas appear white in a *positive* copy: the tones correspond to those of the original. In a *negative* copy, the tone values are reversed. *Positive* and *negative* are also used in another sense, the former to describe an original image with dark letters on a light background; the latter, white letters on a dark background. When a negative-working process is used, the first copy made from a positive original will be a negative copy (tonal values reversed) and must be recopied to get a positive copy. Similarly, if a procedure yields reverse-reading copies, another step is required for getting right-reading copies.

A *direct* process produces a copy directly on a piece of material. A *transfer* process first produces an image on a piece of sensitized material that is used as an intermediate and that then transfers it to another piece of material that becomes the copy.

The sensitized material may be exposed to energy (light or heat, depending on the process) in contact with the original or through a lens (optic). Thus the method of exposure may be called *contact* or *optical.*

Contact exposure can be either *direct* (the light passes through the original to expose the sensitized

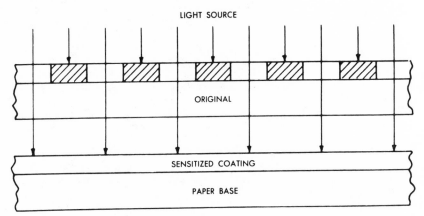

Figure 1. Copying by the direct contact method

Figure 2. Copying by the contact-reflex method

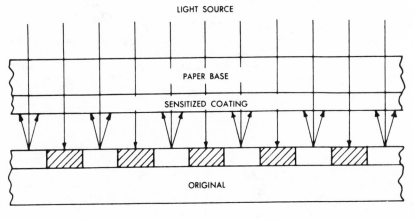

701

material) or *reflex* (the light passes through the sensitized material, to be absorbed by the dark and reflected by the white parts of the original). The *direct-contact* method can be used only for copying originals printed on one side of translucent paper or film, as the light must pass through it to create the image.

The copy will be right-reading or reverse-reading, depending on whether the translucent original is placed face up or face down on the sensitized material. Unless special (autopositive) material is used, the copy will be negative. Originals printed on both sides and on opaque materials can be copied with the *contac-reflex* method. Normally, the copy made by "reflexing" is negative and reverse-reading, and a right-reading copy is then made of it by the direct-contact method.

Contact methods work quite well with loose sheet material, as it is usually possible to bring the original and the sensitized material into the near-perfect contact necessary for satisfactory imaging. The difficulties in using this method with bound volumes, however, are great. The size, thickness, and weight of the book, the variations in paper surface and condition, the stiffness of the binding (as in, for example, oversewn binding), insufficient margins, and other variables can pose problems that might be difficult or impossible to solve.

Although a variety of light-sensitive materials were used with success in the early days of photography in the 1840s, the predominant role in photographic (including reprographic) imaging was soon taken by silver halide systems. Silver halide materials can be fashioned to suit many purposes and processes and yield excellent results. Alternative systems, which have been developing during the past several decades, have so far found a place only in a few special, though important, applications, such as reprography.

At a Paris exhibition in 1900 a camera was shown that was designed to make copies from books on a roll of paper and was equipped with a reversing prism; it was awarded a prize. In 1910 a similar machine, the *Photostat* camera, entered the American market. The Photostat system (and similar apparatus made by other manufacturers) combines a copyboard, a prism-equipped camera capable of making prints up to 18 by 24 inches, a large capacity paper supply, and developing and fixing trays in one machine. There is no need for a darkroom. The first copy is negative, but right-reading, and copy size may be varied from 50 to 200 percent of the original. Various photographic controls may be exercised during exposure and processing; the quality of the product is potentially very high.

One of several important reprographic systems introduced in the 1950s was a new silver halide process: *diffusion-transfer-reversal* (DTR). Thanks to the speedy and simple processing and the one-step production of a positive copy, inexpensive equipment, and numerous fiercely competitive suppliers, DTR became the dominant copying method of the 1950s. Another innovation of the 1950s was Verifax (TM), a *gelatin-dye-transfer* process, which achieves the same result as the DTR process by different means, and which was also popular for a time.

Another important reprographic novelty of the 1950s was Thermo-Fax™—the first practical imaging process operating by the action of heat rather than light. The process is simple, clean, convenient, and very fast. It has the disadvantage, however, that the text of the original must be written, typed, or printed with heat-absorbing (carbon content) ink (dyes do not absorb heat), and that the unexposed parts of the material retain their heat sensitivity and are subject to deterioration. The *dual spectrum* process is a combined photographic-thermographic process introduced a few years later. The original need not absorb heat and, like the Thermo-Fax process it largely replaced, does not need chemicals for processing.

Xerography was another new reprographic process introduced in the 1950s. After a relatively slow start, it has had a more far-reaching effect in the long run than either DTR or thermography. Xerography is based on the behavior of certain materials (photoconductors), which retain an electrostatic charge in the dark, but dissipate it upon exposure to light. If the photoconductor (such as a selenium-coated plate or cylinder) is given an electrostatic charge prior to exposure, the charge is retained or dissipated and a latent image formed according to the pattern of light reflected from the original. Pigment (toner) particles attracted by the retained charge make the latent image visible. The pigment is transferred from the plate or cylinder to some material (such as uncoated paper) and fused by heat or pressure. Xerography is an *electrophotographic transfer* process.

A *direct electrophotographic* process (Electrofax) became commercially available in 1954. In this process the latent image is formed on a thin photoconductive layer coated on the copy paper itself. The coating—zinc oxide—is readily available, inexpensive, nontoxic, and stable. The sensitivity of zinc-oxide paper can be modified and controlled by the addition of dyes to the coating, and with pigment suspended in liquid, very high resolution can be achieved.

By the end of the 1960s, the highly developed, self-contained, automated equipment manufactured for office copying with the electrophotographic method made almost all previous copying processes look obsolete and unquestionably dominated the marketplace.

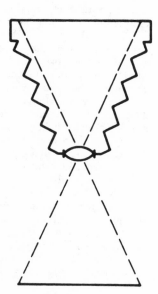

Figure 3. Optical copying (full-size)

Applications. Copying processes are used in libraries for (1) the acquisition, sharing, and preservation of library materials, (2) the assistance of patrons in using library materials, and (3) communication and record management purposes. In the last category, with the possible exception of catalogue card reproduction, the application requirements and procedures are essentially the same in the library as in other organizations. Copying for the purpose of adding something to the collection that is unavailable in the original, making facsimiles of highly prized or fragile items, sharing resources with other libraries without depriving the library's own constituency of potential use, replacing deteriorating items, missing issues, lost pages—these are the principal copying uses in the library, and they have requirements that are often different from and more difficult to meet than those in many other applications of copying technology.

The need for copying is as old as writing. Until the development of photography around the middle of the 19th century, an existing document had to be copied by hand. The new medium's potential for making facsimiles for the purpose of extending the use of literature in hitherto impossible ways was quickly recognized. Microphotocopying was demonstrated in 1839, and the idea of republishing by microphotographic means was first communicated by Sir John Herschel in 1853. During the second half of the century the materials and apparatus of general photography were used for copying. Some of the advantages of specially designed copying equipment were realized at the turn of the century. By then some libraries had installed photographic laboratories.

Photocopying for acquisition and preservation purposes, as well as for patrons' use, was greatly expanded by the introduction of the photostat-type camera, which is well suited to copying library materials. In 1912 photostat-type cameras were installed in the Library of Congress, Chicago's John Crerar Library, and the New York Public Library; by 1929, 42 libraries operated such machines. Until the mid-1930s, when microfilm took over such tasks, libraries used photostats for reprinting rare books in small editions and for the preservation of deteriorating newspaper collections. By 1946 the public demand for copies had increased so much that the New York Public Library produced almost half a million photostat copies in one year.

Photostat services proved valuable to libraries and library users. Yet they required relatively large investment and, in order to be economically efficient, consistently high production levels; thus only a few dozen libraries could afford them. The majority had to wait for simpler and cheaper copying methods. These came about when some major manufacturers decided to concentrate on one segment of the copying market that had the highest sales potential, office records.

The new processes of the 1950s were conceived as office systems, for an input (business letters and records) that was of standard size and of fairly uniform graphic quality, and for an output that satisfied rather modest functional requirements of appearance, legibility, and permanence. Since the machines were cheap and the process simple, any library could afford them. Most did acquire them, in spite of the serious shortcomings of the equipment and materials for library purposes. Copying from bound volumes was difficult and wasted much time and material. Books were subject to far more wear and tear than in photostating or microfilming. Larger books and other "difficult" items could not be handled at all, and the results from even routine materials were normally quite inferior to photostats. But copies were readily available and affordable; "convenience copying" had begun.

In 1959 with the Xerox 914 automated copying reached the market. Copying became easier and faster than at any time previously, and the copies, made on inexpensive plain paper, were usually better. The machine was complex and expensive; the 914, however, was not sold, just leased, with charges based on usage. Under those circumstances, many libraries were able to install these machines and offer a copying service that was faster, cheaper, and for the most part better than before.

Owing to the ease and speed of their operation, and to effective marketing plans, the Xerox and other electrostatic machines quickly and firmly established themselves in libraries. Very low prices and fast service led to such a great expansion in demand that not only were the staff-operated copy services kept busy but also the numerous coin-operated, self-service copiers, which became prevalent in libraries around the mid-1960s. With the advent of these machines, convenience copying increased significantly.

Convenience was also a factor in the use of electrostatic copiers for catalogue-card reproduction. The cards produced on office copiers do not match the appearance and durability of cards made by quality offset printing or from microfilm intermediates on continuous electrostatic printers, but they are instantly available and cheap. The method became popular in many libraries.

When the price of copies fell to a few cents, many library users quit taking notes and copied the entire text of their reading instead. Low-cost, instant copying has thus changed study habits and has been instrumental in the partial conversion of the circulating library into a duplicating library. For libraries there have been several consequences of this development. First, by the early 1970s self-service copying had lowered the volume of work in staff-operated services to the point that some were no longer economically justifiable. Second, electrostatic copiers add to the preservation problems in the library because of wear and tear. Third, a part of the public seems to have developed a sense of unquestionable right to uninterrupted copying in the library. The library user normally copies from relatively difficult-to-handle originals yet often lacks the elementary skills required for operating the copier and seems not to have an understanding of the frailties of the machine. Service interruptions and "bad copies" (often due to failure to use the machine correctly) tend to cause occasionally extreme adverse public reaction.

Legally, it may be argued, most copying in the library seems to constitute "fair use"; legitimate rights of publishers do not appear to be violated by the practice. Nevertheless, the implications of the large expansion in copying, especially for interlibrary loan, were among the hotly debated issues in writing the U.S. Copyright Act of 1976. This law succeeds in fairly balancing private interests with the rights of the public (a basic feature of U.S. copyright from the beginning). It continues to be attacked by some publishers trying to gain economic advantage by replacing the concept of "fair use" with "fee for use."

Telefacsimile. First demonstrated in the 1840s, established for the transmission of wirephotos in the 1930s, in more general use in the 1960s and 1970s, telefacsimile is a reprographic process for transmitting images of documents over communications lines and producing their facsimiles at distant sites.

In a telefacsimile system, a transmission facility (such as a cable or a telephone line) connects a transmitter with a receiver. In the transmitter, a scanning apparatus evaluates the light reflectance of very small areas, called *pixels* or picture elements (from 10,000 to 160,000 per square inch), and converts the image patterns into analogue or digital electric signals. These signals are converted into tone patterns transmittable over communication lines. They are transmitted and then restored to their original form by the facsimile receiver and fed to a printer. The graphic quality of the facsimile is determined by the type of printer (electrothermal, dielectric, photographic, or electrostatic) and by the number of pixels scanned and printed. The higher the number of pixels per square inch, the higher the potential quality of reproduction, the slower the rate of transmission—and the higher the cost.

In spite of the obvious potential of telefacsimile in library applications (such as interlibrary communications and the transmittal of short texts), the pioneering installations of the 1960s and 1970s were largely unsuccessful, as much for the lack of demonstrated need for the speedy delivery provided as for their relatively high costs and some technical problems. In the 1980s, improved equipment, a greater degree of compatibility, increased user familiarity, and relatively reasonable costs led to much more widespread commercial utilization and reawakened library interest in telefacsimile.

New Systems of the 1980s. Advances in digital image processing and in computers and computer-related equipment facilitated the development of new systems for the storage and reproduction of document images. Optical disk systems exemplify this trend, as does the laser copier introduced in 1985. In appearance and size this copier resembles medium-volume conventional copiers; the copies look identical to those made on standard, high-quality copy equipment. Instead of imaging optically, however, the original document is scanned and the copy is printed from digital signals, using a process developed for computer page printers.

The laser copier can do more, however, than just duplicate the product of conventional optical copiers. It can create new images: change the dimensions of the image differentially—that is, to a greater or lesser degree horizontally than vertically; selectively copy part of an image; delete part of an image; automatically center the image on the copy regardless of the position of the original document on the copy glass; shift an image to any position on the copy; and reverse images from positive to negative and vice versa. Acting as an input device is another capability: the

digitized image data may be sent to a word processor or to a computer memory. As an output device, it can receive and print image data from external storage or from a transmission line. The laser copier combines the functions of an optical copier with those of a graphic arts image manipulator, a digital image processor, and a versatile computer peripheral device.

REFERENCES
F. C. Crix, *Reprographic Management Handbook* (1975).
William R. Hawken, *Copying Methods Manual* (1966).
Patrick Firpo, Lester Alexander, and Claudia Katayanagi, *Copyart: The First Complete Guide to the Copy Machine* (1979).
Charles LaHood and Robert C. Sullivan, *Reprographic Services in Libraries: Organization and Administration* (1975).
Library Technology Reports (1965–   ) includes test reports and news about copying equipment.
Peter G. New, *Reprography for Librarians* (1975).

FRANCIS F. SPREITZER

Resource Sharing

Any study of the library literature reveals many concepts of resource sharing and indicates that the range of resource sharing activities encompasses virtually all the functions of a library. At the heart of most uses of the term, however, is a view that, whatever resource is being considered, the sharing of it means not only that a library gives and receives a part of it, but also that the library is involved in the process of determining how the resource should be shared and in the work of its distribution. Resources to be shared may be objects, persons, or funds, and include library materials, library records, staff expertise, storage facilities, and equipment such as computers.

Two definitions, from the American and British library literature, will provide a clearer idea of the concept. First, Allen Kents states:

> Resource sharing denotes a mode of operation whereby library functions are shared in common by a number of libraries. The goals are to provide a positive net effect: (*a*) on the library user in terms of access to more materials or services, and/or (*b*) on the library budget in terms of providing level service at less cost, increased service at level cost, or much more service at less cost than if undertaken individually. (*Encyclopedia of Library and Information Science* [1978], vol. 25, p. 295).

Second, Philip Sewell writes:

> Resource sharing may appear to be nothing more than a new term for the familiar concept of library cooperation. True, many of the same activities are included, but there is a significant difference in approach. The earlier term takes the existence of libraries for granted and describes how they can achieve their objectives better by working together. The new term appears rather to assume a range of physical, intellectual and conceptual resources on the one hand and a body of people on the other, and covers the activities involved in organizing the one into a set of optimum relationships to meet the needs of the other. (*Resource Sharing* [1981], p. 9).

This second definition particularly emphasizes that resource sharing is not an end in itself, but rather a means to improve the services provided to information users.

The need for resource sharing activity is the result of three underlying trends in 20th-century society: (1) the growth of all forms of literature; (2) stemming from this, society's increasing reliance on information to enable it to function effectively; (3) inflation in the cost of materials coupled with increasing availability of technology, which have made it economically imperative to consider sharing resources.

Resource Sharing Activities. The oldest and most common resource sharing activity is almost certainly the provision of access to library materials. Indeed, interlibrary lending of material has been practiced for many years, although the scale of such activity has expanded greatly since the mid-1950s. Interlibrary loan (ILL) arrangements have inherent weaknesses; they fail to extend the total provision of available material unless accompanied by a cooperative acquisition policy. Additionally, they require the construction of union lists of holdings and/or possibly time-consuming and staff-intensive procedures for processing ILL requests. Interlibrary lending may also conflict with a library's obligations to its own users, and in the larger decentralized systems the stage has been reached where the demands imposed on those libraries with richer collections have spawned restrictions and punitive charges. The net results of these weaknesses are low satisfaction rates, delays, high costs, and low confidence.

An alternative is to provide a centralized collection dedicated to the provision of services to other libraries. This is the approach adopted in the United Kingdom, where 75 percent of all interlibrary lending demand is channelled through the British Library Lending Division (BLLD). Such an arrangement avoids some of the weaknesses of decentralized interlending and can result in better provision and more efficient access. However, the crucial factor is whether such an arrangement is a sensible use of funds. Maurice Line asserted (1984) that government funding of centralized collections can be justified:

> If the volume of demand is large enough to result in low unit costs; at least 1,500,000 requests a year need to be received to make a system based on a comprehensive central stock more economic than a co-operative one, though it might be decided to operate with fewer requests than this on the grounds that the better service is worth paying for.

This is in effect a shared resource.

Another means for providing access to materials through resource sharing is the referral of readers themselves to collections likely to be able to supply their particular information needs, a process that may be assisted by the compilation of directories of resources. Other activities may include joint provision of transport arrangements for document supply; cooperative indexing, abstracting, or translation of material; and joint provision of online services to assist exploitation of collections.

Cooperative Acquisition Policies within Groups of Libraries. These feature prominently in many resource sharing arrangements. In some cases, as in the Research Libraries Group, an analysis of existing collection strengths and development policies may be the starting point. Other schemes, such as the British Regional Library Systems subject specialization schemes, may fund cooperative acquisition arrangements to ensure adequate coverage of particular material. Such arrangements, however, are frequently in conflict with the primary responsibility of a library to its own clientele, in that in order to satisfy its obligation to the resource sharing policy the library is purchasing some material of less importance to its own readers, with funds that could otherwise be spent on more relevant material. It is therefore not surprising that cooperative acquisition programs have a checkered history. Both cooperative acquisition and deacquisition—cooperative decisions as to which monographs should be discarded to ensure that adequate coverage is maintained, or which less-used serials each partner should cancel to ensure that at least one copy of each title is held—also rely on union lists and catalogues as do interlending arrangements.

Other extensions of resource sharing to support collection development include the provision of cooperative storage facilities for lesser-used material and a cooperative approach to preservation and binding policies. Both require as much coordination as cooperative acquisition and deacquisition policies, and suffer from the same drawbacks, but the looming preservation crisis will result in greater attention to this aspect of resource sharing.

Record Creation Activities. These comprise a further set of objectives in many resource sharing arrangements. Indeed, despite the establishment of national bibliographies throughout all the developed and much of the developing world, many resource sharing arrangements have their origin in shared cataloguing, largely assisted by the increasing availability of suitable computer technology since the mid-1960s. We have already noted how cooperative collection development policies and interlending may be facilitated by the availability of union listings, but there is a conflict between the needs for successful interlending on the one hand and shared record creation on the other. The latter's efficiency is enhanced by a large overlap of acquisitions between member libraries, whereas interlending is aiming at providing access to as many different titles as possible within the resource sharing arrangement. One extension of cooperative record creation that does facilitate interlending is the sharing of circulation data; information about a particular title's availability on the shelf in another library may be a valuable addition to the services a library can offer to its users.

Staff; Management Information. Finally, two other activities amenable to resource sharing involve staff resources and management information. Resource sharing may incorporate arrangements for cooperative staff training ventures and exchanges of staff, while most successful resource sharing requires a sharing of information for monitoring its activities, including levels of provision and use within each of the cooperating libraries.

Organization and Administration of Programs. Resource sharing can be carried out at any level, from the international to the local, and can be arranged in a variety of ways. Work by Unesco in the 1970s, in cooperation with organizations such as the International Federation of Library Associations and Institutions (IFLA), led to the establishment of two complementary programs later merged: UNISIST, concentrating on the development of a world science information system, and NATIS, identifying the structures required to enable library and information services to play an effective role in national plans for economic and social development. IFLA conducts two major programs, Universal Bibliographic Control (UBC), which seeks to make available basic bibliographic data on all publications issued in all countries, and Universal Availability of Publications (UAP), which aims to improve availability of materials at all levels, including access to new publications and retention of last copies, and which is based on the principle that every country should be able to provide access to its own publications. Both are programs that, if fully developed, will have profound resource sharing implications.

At the national level, the centralized approach to interlibrary lending in the United Kingdom has been described. Plans for the establishment of a National Periodicals Center in the U.S. foundered largely because of disagreement among librarians as to how it should operate, because of the tradition of state autonomy, and because of a lack of federal funding. Resource sharing in the U.S. is largely characterized by privately funded networks such as RLG's Research Libraries Information Network (RLIN), OCLC, and state or regional networks such as the Washington Library Network (WLN) and the Minnesota Interlibrary Telecommunications Exchange (MINITEX). Many local resource sharing ventures have operated for long periods, based on particular cities or conurbations, one such example being the Sheffield Interchange Organization (SINTO) in the U.K.

In developing countries the need for resource sharing may be obvious, but the lack of resources to share may be a fundamental obstacle. Experience suggests that an evolutionary progression, from exchange of accessions lists and compilation of directories of resources to formal establishment of union lists and interlibrary loans (perhaps restricted to particular subject fields) is likely to prove more successful than broader, centralized schemes, such as the Standing Conference of African University Librarians (SCAUL), that have attempted to be comprehensive both in functions and subject coverage.

The arrangements between partners in a resource sharing venture can often be categorized into star, hierarchical, and distributed networks. If most of the funds of the venture are spent on maintaining one or a few major centers it will probably be a highly centralized or "star" network. If requests for information are expected to be routed through particular stages, for example, through a regional center and, if failed, to a larger state library, inherent delays result from such a hierarchical structure. A distributed network of partners of equal status is now becoming a more effective option because of developments in telecommunications and computing, but it is still complex to organize such a network effectively.

Impact on Individual Libraries. Resource sharing activities affect the autonomy of the libraries involved. Dangers arising from that factor can be minimized only by firm and unambiguous arrangements with partners and a clear understanding of the roles of each of the participating libraries. Librarians need to consider responsiblities to their primary clientele and the ways in which resource sharing can enhance their services. Successful sharing will occur only where there is no conflict between obligations made by the resource sharing arrangement and the objectives of the institutions involved.

Membership of networks that involve the sharing of records may have a profound effect on the record creation and automation activities of member libraries. While local discretion is possible in such matters as cataloguing standards, deviations will of themselves consume resources and libraries will reap the maximum benefits only by conforming to agreed standards. The problems of transitional arrangements between new and existing record creation practices may receive attention and retrospective conversion of older records may require consideration. The costs involved in such arrangements should be defined, compared with those of the existing practices, and weighed against the benefit resource sharing is expected to bring.

Resource sharing will require a willingness on the part of those involved to adapt to change and to come to terms with the realization that libraries can no longer be self-sufficient. Users must be educated and consulted in order to build an understanding of the types of material that can be expected to be provided locally and of how to gain access to the resources of other libraries.

Users must also be convinced that they can live with the delays inherent in resource sharing, or special arrangements must be made to meet the extra costs of rapid delivery of documents by such means as facsimile transmission. Sensible predictions about trends in users' needs have to be made so that acquisitions are only reduced in those areas where demands are likely to remain slight. Users will still expect that their primary needs will be met from their own libraries' resources, and large increases in interlending and document supply transactions may adversely affect both the standard and the costs of the service offered.

The effectiveness of any resource sharing arrangement will depend upon efficient and reliable communications and delivery systems between members. Resource sharing is not an end in itself, and there would be more success stories to report in this field if librarians regarded cooperation not only altruistically, but also realistically as a means for the library to improve its standards of services to its users.

Trends and Issues. Many trends will be significant in the development of resource sharing activities in the next decade, but the effects of *technology* are likely to be more profound than all others. The impetus for increased resource sharing has often come in the past from particular technical developments, and this pattern is likely to continue. The first such impetus came from the introduction of cheap and reliable photocoyping equipment, which provided an alternative to interlibrary loan for shorter items such as serial articles. Document supply, a term which has been developed to cover both the loan of originals and the supply of surrogates or copies for retention, will undergo a further transformation when it becomes economic and reliable to transmit images digitally over telecommunication networks. Facsimile transmission has been available to libraries for many years but numerous studies and practical experience have shown that the "Group III" generation of machines available in the mid-1980s is expensive and unsuitable for the mass transmission of library documents; however, there is hope that the forthcoming generation of equipment will change this situation. Telecommunication facilities, including satellites, which enable massive amounts of data, including digital images of documents, to be transmitted from continent to continent are already available and becoming cheaper. Even the existing telecommunication networks of major library networks such as RLG and OCLC have capacity at quiet periods, especially overnight, to transmit images of documents, once the problems of rapidly digitizing the originals and storing them for later transmission have been overcome.

Developments in the technology for storing data are also likely to have a powerful impact on resource sharing networks. Present bibliographic networks have become possible only because of advances already made in the storage of large quantities of machine readable data on magnetic media. The development of optical disk technology appears to offer the prospect of libraries being able to hold far more data on their own computer equipment than at present. It is possible to predict that within only a few years a database of the size of RLIN's can be copied onto optical disks and distributed to member libraries for mounting on their own computers. Such technology also enables libraries to store complete texts online.

Copyright. Publishers throughout the world have argued, with varying degrees of conviction, that library photocopying is damaging their interests and have pressed for legislation to control such activities. Although in the U.S. libraries are now obliged by law to limit their photocopying and a Copyright Clearance Center was established, there has been no change in the legal position in the U.K. or in many other countries. Publishers have not been slow to appreciate the potential benefits of new technology, however, in particular optical disks. Although a consortium of major scientific, technical, and medical publishers known as ADONIS did not proceed with its initial plans, it was indicative of likely future development. The ADONIS system was originally envisaged as a cooperative venture to store on optical disks the full texts of current and recent issues of the approximately 5,000 journals most frequently requested on interlibrary loan. A service for copies of single articles would then be offered by the publishers, possibly bypassing libraries altogether, but more likely using existing document suppliers as agents. The revenues to be gained from such a service might yet tempt the publishers to exploit the single-article market directly, although such activity in the mid-1980s was mainly restricted to licensing commercial document suppliers to provide copies of articles.

The development of electronic publishing, particularly where there is no hardcopy or microform equivalent, may also have a significant effect on resource sharing during the next decade. Publishers will have far greater control over the use made of these texts and are likely to ensure that library users pay royalties.

Conservation. Richard De Gennaro highlighted the issue of conservation in a resource sharing context thus (1980):

> A vast majority of the books printed between 1850 and 1950 will be unusable by the end of this century as a result of the destructive effects of air pollution and the presence

of acid and other harmful chemicals in their paper and binding. When we add to this the destructive effects of careless use, repeated photocopying, and frequent shipment through the mails, we are facing a crisis of monumental proportions.

Clearly, conservation is going to play a more prominent role in resource sharing considerations in the future. On the one hand, libraries will become more cautious about loaning originals, but, on the other, conservation by microfilming, deacidification, or digital storage may all be activities undertaken by resource sharing networks to enable surrogates of fragile material to continue to be used.

Evaluation and Research. Resource sharing will clearly be a continuing element in the provision of library services. It is already one of the most written about topics in library literature, and now has a journal devoted entirely to the subject, *Resource Sharing and Library Networks* (1981–). Yet there has been little evaluation of the results of resource sharing that is useful for professional guidance. There is clearly a need for research in this area, in order that activity may be planned more rationally. This position is passionately argued by Thomas Ballard, who claims (*American Libraries,* 1985): "It would seem that resource sharing needs no objective evidence to support it; being, therefore, dogma, it has no obligation to justify itself." He argues that resource sharing proposals need to estimate the benefits (supported with objective data), build in evaluation, describe the costs, consider cheaper alternatives for accomplishing the same goal, and alternatives to cooperation.

While technological developments may have a substantial effect on resource sharing in the Western Hemisphere, it is not realistic to assume that progress in library provision will be made at the same pace throughout the world. The international dimension of resource sharing, however, will assume greater importance in the future because of current developments in telecommunications. Resource sharing should not be seen as an end in itself. All such activities still need to be assessed in light of overall benefit to the library user.

REFERENCES

Richard De Gennaro, "Resource Sharing in a Network Environment," *Library Journal* (1980).
Maurice Line, "Resource Sharing: the Present Situation and the Likely Effect of Electronic Technology." *The Future of Serials: Publication, Automation and Management* (1984).
Rose Mary Magrill, "The Concept of Resource Sharing," *Canadian Library Journal* (1978).
Philip Sewell, *Resource Sharing.* (1981).
H. D. L. Vervliet, *Resource Sharing of Libraries in Developing Countries.* (1979).

MALCOLM SMITH

Richardson, Ernest C.
(1860–1939)

Exemplar of the scholar-librarian tradition, Ernest Cushing Richardson made enduring contributions to American librarianship. Among his notable accomplishments may be counted the directorship of the Princeton University Library (1890–1920), the development of a classification scheme, the pursuit of cooperative bibliographic arrangements, and the publi-

Ernest C. Richardson

cation of nearly 200 items covering an impressive range of library topics and other scholarly subjects.

Richardson was born on February 9, 1860, in Woburn, Massachusetts. His early years were devoted to school, athletic activites, and frequent use of the local public library. He entered Amherst College in 1876 at 16, the last year of Melvil Dewey's term as Assistant Librarian. Although Richardson became a library student assistant during his freshman year, it is not known if he was capitvated by the charismatic Dewey. Richardson's apprenticeship under Dewey's brilliant successor, Walter S. Biscoe, was a decisive influence on the selection of a career in librarianship.

Deeply religious and committed to a life of scholarship, Richardson entered the Hartford Theological Seminary in 1880. He worked as a student assistant for several years, became Assistant Librarian in 1882, and accepted the position of Director in 1884. During 1884 Richardson traveled to Europe and studied at various university libraries, a journey that he repeated many times in the ensuing years. The European visit marked the beginning of a lifetime concern with international library cooperation. At the Hartford Seminary, Richardson devised and implemented a classification scheme and completed many learned studies. In 1888 he was awarded an honorary doctorate from Washington and Jefferson College for preparation of the *Bibliographical Synopsis of the Ante-Nicene Fathers* (1887), a guide to the literature relating to early Christian leaders.

Although Richardson enjoyed the congenial atmosphere at the Hartford Seminary, the need for salary improvement and the challenge of managing a distinguished research library convinced him to accept the Librarian's position at Princeton University in 1890. One year after his appointment, Richardson married Grace Duncan Ely, a woman of above-average financial means.

For 30 years Richardson struggled to provide the collections, facilities, and services that he believed Princeton needed. By 1900 Princeton had adopted a decimal classification scheme devised by Richardson, and in 1901 the Library became one of the early subscribers to the Library of Congress catalogue cards. That momentous decision was reached in a meeting which included such luminaries as Woodrow Wilson, Grover Cleveland, and John S. Billings. Richardson was perhaps most successful with the acquisitions program; the collection grew from 81,000 volumes in 1890 to approximately 450,000 volumes in 1920.

The reduction of bibliographic complexity was one of Richardson's many crusades that found application at Princeton. He believed in abbreviated cataloguing, an approach that provided the minimum information needed to identify and locate library materials. Richardson's "title-a-bar" theory involved the use of a Linotype machine to print one-line entries for each book in the form of a printed catalogue. That type of catalogue was not uniformly endorsed by the Princeton faculty. Beginning in 1913 the Princeton Library experienced reduced financial support, and salary levels declined. Faculty demands for more services and various complaints led to the appointment of an investigatory committee in 1920. An Associate Librarian, James Gerould, was employed with special authority to institute changes. He immediately abandoned the printed catalogues and be-

gan to reclassify portions of the collection. Administratively dethroned and elevated to figurehead status, Richardson argued bitterly with the university until 1925, when he accepted a position as honorary consultant in bibliography at the Library of Congress. Neither side was without fault, but Richardson was clearly stubborn, unwilling to compromise or concede shortcomings. This unfortunate propensity to pursue a collision course would occur again.

At the Library of Congress Richardson continued to teach as he had done at Princeton and initiated one of the most significant bibliographic projects of that era. For 20 years Richardson had been writing and speaking, primarily through the American Library Institute, a deliberative body affiliated with the American Library Association, about the paucity of resources in research libraries and the lack of systematic bibliographic organization. As Chairman of ALA's Committee on Bibliography, Richardson had laid the groundwork for "Project B," a cooperative cataloguing program to augment and revitalize the national union catalogue at the Library of Congress. Richardson and his staff succeeded in enlarging the union catalogue file from 1,500,000 titles in 1927 to approximately 7,000,000 titles in 1932. Unhappily, Richardson became enmeshed in a debate with the ALA Executive Board over the jurisdiction of another committee, the Cooperative Cataloguing Committee. After a protracted controversy, which erupted in the professional journals, Richardson resigned in 1934 to pursue his many scholarly interests. His commitment to bibliographic control and cooperative arrangements exceeded that of most contemporaries, and "Project B" may be considered the unheralded predecessor of the better-known Farmington Plan of the 1940s.

Foremost a scholar, Richardson published extensively in the fields of librarianship, history, and theology. Significant contributions to the library field included *Classification, Theoretical and Practical* (1901), which influenced such classificationists as England's W. C. Berwick Sayers, *Some Aspects of International Library Cooperation* (1928), *General Library Cooperation and American Research Books* (1930), and *Some Aspects of Cooperative Cataloging* (1934). His writings in library history reveal a serious as well as a whimsical side: *Some Old Egyptian Librarians* (1911), *Biblical Libraries* (1914), and *The Beginnings of Libraries* (1914). Historians remain indebted to his pioneering editorial work on the first volume of *Writings on American History* (1904).

Richardson was an active member and officer of many learned societies and professional groups: American Library Association (President, 1904–05); councillor of the Bibliographical Society of America (1917–37); Chairman of the Bibliography Committee of the American Historical Association (1902–15); and Chairman of the ALA Committee on Bibliography (1922–34). Following World War I his service extended beyond the academy to participation on the United States House Inquiry Commission, a group designated to select and transport documents for the peace conference at Versailles.

After the death of his wife in 1933 and the confrontation with the Executive Board in 1934, Richardson withdrew from library affairs and moved to a cottage near Old Lyme, Connecticut. His scholarly work continued, especially in theology, and he remained actively associated with several institutions of higher education. He died in Old Lyme, Connecticut, June 3, 1939, while engaged in a study of rare books.

Although Richardson does not today enjoy the reputation accorded some early library leaders, his accomplishments were impressive. Few librarians have surpassed his scholarly attainments or pursued more vigorously the goal of bibliographic interdependence. Fittingly, Richardson defined and exemplified the object of library science as the need "to connect a reader, surely and promptly, with the book that he wants to use."

REFERENCES

Lewis C. Branscomb, *A Bio-Bibliographical Study of Ernest Cushing Richardson, 1860–1939,* the standard biography (Ph.D. dissertation, University of Chicago, 1954).

Primary sources are in the Princeton University Library, the Library of Congress, and the Hartford Seminary Foundation Library.

Lewis C. Branscomb, "Richardson, Ernest Cushing," *Dictionary of American Library Biography* (1978).

ARTHUR P. YOUNG

Rider, Arthur Fremont
(1885–1962)

Arthur Fremont Rider, self-described as inquisitive, introverted, and principled, was one of the library profession's most versatile figures. He was an editor, publisher, and writer, associate of Dewey, university librarian, and early microform advocate. Blending the conceptual with the practical was his forte. Rider's bequest to library scholarship is confirmed by the frequent citations to his seminal writings.

Rider was born in Trenton, New Jersey, on May 25, 1885. His childhood years were spent in Middletown, Connecticut, where he first used the Wesleyan University Library, a library he would later direct. Rider graduated from Syracuse University in 1905 and enrolled in the New York State Library School (class of 1907). Before graduating he was invited by Melvil Dewey, a lifelong influence, to work on a revision of the Decimal Classification at the Lake Placid Club. Rider met his first wife, Grace Godfrey, a relative of Dewey, at Lake Placid, and they were married in 1908. Rider was married to Marie Gallup Ambrose in 1951.

Rider began in 1907 the first of many, often overlapping careers. Between 1907 and 1917 he served as Associate Editor of *The Delineator* and Editor of *Monthly Book Review, Publishers' Weekly,* and *Library Journal.* From 1914 to 1932 he was President of Rider Press, a periodical press that printed most of the R. R. Bowker publications. The press failed at the depth of the Depression following a debilitating struggle with a union and the withdrawal of Bowker's patronage. During that period Rider published a series of well-received guidebooks to New York City, Washington, Bermuda, and California. Still not content with those accomplishments, he wrote numerous short stories for popular magazines and dabbled in poetry, drama, and real estate.

Rider's early association with Dewey and library publishing together with business acumen and literary inclinations were valuable assets for the next phase of his career. He was invited to become Librarian of Wesleyan University's Olin Library in 1933, and for the next two decades Rider challenged tradition, experimented, and proselytized new concepts. The results of these reappraisals and other pertinent information about the Wesleyan Library were reported in the Rider-edited periodical, *About Books.* The collection more than doubled during his tenure, largely through en bloc purchases. New cost accounting procedures were introduced; catalogue cards for Wesleyan titles not listed in the Library of Congress catalogue were printed and distributed to many libraries; and cooperative relationships with neighboring libraries were pursued. Faced with limited shelving, Rider initiated a compact shelving program for seldom-used books. The books were shelved, after cropping, on their foreedges. His controversial ideas on compact shelving were published in *Compact Book Storage* (1949). Because of his provocative writings and practical adaptations at Wesleyan, Rider was in constant demand as a speaker and received innumerable requests for advice.

Of his numerous achievements, perhaps his enduring legacy remains his analysis of research library growth and advocacy of microcards espoused in *The Scholar and the Future of the Research Library* (1944). By studying collection growth patterns, Rider concluded that the collections of research libraries double approximately every 16 years. This observation, startling in its time, coupled with the infrequent use of research-level materials, led Rider to propose the microcard as a cost-effective, space-saving solution. Ingeniously, the catalogue card and the relevant document were combined to form a single card with bibliographic description on the front and microtext on the back. His book was reviewed extensively in the library literature and in such nonlibrary journals as the *Columbia Law Review* and the *New England Quarterly.* He invariably received high marks for his trenchant analysis and concise style, but many reviewers questioned the immediate practicability of the idea; however, all would have concurred with William Warner Bishop's remark that Rider had "given librarians much to think about and to think about furiously." Unselfish about the microcard, Rider never patented the concept. Years later, in 1961, he was awarded the annual medal of the National Microfilm Association for his distinguished contribution to microform technology.

Near the end of his library career, in 1951, Rider built the Godfrey Memorial Library, a noncirculating library for the study and promotion of genealogical research. Of major importance to historians and genealogists is the *American Genealogical-Biographical Index* (100+ volumes), issued by that research facility. In 1961, one year before his death, Rider published *Rider's International Classification for the Arrangement of Books on the Shelves of General Libraries.* Reviewers were impressed with the brave attempt but decidedly lukewarm over the results.

Rider's multidimensional career is flamboyantly reconstructed in an often vainglorious autobiography, *And Master of None* (1955), a mine of information, especially about his nonlibrary activities. His contribution to library history was *Melvil Dewey: A Biography* (ALA, 1944); although expectedly favorable toward Dewey, Rider's study was a refreshing

Godfrey Memorial Library
Arthur Fremont Rider

corrective to Grosvenor Dawes's earlier deification of the great pioneer.

Rider died on October 26, 1962, in Middletown, Connecticut. His intellect, vision, and creative applications place him in the front rank of library forebears.

REFERENCE
Wyman W. Parker, "Rider, Arthur Fremont," *Dictionary of American Library Biography* (1978).

ARTHUR P. YOUNG

Joyce Robinson

Robinson, Joyce
(1925-)

Joyce Lilieth Robinson became a leading figure in the development of library services in Jamaica and the Caribbean.

Born in Saint James, Jamaica, July 2, 1925, and educated in Jamaica and in London, Robinson had an impressive record of educational and professional achievement. As the first Jamaican Director of the Jamaica Library Service, she effectively expanded island-wide public and school library services during the 19 years (1957–76) of her administration. A founding member of the Jamaican Library Association, Robinson held offices in JLA and wrote numerous articles and pamphlets on Jamaican library services published in international journals and by the Jamaican press. She participated as a committee member, delegate, or course director in several international library activities. As a volunteer committee member, she became part of many social, educational, and cultural organizations.

In the 1970s she headed JAMAL, (the Jamaican Movement for the Advancement of Literacy), a community-centered basic literacy program for adults 15 years and older. Thousands of volunteer tutors across Jamaica instruct students in reading, writing, and numeracy skills. The curriculum is Jamaican-based, with an emphasis on survival information and reading for pleasure. The program uses island-developed materials that have a strong appeal to both rural and urban readers. JAMAL's experience proved that an adult can be taught to read and write in 400 instruction hours, or six months at three hours daily.

Her background as a librarian led her to a strong conviction that the adult new readers will not maintain their newly acquired skills without continuous access to reading-for-pleasure resources. Stimulating the adult new reader to read for pleasure is the key to preventing the loss of reading skills.

The American Library Association invited Robinson to be its 1979 Carl Milam International Lecturer. She spoke about the role of libraries in the JAMAL effort at several library schools in the United States and Canada. She was awarded an honorary doctorate by Dalhousie University.

JEAN ELLEN COLEMAN*

Rogers, Frank Bradway
(1914-)

Frank Bradway Rogers, military surgeon, trained librarian, and Director of the National Library of Medicine in a crucial period, became one of the de-

ALA
Frank Bradway Rogers

velopers of the first automated database for scientific literature (MEDLARS) and supervised its transfer to medical libraries and hospitals, conceiving a national system for strengthening the provision of biomedical information to health professionals.

Frank "Brad" Rogers was born on December 31, 1914, in Norwood, Ohio. He returned there for his medical training after obtaining an undergraduate degree from Yale University and working for several years at various jobs in New York City and the Midwest. He was private secretary to a professor-turned-congressman—an experience that stood him in good stead later in life when he was trying to persuade congress to pass the Medical Library Assistance Act, advertising agent for a soap firm, and clerk in a food store, all to obtain enough money to see him through medical school, like John Shaw Billings. Rogers joined the Army Medical Corps after graduation from medical school. He took his internship at Letterman General Hospital near San Francisco; later he served in the campaigns in Luzon in the Philippines and in the American Occupation in Japan.

After World War II Rogers accepted a residency in surgery at Walter Reed Army Medical Center. While there he learned that the Army was looking for a physician to be Director of what was then called the Army Medical Library. When the position was offered to him in 1948, he accepted—and thus changed the whole direction of his life.

At that time the Army Medical Library had just undergone a thorough reevaluation, after a long period when it had been allowed to disintegrate to a remarkable degree. Billings, its founder, had given it momentum in the late 19th century through his vision and sense of purpose (aided greatly by the backing and fiscal care bestowed on the Library by the various earlier Surgeons-General of the Army), but the momentum had gradually declined or been halted. When World War II erupted and the armed forces began fighting in exotic areas of the world, encountering exotic diseases, it became obvious that the Army Medical Library could not help the medical officers in their struggles against blackwater fever, jungle rot, tsutsugamushi disease, and unusual tick and bacterial fevers unknown to the physicians in America and western Europe.

Perhaps the most serious example of the inadequacies of the then Army Medical Library was its failure to keep up regular publication of the *Index-Catalogue of the Library of the Surgeon General's Office, Army Medical Library*. Billings had founded the *Index-Catalogue* in the 1870s as a list of the books and journal articles in the Library, the largest medical library in the world. It was arranged and issued alphabetically in a 15- to 20-year cycle—volume 1, for example, contained all the authors and subjects beginning with the letters A to Be; volume 2 went on to Ch; and so on. By 1936 three complete series had been published, but the fourth series was stuck in the middle of the alphabet.

The *Index-Catalogue* had always had a companion publication, the *Index Medicus,* which appeared monthly and brought the alphabetical volumes up to date. By using the two works together, a biomedical worker could obtain a conspectus of some 15 to 20 years of the literature on a topic in one place (the *Index-Catalogue*), then bring it up to date year by year by use of the *Index Medicus*.

This systematic approach to the knowledge of medicine was destroyed when the *Index-Catalogue* was not published on a regular basis and when the *Index Medicus* (after uniting with the American Medical Association's *Quarterly Cumulative Index Medicus*) was not published at all in the 1940s. Neither the older writings of those who had experience with these diseases nor the newer knowledge that was being uncovered in the vast laboratory of World War II medicine was available to military physicians, and it is estimated that, as a result, endemic diseases may have been as lethal to the troops as enemy gunfire.

The need was so obvious something had to be done. The Surgeon-General asked a committee of distinguished librarians from the American Library Association to survey the Library and to recommend needed action. One of their recommendations was for a professionally trained Director of the Library who would be assigned long enough to be able to carry out the needed reforms. Rogers was appointed to this post; he was sent to the library school at Columbia University for a year (1948–49) and then took office. He remained as Director of the Library until August 1963, when he left to become the Librarian of the University of Colorado Medical Center in Denver.

During his term in Washington, Rogers oversaw the transformation of the Library from a sleepy and almost moribund institution to perhaps the most dynamic library, not only for medicine, but for information science as well. He helped arrange the transfer of the Library from the Army alone to the joint Armed Forces, and then from military control to the U.S. Public Health Service, which understood its mission as was central to the purpose of the agency itself. Not surprisingly, Rogers was able to obtain from so understanding an agency a much-needed new Library building, whose form has made it an architectural delight. As the Director of the National Library of Medicine, Rogers defined its role; planned and carried out its reorganization into a Library using 20th-century methods; reinvigorated its classic mission of producing indexes to the medical literature that were extensive in scope and that appeared on time; and began a series of experiments with modern technology (such as time-lapse photography and computer-assisted printing) that has made medicine the best-served field bibliographically speaking, and which has become the model for many other fields and endeavors. The extent of its influence is shown in such achievements as the MEDLARS/MEDLINE system (the precursor to all the automated databases now in use) and the Medical Library Assistance Act, which provided the U.S. for the first time with a national network of medical information centers available to its citizens generally, and which encouraged research and development in this subject fiscally in many national and international centers.

Rogers also saw and acted on the responsibilities of the United States in a period when it had become a world-wide leader. Whether he was co-chairing the First International Congress on Medical Librarianship, in London in 1953, seeing to the myriad details of the Second Congress, held at the new building of the NLM in Bethesda in 1963, or arranging to bring foreign medical librarians to NLM for observation or training, Rogers always had international purposes in mind. He carried out consulting missions in Nigeria and Korea for the Ford and other foundations. When the occasion presented itself, he took over from the National Institutes of Health responsibility for running the medical portion of the translation program under Public Law 480, which used blocked currency from U.S. debtor nations to purchase translations of Russian- and other-language medical research works. He published them in sizable editions and distributed them free to appropriate American institutions.

Rogers was a student of medical history, which he enjoyed examining by himself and which he helped to put on a sound footing again at NLM. He was a craftsman who delighted in the well-bound book, and fitted up a bindery for himself, in which he continued to work after his retirement. His sense of words and their use made all of his writings exact, fitting, and musical. His honors and awards include election to the presidency of the Medical Library Association (which also bestowed on him its Marcia C. Noyes Award) and the American Association of the History of Medicine; the award of the Cyril Barnard Memorial Prize for outstanding service to medical librarianship in 1954; the Melvil Dewey medal of the American Library Association; the U.S. Public Service Distinguished Service Award; and the Horace Hart Award of the Education Council of the Graphic Arts Industry. In 1983 the Frank B. Rogers Information Advancement Award was established by The Institute for Scientific Information in the Medical Library Association.

Rogers's place in the history of the transmission of biomedical information is safe for all time. He came at the right time with Pasteur's "mind prepared," and he left this field immeasurably ahead of where he had found it. A colleague who worked with him for many years described him admiringly as "the civil servant the citizens of the United States don't deserve"; indeed, it was on the basis of Rogers's work there, that the later history of NLM has developed.

REFERENCES
Estelle Brodman, "Frank Bradway Rogers, M.D., President, Medical Library Association, 1962/63," Bulletin of the Medical Library Association (1962).
Wyndham D. Miles, *A History of the National Library of Medicine, The Nation's Treasury of Medical Knowledge* (1982).
ESTELLE BRODMAN

Romania

Romania, a socialist republic of the Balkan Peninsula in southeastern Europe, is bounded by the U.S.S.R. on the north, by the Black Sea on the east, by Bulgaria on the south, and by Yugoslavia and Hungary on the west. Population (1984 est) 22,794,000; area 237,500 sq.km. The official language is Romanian.

History. Monastery and church libraries in Romania, which date back to the 14th century, contain liturgical and patristic manuscripts and books, plus historical and clerical works. Romanian princes maintained court libraries beginning in the 15th century.

Modern public libraries were not developed in Romania until the mid-19th century, when the Central State Library in Bucharest, the Central State Library in Jassy, and the ASTRA Library in Sibiu were established.

National Libraries. Romania has two national libraries, the Central State Library and the Library of the Academy.

Central State Library. The Central State Library of the Socialist Republic of Romania was founded in 1955 as the national library. It continues the traditions of the Central State Library in Bucharest, created in the 1830s and incorporated with the Library of the Romanian Academy in 1901. The collections are encyclopedic in character, and by the mid-1980s they totaled about 7,800,000 bibliographic units, including, besides books and serials, thousands of manuscripts, archive documents, rare and precious books, graphic works, maps, atlases and globes, photographs and illustrated postcards, records, and other items.

The Central State Library acts as the National Center of Bibliographic Information. It provides bibliographic control on the national level by publishing *Bibliografia Republicii Socialiste România,* the national bibliography; it prepares *Anuarul Cărtii,* the cumulative indexes of the national production of printed works; makes up the national union catalogue on cards; and publishes directories and union catalogues of foreign books and serials, among other activities.

The Central State Library also functions as the Documentation Center in Librarianship and Book Restoration. It monitors current literature in the field, publishes some secondary publications, undertakes studies and documentary analyses on subjects regarding research in library science, book preservation and care, and library development in Romania, and makes translations. It also acts as the Documentation Center on Culture and produces secondary publications *(Buletin de informare documentară in cultură)*.

In its capacity as Central Legal Deposit, it receives legal deposit copies and distributes them to the libraries that have this right, provides statistics on the national production of printed works, and controls the way in which the law on legal deposit is brought into operation.

The Central State Library functions as the National Exchange Center of Romania; it receives and redistributes the publications sent on exchange by and to other Romanian institutions, compiles statistics on international exchange, and is concerned with international interlibrary loans, among other activities.

The Methodology Center of the Central State Library provides specialized assistance to the public libraries and other libraries in the country, undertakes sociological studies in library activity and reading, prepares materials on the methodology of book-promotion activities, organizes pioneer libraries and study sessions for exchanges of experience, and assists in professional training of library workers and in offering periodic professional refresher courses.

The Central State Library has several reading rooms specialized by fields of knowledge and by categories of publications and media (such as manuscripts and letters, Romanian bibliophilic books, foreign bibliophilic books, maps, loose sheets, and newspapers); there is also a department for official publications and offices for Unesco publications and publications of other international bodies. Educational activities include organizing exhibitions, meetings with writers and scholars, musical programs, and other events.

Library of the Academy of the Socialist Republic of Romania. This is the second of the two national libraries of the country. It was founded in 1867. Its early growth owed much to private donations and to legal deposit privileges (since 1885). Until 1948 the Library covered almost exclusively humanities and social sciences, but after the reorganization of the Romanian Academy, the Library started collecting works in scientific and technical fields as well.

Holdings total some 8,800,000 volumes; in addition there are thousands of manuscripts, rare books, engravings, maps, about 300,000 letters, archives of important personalities, records, and various categories of other items.

The Library of the Academy is concerned with the publication of the Romanian national retrospective bibliography of books and periodicals from the 16th century. It provides various bibliographic tools and services for its collections. It also administers a major exchange program with publications issued by the Publishing House of the Academy, which are sent to about 10,000 exchange partners in more than 100 countries and fulfill interlibrary loan requests.

Academic Libraries. In the early 1980s there were 43 academic libraries: 3 central university libraries (with general holdings), 4 university libraries, and 36 libraries of the institutes of higher education. These libraries have a rich documentation basis (19,297,00 bibliographic units in the university libraries alone) and include in their holdings Romanian works of great cultural value and outstanding works of the world cultural heritage.

The three central university libraries have also in their collections works by Romanian personalities in manuscript form, private collections of books with dedications, and autographed books. The central university libraries in Bucharest (founded in 1891), Cluj-Napoca (founded in 1872), and Iasi (founded in 1640) have a special status; they are directly subordinated to the Ministry of Education and serve the entire university community on the campus, providing, at the

Central State Library of Romania

Central State Library of Romania, founded 1955. It incorporated the State Central Library in Bucharest with the Library of the Romanian Academy.

same time, support for library activities and for refresher courses for librarians in the university libraries.

The Central University Library in Bucharest acquires foreign publications (books and periodicals) for libraries in the academic network and maintains holdings for the departments of Romanian language, literature, and civilization created abroad.

Academic libraries in Romania are expected to meet not only the requirements of education and research but also those of study and documentation of the specialists on the university campuses they serve. They issue information bulletins, bibliographies, indexes of journals, bibliographic studies on subjects, directories, and other information sources and instruments. They contribute—on the local and national level—to bibliographic and documentary information works and instruct students in library use.

Other libraries include the Library of the Medical and Pharmaceutical Institute (founded in 1857, 848,251 books and 9,447 periodicals), Library of the Polytechnic Institute Gheorghe Gheorghiu-Dej (founded in 1868, 1,310,363 books and periodicals), Central Library of the Academy of Economic Studies (founded in 1913, 1,897,498 volumes), and Central Library of the Nicolae Bălecscu Agronomic Institute (founded in 1948, 468,578 volumes.)

Public Libraries. Romania recognizes three categories: state public libraries, libraries of the trade unions, and libraries of the craftsmen's cooperatives. In 1981, 6,303 public libraries functioned with holdings that add up to 61,095,000 volumes, registering 3,841,269 borrowers and circulating 42,876,510 volumes.

State Public Libraries. Under a decree of the Council of Ministers of December 1951, public libraries were organized according to territorial and administrative criteria. From 1968 each state public library was sponsored by a local administration (such as a county, municipality, town, or village), and was at the same time placed under the guidance and control of the Council of Culture and Socialist Education.

County public libraries have encyclopedic holdings. They gather the printed works issued in the county and works about the county issued outside its boundaries. They draw up local bibliographies, prepare local union catalogues, and edit orientation bibliographies to support the social and economic inter-

ests of the county and its educational program. They organize exhibitions and public meetings, undertake studies on reading, ensure the availability of library materials in reading rooms and lending facilities, and organize libraries for children that work as sections of the county public library. They also organize branch libraries and mobile lending centers, administer interlibrary loans, and provide other services.

Municipal and town libraries function in urban settlements, gather holdings of encyclopedic character, provide library materials to the population in the municipality or town, and participate in various educational programs.

Village libraries cooperate with the school libraries in providing library materials to the population and in supporting the educational programs.

Libraries of the Trade Unions. These libraries belong either to local trade union committees or to the trade union committees of industrial or other economic units. They serve the members of the trade union organization and their families. They carry on—by themselves or in cooperation with the state public libraries and other cultural institutions—activities of an educational character.

Libraries of the Craftsmen's Cooperatives. These libraries belong to the Union of the Craftsmen's Cooperatives and serve the members of the cooperatives and their families.

School Libraries. In Romania school libraries (more than 10,780 in 1981) are organized in each elementary school, gymnasium, secondary school, or vocational school, being sponsored by the local educational bodies or by the corresponding ministries (the technical and vocational schools). They are placed under the guidance and control of the Ministry of Education and Instruction; their holdings contain materials that cover the curriculum requirements and materials concerning problems of children and youth education (50,689,000 volumes in 1981.)

School libraries organize educational activities on their own or cooperate with other cultural institutions in supporting other such activities. They organize circles for children that aim to promote skills of intellectual activity and to instruct them in the techniques of bibliographic and documentary activities. They participate in sociological studies concerned with the reading interests of school children and young people. The Central Pedagogical Library gives methodological guidance to school libraries.

Libraries in Romania (1981)

Type	Administrative units	Service points	Volumes in collections	Annual expenditures (leu)	Population served[a]	Professional staff	Total staff
National[b]	2	--	13,376,000	--	200,916	--	--
Academic[b,c]	43	--	19,297,000	--	252,000	--	--
Public	6,303	--	61,095,000	108,217,000[d]	3,841,269	--	2,231
School	10,782	--	50,689,000	--	2,991,000	--	--
Special[b]	3,948	--	19,279,000	--	843,000	--	--

[a]Registered borrowers.
[b]1980 data.
[c]University libraries only.
[d]Libraries supported by the public authorities only.

Source: Unesco, *Statistical Yearbook,* 1984.

Special Libraries. Special libraries in Romania (3,948 in 1980) belong to research institutes, institutes of higher education, academies, scientific and cultural associations, cultural institutions, institutions of the state administration, industrial units, documentation centers, and offices. Their holdings reflect the specialized character of the fields they serve (19,279,000 volumes in 1980); they serve research workers, engineers, and various specialists. According to the law, such a library may be constituted with no fewer than 3,000 bibliographical units.

The Central Pedagogical Library was founded in 1880 as the library of the Higher Normal School. Its collections are specialized in teaching and number some 345,000 volumes. Its holdings are available to school administrators, university professors, and teachers in all grades of the general obligatory schools or of secondary schools in its own reading rooms or on loan; it publishes educational news and information on methods and makes bibliographic and documentary studies on request; it acts as a forum for the 40 county pedagogical libraries and all school libraries in the country; it also informs other countries on educational achievements and pedagogical research in Romania. It has exchange relations with a number of other countries.

Other libraries include the Library of the National Institute for Information and Documentation, founded in 1949 (holdings of 155,000 books and 6,100 periodicals); the Central Medical Library (1951); and the Central Library of the Academy of Agricultural and Forestry Sciences (1928).

The Profession. The Association of Librarians in the Socialist Republic of Romania was founded in 1957. It contributes to the development of library programs and the drafting of legal documents concerning libraries, participates in activities connected with training and refresher courses for those working in all categories of libraries, and organizes meetings for professional purposes. It became a member of IFLA in 1957 and takes an active part in the life of the international library community.

ANGELA POPESCU-BRĂDICENI*

Rome

There is considerable literary evidence of the private book collections assembled in the latter days of the Republic, thanks successively to Greek stimulation, Roman pride, and military conquest. Much less is known about libraries of a public sort because the archaeological testimony becomes more critical and very little has survived. It is possible that M. T. Varro, a leading Roman of the 1st century B.C., composed a treatise on libraries, but it is established only that Caesar asked him to take charge of a project to build a grand public library, Rome's first, and that nothing came of it directly after Caesar's assassination. Caesar's friend, C. Asinius Pollio, did found near the Forum ("Atrium Libertatis") in the 30s B.C. a library apparently of the sort Caesar had wanted. Reportedly it comprised mainly book booty from the Illyrian campaign of 39 B.C. Latin and Greek sister libraries were formed; the premises were decorated with likenesses of the outstanding writers, Varro being the only living author among the honorees. What became of it is not known.

Several libraries were organized in the imperial capital to memorialize past achievement and nourish national pride. When in 28 B.C. Augustus dedicated a temple of Apollo on the Palatine, Latin and Greek libraries were attached to it. This pairing, as well as the temple nexus, had precedent, but this occasion may have been the first time a practical advantage was manifest, inasmuch as the Latin division was strong in Roman law and the Senate met there occasionally. The Palatine library story is further marked by severe losses from fire, some rebuilding, and leadership by a number of learned men appointed by the emperor; the fire of 363 was apparently the end. The same career and fate seem to have been the lot of the paired libraries begun by Augustus about 25 B.C. on the Campus Martius, named in honor of his sister Octavia. Later emperors also founded libraries, some of which endured: 28 in Constantine's day, it is said (reasonably, although only 10 names are known).

Noteworthy is the Pantheon Library, founded by Emperor Alexander Severus around 230, perhaps the first public library in Rome to have held Eastern religious materials, especially Christian and Jewish writings. It is interesting, and possibly of critical significance, that Julius Africanus, appointed Director, was not only a career soldier and engineer but also a scholar in Christian church chronology and a man of broad enough interests to compile an encyclopedia.

The royal example was followed almost from the start by individuals prominent in letters and well enough off to endow a library—or wealthy and desiring to be remembered as friendly to the world of intellect. We know of a library for the Musicians and Actors Association, and it seems likely that various other associations and institutions had book collections too, whether endowed or not. Were they, like the imperial gifts, placed at temples, public baths, or colonnades?

When chronicler Ammianus Marcellinus complained late in the 4th century that the libraries of Rome were shut up like tombs, he, a Syrian Greek defending Rome against the declining tone in upper-crust Roman life, may well have taken comfort from the vigor outside Rome. From the early 3rd century until the empire's collapse, public libraries were a fairly standard feature of Roman centers in western Europe and North Africa, scattered details being available in the literary records and occasionally from archaeology. Verified information about such institutions in the East is similarly fragmentary, but many of them played a part in the rise and 4th-century triumph of Christianity; of course they were often ecclesiastical rather than really "public." Also, the leading library at Constantinople is apparently the first to have drawn attention in public law, a decree of 372 incorporated in the Theodosian Code.

The first books in a Roman library were most likely to have arrived by arrangement with whoever had donated the building. Such a donation was one recognized means of winning honorable notice, perhaps even from the emperor; it often led to the erection of a statue. The sovereign did not hesitate to ban from these libraries books he considered objectionable, but the general practice was reportedly rather generous, admitting Christian and non-Roman philosophy. Proscription first of Christian and then of anti-Christian materials did not begin until the struggles of the 4th century.

The book trade could be counted on only for ordinary current works, and the copies supplied by dealers were held in low esteem. Libraries tended to make their own, insofar as they could not fill gaps with the help of auctions or other special opportunities; besides, papyrus exposed to the air lasted no more than 200 years. Many libraries public and private, not just the very largest, operated copying rooms. Regulations sometimes called for annual fresh copies of certain works, and there must have been great dependence on a cadre of skilled copyists. We know that in late-4th-century Constantinople the copyists (*antiquarii*) were important individuals, reminiscent of the scribes 2,500 years earlier.

Extant catalogue information indicates beyond serious doubt that titles were listed in subject groups. It seems almost as clear that the shelving of rolls followed the same plan; at least the recorded placement of likenesses of writers also argues for that conclusion. In each cabinet (*armarium*), the rolls were arranged in author-alphabetical order, individually identified by a small stick projecting from the center of the roll (*titulus*). No location number has been found for an individual work. Cabinet doors were kept closed to protect the rolls from light.

For a book owner to allow friends to read on the premises was common, but to loan a book for use elsewhere called for unusual friendship. The public libraries were essentially limited to reading on the premises. Evidence has survived of an oath required of readers in an Athenian library that they would not walk off with the book entrusted to them. Now as then, of course, permission to borrow was granted to a person of known scholarship or exceptional influence.

The daylight hours were obviously of prime importance. Architect Vitruvius urged that a library be arranged so that its windows maximized the availability of sunlight. The Athenian library just mentioned was open, according to an inscription, from sunrise to 6 P.M.

The would-be reader in a public library went first to the catalogue, then applied to the staff for the desired item; only the latter were supposed to go to the book-cabinets. Literary testimony suggests that this procedure was reasonably satisfactory. Some moments were remembered because the catalogue generated either frustration or a pleasant surprise.

Some staff members were imperial slaves assigned to the leading libraries founded in the 1st century A.D.; these are noted, with their library relationship, in many tomb inscriptions. Anonymity absorbed their successors, perhaps in connection with the civil service reforms begun under Hadrian. Library direction was customarily in the hands of scholars: they were among the procurators in the 1st century, but the latter category gradually became transformed primarily into performer of fiscal and other external functions—by the 4th century part of the duties of the city prefect—and the scholars tended to be limited to internal affairs such as book selection.

The division of library labor had by empire days reached the stage of establishing perhaps a dozen Latin verbs for specifically library functions. They included special meanings for terms used in other ways too, like *disponere* ("organize"), and terms peculiar to the library, for example, *commutare* ("replace a poor copy with a better one").

Librarianship as a set of skills attracted some thoughtful attention, but the extant records give greatly varying support on various issues. Least questioned is the tradition of scholarly management and purpose well established in Hellenistic days, especially at Alexandria; the testimony is almost entirely literary. That Varro could have said many useful things in his treatise on libraries, with known ideas and practices to back them up from Hellenistic data, is quite plausible. Unfortunately, not one scrap survives; we cannot be certain that he ever wrote that treatise. Widely accepted as likely, though impossible to prove with archaeological evidence, is the debt of Rome's noted library buildings to whatever the Ptolemaic architects devised at Alexandria. Indications are available from the physical remains at other sites, such as Pergamum. In any case, architect Vitruvius, writing in the late 1st century B.C., advised on library design as an expected topic. The same applies to library catalogues, for whose existence the literary testimony from at least the 1st century A.D. is noticeable though neither routine nor detailed. If the Alexandrian customs were known, they would apparently have been associated with Callimachus's *Pinakes*. The sole regular allusions to libraries surviving from Roman times are those in Suetonius, who names sponsoring emperors, librarians, and the writers of consequence represented in those libraries. The data are scientific materials only in the sense that they give us a proximate source for Aulus Gellius's and Isidor of Seville's passages on libraries.

The story of the Christians' book collections actually begins also during the Roman Empire but falls more naturally with the information on the Middle Ages (*See* Middle Ages, Libraries in the).

SIDNEY L. JACKSON
(d. 1979)

Rovira, Carmen
(1919-   )

Carmen Rovira's experience and pioneering scholarship in the bibliography, classification, and cataloguing of Spanish-language materials, together with many related and significant organizational activities, made her a figure of central importance in Latin American librarianship.

Rovira was born in Santiago de Cuba on June 13, 1919, and her early life was spent in both Spain and Cuba. She received a doctoral degree in Philosophy and Letters from the University of Havana in 1946 and graduated from its Library School in 1952. In 1969 Rovira received a Master's degree in Library Science from the Graduate Library School of the Catholic University of America in Washington, D.C.

In 1942 Rovira began her professional career as Librarian of the Art History Department of the University of Havana. She was appointed library cataloguer at the Catholic University of Saint Thomas of Villanova in 1952; in 1953 she was made head of the library, a post she held until she left Cuba in 1960 after the revolution. Between 1951 and 1960 she gave numerous courses in librarianship in both the summer school and regular sessions of the University of

Havana's Library School, most frequently on the subjects of cataloguing and classification.

From 1960 Rovira worked in the Library Development Program of the Organization of American States, which she headed from 1978 until 1982, when she retired.

Between 1961 and 1966 she compiled, together with Jorge Aguayo, the *Lista de Encabezamientos de Materia para Bibliotecas* ("Subject Heading List for Libraries"), a milestone work that has served the entire Spanish-speaking world since its publication in 1967 as the basic subject-heading list for library materials in Spanish. She also served as a consultant to Forest Press on the Spanish translation of the 18th edition of the Dewey Decimal Classification.

Carmen Rovira's other major publication is *Los Epígrafes en el Catálogo Diccionario* ("Titles in a Dictionary Catalog") (1953; 2nd edition, 1966), the first Spanish-language work on the theory of subject headings. She also served as Director of the professional journal *Cuba Bibliotecológica* ("Cuban Librarianship") in 1953 and again between 1955 and 1957.

MARTHA TOMÉ

Rudomino, Margarita Ivanovna
(1900-   )

Margarita Ivanovna Rudomino founded the All-Union State Library of Foreign Literature in Moscow in 1921, remained its Director for more than 50 years, and had a broad international experience, mainly through the International Federation of Library Associations. She became the principal ambassador of Soviet librarianship abroad.

She was born July 3, 1900, in Bialystok, in what is now Poland, and although orphaned at an early age, she was able to finish secondary school in Saratov, Russia. She was Librarian in the school for foreign studies in the same city four years before being entrusted with the library of foreign literature—known at the time as the Neophilological Library.

The All-Union State Library of Foreign Literature had a modest start in 1921. Initially on the fifth floor of a 19th-century building in the center of Moscow, it moved four times and used several buildings before it finally occupied in 1967 a large modern building, designed as a library by the architect V. Sitnov. At the time of the dedication it had 700 staff members, 55,000 registered readers, and a collection of about 4,000,000 volumes in 128 languages. It became one of the important libraries in the world, while its objective gives it a unique character. It has a number of unusual features, foreign languages being fundamental to the entire operation: language courses in laboratories with sophisticated audiovisual equipment, readings by foreign authors, exhibitions of foreign books, bibliographic control of foreign literatures, and guidance to Soviet libraries with foreign language departments and departments of foreign library literature.

At the dedication ceremonies Rudomino said, "All about this building—both its exterior view and its light reading rooms—create that atmosphere of peace and joy which is so important for thoughtful, thorough study of a book or a manuscript." The architecture contributes to the urban landscape of Moscow both a local ponderousness and an imported elegance, Scandinavian influence being most obvious in the interior design and furniture.

The collections come mainly, but not exclusively, from the West. They are organized according to Western patterns, and an American or European librarian can easily understand its structure. Catalogues and other tools match familiar standards and traditions. Rudomino carefully studied European library techniques, particularly in Denmark.

The founder of the library was still in charge at the celebration of its 50th anniversary in 1972. Rudomino could look back on a brilliant achievement both at home and abroad. She took most of her professional, political, and philological training after she had started the All-Union Library of Foreign Literature. In 1926 she graduated from Moscow University, Philological Department, Romanic-Germanic division, and in 1939 she finished work at the University of Marxism-Leninism. As late as 1955 she completed a postgraduate course at the Moscow State Library Institute. In the meantime she had married a physician, Vasili Moskalienko, and had two children. She retired in 1973.

The many publications that the Library issued over the years are linked to the overall purpose of the Institution: opening up foreign literature, classical and new in all fields, to the Soviet reader—whether expert or beginner—through indexes, reference tools, bio-bibliographic monographs, union catalogues, and so forth. Rudomino took responsibility for them all. The long list of her own writings shows an unfailing interest in Western librarianship. Her articles appeared in Russian and foreign professional journals. She is mainly responsible for introducing Western ideas into Soviet librarianship; now foreign library literature is acquired, analyzed, indexed, summarized, and, when needed, translated into Russian. For many years she edited the Russian version of the *Unesco Bulletin for Libraries*.

Rudomino always believed in two-way traffic, from abroad toward the Soviet Union but also from her home country to the rest of the world. She often officially represented the U.S.S.R. abroad. From the early 1950s she was an active member of the International Federation of Library Associations and was elected Vice-President in 1967, First Vice-President in 1971, and Honorary Vice-President in 1973. She took part in all annual general council meetings of the Federation and was the key figure of the one organized in Moscow in 1970. Several times she was the Soviet representative at library meetings organized by Unesco—such as the Brussels meeting in 1958 on the exchange agreements of library materials and, at Unesco headquarters in Paris, of the International Advisory Committee on Libraries, Archives, and Documentation.

Her leadership position made her a member or chair of domestic professional committees, organizations, or editorial boards. She was close to the Lenin Library, the State Committee on Public Libraries, the Council for Library Service, and many other government agencies. Through her professional interest abroad she played an important role in the Council of Societies for Friendship with Foreign Countries, the U.S.S.R.-Denmark Society, the U.S.S.R.-France Society, and the National Unesco Commission.

Rudomino, interested in the contents of the books that she handled as a librarian, read widely, and although the choice of her authors—mainly foreign—reflected the social system to which she belonged, her critical sense always remained alert. She had friendly relations with many foreign writers, whom she always tried to meet during her numerous trips abroad. She traveled widely in the Communist world, Western Europe, the United States, Canada, and the East. Like many of her countrymen, she demonstrated an outspoken leaning toward a theoretical foundation of all professional and intellectual activities, favoring a view of major issues in a wide historical and methodological perspective. This did not, however, prevent her interest in human influences; biographies of leading figures, in professional and other fields, remained close to her heart. She would have been happy to be the editor of a Russian counterpart of a work like this *Encyclopedia*. In her *dacha*, near Moscow, she worked on a history of her own library and of the International Federation of Library Associations.

HERMAN LIEBAERS

Rwanda

Rwanda, a republic in eastern Africa, is bordered by Uganda on the north, Tanzania on the east, Burundi on the south, and Zaire on the west. Population (1983 est.) 5,644,000; area 26,338 sq.km. The official languages are Kinyarwanda and French.

History. Long before white Europeans introduced writing, Rwandans devised various means of communicating verbal messages. These means were refined generation after generation and, as one might expect, were based principally upon the ability of people to recall and report what they had heard from their elders. Ancient Rwandans evolved various kinds of oral traditions. They included popular tradition; sapient tradition, which called on proverbs and riddles; and dynastic tradition, which was trusted by the monarchic court to some families with a view to conserve and perpetuate it, and included esoteric code, dynastic genealogy, pastoral poetry, war songs, and harp music. Most of these traditions were written down after missionaries arrived in Rwanda and created schools in which local peoples could learn to read and write. Their work was pursued by the colonial German administration for about 20 years, and then was taken over by the Belgians in 1916.

The first libraries were created under Belgian rule. After its foundation in 1929, a Group Scolaire of Butare strove to set up its own library, intended to provide general and technical reading. The present

National University of Rwanda Library/General Secretariat

Library of the National University, Ruhengeri Campus

Library of the Rwandan Institute of Agronomic Sciences (ISAR) dates back to 1932. In 1936 the Major Catholic Seminary of Nyakibanda, which had just been transferred from Kabgayi, opened its Library. The Governor-General of the Belgian Congo, to which Rwanda was attached and ruled under the Belgian trusteeship, was charged in 1931 with organizing public libraries in the colony. In Rwanda, a library for Europeans was created in Kigali between 1932 and 1940. From 1947 to 1954, a single public Library was opened for local people in each one of the 10 administrative districts."

The most important of those libraries was in Kigali, and it counted 2,623 books in 1960. Usually, at least half the members of the administration boards of those libraries had to be Rwandans. Later, between the years 1959 and 1962, the libraries ceased to operate as government-subsidized public libraries, for various reasons in connection with the Rwandese Revolution and the great turn in Rwanda history. After the country became a republic in 1961 and gained independence in 1962, initiatives were generally left up to private or half-private institutions to found public libraries.

The Association Caritas Rwanda played a considerable role in promoting national culture by offering books to newly founded reading clubs, as well as to certain prisons and other institutions.

The Rwandan government worked to set up and extend school and specialized libraries, to increase literacy throughout the country, to promote production

Libraries in Rwanda (1981)

Type	Administrative units	Service points	Volumes in collections	Annual expenditures (franc)	Population served	Professional staff	Total staff
Academic	2	3	132,000	17,030,000	1,417[a]	3	50

[a]Registered borrowers.
Source: Unesco, *Statistical Yearbook*, 1984.

of literary works in the national language, and to train qualified personnel for libraries.

In 1963 the Ministry of Education Library for Pedagogic Documentation was opened in Kigali with the help of Unesco. In 1964 the Library of the National University of Rwanda was built, and two years later it was followed by that of the National Pedagogic Institute. In 1972 an important exhibition of works on national documentation, Trésors de la Nation Rwandaise, was held in Kigali; it was intended to draw attention to the urgency of creating a national library and national archives facilities, and to the necessity of organizing libraries.

In 1978 a service of Archives Nationales was established in the Ministry of National Education, and was attached, the following year, to the President's Office by a Presidential act. An act of November 15, 1983, establishing copyright, was promulgated in 1984.

Two Canadian librarians did great pioneering work both at the National University and throughout the country. One was Albert Lévesque, who was the first Chief Librarian at the National University (1964–69) and the first Director of the Bibliographic Center for Information on Rwanda (1970–72). The other was Paulette Trudeau-Lévesque, who first served as a librarian, and then became Chief Librarian of the same institution (1969–72). They were the first professionals to run a well-organized library efficiently in Rwanda. They greatly contributed to awakening the authorities to the need for training librarians and to the increase of public interest in bibliographic work.

In Rwanda, a developing country that has no access to the ocean—and no long history in library matters—the book and the periodical are precious articles. Documentation is generally kept in small libraries that public authorities and the population are continually trying to improve.

National Library and Archives. There was no national library in Rwanda in the mid-1980s, but the government was considering creating one. The Information and National Archives Service is a service of the President's Office. It contains two sections, the Archives Central Depot and the Pre-archives Section. The Central Depot essentially receives and keeps public archives of the pre-independence period. There are also some small private archives depots. Usually those belong to religious communities that are considered to be well kept. The Archives of the Bishopric of Kabgayi, one example, are mainly concerned with the history of the Catholic Church in Rwanda.

Academic Libraries. The Libraries of the National University of Rwanda constitute the most important system of academic libraries in the country. After the former National University of Rwanda was combined with the former National Pedagogic Institute in 1981, there were two university campuses, with one library on each. The library on the main campus at Butare owned 41,000 books in 1971, but by 1983 it had 115,000 books and 720 periodicals. It consists of the Central Library, the Medical Library, the Law Collection, a Documentation Center, and a bibliographic center for information on Rwanda. The other Library, which is on the campus of Ruhengeri at Nyakinama, serves the teachers and students of the Arts Faculty. It had a collection of about 20,000 books and 49 periodicals in 1983. It has a branch library on the Ruhengeri campus at Butare, mainly used by teachers and students of the Ecole Supérieure des Techniques Modernes and by those from the Faculty of Educational Sciences. The Library of the Ruhengeri campus at Butare had 10,620 books and 50 periodicals in 1983. The University Library on the main campus at Butare occupies a modern functional building and the one on the Ruhengeri campus at Nyakinama is housed in a fairly adequate building.

The Library of the Major Catholic Seminary of Nyakibanda has an important collection that mainly deals with theology and philosophy as well as with the history of the church. It had about 20,000 books in 1983. Two other institutions of higher learning have libraries in Kigali. They are the Ecole Supérieure Militaire and the African and Mauritius Institute of Applied Economy and Statistics. And finally, the Adventist University of Central Africa, created at Mudende near Gisenyi in 1984, was considering opening its own modern library. In general, academic libraries are subsidized and receive various forms of support.

Public Libraries. After Rwanda became independent in 1962, public libraries were gradually opened by embassies, religious institutions, and groups of individuals, and by the National University Extension. The most important of these is the French–Rwandan Cultural Exchange Center Library, opened at Kigali in 1967. In 1983 it had 21,000 books and 45 periodicals and a good collection of films and slides. In 1975 it served about 37,600 readers, 33,700 of them Rwandans, and it lent out almost 18,000 books. In 1980 the number of books it lent rose to 60,000. The Library opened branch libraries at Gisenyi, Butare, and Rwamagana.

Other libraries include the American Cultural Center Library, which was built in Kigali in 1965; the Club Rafiki Library, opened by the Dominican Fathers at Nyamirambo in 1975; the Protestant Center Library (CELTAR); and the Islamic Cultural Center Library, in Kigali. The Public Library of the National University Extension at Butare serves the population of Butare and had 14,000 books with 238 subscribers in 1983. At least 20 other cultural centers and associations operate in various parts of the country. One of their aims is to offer library services to both their members and the general public. About 10 cultural centers are sponsored or run by Catholic parishes.

Public libraries in general have few trained workers, and most documentation is mainly in French or sometimes in English. The percentage of literacy in Rwanda in the early 1980s was about 49, a sharp rise from five percent in 1978.

School Libraries and Media Centers. Secondary schools, in general, have small libraries. Their collections consist chiefly of documents distributed by the Ministry of Primary and Secondary Education and of gifts. The principal school library in the country is found in Groupe Scolaire in Butare. In 1981 it had 18,000 books and 75 periodicals. Its reading room has a sitting capacity of 80 places, and each class schedules one hour for reading in the Library. Secondary schools may use the services of the mobile library and educational films made available by the National University Extension of Butare. In 1983 the mobile library service had 12,000 books and was able

718

to meet the needs of only 30 schools.

Primary schools did not have libraries of their own in the mid-1980s, but they regularly received from the Ministry books that are mainly written in Kinyarwanda. Other means used to help primary schools including broadcasting of school materials (twice a week) and offering refresher courses to teachers. Pupils subscribe in great numbers to a magazine edited for children in Kinyarwanda.

Special Libraries. The Library of the National Scientific Research Institute (INRS) in Butare owns precious works on natural sciences and a good collection of sound materials of great historical and linguistic interest. The Rwandan Institute of Agronomic Sciences, at Rubona, is building a collection in agriculture, breeding, and botany. The Research and Cooperative Formation Center (IWACU) began a library in Kigali for materials on how to run cooperatives.

The National Development Council (Parliament) and most ministries and public institutions have libraries or documentation services of various sizes. Examples include the Ministry of Primary and Secondary Education (14,862 books in 1981); the Ministry of Finance and Economy; the Ministry of Planning (15,000 books in 1982); the Ministry of Justice; the Ministry of Foreign Affairs and Cooperation; the Ministry of Industry, Mines, and Crafts; the Ministry of Public Health and Social Affairs; the Ministry of National Institutions; the Rwandan Office of Information; and the National Bank of Rwanda.

International organizations such as the Economic Community of Great Lakes Countries (CEPGL), whose permanent secretariat is at Gisenyi, and the Akagera Basin Management and Development Organization, whose head office is in Kigali, have documentation centers.

Several libraries belong to religious communities and bishoprics. The best known of these are the Library of the Archbishopric of Kigali, the Library of the Benedictine Fathers at Gihindamuyaga (8,000 books), and the Library of the Dominican Fathers in Kigali, whose collection contained nearly 30,000 books and 60 periodicals in 1983. This latter library deals essentially with theology and philosophy, as well as with documentation and literacy problems in Rwanda.

The Profession. Rwandan professional librarians are trained abroad, especially in Senegal, France, or Canada. Their number, however, is still small, although a certain number of foreign librarians lend their services to some libraries in the country. In the years 1982–83, the government sponsored for the first time a six-month training program, intended for those who were to work in certain libraries, archives, and documentation centers. Opportunities for professional education are still limited, and the country often resorts to sending librarians abroad on short-term training programs for specialization. It allows a number of others to participate in seminars and meetings of professional interest organized inside or outside the country.

REFERENCES

Jean Brock, "Les bibliothèques en Afrique centrale," *Archives et Bibliothèques de Beligque* (1972), a summary of library development problems in Black Africa.

André Guitard, "Etre bibliothécaire au coeur de l'Afrique," *Argus* (July–August 1974), the working conditions of the librarian in Rwanda presented by a Canadian librarian.

Grégoire Hategekimana, "L'information scientifique et technique, la politique de développement et la circulation de l'information nécessaire à l'application de la science et la technique au Rwanda," *Education et Culture* (April-June 1980), a summary of scientific and technical information services in Rwanda.

EMMANUEL SERUGENDO

Sabin, Joseph
(1821–1881)

Joseph Sabin ranks among the preeminent booksellers, auctioneers, and bibliographers of the mid-19th century. His reputation and lasting importance rest upon his *Dictionary of Books Relating to America from its Discovery to the Present Time,* also known as *Bibliotheca Americana,* or simply, "Sabin." It is an alphabetical list by author of books and pamphlets, in any language, that in some way relate to the New World.

Sabin was born in Braunston, Northamptonshire, England, in December 1821. At 14, he was apprenticed to Charles Richards, an Oxford bookseller, to learn bookbinding. Within a few months, Richards saw that Sabin's abilities were better suited to the sales room, and he was instead trained as a bookseller. In 1842, after completing his seven-year apprenticeship, Sabin and a partner set up on their own as booksellers and auctioneers in Oxford. Sabin's first book, *The Thirty-Nine Articles of the Church of England with Scripture Proof and References,* was anonymously published by his firm in 1844.

Sabin emigrated to the United States with his wife and two sons in 1848. He landed in New York, but soon went to Philadelphia, where he took a position with George S. Appleton. Sabin is said to have introduced there the English binding style known as half-leather: a binding with paper-covered sides and leather on the spine and corners. After about two years, Sabin returned to New York to work as a cataloguer for the auction firm of Cooley and Keese, which was sold in 1851 to Lyman and Rawdon. For one of their first auctions, Sabin compiled a large, detailed catalogue of the library of Samuel Farmer Jarvis. A dispute regarding Sabin's payment for the work followed, and Sabin left in 1852 for the rival firm of Bangs, Brother & Co., then becoming one of the most active auction houses in New York. While there, Sabin not only catalogued many large libraries, but also began to see much Americana. He was thus inspired to begin collecting notes and references that would eventually become the *Bibliotheca Americana.* One of the last catalogues Sabin prepared for Bangs was of the library of Edward B. Corwin (sold November 10, 1856), consisting exclusively of Americana.

Early in 1857, Sabin opened a bookshop in New York, but within a year, moved it to Philadelphia. There he began to prosper—particularly with customers from the South. As the Civil War approached, however, the book trade in general, and Sabin's in particular, became severely weakened. He moved back to New York, and in partnership with H. A. Jennings set up an auction firm in 1860. It failed after one auction: that of the library of William E. Burton, in which over 6,000 lots sold for next to nothing. Sabin spent the next few years preparing catalogues of private libraries and freelancing for various auction houses, a practice continued (though more selectively) after he established a bookshop, J. Sabin and Sons, on Nassau Street in 1864.

Nassau Street was the center of the New York book trade, and 1864 marked the beginning of a revival in book collecting. The signal event of the revival was the auction of the library of John Allan in May 1864: it resulted in the highest sales total in the United States to that date. In following years, Sabin would be involved in the sales of other important collections, such as that of John A. Rice (March 1870), who had acquired many books through Sabin; Thomas W. Field (May 1875), rich in material on American Indians and the basis of a bibliography on the subject; and William Menzies (November 1876), a notable collection of Americana. Sabin wrote the catalogues and was auctioneer for all of these sales.

In the midst of this activity, in December 1866, Sabin issued a prospectus announcing the publication of the work for which he is now remembered: his *Dictionary of Books Relating to America.* The first four parts appeared in 1867, and six parts each year thereafter until his death. (The edition totaled 635 copies, with 110 on large paper.) Sabin also published a monthly journal called *The American Bibliopolist* from 1869 until 1877. It featured news of the book trade and auctions, general articles on book collecting and other bookish subjects, and a section of advertising— both lists of books from Sabin's stock and display advertisements from other dealers. Here one can see the broad range of material that Sabin handled—recent English acquisitions (a son had opened the firm's London branch in 1871), prints, portraits, and illustrated books, as well as Americana and literature.

A trend of the 1860s and 70s was the reprinting of rare historical texts. Sabin published over a dozen such works, among them *The Journal of Major George Washington,* and William Smith's *The History of the First Discovery and Settlement of Virginia.* In 1877 Sabin's *Bibliography of Bibliography, or a Handy Book About Books which Relate to Books* was published separately after appearing serially in *The American Bibliopolist.*

In 1879 Sabin retired from the daily operation of his business. The firm changed its name to J. Sabin's Sons, and was run by several members of his family. Sabin, however, continued to work on his *Dictionary* and still did some auctioneering. His last auction was Part Three of the library of George Brinley: an Americana collection that rivalled those of John Carter Brown and James Lenox. The sale was scheduled for March 1881 but was postponed until April because of Sabin's poor health. Lot no. 5839 was Brinley's copy of the Gutenberg Bible: the second Gutenberg Bible brought to the United States and the first to be sold in an American auction.

Joseph Sabin died in Brooklyn, N.Y., June 5, 1881. His *Bibliotheca Americana,* however, did not cease. By the time of his death, Sabin had completed 82 parts. (The last two were published posthumously.) From 1884 to 1892, Wilberforce Eames edited parts 83-116. Publication was then suspended for 35 years. When it resumed in 1927, Eames was still the editor and he continued until 1930 when succeeded by R. W. G. Vail. The final part (no. 172) appeared in 1936. (From 1929 the work was published by the Bibliographical Society of America.) Eames and Vail refined Sabin's all-encompassing definition of Americana; they eliminated ephemeral items and many government publications; they set a cut-off date of 1860 (later changed to 1840), and provided more bibliographically thorough descriptions. At its completion, the *Dictionary* numbered 106,413 entries, many of which include references to more than one work or edition. Vail estimated that more

Courtesy Grolier Club
Library/Jay Cantor, New York
City

Joseph Sabin

than a quarter of a million publications are included in it.

Although it took 70 years to complete, and the work is not without flaws, the *Bibliotheca Americana* remains an invaluable guide to books about America. It certifies Sabin's place in bibliographical history. That he also made important contributions to the book trade, book collecting, and publishing only confirm it.

REFERENCES

Frederick R. Goff., *Joseph Sabin, Bibliographer (1821–1881)*, (1963).

Adolph Growell, *Book-Trade Bibliography in the United States in the XIXth Century* (New York, The Dibdin Club, 1898).

New York Times obituary, June 6, 1881.

William S. Reese, "Joseph Sabin," *American Book Collector* (1984).

R. W. G. Vail, "Sabin's 'Dictionary,'" *Papers of the Bibliographical Society of America* (1937).

ALLEN ASAF

Sabor, Josefa
(1916-   )

Josefa Emilia Sabor, Argentine library educator, administrator, and author, attended many international conferences, lectured in and outside Argentina, and studied libraries, documentation centers, and schools for librarians in Europe and the three Americas. Born November 23, 1916, in Villanueva de Arosa, Spain, she became an Argentine citizen in 1937. She was a high school and normal school teacher, specializing in history in the Faculty of Philosophy and Letters of the University of Buenos Aires and a librarian of the same faculty. She was granted a scholarship by Unesco and the Office of Ibero-American Education to study documentation in Spain, France, Italy, West Germany, and Brazil and received another scholarship from the U.S. State Department's Bureau of Educational and Cultural Affairs to study the teaching of library techniques in 10 U.S. universities.

In 1938 Sabor became a library assistant in the Teaching Institute of the Faculty of Philosophy and Letters of the University of Buenos Aires. She served as Director of the Library and of Bibliography, Library Institute, University of Buenos Aires, from 1943 to 1946, and Director of the Library, Argentine Museum of Natural Sciences, from 1948 until 1952, when she was dismissed for political reasons. From 1955 to 1964 she served as Director of the Central Library of the Faculty of Philosophy and Letters, University of Buenos Aires.

Her teaching activities in Argentina included service from 1947 to 1951 as Professor of Reference in the School for Librarians of the Argentine Social Museum, from 1955 to 1970 as Director of the School for Librarians, Faculty of Philosophy and Letters, University of Buenos Aires, and from 1963 as Associate—later Full—Professor of Bibliography, Reference Services, and Documentation in that faculty. She became Titular Professor in 1969. From 1965 to 1970 she reorganized and directed the Career of Librarianship program in the Faculty of Philosophy and Letters. From 1955 to 1957 she directed and organized the National School of Librarians for the Ministry of Justice and Education, and from 1963 to 1973 she

served as founding Director of the Center for Library Research of the Faculty of Philosophy and Letters in collaboration with Unesco.

She retired from active teaching in 1980 and thereafter dedicated herself to research. She became a researcher in the National Council of Scientific and Technical Research, working on the origins of Argentine bibliography.

Her international activities included contributions as Director of the Library and Publications Department of the Inter-American Living Center, Bogotá, Colombia, for the Organization of American States (1952-53); Unesco expert, consultant, and Professor at the Central Library of the University of Costa Rica (1962); member of the International Consulting Committee for Librarians, Unesco, Paris (1965-69); OAS Visiting Professor at the Inter-American School of Librarianship in Medellín, Colombia (1973-74); and Visiting Professor at the School of Librarianship, National University of Asunción, Paraguay (1975). For the OAS she presented two programs for teachers in the Master's Program in Librarianship, University of Guanajuato, Mexico (1977).

Her publications include *Manual de bibliotecología* ("Manual of Librarianship," with Juan Albani, J. Federico Finó, Carlos Victor Penna, and Emilio Ruiz, 1951, 2nd edition, 1984), *Manual de fuentes de información* ("Manual of Information Sources," 1957, 3rd edition, 1979), *Bibliografía básica de obras de referencia de artes y letras para la Argentina* ("Basic Bibliography of Reference Works in Arts and Letters for Argentina," 1969), *Methods of Teaching Librarianship* (1969), *Las normas y conclusiones de Medellín y la formación de bibliotecarios en América Latina* ("The Medellín Standards and Conclusions and the Training of Librarians in Latin America," 1974), *El planeamiento bibliotecario a través de los congresos y reuniones celebrados en América Latina* ("Library Planning Through Congresses and Meetings in Latin America," 1974), *Desarrollo del planeamiento bibliotecario en América Latina* ("Development of Library Planning in Latin America," 1975), and many articles in library journals.

EMMA LINARES; revised and translated by EDWIN S. GLEAVES

Josefa Sabor

St. John, Francis R.
(1908–1971)

Francis Regis St. John was Director of the Brooklyn Public Library, the position for which he is best known and remembered, from 1949 to 1963.

His life and career were centered in the East from his birth in Northampton, Massachusetts, on June 16, 1908, until his death in Manchester, New Hampshire, on July 19, 1971. His association with libraries began as page and desk assistant at the Northampton Public Library when he was 11 years old and continued through his student years at Amherst (Massachusetts) College (A.B., 1931). Professional education at Catholic University, Washington D.C., followed immediately (B.S., 1932).

His professional career began at the New York Public Library, where he held several professional positions, the last of which was Chief of the Circulation Department. In 1939 he became Assistant Li-

Brooklyn Public Library, Brooklyn Collection

Francis R. St. John

brarian of the Enoch Pratt Free Library under Joseph L. Wheeler.

During World War II, St. John organized the Army Medical Library (1943–45), which later became the National Library of Medicine. Following the war he was the first Director of Library Services for the Veterans Administration. In 1949 he left the VA for the Brooklyn Public Library, where he was to earn his national reputation.

The St. John years at Brooklyn were a time of enormous change and growth for the system. Circulation of materials doubled from over 5,000,000 to more than 10,000,000 annually. The number of branches increased from 38 to 55. There were innovations in service programs as well. The District Library concept, which put strong subject collections and specialists closer to the people, was inaugurated, and the Community Coordinator program, which placed librarians on detached duty in the community to form linkages with agencies and organizations, was begun.

St. John quickly became identified as a manager. The introduction of assembly-line book processing and other management innovations held down operating costs, freeing funds for expanded service programs.

Personal professional activities were diverse and extensive. He was a founding member of the National Book Committee and initiator of the Franklin Books program. His *Survey of Library Service to the Blind, 1956* (1957) is a major document in the development of library services.

Following his retirement from Brooklyn in 1963, St. John opened a private consulting firm. Among the projects undertaken was a statewide library survey for the state of Oklahoma. In the years before his death he served as Consultant to the New Hampshire College and University Council and was also Librarian at Saint Anselm's College in Manchester, New Hampshire.

REFEENCE
Milton S. Byam, "St. John, Francis Regis," *Dictionary of American Library Biography* (1978).

F. WILLIAM SUMMERS

Samper Ortega, Daniel
(1895–1943)

Daniel Samper Ortega, educator, historian, and writer, was the leading promoter of library development in Colombia.

Samper was born in Bogotá, Colombia, November 28, 1895. After graduation from the Military Academy, he wrote four novels, two plays, and several essays. Later he went to Spain to do research for a historical novel and to lecture at a Spanish university. He taught also in the Gimnasio Moderno, a progressive, independent, and private high school founded by his father, one of his uncles, and other businessmen with Agustín Nieto Caballero, an outstanding educator trained in Europe.

In 1930, during the Depression, the Liberal Party came to power after 50 years of Conservative rule in Colombia. There was a spirit of renewal in the country, and in February 1931 Samper Ortega was called by President Olaya Herrera and his Minister of Edu-

cation to become the Director of the National Public Library in Bogotá, a position given traditionally to men of letters who took little serious interest in library development.

The state in which he received the Library was appalling. It was in a dilapidated old colonial house near Plaza de Bolívar, the main square. Books, magazines, and newspapers were thrown on the floors; the rest, unreachable, were piled on dusty shelves. Eighty-seven boxes of exchange publications, sent not only for the National Library but for other institutions in the country, remained unopened, some dated as far back as 1898. In the main room 52,000 volumes were uncatalogued except for a few private collections donated to the Library. Sixteen thousand valuable incunabula and parchment books were found, piled on shelves three volumes deep or on the floor. The final search yielded a total of 85,355 volumes, of which 60 percent were unreachable for lack of shelves.

He undertook a thorough reorganization of the National Library and despite financial limitations turned it into one of the most modern and efficient public libraries of Latin America at that time. By 1934 a total of 192,914 additional reference cards had been made; the exchange system had been organized, and 15,898 volumes had been sent to other libraries; the National Archives were incorporated in the Library and 290,000 historical documents had been organized; and readers had increased to 9,362 a month, an increase of 358 percent from the time the reorganization was started.

Samper organized with Janeiro Brooks (later Schmidt) the first Library School of Colombia. Librarians were trained for the other ministries, the National University, the Central Bank (Banco de la República, which today has the best economic library in the country), and other institutions. By 1938 the National Library had in operation a children's library and theater, which was used as a model for the future satellite libraries.

He conceived the National Library as a dynamic center for the diffusion of education and culture, capable of breaking down provincial and national boundaries. He did not want to wait for the readers to come to the Library; he went out to the readers. The books, to him, were only one of the means to serve the readers. Early in the reorganization he started the National Radio Station, as part of the Library, and a section to produce educational movies. He compiled a 100-volume selection of Colombian literature (*Selección Samper Ortega*), a titanic effort, unparalleled in Colombia and in the rest of Latin America. He started the *Biblioteca Aldeana de Cultura Popular,* a series of manuals prepared for farmers on subjects such as cultivation of various crops, health, care of children, and food, to take culture and education to the rural regions, through the National Library. Finally, in 1934 he started the publication of a monthly journal, *Senderos* ("Paths"), finely designed and printed, for the diffusion of ideas and knowledge as well as of information about the National Library. Later the Ministry of Education assumed those educational services.

The culmination of his seven years of service as Director of the National Library was the inauguration, in August 1938, of a magnificent, large, functional, and complete new building, in a corner of the Park of Independence, planned for a growth of at least a century. The inauguration of the new building was one of the main events with which Colombia celebrated the 400th anniversary of the founding of the city of Bogotá. Samper was at that time a Founding Member of the Academy of Arts, the Permanent Secretary of the Academy of Letters, and the President of the Academy of History. He resigned and became Cultural Counselor of the Colombian embassy in the United States. In Washington, D.C., he displayed his boundless energy for two years, making known the cultural achievements of Colombia, lecturing at the universities, and keeping in touch with educational and professional groups, among them the American Library Association.

He resigned his diplomatic post in 1941 to return to Colombia as Director of the Gimnasio Moderno, a school with which he had sentimental ties. There, with renewed energy, he undertook the task of turning it into a private university. With assistance from the Business School of Harvard University he opened the first College of Business Administration and Economics in Colombia, where the new business executives and economists of the country were trained.

He died in Bogotá on November 3, 1943.

In 1977, at the initiative of the historian Pilar Moreno de Angel, then Director of the National Library, and on the occasion of the 200th anniversary of the library, the Colombian Institute of Culture (Colcultura) of the Ministry of Education remodeled the new building, inaugurated in 1938, and introduced new services. The main reading room was named after Samper.

REFERENCE

Guillermo Hernandez de Alba and Juan Carrasquilla Botero, *Historia de la Biblioteca Nacional de Colombia* (1977), a complete and concise history of the National Library of Colombia. Chapter 24 is dedicated to "Daniel Samper Ortega, the Restorer" and chapter 25 to "Daniel Samper and the new building of the Library."

ARMANDO SAMPER

Sarmiento, Domingo Faustino
(1811–1888)

A man whose activities embraced many interests, including public education, politics, diplomacy, literature, and librarianship, Domingo Faustino Sarmiento has been termed a "universal man" and a "father of public education." He was President of the Argentine Republic, 1868–74. To his own passion for books and popular education he added lessons learned from years of travel and investigations abroad, and he took advantage of the opportunity to act offered by political office.

Born in San Juan City, province of San Juan, Argentina, February 14, 1811, Sarmiento rose quickly in local and national politics, serving in provincial and cabinet posts. In 1840, as a consequence of political events, he was forced to flee. He settled in Chile, involving himself in politics and devoting himself to putting his ideas on public education into practice.

Sarmiento was an indefatigable traveler and a born journalist. In 1845 the Chilean government commissioned him to study the organization of schooling in Europe and the United States. He visited France, Spain, Germany, Switzerland, Holland, Belgium, and Great Britain on the European leg of his tour. Before returning home by way of Cuba, Panama, and Peru, he conducted a survey of educational innovations in the United States. While in the U.S. he cultivated the friendship of Horace Mann. Sarmiento thereafter spread Mann's ideas on education throughout South America.

Sarmiento returned to Chile in February 1848. He founded a well-equipped printing house directed by Julio Belin, who later married Sarmiento's daughter, Faustina, in 1850. Throughout his exile, Sarmiento remained a prolific writer on matters of education, culture, and intellectual interests. His collected works would ultimately amount to 52 volumes. He played a significant role in the overthrow of the Rosas government in 1852, and in December 1863 the President of Argentina appointed Sarmiento Ambassador to the United States. He returned to the U.S. in May 1865. Sarmiento displayed remarkable energy, constantly traveling throughout the land in order to acquaint himself with subjects of practical interest to the development of Argentina. In 1866 he published a biography of his personal hero, Abraham Lincoln, and *Las escuelas como base de la prosperidad de la república en los EEUU* ("Schools as the Basis of Prosperity in the U.S"). He attended an international conference of teachers, and in June 1868 the University of Michigan awarded him an honorary doctorate. Horace Mann's widow, Mary, translated his *Recuerdos de Provincia* (*Reminiscences of a Province*) and introduced Sarmiento in North America.

Sarmiento remained in the U.S. until July 1868, when he was elected President of the Argentine republic, a post he held until 1874. Under his leadership, the first nationally financed schools for the training of teachers were founded in Argentina. He arranged for 65 professional teachers from Mann's state of Massachusetts to establish normal and primary schools in his country and train personnel for them.

Sarmiento quickly acted to assure the parallel development of popular libraries. On September 23, 1870, he signed into law legislation creating the Comisión Protectora de Bibliotecas Populares (Protective Commission of Popular Libraries). Sarmiento later said in reference to this major cornerstone of his education program that "the need for libraries is everywhere felt. It is necessary to create the school library to complement the school and enliven it, serving as an aid to the teacher and an incentive to the child's curiosity." He also noted that it is "not without reason that we include schools and libraries within the same function. The latter complement the former; and as education becomes more generally available so will the number of libraries, occupying the position due them within the scheme of public instruction. Now the library is an integral part of the social organization, just like the free and compulsory schools—something not so before."

He died in Asunción, Paraguay, on September 11, 1888. Though Sarmiento's goals are far from realization in the countries of South America, his ideal remains true.

REINALDO JOSÉ SUÁREZ

Saudi Arabia

Saudi Arabia, a monarchy in southwest Asia, comprises most of the Arabian Peninsula. It is surrounded by Jordan, Iraq, and Kuwait on the north; the Persian Gulf, Qatar, and the United Arab Emirates on the east; Oman, Yemen (Aden), and Yemen (Sana'a) on the south; and the Red Sea on the west. Population (1984 est.) 10,841,000; area 2,240,000 sq.km. The official language is Arabic.

History. The medieval libraries of Saudi Arabia were developed mainly in Mecca and Medina, notably the collections of the Great Mosque of Mecca and the Prophet's Mosque in Medina. Other types of modern libraries—public, academic, school, and special—were not established until after World War II.

National Library. The National Library, established in the capital city of Riyadh in 1963, was placed in 1968 under the auspices of the Department of Public Libraries of the Ministry of Education. Its holdings total some 16,000 volumes. A legal deposit law was not issued. A new building was under construction in the mid-1980s.

The National Library issued a prospective national bibliography under the title *Mujam al-Matbu'at al-Sa'udiyah* (1973) covering commercial and official publications issued in Saudi Arabia. It also publishes a bimonthly bibliography that includes new additions as well as indexing of periodical articles.

Academic Libraries. Modern academic libraries have been established with the emergence of university education in Saudi Arabia. Those universities that have developed in the kingdom since the 1950s have shown special interest in developing their libraries as focal points for teaching. King Sa'ud University in Riyadh, established with only one college in 1957, expanded to include colleges in arts, sciences, commerce, pharmacy, agriculture, education, engineering, and medicine, all with their own libraries. The Central Library of the University was established in 1964; all college libraries and the Central Library were placed under the direction of the Dean of University Library Affairs in 1974. The university libraries possess 791,883 volumes and 11,917 periodical titles.

The King Abdul Aziz University, with campuses in Jeddah and Mecca, was established in 1967. The central library at Jeddah has 434,592 volumes and periodical titles; the library at Mecca possesses about 40,000 volumes and subscribes to some 400 periodicals. The Islamic University in Medina, founded in 1961, has a central library and three college libraries for law, theology, and a secondary institute. The libraries of the Islamic University have 30,000 volumes. The Library of the Islamic University of Imam Muhammad Ibn Sa'ud in Riyadh, founded in 1950 and of university status from 1974, has some 30,000 volumes. The Petroleum and Minerals University in Dharan, founded in 1963 and of university status from 1975, has a library of about 100,000 volumes.

Public Libraries. The Departments of Public Libraries at the Ministry of Education and at the Ministry of Hag and Awqaf are custodians of about 28 public libraries throughout the country. Some of the noteworthy ones are housed in mosques, such as the Holy Mosque Al Harm, Mecca (7,000 volumes), and the Prophet's Mosque in Medina. The Saudi Library in Riyadh has about 15,000 volumes and 200 manuscripts. The Mahmoudia Library, which possesses about 5,000 volumes and 500 manuscripts, and the Arif Hikmat Library, with about 2,000 volumes and 4,500 manuscripts, are in Medina. The Abbas Kattan Library in Mecca has about 8,000 volumes and 200 manuscripts. Other public libraries are found in Saudi towns, such as Taif, Ahsaa, Damman, Buraida, Onaiza, Shakra, Hawdit, and Sidair.

School Libraries. The development of modern school libraries was assigned to the Department

Main entrance to King Saud University Central Library, Riyadh.

King Saud University Libraries

Catalogue, King Saud University Central Library.

King Saud University Libraries

Libraries in Saudi Arabia (1982)

Type	Administrative units	Service points	Volumes in collections	Annual expenditures (riyal)	Population served[a]	Professional staff	Total staff
Special	1	--	20,000	--	250	--	--

[a]Registered borrowers.

Source: Unesco, *Statistical Yearbook*, 1984.

of School Libraries of the Ministry of Education. Efforts are being made to establish, maintain, and staff school libraries for all types and levels of schools in the country. Acquisition and technical processing of library materials are done centrally and delivered to school libraries. Most of the school libraries are staffed with professionally trained librarians recruited from other Arab countries, mainly from Egypt.

Special Libraries. Saudi Arabian ministries, government agencies, organizations, companies, and research centers have shown interest in establishing special libraries to serve their officials. More than 24 special libraries have been founded in Saudi organizations since the mid-1950s. Institutions with well-organized special libraries include government Ministries of Finance and National Economy, Petroleum and Mineral Resources, Labor, and Planning. Others are with the General Statistics Directorate, Arab Saudi Organization for Specification and Measurement, Saudi Fund for Industrial Development, Industrial Research Development Center—Riyadh, General Organization of Petroleum and Minerals, Saudi Monetary Organization, Institute of Applied Geology—Jeddah, Arab American Oil Company, Saudi Airlines, and the Information Center of the Department of Educational Statistics, Research, and Documentation of the Ministry of Education. Many of these libraries have established documentation centers serving specialized needs, such as inquiry services, indexing, abstracting, bibliographical services, translation, and reprography.

MOHAMED M. EL HADI*

Savage, Ernest A.
(1877–1966)

Ernest Albert Savage had one of the most original minds and was one of the most vigorous personalities in the history of the British public library service.

He was born at Croydon, Surrey, March 30, 1877, and began his library career at the recently established Croydon public library at the age of 13. By a fortunate chance he rejoined the Croydon staff, after two years at Watford Public Library, just before the Croydon libraries came under the direction of Louis Stanley Jast. Jast was not only a bold experimenter; he was infectiously enthusiastic. Perceiving that Savage was of more than average ability, he made him his deputy. As Savage later realized, working closely with Jast was a better professional education than going to a library school.

In 1904 Savage became Librarian of Bromley, Kent, and in 1906 Librarian of Wallasey, Cheshire. At each of these towns he planned a Carnegie library, but he did not have a major opportunity to prove his mettle until he became Librarian of Coventry in 1915. As a versatile industrial city of high repute, Coventry was then much concerned with war contracts. It seemed to Savage that its industrial efficiency would be all the greater if its factories had the benefit of a public technical information service. He therefore set about providing one at the central library. Following the success of this novel enterprise, Savage persuaded the Library Association to appoint a special committee to discuss means of improving the supply of technical information throughout the country. Although

this committee, of which Savage was Secretary, failed to secure government support for its ambitious plan for a national technical information service (in suggesting the establishment of a National Lending Library of Science and Technology it was over 30 years ahead of its time), it did encourage the public libraries of several of the larger British industrial cities to provide out of their own resources special library and information services for local industrial and commercial firms.

Savage was also one of the first British librarians to recognize the value of local studies and perceive how public libraries might assist and stimulate them. The Coventry and Warwickshire Collection, which Savage organized and for which he devised a special classification scheme still in use today, was far ahead of the average local collection at that time.

In 1922 Savage was appointed Principal Librarian of Edinburgh city libraries. He took over a library system that, like too many others in the United Kingdom, was suffering from old-fashioned administration, unimaginative policies, and the unavoidable restrictions imposed by World War I.

Savage's career at Edinburgh spanned two decades. During the first he brought the city libraries up to the level of the best in the country; during the second he raised them above it, although not as far as he wished. Lack of resources prevented him from making Edinburgh Central Library the first completely subject departmentalized public library in Britain. The conversion of the city libraries to open access during the first decade was not in itself novel. The adoption of the Library of Congress Classification, which Savage greatly admired, instead of the ubiquitous Decimal Classification, was.

The partial reorganization of the central library into subject departments, during the 1930s, was inspired by the pioneering divisional organization of the U.S. public libraries of Cleveland, Los Angeles, and Baltimore. While Jast was planning a new and unusually large central library at Manchester, which would have offered ample capacity for subject departmentalization had Jast favored it, Savage was struggling with the restrictions of an existing Carnegie library. His establishment of an Edinburgh Historical and Topographical Library, an Economics and Commercial Library, a Music Library, and a Fine Arts Library were steps in the right direction. A more sophisticated pattern of subject specialization was not established in any British public library until after World War II, when George Chandler reorganized the Liverpool Central Library.

Savage's 20 years at Edinburgh were notable also for his outside activities. Early in 1933, at the request of the Carnegie Corporation, Savage went to the West Indies to investigate and report on the various libraries available to the public. Most of the libraries Savage visited were subscription libraries; he recommended the establishment of a public library service modeled after English county libraries. Although Savage's recommendations could not be adopted in their entirety, a public library service was eventually inaugurated at Trinidad and Tobago with the help of the Carnegie Corporation.

Savage believed in the need for the Library Association; though he was always its most vehement critic, he was also its savior. In 1926 Savage attended

ALA

Ernest A. Savage

725

the jubilee meeting of the American Library Association in Atlantic City. Impressed by the ALA's resources, activities, and status within the library profession, he felt that the ALA was "the powerful driving force of the library movement in the States and Canada." He returned to Britain resolved to bring the Library Association out of the doldrums, where it had been becalmed for many years, with a small membership and negligible resources.

The essence of Savage's plan was to engineer amalgamation with the Association of Assistant Librarians and the other independent library associations and to obtain financial aid from the Carnegie United Kingdom Trust (CUKT). When Savage became Honorary Secretary of the LA in 1928, he was in a good position to further his plan. With CUKT funds and the cooperation of the other library associations, the LA was transformed within a few years. By the early 1930s it had a paid secretary, its own headquarters building, and a library. Having piloted the LA through a crucial period in its history, Savage resigned from the honorary secretaryship in February 1934. In 1936 he served as President and for the rest of his life told the LA what it should do.

Savage's retirement in 1942 was purely nominal. Over the next 20 years he published several books and many articles, all of them written in his uniquely pungent, didactic, aphoristic style. Usually he was wise; often he was farsighted. Only in his opposition to the McColvin Report (*The Public Library System of Great Britain,* 1942), which advocated fewer and larger public library authorities, did Savage join forces with the reactionaries. For the most part, his contributions to the *Library Association Record,* the *Library World,* and the *Library Review* during the 1940s and 1950s rank high in the annals of library literature.

Among his books the most notable is *Special Librarianship in General Libraries and Other Papers* (1939). This collection of published and unpublished papers was the most original and stimulating book on librarianship published in Great Britain before World War II. Savage attacked the traditional pattern of public library organization in Britain, the common division of the stock into a general reference library and a general home reading library, and offered sound advice on how to replace them with subject departments. Even more striking, however, was the long essay on "The Training of Librarians," which foreshadowed the establishment of the postwar library schools in Great Britain and their eventual emancipation from the Library Association's unsatisfactory examination system.

Special Librarianship also included two of Savage's best contributions to library history, yet another area in which he excelled. When he was Librarian of Wallasey, he had somehow found time to write an impressive treatise called *Old English Libraries* (1911), which is still in use. In his retirement Savage wrote a fascinating professional autobiography, *A Librarian's Memories: Portraits and Reflections* (1952), which, despite its omissions and its occasional unfair judgments on some of his contemporaries, is likely to survive longer than any of his writings. When Savage published his last essay, in October 1963, he brought to a close a period of 73 years devoted almost entirely to librarianship.

In his day Savage was not appreciated as much

ALA

Frances Clarke Sayers

as he deserved. His abiding and ill-concealed dissatisfaction with so many things in the library world gave him the reputation of a captious schoolmaster, which was not altogether fair. Savage's criticism was always constructive, and he never suggested anything should be done that he was incapable of doing himself. Jast was more endearing as a critic of library practice, and W. C. Berwick Sayers was a more patient mentor, but Savage was the most versatile and, in the end, the most influential public librarian of his day. He died at Edinburgh February 4, 1966.

REFERENCES
The major sources of information on Savage are the detailed, fully documented biography *Ernest A. Savage: Librarian Extraordinary* by James G. Ollé, 2nd revised edition (1978), and Savage's own *A Librarian's Memories,* which provides a vivid picture of his professional life before he went to Coventry.

JAMES G. OLLÉ

Sayers, Frances Clarke
(1897–)

Frances Clarke Sayers contributed to the world of children's literature as author, critic, lecturer, storyteller, and teacher. Perhaps her major contributions have been the sharing of a sense of celebration and enthusiasm for good children's books and the demonstration that children's literature can be not only the lifelong occupation but the object of passionate advocacy of a mature and thinking individual.

Born in Topeka, Kansas, September 4, 1897, she spent her childhood in Galveston, Texas. Summers on the forested shore of Lake Michigan left permanent impressions of the pleasures of reading, the beauties of the natural setting, and the intensity of early experiences. When she was 12 years old, she read an article in *St. Nicholas Magazine* on service to children in the New York Public Library—and she determined immediately to become a children's librarian.

After two years at the University of Texas, she entered Carnegie Library School in Pittsburgh, noted for its devoted staff and belief in taking books to children wherever they were. Anne Carroll Moore, the energetic and stimulating pioneer of library service to children in the United States, invited the young Frances Clarke to join the children's staff at the New York Public Library. This heady environment, with its outstanding personnel and direct access to authors, illustrators, and publishers of children's books, as well as New York's other intellectual and cultural influences, played an important role in developing her abilities as critic, storyteller, and teacher.

After five years' service at the New York Public Library, Frances Clarke left in 1923 to live with her family in California. Two years later she married Alfred H. P. Sayers, an old friend from the New York days. They lived for seven years in Chicago and then in Sausalito, California, near the Golden Gate. During this period she not only retained her close association with children's literature and children's library service, but began to write children's books. In *Bluebonnets for Lucinda,* published by Viking and illustrated by Helen Sewell (1932), a little girl who lived on an offshore Texas island saw for the first time, miles of Texas bluebonnets brightening the earth of the mainland. *Mr. Tidy Paws,* with lithographs by Zhenya Gay (1934), told in a mixture of realism and fantasy how a boy's changeling cat made badly needed money for the boy's grandmother by performing in a dog and pony show. *Tag-Along Tooloo,* illustrated by Helen Sewell (1941), described five-year-old Talluluh's dependence upon her big sister until she became something of a heroine at the circus.

Frances Sayers also began to lecture. Beginning in 1936 she offered a course in children's literature at the Library School of the University of California, Berkeley, where she emphasized high standards of criticism, respect for children and children's books, and delight in storytelling. At the same time, she took her enthusiasm and knowledge of books to schools throughout California.

In 1941 she was named Superintendent of Work with Children at the New York Public Library, succeeding Anne Carroll Moore, a powerful figure to follow; but the new Superintendent "brought to the direction of the room not only first-hand familiarity with its life and tradition, but a vision of her own for a future in which artists and children continue to flourish" (*Illustrators of Children's Books 1744–1945,* The Horn Book, 1947, p. 125). Staff members looked forward to their monthly meetings with her because she always provided something to surprise them and lift their spirits.

During her tenure at the New York Public Library, she wrote two children's books: *Sally Tait,* illustrated by Eileen Evans (1948), an account of the ninth year of a Texas girl, 1912–13, and *Ginny and Custard,* illustrated by Eileen Evans (1951), in which a young New York girl, her parents, and her beloved cat spent a year exploring the country and urban sights in the Los Angeles area.

She also taught a course in writing for children at the New School for Social Research, wrote the script for "The Impressionable Years," a U.S. State Department film on library service to children, and served as a Consultant to the Library of Congress for the reorganization of its Children's Book Collection. Eleven years before it came into being, she recommended the establishment of a Children's Book Section at the Library of Congress.

She retired from the New York Public Library in 1952. *Compton's Pictured Encyclopedia* thereafter sponsored her visits to 25 colleges and universities with library schools or courses in children's literature for teachers. From February 1953 to May 1954, she lectured on the importance and joys of reading for children and told stories as well, leaving "a trail of enthusiasm behind her" (*The Horn Book,* April 1954, p. 81).

By that time she had moved to Los Angeles, where she lived with her sister, Marie Clarke, a librarian at the University of California, Los Angeles. In addition to writing and editing, Frances Sayers was teaching yet again—this time as Senior Lecturer in the English Department of UCLA. When the UCLA School of Library Service opened in 1960, she was invited to offer the course in children's literature there also.

She collaborated with Edna Johnson and Evelyn H. Sickels in producing the third edition of *Anthology of Children's Literature* (1959), a collection of more than 700 stories and poems, divided into approximately 15 categories, each introduced by a critical and historical essay. She later collaborated on a fourth, revised edition.

Summoned by Books (1965), a collection of Sayers' speeches and essays from 1937 through 1961, was edited by a former library school student, Marjeanne Jensen Blinn, with an introduction by Lawrence Clark Powell. The intent of this publication was to preserve for those who had not known her work personally or read her articles in professional periodicals some of Sayers' best contributions to the philosophy of children's library service and to the criticism of children's literature.

In 1965 Sayers retired from UCLA and moved to Ojai, California. She continued to write for professional journals and wrote a children's book, *Oscar Lincoln Busby Stokes,* illustrated by Gunnar Anderson (1970), in which a contemporary boy learned to be proud of his unusual name. She completed a major work, *Anne Carroll Moore: A Biography* (1972), a project that occupied her for 10 years.

During Sayers' long and productive professional life—she was present when Frederick Melcher opened the first Book Week Celebration in 1919—she was honored with many awards; they include the Joseph W. Lippincott Award for Distinguished Service in the Profession of Librarianship (1965); the Clarence Day Award for *Summoned by Books* (1966); a Southern California Council on Literature for Children and Young People's Award (1969); and the Catholic Library Association's Regina Medal (1973).

Her love of books, music, fine art, animals, good food, and all forms of nature are evident throughout her writings. She attributed her eagerness to reach out for new insights and new friendships to the influence of her mother and railroad-official father. All these characteristics she synthesized over the years in becoming a spell-binding storyteller and a Pied Piper of a speaker.

Sayers' professional work was always characterized by a crusading spirit. She continuously spoke forthrightly against shoddiness, faddishness, and didacticism in children's literature, trusting the power of art to give children wisdom. "The awakened and aware spirit is best served by subtlety and indirection—in short, by the arts" (*The Horn Book,* 1972, p. 446), she said. She proved a strong defender of the freedom of ideas.

WINIFRED RAGSDALE

Sayers, W. C. Berwick
(1881–1960)

William Charles Berwick Sayers was one of the most prominent public librarians of his generation in Britain. Indeed, through his textbooks, he influenced the library education of at least two generations after him. His influence was not confined to the development of public librarianship, since as an editor and writer on such pervasive topics as classification he had an important hand in the progress of all types of librarianship during his life. Furthermore, he can be described as a Library Association man. He was a Council member for nearly 50 years, President in

Library Association
W. C. Berwick Sayers

1938, and one of the great figures in the Association's history.

Born on December 23, 1881, at Mitcham, England, he received his early education in Bournemouth and began his career at Bournemouth Public Libraries. He was Sublibrarian there for four years from 1900, and then at the age of 23 he was appointed Deputy Librarian of Croydon under the great Louis Stanley Jast. Jast helped most in the molding of Sayers as a professional librarian. From the viewpoint of his future career, Sayers could not have been at a better age, in a better place, or under a better guide.

Education for librarians was at that time in an embryonic stage in Britain, and aspirants had to enlarge their knowledge as best they could, since there were no library schools. Before going to Croydon, Sayers had already demonstrated his professional ambitions by winning the Greenwood prize in librarianship, and with Jast's encouragement he widened his knowledge by attending lectures organized by the London School of Economics from 1905 to 1908.

At about this time Sayers became interested in the activities of the Library Assistants' Association, which had been formed in 1895. For 10 years, until he became a chief librarian, he worked heart and soul for the LAA, being Honorary Secretary from 1912 to 1915. At the same time his interest in the Library Association was growing. In 1908 he became a Fellow by honors diploma, and in 1912 he was elected to the Council and also became one of the Association's examiners.

In 1915 he was appointed Chief Librarian of Wallasey, where he succeeded Ernest A. Savage. But Sayers was destined to hold his new position for less than a year. Jast, his erstwhile chief at Croydon, was leaving to go to Manchester, and the Croydon authorities, no doubt on Jast's advice, invited Sayers to return to Croydon as chief.

Sayers remained Chief Librarian of Croydon until his retirement in 1947. Although his term of office was affected by two world wars, he instigated the provision of several new branch libraries for the rapidly expanding suburban population. Sayers also saw to it that Croydon remained the professional powerhouse of British librarianship created by Jast. Sayers in his time brought along such later notables as Lionel R. McColvin, Clifford Musgrave, Henry A. Sharp, and L. Montague Harrod.

But Sayers is remembered even more for his influential writings and for his work for the LA and for the National Central Library. In addition to writing hundreds of articles, he was the author of 12 books, as well as being editor of 4 editions of Brown's *Manual of Library Economy.* It was also an open secret that for many years he was the anonymous editor of *The Library World,* the monthly journal Brown had founded in 1898. His first book appeared in 1912; entitled *The Children's Library,* it was later described by Munford as a pioneer British book on the subject. Twenty years after, Sayers was to return to the same theme with a more mature book called *Children's Libraries.*

Sayers was not merely an author on library topics. He wrote books about Croydon and in 1913 published *Over Some Alpine Passes.* He was also a poet and musician. He composed many songs and wrote the definitive biography of the British composer Samuel Coleridge-Taylor. This appeared in 1915, with a later edition in 1927.

Classification was, however, the topic always associated with the name of Sayers. His earliest book on this subject was the *Canons of Classification,* issued in 1915, followed by *An Introduction to Library Classification* in 1918. This latter title achieved no fewer than nine editions in the ensuing 40 years. His magnum opus was undoubtedly the *Manual of Classification,* which appeared in 1926, with second and third editions in 1944 and 1955. Arthur Maltby produced a fourth completely revised edition in 1967 and a fifth edition in 1975.

Sayers added much to our knowledge of the history of classification, and he was a judicious if sometimes biased assessor of modern bibliographical schemes. He favored the enumerative schemes of Dewey, Cutter, the Library of Congress, and Brown but was much less at home with Bliss and with faceted schemes such as that of Ranganathan, his former pupil. Nevertheless, he was an inspiring writer on classification, and lectured on the subject for 32 years at the University of London School of Librarianship.

Although he retired from practicing librarianship in 1947, he remained active and influential until his death in Croydon on October 7, 1960. He had been Chairman of the LA Executive Committee throughout World War II and received the accolade of the Honorary Fellowship in 1947. He continued to serve on the LA Council, being a particularly valuable member of the Education and the Publications Committee and later a Trustee of the National Central Library.

Memorial Volume. The profession was preparing to celebrate Sayers' 80th birthday with a Festschrift edited by D. J. Foskett and B. I. Palmer when Sayers died shortly before his 79th birthday. Work went ahead on the proposed tribute, which eventually appeared in 1961, published by the LA as the *Sayers Memorial Volume.* It contains 16 chapters by various writers, mainly on classification themes, and it proved a fitting tribute to a man who was a tower of strength to the libraries he served, to the Library Association, and to library education and library cooperation in his country. He is still remembered as a gentlemanly librarian, urbane of speech, and possessed of a Churchillian turn of phrase suitable for the big occasion.

K. C. HARRISON

Scandinavian Federation of Research Librarians

The Nordiska Vetenskapliga Bibliotekarieförbundet (NVBF) (Scandinavian Federation of Research Librarians) was established on August 15, 1947, in Copenhagen. The purpose of the Federation was to promote cooperation among the research libraries in the Nordic countries and stimulate the exchange of ideas and experiences of their research librarians.

At the start, the Federation launched two important projects with great impact on Scandinavian library life, the Scandia Plan and the Nordic Union Catalogue for Periodicals (NOSP). The exchange of ideas was also taken into account: a general handbook on librarianship appeared in two editions and the Federation initiated and arranged a number of Round

Table conferences on various subjects.

As time went by the Scandia Plan and NOSP proved to be too heavy a load on the Federation, which was run primarily by unpaid volunteers. During the 1970s library life was more and more professionalized, and official bodies advising on library matters were established in all Scandinavian countries. In 1967 a Nordic Council for Scientific and Technical Information, NORDINFO, was established and, with some relief, NVBF handed over its two great projects—the Scandia Plan and NOSP—to this organization. Since then the question has many times been raised whether the NVBF still has a raison d'être. It is still important as the source of inspiration and ideas for NORDINFO and of mutual benefit for its member organizations as a forum for exchange of knowledge and experiences. The Federation is still strong, issuing publications and arranging Round Table conferences and general meetings.

The members of the Federation are the following research library associations in the Nordic countries: Foreningen af Medarbejdere ved Danmarks Forskningsbiblioteker (Denmark), Finlands Ventenskapliga Bibliotekssamfund (Suomen tieteellinen kirjastoseura, Finland), Deild Bókavaróa Í Íslenskum Rannsóknarbókasfnum (Iceland), Norsk Fagbiblioteksforening (Norway), and the Svenska Bibliotekariesamfundet (Sweden). These member associations nominate two members each to the NVBF board, except the Icelandic association, which nominates one. The chairmanship rotates among the countries on a two-year basis and the custom is for the country next in turn to succeed to the chairmanship and to provide the vice-chairman/treasurer. NVBF is financed by fees from the member associations, sale of publications, and grants for special projects given by NORDINFO.

The individual members of the member associations convene at general meetings every second year. Every second time the general meeting comprises a comparatively modest part of the general Nordic library meeting, which is arranged every fourth year; the other second time NVBF has its own three- or four-day meeting. These meetings are the most important, with invited keynote speakers and opportunities for the individual members to gather in groups of interests. Round Table conferences are held once or twice a year on diverse topics, such as collection and preservation of manuscripts, collection management, marketing of the library, and other issues.

NVBF published during the 1950s a Nordic library handbook, which used to be a cornerstone in Nordic library education. In many parts it is still valid, though it became dated in other parts. A revision was not undertaken, however, as publications issued took on a more specialized character—special handbooks (for example, on library questions about developing countries) and proceedings of meetings and Round Table conferences.

NVBF withdrew as a member association of IFLA, partly for financial reasons, partly because the member associations by themselves are members of IFLA. As to NORDINFO, NVBF takes a role comparable to that IFLA takes with Unesco: NVBF initiates and in many cases executes projects financed by NORDINFO.

LARS-ERIK SANNER

Schellenberg, Theodore R.
(1903–1970)

University of Wisconsin–Madison Archives
Theodore R. Schellenberg

Theodore R. Schellenberg was an archivist whose major influence was less as an archival administrator than as a theoretician, author, and teacher.

Schellenberg was born February 24, 1903, in Harvey County, Kansas. He received his undergraduate degree from Kansas State University and earned a Ph.D. in history at the University of Pennsylvania. In 1934 he moved to Washington to serve as Secretary of the Joint Committee on Materials for Research of the American Council of Learned Societies and the Social Science Research Council, a position that involved him in the early application of microfilm to documentary materials. He then served briefly as Associate National Director of the Survey of Federal Archives before joining the staff of the recently established National Archives in 1935.

Schellenberg began his archival career as a Deputy Examiner, one of a small group of academically trained professionals who advised the Archivist of the United States on the appraisal and disposition of noncurrent government records, determining whether records no longer needed for conducting current business should be preserved in the Archives or destroyed. A concern with this most difficult responsibility of the Archivist became a central theme in Schellenberg's writings and teaching for the next 30 years, and one of his most important contributions to archival theory and practice was his elaboration of the "evidential" and "informational" criteria to be applied in the collective appraisal of institutional records. Schellenberg rose rapidly in the National Archives to the position of Chief of the Agriculture Department Archives, where he contributed to the development of records disposition schedules for federal agencies, which identified and authorized, on a continuing basis, the destruction of those recurring record series without archival value.

After World War II Schellenberg became Records Officer of the Office of Price Administration, where he could participate directly in the development of the subdiscipline of records management. Emphasizing the life-cycle concept of records—from creation or receipt through maintainance and use to preservation as archives or destruction when noncurrent—records management attempts to reduce the quantity and improve the quality of records in their creation-receipt phase, to achieve greater economy and efficiency in the maintenance and use of current records, and to assure an orderly and timely retirement and disposition when records become semicurrent, including their intermediate storage in records centers. In 1948 Schellenberg returned to the National Archives as Program Adviser to the Archivist. He became Director of Archival Management the following year when the National Archives was reorganized as the National Archives and Records Service and in 1962 was appointed Assistant Archivist for a newly established Office of Records Appraisal, a position he held until his retirement from the federal service at the end of 1963.

He prepared the first comprehensive handbook of procedures for the National Archives—covering all professional activities—and wrote a number of staff information papers, bulletins, and journal articles on modern archival theory and practice. He organized and taught training courses for staff members of the National Archives; together with Ernst Posner of the American University, he taught credit courses and short intensive institutes on the preservation and administration of modern archives. In 1954 he was a Fulbright Lecturer in Australia and New Zealand; these lectures were the basis of the manual, published in 1956, *Modern Archives: Principles and Techniques.* The work became the most widely known and influential American publication in the field and formed the basis for Schellenberg's international reputation and influence with its eventual translation into Spanish, Portuguese, German, and Hebrew.

Having provided a theoretical and methodological foundation for the administration of modern public records and archives, Schellenberg then turned to bridging the gaps that had developed between archivists, manuscript curators, and librarians in their increasing specialization. After his retirement he lectured widely and taught courses at several universities. In 1965 he published his second major work, *Management of Archives,* which was based on the conviction that the principles and techniques of administering modern public records and archives are also applicable to those of private institutions and to accumulations of personal papers. He also proposed that chief responsibility for the training of archivists be placed with graduate library schools. Although the book did not have the widespread acceptance and impact of his earlier treatise, it has had a continuing influence on the relations between archivists, manuscript curators, and librarians.

Schellenberg continued to teach and write until shortly before his death on January 14, 1970. In addition to his travels throughout the United States, he was also active internationally, particularly in the Caribbean and Latin America. In 1961 he organized and directed the first Inter-American Archival Council and continued to serve as an adviser on the development of archival programs in this region. In recognition of his contributions to the archival profession worldwide, he was the first American to be elected to honorary membership in the International Council on Archives.

FRANK B. EVANS

Scholarly and Research Services

In the 1812 Act of Incorporation of the American Antiquarian Society, now one of America's leading specialist research libraries, Isaiah Thomas stated that "the collection and preservation of the antiquities of our country . . . have a tendency to enlarge the sphere of human knowledge, aid the progress of science, to perpetuate the history of moral and political events, and to improve and instruct posterity . . . ." Research libraries have historically performed dual but complementary roles, an active role of "enlarging the sphere of human knowledge," and a more passive role of collection, organization, and preservation of the information scholars and researchers use in individual and collective ways to make their own contributions to knowledge.

Large research libraries play an active, if often unrecognized, role in shaping the direction of scholarship itself through their decisions about what is important to preserve for posterity and what is chaff to be discarded. By their decisions on what should be retained and made accessible from the human record, research librarians often set new directions in scholarship or, at the least, affect the extent of those directions.

More specifically, libraries have made their own contributions to knowledge through their support of research, for example in such fields as conservation and preservation (leaf-casting, paper deacidification, binding structures, encapsulation, and optical disk technology), the scholarship of cataloguing (that is, attributions of authorship or date), and library history, a field that has assumed a scholarly life of its own as a subset of institutional history. In addition many research libraries—notably the Library of Congress, the New York Public Library, the Folger Library, and the Huntington Library, to name a few—have supported active publication programs intended to enlarge the sphere of human knowledge and to make that knowledge more accessible to a wider public. Such massive projects as the *National Union Catalog,* the *Union List of Serials,* the *National Union Catalog of Manuscript Collections,* and the development of national bibliographical databases can be considered direct contributions to knowledge in their own right. So too can the publication of catalogues from large institutional collections such as the British Library, the Bibliothèque Nationale, and the New York Public Library. Collaborative efforts to enhance these tools through online access to vast bodies of literature (such as the *Eighteenth-Century Short-Title Catalogue*) are further indications of the active role libraries have played in support of scholarship. Nor is this a new phenomenon: librarian John Shaw Billings, for example, was instrumental in developing *Index Medicus* in the late 19th century.

Several research libraries, especially independent research libraries such as the Newberry Library, the Folger, and the Huntington, have sponsored seminars, lectures, and research-oriented symposia that have also made active contributions to the advancement of learning. Examples of this form of outreach are the American Antiquarian Society's Program in the History of the Book in American Culture, the Folger Library's Institute of Renaissance and Eighteenth-Century Studies, and the Newberry Library's Hermon Dunlap Smith Center for the History of Cartography.

To most users, however, the primary functions of research libraries are the accumulation, cataloguing, and preservation of vast amounts of information in various formats. Some of that information may seem arcane, esoteric, and unimportant until synthesized by the inspired researcher. The French anthropologist Claude Levi-Straus stated somewhat hyperbolically that everything he learned about anthropology he learned during long hours in the Main Reading Room of the New York Public Library during the early 1940s; one can also consider the wide reading by Karl Marx in the British Museum a century earlier.

Collections. The habit of hoarding, often unrelated to imminent use, is predicated on the unpredictability of both the frontiers of knowledge and the demands that might develop for information. Although this assumption may be challenged, as it has been in studies at the University of Pittsburgh, and although the assumption may be more easily demonstrable for retrospective humanistic and historical research than for most scientific inquiry, with its emphasis on currency of information, most large research libraries have traditionally accepted as a necessity the development of comprehensive and vast collections sufficient to meet the unpredictable needs of the scholarly community.

While continuing to assume that necessity, research libraries were faced in the 1980s with an insoluble dilemma created by finite resources in an expanding information world. They operate in an arena in which selectivity, for practical reasons, is an absolute necessity, even though selectivity in acquisition has been called "anathema to future research needs." Despite the continued growth in the demand by researchers for comprehensive collections in their own institutions, economic forces inexorably led research libraries to coordinated distribution of collection responsibility, so that on a national scale the more harmful results of selectivity in the limitation of the scope of research might be minimized.

The development of the Research Libraries Group (RLG) conspectus and its adoption by the Association of Research Libraries in 1983 was intended to address this need by providing standardized and comparable data on collection practices in research libraries.

Preservation. An important component of the scholarly service known as collection development is the preservation of those collections for future use. Physical deterioration of library materials has brought its own uncontrolled selectivity in most libraries. As noted previously, libraries have already made impressive contributions to this field, and research and interest are continuing at an accelerated rate. Some large libraries and specialized collections have diverted sizable funds from other activities, including collecting, to preserve materials already in their collections. Like collecting, however, the task is too great for individual libraries to undertake alone.

The most pressing present need of the mid-1980s, given the widespread deterioration of post-1850 papers, is a coordinated national program for nonduplicative micropreservation. A major work serving that end has been the *National Register of Microform Masters* (NRMM) produced at the Library of Congress since 1965 and cumulated in 1976 in six volumes of almost 6,000 pages, with another cumulation for 1976–82 promised. As a record of past micropreservation activities and as an admittedly imperfect guide to the present availability of preserved materials, the *National Register* has proved to be an extremely valuable tool. Later work at RLG provided online access to current bibliographic data concerning ongoing micropreservation activities. The system allows research libraries to coordinate preservation activities and, like the original *NRMM,* is intended to aid in avoiding duplication of the most expensive step in micropreservation, the creation of a master negative. Initial efforts for the use of this new capability have been directed toward a cooperative program of micropreservation of late 19th-century American imprints. Related to these developments are research and development efforts at the Library of Congress

American Antiquarian Society

American Antiquarian Society, Worcester, Massachusetts.

in optical disk technology—an alternative means of both preservation and access which may well supplant microfilm—and in mass deacidification (see Conservation and Preservation of Library Materials).

No less crucial, though requiring even greater financial resources, is the conservation and preservation of books and manuscripts in their original formats. No libraries have yet made strides in this area commensurate to the scope of the problem. The task of restoring valuable materials is time-consuming and expensive and requires highly skilled craftsmen and technicians. As a result, research libraries have been able to deal with only a minuscule proportion of their problem collections. The most significant gains in recent years have been the growing awareness of the scope and importance of the problem, the development of both institutional programs and regional conservation centers, and the establishment at Columbia University of a training program designed to produce a trained cadre of skilled conservators and preservation administrators able to carry out pragmatic programs of conservation within the fiscal restraints necessitated by other institutional commitments. Students from that program are now entering the preservation field.

Although the environmental conditions in which collections are kept have generally improved since the 1960s, greater preventive measures for protection of materials are needed. In the mid-1980s few research libraries met even minimal standards for proper storage and current costs were likely to make achievement of adequate environmental control even more difficult. Many libraries, including the New York Public Library, invested large sums in conservation and micropreservation, only to return preserved materials to a hostile environment.

Much remains to be done in the entire field of preservation and environmental control. Alexis de Tocqueville in *Democracy in America* complained

Scholarly and Research Services

The Newberry Library

Summer Institute at the Hermon Dunlap Smith Center for the History of Cartography, Newberry Library, Chicago. Participants are examining late 16th century and early 17th century city plans.

about American carelessness in preserving the records of its past:

> The instability of administration has penetrated into the habits of the people; it even appears to suit the general taste, and no one cares for what happened before his time: no methodical system is pursued, no archives are formed, and no documents are brought together when it would be very easy to do so. Where they exist, little store is set upon them. I have among my papers several original public documents which were given to me in the public offices in answer to some of my inquiries.

While the collecting of books and archives has improved immeasurably since de Tocqueville wrote in 1834, our care and custody of those collections has been almost irresponsible.

Organization. Inextricably connected with the primary scholarly service of research libraries in collecting and preserving comprehensively is the task of organizing those collections for use. That task is basically similar in all libraries and need not be covered in detail here, except to note the greater importance of authority control in research library cataloguing practice. This importance is largely a factor of the greater size of research libraries, the retention of virtually all materials received, and the necessity of assuring that the scholar consulting a library's catalogues has access to all of the works available of a given author, on a given subject, or about a particular work. Authority control, by which a library maintains consistency in the bibliographical organization of its collections for use, is a major aid to the scholar, and thus justifies its greater expense in research libraries. The collection of like works in catalogue listings to some extent makes up for the inability to house all like works together on the shelves.

Classification, the attempt to bring like works together physically according to some organizing principle (such as subject or size), has often been seen as a scholarly aid to serendipitous discovery. As a result, open access to bookstacks has always been a valued privilege among American scholars, a privilege not often available to their European counterparts.

However, several pressures are likely to lead large academic research libraries to abandon or severely limit such access. Automated bibliographical systems, with their multiplicity of access points, already provide better means of access to materials than do shelf classification and open stacks. As browsing with the computer develops, the importance of location through subject classification is likely to diminish, at least as a part of the scholarly process. The open-access tradition in American academic libraries has been maintained at the very great but unquantifiable cost of widespread theft and mutilation, as well as at the cost of poor service through the inability of many research libraries to provide access to substantial portions of their collections. Furthermore, classified open access collections require more space and room for growth than closed collections in various forms of compact storage. Despite the increased cost of retrieving materials for patrons, and despite the political problems of withdrawing stack privileges, the advantages of greater security, reduced space needs, greater control and accessibility, and better possibilities for optimum environmental control are likely to lead research libraries to close portions of their general collections from direct public access. Such a movement will also put a higher priority on developing alternate means for retrieval and remote access to stored optical images and other computerized information. The technology is already available for such access through the scholar's workstation.

Other Services. Many services traditionally offered to scholars by research libraries are shared in common with services in most other kinds of libraries. Direct reference services, reference correspondence, interlibrary loan, computerized literature services, and SDI services have become staples of the trade. In addition, research library photoservice departments have greatly aided scholarly access to information, as has cooperation with publishers and commercial microfilmers in producing facsimiles in various formats of vast holdings of interest to researchers. Some libraries have even provided translation services to extend further access to materials in their care. Finally, the 1970s and 80s have seen an increasing preoccupation with educating users, both students and more advanced scholars, in the use of current information services available through research libraries, especially in the area of automated retrieval services.

Libraries are making important contributions to the support of scholarship, not least in the linkages they have established between and among themselves, the world of scholarship and its disciplines, and the universe of developing technology. The decade of the mid-1970s to the mid-1980s provided a sound base on which to build and expand those links.

In the final analysis, collecting and preservation remain the most important functions of research libraries. The National Enquiry into Scholarly Communication (1979) points to inadequate library collections as a major concern of scholars in the humanities who wish to have comprehensive collections available locally. Nonetheless, the Enquiry's report goes on to state that "The sheer growth of written and recorded materials coupled with inevitable limitations on library budgets suggests that the understandable desire of scholars for local self-sufficiency in library resources will increasingly fall short of attainment." These contradictory forces only seem to reemphasize the impossibility of single libraries "of last resort" and the absolute necessity for effective networking among research libraries based on efficient communications and delivery systems.

The need for the book and for comprehensive and coordinated repositories for the book seems secure. The codex remains the best medium for reflective learning and for access to the greatest and most creative works of the human mind. It is also the storehouse of that mind. Until its contents are captured in some other form or until abandoned, there is still compelling need for its retention.

REFERENCES

Albert H. Rubenstein et al., "Search versus Experiment: The Role of the Research Librarian," *College and Research Libraries* (1973).

Scholarly Communication: The Report of the National Enquiry (1979).

David H. Stam, "The Preservation of the Human Record in a Democratic Society: Who Is Responsible? The Role of Libraries," *New York Library Association Bulletin* (1978).

Nancy E. Gwinn and Paul H. Mosher, "Coordinating Collection Development: The RLG Conspectus," *College and Research Libraries* (1983).

DAVID H. STAM

School Libraries/Media Centers

PURPOSES AND OBJECTIVES

School library development in the United States was first promoted in the late 1800s. Around 1895 farsighted high school principals and directors of public libraries in individual and isolated communities began to create school libraries, and by 1900 the first high school librarian, Mary Kingsbury, had been appointed in Brooklyn, New York. The National Education Association (NEA) through its Library Department, the Library Section of the National Council of Teachers of English (NCTE), and the American Library Association (ALA) supported the development of the concept.

In 1915 the New York City District Superintendent of High School said, "It may confidently be asserted that the most potent single agency in the modern cosmopolitan high school is the library." The NEA *Proceedings* for 1912 stated that "the school library will be the proof of the educational value of the new curriculum. . . . the library will be the open door to the opportunity of the present." Mary E. Hall, one of the early leaders in high school library development, said that the modern high school library could be depicted in this fashion (1925):

> The room may fulfill all its pedagogical functions as a reference collection for obtaining information, a training school in the best methods of securing that information, a laboratory for special topic work and collateral reading in connection with the subjects in the curriculum and yet fail one of its highest functions if it fails to be a place of inspiration and recreation as well.

"The old high school library was static," said Hall, "but the new is dynamic. The old was largely for reference and required reading in History and En-

glish; the new is all things to all departments." These earliest statements by educators and librarians indicated a clear vision of what high school library service could become.

The high school library movement continued to expand, but elementary school libraries were slower to develop. *Certain Standards for Elementary School Libraries* was published in 1925, and in 1933 the Department of Elementary School Principals of NEA devoted its yearbook to supporting the concept. But elementary school libraries did not gain prominence until after World War II. The increased birthrate necessitated building a large number of elementary schools; these schools included libraries—often called library resource areas or media centers. Local, state, and federal funds helped to purchase books and nonprint materials, and the elementary schools flourished, as did their libraries. Professional staffs and experimental programs were considered an important part of reading programs as well as other aspects of the instructional curriculum.

Unfortunately, specific legislation was not forthcoming among the states requiring certified libraries in elementary schools similar to requirements for secondary school libraries. Hence, the economic pressures of the 1970s and 1980s produced serious cutbacks and threatened this aspect of school library service in many states. A reevaluation of the values of the elementary school library/media center by librarians, teachers, school administrators, parents, and other citizens is a current necessity, so that these libraries not only will be resuscitated, but also will actually expand into the vital force they could be as basic support for developing educational and leisure-time pursuits for all future adults. Strong state standards that insist on quality as well as quantity of materials and well-educated librarian/media specialists, new efforts at multitype library cooperation, and specific legislation to guarantee support could do much to enhance and solidify the value of school libraries in tomorrow's education program.

Education. "The teacher librarian should meet the requirements for teachers plus training in the use of books and library methods. School librarians

Prince George's County Public Schools, Maryland

Poetry reading in public school, Prince George County, Maryland.

should have more training than the teachers in the schools wherein they serve. To create libraries without training librarians is futile." "One of the cardinal mistakes of the library movement has been to emphasize books more than service, and too often this can lead to a clerical type of library service." "School libraries' activities are fundamentally educational: that they enrich the curriculum; that they stimulate initiative on the part of the pupils and develop healthy minds; that they socialize and democratize values and that they have an important part in character development." These quotations from a 1924 address by Joy Morgan before the NEA's Department of Elementary School Principals epitomize the belief that has prevailed consistently in the library profession—that the school librarian must be both teacher and librarian. There are varying views about the minimum requirements for personnel, which are often influenced directly by state fiat, yet certification codes specify minimum standards in both education and librarianship at the secondary level and in some states at the elementary. The requirement of a Bachelor's degree with a teacher education emphasis plus a Master's degree in librarianship is the preferred level of education for school librarians today. Library and information science educational programs for school libraries/media centers continue to emphasize work with curriculum materials, courses in management/administration, instructional technology, teaching of reading, and child psychology as well as computer utilization. The practicum aspect coordinates librarianship competencies with current educational trends and methodology.

Professional Organization. It was inevitable that with the increased visibility of school libraries a movement would develop within the ALA to recognize this group of libraries. In December 1914 at the ALA Midwinter Meeting, the ALA Council approved a petition from the Round Table of Normal and High School Librarians to form a school library section. The petition was supported on the grounds that there was "likely to be in the near future a rapid and extensive development of activity in this field of library work and the existence of a section . . . especially devoted to its study and discussion should be of material aid to those professionals concerned with it." Likewise, "The work and problems of school librarians are sufficiently different from those other library workers to justify their special organization as a section."

From 1915 to 1944 the School Libraries Section maintained a rather uneventful existence, but in 1941 it was reorganized as a part of the Division of Libraries for Children and Young People and became visible and active at the national level. In 1944 it was renamed the American Association of School Librarians (AASL) and in 1951 it became an autonomous division within ALA. Patricia Pond has noted that AASL achieved three benchmarks in the development of a professional association: (1) forming an association that united members of the same occupation and/or those who wished to promote goals of an occupational group; (2) preparing a statement of goals and objectives; and (3) structuring an organization that provided continuity of leadership, mechanisms for achieving its goals, and representation of the interests of members.

Since 1951 AASL has had a full-time Executive Secretary, published a quarterly journal, set standards for the profession, and functioned as a liaison with state school library/media associations and associations with similar educational concerns and interests.

Guidelines and Standards. Despite changes in curriculum, technological developments, socioeconomic pressures, wars, and depressions, the basic principle that school libraries should participate effectively and completely in the school program has remained constant. This principle has been expressed in guidelines and standards published by the ALA School Library Section as it grew and expanded from 1915 to the present. The changes in interpreting this principle can best be seen by a review of the goals and objectives developed by AASL since the 1940s.

Both the ALA and the NEA constantly supported standards for school libraries. They issued their first significant statement on the subject in 1941 in *Schools and Public Libraries Working Together in School Library Service:*

The school library is an essential element in the school program; the basic purpose of the school library is identical with the basic purpose of the school itself.

School library service, being an essential part of the school program, is basically a responsibility of the board of education.

The distinctive purpose of the school library within the total complex of the work of the school is that of helping children and young people to develop abilities and habits of purposefully using books and libraries in attaining their goals of living.

The school library program should carry out the purposes of sharing in the whole school program and of encouraging the effective use of books and libraries by providing individual service to individual children through reading guidance, ample reading materials, and library experience.

Three essential factors without which a school library does not exist are: (1) the librarian, (2) the book collection, and (3) the library quarters.

A school library does not become effective without the informed and constructive participation of many persons within the school system in addition to the librarian and the pupils, including especially: (1) the superintendent of schools and the central administrative staff, (2) principals of school buildings, and (3) classroom teachers.

School libraries and the public library should work together to provide a coordinated and complete library service to school children without unnecessary duplication of activities.

State leadership, operating under adequate state laws and regulations and working in cooperation with local groups, is essential in performing certain promotional, advisory, administrative, and coordinating services not otherwise available to local school libraries.

The first AASL document, *School Libraries for Today and Tomorrow: Functions and Standards* (1945), was both a qualitative and quantitative effort, restating the purposes of the school library and emphasizing services to pupils and teachers, but also setting specific standards for personnel, resources, facilities, budgets, and administration.

In 1956 AASL unanimously passed a statement, *School Libraries as Instructional Materials Centers,* the first official recognition that the flood of nonprint materials and equipment—beyond the traditional picture file or records and slides—had become an important part of the school's educational program and belonged in the library, where it would be shared by the entire school community. The statement reiterated the role of the school librarian and stressed teacher training requirements:

In summary, the well-trained professional school librarian should anticipate service both as a teacher and as an instructional materials specialist. Where adequate funds and staff are available, the school library can serve as an efficient and economical means of coordinating the instructional materials and equipment needed for a given school program. It should always stand ready to provide informed guidance concerning selection and use of both printed and newer media.

This 1956 declaration was followed by the 1960 *Standards for School Library Programs,* produced by a committee of school librarians in cooperation with representatives from 20 other related school groups and based on good school library practice as determined by a questionnaire sent to 1,400 schools. Those standards expanded the concept of the school library as an educational force:

The school library thus stands as a symbol for the truthful expression of man's knowledge and experiences. The extent to which many children and young people of today will be creative, informed, knowledgeable, and, within their own years, wise, will be shaped by the boundaries of the content of the library resources available within their schools.

This statement represents an enhancement of the 1915 vision. The document's presentation of (1) principles of policy and practice, (2) principles of administration and organization, and (3) specifications for staff, materials, and finances was intended to apply to all types of school libraries. Once again the basic concepts were restated and were interpreted in a manner appropriate for both lay persons and school librarians, and the standards set specific goals toward which all libraries should strive.

Social, educational, and technological developments led in 1969 to a new set of standards, *Standards for School Media Programs.* They constituted a unique cooperative effort by the AASL and the Department of Audiovisual Instruction of NEA and were designed to coordinate standards for both school library and audiovisual programs—a unified program.

The philosophy of a unified program of audiovisual and printed services and resources in the individual school is one that has continuously grown and been strengthened in the last thirty years. This fusion of media resources and services provides optimum service for students and teachers. Many schools now have unified media programs. For those others that have separate audiovisual departments and school libraries, it is recommended that wherever possible, these services be combined, administratively and organizationally, to form a unified media program. New schools should start with a unified media center and program of services.

Since the emphasis in this publication was on the school building's library, it soon became evident that directions were needed for districtwide centers as well. Four major assumptions form the basis for the most recent standards, *Media Programs: District and*

Prince George's County Public Schools, Maryland

Learning how to make books—in a Maryland junior high school library.

School (1975), and further delineate the shift in emphasis with the school library programs: (1) full acceptance of a total media concept; (2) a greater participation in instructional decision making; (3) stress on programmatic activity focused on the "user"; and (4) utilization of pertinent principles of management theory. Here was an even stronger movement away from quantitative standards for resources and a more deliberate emphasis on how such resources would be used.

In this document, published by ALA for AASL and the Association for Educational Communications and Technology (AECT), the media program is considered in light of four functions: design, consultation, information, and administration. Throughout the statement is evidence of the premise that there is an obligation to share implementation of goals as well as operation of programs with the community.

In 1985 a committee representing AASL and AECT was evaluating the old guidelines and preparing a new publication directed toward the future development of the library/media center and reflecting current changes in education.

Program Trends. School library services and programs have always been affected by changes in their educational, cultural, and social environments. The exponential growth in use of personal computers, networking trends, the continuous expansion of high technology and its effect on communication, the impact of censorship, and shifts in federal support for education have particularly influenced the services offered. The *School Library Media Quarterly* (SLMQ), AASL's official publication, helps professionals to keep up with these changes through feature articles on topics such as exceptional children, research, community education, school and public library cooperation, or materials for bilingual youth.

The concerns of the 70s and early 80s have not disappeared. But today school library/media specialists are also trying to determine how they will fit into the next decade and the next century. What will be the relationship with other professional groups, and with ALA as a whole? What will be the best mode or

735

organizational pattern for AASL? How should programs be evaluated? What are the best recommendations to educate the professional of the future? School library programs, and the profession itself, must adjust to the demands of the 21st century.

International. The burgeoning school library in the U.S. during the late 1940s and 1950s was followed by comparable growth and interest in other countries. The Canadian pattern developed along similar lines, and Canadian and American school librarians often share their endeavors through workshops, conferences, and standards. In Europe—particularly Denmark and to a somewhat lesser degree Sweden and the United Kingdom—legislation was passed promoting school libraries, and government funds supported rapid expansion of school libraries in the early 1970s. Denmark has a national mandate for a library in every school staffed by professional teacher-librarians. Australian school librarians quickly followed, requesting legislative and financial support at federal and state levels. By the late 1960s an international interest was evident in the field of education, resulting in a movement to advance school library services in both developed and developing countries. Hong Kong, Indonesia, Japan, Malaysia, New Zealand, Nigeria, the Philippines, and Singapore are all examples of countries where specific efforts to promote such activity can be identified.

One of the interesting international developments is the growth of associations for school librarians, either as independent organizations or as special divisions in national library associations. Some 30 such associations can be identified that have active programs, and most publish journals or newsletters. They organize workshops and institutes for training personnel, promote legislation in support of libraries, and argue for indigenous publications relevant to their children's interest.

For example, the Fiji Library Association helped develop school library programs and urged that pupils have an opportunity to develop language fluency and increase their vocabularies in a second language, encouraging teachers to read books to the children and urging school libraries to purchase materials relevant to their student needs.

A major achievement for the school library profession in Australia has been the establishment of the Australian Schools Catalogue Information Service (ASCIS), a cooperative, shared cataloguing information scheme that will extend to all of the nation's 10,000 schools, even as an online service if desired.

A Philippine Association of School Librarians task force, working on a five-year plan for developing libraries in every school, was pursuing three projects in the mid-1980s: formulation of school library standards; preparation of a basic book collection for elementary/secondary schools; and creation of a staff development program.

The basic problems facing school library development in Third World countries continue to be significant. Competition for funds is far more intense than in the U.S.; education and libraries are often forced to take a second place behind such basic needs as food, clothing, and shelter. Where do books and libraries fit into a country's program when the population increases proportionately faster than the number of teachers, let alone librarians? How can one

move into a computerized society when there is little or no electricity? Such problems are exacerbated by the difficulty of obtaining reading materials of any kind in sufficient quantity, especially in the language of the people, relevant to the culture, or written by indigenous authors. Yet the acceptance of the concept of school library service is still evident. Ministries of education are promoting legislation that will begin to support types of library resource centers and are encouraging the development of a corps of professional librarians to serve as organizers and supervisors. National, regional, and internationl organizations are promoting exchange of information, programs, research, and standards. The impact of school library media and services, and their role and function in education, will continue to grow in all countries.

By 1985 the pressures on the school libraries/media centers were gaining in momentum. The questions being raised about the content or approach of textbooks; such arguments as evolution vs. creationism and how and where to provide sex education; censorship; and shifts in emphasis in historical study—all these are questions the school librarian/media specialist must be aware of. They require ever closer evaluation of choices of materials, the input of all members of the school community in making judgments, and abiding by selection policies. School libraries/media centers have been predicated upon the need to have collections in a wide range of formats that meet the needs of all students and teachers and thus support the educational program of the school. The preservation of this basic objective will be one of the important tasks of the immediate future years.

JEAN E. LOWRIE

SERVICES TO USERS

The concept of the school library as an instructional resource center and laboratory for learning is derived from, but also represents a distinct break from, the U.S. tradition of public library services to children, which took form beginning in the late 19th century as separate library rooms for children, book loan services to schools, summer reading promotions, and the specialization of children's work as a branch of public librarianship. Often established at the initiative of public libraries, book rooms and services in schools had a simple reason for being: to enrich textbook teaching with good books and to introduce children to the wonderful world of imaginative literature through storytelling, book talks, and readers' guidance.

A noticeable break with these traditions occurred during the mid-1950s. A series of public education reforms was precipitated by an extraordinary increase in knowledge and the proliferation of communication technologies. In a few years' time, the advances rendered predominantly textbook-based curricula obsolete, raised doubts about the validity of the printed word as the exclusive communication medium of education, and highlighted the futility of attempting to teach children "everything there is to know" in 12 years of schooling.

Concurrently, educational researchers were advancing new insights on how children learn and why a substantial number do not. Their judgment that all children can learn, though not necessarily at the same rate or in the same way, was an indictment of then-current practices in most American schools. Educators were induced to experiment with a variety of audiovisual equipment and teaching strategies that would allow aberrant learners to be educated in their own way rather than by the methodologies followed in the majority of classrooms. Individualized learning, motivation, and humanizing education became the buzzwords of school reform. The subsequent decades were characterized by revolutionary changes in curriculum content, the introduction of alternate patterns of instructional organization (for example, the open classroom), and many innovative uses of technology borrowed from business and the military.

Libraries emerged as the places where students would learn from a range of information sources, using "discovery" and problem-solving learning procedures. With the help of federal funds, school libraries were established where formerly there had been none, and existing collections were expanded. Motion pictures, sound recordings, videotapes, transparencies, filmstrips and slides, programmed instruction, computer programs, microforms—along with a bewildering array of technologies for projection, reception, recording, magnification, and production—were introduced into library collections.

Libraries were enlarged, wired, and adapted to accept the strange shapes and sizes of nonbook information packages and their hardware. Photo darkrooms, television studios, microform libraries, projection and recording rooms, and AV production centers where students could work creatively with the new media were incorporated into the design of media facilities. Both teachers and librarians were sent off to government-financed workshops to learn how to use the new educational tools. District and regional media resource centers were established.

Dimensions of Services. The result of three decades of school and school library reform has been to move the library and the librarian from the periphery of the instructional program into the mainstream of educational effort. Today the school library/media center serves two publics, teachers and students. The student users may range in age from 5 to 18—younger when prekindergarten programs exist, older if classes of mentally retarded students are housed in the school. Within each age group, students differ from one another in degrees of physical, mental, and emotional maturation, any of which may affect their progress through the educational system. Students are, like all people, fast or slow, eager to learn or stubbornly resistant to schooling. Some are emotionally impaired or learning disabled in ways that require the intervention of specially trained adults, including librarians. The talented and gifted among them, along with those educationally handicapped by reason of cultural, emotional, physical, or economic circumstances, are singled out by law for supplementary, compensatory, or alternative services, many of them media-related.

Teachers also come with individual differences: in age, in experience, in curriculum-area interests and responsibilities, in teaching styles, and in perceptions about what is expected from the school library/media specialist. School administrators, board of education members, and the educational community, consisting of parent-teacher and other organizations for protecting or promoting special educational interests and the

taxpaying public, are also potential users of the library/media center.

Factors Affecting Services. There is frequently a gap between the services that can actually be provided and those that should be. The extent to which library/media centers can provide services to their users depends on resources in personnel, physical facilities, and collections.

The scope of services offered and the number of users that can be accommodated depend primarily on the size and competence of the staff. In many schools the number of professionals and supporting staff is less than that needed to assure a desired range and quality of services.

Similarly, the size and suitability of the facility for the media program and its services also affect services to users, particularly since new communications media have moved into the media center. A facility too small to accommodate the number and variety of materials for its many categories of users, that lacks space for all the people who want to or should use it, or that cannot house the instructional equipment it should have will not meet legitimate expectations for service, no matter how committed its leadership to a philosophy of comprehensive user services.

Finally, the media center's collections and budget must be large enough to support the information requirements of the school's instructional program and the diverse developmental needs of its total student population.

Traditional Services. Despite the many changes in school library services, some remain basic:

Reading. School library/media specialists are advocates of books and reading. In this role they help students acquire an enduring love of books and learning. They tell stories and give book talks. They compile special reading lists, prepare bibliographies, cre-

Greenwich Public Schools

Student filmmakers preparing clay characters for an animation movie, a project in a public school in Greenwich, Connecticut.

737

ate alluring displays, and promote reading clubs. They make the library a reading guidance center in which students, as individuals or in groups with their teachers, find books for information or recreational reading.

Reference. The school library/media center is the information center of the school with a collection of basic reference sources and assistance in locating information. Where resources are inadequate, the library/media specialist calls upon resources outside the school—the public library, museums, historical societies, interlibrary loan, and whatever other information networks are accessible to the school.

Teaching. School library/media specialists are teachers as well as information experts. They know not only how libraries are administered but also how children learn the process of purposeful inquiry. They help students to become confident seekers and organizers of information and increasingly independent library users. Instruction is sequential and classroom-related. For younger students, an information skills lesson may focus on using the table of contents and index of a book or threading a filmstrip viewer. For college-bound high school seniors it may be using the *New York Times Index* as a research tool or using a microcomputer. In the search for knowledge there is no primacy of print or nonprint; students learn to learn from all kinds of information sources and to use the technology they require.

Instructional Support Services. *Curriculum.* Media specialists are instructional materials experts, contributing their professional expertise to the planning, design, and implementation of curricula. They identify, select, and acquire educational materials. They assemble, organize, and list materials, prepare bibliographies, assist in the design of activities, and make other contributions to the fulfillment of educational objectives. They provide alternative materials for the fast, slow, emotionally disturbed, learning disabled, and those with limited competencies in the English language.

Administration. In a well-managed media center a user should be able to know what materials the media center has and, with reasonable effort, be able to find them. Efficient procedures for cataloguing, processing, listing, storage, and circulation ensure ease of access and equitable availability of instructional materials for all users. Equipment is scheduled, distributed, and maintained in good operating order. Hours of opening are planned for the convenience of the users. Facilities are designed and furnished for comfort and suitability to the educational purposes intended. The atmosphere is hospitable, the staff friendly.

Supervision. The library/media specialist manages the media center as a learning laboratory available to individuals and classes for exploring, investigating, and researching their intellectual interests and for becoming acquainted with the means available in the media center for so doing. It is open for self-directed learning or recreational reading, viewing, and listening throughout the school day and before and after school hours. All levels of student interest, ability, academic achievement, maturity, and motivation are matched within it.

Planning. Another instructional support service is the planning and implementation of curriculum-re-lated activities that extend and enrich the classroom experiences of students. This might mean bringing into the school, or arranging telephone conferences with, persons of achievement in the arts, sciences, or public life. Book fairs, career awareness days, art exhibits, and other learning experiences come into the classroom by way of the media center, cutting across all levels and disciplines.

Staff Development. Another category of services contributes to the professional growth of teachers. Wherever possible, a portion of the media center budget is allocated for purchasing professional journals and books on current issues in education. For teachers working on advanced degrees, the media specialist helps locate research materials. In coordination with district or regional centers, the media staff sponsors workshops to introduce to teachers new materials and equipment for improving teaching and learning and to create an awareness of staff development opportunities both in and outside the school and community.

New Technologies. Much of the responsibility for integrating the new communication media into the fabric of instruction falls upon the school media specialist, who identifies, selects, organizes, and makes these resources available to faculty and students. Implicit in this responsibility is the care, maintenance, scheduling, and instruction of the presentation devices needed for their use. The media center staff provides assistance to teachers whose professional education has not included preparation for using audiovisual equipment and materials or computers.

Production. Some of the new technologies are not only sources of information, but also themselves media for communication and vehicles for artistic expression. The fully equipped media center provides a location, equipment, and raw materials for creating, along with a staff with professional expertise for teaching the technology-related communication arts.

Learning Centers. The supervision of skill development or "prescriptive" learning centers is yet another service of library/media centers at both the elementary and secondary levels. Many centers also house, in or adjacent to their own areas, "learning centers" where supplementary teaching staff and instructional equipment may provide remedial experiences for the problem learner, principally in reading and mathematics. Using programmed instruction, media center staff work in a team relationship with the classroom teacher, identifying problems, testing, scheduling, monitoring, recording, and reporting progress. Students for whom English is a second language may find in the media center a place where special language problems are solved. These same centers may offer opportunities for the academically gifted or creative students to undertake projects that lead them into experiences beyond what is offered in the classroom.

Computer Areas. The use of microcomputers in school programs has expanded to such a degree that library/media centers must now have either within or adjacent to them facilities for housing various types of computers. Instruction in utilization is often required and this too should be developed in conjunction with classroom needs by librarian and teacher. Skill in searching for information and references by accessing specific databases is now becoming an integral part of student competencies.

District Services. The consolidation of school districts into larger units for administering educational services has expanded the range of school-level media services and created a new category of services from district or regional centers. The services most commonly provided on a system-wide basis are evaluation of materials, staff development, equipment maintenance and repair, film, television, and computer services, and a professional reference library.

The district media center coordinates the review, evaluation, and purchase of instructional materials. The staff meets with publishers' representatives, arranges for the evaluation of materials by appropriate personnel, and distributes the results of evaluations in order to ensure that the best educational materials available will be purchased.

The district media center provides staff development opportunities for media personnel and teachers on media and media-related topics.

It maintains collections of the more expensive instructional materials, such as 16-mm films, videotapes, and computer programs for use in classrooms and media centers throughout the district. It also provides for the maintenance and repair of instructional equipment on a system-wide, cost-effective basis.

An educational reference library for teachers and the educational community may be found in district media centers. The library will include current titles, journal literature, bibliographies and indexes, and basic reference materials needed for decision making in the management of school facilities and programs.

The district center provides coordination in the management of system-wide communication resources, specifically instructional television and computer systems. In addition, it supervises school-level media programs, ensuring that equitable fiscal support and services are available throughout the system.

Services of the Future. Tomorrow's schools and school library/media centers, in recognition of the tremendous power of the mass communication media in our society, will pay more attention than is now given to "visual literacy," the ability of viewers to be perceptive and judgmental about what they see and hear on the screen and to know when they are being manipulated. More children will become active users of the communication technologies, learning to express ideas and to create art forms in visual and sound formats and becoming skilled in the techniques employed in the communications technologies.

The future will probably see a still greater dependence on machines for individualizing instruction, reinforcing learning with sight and sound, remedying learning deficiencies, and programming instruction for the slow or unmotivated student. As machines become more pervasive in the schools, teachers will become more skilled in their use. There will be greater use of technology for meeting general information needs, and through their media centers schools will be linked to networks supplying computerized information banks and computer-based, computer-managed curriculum materials of many kinds.

It is also likely that there will be a continuing emphasis on teaching children how to learn, to enjoy learning, and to grow up with inquiring minds.

Media centers and the schools they serve will probably also share greater commonality of purpose. In the past the school library has been faulted for functioning as a separate agency within the school, its goals and objectives not always meshed with those that hold together the fabric of the educational enterprise. Understandable from a historical perspective, that condition is no longer tenable. School librarianship is now a discrete branch of library services to children, with its locus in the schools and its allegiance to the educational program and the learner.

ELRIEDA MC CAULEY;
JEAN E. LOWRIE

COLLECTIONS

The changing trends in education that have resulted in the development of new teaching strategies and in a variety of organizational patterns in the school have directly affected the growth of the school library/media center. The shift away from the single-textbook, self-contained classroom mode of teaching to the interdisciplinary, diversified curriculum aimed at individualized instruction has created the demand for a wide range of instructional materials available from a centralized source in the school. The book collection of the traditional library has given way to the multimedia collection of the school library/media center. The collection, together with the center's program of service and instruction, plays a vital role in the attainment of the school's objective of providing a high-quality education for all children and young people.

Collection Building. The school library/media center's program has become an integral part of the instructional program of the school, and its collection of materials is a key factor in the success of the school's program. The basic purpose of the collection is to support and supplement the curriculum and to provide quality recreational reading material for student enrichment. Each collection is unique in size and content and, ideally, is developed to meet the needs and objectives of the individual school program as well as the interests and abilities of the school population. The number of students in the various grade levels, the span of reading levels represented, the curriculum content, the socioeconomic backgrounds of the students, and the resources available in the community are among factors considered in developing a well-balanced, dynamic, useful collection.

In building such collections, standards of excellence will be applied to all forms of materials representing a broad coverage of subjects and varying levels of difficulty. Consideration is given to both the long-range goals and the immediate needs of the instructional program. To support a variety of learning experiences, the collection will include a diversity of media formats, including hardbound and paperback books, pamphlets, periodicals, newspapers, clippings, pictures, audiovisual materials, and other learning aids. *Media Programs: District and School* (1975) provides a detailed listing of the types of media and necessary equipment that may be included in the media center.

By creating a diverse collection the library offers students and teachers the opportunity to use the medium that most effectively meets the needs of a particular learning situation. Reference tools are provided for research work, while suitable materials for viewing and listening activities are available, along with books for pleasure reading and a current, varied collection of professional materials.

Organization. The effectiveness of the media center depends not only on the materials in its collection but also on their accessibility. It is essential that students and teachers be able to find readily and use the desired media as the need arises. The collection must be well organized according to those standard library procedures most suitable for the particular school. A current, viable collection is achieved through careful selection, constant maintenance, and good systems for organization and access.

An integrated approach in organizing materials results in a collection in which all materials, regardless of format, are catalogued and classified according to a single system. The complete index to the collection (whether in card or book form or on a computer terminal) indicates all book and nonbook materials in a single listing, enabling users to identify and locate the media center's holdings on a given subject. Whether the various types of media are placed together on the shelves or stored in separate areas in the center will depend upon the facilities available and the policy of the individual media center. Some materials may even be housed elsewhere in the school.

Ephemeral materials such as pamphlets, clippings, and pictures, which do not warrant the time or cost involved in cataloguing, are housed in filing cabinets and are arranged according to subject headings that correspond to those used for other material in the collection. The media center's catalogue may indicate that information on a particular subject can be found in the pamphlet file, or there may be a separate listing of subjects represented in the file.

Current issues of periodicals and newspapers are usually displayed on special shelving or racks and a list of the titles made available. The policy regarding retention of back issues depends upon storage facilities in the media center; microform copies require minimal space and, with adequate equipment for viewing and copying, can meet the need for periodical information.

The books, audiovisual material, and computer software may be catalogued and classified for the individual school collection by a centralized processing center in the school district, by commercial firms, or through arrangements with other agencies or school districts, because processing at the local level is least desirable in terms of cost effectiveness and staff time. However the cataloguing and physical processing are provided, they must be consistent and meet the specifications of the individual media center and should meet the standards of the field at large.

With the publication in 1978 of the Second Edition of the *Anglo-American Cataloguing Rules,* a standard for cataloguing nonbook materials was established. Book and nonbook materials can be processed with uniformity, with the result of increased potential for sharing resources through systems and networks, thus offering a greater wealth of material to students and teachers.

Continuous reevaluation of the collection for accuracy of information, current interests, and changing curriculum content is important if the collection is to be meaningful and useful.

Weeding is an ongoing process involving the removal from the collection of all forms of material, including books that contain out-of-date information; books that are defaced, dirty, or worn or have discolored or brittle pages; books for which new or revised editions are available; duplicate copies of books no longer needed in quantity; books no longer of interest or that are too easy or too difficult for a changing student body; periodicals, pamphlets, and other materials that are outdated or worn; and audiovisual materials that are outdated, worn, or damaged. As these materials are discarded, procedures for replacement are established as part of the regular selection process.

Collection Policy. In the face of the abundance of library materials available for children and young people, selection of quality materials for the school library media center program is imperative. Each school district should have a written policy statement regarding selection. Professional library staff, administrators, teachers, parents, and school board members often participate in the development of such a statement, which may include the philosophy of the school's educational program, the types of materials to be ordered, criteria for their evaluation, and procedures for handling problems that may arise when material selected is questioned.

Administrators, teachers, students, and parents may be encouraged to recommend materials for the school library/media collection. A school faculty consists of many subject area experts, and they are aware of materials that are needed to supplement the curriculum. Students and parents are aware of needs, interests, and abilities of the students and can be a great help in the selection process. School library/media center budgets will indicate the amount of materials that may be purchased, and the final selection of materials is the responsibility of the principal, who usually delegates the leadership activity to the professionally trained staff of the media center.

Great quantities of library materials are produced each year, and it is difficult to read or preview all materials before ordering them. Faculty members may be able to preview library materials while at-

Hamsters and gerbils keeping students company in library of a St. Paul, Minnesota, elementary school.

Highwood Hills Elementary School, St. Paul School District

tending conferences, and the library staff may also request audiovisual materials for review by a department or a teacher. Excellent selection aids and reviewing media are available for use in choosing materials, and specialized reference tools locate quality materials in particular subjects. Selection guides are used in establishing a new media center collection or in developing balance in an established collection. Reviews of books and audiovisual materials are found in major library periodicals, and discriminating reviews and recognized selection aids are considered more reliable in selecting materials than vendors' catalogues, which are ordinarily only descriptive announcements of materials.

In evaluating books the following general criteria may be considered:

The subject matter is appropriate, desirable, and significant.

The information is accurate, up-to-date, and unbiased.

The characters are not stereotyped.

The author is qualified to write about the particular subject.

The writing has literary quality and style.

The style is suitable for the content and for the reader for whom it is intended.

The illustrations reflect the subject matter with propriety, accuracy, and clarity, and have artistic value.

The format relative to size, binding, paper, margins, type, and spacing is satisfactory.

A recognized list or reviewing tool has included this title.

The material challenges the student's thinking, and he or she is stimulated to search for further information.

The concepts and policies are in keeping with the philosophy and objectives of the educational program of the school.

In evaluating audiovisual materials, these general criteria may be applied:

The subject matter is appropriate, desirable, and significant to the student.

The information provided is accurate, up-to-date, and unbiased.

The material has been previewed, or included in a recognized list, or reviewed in a reliable selection aid.

The material challenges the student's thinking, and he or she is stimulated to search for further information.

The objectives of a particular lesson or problem-solving activity are met by the content and the type of material.

A guide is provided to assist the teacher in making the most effective use of the material.

The technical quality of the material is adequate.

The cost of the material will be justified by its use.

The content is in keeping with the philosophy and objectives of the educational program of the school.

Magazines have a tremendous appeal for children and young people. Local, national, and international newspapers may also be represented in the school library/media center collection to provide supplementary information, serve special interests, and provide

examples of a variety of viewpoints. Audio and video cassettes, laser disks, and other newer media, which school children accept as part of today's communication and information formats, must be included in building a contemporary collection.

Another important consideration in the selection process, and an underlying principle of the selection policy, is the need for a balanced library collection. Balance must be maintained between print and nonprint collections, fiction and nonfiction, paperbacks and hardbound books. Different reading levels among students should be addressed, so books for poor readers, average readers, and superior readers can be provided to meet individual needs. A reference collection adequate for student research should be offered, while a well-rounded professional collection will serve teachers and parents. The professional staff must know the total collection so that gaps can be recognized, popular items needing duplicate copies identified, and replacements for lost items obtained.

WINIFRED E. DUNCAN;
JEAN E. LOWRIE

ADMINISTRATION, GOVERNANCE, AND FINANCE

The Tenth Amendment to the United States Constitution, ratified in 1791, declares that "The powers not delegated to the United States by the constitution, nor prohibited by it to the states, are reserved to the states respectively, or to the people." Since education is not specifically mentioned, such powers are thus the responsibility of state governments. A state legislature elected by the people controls the establishment and maintenance of the schools in each state through a State Board of Education and a State Department of Education. Most states employ professional school library/media staff to develop programs in the schools.

Federal Leadership. Although state governments have responsibility for education, the courts have ruled that under the "general welfare" clause of the Constitution, Congress may enact laws that affect public education; the United States Office of Education (USOE) was made responsible for administering federal efforts in relation to public and private schools.

In January 1938 the first specialist in school and children's libraries in the Office of Education, Nora E. Buest, was employed to serve as consultant to USOE staff members, school superintendents, school board members, trustees of public libraries, library administrators, state departments of education, state library agencies, state and federal government officials, and professional organizations concerned with library services for children and young people. The specialist was responsible for serving libraries in both public and private schools and in children's and young people's departments in public libraries. The charge of the first specialist in school and children's libraries was to promote and assist in the extension and improvement of library service for children and young people and was to include a variety of activities.

Buest served until 1958, when she was succeeded by Mary Helen Mahar, who was given the title of Coordinator of School Libraries. That office has been responsible for the compilation of school library statistics, book lists, bibliographies, and articles on elementary libraries and national trends in school and public libraries service for children and young adults. It had important national leadership responsibilities for developing and communicating and understanding the need for and the role of programs of library services for children and young adults.

In 1980, when the Department of Education was created, the Office for Libraries and Learning Technologies was organized as a part of the Ofice of Education Research and Improvement. A Center of Libraries and Education Improvement was established. But no one was appointed to speak out or be responsible for school library/media center needs and programs, a sad lack in view of the previous strengths and leadership at that level.

In 1958 Congress, spurred by Soviet advances in science and technology, passed the National Defense Education Act (NDEA), to provide federal resources to strengthen and improve various areas of the elementary and secondary education program. Federal interest in aiding elementary and secondary education reached a high point in 1965 with the passage of the Elementary and Secondary Education Act (ESEA); Title II provided grants to states on a formula basis to aid local education agencies in acquiring school library resources, textbooks, and other instructional materials. Between 1966 and 1976 this program provided more than $895,000,000 to public and private schools in the United States.

In addition to federal funds, a number of states, among them North Carolina, Michigan, and Wisconsin, also provided separate funding for the purchase of school library/media materials. Most state aid formulas for schools included salaries for library/media personnel and funds to purchase resources as part of instructional costs.

State Supervision. State school library supervision in the U.S. traces its beginings to the 1890s, when the New York State Education Department established a position for an inspector to "help schools improve their book collections and encourage people's reading." In 1891 the Wisconsin legislature au-

thorized the state superintendent to appoint one clerk to aid in "promoting the establishment and maintenance and control of libraries as provided by the law." In 1904 the Division of School Libraries was established by the Regents of New York State, and a School Library Supervisor position was created. In 1911 Minnesota set up an Office of Supervisor of School Libraries in the Department of Public Instruction, and in 1915 Wisconsin changed the title of the Library Clerk to Supervisor of School Libraries. By 1952 there were 25 states and one Canadian province in which there were one or more persons specifically assigned responsibility for state supervision of school libraries; most of those positions were established after 1940. State school library supervision developed rapidly in the early 1960s as a result of a new set of national standards, an intensive implementation process, and several key publications concerning the need for and the role of professional personnel at the state level.

In the early 1960s Mahar indicated that the responsibilities of the state departments of education toward school libraries fell into six broad categories:

1. Certification of school librarians

2. Standards for school libraries

3. Supervision of school libraries

4. Cooperation for school libraries

5. Statistics and research on school libraries

6. Information on school libraries.

In USOE the ESEA Title II program was administered by the staff responsible for school library programs under a state plan submitted by each state. In many state departments of education, administration of the ESEA Title II program was developed and conducted by people who were themselves school library/media supervisors. The new federal funds coming into the states caused the creation of a number of new positions for school library supervisor-consultants in state education departments; this resulted from the need for staff to administer the new federal program, coupled with a provision in the law for a certain amount of funding to support it. In 1969 Milbrey Jones reported that there were about 120 state library school consultants in 48 states and the District of Columbia and 165 supervisors, consultants, and program administrators in the 50 states, the Trust Territories of the Pacific, Guam, Puerto Rico, the Virgin Islands, and the Bureau of Indian Affairs. A number were assigned other responsibilities besides those related to school library/media programs.

In 1975 David R. Bender examined the state education agencies' roles and functions related to school library/media programs and identified 11 functions that illustrate one state's responsibility for program development:

1. To formulate long-range plans for the development of schoool media programs, including cooperative planning for regional and state services.

2. To provide advisory and consultative service to local school systems, particularly in areas of new media services and technology in school media facilities.

3. To develop standards and guidelines for the improvement of media programs.

Students construct a set and prepare to film a movie at Western Junior High School in Greenwich, Connecticut.

Greenwich Public Schools

4. To provide programs of in-service education on the concepts of the utilization of media to administrators, supervisors, media personnel, and teachers.

5. To develop proposals for needed research in media services.

6. To collect, analyze, and disseminate information on the scope and quality of media programs in the state.

7. To assist in the determination of the qualifications for certification for media personnel.

8. To administer federal funds available for media programs.

9. To provide for the effective coordination of media services with the critical educational concerns of the state and local school systems.

10. To develop coordinated plans and policies with other personnel agencies that will strengthen library/media services for all citizens.

11. To act as a clearinghouse for information on library services in the state and foster interlibrary loans and cooperative arrangements with the school, public, academic, or other libraries.

A National Center for Education Statistics (NCES) survey (1974), *Library General Information Survey* (LIBGIS), showed that a tremendous amount of development had taken place in school library/media centers in the period 1964–74. Library/media centers in 1974 were provided for 50 percent more school children—14,600,000 more—than in 1964. The number of centers increased over the decade from 56,000 in schools of 150 pupils or more to an estimated total of 74,725. To a considerable extent this tremendous expansion must be credited to the dedicated leadership provided by USOE personnel and to state school library/media supervisors, along with federal funds provided mainly by the ESEA Title II program.

Economic difficulties, from local to national level, slowed this progress from the mid-70s to mid-80s, and development has been most uneven where state aid has been cut back most severely. Many states have abolished or amalgamated the position of state school library/media supervisor.

JEAN E. LOWRIE

MEASUREMENT AND EVALUATION

Two fairly recent general surveys exist on the complex topic of measurement and evaluation: Evelyn Daniel's state-of-the-art review in the 1976 volume of *Advances in Librarianship* on performance measures for school librarians and the summer 1975 issue of *School Media Quarterly,* entitled "Evaluation for Accountability." The following account builds on those two studies with an overview, an update, and suggestions for further study.

Terms and Issues. Although there is some disagreement on the shades of meaning in the terms measurement and evaluation, generally speaking, evaluation refers to the larger process of making a considered judgment as to the worth of an object, a person, or an event. It usually involves collecting evidence (formally or informally), analyzing it, and weighing it against one or more implicit or explicit criteria in order to make a value judgment. Measure-

ment, more narrowly, is quantitative in approach, usually referring to the specific act of determining the number or extent of certain phenomena on the basis of which an evaluation, or appraisal of worth, can be made.

It is often pointed out that one can measure quantities precisely, but that one can only infer quality for judgment of value; measurement is considered a science, evaluation an art. In the generally accepted "ideal" model of evaluation, some general goals and specific objectives are developed (or received as givens); some criteria are established as the basis for making judgments; indicators that are observable and can be measured are selected to serve as evidence that the criteria are being met; data are collected on the indicators in ways that are reliable and unbiased; the collected data are compared to some standard of acceptability or excellence; and judgment is passed.

In this statment goals are broad statements of philosophy or direction usually quite general in scope. Objectives describe the expectations and intended accomplishments of an organization or an individual within some specified time. Criteria can be either normative (related to the average performance of some similar phenomena) or absolute (as in a defined, published standard).

Evaluation is often referred to as being either formative or summative in nature. Formative evaluation is ongoing; it occurs during the activity and is intended to guide decision making and to "form" or shape the future of the event or agency being evaluated. Summative evaluation is administerd at a single time, usually at the end of a program or at the end of a cycle; the intent is to "sum up," to grade, to make an overall judgment as to the worth of the phenomena. It relates to the process of accountability. Confirmative evaluation, another term less often seen, relates to a regularly recurring review process toward the end of "confirming" that the project or program should or should not continue.

Thus evaluation involves one or more comparisons. A major political issue becomes who sets the criteria or standards of comparison. In one approach the professional association develops goals and objectives, criteria and indicators, and publishes standards; the individual professional operating as manager in a media center then uses the published standard to establish the criteria against which the performance of the center and that of the media specialist are to be measured. In a bureaucratic situation (as in a school), there may be standardized rules and procedures that govern behavior. In a more political milieu, groups may compete against each other to determine directions and criteria for performance. Where a strong central authority exists, standards for evaluation may be imposed.

A second major issue revolves around a difference of opinion as to whether evaluation should be based on quantitative measures or should be largely subjective and intuitive. Proponents of the latter view suggest that inferring quality from quantity may be dangerously misleading. Ernest DeProspo observed that "any measurement process that generates numbers must overcompensate for a built-in anticipation that larger numbers suggest directly or indirectly more effective and efficient service even if that is not the intended meaning." Yet the trend in the mid-

1980s seemed to be toward a more quantitative approach.

A third issue arises from the differing concerns of the researcher and the practitioner. Fritz Machlup, expressing the frustration he felt when attempting to collect quantitative data on the amount libraries spend each year to acquire materials in various fields, said, "Alas, the librarians did not have the answers and the most I have learned from them is why the answers are not available and how enormously difficult, if not impossible, it would be to obtain them." The methodology that surrounds unbiased data collection and statistical analysis of results is highly sophisticated; the expenditure of time, money, staff, and energy on collecting good assessment data will ordinarily be considered by the practitioner from a managerial perspective, one somewhat different from that of the researcher.

Standards and Statistics Collection. The typical standard or guideline used in the library profession is prescriptive in nature; it describes what ought to be. Publications such as *Media Programs: District and School,* still the standard for school media programs in the first half of the 1980s, are generated by committees made up primarily of professional librarians who attempt through this device to establish acceptable criteria for the elements of a good library program. Some qualities considered necessary for a library standard for evaluation are that each standard be measurable, clearly defined, appropriate, authoritative, and realistic. Some effort is being expended to compile statistical norms for areas being measured.

Critics of library standards point out a number of shortcomings. Standards are more concerned with measuring inputs to the library than outputs, or benefits to the user. The quantitative criteria, although measurable, are often set by arbitrary judgments. They tend to discourage progress, as the minimum set by the standard often becomes the maximum. On the positive side, standards can be useful to the practicing school library/media specialist in the goal-setting, objective-stating process and also as a widely accepted authoritative source for persuading administrators to provide adequate support.

Of all the standards generated by the various types of libraries, the national school library standards are perhaps the most nearly complete and the most satisfactory when compared to the qualities of a good standard as set forth above. Still, it may be helpful for the school media specialist to examine and compare national standards for other types of libraries. In addition, virtually every state in the U.S. has its own standard for school media services, and many state and regional associations also publish standards for service. State and regional standards are usually less ambitious than the national standards.

School accrediting agencies also employ published evaluative criteria for each area of the school program. The AASL Committee on Evaluation of School Media Programs works to maintain contact with the five regional accrediting agencies to monitor the development of new standard criteria and to influence the process of criteria selection for the evaluation of school media programs.

A more quantitative effort to measure the national "health" of libraries is that undertaken by the U.S. government through the National Center for Education Statistics (NCES). Although school libraries are scheduled for collection and reporting of data every three years, there have in fact been only two publications of statistics for public school library media centers: one published in 1964 reporting data from 1962–63 and the other published in 1977 reporting data of 1974. (A good summary of the latter is found in the 1978 *Bowker Annual.*) NCES has also commissioned two studies of interest to school media specialists, a handbook of standard terminology for reporting information about educational technology and another handbook with a similar title that attempts to unify the data collection techniques and categories for all libraries. The National Information Standards Organization reactivated a subcommittee to revise the standard for library statistics published in 1968.

These efforts may seem remote from the work of the individual school media practitioner, but because they are attempts to establish criteria and standards that will have an impact on resources received, it is important to be aware of these activities. The ALA, through the Statistics Section of its Library Administration and Management Association, had eight statistics committees in 1985, including a Statistics for School Library Media Centers Committee, that discuss, critique, and offer suggestions for activities in this area.

Research Efforts. Educational evaluation has become a separate speciality within the field of education. DeProspo and James W. Liesener provide a good overview of some of the major evaluation models in a 1975 report.

The public, academic, and school sectors of librarianship have each had a major research effort in the measurement and evaluation area. The Management Review and Analysis Program (MRAP), designed and operated by the Office of Management Studies of the Association of Research Libraries, is a set of guidelines for an academic library to use in conducting an internal assessment of its management practices. It was originally instituted for large research libraries but is now developing self-improvement techniques for use by small and medium-sized academic libraries. Many of the techniques used in this program are drawn from organizational development (OD) theories.

Ellen Altman, DeProspo, and others mounted the major public library research effort that focused on the development of performance measures that would be easy for practitioners to collect and that would employ good sampling techniques, thus keeping costs of data collection low. Many of the performance measures that have developed have application for the school library/media program.

The major school library research effort shares with MRAP a consensus-building approach. Liesener, a major researcher in this area, views evaluation as only one aspect of the larger problem of program planning and the development of overall goals and objectives. Some research has elaborated service statements useful for evaluating media center services, while other work has been directed to the problem of competency assessment, specifically in the context of media educational preparation programs.

Measurement Techniques. A number of published surveys exist that collectively provide a good overview of the array of measurement techniques, including catalogue use and other use studies, library surveys, and specific evaluation measures for reference, search and retrieval, collections, technical services, and document delivery. Quantitative measures may include measures for document exposure time, indexes of availability or capability, failure analyses, circulation predictors, a number of techniques for collection evaluation, and an attitudinal expectation rate measure in which users estimate their chances of successfully retrieving a given item.

A number of evaluation tools have been published to assist in evaluating school library/media centers; several of these tools have already been mentioned here. A major document, *Evaluating Media Programs,* a publication of the Association for Educational Communications and Technology, uses the national standard *Media Programs: District and School* as its main source of criteria. Through a modular format, the instrument provides a series of checklists and scales for use in a formative evaluation procedure. Courses, workshops, and conferences on measurement and evaluation are offered on a fairly regular basis. Several state school library associations developed their own evaluation guidelines that are useful for comparative techniques and formats.

Uses of Evaluation. Evaluation can be used to improve, to justify or attack, to delay action, or to exert control. Responses to evaluation information can be a change of behavior or opinion, a distortion, rejection, or ignoring of the data. Factors that affect the reception of evaluation information include the adequacy and appropriateness of the methodology used, the need for a value judgment, the timing of the delivery of results, the degree to which the information fits preconceived ideas or supports vested interests, the potential threat involved in acceptance of results, and the acceptability of the motive for undertaking the evaluation.

Before any measurement and evaluation process is undertaken, it is important to recognize that some prior decisions must be made: the purpose of the evaluation, the person or group for whom the evaluation is intended, the question(s) to be answered, the criteria and indicators to be used, the data to be collected and how they are to be analyzed, and the form of the final report.

Because of the variety of uses and users of evaluation information, it may be helpful for an evaluation team to be set up comprised of the major users of evaluation information about the media center. This team might be composed of administrators, peer teachers, media specialist and staff, and students. An examination of consensus and dissensus among these four components can be a useful by-product of this approach.

EVELYN H. DANIEL;
JEAN E. LOWRIE

LIBRARY COOPERATION

The educational philosophy accepted by educators throughout the history of education in the U.S. has had a direct effect upon the type and scope of cooperation between school libraries and other libraries. In the early years secondary school libraries represented the majority of libraries serving students in the public

Greenwich Public Schools

Students at Julian Curtiss School, Greenwich, Connecticut, locating their town on a library globe.

schools, while the public library provided the services now performed by the elementary school library. In some communities the board of education and the public library jointly organized and controlled the school library materials. Minimal use of the school library was directed toward meeting the needs of the school's curriculum during that period.

The NEA and the ALA were forerunners in encouraging the development and functional use of school libraries through jointly sponsored publications and documents. *School and Public Libraries Working Together in Library Service* (1941) asked that local boards of education establish school libraries in every school for the purpose of serving the educational objectives of the school. As the curricular offerings of the nation's schools became more diversified, the educational environment continued to justify the school library's existence.

Resource sharing among school library/media centers was preceded by an era of rapid school library growth that began in the 1950s and accelerated in the 1960s. This growth was stimulated by the first national standards for school libraries, *School Libraries for Today and Tomorrow,* published by ALA in 1945. Cooperation among libraries for the purpose of encouraging continuing education and cultural growth was referred to in these standards and again identified in the 1960 *Standards for School Library Programs,* endorsed by 20 educational and professional organizations as a force for excellence in library programs.

Today school library/media centers represent a wealth of resources and information, including print, visual, auditory, and tactile materials and equipment selected and evaluated acording to school policies that guarantee a balanced collection of instructional materials meeting curriculum goals. In 1974 the NCES reported in its *Statistics of Public School Libraries/Media Centers* that 507,000,000 library books and 68,000,000 titles of audiovisual materials were available to students with central library media centers. Still, it is generally understood and accepted that no one school building or district can provide students with the range of instructional materials and equipment necessary to meet the goal of the National Commission on Libraries and Information Science (NCLIS), which calls for every person in the U.S. to have equal opportunity of access to the total information resources that will satisfy the individual's educational, working, cultural, and leisure-time needs and interests. This goal can be achieved only when schools are involved as full participating members in library networks.

Media Programs: District and School, the 1975 standards of the American Association of School Librarians and the Association for Educational Communications and Technology, modified the singular, self-sufficient role of the school library/media center. For the first time networks were mentioned in published, comprehensive standards for school media programs; networks were cited as avenues of access to information or knowledge not readily available to regional, district, and school programs. Such information is to be transmitted to the schools by such advanced communication techniques as telecommunications, computer systems, and high-speed random-access retrieval systems.

The school library/media center has been required to broaden its vision and responsibilities to include increased interaction and cooperation among personnel, processes, and information sources. In the 1970s many school library/media specialists became convinced that the sharing of resources would result in improved services and communication with other librarians to develop effective library cooperatives. Stimulated in large part by the desire of school media professionals to help users of their programs make more effective use of library resources and services, and by the realization that it is impossible to satisfy all user needs through one library program, resulting cooperative efforts progessed through a series of stages in the 1970s toward sophisticated cooperative programs among various types of libraries.

By the early 1980s real progress had been made toward involving school librarian/media center specialists in library cooperation through regular contracts, legislation, and special budget allocations. Mary Sive's report on a variety of structures and mechanisms in *School Library Media Centers and Networking* (1982) supports this picture of growth.

Single-Type Networks. The single-type network is not new in school librarianship; indeed the most common form of cooperation in this field is the single-type library cooperative, in which a group of centers work together, generally on an information basis, to achieve a mutual goal, such as continuing education or joint book evaluation. *Media Programs: District and School* identifies regional media programs that are developed cooperatively as another level of the single-type library cooperative. This type of cooperative has been preferred because the school libraries involved ordinarily share the same organizational pattern, funding base, governance, and service patterns and the majority of participants are faced with similar problems.

Individual states have organized regional educational service centers that provide sophisticated collections of media program materials for local districts. Regional centers feature large film libraries, evaluation and selection centers, facilities for local production of audiovisual materials, and in-service training for personnel. Examples of intermediate units that contract with local boards of education are found in Iowa, Michigan, New York, Oregon, and Texas.

Multitype Cooperation. Multitype library cooperation gained somewhat more acceptance in the 1970s among school media personnel, though not nearly to the degree gained by the single-type library cooperative. Through this means, school library/media centers share resources, personnel, facilities, and/or programs with a library or libraries of another type having a different legal base. According to G. Flint Purdy, multitype library cooperatives' activities fall into two categories: (1) sharing resources more generously, more systematically, and more expeditiously than they would otherwise be shared; (2) strengthening the resources to be shared. Some specific examples of these activities are union catalogues and lists, reciprocal borrowing and interlibrary loan, centralized processing, and cooperatively sponsored planning and surveys.

The legal basis of multitype library cooperation varies from state to state. The *Report on Interlibrary Cooperation 1978* identifies specific authorization in some states that allows all types of libraries to merge and provide more effective library service. In other states the authorization extends only to designating a state agency that will coordinate and promote cooperative activities. Another basis for authorization used in some states is a blanket law allowing two or more public agencies to enter into agreements with any other agency for joint or cooperative action. Even where specific authorization does not exist, few states have reported legal barriers to statewide participation in multitype library cooperatives.

Many in the library profession have questioned the extent to which school libraries can be involved effectively in cooperative efforts; Anne Marie Falsone identified five reasons why they fail to participate more fully in multitype library cooperation: (1) schools are open only during the school day; (2) collections are chosen to support the curriculum; (3) interjurisdictional loan of school library materials or equipment is sometimes prohibited by school district policy; (4) in some cases there is a lack of such basic communication tools as telephones; and (5) students and teachers have an "immediacy of need" for materials that inhibits interlibrary loan of materials. Other

Library media center in Irmo, South Carolina. It provides equipment and guidance for varions productions, including video news spots.

Irmo Middle School Complex, Irmo, South Carolina

barriers to multitype library cooperation have been inadequate funds and resources to be shared, lack of incentives, lack of time and staff, and negative attitudes of staff members and administrators toward cooperation.

Advocates of inclusion of school media programs in multitype library cooperatives argue that such programs can offer a number of special contributions. Among them are strong audiovisual collections, broad collections of children's and young adult material, expertise in the selection, use, and evaluation of audiovisual materials and equipment, in-depth knowledge of local production of materials, and expertise in developing and implementing effective techniques for carrying out the library's instructional function. In order for these resources to be incorporated effectively into multitype library cooperatives, however, proponents point out that barriers must be eliminated through adequate planning, sufficient money, staff, time, reciprocal agreements, and attitudinal changes.

One form of multitype library cooperation that continues to receive attention is the combining of school and public library services in the same facility. Interest arises from such factors as broader acceptance of the community school concept, decreasing fiscal resources, increased public pressure for most cost-effective library operations, and a growing desire on the part of the public for access to information regardless of format. A *Study of the Combined School Public Library* (1980), conducted for the State Library of Florida by Shirley L. Aaron and Sue O. Smith, concluded that it is unlikely that a community able to support or now supporting separate types of libraries will offer better school and public library service through a combined program because the combination of factors required to promote a successful combined program seldom occurs. Further, when a community is unable to provide minimum library services through separate facilities, and no option for improved services through system membership exists, the combined program presents a possible alternative to limited or nonexistent services under certain conditions. Communities searching for a cheaper way to provide better library service should be aware that the study revealed no documented evidence that economy results from this organizational pattern.

A study prepared by the Interdepartmental Liaison Group on Library Development, Alberta Education Culture (Edmonton), came to a similar conclusion; its 1979 *Statement on Community School Libraries* acknowledges that consolidated operations are unsuccessful in serving the public at large.

Multitype Networks. The informal agreements that characterize many multitype library cooperatives are becoming increasingly inadequate to cope with the complexities of present and projected efforts in this area. Consequently, the trend has been toward the development of multitype library networks. Multitype networks tend to incorporate public, academic, school, institutional, and special libraries into a state network granting full shares in governance, responsibility, and participation to all types of libraries involved. Flexibility is essential in a multitype network where the requirements of the members will vary from one type of library to the other.

A national effort to clarify, delineate, and de-

St. Paul School District, St. Paul, Minnesota

Students sharing a story on tape in a school library in St. Paul, Minnesota.

scribe the role of the school library/media program in networking was developed through a task force established by the National Commission on Libraries and Information Science in cooperation with the American Association of School Librarians. The 1978 *Report of the Task Force on the Role of the School Library Media Program in Networking* identified immediate, intermediate, and long-range recommendations for the purpose of alleviating the psychological, political, funding, communication, and planning problems that have inhibited the full participation of schools in interlibrary networks.

A 1983 survey by Richard J. Sorensen reported changes in school media programs resulting from participation in networking. Respondents represented a wide variety of centers, from building through regional, and with varying perceptions of library networking. Their replies indicated the following:

1. Changes in professional attitude: more confidence in their ability to handle widely differing information; more willingness to borrow from and lend to other resources; losing a sense of isolation plus a strengthening of ties with other librarians; impetus for professional development

2. Staff deployment: professionals less involved in "packaging" and more in searching and contact with other network personnel

3. Facilities and equipment: microcomputers, telephones, index tables, and similar items have been purchased

4. Financial: visible shifts in budgets; easier to replace missing articles through photocopying; shared cataloging and processing services; use of ILL to preview AV materials

5. Collection development: concentration on building complementary collections rather than "a little bit of everything"; economy of group purchase of materials and/or equipment; expanded sources of indexes and periodicals appreciated by users

6. Technical services: closer to accepting more complete

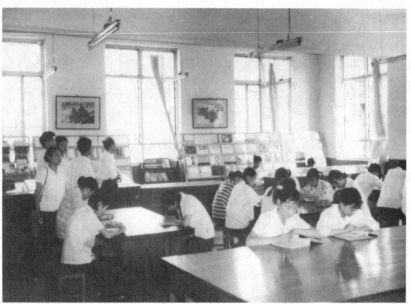

Josephine Riss Fang

Nankai Middle School Library in Tianjing (Tientsin) China.

descriptive cataloguing as required for union lists; bibliographic research upgraded

7. Library skill instruction: expanded into broader area; use of borrower's courtesy cards; collaboration with academic and public libraries to design instruction at secondary level to prepare students better for future library use; conversely, public and academic libraries are helping students more in the use of other reference tools

8. User attitudes: changed students' concepts of what libraries are; understanding or awareness of other resources

9. Relationship with users: significant changes in expectations of what school librarians/media center specialists can do for teachers, students, administrators; beginning to plan research work more in advance; school librarian/ media specialist has improved image, more visibility; promoted better library-to-teacher collaboration and involvements in teaching and curriculum development.

There is reason to believe that such changes will become common in all instructional media programs. Librarians/media specialists will increase their knowledge of available resources. Budgets will include more money for interlibrary loan. Staff and time management changes will be developed more in the area of network maintenance. Sharing will become accepted in word and practice as automation and computer utilization become common and more emphasis is placed on service to the information seeker.

The issue of cooperation among school libraries internationally was addressed at the seventh annual conference of the International Association of School Librarianship in Melbourne, Australia, in 1978. This topic was discussed again in Honolulu in 1984, with special emphais on school/public library cooperation, and on Australia's computerized cataloguing services through a national network with satellite connections to some of the Pacific islands. The fourth Congress of Southeast Asian Librarians met in Bangkok, Thailand, in June 1978 for the purpose of establishing national committees that would work toward the development of regional cooperation in information services. Children's materials and services were identified in projected surveys of user needs.

School library/media professionals are becoming more sensitive to the value of networking. The goal of enhancing information access for schools has promoted enabling legislation in many states and has involved school librarians/media specialists in closer association with all other types of libraries and systems, removing some of the isolation long felt by that group of professionals.

ALICE E. FITE; JEAN E. LOWRIE

LAWS AND LEGISLATION

History. The earliest recorded legislation for school libraries in the U.S. was on the state level. In 1827 Governor DeWitt Clinton of New York began to urge that collections of books be placed in school districts. In 1835 he secured passage of a law permitting the voters of any school district to levy a tax of $20 to start a library and $10 annually to maintain it, but it was unsuccessful for a number of reasons. Permissive legislation did not appeal to the rural taxpayer. There were no library quarters provided; books were kept in the homes of individuals and many were lost. There were no trained librarians, nor were the individuals who held the collections accountable to any authority for the administration of the books. The books were purchased, for the most part, from peddlers and were unsuitable for their potential users. The school curriculum of that time was rigid and did not call for the general use of books. The library collections were more for the people of the community and only secondarily for the school children.

Also in 1835, Massachusetts passed a permissive school district law. Through the efforts of Horace Mann, who had studied the education of the young in Europe, this law set up $30 a year (thereafter) for books. Other states soon began to follow suit. In 1837 Michigan and Rhode Island passed laws allowing each school district to raise $10 for school libraries; in Rhode Island they were to receive the fines levied in cases of breach-of-the-peace laws. The Virginia constitution recommended in 1870 that school libraries be developed. By 1876, 19 states had some legislation providing for school district libraries. In 1894 North Carolina passed the first law permitting state funds for the establishement and maintenance of libraries in rural schools; Georgia enacted similar legislation that same year.

In 1892 New York made distinct advances in school library legislation. Profiting from past mistakes, the state set up district school libraries but this time required that all books be housed in the school building. A school librarian had to be appointed to be responsible for the books. Each school district was required to raise as much money as that provided by the state, and all books purchased had to be approved by the State Superintendent of Public Instruction. The 1890s also proved to be a period of marked effort on the part of public libraries to extend library services to schools.

In 1901 North Carolina appropriated $2,500 to aid in book purchase on a matching basis, $10 for $10 raised locally. The matching idea caught on, and by 1909 Georgia, Texas, South Carolina, Virginia, Kentucky, Tennessee, Louisiana, and Alabama had begun the state matching for funds for books for schools. Alabama, for example, funded $6,700, or $100 per county. For every $1 of state money, $2 had to be raised locally.

The many pieces of state legislation on services, finance, and staff certification that followed cannot be detailed here. Federal legislation has had significant impact on school libraries and must be covered in detail.

National Defense Education Act of 1958. The greatest leap in the growth of school library collections came when the federal government, shocked by the successful launching of Sputnik, passed the National Defense Education Act (NDEA) in August 1958.

Title II provided funds to institutions of higher education for loans to prospective school librarians, teachers of science, and others, and provision was made to encourage teachers to be retrained.

Title III, Financial Assistance for Strengthening Science, Mathematics and Modern Foreign Languages, became known as "the matching fund." It provided for the acquisition of audiovisual materials and equipment and printed materials (other than textbooks) suitable for use in providing education in science, mathematics, or modern foreign languages in public elementary or secondary schools, or both, and minor remodeling of laboratory or other space used for such materials or equipment. Grants to individual public elementary and secondary schools or school systems were based on projects submitted by local school systems to their state departments of education. Funds for nonpublic schools were available as loans.

Title IV provided for National Defense Fellowships. School librarians benefited especially through fellowships to individuals for study in graduate programs approved by the Commissioner of Education. The programs had to be new or expanded programs "for the graduate training of college or university level teachers."

Title V provided for establishing, maintaining, and improving guidance, counseling, and testing in secondary schools. Under this title libraries were able to procure printed and audiovisual materials needed by teachers and students in such programs.

Title VII addressed research and experimentation in more effective use of television, radio, motion picture, and related media for educational purposes. It funded projects for research and enabled library schools to design studies to train school librarians in using newer media.

Title VIII extended the Smith-Hughes Vocational Education Act and the Vocational Education Act of 1946, supporting the purchase of such materials as reference books, visual aids, instructional supplies, and instructional materials, all of which could be a part of the library collection.

Title X provided for improved statistical services of state education agencies. Each state seeking funds was required to submit to the Commissioner of Education an overall basic plan including: priorities of projects, standards for equipment and materials, and expenditures solely for equipment, materials, and minor remodeling. By the end of June 1959, 48 states and territories had developed effective plans.

The Library Services and Construction Act. The Library Services Act of 1956, amended in 1964 and renamed the Library Services and Construction Act (LSCA), primarily supported public library development in the states. The intent of Title III was to establish and maintain local, regional, state, or interstate cooperative networks of libraries for the systematic and effective coordination of the resources of school, public, academic, and special libraries and special information centers. This was an early effort to bring school libraries into the developing network concept.

Elementary and Secondary Education Act of 1965. Congress recognized by 1965 the need for library legislation to "strengthen and improve educational quality and educational opportunities in the nation's schools." The Elementary and Secondary Education Act (ESEA) was a landmark in education legislation because its scope was broad and its possibilities infinite. The appropriations of federal funds for carrying out its provisions during the first year alone were $1,300,000,000; during the second year, $1,464,610,000; and during the third, $1,588,577,000.

Title I provided financial assistance to local educational agencies for the education of children of low-income families, and it was estimated that a large majority of the school districts of the United States would qualify for this aid. In writing plans under Title I, local educational agencies were encouraged to develop new and varied approaches to the education of culturally deprived children. School libraries became involved where their services could be related to the approved plan. There was evidence that among the supposedly ineducable children from lower-income families some were actually highly gifted. Under this title, special educational approaches and methods were developed to identify and encourage potential talent. Programs were developed for strengthening the education of the disadvantaged through instructional materials, books (including textbooks), periodicals, films, and recordings, as well as other types of materials. Title I also provided for

Media equipment in use in school library in Madison, Wisconsin.

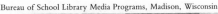

Bureau of School Library Media Programs, Madison, Wisconsin

facilities, staff, equipment, and supplies to provide school library service where not previously available or to strengthen libraries already in operation. Varied kinds of support for school library programs serving the special needs of the disadvantaged were available.

Title II dealt most directly with the improvement of school libraries. It authorized $100,000,000 to the states for school library resources, textbooks, and other instructional materials for the use of children and teachers in public and private elementary and secondary schools. The funds for materials under Title II were not to be considered a substitute for state or local support but would encourage and supplement the state and local funds. The states submitted plans that took into account the relative need of all children and teachers in all the schools of the state and provided assurance that the children and teachers in private schools would receive materials on an equitable basis. State plans also indicated the criteria to be used for making determinations of the adequacy, quality, and quantity of school library resources, textbooks, and other instructional materials. Title II was enacted in response to testimony showing the overwhelming and well-documented need in schools for more and better instructional materials. Singled out for special attention were the number of elementary schools still without libraries and the inability of many schools with centralized libraries to meet ALA standards for materials without federal assistance. In its first year of operation, Title II stimulated the establishment of more than 3,000 new public elementary school libraries serving 1,400,000 children and about 250 new school libraries in public secondary schools enrolling 145,000 children. The 62,000 existing public school library collections that were expanded in the first year served 1,500,000 children. The 17,700 000 volumes acquired with Title II funds, however, added only slightly more than one-third of one school library book per child in the elementary and secondary schools in the U.S. A significant outcome of the inclusion of Title II in ESEA was indirect—it served to focus attention on the essential role that school libraries play in providing quality instruction.

Title III authorized funds for supplementary educational centers and services and sanctioned an unusually broad scope of educational activity. The purpose of these centers was to provide educational services not previously available to children in a particular area, to strengthen services already available, or to develop models of commendable educational programs. Model school libraries could be provided in these centers. Under Title III, special programs representing various subject fields or educational services, such as science or guidance and counseling, could be instituted. Instructional materials and staff to support such programs and to demonstrate model use of the materials could be secured and audiovisual equipment and materials purchased to enrich academic programs.

Title IV provided $100,000,000 to be made available over a five-year period for regional educational research and training facilities. Institutions of higher education and other nonprofit organizations could receive grants for programs to benefit public schools. This title extended the Cooperative Research Act and provided for national and regional research and train-ing laboratories to be located in areas of population concentration. Under this title, school library problems could be thoroughly explored. Each laboratory would come up with its own plan for research to benefit schools.

Title V authorized $25,000,000 to strengthen state departments of education. Two types of grants were available under this title: funds for basic grants made up 85 percent of the authorized funds, and the remainder supported experimental projects or the establishment of services that might contribute to the solution of problems common to other states. In state education agencies 80 new supervisory positions were established in a single year after the passage of ESEA, most of them for school library consultants or media and instructional materials specialists.

Higher Education Act of 1965. The Higher Education Act of 1965 (HEA) authorized a program of federal financial assistance to institutions of higher education. Title II–B covered assistance in training persons in librarianship. Grants were used to assist institutions in covering the costs of courses of training or study and to upgrade or update the competencies of persons serving all types of libraries, information centers, or instructional material centers and those working as educators. Grants were made for fellowships at the master's, post-master's, and doctoral levels for training in librarianship and information science. This legislation was implemented through institutes and fellowships.

Institutes provided education opportunities for librarians and information specialists to retrain, acquire special skills, or keep up to date. The institute has traditionally provided an opportunity for keeping up with educational principles and advances in various subject areas. The HEA institute program amended the portion of the NDEA that specifically authorized institutes for school library personnel, expanding the base of educational opportunities for librarians and information scientists by offering them training in the principles and practices of the library and information sciences.

Education Consolidation and Improvement Act (ECIA). This act was passed in 1981 and implemented in 1982. Chapter 2 includes school library/media resources and instructional materials among its 33 programs. A survey by the American Association of School Administrators indicated that more than 56 percent of the districts surveyed spent their money for books and other instructional materials. Private schools also benefited from an increase in funding.

Other Issues. Other federal programs of special interest to advocates of improved school library/media centers in the mid-1980s were the provisions in the Higher Education Act on training and the provisions in the Library Services and Construction Act on interlibrary cooperation. Both programs eventually received appropriations, despite the Reagan Administration's zero budget recommendations. Bilingual education, education for disadvantaged and handicapped children, and Indian education all received appropriations; in many parts of the country these are of significant interest. In addition it should be noted that many states have passed legislation in the 1980s supporting the concept of networking and library cooperation. Copyright questions continued to be raised with some concern.

The task force report *A Nation at Risk* (198.), commissioned by Secretary of Education Terrel Bell, was of great concern to librarians, particularly school library/media specialists, because it made little mention of the educational services provided by school, academic, or public libraries. In 1984 the ALA responded to *A Nation at Risk* and to the Reagan Administration's position with a strong statement, *Realities: Education Reform in a Learning Society*. One of the four basic realities developed was that "good schools require good school libraries," with specific recommendations for public officials. It was hoped that this statement would help support legislation at both state and national levels to reinforce the valuable contribution made by school library/media personnel and their centers of service.

A further response appeared in *Alliance for Excellence: Librarians Respond to a Nation at Risk,* (1984) prepared by representatives of library associations and chaired by the Director of the Division of Library Programs, U.S. Department of Education. Eight recommendations for strengthening the use of school library/media centers were included, relating to resources, standards, use patterns, staff, and the education of teachers and school administrators who can learn what can happen in a center "where excellence is the rule, rather than the exception." The more than 88,000 public and private school library/media centers in the U.S. can play a significant role in meeting the challenge of *A Nation at Risk* if these recommendations are fully implemented.

REFERENCES

Alliance for Excellence: Librarians Respond to a Nation at Risk. Recommendations and Strategies from Libraries and the Learning Society (1984).

American Association of School Librarians and Association for Educational Communications and Technology, *Media Programs: District and School* (1985).

David R. Bender, "State Educational Agencies: Roles and Functions," *School Library Journal* (1975).

R. A. Davis, *The School Library Media Center: A Force for Educational Excellence,* 2nd edition (1974).

Evelyn H. Daniel, "Performance Measure for School Librarianship: Complexities and Potential," *Advances in Librarianship* (1976).

Ernest R. DeProspo, "Potential Limits and Abuses of Evaluation," *School Media Quarterly* (1975).

Ernest R. DeProspo, Ellen Altman, and Kenneth E. Beasley, *Performance Measures for Public Libraries* (1973).

Ernest R. DeProspo and James W. Liesner, "Media Program Evaluation: A Working Framework," *School Media Quarterly* (1975).

Anne Marie Falsone, "Participation of School Libraries," in Beth A. Hamilton and William R. Ernst, Jr., editors, *Multitype Library Cooperation* (1977).

J. T. Gillespie and D. L. Spirt, *Creating a School Media Program* (1973).

Mary E. Hall, "The Development of the Modern High School," in Martha Wilson, comp., *Selected Articles on School Library Experience* (1978).

Audrey Kolb, "Development and Potential of a Multitype Library Network," *School Media Quarterly* (1977).

Patricia Pond, "Development of a Professional School Library," *School Media Quarterly* (1976).

G. Flint Purdy, "Interrelations among Public, School, and Academic Libraries," *Library Quarterly* (1969).

Realities: Educational Reform in a Learning Society (1984).

Mary R. Sive, "School Libraries and Networking in Selected States," in *School Library Media Annual* (1984).

Richard J. Sorensen, "Changes in School Media Programs Resulting from Participation in Networking," in *School Library Media Annual* (1984).

RUTH WALDROP;
JEAN E. LOWRIE

Scoggin, Margaret C.
(1905–1968)

The New York Public Library
Margaret C. Scoggin

Margaret Clara Scoggin was a pioneer in the establishment of young adult services in public libraries. She designed, opened, and supervised the Nathan Straus Branch of the New York Public Library (NYPL), which was devoted exclusively to patrons 21 and under. As a result of her experience there, she was invited by ALA to help organize the International Youth Library in Munich, Germany, and she toured other European libraries in an advisory capacity for Unesco. As successor to Mabel Williams, Scoggin served as Superintendent of Work with Young People for the New York Public Library from 1952 until 1967. She was the recipient of many awards and honors, most notably the ALA Grolier Award for outstanding service to young people.

Born in Caruthersville, Missouri, April 14, 1905, Margaret Scoggin graduated as high school valedictorian with a record-setting average; she then finished Radcliffe magna cum laude and was elected to Phi Beta Kappa. Her interest in youth work may have started with the classes she taught in a local settlement house during college. In July 1926 Scoggin worked as a summer replacement at NYPL, starting at the Mott Haven Branch and moving around in various branches to gain experience, under the encouraging supervision of Mabel Williams, Supervisor of Work with Schools. Young people's opinions were important to her; she believed that libraries would serve young people best through identifying their interests and through listening carefully to what they had to say. She wrote, "True reading guidance lies in discovering in each boy and girl the interests he has. . . . It calls for tolerance of young people's choices— listening instead of telling." She saw this communication process as one that enhanced the growth of critical judgment in young people through the testing of their ideas in a supportive environment. She created this environment at that time in two ways— through library-based clubs in which young adults discussed books and produced plays and puppet shows, and through skilled one-to-one reading guidance.

After completing a degree at the School of Librarianship at the University of London, Scoggin returned to NYPL to continue her YA work and introduced a teen book review booklet, called *Back Talk,* which included articles on topics of interest to young people as well as reviews. She said, "In school only the best is taken, but the public library takes everything." This attitude continues to distinguish public library YA work from school-related activities.

Although she started a Master's program at Columbia University, Scoggin never completed the degree because of pressures of time and money. In 1935 she was named systemwide Librarian in Charge of Vocational and Industrial Schools of NYPL. In this capacity she spoke at assemblies and arranged class visits and presentations in all parts of the city. She also compiled bibliographies of simple technical books for the vocational school students, because she identified their great need for books on a level they could comprehend. NYPL published *Simple Technical Books* in 1939.

In April 1940, having completed her work with the vocational schools, Scoggin began work with designers on the Nathan Straus Branch Library for Children and Young People. She insisted upon good light, bright colors, a welcoming atmosphere, a collection built around youth interests, and a specially trained staff. The branch opened in 1941, and its success can be measured, in Scoggin's own terms, by comments from patrons of 1943:

> I can get the kind of books I want without wading through a mess of junk that's way over my head.

> The librarians LIKE to help you in any problem you have and they are all very nice.

> You feel as you come in that you are going into your own home.

> I guess I don't dislike anything or anyone in this library.

While supervising Nathan Straus, which quickly became a professional demonstration library in addition to its other mission of service to young people, Scoggin lectured at Saint John's University, served on local agency councils and ALA committees, and was consulted by innumerable literary, publishing, and youthwork groups. During her time at Nathan Straus she also pioneered music library programs for young adults and was a leading advocate of recordings as part of YA collections. The Nathan Straus branch continued from 1941 until 1955, when the YA services and collection were moved to their present location at the Donnell Library Center on 53rd Street.

In 1945, after an interview on New York radio station WMCA, owned by Mrs. Nathan Straus, wife of the philanthropist who gave money for the branch bearing his name, Scoggin was invited to organize a young people's radio review program. The enormously successful program continues on WNYC today. The quality of "The Young Book Reviewers" program was recognized by awards from the Institute of Education by Radio and Television at Ohio State University. When the program moved to WNYC as the library-sponsored "Teen Age Book Talk," it won the George Foster Peabody Broadcasting Award of the Henry W. Grady School of Journalism at the University of Georgia. In 1965 the radio program was judged "Best Radio Program for Youth" as one of the Thomas Alva Edison Foundation's National Mass Media Award Winners.

With her good sense of what really interested young adults, Scoggin produced six anthologies of stories for young people taken primarily from adult books. Two featured humor—*Chucklebait* (1945) and *More Chucklebait* (1949); three adventure—*Lure of Danger* (1945), *Edge of Danger* (1951), and *Escapes and Rescues* (1960); and one true stories from World War II—*Battle Stations* (1953).

Scoggin left a rich body of professional writings. In 1947 she presented "The Library as a Center for Young People in the Community" at the University of Chicago's Symposium, *Youth, Communication and Libraries.* In 1948 she originated "Outlook Tower" in *Horn Book,* a review column of recommended adult books for YA's of which she was editor for almost

20 years. In 1952 Scoggin coedited *Gateways to Readable Books,* a graded, annotated list of books for slow readers in high schools. Her articles were as eloquent as they were entertaining, as this 1952 quote from *ALA Bulletin* shows:

> Young readers need an adult mind to challenge their ideas of books and authors. Let us be sure that the minds we provide as the challenge are both adult and functioning.

Scoggin continued to be a "Renaissance Woman" as Superintendent of Work with Young People. Even in that demanding position, she still managed to find time to teach a weekly course at the Simmons library school. During this period she also initiated annotations as Editor of *Books for the Teenage,* an annual list started in NYPL in 1929.

In postwar Germany the success of an International Book Exhibition organized by Hella Lepman under the American military government led to the idea of a permanent International Youth Library. Such a library would collect the best children's books of the world to help foster international understanding through books. With funds from the Rockefeller Foundation and the Bavarian government, ALA chose Scoggin as its representative because of her work at Nathan Straus. Scoggin spent six gruelling months weeding and classifying 8,000 books from 24 countries and developing programs to lure and keep the young interested in the library. In addition, she toured other European libraries for Unesco and persuaded authorities to include books in CARE packages. After much effort and encouragement, the International Youth Library opened in 1949, and Scoggin continued soliciting materials and equipment for it after she returned home. Because of her work with the Library, the Children's Book Council has established the Margaret Scoggin Memorial Collection there. It includes all the titles on the annual ALA Notable Children's Books and Best Books for Young Adults lists.

Scoggin was active in professional associations in many capacities. She was the first Chair of the newly formed Children's and Young Adult Services Division of the New York Library Association in 1951–52. In ALA she chaired the International Relations Committee and the Young People's Reading Round Table, was elected an ALA Councilor, and received the Grolier Award. From the Women's National Book Association she received the Constance Lindsay Skinner Award.

The full measure of her outstanding contributions to librarianship may be measured, and remembered, by two comments. The first is from "some of her grateful young book reviewers" on a scroll they presented to her:

> To Margaret Scoggin, who has opened the door to the wonderful world of books for many who might not have found the way themselves.

The second is a tribute written after her death in New York City on July 11, 1968, by Dorothy L. Cromien, formerly her assistant at Nathan Straus:

> The professional world is served today in many places by those whom Miss Scoggin encouraged and inspired. The most lasting tribute we can give Margaret Scoggin is to turn with her generosity to the generations we may have scarcely noticed coming up behind us.

REFERENCE

Beverly Lowy, "Margaret C. Scoggin (1905–1968): Her Professional Life and Work in Young Adult Librarianship" (unpublished M.A. thesis, Palmer Graduate Library School, Long Island University, May 1970.)

MARY K. CHELTON

Sears, Minnie Earl

(1873–1933)

Minnie Earl Sears, cataloguer, reference librarian, bibliographer, teacher, and editor of reference books, is best known for her *List of Subject Headings for Small Libraries*.

Sears was born November 17, 1873, in Lafayette, Indiana, and received the B.S. degree from Purdue University in 1891, at the age of 18, the youngest member of her class. Two years later she received the M.S. degree from the same university, and in 1900 she received the B.L.S. degree from the University of Illinois.

Her particular interest was cataloguing. She served as Head Cataloguer at Bryn Mawr College Library, 1903–07, Head Cataloguer at the University of Minnesota Library, 1909–14, and First Assistant of the Reference-Catalogue Division of the New York Public Library, 1914–20.

Isadore Gilbert Mudge, colleague, friend, and co-editor of several works, described her in the January 1934 issue of *Wilson Bulletin for Librarians* as follows: "She had an unusual ability for research work of a high order and, had her tastes turned in that direction, would have made one of the great reference librarians of the country, but from the beginning she was interested especially in the scholarly side of cataloging and cataloging research, and in the problems of subject cataloging."

She also had a strong interest in bibliographic and literary research, evident in the *Thackeray Dictionary* (1910) and the *George Eliot Dictionary* (1924), which she wrote with Mudge.

In 1923 she joined the editorial staff of the H. W. Wilson Company, where she combined her cataloguing expertise with her research ability. In this capacity she was able to use her knowledge and understanding of libraries to assist not just one library but many libraries throughout the country. She edited the third edition of *Children's Catalog* in 1925 and the fourth edition in 1930. Because of her interest and care, this selection tool for juvenile books became a cataloguing and reference tool and also a useful source for teaching in library schools. She edited other similar reference works: the second edition of the ALA *Standard Catalog for High School Libraries* (1932) and the ALA *Standard Catalog for Public Libraries* (1927–33).

One of her goals in compiling the *George Eliot Dictionary* was to identify the songs and musical compositions referred to in George Eliot's works. This task required the use of the resources of the three largest music libraries in the country at that time as well as foreign correspondence. When Sears accepted the task of editing the *Song Index,* she did so with a practical knowledge of the problems involved and an appreciation of the need for such a tool. The *Song Index* was published in 1926.

The plan for *Essay and General Literature Index* (1931–33), which Sears edited with Marion Shaw,

"was based on one of the points of her cataloguing creed upon which she always felt very strongly, that is, the economic waste of analyzing in individual card catalogues material which could be analyzed once for all in a printed catalogue or index," according to Mudge (*Wilson Bulletin for Librarians,* January 1934). Thus the basis for describing titles included in such works as *Essay and General Literature Index* and *Standard Catalog for Public Libraries* was careful cataloguing and the availability of cooperative cataloguing to libraries everywhere.

Her *List of Subject Headings for Small Libraries,* first published in 1923 (12th edition, *Sears List of Subject Headings,* 1982) filled a long-felt need among smaller libraries and soon became a tool for teaching subject heading work in library schools. In the 3rd edition, published in 1933, the last one she edited, she added a chapter entitled "Practical Suggestions for the Beginner in Subject Heading Work." Also published as a separate pamphlet, it contained simple rules with logical explanations about how to assign subject headings, told how new subject headings are established, and gave advice on how to handle subject heading changes. From the start Sears used the Library of Congress form for subject headings. As a result, cataloguers could easily add Library of Congress headings when a subject was not included in the Sears *List*. One exception to this practice was the use of hyphens; in the *Wilson Bulletin* (vol. 2, 1922–26), Sears commented on her preference in the *Sears List* for the more modern usage of less hyphenation.

In a talk to the New York Regional Catalogers Group on "The Teaching of Cataloging" (*Library Journal,* June 1, 1927), she discussed several issues about elementary and advanced cataloguing courses and the continuation of learning about cataloguing that needs to follow library school graduation. One issue that she discussed seems to summarize the essence of her purpose as cataloguer and reference librarian: "Can not more be done to make them [cataloguers] realize that there is no difference between the research work often demanded in cataloging, especially in a large library, and the work that is done as pure reference work? . . . Could something more be done in reference courses to connect practical reference with cataloging and vice versa?"

Sears joined the faculty of the Columbia University School of Library Service in 1927 and served there until 1931. She organized the first graduate course in cataloguing for the Master's degree. She served as Chairman of the ALA Catalog Section, 1927–28, Chairman of the New York Regional Catalog Group, 1931–32, and from 1932 until her death on November 28, 1933, she was a member of the ALA committee advising on the revision of the *ALA Catalog Rules*.

BARBARA GATES

Seminar on the Acquisition of Latin American Library Materials

Founding and Membership. The Seminar on the Acquisition of Latin American Library Materials (SALALM) was born out of a 1956 meeting to consider the problems in acquiring Latin American imprints for North American research libraries. Additional annual meetings were held in the ensuing years, and SALALM was incorporated as a nonprofit organization in January 1968. The organization's international membership combines a range of Latin Americanist constituencies. Selectors, publishers, and bookdealers work together to address overlapping concerns. Scholars and librarians are also represented. The challenges of meeting research needs for a discipline—and area—characterized by diffuse and often idiosyncratic patterns of research and publication have mandated close collaboration among all the affected parties. This alliance has, in turn, enriched each of them.

The membership includes about 300 individuals (1985). Approximately 70 percent are from North America, and the rest divide fairly evenly between Latin America and the rest of the world. There are also about 125 institutional members.

Purpose. SALALM's name denotes one of the organization's primary purposes. Its constitution enumerates the following goals:

> to promote the improvement of library services in support of study and research activities in Latin American and inter-American affairs; to provide an association for study programs in which scholars, librarians, and others interested in book and library resources relating to Latin American and inter-American studies can discuss problems, and carry out programs of common interest; and to promote cooperative efforts to achieve better library services as a means of encouraging and advancing international understanding in the Western Hemisphere.

SALALM's conference programs, publications, and committee structure illuminate its purposes and concerns more fully than any formal statement. All have shifted over time, in an evolution reflecting changes in the Latin American book trade, the organization's successes in improving acquisitions possibilities, an ongoing dialogue with scholars, and the opportunities and demands of new technology.

History. SALALM can date its formation to the June 14–15, 1956, meeting at Chinsegut Hill, Florida. Until its formal incorporation, in 1968, the organization was administered through an Executive Secretary and a Steering Committee. The annual conferences were self-supporting (as they for the most part remain), and the Executive Secretariat was unofficially maintained within the Library Development Program of the Organization of American States, under the tutelage of Marietta Daniels Shepard. After 1968, SALALM gradually constructed a more elaborate governmental apparatus, as mandated by its constitution and bylaws.

Organization. SALALM's Executive Board includes both elected and ex officio members. The President is elected to a one-year term, and serves as Vice-President/President-elect for one year before assuming the presidency. The Executive Board normally meets once or twice a year. The organization is self-supporting. Most income is derived from dues, conference fees, and publication sales. Expenses include Secretariat costs (usually shared by the institution hosting the secretariat), conference charges, and printing and editorial work.

SALALM's committees are the principal locus for the organization's activities. The eight Executive Board Committees are concerned with maintaining the organization per se. The Substantive Committees,

with their affiliated subcommittees, have been responsible for most of SALALM's more public accomplishments. Participation on substantive committees is open without restriction to the entire membership. Individual talents have been readily tapped under that arrangement, while the organization has minimized the formation of cliques. More than a third of SALALM's personal members serve on committees or subcommittees. Committee chairs, one-third of whom change each year, are appointed to three-year terms by the incoming President.

SALALM includes five substantive committees and a host of affiliated subcommittees. The Gifts and Exchanges Subcommittee of the Acquisitions Committee compiled a guide to exchange sources in Latin America that has proved indispensable to institutions using this mechanism to build their collections. The Library-Bookdealer-Publisher Relations Subcommittee addresses the difficulties of international and intercultural business relationships; it compiled a *Directory of Vendors of Latin American Library Materials*. The Acquisitions Committee also oversees the ongoing annual compilation of book cost statistics for Latin Americana.

The Bibliography Committee prepares the annual *Bibliography of Latin American Bibliographies*, which is periodically cumulated as supplements to Arthur Gropp's *A Bibliography of Latin American Bibliographies*. The Committee also addresses techniques for Latin Americanist bibliographic instruction through its similarly named subcommittee. Its Subcommittee on Cuban Bibliography has produced a number of definitive specialized bibliographies. And the Subcommittee on Non-Print Media grapples with the special problems of acquiring and controlling materials in nontraditional formats.

The Committee on Library Operations and Services has pursued closer relationships with Latin American librarians through the Subcommittee on Library Education. Its Subcommittee on Reference Service addresses a host of public service concerns, and the Subcommittee on Cataloguing and Bibliographic Technology focuses on technical processing support for Latin Americana.

The Joint Committee on Official Publications was formed in light of the bibliographic and acquisitions complexities associated with these crucial materials. The Committee on Interlibrary Cooperation, finally, has collaborated in preparing a conspectus for Latin American Library Collections, designed for use by the Research Libraries Group as well as within SALALM, as part of its larger concern with coordinated collection development.

In the mid-1980s major Latin American collections in the United States were divided about evenly between institutions using OCLC as their bibliographic utility and those belonging to the Research Libraries Group (RLG). The SALALM Subcommittees for OCLC Users and RLG Members provide forums for constituents of each bibliographic utility. Since both subcommittees are within the Committee on Interlibrary Cooperation, unified responses to common Latin Americanist concerns are encouraged. Their activities should thus help bridge the gap between utilities.

Programs. SALALM's annual programs, for which the President is responsible, are one of the organization's most obvious manifestations of concerns and vitality. The meetings last for four or five days, and are usually held at centers for Latin American research. SALALM meets outside the U.S. about once every three or four years. The conferences combine sessions based on formal papers with workshops and committee meetings. In most years the substantive committees play a major role in organizing specific sessions.

During SALALM's early years, most conferences emphasized the bibliographic and acquisitions problems of specific countries or subregions. Shifts toward issue-oriented scholarship, in conjunction with improved bibliographic control and dealer service throughout much of Latin America, have more recently resulted in themes that emphasize particular issues or sets of issues. The second conference (1957), for example, dealt with acquiring materials from Mexico; the third (1958), with Chile and Argentina; the fifth (1960), with the Caribbean. By contrast, the 26th meeting (1981) addressed "Latin American Economic Issues"; the 27th (1982), "Public Policy Issues and Latin American Library Resources"; and the 30th (1985), "Latin America's Masses and Minorities: Their Images and Realities." SALALM has paid increasing attention to the twin contexts of Latin American Studies in the academic community and Latin American collections in research libraries. There is fluctuating support for expensive academic and acquisitions programs that sometimes seem peripheral to national research priorities; SALALM thus intensified efforts to understand the area's present, and to anticipate its future.

Publications. SALALM's most prominent publications have always been the collected working papers of its conferences. They summarize findings, list sources, and outline strategies for acquisitions, collection development, and reference service. SALALM has also, through its "Bibliography and Reference Series," published many specific compilations. It prepares the annual *Bibliography of Latin American Bibliographies,* and its *Microfilming Projects Newsletter* reports Latin Americanist microfilming long before entries appear in the *National Register of Microform Masters.* Current announcements and news are disseminated through a quarterly *Newsletter.*

Relations with Other Organizations. SALALM avoided formal alliances with other bodies, but it places a high value on collaborative working relationships. LACAP, the Latin American Cooperative Acquisitions Program, flourished through much of the 1960s as the result of close cooperation between SALALM as a whole, specific member institutions, and the firm of Stechert-Hafner. SALALM'S 1982 meeting was held jointly with the Latin American Studies Association, and for 1987 it planned a joint conference with the Association of Caribbean University and Research Libraries (ACURIL).

SALALM recognizes other significant endeavors by providing meeting time and program support during its annual conferences. The Latin American Microform Project (LAMP) is a voluntary association of institutions, administered through the Center for Research Libraries, which conducts specific microfilming projects throughout the hemisphere. The *Hispanic American Periodicals Index* (HAPI) relies almost exclusively on SALALM volunteers as indexers.

Both enterprises meet in conjunction with SALALM.

SALALM's primary concern remains that which inspired its formation: to make necessary resources available to Latin Americanist students and scholars throughout the world. As scholarly, institutional, and technological contexts have shifted, the specific manifestations of this concern have changed as well. Mainstream Latin Americana is, by now, fairly readily accessible. But the special and esoteric materials essential for current scholarship remain elusive. Equally critical, the balance of forces within North American libraries and academic institutions continues to change, as a result of both new technologies and political and intellectual dynamics.

DAN C. HAZEN

Senegal

Senegal, a republic of West Africa, lies on the Atlantic Ocean and is bounded by Mauritania on the north, Mali on the east, and Guinea and Guinea-Bissau on the south. Population (1984 est.) 6,352,000; area 196,722 sq.km. The official language is French.

History. The history of libraries in Senegal is recent in comparison with that of developed countries. Like most African nations, Senegal is a country of oral traditions. They have a certain documentary value because they convey the social and cultural heritage of peoples, but this source of information was not conserved in a methodical manner. Oral traditions are fragile and perishable, leading Hampaté Bậ to declare that "in Africa when an old man dies, it is a whole library that burns." On the other hand, although these traditions were the monopoly of the *griots* (a caste of praise singers), who acted as guardians of the values of the past by transmitting their knowledge from father to son, the process of transmission was not exempt from alteration.

Aware of the importance of oral tradition as a first-hand source of information, the Senegalese government set up the Direction des Archives Culturelles (Directorate for Cultural Archives, a multimedia archival agency), responsible for collecting, conserving, and studying various forms of cultural expression of the various ethnic groups in the country. Publishers have also gathered oral traditions and have published them in historical novels and in collections of folktales.

With the coming of the printed word, oral traditions had to compete with written sources introduced during colonization. The first libraries established in Senegal made their appearance with the French conquest in Africa. In an effort to promote the French language and to respond to the needs of colonial administrators, the French established the first public, administrative, municipal, and teachers' libraries in Senegal.

With the goal of developing a test for reading by providing the inhabitants of the two largest communes (cities with voting rights) with books for their instruction and entertainment, two public libraries were created in Senegal: the first in Saint-Louis in 1849 and the second in Dakar in 1905.

National Library Services. Three libraries perform the functions of a national library. The Library of the Institut Fondamental d'Afrique Noire (IFAN; Fundamental Institute of Black Africa) was

Photo IFAN/Bibliothèque de l'Université de Dakar

The Faculty of Letters of the University of Dakar.

established in 1938, when it inherited more than 6,000 works from the Library of the government of French West Africa. It later increased its collections more than ten-fold and owns manuscripts, rare books, and newspapers dating back to Colonial times. It received copyright privileges on July 17, 1946. A decree on legal deposit requirements was adopted April 9, 1976. The Library of the Archives Nationales du Sénégal was founded in 1913 and is housed in Dakar. From 1962 it published a bibliographical bulletin (Bibliographie du Sénégal), a first draft toward a national bibliography. From its founding it received official state publications for deposit. The Library of the Centre de Recherche et de Documentation du Sénégal (Center for Research and Documentation of Senegal) in Saint-Louis was founded in 1944 when it acquired the former IFAN Center of Senegal.

Academic Libraries. There is a central library at the University of Dakar, founded in 1952. In addition, there are a number of other institutional and professional school libraries.

Administrative Libraries. After 1904 administrative libraries were created in the *cercles* in order to meet the immediate needs of the colonial administrators who presided over the district tribunals. These libraries contained works on both French and Islamic law. In Dakar, the capital of French West Africa, there was also an administrative library composed mainly of legal works to aid the administrators in governing the colony. This library also contained the first important scientific collection in the federation.

Teachers' Libraries. After 1904 pedagogical or teachers' libraries were set up in the capitals of colonies that were part of French West Africa. Two of these were in Senegal, one in Dakar and one in Saint-Louis. They were established to enable teachers to learn more about the colony and prepare their courses.

Public and Other Library Service. A Municipal Library was created in Louga in 1915. Senegal benefited by acquiring some libraries created during French rule. But the system was not consolidated after Senegal became independent. Many small municipal libraries from the Colonial period disappeared or lost their effectiveness as a result of lack of follow-through and of funding. The Senegalese government

ALA

T. P. Sevensma

was obliged to start anew in creating new, better-adapted services, such as the national documentation center, the directorate for public reading (Direction de la lecture publique), the directorate for archives, and other services; however, other collections inherited by Senegal (such as the University Library, the IFAN Library, the Library at the National Archives, and the basic administrative structure and collections of the archives themselves) placed Senegalese library resources far ahead of those in any other country in Francophone Africa.

The Profession. Since 1967 the training of information professionals has been offered at the University of Dakar by the École des Bibliothécaires, Archivistes et Documentalistes (EBAD, the School for Librarians, Archivists, and Documentalists). This school replaced the Centre régional de formation des bibliothécaires (CRFB), a regional center created to train qualified library personnel in Africa and for Africa. Broader in conception than CRFB (which concentrated solely on library education), EBAD includes two other sections, one for archivists and one for documentalists. Like CRFB, EBAD has a regional vocation because it welcomes students from many countries in Francophone Africa.

EBAD includes two levels of training: an undergraduate program for training intermediate-level personnel in two years; and a graduate program for training higher-level personnel in two years. Admission to the graduate program is gained by competitive examination, reserved for those holding *licences* (university degrees), or professional examination, reserved for those holding undergraduate diplomas from EBAD who have completed at least three years of library or information work. An advanced diploma of information science and communication is awarded on completion of two years of training.

Besides the training offered at EBAD, students may obtain professional education abroad, notably in France (at the École Nationale Supérieure des Bibliothécaires in Lyon or the Institut National des Techniques de la Documentation in Paris) or in Canada (at the University of Montreal).

REFERENCES

Mary Niles Maack. *Libraries in Senegal: Continuity and Change in an Emerging Nation* (1981). Three articles by Maack treat specific aspects of librarianship in Senegal.

"The A.O.F. Archives and the Study of African History," *Bulletin de l'Institut Fondamental d'Afrique Noire, Série B* (1980).

"Libraries for the General Public in French-Speaking Africa: Their Cultural Role," *Journal of Library History* (1981).

"The Colonial Legacy in West African Libraries: A Comparative Analysis," *Advances in Librarianship* (1982).

WALY NDIAYE;
translated by MARY NILES MAACK

Sevensma, T. P.

(1879–1966)

Founder and first President of the Dutch Library Association (Nederlandse Vereiniging van Bibliothecarissen—NVB), and the first General Secretary of the International Federation of Library Associations (IFLA), T(iestse) P(ieter) Sevensma gave distinguished leadership to the international library world for more than 30 years.

Born in 1879 in Sneek, in the northern province of Friesland in the Netherlands, Sevensma gained his principal education at the University of Amsterdam, where he went to take doctoral degrees in both theology and political science. After a brief period as a lecturer in Hebrew at a Rotterdam grammar school, he began his library career in 1908 at the University of Amsterdam. He also compiled booksellers' catalogues for Martinus Nijhoff of The Hague.

In 1913 Sevensma was appointed Librarian of the Commercial University Library in Rotterdam, where he had the experience of organizing the library in a new building. After three years he moved back to Amsterdam as Librarian of the Public Library. This responsibility was combined with that of Librarian of the University of Amsterdam Library in 1929. During 1912–23 Sevensma founded and served as the first President of the Dutch Library Association (NVB).

His academic library experience and impressive linguistic skills made him a natural choice to succeed Florence Wilson of Columbia University as the Librarian of the League of Nations Library in 1927. A new library building in Geneva was completed, with the assistance of an international committee of library experts appointed by the Secretariat. Sevensma directed the transition to the new facility with only one day without service to readers. As Geneva and the League were considered the heart of international influence, the International Federation of Library Associations invited Sevensma to become its first Secretary in June 1929.

Although Sevensma left the League of Nations in 1938 to become Librarian of the oldest university library in the Netherlands, Leiden, he remained Secretary of IFLA until 1958. Appointing Arthur C. Breycha-Vauthier as Assistant Secretary, and Sevensma's successor at the League, IFLA continued to benefit from office subvention by the League. Through the years of World War II Sevensma held fast to the idea of IFLA.

Sevensma maintained an active scholarly life as one of the editors of the fourth edition of Winkler Prins' *Encyclopedia* and as chief editor of a newly created Dutch encyclopedia, *Zoecklicht* ("Searchlight").

Sevensma was honored at 60 by his colleagues who established the Sevensma prize, offered annually by IFLA for the best essay on a selected topic. Active until an advanced age, he died in Hilversum at 87.

ROBERT WEDGEWORTH

Seychelles

Seychelles, a republic in the Indian Ocean off the east coast of Africa, comprises a group of islands of disputed number. The islands were a British colony until 1976; they had been a dependency of the Mauritius Islands until 1903. Population (1984 est.) 65,000; area 443 sq.km. The official languages are English and French. Creole patois is spoken also.

On Mahé, the largest island of the country, is the National Library; of some major importance, it was inherited from the Carnegie Foundation Library. Also on Mahé the Museum Library offers a collection on the life sciences, and the National Archives preserves documents of importance about the history of the Indian Ocean. There are also 11 school libraries with a total of about 11,000 volumes.

J. C. RODA*

Shackleton, Robert
(1919-)

Robert Shackleton, Librarian of the Bodleian Library and author of work of outstanding originality and perception in French 18th-century studies over many years, was Chairman of the Committee on Oxford University Libraries. He resolved the managerial anomalies of the departmental, faculty, and museum collections that had grown up independently over centuries, reconciled local and knowledgeable supervision, selection and spending, under individual committees, with fiscal common sense as enunciated by a Libraries Board, and guided the largest unit, the Bodleian Library, into extension, automation, and shared acquisition policies for materials published abroad.

Shackleton was born in Yorkshire, England, on November 25, 1919. He was an undergraduate at Oriel College (graduated 1940); and his early academic appointments were at Trinity College (Lecturer, 1946–49) and Brasenose College (Fellow, 1946–79; Vice-Principal, 1963–66). From 1948 to 1966 he was Librarian. From University Lecturer in French he proceeded to the Readership in 1965, the year of his heaviest activity as Chairman of the Committee appointed to consider what might be done to exact the greatest utility, scholarly and economic, from the University Libraries, especially those not under the authority of the Curators of the Bodleian Library. "The importance of these may be demonstrated," to quote the report (known generally as the *Parry Report*) of the Committee on Libraries of the University

Bodleian Library

Robert Shackleton

Libraries in Seychelles (1982)

Type	Administrative units	Service points	Volumes in collections	Annual expenditures (rupee)	Population served[b]	Professional staff	Total staff
National	--	--	--	--	--	--	--
Academic	--	--	--	--	--	--	--
Public[a]	1	6	25,000	368,000	8,770	--	16
School	11	11	11,000	--	--	--	--

[a]1981 data.
[b]Registered borrowers.

Source: Unesco, *Statistical Yearbook,* 1984.

Grants Committee, 1967 "by comparing the book resources of Oxford with one of the larger libraries in a provincial university. If the Bodleian complex and all college libraries were destroyed, the remaining libraries would still have a larger stock than that of the largest English university libraries, for example Birmingham or Leeds or Liverpool or Manchester."

The recommendations for common standards and policies and collaboration set forth by Shackleton's committee, published as the *Report of the Committee on University Libraries,* (Supplement No. 1 to the *Oxford University Gazette,* XCVII), appeared in November 1966. It was a model of industry, historical and economic analysis, and tact, and it gained early and, in an Oxford context, surprisingly unacrimonious acceptance. In the year of its publication Shackleton became Bodley's Librarian. Much of the tolerance by faculties and departments of a mildly directive system for library management, which was philosophically at variance with academic self-government and the notion of independence in the university's parts, was owed to the new Librarian's political sense and modest but firm persuasiveness.

In virtue of his office, Shackleton became a member of the Libraries Board, and his quiet reasonableness and avoidance of partisanship helped to set the tone of the new body, and of the meetings of librarians from the extra-Bodleian libraries which rounded the consultative system. For 13 years, within and without the central Library, he guided, thoughtfully and unabrasively, the policies and practice of acquisition, proliferation, funding, and common storage of library materials in Oxford. He saw to a successful conclusion such essential new construction as the underground area of the Radcliffe Science Library and such happy refurbishment as the splendid exterior of Gibbs's Radcliffe Camera. These and like improvements were wholly within the Bodleian operation; to some extent outside it, and to the benefit of the University Libraries at large, were cooperative ventures such as the book repository at Nuneham Courtenay with delivery at a speed held by some librarians if not by their readers to be unseemly. In 1979 Shackleton stood down.

The circumstances of his retirement were felicitous. In the Preface to *Montesquieu: a critical biography* (1961), Shackleton had disclaimed, for himself, the universal competence of his subject. His prudence was a mark of integrity; it was Oxford's fortune that he was able to discard the restraints of specialization in his office as Bodley's Librarian. From the early Brasenose conference on library automation to the increasingly intricate conventions, in the later 1970s, of the International Federation of Library Associations, with little visible diminution of his work in French literature or in Enlightenment studies, Shackleton found his way surely through the technological mazes of innovative and administrative librarianship and was honored not only by learned societies but by professional bodies for librarians also. Yet the highest honor was in his recall to the plow. With a Fellowship at All Souls College, Oxford, he was elected Marshal Foch Professor of French, the first Englishman so appointed.

In this chair, long held by his admired Jean Seznec, and in sustained industry, Shackleton rounded off with distinction the career in letters in which

Bodley's librarianship was an equally distinguished intervention.

Shackleton assembled a superb Montesquieu collection; his wider taste in rare books resulted in his election to the Grolier Club of New York in 1967 and to its pantheon of Honorary Foreign Corresponding Members three years later. As he drew the reader into his work on Montesquieu, Shackleton confessed his unfitness, as he saw it, to discuss the springs of thought and action in one whose mind could still be open to all the sciences and all the arts; but the attempt secured to him a treasury of understanding.

Distinctions conferred on Shackleton include the Fellowships of the British Academy, the Society of Antiquaries, and the Royal Society of Literature, the Presidency of the Society for French Studies, a Visiting Fellowship of the Humanities Research Centre of the Australian National University, the Foreign Honorary Membership of the American Academy of Arts and Sciences, the Lyell Readership and the Zaharoff Lectureship in the University of Oxford, various American visiting professorships, the office of Delegate (board member) of the Oxford University Press, the Presidency of the International Society for 18th Century Studies, a Directorship of the Voltaire Foundation, corresponding membership of the Académie de Bordeaux, and many honorary fellowships in Oxford and honorary doctorates in English-speaking countries. Honors also include the Honorary Doctorate of the University of Bordeaux, the Médaille de la Ville de Paris, the John Brademas Inaugural Award at New York University, and appointment as Chevalier de la Légion d'Honneur.

CLIFFORD CURRIE

Shamurin, E. I.
(1889–1962)

Evgenii Ivanovich Shamurin was one of the most erudite Soviet scholars in librarianship and bibliography. He distinguished himself with excellence in research, prolific writing, and outstanding teaching. Many students and peers were touched by his vast knowledge.

He was born on October 28, 1889, in Erevan, Armenia. After his father, an attorney, died in 1904, the young Shamurin settled in an orphanage in Tambov, where he finished his secondary education in 1908. Following anti-government demonstrations during the Russo-Japanese War (1905), Shamurin was jailed and placed on probation. Soon after that he went to live with his maternal uncle, N. P. Zagoskin, a professor of law at the University of Kazan. He enrolled in the law school there, but also took advantage of broad curricular offerings. In addition to law he took a program in the humanities and the social sciences. This background led him to pursue his interests in the fine arts and literature rather than the practice of law. After graduation he fulfilled the required military service in 1912.

Virtually penniless, he left Kazan for Moscow, where he took some additional training in the arts and music. He began to write for various papers and journals, often using pseudonyms. His activities were interrupted by World War I. He served in the imperial army and was demobilized after the outbreak of the October Revolution.

He served as a jurist and a law lecturer until 1920 in the city of Tomsk. In early 1921 Shamurin began to work in the Bibliography Section of the Tartar State Publishing enterprise. In September 1921 he secured a job at the Russian Central Book Chamber in Moscow. This was a turning point in his career. The next 40 years he devoted to the field of bibliography and librarianship.

In the Book Chamber he held steadily increasing positions of responsibility dealing with such tasks as editorial work, organization of catalogues, descriptive cataloguing, classification, and the problems of terminology. He was active in the organization of two significant all-Russian bibliographic conferences, holding important official posts. He demonstrated his competence at the first conference, delivering a paper "On the Application of the Anglo-American Code in the Russian Bibliographic Practice" and also "On the Measures toward the Standard Title Page," both published in the 1926 conference proceedings.

During the 1920s he joined many professional groups, such as the Russian Bibliographic Society, Russian Society of Decimalists, Society of the Book Friends, and the Ukrainian Bibliological Society. During the 1930s he played many leading roles in the growth, development, and reorganization of the Book Chamber. He was instrumental in launching the journal *Bibliography,* later titled *Soviet Bibliography.*

In 1937 he left the Book Chamber but retained the role of a learned consultant. He participated in the advanced work of the Interlibrary Cataloguing Commission and many other official assignments. During this decade he gathered a wealth of knowledge and materials in the field of classification. His intention was to complete his doctoral studies. In 1943 he defended his 865-page dissertation, "The Library and Bibliographic Classification Abroad and in pre-Revolutionary Russia." In 1944 he was awarded the degree of doctor of pedagogical sciences with the rank of full professor and named chairman of the Department of Collections and Catalogues at the Moscow State Library Institute, where he served from 1940 to 1950.

He steered the project on the new Soviet library-bibliographic classification under the aegis of the Lenin State Library. He also guided the scholarly work of the Book Chamber in the restoration of fire-damaged catalogues, retrospective bibliography, and editorial work.

In 1950 he was sent into early retirement at the age of 61. But the last 12 years of his life proved to be his most productive period. Three of his chief works were published: the monumental *Essays on the History of the Library—Bibliographic Classification* (vol. 1, 1955, vol. 2, 1959; translated into German, 1964-67); *Dictionary of Library Terminology* (1958); and *Methods in the Preparation of Annotations* (1959).

Shamurin died in Moscow, December 1, 1962. A biography was started by Yu. I. Masanov and completed by I. B. Gracheva (1970). A definitive bibliography (1911-62) was prepared by his daughter, Sofiia E. Shamurina, also a librarian. It lists 34 monographs, most of them accompanied by references to book reviews. It also lists 93 of his journal articles, book reviews, contributions to other works, lectures, and speeches. And it lists 49 works edited by him or

under his editorial supervision. For his achievements, Shamurin was awarded the Order of the Red Banner of Labor and a privileged personal pension on retirement. Sidney L. Jackson said: "When every doctor of library science can show some knowledge of Shamurin's achievement, education for librarianship will have taken a long step towards truly professional education."

REFERENCES
Sidney L. Jackson, "In Review," *Journal of Education for Librarianship* (1968).
Yu.I. Masanov and I. B. Gracheva, *E. I. Shamurin, 1889–1962* (1970).
Ray R. Suput, *The Contribution of E. I. Shamurin to Soviet Librarianship* (dissertation, Case Western University, 1972).

RAY R. SUPUT

Katharine Lucinda Sharp

ALA

Sharp, Katharine
(1865–1914)

One of the outstanding library leaders of the late 19th and early 20th centuries, Katharine Lucinda Sharp built the cornerstone of the University of Illinois research libraries and contributed to the acceptance of graduate education for librarianship in the Midwest.

She was born in Elgin, Illinois, on May 21, 1865. The details of her childhood years are largely unrecorded; her mother's death, when Katharine was seven, led to her being housed with relatives while she attained her basic education at the Elgin Academy from 1872 to 1880. She enrolled, in 1881, at Northwestern University, Evanston, Illinois, and graduated in 1885 with a Bachelor of Philosophy degree with honors. At the New York State Library School, Albany, she earned a Bachelor's degree in 1892 and a Master's degree in 1907. Sharp also, in 1899, received a Master of Philosophy degree from Northwestern.

She spent the years from 1888 until 1907 devoted to studying, practicing, and living the profession of librarianship. Until her death at Saranac Lake, New York, June 1, 1914, caused by injuries suffered in an automobile accident May 28 at Lake Placid, she was closely associated with other 19th-century library pioneers, particularly her mentor and friend Melvil Dewey. Sharp studied with Dewey at Albany, and when she left the University of Illinois, in 1907, she found a close circle of friends at his Lake Placid Club in New York, where she served as Vice-President until her death.

Three years after her graduation from Northwestern she accepted her first library position as Assistant Librarian at the public library at Oak Park, Illinois. During the intervening years she had taught at the Elgin Academy. Her first exposure to library work quickly led her to the conclusion that she should enroll in the country's first library school; Dewey later noted, she "was so easily first" there. His recommendation to Frank W. Gunsaulus, President of the newly established Armour Institute in Chicago, brought her appointment, in 1893, as Director of both the Library and the Department of Library Economy. Of special note was the establishment of the library training class, the fourth opened in the United States and the first in the Midwest.

In 1897 she moved to the Champaign/Urbana campus of the University of Illinois; the Armour library class was transferred with her. She was already recognized for her ability and leadership in the emerging library profession. Her students at Armour included other future leaders such as Margaret Mann, Cornelia Marvin Pierce, and Alice Tyler. Sharp also was perceived as a national figure through her activities in the American Library Association and her vibrant advocacy of state library organizations, extension work, and cooperative information systems. At Illinois Sharp was named Head Librarian and Director of the Library School, and she also served as Professor of Library Economy.

In the 10 years of her work at the University of Illinois, Sharp's life was dominated by three concerns: the Illinois State Library School, now the Graduate School of Library and Information Science; the University library itself; and the development of a strong library organization and information network in Illinois. In each area she had extraordinary successes, but in each area she also had many disappointments.

The main interest of Sharp's professional career rested in her personal belief in education for librarianship that was housed in an academic setting. Dewey had broken the pattern of "learning by experience" in his prototype school; Sharp, his protogeé, accepted the philosophy that Dewey promulgated and carried it as far as she could at the University of Illinois. The classes at the Armour Institute and at the University of Illinois were founded to provide a specialization taught in an institution of higher education. At Illinois a combination of three elements, faculty, curriculum, and students, was brought together in such a way as to set a standard of achievement essential to the continuation of formal education for librarianship. The School, under her leadership, moved steadily from a B.L.S. based on a junior and senior year of college work toward acceptance of a graduate program. Although she did not completely achieve that objective, the curriculum evolved from routine "economy" courses in cataloguing, classifi-

cation, and library "techniques" to administration, the study of different kinds of resources such as public documents, library extension, special services, research methods, and new technology.

Sharp arrived at Illinois at a critical period in its history; the University Library was disorganized and lacked a professional perception. Sharp imposed her own distinctive conception of library service on the institution. A logical order and arrangement of the collection was basic; this was followed by an expansion of the services, including reference (which was directed by Isadore Gilbert Mudge) and a modernization of procedures. She enlarged the staff from 3 in 1897 to 15 in 1907, while the number of volumes increased from 37,000 to 96,000—all catalogued, classified, and accessible. She left a sound foundation for her successors.

Sharp's third, closely linked professional concern lay in the extension of the library into the community and the development of an effective political body that could work for the betterment of library services for all citizens. In this larger arena she did attain certain goals but also failed, since her efforts in Illinois to provide a strong authority for the promotion of library interests were not rewarded. An effective state library association was founded and set firmly on its way, but she and her colleagues did not initiate successful legislation to establish a state library commission. Her efforts to centralize library extension at the University also failed, although she did leave behind dedicated followers who continued to stress her philosophy and who mustered library supporters throughout the state.

Although she was not a prolific writer, she published nearly two dozen articles and a monumental compilation on the condition of libraries in Illinois, *Illinois Libraries* (1906–08), a multivolume survey of the current status of public, school, academic, and special libraries. It contained an exhaustive historical study.

Throughout her life Sharp was active in library and professional associations. In each organization she was a major officer, including ALA; she was active on many ALA committees, served 10 years on the Council, and was twice elected Vice-President.

REFERENCES

Laurel A. Grotzinger, *The Power and the Dignity: Librarianship and Katharine Sharp* (1966), the only book-length treatment of Katharine Sharp, contains detailed assessment of her educational preparation, Armour years, University of Illinois contributions, work at Lake Placid, and personal characteristics.

Harriet E. Howe, "Katharine Lucinda Sharp, 1865–1914," in *Pioneering Leaders in Librarianship,* edited by Emily Miller Danton (1953), a memoir, prepared by a former student, which illustrates the strong influence of Sharp on her students and gives examples of her professional contributions.

Laurel A. Grotzinger, "Sharp, Katharine Lucinda," *Dictionary of American Library Biography* (1978).

LAUREL A. GROTZINGER

Shaw, Ralph
(1907–1972)

Ralph Robert Shaw, internationally known library administrator, researcher, educator, and inventor, was one of the most creative librarians to have worked in the United States. He was considered a radical in his early years and a conservative, by some of his colleagues, in his later years. His brilliant mind had the capacity to see a problem, create a solution, then turn it over to colleagues to perfect and implement.

Shaw was born in Detroit, Michigan, May 18, 1907. He secured an A.B. degree from Western Reserve University in 1928, the B.S. and M.S. at Columbia in 1929 and 1931, respectively, and the Ph.D. at the University of Chicago in 1950. His early professional experience included the New York Public Library (1928–29), Engineering Societies Library (1929–36), and service as Chief Librarian, Gary (Indiana) Public Library (1936–40). In 1940 he became Director of Libraries, U.S. Department of Agriculture, a position that he held (with time out to serve in the U.S. armed forces) until 1954, when he went to Rutgers the State University of New Jersey. There he served as Professor in the newly established Graduate School of Library Service, becoming Dean, 1959–61, and Distinguished Service Professor, 1961–64. Finally he became Professor, Dean of Library Activities, and Professor Emeritus at the University of Hawaii in Honolulu until his retirement in 1969, although he continued to lecture occasionally at Rutgers until 1968.

Everywhere Shaw worked, his keen mind attacked the problems of the institution and produced innovative solutions, showing especial interest in the scientific and efficient management of libraries. In Gary he instituted transaction charging, the use of photography in circulation control, and the use of truck cabs coupled with trailers as bookmobiles, which could be left on location for several days or longer. His invention of the rapid selector came during this period, as well as his translation of Georg Schneider's work *Theory and History of Bibliography* (Columbia University Press, 1934). His dissertation at Chicago, revised and published as *Literary Property in the United States* (Scarecrow, 1950), marked the beginning of a continuing concern with copyright problems, evidenced again in one of his last works, "Williams and Wilkins v. the U.S.: A Review of the Commissioner's Report" (*American Libraries,* October 1972).

His work at the U.S. Department of Agriculture offered ample opportunity to continue his interest in the use of machines as tools of management. There he initiated the first study of scientific management as applied to libraries of that department, and later he carried this to Rutgers, where one of the first courses on this subject was introduced in the regular library school curriculum. His concern with bibliography brought his attention to the development of the *Bibliography of Agriculture,* which became a major tool for the dissemination of agricultural information on a worldwide basis.

His interest in international problems was also shown at this time and continued throughout his career. He was active on numerous committees for ALA and Unesco and served as a consultant on major library studies for a variety of governmental agencies. He advised, for example, the Department of State, the National Science Foundation, and the U.S. Veterans Administration, to name only a few. He planned a network of agencies to distribute agricultural information in India (1957), developed the information component of the International Rice Research Institute at Los Baños, Philippines (1962), and worked as well in many Latin American countries through his membership on the advisory committee of the Inter-American Institute of Agricultural Science.

Shaw's continuing service to public libraries was shown through a survey for the Toronto Public Library (*Libraries of Metropolitan Toronto,* 1960); a feasibility study for the Boards of Trustees of the Brooklyn Public Library, New York Public Library, and Queens Borough Public Library (*A Study of the Advantages and Disadvantages of Consolidation,* January 1957); and work at the local level to establish new public libraries, such as the one in Woodbridge, New Jersey. To all of these projects, and many more, he brought enthusiastic commitment, positive support, and expertise seldom matched in an individual librarian.

Publishing, as the other side of the coin of library development, received his attention in 1950 when he established the Scarecrow Press, Inc., on the principle of producing scholarly works and bibliographies in librarianship for which only a small market could be anticipated at a reasonable price, usually printing by offset from plates made from typewritten copy, yet always paying a royalty to authors. Among other experiments he tried miniprint, published especially to meet the needs of scholars in developing countries. With the help of Viola Leff Shaw, whom he had married in 1929 and who died in 1968, he worked from the basement of their homes in Alexandria, Virginia, and New Brunswick, New Jersey, and built a business until it became too large to manage at home and then sold a controlling interest in 1955 to Albert Daub, Sr.; in 1968 it was sold outright to Grolier Educational Corporation. Other similar publishers have used Scarecrow as a model for their operations. In 1969 he was married to Mary McChesney Andrews in Honolulu.

Few who knew Shaw during his days in Washington would have thought of him as having potentiality as a university professor, and yet when he was interviewed at Rutgers by Mason Gross, the President phoned the Dean and said, "We *must* have that man." When Shaw joined the small group of faculty who established the school in 1954, he quickly made an impact as an excellent instructor, an effective colleague in the development of curriculum, and a person deeply sympathetic to students, even though he was tough-minded and frequently dogmatic, could seldom suffer fools gladly, and had a special gift for stirring controversy. He initiated courses new to the library field, was influential in developing the doctoral curriculum, was tireless in seeking support for students and generous to colleagues, but brooked no delay on the part of faculty in responding to deadlines for dissertations and other related responsibilities.

A major contribution to the School and to the profession at this time was his editorship of the State of the Library Art series (Rutgers University Press, 1960–61, 5 vol.), published under a grant from the Council on Library Resources. He also initiated the Shaw/Shoemaker project *American Bibliography: A Preliminary Checklist for 1801–1819* (Scarecrow, 1958–66, 22 vol.) in order to close a 20-year gap left by

ALA

Ralph Shaw

Evans's pioneering work. It was typical of a Shaw project that he conceived the idea of using the "WPA shoe boxes" of cards plus photocopying as a method of expediting the work; as a result he was successful in producing, from a variety of secondary sources, a tool that has a remarkably high record of accuracy. Another contribution to librarianship was his development, as adviser to doctoral students, of a number of related research studies in the field of management as a means of "growing the field," in his words.

In 1964, when he was invited to go to the University of Hawaii, he carried much of the Rutgers curriculum and some of the faculty and doctoral students to establish a new library school there and to breathe new life into its library system. True to form, he experimented there too, particularly using his "visiting professor" idea, begun at Rutgers when such luminaries as Ranganathan, Joseph Wheeler, and Keyes Metcalfe visited and lectured to library school students. At Honolulu he applied this idea to undergraduate students with some success, though limited by the economics of the situation.

Shaw was also always active in professional associations, although he questioned the effectiveness of library meetings. He was President of the Indiana Library Association (1938–39), the New Jersey Library Association (1962–63), and the American Library Association (1956–57), becoming an Honorary Member of that Association in 1971. He was active in committees related to all his many, varied interests but in the ALA especially in association reorganization. It is difficult to set priorities for a presidential year and equally difficult to assess the impact of an ALA President. In Shaw's case, his report to Council at the 1957 Midwinter Conference reflects both his expectations and his frustrations. He criticized ALA at that time for "not approaching its goals, . . . in fact, appearing to go in the opposite direction" ("The President's Report," *ALA Bulletin,* March 1957). In his year as President, however, Shaw could take satisfaction in having eliminated a considerable amount of work from membership record-keeping and in bringing about the consolidation of *Booklist* and *Subscription Books Bulletin.*

One of his colleagues at that time, looking back on his presidency, has stated that "Shaw maintained that A.L.A. was a sprawling, inefficient, wasteful, non-productive organization, badly in need of effective business procedures and more democratic membership control," typical of Shaw's usual incisive analysis. Some of his criticisms are still true today; others have been ameliorated by recent activists.

Shaw's printed publications make up a list of more than a hundred references from 1932 to 1972, with many more unpublished speeches, in-house reports, and the like remaining to be sorted and organized. In addition to those publications already mentioned, a few of his more significant contributions are worthy of special mention. As he was never averse to controversy, one of the more interesting examples arose as a result of Jesse Shera's article "Beyond 1984" (*ALA Bulletin,* March 1967). This exchange on the role of machines in libraries provided an opportunity for Shaw to reiterate his position that "it is just as stupid to hate machines as it is to love them. They are tools which may, used properly, help us to do the library and bibliographical jobs that we are supposed

to do, and if used improperly can waste our resources." Shaw's *Pilot Study on the Use of Scientific Literature by Scientists* (Scarecrow Reprint Corp., 1971), originally published in 1956, was constantly referred to in his teaching as a model for services by librarians and information scientists. His "CAT-CALL: Completely Automated Technique [for] Cataloging [and] Acquisition [of] Literature [for] Libraries" (*College & Research Libraries,* March 1970), in addition to illustrating his addiction to acronyms, also illustrates his forward-looking ability to advocate new and more economic ways of carrying out library procedures, in this case through cooperation with publishers and the book trade; some of the recommendations he made have since been realized, but others still await fulfillment.

Finally, almost on his deathbed, Shaw completed the translation and editing of the monumental work by Richard Muther, *German Book Illustration of the Gothic Period and the Early Renaissance (1460–1530)* (Scarecrow, 1972). In his own words, Shaw's work on this book was intended to illustrate how such early works—"verbose, using various German languages, and tough even if you are a German scholar"—can be reorganized with integrity to the original.

Shaw died in Honolulu on October 14, 1972. Until the end this amazing and unique scholar-librarian continued experimenting and breaking new ground. His greatest impact, however, will be felt through his students, especially those in his doctoral classes, who treasured his Shavian witticisms and aphorisms, crowded his classes to catch every word, and carry on his ideals of research and experimentation. A colleague, Lawrence Thompson, characterized him "as a globe-trotter, raconteur, wit, host, and in some dozens of other capacities . . . approaching the ideal of the Renaissance man" (*College & Research Libraries,* October 1954).

REFERENCES

Norman D. Stevens, editor, *Essays for Ralph Shaw* (1975), contains a tribute to Ralph Shaw (Lowell Martin), "Shaw and the Machine" (Theodore C. Hines), and an "Afterword: The Aphorisms of Ralph Shaw," as well as other more typical *Festschrift* articles by Rutgers doctoral graduates.

Mary V. Gaver, "Ralph Shaw at Rutgers," *Wilson Library Bulletin* (February 1973).

Stanley L. West, "Ralph R. Shaw: The Hawaiian Years," *Hawaii Library Association Journal* (December 1973).

Norman D. Stevens, "Shaw, Ralph Robert," *Dictionary of American Library Biography* (1978).

MARY V. GAVER

Shera, Jesse H.
(1903–1982)

Jesse Hauk Shera, educator, philosopher, and theoretician, considered that perhaps his most significant contribution to librarianship was not a "thing" but a concept—"the concept of librarianship as a totality, a unity in which all the facts are interrelated and interdependent." He consistently held that documentation and information science are an integral part of the totality of librarianship, that librarianship is the generic term, and information science contributes to the theoretical and intellectual base for the librarian's opera-

ALA

Jesse Shera

tions. The role of the librarian, he felt, is to act as mediator between users and graphic records, and "the goal of the librarian is to maximize the social utility of graphic records for the benefit of humanity."

Shera was born December 8, 1903, in Oxford, Ohio. He attended William McGuffey High School in Oxford and went on to Miami University, where he earned an A.B. with honors in English (1925). His graduate work at Yale culminated with an A.M. in English Literature (1927). He received a Ph.D. in Library Science from the University of Chicago in 1944.

Initially, Shera wanted to become a professor of English, but signs of the Depression were already visible when he completed his work at Yale. Opportunities to teach—especially English—were diminishing drastically; Shera felt even more restricted because of his somewhat impaired vision. Thus, when Librarian Edgar King offered him a job in Miami University's Library, he took it. Later King urged him to apply to library school. Shera was accepted at Columbia (King's school) in 1928 but instead decided to work as Bibliographer and Research Assistant of the Scripps Foundation for Population Research at Miami, a position he held until 1938.

Shera's glimmer of interest in the sociological aspects of librarianship—reflected in his master's thesis at Yale and subsequent doctoral work at the Graduate School of the University of Chicago from 1938 to 1940—grew more ardent through his association with Warren S. Thompson, Director of the Scripps Foundation, who held a Ph.D. in sociology from Columbia and had already made a name for himself in demography. So without professional training and education, Shera "backed into library work," as he put it.

At Chicago he encountered ideas about the breadth of librarianship that underscored and affirmed his own thinking. GLS offered a philosophical, theoretical, and interdisciplinary approach to library service. Louis Round Wilson, Douglas Waples, Carleton Joeckel, Ralph Beals, and Pierce Butler, to mention only a few, were among the library leaders he met there.

For several years after Shera completed his course work at GLS and before his degree was conferred, he worked in Washington: first as Chief of the Census Library Project at the Library of Congress, 1940–41, later as Deputy Chief, Central Information Division, Research and Analysis Branch, Office of Strategic Services (OSS), 1941–1944. His first year in Washington was frustrating because of the lack of a clear charge in his assignment, but the experience at OSS was significant. In addition to supervising a conventional library, picture collection, and "intelligence documents" (reports from various armed services), there was something called "censorship intercepts" (taken from the mail by the Office of Censorship). This amorphous mass of material had to be organized to provide easy access, necessitating experimenting with methods of retrieving information. Having had exposure at Scripps to tabulating machines, punched cards, and the like, Shera utilized these same devices for recording, storing, searching, and retrieving information through a system of assigning subject headings (or descriptors). Besides experimenting with these aspects of mechanization, Shera gained valuable experience in administration and an insight into goverment libraries.

While in Washington, Shera continued to work on his dissertation (which was later published) and solidified his friendship with Ralph Beals—a colleague from GLS who was Assistant Director of the Public Library in Washington, D.C., and who helped strengthen and widen Shera's grasp of librarianship. In March 1944 Beals became Director of the University of Chicago libraries and invited Shera to be Associate Director, first in charge of technical services, then of public services; when Beals was appointed Dean of GLS, he asked Shera to teach on a part-time basis. So Shera found his teaching career—though not in English literature—and in 1947 was appointed to the faculty of GLS on a full-time basis. There he taught courses on academic libraries, administration, cataloguing, American library history, and the theory of classification..

With his colleagues at GLS, he pondered the implications of the new technology on library service but would wait a few years before he did anything more concrete with his ideas than to attend conferences, to organize with Margaret Egan in 1950 a conference on bibliographic organization, and to become a charter member of the revived American Documentation Institute (ADI) early in 1952. Later that year Shera was appointed Dean of Western Reserve's School of Library Science (SLS) in Cleveland.

Shera's deanship was one of the most felicitous and fruitful of appointments, for both the individual and the institution. For Shera, Western Reserve provided a setting where he had strong moral support and had time to write and speak. For Western Reserve, especially the SLS, Shera initiated a new era. Probably Shera's greatest single contribution was the establishment of the Center for Documentation and Communication Research (CDCR), which developed a program of teaching and research in the emerging field of information retrieval. In November 1952 Shera and James Perry, then at Battelle Memorial Institute (BMI) in Columbus, agreed to work jointly in the new field and later proposed an international conference to be sponsored by BMI and WRU, held at the latter institution. When conditions soon changed at BMI and Perry left, Shera persuaded him and his associate, Allen Kent, to join WRU, and the CDCR was established in spring 1955.

The CDCR prospered. A three-day International Conference held in January 1956 and known as the PURK Conference (Practical Utilization of Recorded Knowledge) was a huge success, gathering some 700 attendees who represented business, industry, government, and academe, as well as the library world. This was the first in a series of significant conferences, international and interdisciplinary in their appeal, held in the following decade. Perry designed and constructed at WRU a "searching selector," and early in 1959 the University signed a contract with General Electric to build a high-speed electronic counterpart of it for the CDCR (delivered in 1961). Research contracts were made with various scientific societies and government agencies, notably the American Society for Metals to organize and abstract the literature of metallurgy. With all those successes in various operations, the original purpose of the CDCR to promote research in the development and evaluation of new and unconventional methods in information storage and retrieval was greatly diminished, although the educational program was enriched through new courses and seminars. Perry left WRU in 1960 and Kent in 1962. In 1963 Shera appointed A. J. Goldwyn, a senior member of the CDCR staff, Executive Director, and a reorganization of the work of the Center freed the staff from the burden of operations and made possible the creation of a Comparative Systems Laboratory.

In addition to guiding the work of the CDCR and participating actively in its conferences, Shera continued not only to carry the responsibilities of Dean and administrative head of the SLS but also to teach; to plan and execute the observances in connection with the 50th anniversary of the School in 1954; to participate in professional affairs, including holding important offices and making significant addresses; to serve as Editor of the official journal of ADI (1953–60) and of the WRU Press (1954–59); and to write a monthly column for the *Wilson Library Bulletin* (1961–68). Verner Clapp said, "Shera is too many for us." As Dean, Shera increased the number of full-time faculty and made it possible for graduates holding the Bachelor's in Library Science to earn the Master's through additional study and the writing of a master's paper. He also initiated a doctoral program that strengthened work in library and information science with emphasis on research.

Greatly concerned with the foundations of education for librarianship, he held a series of meetings with the faculty on the philosophy and theory of librarianship. In February 1956 he received funding from the Carnegie Corporation for a three-year study. In 1972 the book resulting from this study was published as *Foundations of Education for Librarianship*. It was delayed because of his many activites and other difficulties, but Shera said, "It is by the quality of the finished study that the wisdom of the original investment will be eventually judged." The book was awarded the Scarecrow Press Award in 1974.

Other activities in which Shera engaged during these years were many and varied. His contribution to the Ohio Library Association, for example, was substantial—helping to avert the closing of the State Library, establishing the Office of Executive Secretary for the Association, and initiating a Library Development Committee.

Shera retired as Dean of the CWRU School of Library Science in June 1970. His first year thereafter was spent teaching in the Graduate Library School of the University of Texas, and the next year he returned to Reserve to teach. He continued to teach, both at Reserve and at a number of other schools, sometimes for a week or two, sometimes for a quarter or semester. He continued to write—"It gets in your blood," he said—and to take an active part in professional affairs. [For this Encyclopedia, he contributed "Librarianship, Philosophy of," to the First Edition.] He continued to be in demand as speaker, editor, contributor, or consultant.

Shera became known for his wide range of interests and for his ability to talk with all kinds of people, on all kinds of topics, ranging from football and television to social epistemology and classical music. He won notice for his wit. When Alan Rees told Shera he had been asked to write a personality portrait of him for *Science Information News,* Shera replied, "It seems most appropriate that a publication known as SIN should take some notice of my retirement."

Shera died in Cleveland, Ohio, on March 8, 1982. The Jesse H. Shera Memorial Endowment Fund was established at CWRU to support an assistant professorship in library science education. After the closing of the School in June 1985, the assistant professorship no longer carried library science in its name but rather humanities. Thus Shera's name was perpetuated at CWRU and his broad interests and humanistic concerns recognized.

REFERENCE

The Shera Festschrift, *Toward a Theory of Librarianship: Papers in Honor of Jesse Hauk Shera,* edited by Conrad H. Rawski (1973), provides a bibliography of 381 of Shera's writings compiled through December 1971. Rawski later revised and updated it for publication in the *Encyclopedia of Information and Library Science.*

MARGARET KALTENBACH

Sierra Leone

Sierra Leone, a republic in West Africa, is bounded by Guinea on the north and east, Liberia on the south, and the Atlantic Ocean on the west. Population (1984 est.) 3,805,000; area 71,740 sq.km. The official language is English.

National Library and Public Library Services. In the absence of a national library, the Public Library System performs certain national library functions; for example, by the Publications Ordinance of 1962 the Public Library became one of two copyright libraries (the other is Fourah Bay College Library in Freetown) empowered to produce an Annual List of Publications. Though not a national bibliography, since it is not a comprehensive list of titles published in Sierra Leone, the list is useful in providing information mostly on titles published by the Government Printing Office. The Public Library also provides interlibrary loan service, which is used locally and internationally.

Academic Libraries. The principal academic library is at Fourah Bay College of the University of Sierra Leone. Established in 1827, the College became affiliated with the University of Durham, England, in 1876. By 1968 the College had been granted full university status. A University Act of 1972 established a unified university system connecting it with Njala University College (1964), an agricultural college that also offers degree courses in education. Their combined bookstock totals more than 160,000 volumes, with Fourah Bay housing some 125,000. Four of the university's faculties are at Fourah Bay: Arts, Science, Economics and Social Science, and Engineering; two exist at Njala: Agriculture and Education.

School Libraries. The British Council of the United Kingdom provided books and periodicals through its Book Presentation Programme for secondary schools. To ensure that materials provided under this program are maintained, the local British Council office encourages the appointment of library assistants who serve as the paraprofessional staff. The Ministry of Education provides the salary of library assistants who have acquired educational qualification and have participated in one of the University's library training courses.

Many secondary schools have also appointed teacher/librarians to be in charge of their libraries. These are qualified teachers, often graduates, who are required to attend short library courses organized annually by the University.

The Sierra Leone School Library Association produced minimum standards for secondary school libraries, which were endorsed and accepted by the National Conference of Principals of Secondary Schools.

Special Libraries. The establishment of special libraries is based on the provision of library facilities in government administrative departments and ministries. On the country's independence in 1961, foreign embassies and other parastatal institutions were established, many of which have libraries or information centers serving their individual needs. There are about 20 special libraries in addition to libraries in ministries. Many suffer from lack of funds for the purchase of materials, but the collections are useful.

The National Museum Library's basic collection was formed by Captain Butt-Thompson's Library, donated to the museum. This Library serves as a research library for museum users.

The Profession. The Sierra Leone Library Association was founded in June 1970 and the Sierra Leone School Library Association in 1975. The Sierra Leone Library Association holds workshops, seminars, and conferences to further the general development of libraries in Sierra Leone. It published *The Sierra Leone Library Journal* from 1974 (two issues a year) and a *Directory of Libraries and Information Service* in Sierra Leone. The Sierra Leone School Library Association operates through four regional branches. It holds an annual conference.

GLADYS M. JUSU-SHERIFF*

Singapore

Singapore, a republic on the southern tip of the Malay Peninsula in Southeast Asia, includes the island of Singapore and 50 islets. Population (1984 est.) 2,529,000; area 616 sq.km. The official languages are Chinese, English, Malay, and Tamil.

History. The earliest records are presumed to have been printed on palm leaf, bark, clay, sandstone, and other such materials but few examples have survived, the most notable being fragments of the undeciphered *Singapore Stone,* from about the 13th or 14th century and now in the National Museum.

The history of Singapore libraries began soon after the founding of modern Singapore by Sir Stamford Raffles in 1819 as a trading post of the East India Company. In 1823 Raffles founded the Singapore Institution as a school for promising students, with a library open to parents, teachers, and students. It became the forerunner of the Raffles Library, a subscription library that was eventually reconstituted as the National and Public Library of Singapore from 1958.

The earliest special library was that of the Botanic Gardens, founded in 1859. Most special libraries developed after World War II, particularly governmental libraries devoted to economics, foreign affairs,

The Sierra Leone Library Association

Central Library in Freetown, Sierra Leone, which performs certain national library functions.

education, and industry. There are also a few attached to foreign and regional organizations and to firms in the private sector.

The earliest academic libraries were those of the King Edward VII Medical College (founded in 1905) and Raffles College (founded in 1928), which later formed part of the University of Malaya (founded in 1949). Other academic libraries are those of the Institute of Education (for teacher training) and two polytechnic libraries, the Singapore Polytechnic (founded in 1958) and Ngee Ann Polytechnic (formerly College, founded in 1963). There is also a library attached to the Trinity Theological College.

A number of small school libraries were attached to government and government-aided schools before World War II. School library development was limited owing to priority for the attainment of universal free primary education, which was achieved by 1967, with resources being channelled for school buildings, textbooks and equipment, and teacher training. Pioneer efforts to develop and improve school libraries were made by the Library Association of Singapore from 1962 through courses for teacher-librarians, provision of booklists, and representations to the Ministry of Education. A Standing Committee on School Libraries that operated from 1970 to 1980 drew up recommended standards for secondary school libraries (1972) and for primary school libraries (1974); it organized courses for teacher-librarians and placed bulk orders for school libraries. The first full-time Library Development Officer was appointed by the Ministry of Education in 1973 and by 1984 the School Library Section consisted of five such officers.

The greatest incentive to the development of all types of libraries was the attainment of self-government in 1959, followed by independence in 1965. With the expansion of primary, secondary, and tertiary education since 1959, the literacy rate increased from about 50 percent in 1957 to 84.2 percent by 1980. Previously extant libraries were expanded and new libraries set up to meet educational, informational, and cultural needs.

National Library. The National Library of Singapore was established in 1958 following the passage of the Raffles Library Ordinance of 1957 under which the former Raffles Library, a subscription library, became a public and national library. It was called the Raffles National Library until 1960. The National Library inherited the legal deposit functions that had been in force since 1886 as well as the archival functions that had been added in 1938. With the National Archives and Records Centre Act of 1967, the archives were separated from the Library and administered as a separate department but continued to be housed in the National Library until 1970 and headed by the same Director until 1978. The National Library provides reference services, interlibrary loans and exchanges, reprographic services, and bibliographic services, including the compilation of the national bibliography, periodicals index, and various union catalogues. Its research collection on Southeast Asia is open to local and overseas scholars and researchers.

The National Library's collection totaled 1,860,872 volumes in Malay, Chinese, Tamil, and English in the fiscal year 1983–84, plus more than 97,000 items of special materials, including sheet music and scores, microforms, films, slides, tapes, and recordings.

Academic Libraries. The only university library is at the National University of Singapore. There are two technical colleges, the Singapore Polytechnic and the Ngee Ann Polytechnic (formerly the Ngee Ann Technical College); one teacher training institution, the Institute of Education; and a private theological college, Trinity College.

The University of Singapore was founded in 1949 as the University of Malaya, which amalgamated the former King Edward VII Medical College, founded in 1905, and the Raffles College, founded in 1928. In 1959 the University was split into two autonomous divisions, the University of Malaya in Kuala Lumpur and the University of Malaya in Singapore. From 1962, the former became known as the University of Malaya and the latter the University of Singapore. Nanyang University, founded in 1956 as

a Chinese-language institution, gradually included English as the medium of instruction for some courses. A policy of having its first-year students undergo courses jointly with University of Singapore students at the Bukit Timah campus took effect in 1978. In 1980 the two universities were merged to form the National University of Singapore. The National University of Singapore Library has more than 1,000,000 volumes (including more than 300,000 volumes of the former National University Library), in six constituent libraries—the Main Library; Chinese Library; Architecture, Engineering, and Law Libraries at the Kent Ridge Campus; and the Medical Library in the Faculty of Medicine building at Sepoy Lines.

Public Libraries. The National Library operates the public library system, which includes a central library, four full-time branches, three part-time branches, and 10 bookmobile points. The fourth full-time branch opened in 1982. Loans of books and periodicals totaled more than 6,000,000 in fiscal year 1983, including bulk loans to social welfare homes, community centers, and other agencies. The total number of registered users in fiscal year 1983 was estimated at 25.9 percent of the total population. Young people (aged 12 to 19 years) formed the largest group, with 36 percent of total membership, followed by children under the age of 12 (32.4 percent) and adults (31.6 percent).

School Libraries. All 146 secondary schools, including 11 junior colleges (which provide two years of preuniversity education), had centralized libraries (1985). Of the 274 primary schools (a school conducting both primary and secondary classes is treated as one primary and one secondary school), about 99 percent also have centralized libraries, while the remainder have classroom libraries. All new schools are equipped with libraries, including furniture, equipment, and initial bookstock. School libraries are also developing into resource centers with audiovisual resources and facilities as well as printed materials. An Instructional Materials Library also provides additional audiovisual resources on loan to schools.

In late 1982, a five-year grant of S$27,000,000 was provided to increase collections in school libraries to meet the quantitative standards of British

Libraries in Singapore (1982)

Type	Administrative units	Service points	Volumes in collections	Annual expenditures (Singapore dollar)	Population served	Professional staff	Total staff
National and Public	1	17	1,694,045	9,580,530	2,471,800[a]	83	347
Academic	5	17	1,366,980	8,800,208	40,507	64	318
School	401	--	3,687,787	2,676,865	467,141	7[b]	14[b]
Special[c]	52	63	1,105,308[d]	2,181,420[e]	90,218[f]	49	254[g]

[a]Estimate.
[b]Full-time staff in junior college libraries. Schools are staffed by teacher-librarians and are not included.
[c]1983 data given for one special library, 1984 data for another.
[d]Excludes data for one library. Periodicals included.
[e]In many cases personnel expenses not reported. No expense data available for nine of the special libraries.
[f]Excluded population served by five libraries.
[g]Part-time staff reported by two libraries have been counted as half-time workers.

Source: Replies to questionnaires.

school libraries. However, school library development is still handicapped by the lack of trained or additional manpower for the running of school libraries.

Special Libraries. There are 44 special libraries attached to government departments and statutory boards, including 16 government libraries staffed by professionals and a few others with subprofessional staff. Most serve only the staffs of their agencies, but the Department of Statistics Library is open to the public. In addition there are nine professionally staffed libraries of statutory bodies, including the Civil Aviation Authority and the Institute of Southeast Asian Studies, and 12 libraries attached to such foreign and regional agencies as the American Resource Center, the British Council, the Goethe-Institut, the Regional Language Center, the Colombo Plan Staff College for Technical Education, and the Regional Institute of Higher Education and Development. A few special libraries are attached to banks, newspapers and other firms in the private sector.

The Profession. The library profession is essentially a young and post-World War II profession as there were hardly any qualified librarians earlier.

The Malayan Library Group was founded in 1955 and succeeded by the Library Association of Singapore (LAS). At that time, there were only about a half dozen qualified librarians in Singapore, most of whom were expatriates from Britain, Australia and New Zealand, working mainly at the University of Malaya Library. Since then, the library profession has grown in keeping with library development in Singapore. The LAS membership (March 1985) includes 235 qualified librarians out of a total of 363 members, most of whom are Singapore citizens. Most of them have also been trained abroad, in Australia, Britain, Canada, New Zealand, and the United States. The largest number are employed by the government. Singapore lacks a library school.

The continued shortage of librarians led to provision of a basic part-time Postgraduate Course in Library and Information Science jointly organized by the LAS and the National Library from 1982. The first 21 students who completed the course were graduated in 1984.

Continuing education courses are organized by the National Library and the LAS. The Association publishes *Singapore libraries,* its official journal, annually as well as a quarterly *Newsletter,* a *Directory of libraries in Singapore* (latest edition, 1983), and other occasional publications such as conference proceedings. The Association works closely with the PPM (Library Association of Malaysia), with which it shares a common origin in the Malayan Library Group. Cooperation is fostered through a joint liaison council of the two associations as well as work in various bibliographical and other projects. The LAS and the PPM were also joint sponsors of the Congress (originally Conference) of Southeast Asian Librarians.

HEDWIG ANUAR

Somalia

Somalia is a republic on the Horn of Africa. It lies in the northeastern corner of Africa, bounded by the Gulf of Aden on the north, the Indian Ocean on the east, and Kenya, Ethiopia, and Djibouti on the west. It has the longest coastline in Africa, 3,000 km. Population (1984 est.) 5,423,000, 80 percent of whom are nomads; area 638,000 sq.km. The official languages are Somali and Arabic, but English and Italian are also used in communication.

History. Somali became a written language only in 1972. So written Somali literature is not yet abundant, in spite of the language's rich cultural past. Also, book development is of comparatively recent origin, and adequate printing and production facilities had yet to be organized in the mid-1980s. Paper requirements are met through imports, and research facilities are modest and mainly problem-oriented.

Library facilities in Somalia are in an early stage of development and literature resources in the country are, by and large, scanty, if not poor. Formal education and literacy training did not receive much attention in colonial times, and reading has been of little interest to the majority of the population who are nomads. The lack of qualified staff is a serious barrier to the systematic organization of libraries. The importance of library and information services for supporting national development programs is being recognized. Many government departments and agencies planned to set up library and documentation centers with the help of international organizations such as Unesco, the World Health Organization, and the World Bank. Other countries, among them the United States, the Federal Republic of Germany, Italy, and India, provided technical assistance in the field of librarianship and documentation.

There were no public libraries in 1984; at the most there were a few reading rooms in some regions of the country.

National Library Services. Plans for a national library were begun in 1976 on the initiative provided by Unesco. Proposals were made from time to time to construct a permanent building. The National Library holdings comprised only a few thousand items in the mid-1980s. Under library legislation of 1976, the Ministry of Higher Education and Culture was given responsibility for library development. In spite of the enactment of library legislation and formulation of guidelines for evolving a national library system, there was no strong commitment on the part of the country to undertake development of libraries. Under a five-year development plan (1982–86), however, a permanent building for a National Library was under construction.

Academic Libraries. The university library system under the Somali National University consists of a central library and seven faculty libraries. The central library, organized largely with Italian technical assistance, has a collection of about 28,000 volumes. Among the faculty libraries, the library of the College of Education has good facilities and resources, a result of Indian technical assistance and U.S. AID assistance to the college. The Library of the College of Education has 37,500 volumes, and it includes textbooks in multiple copies. The library of the Faculty of Medicine has 6,000 volumes. The library of the Faculty of Agriculture is also fairly well equipped. Generally speaking, the university library system is far from adequate for supporting instructional and research programs.

School Libraries. School libraries hardly exist. The Women's Education School Library has a collection of 3,000 volumes set up with UN assistance. The library of the American School has excellent facilities, but it is not a Somali institution.

Special Libraries. A few government agencies and ministries have libraries. The Documentation Centre of the Ministry of National Planning, formerly the State Planning Commission, was being developed in 1976 as a UN Development Programme/ Unesco project. This is the only documentation centre well established and organized to meet the documentation and information needs of the country. It caters to the needs of development planners, consultants, missions, ministry staff, students and faculty of the National Institute of Statistics and Applied Economics run by the Ministry of National Planning. The Documentation Centre has a collection totaling some 18,000 volumes and regularly receives about 250 periodicals. Every year around 3,000 documents are added to the collection. Documentation services includes rendering advice on setting up library and documentation centers in the country. The centre has been recognized by the Pan-African Documentation and Information System (PADIS) as a National Information and Documentation Center. It acts as a National Focal Point (INFOTERRA) for dissemination of environmental information.

The Somali Institute for Development Administration and Management, a UN and World Bank project, has a fairly well established library. The Ministry of Foreign Affairs has good physical facilities but lacks qualified staff. The Ministry of Industry developed a technical library in 1983 with the assistance of a United Nations Volunteer (UNV) Librarian. The U.S. AID Mission assists the center, which has a total collection of around 3,500 documents. Various other government ministries, teacher training, military, agricultural, and archival institutions were reorganizing library services in the mid-1980s.

The libraries of foreign missions such as those of the U.S., Italy, France, and India are used by the reading public. The Library of the United Nations Development Programme has a collection of publications on international organizations. The active role of UN Volunteer program and bilateral assistance in the field of librarianship led to establishment of several ministry and agency libraries in the country.

The Profession. Efforts were being made in the mid-1980s to establish a library association and a training center to meet the immediate problems of staffing. Under UN and Unesco auspices a few short-term training programs were conducted in 1979 and in 1980 and 1982. In-service training has been conducted regularly, but there remained a pressing demand for regular training, especially for middle-level staff.

G. THIMME GOWDA

South Africa

South Africa is a republic on the southern tip of Africa. It lies between the Atlantic and Indian oceans; Namibia (South West Africa), Botswana, Zimbabwe, Mozambique, and Swaziland lie to the north. Population (1980 est.) 29,000,000; area 1,140,943 sq.km. The official languages are Afrikaans and English/.

History. Libraries in South Africa have been in existence since the second half of the 18th century. The history of libraries throughout the 18th and 19th centuries is largely that of public libraries. Although the South African Library (now a national library) was founded in 1818 as one of the world's first free tax-supported libraries, the trend in South Africa throughout the 19th century was toward the formation of a number of subscription libraries; some 21 were founded in the Cape Colony between 1828 and 1861. A further six were established in the Natal Colony between 1851 and 1883; another four were formed in the Orange Free State between 1875 and 1897 and four in the Transvaal between 1878 and 1893. All in all, some 71 subscription libraries were formed in South Africa in those early years. Eight South African university libraries were established in the 19th century, as well as a number of school libraries (the latter mostly in the Cape) and six major special libraries.

The modern library movement in South Africa effectively dates from 1928, following the visit of two Carnegie Corporation commissioners (Milton Ferguson and S. A. Pitt); the first national conference on library affairs was held in 1928. It was followed in 1930 by the establishment of the South African Library Association and in 1937 by the Report of the Government's Interdepartmental Committee on the Libraries of the Union of South Africa.

Rural library services were developed in the 1940s following the establishment of provincial library services in each of the four provinces. After World War II there was also considerable growth in university libraries and of school and special libraries and information centers. The 1984 *Directory of Southern African Libraries* listed 1,348 libraries.

National Libraries. South Africa has three national libraries: the South African Library (Cape Town), the State Library (Pretoria), and the National Library for the Print Handicapped (Grahamstown). The South African Library, established in 1818, is the oldest of the three; it has Africana and rare book collections and has concentrated on its functions as a national reference and research library in the humanities. The State Library, founded in 1887, serves as the national lending library, coordinates interlibrary loan activities, maintains the Joint Catalogue of Books (the country's union catalogue), and published the *South African National Bibliography* from 1959. The State Library also developed a major microfiche publishing program. The third national library was founded in 1919 as the South African Library for the Blind and became a national library in 1969. It provides books in braille and on tape.

The country has five legal deposit libraries. Each receives a copy of every work published in the country. In addition to the South African Library and State Library, the three other legal deposit libraries are the Library of Parliament (Cape Town), the Natal Society Library (Pietermaritzburg), and the Bloemfontein Public Library.

Academic Libraries. Library services to academic staff and students are provided at all 22 universities in South Africa: Bophuthatswana, Cape Town, Durban-Westville, Fort Hare, Medunsa, Natal (Durban), Natal (Pietermaritzburg), the North, Orange Free State, Port Elizabeth, Potchefstroom, Pretoria, Rand Afrikaans, Rhodes, South Africa, Stellenbosch, Transkei, Venda, Vista, Western Cape, Witwatersrand, and Zululand.

The older university libraries are distinguished by important research and special collections: notable examples in Africana include the Killie Campbell Collection at the University of Natal Library, Durban; the Gubbins, Humphreys, and Jeffreys collections at the University of the Witwatersrand; the Hugh Solomon Collection at the University of Stellenbosch; and the Cory Library for Historical Research at Rhodes University. Because of their resources, the university libraries are major links in the interlibrary loan system.

The university libraries led in technological development. Some 15 university libraries had been computerized to a considerable extent by the mid-1980s; 8 university libraries were active in online information retrieval. The majority of university libraries are also involved with audiovisual technology. Well-planned and attractively designed library buildings are a feature of many of these universities.

Libraries also exist in teacher training colleges, technical colleges, and colleges for advanced technical education.

Public Libraries. In the South African context public libraries are best considered in two distinct categories, municipal and provincial libraries.

Municipal Libraries. All the larger cities have free, tax-supported public libraries. Some are quite highly developed, such as the Johannesburg Public Library, with its central reference library, some 24 suburban branch libraries, and important subject libraries for Africana, art, music, and local government. One of the largest and most important public libraries, it opens its doors to people of all races.

Provincial Libraries. The majority of public libraries are affiliated to one of the four Provincial Library Services—Cape, Natal, Orange Free State, and Transvaal—established in 1945, 1950, 1948, and 1942, respectively. They provide for the flow of books through regional centers to libraries that are housed and staffed by urban local authorities. In 1981 some 725 public library service points were affiliated with the provincial libraries. Media such as art prints, phonograph records, and films are a feature of these provincial library services.

School Libraries. These have undergone major recent developments in all four provinces of the country. Credit for their development in the Trans-

South African Library

South African Library, Capetown, established in 1818.

vaal belongs to the Transvaal Education Library and Audiovisual Ancillary Service, which has a central teachers' library of more than 200,000 books and which assists teachers with the choice, purchase, and binding of books in school libraries. It also has a number of full-time school library advisers who tour the provinces offering advice and guidance in school library administration. The Transvaal has combined school audiovisual centers and libraries to form media centers. Regular vacation courses are offered, and manuals are published from time to time. The Cape Provincial Education Department has a similar central school library organization, and in Natal Province the Education Department spearheaded the development of resource centers in schools; it established models in the larger cities. School library services to Coloureds, Indians, and Blacks (the South African official population designations) have also developed rapidly in recent years.

Special Libraries. South Africa had more than 660 special libraries in 1984. They are found in the public and private sector, in financial, industrial, and

Libraries in South Africa (1981)

Type	Administrative units	Service points	Volumes in collections[a]	Annual expenditures[b] (rand)	Population served	Professional staff	Total staff
National	3	3	47,435	1,711,904	- -	63.5	212
Academic	73	163[c]	210,238	22,190,015	- -	569	1,394
Public[d]	688	906[c]	1,303,792	34,136,368	- -	723	3,347
School	- -	- -	- -	- -	- -	- -	- -
Special[e]	418	661[c]	659,499	14,420,077	- -	474	1,088

[a]Linear meters (*not* volumes).
[b]Includes personnel and acquisition costs.
[c]Service points.
[d]Includes all public and provincial library services.
[e]Includes government libraries.

Source: *Directory of Southern African Libraries*, 1983.

mining circles; in government and semigovernmental corporations; in museums and art galleries; and elsewhere. Nearly 140, covering many subject fields, are attached to government departments and form part of the Library Services Branch of the Department of National Education.

Bibliographic Records. South Africa has well-developed current and retrospective national and subject bibliographies. There are excellent union catalogues in microfiche of book and periodical holdings and a computerized national register of manuscripts. The country also has a well-developed interlibrary loan and photocopying network, linking the resources found in all the major libraries and in many of the smaller libraries as well. In 1983 the South African Bibliographic and Information Network (SABINET) was established with a membership of 50 institutions. This network supports resource-sharing, computerization, and rationalization of library and information activities by providing for the national and international exchange of machine-readable bibliographic data.

The Profession. The South African Library Association was founded in 1930 and was succeeded by the South African Institute for Librarianship and Information Science (SAILIS) in 1980. In 1984 the Institute had a membership of 2,519; it is open to people of all races. The establishment of the Institute in 1980 thus effectively reversed the decision taken in 1960 to have segregated associations for Blacks, Indians, and Coloureds. The African Library Association, founded in 1964, is affiliated with the Institute, but continues to exist in its own right in order to carry on with its task of improving library services for the Black population of South Africa. The Institute functions through eight geographical branches; its newest is a subject division for law. The branches are coordinated through a central Administrative Council. The Institute organizes an annual conference and produces a quarterly journal, the *South African Journal of Library and Information Science,* published by the Bureau for Scientific Publications, and a monthly newsletter.

Sixteen South African universities offered programs of education for librarianship in the mid-1980s. They lead to the basic professional qualifications—either the four-year degree known as Baccalaureus Bibliothecologiae (B.Bibl.) or the post-graduate Higher Diploma in Librarianship (H.Dip.Lib.), which is pre-

ceded by a three-year degree in almost any field of study. Advanced degrees (Honours, Masters, and Doctoral) are also offered by many of these institutions. Between 1954 and 1982, 103 candidates obtained masters' degrees in librarianship and 22 obtained doctoral degrees in librarianship.

Some universities also offer specialized courses in school librarianship. The teacher training colleges in all four provinces include training in school librarianship in their general teacher training courses, some offering full specialist courses in school librarianship as well as the more general introductory courses. Diplomas designed to train paraprofessional staff in all aspects of the work of a modern library and information center are offered by the colleges for advanced technical education (technikons). Considerable progress has been made with continuing education. A variety of courses and a steadily increasing number of them have been evident in recent years.

REFERENCES
R. Musiker, *Companion to South African Libraries* (Johannesburg, 1985).

REUBEN MUSIKER

Spain

Spain, a monarchy in southwestern Europe, is bordered by France, Andorra, and the Bay of Biscay on the north, the Mediterranean Sea on the east and southeast, the Atlantic Ocean on the northwest and southwest, and Portugal on the west. Its territory includes the Balearic Islands (off the east coast) and the Canary Islands (off the west). Population (1984 est.) 38,435,000; area 504,750 sq. km. The official language is Spanish.

History. The first Spanish libraries were those of Visigoth Spain (5th–8th centuries), the best known of which was that of the Sevillian archbishops San Leandro and San Isidoro. In his book *Etimologías* ("Etymologies"), San Isidoro devoted a section to books and libraries. During the High Middle Ages, libraries, most of them with few books, were found predominantly in monasteries, although in Córdoba in Muslim Spain the Caliph al-Hakem II maintained a collection of 400,000 volumes. In the Late Middle Ages, the best libraries were found in universities, especially the University of Salamanca, where King Al-

Libraries in Spain (1981)

Type	Administrative units	Service points	Volumes in collections	Annual expenditures (peseta)	Population served	Professional staff	Total staff
National[a]	2	3	3,000,000[d]	74,751,000[d]	7,404[b]	100[d]	360[d]
Academic	332	626	8,462,000	837,422,000	319,740[b]	803	2,713
Public[c]	1,396	1,662	11,730,000	1,226,082,000	1,307,938[d]	805	4,648[d]
School	626	626	2,268,000[d]	87,837,000	211,768[b]	154	1,752

[a]Unesco reports 5,209,000 volumes (1979 data).
[b]Registered borrowers.
[c]1980 data.
[d]Data provided by author.

Source: Unesco, *Statistical Yearbook,* 1984.

fonso the Wise, who had established a large private library, provided library and research services. In the 16th century Cardinal Cisneros, after creating the University of Alcalá de Henares, provided the university with an important library; in Seville, Fernando Colón, son of Christopher Columbus, willed his library, the Biblioteca Colombina (Columbus Library), to the city's cathedral; and King Felipe II founded his famous library in the Escorial.

The National Library of Spain was founded in Madrid in 1712 by Felipe V as a public library; it belonged to the Crown until 1836, when it was nationalized and became a governmental unit. In 1896 it was moved to a beautiful and centrally located building covering some 40,000 square meters. In 1856 the School of Diplomacy was founded for the training of those having responsibility for the state libraries and archives; and in 1858 the Faculty of Archivists and Librarians was established, which still maintains responsibility for this area.

In 1939 the General Board of Archivists and Librarians was created within the Ministry of Education, but the Board was dissolved in 1972. Archives now belong to the General Board of Fine Arts and Archives, while libraries are under the General Board of Books and Libraries; both report to the Ministry of Culture. The General Board of Books and Libraries has administrative responsibility for the National Library, the Copyright Office, the International Exchange Center, and the National Documentary and Bibliographic Treasury, which inventories the collections and assures that materials are purchased as they appear on the market. The Hispanic Bibliographic Center oversees legal deposit and prepares the Spanish national bibliography. The Center for Bibliographic and Documentary Studies is primarily a center for training professionals. Provincial public libraries also report to the General Board of Books and Libraries, as did the public libraries associated with the National Reading Center until the approval of the new constitution in 1978. Those libraries, along with the 48 Provincial Coordinating Centers for Libraries and other governmental agencies, have been transferred to the 17 autonomous governments within the country.

National Library. The National Library of Spain contains the largest and richest collection in the country and provides the greatest number of services. It specializes in the humanities, most notably in Spanish culture. The Manuscript Section possesses more than 2,000 medieval codices, some of them dating from the 10th century. In addition to the many Latin and Castillian codices, there are also many excellent ones in Greek, Arab, and Hebrew. Two outstanding collections include codices adorned with miniature paintings, as well as manuscripts of Spanish comedies of the Golden Age, (16th–17th centuries) including original manuscripts of great dramatists such as Lope de Vega and Calderón de la Barca. The Cervantes Collection contains 14,000 books and 3,000 pamphlets. The Incunabula and Rare Books Section maintains a collection of 2,903 incunabula and 40,000 valuable, rare, and unique items. The African Section is important for its holdings on the modern history of North Africa. The Prints and Fine Arts Section features 200,000 prints and engravings and 14,000 drawings of special interests due to their themes or

Biblioteca del Palacio

their artists: Dürer, Velásquez, Rubens, Titian, Rembrandt, and Goya. The Music Section holds 100,000 musical scores and 170,000 records and cassettes; the Map Section, 100,000 maps and plans; and the Periodicals Section, 30,000 titles, of which about 15,000 are currently published.

In all, the National Library possesses more than 3,000,000 volumes. In 1983 the Library acquired 500,000 items, representing 100,000 volumes. Each year a half-million readers utilize more than a million works. More than 130,000 items are loaned annually, and the library's laboratories produce 1,300,000 photocopies and 400,000 microfilms for its readers. Half of the works acquired come in through legal deposit, an advantage the National Library has had since its creation.

Academic Libraries. Great differences exist among Spanish academic libraries in collections, annual acquisitions, financial resources, personnel, and services. The libraries of the 30 universities of the country (1986) occupy a special place among academic libraries. Although the library is considered a unit within the university and each has a director, in reality the libraries are fragmented into different school and departmental libraries; some serve professors exclusively. Even the libraries at the school level are more oriented to meeting the needs of the teachers than the interests of students, who usually lack places for study. Personnel are very scarce in all these libraries, although the number has grown in recent years. Of special interest are the libraries of the Complutense in Madrid, with more than 700,000 volumes, the Central University in Barcelona, and the universities in Valencia, Zaragoza, Vallodolid, and Salamanca. Vallodolid and Salamanca, established in the 13th century, are notable not only for the number of books acquired annually but also for the richness of their historical collections, including valuable medieval manuscripts and incunabula.

Public Libraries. Public libraries are organized into systems called Provincial Coordinating Library Centers, with a central library in the capital of the province and branch libraries in other towns. The

Library of the National Palace, where 300,000 volumes, including manuscripts and incunabula, are preserved.

centers are regulated by boards of trustees and are supported by donations from three sources: the autonomous government, the provincial government, and the municipality. It was difficult in the mid-1980s to obtain reliable data from the autonomous governments concerning the 48 provinces that have a Library Center, but in 1977, according to information provided by the General Board of Books and Libraries, there were 1,245 libraries containing a total of 6,500,000 volumes, with 13,000,000 readers using 18,300,000 volumes. The provincial governments of Navarra and Barcelona maintain their own systems; Barcelona's, which is more than 50 years old, is the more important. The central library contains more than 500,000 books, and its network of 75 branch libraries serves both the neighborhoods of Barcelona and the other towns in the province. In addition to the independent municipal libraries, there are networks of public libraries in a number of provinces supported by savings banks, the most notable of which is the library network of the Old Age and Savings Fund of Catalonia.

School Libraries. There are no school libraries in Spain worthy of the name, although in the Centers for Basic General Education and in the Spanish equivalents of American high schools some collections of books are sufficiently strong to qualify as libraries. The reason is simply that as of the mid-1980s there were no standards to govern their operations, nor were there personal or financial resources. The books that make up these collections consist of occasional gifts from the Ministry of Education.

Special Libraries. The libraries that support research in governmental offices and private firms are many and diverse. One of the most important of the special libraries is the consortium of the Superior Counsel of Scientific Research, with a total of 1,500,000 volumes distributed across two general libraries and 50 others that serve specialized centers in various fields of the sciences, technology, and humanities.

In the field of the humanities, the National Palace Library is especially notable, containing more than 300,000 volumes, among them valuable manuscripts, incunabula, and collections of fine bindings and drawings. Equally important are the libraries of the Royal Academies, especially the History Library, which contains 200,000 volumes and a large collection of historical manuscripts, and the Language Library, with 80,000 volumes. The Military Center Library has a collection of 300,000 specialized works on Spanish history. The libraries of the Church, especially the cathedral libraries, should be mentioned, although specific information on such libraries is scarce.

The Profession. Since the early years of the 20th century, library education has taken place at the University of Madrid, which assumed instructional responsibilities when the School of Diplomacy closed in 1900. Instruction was later offered in other universities. In 1915 the School of Librarians of Barcelona was established; it has been incorporated into the main university of that city. Professional education is also offered at the University of Granada and at the School of Bibliographic and Documentary Studies in Madrid; the latter is a continuation of the courses be-

gun in 1952 by the General Board of Archives and Libraries.

The Asociación de Archiveros, Bibliotecarios, Conservadores de Museos y Documentalistas (Association of Archivists, Librarians, Museum Curators, and Documentalists; ANABAD) was adopted as the name of the original association (ANABA) founded in 1949; new statutes provide memberships for documentalists. The Association organizes conventions and working meetings and publishes some books and a bulletin. Its membership was 1,485 in 1985.

REFERENCES
Hipólito Escolar Sobrino, *Historia del libro* ("History of the Book") (1984).
Escolar Sobrino, *Historia de las bibliotecas* ("History of Libraries") (1985).

HIPOLITO ESCOLAR-SOBRINO;
translated by EDWIN S. GLEAVES

Special Libraries

PURPOSES AND OBJECTIVES

Information service is the raison d'être of special libraries. While other types of libraries may encompass multiple objectives—education, recreation, aesthetic appreciation, or scholarly research—the major, and usually only, objective of a special library is the provision of information in support of the objectives of its parent organization. In 1916 John A. Lapp, a pioneer special librarian, wrote that "Undoubtedly one of the greatest problems of the time is to put the knowledge which we possess at work." From Lapp's statement came the motto of the Special Libraries Association (SLA), "Putting Knowledge to Work," a phrase that succinctly describes the purpose and objectives of the special library.

A special library may have its own goals and objectives regarding the resources, services, and clientele needed or desired to provide such services, but these goals are internal to the library. The parent organization usually has little interest in library service as an end in itself; rather, it is interested in the library and supports it as the means of getting the information it needs. If the special library is to exist, it must provide information—it must provide information more efficiently and economically than could be provided by alternate methods, and it must continually demonstrate to the management of its parent organization that it is doing so. If it does not accomplish this goal, it will not thrive; it may even cease to exist. The ultimate decision as to the practicability, efficiency, and value of the special library and the resources that will be allocated to it is made by the parent organization. Such a decision is not based on how well the library is meeting its own goals; it is based on how well the library is providing information service.

Special libraries exist in a wide variety of organizational settings. They are units of larger organizations whose purposes are usually other than the provision of education or library service. Special libraries are found in private business and industrial organizations such as banks, insurance companies, advertising agencies, public utilities, publishers, chemical and pharmaceutical manufacturers, petroleum producers, engineering firms, and the aerospace and automotive industries, to name a few. Others serve federal, state, county, or municipal government agencies. A significant number of special libraries are in nonprofit institutions such as hospitals and health agencies, social and welfare organizations, and museums, or are parts of trade and professional associations and societies.

Special libraries are often described (and usually associated or organized) along subject lines because they are limited in scope and oriented to a single subject or, more often, a group of related subjects that comprise a field of activity. Their scope is determined by the interests of their parent organizations. The library collects and organizes intensively in its primary subject areas, often at a depth impossible for other types of libraries. While the special library may collect some information peripheral to its primary interests, it depends on resources outside the library and parent organization for material that is little used or out of scope.

Special libraries serve a limited and well-defined clientele. Most frequently, the special library's clientele is limited to its parent organization, and within this limitation the clientele may range from the personnel of a single department to employees throughout the organization, sometimes to employees in other geographic locations. When the clientele is limited to a particular organization, special libraries often develop close working relationships with their users and are able to identify, not only on an organizational basis but also on an individual basis, the type of information needed and how it should be delivered. Thus services can be closely tailored to fit the needs and working habits of the users. Some special libraries, such as those maintained by societies and associations, consider the group's membership or anyone with a serious interest in the subject as their clientele. Most special libraries admit outsiders who have a need to use their resources, although such access is usually within the constraints of organizational and library policy and confidentiality of unpublished or internal materials in the collection.

The special librarian is viewed by some as a distinguishing characteristic of the special library, on the grounds that the special librarian's active role in information service is the main working asset of the library. The special librarian serves as a specialist in the literature of the subject, bringing to the organization professional expertise in the identification, acquisition, organization, evaluation, and interpretation of information. Without the expertise of the special librarian, the organization might have a library, but it would not have information service.

Another characteristic of special libraries that adds to the frame of reference in discussing their nature is size. Some special libraries have scores of employees and hundreds of thousands of volumes in the collections, but most of them are small in staff, space occupied, and size of collection. More than half of all special libraries are estimated to be one-person (librarian) or two-person (librarian and assistant or clerk) operations.

Problems of Definition. The precise definition of special library is one of the unresolved issues of librarianship. The literature is littered with definitions ranging from those based on the logic that the term fits all libraries that are specialized in some way (form, purpose, collection, ownership, or clientele) and therefore may include all libraries, through defi-

National Association of Realtors

nitions based on the presence of a combination of characteristics (special collection, special form, and/or ownership) to definitions that attempt a pragmatic, discrete delineation of a type of library. Even within this relatively narrow definition of the special library as distinct from a public, college and university, or school library, special libraries display such diversity and individuality that descriptions of characteristics and activities must be broad rather than specific.

Another issues arises with nomenclature. While many special libraries use the word "library," others use "information center" or "information service" to identify the unit's purpose more clearly or to avoid what some regard as a passive connotation of the word "library." In theory, "information center" indicates a greater range and depth of services and more advanced technology, but in practice one organization's library may be more sophisticated than another's information center. Whatever the organization calls its information unit, a modifier is commonly added to the noun in order to clarify the unit's scope or its primary clientele. Technical library, business information center, and research information service are typical examples.

U.S. Growth. Special libraries first began to appear in significant numbers in the United States in the first decades of the 20th century. They were a new form of library, sharply differentiated from the mainstream of American librarianship at that time in their singleness of purpose and in their novel methods of collecting and organizing materials. The early special libraries were largely isolated from each other and invisible to the library community until the founding of the Special Libraries Association (SLA) in 1909. SLA provided a focal point for the emerging special libraries and their leadership as the modern special library movement gained momentum.

Vast changes had begun to take place in American business and industry in the late 19th century. Organizations increased in size and complexity as business and industry evolved from smaller enterprises into larger corporations. Governmental units proliferated and increased in size and jurisdiction. In business and industry, interest in efficiency and scientific management developed. In government there was a strong move toward legislative and social re-

Library of the National Association of Realtors, Chicago.

773

form. Professional and trade associations and societies with strong interests in standards and education were formed. All of these interests required information to support their activities. An entirely new business and technical literature, often in nontraditional and ephemeral formats, began to develop along with increases in the collection and publication of statistics, the issuance of government regulations, the publication of financial reports, and the dissemination of business records.

Legislative reference libraries serving state and municipal governments were among the earliest modern special libraries, becoming models for intensive or "amplified" reference service. Special libraries in business and financial organizations next emerged to "manage" business and financial material and also developed high levels of information service for a clientele relatively unfamiliar with literature-based research.

The exigencies of World Wars I and II and the "information explosion" of the post-World War II years contributed to the continuation of an environment hospitable to special libraries. Following both wars there was an expansion in the need for scientific and technical research; research and development became increasingly institutionalized; and the number and size of research departments and organizations grew as team research supplanted individual investigation. This growth was paralleled by the increase and expansion of scientific and technical libraries to support the research and to cope with the ever-increasing flow of published results.

Although efforts have been under way since the late 1950s to develop census statistics for special libraries, there has never been an accurate count of their number. Problems of definition, diversity, and poor visibility because of small size or lack of participation in the library community form strong barriers to compiling accurate statistics for special libraries. Although some segments of the field—medical, law, and government libraries—have been surveyed, a large segment of the special library universe remains unexplored.

Such figures as are available are derived as by-products of directories. For example, the *American Library Directory* (37th edition, 1984) reports almost 9,000 special libraries, including law, medical, government, and religious libraries not affiliated with colleges and universities in the United States and another 1,000 special libraries in Canada. The other principal North American directory, *Directory of Special Libraries and Information Centers* (8th edition, 1983), lists more than 16,000 special libraries, including those affiliated with public and university libraries in the U.S. and Canada. Statistics on special libraries in other countries may be found in this Encyclopedia. Tables accompanying articles on countries give statistics reported by the countries and by Unesco on the number of special libraries by each country's definition.

Despite the inability to document the exact number of special libraries, growth has been one of their outstanding characteristics in the past, and all evidence points to continued growth. The factors that gave rise to the emergence of special libraries in the past have not disappeared; indeed, they are stronger than ever before and spreading in influence as new industries and new organizations evolve. The challenge of putting information to work continues to grow.

Other Countries. While the study of special libraries on an international scale is in its early days, the pattern of the U.S. special library movement has been repeated around the world as special libraries emerge in other nations where industrialization and increased research lead to the need for more information resources.

In France, Germany, the United Kingdom, and other industrialized nations, special libraries were being established in the first decades of the 20th century, and their rate of growth, particularly in the scientific and technical fields, increased to meet the demand for support of postwar research activities. As nations have continued to industrialize and increase their research efforts, special libraries have been established in government ministries and agencies, research institutes, and private business and industry in nations around the world, including the developing countries. Many U.S. corporations with international facilities have libraries in their foreign subsidiaries and affiliates. The interest in special libraries around the world was illustrated by the action of the International Federation of Library Associations (IFLA) in 1976, when the Special Libraries Section was elevated to Divisional status. The Division of Special Libraries currently comprises six sections—administrative libraries, art libraries, biological and medical sciences libraries, geography and map libraries, science and technology libraries, and social science libraries.

SERVICES TO USERS

A special library provides two basic types of information service. The first is that provided in response to requests for information and encompasses reference and research services. The second is information service in anticipation of need and encompasses services designed to keep the library's clientele up to date on new and current information—usually described as current awareness services.

The major effort in the special library is devoted to the dissemination of information through these services; all other functions support information services. Decisions about allocation of the library's resources, particularly staff resources, between acquiring and organizing materials and information service must take this fact into account.

Reference Services. Reference and research services range from answering simple reference questions to undertaking complex research and literature searches. The special librarian may assist users who wish to pursue their own search, but often the librarian, as information expert whose function is to save the inquirer's time, is the primary user of the library, locating requested information and transmitting it in the most useful form.

The special librarian's expertise in information handling may be applied to a reference question that requires a specific answer—a name, an address, a report, article, or book. Most special libraries devote a good deal of time to literature searches, either comprehensive or limited by time period, language, or other parameter. Unless the inquirer requests the information in a certain form, the librarian decides, on the basis of the results of the search and knowledge of the inquirer's preferences, how best to present the information—in a bibliography, copies of relevant materials, a memorandum, or a report.

Some special libraries offer translations, providing in-house service or obtaining them from outside sources. Many serve as the centralized source for ordering publications and subscriptions for the organization to eliminate duplication of materials.

Special librarians, particularly those whose primary clientele is located within an organization, develop a close working relationship with their users. They learn users' ongoing information needs and interests; they learn how to negotiate requests effectively; they learn how the inquirer wants the information delivered. The alert special librarian also tries to anticipate need so that information can be collected and, when desirable, disseminated in advance of need.

Current Awareness Service. Special libraries have developed a wide range of services to keep their clientele informed of new and current developments. Such services may be directed to the organization as a whole or tailored to specific groups or individuals. Some also make their current awareness services available to a secondary clientele—other offices or libraries in the organization, special libraries in other organizations, or fee-paying subscribers.

Routing of current periodicals is one of the most common functions of the special library. The library periodically surveys its clientele as to which periodicals they wish to see on a regular basis, then circulates them to readers as issues arrive. Acquisition bulletins, another common service, may be simple lists of new materials or may include annotations or abstracts. Subject-oriented abstract bulletins, news summaries, and digests are other current awareness services offered by the special library. They may be based on the library's own abstracting or obtained from commercial services or databases. The indexes some libraries prepare to cover unindexed periodicals may be used within the library or may be published as bulletins, combining citations with order forms for users to request indexed materials.

Current awareness may be targeted to individual users through the use of computer-based Selective Dissemination of Information (SDI) systems. In SDI systems, incoming information is matched with individual user-interest profiles; the result is a personalized service for each user. SDI may operate through in-house databases or be obtained from online databases or outside SDI services.

Levels of Function. The nature and extent of information services offered by the individual special library varies according to the working habits and needs of its primary clientele and according to its own resources in staff and collections. If the clientele is very large in proportion to library staff, or if the clientele is made up of users who as part of their jobs perform their own research, then the library staff is generally engaged in ready reference, fact checking, advising on research problems, or conducting research involving unfamiliar subjects or use of outside resources. On the other hand, if the library itself has primary responsibility for documentary research and the provision of information, then its staff themselves become the library's primary users and function at a more intensive level of service.

Harvard Law Art Collection

Langdell Reading Room, Harvard Law School, Cambridge.

Three functional levels are sometimes used to describe the range of information services provided by the special librarian. At the minimum level, the librarian disseminates information and materials, answers reference questions, directs users needing detailed or research information to appropriate sources, and handles such simple current awareness services as periodical routing. At the intermediate level, the special librarian also offers literature searches, bibliography preparation, selection and transmittal of research materials, and additional current awareness services such as acquisition bulletins. At the maximum level, the special librarian adds to or substitutes for the activities already described the synthesis and evaluation of information into written form, preparation of critical bibliographies, evaluative, comprehensive literature searches, and more complex current awareness services such as SDI systems. The information center concept is best exemplified at the maximum level of service.

Most special libraries do not function at a single level of service. The individual library operates situationally at various levels, depending on the varying needs of its clientele. Nevertheless, the special library's ultimate goal is to function at the maximum level of service when given the opportunity and resources to do so.

COLLECTIONS
Special library collections are working collections to support information services, with emphasis on current information and the amount of retrospective material determined by need and use patterns and avail-

able outside resources. While some collections may concentrate on a single format such as pictures, clippings, or maps, special library collections typically include a wide variety of formats. Some, particularly those in scientific and technical areas, will have collections that are largely in the traditional formats of books, journals, and technical reports. Other special libraries' collections are significant for their files of information from business records and ephemeral material. Although it may be physically small, the special library collects in great depth in its primary areas of interest and includes materials that may not be found in other types of libraries.

Some of the larger subject groupings of special library collections include: advertising and marketing, aerospace, biological sciences, business and finance, chemistry, education, engineering, environmental sciences, food and nutrition, insurance, law, metals and materials, nuclear science, petroleum, pharmaceuticals, physics, public utilities, legislative reference, social welfare, and transportation. Even within these broad groups, individual libraries display a wide diversity; a transportation library, for example, may cover all forms of transportation, or focus on automotive, air, railroad, or urban transportation, and further specialize by technical, business, or consumer aspects. Insurance libraries may concentrate on one or more branches of insurance—life, property, health, casualty—and such related areas as actuarial science, insurance law, marketing, and insurance education for employees.

Libraries that serve such organizations as accounting firms, advertising agencies, banks and other financial institutions, law firms, and consultants in many fields will encompass not only accounting, advertising, banking, or law but also the subject areas represented by present and prospective clients.

The subject scope of the collection is not static; it is dynamic and changing. As new products or ser-

Information desk at the National Agricultural Institute's library, Chapingo, Mexico.

United Nations

vices, mergers, or the extension of interdisciplinary methods affect the parent organization, they also affect the subject scope of the special library. The special librarian must therefore be constantly alert to possible new areas and the changing interests of the organization so that the library's collection can respond to changing demands for information.

Special library collections have three major components: the first is published information, the second internally generated information, and the third the information available from sources outside the organization.

Published Information. In most special libraries, periodicals provide the most up-to-date information; in some, they provide the only information. Although books are important in some special libraries, periodicals often form a large and important segment of the collection. Periodical collections include not only research journals but also the many business and trade magazines and newsletters published for specialized audiences.

Special (or "vertical") file materials are another major special library resource. These collections bring together large and small bits of information from such varied sources as clippings, pamphlets, speeches, statistical compilations, advertising brochures, sales literature and samples, trade catalogues, annual reports and financial statements, patents, and government documents.

Technical reports—the results of public and private research and development—are an important and sometimes overwhelming part of the special library collection, especially in scientific and technical fields. Such reports figured largely in the information explosion of the post-World War II period, when special libraries had to scramble frantically to impose some sort of order on the acquisition and control of technical reports. Special indexing and cataloguing techniques were developed, with many special librarians using their organizations' computers to assist them in this effort. The situation has improved since the mid-1960s as various commissions studied producers', users', and governments' needs for bibliographic control and information transfer. Since that time, a number of federal, contract, and private technical information centers and abstracting and indexing services have been established to improve control of and access to reports in scientific and technical fields. A notable development in the control of reports was the creation in 1970 of the National Technical Information Service (NTIS), an agency of the U.S. Department of Commerce. The National Aeronautics and Space Administration's Scientific and Technical Information Facility (NASA/STIF), the Defense Technical Information Center (DTIC), and the Department of Energy's Technical Information Center (DOE/TIC) are other major federal document centers. The Educational Resources Information Center (ERIC) acts as a clearinghouse for the literature of education including library and information science.

Other formats are also found in special library collections, including maps, pictures, audiovisual materials, patents, technical standards and specifications, and realia. Microforms may be used to add retrospective resources and to conserve space. Machine-readable databases have become valuable additions to the libraries' information resources.

Internal Information. The second major component of the collection is information generated internally: research reports, technical memoranda, laboratory notebooks, working papers, correspondence, house organs and newsletters, sales literature, and company and competitive advertising. The library usually makes a conscious decision either to be responsible for all or part of the organization's internal material or to collect only such information as is germane to its primary clientele. The library in a research department may be responsible for that department's complete file of research reports and working papers but may collect from other departments only those reports that are useful to its own department. Some special libraries maintain the corporate archives and some are responsible for records (or information resource) management, the supervision and control of all internal records. With the advent of micro- and minicomputers and progress in database design, some special libraries have expanded their functions to include internal database management.

The presence of internal and proprietary material in the special library is sometimes a barrier to outside use. Such material is either removed before access to the file is granted to outside users or is completely isolated from the general collection and thereby kept confidential.

Outside Resources. Use of resources outside the organization is the third component of the special library collection. While the library may strive to be self-sufficient in its primary subject area or in heavily used materials, it depends on outside resources for information and materials outside its scope. It is said that a special librarian's best friend is the local directory of special libraries; indeed, informal cooperation with other special libraries is a long-standing tradition in special librarianship. Special libraries also use public, academic, and research libraries through more formal interlibrary loan procedures, purchasing memberships or company registrations, paying user fees, and participating in multitype library cooperatives and networks. They also seek information from research organizations, professional and trade associations, individual subject experts, and even commercial firms providing information, the so-called information brokers.

Organization. Special libraries employ a wide spectrum of methods of organization, with an emphasis on flexibility and adaptability to changing needs. Though simple methods of organization are used wherever possible, special libraries will also develop complex and specialized systems where needed. Organization may be the key to efficient use of the collection, but it must also be balanced against the priorities of information service.

Special libraries with small collections and limited staff usually operate at a minimal level of organization. Material is arranged in a simple, logical order—books by author or subject, periodicals by title and date, vertical file materials under broad subject headings, and other material similarly. The catalogue, if there is one, may be limited to one or two entries per item. As collections grow and the need dictates, more formal methods of organization may be employed. The card or book catalogue will become more complex; catalogue records may be obtained from an online bibliographic source such as OCLC. Online catalogues and databases of library holdings may be developed.

Some special libraries adopt or adapt one of the major classification systems, the Dewey Decimal or Library of Congress Classification. Others may use a classification designed for their subject area. Although some special libraries have developed their own classification systems, most find an existing system, with adaptation or expansion, to be suitable.

For alphabetical subject analysis, special libraries can select from one of the large, general subject heading lists, from the many specialized subject heading lists and thesauri, or, again, develop their own. However, even when a thesaurus is available in their subject field, individual special libraries generally choose to adapt and supplement it in order to achieve maximum effectiveness for their areas of interest and to coordinate with their own organization's terminology.

As in information service, special libraries seldom function at a single level of organization, nor do they process each item to the same degree; rather, the maximum organizational effort is devoted to the in-depth subject analysis of the most important information. Any one item, no matter what its form, will be given precisely the amount of processing it needs to be retrieved most efficiently, according to the importance of the information it contains, its probable use, the length of time it will be retained, and the availability of published guides to it. The decision as to what to retain and process is as important as what to acquire. Weeding of outdated, nonessential information goes on constantly, and retention policies are used to control the size of the collection. In spite of such measures, however, collections do tend to grow rapidly; one estimate suggests that a newly established special library will double in size and space requirements within five years.

Another consideration that affects the special library's organization is who actually uses it. If most of the actual physical use is by the library staff itself, many organizational shortcuts can be taken. On the other hand, if a large number of users come to the library, the organization must facilitate their access. Although some adopt an overall organization for the entire collection, most special libraries consist of separate segments, each arranged according to the need and use factors described above.

Retrieval. Abstracting and indexing are of paramount importance in the special library. Special libraries have a long tradition of indexing, first because there were no indexing or abstracting services in their areas of interest and later, as indexes became available, to supplement commercially produced coverage and to cover internal information. Special librarians were among the first to develop newer information retrieval methods in both manual and computer-based applications.

Today, the still increasing availability of commercial abstracting and indexing services in both print and database form has brought some degree of coverage to most subjects. Many special libraries continue their own abstracting and indexing, however, and abstracting and use micro- or minicomputers to construct databases to meet their needs more specifically than external sources can. The purpose of these databases may be to provide deep analysis of important information, to focus on a new subject of vital interest to the organization, or to track material in publications important to the organization but not covered by commercial indexes. Much internal material is indexed in depth, and while reports are most often treated in this way, the library may also index memoranda, minutes, house organs, and other internal documents. A few special libraries make their indexes and databases available outside their parent organizations on a subscription basis.

ADMINISTRATION

Special library administration has two major aspects. One is the library's administrative relationship to its parent organization; the other is its internal administration.

The special library's place in the structure of its parent organization varies according to what part of the organization it serves and how the organization is structured. If the library has been established to serve the entire organization, its optimal location is one directly accessible to its clientele and is one from which it can build and maintain effective, direct communication with all departments. Personnel thus have direct access to the library and need not go through administrative channels to request service. Similarly, the librarian has direct access to the clientele. The library whose primary clientele is a single department or division typically would be located with that department.

The special library may be directly under the cognizance of top management, with the librarian reporting directly to the chief executive officer or to an administrative assistant to that officer. More often, whether it is a separate department or a subunit of a larger department, the library will be part of a division such as research and development, administrative services, public relations or public information, editorial, or information services, reporting to the senior executive in charge of that area.

In addition to the significance that organizational location holds for effective service and communication, the library's place in the hierarchy and its reporting channel are important for facilitating general communication with decision-makers in the organization. The special library must not only provide an effective information service, but also be able to demonstrate to management that it is doing so and, further, must educate management about the resources required to provide such service. While its users may be in the best position to appreciate and understand the library and its needs, they frequently are not among those who determine its support.

The special library within the research and development, editorial, or management information services area operates in a close relationship with those who use information, appreciate its value, and recognize the library as a tool in their work; the executive in charge is likely to be in a good position to understand and endorse the library's needs. On the other hand, the library that is under administrative services (along with the mail room and the cafeteria), or that reports to an administrative assistant, may have direct access to the decision-making level but may be reporting to an executive who has little direct experience with library service and only a vague idea of its contribution to the organization.

Although the practice is not widespread, some special libraries have an advisory committee drawn from the organization's personnel or membership. Advisory committee functions vary; some aid in selection of materials while others may advise on policies, objectives, and administrative matters.

Although most organizations maintain one library, some large organizations have two or more separate libraries. When divisions of an organization are geographically separate, libraries may be established in the various locations. Some organizations consolidate business, technical, legal, and other subjects in one library, but a more common pattern is to provide separate libraries, conveniently located near the appropriate departments. These intraorganizational libraries may operate autonomously, cooperating with each other on an informal basis, or they may be formally coordinated by a senior information officer. A survey of special libraries in large industrial corporations identified five corporations with more than 20 libraries each; the largest maintained 32. One firm had 25 libraries, of which 23 were scientific and technical and 2 were business libraries; of the firm's libraries, 21 were in the United States, 2 in Canada, and 2 in other nations.

Finance. In a few cases, the parent organization may qualify for a grant or other outside assistance, and the special library may obtain some outside funding. In general and for the vast majority of libraries, however, funding comes from the library's parent organization, and accounting and budgeting procedures are set by the organization. Although budgeting and costs are widely discussed by special librarians, concrete cost figures for establishing and maintaining special libraries have not been gathered on a regular basis. The great diversity of budgeting procedures and differing levels of service make standardized reporting difficult, and many libraries are prohibited from revealing such information.

Virtually all organizations classify the cost of the library as an overhead or indirect expense, making the library budget vulnerable to pressures to reduce overhead. A common method of distributing library costs is to allocate library expenses to departments or budgetary units within the organization. The special library may allocate or charge some of its expenses directly; the library in a service organization, for example, may be able to charge project research time to a client, thus transforming part of the overhead to a direct cost. Such charges may include library overhead or may be limited to staff or computer time. While this practice results in a reduction of the cost of the library as an overhead expense, it also increases pressure on the library to bill as much of its time as possible and, correspondingly, to spend less time on nonbillable but still important activities. A few libraries are able to recover some costs by marketing their research services, publications, or databases to outside users.

A special library's operating budget, like that of any other library, ordinarily includes the categories of personnel, materials and database fees, equipment and supplies, and professional dues and meetings. The library may or may not also be responsible for such overhead costs as space, utilities, and other office services. Personnel has generally taken 60 to 80 percent of the special library budget; materials, the major part of the rest. Recent studies of scientific and technical libraries and information centers indicate that this proportion is changing as computer resources figure larger in the budget.

Staff. The special librarian is at once a manager, a librarian, and a subject specialist. In addition to library and subject skills, the special librarian must have a strong motivation toward service, flexibility in procedures, and aggressiveness in promoting the library to the organization. Managerial skills are needed because the librarian functions both as an executive in the organization and as a manager of the library staff. One of the continuing debates in the field is whether the special librarian should be primarily a subject specialist, a librarian, or both. Ideally, the librarian will have a library degree and some education or experience in the organization's areas of interest. Although the special librarian is equipped through a library education to obtain a working knowledge of a subject and its literature, organizations often feel more comfortable with a subject specialist. The organization understands what the subject specialist knows; it is less likely to understand what the librarian knows. The issue of professional staffing commonly arises in organizations seeking to establish a new library, in some smaller special libraries, and sometimes in larger libraries adding professional staff.

About half of all special libraries fall into the categories of one- or two-person libraries; about 65 percent have three or fewer staff members. In the small special library, the librarian must assume all professional responsibilities. Additional professional staff may include reference personnel, cataloguers, indexers, abstractors, literature specialists, or translators. The minimum staffing level for a special library is considered to be one professional and one clerical person. In larger libraries, a ratio of one professional to two clerical assistants may be found, but the ratio varies considerably, depending on the nature of the library's services. The clerical assistant in the small special library works closely with the librarian and frequently gets considerable on-the-job training in reference work, in addition to performing clerical duties. As staff size increases, specialization at the clerical level may evolve into such positions as secretary, acquisitions clerk, file clerk, or typist.

Space. The special library's physical facilities depend on the space the organization itself occupies, and there is often considerable competition within the organization for what may be very expensive floor space. The library's physical facilities should be designed in relation to its role, how it achieves its goals, how its staff operates, and what the future is likely to hold. The contents of the library have a direct bearing on space and furniture requirements, as does the amount of time devoted to the various administrative, bibliographic, information, and clerical functions. The library's space must be physically contiguous and separate from other office uses. While the special library may occupy only a few thousand square feet of floor space, the not infrequent practice of scattering shelving down hallways or in conference and storage rooms ultimately serves to reduce efficiency, accessibility, and control. (An exception is found in records management, where active records may be located throughout the organization and less expensive off-site warehouse space may be obtained for storage of little-used records.) A major factor in space allocation is the nature of use; the library that is primarily used by its staff will allocate less space for browsing and study areas than will the library in which users frequently come in to do research or reading. Finally, space for growth must be provided. Even though the special library weeds its collection of unused, outdated materials and may turn to compact shelving or microforms to conserve space, its collection still grows, and adequate space for expansion must be allowed.

MEASUREMENT AND EVALUATION

The ultimate measure of the special library's value is its continued existence. In profit-making and nonprofit organizations alike, there are competitive pressures for available resources. The library, along with other overhead services, is particularly vulnerable to such pressures, and the special library is continually challenged to demonstrate its contributions. This challenge is made even more difficult in light of the fact that while the lingua franca of many organizations is economic, the economics of information are still but dimly understood. The major concern of both the special library and management has been to evaluate the library and its services according to its effectiveness in meeting its clientele's information needs.

Statistics. Traditional statistical measures of library activity gathered by some special libraries include collection size, processing volume, number of users, and reference questions answered; they are useful measures of library efficiency and workload, but do not reflect the depth, quality, relevance, or effectiveness of information service. Such statistics are time-consuming to collect and are given relatively low priority in the special library with only limited staff time.

Special library collections do not lend themselves well to statistical description. Although some may have significant book collections, in many the journal is predominant, so the size of the periodical collection is far more significant. For many special libraries the number of special file drawers, technical reports, pictures, maps, or clippings may be more significant. In any case, size of the collection and growth rate are not as important as the relevance of the materials and the use made of them. Counts of books catalogued, material processed, or number of items indexed or abstracted may indicate that the library is busy but mean little to management. Similarly circulation statistics (where there is a formal circulation system) do not reflect either use of materials in the library or the output of information in the form of spoken messages, written memoranda, or reports, all of which may be more significant means of information transfer.

Statistics on the number of users and of reference and research requests do relate more directly to information service and, to some extent, indicate who is using the library and what type of information is being sought. The special library can usually identify its potential user population as the total number of employees or members of the organization to whom services of the library are available. User statistics are

Fort Concho Museum Library

Fort Concho Museum Library in San Angelo, Texas. It is housed in one of eight surviving officers' quarters at what is probably the best preserved 19th-century army post in the United States.

ing policies and procedures, system vocabulary, search procedures, and system/user interaction. They have not yet, however, been widely adopted by special libraries and information centers.

The ideal measure of the special library or information center's worth would be cost-benefit analysis. Cost-benefit has been successfully applied to certain special library operations and to specific instances of information service, but while the total cost of maintaining the special library can be identified, it has not yet been demonstrated that it is possible to identify the total benefits of information service in economic terms. Although in some instances the special library may be able to say that the location of a specific bit of information was worth x dollars saved in research costs or that the expenditure of y dollars of library staff time saved a greater dollar value of the user's time, it is not so easy to put a dollar value on such benefits as the general contribution to the knowledge of the staff, improvement in productivity resulting from this knowledge, or time and resources freed for other activities—in other words, the general contribution to business efficiency.

Objectives. Although the diversity of special libraries all but precludes comparison among libraries and development of standards, it has long been recognized that successful special libraries do have certain elements in common. These elements are described in the SLA publication *Objectives for Special Libraries,* first issued in 1964. The *Objectives,* designed to serve as guidelines for both management and librarians, describe the qualities found in the objectives, staff, collection, services, physical facilities, and budgets of successful special libraries. Qualitative rather than quantitative, the *Objectives* provide a conceptual framework for both the design and the evaluation of special library services.

COOPERATION

Cooperation is one of the cornerstones of special librarianship. Pioneer special librarians at the turn of the century recognized that effective and efficient information service depended on extending an individual library's resources through cooperation with other libraries. The specialized library associations proved to be a strong force in facilitating cooperation and in providing leadership in cooperative projects. The SLA and its geographic Chapters and subject Divisions engage in various resource-sharing activities; the most common are exchange of materials and preparation of directories of special libraries and of union lists of serials. Within six months of its founding, the SLA had published its first directory of special libraries (April 1910); over the next 40 years, it published four more editions. Although after the mid-1950s other directories began to serve as national inventories of special libraries, the SLA membership directory continues to be a valuable resource. Local and regional directories of special libraries and their subject specializations are still an important part of Chapter activities. Boston special librarians produced the first regional directory in 1920, and since then most SLA Chapters have done likewise. A number of Chapters have produced local and regional union lists of serial holdings in special libraries, and many coordinate the exchange of materials through duplicate exchanges.

somewhat more difficult to collect since few special libraries have any type of registration and the count of users must take into account on-site use, telephone or written requests, those on routing and distributions lists, and possibly electronic mail or database use. In addition, reference and research statistics, to be at all meaningful, must be based on the relative levels of service provided—how much reference, how many literature searches, bibliographies, memoranda, or reports, and so on.

User Surveys. Special librarians are able to evaluate the effectiveness of information service on an informal basis. Because they have day-to-day interaction with users, they can evaluate how well the library is meeting the information needs of the users and thereby adjust services to meet changing needs. Formal user surveys are undertaken from time to time; such a survey may be conducted by the library itself, management, or an outside consultant, using such methods as interviews or questionnaires. A typical survey covers services used and satisfaction with the quality, relevance, and promptness of service.

The orientation of the user to the library and its information services—obtained either by statistics of use, user surveys, or informal response—is the most generally applied method of evaluating the special library's contribution to the goals of the organization, on the theory that if the special library meets or exceeds the demands of its users, it is providing effective service.

Since the early 1970s there has been interest and research in the use of cost-effectiveness and cost-benefit analyses to evaluate special libraries and information systems. Cost-effectiveness focuses on the relationship between level of performance and the costs of achieving that level; cost-benefit refers to the relationship between the benefits of a particular product or service and the costs of providing it. Research into cost-effectiveness measurement has emphasized the criteria of coverage, recall (the ability to retrieve wanted items), precision (the ability to avoid unwanted items), response time, and amount of effort required of the user. These measures have been developed for single information systems and to compare alternative methods in system coverage, index-

In the United Kingdom, functions and activities comparable to those of SLA are conducted by Aslib, founded in 1924 as the Association of Special Libraries and Information Bureaux. With more than 2,000 institutional and individual members, Aslib publishes several journals and a variety of monographic and reference works. It sponsors frequent seminars, workshops, and training courses.

The need for bibliographic access and control of technical, nontraditional, and specialized subject literature has also been the focus of cooperative efforts. The *Industrial Arts Index* (predecessor of the *Applied Science & Technology Index*) and *Public Affairs Information Service* both had their genesis as cooperative efforts of special librarians. SLA's Engineering-Aeronautical Section began an index of translations in 1946 that evolved into the Translations Center at the John Crerar Library. SLA units also initiated such publications as *Unlisted Drugs, Technical Book Review Index, Scientific Meetings, Dictionary of Report Series Codes,* and countless bibliographies published in *Special Libraries* and as monographs.

Traditionally, informality has been the predominant characteristic of special library cooperation in resource sharing. Such informality has been possible because local groups of special librarians have tended to be small and closely knit, forming "old boy networks" (a phrase that has been described as a complete anomaly, since these old boy networks have forever been created, nurtured, and ruled by the "old girls"). Within these networks special librarians can operate, with some discretion, even though their parent organizations may be in competition. Despite the development of more formal single and multitype networks, informality will probably continue to characterize the cooperative relationships special librarians maintain among themselves, simply because informal cooperation has worked so well.

At the most basic level, cooperation in resource-sharing is on an ad hoc basis, with no long-term commitments. In a number of instances, however, special libraries in physical proximity, ranging from a region of several counties to an area as small as a complex of office buildings, may develop more lasting relationships that are usually based on union lists, sharing responsibility for long-term retention of journals, or, more recently, bibliographic utility user groups.

Cooperative relationships have also been initiated by special libraries within a single company. Although some very large organizations with multiple special libraries in various locations sometimes provide a centralized organizational structure for their library and information services, more often they do not. In such instances the special libraries serving the various units will develop cooperative relationships to share resources and coordinate activities.

Subject-oriented networks have also emerged. An example is the Textile Information Users Council, which works to develop and improve information services related to the textile industry. Its members represent fiber producers, chemical and dyestuff manufacturers, textile companies, textile machinery manufacturers, trade associations, research institutes, and academic textile schools.

Special libraries, despite their contributions to librarianship and access to specialized literature, were for a long time a little known and poorly understood resource, separated from the mainstream of librarianship. In the 1970s significant moves were made to bring special library resources to bear on total information resources and to show the special library to be an effective part of the library community.

In the United States special libraries followed the proceedings of the various government committees and commissions concerned with scientific and technical communications and libraries. Nevertheless, until the establishment of the National Commission on Libraries and Information Science (NCLIS) in 1970, special libraries were often bypassed, except in the role of users, as active contributors to national information resources.

The role that special libraries will play in networks is still evolving, just as networks themselves are still in the process of evolution. However, as experience accumulates, a clearer picture of special libraries' role in and contributions to networking is beginning to emerge. A survey by the NCLIS/SLA Task Force on the role of special libraries in networks found that in 1981 special libraries accounted for 28 percent of network memberships (including bibliographic utilities). It also found that unique resources, service on governing bodies, a willingness to lend resources, and "advanced thinking" were identified by networks as important special library contributions.

Networks have proved to be a valuable tool for special libraries in gaining access to additional resources, as was expected from the early days of networking. Shared cataloguing has proved to be a somewhat unexpected benefit. It was predicted that concern for confidentiality of materials and unwillingness to standardize would be barriers to special library participation in shared cataloguing. However, the number of special libraries joining bibliographic utilities indicates that these barriers are not insurmountable.

Some predicted barriers have been overcome, but other constraints are more difficult to ease. Publicly funded and nonprofit networks potentially endanger their funding or Internal Revenue Service not-for-profit status if private, for-profit organizations are included. Lacking clear Internal Revenue Service guidelines, networks have restricted for-profit memberships to a certain percentage, have relegated them to nonvoting or associate memberships, or have prohibited for-profit organization libraries from participating in network governance. The NCLIS/SLA Task Force has raised the question of possible violation of antitrust laws by the subject networks; although district rulings have been made by the IRS on the former question, no clear precedent has yet emerged, and a review of antitrust laws has yet to be undertaken.

Other barriers or constraints to special library participation in networks come from special libraries themselves. Although their participation in networking is substantial, an estimated 50 percent of special libraries do not participate at all. The NCLIS/SLA Task Force found that many of these libraries were in highly competitive sectors—business and finance, newspapers, engineering, petroleum, chemicals, and insurance—where there was little incentive to share or to advertise what they had acquired. Some libraries are simply too small, have neither resources, time, nor money to contribute, and will always be too small for networking. Finally, many special libraries find that their long-term informal cooperative efforts are comfortable and are reluctant to replace them with the more complex or different methods required by formal networks.

LAWS AND LEGISLATION

Special libraries, nestled within parent organizations that provide financial support, are seldom directly involved in or affected by legislation. There are, of course, exceptions. There are instances of involvement in government regulations and funding among groups of special libraries, notably those in the public sector, government libraries, medical libraries, and libraries whose parent organizations hold government contracts. But until the mid-1970s, most special librarians in the U.S. had not been involved with laws and legislation to the same degree as had their colleagues in other types of libraries. Change came from two directions: the Copyright Law of 1976 and legislation concerning multitype cooperatives and networks.

As revision of copyright moved toward passage in Congress, special librarians become deeply involved in the legislative process as they, individually and through the SLA, joined with five other major U.S. library associations (American Association of Law Libraries, American Library Association, Medical Library Association, Music Library Association, and Association of Research Libraries) in a unified effort to ensure equitable treatment for libraries. After enactment of the new copyright law, SLA continued to represent the special library community on copyright matters and to disseminate information on copyright law implementation and compliance to special librarians.

For all libraries a significant part of the U.S. copyright law has been library reprography and photocopying, specifically Sections 107, governing fair use, and 108, governing reproductions by libraries and archives. Special libraries, particularly those in for-profit organizations, have had some special problems with Section 108 and with the interpretation of "direct or indirect commercial advantage" and "systematic" reproduction.

In implementing provisions of the law, special libraries were faced with the same problems of interlibrary loan procedures, interpretation of fair use, and warning notices as were other types of libraries. The prohibitions against "multiple" and "systematic" photocopying, however, meant that special librarians had to review carefully their current awareness services for possible infringements. Many special librarians, naturally reluctant to embroil their parent organizations in legal difficulties, turned to their firms' lawyers for advice, with the result that each special library developed its own policies, reflecting the varying opinions of legal counsel. In some cases alternative methods have been adopted for disseminating information or copyright clearance has been obtained; some services have simply been dropped, either because of possible infringement or because an efficient, effective alternative could not be found.

Special libraries are affected by legislation concerning multitype library cooperatives and networks. Possible legal problems in the inclusion of special libraries in for-profit organizations were identified early in multitype network planning. At the same time, special libraries were increasingly being given at least lip-service recognition as a part of total library resources. From the position of mobilization of total library resources, federal and state legislation has by and large, implicitly if not explicitly, enabled special libraries to be included in multitype cooperatives and networks. The potential barrier remains at the individual cooperative/network level, where special libraries in for-profit organizations may be excluded from certain networks or network activities. Another concern raised by the NCLIS/SLA Task Force on the role of the special library in networks involves possible antitrust violations by subject-oriented networks that include for-profit libraries.

In recognition of special libraries' increasing interest in legislation, the SLA in 1980 abandoned its deliberate policy of noninvolvement and established a standing Government Relations Committee. This committee developed legislative programs for SLA, focusing on legislation and policies that advance library and information services in the public and private sectors, including copyright, network legislation, government information policies, and telecommunications.

REFERENCES

Janet L. Ahrensfeld, Elin B. Christianson, and David E. King, *Special Libraries: A Guide for Management* (2nd edition, 1981), although brief and intended for a management audience, is a comprehensive introduction to special libraries.

Elizabeth Ferguson and Emily R. Mobley, *Special Libraries at Work* (1984) is also a useful general introduction.

Johan van Halm, *The Development of Special Libraries as an International Phenomenon* (1978) covers special libraries in some 100 countries.

Historical treatments: Anthony T. Kruzas, *Business and Industrial Libraries in the United States, 1820-1940* (1965).

Samuel J. Rothstein, *The Development of Reference Services through Academic Tradition, Public Library Practice and Special Librarianship,* ACRL Monographs, No. 14 (1955).

Bill M. Woods, "The Special Library Concept of Service," *American Libraries* (1972), provides excellent coverage of the two decades following World War II.

Special Libraries, published by the Special Libraries Association, is the principal journal in the field and carries many articles on special libraries, their services, collections, and administration, and on SLA activities and programs.

Special Libraries, the *Journal of the American Society for Information Science* (1949 -), and the *Annual Review of Information Science and Technology* (1966 -) are the principal sources for reports of work on the measurement and evaluation of information systems and special libraries.

The role of the special library in multitype library cooperatives and networks is set forth in Beth A. Hamilton and William B. Ernst, Jr., editors, *Multitype Library Cooperation* (1977).

Robert W. Gibson, Jr., editor, *The Special Library Role in Networks* (1980).

NCLIS/SLA Task Force report, *The Role of the Special Library in Networks and Cooperatives* (1984).

ELIN B. CHRISTIANSON

Spofford, Ainsworth Rand
(1825–1908)

The modern history of the Library of Congress began when Ainsworth Rand Spofford became Librarian, for during his 32-year administration (1865–97) he transformed the LC into an institution of national significance. Spofford permanently joined the legislative and national functions of the Library, first in practice and then, through the 1897 reorganization of the Library, in law. He provided his successors as Librarian with four essential prerequisites for the development of an American national library: (1) firm congressional support for the notion of the LC as both a legislative and a national library; (2) the beginning of a comprehensive collection of Americana; (3) a magnificent new building, itself a national monument; and (4) a strong and independent office of Librarian of Congress. Spofford had the interest, skill, and perseverance to capitalize on the LC's claim to a national role. Each Librarian of Congress since Spofford has shaped the institution in a different manner, but none has wavered from Spofford's fundamental assertion that the Library was both a legislative and a national institution.

Spofford was born in Gilmanton, New Hampshire, on September 12, 1825. He was tutored at home and developed into an avid reader and student. In 1845 he migrated West to Cincinnati and found a job in a bookstore that soon became, thanks to his efforts, the city's leading importer of the books of the New England transcendentalists. From the book business he moved, in 1859, to a new career as Associate Editor of Cincinnati's leading newspaper, the *Daily Commercial;* his first editorial, titled "A Bibliologist," attacked the naive book-buying practices of the city librarian. Two years later the newspaper sent Spofford to Washington, D.C., to report on President Abraham Lincoln's inauguration, a trip that led to his acceptance, in the autumn of 1861, of the position of Assistant Librarian of Congress. On December 31, 1864, President Lincoln named the knowledgeable, industrious, and ambitious Spofford to the post of Librarian of Congress. Located in the west front of the U.S. Capitol, the Library had a staff of seven and a book collection of approximately 82,000 volumes.

Spofford soon proved to be a skilled politician as well as an energetic librarian. Congressmen liked him and the nonpartisan manner in which he administered the Library. As one result, between 1865 and 1870 he obtained support for several legislative acts that ensured the growth of the collections and made the LC the largest library in the United States. The most important new measure was the copyright law of 1870, which centralized all U.S. copyright registration and deposit activities at the Library. The new law brought books, pamphlets, maps, prints, photographs, and music into the institution without substantial cost, thus assuring the future growth of the Americana collections and providing the Library of Congress with an essential and unique national function.

In his annual reports to Congress, Spofford continually emphasized that a national library should be a permanent, comprehensive collection of national literature "representing the complete product of the American mind in every department of science and literature." Comprehensiveness was essential, for in his view the American national library should serve both the American citizenry and its elected representatives. Books and information were needed about all

subjects and, as the library of the American government, the LC was the natural site for such a comprehensive collection.

In 1874, for the first time, the copyright law brought in more books than were obtained through purchase, and three years later Spofford's already cramped library was out of space and more than 70,000 books were "piled on the floor in all directions." The Librarian's struggle for a separate building, which began in 1871, was a crucial part of his national library effort. A separate structure would ensure, once and for all, the unique status of the Library of Congress among American libraries—and would give the U.S. a national library that would equal if not surpass the great national libraries of Europe. The latter argument was a particularly popular one with the Congress. Spofford personally wanted a national monument that would also serve as an efficient, well-functioning building. The new building, however, was not authorized until 1886 and not completed for another decade. Spofford's dream was fulfilled in 1897 when the doors to the ornate new structure across the east plaza from the Capitol, at the time the "largest, safest, and costliest" library building in the world, were finally opened to an admiring public.

For the most part Spofford operated quite independently of the American library movement and the American Library Association. By 1876, when ALA was founded, Spofford's LC was already the leading library in the country, and he was completely absorbed in his struggle for a new building. His independence from other libraries and librarians was accentuated by his idea of a national library as well as by his personal temperament. The national library was a single, enormous accumulation of the nation's literature. He did not view it as a focal point for cooperative library activities and was not inclined to exert leadership in that direction.

Fron November 16 to December 7, 1896, the Joint Committee on the Library held hearings about the LC, its "condition," and its organization. Although Spofford was the principal witness, ALA sent six librarians to testify. The testimony of Melvil Dewey and Herbert Putman on the desirable features of the LC was of special interest; both men avoided direct criticism of Spofford, but it was obvious that their view of the proper functions of the Library differed from that of the aging Librarian. Putnam wholeheartedly endorsed Dewey's description of the necessary role of a national library: "a center to which the libraries of the whole country can turn for inspiration, guidance, and practical help." Centralized cataloguing, interlibrary loan, and a national union catalogue were among the services described.

Immediately after the hearings, Putnam supplemented his comments in a letter in which he summarized the testimony of the ALA witnesses and stated, tactfully, that the time had come for the LC to modernize and to expand its services far beyond those offered by the Library under Spofford.

The hearings resulted in a major reorganization and expansion, effective July 1, 1897. Spofford became Chief Assistant Librarian under a new Librarian of Congress, John Russell Young, and he continued as Chief Assistant under Herbert Putnam, who became the Librarian of Congress in April 1899. Spofford died in Holderness, New Hampshire, on August

Library of Congress
Ainsworth Rand Spofford

11, 1908.

Spofford's professional and personal interests were perhaps most accurately described in the formidable title of his *A Book for All Readers, Designed as an Aid to the Collection, Use, and Preservation of Books and Formation of Public and Private Libraries* (1900). He was respected by librarians, politicians, and the general public, not only because of his accomplishments at the LC, but also because of his fair-mindedness and his continual delight in sharing his views about his favorite subjects—reading, bibliography, and collection-building.

REFERENCES

John Y. Cole, editor, *Ainsworth Rand Spofford: Bookman and Librarian* (1975).

Cole, "Spofford, Ainsworth Rand," *Dictionary of American Library Biography* (1978).

JOHN Y. COLE

Sri Lanka Library Association

Oriental Library in the Temple of the Tooth, Kandy, Sri Lanka. Built in the 17th century, it houses ancient ola *(palm) manuscripts.*

Sri Lanka

Sri Lanka, an island republic in the Indian Ocean, lies off the southeastern coast of India. It occupies the island long called Ceylon. Population (1984 est.) 15,756,00; area 65,610 sq.km. The official language is Sinhalese.

History. Possessing an ancient civilization stretching back over 2,500 years of recorded history, Sri Lanka has a longstanding intellectual tradition and a background of learning and scholarship. Temple libraries were widespread, but not until British colonization and the development of Western-style institutions of education in the 19th century did a modern system of libraries begin to appear. Subscription libraries, subsidized by the government, were established in the early part of the century, and the Government Oriental Library, operated under the Colonial Secretary, was opened in 1870. Over a hundred years of state-sponsored education have provided the stimulus to a growing network of libraries of all kinds serving a population whose general literacy rates are in the region of 75 to 85 percent.

National Library. There was no National Library as of the mid-1980s, but the blueprint for its construction had been accepted, and the foundation stone was laid in 1977. The principal state reference library is the National Museum Library, established in Colombo, the capital city, in 1877. Its collections number 600,000 volumes, including manuscripts, and it served as a legal deposit library as well from 1885.

The Sri Lanka National Library Services Board was begun under an act of 1970. Its primary objectives are to formulate a national library policy, to promote and assist the development of all types of libraries, especially those maintained by state funds, and to set up a National Library. It is responsible for producing the Sri Lanka National Bibliography (begun in 1962) and has been accorded legal deposit privileges for this purpose from 1974.

The Department of National Archives is also a legal deposit library, and the Director of National Archives is the Registrar of Books, Periodicals, Newspapers, and Printing Presses.

Academic Libraries. At the apex of the tertiary (or higher) system of education, established in 1870 with a Ceylon Medical College and in 1921 with the Ceylon University College, are the nine universities and their affiliated colleges and institutes. The oldest and largest of these are the universities of Peradeniya and Colombo. Peradeniya has much the larger library, amounting to 400,000 volumes, excluding its legal deposit materials since 1952. Colombo holds some 140,000 volumes. The collections in the universities alone total nearly a million vol-

Libraries in Sri Lanka (1977)

Type	Administrative units	Service points	Volumes in collections	Annual expenditures (rupee)	Population served[a]	Professional staff	Total staff
National	1	3	13,000	476,000	4,800	4	38
Academic[b]	5	14	540,000	3,401,000	7,184	16	206
Public[c]	650	684	--	5,498,000[d]	197,200	7	952
School[e]	793	--	1,423,000	660,000	4,000,000	60	793[f]
Special[e]	51	--	435,000	2,100,000	3,000	37	185

[a]Registered borrowers.
[b]University libraries only.
[c]1980 data.
[d]Employees and acquisitions.
[e]1976 data.
[f]Includes part-time staff.

Source: Unesco, *Statistical Yearbook*, 1984; Annual reports and personal inquiries.

umes covering all disciplines. There are special collections on Sri Lanka and Oriental subjects in the larger universities. The libraries in technical colleges and institutes are much smaller and of more recent origin.

Public Libraries. Various sorts of subscription libraries existed from early British times, and two of them (the United Services Library and the Colombo Pettah Library) were amalgamated in 1925 to form the Colombo Public Library, which developed into the premier public library in the island. The organization and maintenance of public libraries is not obligatory for local government authorities but is a permissive function. The scope and nature of such libraries vary widely from region to region. The Ministry of Local Government stepped up the provision of library services and elevated the resources of buildings, staff, and books. Most of the local government bodies maintained libraries in 1980.

School Libraries. Despite considerable activity in public education since independence in 1948 and the high participation rate in the free educational stream, the provision of school libraries of sufficient quality lagged behind that of other educational facilities. The Ministry of Education took active steps to remedy this deficiency and to promote the concept of a school library as a center of learning. Most schools have libraries of sorts and, as in public libraries, literature is provided in all three languages—Sinhalese, Tamil, and English—used as media of education and administration.

Special Libraries. Special libraries and documentation centers are located in state corporations, government departments, and private organizations dealing with industry, commerce, scientific research, technology, agriculture, and allied fields. The clientele are select groups of users connected with the institutions, and this class of library service has grown rapidly. The National Science Council of Sri Lanka operates a Science and Technology Information Center.

The Profession. The Sri Lanka Library Association was established in 1960 and conducts part-time classes in librarianship and information studies at various levels. A Department of Library Studies in the University of Kelaniya was begun in 1973.

REFERENCE

I. Corea, editor, *Libraries and People* (Colombo Public Library, 1975), a valuable symposium of articles on all aspects of the library scene in Sri Lanka.

HENRY ALFRED IAN GOONETILEKE*

Standing Conference of African University Libraries (SCAUL)

The Standing Conference of African University Librarians (SCAUL) was formed as a result of the discussions at the Leverhulme Inter-University Conference on the Needs and Problems of University Librarians in Tropical Africa, held in Salisbury, Rhodesia, September 14–23, 1964. At the end of the Conference, a Continuation Committee was appointed and charged with the responsibility of implementing the conference resolutions, one of which recommended that further conferences be held periodically.

Members of the Continuation Committee took the opportunity of the Conference of Librarians from Commonwealth Universities in Africa, sponsored by the Commonwealth Foundation and held in Lusaka, Zambia, August 24–29, 1969, to discuss further the organization of the Standing Conference of African University Librarians. At this conference, the non-Commonwealth Committee members, Ethiopia and Senegal, took part as observers. Some important recommendations concerning the organization of SCAUL were made, and a draft constitution was drawn up.

According to this constitution, full membership in SCAUL would be open to heads of libraries of universities eligible for membership in the Association of African Universities, with associate membership open to university libraries in other parts of the world, SCAUL activities would be developed mainly within Area Organizations of SCAUL. A Central Committee, comprising the Convener/Secretary (Chairman), representatives of Area Organizations, and the Editor of the *Newsletter,* would meet periodically to coordinate the work of the Areas. Each member of SCAUL would be free to choose the Area that it would join and would be allowed to attend as an observer the conferences in the Areas to which it did not belong. Each Area would determine its own membership requirements and draft its own constitution based on that of SCAUL. The *Newsletter* was to be published as the official organ of SCAUL. The name of the organization was changed to Standing Conference of African University Libraries.

These recommendations were subsequently approved in a postal ballot, and the draft constitution was fully discussed at Area meetings in 1971 and 1972 and subsequently approved.

SCAUL now operates through two Area Organizations: the Eastern Area (SCAULEA), headquartered at the library of the University of Nairobi, Kenya, and the Western Area (SCAULWA), at the University of Lagos Library, Lagos, Nigeria. Each of the Area Organizations has both anglophone and francophone countries as members. SCAULEA has held conferences in Addis Ababa (1971), Mauritius (1973), and Nairobi (1977). SCAULWA held conferences in Lagos (1972), Dakar (1974), Accra (1976), Kinshasha (1978), Monrovia (1980), and Lagos (1982).

The aims of SCAUL are (1) to keep members informed of each other's activities and, whenever possible, to correlate such activities in the common interest; and (2) to support and develop university library services in Africa.

SCAUL seeks to advance the development of university libraries by organizing conferences as a forum for discussing the problems of university librarianship in Africa and of the programs of each member library. SCAUL sponsors individual research activities and projects and meetings of specialists on African bibliography, cataloguing, classification, and other library topics.

SCAUL publications include proceedings of the conferences of SCAULEA and SCAULWA and SCAUL *Newsletter.* SCAULWA also publishes *African Journal of Academic Librarianship,* established in 1983 and edited by E. Bejide Bankole.

E. BEJIDE BANKOLE

Sudan

The Democratic Republic of the Sudan, in northeastern Africa, is bounded by Egypt on the north, the Red Sea and Ethiopia on the east, Kenya, Uganda, and Zaire on the south, and the Central African Republic, Chad, and Libya on the west. Population (1984 est.) 21,160,000; area 2,503,890 sq.km. The official language is Arabic; English is widely spoken and is considered the first European language in the school system.

History. The word "Sudan" was used for hundreds of years to refer to the land south of the Great Desert. Its use was first limited to the area of the present Democratic Republic of the Sudan in 1899, at the beginning of the dual role played by Egypt and Britain in that part of Africa.

In 1903 Gordon's Memorial College was set up to train qualified personnel to serve in the government and to teach in schools. The first public library was established in 1947 at Wadmedani. Two comprehensive reports on Sudanese libraries, in 1960 and in 1972, revealed that responsibility for establishing libraries and training librarians was distributed among several authorities. The National Commission of Unesco, which examined the two reports, recommended the establishment of a National Council for Libraries. The Council consists of representatives from various ministries and educational institutions interested in library development.

National Library Service. There is no national library in the Sudan. The University of Khartoum Central Library functions as a national library, receiving publications through legal deposit and maintaining The Sudan Collection. The Collection was established in 1962 to serve scholars and researchers involved in Sudanese studies.

Academic Libraries. There are several university and college libraries in the Sudan. The development of Gordon's Memorial College (1903) into Gordon's University College in 1945 underscored the need for establishing a good library with a comprehensive collection to support advanced studies and to continue to provide students and faculty with adequate reference and reading materials. A new library was established around the collection of Sir Douglas Newbold, who was the Administative Secretary of the Sudanese government. The Library was named after him until 1956.

In 1956 the University College became the University of Khartoum, with the addition of new colleges. The Library of the new University acquired collections from various sources, totaling about 3,000 titles and covering such subjects as the history and topology of the Sudan, African history, agriculture, and medicine. Two more universities and several university colleges were later established and equipped with fairly good libraries.

The University of Khartoum Library is the largest and richest in the country. It uses the Bliss Classification System; some of the college libraries use the Colon Classification. Prior to 1978 the Central Library supervised the various faculty libraries technically and administratively. After 1978 the faculties of Engineering, Law, Medicine, and Agriculture developed their own acquisition and cataloguing programs. Catalogue cards are submitted by these libraries to the Central Library for its Union Catalog. The

book budget for 1983 was set at 675,000 Sudanese pounds, but the actual expenditure was 4,000,000 Sudanese pounds (U.S. $400,000). The Library uses the University's computer center for the computerization of its classified catalogue and serials files.

Circulation statistics at the University of Khartoum show that the Central Library has the highest circulation, followed by Medicine and Agriculture.

Omdurman Islamic University was initially established in 1917 as the Omdurman Religious Insitution to teach Islamic jurisprudence. Through various contributions, from charitable societies and individuals, the institution's Library was developed and its collection augmented. In 1965 the Institution achieved the status of an Islamic university and the old collection formed the core of the University Library's collection. The Library uses the Dewey Decimal Classification.

Public Libraries. Public libraries were introduced in the Sudan at the end of World War II, under the jurisdiction of the Ministry of Local Government. They were known as municipal libraries because they were directly administered by the municipalities set up by the Ministry of Local Government. Supervision was later transferred to the Public Libraries Department in the Ministry of Culture and Information.

Public libraries were established in Wadmedani, Atbara, Port Sudan, Khartoum, and many other towns. They have poor and small collections compared to the size of the population to be served, mainly because of financial constraints, high rates of booktheft, and loss of borrowed books. Their collections tend to emphasize literature and fiction, and little if any attention is paid to the sciences or social sciences. Borrowers are mainly government employees, teachers, and students. There is a marked absence in these libraries of registers of borrowers and books loaned. Catalogues are often outdated.

Several foreign cultural centers have opened their libraries to the Sudanese public, but the majority of titles in those libraries are in foreign languages and require a fair knowledge of those languages by the Sudanese users. Some centers are heavily used by university students, particularly in medicine and sciences and other related fields in which American and European texts are heavily used.

School Libraries and Media Centers. The first primary schools in the Sudan were established in 1863 in Khartoum, Barbar, Dongola, and Kassala and a few years later at Swaken and Sinnar. Preparatory schools were established in 1906 in Barbar, Omdurman, Wadmedani, Khartoum, Swaken, and Halfa. It

Libraries in Sudan (1983)

Type	Administrative units	Volumes in collections
Academic	9	397,472
Public	7	35,528
School	4,676	89,000
Special	35	189,127
Young Peoples'	60	15,020
Mosque	6	10,030
Foreign Cultural Centres	9	75,158
Info. and Docu. Centres	1	5,150

is not known whether school libraries existed before; there are no references to the existence of such libraries. In 1974 the Ministry of Education established a department to plan for and develop school libraries.

At the primary and preparatory school levels, school libraries are no more than collections of books under the control of a particular teacher. However, there are libraries in secondary schools in compliance with a regulation that every secondary school should have a room designated as a library and every school with more than 640 pupils should have a full-time librarian.

In spite of this regulation, the school libraries situation was still poor not only in physical location and facilities but also in collections, as indicated by the ratio of 89,000 volumes against 4,686 schools or only 19 books per school.

Special Libraries. Special libraries have been established in the ministries, banks, research centers, and other sectors in order to meet the objectives of the respective organizations and to serve the needs of their staffs.

The National Documentation Center began as the main documentation center for the National Council for Research (in Science and Technology). It became an autonomous body and took its present name in 1972. The Center publishes abstract bulletins. It has microfiche and microfilm readers and printers but they are not heavily used. As part of an agreement with Unesco the Center received a minicomputer for processing information and creating a local database utilizing the MINISIS software package.

The Sudan News Agency (SUNA) maintains an active Information and Research Department. The Department is divided into two units: the Information and Library Section and the Research Statistics and Follow-up Section. The former compiles data on a variety of topics, including ministries and other governmental departments, corporations, and institutions. The Department also maintains biographical files on all prominent Sudanese and international figures. Its library has more than 1,000 volumes and published a number of research works on oil in the Sudan, regional government in the Sudan, the Western Sahara, and other topics.

Mosque libraries are administered by the Ministry of Religious Affairs and Endowments. The Ministry aims at setting up a library in every large mosque in the country.

The Profession. Sudan launched the first library training courses in 1961, when the University of Khartoum's Department of General Studies organized two permanent training courses for employees in libraries and archives centers. A preliminary training program dealt with acquisition, cataloguing, circulation, and readers' advisory services, followed by an advanced stage of training in library administration, classification, and bibliography. Lecturers for these courses were recruited from the University Library and the Institute of Public Administration. Although the course was for one academic year, it did not lead to a formal degree or certification.

In 1966–67 the Department of Librarianship and Archives was established at Omdurman Islamic University. The undergraduate program is a four-year program. In the first year, students are offered general courses in the humanities and in the social sciences; the other three years are devoted to library and archival studies.

Library training in the southern part of the Sudan began at the University of Juba in 1978 when regional ministries and other institutions were seeking to establish libraries. Short courses in basic librarianship were organized.

The Certificate course for paraprofessionals began in 1981 and is of one-year duration. The objective of the program at the University of Juba is to train library assistants to run small libraries or to work under the guidance of a professional librarian.

The Sudan Library Association, established in 1971, held its first conference in January 1972. The Association ceased to be active in 1979. Both the British Council and the U.S. Information Center maintain close liaison with practicing Sudanese librarians, who are usually invited to attend meetings or colloquia hosted by those active centers.

M. M. AMAN;
SHA'BAN A. KHALIFA

Suriname

Suriname, a republic in northern South America, is bounded by the Atlantic Ocean on the north, French Guiana on the east, Brazil on the south, and Guyana on the west. Population (1984 est.) 352,000; area 163,820 sq.km. The official language is Dutch.

History. Suriname has had a tradition of libraries since the 18th century, when the capital of Paramaribo had a large scientific library comparable to similar libraries in Western Europe and the United States. The library was destroyed in the 19th century by a fire set by the freedom fighters of the time, the Maroons. Various private libraries also date from this period, as do personal libraries. The so-called Volksbibliotheek (People's Library) was set up at the end of the 18th century under the influence of the Maatchappij tot Nut van het Algemeen (Public Benefit Company) in the Netherlands, but that library was also destroyed by fire in 1821.

Between 1821 and 1856 some brief attempts were made to establish loan associations for books on a commercial basis. In 1856 two medical doctors, F. A. G. Dumontier and C. Landré, proposed a plan to set up a library in Paramaribo. Their plan was successful, and on December 1, 1857, the Colonial Library was established under the jurisdiction of the Inspector of Education. This was the first attempt to found a national library, which had to serve as both public and research library. A lack of expert personnel and poor facilities caused the National Library to close in 1957. The collection was distributed among a number of libraries in the Netherlands, including the library of the Royal Institute for the Tropics and the Royal Library. In 1950 the collections for adults and children had already been turned over to the Public Library of the Cultural Centre of Suriname (CCS), which had begun operating in 1949.

Academic Libraries. At the University of Suriname, libraries were established at the Faculty of Law (with holdings of about 10,000 publications), the Faculty of Medicine (10,000), the Faculty of Social and Economic Sciences (3,000), the Engineering Faculty (10,000), the Faculty of Natural Resource Studies

(10,000), and the International Law library (2,000). These faculty libraries primarily serve the university's 1,000 students.

Public Libraries. The Public Library of the CCS was set up on the initiative of the Cultural Committee for Suriname. Pioneering work was performed by M. Nassy, the first Librarian of this institution. It quickly became apparent that an organization of the existing libraries was necessary. From 1950 to 1957 the National Library functioned as a center for reference works and scientific literature, while the CCS library covered belles lettres and services to youth.

The CCS library operates as a central public library and works to set up public libraries in other regions. Until 1975 it was subsidized by STICUSA (Foundation for Cultural Cooperation between the Netherlands, Suriname, and the Netherlands Antilles), but after Suriname's independence in 1975 it was supported by the state. The central library and its six branches and two bookmobiles have a total collection of about 225,000 volumes.

School Libraries. The Ministry of Education and Community Development is largely responsible for school libraries; a Library Affairs Section was attached to the Ministry in 1968. The first library it established was the General Educational Library (1969), a central library for all the school libraries, where expensive research material may be consulted. The Library also provides materials for evening school courses. The Library Affairs Section founded 60 school libraries, with estimated total collections of about 60,000 items. The General Educational Library has about 35,000 publications, with some 75,000 annual loans and visitors.

Special Libraries. Most of the special libraries in Suriname are in ministries. They include the Ministry of Agriculture, Animal Husbandry and Fisheries (37,000 volumes), the Ministry of Justice and Police Affairs, the State Forest Administration, and the Central Bank. Other libraries that are open to a larger public are the library of the Suriname Museum Foundation, which has the largest collection of writings on Suriname (12,000 publications), the Institute for Advanced Teacher Training, and the Scientific Institute Foundation.

The Profession. Most workers in school libraries are teachers who have taken three-week inservice training courses at the Library Affairs Section.

The staff at the Library Affairs Section must have at least four years of practical experience and one year of professional training. There is also a two-year library course at the CCS.

R. CH. W. LONT*

Swaziland

Swaziland, a monarchy based on tribal tradition in southwestern Africa, is bounded on the east by Mozambique and on the north, west, and south by South Africa. Population (1984 est.) 623,000; area 17,364 sq.km. The official languages are English and siSwati.

National Library Services. The functions of a national library, in the absence of such an institution, were assigned to the Swaziland National Library Service and the University of Swaziland Library, which enjoy legal deposit status.

Academic Library. The only academic library is the University of Swaziland Library, founded in 1971 at the devolution of the University of Botswana, Lesotho, and Swaziland and incorporating the Swaziland Agricultural College and University Centre. It consists of the Main Library at Kwaluseni, with 55,000 volumes, and the Faculty of Agriculture Library at Luyengo, with 15,000 volumes. In addition to undergraduate material, the Library has a collection of Swaziana and compiles the *Swaziland National Bibliography* (1976-). It also has deposit status for documents of the Food and Agriculture Organization and the World Bank.

Public Libraries. The Swaziland National Library Service provides public library services, operating a public library in Manzini with several branches, depots, and mobile unit stops. It has holdings of 55,000 volumes and 1,000 current periodicals and an annual circulation of around 120,000; it reaches more than 20 percent of the country's literate population.

School Libraries. The Ministry of Education operates some 500 schools for about 125,000 pupils and distributes books among 48 school libraries, while the Swaziland National Library Service lends books to the schools. A number of secondary and high school libraries operate on their own budgets. The Swaziland College of Technology, the Swaziland Institute of Management and Public Administration, and two teacher training colleges have libraries with more than 10,000 volumes.

Libraries in Suriname (1978)

Type	Administrative units	Service points	Volumes in collections	Annual expenditures (guilder)	Population served[a]	Professional staff	Total staff
National	--	--	--	--	--	--	--
Academic	2	5	29,000	--	--	8	11
Public	2	68	268,000	376,000	53,637	18	52
School	3	49	60,000	200,000	20,447	8	52
Special	27	--	63,000	--	967	--	--
Non-specialized	7	--	129,000	--	--	--	--

[a]Registered borrowers.

Source: Unesco, *Statistical Yearbook, 1984.*

Special Libraries. The Malkerns Research Station and the Lowveld Experimental Farm have libraries with a joint stock of more than 6,000 volumes and more than 200 agricultural journals. There is a 2,500-volume library at the Mananga Agricultural Management Centre, run by the Commonwealth Development Corporation, which provides training for junior and middle level management and extension workers from developing countries of the Commonwealth. A few ministries of government have departmental libraries for their staffs. The Attorney General's Chambers Library serves the Ministry of Justice and the Central Statistical Office Library serves the Government Statistician. The Monetary Authority and the Ministry of Agriculture operate libraries; the National Archives contains a library section devoted to Swaziana. The British High Commission Office and the American embassy run libraries with open membership, while the Mbabane Library Association is a subscription library.

REFERENCES

A. W. Z. Kuzwayo, *Information Systems and National Information Services in Swaziland* (University College of Swaziland Library, 1978), gives quantitative and qualitative assessment.

Wallace Van Jackson, "Library Development in Swaziland," *International Library Review* (1976).

A. W. Z. KUZWAYO*

Sweden

Sweden, a constitutional monarchy, lies on the eastern part of the Scandinavian Peninsula in northern Europe. It is bounded by Norway on the west, Finland on the northeast, the Gulf of Bothnia and the Baltic Sea on the east, and the North Sea on the southwest. Population (1984 est.) 8,341,000; area 449,964 sq.km. The official language is Swedish.

History. Around 3,000 years ago Swedish ancestors left extensive rock carvings in granite as a pictorial script of events occurring in shipping, hunting, and agriculture, and in association with religion and magic. The oral traditions behind these events have been lost, and we can only guess at their meaning. The most famous ones are found in Tanum, Bohuslän. A large megalith calendar can be seen at Kåseberga, Skåne.

Contacts with writing later took place in encounters with the Mediterranean peoples. Ancient Greek cursive characters were taken over or read-

Uppsala-Bild

Uppsala University Library. Founded in 1620, it is the most famous of Sweden's academic libraries. Collections date from early monastic libraries.

justed so that they could be carved on wooden objects as "runes," which start to appear in the 4th century A.D.. Runes are also found in the fragments of the Ulfila's bible, Codex Argenteus, a vellum manuscript now in the Uppsala University Library. Most visible are about 3,000 memorial runestones scattered around the country. One runestone four meters tall is now in the hall of Lund University Library. The Swedish Vikings left behind "graffiti" of carved runes and dragon ornaments on the Lion of Pireus, which has stood since 1687 in front of the Armory of Venice, and in the large mosque of Istanbul. Even though there are numerous runes inscribed on such useful objects as weapons, rings, and coins, runes do not constitute a Swedish book culture.

Books came with the Catholic monks who from the 9th century on traveled to the distant North in their zeal to convert Scandinavian believers in the Aesir (a group of deities) to Christianity. The first libraries were founded in churches and monasteries to serve the needs of the ecclesiastics. The oldest Nordic manuscript, Necrologium Lundense, now in the Lund University Library, started in 1123 as a registry of the dates of death of persons associated with the Diocesan Chapter of the Saint Laurentii Church, Lund. It contains the first library instruction in Sweden, proving that the Chapter at that time had an extant "library in the custody of the Cantor" (in Latin).

Libraries in Sweden (1982)

Type	Administrative units	Service points	Volumes in collections	Annual expenditures (krona)	Population served	Professional staff	Total staff
National	2	12	5,700,000	67,000,000	c.25,000	72	314
Academic	22	66	7,800,000	127,000,000	c.150,000	270	867
Public	407	4,751	41,379,000[a]	1,157,959,000	7,834,410[b]	2,168	5,652
School	77	2,170	--	45,000,000	1,301,000[b]	--	--
Special	567[b]	567	8,127,000	--	--	147[b]	1,314[b]

[a]1981 data.
[b]1980 data.

Sources: *Statistisk årsbok 1984,* Stockholm, 1984; *Bibliotekskalendern 1984,* Lund, 1983; *TLS Handbok 8,* Stockholm, 1980.

Besides cathedral libraries in Linköping, Skara, Strängnäs, and Uppsala, wealthy libraries were found in monasteries. The library of the Abbey of St. Bridget, Vadstena, grew during the Middle Ages to be the largest library in the Nordic countries, holding more than 1,400 manuscripts and books. The Abbey in 1495 set up the first printshop.

The first book printed in Sweden was made by Johan Snell, who in 1483 was called from Lübeck, Germany, to Stockholm to print *Dialogus Creaturarum Moralizatus,* a collection of sermons and fables. Before the end of the century another 14 incunabula were printed.

The judicial arm also needed books, and the oldest manuscript in Swedish, *Västgötalagen,* dates back to the beginning of the 13th century, followed by many similar editions for the law of various lands. Parchment of sheep, goat, or calf played the main role for book material. Paper documents first appeared in Sweden in 1345, but paper manufacturing there did not start until two hundred years later.

The Protestant Reformation that Luther started in 1527 turned out to be a catastrophe for many libraries. They were deprived of most of their collections, and many Latin manuscripts were torn up and used as material in making tax lists and binding records of the emerging national state. Others were placed in the Court library, schools, and private collections.

In contrast to the decline in the 16th century, lively collection-building occurred in the 17th. Sweden as a great power enriched its libraries by booties from royal libraries and monasteries in Northern Europe. Universities were founded with libraries—Uppsala Library in 1620 and Lund Library in 1666. Queen Christina (1632–54) opened up the Royal Library to scholars. In spite of the early government contributions in support of these libraries, the 18th and 19th centuries marked slow progress for them. A new university library was founded in Göteborg in 1861. The 20th century saw a rapid establishment of new universities and colleges with libraries—Umeå (1964), Linköping (1969), Stockholm (1971), and other institutions.

In a sparsely populated, long and narrow country it was difficult for the state to develop adequate library services for the general public. Toward the end of the 18th century a public library movement was begun with the establishment of parish libraries. In 1842 the public school law stated that the vicars "should encourage the setting up and usage of parish libraries and also propose books for that end." In 1868 a total of 1,437 such libraries were recorded; then came a period of decline. Instead, with industrialization there was a swing toward the establishment of town libraries, of which the Dicksonska, Göteborg, founded in 1861, was the most important. These libraries were seen as complements to elementary education in order to promote the general educational level. Workmen's association libraries were started in Stockholm in 1882. Many of the parish, town, and workmen's libraries were later merged with public libraries established in each community.

For long the government was reluctant to support that movement. In 1905 the public libraries were acknowledged by a government grant for their activities. In the 1920s other forms of public libraries, such as hospital and seamen's libraries, got such funding. The Public Library Act of 1930 recognized only one library in each county as eligible for funding, considering it central in assisting the local libraries in their book demands; the municipalities, in the meantime, had to support all of their public and school libraries. A government commission in 1984 proposed a law to the Parliament intended to upgrade the poorest libraries in the municipalities.

National Libraries. Sweden has an archival national library, the Royal Library, which since 1661 has been entitled to receive statutory copies. In 1978 Lund University Library became the national lending library, but it had the mandatory right, dated back to 1698, to receive copyrighted material. These two libraries are obliged to preserve all deposits. Deposit copies of films and sound and video recordings are preserved by the Arkivet för ljud och bild, Stockholm.

The Royal Library in Stockholm also collects foreign publications in the humanities and the social sciences. From 1953 its Bibliographic Institute was responsible for the National Bibliography and the union catalogue of foreign books and periodicals in the research libraries. The predecessors to the National Bibliography date back to the 16th century. A gap from 1700 to 1829 was to be filled by the Institute by the late 1980s. The National Bibliographies are *Svensk Bokkatalog* and *Svensk Bokförteckning.* The union catalogue of foreign acquisitions in the research libraries was started in 1886.

The National Bibliography and the union catalogue are computerized in a network, the LIBRIS (LIBRary Information System), started in the early 1970s and now the responsibility of the Royal Library. Through cooperative input, the database held more than 1,000,000 bibliographic records accessible by terminals by the mid-1980s . LIBRIS is also used for card and microfiche production. Many libraries prefer to download the records needed and produce their own cards in-house. The Royal Library is a government agency directly under the Ministry of Education. Besides its Institute, it has eight divisions, a newspaper film department, and a remote deposit library, Statens biblioteksdepå, Bålsta. Its collections amount to more than 2,000,000 volumes and 10,000,000 other items. Its manuscript collection occupies 1,500 meters of shelving.

The Lund University Library (founded 1666) dates to medieval times, when it took over the books and manuscripts of the former Danish cathedral chapter. It is the largest Swedish library, holding more than 94,000 shelf meters.

The national archive, Riksarkivet (1618), holds earlier medieval archives (about 13,000 parchment documents). Since 1906, it has been the central authority for all archives of government bodies.

Academic Libraries. Besides Lund, the most renowned academic library is the Uppsala University Library, Carolina Rediviva, Uppsala. It was founded in 1620, but it integrated earlier monastic libraries such as that of St. Bridget's monastery. It has a fine collection of manuscripts (2,000 shelf meters), including the Codex Argenteus. The total holdings are more than 90,000 shelf meters. Like the younger university libraries, it is entitled to receive statutory copies of Swedish publications.

The Göteborg University Library (1861), Umeå University Library (1964), Linköping University Library (1969), and Stockholm University Library (1971) have substantial collections. Stockholm University goes back to a private college founded in 1877.

There are many technical libraries in Sweden. The most important are those of the Royal Institute of Technology (KTH) in Stockholm (1826) and the Chalmers University of Technology in Göteborg (1829). The KTH Library is responsible for SDI service from a score of databases. The Medical Information Center (MIC) at the Karolinska Institutet (1810) is the Nordic center for MEDLARS and MEDLINE; a great many terminals in northern Europe are linked to MEDLINE through MIC. The Agricultural University Library, Ultuna, is the central library for agriculture and is responsible for input to AGRIS and the utilization of CAIN. Chalmers Library is noted for its curriculum development to educate library users.

The research libraries early developed interlibrary loans as well as home loans to their patrons. They also serve as back-up libraries for the public and special libraries. Foreign acquisitions in the public libraries are noted in their database system BUMS, for which the public libraries' own cooperative service center, Bibliotekstjänst, Lund, is responsible.

Public Libraries. The communities are responsible for the funding and operation of the public library system. The government supports the central service offered by 24 county libraries. It also gives funds for hospital, prison, and seamen's libraries. The Stockholm Public Library serves 649,000 inhabitants, and counts 8.8 loans per capita. It has 47 branches, 4 bookmobiles, and a number of smaller outlets. The staff of 620 includes 227 qualified librarians. The smallest county library is Gotlands Läns Library, Visby. In Linköping, Skara, Västerås, and Växjö are libraries that combine the functions of public and research libraries. Their origins stem from the medieval diocesan libraries that also served secondary education.

School Libraries. Libraries are compulsory for primary and secondary schools. The most northern media center, Kiruna Läromedelscentral, serves 15 primary schools and 1 secondary school. There is a "book room" or a school library in each primary school. Often these premises have served as a buffer for other purposes. If needed, the library has been taken up by classes for the whole school year, and library activities have been muddled with non-library activities—instruction in handicraft or typewriting or the school nurse services.

For libraries in the secondary schools, government grants cover the initial acquisition of educational media. A basic collection is 4,000 volumes plus 10 volumes per pupil. The minimum annual acquisition rate is 300 titles. In communities where there are no central service or media center, the needed activities are carried out by a public library from which the school buys the service. The librarians in the schools are in most cases teachers.

Special Libraries. The Parliamentary Library (Riksdagsbiblioteket) serves both the Parliamentarians and the civil servants in the central Government. Since 1931 it has been responsible for the current bibliography of government publications, *Sveriges statliga publikationer*. From 1983 this publication was computerized, and it appears in weekly supplements. A central library for technical reports is Studsvik Energiteknik, Nyköping, responsible for input to INIS and ERDA. The Nobel Library of the Swedish Academy provides the members of the Academy with the background material for choosing candidates for the Nobel Prize for literature. The Academy of Sciences Library, now merged with the Stockholm University Library, holds manuscripts by Emanuel Swedenborg, Carl Linnaeus, J. J. Berzelius, and others. Fine examples of a nobleman's library are the Skokloster Castle Library, Uppland, and the Borrestads Library, Skåne.

Special libraries in private companies participate in a union catalogue of foreign periodicals, published by the KTH under the title LIST-TECH and supply photocopies on request.

The Profession. Bibliotekshögskolan Borås (BHS) (founded in 1972) is responsible for the academic preparation of public and research librarians. The curricula cover four terms (80 points), so in order to get a bachelor's degree a student has to take 40 points in other subjects. The school admits 120 students each term, or 240 in a year. From 1985, students with doctorates in other subjects could graduate from a two-term course. It offers courses for continuing education.

For library assistants there is no formal education; the county libraries and others have arranged courses. In 1981 a program in *Informatik* was established at the Stockholm University, providing many special librarians an opportunity to study library and information sciences up to qualification for a doctor's degree. The Tekniska litteratursällskapet, TLS, offers courses for people in special libraries about literature searches, special collections, patents, and related topics. The Riksarkivet holds courses for archivists. Fellowships for studies abroad in the library information field are given by the Delegationen för Vetenskaplig och Teknisk Informationsförsörjning (DFI), a government agency for information policy and the support of research in library information sciences. It was founded in 1979, and its annual budget is Kr. 18,000,000.

Sveriges Allmänna Biblioteksförening (SAB) was founded in 1915, and in 1982 it had 1,500 individual members. It publishes *Biblioteksbladet* (BBL). Svenska Bibliotekariesamfundet (SBF), founded in 1921, has around 600 members and publishes *Bibliotekariesamfundet Meddelar*. Special libraries belong to TLS (1936), which has a membership of 1,300. It publishes *Tidskrift för dokumentation*—"The Nordic Documentation Journal" (TD). These three organizations belong to IFLA. The DFI is the national member of FID.

REFERENCES

Scientific and Technical Information Provision in Sweden. Proposal for New Organization (Report submitted by two Swedish Government commissions) (1977; Summary, Stockholm, 1978).

Folkbibliotek i Sverige. Betänkande av folkbiblioteksutredningen (1984).

BJÖRN TELL

Switzerland

Switzerland, a federal republic in central western Europe, is bounded by the Federal Republic of Germany on the north, Austria and Liechtenstein on the east, Italy on the south, and France on the west. Population (1984 est.) 6,436,000, area 41,293 sq.km. The official languages are French, German, and Italian. The 26 cantons and semi-cantons are responsible for matters of cultural and educational policy. Therefore the historical background and the structure of the public authorities have both exerted a strong influence on the development and organization of Swiss libraries.

History. One of the oldest libraries in the world, the library of the Abbey of St. Gall (Stiftbibliothek) is in Switzerland. The Library was founded at the beginning of the 7th century. Around the year 820, the abbot Gozbert gave the order to draw up a plan of the Abbey. The manuscript has been preserved in the archives of the Abbey, and the collections have remained intact for nearly 1,300 years. Some of the most important Swiss libraries date back to the Renaissance (Basel, 1460) or the Reformation (Bern, 1529, 1537; Geneva, 1559) or the 17th century (Zurich, 1629).

Under the influence of the economic institutions originating from the Enlightenment, which developed in Switzerland during the second half of the 18th century, many libraries were built in less important towns such as Morges, Yverdon, Zofingen, and Neuchâtel.

One of the most beautiful creations in Swiss library history is the Bibliotheca Bodmeriana, founded by Martin Bodmer (1899–1971). He reassembled 150,000 rare and precious books and manuscripts, including the only known manuscripts of the Greek poet Menander, the oldest papyri of the New Testament (2nd century), and the valuable autographs of the poet Rainer Maria Rilke (1875–1926). The collection is organized around five poles: Homer, the Bible, Dante, Shakespeare, and Goethe. This fascinating collection was returned to the Bodmer foundation after the death of Martin Bodmer, and is open to the public.

National Library. The Swiss National Library shows the influence of historical factors through several characteristics. It was not founded until 1895, and initially its role was limited to the acquisition of *Helvetica* (works concerning Switzerland and those of Swiss authorship, as well as works printed in Switzerland) after 1848. Since legal deposit had not been adopted, "free deposit" was established in 1915 between the Library and the two associations of Swiss booksellers and editors, under which the associations submit one copy of each new publication

to the Library. Any Swiss national or any person residing in Switzerland over 15 years of age can borrow books.

Over the years the Library's functions have been augmented. It manages a bookstock of about 1,500,000 items, including publications of official Swiss, as well as international, organizations. It administers the Swiss Union Catalogue, which indexes more than 5,000,000 foreign publications held in 300 libraries. In order to exploit these resources a series of publications have been edited: *Das Schweizer Buch; Das Schweizer Bücherverzeichnis*, the cumulative edition published quinquennially; *Das Schweizer Zeitschriftenverzeichnis; Bibliographie der Schweizergeschichte; Bibliographia scientiae naturalis Helvetica; Jahresverzeichnis des schweizerischen Hochschulschriften;* and *Bibliographie der Schweizer Familiengeschichte.* The library also houses an office responsible for publishing the *Statistische Quellenwerke der Schweiz.*

Academic Libraries. Most of the 10 Swiss university libraries were founded between 1460 (Basel) and 1629 (Zurich). The Fribourg Library was founded in 1848 through the fusion of the old libraries of the dissolved convents—Collège Saint-Michel. The Zurich Federal Polytechnic, founded in 1855, has developed considerably; it possesses a bookstock of more than 3,000,000 items. Swiss academic libraries possess a total of 13,000,000 volumes and approximately 6,000 incunabula. Several of these libraries have a second function. As canton libraries they serve the local population's needs in scientific literature.

Automation. The Bibliothèque cantonale et universitaire of Lausanne (BCU/L) developed a computerized system (SIBIL) (Système informatisé de bibliothèques) based on a format derived from MARC II. It serves needs of lending scheduling by bar code, acquisitions, and online cataloguing. The database acquires nearly 100,000 records a year, originating from about 20 libraries of Fribourg, Geneva, Lausanne, and Neuchâtel. The database (more than 550,000 titles in 1984) is a mainstay of REBUS.

REBUS (Réseau des bibliotheèques utilisant SIBIL) is a network of four databases utilizing the SIBIL system: Lausanne (connecting more than 20 libraries of four universities), Basel (University Library and Law library), Sankt Gallen (cantonal libraries, including the National Library of Liechtenstein), and—in France—Montpellier (university libraries including also the university libraries of Bordeaux, Pau, Grenoble, and the École Polytechnique of Paris). REBUS is designed to connect the four databases and to extend the network to other libraries in France, Belgium, Luxembourg, Spain, and Switzerland.

The library of the Swiss Federal Institute of

Libraries in Switzerland (1982)

Type	Administrative units	Service points	Volumes in collections	Annual expenditures (franc)	Population served	Professional staff	Total staff
National	1	1	1,500,000	6,408,832	6,366,000	29	82
Academic	8	--	13,400,000	49,837,000	66,206	267	624
Public	1,948	--	--	--	6,366,000	--	--
School	2,764	--	--	--	--	--	--
Special	1,276	--	--	--	--	--	--

National Library of Switzerland

The National Library of Switzerland, Bern, founded in 1895.

Technology in Zurich was working in 1985 on its own computerized system (ETHICS), which was to be ready around 1987.

Building. The university library building in Lausanne (150,000 square feet) opened its doors in 1982; it was built according to an American model. It holds 200,000 volumes in an open-access system.

Public Libraries. The earliest public libraries in Switzerland were originally theological libraries established during the Reformation (Bern, 1528; Sankt Gallen, 1551). The first public libraries without theological antecedents were at Berthoud (1729) and Glarus (1758). The development of public libraries gained momentum, however, principally in the 19th century. From 1868 to 1911 the number of these libraries almost tripled.

There are approximately 2,000 public libraries. Those canton libraries not controlled by a university acquire scientific and bibliographic reference works and additionally conserve the local printed production, which is incorporated in its entirety.

Public library networks have been created, notably in Geneva, Zurich (Bibliothek der Pestalozzi-Gesellschaft), and Bern (Berner Volksbücherei). The Schweizerische Volksbibliothek, founded in 1920, has seven regional branches housing 200,000 volumes, which may be lent either to organizations or to individuals.

School Libraries. There are approximately 3,000 school libraries of varying size and importance.

Special Libraries. Approximately 1,300 special libraries may be divided into four categories: (1) 15 libraries of international organizations, among them the United Nations Library (700,000 volumes, 12,000 periodicals), the International Bureau of Education Library/Unesco (60,000 volumes, 800 periodicals), and the International Labour Office Library (300,000 volumes, 10,000 periodicals); (2) 200 libraries belonging to public societies and associations; (3) approximately 100 libraries belonging to private enterprise (industry, banks, and insurance companies), with collections totaling more than 1,200,000 volumes; and (4) 118 archival libraries.

Monastic Libraries. Among numerous libraries meriting citation the following are especially important: the Stiftsbibliothek Sankt Gallen (100,000 volumes, 2,000 manuscripts, 1,650 incunabula), the libraries of Einsiedeln, and those of Engelberg.

Associations. There are three library associations in Switzerland: the Vereinigung Schweizerischer Bibliothekare (VSB) (200 corporate members and 1,000 individual members), the Schweizerische Vereinigung für Dokumentation (SVI) (425 individual members), and the Vereinigung Schweizerischer Archivare (VSA) (35 corporate members and 124 individual members).

JEAN-PIERRE CLAVEL;
J. MÉDIONI

Sylvestre, Guy
(1918-   )

Jean-Guy Sylvestre was second National Librarian of Canada and under him the National Library experienced remarkable growth and development. He reorganized and expanded the institution, took major initiatives in the areas of collection development, bibliographic control, and systems, and created a consultative approach to policy formulation.

Sylvestre was born in Sorel, Quebec, on May 17, 1918. He graduated from the University of Ottawa with a B.A. in 1939, a L.Ph. in 1940, and an M.A. in 1941. Following several years of government service, he became the private secretary to the Prime Minister of Canada, Louis St. Laurent, in 1945. In 1953 he was appointed Assistant Parliamentary Librarian, and in 1956 Associate. He succeeded W. Kaye Lamb as National Librarian in 1968, serving until November 17, 1983. Following retirement, he was Executive Director of the Canadian Institute for Historical Microreproductions.

Sylvestre was the architect of the revised National Library Act (1969), which expanded the mandate of the library by giving it a role as coordinator of federal library services and enabling it to enter into formal agreements with other libraries and educa-

© 1982 Karsh, Ottawa
Guy Sylvestre

793

tional institutions in respect to library services. Through this device, the National Library was able to pursue the goal of a nationwide library network.

Because the National Library was a relatively new institution, established in 1952, its collections were not comprehensive, and consisted mainly of materials received through legal deposit and transferred from the Library of Parliament and other federal libraries. Sylvestre created a Collection Development Branch in 1972 and, a year later, a Rare Books and Manuscripts Division. These agencies accelerated the systematic development of a retrospective collection of Canadiana and of literature in the humanities and social sciences, with the objectives of supporting research and interlibrary loan. Sylvestre's initiative led to the acquisition of many notable private collections and the papers of several major Canadian authors, composers, and musicians. In 1968 Sylvestre established a Resources Survey Office to assess and monitor the development of collections in other Canadian libraries. To facilitate the sharing of these resources, he took several measures to improve interlibrary loan in Canada, including the establishment in 1980 of a Resource Network Committee.

Having responsibility for the compilation of the national bibliography *Canadiana,* Sylvestre understood the importance of the principles of Universal Bibliographic Control. He moved aggressively to establish and implement national and international standards in the context of developing computer-based systems. Special task forces were established in the early 1970s to develop Canadian cataloguing standards and a Canadian MARC format that would accommodate the two official languages, English and French. These and subsequent committees led to the definition and publication of Canadian MARC formats, authorities, and subject headings. The National Library assumed responsibility for the assignment of ISBNs and ISSNs and developed a decentralized system of Cataloguing-In-Publication.

The appointment of a Systems Development Team in 1968 and the establishment of a Research and Planning Branch in 1970 (later reorganized as the Library Systems Centre and the Office for Network Development) led to the acquisition and modification of the DOBIS software in 1976 and its subsequent application to the production of the national bibliography, to the creation of an online cataloguing system for federal libraries, and to the implementation of an automated union catalogue in 1980. In 1982 the National Library was a key participant in a successful experiment in interchanging bibliographic data between autonomous computer systems.

Sylvestre also moved to improve public services, for example by establishing in 1972 a selective dissemination of information service and in 1973 a multilingual biblioservice which provides loan collections to public libraries for the use of Canada's many ethnic groups. Much attention was devoted to the future of the union catalogue location services: location requests shot up from 58,000 in 1968 to 183,000 in 1983. The National Library provides locations for about 78 percent of these requests and fills about 27 percent of them from its own enlarged collections.

Sylvestre made a particular effort to establish liaison with the library community nationally and internationally. He expanded the National Library's publishing program, launching the *National Library News* in 1979 as a vehicle for the regular provision of information. He exploited consultative mechanisms to the fullest extent, involving hundreds of librarians in the work of the National Library Advisory Board and many committees and task forces. He called upon all librarians in Canada to contribute to the development of a long-range plan for the National Library, which was published in 1979. On the international front, he initiated the practice of regular administrative meetings with the Library of Congress, was prominent in the affairs of the International Federation of Library Associations, and was the founder and first Chairman (in 1974) of the Conference of Directors of National Libraries.

Sylvestre was at the same time an active scholar and a man of letters, having published extensively in the fields of French- and English-Canadian literature. He was elected a Fellow of the Royal Society of Canada in 1951, serving as its President in 1973, and was appointed an Officer of the Order of Canada in 1982. He received many honorary degrees and awards, including, in 1983, the government's highest form of recognition, the Outstanding Public Service Award.

REFERENCES
F. Dolores Donnelley, *The National Library of Canada* (1973).
National Library of Canada, *The Future of the National Library of Canada* (1979).
Ian Wees, *The National Library of Canada: Twenty-Five Years After* (1978).

BASIL STUART-STUBBS

Syria

Syria, a republic in southwest Asia, is bounded by Turkey on the north, Iraq on the east, Jordan and Israel on the south, and Lebanon and the Mediterranean Sea on the west. Population (1984 est.) 9,934,000; area 185,180 sq.km. The official language is Arabic.

National Libraries. The two national libraries in the Syrian Arab Republic also function as public libraries. The Al-Zahiriyah National Library in Damascus, founded in 1877, is attached to the Academy of Arabic Language, which is affiliated with the Ministry of Higher Education. The library has about 100,000 books, 65,000 volumes of periodicals, and 13,000 manuscripts and other materials. The main emphasis of the collections is on humanities and social sciences. A department of photography and microfilming has been instituted in the Library. The second National Library is the Al-Maktaba al-Wataniyah in Aleppo, which was founded in 1924. The Library possesses about 30,000 volumes and 50 periodical titles and is mainly directed toward public library services. The legal deposit law of 1963 requires printers to deliver five copies of literary works published in the republic, four copies of nonliterary works, and two copies of books printed in the republic but published abroad to the Ministry of Information, which has to transmit one copy to Al-Zahiriyah National Library. The Al-Zahiriyah National Library issued the Bulletin of Books Published in the Syrian Arab Republic from 1971 as an annual Syrian national bibliography.

A new national library was opened in Damascus, southern Syria, in 1985.

Academic Libraries. The main universities in Syria have established libraries to serve their teaching staff, students, and scholars at large. The oldest and largest is the Central Library of the University of Damascus, founded in 1919. The Central Library and the 16 college branch libraries have more than 150,000 volumes and subscribe to about 1,400 periodical titles. The other academic libraries are those of the University of Aleppo (founded in 1960; 36,000 volumes), the Tichreen University in Latakia (1971), the Damascus Institute of Technology (1963; 6,000 volumes), the Arab University of Damascus (1919; 15,000 volumes), and Al-Baath University (1979; 6,000 volumes).

Public Libraries. Syria has a well-developed public library system. The Directorate of Libraries of the Ministry of Culture, Tourism, and National Guidance administers more than 40 libraries in the Arab Cultural Centers, which are spread throughout the country. People in rural areas have access to public library services through 10 bookmobiles. The Directorate of Libraries supplies materials, technical guidance, and personnel and also publishes a monthly bulletin of ministry publications.

School Libraries. Schools of various types possess libraries, but their use is not incorporated into the teaching process. The majority of school libraries in Syria are administered by part-time teachers who are not professionally trained. Unesco reported 1,984 school libraries in the country in 1980, with total holdings of some 400,000 volumes.

Special Libraries. Many Syrian government agencies, organizations, and research centers established special libraries to serve their officials and the research community. Special libraries are found in the Ministry of Information, the Ministry of Transport, the Directorate of Scientific and Technical Affairs of the Ministry of Industry, the Directorate of Scientific and Technical Affairs of the Ministry of Petroleum and Minerals, the Directorate of Scientific and Agricultural Research of the Ministry of Agriculture, the Higher Council of Sciences (which incorporates the Council Library and the Nuclear Energy Library), the Central Bureau of Statistics, the Organization of Industrial Projects, and the Planning Institute for Economic and Social Development.

Some of these special libraries offer bibliographical services, indexing, abstracting, photocopying, and publishing and inquiry services. Other organizations emphasize documentation and information services, such as the Department of Documentation and Technical Information, attached to the Center of Industrial Testing and Industries (founded in 1967); the Directorate of Scientific Documentation and Information, attached to the Center of Scientific Studies and Research of the Ministry of Defense (1972); and the Educational Documentation Center of the Ministry of Education (1961).

MOHAMED M. EL HADI*

Libraries in the Syrian Arab Republic (1980)

Type	Administrative units	Service points	Volumes in collections	Annual expenditures (pound)	Population served[a]	Professional staff	Total staff
National	1	1	85,000	--	--	1	14
Academic	--	--	--	--	--	--	--
Public	--	--	--	--	--	--	--
School	1,984	--	416,000	5,515,000	422,160	4	844
Special							
Nonspecialized	1	--	1,000	--	--	--	--

[a]Registered borrowers.

Source: Unesco, *Statistical Yearbook,* 1984.

Tanodi, Aurelio Zlatko

(1914-   )

Aurelio Zlatko Tanodi, leading Argentine scholar associated with the development of various scholarly pursuits, including historical research, paleography, and archival studies, conducted many research projects. His work in the organization of archival materials, together with the training of high-level personnel in the discipline, won him special recognition.

Tanodi was born September 1, 1914, in Hum, Zagreb, Croatia, in what is now Yugoslavia. He studied at the National College of Varazdin and in 1937 received a degree in Universal History from the Faculty of Philosophy of Zagreb University.

His work at the Colegio Clasico de Varazdin (Classic College of Varazdin) began with historical research based on medieval documents deposited in the municipal archives of the city. He worked at the National Archive of Croatia in Zagreb and, commissioned by the government of his country, studied at the Secret Archive of the Vatican and the National Archive of Hungary in Budapest. During this period he worked at the National Academy of Arts and Sciences of Croatia, obtaining the title Doctor of History at the University of Zagreb; his thesis, "Bula de Oro de Zagreb" (The Golden Papal Bull of Zagreb) won highest honors.

In 1945 he moved to Austria, continuing studies at the University of Graz. During 1947–48 he worked at the Biblioteca Mayor of the Antonianum University in Rome, simultaneously studying archival management at the Vatican Archive and librarianship at the Vatican Library. Having established residence in Argentina in 1948, Tanodi began a teaching career at the National University of Córdoba in 1953.

He published the *Manual de Archivología Hispanoamericana: teorías y principios* ("Manual of Hispanoamerican Archives: Theories and Principles") in 1961 in the Collectanea Archivistica series. During 1972–73 he visited various Latin American countries under the auspices of the International Archival Council and the Department of Cultural Affairs of the OAS, demonstrating the urgent need for professional training in this area.

Tanodi's work in Argentina was centered at the Escuela de Archiveros (School of Archival Management), part of the National University of Córdoba, of which he became Director in 1959. He also directed the Centro Interamericano de Desarrollo de Archivos (Interamerican Center for the Development of Archives), part of the School of Archival Management, under the auspices of the OAS, from 1972. Aside from administrative and teaching activities, Tanodi also did advisory and consulting work in the area of archival management in various Latin American countries and edited the annual *Boletín Interamericano de Archivos*. He participated in a number of national and international congresses and conferences.

REINALDO J. SUAREZ

Aurelio Zlatko Tanodi

Tanzania

Tanzania, a republic in southeast Africa, comprises two distinct areas. Tanganyika, bordering the Indian Ocean, is surrounded by Kenya, Uganda, Rwanda, Burundi, Zaire, Zambia, Malawi, and Mozambique.

Zanzibar, including Pemba Island, Zanzibar Island, and various small islets, is off the coast. Population (1984 est.) 21,202,000; area 945,087 sq.km. The official languages are English and Swahili.

History. The genesis of a nationwide library system in Tanzania dates to 1960 when Sidney Hockey was invited by the governments of Uganda, Kenya, Tanganyika, and Zanzibar to carry out a survey of their existing library facilities and make recommendations on services to be offered. Tanganyika was the first country to adopt the Hockey report. In 1963 the Tanganyika Library Services Board Act was passed, empowering the Board to promote, establish, equip, manage, maintain, and develop libraries in mainland Tanzania. In 1975 a new act repealed that of 1963. Enacted in the framework of Unesco's NATIS concept, the act empowers the Board to coordinate library and documentation services, arrange facilities for library training, promote literacy campaigns and the development of indigenous literature, and supervise all types of libraries in Tanzania.

National Library. There was no separate national library in the mid-1980s. The National Central Library operates as both a national and a public library. Plans were under way to establish a separate national library in the new capital, Dodoma. The National Central Library was founded in 1965 as a pilot library in temporary premises with a collection of 30,000 books from the East African Literature Bureau and 20,000 from the British Council. The new building was opened by President Mwalimu Julius K. Nyerere on December 9, 1967, and is the headquarters of a nationwide library service. It has public reference and lending service for both adults and children, a central book processing and supply unit, and a central advisory service. Since 1969 Tanzania Library Service has compiled the national bibliography of Tanzania, and it enjoys legal deposit status.

The Service is responsible for the promotion, establishment, and management of all public libraries in the country in both urban and rural areas. By 1984, 15 branch (regional) libraries had been established in major towns in mainland Tanzania, and rural library services were being offered to several areas by bookmobiles and village libraries.

The National Central Library also operates (1) the Tanzania National Documentation Centre (TANDOC), which produces, among other things, *Agricultural Abstracts, Industrial Abstracts,* and *Education Abstracts;* and (2) the National Bibliographic Agency (NBA), which, apart from producing *Tanzania National Bibliography* (TNB), allocates International Standard Book Numbers (ISBNs) and International Standard Serial Numbers (ISSNs) to local publishers and institutions.

With Unesco's assistance, plans were under way in 1985 to automate the National Bibliographic Agency using a microcomputer.

Academic Libraries. Although there are several libraries in teacher training colleges and other institutions of higher education, they are not well developed. The most important academic library is that of the University of Dar es Salaam. The University College, Dar es Salaam, was founded by the Tanganyika Africa National Union (TANU) in October 1961. The College at first was downtown in the building that now houses the Institute of Adult Education. In 1963 it became a constituent College of the University College and Nairobi University College. The University of East Africa was initially affiliated with the University of London. In 1964 the College moved to its present campus on Observation Hill overlooking the city of Dar es Salaam.

On July 1, 1970, an act of Parliament revoked the 1962 Act of the East African Common Service Organization (EACSO), which linked the three constituent Colleges, and consequently the University College of Dar es Salaam ceased to exist. The University of East Africa also terminated activities, and on August 29, 1970, the University of Dar es Salaam was formally inaugurated as an independent university. The University Library was established downtown at the same time as its parent institution in 1961 and moved to its present building in July 1965.

A large quantity of materials, particularly Tanzanian government documents, were acquired under the Library (Deposit of Books) Act of 1962. Also placed in the library are publications of major international organizations. There are other special collections on law and East Africana; of particular importance is the East African Bibliography on punched cards, which includes entries from libraries at Makerere and Nairobi universities. The library has also an excellent collection of maps, mainly of East African countries, and manuscripts. In addition to the main library, branch libraries serve the faculty of medicine at Muhimbili Hospital in Dar es Salaam and the faculty of agriculture and veterinary science at Morogoro.

School Libraries. The Education Libraries Department at the National Central Library provides services to schools and teacher training colleges, including advice on book selection, design and planning of library buildings, library seminars, and actual visits to schools and colleges. There is, in addition, a school mobile library service with a van specially designed for this purpose. Visits are made to secondary schools where books are distributed to libraries to supplement their educational needs.

Special Libraries. The Tanzania Library Service is also responsible for special libraries. Many requests are received from government ministries and from other organizations and institutions for assistance in the organization of their libraries. The Tanzania Library Service gives professional advice and, wherever possible, sends librarians to these institutions.

Tanzania Library Service

National Central Library in Dar Es Salaam, founded in 1965.

The Profession. The Tanzania Library Association (TLA) was formed in 1965 as a branch of the East African Library Association (EALA), established in 1956. In 1971–72 the TLA became an autonomous national association. Since 1968 the TLA has published *Someni* as its official journal. The Association's main functions are: to unite all people working or interested in library work; to encourage the promotion, establishment, and improvement of libraries and library services; and to improve the standard of librarianship.

REFERENCE

E. E. Kaungamno, "The Functions and Activities of Tanzania Library Services within the NATIS Concept," *Unesco Bulletin for Libraries* (1975).

E. E. KAUNGAMNO

Taube, Mortimer
(1910–1965)

Mortimer Taube, information scientist and library consultant, was an innovator and inventor, as well as scholar and business executive. He is widely credited

Libraries in Tanzania (1984)

Type	Administrative units	Service points	Volumes in collections[a]	Annual expenditures (shilling)	Population served	Professional staff	Total staff
National	1	7	187,223	--	1,000,000	34	192
Academic[c]	70	72	382,264	--	26,045	9	217
Public	19	26	453,754	3,000,000[b]	1,105,000	52	410
School	130	16	45,379	--	10,340	1	35
Other	3	3	17,641	--	1,805	--	7

[a]Includes periodicals.
[b]Expenditures for the National Library and public libraries combined.
[c]Excludes the University of Dar es Salaam Main Library.

Source: Tanzania National Documentation Centre.

with the implementation of *coordinate indexing* through the application of "uniterms," a concept that, although initially applied to manual retrieval systems, forms the basis of a significant amount of computerized search strategy.

He was born in Jersey City, New Jersey, on December 6, 1910. He received an A.B. degree from the University of Chicago and was elected to Phi Beta Kappa. He did graduate work at Harvard University in philosophy under Alfred North Whitehead, received a Ph.D. from the University of California at Berkeley in 1935, and followed with a certificate in librarianship at Berkeley in 1936.

Starting in 1936 he held a variety of responsible academic library positions: circulation librarian at Mills College (Oakland, California), cataloguer at Rutgers University (New Brunswick, New Jersey), and Head of the Acquisitions Department at Duke University (Durham, North Carolina) from 1940 to 1944. He joined the Library of Congress in 1944 and served for five years as Assistant Chief of the General Reference and Bibliography Division, Assistant Director of the Acquisitions Department, and Chief of the Science and Technology Project. He left LC to serve, from 1949 to 1952, as Deputy Chief of the Atomic Energy Commission's Technical Information Service.

Taube founded Documentation, Inc., in 1952 and served as its Board Chairman and leader until his death. Documentation, Inc., was the first (and for a long time only) information science corporation in existence. Starting with only a handful of associates, Taube built an organization that, by 1965, numbered over 500. Under his guidance the corporation engaged in a large number of innovative studies for government agencies—including the U.S. Air Force and the National Institutes of Health— and pioneered in the field of information facilities management. The organization administered the first contract-operated national information program, the NASA Scientific and Technical Information Facility, from 1962 to 1968. Persons who worked with and for Taube in the pioneering days at Documentation, Inc. came to comprise a Who's Who of the information science profession.

Throughout his career Taube found the time to lecture and write. He taught at the University of Chicago and Columbia University and flew to New York weekly for seminars at Columbia. He wrote numerous articles and several significant books, including *Studies in Coordinate Indexing,* volumes 1–6 (1953–65) and *Computers and Common Sense: The Myth of Thinking Machines* (1961). He was Editor of *American Documentation,* 1951–52. The Special Libraries Association presented him its Professional Award in 1952, and the American Society for Information Science presented its Award of Merit to him posthumously in 1966.

Taube was indefatigable in his search for truth and honesty. He was often controversial, usually because his ideas were well ahead of their time. A natural teacher and brilliant and witty lecturer, Taube had strong convictions and was not afraid to express them, but he had abiding respect for other opinions if he felt they were honestly and intelligently derived. He was the outspoken foe of shoddy scholarship, meaningless studies, and twisted logic to support pre-

Maurice Tauber

ALA

determined conclusions.

Taube was particularly concerned lest practices designed for manual library systems simply be moved to computers. He feared the library profession would miss the opportunity to reexamine its premises in light of the opportunities computer technology would offer in bibliographic control and analysis.

A person of many talents and interests, Taube worked tirelessly on behalf of religious, political, and numerous charitable interests. He died on September 3, 1965, at the age of 54. At the time of his death he was engaged in one of the many activities that involved him passionately: he was sailing on Chesapeake Bay.

REFERENCE
Jesse H. Shera, "Taube, Mortimer," *Dictionary of American Library Biography* (1978).

HERBERT S. WHITE

Tauber, Maurice
(1908–1980)

Maurice Falcom Tauber was an international leader in library and information science—a prolific writer, biographer, editor, critic, researcher, scholar, educator, administrator, and expert in technical services and library buildings.

He was born on February 14, 1908, in Norfolk, Virginia. In 1925 his family moved to Philadelphia. He studied at Temple University, Philadelphia, where he majored in English and education and earned a Master's degree in sociology (1939). In 1932, while working in the Library of Temple University, he commuted to New York City to take courses at Columbia University School of Library Service. He completed the school's Bachelor of Science program in 1934.

In 1935 he was appointed Head of the Cataloguing Department of Temple University. While there he undertook the reclassification of the Library's holdings from Dewey to Library of Congress. He enrolled in the Graduate Library School of the University of Chicago (Ph.D., 1941), and in 1941 he joined the University Library at Chicago as Head of its Cataloguing Department. Soon after, he was appointed to the faculty of the Graduate Library School as Assistant Professor.

In 1944 Tauber returned to Columbia University as Assistant Director of its Library, in charge of Technical Services, and Assistant Professor at the School of Library Service. He gave up his position at the Library to become a full-time member of the School of Library Service faculty with the rank of Associate Professor in 1946. Tauber was finally able to fulfill his dream of fully dedicating his time to teaching and research. He was awarded a full professorship three years later. In 1954 he was named Melvil Dewey Professor of Library Service. He held that post until his retirement from Columbia in 1976, but it did not make him favor the Dewey Decimal Classification—he spent a lifetime promoting the LC classification and influenced many academic libraries to shift from Dewey to LC.

As a researcher and consultant, Tauber was asked to conduct surveys by a great number of institutions. A bibliography (Marion C. Szigethy, 1974) cites 75 survey reports, of which 5 were on a national level (libraries in Australia); 45 on university, college, and research libraries; 5 on public and school libraries; 11 on special libraries; and 9 on state libraries and library systems. Among the institutions he surveyed were Columbia University (1943 and 1957); Cornell (1947); Dartmouth (1952); Barnard College Library (1954); Boston University (1956); Manhattanville College (1958); University of South Carolina (1958); Montana State University (1959); and Australian libraries (1964).

Szigethy also credits Tauber with 20 monographs; 25 conference papers, proceedings, and reports; and 85 articles and essays. Tauber was Editor of *College and Research Libraries* for 18 years. He was also on the editorial advisory boards of *Library Sources and Technical Services,* the *Journal of Cataloging and Classification,* the *Journal of Documentation,* the *Journal of Higher Education,* and others.

Tauber's first publication was a 17-page monograph, *Brief History of the Library of Temple University* (1934). Among his many publications, *The University Library* (1945), on which he collaborated with Louis Round Wilson, and *Technical Services in Libraries* (1954), stand out as classics. Tauber was interested in all aspects of the library and information profession but distinguished himself as a champion in the specific areas of reclassification and recataloguing.

In technical services, he loudly and clearly sang his song in favor of centralization of services. Academic and research libraries became his main platform. He also became deeply interested in the planning and design of library buildings. Sixteen of his surveys were primarily concerned with design of library buildings. Tauber's interests were not limited to American institutions. In Australia he visited 162 libraries in 1964; his report included approximately 300.

His service to ALA and other professional associations was extensive. He received many national awards, among them the Margaret Mann Citation (1953) and the Melvil Dewey Award and Medal (1955).

As a teacher he won the affection and admiration of many of his students; he opened his house to them, especially to those from foreign lands.

In 1981 the Maurice F. Tauber Foundation was established in New York. It sponsors an annual memorial lecture hosted by library schools throughout the United States, publication of appropriate scholarly works, and an annual award for excellence in library and information science. The first memorial lecture was delivered by Lowell A. Martin at Columbia University, December 12, 1981, on "The Library Surveyor—Innovator or Intruder?"

REFERENCES

Richard L. Darling, "Maurice F. Tauber, 1908–1980," *Library Service News* 41 (Fall, 1980).

Kurt S. Maier, "Maurice F. Tauber," *Leaders in American Academic Librarianship 1925-1975,* edited by Wayne A. Wiegand (Beta Phi Mu, 1983), provides the most comprehensive information.

Marion C. Szigethy, *Maurice Falcom Tauber: A Bibliography 1934–1973* (1974), provides biographical information.

NASSER SHARIFY

Thailand

Thailand, an independent constitutional monarchy in southeastern Asia, is bounded by Laos on the northeast, Kampuchea on the southeast, the South China Sea on the south, and Burma on the west; a section of Thailand extends down the Malay Peninsula to Malaysia on the south and the Indian Ocean on the west. Population (1984 est.) 50,382,000; area 514,000 sq.km. The official language is Thai.

History. The National Library has more than 184,000 Thai manuscripts. Written on palm leaves and Thai paper folded in accordion pleats, they are mainly copies of Buddhist sacred books and other Buddhist literature, literary compositions, and works on medicine, law, history, arts, and astrology. There are 87 stone inscriptions in various ancient languages and scripts of the Southeast Asian region.

National Library. The National Library of Thailand is composed of three libraries: the Vajirayana Library, Vajiravudh Library, and Damrongrajanupharb Library. Established in 1905, the National Library is a division in the Department of Fine Arts of the Ministry of Education.

The present National Library building was opened in May 1966. Its printed book collection is strong in the history and geography of Thailand and totals about 900,000 volumes in Thai and other languages. The Library is entitled by law to receive two copies of every book published in Thailand, but this has not been well enforced. There is no copyright registration in Thailand.

Audiovisual materials include a collection of tapes and Thai folklore, important lectures and discussions, and parliamentary debates and speeches. The library compiles various bibliographies.

Two libraries in addition to the National Library are the Phya Anuman Rajadhon Memorial Library and the Library of King Rama VI. The National Archives was developed along with the National Library and has its own building.

Central Library, Chulalongkorn University

Central Library of Chulalongkorn University, Thailand.

Academic Libraries. Thailand has 11 universities. All have their own libraries, many with more than 100,000 books, most in foreign languages and inadequate in all subjects. Financial support for university libraries varies from one institution to another. In most faculties, lecturers act as librarians along with their teaching.

In 1967 the Thai and U.S. governments set up funds for each university to acquire more books on science, technology, and the social sciences, a project that had ended by the late 1970s. In 1968 the National Council formed the Committee on Development of University Libraries, comprising 10 university librarians and an official of the Council. The Committee planned to compile a union list of serials from all university and some government libraries and a union catalogue of books in all universities. There are incomplete union catalogues at Chulalongkorn and Kasetsart University Central libraries.

The Committee also attempted to promote recognition of higher status for university libraries and librarians and solve other problems. Cooperation among university libraries includes interlibrary loan and duplicate exchanges with hope for cooperative acquisition and cataloguing.

Public Libraries. Public library development has been slow. The government initiated services in 1949. Though more than 300 public libraries were established, most had small reading rooms and an average of 300 volumes and had no professionally trained librarians. The government agencies operating public libraries are the Adult Education Division, Elementary and Adult Education Department, Ministry of Education; the Bangkok Municipality; the National Security Command Community Development Department; and the Ministry of Interior. Each government agency followed its own information policies.

Public libraries of the Bangkok Municipality and the Dhonburi Municipality have trained librarians and adequate budgets. Public libraries under the supervision of the Adult Education Division lack trained librarians, and librarians are placed at the lowest grade of the civil servants. Budgets are too small to bring the public libraries up to the standards set by the Ministry of Education in 1968. Those standards grew out of a 1962 Unesco study.

School Libraries. The Ministry of Education supervises school libraries. Lack of suitable children's books, few professional librarians, and low status accorded the school librarian contributed to limited student use of libraries. Out of some 28,000 schools of all levels, fewer than 10 percent have libraries rendering good services to students.

A committee for library development appointed in 1963 helped improve salary scales for school librarians and led to the adoption of standards. There were later projects to provide all schools with libraries and in-service training for staff. The Comprehensive School Project aims to improve the quality of instruction, library quarters, and book collections of 20 schools throughout Thailand.

Special Libraries. Special libraries in Thailand are found in research institutes, government agencies, professional and trade associations, learned societies, and business firms. Among the libraries that have special resources in the field of science are the Division of Scientific and Technological Information Department of Science Service, Ministry of Science, Technology, and Energy; the Faculty of Science Library, Chulalongkorn University; and the Faculty of Science Library, Mahidol University. Several outstanding libraries in health sciences, such as Siriraj Medical Library of Mahedol University, Chulalongkorn Medical Library, and Ramathibodhi Hospital Library, are part of the medical schools of major universities. A number have had assistance from the China Medical Board and the Rockefeller Foundation.

The Library of the National Institute for Developmental Administration has a collection of about 60,000 volumes. The Thailand Information Center at the Faculty of Political Science, Chulalongkorn University, specializes in information on Thailand, with particular emphasis on the behavioral and social sciences and related disciplines. The Asian Institute of Technology has an engineering library that pioneered in introducing computerized systems to library work. It worked toward becoming a regional information center for science and technology in Southeast Asia.

Other special libraries include the Siam Society Library of Southeast Asian materials, the Bank of Thailand, the Highway Department, and the Department of Technical and Economic Cooperation.

The Thai National Documentation Center supplies scientific and technical information and holds some 126,000 volumes. Other international organizations have libraries in Thailand.

The Profession. The Thai Library Association was founded in 1954 with the help of the Asia Foundation. The Association sponsors workshops, conferences and seminars, radio and television programs, publications, and other activities and has played an important role in the library development of the country.

REFERENCES
Suthilak Ambhanwong, *Libraries and Librarianship in Thai-*

Libraries in Thailand (1981)

Type	Administrative units	Service points	Volumes in collections	Annual expenditures (baht)	Population served	Professional staff	Total staff
National	1	6	1,245,000	13,005,000	--	35	399
Academic	--	--	--	--	--	--	--
Public	--	--	--	--	--	--	--
School	--	--	--	--	--	--	--

Source: Unesco, *Statistical Yearbook,* 1984.

land, Chulalongkorn University Department of Library Science, paper no. 5 (1967).
David Kaser, Walter C. Stone, and Cecil K. Byrd, *Library Development in Eight Asian Countries* (1969).

UTHAI DHUTIYABHODI*

Thorpe, Frederick A.

(1913-)

Frederick A. Thorpe, British publisher, founded large-print book publishing in Britain.

Thorpe was born on October 22, 1913, in Leicester, one of the major English provincial cities, and brought up there. His initial experience in publishing was interrupted by war service in the Royal Air Force from 1940 to 1946. On his return to Leicester he resumed his publishing interests, which developed and expanded to become a highly successful business. In it he gained the experience in every aspect of the book trade and publishing that, like the contacts he made with agents and distributors worldwide, was to prove an apprenticeship for his second career, that of pioneering the publication of books in large print.

In 1963, when he was about to retire from his business, Thorpe was approached by a committee set up in response to the concern expressed by the British Government for the cultural well-being of elderly people. There were books available in abundance, but many elderly people could not easily read normal-size print. The committee sought Thorpe's advice, and he applied his experience in printing and publishing to the problem. He discussed it with the Library Association and learned of the results of earlier investigations into this and similar problems, none of which had produced a solution. He decided that the technical difficulties of printing and producing books in print twice as large as that in normal books, and with an ink density and paper quality that would ensure a sharp contrast, could be solved; he founded the non-profit publishing house of Ulverscroft Large Print Books to produce them.

In selecting the first titles for publication, Thorpe found publishers reluctant to allow their authors' work to appear in a new and untried format from an unknown publisher. His market for large-print books was mainly the elderly who looked for established authors and well-written books. After some initial disappointments he approached Dame Agatha Christie, who gave the project her full support and encouraged other well-known authors to allow their books to appear in the new series. Four thousand copies of each of the first four titles were published in September 1964: *Pocketful of Rye* by Agatha Christie, *I Brought a Mountain* by Thomas Firbank, *The Avenger* by Edgar Wallace, and *The Fettered Past* by Netta Muskett. They established a precedent both in the careful selection of titles that is a hallmark of the firm and in their format. They were printed by offset lithography from photographic enlargements of the normal-size books. Their size, eleven by eight inches, and their distinctive book jackets (blue for romances and historical and romantic suspense; orange for westerns; black for mystery; red for general fiction,

adventure, and suspense; green for nonfiction; and, later, purple for specialist series and brown for individual specialist titles) made them immediately recognizable.

Thorpe decided that the books should be sold directly to libraries and other institutions, not through the book trade, which helped to keep the selling price low. The Library Association sent one book, with a letter supporting the venture, to each library. While orders from libraries reached the expected level, there were few from hospitals and welfare institutions, which had been expected to purchase half the copies. Thorpe therefore sought overseas markets. Through his own international contacts, and others made through the American and Canadian Library Associations, Rotary International, and a number of interested individuals, the sale of Ulverscroft Large Print Books spread throughout the English-speaking world. Thorpe's personal interest, his visits to libraries, and his presence at conference exhibitions made him an internationally recognized figure in librarianship.

The development of large print books from 1963 to 1969 was one of technical experiment to improve quality and overcome the difficulties caused by the photographic enlargement of existing typesetting, especially broken type and uneven inking, which are much more noticeable when enlarged. The solution was to reset the books in large print; this decision, along with the production of a thinner but opaque paper, led in 1969 to a new nine-by-six-inch format, easier for the reader to enjoy and the library to shelve. The new format was greatly appreciated, and Thorpe went on to newer, still thinner papers, producing even longer books in the series that are not uncomfortable to handle.

The 500th title appeared in 1971 and the 1,000th in 1976, an event marked by the publication of a five-volume edition of *War and Peace*. Thorpe introduced the Charnwood Series in 1981 in order to include a wider range of titles to meet the needs of a new generation of large-print readers and began the Linford Series of paperback books in 1983 to help frail elderly readers. By 1984 the number of titles published had reached more than 2,400, and Thorpe had plans for further developments.

The profits from Ulverscroft Large Print Books are covenanted to the Ulverscroft Foundation, a charity that also receives donations from individuals, including many readers of Ulverscroft books. The Foundation is administered by trustees and assists hospitals, schools, and libraries.

The importance of Thorpe's work has been recognized in several ways. In 1969 he was awarded the Order of the British Empire (OBE) by the Queen, in 1972 the ALA's Francis Joseph Campbell Award, in 1973 the Queen's Award to Industry and the Grimshaw Memorial Award from the National Federation of the Blind, in 1976 an ALA Centennial Citation and in 1984 an engrossed resolution of the Council of the Library Association.

Thorpe's achievement is expressed in the title of the book he chose as the 500th Ulverscroft large-print title *A Many-Splendoured Thing*. He had made reading possible for many people by bringing unbounded energy and business experience to the creation of a new and now essential part of the resources of libraries in meeting the needs of the disadvantaged.

REFERENCES
F. A. Thorpe, "Large Print: An Assessment of its Development and Potential," *Library Association Record* (March 1972).
W. A. Munford, "Books for the Partially Sighted," *British Book News* (April 1976).

GEOFFREY SMITH

Tibet

Also known as the Land of Snow, Tibet occupies an area of approximately 1,221,700 sq.km. on the Himalayan plateau and has within its borders some of the highest mountains in the world. The average elevation of its inhabited areas is 16,000 feet (4,876 meters). It is bordered by China on the north and east, India, Bhutan, and Nepal on the south, and Jammu and Kashmir on the west. Lhasa, the capital and former seat of the Dalai Lama, has an elevation of 12,000 feet; Shigatse, the former seat of the Panchen Lama, has an elevation of 9,000 feet. This vast area is but scantily populated; according to a 1980 estimate, the population was about 2,000,000. Most of the people live in the southern valleys. The chief languages are Tibetan and Chinese.

Religion constitutes the principal form of Tibetan cultural life. In the 8th century the native Bon religion was displaced by a tantric form of Buddhism, a form that flourished from the 10th through the 13th centuries and has become known as the *rNin-ma-pa,* or Red Hat sect. In the 15th century, in reaction against the decadent practices of the Red Hat sect, a reform took place that led to the formation of the *dGe-lugs-pa,* or Yellow Hat sect. Quickly the Yellow Hat sect became Tibet's major Buddhist sect and transformed Tibet into a theocratic state under the leadership of the Dalai Lama and the Panchen Lama. Tibet was incorporated into the People's Republic of China in 1951.

No structured library system existed in Tibet prior to 1951. Each monastery had its own library, and some of the major ones, such as Drepung and Sera, also functioned as publishing houses. No information is available on how materials in these monastic libraries were stored and made accessible, nor is there any indication that any monastery functioned as a national library or that material circulated among monasteries. The monasteries gradually disappeared after Tibet's incorporation into China.

Tibet's monastic libraries, however, never played an important role in the country's cultural life, serving more frequently than not as mere storage areas. In spite of a large output of religious literature, Tibet's population was, by and large, illiterate. Most of the monks limited their reading activities to a few basic texts. The degree of change in the country's literacy rate under Chinese rule is difficult to assess because of lack of reliable data. If, however, the experience in China proper can be used as a guide, the situation could have improved considerably. Observers assume that an increase in literacy means knowledge of Chinese rather than knowledge of Tibetan. Indeed, most material published in Tibet in the decades after mid-century was published in Chinese. The country's main newspaper, the *Hsi-tsang Jih-pao* (The Tibet Daily), is exclusively in Chinese. Libraries in

Tibet were likely to be structured along the lines followed in China.

In 1959 Tibet witnessed an uprising against the Chinese in Lhasa that forced many refugees, including the Dalai Lama, to go to India. The majority of them settled in Dharmsala, Himachal Pradesh, where they began a conscious effort to preserve their cultural heritage, encouraged by the Dalai Lama. In this context the Library of the Tibetan Works and Archives was founded in 1971, with the principal purpose of collecting all materials, in printed as well as in manuscript form, dealing directly or indirectly with Tibet. Only scant details about the Library's operation and holdings are readily available. The Library undertook an oral history project and a retranslation project; the former covers the recording of Tibetan oral traditions, the latter the translation of Tibetan Buddhist texts into Sanskrit.

REFERENCE
H. Hoffman, *Tibet: A Handbook,* Indiana University Asian Studies Research Institute, Oriental Series (1977)

LUC KWANTEN*

Togo

Togo, a West African republic, is bounded on the north by Upper Volta, on the east by Benin, on the south by the Gulf of Guinea, and on the west by Ghana. Population (1984 est.) 2,947,000; area 56,785 sq.km. The official language is French.

National Library. The Bibliothèque Nationale in Lomé was decreed a national library on October 1, 1969. Under the directorship of the Ministère de l'éducation nationale, the library originally was established in 1937 as the Service de la documentation générale, a documentation center to study documentation concerns in museums, archives, and libraries. In 1945 it was taken over by the local IFAN Centre (Institut fondamental de l'Afrique noire), and in 1960 that center become the Institut togolais des sciences humaines. The Institut has departments of anthropology, archaeology, history, ethnography, geography, linguistics, and sociology. In the mid-1980s the Library's collection housed approximately 6,000 volumes and 1,000 periodicals; 85 percent of all holdings are in French.

The functions of a national archives are performed by the Institut togolais des sciences humaines and the Archives de la Présidence de la République. Although Togo has some laws relating to legal deposit, they have never been systematically enforced.

Academic Libraries. Togo has one university, the Université du Bénin, which was founded as a college in Lomé in 1965 and attained university status in 1970. All higher education institutions throughout the country are part of the University. The language of instruction is French. The University's libraries are decentralized. Holdings include 50,000 volumes and pamphlets, 90 percent of which are in French. Another institution of higher education is the École nationale d'administration (ENA), founded in Lomé in 1958 to provide a training center for Togolese civil servants. The library has more than 1,000 volumes. There are government-sponsored technical colleges at Lomé and at Sokodé and an agricultural school in Kpalimé with a library of about

Libraries in Togo (1982)

Type	Administrative units	Service points	Volumes in collections	Annual expenditures (C.F.A. franc)	Population served[a]	Professional staff	Total staff
National	1	--	6,000	33,262,000	--	9	40
Academic	1	6	50,000	34,383,000	4,904	7	41
Public	--	--	--	--	--	--	--
School	--	--	--	--	--	--	--

[a]Registered borrowers.

Source: Unesco, *Statistical Yearbook,* 1984.

3,500 volumes. The library of the teacher training college at Atakpamé holds some 6,000 volumes.

Other Services. Togo does not have an organized public library system.

Important collections of specialized research institutes include those of the Institut national de la recherche scientifique and the Office de la recherche scientifique et technique Outre-mer (ORSTOM). The Institut national de la recherche scientifique, Lomé, was founded in 1965 as a coordination center for scientific research. Its library currently holds 6,000 volumes; findings of research activity are published in its quarterly, *Études togolaises.* The Library of ORSTOM, founded in 1948, has more than 2,000 volumes. The library has holdings on child development, geography, sociology, and geophysics.

The Library of the Centre regional d'études et de documentation économiques, founded in 1972 in Lomé, houses more than 3,500 volumes and 100 current periodicals, specializing in economics, labor, and unionism. It publishes *African Trade Union News* in English and French editions.

There are two cultural center libraries in Lomé, the American Cultural Center Library and the Library of the Centre culturel français. The American collection consists of approximately 3,700 volumes; the French, more than 20,000 volumes.

The documentation center of the Institut pédagogique national houses more than 3,000 volumes, specializing in education and educational psychology.

The Profession. A Togo branch of the Association internationale pour le développement de la documentation, des bibliothèques et des archives en Afrique was established in 1959. It has its headquarters at the Library of the Université du Bénin in Lomé. It is affiliated with IFLA.

Trinidad and Tobago

The republic of Trinidad and Tobago comprises two islands off the coast of Venezuela. Population (1984 est.) 1,120,000; area 5,126 sq.km. The official language is English.

History. A former British colony, the country has an education system based on the British pattern.

In 1851 the Trinidad Public Library was founded based on the purchase of a former circulating library. It was supported partly by the colonial (and later also municipal) government and partly by a small subscription from its members.

National Library. Proposals for a national library were published as early as 1869 by the Scientific Association of Trinidad. There was, however, still no officially designated national library in the mid-1980s.

Plans for the development of the national library service, including a national library, were outlined in the government's Draft Plan for Educational Development published in 1968. Approval was subsequently given for the development of an integrated national network, the headquarters of the system to be known as NALIAS—the National Library Information and Archives Service. It was to consist of seven major units: Archives and Heritage Library, Bibliographic Services, Public Libraries, School Libraries, Special Libraries Information Network, Planning and Development, and Administration.

The Library Task Force appointed in 1978 became the interim Board of NALIAS pending the introducion of new legislation. Meanwhile, some national library functions are currently distributed between the Central Library of Trinidad and Tobago and the University of the West Indies Library, which jointly produce the Trinidad and Tobago National Bibliography; the University Library, drawing on the British Library and on its own resources, coordinates interlending services for the nation.

Regional library in Scarborough, Tobago.

Library, University of West Indies

Academic Libraries. The country is one of 14 in the Caribbean served by the regional University of the West Indies from three campuses.

The University Campus in Trinidad was established in 1960 by merger with the former Imperial College of Tropical Agriculture (ICTA) and an extension to its main library was completed in 1983. Emerging from a college library of 30,000 volumes in 1960, it held more than 247,000 volumes in 1983. In addition, more than 474,000 unbound journal parts and nonbook items were in stock. The collection is especially strong in agriculture, engineering, and the natural sciences but has also been developing strengths in the humanities and West Indiana. Other academic libraries on the same campus are those of the Faculty of Education (12,000 volumes), the Hugh Wooding Law School (16,500 volumes), and the Institute of International Relations (14,830 volumes).

Public Libraries. There are three independent public library services in the country, two of which work in close collaboration. The Central Library of Trinidad and Tobago was formally established in 1949 and the Carnegie Free Library opened in 1919. The third service, the Trinidad Public Library, became free in 1951 after serving as a subscription library for a hundred years. It serves workers and residents of the capital city, Port-of-Spain, and operates three suburban branches in addition to the headquarters. The full integration of these three services within NALIAS was envisaged.

In 1983 the Central Library operated 15 branch libraries in the largest towns, but rural bookmobile services (116 service points) remained suspended. A major new facility was opened at Scarborough in Tobago in 1983. Service to children is an important feature of each of the public library services while the Trinidad Public Library maintains a lively adult education program. Readers registered with the three services represent six percent of the population.

School Libraries. A School Libraries Division of the Central Library was established in 1977 to coordinate service to schools. This service is largely confined to the secondary level, and 94 libraries had been established in such schools by 1983. Efforts have been concentrated on the development of suitable collections for senior pupils in the sixth form (ages 17 and 18), and all new government school buildings at that level are provided with library rooms. Services for primary schools are slowly being developed and 32 such schools were equipped with libraries in 1983.

Provision is made for all libraries serving senior pupils in the sixth form to be administered by trained school librarians while those at the lower level are staffed by paraprofessionals.

The Profession. The Department of Library Studies at the University of the West Indies in Jamaica offers a Postgraduate Diploma in Library Studies (one year) and a Bachelor's Degree (three years) but training facilities in North America and the United Kingdom are also used.

The Library Association of Trinidad and Tobago provides some opportunity for continuing education by sponsoring workshops, some of them jointly with the Department of Library Studies. The Association, founded in 1960, provides a useful channel of communication for the body of 135 professionals in the country. Its membership includes other persons interested in promoting its objectives. The Association publishes a bulletin on an irregular basis.

ALMA JORDAN;
BARBARA COMISSIONG

Tropovsky, Lev
(1885–1944)

Lev Naumovich Tropovsky was a Soviet specialist in library science and bibliography noted especially for his work in library classification.

He was born in Kremenchug on February 12 (old style; February 25, new style), 1885. On graduating from secondary school he entered the Faculty of Natural Sciences at Warsaw University. Later he was expelled for taking part in a students' meeting and strike. In 1904 he joined the Polish Socialist-Democratic Party and in 1905 he became a member of the Warsaw Committee of the Military and Revolutionary Organization of the Socialist-Democrats. He was arrested, then emigrated.

While living in Paris, Tropovsky graduated from the Faculty of Natural Sciences of the Sorbonne. In 1917 he returned to Russia, where in 1920 he became a member of the Communist Party of the Soviet Union (Bolsheviks). From 1923 he was chief of the Bibliographic Department of the Central Board of Political and Educational Activities (Glavpolitprosvet), where he worked under the direct guidance of N. K. Krupskaya. In that period he delivered a number of reports at important scientific conferences deal-

Lev Tropovsky

Libraries in Trinidad and Tobago (1983)

Type	Administrative units	Service points	Volumes in collections	Annual expenditures (Trinidad dollar)	Population served	Professional staff	Total staff
National	- -	- -	- -	- -	- -	- -	- -
Academic	4	4	279,552	4,831,772	5,087	24	107
Public	3	15	- -	8,938,133	1,120,000	33	266
School	126	126	104,000	566,000	200,000	24	100
Special	35	54	- -	- -	- -	53	101
Other[a]	12	12	- -	164,500	3,370	1	12

[a]Tertiary education institutes and colleges.

ing with party spirit in bibliography. From 1932 he was Director of the Research Institute of Library Science and Recommendatory Bibliography and Head of the Bibliographic Department of the Moscow State Library Institute. He wrote such educational works as *Library Classification* and *Bibliography of Natural History.* Tropovsky was a member of the editorial board of leading specialized journals and helped make possible collections of articles such as *Bibliography, Bibliography and Library Science,* and *Soviet Bibliography.* He was also a member of the Learned Councils of the State Lenin Library, the All-Union Book Chamber, and the Moscow Library Institute. He died in Moscow on October 26, 1944.

With other library specialists and bibliographers he worked at modifying the UDC in keeping with the needs of Soviet libraries. Glavpolitprosvet introduced a version of the UDC in 1921; the work was the responsibility of a special committee headed by Tropovsky. He substantially revised the decimal classification and introduced a number of amendments and additions into some of its classes, particularly those dealing with questions of philosophy, ideology, and sociopolitical activities. He introduced a new class in the classification—"Marxism-Leninism," in which works by Marx, Engels, Lenin, and leaders of the Communist Party and government were reflected. He also worked out geographical subdivisions for the U.S.S.R. and edited all the classes and subdivisions.

The tables of library classification worked out by Tropovsky were popular and widely used in scientific and public libraries of the Soviet Union. Shortly before his death he also took part in the preparation of a new Soviet classification for books. The work was carried out in the late 1930s and early 1940s under the guidance of the State Lenin Library. In postwar years this work was continued by Tropovsky's pupil, Z. N. Ambartsumian (1903–70). The most important editions of this classification are *Library Classification Tables for Public Libraries,* which ran into three editions (1959, 1961, and 1968), and *Library Classification Tables for Children's Libraries* (1960, 1964, 1974).

The activities of Tropovsky and other Soviet library specialists advanced the preparation of the original Soviet library classification (BBK), the publishing of separate issues of which was begun in 1960. The BBK is a universal classification that embraces all branches of knowledge and areas of human practical activity reflected in printed matter. The BBK was published in 25 issues (30 volumes), the abbreviated version in 5 issues (7 volumes). The version for small public libraries and tables for children's libraries were worked out and published on the basis of the abbreviated tables. The BBK tables are used by more than 300 scientific and special libraries, and they were introduced widely in public library practice.

In Tropovsky's working-out of theoretical and practical problems of bibliography, "recommendatory" bibliography in particular was especially great. He emphasized the importance of giving an estimate of a book in the annotations of bibliographic indexes. Tropovsky showed a marked interest in recommendatory bibliography all his life, and he paid special attention to its political and social role in the Soviet Union.

C. I. ABRAMOV

Tunisia

Tunisia, a republic of North Africa in the most eastern part of the Maghreb, faces the Mediterranean Sea on the north and east and is bounded on the south by Libya and on the west by Algeria. Population (1984 est.) 6,966,173; area 164,150 sq.km. The official language is Arabic; French is widely spoken.

History. Libraries in Tunisia were founded in great number, especially during the Aghlabid and Fatimid ages (800–1171) when they were located in mosques and also in schools. Among the most famous libraries are the Ibdilliyya Library (1393), the Al-Ahmadiyya Library (1840), and the Sadiqiyya Library (1885).

Before independence in 1956, library services were administered by cultural institutions such as the Khalduniyya Library (1909) and Al-Lakmiyya library in Sfax (1931).

There are also a limited number of foreign libraries, notably that of the British Council (1943) and the Library of the American Cultural Center (1948).

The concept of modern library service emerged after independence in 1956. Libraries were given greater attention, and since 1963 the persistent need for raising the standard of library services moved the authorities to plan for libraries in the "Fourth Plan: 1972–1976." As a result of the Fourth and Fifth Plans, several types of libraries are found in Tunisia.

National Library. Known as the French Library and later as the Public Library, the National Library in Tunis was established by law in 1885 under French government sponsorship. Its collection was gathered in individual sporadic efforts and by gifts.

The concept of Dâr Al-Kutub Al-Waṭaniyya, the National Library, however, emerged only after independence in 1956. In 1970 the Tunisian National Library published the first issue of the *Tunisian National Bibliography,* a booklet covering the first period in 1969. From then on the National Library has tried to fulfill the enormous task of publishing current and retrospective bibliographies at the same time, ensuring the link between the past and the present and tracing every single document produced in the area from the introduction of printing in Tunisia (1881) up to independence. By 1983, 13 bibliographies had been issued covering the years from 1956 through 1982.

The *Tunisian National Bibliography* is issued quarterly with an annual cumulation. It covers all documents published in Tunisia and deposited at the National Library. These documents include government and nongovernment publications, university theses, textbooks, and new periodicals. Nonbook material is not covered. The National Library also compiles current bibliographies on special Tunisian and Arabic subjects.

The National Library's collection of manuscripts, which includes some that date from the 5th century, totals 25,000. The National Library also has a collection of about 10,000 current periodicals, more than two-thirds of them in Arabic.

The Library's collection reached about 750,000 volumes by 1984. It suffers from lack of space for users. It serves about 27,000 users a year, even though the number of seats is just 160. The collection is primarily in Arabic and French, but there are considerable holdings in English, and volumes are collected in 12 languages.

The National Library is a depository for Tunisian publications and has an accession rate of about 10,000 volumes a year. The Library's Documentary Department is responsible for legal deposit, but it did not officially have copyright deposit privilege in the mid-1980s.

In December 1984 the government started building a modern library to serve as a National Library. Modern processes and operations will be used for computer applications, nonbook materials, and bibliographic and other services.

Tunisia is one of the few African countries to have an International Serials Data System (ISDS) national center.

Academic Libraries. The University of Tunis was founded in 1960 and academic libraries were established later in the various parts of the republic—Sfax, Sousse, Monastir, Gabès, Gafsa, and Bizerte. The University of Tunis has no central library. Every school, institute, and faculty has its own library. Each functions separately from the others. The Library of the Zitouna mosque (now the Faculty of Theology of the University of Tunis) was established in the 8th century. It was considered important for its Arabic and Islamic collections, attracting students and scholars from various Muslim countries.

There are two types of academic collections: the European and American collections and the Arabic collections. The most important and the largest library of the University of Tunis is the Library of the Faculty of Law, Political Science, and Economics, which had a collection of about 128,180 volumes in 1984, two-thirds in French and the remainder evenly divided into Arabic and other languages, and 800 current periodicals. The library of the Faculty of Letters and Humanities had a collection of more than 124,000 volumes and 1,140 periodicals. The Faculty of Sciences (Mathematics, Physics, and Natural Sciences) had a collection of more than 37,360 volumes and about 438 periodicals. The Library of the Faculty of

Medicine of Tunis had a collection of 12,738 volumes, 600 periodicals, 39,000 foreign theses, and 1,615 Tunisian theses in 1984.

The National School of Administration, founded in 1949 and reorganized in 1964, is run by the Prime Minister and has a collection of 50,000 volumes and 400 periodicals. The Bourguiba Institute of Modern Languages, founded in 1961, has a library created in 1966 with aid from the Ford Foundation; its collection covers linguistics and translation.

Problems affecting library development include lack of professional staff, inadequacy of collections, shortcomings in technical services, and difficulties concerning library automation. Academic libraries in Tunisia are in a state of transition. In 1984 the number of students had grown far more quickly (29,537 students) than the university libraries, which numbered 27.

Public Libraries. Public libraries in Tunisia have developed during the years since independence, and their administration is fully centralized in the Ministry of Cultural Affairs. The public libraries do not, in general, possess large book collections, although as early as 1968 they had a total of 330,000 volumes. By 1970 the circulating stock was nearly 600,000 volumes, 65 percent in Arabic and 35 percent in French. Efforts are being made to develop the collections. Public libraries had a collection of books totaling about 1,314,689 in 1984.

The Central library is in Tunis. Branches are operated throughout the country and are distributed as follows: 63 public libraries for adults, 62 public libraries for children, 76 public libraries for youth, 8 municipal libraries, 46 popular and community libraries, 21 bookmobiles, and 4 regional libraries.

School Libraries. In 1956 the distinction between state schools and religious schools was eliminated, and free education was made available to all pupils of Tunisia. Enrollment increased dramatically in the years following independence: between 1956 and 1984 the number of pupils in primary schools increased from 225,000 to 1,119,408. In secondary

Libraries in Tunisia (1984)

Type	Administrative units	Service points[a]	Volumes in collections	Annual expenditures (dinar)	Population served	Professional staff	Total staff
National	1	2	750,000	200,000	27,000	32	180
Academic	30	33	650,000	861,000[b]	29,573[d]	43	302
				920,000[c]	2,882[e]		
Public	274	274	1,314,689	170,000	2,337,601	75	541
School	100	100	--	--	--	--	--
Special	35	35	--	--	--	--	--
Other	25[f]	25[f]					
	20[g]	20[g]					
	30[h]	30[h]	--	--	--	--	--

[a]Includes figures from previous column.
[b]Collection.
[c]Staff.
[d]Students.
[e]Professors.
[f]Ministry libraries.
[g]Political libraries.
[h]Economic libraries.

schools, the number of students increased from 30,000 in 1956 to approximately 364,492 in 1984. In addition, students were enrolled in vocational schools and in teacher-training programs. The languages of instruction are Arabic and French.

In Tunisia all school libraries are administered by the Minister of Education. The Division of School Libraries is responsible for complete operation of school libraries, including the selection and acquisition of library materials. School libraries in Tunisia are still in an early stage of development. There are a few school libraries in primary schools, and the collections of books in secondary schools are limited principally to textbooks.

Special Libraries. Tunisia has a large number of special libraries and specialized documentation centers. More than 25 special libraries and documentation centers are attached to ministries and government departments. Among the important special libraries are those of the Prime Minister, Justice Ministry, Health Ministry, and the Documentation Center of Cultural Development. Two specialized institutions that should be mentioned are the National Documentation Center and the Agricultural National Documentation Center.

The Tunisian National Documentation Center was established in 1966 to collect, catalogue, analyze, and preserve all government documents, mainly documents on economics, political and social sciences, and cultural affairs published in Tunisia and abroad. In 1975 a terminal was installed with the database called TANIT.

The Agricultural National Documentation Center was established in 1975 to lay out a modern system to collect data on agriculture in Tunisia and analyze it for dissemination. The Center accommodates two automated information systems. One is the National Tunisian Documentation System for Agriculture (TUNAGRI), consisting of a database of analyzed agricultural documents. It has direct communication with the International System for Agriculture (AGRIS), and data are exchanged between the two systems. Current Tunisian Research in Agriculture (CARIST) consists of a database covering subjects, places of current research, and names of researchers in the field of agriculture in all parts of Tunisia.

The Profession. The Tunisian Association of Documentalists, Librarians, and Archivists was established on June 10, 1965, at the Institut Bach Hamba, its headquarters in Tunis. The Association started activities in January 1966. The *Bulletin de L'A.T.D.* (1966-   ), its official journal, is issued approximately four times a year. The A.T.D. is a member of IFLA and the Tunisian Committee of Unesco and UNISIST.

Professional education in the field of library science in Tunisia has undergone several developments since independence in 1956. The origins of these educational programs can be traced to the Bach Hamba Institute in Tunis, which in 1964 offered a six-month study program for 50 students of librarianship. The persistent need for raising the standard of personnel working in libraries prompted the Ministry of Cultural Affairs to plan in 1965 for an educational and training program at the National Library. In fewer than five years two groups of assistant-librarians and four groups of clerical secretaries benefitted from programs offered by the National Library.

Responsibility for educational programs in library science were in 1971 transferred to the National School of Administration under the sponsorship of the Prime Minister's Office. In 1979 the responsibility for professional education in library science was transferred once again, this time to the Institute of Journalism and Information Sciences, which was under the jurisdiction of the Ministry of Higher Education and Scientific Research. In 1981 that program was replaced by a course of studies directed to graduate students with first university degrees in any subject, pending an entrance examination. The students followed a two-year professional program, graduating with bachelor's degrees.

Since 1982 two institutions have taught documentation, library science, and archives subjects. The Institut de Presse et des Sciences de l'Information is affiliated with the University of Tunis and offers a graduate program in library science. As of 1985, there were 100 students enrolled, with 24 staff members. L'Institut Supérieur de Documentation" (ISD) is also affiliated with the University of Tunis, and offers an undergraduate program for students of library science. Students in the latter institution enter upon the successful completion of a secondary school leaving exam, and after two years of professional instruction are graduated as assistant librarians. In 1985, there were 150 students and 10 staff members.

During the academic year 1984–85, the IPSI started a new postgraduate program open to students with B.A. degrees in any subject. They undertake a two-year program leading to a Diplôme de Conservateur.

School libraries face many difficulties of their own. There is a shortage of qualified university teachers capable of teaching in the Arabic language. There is also a shortage of Arabic teaching manuals and materials, as well as shortcomings in technical services.

REFERENCES

Mohammed Abdeljaouad, "La situatuin des B.U. de Tunisie en 1984," *A.T.D. Bulletin* (1984).

Ridha Attia, "National Bibliographies in the Maghreb: a Survey of Their Contents and Perspectives," *IFLA Council* (1984).

Douglas W. Cooper, "Libraries of Tunisia," *Wilson Library Bulletin* (June, 1979).

Hussein Habaili, "Development of Libraries and Information Services in Tunisia" *The Arab Magazine for Information Sciences* (ALESCO, Tunis, 1984).

HUSSEIN HABAILI

Turkey

Turkey, a republic in southeastern Europe and Asia Minor, is bordered by the Black Sea on the north, the U.S.S.R. and Iran on the east, Iraq, Syria, and the Mediterranean Sea on the south, the Aegean Sea on the west, and Greece and Bulgaria on the northwest. Population (1984 est.) 48,591,000; area 779,452 sq.km. The official language is Turkish.

National Libraries. The National Library of Turkey, in the capital of Ankara, was unofficially founded on April 15, 1946, in a basement room in the Ministry of Education. Later that year a government program included provision for a larger, official national library. Finally, in August 1948, the National Library opened to the public. A law of March 23, 1950, set its purpose: to preserve the national culture and to form a basis for cultural research. It is one of six legal depository libraries. The collection totals about 782,000 volumes. In the 1980s construction proceeded on a new building for the Library.

The Turkish Bibliographic Institute was initiated in the National Library in 1952 and was established by law in 1955. It issues the *Turkish National Bibliography* (*Türkiye Bibliyografyasi*, 1928-) and the *Turkish Articles Bibliography* (*Türkiye Makaleler Bibliyografyasi*, 1952-).

The Library of the Turkish Grand National Assembly, born with the Turkish Republic in 1923, serves the legislature with its collections in law, economics, and politics.

TÜRDOK, the National Documentation Centre for Science and Technology, was established in 1966 to disseminate scientific and technical information and to promote and coordinate library and information systems. It issues several periodicals, bibliographies, and reference works.

Academic Libraries. The structure of academic libraries in Turkey varies from one university to another. There were 27 universities in Turkey in the mid-1980s, 13 of which had been founded since 1975. The older ones lack centrally organized library services, and each faculty (college), institute, and department has its own library. The oldest academic library is the Central Library of Istanbul University, established in 1924, with 275,000 volumes, including 18,600 manuscripts. Some of the newer universities have well-organized central library systems, such as the Middle East Technical University, Ankara; the two campuses of Hacettepe University, Ankara; and the Boğaziçi University (formerly Robert College) in Istanbul.

Public Libraries. Under Ottoman rule, before the foundation of the Turkish Republic in 1923, public libraries were developed and governed by individual foundations. By the "Unity of Education" Law enacted in 1924, public library service was recognized as a state function. From 1978 both the National Library and the public libraries were under the General Directorate of Libraries in the Ministry of Culture. In 1945 there were 82 public libraries, and the number of volumes totaled about 660,000. In 35 years the number of public libraries grew to 363,

with a total collection of 5,044,000 volumes.

There are also *manuscript libraries*, which have public library status and which are unique in their holdings, chiefly of manuscripts in Turkish, Persian, and Arabic. The most famous of these is the Süleymaniye (Suleiman) Library in Istanbul, with 70,000 manuscripts; the Library has a book facility where 250 books or as many as 25,000 pages are repaired annually. The total number of manuscripts held by the libraries under the control of the Ministry of Culture is about 162,000.

Problems include unfair regional distribution of public library services, inadequate physical facilities, insufficient allocation of funds, and lack of professional staff. Needed in the 1980s were such projects as establishment of regional public libraries, increasing bookmobile services, centralization of technical processes, a union catalogue of manuscripts, and construction of prefabricated library buildings in rural areas.

School Libraries. Theoretically, there must be a library in each primary or secondary school, but school libraries are far from being adequately developed. They are under the authority of the Ministry of Education, but their development has been limited to the individual efforts of school authorities. Unesco reported 712 school libraries in Turkey in 1981. Generally speaking, the educational system has been indifferent to library services.

Special Libraries. There is no central authority for special libraries, which are established haphazardly. In most cases they are underdeveloped and lack professional staff. Examples of well-organized special libraries exist, however, including the libraries of the Turkish Historical Society, Turkish Linguistic Society, State Planning Organization, and Ankara Nuclear Research and Training Centre (which is also the liaison center for INIS, International Nuclear Information System) in Ankara; the Çekmece Nuclear Research and Training Centre in Istanbul; and the Marmara Scientific and Industrial Research Institute in Gebze, Kocaeli.

Estimates of the number of special libraries range from fewer than 200 to about 250, with a total of about 2,256,000 volumes. The State Planning Organization has included in its Annual Executive Plans enforcing measures for the establishment and development of special libraries in the public and private sectors.

The Profession. Türk Kütüphaneciler Der-

Libraries in Turkey (1980)

Type	Administrative units	Service points	Volumes in collections	Annual expenditures (lira)	Population served[a]	Professional staff	Total staff
National	1	1	782,000	19,905,000	--	18	114
Academic	--	--	--	--	--	--	--
Public	363	647	5,044,000	558,763,000	502,337	115	2,675
School	--	--	--	--	--	--	--
Nonspecialized[b]	2	--	344,000	--	--	--	--

[a]Registered borrowers.
[b]1977 data.

Source: Unesco, *Statistical Yearbook*, 1984.

neği (TKD; Turkish Librarians' Association) was founded in 1949 in Ankara. It has 51 branches and 1,200 members. It publishes the quarterly *Türk Kütüphaneciler Derneği Bülteni* (Bulletin of the Turkish Librarians Association).

Universite Kütüphanecilik Bölümü Mezunlari Derneǐ (KÜT-DER; Association of Library School Graduates) was founded in 1970 and has 250 members. Membership is limited to graduates of library schools. It issues the monthly bibliographical bulletin *Yeni Yayinlar—Aylik Bibliyografya Dergisi* (New Publications—Monthly Bibliographical Journal).

REFERENCES

Irfan Çakin, *The Analysis of the Structure and Function of University Libraries in Turkey* (Ph.D. dissertation, University College, University of London, 1978).

Ilhan Kum and Phyllis Lepon Erdoğan, "Spotlight on Turkey," *Unesco Bulletin for Libraries* (1979).

Lawrence S. Thompson, "The Libraries of Turkey," *Library Quarterly* (1952).

SÖNMEZ TANER*

Tveterås, Harald L.
(1904–)

Harald Ludvig Tveterås, Norwegian library director, influenced Norwegian librarianship as few other members of the profession have done. He extended and modernized the service, put libraries in the middle of teaching and research activity, and improved the relationship with Nordic and international colleagues. Tveterås knew library service from the very bottom and combined the intellectual qualifications of the scholar with the art of the narrative historian.

Tveterås was born in Stavanger, Norway, October 15, 1904. He studied geography, history, and Norwegian language and literature at the University of Oslo and earned his final degree in 1932.

He entered library service at the Royal University Library, Oslo, in 1929, and served that institution for the next 40 years. For a number of years he worked in the National Department. In 1942 he was appointed head of the Foreign Department. By 1951, however, he was back at the National Department as departmental librarian. Soon afterward, in 1953, he took over the office of director of the entire library, which is both the national library of Norway and the center of the research library system of the country. He served in that capacity for 15 years, until in 1969 he became director of the newly established National Office for Research and Special Libraries. He retired in 1974.

In his early career Tveterås was devoted mainly to the duties of the National Department, where he extended his profound knowledge of Norwegian literature and Norwegian publications. He studied popular reading and reading habits in various social communities and contributed a number of studies on social history and sociology.

He also published several bibliographical works. Most important is *Norske tidsskrifter* (1940), a complete registration of Norwegian periodicals, 1760–1920. In a historical introduction, he outlined the development of Norwegian literature seen from a sociological point of view. He was commissioned to write the history of the Norwegian booktrade (*Den norske bokhandels historie*). Two volumes were published (1950 and 1964), a third volume was in press in 1985, and a fourth volume was in preparation. Volume 2 earned him a doctor's degree in 1964. In addition to that monumental contribution, Tveterås wrote a number of monographs and articles about publishers and booksellers in Norway. Furthermore, he wrote many articles and essays on library history, mainly related to Norway and the Nordic countries.

As Library Director, Tveterås had to face the challenge of increasing demands from the rapidly expanding university and a growing number of external users from all parts of the country. In the early postwar years the national government had to give priority to reconstruction, extend the social security system into a modern welfare state, and stimulate and modernize industry and production. Education and research got what was left, and the research libraries suffered badly from insufficient grants for acquisitions of literature. Tveterås took up the problem. He argued vigorously for increased funds and he succeeded. Gradually the grants were increased.

As the university expanded in the 1950s and 1960s Tveterås proposed a plan to extend library service to all the faculty centers and their institutes. The Senate accepted his plan. From 1956 all library collections were included in a total university library system, and the services were coordinated by the university library. The faculty service, as the system was named, was not brought into being at one stroke. It was an ambitious program, which had to be realized during more than a decade. But by 1970 it was fully accepted and organized.

As the number of students, teachers, and scholars steadily grew, an improved information service also became necessary. Tveterås started lectures and courses for students and teaching staff and much attention was given to modeling it as a useful tool and not as a new teaching subject itself. A new information office was staffed and set to work. He also modernized the public catalogues of the library and made them more comprehensive and easier to use. The union catalogue was reorganized in two sections: one for periodicals and another for monographs. The periodical section was issued according to subjects, finally in four parts updated every second year. The union catalogue for monographs remained a card catalogue but was greatly improved.

As Director of by far the greatest library in the country, Tveterås also acted as adviser and consultant for governmental and political authorities. That arrangement proved to be insufficient because of the steadily increasing number of library units within the country and the extended relations with international governmental and nongovernmental organizations, and the Norwegian parliament in 1969 established the National Office for Research and Special Libraries. Tveterås the same year became the first Director of that institution with the title Riksbibliotekar. With great energy Tveterås took up the numerous duties given to the new office. He argued for a better library service at the new regional university colleges; above all he stressed the importance of immediate access to broad collections of relevant research literature.

Tveterås also extended Norwegian participation in international library cooperation. He served for two years as director of the Unesco library in Paris,

Harald Tveterås

and was for several years a member of the Unesco International Advisory Committee on Documentation, Libraries and Archives. He was also chairman of the European Translation Centre, Delft.

Tveterås took an active part in Nordic library cooperation. He carried out the Scandia Plan, a Nordic version of the Farmington Plan, aiming at the most comprehensive acquisition program possible for all Nordic research libraries. A result of his achievement was the nongovernmental documentation organization NORDOK, later replaced by the Nordic Intergovernmental Council for Research Libraries Documentation and Information Services, NORDINFO.

GERHARD MUNTHE

Uganda

Uganda, a land-locked republic in eastern Africa, is bounded by Sudan on the north, Kenya on the east, Tanzania on the south, Rwanda on the southwest, and Zaire on the west. Population (1980 census) 12,636,000; area 241,139 sq.km. The official language is English.

Uganda gained its independence from Britain in 1962 within a two-party system. It became a republic in 1967. Between 1971 and 1979, the country was under military rule. From 1980 it worked toward reverting to the 1962 system of government.

Uganda is 800 km. from the sea by direct route but 1,280 km. by single track railway to Mombasa, Kenya, the port on the Indian Ocean that is the country's principal trade outlet. The economy is predominantly agricultural with production of export crops heavily concentrated in the south. Coffee and cotton are the chief cash crops.

History. Uganda was declared a British protectorate in 1900. From that date, English has been the official language, but there are more than 50 ethnic groups in Uganda, speaking distinct dialects or languages. The indigenous languages, although at first fostered by Britain, were eventually left to sink into oblivion. After independence successive Ugandan governments did not do much better in producing reading materials in indigenous languages, and the number of indigenous people who have come to master Swahili, English, or French has remained small. At the same time, library materials favored foreign languages and cultures. From 60 to 80 percent of adult and potential readers could not comprehend foreign language library materials in Uganda in the 1980s.

Public libraries for all remains an illusory goal until either sufficient indigenous reading materials are produced or a greater proportion of Ugandans master foreign languages, unlikely in the foreseeable future.

Thus Uganda's library services differ from those in developed countries but are comparable with those in many developing countries in Africa. First, there is no national library as such. Some of the conventional functions of a national library are performed by the large academic or special libraries. Second, most library services are funded by the central government, and very few libraries have developed as a result of local initiative. This fact partly explains the marked concentration of large libraries in the capital city of Kampala and other towns where readers have a functional knowledge of English. Rural areas remain hardly touched by public library development.

In 1973 a dark period began for libraries. There was an exodus of traditional users of the existing libraries of all sorts (Asians, Europeans, academicians, research fellows, and associates). A shortage of foreign exchange and a lack of general appreciation of the role of libraries in the priorities of funding authorities, moreover, meant that a considerable number of periodical subscriptions could not be renewed. For example, Makerere University Library system had more than 2,000 exchange partners and regular donors outside Uganda in 1973, mainly in Britain and the United States. But the exchange agreements were cancelled as libraries in Uganda failed to reciprocate. Library budgets dwindled and development almost came to a standstill.

Ugandan libraries in the mid-1980s were painfully trying to recover from their decline and revert to the pre-1973 conditions.

Academic Libraries. The largest academic libraries have been associated with Makerere University, the only university in the country. The origins of the university can be traced as far back as 1922, when it started as a technical school. It was affiliated with the University of London (1948–63), then was a College of the University of East Africa (1964–70). In 1970 it became a full-fledged university. It has a British-style system of organization with 11 faculties, 2 associated schools, and 2 institutes. Its library system is composed of the Main Library, founded in 1940, seven sublibraries, and small department collections. Certain University departments were transferred to Kyambogo (site of Uganda Technical College and National Teachers College) and to Nakawa (site of Uganda College of Commerce). Makerere University acquired campuses in both places. According to 1977 estimates, the system had a stock of 400,000 volumes. The size of the holdings in the 1980s may not differ much from the 1977 estimates, allowing for losses during the period.

The Main Library is one of the legal depository libraries in the country under the Deposit Library Act of 1964. The sublibraries benefit from deposits according to their fields of specialization. The Main Library also has a special collection of Africana with concentration on eastern Africa. Stock was well over 150,000 volumes and 2,000 periodical titles were taken in 1973.

The most important sublibraries are the Albert Cook Medical Library; the Faculty of Education Library; the Centre for Continuing Education Library; the Faculty of Agriculture Library at Kabanyolo; the East African School of Librarianship Library; the Faculty of Veterinary Medicine Library; and the Makerere Institute of Social Research Library. All these enjoy a certain degree of autonomy from the Main Library in their fields of specialization. The oldest and most important is the Albert Cook Medical Library,

Libraries in Uganda (1980)							
Type	Administrative units	Service points	Volumes in collections	Annual expenditures	Population served	Professional staff	Total staff
Public	1	18	73,000	--	156,891[a]	15	103

[a]Registered borrowers.

Source: Unesco, *Statistical Yearbook,* 1984.

Kampala Library, headquarters for branch libraries in Uganda.

language readers throughout the country who did not have access to Kampala Public Library. That Library was founded in 1964 as a branch of the Uganda Library Service. It had originally been known as Kampala Municipal Library and was under the Kampala Municipal Council.

The 1964 Public Library Act provided for a national headquarters and regional libraries under a Public Libraries Board. The Board became responsible for all public libraries in the country, with its headquarters in Kampala. It had a stock of more than 100,000 books, local newspapers, and periodicals intended for circulation throughout its 32 branch libraries in the country in 1973. Before the dark days of 1973 set in, its other functions included a postal lending service to individuals, a book box loan scheme to institutions, and mobile library service.

The British Council and Uganda Library service operated two branch libraries jointly: at Kabarole and at Mbale. The British Council also ran a Teachers Center and Reference Libraries based in Kampala before 1973, when it pulled out. The United States Information Service operated a library based in Kampala but also had to pull out around the same time; it was being reconstituted in the mid-1980s. The Alliance Française, with offices in Kampala, is often of great assistance with French books.

School Libraries. Since the mid-1960s the central government has gradually taken control of the large schools in the country, so that by 1976 all the major schools were either fully or partly financed by the government; that support led to more emphasis on the development of school libraries.

Capital funds from foreign loans were used in establishing or equipping libraries. With funds from the World Bank, a number of new secondary schools were built, and old ones were improved under an Agency for International Development (AID) project; all AID project schools were planned to include libraries. With the phasing out of loan agreements for such projects, however, those libraries often found it difficult to continue their progress.

A study conducted in 1975 and 1976 found that the average high school library contained about 2,000 to 3,000 books. However, because of shortages of funds, many schools cannot buy new editions fast enough to have current collections. Primary schools have less funds, and some do not have libraries of any sort.

Special Libraries. The Uganda Technical College Library is considered to be the leading special library in the country. Whereas its basic role is to serve the Uganda Technical College, it also became an important technical information source for practicing engineers in the country. It houses the Uganda Technical Information Service (UTIS), to which several consulting firms subscribe. It has a stock of more than 16,000 volumes, more than 240 journals, and collections of standards. Practically all government departments and parastatal bodies have tended to establish some sort of working libraries, but private firms, mainly international corporations such as the oil and tobacco companies, have not usually established libraries in Uganda.

The Institute of Public Administration Library, founded in 1968 at Kololo under the Ministry of Public Service and Cabinet Affairs, was accorded legal

founded in 1960. It serves the Mulago Hospital Medical School, with a strong concentration on tropical medicine and research literature on medical problems in eastern Africa. It has been designated a depository of World Health Organization publications. It had a stock of 30,000 volumes and 450 periodical titles were taken in 1973.

The Education Library, founded in 1962 as a separate unit under the auspices of Unesco, issues *Education in East Africa: A Selected Bibliography*, published occasionally.

The Makerere Institute of Social Research Library, founded in 1958 as the East African Institute of Social Research Library, is a center of interdisciplinary and cross-cultural research with a strong regional commitment to eastern Africa. The Library had more than 5,000 volumes entirely dealing with Africa, plus selected government publications, periodicals, conference papers, working papers, reports, and a significant number of unpublished manuscripts in 1973.

The university library system extends its services to serious readers throughout Uganda, inasmuch as there are no comparable libraries in the country. It is undoubtedly the de facto, though not de jure, national reference library.

Public Libraries. Early attempts to provide a public library service were made in the late 1940s as part of postwar efforts to improve conditions in the country. As early as 1923, however, the Uganda Society Library provided services for the reading needs of expatriates in Kampala and Entebbe, who at that time were practically the only people who were literate in English. Under the 10-year development plan (1946–56), social services were emphasized, among them lending libraries, but the project lasted only a few years before it was abandoned. In 1948 the East African Literature Bureau, serving Kenya, Uganda, and Tanzania, started a public libraries program based at Kampala. It was composed of two services: circulating book boxes loaned to subscribing institutions and a postal loan service to subscribing individuals. The East African Literature innovation should be viewed as a venture to reach more of the English-

depository rights. It is also the Uganda National Documentation Center base. The Institute is responsible for in-service training for all Uganda government cadres, the main users of the library. Other notable special libraries include those of the Bank of Uganda, the East African Development Bank, Kawanda Agricultural Research Station, the Geological Survey of Uganda at Entebbe, and the Law Development Center at Makerere.

Many of the special libraries are not professionally staffed because of a shortage of trained personnel and money at all levels. There are also examples of qualified librarians not having sufficient books or facilities.

The Profession. *Education.* The East African School of Librarianship was founded in 1962 with the assistance of Kenya, Uganda, and Tanzania. At the time of the dissolution of the University of East Africa in 1970, leading to the simultaneous creation of independent national universities for each of the countries, the School of Librarianship, established at Makerere, was authorized to continue to serve as a regional institution. The Council for Library Training in East Africa supervises the School. It is the only one of its kind in the region dedicated to the education of library personnel for professional and nonprofessional careers in the field of librarianship.

Before 1973, students went abroad for postgraduate studies in librarianship. As the availability of foreign exchange tightened, and funds for overseas education diminished, they were accommodated in the School. The School has been a traditional training ground for nongraduates, offering candidates a diploma or certificate.

Association. The Uganda Library Association (ULA) was formed in 1972. Earlier it had been the regional branch of the East African Library Association (EALA), which was created in 1958. Under normal circumstances, such as those prevailing before 1973, the Uganda Library Association holds national seminars. It also collaborates with such international organizations as IFLA, the Commonwealth Library Association (COMLA), the International Federation of Documentation (FID), and the Standing Conference of Eastern, Central, and Southern Africa Librarians (SCECSAL). Its journal is *Uganda Libraries.* Membership in the mid-1980s was about 60 individuals.

Cooperation. Shortages of indigenous language materials dictate that the libraries of Uganda must cooperate with external libraries or institutions that are capable of providing foreign language materials, still the mainstay of libraries in developing countries such as Uganda. Such imported resources, mainly through gifts and exchanges, provide a means by which libraries in Uganda can have hope for supplementing small and inadequate library budgets. In addition, informal types of cooperation within the country are often taken on as extra burdens outside their realms of concentration by certain relatively well-endowed libraries.

REFERENCES

Margaret Macpherson, *They Built for the Future: A Chronicle of Makerere University College, 1922–1962* (1964).

B. W. K. Matogo, "Leading Issues in Developing Public Libraries in Emergent Uganda 1960–1970." *Libri* (1975).

BONIFACE M. KAWESA

Unesco

The United Nations Educational, Scientific and Cultural Organization (Unesco) was founded in London on November 16, 1946, by representatives of 20 nations as a specialized agency of the United Nations. It has its headquarters in Paris.

The Preamble to its Constitution, which was largely inspired by British Prime Minister Clement Attlee and the American poet Archibald MacLeish, states that "Since wars begin in the minds of men, it is in the minds of men that the defences of peace must be constructed."

"The Purpose of the Organization is to contribute to peace and security by promoting collaboration among nations through education, science and culture in order to further universal respect for justice, for the rule of law and for the human rights and fundamental freedoms which are affirmed for the peoples of the world, without distinction of race, sex, language or religion by the Charter of the United Nations" (Article 1, paragraph 1 of the Constitution).

The Organization, therefore, is committed to: "(a) collaborate in the work of advancing the mutual knowledge and understanding of peoples through all means of mass communication and, to that end, recommend such international agreements as may be necessary to promote the free flow of ideas by word and image . . . (b) give fresh impulse to popular education and to the spread of culture . . . (c) maintain, increase and diffuse knowledge" (Article 1, paragraph 2 of the Constitution).

To these ends, Unesco's activities, as defined in the Organization's Second Medium Term Plan for

Unesco/D. Roger

Unesco literacy training program in Ethiopia.

1984–89, are carried out by eight Sectors: Education, Natural Sciences, Social and Human Sciences, Culture, Communication, External Relations and Information, General Activities, and Programme Support, and General Administration. In addition, Unesco operates one Principal Regional Office, one Unesco Office for the Pacific States, one Regional Centre and six Liaison Offices (Addis Ababa, Geneva, New York, Venice, Vienna, and Washington). Unesco has nominated 10 Regional Advisers and 12 Sub-Regional Advisers and Unesco Representatives in 24 countries. They are in four regions: (1) Africa, (2) Latin America and the Caribbean, (3) the Arab states, and (4) Asia and the Pacific. Offices in the four regions work under Regional Coordinators.

Membership. Unesco has a membership of 160 states. In 140 of them a Unesco National Commission provides a link between institutions concerned with educational, scientific, cultural, and communication matters and the work of Unesco as a whole.

The supreme body of Unesco is the General Conference, which meets every two years to decide policy and approve the program and budget of the Organization for the next two years. The General Conference, at its 22nd session in 1983, voted a regular budget of $374,410,000 for the 1984–85 biennium.

Between general conferences, the program is implemented by the Secretariat under the supervision of the Executive Board, whose 50 members are elected by the General Conference from among regional groupings.

The Director-General is elected by the General Conference for a period of six years. Amadou Mahtar M'Bow, formerly Senegal's Minister of Education, was elected Director-General in 1974 and elected to a further term of office in 1980.

There are 3,351 members on the Unesco staff, according to figures released in October 1984, coming from 130 countries; 2,446 worked at Headquarters in Paris and 905 in the field and in regional offices. The implementation of all Unesco's activities is carried out within the framework of its Second Medium Term Plan for 1984–89, which was approved by the General Conference at its Fourth Extrordinary Session held in 1982. The Plan is based on an analysis of contemporary world problems. It presents 14 major programs designed to facilitate the discharge of the Organization's five "essential tasks." These tasks are defined as follows: "(1) To contribute to a continuing study of present world problems so as to create a greater awareness of the common destiny which now unites individuals and peoples alike. (2) To help pave the way for the widest participation by individuals and groups in the life of the societies to which they belong and in that of the world community. (3) To assist in strengthening problem-solving capability by fostering the development and democratization of education and the advancement of science, by increasing and developing the creative potential, both scientific and technological, of all peoples by reinforcing aptitudes and abilities, by developing research and training infrastructures and by promoting the free flow of knowledge and know-how. (4) To help to facilitate the changes and transitions that are now recognized as necessary by the in-

ternational community as a whole, in fields where the convergence of aspirations gives rise to a broad consensus. (5) To arouse and encourage a renewal of values within a context of genuine understanding among peoples, thereby advancing the cause of peace and human rights."

PGI. The Division of the General Information Program, often called PGI, the initials of its French name—Programme général d'information—was established in 1976 to provide a focus for Unesco's activities in the fields of specialized information systems, documentation, libraries, and archives. It is committed to promote the dissemination of specialized information of use to economic and social development, especially in the Third World. PGI incorporates the previously launched Unesco/UNISIST program for cooperation in the field of scientific and technological information. Under the UNISIST program, standards, rules, methods, principles, and techniques for the processing and transfer of information are now adopted and applied internationally. The scope of PGI and UNISIST has been extended beyond science and technology to include all fields of specialized information.

An Intergovernmental Council of 30 members, elected by the General Conference, guides the implementation of each biennial programme.

PGI helps Member States to strengthen their national capabilities for handling information by offering assistance in setting up and managing national and regional information systems. It conducts activities designed to help them in: (1) elaborating and implementing national information policies and plans; (2) developing and applying international methods, norms, and standards for information handling; (3) establishing and developing their information infrastructures; and (4) providing education and training facilities for information specialists and users. It works in close cooperation with Member States, intergovernmental and nongovernmental organizations, other Unesco programs, and the United Nations and its other specialized agencies. PGI convenes meetings, consultations, and conferences; sponsors, organizes, or supports education and training courses and seminars; launches projects and organizes consultancy missions; offers study fellowships and equipment grants; conducts research; and issues studies and publications. A bibliography of its publications is issued.

The work of PGI is financed—in addition to its regular budget and participation program—from a variety of sources, including the United Nations Development Programme (UNDP), Funds-in-Trust, and development banks. Its total budget from all sources for the 1984–85 biennium was approximately $16,000,000.

PGI is responsible for the implementation of most of Major Programme VII: Information Systems and Access to Knowledge, one of the organization's 14 major programs. It was evolved in order to: (1) facilitate the access of member states to information and to promote its unimpeded flow; (2) support their development programs; and (3) enhance their capacity to exchange, store, process, and use information. Major Programme VII is based on the principle that member states, particularly the developing countries, should be encouraged to increase their self-reliance and to develop technical cooperation among themselves.

During the mid-1980s emphasis was placed on operational activities; promoting new technology applications in information handling; setting up the systems needed for numerical, statistical, and other factual data; and information analysis, consolidation and repackaging, required in order to meet the needs of a variety of user groups.

The applications of information technology in developing countries, provided for under this major program, include library applications, information service applications, setting up local databases, and online access to remote databases using national and international telecommunication networks. Successful experiments have been carried out with computer messaging systems, electronic mail, teleconferencing, and videotex.

A feature of the activities proposed under this program is the balance that has been achieved between innovative pursuits that take technological changes into account and seek to introduce modern information systems and create databases using computers—particularly microcomputers—and the continuing efforts made to establish and consolidate essential traditional information services. While it is vital to foster the introduction of new informatics and telecommunication technologies on which rapid access to information in fundamental areas now depends, traditional archive and library services (national, university, public, and school libraries) still constitute the irreplaceable means of acquiring knowledge and safeguarding the intellectual heritage of all nations.

Information Policies and Plans. Unesco/PGI organizes and participates in consultations on existing and planned information systems, contributes to study and research on the exchange and transfer of information, both inside and outside the United Nations system. At the national level, liaison between PGI and member states is maintained through 59 Focal Points and 45 UNISIST National Committees. A National Focal Point is a government agency responsible for overall information policy and coordination of national activities; a UNISIST National Committee is a consultative body designated to advise on all aspects of information exchange and in liaison with PGI. Working contacts are maintained with existing information networks and programs, such as those of the Council for Mutual Economic Assistance and the Commission of European Communities.

Member States are assisted in the review of their information needs, with a view to enabling them to make the best possible use of existing information sources. To this end, surveys were undertaken in three member states (Ethiopia, Malaysia, and Panama) to study innovations in planning information policies and removing obstacles to the flow of information. On the basis of these surveys, three seminars on the analysis and evaluation of national information policies and plans were held in Panama, Ethiopia, and Malaysia. Draft guidelines entitled *National Information Policies, Scope, Formulation and Implementation* were prepared and submitted to the International Seminar on National Information Policy held in Dubrovnik, Yugoslavia, in 1984.

PGI helps Member States to create or develop library and information services and to improve the

Unesco/Eric Schwab

Unesco-sponsored primary school in Douala, Cameroon, attended by Europeans and Africans.

access of users to documentation and information. A consultant mission was sent to China to advise on equipping the new building of the Institute of Scientific and Technical Information and another to the United Arab Emirates on establishing a library and records center at the Ministry of Environment and Public Works. At the request of the government of Nepal, and in collaboration with the International Development Research Centre (IDRC) of Canada, consultant services were provided to the Royal Nepal Academy of Science and Technology. Another joint PGI/IDRC mission was sent to Nepal to advise the International Centre on Integrated Mountain Development (ICIMOD) there on setting up its information system.

Within the framework of its assistance program for national, university, research, school, and public library development, Unesco launched a project for the preservation and conservation of thousands of manuscripts and ancient books held in the libraries of Morocco. Equipment and training of local personnel was provided to the value of some $150,000, including setting up a laboratory in Rabat for microfilming manuscripts. PGI continues to support the Unesco Pilot Project on School Library Development in Oceania. Within the framework of this Project, course materials were prepared for the instruction of teachers employed in teacher training colleges on the use of teaching materials. A series of courses, some given via satellite, was organized with the collaboration of the Department of Distance Education of the University of the South Pacific.

Norms and Standards and Their Dissemination. In drawing up and disseminating standards and norms relevant to information work, Unesco/PGI cooperates closely with the International Organization for Standardization (ISO), which is responsible for the ultimate adoption of international standards; with the International Centre for Terminology (Infoterm); and with professional organizations. PGI concentrated its efforts in the mid-1980s on the application of international standards and only to a lesser extent on their elaboration. The promotion of exist-

Unesco/Carracciolo and Banoun

Students in New Delhi, India, participating in a Unesco-sponsored Institute of Film and Television.

ing standards is being ensured by a number of methods, including updating such documents as the *ISO Standards Handbook on Information Transfer* and the *UNISIST Guide to Standards for Information Handling,* which is being broadened to include standards relating to archives administration and records management systems and services. Many educational materials are being prepared and will be made available to Member States in order to promote the adoption of standards. A directory of national standards relating to archives administration and records management systems and services was in preparation in 1985, as were model classification standards and job descriptions concerning the staff of archival and records management services, the latter being intended for use in developing countries.

The Common Communication Format, which was developed to make communication of bibliographic data practicable among computer-based systems throughout the world, has been issued in a preliminary version. It was being tested for the conversion of records in the format of the UNISIST Reference Manual, the Universal MARC Format (UNIMARC), and the International Serials Data System (ISDS) format into the new CCF format and vice versa.

Prior to developing an appropriate strategy for the implementation of its objectives and defining the goals and priorities of a program for the development of microcomputer-based software packages, Unesco, after consulting a number of international experts, defined the general features and specific application requirements that a portable software should have and meet, and subsequently identified at the Institut für Maschinelle Dokumentation (IMD) in Graz, Austria, a package called IV + V (Informationsvermittlung und verarbeitung), which Austria offered to Unesco for use in developing countries. Unesco is currently implementing several projects on a pilot basis to develop specific applications and gain further operational experience. The first of these projects was the development of a comprehensive bibliographic application package using the IV + V system soft-

ware and implenting the *UNISIST Reference Manual for Machine-readable Bibliographic Descriptions* at the Institute of Social Studies in the Netherlands. Other projects are implemented in Thailand, Tanzania, India, and Senegal, and at the United Nations Centre for Human Settlements in Kenya. Unesco intended to prepare a demonstration database on its own microcomputer using IV + V. A first explanatory mission visited five Latin American countries in 1984 to present Unesco's new program to interested institutions in Venezuela, Chile, Argentina, Uruguay, and Brazil with a view to creating local databases and improving regional cooperation in the field of information.

In order to promote the application of available bibliographic standards to the totality of the world's published information, Unesco, in close cooperation with the International Federation of Library Associations and Institutions (IFLA), implements a program designed to assist Member States in achieving Universal Bibliographic Control.

Information Personnel and Information Users. PGI promotes in Member States and at the regional level the creation and reinforcement of educational programs designed to prepare the information scientists, librarians, archivists, and other technical staff required to staff a full range of information systems and services and promote the improvement of information use by a wide range of user groups. It fosters the establishment of new regional or national education and training institutions or the reinforcement of existing ones. It organizes intensive courses in areas such as the new technologies, the establishment of nonconventional information services, and management, with a view to updating the knowledge of practicing teachers, managers, information scientists, and archivists. PGI also prepares and disseminates teaching packages, textbooks, and curricula on a variety of topics including microcomputer use, restoration and preservation, information analysis, numerical data services, and referral services with a view to the training of information professionals. In order to increase public awareness of the value of information and its proper use in pilot sectors, PGI also prepares model user training materials for introduction into the study programs of educational institutions at various levels. It conducts activities designed to improve harmonization of specialized training programs in the information sciences and collects and disseminates information on training opportunities and materials.

PGI's principal long-term goal is to assist in building up in Unesco's Member States the basic facilities needed for the professional education and training of information personnel. It organizes consultant missions to advise Member States on planning and establishing such training facilities, assist in forecasting personnel requirements, or advise on curriculum development or revision. An International Symposium on Harmonization of Theoretical and Practical Training Programmes in Information Science, Librarianship and Archival Studies was held in 1984 and the Ad Hoc Committee on Education and Training Policy and Programme met in 1985. A third revised edition of the *World Guide to Library Schools and Training Courses in Documentation* was in preparation in 1985. This work identifies academic programs for professional training and contains updated information on informal training opportunities, including short courses and fellowships. PGI, with the financial cooperation of UNDP, provides assistance for the Regional Programme of Postgraduate Studies in Information Science for Latin America, with its headquarters in Venezuela.

Development of Regional Information Systems. At the regional level, programs are launched for cooperation in information exchange and the development of information systems, often with the help of funding agencies such as UNDP. For instance, a Regional Network for the Exchange of Information and Experience in Science and Technology in Asia and the Pacific (ASTINFO) was being developed. PGI allocated to it some $200,000 in the 1984–85 biennium, and extra-budgetary sources were being sought. Associated Centres of ASTINFO have been nominated that have specialized capability in providing information services, training, or computer facilities and are willing to share resources with other centers in the implementation of ASTINFO activities.

A similar program of cooperation is being promoted in Latin America and the Caribbean Region, with the participation of Member States and of regional and international nongovernmental and governmental organizations.

In Africa, cooperation is maintained with the Economic Commission for Africa (ECA) in developing the Pan-African Documentation and Information System (PADIS). PGI organized in January 1985 the Fifth Seminar on the African Standing Conference on Bibliographic Control (ASCOBIC) in Lome, Togo.

In the Arab States, the flow of information is promoted through collaboration with the Arab League Educational, Cultural and Scientific Organization (ALECSO).

Records and Archives Management Programme (RAMP). RAMP, which is implemented in consultation with the International Council of Archives (ICA), covers policies, norms and standards, infrastructures, training, research, and other aspects of national, regional, and international archival development. It is being developed on a long-term basis in recognition of the growing importance of records and archives in Member States.

Studies are conducted and guidelines prepared in collaboration with ICA; they include works on records surveys and schedules, the archival appraisal of motion pictures and related records, machine-readable records, and still pictures. Other studies deal with archival records management, legislation, and regulations, and the preservation and restoration of paper records and publications and of photographic materials. A directory of national standards relating to archives administration and records management and services was being compiled in 1985. Model classification standards and job descriptions concerning the personnel of archival and records management services, with particular reference to developing countries, was also in preparation. In addition, the impact of new technologies in information processing and communication on traditional institutional records and archives was being studied.

Participation and Technical Cooperation Programmes. Unesco/PGI is the executive agency for projects financed by sources other than Unesco's regular budget. These sources include UNDP and other United Nations funding agencies such as the United Nations Financing System for Science and Technology for Development. Extra-budgetary resources are also derived from funds-in-trust received from Member States or international, regional, or national governmental and nongovernmental organizations. These funds are intended to enable Unesco to carry out specific activities consistent with the aims and policies of the Organization on behalf of the sponsoring organizations and at their request. Information services, libraries, and archives have benefited from the UNDP assistance within the framework of 11 projects carried out by Unesco. Three funds-in-trust projects were in the course of implementation in the mid-1980s. Extra-budgetary funds have financed projects setting up and strengthening national documentation centers in Albania, the People's Republic of China, Greece, Kenya, the Lao People's Democratic Republic, Senegal, and Vietnam; developing national archives in Burma; establishing a Regional Documentation Centre for the Kagera River Basin Organization; and library work in Burkina Faso and Zimbabwe. All UNDP projects contain a major training component for fellowships, study grants, and in-service training.

In 1984 Unesco had a membership of 161 states; the withdrawal of the United States as a Member State on December 31, 1984, reduced membership to 160.

JACQUES TOCATLIAN

UNICEF

UNICEF (the United Nations International Children's Emergency Fund) came into being in December 1946 when the UNRRA (UN Relief and Rehabilitation Administration) was coming to an end. The council of UNRRA recommended that a fund be created out of its residual assets to continue aid to children through the UN. Voluntary contributions from governments and individuals were to be its continuing source of funding. UNICEF is governed by an Executive Board made up of nations representing major contributing and recipient countries. The Executive Director is appointed by the Secretary General of the United Nations, in consultation with the Executive Board of UNICEF, which meets annually. In 1953 the General Assembly voted to continue UNICEF indefinitely, changed the official name to United Nations Children's Fund (but keeping the old acronym UNICEF), and recommended a change from only emergency aid to long-range programs of benefit to children in developing countries. From the early 1980s, aid was concentrated on the Child Survival Campaign, concerned with lowering infant mortality through low-cost health measures.

UNICEF has its headquarters in New York, with a European office in Geneva and regional offices in Abidjan, Amman, Bangkok, Bogota, Nairobi, and New Delhi. In addition some 100 offices and sub-offices are in major cities in developing countries, and a warehousing and shipping center is in Copenhagen. Total UNICEF staff (international and local) numbers almost 3,300.

Children from a New York City public school viewing materials in the UNICEF Information Center on Children's Cultures.

In order to stimulate funds in the developed countries and to educate their populations about the needs of children in developing countries, national committees were set up, either as private, nonprofit organizations or as semigovernmental agencies. The first was the U.S. Committee for UNICEF, established as a private nonprofit corporation in the state of New York in 1947. There were 33 national committees and 4 national liaison organizations in 1985.

UNICEF maintains at its headquarters a library of informational books and reports related to children in developing countries. There is also a documents section consisting of documents produced in connection with projects in the field, all UNICEF headquarters documents, and related material from other agencies and organizations. Both are essentially for internal staff use.

The Geneva office and the six regional offices also have book and document collections, of varying sizes, with the largest being in New Delhi. The only National Committee maintaining a library is the U.S. Committee for UNICEF, which supports the Information Center on Children's Cultures, established in 1967 and functioning since 1968. The main purpose of the Center is to inform the general public, and specialized segments of it, about the lives of children in developing countries. The Center offers a mail and telephone reference service; initiates or assists with books, products, television programs, and other media about children in developing countries; and compiles and publishes numerous bibliographies and information sheets.

ANNE PELLOWSKI

Union of Soviet Socialist Republics

The Union of Soviet Republics comprises 15 Union Republics: R.S.F.S.R. (Russian), Ukrainian S.S.R., Belorussian S.S.R., Uzbek S.S.R., Kazakh S.S.R., Georgian S.S.R., Azerbaidzhan S.S.R., Lithuanian S.S.R., Moldavian S.S.R., Latvian S.S.R., Kirgiz S.S.R., Tadzhik S.S.R, Armenian S.S.R. Turkmen S.S.R., Estonian S.S.R. Population (1984 est.) 273,400,000; area 22,402,200 sq.km. More than 90 languages are spoken. Russian is the official language.

History. The first famous Russian book repository was founded in about 1037 in the Sofia Cathedral in Kiev. It was the most complete collection of written monuments and government documents of ancient Rus. In the earliest development of oral and written works, the high point of cultural and economic connections of the Russian principalities led to the appearance of libraries in the large Troitse-Sergiev, Solovetsk, and Belozersk monasteries. In the 12th century, book repositories also appeared in Vladimir, Riazan, Chernigov, Suzdal, Rostov, Murom, Polotsk, Smolensk, Pskov, and other cities. In Novgorod, as archaeological excavations show, there were many written collections on birch bark, made from the thin layer of birch-tree bark. Many valuable Slavic manuscripts were preserved there, among which was the first dated, written monument—the celebrated "Ostromir Gospel" (1057).

The invasion of Rus by numerous enemies—from the East the Mongol Hord, from the West the Teutonic Knights—conflagration and civil war, accompanied by the destruction of cities and monasteries, in which were concentrated the written treasures, destroyed thousands of priceless written documents of the past.

Only in the middle of the 16th century, after the appearance in Moscow of the printing press, when in the year 1564 the first Russian book *Apostol* was printed by I. Fedorov, did favorable conditions arise for the development of libraries. From the beginning of book printing to the beginning of the 18th century, only about 1,000 books were produced in Russia. In the epoch of Peter I more than 600 books were printed.

That promoted the appearance of the first large private book collections. For example, the library of Field Marshal B. P. Sheremet'ev numbered more than 25,000 volumes. In 1714 in the capital of the country, St. Petersburg, the first library was born (now the Library of the Academy of Sciences of the U.S.S.R.) and 40 years later the first library appeared in Moscow (now the Lomonosov Library of Moscow State University).

In St. Petersburg in 1795 the beginning of another prominent library was laid—the Imperial (now the Saltykov-Shchedrin State Public Library), which opened for visitors in 1814. Almost a half-century later, in 1862 in the Rumiantsev Museum in Moscow, a public library was also founded (now the Lenin State Library of the U.S.S.R.). Up to that time public libraries were arising in other district towns also, and on the national frontiers of Russia—in Riga, Tallinn, Kishinev, Erevan, Tblisi, Kazan, Tashkent. They preserved in various circumstances the best monuments of the written culture of the peoples of the Baltic, Transcaucasia, and Central Asia.

In prerevolutionary Russia there were altogether no more than 76,000 libraries, of which the vast majority offered small book collections, full of loyal literature permitted for reading by the tsarist censor. At the same time those libraries also held works of A. S. Pushkin, M. Iu. Lermontov, N. V. Gogol, N. A. Nekrasov, F. M. Dostoevsky, L. N. Tolstoy, A. P. Chekhov, and others who enjoyed great popularity.

The Great October Socialist Revolution of October 25, 1917 (O.S.), opened a new stage of development for library work. V. I. Lenin gave libraries special meaning as the most popular and accessible centers for the diffusion of knowledge and the enlightenment of the people. "He considered the elevation of library work to be one of the indicators of the cultural level of a country," wrote N. K. Krupskaya, Lenin's wife and a leader in Soviet library development. On the initiative of Lenin, the Soviet administration issued a series of fundamental directives and decrees, directed toward a basic reorganization of library work on new Socialistic principles. The following decrees, among others, were issued: "On the Preservation of Libraries and Book Repositories of the R.S.F.S.R." (1918), "On the Centralization of Library Work in the R.S.F.S.R." (1920), "On the Transfer of Library Work in the R.S.F.S.R. to the National Commissariat for Education" (1920).

An important event was the reorganization in 1925 of the Library of the Rumiantsev Museum as the Lenin State Library of the U.S.S.R., which helped the process of organizing a unified library system. The first Soviet library law, issued in 1934, "On Library Work in the U.S.S.R.," noted significant successes in libraries: the growth of a network of libraries, the opening of new libraries in factories, construction projects and collectives; and a significant increase in library holdings and numbers of readers.

At the beginning of 1941, there were 277,000 libraries of all types and forms in the U.S.S.R. with book holdings of 520,000,000 items. The overall readership in libraries consisted of 55,000,000. There was one public library for every 2,000 people, and for every 100 people there were 96.5 books.

In the years of World War II, called in the Soviet Union the Great Patriotic War, 1941–45, Hitler's troops, while in occupied regions of the U.S.S.R.,

V. I. Lenin State Library of the U.S.S.R., Moscow.

completely destroyed 43,000 public and hundreds of large libraries and plundered more than 100,000,000 books. In the postwar period special attention was given to the restoration of the network of libraries and their collections. By 1950 the number of libraries surpassed prewar records by 12 percent.

In 1959 the Central Committee (CPSU) issued a directive "On the Condition and Measures for Improvement of Library Work in the Country," and in 1974 one "On the Promotion of the Role of Libraries in Communist Education of the Workers and Scientific-Technical Progress."

The implementation of these party documents characterize the widening of the sphere of influence of libraries, the increase in the number of readers and book lending and the strengthening of interdepartmental connections and the reinforcement of coordination of the activities of various libraries.

In the Soviet Union there were about 329,000

Libraries in the U.S.S.R. (1985)

Type	Number	Volumes in collections	Population served[a]	Professional staff	Total staff
Lenin State Library of the U.S.S.R.	1	32,345,000	220,000	--	--
Saltykov-Schedrin State Public Library	1	25,044,653	185,000	--	--
State libraries of the Union Republics	14	60,039,000	438,600	--	--
Public libraries	133,200	1,945,100,000	148,000,000	--	257,000[b]
Libraries of general-education schools and orphanages	144,000	862,000,000	40,000,000	--	--
Scientific-technical and other special libraries	53,000	2,031,000,000	--	--	--

[a]Readers.
[b]1980 data.

Sources: I Nazmutdinov, Deputy Chief, Library Department, Ministry of Culture of the U.S.S.R., Moscow; Unesco, *Statistical Yearbook, 1984.*

libraries (1985) with book collections of 4,717,000,000 items, used by 224,000,000 readers (see Table).

On March 13, 1984, the Presidium of the Supreme Soviet of the U.S.S.R. ratified by decree "The Regulation of Library Work in the U.S.S.R.," a new legislative law regulating various aspects of activity of Soviet libraries. This document established the social function of libraries as ideological, cultural-educational and scientific-informational institutions whose activity is guided toward the realization of the constitutional rights of the citizens of the U.S.S.R. to an education and to make use of the achievements of culture, recreation, and the freedom of scientific, technical and artistic creation.

"The Regulation of Library Work in the USSR" thus set out to strengthen Lenin's principles of organization of library work in the U.S.S.R.: the joining of libraries into a single system, planned development and the spread of the system, the guarantee of unity of organization and methodological leadership, government planning of the training of library staff, general accessibility, and cost-free library services for the population.

National, All-Union, Republic, Regional, and District Libraries. *Lenin State Library.* In accordance with "The Regulation of Library Work in the U.S.S.R.", the Lenin State Library of the USSR (founded in 1862) functions as the main national library of the country.

The Statute of the Library, ratified in 1985, defines its functions in the system of libraries of the Soviet Union as the overall state universal book repository, the all-union coordination center for scientific research work in the area of librarianship, bibliographic control and book processing, the primary all-union scientific-methodological center for all libraries, regardless of their position in the hierarchy, the center for selected bibliographies and interlibrary loan, and a museum of the book.

The overall size of the collections of the Lenin State Library of the U.S.S.R. (mid-1980s) is 32,345,000 items in 247 languages, of which 20,960,400 (64.8 percent) are in Russian and other languages of the peoples of the U.S.S.R.; 11,384,560 (35.2 percent) are in foreign languages. The annual

Map collection in the Vilnius State Library, Lithuania.

receipts exceed 1,000,000 items. The exchange of literature involves approximately 3,415 libraries and organizations in 105 countries of the world.

The number of readers exceeds 220,000. At their service is a system of reading halls with 2,500 seats. Every day from 9 AM to 10 PM, from 8,000 to 10,000 people visit the library. Annual visits exceed 2,175,000, and book loans 12,000,000, including 335,000 through interlibrary loan.

The library administers various bibliographic projects for display and information (up to 100,000 inquiries are handled annually), provides service for the inquiries of party and government agencies, fulfills the functions of an information center for culture and art, issues reference and review and analysis publications, compiles advisory and retrospective bibliographic sources, and develops standards for various library-bibliographic processes.

Book Chamber. The current national bibliography in the U.S.S.R. is handled by the All-Union Book Chamber (founded in 1917), which registers all kinds of publications: books and brochures, periodical publications, playbills, posters, postcards, music scores, and maps in *Knizhnaia letopis* ("Book Annual") and other annuals, in *Ezhegodnik knigi* ("Annual of the Book"), and also in categorized sets of catalogue cards. The holdings of the Chamber total some 61,000,000 items (mid-1980s). Every year the Chamber receives several hundred thousand newly printed publications, since after appropriate bibliographic preparation, one copy of every type of publication is sent to the State Archive of Publication of the U.S.S.R. for permanent preservation. The Chamber provides centralized cataloguing and statistics of publications, and fulfills the functions of a scientific center in the area of book processing and publishing activities.

State Library of Foreign Literature. The All-Union State Library of Foreign Literature (founded in 1922) in accordance with the statute ratified in 1985, serves in the single system of libraries of the U.S.S.R. the functions of a library of broad humanistic services; satisfying inquiries about foreign literature from scientific research institutions; conducting work in the area of foreign librarianship and book processing; and serving as the center for interlibrary loan of literature in foreign languages. The holdings of the library total 4,394,600 items. The number of readers is 50,000. The annual book loans total 2,500,000. Book exchanges are conducted with more than 1,275 partners in 97 countries of the world.

Saltykov-Shchedrin State Public Library. This library in Leningrad (founded in 1814) became, because it was one of the first to receive an obligatory copy of the printed works in Russia, the holder of a priceless collection of publications in the Russian language. The Library's collections number 25,044,653 items. Annual additions total 280,000 items, book loans 8,882,900. The number of readers is 185,000.

State Libraries. In accordance with national-governmental structure, consolidated in the Constitution of the U.S.S.R. in 1977, the Soviet Union unites 15 union republics, in each of which there is a primary republic library (in the R.S.F.S.R. these functions are fulfilled by the Saltykov-Shchedrin State Public Library). In accordance with the Model Statute of the State Library of the Union Republic, ratified in 1967, they have become generally accessible libraries of universal profile. Their total holdings, excluding the Saltykov-Shchedrin Library, consist of 60,039,000 items; the overall number of readers is 438,600 and book loans total 25,945,300 items. The strongest book collections are concentrated in the State Library of the Armenian S.S.R. (7,100,000 items), Georgian S.S.R (6,616,000), Belorussian S.S.R. (6,140,000), Kazakh (4,294,000), and Uzbek (4,144,000). In the remaining republics there are from 2,500,000 to 4,000,000 items. These libraries devote special attention to collecting literature in the languages of the peoples of the republic and about the republic. They receive an obligatory copy of newly printed publications, and are built on a collection of literature of previous years of publishing, including rare books, and the organization of a system of book exchange. The State Library of the Armenian S.S.R. serves as an illustration—it holds 2,000,000 Armenian books, beginning with the first one printed (1512).

Main Universal Science Libraries. In the administrative centers of 20 autonomous republics, 6 regions, 123 districts, and 8 autonomous districts, these libraries, as fixed by their particular library statute ratified in 1983, render active assistance to local party organizations in Communist education of workers. They promote the achievements of science and technology and deal with concrete problems of the regional production complexes and agro-industrial unified system. Libraries in Gorky, Groznyi, Kazan, Kalinin, Kirov, Kuibyshev, Omsk, Perm, Sverdlovsk, Ufa, and Cheliabinsk each have holdings of more than 2,000,000, and another 70 libraries have upwards of 1,000,000 items. The number of readers in some of these libraries approaches 50,000. There is a special value in the holdings of regional literature about local resources, history, geography, economics, art, and culture. Many libraries, among them, libraries in Archangel, Volgograd, Ordzhonikidze, Tambov, and Tiumen have new buildings.

Public Libraries. The leading place in the system of library service to the people of the U.S.S.R. is held by the 133,200 public libraries in the mid-1980s with book collections of 1,945,100,000 items, which are used by 148,000,000 people, or more than half the population of the country. Readers annually borrow 3,170,000,000 items, 22 books and journals per person in a year. Toward the end of 1980, in accordance with the decree of the Central Committee of the CRSU "On the Promotion of the Role of Libraries in the Communist Education of the Workers and Scientific-Technical Progress" (1974), a reorganization of the work of these libraries was completed on the principles of centralization. Isolated libraries were brought into a system with almost 4,000 strong library associations within the boundaries of separate cities and administrative regions.

The reorganization of the network of public libraries permitted the spread of the sphere of influence of libraries, and satisfied more than half of the population's requirements for books. This was facilitated by many things, including the publication in a special library series of 5,000 titles of the most popular books in a total quantity of 170,000,000 copies, which helped to build up collections of the public libraries.

Children's Libraries and School Libraries. To serve the rising generation of the U.S.S.R. with

U.S.S.R. Ministry of Culture

Saltykov-Schedrin State Public Library in Leningrad, opened in 1814. It holds an extensive collection of 19th-century Russian books and periodicals.

books, more than 10,000 libraries were created for children and young people, including republic, regional, district, and urban libraries, as well as 144,000 school libraries. Their combined book holdings exceed 862,000,000 items, which are regularly replenished with publications of school series, which include the best works of classic and current domestic and foreign literature. The readership of these libraries consists of the 40,000,000 pupils of general-education schools.

Scientific, Technical, and Other Specialized Libraries. There are 53,000 scientific, technical, and other specialized libraries with book holdings of 2,031,000,000 items. These libraries are an integral part of the State Automated System of Scientific-Technical Information (GASNTI) headed by the All-Union Institute of Scientific and Technical Information (VINITI), which works on an immense flow of documents on natural and technical sciences, received from 130 countries of the world in 66 languages.

The most diverse network of scientific-technical libraries exists in such branches of the national economy as the automobile industry, heavy and transport machine construction, rail transport, non-ferrous and ferrous metallurgy, the chemical and coal industry, and others. These libraries possess large numbers of actual scientific and technical literature, periodical publications, special forms and other documents, the use of which serves the advance of scientific and technical progress, the achievement of entire complex programs of development of the national economy, and the realization of economic experiments in various branches of industry.

The main scientific-technical library of the country is the State Public Scientific-Technical Library of the U.S.S.R. (founded in 1958). It carries out library bibliographic and information service for ministries and departments of the U.S.S.R. and Union Republics, enterprises, institutions, and organizations, as well as for individual consumers of information. It conducts analysis and preservation of domestic and foreign sources of information, and searches for information in them. The holdings of the library approach 10,000,000 items, readership is 170,000, and book loans total 7,000,000 items. Every year the holdings are increased by more than 300,000 publications of various kinds.

The Library carries out the coordination of subscriptions to foreign literature on science and technology; from 1964 it annually issued "A List of Foreign Journals, Subscribed to by Organizations of the USSR." It publishes the lists of "New Foreign Books" and "New Foreign Journals," and it prepares advanced information about the contents of the most important foreign journals on science and technology. Since 1968 an information-computer center has existed in the library, provided with new equipment and machines.

The other large scientific-technical library of the country is The State Public Scientific-Technical Library of the Siberian Division of the Academy of Sciences of the U.S.S.R. in Novosibirsk (founded in 1918). The holdings of the library exceed 9,000,000 items: annual additions number 220,000 items.

Academy Libraries. In the system of academic libraries there are the Library of the Academy of Sciences of the U.S.S.R. in Leningrad (founded in 1714), the Library for the Natural Sciences of the Academy of Sciences in Moscow (founded in 1973), and the Library of the Institute of Scientific Information for the Social Sciences (founded in 1969), whose basic direction of activity is the preparation of bibliographic and reference information. The holdings of the Library of this institute exceed 10,000,000 items, more than half of which are foreign publications. The number of readers is 31,000 people; book loans number 3,000,000.

A central library is in operation in each of the 15 Union Republics. The holdings of the Library of the Academy of Sciences of the Latvian S.S.R. (founded in 1524), as one example, exceed 3,000,000 items. The number of readers is 15,000 and book loans total 1,300,000 items.

Agricultural Libraries. The leader is the Central Scientific Agricultural Library of the Lenin All-Union Academy of Agricultural Sciences (founded in 1930). The holdings of the library exceed 3,000,000 items (readers, 40,000, book loans, 2,000,000). From 1948 the library issued a monthly bibliographic list, "Agricultural Literature of the USSR", and from 1961 "New Works in Agricultural Science and Practice." The library is the methodological center for 1,300 libraries of scientific-research institutions, colleges, and technical schools with an agricultural emphasis, and experimental stations with a total holdings of 90,000,000 items, used by 2,000,000 readers.

Medical Libraries. In order to serve the medical workers and specialists in health services, a network of medical libraries was created, headed by the State Central Scientific Medical Library (founded in 1919), the holdings of which equal 2,500,000 items.

Educational Institutions. The students and teachers of nearly 900 universities and higher educational institutions and 4,400 middle-level specialist educational institutions of the country have special libraries at their disposal. Among them the oldest are the Library of Lvov University (founded in 1661), Moscow (1755), Tartu (1802), Vilnius (1803), Kazan (1804), and others. The overall number of reader-students (mid-1980s) is 9,833,000. As the All-Union scientific-methodological center, carrying out the leadership of the network of libraries of higher and middle-level specialist educational institutions, there is the Gorky Research Library of Lomonosov Moscow State University.

Library Cooperation. Libraries in the U.S.S.R. are under the authority of nearly 100 departments. From 1975 the State Interdepartmental Library Commission operated in the country under the control of the Ministry of Culture of the U.S.S.R. In accordance with "The Regulation of Library Work in the U.S.S.R.," it has been charged with the consideration of new regulations for the development of library work and with the determination of the principles of the assignment of libraries in the country, and also the resolution of various questions in accordance with its position as confirmed by the Council of Ministers of the U.S.S.R.. The decisions of this Commission are compulsory for the ministers and government committees, departments, and other organizations that have libraries under their control.

The Profession. The training of professional library workers is conducted in 17 institutions of culture, 43 pedagogical institutions, and 7 universities, as well as in 130 middle-level specialist educational institutions, located in the territory of each of the 15 Union Republics. The students learn on the basis of instructional plans, set forth for the preparation of specialists of broad background, with a specialization in one of the groups of literature (socio-political, artistic, children's, young people's, and so on). Training is conducted in institutes of culture (four years), in other higher educational institutions (five years), or in middle-level specialist educational institutions (three years). In some educational institutions (the Moscow and Leningrad Institutes of Culture), there is a postgraduate course.

The libraries of the Soviet Union in the mid-1980s were preparing "The Fundamental Direction of Their Activities for 1986–1990 and for the Period through 2000," determining the prospects for realization of the decisions of the 27th Congress of the Communist Party of the Soviet Union,

I. NAZMUTDINOV;
Translated by THOMAS L. MANN

United Arab Emirates

The United Arab Emirates—a union of seven former Trucial sheikdoms (Abu Dhabi, Ajman, Dubai, Fujairah, Ras al-Khaimah, Sharjah, and Umm al-Qaiwain) lies on the eastern coast of the Arabian Peninsula on the Persian Gulf. Population (1984 est.) 1,290,000; area 83,600 sq.km. The official language is Arabic.

National Library. There is no national library in the country. The book production is negligible. In 1968 the Center for Documentation and Research was founded. Attached to the Presidential Court, it collects manuscripts, documents, books, maps, and articles relevant to the Gulf States and Arabian Peninsula. The Center also conducts research on subjects related to those areas. Its library contains more than 5,000 volumes in Arabic and foreign languages.

Academic Library. The University of the United Arab Emirates, at Al Ain, founded in 1978, established a central library with its Teachers College

Libraries in the United Arab Emirates (1977)

Type	Administrative units	Service points	Volumes in collections	Annual expenditures (dirham)	Population served[a]	Professional staff	Total staff
National	1	1	818,000	285,000	--	19	120
Academic	4	9	17,000	--	608	4	45
Public	--	--	--	--	--	--	--
School	--	--	--	--	--	--	--

[a]Registered borrowers.

Source: Unesco, *Statistical Yearbook,* 1984.

as its primary focus. The Library has some 28,000 volumes. The University established colleges of Art, Political and Administrative Sciences, Natural Sciences, and Law and Jurisprudence.

Public Libraries. There is a public library in each of the seven emirates. Noteworthy is the Dubai Public Library, with a collection of about 15,000 volumes, mostly in Arabic. The public libraries support adult education in the country.

Special Libraries. Four ministerial libraries contain small collections of books, periodicals, reports, and newspapers. A Gulf Documentation Center in Abu Dhabi is under the supervision of the Ministry of Information and Tourism. The Center collects, processes, and disseminates communications information for the Gulf States and the Arabian Peninsula.

MOHAMED M. EL HADI*

United Kingdom

The United Kingdom, a constitutional monarchy, comprises the island of Great Britain—England, Scotland, and Wales—Northern Ireland, and various islands. Population (1984 est.) 56,236,000; area 244,100 sq.km. The official language is English.

History. The oldest libraries in Britain can trace their origins back a thousand years. They are the ecclesiastical collections, some of which still exist. The next oldest are those of colleges at the universities of Oxford, Cambridge, and St. Andrews. From 1753 to 1973 the national library was the British Museum Library, but it is interesting to note that copyright deposit dates back to 1666 in England. After the union with Scotland in 1707, a Copyright Act of 1709 became the first to extend the practice to Great Britain as a whole. That act required nine copies of every printed publication to be delivered to Stationers' Hall, these being destined for the Royal Library, the two English and four Scottish university libraries, Sion College Library, and the Advocates' Library in Edinburgh.

From the 17th century a few libraries were open to the public, examples being Chetham's Library in Manchester and Archbishop Tenison's Library in Westminster, but public libraries as we know them date only from an act of Parliament passed in 1850. For more than 50 years the whole of Britain has enjoyed a comprehensive public library service, while libraries in other institutions, universities, colleges, polytechnics, schools, and hospitals have steadily ex-

panded. Since 1877 the Library Association has had a great and continuing influence on library progress. Full-time education for librarianship may be said to have begun in Britain in 1919.

NATIONAL LIBRARIES
The British Library. Britain's national library until 1973 was the British Museum Library, which could trace its origins back to 1753, when Sir Hans Sloane bequeathed his outstanding collection of books and manuscripts to the nation. In 1969, however, the Dainton Committee Report drew attention to the need to rationalize the British Museum Library and other related collections. The Library Association strongly urged the government to act on the Dainton Committee Report; in 1972 Parliament passed the British Library Act, and on July 2, 1973, the British Library (BL) came into being. It was formed from the British Museum Library, the Science Reference Library, the Patent Office Library, the National Lending Library for Science and Technology, the National Central Library, and the *British National Bibliography.* The latter, known as BNB, had been formed in 1950, the British Museum and the Library

Theodore F. Welch

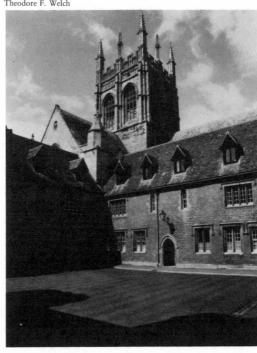

England's oldest surviving college library building is at Oxford University's Merton College, which was founded in 1264.

Association being among the partners that had initiated and supported it.

The British Library derives the bulk of its finances from Parliament, though it receives a considerable proportion of its revenue, about 20 percent in the mid-1980s, from its various activities. It is governed by a Board consisting of a part-time Chairman, nine part-time Members, and the Chief Executive and the Directors General of the three Divisions of the Library. The Chief Executive also acts as Deputy Chairman of the Board.

The British Library includes three main divisions—for Reference, for Lending, and for Bibliographical Services. In addition there is a Central Administration and a Research and Development Department. The main Reference Division is at the old British Museum Library in Great Russell Street, London. Other reference collections belonging to the BL are the Department of Manuscripts, the Department of Oriental Manuscripts and Printed Books, the Library Association Library, the Newspaper Library at Colindale in northwest London, the India Office Library and Records, the Science Reference Library at Holborn and Aldwych, and the National Sound Archive.

British Library Lending Division. The British Library Lending Division (BLLD) is housed at Boston Spa in Yorkshire, more than 200 miles north of London, on the site of the former National Lending Library for Science and Technology. To those collections was added the stock of the former National Central Library. The BLLD has about 2,000,000 volumes, more than 1,000,000 microforms, and more than 50,000 periodicals. It lends to other libraries,

normally by photocopying, though it lends volumes as well. It handles about 3,000,000 requests annually, of which more than 10 percent are from countries outside the United Kingdom. IFLA established an office for International Interlending at the BLLD. The BLLD was renamed the BL Document Supply Centre in December 1985.

Other BL Services. The Bibliographical Services Division continues to produce, among other services, the *British National Bibliography*. The Research and Development Department offers grants to individuals and institutions in varied fields of approved library research. The BL has an effective Press and Public Relations Section, which publishes an *Annual Report* and much other material offering up-to-date information about the BL.

Building Plans. The BL operates from nine separate addresses in London, in addition to the BLLD in Yorkshire. The Central Administration, the Bibliographical Services Division with its attendant Copyright Receipt Office and Marketing and Support Group, as well as the R&D Department and the Press and PR Section, are all situated at 2 Sheraton Street, London. The obvious need is to gather together all the Library's London activities in one adequate and centrally located building. Successive governments recognized the need, and in 1978 the Labour government gave approval for the building of a new library on a nine-and-a-half acre site next to St. Pancras Station on Euston Road. The Conservative government honored that promise, and in 1982 work began on the first of seven phases that will eventually result in a colossal building, one of the world's largest libraries. The first phase, consisting of the foundations, base-

Libraries in United Kingdom (1982)

Type	Administrative units	Service points	Volumes in collections	Annual expenditures (pound)	Population served	Professional staff	Total staff
National							
British Library	5[a]	14[b]	c. 15,000,000	51,522,753	56,340,000[c]	798	2,418
Scotland	1	3	c. 4,500,000	2,749,328		37	200
Wales	1	1	c. 3,000,000	1,863,761		30	165
Academic							
Universities	168[d]	--	--	71,182,000[e]	317,338[f]	--	--
Polytechnic	31	106	9,600,515	26,487,000[g]	180,800[h]	691	1,580
Others	636[i]	--	--	--	--	--	--
Public	167	17,500	--	384,131,197	56,340,000	8,488	29,584
School	--	--	--	--	8,137,315[j]	600[k]	--

[a]Includes three operating Divisions (Bibliographic Services, Lending & Reference), the Research and Development Department, and a Central Administration. A second Department—the National Sound Archive—was added in 1983.
[b]Reading Rooms.
[c]Population of UK according to *Britain . . .: An Official Handbook,* London: H.M.S.O. Ignores the large numbers of foreign visitors using the libraries, and participation in the international loan service.
[d]Includes colleges, schools, and institutes of the federal universities of Oxford, Cambridge, and London.
[e]Excludes capital expenditure on buildings, equipment, furniture, etc.
[f]Staff and students. Many academic libraries also participate heavily in the inter-library loans service.
[g]Recurrent and capital expenditure, from a mean figure.
[h]Academic staff and students, if full-time equivalents.
[i]State-supported institutions only. No figures available for any privately maintained institutions.
[j]Pupils only, staff served not known.
[k]England and Wales only. No figures available for Scotland or Northern Ireland.

Sources: The British Library: *Tenth Annual Report, 1982-83;* Council of Polytechnic Librarians, *Statistics of Polytechnic Libraries, 1982/83; Education Statistics 1982-83,* Actuals, C.I.P.F.A., 1984; National Library of Scotland, *Annual Report, 1982-83;* The National Library of Wales, *Annual Report, 1982-83; Public Library Statistics 1982-83,* Actuals, C.I.P.F.A., 1984; University Grants Committee, *University Statistics 1982-83, vol. 3: Finance;* and information from the various bodies concerned.

ments, and some superstructure, was not due to be finished until 1990–91, and it may well be into the 21st century before the building is finally completed. Even then, it will not include the lending operations, which will continue to be housed in Yorkshire. Fortunately, there is plenty of room for expansion there.

Library Cooperation. The BLLD is the hinge upon which British library cooperation and interlending works, but it was not always so. The idea of library interlending was talked about in Britain as long ago as 1890, but its real genesis took place in 1916 with the start of the Central Library for Students. This followed a Carnegie United Kingdom Trust (CUKT) report written by W. G. S. Adams. The Central Library for Students, set up with CUKT money, was originally designed to help public libraries meet the demands of adult classes for multiple copies of textbooks for study. In 1930 the Central Library for Students was reconstituted as the National Central Library, a result of a government committee report of 1927 known as the Kenyon Report.

Meanwhile, during the 1920s, the country's public libraries had begun to set up schemes of mutual help based upon various regions. They have been very successful, and there are nine Regional Library systems, one for London and southeastern England, six more in the rest of the country, one in Wales, and one in Scotland. Originally, only public libraries were members, but now most of the Regions include academic and special libraries in their membership as well. The systems are financed by subscriptions from the member libraries themselves.

The networks operate as follows. When a reader submits a request for material that is not in the stock of his or her own library, that library passes on the request to the headquarters of the Regional System to which its belongs, and the headquarers tries to satisfy the request from other libraries in the same region. If that attempt proves unsuccessful, the request then goes to the BLLD, which tries to meet it from its own stock or from other Regions or overseas libraries. The Regions usually satisfy about 80 percent of the requests; the BLLD success rate is over 90 percent.

To coordinate the work of the Regional Library systems and to provide for closer liaison between the Regions and the BLLD, there is a National Committee on Regional Library Cooperation, formed in 1931. There are also a number of district systems of library cooperation, based on such industrial centers as Liverpool, Sheffield, Bradford, and a number of other cities and counties.

Other National Libraries. *Scotland.* In addition to the British Library there are two other national libraries in the United Kingdom—the National Library of Scotland, which can trace its origins back to the 17th century, and the more recent National Library of Wales. The National Library of Scotland was founded in 1682 as the Advocates' Library; the Faculty of Advocates presented its collections to the nation in 1925 and Parliament set them up as the National Library. Since 1709 it has been a copyright library; it contains a notable collection of Scottish books and manuscripts. Housed in a building on George IV Bridge, Edinburgh, it includes a fine Reading Room and imposing Exhibition Rooms; the printed accessions number about 100,000 annually.

Joel Lee

Samuel Pepys's Library, dating from the 17th century, preserved at Magdalene College, Cambridge.

There is a card catalogue of printed books and a printed catalogue of manuscripts. A Board of Trustees directs the Library's activities.

Wales. The National Library of Wales is at Aberystwyth, where its building was begun in 1911 and finally completed in 1955. It has three departments: Manuscripts and Records; Printed Books; and Prints, Drawings, and Maps. Classification is by the Library of Congress system. The Library has benefited under the Copyright Act since 1911, but it may demand only certain material, mainly Welsh, under the legal deposit system. It possesses more than 2,000,000 printed books and large collections of other materials. It is the headquarters of the Regional Library System for Wales.

ACADEMIC LIBRARIES

Universities. Britain is well equipped with academic libraries, headed by those of the older universities of Oxford and Cambridge. Oxford is served by the Bodleian Library, which was actually begun in the 14th century but reorganized by Sir Thomas Bodley in 1598. The building was expanded in 1946; it houses well over 2,000,000 volumes and substantial collections of other materials. Like the Cambridge University Library, the Bodleian Library in Oxford has enjoyed copyright deposit privileges since the inception of legal deposit. Cambridge University Library also has collections dating from the 14th century and is of similar size. Its distinctive building was opened in 1934.

Next in importance are the libraries of the University of London. In addition to the Central University of London Library in Malet Street, London, are some 44 other libraries in the group. As a whole, the University of London libraries possess more than 6,000,000 volumes and seat more than 10,000 readers. The main controlling body is the Library Resources Co-ordinating Committee of the University.

Many of the 44 degree-giving universities in Britain are of more recent origin. The 'red-brick' universities, such as Nottingham and Southampton, emerged in the early part of the 20th century, but most of the county universities—such as those of York, Lancaster, Kent, Sussex and others—were formed more recently. The University Grants Committee has provided funds for libraries for these newer institutions. Some notable university library buildings have resulted, including those of the University of Reading, the University of Nottingham, the University of Edinburgh, and the Pilkington Library at the University of Loughborough.

Colleges and Institute Libraries. These also add much luster and value to the British academic library scene, good examples being some of the university college libraries at Oxford, Cambridge, London, Durham, St. Andrews, Belfast, Coleraine, and elsewhere. England's oldest surviving college library building is at Oxford University's Merton College, which was founded in 1264.

The many institute libraries in the University of London also are worthy of mention. Britain has numerous university extramural libraries, as well as libraries in colleges of education. In addition there are 31 polytechnics in England, Wales, and Northern Ireland, all of which possess libraries of growing importance. Just as British university and national librarians have formed themselves into a body known as the Standing Conference of National and University Libraries (SCONUL), so the polytechnic librarians started the Council of Polytechnic Librarians (CO-POL). The Library Association also has been active in producing and revising standards for college and certain other types of academic libraries.

PUBLIC LIBRARIES

History. In 1850 Parliament passed the first Public Libraries Act—a weak, tentative law, permissive and not mandatory. Almost everything was left to local initiative in cities and towns. The counties were not permitted to operate public library services until 1919; the provision of public libraries became a duty imposed on city, town, and county councils in 1964 but by that date complete coverage of the country had already been achieved, apart from one or two small areas.

After 1850 public library progress at first was slow, but from the 1880s it began to accelerate, favorable factors being the grants offered by Andrew Carnegie and the increasing professional influence of the Library Association. British public libraries really began to burgeon in the 1930s. By that time financial limitations had been relaxed, county libraries had been set up, and the library cooperative networks based on the National Central Library and the Regional Library Systems were working more effectively. Attracted by the more efficient services, often operating from new, purpose-planned buildings, new readers began to flock to Britain's public libraries in the days before World War II.

During the war years, in spite of reduced staffs and often in the face of enemy bombardments, the country's public libraries were used more than ever before; their role as purveyors of reference work and information was increasingly recognized. After the war the profession began to build upon its newfound confidence. As soon as conditions permitted, existing services were expanded and new ones, such as the provision of audiovisual materials and the establishment of services to the disadvantaged, were embarked upon.

Until the mid-1960s, however, public library development in Britain was hampered by the fact that there were too many local authorities. They varied greatly in size and financial resources, and too many unacceptable inequalities in the service resulted. Lionel R. McColvin had drawn attention to this problem in his *Report on Public Library Systems in Great Britain (1942),* which had been endorsed by the Library Association. There were more than 600 separate public library authorities in McColvin's time, but a succession of new laws—the London Government Act of 1963, the Public Libraries and Museums Act of 1964, and the Local Government Act of 1973, along with separate legislation for Scotland and Northern Ireland—reduced the number of local library authorities to 167.

Inequalities still persist but are much less noticeable than before; the larger authorities created by mergers and combinations of the older ones are financially more viable and capable of making better all-round provision for ever-widening public library responsibilities and services. Since the dawn of the 1980s, budget cuts have begun to make themselves felt, particularly in the hard-hit industrial areas of Britain, and inequalities of service were beginning once again to be apparent in the mid-1980s. Nevertheless, many public library systems continued to develop through the provision of new library buildings and by the adoption of automated systems integrating the ordering of materials, cataloguing, and loan methods.

Buildings. From about 1958 there was a welcome renaissance of public library building in the country. Hundreds of new branch libraries were erected in cities, towns, and counties. Reflecting the best influences of Scandinavian architecture and design, the attractive buildings appeared up and down the country throughout the 1960s and the first half of the 1970s. There was a mild hiccough in the late 1970s because of fiscal restrictions, but the program by no means came to a halt. New main libraries for the cities and larger towns and new headquarters for county libraries were at first not as common as the smaller branches, but numerous major public library buildings emerged during the two decades from the

British Library Lending Division (BL Document Supply Centre from December 1985) building at Boston Spa, Yorkshire, formerly site of the National Lending Library for Science and Technology.

mid-1960s. These include the great extensions to the Mitchell Library in Glasgow (making it the largest public library in Europe) and new central libraries in such cities and towns as Birmingham, Bradford, Salisbury, and Worthing; in the London area at Camden, Bromley, Sutton, and the City of London; and county library headquarters in Kent, Montgomeryshire, and elsewhere.

Free Principle. Members of the reading public were not slow to use them. Public library services in Britain have been, and remain, free, both for those borrowing books and for those consulting reference material. A loophole in the 1964 Act, however, did permit library authorities to charge for borrowing phonograph records and cassettes, and many, though not all, do so. Some libraries charge for the loan of audio material through an annual subscription; others charge a fee for each borrowing transaction. From time to time the idea of making charges for borrowing books is mooted but so far it has been effectively scotched. All the main political parties are dedicated to the free principle. But a volte-face is always possible, and the Library Association is ready to counteract such a possibility.

Public Lending Right. From 1951 onwards the idea of a public lending right was debated in the United Kingdom. The Library Association agreed that authors should be fairly compensated for their work, but it opposed some of the early projected schemes that would have thrown much extra work upon library staffs and could have had depressing effects upon book funds. After studies by successive governments, a Public Lending Right Scheme went into force in 1982. The first payments were made to authors in 1984.

The Library Association's arguments were taken into account when the law was promulgated; calculations are based on samplings from a limited number of libraries in various parts of the country, and the money, both for the authors' compensation and for the scheme's administration, comes from central government and not the local library authorities. The first year's working of the PLR scheme confirmed the suspicions of librarians—that it does little or nothing for authors of modest standing; it only adds to the income of the already well-off best-selling writers.

Circulation and Special Services. British public libraries are among the best used in the world, the loan figure being about 12 per capita annually—that is, more than 650,000,000 volumes a year. In addition to providing comprehensive lending departments for both adults and children, most lend records, cassettes, and video recordings. Reference and information work is particularly well developed, and there are special services for the housebound, immigrant communities, slow readers, and other special groups. Some, but not all, British public libraries also operate the school, hospital, and prison libraries in their areas. Where that is not done, school libraries are organized by the education authority, hospital libraries either by the Regional Hospital Boards or by voluntary effort, and prison libraries by the Home Office. School, hospital, and prison libraries in the United Kingdom still need to have more rational organization.

The larger British public libraries, especially those of the big cities, often have more in common

© The British Library

Reading Room of the British Library, inside the quadrangle of the British Museum, was completed in 1857. Since 1973, the British Library has been independent of the British Museum.

with research libraries than with smaller public libraries. Many operate important special collections, such as the Shakespeare collection of Birmingham City Libraries, the International Library of Liverpool City Libraries, the Business Library of the City of London Libraries, and the Central Music Library of Westminster City Libraries.

Children's Services. Children's and youth library work is emphasized by most British public libraries. Branch and mobile libraries are generally well provided and relatively few people in the country live more than a mile away from their nearest library service point. Computerized methods of cataloguing and charging systems are increasingly being used and refined; and public relations programs—oral, visual, and printed—are being developed within limitations of staff and finances.

SPECIAL AND INDUSTRIAL LIBRARIES

Although it is possible to cite earlier examples, it is still fair to say that most British special and industrial libraries are phenomena of the post-1920s. Indeed, World War I probably first drew attention to the need for libraries catering to the needs of those concerned with technology, industry, commerce, and statistics. Steady increases in the appearance of such libraries took place between the two World Wars. They were sponsored by government departments; industrial, commercial, and professional organizations; public authorities; research associations; and other bodies. To aid and encourage their development, the Association of Special Libraries and Information Bureaux (Aslib) was formed in 1924, and the Library Association later formed a Reference, Special and Information Libraries Section, as well as an Industrial Group, a Government Libraries Group, and a Medical, Health and Welfare Libraries Group.

World War II gave further impetus to the need for more special and industrial libraries in the United Kingdom, and another fillip was added in 1948 when

Cambridge University Library traces its origins to the 14th century. This building opened in 1934.

Theodore F. Welch

the Royal Society sponsored a Scientific Information Conference, which proved influential in government circles. Aslib's *Handbook of Special Librarianship* has run to many editions and has fostered developments in this field.

Some of the biggest and most important special libraries are government owned, examples being those of the Department of Trade and Industry and of the Department of Education and Science. Important public authority libraries include the many collections owned by the BBC and the libraries of the National Coal Board and the UK Atomic Energy Authority. Outstanding among industrial and commercial libraries are those belonging to the Metal Box Company, ICI Limited, and Boots Pure Drug Company. Professional libraries also abound; important ones include those of the British Medical Association and the Royal Institute of British Architects. There are also collections of great significance belonging to private societies and clubs: among these are the library of the Zoological Society of London, the Royal Commonwealth Society Library, and the MCC (Marylebone Cricket Club) Library at Lord's Cricket Ground in London. Such libraries are invariably made available to bona-fide research workers, even if they are not members of the society or club.

THE PROFESSION

Associations. For many years only one organization was devoted to the development of British libraries and librarianship—the Library Association (LA), founded in 1877, only a year after the formation of the American Library Association. Although the LA had been formed and was supported in its early years by academic and research librarians, its emphasis gradually changed; by the early 1920s it was concerned largely with public librarianship. Since that

time there have sprung up a variety of other associations, in addition to Aslib, such as those for national and university librarians (SCONUL), for polytechnic librarians (COPOL), and for art libraries (ARLIS), among others.

In spite of the proliferation of other organizations, the Library Association has advanced steadily into its second century. Celebrating its centenary in 1977, the LA had more than 24,000 members. Its financial position is sound, its greatest material asset being ownership of the headquarters building in London. Opened in 1965, it houses council and committee rooms, a members' lounge, library, offices, and other facilities.

The LA is governed by a 60-member Council, elected by the membership, and advised by six main committees. The Association is constantly, though rightly, changing its committee structure to take cognizance of changing situations. In addition to the Executive Committee, there are committees for Bibliographic and Information Systems and Standards, for Education, for Manpower and Conditions of Service, for Membership Services, and for Library and Information Services. The LA is also divided into 12 regional Branches and 22 Groups, the latter representing such specialist interests as Cataloguing and Indexing; Information Technology; International and Comparative Librarianship; Training and Education; and Youth Libraries.

Professional Education. For the first 90 years of its existence, the LA was virtually the only body in the United Kingdom to have a concern for education in librarianship. From its earliest years it organized courses for aspiring librarians, planned a syllabus, conducted examinations, and maintained, as it still does, a professional register. It also encouraged the formation of library schools, of which there were 16 in the country in the mid-1980s.

Although the LA's role as an examining body steadily diminished, and was scheduled to disappear entirely in 1985, the Association still plays an important part in continuing professional education and training. It maintains the professional register of Fellows and Associates, organizes an increasing number of short courses on developments in library and information science, and carries on a continuing dialogue with the heads of the library schools.

Library Schools. Of the 16 library schools in the United Kingdom (1985), the oldest is that of University College, London, which was founded in 1919. The remaining schools did not begin to function until 1946 and succeeding years. Five are attached to universities, seven are part of polytechnics, three are attached to colleges of technology or higher education, and one (the College of Librarianship, Wales) is independent. All the library schools offer graduate or postgraduate courses in library and information science, documentation, and archival work. Most of them offer special courses for external students, and some have arranged international library courses and have published occasional papers. Many professors and lecturers from British library schools have had international experience as consultants overseas sponsored by Unesco, the British Council, and other bodies.

Publications. The LA is also actively concerned with conferences and publications. In addition to the

Association's own annual conference, most of the Branches and many of the Groups arrange their own conferences, meetings, and study schools. Printed proceedings frequently result. The LA issues the monthly *Library Association Record*, the quarterly *Journal of Librarianship*, the annual LA *Year Book*, and several serials as well as conference proceedings. The Association also has a vigorous publishing program operating under the Board of Library Association Publishing Ltd. One of its best sellers is Walford's *Guide to Reference Material*. During its centenary year in 1977, LA issued a number of centenary volumes, one of which was a history of the Association by W. A. Munford.

Research. Research and development are also given prominence by the LA. Although it sponsors numerous projects on its own initiative and from its own resources, it often works with other bodies such as Aslib, the British Library, and the library schools in several areas of research.

Aslib and Other Organizations. Aslib was formed as an association for special libraries and information bureaux, and recently changed its name to Aslib, the Association for Information Management. It consists almost entirely of institutional members, of which there are more than 2,000 in 70 countries. Like the LA, it is organized into Branches and Groups; it arranges conferences, meetings, and courses; and it has an active publishing program, including the monthly *Aslib Proceedings*, the quarterly *Journal of Documentation*, as well as the *Aslib Directory* and the *Aslib Year Book*. Aslib publishes *Current Awareness Bulletin* monthly and *Network* and *Information Management Today*, quarterly.

Aslib maintains a library and information service, a consultancy service for its members, a staff employment register, a register of specialist translators and indexers, and an online resources center offering advice on online data management matters. It conducts searches for a fee. Aslib also has a research function funded partly by the British Library.

Among the numerous other bodies devoted to developing various aspects of British library and information science are such organizations as SCONUL, COPOL, and ARLIS, already mentioned, and the Association of British Library and Information Science Schools (ABLISS), to name just a few.

International Librarianship. Britain exercised considerable influence on world librarianship. British librarians have traditionally played important parts in developing IFLA, itself formed after the Library Association's 50th Anniversary Conference, held in Edinburgh in 1927. Both the British Council and the Library Association helped to start library movements in the developing countries of the Commonwealth and have had particular successes in Ghana, India, Jamaica, Kenya, Nigeria, Singapore, and Sri Lanka. The LA also gave invaluable help and encouragement in establishing the Commonwealth Library Association (COMLA) in 1972. Large amounts of money have been fed into many of the developing countries by the Overseas Development Administration and the British Council, and many British librarians have acted as consultants or library advisers for Unesco, the British Council, and other bodies in such countries as Mauritius, Sudan, Tanzania, and the United Arab Emirates. Other members of the profession have given their services through Voluntary Service Overseas (VSO), the British equivalent of the U.S. Peace Corps.

Library Press. Library journalism has flourished in the United Kingdom during the last 100 years. Soon after its foundation the LA communicated with its membership through a publication known as *Monthly Notes*. It lasted from 1880 to 1884, then from that year until 1888 it was succeeded by *The Library Chronicle*. From 1889 to 1898, a monthly journal, *The Library*, was adopted as the official organ of the LA, although it was owned and edited by J. Y. W. MacAlister. Finally, in 1899, the *Library Association Record* became the Association's official journal, and has remained so ever since. Its first editor was Henry Guppy, and it has had many distinguished librarian-editors, including Arundell Esdaile, W. B. Stevenson, J. D. Reynolds, and Edward Dudley. From 1976 it was edited by full-time professional journalists. The LA established the quarterly *Journal of Librarianship* (1969) which features longer and usually more scholarly articles than the *Record*, which is more concerned with current news and events. Several of the LA's Branches and Groups issue regular publications that have established themselves in library literature. Among these are the Scottish Library Association's *SLA News*, the *Book Trolley*, *YLG News*, from the Youth Libraries Group, the *Cataloguer and Indexer*, *Library History*, and others.

There have also been several independent library journals in Britain. One of these, *The Library World*, was founded by James Duff Brown in July 1898, and it thus predates the *Library Association Record* by six months. It has appeared monthly ever since that date, though it changed its title to *New Library World* when it was purchased by the publisher Clive Bingley in 1971. After Duff Brown, its editors have included J. D. Stewart, W. C. Berwick Sayers, and K. C. Harrison. In October 1983 it issued its 1,000th number, with suitable celebratory articles.

Another British independent journal was *The Librarian and Book World*, a monthly started by Alex J. Philip in 1911 and carried on bravely until the 1960s, being taken over after Philip's death by the publishing firm of James Clarke and Company. In 1927 yet another independent publication appeared, the *Library Review*, published in Glasgow and edited by R. D. Macleod. It began as a quarterly devoted to libraries and literature, and throughout its existence it has tended to give prominence to the literary and historical side of librarianship. It devotes much prominence to book reviews in depth, both of professional and general literature, and it frequently features articles on aspects of library history and biography. Owned by Holmes McDougall, it is edited under the direction of a collective of three librarians and a board of consultants.

REFERENCES

S. P. L. Filon, *The National Central Library: an experiment in library cooperation* (1977).

K. C. Harrison, Editor, *Prospects for British Librarianship* (1976).

Thomas Kelly, *A History of Public Libraries in Great Britain, 1847–1975* (1977).

W. A. Munford, *A History of the Library Association, 1877–1977* (1976).

L. J. Taylor, Editor, *British Librarianship and Information Work, 1976–1980*, 2 volumes (1982).
Annual reports published since 1975 by the British Library.

K. C. HARRISON

United States

The United States of America is a federal republic of 50 states; 48 of them, the coterminous states, are bordered by Canada on the north, the Atlantic Ocean on the east, Mexico on the south, and the Pacific Ocean on the west; Alaska is bordered by Canada on the east and the Pacific on the west, and Hawaii is in the mid-Pacific. Population (l984 est.) 236,634,000; area 9,363,571 sq.km.

HISTORY

Colonial Period: Oral Culture. For many years after their arrival in 1607, New World colonists had little time for books and reading. With homes to build, forests to clear, and crops to plant and harvest, these immigrants had to spend most of their energy surviving a new environment and adapting to its unique demands. Any immediate, practical information needs they had were answered most often by the experience of trial and error, on occasion by native Americans, or perhaps not at all. The colonists lived in an oral culture. Literacy was not essential for daily living, and intellectual needs naturally received a low priority. The population—though growing—was neither large nor wealthy enough to support a literary class. The New World lacked prominent aristocrats to patronize authors and artists; and although some members of the medical and theological professions possessed a score or more of books they felt necessary for their vocations, the small minority of colonists who could read required little print information beyond their Bibles, hymnals, and prayer books. Others managed by committing favorite verses to memory to get themselves through church services, or by trusting a friend who could read to interpret important documents.

Private Collections. Despite the dominance of an oral culture, literacy was more widely diffused among the New World populations than in Europe, and eventually libraries began to take root and grow. At first, most collections were private. Until the turn of the 18th century, personal libraries characteristically consisted of 50 to 100 volumes held by ministers or doctors. But several stood apart. By 1639, Connecticut's Governor John Winthrop, Jr., had accumulated more than a thousand volumes in his personal library. Six decades later, Cotton Mather of Massachusetts and William Byrd of Virginia each boasted collections of more than 4,000 volumes.

Several attempts were made during the late 17th century to expand access to print materials beyond private libraries. In 1656 Captain Robert Keayne, a Massachusetts merchant, willed part of his personal collection to establish a public library in Boston, provided that the city construct a suitable building to house it.

Thomas Bray's Libraries. At the turn of the 18th century, the Reverend Thomas Bray, an Anglican clergyman, made more serious efforts to create literary centers for colonists. Operating out of England, Bray set up more than 70 libraries in the Colonies between 1695 and 1704. Five were located in large cities to serve entire provinces; 40 were given for use by the parishioners of specific churches; the remainder were controlled by ministers of the Anglican church and designed to serve laymen. Several colonial legislatures passed laws to maintain and staff the Bray libraries, but they made little provision to add new volumes to the original collections. As a result, the libraries fell into disuse shortly after their sponsor died in 1730.

By that time, the New World was changing. Within a century of the landing at Plymouth Rock, the brush had been cleared from the Eastern seaboard, the forests pushed back, and the threat of Indian raids minimized. Colonists began to find time to reflect upon their current situation. European intellectuals, among them Newton, Locke, and Rousseau, were asking significant questions and offering important observations about human nature and the social and political environment. Literate colonists found themselves thinking less about their religious needs and more about their secular and vocational goals. They desired to expand their interests, and they hungered for access to more information sources that would help them answer questions unique to their New World environment.

Benjamin Franklin and Social Libraries. In 1728 an enterprising Pennsylvania printer named

---

Libraries in the United States (1982)

Type	Administrative units	Service points	Volumes in collections	Annual expenditures (dollar)	Population served	Professional staff	Total staff
National[a]	3	--	22,494,066	305,875,000	--	1,162	5,511
Academic[b]	4,924	1,728	567,826,000	1,941,983,000	--	58,421	23,806
Public[b]	8,768	6,056	509,250,000	2,243,236,000	--	--	--
School[c]	70,854	--	469,700,000	1,385,600,000	47,500,000[e]	--	34,171
Special[b,d]	9,201	--	--	--	--	--	--

[a]Library of Congress, National Library of Medicine, National Agricultural Library.
[b]*Statistical Abstract of the United States*, 1984.
[c]Based on National Center for Education Statistics, *Statistics of Public School Libraries/Media Centers*, Fall, 1982. Statistics cover public schools only.
[d]Also includes medical, government, religious, armed forces, and law libraries.
[e]Public school pupils and teachers.

Benjamin Franklin joined in organizing the Philadelphia Junto, a group of 12 men seeking intellectual stimuli. Franklin suggested that members pool their book holdings and locate them in one place for the benefit of all. Although that scheme failed, the resourceful Franklin did not give up. In 1731 he organized the Library Company of Philadelphia. He asked members to purchase shares of stock (which could be subsequently traded or sold) and promised to use the money they invested to acquire books of interest to all. The newly acquired collections demonstrated the continued trend away from religious reading interests. The Library Company eagerly accumulated volumes on such topics as philosophy, travel, and biography.

The Company's proprietary structure served as a prototype for other kinds of social libraries. Some expanded their holdings by inviting nonshareholders to pay a "subscription" price to utilize library services, thus introducing the "subscription library." Others acquired newspapers and magazines for their collections and, by charging large stock prices and fostering other cultural activities, became known as "athenaeums." A fourth type of social library—the "mechanics" or "mercantile" library—resulted from the philanthropic inclinations of prosperous businessmen and industrialists who wanted to provide white-collar clerks and blue-collar mechanics with opportunities to advance themselves through self-education.

Other Public Library Precursors. Other types of libraries existed along with the social library, but served different purposes. Collections in Sunday school libraries emphasized religious themes designed to provide inspirational messages. Some industries sponsored "apprentice" libraries to foster educational and recreational reading among their employees. The "circulating" library also served those who sought recreational reading; for a small fee, a patron could withdraw books from a library (usually in a printshop or bookstore) whose collection consisted mainly of fiction.

In 1835 the New York state legislature passed a law authorizing school districts to impose a tax on citizens to fund libraries. The legislature approved matching funds three years later, and collections contained some 1,500,000 volumes by 1850. Although several other states passed similar legislation, the success of school district libraries was shortlived. Legislators usually neglected to provide additional funds for staff and quarters, and the book selection procedures were haphazard. Most school district libraries died for lack of interest and attention.

Public Libraries. The changes experienced by libraries in the United States mirrored changes in America's rapidly diversifying socioeconomic structure. By 1850, the United States began to suffer new growing pains. As the nation neared its 100th birthday, it was becoming less dependent upon foreign manufactures to fulfill industrial needs. New industries, which clustered in or near major urban areas, struggled to meet demands created by growing populations. In the process, they created jobs that attracted workers from rural areas (farms were becoming increasingly mechanized and required fewer laborers) and held ever-growing numbers of immigrants who had fled the static and often depressing

The Library of Congress

Jefferson building of the Library of Congress, Washington, D.C. completed in 1897; behind it is the Madison Building (1979).

economic and social conditions of their native lands for the promise of a new life in the United States. Industrialization and urbanization also stimulated the growth of a professional middle class. Its members sought to perpetuate the country's growth patterns and to remove obstacles that threatened to alter radically the socioeconomic structure supporting their endeavors. As members of this class looked upon the manifestations of their nation's growing pains with increased anxiety, they began to search for solutions to perceived problems.

One solution they advocated transformed the nation from an oral to a written culture. Mid-century proponents of universal literacy promised that the United States could correct its social ills only if all its citizens could read and write. They were persuasive enough to convince most states to mandate school attendance; their efforts led to the establishment of institutions that had significant potential for socializing the nation's youth. The American library community was eager to tie itself to this new force. Melvil Dewey, who helped organize the American Library Association and establish the *Library Journal* in 1876, echoed the sentiments of many ALA peers by arguing repeatedly that more tax-supported libraries were needed, and each of these ought to become a "people's university," a place citizens could turn to for self-paced education after the conclusion of their formal schooling. Of course, he noted, librarians would provide the proper direction for this mass educational venture by developing and organizing high-quality collections and supplementing them with valuable personal assistance. The ideology emerging from this perspective helped spark the library movement in the last quarter of the 19th century. In their rush to help educate America, librarians took the institutions for which they held responsiblitiy into new directions.

The transition from the social to the public library that characterized one major direction in the late 19th century traced its roots to Thomas Jefferson's firm belief that a democratic government could not function properly without an informed public. Peterborough, New Hampshire, established the nation's first local library supported by public taxes and open to all its citizens (1834). By the middle of the 19th century, several state legislatures passed laws giving local governments the authority to tax their citizens to support public libraries. New Hampshire was first in 1849, but Massachusetts's 1851 law led directly to the 1854 opening of the Boston Public Library, which became the model for most urban libraries (and many smaller ones) for the remainder of the 19th century.

While city after city established and funded urban public libraries that were developing innovative methods to serve the newer populations flocking to their cities, state after state established library commissions to ensure that similar information services were extended to rural populations by traveling libraries or through the fostering of small-town public libraries.

Carnegie Libraries. Much of this activity was fueled by the philanthropic benefactions of Andrew Carnegie (1835-1919), the steel magnate and philanthropist who perceived the public library as a self-help mechanism particularly well suited to nurturing American democratic ideals. After retiring from industry in 1901, he accelerated his philanthropy, and by 1920 he had dispensed more than $50,000,000 in the constuction of about 2,500 library buildings in various parts of the world. To merit consideration for a grant, municipalities had only to guarantee an annual appropriation of 10 percent of the sum given in order to support the library.

World War I. The war and its effects significantly influenced the American public library. While the American Library Association directed efforts to provide a Library War Service for American troops at home and abroad, public libraries also assisted in obtaining gift books and donating staff services. In addition, they encouraged patriotic organizations to use their facilities, reached out to the new arrivals to their towns who had come to work in war-related industries, and eagerly served as channels for information that the federal government wished to pass along to citizens. By the end of the war in 1918, the public library had matured into a bona fide social service institution.

The 1920s and 1930s. The 1920s contrasted sharply with the previous two decades. Resolution of the social problems that seemed so important and received so much attention during the first two decades of the 20th century appeared to dissipate in an overriding desire to accumulate more personal and corporate wealth. Just as individuals turned more attention to personal concerns, so the public library focused more attention on its internal mechanisms. Some public libraries attempted to reach out to nonuser populations and to harness the momentum of the adult eduation movement, but the nation was not ripe for social crusades.

The next decade brought significant change, however. First, the Great Depression threw millions out of work. Partly to relieve their boredom, partly to improve their chances at reentering the labor market through vocational self-education, Americans began to use libraries more frequently. Circulation increased, and librarians found themselves called upon to meet increasing demands with decreasing budgets for staff and materials. Then, as European and Asian totalitarian governments posed an apparent ever-increasing threat to world stability through a variety of aggressive actions (including such activities as book burnings), American public libraries promoted themselves as "guardians of the people's right to know." This theme persisted through the World War II years, the McCarthy era of the 1950s, and down to the present day.

Later History. By the mid-1950s, the public library augmented its focus on wider service, especially by reaching out to traditional nonuser groups. Fed by the Great Society programs of the mid- and late 1960s, outreach and rural services once again received increased attention. Public libraries attached themselves to the adult education movement and used the influx of new federal dollars to spur more efforts at cooperation and new activities such as information and referral services. Federal dollars also contributed significantly to the construction of new libraries, many of which replaced old Carnegie buildings.

Independent Research Libraries. The late 19th-century public library movement also sparked the birth of several unanticipated offspring. A few wealthy men with bibliophilic propensities donated vast sums of money for the construction and maintenance of private research libraries to answer the needs of a clientele not directly addressed by the new objectives public and academic libraries had defined for themselves. Chicago received a major share of attention in the 1890s when money left by Walter L. Newberry and John Crerar created research libraries that now bear their names. The Lenox and John J. Astor Libraries had performed similar functions for New York City in the mid-19th century, until they were merged into the New York Public Library system during the same decade. In 1919 Henry Huntington founded a library bearing his name in San Marino, California, which built on his substantial rare book collection. The Folger Shakespeare Library was founded in 1932 in Washington, D.C., as a result of the Shakespeare collections and fortune of Henry Clay Folger. Other prominent endowed research libraries established before 1970 include the Hoover Library on War, Revolution and Peace at Stanford University (1919), the Pierpont Morgan Library in New York City (1924), and the Marshall Research Library in Lexington, Virginia (1964).

Academic Libraries. The nation's transformation from an oral to a written culture, coupled with the effects of immigration, urbanization, and industrialization, pressed American academic libraries at the turn of the 20th century into a direction different from that of public libraries. Previously, academic libraries had had a quiet history dating back to 1638, when the Reverend John Harvard donated nearly 300 books—three-fourths of which dealt with theological topics—to establish a New World institution of higher learning. The well-intentioned clergyman did not realize that his gift would reflect three problems that plagued academic libraries for the next two-and-a-half centuries. First, academic institutions struggling to survive were reluctant to commit money for books for their libraries, forcing college librarians to augment their collections largely through donations.

Second, the gift books themselves badly skewed the collections; many donated texts were discards that owners no longer wanted, and most were in the subject areas of theology and the classics. As long as the institution's curriculum demonstrated a theological-classical emphasis, the college library could at least render lip-service to supporting it, but once college curricula began changing during the mid-19th century, the utility of academic library collections became even more marginal. Third, the attitude that characterized college library administrators augmented the libraries' inherent problems. Academic librarians were often faculty members whose library duties were simply added to their regular classroom duties, and the institutions' trustees and administrators normally looked to these caretakers for library security and careful record-keeping. Librarians extended borrowing privileges mostly to faculty, infrequently to upperclassmen, and almost never to undergraduates. They opened their libraries as little as possible and often at inconvenient times. Understandably, students shied away from academic libraries and began to develop their own alternative—the literary society library. Between the American Revolution and 1850, for example, literary society libraries at Ivy League colleges were more accessible, contained more books, were broader in scope, and were much more comfortable than their institutional counterparts.

By mid-19th century, the situation began to change. Charles W. Eliot, President of Harvard from 1869 to 1909, endorsed an elective system that gave students more options, and other institutions followed Harvard's lead. In addition, many American scholars had been trained in German universities that emphasized research; as they took faculty positions in American colleges and universities, they began to demand that academic libraries provide better research facilities for themselves and their students. Finally, members of a new professional middle class demanded that colleges offer courses designed to introduce students to the special knowledge of particular professions.

All of these factors served to persuade college administrators that they needed to provide more funds to alter the traditional patterns of academic library service. Academic libraries began to push for longer hours, services to all members of the academic community, and better catalogues to record their holdings. Most literary society libraries had been absorbed into regular academic library collections by the turn of the 20th century, a fact that suggests that academic libraries were responding more directly to student and faculty needs. The proliferation of seminars, graduate education, and honors and independent study programs all had significant impact on the patterns of academic library use. Librarians instituted closed reserve systems to address the problem of circulating heavily used class-related materials. In the 1930s, several academic library directors began dividing their holdings and service into subject collections, and scholars began to acknowledge that intellectual content worthy of preservation might be found in formats other than print.

Post-World War II. The years after World War II brought changes that, although not as significant as the late 19th century in changes of service, were

United Press Photo

Main Reading Room of the Library of Congress.

much more impressive in numbers. The G.I. Bill provided a tempting invitation to returning veterans to undertake a college education, and institutional enrollments expanded. As veterans and their offspring progressed through the American educational system in the 1950s and 1960s, academic libraries found their collection resources and service capacities sorely tested. The federal government supplied some help; the Higher Education Act of 1965 awarded acquisition grants directly to academic institutions, while other federal acts funded the construction of many new academic library buildings in the 1960s. Standards created by various national, regional, and local accrediting agencies also had significant impact on the development of modern academic library services.

School Libraries. School-library development is largely a 20th-century phenomenon. Although some school libraries had early 18th-century beginnings, significant movement to provide library services to school children did not occur until the last two decades of the 19th century, when many public libraries attempted to serve school curricula by making the schools branch public library stations. While these efforts proved helpful, many members of the National Education Association (NEA) looked for more direct control over school library collections. NEA began seeking more autonomy for the libraries and pressed for acceptance of the concept of separate school libraries that were acquired, staffed, and organized solely for the use of school faculty and students and designed to support the school curriculum. In the 1920s the Association developed standards for elementary and secondary school libraries. State and local governments encouraged this trend by funding school library supervisors and recommended booklists and specially developed handbooks.

The Great Depression of the 1930s temporarily stayed school library development, but the years after

833

World War II saw the growth patterns restored and several new trends. One was more use of nonprint media for instruction. Since someone had to acquire, store, maintain, and circulate media equipment and materials, the school library was gradually transformed into an instructional materials center. Another trend after World War II reflected efforts to establish more elementary school libraries. The movement received tremendous impetus with the passage of the Elementary and Secondary Education Act of 1965. School libraries used the influx of federal dollars to emulate successful demonstration projects that had been supported by the Knapp Foundation and a School Library Development Project organized by the ALA and funded by the Council on Library Resources. The Higher Education Acts of 1965 and 1966 also promoted school librarian training.

Overview. Until the mid-19th century, libraries in the United States experienced slow, sometimes lethargic growth in the midst of a predominantly oral culture. Library development was affected only infrequently by strong individuals of moderate to high means who perceived the institution's value to a society they helped to control. Only after government intervened to supplement or replace private funding with public tax dollars in the last half of the 19th century did library growth accelerate. By the turn of the 20th century the push for universal literacy had produced a momentum that librarians willingly tapped in order to motivate their institutions to improve collections and services. That momentum slowed for several decades following World War I, but received a significant new impetus when Congress authorized President Lyndon B. Johnson's Great Society programs in the mid-1960s. A contemporaneous yet coincidental development—the growth of computer technology and accessibility—combined with this new impetus to launch libraries into the new Information Age.

NATIONAL LIBRARIES

Library of Congress. The United States sponsors numerous governmental libraries, but three qualify as national because of the constituencies they serve. The largest is the Library of Congress (80,000,000 items in 1984), created by law in 1800 to serve the information needs of the Congress. The British destroyed the Library during the War of 1812, but Thomas Jefferson offered to revive it by selling his personal library to the federal government in 1816. After some political haggling, Congress decided to accept Jefferson's offer, subsuming not only his collection but also his classification scheme. The Library of Congress limped along for several decades on minimal budgets and in inadequate quarters, but space needs accelerated when the Smithsonian Institution gave its scientific periodicals collections to the Library in 1866, and Congress authorized the purchase of Peter Force's collection of Americana in 1867. Then, when Congress passed the Copyright Law of 1870, which mandated that two copies of any work copyrighted in the United States be deposited in the Library, the collection really began to swell. Ainsworth Rand Spofford, Librarian of Congress from 1865 to 1897, argued that the Library needed a separate building and, after nearly two decades of constant pressure, finally convinced Congress of the Library's critical situation. Workmen applied the finishing touches to a new structure in 1897, and two major additions followed in the 20th century—the Thomas Jefferson Building in 1939 and the James Madison Building in 1983.

Herbert Putnam became Librarian of Congress in 1899, and under his direction the Library began to flex its muscle as a national library by spearheading efforts to centralize cataloguing processes. What started in the first decade of the 20th century as a service to distribute catalogue cards grew to the printing of the *National Union Catalog* in the fourth decade and ultimately led to Machine Readable Cataloguing (MARC) tapes in the sixth. The Library also plays a role in other national library activities; it is actively involved in investigating better methods for preserving print materials, in sponsoring book exchanges, and in acting as a center for the National Library Services for the Blind and Physically Handicapped. In addition, in 1977 Congress authorized the Library to establish a Center for the Book to focus attention on that medium's traditionally important role.

Medicine and Agriculture. The federal government also supports two other important national libraries. The National Library of Medicine (NLM) emerged in the 1950s directly from its predecessor, the Army Medical Library, and serves America's physicians and medical scientists through MEDLARS (Medical Literature Analysis and Retrieval System), an intricate and sophisticated computerized storage and retrieval system that grew from *Index Medicus*, the Library's paper-copy index to current medical literature. Holdings of the NLM surpassed 3,000,000 catalogued items by the mid-1980s.

The National Agriculture Library grew out of the Department of Agriculture Library. It, too, has led in the development of computerized storage and retrieval of information in its field.

Other Government Libraries. Many federal government agencies have acquired impressive collections. The Department of State began building its library when President George Washington created

National Agricultural Library

Theodore F. Welch

the cabinet post in 1789, and libraries at other cabinet-level agencies have followed State's lead. The National Archives established its own library in 1934 to facilitate use of the millions of documents it houses. Libraries serve both faculty and students at each of the nation's military academies, and the United States supports a presidential library for every Chief Executive since Herbert Hoover; each collects manuscript materials and memorabilia about the president's life and term in office.

STATE LIBRARY AGENCIES AND LOCAL SYSTEMS

Services and collections among state library agencies vary greatly. Although some state libraries were established in the early 1800s, state-supported library services did not expand significantly until the turn of the 20th century when new agencies, often public library commissions, were established outside state library control. Many states consolidated commission and state library functions after World War I, and by 1940 services commonly offered by surviving state library agencies included legislative reference, provisions for traveling libraries, and library promotion. From there, however, functions differ markedly. Some have developed into large research libraries (California and New York), while others act as the center of the state's public library system and serve city and county public libraries through interlibrary loans and traveling exhibits. Since 1956, state library agencies have also acted as conduits for federal library funds.

Local Systems. At the beginning of the 20th century, municipal and local library systems established branch libraries, book stations, bookmobiles, and books-by-mail programs. Later emphasis was placed on the development of local consortia designed to pool resources, distribute costs, share in acquisition, and cooperate in weeding.

ACADEMIC LIBRARIES

Academic libraries have developed individual growth patterns. Harvard's library system represents the largest of the privately supported institutions whose collections and inter-institutional responsibilities have grown geometrically. The University of Wisconsin library system demonstrates a pattern of support by an individual state that looked to the major publicly supported institution within its borders for leadership. Many land-grant institutions of higher education provided indifferently for their libraries until the press of increasing numbers of students and the demand for new services forced changes in the 1960s. Small libraries at institutions such as Earlham College in Richmond, Indiana, have been among the most consistent performers over the past half-century. Although their collections and services have grown to meet the varied needs of more students, such institutions continue to place great emphasis on individualized services. The same may be said of outstanding community college libraries that survived the impact of embryonic periods of growth in the decades from the mid-1950s through the mid-1980s. Many made significant contributions to their students' intellectual and vocational development.

The combination of shrinking budgets and concern for better service sparked several cooperative

Theodore F. Welch

National Technical Information Service

ventures. In 1942 several Boston libraries pooled little-used materials into the New England Depository Library. The Center for Research Libraries, founded in 1949 by 10 Midwestern universities, has large holdings from which its 169 institutional members can withdraw by interlibrary loan. The Online Computer Library Center (OCLC), started originally in 1968 as a cooperative cataloguing effort among a number of academic libraries in Ohio, grew into a national system serving more than 6,000 libraries. The Research Libraries Group (consisting in 1984 of more than 20 major U.S. research institutions) was organized in 1974 to identify collection strengths and minimize wasteful duplication.

PUBLIC LIBRARIES

The 1970s brought a shrinking of federal financial support to public libraries in the United States. Inflation seriously weakened budgets, programs were cancelled, and many services were either curtailed or cut off altogether. The growth patterns characteristic of the 1960s appeared to have been arrested. Despite these difficulties, however, public libraries have continued to provide essential information services to their constituent communities.

For more than a century the local public library has benefited from the widely held Jeffersonian belief that a democracy can survive and prosper only in a society of citizens educated and informed enough to make prudent choices. That citizens in the United States adhere to that belief is evident from their willingness to be taxed (mostly on the basis of real estate ownership) in order to support public libraries. In return, all citizens residing in the taxed community are free to use the public library's services. Traditionally these services fall into four broad categories: basic education (for example, computer and reading literacy programs and story hours), culture (exhibits, lectures, and public forums), information (ready reference queries, referral services for community agencies, and database searches), and leisure (films, concerts, and crafts demonstrations). The distinctions among these categories have tended to blur.

Nearly 13,000 public libraries (ncluding branches) serve U.S. citizens. They range in size from the Boston Public Library (established in 1854, holding more than 5,000,000 volumes, and circulating 1,500,000 items a year in the mid-1980s) to the

Public Library in Elsinore, Wyoming (started in 1980 and holding 13,000 volumes). Twelve-year-old Jason Hardman of Elsinore persuaded the local town government to donate space for a collection he built through donations and staffed with voluntary labor. Like most public libraries, the Boston and the Elsinore Public Libraries answer to local governing boards whose stucture and composition is determined by state laws authorizing localities to establish public libraries and impose taxes to support them.

The future holds many challenges for American public libraries. Automation will alter the way traditional services are delivered, perhaps eliminating a few and certainly creating some new ones. These changes, among others, will force the public library community to address several knotty questions brought by new technological developments. The dilemma of "fee-based" versus "free" data searches with new technologies demonstrates only one of the more pressing problems. Local systems will also explore ways to cooperate on a regional basis to increase efficiency and control costs.

SCHOOL LIBRARIES AND MEDIA CENTERS

More than 75,000 library and media centers can now be found in public and private elementary and secondary schools in the United States. Since World War II their establishment and growth has been stimulated by the development and regular revision of standards defined by the American Association of School Librarians (AASL) and the Association for Educational Communication and Technology (AECT) and endorsed by the NEA and ALA. Even more significant, however, were the federal dollars funneled into the development of libraries and media centers by the National Defense Education Act (1958), the Library Services and Construction Acts (1964, 1965), the Elementary and Secondary Education Act (1965), and the Higher Education Act (1965).

The infusion of federal support, coupled with standards developed by professional associations, allowed libraries and media centers to improve traditional services in the areas of reading, reference, and teaching, and to augment their role in supplying schools with additional instructional support. They have begun to participate actively in designing the computer literacy programs that are rapidly growing in the nation's elementary and secondary schools.

SPECIAL LIBRARIES

Special libraries exist to serve specific clienteles. Because they do not concern themselves with the information needs of larger populations, their collections are usually smaller, many are staffed by library and information science professionals with special training, they offer tailored hours of service, and they reflect different patterns of organization. Some of them are affiliated with larger library systems, such as medical libraries within university systems, but most of them are attached to specific industries or services that have developed a need for quick access to specific kinds of information. The special libraries at AT&T's Bell Laboratories, International Business Machines, and Westinghouse Electric Corporation are examples. Newspapers, advertising agencies, and other busi-

nesses need special libraries for staff research use. For newspapers, these libraries often take the form of a "morgue," a series of file clippings arranged and indexed by subject or topic for quick retrieval. Ready-reference materials are frequently available, especially in the libraries of larger newspaper, magazine, and other publishers. Special libraries also serve educational and professional associations and institutions: the ALA Headquarters Library in Chicago and the Engineering Societies Library in New York City are examples.

Most special libraries receive their support from private sources. They include those at historical and philosophical societies, private schools, hospitals, and banking, investment, law, publishing, research, and scientific institutions. Special libraries at federal, state, and local mental and correctional institutions receive most of their funding from taxes. Most special libraries have developed within the last 75 years.

THE PROFESSION

ALA. One hundred and three people sharing an interest in libraries met in Philadelphia in the fall of 1876 as part of the nation's centennial celebration in that city. Near the end of the meeting, Melvil Dewey moved that the group form the American Library Association and, after his motion was approved, signed himself "No. 1."

In the early years, ALA concerned itself primarily with matters such as cooperative activities, standardization of library procedures and forms, and debating the merits and demerits of stocking fiction. In 1886 the Association established a section to oversee the publication of bibliographical aids, and a $100,000 gift from Andrew Carnegie in 1902 permitted the Publishing Section to expand its program significantly. By the beginning of World War I, the Association had become the national voice for library interests. The war provided ALA with an opportunity it had never before experienced. In organizing the Library War Service under Herbert Putnam's direction, ALA willingly sought to supply the reading needs of U.S. soldiers and sailors at home and abroad. Association members helped to set up camp libraries and to collect books for shipment overseas. After the war ended in 1918, some members of ALA sought to capitalize on the Association's positive wartime experiences and push for an enlarged program designed to expand its activities. But funding agencies and the membership failed to support it, and the proposed program died for lack of interest.

By the end of the war the Association, like the profession it represented, had become highly feminized. In 1870 the Bureau of the Census could locate only 43 female library workers; in 1910 the Bureau found 8,621. A decade later women comprised more than 90 percent of total library employees, a proportion larger than that of social work or teaching. As a female culture based on the Victorian ideal of domesticity began to lose its grip in the late 19th century, women looking for expanded career opportunities found relatively few open to them. Library trustees and employers welcomed them into the profession, in part because they thought a "mother" image and a "domestic touch" promised increased benefits for library services, in part because they realized women provided cheaper labor than men. But most of the prestigious posts in librarianship—and in ALA—continued to go to men. Women's contributions and leadership in American librarianship would remain in historical shadows for decades.

Carl Milam (1884-1963) served as ALA Executive Secretary from 1920 to 1948. He consolidated ALA programs and activities at ALA's Chicago Headquarters (where it continues to reside, despite periodic suggestions that it move elsewhere). He saw ALA through the 1920s, when the Association concerned itself with the adult education movement, the status of library education, and librarians' welfare, and through the 1930s, when many ALA members questioned its management as "undemocratic." He still led its staff in the 1940s, when ALA took up the banner of intellectual freedom. Milam's successor, David Clift (1907-1973), carried that banner through the McCarthy era and into the late 1950s, when the federal government began to provide funds for library services. Robert Wedgeworth, Executive Director from 1972 to 1985, directed his attention toward implementing changes in the dues and organizational structure, controlling budget deficits, rebuilding staff morale at Headquarters, and expanding facilities in a new building. He also emphasized ALA's presence in national and international professional activities. The Association grew significantly from a membership of 69 in 1876 to 1,152 in 1902, 8,848 in 1926, 19,701 in 1951, and more than 42,000 by 1985. (See also American Library Association.)

Other Associations. The American Association of Law Libraries, established in 1906, had more than 3,500 members in 1984. The American Theological Library Association was organized in 1947 to foster cooperation and understanding of a special library's function within a school of theology; membership was more than 600 in 1984. The Art Libraries Society of North America, begun in 1972, provides a forum for art librarians. Institutional and personal members numbered 1,100 in 1984. The Catholic Library Association, organized in 1921, had more than 3,200 members in 1984. The Medical Library Association, begun in 1898, served more than 5,000 institutional and individual members in 1984. The Music Library Association, founded in 1931, had nearly 1,700 members. The Special Libraries Association, established in 1909, served 11,000 members. The Theatre Library Association, established in 1937, had nearly 500 institutional and personal members in 1984.

The Association of Research Libraries, organized in 1932, represents a different type of library association. It consists of 110 member institutions that seek to address problems common to the needs of large research libraries.

U.S. librarians are also served by regional, state, and local library associations. The Pacific Northwest Library Association (with more than 900 members in 1984) began in 1909, the Southeastern Library Association in 1920 (with more than 2,500 members in 1984). Nearly every state in the Union has its own library association, ranging from the largest in New York (3,500 members) to the smallest in Nevada (250 members).

Other associations and agencies heavily involved in library and information activities include the American Society for Information Science (ASIS),

born of the American Documentation Institute (founded in 1937; more than 5,000 members in 1984), and the Society for American Archivists, established in 1936 (membership more than 4,000).

Beta Phi Mu, the international library science honor society founded in 1948, has more than 15,000 members in more than 40 chapters in library schools across the country.

The Freedom to Read Foundation provides legal aid for defendants implicated in First Amendment cases that involve librarians, libraries, and those who use them.

The Continuing Library Education Network and Exchange (CLENE) was organized in 1975 to provide a forum for the discussion of the continuing education needs of library personnel.

The National Commission on Library and Information Science (NCLIS), the Council on Library Resources, and the Urban Libraries Council are among organizations that deserve mention for their efforts to facilitate and improve library services.

The Library Press. Members of the library community in the United States enjoy numerous avenues of communication with their professional colleagues. The library press in the United States can trace its roots to 1876, when the *American Library Journal* published its first issue. Shortly thereafter, it dropped "American" from its title and now acts as an independent voice in library affairs. The *Wilson Library Bulletin* is in the same category. The *Journal of Academic Librarianship* serves an audience with more specific interests.

ALA and its divisions publish important journals. *American Libraries* is ALA's principal publication for communicating with its members and the public. *College and Research Libraries* is published by the Association of College and Research Libraries, a division of ALA. *RQ* is a quarterly sponsored by the Reference and Adult Services Division. Other ALA journals and newsletters also make important contributions to the profession. Most regional, state, and national library and information science associations issue journals, many of which started publication with the founding of their parent organization. Periodicals such as *Library Quarterly* (University of Chicago) and the *Journal of Library History* (University of Texas) provide a forum for professionals of scholarly bent.

Commercial publishers, such as the R. R. Bowker Company, Libraries Unlimited, Scarecrow Press, and the H. W. Wilson Company, issue monographs and reference tools that often prove important and even essential to library services, as does ALA Publishing Services. Academic Press's *Advances in Librarianship* offers an annual review of topics of interest to the library and information science profession. *Library Trends* (University of Illinois) and the *Drexel Library Quarterly* (Drexel University) devote issues to specific topics of current interest.

REFERENCES
Useful surveys include Michael Harris, *History of Libraries in the Western World* (1984), and Howard Winger (editor), "American Library History: 1876-1976," *Library Trends* (1976), entire issue.
Jesse Shera, *Foundations of the Public Library: The Origins of the Public Library Movement in New England, 1629-1855* (1949), remains standard. Dee Garrison, *Apostles of Cul-*

ture: *The Public Librarian and American Society, 1876-1920* (1979), offers a revised look at this subject.

Arthur T. Hamlin, *The University Library in the United States: Its Origins and Development* (1981), Orvin Lee Shiflett, *Origins of American Academic Librarianship* (1981), and Wayne A. Wiegand (editor), *Leaders in American Academic Librarianship, 1925-1975* (1983), provide historical coverage of academic library activities since Colonial times.

Edward G. Holley, "ALA at 100," *The ALA Yearbook* (1976) pp. 1-32, is a still useful if brief survey.

Bohdan S. Wynar (editor), *Dictionary of American Library Biography* (1978), and Michael H. Harris and Donald G. Davis, Jr., *American Library History: A Bibliography* (1978), are invaluable tools to identify sources for further information on the history of library and information services in the United States.

WAYNE A. WIEGAND

Donald John Urquhart

Urquhart, Donald John
(1909-   )

Donald John Urquhart, British librarian, administrator, and information expert, won worldwide recognition for the practical success of his ideas for the National Lending Library in Boston Spa, Yorkshire.

Born November 27, 1909, he was reared in the northeast of England, brought up in Whitley Bay, and educated at Barnard Castle School and Sheffield University. He showed the qualities of determination, directness, and independence of mind that characterize the sons of that part of England and that in his case have marked his approach to librarianship and the work of the librarian.

After taking his B.Sc. and Ph.D. degrees at Sheffield, Urquhart worked from 1934 to 1937 in the Research Department of the English Steel Corporation. In 1938 he joined the library staff of the Science Museum, then under the directorship of Samuel Clement Bradford, the active supporter of the Universal Decimal Classification and one of the founders of the British Society for International Bibliography. Bradford's work and that of his successor, Lancaster-Jones, was of great significance in the library field and in the new field of "documentation." During World War II Urquhart worked in several government departments, most importantly in the Ministry of Supply, all of which were crucially concerned with the supply of scientific and industrial information and

were grievously embarrassed by the consequences of past neglect of this vital aspect of library information work. The war had brought home to scientists and industrialists the significance of information in the day-to-day activities of an industrial society, and it was becoming clear that the speed at which new knowledge and ideas were made available was governed by the effectiveness of information services. Management also needed up-to-date assessments of raw materials, supply and production processes, and equipment design.

These problems prompted several conferences at which scientific information services were discussed in considerable detail, notably the Royal Society Empire Scientific Conference (1946), the Royal Society Scientific Information Conference (1948), and the 27th annual conference of Aslib, the Association of Special Libraries and Information Bureaux (1952). At this last meeting Urquhart, who by this time had become attached to the Department of Scientific and Industrial Research (DSIR) and thereby much concerned with the results of the Scientific Information Conference, reviewed the results of the conference with special reference to the part played by DSIR in implementing them. He was able to point to the publication of a number of guides to sources of information, but the most important question to be resolved was how to ensure that the United Kingdom would have an adequate system of scientific libraries.

The first attempt at solving this problem centered on the possibility of extending the Patent Office Library and the Science Museum Library to include every publication containing material of value to science and technology. The final answer, however, was to establish and develop in DSIR itself, under Urquhart's direction, a so-called Lending Library Unit, which afterward became the National Lending Library for Science and Technology, a division of the British Library.

The National Lending Library embodies many of the ideas that Urquhart had strenuously advocated during the years of discussion after the Royal Society Conference in 1948. For example, the location of the Library in Boston Spa in Yorkshire was to a considerable extent conditioned by his belief that such a library should be a purely practical institution without elaborate architectural features or adornment, that it should be within easy postal reach of all parts of the country, and that it should have space to enable it to respond to all requests by return mail.

SIR FRANK FRANCIS

Uruguay

Uruguay, a republic in southern South America, is bounded by Brazil on the north and east, the Atlantic Ocean on the southeast, the Rio de la Plata on the south, and Argentina on the west. Population (1984 est.) 3,013,000; area 176,215 sq.km. The official language is Spanish.

History and National Library. The National Library was founded in Montevideo on May 26, 1816, by decree of General José Artigas. Eight months later invading Portuguese forces destroyed its collections. The Library reopened on July 18, 1838, and has served as the repository of the national documentary and bibliographic production; it maintains legal deposit and is responsible for bibliographical and information services through its Information and Consultative Section and the Center of Scientific, Technical, and Economic Documentation. It compiles the national bibliography, *Uruguayan Bibliographical Annual*.

The collection consists of 900,000 books, 800,000 manuscripts and related items, 35,000 pamphlets, and other special material. Inaugurated May 26, 1978, its Children's Section caters to the particular needs of children aged 3 to 12.

Academic Libraries. Each of the 10 faculties of the University of the Republic has its own departmental library in the field of its specialty. They function under the direction of a librarian and are the best-organized libraries in the country, conducting cooperative programs with related divisions. Holdings are estimated at approximately 900,000.

Public Libraries. The principal network of public libraries consists of 18 branches in the municipality of Montevideo, distributed by city wards. There are also public libraries in the capitals of departments. Rarely are they staffed by professional librarians and, in general, the collections are inadequate.

School Libraries. Libraries are not a part of the national school system, and such services have not been included in the educational structure of the country. Collections are inadequate in size and quality and are composed largely of donations.

Special Libraries. As a rule, special libraries in Uruguay are quite well organized, with adequate financial resources. They are found in branches of official agencies and in polytechnic and other schools of higher education. Others are maintained by banks and private businesses, by embassies, and by regional and international organizations. The Uruguayan Institute of Conservation, founded in June 1977, is dedicated to the study and development of natural resources and the restoration of national roots through the exchange of techniques at national and international levels.

The Profession. The Association of Librarians of Uruguay, active in the years 1945–73, contributed to the status of librarians. The Uruguayan Institute of Library Research, founded in 1977, addresses the study of the many branches of librarianship and promotes technical standards and cooperation.

ERMELINDA ACERENZA*

Utley, George Burwell
(1876–1946)

George Burwell Utley was Secretary of the American Library Assocation and Director of the Newberry Library. His pioneering work in librarianship, managerial legacy to ALA, and pursuit of scholarly excellence for the Newberry attest to a significant career in librarianship.

Utley was born during the U.S. centennial year on December 3, 1876, in Hartford, Connecticut. His parents were George Tyler Utley and Harriet Ella Burwell Utley. His father, whose English forebears settled in the Connecticut valley in the 17th century, was a businessman and longtime Secretary of the Connecticut Railroad Commission. His mother died before George was three, and he was raised by maternal aunts in Pleasant Valley, about 25 miles from Hartford. Utley was deeply attached to his childhood home and in retirement he returned to "Burwell Heights" for the remainder of his years.

He prepared for college at Vermont Academy, near Brattleboro, and after a year at Colgate transferred to Brown, where he majored in English literature and received a Ph.B. in 1899. Unable to secure a teaching position after graduation, he worked briefly for a Hartford insurance firm. He was soon persuaded by Librarian Frank B. Gay of the Watkinson Library in Hartford to join the staff. His apprenticeship enabled him to satisfy his scholarly inclinations in a congenial setting. It was the begining of a significant and enormously productive career in librarianship.

In 1901 Utley married Lou Mabel Gilbert, who remained his close companion for the next 45 years. That same year he accepted an offer to head the Maryland Diocesan Library of the Protestant Episcopal Church in Baltimore. Utley, a Baptist, stayed in Baltimore for four years and while there began to research and write the first of many contributions to the professional and historical literature. Perhaps his earliest publication was a biographical sketch of genealogist Edmund J. Cleveland in the proceedings of the *New England Historical and Genealogical Society* (1903). Research for his first book, *The Life and Times of Thomas John Claggett, First Bishop of Maryland* (1913), was completed at the Maryland Library.

To enlarge his sphere of experience, Utley became Director of the Jacksonville (Florida) Public Li-

ALA

George Burwell Utley

Libraries in Uruguay (1980)

Type	Administrative units	Service points	Volumes in collections	Annual expenditures (peso)	Population served	Professional staff	Total staff
National	1	1	860,000	--	--	44	204
Academic[a]	55	--	900,000	--	400,000	150	--
Public[a]	72	--	166,000	--	87,500	--	--
School[a]	51	--	39,000	--	10,000	--	--
Special[a]	40	--	--	--	--	--	--
Others[a]	107	--	760,000	--	270,000	--	--

[a]1976 data.

Source: Unesco, *Statistical Yearbook,* 1984; Biblioteca Palacio Legislativo, *Bibliotecas del Uruguay* (1978).

brary in 1905. Awarded a Carnegie building grant in 1902, the Jacksonville Public Library became the state's first tax-supported public library. With limited resources Utley organized the new library, upgraded its resources, and expanded services. His receptive manner, scholarly approach, and administrative finesse all contributed to a successful tenure at Jacksonville. Evidence of his social conscience may be gleaned from an article he wrote on black library patrons for *The Critic* in 1906. Long before most white librarians became sensitive to the needs of black citizens, Utley related the positive accomplishments of Jacksonville's "colored department" and emphasized the serious literature read by the black community.

Utley's achievements were noted outside Florida, and in 1911 he was invited to become Secretary of the American Library Association, a post he filled with distinction until 1920. He moved to Chicago to work in the Association's quarters in the Chicago Public Library, and he was soon immersed in the work of answering correspondence, traveling to state association meetings, speaking at library schools, expanding the membership, and improving the publicity and publication programs. The membership doubled during his term of office. Recognition of Utley's accomplishments and the Association's emerging status as the national voice for library affairs came in 1917 when he was appointed by the U.S. Commissioner of Education to a national committee to study Americanization.

From 1917 to 1920, ALA was engaged in a global book crusade, a program to furnish library materials and services to several million American soldiers. Designated the Library War Service, the project was headquartered at the Library of Congress and directed by Herbert Putnam and later by Carl H. Milam. Utley also served ably as Secretary of the wartime program and spent much of this period in Washington, D.C. Utley's personal qualities were succinctly captured in the Association's farewell resolution that referred to his "agreeable manner, abounding good nature, unfailing patience and clear voice."

After the war Utley was a supporter of the Enlarged Program, an unsuccessful attempt to extend ALA's postwar services and influence. He was recognized for his contributions to ALA by election as President in 1922. In his presidential address Utley urged the Association to press for library extension at all levels and, sensing the evolving bureaucratization of the profession, admonished the members never to forget their primary clients, the public. He continued to serve on various ALA committees for the next 20 years.

Another job offer, this one from the Newberry Library, enticed Utley to leave ALA in 1920. For the next 22 years Utley directed the Newberry in Chicago, a premier private library specializing in history, literature, genealogy, music, and the typographic arts. Under his direction the Library's staff, resources, and services to readers made impressive gains. To extend the Library's usefulness, Utley issued checklists of its holdings and revitalized services to the scholarly community. For his sponsorship of the Library's Dante exhibition, Utley was decorated by the Italian Monarch with the Order of the Crown of Italy in 1922. Eight years later he was appointed by the American Booksellers Association to a blue-ribbon committee that selected books for the White House Library. His wish to serve the Newberry for a quarter of a century was not realized; retirement at 65 was mandatory, and so he returned to his beloved Pleasant Valley in 1942.

Befitting his long career in prominent positions, Utley was a member of many organizations. His library affiliations included the Illinois Library Association (President, 1924–25) and the American Library Institute (President, 1937–39). Deeply committed to his adopted Chicago, Utley served as President of Chicago's Geographic Society (1929–31), Literary Club (1935–36), and Writer's Guild (1935–36). He was the author of over 60 publications, his writings appearing in such diverse periodicals as *Library Journal, The Touchstone, the Mississippi Valley Historical Review,* and *Survey.* Among his 10 biographical sketches for the *Dictionary of American Biography* were vignettes of Katharine Lucinda Sharp, Walter Loomis Newberry, and Obadiah Rich. Utley's *Fifty Years of the American Library Association* (ALA, 1926) is a noninterpretive but informative reconstruction of ALA's first half-century.

Retirement in Pleasant Valley afforded Utley the opportunity for gardening, stamp collecting, and resumption of a project that had been deferred for more than two decades. When he died in Pleasant Valley, Connecticut, on October 4, 1946, he had nearly finished *The Librarians' Conference of 1853;* published in 1951 by ALA, this study remains the definitive history of America's first library convention.

Utley was an effective administrator and esteemed by his contemporaries. William Warner Bishop, an ALA President (1918–19) and ardent internationalist, lauded Utley in his reminiscences: "There are not so very many men who improve on closer acquaintance, but Utley was one of them." Utley's characterization of the purpose of libraries—"to induce people to read and to furnish ample and generous facilities for independent study and unrestrained mental activity"—was a goal measurably advanced by his achievements.

REFERENCES

Materials covering the Florida years are available in the Jacksonville Public Library. His ALA correspondence, especially for the World War I period, is in the ALA Archives, University of Illinois Library, Urbana. Utley's Newberry papers are held by that library.

ARTHUR P. YOUNG

Venezuela

Venezuela, a republic of northern South America, is bordered on the north by the Caribbean Sea and the Atlantic Ocean, on the east by Guyana, on the south by Brazil, and on the southwest and west by Colombia. Population (1984 est.) 15,601,000; area 912,050 sq.km. The official language is Spanish.

History. The country won its independence from Spain in 1821 under Simón Bolívar, who was born in Caracas in 1783. The first imprint in Caracas, the capital, was dated October 24, 1808; the book was printed on a press acquired from Trinidad. In 1917 oil was discovered at Maracaibo. What had been an agrarian country with limited public services thereafter enjoyed a comparatively high standard of living. Library services in urban areas greatly improved.

In the years following adherence to the Unesco NATIS Program in 1974, the National Commission for Library and Information Services (SINASBI) was created by presidential decree in 1976 and reformed in 1978. Structured to coordinate all aspects of library, archival, and information services in the country, it had ceased to exist for all practical purposes by the mid-1980s and many of its functions were absorbed by the National Library. Others were simply allowed to disintegrate. The lack of a national policy and strategy in information accentuated strengths and weaknesses of individual institutions and services.

National Library. The Biblioteca Nacional de Venezuela was founded by decree in 1833. Its scope of responsibilities was expanded by law in 1977 to encompass the public library system and a broad array of information services. Its full name is Instituto Autónomo Biblioteca Nacional y de Servicios de Bibliotecas.

Under the leadership of Virginia Betancourt, Director from 1974, this institution has been the renovator of library and information services in the country, reaching out to a population new to library services. It is organized around three main programs: the National Library as such, the National Public Library System, and a Technical Services support program covering all holdings.

By 1981 the National Library housed close to 805,000 books and 2,000,000 periodicals, mostly on Venezuelan topics, and a microfilm collection of just over 2,500,000 frames, 1,800,000 of which pertain to official publications. Some 132,388 additional items

include maps, video and movie tapes, musical scores, and graphic designs.

The Venezuelan Legal Deposit Law was amended in 1982 to broaden its scope; the number of copies of official publications sent to the National Library was set at 25 percent. In practice the law proved an effective means of enriching holdings and specifically served to enhance the base for the National Union Catalogue.

Publications of the National Library include the *Anuario Bibliográfico Venezolano,* now known as *Bibliografía Venezolana,* which lists books and pamphlets, official publications, academic theses and dissertations, and musical scores published from approximately 1942. Others are the *Catálogo General;* the *Índice Bibliográfico; Fuentes para el Estudio de los Partidos Politicos Venezolanos del Siglo XX* ("Sources for the Study of Venezuelan Political Parties in the 20th Century"); *Catálogo de la Prensa Venezolana del Siglo XIX* ("Catalogue of the Venezuelan Press in the 19th Century"); *La Bibliografía Indigenista Venezolana* ("Bibliography of Indigenous Venezueliana"); *La Bibliografía Afro-Venezolana;* plus a series of bibliographies for the states of Miranda, Zulia, Monagas, and Sucre.

In 1978 the National Library signed an agreement with Northwestern University of Evanston, Illinois, for the use in Venezuela of its NOTIS computerized library system. That date marks the beginning of automation of processing and other functions in the National Library framework. In 1981 and 1982 services were extended with the use of Documaster software to the Supreme Court of Justice and the main library of the Central University, both in Caracas.

Construction of a new National Library building was under way in the mid-1980s at the Foro Libertador in Caracas, where 80,000 square meters would provide an excellent opportunity to improve services for a broad patron base. Occupancy was expected, at least in part, by 1988.

The Archivo General de la Nación, founded in 1888, is responsible for historical, religious, and public administration archives. Its collections are divided into three sections: La Colonia (1535–1810), La Revolución (1810–1830), and La República (1830 to about 1950). It was given legal standing in 1945, but updating did not follow and its role remains largely within the historical sphere. However, a new building of 20,000 square meters was also under construction at

Libraries in Venezuela (1982)

Type	Administrative units	Service points	Volumes in collections	Annual expenditures (bolivar)	Population served[a]	Professional staff	Total staff
National	1	3	804,951[a]	47,480,490	56,563[b]	45	407
Academic	167	– –	1,367,477[c]	16,117,100[c]	1,319,412[c]	131[c]	692[c]
Public	23	395	1,130,000	70,800,000	3,999,738[b]	70[d]	973[d]
School[c]	235	– –	352,500	9,300,000	241,520	11	470
Special	206	– –	224,072[c]	4,048,099	80,869	48[c]	222[c]

[a]1981 data, excludes periodical and audiovisual collections.
[b]Requests attended.
[c]1977 data.
[d]1983 data.

National Library of Venezuela, Caracas, established in 1833 and expanded in 1977.

Theodore F. Welch

the Foro Libertador site in the mid-1980s. The National Archives publishes a biannual bulletin.

Public Libraries. The Public library system in Venezuela experienced a period of sustained growth in the early 1980s. For administrative purposes the country was divided into nine geographical regions, the largest services being provided for the Metropolitan Caracas and Federal District System, which serves the capital city. Each state has a central public library that follows the technical directives of the National Library, although all personnel and expenses are covered by the individual states. By 1982 there were 396 public libraries throughout the nation, covering 81 percent of all districts. Additionally, all states except one enjoyed bookmobile service. Patron requests increased from fewer than 3,000,000 in 1980 to more than 5,000,000 in 1983.

During the period 1979 to 1982, reader facilities doubled to 18,225 seats and holdings jumped about one-and-a-half times, from 776,000 volumes to 1,130,000. Personnel increased 25 percent to 973 employees and budgets more than doubled to 70,800,000 bolivars. The metropolitan public library system alone served 637,271 patrons, an increase of more than 30 percent compared with 1981. In 1982 special coverage was extended to three homes for the aged, in keeping with Unesco's recognition of the Year of the Aged.

Another important institution, the Banco del Libro, originally created in 1960 to provide a textbook exchange facility, was expanded into a research center for public library services directed toward children. It promotes reading techniques and materials. It maintains Ediciónes Ekare, a children's book publishing house started in 1978 and known for its beautiful illustrations and dissemination of folktales and poems of Venezuelan origin. It also trains schoolteachers in library services, and the National Library designated it to select children's books for all public libraries in the country.

From 1980, Banco del Libro published *Parapara,* the only journal on children's literature in all of Latin America. It is also the center for the Interamerican

Project on Children's Literature sponsored by the Organization of American States. The Banco del Libro operates two libraries in Caracas and four in Ciudad Guayana, Bolívar state, as testing grounds for its research.

School Libraries. The school library system covered 235 primary and secondary schools and served some 241,530 pupils in the mid-1980s. A typical collection comprises 45 percent texts, 20 percent recreative literature, 5 percent reference works, 5 percent teaching materials, and the remaining 25 percent complementary titles to the scholastic program. Coordination, planning, and follow-up are managed through the education authorities in each state, who are accountable to a centralized body at the Ministry of Education.

Two school library networks, one in Caracas (Valle-Coche) and another in Maracaibo (Zulia State), served as experimental models to try out new techniques and services prior to their extension throughout the system. The Valle-Coche network was integrated into the national system; the Maracaibo network was retained for testing.

Special Libraries. The Consejo Nacional de Investigaciónes Científicas y Tecnológicas (CONICIT, the National Scientific and Technological Research Council), created in 1967, coordinates scientific and technological information networks. Cooperative information networks in the early 1980s included Biomedical Information; (52,284 users); Agricultural Sciences (REDIAGRO) (989); Engineering and Architecture (REDINARA) (2,523); Social and Economic (REDINSE) (532); Housing and Urban Planning (20,390); and Technology and Industry.

CONICIT authorized a feasibility study on a countrywide automated data transmission information system called Sistema Automatizado de Información Científica y Tecnológica (SAICYT). Strategically placed nodes would link most heavily industrialized regions, and the Caracas node would connect to an international network. Emphasis was placed on providing training on database searching, mainly in conjunction with U.S. vendors, and developing expertise in creating local databases and indexing systems. Venezuela participates in the Andean Technological Information System (SAIT) and the Latin-American Technological Information Network (RITLA).

In 1978 CONICIT published *Catálogo Colectivo de Publicaciónes Periodicas en Ciencias y Tecnología de Venezuela* ("Union Catalogue of Venezuelan Periodicals in Science and Technology"), which included more than 15,000 entries and identified libraries holding such publications.

In addition, there are many institutions with specialized libraries in science and technology. One is the Venezuelan Institute of Scientific Research (IVIC). INTEVEP is the Center for Research and Development of the Venezuelan nationalized oil industry. IVIC's scientific periodical holdings are the largest in Venezuela with some 4,500 titles. INTEVEP organized the first automated information network with national coverage, linking information centers in the oil industry to a centralized database resident at the company's Los Teques headquarters. This system is MARC compatible, as is the one at the National Library, thus creating a de facto national standard.

The Petroleum and Petrochemical Information Network (RIPPET) by 1983 covered 33 oil industry information centers, 19 of which were interconnected to the automated library system through 52 terminals. The Periodicals Collective Catalogue listed 1,800 titles, 131,000 technical reports, 82,000 books, and 213,500 other items such as microforms, maps, industrial drawings, and so forth. Document requests totaled 76,000 in 1982. INTEVEP's Technological Information Center (CIT), the coordinating body of RIPPET, was the first Venezuelan information center to offer access to international database searching (1978).

The Profession. The Colegio de Bibliotecologos y Archivologos de Venezuela is the main national organization for professional librarians and archivists. It was founded in 1952 to promote the welfare and professional competency of its members, which number more than 500. The library community is represented in many international organizations and participates in Unesco's General Information Programme, FID, IFLA, and ACURIL, and attends the yearly ALA Convention.

MORRIS MATZA

Verona, Eva

Eva Verona, Yugoslav university librarian, has been highly influential in the areas of international bibliographic control in general and of the role of corporate entry in cataloguing in particular. With a background in mathematics and physics, she brought to the field a logical mind, a disciplined scholarship, and the ability to communicate, not only in her own country but in international circles as well.

She first appeared in meetings of the International Federation of Library Associations in 1952; for the ensuing 25 years she was an active member, eventually serving both as member and chairman of the Association's Committee on Cataloguing. During that time, she had become head of two departments in the National and University Library in Zagreb, and, 1966, she held the position of Senior Lecturer in the Postgraduate Study of Librarianship, Documentation and Information Sciences, at the University of Zagreb.

For a long time she had been keenly interested in the area of corporate entry in cataloguing, particularly in logical aspects of the formats developed in this area. A lengthy article entitled "A historical approach to corporate entries," appeared in *LIBRI* in 1957. It was followed by a series of books and articles in Croatian.

The major part of those contributions came about as a result of involvement in the international discussions about codes for descriptive cataloguing taking place in the 1960s and 1970s. Verona's most significant work prior to 1975 was the *Statement of Principles Adopted at the International Conference on Cataloguing Principles, Paris, 1961* (Annotated Edition, with Commentary and Examples, IFLA Committee on Cataloguing, 1971). In preparing that monograph she was assisted by Franz Georg Kaltwasser, P. R. Lewis, and Roger Pierrot. At that time she was also caught up in the general movement toward the creation of a means for achieving international bibliographic control. This movement produced the suc-

cessful International Standard Description for Monographs (ISBD–M) as a means for obtaining a standardized format suitable for both acquisitions and cataloguing. An International Standard Book Number had already been developed in Britain. Other similar standards followed, but these were the most freely adopted.

The 1970s in particular saw much discussion of the principles of authorship, in particular the notion of corporate authorship. This had been controversial in the past and probably will continue to be in the future. Nevertheless, Verona, who had been interested in the problems involved in considering a corporate body as the *author* of its works, now produced highly significant research on the topic, entitled *Corporate Headings: Their Use in Library Catalogues and National Bibliographies* (1971). This major work strongly influenced the treatment of corporate bodies in the second edition of *Anglo-American Cataloguing Rules,* (1978).

Verona's *Corporate Headings* defines corporate authorship as follows:

A work should be considered to be of corporate authorship if it may be concluded by its character or nature that it is the result of creative and/or organizational activity of a corporate body as a whole, and not the result of an independent creative activity of the individual(s) who drafted it.

The 1970s witnessed a rethinking of the principles of authorship, and much serious discussion of corporate authorship. The 1978 Anglo-American code greatly altered the interpretation of "the result of creative and/or organizational activity of a corporate body as a whole." In fact, the limitations described in its 21st chapter are more organizational than creative activity.

The advent of the computer, it has been argued, has made the concept of *main entry* obsolete and in that respect much of the argument over entry (any kind of entry) is unnecessary because one can now use as many entries as the topic requires—something that was impossible with card catalogues and very difficult with book catalogues. While Verona's argument is significant, a dissertation by Michael Carpenter (published 1981) suggests that, philosophically speaking, one can still make a fair argument for corporate entry, under limited conditions.

In 1976 Verona received the Margaret Mann Citation from the ALA's Resources and Technical Services Division, a well-deserved award for what clearly has become a definitive work on the subject.

REFERENCES
Eva Verona, "A Historical Approach to Corporate Entries," *LIBRI* (1957).
Eva Verona, *Corporate Headings: Their Use in Library Catalogues and National Bibliographies: a Comparative and Critical Study. (IFLA Committee on Cataloguing, 1971).*

PHYLLIS A. RICHMOND

Vickery, Brian
(1918-)

Brian Campbell Vickery, British information scientist, is known—particularly to those outside the United Kingdom—as an accomplished theoretician of information retrieval.

Vickery was born in Sydney, Australia, on September 11, 1918. He was educated in England at the King's School, Canterbury, and Oxford University, where he majored in chemistry. During World War II he worked at the Royal Ordnance Factory in Somerset.

After a brief period as a technical journalist, Vickery joined the Ackers Research Laboratory of Imperial Chemical Industries (ICI) as its Librarian in 1946, and he remained there for 14 years. As an active member of the (UK) Classification Research Group, he began his investigations in classification and indexing and the newly emerging discipline of information retrieval. Two major monographs emerged, both early recognized as significant contributions and now considered classics: *Classification and Indexing in Science* (1958) and *On Retrieval System Theory* (1970). Both works have been translated into other languages and both have been reissued.

Vickery gained an international reputation as a theoretician. While such a reputation is wholly justified, his undoubted abilities as a practitioner of information science are perhaps less appreciated. In fact, his career demonstrated a perhaps unusual capacity to contribute both to the fundamental understanding of the nature of information science and to the development of practical services as a result of such insights. His early appreciation of Bradford's Law of scattering led, for example, to one of the first recorded applications of it in an industrial special library.

Vickery's wide-ranging abilities were recognized by D. J. Urqhart, who recruited him as Principal Scientific Officer to the newly created National Lending Library for Science and Technology (later to be absorbed into the British Library as its Lending Division). From 1960 to 1964 he worked there, during the formative years of that unique and universally respected institution, and served subsequently on its Advisory Committee.

From 1964 to 1966 he was the Librarian of the Manchester Institute of Science and Technology, an institute with a formidable international reputation in the development of computer technology. Two major monographs were to emerge during his period as Director of Research at Aslib, London, from 1966 to 1973: *Techniques of Information Retrieval* (1970) and *Information Systems* (1973). These reflected an increasing involvement in research and consultancy on systems development and evaluation, and particularly on automated systems. Two major development studies at that time were concerned with the Commonwealth Agricultural Bureaux and the House of Commons Library.

In 1973 he was appointed Professor and Director of the School of Library, Archives and Information Studies at University College, London, where he remained until his retirement in 1983. There he expanded teaching in the areas of computer applications and communications technology, and also in techniques for the investigation and evaluation of libraries and information services. With his second wife, Alina, the Director of the Central Information Services at London University (Senate House), he formed an axis for the rational development of library and information services within the University. He remained an active Honorary Research Fellow of the College.

His more than 100 publications in the professional literature cover a wide variety of topics—information retrieval, systems development and management, information systems dynamic modeling, library procedures, online search services, microcomputers, and the social aspects of information—and reflect his breadth of interests and experience. He was also much sought after as a reviewer because of his authority and fairness, qualities consistent with his lack of identification with any particular faction or school of thought. He became a Fellow both of the Library Association and the Institute of Information Scientists.

HARRY EAST

Vietnam

Vietnam, a socialist republic of southeast Asia, is bounded by China on the north, the South China Sea on the east, and Cambodia and Laos on the west. Population (1984 est.) 48,280,000; area 338,392 sq.km. Vietnamese is the official language; French and English are also spoken. The former North Vietnam and South Vietnam were merged after the end of the war in 1975.

History and National Library. The National Library of the Socialist Republic of Vietnam (SRV) in the capital city of Hanoi was first established by the French in 1919 as the Bibliothèque Centrale of Indochina. From 1921 until about 1941 it was the legal deposit library and officially received one copy of each publication produced in Indochina. By the 1950s its collections included 150,000 books and 2,300 periodicals. In 1954 the French took a portion of the collection to Saigon and Paris (approximately 50,000 books and 400 periodicals).

The Democratic Republic of Vietnam (DRV) quickly began to rebuild the central collections, adding more than 20,000 items accumulated in the hills and filling out the missing items. A decree required that 10 copies of all new publications go into the Library. By the 1970s the Library possessed more than 1,200,000 books and 70,000 bound volumes of periodicals. Besides the growing Vietnamese collection, it has good French, Russian, Chinese, English, and German collections. Special collections include Asian languages, ethnic minority material, maps, engravings, phonograph records, and children's books. It produces a national bibliography, bibliographies of periodical and newspaper articles, and lists of recommended reading.

The National Library of the Republic in the former Saigon is now the General Scientific Library of Ho Chi Minh City, attached to the city's cultural office; it holds some 600,000 volumes.

Academic Libraries. The main research library is the Central Scientific Library in Hanoi, founded in 1959 and based on and located in the old library of the École Française d'Extreme Orient

(1898). Holdings total some 255,000 volumes and 2,550 periodicals. It too is a legal deposit for all Vietnamese publications and has two sections, natural and social sciences, which have a number of research institutes under them (such as those of Archaeology, History, Literature, and Philosophy). Each Institute possesses its own collection.

Hanoi University, re-founded in 1956, has a library containing approximately 62,000 volumes.

Public Libraries. These are state libraries rather than "public" in the usual Western sense. From 1956 the DRV set up a series of provincial and municipal libraries. The provincial libraries, the largest in Hanoi, Haiphong, and Nam Dinh, were meant to coordinate the use of written materials in their areas. By the 1970s there were 34 libraries in cities and provinces, 102 city or town reading rooms, and more than 20,000 libraries across the countryside. Their books totaled more than 6,000,000. More than 4,000 trade union libraries were established in work locations to provide both technical detail and recreational reading. The general public has access to books through factory, union, or village. All this helped push the major DRV literacy campaign.

In addition, collections of more than 500,000 items were made before 1975 to add to southern libraries upon unification. The latter thus joined the already existing network. Unesco reported 316 public libraries in Vietnam in 1977 with total holdings of 4,879,000 volumes.

School Libraries. Various units of government, such as the Ministries of Defense and Agriculture, have their own libraries. In the South before 1975 there were the collections of the National Institutes of Administration and of Statistics, the Industrial Development Center, and the Ministry of Information, all in Saigon. In Dalat existed an irreplaceable collection of 19th-century imperial and land records. Where these collections were later located is uncertain.

The Profession. There is an Association of Vietnamese Library Workers.

REFERENCES

J. Rowlands, *Libraries in Indochina: A Brief Survey of Libraries in Laos, North Vietnam, South Vietnam* (1973), good summary of existing information.

J. K. Whitmore, "Vietnamese Retrospective Materials," *Foreign Acquisitions Newsletter* (Fall 1973), an examination of historical materials.

D. Kaser et al., *Library Development in Eight Asian Countries* (1969), a detailed, but early, description of the South.

JOHN K. WHITMORE*

Vosper, Robert G.
(1913-)

Robert G. Vosper

Robert Gordon Vosper, university librarian and educator, gained recognition as a force in general support of librarianship in the United States and throughout the world.

Born in Portland, Oregon, on June 21, 1913, he early set a goal of pursuing scholarship in classics. After finishing his B.A. (1937) and M.A. degrees (1939) at the University of Oregon, he enrolled in the School of Librarianship at the University of California, Berkeley, as a logical next step when the pressures of the Depression foreclosed his first option. With an offer of a job as a student employee of the University Library, Vosper was successful in winning admittance to the School, beginning a long and outstanding career.

After completing his library studies at Berkeley in 1940, Vosper served as a Reference Librarian there, and then as an Assistant Reference Librarian at Stanford, 1942–44. There he was associated with Nathan van Patten, Director of the Library and an outstanding expert in the field of acquisitions for academic libraries. With van Patten's encouragement and assistance, Vosper moved to the University of California at Los Angeles in 1944 to head the acquisitions department under the direction of University Librarian Lawrence Clark Powell. He soon began to show his penchant for action under pressure in the building of research libraries and particularly their collections as UCLA continued its march from being the southern branch of the University of California to being a leading research agency.

Vosper quickly rose to the rank of Assistant, then Associate, Librarian under Powell before becoming the head of the University of Kansas Library in 1952. Kansas recognized that it needed a much-expanded library in order to become a first-rate research institution. Its new President, the young Franklin Murphy, former Dean of Medicine, was the chief advocate of the Library. With Vosper, he toured the state and proselytized the legislators with great success to obtain funds for the Library. Vosper enlisted the faculty's help in selecting materials and began to build a core of specialists in the Library to guide the development of the collections. In this manner, Vosper may be considered the agent who gave credibility and visibility to the position of "bibliographer" in libraries.

Murphy moved to become Chancellor at UCLA in 1960. The regents of the University of California

Libraries in Vietnam (1977)

Type	Administrative units	Service points	Volumes in collections	Annual expenditures (dong)	Population served	Professional staff	Total staff
National	1	1	818,000	285,000	--	19	120
Academic	--	58	2,922,000	--	--	--	--
Public	--	316	4,879,000	--	--	--	--
School	--	--	--	--	--	--	--
Special	--	44	1,070,000	--	--	--	--

Source: Unesco, *Statistical Yearbook,* 1984.

had decided that UCLA's library should reach parity with Berkeley, and once again Murphy turned to Vosper to guide the Library's development. Vosper became University Librarian at UCLA in 1961, succeeding Powell, who was devoting his time to the establishment of a library school. Vosper thus returned to work with many of the people who knew him from his earlier term at UCLA, and at a time when the regents not only had approved the growth of the Library, but also had appropriated funds for a new central library building.

Under Vosper's direction the UCLA library grew by nearly 2,000,000 volumes. Vosper retired as University Librarian in 1973 and assumed full-time teaching duties as professor in the UCLA Graduate School of Library and Information Science. At the same time he continued to serve as Director of UCLA's Clark Library, a prestigious segment of the system, devoted to many aspects of English literature, including the works of John Dryden and Oscar Wilde. He retired from active University service in 1984, with the rank of University Librarian and Professor Emeritus. He continued his contribution to university work by serving as President of the UCLA Emeriti Association and on various committees within the University.

Vosper was President of the Association of College and Research Libraries, 1955–56, and of the American Library Association, 1965–66. As Chairman of the Association of Research Libraries Board of Directors in 1963–64, he directed the opening of membership of that organization to include the many schools that were achieving research status and had problems in common to solve, making membership in ARL a powerful status for their solution. He also led the way to section status for the rare books and manuscripts librarians in ACRL. His commanding view led to his membership on the Board of Directors of the Council on Library Resources from 1968. He also served as a consultant, external reviewer, and member of the boards of many prominent agencies, including the Center for Research Libraries, the American Chemical Society, the National Library of Medicine, and Stanford University.

Vosper proved always an advocate for the recognition of the rights of librarians as partners in a scholarly enterprise. Through his leadership while in library school, students from the school who were employees of the library were recognized as professionals. While Vosper was at Kansas, librarians gained faculty status, although Vosper believed that status as librarians was reward in itself and should not be confused with that of traditional faculty members. Even in a position which accrues power such as he had at UCLA he was able to recruit managers who could give evidence of faith in the abilities of librarians to apply their own judgment in conducting the work of the library.

Vosper's work in international librarianship earned him high honors. Foreign acquisitions are major elements of academic research libraries, hence his interest was attracted early in his career. He attended the Princeton Conference on International, Cultural, Educational, and Scientific Exchanges in 1946. The conference led to the formation of the Farmington Plan, administered by the Association of Research Libraries, to increase the foreign holdings of academic libraries. In 1957 Vosper conducted a study of the Plan, leading to important changes in its administration nationwide.

On a Guggenheim tour of Europe in 1959 Vosper noted many features of librarianship that should have been attractive to American academic libraries. He arranged for a meeting of the Association of Research Libraries with its British counterpart. This led to Vosper's attraction to the work of the International Federation of Library Associations, a tie he strengthened during a Fulbright tour in Italy. He was the IFLA Vice-President from 1971 to 1976, Chairman of the Steering Committee for Universal Bibliographic Control, and Chairman of the program committee for the 50th anniversary celebration in Brussels in 1977. He received the Order of the Belgian Crown for that work, and was honored with the rank of Fellow of IFLA. He was a member of the U.S. State Department's Government Advisory Committee on Overseas Book and Library Programs from 1970 to 1975. From 1968 to 1973 he was a member of the U.S. National Commission on Unesco.

During the years of student unrest on university campuses in the late 1960s his commitment to libraries was a beacon for campus guidance. His words were posted in the library:

> The Library is an open intellectual sanctuary. It is devoted to individual intellectual inquiry. Its function is to provide free access to ideas and information. It is a calm and peaceful haven of privacy, a source of both cultural and intellectual sustenance for the individual reader. Since it is thus committed to free and open inquiry on a personal basis, the Library must remain open, with access to it always guaranteed.

This view gave staff the strength it needed, not only to deal with crises, but also to develop new programs in the service of the University. His influence on individuals was extended through his teaching career, not only on the faculty at UCLA, but also as a faculty member and lecturer at Columbia University and the Universities of Minnesota and Tennessee.

When he retired as University Librarian, a quotation from his writings was engraved for permanent display in the Library:

> If we mean, as we do, to support creative, imaginative research and inspired scholarship, UCLA must have a library rich in the whole history of man's intellectual and cultural life as it is crystallized and presented in books.

Vosper was given the LL.D. degree by Hofstra University in 1967 and was honored with the Joseph D. Lippincott award by the American Library Association in 1985. His citation reads: "through his patient and quiet leadership in the belief that libraries are collections and people, not systems, Robert G. Vosper has had a major impact on our profession."

REFERENCES
Alexandra Mason, "Rare Books in the Great American Desert," *Antiquarian Bookman* (1982).
Betty Milum, "Robert G. Vosper," *Leaders in American Academic Librarianship: 1925–1975* (1983)

RUSSELL SHANK

Walford, A. J.
(1906-   )

Albert John Walford, English reference librarian and editor, is known primarily as compiler and editor of various widely used bibliographical publications, especially the *Guide to Reference Material,* the British reference librarian's bible.

Born August 3, 1906, in Bermondsey, he spent his early years in the southeastern part of Greater London and graduated from London University. He began his library career as a senior assistant at Stoke Newington Public Library and continued it at Lambeth Public Libraries, where he was chief assistant from 1932 to 1946, apart from the period when he was on war service. When, toward the end of World War II, the War Office inaugurated a network of libraries to support the Army's educational activities, Walford became supervisor of the command libraries in North Africa and Italy. Soon after demobilization he became one of the first librarians to leave the public library service for senior posts in the expanding libraries of the central government departments, which were in need of reorganization by qualified and experienced staff. From 1946 to 1973 he was employed at the Ministry of Defence.

Walford's retirement from the Ministry proved to be purely nominal. In various ways he contrived to remain active in matters bibliographical and bibliothecal. His particular concern was the preparation of new editions of his well-known *Guide to Reference Material.*

From the 1930s he was at pains to communicate his wide-ranging knowledge of classification, reference techniques, and subject bibliography to others. He first became known in the profession for his articles and pamphlets on problems encountered by students of librarianship, guidance particularly welcome when attendance at a library school was available to only a few students in the U.K. The 1950s saw him engaged simultaneously on two of his major part-time activities. During the period 1953–59 he edited the monthly *Library Association Record* and planned and compiled the first edition of his *Guide to Reference Material,* published by the LA in 1959.

The *Guide* was not an entirely new kind of subject bibliography. The American Library Association's classic *Guide to Reference Books*—which *Walford* complements more than it rivals—had first appeared in 1902. The LA itself had published *Reference Books: a Classified and Annotated Guide,* compiled by John Minto, in 1929. Unfortunately, through lack of support from British libraries, for whom it had been expressly compiled, Minto's bibliography faded away after the publication of one supplement. The new LA *Guide,* published when reference and special libraries had become more numerous and active, was cordially received. Although, like the earlier *Guide,* it favored British publications, its scope was wide and every title listed was given a helpful descriptive annotation. Walford's declared purpose, which remains unchanged, was "to provide a signpost to reference books and bibliographies published mainly in recent years . . . for librarians, in the building up and revision of reference library stock; for use in general and special enquiry work; as an aid to students taking examinations in librarianship; and for research workers, in the initial stages of research" (Introduction).

The second edition of the *Guide* was in three volumes— Volume 1: *Science and Technology;* volume 2: *Social and Historical Sciences, Philosophy and Religion;* volume 3: *Generalities, Languages, the Arts and Literature.* They appeared between 1966 and 1970. The first volume of the fourth edition appeared in 1980.

Walford won a reputation as a librarian whose knowledge is matched by his energy, both prodigious. In the compilation of the *Guide* he had the cooperation of many colleagues in the library profession who have specialized knowledge. But in the planning and routine of compilation, his has been the mastermind, even though the editorial labors were later shared. In the fourth edition the title was changed to *Walford's Guide to Reference Material,* and an abridgment, first published by the LA in 1981, is called *Walford's Concise Guide to Reference Material. Walford's Guide to Current British Periodicals in the Humanities and Social Sciences,* first edition, was published by the LA in 1985.

REFERENCE
A. J. Walford, "Compiling the *Guide to Reference Material,*" *Journal of Librarianship* (1978).

JAMES G. OLLÉ

Waples, Douglas
(1893–1978)

Douglas Waples was a man whose roots were in literature, culture, research, and educational psychology, and who grew with and contributed to the growth of theory in the field of communications, the central core of his professional attention. His work in army intelligence and psychological warfare while serving in the U.S. Army during two world wars and as a consultant to the U.S. Department of State was tied closely to his interest in international communications. Recruited to library education as a specialist in educational method and in research, Waples studied librarianship and library education with a fine glass and saw librarianship as having high potential but never thought of himself as a librarian. Critical and stimulating in his objective clarity, Waples was always an outsider in relation to the field he served so well. He was not only an interdisciplinary scholar but also an exemplar of the post-World War II international perspective.

Born on March 3, 1893, in Philadelphia, Douglas Waples was the only child of Rufus Waples and Christine Beach Isham Waples; his mother, who suffered from tuberculosis, took him with her to Colorado Springs, Mexico City, and El Paso for the first five years of his life. Upon his mother's death in 1898, he returned to Pennsylvania, living in Wayne and attending Miss Miel's school. With his father's marriage in 1901, Douglas entered Radnor public school and sang in the Saint Mary's Protestant Episcopal Church boys' choir. In 1904 he entered Haverford School and became enamored of athletics, English, Latin, and Greek. Vactioning in New England and Michigan meant sports and the out-of-doors over the years, with a three-week canoe trip on the French River in Canada a memorable highlight. Thus early in life, Waples established his devotion to music, sports, and literature. A bassoonist, Waples later played with equal pleasure in the University Orchestra and in a woodwind quartet in Chicago. Former students recall him jogging regularly around the Midway in his later years on the Chicago campus.

Four years at Haverford College culminated in 1914 with election to Phi Beta Kappa, some literary prizes, and a bid to the 1914 Olympics. Teaching English and athletics in the Gilman School in Baltimore led him back to study, this time at Harvard, from which he earned an M.A. in June 1917, the same month he married Eleanor Cary. His doctorate came three years and a world war later, a Ph.D. degree in Educational Psychology from the University of Pennsylvania in 1920, the same spring as the birth of his first child.

His family and his career were launched with a position as Assistant Professor of Psychology and Education at Tufts in Boston, from which he continued studies at Harvard. In 1923 Waples moved to the University of Pittsburgh, where W. W. Charters was a colleague. When Charters moved to the University of Chicago in 1925, he saw that Waples also was added to that faculty. On his retirement in 1957, Washington Island, Wisconsin, become home base for him and Dorothy (Blake) Waples, his wife since 1947. Their Fulbright research trips to India and Peru sustained Waples's activity in public communication research until a debilitating stroke in 1960 severely limited his activity. He died on Washington Island April 25, 1978.

University of Chicago. Waples's 15 years (1928–42) on the faculty of the Graduate Library School of the University of Chicago spread his influence among his students and brought three of his major interests to bear on librarianship: scholarship, research, and reading behavior—all related to his central focus on public communication.

Waples's writings in the area of scholarship dealt often with the international exchange of ideas. *National Libraries and Foreign Scholarship,* written with Harold D. Lasswell (1936), and Waples's later article "Belgian Scholars and Their Libraries," *Library Quarterly* (1940), described the interaction between political nationalism and the importation of foreign social science literature and detailed the significance of broad general research collections in the development of scholarship.

Research was central to Waples's professional life. Each of his five important contributions to secondary education published between 1924 and 1930 made the research orientation central to curriculum evaluation, teaching methods, or supervision. Waples wrote with Ralph W. Tyler (1930) a textbook for teachers on the use of research methods that was precursor to Waples's later volume on research methods applied to librarianship, *Investigating Library Problems* (1939), which stressed the importance of building a research-based body of knowledge for librarianship. This emphasis made Waples, equally with Pierce Butler (*Introduction to Library Science,* 1934), spokesman for the unique research orientation of the Graduate Library School from 1928 to 1942.

Waples's studies of reading behavior, however, were then and remain his most substantive contribution to librarianship. He provided insight into the "hierarchy" of choices of reading materials: accessibility, readability, and subject interest in "The Rela-

tion of Subject Interests to Actual Reading," *Library Quarterly* (1932). "People versus Print," in L. R. Wilson's *Library Trends* (1936), with its corollary perspective on the library's role in making accessible the socially significant materials of an era, has had strong impact on American librarianship.

Waples's sheer intellectual power in grouping and analyzing data, in generating hypotheses, and in giving order to the chaos of perceived significance in reading studies is demonstrated in the unmatched series of publications that use sociological research strategies to explore his psychological hypotheses in the area of adult reading. *What People Want to Read About,* written with Ralph W. Tyler (1931), was even more significant for its methodology and its analysis of the field of reading research problems than it was for the findings on subject interests of a wide diversity of adult groups. Similarly, his monograph *People and Print* (1936) studies the "social aspects of reading in the depression," opening research into the relationship of the larger trends and critical events in society and the use of library resources. Market analysis, special publics, advertising, and cost efficiency in various types of book service were explored. But the compelling problem was still seen as that of effective description of readers "to present why they read as they do." Waples always sought methods of investigation that would allow penetration of this problem below the superficial level, and this search represents his major contribution. *Libraries and Readers in the State of New York,* which he wrote with Leon Carnovsky (1939), was the first study of research in total communities in an experimental design.

His research report, with Bernard Berelson and Franklyn R. Bradshaw, *What Reading Does to People* (1940), was notable not only for his full statement of "the five effects of reading," the record of reading as social history; it was also notable for a summation of the field of research in the social effects of reading and for recommendations on the methodology of content analysis and case studies. A brilliant conceptualizer, and skilled practitioner in research design, Waples has not had his equal in the area of adult reading studies.

Following World War II, Waples devoted himself to his public-communications studies outside the context of the Graduate Library School. He was Chairman of the University's Committee in Communication from 1951 to his retirement in 1957. Waples was one of that small group of major figures at GLS who shared in establishing a base for library science and a research orientation to library education.

MARGARET E. MONROE

Wheeler, Joseph L.
(1884–1970)

When the Enoch Pratt Free Library of Baltimore celebrated the 30th anniversary of the famous central building on February 15, 1963, the man responsible for making it a model of its kind was present. He saw carved on the marble entrance to the auditorium named in his honor, "Joseph L. Wheeler, 1926–1945. Under His Leadership the Enoch Pratt Free Library Became One of the Notable Libraries of the World." A skilled publicist, he had an eye for potential talent and the ability to inspire his staff, many of whom went on to major positions.

Wheeler was born March 16, 1884, in Dorchester, Massachusetts. After public schooling in Bridgewater and frequent visits to the local library, he studied engineering at Brown University and worked at the Providence Public Library. He switched courses, taking a Bachelor of Philosophy degree and a Master's degree in Social and Political Science from Brown. Later he completed the course at the New York State Library School in Albany.

Wheeler's professional progress was rapid and steady. Beginning at the Washington, D.C., Public Library, he held positions of increasing responsibility in public libraries of Jacksonville, Florida; Los Angeles; and Youngstown, Ohio.

He was 42 years old, energetic, seasoned, and boiling with ideas when he took over as Librarian of Baltimore's unexciting public library in 1926. Wheeler breathed life into the institution, using his skills in publicity and personnel development. He motivated and prodded trustees, staff, and officials of the city. The Pratt quickly earned a reputation for being in the van of public library organization and service.

Service to the public was Wheeler's obsession, as shown in the Pratt's building design. It was the first large public library with a street-level entrance, big display windows, and collections easily accessible to the public. Staff stations were strategically placed for assistance to readers.

Recognition of the Pratt Library for excellence and the proven efficiency of the central library created a nationwide demand for Wheeler's services as a consultant. After leaving Baltimore in 1944, he advised numerous libraries. He had completed more that 225 studies and surveys by the time of his death in Benson, Vermont, on December 3, 1970.

REFERENCE

Lee H. Warner, "Wheeler, Joseph Lewis," *Dictionary of American Library Biography* (1978).

EDWIN CASTAGNA
(d. 1983)

Wijasuriya, D. E. K.
(1934-)

Donald Earlian Kingsley Wijasuriya, a pioneer of the library profession in Malaysia, was born in Kuala Lumpur, Malaysia, on November 22, 1934. In Sri Lanka he obtained a B.A. degree from the University of Ceylon in Paradeniya in 1959. He joined the University of Malaya Library as a library assistant, and after spending a year there was sent by the University to the North-Western Polytechnic in London for professional studies in library science, 1961–63. He was admitted as an Associate of the Library Association, London, in 1962. Three years later, he was admitted by examination as a Fellow of the Library Association. In 1980 he received a doctorate from Loughborough University in the United Kingdom. In 1984 he was admitted as an Associate of the Australian Library Association.

He served the University of Malaya Library for more than 13 years, as Head of the Readers Services Division, Head of the Serials Division, and Deputy Librarian. At times he was Acting Librarian (1970–72). In 1972 Wijasuriya left the premier university library of the country to take a position with the young national library, still in its formative years. He was seconded from the University of Malaya Library and became the Deputy Director General of the National Library of Malaysia. It was the highest professional position in the National Library; the position of the Director General was traditionally filled by a senior civil servant from the administrative or diplomatic service. From May 1983, however, he acted as the Director General of the National Library.

He served on the Council of the Library Association of Malaysia from 1964 to 1979, during which time he was Secretary (1964–65), Vice-President (1970–71), and President (1972, 1973, 1975) of the Library Association of Malaysia. He also served on several committees of the Association in various capacities.

Public library service in Malaysia came to owe much to the efforts of Wijasuriya. In the 1970s he worked unceasingly with state library committees and provided valuable advice and guidelines in formulating their legal enactments setting up the state public library services. The Sultan of the State of Kedah awarded him the Kedah Distinguished Service Star in 1979 in recognition of his public library contributions. In the same year the King of Malaysia made him an Officer of the Most Distinguished Order of the Defender of the Realm for his services to the nation.

Under Wijasuriya's leadership, the National Library, from humble beginnings as a section of the National Archives with a collection of about 4,000 volumes, went through a period of spectacular growth and development after 1972. In 1977 it was established as an independent department of the federal government with its own identity, and by the mid-1980s had a collection of more than half a million volumes and a staff of about 240, of whom more than a quarter were professionals. The operational budget of the National Library increased by about twenty-fold. Wijasuriya was the moving force behind most of the services developed in the National Library, including the *National Bibliography, Index to Malaysian Periodicals, The Malaysian Newspaper Index,* and *The Malaysian Conference Index* as well as a na-

The Baltimore Sunpapers

Joseph Lewis Wheeler

D. E. K. Wijasuriya

tional postal loan service and the branch and mobile library services in the Federal Territory.

The establishment of a network of the four university libraries in the country and the national library to ensure optimum resource-sharing was initiated by Wijasuriya. With the assistance of Unesco, that project led to the development of the MALMARC database, which had about 250,000 records of holdings of all the participating libraries in the mid-1980s.

Active in the Conference of South East Aisan Librarians (CONSAL), he served on its Board from 1974 and was Chairman of the Board, 1979–81, when Malaysia was host to CONSAL.

In 1984 the government set up a task force chaired by Wijasuriya to formulate a national policy for library and information services in Malaysia.

J. S. SOOSAI

Wijnstroom, Margreet
(1922–   )

Margreet Wijnstroom

Margreet Wijnstroom, Dutch librarian and association leader, became known to the international library world as the Secretary General of IFLA (the International Federation of Library Associations and Institutions).

She was born August 26, 1922 in Bloemendaal in the Netherlands. To her as well as to many others of the same generation, World War II caused changes in the plans for a future career. She had decided to study law, but during the war students who wanted to enter a university had to sign a declaration of loyalty decreed by the Nazis. She, like many others, found that unacceptable. Instead, she took up librarianship, which was taught in courses organized by the Dutch Library Association and received her practical training in the City Library in Haarlem. For a short period thereafter she worked in The Hague Public Library. For the rest of the war she worked illegally in Haarlem, as official jobs were reserved for friends of the occupation forces.

In 1945–46 she followed the course for future directors of public libraries in The Hague. She could not, however, completely give up the idea of studying law and started her studies at the University of Amsterdam in 1947. She obtained her degree in 1954 but nevertheless continued in the library field as a public relations librarian at the Public Library in Amsterdam, 1954–57.

Margreet Wijnstroom stood up for women's rights to an extent hard to credit today, but the need was urgent in the 1950s. Thus she could not resist applying for the job as Secretary of the Dutch Public Library Association, although the position was advertised for men only. She received the job, luckily for the library world at large, and this soon revealed her outstanding ability to run a professional organization. During the period that she was in charge, 1954–1971, the staff of the Association increased from 6 to 80 and a number of new activities were launched, so that the Association also became what in many other countries is known as a library center. She was asked to join IFLA as the first full-time Secretary General in 1971. Her experience in the library field as well as her background in law proved an excellent

combination. Her citizenship in a small country, where people are known for their international interests and contacts, was of equal importance. To make an international organization prosper is not merely a question of increasing the membership, but it also requires the person in charge to be able to create an atmosphere of trust among members from all over the world.

IFLA's growth since 1971 soon made it necessary for the Federation to revise its statutes. This was far from a painless operation. The proposal put forward to the Council in 1975 was found unacceptable by the membership and for a time IFLA's future situation was unclear. That the new statutes were eventually adopted in the following year was to a great extent due to the Secretary General, who, in addition to being familiar with the juridical formalities governing such an international organization, had also the feeling of what might be accepted by the members, who based themselves on their national organization systems. The former "gentlemen's club" then really changed into a workable organization, inspiring new generations of librarians to take interest in joining IFLA and working in specialized areas toward the common goal of promoting librarianship.

Though the membership grows continuously, this does not necessarily mean that more money can be put at the disposal of the Secretariat. This is due to the differentiated fee system. The Secretary General, delighted that so many new members from the Third World have joined IFLA, thereby making it a truly global organization, came to face a constant challenge for finding ways to make ends meet.

Margreet Wijnstroom has announced her retirement in 1987. However, she will have no trouble in filling her spare time. In her youth she was an international field hockey player, captaining the Dutch team for a decade. She is still assisting the Dutch Field Hockey Association as member/chair of various committees, and has designed a new legal penalty system for the Hockey Association. She is a well-known critical reviewer in Holland of Dutch and foreign mystery literature, and plans to continue this activity and her DFHA activities when she retires. Honors she received include Officer in the Order of Oranje Nassau (Netherlands), Officer in the Crown Order of Belgium, and a Special Citation of the U.S. National Commission on Library and Information Science.

Margreet Wijnstroom wrote *De Openbare Bibliotheek In Europe* ("The Public Library in Europe") and contributed many professional articles in library journals.

ELSE GRANHEIM

Williamson, Charles C.
(1877–1965)

Charles Clarence Williamson, U.S. librarian, is most widely known for his landmark study, *Training for Library Service,* yet his many achievements as a special librarian, academic librarian, and dean were also major contributions to the emerging field of librarianship.

Williamson was born in Salem, Ohio, on January 26, 1877. In June 1897 he graduated from the

Salem high school first in his class. He had to work while studying for his A.B. degree and, after one year of study at Ohio Wesleyan University, he returned to Salem in 1899 and became a first grade teacher; he later became principal as well. In 1901 Williamson, anxious to resume his college education, accepted a part-time job from the President of Western Reserve University, Charles F. Thwing. The job provided an opportunity for Williamson to resume his college education at Western Reserve. He majored in economics and graduated in 1903 *magna cum laude* and was elected to Phi Beta Kappa. He then assisted and studied under Richard T. Ely at the University of Wisconsin, checking bibliographies and making recommendations for the purchase of books in economics and related subjects. In 1906, at the end of the academic year, Ely went to Columbia University in New York City, and Williamson, who had been awarded a fellowship, also transferred to Columbia, from which he received his Ph.D. degree in 1907.

Williamson demonstrated, for almost four decades, that "he was a man of many interests and possessed an innate interest in almost every thing. This is revealed in his life, work, writings, and contributions; support of professional and scholarly groups; bibliographical activities; activities in professional library associations; and a career which included work as a teacher, principal, secretary, economist, associate professor, political scientist, librarian, statistician, foundation executive, library director, dean, library educator, professor, author, editor, bibliographer, compiler, surveyor, and consultant." (Paul Winckler).

John Shaw Billings, acting on the advice of Edwin R. Seligman, one of Williamson's former professors, appointed him Chief of the new Division of Economics and Sociology at the New York Public Library with the understanding that it would be available to the public on the opening day of the new building at Fifth Avenue and 42nd Street. Williamson was then a professor at Bryn Mawr College (Pennsylvania). The new library opened on May 23, 1911, before Williamson could leave Bryn Mawr. He nonetheless completed all the planning and organization required for the Division of Economics and Sociology to open as scheduled.

The Economics Division quickly became one of the library's most important and heavily used centers of research and scholarship. Williamson and his staff provided a wide range of information services and aggressive promotion; they also added more than 100,000 volumes to the collection by 1914. Williamson then took on a second major challenge: he became the Municipal Reference Librarian of New York City on October 19, 1914. The relatively new library was in disarray because of the poor performance of the previous head librarian, who had been dismissed. In fewer than four years, Williamson developed the Municipal Reference Library into a model of efficiency and effectiveness in the delivery of information and reference services to the city's employees and officials. He established the practice of aggressively supplying city employees and officials with pertinent data. He started *Municipal Reference Notes,* which was sent to city employees and policymakers to alert them to recent useful information. Thus from Williamson came a forerunner of today's

selected dissemination of information.

Williamson also acted to provide facts about the entire government of New York City; he did so by compiling and publishing the *Municipal Year Book of the City of New York;* later he described the need and helped to secure funding for the publication of the *Minutes of the Common Council of the City of New York, 1784-1831;* he further contributed to this work by serving as Secretary to the Publications Committee. But perhaps of even greater importance, Williamson envisioned a greater role for *Public Affairs Information Service* and worked to make it a reality. Williamson's landmark achievements at the Municipal Reference Library were all the more remarkable considering that the political environment in which he accomplished so much was only minimally hospitable to him. With no small relief, he accepted a new and entirely different assignment with the Carnegie Corporation in 1918. One year later, after he had completed his part of the Corporation's "Study of the Methods of Americanization," Williamson returned to his position as Chief of the Division of Economics and Sociology at the NYPL in 1919.

During his second tenure at the NYPL, Williamson began to focus his attention on education for librarianship. The Carnegie Corporation commissioned him to do his pioneering study of the institutions that were preparing librarians to operate the nation's libraries. As early as 1914, Henry S. Pritchett, President of the Board of the Carnegie Corporation, had expressed his uneasiness ". . . about the activities of the corporation in planting libraries" around the country, and he had obtained the services of Alvin Johnson to survey the Corporation's library building program. Johnson stated his belief that "Not buildings nor even book collections, but trained, intelligent, enterprising library service makes a real library." Hence he recommended that the Corporation ". . . divert as much as practicable of available library funds to the promotion and support of library training." Following World War I, the Corporation's and Williamson's interests in library training matched; the result was *Training for Library Service, A Report Prepared for the Carnegie Corporation of New York* (1923). This report laid the foundation for today's strong library schools. The Report also assured Williamson a prominent place in the history of professional education along with Abraham Flexner, who had submitted a set of recommendations that revolutionized medical education in America almost two decades earlier.

In 1921 Williamson left the NYPL and joined the staff of the Rockefeller Foundation. He became its Information Officer and had administrative responsibility for the Foundation's library. Williamson managed the Library and the Foundation's public relations with his usual care and thoroughness until 1926.

On May 1, 1926, he was appointed Director of the Libraries and of the School of Library Service at Columbia University. Williamson's performance became further testimony of his uncommon skills as a planner and organizer. By the time he retired in 1943, Columbia was ranked among the top library schools in the nation; Williamson had carried out the decision to merge the Library School of the New York Public Library and the New York State Library School. The libraries, which were scattered around Columbia

University's campus, were operating in a well-coordinated system before he retired. The Library Administration and the Library School were both housed in a handsome new library building Williamson had planned. Of the building Keyes Metcalf said: "It was a great university library building; and, in spite of monumental features, it cost just about one-half as much as Yale's Sterling Library, which was built at the same time, had the same number of square feet, and was designed by the same architect." Later named Butler Library, it contained the forerunner of undergraduate libraries that were later popular.

Williamson found time to play key roles in a wide range of other interests. He was a leader for many years of the Conference of Eastern Librarians; the French government awarded him the Chevalier of the Legion of Honor for the important part he played in the publication of the printed catalogue of the Bibliothèque Nationale; he also served as an officer of the Special Libraries Association, the American Library Association, the Association of American Library Schools, and the American Library Institute. And he was an active member of the Association of Research Libraries. Williamson was, moreover, a participant in other associations, among them the Bibliographical Society of America, the American Economic Association, the Political Science Association, and the American Sociological Society.

Few librarians have been able to make so many important contributions directly to the advancement of librarianship and in many other areas of service as Williamson did. He died on January 11, 1965, in Greenwich, Connecticut.

REFERENCES

Paul A. Winckler, "Charles Clarence Williamson (1877-1965): His Professional Life and Work in Librarianship and Library Education in the United States" (Ph.D. dissertation, New York University, 1968).
Keyes D. Metcalf, "Six Influential Academic and Research Librarians," *College and Research Libraries* (July 1976).

CHARLES D. CHURCHWELL

Wilson, H. W.
(1868–1954)

Halsey William Wilson's contributions to librarianship cannot easily be overstated. It is hardly possible to imagine American libraries without the indexes and bibliographies he created as bookseller, publisher, and founder of the company that bears his name.

Son of Althea Dunnell Wilson and John Thompson Wilson, a stonecutter, H. W. Wilson was born in Wilmington, Vermont, on May 12, 1868. He was a descendant of Roger Williams, Anne Hutchinson, and Mary Dyer, the Quaker martyr. Orphaned before the age of three, Wilson was brought up by his maternal grandparents in rural Massachusetts and later by an aunt and uncle in Iowa. He soon developed his legendary capacity for work and began to exercise his talent for simultaneous activity. He gained his formal education at a Beloit, Wisconsin, boarding school and the University of Minnesota. While attending the university intermittently between 1885 and 1892, he delivered newspapers, worked as a church custodian, ran a small job printing business, studied music in hope of becoming an organist,

ALA

H. W. Wilson

worked weekends at the Minneapolis Public Library, and, with his roommate, Henry S. Morris, acted as book agent for faculty and students.

In December 1889 the two young men pooled their modest resources, $200, and opened a campus bookstore in the main university building. The firm of Morris and Wilson began on a small scale, furnishing textbooks and supplies and printing syllabuses. After Morris's graduation in 1891, Wilson continued the business, bought out his partner, and soon built it up into the best bookstore in Minneapolis. At one period the store had a bicycle section and managed the university post office, ensuring that everyone on campus made a daily visit to the bookstore. The success of the business enabled Wilson to marry, on August 12, 1895, Justine Leavitt, a graduate student. She was closely associated with the bookstore and the publishing firm until about 1913, when she turned her full attention to civic matters, especially the women's suffrage movement.

As a bookseller, Wilson became aware of the need for an accurate, up-to-date source for locating books in print. *Publishers' Weekly* had published semi-annual cumulations of its weekly lists, but discontinued them in 1897 because of rising costs. Wilson, spurred on by what he later called the "bibliographic urge," conceived the idea of a monthly listing of new books, to be cumulated into a permanent record of American book publishing. Thus was born *Cumulative Book Index* (CBI), which first appeared in February 1898. CBI embodied the now familiar Wilson bibliographical features: author, title, and subject entries arranged in one alphabet. The success, limited at first, of CBI led Wilson to produce the first *United States Catalog, Books in Print,* in 1899. Hard on the heels of this came the most familiar of all the Wilson publications, *Readers' Guide to Periodical Literature,* which first appeared in 1901, indexing the contents of 20 general periodicals. These early publications were cumulated by another Wilson innovation: bibliographic entries on Linotype slugs that could be kept and rearranged at will before each printing.

In 1903 Wilson incorporated his bookstore-publishing firm, offering stock in the H. W. Wilson Company to friends in the academic, bookselling, and library communities. Thus began the company's continuing association with librarians. The first product of the new firm was the *Book Review Digest* (1905), edited by Mrs. Wilson. Over the next several years, some half-dozen periodical indexes, forerunners of now standard titles, appeared under the Wilson imprint, as well as two cumulative editions of *Readers' Guide,* two revisions of the *United States Catalog,* and a number of other library-oriented publications. The firm also issued dozens of titles as the unofficial University of Minnesota Press.

Early in his career, Wilson evolved a method of pricing *Readers' Guide* on a sliding scale, the "service basis," which made it possible for almost all libraries to afford this valuable reference source. He conceived the index as a *service:* the price depended upon a library's periodical holdings and thus the index's usefulness to that library. The more titles indexed for a library, the more useful *Readers' Guide* was; and each library was charged accordingly. Similar but more complex scales were developed for the specialized Wilson indexes, involving not only the number of periodical titles held but also the number of indexing entries per title. The service basis, though criticized from time to time, has served both the company and its subscribers well.

As the firm flourished, Wilson recognized the need to be located on the East Coast, closer to the publishing world and the majority of his subscribers. In 1913 he moved the firm to White Plains, New York. From White Plains came *Industrial Arts Index* (1913), *Agricultural Index* (1916), and still more library-oriented reference books. A house organ begun in this period evolved into *Wilson Library Bulletin*. After four years in White Plains, Wilson moved the firm even closer to New York City. In 1917, on a site in the Bronx overlooking the Hudson River, he built the first building of a complex that ultimately included four large structures. He also built the 30-foot lighthouse that became the company's colophon.

From the familiar 950 University Avenue address, the Wilson Company developed additional specialized periodical indexes, among them *Art Index* (1929), *Education Index* (1929), *Library Literature* (1936), and *Bibliographic Index* (1938). Other specialized reference guides from this period are *Essay and General Literature Index* (1934), *Vertical File Index* (1932), *Current Biography* (1940), and *Biography Index* (1946). The Standard Catalog series was developed fully in this period. The first *Union List of Serials in Libraries of the United States and Canada* (1928) was the result of cooperation between the Wilson Company, the American Library Association, and participating libraries. Wilson later provided a feasibility study for the continuation of the Library of Congress's *Catalog of Books Represented by Library of Congress Printed Cards, issue to July 31, 1942,* which contributed in large measure to its continuation as the *National Union Catalog.*

Wilson realized quite early that the success of his firm, with its market limited mostly to libraries, depended upon close cooperation with librarians. The firm employed many librarians in its indexing operations. Practicing librarians were consulted at every step about the company's services and activities, even to the point of making decisions about the scope and content of many Wilson publications. To facilitate cooperation, Wilson attended more than 40 American Library Association national meetings, as many Midwinter meetings, and hundreds of regional, state, and local meetings of librarians. He also participated in and sponsored national and international bibliographical projects, created library awards, and placed librarians on his board of directors. The Wilson staff was encouraged to participate in library association activites and allowed generous time for committee work. Over the years these close ties to the library community led to a steady stream of Wilson publications, each geared to some specific library need.

In 1948 Wilson summed up his method of creating new publications, emphasizing the importance of listening to and talking with librarians.

First, listen to the advice of prospective supporters of a project. If the project is important it will be discussed in librarians' meetings and journals. Then scan the field and study what has been done and why there may have been successes and failures. Consult and secure advice from librarians who may be expected to have an interest in the project. Then the final question: "If this is a good plan and if we proceed with it, will you plan to subscribe for it?"

While Wilson's business methods and bibliographical innovations were quite modern, his managerial approach was that of the paternalistic Yankee individualist. Though he grew to manhood in the age of Rockefeller, Carnegie, Gould, and Fisk, he became a Wilsonian Democrat in his middle years. An admirer of Henry Ford, he disliked the income tax, loathed Franklin D. Roosevelt and the New Deal, and unsuccessfully resisted unions in the firm. From the beginning, the staff of the Wilson Company was like a family, and this feeling never entirely disappeared as the firm grew. Though salaries were skimpy, Wilson provided such fringe benefits as stock sharing, pensions for older employees, cumulative sick leave, and hospitalization at a time when few American business firms did so. He encouraged vacations, though rarely taking them himself; employed women and placed them in positions of responsibility; and pioneered in the hiring of the physically handicapped.

Wilson began developing his publications at a time when the need for bibliographical control of an expanding world of print was becoming acute. Extension of secondary and higher education, growth of the book and periodical publishing industry, the Carnegie-inspired revolution in library expansion, the rise of scholarly and scientific publication and research, all had created a flood of information and generated a need for indexes to make this information easily accessible. Wilson's knowledge of the needs of libraries, his high standards of indexing, his pricing systems to make his indexes widely available, his publication of a broad range of indexes and services, and his continuing modernization of his publications ultimately made for a unique, satisfying, and profitable bibliographical publishing career.

In person Wilson was a stocky, robust figure. His round features and a twinkle in the eye relieved an otherwise stolid but not forbidding appearance. Though personally abstemious (he neither smoked nor drank alcohol), he did indulge a stupendous sweet tooth and a wry sense of humor. He was addicted to puns, and the wary soon learned to spot the signs that a particularly horrendous one was on the way. Fond of after-dinner stories, he published, under the transparent pseudonym Harold Workman Williams, three collections of jokes, stories, and quotations for all occasions.

Wilson was much honored in his lifetime. Brown University presented him an honorary Doctor of Letters degree in 1939; in 1948 the University of Minnesota honored him with its first Outstanding Achievement award. The American Library Association and the Special Libraries Association made special presentations on the 50th anniversary of the Wilson Company in 1948. In 1950 he received the American Library Association's Joseph W. Lippincott Award. In his turn, Wilson honored the library community. In 1946 the firm began to sponsor library awards, the most prestigious of which is the annual John Cotton Dana Library Publicity Award.

Wilson resigned as President of the firm in December 1952 but continued as Chairman of the Board until his death at his home in Yorktown Heights,

New York, on March 1, 1954. He died exactly 60 years to the day after the death of an earlier bibliographer and periodical indexer, William Frederick Poole. After Mrs. Wilson's death in 1955, the Wilson estate was turned over to the H. W. Wilson Foundation, to be used primarily for the benefit of former employees. Grants were made for such purposes as library school scholarships, National Library Week, the activities of several library associations, and programs for the blind and physically handicapped.

REFERENCE
Arthur Plotnik, "Wilson, Halsey William," *Dictionary of American Library Biography* (1978).

A. E. SKINNER
(d. 1985)

ALA

Louis Round Wilson

Wilson, Louis Round
(1876–1979)

Louis Round Wilson was Librarian of the University of North Carolina at Chapel Hill, 1901–32, and Dean of the Graduate Library School of the University of Chicago, 1932–42. His career as librarian, teacher, writer, and editor and his active and influential participation in library associations exemplify the emergence of the professional university library administrator in the United States.

Born in Lenoir, North Carolina, on December 27, 1876, Wilson was educated in Lenoir schools, attended Haverford (Pennsylvania) College, and was graduated from the University of North Carolina at Chapel Hill in 1899. He taught in private academies in North Carolina for two years before returning to Chapel Hill as University Librarian in 1901. He also pursued graduate study and received a Master's degree in English in 1902 and a Ph.D. in 1905. Though Wilson had expected to become a professor of English, he decided instead to remain with the University of North Carolina as its Librarian, a decision that influenced his own life and made an indelible impact on the library profession.

Wilson foresaw the growth and development of the University of North Carolina into one of the major universities in the United States and endeavored to build a library collection that would support graduate study and research. Working with the university's academic departments, he acquired books, periodicals, and bibliographic materials that greatly expanded the holdings of the main library. Wilson was especially interested in the special collections of the library; acknowledging the regional quality of the University, he envisioned a manuscript collection that would serve historians of the South. He lived to see the Southern Historical Collection take its place among the major manuscript repositories in the U.S. He encouraged the development of a collection of North Caroliniana and sought and gained financial support from friends and alumni of the University for the purchase and preservation of rare books and incunabula.

Wilson supervised the construction of two library buildings. A Carnegie building was completed in 1907, and the present special collections library, which bears his name, was dedicated in 1929. With the growth of the collections and the expanded physical facilities came an increase in the number of trained librarians on Wilson's staff. In 1907 when the Carnegie library was opened, Wilson ran the library with the aid of only one trained librarian and a few student assistants; by 1932 there were 23 librarians on the staff.

Wilson taught his first course in librarianship in the summer session of 1904. In 1907 courses in library administration were offered in the regular session, and Wilson was made an Assistant Professor of Library Administration. In 1920 Wilson was made a Kenan Professor of Library Science; the Kenan professorships are the University of North Carolina's oldest and most distinguished endowed professorships. Wilson taught courses in library science until he left the University and was vigorous and successful in campaigning for a School of Library Science, which opened in 1931 with Wilson as its first Dean.

As a member of the faculty of the University, Wilson assumed many additional duties. As Chairman of the Committee on Extension from 1912 to 1920, he drew the library heavily into extension work; through the Library Extension Department books were circulated to the people of North Carolina for more than 40 years. Wison was Editor of the *Alumni Review,* 1912–24, and co-founder and Director of the University Press, 1922–32.

In 1932 Wilson accepted the position of Dean of the Graduate Library School of the University of Chicago. As Dean of the seven-year-old school, he led the faculty in developing a curriculum designed to produce librarians who would be specialists in administration of various types of libraries. Wilson taught courses in university library administration and library trends. He organized teams of students and faculty members to study current problems in librarianship and began institutes that explored new directions for the profession. Many of these studies resulted in books that were published as part of the University of Chicago Studies in Library Science series, of which Wilson was General Editor.

Wilson's own volume in the series, *The Geography of Reading* (1938), reflects his long-standing interest in the phenomenon of reading. As early as 1922 he was studying the reading habits of North Carolinians, and in the 1930s he extended this interest in reading and public libraries to the entire country.

In 1942 Wilson returned to North Carolina, where he rejoined the faculty of the School of Library Science. In 1945 he and Maurice F. Tauber published *The University Library,* a significant addition to the literature of library administration. After retiring from the faculty at 83 in 1959, Wilson continued in service to the University as a consultant to the President of the university system until 1969.

Throughout his career Wilson served as a library consultant and surveyor. His opinions on academic libraries, library buildings, and possible sites for library schools were sought by the Carnegie Corporation, the General Education Board, and the Board of Education for Librarianship of the American Library Association. In the mid-1930s Wilson and Edgar A. Wight surveyed county libraries in the Southeast, and in 1941 and 1946 Wilson conducted surveys for the Tennessee Valley Authority and the Tennessee Valley Library Council, with a view to increasing library service to the Tennessee Valley region under the aegis of the Tennessee Valley Authority.

Wilson's participation in professional associations began when he joined ALA in 1904. As President of ALA, 1935–36, he led a successful campaign for adoption of a statement in support of federal aid to libraries. He helped to found the North Carolina Library Association in 1904 and was its President in 1910 and again in 1930–31. Wilson was President of the Southeast Library Association (SELA), 1924–26, and endeavored to join the efforts of SELA and the Southern Association of Colleges and Secondary Schools in providing standards for school and college libraries. Always mindful of the needs of the people of the state, Wilson helped to draft the legislation that created the North Carolina Library Commission in 1909 and served as Chairman of the Commission from 1909 until 1916. He was active in the Citizen's Library Movement in 1927.

Wilson's career demonstrates his belief in the role of the library as a service organization. He saw the library as an active force in American society and never ceased in his efforts to bring the library into active service to the people. He knew that the library was a vital and necessary adjunct to the school and college, but he also believed that the librarian must reach out beyond the walls of the library in bringing the materials of the library to the people.

Wilson was married in 1909 to Penelope Bryan Wright. They had four children. He built a house in Chapel Hill in 1911. His oldest two daughters lived with him until his death in Chapel Hill, December 10, 1979, at the age of 102.

REFERENCES

Louis Round Wilson Bibliography: A Chronological List of Works and Editorial Activities (1976).

Maurice F. Tauber, *Louis Round Wilson: Librarian and Administrator* (1967).

Frances A. Weaver, *Louis Round Wilson, The Years since 1955* (1976).

Edward G. Holley, "The Centenary of a Giant of Librarianship: Louis Round Wilson" (illustrated), *The ALA Yearbook* (1977).

John V. Richardson, Jr. "Louis Round Wilson," *Leaders in American Academic Librarianship* (1983).

FRANCES A. WEAVER

Winchell, Constance M.
(1896–1984)

Constance Mabel Winchell, a member of the reference staff at Columbia University Library for 38 years, was responsible for the seventh and eighth editions of *A Guide to Reference Books.*

Winchell was born on November 2, 1896, in Northampton, Massachusetts, where her aunt was a librarian in the historic Forbes Library directed by Charles A. Cutter. Winchell earned a Bachelor of Arts degree from the University of Michigan, where she "filed her way through college" with a job in the university library. Upon graduation Winchell began her career as a librarian at the Central High School in Duluth, Minnesota. She had prepared for such a post by attending the "library summer school" sessions conducted at Michigan by the Director of the University Library, William Warner Bishop, following her junior and senior years. Unlike many who become librarians after trying some other profession,

Constance M. Winchell

ALA

Winchell wanted that career from the beginning. In an interview she once remarked: "It never entered my mind that I was not going to be a librarian. I had always intended to be a librarian, always."

On Bishop's advice, she attended the Library School at New York Public Library and received a certificate in 1920. She then worked for the U.S. Merchant Marine in New York City and was responsible for libraries in lighthouses. Five months later Winchell returned to Ann Arbor, where she worked first as a reviser in the catalogue department of the university library and then as a reference assistant. She wanted to do reference work immediately, but Bishop advised that any reference librarian should have cataloguing experience.

In 1924 Winchell went to the American Library in Paris as Head Cataloguer. Bishop disapproved, but Winchell wanted the experience of life in another country. She returned to the United States in 1925 and joined the reference staff of the Columbia University Library. Winchell stayed there for 38 years, rising from Reference Assistant to Assistant Reference Librarian to Reference Librarian—taking that post when Isadore Gilbert Mudge retired in 1941.

Mudge was Head of the Reference Department during Winchell's early years at Columbia and was also Winchell's teacher in the Columbia School of Library Service, where Winchell earned an M.S. in 1930. Mudge suggested and then supervised the preparation of Winchell's Master's essay, published as *Locating Books for Interlibrary Loan* (H. W. Wilson, 1930). The work incorporates many of the techniques and concepts Mudge had developed through 20 years of work with interlibrary loan problems. Winchell's lucid explication of practices at Columbia stood for many years as the standard guide for interlibrary loan operations, which were then expanding in all parts of the country.

The value of this work was noted when Winchell received the Isadore Gilbert Mudge Citation for distinguished contributions to reference librarianship in 1960. Winchell was the second person to receive this award, established by the Reference Services Division of ALA in 1959. Winchell received it for "her constructive service to the Library of Columbia University in building its reference collection and . . . her trail-blazing book, *Locating Books for Interlibrary Loan,* which has been an effective aid to the development of interlibrary loan in this country and which continues to be useful as a systematic guide to finding the location of a needed book [and for] . . . that bible of the librarian, *A Guide to Reference Books*."

A Guide to Reference Books was started by Alice Bertha Kroeger, who was responsible for the first edition in 1902, the five annual supplements that were published in *Library Journal,* and the second edition published in 1908. Isadore Gilbert Mudge prepared supplements to the second edition and was responsible for the third, fourth, fifth, and sixth editions and all the supplements in between. When Mudge retired in 1941, she turned over the *Guide* to Winchell, who had been involved in it ever since she helped with *Reference Books of 1929,* a supplement to the fifth edition. After Mudge's retirement, Winchell produced supplements to the sixth edition and both the seventh and eighth editions—the last published five years after her own retirement from Columbia. Reviewers of these volumes have praised Winchell's skill in making good use of the work of her predecessors while introducing significant and useful changes in the *Guide.*

Winchell not only knew the contents of reference books; she also understood what good reference service should be. When she retired in 1962, the Director of Libraries at Columbia, Richard Logdson, wrote a brief tribute in *College and Research Libraries:*

> Miss Winchell's standards of excellence, her almost uncanny skill in unraveling bibliographic snarls, her zeal in learning new tools to improve existing techniques, and her thorough training of younger assistants have characterized her work through the years. She possessed these qualities, desired in all good reference chiefs, to the highest degree, but beyond these were two deserving special mention. The first is Miss Winchell's concept of a university library as part of the university, not as an island alone. . . . Finally there is Miss Winchell's devotion to duty nurtured by such a profoundly kind heart that she had found it impossible to appear impatient, or bored, or irritated with a reader. . . .

Before she retired, Winchell took a four-month leave of absence for an extensive tour of Asia. Her interest in faraway places was reflected in the many post cards that decorated the home in New Paltz, in upstate New York, where she moved after completion of the eighth edition of the *Guide.* She died there on May 23, 1984.

REFERENCES

Mary Jo Lynch, "Women in Reference Service," in *Women in the Library Profession: Leadership Roles and Contributions* (1971).

Constance M. Winchell, "The Reminiscences of Constance Mabel Winchell," transcript of an interview with Elizabeth Rumics in 1963, on file in the Oral History Collection, Columbia University Library.

MARY JO LYNCH

Wing, Donald Goddard
(1904–1972)

Donald Goddard Wing, who was associated for over 40 years with the Yale University Library, compiled an indispensable tool for librarians and the book trade, the *Short-Title Catalogue* of books printed in English in the 17th century.

Wing was born in Athol, Massachusetts, on August 18, 1904. His interest in literature and books developed early; while in school in Athol he read and collected the *Smart Set* and other "little magazines." From Athol he went to Yale, where he studied English, added a book a day to his collection, and was elected to the Elizabethan Club. After graduating in 1926, he spent a year at Trinity College, Cambridge, tutored by George Rylands. A member of the Bloomsbury group, Rylands confirmed Wing's passion for contemporary poetry and literature. Wing traveled widely during his year abroad, and when he returned to the United States he had his copy of the still-banned *Ulysses* hidden in his laundry bag. After a year at Harvard to earn his M.A., Wing returned to Yale, remaining there until the end of his life. He received his Ph.D. in English from Yale in 1932 for his dissertation on "Origins of the Comedy of Humours."

At Yale University, Wing served as Head of Accessions (1939–45), Associate Librarian (1945–65), and Associate Librarian for Collections of the Libraries (1966–70). The Yale Library grew tremendously during those years and gained international prominence. Wing's remarkable memory and intimate knowledge of the Yale collections, combined with his diverse intellectual interests, significantly contributed to the Library's expansion. He loved books and delighted in American libraries' "delirious, exhilarating race toward adequacy."

Wing's great and enduring contribution to bibliography is his *Short-Title Catalogue of Books Printed in England, Scotland, Ireland, Wales and British America and of English Books Printed in Other Countires, 1641–1700.* It was issued in three volumes by the Index Society from 1945 to 1951. His work served as a continuation of Pollard and Redgrave's *Short-Title Catalogue of Books . . . 1475–1640.* Wing surveyed a greater range of libraries than Pollard and Redgrave had; he provided more cross references, gave longer imprints, and indicated by ellipsis the shortening of titles. In addition, he dealt with about 90,000 titles, about three times as many as the earlier STC. Remarkably, Wing compiled his STC during his spare time, except for a year in England in 1936 on a Guggenheim Fellowship.

Yale's acquisition of Falconer Madan's personal collection of Oxford books, and the need to make sense of Yale's holdings of early English books, provided Wing with reason to begin collecting notes while still in his 20s. He wrote out a slip for each title; on it he noted author, short-title, imprint, format, edition, and number of pages. He listed the location of copies, giving the British Museum and Yale shelf numbers and noting unusual provenance. He examined bibliographical reference works and added specific citations for each book. He searched sale catalogues from the 19th century for rare titles and noted the appearance of uncommon items at auction or in booksellers' catalogues in his own day. He not only looked at each tract in the Thomason Collection at the British Museum but also examined at least one copy of the great majority of the titles he listed. To fill in details, he corresponded with librarians and scholars.

Wing's achievement was astonishing. In little over a decade, he produced what quickly became an indispensable tool. Soon librarians and booksellers spoke of "Wing books," and many used "Wing numbers" for identifying, selling, cataloguing, and shelving "Wing period" titles. Librarians were able to measure the strength of their collections and to plot acquisition policy; booksellers could determine at a glance relative rarity and set prices accordingly; and scholars could refer to lists of an author's work or search for pamphlets on a similar theme or subject.

During the remainder of his career, Wing kept his slips up to date with the goal of preparing a revised edition. His *A Gallery of Ghosts* (1967) was based on his search list for 5,000 titles or editions that had appeared at auction or in a bookseller's catalogue or were listed in a previous bibliographer's work but for which no copy was found. Wing received a gratifying response; over half of his ghosts were quickly identified or laid to rest. With the benefit of a sabbatical year, the first granted to a Yale librarian, Wing prepared his revision of the first volume for publication in 1972.

The period 1641 to 1700 comprised only part of Wing's interests. Although he put together an excellent collection of the works of James Howell, a prolific Wing period author, he also collected and read Henry James, Ronald Firbank, Marcel Proust, Edith Wharton, Ezra Pound (whom he first met, appropriately, in the Laurentian library in Florence), Ellen Glasgow, Wyndham Lewis, E. M. Forster, André Gide, all the Sitwells, and Virginia Woolf.

Wing was a member of the Grolier Club and of the Bibliographical Societies of America, London, Cambridge, Oxford, and Edinburgh. He wrote articles and reviews for the *Yale University Library Gazette,* the *Yale Review,* the *Saturday Review of Literature,* and the *William and Mary Quarterly.* He died in Woodbridge, Connecticut, on October 8, 1972.

His research notes are available to scholars in the Yale Library; they form the basis of the revision of his STC, sponsored by the Modern Language Association of America.

REFERENCE

Katherine Cveljo, "Wing, Donald Goddard," *Dictionary of American Library Biography* (1978).

TIMOTHY J. CRIST

Winsor, Justin
(1831–1897)

Justin Winsor, American librarian and historian, is probably best remembered for his efforts to make libraries more accessible to their users. He was a founder and first President of the American Library Association.

Winsor was born in Boston, Massachusetts, on January 2, 1831, one of five children of Nathaniel Winsor, a prosperous merchant. Descendents of English settlers, the Winsor family had lived in the Boston area since the early 1700s. As a child Justin was somewhat introverted and very fond of reading; he was also quite independent and inclined to rebel against authority. As a result, he was often in difficulty at school and was sent to a boarding school at the age of 10 with the hope that a more structured situation would benefit him.

Winsor, however, intensely disliked the uniformity that prevailed there and enjoyed neither his boarding school days nor his later studies at the Boston Latin School. Although intelligent, he was judged a poor student since he preferred to concentrate on his own projects rather than school assignments. He developed an aversion to memorization from textbooks that lasted throughout his life. Similarly, Winsor's student days at Harvard College were not distinguished. His rejection of the prescribed curriculum led to his leaving in January 1852 without graduating, though 15 years later he was awarded a degree in recognition of his scholarly writings.

His career as a historian began in 1849 with the publication, during his freshman year at Harvard, of *A History of the Town of Duxbury, Massachusetts . . . .* The material for this work had been collected on family trips to Duxbury while visiting relatives. On those visits Winsor not only gathered information but also drew maps of the town to scale. He showed an early interest in cartography, a field in which he later became a recognized authority.

After leaving Harvard, Winsor traveled and studied in Europe for almost a year. He settled in Boston, devoting his time to writing poetry, short pieces of fiction, and literary criticism. Upon his return from Europe, Winsor became engaged to Caroline Tufts Barker, of his Harvard class of 1853; they were married on December 18, 1855. Marriage tended to expand his somewhat limited social contacts, and although he had never enjoyed churchgoing in his youth, he began to attend the Church of the Unity (Unitarian) in Boston and even compiled a small volume of hymns to be used by the congregation.

Boston Public Library. Rejected for military service during the Civil War because of poor eyesight, Winsor continued to spend most of his time in literary pursuits, becoming well known in Boston and New York for his critical writing, which appeared regularly in leading newspapers and periodicals. In large part because of this prominence he was appointed to the Board of Trustees of the Boston Public Library in 1867 and, at 36, he was its youngest member.

The Boston Public Library, founded 12 years earlier, was the first large American library wholly supported by city taxes. It was then the yearly practice of the Board to appoint an Examining Committee of five city residents, chaired by a Trustee, to analyze and make recommendations on the operations of the library. Winsor was chosen to head the 1867 Committee.

Always a forthright person, Winsor presented clearly and concisely what he felt were the positive and negative aspects of the library operations. He commended the staff on the size of the collection and rate of accessions but noted the crowded conditions in the building, the lack of proper workrooms, and poor ventilation and insufficient lighting. Winsor also was greatly concerned over the circulation of books, which he felt was too low, and over the nature of the collection as compared with the nature of the reading public. Whereas fiction constituted only one-fourth of the collection, it accounted for two-thirds of the circulation at the time. He recommended setting up branch libraries to increase circulation and purchasing

ALA

Justin Winsor

more and better fiction titles to satisfy patron needs.

Charles Coffin Jewett, then Superintendent of the Library, died suddenly in January 1868; since the Assistant Superintendent was in poor health and could not assume control, the Trustees appointed Winsor as Temporary Superintendent. He took over the library administration so energetically and effectively, however, that they confirmed a regular appointment in February.

Winsor was by education a historian, with no experience or training as a librarian, but he had learned much in his few months as a Trustee. Always a humble person, he realized that he had risen rapidly considering his lack of training. The Trustees, however, had obtained a man with great administrative and executive talents, and the Boston Public Library expanded its services extensively during his leadership.

Among the innovations he brought to the library were the initiation of studies to identify the readers and what they read, in order better to serve their needs. Interlibrary loan procedures were instituted to obtain additional materials. He also supervised the repair and renovation of the existing building and established six branches.

Winsor's creation of a "shelf list" in card form in place of an accession ledger was widely adopted by other libraries, as was his system of "continuous inventory," which made unnecessary the closing of the library for a one-month inventory, as had been the earlier practice. He also opened the library on Sundays and reduced the age limit for borrowers. His guiding principle was always more and better service for the readers.

Harvard. Winsor's career as Superintendent came to an abrupt end when the City Council, exceeding its authority, reduced the salaries of all library staff members, including Winsor's. Winsor had received an offer of the post of Librarian at Harvard to replace the retiring John Langdon Sibley, and when some of the Boston City Council members reneged on the terms of a proposed salary designed to keep him at the Public Library, he resigned, annoyed, and accepted the Harvard position on July 11, 1877.

In his first annual report at Harvard, Winsor stated the principle that was to guide his work for the next 20 years: "I consider nothing more important than the provision of large classes of books to which unrestricted access can be had." Accordingly, he opened the stacks to students, an unusual practice at the time, and greatly extended the reserved-book system begun by Sibley.

He began to keep precise records of circulation, including them in his annual reports to the President. He had studies made of book use by the students and in 1887, ten years after he had become Librarian, could report that nine out of ten students were using the library, in contrast to five out of ten in 1876. Winsor pioneered in that kind of statistical analysis in library administration.

Other notable accomplishments at Harvard included designing call slips to be filled out by borrowers, thus speeding up circulation; initiating instruction in library use; devising a compact metal stack storage plan for the collections; promoting more effective participation of the faculty in book selection; exchanging serials holdings lists with other libraries; and reorganizing the administrative structure of the library to delegate more responsibility to each staff member.

An early advocate of the employment of women in libraries, Winsor, at a conference in 1877, urged his British colleagues to train more women for library work. He stated that graduates of Vassar and Wellesley, skilled in languages, were finding challenging positions within the American library system.

Winsor believed a university librarian should be both an administrator and a scholar, and his own career illustrated his philosophy. He continued to do historical research and to write and was considered a leading cartographer. While at Harvard he edited two important historical works: *The Memorial History of Boston* (four volumes, 1880–81) and *A Narrative and Critical History of America* (eight volumes, 1889). The more important of his own works include *Reader's Handbook of the American Revolution* (1879); *Christopher Columbus and How He Received and Imparted the Spirit of Discovery* (1891); *Cartier to Frontenac—Geographical Discovery in the Interior of North America in its Historical Relations, 1534–1700* (1894); *The Mississippi Basin* (1895); and *The Westward Movement* (1897).

Always active in professional organizations, Winsor was the American Library Association's first President, from 1876 to 1885, and President again in 1897, the year he died. He also helped found the *Library Journal*. Winsor foresaw a future in which librarians would be purveyors as well as preservers of knowledge, and his work in the profession was always directed toward that end.

Winsor died in Boston on October 22, 1897.

REFERENCES

Joseph A. Borome, "The Life and Letters of Justin Winsor" (Ph.D. dissertation, Columbia University, 1950). The most complete study of Winsor available, it presents Winsor's life history, treating in some detail his library career, and contains an extensive bibliography of periodical articles by and about Winsor.

Kenneth J. Brough, *Scholar's Workshop: Evolving Conceptions of Library Service* (1953). Details the history of four university libraries, covering the period of Winsor's tenure as Librarian at Harvard.

Robert E. Brundin, "Justin Winsor and the Liberalizing of the College Library," *Journal of Library History* (January 1975), pp. 57-70.

Wayne Cutler and Michael H. Harris, "Winsor, Justin," *Dictionary of American Library Biography* (1978).

Walter Muir Whitehill, *Boston Public Library: A Centennial History* (1956). Contains a 29-page chapter dealing with the decade of Winsor's superintendency of the Library.

Winsor, Justin, *Justin Winsor: Scholar-Librarian* (1980).

ROBERT E. BRUNDIN

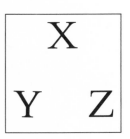

Yemen (Aden)

Yemen (Aden), a democratic people's republic in the Arabian Peninsula, is bounded by Yemen (Sana'a) on the west and northwest, Saudi Arabia on the north, Oman on the east, and the Gulf of Aden and the Arabian Sea on the south. Population (1984 est.) 2,147,000; area 287,680 sq.km. The official language is Arabic.

National Library Services. A law of 1976 established the Yemeni Center for Cultural Research, which aims at offering some functions of a national library. Among the objectives of the Center are the collection and publication of the Yemeni national heritage; the gathering and preservation of manuscripts, documents, periodicals, and other materials relating to Yemeni culture and history; and administering a central library. The Center is organized into sections for manuscripts, microfilming, publishing, printing, museums, and the library. The Center's Library possesses about 2,000 volumes on Yemeni affairs.

Academic Libraries. Aden University has five college libraries and a central library in an early stage of development. The Central Library has a collection of about 2,000 volumes. The Library of the Higher College of Education, founded in 1970, possesses about 15,000 volumes, of which 10,000 are in Arabic. The Library of the College of Medicine, established in 1975, has 5,000 volumes, mostly in Spanish, a language not spoken in the country. The Library of the Higher Technical Institute, established in 1952, maintains a collection of some 10,000 volumes that are mostly duplicate copies. The Library of Nasser College for Agricultural Sciences, founded in 1972, possesses about 6,000 volumes. The Library of the College of Economics and Administration contains 2,000 volumes. The academic libraries in Aden University are staffed by nonprofessional personnel. Most of the library holdings are not processed; its collections are not catalogued but only registered. The libraries began to reclassify their collections according to the Dewey Decimal Classification.

Public Libraries. The public library system is not well developed enough to support the adult education campaign in the country. The Miswat Public Library in Aden and the People's Library at Al-Mukalla, Hadramawt, are the largest public libraries. The Miswat Public Library, with a collection of about 30,000 volumes, was established in 1953 and is administered by Aden Municipality. The People's Library of Hadramawt, established in 1930, is administered by the Ministry of Culture.

School Libraries. Although some secondary schools possess sizable collections of books, they are not well organized because of the lack of qualified school librarians in the country.

Special Libraries. The Educational Research Center of the Ministry of Education established a Section for Documentation and Libraries that collects and exchanges educational documents. The Teachers' Club has a library of more than 2,000 volumes.

MOHAMED M. EL HADI*

Yemen (Sana'a)

Yemen (Sana'a), a republic in the Arabian Peninsula, is surrounded by Saudi Arabia on the north and east,

Yemen (Aden) on the south, and the Red Sea on the west. Population (1984 est.) 6,375,000; area 200,000 sq.km. The official language is Arabic.

National Library. The National Library in Sana'a was founded in 1968 with the establishment of the General Organization for Antiquities and National Library and is under the auspices of the presidency of the Yemen Arab Republic. All printed books that were found in the palaces of the deposed kingdom were transferred to this library, while the Arabic manuscripts remained in the Library of the Great Mosque in Sana'a (not open to the public). The country lacked a deposit law and a national bibliography; the publishing industry was almost nonexistent in the 1980s.

Academic Library. The only academic library is that of the Sana's University, established in 1971 with financial aid from the Kuwaiti government. The Central Library and the college libraries of the University are being developed. A few recruited personnel from other Arab countries direct and organize the book collections in these libraries.

Public Libraries. The General Organization of Antiquities and National Library is responsible for all public libraries in the country. The Library of the Great Mosque, founded by Iman Ahmed in 1925, was the first public library and was known as Al-Awqaf Library. After the Yemeni Revolution of 1962, the private library of Iman Yehia and all manuscripts in the libraries housed in the palaces of deposed princes were transferred and preserved in the Library of the Great Mosque. The Library's manuscript collection totals about 10,000 volumes and is microfilmed by the Arab League with the aid of Unesco. Other public libraries are in such cities as Taiz, Hijah, and Al-Hudayduh.

School Libraries. Few secondary schools have book collections for their students. School librarianship was not developed because of the lack of adequate funding and professional library education.

Special Libraries. The Central Library of the Ministry of Education, the Library of the Central Planning Agency, founded in 1976, and the Library of the National Institute of Public Administration, founded in 1973, offer special library services to their employees and to all those interested in their collections.

MOHAMED M. EL HADI*

Young Adult Services

HISTORY

Young adult services emerged as a specialty in public libraries in the early 20th century because pioneer children's librarians became concerned that all their personalized work to encourage reading and lifelong learning in the newly established children's rooms would be undermined once their young patrons went on to the adult sections of the library. Compulsory formal schooling ended for most adolescents at 8th grade, leaving the public library as their only adult educational option. Increased numbers of young people were drawn to urban areas by immigration and industrialization. In accord with the social philosophy of the Progressive Era reformers, these early advocates of library services to young people saw the public library as a place where immigrant youth could become "Americanized" and where all idle youth could find a cultured haven from the frequent vicissitudes of urban street life.

The first viable young adult program in the United States was begun at the New York Public Library under the direction of Mabel Williams, an adult reference librarian recruited in New England by New York Public's first children's services coordinator, Anne Carroll Moore. Looking forward to the era of compulsory secondary schooling, Williams's department was initially called Work with Schools. Her job, much like that of any contemporary YA librarian's, was to see that the emerging school-related needs of high-school students were met in the adult sections of the New York Public Library and, at the same time, to call teachers' and adolescents' attention to the rich resources available to them in the Library.

Williams established in 1929 a publication that continues today—*Books for Young People* (now *Books for the Teenage*). Her philosophy, as stated in the preface to that first list, still delineates the essential difference between young adult services in the public library and those in the school library:

This list is primarily for use in the adult sections of the Library, to suggest books to boys and girls when they are first transferred from the Children's Rooms. It is not expected to replace any of the lists now used by the schools. High School lists are naturally affected by curriculum and the desire to give pupils an opportunity of knowing all forms of literature before leaving school. Furthermore, their use is dependent not only on inclination but also on compulsion, because of the various checking-up methods used in the schools. This list, on the other hand, includes only those books which boys and girls are known to have enjoyed either through their own discovery or the suggestion of a friend, a teacher, a librarian, or through the impetus received from book talks or reading clubs (*Branch Library Book News,* October 1929, p 114).

Ultimately, Williams's program, enchanced by her successor, Margaret Scoggin, through the establishment of the Nathan Straus Branch Library for Children and Young People, emerged as a fully developed separate department, widely emulated elsewhere in large urban and suburban public library systems.

Definitions. A young adult is formally defined nationally by YASD as "a person who no longer sees him/herself as a child, but whom society does not yet see as an adult." The "statistical invisibility" of this client group in public libraries led to discussions about a national definition based on grade in school or chronological age or both. For practical purposes, young adults are adolescents, defined as "persons in the second decade of human life" by *Adolescence,* the oldest interdisciplinary research journal devoted to this part of the life span.

Young adult services is a cross-functional specialty concept that attempts to apply all the technical skills of contemporary librarianship to the interrelated developmental and informational needs of adolescents, regardless of setting, so as to

promote the healthy development of adolescents through organized exposure to materials and information experiences related to this part of the life cycle, to help create the circumstances under which adolescents might become functioning adults at home with themselves, their communities, and the world (Mary K. Chelton, "Develop-

mentally Based Performance Measures for Young Adult Services," *Top of the News,* Fall 1984, p. 43).

Recognizing that the social and interpersonal context in which learning takes place is vital during the rapid changes of adolescence, and that this is not only the period during which many major life decisions are made, but also the period during which library usage frequently stops for good, YA services emphasize the availability of a mature, technically skilled, professionally trained librarian who likes and understands the age group. Services based on Williams's model that mistakenly emphasized facilities and the location of the collection over the personality and skill of the librarian providing this service have failed regularly. The young adult librarian is considered pivotal in young adult services.

The term "young adult novel," often used interchangeably with "adolescent novel," "teen novel," "junior novel," "adolescent fiction," and "adolescent literature," refers to a particular genre of realistic fiction usually told in the first person by an adolescent protagonist who is attempting to work through some sort of adolescent problem, usually with minimal help from adults. Despite its wide usage in library and English education literature, the term in no way encompasses all the genres of possible interest to adolescents, and the context in which it is used should be noted.

A "young adult program," as opposed to the *total* YA service program of which any individual program would be a part, is defined as a library-sponsored or cosponsored event, inside or outside the library itself, which appeals to a group rather than an individual. A program may be informational or recreational in nature and can be combined with or totally divorced from traditional print materials promotions and other traditional library activities.

Materials. Contemporary young adult materials cut across all formats and media categories, depending on why, how, and for what setting they are chosen. What they have in common is an immediate, topical, personal appeal for the adolescent user. As one critic has eloquently put it:

Teenagers are not just older children. With the onset of puberty comes a shift in their relationship to information. Where before they had accepted almost everything adults said, now they come to a point where they must sort out the data they have collected—reject some of what they have been told, accept other ideas as their own, and begin to put it all into a coherent whole that expresses who they are. This process is maddening to adults, but absolutely necessary if young adults are not going to end up puddings on legs. Remember always that the basic YA question is "Who am I, and what am I going to do about it?" In the turmoil of adolescence, the young adult no longer has much patience for new factual data, for the classics, for anything which doesn't bear on the answer to The Question (Patty Campbell, *Top of the News,* Winter 1979, pp. 161-162).

When young adult services began, libraries consisted primarily of hardback books, and the challenge was to identify titles from the adult collection that provided a conceptual "bridge" to adult reading and interests. While that is still true to some extent, the emergence of a flourishing paperback publishing industry, coupled with an increasing number of skilled writers and editors in juvenile publishing departments interested in adolescents, has made the YA librarians' job of book selection easier. The overwhelming popularity of the mass market paperback format has made "young adult" synonymous with "paperback" in both the publishing industry and libraries.

While the forerunners of the modern adolescent novel can be traced back to popular literature of the 19th century, the two novels which have most influenced the genre are *The Pilgrim* by Paul Zindel and *The Outsiders* by S. E. Hinton. The overwhelming, continued popularity of these stories with adolescents makes them contemporary classics, with literary conventions widely and successfully imitated, and in some cases surpassed by succeeding authors. Furthermore, Hinton's youth as a first novelist has spawned a continual search for another adolescent writer as good as she was at the same age. Some particularly interesting examples of the genre include *The Chocolate War* by Robert Cormier, *Fast Sam, Cool Clyde and Stuff* by Walter Dean Myers, *Forever* and *Tiger Eyes* by Judy Blume, *Ludell and Willie* by Brenda Wilkinson, *Center Line* by Joyce Sweeney, *Hold Fast* by Kevin Major, *Father Figure* by Richard Peck, *Home Before Dark* by Sue Ellen Bridgers, *Someone to Love* by Norma Fox Mazer, *Running Loose* by Chris Crutcher, *Is That You, Miss Blue?* by M. E. Kerr, *Annie on My Mind* by Nancy Garden, *The Last Mission* by Harry Mazer, *Killing Mr. Griffin* by Lois Duncan, and *The Great Santini* by Pat Conroy.

Besides an increased interest in real life problems seen in the mature themes of contemporary adolescent novels, young adults enjoy testing their newly developing thinking abilities by reading speculative fiction genres—science fiction, fantasy, and mysteries. One critic has even said that "The Golden Age of science fiction is twelve (David Hartwell, *Top of the News,* Fall 1982, pp. 39-53)." Attracted by good plotting, technical ingenuity, and the romantic optimism of most science fiction, the very brightest and most literate young adult readers are inevitably fans, and frequently amateur writers, of the genre. This interest spills over into fantasy role-playing games such as *Dungeons and Dragons,* which are not only borrowed from but played in many libraries. Interest in science fiction and fantasy is further fed through media tie-ins such as *Dune, Star Wars, E.T.,* and *2001.*

Mysteries and the occult seem to provide a transition between the purely realistic and the purely speculative, with the popularity of adult author Stephen King paramount. Several publishers have tried formula-written series with elements of both adolescent novels and adult horror fantasy, in an attempt to appeal to YA interests while appeasing adult concerns over language and themes, but adolescent interest in the gruesome continues unabated if the average age of movie audiences for *Halloween, Prom Night,* and *Friday the 13th* is any example.

(Top) Ninth-grade students preparing a social studies report using microfilmed resources from school library media center. An Irving, Texas, Public librarian helping students use a periodical index (center). While a student videotapes (right) a parent volunteer at West Frederick Junior High in Maryland leads a book discussion.

No group among any library's clientele is more rabidly addicted to music as a shared generational experience than young adults, fed by cable television's music video stations and several enormously successful commercial films with musical scores about adolescent "outsiders," such as *Saturday Night Fever* and *Footloose*. With the major moviegoing audience in the U.S. under 30, relevant library materials for young adults must now include now only popular music in audio but video formats, as well as videocassettes of motion pictures. A good example of an ideal YA videocassette is *The Making of Michael Jackson's Thriller*.

Adolescent fascination with computers has been fueled by video games, increased emphasis on computer literacy and instruction in schools, a massive increase in home computer ownership, and computer camps specifically designed for young people. School libraries particularly reflect this change, with an increased proportion of collection development, attention, and resources going to instructional computer software such as *Magic Windows*. Computer mania has also spawned various series of "programmable" books in which YA readers can choose to direct the storyline for themselves. The most famous of these is called, appropriately, *Choose Your Own Adventure*.

In a reaction both to the frequently depressing realism of the adolescent novels of the 1970s and to declining library budgets, formula "squeaky clean" paperback romances for teenagers marketed directly to trade outlets emerged in the 1980s, creating dismay among YA librarians who were upset at their popularity among teenage girls and at the inadequacy of previously accepted selection criteria to accommodate them. It is obvious, however, that any library not circulating teen romances is ignoring a major female adolescent interest. Unfortunately, nothing with equally predictable male appeal at the same reading level has appeared.

Self-help materials, especially those concerning sexuality, body image, and relationships, are perennially popular, often in inexpensive pamphlet formats such as *What's Happening Now*. The self-help genre has also come to include short "trigger" films depicting open-ended situations designed to promote YA group discussion of sexual decision making. Other major self-help categories include very topical subjects such as how to do specific dances or play specific games, as well as all the career and college choice materials, many of which now have computerized versions. One publisher offers hundreds of college catalogues to libraries on microfiche.

While religion has always been of interest to adolescents, it has usually only been represented in library collections in the popular true stories of people, frequently sports figures who overcome disabilities through religious faith. The resurgence of religious interest in the 1970s has led to more serious consideration of materials from religious presses depicting not only the traditional overcoming odds stories such as *Joni*, but also conversion experiences such as John Benton's series from Revell, or the engaging *What Now, McBride?* by Gary Davis from Randall. Jewish survival stories from World War II continue as staples in YA collections.

Facilities. Accepted guidelines for YA-serving facilities are few but basic. YA specialists advise that a YA collection should never be in or near the children's room in a public library and elementary and secondary school libraries should never be merged, if possible. For a group who "no longer see themselves as children," such juxtapositions are doomed to failure. Except for brief periods, it is inappropriate in public libraries to segregate adolescents totally from patrons of other ages and thus reinforce the age segregation forced on them in schools and the larger culture. Since peer relationships are of paramount developmental importance in adolescence, facilities should be planned primarily for groups as opposed to individuals, except for the early adolescent seeking a respite from rapid growth, or the student who cannot study in a noisy home. Mass market paperbacks are the most appealing print format for young adults outside comics, and publishing sales wisdom advises displaying them on racks with the covers out. Given a knowledgeable, hospitable staff, and the right materials in the right formats, almost any facilities based on these guidelines will work with young adults.

Services. Young adult services are by definition intended to be developmentally responsive to the needs of adolescents, and the functional form they take at any particular time depends on the particular library and user. Historically, YA services were first seen predominantly as readers' advisory—the right book for the right kid at the right time—preferably something slightly more enriching, "adult," and world-expanding than what was previously read. An arsenal of promotional techniques—booktalking, reading clubs, reading lists, discussion groups, radio spots, and so on—buttress this aspect of YA services to this day. As compulsory secondary schooling came to dominate the adolescent experience, however, school-related reference services were offered to students and their teachers, supported by class visits, one-to-one and group library instruction, topical "pathfinders" on frequently requested topics, and most recently homework hotlines and tutors. With the emergence of alternative services for troubled youths in the 1960s, and a greater awareness of the supportive help needed desperately by a minority of adolescents, libraries responded with information and referral services. While various group discussions and presentations have always been part of YA services, these "programs" did not come to be seen as an information end in themselves, rather than a means of encouraging more traditional library book use, until the 1960s. Similarly, the passage of a youth participation resolution at the 1978 White House Conference on Libraries and the subsequent publication of *Youth Participation in School and Public Libraries* enhanced awareness of the value of youth participation as a social learning process and helped to make it part of the young adult services concept.

Programs. Young adult programs are presented for many reasons, the most common of which are to promote a more favorable image of the library as a place interested in adolescents, to offer information in a shared group setting that may not be available to young adults in any other form, and to use the program as a showcase for YA talent and energy. Generic types of programs are discussion groups, workshops, talks, clubs, film showings, concerts, and large-scale galas, often merged with one another in a one-time presentation or as a series.

Examples of just a few successful programs reported in library literature include the King Arthur Festival at the Virginia Beach (Virginia) Public Library, the annual Golden Pen Awards chosen by the Young Adult Advisory Committee of the Spokane Public Library to honor favorite authors, Enoch Pratt Free Library's Bookjack summer reading game program in Baltimore, the Bop Till You Drop Readathon at the Albany (New York) Public Library, the Kansas oral history program of the Topeka West High School Library, the fantasy games playing clubs in the Contra Costa County (California) Library System and the Mesa (Arizona) Public Library, the computer tutor program at the Fairport (New York) Public Library, and the after-school survival skills program at the Hillsborough (North Carolina) Public Library.

Education and Research. Public library positions tend to be broadly classified without reference to a particular clientele, or rigidly defined only by technical function, and librarians serving young adults in public libraries almost inevitably feel underprepared for the experience. They clamor repeatedly for more attention to adolescent psychology in library schools. Schools accredited under the 1972 Standards adopted by ALA's Committee on Accreditation continue to emphasize the general body of knowledge any librarian needs, and specialized YA services are usually relegated to the status of electives, often not taught by fulltime faculty, for all students except those intending to be school librarians. School library media certification requirements vary widely by state, and may be awarded by non-ALA-accredited schools.

The Education Committee of ALA's Young Adult Services Division prepared a list of competencies anyone being trained for any entry-level YA position should be able to demonstrate, regardless of how or where they got them. The document reiterates the necessity of having a person with a high level of general technical skill combined with a specific knowledge of how to apply it to this age group.

Young adult services remain the least researched area of librarianship, largely because of the lack of a national quantitative definition of "young adults," an indifferent audience for research reporting, and few resources in library schools or among practitioners to support such research. Despite these problems, YA studies exist that examine reading preferences, library usage patterns, library cooperation patterns, information-seeking behavior, historical development of the YA specialty, and local service definitions and resource allocations.

Trends and Issues. The most famous censorship attempts inevitably occur in the young adult services area, especially in schools. Unless the nature of adolescence or materials and subjects of interest to adolescents change dramatically, this is likely to continue. The censorship attempts usually reflect value or generational struggles within the larger culture, specific communities, or individual families, the library becoming a scapegoat or the means toward a larger political agenda.

Budget-cutting initiatives may force school and public library cooperation to the point of common facilities, unless better voluntary cooperation can be documented or a better case made for supporting two seemingly similar institutions with very different service missions for a shared clientele.

Momentum toward making all public library positions "generalist" may eradicate the young adult services specialty, unless some means of providing replacement leadership, at least in those libraries, is found. Probably some "generalists" will favor adolescents and attempt to serve them well regardless of job title, much as adult reference and children's librarians do now. The "generalist" movement dramatizes the need for written documentation of YA services in professional literature so that carefully developed knowledge is not entirely lost, or assigned arbitrarily only to school librarians.

Fertility was down in all the developed countries in the first half of the 1980s, making youth an ever smaller proportion of their populations. Fertility rates among ethnic groups vary dramatically, however, and services designed for a group now in the majority may have to be rethought for others considered minorities. If current trends continue in the U.S., for example, the young adult services population of the next century will be overwhelmingly Black and Hispanic, and in the Soviet Union primarily Asian and not European. The effects of these fertility shifts have yet to be fully felt by the YA services community, but they are sure to be dramatic.

REFERENCES

Miriam Braverman. *Youth, Society, and the Public Library* (1979).
Dorothy Broderick. *Librarians' Guide to Young Adult Paperbacks* (1982).
Margaret Edwards. *The Fair Garden and the Swarm of Beasts, the Library and the Young Adult* (1974).
Amelia H. Munson. *An Ample Field* (1950).
Voice of Youth Advocates (bimonthly).
Youth Participation in School and Public Libraries (1983).

MARY K. CHELTON

Yuan, T'ung-li
(1895–1965)

Yuan T'ung-li, Chinese librarian, educator, and library administrator, was a pioneer in the modern library movement and an exponent of closer cultural ties between East and West. He proposed large-scale exchange programs not only for librarians but also for students.

Yuan T'ung-li was born in 1895, the second son of a government official in Hsushui, Hebei, China. At an early age Yuan showed an avid interest in books and scholarship. He graduated from National Beijing (then Peking) University in 1916 and immediately began work as Assistant Librarian at Tsinghua College. He became Acting Librarian the following year and was largely responsible for construction of the College's new library building.

In 1920 Yuan went to the United States for advanced studies; he received the A.B. degree from Columbia University in 1922 and the B.L.S. degree in 1923 from New York State Library School in Albany. He also spent a year doing postgraduate work at the University of London's Institute of Historical Research. During this period he spent three summers at the Library of Congress helping to catalogue its Chinese collections. In 1924 he returned to China to become Librarian of Guandong (then Kwangtung) University. He became Librarian and Professor of

Bibliography at Beijing University in 1925, and when the Beijing National Library was organized in 1926, he became its Librarian, with Liang Ch'i-ch'ao as Director. In 1929 the Metropolitan Library and the old National Library were merged to form the National Library of Beijing, and Ts'ai Yuan-p'ei was made its Director, with Yuan as Associate Director. Later Yuan served successively as Acting Director and Director, helping to build it into the largest library in China and one of the largest in the world.

Many library activities in China were disrupted by the Sino-Japanese War, and in 1942 Yuan T'ung-li moved to China's wartime capital, Chongqing (then Chungking), where he set up an office of the National Library of Beijing. There he also engaged in many cultural cooperation projects with Great Britain and the U.S. on behalf of the Chinese government. In 1945 he was an adviser to the Chinese delegation to the United Nations Conference on International Organization in San Francisco, and in May of that year he received an honorary degree from the University of Pittsburgh.

During the 1920s and 1930s he was credited with the discovery of rare works and manuscripts of Chinese literature, including the remains of a vast encyclopedia from the Ming Dynasty, the *Yung lo ta tien*, long thought to have been destroyed, but of which he compiled successive censuses of surviving extant volumes. Among his most important contributions to the library profession was his introduction to China of such Western practices as interlibrary loan, a photocopying service, exchange of materials with foreign countries, and the compilation of union catalogues and serial lists.

In 1949 Yuan went to the United States, and from 1951 to 1953 he served as Chief Bibliographer of Stanford Research Institute. He rejoined the Library of Congress in 1957 in the Descriptive Cataloging Division and served in the Subject Cataloging Division from 1958 to the time of his retirement on January 15, 1965. His service with the Library of Congress totaled eight and a half years but spanned more than 43. He died in Washington, D.C., February 6, 1965.

Among his more significant publications are *China in Western Literature* (1958), *Russian Works on China, 1918–1960, in American Libraries* (1961), and various guides to doctoral dissertations by Chinese students.

CHI WANG

Yugoslavia

Yugoslavia, a socialist federal republic in eastern Europe, is bordered by Austria and Hungary on the north, Romania on the northeast, Bulgaria on the east, Greece on the south, Albania and the Adriatic Sea on the southwest, and Italy on the west. Population (1984 est.) 23,053,000; area 255,804 sq.km. Yugoslavia comprises six republics: Bosnia-Hercegovina, Croatia, Macedonia, Montenegro, Serbia, and Slovenia. The official languages are Serbo-Croatian, Slovenian, and Macedonian.

History. In Yugoslavia, as in other nations, the development of libraries came under the aegis of the Church during the Middle Ages. In monasteries and bishoprics books were written, copied, and illuminated primarily for the Church and then for secular purposes. Many monasteries existed in Serbia, among them Studenica, which was founded in the second half of the 12th century, Žiča dating from the first half of the 13th century, Dečani (1327-1335), where a remainder of the library still exists, and Manasija (1407-1418). In Croatia there was the famous Benedictine Abbey in Zadar (986). In Slovenia the Cistercian convents at Stična (1136), Konstajevica (1234), and Bistra (1260) served as libraries in the Middle Ages. Among medieval bishoprics in Croatia, the Zagreb See with its old Chapter library is still in existence. The Turkish invaders of the 15th century greatly limited the growth of libraries in areas under their domination. In Bosnia, where some of the people embraced Islam, Muslim cultural institutions appeared. In 1537 Gazi Husrevbeg set up a library for the medresa (school) he had founded in Sarajevo.

During the 19th century the Southern Slavs experienced a national revival and with it a new growth in libraries. In 1832 the Serbs founded the National Library in Beograd (Belgrade). By 1816 the Academy Library in Zagreb, Croatia, was taking on the role of a national library. In Slovenia the Ljubljana Library had already developed in to the main and central library for Carniola. In Montenegro the State Library was founded in 1896 at Cetinje.

National Libraries. Each of the six republics has a national library. These are: in Bosnia and Hercegovina, the National and University Library of Bosnia and Hercegovina, Sarajevo; Croatia, the National and University Library, Zagreb; Macedonia, the National and University Library Kliment Ohridski, Skopje; Montenegro, the Central National Library Djordje Crnojevic, Cetinje; Serbia, the National Library of Serbia, Beograd; Slovenia, the National and University Library, Ljubljana. The two autonomous provinces also have national libraries: Kosovo, the National Library of Kosovo, in Priština and Vojvodina, the Library of Matica Srpska, Novi Sad.

All the national libraries build up their collections by legal deposits of all published works throughout the whole country. The national library of each republic or province takes special care about the completeness of issues from its own area as well as materials referring to its area found in libraries of other republics and abroad. National libraries also purchase the outstanding works of world literature and sources in all branches of science.

The Yugoslav Bibliographical Institute develops the bibliography of Yugoslavia, covering books, pamphlets, and music from 1950 and serial publications from 1956. Series A includes articles from the social sciences; Series B, natural, applied, medical, and technical sciences; and Series C, arts, philology, and literature. The national libraries of all republics and provinces deal with bibliography, producing mainly national retrospective bibliographies. The National and University Library in Ljubljana, Slovenia, issues the "Slovenian Bibliography of Journals and Books"; the National and University Library in Zagreb, Croatia, maintains its national bibliography; as does the National and University Library Kliment Ohridski in Skopje, Macedonia.

Academic Libraries. National libraries are at the same time central university libraries except in

Serbia, Vojvodina, and Montenegro. There are a large number of academic libraries in each of the republics: central faculty libraries, seminar libraries, and libraries at research institutions with extensive book holdings of domestic and foreign scientific literature. Scientific libraries include those under the scope of republican academies of sciences, such as the Library of the Serbian Academy of Sciences and Arts in Belgrade, Library of the Yugoslav Academy of Sciences and Arts in Zagreb, Library of the Academy of Sciences and Arts of Slovenia in Ljubljana, Library of the Macedonian Academy of Sciences and Arts in Skopje, Library of the Association of Science and Arts of Montenegro in Titograd, and Library of the Academy of Sciences and Arts of Bosnia and Hercegovina in Sarajevo. These libraries collect publications issued by academies of sciences, universities, and scientific and professional associations in all parts of the world.

Public Libraries. Public libraries provide the basic library service in the areas they serve—in regions, communities, and local communities. These libraries provide at the same time the institutional support for educational and cultural activities. More than 2,000 public libraries held more than 24,000,000 volumes in the early 1980s.

Special Libraries. Special libraries are attached to industrial, social, scientific, and cultural institutions and organizations. In Yugoslavia at the beginning of the 1980s there were more than 1,000 special libraries collecting scientific and technical literature from all branches of science.

The Profession. There are five major library associations for librarians and library workers in Yugoslavia: Savez društava bibliogrkara Jugoslavije (Federation of Library Associations) in Sarajevo; Savez bibliotečkih radnika Srbije (Union of Serbian Library Workers), in Belgrade; Croatian Library Association, National and University Library, in Zagreb; Društvo Bibliotekara BiH (Librarian's Society of Bosnia and Hercegovina); and Sojuz na Društvata na Bibliotekarite na Makedonija (Union of Librarians' Associations of Macedonia), Skopje. Librarians from all republic and provincial libraries are through their associations members of the League of the Librarians Association of Yugoslavia. The seat of the League is changed every two years. National libraries of all the republics and provinces together with the Yugoslav

Bibliographical Institute are associated in the League of Yugoslav National Libraries. Its seat is changed every two years also. The Association joins forces active in establishing a library-information network at the Yugoslav level. National libraries provide complete coverage of the network. Consideration is given to recommendations of international organizations of which Yugoslavia is a member (Unesco, ISO, IFLA, FID, and others), and they are modified according to Yugoslav social, economical, cultural, and other local conditions. The National Library of Serbia, for instance, maintained a computerized union catalogue of foreign periodicals in the libraries of Serbia.

RICHARD L. KORT

Zaire

Zaire, a republic of equatorial Africa (formerly the Democratic Republic of the Congo, which was a Belgian colony until 1960), is bordered on the north by the Central African Republic and the Sudan, on the east by Uganda, Rwanda, Burundi, and Tanzania, on the south by Zambia and Angola, and on the west by the Congo, the Cabinda enclave of Angola, and the Atlantic Ocean. Population (1984 est.) 32,084,000; area 2,344,885 sq.km. Although the official language is French, four national languages are recognized: Swahili, Tshiluba, Lingala, and Kikongo. More than 200 Pygmy, Bantu, and Nilo-Saharan languages and dialects are spoken throughout the country.

National Library. The Bibliothèque centrale du Congo, founded in 1949, became the Bibliothèque Nationale after independence in 1960. The National Library, in Kinshasa-Gombe, is both a governmental library and a public library. Works published in or about Zaire are required by law to be deposited there. In addition, as of February 1950, two copies of all government publications had to be deposited. Although government publications comprise a large share of the total number of volumes, the Library also has an important Africana collection and extensive holdings in economics, social sciences, and law. During fighting in the area, many libraries lost much of their stock. In 1980 holdings totaled some 146,000 volumes. The Archives Nationales, a section connected to the national library, attempts to acquire all administrative and historical archives relating to

Libraries in Yugoslavia (1980)

Type	Administrative units	Service points	Volumes in collections	Annual expenditures (dinar)	Population served[a]	Professional staff	Total staff
National	8	--	8,103,000	12,061,639,000	103,836	343	684
Academic	398	411	10,647,000	226,476,000[b]	682,643	861[c]	1,030[c]
Public	2,101	--	24,123,000	--	4,367,686	672	2,639
School	8,458	8,458	29,981,000	--	4,200,000	--	--
Special	1,072	--	10,881,000	--	313,831	--	--
Nonspecialized	11	11	3,485,000	--	17,201	--	--

[a]Registered borrowers.
[b]Acquisitions only. Expenditure measured in millions.
[c]Excludes part-time staff.

Source: Unesco, *Statistical Yearbook*, 1984.

Zaire. In 1955 the Library began a monthly accessions list, which later become the *Bibliographie nationale*. The Library also issued a retrospective national bibliography of its acquisitions that had been published between 1871 and 1960. Efforts were begun to establish a union catalogue of all the libraries of Zaire, but political turmoil curtailed such library activities. Book publishing in Zaire is limited.

Academic Libraries. In 1971 the three universities of Zaire were incorporated into the Université Nationale du Zaire (UNAZA): the Université Lovanium in Kinshasa, founded in 1949; the Université libre du Congo in Kisangani (1963); and the Université officielle du Congo in Lubumbashi (1956). Each campus has a central library; those at Kinshasa and Lubumbashi also have many departmental libraries. The library at Kisangani has, in addition to its central library, faculty libraries of Science and Education. The Bibliothèque centrale, Kinshasa, holds approximately 300,000 volumes; the Bibliothèque centrale, Kisangani, 46,000 volumes; and the Bibliothèque centrale, Lubumbashi, 93,000 volumes. Holdings are primarily in French, with a considerably smaller number of volumes in English and in African and Arabic languages. The many departmental libraries are of varying sizes and are all catalogued at the central libraries. Interlibrary loans are available among the university libraries, research centers, and specialized libraries.

Public Libraries. There is no centralized public library system in Zaire. Individual public libraries throughout the provinces are administered through the local offices of the Ministry of Fine Arts and Cultural Affairs, which is actually a division of the Bibliothèque Nationale. Most of these libraries are subscription libraries, which require a fee for use of their materials. Holdings are very limited and, for the most part, are not widely used. The illiteracy rate is high. A list of public libraries was published by the Ministry: *Liste des bibliothèques publiques* (1971). The size of the country and limited communication systems, as well as political unrest, worked against the establishment of effective public library service.

Most schools in Zaire have been established through the missions, particularly the Catholic missions. Statistical and detailed information concerning existing libraries for school students were not available in the mid-1980s. Most schools did not have libraries.

Special Libraries. Most special libraries were established prior to independence in 1960. Many of the governmental ministries have their own libraries, with collections of works on Africa and on Zaire in particular. These libraries are especially important to researchers, as are those attached to major research centers, such as the Institut national pour l'étude et la recherche agronomique (INERA) at Yangambi, founded in 1933. The Library's holdings consist of approximately 44,000 technical and scientific volumes, 2,300 current periodicals, and about 3,000 maps and photographs. That library serves the agriculture department at the Kisangani campus. The Institut maintains several regional libraries. Also of importance are the libraries of the Institut de recherche scientifique. The Library, Documentation, and Publications section of the Institut Makanda Kabobi (IMK), established in 1974 in Kinshasa, houses approximately 10,000 volumes and has extensive newspaper clippings that relate to the Institute's work. The IMK was founded to train executive personnel, but its library is open to the public. Its collection is particularly strong in the humanities. Many of the institutes connected with the universities have extensive libraries. The central library of the Institut pedagogique national (IPN), founded in Kinshasa in 1961, houses approximately 37,000 volumes, primarily in French and English. The Instituts supérieurs pédagogiques (ISP) have libraries in at least ten provinces, many of which were established in the late 1960s. In addition, many libraries are affiliated with private companies, independent research institutes, and cultural centers of embassies and consulates.

The Profession. The Zairian Association of Archivists, Librarians, and Documentalists was established in Kinshasa on October 5, 1968. Its purpose is to promote library and documentation centers throughout the country and to establish technology and information science centers in Zaire. It is affiliated with IFLA, AIDBA, and FID. Meetings are held every three years. The Association publishes an official journal, *Mukanda: Bulletin des archives, bibliothèques et documentation du Zaire* (1975-), and issues proceedings of seminars and conferences.

Libraries in Zaire (1980)

Type	Administrative units	Service points	Volumes in collections	Annual expenditures (zaire)	Population served	Professional staff	Total staff
National	1	1	146,000	--	--	--	17
Academic	--	--	--	--	--	--	--
Public[a]	8	31	6,000	54,000[b]	9,238	--	45
School	--	--	--	--	--	--	--

[a]1977 data.
[b]Acquisitions only.

Source: Unesco, *Statistical Yearbook*, 1984.

Zambia

Zambia, a republic in south-central Africa, is bounded on the north by Zaire and Tanzania, on the east by Malawi, on the southeast by Mozambique, on the south by Zimbabwe, Botswana, and Namibia, and on the west by Zaire. Population (1978 est.) 5,514,000; area 752,614 sq.km. Many Bantu languages are spoken. Four major languages are Tonga, Bemba, Nyanja, and Lozi. The language of the administration is English.

History. The history of libraries in Zambia is linked with the colonial history of the country. Cultural traditions and beliefs of various ethnic groups were preserved through memory and repeated orally from generation to generation. The changeover from oral to the written word came with the arrival of missionaries who introduced Western education with its emphasis on reading and writing skills. The first missionary to arrive in Zambia, David Livingstone, introduced the first prototype library. Known as the "tin-truck" portable library, it was carried around during his travels in Zambia between 1853 and 1873.

The Livingstone subscription library was one among the first libraries established in Livingstone about 1908; and in the 1920s a number of small subscription libraries were set up in the townships such as Chipata, Kasama, Mongu, Mansa, Lusaka, Luanshya, Choma, and Ndola. Those libraries were used mostly by Europeans who could afford to pay membership and subscription fees.

The British South Africa Company, founded by Cecil Rhodes in 1889, ruled Zambia (formerly Northern Rhodesia) until 1924, and did almost nothing to provide and develop library services for the Africans. Similarly, the British colonial government, which ruled Zambia from 1924 to 1964, did not do much either except that some money from its Colonial Development and Welfare Fund was used to establish the Northern Rhodesia Publications Bureau in 1947. The Bureau, renamed Joint Publications Bureau of Northern Rhodesia and Nyasaland in 1948, introduced a country book-box library scheme in 1959 that provided the majority of Africans their first access to library services. In 1960 the Joint Publications Bureau received a grant-in-aid from the Ford Foundation toward the development of country-wide public library service in Zambia. This led to the establishment in 1962 of the Northern Rhodesia Library Service, which was subsequently renamed the Zambia Library Service.

Public library service in Zambia received very little government support and suffered from lack of public library legislation. Further contributing factors to disappointing development were unfavorable economic and environmental conditions resulting in the

National Archives of Zambia

Library of the National Archives of Zambia, Lusaka.

fall of prices of exports and rise in costs of imports; inadequate transport facilities; unproductive farming; lack of foreign exchange; and mounting inflation.

National Library and Archives. Although no national library was established by legislation, the University of Zambia (UNZA) Library serves the functions of a national library. Wherever possible, it extends its facilities and services to scientists and researchers beyond the University community from its holdings of 300,000 volumes. It is a depository for government and international publications and repository of printed official documents of the United Nations and its agencies. The Library has extensive collections of East African government publications, Zambiana (including oral history and archival materials), Africana, Livingstoniana, and material on former Portuguese territories in Southern and Central Africa, the Simon's Collection on African law, and University theses.

The Library of the National Archives of Zambia in Lusaka was developed into a relatively advanced reference and research center for the country. It has record centers in the nine provinces of the country. Its origin can be traced back to 1935 when the Archives of Zimbabwe was inaugurated and its services extended to Malawi and Zambia in 1946. An act establishing the National Archives of Zambia was passed in 1969.

The Archives Library has a total of 13,485

Libraries in Zambia (1982)

Type	Administrative units	Service points	Volumes in collections	Annual expenditures	Population served	Professional staff	Total staff
Academic	42	3	584,154	--	--	80	190
Public	24	15	866,913	--	--	58	245
Special	65	22	295,017	--	--	39	75

Source: Nawa Mwiya, *A Directory of Libraries in Zambia,* 3rd ed. (unpublished).

books, 360 foreign periodicals, 310 Zambian periodicals, and more than 20,000 archival files. The historical manuscripts in the archives include private papers of explorers, missionaries, administrators, and political figures dating back to 1877. Among the important collections are the papers and diaries of President Kenneth David Kaunda of the Republic of Zambia.

The Library has legal deposit rights and all the books and periodicals so received are registered and compiled annually into a *National Bibliography of Zambia,* published since 1970.

Academic Libraries. Almost all academic libraries of note are financed by the government of Zambia. The largest is that attached to the University of Zambia, established by an act of Parliament in 1965. The UNZA library system consists of the Main Library in Lusaka (250,000 volumes and 2,170 serials); the Medical Library, also in Lusaka (21,000 volumes and 283 periodicals); and the Ndola Campus Library established in 1978 some 320 kilometres from Lusaka (10,000 volumes and 200 serials) specializing in business, industrial, and environmental collections. A new library was being established in the mid-1980s at UNZA School of Veterinary Medicine in Lusaka.

Other academic libraries are those attached to institutions of higher learning, such as the Natural Resources Development College founded in Lusaka in 1964 (20,000 volumes, 1,500 serials, and 10,000 technical reports); Nkrumah Teachers College established in 1967 in Kabwe (19,000 volumes and 12 serials); Dag Hammarskjold Memorial Library established in 1963 at Mindolo Ecumenical Foundation in Kitwe (18,000 volumes and 60 serials); Zambia Institute of Technology, also in Kitwe, established in 1970 (17,000 volumes, 150 serials, and 800 technical reports); and David Livingstone Teachers College Resource Center established in 1978 in Livingstone (14,600 volumes, 16 serials, and 75 technical reports).

Public Libraries. The birth of the Zambia Library Service (Z.L.S.) in 1962 marks the rise and development of nationwide public Library service in Zambia. Its Headquarters Library is in Lusaka; there are seven regional libraries, in Chipata, Monze, Mansa, Kasama, Solwezi, Choma, and Mongu, and a branch library at Solwezi. The Headquarters Library contains 150,000 volumes and 200 serials. The average stock in each of the regional (provincial) libraries is 37,500 volumes and 10 serials. Z.L.S. serves 931 centers each with a collection ranging from 100 to 250 books in schools, governmental, and parastatal organizations in urban and rural areas.

Despite shortcomings in the development of public libraries, the Z.L.S. through a network of provincial libraries, district libraries, and library centers makes books freely available on loan wherever possible in urban and rural areas.

Zambia also has municipal public libraries that operate autonomously serving the residents of the urban areas of Lusaka, Kabwe, Livingstone, Luanshya, and Chingola. Although the municipal libraries are administered and operated separately from the Z.L.S., they both receive funds from the central government. The municipal libraries are financed by the Ministry of Local Government and the Z.L.S. by the Ministry of Education. The services of both are available to all in the country.

The services of the municipal libraries and the Z.L.S. are supplemented by the libraries run by the United States Information Service in Lusaka (15,000 volumes and 100 serials) and the British Council libraries in Lusaka and Ndola (25,000 volumes and 200 serials). These libraries are administered and financed separately by their respective governments and serve as both public and special libraries. They are popular with schoolchildren and with professional men and women.

School Libraries and Media Centers. The 931 centers served by the Z.L.S. provide library services to elementary and secondary schools. The municipal libraries in urban areas link their services to schools by providing mobile libraries, and the city of Lusaka Public Library has branches in the residential areas to attract schoolchildren to their libraries. In a survey carried out in December 1977, questionnaires were sent to 119 schools out of which only 81 replied, probably because 38 out of 119 schools did not have school libraries. Just over 51 percent (41) out of 78 responding schools had between 500 and 1,000 pupils. Almost the same number (39) had between 1,000 and 3,000 books. Taking the mean of both sets of figures would indicate approximately three times as many books as pupils. This situation has not changed much.

Special Libraries. Most of Zambia's 65 special libraries are owned and financed by the various government ministries. They enjoy good informal interlibrary cooperation with the University of Zambia libraries. They specialize in subjects such as natural sciences, agriculture, law, education, banking, and mining, all of great economic importance to the country. The Library of the National Council for Scientific Research and Documentation (10,000 volumes) established in 1967 in Lusaka specializes in natural sciences, and in the mid-1980s had the potential for becoming the principal documentation and information center for the country. The Department of Agriculture Library established in 1953 at Mount Makulu Research Station has service points at 11 regional stations and contains special collections in agriculture and related sciences (10,000 volumes, 200 serials, 2,000 FAO Reports). Livingstone Museum Research Library, established 1951 in Livingstone (22,000 volumes and 400 reports), produces a museum journal and museum guide and contains materials on archaeology, ethnography, history, anthropology, and Africana. The Geological Survey library in Lusaka (34,645 volumes) has publications on geology, mining, metallurgy, and allied scientific and engineering subjects. In the Copperbelt, the mining industries maintain special libraries in Kitwe and Ndola that contain materials on all aspects of mining in Zambia. The Bank of Zambia Library established in 1967 in Lusaka (2,500 volumes, 468 serials) has materials on economics, the International Monetary Fund, World Bank, the United Nations, and financial and nonfinancial institutions of Zambia.

Other libraries with special collections are the Parliamentary Information and Research library of the National Assembly (23,000 volumes); the Library at Highcourt in Zambia (7,000 volumes, 30 serials); Radio Zambia Record and Reference Library in Lusaka with branch at Kitwe studios (75,000 discs, 23,000 tapes); Zambia Information Service Film Library (7,000 films); Zambia Standard Institute Technical Reference Library (8,000 volumes); United National Independence Party (UNIP) Library established in 1975 (5,000 volumes, 70 serials); and Civil Aviation Technical Library (1,300 volumes). Libraries with religious collections are found at the United Church of Zambia Theological College Library in Kitwe and Jesuit Theological Library and Islamic Library in Lusaka.

The Profession. The Department of Library Studies in the University of Zambia offers a four-year B.A. in Library Studies (B.A.L.S.) and a two-year nongraduate Diploma in Librarianship (Dip. Lib.). From its inception in 1967 until 1984 the Department trained 115 graduates with the B.A.L.S. and 59 with the Dip. Lib. In addition, the Department offers a course in School Librarianship to fourth-year B.A. and B.Sc. education students who wish to become teacher-librarians in schools. Plans were under way in the mid-1980s to introduce a Master's degree in Library Science. The publications of the Department include its *Handbook,* published annually, and *Zambian Libraries,* a journal whose first issue came out in March 1984.

The Posts and Telecommunication Training College in Ndola offers a six-month subprofessional course called the Certificate Course in Librarianship.

The Zambia Library Association (ZLA) was established in 1967 with the Zambia Library Association Council as its governing body. Separate committees within the ZLA deliberate and make recommendations on topics such as establishing the National Information System (NATIS), compilation of a National Union Catalogue, and employment of librarians in Zambia. ZLA takes an active interest in the development of regional information and documentation services for the countries in Eastern, Central, and Southern Africa. The *Zambian Library Association Journal* was issued quarterly from 1968, but changed to biannual publication in 1979. The *Zambia Library Association Newsletter,* a bimonthly, was inaugurated in April 1979. From 1983, however, the frequency of publication and appearance of those publications were irregular.

O. N. MOHAMEDALI

Zimbabwe

Zimbabwe, a republic in southwestern Africa, is bordered by Zambia on the north, Mozambique on the northeast and east, South Africa on the south, and Botswana on the southwest and west. Population (1984 est.) 8,060,000; area 390,759 sq.km. The official language is English and the principal national languages are Shona and Ndebele.

History. Writing was introduced into what is now Zimbabwe by missionaries in the 19th century, and libraries were first established by colonists from the mid-1890s. After an initial pioneer phase, development was slow.

National Libraries. The Library of the National Archives of Zimbabwe, founded in the capital city of Salisbury (now Harare) in 1935 as a department of the Central African Archives, is the principal legal deposit library, the foremost center for research on South-Central Africa and its history, and the chief bibliographical services center. Its collections, which

National Archives of Zimbabwe

National Archives of Zimbabwe, Harare.

comprise all works published in Zimbabwe, works by Zimbabwean authors, and works on Zimbabwe published elsewhere with wide coverage of Southern, Central, and Eastern African subjects, totaled 35,850 monographs, 36,000 audiovisual materials, and 6,000 current serials in 1984. The Library publishes the *Zimbabwe National Bibliography,* maintains a *Directory of Zimbabwean Libraries,* administers the allocation of international standard book numbers, and is the Unesco deposit library for Zimbabwe.

The national lending library, national center for interlibrary loans, and central library for students is the National Free Library of Zimbabwe, founded at Bulawayo in 1944. It maintained a national union catalogue of monographs between 1956 and 1972 and coordinates the incorporation of the record of Zimbabwean library holdings in Southern African union catalogues published on microfiche from 1972. Its collections, which totaled 85,000 monographs, 15,000 technical specifications, and 500 current periodicals in 1984, supplement the public library service in academic, scientific, technical, and cultural books and information.

Archives holdings in Zimbabwe totaled 2,750 cubic meters in 1982, and annual expenditures were 140,000 Zimbabwean dollars. Staff totaled 56 (10 professionals).

University Library. The largest library in Zimbabwe is the Library of the University of Zimbabwe at Harare, founded in 1957 as the University College of Rhodesia and Nyasaland. It lends generously through interlibrary loans from its collections, which totaled 350,000 monographs and 5,000 current periodicals in 1984. It comprises a main library, extended in 1983–84 to accommodate a rapidly expanding student body, and law, medical, education, and map libraries, with special collections of Zimbabweana and African languages.

Public Libraries. Zimbabwe inherited from the colonial era (1890–1980) a dual system of grant-aided public subscription libraries in the main urban centers and municipal library services in high-density suburbs. The largest public libraries are the Harare City Library, founded in 1902 as the Queen Victoria

Memorial Library, with 75,000 volumes and five branch libraries; the Bulawayo Public Library, founded in 1896, with 80,000 volumes, three branch libraries, and a mobile library service; and the Bulawayo Municipal Libraries, with 70,000 volumes and seven branch libraries (1984). The Bulawayo Public Library is the country's second legal deposit library, and maintains a Historic Reference Collection at the Bulawayo City Hall.

Moves sponsored by the Carnegie Corporation of New York to foster a free public library system failed in 1929 for want of finance, but resulted in the foundation of the National Free Library in 1944. The Varley Report (1951), commissioned by the Central African Branch of the South African Library Association, recommended a national library service for the two Rhodesias and Nyasaland. The Rhodesia Library Commission (1970) reported serious deficiencies in the public library system and proposed the establishment of a nationwide free public library service. Neither report was implemented.

The coming of independence in 1980 brought with it a new impetus for library development planning. At government request the British Council sponsored a survey by W. A. G. Alison, Director of Libraries of the City of Glasgow, Scotland, who recommended in 1981 the establishment of a national library service uniting government, education, and public libraries. In 1982 a Swedish Library Mission recommended the inclusion of a national information and documentation center and supplied a blueprint for a library school. In January 1984 ground was broken for a new National Library and Documentation Service headquarters at Harare, and the third draft of an NLDS bill was prepared in June 1984 for presentation to the Parliament. Plans envisaged a central administration, 8 regional centers, and rural library service by bookmobile and through 55 district libraries. The National Free Library would be incorporated as a constituent library and urban public libraries invited to affiliate to the service.

School and College Libraries. School libraries, coordinated by the School Libraries Section of the Ministry of Education and supported by a per capita grant from the Ministry, are provided in most secondary schools. College libraries are established at teachers' colleges, technical colleges, and agricultural colleges.

Special Libraries. Most special libraries are in government departments and state-related bodies. Libraries are coordinated by the Government Library Service based at the National Archives. Foremost is the Library of Parliament, Harare, founded in 1897 as the Library of the Legislative Council, with collections that totaled 70,000 monographs and 276 current periodicals in 1981. The Central Library of the Ministry of Agriculture, which had collections totaling 3,170 monographs, 3,900 microforms, and 500 current periodicals in 1981, was being strengthened in the mid-1980s to become a resource for the Southern African Development Coordination Conference (SADCC) region. The British Council and the United States Information Service operate lending and study libraries in Harare. Notable libraries of international standing are those of the National Museums and Monuments of Zimbabwe and the Tobacco Research Board.

The Profession. The Zimbabwe Library Association was founded in 1959 as the Library Association of Rhodesia and Nyasaland. It publishes the *Zimbabwe Librarian*. Its membership in 1984 was 140 institutional and 122 personal members.

REFERENCES

Douglas Harold Varley, *Library Services in the Rhodesias and Nyasaland* (1951).

Sir Cornelius Greenfield (Chairman). *Report of the Rhodesia Library Commission, 1970* (1971).

Norman Johnson, "Library Development in Rhodesia," *Give the People Light: Essays in Honour of Matthew Miller Stirling* (1972). William A. G. Alison, *A National Library Service for Zimbabwe: A Report to the British Council* (1981).

Chagan Lalloo, Kerstin Jonsson, and Nina Bergstrom. *Zimbabwe: National Library and Documentation Service: Report of the Swedish Library Mission* (1982).

NORMAN JOHNSON

Libraries in Zimbabwe (1982)

Type	Administrative units	Service points[a]	Volumes in collections	Annual expenditures (Zimbabwean dollar)	Population served	Professional staff	Total staff
National	2	2	129,200	214,000	7,539,326	12	28
University	1	5	331,000	912,300	4,700	20	67
College	16	17	--	215,000	15,200	16	49
Public[b]	60	80	503,000	--	--	--	--
School	--	--	--	--	--	--	--
Special	--	--	--	--	--	--	--
Government	42	42	--	262,900	--	20	46

[a]Figures include main libraries.
[b]1981 data.

Sources: *Directory of Zimbabwean Libraries;* replies to questionnaires.

Index

PAMELA HORI, INDEXER

Index

ERRATA: *The following indexing follows the letter H on page 881.*

I

ISBN 0-8389-0427-0
ISBN 0-7449-0003-4

School Libraries for Today and Tomorrow 745

School of Documentalists, National Library of Spain (Madrid), European archival school 72

Schweizerische Vereinigung fur Dokumentation (SVI), Swiss Association of Documentalists 793

Science Citation Index 299

Scoggin, Margaret C., U.S. librarian, 71–753, photo 751

SCOLE: *see* Standing Committee on Library Education

SCONUL: *see* Standing Committee of National and University Libraries (Israel)

SCONUL: *see* Standing Conference of National and University Libraries (U.K.)

Scott, Marianne, National Librarian of Canada, 158

scriptorium, monastery facility for copying or writing manuscripts 389

SDC: *see* Systems Development Corporation

SDI (Selective Dissemination of Information) systems, personalized information service 503, 775

SEAFDEC: *see* Southeast Asian Fisheries Development Center

search room, archival repository of equivalent of library reading room 67–68

Sears, Minnie Earl, U.S. cataloguer, bibliographer, editor, 753

SELA: *see* Southeastern Library Association

Selected Bibliography on Kuwait and Arabian Gulf, Kuwait National Bibliography 426

selection of materials: *see* Collection Development

Selective Dissemination of Information Systems: *see* SDI Systems

Self-Study: A Guide to the Process and to the Preparation of a Report for the Committee on Accreditation 28

Semiconductor Chip Protection Act (1984), U.S., law to protect patterns on semiconductors from unauthorized reproduction 228

Seminar on the Acquisition of Latin American Library Materials (SALALM), U.S. 753–755

Senegal 755–756, photo 756

Serial Publications: Their Place and Treatment in Libraries 625

serials
    law libraries 435
    medical libraries 528

series, body of archival file units 54, 1–62

services to users: *see* library services

Serving Adult Learners 33

Sevensma, T. P., Dutch librarian and administrator, 756–757, photo 756

Sevensma Prize, essay award offered by IFLA 757

Seychelles 757, table 757

Shakleton, Robert, British librarian, administrator, teacher, 757–758, illus 757

Shamurin, E. I., Soviet scholar, teacher, 758–759

(I. P.) Sharp, Canadian computer time-sharing company 614

Sharp, Katharine, U.S. librarian, 759–760, illus 759

Shaw, Ralph, U.S. library administrator, educator, 760–762, photo 761

(Ralph R.) Shaw Award, U.S. award for contribution to library literature 295

shelf list, record of materials in shelf order 858

shelving, innovations in 709

Shera, Jesse H., U.S. librarian, educator, administrator, 762–764, photo 762

    on Butler 149

Short-Title Catalogue of Books Printed in England, Scotland, Ireland, Wales and British America and of English Books Printed in Other Countries, 1641–1700 651, 856

SIBIL (Système informatisé de bibliothèques), Swiss computerized library system based on MARC II 792

SIDES: *see* Sistema de Información y Documentación para la Educación Superior

Sierra Leone 764–765, photo 765

Sierra Leone Library Association 765

Sierra Leone Publications, National Bibliography of Sierra Leone 579

Silver Anvil, award given by Public Relations Society of America 683, 684

silver halide film, light-sensitive photographic material 702

Singapore 765–767, table 766
    continuing education 481

Singapore National Bibliography 579

SINTO, Polish national scientific, tech-